2011
Getting
Financial Aid

2011
Getting
Financial Aid

CollegeBoard

Fifth Edition

The College Board, New York

The College Board

The College Board is a not-for-profit membership association whose mission is to connect students to college success and opportunity. Founded in 1900, the College Board is composed of more than 5,700 schools, colleges, universities and other educational organizations. Each year, the College Board serves seven million students and their parents, 23,000 high schools, and 3,800 colleges through major programs and services in college readiness, college admission, guidance, assessment, financial aid and enrollment. Among its widely recognized programs are the SAT®, the PSAT/NMSQT®, the Advanced Placement Program® (AP®), SpringBoard® and ACCUPLACER®. The College Board is committed to the principles of excellence and equity, and that commitment is embodied in all of its programs, services, activities and concerns.

For further information, visit www.collegeboard.com.

Editorial inquiries concerning this book should be directed to College Planning Services, College Board, 45 Columbus Avenue, New York, NY 10023-6992.

Copies of this book are available from your local bookseller or may be ordered from College Board Publications, P.O. Box 8670, Reston, VA 20195. The book may also be ordered online through the College Board Store at www.collegeboard.com. The price is $21.99.

ISBN: 978-0-87447-905-8

Printed in the United States of America

Distributed by Macmillan

Contents

List of Figures

List of Tables

List of Worksheets

Preface

Financial aid is a great equalizer. In 2009, over $168 billion in aid was awarded from government and private sources. Coupled with the wide range of lower-cost college options available, financial aid should make a college education affordable for just about everyone.

Yet a recent study by the American Council on Education shows that each year almost *two million* students who are eligible for this boon don't even apply for it. We assume these students are either unaware of the possibility of aid, or mistakenly believe financial aid is not for them.

And many parents and students who apply for financial aid find the process to be confusing, even intimidating. Like the tax code, the forms and guidelines appear to be full of exceptions, convolutions and incomprehensible terms.

But it doesn't have to be that way. A central aim of this book is to take the confusion and intimidation out of the process by giving clear and direct explanations of what financial aid is all about and simple, step-by-step directions for how to get it. By combining these explanations and directions with costs and financial aid facts for every accredited college that reports this data, we hope this book will achieve our ultimate goal of connecting students to colleges that match both their needs and their means.

Acknowledgments

We gratefully acknowledge the contributions of the many individuals who helped bring the first edition of this book into being. George Ochoa, our writer for Part I of this book, "Financial Aid, Step by Step," transformed a complicated and intricate subject into clear and simple prose. Without his talent, the purpose of this guide could not have been achieved.

Renée Gernand provided leadership and editorial guidance throughout the project. Kathie Little and Jack Joyce, our resident experts on financial aid, reviewed the content and kept our course true, as did Sandy Baum, Cindy Bailey, Myra Baas Smith and Linda Peckham. Kate Crane copyedited the manuscript, and Betty Keim proofread the finished book.

While we had the advantage of many "in-house" resources, we also relied upon the knowledge and advice of seven financial aid officers who took time from their busy schedules to give us interviews: Vincent Amoroso of the University of North Carolina at Chapel Hill (now at Johns Hopkins University), Bonnie Lee Behm of Villanova University, Elizabeth Bickford of the University of Oregon, Joe Paul Case of Amherst College, Mary San Agustin of Palomar College, Mike Scott of Texas Christian University and Forrest Stuart of Rhodes College (now at Furman University). We hope you will find their insight and advice, quoted throughout Part I, as illuminating as we did.

For the current edition, we relied on the our resident experts Myra Smith, Ami Boshardt and Cindy Shelberg for help with updating the information in Parts I and II. The descriptions of colleges presented in Part III, "Financial Aid, College by College," were compiled from the College Board's Annual Survey of Colleges. The college data were collected, edited and verified by a team of editors led by Connie Betterton and Stan Bernstein, with the assistance of Cathy Serico, Andrew Costello, Renée Gernand, Roger Harris and Doris Chow. Mary Anne Blazier, May Cooper, Marci Harman, Christina Latimer, Diana McDermott, Randy Peery, Leah Swaggerty, Jenny Xie and Katrina Kingdon did the hard work. Finally, we would like to thank the team of programmers and composers at Content Data Solutions, Inc., who converted the database into readable pages.

Tom Vanderberg, Senior Editor
College Planning Services

Michael Polizzi, Assistant Editor

How to Use This Book

Part I: Financial Aid, Step by Step

The first chapter, "Yes, You Can Afford College," establishes our central point: a college can be found to fit any budget. If you are skeptical about that, please start here — we think we make a strong case.

Steps 1 through 11 provide easy-to-follow directions on how to get financial aid, including what you need to know, what you need to do, and when you need to do it.

These "steps" are presented in a logical sequence. But depending upon your own circumstances — where you are in the college application process, your family's finances, what kinds of colleges you're applying to, and the policies of those individual colleges — you may need to take the steps in a slightly different order, skip some steps, or do some steps simultaneously. To keep track of what should be done when, consult the planning calendar on the inside front cover.

Financial aid officers and the forms you need to fill out often use jargon that can at times seem vague or confusing. Terms like "need" and "cost of attendance" have specific meanings that might not be the same as what you would assume. Throughout Part I, you'll find key terms defined in "Know the Lingo" sidebars (you'll also find a detailed, comprehensive glossary at the end of this book). Other sidebars emphasize or illustrate the main points of each step.

Throughout Part I, you'll find graphs and charts that also illustrate key points, and tables that summarize information and let you compare different financial aid options. You'll also find checklists and prefilled sample worksheets that will help you plan and keep track of your applications. Blank copies of those worksheets for you to fill in are in Part II.

Part II: Tables and Worksheets

One of the worksheets that you'll find in Part II will help you compare the financial aid award letters that you'll receive from colleges. To drive home the point that no two award letters are alike, we've included two samples in Part II, immediately after the comparison worksheet. These are actual award letters that were sent to the same aid applicant by two different universities, the names of which we've changed.

Part II also includes a series of worksheets that you can use to estimate how much the federal government will say you should pay for college out of pocket — that's your "expected family contribution" (EFC) used by colleges to award financial aid. (You'll learn more about the EFC and how it's calculated in Part I.) These worksheets are designed for dependent students and their parents. If you are an independent student, you can do the same thing with the online tools at the collegeboard.com website. In addition to worksheets, Part II includes a sample of the preapplication worksheet for the Free Application for Federal Student Aid (FAFSA). This worksheet shows all of the questions included on *last year's* FAFSA; it may be that some questions will change somewhat in the year you fill this out. Finally, in Part II you'll find lists of state aid programs, state-sponsored 529 college savings plans and other useful places to find more information.

Part III: Financial Aid College by College

This is where we help you get the "financial aid picture" at specific colleges, including scholarships the colleges offer to entering students, and required forms and deadlines. To place this picture in context, we give you brief facts about the kind of college it is, and its basic costs. This information can help you compare the colleges you are considering and find colleges that look affordable. But keep in mind that the financial aid figures are mostly based on averages, meaning many students will be above or below these benchmarks.

The college descriptions in Part III are arranged alphabetically by state or territory. Running headers at the top of each page will help you orient yourself and find schools quickly. An alphabetical index of all the colleges in the book appears in Part IV.

Every college described in this book is accredited by an agency recognized by the U.S. Department of Education. Accreditation is a process in which an outside agency ensures that a college meets certain basic standards — it's a stamp of approval on the college's teaching, facilities and administration. For financial aid purposes, accreditation by a federally recognized agency means that federal student aid dollars can be used to attend the institution.

The College Board College Handbook also includes full descriptions of the colleges in this book, going beyond the cost and financial aid details presented here to include information about admissions requirements, academics, housing, student life, athletics and more.

Where the College Information Comes From

The information in the college descriptions comes from the College Board's most recent Annual Survey of Colleges, which was conducted in the spring of 2010. Every college reported its own cost and financial aid information to us. Where possible, our staff of editors verified the information by consulting third-party sources, including public university system or district offices, state education departments and the federal government's Integrated Postsecondary Educational Database System. The information presented was current at the time this book went to press in May 2010 — but be warned that it may have changed by the time you're reading this. Once you have narrowed down a list of colleges that you're interested in, you should confirm critical information, such as financial aid application deadlines and requirements, by visiting the colleges' websites or contacting their financial aid offices.

What's in the College Descriptions

Each college description begins with a shaded box that contains the name of the college, the city or town where it's located, and its website address. For every college, its six-digit "federal code" — the code you will need in order to have your FAFSA information sent to the college — appears in this box. If a college requires the College Board's CSS/Financial Aid PROFILE®, its four-digit CSS code also appears in this box. (The CSS code is the same code you use to send SAT® and SAT Subject Tests™ scores and AP® Exam scores to a college; the federal code is only used for the FAFSA.)

Below the college name box you'll find a brief summary of what type of college it is — whether it's a four-year private university, a two-year community college or a four-year culinary school run on a for-profit basis. (Definitions of all the different types of schools you might find here are in the glossary.) You'll also find information about the number of students who were enrolled in the 2009-10 school year, and the relative difficulty of obtaining admission to the college.

BASIC COSTS

"Basic Costs" lists the tuition, fees, room and board charged by the college. The date indicates the school year for which these numbers apply — if the college was unable to report final or projected figures for the upcoming school year, last year's figures are given. If the college combines tuition, fees, and room and board expenses, that single figure is given as a comprehensive fee.

xii How to Use This Book

It's important to note that these figures do not include other out-of-pocket costs, such as books, supplies, transportation and personal expenses. These costs can be substantial, depending upon where and how you live, and what you study. But since these costs vary widely from student to student, we felt it would be misleading to display average amounts.

FINANCIAL AID PICTURE

The core of each college's description is the information about the financial aid it offers. Again, the date indicates the school year for which the college reported numbers — either the current year or the prior year. Depending on the aid programs offered by the college and the figures they reported, you may see one or several of these elements of the financial aid picture:

- **Students with Need.** This shows how financial aid was given to students who could not afford the full cost of attending the college on their own (a full explanation of how "need" is determined is found in Part I, Step 1). The focus is on the entering freshman class but, if a college was unable to provide that breakdown, the numbers are for all undergraduates. Most colleges disclosed the average percentage of need met by financial aid packages, and the relative proportion of aid given as scholarships and grants as opposed to loans or work-study jobs. Use this data to get a sense of how likely a college is to meet your full need, and how much aid will probably come in the form of loans.

- **Students Without Need.** Even though a student does not need financial aid, it's still possible that a college will provide aid based on merit or other criteria, such as alumni affiliation or minority status. That's what is shown here. If a college has a policy of only awarding aid to students who have need, this is also stated here.

- **Scholarships Offered.** This gives details on merit scholarships offered by the college and their criteria for being awarded. Here you can get a sense of whether your GPA or SAT scores put you in the right ballpark for a merit-based grant. You'll also find information about the number of student-athletes who were given a scholarship by the college, and the average award.

- **Cumulative Student Debt.** This tells you how many students borrowed money to pay for college and how much they owed, on average, when they graduated. This is another way for you to measure how much of a college's aid will be loan based. The numbers here only include student loans taken out through the college — not PLUS loans, private education loans or other borrowing done through a third-party lender.

FINANCIAL AID PROCEDURES

The financial aid application forms required by the college, and the priority date and/or deadlines that the financial aid office has set, appear here. This section also includes information about notification — that is, when you can expect to hear back from the financial aid office after applying, and by when they will need your final answer about whether you'll be attending. Unless otherwise noted, all dates given in this section are for applicants who intend to enroll in the fall of 2011. If you plan to apply for admission to the spring 2012 term, contact the college's financial aid office to find out about their policies and deadlines.

CONTACT

The final section of each college description lists the mailing address of the school's financial aid office.

Part IV: Scholarship Lists

If you want to zero in on colleges that offer scholarships for your particular talents and interests, the lists in Part IV will help you do that. Arranged alphabetically by state, these lists will point you to colleges that offer scholarships for a variety of achievements. Please note that, in many cases, merit is not the only criterion used by the college when awarding aid: It may require recipients to also demonstrate financial need by submitting the FAFSA or another financial aid form.

At some colleges, every applicant is automatically considered for merit scholarships. At others, you have to specifically apply for a given scholarship. And in some cases, a scholarship is only open to you if you've been recommended by your principal, school counselor or teacher.

What's in the Scholarship Lists

Each list points to colleges that offer aid for a specific talent or area of interest.

Academics. This list names colleges that offer merit aid for academic achievement. Typical criteria include the classes you've taken, your GPA and your standardized test scores.

Art. This list includes colleges that offer merit aid for artistic ability, as reflected by grades in art classes, teacher recommendations and/or a portfolio you submit to the college.

Athletics. If a college offers scholarships for a certain sport, it will be listed here. The letters "M" and "W" indicate whether the scholarship is available to men, women or both. Please note that, at most colleges, only a very few athletes receive significant scholarships. No one should rely on athletic achievements alone to get into college or to pay for it. Instead, make sure your academic record is solid, and be sure to apply for need-based financial aid by submitting the FAFSA and any other required forms.

Music/Drama. This list includes colleges and conservatories that offer merit aid for talent in the performing arts, as reflected by grades in music, dance or drama classes; teacher recommendations; and/or an audition or a submitted tape.

ROTC. Three lists are included here, one each for the Air Force, Army and Naval Reserve Officers' Training Corps. (Marine Corps ROTC is included in Naval ROTC; the Coast Guard and Merchant Marine do not have ROTC programs.) The schools listed may not necessarily have all their ROTC programs on campus; they may have a sponsorship agreement with a neighboring college or university instead. If you enroll in ROTC, you will need to apply separately for the actual ROTC scholarship from the service branch you've chosen — the money doesn't come automatically. (For information on how much money is awarded and how to apply, consult *The College Board Scholarship Handbook,* or visit your local recruiting station.) Some colleges offer additional institutional scholarships for ROTC candidates from their own funds, beyond what's awarded by the Department of Defense.

Part I

Financial Aid Step by Step

Yes, You Can Afford College

Yes, you can afford college. How do we know? Because most colleges are not as expensive as you think. Because if a college wants you as a student, it will try to help you with financial aid. Because most students get financial aid. And because there are ways to reduce the amount you have to pay now, including working part-time and taking out loans.

This is not what everyone will tell you. You may hear discouraging words like, "Most colleges are expensive" and "You won't qualify for financial aid." People may hint that college is not worth all the trouble. The financial aid forms may look complicated and confusing.

We will show you how to get past these doubts. You *can* afford college, and we will show you how. College is worth the expense; you should apply for financial aid. With our step-by-step guide through the process, you'll sidestep confusion and be able to focus on the important decisions in front of you.

This book will help you if you have already saved some money for college — and also if you have not. It will help if you are a student, or a parent of a student. It will help if you have already decided what colleges to apply to, and also if you are not sure where you'd like to go. You may be the first in your family to consider college, or the latest in a family tradition. You might think your family doesn't make enough money to afford college, or that it makes too much to be awarded financial aid. You may have an expensive "dream college" you hope to attend, or you may be looking only for the best buy. You may plan to work or not to work, commute or live on campus, rely on your parents' money or pay your own way. No matter what your situation, you can afford college and we will help you do it.

Why You Can Afford College

Despite media hype about pricey colleges and the soaring cost of higher education, most colleges are not as expensive as you might think. In addition, the published prices of many colleges, though high, are not the whole story. If a college wants you as a student, and if you and your parents don't have enough money, the college will usually offer help so you can attend. That help is financial aid — and because of it, **a college's published tuition and fees are not what most people pay.**

Financial aid is a great equalizer, and most students benefit from it. More than two-thirds of all full-time college students receive grants or scholarships to help them foot the bill. Those grants come either from the government, the college or both, and do not have to be paid back. Many students also receive other forms of help, including federal tax credits and deductions that allow their families to keep more of their money at tax time. Thanks to all this assistance, full-time college students pay, on average, much less than the advertised price of their education. In 2009-10, for example, students at four-year private colleges paid an average net price of $11,900 in tuition and fees instead of the published price of $26,273. Students at four-year public universities received a proportionally similar discount.

Even expensive colleges are less costly than you might think because they offer more financial aid. Since a high-priced college often awards more assistance than a low-priced one, a particular student might end up paying the same out-of-pocket cost at both, or even less at the college with a higher sticker price. **That's why you shouldn't rule out your "dream college" as too expensive until you find out if it wants you and what kind of financial aid package it will give you.**

That said, there are great deals to be found. At a public college — one supported by a state or local government — the average tuition and fees in 2009-10 were $7,020 a year. That's a 74 percent saving over the $26,273 a year charged by private colleges. Another way to save money is to spend your first two years at a community college, which is a public college that specializes in two-year education programs. Published tuition and fees at community colleges averaged just over $2,500 a year — a 64 percent saving over the average at a public four-year college.

Here's one last reason you can afford college: you don't have to pay every penny up front. You can borrow money at a low interest rate and pay it back after your studies are over. There are also ways to reduce the amount you have to pay right now. (*See Step 11 for more on these "out-of-pocket" options.*)

Figure 1:
Total Tuition, Fees, Room and Board Charges, 2009-10

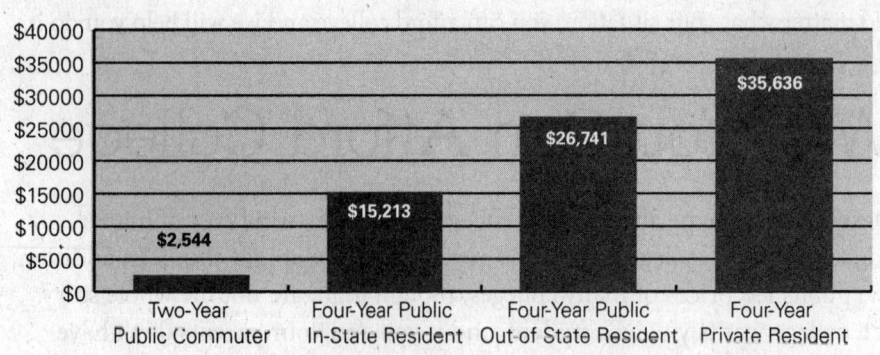

See Step 3 for more about the components of college costs.

Is College Worth It?

Even if you can afford college, is it a good idea? No matter how much financial aid you get, college will still require a sacrifice of money, time, and effort. Kids who go straight to work after high school have more spending money sooner. Does college give enough bang for the buck?

The answer is yes for many reasons including money, job insurance and personal growth.

In terms of money, college clearly pays. The difference in earnings between college graduates and high school graduates has increased sharply over the past three decades. The typical male college graduate now earns 65 percent more than the typical male high school graduate; for women, the difference is 60 percent. **College graduates earn an average of $1 million more over their careers than high school graduates**. Even if you borrow to pay for part of your education, it's still worth it. Provided you borrow intelligently, your increased earnings will help you pay back the loan. (*See Step 11 for more about loans.*)

You might think that the increased earnings from your college education won't make up for the total costs and the years that you won't be in the work force. But Figure 3 on the next page shows otherwise. The grey line shows the cumulative earnings at each age for the average high school graduate

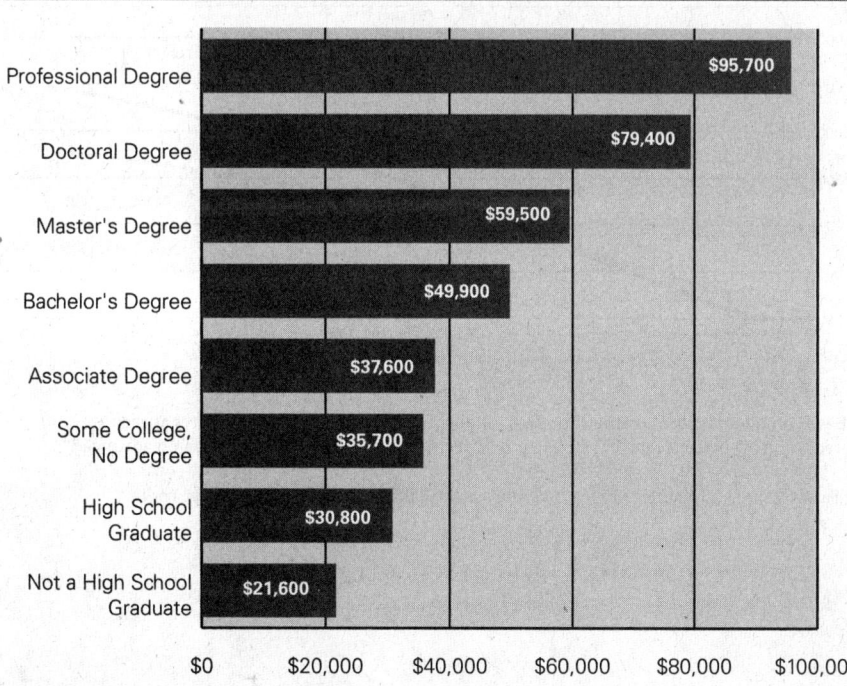

Figure 2:
Median Annual Earnings by Education Level

Note: Includes full-time, year-round workers age 25 and older.
Sources: U.S. Census Bureau, 2006, PINC-03; Internal Revenue Service, 2006; McIntyre, et al., 2003; calculations by the authors.

who enters the workforce full time at the age of 18. The black line shows the cumulative earnings at each age for the average college graduate who enters the workforce at age 22, after subtracting average tuition and fees paid over four years at a public college or university. As you can see, by age 32 the lines intersect. From that point on, the investment in college pays off.

College also provides job insurance in a world whose economy is constantly changing. As new industries develop and many jobs are outsourced to foreign countries, you can compete better with a college degree. A college degree teaches you how to acquire knowledge and put it to use no matter what the circumstances. In fact, some higher-education credential — at least an associate degree — is a minimum to stay employed in the "knowledge economy" of the 21st century. **A mere high school diploma is obsolete; college helps to ensure employment**.

But the value of college can't be reduced to dollars alone. It involves intangibles, things you can't touch directly: how you value yourself, your dreams and your ambitions. If you are an artist, a musician, a writer, a builder, a scientist or a thinker, college will help you cultivate those talents. If you are hoping to find yourself, meet people who are more like you, and meet people who are different and interesting, college can contribute to that search too. College provides rich ground for personal growth.

On every front, as a matter of value for dollars, college is a good buy. You can afford college — and it is worth the price.

Figure 3:
Estimated Cumulative Earnings Minus College Costs

Notes: Based on median 2005 earnings for high school graduates and college graduates at each age and discounted using a 3 percent rate. Earnings for B.A. recipients include only those with no advanced degree.
Source: Sandy Baum and Kathleen Payea, *Education Pays 2007*, The College Board, New York.

How This Book Will Help You

KEEP IN MIND

Don't approach the chronology of this book too rigidly — **not all steps have to come in this order.** For example, Step 9, "Look for Other Sources of Money," can be done at any time. Since outside scholarships aren't tied to a particular college, you can start researching and applying for them before you've even made a short list of schools. In fact, this is a good idea because the application deadline for these scholarships may be as early as Nov. 1, before most college admissions applications are due.

Through this book, you will learn how to make college affordable for you. You'll find out exactly what you need to know so you can apply for financial aid, choose an affordable college and control costs while at college. In Part I, we will walk you step-by-step through the process. There are 11 steps in all:

- **Step 1:** You'll find out the key facts about financial aid.

- **Step 2:** You'll get an idea of how much financial aid you can get.

- **Step 3:** You'll see how and why college costs vary.

- **Step 4:** You'll figure out which forms you need to fill out, and when.

- **Step 5:** You'll learn how to fill out the Free Application for Federal Student Aid (FAFSA).

- **Step 6:** You'll find out how to complete the CSS/Financial Aid PROFILE® application (called the PROFILE for short), if your colleges require it.

- **Step 7:** You'll learn how to fill out any other forms a particular college might require.

- **Step 8:** If your family has special circumstances, you'll find out the best way to explain them to colleges.

- **Step 9:** You'll learn about scholarships and other aid you can get from sources outside of a college.

- **Step 10:** You'll learn how to compare award letters from colleges and decide which offer is best for you.

- **Step 11:** You'll learn how to pay your share of the cost of college through work, loans and other means.

In Part II of the book, tables and worksheets will help you make informed decisions and stay in control of the financial aid process. Part III will paint a clear picture of the financial facts about each college you might want to investigate. That includes its costs and its approach to financial aid.

No one will tell you that paying for college is fun. But what you're getting — a college education — is worth it and is within reach. College is a big-ticket purchase that requires careful thought and preparation, like a house or a car. And it shouldn't be done in the dark. This book will guide you into one of the most important purchases you'll ever make — with your eyes wide open.

Step 1: Let's Go Over the Basics

QUICK OVERVIEW

The first step to getting financial aid is to understand the basic facts about it. In this step we will explain what financial aid is (money to help you pay for college), what types there are (the kind that comes free and the kind that doesn't), who gets it and where it comes from.

The most important point: almost everyone qualifies for at least one form of financial aid. As long as you apply, the chances are excellent that you will get some.

Just What Is Financial Aid?

KNOW THE LINGO

Grant — Money that is given away for free, usually on the basis of who needs it

Merit scholarship — Money that is given away for free on the basis of academic qualifications or special talents

Subsidized loan — Money that you have to pay back with interest; however, the federal government pays the interest for you while you are in college

Work-study — A program in which you take a part-time job to earn money for your education; the federal government pays part of your salary

Financial aid package — What a college offers to an accepted student who has applied for aid. Usually a mix of grants, loans and/or work-study.

Financial aid is money given or loaned to you to help you pay for college. Different forms have different rules. The vast majority of aid comes from the federal government, and most of it consists of loans that you must pay back. However, some aid does not require repayment — which makes it the best kind of aid to get.

If you qualify for financial aid, your college will put together an aid "package," usually with different types of aid bundled together. You and your parents will almost certainly still have to pay something, but the aid package will help. Most students qualify for some form of financial aid, so it makes sense to apply for it.

You'll apply for financial aid either at the same time or soon after you apply for admission. You may have to fill out more than one application. At the very least you will fill out the FAFSA, or federal government form. You may also fill out another form, the PROFILE, which many colleges require. And some colleges and state aid agencies require their own financial aid forms, too. The colleges to which you apply will use the forms to figure out what your family can afford to pay and what your "need" is — that is, the difference between what you can pay and what the college actually costs. If the school wants you as a student but sees that you can't handle the whole bill, it will make you a financial aid offer to help you meet your need. If you accept, that financial aid package is your award.

You will need to apply for financial aid every year that you are in college, mainly because your family's financial situation changes yearly. As a result, your financial aid package will probably be somewhat different from year to year.

Financial aid is a helping hand, not a free pass. In the United States, everyone has a right to a free public school education, but not to a free college education. The federal government and most colleges agree that students and their parents are the ones most responsible for paying for college. "The primary responsibility of paying for the student's education lies with the student and his or her parents," says Forrest M. Stuart, the director of financial aid at Furman University in Greenville, S.C. "Financial aid comes in to fill that gap, if you will, between what they can afford and what the college costs." Even so, financial aid can be the deciding factor in whether or not a student attends college.

Types of Aid

Financial aid may come in many forms. However, all forms can be grouped into two major categories: gift aid and self-help aid.

GIFT AID

Gift aid is free money, money that you don't have to pay back or work for. Naturally, this is the kind of aid most people want. It can take the form of grants or scholarships.

The terms "grant" and "scholarship" are often used interchangeably to mean free money. But here's the difference. A grant is usually given only on the basis of need, or your family's inability to pay the full cost of college. Scholarships are usually awarded only to those who have "merit," such as proven ability in academics, the arts or athletics. Once you're in college, you may have to maintain a minimum GPA or take certain courses to continue receiving a scholarship.

SELF-HELP AID

Self-help aid is money that requires a contribution from you. That can mean paying back the money (if the aid is a loan) or working for the money (if the aid is a work-study job).

The most common form of self-help aid is also the most common of any form of financial aid: the loan. A loan is money that you have to pay back with interest. In light of that, you might not consider this aid at all. But it is — a loan means you don't have to pay the full price of college all at once: You can stretch the payments over time, as you would when buying a house or a car. Furthermore, some student loans are subsidized by the federal government. With these loans, you don't have to pay the interest that comes due while you're in college. The federal government subsidizes, or helps to pay, the loan by paying that interest while you're enrolled and for the first few months after you graduate.

Subsidized loans, which are awarded based on need and administered by the college, are the best kind. But you can also take out unsubsidized student loans and parent loans, which are not packaged by most colleges. However, be careful not to take on more debt than necessary. No matter what kind of loan you take out, you will have to pay it back.

Another form of self-help is work-study. This is financial aid in the form of a job. Since you earn the money through your work, this too may not seem like aid. But it is, because the federal work-study program pays most of your wages. And work-study jobs are usually available right on campus, with limits on your hours so that you won't be unduly distracted from studying.

Aid can also come in the form of tax cuts — income tax deductions and credits for education. But colleges don't award this variety, and you don't apply for it in the same way as you would loans or grants, so we will discuss it separately, in Step 11.

Who Gets Aid?

Grants and loans are not just for the poorest of the poor, nor are scholarships only for the smartest of the smart. The truth about who gets financial aid is somewhat different from what many people think.

Those Who Need It

Most financial aid is based on need, not merit. There is money for merit, but since the 1950s most colleges in the United States have focused their financial aid packages on meeting financial need.

However, there is a lot of confusion about what need means. Many people think it means a state of dire poverty, so that no working-class or middle-class student need apply. "A lot of people think that they either have to be on welfare or Social Security — really poor — to get financial aid, and that's not correct," says Mary San Agustin, director of financial aid and scholarships at Palomar College in San Marcos, Calif. On the other hand, some rich families mistakenly think they are needy because their high living expenses leave them little money for college. "It's this expectation of, I pay my taxes, so my kid should be entitled to some federal financial aid regardless of how much money I make," says Ms. San Agustin.

Need simply means that your family can't afford to pay the full cost of a particular college. The *amount* of your need will vary from college to college, because it depends on the cost of attending an individual college. Whether your family has need is determined not by whether you think you are rich or poor, but by the financial aid forms you fill out.

Just fill out the forms. If you do have need, you will be considered for financial aid.

Those Who Don't

Despite the overall emphasis on need, many colleges do give away money on the basis of merit. They do this to attract the students they want most, and they may award this money even if it is more than the student needs. However, in many cases, the student both needs the money and has earned it on the basis of merit.

Don't think that only geniuses get merit aid. At many colleges a "B"-average GPA can put you in the running for merit money. Sometimes a separate application for merit aid is required to put you into consideration; sometimes your application for admission is enough. In either case, don't count yourself out by not applying; apply and let the college decide.

Grants are sometimes awarded based on neither need nor merit. For example, you may get a grant if you are in a certain field of study, are a resident of the state or are a student from the same town as the college. (*See Step 9 for more about grants and scholarships.*)

Part-Time Students

Some kinds of aid are only available to students enrolled in college full time — usually 12 or more credit hours of courses per semester. But part-time students are eligible for some financial aid. For example, federal programs such as the Stafford loan require only that students be enrolled at least half-time, whereas others, like the Pell Grant, are available to students enrolled less than half-time. Also, some employers offer tuition reimbursement benefits to students who work full time and go to college part time.

Where the Money Comes From

Financial aid comes from three basic sources: governments (both federal and state), colleges and outside benefactors.

From the Government

The lion's share of total financial aid awarded in this country comes from the federal government. Fully 69 percent of all student aid is sent from Washington. The largest chunk of that consists of federal loans, which total $83.9 billion a year and represent 45 percent of all student aid. The loans take multiple shapes. Perkins and Stafford loans are for students, while parents may take out a PLUS loan to help pay for their children's educations.

The federal government also funds several grants, including the Pell Grant, the Supplemental Educational Opportunity Grant (SEOG), the Academic Competitiveness Grant and the SMART Grant. The Pell and SEOG are strictly needbased, while the last two are based on both need and academic criteria. The government also funds the federal work-study program.

KNOW THE LINGO

Merit aid — Aid awarded on the basis of academics, character or talent

Need-based aid — Aid awarded on the basis of a family's inability to pay the cost of attending a particular college

Non-need-based aid — Aid awarded on some basis other than need or merit, such as grants with eligibility requirements related to field of study or state residence

A much smaller piece of the financial aid pie (7 percent) comes from individual state governments. Most of this aid is for use only at colleges within the state, though a few states offer "portable" aid, which state residents can take with them to a college in another state.

From the College

A great deal of financial aid comes from individual colleges, using their own "institutional" funds. In fact, colleges award nearly half of all grants. Many, though not all, award merit scholarships as well as need-based grants. They may also offer on-campus job opportunities and loans.

Private colleges give more financial aid than public ones, but their tuition is usually higher as well. Public colleges award less aid, but taxpayer support keeps their tuition lower.

Outside Grants and Scholarships

Outside grants and scholarships come from sources other than the government or the college. These sources may include corporations like Coca-Cola or community groups like the Elks Club. Some are well known, such as the National Merit Scholarship, but altogether they are the smallest piece of the financial aid pie: **only 6 percent of all student aid comes from this source.** Pursue them, but don't expect them to outweigh the other aid you will get.

Bear in mind also that your outside scholarship is unlikely to expand the total aid you receive. Most colleges will use an outside scholarship to substitute for some other piece of aid rather than increase the total aid package. Think of your financial aid package as a barrel: when the barrel is full, no more can be added unless something is taken away. The last thing colleges will take away is whatever sum of money your family is expected to contribute. However, at many colleges, the first thing taken away is self-help aid such as loans. Since that could reduce the total amount you will have to

Figure 4:

Undergraduate Student Aid (in billions) by Source, 2008-09

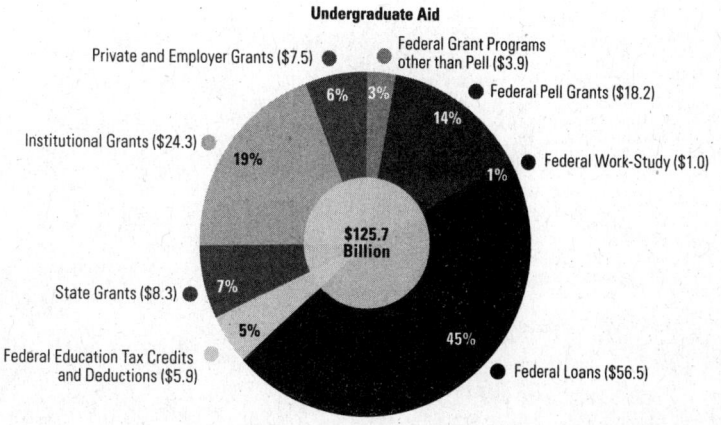

pay back later, it is worth applying for outside scholarships. (*See Step 9 for more on these sources of aid.*)

There is a lot of financial aid out there, in many forms. Apply for it — there is a good chance you will get some. These are the main things to know about financial aid:

QUICK RECAP

- It is money to help you pay for college.
- It may come in the form of a gift (grants and scholarships) or in the form of self-help (loans and work-study).
- Most people get it because they need it, though some get it solely because of merit.
- The federal government funds most of it, but states, colleges and outside sources also help.

Step 2: Estimate How Financial Aid Will Work for You

QUICK OVERVIEW

Only rarely does a student get a "free ride" scholarship. You and your parents will have to contribute some money to your education — the precise amount will be determined by the college's analysis of financial aid forms you'll fill out. But even before you fill out the forms, you can estimate your share of the cost and begin planning for how to pay it.

Don't Count Yourself Out

Most college students get some financial aid, but few receive exactly the same financial aid package. Financial aid packages are as individual as the financial circumstances of the students who apply. One family makes $50,000 a year and has two children, a house and a savings account; another makes $50,000 a year but has only one child, a rented apartment and no savings. What financial aid package will each family receive? The answer: It depends on several factors. Families must first submit their applications for consideration by the colleges.

"Probably the question I'm most often asked is, 'Is there a cutoff?'" says Joe Paul Case, the dean and director of financial aid at Amherst College in Amherst, Mass. Financial aid officers agree that there is no single salary cutoff for financial aid — no one income figure that will definitely exclude a student from receiving financial aid. Income is only one criterion for giving out aid: Colleges also consider such factors as family size, number of children in college, and savings. Many students who would be eligible for financial aid fail to apply because they don't realize this.

"I always tell families, don't cut yourself off from the application process," says Bonnie Lee Behm, the director of financial assistance at Villanova University in Villanova, Pa. "Apply and let it work through the system."

Even if you feel absolutely sure that your family doesn't qualify for financial aid, fill out the forms. Your family circumstances might change suddenly — a lost job, health problems, a new child. Then you may need financial aid, and it will help to be in the system already. A college can assist you faster if your financial aid application is on file.

EXPERT ADVICE

"We always encourage students to **go ahead and apply** for financial aid even though you may not qualify for anything but a student loan. **At least get the paperwork in**, because if something happens in the middle of the year, we already have the financial aid data we need to make adjustments."

— Forrest M. Stuart, director of financial aid, Furman University, Greenville, S.C.

What "Expected Family Contribution" Means

Even though you probably will qualify for some financial aid, it's very unlikely that you will get the fabled "full ride." Colleges do sometimes award full tuition — or even full room and board — to a student they greatly want to attract, but that is rare. Almost always, the family is expected to contribute some money. The exact dollar amount will be based on the family's ability to pay. That dollar amount is the expected family contribution, or EFC.

The EFC is carefully calculated to be your "fair share." It is what you can afford to pay based on your financial circumstances — no more and no less. The formulas that the federal government and colleges use to calculate EFC are ultimately intended to make sure that the EFC is fair.

In some ways, the concept of EFC works in your favor. No matter what a college costs, so long as it awards you the full financial aid you need you won't have to pay more than your EFC — the amount your family is able to pay. Say your EFC is $8,000. At a college with a total cost of attendance of $11,000, you could get up to $3,000 in financial aid. At a college where the total cost is $25,000, you could get up to $17,000 in aid. **Because of financial aid, any college is at least worth considering; no college should be ruled out in advance as too expensive.**

On the other hand, even though the expected family contribution is based on ability to pay, that does not simply mean how much the family would like to pay. For any purchase, most people would *like* to pay zero dollars. But what they are *able* to pay is how much money they have minus how much they need to keep for other things, such as food, rent, heat and retirement. When colleges award financial aid, they calculate your ability to pay by looking at your income and financial assets as you lay them out in your financial aid application. Using what are called need-analysis formulas, they analyze your data to see how much of the college costs you are able to pay (your EFC) and how much you are unable to pay (your need). How much you would like to pay is not part of the calculation.

Costs – EFC = Need

Your expected family contribution is your family's share of college costs. Any cost greater than that is your need. Need varies from college to college because it depends on the cost of the individual college. **It's simple arithmetic: College costs minus your EFC equals the amount of aid you need.** At colleges that award enough financial aid to meet your need, the aid package will equal the amount of your need. Costs minus aid equals what you pay.

Unmet Need (a.k.a. "Gap")

Unfortunately, not all colleges will award enough aid to meet your full need. Some colleges may "gap" your package — that is, not meet your full need. Economics plays a part here. While some colleges may have enough aid dollars available to meet every student's full need, some colleges lack such funds. If your college cannot meet your full need, costs minus aid will still equal what you pay. But what you pay will be more than your EFC. (*See Step 11 for more information on loans* and other ways to help fill such a gap.)

If you do encounter a "gap" in your award, compare the package with the ones you've gotten from other schools, and consider your priorities. Do you want to go to that college, no matter the cost? Or does cost matter more? (*For more on this topic, see Step 10.*)

It Depends on the College

The amount of aid you get — along with the kind of aid you get, whether gift or self-help — ultimately depends on the college. Formulas and forms are important, but so is the professional judgment of the financial aid officer. And so is the desire of the college to attract you to its campus.

How Colleges Calculate Your Need

As you saw in Step 1, financial aid comes from two main sources: government money (usually in the form of loans and work-study), and the college's own "institutional" money — usually in the form of grants and scholarships. Your financial aid package will probably contain money from both sources.

Just as there are two main sources of aid, there are two main formulas that colleges use to figure out how much aid you should get. One is called the "Federal Methodology," used for aid coming from government money. Most colleges use it to award their own institutional funds as well. The Federal Methodology is based on the FAFSA, the federal financial aid form.

For aid coming out of their own money, some colleges and scholarship programs use a different formula called the "Institutional Methodology." This is based on the PROFILE (more formally known as the College Board's CSS/Financial Aid PROFILE application) and/or the college's own financial aid application form. (*For more about these forms, see Steps 6 and 7.*) Colleges that use the Institutional Methodology do so because they think it presents a fuller picture of your family's financial situation. "I just think it does a much better job of measuring ability to pay," says Forrest M. Stuart, whose institution, Furman University, requires the PROFILE.

So what does all this mean to you? The differences between the two formulas make it possible that your expected family contribution will be lower under

KEEP IN MIND

If a college offers you a financial aid award that doesn't meet your full need, you may be able to fill the "gap" in your package with an **outside scholarship**. For more on outside scholarships, see Step 9.

one or the other; it all depends on your individual family circumstances, and the individual college(s) you are applying to. You don't have to know how these formulas work or remember what they are called. The thing to remember is that if you apply to several colleges, because of these different formulas you might end up with a different EFC for one college than you do for another.

Will College Savings Count Against You?

While some families save diligently for their children's college educations, others think this is a mistake. They worry that having a lot of savings will keep colleges from awarding financial aid. **But savings help you more than they hurt you**, and here is why.

When calculating your EFC, colleges subtract what they call an "asset protection allowance" from the amount you have saved. This "allowance" is the amount of money considered reasonable to set aside for educational savings and family emergencies. These "free" savings are not assessed at all. In Federal Methodology, the allowance varies based on the age of the oldest parent, and it can be several tens of thousands of dollars for a married couple in their 40s or 50s. These savings are clearly worth having, since they aren't included when calculating your EFC. (See Table 12 on page 136 to get an estimate of what your parents' asset protection allowance may be.)

Even if your family saves more than the asset protection allowance, those savings will be assessed at a maximum rate of only 5.6 percent. So even if 5.6 percent of your excess savings count "against" you when it comes to federal need determination, 94.4 percent count "for" you. You can use them to meet your expected contribution, whatever it turns out to be. That's good news, because your family will be expected to pay much more out of income than out of savings. Most colleges will expect your parents to contribute between 22 and 47 percent of their income toward your EFC.

Essentially, your family will be expected to pay some part of your college costs out of pocket, and if you have savings, you have a pot to draw from. The alternatives are to pay it out of your monthly income or to borrow it — both of which are less appealing choices than using savings. "If I were preparing to send a son or daughter off to school, I would want to have as much savings available to me as I realistically could," says Vincent Amoroso, director of the Office of Student Financial Services at Johns Hopkins University. "The reason is because, just like in other situations, having money on hand makes it easier for me to make choices that are good for myself and my child."

To be sure, there are other factors your family should consider before saving for college, such as whether they have enough money to save for retirement. But if they can put away any money for college, they should do so without hesitating. (*See Step 11 for information on tax-free college savings plans.*)

KNOW THE LINGO

EFC (Expected Family Contribution) — How much money a family is expected to pay for college.

Need — The difference between your EFC and the cost of attending a particular college you've chosen. Financial aid is designed to meet your need, not your EFC.

Unmet need — The difference (if any) between the your need and the financial aid offered by a particular college. Informally, unmet need is also called a **gap**.

Asset protection allowance — The amount of money considered reasonable to set aside for educational savings and emergencies, and is therefore not part of your EFC.

Responsibilities Within the Family

Who should pay for college? Is it entirely the parents' duty, or should the student be responsible? If both, which combination of both? There is no single right answer to questions like these. But families need to discuss the topic, and the sooner the better. Your college will expect someone in the family to make a contribution, and you and your parents should figure out who that is before the bill comes due.

"Families should discuss college costs, family budget, financial aid and financing options at the beginning of the college application process, not at the end," says Carlene Riccelli, a college adviser at Amherst Regional High School in Amherst, Mass. Try to reach decisions that are as specific as possible, so that you each know what's expected of you. Try to make the decisions fair, so that no one feels used. What portion of your summer job income should go toward college? If your family takes out loans, should they be in your name your parents' name or both? Don't forget to discuss ways of keeping costs down, such as living at home and taking community college courses.

If your family is nontraditional, the discussion should include all adults involved in your care. When considering the financial need of students with divorced parents, for example, some colleges that use the Institutional Methodology will assess the income and assets of both natural parents. It will be up to the family to decide how to pay the expected family contribution, but part of that contribution will be based on the income and assets of the parent without custody. (*See Step 8 for more about parental custody and financial aid.*)

While it's important to talk about money, your family also needs to talk about other aspects of choosing a college, such as its academic and social environment. Some of the discussion will have nothing to do with money, but others will have financial aspects: for example, going away to an expensive college versus staying home and commuting to a cheaper one. Step 3 will further explore how to think about these issues. But the important thing is to start having the discussions — financial and otherwise — as early as possible.

Crunch Some Numbers

If you want a sneak peek at what your expected family contribution will be, crunch some numbers. Part II contains worksheets and tables that you can use to calculate the EFC of a "typical" family under the Federal Methodology. Use the worksheets to add up your income, then subtract deductions and allowances. Total up your assets, too. Apply the formulas in the worksheets to calculate the contribution that is expected from you as a student. Then use the next set of worksheets and tables to calculate your parents' expected contribution. When you're finished, you will have your estimated EFC.

The figure you come up with will only be an estimate. Your actual EFC may be higher or lower, depending on the exact data you ultimately submit and the particular college's financial aid policies. But at least this exercise will give you a ballpark figure for what you can expect to pay.

Online Calculators

If you'd prefer to estimate your EFC online, there are several websites with special calculators. They include:

- **collegeboard.com** — Our Financial Aid EasyPlanner lets you "Do the Math" not only on EFC but on college costs, savings and loans.
- **College and university websites** — These sites sometimes include calculators geared to their individual financial aid policies.

Figure 5:

Sample EFC Illustration

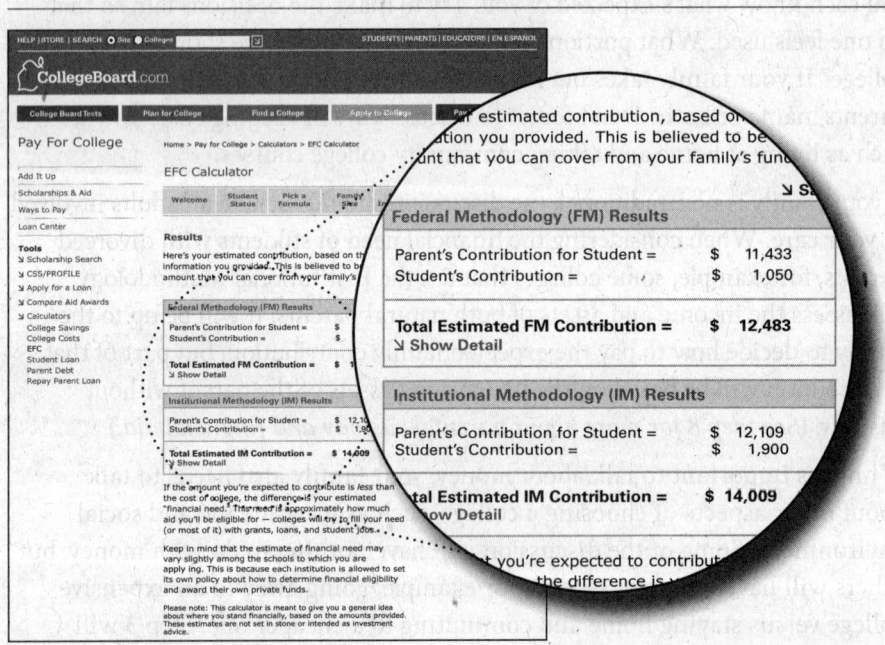

Online calculators like the one at www.collgeboard.com can help you estimate your expected family contribution.

Your Unique Situation Counts Too

Colleges expect families to contribute some money toward students' education, and the amount they expect is your EFC. But colleges are not just faceless buildings of stone, and your EFC is not fixed in cement. The financial aid officer in charge of distributing a college's financial aid is a human being, and he or she does have some room to adjust how the EFC calculations are made based on your individual circumstances.

Step 8 will go into greater detail on how to notify your college about changes in your family's financial situation, such as a lost job. And Step 10 will discuss how to appeal if you think the college hasn't taken all your circumstances into account. Generally, financial aid officers are sympathetic if you are struggling with problems such as caring for an elderly parent or a lost job. They will be less sympathetic if it seems that you've chosen your financial problems — such as buying a new motorcycle with money that could have gone to pay your college bill. Still, financial aid officers are not heartless, and they will try to help when there is genuine distress.

QUICK RECAP

The American education system expects families to bear as much responsibility for the costs of higher education as they can, but not more. Your family will have to contribute to your college costs, but will also receive help.

- Your family will be required to pay an expected family contribution, or EFC.
- The costs of the college you attend minus the financial aid you receive equals what you pay.
- College savings will not be held against you.

Step 3: Choosing Colleges, Thinking Costs

QUICK
OVERVIEW

This step shows you how to think about cost when choosing a college. You'll see why you shouldn't exclude any college from consideration just because of its price. You'll learn what your different college expenses will be, from tuition to pizza money; how costs can vary from college to college; and how to factor in the financial aid package the college is likely to give.

How to Think About College Costs

KNOW THE LINGO

Total cost of attendance — Not just tuition, but also all fees, room and board, transportation, books and supplies, and personal expenses.

Public college — A college or university that is subsidized by taxes and other public revenues and governed by a county, state or federal government agency.

Community college — A two-year public college subsidized by a local government, such as a county or city.

Out-of-state tuition — What public colleges charge students from other states; often more than double the rate for in-state residents.

Reciprocity agreement — A deal between neighboring states that allows residents to attend a public college in either state at the in-state tuition rate.

When you're thinking about where to apply for college, its "list price" should not be the main consideration. Because financial aid will probably be available to help meet your need, even a college that appears exorbitant may in fact be within reach. A college's published costs are only one part of the equation when it comes to what you'll actually pay. **Until you've applied for and received an offer of financial aid, you won't know the real cost to your family.**

Remember that financial aid works like this: Total cost of attendance *minus* your family's expected family contribution (EFC) *equals* your financial need. As long as the college meets your need, the amount you pay stays the same whatever the price of the college. "I don't think college cost really should be a factor in where students apply for admission," says Vincent Amoroso of Johns Hopkins University. "I say that because your family contribution, in theory, is the same whether you apply to a school that costs $4,000 or to a school that costs $40,000."

In practice, your expected family contribution may actually vary somewhat from college to college. As noted in Step 2, a college using the Federal Methodology to assess your ability to pay might calculate a higher or lower EFC than a college that uses the Institutional Methodology. Even two institutions using the same methodology might calculate slightly different EFCs, depending on how they have treated any special circumstances that may apply to your family. (*See Step 8 for more on special circumstances.*) But in general, the principle holds that your EFC will be constant from college to college, while your need will vary depending on the price of each college.

The main thing to consider when applying for college is whether you and that school will be a good fit. Look for the academic and social aspects that are likely to make you happy and successful there. Are you artistic? Are you mathematical? Do you love to learn for learning's sake? Do you have strong career ambitions in a particular field? Do you long to get away and see the world? Or does it matter more to stay near your family and the place where you grew up? "Students should not just look at a school because it's affordable," says Bonnie Lee Behm of Villanova University. "They should look at a school because it's the right fit for them academically, socially, spiritually and physically. Is cost an important part? Yes. It's a consideration, but only one among many." **And remember — you can find a good fit at more than one college.**

To discover what specific colleges have to offer, research them. You can find a lot of information about majors offered, the composition of the student body, academic policies, and extracurricular and athletic offerings in *The College Board College Handbook*. You can also learn more on the College Search engine on collegeboard.com, and from college guidebooks and websites. If you know people who have gone to the colleges you're considering, talk to them and get their opinions.

So, when deciding which colleges to apply to, don't focus too much on cost. But do be aware of what the costs are; cost may become a factor depending on what financial aid packages you are ultimately offered. Even though your EFC should in principle be the same at all colleges, not all schools always meet full need. And even those that do may meet it with different packages — some with more loans, others with more grants. It makes sense to know what kinds of packages a particular school is likely to give.

By using Part III of this book as a guide, and also by contacting the admissions and financial aid offices of the colleges you're considering, gather as much information as you can about the costs of the school and the type of aid they offer. The rest of Step 3 suggests the kinds of information you should be seeking from each school.

Choosing Colleges

Both you and your parents should be involved in the discussion about where to apply for college. You will share the responsibility for paying for college, so you should all have a voice. Furthermore, your parents can give you good advice about what colleges to consider based on their life experiences, their knowledge of you, and their understanding of the family finances — even if they themselves have never been to college. The deciding vote, however, should be yours. You are the one who will have to start and finish college, and you are more likely to do so successfully if you have chosen the college yourself. "Only the student knows the fit that he or she will have at a particular institution academically, socially and financially as well," says Forrest Stuart of Furman University.

When you begin choosing where to apply, don't exclude any college. Let every college be on the table, even if it seems too difficult academically or financially. Aim high. Shop around. The best colleges for you may not be the ones that occur to you first.

If a college is a good fit for you, there is probably a way to make it work financially. "Apply to those colleges that you think, okay, maybe we could afford these, but also apply above that level, because some schools may be much more manageable than you expect," says Bonnie Lee Behm of Villanova University.

Do Consider a "Financial Safety"

Even though all colleges should be on the drawing board, you should also consider applying to a financial "safety" school — one that is a good academic fit and that you feel fairly confident you can afford. Your financial safety school is one you would be happy attending and that has either low published costs or will almost certainly offer enough grant money to make attendance affordable. A public university in your state, a local community college or a private university where you are highly likely to win a merit scholarship might all be financial safeties.

A financial safety is a good idea because your top choices may not give you as much financial aid as you want. "We know students who are really strong academically, but they're not at the top of their class, and they apply to the college of their dreams," says Elizabeth Bickford, director of the Office of Student Financial Aid and Scholarships at the University of Oregon in Eugene. Despite their hopes for a full merit scholarship, such students may find that they can enroll only if they are willing to take out a large amount in unsubsidized loans — something their family may not be willing to do.

In these and other situations, a financial safety is a good backup. For example, if you accept admission to a far-off university, but find that you can't get used to it and want to come back to the financial safety school near home, it will be easier to transfer if you've already applied and been admitted. Still, Elizabeth Bickford says she encourages students to "dream large, because it's your one opportunity. When you go from high school to that first year in college, that's where most of the scholarships are — for entering freshmen. It's your opportunity to make that big step away from home."

KNOW THE LINGO

Need-blind admission — If a college has a "need-blind admission" policy, this means that it will admit a student solely on the basis of his or her academic merit or other characteristics, regardless of their ability to pay. However, it does not mean the college guarantees to meet full need. You may be admitted, but the college may be unable to offer a financial aid package equal to your need.

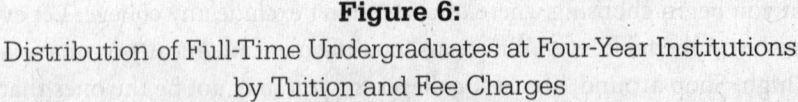

Figure 6:
Distribution of Full-Time Undergraduates at Four-Year Institutions
by Tuition and Fee Charges

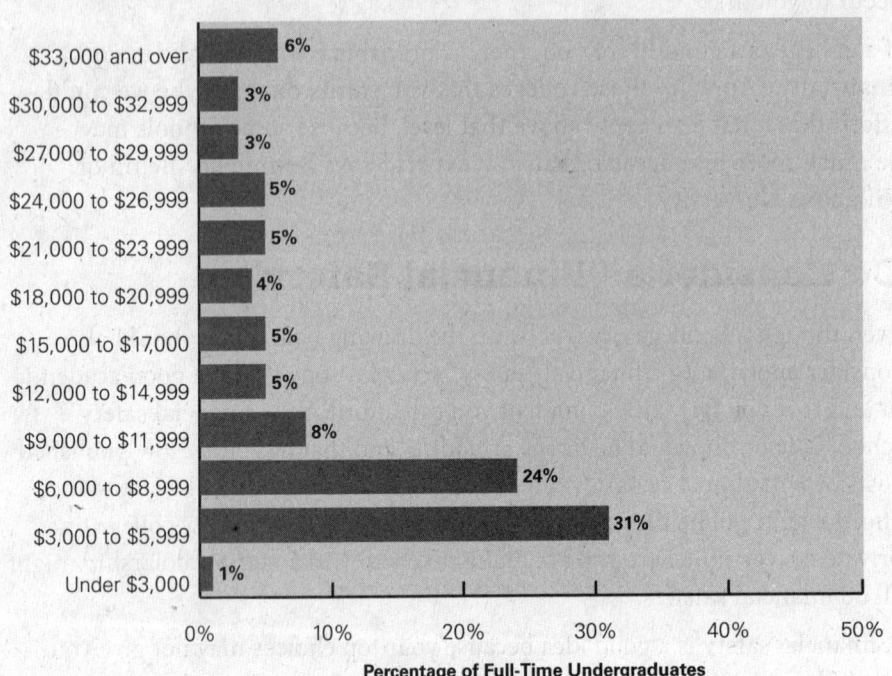

Fifty-three percent of full-time undergraduates attend colleges with published tuition and fee charges of under $9,000. After financial aid, many of those students pay an even lower "net price" for tuition.

Source: *Annual Survey of Colleges*, The College Board, New York

Components of College Costs

The price of a college education has several parts. The most obvious is tuition, the cost of taking courses. Tuition varies depending on how many courses you take, but full time students pay a flat rate for a full schedule of courses. If you attend part time, you will likely pay by credit hours, a measure of how long each class is. Most courses are three credit hours apiece, which usually translates to three one-hour classes each week. Most full-time students take an average of four or five courses per semester, for a total of 12 to 15 credit hours per semester for a full load.

Fees are another component of college costs. Fees are usually billed to all students as funding for the college's general expenses, such as the library or student activities. But there may be additional special fees for students enrolled in certain classes or activities. A chemistry student may pay lab fees, for example.

Tuition and fees are just one part of what you'll pay for college, and often not even half. Another large component is room and board. "Room" is the cost of housing you, and "board" is the cost of food. You may live in a dorm on campus, or off campus — in an apartment or a house with other students or at home with your parents. You may be on a meal plan where all your meals are prepared for you for one price, or you may fend for yourself, buying groceries and cooking meals. Either way, these basic living expenses are your room and board.

Taken together, tuition, fees, room and board are the largest chunk of college costs. On average, at four-year public colleges across the nation, these elements together make up 78 percent of what students pay for college — tuition and fees 36 percent, room and board 42 percent. Yet there is still another 22 percent of costs to be accounted for. These include:

- Books and supplies — class expenses that are not covered by tuition and will vary depending on the courses you take.

- Transportation expenses — for on-campus students, this is the cost of trips home during holidays; for commuters, this is the cost of either mass transit or a car. Car costs include parking, gas, insurance and maintenance.

- Computer equipment costs — if required by the college. Some colleges may insist that you buy a certain model of computer, or bring your own computer but have special hardware and software installed to make it work on the campus network.

- Personal expenses — everything from snacks outside the meal plan to newspaper subscriptions to haircuts and toothpaste to membership fees for student groups.

How Costs Can Vary

Each college has different price tags for each of the cost components. For example, on average, books and supplies cost $900 for the first year at the University of Nebraska, but $1,500 at the Kansas City Art Institute. Table 1 on page 28 shows national averages for cost components.

To get specifics for a particular college that you're considering, check its website and look for the school's published estimate of what the average student spends on the different expense categories. The college will use these averages as part of the calculation of your "total cost of attendance," which will partly determine how much aid you're awarded. You can also consult Part III of this book for a school-by-school summary of costs.

However, remember that these average costs are only averages. You are an individual, and you may pay more or less than average, depending on your individual circumstances. For example, if you attend college in California but your family lives in New York, you will pay more for traveling to and from home than if your family is also in California.

Textbook and supply costs can also vary widely depending on your major. If you are an architecture or drafting student, you might have to buy an expensive computer-aided design program that your English major friends won't need. Science students might need to buy a statistical-modeling software package; studio artists a graphic-design suite. At least software like this only has to be bought once and is then used to do work for several classes; furthermore, educational discounts may be available for such purchases. In some programs, students might have to buy supplies that frequently get used up and must be replenished, such as brushes and paints for art students.

Rooming costs will vary a little between different dorm complexes on campus — for example, newer dorms may cost more, and a single room is always more expensive than one shared with a roommate. There will also be differences between various off-campus rooming locations.

Finally, your personal expenses may be higher or lower than average depending on lifestyle factors — but they will almost always be higher than you think. As James Schembari wrote in the *New York Times*, there is always a need for "pizza money" — money to buy pizza, go on a road trip, or hang out at the student union. Books, supplies, travel and everyday expenses "can add $3,000 or more a year, depending on parents' generosity and where their child goes to college," wrote Mr. Schembari.

Table 1:
Average Estimated Undergraduate Budgets, 2009-10

SECTOR	TUITION AND FEES	BOOKS AND SUPPLIES	ROOM AND BOARD	TRANSPOR-TATION	OTHER EXPENSES	TOTAL EXPENSES*
Public Two-Year						
Resident	$2,544	$1,098	$7,202	$1,079	$1,974	$13,897
Commuter	$2,544	$1,098	—	$1,445	$1,996	$7,083
Public Four-Year						
Resident	$7,020	$1,122	$8,193	$1,079	$1,974	$19,388
Commuter	$7,020	$1,122	—	$1,445	$1,996	$11,583
Out-of-State	$18,548	$1,122	$8,193	$1,079	$1,974	$30,916
Private Four-Year						
Resident	$26,273	$1,116	$9,363	$849	$1,427	$39,028
Commuter	$26,273	$1,116	—	$1,445	$1,996	$30,830

Note: Estimates of individual budget items are based on reporting by institutional financial aid offices.
Source: *Annual Survey of Colleges*, The College Board, New York, N.Y.

Ways to Reduce Costs

There are a few time-tested ways of saving money on some of the major cost components of college. To save money on tuition and fees, many students have attended public colleges and community colleges. To save money on room and board, many have commuted rather than roomed on campus. Here are the pros and cons for these money-saving techniques.

Public vs. Private, In-State vs. Out-of-State

Attending a public college in your own state is an excellent way to save money on tuition and fees. Public colleges are subsidized by state taxes, so their tuition and fees for state residents are usually much less than at private colleges — 74 percent less, on average. Depending on the school, the quality of education may be as good or even better than what you would get at a private college.

On the other hand, the true cost picture is more complicated than it looks. Even though private colleges charge more for tuition and fees, most of them also give more scholarships and grants than public colleges do, which helps to even out the costs. "There's an adage that the more expensive the school, the more money they give away," says Mike Scott of Texas Christian University, a private institution.

Cost isn't everything. If a particular private school has some valuable characteristic that you want — smaller classes, professors with whom you want to study — it may be worth the extra tuition money. But cost is a factor to consider. If a certain state school can give you all that you want from college, why not go there and save some money?

If you would like to study at a public college or university in another state, be aware that most public schools charge higher tuition to students from out of state than they do to in-state students. Public colleges currently charge an average of $7,020 in tuition and fees to a state resident, but $18,548 to an out-of-state student. The in- and out-of-state rates for specific public colleges and universities are listed in Part III.

PAYING IN-STATE RATES IN ANOTHER STATE

It is sometimes possible to get the in-state tuition rate, or at least a lowered tuition rate, even if you are an out-of-state student. For example, some state universities have "reciprocity agreements" with neighboring states. South Dakota residents pay tuition rates comparable to state residents at the University of Minnesota and vice versa. There are also discipline-based "consortiums" of public colleges that let you get the in-state tuition rate at another state's public college if your desired major is not available at any public college in your own state.

Your school counselor and state board of education website can give you more information about programs for paying in-state rates in another state.

Community Colleges

Community colleges are another great way of saving money on tuition and fees. A community college is a two-year school subsidized by a state, county or city. Its cost for tuition and fees is usually much lower than that of a four-year institution — 64 percent lower, on average, than a public four-year college. Community colleges often charge tuition in three tiers — in district, in state and out of state — with the lowest price for those who live in the local district. Though most community colleges do not offer a four-year bachelor's degree (though the number that do are on the rise), they do provide courses whose credits can be transferred toward a bachelor's degree at another college. Because those courses cost much less, this can be a way to save money in your first two years of college — money you can use to help pay for the last two years. Four out of 10 college-bound high school graduates start their college education this way.

There are other reasons to attend a community college besides saving money. If you aren't sure whether you want to go to a four-year college, a community college will give you a sense of what the college experience is like. If you don't know what kind of program you want to pursue — science, art, business or something else — you can explore different subject areas at a community college before committing to a program. And if you need to be able to work, perhaps to support a family, you can work out a more flexible schedule at a community college, where many students work full time and attend classes at night and on weekends.

A community college is also a golden opportunity for students who didn't do well enough in high school to win admission to the college of their choice. Community colleges are open to everyone, and some have agreements with four-year colleges that guarantee admission in the third year for students who have maintained good grades. This is the case in California, according to Mary San Agustin of Palomar College, a community college. If students, she says, "have their heart set in going, let's say, to Stanford or U.C. Berkeley, we have an excellent articulation program that allows them to take the two-year required courses and get guaranteed admissions in their junior year at those schools that they prefer to go to." In this way, **a community college can open the door to a four-year college for you.**

Of course, there are advantages to entering a four-year college as a freshman rather than two years later as a transfer from a community college. Socially and academically, you may enjoy a fuller college experience. "It's all the things that you can't quite name," says Elizabeth Bickford of the University of Oregon. "There is something that you do lose in that transition as an 18- or 19-year-old." But those factors have to be balanced against financial realities, as Ms. Bickford found when she was making her own college decisions. "I'm a community college transfer to a four-year myself. So is my husband. We wouldn't have financially been able to make it if we hadn't done it that way. I think it's a good way to make it if all the support isn't there."

Living at Home

A good way to save money on room and board is to commute. Instead of paying for campus housing and meals — an average cost of $9,363 a year for private colleges — you continue to live at home. There your housing and meal costs remain whatever they have been, and you commute to campus daily by train, bus, car or other means. This will probably be more inconvenient than living on campus, where you would only have to walk a few steps from your dorm to the classroom. But you will almost certainly save a lot of money.

However, commuting has hidden costs. You will have transportation expenses that you wouldn't have if you lived on campus. If you can use mass transit, these costs will probably be low enough to make economic sense. But if you have to buy a car and pay for gas and insurance, your transportation costs might end up being close to the costs of on-campus room and board. And if you're thinking of relying on family and friends for rides to and from campus, remember that their schedules may not overlap with yours. Your own schedule may change day to day and semester to semester, depending on your classes and activities. You probably will need your own car if mass transit isn't available.

Also, don't forget that you cost money at home, too. You're still eating and using utilities at home, and you'll inevitably add pick-up meals on campus to those costs. Financial aid packages usually offer help in paying for room and board as well as tuition and fees, so your actual cost for living on campus would probably not be as high as the published price.

We're not saying that commuting isn't a bargain — it usually is. (There are other good reasons to live at home, too.) But if you are thinking of commuting just to save money, don't commit to it until you weigh all the costs and assess the financial aid offers from any "live away" colleges to which you may apply.

Living Off-Campus

If you don't want to commute but still want to save money on room and board, you might want to consider living off-campus. By residing near campus in an apartment that you share with classmates, you may be able to live more cheaply than you could in the dorms. **But be sure to check the college's policies** — many do not allow freshmen to live off campus if they're under 21 and not living with their parents.

How to Factor in Financial Aid

Every college publishes an average price for the various cost components, but that published price is probably not the price you will end up paying. Your financial aid package will reduce your actual costs. Yet financial aid packages vary from college to college as much as costs do. In thinking about where you will apply, you need to find out some financial aid basics about each college on your short list. How great a percentage of need does it usually meet? How much aid does it award in grants and how much in loans? Does the college offer any merit scholarships or other forms of aid not based on need?

Part III of this book, "Financial Aid College by College," gives you these financial aid basics, along with a number of other essential facts. These include:

- the school's Web address
- what type of school it is, such as public or private
- how many students are enrolled
- how selective the school is
- basic costs, including tuition, fees, room and board
- financial aid application procedures, including deadlines and required forms
- contact information for the financial aid office

In addition, the "Financial Aid Picture" section of each college's profile tells you how much aid is being distributed to how many students and in what form. This information is useful, but note that it only shows averages. Since few families are "average," the numbers in the financial aid profile shouldn't be considered a guarantee of what you'll get or how much you'll have to pay. For example, in-state students at public colleges usually borrow much less than the average debt per student listed in the profiles, while out-of-state students usually borrow more. You can, however, use the profiles to compare colleges: This college meets a greater percentage of need than most; this college awards a relatively large portion of aid in grants.

Check with the Financial Aid Office Before You Apply

Before you apply for financial aid, check with the financial aid offices of the colleges to which you're planning to apply for admission — by simply visiting their website, or by talking to them on the phone or in person. Confirm which forms you need to complete and the deadlines. Better to get these details right before you get started than to find out after the fact that you filed too late or didn't file the proper form.

Bear in mind also that each college has its own financial aid policies, such as how outside scholarships are treated and whether or not aid awards can be appealed. When you contact the office, whether long distance or in a campus visit, find out as much as you can about these policies, along with facts about costs and the financial aid process. If possible, schedule an interview with a member of the financial aid staff. They'll give you a lot of information, but don't expect them to offer you aid until they've seen your forms.

KEEP IN MIND

The **college profiles in Part III** of this book give the "financial aid picture" for each college, based on averages. Use these profiles to **compare colleges only**; the aid you would get at any college is based on your own individual circumstances, so the amount might be higher or lower than the average for that college.

Questions to Ask Colleges

Here are some questions worth asking the aid office:

✔ What are your average costs for the first year for:
- tuition and fees
- room and board
- books and supplies
- transportation
- other personal expenses

✔ What is the range of costs for:
- rooms (single, double)
- board (different meal plans)
- tuition rates (flat rate, per credit, etc.)

✔ By how much will total costs increase each year?

✔ How much have tuition and fees and room and board increased over the past three to five years?

✔ Does financial need have an impact on admission decisions?

✔ Does the school offer both need-based and merit-based financial aid?

✔ Do I need to file a separate application for merit-based scholarships?

✔ If the financial aid package isn't enough, under what conditions, if any, will the aid office reconsider the offer?

✔ How will the aid package change from year to year?

✔ What will happen if my family's financial situation changes?

✔ What are the terms and conditions of your aid programs? For example, what are the academic requirements or other conditions for renewing financial aid from year to year?

✔ When can we expect to receive bills from the college? Is there an option to spread the yearly payment over equal monthly installments?

QUICK RECAP

When deciding where to apply to college, cost is a factor, but not the most important factor. Don't exclude any college from consideration because of its "sticker price" — what you will actually pay might be much less. Remember:

- Each school has different costs and financial aid policies.
- When choosing colleges to apply to, consider a "financial safety."
- Your costs might vary from the published averages.
- You might be able to save money at a public college or community college or by commuting — but there are pros and cons to all those strategies.
- Research the colleges you're considering and contact their financial aid offices early.

Step 4: Get Ready for the Forms

QUICK OVERVIEW

Depending on where you'll apply, you may need to file up to three kinds of forms to get financial aid: the FAFSA, the CSS/Financial Aid PROFILE and forms for individual colleges or states. Step 4 gets you ready for those forms. There are two main things to remember. First, file before the deadlines. The early bird — or at least the timely bird — gets the worm. Second, don't be intimidated. The forms are easier to fill out than they look.

Forms You'll Fill Out

Applying for financial aid is basically a matter of filling out a few financial aid forms on time. The forms may look complicated and be hard to face, but they are simpler than they look, and millions of people fill them out every year. We will guide you through them so they make sense.

The three steps that follow this one walk you through the forms you may need to complete: the FAFSA (Step 5), the PROFILE (Step 6) and whatever forms your individual colleges may require (Step 7). This step will help you create a timeline of which colleges require which forms when.

You may not need to fill out all the forms we describe. Most colleges require only one form, the FAFSA. If you do need to fill out more than one form, take heart. Most of the other forms ask for information similar to what the FAFSA requests. Repeating that information may be annoying, but it isn't hard.

FAFSA: The Federal Form

This is the big one. The FAFSA, or Free Application for Federal Student Aid, must be completed by everyone who wants federal government aid. Just about every college financial aid program requires it, even if they also require other forms. Most schools and states use nothing but the FAFSA to determine eligibility for aid.

There is no charge for completing the FAFSA, which you should fill out online if possible at www.fafsa.ed.gov.

KEEP IN MIND

Even though this book presents the financial aid forms in order of FAFSA, PROFILE and institutional forms, **you may need to submit these forms in a different order** depending on the financial aid deadlines of your colleges. In some cases, you may have to file PROFILE a few weeks before FAFSA, or the institutional form on the same day as FAFSA.

FILING THE FAFSA

You cannot file the FAFSA before Jan. 1 of the year for which you're seeking aid. For example, if you will start college in September 2011, you cannot file the FAFSA before Jan. 1, 2011. If you want a head start, visit the FAFSA website earlier so you can familiarize yourself with the form and start working on your application as soon after Jan. 1 as possible.

Once it's Jan. 1, however, you should aim to file your FAFSA as soon as possible. Don't be fooled by the federal filing deadline (June 30). **Most college deadlines for financial aid are in February or March**, and they need your FAFSA information by then. The window of time between Jan. 1 and the financial aid deadlines, some of which fall as early as Feb. 1, isn't big. So, come January, the earlier that you start working on the FAFSA, the better. **Don't worry about filing your tax return first**: If you don't have all your tax documents together before you need to file your FAFSA, you can estimate your tax information using your end-of-year pay stubs and last year's income tax returns (see "Get Your Stuff Together" on page 41). You can correct your FAFSA with actual tax figures later.

The most important thing is to leave time for your FAFSA to be processed after it's filed. If you're filing on paper, leave at least four weeks before your earliest college or state deadline. If you're filing online, you can wait until only a week before the earliest deadline.

The FAFSA may seem complicated, but it's a lot easier than it looks. We'll walk you through it in Step 5.

On the FAFSA, you'll provide financial information about yourself and also about your parents, if you're a dependent student. The information will be based on your income tax returns plus your own reporting of your financial assets, such as bank accounts and savings bonds. The federal government will use that data to calculate your Expected Family Contribution, or EFC.

Soon after you've submitted the FAFSA, you'll receive the Student Aid Report (SAR). This lists the information you reported on your FAFSA and tells you what your EFC is. This report is important. Check it over as soon as possible and, if necessary, update it with your family's latest tax return information. **Don't sit on the SAR: keep the process moving quickly**.

WHERE TO GET A PAPER FAFSA

If you don't have Internet access or just prefer to work on paper, you can request the paper FAFSA by calling 800-433-3243. After you submit the paper FAFSA you'll have to allow at least four weeks for mailing and processing before your earliest deadline.

If you use the paper FAFSA, you can only list four colleges to receive your information. You can add up to six more later, but you'll have to wait until your FAFSA is processed and you've received your Student Aid Report (SAR).

GOOD TO KNOW

If you're filing both the PROFILE and the FAFSA, it might help to **do the PROFILE first**. One feature of the PROFILE website is that once you've completed your application, it will create a worksheet you can use to fill out the FAFSA.

KNOW THE LINGO

FAFSA (Free Application for Federal Student Aid) — The form that must be completed by everyone applying for federal government aid.

PROFILE (CSS/Financial Aid PROFILE) — A Web-based form offered by the College Board and used by some colleges and scholarship programs to award their own financial aid.

PIN (Personal Identification Number) — A number that serves as your electronic signature for filing the FAFSA on the Web.

SAR (Student Aid Report) — A report based on the information you provided in your FAFSA that reports your federally calculated EFC. The SAR is sent to every student who files a FAFSA.

Priority date — The date by which applications for financial aid must be received in order to be offered the best possible package. After the priority date, applicants are considered on a first-come, first-served basis, and are offered grants, scholarships and work-study only if the college still has money remaining.

PROFILE

In addition to the FAFSA, some colleges and scholarship programs also require that you fill out the CSS/Financial Aid PROFILE to award their own nonfederal funds. They believe this form gives a more complete picture of students' financial circumstances, allowing them to allocate money as fairly as possible. The PROFILE service is administered by the College Board, though the College Board itself does not give out any need-based scholarships.

A few colleges require PROFILE only if you're applying for early decision or early action. Others require it for all applicants. If your college requires it and you're applying early, it is often the first form to fill out — ahead of even FAFSA. To find out if your colleges require PROFILE, look them up in Part III of this book or refer to the college's websites.

PROFILE is online only; there are no paper forms. You can register for PROFILE at www.collegeboard.com beginning Oct. 1 of the year before you intend to start college. Once you register, you can either complete your application then and there or return to it at a later time. It's best if you submit it at least one week before your earliest college financial aid deadline. You can use the same application for multiple colleges, and you'll receive an online acknowledgment confirming the schools to which you're sending the information.

There is a $25 fee to send your PROFILE to one college, plus a fee of $16 for each additional institution. However, depending on the information you submit, you may qualify for a fee waiver. Automatically awarded to low-income, first-time applicants, the fee waiver covers the costs of the PROFILE registration and up to six school reports.

College Forms

Some colleges — most of them private — require you to complete their own financial aid form as well as the FAFSA. Usually the forms are not complicated, and filling them out is not a big deal. Mike Scott of Texas Christian University says, "We have a very simple online form, where we just ask a couple of extra questions." Some of the questions are about projected enrollment: "Are they going to be full time or part time? When do they think they're going to graduate?" Others are aimed at matching students to outside sources of aid.

Find out if your colleges require you to file their own form, and if they do, file them on time.

State Forms

Most states offer need-based financial aid to their residents, and most colleges will require you to apply for it. Ask your school counselor for information on what form you need to complete to apply for state scholarship or grant programs. In many states, the FAFSA alone is enough to establish eligibility for state aid — but some states require their own form. If your state does, find out the deadline and add it to your master timeline for applying for aid. (*A table showing the deadlines for state aid, and which forms each state requires, appears on page 72 of this book.*)

Know the Deadlines!

Deadlines count. If you're on time, the colleges to which you've applied will have more money to give you; if you're late, they will have less money — or even none. **Late means less money, so be on time!** That means knowing and keeping track of all the financial aid deadlines you have to meet.

This can be tricky, because the deadlines are not all the same. Many schools and states may require you to fill out their own financial aid forms, and those forms may have deadlines that differ from those of the FAFSA or PROFILE. And **keep in mind that a college's due date for financial aid applications is typically different from its due date for admissions applications.**

Many colleges have no firm deadline or closing date for applying for financial aid; rather, they have a "priority" date. Often falling in February or March, the priority date is the date by which the school needs to receive your application to make its most attractive aid offer. After that date, funds may be limited or used up, and you may not get as much aid as you need. "I urge my students to apply for aid by the priority date," says Lauri Benton, a counselor at Columbia High School in Decatur, Ga. "They are more likely to get the aid they need early in the process, when the colleges have ample money to award."

Some colleges accept financial aid applications on a "rolling" basis. This means that applications are reviewed as they come in on a first-come, first-reviewed basis. Applicants are notified — that is, sent a financial aid award letter — a few weeks after they submit their forms. Most colleges that have a priority date will review late applications on a rolling basis. If you're applying to a rolling-applications college that doesn't have any set deadlines or priority dates, you're best off applying by mid-February or early March, when they will probably still have enough money available to meet your need.

Part III of this book, "Financial Aid College by College," lists deadlines and priority dates for colleges, along with their required forms. But it is worth confirming this information with the schools to which you're applying — at least by visiting their websites in November or December. Remember: Time is money. To get the most aid available, apply by the priority date. (*See also "Do You Get More Money If You Apply Early?" on page 40.*)

Creating a Timeline for Aid Applications

There are a lot of dates to remember as you apply for financial aid, but they don't have to be overwhelming. You can stay on top of them by making a timeline.

When you've found out the priority dates of the colleges and scholarship programs to which you're applying, as well as those of your state financial aid agency, list them in chronological order. Make that list part of a month-by-month timeline. Don't worry about the past; start the timeline with whatever month you're in now. The chart on the opposite page is an example of the sort of timeline you might construct. (*A blank copy of this chart for you to fill in appears in Part II on page 123.*)

SAMPLE WORKSHEET 1:
Meet Your Application Deadlines

		COLLEGE 1:	COLLEGE 2:	COLLEGE 3:
	College Name	*1st Choice Univ.*	*Private Univ.*	*Financial Safety*
FORMS REQUIRED	FAFSA	*Yes*	*Yes*	*Yes*
	PROFILE	*For ED (by 11/1)*	*Yes*	*No*
	State form	*Yes*	*No*	*Yes*
	Institutional form	*No*	*Laptop loaner*	*Yes*
	Tax returns	*Verification only*	*Verification only*	*Yes*
	Other			
SCHOOL CODES	Federal code	*999999*	*888888*	*777777*
	CSS code	*999Z*	*999X*	
PRIORITY DATE		*3/1 (FAFSA, State Form)*	*2/1*	*3/15*
CLOSING DATE		*None*	*2/15*	*None*
AFTER APPLYING	Need to send letter?			
	Documentation required?			
COMPARE AWARDS	Notification date	*12/15*	*4/1*	*2 weeks after applying*
	Reply-by date	*Immediately (if accepted ED)*	*5/1*	*4 weeks after notification*

For a blank version of this worksheet that you can photocopy for your own use, see page 123.

Throughout the period that you're applying for aid, keep your timeline where you can see it, check off what you've done, and remind yourself of what to do next. This will put the deadlines in your control. (*See the inside front cover of this book for a calendar of important dates and reminders.*)

Do You Get More Money If You Apply Early?

No. If you apply for financial aid Tuesday and another student applies Wednesday, you don't get more money than that student — so long as both of you apply by the deadline (or the priority date). However, when it comes to the college's own funds, and certain "campus-based" federal student aid programs (such as federal work-study), aid is distributed first-come, first-served once that date has passed. If you apply for aid after the college's deadline or priority date, the pool of funds may be used up. So always apply on time.

WHAT ABOUT EARLY DECISION?

Many schools allow students to apply for admission under early-decision or early-action programs. Whether early acceptance to a school affects the student's financial aid package varies from school to school. Depending on the college, the student accepted early may get more financial aid, less, or the same.

If you are considering early-decision programs, ask each school's financial aid officer: How is financial aid affected if I apply early decision? You may not know exactly what aid you'll get until after you accept. Don't panic: The rules of early decision allow you to turn down the college's acceptance offer if it doesn't offer you enough aid. Just don't put all your eggs into one basket — be sure to apply to a "financial safety school" as well.

The Benefits of Web-Based Applications

The FAFSA can be filled out and submitted online at www.fafsa.ed.gov. A limited number of paper FAFSAs are available for students who do not have access to a computer (see page 36 for information) but it is better to file online. Doing so cuts processing time by several weeks — essential if you're running late. It can also reduce delays due to errors because the site edits your information before you submit it, allowing you to correct it before submitting. Also, once you have submitted the form online, you will instantly get your EFC back from the website, which reduces some of the anxiety in the process. The FAFSA website gives lots of help in completing the form.

If you do file online, save and print out a hard copy of the confirmation you'll receive after submitting your application. If you file a paper form, make a photocopy for your records.

KEEP IN MIND

When you fill out the FAFSA, both you and one of your parents need a **Personal Identification Number**. This is important: the PIN will allow you to sign your FAFSA electronically, which will cut down your processing time. **You and one of your parents must each request a PIN** at **www.pin.ed.gov**. You should register for your PINs **before you fill out the FAFSA**. A good time to ask for your PINs is November of your senior year. **Remember your PIN and write it down in a safe place:** If you forget it, the government can't "remind" you of it later on.

PROFILE is only available online. If you don't have a computer at home, find out if one of your parents can use a computer at work, or use a computer at your school's guidance office or the library. After you register for the PROFILE, you can print a customized preapplication worksheet to help you gather the information you'll need, then complete the application online.

Figure 7:
FAFSA PIN Site

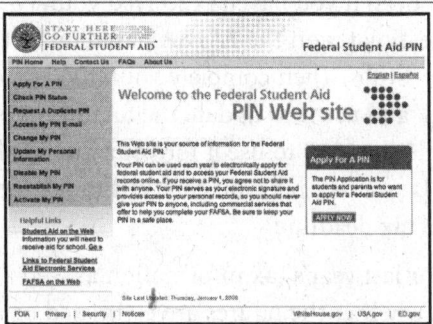

Get Your Stuff Together

For maximum efficiency, gather all the records you need to complete the forms before you sit down to work on them. That will save you a lot of time getting up, hunting around and forgetting where you left off. For both you and your parents, you'll probably need tax returns and related documents (such as W-2 forms) for the year that just ended, as well as end-of-year pay stubs, bank statements and other financial records. If you're filling out the PROFILE, you will also need tax documents from the previous year. If your parents own their home, you will need current value and mortgage information to fill out the PROFILE.

The FAFSA and PROFILE preapplication worksheets are basically a way to help you gather your information before filling out the actual application. Use them that way. Add a list of all the records you need to assemble. It should be comprehensive and indicate which records are for all forms and which are for PROFILE only.

Establish Eligibility

To be eligible for federal financial aid, among other requirements, you'll have to:

- be a U.S. citizen or eligible noncitizen
- have a valid Social Security number
- not have been convicted of sale or possession of drugs
- if male and at least 18 years old, be registered with the Selective Service (in most cases)

Most of these requirements will not require extra work for most students. But two of them may. If you don't have a Social Security number, get one as soon as possible (go to www.ssa.gov to learn how), and certainly before you file your

FAFSA. And if you are male, you can register for the Selective Service through the FAFSA application if you haven't already. If you do have a drug conviction, you may still be able to establish eligibility by completing a treatment program.

Tax Forms and Other Records

Income tax returns are due on April 15, but most colleges want your financial aid forms much sooner. **Don't wait until your taxes are done to file your financial aid forms.** Even if you haven't received your W-2s yet, you can still file the FAFSA. Use estimates on the FAFSA based on last year's return and your current-year pay stubs. Then complete your 1040 tax return as soon as possible afterward, and use it to update the SAR if necessary. You don't necessarily have to file the 1040 to use it for your financial aid forms; you just need to complete it. If you owe tax, you can wait to file the tax return until closer to the April 15 tax deadline.

PROFILE asks you for last year's tax information as well as for this year's. For this year, it asks you whether the figures are estimated or final. It also asks for estimated income for next year, which you can base on this year's information.

You'll have to file some forms to get financial aid, but they aren't as difficult as they might look. The main forms are FAFSA and PROFILE, plus whatever other forms your colleges or state may require.

- File on time — filing late can cost you money.

- File your FAFSA online. Get a PIN for yourself and for one of your parents early — and don't lose them.

- Make a timeline to keep track of your deadlines, including college priority dates.

- As early as possible, check with your colleges to be sure you know what forms they each require.

- Gather together the records you need to fill out the forms.

- If you don't have one already, get a Social Security number.

QUICK RECAP

Step 5: Fill Out the FAFSA

The FAFSA may look intimidating, but it's actually pretty easy to fill out. The questions mainly concern your income and assets and those of your parents, but they also touch on other matters, such as your citizenship status and the schools to which you want the FAFSA to be sent. We'll walk you through it, and give you tips about how to avoid delays. Above all: File on time!

General Advice

Nobody likes to fill out forms. And no one enjoys having to share information about family finances. But the potential result — money to help you pay for college — is well worth it. And you will see in this step that the FAFSA is really pretty simple. While the form for 2010-11 has seven sections, only one requires financial information, and another is, essentially, "sign here." The online FAFSA also has "skip logic" so you don't have to see questions that don't pertain to you.

Again, remember that you don't have to do the steps in this book in exactly the order presented. If the colleges require you to submit the PROFILE before the FAFSA, then do the PROFILE first, even though we present the FAFSA first. In fact, one nice thing about the PROFILE is that, after you've submitted it, you'll receive a worksheet that you can use to fill out the FAFSA, making this step much easier.

Help is available by phone and online if you have questions about FAFSA (see the "Good to Know" sidebar on page 45). And don't be afraid to call the financial aid offices of the colleges to which you're applying. If you're confused about this or any other aspect of the financial aid process, these offices can help. "People look at the FAFSA and they find it a bit overwhelming initially," says Vincent Amoroso of Johns Hopkins University. "They come to us seeking guidance and reassurance on how to get through the application process. We show them that it's not as complicated as it looks."

EXPERT ADVICE

"Our job is to get students through this maze. You'd call a mechanic if your car is broken. Well, why not call us if you have a question about financial aid applications? That's our job — to get you through the process."

— *Bonnie Lee Behm, director of financial assistance, Villanova University*

Apply on Time

You can't file your FAFSA before Jan. 1 of the year you're applying for aid. Most college deadlines for financial aid are in March, and some fall as early as February, so the window for filing is narrow. You have to leave time for your FAFSA to be processed. Be sure to file your online form at least one week before the earliest deadline.

Don't wait until the April 15 tax deadline to file your FAFSA. Most priority dates will be long over by then. If your earliest deadline doesn't fall until March, you can wait for W-2s, 1099s and other official tax documents to arrive from employers and banks and then complete draft income tax returns. You don't have to file those draft returns with the IRS, but you can use the information from them on your FAFSA. The advantage of using draft tax returns this way is that you probably won't have to correct your FAFSA after you've submitted it, and it will be easier to answer the questions on the form that refer directly to lines on the 1040.

If your earliest deadline falls in February, however, you should have a backup plan in case W-2s don't arrive in time. The best thing to do in this case is to use end-of-year pay stubs, quarterly bank statements and similar records to estimate your and your parents' income. You can also use 1040 forms for the previous year as a frame of reference, but don't just plug in the information from last year's returns into the FAFSA — you really do need to estimate the current information, not duplicate old information. (Also, be warned that the numbers assigned to each line of the 1040 tend to change whenever the IRS adds new credits or deductions, so the references on the FAFSA you're filling out may not match old 1040s.)

No matter how you derive the numbers, remember this above all: Get the FAFSA in on time.

Read Instructions Carefully; Fill Out the Form Accurately

With the FAFSA as with all financial aid forms, accuracy is vital. Read the directions. Understand the terms that are being used. Many terms, such as "date of birth," are straightforward, but others, such as "investments," require you to read the instructions carefully so you know what they mean in this context. Even the term "parent," as discussed below, has a special meaning on the FAFSA.

Be as complete and accurate as you can about your financial circumstances. If you submit incorrect data, you might create delays that could endanger your aid. By avoiding errors, you will increase your chances of getting all the aid for which you are eligible.

The top right corner.

Keep Track of Your Pin and Password

You can submit a paper FAFSA, but it's easier and faster to submit your FAFSA online at www.fafsa.ed.gov. Filing the FAFSA on the Web can reduce processing time by a couple of weeks. It also reduces delays due to errors: The site edits your information before you submit it, so if you made errors or left out information, you can correct it before submitting it.

You don't have to complete the FAFSA on the Web in one sitting. At the start, you'll supply a password that will allow you to leave the application before completing it and to return later, so long as you come back within 45 days.

Get PINs ahead of time for both yourself and for one of your parents so you can sign the form electronically. The PINs can be ordered at www.pin.ed.gov. You should do this in advance because it will take a week to get the PINs — a delay you may not be able to afford later in the process. Write down the PIN in a safe place; if you forget it, that could make you miss your deadline.

Figure 8:
FAFSA on the Web

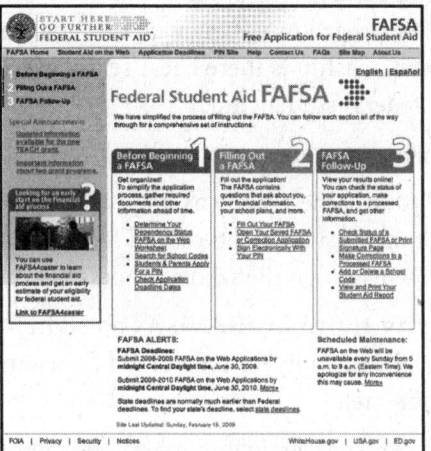

Let's Walk Through It

The FAFSA has six sections that ask questions, each with a common theme. The exact order or wording of these questions may change from year to year (last year's preapplication worksheet is in Part II), but the substance remains more or less the same. And the purpose never changes: to provide information about yourself and your family that colleges will use to figure out how much federal student aid you qualify for.

There are a few general tips to keep in mind while filling out the FAFSA:

- The word "you" always means you, the student.
- The word "college" means a college, university, community college or any other school beyond high school.

- The phrase "net worth" means the current value of an asset (such as a business) minus the amount of debt owed on it.

- Questions about income are for the previous year; questions about assets ask for their value as of the day you fill out the form.

- When entering dollar figures, round to the nearest dollar and don't use commas or decimal points.

- If you have special financial circumstances that you need to explain, you can't do it on the FAFSA. Instead, write to your colleges directly. (*See Step 8 of this book, "Make Your Special Circumstances Known."*)

Here is a step-by-step walk–through of the key questions on the FAFSA. Since the online form is interactive, it will automatically skip over some questions or sections depending on how you answer. For example, if you say that you're not married, you won't be asked questions about your spouse. For that reason, you might not see all the questions described here.

FAFSA Step One: About Yourself

These questions gather basic information used to identify you and determine which federal and state programs you may qualify for. For example, the question about your citizenship is there because only U.S. citizens (or eligible noncitizens) can get federal student aid.

Here's the main information this section will ask for:

Your name. Enter your name exactly as it appears on your Social Security card. If the two don't match, you will be asked for more documentation through the mail, slowing down the whole process.

Your Social Security number (SSN). As noted in Step 4 of this book, you need to have an SSN to apply for federal aid (you can't even open the online FAFSA without one).

Your date of birth. Enter as straight numbers with zeros, for example, May 3, 1980, would be entered as 05031980.

Whether you're male or female. If you are male and you haven't registered with the Selective Service yet, you'll have the option of registering now via the FAFSA. To get federal aid, male students 18 years or older must be registered with the Selective Service, the agency responsible for providing drafted men to the armed forces in an emergency.

Where you live. Use a permanent home mailing address here, not a school or office address.

The state in which you legally reside. You will be asked this question if you have lived in your state for less than five years. Your answer will determine whether you're eligible for scholarships and grants from your state. In some cases, your state of legal residence might be different from the state where you're actually living at the time you fill out the FAFSA. This might be the case if you've recently moved or one of your parents is in the military.

Your permanent telephone number. Use a permanent home or cell phone number, not a school or office number.

Your e-mail address. This is optional, but if you provide it, the government can send your Student Aid Report (SAR) by e-mail instead of snail mail, so it will reach you faster.

Whether you are a citizen or an eligible noncitizen. You are a citizen if you were born in this country or became a citizen through the naturalization process. An eligible noncitizen is someone such as a U.S. permanent resident holding a green card (Permanent Resident Card), or someone who has refugee status who is allowed to live permanently in the United States. It is not someone visiting on a student visa. If you're an eligible noncitizen, you'll have to fill in your Alien Registration Number. If you're neither a citizen nor an eligible noncitizen, you can't get federal aid, but you may be eligible for state or college aid — so you should still fill out the FAFSA, unless you don't have a Social Security number. In that case, call your colleges.

Whether you've ever been convicted of possessing or selling illegal drugs. Say "yes" only if the offense occurred while you were receiving federal student aid (unlikely if this is your first FAFSA, in which case you won't even see this question online), it's still on your record, and you were tried as an adult.

Your high school completion status next year. Before you can get federal financial aid, you must have completed high school or its equivalent. Select "High school diploma" if you will have graduated from a public or private high school before you enter college; "General Educational Development (GED) if you have the GED diploma or expect to pass the GED exam; or "Home schooled" if you will have satisfied you state's requirements for successfully completing home schooling at the high school level. If you must select "None of the above," contact the financial aid office at the colleges you want to attend.

What year of college you'll be in next year. Your answer determines the aid programs for which you qualify. For example, the SMART grant is only available to students in their junior or senior year of college.

What degree will you be working on in the next school year. Some aid programs are not available for graduate study, a second bachelor's degree or nondegree study. If you are undecided about what type of degree you will be pursuing (for example, if you're applying to both two-year and four-year colleges), check "undecided," but be sure to follow up with each college you're applying to after you've submitted the FAFSA.

The highest level of education completed by your father and mother. This won't affect your federal aid, but some states use this information to award scholarships to students who are the first in their family to attend college.

FAFSA Step Two: School Selection

This is where you indicate which colleges should receive your FAFSA information. You list the colleges, and the government will send the processed information to them for free.

You can list up to 10 colleges online; but if you are using the paper FAFSA, you can only list four. In either case you can add additional schools later, when you get your Student Aid Report (SAR). In choosing which colleges to list first, *pick the ones whose financial aid deadlines come first.*

Identify each college by its federal school code. You can find the federal school code in Part III of this book (see Figure 9 below). You can also search for it on the FAFSA Web page.

For each college, you have to say whether you plan to live on campus, off campus or with your parents. Your answer will affect the housing costs that the school will estimate for you, and therefore your financial need. If you haven't made a decision yet, assume you'll live on campus.

You don't need to request that your information be sent to a state agency; the government will automatically send your processed information to the agency of your state government that administers financial aid programs for state residents, whether scholarships, grants or loans. Do be aware, however, that some states require an additional financial aid form, as discussed in Step 7 of this book.

Figure 9:
Finding a College's Federal Code

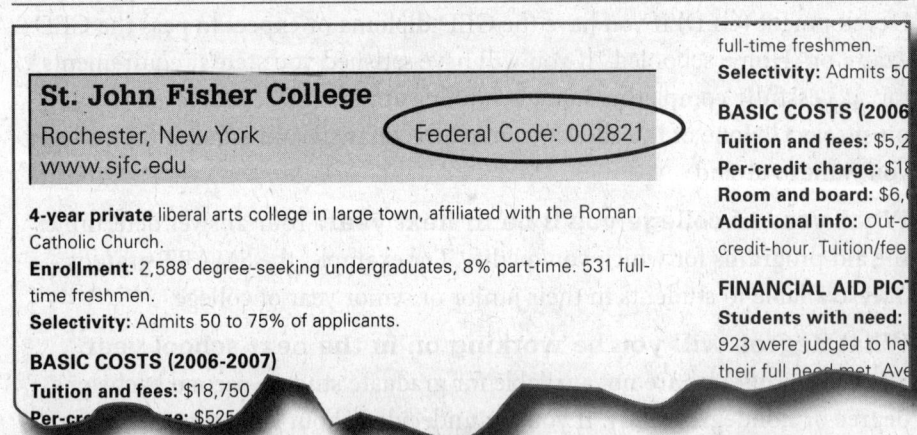

The Federal Code for each college in Part III of this book can be found in its college description.

Your enrollment status next school year. Most aid programs are not available to students who will be attending less than half-time (that is, taking fewer than six credits per semester). Some are only available for full-time students. If you're not sure how many credits you will take, check "undecided," but be sure to follow up with each college you're applying to after you've submitted the FAFSA.

Whether you're interested in loans, work-study or the TEACH program. It's best to preserve your options and check "yes" to loans and work-study, and the TEACH program too if you are even remotely interested. (The TEACH program provides grants to students who want to become high school teachers, and are willing to commit to teaching in a low-income school for four years after college.) It doesn't matter if you aren't sure. Saying you are interested in all three won't affect your chances for other types of aid, and you can always change your mind later.

FAFSA Step Three: Are You Independent?

The questions in this step determine whether or not you're an independent student. To be considered independent for the purpose of federal student aid eligibility, it doesn't matter if you feel independent, have a job or even live on your own. It also has nothing to do with whether your parents claim you as a dependent on their tax return. But if you can truthfully answer "yes" to at least one of the questions in this step, you will be considered independent.

The things that would classify you as independent are:

- You turn age 24 or older in the year you start college.

- You'll be enrolled in a graduate degree program in the year for which you're seeking aid.

- You're married.

- You have children who get more than half of their support from you.

- You have dependents other than your children or spouse who live with you and get more than half their support from you.

- You're an orphan, or you've been a ward/dependent of the court.

- You're currently serving in, or are a veteran of, the active-duty U.S. armed forces. (If you served only as a reservist and were never activated for reasons other than training, answer "no.")

If you are independent, then you can skip the section about your parents' income and assets. But there are certain cases where a college financial aid office will want to know about your parents' finances even if you are an independent. If you do meet one of the criteria on the list above, it's a good idea to ask the colleges to which you're applying whether they'll consider you fully independent for the purpose of awarding their own institutional funds. If one or more of them won't, you should fill out the parent section. The online application will ask you whether you want to fill it out or skip it.

Are you unable to obtain information about your parents? Even if it is determined that you are a dependent, you might be able to show special circumstances that will allow you to submit your FAFSA without parental information. Follow the instructions on the FAFSA carefully, and then follow up immediately with the financial aid office at each college you want to attend.

FAFSA Step Four: Information About Your Parents

If you're a dependent student, you have to answer these questions even if you don't live with your parents. When you're ready to submit the application, you will also need one of your parents to sign it, either on the paper form or by using a PIN on the electronic version.

Modern family life can make the definition of "parent" complicated. But the FAFSA definitions are fairly clear:

- If both your parents are living and married to each other, answer the questions about both of them.

- If only one of your parents is living, answer the questions about him or her.

- If your widowed parent remarried, answer the questions about your stepparent too.

- If you were raised by a single parent, answer the questions about him or her.

- If your parents are divorced or separated, answer the questions about the parent you lived with the most during the past 12 months.

- If that parent remarried, answer the questions about your stepparent, too.

- Don't provide information about grandparents, legal guardians or foster parents. FAFSA doesn't consider them your parents unless they have legally adopted you.

This step is the most work, but it's not hard. Here's a run-down of the important questions:

Their Social Security numbers: Unlike you, your parents are not required to have Social Security numbers in order for you to file the FAFSA (but in that case you have to enter zeroes). But if they do have Social Security numbers, they must provide them.

Their names: Again, if they have social security cards, their names must exactly match.

The number of people in your parents' household: These include you and your parents. The number who will be in college during the next year is also asked for: that also includes you (but not your parents). These questions affect how much money your parents will be expected to contribute to your education.

FAFSA Step Five: Parents' Financial Information

OK, this is usually the most complicated part of the FAFSA. But this section has been greatly simplified. For the most part, it asks for the same information that your parents must provide on their federal income tax form, and even points out exactly where they can find that information.

EXPERT ADVICE

"**Some people overthink the FAFSA** questions. They'll get to what we would see as straightforward questions: 'How many are in your household?' And then 'How many in your household go to college?' Well, some families will list every person who's ever lived in the household and then every member who has ever attended college. And actually **what we want to know** is, how many are living in your household now, and how many of them are in college now."

— Elizabeth Bickford, director, Office of Student Financial Aid and Scholarships, University of Oregon, Eugene

Whether they've completed a tax return for the past year. This means the return that is due the coming April 15.

Whether they're eligible to file the 1040A or 1040EZ tax form. It's to your advantage if they can answer yes, they're eligible to file this form. If they would normally file the 1040A but filed the full 1040 only to take advantage of an education tax benefit relating to a child already in college, they can still check this box.

If either of your parents is a "dislocated worker." Answer "yes" if one (or both) of your parents has been laid off or has lost their business due to the economic downturn, and is still unemployed. "Dislocated worker" also includes a stay-at-home mom or dad who no longer receives support from a spouse and can't find a job. If you answer "yes" to this question, you should also contact the financial aid office at each college you are applying to. *(See Step 8, "Make Your Special Circumstances Known.")*

Their income tax information: These questions are easy to answer if they've already completed a draft of their tax return. But if they haven't, ask them to give estimates, using W-2s or pay stubs, bank statements, and last year's return. **Don't miss any college deadlines or priority dates because your parents haven't done their taxes yet.** After you submit your FAFSA, you'll be able to correct the estimated figures on your SAR.

What their untaxed income and benefits are. These include items like earned income credits, welfare benefits, Social Security benefits, child support and other money that didn't get taxed. It also includes any contributions your parents made for the last tax year to deductible Individual Retirement Accounts (IRAs) or employer-sponsored retirement plans such as 401(k)s or 403(b)s. Add this up on worksheets and fill in the totals on the FAFSA. If you're filling out the worksheets online, the information will appear on the confirmation page you'll see after submitting, which you should print out and keep on file in case a financial aid administrator asks about them later.

What their assets are. These include cash, savings and the value of investments, such as stocks and bonds. The amounts to put down are "as of" the day you fill out the FAFSA. Often that is just a best guess, using the most recent bank statements. (Keep in mind that the amount of aid you are entitled to is based much more on family income than on assets.) They do *not* include the home where your parents primarily live (a summer cottage would be included), a family-owned business of less than 100 employees, or a family farm that they live on and operate. However, if your parents own more than one home — a summer cottage, for example, or an investment property — they also should report their equity in that home on the "investments" line. If they own a farm that they don't live on, they also should report the value of that farm as a business. Another thing your parents do not need to include here is any money they have in tax-advantaged retirement accounts, such as IRAs, 401(k)s, 403(b)s and the like.

GOOD TO KNOW

The FAFSA asks both you and your parents to report the amount of income tax you will have to pay on last year's income. The **amount they want here is only the federal income tax amount** — don't include Social Security, Medicare, or any of the taxes that are reported in the "other taxes" section of Form 1040. If you or one of your parents is self-employed or has to self-report tip income from a restaurant job, you should keep this in mind.

FAFSA Step Six: Your Own Income and Assets

These questions ask about *your* income and assets — the student's. Income is how much money you made last year; assets are what you own and the savings you have. If you are married, they also want to know about your spouse's income and assets.

These are the main things that this section asks for:

Whether you've completed a tax return for the past year. This means the return that is due the coming April 15, not the one you filed a year ago. If you have filed a return or plan to file one, they will ask what form you're using, for example, the 1040 or 1040A. If you're not going to file any tax return, they will still ask how much you (and, if you have one, your spouse) earned from working.

Whether you're eligible to file the 1040A or 1040EZ tax form. The instructions on the FAFSA explain who can file these forms. Most students can. If you can, say yes.

What income and tax information you and your spouse will report on your tax returns. Again, these questions are easy to answer if you've already completed a draft of your tax return. But if you haven't completed your tax return yet, you should estimate what the information on the completed return will be and update the information later. Use pay stubs and, if you have one, your prior-year tax return to make the income estimates. Just don't put off filing the FAFSA because you haven't done your taxes yet. **You're not required to file your tax return before completing the FAFSA.**

The number of people in your household: This question refers to the number of people in *your* household, if you have one — not your parents'.

What your untaxed income and benefits are. Once again, these include items like earned income credits, welfare benefits, Social Security benefits, child support and other money that came to you without being taxed. You will be asked about these in a series of questions on screen. (If you are filling out the paper FAFSA, you should use the worksheets that come with the form to add them all up, then fill in the totals on your FAFSA. Don't submit the worksheets, but keep copies of them on file. A financial aid office may want those details later.)

What your assets are. This question is meant to provide a snapshot of your assets, the money or property you currently own. Using current banking statements and investment records, say how much cash and savings you have, as well the total value of any stocks, other investments or investment properties that you might own. If you're still in high school, chances are that you only have a small savings or checking account, which you should report on the line asking for "cash, savings accounts and checking accounts." You may also have some government savings bonds, certificates of deposit (CDs) or a few shares of stock; those should be reported on the line asking about "investments."

GOOD TO KNOW

Most students are eligible to file IRS Form 1040EZ or 1040A as their tax return. Some parents can, too. (The rules determining whether you can are explained in the FAFSA instructions.) **If both you and your parents are eligible to file the 1040A or 1040EZ**, you may qualify for a "simplified needs analysis," wherein only your income (not your assets) will be assessed when calculating your expected family contribution.

Don't include any college savings accounts in this step unless you are independent (you answered "yes" to any question in FAFSA Step Three) and they are owned by you in your own name.

FAFSA Step Seven: Review Your Answers, Then Sign and Submit

This is easy, but it's still an important step. Take the time to carefully review all your answers for accuracy and spelling — even your name. Be sure to print out your FAFSA if you're filling it out online.

Preparer's information. If you or your family paid a fee to someone to fill out your FAFSA, or to advise you on how to fill it out, that person must provide his or her Social Security number or Employment Identification Number (EIN), and must also sign and date the form. This requirement does not apply to school counselors, financial aid administrators, friends or mentors who helped but did not charge a fee.

Pay heed to this warning from the FAFSA website: "Be wary of organizations that charge a fee to submit your application, or to find you money for school. Some are legitimate and some are scams. Generally, **any help that you pay for can be received free** from your school or Federal Student Aid."

Terms to read before signing. You'll see a list of terms you must agree to by signing. There is nothing onerous here, but there is a scary-sounding penalty for giving "false or misleading information." This does *not* mean honest mistakes or estimates that turn out to be way off; they're talking about intentional fraud.

If your parents provided financial information, one of them also needs to sign. Use your PINs to sign electronically — don't use the "print signature page and mail" option. It just wastes time.

Be sure to keep clicking on "next" until you get to the confirmation page! Your FAFSA is not truly submitted until then.

FAFSA Step Eight: Confirmation

You're done! Be sure to print the confirmation page, and save it to your hard drive as well. If you don't have a printer, write down the confirmation number, date and time. This is your proof that your FAFSA was received.

If you file using the paper form, make a photocopy of it before mailing it, and keep that photocopy together with the worksheets you filled out and all the records you used.

KEEP IN MIND

You have to leave time for your FAFSA to be processed. If you're filing on paper, allow at least four weeks before your earliest college or state deadline. If you're filing online, leave at least one week before the earliest deadline.

Check Your Student Aid Report!

After you submit your FAFSA, you'll receive your Student Aid Report, or SAR. How long it will take for you to receive it, and in what form, will depend on how you filed the FAFSA. If you filed FAFSA on the Web and signed it with your PIN, you should recieve it immediately, or at most within one to three days. If you filed a paper FAFSA and did not provide an e-mail address, you'll receive a paper SAR within about four weeks.

In whatever form the SAR reaches you, check it over carefully. It will include a summary detailing the information you supplied on the FAFSA. Make sure this information is correct. If not, then you must make corrections. It's easy to do — just go back to www.fafsa.ed.gov and follow the link under "FAFSA Follow Up."

Make corrections only if the data on the SAR doesn't accurately represent your family's financial situation at the time the FAFSA was originally filed. For example, if you estimated the previous year's income but have since filed a tax return with exact figures, substitute those figures now. Or if you mistyped a number, or if the federal data-entry clerk misread your handwriting, correct that. But **don't make changes that reflect changes to your income or assets since you filed the FAFSA**. If important changes of that sort have happened — such as a lost job — inform your colleges individually rather than through the FAFSA. (*See Step 8, "Make Your Special Circumstances Known."*)

At the top of the SAR's front page, you should also see an estimate of your EFC: the amount of money your family is expected to contribute toward college costs. The only reason you won't see it is if your SAR has been rejected because you didn't provide required signatures, valid Social Security numbers or enough data to calculate the EFC. If that happens to you, submit the necessary corrections and you'll get your EFC estimate. **The actual EFC calculated by a given college may be different than what you'll see here**, especially if that college uses a different formula, or if its financial aid office has adjusted your EFC based on special circumstances that you brought to the college's attention.

The colleges you requested to receive your FAFSA information will automatically get your SAR. At the corrections stage, you'll have an opportunity to add more colleges to receive your FAFSA information. You can also give a school permission to add itself to the list. Just provide the college with the Data Release Number (DRN) at the bottom-left corner of the first page of the SAR. The school will use your DRN to access your application record.

The SAR gives you an estimate of how much money your family is expected to pay for college, but not how much financial aid you'll receive. You'll find that out when your individual colleges send you their award letters. Even so, by filing your FAFSA, you've taken a big step toward getting those letters.

KEEP IN MIND

Eligibility for **federal student aid does not automatically continue** from one year to the next. You have to reapply every year that you're in college. Do that by filling out a **Renewal FAFSA**. This is a partially preformatted version of the FAFSA that you can use so long as you applied for federal aid the previous year.

If the expected family contribution (EFC) indicated on the SAR looks too high for your family to afford, you should talk to your parents and discuss other financing options with them. (*See Step 11, "Consider Your Out-of-Pocket Options."*) It could also mean that you need to explain some special financial circumstances to the colleges to which you've applied (see Step 8).

QUICK RECAP

The FAFSA is easier than it looks. Most of it is about your income and assets, and that of your parents. It's organized in seven steps. Remember:

- File on time. Submit your FAFSA as soon as possible, beginning Jan. 1 of the year you'll start college.
- It helps to have your tax return finished first, but don't let that delay you. You can estimate your figures and correct them later.
- Read instructions.
- Be accurate.
- Reapply every year.

Step 6: Fill Out the PROFILE (If Required)

QUICK OVERVIEW

Whether you have to fill out the CSS/Financial Aid PROFILE depends on the colleges to which you're applying. If you do, you'll find it mainly asks for "more of the same" — information about your family's income, expenses and assets — rather than something completely new. The online form is customized to your situation, so you won't be presented with too many questions that don't apply to you. However, the application does take time to fill out, so leave yourself plenty of time to submit it before your colleges' deadlines.

General Advice

Step 6 is to fill out the CSS/Financial Aid PROFILE® — but only if you need to. If the schools to which you're applying don't require this financial aid form, you don't have to complete it. Find out if they require it by checking Part III of this book or the colleges' websites.

The PROFILE is administered by the College Board, a not-for-profit association of schools and colleges (and the publisher of this book). It is available online only: You can't file on paper. The upside of this is that PROFILE is available 24 hours a day, seven days a week. Furthermore, its system of online edits alerts you to missing or incorrect information before you submit the application, eliminating a potential source of delays. Firewall protection and data encryption protect the information you submit about your family and their finances. The downside is that if you don't have a computer with Internet access at home, you will have to use one at your school, a library or a parent's workplace.

The PROFILE doesn't replace the FAFSA: You still need to complete that, too, because that's the form required for federal student aid, which any college will expect you to seek before they give away their own institutional funds. The schools that require the PROFILE do so because they believe it gives a more complete account of your financial situation to guide them in awarding their own funds. The College Board provides the colleges with your PROFILE information, and the colleges use it to calculate your expected family contribution and your need.

Since it's designed to give a more complete picture of your finances, it is not surprising that the PROFILE is longer than the FAFSA. It's the same general concept, but you'll need to gather more records to answer all the questions, and it will take more time to fill out.

Figure 10:
CSS/Financial Aid PROFILE Online

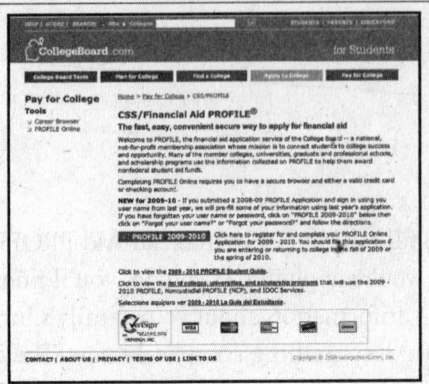

EXPERT ADVICE

"Chapel Hill is no different than most schools that require the PROFILE and use it when they're investing a lot of their own institutional dollars into need-based programs. We use it because **the PROFILE gives us an added, more in-depth look** at a family's financial strength. Our ultimate goal is to give the right dollars to the right students at the right time, and this PROFILE application helps us do that."

— Vincent Amoroso, director, Office of Student Financial Services, Johns Hopkins University

Register and File Early

Because the PROFILE form is more involved, and because colleges may ask for additional information even after the form is filed, register well before your colleges' deadlines and leave yourself lots of time to fill out the application. The College Board usually processes your PROFILE information overnight, but delays can happen — especially in late January and early February. Also, don't assume it can all be completed in one session; you may need to gather additional information to complete the form (especially if a college asks for additional information in section SQ). Fortunately, you can go back and forth to your application online, rather than having to finish it in one sitting.

It's best to submit the PROFILE at least one week before your earliest financial aid priority date. Remember, colleges use PROFILE information to determine who gets their limited grant dollars. If you file late, you will have to make do with whatever funds, if any, are left over.

You may need to submit the PROFILE ahead of the FAFSA, depending on the deadlines your colleges set. In fact, some of the colleges that require the PROFILE will ask you to submit it before you submit your FAFSA. This is especially likely if you're applying early decision or early action for admission to the college. If a college requires the PROFILE before Jan. 1, you can submit a PROFILE with estimated income figures for this year based on your year-to-date pay stubs and your previous year's tax return, then send corrections to the college later if necessary.

Even if college deadlines don't require the PROFILE first, it may save you time to complete it before the FAFSA. The PROFILE collects all the information asked for by the FAFSA, and when you complete the application, PROFILE will generate a worksheet that you can print out and use to complete the FAFSA.

Preparing for the PROFILE

You can get ready to complete the PROFILE with the Pre-Application Worksheet, available from the PROFILE site at collegeboard.com. (The worksheet is customized for you after you have registered.) You can also download and print out the PROFILE Registration Guide and Application Instructions from the same site.

The Pre-Application Worksheet can save you a lot of time by helping you gather all your necessary family financial information before starting the application. Filling it out on paper can also speed your way if you have to file the application on a computer where your log-in time is limited, such as at school or a library.

Whether you're filling out the Pre-Application Worksheet or the PROFILE itself, you'll need to gather more records to fill out the PROFILE than you will for the FAFSA. For example, in addition to asking about your parents' income for the year before you plan to enter college, the PROFILE asks about their income the year before that, as well as their projected income in the year to come. There are also questions about your projected summer and school-year earnings during your first year in college. The purpose of this is to give financial aid officers a better idea of whether last year's income was typical or unusually low or high. But it also means that you must collect more documents, such as tax returns for the prior year, and you'll need to estimate future income.

Documents You'll Need Before You Fill Out Your PROFILE

It's a good idea to gather the necessary records before you start and have them handy as you work on the PROFILE. You'll need records for both yourself and your parents.

- ✔ Federal income tax return for the year before you start college, if completed, or pay stubs and other income-related records for estimates
- ✔ Federal income tax return for the year before that
- ✔ W-2 forms and other records of money earned the year before you start college
- ✔ Records of untaxed income for those two years
- ✔ Current bank statements and mortgage information
- ✔ Records of stocks, bonds, trusts and other investments

As with the FAFSA, it's easiest if you've already completed your tax return for the most recent tax year before you start filling out the PROFILE. But don't let that hold you up. Estimate your tax return information if you haven't completed your return by the time you need to file the PROFILE. (There are tools on the PROFILE site to help you and your parents estimate this information.) You can correct PROFILE information, if necessary, directly with the colleges after filing your return.

How to Register/File on the Web

Just like registering ahead of time for a FAFSA PIN, **it's best to register for the PROFILE well before the first college's deadline**. Since the PROFILE is entirely Web based, you do this online at www.collegeboard.com. You'll need to create a collegeboard.com account (with a username and password) before you can file; setting up the account is free. (If you previously registered online for the SAT, you already have this account: It's the same one you used then.) If you don't have Internet access at home, ask your school counselor or librarian if you can use one of the school's computers.

It's smart to register for PROFILE as soon as you're sure about where you'll be applying for aid, but in any case at least one week before the earliest financial aid filing date you need to meet. Registrations are accepted beginning Oct. 1 of the year before you intend to start college. Once you register, you can either complete your application then and there or return to it at a later time. Your PROFILE application will be customized to your circumstances based on the information you give when you register.

Most families will have to pay a fee of $25 to have their PROFILE sent to one college, plus $16 for each additional college. The fee can be paid with most major credit cards, with some bank debit cards or by an electronic withdrawal from your checking account. Low-income families applying for the first time may qualify for a fee waiver (see sidebar).

Registration will involve providing some preliminary information such as your date of birth; mailing address; the year in school for which you're seeking aid; whether you are a U.S. citizen, a veteran or an orphan; whether you have dependents or have separated or divorced parents; and whether your parents own a home, or all or part of a business or farm. The questions usually won't involve looking up documents; just answer them straightforwardly. Some of them (such as the questions about date of birth and being a veteran) are intended to clarify whether you're a dependent or an independent student.

GOOD TO KNOW

If your family's income and assets are very low, and you are applying for financial aid for the first time, **you may be eligible for a fee waiver** covering registration costs and up to six school reports. Whether you qualify will be determined based on the information that you provide in the PROFILE form itself. **You will automatically get the fee waiver if you qualify** — you don't have to apply for it separately.

Figure 11:

Finding a College's CSS code

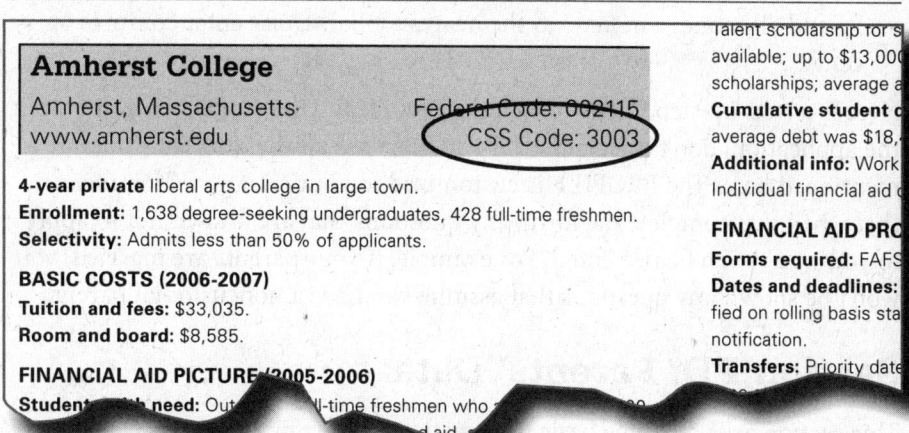

The College Scholarship Service (CSS) Code for each college in Part III of this book can be found in its college description.

During registration you will also be asked a few very basic questions about your family's finances; these determine whether you will be asked certain questions that usually don't apply to low-income families. For example, if your parents rent their house, they won't be asked about home equity in the Parents' Assets section.

You will also have to select the colleges or scholarship programs to which you would like to have your PROFILE report sent. Colleges and programs can be selected on collegeboard.com by name, code or state. You can add more colleges or programs to this list after you register, or even after filing your application. (See "After Submitting Your PROFILE" on page 67.)

Let's Walk Through It

Your PROFILE application may contain up to 18 sections, depending on your family's situation. The application includes questions about you and your finances and questions about your parents and their finances. There is a place for you to explain in writing any special financial circumstances (section ES) and a place for any additional questions that may be required by one or more of the schools to which you're applying (section SQ). In addition, if your parents are divorced or separated, your noncustodial parent might need to complete an online Noncustodial PROFILE.

To help you fill out the PROFILE, there are instructions online that you can follow, along with other avenues for help (see sidebar on page 59). A few general points to keep in mind:

- If a financial question (such as one about income or assets) doesn't apply to you, enter a zero (0).

- If a nonfinancial question (such as a year or a name) doesn't apply to you, leave it blank.

- Round all money amounts to the nearest dollar. Don't enter commas or cents.

Here is a step-by-step walk through the PROFILE. However, when you fill out the application, don't be surprised if you don't see all the questions that are mentioned here. The PROFILE is customized to your situation. That means that when you complete the form, any questions that are known not to apply to you won't even be presented. For example, if your parents are married, you won't be shown any questions that assume you have a noncustodial parent.

Section PD: Parents' Data

This section asks for some basic information from your parents. The term "parents" as PROFILE understands it might need some defining. It basically means your custodial parents, the people with whom you live. If both your parents are living, married to each other and have custody of you, answer the questions about both of them. But if that isn't the case, follow these rules:

- If your birth or adoptive parents are divorced, separated or were never married, then you only need to provide information about the parent with whom you live. If you lived with both equally in the past 12 months, answer the questions about the parent who provided most of your financial support.

- If you have a widowed or single parent or a legal guardian, answer the questions only about that person.

- If your parent (as defined above) has married or remarried, include information about your stepparent too.

Your parents should use this section to provide information about themselves, including name, date of birth, employment status, and whether they themselves are in college or graduate school. Some of these questions have to do with clarifying financial strength — for example, the question about what kind of retirement plans your parents have. Some are just matters of housekeeping, such as their preferred daytime telephone number in case they need to be contacted.

Section PH: Parents' Household Information

Here your parents give basic information about their household, such as how many members are in their household and how many of them will be in college. The more dependents your parents have, and the more college educations they have to pay for, the less they will be expected to contribute to your own college education.

Section PI: Parents' Income and Benefits for the Previous Year

In this section, your parents report their income and benefits for the year before you intend to start college. Just as with the section about your income, this is important in establishing the resources they have available to pay for college.

If your parents have a completed tax return, filling in this section is mostly a matter of copying from the right lines. If they haven't filed a return but will do so later, they'll need to estimate the amounts. If they don't plan to file a return, they still have to report income. Again they have to list untaxed income and benefits, such as Social Security benefits or child support.

Section PP: Parents' Income and Benefits for the Year Before Last

Here your parents are asked to give information about income and benefits not for the year before you intend to start college, but the year before that year. Together with sections PI and PF, this is meant to give the PROFILE colleges a long-term view of your family's finances in order to clarify whether or not last year was typical. This section is fairly easy to fill out: for most of the questions — e.g., adjusted gross income, income taxes and itemized deductions — your family has only to look up their tax return for that year. You also have to calculate any untaxed income and benefits, using a worksheet that's provided.

Section PF: Parents' Expected Income and Benefits for This Year

Here your parents have to estimate how much they expect to receive in income and benefits during the year in which you start college. Again, the idea is to establish as clear a picture as possible about your family's finances in the long term, and to show whether the year before you started college was typical or not. Your parents will have to estimate work income, other taxable income, and untaxed income and benefits. In Section ES, explain any unusual increases or decreases in income and benefits (10 percent or more) from last year.

Section PA: Parents' Assets

This section asks about your parents' assets because these are resources that can help them finance college. There are questions about cash and savings and checking accounts (with their value as of the day you fill out the form). If they own their home, there are questions to determine home equity, the difference between the current market value of their home and the outstanding mortgage debt.

There are also questions about the current market value of any other assets they own, including investments and other real estate. They also need to include educational savings accounts, such as 529 prepaid tuition or college savings plans or Coverdell savings accounts that they've opened for you or your siblings.

Sections BA and FA: Business Assets and Farm Assets

These sections will only appear if your parents indicated ownership in a business or farm. There will be questions about value, debt, number of employees, tax form filed and if you live on the farm.

Section PE: Parents' Expenses

This section asks about certain special expenses your parents might have. These are not just any expenses, such as grocery bills or vacation airfare, but specific costs that might legitimately affect their ability to pay for college. Included here are child support payments, certain educational costs, and medical and dental expenses not covered by insurance.

Section NP: Information About a Noncustodial Parent

If your parents are divorced or separated, this section asks for information about the parent who doesn't have custody of you. But it should be filled out by your custodial parent. If for any reason you can't get sufficient information about the noncustodial parent, explain why in Section ES. Many colleges want this information because they believe it is the responsibility of both your biological or adoptive parents to pay for your college costs, even if they no longer live together, and even if the parent who does have custody of you has remarried. That's why, after you've filled out this section and submitted your PROFILE, they may request that your noncustodial parent fill out a supplemental form, the Noncustodial PROFILE. (See "After Submitting Your PROFILE" on page 67.) The section you're filling out here is not that supplemental form; your noncustodial parent will fill out that form if it's required.

Section SD: Student's Data

This is the beginning of the part of PROFILE that focuses on you, the student applying for aid. In Section SD, you provide some basic information about yourself. Much like on the FAFSA, you'll be asked to name your current legal state of residence, which may not be the same as the state you're actually living in now (see page 46).

Section SI: Student's Income and Benefits for the Previous Year

This section asks about your income and benefits in the year before you intend to start college.

If you have a completed tax return for that year, this section is mostly a matter of copying the amounts from the correct lines, such as the adjusted gross income and income tax paid. If you haven't filed a return but plan to do so later, you'll have to fill in estimates. If you don't plan to file a return but you did make some money last year, you'll have to report it. Untaxed income also goes in this section. A worksheet is available for you to tally it up.

Section SR: Student's Expected Summer/ School-Year Resources for the Coming School Year

Here you're asked to state your expected resources for this coming summer and this coming school year. You're also asked about scholarships you expect to get from sources other than the colleges to which you're applying and how much money your parents think they'll be able to pay for your college expenses.

This may seem like a strange series of questions, especially if you don't know yet where you'll be going to college next year, or where (even if) you'll be working. But colleges that use the PROFILE want to have as clear a picture as possible of your future resources, not just your past ones. For example, if you currently have an after-school job but will leave that job when you graduate, the financial aid offices need to know that the income from that job won't be available to you anymore once you've started college.

Do the best you can to estimate these figures. If you're not sure how to answer in your particular case, check the PROFILE help online or contact the financial aid office at the college to which you're applying.

Section SA: Student's Assets

This section asks about your assets — the money or property you, the student, currently own. These too affect your ability to pay for college. You need to list any cash you have and any checking or savings accounts in your name. Give their value as of the day you're filling out the application. You should also include any investments, such as certificates of deposit, savings bonds, stocks or real estate that you own. If you have any Individual Retirement Accounts (IRAs) or other tax-advantaged retirement accounts, you should also list them here.

If you're an independent student, then any money you have in 529 prepaid tuition or college savings plans or Coverdell savings accounts should be included here. If you're a dependent, those will be considered your parents' assets, and the information about them should go in Section PA.

This section will also ask you to answer questions about any trust accounts your parents or other relatives may have established for you. A trust account is money that is held for you by somebody else until you reach a certain age, at which point it becomes yours. Colleges want to know about this because if you have a trust, that money will eventually reach your hands, lowering your ultimate financial need. If you have any trust accounts, list their value here and answer the questions about them. But don't include money in Section 529 plans; those aren't the same as trusts.

Section SE: Student's Expenses for the Previous Year

You'll only see these questions if you're an independent student. If you are, you'll be asked about any child support you or your spouse paid to a former spouse and any medical and dental expenses you had last year that weren't covered by insurance. Most colleges will consider these expenses in determining your financial need.

Section FM: Dependent Family Member Listing

This section asks questions about other dependent members of your household. If you're an independent student, the household in question here is the one you described in Section SD; if you're a dependent, it's your parents' household as described in Section PD.

The questions in Section FM ask for more information about these household members: their names, how they're related to you, their ages, and to what extent you or your parents are required to pay for their school or college education last year and next year. The reason for these questions is that if household members other than you are enrolled in college, and your family is paying heavily to fund those educations, the colleges may take this into account when they determine the expected family contribution (EFC) to your own education. If there are younger children in the family, the colleges will assume that a certain portion of the household's income and assets need to be saved for their college educations, which will also affect your EFC.

Section ES: Explanations/ Special Circumstances

This is the one free-form part of the PROFILE, where you write rather than fill in boxes. This section gives you a chance to explain anything unusual in your application or any special circumstances that affect your family's ability to pay for college. You can mention, for example, reasons for unusually high medical or dental expenses, steep rises or falls in income from year to year, or loss of employment. You should also give information about any outside scholarships you've been awarded. This allows the PROFILE colleges to better understand your financial picture.

In addition to telling the colleges about anything you think it's important that they know about, you should also use this section to expand on your answers to certain questions in previous sections, per the instructions that you'll find on the PROFILE website. For example, if there are more than six dependent members of your household, you won't be able to list them all in section FM. The instructions will tell you to list the additional members here.

You're limited to 27 lines of information in this section. If you need more space, send the information on paper directly to your colleges, including your name and Social Security number on all correspondence. (**See Step 8 for tips on how to let your college know about your special circumstances.**)

Section SQ: Supplemental Information

Section SQ may not be included in your application. You will only see it if one or more of the colleges to which you're applying requires more information. In that case, you'll see additional questions here. Your answers to these questions will be used only by the colleges that ask for them. Some of the questions colleges ask here are used to determine your eligibility for purely need-based financial aid; others are used to determine if you're eligible for scholarships that have non-need-based criteria.

Here are some examples of the types of questions you might see:

- What is the year, make and model of the family's primary car?

- Do you or either of your parents receive free food or housing as a job benefit?

- What is your family's religious denomination? (This information will be used to determine scholarship eligibility.)

- In what field of study do you plan to major?

After Submitting Your PROFILE

After you complete your PROFILE, you'll receive an online PROFILE acknowledgment that confirms the colleges to which you're sending the information and gives you the opportunity to correct any data you submitted. You should print the acknowledgment, which includes the list of colleges and the data you entered on the form. Once you submit your PROFILE, you can't revise your information online for the colleges you selected. Use the printed acknowledgment to make changes, if necessary, to the PROFILE information, and send those corrections directly to your colleges.

The College Board analyzes your data and reports it to the colleges to which you're applying. The schools then apply their own institutional policies to figure out your expected family contribution (EFC). From this analysis, they determine how great your need is and how much institutional financial aid to give you.

SENDING YOUR PROFILE TO ADDITIONAL COLLEGES

You can delete colleges from your list of schools only before you submit the application. After that, all the listed colleges will get your information. But you can add colleges whenever you want, even after you submit the application. Just go to the PROFILE website and click on "Add Colleges to Submitted Application." The fee is $16 for each additional college or program to which you want your information sent.

GOOD TO KNOW

If only one of your birth parents has custody of you, your college may still require information from both parents. If that happens, the main PROFILE application collects information from one parent, and the **Noncustodial PROFILE** collects information from the other. After the information is processed, the college will complete the EFC calculation. How to divide up payment of the EFC among you and your parents is a family decision.

When you add additional colleges, you will also be given the opportunity to update or correct any of the information on your original application. Please note, however, that this new information will only be sent to the colleges you're adding. You should directly contact the colleges to which you submitted your original application to update your information with them.

SUPPLEMENTAL PROFILE FORMS

Some colleges require supplemental information that's not on the PROFILE application. For example, a college may require a Noncustodial PROFILE if you don't live with both of your birth parents. When you register for the PROFILE and indicate that your biological or adoptive parents are not married, you will receive an e-mail with instructions, a temporary password and a link to an application that you should forward to your noncustodial parent to complete. This form can be completed only by the noncustodial parent.

Be aware that these follow-ups take additional time. All the more reason to leave yourself plenty of time to file the PROFILE before your college financial aid deadlines.

Since the PROFILE form is customized, the application may not necessarily be the same length as the FAFSA. In some cases the PROFILE will contain more questions than the FAFSA and in some cases it will contain fewer. The main difference is that it tries to get a more complete picture of your family's finances. A few points to keep in mind:

- File early.
- The PROFILE is online only, so you have to submit it on a computer.
- Prepare by using the Pre-Application Worksheet.
- There are fees, but students from low-income families may qualify for a fee waiver.
- After you submit your PROFILE, you'll get an online acknowledgment confirming that you submitted it. To make corrections to your information, you should write your colleges directly.
- Depending on your circumstances, you or one of your parents may have to submit supplemental information to one or more of your colleges.

**QUICK
RECAP**

Step 7: Fill Out Any Other Required Forms

QUICK OVERVIEW

The FAFSA and PROFILE are the big ones, but don't forget to file any other forms that may be required by your state or by the colleges to which you're applying. You don't want to have your application for financial aid marked "incomplete" because you didn't file a one-page form. These forms can vary widely from college to college, and from state to state.

Some Colleges Have Their Own Financial Aid Application

Some colleges have their own forms that you have to submit in addition to the FAFSA and the PROFILE. A purpose of the form may be to get more information about your finances, or to find out if you're a member of a particular group that is eligible for a special scholarship or grant. If a college requires such a form from all first-time applicants, its description in Part III of the book will say "institutional form required" under the "application procedures" section. Contact the financial aid office at your colleges to find out more.

The good news is that these forms are generally not long or complicated — they are usually just a page or two in length. They manage to stay short because they are intended not to duplicate the FAFSA or PROFILE forms but to supplement them and help the financial aid office keep track of applications. Such a "one pager" might, for example, ask for basic identifying information, some demographic facts and whether you are interested in loans and work-study. This kind of form is typical at community colleges and most four-year public colleges. "It's almost like an update form," Mary San Agustin says of the institutional form currently in use at her institution, Palomar College. "It's basically just a supplemental form in case any changes occurred since the time the student applied for admission or completed the FAFSA."

Sometimes a college might require a longer form that asks questions about your finances that are about as broad and deep as the FAFSA or PROFILE. Usually this only happens with colleges that use their own formulas to calculate need, but choose not to use the PROFILE to help them with it.

Another reason a college might require its own financial aid form is if it requires every student to have a computer on campus. Such schools sometimes have a supplemental form that qualifies needy applicants for a stipend to buy a computer, or places them in a "loaner" program so they can borrow one. The University of Virginia has two forms that deal with computers. One form is for its "laptop loaner" program, and a different form is for a "one-time computer expense" that allows students who want to buy a laptop to add the purchase price to their cost of attendance; that way their aid package may cover the cost.

Still another kind of institutional form is one for early decision applicants. Such a form works as a sort of "pre-read" meant to help students get an early estimate of their expected family contribution and the financial aid package they will receive if they accept an early-decision offer. (The rules of early decision require them to accept the offer if the college offers enough financial aid for them to attend.) Some schools offer a similar pre-read form for student athletes who are being recruited by a coach.

Scholarship and Grant Forms

Some colleges require a separate form for students applying for merit scholarships. This isn't always the case: At many schools, every student who applies for admission is automatically considered for merit scholarships. But at some schools, you must file a separate application for merit scholarships. The rules may even differ from department to department, depending on your major. "Theater majors may have to audition," says Bonnie Lee Behm of Villanova University. "Or a film major may need to send in a tape." Contact the financial aid office at your colleges for more details, and check with the department in which you're interested in majoring.

Some institutional forms ask questions to find out if you qualify for financial aid funds set aside for students with particular characteristics. For example, the college might offer grants that are only available to children of alumni or descendants of the town's founding families. At most colleges, these grants are part of the need-based aid program, so you have to demonstrate need through the FAFSA along with proving you have the right qualifications for the grant.

Verification of Your Tax Return

Some colleges require you to send copies of your family's federal or state tax returns. They may tell you to mail them with your initial application, or they may require them for only a few applicants who have been selected for verification.

"Verification" doesn't mean that you did something wrong. It's not like an IRS audit, where only suspicious tax returns are selected for special scrutiny. Since colleges disburse federal money — in the form of grants, work-study and loans — they are required by law to check the information that a certain percentage of financial aid applicants have submitted. Some colleges exceed this minimum requirement and, for the sake of safety and fairness, verify all applications.

If you are selected for verification by one or more colleges, you'll have to submit tax documents: for example, the 1040 and any attached schedules, along with the W-2s or 1099s you received from employers and banks. Usually you'll also have to fill out a form that allows colleges to confirm details, like how many of your siblings are enrolled in college. The college may ask you to send your documents directly to the financial aid office, or it might ask you to send them to the College Board's Institutional Documentation (IDOC) service.

Some colleges will request verification if the data you submitted on the FAFSA looks unusual. As an extreme example, people who reported that they had no income last year may be asked how they supported themselves.

State Forms

Most states rely on the FAFSA to award their need-based grants and loans to students. But a few states have their own financial aid forms. For example, New York State has an application for its Tuition Assistance Program (TAP) that is sent to eligible students who submit a FAFSA.

Even though the thought of filling out yet another form may seem burdensome, and you feel sure that you won't qualify for the state aid program, fill it out. If you don't, your application might be marked "incomplete" at your colleges. These state forms are usually short and don't take long to fill out, especially once you do the prep work of filling out the FAFSA. **When you file the FAFSA online, you'll be automatically directed to your state's form.** (If you file the FAFSA paper form, you'll usually have to send away for a paper copy of your state form.)

PART I: FINANCIAL AID STEP BY STEP

Table 2:
State Aid Deadlines

STATE	FORM(S) REQUIRED	DEADLINE	NOTES
Alaska	FAFSA	4/15	
Arkansas	FAFSA	6/1	Higher Education Opportunity Grant Academic Challenge awards
California	FAFSA, state form	3/2	Initial awards
		9/2	Additional community college awards
Connecticut	FAFSA	2/15	
Delaware	FAFSA	4/15	
District of Columbia	FAFSA, DC form	6/30	
Florida	FAFSA	5/15	
Idaho	FAFSA, state form	3/1	
Illinois	FAFSA	1/1	Priority date
Indiana	FAFSA	3/10	
Iowa	FAFSA	7/1	
Kansas	FAFSA, state form	4/1	
Kentucky	FAFSA	3/15	
Louisiana	FAFSA	7/1	Closing date
Maine	FAFSA	5/1	
Maryland	FAFSA	3/1	
Massachusetts	FAFSA	5/1	
Michigan	FAFSA	3/1	
Minnesota	FAFSA	30 days after start of term	
Missouri	FAFSA	4/1	
Montana	FAFSA	3/1	
New Hampshire	FAFSA	5/1	
New Jersey	FAFSA	6/1	Tuition Aid Grant applicants
		10/1	All other applicants
		3/1	Spring-term applicants only
New York	FAFSA, state form	5/1	
North Dakota	FAFSA	3/15	
Ohio	FAFSA	10/1	
Oklahoma	FAFSA	4/15	Priority date
Oregon	FAFSA	3/1	OSAC scholarship
Pennsylvania	FAFSA, state form	5/1	Degree program candidates
		8/1	Other applicants
Rhode Island	FAFSA	3/1	
South Carolina	FAFSA	6/30	
Tennessee	FAFSA	2/15	State grant
West Virginia	FAFSA, state form	4/15	

Residents of states not listed in this table should contact their state aid office directly. See page 137 for a list of addresses, phone numbers and websites for each state's aid office.

In addition to the FAFSA and PROFILE, some states and colleges have financial aid forms of their own. Here's what to know about them:

QUICK RECAP

- They're usually short.
- Their questions vary from school to school and from state to state.
- They may determine if you're eligible for special grants.
- They may help verify your financial information, perhaps through questions about your tax returns.
- If state aid is available, apply for it, or your colleges might consider your financial aid application incomplete.
- If one of your colleges requires an institutional application, fill it out, or you'll disqualify yourself from financial aid.

Step 8: Make Your Special Circumstances Known

QUICK OVERVIEW

If something in your family's financial life can't be explained on the financial aid forms, make sure your colleges know about it. These "special circumstances" may include a lost job, high medical expenses or supporting an extended family. Colleges are willing to listen and, if you make your case, may be able to improve your financial aid package by taking those circumstances into account. This step is about how to prepare your case.

Be a Person, Not Just a Form

Sometimes the financial aid forms you fill out don't tell the whole story. They may not show that your family sends money every month to support relatives in another country. Since the forms are based on last year's tax forms, they may not reveal this year's events: how one of your parents just lost a job, or will be shifting from full-time to half-time work. When the forms don't adequately report a special circumstance that affects your family's ability to pay for college, let your college know — it may change how much financial aid you get!

Even if you're not sure your circumstance qualifies as special, speak up. The financial aid office will let you know whether it qualifies. Don't think you're limited to communicating with your college only through the financial aid forms. If there's any doubt in your mind about whether those forms give a true picture of your family's situation, feel free to go beyond the form and contact the financial aid office. **Be a person, not just a form**. There are two reasons to do this: It guarantees that the college knows how much you are able to pay, and it shows that you're interested in the college — which may affect the lengths to which they'll go to help you.

Using the Financial Aid Forms

In some cases, you can inform your colleges of special circumstances through the financial aid forms themselves — the FAFSA, PROFILE and institutional forms (Steps 5, 6 and 7, respectively, of this book). If you're supporting children, if you've been in the military, or if your parents are divorced, your FAFSA will make that clear. For colleges requiring PROFILE, you can use Section ES of that form to describe special financial circumstances. Elsewhere on the PROFILE form, you can list special family expenses, such as your family's medical and dental expenses, or any private school tuition that your parents might pay for your younger siblings. While forms may serve well enough, it may still be a good idea to write a letter or schedule a visit. If there's any doubt in your mind about whether forms convey your situation, definitely contact the college.

Going Beyond the Forms

You may have special circumstances that aren't covered by the forms. Or financially significant events may happen after you submit the forms — events that may be too complicated to explain in a simple correction. If that happens, communicate with the aid office as soon as possible after you realize you have special circumstances or after any financial hardships arise. The sooner you act, the sooner the college can adjust your award — and the more likely they are to still have the funds available to do so.

Even after you start college, if a financial emergency occurs, let the school know. The financial aid director can often help needy students with unusual expenses, such as medical costs, emergency trips home or funding to allow them to take an unpaid internship in the summer instead of working for money.

How to Contact the College

A letter to the financial aid office explaining your circumstances is often the best way to state your case. Some schools have a form specifically for explaining special circumstances; it's worth asking your colleges what they prefer. The more closely you follow their procedures, the more likely you are to be heard.

No matter how you communicate with your college, be polite, clear and specific. There's no need for a despairing or bullying tone. **Remember, you're trying to put a face to the form, so make it a friendly one.** You'll get further by calmly presenting your situation and giving as many relevant specifics as possible. A school will want to know not only that a parent got laid off, but what the prospects for reemployment might be, whether the parent has filed for unemployment benefits and, if so, the amount of the benefit payments awarded to the parent. Don't be surprised or offended if the college responds to you with a request for documentation, such as a copy of your tax return or a recent pay stub.

The Special Circumstances Form

Some colleges have a form through which you can let them know about special circumstances. At Furman University, it's called the Special Financial Circumstances Form, and it is available on the school's website. "The purpose of the form is not to make everybody jump through a hoop," says Forrest

Stuart, the director of financial aid at Furman. "It's to help the parents and the student put on paper all the information we need to help them out."

The form asks the student for the specific data — such as about changes in income and expenses — that the financial aid office will need to reach a decision about their case. It helps the school treat students equally, and it prevents the vagueness that might be found in a letter. "A lot of time we'll just get letters — I've lost my job, I need more aid," says Stuart. "Well, that doesn't tell me a whole lot. But if I can see some concrete information, then that gives me an idea of how I can help this student."

Communicating by Letter

With many schools, the best way to contact the aid office is in a letter. Often, it can strengthen your case to enclose photocopies of supporting documentation with the letter — for example, a paper showing your parent was laid off. The aid officer may also ask you for specific documentation.

After sending your letter, follow up with the financial aid office a week or two later to make sure they received it and to see if they have any questions. You can do this by e-mail or telephone. If you live close by, or have scheduled a campus visit, you should also visit the aid office, but call first to make an appointment.

E-Mail

Some colleges prefer to have you contact them by e-mail. At the University of Oregon, applicants can communicate their special financial circumstances through the school's website, where they can find an e-mail address for the financial aid office. "That way, they can do it whenever they think about it," says Elizabeth Bickford, the financial aid director.

Examples of Special Situations

Many circumstances can affect your family's ability to pay for college. They may include a change in your financial situation from what was reported in the financial aid forms, such as a lost job, emergency expenses, health problems or even a windfall that misrepresents your usual level of income.

Family ties can also have financial implications, such as supporting an extended family or going through a divorce. And if you've served in the military, there are some special instructions you need to follow on the financial aid forms.

Change in Financial Situation

Financial aid officers want to know not only that your financial aid situation changed, but why it changed. Certain types of changes are more likely than others to persuade them to give you more financial aid. Generally, aid officers will look more kindly on circumstances that are beyond your control, rather than the result of poor planning. For example, if your father gets laid off because his company has fallen on hard times, that is more likely to get attention than if he retires early to spend more time golfing. And the college is more likely to turn a sympathetic eye to necessary roof repairs than a loan to install a backyard Jacuzzi.

LOST JOB OR LOST INCOME

If you or your parents had a job when you filled out the FAFSA, and now don't, that will clearly affect your ability to pay. Even if you receive a severance package or collect unemployment benefits, your long-term ability to pay will still be reduced. This is information your financial aid office needs to know. For Palomar College, you would fill out a form that allows the financial aid office to override the FAFSA data with the new data. "You have to still report the prior year's income," according to Palomar's Mary San Agustin, "but we override it with the current-year income."

The FAFSA form for 2010-11 asks if you or a parent is a "dislocated worker." But don't think answering "yes" to that question is sufficient to alert colleges to the problem. They will want to know more, and the more information you give them, the more likely they can help you. And given the large number of job losses caused by the current recession, you should try to give them this information as soon as possible. Remember, there is a limit to the amount of financial aid funds available.

Equally important are unusual changes in other sources of income besides wages and salaries. For example, suppose a student's mother becomes disabled in August and has to stop working, and her employer's disability insurance plan gives her a large percentage of her salary for the first six months (through February), but a much lower percentage afterward. The FAFSA will show a larger income than she will be receiving once the student arrives in college. This change in disability benefits, like a lost job, needs to be explained to the college.

EMERGENCY SAVINGS DRAWDOWN

An emergency may force your family to spend some of the savings that you reported on the financial aid forms. For example, suppose your house is damaged by a fire the day after you submit the FAFSA. Your family needs to spend a large amount of money to pay for the repairs. Depending on where the money comes from — regular savings, a retirement account, borrowing through a home-equity loan — this will have different effects on your need calculation. But no matter what the emergency or the source of the money you wind up spending is, you should tell the aid office.

Sometimes one crisis will have several different effects. Hurricane Katrina in 2005 might not only have destroyed an applicant's home in Louisiana, but put the family breadwinners temporarily out of work. In such a case, make sure the aid office knows about all the different effects on your financial situation.

GOOD TO KNOW

If you're explaining your special financial circumstances by letter, it's best to send it to the financial aid office via mail or fax, so that it can be **easily incorporated into your file**. Write and format it as a standard business letter. **Put your name and Social Security Number** in the first paragraph, so the financial aid office won't have trouble matching the letter to your file.

HEALTH PROBLEMS

A serious health problem in your family can have financial as well as medical effects. It may involve both an emergency savings drawdown to pay for medical expenses, and loss of income if the patient is too sick to work. If someone in your family has recently become disabled, developed a chronic illness or had major surgery, this has a clear impact on your family's ability to pay for college. Your college's financial aid office should be able to help.

A letter, or the school's own "special circumstances" form (if they have one), is a good way to let a college know about your family's medical problem. But the financial aid forms provide some paths as well. The PROFILE form allows you to list medical expenses that weren't covered by insurance last year, and estimate the same for this year. You can also explain high medical expenses in the "Explanations/Special Circumstances" box (Section ES). The FAFSA, on the other hand, doesn't ask specifically about medical expenses. If your college only uses the FAFSA, and you have unusually high medical expenses, a letter to the college makes sense.

WINDFALL

In financial terms, a windfall is a sum of money you didn't expect to get, which is normally a good thing — but even a windfall can have its downside. On your financial aid forms, if you received a windfall last year, that makes your annual income look higher than it normally is, which will tend to raise your expected family contribution (EFC).

Some windfalls are better than others. A windfall is usually understood as a genuine, one-time boost to your finances. It might be an inheritance from an aunt you never knew or an unusually high year-end bonus from your job. If you get such a windfall, inform the aid office that your income was higher than usual last year, and that they shouldn't expect a repeat performance next year.

But some windfalls not only make your annual income look bigger than it is, but represent an overall loss to your financial position. Examples include a severance package on losing your job, or an early withdrawal from a retirement plan, such as an IRA, to cover an emergency. In both situations, your records for that year show a boost in income, but that apparent good news conceals bad financial news — that you lost your job in one case, and suffered a massive hit to your retirement savings in the other. If you experience this kind of windfall, explain the reality to your aid office.

Family Ties

Not every family has two parents married to each other. And some families have stronger ties to grandparents, uncles, aunts and cousins than others. Different families live in different ways. The way your family lives may have financial implications that your financial aid office should recognize.

SUPPORTING EXTENDED FAMILY

The financial aid forms tell the colleges about how many people live in your household, including you, your parents and your siblings. But many families give financial support to an extended family of relatives who live outside the household. Immigrant families, for example, often send money regularly to grandparents, aunts or uncles in another country. Since that decreases the amount you have available to pay for college, make sure the financial aid office knows about it.

DIVORCED OR SEPARATED PARENTS

If your parents have divorced or separated, make sure the colleges know how that has affected your ability to pay. To do this, follow the rules on the financial aid forms. For the FAFSA, provide only the information about the parent you lived with more during the past 12 months (your custodial parent) — and, if that parent has remarried, your stepparent. For the PROFILE, provide not only that data but also information on your other parent, the one who does not have custody of you — your noncustodial parent. That information goes in Section NP of the PROFILE.

Some colleges that use PROFILE will also want your noncustodial parent to submit information separately on the Noncustodial PROFILE. That information will be confidential; you and your custodial parent won't be able to see the data the other parent provides, nor will that parent see yours. However, the information submitted by your noncustodial parent will affect the college's calculation of your total expected family contribution (EFC). If you don't think it will be possible to get your noncustodial parent to fill out the form, let the college know. However, the school isn't likely to waive its requirement for the form for anything less than a significant reason.

In the parent-income section of either the FAFSA or PROFILE, a custodial parent who is receiving alimony or child support payments should report only what he or she received, not what he or she was supposed to receive. In certain circumstances, documented evidence that your noncustodial parent is behind in payments could help support your case if you appeal your award.

Military Service

If you're currently serving in the active-duty military or the reserves, or if you are a veteran, don't assume that your military benefits alone will meet your full financial need. At most institutions, they no longer will. Benefits or not, you should apply for financial aid by submitting the FAFSA and any other required forms.

When filling out these forms, there are a few points to remember. Read the instructions carefully to make sure you qualify as a veteran for purposes of federal student aid. You should report housing allowances, subsistence allowances and untaxed combat pay as income. But don't include veterans' education benefits or ROTC scholarships when answering the questions about your untaxed income. The colleges consider them outside resources to be reported separately. (*See Step 9 for more information on outside resources.*)

Veterans are as liable as anyone to the special situations discussed earlier, from lost jobs to medical crises. That includes windfalls. For example, if you received a lot of combat pay last year but have now been discharged and won't receive it again, you should explain that to the colleges.

For more information on the intricacies of how veterans' benefits affect the FAFSA, see www.gibill.va.gov.

QUICK RECAP

If there are special circumstances that affect your ability to pay for college, let your college know.

- Tell the college financial aid office as soon as you know about your special circumstances — either before you get your award or afterward.
- If you have to go beyond the forms, write a letter, e-mail, call or visit.
- Explain your situation clearly, documenting it where appropriate.
- The situations that may affect your ability to pay range from a lost job or high medical bills to status as a veteran or an undocumented immigrant.

Step 9: Look for Scholarships

QUICK OVERVIEW

It's worth it to look for financial aid beyond what you'll get from colleges and federal student aid programs. This "outside money" probably won't amount to a "full ride," but it can help. Begin your search for outside scholarships around the time you start looking for a college because many scholarships have early deadlines.

Scholarships Colleges Give You vs. Scholarships You Get on Your Own

KNOW THE LINGO

Outside money — Grants and scholarships that come from sources other than colleges or the federal government, such as states and private organizations.

Portable money — Grants and scholarships that you can take with you to whichever college you attend.

College-offered money — Grants and scholarships that colleges award from their own funds.

Financial aid doesn't come only from the government and colleges. It also comes in the form of scholarships from outside sources, including states and private donors. This money doesn't come looking for you: You have to find the programs that fit you and apply. You will have to qualify for the scholarship in some way, whether through academic merit, artistic talent or fitting some set of criteria, such as being a person of Japanese descent living in either Connecticut, New York or New Jersey. **Very few outside scholarships offer anything close to full tuition, fees, room and board**. But they're worth the search because every little bit helps.

The scholarships you can get from outside sources are not exactly like the scholarships you might get from your college. These are the basic facts to know about each type.

College-Offered Scholarships

In most cases, you don't have to apply separately for the scholarships that colleges award. You're automatically considered for them when you apply to the school. If you qualify, the college will include the scholarship in your financial aid package as they see fit. However, some colleges have merit-based scholarships for which you must apply separately.

To find out what the rules are for scholarship aid at your colleges, contact the schools or look at their websites, which usually describe the process for applying for scholarships under "admission" and then under "financial aid." Be sure to do this research *before* you submit your application for admission. At some colleges, you have to indicate on your admissions application that you are applying for a special scholarship; for example, this is true of Boston University's Trustee Scholar Program. At others, you don't have to apply for special scholarships until after you've submitted your application for admission.

Many college merit scholarships have to be renewed from year to year. To make sure yours is renewed, know the school's criteria for keeping it — for example, maintaining a certain GPA. Different scholarships will have different criteria at each college.

Outside Scholarships: State Sources

Almost every state offers scholarships to their residents. These scholarships are usually available only for state residents attending colleges within the state, though a few states offer "portable" aid that a state resident can take to a college in another state.

Take the time to research scholarships and grants in your state. Almost every state has a department of education website that describes state scholarships and how to apply for them. These are usually separate from the state-sponsored, need-based financial aid programs for which you apply through the FAFSA or the state's own financial aid form, such as the Tuition Assistance Program (TAP) in New York State. An example of a state-sponsored, merit-based scholarship program with a separate application process is Florida's Merit Scholars Award, for which applicants must show high academic achievement.

Outside Scholarships: Private Sources

Private scholarships are offered by many sources, including foundations, corporations, civic groups, religious organizations, veterans' associations and the military. The Society of Women Engineers offers the Bechtel Corporation Scholarship to high-achieving female students of engineering. United Methodist Scholarships are available to students who belong to that Christian denomination. The Senator George J. Mitchell Scholarship Research Institute offers awards to Maine residents studying in state.

Don't assume you have to be a genius to get a private scholarship. Although many scholarship programs consider academic merit, a range of conditions may qualify you for a scholarship, including interests, ethnic background and community work. The Los Padres Foundation grants scholarships to low-income Latino students. California students pursuing a career in agriculture are eligible for a California Farm Bureau Scholarship.

Most scholarships come with limits. Though a few programs will pay full tuition, the amount of most awards is much smaller, as little as $500 or $1,000.

Myth: "Untold millions" of scholarship dollars are available for use every year.

Fact: Private scholarships are only a small segment of the overall money available for college — **just 6 percent**. True, that share amounts to $7.5 billion a year, but that's dwarfed by the $125.6 billion paid out by other sources. Money from federal, college-granted and state funds, in that order, are likely to be much more important in your overall financial aid package. It's worth looking for private scholarships, but don't count on them as your sole source of funding.

Many awards are limited to the freshman year of study. Fortunately, other scholarships are only for later years. The Bechtel Corporation Scholarship, for example, is just for women in their sophomore, junior or senior year of study. And once you've declared a major you may find yourself eligible for a scholarship that is aimed only at students in your academic discipline.

Searching for Scholarships

Searching for private scholarships takes effort. But there are a number of Web-based scholarship search engines, like the ones on collegeboard.com and fastweb.com, that can help you zero in on scholarships for which you may qualify. If you like using this book, you might prefer to search for scholarships using the *College Board Scholarship Handbook*. It describes more than 2,100 outside scholarships, internships and loan programs, and is indexed by eligibility requirements — such as minority status, religious affiliation and state of residence — to help you match yourself to the programs.

Beware of commercial scholarship search companies that offer to help you find scholarships for a fee. Some do a responsible job, but many charge exorbitant fees and make fraudulent claims. For example, if they "guarantee" you a scholarship or promise to "do all the work for you," they are probably lying. Getting a scholarship is never guaranteed and, no matter what, you are going to have to do some work to apply.

Your school counselor may be of more help. Many private scholarships send application forms directly to school counselors. Tell your counselor in your junior year or early in your senior year that you are interested in applying for private scholarships.

Figure 12:
collegboard.com's Scholarship Search

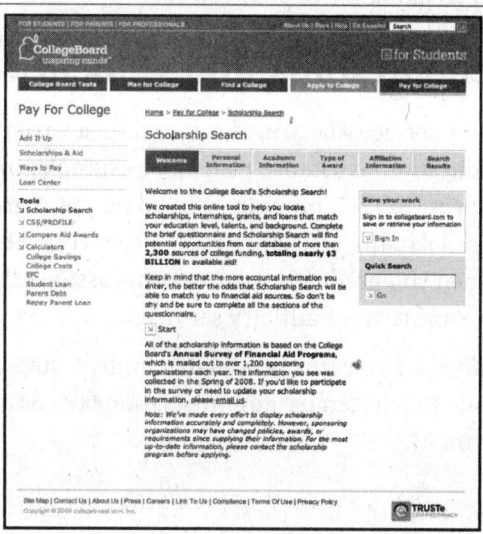

Start researching options as soon as possible. You'll need time to learn about scholarships, request information and application materials, and complete your application. Some programs, such as the Discover Card Tribute Award Scholarship (see sidebar on page 89), are looking only for students in their junior year of high school. Even if you're past that point, look as soon as you can — in the summer before your senior year, or by October or November of that year.

Look Locally

The national and state programs that you'll find on Web-based scholarship search engines and in print directories are good sources of scholarship aid. But don't forget to look even closer to home: your own county, city, town, employer or church. When looking for scholarships, it pays to look locally.

The fact is, you are more likely to obtain a scholarship from a local organization than from a state or national one. On the local level, you will be competing with a smaller pool of applicants and are more likely to have characteristics that interest the donors. Again, your school counselor can help. The counseling office will have a file of local scholarships — from banks, the Kiwanis, the local garden club and other groups. Let your counselor know you are looking for scholarships; stop by the counseling office regularly to read the scholarship files or check the scholarship bulletin board. The office may also use Internet announcements, e-mail postings or newsletters to spread the word about scholarship programs to interested students.

Employers can also be a source of scholarship money. If you have a part-time job after school or a summer job, check to see if the company that employs you has a scholarship program or offers tuition assistance. For example, Chick-fil-A has a well-known scholarship program for its restaurant employees. Some companies provide their employees with a dependent tuition-assistance benefit. That means one of your parents might be able to get his or her employer to pay some of your tuition.

Military Scholarships and Education Benefits

In return for military service, the armed forces offer a variety of college scholarships and education-assistance plans. For example, in the Reserve Officer Training Corps (ROTC) program offered by the Army, Navy and Air Force, you get scholarship assistance for college while being trained as a military officer. When you graduate, you are commissioned as an officer in the reserves and begin your term of military service.

Educational assistance for veterans is available in most states. If you're a veteran, contact your state veterans' administration for complete information and application forms.

Applying for Scholarships

Once you find the programs for which you qualify, you have to apply. This may mean not only another form to fill out, but compiling supporting documents, such as transcripts, recommendations and an essay. Depending on the program, you may have to provide evidence of leadership, patriotism, depth of character, desire to serve or financial need. Get to know the requirements of each scholarship as early as possible, so you can do any necessary extra work on time.

A few pointers to remember:

Apply early! Apply as early as possible to scholarship programs. If you can, do it in the fall of your senior year, even if the deadlines aren't until February or March. Very often, scholarship programs will have awarded all their funds for the year on a first-come, first-served basis before their stated deadline.

Follow directions. Read instructions carefully and do what they say. Scholarship programs receive hundreds and even thousands of applications. Don't lose out because of failure to submit a typewritten essay versus a handwritten one if required, or to provide appropriate recommendations. If you have a question about your eligibility for a particular scholarship or how to complete the application, contact the scholarship sponsors.

Be organized. It's a good idea to create a separate file for each scholarship and sort them by their due dates. Track application deadlines and requirements using Worksheet 2 (**a blank copy of this worksheet appears on page 124**). In one place, store the different supporting documents you may need, such as transcripts, standardized test scores and letters of recommendation.

Check your work. Proofread your applications for spelling or grammatical errors, fill in all blanks, and make sure your handwriting is legible.

Keep copies of everything. If application materials get lost, having copies on file will make it easier to resend the application quickly.

Reapply. Some programs only offer money for the first year of college, but others can be renewed each subsequent year. If your program is one of them, it pays to reapply once you're in college.

SAMPLE WORKSHEET 2:
Scholarship Application Planner

	PROGRAM 1	PROGRAM 2	PROGRAM 3
PROGRAM/SPONSOR	National Merit Scholarship	Young Epidemiology Scholars	First Bank
ELIGIBILITY REQUIREMENTS	Academic merit	Academic merit	Need, local residency
TYPE OF AWARD	Scholarship	Scholarship	Internship
AMOUNT OF AWARD	$2,500	$1,000 or more	$2,500
CAN BE USED FOR	Tuition/fees	Any expense	Any expense
CAN BE USED AT	First-choice college	Any college	In-state colleges
DEADLINE	Oct. 1 (give essay to English teacher for review)	Feb. 1	April 1
FORMS REQUIRED	NMSC application	Web form	Application (includes need analysis)
TEST SCORES REQUIRED	PSAT/NMSQT (already took), SAT (by December)	None	SAT
ESSAY OR ACADEMIC SAMPLE	Personal statement, academic transcript	Essay, research project	None required
RECOMMENDATIONS	Principal	None	One teacher (Mr. Filmer), Local branch manager
NOTIFICATION BEGINS	February	Not sure	May 15
REQUIREMENTS TO KEEP AFTER FRESHMAN YEAR	One-time payment only	One-time payment only	Based on performance during internship

For a blank version of this worksheet that you can photocopy for your own use, see page 124.

How a Scholarship Can Affect Your Financial Aid Package

If a college to which you're applying hasn't met your full need — that is, if there's a "gap" in your financial aid award — outside scholarships can be used to fill that gap. That will make the college much more affordable and give you more choices when it comes time to decide which college you want to attend.

If, on the other hand, a college is already meeting your full need, it works a little differently. It would be nice if your outside scholarship were added on top of all your other financial aid to make your total aid package even bigger. But it probably won't be. Following federal policy, your college will most likely count any outside scholarship or tuition assistance you receive as an "outside resource" that decreases your aid package dollar for dollar. So the total amount of your financial aid package will be exactly the same.

You might think this is unfair: This is money you found and, in the case of employer tuition assistance and veteran's benefits, money you earned. On the other hand, it is money that's available to pay for your education without your having to dip into your income and assets. The philosophy behind financial aid is that everyone should pay what they can out of income and assets (your expected family contribution, or EFC), and then financial aid, including any outside resources, makes up the difference. The only way you can pay less than your EFC is if you get so many outside scholarships that they exceed your financial need. This is highly unlikely.

However, **it is still worth getting outside scholarships**. For one thing, it increases your freedom to choose a college regardless of cost. "If I'm a student, the more money that I can bring to the table for myself, the better position I'm going to be in to exercise choices that I might want to make," says Vincent Amoroso of Johns Hopkins University. For another thing, many colleges will use your outside scholarship money to reduce the self-help part of your aid package first — loans and work-study. This can significantly reduce the amount of money you'll owe after college or the time you'll need to spend working during college.

At some colleges, your outside scholarships will not be used to reduce your gift aid (grants and scholarships) unless the amount exceeds your self-help aid. Others use a formula in which at least a portion of your outside money will be used to decrease loans. For example, the first $500 in outside scholarships might be used to reduce your loans, then any funds remaining would be split 50/50 between reducing loans and cutting grants. Colleges that don't meet your full financial need may first apply outside scholarships toward filling the gap. Most colleges decide these issues on a case-by-case basis, but a few have stated policies that they publish on their financial aid Web page or will share with you if asked.

No matter what their policies, colleges welcome outside scholarships because they may reduce the amounts of college funds that have to be spent. Indeed, some schools encourage students to look for outside scholarships. According to Vincent Amoroso, the institutional financial aid form at his college asks students for data related to outside sources of financial aid, including global foundations, to "help us know [if] the student might match up to one of these other foundations that's awarding money."

In making admission decisions, admission offices are likely to look on outside scholarships favorably. Students who have searched for and found outside scholarships on their own will probably be seen as students with initiative and a sense of responsibility. That makes the student a stronger candidate for admission.

If you win a scholarship after you've already submitted your FAFSA and/or PROFILE, tell the colleges to which you've applied. Many schools have a special form specifically designed for you to submit this information. If you don't tell the colleges about a scholarship, it could jeopardize your eligibility for federal aid.

Tax Effects

Your outside scholarship may be taxed as income — this depends on the use for which it's designated by the program that awards the scholarship. Generally, scholarship dollars used for costs that are purely educational, such as tuition and fees, will be tax free. But money used for living expenses, transportation or books will be taxed as unearned income. The scholarship program will let you know how much (if any) of your award is taxable, and will send you a copy of the IRS's Form 1098 at the end of each tax year.

If your employer gives you tuition assistance, it's tax free up to $5,250 a year. After that amount, it's taxable. If you get tuition assistance from your parent's employer, the entire amount will be added to your parents' taxable income, but they might be able to deduct some of that amount (see Table 7 on page 112 for more info.)

It takes work to hunt down and apply for outside scholarships, but it's worth it. Just remember:

- Outside scholarships will probably provide only a small part of the money you need for college, but every little bit helps.
- There are national and statewide scholarships programs, but look locally too.
- Websites, books and your school counselor can help you match outside scholarships to your qualifications.
- Search and apply early, and follow instructions.
- Your outside scholarship may affect the financial aid package awarded by your college, and it may be taxable as income.

QUICK RECAP

Step 10: Weigh the Offers

QUICK OVERVIEW

After you've submitted all the financial aid forms, you'll receive offers of financial aid from the colleges that have accepted you. This step will help you weigh these award letters and make an informed decision based on an "apples to apples" comparison of the packages. If an award leaves you with a larger out-of-pocket share than you think your family can handle, you can appeal.

Comparing Award Letters from Colleges

Sometime after a college accepts you for admission, it will send you a financial aid award letter. The letter will detail your award — the financial aid package the college is offering you. It will contain an outline of the expected costs you will incur during a year at the college, your expected family contribution (EFC) toward those costs, and the types and amounts of financial aid the college is offering to make up the difference between the costs and the EFC.

The letter will also contain instructions on how to accept the aid package and how to contact the aid office if you have any questions or want to appeal the award. Often, the award letter will come with a thick packet of supplementary documents, including promissory notes for any loans offered and information about work-study jobs, if you've been offered those.

It's best to wait until you have the award letters from all the different colleges that have accepted you before deciding which one to accept. If you have questions, wait until you've gotten answers from all the financial aid offices involved before you decide.

The offers in your award letters will differ. The amount and type of aid given will vary, and the letters may also differ in format, especially in how they itemize costs. In weighing the offers, the important thing is to compare apples to apples and not apples to oranges. For example, just because School A offers $10,000 in financial aid while School B only offers $8,000 doesn't necessarily

KNOW THE LINGO

Aid package — The total amount of all financial aid being offered to a student by a college.

Award letter — A document that a college sends to a student detailing the financial aid package. It indicates the type and amount of each scholarship, grant, loan or work-study opportunity being offered.

Appeal — A request that a college reconsider its financial aid package.

SAMPLE WORKSHEET 3:
Compare Your Awards

	COLLEGE 1	COLLEGE 2	COLLEGE 3
Step 1. List the name of each college you want to consider attending, the award deadline, and the total cost of attendance. This figure should be in your award letter. If not, refer to the college catalog or contact the college financial aid office.			
Name of college	*Private Univ.*	*Small College*	*Regional State*
Award deadline date	*5/1*	*5/1*	*4 weeks*
Total cost of attendance	*$31,825*	*$33,410*	*$15,566*
Step 2. List the financial aid awards each school is offering. Don't forget that grants, scholarships and work-study do not have to be repaid, while all loans must be repaid.			
Grants and scholarships			
• Pell Grant (federal)			
• SEOG (federal)			
• State	*can't use*	*$2,000*	*$2,000*
• College	*$12,700*	*$13,785*	*$941*
• Other			
Total grants/scholarships	*$12,700*	*$15,785*	*$2,941*
Percentage of package that is grant/scholarship	*60%*	*74%*	*53%*
Work-study opportunities	*$2,000*	*$1,000*	
Loans			
• Stafford-Direct (federal)	*$2,625*	*$2,625*	*$2,625*
• Perkins (federal)	*$4,000*	*$2,000*	
• Other			
Total loans	*$6,625*	*$4,625*	*$2,625*
Percentage of package that is work or loans	*40%*	*26%*	*47%*
Total financial aid award	*$21,325*	*$21,410*	*$5,566*
Grants and scholarships + work-study + loans			
Step 3. Calculate what it will cost you to attend each college you are considering. For each college, enter the total cost of attendance. Then, subtract the total financial aid award from the total cost of attendance. That number is the net cost, or what it will cost you to attend that college.			
a) Total cost of attendance	*$31,825*	*$33,410*	*$15,566*
b) Total financial aid award	*$21,325*	*$21,410*	*$5,566*
c) Net cost to attend (a minus b)	*$10,500*	*$12,000*	*$10,000*

For a blank version of this worksheet that you can photocopy for your own use, see page 125.

EXPERT ADVICE

"It's **not simply the dollar amount of the grant or scholarship** that families should focus on. They need to **lay out, side by side, the full picture**. What's the cost of attendance, including out-of-pocket expenses? What's the family contribution? What are the elements of aid? What's going to happen with loans, with work?"

— *Joe Paul Case, dean and director of financial aid, Amherst College, Amherst, Mass.*

mean School A has the better deal. If School A's aid package has $3,000 in grants and $7,000 in loans, but School B has $6,000 in grants and $2,000 in loans, School B is offering you more free money (grants) than School A.

There is another reason why a financial aid package may not be as big as it seems: higher costs. If one school's costs are higher than another's, you may be left with a higher out-of-pocket expense even after subtracting a "bigger" aid package. **Don't be dazzled by a large award. Instead, look for the bottom line: your net cost to attend the school.**

Here's a true story to illustrate this further. **Two sample award letters appear in Part II** (see pages 126, 127). These were taken from actual letters received by a student. Only the names of the colleges involved have been changed, to "Blue University" and "Green University." The student's first-choice college was Blue U, which cost about $2,000 more than Green U. When she first compared the letters, she was very upset because it looked like Green U was giving her a much bigger scholarship, and much more total aid.

But her school counselor showed her that Blue U was actually offering the better deal. First of all, the grants and scholarship from Green U only looked bigger because they were presented as a total. Secondly, the student loans offered by Blue U (Stafford and Perkins) were subsidized, while the Stafford loan offered by Green U was not. That meant at Green U she would have to pay interest on the loan while she was in college. And third, the $14,810 Green U was "offering" as a parent PLUS loan wasn't really aid at all, but just an option for how her family could pay for their contribution. Bottom line, the true cost to her would be about the same at both colleges, even though Blue U is more expensive.

Collegeboard.com has an online "Compare Your Aid Awards" tool that lets you do this kind of side-by-side comparison of your awards. You can also use Worksheet 3 to break out the different components of costs and aid packages and compare them side by side (a blank copy of this worksheet appears on page 125). When doing this analysis, keep an eye out for both quantity and quality. On the quantity side, for example, the "Family Share of Costs" figure tells you the amount of money your family will be expected to contribute. Your family will need to decide whether this amount is affordable. Look especially for evidence of "gapping," the practice of leaving a gap between the cost of attendance and the money accounted for by aid and EFC. You will be expected to fill that gap — in effect increasing your EFC.

On the quality side, consider the figures for "% of Award That Is Gift Aid" and "% of Award That Is Loan." The higher the proportion of gift aid (grant or scholarships) to loans, the better the award.

Loans vs. Grants

All other things being equal, it's better to receive a grant or scholarship than a loan. For that reason, a financial aid package with a high percentage of gift aid is more attractive, on the face of it, than one with a high percentage of loans. But there are circumstances where you might take the award that offers more loans and less gift aid: For example, if that college is a better fit for you overall.

In any event, don't be surprised if your award includes loans. Most aid packages contain them. Loans are optional; you don't have to take them out. But if offered as part of a need-based aid package, they can be an excellent way to help finance your education. The alternative — taking only grant aid and trying to pay the costs that the loans would cover out of pocket — could put your family under much more financial stress than the loan would.

It's usually in your best interest to accept subsidized Stafford and Perkins loans that are part of the aid package: The repayment terms are good and the government pays the interest while you're in school. Unsubsidized loans — such as unsubsidized Stafford, PLUS loan and private loans from a bank — should be studied more carefully to make sure the terms are acceptable. You should understand the specific terms of each loan, including its interest rate, the origination fee, the term of the loan and the grace period before repayment begins. You should also realize that unsubsidized loans are not need based and are typically used to help your families pay their EFC. If a college offers them as part of your aid package, consider them as an option, but don't weigh them equally with subsidized loans in the package.

Work-study jobs are also optional, but if you're offered one and you can manage the time, take it. Having a job on campus brings in income, expands your social networks, allows you to make contacts with professors and administrators, and gives you experience that can improve your résumé.

Appealing Your Award

Even though your award letters are printed in black and white, they aren't necessarily the last word. It is possible to appeal the awards: to ask the colleges to reconsider their aid packages. There is no guarantee that they will grant your request, but there are circumstances where it's worth trying.

One reason you might appeal a package is if it has a lot of unsubsidized loans. However, bear in the mind that the college probably offered those loans because there wasn't enough gift aid to go around. Another reason to appeal is if you don't think you can afford the expected family contribution. You will need to have evidence to make that case. The college based its calculation of your EFC on the financial information you submitted. If you think this calculation was wrong, ask the financial aid office how it was made and see if you can find out if a mistake occurred. It will help if you have special circumstances that weren't communicated in your financial aid forms, such as a recent layoff; situations like this will clearly demonstrate why your family would have difficulty paying its EFC. (*See Step 8, "Make Your Special Circumstances Known."*)

"I've changed financial aid packages on appeal if somebody can demonstrate why they can't afford it," says Forrest Stuart of Furman University. "It may be the need analysis just didn't take some things into account. If they can show me where there's a real problem, even to the point where they show me their monthly

KEEP IN MIND

Just because you're awarded a loan to pay part of your college costs **doesn't mean you have to accept it**. If your family has funds available in savings or current income, you can use these funds if you prefer. The downside is that you'll have less money available now, which could put your family under financial stress. The upside is that you won't have to pay the money back later with interest.

KNOW THE LINGO

There are three types of federal loans for educational expenses:

Stafford — Loan to students. May be subsidized (if student demonstrates need) or unsubsidized. If subsidized, the government pays the interest on the loan while the student is in college.

PLUS — A federal loan for parents to cover college costs not met by financial aid. Not subsidized.

Perkins — Subsidized loan to students with exceptional need. Perkins-loan debt may be forgiven if the borrower enters a career in the public service.

Questions to Ask About Your Award

These are some questions to ask your college financial aid office if you're awarded gift aid:

✔ What do I have to do to keep my scholarship — do I have to do anything more than maintain satisfactory academic progress?

✔ Is there a minimum GPA or other condition?

✔ Is the scholarship renewable in subsequent years?

✔ If I win an outside scholarship, what happens to my aid?

Questions to ask if you're awarded a loan:

✔ What are the terms of my loan?

✔ What is the interest rate, and when do I start repayment?

✔ How much will I owe by the time I graduate?

✔ What will my monthly repayment be?

✔ By how much will my loan increase after my first year?

Questions to ask if you're awarded work-study:

✔ Do I have a "guaranteed" job, or will I have to find one?

✔ How are jobs assigned?

✔ How many hours per week will I be expected to work?

✔ What is the hourly wage?

✔ How often will I be paid?

✔ Will I be paid directly, or will my student account get credited?

budget, I might say, 'Man, you are right. You've got these medical expenses or you've got this and that. Let me see if I can help you.' I am not perfect, and the need analysis is not perfect, and we'll sometimes overlook something."

Still another reason for appealing an award is if you have better offers from other colleges, and would like to see if this college can match them. Some aid offices will consider matching a better offer from another college. But most will only hear an appeal that's based on your family's financial circumstances. "We don't bargain," says Mike Scott of Texas Christian University. "We just don't want to play that game of, 'Well, we'll give you more money simply because another school gave you more money.'"

You might see the entire appeal process as essentially negotiation or bargaining — trying to get as much as possible from the school you'd like to attend. However, most financial aid officers loathe the term "negotiate." Your appeal will have a better chance of success if it appears not a matter of haggling but of providing information not previously available to the financial aid office.

It will also help your cause if you are obviously doing your part to fund your education. A student who accepts the self-help components of a school's financial aid package will be more likely to get extra help than one who declined them. "If the student is not willing to somehow contribute, either by working or taking out a student loan, then we are very unlikely to give them any extra money," says Mike Scott.

A phone call is a good way to start the appeal process, even though most colleges will want you to put your reasons for an appeal in writing. Some have a specific form for appeals; others would like for you to state your case in a letter. Find out the college's preferred procedure by calling or checking their website. No matter how you file your appeal, your case will be stronger if you can provide data to back it up. A few days after filing your appeal, follow up with a phone call or, if possible, by visiting the aid office. Within a short time, the college will let you know its decision.

If you receive a revised award, take the new award letter and compare it to your other aid packages. **It's best not to decide where to enroll until you've received the final offer from each college**. But keep in mind the deadline set by each college for acceptance of its award. If you miss the deadline, you could lose the package. If you do need more time, try asking the college for an extension.

Follow Up: Accepting an Award

Once you've compared all the awards and any appeals have been ruled upon, you and your family will have to decide on a college. Many factors, including costs and financial aid, will be in play. If your first-choice college has accepted you but not given as much aid as you'd hoped, the choice may be difficult. Do you go to your first-choice college even though it's a financial risk for your family, or to a second-choice college your family can safely afford? In the end, your own preferences should have the greatest weight. Most of the loan debt, payable after graduation, will be on your shoulders. And your personal happiness at the school will have a major influence on whether you graduate successfully. If your family can put together a sensible financial plan to pay the costs, the best choice is the one that fits you best academically and personally.

Once you've decided which offer to accept, it's polite to send a note declining the offers of the colleges you're rejecting. That way any funds they offered you can be made available to other students. As for the offer you're accepting, follow whatever instructions came in the award packet. If you're being asked for more information, send it. Complete any forms that came with the award letter. Sign the letter and return it by the due date.

EXPERT ADVICE

"I tell families **not to use the word 'negotiate.'** If an aid package is much lower than what's being offered by similar institutions, families should call and ask if there is additional information that may make a difference."

— *Carlene Riccelli, college adviser, Amherst Regional High School, Amherst, Mass.*

When you receive your award letters from colleges, you'll have to decide which offer to accept.

QUICK RECAP

- Compare apples to apples, analyzing the awards to see what the real costs and financial aid elements are.
- Just because loans are offered, you don't have to accept them. But they're worth considering, especially if they're subsidized loans.
- If you appeal an award, you'll be on stronger ground if you can demonstrate circumstances that weren't previously made clear to the school.
- Your decision about which offer to accept should be based not just on cost but on how well the college fits you academically, socially and personally.

Step 11: Consider Your Out-of-Pocket Options

Financial aid is intended to cover the difference between your expected family contribution (EFC) and the total cost of college. However, you still have to pay your EFC and whatever gap there might be between the aid you received and your financial need. This step is about ways to meet those out-of-pocket costs.

Making Up the Difference

For almost every family, college is going to cost money. Even a generous financial aid package will usually leave you with some bills to pay. Some packages will meet less than your full need and leave you spending more than your EFC. You can afford to make up this difference between the total cost of attendance and the aid you're receiving if you take advantage of the various resources available to you. Most families use a combination of savings, current income and loans to pay their out-of-pocket costs. You'll have to decide how to do that in a way that fits your own particular situation. But you'll have help, because there are a number of programs and strategies that can help you save, pay or borrow for college.

Save for It

You shouldn't spend your entire family savings on college: You need to leave some for other uses, such as retirement and emergency medical costs. But it makes sense to use some of your savings for college.

Don't worry if your family doesn't already have a huge sum of money saved for college. **Every little bit helps, and it's never too late to start saving.** Even while you're applying to college, your family can start saving. Try to save as much as you can from summer and after-school jobs, and encourage your parents to set aside some money from every paycheck. Talk with your parents about how much money you and they already have saved for your college costs, and discuss how your family can afford the rest of the bill.

KNOW THE LINGO

EFC (Expected Family Contribution) — How much money a family is expected to pay for college out of pocket, based on the family's ability to pay.

Need — The difference between your EFC and the cost of attending a particular college you've chosen. Financial aid is designed to meet your need, not your EFC.

Unmet need — The difference (if any) between your need and the financial aid offered by a particular college. Informally, unmet need is also called a **gap**.

Don't believe anyone who says you shouldn't save for college because it will reduce your chances of getting financial aid. As noted in Step 2, savings are worth having so you can pay out-of-pocket costs without having to borrow. Very little, if any, of your parents' savings are counted against you when your financial need is determined. "Parents should not avoid saving because, frankly, a family that has saved has a resource to draw on, whereas a family that hasn't is totally dependent on current income and loans," says Joe Paul Case, dean and director of financial aid at Amherst College in Amherst, Mass.

There are a number of places families can put their savings. The most traditional is a regular bank savings account, which pays a little interest and offers freedom to withdraw and deposit money at any time. A certificate of deposit (CD) has stricter rules about when you can withdraw money, but it usually pays higher interest than a savings account. Both of these options are good for short-term, flexible savings. But neither has any tax incentives — tax breaks that make them especially attractive for college savings.

The following savings vehicles do come with tax breaks. For more details, see Table 3 on page 102:

529 college savings plan. Also known as the QTP (Qualified Tuition Program), these are tax-advantaged accounts sponsored by the various states. Interest earned in these plans is not taxed as income, and some states also offer a state income-tax deduction for contributions their residents make to the state's plan. There are no income restrictions, and contribution limits are high. Grandparents, uncles and aunts are also allowed to contribute to the plan, even if they don't live in the same state as you and your parents — in fact, you don't have to be a resident of a state to contribute to its plan, and you can withdraw funds from a state's plan to pay for expenses at a college in another state. Most plans offer a few different investment types, such as a fund that invests in stocks or one that invests in bonds.

Coverdell Education Savings Account. These tax-free trust or custodial accounts are similar to 529s, but they're sponsored by banks and brokerage houses instead of states, and therefore offer a greater range of investment choices. They can be used to pay private elementary and high school costs as well as college costs, unlike 529s, which can only be used for college costs. Total contributions for the student can't be more than $2,000 in a given year, and your family income has to be less than $110,000 (for single filers) or $220,000 (for joint filers). You can contribute to both a 529 and a Coverdell in the same year for the same student.

529 prepaid tuition plan. Like the 529 college savings plans, these are sponsored by the states, but they work differently. A 529 prepaid tuition plan lets a family make advance tuition payments years before their children will enter college. That allows them to "lock in" today's tuition rates instead of paying the higher rates likely to prevail years from now. Provided the student is admitted, the plans are guaranteed to be honored by public universities and some private colleges in the state that sponsors the plan. However, these plans have drawbacks. They can only be used for tuition and fees, not for room, board or other supplemental costs. When that's combined with the fact that the tuition rates are only locked in for in-state colleges, most parents prefer the more flexible 529 savings plans.

Independent 529 prepaid tuition plan. This is a special 529 prepaid tuition plan sponsored by a group of private colleges and universities and administered by TIAA-CREF. For more information, visit www.independent529plan.org.

U.S. savings bonds. If your parents pay for some of your college costs by cashing in U.S. government savings bonds, the interest that has accumulated on the bond may be tax exempt. That means the interest won't be taxed as income and your tax bill will be smaller. There's a penalty if you cash in the bonds less than five years after the date of issue, and there are some restrictions on the tax exemption. The bond must be issued after 1989 and your parent must have been age 24 or older when the bond was issued. This deduction can't overlap with any other education tax break. You can't use two different tax breaks to pay for the same expense. The family income must be less than $82,100 (for single filers) or $130,650 (for joint filers).

Uniform Gifts to Minors Act (UGMA) or Uniform Transfers to Minors Act (UTMA) account. These accounts allow parents to put money in the child's name so it will receive preferential tax treatment. Much of the earnings are taxed at the child's rate rather than the parent's rate. Such accounts were popular in the 1980s, but the advent of tax-free 529s and Coverdells has made them nearly obsolete as a college-savings vehicle.

Individual Retirement Account (IRA). Generally, it's not a good idea to raid the family retirement funds, such as IRAs, to pay for college. "We tell parents all the time, you can borrow money to pay for your kid's education. You cannot borrow money to retire with," says Mike Scott of Texas Christian University. It's usually better to take out a PLUS loan than to diminish retirement assets. Still, if your family does need to go into an IRA to pay college expenses, the government doesn't charge the 10 percent additional tax you would ordinarily have to pay for breaking open an IRA before age 59½.

Table 3:
Comparison of Education Savings Options

	COVERDELL EDUCATION SAVINGS ACCOUNT	529 COLLEGE SAVINGS PLAN (QUALIFIED TUITION PROGRAM)	529 PREPAID TUITION PLAN	U.S. GOVERNMENT SAVINGS BONDS	UNIFORM GIFTS TO MINORS ACT ACCOUNT	INDIVIDUAL RETIREMENT ACCOUNT
Tax advantages	Earnings in account not taxed as income	Earnings in account not taxed as income Some states allow residents to deduct contributions for state income tax purposes	Earnings in account not taxed as income Some states allow residents to deduct contributions for state income tax purposes	Interest earned is not taxed if used for qualified expenses	Interest earned is taxed at child's rate	Exception to the 10% early withdrawal penalty rule
Expenses that qualify	• Tuition & fees • Books & supplies • Room & board (if at least half-time) • Expenses for special needs services • K-12 education expenses	• Tuition & fees • Books & supplies • Room & board (if at least half-time) • Computer • Special needs services	Tuition & fees	• Tuition & fees • Contributions to a Coverdell or 529	Any expense (not limited to education)	• Tuition & fees • Books & supplies • Room & board (if at least half-time) • Special needs services
Contribution limits	$2,000 per year	None	None	None	None	$4,000 per year ($5,000 if over 50)
Income phaseout for benefits	$95,000–$110,000 (single filers) $190,000–$220,000 (joint filers)	None	None	$69,950–$84,950 (single filers) $104,900–$134,900 (joint filers)	None	Varies by type of account
Other limitations	Assets must be distributed by age 30 Must pay 10% penalty if distributions not used for qualified expenses	Must pay 10% penalty if distributions not used for qualified expenses	Benefits may only be used at colleges that participate in the plan Must pay 10% penalty if distributions not used for qualified expenses	Applies only to Series EE or Series I bonds issued after 1989 and purchased after owner turned 24	Counted as student asset for financial aid purposes	Interest earned will still be taxed at your regular rate

Work for It

Besides a summer job, you might also want to consider working during the school year to help meet expenses. There are two basic approaches. You can go to college full time while working part time, or you can hold a full-time job while attending college part time.

Full-Time Student, Part-Time Job

If you're offered a work-study job as part of your financial aid package, the earnings from that job will go toward your college costs. Even if you're not offered work-study, you may still be able to find a part-time job on or near campus. You can also work during the summer to make money to put toward college.

Work has benefits beyond the extra income it generates. It can help you structure your time, which can make you a more disciplined student. Studies have shown that students who work part time get better grades and are more likely to finish college than those who don't work at all. If the job is on campus, it enhances the college experience by connecting students more closely with the school and giving them a chance to meet people they wouldn't meet in classes.

On the other hand, don't work so many hours that you jeopardize your ability to get through college. **If you're going to college full time, the recommended workload is about 10 to 15 hours a week**. If you work more than 20 hours a week, you're likely to get overloaded and put yourself at risk of dropping out. If you take fewer courses to make time for work, you may drop below full-time status, which could make you ineligible for many grants and scholarships. If your financial situation makes you feel that you have to work more hours, it might be better to borrow more money so you don't have to work so much.

Part-Time Student, Full-Time Job

A different (and much more difficult) way of approaching work is to be a full-time worker who goes to college part time. This is possible as long as you don't take too many credits in one semester. If you try for more than six to eight credits (two courses) while working full time, you'll probably have trouble getting everything done. On the other hand, if you take fewer than six credits a semester, you won't be eligible for need-based subsidized Stafford or Perkins loans or a Pell Grant.

Working full time while going to school part time is an especially attractive way to pay for an associate degree or a vocational certificate. Most community colleges cater to working students and offer classes at night to meet their needs. If you take six credits per semester, you can probably earn an associate degree in four or five years.

If you're planning on earning a bachelor's degree, however, you should strongly consider attending college full time and borrowing money to replace the income that you won't be earning through a job. Why? If you take only six credits a semester, it will take 10 years to earn a bachelor's! You will probably

---

EXPERT ADVICE

"**Work gives students structure.** First, they have to be somewhere. They have to be doing something at certain times of the week, which helps them manage their time. Second, if the job is on campus, they get involved with an office or a department or a faculty member, and that helps to **strengthen that student's connection with that school**, which always enhances the academic experience."

— *Vincent Amoroso, director, Office of Student Financial Services, Johns Hopkins University* earn more money in the long run if you get that bachelor's in the usual four or five years, and concentrate on your career after you've earned that degree.

Some employers offer tuition assistance or scholarship money to employees who are attending college. Check to see if your employer is one of them. For a typical educational assistance program, up to $5,250 of those benefits will be tax free each year.

Co-op and Internship Programs

Many colleges sponsor internships or "co-op" (cooperative) programs with local employers. Some interns and almost all co-op participants receive payment from their employers along with academic credit. In co-op programs, you may be able to alternate periods of full-time work and full-time study. Often the business at which you intern hires you after graduation, or at least recommends you to others. Internship and co-op programs can help you make money, get academic credit, gain job experience and make contacts with potential employers.

Promising to Work Later

Holding a job during college is not the only way of using work to pay your college costs. There are several programs that allow you to commit to work in public service after graduation in exchange for either a non-need-based scholarship while in college or a stipend that can be used to repay student loans after college. The ROTC program is an example of the former, and AmeriCorps is an example of the latter.

ROTC

In return for military service, the armed forces offer career training and a number of educational benefits to help pay for college, including full college scholarships and education assistance plans. If you're interested in training to be a military officer during college in return for educational benefits, check with the Reserve Officers' Training Corps (ROTC) office at your high school or on your college campus. Each branch of the military offers ROTC training. Part IV of this book contains lists of colleges that offer ROTC programs for each service branch.

OTHER SERVICE PROGRAMS

AmeriCorps is a network of national service programs for which you can work as a volunteer, full or part time, for up to a year. After completing a term of service with AmeriCorps, you're eligible for an education award, which can be used either to repay student loans or to pay for college tuition. The amount of the award depends on how long you worked for the program, and for how many hours each week. (Currently, completion of one year's full-time service earns an award of $4,725.) For more information, go to www.americorps.org.

Another type of program is one that hinges on your financial aid package and the profession you choose after college. If you received a Perkins loan as part of your package, the loan may be forgiven if you enter certain professions serving the public, such as teaching, nursing or law enforcement.

KEEP IN MIND

As noted in Step 2, you will be **expected to contribute** a larger percentage of your **work income to college costs** than your parents will. This is because it is expected that you have fewer financial responsibilities and will benefit more from college than your parents will. In general, you will be expected to pay about 50 percent of your earnings toward the EFC.

Borrow It

To borrow money is to spend today what you'll earn in the future. You will have to pay the loan back, with interest, when you start earning money after college. A loan can be intimidating because it assumes you'll have the money for repayment, and you may not feel sure of that. But rest assured that college will increase your earning power, which will make it possible to repay your loans.

There are many forms of "bad debt" in our society, such as credit card debt, where you borrow money on unfavorable terms to buy consumer goods that will have little or no value in a year. By comparison, an education loan is a "good debt." You are borrowing money on favorable terms to achieve an outcome — higher lifetime earnings — that will more than pay back the loan.

Subsidized Stafford loans, Perkins loans and need-based state loans all have excellent terms that make them worth considering. Some institutions also offer their own need-based loans to qualified students. However, these loans are intended as financial aid to cover your need. In general, you won't be able to use them towards your expected family contribution.

However, loans are available that are not based on need and that your family can use to borrow money to meet their EFC. The terms are not as favorable as the need-based loans, but the loans may be helpful just the same. The most common types are the unsubsidized Stafford and the PLUS loan, both of which are guaranteed by the federal government, but there are also state and private sources.

How Much Should You Borrow?

If your family decides to borrow money to pay for college, they should consider the total debt that you will carry after graduation. That total debt includes any subsidized, need-meeting loans that you accept as part of the college's aid package as well as any non-need-based loans your family takes out to meet the EFC. When you pay back that debt, you'll do so in the form of monthly payments, and those payments should be reasonable ones that you can afford to pay from the income you're likely to have. The total monthly payment will usually be similar to a car payment — $200 to $300 a month. But the amount will vary with the amount borrowed and interest rate offered. See Table 4 on the next page for help in determining what your monthly payment will be. It shows monthly repayment over 10 years for a loan of $10,000 at various interest rates. To calculate a monthly payment for a loan amount not listed on the table, multiply the amount borrowed by the repayment factor for your interest rate. For example, if you borrowed $12,500 at 7.5 percent, your monthly payment would be $148.46 ($12,500 × .0118770).

There are some ways to make your repayment burden lighter after college. Many lenders will offer to cut your interest rate a bit if you make your first 12 monthly payments on time. If you borrow from multiple federal loan programs, such as the Perkins, subsidized Stafford and unsubsidized Stafford, you can consolidate these loans after graduation, which will simplify things by allowing you to make only one payment a month. Consolidation also gives you the option of "re-amortizing" your loans — that means stretching your payments over a longer period of time than you would normally have left to repay the debt. If you re-amortize when you consolidate, you will usually have a lower monthly payment, but will pay more interest over the total life of all the loans.

Table 4:

Calculating Your Monthly Loan Payment

AMOUNT OF LOAN	INTEREST RATE	REPAYMENT FACTOR	MONTHLY PAYMENT
$10,000	4.00%	.010125	$101.25
	4.50%	.010364	$103.64
	5.00%	.010607	$106.07
	5.50%	.010853	$108.53
	6.00%	.011102	$111.02
	6.50%	.011355	$113.55
	7.00%	.011611	$116.11
	7.50%	.011870	$118.70
	8.00%	.012133	$121.33
	8.50%	.012399	$123.99
	9.00%	.012668	$126.68

GOOD TO KNOW

When you start paying back your educational loan, remember that the **interest may be tax deductible**. To a maximum of $2,500 per year, you can deduct the interest you pay from your income, which will lower your tax bite. In effect, the government will be subsidizing your loan. This is true for every kind of education loan, including PLUS loans.

Types of Non-Need-Based Loans

There are three basic types of loans you can use to pay your out-of-pocket costs: federal, state and private.

FEDERAL LOANS

Federal loans have relatively low interest rates and are guaranteed by the federal government. This means that if you don't pay your loan back to the lender (though, of course, you should), the federal government will. That encourages lenders to lend you money even if you're a student with no credit history and little employment record.

Two basic kinds of federal loans are used for paying an EFC, one for students, one for parents:

- **Student Loans (Unsubsidized Stafford).** With an unsubsidized Stafford loan, you borrow money through participating colleges or directly from a bank or other lender. You'll be charged only interest while you're in school, and can either pay it while you're in school or let it accrue (accumulate) for payment after school. If you let the interest accrue, the bank will "capitalize" it into the principal of the loan when you start sending them payments after graduation. Table 5 shows the effects of interest accrual. The calculations on the table are for example only — they assume that you borrow $3,500 at the beginning of your freshman year and don't borrow any more to fund subsequent years of education. With this amount and the interest rate shown, letting the interest accrue saves you a $20 monthly payment while you're in college, but it ends up costing you about $407 more over the life of the loan. Whether or not you let interest accrue, six months after leaving school (your grace period), you have to begin paying back both the principal and the interest. To apply for an unsubsidized Stafford loan, ask your college financial aid office; they will refer you to lenders.

Table 5:

Effects of Letting Interest Accrue While You're in College

	INTEREST RATE IN COLLEGE	MONTHLY PAYMENT IN COLLEGE	DEBT REMAINING AFTER COLLEGE	INTEREST RATE AFTER COLLEGE*	MONTHLY PAYMENT AFTER COLLEGE	TOTAL INTEREST PAID OVER LIFE OF THE LOAN
Subsidized Stafford	0%	$0	$3,500.00	3.4%	$34.45	$634.00
Unsubsidized Stafford (no interest accrual)	6.8%	$19.83	$3,500.00	6.8%	$40.28	$2,404.60
Unsubsidized Stafford (interest accrual option)	6.8%	$0	$4,571.00	6.8%	$52.60	$2,812.00

*From July 1, 2011, to July 1, 2012

- **Parent Loans (PLUS).** With a PLUS loan, your parents borrow money to pay for your education either through the school or a third-party lender. They can borrow any amount up to the student's total cost of attendance minus the financial aid you receive. To get a PLUS loan, your parents have to fill out an application and pass a credit review. They will have to start making payments on the entire debt — both the principal and the interest — as soon as the loan money is disbursed to the school.

If you take out a federal loan, you'll receive a loan repayment schedule that spells out when your first payment is due and the number, frequency and amounts of the payments. You'll have to pay back the loan on schedule or go into default, an official state of failure to repay a loan. That would hurt your credit rating — your ability to borrow more money later.

Under certain circumstances, such as economic hardship, you can postpone repayment of a federal student loan by applying for a deferment (during which no interest accumulates) or forbearance (during which it does). Under exceptional circumstances, such as total disability or teaching in a designated low-income school, some borrowers get a loan discharge, or cancellation of the debt. These rules apply to all federal student loans, but not to PLUS loans.

STATE LOANS

Some states sponsor loan programs for students and parents in their state. These loans are usually neither subsidized nor based on need. Check with your state financial aid agency to find out more.

PRIVATE LOANS

Many banks, credit unions and other organizations offer their own education loans. These usually have slightly higher interest rates than federal loans, but they have lower interest rates than other consumer borrowing options, and may have attractive features, such as deferred repayment while in school. The borrowers — usually parents — have to prove their creditworthiness to get these loans.

HOME-EQUITY LOANS

Many parents consider taking out a loan against their home equity to pay for their children's higher education. While this may be an attractive option for your family, you should keep in mind that, unlike PLUS loans and other education loans, home-equity loans do come with the condition that if you can't pay back the loan, the bank can foreclose on your house.

Table 6:
Comparison of Education Loan Options

	SUBSIDIZED STAFFORD	PERKINS	UNSUBSIDIZED STAFFORD	PLUS	PRIVATE/ ALTERNATIVE EDUCATION LOAN	HOME EQUITY LOAN OR LINE OF CREDIT
BORROWING LIMIT	$3,500 first year $4,500 second year $5,500 third and fourth years Higher limits for independent students and for graduate study	$5,500/year $27,500 undergraduate maximum	$5,500 first year $6,500 second year $7,500 third and fourth years Higher limits if parents were denied a PLUS loan	Maximum is difference between total cost of attendance and financial aid awarded	Depends on credit check Maximum is difference between total cost of attendance and financial aid awarded	Depends on credit check and home equity
INTEREST RATES FOR 2011-12	In school: 0% In repayment: 3.4% (fixed)	In school: 0% In repayment: 5% (fixed)	In school: 6.8% (fixed) In repayment: 6.8% (fixed)	8.5% (fixed)	Depends on lender and credit check; range from 7% to 12%; may be fixed or variable	Depends on lender and credit check; may be fixed or variable
PROS	Interest that accumulates while you're in college paid by federal government	No origination fee Interest that accumulates while you're in college paid by federal government Debt may be forgiven if you enter a career in the public service	Option of not making payments during college and "capitalizing" accrued interest into the loan upon graduation Same deferment, and forbearance rules as subsidized loans	No collateral required	Available for nondegree programs and adult continuing education Repayment term may be longer than for federal loans	Can use money for noneducational purposes Repayment term may be longer than for federal loans
CONS	Only available to students with financial need 2% origination fee (may be discounted by lender)	Only available to students with financial need Amount of loan you're offered subject to college financial aid office's discretion	4% origination fee (may be discounted by lender)	Parents must pass credit check to take out loan Parents must begin paying interest immediately 4% origination fee	Student must pass credit check Parents may have to cosign promissory note May have high origination fees	Home used as collateral for loan Can take several months to secure loan; may need to have house appraised

Cut It

In addition to spending past, present and future resources to pay your college bill, you can also take steps to make that bill smaller. This is an especially smart move if it looks like college won't be affordable otherwise, even when you contribute all you can from savings, current income and loans. But some strategies to cut college costs are worth using even if your family is financially comfortable.

Tuition "On the Cheap"

Tuition, the cost of taking classes, is usually high at four-year colleges. But you can get a reduced rate on those classes by taking them ahead of time at your own high school or a community college. By doing this, you may also be able to reduce the number of semesters you have to spend in college, which will cut not only your tuition costs but all other costs, such as room and board. Some colleges offer accelerated programs that will help you do that.

AP®/CLEP®

Several programs let you earn college credit or advanced placement. They include the Advanced Placement Program® (AP®) and the College-Level Examination Program® (CLEP®), which are sponsored by the College Board. The programs differ in various ways. For example, students take AP courses as part of their high school curriculum, but they can prepare to take the CLEP examinations by any number of means — in school, on the job or by just reading books in their spare time. These programs are similar, however, in that you earn credit by taking an examination and receiving a score that your college accepts.

Colleges differ as to which programs, courses and scores they accept and how much credit they grant. But every credit you receive means a credit you don't have to pay for in college. Depending on your exam scores and your college's policies, you may be able to graduate a semester or even a year early if you've taken enough AP Exams.

CLEP exams can be taken on your campus or at a nearby campus, and can be used to bypass introductory-level courses. For more information go to collegeboard.com/clep. To find out about your college's policy on AP credit, go to collegeboard.com and use the AP Credit Policy Info tool.

TAKE COMMUNITY COLLEGE CLASSES OVER THE SUMMER

Courses at a community college usually cost much less than at a four-year college. Find out if there are courses you can take at a local community college in the summers and transfer to your four-year college. For example, if you don't have the knowledge of a certain subject that you need to pass a CLEP exam, you may still be able to take that course at a community college over the summer and transfer the credit to your four-year college.

OTHER ACCELERATED PROGRAMS

Some colleges offer an "accelerated program" designed for students who want to graduate in three years. These programs require a lot of work and dedication, but they will cut your college costs substantially by eliminating an entire year of expenses. It's possible to get through these programs if you're determined.

Cutting Other Expenses

Tuition is not the only college cost you can cut. Room, board, books, supplies, transportation — all of these add substantially to your total college bill. (Most people are shocked at what college textbooks cost these days.) Here are some suggestions to reduce these expenses:

BOOKS

- ✔ Buy used textbooks instead of new ones.
- ✔ Comparison shop for textbooks online.
- ✔ Sell your textbooks at the end of the semester.

ROOM AND BOARD

- ✔ Live off campus in a house or apartment that you share with classmates. That can be cheaper than a college dorm. (But check the policy at the college you want to attend — many require freshmen to live on campus.)
- ✔ If you plan to live in a dorm in your sophomore year and beyond, try to get a position as a resident adviser and the free room and board that comes with it.

TRANSPORTATION

- ✔ If you're commuting to school, carpool with a classmate from your area.

Education Tax Breaks

Federal student aid isn't the only way that Uncle Sam can help you pay for college. There are also tax breaks available for higher-education costs. By reducing the amount your family has to pay the government at tax time, these programs amount to federal subsidies for out-of-pocket costs. Some of them take the form of tax credits, which cut your taxes dollar for dollar: That is, a $1 tax credit would make your tax bill $1 smaller. Others take the form of tax

GOOD TO KNOW

The information about higher-education tax breaks printed here is current as of early 2010. **To make sure you qualify for a deduction or credit** before you file, download IRS Publication 970, "Tax Benefits for Education," from www.irs.gov.

deductions, which lower the amount of your income that is subject to tax, indirectly lowering your tax bill.

There are three federal income tax credits for college expenses: the **American Opportunity credit**, the **Hope credit**, and the **Lifetime Learning credit**. All of these tax credits let your family reduce the taxes they pay dollar-for dollar, but each credit is for a different amount and has different requirements. And for any one student, a family can only elect to use only one of these credits on the same tax return.

The American Opportunity credit is worth up to $2,500 per year for each eligible student in the family. Unlike the other two credits, if the amount of the American Opportunity credit is more than the amount of tax owed, all or a portion of the excess may be received as a refund. This credit is available for the *first four years* of college. To be eligible, a student must be enrolled at least half-time; and the credit can only be claimed for four tax years for each student in the family. If a family has more than one student in college, it can claim the American Opportunity credit for one student and the Lifetime Learning credit (but not the Hope credit) for another student in the same tax year.

For most taxpayers, the Hope tax credit has been replaced by the American Opportunity credit. However the Hope credit is still available for families who have at least one student attending college in a Midwestern disaster area in the states of Arkansas, Illinois, Indiana, Iowa, Missouri, Nebraska and Wisconsin. The credit is worth up to $3,600 per year for each student attending college in the Midwestern disaster area, and up to $1,800 for each student attending college elsewhere. The credit is limited to students in the *first two years* of an undergraduate program. To be eligible, a student must be enrolled at least half-time; but the credit can only be claimed for two tax years for each student in the family. If a family has more than one student in college and wants to claim the Hope credit for one student, it can't also claim the American Opportunity credit for *any* student that year.

The Lifetime Learning credit is worth up to $2,000 per year ($4,000 for students attending college in the Midwestern disaster area) for each eligible student in the family. There is *no limit on the number of years* this credit can be claimed for each student. If a family has more than one student in college, it can claim an education tax credit on a per-student, per-year basis. In other words, it can claim the American Opportunity credit or the Hope credit for one student, and the Lifetime Learning credit for another student in the same year.

For each of these tax credits, the amount of the credit depends on your family's income. The American Opportunity credit is gradually reduced if your family's adjusted gross income is between $160,000 and $180,000 if you have two parents filing a joint return and between $80,000 and $90,000 for a parent filing singly. The Hope and Lifetime Learning credits both phase out between $100,000 and $120,000 for joint returns and $50,000 and $60,000 for single returns.

If your family's income is too high to qualify for any of these tax credits, there's also a tax deduction that may help. With the tuition and fees deduction, you can deduct up to $4,000 of college tuition and fees as long as your family income isn't more than $80,000 (for single filers) or $160,000 (for joint filers). If you claim this deduction, you can't claim the American Opportunity, Hope or Lifetime Learning credits for the same student that year.

Interest paid on student loans is tax deductible to a maximum of $2,500 per year. This benefit applies to all loans used to pay for college, including PLUS loans. To be eligible for this deduction, your income has to be lower than $75,000 (for single filers) or $150,000 (for joint filers). The tax break is only for the amount of interest you paid, not the amount you borrowed. If you take out a student loan, the lender will send a 1098 form to you at the end of each tax year telling you how much of your payments were for interest that year.

Some states also allow you to take tax credits or deductions from your state income taxes. Find out about yours from your state government.

Table 7:
Federal Income Tax Benefits for Higher Education

	AMERICAN OPPORTUNITY CREDIT	HOPE EDUCATION CREDIT	LIFETIME LEARNING CREDIT	TUITION AND FEES DEDUCTION	STUDENT LOAN INTEREST DEDUCTION
AVAILABLE FOR	Tuition, fees, books, supplies and equipment 1st four years of undergraduate study only Associate and bachelor's degree programs only	Tuition and fees only 1st two years of undergraduate study only Associate and bachelor's degree programs only	Tuition and fees only All years of study Any degree program, also nondegree courses to acquire job skills	Tuition and fees only All years of study Attendance at any postsecondary institution participating in a federal student aid program	Any higher education cost All years of study Any degree program
MAXIMUM VALUE	$2,500 credit per student	$1,800 credit per student	$2,000 credit per family	$4,000 deduction taken as an adjustment to gross income	$2,500 deduction from taxable income
MAXIMUM INCOME FOR ELIGIBILITY	$80,000–$90,000 (single filers) $160,000–$180,000 (joint filers)	$50,000–$60,000 (single filers) $100,000–$120,000 (joint filers)		$80,000 (single filers) $160,000 (joint filers)	$60,000–$75,000 (single filers) $120,000–$150,000 (joint filers)
CONDITIONS	Student must be enrolled at least half-time Cannot claim Hope credit on same return	Student must be enrolled at least half-time At least one student must be in Midwestern disaster area Can be claimed for only two tax years for each student Cannot claim American Opportunity credit on same return	No other conditions	Cannot claim an education tax credit for same student in the same year	Student must have been enrolled at least half-time

**QUICK
RECAP**

To deal with out-of-pocket college costs, you have several options. You can draw on savings or current income to pay, or you can borrow some portion of the total bill. And you can cut the costs.

- Several savings options, including U.S. savings bonds, 529s and Coverdell accounts, have tax benefits that can also help.
- You can work during college or promise to work later through programs like ROTC or AmeriCorps.
- You can borrow through student or parent loans.
- You can reduce your costs by such means as taking college-level courses for credit before you enter college.
- Tax breaks can help you meet college costs.

Once You're in College

QUICK OVERVIEW

Once you're in college, you shouldn't be preoccupied with paying for it. Academics, extracurricular activities and making friends are more important. But there are some things you need to do to stay on target financially. This chapter will tell you what they are.

Reapply for Aid Each Year!

Don't forget to reapply to renew your aid package every year! Check at your financial aid office to make sure you have the right forms and know what the deadlines are. Most colleges have a renewal deadline for financial aid that's a week or two later than the deadline for new applicants.

When you renew, don't expect your aid package to stay exactly the same. It may become more loan heavy each year, with more money in subsidized loans. The borrowing limits on the subsidized Stafford loan are higher for sophomores than for freshmen, and even higher for juniors and seniors. Also, keep in mind that some scholarships and grants are for freshmen only.

While you're reapplying for the financial aid you already have, keep an eye out for new opportunities. As you move on to higher grades and declare a major, you may become eligible for outside scholarships that weren't open to you in the past. Follow the guidelines in Step 9 to look for outside sources of money.

EXPERT ADVICE

"There are students who tell me that the reason they didn't pass their class was they're **too busy working**, because they need the money to support themselves. And I tell them, you need to determine your priorities. There's a limit of how much financial aid I can give you to help offset that."

— *Mary San Agustin, director of financial aid and scholarships, Palomar College, San Marcos, Calif.*

Stay on Track

The next thing to keep in mind is that you have to maintain eligibility for financial aid. For federal student aid, stay in school at least half-time, and avoid illegal drugs. A drug-related conviction can lead to suspension or revocation of your federal-aid eligibility.

You don't have to maintain a particular GPA to maintain federal eligibility (though you do have to meet your individual school's standards for "satisfactory academic progress"). But the financial aid your college gives you, such as scholarships, may have specific academic requirements. Do your best in all your classes and stay on track academically, not only because it will help you get the most out of college but because it will help you keep your financial aid. To maintain or establish eligibility for academic scholarships, an on-campus job such as a teaching or research assistant, or a "co-op" program between your department and a local employer, you'll need to be in good academic standing.

Maintain Grades

To keep up your grades, you'll have to make decisions about how to spend your time. It's important to build social relationships, pursue extracurricular activities, and earn money through work, but balance those against the need to maintain a good academic record. If you have a job, don't work so hard at it that you jeopardize your aid eligibility. (See "Expert Advice" sidebar on page 11.)

Don't Stay Too Long (Pick a Major, Any Major)

Did you know that only about one-third of all students who enter a four-year college graduate in four years? Most take six or more years to earn a bachelor's degree. Obviously, the longer you stay in college, the more it's going to cost you — not only in tuition, fees, room, board and other expenses, but also in lost earnings from a delayed career.

Make it a goal to graduate on time. Make sure you are on track to complete your college's core requirements, as well as the core requirements for your major.

Speaking of majors, don't feel that you need to rush into choosing one. Except for some very specialized career and technical institutes, most colleges and universities allow you to take time during your first two years to take classes in different fields and make sure you know enough to choose a major that fits your interests and abilities. On the other hand, don't wait so long that you neglect to take the courses that are requirements for a major. You don't want to have to pay for an extra semester to get your biology degree because you didn't take that required organic chemistry course your sophomore year.

Transferring from a Community College

If you're going to a community college, and plan to transfer to a four-year college, **make sure you know all the transfer requirements** — including whatever courses are needed for the major you intend to declare. It helps if your community college has an articulation agreement with the four-year college specifying exactly what courses are required for transfer. Almost all community colleges have a transfer adviser on staff who can help you make sure you're on track. Get to know your adviser and check in with him or her regularly.

MYTH/FACT

Myth: Only certain majors will lead to high earnings after graduation.

Fact: Don't be fooled. If you're not drawn to the major, you probably won't like the work and will leave that field before you ever reach the high earnings. Instead, **choose a major based on your interests and talents**, not on someone else's predictions of industrial trends. And remember that many of today's highest paying fields — such as marketing and software engineering — require critical thinking skills that you will acquire in courses like anthropology and philosophy. To learn more about specific academic fields and what it's like to major in them, read the College Board's *Book of Majors*.

Watch Your Personal Expenses

The purpose of financial aid is to give you the money you need to pay for college costs. But that aid can quickly become too little if you spend too much. To avoid overspending, live within your means and don't run up frivolous debt. That means sticking to a budget and avoiding credit cards.

Student Budgeting

To live within your means, all you have to do is not spend more than you receive in income. The best way to do that is to create a budget at the beginning of each semester and stick to it. Your budget should list the funds you will receive (such as money from parents, savings, work, grants and loans), subtract how much money you plan to spend on given items (such as tuition, fees, room, board, books, clothes and recreation) and calculate the difference — the bottom line. If the bottom line is a negative number — that is, if your expenses exceed your income — you're overspending. Once you have a budget where your income is equal to or greater than your expenses, follow it, and you'll be living within your means.

To create a budget, first examine what you have actually been spending, then **set priorities if you're spending too much**. That alone can help you to spend less, as you realize you can make do with one latte a day instead of two. "You start making conscious decisions about what it is that you want to do," says Elizabeth Bickford of the University of Oregon at Eugene. "You're actually just taking control over your financial spending."

By all means have fun, but don't spend too much money on nonessential items like DVDs, high-end clothes or trips to the beach. Some of your friends at college may have more money than you, but don't let social pressure push you into trying to spend like they do. Learn to suggest ordering pizza from the local hangout instead of driving to an expensive restaurant.

Save money wherever you can — for example, limit your cell phone use to free times. Comparison shop for groceries and supplies. And don't visit the ATM too often: It's too easy to withdraw money and overspend. See collegeboard.com for more advice on budgeting and financial planning.

Credit Card Debt

Be especially careful with your credit cards. They can be convenient for paying for big-ticket items like textbooks and airplane tickets, if you use them sparingly and pay off the entire amount when you get the bill. But if you abuse them, they can land you in a world of trouble.

A credit card is essentially a high-interest loan. Pulling it out at a cash register to make an impulse purchase may give you a feeling of freedom, but you won't feel free once you get the bill — especially when you're still paying interest on that impulse purchase months or years later. If you let the debt accumulate, it may swell so much that you won't be able to pay down the debt. This can affect your future academic career. If you miss payments on your credit cards, or if your credit card debt is high, you can hurt your credit rating. A bad credit rating can harm your chances of getting student loans to pay for graduate school, or a car loan when you start working. It can even prevent you from getting a job with certain security-conscious employers, such as banks or government agencies.

Use credit cards only when you know you can repay the debt promptly. Save them for emergencies. (A spring-break vacation is not an emergency.) Think through each credit card purchase before you spend. If you do get in over your head with credit card use, cut your expenses and talk to your family and financial aid administrator for more guidance.

Saving for Future Needs

While you're trying to live within your means, it's also wise to save for the future. Savings will give you greater freedom to cope with college and personal costs to come. If at all possible, make sure your budget includes money set aside for future needs. Your parents, of course, should do the same.

Try to save what you can from the jobs you have during the school year and in the summer. Think about the following as goals for your savings:

Students should think about …

- ✔ Next year's college expenses
- ✔ Application fees and tuition for graduate school
- ✔ A vacation with friends after you graduate
- ✔ Moving to another city after you graduate
- ✔ The unexpected (such as traveling to a friend's wedding or a family funeral)

Parents should think about …

- ✔ Next year's college expenses
- ✔ College expenses for younger children (if any)
- ✔ Retirement
- ✔ The unexpected (such as making it through a layoff or paying for a child's wedding)

Final Thoughts

Once you're in college, you may sometimes wonder if it's worth it. Can your family afford the expense? Will you be able to repay your student loans? If you've made reasonable choices along the way, the answer is yes. If you ever have doubts, visit your school's career center and do some research into the fields of work you might enter. Find out how much money you're likely to be earning when you first graduate, and how much five years later. A light might go on for you, as Elizabeth Bickford has often observed with other students. "When they see that relationship, many students say, 'Oh, wait a second, I can do that.'"

You will be able to pay back your student loans. College is a sound investment. You can afford college!

QUICK RECAP

Once you're in college, make sure you stay on track financially.

- Reapply for aid every year.
- Maintain your federal eligibility by staying in school the right number of hours and avoiding illegal drugs.
- Keep up your grades. Don't let them get derailed by too much time spent on work or other nonacademic activities.
- Declare a major at a suitable time.
- Make a budget and stick to it.
- Be wary of credit cards.
- Save for future expenses.
- Keep an eye out for new sources of outside scholarships.
- Remember that college is worth it!

Part II

Tables and Worksheets

WORKSHEET 1:
Meet Your Application Deadlines

		COLLEGE 1:	COLLEGE 2:	COLLEGE 3:
	College Name	*1st Choice Univ.*	*Private Univ.*	*Financial Safety*
FORMS REQUIRED	FAFSA			
	PROFILE			
	State form			
	Institutional form			
	Tax returns			
	Other			
SCHOOL CODES	Federal code			
	CSS code			
PRIORITY DATE				
CLOSING DATE				
AFTER APPLYING	Need to send letter?			
	Documentation required?			
COMPARE AWARDS	Notification date			
	Reply-by date			

WORKSHEET 2:
Scholarship Application Planner

	PROGRAM 1	PROGRAM 2	PROGRAM 3
PROGRAM/SPONSOR			
ELIGIBILITY REQUIREMENTS			
TYPE OF AWARD			
AMOUNT OF AWARD			
CAN BE USED FOR			
CAN BE USED AT			
DEADLINE			
FORMS REQUIRED			
TEST SCORES REQUIRED			
ESSAY OR ACADEMIC SAMPLE			
RECOMMENDATIONS			
NOTIFICATION BEGINS			
REQUIREMENTS TO KEEP AFTER FRESHMAN YEAR			

WORKSHEET 3:
Compare Your Awards

	COLLEGE 1	COLLEGE 2	COLLEGE 3
Step 1. List the name of each college you want to consider attending, the award deadline and the total cost of attendance. This figure should be in your award letter. If not, refer to the college catalog or contact the college financial aid office.			
Name of college			
Award deadline date			
Total cost of attendance			
Step 2. List the financial aid awards each school is offering. Don't forget that grants, scholarships and work-study do not have to be repaid, while all loans must be repaid.			
Grants and scholarships			
• Pell Grant (federal)			
• SEOG (federal)			
• State			
• College			
• Other			
Total grants/scholarships			
Percentage of package that is grant/scholarship			
Work-study opportunities			
Loans			
• Stafford-Direct (federal)			
• Perkins (federal)			
• Other			
Total loans			
Percentage of package that is work or loans			
Total financial aid award			
Grants and scholarships + work-study + loans			
Step 3. Calculate what it will cost you to attend each college you are considering. For each college, enter the total cost of attendance. Then, subtract the total financial aid award from the total cost of attendance. That number is the net cost, or what it will cost you to attend that college.			
a) Total cost of attendance			
b) Total financial aid award			
c) Net cost to attend (a minus b)			

Figure 13:
Sample Financial Aid Award Letter 1

Blue University   Cost of Attendance: $ 28,706.00

CLASS: 01

March 22, 2008

TENTATIVE
FINANCIAL AWARD NOTIFICATION FOR 2008-2009

Based on the information that you submitted on your FAFSA and to our office,
Blue University can offer you the following TENTATIVE awards.

This package is based on an award period from 09/10/08 to 06/06/09.

AID AWARD	ACCEPT AWARD		OFFERED AMOUNT
	Yes	NO	
FEDERAL PERKINS LOAN	_____	_____	$1,143
STATE WORK-STUDY	_____	_____	$2,400
BLUE EDUCATIONAL GRANT	_____	_____	$3,538
UNIVERSITY SCHOLARSHIP	_____	_____	$2,000
RESIDENCE HALL GRANT	_____	_____	$2,000
FEDERAL STAFFORD LOAN – SUB.	_____	_____	$2,625

Finalize your financial aid award as soon as possible by forwarding to our office the forms listed on
the Missing Documents Form included with this letter.

Please read the important information pamphlet! Indicate your intent by checking whether or not you
accept each aid award, then sign and return this letter in order to reserve your award(s).

Please refer to the Cost Worksheet to help determine your expenses for the academic year.

If direct loan amounts desired are less than above, please indicate below:

     Requested Federal Stafford Loan (Sub.) $ _____
     Requested Federal Perkins Loan $ _____

I acknowledge that I have read and will comply with all the supporting information in the Important
Information Pamphlet. Furthermore, if I receive any financial assistance not included in this award
letter, including tuition waivers or employer reimbursement, I will notify your office immediately.

Signature _____   Date _____

Figure 14:
Sample Financial Aid Award Letter 2

PART II: TABLES AND WORKSHEETS

Green University | **Office of Student Financial Planning**

Cost of Attendance: $ 26,005.00

March 1, 2011

Step 1. Circle A for Accept or D for Decline for each individual award where indicated below:

	Fall 2008	Spring 2009	Total	A / D
Presidential Freshman Scholarship	$3,250	$3,250	$6,500	A / D
Green University Grant	$705	$705	$1,410	A / D
Total Grants and Scholarships			**$7,910**	
Federal Unsubsidized Stafford Loan	$1,313	$1,312	$2,625	A / D
Total Student Loans			**$2,625**	
Federal College Work-Study	$330	$330	$660	A / D
Federal PLUS Loan and/or Green Partnership Loan	$7,405	$7,405	$14,810	

Step 2. Please note the following:

Your awards are based on full-time enrollment for the fall and spring terms and residence hall occupancy for the fall and spring terms (for financial aid purposes, full-time is defined as 12 credits or more per term).

You have been offered loan(s) that require separate loan materials.

The amount of your Green University Grant was based upon residence hall occupancy for the fall and spring terms. A change in housing status may result in a reduction of this award.

Step 3. Please list other financial assistance, scholarships, or loans you will receive not indicated above. List the scholarship/donor name and the expected amount (example: Elks Club $100).

Name	Amount

Step 4. Attention: Your awards are not final until you complete the items on the ACTION REQUESTED page.

2010–2011
FAFSA ON THE WEB WORKSHEET
www.fafsa.gov

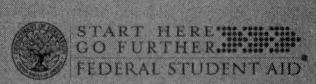

START HERE
GO FURTHER
FEDERAL STUDENT AID

DO NOT MAIL THIS WORKSHEET.

You must complete and submit a *Free Application for Federal Student Aid* (FAFSA) to apply for federal student aid and to apply for most state and college aid. Applying online with *FAFSA on the Web* at **www.fafsa.gov** is faster and easier than using a paper FAFSA.

This worksheet has been designed to provide a preview of the questions that you may be asked on *FAFSA on the Web*. Write down notes to help you easily complete your FAFSA anytime after January 1, 2010.

See the table to the right for state deadlines. Check with your high school counselor or your college's financial aid administrator about other deadlines.

- **This Worksheet is optional and should only be completed if you plan to use *FAFSA on the Web.***

- **Sections in grey are for parent information.**

- **This Worksheet does not include all the questions from the FAFSA. The questions that are included are ordered as they appear on *FAFSA on the Web*. When you are online you may be able to skip some questions based on your answers to earlier questions.**

Apply Faster—Sign your FAFSA with a Federal Student Aid PIN.

If you do not have a PIN, you can apply for one at **www.pin.ed.gov**. Your PIN allows you to electronically sign when you submit your FAFSA. If you are providing parent information, one parent must also sign your FAFSA. To sign electronically, your parent should also apply for a PIN.

You do not have to pay to get help or submit your FAFSA. Submit your FAFSA for **free** online at **www.fafsa.gov**. Federal Student Aid provides **free** help online at **www.fafsa.gov** or you can call 1-800-4-FED-AID. TTY users (hearing impaired) may call 1-800-730-8913.

NOTES:

STATE AID DEADLINES

Check with your financial aid administrator for these states and territories:

AL, AS *, AZ, CO, FM *, GA, GU *, HI *, MH *, MP *, NC, NE, NM, NV *, PR, PW *, SD *, TX *, UT, VA *, VI *, VT *, WA, WI and WY *.

Pay attention to the symbols that may be listed after your state deadline.

AK	April 15, 2010 *(date received)*
AR	Academic Challenge - June 1, 2010 *(date received)*
	Workforce Grant - Contact the financial aid office.
	Higher Education Opportunity Grant
	- June 1, 2010 (fall term) *(date received)*
	- November 1, 2010 (spring term) *(date received)*
CA	Initial awards - March 2, 2010 + *
	Additional community college awards
	- September 2, 2010 *(date postmarked)* + *
CT	February 15, 2010 *(date received)* # *
DC	June 30, 2010 *(date received by state)* # *
DE	April 15, 2010 *(date received)*
FL	May 15, 2010 *(date processed)*
IA	July 1, 2010 *(date received)*
ID	Opportunity Grant - March 1, 2010 *(date received)* # *
IL	As soon as possible after 1/1/2010. Awards made until funds are depleted.
IN	March 10, 2010 *(date received)*
KS	April 1, 2010 *(date received)* # *
KY	March 15, 2010 *(date received)* #
LA	July 1, 2010 *(date received)*
MA	May 1, 2010 *(date received)* #
MD	March 1, 2010 *(date received)*
ME	May 1, 2010 *(date received)*
MI	March 1, 2010 *(date received)*
MN	30 days after term starts *(date received)*
MO	April 1, 2010 *(date received)* #
MS	MTAG and MESG Grants - September 15, 2010 *(date received)* #
	HELP Scholarship - March 31, 2010 *(date received)* #
MT	March 1, 2010 *(date received)* #
ND	March 15, 2010 *(date received)*
NH	May 1, 2010 *(date received)*
NJ	2009-2010 Tuition Aid Grant recipients - June 1, 2010 *(date received)*
	All other applicants
	- October 1, 2010, fall & spring terms *(date received)*
	- March 1, 2011, spring term only *(date received)*
NY	May 1, 2011 *(date received)* + *
OH	October 1, 2010 *(date received)*
OK	April 15, 2010 *(date received)* #
OR	OSAC Scholarship - March 1, 2010
	Oregon Opportunity Grant - Contact the financial aid office.
PA	All 2009-2010 State Grant recipients & all non-2009-2010 State Grant recipients in degree program - May 1, 2010 *(date received)* *
	All other applicants - August 1, 2010 *(date received)* *
RI	March 1, 2010 *(date received)* #
SC	Tuition Grants - June 30, 2010 *(date received)*
	SC Commission on Higher Education - no deadline
TN	State Grant - February 15, 2010 *(date received)* #
	State Lottery - September 1, 2010 *(date received)* #
WV	April 15, 2010 *(date received)* # *

\# For priority consideration, submit application by date specified.
\+ Applicants encouraged to obtain proof of mailing.
* Additional form may be required.

SECTION 1 - STUDENT INFORMATION

After you are online, you can add up to ten colleges on your FAFSA. The colleges will receive the information from your processed FAFSA.

Student's Last Name	First Name	Social Security Number

Student Citizenship Status (check one of the following)

❑ U.S. citizen (U.S. national)   ❑ Neither citizen nor eligible noncitizen

❑ Eligible noncitizen (Enter your Alien Registration Number in the box to the right.)

Your Alien Registration Number

Generally, you are an eligible noncitizen if you are:
- A permanent U.S. resident with a Permanent Resident Card (I-551);
- A conditional permanent resident (I-551C); or
- The holder of an Arrival-Departure Record (I-94) from the Department of Homeland Security showing any of the following designations: "Refugee," "Asylum Granted," "Parolee" (I-94 confirms paroled for a minimum of one year and status has not expired), "Victim of human trafficking," T-Visa holder (T-1, T-2, T-3, etc.) or "Cuban-Haitian Entrant."

A [ ] [ ] [ ] [ ] [ ] [ ] [ ] [ ]

Student Marital Status (check one of the following)

❑ Single   ❑ Married or remarried   ❑ Separated   ❑ Divorced or widowed

You will be asked to provide information about your spouse if you are married or remarried.

Selective Service Registration

If you are male and 25 or younger, you can use the FAFSA to register with Selective Service.

Student Aid Eligibility Drug Convictions

❑ I have never attended college   ❑ I have never received federal student aid   ❑ I have never had a drug conviction

If you did not check any of these boxes, you will be asked more questions online.

Highest school your father completed	❑ Middle school/Jr. high ❑ High school	❑ College or beyond ❑ Other/unknown
Highest school your mother completed	❑ Middle school/Jr. high ❑ High school	❑ College or beyond ❑ Other/unknown

SECTION 2 - STUDENT DEPENDENCY STATUS

If you can check ANY of the following boxes, you will not have to provide parental information. Skip to page 4.

If you check NONE of the following boxes, you will be asked to provide parental information. Go to the next page.

❑ I was born before January 1, 1987	❑ I am married	❑ I will be working on a master's or doctorate program (e.g., MA, MBA, MD, JD, PhD, EdD, graduate certificate)
❑ I am serving on active duty in the U.S. Armed Forces	❑ I am a veteran of the U.S. Armed Forces	❑ I have children and I provide more than half of their support
❑ Since I turned age 13, both of my parents were deceased	❑ I was in foster care since turning age 13	❑ I have dependents (other than children or my spouse) who live with me and I provide more than half of their support
❑ I was a dependent or ward of the court since turning age 13	❑ I am currently or I was an emancipated minor	❑ I am currently or I was in legal guardianship	❑ I am homeless or I am at risk of being homeless

NOTES:

PART II: TABLES AND WORKSHEETS

SECTION 3 - PARENT INFORMATION

Who is considered a parent? "Parent" refers to a biological or adoptive parent. Grandparents, foster parents, legal guardians, older siblings, and uncles or aunts are **not** considered parents on this form unless they have legally adopted you. In case of divorce or separation, give information about the parent you lived with most in the last 12 months. If you did not live with one parent more than the other, give information about the parent who provided you the most financial support during the last 12 months or during the most recent year you received support. If your divorced or widowed parent has remarried, also provide information about your stepparent.

Providing your father's information? You will need:	**Providing your mother's information? You will need:**
Father's/Stepfather's Social Security Number	Mother's/Stepmother's Social Security Number
Father's/Stepfather's name	Mother's/Stepmother's name
Father's/Stepfather's date of birth	Mother's/Stepmother's date of birth
❏ Check here if your father/stepfather is a dislocated worker	❏ Check here if your mother/stepmother is a dislocated worker

Did your parents file or will they file a 2009 income tax return?
- ❏ My parents have already completed a tax return
- ❏ My parents will file, but have not yet completed a tax return
- ❏ My parents are not going to file an income tax return

Your parents will need their tax returns and/or W-2 forms to complete the FAFSA.

What was your parents' adjusted gross income for 2009?

Skip this question if your parents did not file taxes. Adjusted gross income is on IRS Form 1040—Line 37; 1040A—line 21; or 1040EZ—line 4. $ _____

The following questions ask about earnings (wages, salaries, tips, etc.) in 2009. Answer the questions whether or not a tax return was filed. This information may be on the W-2 forms, or on the IRS Form 1040—Line 7 + 12 + 18 + Box 14 of IRS Schedule K-1 (Form 1065); 1040A—line 7; or 1040EZ—line 1

How much did your father/stepfather earn from working in 2009? $ _____

How much did your mother/stepmother earn from working in 2009? $ _____

In 2008 or 2009, did anyone in your parents' household receive:

- ❏ Supplemental Security Income
- ❏ Food Stamps
- ❏ Free or Reduced Price School Lunch
- ❏ Temporary Assistance for Needy Families (TANF)
- ❏ Special Supplemental Nutrition Program for Women, Infants and Children (WIC)

Note: Food Stamps and TANF may have a different name in your state. Call 1-800-4-FED-AID to find out the name of the state's program.

Did your parents have any of the following items in 2009?
Check all that apply. Once online, you may be asked to report amounts paid or received by your parents.

Additional Financial Information	**Untaxed Income**	
❏ Hope and Lifetime Learning tax credits	❏ Payments to tax-deferred pension and savings plans	❏ Untaxed portions of pensions
❏ Child support paid	❏ Child support received	❏ Housing, food and other living allowances paid to members of the military, clergy and others
❏ Taxable earnings from work-study, assistantships or fellowships	❏ IRA deductions and payments to self-employed SEP, SIMPLE and Keogh	❏ Veterans noneducation benefits
❏ Grant and scholarship aid reported to the IRS	❏ Tax exempt interest income	❏ Other untaxed income not reported, such as workers' compensation or disability
❏ Combat pay or special combat pay	❏ Untaxed portions of IRA distributions	
❏ Cooperative education program earnings		

Your parents may be asked to provide more information about their assets.
Your parents may need to report the net worth of their current businesses and/or investment farms.

NOTES:

Blue University   Cost of Attendance: $ 28,706.00

CLASS: 01

March 22, 2008

PART II: TABLES AND WORKSHEETS

TENTATIVE
FINANCIAL AWARD NOTIFICATION FOR 2008-2009

Based on the information that you submitted on your FAFSA and to our office,
Blue University can offer you the following TENTATIVE awards.

This package is based on an award period from 09/10/08 to 06/06/09.

AID AWARD	ACCEPT AWARD		OFFERED AMOUNT
	Yes	NO	
FEDERAL PERKINS LOAN	_____	_____	$1,143
STATE WORK-STUDY	_____	_____	$2,400
BLUE EDUCATIONAL GRANT	_____	_____	$3,538
UNIVERSITY SCHOLARSHIP	_____	_____	$2,000
RESIDENCE HALL GRANT	_____	_____	$2,000
FEDERAL STAFFORD LOAN – SUB.	_____	_____	$2,625

Finalize your financial aid award as soon as possible by forwarding to our office the forms listed on the Missing Documents Form included with this letter.

Please read the important information pamphlet! Indicate your intent by checking whether or not you accept each aid award, then sign and return this letter in order to reserve your award(s).

Please refer to the Cost Worksheet to help determine your expenses for the academic year.

If direct loan amounts desired are less than above, please indicate below:

      Requested Federal Stafford Loan (Sub.) $ _____
      Requested Federal Perkins Loan $ _____

I acknowledge that I have read and will comply with all the supporting information in the Important Information Pamphlet. Furthermore, if I receive any financial assistance not included in this award letter, including tuition waivers or employer reimbursement, I will notify your office immediately.

Signature _____   Date _____

Estimate Your EFC
Under Federal Methodology

WORKSHEET 4A:
Estimate a Dependent Student's
Expected Contribution

STUDENT'S INCOME	
1. Taxable income ("adjusted gross income" from IRS Form 1040)	$
2. Untaxed income/benefits	+
3. Taxable student aid	-
4. Total student's income (sum of lines 1 and 2, minus line 3)	=
Allowances	
5. U.S. income tax paid (from IRS Form 1040)	
6. State taxes paid (% from Table 8 x line 4)	+
7. F.I.C.A. (Table 9)	+
8. Income protection allowance	$3,000
9. Parents' negative available income offset (line 11 of parents' worksheet, if negative)	+
10. Total allowances (sum of lines 5-9)	=
11. Available income (line 4 minus line 10)	=
12. Available income assessment rate	x 0.50
13. Contribution from income (line 11 x line 12; if negative, enter $0)	=
Student's Assets*	
14. Cash, savings and checking accounts	
15. Other real estate/investment equity	+
16. Business/nonfamily farm equity	+
17. Net assets (sum of lines 14-16)	=
18. Asset assessment rate	x 0.20
19. Contribution from assets (line 17 x line 18; if simple needs test or negative, enter $0)	=
Contribution**	
20. Total Student Contribution (sum of lines 13 and 19)	=

* If you are eligible to file an IRS 1040A or 1040EZ form, or you are not required to file a tax return, and your parents' taxable income is less than $50,000, no assets are included in the methodology.

** If your parents' adjusted gross income is $30,000 or less, and they file or are eligible to file an IRS 1040A or 1040EZ form, no contribution is expected.

WORKSHEET 4B:
Estimate the Parents' Expected Contribution

Parents' Income	
1. Taxable income ("adjusted gross income" from IRS Form 1040)	$
2. Untaxed income/benefits	+
3. Income exclusions (child support paid + education tax credits + taxable combat pay)	-
4. Total parents' income (sum of lines 1 and 2, minus line 3)	=
Allowances	
5. U.S. income tax paid (from IRS Form 1040)	
6. State taxes paid (% from Table 8 x line 4)	+
7. F.I.C.A. paid (Table 9)	+
8. Employment allowance (Table 9)	+
9. Income protection allowance (Table 10)	+
10. Total allowances (sum of lines 5-9)	=
11. Available income (line 4 minus line 10; may be negative)	=
Parents' Assets*	
12. Cash, savings and checking accounts	
13. Other real estate/investment equity	+
14. Adjusted business/nonfamily farm equity (Table 11)	+
15. Net worth (sum of lines 12-14)	=
16. Education Savings and Asset protection allowance (Table 12)	-
17. Discretionary net worth (line 15 minus line 16)	=
18. Conversion percentage	x 12%
19. Contribution from assets (line 17 x line 18; if simple needs test or negative, enter $0)	=
20. Adjusted available income (sum of line 11 and line 19; may be negative)	=
Contribution**	
21. Total contribution (calculate using line 20 and Table 13)	=
22. Number of dependent children in college at least half time	÷
23. Parents' contribution for student (line 21 divided by line 22; if negative, enter $0)	=

* If your parents are eligible to file an IRS 1040A or 1040EZ form, or are not required to file a tax return and their taxable income is less than $50,000, no assets are included in the methodology.

** If your parents' adjusted gross income is $30,000 or less, and they are eligible to file an IRS 1040A or 1040EZ form, or are not required to file a tax return, no contribution is expected.

TABLE 8: 2010-2011 Federal EFC Allowances for State Taxes

PART II: TABLES AND WORKSHEETS

	Parents		Student			Parents		Student
	TOTAL INCOME		TOTAL INCOME			TOTAL INCOME		TOTAL INCOME
	$ 0-14,999	$15,000 or more	Any amount			$ 0-14,999	$15,000 or more	Any amount
Alabama (AL)	3%	2%	2%		North Dakota (ND)	3%	2%	1%
Alaska (AK)	2	1	0		Northern Mariana Islands (MP)	3	2	2
American Samoa (AS)	3	2	2		Ohio (OH)	6	5	4
Arizona (AZ)	4	3	3		Oklahoma (OK)	4	3	3
Arkansas (AR)	4	3	3		Oregon (OR)	7	6	5
California (CA)	9	8	5		Palau (PW)	3	2	2
Canada (CN)	3	2	2		Pennsylvania (PA)	5	4	3
Colorado (CO)	5	4	3		Puerto Rico (PR)	3	2	2
Connecticut (CT)	8	7	4		Rhode Island (RI)	7	6	4
Delaware (DE)	5	4	3		South Carolina (SC)	5	4	3
District of Columbia (DC)	7	6	6		South Dakota (SD)	2	1	1
Federated States of Micronesia (FM)	3	2	2		Tennessee (TN)	2	1	1
Florida (FL)	4	3	1		Texas (TX)	3	2	1
Georgia (GA)	5	4	4		Utah (UT)	5	4	4
Guam (GU)	3	2	2		Vermont (VT)	6	5	3
Hawaii (HI)	5	4	4		Virgin Islands (VI)	3	2	2
Idaho (ID)	5	4	4		Virginia (VA)	7	6	4
Illinois (IL)	6	5	2		Washington (WA)	3	2	1
Indiana (IN)	4	3	3		West Virginia (WV)	3	2	2
Iowa (IA)	5	4	3		Wisconsin (WI)	7	6	4
Kansas (KS)	5	4	3		Wyoming (WY)	2	1	1
Kentucky (KY)	5	4	4		Not Reported (NR)	3	2	2
Louisiana (LA)	3	2	2					
Maine (ME)	6	5	4					
Marshall Islands (MH)	3	2	2					
Maryland (MD)	8	7	5					
Massachusetts (MA)	7	6	4					
Mexico (MX)	3	2	2					
Michigan (MI)	5	4	3					
Minnesota (MN)	6	5	4					
Mississippi	3	2	2					
Missouri (MO)	5	4	3					
Montana (MT)	5	4	3					
Nebraska (NE)	5	4	3					
Nevada (NV)	3	2	1					
New Hampshire (NH)	5	4	1					
New Jersey (NJ)	9	8	4					
New Mexico (NM)	3	2	3					
New York (NY)	10	9	6					
North Carolina (NC)	6	5	4					

TABLE 9: Federal EFC Allowances for FICA and Employment

FICA: WAGES

$1 to $106,800	7.65% of income earned by each wage earner (maximum $8,170.20 per person)
$106,801 or more	$8,170.20 + 1.45% of income earned above $106,800 by each wage earner

EMPLOYMENT ALLOWANCE	35% of lesser earned income to a maximum $3,500 (single parent: 35% of earned income to a maximum of $3,500)

TABLE 10: Federal EFC Income Protection Allowance for Parents

Family Size (including student)	Number in College				
	1	2	3	4	5
2	$ 19,690	$ 16,330			
3	24,510	21,160	$ 17,800		
4	30,280	26,910	23,560	$ 20,190	
5	35,730	32,350	29,000	25,640	$ 22,290
6	41,780	38,410	35,080	31,690	28,350

For each additional family member, add $4,710.
For each additional college student, subtract $3,350.

TABLE 11: Federal EFC Adjusted Net Worth of a Business or Farm

NET WORTH	ADJUSTED NET WORTH		
Less than $1	$ 0		
$1 to 115,000	$ 0	+	40% of net worth
$115,001 to 345,000	$ 46,000	+	50% of net worth over $115,000
$345,001 to 580,000	$ 161,000	+	60% of net worth over $345,000
$580,001 or more	$ 302,000	+	100% of net worth over $580,000

PART II: TABLES AND WORKSHEETS

TABLE 12: Federal EFC Education Savings and Asset Protection Allowance for Parents

AGE OF OLDER PARENT OR STUDENT	COUPLE/ MARRIED	UNMARRIED/ SINGLE
25 or under	$ 0	$ 0
26	2,800	1,100
27	5,500	2,200
28	8,300	3,300
29	11,100	4,400
30	13,800	5,500
31	16,600	6,600
32	19,400	7,700
33	22,100	8,700
34	24,900	9,800
35	27,700	10,900
36	30,400	12,000
37	33,200	13,100
38	36,000	14,200
39	38,700	15,300
40	41,500	16,400
41	42,200	16,700
42	43,300	17,100
43	44,400	17,500
44	45,500	17,900
45	46,600	18,300
46	47,700	18,700
47	48,900	19,100
48	50,100	19,600
49	51,300	20,100
50	52,900	20,500
51	54,200	21,000
52	55,500	21,500
53	57,100	22,000
54	58,500	22,600
55	60,200	23,200
56	62,000	23,700
57	63,500	24,300
58	65,300	25,000
59	67,200	25,600
60	69,200	26,300
61	71,200	27,000
62	73,200	27,800
63	75,600	28,500
64	77,700	29,300
65 or over	80,300	30,100

TABLE 13: Federal EFC Parents' Contribution from Adjusted Available Income (AAI)

ADJUSTED AVAILABLE INCOME (AAI)	TOTAL CONTRIBUTIONS FROM INCOME
Less than $ -3,409 (3,409)	$ -750
$(3,409) to 14,500	22% of AI
$ 14,501 to 18,200	$ 3,190 + 25% of AAI over $ 14,500
$ 18,201 to 21,900	$ 4,115 + 29% of AAI over $ 18,200
$ 21,901 to 25,600	$ 5,188 + 34% of AAI over $ 21,900
$ 25,601 to 29,300	$ 6,446 + 40% of AAI over $ 25,600
$ 29,301 or more	$ 7,926 + 47% of AAI over $ 29,300

Contact Information for State Aid Programs

ALABAMA
Alabama Commission on Higher Education
P.O. Box 302000
Montgomery, AL 36130-2000
334-242-1998
www.ache.state.al.us

ALASKA
Alaska Commission on Postsecondary Education
P.O. Box 110505
Juneau, AK 99811-0505
800-441-2962
www.state.ak.us/acpe

ARIZONA
Arizona Department of Education
1535 West Jefferson Street
Phoenix, AZ 85007
800-352-4558
www.ade.state.az.us

ARKANSAS
Arkansas Department of Higher Education
114 East Capitol Avenue
Little Rock, AR 72201
501-371-2000
www.adhe.edu

CALIFORNIA
California Student Aid Commission
P.O. Box 419026
Rancho Cordova, CA 95741-9026
888-224-7268
www.csac.ca.gov

COLORADO
Colorado Department of Education
201 East Colfax Avenue
Denver, CO 80203-1799
303-866-6600
www.cde.state.co.us

CONNECTICUT
Connecticut Department of Higher Education
61 Woodland Street
Hartford, CT 06105-2326
860-947-1800
www.ctdhe.org

DELAWARE
Delaware Higher Education Commission
Carvel State Office Building, 5th floor
820 North French Street
Wilmington, DE 19801-3509
800-292-7935
www.doe.state.de.us/high-ed

DISTRICT OF COLUMBIA
Office of the State Superintendent
of Education
810 First Street, NE, 9th Floor
Washington, DC 20002
202-727-6436
www.seo.dc.gov

FLORIDA
Florida Department of Education
Office of Student Financial Aid
1940 North Monroe Street, Suite 70
Tallahassee, FL 32303-4759
888-827-2004
www.floridastudentfinancialaid.org

GEORGIA
Georgia Student Finance Commission
2082 East Exchange Place
Tucker, GA 30084
800-505-4732
www.gsfc.org

HAWAII
Hawaii State Department of Education
P.O. Box 2360
Honolulu, HI 96804
808-586-3230
www.doe.k12.hi.us

IDAHO
Idaho State Department of Education
650 West State Street
P.O. Box 83720
Boise, ID 83720-0027
800-432-4601
www.sde.idaho.gov

ILLINOIS
Illinois Student Assistance Commission
1755 Lake Cook Road
Deerfield, IL 60015-5209
800-899-4722
www.collegezone.com

INDIANA
State Student Assistance Commission of Indiana
W462 Indiana Government
Center South
402 West Washington Street
Indianapolis, IN 46204
317-232-2350
www.in.gov/ssaci

IOWA
Iowa College Student Aid Commission
200 10th Street, Fourth Floor
Des Moines, IA 50309-3609
877-272-4456
www.iowacollegeaid.org

KANSAS
Kansas Board of Regents
1000 SW Jackson Street, Suite 520
Topeka, KS 66612-1368
785-296-3421
www.kansasregents.org

KENTUCKY
KHEAA Student Aid Branch
P.O. Box 798
Frankfort, KY 40602
800-928-8926
www.kheaa.com

LOUISIANA
Louisiana Office of Student Financial Assistance
P.O. Box 91202
Baton Rouge, LA 70821-9202
800-259-5626
www.osfa.state.la.us

MAINE
Finance Authority of Maine
Education Assistance Division
P.O. Box 949
5 Community Drive
Augusta, ME 04332
800-228-3734
www.famemaine.com

MARYLAND
Maryland Higher Education Commission
Office of Student Financial Assistance
839 Bestgate Road, Suite 400
Annapolis, MD 21401
800-974-0203
www.mhec.state.md.us

MASSACHUSETTS
Massachusetts Board of Higher Education
Office of Student Financial Assistance
454 Broadway, Suite 200
Revere, MA 02151-3034
617-727-9420
www.osfa.mass.edu

MICHIGAN
Michigan Higher Education Assistance Authority
Office of Scholarships and Grants
P.O. Box 30462
Lansing, MI 48909-7962
888-447-2687
www.michigan.gov/mistudentaid

MINNESOTA
Minnesota Office of Higher Education
1450 Energy Park Drive, Suite 350
St. Paul, MN 55108-5227
800-657-3866
www.ohe.state.mn.us

MISSISSIPPI
Mississippi Office of Student Financial Aid
3825 Ridgewood Road
Jackson, MS 39211-6453
800-327-2980
www.ihl.state.ms.us/financialaid

MISSOURI
Missouri Department of Higher Education
3515 Amazonas Drive
Jefferson City, MO 65109-5717
800-473-6757
www.dhe.mo.gov

MONTANA
Montana Board of Regents
P.O. Box 203201
2500 Broadway Street
Helena, MT 59620-3201
406-444-6570
www.mus.edu

NEBRASKA
Nebraska Coordination Commission for Postsecondary
Education
P.O. Box 95005
Lincoln, NE 68509-5005
402-471-2847
www.ccpe.state.ne.us

NEVADA
Nevada Department of Education
700 East Fifth Street
Carson City, NV 89701
775-687-9220
www.doe.nv.gov

NEW HAMPSHIRE
New Hampshire Postsecondary Education Commission
3 Barrell Court, Suite 300
Concord, NH 03301-8543
603-271-2555
www.nh.gov/postsecondary

NEW JERSEY
New Jersey Higher Education Student Assistance
Authority
P.O. Box 540
Trenton, NJ 08625
800-792-8670
www.hesaa.org

NEW MEXICO
New Mexico Higher Education Department
2048 Galisteo Street
Santa Fe, NM 87505
505-476-8400
www.hed.state.nm.us

NEW YORK
New York State Higher Education Services Corporation
99 Washington Avenue
Albany, NY 12255
800-697-4372
www.hesc.state.ny.us

NORTH CAROLINA
North Carolina State Education Assistance Authority
P.O. Box 14103
Research Triangle Park, NC 27709
919-549-8614
www.ncseaa.edu

NORTH DAKOTA
North Dakota University System
10th floor State Capitol
600 East Boulevard Ave, Dept. 215
Bismarck, ND 58505-0230
701-328-2960
www.ndus.nodak.edu

OHIO
Ohio Board of Regents
30 East Broad Street, 36th Floor
Columbus, OH 43215-3414
614-466-6000
www.regents.ohio.gov

OKLAHOMA
Oklahoma State Regents for Higher Education
Tuition Aid Grant Program
655 Research Parkway, Suite 200
Oklahoma City, OK 73104
405-225-9100
www.okhighered.org

OREGON
Oregon Student Assistance Commission
1500 Valley River Drive, Suite 100
Eugene, OR 97401
800-452-8807
www.osac.state.or.us

PENNSYLVANIA
Pennsylvania Higher Education Assistance Agency
1200 North Seventh Street
Harrisburg, PA 17102-1444
800-233-0557
www.pheaa.org

PUERTO RICO
Departmento de Educacion
P.O. Box 190759
San Juan, PR 00919-0759
787-759-2000
www.de.gobierno.pr

RHODE ISLAND
Rhode Island Higher Education Assistance Authority
560 Jefferson Boulevard, Suite 100
Warwick, RI 02886
401-736-1100
www.riheaa.org

SOUTH CAROLINA
South Carolina Commission on Higher Education
1333 Main Street, Suite 200
Columbia, SC 29201
803-737-2260
www.che.sc.gov

SOUTH DAKOTA
South Dakota Department of Education
Office of Finance and Management
700 Governors Drive
Pierre, SD 57501
605-773-3134
www.doe.sd.gov/stateaid

TENNESSEE
Tennessee Student Assistance Corporation
404 James Robertson Parkway,
Suite 1510, Parkway Towers
Nashville, TN 37243-0820
800-342-1663
www.state.tn.us/tsac

TEXAS
Texas Higher Education Coordinating Board
Division of Student Services
P.O. Box 12788, Capital Station
Austin, TX 78711
800-242-3062
www.hhloans.com

UTAH
Utah Higher Education Assistance Authority
Board of Regents Building, The Gateway
60 South 400 West
Salt Lake City, UT 84101-1284
877-336-7378
www.uheaa.org

VERMONT
Vermont Student Assistance Corporation
P.O. Box 999
Winooski, VT 05404
800-798-8722
www.vsac.org

VIRGINIA
State Council of Higher Education for Virginia
James Monroe Building
101 North 14th Street
Richmond, VA 23219
804-225-2600
www.schev.edu

WASHINGTON
Washington Higher Education Coordination Board
917 Lakeridge Way
P.O. Box 43430
Olympia, WA 98504-3430
360-753-7800
www.hecb.wa.gov

WEST VIRGINIA
West Virginia Higher Education Policy Commission
Central Office, Higher Education Grant Program
1018 Kanawha Boulevard East, Suite 700
Charleston, WV 25301-2800
304-558-4614
www.hepc.wvnet.edu

WISCONSIN
Wisconsin Higher Educational Aids Board
P. O. Box 7885
Madison, WI 53707
608-267-2206
www.heab.state.wi.us

WYOMING
Wyoming Department of Education
2300 Capitol Avenue
Hathaway Building, Second Floor
Cheyenne, WY 82002-0050
307-777-7690
www.k12.wy.us

GUAM
University of Guam
Student Financial Aid Office
UOG Station
Mangilao, GU 96923
671-735-2284
www.uog.edu

VIRGIN ISLANDS
Financial Aid Office, Virgin Islands Board of Education
P.O. Box 11900
St. Thomas, VI 00801
340-774-4546

Part III

Financial Aid
College by College

Alabama

Alabama Agricultural and Mechanical University
Huntsville, Alabama
www.aamu.edu   Federal Code: 001002

4-year public university and agricultural college in small city.
Enrollment: 4,489 undergrads, 8% part-time. 973 full-time freshmen.
Selectivity: Admits less than 50% of applicants.

BASIC COSTS (2009-2010)
Tuition and fees: $5,322; out-of-state residents $10,272.
Per-credit charge: $165; out-of-state residents $330.
Room and board: $5,350.
Additional info: Tuition/fee waivers available for minority students.

FINANCIAL AID PICTURE
Students with need: Need-based aid available for full-time and part-time students. Work study available weekends and for part-time students.
Students without need: No-need awards available for athletics, minority status.
Scholarships offered: Presidential Scholarship; full tuition, course fees, room and board, $1,000 for books and supplies per semester; for students with 3.5 GPA or higher. Provost Scholarship; full tuition, course fees, room and board, $800 for books and supplies per semester; for students with 3.4 GPA or higher. Dean's Scholarship; full tuition, course fees, room and board, $500 for books and supplies per semester; for students with 3.3 GPA or higher.

FINANCIAL AID PROCEDURES
Forms required: FAFSA, institutional form.
Dates and Deadlines: Applicants notified on a rolling basis; must reply within 2 week(s) of notification.

CONTACT
Sybrenna Harris, Director of Financial Aid
Box 908, Normal, AL 35762
(256) 372-4862

Alabama State University
Montgomery, Alabama
www.alasu.edu   Federal Code: 001005

4-year public university in small city.
Enrollment: 4,614 undergrads, 9% part-time. 1,221 full-time freshmen.
Selectivity: Admits 50 to 75% of applicants.

BASIC COSTS (2009-2010)
Tuition and fees: $6,132; out-of-state residents $11,412.
Per-credit charge: $220; out-of-state residents $440.
Room and board: $4,800.

FINANCIAL AID PICTURE (2009-2010)
Students with need: Out of 1,159 full-time freshmen who applied for aid, 1,136 were judged to have need. Of these, 1,088 received aid, and 135 had their full need met. Average financial aid package met 60% of need; average scholarship/grant was $5,011; average loan was $3,263. For part-time students, average financial aid package was $10,468.
Students without need: 4 full-time freshmen who did not demonstrate need for aid received scholarships/grants; average award was $10,726. No-need awards available for academics, alumni affiliation, art, athletics, job skills, leadership, minority status, music/drama, ROTC, state/district residency.

Scholarships offered: 52 full-time freshmen received athletic scholarships; average amount $11,709.
Cumulative student debt: 90% of graduating class had student loans; average debt was $31,317.

FINANCIAL AID PROCEDURES
Forms required: FAFSA.
Dates and Deadlines: Priority date 4/1; no closing date. Applicants notified on a rolling basis starting 5/1.
Transfers: Applicants notified on a rolling basis starting 5/1.

CONTACT
Dorenda Adams, Director of Financial Aid
PO Box 271, Montgomery, AL 36101-0271
(334) 229-4323

Amridge University
Montgomery, Alabama
www.amridgeuniversity.edu   Federal Code: 016885

4-year private virtual university in small city, affiliated with Church of Christ.
Enrollment: 385 undergrads, 37% part-time.
Selectivity: Open admission; but selective for some programs.

BASIC COSTS (2010-2011)
Additional info: $315 per-semester-hour charge; full-time students receive a $150 credit per semester. New students receive an additional one-time $150 credit their first semester.

FINANCIAL AID PICTURE (2008-2009)
Students with need: Need-based aid available for full-time and part-time students.
Students without need: No-need awards available for academics, leadership.

FINANCIAL AID PROCEDURES
Forms required: FAFSA, institutional form.
Dates and Deadlines: Priority date 5/1; closing date 6/30. Must reply by 8/15 or within 2 week(s) of notification.
Transfers: No deadline.

CONTACT
Louise Hicks, Financial Aid Officer
PO Box 240240, Montgomery, AL 36124-0240
(800) 351-4040 ext. 7525

Athens State University
Athens, Alabama
www.athens.edu   Federal Code: 001008

Upper-division public business and liberal arts and teachers college in large town.
Enrollment: 3,276 undergrads, 52% part-time.
Selectivity: Open admission.

BASIC COSTS (2009-2010)
Tuition and fees: $4,350; out-of-state residents $7,950.
Per-credit charge: $120; out-of-state residents $240.

FINANCIAL AID PICTURE (2008-2009)
Students with need: Need-based aid available for full-time and part-time students. Work study available nights, weekends, and for part-time students.
Students without need: No-need awards available for academics, alumni affiliation, art, athletics, leadership, minority status.

FINANCIAL AID PROCEDURES
Forms required: FAFSA.

Dates and Deadlines: No deadline. Applicants notified on a rolling basis starting 6/1; must reply within 3 week(s) of notification.

CONTACT

Sarah McAbee, Director, Student Financial Services
300 North Beaty Street, Athens, AL 35611
(256) 233-8122

Auburn University
Auburn, Alabama
www.auburn.edu   Federal Code: 001009

4-year public university in large town.
Enrollment: 19,916 undergrads, 8% part-time. 3,984 full-time freshmen.
Selectivity: Admits over 75% of applicants.

BASIC COSTS (2009-2010)
Tuition and fees: $6,960; out-of-state residents $19,440.
Per-credit charge: $258; out-of-state residents $774.
Room and board: $8,972.

FINANCIAL AID PICTURE (2008-2009)
Students with need: Out of 2,097 full-time freshmen who applied for aid, 1,093 were judged to have need. Of these, 1,093 received aid, and 244 had their full need met. Average financial aid package met 56% of need; average scholarship/grant was $6,195; average loan was $3,254. For part-time students, average financial aid package was $6,160.
Students without need: 964 full-time freshmen who did not demonstrate need for aid received scholarships/grants; average award was $4,474.
Scholarships offered: *Merit:* Freshmen and General Scholarships; up to full-tuition; require 28 ACT/1240 SAT and 3.25 GPA. National Merit and National Achievement Finalists; full-tuition plus additional benefits. *Athletic:* 86 full-time freshmen received athletic scholarships; average amount $22,020.
Additional info: State of Alabama has pre-paid college tuition plan for residents.

FINANCIAL AID PROCEDURES
Forms required: FAFSA.
Dates and Deadlines: Priority date 3/1; no closing date. Applicants notified on a rolling basis.
Transfers: No deadline. Applicants notified on a rolling basis; must reply within 2 week(s) of notification.

CONTACT
Mike Reynolds, Director, Student Financial Services
Quad Center, Auburn, AL 36849-5111
(334) 844-4080

Auburn University at Montgomery
Montgomery, Alabama
www.aum.edu   Federal Code: 008310

4-year public university in small city.
Enrollment: 4,525 undergrads, 31% part-time. 734 full-time freshmen.
Selectivity: Admits over 75% of applicants.

BASIC COSTS (2009-2010)
Tuition and fees: $5,970; out-of-state residents $17,250.
Per-credit charge: $188; out-of-state residents $564.
Room only: $3,720.

FINANCIAL AID PICTURE (2009-2010)
Students with need: Need-based aid available for part-time students.
Students without need: No-need awards available for academics, alumni affiliation, art, athletics, job skills, leadership, minority status, music/drama, religious affiliation, ROTC.

FINANCIAL AID PROCEDURES
Forms required: FAFSA.
Dates and Deadlines: Priority date 3/1; no closing date. Applicants notified on a rolling basis starting 6/1; must reply within 2 week(s) of notification.
Transfers: Aid awarded based on need and the availability of funds.

CONTACT
Anthony Richey, Director of Financial Aid
7400 East Drive, Room 139 Taylor Center, Montgomery, AL 36124-4023
(334) 244-3571

Bevill State Community College
Jasper, Alabama
www.bscc.edu   Federal Code: 005733

2-year public community college in small town.
Enrollment: 4,376 undergrads, 42% part-time. 941 full-time freshmen.
Selectivity: Open admission; but selective for some programs.

BASIC COSTS (2009-2010)
Tuition and fees: $2,730; out-of-state residents $4,860.
Per-credit charge: $71; out-of-state residents $142.
Room only: $1,350.
Additional info: Tuition/fee waivers available for unemployed or children of unemployed.

FINANCIAL AID PICTURE (2008-2009)
Students with need: Need-based aid available for part-time students.
Students without need: No-need awards available for academics, athletics, leadership, music/drama.

FINANCIAL AID PROCEDURES
Forms required: FAFSA.
Dates and Deadlines: Priority date 5/1; no closing date. Applicants notified on a rolling basis starting 7/1.

CONTACT
SuZanne Bush, Assistant to the Dean of Student Services
1411 Indiana Avenue, Jasper, AL 35501
(205) 387-0511 ext. 5814

Birmingham-Southern College
Birmingham, Alabama
www.bsc.edu   Federal Code: 001012

4-year private liberal arts college in very large city, affiliated with United Methodist Church.
Enrollment: 1,508 undergrads, 2% part-time. 424 full-time freshmen.
Selectivity: Admits 50 to 75% of applicants.

BASIC COSTS (2010-2011)
Tuition and fees: $27,890.
Per-credit charge: $1,121.
Room and board: $9,320.

FINANCIAL AID PICTURE (2009-2010)
Students with need: Out of 328 full-time freshmen who applied for aid, 263 were judged to have need. Of these, 263 received aid, and 130 had their full need met. Average financial aid package met 98% of need; average scholarship/grant was $8,792; average loan was $3,866. For part-time students, average financial aid package was $18,517.
Students without need: 154 full-time freshmen who did not demonstrate need for aid received scholarships/grants; average award was $13,573. No-need awards available for academics, alumni affiliation, art, job skills, leadership, minority status, music/drama, religious affiliation, state/district residency.

Scholarships offered: Neal and Anne Berte Scholarship; full tuition; based on academic achievement; 1 awarded. Blount-Monaghan/Vulcan Materials Company Scholarship; full tuition; based on academic achievement; 1 awarded. William Jones and Elizabeth Perry Rushton Scholarship; full tuition, room and board, fees, books, $2,000 travel stipend; based on academic achievement; 1 awarded. Phi Beta Kappa; full tuition; based on academic achievement. United Methodist Scholarship; $1,000-$2,500; awarded to United Methodist with recommendation from senior United Methodist Minister.

Additional info: Auditions required for music, theatre, dance applicants seeking scholarships. Portfolios required for art applicants seeking scholarships, and essays recommended for all applicants seeking scholarships.

FINANCIAL AID PROCEDURES

Forms required: FAFSA.

Dates and Deadlines: Closing date 3/1. Applicants notified on a rolling basis starting 3/1; must reply by 8/21.

Transfers: No deadline. Applicants notified on a rolling basis starting 3/1; must reply within 2 week(s) of notification.

CONTACT

Fred Carter, Director of Financial Aid Services
900 Arkadelphia Road, Birmingham, AL 35254
(205) 226-4688

Central Alabama Community College
Childersburg, Alabama
www.cacc.cc.al.us   Federal Code: 001007

2-year public community college in large town.

Enrollment: 2,444 undergrads.

Selectivity: Open admission; but selective for some programs.

BASIC COSTS (2009-2010)

Tuition and fees: $2,700; out-of-state residents $4,830.

Per-credit charge: $71; out-of-state residents $142.

FINANCIAL AID PICTURE (2009-2010)

Students with need: 77% of average financial aid package awarded as scholarships/grants, 23% awarded as loans/jobs.

Students without need: No-need awards available for academics, athletics, state/district residency.

FINANCIAL AID PROCEDURES

Forms required: FAFSA, institutional form.

Dates and Deadlines: Priority date 7/15; no closing date. Applicants notified on a rolling basis.

CONTACT

Cindy Entrekin, Financial Aid Officer
34091 US Highway 280 South, Childersburg, AL 35044
(256) 234-6346 ext. 4251

Chattahoochee Valley Community College
Phenix City, Alabama
www.cv.edu   Federal Code: 012182

2-year public community college in small city.

Enrollment: 1,907 undergrads, 30% part-time.

Selectivity: Open admission; but selective for some programs.

BASIC COSTS (2009-2010)

Tuition and fees: $2,940; out-of-state residents $5,070.

Per-credit charge: $71; out-of-state residents $142.

FINANCIAL AID PICTURE (2008-2009)

Students with need: Need-based aid available for full-time and part-time students. Work study available nights, weekends, and for part-time students.

Students without need: No-need awards available for academics, art, athletics, leadership, music/drama.

FINANCIAL AID PROCEDURES

Forms required: FAFSA.

Dates and Deadlines: Priority date 7/1; no closing date. Applicants notified on a rolling basis; must reply within 1 week(s) of notification.

CONTACT

Joan Waters, Director of Financial Aid
2602 College Drive, Phenix City, AL 36869
(334) 291-4915

Faulkner University
Montgomery, Alabama
www.faulkner.edu   Federal Code: 001003

4-year private university and liberal arts college in large city, affiliated with Church of Christ.

Enrollment: 2,753 undergrads, 25% part-time. 344 full-time freshmen.

Selectivity: Admits 50 to 75% of applicants.

BASIC COSTS (2010-2011)

Tuition and fees: $14,810.

Per-credit charge: $480.

Room and board: $6,500.

Additional info: Tuition/fee waivers available for adults, minority students, unemployed or children of unemployed.

FINANCIAL AID PICTURE (2009-2010)

Students with need: Out of 316 full-time freshmen who applied for aid, 247 were judged to have need. Of these, 247 received aid, and 22 had their full need met. Average financial aid package met 60% of need; average scholarship/grant was $2,650; average loan was $3,500. For part-time students, average financial aid package was $3,900.

Students without need: No-need awards available for academics, alumni affiliation, art, athletics, leadership, music/drama, religious affiliation, ROTC, state/district residency.

Cumulative student debt: 89% of graduating class had student loans; average debt was $21,000.

FINANCIAL AID PROCEDURES

Forms required: FAFSA, state aid form, institutional form.

Dates and Deadlines: Priority date 5/1; no closing date. Applicants notified on a rolling basis starting 6/1; must reply within 3 week(s) of notification.

Transfers: No deadline. Applicants notified on a rolling basis; must reply within 3 week(s) of notification.

CONTACT

William Jackson, Director of Financial Aid
5345 Atlanta Highway, Montgomery, AL 36109-3398
(334) 386-7195

Gadsden State Community College
Gadsden, Alabama
www.gadsdenstate.edu   Federal Code: 001017

2-year public community and technical college in small city.

Enrollment: 6,494 undergrads, 37% part-time. 3,147 full-time freshmen.

Selectivity: Open admission; but selective for some programs.

BASIC COSTS (2009-2010)

Tuition and fees: $2,700; out-of-state residents $4,830.

Per-credit charge: $71; out-of-state residents $142.

Room and board: $3,200.

Additional info: Tuition/fee waivers available for minority students, unemployed or children of unemployed.

FINANCIAL AID PICTURE (2008-2009)

Students with need: Need-based aid available for full-time and part-time students.

Students without need: No-need awards available for academics, alumni affiliation, art, athletics, job skills, leadership, minority status, music/drama, state/district residency.

FINANCIAL AID PROCEDURES

Forms required: FAFSA, institutional form.

Dates and Deadlines: Priority date 4/15; no closing date. Applicants notified on a rolling basis starting 6/10.

CONTACT

Jacqueline Henderson, Director of Financial Services

1001 George Wallace Drive, Gadsden, AL 35902-0227

(256) 549-8267

Heritage Christian University
Florence, Alabama
www.hcu.edu   Federal Code: 015370

4-year private Bible college in large town, affiliated with Church of Christ.

Enrollment: 83 undergrads.

BASIC COSTS (2010-2011)

Tuition and fees: $11,130.

Per-credit charge: $355.

Room only: $3,000.

Additional info: Housing consists of on-campus three-bedroom/three-bathroom apartments with full kitchen and common living area; typically, three students per unit, each with his/her own bedroom and bathroom. On-campus meal plan covers ten meals per week, $650 for academic year.

FINANCIAL AID PICTURE (2009-2010)

Students with need: Need-based aid available for full-time and part-time students.

FINANCIAL AID PROCEDURES

Forms required: FAFSA.

Dates and Deadlines: Priority date 6/1; no closing date. Applicants notified on a rolling basis starting 6/1; must reply by 7/28 or within 2 week(s) of notification.

Transfers: No deadline. Applicants notified on a rolling basis; must reply by 7/28 or within 3 week(s) of notification.

CONTACT

Mechelle Thompson, Financial Aid Counselor

3625 Helton Drive, Florence, AL 35630

(256) 766-6610 ext. 224

Herzing University
Birmingham, Alabama
www.herzing.edu   Federal Code: 010193

4-year for-profit business and technical college in very large city.

Enrollment: 406 undergrads.

Selectivity: Admits over 75% of applicants.

BASIC COSTS (2009-2010)

Additional info: $340 to $490 per credit hour depending on program.

FINANCIAL AID PICTURE

Students with need: Need-based aid available for full-time students.

Students without need: This college awards aid only to students with need.

FINANCIAL AID PROCEDURES

Forms required: FAFSA.

CONTACT

Kentray Sims, Director of Financial Services

280 West Valley Avenue, Birmingham, AL 35209

(205) 916-2800

Huntingdon College
Montgomery, Alabama
www.huntingdon.edu   Federal Code: 001019

4-year private liberal arts college in small city, affiliated with United Methodist Church.

Enrollment: 1,067 undergrads, 20% part-time. 237 full-time freshmen.

Selectivity: Admits 50 to 75% of applicants.

BASIC COSTS (2009-2010)

Tuition and fees: $20,990.

Per-credit charge: $830.

Room and board: $7,500.

Additional info: Tuition at time of enrollment locked for 4 years.

FINANCIAL AID PICTURE (2009-2010)

Students with need: Out of 213 full-time freshmen who applied for aid, 191 were judged to have need. Of these, 191 received aid, and 28 had their full need met. Average financial aid package met 73% of need; average scholarship/grant was $14,071; average loan was $2,983. For part-time students, average financial aid package was $3,010.

Students without need: 46 full-time freshmen who did not demonstrate need for aid received scholarships/grants; average award was $11,076. No-need awards available for academics, alumni affiliation, leadership, music/drama, religious affiliation, ROTC, state/district residency.

Cumulative student debt: 58% of graduating class had student loans; average debt was $14,034.

FINANCIAL AID PROCEDURES

Forms required: institutional form.

Dates and Deadlines: Priority date 4/15; no closing date. Applicants notified on a rolling basis; must reply by 5/1 or within 2 week(s) of notification.

Transfers: Transfer student should be in good academic standing at previous institution and cannot be in default on any previous student loans. While Academic Transfer scholarships are merit-based according to GPA, need-based aid (i.e. FAFSA) contingent upon eligibility and good-standing within Title IV.

CONTACT

Belinda Duett, Director of Student Financial Services

1500 East Fairview Avenue, Montgomery, AL 36106-2148

(334) 833-4428

Jacksonville State University
Jacksonville, Alabama
www.jsu.edu   Federal Code: 001020

4-year public university in small town.

Enrollment: 7,553 undergrads, 22% part-time. 1,220 full-time freshmen.

Selectivity: Admits over 75% of applicants.

BASIC COSTS (2009-2010)

Tuition and fees: $6,240; out-of-state residents $12,480.

Per-credit charge: $208; out-of-state residents $416.

Room and board: $5,000.

FINANCIAL AID PICTURE (2008-2009)
Students with need: Need-based aid available for full-time and part-time students. Work study available nights, weekends, and for part-time students.
Students without need: No-need awards available for academics, alumni affiliation, art, athletics, music/drama, ROTC.
Scholarships offered: 4-year tuition scholarship; for entering freshmen from Alabama with 28 ACT or 1230 SAT.

FINANCIAL AID PROCEDURES
Forms required: FAFSA, institutional form.
Dates and Deadlines: Priority date 3/15; no closing date. Applicants notified on a rolling basis starting 5/15; must reply within 2 week(s) of notification.

CONTACT
Vickie Adams, Director of Financial Aid
700 Pelham Road North, Jacksonville, AL 36265-1602
(256) 782-5006

Jefferson Davis Community College
Brewton, Alabama
www.jdcc.edu   Federal Code: 001021

2-year public nursing and community college in small town.
Enrollment: 1,292 undergrads, 48% part-time. 329 full-time freshmen.
Selectivity: Open admission; but selective for some programs.

BASIC COSTS (2009-2010)
Tuition and fees: $2,700; out-of-state residents $4,830.
Per-credit charge: $71; out-of-state residents $142.
Room only: $1,866.

FINANCIAL AID PICTURE (2008-2009)
Students with need: Need-based aid available for full-time and part-time students. Work study available nights.
Students without need: No-need awards available for academics, athletics, leadership.

FINANCIAL AID PROCEDURES
Forms required: FAFSA.
Dates and Deadlines: Priority date 5/8; no closing date. Applicants notified on a rolling basis; must reply within 2 week(s) of notification.
Transfers: Must reply within 2 week(s) of notification.

CONTACT
Vanessa Kyles, Director of Financial Aid
PO Box 958, Brewton, AL 36427
(251) 809-1516

Jefferson State Community College
Birmingham, Alabama
www.jeffstateonline.com   Federal Code: 001022

2-year public community college in very large city.
Enrollment: 7,098 undergrads, 57% part-time. 1,037 full-time freshmen.
Selectivity: Open admission; but selective for some programs.

BASIC COSTS (2010-2011)
Tuition and fees: $3,480; out-of-state residents $6,030.
Per-credit charge: $85; out-of-state residents $170.

FINANCIAL AID PICTURE (2009-2010)
Students with need: Need-based aid available for full-time and part-time students. Work study available nights.
Students without need: No-need awards available for academics, art, athletics, leadership, music/drama.

Additional info: Any Alabama resident over age 60 may attend classes tuition free, on a space available basis.

FINANCIAL AID PROCEDURES
Forms required: FAFSA, institutional form.
Dates and Deadlines: Priority date 5/1; no closing date. Applicants notified on a rolling basis starting 6/1.
Transfers: Transfer students not eligible for academic scholarships until 12 hours have been completed on campus.

CONTACT
Tracy Adams, Director, Financial Aid
2601 Carson Road, Birmingham, AL 35215-3098
(205) 856-8509

Judson College
Marion, Alabama
www.judson.edu   Federal Code: 001023

4-year private liberal arts college for women in small town, affiliated with Baptist faith.
Enrollment: 297 undergrads, 16% part-time. 69 full-time freshmen.
Selectivity: Admits over 75% of applicants.

BASIC COSTS (2009-2010)
Tuition and fees: $12,890.
Per-credit charge: $409.
Room and board: $7,970.

FINANCIAL AID PICTURE (2009-2010)
Students with need: Out of 61 full-time freshmen who applied for aid, 60 were judged to have need. Of these, 60 received aid, and 10 had their full need met. Average financial aid package met 69% of need; average scholarship/grant was $5,835; average loan was $3,471. For part-time students, average financial aid package was $2,882.
Students without need: 7 full-time freshmen who did not demonstrate need for aid received scholarships/grants; average award was $11,297. No-need awards available for academics, alumni affiliation, art, athletics, music/drama, religious affiliation, state/district residency.
Scholarships offered: *Merit:* Full Tuition Scholarship; given to National Merit Finalists or students with 29 ACT and 3.5 GPA; up to 5 awarded. Honor Scholarships; 1 for full-tuition, 2 for $2,500, 3 for $2,000; awarded based on exam scores. Music scholarships; $1,500; awarded based on audition. *Athletic:* 1 full-time freshmen received athletic scholarships; average amount $4,000.
Cumulative student debt: 60% of graduating class had student loans; average debt was $17,563.

FINANCIAL AID PROCEDURES
Forms required: FAFSA, state aid form, institutional form.
Dates and Deadlines: Priority date 3/1; no closing date. Applicants notified on a rolling basis starting 3/1; must reply within 2 week(s) of notification.
Transfers: No deadline. Applicants notified on a rolling basis starting 3/1; must reply within 2 week(s) of notification.

CONTACT
Doris Wilson, Director of Financial Aid
302 Bibb Street, Marion, AL 36756
(334) 683-5157

Lawson State Community College
Birmingham, Alabama
www.lawsonstate.edu   Federal Code: 001059

2-year public community college in small city.
Enrollment: 4,354 undergrads.

Selectivity: Open admission; but selective for some programs.

BASIC COSTS (2009-2010)

Tuition and fees: $3,000; out-of-state residents $5,130.
Per-credit charge: $71; out-of-state residents $142.
Room and board: $2,000.

FINANCIAL AID PICTURE (2009-2010)

Students with need: 97% of average financial aid package awarded as scholarships/grants, 3% awarded as loans/jobs. Need-based aid available for part-time students. Work study available nights.
Students without need: This college awards aid only to students with need.

FINANCIAL AID PROCEDURES

Forms required: FAFSA.
Dates and Deadlines: Priority date 6/1; no closing date. Applicants notified on a rolling basis starting 8/1; must reply within 2 week(s) of notification.

CONTACT

Cassandra Byrd, Director of Student Financial Services
3060 Wilson Road SW, Birmingham, AL 35221-1717
(205) 929-6380

Miles College
Birmingham, Alabama
www.miles.edu   Federal Code: 001028

4-year private liberal arts college in very large city, affiliated with Christian Methodist Episcopal Church.
Enrollment: 1,900 undergrads.
Selectivity: Open admission; but selective for some programs.

BASIC COSTS (2009-2010)

Tuition and fees: $9,164.
Per-credit charge: $358.
Room and board: $6,000.

FINANCIAL AID PICTURE (2008-2009)

Students with need: Need-based aid available for full-time and part-time students.
Students without need: This college awards aid only to students with need.

FINANCIAL AID PROCEDURES

Forms required: FAFSA, state aid form.
Dates and Deadlines: Priority date 4/15; no closing date. Applicants notified on a rolling basis starting 7/15; must reply within 2 week(s) of notification.

CONTACT

Percy Lanier, Director of Financial Aid
5500 Myron-Massey Boulevard, Fairfield, AL 35064
(205) 929-1665

Northeast Alabama Community College
Rainsville, Alabama
www.nacc.edu   Federal Code: 001031

2-year public community college in rural community.
Enrollment: 2,100 undergrads.
Selectivity: Open admission; but selective for some programs.

BASIC COSTS (2009-2010)

Tuition and fees: $2,850; out-of-state residents $4,980.
Per-credit charge: $71; out-of-state residents $142.

FINANCIAL AID PICTURE

Students with need: Need-based aid available for full-time and part-time students.
Students without need: No-need awards available for academics, art, leadership, minority status, music/drama.

FINANCIAL AID PROCEDURES

Forms required: FAFSA.
Dates and Deadlines: No deadline. Applicants notified on a rolling basis.

CONTACT

Nixon Willmon, Director of Financial Aid
Admissions Office, NACC, Rainsville, AL 35986-0159
(256) 228-6001 ext. 327

Northwest-Shoals Community College
Muscle Shoals, Alabama
www.nwscc.edu   Federal Code: 005697

2-year public community and technical college in large town.
Enrollment: 3,908 undergrads, 38% part-time. 923 full-time freshmen.
Selectivity: Open admission; but selective for some programs.

BASIC COSTS (2009-2010)

Tuition and fees: $2,880; out-of-state residents $5,010.
Per-credit charge: $71; out-of-state residents $142.
Room only: $1,600.
Additional info: Tuition/fee waivers available for minority students, unemployed or children of unemployed.

FINANCIAL AID PICTURE (2008-2009)

Students with need: 54% of average financial aid package awarded as scholarships/grants, 46% awarded as loans/jobs. Need-based aid available for part-time students. Work study available nights.
Students without need: No-need awards available for academics, art, athletics, leadership, minority status, music/drama.

FINANCIAL AID PROCEDURES

Forms required: FAFSA, institutional form.
Dates and Deadlines: Priority date 4/1; closing date 8/1. Applicants notified on a rolling basis; must reply within 2 week(s) of notification.
Transfers: No deadline. Applicants notified on a rolling basis; must reply within 2 week(s) of notification. Students without 1-year Alabama residency before fall term ineligible for state grant.

CONTACT

Joel Parris, Director of Student Financial Aid Services
PO Box 2545, Muscle Shoals, AL 35662
(256) 331-5368

Oakwood University
Huntsville, Alabama
www.oakwood.edu   Federal Code: 001033

4-year private liberal arts college in small city, affiliated with Seventh-day Adventists.
Enrollment: 1,800 undergrads.
Selectivity: Admits 50 to 75% of applicants.

BASIC COSTS (2009-2010)

Tuition and fees: $13,834.
Room and board: $8,464.

FINANCIAL AID PICTURE

Students with need: Need-based aid available for full-time students.
Students without need: No-need awards available for academics, leadership, religious affiliation, state/district residency.

FINANCIAL AID PROCEDURES

Forms required: FAFSA, state aid form.

Dates and Deadlines: Priority date 3/31; no closing date. Applicants notified on a rolling basis starting 4/1.

CONTACT

Compton Brathwaite, Director of Financial Aid

7000 Adventist Boulevard, NW, Huntsville, AL 35896

(256) 726-7208

Prince Institute of Professional Studies

Montgomery, Alabama

www.princeinstitute.edu   Federal Code: 022960

2-year for-profit technical and career college in large city.

Enrollment: 96 undergrads.

Selectivity: Open admission.

BASIC COSTS (2009-2010)

Tuition and fees: $8,095.

FINANCIAL AID PICTURE (2009-2010)

Students with need: Need-based aid available for full-time and part-time students.

Students without need: This college awards aid only to students with need.

FINANCIAL AID PROCEDURES

Forms required: FAFSA.

Dates and Deadlines: No deadline.

CONTACT

Reginald James, Financial Aid Administrator

7735 Atlanta Highway, Montgomery, AL 36117-4231

(334) 271-1670

Remington College: Mobile

Mobile, Alabama

www.remingtoncollege.edu   Federal Code: 026055

2-year for-profit career college in large city.

Enrollment: 150 undergrads.

Selectivity: Open admission.

BASIC COSTS (2009-2010)

Additional info: Associate degree program annual tuition $39,900 plus $50 fees. 8-month diploma program full tuition $13,900 plus $50 fees. Tuition includes textbooks and supplies.

FINANCIAL AID PICTURE (2008-2009)

Students with need: Need-based aid available for full-time students. Work study available nights.

Students without need: This college awards aid only to students with need.

FINANCIAL AID PROCEDURES

Forms required: FAFSA.

CONTACT

Linda Calvanese, Financial Aid Director

828 Downtowner Loop West, Mobile, AL 36609-5404

(251) 343-8200

Samford University

Birmingham, Alabama

www.samford.edu   Federal Code: 001036

4-year private university in small city, affiliated with Southern Baptist Convention.

Enrollment: 2,879 undergrads, 6% part-time. 708 full-time freshmen.

Selectivity: Admits over 75% of applicants.

BASIC COSTS (2010-2011)

Tuition and fees: $21,942.

Per-credit charge: $726.

Room and board: $7,024.

Additional info: Other expenses $3,005.

FINANCIAL AID PICTURE (2008-2009)

Students with need: Out of 511 full-time freshmen who applied for aid, 329 were judged to have need. Of these, 329 received aid, and 51 had their full need met. Average financial aid package met 80% of need; average scholarship/grant was $11,672; average loan was $4,402. For part-time students, average financial aid package was $7,083.

Students without need: 174 full-time freshmen who did not demonstrate need for aid received scholarships/grants; average award was $4,795. No-need awards available for academics, alumni affiliation, art, athletics, leadership, music/drama, religious affiliation, ROTC, state/district residency.

Scholarships offered: 40 full-time freshmen received athletic scholarships; average amount $18,292.

Cumulative student debt: 38% of graduating class had student loans; average debt was $15,702.

FINANCIAL AID PROCEDURES

Forms required: FAFSA, state aid form.

Dates and Deadlines: Priority date 3/1; no closing date.

CONTACT

Lane Smith, Director of Financial Aid

800 Lakeshore Drive, Birmingham, AL 35229

(205) 726-2905

Shelton State Community College

Tuscaloosa, Alabama

www.sheltonstate.edu   Federal Code: 005691

2-year public community and technical college in small city.

Enrollment: 5,834 undergrads.

Selectivity: Open admission.

BASIC COSTS (2009-2010)

Tuition and fees: $2,700; out-of-state residents $4,830.

Per-credit charge: $71; out-of-state residents $142.

FINANCIAL AID PICTURE

Students with need: Need-based aid available for full-time and part-time students. Work study available nights.

Students without need: This college awards aid only to students with need.

FINANCIAL AID PROCEDURES

Forms required: FAFSA.

Dates and Deadlines: Priority date 6/30; no closing date. Applicants notified on a rolling basis starting 7/30.

CONTACT

JoeAnn Cousette, Financial Aid Director

9500 Old Greensboro Road, Tuscaloosa, AL 35405-8522

(205) 391-2376

Snead State Community College

Boaz, Alabama
www.snead.edu

Federal Code: 001038

2-year public community college in small town.
Enrollment: 2,483 undergrads.
Selectivity: Open admission; but selective for some programs.

BASIC COSTS (2009-2010)
Tuition and fees: $2,820; out-of-state residents $4,950.
Per-credit charge: $71; out-of-state residents $142.
Room and board: $3,190.

FINANCIAL AID PICTURE
Students with need: Need-based aid available for full-time and part-time students. Work study available nights.
Students without need: No-need awards available for academics, alumni affiliation, art, athletics, leadership, music/drama.

FINANCIAL AID PROCEDURES
Forms required: FAFSA.
Dates and Deadlines: Closing date 4/15. Applicants notified on a rolling basis starting 4/15.

CONTACT
Amanda Harbison, Financial Aid Officer
PO Box 734, Boaz, AL 35957-0734
(256) 840-4127

South University: Montgomery

Montgomery, Alabama
www.southuniversity.edu

Federal Code: 004463

4-year for-profit university in small city.
Enrollment: 598 undergrads, 40% part-time. 59 full-time freshmen.

BASIC COSTS (2009-2010)
Tuition and fees: $14,985.

FINANCIAL AID PICTURE (2009-2010)
Students with need: Need-based aid available for full-time and part-time students.
Students without need: This college awards aid only to students with need.

FINANCIAL AID PROCEDURES
Forms required: FAFSA.
Dates and Deadlines: No deadline. Applicants notified on a rolling basis starting 6/1.
Transfers: No deadline. Applicants notified on a rolling basis.

CONTACT
Yvonne Miller, Director of Financial Aid
5355 Vaughn Road, Montgomery, AL 36116-1120
(334) 395-8800

Southeastern Bible College

Birmingham, Alabama
www.sebc.edu

Federal Code: 013857

4-year private Bible college in very large city, affiliated with nondenominational tradition.
Enrollment: 203 undergrads, 10% part-time. 18 full-time freshmen.
Selectivity: Admits over 75% of applicants.

BASIC COSTS (2009-2010)
Tuition and fees: $10,930.
Per-credit charge: $360.
Room only: $2,450.

FINANCIAL AID PICTURE (2008-2009)
Students with need: Out of 15 full-time freshmen who applied for aid, 12 were judged to have need. Of these, 12 received aid. Average financial aid package met 65% of need; average scholarship/grant was $4,500; average loan was $3,500. Need-based aid available for part-time students.
Students without need: 2 full-time freshmen who did not demonstrate need for aid received scholarships/grants; average award was $1,000. No-need awards available for academics, music/drama.
Cumulative student debt: 100% of graduating class had student loans; average debt was $29,165.

FINANCIAL AID PROCEDURES
Forms required: FAFSA, institutional form.
Dates and Deadlines: Priority date 4/1; no closing date. Applicants notified on a rolling basis starting 1/1.
Transfers: No deadline. Applicants notified on a rolling basis.

CONTACT
Ann Campbell, Director of Financial Aid
2545 Valleydale Road, Birmingham, AL 35244-2083
(205) 970-9215

Southern Union State Community College

Wadley, Alabama
www.suscc.edu

Federal Code: 001040

2-year public community and technical college in small city.
Enrollment: 5,000 undergrads.
Selectivity: Open admission; but selective for some programs.

BASIC COSTS (2009-2010)
Tuition and fees: $2,700; out-of-state residents $4,830.
Per-credit charge: $71; out-of-state residents $142.
Room and board: $3,200.

FINANCIAL AID PICTURE (2009-2010)
Students with need: Need-based aid available for full-time and part-time students.

FINANCIAL AID PROCEDURES
Forms required: FAFSA.
Dates and Deadlines: Priority date 4/1; no closing date. Applicants notified on a rolling basis.

CONTACT
Ellen Canada, Director of Financial Aid
750 Roberts Street, Wadley, AL 36276
(256) 395-2215

Spring Hill College

Mobile, Alabama
www.shc.edu

Federal Code: 001041

4-year private liberal arts college in large city, affiliated with Roman Catholic Church.
Enrollment: 1,304 undergrads, 9% part-time. 353 full-time freshmen.
Selectivity: Admits 50 to 75% of applicants.

BASIC COSTS (2010-2011)
Tuition and fees: $26,730.
Per-credit charge: $890.
Room and board: $10,250.

FINANCIAL AID PICTURE (2009-2010)

Students with need: Out of 310 full-time freshmen who applied for aid, 252 were judged to have need. Of these, 252 received aid, and 73 had their full need met. Average financial aid package met 85% of need; average scholarship/grant was $17,633; average loan was $4,471. For part-time students, average financial aid package was $6,556.

Students without need: 96 full-time freshmen who did not demonstrate need for aid received scholarships/grants; average award was $14,332. No-need awards available for academics, alumni affiliation, athletics, job skills, leadership, minority status, state/district residency.

Scholarships offered: *Merit:* Spring Hill Scholars scholarships: full tuition and fees for 4 years; based on leadership, service, 3.5 GPA and 27 ACT/1200 SAT; 5 awarded. Trustee Honors Scholarship: $16,000-$18,000 annually; based on 3.5 GPA and 27 ACT/1200 SAT. Presidential Honors Scholarship: $16,000-$18,000 annually; based on grades, test scores, and leadership potential. Portier Scholarship: $12,000-$16,000 annually; based on grades, test scores, and leadership potential. Ignatian Leadership Award; $10,000-$12,500 annually; based on grades, test scores, and leadership potential. Gautrelet Award; $5,000-$10,000 annually; based on leadership, service, and potential contributions to the college community. ***Athletic:*** 30 full-time freshmen received athletic scholarships; average amount $3,310.

Cumulative student debt: 72% of graduating class had student loans; average debt was $13,775.

FINANCIAL AID PROCEDURES

Forms required: FAFSA, state aid form.

Dates and Deadlines: Priority date 3/1; no closing date. Applicants notified on a rolling basis starting 2/15; must reply by 5/1 or within 2 week(s) of notification.

Transfers: No deadline. Applicants notified on a rolling basis starting 3/1; must reply within 2 week(s) of notification. Transfer scholarships awarded to students transferring from accredited college or university with 3.0 GPA. Scholarships range from $5,000-$10,000 annually and are renewable with 2.5 GPA. Transfer students who are members of Phi Theta Kappa and/or transfer students who plan to pursue degree in nursing may receive additional scholarship funding.

CONTACT

Ellen Foster, Director of Financial Aid
4000 Dauphin Street, Mobile, AL 36608-1791
(251) 380-3460

Stillman College

Tuscaloosa, Alabama
www.stillman.edu   Federal Code: 001044

4-year private liberal arts college in small city, affiliated with Presbyterian Church (USA).

Enrollment: 1,075 undergrads.

Selectivity: Admits less than 50% of applicants.

BASIC COSTS (2009-2010)

Tuition and fees: $13,430.
Per-credit charge: $503.
Room and board: $6,336.

FINANCIAL AID PICTURE (2008-2009)

Students with need: Need-based aid available for full-time and part-time students. Work study available nights, weekends, and for part-time students.
Students without need: This college awards aid only to students with need.

FINANCIAL AID PROCEDURES

Forms required: FAFSA, institutional form.
Dates and Deadlines: No deadline. Applicants notified on a rolling basis; must reply within 4 week(s) of notification.
Transfers: Priority date 3/15; no deadline. Applicants notified by 11/15.

CONTACT

Jacqueline Morris, Director of Financial Aid
3600 Stillman Boulevard, Tuscaloosa, AL 35403
(205) 366-8950

Talladega College

Talladega, Alabama   Federal Code: 001046
www.talladega.edu   CSS Code: 1800

4-year private liberal arts college in large town, affiliated with United Church of Christ.

Enrollment: 700 undergrads.

Selectivity: Open admission; but selective for some programs.

BASIC COSTS (2009-2010)

Tuition and fees: $8,940.
Per-credit charge: $271.
Room and board: $5,324.

FINANCIAL AID PICTURE (2009-2010)

Students with need: Need-based aid available for full-time and part-time students.
Students without need: This college awards aid only to students with need.

FINANCIAL AID PROCEDURES

Forms required: FAFSA, CSS PROFILE, state aid form, institutional form.
Dates and Deadlines: Priority date 4/15; no closing date. Applicants notified on a rolling basis; must reply within 2 week(s) of notification.
Transfers: No deadline. Applicants notified on a rolling basis.

CONTACT

Michelle Burwell, Director of Financial Aid
627 West Battle Street, Talladega, AL 35160
(256) 761-6256

Troy University

Troy, Alabama
www.troy.edu   Federal Code: 001047

4-year public university in large town.

Enrollment: 22,029 undergrads, 50% part-time. 1,997 full-time freshmen.

Selectivity: Admits 50 to 75% of applicants.

BASIC COSTS (2009-2010)

Tuition and fees: $6,400; out-of-state residents $12,190.
Per-credit charge: $193; out-of-state residents $386.
Room and board: $5,440.

FINANCIAL AID PICTURE (2009-2010)

Students with need: For part-time students, average financial aid package was $4,939.
Students without need: No-need awards available for academics, alumni affiliation, art, athletics, leadership, minority status, music/drama, ROTC.

FINANCIAL AID PROCEDURES

Forms required: FAFSA, institutional form.
Dates and Deadlines: Closing date 5/1. Applicants notified on a rolling basis starting 5/1; must reply within 2 week(s) of notification.

CONTACT

Carol Supri, Director, Financial Aid
University Avenue, Adams Administration 111, Troy, AL 36082
(334) 670-3186

Tuskegee University

Tuskegee, Alabama
www.tuskegee.edu
Federal Code: 001050
CSS Code: 1813

4-year private university in small town.
Enrollment: 965 undergrads. 689 full-time freshmen.
Selectivity: Admits 50 to 75% of applicants.

BASIC COSTS (2010-2011)
Tuition and fees: $16,750.
Per-credit charge: $665.
Room and board: $7,570.

FINANCIAL AID PICTURE (2008-2009)
Students with need: 37% of average financial aid package awarded as scholarships/grants, 63% awarded as loans/jobs. Need-based aid available for part-time students.
Students without need: No-need awards available for academics, athletics, ROTC, state/district residency.

FINANCIAL AID PROCEDURES
Forms required: FAFSA, CSS PROFILE, institutional form.
Dates and Deadlines: Closing date 3/31. Applicants notified on a rolling basis starting 5/15; must reply within 2 week(s) of notification.

CONTACT
Advergus James, Director of Financial Aid Services
102 Old Administration Building, Tuskegee, AL 36088
(334) 724-4733

University of Alabama

Tuscaloosa, Alabama
www.ua.edu
Federal Code: 001051

4-year public university in small city.
Enrollment: 23,296 undergrads, 7% part-time. 5,034 full-time freshmen.
Selectivity: Admits 50 to 75% of applicants.

BASIC COSTS (2009-2010)
Tuition and fees: $7,000; out-of-state residents $19,200.
Room and board: $7,796.

FINANCIAL AID PICTURE (2008-2009)
Students with need: Out of 2,309 full-time freshmen who applied for aid, 1,702 were judged to have need. Of these, 1,702 received aid, and 237 had their full need met. Average financial aid package met 55% of need; average scholarship/grant was $7,063; average loan was $3,621. For part-time students, average financial aid package was $6,135.
Students without need: 1,195 full-time freshmen who did not demonstrate need for aid received scholarships/grants; average award was $6,119. No-need awards available for academics, alumni affiliation, art, athletics, leadership, minority status, music/drama, ROTC, state/district residency.
Scholarships offered: 97 full-time freshmen received athletic scholarships; average amount $19,271.
Cumulative student debt: 52% of graduating class had student loans; average debt was $23,964.

FINANCIAL AID PROCEDURES
Forms required: FAFSA.
Dates and Deadlines: Priority date 3/1; no closing date. Applicants notified on a rolling basis starting 4/1; must reply within 3 week(s) of notification.
Transfers: No deadline. Applicants notified on a rolling basis. Scholarship opportunities for transfer students.

CONTACT
Jeanetta Allen, Director, Student Financial Aid
Box 870132, Tuscaloosa, AL 35487-0132
(205) 348-6756

University of Alabama at Birmingham

Birmingham, Alabama
www.uab.edu
Federal Code: 001052

4-year public university in very large city.
Enrollment: 10,265 undergrads, 23% part-time. 1,247 full-time freshmen.
Selectivity: Admits over 75% of applicants.

BASIC COSTS (2009-2010)
Tuition and fees: $6,152; out-of-state residents $14,072.
Per-credit charge: $176; out-of-state residents $440.
Room and board: $8,142.

FINANCIAL AID PICTURE (2008-2009)
Students with need: Out of 817 full-time freshmen who applied for aid, 564 were judged to have need. Of these, 554 received aid, and 115 had their full need met. Average financial aid package met 49% of need; average scholarship/grant was $4,759; average loan was $3,870. For part-time students, average financial aid package was $6,269.
Students without need: 374 full-time freshmen who did not demonstrate need for aid received scholarships/grants; average award was $6,778. No-need awards available for academics, alumni affiliation, art, athletics, leadership, minority status, music/drama, ROTC.
Scholarships offered: *Merit:* Presidential Scholarship; full tuition, fees, and housing (up to 15 credit hours); based on 33-36 ACT and 3.0 GPA. Golden Excellence Scholarship; $6,000; based on 28-32 ACT and 3.3 GPA. Collegiate Honors Scholarship; $3,000; based on 25-27 ACT and 3.5 GPA. UAB Breakthrough Scholarship; $2,000; based on 24 ACT and 3.5 GPA. UAB Academic Achievement Scholarship; $1,000; based on 24-27 ACT and 3.0-3.49 GPA or 28-32 ACT and 3.0-3.29 GPA. Blazer Elite; $9,000; based on 28 ACT and 3.8 GPA; awarded to out-of-state students. Blazer Gold; $5,500; based on 26 ACT and at least 3.5 GPA, awarded to out-of-state students. Blazer Achievement; $3,500; based on 26 ACT and 3.0 GPA; awarded to out-of-state students. Blazer Pride; $2,500; based on 24 ACT and 3.0 GPA; awarded to out-of-state students. *Athletic:* 53 full-time freshmen received athletic scholarships; average amount $13,059.

FINANCIAL AID PROCEDURES
Forms required: FAFSA, institutional form.
Dates and Deadlines: Priority date 4/1; no closing date. Applicants notified on a rolling basis starting 4/1; must reply within 4 week(s) of notification.
Transfers: Must reply within 4 week(s) of notification.

CONTACT
Jan May, Director of Financial Aid
HUC 260, 1530 Third Avenue South, Birmingham, AL 35294-1150
(205) 934-8223

University of Alabama in Huntsville

Huntsville, Alabama
www.uah.edu
Federal Code: 001055

4-year public university in small city.
Enrollment: 5,956 undergrads, 23% part-time. 775 full-time freshmen.
Selectivity: Admits 50 to 75% of applicants.

BASIC COSTS (2009-2010)
Tuition and fees: $6,510; out-of-state residents $15,628.
Per-credit charge: $213; out-of-state residents $512.
Room and board: $7,208.

Additional info: Per-credit-hour rate decreases as number of hours registered increases.

FINANCIAL AID PICTURE (2009-2010)

Students with need: Out of 707 full-time freshmen who applied for aid, 364 were judged to have need. Of these, 363 received aid, and 62 had their full need met. Average financial aid package met 62% of need; average scholarship/grant was $6,236; average loan was $5,340. For part-time students, average financial aid package was $6,342.

Students without need: 252 full-time freshmen who did not demonstrate need for aid received scholarships/grants; average award was $4,470. No-need awards available for academics, art, athletics, leadership, minority status, music/drama, ROTC.

Scholarships offered: *Merit:* Application deadline for institutional scholarships is December 1st. *Athletic:* 39 full-time freshmen received athletic scholarships; average amount $7,851.

Cumulative student debt: 26% of graduating class had student loans; average debt was $24,938.

FINANCIAL AID PROCEDURES

Forms required: FAFSA.

Dates and Deadlines: Priority date 4/1; closing date 7/31. Applicants notified on a rolling basis starting 4/1; must reply within 2 week(s) of notification.

Transfers: First-time regularly admitted transfer students who have earned transfer credits from an accredited 2-year institution of higher learning considered for one-time transfer scholarship award. Preference given to students who have demonstrated academic potential and leadership and are members of Phi Theta Kappa. Super Scholar Transfer Scholarship requires 3.75 college GPA and is currently valued at $2,000 plus a $500 textbook scholarship, renewable for an additional year. UAH Transfer Merit Scholarship requires 3.25 college GPA and is currently valued at $1,000 plus a $500 textbook scholarship, renewable for an additional year. Eligible students should submit the UAH Scholarship Application to apply.

CONTACT

Andy Weaver, Director of Student Financial Services
UAH Office of Undergraduate Admissions, Huntsville, AL 35899
(256) 824-6241

University of Mobile

Mobile, Alabama
www.umobile.edu
Federal Code: 001029

4-year private university and liberal arts college in small city, affiliated with Baptist faith.

Enrollment: 1,417 undergrads, 11% part-time. 221 full-time freshmen.

Selectivity: Admits over 75% of applicants.

BASIC COSTS (2010-2011)

Tuition and fees: $16,120.

Per-credit charge: $555.

Room and board: $7,980.

FINANCIAL AID PICTURE (2009-2010)

Students with need: Out of 221 full-time freshmen who applied for aid, 198 were judged to have need. Of these, 189 received aid. Average financial aid package met 62% of need; average scholarship/grant was $10,666; average loan was $4,097. For part-time students, average financial aid package was $6,919.

Students without need: 32 full-time freshmen who did not demonstrate need for aid received scholarships/grants; average award was $6,160. No-need awards available for academics, alumni affiliation, athletics, music/drama, religious affiliation, ROTC.

Scholarships offered: 6 full-time freshmen received athletic scholarships; average amount $11,643.

Cumulative student debt: 25% of graduating class had student loans; average debt was $18,840.

FINANCIAL AID PROCEDURES

Forms required: FAFSA, state aid form.

Dates and Deadlines: No deadline. Applicants notified on a rolling basis starting 2/1; must reply within 2 week(s) of notification.

CONTACT

Marie Batson, Associate Vice President for Enrollment Management
5735 College Parkway, Mobile, AL 36613-2842
(251) 442-2252

University of Montevallo

Montevallo, Alabama
www.montevallo.edu
Federal Code: 001004

4-year public university and liberal arts college in small town.

Enrollment: 2,547 undergrads, 11% part-time. 409 full-time freshmen.

Selectivity: Admits 50 to 75% of applicants.

BASIC COSTS (2009-2010)

Tuition and fees: $7,010; out-of-state residents $13,550.

Per-credit charge: $217; out-of-state residents $434.

Room and board: $4,440.

FINANCIAL AID PICTURE (2008-2009)

Students with need: Need-based aid available for full-time and part-time students.

Students without need: No-need awards available for academics, art, athletics, job skills, leadership, minority status, music/drama, religious affiliation, ROTC.

FINANCIAL AID PROCEDURES

Forms required: FAFSA.

Dates and Deadlines: Priority date 4/1; no closing date. Applicants notified on a rolling basis starting 4/20; must reply within 2 week(s) of notification.

CONTACT

Maria Parker, Director of Financial Aid
Station 6030, Montevallo, AL 35115-6030
(205) 665-6050

University of North Alabama

Florence, Alabama
www.una.edu
Federal Code: 001016

4-year public university in large town.

Enrollment: 5,814 undergrads, 14% part-time. 1,050 full-time freshmen.

Selectivity: Admits over 75% of applicants.

BASIC COSTS (2009-2010)

Tuition and fees: $6,018; out-of-state residents $11,028.

Per-credit charge: $167; out-of-state residents $334.

Room and board: $4,783.

FINANCIAL AID PICTURE (2008-2009)

Students with need: Out of 689 full-time freshmen who applied for aid, 522 were judged to have need. Of these, 505 received aid, and 240 had their full need met. Average financial aid package met 61% of need; average scholarship/grant was $4,060; average loan was $2,115. For part-time students, average financial aid package was $3,773.

Students without need: 340 full-time freshmen who did not demonstrate need for aid received scholarships/grants; average award was $2,726. No-need awards available for academics, art, athletics, leadership, minority status, music/drama, ROTC, state/district residency.

Scholarships offered: 67 full-time freshmen received athletic scholarships; average amount $4,150.

Cumulative student debt: 64% of graduating class had student loans; average debt was $24,500.

FINANCIAL AID PROCEDURES

Forms required: FAFSA.

Dates and Deadlines: Priority date 6/1; no closing date. Applicants notified on a rolling basis starting 6/30; must reply within 2 week(s) of notification.

CONTACT

Ben Baker, Director of Student Financial Services

One Harrison Plaza, UNA Box 5011, Florence, AL 35632-0001

(256) 765-4590

University of South Alabama

Mobile, Alabama

www.southalabama.edu   Federal Code: 001057

4-year public university in small city.

Enrollment: 11,250 undergrads, 24% part-time. 1,753 full-time freshmen.

Selectivity: Admits over 75% of applicants.

BASIC COSTS (2009-2010)

Tuition and fees: $5,962; out-of-state residents $10,822.

Per-credit charge: $162; out-of-state residents $324.

Room and board: $5,308.

Additional info: Tuition/fee waivers available for minority students.

FINANCIAL AID PICTURE (2008-2009)

Students with need: Need-based aid available for full-time and part-time students.

Students without need: No-need awards available for academics, alumni affiliation, art, athletics, minority status, music/drama, ROTC, state/district residency.

FINANCIAL AID PROCEDURES

Forms required: FAFSA, institutional form.

Dates and Deadlines: Priority date 5/1; no closing date. Applicants notified on a rolling basis starting 5/15.

CONTACT

Emily Johnston, Director of Financial Aid

Meisler Hall, Suite 2500, Mobile, AL 36688-0002

(251) 460-6231

University of West Alabama

Livingston, Alabama

www.uwa.edu   Federal Code: 001024

4-year public university in small town.

Enrollment: 1,945 undergrads, 21% part-time. 243 full-time freshmen.

Selectivity: Admits 50 to 75% of applicants.

BASIC COSTS (2009-2010)

Tuition and fees: $5,560; out-of-state residents $10,620.

Per-credit charge: $215; out-of-state residents $430.

Room and board: $4,416.

FINANCIAL AID PICTURE (2009-2010)

Students with need: Need-based aid available for full-time and part-time students. Work study available nights, weekends, and for part-time students.

Students without need: No-need awards available for academics, alumni affiliation, athletics, leadership, music/drama, state/district residency.

FINANCIAL AID PROCEDURES

Forms required: FAFSA.

Dates and Deadlines: Priority date 4/1; no closing date. Applicants notified on a rolling basis starting 6/1; must reply within 2 week(s) of notification.

CONTACT

Don Rainer, Director of Financial Aid

Station 4, Livingston, AL 35470

(205) 652-3576

Wallace State Community College at Hanceville

Hanceville, Alabama

www.wallacestate.edu   Federal Code: 007871

2-year public health science and community college in rural community.

Enrollment: 3,100 full-time undergrads.

Selectivity: Open admission; but selective for some programs.

BASIC COSTS (2009-2010)

Tuition and fees: $2,700; out-of-state residents $4,830.

Per-credit charge: $71; out-of-state residents $142.

Room only: $1,650.

FINANCIAL AID PICTURE

Students with need: Need-based aid available for full-time and part-time students. Work study available nights.

Students without need: This college awards aid only to students with need.

FINANCIAL AID PROCEDURES

Forms required: FAFSA.

Dates and Deadlines: Priority date 5/1; no closing date. Applicants notified on a rolling basis starting 7/15; must reply within 2 week(s) of notification.

Transfers: No deadline.

CONTACT

Becky Graves, Director of Student Financial Aid

PO Box 2000, Hanceville, AL 35077-2000

(256) 352-8182

Alaska

Alaska Pacific University

Anchorage, Alaska

www.alaskapacific.edu   Federal Code: 001061

4-year private university and liberal arts college in large city, affiliated with United Methodist Church.

Enrollment: 427 undergrads, 41% part-time. 27 full-time freshmen.

Selectivity: Admits less than 50% of applicants.

BASIC COSTS (2010-2011)

Tuition and fees: $26,360.

Per-credit charge: $1,100.

Room and board: $9,300.

Additional info: Tuition at time of enrollment locked for 4 years.

FINANCIAL AID PICTURE (2009-2010)

Students with need: Average financial aid package met 89% of need; average scholarship/grant was $7,500; average loan was $3,375. For part-time students, average financial aid package was $4,251.

Students without need: No-need awards available for academics, alumni affiliation, art, leadership, music/drama, religious affiliation, state/district residency.

Cumulative student debt: 32% of graduating class had student loans; average debt was $44,398.

FINANCIAL AID PROCEDURES

Forms required: FAFSA.

Dates and Deadlines: Priority date 4/15; no closing date. Applicants notified on a rolling basis starting 2/1; must reply within 4 week(s) of notification.
Transfers: Priority date 6/1; no deadline. Applicants notified on a rolling basis starting 2/1; must reply within 2 week(s) of notification.

CONTACT
Jo Holland, Director, Student Financial Services
4101 University Drive, Anchorage, AK 99508-3051
(907) 564-8341

Ilisagvik College
Barrow, Alaska
www.ilisagvik.cc   Federal Code: 034613

2-year public Tribal Community College in rural community.
Enrollment: 94 undergrads, 56% part-time. 12 full-time freshmen.
Selectivity: Open admission.

BASIC COSTS (2009-2010)
Tuition and fees: $2,820; out-of-state residents $4,020.
Per-credit charge: $100; out-of-state residents $150.
Room and board: $10,650.

FINANCIAL AID PICTURE (2008-2009)
Students with need: 77% of average financial aid package awarded as scholarships/grants, 23% awarded as loans/jobs.

FINANCIAL AID PROCEDURES
Dates and Deadlines: No deadline.

CONTACT
Fred Miller, Director of Financial Aid
100 Stevenson Road, Barrow, AK 99723
(907) 852-1708

Prince William Sound Community College
Valdez, Alaska
www.pwscc.edu   Federal Code: 011462

2-year public community college in small town.
Enrollment: 170 undergrads.
Selectivity: Open admission.

BASIC COSTS (2009-2010)
Tuition and fees: $4,170.
Per-credit charge: $122.
Room only: $4,970.

FINANCIAL AID PICTURE
Students with need: Need-based aid available for full-time and part-time students.
Students without need: No-need awards available for state/district residency.

FINANCIAL AID PROCEDURES
Forms required: FAFSA.
Dates and Deadlines: Priority date 6/30; no closing date. Applicants notified on a rolling basis.
Transfers: Priority date 4/1; closing date 5/1.

CONTACT
Gianna Thornton, Assistant to the Director of Student Services
Box 97, Valdez, AK 99686
(907) 834-1666

University of Alaska Anchorage
Anchorage, Alaska
www.uaa.alaska.edu   Federal Code: 011462

4-year public university in large city.
Enrollment: 11,878 undergrads, 42% part-time. 1,417 full-time freshmen.
Selectivity: Open admission; but selective for some programs.

BASIC COSTS (2009-2010)
Tuition and fees: $4,806; out-of-state residents $14,706.
Per-credit charge: $141; out-of-state residents $471.
Room and board: $8,605.

FINANCIAL AID PICTURE
Students with need: Need-based aid available for full-time and part-time students. Work study available nights, weekends, and for part-time students.
Students without need: No-need awards available for academics, athletics.

FINANCIAL AID PROCEDURES
Forms required: FAFSA, institutional form.
Dates and Deadlines: Priority date 4/1; closing date 8/1. Applicants notified on a rolling basis starting 3/15; must reply within 4 week(s) of notification.
Transfers: Closing date 4/15.

CONTACT
Ted Malone, Director of Financial Aid
PO Box 141629, Anchorage, AK 99514-1629
(907) 786-1586

University of Alaska Fairbanks
Fairbanks, Alaska
www.uaf.edu   Federal Code: 001063

4-year public university in small city.
Enrollment: 5,273 undergrads, 34% part-time. 763 full-time freshmen.
Selectivity: Admits 50 to 75% of applicants. GED not accepted.

BASIC COSTS (2009-2010)
Tuition and fees: $5,133; out-of-state residents $15,033.
Per-credit charge: $141; out-of-state residents $471.
Room and board: $7,360.
Additional info: Estimated course and lab fees: $500 per year.

FINANCIAL AID PICTURE (2008-2009)
Students with need: Out of 577 full-time freshmen who applied for aid, 353 were judged to have need. Of these, 338 received aid, and 142 had their full need met. Average financial aid package met 56% of need; average scholarship/grant was $5,574; average loan was $8,377. For part-time students, average financial aid package was $8,816.
Students without need: 219 full-time freshmen who did not demonstrate need for aid received scholarships/grants; average award was $7,834. No-need awards available for academics, art, athletics, leadership, minority status, music/drama, ROTC, state/district residency.
Scholarships offered: 17 full-time freshmen received athletic scholarships; average amount $13,279.
Cumulative student debt: 54% of graduating class had student loans; average debt was $29,485.

FINANCIAL AID PROCEDURES
Forms required: FAFSA.
Dates and Deadlines: Priority date 2/15; closing date 7/1. Applicants notified on a rolling basis starting 3/1; must reply within 2 week(s) of notification.

CONTACT
Deanna Dieringer, Director of Financial Aid
PO Box 757480, Fairbanks, AK 99775-7480
(888) 474-7256

University of Alaska Southeast
Juneau, Alaska
www.uas.alaska.edu   Federal Code: 001065

4-year public university and liberal arts college in large town.
Enrollment: 1,503 undergrads, 55% part-time. 160 full-time freshmen.
Selectivity: Admits over 75% of applicants.

BASIC COSTS (2009-2010)
Tuition and fees: $5,017; out-of-state residents $14,917.
Per-credit charge: $141; out-of-state residents $471.
Room and board: $6,430.
Additional info: Tuition reported is for lower division offerings.

FINANCIAL AID PICTURE (2008-2009)
Students with need: Out of 155 full-time freshmen who applied for aid, 72 were judged to have need. Of these, 69 received aid, and 7 had their full need met. Average financial aid package met 46% of need; average scholarship/grant was $1,177; average loan was $1,682. For part-time students, average financial aid package was $4,214.
Students without need: 27 full-time freshmen who did not demonstrate need for aid received scholarships/grants; average award was $1,326. No-need awards available for academics, job skills, leadership, music/drama, state/district residency.
Cumulative student debt: 75% of graduating class had student loans; average debt was $2,763.
Additional info: Transfer, continuing, and freshman scholarship deadline March 1.

FINANCIAL AID PROCEDURES
Forms required: FAFSA.
Dates and Deadlines: Priority date 4/15; no closing date. Applicants notified on a rolling basis starting 3/1; must reply within 3 week(s) of notification.

CONTACT
Barbara Burnett, Director of Financial Aid
11120 Glacier Highway, Juneau, AK 99801-8681
(907) 796-6255

Arizona

Anthem College
Phoenix, Arizona
www.hightechinstitute.edu   Federal Code: 022631

2-year for-profit technical college in very large city.
Enrollment: 2,500 undergrads.
Selectivity: Open admission.

BASIC COSTS (2009-2010)
Additional info: Costs for diploma programs range from $12,150 to $25,850. Fees, books, uniforms and tools included.

FINANCIAL AID PICTURE
Students with need: Need-based aid available for full-time students.
Students without need: This college awards aid only to students with need.

FINANCIAL AID PROCEDURES
Dates and Deadlines: No deadline.

CONTACT
Joshua Esquivel, Financial Aid Director
1515 East Indian School Road, Phoenix, AZ 85014-4901
(602) 279-9700

Arizona State University
Tempe, Arizona
www.asu.edu   Federal Code: 001081

4-year public university in very large city.
Enrollment: 53,902 undergrads, 16% part-time. 8,261 full-time freshmen.
Selectivity: Admits over 75% of applicants.

BASIC COSTS (2009-2010)
Tuition and fees: $6,334; out-of-state residents $18,919.
Per-credit charge: $428; out-of-state residents $774.
Room and board: $9,210.

FINANCIAL AID PICTURE (2008-2009)
Students with need: Need-based aid available for full-time and part-time students.
Students without need: No-need awards available for academics, art, athletics, leadership, music/drama, ROTC.

FINANCIAL AID PROCEDURES
Forms required: FAFSA.
Dates and Deadlines: Priority date 3/1; no closing date. Applicants notified on a rolling basis.

CONTACT
Craig Fennell, Director of Student Financial Assistance
Box 870112, Tempe, AZ 85287-0112
(480) 965-3355

Arizona Western College
Yuma, Arizona
www.azwestern.edu   Federal Code: 001071

2-year public community college in small city.
Enrollment: 7,269 undergrads, 64% part-time. 48 full-time freshmen.
Selectivity: Open admission; but selective for some programs.

BASIC COSTS (2009-2010)
Tuition and fees: $1,800; out-of-state residents $6,360.
Per-credit charge: $60; out-of-state residents $212.
Room and board: $5,140.

FINANCIAL AID PICTURE (2009-2010)
Students with need: Need-based aid available for full-time and part-time students. Work study available nights, weekends, and for part-time students.
Students without need: No-need awards available for academics, athletics.

FINANCIAL AID PROCEDURES
Forms required: FAFSA, institutional form.
Dates and Deadlines: Priority date 4/1; no closing date. Applicants notified on a rolling basis starting 5/1.

CONTACT
Lisa Seale, Director of Financial Aid
PO Box 929, Yuma, AZ 85366-0929
(928) 344-7634

Art Center Design College
Tucson, Arizona
www.theartcenter.edu   Federal Code: 024915

4-year for-profit visual arts college in very large city.
Enrollment: 349 undergrads, 32% part-time. 27 full-time freshmen.

BASIC COSTS (2009-2010)
Tuition and fees: $16,800.
Per-credit charge: $700.

FINANCIAL AID PICTURE
Students with need: Need-based aid available for full-time and part-time students. Work study available nights, weekends, and for part-time students.
Students without need: This college awards aid only to students with need.
Scholarships offered: Board of Trustees Scholarship, Transfer Student Scholarship, Scholarship for Continuing Students.

FINANCIAL AID PROCEDURES
Forms required: FAFSA.
Dates and Deadlines: No deadline.
Transfers: No deadline. Applicants notified on a rolling basis.

CONTACT
Amy Woods, Director of Student Services
2525 North Country Club Road, Tucson, AZ 85716
(520) 325-0123

Art Institute of Phoenix
Phoenix, Arizona
www.artinstitutes.edu/phoenix   Federal Code: 040513

3-year for-profit culinary school and visual arts college in very large city.
Enrollment: 1,125 undergrads.

FINANCIAL AID PICTURE
Students with need: Need-based aid available for full-time and part-time students.

FINANCIAL AID PROCEDURES
Forms required: FAFSA.
Dates and Deadlines: No deadline.

CONTACT
Lori Ryan, Director of Administrative and Financial Services
2233 West Dunlap Avenue, Phoenix, AZ 85021-2859

Brookline College: Phoenix
Phoenix, Arizona
www.brooklinecollege.edu   Federal Code: 022188

2-year for-profit career college in very large city.
Enrollment: 1,186 undergrads.
Selectivity: Open admission; but selective for some programs.

BASIC COSTS (2010-2011)
Tuition and fees: $13,000.
Additional info: Tuition shown is an average, actual tuition and fees may vary by program. $100 Technology fee per term for programs taken online.

FINANCIAL AID PICTURE
Students with need: Need-based aid available for full-time students.
Students without need: This college awards aid only to students with need.

FINANCIAL AID PROCEDURES
Forms required: FAFSA, institutional form.
Dates and Deadlines: No deadline.

CONTACT
Genna Gillary, Corporate Director of Financial Aid
2445 West Dunlap Avenue, Suite 100, Phoenix, AZ 85021-5820
(602) 644-7110

Brookline College: Tempe
Tempe, Arizona
www.brooklinecollege.edu   Federal Code: 022188

2-year for-profit branch campus and career college in very large city.
Enrollment: 301 undergrads.
Selectivity: Open admission; but selective for some programs.

BASIC COSTS (2010-2011)
Tuition and fees: $13,000.
Additional info: Tuition shown is an average, actual tuition and fees may vary by program.

FINANCIAL AID PICTURE
Students with need: Need-based aid available for full-time students.
Students without need: This college awards aid only to students with need.

FINANCIAL AID PROCEDURES
Forms required: FAFSA, institutional form.
Dates and Deadlines: No deadline.

CONTACT
Genna Gillary, Corporate Director of Financial Aid
1140-1150 South Priest Drive, Tempe, AZ 85281-5240
(480) 545-8755

Brookline College: Tucson
Tucson, Arizona
www.brooklinecollege.edu   Federal Code: 022188

2-year for-profit branch campus and career college in very large city.
Enrollment: 598 undergrads.
Selectivity: Open admission; but selective for some programs.

BASIC COSTS (2010-2011)
Tuition and fees: $13,000.
Additional info: Tuition shown is an average, actual tuition and fees may vary by program.

FINANCIAL AID PICTURE
Students with need: Need-based aid available for full-time and part-time students.
Students without need: This college awards aid only to students with need.

FINANCIAL AID PROCEDURES
Forms required: FAFSA, institutional form.
Dates and Deadlines: No deadline.

CONTACT
Genna Gillary, Corporate Director of Financial Aid
5441 East 22nd Street, Suite 125, Tucson, AZ 85711-5444
(602) 644-7090

Central Arizona College
Coolidge, Arizona
www.centralaz.edu/   Federal Code: 007283

2-year public community college in rural community.
Enrollment: 5,282 undergrads, 67% part-time. 604 full-time freshmen.
Selectivity: Open admission; but selective for some programs.

BASIC COSTS (2009-2010)
Tuition and fees: $1,736; out-of-state residents $7,728.
Per-credit charge: $62; out-of-state residents $120.

Room and board: $4,900.

FINANCIAL AID PICTURE

Students with need: Need-based aid available for full-time and part-time students. Work study available nights, weekends, and for part-time students.

FINANCIAL AID PROCEDURES

Forms required: FAFSA.

Dates and Deadlines: Priority date 5/1; closing date 7/15. Must reply within 3 week(s) of notification.

CONTACT

Russ Banta, Vice President Finance & Administration and Chief Financial Officer
Admissions Office, Coolidge, AZ 85128-9030
(520) 494-5425

Chandler-Gilbert Community College: Pecos

Chandler, Arizona
www.cgc.maricopa.edu   Federal Code: 030722

2-year public community college in small city.
Enrollment: 4,127 undergrads, 62% part-time. 825 full-time freshmen.
Selectivity: Open admission.

BASIC COSTS (2009-2010)

Tuition and fees: $2,145; out-of-state residents $8,595.
Per-credit charge: $71; out-of-state residents $286.

FINANCIAL AID PICTURE (2009-2010)

Students with need: Work study available nights, weekends, and for part-time students.

CONTACT

Doug Bullock, Director of Financial Aid
2626 East Pecos Road, Chandler, AZ 85225

Cochise College

Douglas, Arizona
www.cochise.edu   Federal Code: 001072

2-year public community college in large town.
Enrollment: 3,512 undergrads, 69% part-time. 275 full-time freshmen.
Selectivity: Open admission; but selective for some programs.

BASIC COSTS (2009-2010)

Tuition and fees: $1,630; out-of-state residents $8,770.
Per-credit charge: $52; out-of-state residents $290.
Room and board: $4,600.

FINANCIAL AID PICTURE (2008-2009)

Students with need: Out of 220 full-time freshmen who applied for aid, 192 were judged to have need. Of these, 190 received aid. For part-time students, average financial aid package was $4,450.
Students without need: 9 full-time freshmen who did not demonstrate need for aid received scholarships/grants; average award was $675. No-need awards available for academics, athletics.
Cumulative student debt: 15% of graduating class had student loans; average debt was $7,385.

FINANCIAL AID PROCEDURES

Forms required: FAFSA, institutional form.
Dates and Deadlines: Closing date 4/15. Applicants notified on a rolling basis starting 6/15; must reply within 2 week(s) of notification.
Transfers: Priority date 4/15; no deadline. Applicants notified on a rolling basis.

CONTACT

Dartle Atherton, Director of Financial Aid
901 North Colombo Avenue, Sierra Vista, AZ 85635
(520) 515-5417

Coconino County Community College

Flagstaff, Arizona
www.coconino.edu   Federal Code: 031004

2-year public community college in small city.
Enrollment: 2,742 undergrads.
Selectivity: Open admission; but selective for some programs.

BASIC COSTS (2009-2010)

Tuition and fees: $1,800; out-of-state residents $6,000.
Per-credit charge: $75; out-of-state residents $250.

FINANCIAL AID PICTURE (2008-2009)

Students with need: 21% of average financial aid package awarded as scholarships/grants, 79% awarded as loans/jobs.

FINANCIAL AID PROCEDURES

Dates and Deadlines: Priority date 4/15; closing date 6/30.

CONTACT

Bob Voytek, Director for Student Support Services and Financial Assistance
2800 South Lone Tree Road, Flagstaff, AZ 86001
(928) 226-4219

DeVry University: Phoenix

Phoenix, Arizona
www.devry.edu   Federal Code: 008322

4-year for-profit university in large city.
Enrollment: 1,339 undergrads, 39% part-time. 212 full-time freshmen.

BASIC COSTS (2009-2010)

Tuition and fees: $14,160.
Per-credit charge: $550.

FINANCIAL AID PICTURE (2008-2009)

Students with need: Need-based aid available for full-time and part-time students.
Students without need: This college awards aid only to students with need.

FINANCIAL AID PROCEDURES

Forms required: FAFSA.
Dates and Deadlines: No deadline. Applicants notified on a rolling basis.

CONTACT

Kathy Wyse, Dean of Student Finances
2149 West Dunlap Avenue, Phoenix, AZ 85021-2995
(602) 870-9229

Dine College

Tsaile, Arizona
www.dinecollege.edu   Federal Code: 008246

2-year public community college in rural community.
Enrollment: 600 full-time undergrads.
Selectivity: Open admission.

BASIC COSTS (2009-2010)

Tuition and fees: $850.
Room and board: $4,472.

PART III: FINANCIAL AID COLLEGE BY COLLEGE

FINANCIAL AID PICTURE (2008-2009)
Students with need: Need-based aid available for full-time and part-time students.
Students without need: This college awards aid only to students with need.

FINANCIAL AID PROCEDURES
Forms required: FAFSA, institutional form.
Dates and Deadlines: Priority date 4/15; no closing date. Applicants notified on a rolling basis starting 5/1; must reply within 4 week(s) of notification.
Transfers: Priority date 3/1; no deadline. Applicants notified on a rolling basis starting 1/1; must reply within 6 week(s) of notification.

CONTACT
Gary Segay, Director of Financial Aid
Box 67, Tsaile, AZ 86556
(928) 724-6738

Eastern Arizona College
Thatcher, Arizona
www.eac.edu   Federal Code: 001073

2-year public community college in large town.
Enrollment: 4,470 undergrads, 55% part-time. 648 full-time freshmen.
Selectivity: Open admission; but selective for some programs.

BASIC COSTS (2009-2010)
Tuition and fees: $1,520; out-of-state residents $8,120.
Per-credit charge: $65; out-of-state residents $140.
Room and board: $4,795.

FINANCIAL AID PICTURE (2009-2010)
Students with need: Average financial aid package met 37% of need; average scholarship/grant was $5,012. For part-time students, average financial aid package was $35.
Students without need: No-need awards available for academics, art, athletics, leadership, music/drama, state/district residency.
Scholarships offered: Departmental Scholarships; in-state tuition; based on 2.5 GPA. Academic Scholarships; in-state tuition; based on 3.0 GPA. Performing Arts Scholarships; amounts vary; based on 2.5 GPA and audition.
Additional info: Limited number of tuition waivers for New Mexico residents. Unlimited number of waivers for those meeting WUE requirements.

FINANCIAL AID PROCEDURES
Forms required: FAFSA, institutional form.
Dates and Deadlines: Priority date 3/1; no closing date. Applicants notified on a rolling basis starting 3/15.
Transfers: No deadline. Applicants notified on a rolling basis starting 3/15.

CONTACT
Sharon Montoya, Director of Financial Aid
615 North Stadium Avenue, Thatcher, AZ 85552-0769
(928) 428-8287

Embry-Riddle Aeronautical University: Prescott Campus
Prescott, Arizona
www.embryriddle.edu   Federal Code: 014797

4-year private university in large town.
Enrollment: 1,613 undergrads, 7% part-time. 318 full-time freshmen.

BASIC COSTS (2010-2011)
Tuition and fees: $28,948.
Per-credit charge: $1,170.
Room and board: $8,790.

FINANCIAL AID PICTURE (2009-2010)
Students with need: Need-based aid available for full-time and part-time students.
Students without need: No-need awards available for academics, alumni affiliation, athletics, leadership, ROTC.

FINANCIAL AID PROCEDURES
Forms required: FAFSA.
Dates and Deadlines: No deadline. Applicants notified on a rolling basis starting 3/1; must reply within 4 week(s) of notification.

CONTACT
Barbara Dryden, Director of Financial Aid
3700 Willow Creek Road, Prescott, AZ 86301-3720
(928) 777-3765

Estrella Mountain Community College
Avondale, Arizona
www.estrellamountain.edu   Federal Code: 031563

2-year public community college in small city.
Enrollment: 3,390 undergrads, 71% part-time. 457 full-time freshmen.
Selectivity: Open admission.

BASIC COSTS (2009-2010)
Tuition and fees: $2,145; out-of-state residents $8,985.
Per-credit charge: $71; out-of-state residents $286.

FINANCIAL AID PICTURE (2008-2009)
Students with need: Need-based aid available for full-time and part-time students. Work study available nights.
Students without need: No-need awards available for leadership.

FINANCIAL AID PROCEDURES
Dates and Deadlines: Priority date 4/1; no closing date. Applicants notified on a rolling basis starting 4/15.

CONTACT
Rosanna Short, Director, Financial Aid
3000 North Dysart Road, Avondale, AZ 85392
(623) 935-8930

GateWay Community College
Phoenix, Arizona
www.gatewaycc.edu   Federal Code: 008303

2-year public community and technical college in very large city.
Enrollment: 7,076 undergrads.
Selectivity: Open admission; but selective for some programs.

BASIC COSTS (2009-2010)
Tuition and fees: $2,145; out-of-state residents $8,085.
Per-credit charge: $71; out-of-state residents $269.

FINANCIAL AID PICTURE (2008-2009)
Students with need: Need-based aid available for full-time and part-time students. Work study available nights, weekends, and for part-time students.
Students without need: No-need awards available for athletics.

FINANCIAL AID PROCEDURES
Forms required: FAFSA, institutional form.
Dates and Deadlines: Priority date 4/15; no closing date. Applicants notified on a rolling basis; must reply within 4 week(s) of notification.

CONTACT
Suzanne Ringle, Director of Financial Aid
108 North 40th Street, Phoenix, AZ 85034
(602) 286-8115

Glendale Community College
Glendale, Arizona
www.gccaz.edu   Federal Code: 001076

2-year public community college in small city.
Enrollment: 8,438 undergrads, 59% part-time.
Selectivity: Open admission; but selective for some programs.

BASIC COSTS (2009-2010)
Tuition and fees: $2,145; out-of-state residents $9,375.
Per-credit charge: $7; out-of-state residents $312.

FINANCIAL AID PICTURE (2008-2009)
Students with need: 52% of average financial aid package awarded as scholarships/grants, 48% awarded as loans/jobs. Need-based aid available for part-time students. Work study available nights, weekends, and for part-time students.

FINANCIAL AID PROCEDURES
Forms required: FAFSA.
Dates and Deadlines: Priority date 4/30; closing date 7/31. Applicants notified on a rolling basis starting 5/1.

CONTACT
Ellen Neel, Director of Financial Aid
6000 West Olive Avenue, Glendale, AZ 85302
(623) 845-3366

Grand Canyon University
Phoenix, Arizona
www.gcu.edu/clgbrd   Federal Code: 001074

4-year for-profit university in very large city.
Enrollment: 2,835 full-time undergrads.

BASIC COSTS (2009-2010)
Tuition and fees: $17,050.
Per-credit charge: $687.
Room and board: $12,400.

FINANCIAL AID PICTURE (2009-2010)
Students with need: Need-based aid available for full-time and part-time students. Work study available nights, weekends, and for part-time students.
Students without need: No-need awards available for academics, alumni affiliation, athletics, leadership, religious affiliation, ROTC.

FINANCIAL AID PROCEDURES
Forms required: FAFSA.
Dates and Deadlines: No deadline. Applicants notified on a rolling basis.
Transfers: No deadline. Applicants notified on a rolling basis.

CONTACT
David Weems, Director of Financial Aid
3300 West Camelback Road, Phoenix, AZ 85017
(602) 639-6522

Lamson College
Tempe, Arizona
www.lamsoncollege.com   Federal Code: 005186

2-year for-profit junior and technical college in very large city.
Enrollment: 643 full-time undergrads.
Selectivity: Open admission.

BASIC COSTS (2009-2010)
Additional info: Per-credit-hour charges vary according to program: $250 to $271; cost of books and supplies ranges from $995 to $3,000, depending on program of study.

FINANCIAL AID PICTURE
Students with need: Need-based aid available for full-time and part-time students.

FINANCIAL AID PROCEDURES
Forms required: FAFSA.
Dates and Deadlines: No deadline. Applicants notified on a rolling basis.

CONTACT
Massus Lindsley, Director of Financial Aid
1126 North Scottsdale Road, Suite 17, Tempe, AZ 85281-1700
(480) 898-7000

Mohave Community College
Kingman, Arizona
www.mohave.edu   Federal Code: 011864

2-year public community college in small city.
Enrollment: 6,010 undergrads.
Selectivity: Open admission; but selective for some programs.

BASIC COSTS (2009-2010)
Tuition and fees: $2,020; out-of-state residents $4,516.
Per-credit charge: $64; out-of-state residents $192.

FINANCIAL AID PICTURE (2009-2010)
Students with need: Need-based aid available for full-time and part-time students. Work study available nights.

FINANCIAL AID PROCEDURES
Forms required: FAFSA, institutional form.
Dates and Deadlines: Priority date 4/15; no closing date. Applicants notified on a rolling basis starting 5/1; must reply within 2 week(s) of notification.

CONTACT
Bill Osbom, Director of Financial Aid
1971 Jagerson Avenue, Kingman, AZ 86409
(866) 664-2832

Northern Arizona University
Flagstaff, Arizona
www.nau.edu   Federal Code: 001082

4-year public university in small city.
Enrollment: 18,044 undergrads, 15% part-time. 3,309 full-time freshmen.
Selectivity: Admits 50 to 75% of applicants.

BASIC COSTS (2009-2010)
Tuition and fees: $6,676; out-of-state residents $17,902.
Per-credit charge: $410; out-of-state residents $703.
Room and board: $7,872.
Additional info: Tuition at time of enrollment locked for 4 years.

FINANCIAL AID PICTURE (2008-2009)
Students with need: Out of 2,611 full-time freshmen who applied for aid, 1,619 were judged to have need. Of these, 1,546 received aid, and 306 had their full need met. Average financial aid package met 69% of need; average scholarship/grant was $6,074; average loan was $3,295. For part-time students, average financial aid package was $6,565.
Students without need: 733 full-time freshmen who did not demonstrate need for aid received scholarships/grants; average award was $3,530. No-

need awards available for academics, alumni affiliation, art, athletics, leadership, minority status, music/drama, ROTC, state/district residency.
Scholarships offered: 58 full-time freshmen received athletic scholarships; average amount $13,155.
Cumulative student debt: 50% of graduating class had student loans; average debt was $16,703.

FINANCIAL AID PROCEDURES
Forms required: FAFSA.
Dates and Deadlines: Priority date 2/14; no closing date. Applicants notified on a rolling basis starting 3/15.
Transfers: Priority date 2/15. Applicants notified on a rolling basis.

CONTACT
Michelle Castillo, Director of Financial Aid
PO Box 4084, Flagstaff, AZ 86011-4084
(928) 523-4951

Northland Pioneer College
Holbrook, Arizona
www.npc.edu   Federal Code: 011862

2-year public community and technical college in small town.
Enrollment: 1,684 undergrads, 70% part-time. 175 full-time freshmen.
Selectivity: Open admission; but selective for some programs.

BASIC COSTS (2009-2010)
Tuition and fees: $1,595; out-of-state residents $7,535.
Per-credit charge: $52; out-of-state residents $85.

FINANCIAL AID PICTURE (2009-2010)
Students with need: Need-based aid available for full-time and part-time students. Work study available nights, weekends, and for part-time students.
Students without need: No-need awards available for academics, art, job skills, leadership, minority status, music/drama, state/district residency.

FINANCIAL AID PROCEDURES
Forms required: FAFSA, institutional form.
Dates and Deadlines: Priority date 6/1; no closing date. Applicants notified on a rolling basis starting 5/15; must reply within 2 week(s) of notification.
Transfers: No deadline. Applicants notified on a rolling basis.

CONTACT
Beaulah Bob-Pennypacker, Financial Aid Coordinator
PO Box 610, Holbrook, AZ 86025-0610
(928) 524-7626

Paradise Valley Community College
Phoenix, Arizona
www.pvc.maricopa.edu   Federal Code: 026236

2-year public community college in very large city.
Enrollment: 3,790 undergrads.
Selectivity: Open admission.

BASIC COSTS (2009-2010)
Tuition and fees: $2,160; out-of-state residents $8,610.
Per-credit charge: $71; out-of-state residents $286.

FINANCIAL AID PICTURE (2008-2009)
Students with need: 35% of average financial aid package awarded as scholarships/grants, 65% awarded as loans/jobs. Need-based aid available for part-time students.

FINANCIAL AID PROCEDURES
Forms required: FAFSA.

Dates and Deadlines: No deadline. Applicants notified on a rolling basis starting 6/1.

CONTACT
Ken Clarke, Interim Director of Financial Aid
18401 North 32nd Street, Phoenix, AZ 85032
(602) 787-7100

Phoenix College
Phoenix, Arizona
www.pc.maricopa.edu   Federal Code: 001078

2-year public community college in very large city.
Enrollment: 2,496 full-time undergrads.
Selectivity: Open admission; but selective for some programs.

BASIC COSTS (2009-2010)
Tuition and fees: $2,160; out-of-state residents $9,390.
Per-credit charge: $71; out-of-state residents $312.

FINANCIAL AID PICTURE
Students with need: Work study available weekends and for part-time students.

FINANCIAL AID PROCEDURES
Forms required: FAFSA.
Dates and Deadlines: Priority date 6/30; no closing date. Applicants notified on a rolling basis starting 5/1.

CONTACT
Genevieve Watson, Director of Financial Aid
1202 West Thomas Road, Phoenix, AZ 85013
(602) 285-7404

Pima Community College
Tucson, Arizona
www.pima.edu   Federal Code: 007266

2-year public community and technical college in very large city.
Enrollment: 33,232 undergrads, 65% part-time. 3,146 full-time freshmen.
Selectivity: Open admission; but selective for some programs.

BASIC COSTS (2009-2010)
Tuition and fees: $1,685; out-of-state residents $7,910.
Per-credit charge: $52; out-of-state residents $87.

FINANCIAL AID PICTURE
Students with need: Need-based aid available for full-time and part-time students.
Students without need: No-need awards available for academics, alumni affiliation, art, athletics, minority status, music/drama.

FINANCIAL AID PROCEDURES
Forms required: FAFSA.
Dates and Deadlines: Priority date 3/15; no closing date. Applicants notified on a rolling basis starting 7/1; must reply within 2 week(s) of notification.

CONTACT
Anna Reese, Executive Director of Financial Aid
4905B East Broadway, Tucson, AZ 85709-1120
(520) 206-4950

Prescott College
Prescott, Arizona
www.prescott.edu   Federal Code: 013659

4-year private liberal arts college in large town.
Enrollment: 763 undergrads, 17% part-time. 73 full-time freshmen.
Selectivity: Admits over 75% of applicants.

BASIC COSTS (2009-2010)
Tuition and fees: $23,643.
Room only: $3,630.
Additional info: Health insurance is required; cost of school's health insurance is $482 for fall term and $675 for spring term.

FINANCIAL AID PICTURE (2009-2010)
Students with need: Average financial aid package met 58% of need; average scholarship/grant was $12,131; average loan was $3,349. For part-time students, average financial aid package was $9,603.
Students without need: No-need awards available for academics, alumni affiliation, minority status, state/district residency.
Cumulative student debt: 67% of graduating class had student loans; average debt was $14,947.

FINANCIAL AID PROCEDURES
Forms required: FAFSA.
Dates and Deadlines: Priority date 3/1; no closing date. Applicants notified on a rolling basis starting 3/15; must reply within 12 week(s) of notification.
Transfers: No deadline. Applicants notified on a rolling basis; must reply within 12 week(s) of notification.

CONTACT
Mary Frances Causey, Director of Financial Aid
220 Grove Avenue, Prescott, AZ 86301
(928) 776-5225

Rio Salado College
Tempe, Arizona
www.riosalado.edu   Federal Code: 014483

2-year public virtual community college in very large city.
Enrollment: 1,223 undergrads.
Selectivity: Open admission; but selective for some programs.

BASIC COSTS (2009-2010)
Tuition and fees: $2,160; out-of-state residents $9,390.
Per-credit charge: $71; out-of-state residents $312.

FINANCIAL AID PICTURE (2008-2009)
Students with need: Need-based aid available for full-time and part-time students.
Students without need: This college awards aid only to students with need.

FINANCIAL AID PROCEDURES
Forms required: FAFSA, institutional form.
Dates and Deadlines: Priority date 6/30; no closing date. Applicants notified on a rolling basis starting 6/30.

CONTACT
Ryan Chase, Director of Financial Aid
2323 West 14th Street, Tempe, AZ 85281
(480) 517-8310

Southwestern College
Phoenix, Arizona
www.swcaz.edu   Federal Code: 007113

4-year private Bible and liberal arts college in very large city, affiliated with Baptist faith.
Enrollment: 300 full-time undergrads.
Selectivity: Admits 50 to 75% of applicants.

BASIC COSTS (2009-2010)
Tuition and fees: $15,094.
Per-credit charge: $600.
Room and board: $6,668.

FINANCIAL AID PICTURE
Students with need: Need-based aid available for full-time and part-time students.
Students without need: No-need awards available for academics, alumni affiliation, athletics, leadership, minority status, music/drama, religious affiliation.

FINANCIAL AID PROCEDURES
Forms required: FAFSA, state aid form, institutional form.
Dates and Deadlines: Priority date 3/15; closing date 8/31. Applicants notified on a rolling basis.

CONTACT
Cheryl Hansen, Director of Financial Aid
2625 East Cactus Road, Phoenix, AZ 85032-7042
(602) 489-5500 ext. 115

Tohono O'odham Community College
Sells, Arizona
www.tocc.cc.az.us   Federal Code: 037844

2-year public community college in rural community.
Enrollment: 25 full-time undergrads.
Selectivity: Open admission.

FINANCIAL AID PICTURE (2008-2009)
Students with need: Need-based aid available for full-time and part-time students.
Students without need: This college awards aid only to students with need.

FINANCIAL AID PROCEDURES
Forms required: FAFSA, institutional form.
Dates and Deadlines: No deadline. Applicants notified on a rolling basis.

CONTACT
Alvaro Rivera, Financial Aid Director
PO Box 3129, Sells, AZ 85634-3129
(520) 383-8401 ext. 41

University of Advancing Technology
Tempe, Arizona
www.uat.edu   Federal Code: 017188

4-year for-profit university in very large city.
Enrollment: 1,090 undergrads. 152 full-time freshmen.

BASIC COSTS (2009-2010)
Tuition and fees: $17,900.
Room and board: $10,348.

FINANCIAL AID PICTURE (2008-2009)

Students with need: 58% of average financial aid package awarded as scholarships/grants, 42% awarded as loans/jobs. Need-based aid available for part-time students.

FINANCIAL AID PROCEDURES

Forms required: FAFSA.

Dates and Deadlines: Priority date 4/15; no closing date. Applicants notified on a rolling basis; must reply within 2 week(s) of notification.

Transfers: No deadline. Must reply within 2 week(s) of notification. Loan periods may not overlap.

CONTACT

Robert Conlon, Senior Financial Aid Administrator
2625 West Baseline Road, Tempe, AZ 85283-1056
(602) 383-8217

University of Arizona

Tucson, Arizona
www.arizona.edu   Federal Code: 001083

4-year public university in very large city.

Enrollment: 30,333 undergrads, 11% part-time. 6,331 full-time freshmen.

Selectivity: Admits over 75% of applicants.

BASIC COSTS (2009-2010)

Tuition and fees: $6,855; out-of-state residents $22,264.

Per-credit charge: $357; out-of-state residents $943.

Room and board: $8,614.

Additional info: Tuition/fee waivers available for minority students.

FINANCIAL AID PICTURE (2008-2009)

Students with need: Out of 4,048 full-time freshmen who applied for aid, 2,476 were judged to have need. Of these, 2,401 received aid, and 321 had their full need met. Average financial aid package met 65% of need; average scholarship/grant was $7,794; average loan was $3,376. For part-time students, average financial aid package was $6,996.

Students without need: 2,200 full-time freshmen who did not demonstrate need for aid received scholarships/grants; average award was $4,586. No-need awards available for academics, art, music/drama.

Scholarships offered: *Merit:* Various merit scholarships available. National Merit scholarship; $6,000-$10,000 a year. *Athletic:* 57 full-time freshmen received athletic scholarships; average amount $14,405.

Cumulative student debt: 43% of graduating class had student loans; average debt was $18,712.

Additional info: Arizona Assurance Program: provides housing, books, and tuition for all new, incoming resident freshmen; must be Pell-eligible with combined family income less than $42,500; funding provided as grants, scholarships, and federal work-study.

FINANCIAL AID PROCEDURES

Forms required: FAFSA.

Dates and Deadlines: Priority date 3/1; no closing date. Applicants notified on a rolling basis starting 4/1; must reply within 3 week(s) of notification.

Transfers: Some waivers available for Arizona Community College transfer students with 3.2 GPA who are Arizona residents.

CONTACT

John Nametz, Director of Student Financial Aid
Robert L. Nugent Building, Tucson, AZ 85721-0040
(520) 621-1858

University of Phoenix

Phoenix, Arizona
www.phoenix.edu   Federal Code: 014593

4-year for-profit virtual university in very large city.

Enrollment: 390,487 undergrads. 49,077 full-time freshmen.

Selectivity: Open admission; but selective for some programs.

BASIC COSTS (2009-2010)

Tuition and fees: $11,937.

Per-credit charge: $398.

FINANCIAL AID PICTURE

Students with need: Need-based aid available for full-time students.

FINANCIAL AID PROCEDURES

Forms required: FAFSA, institutional form.

Dates and Deadlines: No deadline. Applicants notified on a rolling basis.

CONTACT

Robert Collins, Vice President, Student Financial Aid
4035 South Riverpoint Parkway, Phoenix, AZ 85040-0723
(480) 804-7600

Western International University

Phoenix, Arizona
www.west.edu   Federal Code: 014970

4-year for-profit university and business college in very large city.

Enrollment: 1,957 undergrads. 37 full-time freshmen.

Selectivity: Admits over 75% of applicants.

BASIC COSTS (2010-2011)

Tuition and fees: $11,250.

Per-credit charge: $375.

FINANCIAL AID PICTURE (2008-2009)

Students with need: Average financial aid package for all full-time undergraduates was $10,500.

Students without need: This college awards aid only to students with need.

FINANCIAL AID PROCEDURES

Forms required: FAFSA, institutional form.

Dates and Deadlines: No deadline. Applicants notified on a rolling basis.

Transfers: No deadline. Applicants notified on a rolling basis.

CONTACT

Ella Owen, Associate Director of Financial Services
9215 North Black Canyon Highway, Phoenix, AZ 85021-2718
(602) 943-2311

Arkansas

Arkansas Baptist College

Little Rock, Arkansas
www.arkansasbaptist.edu   Federal Code: 001087

4-year private liberal arts college in small city, affiliated with American Baptist Churches in the USA.

Enrollment: 734 undergrads, 19% part-time. 152 full-time freshmen.

Selectivity: Open admission.

BASIC COSTS (2009-2010)
Tuition and fees: $7,018.
Per-credit charge: $317.
Room and board: $7,606.

FINANCIAL AID PICTURE
Students with need: Need-based aid available for full-time and part-time students.
Students without need: This college awards aid only to students with need.

FINANCIAL AID PROCEDURES
Forms required: FAFSA.
Dates and Deadlines: Closing date 5/1. Applicants notified on a rolling basis starting 6/15.

CONTACT
Rosie Toney, Director of Admissions and Financial Aid
1621 Dr. Martin Luther King Drive, Little Rock, AR 72202
(501) 374-6135

Arkansas Northeastern College
Blytheville, Arkansas
www.anc.edu   Federal Code: 012860

2-year public community college in small town.
Enrollment: 1,340 undergrads.
Selectivity: Open admission; but selective for some programs.

BASIC COSTS (2009-2010)
Tuition and fees: $1,780; out-of-district residents $2,080; out-of-state residents $3,580.
Per-credit charge: $52; out-of-district residents $62; out-of-state residents $112.

FINANCIAL AID PICTURE (2009-2010)
Students with need: Need-based aid available for full-time and part-time students.
Students without need: No-need awards available for academics, art, minority status, music/drama, state/district residency.

FINANCIAL AID PROCEDURES
Forms required: FAFSA, institutional form.
Dates and Deadlines: Priority date 4/15; no closing date. Applicants notified on a rolling basis starting 5/1; must reply within 2 week(s) of notification.

CONTACT
Laura Yarbrough, Director of Financial Aid
Box 1109, Blytheville, AR 72316-1109
(870) 762-1020

Arkansas State University
State University, Arkansas
www.astate.edu   Federal Code: 001090

4-year public university in small city.
Enrollment: 9,441 undergrads, 19% part-time. 1,650 full-time freshmen.
Selectivity: Admits over 75% of applicants.

BASIC COSTS (2009-2010)
Tuition and fees: $6,370; out-of-state residents $14,290.
Per-credit charge: $163; out-of-state residents $427.
Room and board: $5,856.

FINANCIAL AID PICTURE (2009-2010)
Students with need: Out of 1,444 full-time freshmen who applied for aid, 1,235 were judged to have need. Of these, 1,235 received aid, and 413 had their full need met. Average financial aid package met 61% of need; average scholarship/grant was $6,850; average loan was $3,500. Need-based aid available for part-time students.
Students without need: 120 full-time freshmen who did not demonstrate need for aid received scholarships/grants; average award was $5,200. No-need awards available for academics, alumni affiliation, art, athletics, leadership, minority status, music/drama, ROTC, state/district residency.
Scholarships offered: 65 full-time freshmen received athletic scholarships; average amount $8,820.
Cumulative student debt: 68% of graduating class had student loans; average debt was $18,900.

FINANCIAL AID PROCEDURES
Forms required: FAFSA, institutional form.
Dates and Deadlines: Priority date 2/15; closing date 7/1. Applicants notified on a rolling basis starting 6/1; must reply within 2 week(s) of notification.
Transfers: Applicants notified on a rolling basis starting 6/1; must reply within 2 week(s) of notification.

CONTACT
Terry Finney, Director of Financial Aid and Scholarships
PO Box 1630, State University, AR 72467-1630
(870) 972-2310

Arkansas State University: Beebe
Beebe, Arkansas
www.asub.edu   Federal Code: 001090

2-year public community college in small town.
Enrollment: 3,663 undergrads, 30% part-time. 949 full-time freshmen.
Selectivity: Open admission.

BASIC COSTS (2009-2010)
Tuition and fees: $2,670; out-of-state residents $4,350.
Per-credit charge: $78; out-of-state residents $134.
Room and board: $3,150.

FINANCIAL AID PICTURE (2008-2009)
Students with need: Need-based aid available for full-time and part-time students. Work study available nights, weekends, and for part-time students.
Students without need: No-need awards available for academics, leadership, music/drama.

FINANCIAL AID PROCEDURES
Forms required: FAFSA, institutional form.
Dates and Deadlines: Priority date 6/1; no closing date. Applicants notified on a rolling basis starting 6/1; must reply within 2 week(s) of notification.
Transfers: No deadline. Applicants notified on a rolling basis.

CONTACT
Linda Yelder, Director of Financial Aid
PO Box 1000, Beebe, AR 72012-1000
(501) 882-8245

Arkansas State University: Mountain Home
Mountain Home, Arkansas
www.asumh.edu   Federal Code: 901090

2-year public community and technical college in large town.
Enrollment: 1,437 undergrads, 36% part-time. 259 full-time freshmen.
Selectivity: Open admission; but selective for some programs.

BASIC COSTS (2009-2010)
Tuition and fees: $2,760; out-of-state residents $4,410.
Per-credit charge: $77; out-of-state residents $132.

FINANCIAL AID PICTURE (2008-2009)
Students with need: 84% of average financial aid package awarded as scholarships/grants, 16% awarded as loans/jobs. Need-based aid available for part-time students.
Students without need: No-need awards available for academics, alumni affiliation, state/district residency.

FINANCIAL AID PROCEDURES
Forms required: FAFSA, institutional form.
Dates and Deadlines: Priority date 7/1; no closing date. Applicants notified on a rolling basis starting 5/1; must reply within 2 week(s) of notification.
Transfers: No deadline. Must reply within 5 week(s) of notification.

CONTACT
John Davidson, Vice Chancellor Administrative Affairs
1600 South College Street, Mountain Home, AR 72653
(870) 508-6195

Arkansas Tech University
Russellville, Arkansas
www.atu.edu   Federal Code: 001089

4-year public university and liberal arts college in large town.
Enrollment: 7,331 undergrads, 13% part-time. 1,452 full-time freshmen.
Selectivity: Admits over 75% of applicants.

BASIC COSTS (2009-2010)
Tuition and fees: $5,610; out-of-state residents $10,620.
Per-credit charge: $167; out-of-state residents $334.
Room and board: $5,156.

FINANCIAL AID PICTURE (2008-2009)
Students with need: Out of 1,170 full-time freshmen who applied for aid, 896 were judged to have need. Of these, 870 received aid, and 206 had their full need met. Average financial aid package met 73% of need; average scholarship/grant was $4,064; average loan was $2,835. For part-time students, average financial aid package was $5,215.
Students without need: 351 full-time freshmen who did not demonstrate need for aid received scholarships/grants; average award was $6,916. No-need awards available for academics, athletics, leadership, music/drama, ROTC, state/district residency.
Scholarships offered: 53 full-time freshmen received athletic scholarships; average amount $3,203.
Cumulative student debt: 51% of graduating class had student loans; average debt was $12,562.

FINANCIAL AID PROCEDURES
Forms required: FAFSA, institutional form.
Dates and Deadlines: Priority date 4/15; no closing date. Applicants notified on a rolling basis starting 5/1; must reply within 2 week(s) of notification.

CONTACT
Shirley Goines, Director of Student Financial Aid
1605 Coliseum Drive Suite 141, Russellville, AR 72801-2222
(479) 968-0399

Central Baptist College
Conway, Arkansas
www.cbc.edu   Federal Code: 001093

4-year private Bible and junior college in large town, affiliated with Baptist faith.
Enrollment: 621 undergrads, 16% part-time. 125 full-time freshmen.

Selectivity: Admits over 75% of applicants.
BASIC COSTS (2009-2010)
Tuition and fees: $10,010.
Room and board: $5,500.

FINANCIAL AID PICTURE
Students with need: Need-based aid available for full-time and part-time students.
Students without need: No-need awards available for academics, athletics, music/drama, religious affiliation.

FINANCIAL AID PROCEDURES
Forms required: FAFSA.
Dates and Deadlines: Priority date 7/1; closing date 8/1. Applicants notified on a rolling basis starting 4/1.
Transfers: No deadline.

CONTACT
Christi Bell, Director of Financial Aid
1501 College Avenue, Conway, AR 72034
(501) 329-6872 ext. 185

Cossatot Community College of the University of Arkansas
De Queen, Arkansas
www.cccua.edu   Federal Code: 012432

2-year public community college in small town.
Enrollment: 1,486 undergrads.
Selectivity: Open admission; but selective for some programs.

BASIC COSTS (2009-2010)
Tuition and fees: $1,840; out-of-district residents $2,140; out-of-state residents $4,900.
Per-credit charge: $48; out-of-district residents $58; out-of-state residents $150.
Additional info: Residents of bordering out-of-state counties may qualify for in-state tuition.

FINANCIAL AID PICTURE (2008-2009)
Students with need: Need-based aid available for full-time and part-time students. Work study available nights.
Additional info: Active or honorably discharged military and their dependents receive tuition discounts.

FINANCIAL AID PROCEDURES
Forms required: FAFSA, institutional form.
Dates and Deadlines: Priority date 5/1; no closing date. Applicants notified on a rolling basis starting 3/1.
Transfers: Applicants notified on a rolling basis starting 3/1.

CONTACT
Denise Hammond, Director of Financial Aid
183 Highway 399, De Queen, AR 71832
(870) 584-4471

Crowley's Ridge College
Paragould, Arkansas
www.crowleysridgecollege.edu   Federal Code: 001095

2-year private junior college in large town, affiliated with Church of Christ.
Enrollment: 138 undergrads.
Selectivity: Open admission.

BASIC COSTS (2009-2010)
Tuition and fees: $8,710.
Per-credit charge: $255.
Room and board: $5,500.
Additional info: Tuition/fee waivers available for adults.

FINANCIAL AID PICTURE (2009-2010)
Students with need: Work study available nights, weekends, and for part-time students.
Students without need: No-need awards available for academics, leadership; music/drama.

FINANCIAL AID PROCEDURES
Forms required: FAFSA.
Dates and Deadlines: No deadline.

CONTACT
David Goff, Director of Financial Aid
100 College Drive, Paragould, AR 72450
(870) 236-6901

East Arkansas Community College
Forrest City, Arkansas
www.eacc.edu   Federal Code: 012260

2-year public community college in large town.
Enrollment: 1,303 undergrads, 36% part-time. 293 full-time freshmen.
Selectivity: Open admission; but selective for some programs.

BASIC COSTS (2009-2010)
Tuition and fees: $2,040; out-of-district residents $2,280; out-of-state residents $2,700.
Per-credit charge: $60; out-of-district residents $68; out-of-state residents $82.

FINANCIAL AID PICTURE
Students with need: Need-based aid available for full-time and part-time students.
Students without need: This college awards aid only to students with need.

FINANCIAL AID PROCEDURES
Forms required: FAFSA.
Dates and Deadlines: Priority date 3/1; closing date 7/1. Applicants notified on a rolling basis starting 5/15; must reply within 2 week(s) of notification.

CONTACT
Alvin Coleman, Director of Financial Aid
1700 Newcastle Road, Forrest City, AR 72335-9598
(870) 633-4480 ext. 225

Ecclesia College
Springdale, Arkansas
www.ecollege.edu   Federal Code: 038553

4-year private Bible and liberal arts college in large town, affiliated with inter-denominational tradition.
Enrollment: 123 undergrads.
Selectivity: Open admission; but selective for some programs.

BASIC COSTS (2009-2010)
Tuition and fees: $15,050.
Per-credit charge: $475.
Room and board: $5,010.
Additional info: Full-time students not living on campus may be subject to additional $750 nonresidents fee/semester. Tuition/fee waivers available for adults.

FINANCIAL AID PICTURE (2009-2010)
Students with need: Need-based aid available for full-time and part-time students. Work study available nights, weekends, and for part-time students.
Students without need: No-need awards available for academics, athletics, leadership, music/drama.

FINANCIAL AID PROCEDURES
Forms required: FAFSA.
Dates and Deadlines: No deadline. Applicants notified on a rolling basis starting 7/1.
Transfers: No deadline. Applicants notified on a rolling basis; must reply within 4 week(s) of notification.

CONTACT
Jesse Wadkins, Financial Aid Officer
9653 Nations Drive, Springdale, AR 72762
(479) 248-7236 ext. 204

Harding University
Searcy, Arkansas
www.harding.edu   Federal Code: 001097

4-year private university in large town, affiliated with Church of Christ.
Enrollment: 4,052 undergrads, 6% part-time. 981 full-time freshmen.
Selectivity: Admits 50 to 75% of applicants.

BASIC COSTS (2010-2011)
Tuition and fees: $13,974.
Per-credit charge: $451.
Room and board: $5,988.

FINANCIAL AID PICTURE (2008-2009)
Students with need: Out of 732 full-time freshmen who applied for aid, 516 were judged to have need. Of these, 514 received aid, and 198 had their full need met. Average financial aid package met 83% of need; average scholarship/grant was $7,557; average loan was $4,163. For part-time students, average financial aid package was $6,756.
Students without need: 175 full-time freshmen who did not demonstrate need for aid received scholarships/grants; average award was $5,399. No-need awards available for academics, alumni affiliation, art, athletics, leadership, music/drama, religious affiliation, ROTC, state/district residency.
Scholarships offered: 43 full-time freshmen received athletic scholarships; average amount $6,420.
Cumulative student debt: 70% of graduating class had student loans; average debt was $31,730.
Additional info: Music scholarships available, audition required.

FINANCIAL AID PROCEDURES
Forms required: FAFSA.
Dates and Deadlines: Priority date 4/15; no closing date. Applicants notified on a rolling basis starting 2/15; must reply within 2 week(s) of notification.
Transfers: No deadline.

CONTACT
Jon Roberts, Director of Student Financial Services
915 East Market Avenue, Searcy, AR 72149-2255
(501) 279-4257

Henderson State University
Arkadelphia, Arkansas
www.getreddie.com   Federal Code: 001098

4-year public university and liberal arts college in large town.
Enrollment: 3,073 undergrads, 10% part-time. 628 full-time freshmen.
Selectivity: Admits 50 to 75% of applicants.

BASIC COSTS (2009-2010)

Tuition and fees: $6,204; out-of-state residents $11,304.
Room and board: $4,964.

FINANCIAL AID PICTURE (2009-2010)

Students with need: Out of 593 full-time freshmen who applied for aid, 478 were judged to have need. Of these, 475 received aid, and 19 had their full need met. Average financial aid package met 83% of need; average scholarship/grant was $11,558; average loan was $3,500. For part-time students, average financial aid package was $8,794.

Students without need: 83 full-time freshmen who did not demonstrate need for aid received scholarships/grants; average award was $9,354. No-need awards available for academics, alumni affiliation, art, athletics, leadership, minority status, music/drama, state/district residency.

Scholarships offered: 6 full-time freshmen received athletic scholarships; average amount $2,816.

FINANCIAL AID PROCEDURES

Forms required: FAFSA.

Dates and Deadlines: Priority date 4/15; no closing date. Applicants notified on a rolling basis starting 3/1; must reply within 2 week(s) of notification.

Transfers: No deadline. Applicants notified on a rolling basis starting 3/1; must reply within 2 week(s) of notification.

CONTACT

Vicki Taylor, Director of Financial Aid
1100 Henderson Street, Arkadelphia, AR 71999-0001
(870) 230-5094

Hendrix College
Conway, Arkansas
www.hendrix.edu   Federal Code: 001099

4-year private liberal arts college in small city, affiliated with United Methodist Church.

Enrollment: 1,454 undergrads, 1% part-time. 413 full-time freshmen.
Selectivity: Admits over 75% of applicants.

BASIC COSTS (2010-2011)

Tuition and fees: $32,040.
Per-credit charge: $1,197.
Room and board: $9,086.

FINANCIAL AID PICTURE (2009-2010)

Students with need: Out of 338 full-time freshmen who applied for aid, 244 were judged to have need. Of these, 244 received aid, and 106 had their full need met. Average financial aid package met 87% of need; average scholarship/grant was $20,593; average loan was $4,219. For part-time students, average financial aid package was $5,045.

Students without need: 166 full-time freshmen who did not demonstrate need for aid received scholarships/grants; average award was $17,466. No-need awards available for academics, art, leadership, music/drama, religious affiliation.

Scholarships offered: Hays Memorial Scholarship: full tuition, room, board, mandatory fees; based on academic excellence. Visual and Performing Arts Scholarships (music, theatre, art): $2,000 to $5,000 per year; auditions/portfolios required. Leadership and United Methodist (UMYF) scholarships: $2,000 to $3,500.

Cumulative student debt: 87% of graduating class had student loans; average debt was $17,641.

FINANCIAL AID PROCEDURES

Forms required: FAFSA.

Dates and Deadlines: Priority date 2/15; no closing date. Applicants notified on a rolling basis starting 2/15; must reply by 5/1 or within 4 week(s) of notification.

Transfers: Applicants notified by 2/15; must reply by 5/1.

CONTACT

Mark Bandre, Director of Financial Aid
1600 Washington Avenue, Conway, AR 72032-3080
(501) 450-1368

John Brown University
Siloam Springs, Arkansas
www.jbu.edu   Federal Code: 001100

4-year private liberal arts college in large town, affiliated with interdenominational tradition.

Enrollment: 1,691 undergrads, 19% part-time. 306 full-time freshmen.
Selectivity: Admits 50 to 75% of applicants.

BASIC COSTS (2010-2011)

Tuition and fees: $19,730.
Per-credit charge: $752.
Room and board: $7,186.
Additional info: Tuition/fee waivers available for adults.

FINANCIAL AID PICTURE (2009-2010)

Students with need: Out of 245 full-time freshmen who applied for aid, 126 were judged to have need. Of these, 126 received aid, and 10 had their full need met. Average financial aid package met 50% of need; average scholarship/grant was $7,061; average loan was $3,042. For part-time students, average financial aid package was $6,437.

Students without need: 39 full-time freshmen who did not demonstrate need for aid received scholarships/grants; average award was $6,269. No-need awards available for academics, alumni affiliation, art, athletics, leadership, music/drama.

Scholarships offered: 10 full-time freshmen received athletic scholarships; average amount $17,291.

Cumulative student debt: 60% of graduating class had student loans; average debt was $19,991.

FINANCIAL AID PROCEDURES

Forms required: FAFSA.

Dates and Deadlines: Priority date 3/1; no closing date. Applicants notified on a rolling basis starting 3/1; must reply within 4 week(s) of notification.

Transfers: No deadline. Applicants notified on a rolling basis; must reply within 4 week(s) of notification.

CONTACT

Kim Eldridge, Director of Financial Aid
2000 West University Street, Siloam Springs, AR 72761-2121
(877) 528-4636

Lyon College
Batesville, Arkansas
www.lyon.edu   Federal Code: 001088

4-year private liberal arts college in small town, affiliated with Presbyterian Church (USA).

Enrollment: 592 undergrads, 2% part-time. 217 full-time freshmen.
Selectivity: Admits 50 to 75% of applicants.

BASIC COSTS (2010-2011)

Tuition and fees: $21,644.
Per-credit charge: $790.
Room and board: $7,340.

FINANCIAL AID PICTURE (2009-2010)

Students with need: Out of 198 full-time freshmen who applied for aid, 165 were judged to have need. Of these, 165 received aid, and 34 had their full need met. Average financial aid package met 84% of need; average scholarship/grant was $14,519; average loan was $3,166. For part-time students, average financial aid package was $8,620.

Students without need: 54 full-time freshmen who did not demonstrate need for aid received scholarships/grants; average award was $10,757. No-need awards available for academics, art, athletics, leadership, minority status, music/drama, religious affiliation, state/district residency.

Scholarships offered: *Merit:* Brown Scholarship; tuition, room, board, mandatory fees and books; based on high school record, standardized test scores; 4 awarded. Anderson Scholarship; tuition, mandatory fees and books; based on high school record, test scores; 4 awarded. Lyon Fellowship; $10,000; based on high school record, test scores, with a preference for students with a career interest in business or public service or a strong academic interest in computer science or the fine arts; up to 8 awarded. *Athletic:* 20 full-time freshmen received athletic scholarships; average amount $11,638.

Cumulative student debt: 61% of graduating class had student loans; average debt was $19,642.

FINANCIAL AID PROCEDURES

Forms required: FAFSA.

Dates and Deadlines: Priority date 3/15; no closing date. Applicants notified on a rolling basis starting 3/1; must reply by 8/15.

Transfers: No deadline. Applicants notified on a rolling basis starting 3/1; must reply within 2 week(s) of notification.

CONTACT

Tommy Tucker, Director of Student Financial Assistance
PO Box 2317, Batesville, AR 72503-2317
(870) 307-7257

Mid-South Community College

West Memphis, Arkansas
www.midsouthcc.edu   Federal Code: 015862

2-year public community and junior college in large town.
Enrollment: 1,567 undergrads.
Selectivity: Open admission.

BASIC COSTS (2009-2010)

Tuition and fees: $2,120; out-of-district residents $2,570; out-of-state residents $4,370.
Per-credit charge: $60; out-of-district residents $75; out-of-state residents $135.

FINANCIAL AID PICTURE (2008-2009)

Students with need: Need-based aid available for full-time and part-time students. Work study available nights.
Students without need: No-need awards available for academics, state/district residency.

FINANCIAL AID PROCEDURES

Forms required: FAFSA, institutional form.
Dates and Deadlines: No deadline. Applicants notified on a rolling basis starting 6/1; must reply within 2 week(s) of notification.

CONTACT

Jackie Brubaker, Director of Financial Aid
2000 West Broadway, West Memphis, AR 72301
(870) 733-6741

National Park Community College

Hot Springs, Arkansas
www.npcc.edu   Federal Code: 012105

2-year public liberal arts and technical college in large town.
Enrollment: 3,257 undergrads, 44% part-time. 527 full-time freshmen.
Selectivity: Open admission; but selective for some programs.

BASIC COSTS (2009-2010)

Tuition and fees: $2,075; out-of-district residents $2,375; out-of-state residents $4,145.
Per-credit charge: $65; out-of-district residents $75; out-of-state residents $134.

FINANCIAL AID PICTURE

Students with need: Need-based aid available for full-time and part-time students. Work study available nights, weekends, and for part-time students.
Students without need: No-need awards available for academics, minority status, music/drama, state/district residency.

FINANCIAL AID PROCEDURES

Forms required: FAFSA, institutional form.
Dates and Deadlines: Priority date 7/1; no closing date. Applicants notified on a rolling basis.
Transfers: Transfer applicants must furnish evidence of good standing at previous institution to qualify for financial aid.

CONTACT

Lisa Hopper, Director, Financial Aid
101 College Drive, Hot Springs, AR 71913
(501) 760-4235

North Arkansas College

Harrison, Arkansas
www.northark.edu   Federal Code: 012261

2-year public community and technical college in large town.
Enrollment: 2,107 undergrads, 30% part-time. 502 full-time freshmen.
Selectivity: Open admission; but selective for some programs.

BASIC COSTS (2009-2010)

Tuition and fees: $1,800; out-of-district residents $2,460; out-of-state residents $4,590.
Per-credit charge: $60; out-of-district residents $82; out-of-state residents $153.
Additional info: Residents of contiguous Missouri counties (Barry, Stone, Taney, Ozark) pay $102 per credit hour and $3,060 full-time tuition.

FINANCIAL AID PICTURE (2008-2009)

Students with need: Need-based aid available for full-time and part-time students. Work study available nights.
Students without need: No-need awards available for academics, athletics, state/district residency.

FINANCIAL AID PROCEDURES

Forms required: FAFSA, institutional form.
Dates and Deadlines: Priority date 5/1; no closing date. Applicants notified on a rolling basis starting 5/1.
Transfers: No deadline. Applicants notified on a rolling basis starting 5/1.

CONTACT

Jennifer Haddock, Director of Financial Aid
1515 Pioneer Drive, Harrison, AR 72601
(870) 391-3266

Northwest Arkansas Community College

Bentonville, Arkansas
www.nwacc.edu   Federal Code: 030633

2-year public community college in small city.
Enrollment: 6,188 undergrads, 56% part-time. 797 full-time freshmen.
Selectivity: Open admission; but selective for some programs.

BASIC COSTS (2010-2011)
Tuition and fees: $2,493; out-of-district residents $3,603; out-of-state residents $4,863.
Per-credit charge: $66; out-of-district residents $103; out-of-state residents $145.

FINANCIAL AID PICTURE
Students with need: Need-based aid available for full-time and part-time students. Work study available nights, weekends, and for part-time students.
Students without need: No-need awards available for academics, leadership, music/drama, state/district residency.

FINANCIAL AID PROCEDURES
Forms required: FAFSA, institutional form.
Dates and Deadlines: Priority date 4/1; no closing date. Applicants notified on a rolling basis starting 4/1; must reply within 2 week(s) of notification.

CONTACT
Michelle Cordell, Director of Financial Aid
One College Drive, Bentonville, AR 72712
(479) 619-4129

Ouachita Baptist University

Arkadelphia, Arkansas
www.obu.edu   Federal Code: 001102

4-year private liberal arts college in large town, affiliated with Southern Baptist Convention.
Enrollment: 1,421 undergrads, 1% part-time. 404 full-time freshmen.
Selectivity: Admits 50 to 75% of applicants.

BASIC COSTS (2010-2011)
Tuition and fees: $19,820.
Per-credit charge: $560.
Room and board: $5,840.

FINANCIAL AID PICTURE (2008-2009)
Students with need: Out of 333 full-time freshmen who applied for aid, 269 were judged to have need. Of these, 269 received aid, and 123 had their full need met. Average financial aid package met 88% of need; average scholarship/grant was $13,230; average loan was $4,456. For part-time students, average financial aid package was $3,998.
Students without need: 131 full-time freshmen who did not demonstrate need for aid received scholarships/grants; average award was $7,981. No-need awards available for academics, alumni affiliation, art, athletics, job skills, leadership, minority status, music/drama, religious affiliation, ROTC, state/district residency.
Scholarships offered: 26 full-time freshmen received athletic scholarships; average amount $9,077.
Cumulative student debt: 61% of graduating class had student loans; average debt was $16,230.

FINANCIAL AID PROCEDURES
Forms required: FAFSA.
Dates and Deadlines: Priority date 1/15; closing date 6/1. Applicants notified on a rolling basis; must reply by 5/1.

CONTACT
Chris Kear, Director of Student Financial Services
OBU Box 3776, Arkadelphia, AR 71998-0001
(870) 245-5570

Ouachita Technical College

Malvern, Arkansas
www.otcweb.edu   Federal Code: 009976

2-year public community and technical college in small town.
Enrollment: 837 undergrads, 35% part-time. 133 full-time freshmen.
Selectivity: Open admission; but selective for some programs.

BASIC COSTS (2009-2010)
Tuition and fees: $2,240; out-of-state residents $4,010.
Per-credit charge: $59; out-of-state residents $118.

FINANCIAL AID PICTURE (2008-2009)
Students with need: 69% of average financial aid package awarded as scholarships/grants, 31% awarded as loans/jobs. Need-based aid available for part-time students. Work study available nights.

FINANCIAL AID PROCEDURES
Forms required: FAFSA.
Dates and Deadlines: Closing date 6/30. Applicants notified on a rolling basis starting 7/1; must reply within 6 week(s) of notification.

CONTACT
Teresa Avery, Director of Financial Aid
One College Circle, Malvern, AR 72104
(501) 337-5000 ext. 1122

Ozarka College

Melbourne, Arkansas
www.ozarka.edu   Federal Code: 013217

2-year public community and technical college in rural community.
Enrollment: 1,291 undergrads.
Selectivity: Open admission; but selective for some programs.

BASIC COSTS (2009-2010)
Tuition and fees: $2,620; out-of-state residents $5,560.
Per-credit charge: $70; out-of-state residents $168.

FINANCIAL AID PICTURE (2009-2010)
Students with need: Need-based aid available for full-time and part-time students.

FINANCIAL AID PROCEDURES
Forms required: FAFSA.
Dates and Deadlines: No deadline. Applicants notified on a rolling basis; must reply within 2 week(s) of notification.

CONTACT
Joyce Goff, Financial Aid Officer
218 College Drive, Melbourne, AR 72556-0010
(870) 368-7371 ext. 2010

Philander Smith College

Little Rock, Arkansas
www.philander.edu   Federal Code: 001103

4-year private liberal arts college in small city, affiliated with United Methodist Church.
Enrollment: 665 undergrads.

Selectivity: Admits 50 to 75% of applicants.

BASIC COSTS (2009-2010)

Tuition and fees: $9,000.
Room and board: $6,850.

FINANCIAL AID PICTURE (2009-2010)

Students with need: Need-based aid available for full-time and part-time students.
Students without need: This college awards aid only to students with need.

FINANCIAL AID PROCEDURES

Forms required: FAFSA, institutional form.
Dates and Deadlines: Priority date 3/1; no closing date. Applicants notified on a rolling basis starting 5/1; must reply within 2 week(s) of notification.
Transfers: Closing date 6/30.

CONTACT

David Page, Director of Financial Aid
900 West Daisy Bates Drive, Little Rock, AR 72202-3718
(501) 370-5350

Phillips Community College of the University of Arkansas

Helena, Arkansas
www.pccua.edu   Federal Code: 001104

2-year public community college in large town.
Enrollment: 1,285 undergrads, 36% part-time. 216 full-time freshmen.
Selectivity: Open admission; but selective for some programs.

BASIC COSTS (2009-2010)

Tuition and fees: $2,030; out-of-district residents $2,300; out-of-state residents $3,440.
Per-credit charge: $55; out-of-district residents $64; out-of-state residents $102.

FINANCIAL AID PICTURE (2008-2009)

Students with need: Out of 185 full-time freshmen who applied for aid, 185 were judged to have need. Of these, 185 received aid. For part-time students, average financial aid package was $2,238.
Students without need: This college awards aid only to students with need.
Additional info: Tuition waivers are given to firefighters and law enforcement officers.

FINANCIAL AID PROCEDURES

Forms required: FAFSA.
Dates and Deadlines: Priority date 4/1; closing date 6/30. Applicants notified on a rolling basis starting 4/1; must reply within 2 week(s) of notification.

CONTACT

Barbra Stevenson, Director of Financial Aid
1000 Campus Drive, Helena, AR 72342
(870) 338-6474 ext. 1160

Pulaski Technical College

North Little Rock, Arkansas
www.pulaskitech.edu   Federal Code: 014167

2-year public community and technical college in small city.
Enrollment: 9,187 undergrads.
Selectivity: Open admission; but selective for some programs.

BASIC COSTS (2009-2010)

Tuition and fees: $2,790; out-of-state residents $4,320.
Per-credit charge: $80; out-of-state residents $131.

FINANCIAL AID PICTURE (2009-2010)

Students with need: Need-based aid available for full-time and part-time students.

FINANCIAL AID PROCEDURES

Forms required: FAFSA, institutional form.
Dates and Deadlines: Closing date 5/15. Applicants notified on a rolling basis starting 5/1; must reply within 2 week(s) of notification.

CONTACT

Kris Burford, Director Financial Aid
3000 West Scenic Drive, North Little Rock, AR 72118-3347
(501) 812-2289

Rich Mountain Community College

Mena, Arkansas
www.rmcc.edu   Federal Code: 012435

2-year public community college in small town.
Enrollment: 638 undergrads.
Selectivity: Open admission; but selective for some programs.

BASIC COSTS (2009-2010)

Tuition and fees: $1,620; out-of-district residents $2,010; out-of-state residents $5,190.
Per-credit charge: $51; out-of-district residents $64; out-of-state residents $170.

FINANCIAL AID PICTURE (2008-2009)

Students with need: Need-based aid available for full-time and part-time students.
Students without need: No-need awards available for academics.

FINANCIAL AID PROCEDURES

Forms required: FAFSA, institutional form.
Dates and Deadlines: Priority date 7/1; no closing date. Applicants notified on a rolling basis starting 6/1; must reply within 2 week(s) of notification.

CONTACT

Mary Standerfer, Director of Financial Aid
1100 College Drive, Mena, AR 71953
(479) 394-7622 ext. 1420

South Arkansas Community College

El Dorado, Arkansas
www.southark.edu   Federal Code: 013858

2-year public community and junior college in large town.
Enrollment: 1,526 undergrads.
Selectivity: Open admission.

BASIC COSTS (2009-2010)

Tuition and fees: $2,240; out-of-district residents $2,480; out-of-state residents $4,370.
Per-credit charge: $68; out-of-district residents $76; out-of-state residents $139.
Additional info: $25 lab fee for most courses.

FINANCIAL AID PICTURE (2008-2009)

Students with need: Need-based aid available for full-time and part-time students.

FINANCIAL AID PROCEDURES

Forms required: FAFSA, institutional form.

Dates and Deadlines: Closing date 8/1. Applicants notified on a rolling basis starting 7/1; must reply within 2 week(s) of notification.

CONTACT
Veronda Tatum, Director of Financial Aid
Box 7010, El Dorado, AR 71731-7010
(870) 864-7133

Southeast Arkansas College
Pine Bluff, Arkansas
www.seark.edu   Federal Code: 005707

2-year public community and technical college in small city.
Enrollment: 1,688 undergrads, 37% part-time. 275 full-time freshmen.
Selectivity: Open admission; but selective for some programs.

BASIC COSTS (2009-2010)
Tuition and fees: $2,290; out-of-state residents $4,330.
Per-credit charge: $68; out-of-state residents $136.

FINANCIAL AID PICTURE (2008-2009)
Students with need: 76% of average financial aid package awarded as scholarships/grants, 24% awarded as loans/jobs. Need-based aid available for part-time students. Work study available nights.
Students without need: No-need awards available for academics, leadership, state/district residency.

FINANCIAL AID PROCEDURES
Forms required: FAFSA.
Dates and Deadlines: Priority date 6/1; no closing date. Applicants notified on a rolling basis starting 5/1; must reply within 2 week(s) of notification.

CONTACT
Donna Cox, Director of Financial Aid
1900 Hazel Street, Pine Bluff, AR 71603
(870) 543-5909

Southern Arkansas University
Magnolia, Arkansas
www.saumag.edu   Federal Code: 001107

4-year public university in large town.
Enrollment: 2,647 undergrads, 10% part-time. 617 full-time freshmen.
Selectivity: Admits 50 to 75% of applicants.

BASIC COSTS (2009-2010)
Tuition and fees: $6,056; out-of-state residents $8,696.
Per-credit charge: $170; out-of-state residents $258.
Room and board: $4,460.

FINANCIAL AID PICTURE (2008-2009)
Students with need: 41% of average financial aid package awarded as scholarships/grants, 59% awarded as loans/jobs. Need-based aid available for part-time students. Work study available nights, weekends, and for part-time students.
Students without need: No-need awards available for academics, alumni affiliation, art, athletics, leadership, minority status, music/drama, state/district residency.

FINANCIAL AID PROCEDURES
Forms required: FAFSA.
Dates and Deadlines: Priority date 7/1; no closing date. Applicants notified on a rolling basis starting 4/15; must reply within 2 week(s) of notification.

CONTACT
Bronwyn Sneed, Director of Financial Aid
Box 9382, Magnolia, AR 71754-9382
(870) 235-4023

Southern Arkansas University Tech
Camden, Arkansas
www.sautech.edu   Federal Code: 007738

2-year public community and technical college in large town.
Enrollment: 981 undergrads. 221 full-time freshmen.
Selectivity: Open admission; but selective for some programs.

BASIC COSTS (2009-2010)
Tuition and fees: $3,180; out-of-state residents $4,500.
Per-credit charge: $85; out-of-state residents $129.

FINANCIAL AID PICTURE (2008-2009)
Students with need: Need-based aid available for full-time and part-time students. Work study available nights, weekends, and for part-time students.
Students without need: No-need awards available for academics, state/district residency.

FINANCIAL AID PROCEDURES
Forms required: FAFSA.
Dates and Deadlines: Priority date 6/1; no closing date. Applicants notified on a rolling basis starting 5/1.
Transfers: Priority date 4/15; closing date 6/1. Applicants notified on a rolling basis starting 5/1.

CONTACT
John Jefferson, Director of Financial Aid
PO Box 3499, Camden, AR 71711-1599
(870) 574-4511

University of Arkansas
Fayetteville, Arkansas
www.uark.edu   Federal Code: 001108

4-year public university in small city.
Enrollment: 15,347 undergrads, 12% part-time. 2,979 full-time freshmen.
Selectivity: Admits 50 to 75% of applicants.

BASIC COSTS (2009-2010)
Tuition and fees: $6,459; out-of-state residents $15,337.
Per-credit charge: $167; out-of-state residents $463.
Room and board: $7,806.

FINANCIAL AID PICTURE (2008-2009)
Students with need: Out of 1,856 full-time freshmen who applied for aid, 1,211 were judged to have need. Of these, 1,187 received aid, and 288 had their full need met. Average financial aid package met 68% of need; average scholarship/grant was $6,550; average loan was $3,458. For part-time students, average financial aid package was $5,303.
Students without need: 527 full-time freshmen who did not demonstrate need for aid received scholarships/grants; average award was $5,536. No-need awards available for academics, alumni affiliation, art, athletics, leadership, minority status, music/drama, ROTC, state/district residency.
Scholarships offered: *Merit:* Sturgis Fellowship: $11,500, based on exceptional academic performance, 10 awards available to arts and sciences majors. Bodenhamer Fellowship: $11,000, based on strong academic performance and leadership. Chancellor's Scholarships: tuition, fees, room and board. University Scholarships: $4,000, based on rank in top 5-10% of high school class. Non-resident Tuition Award: non-resident tuition, for entering freshmen from neighboring states, based on minimum ACT score of 25 or

SAT of 1130 (exclusive of writing) and 3.5 high school GPA. *Athletic:* 79 full-time freshmen received athletic scholarships; average amount $8,033.
Cumulative student debt: 43% of graduating class had student loans; average debt was $19,439.

FINANCIAL AID PROCEDURES
Forms required: FAFSA.
Dates and Deadlines: Priority date 3/15; no closing date. Applicants notified on a rolling basis starting 4/1; must reply within 4 week(s) of notification.

CONTACT
Kattie Wing, Director of Student Financial Services
232 Silas Hunt Hall, Fayetteville, AR 72701
(479) 575-3806

University of Arkansas at Fort Smith
Fort Smith, Arkansas
www.uafortsmith.edu   Federal Code: 001110

4-year public university in small city.
Enrollment: 6,582 undergrads, 25% part-time. 1,191 full-time freshmen.
Selectivity: Open admission; but selective for some programs.

BASIC COSTS (2009-2010)
Tuition and fees: $4,600; out-of-state residents $10,000.
Per-credit charge: $114; out-of-state residents $294.
Room only: $4,789.

FINANCIAL AID PICTURE (2008-2009)
Students with need: Out of 938 full-time freshmen who applied for aid, 777 were judged to have need. Of these, 759 received aid, and 189 had their full need met. Average financial aid package met 69% of need; average scholarship/grant was $4,403; average loan was $3,018. For part-time students, average financial aid package was $5,288.
Students without need: 240 full-time freshmen who did not demonstrate need for aid received scholarships/grants; average award was $3,099. No-need awards available for academics, athletics, job skills, leadership, music/drama.
Scholarships offered: 23 full-time freshmen received athletic scholarships; average amount $5,145.
Cumulative student debt: 47% of graduating class had student loans; average debt was $15,003.

FINANCIAL AID PROCEDURES
Forms required: FAFSA.
Dates and Deadlines: Priority date 6/15; no closing date. Applicants notified on a rolling basis starting 3/1; must reply within 4 week(s) of notification.
Transfers: No deadline. Applicants notified on a rolling basis starting 3/1; must reply within 4 week(s) of notification.

CONTACT
Alan Pixley, Director of Financial Aid
PO Box 3649, Fort Smith, AR 72913-3649
(479) 788-7090

University of Arkansas at Little Rock
Little Rock, Arkansas
www.ualr.edu   Federal Code: 001161

4-year public university in small city.
Enrollment: 10,200 undergrads.
Selectivity: Admits over 75% of applicants.

BASIC COSTS (2009-2010)
Tuition and fees: $6,332; out-of-state residents $14,799.
Per-credit charge: $168; out-of-state residents $450.

Room only: $3,100.

FINANCIAL AID PICTURE
Students with need: Need-based aid available for full-time and part-time students.

FINANCIAL AID PROCEDURES
Forms required: FAFSA.
Dates and Deadlines: Closing date 8/1. Applicants notified on a rolling basis starting 5/1.

CONTACT
Tammy Harrison, Director of Admissions and Financial Aid
2801 South University Avenue, Little Rock, AR 72204
(501) 569-3035

University of Arkansas at Monticello
Monticello, Arkansas
www.uamont.edu   Federal Code: 001085

4-year public university and technical college in large town.
Enrollment: 2,976 undergrads, 17% part-time. 742 full-time freshmen.
Selectivity: Admits 50 to 75% of applicants.

BASIC COSTS (2009-2010)
Tuition and fees: $4,750; out-of-state residents $9,010.
Per-credit charge: $117; out-of-state residents $259.
Room and board: $4,070.

FINANCIAL AID PICTURE (2008-2009)
Students with need: Need-based aid available for full-time and part-time students. Work study available nights, weekends, and for part-time students.
Students without need: No-need awards available for academics, athletics, job skills, leadership, music/drama, ROTC, state/district residency.

FINANCIAL AID PROCEDURES
Forms required: FAFSA, institutional form.
Dates and Deadlines: Priority date 5/1; no closing date. Applicants notified on a rolling basis starting 4/1; must reply within 2 week(s) of notification.

CONTACT
Susan Brewer, Director of Financial Aid
Box 3600, Monticello, AR 71656
(870) 460-1050

University of Arkansas at Pine Bluff
Pine Bluff, Arkansas
www.uapb.edu   Federal Code: 001086

4-year public university in small city.
Enrollment: 3,624 undergrads, 9% part-time. 960 full-time freshmen.
Selectivity: Admits less than 50% of applicants.

BASIC COSTS (2009-2010)
Tuition and fees: $4,796; out-of-state residents $9,476.
Per-credit charge: $118; out-of-state residents $274.
Room and board: $6,168.
Additional info: Tuition/fee waivers available for minority students.

FINANCIAL AID PICTURE (2008-2009)
Students with need: Need-based aid available for full-time and part-time students. Work study available weekends and for part-time students.
Students without need: No-need awards available for academics, alumni affiliation, art, athletics, leadership, minority status, music/drama, religious affiliation, ROTC, state/district residency.

FINANCIAL AID PROCEDURES
Forms required: FAFSA.

Dates and Deadlines: Priority date 4/15; no closing date. Applicants notified on a rolling basis starting 3/1.
Transfers: Must supply financial aid transcript from prior college or university.

CONTACT
Janice Kearney, Director of Financial Aid
1200 North University Drive, Mail Slot 4981, Pine Bluff, AR 71601-2799
(870) 575-8302

University of Arkansas Community College at Morrilton

Morrilton, Arkansas
www.uaccm.edu
Federal Code: 005245
CSS Code: 3881

2-year public community college in small town.
Enrollment: 2,375 undergrads, 32% part-time. 599 full-time freshmen.
Selectivity: Admits 50 to 75% of applicants.

BASIC COSTS (2009-2010)
Tuition and fees: $2,640; out-of-district residents $2,850; out-of-state residents $3,900.
Per-credit charge: $70; out-of-district residents $77; out-of-state residents $112.

FINANCIAL AID PICTURE (2008-2009)
Students with need: Out of 476 full-time freshmen who applied for aid, 413 were judged to have need. Of these, 387 received aid, and 30 had their full need met. Average financial aid package met 46% of need; average scholarship/grant was $2,895; average loan was $2,264. For part-time students, average financial aid package was $5,067.
Students without need: 7 full-time freshmen who did not demonstrate need for aid received scholarships/grants; average award was $458. No-need awards available for academics, leadership, state/district residency.

FINANCIAL AID PROCEDURES
Forms required: FAFSA, CSS PROFILE, institutional form.
Dates and Deadlines: Priority date 7/1; no closing date.
Transfers: Applicants notified on a rolling basis starting 5/1.

CONTACT
Teresa Cash, Director of Financial Aid
1537 University Boulevard, Morrilton, AR 72110
(501) 977-2055

University of Arkansas: Community College at Batesville

Batesville, Arkansas
www.uaccb.edu
Federal Code: 020735

2-year public community college in small town.
Enrollment: 1,547 undergrads.
Selectivity: Open admission; but selective for some programs.

BASIC COSTS (2009-2010)
Tuition and fees: $2,210; out-of-district residents $2,570; out-of-state residents $4,190.
Per-credit charge: $54; out-of-district residents $66; out-of-state residents $120.

FINANCIAL AID PICTURE
Students with need: Need-based aid available for full-time students. Work study available nights, weekends, and for part-time students.
Students without need: This college awards aid only to students with need.

FINANCIAL AID PROCEDURES
Forms required: FAFSA.
Dates and Deadlines: No deadline. Applicants notified on a rolling basis starting 3/1; must reply within 2 week(s) of notification.

CONTACT
Gayle Cooper, Vice Chancellor for Finance and Administration
Box 3350, Batesville, AR 72503
(870) 612-2036

University of Arkansas: Community College at Hope

Hope, Arkansas
www.uacch.edu
Federal Code: 005732

2-year public community and technical college in small town.
Enrollment: 1,358 undergrads.
Selectivity: Open admission; but selective for some programs.

BASIC COSTS (2009-2010)
Tuition and fees: $1,790; out-of-district residents $1,940; out-of-state residents $3,620.
Per-credit charge: $54; out-of-district residents $59; out-of-state residents $115.

FINANCIAL AID PICTURE (2008-2009)
Students with need: Need-based aid available for full-time and part-time students. Work study available nights.
Students without need: No-need awards available for academics.

FINANCIAL AID PROCEDURES
Forms required: FAFSA, institutional form.
Dates and Deadlines: Closing date 7/6. Applicants notified on a rolling basis starting 1/1; must reply within 4 week(s) of notification.

CONTACT
Becky Wilson, Director of Financial Aid
2500 South Main, Hope, AR 71802-0140
(870) 722-8264

University of Central Arkansas

Conway, Arkansas
www.uca.edu
Federal Code: 001092

4-year public university in small city.
Enrollment: 9,224 undergrads.
Selectivity: Admits over 75% of applicants.

BASIC COSTS (2009-2010)
Tuition and fees: $6,450; out-of-state residents $11,640.
Per-credit charge: $174; out-of-state residents $347.
Room and board: $4,880.

FINANCIAL AID PICTURE (2008-2009)
Students with need: Need-based aid available for full-time students. Work study available nights, weekends, and for part-time students.
Students without need: No-need awards available for academics, art, athletics, leadership, minority status, music/drama, ROTC, state/district residency.
Additional info: Room and board may be paid monthly.

FINANCIAL AID PROCEDURES
Forms required: FAFSA.
Dates and Deadlines: Priority date 4/15; closing date 7/1. Applicants notified on a rolling basis starting 5/4.

CONTACT

Cheryl Lyons, Director of Financial Aid
201 Donaghey Avenue, Conway, AR 72035
(501) 450-3140

University of the Ozarks

Clarksville, Arkansas
www.ozarks.edu　　　　　　　Federal Code: 001094

4-year private university and liberal arts college in small town, affiliated with Presbyterian Church (USA).
Enrollment: 595 undergrads, 1% part-time. 195 full-time freshmen.
Selectivity: Admits over 75% of applicants.

BASIC COSTS (2009-2010)

Tuition and fees: $18,900.
Per-credit charge: $766.
Room and board: $6,050.
Additional info: Tuition/fee waivers available for minority students.

FINANCIAL AID PICTURE (2008-2009)

Students with need: Out of 155 full-time freshmen who applied for aid, 143 were judged to have need. Of these, 143 received aid, and 35 had their full need met. Average financial aid package met 87% of need; average scholarship/grant was $15,183; average loan was $6,476. For part-time students, average financial aid package was $11,161.
Students without need: 44 full-time freshmen who did not demonstrate need for aid received scholarships/grants; average award was $15,077. No-need awards available for academics, alumni affiliation, art, leadership, minority status, music/drama, religious affiliation, state/district residency.
Cumulative student debt: 44% of graduating class had student loans; average debt was $16,852.
Additional info: Walton International Scholarship Program provides full scholarships to selected Central American and Mexican residents.

FINANCIAL AID PROCEDURES

Forms required: FAFSA.
Dates and Deadlines: Priority date 2/15; no closing date. Applicants notified on a rolling basis starting 3/1; must reply within 2 week(s) of notification.

CONTACT

Jana Hart, Dean of Admissions and Financial Aid
415 North College Avenue, Clarksville, AR 72830-2880
(479) 979-1221

Williams Baptist College

Walnut Ridge, Arkansas
www.wbcoll.edu　　　　　　　Federal Code: 001106

4-year private liberal arts college in small town, affiliated with Southern Baptist Convention.
Enrollment: 509 undergrads, 3% part-time. 145 full-time freshmen.
Selectivity: Admits 50 to 75% of applicants.

BASIC COSTS (2010-2011)

Tuition and fees: $12,020.
Per-credit charge: $470.
Room and board: $5,400.

FINANCIAL AID PICTURE (2008-2009)

Students with need: Out of 112 full-time freshmen who applied for aid, 64 were judged to have need. Of these, 64 received aid. For part-time students, average financial aid package was $5,338.
Students without need: No-need awards available for academics, art, athletics, leadership, minority status, music/drama, religious affiliation, state/district residency.

Scholarships offered: *Merit:* Trustee's Scholarship: up to full tuition and room and board; based on minimum ACT composite score of 30 and minimum 3.5 high school GPA; 1 awarded; deadline March 1, renewable for 4 years with 3.25 cumulative GPA on at least 15 credit hours per semester. ***Athletic:*** 67 full-time freshmen received athletic scholarships; average amount $3,765.
Cumulative student debt: 80% of graduating class had student loans; average debt was $16,838.
Additional info: Art scholarship applicants must submit portfolio.

FINANCIAL AID PROCEDURES

Forms required: FAFSA.
Dates and Deadlines: Priority date 5/1; no closing date. Applicants notified on a rolling basis starting 4/1; must reply within 2 week(s) of notification.
Transfers: Priority date 4/1; no deadline. Applicants notified on a rolling basis starting 4/1; must reply within 2 week(s) of notification.

CONTACT

Barbara Turner, Director of Financial Aid
PO Box 3665, Walnut Ridge, AR 72476
(870) 759-4112

California

Academy of Art University

San Francisco, California
www.academyart.edu　　　　　　Federal Code: 007531

4-year for-profit university and visual arts college in very large city.
Enrollment: 10,724 undergrads, 40% part-time. 832 full-time freshmen.
Selectivity: Open admission.

BASIC COSTS (2010-2011)

Tuition and fees: $22,490.
Per-credit charge: $740.
Room and board: $13,400.
Additional info: $500 tuition deposit (non-refundable) required for international applicants.

FINANCIAL AID PICTURE (2008-2009)

Students with need: Out of 605 full-time freshmen who applied for aid, 505 were judged to have need. Of these, 496 received aid. For part-time students, average financial aid package was $4,885.
Students without need: No-need awards available for academics, art.
Scholarships offered: 48 full-time freshmen received athletic scholarships.
Additional info: Numerous summer grant programs available.

FINANCIAL AID PROCEDURES

Forms required: FAFSA, institutional form.
Dates and Deadlines: Priority date 7/10; no closing date. Applicants notified on a rolling basis.
Transfers: Priority date 3/1; no deadline. Applicants notified on a rolling basis.

CONTACT

Joe Vollaro, Executive Vice President for Financial Aid/Compliance
79 New Montgomery Street, San Francisco, CA 94105-3410
(415) 618-6273

Allan Hancock College

Santa Maria, California
www.hancockcollege.edu　　　　　Federal Code: 001111

2-year public community college in small city.
Enrollment: 5,330 undergrads, 67% part-time. 548 full-time freshmen.

Selectivity: Open admission; but selective for some programs.

BASIC COSTS (2009-2010)

Tuition and fees: $824; out-of-state residents $6,524.
Per-credit charge: $26; out-of-state residents $216.

FINANCIAL AID PICTURE

Students with need: Need-based aid available for full-time and part-time students.
Students without need: This college awards aid only to students with need.

FINANCIAL AID PROCEDURES

Forms required: FAFSA.
Dates and Deadlines: Priority date 5/1; no closing date. Applicants notified on a rolling basis starting 6/1.

CONTACT

Robert Parisi, Financial Aid Director
800 South College Drive, Santa Maria, CA 93454-6399
(805) 922-6966 ext. 3200

Alliant International University

San Diego, California
www.alliant.edu   Federal Code: 011117

Upper-division private university in very large city.
Enrollment: 151 undergrads, 68% part-time.

BASIC COSTS (2010-2011)

Tuition and fees: $16,350.
Per-credit charge: $600.
Room only: $7,204.
Additional info: Tuition/fee waivers available for minority students.

FINANCIAL AID PICTURE (2009-2010)

Students with need: Need-based aid available for full-time and part-time students. Work study available nights, weekends, and for part-time students.
Students without need: No-need awards available for academics, alumni affiliation, athletics, leadership.
Scholarships offered: Grants and scholarships available based on GPA and SAT/ACT scores.

FINANCIAL AID PROCEDURES

Forms required: FAFSA.
Dates and Deadlines: Priority date 3/2; no closing date. Applicants notified on a rolling basis starting 2/1; must reply within 3 week(s) of notification.

CONTACT

Deborah Spindler, Director of Financial Aid
10455 Pomerado Road, San Diego, CA 92131-1799
(858) 635-4559

American Jewish University

Los Angeles, California
www.ajula.edu   Federal Code: 002741

4-year private university and liberal arts college in very large city, affiliated with Jewish faith.
Enrollment: 112 undergrads, 4% part-time. 23 full-time freshmen.
Selectivity: Admits over 75% of applicants.

BASIC COSTS (2010-2011)

Tuition and fees: $24,512.
Per-credit charge: $982.
Room and board: $11,778.

FINANCIAL AID PICTURE (2009-2010)

Students with need: Out of 23 full-time freshmen who applied for aid, 23 were judged to have need. Of these, 23 received aid. Average financial aid package met 87% of need; average scholarship/grant was $13,220; average loan was $3,070. Need-based aid available for part-time students.
Students without need: 23 full-time freshmen who did not demonstrate need for aid received scholarships/grants; average award was $10,000. No-need awards available for leadership, minority status, music/drama, state/district residency.
Cumulative student debt: 75% of graduating class had student loans; average debt was $66,000.

FINANCIAL AID PROCEDURES

Forms required: FAFSA, institutional form.
Dates and Deadlines: No deadline. Applicants notified on a rolling basis starting 1/1; must reply by 6/30.
Transfers: Priority date 7/1; no deadline. Applicants notified on a rolling basis; must reply within 3 week(s) of notification.

CONTACT

Larisa Zadoyen, Director of Financial Aid
Office of Undergraduate Admissions, Los Angeles, CA 90077
(310) 476-9777 ext. 252

American River College

Sacramento, California
www.arc.losrios.edu   Federal Code: 001232

2-year public community college in large city.
Enrollment: 40,144 undergrads.
Selectivity: Open admission; but selective for some programs.

BASIC COSTS (2009-2010)

Tuition and fees: $812; out-of-state residents $6,512.
Per-credit charge: $26; out-of-state residents $216.
Additional info: Tuition/fee waivers available for minority students.

FINANCIAL AID PICTURE

Students with need: Need-based aid available for full-time and part-time students.
Students without need: This college awards aid only to students with need.

FINANCIAL AID PROCEDURES

Forms required: FAFSA.
Dates and Deadlines: Priority date 3/2; no closing date. Applicants notified on a rolling basis starting 7/1; must reply within 2 week(s) of notification.

CONTACT

Roy Beckhorn, Financial Aid Supervisor
4700 College Oak Drive, Sacramento, CA 95841
(916) 484-8437

Antelope Valley College

Lancaster, California
www.avc.edu   Federal Code: 001113

2-year public community college in large city.
Enrollment: 12,069 undergrads.
Selectivity: Open admission; but selective for some programs.

BASIC COSTS (2009-2010)

Tuition and fees: $782; out-of-state residents $6,482.
Per-credit charge: $26; out-of-state residents $216.

FINANCIAL AID PICTURE

Students with need: Need-based aid available for full-time and part-time students.

FINANCIAL AID PROCEDURES

Forms required: FAFSA, state aid form, institutional form.
Dates and Deadlines: Priority date 3/2; no closing date. Applicants notified on a rolling basis starting 7/15; must reply within 2 week(s) of notification.

CONTACT

Sherrie Padilla, Director of Financial Aid
3041 West Avenue K, Lancaster, CA 93536-5426
(661) 722-6336

Antioch University Santa Barbara

Santa Barbara, California
www.antiochsb.edu   Federal Code: 003010

Upper-division private university and liberal arts college in small city.
Enrollment: 48 undergrads.

BASIC COSTS (2010-2011)

Tuition and fees: $16,614.
Per-credit charge: $546.

FINANCIAL AID PICTURE (2008-2009)

Students with need: Need-based aid available for full-time and part-time students. Work study available nights, weekends, and for part-time students.

FINANCIAL AID PROCEDURES

Forms required: FAFSA, institutional form.
Dates and Deadlines: Priority date 4/15; no closing date. Applicants notified on a rolling basis; must reply within 4 week(s) of notification.
Transfers: Priority date 4/1; no deadline.

CONTACT

Cecilia Schneider, Financial Aid Director
801 Garden Street, Suite 101, Santa Barbara, CA 93101-1581
(805) 962-8179 ext. 108

Art Center College of Design

Pasadena, California
www.artcenter.edu   Federal Code: 001116

4-year private visual arts college in small city.
Enrollment: 1,470 undergrads, 9% part-time. 554 full-time freshmen.
Selectivity: Admits 50 to 75% of applicants.

BASIC COSTS (2010-2011)

Tuition and fees: $32,168.
Per-credit charge: $1,131.

FINANCIAL AID PICTURE (2008-2009)

Students with need: Out of 255 full-time freshmen who applied for aid, 240 were judged to have need. Of these, 231 received aid. Need-based aid available for part-time students.
Students without need: 21 full-time freshmen who did not demonstrate need for aid received scholarships/grants; average award was $7,692.
Additional info: Students may apply for scholarships after they enroll while progressing through the program.

FINANCIAL AID PROCEDURES

Forms required: FAFSA.
Dates and Deadlines: Priority date 3/1; no closing date. Applicants notified on a rolling basis starting 5/15.
Transfers: Applicants notified on a rolling basis starting 1/1.

CONTACT

Clema McKenzie, Director of Financial Aid
1700 Lida Street, Pasadena, CA 91103
(626) 396-2215

Art Institute of California: Hollywood

North Hollywood, California
www.artinstitutes.edu/hollywood   Federal Code: 031254

4-year for-profit culinary school and visual arts college in very large city.
Enrollment: 1,256 undergrads, 50% part-time. 97 full-time freshmen.
Selectivity: Open admission.

BASIC COSTS (2009-2010)

Per-credit charge: $503.
Additional info: Cost for 7-quarter continuous enrollment associate degree program $56,486; cost for 12-quarter continuous enrollment bachelor's degree program $96,726. Fees vary by program.

FINANCIAL AID PICTURE (2009-2010)

Students with need: Need-based aid available for full-time and part-time students.

CONTACT

Adis Ceballos, Director of Student Financial Services
5250 Lankershim Boulevard, North Hollywood, CA 91601
(818) 299-5151

Art Institute of California: Los Angeles

Santa Monica, California
www.artinstitutes.edu/losangeles   Federal Code: 007470

2-year for-profit visual arts college in small city.
Enrollment: 2,159 undergrads.

BASIC COSTS (2009-2010)

Tuition and fees: $24,244.
Per-credit charge: $503.
Additional info: Apartment-style housing: $2,994/quarter for 2-bedroom.

FINANCIAL AID PICTURE (2009-2010)

Students with need: Need-based aid available for full-time and part-time students. Work study available nights, weekends, and for part-time students.
Students without need: No-need awards available for academics.

FINANCIAL AID PROCEDURES

Forms required: FAFSA.
Dates and Deadlines: No deadline. Applicants notified on a rolling basis.

CONTACT

Director of Student Financial Services
2900 31st Street, Santa Monica, CA 90405-3035
(310) 752-4700

Art Institute of California: Orange County

Santa Ana, California
www.artinstitutes.edu/orangecounty Federal Code: 007236

3-year for-profit culinary school and visual arts college in very large city.
Enrollment: 1,873 undergrads.
Selectivity: Open admission; but selective for some programs.

BASIC COSTS (2009-2010)

Tuition and fees: $24,344.
Per-credit charge: $503.

Room only: $2,997.
Additional info: Typical full-time load 16 credit hours per quarter. Culinary lab fee $315 per quarter, online fee $100 per class per quarter.

FINANCIAL AID PICTURE
Students with need: Need-based aid available for full-time and part-time students. Work study available nights, weekends, and for part-time students.
Students without need: No-need awards available for academics, art, minority status.

FINANCIAL AID PROCEDURES
Forms required: FAFSA, state aid form.
Dates and Deadlines: No deadline. Applicants notified on a rolling basis; must reply within 2 week(s) of notification.

CONTACT
Silvia Guzman, Director of Student Financial Services
3601 West Sunflower Avenue, Santa Ana, CA 92704-7931
(714) 830-0202

Art Institute of California: San Diego
San Diego, California
www.artinstitutes.edu/sandiego   Federal Code: 016471

3-year for-profit visual arts college in very large city.
Enrollment: 2,053 undergrads.
Selectivity: Admits less than 50% of applicants.

BASIC COSTS (2009-2010)
Tuition and fees: $24,144.
Per-credit charge: $503.

FINANCIAL AID PICTURE
Students with need: Need-based aid available for full-time students.

FINANCIAL AID PROCEDURES
Forms required: FAFSA.
Dates and Deadlines: No deadline.

CONTACT
Director of Student Financial Services
7650 Mission Valley Road, San Diego, CA 92108-4423

Azusa Pacific University
Azusa, California
www.apu.edu   Federal Code: 001117

4-year private university in small city, affiliated with interdenominational tradition.
Enrollment: 4,874 undergrads, 15% part-time. 1,090 full-time freshmen.
Selectivity: Admits 50 to 75% of applicants.

BASIC COSTS (2010-2011)
Tuition and fees: $27,750.
Per-credit charge: $1,123.
Room and board: $8,314.
Additional info: Tuition/fee waivers available for minority students.

FINANCIAL AID PICTURE (2008-2009)
Students with need: Out of 1,020 full-time freshmen who applied for aid, 718 were judged to have need. Of these, 717 received aid, and 171 had their full need met. Average financial aid package met 67% of need; average scholarship/grant was $15,616; average loan was $4,068. For part-time students, average financial aid package was $10,079.
Students without need: 269 full-time freshmen who did not demonstrate need for aid received scholarships/grants; average award was $8,103. No-

need awards available for academics, athletics, leadership, minority status, music/drama, religious affiliation, ROTC.
Scholarships offered: 23 full-time freshmen received athletic scholarships; average amount $13,101.

FINANCIAL AID PROCEDURES
Forms required: FAFSA, institutional form.
Dates and Deadlines: Priority date 3/2; closing date 7/1. Applicants notified on a rolling basis starting 3/1; must reply within 3 week(s) of notification.
Transfers: Cal Grants not available to first time applicants who are seniors.

CONTACT
Todd Ross, Director of Student Financial Services
901 East Alosta Avenue, Azusa, CA 91702-7000
(626) 812-3009

Barstow Community College
Barstow, California
www.barstow.edu   Federal Code: 001119

2-year public community college in large town.
Enrollment: 5,087 undergrads.
Selectivity: Open admission.

BASIC COSTS (2009-2010)
Tuition and fees: $780; out-of-state residents $6,120.
Per-credit charge: $26; out-of-state residents $204.

FINANCIAL AID PICTURE (2008-2009)
Students with need: 96% of average financial aid package awarded as scholarships/grants, 4% awarded as loans/jobs. Need-based aid available for part-time students.
Students without need: This college awards aid only to students with need.

FINANCIAL AID PROCEDURES
Forms required: FAFSA.
Dates and Deadlines: Closing date 6/17. Applicants notified on a rolling basis starting 7/1.

CONTACT
Danielle Cordova, Financial Aid Officer
2700 Barstow Road, Barstow, CA 92311-9984
(760) 252-2411 ext. 7205

Berkeley City College
Berkeley, California
www.berkeleycitycollege.edu   Federal Code: 014311

2-year public community college in small city.
Enrollment: 7,300 undergrads.
Selectivity: Open admission.

BASIC COSTS (2009-2010)
Tuition and fees: $814; out-of-state residents $6,514.
Per-credit charge: $26; out-of-state residents $216.
Additional info: Tuition/fee waivers available for adults, minority students, unemployed or children of unemployed.

FINANCIAL AID PICTURE
Students with need: Need-based aid available for full-time and part-time students.
Students without need: This college awards aid only to students with need.

FINANCIAL AID PROCEDURES
Dates and Deadlines: No deadline. Applicants notified on a rolling basis.

CONTACT
Financial Aid Program Supervisor
2050 Center Street, Berkeley, CA 94704
(510) 981-2878

Bethany University
Scotts Valley, California
www.bethany.edu   Federal Code: 001121

4-year private Bible and liberal arts college in small town, affiliated with Assemblies of God.
Enrollment: 421 undergrads, 15% part-time. 75 full-time freshmen.
Selectivity: Admits less than 50% of applicants.

BASIC COSTS (2010-2011)
Tuition and fees: $18,750.
Per-credit charge: $764.
Room and board: $7,600.

FINANCIAL AID PICTURE (2009-2010)
Students with need: Need-based aid available for full-time and part-time students. Work study available nights, weekends, and for part-time students.
Students without need: No-need awards available for academics, alumni affiliation, athletics, leadership, minority status, music/drama, religious affiliation.

FINANCIAL AID PROCEDURES
Forms required: FAFSA, institutional form.
Dates and Deadlines: Priority date 3/2; no closing date. Applicants notified on a rolling basis starting 4/15; must reply within 2 week(s) of notification.

CONTACT
Debi Snow, Director of Financial Aid
800 Bethany Drive, Scotts Valley, CA 95066-2898
(831) 438-3800

Bethesda Christian University
Anaheim, California
www.bcu.edu   Federal Code: 032663

4-year private university in large city, affiliated with Christian Church.
Enrollment: 181 undergrads.
Selectivity: Open admission. GED not accepted.

BASIC COSTS (2010-2011)
Tuition and fees: $7,160.
Per-credit charge: $231.
Room and board: $3,200.

FINANCIAL AID PICTURE (2009-2010)
Students with need: Need-based aid available for full-time and part-time students.
Students without need: This college awards aid only to students with need.

FINANCIAL AID PROCEDURES
Forms required: FAFSA, institutional form.
Dates and Deadlines: Closing date 3/14. Applicants notified on a rolling basis starting 6/30.
Transfers: No deadline.

CONTACT
Tony Chiang, Director of Financial Aid
730 North Euclid Street, Anaheim, CA 92801
(714) 517-1945

Biola University
La Mirada, California
www.biola.edu   Federal Code: 001122

4-year private university and Bible college in large town, affiliated with inter-denominational tradition.
Enrollment: 3,888 undergrads, 9% part-time. 901 full-time freshmen.
Selectivity: Admits over 75% of applicants.

BASIC COSTS (2009-2010)
Tuition and fees: $27,744.
Per-credit charge: $1,156.
Room and board: $8,080.
Additional info: Tuition/fee waivers available for minority students.

FINANCIAL AID PICTURE (2008-2009)
Students with need: Need-based aid available for full-time and part-time students.
Students without need: No-need awards available for academics, alumni affiliation, art, athletics, leadership, minority status, music/drama, state/district residency.
Scholarships offered: Scholarships for Underrepresented Groups of Ethnicity: up to $6,500; based on GPA and ethnicity. Community Service Scholarship: $2,700; based on demonstration of outstanding spiritual leadership. Alumni Dependent Scholarship: $500; given to students whose parents completed 30 units of coursework at Biola University.

FINANCIAL AID PROCEDURES
Forms required: FAFSA, state aid form.
Dates and Deadlines: Priority date 1/1; no closing date. Applicants notified on a rolling basis starting 3/1.
Transfers: No deadline. Applicants notified on a rolling basis starting 3/1.

CONTACT
Jonathan Choy, Director of Financial Aid
13800 Biola Avenue, La Mirada, CA 90639-0001
(562) 903-4742

Cabrillo College
Aptos, California
www.cabrillo.edu   Federal Code: 001124

2-year public community college in large town.
Enrollment: 4,751 full-time undergrads.
Selectivity: Open admission; but selective for some programs.

BASIC COSTS (2009-2010)
Tuition and fees: $826; out-of-state residents $6,646.
Per-credit charge: $26; out-of-state residents $220.

FINANCIAL AID PICTURE (2008-2009)
Students with need: Need-based aid available for full-time and part-time students.

FINANCIAL AID PROCEDURES
Forms required: FAFSA, institutional form.
Dates and Deadlines: No deadline. Applicants notified on a rolling basis starting 7/31; must reply within 3 week(s) of notification.
Transfers: Academic transcript required.

CONTACT
Debbie Soria, Director of Financial Aid and Scholarships
6500 Soquel Drive, Aptos, CA 95003
(831) 479-6100

California Baptist University

Riverside, California
www.calbaptist.edu   Federal Code: 001125

4-year private university and liberal arts college in large city, affiliated with Southern Baptist Convention.

Enrollment: 3,212 undergrads, 14% part-time. 391 full-time freshmen.
Selectivity: Admits 50 to 75% of applicants.

BASIC COSTS (2010-2011)

Tuition and fees: $24,654.
Per-credit charge: $879.
Room and board: $8,370.

FINANCIAL AID PICTURE (2008-2009)

Students with need: Out of 391 full-time freshmen who applied for aid, 281 were judged to have need. Of these, 273 received aid, and 182 had their full need met. Average financial aid package met 48% of need; average scholarship/grant was $5,294; average loan was $1,429. For part-time students, average financial aid package was $4,235.

Students without need: 52 full-time freshmen who did not demonstrate need for aid received scholarships/grants; average award was $6,528. No-need awards available for academics, art, athletics, leadership, music/drama, religious affiliation, ROTC.

Scholarships offered: *Merit:* Matching room and board scholarship for recipients of the ROTC scholarships. Yellow Ribbon Scholarship for qualified veterans. *Athletic:* 71 full-time freshmen received athletic scholarships; average amount $3,865.

Cumulative student debt: 82% of graduating class had student loans; average debt was $35,550.

FINANCIAL AID PROCEDURES

Forms required: FAFSA, state aid form.
Dates and Deadlines: Priority date 3/2; no closing date. Applicants notified on a rolling basis starting 3/2; must reply by 5/1 or within 3 week(s) of notification.
Transfers: No deadline. Applicants notified on a rolling basis starting 12/15.

CONTACT

Rebecca Sanchez, Director of Financial Aid
8432 Magnolia Avenue, Riverside, CA 92504-3297
(951) 343-4236

California College of the Arts

San Francisco, California
www.cca.edu   Federal Code: 001127

4-year private visual arts college in very large city.
Enrollment: 1,362 undergrads, 7% part-time. 239 full-time freshmen.
Selectivity: Admits 50 to 75% of applicants.

BASIC COSTS (2010-2011)

Tuition and fees: $35,222.
Per-credit charge: $1,453.
Room only: $7,000.
Additional info: No meal plan offered. Residence halls equipped with kitchens on each floor. Estimated food cost: $2850.

FINANCIAL AID PICTURE (2008-2009)

Students with need: Out of 178 full-time freshmen who applied for aid, 160 were judged to have need. Of these, 159 received aid, and 7 had their full need met. Average financial aid package met 58% of need; average scholarship/grant was $17,554; average loan was $3,484. For part-time students, average financial aid package was $11,067.

Students without need: 51 full-time freshmen who did not demonstrate need for aid received scholarships/grants; average award was $7,559. No-need awards available for academics, art.
Scholarships offered: Creative Achievement Scholarship: up to $20,000 annually; renewable; based on academic achievement and strength of admissions portfolios.
Cumulative student debt: 64% of graduating class had student loans; average debt was $34,518.
Additional info: Application deadline for merit scholarships February 1.

FINANCIAL AID PROCEDURES

Forms required: FAFSA.
Dates and Deadlines: Priority date 3/1; no closing date. Applicants notified on a rolling basis starting 3/15; must reply by 5/1 or within 3 week(s) of notification.
Transfers: No deadline. Applicants notified on a rolling basis starting 3/15; must reply by 5/1 or within 3 week(s) of notification. Scholarships available for community college transfer students.

CONTACT

Silvia Marquez, Director of Financial Aid
1111 Eighth Street, San Francisco, CA 94107-2247
(415) 703-9528

California Culinary Academy

San Francisco, California
www.caculinary.edu   Federal Code: 015698

2-year for-profit culinary school and career college in very large city.
Enrollment: 775 undergrads.
Selectivity: Open admission.

BASIC COSTS (2009-2010)

Tuition and fees: $37,285.
Additional info: Tuition quoted is for 12 months.

FINANCIAL AID PICTURE

Students with need: Need-based aid available for full-time students.

FINANCIAL AID PROCEDURES

Forms required: FAFSA, state aid form.
Dates and Deadlines: No deadline. Applicants notified on a rolling basis; must reply within 1 week(s) of notification.

CONTACT

I Chen, Director of Financial Aid
350 Rhode Island, San Francisco, CA 94103
(415) 771-3500

California Institute of Integral Studies

San Francisco, California
www.ciis.edu   Federal Code: 012154

Upper-division private liberal arts college in very large city.
Enrollment: 70 undergrads, 13% part-time.

BASIC COSTS (2010-2011)

Tuition and fees: $14,950.
Per-credit charge: $620.
Additional info: Cost quoted for 2 semesters; 3-semester attendance mandatory.

FINANCIAL AID PICTURE (2008-2009)

Students with need: Average financial aid package for all full-time undergraduates was $9,486; for part-time $8,164. 24% awarded as scholarships/grants, 76% awarded as loans/jobs. Work study available nights, weekends, and for part-time students.

Students without need: No-need awards available for academics, alumni affiliation, art, job skills, leadership, minority status, music/drama, ROTC, state/district residency.
Cumulative student debt: 100% of graduating class had student loans; average debt was $23,000.

FINANCIAL AID PROCEDURES

Dates and Deadlines: Closing date 4/15.
Transfers: Priority date 4/15; no deadline.

CONTACT

Marisol Mendoza, Financial Aid Director
1453 Mission Street, San Francisco, CA 94103
(415) 575-6156

California Institute of Technology

Pasadena, California   Federal Code: 001131
www.caltech.edu   CSS Code: 4034

4-year private university in small city.
Enrollment: 951 undergrads. 252 full-time freshmen.
Selectivity: Admits less than 50% of applicants.

BASIC COSTS (2010-2011)

Tuition and fees: $36,282.
Room and board: $11,397.

FINANCIAL AID PICTURE (2009-2010)

Students with need: Out of 176 full-time freshmen who applied for aid, 144 were judged to have need. Of these, 144 received aid, and 144 had their full need met. Average financial aid package met 100% of need; average scholarship/grant was $28,991; average loan was $2,900.
Students without need: 3 full-time freshmen who did not demonstrate need for aid received scholarships/grants; average award was $16,849.
Cumulative student debt: 42% of graduating class had student loans; average debt was $8,218.

FINANCIAL AID PROCEDURES

Forms required: FAFSA, CSS PROFILE, state aid form, institutional form.
Dates and Deadlines: Closing date 1/15. Applicants notified by 4/1; must reply by 5/1.
Transfers: Priority date 3/1; no deadline.

CONTACT

Don Crewell, Director of Financial Aid
1200 East California Boulevard, MC 1-94, Pasadena, CA 91125
(626) 395-6280

California Institute of the Arts

Valencia, California
www.calarts.edu   Federal Code: 001132

4-year private visual arts and performing arts college in small city.
Enrollment: 888 undergrads, 1% part-time. 160 full-time freshmen.
Selectivity: Admits less than 50% of applicants.

BASIC COSTS (2010-2011)

Tuition and fees: $36,742.
Room and board: $9,293.

FINANCIAL AID PICTURE (2009-2010)

Students with need: Out of 132 full-time freshmen who applied for aid, 108 were judged to have need. Of these, 105 received aid, and 5 had their full need met. Average financial aid package met 71% of need; average scholarship/grant was $14,771; average loan was $4,502. Need-based aid available for part-time students.

Students without need: 13 full-time freshmen who did not demonstrate need for aid received scholarships/grants; average award was $4,554. No-need awards available for academics, art, minority status, music/drama.
Cumulative student debt: 67% of graduating class had student loans; average debt was $39,286.

FINANCIAL AID PROCEDURES

Forms required: FAFSA.
Dates and Deadlines: Priority date 3/2; no closing date. Applicants notified on a rolling basis starting 4/1; must reply by 5/1 or within 3 week(s) of notification.

CONTACT

Bobbi Heuer, Financial Aid Director
24700 McBean Parkway, Valencia, CA 91355
(661) 253-7869

California Lutheran University

Thousand Oaks, California
www.callutheran.edu   Federal Code: 001133

4-year private university and liberal arts college in small city, affiliated with Evangelical Lutheran Church in America.
Enrollment: 2,344 undergrads, 3% part-time. 464 full-time freshmen.
Selectivity: Admits 50 to 75% of applicants.

BASIC COSTS (2010-2011)

Tuition and fees: $31,000.
Per-credit charge: $990.
Room and board: $10,580.

FINANCIAL AID PICTURE (2009-2010)

Students with need: Out of 455 full-time freshmen who applied for aid, 323 were judged to have need. Of these, 323 received aid, and 81 had their full need met. Average financial aid package met 88% of need; average scholarship/grant was $17,600; average loan was $3,400. For part-time students, average financial aid package was $10,690.
Students without need: 141 full-time freshmen who did not demonstrate need for aid received scholarships/grants; average award was $12,400. No-need awards available for academics, alumni affiliation, art, leadership, minority status, music/drama, religious affiliation, state/district residency.
Scholarships offered: Academic Scholarships: range from $3,000 up to $15,000 per year; based on GPA, test scores, and class rank at time of Admission. Presidential Scholarship Program: $17,000 up to full tuition; additional application required. UC Guarantee: 2008-2009 amount was $15,994; student must be admitted to CLU and UCLA or UCSB. Visual and Performing Arts Scholarships: $1,000-$6,000; application deadline of February 1 and audition with department deadline of February 22.

FINANCIAL AID PROCEDURES

Forms required: FAFSA.
Dates and Deadlines: Priority date 3/1; no closing date. Applicants notified on a rolling basis starting 3/15; must reply within 2 week(s) of notification.
Transfers: No deadline. Applicants notified on a rolling basis starting 3/15; must reply within 2 week(s) of notification.

CONTACT

Rebecca Keenan, Associate Director of Financial Aid/Scholarships
60 West Olsen Road #1350, Thousand Oaks, CA 91360-2787
(805) 493-3115

California Maritime Academy

Vallejo, California
www.csum.edu   Federal Code: 001134

4-year public university and maritime college in small city.
Enrollment: 825 undergrads.
Selectivity: Admits 50 to 75% of applicants.

BASIC COSTS (2009-2010)

Tuition and fees: $5,090; out-of-state residents $16,250.
Room and board: $9,360.
Additional info: Each student participates in at least one cruise and one internship prior to graduation. Some majors have additional cruise requirements. The cost for a cruise is $3,900. The cost for an internship/co-op is $225. Additionally, each incoming student must purchase a uniform. Prices range from $1,550-$1,785 depending on the major. Reduced out-of-state tuition for residents of AK, AZ, CO, HI, ID, MT, NV, NM, ND, OR, SD, UT, WA, WY available under the Western Undergraduate Exchange (WUE) program. WUE students pay one-and-a half the State University Fee ($3,354 this year), which is $5,031.

FINANCIAL AID PICTURE (2009-2010)

Students with need: Need-based aid available for full-time and part-time students.
Students without need: This college awards aid only to students with need.
Additional info: US Maritime Administration provides annual incentive payment of $3,000 per student, with certain conditions. Tuition waiver for children of deceased or disabled California veterans.

FINANCIAL AID PROCEDURES

Forms required: FAFSA.
Dates and Deadlines: Priority date 3/2; no closing date. Applicants notified on a rolling basis starting 4/1.

CONTACT

Ken Walsh, Director of Financial Aid
200 Maritime Academy Drive, Vallejo, CA 94590
(707) 654-1275

California Polytechnic State University: San Luis Obispo

San Luis Obispo, California
www.calpoly.edu   Federal Code: 001143

4-year public university in large town.
Enrollment: 18,239 undergrads, 4% part-time. 3,449 full-time freshmen.
Selectivity: Admits less than 50% of applicants.

BASIC COSTS (2009-2010)

Tuition and fees: $6,498; out-of-state residents $17,658.
Room and board: $9,846.
Additional info: Required fees vary by program.

FINANCIAL AID PICTURE (2008-2009)

Students with need: Out of 2,401 full-time freshmen who applied for aid, 1,168 were judged to have need. Of these, 1,055 received aid, and 168 had their full need met. Average financial aid package met 66% of need; average scholarship/grant was $2,050; average loan was $3,149. For part-time students, average financial aid package was $5,515.
Students without need: 201 full-time freshmen who did not demonstrate need for aid received scholarships/grants; average award was $2,018. No-need awards available for academics, alumni affiliation, art, athletics, job skills, leadership, music/drama, ROTC, state/district residency.
Scholarships offered: 85 full-time freshmen received athletic scholarships; average amount $2,324.

Additional info: College-administered financial aid is not available for undergraduate international students.

FINANCIAL AID PROCEDURES

Forms required: FAFSA.
Dates and Deadlines: Priority date 3/2; no closing date. Applicants notified on a rolling basis starting 4/1.

CONTACT

Lois Kelly, Director, Financial Aid
Admissions Office, Cal Poly, San Luis Obispo, CA 93407-0031
(805) 756-2927

California School of Culinary Arts

Pasadena, California
www.chefs.edu/los-angeles/#   Federal Code: 032103

2-year for-profit culinary school in very large city.
Enrollment: 1,355 undergrads.
Selectivity: Open admission.

BASIC COSTS (2009-2010)

Additional info: Diploma programs vary in cost. Associate of Occupational Studies in culinary arts program tuition: $43,950, fees $2,800. Associate of Occupational Studies in hospitality/restaurant management tuition: $31,000, fees $3,470. Associate of Occupational Studies in patisserie and baking program tuition: $35,750, fees $ 2,760.

FINANCIAL AID PICTURE (2008-2009)

Students with need: Need-based aid available for full-time and part-time students. Work study available nights, weekends, and for part-time students.

FINANCIAL AID PROCEDURES

Forms required: FAFSA.
Dates and Deadlines: No deadline. Applicants notified on a rolling basis.
Transfers: No deadline.

CONTACT

Kristin Hanle, Director of Student Finance
530 East Colorado Boulevard, Pasadena, CA 91101
(626) 229-1300

California State Polytechnic University: Pomona

Pomona, California
www.csupomona.edu   Federal Code: 001144

4-year public university in small city.
Enrollment: 20,136 undergrads, 17% part-time. 2,728 full-time freshmen.
Selectivity: Admits 50 to 75% of applicants.

BASIC COSTS (2009-2010)

Tuition and fees: $4,551; out-of-state residents $15,711.
Room and board: $9,570.

FINANCIAL AID PICTURE (2009-2010)

Students with need: Out of 2,122 full-time freshmen who applied for aid, 1,485 were judged to have need. Of these, 1,338 received aid, and 356 had their full need met. Average financial aid package met 79% of need; average scholarship/grant was $9,318; average loan was $3,036. For part-time students, average financial aid package was $9,310.
Students without need: 3 full-time freshmen who did not demonstrate need for aid received scholarships/grants; average award was $2,192. No-need awards available for academics, alumni affiliation, athletics, leadership, state/district residency.
Scholarships offered: 32 full-time freshmen received athletic scholarships; average amount $3,395.

Cumulative student debt: 36% of graduating class had student loans; average debt was $14,035.

FINANCIAL AID PROCEDURES
Forms required: FAFSA.
Dates and Deadlines: Priority date 3/2; no closing date. Applicants notified on a rolling basis starting 4/1; must reply within 2 week(s) of notification.

CONTACT
Diana Minor, Director of Financial Aid
3801 West Temple Avenue, Pomona, CA 91768-4019
(909) 869-3700

California State University: Bakersfield
Bakersfield, California
www.csub.edu   Federal Code: 007993

4-year public university and liberal arts college in small city.
Enrollment: 6,494 undergrads.

BASIC COSTS (2009-2010)
Tuition and fees: $5,091; out-of-state residents $16,251.
Room and board: $6,678.
Additional info: Reduced out-of-state tuition for residents of AK, AZ, CO, HI, ID, MT, NV, NM, ND, OR, SD, UT, WA, WY available under the Western Undergraduate Exchange (WUE) program. WUE students pay one-and-a half the State University Fees plus campus-based fees, which is $6,096 for the 2008/2009 academic year.

FINANCIAL AID PICTURE (2008-2009)
Students with need: Need-based aid available for full-time and part-time students.
Students without need: This college awards aid only to students with need.

FINANCIAL AID PROCEDURES
Forms required: FAFSA.
Dates and Deadlines: Priority date 3/2; closing date 4/1. Applicants notified on a rolling basis; must reply within 2 week(s) of notification.

CONTACT
Ron Radney, Director of Financial Aid & Scholarships
9001 Stockdale Highway, Bakersfield, CA 93311-1099
(661) 664-2011

California State University: Channel Islands
Camarillo, California
www.csuci.edu   Federal Code: 039803

4-year public university in small city.
Enrollment: 3,575 undergrads, 17% part-time. 710 full-time freshmen.
Selectivity: Admits less than 50% of applicants.

BASIC COSTS (2009-2010)
Tuition and fees: $4,881; out-of-state residents $16,041.
Room and board: $10,780.

FINANCIAL AID PICTURE (2008-2009)
Students with need: Out of 551 full-time freshmen who applied for aid, 420 were judged to have need. Of these, 420 received aid, and 13 had their full need met. Average financial aid package met 30% of need; average scholarship/grant was $5,551; average loan was $3,212. For part-time students, average financial aid package was $5,466.
Students without need: 24 full-time freshmen who did not demonstrate need for aid received scholarships/grants; average award was $1,725. No-need awards available for academics, leadership, state/district residency.

Cumulative student debt: 34% of graduating class had student loans; average debt was $20,680.

FINANCIAL AID PROCEDURES
Forms required: FAFSA.
Dates and Deadlines: Priority date 3/2; no closing date. Applicants notified by 4/7.

CONTACT
Richard Montiel, Assistant Director of Financial Aid
One University Drive, Camarillo, CA 93012
(805) 437-8530

California State University: Chico
Chico, California
www.csuchico.edu   Federal Code: 001146

4-year public university and liberal arts college in small city.
Enrollment: 15,617 undergrads, 8% part-time. 2,468 full-time freshmen.
Selectivity: Admits over 75% of applicants.

BASIC COSTS (2009-2010)
Tuition and fees: $5,336; out-of-state residents $16,496.
Room and board: $9,996.
Additional info: Reduced out-of-state tuition for residents of AK, AZ, CO. HI, ID, MT, NV, NM, ND, OR, SD, UT, WA, WY may be available under the Western Undergraduate Exchange (WUE) program.

FINANCIAL AID PICTURE (2009-2010)
Students with need: Need-based aid available for full-time and part-time students. Work study available nights, weekends, and for part-time students.
Students without need: No-need awards available for academics, art, athletics, leadership, minority status, music/drama, religious affiliation.
Scholarships offered: President's Scholar Award: 10 awards at $12,000 each; 12 awards at $1,000 each.

FINANCIAL AID PROCEDURES
Forms required: FAFSA.
Dates and Deadlines: Priority date 3/2; no closing date. Applicants notified on a rolling basis starting 3/2.

CONTACT
Dan Reed, Director of Financial Aid
400 West First Street, Chico, CA 95929-0722
(530) 898-6451

California State University: Dominguez Hills
Carson, California
www.csudh.edu   Federal Code: 001141

4-year public university in small city.
Enrollment: 10,222 undergrads, 34% part-time. 1,069 full-time freshmen.
Selectivity: Admits over 75% of applicants.

BASIC COSTS (2009-2010)
Tuition and fees: $4,645; out-of-state residents $15,805.
Room and board: $9,970.
Additional info: Reduced out-of-state tuition for residents of AK, AZ, CO, HI, ID, MT, NV, NM, ND, OR, SD, UT, WA, WY available under the Western Undergraduate Exchange (WUE) program. Tuition/fee waivers available for adults.

FINANCIAL AID PICTURE (2009-2010)

Students with need: Out of 984 full-time freshmen who applied for aid, 902 were judged to have need. Of these, 867 received aid, and 11 had their full need met. Average financial aid package met 34% of need; average scholarship/grant was $4,454; average loan was $1,637. For part-time students, average financial aid package was $3,915.

Students without need: 48 full-time freshmen who did not demonstrate need for aid received scholarships/grants; average award was $2,629. No-need awards available for academics, alumni affiliation, art, athletics, leadership, music/drama.

Scholarships offered: 1 full-time freshmen received athletic scholarships; average amount $1,000.

Cumulative student debt: 56% of graduating class had student loans; average debt was $7,946.

FINANCIAL AID PROCEDURES

Forms required: FAFSA.

Dates and Deadlines: Priority date 3/2; no closing date. Applicants notified on a rolling basis starting 2/28; must reply within 4 week(s) of notification.

CONTACT

Delores Lee, Director of Financial Aid
1000 East Victoria Street, Carson, CA 90747
(310) 243-3696

California State University: East Bay
Hayward, California
www.csueastbay.edu   Federal Code: 001138

4-year public university in small city.
Enrollment: 11,086 undergrads, 17% part-time. 1,436 full-time freshmen.
Selectivity: Open admission; but selective for some programs.

BASIC COSTS (2009-2010)

Tuition and fees: $4,872; out-of-state residents $16,032.
Room and board: $10,029.
Additional info: Quoted freshman room-only charge is for suite shared by 6 to 8 students. Additional $3,200 advance purchase of flexible retail meal credits required. (Standard meal plans not available).

FINANCIAL AID PICTURE (2008-2009)

Students with need: Need-based aid available for full-time and part-time students.
Students without need: No-need awards available for athletics, music/drama.

FINANCIAL AID PROCEDURES

Forms required: FAFSA.
Dates and Deadlines: Priority date 3/2; no closing date. Applicants notified on a rolling basis; must reply within 3 week(s) of notification.

CONTACT

Rhonda Johnson, Financial Aid Department
25800 Carlos Bee Boulevard, Hayward, CA 94542-3095
(510) 885-3018

California State University: Fresno
Fresno, California
www.csufresno.edu   Federal Code: 001147

4-year public university in very large city.
Enrollment: 18,216 undergrads, 15% part-time. 2,620 full-time freshmen.
Selectivity: Admits 50 to 75% of applicants.

BASIC COSTS (2009-2010)

Tuition and fees: $4,672; out-of-state residents $15,832.
Room and board: $9,652.
Additional info: Tuition/fee waivers available for adults, minority students, unemployed or children of unemployed.

FINANCIAL AID PICTURE (2009-2010)

Students with need: Out of 2,153 full-time freshmen who applied for aid, 1,771 were judged to have need. Of these, 1,699 received aid, and 255 had their full need met. Average financial aid package met 74% of need; average scholarship/grant was $9,888; average loan was $2,944. For part-time students, average financial aid package was $8,981.

Students without need: 76 full-time freshmen who did not demonstrate need for aid received scholarships/grants; average award was $2,609. No-need awards available for academics, art, athletics, leadership, music/drama, ROTC, state/district residency.

Scholarships offered: 84 full-time freshmen received athletic scholarships; average amount $9,098.

Cumulative student debt: 65% of graduating class had student loans; average debt was $10,406.

FINANCIAL AID PROCEDURES

Forms required: FAFSA.
Dates and Deadlines: Priority date 3/3; no closing date. Applicants notified on a rolling basis starting 4/1; must reply within 3 week(s) of notification.

CONTACT

Maria Hernandez, Director of Financial Aid
5150 North Maple Avenue, M/S JA 57, Fresno, CA 93740-8026
(559) 278-2182

California State University: Fullerton
Fullerton, California
www.fullerton.edu   Federal Code: 001137

4-year public university in small city.
Enrollment: 30,670 undergrads, 25% part-time. 4,519 full-time freshmen.
Selectivity: Admits 50 to 75% of applicants.

BASIC COSTS (2009-2010)

Tuition and fees: $4,662; out-of-state residents $15,622.
Room and board: $9,082.

FINANCIAL AID PICTURE (2008-2009)

Students with need: Out of 3,157 full-time freshmen who applied for aid, 2,004 were judged to have need. Of these, 1,750 received aid. Average financial aid package met 68% of need; average scholarship/grant was $7,039; average loan was $2,919. For part-time students, average financial aid package was $6,578.

Students without need: 548 full-time freshmen who did not demonstrate need for aid received scholarships/grants; average award was $3,827. No-need awards available for academics.

Scholarships offered: 57 full-time freshmen received athletic scholarships; average amount $6,310.

Cumulative student debt: 39% of graduating class had student loans; average debt was $14,626.

Additional info: Fee waiver for children of veterans killed in action or with service-connected disability whose annual income is $5,000 or less.

FINANCIAL AID PROCEDURES

Forms required: FAFSA.
Dates and Deadlines: Priority date 3/2; no closing date. Applicants notified on a rolling basis starting 4/22; must reply within 4 week(s) of notification.
Transfers: No deadline. Applicants notified on a rolling basis starting 4/22; must reply within 4 week(s) of notification.

CONTACT

Jessica Schutte, Director of Financial Aid
800 North State College Boulevard, Langsdorf Hall-114, Fullerton, CA 92831-6900
(657) 278-3125

California State University: Long Beach

Long Beach, California
www.csulb.edu   Federal Code: 001139

4-year public university in large city.
Enrollment: 29,226 undergrads, 19% part-time. 3,473 full-time freshmen.
Selectivity: Admits less than 50% of applicants.

BASIC COSTS (2009-2010)

Tuition and fees: $4,370; out-of-state residents $15,530.
Room and board: $10,832.

FINANCIAL AID PICTURE (2009-2010)

Students with need: Need-based aid available for full-time and part-time students.
Students without need: No-need awards available for academics, art, athletics, music/drama.
Scholarships offered: President's Scholar Award: full tuition and fees, campus housing, books.

FINANCIAL AID PROCEDURES

Forms required: FAFSA.
Dates and Deadlines: Priority date 3/2; no closing date. Applicants notified on a rolling basis starting 3/30; must reply within 3 week(s) of notification.
Transfers: Community college EOP students may be eligible for grant.

CONTACT

Nicholas Valdivia, Director of Financial Aid
1250 Bellflower Boulevard, Long Beach, CA 90840-0106
(562) 985-4641

California State University: Los Angeles

Los Angeles, California
www.calstatela.edu   Federal Code: 001140

4-year public university in very large city.
Enrollment: 15,734 undergrads, 25% part-time. 1,870 full-time freshmen.
Selectivity: Admits 50 to 75% of applicants.

BASIC COSTS (2009-2010)

Tuition and fees: $4,640; out-of-state residents $15,800.
Room and board: $13,179.

FINANCIAL AID PICTURE (2009-2010)

Students with need: Out of 1,539 full-time freshmen who applied for aid, 1,417 were judged to have need. Of these, 1,325 received aid, and 317 had their full need met. Average financial aid package met 77% of need; average scholarship/grant was $7,872; average loan was $3,350. For part-time students, average financial aid package was $7,900.
Students without need: 3 full-time freshmen who did not demonstrate need for aid received scholarships/grants; average award was $1,906.
Scholarships offered: 2 full-time freshmen received athletic scholarships; average amount $4,034.

FINANCIAL AID PROCEDURES

Forms required: FAFSA.
Dates and Deadlines: Priority date 3/1; no closing date. Applicants notified on a rolling basis starting 4/1; must reply within 3 week(s) of notification.

CONTACT

Tamie Nguyen, Director of Center for Student Financial Aid
5151 State University Drive SA101, Los Angeles, CA 90032
(323) 343-6260

California State University: Monterey Bay

Seaside, California
www.csumb.edu   Federal Code: 032603

4-year public liberal arts and teachers college in large town.
Enrollment: 4,278 undergrads, 8% part-time. 944 full-time freshmen.
Selectivity: Admits over 75% of applicants.

BASIC COSTS (2009-2010)

Tuition and fees: $4,512; out-of-state residents $15,672.
Room and board: $8,290.
Additional info: Tuition/fee waivers available for unemployed or children of unemployed.

FINANCIAL AID PICTURE (2009-2010)

Students with need: Out of 763 full-time freshmen who applied for aid, 503 were judged to have need. Of these, 470 received aid, and 111 had their full need met. Average financial aid package met 70% of need; average scholarship/grant was $9,244; average loan was $3,288. For part-time students, average financial aid package was $7,259.
Students without need: No-need awards available for academics, alumni affiliation, athletics, leadership, state/district residency.
Scholarships offered: 32 full-time freshmen received athletic scholarships; average amount $2,169.
Cumulative student debt: 63% of graduating class had student loans; average debt was $15,254.

FINANCIAL AID PROCEDURES

Forms required: FAFSA, state aid form.
Dates and Deadlines: Priority date 3/2; no closing date. Applicants notified by 3/1.

CONTACT

Angeles Fuentes, Director of Financial Aid
100 Campus Center, Building 47, Seaside, CA 93955-8001
(831) 582-5100

California State University: Northridge

Northridge, California
www.csun.edu   Federal Code: 001153

4-year public university in very large city.
Enrollment: 29,275 undergrads, 26% part-time. 4,513 full-time freshmen.
Selectivity: Admits 50 to 75% of applicants.

BASIC COSTS (2009-2010)

Tuition and fees: $4,801; out-of-state residents $15,961.
Room and board: $10,872.

FINANCIAL AID PICTURE (2008-2009)

Students with need: Out of 3,472 full-time freshmen who applied for aid, 2,991 were judged to have need. Of these, 2,991 received aid. For part-time students, average financial aid package was $9,197.
Students without need: 86 full-time freshmen who did not demonstrate need for aid received scholarships/grants; average award was $1,462. No-need awards available for academics, athletics, state/district residency.
Scholarships offered: 42 full-time freshmen received athletic scholarships; average amount $5,605.
Cumulative student debt: 39% of graduating class had student loans; average debt was $14,691.

FINANCIAL AID PROCEDURES
Forms required: FAFSA.
Dates and Deadlines: Priority date 3/2; no closing date. Applicants notified on a rolling basis starting 4/1.

CONTACT
Lili Vidal, Director of Financial Aid
18111 Nordhoff Street, Northridge, CA 91328-8207
(818) 677-4085

California State University: Sacramento
Sacramento, California
www.csus.edu   Federal Code: 001233

4-year public university in very large city.
Enrollment: 23,190 undergrads, 18% part-time. 2,714 full-time freshmen.
Selectivity: Admits over 75% of applicants.

BASIC COSTS (2009-2010)
Tuition and fees: $4,900; out-of-state residents $16,060.
Room and board: $11,332.

FINANCIAL AID PICTURE (2008-2009)
Students with need: Out of 2,608 full-time freshmen who applied for aid, 2,274 were judged to have need. Of these, 1,554 received aid, and 167 had their full need met. Average financial aid package met 53% of need; average scholarship/grant was $3,871; average loan was $1,716. For part-time students, average financial aid package was $3,954.
Students without need: 6 full-time freshmen who did not demonstrate need for aid received scholarships/grants; average award was $646.
Cumulative student debt: 35% of graduating class had student loans; average debt was $12,473.

FINANCIAL AID PROCEDURES
Forms required: FAFSA.
Dates and Deadlines: Applicants notified on a rolling basis starting 4/1; must reply within 4 week(s) of notification.

CONTACT
Craig Yamamoto, Financial Aid Director
6000 J Street, Sacramento, CA 95819-6048
(916) 278-6554

California State University: San Bernardino
San Bernardino, California
www.csusb.edu   Federal Code: 001142

4-year public university and liberal arts college in small city.
Enrollment: 14,416 undergrads, 15% part-time. 1,917 full-time freshmen.
Selectivity: Admits 50 to 75% of applicants.

BASIC COSTS (2009-2010)
Tuition and fees: $4,839; out-of-state residents $15,999.
Room and board: $9,432.
Additional info: Substantial tuition reduction depending on SAT scores.

FINANCIAL AID PICTURE (2009-2010)
Students with need: Out of 1,610 full-time freshmen who applied for aid, 1,407 were judged to have need. Of these, 1,679 received aid, and 30 had their full need met. Average financial aid package met 69% of need; average scholarship/grant was $8,602; average loan was $2,879. For part-time students, average financial aid package was $6,880.
Students without need: 6 full-time freshmen who did not demonstrate need for aid received scholarships/grants; average award was $2,900.

Scholarships offered: 14 full-time freshmen received athletic scholarships; average amount $8,821.

FINANCIAL AID PROCEDURES
Forms required: FAFSA.
Dates and Deadlines: Priority date 3/2; no closing date. Applicants notified on a rolling basis starting 4/1.

CONTACT
Roseanna Ruiz, Director of Financial Aid
5500 University Parkway, San Bernardino, CA 92407-2397
(909) 537-7800

California State University: Stanislaus
Turlock, California
www.csustan.edu   Federal Code: 001157

4-year public business and liberal arts college in small city.
Enrollment: 7,067 undergrads, 31% part-time. 798 full-time freshmen.
Selectivity: Admits 50 to 75% of applicants.

BASIC COSTS (2009-2010)
Tuition and fees: $4,840; out-of-state residents $16,000.
Room and board: $8,820.
Additional info: Tuition/fee waivers available for adults.

FINANCIAL AID PICTURE (2009-2010)
Students with need: Need-based aid available for full-time and part-time students. Work study available nights, weekends, and for part-time students.
Students without need: No-need awards available for academics, alumni affiliation, art, athletics, leadership, minority status, music/drama, state/district residency.
Scholarships offered: President's Scholarships: $12,500, renewable for up to 4 years, awards based on GPA minimum of 3.8 and SAT of at least 1350 or ACT of at least 30, 20 available; Provost's Scholarships: $3,500, renewable for up to 4 years, awards based on GPA minimum of 3.5 and SAT of at least 1250 or ACT of at least 28, 20 available; Provost's Achievement Award for community college transfers: $2,000, renewable for up to 2 years, awards based on GPA minimum of 3.5 and completion of at least 45 transferable credits at time of application, 10 available.

FINANCIAL AID PROCEDURES
Forms required: FAFSA.
Dates and Deadlines: Priority date 3/2; no closing date. Applicants notified on a rolling basis starting 3/15; must reply within 3 week(s) of notification.
Transfers: No deadline. Applicants notified on a rolling basis; must reply within 3 week(s) of notification.

CONTACT
Noelia Gonzales, Director of Financial Aid
One University Circle, Turlock, CA 95382-0256
(209) 667-3336

Cerro Coso Community College
Ridgecrest, California
www.cerrocoso.edu   Federal Code: 010111

2-year public community college in large town.
Enrollment: 5,506 undergrads.
Selectivity: Open admission.

BASIC COSTS (2009-2010)
Tuition and fees: $780; out-of-state residents $6,810.
Per-credit charge: $26; out-of-state residents $227.

FINANCIAL AID PICTURE
Students with need: Need-based aid available for full-time and part-time students. Work study available nights.

FINANCIAL AID PROCEDURES
Forms required: FAFSA.
Dates and Deadlines: Priority date 5/15; no closing date. Applicants notified on a rolling basis starting 6/1; must reply within 2 week(s) of notification.

CONTACT
JoAnn Spiller, Director of Financial Aid and Scholarships
3000 College Heights Boulevard, Ridgecrest, CA 93555-7777
(760) 384-6221

Chabot College
Hayward, California
www.chabotcollege.edu   Federal Code: 001162

2-year public community college in large city.
Enrollment: 9,091 undergrads, 63% part-time. 892 full-time freshmen.
Selectivity: Open admission.

BASIC COSTS (2009-2010)
Tuition and fees: $808; out-of-state residents $6,508.
Per-credit charge: $26; out-of-state residents $216.

FINANCIAL AID PICTURE
Students with need: Work study available nights, weekends, and for part-time students.
Additional info: Tuition and/or fee waivers for low-income students.

FINANCIAL AID PROCEDURES
Forms required: FAFSA, institutional form.
Dates and Deadlines: Priority date 8/1; no closing date. Applicants notified on a rolling basis.

CONTACT
Kathryn Linzmeyer, Director of Financial Aid
25555 Hesperian Boulevard, Hayward, CA 94545
(510) 723-6746

Chaffey College
Rancho Cucamonga, California
www.chaffey.edu   Federal Code: 001163

2-year public community college in small city.
Enrollment: 20,893 undergrads.
Selectivity: Open admission.

BASIC COSTS (2009-2010)
Tuition and fees: $814; out-of-state residents $6,514.
Per-credit charge: $26; out-of-state residents $216.
Additional info: Tuition/fee waivers available for adults.

FINANCIAL AID PICTURE
Students with need: Need-based aid available for full-time and part-time students.
Students without need: No-need awards available for academics.
Additional info: State of California Board of Governors fee waivers to qualified state residents. Criteria for eligibility: households which receive public assistance, meet state's low income guidelines, and demonstrate need as defined by Title IV programs.

FINANCIAL AID PROCEDURES
Forms required: FAFSA.
Dates and Deadlines: No deadline. Applicants notified on a rolling basis starting 7/15; must reply within 2 week(s) of notification.

CONTACT
Karen Sanders, Financial Aid Supervisor
5885 Haven Avenue, Rancho Cucamonga, CA 91701-3002
(909) 652-6006

Chapman University
Orange, California
www.chapman.edu   Federal Code: 001164

4-year private university and liberal arts college in very large city, affiliated with Christian Church (Disciples of Christ).
Enrollment: 4,437 undergrads, 4% part-time. 961 full-time freshmen.
Selectivity: Admits 50 to 75% of applicants.

BASIC COSTS (2010-2011)
Tuition and fees: $38,524.
Per-credit charge: $1,170.
Room and board: $12,957.

FINANCIAL AID PICTURE (2008-2009)
Students with need: Out of 858 full-time freshmen who applied for aid, 574 were judged to have need. Of these, 574 received aid, and 574 had their full need met. Average financial aid package met 100% of need; average scholarship/grant was $23,978; average loan was $4,282. For part-time students, average financial aid package was $14,376.
Students without need: 163 full-time freshmen who did not demonstrate need for aid received scholarships/grants; average award was $17,893. No-need awards available for academics, alumni affiliation, art, music/drama, religious affiliation, ROTC.
Cumulative student debt: 64% of graduating class had student loans; average debt was $23,917.

FINANCIAL AID PROCEDURES
Forms required: FAFSA, state aid form.
Dates and Deadlines: Priority date 3/2; no closing date. Applicants notified on a rolling basis starting 3/15; must reply within 3 week(s) of notification.
Transfers: No deadline. Applicants notified on a rolling basis starting 3/15; must reply within 3 week(s) of notification.

CONTACT
Gregory Ball, Director of Financial Aid
One University Drive, Orange, CA 92866
(714) 997-6815

Charles Drew University of Medicine and Science
Los Angeles, California
www.cdrewu.edu

4-year private university and health science college in very large city.
Enrollment: 226 undergrads.
Selectivity: Open admission; but selective for some programs.

BASIC COSTS (2010-2011)
Tuition and fees: $11,402.

FINANCIAL AID PICTURE (2008-2009)
Students with need: 18% of average financial aid package awarded as scholarships/grants, 82% awarded as loans/jobs. Work study available nights, weekends, and for part-time students.

CONTACT
Pierre Flood, Director of Financial Aid
1731 East 120th Street, Los Angeles, CA 90059
(323) 563-4824

Citrus College

Glendora, California
www.citruscollege.edu   Federal Code: 001166

2-year public community college in large town.
Enrollment: 12,769 undergrads.
Selectivity: Open admission.

BASIC COSTS (2009-2010)

Tuition and fees: $814; out-of-state residents $6,484.
Per-credit charge: $26; out-of-state residents $215.

FINANCIAL AID PICTURE (2009-2010)

Students with need: Need-based aid available for full-time and part-time students. Work study available nights, weekends, and for part-time students.

FINANCIAL AID PROCEDURES

Forms required: FAFSA.
Dates and Deadlines: Priority date 3/1; no closing date. Applicants notified on a rolling basis; must reply within 2 week(s) of notification.

CONTACT

Lilia Medina, Director of Financial Aid
1000 West Foothill Boulevard, Glendora, CA 91741-1899
(626) 914-8592

City College of San Francisco

San Francisco, California
www.ccsf.edu   Federal Code: 012874

2-year public community college in very large city.
Enrollment: 25,421 undergrads, 63% part-time. 1,659 full-time freshmen.
Selectivity: Open admission; but selective for some programs.

BASIC COSTS (2009-2010)

Tuition and fees: $802; out-of-state residents $6,172.
Per-credit charge: $26; out-of-state residents $205.
Additional info: Tuition/fee waivers available for unemployed or children of unemployed.

FINANCIAL AID PICTURE

Students with need: Work study available nights, weekends, and for part-time students.
Additional info: Board of Governor fee waiver for low income students.

FINANCIAL AID PROCEDURES

Forms required: FAFSA.
Dates and Deadlines: Priority date 3/1; no closing date. Applicants notified on a rolling basis starting 7/1.

CONTACT

Jorge Bell, Dean, Financial Aid
Office of Admissions and Records E-107, San Francisco, CA 94112
(415) 239-3576

Claremont McKenna College

Claremont, California   Federal Code: 001170
www.claremontmckenna.edu   CSS Code: 4054

4-year private liberal arts college in large town.
Enrollment: 1,210 undergrads. 282 full-time freshmen.
Selectivity: Admits less than 50% of applicants.

BASIC COSTS (2010-2011)

Tuition and fees: $40,230.
Room and board: $13,000.

FINANCIAL AID PICTURE (2009-2010)

Students with need: Need-based aid available for full-time and part-time students. Work study available nights, weekends, and for part-time students.
Students without need: No-need awards available for academics.
Scholarships offered: McKenna Achievement Award: $10,000; based on strong academic record and outstanding leadership and involvement; 9 are awarded, renewable for total of 4 years. The Frank Seaver Leadership Scholarship: full tuition; awarded to students who demonstrate exceptional promise to become leaders intent on making a positive impact in the world; renewable for 4 years. Interdisciplinary Science Scholarship: full tuition for all four years; awarded to students who want to major in science and a non-science.

FINANCIAL AID PROCEDURES

Forms required: FAFSA, CSS PROFILE.
Dates and Deadlines: Closing date 2/1. Applicants notified by 4/1; must reply by 5/1.
Transfers: Closing date 3/2. Applicants notified by 5/15.

CONTACT

Georgette DeVeres, Associate Vice President of Admission & Financial Aid
890 Columbia Avenue, Claremont, CA 91711-6425
(909) 621-8088

Coastline Community College

Fountain Valley, California
www.coastline.edu   Federal Code: 013536

2-year public community college in small city.
Enrollment: 14,011 undergrads.
Selectivity: Open admission.

BASIC COSTS (2009-2010)

Tuition and fees: $806; out-of-state residents $6,506.
Per-credit charge: $26; out-of-state residents $216.
Additional info: Students who attend one of the three main learning centers are required to pay for a parking decal: Fall/Spring semester $10; Summer $5. Tuition/fee waivers available for unemployed or children of unemployed.

FINANCIAL AID PICTURE (2008-2009)

Students with need: Need-based aid available for full-time and part-time students.
Students without need: This college awards aid only to students with need.
Additional info: Board of Governor's Grant: statewide fee waiver program for students or dependents receiving HFOL/TANF, SSI, General Relief, or whose income meets set standards or who are considered eligible through Federal needs analysis.

FINANCIAL AID PROCEDURES

Forms required: FAFSA, institutional form.
Dates and Deadlines: Priority date 3/2; no closing date. Applicants notified on a rolling basis starting 8/1; must reply within 2 week(s) of notification.

CONTACT

Cynthia Pienkowski, Director of Financial Aid
11460 Warner Avenue, Fountain Valley, CA 92708
(714) 241-6239

Cogswell Polytechnical College

Sunnyvale, California
www.cogswell.edu   Federal Code: 001177

4-year private visual arts and engineering and technical college in small city.
Enrollment: 199 undergrads, 43% part-time. 21 full-time freshmen.
Selectivity: Admits over 75% of applicants.

PART III: FINANCIAL AID COLLEGE BY COLLEGE

BASIC COSTS (2010-2011)
Tuition and fees: $18,924.
Per-credit charge: $781.
Room and board: $7,900.

FINANCIAL AID PICTURE (2008-2009)
Students with need: Need-based aid available for full-time and part-time students.
Students without need: No-need awards available for academics.

FINANCIAL AID PROCEDURES
Forms required: FAFSA.
Dates and Deadlines: Priority date 3/2; no closing date. Applicants notified on a rolling basis starting 4/30; must reply within 4 week(s) of notification.
Transfers: No deadline. Applicants notified by 4/1; must reply within 4 week(s) of notification.

CONTACT
Andrew Hagedorn, Director of Financial Aid
1175 Bordeaux Drive, Sunnyvale, CA 94089-1299
(408) 541-0100

College of Marin: Kentfield
Kentfield, California
www.marin.edu   Federal Code: 001178

2-year public community college in small town.
Enrollment: 7,460 undergrads.
Selectivity: Open admission.

BASIC COSTS (2009-2010)
Tuition and fees: $816; out-of-state residents $6,516.
Per-credit charge: $26; out-of-state residents $216.

FINANCIAL AID PICTURE
Students with need: Need-based aid available for full-time and part-time students.
Students without need: This college awards aid only to students with need.

FINANCIAL AID PROCEDURES
Forms required: FAFSA.
Dates and Deadlines: Priority date 3/1; no closing date. Applicants notified on a rolling basis starting 5/15.

CONTACT
David Cook, Director of Financial Aid
835 College Avenue, Kentfield, CA 94904
(415) 457-8811 ext. 7405

College of the Canyons
Santa Clarita, California
www.canyons.edu   Federal Code: 008903

2-year public community college in large city.
Enrollment: 5,040 full-time undergrads. 320 full-time freshmen.
Selectivity: Open admission; but selective for some programs.

BASIC COSTS (2009-2010)
Tuition and fees: $808; out-of-state residents $5,788.
Per-credit charge: $26; out-of-state residents $192.

FINANCIAL AID PICTURE (2008-2009)
Students with need: 70% of average financial aid package awarded as scholarships/grants, 30% awarded as loans/jobs. Need-based aid available for part-time students. Work study available nights, weekends, and for part-time students.

Students without need: No-need awards available for academics, alumni affiliation, art, leadership, minority status, music/drama, state/district residency.

FINANCIAL AID PROCEDURES
Forms required: FAFSA, state aid form.
Dates and Deadlines: Closing date 3/2. Applicants notified on a rolling basis starting 6/1; must reply within 4 week(s) of notification.
Transfers: No deadline.

CONTACT
Thomas Bilbruck, Director, Financial Aid and Scholarships
26455 Rockwell Canyon Road, Santa Clarita, CA 91355
(661) 362-3242

College of the Desert
Palm Desert, California
www.collegeofthedesert.edu   Federal Code: 001182

2-year public community college in small city.
Enrollment: 12,213 undergrads.
Selectivity: Open admission; but selective for some programs.

BASIC COSTS (2009-2010)
Tuition and fees: $810; out-of-state residents $6,000.
Per-credit charge: $26; out-of-state residents $199.
Additional info: Tuition/fee waivers available for adults, minority students, unemployed or children of unemployed.

FINANCIAL AID PICTURE (2008-2009)
Students with need: 93% of average financial aid package awarded as scholarships/grants, 7% awarded as loans/jobs. Need-based aid available for part-time students. Work study available weekends and for part-time students.
Students without need: This college awards aid only to students with need.

FINANCIAL AID PROCEDURES
Forms required: FAFSA.
Dates and Deadlines: Priority date 3/2; no closing date. Applicants notified on a rolling basis starting 7/1.

CONTACT
Heidi Granger, Director of Financial Aid
43-500 Monterey Avenue, Palm Desert, CA 92260
(760) 773-2532

College of the Redwoods
Eureka, California
www.redwoods.edu   Federal Code: 001185

2-year public community college in large town.
Enrollment: 8,614 undergrads, 55% part-time. 1,481 full-time freshmen.
Selectivity: Open admission; but selective for some programs.

BASIC COSTS (2009-2010)
Tuition and fees: $804; out-of-state residents $7,584.
Per-credit charge: $26; out-of-state residents $252.
Room and board: $6,558.

FINANCIAL AID PICTURE (2009-2010)
Students with need: Need-based aid available for full-time and part-time students.

FINANCIAL AID PROCEDURES
Forms required: FAFSA, institutional form.

Dates and Deadlines: Priority date 4/15; no closing date. Applicants notified on a rolling basis starting 5/1; must reply within 6 week(s) of notification.

CONTACT
Lynn Thiesen, Director of Financial Aid
7351 Tompkins Hill Road, Eureka, CA 95501-9300
(707) 476-4182

College of the Sequoias
Visalia, California
www.cos.edu   Federal Code: 001186

2-year public community college in small city.
Enrollment: 6,568 undergrads, 56% part-time. 1,002 full-time freshmen.
Selectivity: Open admission; but selective for some programs.

BASIC COSTS (2009-2010)
Tuition and fees: $841; out-of-state residents $7,531.
Per-credit charge: $26; out-of-state residents $249.

FINANCIAL AID PICTURE (2008-2009)
Students with need: 97% of average financial aid package awarded as scholarships/grants, 3% awarded as loans/jobs.

FINANCIAL AID PROCEDURES
Forms required: FAFSA, institutional form.
Dates and Deadlines: Priority date 3/2; no closing date. Applicants notified on a rolling basis starting 6/1; must reply within 2 week(s) of notification.

CONTACT
Tamara Ravalin, Dean of Student Services
915 South Mooney Boulevard, Visalia, CA 93277
(559) 730-3879

College of the Siskiyous
Weed, California
www.siskiyous.edu   Federal Code: 001187

2-year public community and junior college in small town.
Enrollment: 3,352 undergrads.
Selectivity: Open admission; but selective for some programs.

BASIC COSTS (2009-2010)
Tuition and fees: $810; out-of-state residents $6,780.
Per-credit charge: $26; out-of-state residents $225.
Room and board: $7,984.
Additional info: Oregon residents with interstate exchange program: $42 per unit (no enrollment fee).

FINANCIAL AID PICTURE (2008-2009)
Students with need: Need-based aid available for full-time and part-time students. Work study available nights, weekends, and for part-time students.
Students without need: This college awards aid only to students with need.

FINANCIAL AID PROCEDURES
Forms required: FAFSA.
Dates and Deadlines: Priority date 4/30; no closing date. Applicants notified on a rolling basis starting 6/1; must reply within 2 week(s) of notification.
Transfers: No deadline. Applicants notified on a rolling basis. Academic transcripts required.

CONTACT
Vicki Wrobel, Director of Student Financial Aid & Veterans Services
800 College Avenue, Weed, CA 96094-2899
(530) 938-5209

Columbia College
Sonora, California
www.gocolumbia.edu   Federal Code: 007707

2-year public community college in small town.
Enrollment: 4,302 undergrads.
Selectivity: Open admission.

BASIC COSTS (2009-2010)
Tuition and fees: $826; out-of-state residents $6,526.
Per-credit charge: $26; out-of-state residents $216.

FINANCIAL AID PICTURE (2009-2010)
Students with need: Need-based aid available for full-time and part-time students.
Students without need: No-need awards available for academics.

FINANCIAL AID PROCEDURES
Forms required: FAFSA, state aid form, institutional form.
Dates and Deadlines: Priority date 3/2; no closing date. Applicants notified on a rolling basis starting 6/15; must reply within 2 week(s) of notification.

CONTACT
Marnie Shively, Financial Aid Specialist
11600 Columbia College Drive, Sonora, CA 95370
(209) 588-5105

Concordia University
Irvine, California
www.cui.edu   Federal Code: 013885

4-year private university and liberal arts college in small city, affiliated with Lutheran Church - Missouri Synod.
Enrollment: 1,423 undergrads, 4% part-time. 300 full-time freshmen.
Selectivity: Admits 50 to 75% of applicants.

BASIC COSTS (2010-2011)
Tuition and fees: $26,000.
Per-credit charge: $775.
Room and board: $8,380.

FINANCIAL AID PICTURE (2009-2010)
Students with need: Out of 267 full-time freshmen who applied for aid, 212 were judged to have need. Of these, 212 received aid, and 44 had their full need met. Average financial aid package met 68% of need; average scholarship/grant was $13,075; average loan was $3,356. For part-time students, average financial aid package was $13,204.
Students without need: 67 full-time freshmen who did not demonstrate need for aid received scholarships/grants; average award was $6,895. No-need awards available for academics, athletics, music/drama, religious affiliation.
Scholarships offered: *Merit:* Presidential Honors: up to full tuition; based on 3.9 - 4.0 GPA and 1300 SAT or 29 ACT. Regent: up to $11,500; based on 3.8 - 4.0 GPA. Provost: up to $9,500; based on 3.4 - 3.79 GPA. Dean's: up to $7,000; based on 3.0 - 3.39 GPA. Phi Theta Kappa: up to $5,000; based on 2.50-4.00 GPA. ***Athletic:*** 24 full-time freshmen received athletic scholarships; average amount $12,018.
Cumulative student debt: 68% of graduating class had student loans; average debt was $23,114.

FINANCIAL AID PROCEDURES
Forms required: FAFSA, state aid form.
Dates and Deadlines: Closing date 2/1. Applicants notified on a rolling basis starting 3/15; must reply within 4 week(s) of notification.
Transfers: Applicants notified on a rolling basis starting 3/15; must reply within 4 week(s) of notification.

CONTACT

Lori McDonald, Executive Director, Student Financial Services

1530 Concordia West, Irvine, CA 92612-3203

(949) 854-8002 ext. 1136

Copper Mountain College

Joshua Tree, California

www.cmccd.edu   Federal Code: 035424

2-year public community college in small town.

Enrollment: 2,329 undergrads.

Selectivity: Open admission.

BASIC COSTS (2009-2010)

Tuition and fees: $782; out-of-state residents $6,482.

Per-credit charge: $26; out-of-state residents $216.

FINANCIAL AID PICTURE (2008-2009)

Students with need: Need-based aid available for full-time and part-time students.

FINANCIAL AID PROCEDURES

Forms required: FAFSA.

Dates and Deadlines: Priority date 3/2; no closing date.

CONTACT

Brian Heinemann, Director of Financial Aid

6162 Rotary Way, Joshua Tree, CA 92252

(866) 366-3791 ext. 4235

Crafton Hills College

Yucaipa, California

www.craftonhills.edu   Federal Code: 009272

2-year public community college in large town.

Enrollment: 6,703 undergrads.

Selectivity: Open admission.

BASIC COSTS (2009-2010)

Tuition and fees: $808; out-of-state residents $6,628.

Per-credit charge: $26; out-of-state residents $220.

Additional info: Tuition/fee waivers available for adults, minority students, unemployed or children of unemployed.

FINANCIAL AID PICTURE

Students with need: Need-based aid available for full-time and part-time students. Work study available nights.

Students without need: This college awards aid only to students with need.

FINANCIAL AID PROCEDURES

Forms required: FAFSA, institutional form.

Dates and Deadlines: Priority date 4/15; closing date 6/2. Applicants notified on a rolling basis starting 7/31; must reply within 2 week(s) of notification.

Transfers: Priority date 1/2; closing date 3/2.

CONTACT

John Muskavitch, Director of Financial Aid

11711 Sand Canyon Road, Yucaipa, CA 92399-1799

(909) 794-2161 ext. 3242

Cuyamaca College

El Cajon, California

www.cuyamaca.net   Federal Code: 014435

2-year public community college in small city.

Enrollment: 9,230 undergrads.

Selectivity: Open admission.

BASIC COSTS (2009-2010)

Tuition and fees: $820; out-of-state residents $6,520.

Per-credit charge: $26; out-of-state residents $216.

FINANCIAL AID PICTURE (2008-2009)

Students with need: Work study available nights, weekends, and for part-time students.

FINANCIAL AID PROCEDURES

Forms required: FAFSA.

Dates and Deadlines: Priority date 3/2; no closing date. Applicants notified on a rolling basis; must reply within 2 week(s) of notification.

CONTACT

Ray Reyes, Financial Aid Director

900 Rancho San Diego Parkway, El Cajon, CA 92019-4304

(619) 660-4201

De Anza College

Cupertino, California

www.deanza.edu   Federal Code: 004480

2-year public community college in large town.

Enrollment: 24,000 undergrads.

Selectivity: Open admission; but selective for some programs.

BASIC COSTS (2009-2010)

Tuition and fees: $855; out-of-state residents $6,345.

Per-credit charge: $17; out-of-state residents $139.

FINANCIAL AID PICTURE

Students with need: Need-based aid available for full-time and part-time students.

Students without need: This college awards aid only to students with need.

FINANCIAL AID PROCEDURES

Forms required: FAFSA.

Dates and Deadlines: No deadline. Applicants notified on a rolling basis starting 5/15; must reply within 2 week(s) of notification.

CONTACT

Cindy Castillo, Director of Financial Aid

21250 Stevens Creek Boulevard, Cupertino, CA 95014

(408) 864-8718

Deep Springs College

Dyer, Nevada

www.deepsprings.edu   Federal Code: 015483

2-year private liberal arts college for men in rural community.

Enrollment: 24 undergrads.

Selectivity: Admits less than 50% of applicants.

BASIC COSTS (2009-2010)

Additional info: All students receive full scholarship covering tuition, room, and board valued at $50,000. Tuition at time of enrollment locked for 2 years.

FINANCIAL AID PICTURE (2008-2009)
Students with need: Work study available nights, weekends, and for part-time students.
Students without need: No-need awards available for academics.

FINANCIAL AID PROCEDURES
Dates and Deadlines: No deadline.

CONTACT
David Neidorf, President
Applications Committee, Dyer, NV 89010-9803
(760) 872-2000 ext. 45

DeVry University: Fremont
Fremont, California
www.devry.edu   Federal Code: 008322

4-year for-profit university in small city.
Enrollment: 1,339 undergrads, 44% part-time. 175 full-time freshmen.

BASIC COSTS (2009-2010)
Tuition and fees: $14,800.
Per-credit charge: $575.

FINANCIAL AID PICTURE (2008-2009)
Students with need: Need-based aid available for full-time and part-time students.
Students without need: This college awards aid only to students with need.

FINANCIAL AID PROCEDURES
Forms required: FAFSA.
Dates and Deadlines: No deadline. Applicants notified on a rolling basis.

CONTACT
Kim Kane, Director of Financial Aid
6600 Dumbarton Circle, Fremont, CA 94555-3615
(510) 574-1120

DeVry University: Long Beach
Long Beach, California
www.devry.edu   Federal Code: 023329

4-year for-profit university in large town.
Enrollment: 915 undergrads, 56% part-time. 83 full-time freshmen.

BASIC COSTS (2009-2010)
Tuition and fees: $14,160.
Per-credit charge: $550.

FINANCIAL AID PICTURE (2008-2009)
Students with need: Need-based aid available for full-time and part-time students.
Students without need: This college awards aid only to students with need.

FINANCIAL AID PROCEDURES
Forms required: FAFSA.
Dates and Deadlines: No deadline. Applicants notified on a rolling basis.

CONTACT
Brenda Woods, Associate Director of Student Finance
3880 Kilroy Airport Way, Long Beach, CA 90806
(562) 427-0861

DeVry University: Pomona
Pomona, California
www.devry.edu   Federal Code: 023329

4-year for-profit university in small city.
Enrollment: 2,018 undergrads, 56% part-time. 143 full-time freshmen.

BASIC COSTS (2009-2010)
Tuition and fees: $14,160.
Per-credit charge: $550.

FINANCIAL AID PICTURE (2008-2009)
Students with need: Need-based aid available for full-time and part-time students.
Students without need: This college awards aid only to students with need.

FINANCIAL AID PROCEDURES
Forms required: FAFSA.
Dates and Deadlines: No deadline. Applicants notified on a rolling basis.

CONTACT
Kathy Odom, Director of Financial Aid
901 Corporate Center Drive, Pomona, CA 91768-2642

DeVry University: Sherman Oaks
Sherman Oaks, California
www.devry.edu   Federal Code: 016219

4-year for-profit university in large city.
Enrollment: 728 undergrads, 37% part-time. 96 full-time freshmen.

BASIC COSTS (2009-2010)
Tuition and fees: $14,160.
Per-credit charge: $550.

FINANCIAL AID PICTURE (2008-2009)
Students with need: Need-based aid available for full-time and part-time students.
Students without need: This college awards aid only to students with need.

FINANCIAL AID PROCEDURES
Forms required: FAFSA.
Dates and Deadlines: No deadline. Applicants notified on a rolling basis.

CONTACT
Lou LaSota, Director of Financial Aid
15301 Ventura Boulevard, D-100, Sherman Oaks, CA 91403
(818) 932-3111

Diablo Valley College
Pleasant Hill, California
www.dvc.edu   Federal Code: 001191

2-year public community college in large town.
Enrollment: 9,228 undergrads.
Selectivity: Open admission.

BASIC COSTS (2009-2010)
Tuition and fees: $780; out-of-state residents $6,030.
Per-credit charge: $26; out-of-state residents $201.

FINANCIAL AID PICTURE (2008-2009)
Students with need: 90% of average financial aid package awarded as scholarships/grants, 10% awarded as loans/jobs. Need-based aid available for part-time students.

FINANCIAL AID PROCEDURES

Forms required: FAFSA, state aid form, institutional form.
Dates and Deadlines: Priority date 3/2; closing date 5/1. Applicants notified on a rolling basis starting 6/1; must reply within 2 week(s) of notification.

CONTACT

Brenda Jerez, Financial Aid Director
321 Golf Club Road, Pleasant Hill, CA 94523-1529
(925) 685-1230 ext. 2290

Dominican University of California
San Rafael, California
www.dominican.edu   Federal Code: 001196

4-year private university and liberal arts college in small city.
Enrollment: 1,408 undergrads, 17% part-time. 267 full-time freshmen.
Selectivity: Admits 50 to 75% of applicants.

BASIC COSTS (2009-2010)

Tuition and fees: $33,840.
Per-credit charge: $1,400.
Room and board: $13,150.

FINANCIAL AID PICTURE (2008-2009)

Students with need: Out of 246 full-time freshmen who applied for aid, 217 were judged to have need. Of these, 217 received aid, and 27 had their full need met. Average financial aid package met 67% of need; average scholarship/grant was $20,065; average loan was $3,837. For part-time students, average financial aid package was $6,892.
Students without need: 43 full-time freshmen who did not demonstrate need for aid received scholarships/grants; average award was $11,767. No-need awards available for academics, alumni affiliation, athletics, leadership, minority status, music/drama.
Scholarships offered: 9 full-time freshmen received athletic scholarships; average amount $5,662.
Cumulative student debt: 84% of graduating class had student loans; average debt was $26,176.
Additional info: 4-year guarantee program.

FINANCIAL AID PROCEDURES

Forms required: FAFSA, institutional form.
Dates and Deadlines: Priority date 3/2; no closing date. Applicants notified on a rolling basis starting 3/15; must reply within 2 week(s) of notification.
Transfers: Must reply within 2 week(s) of notification.

CONTACT

Shanon Little, Interim Director of Financial Aid
50 Acacia Avenue, San Rafael, CA 94901-2298
(415) 257-1350

East Los Angeles College
Monterey Park, California
www.elac.edu   Federal Code: 001222

2-year public community college in very large city.
Enrollment: 12,473 undergrads, 66% part-time. 1,059 full-time freshmen.
Selectivity: Open admission; but selective for some programs.

BASIC COSTS (2009-2010)

Tuition and fees: $802; out-of-state residents $6,442.
Per-credit charge: $26; out-of-state residents $214.
Additional info: Tuition/fee waivers available for adults, minority students.

FINANCIAL AID PICTURE (2008-2009)

Students with need: Need-based aid available for full-time and part-time students. Work study available nights, weekends, and for part-time students.

Students without need: This college awards aid only to students with need.
Additional info: Need-based enrollment fee waivers available through a state aid program.

FINANCIAL AID PROCEDURES

Forms required: FAFSA.
Dates and Deadlines: Closing date 3/2.
Transfers: No deadline.

CONTACT

Lindy Fong, Director of Financial Aid
1301 Avenida Cesar Chavez, Monterey Park, CA 91754
(323) 265-8738

El Camino College
Torrance, California
www.elcamino.edu   Federal Code: 001197

2-year public community and junior college in very large city.
Enrollment: 26,398 undergrads.
Selectivity: Open admission.

BASIC COSTS (2009-2010)

Tuition and fees: $815; out-of-state residents $6,515.
Per-credit charge: $26; out-of-state residents $216.
Additional info: Tuition/fee waivers available for adults.

FINANCIAL AID PICTURE (2008-2009)

Students with need: 86% of average financial aid package awarded as scholarships/grants, 14% awarded as loans/jobs. Need-based aid available for part-time students.
Students without need: No-need awards available for academics, art, athletics, leadership, music/drama.
Additional info: Students may apply for Pell grants until June 30.

FINANCIAL AID PROCEDURES

Forms required: FAFSA, institutional form.
Dates and Deadlines: Priority date 3/2; closing date 6/30. Applicants notified on a rolling basis starting 7/15.
Transfers: Outside scholarships must be reported to financial aid office.

CONTACT

Hortense Cooper, Director of Financial Aid
16007 Crenshaw Boulevard, Torrance, CA 90506
(310) 660-3593 ext. 3493

Empire College
Santa Rosa, California
www.empcol.edu   Federal Code: 009032

2-year for-profit business college in small city.
Enrollment: 119 undergrads. 119 full-time freshmen.
Selectivity: Open admission.

BASIC COSTS (2009-2010)

Tuition and fees: $9,000.

FINANCIAL AID PICTURE (2009-2010)

Students with need: Need-based aid available for full-time students.
Students without need: This college awards aid only to students with need.
Scholarships offered: Dean's Scholarship for high school seniors: 10 awarded; range from $250-$1,500. Dean's Scholarships for Empire College students: 7 awarded; range from $250-$1,000. Based on academic achievement, letter of intent, extracurricular activities and letter of recommendation.

FINANCIAL AID PROCEDURES
Forms required: FAFSA.
Dates and Deadlines: No deadline. Applicants notified on a rolling basis.

CONTACT
Mary O'Brien, Financial Aid Officer
3035 Cleveland Avenue, Santa Rosa, CA 95403-2100
(707) 546-4000

Feather River College
Quincy, California
www.frc.edu   Federal Code: 008597

2-year public community and liberal arts college in small town.
Enrollment: 781 undergrads. 307 full-time freshmen.
Selectivity: Open admission.

BASIC COSTS (2009-2010)
Tuition and fees: $859; out-of-state residents $6,559.
Per-credit charge: $26; out-of-state residents $216.
Room and board: $7,824.
Additional info: Tuition/fee waivers available for adults, unemployed or children of unemployed.

FINANCIAL AID PICTURE (2008-2009)
Students with need: 63% of average financial aid package awarded as scholarships/grants, 37% awarded as loans/jobs. Need-based aid available for part-time students. Work study available nights, weekends, and for part-time students.
Students without need: This college awards aid only to students with need.

FINANCIAL AID PROCEDURES
Forms required: FAFSA.
Dates and Deadlines: Priority date 3/2; no closing date. Applicants notified on a rolling basis starting 4/1; must reply within 3 week(s) of notification.

CONTACT
Barbara Cormack, Financial Aid Director
570 Golden Eagle Avenue, Quincy, CA 95971
(530) 283-0202 ext. 283

Foothill College
Los Altos Hills, California
www.foothill.edu   Federal Code: 001199

2-year public community college in large town.
Enrollment: 19,107 undergrads.
Selectivity: Open admission; but selective for some programs.

BASIC COSTS (2009-2010)
Tuition and fees: $808; out-of-state residents $6,298.
Per-credit charge: $17; out-of-state residents $139.

FINANCIAL AID PICTURE
Students with need: Need-based aid available for full-time and part-time students.
Students without need: This college awards aid only to students with need.
Scholarships offered: Chancellor's Scholarship for first-time freshmen who graduate in the top 20 percent of high school class as Chancellor's Scholar; $1,200 for two years.

FINANCIAL AID PROCEDURES
Forms required: FAFSA, institutional form.
Dates and Deadlines: Priority date 3/30; no closing date. Applicants notified on a rolling basis; must reply within 2 week(s) of notification.

Transfers: Application required for CDL grants, March 2 due date for CAL grant application.

CONTACT
Kevin Harral, Director, Financial Aid
12345 El Monte Road, Los Altos Hills, CA 94022
(650) 949-7245

Fremont College
Cerritos, California
www.fremont.edu   Federal Code: 030399

2-year for-profit health science and career college in very large city.
Enrollment: 243 undergrads.
Selectivity: Open admission; but selective for some programs.

BASIC COSTS (2009-2010)
Additional info: Paralegal: $24,200. Sports therapy: $21,800. Massage Therapy: $15,200. Tuition/fee waivers available for unemployed or children of unemployed.

FINANCIAL AID PICTURE (2008-2009)
Students with need: Need-based aid available for full-time students.
Students without need: This college awards aid only to students with need.

FINANCIAL AID PROCEDURES
Forms required: FAFSA, institutional form.

CONTACT
Neeyah Francois, Director of Financial Aid
18000 Studebaker Road, 900A, Cerritos, CA 90703-5342
(562) 809-5100

Fresno City College
Fresno, California
www.fresnocitycollege.edu   Federal Code: 001307

2-year public community and liberal arts college in large city.
Enrollment: 25,574 undergrads.
Selectivity: Open admission; but selective for some programs.

BASIC COSTS (2009-2010)
Tuition and fees: $814; out-of-state residents $6,514.
Per-credit charge: $26; out-of-state residents $216.
Additional info: Tuition/fee waivers available for adults, minority students, unemployed or children of unemployed.

FINANCIAL AID PICTURE (2008-2009)
Students with need: 86% of average financial aid package awarded as scholarships/grants, 14% awarded as loans/jobs. Need-based aid available for part-time students.
Students without need: This college awards aid only to students with need.
Additional info: Board of Governors Grant Program to offset enrollment fees based on untaxed income, low income, or calculated need. Students qualifying for program also automatically exempt from health fees. March 2 application deadline for California grants.

FINANCIAL AID PROCEDURES
Forms required: FAFSA, state aid form.
Dates and Deadlines: Priority date 4/15; closing date 6/30. Applicants notified on a rolling basis starting 4/1.

CONTACT

Frank Ramon, Financial Aid Director
1101 East University Avenue, Fresno, CA 93741
(559) 442-8279

Fresno Pacific University

Fresno, California
www.fresno.edu   Federal Code: 001253

4-year private university and liberal arts college in large city, affiliated with Mennonite Brethren Church.

Enrollment: 1,798 undergrads, 15% part-time. 157 full-time freshmen.
Selectivity: Admits 50 to 75% of applicants.

BASIC COSTS (2009-2010)

Tuition and fees: $23,898.
Per-credit charge: $845.
Room and board: $6,180.

FINANCIAL AID PICTURE (2008-2009)

Students with need: Out of 144 full-time freshmen who applied for aid, 124 were judged to have need. Of these, 123 received aid, and 18 had their full need met. Average financial aid package met 75% of need; average scholarship/grant was $11,984; average loan was $5,921. For part-time students, average financial aid package was $14,570.
Students without need: 2 full-time freshmen who did not demonstrate need for aid received scholarships/grants; average award was $7,846. No-need awards available for academics, athletics, music/drama.
Scholarships offered: *Merit:* Paragon Scholarship; 2 awarded; full tuition; requires 3.65 GPA, demonstrated Christian leadership, SAT 1150 or higher. President's Scholarship; 40 awarded; $6,500-$9,500; requires 3.65 GPA, demonstrated Christian leadership, SAT 1150 or higher. Provost Scholarship; 20 awarded; $4,000-$8,000; for transfer students with 3.5 GPA and demonstrated Christian leadership. SAT scores exclusive of Writing. *Athletic:* 35 full-time freshmen received athletic scholarships; average amount $9,455.
Cumulative student debt: 82% of graduating class had student loans; average debt was $20,416.

FINANCIAL AID PROCEDURES

Forms required: FAFSA, institutional form.
Dates and Deadlines: Priority date 3/2; no closing date. Applicants notified on a rolling basis starting 3/2; must reply by 7/30 or within 3 week(s) of notification.
Transfers: No deadline.

CONTACT

Ken Isaak, Director of Student Financial Services
1717 South Chestnut Avenue, Fresno, CA 93702-4709
(559) 453-2041

Glendale Community College

Glendale, California
www.glendale.edu   Federal Code: 001203

2-year public community college in small city.
Enrollment: 23,449 undergrads. 920 full-time freshmen.
Selectivity: Open admission; but selective for some programs.

BASIC COSTS (2009-2010)

Tuition and fees: $813; out-of-state residents $6,243.
Per-credit charge: $26; out-of-state residents $207.

FINANCIAL AID PICTURE (2008-2009)

Students with need: Need-based aid available for full-time and part-time students. Work study available nights, weekends, and for part-time students.

Students without need: This college awards aid only to students with need.

FINANCIAL AID PROCEDURES

Forms required: FAFSA, institutional form.
Dates and Deadlines: Priority date 4/15; no closing date. Applicants notified on a rolling basis starting 6/15; must reply within 2 week(s) of notification.
Transfers: No deadline.

CONTACT

Patricia Hurley, Director of Financial Aid
1500 North Verdugo Road, Glendale, CA 91208-2809
(818) 240-1000 ext. 5916

Golden Gate University

San Francisco, California
www.ggu.edu   Federal Code: 001205

4-year private university in very large city.
Enrollment: 404 undergrads, 81% part-time. 2 full-time freshmen.
Selectivity: Admits over 75% of applicants.

BASIC COSTS (2010-2011)

Tuition and fees: $17,100.
Per-credit charge: $570.

FINANCIAL AID PICTURE (2009-2010)

Students with need: Need-based aid available for full-time and part-time students. Work study available nights.
Students without need: This college awards aid only to students with need.

FINANCIAL AID PROCEDURES

Forms required: FAFSA, institutional form.
Dates and Deadlines: Priority date 1/2; no closing date. Applicants notified on a rolling basis; must reply within 3 week(s) of notification.
Transfers: Priority date 6/14; no deadline. Applicants notified on a rolling basis starting 1/2; must reply within 3 week(s) of notification.

CONTACT

Louis Riccardi
536 Mission Street, San Francisco, CA 94105-2968
(415) 442-7270

Grossmont College

El Cajon, California
www.grossmont.edu   Federal Code: 001208

2-year public community college in small city.
Enrollment: 20,371 undergrads.
Selectivity: Open admission; but selective for some programs.

BASIC COSTS (2009-2010)

Tuition and fees: $810; out-of-state residents $6,510.
Per-credit charge: $26; out-of-state residents $216.

FINANCIAL AID PICTURE (2008-2009)

Students with need: Need-based aid available for full-time and part-time students. Work study available nights, weekends, and for part-time students.
Students without need: This college awards aid only to students with need.

FINANCIAL AID PROCEDURES

Forms required: FAFSA.
Dates and Deadlines: Closing date 6/30. Applicants notified on a rolling basis starting 7/15; must reply within 2 week(s) of notification.

CONTACT

Michael Copenhaver, Director of Financial Aid
8800 Grossmont College Drive, El Cajon, CA 92020
(619) 644-7129

Harvey Mudd College

Claremont, California
www.hmc.edu

Federal Code: 001171
CSS Code: 4341

4-year private engineering and liberal arts college in small city.
Enrollment: 757 undergrads. 207 full-time freshmen.
Selectivity: Admits less than 50% of applicants.

BASIC COSTS (2010-2011)

Tuition and fees: $40,390.
Room and board: $13,198.
Additional info: Room and board expense covers 16-meal plan.

FINANCIAL AID PICTURE (2009-2010)

Students with need: Out of 150 full-time freshmen who applied for aid, 124 were judged to have need. Of these, 124 received aid, and 124 had their full need met. Average financial aid package met 100% of need; average scholarship/grant was $29,400; average loan was $3,587. Need-based aid available for part-time students.
Students without need: 37 full-time freshmen who did not demonstrate need for aid received scholarships/grants; average award was $9,842. No-need awards available for academics.
Scholarships offered: Harvey S. Mudd Scholarship: for first-time freshmen in science and technology programs; $10,000 annually for 4 years; must maintain minimum 2.75 GPA. Harvey Mudd College-sponsored National Merit Scholarships: from $750 to $2,000 based on need.
Cumulative student debt: 59% of graduating class had student loans; average debt was $16,384.

FINANCIAL AID PROCEDURES

Forms required: FAFSA, CSS PROFILE, state aid form.
Dates and Deadlines: Closing date 2/1. Applicants notified by 4/1; must reply by 5/1 or within 2 week(s) of notification.
Transfers: Closing date 3/2. Applicants notified by 5/15; must reply by 6/10 or within 2 week(s) of notification.

CONTACT

Gilma Lopez, Director of Financial Aid
301 Platt Boulevard, Claremont, CA 91711-5901
(909) 621-8055

Heald College: Concord

Concord, California
www.heald.edu

Federal Code: 030693

2-year for-profit business and technical college in small city.
Enrollment: 1,250 undergrads.
Selectivity: Open admission; but selective for some programs.

BASIC COSTS (2009-2010)

Additional info: Full time students on 2-year plan pay $3,060 per quarter for 4 quarters ($12,240 per year).

FINANCIAL AID PICTURE

Students with need: Need-based aid available for full-time and part-time students. Work study available nights, weekends, and for part-time students.
Students without need: This college awards aid only to students with need.

FINANCIAL AID PROCEDURES

Forms required: FAFSA.
Dates and Deadlines: No deadline. Applicants notified on a rolling basis.

CONTACT

Maria Duenas, Director of Financial Aid
5130 Commercial Circle, Concord, CA 94520
(925) 288-5800

Heald College: Hayward

Hayward, California
www.heald.edu

Federal Code: 008532

2-year for-profit technical and career college in small city.
Enrollment: 953 undergrads.
Selectivity: Open admission.

BASIC COSTS (2009-2010)

Additional info: Full time students on 2-year plan pay $3,060 per quarter for 4 quarters ($12,240 per year).

FINANCIAL AID PICTURE

Students with need: Need-based aid available for full-time and part-time students. Work study available nights, weekends, and for part-time students.
Students without need: This college awards aid only to students with need.

FINANCIAL AID PROCEDURES

Forms required: FAFSA.
Dates and Deadlines: No deadline.

CONTACT

Wylodin Banez, Director of Financial Aid
25500 Industrial Boulevard, Hayward, CA 94545
(510) 783-2100

Heald College: Rancho Cordova

Rancho Cordova, California
www.heald.edu

Federal Code: 025931

2-year for-profit technical college in large city.
Enrollment: 850 undergrads.

BASIC COSTS (2009-2010)

Additional info: Full time students on 2-year plan pay $3,060 per quarter for 4 quarters ($12,240 per year).

FINANCIAL AID PICTURE

Students with need: Need-based aid available for full-time and part-time students. Work study available nights, weekends, and for part-time students.
Students without need: This college awards aid only to students with need.

FINANCIAL AID PROCEDURES

Forms required: FAFSA.
Dates and Deadlines: No deadline.

CONTACT

James Wilson, Director of Financial Aid
2910 Prospect Park Drive, Rancho Cordova, CA 95670
(916) 414-2700

Heald College: Roseville
Roseville, California
www.heald.edu

2-year for-profit career college in small city.
Enrollment: 1,020 undergrads.
Selectivity: Open admission.

BASIC COSTS (2010-2011)
Additional info: Students completing program in 6 quarters are charged $4,080 per quarter. Students completing program longer than 6 quarters are charged $3,060 per quarter.

FINANCIAL AID PICTURE
Students with need: Need-based aid available for full-time and part-time students. Work study available nights, weekends, and for part-time students.
Students without need: This college awards aid only to students with need.

FINANCIAL AID PROCEDURES
Forms required: FAFSA.
Dates and Deadlines: No deadline.

CONTACT
Rhonda Shaw, Director of Financial Aid
7 Sierra Gate Plaza, Roseville, CA 95678
(916) 789-8600

Heald College: Salinas
Salinas, California
www.heald.edu   Federal Code: 030340

2-year for-profit business college in small city.
Enrollment: 1,000 undergrads.

BASIC COSTS (2010-2011)
Additional info: Full-time students on a 2-year plan pay $4,080 per quarter for 4 quarters ($16,320 per year).

FINANCIAL AID PICTURE
Students with need: Need-based aid available for full-time and part-time students. Work study available nights, weekends, and for part-time students.
Students without need: This college awards aid only to students with need.

FINANCIAL AID PROCEDURES
Forms required: FAFSA.
Dates and Deadlines: No deadline.

CONTACT
Heloise Mata, Director of Financial Aid
1450 North Main Street, Salinas, CA 93906
(831) 443-1700

Heald College: San Francisco
San Francisco, California
www.heald.edu   Federal Code: 007234

2-year for-profit business college in very large city.
Enrollment: 800 undergrads.

BASIC COSTS (2009-2010)
Additional info: Full time students on 2-year plan pay $3,060 per quarter for 4 quarters ($12,240 per year).

FINANCIAL AID PICTURE
Students with need: Need-based aid available for full-time and part-time students. Work study available nights, weekends, and for part-time students.
Students without need: This college awards aid only to students with need.

FINANCIAL AID PROCEDURES
Forms required: FAFSA.
Dates and Deadlines: No deadline.

CONTACT
Judy Bacchus, Director of Financial Aid
350 Mission Street, San Francisco, CA 94105
(415) 808-3000

Heald College: San Jose
Milpitas, California
www.heald.edu   Federal Code: 025932

2-year for-profit business college in very large city.
Enrollment: 1,119 undergrads.

BASIC COSTS (2009-2010)
Additional info: Full time students on 2-year plan pay $3,060 per quarter for 4 quarters ($12,240 per year).

FINANCIAL AID PICTURE
Students with need: Need-based aid available for full-time and part-time students. Work study available nights, weekends, and for part-time students.
Students without need: This college awards aid only to students with need.

FINANCIAL AID PROCEDURES
Forms required: FAFSA.
Dates and Deadlines: No deadline. Applicants notified on a rolling basis starting 6/15; must reply within 2 week(s) of notification.

CONTACT
Lidia Hurtado, Director of Financial Aid
341 Great Mall Parkway, Milpitas, CA 95035
(408) 934-4900

Heald College: Stockton
Stockton, California
www.heald.edu   Federal Code: 025933

2-year for-profit career college in large city.
Enrollment: 913 undergrads.
Selectivity: Open admission.

BASIC COSTS (2009-2010)
Additional info: Full time students on 2-year plan pay $3,060 per quarter for 4 quarters ($12,240 per year).

FINANCIAL AID PICTURE
Students with need: Need-based aid available for full-time students.

FINANCIAL AID PROCEDURES
Forms required: FAFSA.
Dates and Deadlines: No deadline.

CONTACT
Valerie Edwards-Bendy, Director of Financial Aid
1605 East March Lane, Stockton, CA 95210
(209) 473-5200

Holy Names University
Oakland, California
www.hnu.edu   Federal Code: 001183

4-year private university in large city, affiliated with Roman Catholic Church.
Enrollment: 578 undergrads; 26% part-time. 103 full-time freshmen.
Selectivity: Admits over 75% of applicants.

BASIC COSTS (2010-2011)
Tuition and fees: $28,350.
Room and board: $9,780.

FINANCIAL AID PICTURE (2008-2009)
Students with need: Need-based aid available for full-time and part-time
students.
Students without need: No-need awards available for academics, athletics,
leadership, music/drama, religious affiliation.
Scholarships offered: Aspiring Leadership Grant: $5,500 annually; based on
2.70-2.99 GPA. Honors Scholarship: $8,500 annually; based on 3.00-3.29
GPA. Dean's Scholarship: $9,500 annually; based on 3.30-3.49 GPA. Presi-
dent's Scholarship: $11,000 annually; based on 3.50-3.74 GPA. Regent's
Scholarship: $12,000 annually; based on 3.75+ GPA. Durocher Scholarship:
full tuition; campus residency required; based on evidence of leadership, contributions to school and/or community and academic achievement, minimum
GPA 3.75, minimum SAT 1100 (exclusive of Writing); 1 awarded per year.

FINANCIAL AID PROCEDURES
Forms required: FAFSA, state aid form.
Dates and Deadlines: Priority date 3/2; closing date 6/30. Applicants notified
on a rolling basis starting 9/1; must reply by 5/1 or within 2 week(s) of notification.
Transfers: Applicants notified on a rolling basis starting 9/1; must reply by
5/1 or within 2 week(s) of notification.

CONTACT
Murad Dibbini, Dean of Enrollment Services
3500 Mountain Boulevard, Oakland, CA 94619-1699
(510) 436-1327

Hope International University
Fullerton, California
www.hiu.edu   Federal Code: 001252

4-year private university and liberal arts college in small city, affiliated with
Independent Christian Churches and Churches of Christ.
Enrollment: 690 undergrads.
Selectivity: Admits less than 50% of applicants.

BASIC COSTS (2010-2011)
Tuition and fees: $23,190.
Per-credit charge: $850.
Room and board: $7,400.

FINANCIAL AID PICTURE (2009-2010)
Students with need: Need-based aid available for full-time and part-time
students. Work study available nights, weekends, and for part-time students.
Students without need: No-need awards available for academics, job skills,
leadership, music/drama, state/district residency.

FINANCIAL AID PROCEDURES
Forms required: FAFSA, institutional form.
Dates and Deadlines: Closing date 3/2. Applicants notified on a rolling basis
starting 3/15; must reply within 2 week(s) of notification.
Transfers: Priority date 3/2; no deadline. Applicants notified on a rolling basis
starting 4/1; must reply within 2 week(s) of notification.

CONTACT
Shannon O'Shields, Director of Student Financial Aid
2500 East Nutwood Avenue, Fullerton, CA 92831-3199
(714) 879-3901 ext. 2232

Humboldt State University
Arcata, California
www.humboldt.edu   Federal Code: 001149

4-year public university and liberal arts college in large town.
Enrollment: 7,093 undergrads, 9% part-time. 1,168 full-time freshmen.
Selectivity: Admits over 75% of applicants.

BASIC COSTS (2009-2010)
Tuition and fees: $5,166; out-of-state residents $16,326.
Room and board: $9,510.

FINANCIAL AID PICTURE (2008-2009)
Students with need: Out of 942 full-time freshmen who applied for aid, 649
were judged to have need. Of these, 592 received aid, and 32 had their full
need met. Average financial aid package met 71% of need; average scholar-
ship/grant was $4,630; average loan was $295. For part-time students, average financial aid package was $7,277.
Students without need: 11 full-time freshmen who did not demonstrate
need for aid received scholarships/grants; average award was $1,668. No-
need awards available for academics, athletics.
Scholarships offered: 20 full-time freshmen received athletic scholarships;
average amount $2,664.
Cumulative student debt: 47% of graduating class had student loans; average debt was $17,302.

FINANCIAL AID PROCEDURES
Forms required: FAFSA.
Dates and Deadlines: Priority date 3/2; no closing date. Applicants notified
on a rolling basis starting 4/15; must reply within 6 week(s) of notification.
Transfers: Need is most salient factor for some programs.

CONTACT
Kim Coughlin-Lamphear, Director of Financial Aid
One Harpst Street, Arcata, CA 95521-8299
(707) 826-4321

Humphreys College
Stockton, California
www.humphreys.edu   Federal Code: 001212

4-year private business and liberal arts college in large city.
Enrollment: 718 undergrads.
Selectivity: Open admission.

BASIC COSTS (2009-2010)
Tuition and fees: $9,648.
Per-credit charge: $268.
Room only: $6,282.
Additional info: School-controlled apartment housing cost quoted, not in-
cluding utilities.

FINANCIAL AID PICTURE (2009-2010)
Students with need: Need-based aid available for full-time and part-time
students. Work study available nights, weekends, and for part-time students.
Students without need: No-need awards available for academics, state/dis-
trict residency.

FINANCIAL AID PROCEDURES
Forms required: FAFSA.

Dates and Deadlines: Closing date 6/30. Applicants notified on a rolling basis; must reply within 2 week(s) of notification.

CONTACT

Judi Lafeber, Director of Financial Aid
6650 Inglewood Avenue, Stockton, CA 95207-3896
(209) 478-0800 ext. 3

Imperial Valley College

Imperial, California
www.imperial.edu   Federal Code: 001214

2-year public community college in large town.
Enrollment: 3,866 full-time undergrads.
Selectivity: Open admission; but selective for some programs.

BASIC COSTS (2009-2010)
Tuition and fees: $810; out-of-state residents $6,510.
Per-credit charge: $26; out-of-state residents $216.

FINANCIAL AID PICTURE (2008-2009)
Students with need: 95% of average financial aid package awarded as scholarships/grants, 5% awarded as loans/jobs. Need-based aid available for part-time students.

FINANCIAL AID PROCEDURES
Forms required: FAFSA.
Dates and Deadlines: Priority date 3/2; closing date 6/30. Applicants notified on a rolling basis.
Transfers: Closing date 3/2. Academic transcripts from previous institutions required.

CONTACT

Janis Magno, Dean of Financial Aid & State Programs
Box 158, Imperial, CA 92251-0158
(760) 355-6266

Irvine Valley College

Irvine, California
www.ivc.edu   Federal Code: 025395

2-year public community college in small city.
Enrollment: 15,710 undergrads.
Selectivity: Open admission.

BASIC COSTS (2009-2010)
Tuition and fees: $814; out-of-state residents $6,514.
Per-credit charge: $26; out-of-state residents $216.
Additional info: Tuition/fee waivers available for minority students.

FINANCIAL AID PICTURE (2008-2009)
Students with need: Need-based aid available for full-time and part-time students. Work study available nights.
Students without need: This college awards aid only to students with need.

FINANCIAL AID PROCEDURES
Forms required: FAFSA, state aid form, institutional form.
Dates and Deadlines: No deadline. Applicants notified on a rolling basis starting 4/30.

CONTACT

Darryl Cox, Director of Financial Aid
5500 Irvine Center Drive, Irvine, CA 92618-4399
(949) 451-5287

John F. Kennedy University

Pleasant Hill, California
www.jfku.edu   Federal Code: 004484

Upper-division private university in large town.
Enrollment: 280 undergrads.
Selectivity: Open admission; but selective for some programs.

BASIC COSTS (2010-2011)
Tuition and fees: $17,232.
Per-credit charge: $380.

FINANCIAL AID PICTURE (2008-2009)
Students with need: Need-based aid available for full-time and part-time students.
Students without need: This college awards aid only to students with need.

FINANCIAL AID PROCEDURES
Forms required: FAFSA, institutional form.
Dates and Deadlines: Priority date 3/2; no closing date. Applicants notified on a rolling basis; must reply within 4 week(s) of notification.
Transfers: Priority date 4/1.

CONTACT

Mindy Bergeron, Director of Financial Aid
100 Ellinwood Way, Pleasant Hill, CA 94523-4817
(925) 969-3385

Kaplan College: Panorama City

Panorama City, California
www.panorama-city.kaplancollege.com/ Federal Code: 030445

2-year for-profit junior and technical college in very large city.
Enrollment: 45 undergrads.
Selectivity: Open admission.

BASIC COSTS (2009-2010)
Additional info: Tuition varies by program from $13,090 (fees $45) to $30,205 (fees $45).

FINANCIAL AID PICTURE
Students with need: Need-based aid available for full-time students. Work study available nights.
Students without need: This college awards aid only to students with need.

FINANCIAL AID PROCEDURES
Forms required: FAFSA, institutional form.
Dates and Deadlines: No deadline.
Transfers: No deadline.

CONTACT

Cynthia Arevalo
14355 Roscoe Boulevard, Panorama City, CA 91402
(818) 672-8907

The King's College and Seminary

Van Nuys, California
www.kingsseminary.edu

4-year private Bible and seminary college in very large city, affiliated with non-denominational tradition.
Enrollment: 473 undergrads.
Selectivity: Admits over 75% of applicants.

BASIC COSTS (2010-2011)
Tuition and fees: $9,150.
Per-credit charge: $195.
Additional info: Tuition/fee waivers available for adults.

FINANCIAL AID PICTURE
Students with need: Need-based aid available for full-time and part-time students. Work study available nights, weekends, and for part-time students.
Students without need: No-need awards available for academics.
Additional info: Specific scholarships may require specific essays.

FINANCIAL AID PROCEDURES
Forms required: FAFSA.
Dates and Deadlines: No deadline. Applicants notified on a rolling basis; must reply within 4 week(s) of notification.

CONTACT
Norman Stoppenbrink, Financial Aid Director
14800 Sherman Way, Van Nuys, CA 91405-2233
(818) 779-8040

La Sierra University
Riverside, California
www.lasierra.edu   Federal Code: 001215

4-year private university in large city, affiliated with Seventh-day Adventists.
Enrollment: 1,455 undergrads, 11% part-time. 302 full-time freshmen.
Selectivity: Admits 50 to 75% of applicants.

BASIC COSTS (2009-2010)
Tuition and fees: $24,573.
Per-credit charge: $660.
Room and board: $6,990.

FINANCIAL AID PICTURE (2008-2009)
Students with need: Out of 258 full-time freshmen who applied for aid, 212 were judged to have need. Of these, 210 received aid, and 42 had their full need met. Average financial aid package met 70% of need; average scholarship/grant was $16,872; average loan was $3,392. For part-time students, average financial aid package was $7,277.
Students without need: 88 full-time freshmen who did not demonstrate need for aid received scholarships/grants; average award was $10,352. No-need awards available for academics, leadership, music/drama, religious affiliation.
Cumulative student debt: 73% of graduating class had student loans; average debt was $36,946.

FINANCIAL AID PROCEDURES
Forms required: FAFSA, state aid form.
Dates and Deadlines: Priority date 3/2; no closing date. Applicants notified on a rolling basis starting 4/15; must reply by 9/1.
Transfers: No deadline. Applicants notified on a rolling basis.

CONTACT
Esther Kinzer, Director of Student Financial Services
4500 Riverwalk Parkway, Riverside, CA 92515-8247
(951) 785-2175

Laney College
Oakland, California
www.laney.peralta.edu   Federal Code: 001266

2-year public community college in large city.
Enrollment: 14,541 undergrads.
Selectivity: Open admission.

BASIC COSTS (2009-2010)
Tuition and fees: $814; out-of-state residents $6,514.
Per-credit charge: $26; out-of-state residents $216.
Additional info: Tuition/fee waivers available for unemployed or children of unemployed.

FINANCIAL AID PICTURE (2008-2009)
Students with need: 96% of average financial aid package awarded as scholarships/grants, 4% awarded as loans/jobs.

FINANCIAL AID PROCEDURES
Forms required: FAFSA, institutional form.
Dates and Deadlines: Priority date 4/1; no closing date. Applicants notified on a rolling basis; must reply within 2 week(s) of notification.

CONTACT
Judith Cohen, Financial Aid Director
900 Fallon Street, Oakland, CA 94607
(510) 464-3414

Las Positas College
Livermore, California
www.laspositascollege.edu   Federal Code: 030357

2-year public community college in small city.
Enrollment: 9,691 undergrads.
Selectivity: Open admission.

BASIC COSTS (2009-2010)
Tuition and fees: $810; out-of-state residents $6,510.
Per-credit charge: $26; out-of-state residents $216.
Additional info: Tuition/fee waivers available for unemployed or children of unemployed.

FINANCIAL AID PICTURE (2008-2009)
Students with need: Need-based aid available for full-time students.

FINANCIAL AID PROCEDURES
Forms required: institutional form.
Dates and Deadlines: Priority date 5/1; no closing date. Applicants notified on a rolling basis starting 7/1; must reply within 2 week(s) of notification.

CONTACT
Andi Schreibman, Financial Aid Officer
3033 Collier Canyon Road, Livermore, CA 94551
(925) 424-1580

Life Pacific College
San Dimas, California
www.lifepacific.edu   Federal Code: 016029

4-year private Bible college in large town, affiliated with Christian - The Foursquare Church.
Enrollment: 400 undergrads. 6 full-time freshmen.
Selectivity: Open admission; but selective for some programs.

BASIC COSTS (2010-2011)
Tuition and fees: $12,250.
Per-credit charge: $400.
Room and board: $6,000.

FINANCIAL AID PICTURE (2008-2009)
Students with need: Out of 6 full-time freshmen who applied for aid, 6 were judged to have need. Of these, 6 received aid. Average financial aid package met 7% of need; average scholarship/grant was $1,080; average loan was $2,143. For part-time students, average financial aid package was $3,976.

Students without need: No-need awards available for academics, alumni affiliation.

FINANCIAL AID PROCEDURES

Forms required: FAFSA.

Dates and Deadlines: No deadline. Applicants notified on a rolling basis starting 6/1.

CONTACT

Becky Huyck, Director of Financial Aid
Attn: Admissions, San Dimas, CA 91773
(909) 599-5433 ext. 325

Lincoln University
Oakland, California
www.lincolnuca.edu   Federal Code: 006975

4-year private university and business college in very large city.

Enrollment: 83 undergrads, 28% part-time. 7 full-time freshmen.

Selectivity: Admits 50 to 75% of applicants.

BASIC COSTS (2009-2010)

Tuition and fees: $8,920.

Per-credit charge: $335.

Additional info: Tuition for Intensive English program $2,860 per 16 weeks.

FINANCIAL AID PICTURE (2008-2009)

Students with need: Out of 7 full-time freshmen who applied for aid, 7 were judged to have need. Of these, 7 received aid, and 7 had their full need met. Average financial aid package met 100% of need; average scholarship/grant was $5,350; average loan was $3,720. For part-time students, average financial aid package was $9,500.

Students without need: This college awards aid only to students with need.

Cumulative student debt: 90% of graduating class had student loans; average debt was $16,400.

FINANCIAL AID PROCEDURES

Forms required: FAFSA.

Dates and Deadlines: Priority date 3/22; closing date 8/22. Applicants notified by 12/1; must reply by 1/2.

Transfers: Applicants notified by 12/1; must reply by 1/1.

CONTACT

James Peterson, Chief Financial Aid Director
401 15th Street, Oakland, CA 94612
(510) 628-8023

Loma Linda University
Loma Linda, California
www.llu.edu   Federal Code: 001218

3-year private university and health science college in large town, affiliated with Seventh-day Adventists.

Enrollment: 1,054 undergrads, 12% part-time.

BASIC COSTS (2009-2010)

Tuition and fees: $25,164.

Per-credit charge: $525.

Room only: $2,520.

Additional info: Tuition quoted for nursing program. Full-time tuition for dental hygiene program: $23,833 plus $1,590 fees. For allied health program $450/credit hour; for certificate programs, $338/credit. Application fee may vary by program; tuition may vary by grade level in program.

FINANCIAL AID PICTURE (2008-2009)

Students with need: Need-based aid available for full-time and part-time students.

FINANCIAL AID PROCEDURES

Forms required: FAFSA.

Transfers: Priority date 3/2; no deadline. Applicants notified on a rolling basis starting 4/1; must reply within 4 week(s) of notification.

CONTACT

Verdell Schaefer, Director of Financial Aid
Admissions Processing, Loma Linda, CA 92350
(909) 558-4509

Long Beach City College
Long Beach, California
www.lbcc.edu   Federal Code: 001219

2-year public community college in large city.

Enrollment: 31,275 undergrads.

Selectivity: Open admission.

BASIC COSTS (2009-2010)

Tuition and fees: $808; out-of-state residents $6,508.

Per-credit charge: $26; out-of-state residents $216.

FINANCIAL AID PICTURE

Students with need: Need-based aid available for full-time and part-time students.

Students without need: This college awards aid only to students with need.

FINANCIAL AID PROCEDURES

Forms required: FAFSA, institutional form.

Dates and Deadlines: Priority date 5/6; no closing date. Applicants notified on a rolling basis starting 7/6; must reply within 2 week(s) of notification.

CONTACT

Mike MacCallum, Director of Financial Aid and Veterans Affairs
4901 East Carson Street, Long Beach, CA 00000
(562) 938-4257

Los Angeles City College
Los Angeles, California
www.lacitycollege.edu   Federal Code: 001223

2-year public community college in very large city.

Enrollment: 17,636 undergrads.

Selectivity: Open admission.

BASIC COSTS (2009-2010)

Tuition and fees: $802; out-of-state residents $6,442.

Per-credit charge: $26; out-of-state residents $214.

FINANCIAL AID PICTURE (2008-2009)

Students with need: Need-based aid available for full-time and part-time students.

Students without need: This college awards aid only to students with need.

Additional info: Fee waivers available for public assistance and Social Security insurance recipients; fee credits available for low income families.

FINANCIAL AID PROCEDURES

Forms required: FAFSA.

Dates and Deadlines: Priority date 3/2; no closing date. Applicants notified on a rolling basis starting 7/6; must reply within 2 week(s) of notification.

Transfers: No deadline. Applicants notified by 7/1.

CONTACT

Jeremy Villar, Dean of Student Services

855 North Vermont Avenue, Los Angeles, CA 90029-3589

(323) 953-4000 ext. 2025

Los Angeles Harbor College

Wilmington, California

www.lahc.edu   Federal Code: 001224

2-year public community college in small city.

Enrollment: 10,626 undergrads.

Selectivity: Open admission.

BASIC COSTS (2009-2010)

Tuition and fees: $802; out-of-state residents $6,442.

Per-credit charge: $26; out-of-state residents $214.

Additional info: Tuition at time of enrollment locked for 2 years.

FINANCIAL AID PICTURE (2009-2010)

Students with need: 4% of average financial aid package awarded as scholarships/grants, 96% awarded as loans/jobs. Need-based aid available for part-time students. Work study available nights, weekends, and for part-time students.

Students without need: This college awards aid only to students with need.

FINANCIAL AID PROCEDURES

Forms required: FAFSA, institutional form.

Dates and Deadlines: Priority date 3/2; no closing date. Applicants notified on a rolling basis; must reply within 2 week(s) of notification.

Transfers: Closing date 5/15.

CONTACT

Sheila Millman, Financial Aid Manager

1111 Figueroa Place, Wilmington, CA 90744-2397

(310) 233-4320

Los Angeles Pierce College

Woodland Hills, California

www.piercecollege.edu   Federal Code: 001226

2-year public community college in very large city.

Enrollment: 22,133 undergrads.

Selectivity: Open admission; but selective for some programs.

BASIC COSTS (2009-2010)

Tuition and fees: $802; out-of-state residents $6,442.

Per-credit charge: $26; out-of-state residents $214.

Additional info: International Students are charged additional fees: $35 Application Fee + $25 SEVIS Processing Fee.

FINANCIAL AID PICTURE (2009-2010)

Students with need: Need-based aid available for full-time and part-time students. Work study available nights, weekends, and for part-time students.

Students without need: This college awards aid only to students with need.

FINANCIAL AID PROCEDURES

Forms required: FAFSA, institutional form.

Dates and Deadlines: Priority date 3/2; no closing date. Applicants notified on a rolling basis starting 8/1.

CONTACT

Anafe Robinson, Director of Financial Aid, Scholarships & Veterans

6201 Winnetka Avenue, Woodland Hills, CA 91371

(818) 719-6428

Los Angeles Southwest College

Los Angeles, California

www.lasc.edu   Federal Code: 007047

2-year public community college in very large city.

Enrollment: 7,585 undergrads.

Selectivity: Open admission; but selective for some programs.

BASIC COSTS (2009-2010)

Tuition and fees: $802; out-of-state residents $6,442.

Per-credit charge: $26; out-of-state residents $214.

FINANCIAL AID PICTURE

Students with need: Need-based aid available for full-time and part-time students.

Additional info: Board of Governors Enrollment Fee Waiver available to students receiving AFDC, SSI/SSP, or General Assistance. May also qualify on basis of income.

FINANCIAL AID PROCEDURES

Forms required: FAFSA.

Dates and Deadlines: No deadline. Applicants notified on a rolling basis; must reply within 2 week(s) of notification.

CONTACT

Oscar Cobian, Dean, TRIO Programs

1600 West Imperial Highway, Los Angeles, CA 90047-4899

(323) 241-5328

Los Angeles Trade and Technical College

Los Angeles, California

www.lattc.edu   Federal Code: 001227

2-year public community and technical college in very large city.

Enrollment: 15,477 undergrads.

Selectivity: Open admission.

BASIC COSTS (2009-2010)

Tuition and fees: $802; out-of-state residents $6,442.

Per-credit charge: $26; out-of-state residents $214.

FINANCIAL AID PICTURE

Students with need: Need-based aid available for full-time and part-time students. Work study available nights, weekends, and for part-time students.

Students without need: This college awards aid only to students with need.

FINANCIAL AID PROCEDURES

Forms required: FAFSA.

Dates and Deadlines: Priority date 5/1; no closing date. Applicants notified on a rolling basis.

Transfers: No deadline.

CONTACT

Leann Roque, Financial Aid Manager

400 West Washington Boulevard, Los Angeles, CA 90015-4181

(213) 744-9016

Los Angeles Valley College

Valley Glen, California

www.lavc.edu   Federal Code: 001228

2-year public community college in very large city.

Enrollment: 19,619 undergrads.

Selectivity: Open admission; but selective for some programs.

BASIC COSTS (2009-2010)

Tuition and fees: $804; out-of-state residents $6,444.

Per-credit charge: $26; out-of-state residents $214.

FINANCIAL AID PICTURE (2009-2010)

Students with need: Need-based aid available for full-time and part-time students.

Students without need: This college awards aid only to students with need.

FINANCIAL AID PROCEDURES

Forms required: FAFSA.

Dates and Deadlines: Priority date 3/2; closing date 5/1. Applicants notified on a rolling basis.

CONTACT

Barbara Ralston, Associate Dean of Financial Aid

5800 Fulton Avenue, Valley Glen, CA 91401-4096

(818) 947-2412

Loyola Marymount University

Los Angeles, California   Federal Code: 001234

www.lmu.edu   CSS Code: 4403

4-year private university in very large city, affiliated with Roman Catholic Church.

Enrollment: 5,667 undergrads, 3% part-time. 1,261 full-time freshmen.

Selectivity: Admits 50 to 75% of applicants.

BASIC COSTS (2010-2011)

Tuition and fees: $36,404.

Per-credit charge: $1,490.

Room and board: $13,930.

FINANCIAL AID PICTURE (2008-2009)

Students with need: Out of 952 full-time freshmen who applied for aid, 693 were judged to have need. Of these, 690 received aid, and 259 had their full need met. Average financial aid package met 82% of need; average scholarship/grant was $20,562; average loan was $5,217. For part-time students, average financial aid package was $11,545.

Students without need: 150 full-time freshmen who did not demonstrate need for aid received scholarships/grants; average award was $12,527. No-need awards available for academics, alumni affiliation, art, athletics, music/drama, religious affiliation, ROTC.

Scholarships offered: 48 full-time freshmen received athletic scholarships; average amount $22,493.

Cumulative student debt: 61% of graduating class had student loans; average debt was $28,596.

FINANCIAL AID PROCEDURES

Forms required: FAFSA, CSS PROFILE.

Dates and Deadlines: Priority date 2/1; closing date 5/15. Applicants notified on a rolling basis starting 3/15; must reply by 5/1 or within 4 week(s) of notification.

CONTACT

Catherine Graham, Director of Financial Aid

Admissions, One LMU Drive, Los Angeles, CA 90045-8350

(310) 338-2700

Marymount College

Rancho Palos Verdes, California

www.marymountpv.edu   Federal Code: 010474

2-year private junior and liberal arts college in large town, affiliated with Roman Catholic Church.

Enrollment: 561 undergrads, 1% part-time. 298 full-time freshmen.

Selectivity: Admits 50 to 75% of applicants.

BASIC COSTS (2010-2011)

Tuition and fees: $25,474.

Per-credit charge: $950.

Room and board: $11,078.

FINANCIAL AID PICTURE (2009-2010)

Students with need: 71% of average financial aid package awarded as scholarships/grants, 29% awarded as loans/jobs.

Students without need: No-need awards available for academics.

Scholarships offered: President's Scholarship: $8,000; Academic GPA: 3.30 and above; SAT 1530 or ACT 22. Dean's Scholarship: $6,000; Academic GPA 3.00-3.29; SAT 1410 or ACT 20. Achievement Scholarship: $4,500; Academic GPA 2.80-2.99; SAT 1210 or ACT 17. Deadline May 1. All admitted students considered. Renewable for one additional, consecutive year.

FINANCIAL AID PROCEDURES

Forms required: FAFSA.

Dates and Deadlines: Priority date 3/1; no closing date. Applicants notified on a rolling basis starting 2/1; must reply by 5/1 or within 4 week(s) of notification.

CONTACT

Barbara Layne, Director of Financial Aid

30800 Palos Verdes Drive East, Rancho Palos Verdes, CA 90275-6299

(310) 303-7282

The Master's College

Santa Clarita, California

www.masters.edu   Federal Code: 001220

4-year private liberal arts and seminary college in small city, affiliated with Christian, Protestant, Conservative Evangelical.

Enrollment: 986 undergrads, 11% part-time. 177 full-time freshmen.

Selectivity: Admits over 75% of applicants.

BASIC COSTS (2010-2011)

Tuition and fees: $25,640.

Per-credit charge: $1,055.

Room and board: $8,320.

FINANCIAL AID PICTURE (2008-2009)

Students with need: Need-based aid available for full-time and part-time students. Work study available nights, weekends, and for part-time students.

Students without need: No-need awards available for academics, alumni affiliation, art, athletics, leadership, music/drama.

FINANCIAL AID PROCEDURES

Forms required: FAFSA, state aid form, institutional form.

Dates and Deadlines: Priority date 3/2; no closing date. Applicants notified on a rolling basis starting 2/18; must reply by 5/1 or within 2 week(s) of notification.

Transfers: Closing date 3/2.

CONTACT

Gary Edwards, Director of Financial Aid

21726 Placerita Canyon Road, Santa Clarita, CA 91321-1200

(661) 259-3540 ext. 3391

Mendocino College

Ukiah, California

www.mendocino.edu   Federal Code: 011672

2-year public community college in large town.

Enrollment: 2,358 undergrads, 57% part-time. 270 full-time freshmen.

Selectivity: Open admission.

BASIC COSTS (2009-2010)

Tuition and fees: $800; out-of-state residents $6,500.

Per-credit charge: $26; out-of-state residents $216.

Additional info: Tuition/fee waivers available for unemployed or children of unemployed.

FINANCIAL AID PICTURE (2008-2009)

Students with need: Out of 178 full-time freshmen who applied for aid, 178 were judged to have need. Of these, 178 received aid. Average financial aid package met 100% of need; average scholarship/grant was $1,735; average loan was $1,678. For part-time students, average financial aid package was $532.

Students without need: No-need awards available for academics, leadership, music/drama, state/district residency.

FINANCIAL AID PROCEDURES

Forms required: FAFSA.

Dates and Deadlines: Priority date 5/31; no closing date. Applicants notified on a rolling basis starting 7/1; must reply within 2 week(s) of notification.

CONTACT

Jacqueline Bradley, Director of Financial Aid

1000 Hensley Creek/Box 3000, Ukiah, CA 95482

(707) 468-3110

Menlo College

Atherton, California

www.menlo.edu   Federal Code: 001236

4-year private business and liberal arts college in small city.

Enrollment: 594 undergrads, 4% part-time. 136 full-time freshmen.

Selectivity: Admits 50 to 75% of applicants.

BASIC COSTS (2010-2011)

Tuition and fees: $33,550.

Per-credit charge: $1,381.

Room and board: $11,330.

FINANCIAL AID PICTURE (2009-2010)

Students with need: Out of 101 full-time freshmen who applied for aid, 86 were judged to have need. Of these, 86 received aid, and 10 had their full need met. Average financial aid package met 73% of need; average scholarship/grant was $25,343; average loan was $2,671. For part-time students, average financial aid package was $15,012.

Students without need: 39 full-time freshmen who did not demonstrate need for aid received scholarships/grants; average award was $11,525. No-need awards available for academics.

Cumulative student debt: 76% of graduating class had student loans; average debt was $25,696.

FINANCIAL AID PROCEDURES

Forms required: FAFSA, state aid form.

Dates and Deadlines: Priority date 3/2; closing date 8/1. Applicants notified on a rolling basis starting 12/15; must reply by 5/1 or within 2 week(s) of notification.

Transfers: No deadline. Applicants notified on a rolling basis starting 12/1; must reply by 5/1 or within 2 week(s) of notification.

CONTACT

Anne Heaton-Dunlap, Director, Office of Financial Aid

1000 El Camino Real, Atherton, CA 94027

(650) 543-3880

Merritt College

Oakland, California

www.merritt.edu   Federal Code: 001267

2-year public community college in large city.

Enrollment: 7,797 undergrads.

Selectivity: Open admission.

BASIC COSTS (2009-2010)

Tuition and fees: $784; out-of-state residents $6,484.

Per-credit charge: $26; out-of-state residents $216.

Additional info: Tuition/fee waivers available for unemployed or children of unemployed.

FINANCIAL AID PICTURE

Students with need: Need-based aid available for full-time and part-time students.

FINANCIAL AID PROCEDURES

Forms required: FAFSA, institutional form.

Dates and Deadlines: Priority date 4/1; closing date 6/30. Applicants notified on a rolling basis starting 6/1.

CONTACT

Alice Freeman, Financial Aid Coordinator

12500 Campus Drive, Oakland, CA 94619

(510) 436-2465

Mills College

Oakland, California

www.mills.edu   Federal Code: 001238

4-year private liberal arts college for women in large city.

Enrollment: 914 undergrads, 5% part-time. 187 full-time freshmen.

Selectivity: Admits 50 to 75% of applicants.

BASIC COSTS (2010-2011)

Tuition and fees: $37,605.

Per-credit charge: $6,072.

Room and board: $10,924.

FINANCIAL AID PICTURE (2009-2010)

Students with need: Out of 183 full-time freshmen who applied for aid, 171 were judged to have need. Of these, 171 received aid, and 72 had their full need met. Average financial aid package met 87% of need; average scholarship/grant was $27,283; average loan was $5,125. For part-time students, average financial aid package was $10,265.

Students without need: 23 full-time freshmen who did not demonstrate need for aid received scholarships/grants; average award was $17,345. No-need awards available for academics, leadership, minority status, music/drama.

Cumulative student debt: 97% of graduating class had student loans; average debt was $24,255.

FINANCIAL AID PROCEDURES

Forms required: FAFSA, institutional form.

Dates and Deadlines: Priority date 2/15; no closing date. Applicants notified on a rolling basis starting 3/1; must reply by 5/1 or within 2 week(s) of notification.

Transfers: Priority date 3/2. Applicants notified on a rolling basis starting 4/15; must reply by 5/1 or within 2 week(s) of notification. Applications by March 2 for California residents, April 1 for out-of-state students.

CONTACT

David Gin, Associate Vice President for Student Finance and Administration Services

5000 MacArthur Boulevard, Oakland, CA 94613

(510) 430-2000

MiraCosta College

Oceanside, California

www.miracosta.edu   Federal Code: 001239

2-year public community college in large city.

Enrollment: 9,115 undergrads, 60% part-time. 969 full-time freshmen.

Selectivity: Open admission; but selective for some programs.

BASIC COSTS (2009-2010)

Tuition and fees: $824; out-of-state residents $6,524.

Per-credit charge: $26; out-of-state residents $216.

FINANCIAL AID PICTURE (2008-2009)

Students with need: 11% of average financial aid package awarded as scholarships/grants, 89% awarded as loans/jobs. Need-based aid available for part-time students. Work study available nights.

Additional info: Waiver of in-state fees for eligible low-income students.

FINANCIAL AID PROCEDURES

Forms required: FAFSA, state aid form, institutional form.

Dates and Deadlines: Priority date 4/10; no closing date. Applicants notified on a rolling basis; must reply within 4 week(s) of notification.

CONTACT

JoAnn Bernard, Financial Aid Director

One Barnard Drive, Oceanside, CA 92056-3899

(760) 795-6711

Modesto Junior College

Modesto, California

www.mjc.edu   Federal Code: 001240

2-year public community college in small city.

Enrollment: 19,522 undergrads.

Selectivity: Open admission.

BASIC COSTS (2009-2010)

Tuition and fees: $826; out-of-state residents $6,526.

Per-credit charge: $26; out-of-state residents $216.

FINANCIAL AID PICTURE (2009-2010)

Students with need: Need-based aid available for full-time and part-time students. Work study available nights, weekends, and for part-time students.

Students without need: This college awards aid only to students with need.

Additional info: Modesto Junior College scholarship priority deadline 12/15.

FINANCIAL AID PROCEDURES

Forms required: FAFSA, state aid form, institutional form.

Dates and Deadlines: Priority date 3/2; no closing date. Applicants notified on a rolling basis starting 5/1; must reply within 2 week(s) of notification.

CONTACT

Myra Rush, Director of Financial Aid and Scholarships

435 College Avenue, Modesto, CA 95350-5800

(209) 575-6023

Monterey Peninsula College

Monterey, California

www.mpc.edu   Federal Code: 001242

2-year public community college in large town.

Enrollment: 12,992 undergrads.

Selectivity: Open admission.

BASIC COSTS (2009-2010)

Tuition and fees: $844; out-of-state residents $6,544.

Per-credit charge: $26; out-of-state residents $216.

Additional info: Tuition/fee waivers available for adults, minority students, unemployed or children of unemployed.

FINANCIAL AID PICTURE

Students with need: Need-based aid available for full-time and part-time students.

FINANCIAL AID PROCEDURES

Forms required: FAFSA, institutional form.

Dates and Deadlines: Closing date 6/30. Applicants notified on a rolling basis starting 6/1.

CONTACT

Claudia Martin, Director of Financial Aid

980 Fremont Street, Monterey, CA 93940-4799

(831) 646-4000

Mount St. Mary's College

Los Angeles, California

www.msmc.la.edu   Federal Code: 001243

4-year private liberal arts college for women in very large city, affiliated with Roman Catholic Church.

Enrollment: 1,969 undergrads, 25% part-time. 367 full-time freshmen.

Selectivity: Admits over 75% of applicants.

BASIC COSTS (2010-2011)

Tuition and fees: $30,303.

Per-credit charge: $1,218.

Room and board: $9,830.

FINANCIAL AID PICTURE (2009-2010)

Students with need: Out of 367 full-time freshmen who applied for aid, 367 were judged to have need. Of these, 367 received aid, and 27 had their full need met. Average financial aid package met 92% of need; average scholarship/grant was $1,421; average loan was $3,496. For part-time students, average financial aid package was $17,242.

Students without need: 6 full-time freshmen who did not demonstrate need for aid received scholarships/grants; average award was $11,973. No-need awards available for academics, alumni affiliation.

Cumulative student debt: 90% of graduating class had student loans; average debt was $33,030.

FINANCIAL AID PROCEDURES

Forms required: FAFSA.

Dates and Deadlines: Priority date 2/15; no closing date. Applicants notified on a rolling basis starting 3/15; must reply by 5/1.

Transfers: No deadline.

CONTACT

La Royce Dodd, Director of Student Financing

12001 Chalon Road, Los Angeles, CA 90049

(310) 954-4195

Mount San Antonio College

Walnut, California
www.mtsac.edu   Federal Code: 001245

2-year public community college in small city.
Enrollment: 38,563 undergrads.
Selectivity: Open admission.

BASIC COSTS (2009-2010)
Tuition and fees: $836; out-of-state residents $6,536.
Per-credit charge: $26; out-of-state residents $216.

FINANCIAL AID PICTURE
Students with need: Need-based aid available for full-time and part-time students.
Students without need: This college awards aid only to students with need.

FINANCIAL AID PROCEDURES
Forms required: FAFSA, institutional form.
Dates and Deadlines: Closing date 3/2. Applicants notified on a rolling basis starting 6/1; must reply within 4 week(s) of notification.

CONTACT
Susanna Jones, Director Financial Aid
1100 North Grand Avenue, Walnut, CA 91789
(909) 594-5611

Mount San Jacinto College

San Jacinto, California
www.msjc.edu   Federal Code: 001246

2-year public community college in small city.
Enrollment: 18,532 undergrads.
Selectivity: Open admission; but selective for some programs.

BASIC COSTS (2009-2010)
Tuition and fees: $780; out-of-state residents $6,210.
Per-credit charge: $26; out-of-state residents $207.

FINANCIAL AID PICTURE
Students with need: Need-based aid available for full-time and part-time students. Work study available nights.
Students without need: No-need awards available for academics, music/drama.
Additional info: Board of Governors Grant Program for state residents to defray cost of enrollment fees.

FINANCIAL AID PROCEDURES
Forms required: FAFSA, institutional form.
Dates and Deadlines: Priority date 3/2; no closing date. Applicants notified on a rolling basis starting 5/1; must reply within 3 week(s) of notification.
Transfers: No deadline.

CONTACT
Lisa Navarro, Financial Aid Supervisor
1499 North State Street, San Jacinto, CA 92583
(951) 487-3245

Mt. Sierra College

Monrovia, California
www.mtsierra.edu   Federal Code: 031287

3-year for-profit visual arts and technical college in large city.
Enrollment: 467 undergrads.
Selectivity: Open admission.

BASIC COSTS (2009-2010)
Tuition and fees: $14,840.
Per-credit charge: $327.
Additional info: Additional lab fees may apply. Fees vary by program.

FINANCIAL AID PICTURE (2008-2009)
Students with need: Need-based aid available for full-time and part-time students.

FINANCIAL AID PROCEDURES
Forms required: FAFSA.

CONTACT
Albert Prado, Financial Aid Director
101 East Huntington Drive, Monrovia, CA 91016
(626) 873-2100

MTI College

Sacramento, California
www.mticollege.edu   Federal Code: 012912

2-year for-profit business and technical college in large city.
Enrollment: 300 undergrads.

BASIC COSTS (2009-2010)
Tuition and fees: $11,245.

FINANCIAL AID PICTURE
Students with need: Need-based aid available for full-time students. Work study available nights.

CONTACT
Paula Perez, Director of Financial Aid
5221 Madison Avenue, Sacramento, CA 95841
(916) 339-1500

National Polytechnic College of Science

San Diego, California
www.natpoly.edu   Federal Code: 011696

2-year private health science and maritime college in large city.
Enrollment: 185 undergrads.
Selectivity: Open admission.

BASIC COSTS (2009-2010)
Additional info: Associate degree program charge (covering 12 months), $28,612; per-credit-hour charge, $311. Academic year is comprised of 30 weeks (36 quarter credits), with courses offered in five-week sessions. Undergraduate courses are scheduled, typically, for eight to ten hours per day (two days each week, five-week period). Some courses require basic supplies (e.g., wet suit, fins, weights, work boots) that are not covered by tuition; additional cost of these supplies could amount to $800 or more.

FINANCIAL AID PICTURE
Students with need: Need-based aid available for full-time students.
Additional info: Work-study programs available.

FINANCIAL AID PROCEDURES
Forms required: FAFSA, institutional form.
Dates and Deadlines: No deadline. Applicants notified on a rolling basis; must reply within 3 week(s) of notification.

CONTACT
Lida Castillo, Financial Aid Officer
3580 Aero Court, San Diego, CA 92123
(858) 309-3508

National University
La Jolla, California
www.nu.edu   Federal Code: 011460

4-year private university in very large city.
Enrollment: 7,756 undergrads, 75% part-time. 29 full-time freshmen.
Selectivity: Open admission; but selective for some programs.

BASIC COSTS (2009-2010)
Tuition and fees: $10,728.

FINANCIAL AID PICTURE (2008-2009)
Students with need: 30% of average financial aid package awarded as scholarships/grants, 70% awarded as loans/jobs. Need-based aid available for part-time students.

FINANCIAL AID PROCEDURES
Forms required: FAFSA, state aid form, institutional form.
Dates and Deadlines: No deadline. Applicants notified on a rolling basis.
Transfers: No deadline.

CONTACT
Valerie Ryan, Director of Financial Aid
11255 North Torrey Pines Road, La Jolla, CA 92037-1011
(858) 642-8500

NewSchool of Architecture & Design
San Diego, California
www.newschoolarch.edu   Federal Code: 030439

5-year for-profit visual arts and liberal arts college in very large city.
Enrollment: 352 undergrads.
Selectivity: Open admission.

BASIC COSTS (2009-2010)
Tuition and fees: $21,225.
Per-credit charge: $635.

FINANCIAL AID PICTURE (2009-2010)
Students with need: Work study available nights.
Students without need: No-need awards available for academics.
Scholarships offered: Presidential Scholarship; $5,000 annually for 2 years; for incoming freshmen based on GPA, activity, recommendations, portfolio; 15 recipients.

FINANCIAL AID PROCEDURES
Forms required: FAFSA.
Dates and Deadlines: No deadline. Applicants notified on a rolling basis.
Transfers: Priority date 4/1; no deadline.

CONTACT
Matt Wakeman, Director of Financial Aid
1249 F Street, San Diego, CA 92101
(619) 235-4100 ext. 206

Notre Dame de Namur University
Belmont, California
www.ndnu.edu   Federal Code: 001179

4-year private university and liberal arts college in large town, affiliated with Roman Catholic Church.
Enrollment: 873 undergrads, 40% part-time. 116 full-time freshmen.
Selectivity: Admits over 75% of applicants.

BASIC COSTS (2010-2011)
Tuition and fees: $28,480.
Per-credit charge: $700.
Room and board: $11,720.

FINANCIAL AID PICTURE (2009-2010)
Students with need: Out of 95 full-time freshmen who applied for aid, 91 were judged to have need. Of these, 91 received aid, and 5 had their full need met. Average financial aid package met 69% of need. For part-time students, average financial aid package was $7,861.
Students without need: No-need awards available for academics, alumni affiliation, athletics, leadership, music/drama, religious affiliation.
Scholarships offered: Presidential Scholarships: up to $12,000 per semester; based on academic merit and leadership. Emerging Artist Scholarship: up to $9,500 annually; based on demonstrated talent in the performing and fine arts. Belmont Scholarships: up to $9,000 annually; based on merit. Bay Area Catholic High School: up to $7,500 per year to one student from each of Bay Area Catholic high schools.
Cumulative student debt: 82% of graduating class had student loans; average debt was $21,758.

FINANCIAL AID PROCEDURES
Forms required: FAFSA. CSS PROFILE accepted but not required.
Dates and Deadlines: Priority date 3/2; no closing date. Applicants notified on a rolling basis starting 1/15.

CONTACT
Susan Pace, Director of Financial Aid
1500 Ralston Avenue, Belmont, CA 94002-1908
(650) 508-3600

Occidental College
Los Angeles, California
www.oxy.edu   Federal Code: 001249
                         CSS Code: 4581

4-year private liberal arts college in very large city, affiliated with nondenominational tradition.
Enrollment: 1,959 undergrads, 1% part-time. 487 full-time freshmen.
Selectivity: Admits less than 50% of applicants.

BASIC COSTS (2009-2010)
Tuition and fees: $38,922.
Room and board: $10,780.

FINANCIAL AID PICTURE (2008-2009)
Students with need: Out of 322 full-time freshmen who applied for aid, 255 were judged to have need. Of these, 253 received aid, and 253 had their full need met. Average financial aid package met 100% of need; average scholarship/grant was $28,936; average loan was $4,827. For part-time students, average financial aid package was $14,101.
Students without need: 103 full-time freshmen who did not demonstrate need for aid received scholarships/grants; average award was $8,441. No-need awards available for academics, leadership, music/drama, state/district residency.
Scholarships offered: Margaret Bundy Scott Scholarship: $20,000. President's Scholarship: $15,000; awarded to top 10-15% of incoming class based on academic achievement, leadership, and citizenship.
Cumulative student debt: 73% of graduating class had student loans; average debt was $20,381.

FINANCIAL AID PROCEDURES
Forms required: FAFSA, CSS PROFILE, state aid form.
Dates and Deadlines: Closing date 2/1. Applicants notified by 4/1; must reply by 5/1.
Transfers: Closing date 3/15. Applicants notified on a rolling basis; must reply within 2 week(s) of notification. California residents must apply for Cal Grant by completing FAFSA and CSAC's GPA verification form by March 2.

CONTACT
Maureen McRae, Director of Financial Aid
1600 Campus Road, Los Angeles, CA 90041
(323) 259-2548

Ohlone College
Fremont, California
www.ohlone.edu   Federal Code: 004481

2-year public community college in large city.
Enrollment: 10,909 undergrads.
Selectivity: Open admission.

BASIC COSTS (2009-2010)
Tuition and fees: $834; out-of-state residents $6,534.
Per-credit charge: $26; out-of-state residents $216.
Additional info: Tuition/fee waivers available for adults, minority students, unemployed or children of unemployed.

FINANCIAL AID PICTURE
Students with need: Need-based aid available for full-time and part-time students.
Students without need: No-need awards available for academics.

FINANCIAL AID PROCEDURES
Forms required: FAFSA, state aid form, institutional form.
Dates and Deadlines: Priority date 7/1; no closing date. Applicants notified on a rolling basis starting 7/30; must reply within 2 week(s) of notification.

CONTACT
Debra Griffin, Financial Aid Director
43600 Mission Boulevard, Fremont, CA 94539-0390
(510) 659-6150

Orange Coast College
Costa Mesa, California
www.orangecoastcollege.edu   Federal Code: 001250

2-year public community college in small city.
Enrollment: 23,399 undergrads, 59% part-time. 1,147 full-time freshmen.
Selectivity: Open admission.

BASIC COSTS (2009-2010)
Tuition and fees: $812; out-of-state residents $6,512.
Per-credit charge: $26; out-of-state residents $216.
Additional info: Tuition/fee waivers available for adults, minority students, unemployed or children of unemployed.

FINANCIAL AID PICTURE (2008-2009)
Students with need: Out of 1,146 full-time freshmen who applied for aid, 1,131 were judged to have need. Of these, 1,127 received aid, and 7 had their full need met. Average financial aid package met 33% of need; average scholarship/grant was $3,858; average loan was $2,972. For part-time students, average financial aid package was $3,542.
Students without need: No-need awards available for academics.
Cumulative student debt: 90% of graduating class had student loans; average debt was $6,711.

FINANCIAL AID PROCEDURES
Forms required: FAFSA, institutional form.
Dates and Deadlines: Priority date 3/2; closing date 5/25. Applicants notified on a rolling basis; must reply within 2 week(s) of notification.

CONTACT
Melissa Moser, Financial Aid Director
2701 Fairview Road, Costa Mesa, CA 92628-5005
(714) 432-5508

Otis College of Art and Design
Los Angeles, California
www.otis.edu   Federal Code: 001251

4-year private visual arts college in very large city.
Enrollment: 1,150 undergrads, 1% part-time. 173 full-time freshmen.
Selectivity: Admits less than 50% of applicants.

BASIC COSTS (2009-2010)
Tuition and fees: $32,060.
Per-credit charge: $1,022.

FINANCIAL AID PICTURE (2009-2010)
Students with need: Out of 149 full-time freshmen who applied for aid, 121 were judged to have need. Of these, 121 received aid, and 5 had their full need met. Average financial aid package met 49% of need; average scholarship/grant was $15,662; average loan was $3,351. For part-time students, average financial aid package was $4,159.
Students without need: 30 full-time freshmen who did not demonstrate need for aid received scholarships/grants; average award was $7,078. No-need awards available for academics, art.
Cumulative student debt: 66% of graduating class had student loans; average debt was $27,903.

FINANCIAL AID PROCEDURES
Forms required: FAFSA, state aid form.
Dates and Deadlines: Priority date 2/15; no closing date. Applicants notified on a rolling basis starting 3/1; must reply within 2 week(s) of notification.

CONTACT
Ji Choi, Director of Financial Aid
9045 Lincoln Boulevard, Los Angeles, CA 90045-9785
(310) 665-6880

Pacific Oaks College
Pasadena, California
www.pacificoaks.edu   Federal Code: 001255

Upper-division private teachers college in small city.
Enrollment: 84 undergrads.

BASIC COSTS (2009-2010)
Tuition and fees: $26,100.
Per-credit charge: $868.

FINANCIAL AID PICTURE (2009-2010)
Students with need: Need-based aid available for full-time and part-time students. Work study available nights, weekends, and for part-time students.
Students without need: This college awards aid only to students with need.

FINANCIAL AID PROCEDURES
Dates and Deadlines: Priority date 4/15; no closing date. Applicants notified on a rolling basis starting 5/1; must reply by 5/15 or within 4 week(s) of notification.

CONTACT
Seph Rodriguez, Director of Financial Aid
5 Westmoreland Place, Pasadena, CA 91103
(626) 397-1350

Pacific States University
Los Angeles, California
www.psuca.edu   Federal Code: 031633

4-year private university in very large city.
Enrollment: 13 undergrads.
Selectivity: Open admission; but selective for some programs.

BASIC COSTS (2010-2011)
Tuition and fees: $23,280.
Per-credit charge: $380.
Additional info: Tuition at time of enrollment locked for 4 years.

FINANCIAL AID PICTURE
Students with need: Need-based aid available for full-time and part-time students.
Students without need: No-need awards available for academics.

FINANCIAL AID PROCEDURES
Forms required: FAFSA, institutional form.
Dates and Deadlines: No deadline.

CONTACT
Min Kim, Financial Aid Officer
1516 South Western Avenue, Los Angeles, CA 90006
(323) 731-2383 ext. 14

Pacific Union College
Angwin, California
www.puc.edu   Federal Code: 001258

4-year private liberal arts college in small town, affiliated with Seventh-day Adventists.
Enrollment: 1,515 undergrads, 10% part-time. 323 full-time freshmen.
Selectivity: Admits 50 to 75% of applicants.

BASIC COSTS (2009-2010)
Tuition and fees: $23,979.
Room and board: $6,750.

FINANCIAL AID PICTURE (2009-2010)
Students with need: Need-based aid available for full-time and part-time students.
Students without need: No-need awards available for leadership, religious affiliation.

FINANCIAL AID PROCEDURES
Forms required: FAFSA, state aid form, institutional form.
Dates and Deadlines: No deadline. Applicants notified on a rolling basis; must reply within 3 week(s) of notification.

CONTACT
Laurie Wheeler, Director of Student Financial Services
One Angwin Avenue, Angwin, CA 94508
(707) 965-7200

Palo Verde College
Blythe, California
www.paloverde.edu   Federal Code: 001259

2-year public community college in large town.
Enrollment: 1,672 undergrads.
Selectivity: Open admission; but selective for some programs.

BASIC COSTS (2009-2010)
Tuition and fees: $780; out-of-state residents $6,480.
Per-credit charge: $26; out-of-state residents $216.

FINANCIAL AID PICTURE (2008-2009)
Students with need: 98% of average financial aid package awarded as scholarships/grants, 2% awarded as loans/jobs. Need-based aid available for part-time students. Work study available nights.
Students without need: This college awards aid only to students with need.

FINANCIAL AID PROCEDURES
Forms required: FAFSA, institutional form.
Dates and Deadlines: No deadline. Applicants notified on a rolling basis starting 7/1; must reply within 4 week(s) of notification.

CONTACT
Linda Pratt, Financial Aid Officer
One College Drive, Blythe, CA 92225
(760) 921-5410

Palomar College
San Marcos, California
www.palomar.edu   Federal Code: 001260

2-year public community college in large town.
Enrollment: 28,182 undergrads.
Selectivity: Open admission; but selective for some programs.

BASIC COSTS (2009-2010)
Tuition and fees: $824; out-of-state residents $6,524.
Per-credit charge: $26; out-of-state residents $216.

FINANCIAL AID PICTURE
Students with need: Need-based aid available for full-time and part-time students. Work study available nights.
Students without need: This college awards aid only to students with need.

FINANCIAL AID PROCEDURES
Forms required: FAFSA, institutional form.
Dates and Deadlines: Priority date 4/1; no closing date. Applicants notified on a rolling basis starting 6/1.
Transfers: No deadline.

CONTACT
Mary San Agustin, Financial Aid Director
1140 West Mission Road, San Marcos, CA 92069-1487
(760) 744-1150

Patten University
Oakland, California
www.patten.edu   Federal Code: 004490

4-year private university and liberal arts college in large city, affiliated with interdenominational tradition.
Enrollment: 995 undergrads.

BASIC COSTS (2010-2011)
Tuition and fees: $13,440.
Per-credit charge: $560.
Room and board: $7,090.

FINANCIAL AID PICTURE
Students with need: Need-based aid available for full-time and part-time students.

Students without need: No-need awards available for academics, athletics, state/district residency.

FINANCIAL AID PROCEDURES

Forms required: FAFSA, institutional form.
Dates and Deadlines: Priority date 3/31; no closing date. Applicants notified on a rolling basis starting 5/31.
Transfers: No deadline.

CONTACT

Dennis Clark, Financial Aid Director
2433 Coolidge Avenue, Oakland, CA 94601-2699
(510) 261-8500 ext. 7747

Pepperdine University

Malibu, California
www.pepperdine.edu   Federal Code: 001264

4-year private university and liberal arts college in small city, affiliated with Church of Christ.
Enrollment: 3,427 undergrads, 11% part-time. 729 full-time freshmen.
Selectivity: Admits less than 50% of applicants.

BASIC COSTS (2010-2011)

Tuition and fees: $39,080.
Per-credit charge: $1,210.
Room and board: $11,390.

FINANCIAL AID PICTURE (2009-2010)

Students with need: Out of 559 full-time freshmen who applied for aid, 464 were judged to have need. Of these, 462 received aid, and 146 had their full need met. Average financial aid package met 87% of need; average scholarship/grant was $28,952; average loan was $3,572. For part-time students, average financial aid package was $16,088.
Students without need: 81 full-time freshmen who did not demonstrate need for aid received scholarships/grants; average award was $21,015. No-need awards available for academics, art, athletics, minority status, music/drama, religious affiliation.
Scholarships offered: 14 full-time freshmen received athletic scholarships; average amount $39,132.
Cumulative student debt: 58% of graduating class had student loans; average debt was $28,299.

FINANCIAL AID PROCEDURES

Forms required: FAFSA.
Dates and Deadlines: Closing date 2/15. Applicants notified by 4/15; must reply within 2 week(s) of notification.

CONTACT

Janet Lockhart, Director of Financial Assistance
24255 Pacific Coast Highway, Malibu, CA 90263-4392
(310) 506-4301

Pitzer College

Claremont, California   Federal Code: 001172
www.pitzer.edu   CSS Code: 4619

4-year private liberal arts college in large town.
Enrollment: 1,043 undergrads, 5% part-time. 250 full-time freshmen.
Selectivity: Admits less than 50% of applicants.

BASIC COSTS (2010-2011)

Tuition and fees: $41,130.
Room and board: $11,950.
Additional info: $4,690 per course.

FINANCIAL AID PICTURE (2009-2010)

Students with need: Out of 130 full-time freshmen who applied for aid, 104 were judged to have need. Of these, 104 received aid, and 104 had their full need met. Average financial aid package met 100% of need; average scholarship/grant was $32,831; average loan was $2,614. For part-time students, average financial aid package was $19,894.
Students without need: 9 full-time freshmen who did not demonstrate need for aid received scholarships/grants; average award was $5,000. No-need awards available for academics, leadership.
Scholarships offered: Trustee Community Scholar Award; $10,000 per year; based on extraordinary academic achievement, outstanding leadership or exceptional community service; 20 awarded.
Cumulative student debt: 45% of graduating class had student loans; average debt was $20,448.

FINANCIAL AID PROCEDURES

Forms required: FAFSA, CSS PROFILE, state aid form.
Dates and Deadlines: Closing date 2/1. Applicants notified by 4/1; must reply by 5/1.
Transfers: Closing date 3/1. Applicants notified by 5/15; must reply by 6/15.

CONTACT

Margaret Carothers, Director of Financial Aid
1050 North Mills Avenue, Claremont, CA 91711-6101
(909) 621-8208

Platt College: Los Angeles

Alhambra, California
www.plattcollege.edu   Federal Code: 030627

2-year for-profit visual arts and technical college in very large city.
Enrollment: 211 undergrads.

BASIC COSTS (2009-2010)

Additional info: Cost varies by program. Associate degree cost ranges from $24,915 to $34,955. Bachelor's degree cost ranges from $69,930 to $73,930.

FINANCIAL AID PICTURE

Students with need: Need-based aid available for full-time and part-time students. Work study available nights.

FINANCIAL AID PROCEDURES

Forms required: FAFSA, institutional form.
Dates and Deadlines: Priority date 3/2; no closing date. Applicants notified on a rolling basis starting 1/1.

CONTACT

Remie Pascual, Financial Aid Director
1000 South Fremont Avenue A9W, Alhambra, CA 91803
(626) 300-5444 ext. 230

Platt College: Ontario

Ontario, California
www.plattcollege.edu   Federal Code: 030627

4-year for-profit branch campus and technical college in small city.
Enrollment: 385 undergrads.

BASIC COSTS (2009-2010)

Additional info: Cost varies by program. Associate degree cost ranges from $24,915 to $34,955. Bachelor's degree cost ranges from $69,930 to $73,930.

FINANCIAL AID PICTURE

Students with need: Need-based aid available for full-time and part-time students. Work study available nights.

Scholarships offered: Presidential Scholarship, CAPPS Scholarship, Imagine America Scholarship: $1,000 each; based on application and essay; approximately 100 plus available per calendar year.

FINANCIAL AID PROCEDURES
Forms required: FAFSA, institutional form.
Dates and Deadlines: Priority date 3/2; no closing date. Applicants notified on a rolling basis starting 1/1.
Transfers: No deadline.

CONTACT
Rosemarie Young, Regional Director of Compliance and Civil Rights
3700 Inland Empire Boulevard, Ontario, CA 91764
(909) 941-9410

Platt College: San Diego
San Diego, California
www.platt.edu   Federal Code: 023043

4-year for-profit visual arts and technical college in very large city.
Enrollment: 292 undergrads. 113 full-time freshmen.
Selectivity: Open admission; but selective for some programs and for out-of-state students.

BASIC COSTS (2009-2010)
Tuition and fees: $15,310.
Per-credit charge: $507.
Additional info: Total costs range from $17,910 to $36,310, depending on program.

FINANCIAL AID PICTURE (2008-2009)
Students with need: Need-based aid available for full-time and part-time students.

FINANCIAL AID PROCEDURES
Forms required: FAFSA, state aid form, institutional form.
Dates and Deadlines: Closing date 3/2. Applicants notified on a rolling basis; must reply within 1 week(s) of notification.

CONTACT
Opel Olivor, Director of Financial Aid
6250 El Cajon Boulevard, San Diego, CA 92115
(619) 265-0107

Point Loma Nazarene University
San Diego, California
www.pointloma.edu   Federal Code: 001262

4-year private university and liberal arts college in very large city, affiliated with Church of the Nazarene.
Enrollment: 2,367 undergrads, 3% part-time. 535 full-time freshmen.
Selectivity: Admits 50 to 75% of applicants.

BASIC COSTS (2010-2011)
Tuition and fees: $27,100.
Per-credit charge: $1,105.
Room and board: $8,600.

FINANCIAL AID PICTURE (2009-2010)
Students with need: Out of 447 full-time freshmen who applied for aid, 343 were judged to have need. Of these, 340 received aid, and 62 had their full need met. Average financial aid package met 65% of need; average scholarship/grant was $13,188; average loan was $4,226. For part-time students, average financial aid package was $13,171.
Students without need: 67 full-time freshmen who did not demonstrate need for aid received scholarships/grants; average award was $6,472. No-need awards available for academics, athletics, leadership, music/drama.

Scholarships offered: 20 full-time freshmen received athletic scholarships; average amount $10,641.
Cumulative student debt: 87% of graduating class had student loans; average debt was $29,491.

FINANCIAL AID PROCEDURES
Forms required: FAFSA, institutional form.
Dates and Deadlines: Priority date 3/2; no closing date. Applicants notified on a rolling basis starting 3/1.

CONTACT
Pam Macias, Director of Financial Aid
3900 Lomaland Drive, San Diego, CA 92106-2899
(619) 849-2068

Pomona College
Claremont, California   Federal Code: 001173
www.pomona.edu   CSS Code: 4607

4-year private liberal arts college in large town.
Enrollment: 1,531 undergrads. 382 full-time freshmen.
Selectivity: Admits less than 50% of applicants.

BASIC COSTS (2010-2011)
Tuition and fees: $38,394.
Room and board: $12,936.

FINANCIAL AID PICTURE (2008-2009)
Students with need: Out of 240 full-time freshmen who applied for aid, 193 were judged to have need. Of these, 193 received aid, and 193 had their full need met. Average financial aid package met 100% of need; average scholarship/grant was $34,389. Need-based aid available for part-time students.
Students without need: This college awards aid only to students with need.
Cumulative student debt: 47% of graduating class had student loans; average debt was $8,776.

FINANCIAL AID PROCEDURES
Forms required: FAFSA, CSS PROFILE.
Dates and Deadlines: Closing date 2/1. Applicants notified by 4/1; must reply by 5/1.
Transfers: Closing date 3/1. Candidates required to submit finanical aid transcript from previous institution directly to the college.

CONTACT
Mary Booker, Director of Financial Aid
333 North College Way, Claremont, CA 91711-6312
(909) 621-8205

Professional Golfers Career College
Temecula, California
www.golfcollege.edu   Federal Code: 033673

2-year for-profit golf academy in small city.
Enrollment: 130 undergrads.
Selectivity: Open admission.

BASIC COSTS (2009-2010)
Additional info: Tuition $5,590/semester for domestic students and $5,890/semester for international students; program lasts 4 semesters.

FINANCIAL AID PICTURE
Students with need: Need-based aid available for full-time students.

FINANCIAL AID PROCEDURES
Dates and Deadlines: No deadline.
Transfers: No deadline.

CONTACT
Maria Fons, FAO
26109 Ynez Road, Temecula, CA 92591
(800) 877-4380

Reedley College
Reedley, California
www.reedleycollege.edu   Federal Code: 001308

2-year public community college in large town.
Enrollment: 15,234 undergrads.
Selectivity: Open admission.

BASIC COSTS (2009-2010)
Tuition and fees: $814; out-of-state residents $6,514.
Per-credit charge: $26; out-of-state residents $216.
Room and board: $5,504.
Additional info: Tuition/fee waivers available for adults, minority students, unemployed or children of unemployed.

FINANCIAL AID PICTURE (2008-2009)
Students with need: Need-based aid available for full-time and part-time students.
Students without need: This college awards aid only to students with need.
Additional info: Board of Governors fee waiver available for low-income students. Book voucher available for EOPS students.

FINANCIAL AID PROCEDURES
Forms required: FAFSA, state aid form.
Dates and Deadlines: Priority date 3/2; no closing date. Applicants notified on a rolling basis starting 3/2; must reply within 3 week(s) of notification.
Transfers: Priority date 4/15. March 2 deadline for California grants.

CONTACT
Chris Cortes, Director of Financial Aid
995 North Reed Avenue, Reedley, CA 93654
(559) 638-3641

Rio Hondo College
Whittier, California
www.riohondo.edu   Federal Code: 001269

2-year public community college in small city.
Enrollment: 11,561 undergrads, 44% part-time. 1,511 full-time freshmen.
Selectivity: Open admission; but selective for some programs.

BASIC COSTS (2009-2010)
Tuition and fees: $803; out-of-state residents $6,293.
Per-credit charge: $26; out-of-state residents $209.

FINANCIAL AID PICTURE (2008-2009)
Students with need: Need-based aid available for full-time and part-time students.

FINANCIAL AID PROCEDURES
Forms required: FAFSA.
Dates and Deadlines: Priority date 7/15; no closing date. Applicants notified on a rolling basis.

CONTACT
Elizabeth Coria, Director Financial Aid
3600 Workman Mill Road, Whittier, CA 90601-1699
(562) 908-3411

Riverside Community College
Riverside, California
www.rcc.edu   Federal Code: 001270

2-year public community college in large city.
Enrollment: 37,254 undergrads.
Selectivity: Open admission.

BASIC COSTS (2009-2010)
Tuition and fees: $814; out-of-state residents $6,244.
Per-credit charge: $26; out-of-state residents $207.
Additional info: Tuition/fee waivers available for adults, unemployed or children of unemployed.

FINANCIAL AID PICTURE (2008-2009)
Students with need: Need-based aid available for full-time and part-time students. Work study available nights, weekends, and for part-time students.
Students without need: No-need awards available for academics, alumni affiliation, art, leadership, minority status, music/drama, state/district residency.

FINANCIAL AID PROCEDURES
Forms required: FAFSA, institutional form.
Dates and Deadlines: Priority date 3/1; no closing date. Applicants notified on a rolling basis starting 7/1.
Transfers: Students who received financial aid at another institution and earned less than 2.0 GPA ineligible for aid during first semester. Students must complete 6 units and earn 2.0 GPA to be eligible.

CONTACT
Eugenia Vincent, District Dean of Student Financial Services
4800 Magnolia Avenue, Riverside, CA 92506
(951) 222-8709

Sacramento City College
Sacramento, California
www.scc.losrios.edu   Federal Code: 001233

2-year public community college in large city.
Enrollment: 26,412 undergrads.
Selectivity: Open admission.

BASIC COSTS (2009-2010)
Tuition and fees: $812; out-of-state residents $6,512.
Per-credit charge: $26; out-of-state residents $216.

FINANCIAL AID PICTURE
Students with need: Need-based aid available for full-time and part-time students. Work study available nights, weekends, and for part-time students.

FINANCIAL AID PROCEDURES
Forms required: FAFSA, state aid form.
Dates and Deadlines: Priority date 3/2; no closing date. Applicants notified on a rolling basis starting 7/1; must reply within 2 week(s) of notification.
Transfers: Priority date 5/30.

CONTACT
Kimberly Cortijo, Financial Aid Supervisor
3835 Freeport Boulevard, Sacramento, CA 95822
(916) 558-2546

Saddleback College

Mission Viejo, California
www.saddleback.edu   Federal Code: 008918

2-year public community college in small city.
Enrollment: 28,104 undergrads.
Selectivity: Open admission; but selective for some programs.

BASIC COSTS (2009-2010)
Tuition and fees: $814; out-of-state residents $6,514.
Per-credit charge: $26; out-of-state residents $216.

FINANCIAL AID PICTURE (2008-2009)
Students with need: Need-based aid available for full-time and part-time students.
Students without need: This college awards aid only to students with need.

FINANCIAL AID PROCEDURES
Forms required: FAFSA.
Dates and Deadlines: Closing date 6/30. Applicants notified on a rolling basis starting 4/1.

CONTACT
Mary Hall, Director, Financial Aid
28000 Marguerite Parkway, Mission Viejo, CA 92692
(949) 582-4860

St. Mary's College of California

Moraga, California
www.stmarys-ca.edu   Federal Code: 001302

4-year private liberal arts college in large town, affiliated with Roman Catholic Church.
Enrollment: 2,379 undergrads, 4% part-time. 573 full-time freshmen.
Selectivity: Admits over 75% of applicants.

BASIC COSTS (2010-2011)
Tuition and fees: $35,430.
Per-credit charge: $1,440.
Room and board: $12,350.

FINANCIAL AID PICTURE (2009-2010)
Students with need: Out of 513 full-time freshmen who applied for aid, 481 were judged to have need. Of these, 479 received aid, and 8 had their full need met. Average financial aid package met 85% of need; average scholarship/grant was $24,254; average loan was $3,864. For part-time students, average financial aid package was $5,911.
Students without need: 24 full-time freshmen who did not demonstrate need for aid received scholarships/grants; average award was $14,333. No-need awards available for academics, alumni affiliation, athletics, leadership.
Scholarships offered: *Merit:* Honors at Entrance Scholarship Awards: $12,000 annually; freshman students admitted with a GPA of at least 3.7 or higher and a combined SAT score of at least 1200 exclusive of Writing (or a 27 on the ACT); transfers with 30 + transferable academic semester units and 3.5 GPA. Honors at Entrance Scholarship Awards: $10,000 annually; fall term applicants; must be admitted by March 1. Presidential Scholars Scholarships: $10,000 annually; freshmen with 3.8 GPA or higher and combined SAT score of at least 1350 (exclusive of writing). Students who receive Presidential Scholarship will also receive Honors at Entrance Scholarship for total of $22,000 annually. *Athletic:* 29 full-time freshmen received athletic scholarships; average amount $32,512.
Cumulative student debt: 80% of graduating class had student loans; average debt was $31,330.

FINANCIAL AID PROCEDURES
Forms required: FAFSA, state aid form.

Dates and Deadlines: Priority date 2/15; no closing date. Applicants notified on a rolling basis starting 3/15; must reply by 5/1 or within 2 week(s) of notification.
Transfers: To receive consideration for all types of financial aid, transfer students must be admitted by March 1 prior to enrolling in the following fall term.

CONTACT
Priscilla Muha, Director of Financial Aid
Box 4800, Moraga, CA 94575-4800
(925) 631-4370

Samuel Merritt University

Oakland, California
www.samuelmerritt.edu   Federal Code: 007012

Upper-division private health science and nursing college in large city.
Enrollment: 517 undergrads, 1% part-time.
Selectivity: GED not accepted.

BASIC COSTS (2009-2010)
Tuition and fees: $35,398.
Per-credit charge: $1,439.
Additional info: $2,958 per semester health insurance mandatory unless student covered by existing insurance.

FINANCIAL AID PICTURE (2008-2009)
Students with need: Need-based aid available for full-time and part-time students. Work study available nights, weekends, and for part-time students.
Students without need: No-need awards available for academics, leadership, minority status.
Additional info: Ongoing private scholarships available. Students eligible to work in Medical Center (associated with college).

FINANCIAL AID PROCEDURES
Dates and Deadlines: No deadline.
Transfers: Priority date 3/2; no deadline. Applicants notified on a rolling basis; must reply within 3 week(s) of notification.

CONTACT
Mary Robinson, Director of Financial Aid
370 Hawthorne Avenue, Oakland, CA 94609-9954
(510) 869-1550

San Diego Christian College

El Cajon, California
www.sdcc.edu   Federal Code: 012031

4-year private liberal arts college in small city, affiliated with nondenominational tradition.
Enrollment: 420 undergrads, 8% part-time. 62 full-time freshmen.
Selectivity: Admits 50 to 75% of applicants.

BASIC COSTS (2009-2010)
Tuition and fees: $21,610.
Per-credit charge: $833.
Room and board: $8,000.

FINANCIAL AID PICTURE (2009-2010)
Students with need: Out of 54 full-time freshmen who applied for aid, 48 were judged to have need. Of these, 48 received aid, and 15 had their full need met. Average financial aid package met 52% of need; average scholarship/grant was $8,957; average loan was $2,493. For part-time students, average financial aid package was $5,658.
Students without need: 5 full-time freshmen who did not demonstrate need for aid received scholarships/grants; average award was $4,400. No-

need awards available for academics, alumni affiliation, athletics, leadership, music/drama, state/district residency.

Scholarships offered: 15 full-time freshmen received athletic scholarships; average amount $7,865.

Cumulative student debt: 74% of graduating class had student loans; average debt was $27,047.

FINANCIAL AID PROCEDURES

Forms required: FAFSA, state aid form, institutional form.

Dates and Deadlines: Priority date 3/2; closing date 7/15. Applicants notified on a rolling basis starting 4/1; must reply by 5/1 or within 4 week(s) of notification.

CONTACT

Susie Parks, Director of Enrollment Services
2100 Greenfield Drive, El Cajon, CA 92019-1157
(619) 201-8730

San Diego City College
San Diego, California
www.sdccd.edu   Federal Code: 001273

2-year public community and junior college in very large city.

Enrollment: 9,956 undergrads.

Selectivity: Open admission.

BASIC COSTS (2009-2010)

Tuition and fees: $814; out-of-state residents $6,514.

Per-credit charge: $26; out-of-state residents $216.

Additional info: Tuition/fee waivers available for unemployed or children of unemployed.

FINANCIAL AID PICTURE (2008-2009)

Students with need: Need-based aid available for full-time and part-time students.

Students without need: This college awards aid only to students with need.

FINANCIAL AID PROCEDURES

Forms required: FAFSA.

Dates and Deadlines: Priority date 4/15; no closing date. Applicants notified on a rolling basis starting 7/1; must reply within 4 week(s) of notification.

Transfers: No deadline. Aid is limited to remaining eligibility based on receipt of aid from previous college.

CONTACT

Greg Sanchez, Director of Financial Aid
1313 Park Boulevard, San Diego, CA 92101-4787
(619) 388-3501

San Diego Miramar College
San Diego, California
www.miramarcollege.net   Federal Code: 014172

2-year public community college in very large city.

Enrollment: 11,637 undergrads.

Selectivity: Open admission.

BASIC COSTS (2009-2010)

Tuition and fees: $814; out-of-state residents $6,514.

Per-credit charge: $26; out-of-state residents $216.

Additional info: Tuition/fee waivers available for unemployed or children of unemployed.

FINANCIAL AID PICTURE (2008-2009)

Students with need: Need-based aid available for full-time and part-time students.

Additional info: Private scholarships available.

FINANCIAL AID PROCEDURES

Forms required: FAFSA.

Dates and Deadlines: Priority date 3/2; no closing date. Applicants notified on a rolling basis; must reply within 3 week(s) of notification.

Transfers: No deadline. Transfers advised to apply early.

CONTACT

Teresa Vilaboy, Financial Aid Officer
10440 Black Mountain Road, San Diego, CA 92126-2999
(619) 388-7864

San Diego State University
San Diego, California
www.sdsu.edu   Federal Code: 001151

4-year public university in very large city.

Enrollment: 27,537 undergrads, 16% part-time. 3,291 full-time freshmen.

Selectivity: Admits less than 50% of applicants.

BASIC COSTS (2009-2010)

Tuition and fees: $4,902; out-of-state residents $16,062.

Room and board: $11,485.

FINANCIAL AID PICTURE (2009-2010)

Students with need: Out of 3,200 full-time freshmen who applied for aid, 2,000 were judged to have need. Of these, 2,000 received aid, and 400 had their full need met. Average financial aid package met 71% of need; average scholarship/grant was $7,900; average loan was $3,000. For part-time students, average financial aid package was $6,400.

Students without need: 150 full-time freshmen who did not demonstrate need for aid received scholarships/grants; average award was $2,400. No-need awards available for academics, alumni affiliation, art, athletics, leadership, music/drama, ROTC, state/district residency.

Scholarships offered: *Merit:* Various departmental scholarships are open to first time freshman with declared majors. Brian Schultz Memorial Scholarship, amount varies (1 awarded); recipient must be a cancer survivor or have been affected by cancer. *Athletic:* 90 full-time freshmen received athletic scholarships; average amount $13,600.

Cumulative student debt: 44% of graduating class had student loans; average debt was $14,700.

FINANCIAL AID PROCEDURES

Forms required: FAFSA, state aid form.

Dates and Deadlines: Closing date 3/2. Applicants notified on a rolling basis starting 2/14.

Transfers: No deadline. Applicants notified on a rolling basis.

CONTACT

Chrys Dutton, Director of Financial Aid
5500 Campanile Drive, San Diego, CA 92182-7455
(619) 594-6323

San Francisco Art Institute
San Francisco, California
www.sfai.edu   Federal Code: 003948

4-year private visual arts college in very large city.

Enrollment: 304 undergrads, 9% part-time. 56 full-time freshmen.

Selectivity: Admits over 75% of applicants.

BASIC COSTS (2010-2011)

Tuition and fees: $32,894.

Per-credit charge: $1,378.

Room and board: $10,300.

FINANCIAL AID PICTURE (2008-2009)
Students with need: Need-based aid available for full-time and part-time students.
Students without need: No-need awards available for academics, art.
Scholarships offered: Several awards based on portfolio reviews during application for admissions process.

FINANCIAL AID PROCEDURES
Forms required: FAFSA.
Dates and Deadlines: Priority date 3/1; closing date 5/31. Applicants notified on a rolling basis starting 4/15; must reply within 3 week(s) of notification.
Transfers: Priority date 3/2; no deadline. Applicants notified on a rolling basis starting 4/1; must reply within 3 week(s) of notification.

CONTACT
Director of Financial Aid
800 Chestnut Street, San Francisco, CA 94133-2299
(415) 749-4520

San Francisco Conservatory of Music
San Francisco, California
www.sfcm.edu   Federal Code: 001278

4-year private music college in very large city.
Enrollment: 203 undergrads, 2% part-time. 54 full-time freshmen.
Selectivity: Admits 50 to 75% of applicants.

BASIC COSTS (2010-2011)
Tuition and fees: $35,430.
Per-credit charge: $1,540.
Room and board: $10,800.

FINANCIAL AID PICTURE (2009-2010)
Students with need: Out of 51 full-time freshmen who applied for aid, 51 were judged to have need. Of these, 51 received aid, and 10 had their full need met. Average financial aid package met 85% of need; average scholarship/grant was $17,675; average loan was $3,132. For part-time students, average financial aid package was $8,015.
Students without need: 8 full-time freshmen who did not demonstrate need for aid received scholarships/grants; average award was $6,030. No-need awards available for music/drama.
Scholarships offered: 8 full-time freshmen received athletic scholarships; average amount $15,583.
Cumulative student debt: 95% of graduating class had student loans; average debt was $27,000.

FINANCIAL AID PROCEDURES
Forms required: FAFSA, institutional form.
Dates and Deadlines: Priority date 3/1; no closing date. Applicants notified on a rolling basis starting 3/15; must reply by 5/1 or within 2 week(s) of notification.
Transfers: Priority date 2/1; closing date 4/1. Applicants notified on a rolling basis starting 4/1; must reply by 5/1 or within 2 week(s) of notification.

CONTACT
Doris Howard, Financial Aid Officer
50 Oak Street, San Francisco, CA 94102
(415) 503-6235

San Francisco State University
San Francisco, California
www.sfsu.edu   Federal Code: 001154

4-year public university in very large city.
Enrollment: 25,001 undergrads, 20% part-time. 3,755 full-time freshmen.
Selectivity: Admits 50 to 75% of applicants.

BASIC COSTS (2009-2010)
Tuition and fees: $4,740; out-of-state residents $15,900.
Room and board: $11,970.

FINANCIAL AID PICTURE (2009-2010)
Students with need: Out of 2,895 full-time freshmen who applied for aid, 2,174 were judged to have need. Of these, 2,067 received aid, and 160 had their full need met. Average financial aid package met 65% of need; average scholarship/grant was $9,357; average loan was $2,567. For part-time students, average financial aid package was $8,427.
Students without need: This college awards aid only to students with need.
Scholarships offered: *Merit:* Presidential Scholarship: 3.8 GPA and California residency required. *Athletic:* 18 full-time freshmen received athletic scholarships; average amount $2,322.
Cumulative student debt: 39% of graduating class had student loans; average debt was $15,636.

FINANCIAL AID PROCEDURES
Forms required: FAFSA.
Dates and Deadlines: Priority date 3/2; no closing date. Applicants notified on a rolling basis starting 2/1; must reply within 2 week(s) of notification.

CONTACT
Barbara Hubler, Director of Financial Aid
1600 Holloway Avenue, San Francisco, CA 94132
(415) 338-7000

San Joaquin Delta College
Stockton, California
www.deltacollege.edu   Federal Code: 001280

2-year public community college in large city.
Enrollment: 7,927 full-time undergrads.
Selectivity: Open admission; but selective for some programs.

BASIC COSTS (2009-2010)
Tuition and fees: $782; out-of-state residents $6,482.
Per-credit charge: $26; out-of-state residents $216.

FINANCIAL AID PICTURE (2008-2009)
Students with need: Need-based aid available for full-time and part-time students. Work study available nights, weekends, and for part-time students.
Students without need: No-need awards available for academics, athletics.
Additional info: Enrollment fee waivers available for low-income California residents.

FINANCIAL AID PROCEDURES
Forms required: FAFSA, institutional form.
Dates and Deadlines: Closing date 6/30. Applicants notified on a rolling basis starting 5/1; must reply within 3 week(s) of notification.
Transfers: No deadline.

CONTACT
Denise Donn, Director of Financial Aid
5151 Pacific Avenue, Stockton, CA 95207-6370
(209) 954-5115

San Joaquin Valley College
Visalia, California
www.sjvc.edu   Federal Code: 021207

2-year for-profit junior college in small city.
Enrollment: 1,000 undergrads.
Selectivity: Open admission; but selective for some programs.

BASIC COSTS (2009-2010)

Tuition and fees: $12,450.

Additional info: Costs may vary by program, annual tuition includes text-books and supplies.

FINANCIAL AID PICTURE

Students with need: Need-based aid available for full-time students.

FINANCIAL AID PROCEDURES

Forms required: FAFSA, state aid form, institutional form.

Dates and Deadlines: No deadline.

CONTACT

Kevin Robinson, Vice President of Student Financial Services
8400 West Mineral King Avenue, Visalia, CA 93291-9283
(559) 651-2500

San Jose State University
San Jose, California
www.sjsu.edu   Federal Code: 001155

4-year public university and liberal arts college in very large city.

Enrollment: 24,273 undergrads, 25% part-time. 4,708 full-time freshmen.

Selectivity: Admits 50 to 75% of applicants.

BASIC COSTS (2009-2010)

Tuition and fees: $5,054; out-of-state residents $16,214.

Room and board: $10,438.

FINANCIAL AID PICTURE (2008-2009)

Students with need: Out of 2,311 full-time freshmen who applied for aid, 2,112 were judged to have need. Of these, 2,035 received aid, and 706 had their full need met. Average financial aid package met 87% of need; average scholarship/grant was $5,864; average loan was $5,632. For part-time students, average financial aid package was $8,791.

Students without need: This college awards aid only to students with need.

Scholarships offered: 5 full-time freshmen received athletic scholarships; average amount $9,234.

FINANCIAL AID PROCEDURES

Forms required: FAFSA.

Dates and Deadlines: Priority date 3/2; closing date 6/12. Applicants notified on a rolling basis starting 4/10; must reply within 2 week(s) of notification.

CONTACT

Colleen Brown, Director of Financial Aid & Scholarships
One Washington Square, San Jose, CA 95192-0011
(408) 283-7500

Santa Ana College
Santa Ana, California
www.sac.edu   Federal Code: 001284

2-year public community college in large city.

Enrollment: 10,536 undergrads. 474 full-time freshmen.

Selectivity: Open admission.

BASIC COSTS (2009-2010)

Tuition and fees: $808; out-of-state residents $6,508.

Per-credit charge: $26; out-of-state residents $216.

FINANCIAL AID PICTURE (2008-2009)

Students with need: Out of 474 full-time freshmen who applied for aid, 469 were judged to have need. Of these, 463 received aid, and 5 had their full need met. Average financial aid package met 46% of need; average scholarship/grant was $4,459; average loan was $1,724. For part-time students, average financial aid package was $3,187.

FINANCIAL AID PROCEDURES

Forms required: FAFSA.

Dates and Deadlines: Priority date 6/30; no closing date. Applicants notified on a rolling basis starting 6/1; must reply within 2 week(s) of notification.

CONTACT

Robert Manson, Associate Dean of Financial Aid
1530 West 17th Street, Santa Ana, CA 92706
(714) 564-6242

Santa Barbara City College
Santa Barbara, California
www.sbcc.edu   Federal Code: 001285

2-year public community college in small city.

Enrollment: 20,448 undergrads.

Selectivity: Open admission; but selective for some programs.

BASIC COSTS (2009-2010)

Tuition and fees: $866; out-of-state residents $6,566.

Per-credit charge: $26; out-of-state residents $216.

Additional info: Tuition/fee waivers available for unemployed or children of unemployed.

FINANCIAL AID PICTURE (2009-2010)

Students with need: Need-based aid available for full-time and part-time students.

Additional info: California residents may qualify for Board of Governor's Financial Assistance Program, which will allow institutions to waive enrollment fee.

FINANCIAL AID PROCEDURES

Forms required: FAFSA.

Dates and Deadlines: No deadline. Applicants notified on a rolling basis starting 5/1; must reply within 2 week(s) of notification.

CONTACT

Brad Hardison, Director, Financial Aid
721 Cliff Drive, Santa Barbara, CA 93109-2394
(805) 965-0581 ext. 2716

Santa Clara University
Santa Clara, California   Federal Code: 001326
www.scu.edu   CSS Code: 4851

4-year private university in small city, affiliated with Roman Catholic Church.

Enrollment: 5,158 undergrads, 2% part-time. 1,085 full-time freshmen.

Selectivity: Admits 50 to 75% of applicants. GED not accepted.

BASIC COSTS (2010-2011)

Tuition and fees: $37,368.

Per-credit charge: $1,038.

Room and board: $11,742.

FINANCIAL AID PICTURE (2009-2010)

Students with need: Out of 714 full-time freshmen who applied for aid, 506 were judged to have need. Of these, 489 received aid, and 206 had their full need met. Average financial aid package met 74% of need; average scholarship/grant was $22,031; average loan was $3,289. Need-based aid available for part-time students.

Students without need: 272 full-time freshmen who did not demonstrate need for aid received scholarships/grants; average award was $10,373. No-need awards available for academics, alumni affiliation, athletics, music/drama, ROTC.

Scholarships offered: *Merit:* Presidential Scholar at Entry: full tuition; 10 students awarded; admitted with distinction. Provost Scholar: half tuition; 40 students awarded; admitted with distinction. National Merit Scholarship: $2,000; 4 students awarded. Dean's Scholarship: $3,000 to $12,000; admitted with distinction. Honors Program Scholarship: $2,000; by invitation and based on high academic achievement. Bannan Merit Scholarship: amount varies; based on high academic achievement. Jesuit Ignation Award: amount varies, to students of Jesuit high schools. *Athletic:* 75 full-time freshmen received athletic scholarships; average amount $26,264.

Cumulative student debt: 43% of graduating class had student loans; average debt was $23,909.

FINANCIAL AID PROCEDURES

Forms required: FAFSA, CSS PROFILE.

Dates and Deadlines: Priority date 2/1; no closing date. Applicants notified by 4/1; must reply by 5/1 or within 2 week(s) of notification.

Transfers: No deadline. Applicants notified on a rolling basis starting 4/1; must reply by 5/1 or within 2 week(s) of notification.

CONTACT

Richard Toomey, Dean of Financial Services
500 El Camino Real, Santa Clara, CA 95053
(408) 554-4505

Santa Monica College
Santa Monica, California
www.smc.edu   Federal Code: 001286

2-year public community college in small city.

Enrollment: 31,211 undergrads, 63% part-time. 3,875 full-time freshmen.

Selectivity: Open admission; but selective for some programs.

BASIC COSTS (2009-2010)

Tuition and fees: $826; out-of-state residents $6,526.

Per-credit charge: $26; out-of-state residents $216.

FINANCIAL AID PICTURE (2008-2009)

Students with need: Need-based aid available for full-time and part-time students.

FINANCIAL AID PROCEDURES

Forms required: FAFSA, institutional form.

Dates and Deadlines: No deadline. Applicants notified on a rolling basis starting 7/1; must reply within 2 week(s) of notification.

Transfers: No deadline.

CONTACT

Steve Myrow, Director of Financial Aid
1900 Pico Boulevard, Santa Monica, CA 90405-1628
(310) 434-4871

Santa Rosa Junior College
Santa Rosa, California
www.santarosa.edu   Federal Code: 001287

2-year public community college in small city.

Enrollment: 25,319 undergrads.

Selectivity: Open admission; but selective for some programs.

BASIC COSTS (2009-2010)

Tuition and fees: $814; out-of-state residents $6,514.

Per-credit charge: $26; out-of-state residents $216.

FINANCIAL AID PICTURE (2009-2010)

Students with need: 77% of average financial aid package awarded as scholarships/grants, 23% awarded as loans/jobs. Need-based aid available for part-time students. Work study available nights.

Students without need: No-need awards available for academics, art, leadership, music/drama, state/district residency.

Additional info: California's Board of Governors Program provides fee waivers for applicants with need.

FINANCIAL AID PROCEDURES

Forms required: FAFSA.

Dates and Deadlines: Priority date 3/1; no closing date. Applicants notified on a rolling basis starting 4/15.

CONTACT

Kristin Shear, Director of Financial Services
1501 Mendocino Avenue, Santa Rosa, CA 95401-4395
(707) 527-4471

Santiago Canyon College
Orange, California
www.sccollege.edu

2-year public community college in small city.

Enrollment: 5,555 undergrads. 177 full-time freshmen.

Selectivity: Open admission.

BASIC COSTS (2009-2010)

Tuition and fees: $808; out-of-state residents $6,508.

Per-credit charge: $26; out-of-state residents $216.

Additional info: Tuition/fee waivers available for adults, minority students, unemployed or children of unemployed.

FINANCIAL AID PICTURE (2008-2009)

Students with need: Out of 177 full-time freshmen who applied for aid, 150 were judged to have need. Of these, 147 received aid, and 2 had their full need met. Average financial aid package met 43% of need; average scholarship/grant was $3,120; average loan was $2,110. For part-time students, average financial aid package was $3,079.

Students without need: This college awards aid only to students with need.

FINANCIAL AID PROCEDURES

Forms required: FAFSA, state aid form, institutional form.

Dates and Deadlines: Priority date 7/1; no closing date. Applicants notified on a rolling basis starting 6/1.

Transfers: No deadline. Applicants notified by 6/1.

CONTACT

Syed Rizvi, Associate Dean of Fiancial Aid
8045 East Chapman Avenue, Orange, CA 92869
(714) 628-4876

School of Urban Missions: Oakland
Oakland, California
www.sum.edu   Federal Code: 037524

4-year private Bible college in very large city, affiliated with Assemblies of God.

Enrollment: 139 undergrads, 4% part-time. 40 full-time freshmen.

Selectivity: Admits 50 to 75% of applicants.

BASIC COSTS (2010-2011)

Tuition and fees: $7,830.

Per-credit charge: $255.

Room only: $2,400.

FINANCIAL AID PICTURE (2008-2009)

Students with need: Need-based aid available for full-time and part-time students.

Students without need: No-need awards available for academics, leadership, religious affiliation.

FINANCIAL AID PROCEDURES

Forms required: FAFSA.

Dates and Deadlines: No deadline.

Transfers: No deadline. Applicants notified on a rolling basis.

CONTACT

Dave Wallace, Financial Aid Director

735 105th Avenue, Oakland, CA 94603

(510) 567-6174

Scripps College

Claremont, California
www.scrippscollege.edu

Federal Code: 001174
CSS Code: 4693

4-year private liberal arts college for women in large town.

Enrollment: 898 undergrads. 252 full-time freshmen.

Selectivity: Admits less than 50% of applicants.

BASIC COSTS (2010-2011)

Tuition and fees: $40,450.

Per-credit charge: $1,258.

Room and board: $12,450.

FINANCIAL AID PICTURE (2008-2009)

Students with need: Out of 104 full-time freshmen who applied for aid, 73 were judged to have need. Of these, 73 received aid, and 73 had their full need met. Average financial aid package met 100% of need; average scholarship/grant was $30,601; average loan was $2,313. Need-based aid available for part-time students.

Students without need: 17 full-time freshmen who did not demonstrate need for aid received scholarships/grants; average award was $16,153. No-need awards available for academics, leadership.

Scholarships offered: James E. Scripps Scholarship; variable amount up to half-tuition; renewable; for distinguished young women whose intellectual and personal promise can be developed with a Scripps education.

Cumulative student debt: 38% of graduating class had student loans; average debt was $11,270.

FINANCIAL AID PROCEDURES

Forms required: FAFSA, CSS PROFILE, state aid form.

Dates and Deadlines: Closing date 2/1. Applicants notified by 4/1; must reply by 5/1.

Transfers: Priority date 4/1; closing date 4/1. Applicants notified by 5/1; must reply by 6/1 or within 2 week(s) of notification. Students applying for admission as a transfer student should be aware that financial aid may be limited or unavailable.

CONTACT

David Levy, Director of Financial Aid

1030 Columbia Avenue, Claremont, CA 91711-3905

(909) 621-8275

Shasta Bible College and Graduate School

Redding, California
www.shasta.edu

Federal Code: 016802

4-year private Bible college in small city, affiliated with Baptist faith.

Enrollment: 47 undergrads, 26% part-time. 10 full-time freshmen.

Selectivity: Admits over 75% of applicants.

BASIC COSTS (2010-2011)

Tuition and fees: $8,870.

Per-credit charge: $275.

Room and board: $2,400.

FINANCIAL AID PICTURE (2008-2009)

Students with need: 100% of average financial aid package awarded as scholarships/grants, 0% awarded as loans/jobs. Need-based aid available for part-time students.

Students without need: No-need awards available for music/drama.

FINANCIAL AID PROCEDURES

Forms required: FAFSA.

Dates and Deadlines: No deadline. Applicants notified on a rolling basis.

CONTACT

Connie Barton, Financial Aid Director

2951 Goodwater Avenue, Redding, CA 96002

Shasta College

Redding, California
www.shastacollege.edu

Federal Code: 001289

2-year public community and junior college in small city.

Enrollment: 13,034 undergrads.

Selectivity: Open admission; but selective for some programs.

BASIC COSTS (2009-2010)

Tuition and fees: $855; out-of-state residents $6,645.

Per-credit charge: $26; out-of-state residents $219.

Room only: $2,610.

FINANCIAL AID PICTURE (2008-2009)

Students with need: 74% of average financial aid package awarded as scholarships/grants, 26% awarded as loans/jobs. Need-based aid available for part-time students.

Students without need: This college awards aid only to students with need.

FINANCIAL AID PROCEDURES

Forms required: FAFSA, institutional form.

Dates and Deadlines: Priority date 3/2; no closing date. Applicants notified on a rolling basis starting 7/1.

CONTACT

Benna Starrett, Director of Financial Aid

Box 496006, Redding, CA 96049-6006

(530) 225-4735

Sierra College

Rocklin, California
www.sierracollege.edu

Federal Code: 001290

2-year public community college in small city.

Enrollment: 21,373 undergrads.

Selectivity: Open admission; but selective for some programs.

BASIC COSTS (2009-2010)

Tuition and fees: $836; out-of-state residents $6,536.

Per-credit charge: $26; out-of-state residents $216.

Room and board: $6,700.

Additional info: Tuition/fee waivers available for unemployed or children of unemployed.

FINANCIAL AID PICTURE (2009-2010)

Students with need: 68% of average financial aid package awarded as scholarships/grants, 32% awarded as loans/jobs. Need-based aid available for part-time students. Work study available nights, weekends, and for part-time students.

FINANCIAL AID PROCEDURES

Forms required: FAFSA.

Dates and Deadlines: Priority date 3/2; no closing date. Applicants notified on a rolling basis starting 5/15.

Transfers: No deadline.

CONTACT

Linda Williams, Financial Aid Program Manager
5000 Rocklin Road, Rocklin, CA 95677
(916) 660-7310

Simpson University

Redding, California
www.simpsonu.edu   Federal Code: 001291

4-year private liberal arts college in small city, affiliated with Christian and Missionary Alliance.

Enrollment: 953 undergrads, 3% part-time. 144 full-time freshmen.

Selectivity: Admits 50 to 75% of applicants.

BASIC COSTS (2010-2011)

Tuition and fees: $21,000.

Per-credit charge: $875.

Room and board: $7,000.

Additional info: Tuition/fee waivers available for minority students.

FINANCIAL AID PICTURE (2009-2010)

Students with need: Out of 144 full-time freshmen who applied for aid, 134 were judged to have need. Of these, 134 received aid. Need-based aid available for part-time students.

Students without need: 10 full-time freshmen who did not demonstrate need for aid received scholarships/grants. No-need awards available for academics, alumni affiliation, athletics, leadership, minority status, music/drama, religious affiliation, state/district residency.

Scholarships offered: Academic awards; up to full tuition for 4.0 GPA and 1200 minimum SAT (exclusive of Writing).

Additional info: Work-study programs available.

FINANCIAL AID PROCEDURES

Forms required: FAFSA, institutional form.

Dates and Deadlines: Priority date 3/2; no closing date. Applicants notified on a rolling basis starting 3/1; must reply within 4 week(s) of notification.

Transfers: No deadline. Applicants notified on a rolling basis starting 3/1; must reply within 4 week(s) of notification.

CONTACT

Melissa Hudson, Director of Financial Aid
2211 College View Drive, Redding, CA 96003-8606
(530) 226-4111

Skyline College

San Bruno, California
www.skylinecollege.edu   Federal Code: 007713

2-year public community college in small city.

Enrollment: 2,929 undergrads, 70% part-time.

Selectivity: Open admission; but selective for some programs.

BASIC COSTS (2009-2010)

Tuition and fees: $842; out-of-state residents $6,572.

Per-credit charge: $26; out-of-state residents $217.

FINANCIAL AID PICTURE

Students with need: Need-based aid available for full-time and part-time students.

FINANCIAL AID PROCEDURES

Forms required: FAFSA, institutional form.

Dates and Deadlines: Priority date 5/2; no closing date. Applicants notified on a rolling basis starting 5/1; must reply within 2 week(s) of notification.

CONTACT

Maria Escobar, Director of Financial Aid
3300 College Drive, San Bruno, CA 94066-1662
(650) 738-4484

Soka University of America

Aliso Viejo, California
www.soka.edu   Federal Code: 038144

4-year private university and liberal arts college in large town.

Enrollment: 439 undergrads.

BASIC COSTS (2010-2011)

Tuition and fees: $25,344.

Room and board: $9,640.

Additional info: Reported tuition and fees include a laptop computer.

FINANCIAL AID PICTURE (2008-2009)

Students with need: Need-based aid available for full-time and part-time students.

Students without need: No-need awards available for academics, athletics.

FINANCIAL AID PROCEDURES

Forms required: FAFSA.

Dates and Deadlines: Closing date 3/1. Applicants notified on a rolling basis starting 3/15; must reply within 4 week(s) of notification.

CONTACT

Christopher Brown, Director of Admission and Financial Aid
One University Drive, Aliso Viejo, CA 92656-8081
(949) 480-4150

Sonoma State University

Rohnert Park, California
www.sonoma.edu   Federal Code: 001156

4-year public university and liberal arts college in large town.

Enrollment: 7,483 undergrads, 12% part-time. 1,629 full-time freshmen.

Selectivity: Admits over 75% of applicants.

BASIC COSTS (2009-2010)

Tuition and fees: $5,290; out-of-state residents $16,450.

Room and board: $10,418.

FINANCIAL AID PICTURE (2008-2009)

Students with need: Out of 679 full-time freshmen who applied for aid, 394 were judged to have need. Of these, 336 received aid, and 98 had their full need met. Average financial aid package met 64% of need; average scholarship/grant was $8,264; average loan was $3,156. For part-time students, average financial aid package was $6,795.

Students without need: 23 full-time freshmen who did not demonstrate need for aid received scholarships/grants; average award was $1,498. No-need awards available for academics, alumni affiliation, art, athletics, leadership, minority status, music/drama.

Scholarships offered: 16 full-time freshmen received athletic scholarships; average amount $1,867.

FINANCIAL AID PROCEDURES

Forms required: FAFSA.

Dates and Deadlines: Priority date 1/31; no closing date. Applicants notified on a rolling basis starting 3/15; must reply within 2 week(s) of notification.

CONTACT

Susan Gutierrez, Director, Financial Aid
1801 East Cotati Avenue, Rohnert Park, CA 94928-3609
(707) 664-2389

Southern California Institute of Architecture

Los Angeles, California
www.sciarc.edu   Federal Code: 014073

5-year private visual arts college in very large city.

Enrollment: 245 undergrads. 43 full-time freshmen.

Selectivity: Admits over 75% of applicants.

BASIC COSTS (2010-2011)

Tuition and fees: $27,850.

FINANCIAL AID PICTURE (2008-2009)

Students with need: 11% of average financial aid package awarded as scholarships/grants, 89% awarded as loans/jobs. Need-based aid available for part-time students. Work study available nights, weekends, and for part-time students.

Students without need: No-need awards available for academics, state/district residency.

Cumulative student debt: 70% of graduating class had student loans; average debt was $11,200.

FINANCIAL AID PROCEDURES

Forms required: FAFSA, institutional form.

Dates and Deadlines: Priority date 3/1; closing date 5/2. Applicants notified on a rolling basis starting 4/15; must reply by 5/30.

Transfers: Priority date 3/2. Applicants notified on a rolling basis starting 4/15.

CONTACT

Helen Lara, Financial Aid Director
960 East Third Street, Los Angeles, CA 90013
(213) 613-2200 ext. 326

Southwestern College

Chula Vista, California
www.swccd.edu   Federal Code: 001294

2-year public community college in small city.

Enrollment: 23,283 undergrads.

Selectivity: Open admission; but selective for some programs.

BASIC COSTS (2009-2010)

Tuition and fees: $824; out-of-state residents $6,524.

Per-credit charge: $26; out-of-state residents $216.

FINANCIAL AID PICTURE

Students with need: Need-based aid available for full-time and part-time students. Work study available nights, weekends, and for part-time students.

FINANCIAL AID PROCEDURES

Forms required: FAFSA, state aid form.

Dates and Deadlines: Closing date 3/2. Applicants notified on a rolling basis starting 7/1.

CONTACT

Linda Thrower, Director of Financial Aid
900 Otay Lakes Road, Chula Vista, CA 91910-7297
(619) 482-6357

Stanford University

Stanford, California   Federal Code: 001305
www.stanford.edu   CSS Code: 4704

4-year private university in small city.

Enrollment: 6,564 undergrads. 1,703 full-time freshmen.

Selectivity: Admits less than 50% of applicants.

BASIC COSTS (2010-2011)

Tuition and fees: $38,700.

Room and board: $11,876.

FINANCIAL AID PICTURE (2008-2009)

Students with need: Out of 1,051 full-time freshmen who applied for aid, 863 were judged to have need. Of these, 859 received aid, and 824 had their full need met. Average financial aid package met 100% of need; average scholarship/grant was $38,037; average loan was $2,614. Need-based aid available for part-time students.

Students without need: This college awards aid only to students with need.

Scholarships offered: 183 full-time freshmen received athletic scholarships; average amount $15,868.

Cumulative student debt: 36% of graduating class had student loans; average debt was $16,219.

Additional info: For parents with total annual income below $60,000 and typical assets for this income range, Stanford will not expect a parent contribution toward educational costs. Students will still be expected to contribute toward their own expenses from their summer income, part-time work during the school year, and their own savings. For parents with total annual income below $100,000 and typical assets for this income range, Stanford will ensure that all tuition charges are covered with need-based scholarship, federal and state grants, and/or outside scholarship funds.

FINANCIAL AID PROCEDURES

Forms required: FAFSA, CSS PROFILE.

Dates and Deadlines: Priority date 2/15; no closing date. Applicants notified on a rolling basis starting 4/3; must reply by 5/1.

Transfers: Priority date 3/15.

CONTACT

Karen Cooper, Director, Financial Aid
Montag Hall, Stanford, CA 94305-6106
(650) 723-3058

Taft College

Taft, California
www.taftcollege.edu   Federal Code: 001309

2-year public community college in small town.

Enrollment: 13,247 undergrads.

Selectivity: Open admission.

BASIC COSTS (2009-2010)

Tuition and fees: $780; out-of-state residents $6,480.

Per-credit charge: $26; out-of-state residents $216.

Room and board: $3,824.

FINANCIAL AID PICTURE (2008-2009)

Students with need: 96% of average financial aid package awarded as scholarships/grants, 4% awarded as loans/jobs. Need-based aid available for part-time students. Work study available nights.

Students without need: No-need awards available for academics.

Scholarships offered: Taft College Merit Awards: $250; for students from local high schools; available for 2 years; based on GPA of 3.0 or higher. Taft College High School Merit Award: $600; for students from local high schools. Taft College Nonresident Awards: $4,230; applied to nonresident tuition; available for 1 year; based on GPA of 3.0 or higher.

FINANCIAL AID PROCEDURES

Forms required: FAFSA, institutional form.

Dates and Deadlines: No deadline. Applicants notified on a rolling basis; must reply within 4 week(s) of notification.

Transfers: No deadline.

CONTACT

Gayle Roberts, Director of Financial Aid
29 Emmons Park Drive, Taft, CA 93268
(661) 763-7762

Thomas Aquinas College
Santa Paula, California
www.thomasaquinas.edu   Federal Code: 023580

4-year private liberal arts college in rural community, affiliated with Roman Catholic Church.

Enrollment: 345 undergrads. 102 full-time freshmen.

Selectivity: Admits over 75% of applicants.

BASIC COSTS (2010-2011)

Tuition and fees: $22,400.

Room and board: $7,400.

FINANCIAL AID PICTURE (2008-2009)

Students with need: 62% of average financial aid package awarded as scholarships/grants, 38% awarded as loans/jobs. Work study available nights, weekends, and for part-time students.

Students without need: This college awards aid only to students with need.

FINANCIAL AID PROCEDURES

Forms required: FAFSA, state aid form, institutional form.

Dates and Deadlines: Closing date 3/2. Applicants notified on a rolling basis starting 1/1; must reply by 5/1 or within 2 week(s) of notification.

CONTACT

Gregory Becher, Director of Financial Aid
10000 North Ojai Road, Santa Paula, CA 93060-9621
(800) 634-9797

University of California: Berkeley
Berkeley, California
www.berkeley.edu   Federal Code: 001312

4-year public university in small city.

Enrollment: 25,530 undergrads.

Selectivity: Admits less than 50% of applicants.

BASIC COSTS (2009-2010)

Tuition and fees: $8,325; out-of-state residents $30,346.

Room and board: $15,308.

FINANCIAL AID PICTURE (2009-2010)

Students with need: Need-based aid available for full-time and part-time students.

Students without need: No-need awards available for academics.

Scholarships offered: University Scholarship, President's Undergraduate Fellowships, Regents and Chancellor's Scholarships, Alumni Scholarships.

FINANCIAL AID PROCEDURES

Forms required: FAFSA, state aid form.

Dates and Deadlines: Closing date 3/2. Applicants notified by 4/15.

Transfers: Closing date 3/2. Applicants notified by 4/15.

CONTACT

Cheryl Resh, Assistant Vice Chancellor of Financial Aid and Scholarships
110 Sproul Hall, #5800, Berkeley, CA 94720-5800
(510) 642-6000

University of California: Davis
Davis, California
www.ucdavis.edu   Federal Code: 001313

4-year public university in small city.

Enrollment: 24,453 undergrads, 1% part-time. 4,413 full-time freshmen.

Selectivity: Admits less than 50% of applicants.

BASIC COSTS (2009-2010)

Tuition and fees: $9,364; out-of-state residents $32,033.

Room and board: $12,361.

Additional info: Non-resident undergraduates pay an additional $648 in educational fees.

FINANCIAL AID PICTURE (2009-2010)

Students with need: Need-based aid available for full-time and part-time students. Work study available nights, weekends, and for part-time students.

Students without need: This college awards aid only to students with need.

FINANCIAL AID PROCEDURES

Forms required: FAFSA.

Dates and Deadlines: Priority date 3/2; no closing date. Applicants notified on a rolling basis starting 3/12.

CONTACT

Kathryn Maloney, Interim Director of Financial Aid
One Shields Ave, Davis, CA 95616
(530) 752 2390

University of California: Irvine
Irvine, California
www.uci.edu   Federal Code: 001314

4-year public university in small city.

Enrollment: 22,226 undergrads, 2% part-time. 4,561 full-time freshmen.

Selectivity: Admits less than 50% of applicants.

BASIC COSTS (2009-2010)

Tuition and fees: $9,399; out-of-state residents $32,068.

Room and board: $11,291.

Additional info: Tuition not charged to in-state residents.

FINANCIAL AID PICTURE (2008-2009)

Students with need: Out of 3,578 full-time freshmen who applied for aid, 2,376 were judged to have need. Of these, 2,268 received aid, and 1,162 had their full need met. Average financial aid package met 84% of need; average scholarship/grant was $10,946; average loan was $5,889. For part-time students, average financial aid package was $11,403.

Students without need: 148 full-time freshmen who did not demonstrate need for aid received scholarships/grants; average award was $6,325. No-need awards available for academics, art, athletics, job skills, leadership, music/drama, state/district residency.

Scholarships offered: 43 full-time freshmen received athletic scholarships; average amount $9,796.

Cumulative student debt: 46% of graduating class had student loans; average debt was $14,323.

FINANCIAL AID PROCEDURES

Forms required: FAFSA, state aid form.
Dates and Deadlines: Priority date 5/3; closing date 6/30.

CONTACT

Christopher Shultz, Director of Financial Aid
204 Aldrich Hall, Irvine, CA 92697-1075
(949) 824-8262

University of California: Los Angeles
Los Angeles, California
www.ucla.edu   Federal Code: 001315

4-year public university in very large city.
Enrollment: 26,687 undergrads, 3% part-time. 4,442 full-time freshmen.
Selectivity: Admits less than 50% of applicants.

BASIC COSTS (2009-2010)
Tuition and fees: $9,151; out-of-state residents $31,820.
Room and board: $13,314.

FINANCIAL AID PICTURE (2008-2009)
Students with need: Need-based aid available for full-time and part-time students.
Students without need: No-need awards available for academics, alumni affiliation, athletics, ROTC.

FINANCIAL AID PROCEDURES
Forms required: FAFSA.
Dates and Deadlines: Priority date 3/2; no closing date. Applicants notified on a rolling basis starting 3/15; must reply within 3 week(s) of notification.

CONTACT
Ronald Johnson, Director, Financial Aid Office
1147 Murphy Hall, Los Angeles, CA 90095-1436
(310) 206-0400

University of California: Merced
Merced, California
www.ucmerced.edu   Federal Code: 041271

4-year public university in small city.
Enrollment: 3,190 undergrads, 1% part-time. 1,127 full-time freshmen.
Selectivity: Admits over 75% of applicants.

BASIC COSTS (2009-2010)
Tuition and fees: $8,411; out-of-state residents $31,080.
Room and board: $12,211.

FINANCIAL AID PICTURE (2009-2010)
Students with need: Need-based aid available for full-time and part-time students. Work study available nights, weekends, and for part-time students.
Students without need: No-need awards available for academics.
Scholarships offered: Regents' Scholarships: based on strength and breadth of academic program, grades, personal statement, extracurricular activities, community activities, first-generation status, other indicators of academic excellence and promise.

FINANCIAL AID PROCEDURES
Forms required: FAFSA.
Dates and Deadlines: Priority date 3/2; no closing date. Applicants notified on a rolling basis starting 3/2.
Transfers: Applicants notified on a rolling basis starting 3/2.

CONTACT
Diana Ralls, Director of Financial Aid & Scholarships
5200 North Lake Road, Merced, CA 95343-5603
(209) 228-4243

University of California: Riverside
Riverside, California
www.ucr.edu   Federal Code: 001316

4-year public university in large city.
Enrollment: 16,996 undergrads, 3% part-time. 4,272 full-time freshmen.
Selectivity: Admits over 75% of applicants.

BASIC COSTS (2009-2010)
Tuition and fees: $8,507; out-of-state residents $31,178.
Room and board: $10,900.

FINANCIAL AID PICTURE (2009-2010)
Students with need: Out of 3,717 full-time freshmen who applied for aid, 3,014 were judged to have need. Of these, 2,957 received aid, and 1,436 had their full need met. Average financial aid package met 91% of need; average scholarship/grant was $14,081; average loan was $4,761. For part-time students, average financial aid package was $14,326.
Students without need: 56 full-time freshmen who did not demonstrate need for aid received scholarships/grants; average award was $6,221. No-need awards available for academics, art, athletics, job skills, leadership, music/drama, state/district residency.
Scholarships offered: *Merit:* Regents and Chancellor's Scholarships: available to top-ranked incoming freshmen, including international and home-schooled admits. *Athletic:* 26 full-time freshmen received athletic scholarships; average amount $11,680.
Cumulative student debt: 62% of graduating class had student loans; average debt was $16,398.

FINANCIAL AID PROCEDURES
Forms required: FAFSA, state aid form.
Dates and Deadlines: Closing date 3/2. Applicants notified on a rolling basis starting 3/1; must reply by 5/1 or within 3 week(s) of notification.
Transfers: Deadlines may be extended for mid-year admissions.

CONTACT
Sheryl Hayes, Director of Financial Aid
Admissions Office, Riverside, CA 92521
(951) 827-3878

University of California: San Diego
La Jolla, California
www.ucsd.edu   Federal Code: 001317

4-year public university in large town.
Enrollment: 24,817 undergrads. 4,288 full-time freshmen.
Selectivity: Admits less than 50% of applicants.

BASIC COSTS (2009-2010)
Tuition and fees: $8,798; out-of-state residents $31,467.
Room and board: $11,057.

FINANCIAL AID PICTURE (2008-2009)
Students with need: Out of 3,450 full-time freshmen who applied for aid, 2,472 were judged to have need. Of these, 2,380 received aid, and 450 had their full need met. Average financial aid package met 85% of need; average scholarship/grant was $12,310; average loan was $4,971. For part-time students, average financial aid package was $12,587.
Students without need: 133 full-time freshmen who did not demonstrate need for aid received scholarships/grants; average award was $8,708. No-

need awards available for academics, art, athletics, leadership, minority status, music/drama.

Scholarships offered: 116 full-time freshmen received athletic scholarships; average amount $522.

Cumulative student debt: 50% of graduating class had student loans; average debt was $16,317.

FINANCIAL AID PROCEDURES

Forms required: FAFSA, state aid form.

Dates and Deadlines: Priority date 3/2; closing date 6/1. Applicants notified on a rolling basis starting 3/15; must reply within 3 week(s) of notification.

Transfers: Applicants notified on a rolling basis; must reply within 3 week(s) of notification.

CONTACT

Ann Klein, Director of Financial Aid
9500 Gilman Drive, 0021, La Jolla, CA 92093-0021
(858) 534-4480

University of California: Santa Barbara
Santa Barbara, California
www.ucsb.edu   Federal Code: 001320

4-year public university in small city.

Enrollment: 19,793 undergrads, 2% part-time. 4,362 full-time freshmen.

Selectivity: Admits less than 50% of applicants.

BASIC COSTS (2009-2010)

Tuition and fees: $9,077; out-of-state residents $31,746.

Room and board: $12,405.

FINANCIAL AID PICTURE (2008-2009)

Students with need: Out of 3,389 full-time freshmen who applied for aid, 2,361 were judged to have need. Of these, 2,202 received aid, and 643 had their full need met. Average financial aid package met 82% of need; average scholarship/grant was $14,219; average loan was $4,935. For part-time students, average financial aid package was $14,329.

Students without need: 75 full-time freshmen who did not demonstrate need for aid received scholarships/grants; average award was $6,105. No-need awards available for academics, athletics.

Scholarships offered: 63 full-time freshmen received athletic scholarships; average amount $9,589.

Cumulative student debt: 47% of graduating class had student loans; average debt was $17,107.

FINANCIAL AID PROCEDURES

Dates and Deadlines: Priority date 3/2; closing date 5/31. Must reply within 2 week(s) of notification.

Transfers: California residents must apply for a CAL grant from the California Student Aid Commission; must complete and submit FAFSA by March 2.

CONTACT

Mike Miller, Director of Financial Aid
1210 Cheadle Hall, Santa Barbara, CA 93106-2014
(805) 893-2432

University of California: Santa Cruz
Santa Cruz, California
www.ucsc.edu   Federal Code: 001321

4-year public university in small city.

Enrollment: 15,206 undergrads, 1% part-time. 3,954 full-time freshmen.

Selectivity: Admits 50 to 75% of applicants.

BASIC COSTS (2009-2010)

Tuition and fees: $10,095; out-of-state residents $22,071.

Room and board: $13,641.

Additional info: Tuition/fee waivers available for unemployed or children of unemployed.

FINANCIAL AID PICTURE (2008-2009)

Students with need: Out of 3,039 full-time freshmen who applied for aid, 2,048 were judged to have need. Of these, 1,927 received aid, and 641 had their full need met. Average financial aid package met 85% of need; average scholarship/grant was $12,009; average loan was $5,033. For part-time students, average financial aid package was $12,114.

Students without need: 60 full-time freshmen who did not demonstrate need for aid received scholarships/grants; average award was $9,745. No-need awards available for academics, alumni affiliation, art, leadership, music/drama.

Cumulative student debt: 53% of graduating class had student loans; average debt was $15,918.

FINANCIAL AID PROCEDURES

Forms required: FAFSA, state aid form.

Dates and Deadlines: Closing date 3/2. Applicants notified on a rolling basis starting 4/1; must reply within 4 week(s) of notification.

CONTACT

Ann Draper, Director of Financial Aid
Cook House, 1156 High Street, Santa Cruz, CA 95064
(831) 459-2963

University of La Verne
La Verne, California
www.laverne.edu   Federal Code: 001216

4-year private university and liberal arts college in large town.

Enrollment: 1,507 undergrads, 5% part-time. 329 full-time freshmen.

Selectivity: Admits 50 to 75% of applicants.

BASIC COSTS (2010-2011)

Tuition and fees: $29,800.

Per-credit charge: $845.

Room and board: $10,440.

FINANCIAL AID PICTURE (2009-2010)

Students with need: Need-based aid available for full-time and part-time students.

Students without need: No-need awards available for academics, alumni affiliation, art, leadership, minority status, music/drama, religious affiliation.

FINANCIAL AID PROCEDURES

Forms required: FAFSA, state aid form.

Dates and Deadlines: Priority date 3/2; no closing date. Applicants notified on a rolling basis starting 3/17; must reply within 2 week(s) of notification.

Transfers: No deadline.

CONTACT

Leatha Webster, Director of Financial Aid
1950 Third Street, La Verne, CA 91750
(800) 649-0160

University of Redlands
Redlands, California
www.redlands.edu   Federal Code: 001322

4-year private university and liberal arts college in small city.

Enrollment: 2,928 undergrads, 23% part-time. 561 full-time freshmen.

Selectivity: Admits 50 to 75% of applicants.

BASIC COSTS (2010-2011)

Tuition and fees: $35,540.

Per-credit charge: $1,101.

Room and board: $10,832.

FINANCIAL AID PICTURE (2009-2010)

Students with need: Out of 491 full-time freshmen who applied for aid, 455 were judged to have need. Of these, 449 received aid, and 85 had their full need met. Average financial aid package met 71% of need; average scholarship/grant was $25,240; average loan was $4,979. For part-time students, average financial aid package was $21,276.

Students without need: 73 full-time freshmen who did not demonstrate need for aid received scholarships/grants; average award was $14,297. No-need awards available for academics, art, music/drama.

Cumulative student debt: 70% of graduating class had student loans; average debt was $17,290.

FINANCIAL AID PROCEDURES

Forms required: FAFSA, state aid form.

Dates and Deadlines: Priority date 2/15; no closing date. Applicants notified on a rolling basis starting 2/28; must reply by 5/1.

Transfers: No deadline.

CONTACT

Bethann Corey, Financial Aid Director

1200 East Colton Avenue, Redlands, CA 92373-0999

(909) 748-8047

University of San Diego

San Diego, California

www.sandiego.edu   Federal Code: 010395

4-year private university in very large city, affiliated with Roman Catholic Church.

Enrollment: 5,066 undergrads, 4% part-time. 1,260 full-time freshmen.

Selectivity: Admits less than 50% of applicants.

BASIC COSTS (2010-2011)

Tuition and fees: $37,378.

Per-credit charge: $1,275.

Room and board: $11,602.

FINANCIAL AID PICTURE (2008-2009)

Students with need: Out of 743 full-time freshmen who applied for aid, 591 were judged to have need. Of these, 591 received aid, and 115 had their full need met. Average financial aid package met 75% of need; average scholarship/grant was $21,463; average loan was $5,528. For part-time students, average financial aid package was $14,591.

Students without need: 234 full-time freshmen who did not demonstrate need for aid received scholarships/grants; average award was $13,952. No-need awards available for academics, athletics, leadership, music/drama, religious affiliation, ROTC.

Scholarships offered: 23 full-time freshmen received athletic scholarships; average amount $28,762.

Cumulative student debt: 57% of graduating class had student loans; average debt was $27,999.

FINANCIAL AID PROCEDURES

Forms required: FAFSA.

Dates and Deadlines: Priority date 3/2; no closing date. Applicants notified on a rolling basis starting 3/1; must reply by 5/1 or within 3 week(s) of notification.

Transfers: No deadline. Entering transfer students not eligible for institutional merit-based scholarships.

CONTACT

Judith Lewis Logue, Director of Financial Aid Services

5998 Alcala Park, San Diego, CA 92110

(619) 260-4514

University of San Francisco

San Francisco, California

www.usfca.edu   Federal Code: 001325

4-year private university in very large city, affiliated with Roman Catholic Church.

Enrollment: 5,000 undergrads, 3% part-time. 1,072 full-time freshmen.

Selectivity: Admits 50 to 75% of applicants.

BASIC COSTS (2010-2011)

Tuition and fees: $36,380.

Per-credit charge: $1,280.

Room and board: $11,990.

FINANCIAL AID PICTURE (2009-2010)

Students with need: Need-based aid available for full-time and part-time students.

Students without need: No-need awards available for academics, athletics, ROTC.

Scholarships offered: University Scholars Program: $19,500 per year for 4 years; must have 3.8 weighted GPA and combined SAT of 1320 on Critical Reading and Math sections or ACT composite of 30. Applicants must apply for admission by November 15.

Additional info: Individualized installment plans available.

FINANCIAL AID PROCEDURES

Forms required: FAFSA.

Dates and Deadlines: Priority date 2/1; no closing date. Applicants notified on a rolling basis starting 4/1; must reply within 4 week(s) of notification.

CONTACT

Susan Murphy, Senior Associate Dean, Director, Enrollment and Financial Services

2130 Fulton Street, San Francisco, CA 94117-1046

(415) 422-6303

University of Southern California

Los Angeles, California   Federal Code: 001328

www.usc.edu   CSS Code: 4852

4-year private university in very large city.

Enrollment: 16,445 undergrads, 3% part-time. 2,766 full-time freshmen.

Selectivity: Admits less than 50% of applicants. GED not accepted.

BASIC COSTS (2009-2010)

Tuition and fees: $39,274.

Room and board: $11,458.

FINANCIAL AID PICTURE (2009-2010)

Students with need: Out of 1,761 full-time freshmen who applied for aid, 1,185 were judged to have need. Of these, 1,185 received aid, and 1,153 had their full need met. Average financial aid package met 100% of need; average scholarship/grant was $25,657; average loan was $3,757. For part-time students, average financial aid package was $13,941.

Students without need: 688 full-time freshmen who did not demonstrate need for aid received scholarships/grants; average award was $15,726. No-need awards available for academics, alumni affiliation, art, athletics, leadership, music/drama, ROTC.

Scholarships offered: *Merit:* Trustee Scholarship: full tuition; approximately 100 awards annually; finalists invited to a mandatory interview. Presidential Scholarship: one-half tuition; approximately 200 awarded annually; finalists invited to a mandatory interview. National Merit Presidential Scholarship: one-half tuition; number of awards varies; admitted Freshmen who are National Merit Finalists and who designate USC as their first-choice college will receive this award. Deans Scholarship: one-quarter tuition; approximately 50 awards annually. *Athletic:* 102 full-time freshmen received athletic scholarships; average amount $34,146.

Cumulative student debt: 45% of graduating class had student loans; average debt was $30,097.

FINANCIAL AID PROCEDURES

Forms required: FAFSA, CSS PROFILE.

Dates and Deadlines: Priority date 2/2; no closing date. Applicants notified on a rolling basis starting 3/15; must reply by 5/1.

Transfers: Applicants notified by 5/1.

CONTACT

Susan Ikerd, Associate Dean and Director
Office of Admission, Los Angeles, CA 90089-0911
(213) 740-1111

University of the Pacific
Stockton, California
www.pacific.edu   Federal Code: 001329

4-year private university in large city.

Enrollment: 3,489 undergrads, 3% part-time. 892 full-time freshmen.

Selectivity: Admits less than 50% of applicants.

BASIC COSTS (2009-2010)

Tuition and fees: $30,880.

Per-credit charge: $1,048.

Room and board: $10,118.

FINANCIAL AID PICTURE (2009-2010)

Students with need: Out of 786 full-time freshmen who applied for aid, 665 were judged to have need. Of these, 664 received aid, and 245 had their full need met. For part-time students, average financial aid package was $23,071.

Students without need: 148 full-time freshmen who did not demonstrate need for aid received scholarships/grants; average award was $8,824. No-need awards available for academics, athletics, leadership, music/drama, religious affiliation.

Scholarships offered: 26 full-time freshmen received athletic scholarships; average amount $27,355.

FINANCIAL AID PROCEDURES

Forms required: FAFSA.

Dates and Deadlines: Priority date 2/15; no closing date. Applicants notified on a rolling basis starting 3/15.

CONTACT

Lynn Fox, Director of Financial Aid
3601 Pacific Avenue, Stockton, CA 95211-0197
(209) 946-2011

Vanguard University of Southern California
Costa Mesa, California
www.vanguard.edu   Federal Code: 001293

4-year private university and liberal arts college in small city, affiliated with Assemblies of God.

Enrollment: 1,565 undergrads, 18% part-time. 276 full-time freshmen.

Selectivity: Admits over 75% of applicants.

BASIC COSTS (2010-2011)

Tuition and fees: $26,342.

Per-credit charge: $1,098.

Room and board: $8,280.

FINANCIAL AID PICTURE (2008-2009)

Students with need: Out of 248 full-time freshmen who applied for aid, 206 were judged to have need. Of these, 206 received aid, and 36 had their full need met. Average financial aid package met 73% of need; average scholarship/grant was $9,424; average loan was $3,864. For part-time students, average financial aid package was $11,867.

Students without need: 58 full-time freshmen who did not demonstrate need for aid received scholarships/grants; average award was $8,069. No-need awards available for academics, athletics, music/drama, religious affiliation.

Scholarships offered: 21 full-time freshmen received athletic scholarships; average amount $10,097.

FINANCIAL AID PROCEDURES

Forms required: FAFSA, state aid form.

Dates and Deadlines: Priority date 3/2; closing date 3/2. Applicants notified on a rolling basis starting 4/1; must reply within 3 week(s) of notification.

Transfers: Applicants notified on a rolling basis.

CONTACT

Robyn Fournier, Director of Financial Aid
55 Fair Drive, Costa Mesa, CA 92626-9601
(714) 556-3610 ext. 4250

Ventura College
Ventura, California
www.venturacollege.edu   Federal Code: 001334

2-year public community college in small city.

Enrollment: 14,754 undergrads.

Selectivity: Open admission; but selective for some programs.

BASIC COSTS (2009-2010)

Tuition and fees: $822; out-of-state residents $6,492.

Per-credit charge: $26; out-of-state residents $215.

FINANCIAL AID PICTURE

Students with need: Need-based aid available for full-time and part-time students.

FINANCIAL AID PROCEDURES

Forms required: FAFSA, state aid form.

Dates and Deadlines: Priority date 3/2; no closing date. Applicants notified on a rolling basis.

CONTACT

Dora Washington, Director, Financial Aid
4667 Telegraph Road, Ventura, CA 93003
(805) 654-6369

Victor Valley College
Victorville, California   Federal Code: 001335
www.vvc.edu   CSS Code: 4932

2-year public community college in small city.

Enrollment: 5,955 undergrads.

Selectivity: Open admission; but selective for some programs.

BASIC COSTS (2009-2010)

Tuition and fees: $790; out-of-state residents $6,490.

Per-credit charge: $26; out-of-state residents $216.

Additional info: Nevada residents may qualify for tuition reduction program as part of Good Neighbor policy.

FINANCIAL AID PICTURE

Students with need: Need-based aid available for full-time and part-time students.

Additional info: Board of Governors grant pays enrollment fee in full for low-income students.

FINANCIAL AID PROCEDURES

Forms required: FAFSA, CSS PROFILE, state aid form, institutional form.
Dates and Deadlines: Priority date 3/2; no closing date. Applicants notified on a rolling basis starting 8/1; must reply within 4 week(s) of notification.

CONTACT

Greg Ryan, Associate Director, Office of Financial Aid
18422 Bear Valley Road, Victorville, CA 92392-5850
(760) 245-4271 ext. 2377

West Hills College: Coalinga

Coalinga, California
www.westhillscollege.com   Federal Code: 001176

2-year public community college in small town.
Enrollment: 2,786 undergrads.
Selectivity: Open admission.

BASIC COSTS (2009-2010)

Tuition and fees: $780; out-of-state residents $6,480.
Per-credit charge: $26; out-of-state residents $216.
Room and board: $5,321.
Additional info: Additional $250 refundable deposit for room and board plan. Tuition/fee waivers available for unemployed or children of unemployed.

FINANCIAL AID PICTURE

Students with need: Need-based aid available for full-time and part-time students.

FINANCIAL AID PROCEDURES

Forms required: FAFSA.
Dates and Deadlines: Priority date 3/2; no closing date. Applicants notified on a rolling basis starting 6/1.

CONTACT

Dolores Smith, District Director of Financial Aid
300 Cherry Lane, Coalinga, CA 93210
(559) 934-2310

West Los Angeles College

Culver City, California
www.wlac.edu   Federal Code: 008596

2-year public community college in large town.
Enrollment: 11,440 undergrads.
Selectivity: Open admission.

BASIC COSTS (2009-2010)

Tuition and fees: $802; out-of-state residents $6,442.
Per-credit charge: $26; out-of-state residents $214.
Additional info: Tuition/fee waivers available for unemployed or children of unemployed.

FINANCIAL AID PICTURE (2009-2010)

Students with need: Need-based aid available for full-time and part-time students.
Students without need: This college awards aid only to students with need.
Additional info: California residents may qualify for Board of Governors Grant Program.

FINANCIAL AID PROCEDURES

Forms required: FAFSA.

Dates and Deadlines: No deadline. Applicants notified on a rolling basis; must reply within 4 week(s) of notification.
Transfers: No deadline.

CONTACT

Glenn Schenk, Financial Aid Manager
9000 Overland Avenue, Culver City, CA 90230
(310) 287-4533

West Valley College

Saratoga, California
www.westvalley.edu   Federal Code: 001338

2-year public community college in large town.
Enrollment: 12,233 undergrads.
Selectivity: Open admission.

BASIC COSTS (2009-2010)

Tuition and fees: $850; out-of-state residents $6,280.
Per-credit charge: $26; out-of-state residents $207.
Additional info: Tuition/fee waivers available for unemployed or children of unemployed.

FINANCIAL AID PICTURE

Students with need: Need-based aid available for full-time and part-time students.
Students without need: This college awards aid only to students with need.

FINANCIAL AID PROCEDURES

Forms required: FAFSA.
Dates and Deadlines: Priority date 5/31; no closing date. Applicants notified on a rolling basis starting 7/1.

CONTACT

Maritza Cantarero, Director of Financial Aid
14000 Fruitvale Avenue, Saratoga, CA 95070-5698
(408) 867-2200

Western Career College: Emeryville

Emeryville, California
www.westerncollege.edu

4-year for-profit technical college in small town.
Enrollment: 204 undergrads.
Selectivity: Open admission.

BASIC COSTS (2009-2010)

Additional info: ASHS: tuition $11,748, fees $1,439; CJD: tuition $24,825, fees $2,326; GD: tuition $20,745, fees $382; GDD: tuition $29,289, fees $1,384; HCA: tuition $16,596, fees $796; HCAD: tuition $28,344, fees $2,235; HIT: tuition $16,596, fees $1,306; HITD: tuition $28,344, fees $2,745; MA: tuition $16,596, fees $411; MAD: tuition $28,344, fees $1,850; PTD: tuition $24,825, fees $1,825. Registration fee $100.

FINANCIAL AID PICTURE

Students with need: Need-based aid available for full-time students.

FINANCIAL AID PROCEDURES

Forms required: FAFSA.
Dates and Deadlines: Applicants notified on a rolling basis.

CONTACT

6001 Shellmound, #145, Emeryville, CA 94608
(510) 601-0133

Westmont College

Santa Barbara, California
www.westmont.edu
Federal Code: 001341

4-year private liberal arts college in small city, affiliated with nondenominational tradition.

Enrollment: 1,293 undergrads. 332 full-time freshmen.

Selectivity: Admits over 75% of applicants.

BASIC COSTS (2009-2010)

Tuition and fees: $33,190.

Room and board: $10,550.

FINANCIAL AID PICTURE (2009-2010)

Students with need: Out of 252 full-time freshmen who applied for aid, 206 were judged to have need. Of these, 206 received aid, and 21 had their full need met. Average financial aid package met 71% of need; average scholarship/grant was $20,396; average loan was $4,070.

Students without need: 101 full-time freshmen who did not demonstrate need for aid received scholarships/grants; average award was $9,769. No-need awards available for academics, art, athletics, leadership, minority status, music/drama.

Scholarships offered: *Merit:* Scholarships automatically awarded to entering students based on GPA and SAT or ACT scores (first-year students) or college academic GPA (transfers): renewable annually; unlimited number awarded until class is full. First-year scholarships: Presidential ($14,000), must maintain 3.25 GPA; Provost ($12,000), must maintain 3.0 GPA; Dean's ($10,000), must maintain 2.75 GPA. ***Athletic:*** 11 full-time freshmen received athletic scholarships; average amount $20,652.

Cumulative student debt: 61% of graduating class had student loans; average debt was $25,565.

FINANCIAL AID PROCEDURES

Forms required: FAFSA.

Dates and Deadlines: Priority date 3/1; no closing date. Applicants notified on a rolling basis starting 3/15; must reply by 5/1 or within 2 week(s) of notification.

Transfers: Applicants notified on a rolling basis starting 4/1; must reply by 5/1 or within 2 week(s) of notification. Transfer students may qualify for academic merit scholarships.

CONTACT

Diane Horvath, Director of Financial Aid
955 La Paz Road, Santa Barbara, CA 93108-1089
(888) 963-4624

Westwood College: Inland Empire

Upland, California
www.westwood.edu
Federal Code: 007548

3-year for-profit business and technical college in small city.

Enrollment: 1,200 undergrads.

BASIC COSTS (2009-2010)

Tuition and fees: $14,763.

Per-credit charge: $410.

Additional info: Approximately 368 per unit for degree completers (transfer in 24.5 units or more).

FINANCIAL AID PICTURE

Students with need: Need-based aid available for full-time and part-time students. Work study available nights, weekends, and for part-time students.

Students without need: No-need awards available for academics.

FINANCIAL AID PROCEDURES

Forms required: FAFSA, institutional form.

Dates and Deadlines: No deadline. Must reply within 1 week(s) of notification.

Transfers: No deadline.

CONTACT

Erin Vargas, Director of Student Finance and Business Office
20 West Seventh Street, Upland, CA 91786
(909) 931-7599

Whittier College

Whittier, California
www.whittier.edu
Federal Code: 001342

4-year private liberal arts college in small city.

Enrollment: 1,361 undergrads, 1% part-time. 355 full-time freshmen.

Selectivity: Admits 50 to 75% of applicants.

BASIC COSTS (2010-2011)

Tuition and fees: $35,442.

Per-credit charge: $1,490.

Room and board: $10,026.

FINANCIAL AID PICTURE (2009-2010)

Students with need: Out of 355 full-time freshmen who applied for aid, 256 were judged to have need. Of these, 256 received aid, and 68 had their full need met. Average financial aid package met 89% of need; average scholarship/grant was $12,698; average loan was $9,384. For part-time students, average financial aid package was $31,060.

Students without need: 77 full-time freshmen who did not demonstrate need for aid received scholarships/grants; average award was $16,474. No-need awards available for academics, alumni affiliation, art, leadership, minority status.

Cumulative student debt: 78% of graduating class had student loans; average debt was $40,220.

Additional info: Auditions required for talent scholarship applicants in art, music, and theater.

FINANCIAL AID PROCEDURES

Forms required: FAFSA, institutional form.

Dates and Deadlines: Priority date 3/1; closing date 6/30. Applicants notified on a rolling basis starting 2/15; must reply within 2 week(s) of notification.

Transfers: Priority date 2/1. Applicants notified on a rolling basis starting 3/1; must reply by 6/1 or within 2 week(s) of notification.

CONTACT

David Carnevale, Director of Student Financing
13406 East Philadelphia Street, Whittier, CA 90608-0634
(562) 907-4285

William Jessup University

Rocklin, California
www.jessup.edu
Federal Code: 001281

4-year private Bible and liberal arts college in small city, affiliated with nondenominational tradition.

Enrollment: 539 undergrads, 24% part-time. 89 full-time freshmen.

Selectivity: Admits over 75% of applicants.

BASIC COSTS (2010-2011)

Tuition and fees: $19,980.

Per-credit charge: $850.

Room and board: $8,230.

FINANCIAL AID PICTURE (2009-2010)

Students with need: Out of 79 full-time freshmen who applied for aid, 70 were judged to have need. Of these, 70 received aid, and 7 had their full need met. Average financial aid package met 77% of need; average scholarship/grant was $16,199; average loan was $2,605. For part-time students, average financial aid package was $7,094.

Students without need: 13 full-time freshmen who did not demonstrate need for aid received scholarships/grants; average award was $6,041. No-need awards available for academics, athletics, leadership, minority status, music/drama, religious affiliation, state/district residency.

Scholarships offered: 11 full-time freshmen received athletic scholarships; average amount $3,830.

Cumulative student debt: 67% of graduating class had student loans; average debt was $17,389.

FINANCIAL AID PROCEDURES

Forms required: FAFSA.

Dates and Deadlines: Priority date 3/2; no closing date. Applicants notified on a rolling basis starting 3/2; must reply within 3 week(s) of notification.

CONTACT

Korey Compaan, Director of Financial Aid
333 Sunset Boulevard, Rocklin, CA 95765
(916) 577-2233

Woodbury University
Burbank, California
www.woodbury.edu   Federal Code: 001343

4-year private university in very large city.

Enrollment: 1,269 undergrads, 17% part-time. 135 full-time freshmen.

Selectivity: Admits less than 50% of applicants.

BASIC COSTS (2010-2011)

Tuition and fees: $28,855.

Per-credit charge: $965.

Room and board: $9,293.

FINANCIAL AID PICTURE (2008-2009)

Students with need: Out of 113 full-time freshmen who applied for aid, 107 were judged to have need. Of these, 107 received aid, and 5 had their full need met. Average financial aid package met 58% of need; average scholarship/grant was $15,303; average loan was $3,792. For part-time students, average financial aid package was $8,278.

Students without need: 28 full-time freshmen who did not demonstrate need for aid received scholarships/grants; average award was $6,753. No-need awards available for academics.

Cumulative student debt: 91% of graduating class had student loans; average debt was $47,059.

FINANCIAL AID PROCEDURES

Forms required: FAFSA, institutional form.

Dates and Deadlines: Priority date 3/2; no closing date. Applicants notified on a rolling basis starting 3/15; must reply within 2 week(s) of notification.

Transfers: No deadline. Applicants notified on a rolling basis starting 3/15; must reply by 5/1 or within 2 week(s) of notification.

CONTACT

Celeastia Williams, Director of Enrollment Services
7500 Glenoaks Boulevard, Burbank, CA 91510-7846
(818) 767-0888 ext. 273

Yeshiva Ohr Elchonon Chabad/West Coast Talmudical Seminary
Los Angeles, California   Federal Code: 015975

4-year private rabbinical college for men in very large city, affiliated with Jewish faith.

Enrollment: 132 undergrads. 49 full-time freshmen.

Selectivity: Open admission; but selective for some programs.

BASIC COSTS (2010-2011)

Tuition and fees: $11,500.

Room and board: $7,000.

Additional info: $200 book fee. Tuition/fee waivers available for minority students.

FINANCIAL AID PICTURE (2008-2009)

Students with need: 100% of average financial aid package awarded as scholarships/grants, 0% awarded as loans/jobs.

Students without need: This college awards aid only to students with need.

FINANCIAL AID PROCEDURES

Forms required: FAFSA, state aid form, institutional form.

Dates and Deadlines: Priority date 1/15; closing date 6/30. Applicants notified by 5/1; must reply by 7/1.

CONTACT

Hendy Tauber, Financial Aid Administrator
7215 Waring Avenue, Los Angeles, CA 90046
(323) 937-3763 ext. 12

Yuba Community College District
Marysville, California
www.yccd.edu   Federal Code: 001344

2-year public community college in small city.

Enrollment: 2,864 full-time undergrads.

Selectivity: Open admission; but selective for some programs.

BASIC COSTS (2009-2010)

Tuition and fees: $792; out-of-state residents $6,492.

Per-credit charge: $26; out-of-state residents $216.

Additional info: Tuition/fee waivers available for adults.

FINANCIAL AID PICTURE

Students with need: Need-based aid available for full-time and part-time students.

Students without need: No-need awards available for academics, athletics, job skills, minority status, music/drama.

Additional info: Tuition fee waiver based on Board of Governors Grant.

FINANCIAL AID PROCEDURES

Forms required: FAFSA.

Dates and Deadlines: Closing date 3/1. Applicants notified on a rolling basis starting 4/1.

CONTACT

Marisela Arce, Dean for EOP&S and Financial Aid
2088 North Beale Road, Marysville, CA 95901
(530) 741-6781

Colorado

Adams State College
Alamosa, Colorado
www.adams.edu   Federal Code: 001345

4-year public liberal arts college in small town.
Enrollment: 2,347 undergrads, 18% part-time. 463 full-time freshmen.
Selectivity: Admits 50 to 75% of applicants.

BASIC COSTS (2009-2010)
Tuition and fees: $4,454; out-of-state residents $13,598.
Room and board: $7,020.

FINANCIAL AID PICTURE (2008-2009)
Students with need: Out of 436 full-time freshmen who applied for aid, 345 were judged to have need. Of these, 341 received aid, and 2 had their full need met. Average financial aid package met 51% of need; average scholarship/grant was $50,844; average loan was $2,841. For part-time students, average financial aid package was $5,306.
Students without need: 18 full-time freshmen who did not demonstrate need for aid received scholarships/grants; average award was $2,377. No-need awards available for academics, alumni affiliation, art, athletics, leadership, minority status, music/drama, state/district residency.
Scholarships offered: 33 full-time freshmen received athletic scholarships; average amount $3,723.
Cumulative student debt: 65% of graduating class had student loans; average debt was $21,211.

FINANCIAL AID PROCEDURES
Forms required: FAFSA.
Dates and Deadlines: Priority date 3/1; closing date 4/15. Applicants notified on a rolling basis starting 4/30; must reply within 4 week(s) of notification.
Transfers: No deadline. Applicants notified on a rolling basis starting 4/30; must reply within 4 week(s) of notification.

CONTACT
Philip Schroeder, Director of Financial Aid
208 Edgemont Boulevard, Alamosa, CO 81102
(719) 587-7306

Aims Community College
Greeley, Colorado
www.aims.edu   Federal Code: 007582

2-year public community college in small city.
Enrollment: 4,041 undergrads.
Selectivity: Open admission; but selective for some programs.

BASIC COSTS (2009-2010)
Tuition and fees: $2,265; out-of-district residents $3,135; out-of-state residents $12,045.
Per-credit charge: $60; out-of-district residents $89; out-of-state residents $386.
Additional info: Tuition/fee waivers available for adults.

FINANCIAL AID PICTURE (2008-2009)
Students with need: Need-based aid available for full-time students.

FINANCIAL AID PROCEDURES
Forms required: FAFSA.
Dates and Deadlines: Priority date 4/15; no closing date. Applicants notified on a rolling basis starting 6/1.

CONTACT
Teri Dorchuck, Financial Aid Director
5401 West 20th Street, Greeley, CO 80632
(970) 330-8008 ext. 6304

Anthem College
Aurora, Colorado
www.cambridgecollege.com   Federal Code: 021829

2-year for-profit technical college in small city.
Enrollment: 600 undergrads.

BASIC COSTS (2009-2010)
Additional info: Tuition for associate degree programs $22,950 to $24,500 depending on program; tuition for diploma programs $12,450 to $23,850.

FINANCIAL AID PICTURE
Students with need: Need-based aid available for full-time students.
Students without need: This college awards aid only to students with need.

FINANCIAL AID PROCEDURES
Forms required: FAFSA, institutional form.
Dates and Deadlines: No deadline. Applicants notified on a rolling basis.

CONTACT
Gerry Major, Director of Financial Aid
350 Blackhawk Street, Aurora, CO 80011
(720) 859-7900

Arapahoe Community College
Littleton, Colorado
www.arapahoe.edu   Federal Code: 001346

2-year public community college in large town.
Enrollment: 8,226 undergrads.
Selectivity: Open admission; but selective for some programs.

BASIC COSTS (2009-2010)
Tuition and fees: $2,811; out-of-state residents $11,979.
Per-credit charge: $88; out-of-state residents $394.
Additional info: In-state tuition based upon assumption of Colorado Opportunity Fund waiver of $68 per-credit-hour.

FINANCIAL AID PICTURE (2008-2009)
Students with need: 47% of average financial aid package awarded as scholarships/grants, 53% awarded as loans/jobs. Need-based aid available for part-time students. Work study available nights, weekends, and for part-time students.
Students without need: No-need awards available for academics, leadership, state/district residency.
Scholarships offered: President's Scholarship; based on 3.0 GPA, references. College Bound Scholarship; based on high GED score. All awards $750 for full-time students, $375 for half-time, $563 for three-quarters time. Awards made on first-come first-served basis.

FINANCIAL AID PROCEDURES
Forms required: FAFSA, institutional form.
Dates and Deadlines: Priority date 5/1; no closing date. Applicants notified on a rolling basis starting 5/1; must reply within 3 week(s) of notification.
Transfers: No deadline. Applicants notified on a rolling basis starting 5/1.

CONTACT
Thad Spaulding, Associate Director of Financial Aid
PO Box 9002, Littleton, CO 80160-9002
(303) 797-5661

Art Institute of Colorado
Denver, Colorado
www.artinstitutes.edu/denver Federal Code: 013961

4-year for-profit culinary school and visual arts college in very large city.
Enrollment: 2,320 undergrads, 37% part-time. 460 full-time freshmen.

BASIC COSTS (2010-2011)
Tuition and fees: $24,796.
Per-credit charge: $473.
Additional info: Supply kit $565-$2,280 depending on program.

FINANCIAL AID PICTURE (2008-2009)
Students with need: 15% of average financial aid package awarded as scholarships/grants, 85% awarded as loans/jobs. Need-based aid available for part-time students. Work study available nights, weekends, and for part-time students.

FINANCIAL AID PROCEDURES
Forms required: FAFSA, institutional form.
Dates and Deadlines: No deadline. Applicants notified on a rolling basis.
Transfers: No deadline.

CONTACT
Shannon May, Director of Student Financial Services
1200 Lincoln Street, Denver, CO 80203-2983
(303) 824-4889

Bel-Rea Institute of Animal Technology
Denver, Colorado
www.bel-rea.com Federal Code: 012670

2-year for-profit technical college in very large city.
Enrollment: 630 undergrads.
Selectivity: Admits 50 to 75% of applicants.

BASIC COSTS (2009-2010)
Additional info: Tuition for full associate program $24,250.

FINANCIAL AID PICTURE
Students with need: Need-based aid available for full-time students.
Students without need: This college awards aid only to students with need.

FINANCIAL AID PROCEDURES
Forms required: FAFSA.
Dates and Deadlines: Priority date 8/31; no closing date. Applicants notified on a rolling basis starting 8/15.
Transfers: No deadline.

CONTACT
Stasi Botinelli, Financial Aid Director
1681 South Dayton Street, Denver, CO 80247
(303) 751-8700

Boulder College of Massage Therapy
Boulder, Colorado
www.bcmt.org Federal Code: 030131

2-year private health science college in small city.
Enrollment: 165 undergrads.
Selectivity: Open admission; but selective for some programs.

BASIC COSTS (2009-2010)
Additional info: Program costs range from $13,700-$17,500.

FINANCIAL AID PICTURE
Students with need: Need-based aid available for full-time and part-time students.
Students without need: This college awards aid only to students with need.

FINANCIAL AID PROCEDURES
Forms required: FAFSA.
Dates and Deadlines: No deadline.

CONTACT
Debbie Clarke, Director of Financial Aid
6255 Longbow Drive, Boulder, CO 80301
(303) 530-2100 ext. 106

CollegeAmerica: Denver
Denver, Colorado
www.collegeamerica.com Federal Code: 025943

2-year for-profit technical college in very large city.
Enrollment: 645 undergrads.
Selectivity: Open admission.

BASIC COSTS (2009-2010)
Additional info: Tuition, fees, books, and supplies: $37,500 for associate degree programs; $66,100 for bachelor's degree programs.

FINANCIAL AID PICTURE (2009-2010)
Students with need: Need-based aid available for full-time students.
Students without need: This college awards aid only to students with need.
Scholarships offered: High School Academic Scholarship.

FINANCIAL AID PROCEDURES
Forms required: FAFSA, institutional form.
Dates and Deadlines: No deadline. Applicants notified on a rolling basis; must reply within 4 week(s) of notification.
Transfers: No deadline. Applicants notified on a rolling basis.

CONTACT
Ruby Rowe, Corporate Director of Financial Aid
1385 South Colorado Boulevard, 5th Floor, Denver, CO 80222-1912
(303) 691-9756

Colorado Christian University
Lakewood, Colorado
www.ccu.edu Federal Code: 009401

4-year private university and liberal arts college in large city, affiliated with non-denominational tradition.
Enrollment: 2,031 undergrads, 36% part-time. 302 full-time freshmen.
Selectivity: Admits less than 50% of applicants.

BASIC COSTS (2010-2011)
Tuition and fees: $22,040.
Per-credit charge: $950.
Room and board: $9,120.

FINANCIAL AID PICTURE (2008-2009)
Students with need: 13% of average financial aid package awarded as scholarships/grants, 87% awarded as loans/jobs. Need-based aid available for part-time students. Work study available nights, weekends, and for part-time students.
Students without need: No-need awards available for academics, athletics, leadership, music/drama.

FINANCIAL AID PROCEDURES

Forms required: FAFSA.

Dates and Deadlines: Priority date 3/15; no closing date. Applicants notified on a rolling basis starting 4/1; must reply by 5/1 or within 4 week(s) of notification.

Transfers: Priority date 3/1; no deadline. Applicants notified by 3/10; must reply within 4 week(s) of notification.

CONTACT

Steve Woodburn, Director of Student Financial Aid
8787 West Alameda Avenue, Lakewood, CO 80226
(303) 963-3230

Colorado College

Colorado Springs, Colorado   Federal Code: 001347
www.coloradocollege.edu   CSS Code: 4072

4-year private liberal arts college in large city.

Enrollment: 1,966 undergrads. 526 full-time freshmen.

Selectivity: Admits less than 50% of applicants.

BASIC COSTS (2010-2011)

Tuition and fees: $38,698.

Per-credit charge: $1,200.

Room and board: $10,200.

FINANCIAL AID PICTURE (2009-2010)

Students with need: Need-based aid available for full-time and part-time students. Work study available nights, weekends, and for part-time students.

Students without need: No-need awards available for academics, athletics.

Scholarships offered: Barnes Scholarship; full tuition; available in all natural sciences; 4 or 5 awarded in chemistry, 4 available in remaining natural sciences. Trustee Scholarship; $7,000; based on highly rated entering students; 10 awarded. Merit Awards; up to $2,000; for National Merit finalists. Men's Ice Hockey and Women's Soccer merit awards. Colorado College Scholars; 10 merit awards for highly rated entering students from Colorado.

Additional info: Need-based financial aid available only to students enrolled half-time or more.

FINANCIAL AID PROCEDURES

Forms required: FAFSA, CSS PROFILE.

Dates and Deadlines: Closing date 2/15. Applicants notified by 3/20; must reply by 5/1.

Transfers: Closing date 4/1. Transfer students might not receive full-need package during first year.

CONTACT

James Swanson, Director of Financial Aid
14 East Cache La Poudre Street, Colorado Springs, CO 80903-9854
(719) 389-6651

Colorado Heights University

Denver, Colorado
www.chu.edu   Federal Code: 032893

4-year private business and liberal arts college in very large city.

Enrollment: 360 full-time undergrads.

Selectivity: Admits 50 to 75% of applicants.

FINANCIAL AID PICTURE

Students with need: Need-based aid available for full-time and part-time students. Work study available nights.

FINANCIAL AID PROCEDURES

Forms required: FAFSA.

Dates and Deadlines: No deadline.

CONTACT

Agustina Giron
3001 South Federal Boulevard, Denver, CO 80236
(303) 937-4538

Colorado Mountain College

Glenwood Springs, Colorado
www.coloradomtn.edu   Federal Code: 004506

2-year public community and liberal arts college in small town.

Enrollment: 5,095 undergrads.

Selectivity: Open admission; but selective for some programs.

BASIC COSTS (2009-2010)

Tuition and fees: $1,550; out-of-district residents $2,450; out-of-state residents $7,250.

Per-credit charge: $45; out-of-district residents $75; out-of-state residents $235.

Room and board: $7,400.

FINANCIAL AID PICTURE (2008-2009)

Students with need: Need-based aid available for full-time and part-time students. Work study available nights, weekends, and for part-time students.

Students without need: This college awards aid only to students with need.

FINANCIAL AID PROCEDURES

Forms required: FAFSA.

Dates and Deadlines: Priority date 3/31; no closing date. Applicants notified on a rolling basis starting 5/15; must reply within 4 week(s) of notification.

Transfers: Transfer scholarships available for Colorado residents with 3.0 GPA and minimum 20 credit hours from previous schools.

CONTACT

Gary Lewis, Director of Student Financial Aid
831 Grand Avenue, Glenwood Springs, CO 81601
(970) 947-8277

Colorado Northwestern Community College

Rangely, Colorado
www.cncc.edu   Federal Code: 001359

2-year public community college in rural community.

Enrollment: 748 undergrads, 42% part-time. 148 full-time freshmen.

Selectivity: Open admission; but selective for some programs.

BASIC COSTS (2009-2010)

Tuition and fees: $2,875; out-of-state residents $5,676.

Per-credit charge: $88; out-of-state residents $182.

Room and board: $5,868.

Additional info: In-state tuition based upon assumption of Colorado Opportunity Fund waiver of $68 per-credit-hour.

FINANCIAL AID PICTURE (2008-2009)

Students with need: Need-based aid available for full-time and part-time students. Work study available nights, weekends, and for part-time students.

Students without need: No-need awards available for academics, athletics, state/district residency.

Scholarships offered: Academic Scholarships; $200-$1,000; for Colorado residents based on grades, specific talent, area of study; requires application, essay, informal interview, 2.5 GPA.

FINANCIAL AID PROCEDURES

Forms required: FAFSA, institutional form.

Dates and Deadlines: Priority date 5/1; no closing date. Applicants notified on a rolling basis starting 5/15; must reply within 4 week(s) of notification.
Transfers: No deadline.

CONTACT

Merrie Byers, Financial Aid Technician
500 Kennedy Drive, Rangely, CO 81648
(970) 675-3204

Colorado School of Healing Arts

Lakewood, Colorado
www.csha.net   Federal Code: 035844

2-year for-profit career college in small city.
Enrollment: 200 undergrads.
Selectivity: Open admission.

BASIC COSTS (2009-2010)
Tuition and fees: $12,379.
Per-credit charge: $166.
Additional info: Books, massage table package, materials fees, and insurance are included in required fees.

FINANCIAL AID PICTURE (2008-2009)
Students with need: Need-based aid available for full-time and part-time students.
Students without need: This college awards aid only to students with need.

FINANCIAL AID PROCEDURES
Forms required: FAFSA.
Dates and Deadlines: No deadline.

CONTACT

Gina Simpson, Director of Financial Aid
7655 West Mississippi Avenue, Suite 100, Lakewood, CO 80226
(303) 986-2320

Colorado School of Mines

Golden, Colorado
www.mines.edu   Federal Code: 001348

4-year public university and engineering college in large town.
Enrollment: 3,605 undergrads, 4% part-time. 848 full-time freshmen.
Selectivity: Admits 50 to 75% of applicants.

BASIC COSTS (2009-2010)
Tuition and fees: $12,244; out-of-state residents $26,404.
Per-credit charge: $353; out-of-state residents $825.
Room and board: $8,120.

FINANCIAL AID PICTURE (2008-2009)
Students with need: Out of 689 full-time freshmen who applied for aid, 443 were judged to have need. Of these, 443 received aid, and 165 had their full need met. Average financial aid package met 84% of need; average scholarship/grant was $7,357; average loan was $4,471. For part-time students, average financial aid package was $8,619.
Students without need: 138 full-time freshmen who did not demonstrate need for aid received scholarships/grants; average award was $4,408. No-need awards available for academics, athletics.
Scholarships offered: 97 full-time freshmen received athletic scholarships; average amount $5,237.
Cumulative student debt: 62% of graduating class had student loans; average debt was $22,500.

FINANCIAL AID PROCEDURES
Forms required: FAFSA.

Dates and Deadlines: Priority date 2/1; no closing date. Applicants notified on a rolling basis starting 3/1.
Transfers: Applicants notified on a rolling basis starting 3/15. Federal aid only (Pell grant and Stafford loan) available for second undergraduate degree candidates.

CONTACT

Jill Robertson, Director of Financial Aid
Undergraduate Admissions, Golden, CO 80401
(303) 384-2252

Colorado School of Trades

Lakewood, Colorado
www.schooloftrades.com   Federal Code: 013513

2-year for-profit technical college in small city.
Enrollment: 148 undergrads.
Selectivity: Open admission.

BASIC COSTS (2010-2011)
Additional info: For gunsmithing program: tuition, $18,900; tools $3,000; miscellaneous $161.

FINANCIAL AID PICTURE (2009-2010)
Students with need: Need-based aid available for full-time students.

FINANCIAL AID PROCEDURES
Forms required: FAFSA, institutional form.

CONTACT

Robert Martin, President
1575 Hoyt Street, Lakewood, CO 80215-2945
(303) 233-4697 ext. 14

Colorado State University

Fort Collins, Colorado
www.colostate.edu   Federal Code: 001350

4-year public university in small city.
Enrollment: 21,204 undergrads, 7% part-time. 4,351 full-time freshmen.
Selectivity: Admits 50 to 75% of applicants.

BASIC COSTS (2009-2010)
Tuition and fees: $6,318; out-of-state residents $22,240.
Per-credit charge: $241; out-of-state residents $1,037.
Room and board: $8,378.

FINANCIAL AID PICTURE (2008-2009)
Students with need: Out of 3,152 full-time freshmen who applied for aid, 1,720 were judged to have need. Of these, 1,720 received aid, and 750 had their full need met. Average financial aid package met 73% of need; average scholarship/grant was $6,728; average loan was $4,595. For part-time students, average financial aid package was $7,037.
Students without need: 497 full-time freshmen who did not demonstrate need for aid received scholarships/grants; average award was $2,970. No-need awards available for academics, art, athletics, leadership, music/drama, ROTC, state/district residency.
Scholarships offered: 48 full-time freshmen received athletic scholarships; average amount $15,801.
Cumulative student debt: 57% of graduating class had student loans; average debt was $20,432.

FINANCIAL AID PROCEDURES
Forms required: FAFSA.
Dates and Deadlines: Priority date 3/1; no closing date. Applicants notified on a rolling basis starting 3/1.

CONTACT
Sandra Calhoun, Director of Student Financial Aid/Registrar
Office of Admissions/Colorado State University, Fort Collins, CO 80523-1062
(970) 491-6321

Colorado State University: Pueblo
Pueblo, Colorado
www.colostate-pueblo.edu   Federal Code: 001365

4-year public university in small city.
Enrollment: 4,735 undergrads, 18% part-time. 1,004 full-time freshmen.
Selectivity: Admits over 75% of applicants.

BASIC COSTS (2009-2010)
Tuition and fees: $5,210; out-of-state residents $15,602.
Room and board: $6,750.
Additional info: WUE tuition is $2,551 less per semester than out-of-state rate (15 credits per semester). Differential tuition charged for business, nursing, computer information systems, and engineering courses at $18.65 more per-credit-hour.

FINANCIAL AID PICTURE (2009-2010)
Students with need: Average financial aid package met 62% of need; average scholarship/grant was $5,871; average loan was $2,695. For part-time students, average financial aid package was $5,519.
Students without need: No-need awards available for academics, alumni affiliation, art, athletics, job skills, leadership, minority status, music/drama, ROTC, state/district residency.
Cumulative student debt: 46% of graduating class had student loans; average debt was $16,954.

FINANCIAL AID PROCEDURES
Forms required: FAFSA, institutional form.
Dates and Deadlines: Priority date 3/1; no closing date. Applicants notified on a rolling basis starting 3/13; must reply within 3 week(s) of notification.

CONTACT
Sean McGivney, Director of Financial Aid
2200 Bonforte Boulevard, Pueblo, CO 81001-4901
(719) 549-2753

Colorado Technical University
Colorado Springs, Colorado
www.coloradotech.edu   Federal Code: 010148

4-year for-profit university and technical college in large city.
Enrollment: 1,400 undergrads.
Selectivity: Open admission; but selective for some programs.

BASIC COSTS (2009-2010)
Tuition and fees: $13,340.

FINANCIAL AID PICTURE
Students with need: Need-based aid available for full-time and part-time students. Work study available nights, weekends, and for part-time students.
Students without need: No-need awards available for academics, ROTC.

FINANCIAL AID PROCEDURES
Forms required: FAFSA.
Dates and Deadlines: No deadline. Applicants notified on a rolling basis starting 6/30.
Transfers: No deadline.

CONTACT
Cindy Rubek, Director of Student Financial Services
4435 North Chestnut Street, Colorado Springs, CO 80907
(719) 598-0200

Community College of Aurora
Aurora, Colorado
www.ccaurora.edu   Federal Code: 016058

2-year public community college in large city.
Enrollment: 6,358 undergrads.
Selectivity: Open admission.

BASIC COSTS (2009-2010)
Tuition and fees: $2,805; out-of-state residents $11,973.
Per-credit charge: $88; out-of-state residents $394.
Additional info: In-state tuition based upon assumption of Colorado Opportunity Fund waiver of $68 per-credit-hour.

FINANCIAL AID PICTURE
Students with need: Need-based aid available for full-time and part-time students. Work study available nights.

FINANCIAL AID PROCEDURES
Forms required: FAFSA, institutional form.
Dates and Deadlines: Priority date 6/1; no closing date. Applicants notified on a rolling basis starting 7/15.

CONTACT
John Young, Executive Director, Financial Aid
16000 East CentreTech Parkway, Aurora, CO 80011-9036
(303) 360-4709

Community College of Denver
Denver, Colorado
www.ccd.edu   Federal Code: 009542

2-year public community college in very large city.
Enrollment: 5,257 undergrads, 68% part-time. 571 full-time freshmen.
Selectivity: Open admission; but selective for some programs.

BASIC COSTS (2009-2010)
Tuition and fees: $3,194; out-of-state residents $12,362.
Per-credit charge: $88; out-of-state residents $394.
Additional info: In-state tuition based upon assumption of Colorado Opportunity Fund waiver of $68 per-credit-hour.

FINANCIAL AID PICTURE (2008-2009)
Students with need: 58% of average financial aid package awarded as scholarships/grants, 42% awarded as loans/jobs. Need-based aid available for part-time students.
Students without need: No-need awards available for academics, leadership, state/district residency.

FINANCIAL AID PROCEDURES
Forms required: FAFSA, institutional form.
Dates and Deadlines: Priority date 3/1; no closing date. Applicants notified on a rolling basis.

CONTACT
Karla Nash, Director of Financial Aid
Campus Box 201, PO Box 173363, Denver, CO 80217-3363
(303) 556-2420

DeVry University: Westminster
Westminster, Colorado
www.devry.edu   Federal Code: 014831

4-year for-profit university in very large city.
Enrollment: 856 undergrads, 63% part-time. 53 full-time freshmen.

BASIC COSTS (2009-2010)

Tuition and fees: $14,160.

Per-credit charge: $550.

FINANCIAL AID PICTURE (2008-2009)

Students with need: Need-based aid available for full-time and part-time students.

Students without need: This college awards aid only to students with need.

FINANCIAL AID PROCEDURES

Forms required: FAFSA.

Dates and Deadlines: No deadline. Applicants notified on a rolling basis.

CONTACT

Terry Bargas, Director of Financial Aid .

1870 West 122 Avenue, Westminster, CO 80234-2010

(303) 329-3340

Fort Lewis College

Durango, Colorado

www.fortlewis.edu   Federal Code: 001353

4-year public liberal arts college in large town.

Enrollment: 3,571 undergrads, 7% part-time. 784 full-time freshmen.

Selectivity: Admits 50 to 75% of applicants.

BASIC COSTS (2009-2010)

Tuition and fees: $4,645; out-of-state residents $17,615.

Per-credit charge: $155; out-of-state residents $803.

Room and board: $7,444.

Additional info: Tuition/fee waivers available for minority students.

FINANCIAL AID PICTURE (2008-2009)

Students with need: Out of 548 full-time freshmen who applied for aid, 380 were judged to have need. Of these, 376 received aid, and 84 had their full need met. Average financial aid package met 66% of need; average scholarship/grant was $3,315; average loan was $3,062. For part-time students, average financial aid package was $4,997.

Students without need: 238 full-time freshmen who did not demonstrate need for aid received scholarships/grants; average award was $1,034. No-need awards available for academics, alumni affiliation, art, athletics, job skills, leadership, minority status, music/drama, state/district residency.

Scholarships offered: *Merit:* Presidential Scholarship; $8,000 out-of-state, $2,000 in-state; 121 admission index required. Provost Scholarship; $7,000 out-of-state, $1,500 in-state; 110-120 admission index required. Dean's Scholarship; $6,000 out-of-state, $1,000 in-state; 101-109 admission index required. Academic Promise Scholarship; $4,000 out-of-state, $750 in-state; 92-100 admission index required. New Mexico Reciprocal Scholarship; New Mexico residents are given in-state tuition rates; must have 3.5 GPA or higher; number of awards limited. *Athletic:* 52 full-time freshmen received athletic scholarships; average amount $5,056.

Cumulative student debt: 54% of graduating class had student loans; average debt was $15,962.

Additional info: Tuition waived for Native Americans of federally recognized tribes; census number and Certificate of Indian Blood must accompany application.

FINANCIAL AID PROCEDURES

Forms required: FAFSA.

Dates and Deadlines: Priority date 2/15; no closing date. Applicants notified on a rolling basis starting 3/15; must reply within 2 week(s) of notification.

Transfers: Closing date 2/15. Applicants notified on a rolling basis starting 3/15; must reply within 2 week(s) of notification.

CONTACT

Elaine Redwine, Director of Financial Aid

1000 Rim Drive, Durango, CO 81301-3999

(970) 247-7142

Front Range Community College

Westminster, Colorado

www.frontrange.edu   Federal Code: 007933

2-year public community college in large city.

Enrollment: 12,857 undergrads, 62% part-time. 1,394 full-time freshmen.

Selectivity: Open admission.

BASIC COSTS (2009-2010)

Tuition and fees: $2,893; out-of-state residents $12,061.

Per-credit charge: $88; out-of-state residents $394.

Additional info: In-state tuition based upon assumption of Colorado Opportunity Fund waiver of $68 per-credit-hour.

FINANCIAL AID PICTURE (2008-2009)

Students with need: 41% of average financial aid package awarded as scholarships/grants, 59% awarded as loans/jobs. Need-based aid available for part-time students. Work study available nights, weekends, and for part-time students.

Students without need: No-need awards available for academics, job skills, leadership, ROTC, state/district residency.

FINANCIAL AID PROCEDURES

Forms required: FAFSA, institutional form.

Dates and Deadlines: Priority date 5/1; no closing date. Applicants notified on a rolling basis starting 7/1; must reply within 3 week(s) of notification.

CONTACT

Director of Financial Aid

3645 West 112th Avenue, Westminster, CO 80031

(303) 439-9454

Johnson & Wales University: Denver

Denver, Colorado

www.jwu.edu   Federal Code: 003404

4-year private university in large city.

Enrollment: 1,461 undergrads, 2% part-time. 400 full-time freshmen.

Selectivity: Admits 50 to 75% of applicants.

BASIC COSTS (2010-2011)

Tuition and fees: $24,429.

Per-credit charge: $152.

Room and board: $8,904.

FINANCIAL AID PICTURE (2009-2010)

Students with need: Need-based aid available for full-time and part-time students.

Students without need: No-need awards available for academics, alumni affiliation, job skills, leadership, state/district residency.

FINANCIAL AID PROCEDURES

Forms required: FAFSA.

Dates and Deadlines: No deadline. Applicants notified on a rolling basis starting 3/1; must reply within 2 week(s) of notification.

CONTACT

Lynn Robinson, Chief Financial Aid Officer

7150 Montview Boulevard, Denver, CO 80220

(800) 342-5598 ext. 4648

Lamar Community College
Lamar, Colorado
www.lamarcc.edu   Federal Code: 001355

2-year public community college in large town.
Enrollment: 611 undergrads.
Selectivity: Open admission; but selective for some programs.

BASIC COSTS (2009-2010)
Tuition and fees: $2,863; out-of-state residents $5,844.
Per-credit charge: $88; out-of-state residents $182.
Room and board: $5,190.
Additional info: In-state tuition based upon assumption of Colorado Opportunity Fund waiver of $68 per-credit-hour.

FINANCIAL AID PICTURE
Students with need: Need-based aid available for full-time and part-time students.

FINANCIAL AID PROCEDURES
Forms required: FAFSA, institutional form.
Dates and Deadlines: Priority date 4/1; no closing date. Applicants notified on a rolling basis starting 7/1.
Transfers: No deadline.

CONTACT
Matt Martinez, Director of Financial Aid
2401 South Main Street, Lamar, CO 81052-3999

Mesa State College
Grand Junction, Colorado
www.mesastate.edu   Federal Code: 001358

4-year public community and liberal arts college in small city.
Enrollment: 6,375 undergrads, 21% part-time. 1,089 full-time freshmen.
Selectivity: Admits over 75% of applicants.

BASIC COSTS (2009-2010)
Tuition and fees: $5,374; out-of-state residents $14,340.
Per-credit charge: $168; out-of-state residents $488.
Room and board: $7,507.

FINANCIAL AID PICTURE (2008-2009)
Students with need: Out of 867 full-time freshmen who applied for aid, 629 were judged to have need. Of these, 586 received aid, and 43 had their full need met. Average financial aid package met 59% of need; average scholarship/grant was $4,460; average loan was $3,109. For part-time students, average financial aid package was $4,099.
Students without need: 102 full-time freshmen who did not demonstrate need for aid received scholarships/grants; average award was $2,099. No-need awards available for academics, art, athletics, leadership, music/drama.
Scholarships offered: 41 full-time freshmen received athletic scholarships; average amount $2,983.
Cumulative student debt: 53% of graduating class had student loans; average debt was $18,834.

FINANCIAL AID PROCEDURES
Forms required: FAFSA.
Dates and Deadlines: Priority date 3/1; no closing date. Applicants notified on a rolling basis starting 4/1; must reply within 5 week(s) of notification.

CONTACT
Curt Martin, Director of Financial Aid
1100 North Avenue, Grand Junction, CO 81501
(970) 248-1396

Metropolitan State College of Denver
Denver, Colorado
www.mscd.edu   Federal Code: 001360

4-year public liberal arts college in very large city.
Enrollment: 21,882 undergrads.

BASIC COSTS (2009-2010)
Tuition and fees: $3,639; out-of-state residents $13,132.
Per-credit charge: $119; out-of-state residents $514.

FINANCIAL AID PICTURE (2008-2009)
Students with need: Need-based aid available for full-time and part-time students.
Students without need: No-need awards available for academics, art, athletics, job skills, music/drama, state/district residency.

FINANCIAL AID PROCEDURES
Forms required: FAFSA.
Dates and Deadlines: Priority date 2/15; no closing date. Applicants notified on a rolling basis starting 3/1.
Transfers: No deadline.

CONTACT
Cindy Hejl, Director of Financial Aid
Campus Box 16, Denver, CO 80217

Morgan Community College
Fort Morgan, Colorado
www.morgancc.edu   Federal Code: 009981

2-year public community college in large town.
Enrollment: 1,671 undergrads.
Selectivity: Open admission; but selective for some programs.

BASIC COSTS (2009-2010)
Tuition and fees: $2,819; out-of-state residents $11,987.
Per-credit charge: $88; out-of-state residents $394.
Additional info: In-state tuition based upon assumption of Colorado Opportunity Fund waiver of $68 per-credit-hour.

FINANCIAL AID PICTURE (2009-2010)
Students with need: Need-based aid available for full-time and part-time students. Work study available nights, weekends, and for part-time students.

FINANCIAL AID PROCEDURES
Forms required: FAFSA.
Dates and Deadlines: Priority date 6/1; no closing date. Applicants notified on a rolling basis.

CONTACT
Sally Nestor, Director of Financial Aid
920 Barlow Road, Fort Morgan, CO 80701
(970) 542-3100

Naropa University
Boulder, Colorado
www.naropa.edu   Federal Code: 014652

4-year private university and liberal arts college in small city.
Enrollment: 464 undergrads, 8% part-time. 43 full-time freshmen.
Selectivity: Admits over 75% of applicants.

BASIC COSTS (2010-2011)
Tuition and fees: $25,100.
Per-credit charge: $810.

Room only: $5,076.

FINANCIAL AID PICTURE (2009-2010)

Students with need: Out of 32 full-time freshmen who applied for aid, 29 were judged to have need. Of these, 29 received aid, and 3 had their full need met. Average financial aid package met 86% of need; average scholarship/grant was $16,225; average loan was $7,547. For part-time students, average financial aid package was $13,307.

Students without need: This college awards aid only to students with need.

Cumulative student debt: 71% of graduating class had student loans; average debt was $23,717.

FINANCIAL AID PROCEDURES

Forms required: FAFSA.

Dates and Deadlines: Priority date 3/1; no closing date. Applicants notified on a rolling basis starting 3/1; must reply within 3 week(s) of notification.

Transfers: No deadline. Applicants notified on a rolling basis starting 1/15; must reply within 4 week(s) of notification.

CONTACT

Cheryl Barbour, Assistant Vice President of Student Administrative Services
2130 Arapahoe Avenue, Boulder, CO 80302-6697
(303) 546-3534

Nazarene Bible College

Colorado Springs, Colorado
www.nbc.edu   Federal Code: 013007

4-year private Bible college in very large city, affiliated with Church of the Nazarene.

Enrollment: 665 undergrads, 68% part-time.

Selectivity: Open admission; but selective for some programs.

BASIC COSTS (2010-2011)

Tuition and fees: $10,050.

Per-credit charge: $315.

FINANCIAL AID PICTURE (2008-2009)

Students with need: Need-based aid available for full-time and part-time students.

Students without need: No-need awards available for religious affiliation.

Additional info: Tuition waiver available to students serving as student body officers.

FINANCIAL AID PROCEDURES

Forms required: FAFSA.

Dates and Deadlines: Priority date 6/1; no closing date. Applicants notified on a rolling basis starting 6/15; must reply within 2 week(s) of notification.

CONTACT

Mal Britton, Director of Financial Aid
1111 Academy Park Loop, Colorado Springs, CO 80910-3704
(719) 884-5050

Northeastern Junior College

Sterling, Colorado
www.njc.edu   Federal Code: 001361

2-year public community and junior college in large town.

Enrollment: 1,282 undergrads, 26% part-time. 353 full-time freshmen.

Selectivity: Open admission; but selective for some programs.

BASIC COSTS (2009-2010)

Tuition and fees: $3,244; out-of-state residents $10,046.

Per-credit charge: $88; out-of-state residents $315.

Room and board: $5,654.

Additional info: In-state tuition based upon assumption of Colorado Opportunity Fund waiver of $68 per-credit-hour. Tuition/fee waivers available for adults, minority students.

FINANCIAL AID PICTURE (2008-2009)

Students with need: 54% of average financial aid package awarded as scholarships/grants, 46% awarded as loans/jobs. Need-based aid available for part-time students.

Students without need: No-need awards available for academics, alumni affiliation, art, athletics, job skills, leadership, music/drama, state/district residency.

Additional info: Need-based financial aid available to part-time students taking 6 credits or more per semester.

FINANCIAL AID PROCEDURES

Forms required: FAFSA, institutional form.

Dates and Deadlines: Priority date 3/1; no closing date. Applicants notified on a rolling basis starting 4/15; must reply within 3 week(s) of notification.

Transfers: No deadline. Applicants notified on a rolling basis starting 4/15; must reply within 3 week(s) of notification.

CONTACT

Alice Weingardt, Financial Aid Director
100 College Avenue, Sterling, CO 80751
(970) 521-6800

Otero Junior College

La Junta, Colorado
www.ojc.edu   Federal Code: 001362

2-year public community and junior college in small town.

Enrollment: 800 full-time undergrads.

Selectivity: Open admission; but selective for some programs.

BASIC COSTS (2009-2010)

Tuition and fees: $2,855; out-of-state residents $5,656.

Per-credit charge: $88; out-of-state residents $182.

Room and board: $5,172.

Additional info: In-state tuition based upon assumption of Colorado Opportunity Fund waiver of $68 per-credit-hour.

FINANCIAL AID PICTURE (2009-2010)

Students with need: Need-based aid available for full-time and part-time students. Work study available nights, weekends, and for part-time students.

Students without need: No-need awards available for academics, athletics, state/district residency.

FINANCIAL AID PROCEDURES

Forms required: FAFSA.

Dates and Deadlines: Priority date 4/15; no closing date. Applicants notified on a rolling basis starting 4/15; must reply within 2 week(s) of notification.

Transfers: No deadline. Applicants notified on a rolling basis starting 4/15; must reply within 2 week(s) of notification.

CONTACT

Janet Carrillo, Financial Aid Director
1802 Colorado Avenue, La Junta, CO 81050
(719) 384-6834

Pikes Peak Community College

Colorado Springs, Colorado
www.ppcc.edu   Federal Code: 008896

2-year public community college in large city.

Enrollment: 11,510 undergrads.

Selectivity: Open admission.

BASIC COSTS (2009-2010)

Tuition and fees: $2,897; out-of-state residents $12,065.

Per-credit charge: $88; out-of-state residents $394.

Additional info: In-state tuition based upon assumption of Colorado Opportunity Fund waiver of $68 per-credit-hour.

FINANCIAL AID PICTURE

Students with need: Need-based aid available for full-time and part-time students. Work study available nights.

FINANCIAL AID PROCEDURES

Forms required: FAFSA.

Dates and Deadlines: Priority date 7/1; no closing date. Applicants notified on a rolling basis starting 8/1; must reply within 2 week(s) of notification.

CONTACT

Sherri McCullough, Assistant Director of Financial Aid

5675 South Academy Boulevard, Colorado Springs, CO 80906-5498

(719) 502-3000

Platt College: Aurora

Aurora, Colorado

www.plattcolorado.edu   Federal Code: 030149

4-year for-profit visual arts and nursing college in very large city.

Enrollment: 180 undergrads.

Selectivity: Open admission; but selective for some programs.

BASIC COSTS (2009-2010)

Additional info: Visual and Performing Arts: associate program $34,000; bachelor's program $50,107. Nursing program (RN) $68,000. Costs include tuition, registration fee, lab fees, supplies. Cost of books, art kit vary with program.

FINANCIAL AID PICTURE

Students with need: Need-based aid available for full-time students.

Students without need: This college awards aid only to students with need.

FINANCIAL AID PROCEDURES

Forms required: FAFSA, institutional form.

Dates and Deadlines: No deadline. Applicants notified on a rolling basis.

CONTACT

Margie Rose, Director of Financial Aid

3100 South Parker Road, Aurora, CO 80014-3141

(303) 369-5151

Pueblo Community College

Pueblo, Colorado

www.pueblocc.edu   Federal Code: 014829

2-year public community college in small city.

Enrollment: 5,484 undergrads, 55% part-time. 555 full-time freshmen.

Selectivity: Open admission; but selective for some programs.

BASIC COSTS (2009-2010)

Tuition and fees: $2,992; out-of-state residents $12,160.

Per-credit charge: $88; out-of-state residents $394.

Additional info: In-state tuition based upon assumption of Colorado Opportunity Fund waiver of $68 per-credit-hour.

FINANCIAL AID PICTURE (2008-2009)

Students with need: Out of 480 full-time freshmen who applied for aid, 405 were judged to have need. Of these, 388 received aid, and 20 had their full need met. Average financial aid package met 50% of need; average scholarship/grant was $3,000; average loan was $2,000. For part-time students, average financial aid package was $3,000.

Students without need: 20 full-time freshmen who did not demonstrate need for aid received scholarships/grants; average award was $300. No-need awards available for academics, art, job skills, leadership, music/drama.

Cumulative student debt: 65% of graduating class had student loans; average debt was $12,000.

FINANCIAL AID PROCEDURES

Forms required: FAFSA.

Dates and Deadlines: Priority date 3/15; no closing date. Applicants notified on a rolling basis starting 4/1.

Transfers: No deadline. Applicants notified on a rolling basis starting 4/1.

CONTACT

Ron Swartwood, Director of Financial Aid

900 West Orman Avenue, Pueblo, CO 81004-1499

(719) 549-3020

Red Rocks Community College

Lakewood, Colorado

www.rrcc.edu   Federal Code: 009543

2-year public community college in small city.

Enrollment: 7,179 undergrads, 63% part-time. 680 full-time freshmen.

Selectivity: Open admission.

BASIC COSTS (2009-2010)

Tuition and fees: $2,946; out-of-state residents $12,114.

Per-credit charge: $88; out-of-state residents $394.

Additional info: In-state tuition based upon assumption of Colorado Opportunity Fund waiver of $68 per-credit-hour.

FINANCIAL AID PICTURE (2008-2009)

Students with need: Need-based aid available for full-time and part-time students. Work study available nights, weekends, and for part-time students.

FINANCIAL AID PROCEDURES

Forms required: FAFSA, institutional form.

Dates and Deadlines: Priority date 4/1; no closing date. Applicants notified on a rolling basis starting 6/1; must reply within 2 week(s) of notification.

CONTACT

Linda Crook, Director of Financial Aid

13300 West Sixth Avenue, Lakewood, CO 80228-1255

(303) 914-6256

Redstone College

Broomfield, Colorado

www.redstonecollege.com   Federal Code: 007297

2-year for-profit technical college in small city.

Enrollment: 581 undergrads.

Selectivity: Open admission.

BASIC COSTS (2009-2010)

Additional info: Tuition for entire associate degree ranges from $32,000 to $38,000 depending on program.

FINANCIAL AID PICTURE (2009-2010)

Students with need: Need-based aid available for full-time students.

Students without need: This college awards aid only to students with need.

FINANCIAL AID PROCEDURES

Forms required: FAFSA, state aid form.
Dates and Deadlines: No deadline. Applicants notified on a rolling basis; must reply within 2 week(s) of notification.

CONTACT

Alicia Harbin, Financial Aid Director
10851 West 120th Avenue, Broomfield, CO 80021-3401

Regis University

Denver, Colorado
www.regis.edu   Federal Code: 001363

4-year private university and liberal arts college in very large city, affiliated with Roman Catholic Church.
Enrollment: 1,503 undergrads, 2% part-time. 362 full-time freshmen.
Selectivity: Admits over 75% of applicants.

BASIC COSTS (2009-2010)

Tuition and fees: $29,700.
Per-credit charge: $919.
Room and board: $9,400.
Additional info: Tuition-free for any student who does not graduate in 4 years while maintaining required amount of credit hours.

FINANCIAL AID PICTURE (2008-2009)

Students with need: 24% of average financial aid package awarded as scholarships/grants, 76% awarded as loans/jobs. Need-based aid available for part-time students. Work study available nights, weekends, and for part-time students.
Students without need: No-need awards available for academics, athletics, leadership, minority status, religious affiliation, ROTC, state/district residency.

FINANCIAL AID PROCEDURES

Forms required: FAFSA.
Dates and Deadlines: Priority date 3/1; no closing date. Applicants notified on a rolling basis starting 3/15.

CONTACT

Ellie Miller, Director of Financial Aid
3333 Regis Boulevard, Mail Code B20, Denver, CO 80221-1099
(800) 388-2366 ext. 4126

Remington College: Colorado Springs

Colorado Springs, Colorado
www.remingtoncollege.edu   Federal Code: 030121

2-year for-profit technical college in very large city.
Enrollment: 121 undergrads. 106 full-time freshmen.
Selectivity: Open admission; but selective for some programs.

BASIC COSTS (2009-2010)

Additional info: Cost of entire program leading to diploma, associate, and bachelor's degrees ranges from $14,450 to $39,950; includes books and supplies.

FINANCIAL AID PICTURE (2009-2010)

Students with need: Need-based aid available for full-time and part-time students.
Students without need: This college awards aid only to students with need.

FINANCIAL AID PROCEDURES

Forms required: FAFSA.
Dates and Deadlines: No deadline. Applicants notified on a rolling basis; must reply within 3 week(s) of notification.
Transfers: No deadline. Applicants notified on a rolling basis.

CONTACT

Reid Allison, Chief Financial Officer
6050 Erin Park Drive, Colorado Springs, CO 80918
(407) 562-5761

Rocky Mountain College of Art & Design

Denver, Colorado
www.rmcad.edu   Federal Code: 013991

4-year for-profit visual arts college in very large city.
Enrollment: 576 undergrads, 9% part-time. 131 full-time freshmen.
Selectivity: Admits over 75% of applicants.

BASIC COSTS (2009-2010)

Tuition and fees: $24,840.
Per-credit charge: $1,035.
Additional info: Flat fee of $12,420 per term for students taking 12 to 18 credits.

FINANCIAL AID PICTURE (2009-2010)

Students with need: Out of 120 full-time freshmen who applied for aid, 113 were judged to have need. Of these, 113 received aid, and 8 had their full need met. Average financial aid package met 71% of need; average scholarship/grant was $4,462; average loan was $3,353. For part-time students, average financial aid package was $12,887.
Students without need: 17 full-time freshmen who did not demonstrate need for aid received scholarships/grants; average award was $5,934. No-need awards available for academics, art, state/district residency.
Cumulative student debt: 78% of graduating class had student loans; average debt was $29,174.

FINANCIAL AID PROCEDURES

Forms required: FAFSA.
Dates and Deadlines: Priority date 3/15; no closing date. Applicants notified on a rolling basis starting 4/5; must reply within 2 week(s) of notification.
Transfers: Must reply within 2 week(s) of notification.

CONTACT

Tammy Dybdahl, Director of Financial Aid
1600 Pierce Street, Denver, CO 80214
(303) 753-6046

Trinidad State Junior College

Trinidad, Colorado
www.trinidadstate.edu   Federal Code: 001368

2-year public community and junior college in small town.
Enrollment: 1,740 undergrads.
Selectivity: Open admission; but selective for some programs.

BASIC COSTS (2009-2010)

Tuition and fees: $3,054; out-of-state residents $5,855.
Per-credit charge: $88; out-of-state residents $182.
Room and board: $4,874.
Additional info: In-state tuition based upon assumption of Colorado Opportunity Fund waiver of $68 per-credit-hour.

FINANCIAL AID PICTURE (2008-2009)

Students with need: Need-based aid available for full-time and part-time students. Work study available nights.
Students without need: No-need awards available for academics, athletics, state/district residency.

FINANCIAL AID PROCEDURES

Forms required: FAFSA, institutional form.

Dates and Deadlines: Priority date 5/1; no closing date. Applicants notified on a rolling basis starting 6/15.

CONTACT

Wilma Atencio, Financial Aid Director

600 Prospect Street, Trinidad, CO 81082

(719) 846-5553

United States Air Force Academy

USAF Academy, Colorado

www.academyadmissions.com   Federal Code: 001369

4-year public university and military college in large city.

Enrollment: 4,620 undergrads. 1,316 full-time freshmen.

Selectivity: Admits less than 50% of applicants.

BASIC COSTS (2009-2010)

Additional info: Tuition, room, board, medical and dental care paid by U.S. Government. Each cadet receives monthly salary to pay for uniforms, supplies and personal expenses. A government loan is advanced to each member of the freshman class.

CONTACT

HQ USAF/RRS, 2304 Cadet Drive, Suite 2400, USAF Academy, CO 80840

University of Colorado at Boulder

Boulder, Colorado

www.colorado.edu   Federal Code: 001370

4-year public university in small city.

Enrollment: 26,405 undergrads, 6% part-time. 5,527 full-time freshmen.

Selectivity: Admits over 75% of applicants.

BASIC COSTS (2009-2010)

Tuition and fees: $7,932; out-of-state residents $28,186.

Room and board: $10,378.

Additional info: One-time new student fee of $182.

FINANCIAL AID PICTURE (2009-2010)

Students with need: Out of 4,941 full-time freshmen who applied for aid, 2,181 were judged to have need. Of these, 2,177 received aid, and 1,582 had their full need met. Average financial aid package met 92% of need; average scholarship/grant was $7,508; average loan was $5,715. For part-time students, average financial aid package was $14,301.

Students without need: 2,487 full-time freshmen who did not demonstrate need for aid received scholarships/grants; average award was $4,694. No-need awards available for academics, alumni affiliation, art, athletics, leadership, music/drama, ROTC, state/district residency.

Scholarships offered: *Merit:* Presidential Scholars Program; $15,000 per year during freshman and sophomore years, $12,500 per year during junior and senior years; for entering nonresident freshmen in the top 3-5% of admitted nonresident freshman class, based on high school GPA, class rank, and test scores; must maintain 2.75 GPA for renewal. Chancellor's Achievement Scholarship; $5,000 per year during freshman and sophomore years and $2,500 per year during junior and senior years; for top 25% of out-of-state admitted students, based on high school GPA and test scores; must maintain 2.75 GPA for renewal. CU Parents Association Freshmen Scholarship; $1,000; based on full-time entering freshman status with 3.5 GPA, academic excellence and extracurricular activities; 10-20 awarded annually; non-renewable. Norlin Scholars Program; $3,000; based on excellent academic or creative ability; 20-30 annual awards; renewable for 2 or 4 years contingent upon academic progress. *Athletic:* 60 full-time freshmen received athletic scholarships; average amount $15,783.

Cumulative student debt: 42% of graduating class had student loans; average debt was $19,211.

FINANCIAL AID PROCEDURES

Forms required: FAFSA.

Dates and Deadlines: Priority date 4/1; no closing date. Applicants notified on a rolling basis starting 3/1; must reply within 3 week(s) of notification.

Transfers: Some financial aid programs available exclusively to transfer students.

CONTACT

Gwen Pomper, Director of Financial Aid

552 UCB, Boulder, CO 80309-0552

(303) 492-5091

University of Colorado at Colorado Springs

Colorado Springs, Colorado

www.uccs.edu   Federal Code: 004509

4-year public university in large city.

Enrollment: 6,760 undergrads, 20% part-time. 822 full-time freshmen.

Selectivity: Admits 50 to 75% of applicants.

BASIC COSTS (2009-2010)

Tuition and fees: $7,076; out-of-state residents $16,973.

Room and board: $7,490.

Additional info: Tuition varies by program. One-time matriculation fee of $25 required.

FINANCIAL AID PICTURE (2008-2009)

Students with need: Out of 713 full-time freshmen who applied for aid, 385 were judged to have need. Of these, 375 received aid, and 70 had their full need met. Average financial aid package met 57% of need; average scholarship/grant was $4,787; average loan was $3,119. For part-time students, average financial aid package was $5,056.

Students without need: 127 full-time freshmen who did not demonstrate need for aid received scholarships/grants; average award was $1,284. No-need awards available for academics, alumni affiliation, athletics, state/district residency.

Scholarships offered: *Merit:* College Opportunity Fund for in-state undergraduates. *Athletic:* 11 full-time freshmen received athletic scholarships; average amount $2,386.

Cumulative student debt: 60% of graduating class had student loans; average debt was $18,725.

FINANCIAL AID PROCEDURES

Forms required: FAFSA.

Dates and Deadlines: Priority date 4/1; no closing date. Applicants notified on a rolling basis starting 4/15.

CONTACT

Robert Bode, Director of Financial Aid

1420 Austin Bluffs Parkway, Colorado Springs, CO 80933-7150

(719) 255-3460

University of Colorado at Denver

Denver, Colorado

www.ucdenver.edu   Federal Code: 006740

4-year public university in very large city.

Enrollment: 9,060 undergrads, 27% part-time. 744 full-time freshmen.

Selectivity: Admits 50 to 75% of applicants.

BASIC COSTS (2009-2010)

Tuition and fees: $6,657; out-of-state residents $19,689.

Additional info: Tuition varies by program. One-time matriculation fee of $115 required.

FINANCIAL AID PICTURE (2008-2009)

Students with need: Out of 688 full-time freshmen who applied for aid, 555 were judged to have need. Of these, 555 received aid, and 55 had their full need met. Average financial aid package met 59% of need; average scholarship/grant was $6,292; average loan was $3,074. For part-time students, average financial aid package was $5,508.

Students without need: 101 full-time freshmen who did not demonstrate need for aid received scholarships/grants; average award was $3,699. No-need awards available for academics, alumni affiliation, art, job skills, leadership, music/drama, ROTC, state/district residency.

Cumulative student debt: 66% of graduating class had student loans; average debt was $21,264.

FINANCIAL AID PROCEDURES

Forms required: FAFSA, institutional form.

Dates and Deadlines: Priority date 4/1; no closing date. Applicants notified on a rolling basis starting 5/1.

CONTACT

Patrick McTee, Director of Financial Aid
Box 173364, Campus Box 167, Denver, CO 80217-3364
(303) 556-2886

University of Denver

Denver, Colorado
www.du.edu
Federal Code: 001371
CSS Code: 4842

4-year private university in very large city, affiliated with United Methodist Church.
Enrollment: 5,314 undergrads, 10% part-time. 1,198 full-time freshmen.
Selectivity: Admits 50 to 75% of applicants.

BASIC COSTS (2010-2011)

Tuition and fees: $36,501.
Per-credit charge: $989.
Room and board: $10,224.

FINANCIAL AID PICTURE (2008-2009)

Students with need: Need-based aid available for full-time and part-time students.

Students without need: No-need awards available for academics, art, athletics, leadership, music/drama, state/district residency.

FINANCIAL AID PROCEDURES

Forms required: FAFSA, CSS PROFILE.
Dates and Deadlines: Priority date 3/1; no closing date.

CONTACT

Shawn Murphy, Associate Director, Financial Aid Programs
2197 South University Boulevard, Denver, CO 80208
(303) 871-4020

University of Northern Colorado

Greeley, Colorado
www.unco.edu
Federal Code: 001349

4-year public university in small city.
Enrollment: 9,710 undergrads, 8% part-time. 2,066 full-time freshmen.
Selectivity: Admits over 75% of applicants.

BASIC COSTS (2009-2010)

Tuition and fees: $5,116; out-of-state residents $15,364.
Per-credit charge: $179; out-of-state residents $606.
Room and board: $8,370.
Additional info: Costs reflect student share of tuition after the Colorado College Opportunity Fund.

FINANCIAL AID PICTURE (2008-2009)

Students with need: Out of 1,810 full-time freshmen who applied for aid, 961 were judged to have need. Of these, 915 received aid, and 565 had their full need met. Average financial aid package met 100% of need; average scholarship/grant was $5,230; average loan was $3,547. For part-time students, average financial aid package was $9,937.

Students without need: 558 full-time freshmen who did not demonstrate need for aid received scholarships/grants; average award was $2,520. No-need awards available for academics, athletics, music/drama.

Scholarships offered: 12 full-time freshmen received athletic scholarships; average amount $7,232.

FINANCIAL AID PROCEDURES

Forms required: FAFSA.

Dates and Deadlines: Priority date 3/1; no closing date. Applicants notified on a rolling basis starting 4/15; must reply within 4 week(s) of notification.

CONTACT

Donni Clark, Director of Financial Aid
1862 10th Avenue, Campus Box 10, Greeley, CO 80639
(970) 351-2502

Western State College of Colorado

Gunnison, Colorado
www.western.edu
Federal Code: 001372

4-year public liberal arts college in small town.
Enrollment: 2,193 undergrads.
Selectivity: Admits 50 to 75% of applicants.

BASIC COSTS (2009-2010)

Tuition and fees: $4,064; out-of-state residents $13,260.
Per-credit charge: $131; out-of-state residents $514.
Room and board: $8,324.
Additional info: Tuition/fee waivers available for unemployed or children of unemployed.

FINANCIAL AID PICTURE (2009-2010)

Students with need: Need-based aid available for full-time students. Work study available nights, weekends, and for part-time students.

Students without need: No-need awards available for academics, alumni affiliation, art, athletics, leadership, music/drama.

Scholarships offered: Academic Excellence Award; $1,000; based on 3.5 GPA and 22 ACT/1010 SAT. Non-resident Leadership Award; $2,500; based on 3.2 GPA, 990 SAT, leadership activities. SAT scores exclusive of Writing.

FINANCIAL AID PROCEDURES

Forms required: FAFSA.

Dates and Deadlines: Priority date 4/1; no closing date. Applicants notified on a rolling basis starting 4/1; must reply within 4 week(s) of notification.

CONTACT

Marty Somero, Director of Financial Aid
600 North Adams Street, Gunnison, CO 81231
(970) 943-3085

Westwood College: Denver North

Denver, Colorado
www.westwood.edu/locations/colorado/denver-north-campus
Federal Code: 007548

4-year for-profit technical college in very large city.
Enrollment: 4,215 full-time undergrads.

BASIC COSTS (2009-2010)
Additional info: Full-time tuition per 10-week term, $4,921 for most programs.

FINANCIAL AID PICTURE
Students with need: Need-based aid available for full-time and part-time students. Work study available nights.
Students without need: No-need awards available for academics, state/district residency.

FINANCIAL AID PROCEDURES
Forms required: FAFSA, state aid form, institutional form.
Dates and Deadlines: No deadline. Applicants notified on a rolling basis starting 1/1; must reply within 2 week(s) of notification.
Transfers: No deadline.

CONTACT
Amy Argyris, Director, Financial Aid
7350 North Broadway, Denver, CO 80221
(303) 426-7000

Westwood College: Denver South
Denver, Colorado
www.westwood.edu/locations/colorado/denver-south-campus
Federal Code: 007548

4-year for-profit technical and career college in very large city.
Enrollment: 455 undergrads.
Selectivity: Open admission.

BASIC COSTS (2009-2010)
Tuition and fees: $25,580.
Additional info: Tuition and fees may vary by program.

FINANCIAL AID PICTURE (2008-2009)
Students with need: Need-based aid available for full-time and part-time students. Work study available nights.

FINANCIAL AID PROCEDURES
Forms required: FAFSA, state aid form, institutional form.
Dates and Deadlines: No deadline. Applicants notified on a rolling basis; must reply within 2 week(s) of notification.

CONTACT
Maureen Wallace, Director of Campus Operations
3150 South Sheridan Boulevard, Denver, CO 80227-5507
(303) 934-1122

Connecticut

Albertus Magnus College
New Haven, Connecticut
www.albertus.edu
Federal Code: 001374

4-year private liberal arts college in small city, affiliated with Roman Catholic Church.
Enrollment: 1,635 undergrads, 8% part-time. 1,021 full-time freshmen.
Selectivity: Admits over 75% of applicants.

BASIC COSTS (2009-2010)
Tuition and fees: $23,126.
Per-credit charge: $944.
Room and board: $9,914.

FINANCIAL AID PICTURE (2008-2009)
Students with need: Out of 665 full-time freshmen who applied for aid, 443 were judged to have need. Of these, 399 received aid, and 31 had their full need met. Average financial aid package met 52% of need; average scholarship/grant was $12,529; average loan was $3,416. For part-time students, average financial aid package was $5,670.
Students without need: 27 full-time freshmen who did not demonstrate need for aid received scholarships/grants; average award was $5,353. No-need awards available for academics, art, job skills, leadership, music/drama, religious affiliation, state/district residency.
Cumulative student debt: 93% of graduating class had student loans; average debt was $18,733.

FINANCIAL AID PROCEDURES
Forms required: FAFSA.
Dates and Deadlines: Priority date 2/28; no closing date. Applicants notified on a rolling basis starting 3/1; must reply within 2 week(s) of notification.
Transfers: No deadline. Must reply within 2 week(s) of notification.

CONTACT
Andrew Foster, Director of Financial Aid
700 Prospect Street, New Haven, CT 06511-1189
(203) 773-8508

Asnuntuck Community College
Enfield, Connecticut
www.acc.commnet.edu
Federal Code: 011150

2-year public community and technical college in large town.
Enrollment: 1,213 undergrads, 46% part-time. 268 full-time freshmen.
Selectivity: Open admission.

BASIC COSTS (2009-2010)
Tuition and fees: $3,200; out-of-state residents $9,560.
Per-credit charge: $118; out-of-state residents $354.

FINANCIAL AID PICTURE (2008-2009)
Students with need: Need-based aid available for full-time and part-time students. Work study available nights, weekends, and for part-time students.
Students without need: This college awards aid only to students with need.

FINANCIAL AID PROCEDURES
Forms required: FAFSA, institutional form.
Dates and Deadlines: Priority date 6/1; no closing date. Applicants notified on a rolling basis starting 7/1; must reply within 2 week(s) of notification.
Transfers: Financial aid transcript required.

CONTACT
Donna Jones-Searle, Director of Financial Aid
170 Elm Street, Enfield, CT 06082
(860) 253-3000 ext. 3030

Capital Community College
Hartford, Connecticut
www.ccc.commnet.edu
Federal Code: 007635

2-year public community and technical college in small city.
Enrollment: 3,748 undergrads, 68% part-time. 377 full-time freshmen.
Selectivity: Open admission; but selective for some programs.

BASIC COSTS (2009-2010)
Tuition and fees: $3,200; out-of-state residents $9,560.
Per-credit charge: $118; out-of-state residents $354.
Additional info: Tuition/fee waivers available for minority students.

FINANCIAL AID PICTURE

Students with need: Need-based aid available for full-time and part-time students. Work study available nights, weekends, and for part-time students.
Students without need: This college awards aid only to students with need.

FINANCIAL AID PROCEDURES

Forms required: FAFSA.
Dates and Deadlines: Closing date 7/15. Applicants notified on a rolling basis starting 7/15; must reply within 2 week(s) of notification.
Transfers: Closing date 7/1.

CONTACT

Margaret Wolf, Director of Financial Aid
950 Main Street, Hartford, CT 06103-1207
(860) 906-5127

Central Connecticut State University
New Britain, Connecticut
www.ccsu.edu   Federal Code: 001378

4-year public university in small city.
Enrollment: 9,570 undergrads, 18% part-time. 1,281 full-time freshmen.
Selectivity: Admits 50 to 75% of applicants.

BASIC COSTS (2009-2010)
Tuition and fees: $7,414; out-of-state residents $17,106.
Room and board: $9,122.

FINANCIAL AID PICTURE (2008-2009)
Students with need: Need-based aid available for full-time and part-time students. Work study available nights, weekends, and for part-time students.
Students without need: No-need awards available for academics, athletics, minority status.

FINANCIAL AID PROCEDURES
Forms required: FAFSA.
Dates and Deadlines: Priority date 3/1; closing date 9/15. Applicants notified on a rolling basis starting 3/30; must reply within 2 week(s) of notification.

CONTACT
Richard Bishop, Director of Financial Aid
1615 Stanley Street, New Britain, CT 06050
(860) 832-2200

Charter Oak State College
New Britain, Connecticut
www.charteroak.edu   Federal Code: 032343

4-year public virtual liberal arts college in small city.
Enrollment: 1,685 undergrads, 91% part-time.

BASIC COSTS (2009-2010)
Per-credit charge: $295; out-of-state residents $265.
Additional info: Academic Services Fee: In-state associate degree or bachelor's degree, $1,055; out-of-state $1,390. Books and supplies $1,000. Cost of education varies due to students having option to take courses at other institutions.

FINANCIAL AID PICTURE (2008-2009)
Students with need: 30% of average financial aid package awarded as scholarships/grants, 70% awarded as loans/jobs. Need-based aid available for part-time students.
Students without need: This college awards aid only to students with need.

FINANCIAL AID PROCEDURES
Forms required: FAFSA, institutional form.
Dates and Deadlines: No deadline. Applicants notified on a rolling basis starting 8/23.

CONTACT
Deborah Flinn, Director of Financial Aid
55 Paul Manafort Drive, New Britain, CT 06053-2150
(860) 832-3872

Connecticut College
New London, Connecticut   Federal Code: 001379
www.conncoll.edu   CSS Code: 3284

4-year private liberal arts college in large town.
Enrollment: 1,777 undergrads. 502 full-time freshmen.
Selectivity: Admits less than 50% of applicants.

BASIC COSTS (2010-2011)
Tuition and fees: $43,990.
Room and board: $9,120.

FINANCIAL AID PICTURE (2009-2010)
Students with need: Out of 297 full-time freshmen who applied for aid, 237 were judged to have need. Of these, 237 received aid, and 237 had their full need met. Average financial aid package met 100% of need; average scholarship/grant was $31,051; average loan was $2,961. For part-time students, average financial aid package was $7,851.
Students without need: This college awards aid only to students with need.
Cumulative student debt: 34% of graduating class had student loans; average debt was $22,038.

FINANCIAL AID PROCEDURES
Forms required: FAFSA, CSS PROFILE.
Dates and Deadlines: Closing date 2/1. Applicants notified by 4/1; must reply by 5/1.
Transfers: Closing date 4/1.

CONTACT
Elaine Solinga, Director of Financial Aid
270 Mohegan Avenue, New London, CT 06320-4196
(860) 439-2058

Eastern Connecticut State University
Willimantic, Connecticut
www.easternct.edu   Federal Code: 001425

4-year public university and liberal arts college in large town.
Enrollment: 5,025 undergrads, 14% part-time. 944 full-time freshmen.
Selectivity: Admits 50 to 75% of applicants.

BASIC COSTS (2009-2010)
Tuition and fees: $7,813; out-of-state residents $17,505.
Room and board: $9,620.

FINANCIAL AID PICTURE (2008-2009)
Students with need: Need-based aid available for full-time and part-time students. Work study available nights, weekends, and for part-time students.
Students without need: No-need awards available for academics.
Additional info: Tuition waiver for veterans and members of National Guard.

FINANCIAL AID PROCEDURES
Forms required: FAFSA.
Dates and Deadlines: Priority date 3/15; no closing date. Applicants notified on a rolling basis starting 2/15; must reply within 2 week(s) of notification.
Transfers: Must reply within 2 week(s) of notification.

CONTACT

Mona Lucas, Director of Financial Aid
83 Windham Street, Willimantic, CT 06226-2295
(860) 465-5286

Fairfield University

Fairfield, Connecticut — Federal Code: 001385
www.fairfield.edu — CSS Code: 3390

4-year private university in small city, affiliated with Roman Catholic Church.
Enrollment: 3,623 undergrads, 9% part-time. 849 full-time freshmen.
Selectivity: Admits 50 to 75% of applicants. GED not accepted.

BASIC COSTS (2010-2011)

Tuition and fees: $39,040.
Per-credit charge: $525.
Room and board: $12,390.
Additional info: 12- and 14-meal plans available. Proof of health insurance required in order to waive health insurance fee.

FINANCIAL AID PICTURE (2009-2010)

Students with need: Out of 624 full-time freshmen who applied for aid, 493 were judged to have need. Of these, 484 received aid, and 107 had their full need met. Average financial aid package met 92% of need; average scholarship/grant was $24,000; average loan was $4,012. For part-time students, average financial aid package was $6,309.
Students without need: 59 full-time freshmen who did not demonstrate need for aid received scholarships/grants; average award was $17,000. No-need awards available for academics, alumni affiliation, art, athletics, leadership, music/drama.
Scholarships offered: *Merit:* Magis scholarship; $20,000; based on academics and exceptional leadership in high school, community or church activities; renewable for 4 years with 3.0 GPA; 70-75 awarded annually. *Athletic:* 53 full-time freshmen received athletic scholarships; average amount $20,286.
Cumulative student debt: 60% of graduating class had student loans; average debt was $35,161.
Additional info: Free tuition to any eligible student from Bridgeport with family income below $50,000. Enhanced financial aid available for veterans.

FINANCIAL AID PROCEDURES

Forms required: FAFSA, CSS PROFILE.
Dates and Deadlines: Closing date 2/15. Applicants notified by 4/1; must reply by 5/1.
Transfers: Closing date 5/1. Applicants notified on a rolling basis starting 5/1; must reply within 3 week(s) of notification.

CONTACT

Erin Chiaro, Director of Financial Aid
1073 North Benson Road, Fairfield, CT 06824-5195
(203) 254-4125

Gateway Community College

New Haven, Connecticut
www.gwcc.commnet.edu — Federal Code: 008303

2-year public community college in small city.
Enrollment: 5,764 undergrads, 58% part-time. 879 full-time freshmen.
Selectivity: Open admission; but selective for some programs.

BASIC COSTS (2009-2010)

Tuition and fees: $3,200; out-of-state residents $9,560.
Per-credit charge: $118; out-of-state residents $354.

FINANCIAL AID PICTURE

Students with need: Need-based aid available for full-time and part-time students. Work study available nights, weekends, and for part-time students.

Students without need: This college awards aid only to students with need.

FINANCIAL AID PROCEDURES

Forms required: FAFSA, institutional form.
Dates and Deadlines: No deadline. Applicants notified on a rolling basis; must reply within 2 week(s) of notification.

CONTACT

Raymond Zeek, Director of Financial Aid
60 Sargent Drive, New Haven, CT 06511-5970
(203) 285-2013

Goodwin College

East Hartford, Connecticut
www.goodwin.edu — Federal Code: 015833

2-year private health science and career college in small city.
Enrollment: 2,052 undergrads, 75% part-time. 235 full-time freshmen.
Selectivity: Open admission; but selective for some programs.

BASIC COSTS (2009-2010)

Tuition and fees: $17,600.
Per-credit charge: $530.

FINANCIAL AID PICTURE (2008-2009)

Students with need: 41% of average financial aid package awarded as scholarships/grants, 59% awarded as loans/jobs. Need-based aid available for part-time students. Work study available nights.
Students without need: This college awards aid only to students with need.

FINANCIAL AID PROCEDURES

Forms required: FAFSA.
Dates and Deadlines: No deadline. Applicants notified on a rolling basis starting 8/1.
Transfers: No deadline. Applicants notified on a rolling basis starting 8/1.

CONTACT

Bill Mangini, Director of Financial Aid
One Riverside Drive, East Hartford, CT 06118
(860) 727-6723

Holy Apostles College and Seminary

Cromwell, Connecticut
www.holyapostles.edu — Federal Code: 001389

4-year private liberal arts and seminary college in large town, affiliated with Roman Catholic Church.
Enrollment: 46 undergrads, 30% part-time. 5 full-time freshmen.
Selectivity: Admits over 75% of applicants.

BASIC COSTS (2009-2010)

Tuition and fees: $9,360.
Per-credit charge: $390.

FINANCIAL AID PICTURE (2009-2010)

Students with need: 4% of average financial aid package awarded as scholarships/grants, 96% awarded as loans/jobs. Need-based aid available for part-time students.
Students without need: This college awards aid only to students with need.

FINANCIAL AID PROCEDURES

Forms required: FAFSA, institutional form.
Dates and Deadlines: Priority date 7/11; no closing date. Applicants notified on a rolling basis starting 8/25; must reply within 2 week(s) of notification.

Transfers: No deadline. Applicants notified on a rolling basis; must reply within 2 week(s) of notification.

CONTACT
Henry Miller, Financial Aid Director
33 Prospect Hill Road, Cromwell, CT 06416-2005
(860) 632-8120

Housatonic Community College
Bridgeport, Connecticut
www.hcc.commnet.edu   Federal Code: 004513

2-year public community college in small city.
Enrollment: 3,266 undergrads.
Selectivity: Open admission; but selective for some programs.

BASIC COSTS (2009-2010)
Tuition and fees: $3,200; out-of-state residents $9,560.
Per-credit charge: $118; out-of-state residents $354.

FINANCIAL AID PICTURE (2008-2009)
Students with need: Need-based aid available for full-time and part-time students.
Students without need: This college awards aid only to students with need.

FINANCIAL AID PROCEDURES
Forms required: FAFSA.
Dates and Deadlines: Priority date 11/1; closing date 5/1. Applicants notified on a rolling basis starting 6/1.

CONTACT
Barbara Surowiec, Director of Financial Aid
900 Lafayette Boulevard, Bridgeport, CT 06604-4704
(203) 332-5047

Lincoln College of New England: Briarwood
Southington, Connecticut
www.briarwood.edu   Federal Code: 009407

2-year for-profit junior college in large town.
Enrollment: 772 undergrads.
Selectivity: Open admission; but selective for some programs.

BASIC COSTS (2009-2010)
Tuition and fees: $18,490.
Per-credit charge: $590.
Room only: $4,200.

FINANCIAL AID PICTURE
Students with need: Need-based aid available for full-time and part-time students. Work study available nights, weekends, and for part-time students.
Students without need: No-need awards available for academics, alumni affiliation, leadership.

FINANCIAL AID PROCEDURES
Forms required: FAFSA.
Dates and Deadlines: Priority date 4/30; no closing date. Applicants notified on a rolling basis starting 3/15; must reply within 2 week(s) of notification.
Transfers: Priority date 4/15.

CONTACT
Gina Swenton, Assistant Director of Student Financial Services
2279 Mount Vernon Road, Southington, CT 06489-1057
(860) 628-4751 ext. 213

Lincoln College of New England: Suffield
Suffield, Connecticut
http://lincolncollegene.edu

2-year for-profit culinary school and business college in small town.
Enrollment: 102 undergrads.

BASIC COSTS (2009-2010)
Tuition and fees: $14,648.
Room and board: $5,808.
Additional info: Culinary student pay an extra $943 for cutlery and tools.

FINANCIAL AID PICTURE
Students with need: Need-based aid available for full-time and part-time students. Work study available nights, weekends, and for part-time students.
Students without need: No-need awards available for academics.

FINANCIAL AID PROCEDURES
Dates and Deadlines: No deadline. Applicants notified on a rolling basis starting 1/1.

CONTACT
Joanne Seymour, Director of Financial Aid
1760 Mapleton Avenue, Suffield, CT 06078
(860) 668-3515

Lyme Academy College of Fine Arts
Old Lyme, Connecticut
www.lymeacademy.edu   Federal Code: 030794

4-year private visual arts college in small town.
Enrollment: 75 undergrads, 15% part-time. 9 full-time freshmen.
Selectivity: Admits over 75% of applicants.

BASIC COSTS (2010-2011)
Tuition and fees: $24,684.
Per-credit charge: $974.

FINANCIAL AID PICTURE (2009-2010)
Students with need: Need-based aid available for full-time and part-time students. Work study available nights, weekends, and for part-time students.
Students without need: No-need awards available for academics, art, leadership.

FINANCIAL AID PROCEDURES
Forms required: FAFSA.
Dates and Deadlines: Priority date 2/15; closing date 4/15. Applicants notified on a rolling basis starting 3/1; must reply by 5/1 or within 2 week(s) of notification.
Transfers: Closing date 7/31. Applicants notified on a rolling basis starting 2/15; must reply by 5/1 or within 2 week(s) of notification.

CONTACT
Jim Falconer, Director of Financial Aid
84 Lyme Street, Old Lyme, CT 06371
(860) 434-3571 ext. 114

Manchester Community College
Manchester, Connecticut
www.mcc.commnet.edu   Federal Code: 001392

2-year public community college in small city.
Enrollment: 6,502 undergrads, 49% part-time. 1,244 full-time freshmen.
Selectivity: Open admission; but selective for some programs.

BASIC COSTS (2009-2010)

Tuition and fees: $3,200; out-of-state residents $9,560.
Per-credit charge: $118; out-of-state residents $354.

FINANCIAL AID PICTURE (2009-2010)

Students with need: Need-based aid available for full-time and part-time students.

FINANCIAL AID PROCEDURES

Forms required: FAFSA.
Dates and Deadlines: Priority date 5/15; no closing date. Applicants notified on a rolling basis starting 5/1; must reply within 2 week(s) of notification.

CONTACT

Ivette Rivera-Dreyer, Director of Financial Aid
Great Path PO Box 1046, MS 12, Manchester, CT 06040-1046
(860) 512-3380

Middlesex Community College
Middletown, Connecticut
www.mxcc.commnet.edu   Federal Code: 008038

2-year public community college in large town.
Enrollment: 2,233 undergrads, 49% part-time. 425 full-time freshmen.
Selectivity: Open admission; but selective for some programs.

BASIC COSTS (2009-2010)

Tuition and fees: $3,200; out-of-state residents $9,560.
Per-credit charge: $118; out-of-state residents $354.
Additional info: Out-of-state tuition includes fees.

FINANCIAL AID PICTURE

Students with need: Need-based aid available for full-time and part-time students.
Students without need: This college awards aid only to students with need.
Additional info: Tuition and/or fee waiver for veterans.

FINANCIAL AID PROCEDURES

Forms required: FAFSA, institutional form.
Dates and Deadlines: Priority date 6/1; no closing date. Applicants notified on a rolling basis starting 7/1; must reply within 2 week(s) of notification.
Transfers: Closing date 9/1.

CONTACT

Irene Martin, Director of Financial Aid
100 Training Hill Road, Middletown, CT 06457-4889
(860) 343-5741

Mitchell College
New London, Connecticut
www.mitchell.edu   Federal Code: 001393

4-year private liberal arts college in small city.
Enrollment: 872 undergrads, 6% part-time. 259 full-time freshmen.
Selectivity: Admits over 75% of applicants.

BASIC COSTS (2009-2010)

Tuition and fees: $25,627.
Per-credit charge: $275.
Room and board: $11,548.

FINANCIAL AID PICTURE (2009-2010)

Students with need: Out of 213 full-time freshmen who applied for aid, 186 were judged to have need. Of these, 186 received aid, and 10 had their full need met. Average financial aid package met 66% of need; average scholarship/grant was $11,474; average loan was $3,607. For part-time students, average financial aid package was $3,534.
Students without need: 52 full-time freshmen who did not demonstrate need for aid received scholarships/grants; average award was $5,708. No-need awards available for academics, alumni affiliation, art, leadership.
Cumulative student debt: 76% of graduating class had student loans; average debt was $29,506.

FINANCIAL AID PROCEDURES

Forms required: FAFSA.
Dates and Deadlines: Priority date 3/1; no closing date. Applicants notified on a rolling basis starting 2/15; must reply within 3 week(s) of notification.

CONTACT

Jacklyn Stoltz, Director of Financial Aid
437 Pequot Avenue, New London, CT 06320-4498
(860) 701-5040

Naugatuck Valley Community College
Waterbury, Connecticut
www.nvcc.commnet.edu   Federal Code: 006982

2-year public community and technical college in small city.
Enrollment: 5,766 undergrads, 54% part-time. 951 full-time freshmen.
Selectivity: Open admission; but selective for some programs.

BASIC COSTS (2009-2010)

Tuition and fees: $3,200; out-of-state residents $9,560.
Per-credit charge: $118; out-of-state residents $354.
Additional info: Non-resident fees $1,064.

FINANCIAL AID PICTURE (2008-2009)

Students with need: Need-based aid available for full-time and part-time students.
Students without need: This college awards aid only to students with need.

FINANCIAL AID PROCEDURES

Forms required: FAFSA.
Dates and Deadlines: Priority date 4/1; no closing date. Applicants notified on a rolling basis starting 6/1.
Transfers: Financial aid transcripts required from all previous schools attended.

CONTACT

Catherine Hardy, Director of Financial Aid Services
750 Chase Parkway, Waterbury, CT 06708-3089
(203) 575-8006

Norwalk Community College
Norwalk, Connecticut
www.ncc.commnet.edu   Federal Code: 001399

2-year public community and technical college in small city.
Enrollment: 4,829 undergrads.
Selectivity: Open admission; but selective for some programs.

BASIC COSTS (2009-2010)

Tuition and fees: $3,200; out-of-state residents $9,560.
Per-credit charge: $118; out-of-state residents $354.
Additional info: New England Regional Student Program: $177 per credit hour plus fees.

FINANCIAL AID PICTURE
Students with need: Need-based aid available for full-time and part-time students.
Students without need: No-need awards available for academics, alumni affiliation.

FINANCIAL AID PROCEDURES
Forms required: FAFSA, institutional form.
Dates and Deadlines: Priority date 7/1; no closing date. Applicants notified on a rolling basis starting 7/1; must reply within 2 week(s) of notification.

CONTACT
Norma McNerney, Director of Financial Aid
188 Richards Avenue, Norwalk, CT 06854-1655
(203) 857-7023

Paier College of Art
Hamden, Connecticut
www.paiercollegeofart.edu   Federal Code: 007459

4-year for-profit visual arts college in small city.
Enrollment: 204 undergrads, 27% part-time. 22 full-time freshmen.
Selectivity: Admits 50 to 75% of applicants.

BASIC COSTS (2010-2011)
Tuition and fees: $12,965.
Per-credit charge: $400.

FINANCIAL AID PICTURE (2008-2009)
Students with need: Out of 13 full-time freshmen who applied for aid, 10 were judged to have need. Of these, 10 received aid, and 2 had their full need met. Average financial aid package met 70% of need; average scholarship/grant was $3,561; average loan was $3,506. For part-time students, average financial aid package was $7,156.
Cumulative student debt: 80% of graduating class had student loans; average debt was $18,265.

FINANCIAL AID PROCEDURES
Forms required: FAFSA.
Dates and Deadlines: Priority date 4/15; no closing date. Applicants notified on a rolling basis starting 6/1; must reply within 3 week(s) of notification.
Transfers: No deadline. Applicants notified on a rolling basis starting 6/1; must reply within 3 week(s) of notification.

CONTACT
John DeRose, Director of Financial Aid
20 Gorham Avenue, Hamden, CT 06514-3902
(203) 287-3034

Post University
Waterbury, Connecticut
www.post.edu   Federal Code: 001401

4-year for-profit university and business college in small city.
Enrollment: 670 undergrads, 6% part-time. 251 full-time freshmen.
Selectivity: Admits 50 to 75% of applicants.

BASIC COSTS (2009-2010)
Tuition and fees: $24,200.
Per-credit charge: $775.
Room and board: $9,400.

FINANCIAL AID PICTURE (2009-2010)
Students with need: Out of 251 full-time freshmen who applied for aid, 251 were judged to have need. Of these, 251 received aid, and 1 had their full need met. Average financial aid package met 71% of need; average scholarship/grant was $4,310; average loan was $3,561. For part-time students, average financial aid package was $8,009.
Cumulative student debt: 79% of graduating class had student loans; average debt was $18,000.
Additional info: Academic merit scholarships available based on GPA and test scores. Renewable contingent upon maintaining specific GPA.

FINANCIAL AID PROCEDURES
Forms required: FAFSA.
Dates and Deadlines: Priority date 3/15; no closing date. Applicants notified on a rolling basis starting 4/15; must reply by 5/1 or within 3 week(s) of notification.
Transfers: No deadline. Applicants notified on a rolling basis starting 4/15; must reply within 1 week(s) of notification.

CONTACT
Claire Dwyer, Director of Office of Student Finance
800 Country Club Road, Waterbury, CT 06723-2540
(203) 596-4571

Quinebaug Valley Community College
Danielson, Connecticut
www.qvcc.commnet.edu   Federal Code: 010530

2-year public community and technical college in large town.
Enrollment: 1,873 undergrads, 60% part-time. 299 full-time freshmen.
Selectivity: Open admission.

BASIC COSTS (2009-2010)
Tuition and fees: $3,200; out-of-state residents $9,560.
Per-credit charge: $118; out-of-state residents $354.

FINANCIAL AID PICTURE (2009-2010)
Students with need: 96% of average financial aid package awarded as scholarships/grants, 4% awarded as loans/jobs. Need-based aid available for part-time students. Work study available nights.
Students without need: This college awards aid only to students with need.

FINANCIAL AID PROCEDURES
Forms required: FAFSA.
Dates and Deadlines: Closing date 10/1. Applicants notified on a rolling basis starting 5/1.

CONTACT
Alfred Williams, Director of Financial Aid
742 Upper Maple Street, Danielson, CT 06239-1440
(860) 412-7208

Quinnipiac University
Hamden, Connecticut
www.quinnipiac.edu   Federal Code: 001402

4-year private university in small city.
Enrollment: 5,888 undergrads, 3% part-time. 1,586 full-time freshmen.
Selectivity: Admits 50 to 75% of applicants.

BASIC COSTS (2010-2011)
Tuition and fees: $34,250.
Per-credit charge: $760.
Room and board: $12,730.

FINANCIAL AID PICTURE (2009-2010)

Students with need: Out of 1,263 full-time freshmen who applied for aid, 975 were judged to have need. Of these, 972 received aid, and 130 had their full need met. Average financial aid package met 68% of need; average scholarship/grant was $15,499; average loan was $3,515. For part-time students, average financial aid package was $7,380.

Students without need: 257 full-time freshmen who did not demonstrate need for aid received scholarships/grants; average award was $10,748. No-need awards available for academics, athletics.

Scholarships offered: *Merit* Scholarships; $4,000-$18,000 per year; based on class rank and SAT/ACT scores; renewable with full-time status and 3.0 GPA. *Athletic:* 63 full-time freshmen received athletic scholarships; average amount $29,517.

Cumulative student debt: 69% of graduating class had student loans; average debt was $34,621.

FINANCIAL AID PROCEDURES

Forms required: FAFSA.

Dates and Deadlines: Priority date 3/1; no closing date. Applicants notified on a rolling basis starting 2/15; must reply by 5/1 or within 2 week(s) of notification.

Transfers: No deadline. Applicants notified on a rolling basis starting 3/1; must reply by 5/1 or within 2 week(s) of notification. Students transferring with 2 years of full-time college work and 3.5 GPA may be eligible for transfer scholarship.

CONTACT

Dominic Yoia, Director of Financial Aid
275 Mount Carmel Avenue, Hamden, CT 06518-1908
(800) 462-1944

Sacred Heart University
Fairfield, Connecticut   Federal Code: 001403
www.sacredheart.edu   CSS Code: 3780

4-year private university and liberal arts college in large town, affiliated with Roman Catholic Church.

Enrollment: 4,123 undergrads, 14% part-time. 909 full-time freshmen.
Selectivity: Admits 50 to 75% of applicants.

BASIC COSTS (2009-2010)

Tuition and fees: $30,298.
Per-credit charge: $460.
Room and board: $11,684.
Additional info: Tuition/fee waivers available for minority students.

FINANCIAL AID PICTURE (2009-2010)

Students with need: Need-based aid available for full-time and part-time students. Work study available nights, weekends, and for part-time students.
Students without need: No-need awards available for academics, alumni affiliation, art, athletics, leadership, minority status, music/drama.
Additional info: Financial aid covers 100% tuition for first-year, full-time students from Fairfield County, CT who have family income at or below $50,000.

FINANCIAL AID PROCEDURES

Forms required: FAFSA, CSS PROFILE.
Dates and Deadlines: Priority date 2/15; no closing date. Applicants notified on a rolling basis starting 3/1; must reply within 2 week(s) of notification.
Transfers: Priority date 5/1; no deadline. Applicants notified on a rolling basis.

CONTACT

Julie Savino, Dean of University Financial Assistance
5151 Park Avenue, Fairfield, CT 06825
(203) 371-7980

Saint Joseph College
West Hartford, Connecticut
www.sjc.edu   Federal Code: 001409

4-year private liberal arts and career college for women in small city, affiliated with Roman Catholic Church.

Enrollment: 947 undergrads, 19% part-time. 184 full-time freshmen.
Selectivity: Admits over 75% of applicants.

BASIC COSTS (2010-2011)

Tuition and fees: $28,530.
Per-credit charge: $625.
Room and board: $12,940.

FINANCIAL AID PICTURE (2009-2010)

Students with need: Out of 178 full-time freshmen who applied for aid, 164 were judged to have need. Of these, 164 received aid, and 16 had their full need met. Average financial aid package met 79% of need; average scholarship/grant was $18,987; average loan was $3,332. For part-time students, average financial aid package was $6,593.

Students without need: 19 full-time freshmen who did not demonstrate need for aid received scholarships/grants; average award was $10,158. No-need awards available for academics.

Cumulative student debt: 82% of graduating class had student loans; average debt was $39,743.

FINANCIAL AID PROCEDURES

Forms required: FAFSA.
Dates and Deadlines: Priority date 2/15; no closing date. Applicants notified on a rolling basis starting 3/1.
Transfers: No deadline. Applicants notified on a rolling basis starting 3/1.

CONTACT

Elizabeth Baker, Director of Financial Aid
1678 Asylum Avenue, West Hartford, CT 06117
(866) 442-8752

Southern Connecticut State University
New Haven, Connecticut
www.southernct.edu   Federal Code: 001406

4-year public university in small city.

Enrollment: 8,594 undergrads, 14% part-time. 1,237 full-time freshmen.
Selectivity: Admits 50 to 75% of applicants.

BASIC COSTS (2009-2010)

Tuition and fees: $7,428; out-of-state residents $17,120.
Room and board: $9,469.

FINANCIAL AID PICTURE (2008-2009)

Students with need: Need-based aid available for full-time and part-time students. Work study available nights, weekends, and for part-time students.
Scholarships offered: General Academic Achievement Awards; 90 awarded. Presidential Scholarships, Trustees Scholarships available.

FINANCIAL AID PROCEDURES

Dates and Deadlines: Priority date 3/6; no closing date. Must reply within 2 week(s) of notification.
Transfers: Applicants notified on a rolling basis starting 6/15; must reply within 2 week(s) of notification.

CONTACT

Avon Dennis, Director, Financial Aid & Scholarships
131 Farnham Avenue, New Haven, CT 06515-1202
(203) 392-5222

Three Rivers Community College

Norwich, Connecticut
www.trcc.commnet.edu   Federal Code: 009765

2-year public community and liberal arts college in large town.
Enrollment: 4,186 undergrads, 64% part-time. 594 full-time freshmen.
Selectivity: Open admission; but selective for some programs.

BASIC COSTS (2009-2010)
Tuition and fees: $3,200; out-of-state residents $9,560.
Per-credit charge: $118; out-of-state residents $354.
Additional info: Out-of-state required fees $1,064. New England state students pay $4,248 for tuition and $542 for fees.

FINANCIAL AID PICTURE (2008-2009)
Students with need: Average financial aid package met 50% of need; average scholarship/grant was $3,378; average loan was $3,376. For part-time students, average financial aid package was $1,176.
Students without need: This college awards aid only to students with need.
Scholarships offered: Various scholarships; $75 to $500.

FINANCIAL AID PROCEDURES
Forms required: FAFSA.
Dates and Deadlines: Priority date 7/15; no closing date. Applicants notified on a rolling basis; must reply within 2 week(s) of notification.
Transfers: No deadline.

CONTACT
Hong-Yu Kovic, Financial Aid Counselor
574 New London Turnpike, Norwich, CT 06360-6598
(860) 823-2870

Trinity College

Hartford, Connecticut   Federal Code: 001414
www.trincoll.edu   CSS Code: 3899

4-year private liberal arts college in large city.
Enrollment: 2,234 undergrads, 2% part-time. 573 full-time freshmen.
Selectivity: Admits less than 50% of applicants.

BASIC COSTS (2010-2011)
Tuition and fees: $42,370.
Room and board: $10,960.
Additional info: One-time $25 transcript fee for new students only. Tuition/fee waivers available for adults.

FINANCIAL AID PICTURE (2009-2010)
Students with need: Out of 279 full-time freshmen who applied for aid, 247 were judged to have need. Of these, 247 received aid, and 247 had their full need met. Average financial aid package met 100% of need; average scholarship/grant was $33,695; average loan was $3,691. Need-based aid available for part-time students.
Students without need: 1 full-time freshmen who did not demonstrate need for aid received scholarships/grants; average award was $38,900. No-need awards available for academics, leadership.
Cumulative student debt: 42% of graduating class had student loans; average debt was $20,174.

FINANCIAL AID PROCEDURES
Forms required: FAFSA, CSS PROFILE.
Dates and Deadlines: Priority date 2/1; closing date 3/1. Applicants notified by 4/1; must reply by 5/1 or within 2 week(s) of notification.
Transfers: Closing date 4/1. Applicants notified on a rolling basis starting 5/15; must reply within 2 week(s) of notification.

CONTACT
Kelly O'Brien, Director of Financial Aid
300 Summit Street, Hartford, CT 06106
(860) 297-2046

Tunxis Community College

Farmington, Connecticut
www.tunxis.commnet.edu   Federal Code: 009764

2-year public community college in large town.
Enrollment: 3,560 undergrads, 51% part-time. 581 full-time freshmen.
Selectivity: Open admission; but selective for some programs.

BASIC COSTS (2009-2010)
Tuition and fees: $3,200; out-of-state residents $9,560.
Per-credit charge: $118; out-of-state residents $354.
Additional info: Out-of-state required fees: $1,064.

FINANCIAL AID PICTURE (2008-2009)
Students with need: Need-based aid available for full-time and part-time students. Work study available nights, weekends, and for part-time students.
Students without need: No-need awards available for academics, leadership.
Additional info: Financial aid available to all students showing need. Part-time students encouraged to apply.

FINANCIAL AID PROCEDURES
Forms required: FAFSA.
Dates and Deadlines: Priority date 6/1; no closing date. Applicants notified on a rolling basis starting 3/1.

CONTACT
David Welsh, Director of Financial Aid
271 Scott Swamp Road, Farmington, CT 06032-3187
(860) 255-3555

United States Coast Guard Academy

New London, Connecticut
www.uscga.edu   Federal Code: 001415

4-year public engineering and maritime college in small city.
Enrollment: 973 undergrads. 274 full-time freshmen.
Selectivity: Admits less than 50% of applicants.

BASIC COSTS (2010-2011)
Additional info: All tuition, room and board for U.S. residents paid for by U.S. Government. Students make one-time entrance deposit of $3,000 to help defray the cost of uniforms, books, supplies and personal computer. All students paid a monthly stipend of $929.40. Cost of instruction for non-resident alien cadets is $71,349 per year. Before an international cadet is enrolled at the Academy, sponsoring country must agree to reimburse the U.S. Coast Guard for cost of instruction. Countries not listed on World Bank list would be eligible for partial tuition costs of $16,300 annually.

FINANCIAL AID PROCEDURES
Dates and Deadlines: No deadline.

CONTACT
31 Mohegan Avenue, New London, CT 06320
(860) 444-8309

University of Bridgeport
Bridgeport, Connecticut
www.bridgeport.edu   Federal Code: 001416

4-year private university in small city.
Enrollment: 2,248 undergrads, 33% part-time. 436 full-time freshmen.
Selectivity: Admits 50 to 75% of applicants.

BASIC COSTS (2009-2010)
Tuition and fees: $25,465.
Per-credit charge: $780.
Room and board: $11,080.

FINANCIAL AID PICTURE (2009-2010)
Students with need: Out of 405 full-time freshmen who applied for aid, 390 were judged to have need. Of these, 390 received aid, and 43 had their full need met. Average financial aid package met 65% of need; average scholarship/grant was $8,261; average loan was $5,294. For part-time students, average financial aid package was $7,614.
Students without need: 22 full-time freshmen who did not demonstrate need for aid received scholarships/grants; average award was $17,546. No-need awards available for academics, athletics, leadership, music/drama, state/district residency.
Scholarships offered: *Merit:* Academic Excellence and Leadership Scholarship; up to full tuition, room, and board; for students ranking in the top quarter of high school class with 1200 SAT. Academic Scholarship; up to full tuition; for students in the top quarter of class and 1100 SAT. Academic Grant; up to half-tuition; for students in top half of class and 1100 SAT. Challenge Grant; $3,000; for students in the top half of class and 1000 SAT. All SAT scores exclusive of Writing. *Athletic:* 20 full-time freshmen received athletic scholarships; average amount $16,408.

FINANCIAL AID PROCEDURES
Forms required: FAFSA.
Dates and Deadlines: Priority date 4/1; no closing date. Applicants notified on a rolling basis starting 4/1; must reply within 4 week(s) of notification.
Transfers: No deadline. Applicants notified on a rolling basis starting 4/1.

CONTACT
Kathleen Gailor, Director of Financial Aid
126 Park Avenue, Bridgeport, CT 06604
(203) 576-4568

University of Connecticut
Storrs, Connecticut
www.uconn.edu   Federal Code: 007997

4-year public university in large town.
Enrollment: 16,691 undergrads, 3% part-time. 3,215 full-time freshmen.
Selectivity: Admits less than 50% of applicants.

BASIC COSTS (2010-2011)
Tuition and fees: $10,416; out-of-state residents $26,880.
Per-credit charge: $336; out-of-state residents $1,022.
Room and board: $10,782.

FINANCIAL AID PICTURE (2009-2010)
Students with need: Out of 2,694 full-time freshmen who applied for aid, 1,767 were judged to have need. Of these, 1,735 received aid, and 322 had their full need met. Average financial aid package met 71% of need; average scholarship/grant was $8,071; average loan was $3,446. For part-time students, average financial aid package was $7,074.
Students without need: 322 full-time freshmen who did not demonstrate need for aid received scholarships/grants; average award was $6,866. No-need awards available for academics, art, athletics, leadership, minority status, music/drama.

Scholarships offered: 92 full-time freshmen received athletic scholarships; average amount $22,612.
Cumulative student debt: 61% of graduating class had student loans; average debt was $21,257.
Additional info: Institution offers variety of need-based financial aid programs. Financial assistance packages may include grants, loans and work-study awards.

FINANCIAL AID PROCEDURES
Forms required: FAFSA.
Dates and Deadlines: Priority date 3/1; no closing date. Applicants notified on a rolling basis starting 3/1; must reply within 4 week(s) of notification.

CONTACT
Jean Main, Director of Financial Aid
2131 Hillside Road, Unit 3088, Storrs, CT 06269-3088
(860) 486-2819

University of Hartford
West Hartford, Connecticut
www.hartford.edu   Federal Code: 001422

4-year private university in small city.
Enrollment: 5,229 undergrads, 11% part-time. 1,453 full-time freshmen.
Selectivity: Admits 50 to 75% of applicants.

BASIC COSTS (2010-2011)
Tuition and fees: $29,852.
Room and board: $11,572.
Additional info: Tuition/fee waivers available for minority students.

FINANCIAL AID PICTURE (2008-2009)
Students with need: Out of 1,072 full-time freshmen who applied for aid, 1,072 were judged to have need. Of these, 1,072 received aid, and 539 had their full need met. Average financial aid package met 79% of need; average scholarship/grant was $14,465; average loan was $6,561. Need-based aid available for part-time students.
Students without need: 404 full-time freshmen who did not demonstrate need for aid received scholarships/grants; average award was $7,291. No need awards available for academics, art, athletics, music/drama.
Scholarships offered: 21 full-time freshmen received athletic scholarships; average amount $30,950.
Cumulative student debt: 78% of graduating class had student loans; average debt was $34,385.

FINANCIAL AID PROCEDURES
Forms required: FAFSA, institutional form.
Dates and Deadlines: Priority date 2/1; no closing date. Applicants notified on a rolling basis starting 3/1; must reply by 5/1.

CONTACT
Jennifer Fuhrmann, Director of Student Financial Assistance
Bates House, West Hartford, CT 06117-1599
(860) 768-4296

University of New Haven
West Haven, Connecticut
www.newhaven.edu   Federal Code: 001397

4-year private university in small city.
Enrollment: 3,972 undergrads, 11% part-time. 1,252 full-time freshmen.
Selectivity: Admits 50 to 75% of applicants.

BASIC COSTS (2009-2010)
Tuition and fees: $29,470.
Per-credit charge: $940.

Room and board: $12,372.

FINANCIAL AID PICTURE (2009-2010)

Students with need: Out of 1,145 full-time freshmen who applied for aid, 1,035 were judged to have need. Of these, 1,035 received aid, and 154 had their full need met. Average financial aid package met 68% of need; average scholarship/grant was $17,221; average loan was $3,464. For part-time students, average financial aid package was $5,121.

Students without need: 167 full-time freshmen who did not demonstrate need for aid received scholarships/grants; average award was $10,430. No-need awards available for academics, alumni affiliation, athletics, leadership.

Scholarships offered: *Merit:* Presidential Scholarship; half-tuition; for applicants in top 15% of class with 1200 SAT (exclusive of Writing) or ACT equivalent. Academic Achievement Awards. *Athletic:* 17 full-time freshmen received athletic scholarships; average amount $14,827.

Cumulative student debt: 86% of graduating class had student loans; average debt was $36,272.

FINANCIAL AID PROCEDURES

Forms required: FAFSA.

Dates and Deadlines: Closing date 3/1. Applicants notified on a rolling basis starting 3/1; must reply by 5/1 or within 2 week(s) of notification.

CONTACT

Karen Flynn, Director of Financial Aid
300 Boston Post Road, West Haven, CT 06516
(203) 932-7315

Wesleyan University

Middletown, Connecticut
www.wesleyan.edu   CSS Code: 3959

4-year private university and liberal arts college in large town.

Enrollment: 2,766 undergrads. 715 full-time freshmen.

Selectivity: Admits less than 50% of applicants.

BASIC COSTS (2009-2010)

Tuition and fees: $40,392.

Room and board: $11,040.

FINANCIAL AID PICTURE (2008-2009)

Students with need: Out of 405 full-time freshmen who applied for aid, 335 were judged to have need. Of these, 335 received aid, and 335 had their full need met. Average financial aid package met 100% of need; average scholarship/grant was $32,975; average loan was $2,496.

Students without need: This college awards aid only to students with need.

Scholarships offered: Freeman Asian Scholars; for international first-year applicants from select East and Southeast Asian countries; 22 awarded.

Cumulative student debt: 44% of graduating class had student loans; average debt was $29,174.

FINANCIAL AID PROCEDURES

Forms required: FAFSA, CSS PROFILE, state aid form.

Dates and Deadlines: Closing date 2/15. Applicants notified by 4/1; must reply by 5/1.

Transfers: Priority date 2/15; closing date 3/15. Applicants notified by 5/15; must reply by 6/1 or within 2 week(s) of notification. No financial aid available for international transfer candidates.

CONTACT

Jennifer Lawton, Director of Financial Aid
70 Wyllys Avenue, Middletown, CT 06459-0260
(860) 685-2800

Western Connecticut State University

Danbury, Connecticut
www.wcsu.edu   Federal Code: 001380

4-year public university in small city.

Enrollment: 5,521 undergrads, 14% part-time. 930 full-time freshmen.

Selectivity: Admits 50 to 75% of applicants.

BASIC COSTS (2010-2011)

Tuition and fees: $7,909; out-of-state residents $16,906.

Room and board: $10,130.

FINANCIAL AID PICTURE (2008-2009)

Students with need: Out of 758 full-time freshmen who applied for aid, 675 were judged to have need. Of these, 572 received aid, and 232 had their full need met. Average financial aid package met 57% of need; average scholarship/grant was $2,362; average loan was $9,230. For part-time students, average financial aid package was $3,797.

Students without need: 28 full-time freshmen who did not demonstrate need for aid received scholarships/grants; average award was $1,281. No-need awards available for academics.

Cumulative student debt: 36% of graduating class had student loans; average debt was $26,024.

FINANCIAL AID PROCEDURES

Forms required: FAFSA, institutional form.

Dates and Deadlines: Priority date 3/15; closing date 4/15. Applicants notified on a rolling basis starting 4/15; must reply by 5/1 or within 2 week(s) of notification.

CONTACT

Nancy Barton, Director, Financial Aid/Veterans Affairs
181 White Street, Danbury, CT 06810-6826
(203) 837-8580

Yale University

New Haven, Connecticut   Federal Code: 001426
www.yale.edu   CSS Code: 3987

4-year private university in small city.

Enrollment: 5,258 undergrads. 1,305 full-time freshmen.

Selectivity: Admits less than 50% of applicants.

BASIC COSTS (2010-2011)

Tuition and fees: $38,300.

Room and board: $11,500.

FINANCIAL AID PICTURE (2008-2009)

Students with need: Need-based aid available for full-time and part-time students. Work study available nights, weekends, and for part-time students.

Students without need: This college awards aid only to students with need.

Additional info: All scholarships based on demonstrated need.

FINANCIAL AID PROCEDURES

Forms required: FAFSA, CSS PROFILE.

Dates and Deadlines: Closing date 3/1. Applicants notified by 4/1; must reply by 5/1 or within 1 week(s) of notification.

CONTACT

Caesar Storlazzi, Director of University Financial Aid
Box 208234, New Haven, CT 06520-8234
(203) 432-2700

Delaware

Delaware State University
Dover, Delaware
www.desu.edu   Federal Code: 001428

4-year public university in large town.
Enrollment: 3,222 undergrads, 13% part-time. 739 full-time freshmen.
Selectivity: Admits less than 50% of applicants.

BASIC COSTS (2009-2010)
Tuition and fees: $6,481; out-of-state residents $13,742.
Per-credit charge: $230; out-of-state residents $540.
Room and board: $9,386.

FINANCIAL AID PICTURE (2008-2009)
Students with need: Need-based aid available for full-time and part-time students.
Students without need: This college awards aid only to students with need.
Additional info: Students must file FAFSA by March 17 every year.

FINANCIAL AID PROCEDURES
Forms required: FAFSA.
Dates and Deadlines: Priority date 3/1; closing date 7/1. Applicants notified on a rolling basis starting 4/1; must reply by 8/20.
Transfers: Closing date 2/15.

CONTACT
Lynn Iocono, Executive Director of Student Financial Services
1200 North DuPont Highway, Dover, DE 19901
(302) 857-6250

Delaware Technical and Community College: Owens
Georgetown, Delaware
www.dtcc.edu   Federal Code: 007053

2-year public community and technical college in small town.
Enrollment: 4,170 undergrads, 46% part-time. 630 full-time freshmen.
Selectivity: Open admission; but selective for some programs.

BASIC COSTS (2009-2010)
Tuition and fees: $2,763; out-of-state residents $6,471.
Per-credit charge: $103; out-of-state residents $258.

FINANCIAL AID PICTURE
Students with need: Need-based aid available for full-time and part-time students.
Students without need: This college awards aid only to students with need.

FINANCIAL AID PROCEDURES
Forms required: FAFSA.
Dates and Deadlines: Priority date 6/15; no closing date. Applicants notified on a rolling basis; must reply within 2 week(s) of notification.

CONTACT
Veronica Oney, Financial Aid Officer
PO Box 610, Georgetown, DE 19947
(302) 855-5692

Delaware Technical and Community College: Stanton/Wilmington
Newark, Delaware
www.dtcc.edu   Federal Code: 021449

2-year public community and technical college in small city.
Enrollment: 6,894 undergrads, 56% part-time. 1,046 full-time freshmen.
Selectivity: Open admission; but selective for some programs.

BASIC COSTS (2009-2010)
Tuition and fees: $2,763; out-of-state residents $6,471.
Per-credit charge: $103; out-of-state residents $258.

FINANCIAL AID PICTURE
Students with need: Need-based aid available for full-time and part-time students.
Students without need: This college awards aid only to students with need.

FINANCIAL AID PROCEDURES
Forms required: FAFSA.
Dates and Deadlines: Priority date 6/15; no closing date. Applicants notified on a rolling basis; must reply within 2 week(s) of notification.

CONTACT
Debra Troxler, Student Financial Aid Officer
400 Stanton-Christiana Road, Newark, DE 19713
(302) 571-5380

Delaware Technical and Community College: Terry
Dover, Delaware
www.dtcc.edu   Federal Code: 011727

2-year public community and technical college in large town.
Enrollment: 3,214 undergrads, 53% part-time. 549 full-time freshmen.
Selectivity: Open admission; but selective for some programs.

BASIC COSTS (2009-2010)
Tuition and fees: $2,763; out-of-state residents $6,471.
Per-credit charge: $103; out-of-state residents $258.

FINANCIAL AID PICTURE
Students with need: Need-based aid available for full-time and part-time students.
Students without need: This college awards aid only to students with need.

FINANCIAL AID PROCEDURES
Forms required: FAFSA.
Dates and Deadlines: Priority date 6/15; no closing date. Applicants notified on a rolling basis starting 7/1; must reply within 2 week(s) of notification.

CONTACT
Jennifer Grunden, Financial Aid Director
100 Campus Drive, Dover, DE 19901
(302) 857-1040

Goldey-Beacom College
Wilmington, Delaware
www.gbc.edu   Federal Code: 001429

4-year private business college in small city.
Enrollment: 709 undergrads, 31% part-time. 80 full-time freshmen.

BASIC COSTS (2010-2011)

Tuition and fees: $18,660.
Per-credit charge: $612.
Room only: $5,021.

FINANCIAL AID PICTURE (2009-2010)

Students with need: Average financial aid package met 40% of need; average scholarship/grant was $8,205; average loan was $4,243. For part-time students, average financial aid package was $6,795.
Students without need: No-need awards available for academics.
Cumulative student debt: 80% of graduating class had student loans; average debt was $24,670.

FINANCIAL AID PROCEDURES

Forms required: FAFSA.
Dates and Deadlines: Priority date 4/1; no closing date. Applicants notified on a rolling basis starting 3/1; must reply within 2 week(s) of notification.
Transfers: No deadline. Applicants notified on a rolling basis starting 3/1; must reply within 2 week(s) of notification.

CONTACT

Jane Lysle, Dean of Enrollment Management
4701 Limestone Road, Wilmington, DE 19808
(302) 225-6265

University of Delaware

Newark, Delaware
www.udel.edu   Federal Code: 001431

4-year public university in large town.
Enrollment: 15,757 undergrads, 5% part-time. 3,716 full-time freshmen.
Selectivity: Admits 50 to 75% of applicants.

BASIC COSTS (2009-2010)

Tuition and fees: $9,486; out-of-state residents $23,186.
Per-credit charge: $356; out-of-state residents $927.
Room and board: $9,436.

FINANCIAL AID PICTURE (2008-2009)

Students with need: Out of 3,319 full-time freshmen who applied for aid, 1,872 were judged to have need. Of these, 1,793 received aid, and 998 had their full need met. Average financial aid package met 78% of need; average scholarship/grant was $7,156; average loan was $6,075. For part-time students, average financial aid package was $8,128.
Students without need: This college awards aid only to students with need.
Scholarships offered: *Merit:* All freshman applicants evaluated for a wide range of merit scholarships ranging from $1,000 to full cost of education.
Athletic: 142 full-time freshmen received athletic scholarships; average amount $9,239.
Cumulative student debt: 44% of graduating class had student loans; average debt was $17,200.
Additional info: December 15 application deadline to receive scholarship consideration. Sibling/parent tuition credit plan. Senior citizen tuition credit for state residents over 60.

FINANCIAL AID PROCEDURES

Forms required: FAFSA.
Dates and Deadlines: Priority date 2/1; closing date 3/15. Applicants notified on a rolling basis starting 3/15; must reply by 5/1 or within 3 week(s) of notification.
Transfers: No deadline. Aid usualy limited to federal and state programs.

CONTACT

Johnie Burton, Director of Financial Aid
210 South College Avenue, Newark, DE 19716
(302) 831-8761

Wesley College

Dover, Delaware
www.wesley.edu   Federal Code: 001433

4-year private liberal arts college in large town, affiliated with United Methodist Church.
Enrollment: 2,030 undergrads.
Selectivity: Admits 50 to 75% of applicants.

BASIC COSTS (2009-2010)

Tuition and fees: $19,830.
Per-credit charge: $800.
Room and board: $9,000.

FINANCIAL AID PICTURE (2008-2009)

Students with need: Need-based aid available for full-time and part-time students. Work study available nights, weekends, and for part-time students.
Students without need: This college awards aid only to students with need.

FINANCIAL AID PROCEDURES

Forms required: FAFSA, institutional form.
Dates and Deadlines: Priority date 2/1; no closing date. Applicants notified on a rolling basis starting 1/1; must reply within 2 week(s) of notification.
Transfers: No deadline. Applicants notified on a rolling basis; must reply within 2 week(s) of notification.

CONTACT

Michael Hall, Director of Student Financial Planning
120 North State Street, Dover, DE 19901-3875
(302) 736-2334

Wilmington University

New Castle, Delaware
www.wilmu.edu   Federal Code: 007948

4-year private liberal arts college in large town.
Enrollment: 6,000 undergrads, 46% part-time. 327 full-time freshmen.
Selectivity: Open admission.

BASIC COSTS (2009-2010)

Tuition and fees: $9,030.
Per-credit charge: $301.

FINANCIAL AID PICTURE

Students with need: Need-based aid available for full-time and part-time students. Work study available nights, weekends, and for part-time students.
Students without need: No-need awards available for academics, athletics.

FINANCIAL AID PROCEDURES

Forms required: FAFSA.
Dates and Deadlines: Priority date 4/30; no closing date. Applicants notified on a rolling basis starting 8/5; must reply within 2 week(s) of notification.

CONTACT

Trudy Hite, Director of Student Financial Services
320 Dupont Highway, New Castle, DE 19720
(302) 328-9401 ext. 107

PART III: FINANCIAL AID COLLEGE BY COLLEGE

District of Columbia

American University
Washington, District of Columbia
www.american.edu   Federal Code: 001434

4-year private university in very large city, affiliated with United Methodist Church.
Enrollment: 6,430 undergrads, 3% part-time. 1,533 full-time freshmen.
Selectivity: Admits 50 to 75% of applicants.

BASIC COSTS (2010-2011)
Tuition and fees: $36,697.
Per-credit charge: $1,205.
Room and board: $13,468.

FINANCIAL AID PICTURE (2009-2010)
Students with need: Out of 1,144 full-time freshmen who applied for aid, 849 were judged to have need. Of these, 849 received aid, and 255 had their full need met. Average financial aid package met 93% of need; average scholarship/grant was $17,325; average loan was $4,180. For part-time students, average financial aid package was $19,399.
Students without need: This college awards aid only to students with need.
Scholarships offered: *Merit:* United Methodist scholarship; supplemental application required. ***Athletic:*** 30 full-time freshmen received athletic scholarships; average amount $23,016.
Cumulative student debt: 54% of graduating class had student loans; average debt was $40,966.
Additional info: Early decision applicants must submit estimated AU institutional financial aid application by 11/15 and a FASFA as soon as possible after Jan 1.

FINANCIAL AID PROCEDURES
Forms required: FAFSA, institutional form.
Dates and Deadlines: Closing date 2/15. Applicants notified by 4/1; must reply by 5/1 or within 4 week(s) of notification.
Transfers: Priority date 3/1. Phi Theta Kappa scholarship available.

CONTACT
Brian Lee-Sang, Director of Financial Aid
4400 Massachusetts Avenue NW, Washington, DC 20016-8001
(202) 885-6100

Catholic University of America
Washington, District of Columbia
www.cua.edu   Federal Code: 001437

4-year private university in very large city, affiliated with Roman Catholic Church.
Enrollment: 3,422 undergrads, 6% part-time. 813 full-time freshmen.
Selectivity: Admits over 75% of applicants.

BASIC COSTS (2010-2011)
Tuition and fees: $34,205.
Per-credit charge: $1,315.
Room and board: $12,742.
Additional info: Full-time tuition for the School of Architecture and the School of Engineering is $33,860. Per-credit-hour charges for the School of Architecture and the School of Engineering are $1,315 per credit hour. Tuition/fee waivers available for adults.

FINANCIAL AID PICTURE (2009-2010)
Students with need: Out of 659 full-time freshmen who applied for aid, 525 were judged to have need. Of these, 525 received aid, and 258 had their full need met. Average financial aid package met 86% of need; average scholarship/grant was $16,752; average loan was $3,416. For part-time students, average financial aid package was $5,575.
Students without need: 230 full-time freshmen who did not demonstrate need for aid received scholarships/grants; average award was $10,317. No-need awards available for academics, alumni affiliation, music/drama, religious affiliation.

FINANCIAL AID PROCEDURES
Forms required: FAFSA.
Dates and Deadlines: Priority date 2/15; closing date 4/10. Applicants notified on a rolling basis starting 4/1; must reply by 5/1 or within 2 week(s) of notification.
Transfers: Applicants notified on a rolling basis starting 4/1; must reply by 5/1 or within 2 week(s) of notification.

CONTACT
Donald Bosse, Director of Financial Aid
102 McMahon Hall, Washington, DC 20064
(202) 319-5307

Corcoran College of Art and Design
Washington, District of Columbia
www.corcoran.edu   Federal Code: 011950

4-year private visual arts college in very large city.
Enrollment: 350 undergrads.
Selectivity: Admits 50 to 75% of applicants.

BASIC COSTS (2009-2010)
Tuition and fees: $27,960.
Room only: $9,700.

FINANCIAL AID PICTURE (2008-2009)
Students with need: Need-based aid available for full-time and part-time students. Work study available nights, weekends, and for part-time students.
Students without need: No-need awards available for academics, art.

FINANCIAL AID PROCEDURES
Forms required: FAFSA, institutional form.
Dates and Deadlines: Priority date 3/15; no closing date. Applicants notified on a rolling basis starting 4/15; must reply by 5/1 or within 2 week(s) of notification.
Transfers: No deadline. Applicants notified on a rolling basis; must reply within 2 week(s) of notification.

CONTACT
Diane Morris, Director of Financial Aid
500 17th Street, NW, Washington, DC 20006-4804
(202) 639-1816

Gallaudet University
Washington, District of Columbia
www.gallaudet.edu   Federal Code: 001443

4-year private university and liberal arts college in very large city.
Enrollment: 1,053 undergrads, 5% part-time. 180 full-time freshmen.
Selectivity: Admits 50 to 75% of applicants.

BASIC COSTS (2010-2011)
Tuition and fees: $11,226.
Per-credit charge: $542.
Room and board: $9,660.

FINANCIAL AID PICTURE (2008-2009)

Students with need: Out of 169 full-time freshmen who applied for aid, 138 were judged to have need. Of these, 138 received aid, and 54 had their full need met. Average financial aid package met 84% of need; average scholarship/grant was $16,069; average loan was $2,788. Need-based aid available for part-time students.

Students without need: 17 full-time freshmen who did not demonstrate need for aid received scholarships/grants; average award was $7,297. No-need awards available for academics, leadership, minority status.

Cumulative student debt: 54% of graduating class had student loans; average debt was $13,484.

Additional info: Institution receives substantial aid from state vocational rehabilitation agencies, supplemented by institutional grants when needed.

FINANCIAL AID PROCEDURES

Forms required: FAFSA, institutional form.

Dates and Deadlines: Priority date 7/1; no closing date. Applicants notified on a rolling basis starting 3/1; must reply within 4 week(s) of notification.

CONTACT

Nancy Goodman, Director of Financial Aid
800 Florida Avenue, NE, Washington, DC 20002
(202) 651-5290

George Washington University

Washington, District of Columbia   Federal Code: 001444
www.gwu.edu/explore/   CSS Code: 5246

4-year private university in very large city.

Enrollment: 10,225 undergrads, 6% part-time. 2,582 full-time freshmen.

Selectivity: Admits less than 50% of applicants. GED not accepted.

BASIC COSTS (2010-2011)

Tuition and fees: $42,905.

Room and board: $10,120.

Additional info: Tuition stays fixed until student graduates, for a maximum of five years.

FINANCIAL AID PICTURE (2009-2010)

Students with need: Average financial aid package met 94% of need; average scholarship/grant was $25,467; average loan was $4,649. For part-time students, average financial aid package was $9,856.

Students without need: No-need awards available for academics, art, athletics, music/drama, ROTC.

Cumulative student debt: 47% of graduating class had student loans; average debt was $31,299.

Additional info: Auditions required for performing arts scholarships.

FINANCIAL AID PROCEDURES

Forms required: FAFSA, CSS PROFILE.

Dates and Deadlines: Closing date 2/1. Applicants notified on a rolling basis starting 3/24; must reply by 5/1.

Transfers: Priority date 4/1; closing date 5/1.

CONTACT

Daniel Small, Director of Student Financial Assistance
2121 I Street NW, Suite 201, Washington, DC 20052
(202) 994-6620

Georgetown University

Washington, District of Columbia   Federal Code: 001445
www.georgetown.edu   CSS Code: 5244

4-year private university in very large city, affiliated with Roman Catholic Church.

Enrollment: 7,092 undergrads, 3% part-time. 1,571 full-time freshmen.

Selectivity: Admits less than 50% of applicants.

BASIC COSTS (2009-2010)

Tuition and fees: $39,036.

Per-credit charge: $1,609.

Room and board: $13,125.

FINANCIAL AID PICTURE (2008-2009)

Students with need: Out of 850 full-time freshmen who applied for aid, 632 were judged to have need. Of these, 632 received aid, and 632 had their full need met. Average financial aid package met 100% of need; average scholarship/grant was $28,100; average loan was $3,000. Need-based aid available for part-time students.

Students without need: No-need awards available for athletics.

Scholarships offered: 75 full-time freshmen received athletic scholarships; average amount $21,000.

Cumulative student debt: 44% of graduating class had student loans; average debt was $23,333.

FINANCIAL AID PROCEDURES

Forms required: FAFSA, CSS PROFILE.

Dates and Deadlines: Closing date 2/1. Applicants notified by 4/1; must reply by 5/1 or within 2 week(s) of notification.

Transfers: Priority date 3/1. Applicants notified by 5/15; must reply by 5/30 or within 2 week(s) of notification.

CONTACT

Patricia McWade, Dean of Student Financial Services
103 White-Gravenor, Washington, DC 20057-1002
(202) 687-4547

Howard University

Washington, District of Columbia
www.howard.edu   Federal Code: 001448

4-year private university in very large city.

Enrollment: 7,029 undergrads.

Selectivity: Admits 50 to 75% of applicants.

BASIC COSTS (2010-2011)

Tuition and fees: $18,123.

Room and board: $8,500.

FINANCIAL AID PICTURE (2008-2009)

Students with need: Need-based aid available for full-time and part-time students.

Students without need: No-need awards available for academics, art, athletics, music/drama.

FINANCIAL AID PROCEDURES

Forms required: FAFSA, institutional form.

Dates and Deadlines: Priority date 2/15; closing date 8/15. Applicants notified on a rolling basis starting 4/1; must reply by 8/1 or within 4 week(s) of notification.

CONTACT

Marcus DeCosta, Associate Director, Office of Financial Aid, Scholarships, and Student Employment
2400 Sixth Street NW, Washington, DC 20059
(202) 806-2820

Potomac College

Washington, District of Columbia
www.potomac.edu   Federal Code: 032183

3-year for-profit business college in very large city.

Enrollment: 450 undergrads.

Selectivity: Open admission.

BASIC COSTS (2009-2010)
Tuition and fees: $13,480.
Per-credit charge: $445.

FINANCIAL AID PICTURE (2008-2009)
Students with need: Need-based aid available for full-time and part-time students.

FINANCIAL AID PROCEDURES
Forms required: FAFSA, institutional form.
Dates and Deadlines: No deadline. Applicants notified on a rolling basis; must reply within 4 week(s) of notification.

CONTACT
Meliva Carty, Director of Financial Aid
4000 Chesapeake Street NW, Washington, DC 20016
(202) 686-0876

Trinity Washington University
Washington, District of Columbia
www.trinitydc.edu   Federal Code: 001460

4-year private liberal arts college in very large city, affiliated with Roman Catholic Church.
Enrollment: 1,127 undergrads.
Selectivity: Admits 50 to 75% of applicants.

BASIC COSTS (2009-2010)
Tuition and fees: $19,520.
Per-credit charge: $620.
Room and board: $8,850.
Additional info: Mandatory health insurance.

FINANCIAL AID PICTURE (2009-2010)
Students with need: Need-based aid available for full-time and part-time students.
Students without need: No-need awards available for academics, alumni affiliation, leadership.

FINANCIAL AID PROCEDURES
Forms required: FAFSA.
Dates and Deadlines: Priority date 3/1; no closing date. Applicants notified on a rolling basis starting 2/1; must reply within 2 week(s) of notification.

CONTACT
Catherine Geier, Director of Financial Aid
125 Michigan Avenue, NE, Washington, DC 20017
(202) 884-9530

University of the District of Columbia
Washington, District of Columbia
www.udc.edu   Federal Code: 007015

4-year public university and liberal arts college in very large city.
Enrollment: 4,918 undergrads, 53% part-time. 654 full-time freshmen.
Selectivity: Open admission; but selective for some programs.

BASIC COSTS (2009-2010)
Tuition and fees: $3,899; out-of-state residents $12,300.
Per-credit charge: $198; out-of-state residents $487.

FINANCIAL AID PICTURE
Students with need: Need-based aid available for full-time and part-time students. Work study available nights, weekends, and for part-time students.
Students without need: This college awards aid only to students with need.

FINANCIAL AID PROCEDURES
Forms required: FAFSA.
Dates and Deadlines: Priority date 3/15; no closing date. Applicants notified on a rolling basis starting 5/1; must reply within 2 week(s) of notification.

CONTACT
Willis Parker, Director of Financial Aid
4200 Connecticut Avenue NW, Washington, DC 20008
(202) 274-5060

Florida

Angley College
Deland, Florida
www.angley.edu   Federal Code: 035954

2-year for-profit technical and career college in small city.
Enrollment: 251 undergrads. 251 full-time freshmen.
Selectivity: Admits 50 to 75% of applicants.

BASIC COSTS (2009-2010)
Tuition and fees: $15,900.
Per-credit charge: $323.
Additional info: Textbooks included in program cost.

FINANCIAL AID PICTURE (2008-2009)
Students with need: 76% of average financial aid package awarded as scholarships/grants, 24% awarded as loans/jobs.

CONTACT
Michael Kirchmaeir, Financial Aid Director
1700 Woodland Boulevard, Deland, FL 32720-4289

Art Institute of Fort Lauderdale
Fort Lauderdale, Florida
www.aifl.edu   Federal Code: 010195

4-year for-profit visual arts and technical college in large city.
Enrollment: 3,063 undergrads, 42% part-time. 542 full-time freshmen.
Selectivity: Admits less than 50% of applicants.

BASIC COSTS (2010-2011)
Tuition and fees: $22,505.
Per-credit charge: $499.

FINANCIAL AID PICTURE (2008-2009)
Students with need: 23% of average financial aid package awarded as scholarships/grants, 77% awarded as loans/jobs. Need-based aid available for part-time students. Work study available nights, weekends, and for part-time students.
Students without need: No-need awards available for academics.
Scholarships offered: Art Institute's International Excellence Award: $200-$300 per quarter; based on GPA.
Additional info: Internal scholarships available. Financial planning program allows personalized service to budget and meet college costs through individualized payment plans.

FINANCIAL AID PROCEDURES
Forms required: FAFSA.
Dates and Deadlines: No deadline.

CONTACT
Joy Cummings, Director of Student Financial Service
1799 SE 17th Street, Fort Lauderdale, FL 33316
(954) 308-2165

ATI College of Health
Miami, Florida
www.aticareertraining.edu
Federal Code: 014612
CSS Code: 3183

2-year for-profit health science and technical college in very large city.
Enrollment: 1,119 undergrads. 770 full-time freshmen.
Selectivity: Open admission; but selective for some programs.

BASIC COSTS (2009-2010)
Additional info: $44,520 tuition for diagnostic ultrasound program and respiratory therapist program; $31,102 for dental and health information technology.

FINANCIAL AID PICTURE
Students with need: Need-based aid available for full-time and part-time students.
Students without need: This college awards aid only to students with need.

FINANCIAL AID PROCEDURES
Forms required: FAFSA, CSS PROFILE, institutional form.
Dates and Deadlines: No deadline. Applicants notified on a rolling basis.

CONTACT
Financial Aid Director
1395 NW 167th Street, Miami, FL 33169-5745
(305) 628-1000

Baptist College of Florida
Graceville, Florida
www.baptistcollege.edu
Federal Code: 013001

4-year private Bible and teachers college in small town, affiliated with Southern Baptist Convention.
Enrollment: 546 undergrads, 24% part-time. 89 full-time freshmen.
Selectivity: Admits 50 to 75% of applicants.

BASIC COSTS (2009-2010)
Tuition and fees: $8,450.
Per-credit charge: $270.
Room and board: $4,066.

FINANCIAL AID PICTURE (2008-2009)
Students with need: Out of 74 full-time freshmen who applied for aid, 57 were judged to have need. Of these, 49 received aid, and 6 had their full need met. Average financial aid package met 49% of need; average scholarship/grant was $4,808; average loan was $2,752. For part-time students, average financial aid package was $5,109.
Students without need: 6 full-time freshmen who did not demonstrate need for aid received scholarships/grants; average award was $1,333. No-need awards available for academics, minority status, music/drama, religious affiliation.

FINANCIAL AID PROCEDURES
Forms required: FAFSA, state aid form, institutional form.
Dates and Deadlines: Priority date 4/1; closing date 4/15. Applicants notified on a rolling basis starting 6/15; must reply within 4 week(s) of notification.
Transfers: No deadline.

CONTACT
Angela Rathel, Director of Financial Aid
5400 College Drive, Graceville, FL 32440-3306
(850) 263-3261 ext. 461

Barry University
Miami Shores, Florida
www.barry.edu
Federal Code: 001466

4-year private university in large town, affiliated with Roman Catholic Church.
Enrollment: 4,990 undergrads, 17% part-time. 648 full-time freshmen.
Selectivity: Admits 50 to 75% of applicants.

BASIC COSTS (2010-2011)
Tuition and fees: $27,200.
Per-credit charge: $815.
Room and board: $9,002.

FINANCIAL AID PICTURE (2008-2009)
Students with need: Out of 582 full-time freshmen who applied for aid, 556 were judged to have need. Of these, 549 received aid, and 32 had their full need met. Average financial aid package met 72% of need; average scholarship/grant was $9,435; average loan was $3,494. For part-time students, average financial aid package was $6,519.
Students without need: 69 full-time freshmen who did not demonstrate need for aid received scholarships/grants; average award was $8,906. No-need awards available for academics, art, athletics, music/drama.
Scholarships offered: 26 full-time freshmen received athletic scholarships; average amount $13,692.

FINANCIAL AID PROCEDURES
Forms required: FAFSA.
Dates and Deadlines: No deadline. Applicants notified on a rolling basis starting 1/25.

CONTACT
H. Dart Humeston, Director of Financial Aid
11300 NE Second Avenue, Miami Shores, FL 33161-6695
(305) 899-3673

Beacon College
Leesburg, Florida
www.beaconcollege.edu
Federal Code: 033733

4-year private liberal arts college in large town.
Enrollment: 125 undergrads. 29 full-time freshmen.
Selectivity: Admits over 75% of applicants.

BASIC COSTS (2010-2011)
Tuition and fees: $28,460.
Per-credit charge: $510.
Room and board: $8,150.
Additional info: Tuition/fee waivers available for minority students, unemployed or children of unemployed.

FINANCIAL AID PICTURE (2008-2009)
Students with need: Need-based aid available for full-time and part-time students. Work study available nights.
Students without need: This college awards aid only to students with need.
Scholarships offered: Paul and Dorothy Heim Civic Award: $500; awarded annually. Ehil E. Brodbeck Book Scholarship: pays complete book costs for 1 semester; awarded annually based on merit or financial need.
Additional info: Work-study programs offered based on financial need.

FINANCIAL AID PROCEDURES
Forms required: FAFSA, state aid form, institutional form.
Dates and Deadlines: Priority date 4/1; no closing date. Applicants notified on a rolling basis starting 4/1; must reply within 2 week(s) of notification.
Transfers: No deadline. Applicants notified on a rolling basis starting 4/1; must reply within 2 week(s) of notification.

CONTACT

Kimberly Baggett, Financial Aid Coordinator
105 East Main Street, Leesburg, FL 34748
(352) 787-7660

Bethune-Cookman University

Daytona Beach, Florida
www.cookman.edu   Federal Code: 001467

4-year private liberal arts college in small city, affiliated with United Methodist Church.
Enrollment: 3,587 undergrads, 4% part-time. 1,019 full-time freshmen.
Selectivity: Admits 50 to 75% of applicants.

BASIC COSTS (2010-2011)

Tuition and fees: $13,452.
Per-credit charge: $561.
Room and board: $7,980.
Additional info: Tuition at time of enrollment locked for 4 years.

FINANCIAL AID PICTURE (2009-2010)

Students with need: Need-based aid available for full-time and part-time students. Work study available nights, weekends, and for part-time students.
Students without need: This college awards aid only to students with need.

FINANCIAL AID PROCEDURES

Forms required: FAFSA.
Dates and Deadlines: Priority date 4/1; no closing date. Applicants notified on a rolling basis starting 4/1; must reply within 3 week(s) of notification.

CONTACT

Joseph Coleman, Director of Financial Aid
Dr. Mary McLeod Bethune Boulevard, Daytona Beach, FL 32114-3099
(800) 553-9369

Brevard Community College

Cocoa, Florida
www.brevardcc.edu   Federal Code: 001470

2-year public community college in large town.
Enrollment: 16,723 undergrads, 58% part-time. 1,997 full-time freshmen.
Selectivity: Open admission; but selective for some programs.

BASIC COSTS (2009-2010)

Tuition and fees: $2,685; out-of-state residents $9,675.

FINANCIAL AID PICTURE (2008-2009)

Students with need: Need-based aid available for full-time and part-time students.
Students without need: No-need awards available for academics, athletics.

FINANCIAL AID PROCEDURES

Forms required: FAFSA.
Dates and Deadlines: Priority date 4/15; closing date 6/30. Applicants notified on a rolling basis starting 6/1; must reply within 2 week(s) of notification.
Transfers: Transfer students must complete at least 15 credit hours with 3.5 GPA to be considered for merit scholarship.

CONTACT

Indira Dzadovsky, Director of Financial Aid/ Veteran Affairs
1519 Clearlake Road, Cocoa, FL 32922-9987
(321) 433-5530

Broward College

Fort Lauderdale, Florida
www.broward.edu   Federal Code: 001500

2-year public community college in small city.
Enrollment: 32,727 undergrads, 61% part-time. 3,714 full-time freshmen.
Selectivity: Open admission; but selective for some programs.

BASIC COSTS (2009-2010)

Tuition and fees: $2,518; out-of-state residents $9,081.
Additional info: Tuition/fee waivers available for adults, minority students.

FINANCIAL AID PICTURE (2008-2009)

Students with need: 73% of average financial aid package awarded as scholarships/grants, 27% awarded as loans/jobs. Need-based aid available for part-time students. Work study available nights, weekends, and for part-time students.
Students without need: No-need awards available for academics, athletics, leadership, state/district residency.

FINANCIAL AID PROCEDURES

Forms required: FAFSA, institutional form.
Dates and Deadlines: Priority date 4/15; no closing date. Applicants notified on a rolling basis starting 6/1.
Transfers: No deadline.

CONTACT

Marcia Conliffe, Student Success and Enrollment Management Services
225 East Las Olas Boulevard, Fort Lauderdale, FL 33301
(954) 201-7635

Carlos Albizu University

Miami, Florida
www.albizu.edu   Federal Code: 010724

4-year private university in very large city.
Enrollment: 425 undergrads.
Selectivity: Open admission; but selective for some programs.

BASIC COSTS (2009-2010)

Tuition and fees: $14,469.
Additional info: Reported tuition and fees are for bachelor's degree program in business. Other programs individually priced.

FINANCIAL AID PICTURE

Students with need: Need-based aid available for full-time and part-time students. Work study available nights.
Students without need: This college awards aid only to students with need.

FINANCIAL AID PROCEDURES

Forms required: FAFSA, institutional form.
Dates and Deadlines: Priority date 6/1; no closing date. Applicants notified on a rolling basis starting 2/1.
Transfers: No deadline. Applicants notified on a rolling basis.

CONTACT

Ramona Morales, Financial Aid Director
2173 NW 99th Avenue, Miami, FL 33172
(305) 593-1223 ext. 153

Central Florida College

Winter Park, Florida
www.centralfloridacollege.edu   Federal Code: 022455

2-year for-profit technical college in very large city.
Enrollment: 500 undergrads.
Selectivity: Open admission.

FINANCIAL AID PICTURE
Students with need: Need-based aid available for full-time students.
Students without need: This college awards aid only to students with need.

FINANCIAL AID PROCEDURES
Forms required: FAFSA.
Dates and Deadlines: No deadline.

CONTACT
Cathy Lane, Corporate Finance Director
1573 West Fairbanks Avenue, Winter Park, FL 32789
(407) 843-3984

Central Florida Community College

Ocala, Florida
www.cf.edu   Federal Code: 001471

2-year public community college in small city.
Enrollment: 7,830 undergrads, 62% part-time. 845 full-time freshmen.
Selectivity: Open admission; but selective for some programs.

BASIC COSTS (2009-2010)
Tuition and fees: $2,587; out-of-state residents $9,728.
Additional info: Tuition/fee waivers available for minority students.

FINANCIAL AID PICTURE (2008-2009)
Students with need: Need-based aid available for full-time and part-time students.
Students without need: No-need awards available for academics, athletics, minority status, music/drama, state/district residency.

FINANCIAL AID PROCEDURES
Forms required: FAFSA.
Dates and Deadlines: No deadline.

CONTACT
Walter Fleming, Director, Financial Aid
3001 SW College Road, Ocala, FL 34474-4415
(352) 873-5803 ext. 1340

Chipola College

Marianna, Florida
www.chipola.edu   Federal Code: 001472

4-year public community and junior college in small town.
Enrollment: 1,647 undergrads, 42% part-time. 226 full-time freshmen.
Selectivity: Open admission; but selective for some programs.

BASIC COSTS (2009-2010)
Tuition and fees: $2,550; out-of-state residents $7,314.

FINANCIAL AID PICTURE (2008-2009)
Students with need: 92% of average financial aid package awarded as scholarships/grants, 8% awarded as loans/jobs. Need-based aid available for part-time students. Work study available nights.
Students without need: No-need awards available for academics, alumni affiliation, art, athletics, job skills, leadership, minority status, music/drama.

FINANCIAL AID PROCEDURES
Forms required: FAFSA, institutional form.
Dates and Deadlines: Priority date 5/1; no closing date. Applicants notified on a rolling basis starting 1/2; must reply within 2 week(s) of notification.

CONTACT
Sybil Cloud, Director of Financial Aid
3094 Indian Circle, Marianna, FL 32446
(850) 718-2223

City College: Miami

Miami, Florida
www.citycollege.edu   Federal Code: 025154

2-year for-profit business and health science college in large city.
Enrollment: 270 undergrads.
Selectivity: Admits 50 to 75% of applicants.

BASIC COSTS (2009-2010)
Tuition and fees: $13,680.

FINANCIAL AID PICTURE
Students with need: Need-based aid available for full-time and part-time students.
Students without need: This college awards aid only to students with need.

FINANCIAL AID PROCEDURES
Forms required: FAFSA, institutional form.
Dates and Deadlines: No deadline. Applicants notified on a rolling basis.

CONTACT
Armando Rios, President
9300 South Dadeland Boulevard, Miami, FL 33156
(305) 666-9242

Clearwater Christian College

Clearwater, Florida
www.clearwater.edu   Federal Code: 015025

4-year private liberal arts college in small city, affiliated with nondenominational tradition.
Enrollment: 561 undergrads, 1% part-time. 157 full-time freshmen.
Selectivity: Admits over 75% of applicants.

BASIC COSTS (2009-2010)
Tuition and fees: $14,710.
Per-credit charge: $580.
Room and board: $6,740.

FINANCIAL AID PICTURE (2009-2010)
Students with need: 61% of average financial aid package awarded as scholarships/grants, 39% awarded as loans/jobs. Need-based aid available for part-time students. Work study available nights, weekends, and for part-time students.
Students without need: No-need awards available for academics, alumni affiliation, leadership, music/drama, religious affiliation, ROTC.
Additional info: Special consideration given to children of Christian service workers; need-based scholarships available to first-generation students; scholarships up to $3,000 available to dual-enrolled students.

FINANCIAL AID PROCEDURES
Forms required: FAFSA, state aid form, institutional form.
Dates and Deadlines: Priority date 3/15; no closing date. Applicants notified on a rolling basis starting 4/15; must reply within 2 week(s) of notification.

Transfers: Transfer academic scholarship of $750 per semester awarded to sophomore or junior transfer with at least 3.25 cumulative GPA. After transferring, student must maintain 3.5 GPA.

CONTACT
Ruth Strum, Director of Financial Aid
3400 Gulf-to-Bay Boulevard, Clearwater, FL 33759-4595
(727) 726-1153 ext. 214

College of Business and Technology: Flagler
Miami, Florida
www.cbt.edu   Federal Code: 030716

2-year for-profit junior and technical college in very large city.
Enrollment: 150 undergrads.
Selectivity: Open admission.

BASIC COSTS (2009-2010)
Tuition and fees: $14,904.
Per-credit charge: $414.

FINANCIAL AID PICTURE
Students with need: Need-based aid available for full-time and part-time students. Work study available nights.
Students without need: This college awards aid only to students with need.

FINANCIAL AID PROCEDURES
Forms required: FAFSA.
Dates and Deadlines: No deadline.

CONTACT
Yazmin Palma, Financial Aid Director
8230 West Flagler Street, Miami, FL 33144

Daytona State College
Daytona Beach, Florida
www.daytonastate.edu   Federal Code: 001475

2-year public community and technical college in large city.
Enrollment: 15,205 undergrads, 53% part-time. 1,718 full-time freshmen.
Selectivity: Open admission; but selective for some programs.

BASIC COSTS (2009-2010)
Tuition and fees: $2,624; out-of-state residents $9,942.

FINANCIAL AID PICTURE (2008-2009)
Students with need: Need-based aid available for full-time and part-time students.
Students without need: No-need awards available for athletics, leadership, music/drama.

FINANCIAL AID PROCEDURES
Forms required: FAFSA.
Dates and Deadlines: No deadline. Applicants notified on a rolling basis starting 2/15.

CONTACT
Aileen Morrissey, Director of Financial Aid
Daytona State College Admissions Office, Daytona Beach, FL 32114-2811
(386) 506-3000 ext. 3015

DeVry University: Miramar
Miramar, Florida
www.devry.edu

4-year for-profit university in large town.
Enrollment: 1,099 undergrads, 53% part-time. 104 full-time freshmen.

BASIC COSTS (2009-2010)
Tuition and fees: $14,160.
Per-credit charge: $550.

FINANCIAL AID PICTURE (2008-2009)
Students with need: Need-based aid available for full-time and part-time students.
Students without need: This college awards aid only to students with need.

FINANCIAL AID PROCEDURES
Forms required: FAFSA.
Dates and Deadlines: No deadline. Applicants notified on a rolling basis.

CONTACT
Scott Howard, Assistant Director of Student Finance
2300 SW 145th Avenue, Miramar, FL 33027
(954) 499-9700

DeVry University: Orlando
Orlando, Florida
www.devry.edu   Federal Code: 022966

4-year for-profit university in very large city.
Enrollment: 1,727 undergrads, 48% part-time. 186 full-time freshmen.

BASIC COSTS (2009-2010)
Tuition and fees: $14,160.
Per-credit charge: $550.

FINANCIAL AID PICTURE (2008-2009)
Students with need: Need-based aid available for full-time and part-time students.
Students without need: This college awards aid only to students with need.

FINANCIAL AID PROCEDURES
Forms required: FAFSA.
Dates and Deadlines: No deadline. Applicants notified on a rolling basis.

CONTACT
Estrella Velasquez Domenech, Director of Student Finance
4000 Millennia Boulevard, Orlando, FL 32839-2426
(407) 345-2800

Eckerd College
St. Petersburg, Florida
www.eckerd.edu   Federal Code: 001487

4-year private liberal arts college in large city, affiliated with Presbyterian Church (USA).
Enrollment: 1,847 undergrads, 1% part-time. 504 full-time freshmen.
Selectivity: Admits 50 to 75% of applicants.

BASIC COSTS (2010-2011)
Tuition and fees: $33,228.
Per-credit charge: $1,134.
Room and board: $9,326.

FINANCIAL AID PICTURE (2009-2010)

Students with need: Need-based aid available for full-time and part-time students.

Students without need: No-need awards available for academics, art, athletics, music/drama.

Scholarships offered: Academic scholarships: ranging from $7,500 to $13,000 per year; available to entering freshmen regardless of financial need. Trustee, Presidential, and Dean's Scholarships: range from $13,000 to $25,000 awarded to outstanding freshmen with strong scholastic records and leadership potential. Limited number of Artistic Achievement Awards in music, theater, visual art and creative writing also available through separate application process.

FINANCIAL AID PROCEDURES

Forms required: FAFSA.

Dates and Deadlines: Priority date 3/1; no closing date. Applicants notified on a rolling basis starting 2/1.

CONTACT

Patricia Watkins, Director of Financial Aid
4200 54th Avenue South, St. Petersburg, FL 33711-4700
(727) 864-8334

Edison State College

Fort Myers, Florida
www.edison.edu   Federal Code: 001477

4-year public liberal arts college in very large city.

Enrollment: 16,034 undergrads.

Selectivity: Open admission; but selective for some programs.

BASIC COSTS (2009-2010)

Tuition and fees: $2,636; out-of-state residents $9,942.

FINANCIAL AID PICTURE

Students with need: Need-based aid available for full-time and part-time students. Work study available nights, weekends, and for part-time students.

Students without need: No-need awards available for art, music/drama.

FINANCIAL AID PROCEDURES

Forms required: FAFSA.

Dates and Deadlines: Priority date 5/1; no closing date. Applicants notified on a rolling basis starting 6/1; must reply within 2 week(s) of notification.

CONTACT

Cindy Lewis, District Director of Financial Aid
Box 60210, Fort Myers, FL 33906-6210
(239) 489-9346

Edward Waters College

Jacksonville, Florida
www.ewc.edu   Federal Code: 001478

4-year private liberal arts college in very large city, affiliated with African Methodist Episcopal Church.

Enrollment: 812 undergrads.

Selectivity: Admits less than 50% of applicants.

BASIC COSTS (2009-2010)

Tuition and fees: $9,990.

Per-credit charge: $416.

Room and board: $6,439.

FINANCIAL AID PICTURE (2008-2009)

Students with need: Need-based aid available for full-time and part-time students. Work study available nights, weekends, and for part-time students.

FINANCIAL AID PROCEDURES

Forms required: FAFSA.

Dates and Deadlines: Closing date 4/15. Applicants notified on a rolling basis starting 5/1; must reply within 2 week(s) of notification.

CONTACT

James Washburn, Vice President for Business and Finance
1658 Kings Road, Jacksonville, FL 32209
(904) 470-8190

Embry-Riddle Aeronautical University

Daytona Beach, Florida
www.embryriddle.edu   Federal Code: 001479

4-year private university in small city.

Enrollment: 4,430 undergrads, 6% part-time. 857 full-time freshmen.

Selectivity: Admits over 75% of applicants.

BASIC COSTS (2010-2011)

Tuition and fees: $29,720.

Per-credit charge: $1,190.

Room and board: $10,320.

FINANCIAL AID PICTURE (2009-2010)

Students with need: Out of 699 full-time freshmen who applied for aid, 604 were judged to have need. Of these, 601 received aid. For part-time students, average financial aid package was $8,961.

Students without need: No-need awards available for academics, alumni affiliation, athletics, leadership, ROTC.

Scholarships offered: 27 full-time freshmen received athletic scholarships; average amount $11,424.

FINANCIAL AID PROCEDURES

Forms required: FAFSA.

Dates and Deadlines: No deadline. Applicants notified on a rolling basis starting 3/1; must reply within 4 week(s) of notification.

CONTACT

Barbara Dryden, Director of Financial Aid
600 South Clyde Morris Boulevard, Daytona Beach, FL 32114-3900
(386) 226-6300

Embry-Riddle Aeronautical University: Worldwide Campus

Daytona Beach, Florida
www.embryriddle.edu   Federal Code: 001479

4-year private university in small city.

Enrollment: 10,988 undergrads, 81% part-time. 81 full-time freshmen.

BASIC COSTS (2010-2011)

Additional info: Per credit hour charges range from $230 - $321.

FINANCIAL AID PICTURE (2009-2010)

Students with need: Out of 20 full-time freshmen who applied for aid, 17 were judged to have need. Of these, 17 received aid. For part-time students, average financial aid package was $5,596.

Students without need: No-need awards available for academics.

FINANCIAL AID PROCEDURES

Forms required: FAFSA.

Dates and Deadlines: Priority date 4/15; no closing date. Applicants notified on a rolling basis starting 3/1; must reply within 4 week(s) of notification.

CONTACT

Barbara Dryden, Director of Financial Aid

600 South Clyde Morris Boulevard, Daytona Beach, FL 32114-3900

(386) 226-6300

Everglades University: Boca Raton

Boca Raton, Florida

www.EvergladesUniversity.edu   Federal Code: 031085

4-year private university in small city.

Enrollment: 1,000 undergrads.

BASIC COSTS (2009-2010)

Additional info: $1,600 education fee for online students.

FINANCIAL AID PICTURE

Students with need: Need-based aid available for full-time students.

FINANCIAL AID PROCEDURES

Forms required: FAFSA.

Dates and Deadlines: No deadline. Applicants notified on a rolling basis.

CONTACT

Seeta Singh-Moonilall, Director of Financial Aid

5002 T-REX Avenue, Suite 100, Boca Raton, FL 33431

(561) 912-1211 ext. 114

Flagler College

Saint Augustine, Florida

www.flagler.edu   Federal Code: 007893

4-year private liberal arts college in large town.

Enrollment: 2,706 undergrads, 3% part-time. 564 full-time freshmen.

Selectivity: Admits less than 50% of applicants.

BASIC COSTS (2010-2011)

Tuition and fees: $13,860.

Per-credit charge: $465.

Room and board: $7,590.

FINANCIAL AID PICTURE (2009-2010)

Students with need: Out of 460 full-time freshmen who applied for aid, 333 were judged to have need. Of these, 333 received aid, and 28 had their full need met. Average financial aid package met 61% of need; average scholarship/grant was $5,378; average loan was $3,213. For part-time students, average financial aid package was $5,724.

Students without need: 10 full-time freshmen who did not demonstrate need for aid received scholarships/grants; average award was $4,000. No-need awards available for academics, art, athletics, job skills, leadership, minority status, music/drama, state/district residency.

Scholarships offered: 36 full-time freshmen received athletic scholarships; average amount $6,071.

Cumulative student debt: 55% of graduating class had student loans; average debt was $18,190.

FINANCIAL AID PROCEDURES

Forms required: FAFSA, state aid form, institutional form.

Dates and Deadlines: Priority date 4/1; no closing date. Applicants notified on a rolling basis starting 4/1; must reply within 2 week(s) of notification.

Transfers: No deadline. Applicants notified on a rolling basis starting 3/1; must reply within 2 week(s) of notification. Transfer students receiving Florida-sponsored aid must notify Florida Office of Student Financial Assistance of their transfer.

CONTACT

Christopher Haffner, Director of Financial Aid

74 King Street, St. Augustine, FL 32084

(800) 304-4208

Florida Agricultural and Mechanical University

Tallahassee, Florida

www.famu.edu   Federal Code: 001480

4-year public university in small city.

Enrollment: 10,097 undergrads, 8% part-time. 2,092 full-time freshmen.

Selectivity: Admits 50 to 75% of applicants.

BASIC COSTS (2009-2010)

Tuition and fees: $4,120; out-of-state residents $15,513.

Room and board: $6,976.

FINANCIAL AID PICTURE (2008-2009)

Students with need: Out of 1,006 full-time freshmen who applied for aid, 994 were judged to have need. Of these, 975 received aid, and 154 had their full need met. Average financial aid package met 75% of need; average scholarship/grant was $5,812; average loan was $3,166. For part-time students, average financial aid package was $8,955.

Students without need: 135 full-time freshmen who did not demonstrate need for aid received scholarships/grants; average award was $5,479. No-need awards available for academics, art, athletics, leadership, music/drama.

Scholarships offered: 45 full-time freshmen received athletic scholarships; average amount $8,936.

Cumulative student debt: 81% of graduating class had student loans; average debt was $27,253.

FINANCIAL AID PROCEDURES

Forms required: FAFSA.

Dates and Deadlines: Priority date 3/1; no closing date. Applicants notified by 4/15.

Transfers: No deadline. Applicants notified on a rolling basis starting 4/15.

CONTACT

Marcia Boyd, Director of Financial Aid

FHAC, G-9, Tallahassee, FL 32307-3200

(850) 599-3730

Florida Atlantic University

Boca Raton, Florida

www.fau.edu   Federal Code: 001481

4-year public university in small city.

Enrollment: 21,620 undergrads, 40% part-time. 2,582 full-time freshmen.

Selectivity: Admits less than 50% of applicants.

BASIC COSTS (2009-2010)

Tuition and fees: $4,187; out-of-state residents $17,532.

Room and board: $9,582.

FINANCIAL AID PICTURE (2008-2009)

Students with need: Out of 1,736 full-time freshmen who applied for aid, 1,179 were judged to have need. Of these, 1,156 received aid, and 146 had their full need met. Average financial aid package met 85% of need; average scholarship/grant was $6,740; average loan was $2,929. For part-time students, average financial aid package was $5,537.

Students without need: No-need awards available for academics, athletics, music/drama, state/district residency.

FINANCIAL AID PROCEDURES

Forms required: FAFSA.

Dates and Deadlines: Priority date 3/1; no closing date. Applicants notified on a rolling basis starting 4/1; must reply within 3 week(s) of notification.

CONTACT
Carol Pfeilsticker, Director of Financial Aid
777 Glades Road, Boca Raton, FL 33431
(561) 297-2738

Florida Christian College
Kissimmee, Florida
www.fcc.edu   Federal Code: 015192

4-year private Bible and teachers college in small city, affiliated with Christian Churches and Churches of Christ.
Enrollment: 226 undergrads, 28% part-time. 27 full-time freshmen.

BASIC COSTS (2009-2010)
Tuition and fees: $11,170.
Per-credit charge: $350.
Room only: $2,520.

FINANCIAL AID PICTURE (2009-2010)
Students with need: Need-based aid available for full-time and part-time students. Work study available nights, weekends, and for part-time students.
Students without need: No-need awards available for academics, alumni affiliation, leadership, music/drama, religious affiliation, state/district residency.

FINANCIAL AID PROCEDURES
Forms required: FAFSA, institutional form.
Dates and Deadlines: Priority date 5/1; closing date 7/15. Applicants notified on a rolling basis starting 3/1.
Transfers: Available only if funding remains.

CONTACT
Kellie Adams, Director of Student Financial Aid
1011 Bill Beck Boulevard, Kissimmee, FL 34744-4402
(407) 569-1365

Florida College
Temple Terrace, Florida
www.floridacollege.edu   Federal Code: 001482

4-year private liberal arts college in large town.
Enrollment: 467 undergrads, 3% part-time. 172 full-time freshmen.
Selectivity: Admits 50 to 75% of applicants.

BASIC COSTS (2010-2011)
Tuition and fees: $12,350.
Per-credit charge: $485.
Room and board: $7,100.

FINANCIAL AID PICTURE (2008-2009)
Students with need: Out of 92 full-time freshmen who applied for aid, 87 were judged to have need. Of these, 87 received aid, and 3 had their full need met. Average financial aid package met 27% of need; average scholarship/grant was $4,972; average loan was $3,294. For part-time students, average financial aid package was $3,104.
Students without need: 29 full-time freshmen who did not demonstrate need for aid received scholarships/grants; average award was $1,186. No-need awards available for academics, athletics, music/drama, state/district residency.
Scholarships offered: 8 full-time freshmen received athletic scholarships; average amount $4,438.

FINANCIAL AID PROCEDURES
Forms required: FAFSA, state aid form, institutional form.

Dates and Deadlines: Applicants notified on a rolling basis starting 3/1; must reply within 2 week(s) of notification.
Transfers: No deadline.

CONTACT
Lisa McClister, Financial Aid Director
119 North Glen Arven Avenue, Temple Terrace, FL 33617
(813) 849-6720

Florida College of Natural Health: Miami
Miami, Florida
www.fcnh.com   Federal Code: 030086

2-year for-profit branch campus and community college in very large city.
Enrollment: 321 undergrads.

BASIC COSTS (2009-2010)
Tuition and fees: $21,697.
Additional info: Non-degree programs from $4,870 to $11,379 for tuition, plus $850 for books and supplies.

FINANCIAL AID PICTURE
Students with need: Need-based aid available for full-time students.
Students without need: This college awards aid only to students with need.

FINANCIAL AID PROCEDURES
Forms required: FAFSA.
Dates and Deadlines: No deadline. Applicants notified on a rolling basis.

CONTACT
Jorge Villasante, Director of Financial Aid
7925 Northwest 12th Street, Suite 201, Miami, FL 33126
(954) 975-6400

Florida Gulf Coast University
Ft. Myers, Florida
www.fgcu.edu   Federal Code: 032553

4-year public university in small city.
Enrollment: 9,493 undergrads, 17% part-time. 1,837 full-time freshmen.
Selectivity: Admits 50 to 75% of applicants.

BASIC COSTS (2009-2010)
Tuition and fees: $4,427; out-of-state residents $19,768.
Room and board: $7,950.

FINANCIAL AID PICTURE (2008-2009)
Students with need: Out of 1,579 full-time freshmen who applied for aid, 586 were judged to have need. Of these, 586 received aid, and 61 had their full need met. Average financial aid package met 63% of need; average scholarship/grant was $4,456; average loan was $3,912. For part-time students, average financial aid package was $5,212.
Students without need: 85 full-time freshmen who did not demonstrate need for aid received scholarships/grants; average award was $3,440. No-need awards available for academics, alumni affiliation, athletics, leadership, minority status, music/drama, religious affiliation, state/district residency.
Scholarships offered: 43 full-time freshmen received athletic scholarships; average amount $9,883.

FINANCIAL AID PROCEDURES
Forms required: FAFSA.
Dates and Deadlines: Priority date 3/1; closing date 6/30. Applicants notified on a rolling basis starting 2/15.
Transfers: Applicants notified on a rolling basis.

CONTACT

Jorge Lopez-Rosado, Director, Student Financial Aid
10501 FGCU Boulevard South, Ft. Myers, FL 33965-6565
(239) 590-7920

Florida Institute of Technology

Melbourne, Florida
www.fit.edu   Federal Code: 001469

4-year private university in small city.
Enrollment: 4,839 undergrads, 19% part-time. 539 full-time freshmen.
Selectivity: Admits 50 to 75% of applicants.

BASIC COSTS (2010-2011)

Tuition and fees: $32,294.
Per-credit charge: $950.
Room and board: $11,210.

FINANCIAL AID PICTURE (2009-2010)

Students with need: Out of 417 full-time freshmen who applied for aid, 374 were judged to have need. Of these, 374 received aid, and 88 had their full need met. Average financial aid package met 83% of need; average scholarship/grant was $20,802; average loan was $3,501. For part-time students, average financial aid package was $10,662.
Students without need: 151 full-time freshmen who did not demonstrate need for aid received scholarships/grants; average award was $11,189. No-need awards available for academics, alumni affiliation, athletics, ROTC, state/district residency.
Scholarships offered: 10 full-time freshmen received athletic scholarships; average amount $21,188.
Cumulative student debt: 69% of graduating class had student loans; average debt was $40,630.

FINANCIAL AID PROCEDURES

Forms required: FAFSA, state aid form.
Dates and Deadlines: Priority date 3/1; no closing date. Applicants notified on a rolling basis starting 2/15; must reply by 5/1 or within 4 week(s) of notification.
Transfers: No deadline. Applicants notified on a rolling basis starting 2/15; must reply by 5/1 or within 4 week(s) of notification.

CONTACT

Jay Lally, Director of Financial Aid
150 West University Boulevard, Melbourne, FL 32901-6975
(321) 674-8070

Florida International University

Miami, Florida
www.fiu.edu   Federal Code: 009635

4-year public university in very large city.
Enrollment: 30,936 undergrads, 28% part-time. 2,741 full-time freshmen.
Selectivity: Admits less than 50% of applicants.

BASIC COSTS (2009-2010)

Tuition and fees: $4,580; out-of-state residents $16,980.
Room and board: $11,946.

FINANCIAL AID PICTURE (2008-2009)

Students with need: Need-based aid available for full-time and part-time students.
Students without need: No-need awards available for academics, art, athletics, minority status, music/drama, state/district residency.

FINANCIAL AID PROCEDURES

Forms required: FAFSA.

Dates and Deadlines: Priority date 3/1; closing date 5/15. Applicants notified on a rolling basis; must reply by 5/1 or within 4 week(s) of notification.

CONTACT

Francisco Valines, Director of Financial Aid
University Park Campus, PC 140, Miami, FL 33199
(305) 348-7272

Florida Keys Community College

Key West, Florida
www.fkcc.edu   Federal Code: 001485

2-year public nursing and community college in large town.
Enrollment: 1,407 undergrads.
Selectivity: Open admission; but selective for some programs.

BASIC COSTS (2009-2010)

Tuition and fees: $2,677; out-of-state residents $9,401.

FINANCIAL AID PICTURE

Students with need: Need-based aid available for full-time and part-time students.
Students without need: No-need awards available for academics, art, leadership, minority status.

FINANCIAL AID PROCEDURES

Forms required: FAFSA, institutional form.
Dates and Deadlines: Priority date 5/1; no closing date. Applicants notified on a rolling basis starting 6/15; must reply within 2 week(s) of notification.
Transfers: Closing date 5/1. Florida Student Assistance Grant available to students paying Florida resident tuition.

CONTACT

Lynn Burris, Financial Aid Director
5901 College Road, Key West, FL 33040
(305) 809-3523

Florida Memorial University

Miami Gardens, Florida
www.fmuniv.edu   Federal Code: 001486

4-year private liberal arts college in very large city, affiliated with American Baptist Churches in the USA.
Enrollment: 1,933 undergrads.
Selectivity: Admits less than 50% of applicants.

BASIC COSTS (2009-2010)

Tuition and fees: $13,181.
Per-credit charge: $472.
Room and board: $5,554.

FINANCIAL AID PICTURE

Students with need: Need-based aid available for full-time and part-time students.
Additional info: Need-based financial aid available to part-time students taking 6 credits or more per semester.

FINANCIAL AID PROCEDURES

Dates and Deadlines: No deadline. Applicants notified on a rolling basis; must reply within 2 week(s) of notification.
Transfers: Priority date 3/15; closing date 4/15.

CONTACT

Brian Phillip, Director of Financial Aid
15800 NW 42nd Avenue, Miami Gardens, FL 33054
(305) 430-1168

Florida National College

Hialeah, Florida
www.fnc.edu   Federal Code: 017069

2-year for-profit junior college in very large city.
Enrollment: 2,744 undergrads, 27% part-time. 623 full-time freshmen.
Selectivity: Open admission.

BASIC COSTS (2010-2011)
Tuition and fees: $17,100.
Per-credit charge: $525.

FINANCIAL AID PICTURE (2008-2009)
Students with need: Out of 616 full-time freshmen who applied for aid, 609 were judged to have need. Of these, 609 received aid. Need-based aid available for part-time students.
Students without need: This college awards aid only to students with need.

FINANCIAL AID PROCEDURES
Forms required: FAFSA, institutional form.
Dates and Deadlines: No deadline.

CONTACT
Omar Sanchez, Vice President for Planning and Research
4425 West 20th Avenue, Hialeah, FL 33012
(305) 821-3333 ext. 1003

Florida Southern College

Lakeland, Florida
www.flsouthern.edu   Federal Code: 001488

4-year private liberal arts college in small city, affiliated with United Methodist Church.
Enrollment: 1,881 undergrads, 3% part-time. 553 full-time freshmen.
Selectivity: Admits 50 to 75% of applicants.

BASIC COSTS (2010-2011)
Tuition and fees: $24,662.
Per-credit charge: $700.
Room and board: $8,310.

FINANCIAL AID PICTURE (2009-2010)
Students with need: Out of 489 full-time freshmen who applied for aid, 423 were judged to have need. Of these, 421 received aid, and 131 had their full need met. Average financial aid package met 68% of need; average scholarship/grant was $6,470; average loan was $3,325. For part-time students, average financial aid package was $6,855.
Students without need: 69 full-time freshmen who did not demonstrate need for aid received scholarships/grants; average award was $9,590. No-need awards available for academics, alumni affiliation, art, athletics, job skills, leadership, minority status, music/drama, religious affiliation, ROTC, state/district residency.
Scholarships offered: *Merit:* McClug Scholarship: awarded annually to three first-time students; minimum SAT score of 1300 (math and verbal sections) or ACT of 29; be in the top 5% of class. The Hollingsworth Scholarship: up to $10,000 towards tuition and fees; must have a minimum 1270 SAT (math and verbal sections) or 28 ACT and minimum high school GPA of 3.5. The Alderman Scholarship: up to $9,000 towards tuition and fees ; based on high school GPA and SAT/ACT test scores. *Athletic:* 57 full-time freshmen received athletic scholarships; average amount $7,562.
Cumulative student debt: 63% of graduating class had student loans; average debt was $22,910.

FINANCIAL AID PROCEDURES
Forms required: FAFSA, institutional form.

Dates and Deadlines: Priority date 3/1; closing date 7/1. Applicants notified on a rolling basis starting 3/1; must reply within 3 week(s) of notification.
Transfers: No deadline. Applicants notified on a rolling basis; must reply within 2 week(s) of notification.

CONTACT
William Healy, Director of Financial Aid
111 Lake Hollingsworth Drive, Lakeland, FL 33801-5698
(863) 680-4140

Florida State College at Jacksonville

Jacksonville, Florida
www.fscj.edu   Federal Code: 001484

2-year public junior college in very large city.
Enrollment: 20,135 undergrads, 61% part-time. 2,003 full-time freshmen.
Selectivity: Open admission; but selective for some programs.

BASIC COSTS (2009-2010)
Tuition and fees: $2,511; out-of-state residents $9,703.

FINANCIAL AID PICTURE (2009-2010)
Students with need: Need-based aid available for full-time and part-time students. Work study available nights, weekends, and for part-time students.
Students without need: No-need awards available for academics, alumni affiliation, art, athletics, job skills, leadership, minority status, music/drama.

FINANCIAL AID PROCEDURES
Forms required: FAFSA, institutional form.
Dates and Deadlines: Priority date 8/1; no closing date.

CONTACT
Yvonne Horner, Associate Vice President of Financial Services
501 West State Street, Jacksonville, FL 32202
(904) 632-3352

Florida State University

Tallahassee, Florida
www.fsu.edu   Federal Code: 001489

4-year public university in small city.
Enrollment: 30,251 undergrads, 9% part-time. 5,942 full-time freshmen.
Selectivity: Admits 50 to 75% of applicants.

BASIC COSTS (2009-2010)
Tuition and fees: $4,566; out-of-state residents $19,011.
Room and board: $8,730.

FINANCIAL AID PICTURE (2009-2010)
Students with need: Need-based aid available for full-time and part-time students.
Students without need: No-need awards available for academics, athletics, state/district residency.

FINANCIAL AID PROCEDURES
Forms required: FAFSA.
Dates and Deadlines: No deadline. Applicants notified on a rolling basis starting 3/15.

CONTACT
Darryl Marshall, Director of Financial Aid
PO Box 3062400, Tallahassee, FL 32306-2400
(850) 644-0539

Full Sail University
Winter Park, Florida
www.fullsail.edu   Federal Code: 016812

4-year for-profit visual arts and technical college in very large city.
Enrollment: 7,379 undergrads.
Selectivity: Open admission; but selective for some programs.

BASIC COSTS (2010-2011)
Additional info: Programs leading to an associate or bachelor's degree range from $36,775 - $75,775, including books and supplies.

FINANCIAL AID PICTURE
Students with need: Need-based aid available for full-time students. Work study available nights, weekends, and for part-time students.

FINANCIAL AID PROCEDURES
Forms required: FAFSA.
Dates and Deadlines: No deadline. Applicants notified on a rolling basis; must reply within 2 week(s) of notification.

CONTACT
3300 University Boulevard, Winter Park, FL 32792-7429
(407) 679-0100 ext. 2300

Gulf Coast Community College
Panama City, Florida
www.gulfcoast.edu   Federal Code: 001490

2-year public community college in small city.
Enrollment: 4,757 undergrads, 56% part-time. 456 full-time freshmen.
Selectivity: Open admission; but selective for some programs.

BASIC COSTS (2009-2010)
Tuition and fees: $2,439; out-of-state residents $9,151.

FINANCIAL AID PICTURE
Students with need: Need-based aid available for full-time and part-time students. Work study available nights, weekends, and for part-time students.
Students without need: No-need awards available for academics, athletics, job skills, leadership, minority status, music/drama, state/district residency.

FINANCIAL AID PROCEDURES
Forms required: FAFSA.
Dates and Deadlines: Priority date 5/15; closing date 7/1. Applicants notified on a rolling basis starting 7/1.
Transfers: Priority date 11/1; no deadline.

CONTACT
Chris Westlake, Director of Financial Aid
5230 West US Highway 98, Panama City, FL 32401
(850) 872-3845

Hillsborough Community College
Tampa, Florida
www.hccfl.edu   Federal Code: 007870

2-year public community college in large city.
Enrollment: 21,175 undergrads, 55% part-time. 2,890 full-time freshmen.
Selectivity: Open admission; but selective for some programs.

BASIC COSTS (2009-2010)
Tuition and fees: $2,621; out-of-state residents $9,550.

FINANCIAL AID PICTURE (2008-2009)
Students with need: 88% of average financial aid package awarded as scholarships/grants, 12% awarded as loans/jobs. Need-based aid available for part-time students. Work study available nights, weekends, and for part-time students.
Students without need: No-need awards available for academics, art, athletics, minority status, music/drama.

FINANCIAL AID PROCEDURES
Forms required: FAFSA, institutional form.
Dates and Deadlines: Priority date 5/15; closing date 6/30. Applicants notified on a rolling basis.
Transfers: No deadline. Transfer students must submit academic transcripts prior to obtaining student loans at sophomore level.

CONTACT
Charlotte Johns-Rich, Director of Financial Aid
Box 31127, Tampa, FL 33631-3127
(813) 253-7235

Hobe Sound Bible College
Hobe Sound, Florida
www.hsbc.edu   Federal Code: 015463

4-year private Bible college in small town, affiliated with interdenominational tradition.
Enrollment: 234 undergrads.

BASIC COSTS (2009-2010)
Tuition and fees: $5,200.
Per-credit charge: $205.
Room and board: $4,680.

FINANCIAL AID PICTURE (2009-2010)
Students with need: Need-based aid available for full-time and part-time students.
Students without need: No-need awards available for academics, leadership.

FINANCIAL AID PROCEDURES
Forms required: FAFSA.
Dates and Deadlines: Closing date 8/1.

CONTACT
John Churchill, Director of Financial Aid
Box 1065, Hobe Sound, FL 33475
(772) 546-5534 ext. 1003

Hodges University
Naples, Florida
www.hodges.edu   Federal Code: 030375

4-year private university and business college in small city.
Enrollment: 2,032 undergrads, 22% part-time. 262 full-time freshmen.
Selectivity: Admits over 75% of applicants.

BASIC COSTS (2009-2010)
Tuition and fees: $14,330.
Per-credit charge: $465.

FINANCIAL AID PICTURE (2009-2010)
Students with need: Out of 246 full-time freshmen who applied for aid, 214 were judged to have need. Of these, 214 received aid, and 45 had their full need met. Average financial aid package met 66% of need; average scholarship/grant was $2,600; average loan was $2,800. For part-time students, average financial aid package was $6,300.

Students without need: 47 full-time freshmen who did not demonstrate need for aid received scholarships/grants; average award was $400. No-need awards available for academics.

Cumulative student debt: 84% of graduating class had student loans; average debt was $18,600.

FINANCIAL AID PROCEDURES

Forms required: FAFSA.

Dates and Deadlines: Priority date 9/7; no closing date. Applicants notified on a rolling basis starting 7/7.

Transfers: No deadline. Applicants notified on a rolling basis.

CONTACT

Joe Gilchrist, Vice President of Student Financial Assistance

2655 Northbrooke Drive, Naples, FL 34119

(239) 513-1122

Indian River State College

Fort Pierce, Florida

www.irsc.edu   Federal Code: 001493

2-year public community college in small city.

Enrollment: 9,517 undergrads, 58% part-time. 1,188 full-time freshmen.

Selectivity: Open admission; but selective for some programs.

BASIC COSTS (2009-2010)

Tuition and fees: $2,543; out-of-state residents $9,471.

FINANCIAL AID PICTURE (2008-2009)

Students with need: 80% of average financial aid package awarded as scholarships/grants, 20% awarded as loans/jobs. Need-based aid available for part-time students.

Students without need: No-need awards available for academics, athletics, minority status, music/drama, state/district residency.

FINANCIAL AID PROCEDURES

Forms required: FAFSA, institutional form.

Dates and Deadlines: Priority date 7/18; no closing date. Applicants notified on a rolling basis starting 5/15.

CONTACT

Mary Lewis, Director of Financial Aid

3209 Virginia Avenue, Fort Pierce, FL 34981-5596

(772) 462-7450

International Academy of Design and Technology: Tampa

Tampa, Florida

www.academy.edu   Federal Code: 030314

4-year for-profit visual arts and technical college in very large city.

Enrollment: 2,561 undergrads.

Selectivity: Open admission.

BASIC COSTS (2009-2010)

Tuition and fees: $18,780.

Per-credit charge: $385.

Additional info: Required fees vary from $300-$600.

FINANCIAL AID PICTURE (2008-2009)

Students with need: Need-based aid available for full-time and part-time students. Work study available nights, weekends, and for part-time students.

Students without need: No-need awards available for academics.

FINANCIAL AID PROCEDURES

Forms required: FAFSA.

Dates and Deadlines: No deadline.

CONTACT

Tim Coppola, Vice President of Finance

5104 Eisenhower Boulevard, Tampa, FL 33634

(813) 880-8056

Jacksonville University

Jacksonville, Florida

www.ju.edu   Federal Code: 001495

4-year private university and liberal arts college in very large city.

Enrollment: 3,084 undergrads, 25% part-time. 664 full-time freshmen.

Selectivity: Admits 50 to 75% of applicants.

BASIC COSTS (2009-2010)

Tuition and fees: $25,300.

Per-credit charge: $840.

Room and board: $9,060.

Additional info: $540 mandatory health insurance fee charged unless proof of other coverage is provided.

FINANCIAL AID PICTURE (2009-2010)

Students with need: Need-based aid available for full-time and part-time students. Work study available nights, weekends, and for part-time students.

Students without need: No-need awards available for academics, art, athletics, job skills, leadership, music/drama, ROTC, state/district residency.

FINANCIAL AID PROCEDURES

Forms required: FAFSA, state aid form, institutional form.

Dates and Deadlines: Priority date 3/15; no closing date. Applicants notified on a rolling basis starting 2/15.

Transfers: No deadline. Applicants notified on a rolling basis.

CONTACT

Catherine Huntress, Financial Aid Director

2800 University Boulevard North, Jacksonville, FL 32211-3394

(904) 256-7060

Johnson & Wales University: North Miami

North Miami, Florida

www.jwu.edu   Federal Code: 003404

4-year private university in large city.

Enrollment: 2,033 undergrads, 3% part-time. 588 full-time freshmen.

Selectivity: Admits 50 to 75% of applicants.

BASIC COSTS (2010-2011)

Tuition and fees: $24,429.

Room and board: $8,904.

FINANCIAL AID PICTURE (2009-2010)

Students with need: Need-based aid available for full-time and part-time students.

Students without need: No-need awards available for academics, alumni affiliation, job skills, leadership, state/district residency.

FINANCIAL AID PROCEDURES

Forms required: FAFSA.

Dates and Deadlines: No deadline. Applicants notified on a rolling basis starting 3/1; must reply within 2 week(s) of notification.

CONTACT

Lynn Robinson, Director, Financial Aid

1701 Northeast 127th Street, North Miami, FL 33181

(800) 342-5598

Jones College
Jacksonville, Florida
www.jones.edu   Federal Code: 001497

4-year private business and teachers college in very large city.
Enrollment: 724 undergrads, 66% part-time. 19 full-time freshmen.
Selectivity: Open admission.

BASIC COSTS (2010-2011)
Tuition and fees: $9,150.
Per-credit charge: $305.

FINANCIAL AID PICTURE
Students with need: Need-based aid available for full-time and part-time students. Work study available nights, weekends, and for part-time students.
Students without need: This college awards aid only to students with need.

FINANCIAL AID PROCEDURES
Forms required: FAFSA.
Dates and Deadlines: No deadline. Applicants notified on a rolling basis.

CONTACT
Becky Davis, Financial Assistant Director
5353 Arlington Expressway, Jacksonville, FL 32211
(904) 743-1122 ext. 100

Lake City Community College
Lake City, Florida
www.lakecitycc.edu   Federal Code: 001501

2-year public community college in large town.
Enrollment: 3,070 undergrads, 59% part-time. 363 full-time freshmen.
Selectivity: Open admission; but selective for some programs.

BASIC COSTS (2009-2010)
Tuition and fees: $2,448; out-of-state residents $9,571.
Additional info: Tuition/fee waivers available for minority students.

FINANCIAL AID PICTURE
Students with need: Need-based aid available for full-time and part-time students.
Students without need: No-need awards available for academics.

FINANCIAL AID PROCEDURES
Forms required: FAFSA, institutional form.
Dates and Deadlines: Priority date 6/1; no closing date. Applicants notified on a rolling basis starting 6/1; must reply within 2 week(s) of notification.

CONTACT
Debberin Tunsil, Director of Financial Aid
149 SE College Place, Lake City, FL 32025-8703
(386) 754-4282

Lake-Sumter Community College
Leesburg, Florida
www.lscc.edu   Federal Code: 001502

2-year public community college in small city.
Enrollment: 3,756 undergrads, 62% part-time. 458 full-time freshmen.
Selectivity: Open admission; but selective for some programs.

BASIC COSTS (2009-2010)
Tuition and fees: $2,556; out-of-state residents $9,627.

FINANCIAL AID PICTURE (2009-2010)
Students with need: For part-time students, average financial aid package was $1,910.
Students without need: No-need awards available for academics, athletics, minority status, state/district residency.

FINANCIAL AID PROCEDURES
Forms required: FAFSA, institutional form.
Dates and Deadlines: Priority date 6/1; no closing date. Applicants notified on a rolling basis starting 7/1.

CONTACT
Audrey Williams, Financial Aid Director
9501 U.S. Highway 441, Leesburg, FL 34788-8751
(352) 365-3512

Lynn University
Boca Raton, Florida
www.lynn.edu   Federal Code: 001505

4-year private university in small city.
Enrollment: 1,737 undergrads, 9% part-time. 344 full-time freshmen.
Selectivity: Admits 50 to 75% of applicants.

BASIC COSTS (2010-2011)
Tuition and fees: $30,900.
Room and board: $11,950.

FINANCIAL AID PICTURE (2009-2010)
Students with need: Out of 237 full-time freshmen who applied for aid, 161 were judged to have need. Of these, 158 received aid, and 156 had their full need met. Average financial aid package met 64% of need; average scholarship/grant was $15,484; average loan was $4,497. For part-time students, average financial aid package was $6,341.
Students without need: 64 full-time freshmen who did not demonstrate need for aid received scholarships/grants; average award was $11,934. No-need awards available for academics, athletics, leadership, music/drama, religious affiliation, state/district residency.
Scholarships offered: 41 full-time freshmen received athletic scholarships; average amount $8,771.
Cumulative student debt: 43% of graduating class had student loans; average debt was $34,075.

FINANCIAL AID PROCEDURES
Forms required: FAFSA, institutional form.
Dates and Deadlines: Priority date 3/1; no closing date. Applicants notified on a rolling basis starting 2/1; must reply within 2 week(s) of notification.
Transfers: Scholarships and grants available.

CONTACT
Chan Park, Director of Student Financial Assistance
3601 North Military Trail, Boca Raton, FL 33431-5598
(561) 237-7185

Miami Dade College
Miami, Florida
www.mdc.edu/main/   Federal Code: 001506

2-year public community college in very large city.
Enrollment: 51,369 undergrads, 59% part-time. 9,716 full-time freshmen.
Selectivity: Open admission; but selective for some programs.

BASIC COSTS (2009-2010)
Tuition and fees: $2,585; out-of-state residents $9,377.

FINANCIAL AID PICTURE (2008-2009)

Students with need: Out of 6,149 full-time freshmen who applied for aid, 6,098 were judged to have need. Of these, 5,996 received aid, and 4,415 had their full need met. Average financial aid package met 67% of need; average scholarship/grant was $2,925; average loan was $973. For part-time students, average financial aid package was $1,089.

Students without need: 171 full-time freshmen who did not demonstrate need for aid received scholarships/grants; average award was $1,145. No-need awards available for academics, art, athletics, music/drama, state/district residency.

Scholarships offered: 13 full-time freshmen received athletic scholarships; average amount $12,435.

FINANCIAL AID PROCEDURES

Forms required: FAFSA.

Dates and Deadlines: Priority date 3/15; closing date 6/30. Applicants notified on a rolling basis starting 5/15.

Transfers: No deadline. Applicants notified on a rolling basis.

CONTACT

Mercedes Amaya, Collegewide Director of Financial Aid
11011 SW 104th Street, Miami, FL 33176-3393
(305) 237-0382

New College of Florida

Sarasota, Florida
www.ncf.edu   Federal Code: 039574

4-year public liberal arts college in small city.

Enrollment: 825 undergrads. 218 full-time freshmen.

Selectivity: Admits 50 to 75% of applicants.

BASIC COSTS (2009-2010)

Tuition and fees: $4,784; out-of-state residents $26,386.

Room and board: $7,783.

FINANCIAL AID PICTURE (2009-2010)

Students with need: Out of 172 full-time freshmen who applied for aid, 108 were judged to have need. Of these, 108 received aid, and 72 had their full need met. Average financial aid package met 96% of need; average scholarship/grant was $11,297; average loan was $2,942.

Students without need: 109 full-time freshmen who did not demonstrate need for aid received scholarships/grants; average award was $2,964. No-need awards available for academics, state/district residency.

Cumulative student debt: 41% of graduating class had student loans; average debt was $14,794.

FINANCIAL AID PROCEDURES

Forms required: FAFSA.

Dates and Deadlines: Priority date 2/15; no closing date. Applicants notified on a rolling basis starting 10/1; must reply by 5/1 or within 4 week(s) of notification.

Transfers: No deadline. Applicants notified on a rolling basis starting 10/1; must reply by 5/1 or within 4 week(s) of notification.

CONTACT

Monica Baldwin, Director of Financial Aid
5800 Bay Shore Road, Sarasota, FL 34243-2109
(941) 487-5001

North Florida Community College

Madison, Florida
www.nfcc.edu   Federal Code: 001508

2-year public community college in rural community.

Enrollment: 925 undergrads.

Selectivity: Open admission; but selective for some programs.

BASIC COSTS (2009-2010)

Tuition and fees: $2,406; out-of-state residents $9,240.

FINANCIAL AID PICTURE (2008-2009)

Students with need: Need-based aid available for full-time and part-time students. Work study available nights, weekends, and for part-time students.

Students without need: This college awards aid only to students with need.

FINANCIAL AID PROCEDURES

Forms required: FAFSA.

Dates and Deadlines: Priority date 5/15; no closing date. Applicants notified on a rolling basis starting 6/20; must reply within 2 week(s) of notification.

CONTACT

Amelia Mulkey, Director of Financial Aid
325 NW Turner Davis Drive, Madison, FL 32340
(850) 973-1621

Northwest Florida State College

Niceville, Florida
www.nwfsc.edu   Federal Code: 001510

4-year public business and community college in large town.

Enrollment: 7,556 undergrads.

Selectivity: Open admission.

BASIC COSTS (2009-2010)

Tuition and fees: $2,272; out-of-state residents $9,197.

Additional info: Tuition/fee waivers available for minority students.

FINANCIAL AID PICTURE (2008-2009)

Students with need: Need-based aid available for full-time and part-time students. Work study available nights.

Students without need: No-need awards available for academics, art, athletics, leadership, minority status, music/drama.

FINANCIAL AID PROCEDURES

Forms required: FAFSA, institutional form.

Dates and Deadlines: Priority date 4/1; no closing date. Applicants notified on a rolling basis starting 2/1; must reply within 2 week(s) of notification.

Transfers: Academic transcript evaluated to determine student eligibility for financial aid.

CONTACT

Pat Bennett, Director of Financial Aid
100 College Boulevard, Niceville, FL 32578-1295
(850) 678-5111

Northwood University: Florida

West Palm Beach, Florida
www.northwood.edu   Federal Code: 013040

4-year private university and business college in small city.

Enrollment: 575 undergrads, 4% part-time. 96 full-time freshmen.

Selectivity: Admits 50 to 75% of applicants.

BASIC COSTS (2010-2011)

Tuition and fees: $19,272.

Per-credit charge: $715.

Room and board: $9,076.

FINANCIAL AID PICTURE (2009-2010)

Students with need: Out of 69 full-time freshmen who applied for aid, 58 were judged to have need. Of these, 58 received aid, and 7 had their full need met. Average financial aid package met 60% of need; average scholarship/grant was $6,941; average loan was $3,181. For part-time students, average financial aid package was $8,740.

Students without need: 11 full-time freshmen who did not demonstrate need for aid received scholarships/grants; average award was $9,392. No-need awards available for academics, athletics, leadership, minority status, state/district residency.

Scholarships offered: 15 full-time freshmen received athletic scholarships; average amount $7,736.

Cumulative student debt: 55% of graduating class had student loans; average debt was $29,264.

FINANCIAL AID PROCEDURES

Forms required: FAFSA, state aid form.

Dates and Deadlines: No deadline. Applicants notified on a rolling basis starting 3/1.

Transfers: No deadline. Applicants notified on a rolling basis starting 3/1.

CONTACT

Teresa Palmer, Director of Financial Aid
2600 North Military Trail, West Palm Beach, FL 33409-2911
(561) 478-5590

Nova Southeastern University
Fort Lauderdale, Florida
www.nova.edu   Federal Code: 001509

4-year private university in small city.

Enrollment: 5,868 undergrads.

Selectivity: Admits less than 50% of applicants.

BASIC COSTS (2010-2011)

Tuition and fees: $22,150.

Per-credit charge: $720.

Room and board: $9,086.

FINANCIAL AID PICTURE (2008-2009)

Students with need: Need-based aid available for full-time and part-time students. Work study available nights, weekends, and for part-time students.

Students without need: No-need awards available for academics, athletics, leadership, music/drama.

FINANCIAL AID PROCEDURES

Forms required: FAFSA, state aid form.

Dates and Deadlines: Priority date 4/15; no closing date. Applicants notified on a rolling basis starting 3/15.

CONTACT

Stephanie Brown, Associate Vice President, Enrollment and Student Services
3301 College Avenue, Fort Lauderdale, FL 33314
(954) 262-3380

Palm Beach Atlantic University
West Palm Beach, Florida
www.pba.edu   Federal Code: 008849

4-year private university and liberal arts college in large city, affiliated with non-denominational tradition.

Enrollment: 2,419 undergrads, 7% part-time. 424 full-time freshmen.

Selectivity: Admits 50 to 75% of applicants.

BASIC COSTS (2009-2010)

Tuition and fees: $22,700.

Room and board: $8,220.

FINANCIAL AID PICTURE (2008-2009)

Students with need: Out of 351 full-time freshmen who applied for aid, 287 were judged to have need. Of these, 287 received aid, and 22 had their full need met. Average financial aid package met 28% of need; average scholarship/grant was $2,775; average loan was $3,195. Need-based aid available for part-time students.

Students without need: 63 full-time freshmen who did not demonstrate need for aid received scholarships/grants; average award was $7,267. No-need awards available for academics, alumni affiliation, athletics, minority status, music/drama, state/district residency.

Cumulative student debt: 69% of graduating class had student loans; average debt was $19,420.

FINANCIAL AID PROCEDURES

Forms required: FAFSA.

Dates and Deadlines: Priority date 2/1; closing date 8/1. Applicants notified on a rolling basis starting 2/15; must reply within 4 week(s) of notification.

Transfers: Applicants notified on a rolling basis starting 3/1; must reply within 3 week(s) of notification. Florida residential undergraduate students eligible for grant from state if enrolled on full-time basis.

CONTACT

Becky Moore, Director, Student Financial Planning
PO Box 24708, West Palm Beach, FL 33416-4708
(561) 803-2126

Palm Beach Community College
Lake Worth, Florida
www.pbcc.edu   Federal Code: 001512

2-year public community college in large town.

Enrollment: 21,774 undergrads, 57% part-time. 2,362 full-time freshmen.

Selectivity: Open admission; but selective for some programs.

BASIC COSTS (2009-2010)

Tuition and fees: $2,475; out-of-state residents $8,980.

FINANCIAL AID PICTURE (2009-2010)

Students with need: 75% of average financial aid package awarded as scholarships/grants, 25% awarded as loans/jobs. Work study available nights, weekends, and for part-time students.

Students without need: No-need awards available for academics, alumni affiliation, athletics, leadership, state/district residency.

FINANCIAL AID PROCEDURES

Forms required: FAFSA, institutional form.

Dates and Deadlines: Priority date 7/1; no closing date. Applicants notified on a rolling basis; must reply within 2 week(s) of notification.

CONTACT

David Bodwell, Director of Student Financial Aid
4200 Congress Avenue, Lake Worth, FL 33461
(561) 868-3330

Pasco-Hernando Community College
New Port Richey, Florida
www.phcc.edu   Federal Code: 010652

2-year public community college in large town.

Enrollment: 9,186 undergrads.

Selectivity: Open admission; but selective for some programs.

BASIC COSTS (2009-2010)

Tuition and fees: $2,419; out-of-state residents $9,272.

FINANCIAL AID PICTURE

Students with need: Need-based aid available for full-time and part-time students. Work study available nights, weekends, and for part-time students.

Students without need: No-need awards available for academics, athletics, minority status.

Additional info: Childcare assistance grants available to eligible students.

FINANCIAL AID PROCEDURES

Forms required: FAFSA.

Dates and Deadlines: No deadline. Applicants notified on a rolling basis.

CONTACT

Rebecca Shanafelt, Director of Financial Aid/Veterans Services
10230 Ridge Road, New Port Richey, FL 34654-5199
(727) 816-3463

Polk State College
Winter Haven, Florida
www.polk.edu   Federal Code: 001514

2-year public community college in large town.

Enrollment: 7,968 undergrads, 63% part-time. 877 full-time freshmen.

Selectivity: Open admission; but selective for some programs.

BASIC COSTS (2009-2010)

Tuition and fees: $2,585; out-of-state residents $9,596.

FINANCIAL AID PICTURE

Students with need: Need-based aid available for full-time and part-time students. Work study available nights, weekends, and for part-time students.

Students without need: No-need awards available for academics, athletics, leadership, state/district residency.

FINANCIAL AID PROCEDURES

Forms required: FAFSA.

Dates and Deadlines: Priority date 5/15; no closing date. Applicants notified on a rolling basis.

CONTACT

Olivia Maultsby, Director of Financial Aid
999 Avenue H NE, Winter Haven, FL 33881-4299
(863) 297-1004

Rasmussen College: Ocala
Ocala, Florida
www.rasmussen.edu   Federal Code: 008501

4-year for-profit career college in small city.

Enrollment: 1,212 undergrads.

Selectivity: Open admission; but selective for some programs.

BASIC COSTS (2009-2010)

Additional info: Per credit hour charges vary from $365 to $450 leading to degree programs.

FINANCIAL AID PICTURE

Students with need: Need-based aid available for full-time and part-time students.

FINANCIAL AID PROCEDURES

Forms required: FAFSA, institutional form.

Dates and Deadlines: No deadline. Applicants notified on a rolling basis.

CONTACT

Kristen Corrigan, Director of Financial Aid
2221 Southwest 19th Avenue Road, Ocala, FL 34471
(352) 629-1941 ext. 130

Rasmussen College: Pasco County
Holiday, Florida
www.rasmussen.edu   Federal Code: 008501

4-year for-profit career college in small city.

Enrollment: 883 undergrads.

Selectivity: Open admission; but selective for some programs.

BASIC COSTS (2009-2010)

Additional info: Per credit hour charges vary from $365 to $450 leading to degree programs.

FINANCIAL AID PICTURE

Students with need: Need-based aid available for full-time and part-time students.

FINANCIAL AID PROCEDURES

Forms required: FAFSA, institutional form.

Dates and Deadlines: No deadline. Applicants notified on a rolling basis.

CONTACT

Tina Fisher, Director of Student Financial Services
2127 Grand Boulevard, Holiday, FL 34690
(727) 942-0069

Ringling College of Art and Design
Sarasota, Florida
www.ringling.edu   Federal Code: 012574

4-year private visual arts college in small city.

Enrollment: 1,318 undergrads, 4% part-time. 319 full-time freshmen.

Selectivity: Admits 50 to 75% of applicants.

BASIC COSTS (2010-2011)

Tuition and fees: $32,289.

Per-credit charge: $1,389.

Room and board: $10,890.

FINANCIAL AID PICTURE (2009-2010)

Students with need: Average financial aid package met 41% of need; average scholarship/grant was $9,020; average loan was $7,393. For part-time students, average financial aid package was $9,375.

Students without need: No-need awards available for academics, art.

Scholarships offered: Presidential Scholarship: amount determined annually; based on portfolio; up to 4 awards.

Cumulative student debt: 94% of graduating class had student loans; average debt was $51,994.

FINANCIAL AID PROCEDURES

Forms required: FAFSA.

Dates and Deadlines: Priority date 3/1; no closing date. Applicants notified on a rolling basis starting 4/1; must reply within 2 week(s) of notification.

Transfers: No deadline. Applicants notified on a rolling basis; must reply within 2 week(s) of notification.

CONTACT

Kurt Wolf, Director of Financial Aid
2700 North Tamiami Trail, Sarasota, FL 34234-5895
(941) 359-7534

Rollins College
Winter Park, Florida
www.rollins.edu — Federal Code: 001515

4-year private liberal arts college in large town.
Enrollment: 1,773 undergrads. 464 full-time freshmen.
Selectivity: Admits 50 to 75% of applicants.

BASIC COSTS (2010-2011)
Tuition and fees: $37,640.
Room and board: $11,760.

FINANCIAL AID PICTURE (2009-2010)
Students with need: Out of 293 full-time freshmen who applied for aid, 246 were judged to have need. Of these, 246 received aid, and 75 had their full need met. Average financial aid package met 89% of need; average scholarship/grant was $21,550; average loan was $3,982.
Students without need: 79 full-time freshmen who did not demonstrate need for aid received scholarships/grants; average award was $16,380. No-need awards available for academics, art, athletics, leadership, music/drama, state/district residency.
Scholarships offered: *Merit:* Presidential, Alonzo Rollins: $4,000-$15,000 per year; based on academic record; 130 available per year. Donald Cram: $3,000-$5,000 per year; based on academic record, science major; 10 available per year. *Athletic:* 10 full-time freshmen received athletic scholarships; average amount $25,153.
Cumulative student debt: 48% of graduating class had student loans; average debt was $21,789.
Additional info: Audition required for theater arts and music scholarship applicants. Portfolio required for art scholarships.

FINANCIAL AID PROCEDURES
Forms required: FAFSA, institutional form.
Dates and Deadlines: Closing date 3/1. Applicants notified on a rolling basis starting 3/1.
Transfers: Priority date 4/15; no deadline.

CONTACT
Steve Booker, Director of Financial Aid
1000 Holt Avenue, Winter Park, FL 32789
(407) 646-2395

Saint Johns River Community College
Palatka, Florida
www.sjrcc.edu — Federal Code: 001523

2-year public community college in large town.
Enrollment: 5,826 undergrads.
Selectivity: Open admission; but selective for some programs.

BASIC COSTS (2009-2010)
Tuition and fees: $2,550; out-of-state residents $9,585.

FINANCIAL AID PICTURE (2008-2009)
Students with need: Need-based aid available for full-time and part-time students.

FINANCIAL AID PROCEDURES
Forms required: FAFSA.
Dates and Deadlines: Priority date 5/15; no closing date. Applicants notified on a rolling basis.

CONTACT
Wayne Bodiford, Director of Financial Aid
5001 St. Johns Avenue, Palatka, FL 32177-3897
(386) 312-4040

Saint Leo University
Saint Leo, Florida
www.saintleo.edu — Federal Code: 001526

4-year private university in rural community, affiliated with Roman Catholic Church.
Enrollment: 1,735 undergrads, 5% part-time. 487 full-time freshmen.
Selectivity: Admits over 75% of applicants.

BASIC COSTS (2009-2010)
Tuition and fees: $17,646.
Room and board: $8,724.

FINANCIAL AID PICTURE (2009-2010)
Students with need: Out of 455 full-time freshmen who applied for aid, 379 were judged to have need. Of these, 379 received aid, and 98 had their full need met. Average financial aid package met 80% of need; average scholarship/grant was $12,865; average loan was $3,327. For part-time students, average financial aid package was $12,858.
Students without need: No-need awards available for academics, alumni affiliation, athletics, leadership, minority status, music/drama, religious affiliation, state/district residency.
Scholarships offered: 10 full-time freshmen received athletic scholarships; average amount $7,700.
Cumulative student debt: 63% of graduating class had student loans; average debt was $23,787.

FINANCIAL AID PROCEDURES
Forms required: FAFSA.
Dates and Deadlines: Priority date 3/1; no closing date. Applicants notified on a rolling basis starting 1/31.

CONTACT
Brenda Wright, Assistant Vice President, Student Financial Services
Office of Admission, Saint Leo, FL 33574-6665
(800) 240-7658

St. Petersburg College
St. Petersburg, Florida
www.spcollege.edu — Federal Code: 001528

2-year public community college in large city.
Enrollment: 20,964 undergrads, 64% part-time. 2,374 full-time freshmen.
Selectivity: Open admission; but selective for some programs.

BASIC COSTS (2009-2010)
Tuition and fees: $2,614; out-of-state residents $9,491.

FINANCIAL AID PICTURE
Students with need: Need-based aid available for full-time and part-time students. Work study available nights, weekends, and for part-time students.
Students without need: No-need awards available for academics, art, athletics, minority status, music/drama.

FINANCIAL AID PROCEDURES
Forms required: FAFSA, state aid form.
Dates and Deadlines: Priority date 4/15; no closing date. Applicants notified on a rolling basis starting 5/15; must reply within 2 week(s) of notification.

CONTACT
Michael Bennett, Associate Vice-President FAS
Box 13489, St. Petersburg, FL 33733-3489
(727) 791-2485

Saint Thomas University
Miami Gardens, Florida
www.stu.edu   Federal Code: 001468

4-year private university in very large city, affiliated with Roman Catholic Church.
Enrollment: 1,176 undergrads, 6% part-time. 238 full-time freshmen.
Selectivity: Admits 50 to 75% of applicants.

BASIC COSTS (2009-2010)
Tuition and fees: $21,690.
Per-credit charge: $723.
Room and board: $6,516.

FINANCIAL AID PICTURE (2009-2010)
Students with need: Out of 215 full-time freshmen who applied for aid, 198 were judged to have need. Of these, 198 received aid, and 37 had their full need met.
Students without need: 38 full-time freshmen who did not demonstrate need for aid received scholarships/grants; average award was $8,737. No-need awards available for academics, athletics, leadership, music/drama, religious affiliation, state/district residency.
Scholarships offered: 33 full-time freshmen received athletic scholarships; average amount $5,143.

FINANCIAL AID PROCEDURES
Forms required: FAFSA, state aid form.
Dates and Deadlines: Priority date 4/1; no closing date. Applicants notified on a rolling basis starting 3/1.
Transfers: Priority date 4/15.

CONTACT
Ahn Do, Director of Financial Aid
16401 Northwest 37th Avenue, Miami Gardens, FL 33054-6459
(305) 628-6547

Santa Fe College
Gainesville, Florida
www.sfcollege.edu   Federal Code: 001519

2-year public community college in small city.
Enrollment: 13,606 undergrads, 54% part-time. 1,382 full-time freshmen.
Selectivity: Open admission; but selective for some programs.

BASIC COSTS (2009-2010)
Tuition and fees: $2,537; out-of-state residents $9,495.
Additional info: Tuition/fee waivers available for minority students.

FINANCIAL AID PICTURE
Students with need: Need-based aid available for full-time and part-time students.
Students without need: No-need awards available for academics, art, athletics, leadership, minority status, music/drama, state/district residency.

FINANCIAL AID PROCEDURES
Forms required: FAFSA.
Dates and Deadlines: Priority date 3/15; closing date 6/30. Applicants notified by 8/1.
Transfers: Must have minimum 2.0 GPA to be eligible for financial aid.

CONTACT
Werts Peggy, Director of Financial Aid
3000 NW 83rd Street, R-112, Gainesville, FL 32606-6210
(352) 395-5480

Schiller International University
Largo, Florida
www.schiller.edu   Federal Code: 023141

4-year for-profit university in small city.
Enrollment: 110 undergrads.
Selectivity: Open admission.

FINANCIAL AID PICTURE (2008-2009)
Students with need: Need-based aid available for full-time and part-time students. Work study available nights, weekends, and for part-time students.
Students without need: No-need awards available for academics, alumni affiliation, leadership, minority status, state/district residency.
Scholarships offered: Fifty one-fourth tuition awards available to students possessing an outstanding academic record and who exhibit excellent potential for academic achievement. This award is available for one or two semesters. Twenty one-quarter Knowledge Tuition Awards available for two semesters to students who with good academic records and financial need.
Additional info: Special scholarship program for US students studying abroad at European campuses of Schiller. Work-study available to students taking 2 or more courses.

FINANCIAL AID PROCEDURES
Forms required: FAFSA, state aid form, institutional form.
Dates and Deadlines: Closing date 4/1. Applicants notified on a rolling basis starting 5/1; must reply within 3 week(s) of notification.
Transfers: No deadline. Applicants notified on a rolling basis.

CONTACT
Jennifer Fraser, Director of Financial Aid
300 East Bay Drive, Largo, FL 33770-3716
(727) 736-5082 ext. 253

Seminole Community College
Sanford, Florida
www.scc-fl.edu   Federal Code: 001520

2-year public Seminole State College is offering a new Bachelor of Applied Science degree (B.A.S.) in Interior Design. in large town.
Enrollment: 14,505 undergrads, 52% part-time. 2,018 full-time freshmen.
Selectivity: Open admission; but selective for some programs.

BASIC COSTS (2009-2010)
Tuition and fees: $2,636; out-of-state residents $9,640.

FINANCIAL AID PICTURE (2008-2009)
Students with need: 43% of average financial aid package awarded as scholarships/grants, 57% awarded as loans/jobs. Need-based aid available for part-time students.
Students without need: No-need awards available for academics, art, athletics, leadership, minority status, music/drama, state/district residency.

FINANCIAL AID PROCEDURES
Forms required: FAFSA.
Dates and Deadlines: Priority date 7/1; no closing date. Applicants notified on a rolling basis starting 4/1.
Transfers: No deadline. Applicants notified on a rolling basis starting 4/1.

CONTACT
Robert Lynn, Director of Financial Aid
100 Weldon Boulevard, Sanford, FL 32773-6199
(407) 708-4722 ext. 3422

South Florida Community College

Avon Park, Florida
www.southflorida.edu   Federal Code: 001522

2-year public community and technical college in small town.
Enrollment: 2,441 undergrads, 60% part-time. 308 full-time freshmen.
Selectivity: Open admission; but selective for some programs.

BASIC COSTS (2009-2010)
Tuition and fees: $2,561; out-of-state residents $9,667.
Additional info: Tuition/fee waivers available for minority students.

FINANCIAL AID PICTURE (2008-2009)
Students with need: 92% of average financial aid package awarded as scholarships/grants, 8% awarded as loans/jobs. Need-based aid available for part-time students.
Students without need: No-need awards available for academics, athletics, leadership, minority status, music/drama, state/district residency.

FINANCIAL AID PROCEDURES
Forms required: FAFSA.
Dates and Deadlines: Priority date 4/15; no closing date. Applicants notified on a rolling basis starting 4/1.
Transfers: Students must maintain satisfactory academic progress.

CONTACT
Susie Johnson, Director of Financial Aid
600 West College Drive, Avon Park, FL 33825
(863) 453-6661 ext. 7254

South University: West Palm Beach

West Palm Beach, Florida
www.southuniversity.edu

4-year for-profit university in large city.
Enrollment: 814 undergrads, 29% part-time. 71 full-time freshmen.

BASIC COSTS (2009-2010)
Tuition and fees: $14,985.

FINANCIAL AID PICTURE
Students with need: Need-based aid available for full-time and part-time students. Work study available nights.

FINANCIAL AID PROCEDURES
Forms required: FAFSA.
Dates and Deadlines: No deadline. Applicants notified on a rolling basis; must reply within 2 week(s) of notification.

CONTACT
Kacey Atkinson, Director of Student Financial Services
1760 North Congress Avenue, West Palm Beach, FL 33409-5178
(561) 697-9200

Southeastern University

Lakeland, Florida
www.seuniversity.edu   Federal Code: 001521

4-year private liberal arts and teachers college in small city, affiliated with Assemblies of God.
Enrollment: 2,497 undergrads, 6% part-time. 556 full-time freshmen.
Selectivity: Open admission; but selective for some programs.

BASIC COSTS (2010-2011)
Tuition and fees: $16,430.
Per-credit charge: $660.

Room and board: $7,900.

FINANCIAL AID PICTURE (2008-2009)
Students with need: Out of 473 full-time freshmen who applied for aid, 397 were judged to have need. Of these, 397 received aid, and 64 had their full need met. Average financial aid package met 62% of need; average scholarship/grant was $10,191; average loan was $3,450. For part-time students, average financial aid package was $6,098.
Students without need: 79 full-time freshmen who did not demonstrate need for aid received scholarships/grants; average award was $4,049. No-need awards available for academics, athletics, leadership, music/drama, ROTC.
Scholarships offered: 6 full-time freshmen received athletic scholarships; average amount $2,500.
Cumulative student debt: 100% of graduating class had student loans; average debt was $17,044.

FINANCIAL AID PROCEDURES
Forms required: FAFSA, state aid form, institutional form.
Dates and Deadlines: Priority date 4/15; no closing date. Applicants notified on a rolling basis starting 1/1; must reply within 6 week(s) of notification.
Transfers: Must reply within 6 week(s) of notification.

CONTACT
Carol Bradley, Financial Aid Director
1000 Longfellow Boulevard, Lakeland, FL 33801-6034
(863) 667-5024

Southwest Florida College

Ft. Myers, Florida
www.swfc.edu   Federal Code: 016068

2-year private career college in large city.
Enrollment: 1,810 undergrads, 16% part-time. 418 full-time freshmen.
Selectivity: Open admission; but selective for some programs.

BASIC COSTS (2009-2010)
Tuition and fees: $14,175.
Per-credit charge: $290.
Additional info: Required fees do not include lab or online fees.

FINANCIAL AID PICTURE
Students with need: Need-based aid available for full-time and part-time students. Work study available nights, weekends, and for part-time students.

FINANCIAL AID PROCEDURES
Forms required: FAFSA.
Dates and Deadlines: No deadline. Applicants notified on a rolling basis.
Transfers: No deadline. Applicants notified on a rolling basis.

CONTACT
Laura Selvey, Director of Financial Aid
1685 Medical Lane, Ft. Myers, FL 33907-1108
(813) 630-4401

State College of Florida, Manatee-Sarasota

Bradenton, Florida
www.mccfl.edu   Federal Code: 001504

4-year public nursing and community college in small city.
Enrollment: 10,113 undergrads, 49% part-time. 1,281 full-time freshmen.
Selectivity: Open admission; but selective for some programs.

BASIC COSTS (2009-2010)
Tuition and fees: $2,636; out-of-state residents $9,942.

FINANCIAL AID PICTURE (2009-2010)

Students with need: Out of 983 full-time freshmen who applied for aid, 803 were judged to have need. Of these, 803 received aid, and 732 had their full need met. Need-based aid available for part-time students.

Students without need: 243 full-time freshmen who did not demonstrate need for aid received scholarships/grants; average award was $2,725. No-need awards available for academics, art, athletics, music/drama, state/district residency.

FINANCIAL AID PROCEDURES

Forms required: FAFSA.

Dates and Deadlines: Priority date 6/1; closing date 7/28. Applicants notified on a rolling basis starting 3/15.

CONTACT

Anders Nilsen, Director of Financial Aid
Box 1849, Bradenton, FL 34206-1849
(941) 752-5037

Stetson University
DeLand, Florida
www.stetson.edu   Federal Code: 001531

4-year private university in large town.
Enrollment: 2,151 undergrads, 4% part-time. 502 full-time freshmen.
Selectivity: Admits 50 to 75% of applicants.

BASIC COSTS (2010-2011)

Tuition and fees: $33,424.
Per-credit charge: $960.
Room and board: $9,805.

FINANCIAL AID PICTURE (2009-2010)

Students with need: Out of 420 full-time freshmen who applied for aid, 358 were judged to have need. Of these, 358 received aid, and 90 had their full need met. Average financial aid package met 85% of need; average scholarship/grant was $23,402; average loan was $4,159. For part-time students, average financial aid package was $10,785.

Students without need: 118 full-time freshmen who did not demonstrate need for aid received scholarships/grants; average award was $12,201. No-need awards available for academics, alumni affiliation, art, athletics, leadership, minority status, music/drama, religious affiliation, ROTC, state/district residency.

Scholarships offered: 15 full-time freshmen received athletic scholarships; average amount $27,919.

Cumulative student debt: 83% of graduating class had student loans; average debt was $30,914.

FINANCIAL AID PROCEDURES

Forms required: FAFSA, institutional form.

Dates and Deadlines: Priority date 3/15; no closing date. Applicants notified on a rolling basis starting 2/15.

CONTACT

Belem Lopez, Associate Director of Financial Aid
Campus Box 8378, DeLand, FL 32723
(386) 822-7120

Tallahassee Community College
Tallahassee, Florida
www.tcc.fl.edu   Federal Code: 001533

2-year public community college in small city.
Enrollment: 13,127 undergrads, 44% part-time. 2,549 full-time freshmen.
Selectivity: Open admission; but selective for some programs.

BASIC COSTS (2009-2010)

Tuition and fees: $2,220; out-of-state residents $7,836.

FINANCIAL AID PICTURE (2008-2009)

Students with need: Need-based aid available for full-time and part-time students.

Students without need: No-need awards available for academics, art, athletics, leadership, music/drama, state/district residency.

FINANCIAL AID PROCEDURES

Forms required: FAFSA, institutional form.

Dates and Deadlines: Priority date 5/1; no closing date. Applicants notified on a rolling basis starting 5/15.

CONTACT

William Spiers, Director of Financial Aid
444 Appleyard Drive, Tallahassee, FL 32304
(850) 201-8399

Trinity College of Florida
Trinity, Florida
www.trinitycollege.edu   Federal Code: 030282

4-year private Bible college in small city, affiliated with interdenominational tradition.
Enrollment: 210 undergrads, 12% part-time. 31 full-time freshmen.
Selectivity: Admits over 75% of applicants.

BASIC COSTS (2010-2011)

Tuition and fees: $11,824.
Per-credit charge: $430.
Room and board: $6,656.

FINANCIAL AID PICTURE (2008-2009)

Students with need: Out of 27 full-time freshmen who applied for aid, 24 were judged to have need. Of these, 24 received aid, and 2 had their full need met. Average financial aid package met 73% of need; average scholarship/grant was $2,273; average loan was $1,750. For part-time students, average financial aid package was $2,643.

Students without need: 4 full-time freshmen who did not demonstrate need for aid received scholarships/grants; average award was $591. No-need awards available for academics.

Cumulative student debt: 80% of graduating class had student loans; average debt was $20,523.

FINANCIAL AID PROCEDURES

Forms required: FAFSA, institutional form.

Dates and Deadlines: Priority date 3/15; closing date 8/26. Applicants notified on a rolling basis; must reply within 2 week(s) of notification.

Transfers: No deadline. Applicants notified on a rolling basis; must reply within 2 week(s) of notification.

CONTACT

Sue Wayne, Financial Aid Director
2430 Welbilt Boulevard, Trinity, FL 34655-4401
(727) 569-1413

University of Central Florida
Orlando, Florida
www.ucf.edu   Federal Code: 003954

4-year public university in very large city.
Enrollment: 45,048 undergrads, 24% part-time. 6,148 full-time freshmen.
Selectivity: Admits less than 50% of applicants.

BASIC COSTS (2009-2010)

Tuition and fees: $4,526; out-of-state residents $20,005.

Room and board: $8,574.

FINANCIAL AID PICTURE (2008-2009)

Students with need: Out of 4,441 full-time freshmen who applied for aid, 2,540 were judged to have need. Of these, 2,510 received aid, and 485 had their full need met. Average financial aid package met 71% of need; average scholarship/grant was $5,018; average loan was $3,379. For part-time students, average financial aid package was $5,310.

Students without need: 662 full-time freshmen who did not demonstrate need for aid received scholarships/grants; average award was $2,330. No-need awards available for academics, alumni affiliation, athletics, leadership, ROTC, state/district residency.

Scholarships offered: *Merit:* Academic scholarships: $2,000-$24,000 over 4-year period, freshmen automatically considered. *Athletic:* 55 full-time freshmen received athletic scholarships; average amount $8,804.

Cumulative student debt: 41% of graduating class had student loans; average debt was $17,044.

FINANCIAL AID PROCEDURES

Forms required: FAFSA.

Dates and Deadlines: Priority date 3/1; closing date 6/30. Applicants notified on a rolling basis starting 3/15; must reply within 3 week(s) of notification.

CONTACT

Mary McKinney, Executive Director of Financial Aid

Box 160111, Orlando, FL 32816-0111

(407) 823-2827

University of Florida

Gainesville, Florida

www.ufl.edu   Federal Code: 001535

4-year public university in small city.

Enrollment: 33,038 undergrads, 6% part-time. 6,229 full-time freshmen.

Selectivity: Admits less than 50% of applicants.

BASIC COSTS (2009-2010)

Tuition and fees: $4,373; out-of-state residents $23,744.

Per-credit charge: $146; out-of-state residents $792.

Room and board: $7,500.

FINANCIAL AID PICTURE (2008-2009)

Students with need: Need-based aid available for full-time and part-time students. Work study available nights, weekends, and for part-time students.

Students without need: No-need awards available for academics, art, athletics, leadership, minority status, music/drama, ROTC, state/district residency.

FINANCIAL AID PROCEDURES

Forms required: FAFSA.

Dates and Deadlines: Priority date 3/15; no closing date. Applicants notified on a rolling basis starting 4/1.

Transfers: Priority date 3/15; no deadline. Applicants notified on a rolling basis starting 4/1. NA.

CONTACT

Karen Fooks, Director of Student Financial Aid

201 Criser Hall-PO Box 114000, Gainesville, FL 32611-4000

(352) 392-1275

University of Miami

Coral Gables, Florida

www.miami.edu   Federal Code: 001536

4-year private university in small city.

Enrollment: 9,855 undergrads, 6% part-time. 1,905 full-time freshmen.

Selectivity: Admits less than 50% of applicants.

BASIC COSTS (2010-2011)

Tuition and fees: $37,836.

Per-credit charge: $1,538.

Room and board: $11,062.

FINANCIAL AID PICTURE (2009-2010)

Students with need: Out of 1,223 full-time freshmen who applied for aid, 924 were judged to have need. Of these, 924 received aid, and 323 had their full need met. Average financial aid package met 83% of need; average scholarship/grant was $23,904; average loan was $3,934. For part-time students, average financial aid package was $18,628.

Students without need: 328 full-time freshmen who did not demonstrate need for aid received scholarships/grants; average award was $20,279. No-need awards available for academics, athletics, music/drama, ROTC.

Scholarships offered: 48 full-time freshmen received athletic scholarships; average amount $23,816.

Cumulative student debt: 55% of graduating class had student loans; average debt was $24,396.

FINANCIAL AID PROCEDURES

Forms required: FAFSA.

Dates and Deadlines: Priority date 2/1; no closing date. Applicants notified on a rolling basis starting 3/1.

Transfers: Priority date 3/1.

CONTACT

James Bauer, Assistant Vice President of Enrollment Management and Executive Director of Financial Services

132 Ashe Building, Coral Gables, FL 33124-4616

(305) 284-5212

University of North Florida

Jacksonville, Florida

www.unf.edu   Federal Code: 009841

4-year public university in very large city.

Enrollment: 14,216 undergrads, 27% part-time. 1,925 full-time freshmen.

Selectivity: Admits 50 to 75% of applicants.

BASIC COSTS (2009-2010)

Tuition and fees: $4,193; out-of-state residents $17,582.

Room and board: $7,872.

FINANCIAL AID PICTURE (2009-2010)

Students with need: Out of 1,416 full-time freshmen who applied for aid, 922 were judged to have need. Of these, 909 received aid, and 135 had their full need met. Average financial aid package met 91% of need; average scholarship/grant was $1,080; average loan was $1,609. For part-time students, average financial aid package was $2,050.

Students without need: 139 full-time freshmen who did not demonstrate need for aid received scholarships/grants; average award was $1,127. No-need awards available for academics, athletics, leadership, minority status, music/drama, state/district residency.

Scholarships offered: 42 full-time freshmen received athletic scholarships; average amount $2,503.

Cumulative student debt: 41% of graduating class had student loans; average debt was $15,619.

FINANCIAL AID PROCEDURES

Forms required: FAFSA.

Dates and Deadlines: Priority date 4/1; no closing date. Applicants notified on a rolling basis starting 3/15; must reply within 2 week(s) of notification.

Transfers: Must reply within 2 week(s) of notification. Students must submit financial aid transcripts from previous institutions attended.

CONTACT

Anissa Agne, Director of Financial Aid
1 UNF Drive, Jacksonville, FL 32224-7699
(904) 620-2604

University of South Florida

Tampa, Florida
www.usf.edu   Federal Code: 001537

4-year public university in very large city.

Enrollment: 35,750 undergrads, 28% part-time. 4,399 full-time freshmen.

Selectivity: Admits less than 50% of applicants.

BASIC COSTS (2009-2010)

Tuition and fees: $4,577; out-of-state residents $16,708.

Room and board: $8,750.

Additional info: Tuition/fee waivers available for unemployed or children of unemployed.

FINANCIAL AID PICTURE (2008-2009)

Students with need: Out of 3,372 full-time freshmen who applied for aid, 2,479 were judged to have need. Of these, 2,462 received aid, and 281 had their full need met. Average financial aid package met 49% of need; average scholarship/grant was $6,451; average loan was $2,949. For part-time students, average financial aid package was $5,237.

Students without need: 1,137 full-time freshmen who did not demonstrate need for aid received scholarships/grants; average award was $1,932. No-need awards available for academics, alumni affiliation, art, athletics, job skills, leadership, minority status, music/drama, religious affiliation, ROTC, state/district residency.

Scholarships offered: 89 full-time freshmen received athletic scholarships; average amount $6,125.

Cumulative student debt: 52% of graduating class had student loans; average debt was $19,963.

Additional info: Deferred tuition payment plan available for late financial aid recipients.

FINANCIAL AID PROCEDURES

Forms required: FAFSA.

Dates and Deadlines: Priority date 3/1; no closing date. Applicants notified on a rolling basis starting 3/15.

Transfers: Priority date 3/1.

CONTACT

Billie Hamilton, Director of Financial Aid
4202 East Fowler Avenue, SVC 1036, Tampa, FL 33620-9951
(813) 974-4700

University of Tampa

Tampa, Florida
www.ut.edu   Federal Code: 001538

4-year private university and liberal arts college in large city.

Enrollment: 5,518 undergrads, 6% part-time. 1,413 full-time freshmen.

Selectivity: Admits 50 to 75% of applicants.

BASIC COSTS (2010-2011)

Tuition and fees: $23,218.

Per-credit charge: $470.

Room and board: $8,710.

FINANCIAL AID PICTURE (2009-2010)

Students with need: Out of 1,085 full-time freshmen who applied for aid, 838 were judged to have need. Of these, 838 received aid, and 175 had their full need met. Average financial aid package met 71% of need; average scholarship/grant was $6,679; average loan was $3,875. For part-time students, average financial aid package was $5,601.

Students without need: 243 full-time freshmen who did not demonstrate need for aid received scholarships/grants; average award was $6,160. No-need awards available for academics, alumni affiliation, art, athletics, leadership, music/drama, ROTC, state/district residency.

Scholarships offered: *Merit:* Presidential Scholarships: up to $9,000; 3.5 GPA. Dean's Scholarships: up to $8,000; 3.2 GPA. Departmental scholarships also awarded. *Athletic:* 1 full-time freshmen received athletic scholarships; average amount $10,000.

Cumulative student debt: 62% of graduating class had student loans; average debt was $24,812.

Additional info: Early aid estimator service.

FINANCIAL AID PROCEDURES

Forms required: FAFSA, state aid form.

Dates and Deadlines: No deadline. Applicants notified on a rolling basis starting 2/1; must reply within 3 week(s) of notification.

Transfers: No deadline. Must reply within 3 week(s) of notification. Transfer scholarships available; Phi Theta Kappa Scholarships.

CONTACT

John Marsh, Director of Financial Aid
401 West Kennedy Boulevard, Tampa, FL 33606-1490
(813) 253-6239

University of West Florida

Pensacola, Florida
www.uwf.edu   Federal Code: 003955

4-year public university in small city.

Enrollment: 8,718 undergrads, 26% part-time. 1,113 full-time freshmen.

Selectivity: Admits 50 to 75% of applicants.

BASIC COSTS (2009-2010)

Tuition and fees: $4,190; out-of-state residents $16,478.

Room and board: $7,576.

FINANCIAL AID PICTURE (2008-2009)

Students with need: 46% of average financial aid package awarded as scholarships/grants, 54% awarded as loans/jobs. Need-based aid available for part-time students. Work study available nights, weekends, and for part-time students.

Students without need: No-need awards available for academics, alumni affiliation, art, athletics, minority status, music/drama, ROTC.

Scholarships offered: John C. Pace Scholars: $16,000; based on high school record and leadership; 8 awards. John C. Pace Honors and Presidential Scholarships: $4,000; based on high school record. Both available to Florida residents only. Non-Florida tuition reduction scholarships available to non-residents.

FINANCIAL AID PROCEDURES

Forms required: FAFSA, institutional form.

Dates and Deadlines: Priority date 3/1; no closing date. Applicants notified on a rolling basis starting 2/1.

CONTACT

Cathy Brown, Director of Student Financial Aid
11000 University Parkway, Pensacola, FL 32514-5750
(850) 474-2400

Valencia Community College

Orlando, Florida
www.valenciacc.edu   Federal Code: 006750

2-year public community college in very large city.
Enrollment: 31,845 undergrads, 49% part-time. 5,239 full-time freshmen.
Selectivity: Open admission; but selective for some programs.

BASIC COSTS (2009-2010)
Tuition and fees: $2,621; out-of-state residents $9,926.

FINANCIAL AID PICTURE (2009-2010)
Students with need: Need-based aid available for full-time and part-time students. Work study available nights.

FINANCIAL AID PROCEDURES
Forms required: FAFSA.
Dates and Deadlines: Closing date 3/15. Applicants notified on a rolling basis starting 4/2; must reply within 2 week(s) of notification.
Transfers: No deadline.

CONTACT
Brad Honious, Director, Financial Aid
PO Box 3028, Orlando, FL 32802-3028
(407) 299-5000

Warner University

Lake Wales, Florida
www.warner.edu   Federal Code: 008848

4-year private liberal arts college in large town, affiliated with Church of God.
Enrollment: 946 undergrads, 11% part-time. 138 full-time freshmen.
Selectivity: Admits less than 50% of applicants.

BASIC COSTS (2009-2010)
Tuition and fees: $15,320.
Room and board: $6,815.
Additional info: One-time $50 security deposit for incoming freshmen living on campus.

FINANCIAL AID PICTURE (2008-2009)
Students with need: Need-based aid available for full-time and part-time students.
Students without need: No-need awards available for academics, alumni affiliation, art, athletics, leadership, music/drama, religious affiliation, state/district residency.

FINANCIAL AID PROCEDURES
Forms required: FAFSA, state aid form.
Dates and Deadlines: Priority date 5/1; no closing date. Applicants notified on a rolling basis starting 3/15; must reply within 2 week(s) of notification.
Transfers: Priority date 10/1; closing date 5/15. Applicants notified on a rolling basis; must reply within 2 week(s) of notification.

CONTACT
Lorrie Steedley, Financial Aid Director
13895 Highway 27, Lake Wales, FL 33859
(863) 638-7202

Webber International University

Babson Park, Florida
www.webber.edu   Federal Code: 001540

4-year private university and business college in rural community.
Enrollment: 603 undergrads, 8% part-time. 172 full-time freshmen.
Selectivity: Admits over 75% of applicants.

BASIC COSTS (2010-2011)
Tuition and fees: $18,742.
Per-credit charge: $259.
Room and board: $7,164.
Additional info: Tuition/fee waivers available for adults.

FINANCIAL AID PICTURE (2009-2010)
Students with need: 54% of average financial aid package awarded as scholarships/grants, 46% awarded as loans/jobs. Need-based aid available for part-time students. Work study available nights, weekends, and for part-time students.
Students without need: No-need awards available for academics, alumni affiliation, athletics, leadership, state/district residency.

FINANCIAL AID PROCEDURES
Forms required: FAFSA, state aid form.
Dates and Deadlines: Priority date 5/1; closing date 8/1. Applicants notified on a rolling basis starting 4/1; must reply within 4 week(s) of notification.
Transfers: Eligibility for academic scholarships predicated on 12 hours of transferable credit.

CONTACT
Kathleen Wilson, Registrar
1201 North Scenic Highway, Babson Park, FL 33827-0096
(863) 638-2930

Georgia

Agnes Scott College

Decatur, Georgia
www.agnesscott.edu   Federal Code: 001542

4-year private liberal arts college for women in very large city, affiliated with Presbyterian Church (USA).
Enrollment: 784 undergrads, 1% part-time. 237 full-time freshmen.
Selectivity: Admits less than 50% of applicants.

BASIC COSTS (2010-2011)
Tuition and fees: $31,283.
Per-credit charge: $1,294.
Room and board: $9,850.

FINANCIAL AID PICTURE (2009-2010)
Students with need: Out of 200 full-time freshmen who applied for aid, 182 were judged to have need. Of these, 182 received aid, and 54 had their full need met. Average financial aid package met 91% of need; average scholarship/grant was $54,448; average loan was $3,293. For part-time students, average financial aid package was $10,722.
Students without need: 55 full-time freshmen who did not demonstrate need for aid received scholarships/grants; average award was $15,821. No-need awards available for academics, leadership, minority status, music/drama, religious affiliation, state/district residency.
Scholarships offered: Presidential and Honor Scholarships; $8,750 to full tuition, room and board. College will match HOPE Scholarship for HOPE-eligible Georgia residents who meet college admission criteria. Leadership and community service awards also available.
Cumulative student debt: 69% of graduating class had student loans; average debt was $23,176.
Additional info: Middle Income Assistance Grants available. Auditions required for music scholarship applicants.

FINANCIAL AID PROCEDURES
Forms required: FAFSA.
Dates and Deadlines: Priority date 2/15; closing date 5/1. Applicants notified on a rolling basis starting 3/1; must reply within 3 week(s) of notification.

Transfers: Must reply by 5/1 or within 2 week(s) of notification. Merit scholarships available.

CONTACT

Patrick Bonones, Director of Financial Aid
141 East College Avenue, Decatur, GA 30030-3797
(404) 471-6395

Albany State University

Albany, Georgia
www.asurams.edu/   Federal Code: 001544

4-year public university and liberal arts college in small city.
Enrollment: 3,988 undergrads, 16% part-time. 718 full-time freshmen.
Selectivity: Admits less than 50% of applicants.

BASIC COSTS (2009-2010)
Tuition and fees: $4,786; out-of-state residents $16,400.
Room and board: $5,290.

FINANCIAL AID PICTURE (2008-2009)
Students with need: Need-based aid available for full-time and part-time students. Work study available nights, weekends, and for part-time students.
Students without need: No-need awards available for academics, alumni affiliation, art, athletics, music/drama, ROTC.

FINANCIAL AID PROCEDURES
Forms required: FAFSA, state aid form.
Dates and Deadlines: Priority date 4/15; closing date 4/30. Applicants notified on a rolling basis; must reply within 2 week(s) of notification.
Transfers: Must reply within 2 week(s) of notification.

CONTACT
Thomas Harris, Director of Financial Aid
504 College Drive, Albany, GA 31705-2796
(229) 430-4649

Albany Technical College

Albany, Georgia
www.albanytech.edu   Federal Code: 005601

2-year public technical college in small city.
Enrollment: 3,671 undergrads, 32% part-time. 659 full-time freshmen.
Selectivity: Open admission; but selective for some programs.

BASIC COSTS (2009-2010)
Tuition and fees: $2,043; out-of-state residents $3,843.
Per-credit charge: $40; out-of-state residents $80.

FINANCIAL AID PICTURE (2009-2010)
Students with need: Need-based aid available for full-time and part-time students. Work study available nights.
Students without need: No-need awards available for academics, state/district residency.

FINANCIAL AID PROCEDURES
Forms required: FAFSA, state aid form.
Dates and Deadlines: No deadline. Applicants notified on a rolling basis starting 5/1.

CONTACT
Helen Catt, Financial Aid Director
1704 South Slappy Boulevard, Albany, GA 31701-3514
(229) 430-3506

Andrew College

Cuthbert, Georgia
www.andrewcollege.edu   Federal Code: 001545

2-year private junior and liberal arts college in small town, affiliated with United Methodist Church.
Enrollment: 227 undergrads.
Selectivity: Admits 50 to 75% of applicants.

BASIC COSTS (2009-2010)
Tuition and fees: $11,416.
Room and board: $7,170.

FINANCIAL AID PICTURE
Students with need: Need-based aid available for full-time and part-time students.
Students without need: No-need awards available for academics, art, athletics, leadership, music/drama, religious affiliation, state/district residency.

FINANCIAL AID PROCEDURES
Forms required: FAFSA, state aid form, institutional form.
Dates and Deadlines: Priority date 4/1; closing date 8/1. Applicants notified on a rolling basis starting 4/15.

CONTACT
Amy Thompson, Financial Aid Administrator
501 College Street, Cuthbert, GA 39840-1395
(229) 732-5938

Armstrong Atlantic State University

Savannah, Georgia
www.armstrong.edu   Federal Code: 001546

4-year public university in small city.
Enrollment: 6,587 undergrads, 30% part-time. 968 full-time freshmen.
Selectivity: Admits 50 to 75% of applicants.

BASIC COSTS (2009-2010)
Tuition and fees: $4,802; out-of-state residents $16,416.
Per-credit charge: $130; out-of-state residents $517.
Room only: $5,350.
Additional info: Declining balance meal plans available.

FINANCIAL AID PICTURE (2009-2010)
Students with need: Out of 872 full-time freshmen who applied for aid, 654 were judged to have need. Of these, 490 received aid, and 401 had their full need met. Average financial aid package met 82% of need; average scholarship/grant was $4,000; average loan was $4,500. For part-time students, average financial aid package was $6,500.
Students without need: 198 full-time freshmen who did not demonstrate need for aid received scholarships/grants; average award was $3,000. No-need awards available for academics, alumni affiliation, art, athletics, leadership, minority status, music/drama, state/district residency.
Scholarships offered: 37 full-time freshmen received athletic scholarships; average amount $6,000.

FINANCIAL AID PROCEDURES
Forms required: FAFSA.
Dates and Deadlines: Priority date 3/15; no closing date. Applicants notified on a rolling basis starting 2/1; must reply by 4/15 or within 2 week(s) of notification.

CONTACT
LeeAnn Kirkland, Financial Aid Director
11935 Abercorn Street, Savannah, GA 31419-1997
(912) 344-3266

Art Institute of Atlanta
Atlanta, Georgia
www.artinstitutes.edu/atlanta/   Federal Code: 009270

4-year for-profit culinary school and visual arts college in very large city.
Enrollment: 3,839 undergrads, 16% part-time. 1,208 full-time freshmen.

BASIC COSTS (2010-2011)
Tuition and fees: $23,535.
Per-credit charge: $472.
Room only: $9,984.

FINANCIAL AID PICTURE
Students with need: Need-based aid available for full-time and part-time students. Work study available nights, weekends, and for part-time students.
Students without need: No-need awards available for academics, art, state/district residency.
Scholarships offered: Art Institutes Scholarship Competition awards $2,000 - $56,064 depending on program to winning high school seniors selected on merits of written essay, original artwork, resume, letter(s) of recommendation, and high school academic achievement; up to 1 full-tuition, 2 half-tuition, and 24 partial-tuition scholarships available. Art Institutes Culinary Scholarship Competition awards $2,000 - $32,704 to winning high school seniors selected through three-part elimination-style competition to prove academic ability, culinary expertise, and commitment to succeed; up to 1 full-tuition or 2 partial-tuition scholarships available. Various other scholarships and awards available.

FINANCIAL AID PROCEDURES
Forms required: FAFSA, state aid form.
Dates and Deadlines: No deadline. Applicants notified on a rolling basis starting 3/15.

CONTACT
Chris Schwarzer, Director of Administrative and Financial Services
6600 Peachtree Dunwoody Road, NE, Atlanta, GA 30328
(770) 394-8300

Athens Technical College
Athens, Georgia
www.athenstech.edu   Federal Code: 005600

2-year public technical college in small city.
Enrollment: 4,555 undergrads, 58% part-time. 481 full-time freshmen.
Selectivity: Open admission; but selective for some programs.

BASIC COSTS (2009-2010)
Tuition and fees: $2,043; out-of-state residents $3,843.
Per-credit charge: $40; out-of-state residents $80.

FINANCIAL AID PICTURE (2008-2009)
Students with need: Need-based aid available for full-time and part-time students.
Students without need: No-need awards available for academics, leadership.

FINANCIAL AID PROCEDURES
Forms required: FAFSA.
Dates and Deadlines: No deadline. Applicants notified on a rolling basis starting 6/15; must reply within 2 week(s) of notification.

CONTACT
Patrick Harris, Director of Financial Aid
800 US Highway 29 North, Athens, GA 30601-1500
(706) 355-5009

Atlanta Christian College
East Point, Georgia
www.acc.edu   Federal Code: 001547

4-year private Bible and liberal arts college in small city, affiliated with Christian Church.
Enrollment: 683 undergrads, 3% part-time. 70 full-time freshmen.
Selectivity: Admits 50 to 75% of applicants.

BASIC COSTS (2010-2011)
Tuition and fees: $15,902.
Room and board: $5,670.

FINANCIAL AID PICTURE (2008-2009)
Students with need: 44% of average financial aid package awarded as scholarships/grants, 56% awarded as loans/jobs. Need-based aid available for part-time students.

FINANCIAL AID PROCEDURES
Forms required: FAFSA.
Dates and Deadlines: Priority date 6/1; closing date 8/1. Applicants notified on a rolling basis starting 3/1; must reply within 3 week(s) of notification.

CONTACT
Anna English, Director Financial Aid
2605 Ben Hill Road, East Point, GA 30344
(404) 460-2462

Atlanta Metropolitan College
Atlanta, Georgia
www.atlm.edu   Federal Code: 012165

2-year public junior college in very large city.
Enrollment: 2,663 undergrads, 39% part-time. 396 full-time freshmen.
Selectivity: Admits 50 to 75% of applicants.

BASIC COSTS (2009-2010)
Tuition and fees: $2,728; out-of-state residents $9,606.
Per-credit charge: $77; out-of-state residents $306.

FINANCIAL AID PICTURE (2008-2009)
Students with need: Need-based aid available for full-time and part-time students. Work study available nights, weekends, and for part-time students.
Students without need: This college awards aid only to students with need.

FINANCIAL AID PROCEDURES
Forms required: FAFSA, state aid form.
Dates and Deadlines: Closing date 6/1. Applicants notified on a rolling basis; must reply by 6/30.
Transfers: Priority date 6/1; closing date 6/30. Applicants notified on a rolling basis; must reply by 6/30.

CONTACT
Alicia Scott, Director
1630 Metropolitan Parkway, SW, Atlanta, GA 30310-4498
(404) 756-4002

Atlanta Technical College
Atlanta, Georgia
www.atlantatech.edu

2-year public community and technical college in very large city.
Enrollment: 3,671 undergrads, 32% part-time. 659 full-time freshmen.
Selectivity: Open admission; but selective for some programs.

BASIC COSTS (2009-2010)
Tuition and fees: $2,046; out-of-state residents $3,846.
Per-credit charge: $40; out-of-state residents $80.

FINANCIAL AID PICTURE (2009-2010)
Students with need: Need-based aid available for full-time and part-time students. Work study available nights.

FINANCIAL AID PROCEDURES
Forms required: state aid form.
Dates and Deadlines: Priority date 3/1; no closing date. Applicants notified on a rolling basis starting 4/15.

CONTACT
Deborah Clark, Director of Financial Aid
1560 Metropolitan Parkway, SW, Atlanta, GA 30310-4446

Augusta State University
Augusta, Georgia
www.aug.edu   Federal Code: 001552

4-year public liberal arts and teachers college in small city.
Enrollment: 5,394 undergrads.

BASIC COSTS (2009-2010)
Tuition and fees: $4,634; out-of-state residents $16,248.

FINANCIAL AID PICTURE (2008-2009)
Students with need: Need-based aid available for full-time and part-time students. Work study available nights, weekends, and for part-time students.
Students without need: No-need awards available for academics, art, athletics, leadership, minority status, music/drama, ROTC, state/district residency.

FINANCIAL AID PROCEDURES
Forms required: FAFSA, institutional form.
Dates and Deadlines: Closing date 6/1. Applicants notified on a rolling basis starting 3/1; must reply within 4 week(s) of notification.

CONTACT
Willene Holmes, Director of Financial Aid
2500 Walton Way, Augusta, GA 30904-2200
(706) 737-1431

Bainbridge College
Bainbridge, Georgia
www.bainbridge.edu   Federal Code: 011074

2-year public community and technical college in large town.
Enrollment: 3,557 undergrads, 51% part-time. 530 full-time freshmen.
Selectivity: Admits over 75% of applicants.

BASIC COSTS (2009-2010)
Tuition and fees: $2,886; out-of-state residents $9,764.
Per-credit charge: $77; out-of-state residents $308.

FINANCIAL AID PICTURE (2008-2009)
Students with need: Need-based aid available for full-time and part-time students.
Students without need: This college awards aid only to students with need.
Scholarships offered: Small number of merit scholarships available.
Additional info: 30-day loans available for tuition and fees.

FINANCIAL AID PROCEDURES
Forms required: FAFSA, institutional form.
Dates and Deadlines: Priority date 6/1; closing date 8/1. Applicants notified on a rolling basis starting 6/1; must reply within 2 week(s) of notification.

Transfers: Priority date 6/11.

CONTACT
Debra Turner, Director of Financial Aid
2500 East Shotwell Street, Bainbridge, GA 39818-0990
(229) 248-2505

Berry College
Mount Berry, Georgia
www.berry.edu   Federal Code: 001554

4-year private liberal arts college in large town.
Enrollment: 1,756 undergrads, 1% part-time. 569 full-time freshmen.
Selectivity: Admits 50 to 75% of applicants.

BASIC COSTS (2010-2011)
Tuition and fees: $24,620.
Per-credit charge: $814.
Room and board: $8,724.

FINANCIAL AID PICTURE (2009-2010)
Students with need: Out of 528 full-time freshmen who applied for aid, 416 were judged to have need. Of these, 416 received aid, and 94 had their full need met. Average financial aid package met 85% of need; average scholarship/grant was $16,818; average loan was $2,968. For part-time students, average financial aid package was $6,560.
Students without need: 153 full-time freshmen who did not demonstrate need for aid received scholarships/grants; average award was $10,453. No-need awards available for academics, art, athletics, leadership, minority status, music/drama, state/district residency.
Scholarships offered: HOPE Scholarship: $3,500 annually; for entering freshmen based on legal residence in Georgia and graduation from eligible high school with at least a B average in college preparatory coursework.
Cumulative student debt: 82% of graduating class had student loans; average debt was $17,502.
Additional info: Students are encouraged to work on-campus up to 20 hours per week.

FINANCIAL AID PROCEDURES
Forms required: FAFSA.
Dates and Deadlines: Priority date 4/1; no closing date. Applicants notified on a rolling basis starting 2/1.
Transfers: No deadline. Applicants notified on a rolling basis starting 4/1.

CONTACT
Marcia McConnell, Director of Financial Aid
PO Box 490159, Mount Berry, GA 30149-0159
(706) 236-1714

Brenau University
Gainesville, Georgia
www.brenau.edu   Federal Code: 001556

4-year private liberal arts college for women in small city.
Enrollment: 794 undergrads, 4% part-time. 157 full-time freshmen.
Selectivity: Admits less than 50% of applicants.

BASIC COSTS (2009-2010)
Tuition and fees: $19,356.
Per-credit charge: $636.
Room and board: $9,772.

FINANCIAL AID PICTURE (2009-2010)

Students with need: Out of 146 full-time freshmen who applied for aid, 129 were judged to have need. Of these, 128 received aid, and 31 had their full need met. Average financial aid package met .79% of need; average scholarship/grant was $16,666; average loan was $3,257. For part-time students, average financial aid package was $5,479.

Students without need: 21 full-time freshmen who did not demonstrate need for aid received scholarships/grants; average award was $10,924. No-need awards available for academics, art, athletics, leadership, minority status, music/drama.

Scholarships offered: 7 full-time freshmen received athletic scholarships; average amount $15,579.

Cumulative student debt: 64% of graduating class had student loans; average debt was $17,999.

FINANCIAL AID PROCEDURES

Forms required: FAFSA, state aid form.

Dates and Deadlines: Priority date 3/15; no closing date. Applicants notified on a rolling basis starting 3/1.

CONTACT

Pam Barrett, Director of Financial Aid
500 Washington Street SE, Gainesville, GA 30501
(770) 534-6152

Brewton-Parker College
Mount Vernon, Georgia
www.bpc.edu   Federal Code: 001557

4-year private liberal arts college in small town, affiliated with Southern Baptist Convention.

Enrollment: 1,030 undergrads, 26% part-time. 242 full-time freshmen.

Selectivity: Admits 50 to 75% of applicants.

BASIC COSTS (2010-2011)

Tuition and fees: $15,845.

Per-credit charge: $455.

Room and board: $6,840.

FINANCIAL AID PICTURE (2008-2009)

Students with need: Out of 191 full-time freshmen who applied for aid, 171 were judged to have need. Of these, 170 received aid, and 32 had their full need met. Average financial aid package met 73% of need; average scholarship/grant was $9,501; average loan was $2,782. For part-time students, average financial aid package was $6,127.

Students without need: 27 full-time freshmen who did not demonstrate need for aid received scholarships/grants; average award was $4,011. No-need awards available for academics, athletics, music/drama, religious affiliation, state/district residency.

Scholarships offered: *Merit:* Scholarships available for academic achievement and SAT scores for incoming freshman transfer students, ranging from $1,500-$3,000 per academic year, available for four years. *Athletic:* 18 full-time freshmen received athletic scholarships; average amount $3,005.

Cumulative student debt: 89% of graduating class had student loans; average debt was $28,231.

FINANCIAL AID PROCEDURES

Forms required: FAFSA, state aid form.

Dates and Deadlines: Priority date 5/1; no closing date. Applicants notified on a rolling basis; must reply within 2 week(s) of notification.

CONTACT

Jackie White, Assistant Director of Financial Aid
Brewton-Parker College # 2011, Mount Vernon, GA 30445
(912) 583-2241 ext. 209

Central Georgia Technical College
Macon, Georgia
www.cgtcollege.edu   Federal Code: 005763

2-year public community and technical college in small city.

Enrollment: 6,687 undergrads, 42% part-time. 942 full-time freshmen.

Selectivity: Open admission; but selective for some programs.

BASIC COSTS (2009-2010)

Tuition and fees: $2,043; out-of-state residents $3,843.

Per-credit charge: $40; out-of-state residents $80.

FINANCIAL AID PICTURE (2008-2009)

Students with need: Need-based aid available for full-time and part-time students.

FINANCIAL AID PROCEDURES

Forms required: FAFSA, state aid form, institutional form.

Dates and Deadlines: Closing date 7/14.

CONTACT

Pennie Strong, Director, Financial Aid
3300 Macon Tech Drive, Macon, GA 31206
(478) 757-3422

Chattahoochee Technical College
Marietta, Georgia
www.chattahoocheetech.edu   Federal Code: 005620

2-year public technical college in large city.

Enrollment: 10,534 undergrads, 52% part-time. 3,772 full-time freshmen.

Selectivity: Open admission; but selective for some programs.

BASIC COSTS (2009-2010)

Tuition and fees: $2,064; out-of-state residents $3,864.

Per-credit charge: $40; out-of-state residents $80.

FINANCIAL AID PICTURE (2008-2009)

Students with need: Need-based aid available for full-time and part-time students. Work study available nights, weekends, and for part-time students.

Students without need: No-need awards available for state/district residency.

FINANCIAL AID PROCEDURES

Forms required: FAFSA, institutional form.

Dates and Deadlines: No deadline. Applicants notified on a rolling basis.

CONTACT

Lori Burnette, Director of Financial Aid
980 South Cobb Drive, SE, Marietta, GA 30060-3300
(770) 528-4531

Clark Atlanta University
Atlanta, Georgia
www.cau.edu   Federal Code: 001559

4-year private university in very large city, affiliated with United Methodist Church.

Enrollment: 3,202 undergrads, 4% part-time. 702 full-time freshmen.

Selectivity: Admits 50 to 75% of applicants.

BASIC COSTS (2010-2011)

Tuition and fees: $17,954.

Per-credit charge: $719.

Room and board: $7,540.

FINANCIAL AID PICTURE (2009-2010)

Students with need: Need-based aid available for full-time and part-time students.

Students without need: No-need awards available for academics, art, athletics, leadership, minority status, music/drama, religious affiliation, ROTC, state/district residency.

FINANCIAL AID PROCEDURES

Forms required: FAFSA, state aid form.

Dates and Deadlines: Priority date 3/1; no closing date. Applicants notified on a rolling basis starting 4/1.

CONTACT

Director
223 James P. Brawley Drive, SW, Atlanta, GA 30314-4391
(404) 880-6018

Clayton State University
Morrow, Georgia
www.clayton.edu   Federal Code: 008976

4-year public liberal arts and technical college in small city.
Enrollment: 6,412 undergrads, 43% part-time. 314 full-time freshmen.
Selectivity: Admits 50 to 75% of applicants.

BASIC COSTS (2009-2010)

Tuition and fees: $4,848; out-of-state residents $16,462.
Per-credit charge: $130; out-of-state residents $517.
Room and board: $8,078.
Additional info: Tuition at time of enrollment locked for 4 years.

FINANCIAL AID PICTURE (2008-2009)

Students with need: Out of 288 full-time freshmen who applied for aid, 246 were judged to have need. Of these, 245 received aid, and 24 had their full need met. Average financial aid package met 18% of need; average scholarship/grant was $4,424; average loan was $3,342. For part-time students, average financial aid package was $2,997.

Students without need: 12 full-time freshmen who did not demonstrate need for aid received scholarships/grants; average award was $1,067. No-need awards available for academics, athletics, music/drama.

Scholarships offered: 14 full-time freshmen received athletic scholarships; average amount $3,463.

FINANCIAL AID PROCEDURES

Forms required: FAFSA, state aid form.

Dates and Deadlines: Priority date 7/1; no closing date. Applicants notified on a rolling basis.

CONTACT

Patricia Barton, Director of Financial Aid
2000 Clayton State Boulevard, Morrow, GA 30260-0285
(678) 466-4185

College of Coastal Georgia
Brunswick, Georgia
www.ccga.edu   Federal Code: 001558

2-year public liberal arts college in large town.
Enrollment: 2,971 undergrads, 51% part-time. 617 full-time freshmen.
Selectivity: Open admission; but selective for some programs.

BASIC COSTS (2009-2010)

Tuition and fees: $2,860; out-of-state residents $10,342.
Additional info: Costs may vary among students.

FINANCIAL AID PICTURE (2008-2009)

Students with need: Need-based aid available for full-time and part-time students. Work study available nights, weekends, and for part-time students.

Students without need: No-need awards available for academics, athletics, leadership, state/district residency.

FINANCIAL AID PROCEDURES

Forms required: FAFSA.

Dates and Deadlines: Priority date 5/1; no closing date. Applicants notified on a rolling basis starting 7/1.

Transfers: No deadline. Applicants notified on a rolling basis.

CONTACT

Rodney Clements, Financial Aid Director
3700 Altama Avenue, Brunswick, GA 31520
(912) 279-5722

Columbus State University
Columbus, Georgia
www.colstate.edu   Federal Code: 001561

4-year public university and liberal arts college in large city.
Enrollment: 6,760 undergrads, 28% part-time. 1,166 full-time freshmen.
Selectivity: Admits 50 to 75% of applicants. GED not accepted.

BASIC COSTS (2009-2010)

Tuition and fees: $5,024; out-of-state residents $16,638.
Per-credit charge: $130; out-of-state residents $517.
Room and board: $7,090.

FINANCIAL AID PICTURE (2009-2010)

Students with need: Out of 1,023 full-time freshmen who applied for aid, 797 were judged to have need. Of these, 785 received aid, and 132 had their full need met. Average financial aid package met 72% of need; average scholarship/grant was $4,984; average loan was $3,214. For part-time students, average financial aid package was $6,971.

Students without need: 38 full-time freshmen who did not demonstrate need for aid received scholarships/grants; average award was $1,721. No-need awards available for academics, alumni affiliation, art, athletics, job skills, leadership, minority status, music/drama, ROTC.

Scholarships offered: 40 full-time freshmen received athletic scholarships; average amount $4,475.

Cumulative student debt: 64% of graduating class had student loans; average debt was $21,538.

FINANCIAL AID PROCEDURES

Forms required: FAFSA.

Dates and Deadlines: Priority date 5/1; no closing date. Applicants notified on a rolling basis starting 5/15; must reply within 4 week(s) of notification.

Transfers: No deadline. Applicants notified by 5/15.

CONTACT

Janis Bowles, Director of Financial Aid
4225 University Avenue, Columbus, GA 31907-5645
(706) 507-8800

Columbus Technical College
Columbus, Georgia
www.columbustech.org   Federal Code: 005624

2-year public technical college in small city.
Enrollment: 4,100 undergrads, 56% part-time. 478 full-time freshmen.
Selectivity: Open admission; but selective for some programs.

BASIC COSTS (2009-2010)

Tuition and fees: $2,043; out-of-state residents $3,843.
Per-credit charge: $40; out-of-state residents $80.

FINANCIAL AID PICTURE

Students with need: Need-based aid available for full-time and part-time students.

FINANCIAL AID PROCEDURES

Forms required: FAFSA.
Dates and Deadlines: No deadline. Applicants notified on a rolling basis.

CONTACT

Debbie Henshaw, Director, Financial Aid
928 Manchester Expressway, Columbus, GA 31904
(706) 649-1859

Covenant College
Lookout Mountain, Georgia
www.covenant.edu   Federal Code: 003484

4-year private liberal arts college in small city, affiliated with Presbyterian Church in America.
Enrollment: 976 undergrads, 1% part-time. 267 full-time freshmen.
Selectivity: Admits 50 to 75% of applicants.

BASIC COSTS (2010-2011)

Tuition and fees: $26,226.
Per-credit charge: $1,065.
Room and board: $7,450.

FINANCIAL AID PICTURE (2008-2009)

Students with need: Out of 226 full-time freshmen who applied for aid, 178 were judged to have need. Of these, 178 received aid, and 62 had their full need met. Average financial aid package met 83% of need; average scholarship/grant was $12,928; average loan was $4,830. For part-time students, average financial aid package was $3,893.
Students without need: 45 full-time freshmen who did not demonstrate need for aid received scholarships/grants; average award was $6,980. No-need awards available for academics, alumni affiliation, art, athletics, job skills, leadership, minority status, music/drama, religious affiliation, state/district residency.
Scholarships offered: *Merit:* Maclellan Scholars Program; minimum SAT 1200 (exclusive of Writing) or ACT 27, high school GPA 3.3. Presidential Scholarship; based on GPA, leadership, Christian commitment, extracurricular activities, work experience, references. *Athletic:* 28 full-time freshmen received athletic scholarships; average amount $4,198.
Cumulative student debt: 64% of graduating class had student loans; average debt was $17,824.

FINANCIAL AID PROCEDURES

Forms required: FAFSA, state aid form.
Dates and Deadlines: No deadline. Applicants notified on a rolling basis starting 2/1; must reply within 3 week(s) of notification.
Transfers: Some scholarships may be depleted for mid-semester transfers, such as athletic, diversity or music.

CONTACT

Brenda Rapier, Director of Financial Aid
14049 Scenic Highway, Lookout Mountain, GA 30750
(706) 419-1126

Dalton State College
Dalton, Georgia
www.daltonstate.edu   Federal Code: 003956

4-year public liberal arts and teachers college in large town.
Enrollment: 5,722 undergrads, 40% part-time. 1,164 full-time freshmen.
Selectivity: Admits 50 to 75% of applicants.

BASIC COSTS (2009-2010)

Tuition and fees: $2,900; out-of-state residents $10,382.

FINANCIAL AID PICTURE (2009-2010)

Students with need: Need-based aid available for full-time and part-time students.
Students without need: No-need awards available for academics, leadership, minority status, state/district residency.

FINANCIAL AID PROCEDURES

Forms required: FAFSA, state aid form, institutional form.
Dates and Deadlines: Priority date 7/1; no closing date. Applicants notified on a rolling basis starting 7/1.
Transfers: No deadline. Applicants notified on a rolling basis.

CONTACT

Holli Woods, Director of Student Financial Aid
650 College Drive, Dalton, GA 30720
(706) 272-4545

Darton College
Albany, Georgia
www.darton.edu   Federal Code: 001543

2-year public community college in small city.
Enrollment: 4,651 undergrads, 45% part-time. 1,006 full-time freshmen.
Selectivity: Open admission; but selective for some programs.

BASIC COSTS (2009-2010)

Tuition and fees: $2,992; out-of-state residents $9,870.
Per-credit charge: $77; out of state residents $306.

FINANCIAL AID PICTURE (2008-2009)

Students with need: 99% of average financial aid package awarded as scholarships/grants, 1% awarded as loans/jobs. Need-based aid available for part-time students. Work study available nights, weekends, and for part-time students.
Students without need: No-need awards available for academics, alumni affiliation, art, athletics, music/drama, state/district residency.
Additional info: Auditions, portfolios, essays, extracurricular activities impact scholarship decisions.

FINANCIAL AID PROCEDURES

Forms required: FAFSA, state aid form, institutional form.
Dates and Deadlines: No deadline. Applicants notified on a rolling basis; must reply within 3 week(s) of notification.

CONTACT

Martha Whittle, Director of Financial Aid
2400 Gillionville Road, Albany, GA 31707-3098
(229) 317-6746

DeKalb Technical College
Clarkston, Georgia
www.dekalbtech.edu   Federal Code: 016582

2-year public technical college in large city.
Enrollment: 4,664 undergrads, 58% part-time. 483 full-time freshmen.

Selectivity: Open admission; but selective for some programs.

BASIC COSTS (2009-2010)
Tuition and fees: $2,091; out-of-state residents $3,891.
Per-credit charge: $40; out-of-state residents $80.
Additional info: Truck driving and flight technology are higher cost programs.

FINANCIAL AID PICTURE (2009-2010)
Students with need: Need-based aid available for full-time and part-time students. Work study available nights, weekends, and for part-time students.

FINANCIAL AID PROCEDURES
Forms required: FAFSA.
Dates and Deadlines: Closing date 8/20. Applicants notified on a rolling basis.
Transfers: No deadline.

CONTACT
John Gottardy, Director of Financial Aid
495 North Indian Creek Drive, Clarkston, GA 30021-2397
(404) 297-9522 ext. 1166

DeVry University: Alpharetta
Alpharetta, Georgia
www.devry.edu   Federal Code: 009224

4-year for-profit university in large town.
Enrollment: 709 undergrads, 52% part-time. 61 full-time freshmen.

BASIC COSTS (2009-2010)
Tuition and fees: $14,160.
Per-credit charge: $550.

FINANCIAL AID PICTURE (2008-2009)
Students with need: Need-based aid available for full-time and part-time students.
Students without need: This college awards aid only to students with need.

FINANCIAL AID PROCEDURES
Forms required: FAFSA.
Dates and Deadlines: No deadline. Applicants notified on a rolling basis.

CONTACT
David Pickett, Assistant Director of Financial Aid
2555 Northwinds Parkway, Alpharetta, GA 30004
(770) 521-4900

DeVry University: Decatur
Decatur, Georgia
www.devry.edu   Federal Code: 009224

4-year for-profit university in large town.
Enrollment: 2,759 undergrads, 53% part-time. 209 full-time freshmen.

BASIC COSTS (2009-2010)
Tuition and fees: $14,160.
Per-credit charge: $550.

FINANCIAL AID PICTURE (2008-2009)
Students with need: Need-based aid available for full-time and part-time students.
Students without need: This college awards aid only to students with need.

FINANCIAL AID PROCEDURES
Forms required: FAFSA.
Dates and Deadlines: No deadline. Applicants notified on a rolling basis.

CONTACT
Robin Winston, Director of Financial Aid
One West Court Square, Suite 100, Decatur, GA 30030-2556
(404) 292-7900

East Georgia College
Swainsboro, Georgia
www.ega.edu   Federal Code: 010997

2-year public community and junior college in small town.
Enrollment: 2,754 undergrads.

BASIC COSTS (2009-2010)
Tuition and fees: $2,767; out-of-state residents $9,645.
Per-credit charge: $77; out-of-state residents $306.

FINANCIAL AID PICTURE
Students with need: Need-based aid available for full-time and part-time students.
Students without need: No-need awards available for academics, leadership, state/district residency.

FINANCIAL AID PROCEDURES
Forms required: FAFSA, institutional form.
Dates and Deadlines: Priority date 6/1; no closing date. Applicants notified on a rolling basis starting 6/1; must reply within 2 week(s) of notification.

CONTACT
Cynthia Parks, Director of Financial Aid
131 College Circle, Swainsboro, GA 30401-2699
(478) 289-2009

Emmanuel College
Franklin Springs, Georgia
www.ec.edu   Federal Code: 001563

4-year private liberal arts and teachers college in rural community, affiliated with Pentecostal Holiness Church.
Enrollment: 685 undergrads, 4% part-time. 157 full-time freshmen.
Selectivity: Admits less than 50% of applicants.

BASIC COSTS (2010-2011)
Tuition and fees: $13,520.
Per-credit charge: $560.
Room and board: $5,720.

FINANCIAL AID PICTURE (2009-2010)
Students with need: Out of 150 full-time freshmen who applied for aid, 138 were judged to have need. Of these, 138 received aid, and 16 had their full need met. Average financial aid package met 89% of need; average scholarship/grant was $9,024; average loan was $3,178. For part-time students, average financial aid package was $7,062.
Students without need: 19 full-time freshmen who did not demonstrate need for aid received scholarships/grants; average award was $4,583. No-need awards available for academics, art, athletics, job skills, leadership, music/drama, religious affiliation, state/district residency.
Scholarships offered: 7 full-time freshmen received athletic scholarships; average amount $3,786.
Cumulative student debt: 77% of graduating class had student loans; average debt was $25,321.

FINANCIAL AID PROCEDURES
Forms required: FAFSA, state aid form, institutional form.

Dates and Deadlines: Priority date 5/1; closing date 7/1. Applicants notified on a rolling basis starting 3/1; must reply within 2 week(s) of notification.
Transfers: Students on probation at previous institution may be accepted and funded for one semester. Continued funding dependent on satisfactory performance.

CONTACT
Gloria Hambrick, Director of Financial Aid
181 Spring Street, Franklin Springs, GA 30639-0129
(706) 245-2843

Emory University

Atlanta, Georgia
www.emory.edu

Federal Code: 001564
CSS Code: 5187

4-year private university in very large city, affiliated with United Methodist Church.
Enrollment: 5,223 undergrads.
Selectivity: Admits less than 50% of applicants. GED not accepted.

BASIC COSTS (2010-2011)
Tuition and fees: $39,158.
Per-credit charge: $1,608.
Room and board: $11,198.

FINANCIAL AID PICTURE (2009-2010)
Students with need: Average financial aid package met 100% of need; average scholarship/grant was $30,448; average loan was $3,288. Need-based aid available for part-time students.
Students without need: No-need awards available for academics, art, leadership, music/drama, religious affiliation, state/district residency.
Scholarships offered: Emory and Goizueta Scholars programs: two-thirds tuition to full cost; based on academic merit of incoming first-year students, requires nomination by appropriate high school official by November 1 of senior year; renewable for four years of undergraduate study.
Cumulative student debt: 42% of graduating class had student loans; average debt was $25,865.
Additional info: Loan replacement grant and loan cap program available to students from families with total annual incomes of $100,000 or less who demonstrate need for financial aid.

FINANCIAL AID PROCEDURES
Forms required: FAFSA, CSS PROFILE.
Dates and Deadlines: Priority date 2/15; closing date 3/1. Applicants notified by 4/1; must reply by 5/1 or within 4 week(s) of notification.
Transfers: No deadline. Applicants notified on a rolling basis. Limitations on aid available to transfer students. Financial aid filing deadline for transfers is 30 days following transfer student admission date.

CONTACT
Dean Bentley, Director of Financial Aid
200 Dowman Drive, B Jones Center, Atlanta, GA 30322
(800) 727-6039

Fort Valley State University

Fort Valley, Georgia
www.fvsu.edu

Federal Code: 001566

4-year public liberal arts and teachers college in small town.
Enrollment: 3,421 undergrads, 12% part-time. 960 full-time freshmen.
Selectivity: Admits less than 50% of applicants.

BASIC COSTS (2009-2010)
Tuition and fees: $5,012; out-of-state residents $16,626.
Per-credit charge: $130; out-of-state residents $517.
Room and board: $6,538.

FINANCIAL AID PICTURE (2009-2010)
Students with need: Average financial aid package met 97% of need; average scholarship/grant was $2,300; average loan was $2,500. For part-time students, average financial aid package was $450.
Students without need: No-need awards available for academics, alumni affiliation, athletics, ROTC.
Cumulative student debt: 98% of graduating class had student loans; average debt was $3,700.
Additional info: Loans decreased and grant aid offered to make institution more affordable. Financial aid transcripts must be received from former institutions before application for aid will be considered complete and reviewed for awards.

FINANCIAL AID PROCEDURES
Forms required: FAFSA, state aid form.
Dates and Deadlines: Priority date 4/15; closing date 6/30. Applicants notified on a rolling basis starting 7/1; must reply within 1 week(s) of notification.

CONTACT
Eula Solomon, Director of Financial Aid
1005 State University Drive, Fort Valley, GA 31030-4313
(478) 825-6351

Gainesville State College

Gainesville, Georgia
www.gsc.edu

Federal Code: 001567

2-year public junior college in large town.
Enrollment: 8,565 undergrads.

BASIC COSTS (2009-2010)
Tuition and fees: $2,948; out-of-state residents $10,430.

FINANCIAL AID PICTURE (2008-2009)
Students with need: Need-based aid available for full-time and part-time students. Work study available nights, weekends, and for part-time students.
Students without need: No-need awards available for academics, art, leadership, music/drama.

FINANCIAL AID PROCEDURES
Forms required: FAFSA.
Dates and Deadlines: Closing date 6/1. Applicants notified on a rolling basis starting 5/1; must reply within 2 week(s) of notification.
Transfers: No deadline. Applicants notified on a rolling basis starting 5/1; must reply within 2 week(s) of notification. Must have minimum 2.0 GPA to be eligible for financial aid.

CONTACT
Susan Smith, Financial Aid Director
PO Box 1358, Gainesville, GA 30503
(678) 717-3642

Georgia College and State University

Milledgeville, Georgia
www.gcsu.edu

Federal Code: 001602

4-year public university and liberal arts college in large town.
Enrollment: 5,603 undergrads, 9% part-time. 1,088 full-time freshmen.
Selectivity: Admits 50 to 75% of applicants.

BASIC COSTS (2009-2010)
Tuition and fees: $6,902; out-of-state residents $23,940.
Per-credit charge: $190; out-of-state residents $758.
Room and board: $8,228.

FINANCIAL AID PICTURE (2008-2009)

Students with need: Out of 1,044 full-time freshmen who applied for aid, 420 were judged to have need. Of these, 378 received aid. Average financial aid package met 34% of need; average scholarship/grant was $3,620; average loan was $3,191. For part-time students, average financial aid package was $5,245.

Students without need: 11 full-time freshmen who did not demonstrate need for aid received scholarships/grants; average award was $1,047. No-need awards available for academics, alumni affiliation, art, athletics, job skills, leadership, minority status, music/drama, religious affiliation, ROTC, state/district residency.

Scholarships offered: *Merit:* Trustee Scholarships: $6,000 per year for four years. Presidential Scholarships: $4,000 per year for four years; both offered to freshman with superior academic accomplishments; include stipends to be used toward study abroad programs. *Athletic:* 35 full-time freshmen received athletic scholarships; average amount $2,699.

Cumulative student debt: 52% of graduating class had student loans; average debt was $14,312.

FINANCIAL AID PROCEDURES

Forms required: FAFSA, institutional form.

Dates and Deadlines: Priority date 3/1; no closing date. Applicants notified on a rolling basis starting 3/1; must reply within 2 week(s) of notification.

Transfers: No deadline. Applicants notified on a rolling basis starting 3/1; must reply within 2 week(s) of notification.

CONTACT

Cathy Crawley, Director of Financial Aid
Campus Box 23, Milledgeville, GA 31061-0490
(478) 445-5149

Georgia Highlands College

Rome, Georgia
www.highlands.edu   Federal Code: 009507

2-year public community and liberal arts college in large city.

Enrollment: 5,237 undergrads, 39% part-time. 1,406 full-time freshmen.

Selectivity: Admits over 75% of applicants.

BASIC COSTS (2009-2010)

Tuition and fees: $2,644; out-of-state residents $9,514.

Per-credit charge: $77; out-of-state residents $306.

FINANCIAL AID PICTURE (2008-2009)

Students with need: 41% of average financial aid package awarded as scholarships/grants, 59% awarded as loans/jobs. Need-based aid available for part-time students. Work study available nights.

Students without need: No-need awards available for academics, art.

FINANCIAL AID PROCEDURES

Forms required: FAFSA.

Dates and Deadlines: Closing date 4/1. Applicants notified on a rolling basis starting 4/1; must reply within 2 week(s) of notification.

CONTACT

Donna Childres, Director of Financial Aid
3175 Cedartown Highway, Rome, GA 30161
(706) 295-6311

Georgia Institute of Technology

Atlanta, Georgia
www.gatech.edu   Federal Code: 001569

4-year public university in very large city.

Enrollment: 12,942 undergrads, 5% part-time. 2,640 full-time freshmen.

Selectivity: Admits 50 to 75% of applicants.

BASIC COSTS (2009-2010)

Tuition and fees: $7,506; out-of-state residents $25,916.

Room and board: $8,204.

FINANCIAL AID PICTURE (2008-2009)

Students with need: Out of 1,974 full-time freshmen who applied for aid, 897 were judged to have need. Of these, 872 received aid, and 388 had their full need met. Average financial aid package met 74% of need; average scholarship/grant was $9,512; average loan was $3,526. For part-time students, average financial aid package was $5,557.

Students without need: 234 full-time freshmen who did not demonstrate need for aid received scholarships/grants; average award was $4,025. No-need awards available for academics, athletics, leadership, music/drama, ROTC, state/district residency.

Scholarships offered: *Merit:* President's Scholarship Program; 4-year awards range from half to full tuition; for freshmen with outstanding academic/leadership qualities. *Athletic:* 50 full-time freshmen received athletic scholarships; average amount $10,430.

Cumulative student debt: 72% of graduating class had student loans; average debt was $13,445.

Additional info: Scholarships, grants, and job opportunities combined to help eliminate student loan debt. Available to Georgia residents whose families have an annual income of less than $33,300 and are pursuing their first undergraduate degree including incoming freshmen, transfer, and currently enrolled students who meet the eligibility requirements.

FINANCIAL AID PROCEDURES

Forms required: FAFSA, institutional form.

Dates and Deadlines: Closing date 3/1. Applicants notified by 4/1; must reply by 5/1.

Transfers: Closing date 5/1. Applicants notified on a rolling basis starting 6/1. Student must be officially admitted, all final transcripts must be received, and transcripts must be articulated.

CONTACT

Marie Mons, Director of Student Financial Planning and Services
Georgia Institute of Technology, Atlanta, GA 30332-0320
(404) 894-4160

Georgia Military College

Milledgeville, Georgia
www.gmc.cc.ga.us   Federal Code: 001571

2-year public community and military college in large town.

Enrollment: 5,854 undergrads, 30% part-time. 2,675 full-time freshmen.

Selectivity: Open admission; but selective for some programs.

BASIC COSTS (2009-2010)

Tuition and fees: $5,513.

Per-credit charge: $105.

Room and board: $5,535.

Additional info: Tuition and fees for cadet students: $12,150 with $1,150 additional for uniforms.

FINANCIAL AID PICTURE (2008-2009)

Students with need: Need-based aid available for full-time and part-time students. Work study available nights.

Students without need: No-need awards available for athletics, leadership, ROTC, state/district residency.

Additional info: Institutional aid offered to those enrolled in Cadet Corps who reside on campus.

FINANCIAL AID PROCEDURES

Forms required: FAFSA, state aid form.

Dates and Deadlines: No deadline. Applicants notified on a rolling basis starting 3/1.

CONTACT

Alisa Stephens, Director of Financial Aid
201 East Greene Street, Milledgeville, GA 31061
(478) 445-0840

Georgia Perimeter College
Clarkston, Georgia
www.gpc.edu   Federal Code: 001562

2-year public junior and liberal arts college in very large city.
Enrollment: 22,814 undergrads, 50% part-time. 3,222 full-time freshmen.
Selectivity: Admits 50 to 75% of applicants.

BASIC COSTS (2009-2010)
Tuition and fees: $2,908; out-of-state residents $9,786.

FINANCIAL AID PICTURE (2009-2010)
Students with need: 59% of average financial aid package awarded as scholarships/grants, 41% awarded as loans/jobs. Need-based aid available for part-time students. Work study available nights, weekends, and for part-time students.

FINANCIAL AID PROCEDURES
Forms required: FAFSA.
Dates and Deadlines: Closing date 6/1. Applicants notified on a rolling basis; must reply within 3 week(s) of notification.
Transfers: Priority date 6/1; no deadline.

CONTACT
Sheletha Champion, Director, Student Financial Services
555 North Indian Creek Drive, Clarkston, GA 30021-2361
(678) 891-3400

Georgia Southern University
Statesboro, Georgia
www.georgiasouthern.edu   Federal Code: 001572

4-year public university in large town.
Enrollment: 15,626 undergrads, 6% part-time. 3,109 full-time freshmen.
Selectivity: Admits 50 to 75% of applicants. GED not accepted.

BASIC COSTS (2009-2010)
Tuition and fees: $5,440; out-of-state residents $17,416.
Room and board: $7,900.

FINANCIAL AID PICTURE (2008-2009)
Students with need: Out of 2,842 full-time freshmen who applied for aid, 1,640 were judged to have need. Of these, 1,601 received aid, and 268 had their full need met. Average financial aid package met 60% of need; average scholarship/grant was $6,145; average loan was $3,287. For part-time students, average financial aid package was $5,476.
Students without need: 154 full-time freshmen who did not demonstrate need for aid received scholarships/grants; average award was $2,049. No-need awards available for academics, alumni affiliation, art, athletics, leadership, minority status, music/drama, ROTC, state/district residency.
Scholarships offered: *Merit:* 1906 Scholars: tuition for 4 years; 18 awards annually. UHP Scholarships: $1,500 for 4 years; 30 awards annually. Foundation Scholars: $1,500 for 4 years; 4 awards annually. *Athletic:* 36 full-time freshmen received athletic scholarships; average amount $6,458.
Cumulative student debt: 65% of graduating class had student loans; average debt was $18,618.
Additional info: Majority of available scholarships are need-blind.

FINANCIAL AID PROCEDURES
Forms required: FAFSA.

Dates and Deadlines: Priority date 4/20; no closing date. Applicants notified on a rolling basis starting 4/20.
Transfers: No deadline. Applicants notified on a rolling basis starting 4/20.

CONTACT
Connie Murphey, Director of Financial Aid
PO Box 8024, Statesboro, GA 30460
(912) 478-5413

Georgia Southwestern State University
Americus, Georgia
www.gsw.edu   Federal Code: 001573

4-year public university and liberal arts college in large town.
Enrollment: 2,594 undergrads, 26% part-time. 435 full-time freshmen.
Selectivity: Admits 50 to 75% of applicants.

BASIC COSTS (2009-2010)
Tuition and fees: $4,762; out-of-state residents $16,376.
Per-credit charge: $130; out-of-state residents $517.
Room and board: $5,950.

FINANCIAL AID PICTURE (2008-2009)
Students with need: Need-based aid available for full-time and part-time students.
Students without need: No-need awards available for academics, athletics, leadership.
Scholarships offered: Wheatley Scholarship: $2,000-2,500; 3.0 in college preparatory course and either 1100 SAT (exclusive of Writing) or 24 ACT.

FINANCIAL AID PROCEDURES
Forms required: FAFSA, institutional form.
Dates and Deadlines: Priority date 4/1; closing date 6/1. Applicants notified on a rolling basis starting 3/1.

CONTACT
Angela Bryant, Director of Financial Aid
800 Georgia Southwestern State University Drive, Americus, GA 31709-9957
(229) 928-1378

Georgia State University
Atlanta, Georgia
www.gsu.edu   Federal Code: 001574

4-year public university in very large city.
Enrollment: 21,727 undergrads, 22% part-time. 2,588 full-time freshmen.
Selectivity: Admits less than 50% of applicants.

BASIC COSTS (2009-2010)
Tuition and fees: $7,298; out-of-state residents $25,508.
Room only: $7,740.
Additional info: Tuition at time of enrollment locked for 4 years.

FINANCIAL AID PICTURE (2008-2009)
Students with need: Out of 2,541 full-time freshmen who applied for aid, 2,412 were judged to have need. Of these, 2,412 received aid, and 412 had their full need met. Average financial aid package met 27% of need; average scholarship/grant was $2,684; average loan was $2,438. For part-time students, average financial aid package was $9,841.
Students without need: 659 full-time freshmen who did not demonstrate need for aid received scholarships/grants; average award was $3,263. No-need awards available for academics.
Scholarships offered: 38 full-time freshmen received athletic scholarships; average amount $12,389.
Cumulative student debt: 54% of graduating class had student loans; average debt was $15,950.

FINANCIAL AID PROCEDURES

Forms required: FAFSA, institutional form.

Dates and Deadlines: Priority date 4/1; closing date 11/1. Must reply by 4/1 or within 2 week(s) of notification.

Transfers: Closing date 4/1. Applicants notified by 3/1; must reply by 4/1 or within 2 week(s) of notification.

CONTACT

Louis Scott, Director of Student Financial Aid
Box 4009, Atlanta, GA 30302-4009
(404) 413-2400

Gordon College
Barnesville, Georgia
www.gdn.edu   Federal Code: 001575

2-year public junior and teachers college in small town.

Enrollment: 4,545 undergrads.

Selectivity: Admits 50 to 75% of applicants.

BASIC COSTS (2009-2010)

Tuition and fees: $2,962; out-of-state residents $10,444.

Per-credit charge: $84; out-of-state residents $333.

Room and board: $4,940.

FINANCIAL AID PICTURE (2008-2009)

Students with need: Need-based aid available for full-time and part-time students. Work study available nights, weekends, and for part-time students.

Students without need: No-need awards available for academics, athletics, music/drama, state/district residency.

FINANCIAL AID PROCEDURES

Forms required: FAFSA, institutional form.

Dates and Deadlines: Priority date 5/1; no closing date. Applicants notified on a rolling basis starting 5/1.

CONTACT

Larry Mitcham, Director of Financial Aid
419 College Drive, Barnesville, GA 30204
(678) 359-5990

Gupton Jones College of Funeral Service
Decatur, Georgia
www.gupton-jones.edu   Federal Code: 010771

2-year private technical college in very large city.

Enrollment: 172 undergrads. 120 full-time freshmen.

Selectivity: Open admission.

BASIC COSTS (2009-2010)

Tuition and fees: $9,000.

Per-credit charge: $200.

Additional info: Tuition costs include all textbooks and supplies needed.

FINANCIAL AID PICTURE

Students with need: Need-based aid available for full-time and part-time students.

Students without need: This college awards aid only to students with need.

FINANCIAL AID PROCEDURES

Forms required: FAFSA.

Dates and Deadlines: No deadline. Applicants notified on a rolling basis.

CONTACT

James Hinz, Dean
5141 Snapfinger Woods Drive, Decatur, GA 30035
(770) 593-2257

Gwinnett College
Lilburn, Georgia
www.gwinnettcollege.edu   Federal Code: 025830

2-year for-profit junior and career college in large city.

Enrollment: 275 undergrads.

Selectivity: Open admission; but selective for some programs.

BASIC COSTS (2010-2011)

Tuition and fees: $9,325.

FINANCIAL AID PICTURE (2009-2010)

Students with need: Need-based aid available for full-time and part-time students.

FINANCIAL AID PROCEDURES

Forms required: FAFSA.

CONTACT

James Davidson, Director of Financial Aid
4230 Highway 29, Lilburn, GA 30047
(770) 381-7200

Gwinnett Technical College
Lawrenceville, Georgia
www.gwinnetttech.edu   Federal Code: 016139

2-year public technical college in large town.

Enrollment: 6,392 undergrads, 53% part-time. 678 full-time freshmen.

Selectivity: Open admission; but selective for some programs.

BASIC COSTS (2009-2010)

Tuition and fees: $2,109; out-of-state residents $3,909.

Per-credit charge: $40; out-of-state residents $80.

FINANCIAL AID PICTURE (2009-2010)

Students with need: Need-based aid available for full-time and part-time students.

FINANCIAL AID PROCEDURES

Forms required: FAFSA.

Dates and Deadlines: Closing date 7/1.

Transfers: Priority date 7/1; no deadline.

CONTACT

Stephen Whitaker, Director of Financial Aid
5150 Sugarloaf Parkway, Lawrenceville, GA 30243
(770) 962-7580 ext. 6637

Herzing University
Atlanta, Georgia
www.herzing.edu   Federal Code: 014030

3-year for-profit business and technical college in very large city.

Enrollment: 609 undergrads.

Selectivity: Open admission; but selective for some programs.

BASIC COSTS (2009-2010)

Additional info: Costs may vary by program.

FINANCIAL AID PICTURE

Students with need: Need-based aid available for full-time and part-time students. Work study available nights.
Students without need: No-need awards available for academics.

FINANCIAL AID PROCEDURES

Forms required: FAFSA, institutional form.
Dates and Deadlines: No deadline. Applicants notified on a rolling basis.

CONTACT

Stephanie Gunby, Director of Financial Services
3393 Peachtree Road NE, Suite 1003, Atlanta, GA 30326
(404) 816-4533

Kennesaw State University
Kennesaw, Georgia
www.kennesaw.edu   Federal Code: 001577

4-year public university in large town.
Enrollment: 20,237 undergrads, 23% part-time. 2,650 full-time freshmen.
Selectivity: Admits 50 to 75% of applicants. GED not accepted.

BASIC COSTS (2009-2010)

Tuition and fees: $5,142; out-of-state residents $17,118.
Room only: $5,100.

FINANCIAL AID PICTURE (2009-2010)

Students with need: Need-based aid available for full-time and part-time students. Work study available nights.
Students without need: No-need awards available for academics, alumni affiliation, art, athletics, job skills, leadership, minority status, music/drama, ROTC, state/district residency.

FINANCIAL AID PROCEDURES

Forms required: FAFSA.
Dates and Deadlines: Priority date 4/1; closing date 7/1. Applicants notified on a rolling basis starting 5/15.
Transfers: No deadline. Applicants notified on a rolling basis starting 5/15.

CONTACT

Ron Day, Director of Financial Aid
1000 Chastain Road, Kennesaw, GA 30144-5591
(770) 423-6074

LaGrange College
LaGrange, Georgia
www.lagrange.edu   Federal Code: 001578

4-year private liberal arts college in large town, affiliated with United Methodist Church.
Enrollment: 860 undergrads, 10% part-time. 155 full-time freshmen.
Selectivity: Admits 50 to 75% of applicants.

BASIC COSTS (2009-2010)

Tuition and fees: $21,094.
Per-credit charge: $869.
Room and board: $8,576.

FINANCIAL AID PICTURE (2008-2009)

Students with need: Out of 140 full-time freshmen who applied for aid, 116 were judged to have need. Of these, 116 received aid, and 36 had their full need met. Average financial aid package met 82% of need; average scholarship/grant was $12,175; average loan was $3,536. For part-time students, average financial aid package was $6,580.
Students without need: 35 full-time freshmen who did not demonstrate need for aid received scholarships/grants; average award was $10,853. No-

need awards available for academics, art, leadership, music/drama, religious affiliation, state/district residency.
Scholarships offered: Presidential: tuition, room and board. Fellows: $12,000 per year. Deans: $10,000 per year. Founders: $8,000 per year. Lafayette: $ 6,000 per year. Quadrangle: $ 4,500 per year. All competitive.
Cumulative student debt: 75% of graduating class had student loans; average debt was $23,106.

FINANCIAL AID PROCEDURES

Forms required: FAFSA, state aid form.
Dates and Deadlines: Priority date 3/1; no closing date. Applicants notified on a rolling basis starting 3/15; must reply by 8/15 or within 2 week(s) of notification.
Transfers: No deadline. Applicants notified on a rolling basis; must reply within 2 week(s) of notification.

CONTACT

Sylvia Smith, Director of Financial Aid
601 Broad Street, LaGrange, GA 30240-2999
(706) 880-8241

Life University
Marietta, Georgia
www.life.edu   Federal Code: 014170

4-year private university in very large city.
Enrollment: 726 undergrads, 27% part-time. 208 full-time freshmen.
Selectivity: Admits over 75% of applicants.

BASIC COSTS (2009-2010)

Tuition and fees: $8,352.
Per-credit charge: $169.

FINANCIAL AID PICTURE (2009-2010)

Students with need: Out of 112 full-time freshmen who applied for aid, 99 were judged to have need. Of these, 94 received aid. For part-time students, average financial aid package was $7,350.
Students without need: No-need awards available for academics.
Scholarships offered: 20 full-time freshmen received athletic scholarships; average amount $6,200.
Cumulative student debt: 60% of graduating class had student loans; average debt was $17,600.

FINANCIAL AID PROCEDURES

Forms required: FAFSA.
Dates and Deadlines: No deadline. Applicants notified on a rolling basis starting 5/1.

CONTACT

Michelle Nixon, Director of Financial Aid
1269 Barclay Circle, Marietta, GA 30060
(770) 426-2901

Macon State College
Macon, Georgia
www.maconstate.edu   Federal Code: 007728

4-year public College of Information Technology in small city.
Enrollment: 6,537 undergrads.
Selectivity: Open admission.

BASIC COSTS (2009-2010)

Tuition and fees: $2,782; out-of-state residents $10,264.

FINANCIAL AID PICTURE (2008-2009)

Students with need: Need-based aid available for full-time and part-time students. Work study available nights, weekends, and for part-time students.

Students without need: This college awards aid only to students with need.

FINANCIAL AID PROCEDURES
Forms required: FAFSA.
Dates and Deadlines: Priority date 4/1; no closing date. Applicants notified on a rolling basis starting 4/15; must reply within 2 week(s) of notification.

CONTACT
Pat Simmons, Director of Financial Aid
100 College Station Drive, Macon, GA 31206-5145
(478) 803-1200

Medical College of Georgia
Augusta, Georgia
www.mcg.edu   Federal Code: 001579

Upper-division public health science college in large city.
Enrollment: 533 undergrads, 6% part-time.

BASIC COSTS (2009-2010)
Tuition and fees: $6,782; out-of-state residents $24,992.
Room only: $1,912.
Additional info: Declining balance account available for meals.

FINANCIAL AID PICTURE (2009-2010)
Students with need: Need-based aid available for full-time and part-time students. Work study available nights, weekends, and for part-time students.
Students without need: No-need awards available for academics, state/district residency.
Additional info: State Hope scholarships only available to Georgia residents.

FINANCIAL AID PROCEDURES
Forms required: FAFSA, state aid form, institutional form.
Dates and Deadlines: No deadline. Applicants notified on a rolling basis; must reply within 2 week(s) of notification.
Transfers: Priority date 3/31; closing date 5/30. Applicants notified on a rolling basis; must reply within 2 week(s) of notification.

CONTACT
Beverly Boggs, Executive Director, Academic Admissions and Student Financial Aid
Office of Academic Admissions, Room 170 Kelly Building, Augusta, GA 30912-7310
(706) 721-4901

Mercer University
Macon, Georgia
www.mercer.edu   Federal Code: 001580

4-year private university in small city, affiliated with Baptist faith.
Enrollment: 2,295 undergrads, 2% part-time. 616 full-time freshmen.
Selectivity: Admits 50 to 75% of applicants. GED not accepted.

BASIC COSTS (2009-2010)
Tuition and fees: $29,540.
Per-credit charge: $978.
Room and board: $8,788.

FINANCIAL AID PICTURE (2009-2010)
Students with need: Out of 542 full-time freshmen who applied for aid, 475 were judged to have need. Of these, 474 received aid, and 247 had their full need met. Average financial aid package met 88% of need; average scholarship/grant was $21,619; average loan was $6,956. For part-time students, average financial aid package was $12,218.
Students without need: 140 full-time freshmen who did not demonstrate need for aid received scholarships/grants; average award was $21,673. No-

need awards available for academics, art, athletics, job skills, leadership, music/drama, religious affiliation, ROTC, state/district residency.
Scholarships offered: *Merit:* Various scholarships: primarily based on high school GPA, SAT/ACT scores, and personal interview (for some); early applications given highest consideration. National Merit finalists and semi-finalists guaranteed full-tuition scholarships. *Athletic:* 33 full-time freshmen received athletic scholarships; average amount $12,787.
Cumulative student debt: 58% of graduating class had student loans; average debt was $29,065.

FINANCIAL AID PROCEDURES
Forms required: FAFSA, state aid form, institutional form.
Dates and Deadlines: Priority date 4/1; no closing date. Applicants notified on a rolling basis starting 3/15; must reply within 2 week(s) of notification.
Transfers: No deadline. Applicants notified on a rolling basis starting 3/15; must reply within 2 week(s) of notification.

CONTACT
Carol Williams, Associate Vice President, Student Financial Planning
1400 Coleman Avenue, Macon, GA 31207-0001
(478) 301-2670

Middle Georgia College
Cochran, Georgia
www.mgc.edu   Federal Code: 001581

2-year public junior college in small town.
Enrollment: 3,498 undergrads.
Selectivity: Admits over 75% of applicants.

BASIC COSTS (2009-2010)
Tuition and fees: $2,968; out-of-state residents $10,450.
Room and board: $6,060.

FINANCIAL AID PICTURE (2008-2009)
Students with need: Need-based aid available for full-time and part-time students. Work study available nights, weekends, and for part-time students.
Students without need: No-need awards available for academics, alumni affiliation, art, athletics, job skills, leadership, minority status, music/drama, state/district residency.

FINANCIAL AID PROCEDURES
Forms required: FAFSA.
Dates and Deadlines: Priority date 4/1; no closing date. Applicants notified on a rolling basis starting 5/1.

CONTACT
Jon Finkelstein, Director of Financial Aid
1100 Second Street SE, Cochran, GA 31014
(478) 934-3133

Morehouse College
Atlanta, Georgia   Federal Code: 001582
www.morehouse.edu   CSS Code: 5415

4-year private liberal arts college for men in very large city.
Enrollment: 2,673 undergrads, 6% part-time. 700 full-time freshmen.
Selectivity: Admits 50 to 75% of applicants.

BASIC COSTS (2010-2011)
Tuition and fees: $22,444.
Per-credit charge: $850.
Room and board: $11,494.

FINANCIAL AID PICTURE (2008-2009)

Students with need: Out of 685 full-time freshmen who applied for aid, 653 were judged to have need. Of these, 653 received aid, and 38 had their full need met. Average financial aid package met 25% of need; average scholarship/grant was $9,250; average loan was $3,500. Need-based aid available for part-time students.

Students without need: No-need awards available for academics, alumni affiliation, art, athletics, leadership, music/drama, ROTC, state/district residency.

Cumulative student debt: 90% of graduating class had student loans; average debt was $32,125.

FINANCIAL AID PROCEDURES

Forms required: FAFSA, CSS PROFILE, state aid form, institutional form.

Dates and Deadlines: Priority date 2/15; closing date 4/1. Must reply by 5/1 or within 4 week(s) of notification.

Transfers: Applicants notified by 4/1; must reply by 5/1.

CONTACT

James Stotts, Director of Financial Aid

830 Westview Drive SW, Atlanta, GA 30314

(404) 215-2638

North Georgia College & State University

Dahlonega, Georgia

www.northgeorgia.edu   Federal Code: 001585

4-year public university and military college in small town.

Enrollment: 5,014 undergrads, 18% part-time. 814 full-time freshmen.

Selectivity: Admits 50 to 75% of applicants.

BASIC COSTS (2009-2010)

Tuition and fees: $5,036; out-of-state residents $16,650.

Per-credit charge: $130; out-of-state residents $517.

Room and board: $5,544.

FINANCIAL AID PICTURE (2008-2009)

Students with need: Need-based aid available for full-time and part-time students.

Students without need: No-need awards available for academics, alumni affiliation, art, athletics, job skills, leadership, minority status, music/drama, religious affiliation, ROTC, state/district residency.

FINANCIAL AID PROCEDURES

Forms required: FAFSA, state aid form.

Dates and Deadlines: Priority date 3/17; no closing date. Applicants notified on a rolling basis starting 3/1; must reply within 3 week(s) of notification.

CONTACT

Jill Rayner, Director of Financial Aid

82 College Circle, Dahlonega, GA 30597

(706) 864-1412

North Georgia Technical College

Clarkesville, Georgia

www.northgatech.edu   Federal Code: 005619

2-year public community and technical college in large town.

Enrollment: 2,777 undergrads, 36% part-time. 635 full-time freshmen.

Selectivity: Open admission; but selective for some programs.

BASIC COSTS (2009-2010)

Tuition and fees: $2,070; out-of-state residents $3,870.

Per-credit charge: $40; out-of-state residents $80.

Additional info: Higher per-credit-hour charges for some programs. Cost of complete CDL program: $2784;. Tuition/fee waivers available for unemployed or children of unemployed.

FINANCIAL AID PICTURE

Students with need: Need-based aid available for full-time and part-time students. Work study available nights, weekends, and for part-time students.

CONTACT

Kim Kelley, Director of Financial Aid

1500 Highway 197 North, Clarkesville, GA 30523

Oglethorpe University

Atlanta, Georgia

www.oglethorpe.edu   Federal Code: 001586

4-year private liberal arts college in very large city.

Enrollment: 974 undergrads, 9% part-time. 232 full-time freshmen.

Selectivity: Admits less than 50% of applicants.

BASIC COSTS (2010-2011)

Tuition and fees: $27,950.

Room and board: $9,990.

FINANCIAL AID PICTURE (2009-2010)

Students with need: Need-based aid available for full-time students.

Students without need: No-need awards available for academics, music/drama.

FINANCIAL AID PROCEDURES

Forms required: FAFSA, institutional form.

Dates and Deadlines: Priority date 2/1; no closing date. Applicants notified on a rolling basis starting 3/1; must reply by 5/1 or within 3 week(s) of notification.

Transfers: No deadline.

CONTACT

Meg McGinness, Director of Financial Aid

4484 Peachtree Road NE, Atlanta, GA 30319-2797

(404) 304-8350

Oxford College of Emory University

Oxford, Georgia   Federal Code: 001565

www.oxford.emory.edu   CSS Code: 5186

2-year private branch campus and liberal arts college in large town, affiliated with United Methodist Church.

Enrollment: 756 undergrads. 432 full-time freshmen.

Selectivity: Admits 50 to 75% of applicants. GED not accepted.

BASIC COSTS (2010-2011)

Tuition and fees: $33,262.

Room and board: $9,472.

FINANCIAL AID PICTURE (2008-2009)

Students with need: Out of 285 full-time freshmen who applied for aid, 232 were judged to have need. Of these, 232 received aid. Average financial aid package met 100% of need; average scholarship/grant was $19,385; average loan was $3,500. Need-based aid available for part-time students.

Students without need: 31 full-time freshmen who did not demonstrate need for aid received scholarships/grants; average award was $19,289. No-need awards available for academics, leadership, religious affiliation, state/district residency.

Scholarships offered: Woodruff Scholarships; full tuition, room and board for 4 years. Dean's Scholarship; full tuition for 4 years. Faculty Scholarships; half tuition for 4 years. 2-year scholarships; range from $8,000-$10,000 a year.

Cumulative student debt: 41% of graduating class had student loans; average debt was $11,382.
Additional info: Deadline of November 1 to apply for Oxford College Scholars Program.

FINANCIAL AID PROCEDURES
Forms required: FAFSA, CSS PROFILE, state aid form.
Dates and Deadlines: Priority date 2/15; closing date 3/1. Applicants notified by 4/1; must reply by 5/1 or within 2 week(s) of notification.

CONTACT
Jennifer Taylor, Dean of Enrollment Services
100 Hamill Street, Oxford, GA 30054-1418
(770) 784-8303

Paine College
Augusta, Georgia
www.paine.edu
Federal Code: 001587

4-year private liberal arts college in large city, affiliated with Christian Methodist Episcopal Church and United Methodist Church.
Enrollment: 901 undergrads, 5% part-time. 280 full-time freshmen.
Selectivity: Admits less than 50% of applicants.

BASIC COSTS (2009-2010)
Tuition and fees: $11,794.
Per-credit charge: $454.
Room and board: $5,748.

FINANCIAL AID PICTURE (2009-2010)
Students with need: Out of 277 full-time freshmen who applied for aid, 264 were judged to have need. Of these, 262 received aid, and 12 had their full need met. Average financial aid package met 54% of need; average scholarship/grant was $7,054; average loan was $3,342. For part-time students, average financial aid package was $5,637.
Students without need: 3 full-time freshmen who did not demonstrate need for aid received scholarships/grants; average award was $2,000. No-need awards available for academics, alumni affiliation, athletics, music/drama, religious affiliation, ROTC.
Scholarships offered: 6 full-time freshmen received athletic scholarships; average amount $6,343.
Cumulative student debt: 97% of graduating class had student loans; average debt was $27,121.

FINANCIAL AID PROCEDURES
Forms required: FAFSA, state aid form.
Dates and Deadlines: Priority date 3/1; no closing date. Applicants notified on a rolling basis starting 5/1; must reply within 2 week(s) of notification.

CONTACT
Gerri Bogan, Director of Financial Aid
1235 15th Street, Augusta, GA 30901-3182
(706) 821-8262

Piedmont College
Demorest, Georgia
www.piedmont.edu
Federal Code: 001588

4-year private liberal arts and teachers college in rural community, affiliated with United Church of Christ.
Enrollment: 1,232 undergrads, 9% part-time. 235 full-time freshmen.
Selectivity: Admits 50 to 75% of applicants.

BASIC COSTS (2010-2011)
Tuition and fees: $18,000.
Per-credit charge: $750.

Room and board: $6,000.
Additional info: Tuition/fee waivers available for adults.

FINANCIAL AID PICTURE (2009-2010)
Students with need: Out of 183 full-time freshmen who applied for aid, 151 were judged to have need. Of these, 143 received aid, and 51 had their full need met. Average financial aid package met 62% of need; average scholarship/grant was $1,024; average loan was $3,546. For part-time students, average financial aid package was $6,140.
Students without need: 61 full-time freshmen who did not demonstrate need for aid received scholarships/grants; average award was $9,040. No-need awards available for academics, art, leadership, music/drama, religious affiliation, state/district residency.
Scholarships offered: Highest academic scholarships awarded to high school seniors superior in academics, leadership, and extracurricular activities.
Cumulative student debt: 71% of graduating class had student loans; average debt was $16,986.
Additional info: College meets 100% of unmet direct financial need for early applicants through grants, scholarships, and loan programs.

FINANCIAL AID PROCEDURES
Forms required: FAFSA, state aid form, institutional form.
Dates and Deadlines: Priority date 5/1; no closing date. Applicants notified on a rolling basis; must reply within 2 week(s) of notification.
Transfers: Priority date 4/1. Must reply within 2 week(s) of notification.

CONTACT
Kimberly Lovell, Director of Financial Aid
165 Central Avenue, Demorest, GA 30535-0010
(706) 776-0114 ext. 1191

Reinhardt College
Waleska, Georgia
www.reinhardt.edu
Federal Code: 001589

4-year private business and teachers college in rural community, affiliated with United Methodist Church.
Enrollment: 1,026 undergrads, 7% part-time. 246 full-time freshmen.
Selectivity: Admits 50 to 75% of applicants.

BASIC COSTS (2009-2010)
Tuition and fees: $16,670.
Per-credit charge: $550.
Room and board: $6,496.

FINANCIAL AID PICTURE (2008-2009)
Students with need: Out of 196 full-time freshmen who applied for aid, 157 were judged to have need. Of these, 157 received aid, and 28 had their full need met. Average financial aid package met 58% of need; average scholarship/grant was $9,375; average loan was $2,782. For part-time students, average financial aid package was $7,463.
Students without need: 79 full-time freshmen who did not demonstrate need for aid received scholarships/grants; average award was $4,624. No-need awards available for academics, art, athletics, leadership, music/drama, religious affiliation, state/district residency.
Scholarships offered: 23 full-time freshmen received athletic scholarships; average amount $2,618.
Cumulative student debt: 94% of graduating class had student loans; average debt was $6,942.

FINANCIAL AID PROCEDURES
Forms required: FAFSA, state aid form.
Dates and Deadlines: Priority date 5/1; no closing date. Applicants notified on a rolling basis starting 2/1; must reply within 2 week(s) of notification.
Transfers: No deadline.

CONTACT

Robert Gregory, Director of Financial Aid
7300 Reinhardt College Circle, Waleska, GA 30183-2981
(770) 720-5667

Savannah College of Art and Design

Savannah, Georgia
www.scad.edu   Federal Code: 015022

4-year private visual arts and performing arts college in small city.
Enrollment: 8,056 undergrads, 11% part-time. 1,628 full-time freshmen.
Selectivity: Admits 50 to 75% of applicants.

BASIC COSTS (2010-2011)

Tuition and fees: $29,570.
Per-credit charge: $646.
Room and board: $11,750.

FINANCIAL AID PICTURE (2009-2010)

Students with need: Need-based aid available for full-time and part-time students. Work study available nights, weekends, and for part-time students.
Students without need: No-need awards available for academics, art, athletics, music/drama.
Additional info: Degree-seeking students may be awarded maximum of one scholarship from college, but may receive additional scholarships from other sources, as well as additional forms of financial aid. Scholarships based on academic achievement are awarded through admission office.

FINANCIAL AID PROCEDURES

Forms required: FAFSA, state aid form, institutional form.
Dates and Deadlines: Priority date 2/15; no closing date. Applicants notified on a rolling basis starting 6/1.
Transfers: Priority date 4/1; no deadline. Applicants notified on a rolling basis. Transfer students eligible to apply for academic and portfolio scholarships.

CONTACT

Brenda Clark, Director of Financial Aid
PO Box 2072, Savannah, GA 31402-2072
(912) 525-5000

Savannah Technical College

Savannah, Georgia
www.savannahtech.edu   Federal Code: 005618

2-year public technical college in large city.
Enrollment: 4,902 undergrads, 53% part-time. 653 full-time freshmen.
Selectivity: Open admission; but selective for some programs.

BASIC COSTS (2009-2010)

Tuition and fees: $2,043; out-of-state residents $3,843.
Per-credit charge: $40; out-of-state residents $80.

FINANCIAL AID PICTURE (2008-2009)

Students with need: Need-based aid available for part-time students.
Students without need: No-need awards available for academics, leadership, minority status, state/district residency.

FINANCIAL AID PROCEDURES

Forms required: FAFSA.
Dates and Deadlines: No deadline. Applicants notified on a rolling basis.

CONTACT

Timothy Cranford, Financial Aid Director
5717 White Bluff Road, Savannah, GA 31401-5521
(912) 443-5705

Shorter College

Rome, Georgia
www.shorter.edu   Federal Code: 001591

4-year private liberal arts college in large town, affiliated with Southern Baptist Convention.
Enrollment: 1,194 undergrads, 3% part-time. 333 full-time freshmen.
Selectivity: Admits 50 to 75% of applicants.

BASIC COSTS (2010-2011)

Tuition and fees: $17,070.
Per-credit charge: $460.
Room and board: $8,200.

FINANCIAL AID PICTURE (2009-2010)

Students with need: Out of 304 full-time freshmen who applied for aid, 260 were judged to have need. Of these, 260 received aid, and 67 had their full need met. Average financial aid package met 75% of need; average scholarship/grant was $12,687; average loan was $3,058. For part-time students, average financial aid package was $6,400.
Students without need: 54 full-time freshmen who did not demonstrate need for aid received scholarships/grants; average award was $5,800. No-need awards available for academics, art, athletics, music/drama, religious affiliation.
Scholarships offered: 39 full-time freshmen received athletic scholarships; average amount $11,092.
Additional info: Cost is reduced for all in-state students by state tuition equalization grant program. College matches for out-of-state full-time students.

FINANCIAL AID PROCEDURES

Forms required: FAFSA, state aid form, institutional form.
Dates and Deadlines: Priority date 4/1; no closing date. Applicants notified on a rolling basis starting 4/1; must reply within 2 week(s) of notification.
Transfers: Priority date 4/15; no deadline. Applicants notified on a rolling basis starting 3/31; must reply within 2 week(s) of notification.

CONTACT

Tara Jones, Director of Financial Aid
315 Shorter Avenue, Rome, GA 30165
(706) 233-7227

South Georgia College

Douglas, Georgia
www.sgc.edu   Federal Code: 001592

2-year public community and junior college in large town.
Enrollment: 2,000 undergrads, 26% part-time. 718 full-time freshmen.

BASIC COSTS (2009-2010)

Tuition and fees: $2,958; out-of-state residents $9,836.
Per-credit charge: $77; out-of-state residents $306.
Room and board: $7,670.

FINANCIAL AID PICTURE

Students with need: Need-based aid available for full-time and part-time students.
Students without need: No-need awards available for academics.

FINANCIAL AID PROCEDURES

Forms required: FAFSA, institutional form.
Dates and Deadlines: Priority date 4/1; no closing date. Applicants notified on a rolling basis starting 7/6; must reply within 2 week(s) of notification.

CONTACT
Wes Brown, Director of Financial Aid
100 West College Park Drive, Douglas, GA 31533-5098
(912) 260-4282

South University: Savannah
Savannah, Georgia
www.southuniversity.edu   Federal Code: 013039

4-year for-profit university in small city.
Enrollment: 804 undergrads, 32% part-time. 97 full-time freshmen.

BASIC COSTS (2009-2010)
Tuition and fees: $14,985.
Additional info: Additional cost for nursing program.

FINANCIAL AID PICTURE
Students with need: Need-based aid available for full-time students.

FINANCIAL AID PROCEDURES
Forms required: FAFSA, state aid form.
Dates and Deadlines: No deadline. Applicants notified on a rolling basis starting 9/1.

CONTACT
Tressa Brush, Director of Financial Aid
709 Mall Boulevard, Savannah, GA 31406
(912) 201-8000

Southeastern Technical College
Vidalia, Georgia
www.southeasterntech.edu   Federal Code: 030665

2-year public technical college in large town.
Enrollment: 1,757 undergrads, 49% part-time. 538 full-time freshmen.
Selectivity: Open admission; but selective for some programs.

BASIC COSTS (2009-2010)
Tuition and fees: $2,043; out-of-state residents $3,843.
Per-credit charge: $40; out-of-state residents $80.

FINANCIAL AID PICTURE (2008-2009)
Students with need: Need-based aid available for full-time and part-time students. Work study available nights.
Students without need: No-need awards available for state/district residency.

FINANCIAL AID PROCEDURES
Forms required: FAFSA, state aid form, institutional form.
Dates and Deadlines: No deadline. Applicants notified on a rolling basis starting 4/6.

CONTACT
Mitchell Fagler, Executive Director of Student Affairs/Financial Aid
3001 East First Street, Vidalia, GA 30474
(478) 289-2268

Southern Polytechnic State University
Marietta, Georgia
www.spsu.edu   Federal Code: 001570

4-year public university and engineering college in small city.
Enrollment: 4,450 undergrads, 26% part-time. 583 full-time freshmen.
Selectivity: Admits 50 to 75% of applicants. GED not accepted.

BASIC COSTS (2009-2010)
Tuition and fees: $5,374; out-of-state residents $18,494.
Per-credit charge: $146; out-of-state residents $584.
Room and board: $5,950.

FINANCIAL AID PICTURE (2008-2009)
Students with need: Out of 469 full-time freshmen who applied for aid, 469 were judged to have need. Of these, 460 received aid, and 170 had their full need met. Average financial aid package met 76% of need; average scholarship/grant was $2,893; average loan was $3,095. For part-time students, average financial aid package was $2,742.
Students without need: 3 full-time freshmen who did not demonstrate need for aid received scholarships/grants; average award was $8,855. No-need awards available for academics, athletics, minority status.
Scholarships offered: 7 full-time freshmen received athletic scholarships; average amount $2,672.
Cumulative student debt: 43% of graduating class had student loans; average debt was $13,567.

FINANCIAL AID PROCEDURES
Forms required: FAFSA.
Dates and Deadlines: Priority date 3/1; no closing date. Applicants notified on a rolling basis starting 4/1.
Transfers: No deadline. Applicants notified on a rolling basis starting 5/1.

CONTACT
Gary Bush, Director of Financial Aid
1100 South Marietta Parkway, Marietta, GA 30060-2896
(678) 915-7290

Southwest Georgia Technical College
Thomasville, Georgia
www.southwestgatech.edu   Federal Code: 005615

2-year public technical college in large town.
Enrollment: 1,522 undergrads, 55% part-time. 161 full-time freshmen.
Selectivity: Open admission; but selective for some programs.

BASIC COSTS (2009-2010)
Tuition and fees: $2,043; out-of-state residents $3,843.
Per-credit charge: $40; out-of-state residents $80.
Additional info: Truck driving and flight technology are higher cost programs.

FINANCIAL AID PICTURE (2008-2009)
Students with need: Need-based aid available for full-time and part-time students. Work study available nights.
Students without need: No-need awards available for state/district residency.
Scholarships offered: Hope Scholarship; full tuition; available to GA residents with 3.0 minimum GPA.

FINANCIAL AID PROCEDURES
Forms required: FAFSA, institutional form.
Dates and Deadlines: No deadline. Applicants notified on a rolling basis starting 7/1.

CONTACT
Michael Rayburn, Director of Financial Aid
15689 US Highway 19N, Thomasville, GA 31792
(229) 227-2687

Spelman College
Atlanta, Georgia
www.spelman.edu   Federal Code: 001594

4-year private liberal arts college for women in very large city.
Enrollment: 2,229 undergrads, 5% part-time. 540 full-time freshmen.
Selectivity: Admits less than 50% of applicants.

BASIC COSTS (2010-2011)
Tuition and fees: $22,010.
Room and board: $10,464.

FINANCIAL AID PICTURE (2008-2009)
Students with need: Out of 510 full-time freshmen who applied for aid, 431 were judged to have need. Of these, 429 received aid, and 155 had their full need met. Average financial aid package met 42% of need; average scholarship/grant was $12,107; average loan was $3,545. For part-time students, average financial aid package was $9,624.
Students without need: 1 full-time freshmen who did not demonstrate need for aid received scholarships/grants; average award was $200. No-need awards available for academics, alumni affiliation, leadership, music/drama, state/district residency.

FINANCIAL AID PROCEDURES
Forms required: FAFSA, institutional form.
Dates and Deadlines: Priority date 3/1; no closing date. Applicants notified on a rolling basis starting 2/15; must reply within 2 week(s) of notification.
Transfers: Closing date 10/1. No special aid for transfer students for the first year.

CONTACT
Lenora Jackson, Director of Student Financial Services
350 Spelman Lane SW, Campus Box 277, Atlanta, GA 30314
(404) 270-5212

Toccoa Falls College
Toccoa Falls, Georgia
www.tfc.edu   Federal Code: 001596

4-year private Bible and liberal arts college in large town, affiliated with Christian and Missionary Alliance.
Enrollment: 797 undergrads, 4% part-time. 167 full-time freshmen.
Selectivity: Admits 50 to 75% of applicants.

BASIC COSTS (2009-2010)
Tuition and fees: $15,575.
Per-credit charge: $644.
Room and board: $5,650.

FINANCIAL AID PICTURE (2008-2009)
Students with need: Need-based aid available for full-time and part-time students.
Students without need: No-need awards available for academics, alumni affiliation, leadership, music/drama, religious affiliation, state/district residency.
Scholarships offered: Trustee: $7,500; ACT score of 28 or SAT score of 1250 and high school GPA of 3.8; renewable with GPA of 3.5. President: $6,000; ACT score of 26 or SAT score 1200 and high school GPA of 3.5; renewable with GPA of 3.25. Dean: $4,500; ACT score of 25 or SAT score of 1150 and high school GPA of 3.2; renewable with GPA of 3.0. Director: $4,000; ACT score of 21 or SAT score of 1000 and high school GPA of 3.0; renewable with GPA of 2.75. Faculty: $5,000; have earned at least 24 college credits and college GPA of 3.5; renewable with GPA of 3.5. Home School: $5,500; ACT score of 26 or SAT score of 1200 and home school GPA of 3.0; renewable with a GPA of 3.0. Leadership: $6,000; ACT score of 22 or SAT score of 1050 and high school GPA of 3.00 and two letters of recommenda-

tion, personal essay, application by April 1; 10 available, renewable by maintaining leadership standards and a GPA of 2.75. Music: $5,000; ACT score of 22 or SAT score of 1050 and high school GPA of 3.0 and audition, May 1 deadline; 8 available, renewable by maintaining music standards and a GPA of 2.75.

FINANCIAL AID PROCEDURES
Forms required: FAFSA, institutional form.
Dates and Deadlines: Priority date 5/1; closing date 8/1. Applicants notified on a rolling basis starting 3/1; must reply within 2 week(s) of notification.
Transfers: Priority date 12/15; no deadline. Applicants notified on a rolling basis starting 10/1; must reply within 2 week(s) of notification.

CONTACT
Truitt Franklin, Director of Financial Aid
PO Box 800899, Toccoa Falls, GA 30598-0368
(706) 886-6831 ext. 5435

Truett-McConnell College
Cleveland, Georgia
www.truett.edu   Federal Code: 001597

4-year private liberal arts college in small town, affiliated with Southern Baptist Convention.
Enrollment: 373 undergrads, 4% part-time. 133 full-time freshmen.
Selectivity: Admits 50 to 75% of applicants.

BASIC COSTS (2010-2011)
Tuition and fees: $14,540.
Per-credit charge: $468.
Room and board: $5,900.

FINANCIAL AID PICTURE
Students with need: Need-based aid available for full-time and part-time students.
Students without need: No-need awards available for academics, athletics, music/drama, religious affiliation, state/district residency.

FINANCIAL AID PROCEDURES
Forms required: FAFSA, state aid form, institutional form.
Dates and Deadlines: Priority date 6/1; no closing date. Applicants notified on a rolling basis starting 4/1; must reply within 2 week(s) of notification.

CONTACT
Becky Moore, Director of Financial Aid
100 Alumni Drive, Cleveland, GA 30528
(800) 226-8621

University of Georgia
Athens, Georgia
www.uga.edu   Federal Code: 001598

4-year public university in small city.
Enrollment: 25,882 undergrads, 5% part-time. 4,673 full-time freshmen.
Selectivity: Admits 50 to 75% of applicants.

BASIC COSTS (2009-2010)
Tuition and fees: $7,530; out-of-state residents $25,740.
Room and board: $8,046.
Additional info: Tuition at time of enrollment locked for 4 years.

FINANCIAL AID PICTURE (2009-2010)
Students with need: Out of 3,359 full-time freshmen who applied for aid, 1,659 were judged to have need. Of these, 1,648 received aid, and 474 had their full need met. Average financial aid package met 83% of need; average scholarship/grant was $9,976; average loan was $2,834. For part-time students, average financial aid package was $6,788.

Students without need: 274 full-time freshmen who did not demonstrate need for aid received scholarships/grants; average award was $1,507. No-need awards available for academics, athletics, ROTC, state/district residency.

Scholarships offered: 77 full-time freshmen received athletic scholarships; average amount $13,457.

Cumulative student debt: 44% of graduating class had student loans; average debt was $14,766.

FINANCIAL AID PROCEDURES

Forms required: FAFSA.

Dates and Deadlines: Priority date 3/1; no closing date. Applicants notified on a rolling basis starting 5/15; must reply within 2 week(s) of notification.

CONTACT

Bonnie Joerschke, Director of Student Financial Aid
Office of Undergraduate Admissions, Athens, GA 30602-1633
(706) 542-6147

University of West Georgia

Carrollton, Georgia
www.westga.edu   Federal Code: 001601

4-year public university in large town.

Enrollment: 9,622 undergrads, 16% part-time. 1,949 full-time freshmen.

Selectivity: Admits 50 to 75% of applicants. GED not accepted.

BASIC COSTS (2009-2010)

Tuition and fees: $5,382; out-of-state residents $17,358.

Per-credit charge: $134; out-of-state residents $533.

Room and board: $6,504.

Additional info: Tuition/fee waivers available for adults, minority students.

FINANCIAL AID PICTURE (2009-2010)

Students with need: Out of 1,686 full-time freshmen who applied for aid, 1,269 were judged to have need. Of these, 1,248 received aid, and 278 had their full need met. Average financial aid package met 65% of need; average scholarship/grant was $6,614; average loan was $3,232. For part-time students, average financial aid package was $7,007.

Students without need: 42 full-time freshmen who did not demonstrate need for aid received scholarships/grants; average award was $2,125. No-need awards available for academics, alumni affiliation, art, athletics, leadership, minority status, music/drama, religious affiliation, state/district residency.

Scholarships offered: 41 full-time freshmen received athletic scholarships; average amount $5,382.

FINANCIAL AID PROCEDURES

Forms required: FAFSA.

Dates and Deadlines: No deadline. Applicants notified on a rolling basis starting 6/1; must reply within 4 week(s) of notification.

CONTACT

Kimberly Jordan, Director of Financial Aid
1601 Maple Street, Carrollton, GA 30118
(678) 839-6421

Valdosta State University

Valdosta, Georgia
www.valdosta.edu   Federal Code: 001599

4-year public university in small city.

Enrollment: 10,275 undergrads, 12% part-time. 2,086 full-time freshmen.

Selectivity: Admits 50 to 75% of applicants. GED not accepted.

BASIC COSTS (2009-2010)

Tuition and fees: $5,506; out-of-state residents $17,482.

Per-credit charge: $134; out-of-state residents $533.

Room and board: $6,670.

FINANCIAL AID PICTURE (2008-2009)

Students with need: Out of 1,781 full-time freshmen who applied for aid, 1,296 were judged to have need. Of these, 1,286 received aid, and 679 had their full need met. Average financial aid package met 90% of need; average scholarship/grant was $5,725; average loan was $4,457. For part-time students, average financial aid package was $11,854.

Students without need: 32 full-time freshmen who did not demonstrate need for aid received scholarships/grants; average award was $2,366. No-need awards available for academics, alumni affiliation, art, athletics, minority status, music/drama, ROTC, state/district residency.

Scholarships offered: 10 full-time freshmen received athletic scholarships; average amount $4,497.

Cumulative student debt: 65% of graduating class had student loans; average debt was $18,221.

FINANCIAL AID PROCEDURES

Forms required: FAFSA.

Dates and Deadlines: Priority date 5/1; no closing date. Applicants notified on a rolling basis starting 5/15.

CONTACT

Doug Tanner, Director of Financial Aid
1500 North Patterson Street, Valdosta, GA 31698-0170
(229) 333-5935

Waycross College

Waycross, Georgia
www.waycross.edu   Federal Code: 013537

2-year public community and liberal arts college in large town.

Enrollment: 1,100 undergrads.

Selectivity: Open admission.

BASIC COSTS (2009-2010)

Tuition and fees: $2,772; out-of-state residents $9,650.

Additional info: Tuition/fee waivers available for adults.

FINANCIAL AID PICTURE (2008-2009)

Students with need: Need-based aid available for full-time and part-time students. Work study available nights.

Students without need: No-need awards available for academics, alumni affiliation, leadership.

FINANCIAL AID PROCEDURES

Forms required: FAFSA, institutional form.

Dates and Deadlines: Priority date 6/1; no closing date. Applicants notified on a rolling basis; must reply within 2 week(s) of notification.

CONTACT

Debbie Howard, Director of Financial Aid
2001 South Georgia Parkway, Waycross, GA 31503
(912) 449-7600

Wesleyan College

Macon, Georgia
www.wesleyancollege.edu   Federal Code: 001600

4-year private liberal arts college for women in small city, affiliated with United Methodist Church.

Enrollment: 610 undergrads, 37% part-time. 83 full-time freshmen.

Selectivity: Admits 50 to 75% of applicants.

BASIC COSTS (2010-2011)
Tuition and fees: $18,000.
Room and board: $8,100.
Additional info: Tuition/fee waivers available for adults.

FINANCIAL AID PICTURE (2009-2010)
Students with need: Out of 81 full-time freshmen who applied for aid, 72 were judged to have need. Of these, 72 received aid, and 20 had their full need met. Average financial aid package met 83% of need; average scholarship/grant was $14,881; average loan was $3,471. For part-time students, average financial aid package was $6,081.
Students without need: 34 full-time freshmen who did not demonstrate need for aid received scholarships/grants; average award was $13,513. No-need awards available for academics, alumni affiliation, art, job skills, leadership, minority status, music/drama, religious affiliation, state/district residency.
Scholarships offered: Academic Scholarships: $1,000 to $16,000; based on minimum 1100 SAT (exclusive of Writing) or 25 ACT and 3.75 GPA, or 1200 SAT (exclusive of Writing) or 27 ACT and 3.5 GPA. Leadership Awards and scholarships for music, art and theater: range from $1,000-$3,000.
Cumulative student debt: 80% of graduating class had student loans; average debt was $31,473.

FINANCIAL AID PROCEDURES
Forms required: FAFSA, state aid form, institutional form.
Dates and Deadlines: Priority date 2/15; closing date 6/3. Applicants notified on a rolling basis starting 3/1; must reply by 5/1 or within 3 week(s) of notification.
Transfers: Fellowships available based on number of hours and GPA transferred in, with minimum 30 semester or 45 quarter hours and 3.0 GPA required.

CONTACT
Richard Maier, Vice President for Enrollment Services
4760 Forsyth Road, Macon, GA 31210-4462
(478) 757-3902

West Georgia Technical College
Waco, Georgia
www.westgatech.edu   Federal Code: 005614

2-year public technical college in small city.
Enrollment: 6,791 undergrads, 60% part-time. 1,864 full-time freshmen.
Selectivity: Open admission; but selective for some programs.

BASIC COSTS (2009-2010)
Tuition and fees: $2,043; out-of-state residents $3,843.
Per-credit charge: $40; out-of-state residents $80.
Additional info: Tuition reciprocity with bordering states. Commercial truck driving program is $258 per-credit-hour. EMT programs are $73 per-credit-hour.

FINANCIAL AID PICTURE
Students with need: Need-based aid available for full-time and part-time students. Work study available nights.
Students without need: No-need awards available for state/district residency.

FINANCIAL AID PROCEDURES
Forms required: FAFSA, state aid form, institutional form.
Dates and Deadlines: No deadline. Applicants notified on a rolling basis; must reply within 1 week(s) of notification.
Transfers: Aid must be in order or cash paid at registration for classes.

CONTACT
Dorothy Cantor, Financial Aid Coordinator
176 Murphy Campus Boulevard, Waco, GA 30182
(706) 845-4323

Young Harris College
Young Harris, Georgia
www.yhc.edu   Federal Code: 001604

2-year private liberal arts college in rural community, affiliated with United Methodist Church.
Enrollment: 693 undergrads.

BASIC COSTS (2010-2011)
Tuition and fees: $20,775.
Per-credit charge: $650.
Room and board: $7,084.

FINANCIAL AID PICTURE (2008-2009)
Students with need: Need-based aid available for full-time and part-time students. Work study available nights.
Students without need: No-need awards available for academics, art, athletics, job skills, music/drama, state/district residency.
Scholarships offered: Academic Scholarships; $3,500-$8,500; based on index including GPA and SAT/ACT. Additional awards to a percentage of recipients range from additional $1,000 to full tuition, room and board.

FINANCIAL AID PROCEDURES
Forms required: FAFSA, state aid form, institutional form.
Dates and Deadlines: Priority date 4/1; no closing date. Applicants notified on a rolling basis starting 3/1; must reply within 2 week(s) of notification.

CONTACT
Wade Benson, Vice President for Finance
PO Box 116, Young Harris, GA 30582-0116
(706) 379-3111

Hawaii

Chaminade University of Honolulu
Honolulu, Hawaii
www.chaminade.edu   Federal Code: 001605

4-year private university in large city, affiliated with Roman Catholic Church.
Enrollment: 1,013 undergrads, 4% part-time. 263 full-time freshmen.
Selectivity: Admits over 75% of applicants.

BASIC COSTS (2010-2011)
Tuition and fees: $17,740.
Per-credit charge: $587.
Room and board: $10,490.

FINANCIAL AID PICTURE (2009-2010)
Students with need: Need-based aid available for full-time and part-time students.
Students without need: No-need awards available for academics, art, athletics, leadership, religious affiliation, ROTC, state/district residency.
Additional info: For students whose eligibility for federal and institutional aid does not meet entire costs, alternative student loans may be secured for eligible applicants.

FINANCIAL AID PROCEDURES
Forms required: FAFSA.
Dates and Deadlines: Priority date 2/15; no closing date. Applicants notified on a rolling basis starting 2/15; must reply within 4 week(s) of notification.

CONTACT
Eric Nemoto, Associate Dean of Enrollment Management
3140 Waialae Avenue, Honolulu, HI 96816
(808) 735-4780

Hawaii Pacific University
Honolulu, Hawaii
www.hpu.edu   Federal Code: 007279

4-year private university and liberal arts college in large city.
Enrollment: 6,342 undergrads, 43% part-time. 598 full-time freshmen.
Selectivity: Admits 50 to 75% of applicants.

BASIC COSTS (2010-2011)
Tuition and fees: $15,820.
Per-credit charge: $655.
Room and board: $11,648.

FINANCIAL AID PICTURE (2009-2010)
Students with need: 15% of average financial aid package awarded as scholarships/grants, 85% awarded as loans/jobs. Need-based aid available for part-time students. Work study available nights, weekends, and for part-time students.
Students without need: No-need awards available for academics, alumni affiliation, athletics, job skills, leadership, music/drama, religious affiliation, ROTC.
Scholarships offered: Makana Scholarship: $2,600; 3.5 GPA or higher. Phi Theta Kappa Scholarship: $6,500; for member of Phi Theta Kappa.

FINANCIAL AID PROCEDURES
Forms required: FAFSA.
Dates and Deadlines: Priority date 3/1; no closing date. Applicants notified on a rolling basis starting 4/1; must reply within 3 week(s) of notification.

CONTACT
Adam Hatch, Director of Financial Aid
1164 Bishop Street, Suite 200, Honolulu, HI 96813
(808) 544-0253

Heald College: Honolulu
Honolulu, Hawaii
www.heald.edu   Federal Code: E00886

2-year for-profit technical and career college in very large city.
Enrollment: 1,367 undergrads.
Selectivity: Open admission.

BASIC COSTS (2009-2010)
Additional info: Full time students on 2-year plan pay $3,060 per quarter for 4 quarters ($12,240 per year).

FINANCIAL AID PICTURE
Students with need: Need-based aid available for full-time and part-time students. Work study available nights, weekends, and for part-time students.
Students without need: This college awards aid only to students with need.

FINANCIAL AID PROCEDURES
Forms required: FAFSA.
Dates and Deadlines: No deadline.

CONTACT
Candice Wong, Director of Financial Aid
1500 Kapiolani Boulevard, Honolulu, HI 96814-3715
(808) 955-1500 ext. 504

University of Hawaii at Hilo
Hilo, Hawaii
www.uhh.hawaii.edu   Federal Code: 001611

4-year public university in large town.
Enrollment: 3,317 undergrads, 15% part-time. 429 full-time freshmen.
Selectivity: Admits 50 to 75% of applicants.

BASIC COSTS (2009-2010)
Tuition and fees: $4,888; out-of-state residents $14,392.
Per-credit charge: $191; out-of-state residents $587.
Room and board: $7,014.

FINANCIAL AID PICTURE (2008-2009)
Students with need: Out of 273 full-time freshmen who applied for aid, 272 were judged to have need. Of these, 272 received aid, and 35 had their full need met. Average financial aid package met 54% of need; average scholarship/grant was $4,583; average loan was $3,171. Need-based aid available for part-time students.
Scholarships offered: 14 full-time freshmen received athletic scholarships; average amount $3,307.
Additional info: Hawaii student incentive grants and tuition waivers (merit and need-based) available to Hawaii residents at participating institutions.

FINANCIAL AID PROCEDURES
Forms required: FAFSA.
Dates and Deadlines: Priority date 3/1; no closing date. Applicants notified on a rolling basis starting 4/15; must reply within 2 week(s) of notification.

CONTACT
Jeff Schofield, Financial Aid Director
200 West Kawili Street, Hilo, HI 96720-4091
(808) 974-7324

University of Hawaii at Manoa
Honolulu, Hawaii
www.manoa.hawaii.edu   Federal Code: 001610

4-year public university in very large city.
Enrollment: 13,583 undergrads, 18% part-time. 1,702 full-time freshmen.
Selectivity: Admits 50 to 75% of applicants.

BASIC COSTS (2009-2010)
Tuition and fees: $7,168; out-of-state residents $19,216.
Per-credit charge: $282; out-of-state residents $784.
Room and board: $8,493.
Additional info: Tuition/fee waivers available for minority students.

FINANCIAL AID PICTURE (2008-2009)
Students with need: Out of 1,330 full-time freshmen who applied for aid, 671 were judged to have need. Of these, 589 received aid, and 151 had their full need met. Average financial aid package met 62% of need; average scholarship/grant was $5,707; average loan was $3,035. For part-time students, average financial aid package was $3,876.
Students without need: 330 full-time freshmen who did not demonstrate need for aid received scholarships/grants; average award was $6,794. No-need awards available for academics, alumni affiliation, art, athletics, job skills, leadership, minority status, music/drama, religious affiliation, ROTC, state/district residency.
Scholarships offered: 38 full-time freshmen received athletic scholarships; average amount $6,761.
Cumulative student debt: 35% of graduating class had student loans; average debt was $14,835.
Additional info: Hawaii student incentive grants and tuition waivers (merit and need-based) available to Hawaii residents at participating institutions.

FINANCIAL AID PROCEDURES

Forms required: FAFSA.

Dates and Deadlines: Priority date 3/1; no closing date. Applicants notified on a rolling basis starting 3/15; must reply within 4 week(s) of notification.

Transfers: No deadline. Applicants notified on a rolling basis starting 3/15; must reply within 4 week(s) of notification.

CONTACT

Jodie Kuba, Director of Financial Aid
2600 Campus Road, QLC Rm 001, Honolulu, HI 96822
(808) 956-7251

University of Hawaii: Hawaii Community College

Hilo, Hawaii
www.hawcc.hawaii.edu   Federal Code: 005258

2-year public community college in small city.
Enrollment: 2,804 undergrads.
Selectivity: Open admission.

BASIC COSTS (2009-2010)

Tuition and fees: $2,504; out-of-state residents $8,294.
Per-credit charge: $79; out-of-state residents $272.

FINANCIAL AID PICTURE

Students with need: Need-based aid available for full-time and part-time students.
Students without need: This college awards aid only to students with need.
Additional info: Hawaii student incentive grants and tuition waivers (merit and need-based) available to Hawaii residents.

FINANCIAL AID PROCEDURES

Forms required: FAFSA.
Dates and Deadlines: Priority date 4/1; no closing date. Applicants notified on a rolling basis starting 5/1; must reply within 2 week(s) of notification.
Transfers: Residents of Guam, Federated States of Micronesia, Palau, Marianas Islands and certain other island nations considered residents for tuition purpose.

CONTACT

Sheryl Lundberg-Spregue, Financial Aid Officer
200 West Kawili Street, Hilo, HI 96720-4091
(808) 974-7663

University of Hawaii: Honolulu Community College

Honolulu, Hawaii
www.honolulu.hawaii.edu   Federal Code: 001612

2-year public community and technical college in very large city.
Enrollment: 3,458 undergrads.
Selectivity: Open admission; but selective for out-of-state students.

BASIC COSTS (2009-2010)

Tuition and fees: $2,400; out-of-state residents $8,190.
Per-credit charge: $79; out-of-state residents $272.

FINANCIAL AID PICTURE (2008-2009)

Students with need: Need-based aid available for full-time and part-time students.
Students without need: No-need awards available for academics, state/district residency.
Additional info: Hawaii student incentive grants and tuition waivers (merit and need-based) available to Hawaii residents at participating institutions.

FINANCIAL AID PROCEDURES

Forms required: FAFSA.

Dates and Deadlines: Priority date 4/1; no closing date. Applicants notified on a rolling basis starting 7/1; must reply within 3 week(s) of notification.

CONTACT

Jannine Oyama, Financial Aid Officer
874 Dillingham Boulevard, Honolulu, HI 96817
(808) 845-9116

University of Hawaii: Kapiolani Community College

Honolulu, Hawaii
www.kcc.hawaii.edu   Federal Code: 001613

2-year public community college in very large city.
Enrollment: 6,119 undergrads.
Selectivity: Open admission; but selective for some programs.

BASIC COSTS (2009-2010)

Tuition and fees: $2,430; out-of-state residents $8,220.
Per-credit charge: $79; out-of-state residents $272.

FINANCIAL AID PICTURE (2009-2010)

Students with need: Need-based aid available for full-time and part-time students.
Students without need: This college awards aid only to students with need.
Additional info: Hawaii student incentive grants and tuition waivers (merit and need-based) available to Hawaii residents.

FINANCIAL AID PROCEDURES

Forms required: FAFSA.
Dates and Deadlines: Priority date 4/1; no closing date. Applicants notified on a rolling basis; must reply within 2 week(s) of notification.

CONTACT

Jennifer Bradley, Financial Aid Manager
4303 Diamond Head Road, Honolulu, HI 96816-4421
(808) 734-9555

University of Hawaii: Kauai Community College

Lihue, Hawaii
www.kauai.hawaii.edu   Federal Code: 001614

2-year public community college in small city.
Enrollment: 686 undergrads.
Selectivity: Open admission; but selective for out-of-state students.

BASIC COSTS (2009-2010)

Tuition and fees: $2,430; out-of-state residents $8,220.
Per-credit charge: $79; out-of-state residents $272.

FINANCIAL AID PICTURE (2009-2010)

Students with need: Work study available nights.
Additional info: Hawaii student incentive grants and tuition waivers (merit and need-based) available to Hawaii residents.

FINANCIAL AID PROCEDURES

Forms required: FAFSA, institutional form.
Dates and Deadlines: Priority date 3/1; closing date 5/1. Applicants notified on a rolling basis starting 5/1.
Transfers: Academic transcript evaluation by end of first semester is required.

CONTACT

Edward Sanchez, Financial Aid Director

3-1901 Kaumualii Highway, Lihue, HI 96766-9500

(808) 245-8360

University of Hawaii: Leeward Community College

Pearl City, Hawaii

www.lcc.hawaii.edu   Federal Code: 004549

2-year public community college in large town.

Enrollment: 7,484 undergrads.

Selectivity: Open admission.

BASIC COSTS (2009-2010)

Tuition and fees: $2,430; out-of-state residents $8,220.

Per-credit charge: $79; out-of-state residents $272.

FINANCIAL AID PICTURE

Students with need: Need-based aid available for full-time and part-time students.

Additional info: Leveraging Educational Assistance Partnership (LEAP) funds or tuition waivers available to students with financial need.

FINANCIAL AID PROCEDURES

Forms required: FAFSA.

Dates and Deadlines: Priority date 4/15; no closing date. Applicants notified on a rolling basis starting 6/1; must reply within 2 week(s) of notification.

CONTACT

Aileen Lum-Akana, Financial Aid Director

96-045 Ala Ike, Pearl City, HI 96782

(808) 455-0606

University of Hawaii: Maui Community College

Kahului, Hawaii

www.maui.hawaii.edu

2-year public community college in small city.

Enrollment: 3,675 undergrads, 56% part-time. 523 full-time freshmen.

Selectivity: Open admission; but selective for some programs.

BASIC COSTS (2009-2010)

Tuition and fees: $2,496; out-of-state residents $12,126.

Per-credit charge: $79; out-of-state residents $400.

Additional info: Tuition/fee waivers available for minority students.

FINANCIAL AID PICTURE (2008-2009)

Students with need: Need-based aid available for full-time and part-time students. Work study available nights.

FINANCIAL AID PROCEDURES

Forms required: FAFSA, institutional form.

Dates and Deadlines: Priority date 4/1; no closing date. Applicants notified on a rolling basis starting 6/1; must reply within 4 week(s) of notification.

CONTACT

Cathy Bio, Financial Aid Officer

310 West Kaahumanu Avenue, Kahului, HI 96732-1617

(808) 984-3277

University of Hawaii: West Oahu

Pearl City, Hawaii

www.uhwo.hawaii.edu   Federal Code: 014315

4-year public liberal arts and teachers college in large town.

Enrollment: 1,253 undergrads, 68% part-time. 28 full-time freshmen.

Selectivity: Admits over 75% of applicants.

BASIC COSTS (2009-2010)

Tuition and fees: $4,186; out-of-state residents $12,970.

Per-credit charge: $174; out-of-state residents $540.

Additional info: Foreign students pay out-of-state tuition rates. However, citizens of an eligible Pacific island district, commonwealth, territory or insular jurisdiction, state or nation which does not provide public institutions that grant baccalaureate degrees may be allowed to pay 150% of the resident tuition.

FINANCIAL AID PICTURE (2008-2009)

Students with need: 42% of average financial aid package awarded as scholarships/grants, 58% awarded as loans/jobs. Need-based aid available for part-time students.

Students without need: No-need awards available for academics, alumni affiliation, leadership, state/district residency.

FINANCIAL AID PROCEDURES

Forms required: FAFSA.

Dates and Deadlines: Priority date 4/1; no closing date. Applicants notified on a rolling basis starting 4/1.

Transfers: No deadline. Applicants notified by 7/1.

CONTACT

Jodie Kuba, Financial Aid Officer

96-129 Ala Ike, Pearl City, HI 96782

(808) 454-4700

University of Hawaii: Windward Community College

Kaneohe, Hawaii

www.wcc.hawaii.edu   Federal Code: 010390

2-year public community college in small city.

Enrollment: 1,769 undergrads.

Selectivity: Open admission.

BASIC COSTS (2009-2010)

Tuition and fees: $2,410; out-of-state residents $8,200.

Per-credit charge: $79; out-of-state residents $272.

Additional info: Tuition/fee waivers available for minority students.

FINANCIAL AID PICTURE

Students with need: Need-based aid available for full-time and part-time students.

Additional info: Hawaii student incentive grants and tuition waivers (merit and need-based) available to Hawaii residents.

FINANCIAL AID PROCEDURES

Forms required: FAFSA.

Dates and Deadlines: Priority date 4/1; no closing date. Applicants notified on a rolling basis starting 3/15; must reply within 2 week(s) of notification.

CONTACT

Steven Chigawa, Financial Aid Officer

45-720 Kea'ahala Road, Kaneohe, HI 96744

(808) 235-7449

Idaho

Boise Bible College
Boise, Idaho
www.boisebible.edu   Federal Code: 015783

4-year private Bible college in small city, affiliated with nondenominational tradition.

Enrollment: 173 undergrads.

BASIC COSTS (2009-2010)
Tuition and fees: $8,750.
Per-credit charge: $360.
Room and board: $5,832.

FINANCIAL AID PICTURE
Students with need: Need-based aid available for full-time and part-time students.
Students without need: No-need awards available for academics, leadership, music/drama, religious affiliation.

FINANCIAL AID PROCEDURES
Forms required: FAFSA, institutional form.
Dates and Deadlines: Priority date 5/1; no closing date. Applicants notified on a rolling basis starting 5/2; must reply by 8/1 or within 2 week(s) of notification.
Transfers: Financial aid and academic transcripts must be on file before federal aid is awarded.

CONTACT
Joyce Anderson, Financial Aid Officer
8695 West Marigold Street, Boise, ID 83714-1220
(800) 893-7755

Boise State University
Boise, Idaho
www.boisestate.edu   Federal Code: 001616

4-year public university in small city.
Enrollment: 15,997 undergrads, 24% part-time. 2,007 full-time freshmen.
Selectivity: Admits over 75% of applicants.

BASIC COSTS (2009-2010)
Tuition and fees: $4,865; out-of-state residents $13,868.
Per-credit charge: $252; out-of-state residents $332.
Room and board: $5,114.
Additional info: Out-of-state students (undergraduate and graduate) taking less than 8 credit hours pay in-state rate.

FINANCIAL AID PICTURE (2009-2010)
Students with need: Average financial aid package met 19% of need; average scholarship/grant was $3,807; average loan was $4,902. For part-time students, average financial aid package was $6,091.
Students without need: No-need awards available for academics, athletics, music/drama, ROTC, state/district residency.
Cumulative student debt: 64% of graduating class had student loans; average debt was $23,256.

FINANCIAL AID PROCEDURES
Forms required: FAFSA.
Dates and Deadlines: Priority date 4/1; no closing date. Applicants notified on a rolling basis starting 6/1; must reply within 2 week(s) of notification.
Transfers: Financial aid transcripts required from all postsecondary schools attended whether or not financial aid was received.

CONTACT
David Tolman, Director of Financial Aid
1910 University Drive, Boise, ID 83725
(208) 426-1664

Brigham Young University-Idaho
Rexburg, Idaho
www.byui.edu   Federal Code: 001625

4-year private university in large town, affiliated with Church of Jesus Christ of Latter-day Saints.
Enrollment: 14,944 undergrads.
Selectivity: Admits over 75% of applicants.

BASIC COSTS (2009-2010)
Tuition and fees: $3,580.
Per-credit charge: $136.
Room and board: $7,550.
Additional info: Tuition for students who are not members of The Church of Jesus Christ of Latter-day Saints is $6,560 for academic year.

FINANCIAL AID PICTURE (2008-2009)
Students with need: Need-based aid available for full-time and part-time students.
Students without need: No-need awards available for academics, athletics, leadership.
Additional info: Application deadline for merit scholarships 3/1.

FINANCIAL AID PROCEDURES
Forms required: FAFSA.
Dates and Deadlines: Priority date 5/1; no closing date. Applicants notified on a rolling basis starting 2/1.

CONTACT
Aaron Sanns, Financial Aid and Scholarship Director
120 Kimball Building, Rexburg, ID 83460-1615
(208) 496-1015

College of Idaho
Caldwell, Idaho
www.collegeofidaho.edu   Federal Code: 001617

4-year private liberal arts college in large town.
Enrollment: 990 undergrads, 5% part-time. 287 full-time freshmen.
Selectivity: Admits 50 to 75% of applicants.

BASIC COSTS (2010-2011)
Tuition and fees: $21,380.
Per-credit charge: $850.
Room and board: $7,700.
Additional info: Tuition/fee waivers available for adults.

FINANCIAL AID PICTURE (2009-2010)
Students with need: Average financial aid package met 86% of need; average scholarship/grant was $6,165; average loan was $3,727. For part-time students, average financial aid package was $9,857.
Students without need: No-need awards available for academics, alumni affiliation, art, athletics, leadership, minority status, music/drama, religious affiliation, ROTC.
Scholarships offered: Heritage Scholars, $19,300/year, minimum 3.85-4.0 GPA and 31-33 ACT or 1380-1470 SAT. Presidential Scholar, $11,000/year, 2.9 GPA and 36 ACT or 1590 SAT to 4.0 GPA and 29 ACT or 1280 SAT. Trustee Scholar, $9,000/year, 2.50 GPA and 36 ACT or 1590 SAT to 4.0 GPA and 25 ACT or 1125 SAT. Dean Scholar, $7,000/year, 2.5 GPA and 32 ACT or 1400 SAT to 4.0 GPA and 24 ACT or 1090 SAT. Alumni Scholarship $4,000, 2.5 GPA and 27 ACT or 1200 SAT. All SAT scores exclusive of Writing.

Cumulative student debt: 76% of graduating class had student loans; average debt was $19,976.

FINANCIAL AID PROCEDURES

Forms required: FAFSA, institutional form.
Dates and Deadlines: Priority date 2/15; no closing date. Applicants notified on a rolling basis starting 2/1; must reply within 3 week(s) of notification.
Transfers: No deadline. Applicants notified on a rolling basis starting 1/31; must reply within 3 week(s) of notification.

CONTACT

Juanitta Pearson, Director of Student Financial Aid Services
2112 Cleveland Boulevard, Caldwell, ID 83605-4432
(208) 459-5307

Eastern Idaho Technical College
Idaho Falls, Idaho
www.eitc.edu   Federal Code: 011133

2-year public technical college in small city.
Enrollment: 865 undergrads:
Selectivity: Open admission; but selective for some programs.

BASIC COSTS (2009-2010)
Tuition and fees: $1,750; out-of-state residents $6,928.
Per-credit charge: $84; out-of-state residents $168.
Additional info: Fees may vary according to the program of study.

FINANCIAL AID PICTURE

Students with need: Need-based aid available for full-time and part-time students.
Students without need: No-need awards available for academics, job skills, state/district residency.

FINANCIAL AID PROCEDURES

Forms required: FAFSA, institutional form.
Dates and Deadlines: Priority date 6/1; no closing date. Applicants notified on a rolling basis starting 6/6; must reply within 4 week(s) of notification.

CONTACT

Shayna Sharp, Director of Financial Aid
1600 South 25th East, Idaho Falls, ID 83404-5788
(208) 524-3000 ext. 3389

Idaho State University
Pocatello, Idaho
www.isu.edu   Federal Code: 001620

4-year public university in small city.
Enrollment: 10,034 undergrads, 24% part-time. 1,540 full-time freshmen.
Selectivity: Admits 50 to 75% of applicants.

BASIC COSTS (2009-2010)
Tuition and fees: $4,968; out-of-state residents $14,770.
Per-credit charge: $253; out-of-state residents $393.
Room and board: $5,050.
Additional info: $1,046 refundable health insurance.

FINANCIAL AID PICTURE (2008-2009)

Students with need: Need-based aid available for full-time and part-time students. Work study available nights, weekends, and for part-time students.
Students without need: No-need awards available for academics, alumni affiliation, art, athletics, leadership, minority status, music/drama, ROTC, state/district residency.

FINANCIAL AID PROCEDURES

Forms required: FAFSA.

Dates and Deadlines: Priority date 3/1; no closing date. Applicants notified on a rolling basis starting 4/1.
Transfers: Closing date 3/1. Applicants notified on a rolling basis starting 3/1.

CONTACT

Kent Larson, Director of Financial Aid
921 South 8th Stop 8270, Pocatello, ID 83209-8270
(208) 282-2756

Lewis-Clark State College
Lewiston, Idaho
www.lcsc.edu   Federal Code: 001621

4-year public liberal arts and technical college in small city.
Enrollment: 3,239 undergrads, 22% part-time. 592 full-time freshmen.
Selectivity: Admits over 75% of applicants.

BASIC COSTS (2009-2010)
Tuition and fees: $4,596; out-of-state residents $12,874.
Per-credit charge: $234.
Room and board: $5,900.

FINANCIAL AID PICTURE (2008-2009)

Students with need: Out of 473 full-time freshmen who applied for aid, 371 were judged to have need. Of these, 356 received aid, and 29 had their full need met. Average financial aid package met 8% of need; average scholarship/grant was $3,434; average loan was $2,870. For part-time students, average financial aid package was $5,621.
Students without need: 110 full-time freshmen who did not demonstrate need for aid received scholarships/grants; average award was $1,792. No-need awards available for academics, alumni affiliation, art, athletics, leadership, minority status, music/drama.
Scholarships offered: 46 full-time freshmen received athletic scholarships; average amount $8,023.

FINANCIAL AID PROCEDURES

Forms required: FAFSA.
Dates and Deadlines: Priority date 3/1; no closing date. Applicants notified on a rolling basis starting 4/15; must reply within 2 week(s) of notification.

CONTACT

Laura Hughes, Director of Financial Aid
500 Eighth Avenue, Lewiston, ID 83501-2698
(208) 792-2224

North Idaho College
Coeur d'Alene, Idaho
www.nic.edu   Federal Code: 001623

2-year public community college in large town.
Enrollment: 4,705 undergrads, 36% part-time. 896 full-time freshmen.
Selectivity: Open admission; but selective for some programs.

BASIC COSTS (2009-2010)
Tuition and fees: $2,514; out-of-district residents $3,514; out-of-state residents $7,066.
Room and board: $5,750.
Additional info: Tuition/fee waivers available for minority students.

FINANCIAL AID PICTURE (2008-2009)

Students with need: Need-based aid available for full-time and part-time students. Work study available weekends and for part-time students.
Students without need: No-need awards available for academics, art, athletics, leadership, minority status, music/drama, state/district residency.

FINANCIAL AID PROCEDURES

Forms required: FAFSA.

Dates and Deadlines: Priority date 3/15; no closing date. Applicants notified on a rolling basis starting 4/1; must reply within 2 week(s) of notification.

CONTACT

Director of Financial Aid
1000 West Garden Avenue, Coeur d'Alene, ID 83814-2199
(208) 769-3368

Northwest Nazarene University

Nampa, Idaho
www.nnu.edu   Federal Code: 001624

4-year private university in small city, affiliated with Church of the Nazarene.
Enrollment: 1,257 undergrads, 6% part-time. 279 full-time freshmen.

BASIC COSTS (2009-2010)

Tuition and fees: $22,250.
Per-credit charge: $950.
Room and board: $5,830.

FINANCIAL AID PICTURE (2009-2010)

Students with need: Need-based aid available for full-time and part-time students. Work study available nights, weekends, and for part-time students.
Students without need: No-need awards available for academics, alumni affiliation, art, athletics, leadership, minority status, music/drama, religious affiliation, ROTC.
Scholarships offered: Merit scholarships for freshmen based primarily on cumulative high school GPA and ACT test scores.

FINANCIAL AID PROCEDURES

Forms required: FAFSA, institutional form.
Dates and Deadlines: Priority date 3/1; no closing date. Applicants notified on a rolling basis starting 3/1; must reply within 3 week(s) of notification.

CONTACT

Wes Maggard, Director of Financial Aid
623 Holly Street, Nampa, ID 83686-5897
(208) 467-8347

University of Idaho

Moscow, Idaho
www.uidaho.edu   Federal Code: 001626

4-year public university in large town.
Enrollment: 8,757 undergrads, 6% part-time. 1,744 full-time freshmen.
Selectivity: Admits over 75% of applicants.

BASIC COSTS (2009-2010)

Tuition and fees: $4,932; out-of-state residents $15,012.
Per-credit charge: $251; out-of-state residents $755.
Room and board: $6,850.
Additional info: Tuition/fee waivers available for minority students.

FINANCIAL AID PICTURE (2008-2009)

Students with need: Out of 1,354 full-time freshmen who applied for aid, 992 were judged to have need. Of these, 974 received aid, and 294 had their full need met. Average financial aid package met 79% of need; average scholarship/grant was $3,631; average loan was $5,173. For part-time students, average financial aid package was $8,606.
Students without need: 547 full-time freshmen who did not demonstrate need for aid received scholarships/grants; average award was $4,060. No-need awards available for academics, alumni affiliation, art, athletics, leadership, minority status, music/drama, ROTC, state/district residency.
Scholarships offered: 55 full-time freshmen received athletic scholarships; average amount $15,877.

Cumulative student debt: 66% of graduating class had student loans; average debt was $21,702.

FINANCIAL AID PROCEDURES

Forms required: FAFSA.
Dates and Deadlines: Priority date 2/15; no closing date. Applicants notified on a rolling basis starting 3/30; must reply within 4 week(s) of notification.
Transfers: No deadline. Applicants notified on a rolling basis starting 3/30; must reply within 4 week(s) of notification.

CONTACT

Daniel Davenport, Director of Admissions and Student Financial Aid
PO Box 444264, Moscow, ID 83844-4264
(208) 885-6312

Illinois

Augustana College

Rock Island, Illinois
www.augustana.edu   Federal Code: 001633

4-year private liberal arts college in large city, affiliated with Evangelical Lutheran Church in America.
Enrollment: 2,457 undergrads, 1% part-time. 639 full-time freshmen.
Selectivity: Admits 50 to 75% of applicants.

BASIC COSTS (2009-2010)

Tuition and fees: $31,326.
Per-credit charge: $1,350.
Room and board: $7,950.

FINANCIAL AID PICTURE (2008-2009)

Students with need: Out of 548 full-time freshmen who applied for aid, 431 were judged to have need. Of these, 431 received aid, and 193 had their full need met. Average financial aid package met 86% of need; average scholarship/grant was $15,396; average loan was $6,025.
Students without need: 198 full-time freshmen who did not demonstrate need for aid received scholarships/grants; average award was $11,772. No-need awards available for academics, alumni affiliation, art, leadership, music/drama, religious affiliation.
Scholarships offered: Presidential Scholarship: $10,000 to full tuition; 28 ACT composite score (1260 combined SAT score in critical reading and mathematics) and rank in the top ten percent of high school class. Dean's Scholarship: $7,750-$9,000; 25 ACT composite score or above (1140 combined SAT score in critical reading and mathematics) and rank in the top 20 percent of their high school class. Founders Scholarship: $5,000-$7,500; must plan to enroll full-time. Transfer Scholarship: $3,000-$6,000; demonstrated outstanding academic performance in previous college studies.

FINANCIAL AID PROCEDURES

Forms required: FAFSA, institutional form.
Dates and Deadlines: Priority date 4/1; no closing date. Applicants notified on a rolling basis.
Transfers: Priority date 5/1. Financial aid transcripts from previous institutions required.

CONTACT

Sue Standley, Director of Financial Assistance
639 38th Street, Rock Island, IL 61201-2296
(309) 794-7207

Aurora University
Aurora, Illinois
www.aurora.edu   Federal Code: 001634

4-year private university in small city.
Enrollment: 2,377 undergrads, 13% part-time. 416 full-time freshmen.
Selectivity: Admits 50 to 75% of applicants.

BASIC COSTS (2010-2011)
Tuition and fees: $18,700.
Per-credit charge: $550.
Room and board: $8,170.
Additional info: Course laboratory/clinical fees in lab sciences, photography, nursing, physical education and student teaching. Tuition will vary for several adult degree completion programs.

FINANCIAL AID PICTURE (2009-2010)
Students with need: Out of 395 full-time freshmen who applied for aid, 352 were judged to have need. Of these, 352 received aid, and 130 had their full need met. Average financial aid package met 90% of need; average scholarship/grant was $7,450; average loan was $3,301. For part-time students, average financial aid package was $7,132.
Students without need: 63 full-time freshmen who did not demonstrate need for aid received scholarships/grants; average award was $9,238. No-need awards available for academics, alumni affiliation, art, music/drama, religious affiliation, ROTC, state/district residency.
Scholarships offered: Board of Trustees scholarships: $10,000. James E. Crimi Presidential Scholarships: $9,500. Dean's Scholarships: $8,500. Aurora University Opportunity Grants: $7,000. AU Promise Grant: $2,000.
Cumulative student debt: 75% of graduating class had student loans; average debt was $23,935.

FINANCIAL AID PROCEDURES
Forms required: FAFSA.
Dates and Deadlines: Priority date 4/15; no closing date. Applicants notified on a rolling basis starting 3/1; must reply by 5/1 or within 3 week(s) of notification.

CONTACT
Heather McKane, Dean of Student Financial Services
347 South Gladstone Avenue, Aurora, IL 60506-4892
(630) 844-6190

Benedictine University
Lisle, Illinois
www.ben.edu   Federal Code: 001767

4-year private university and liberal arts college in large town, affiliated with Roman Catholic Church.
Enrollment: 3,244 undergrads, 31% part-time. 452 full-time freshmen.
Selectivity: Admits over 75% of applicants.

BASIC COSTS (2009-2010)
Tuition and fees: $22,310.
Per-credit charge: $720.
Room and board: $6,945.
Additional info: Tuition/fee waivers available for adults, minority students.

FINANCIAL AID PICTURE (2008-2009)
Students with need: Need-based aid available for full-time and part-time students. Work study available nights, weekends, and for part-time students.
Students without need: No-need awards available for academics, alumni affiliation, minority status, music/drama, ROTC, state/district residency.

FINANCIAL AID PROCEDURES
Forms required: FAFSA.

Dates and Deadlines: Priority date 4/15; no closing date. Applicants notified on a rolling basis starting 2/15; must reply within 2 week(s) of notification.
Transfers: No deadline. Applicants notified on a rolling basis; must reply within 2 week(s) of notification.

CONTACT
Diane Battistella, Associate Dean
5700 College Road, Lisle, IL 60532
(630) 829-6100

Black Hawk College
Moline, Illinois
www.bhc.edu   Federal Code: 001638

2-year public community college in large town.
Enrollment: 4,338 undergrads, 43% part-time. 490 full-time freshmen.
Selectivity: Open admission; but selective for some programs.

BASIC COSTS (2009-2010)
Tuition and fees: $2,685; out-of-district residents $5,985; out-of-state residents $8,475.
Per-credit charge: $81; out-of-district residents $191; out-of-state residents $274.
Additional info: Agreement with 5 contiguous Iowa counties for special tuition rate of $115 per credit plus required fees. Online courses (tuition only) are $95 per credit hour in-state; $115, out-of-state.

FINANCIAL AID PICTURE (2008-2009)
Students with need: Need-based aid available for full-time and part-time students.
Students without need: No-need awards available for academics, art, athletics, leadership, music/drama, state/district residency.
Scholarships offered: Scholarship program; based on need and/or merit. Tuition awards; awarded to students who graduate in the top 10% of their class.
Additional info: 5/15 deadline for scholarships.

FINANCIAL AID PROCEDURES
Forms required: FAFSA.
Dates and Deadlines: Priority date 5/15; no closing date. Applicants notified on a rolling basis starting 5/1.

CONTACT
Joanna Dye, Director, Financial Aid
6600 34th Avenue, Moline, IL 61265-5899
(309) 796-5400

Blackburn College
Carlinville, Illinois
www.blackburn.edu   Federal Code: 001639

4-year private liberal arts college in small town, affiliated with Presbyterian Church (USA).
Enrollment: 595 undergrads.

BASIC COSTS (2009-2010)
Tuition and fees: $14,286.
Per-credit charge: $472.
Room and board: $4,581.
Additional info: All on-campus students participate in a work program which reduces net tuition costs.

FINANCIAL AID PICTURE (2009-2010)
Students with need: Need-based aid available for full-time and part-time students.

Students without need: No-need awards available for academics, state/district residency.

Additional info: Each resident student works 160 hours per semester.

FINANCIAL AID PROCEDURES

Forms required: FAFSA.

Dates and Deadlines: Priority date 4/1; no closing date. Applicants notified on a rolling basis starting 3/1; must reply within 4 week(s) of notification.

Transfers: No deadline. Applicants notified on a rolling basis; must reply within 4 week(s) of notification.

CONTACT

Jane Kelsey, Director of Financial Aid

700 College Avenue, Carlinville, IL 62626

(217) 854-3231 ext. 4283

Blessing-Rieman College of Nursing

Quincy, Illinois

www.brcn.edu   Federal Code: 006214

4-year private nursing college in small city.

Enrollment: 212 undergrads, 12% part-time.

Selectivity: Admits 50 to 75% of applicants.

BASIC COSTS (2010-2011)

Tuition and fees: $22,775.

Per-credit charge: $510.

Room and board: $8,180.

FINANCIAL AID PICTURE (2009-2010)

Students with need: Need-based aid available for full-time and part-time students.

Additional info: Financial aid for freshmen and sophomores administered by Culver-Stockton College and Quincy University.

FINANCIAL AID PROCEDURES

Forms required: FAFSA.

Dates and Deadlines: No deadline.

CONTACT

Sara Brehm, Financial Aid Officer

PO Box 7005, Quincy, IL 62305-7005

(217) 228-5520 ext. 6993

Bradley University

Peoria, Illinois

www.bradley.edu   Federal Code: 001641

4-year private university in large city.

Enrollment: 5,049 undergrads, 5% part-time. 1,032 full-time freshmen.

Selectivity: Admits 50 to 75% of applicants.

BASIC COSTS (2009-2010)

Tuition and fees: $24,224.

Room and board: $7,650.

FINANCIAL AID PICTURE (2008-2009)

Students with need: Out of 876 full-time freshmen who applied for aid, 708 were judged to have need. Of these, 708 received aid, and 241 had their full need met. Average financial aid package met 78% of need; average scholarship/grant was $12,430; average loan was $3,669. Need-based aid available for part-time students.

Students without need: 189 full-time freshmen who did not demonstrate need for aid received scholarships/grants; average award was $9,476. No-need awards available for academics, alumni affiliation, art, athletics, leadership, music/drama.

Scholarships offered: 11 full-time freshmen received athletic scholarships; average amount $10,941.

FINANCIAL AID PROCEDURES

Forms required: FAFSA.

Dates and Deadlines: Priority date 3/1; no closing date. Applicants notified on a rolling basis starting 2/15.

CONTACT

Dave Pardieck, Financial Assistance Director

1501 West Bradley Avenue, Peoria, IL 61625

(309) 677-3089

Carl Sandburg College

Galesburg, Illinois

www.sandburg.edu   Federal Code: 007265

2-year public community college in large town.

Enrollment: 2,011 undergrads.

Selectivity: Open admission; but selective for some programs.

BASIC COSTS (2009-2010)

Tuition and fees: $3,930; out-of-district residents $4,830; out-of-state residents $6,570.

FINANCIAL AID PICTURE (2008-2009)

Students with need: Need-based aid available for full-time students.

Students without need: No-need awards available for academics, art, athletics, music/drama.

FINANCIAL AID PROCEDURES

Forms required: FAFSA, institutional form.

Dates and Deadlines: Priority date 5/1; no closing date. Applicants notified on a rolling basis starting 5/1; must reply by 8/25 or within 2 week(s) of notification.

Transfers: Must reply by 8/25. Tuition guarantee provides no increase in tuition up to three years as long as enrolled full-time.

CONTACT

Lisa Hanson, Director of Financial Aid

2400 Tom L. Wilson Boulevard, Galesburg, IL 61401

(309) 341-5283

City Colleges of Chicago: Harold Washington College

Chicago, Illinois

www.ccc.edu   Federal Code: 001652

2-year public community college in very large city.

Enrollment: 8,059 undergrads.

Selectivity: Open admission; but selective for some programs.

BASIC COSTS (2009-2010)

Tuition and fees: $2,720; out-of-district residents $8,125; out-of-state residents $9,397.

Per-credit charge: $79; out-of-district residents $259; out-of-state residents $302.

FINANCIAL AID PICTURE

Students with need: Need-based aid available for full-time and part-time students. Work study available nights.

Students without need: This college awards aid only to students with need.

FINANCIAL AID PROCEDURES

Forms required: FAFSA.

Dates and Deadlines: Priority date 5/1; closing date 6/30. Applicants notified on a rolling basis starting 7/1; must reply within 2 week(s) of notification.

CONTACT

Francois Hasouk, Director of Financial Aid
30 East Lake Street, Chicago, IL 60601
(312) 553-6041

City Colleges of Chicago: Kennedy-King College

Chicago, Illinois
www.ccc.edu   Federal Code: 001654

2-year public community college in very large city.
Enrollment: 4,791 undergrads.
Selectivity: Open admission.

BASIC COSTS (2009-2010)

Tuition and fees: $2,720; out-of-district residents $8,125; out-of-state residents $9,397.
Per-credit charge: $79; out-of-district residents $259; out-of-state residents $302.
Additional info: Lab fee of $30 for technical and vocational courses.

FINANCIAL AID PICTURE

Students with need: Need-based aid available for full-time and part-time students.
Students without need: This college awards aid only to students with need.

FINANCIAL AID PROCEDURES

Forms required: FAFSA.
Dates and Deadlines: Priority date 8/1; no closing date. Applicants notified on a rolling basis starting 8/15; must reply within 2 week(s) of notification.

CONTACT

Alicia Williams, Financial Aid Supervisor
6800 South Wentworth Avenue, Chicago, IL 60621
(773) 602-5133

City Colleges of Chicago: Malcolm X College

Chicago, Illinois
www.malcolmx.ccc.edu   Federal Code: 001650

2-year public community and junior college in very large city.
Enrollment: 4,328 undergrads.
Selectivity: Open admission; but selective for some programs.

BASIC COSTS (2009-2010)

Tuition and fees: $2,720; out-of-district residents $8,125; out-of-state residents $9,397.
Per-credit charge: $79; out-of-district residents $259; out-of-state residents $302.
Additional info: Some courses require a $30 lab fee.

FINANCIAL AID PICTURE

Students with need: Need-based aid available for full-time and part-time students. Work study available nights, weekends, and for part-time students.
Students without need: This college awards aid only to students with need.

FINANCIAL AID PROCEDURES

Forms required: FAFSA, institutional form.
Dates and Deadlines: Priority date 7/1; no closing date. Applicants notified on a rolling basis starting 7/1; must reply within 2 week(s) of notification.

CONTACT

Patricia Burke, Director, Financial Aid
1900 West Van Buren Street, Chicago, IL 60612
(312) 850-7146

City Colleges of Chicago: Olive-Harvey College

Chicago, Illinois
www.ccc.edu   Federal Code: 009767

2-year public community college in very large city.
Enrollment: 3,216 undergrads.
Selectivity: Open admission; but selective for some programs.

BASIC COSTS (2009-2010)

Tuition and fees: $2,720; out-of-district residents $8,125; out-of-state residents $9,397.
Per-credit charge: $79; out-of-district residents $259; out-of-state residents $302.

FINANCIAL AID PICTURE

Students with need: Need-based aid available for full-time and part-time students.

FINANCIAL AID PROCEDURES

Forms required: FAFSA.
Dates and Deadlines: Priority date 8/15; no closing date. Applicants notified on a rolling basis; must reply within 3 week(s) of notification.

CONTACT

Michael Shields, Director of Financial Aid
10001 South Woodlawn Avenue, Chicago, IL 60628
(773) 291-6391

College of DuPage

Glen Ellyn, Illinois
www.cod.edu   Federal Code: 006656

2-year public community college in large town.
Enrollment: 21,978 undergrads. 2,143 full-time freshmen.
Selectivity: Open admission; but selective for some programs.

BASIC COSTS (2009-2010)

Tuition and fees: $3,475; out-of-district residents $9,145; out-of-state residents $11,095.
Per-credit charge: $92; out-of-district residents $281; out-of-state residents $346.

FINANCIAL AID PICTURE (2008-2009)

Students with need: Out of 1,044 full-time freshmen who applied for aid, 741 were judged to have need. Of these, 592 received aid, and 84 had their full need met. Average financial aid package met 72% of need; average scholarship/grant was $4,684; average loan was $2,828. For part-time students, average financial aid package was $5,928.
Students without need: 111 full-time freshmen who did not demonstrate need for aid received scholarships/grants; average award was $1,710. No-need awards available for academics, art, leadership, minority status, music/drama, state/district residency.

FINANCIAL AID PROCEDURES

Forms required: FAFSA.
Dates and Deadlines: Priority date 4/30; no closing date. Applicants notified on a rolling basis starting 6/1; must reply within 2 week(s) of notification.
Transfers: No deadline. Applicants notified on a rolling basis; must reply within 2 week(s) of notification. Must have financial aid application on file indicating previous institutions attended.

CONTACT

Mark Holysz, Director of Student Financial Aid
425 Fawell Boulevard, Glen Ellyn, IL 60137-6599
(630) 942-2251

College of Lake County

Grayslake, Illinois
www.clcillinois.edu   Federal Code: 007694

2-year public community college in large town.
Enrollment: 13,175 undergrads, 62% part-time. 1,459 full-time freshmen.
Selectivity: Open admission; but selective for some programs.

BASIC COSTS (2010-2011)

Tuition and fees: $2,660; out-of-district residents $6,160; out-of-state residents $8,148.
Per-credit charge: $81; out-of-district residents $206; out-of-state residents $277.
Additional info: Tuition/fee waivers available for minority students.

FINANCIAL AID PICTURE

Students with need: Need-based aid available for full-time and part-time students. Work study available nights.
Students without need: No-need awards available for academics, alumni affiliation, art, athletics, leadership, minority status, music/drama.
Scholarships offered: Academic Achievement Scholarship: based on GPA and student essay; tuition and fees.

FINANCIAL AID PROCEDURES

Forms required: FAFSA.
Dates and Deadlines: Priority date 6/5; no closing date. Applicants notified on a rolling basis starting 6/15; must reply within 2 week(s) of notification.

CONTACT

Karen Hlavin, Assistant Vice President, Student Development
19351 West Washington Street, Grayslake, IL 60030-1198
(847) 543-2062

College of Office Technology

Chicago, Illinois
www.cot.edu   Federal Code: 017378

2-year for-profit career college in very large city.
Enrollment: 276 undergrads.
Selectivity: Open admission.

FINANCIAL AID PICTURE (2008-2009)

Students with need: Average financial aid package for all full-time undergraduates was $10,231. 54% awarded as scholarships/grants, 46% awarded as loans/jobs. Need-based aid available for part-time students.
Students without need: This college awards aid only to students with need.
Cumulative student debt: 73% of graduating class had student loans; average debt was $7,500.

FINANCIAL AID PROCEDURES

Forms required: FAFSA.
Dates and Deadlines: No deadline. Applicants notified on a rolling basis.

CONTACT

Paula Terronez, Educational Operations and Financial Aid Director
1520 West Division Street, Chicago, IL 60642-3312
(773) 278-0042

Columbia College Chicago

Chicago, Illinois
www.colum.edu   Federal Code: 001665

4-year private visual arts and liberal arts college in very large city.
Enrollment: 11,465 undergrads, 9% part-time. 2,333 full-time freshmen.
Selectivity: Open admission; but selective for some programs.

BASIC COSTS (2009-2010)

Tuition and fees: $18,970.
Per-credit charge: $639.
Room and board: $12,000.

FINANCIAL AID PICTURE (2008-2009)

Students with need: Out of 1,837 full-time freshmen who applied for aid, 1,543 were judged to have need. Of these, 1,528 received aid, and 1,122 had their full need met. Average financial aid package met 23% of need; average scholarship/grant was $1,834; average loan was $3,408. For part-time students, average financial aid package was $7,792.
Students without need: No-need awards available for academics, art, leadership, music/drama, state/district residency.

FINANCIAL AID PROCEDURES

Forms required: FAFSA, institutional form.
Dates and Deadlines: Priority date 5/1; no closing date. Applicants notified on a rolling basis.

CONTACT

Jennifer Waters, Executive Director of Student Financial Services
600 South Michigan Avenue, Chicago, IL 60605-1996
(866) 705-0200

Concordia University Chicago

River Forest, Illinois
www.cuchicago.edu   Federal Code: 001666

4-year private university and teachers college in large town, affiliated with Lutheran Church - Missouri Synod.
Enrollment: 1,232 undergrads, 4% part-time. 249 full-time freshmen.
Selectivity: Admits over 75% of applicants.

BASIC COSTS (2010-2011)

Tuition and fees: $24,581.
Per-credit charge: $747.
Room and board: $8,000.

FINANCIAL AID PICTURE (2008-2009)

Students with need: Out of 235 full-time freshmen who applied for aid, 205 were judged to have need. Of these, 204 received aid, and 45 had their full need met. Average financial aid package met 77% of need; average scholarship/grant was $13,670; average loan was $3,644. For part-time students, average financial aid package was $12,042.
Students without need: 44 full-time freshmen who did not demonstrate need for aid received scholarships/grants; average award was $9,634. No-need awards available for academics, alumni affiliation, music/drama, religious affiliation, state/district residency.
Scholarships offered: Presidential Honors: full tuition; selection by essay; 5 per year. Presidential Scholarships: up to $12,000; selection by ACT and GPA. Community Awards: up to $7000; selection by ACT and GPA. Transfer Honors: up to $10,000; selection by GPA. Music Scholarships: amount varies; selection by audition.
Cumulative student debt: 82% of graduating class had student loans; average debt was $21,086.

FINANCIAL AID PROCEDURES

Forms required: FAFSA.

Dates and Deadlines: Priority date 4/1; no closing date. Applicants notified on a rolling basis starting 3/1; must reply within 4 week(s) of notification.
Transfers: No deadline. Applicants notified on a rolling basis; must reply within 4 week(s) of notification.

CONTACT
Aida Asencio-Pinto, Director of Student Financial Planning
7400 Augusta Street, River Forest, IL 60305-1499
(708) 209-3113

Cooking & Hospitality Institute of Chicago
Chicago, Illinois
www.chic.edu   Federal Code: 016758

2-year for-profit culinary school in very large city.
Enrollment: 1,050 undergrads, 1% part-time. 188 full-time freshmen.
Selectivity: Open admission.

BASIC COSTS (2009-2010)
Additional info: Tuition for associate of applied science in Le Cordon Bleu Culinary Arts: $39,950; associate of applied science in Le Cordon Bleu Patisserie and Baking: $38,500; certificate in Le Cordon Bleu Culinary Arts: $15,980; required fees of $400.

FINANCIAL AID PICTURE
Students with need: Need-based aid available for full-time and part-time students. Work study available nights.

FINANCIAL AID PROCEDURES
Forms required: FAFSA, institutional form.
Dates and Deadlines: No deadline. Applicants notified on a rolling basis.
Transfers: No deadline. Applicants notified on a rolling basis.

CONTACT
Nathan Nimrick, Director of Student Finance
361 West Chestnut, Chicago, IL 60610-3050
(312) 944-0882

Danville Area Community College
Danville, Illinois
www.dacc.edu   Federal Code: 001669

2-year public community college in large town.
Enrollment: 3,225 undergrads, 55% part-time. 494 full-time freshmen.
Selectivity: Open admission.

BASIC COSTS (2009-2010)
Tuition and fees: $2,730; out-of-district residents $4,860; out-of-state residents $4,860.
Per-credit charge: $74; out-of-district residents $150; out-of-state residents $150.

FINANCIAL AID PICTURE (2008-2009)
Students with need: 79% of average financial aid package awarded as scholarships/grants, 21% awarded as loans/jobs. Need-based aid available for part-time students. Work study available nights, weekends, and for part-time students.
Students without need: No-need awards available for academics, art, athletics, leadership, minority status, music/drama, state/district residency.

FINANCIAL AID PROCEDURES
Forms required: FAFSA, institutional form.
Dates and Deadlines: Priority date 7/1; no closing date. Applicants notified on a rolling basis starting 4/1.
Transfers: NSLDS reviewed before aid disbursed.

CONTACT
Janet Ingargiola, Director of Financial Aid
2000 East Main Street, Danville, IL 61832
(217) 443-8891

DePaul University
Chicago, Illinois
www.depaul.edu   Federal Code: 001671

4-year private university in very large city, affiliated with Roman Catholic Church.
Enrollment: 15,821 undergrads, 17% part-time. 2,531 full-time freshmen.
Selectivity: Admits 50 to 75% of applicants.

BASIC COSTS (2010-2011)
Tuition and fees: $28,858.
Per-credit charge: $490.
Room and board: $10,955.

FINANCIAL AID PICTURE (2009-2010)
Students with need: Out of 2,291 full-time freshmen who applied for aid, 1,825 were judged to have need. Of these, 1,780 received aid, and 205 had their full need met. Average financial aid package met 72% of need; average scholarship/grant was $16,124; average loan was $3,457. For part-time students, average financial aid package was $10,531.
Students without need: 189 full-time freshmen who did not demonstrate need for aid received scholarships/grants; average award was $9,314. No-need awards available for academics, art, athletics, leadership, music/drama, ROTC, state/district residency.
Scholarships offered: *Merit:* Various scholarships; based on top 10% of class, 1100 SAT (exclusive of writing) or 26 ACT, and active in student/community organizations. *Athletic:* 45 full-time freshmen received athletic scholarships; average amount $18,865.
Cumulative student debt: 64% of graduating class had student loans; average debt was $19,072.

FINANCIAL AID PROCEDURES
Forms required: FAFSA.
Dates and Deadlines: Priority date 3/1; no closing date. Applicants notified on a rolling basis starting 3/15.
Transfers: Closing date 4/1. Applicants notified on a rolling basis starting 5/1; must reply by 8/1. 5 different scholarships awarded to fall incoming transfer students who have been admitted and have submitted scholarship application by April 1. Scholarships range from $2,000-$7,000, and vary based on competitiveness of pool and student's qualifications.

CONTACT
Paula Luff, Director of Financial Aid
One East Jackson Boulevard, Chicago, IL 60604-2287
(312) 362-8091

DeVry University: Addison
Addison, Illinois
www.devry.edu   Federal Code: 016219

4-year for-profit university in large town.
Enrollment: 1,504 undergrads, 39% part-time. 156 full-time freshmen.

BASIC COSTS (2009-2010)
Tuition and fees: $14,160.
Per-credit charge: $550.

FINANCIAL AID PICTURE (2008-2009)
Students with need: Need-based aid available for full-time and part-time students.
Students without need: This college awards aid only to students with need.

FINANCIAL AID PROCEDURES

Forms required: FAFSA.

Dates and Deadlines: No deadline. Applicants notified on a rolling basis.

CONTACT

Sajel Anin, Director of Student Finance

1221 North Swift Road, Addison, IL 60101-6106

(630) 953-1300

DeVry University: Chicago

Chicago, Illinois

www.devry.edu   Federal Code: 010727

4-year for-profit university in very large city.

Enrollment: 2,063 undergrads, 43% part-time. 220 full-time freshmen.

BASIC COSTS (2009-2010)

Tuition and fees: $14,160.

Per-credit charge: $550.

FINANCIAL AID PICTURE (2008-2009)

Students with need: Need-based aid available for full-time and part-time students.

Students without need: This college awards aid only to students with need.

FINANCIAL AID PROCEDURES

Forms required: FAFSA.

Dates and Deadlines: No deadline. Applicants notified on a rolling basis.

CONTACT

Milena Dobrina, Director of Financial Aid

3300 North Campbell Avenue, Chicago, IL 60618-5994

(773) 929-8509

DeVry University: Tinley Park

Tinley Park, Illinois

www.devry.edu   Federal Code: 022966

4-year for-profit university in large town.

Enrollment: 1,131 undergrads, 48% part-time. 85 full-time freshmen.

BASIC COSTS (2009-2010)

Tuition and fees: $14,160.

Per-credit charge: $550.

FINANCIAL AID PICTURE (2008-2009)

Students with need: Need-based aid available for full-time and part-time students.

Students without need: This college awards aid only to students with need.

FINANCIAL AID PROCEDURES

Forms required: FAFSA.

Dates and Deadlines: No deadline. Applicants notified on a rolling basis.

CONTACT

Sejal Amin, Director of Student Finance

18624 West Creek Drive, Tinley Park, IL 60477-6243

(708) 342-3219

Dominican University

River Forest, Illinois

www.dom.edu   Federal Code: 001750

4-year private university and liberal arts college in large town, affiliated with Roman Catholic Church.

Enrollment: 1,769 undergrads, 7% part-time. 405 full-time freshmen.

Selectivity: Admits 50 to 75% of applicants.

BASIC COSTS (2010-2011)

Tuition and fees: $25,810.

Per-credit charge: $852.

Room and board: $8,000.

FINANCIAL AID PICTURE (2009-2010)

Students with need: Need-based aid available for full-time and part-time students. Work study available nights, weekends, and for part-time students.

Students without need: No-need awards available for academics, alumni affiliation, leadership.

Scholarships offered: Presidential Scholarships: $14,000. Dean's Scholarships: $12,000. University Honor Scholarships: $10,000. Achievement Scholarships: $8,000. All based on ACT/SAT scores and class rank. Ida Brechtel Scholarships: $7,500 up to full tuition; for students majoring in chemistry or biology/chemistry.

FINANCIAL AID PROCEDURES

Forms required: FAFSA.

Dates and Deadlines: Priority date 6/1; no closing date. Applicants notified on a rolling basis starting 2/15; must reply within 2 week(s) of notification.

Transfers: No deadline. Applicants notified on a rolling basis starting 3/15; must reply within 3 week(s) of notification. Merit scholarships available to full-time students with GPA of 3.3 from previous institution. Phi Theta Kappa scholarships available to PTK members.

CONTACT

Michael Shields, Director of Financial Aid

7900 West Division Street, River Forest, IL 60305-1099

(708) 524-6809

East-West University

Chicago, Illinois

www.eastwest.edu   Federal Code: 015310

4-year private university in very large city.

Enrollment: 1,040 full-time undergrads.

Selectivity: Open admission; but selective for some programs.

BASIC COSTS (2009-2010)

Tuition and fees: $15,795.

FINANCIAL AID PICTURE

Students with need: Need-based aid available for full-time and part-time students.

Students without need: No-need awards available for academics.

Additional info: Foreign students eligible for institutional scholarship.

FINANCIAL AID PROCEDURES

Forms required: FAFSA

Dates and Deadlines: No deadline. Applicants notified on a rolling basis starting 1/4; must reply within 4 week(s) of notification.

Transfers: Closing date 4/1.

CONTACT

Elizabeth Guzman, Director of Financial Aid

816 South Michigan Avenue, Chicago, IL 60605

(312) 939-0111

Eastern Illinois University
Charleston, Illinois
www.eiu.edu   Federal Code: 001674

4-year public university and teachers college in large town.

Enrollment: 10,055 undergrads, 10% part-time. 1,637 full-time freshmen.

Selectivity: Admits 50 to 75% of applicants.

BASIC COSTS (2009-2010)
Tuition and fees: $9,429; out-of-state residents $23,769.
Per-credit charge: $239; out-of-state residents $717.
Room and board: $8,078.

FINANCIAL AID PICTURE (2009-2010)
Students with need: Out of 1,455 full-time freshmen who applied for aid, 902 were judged to have need. Of these, 863 received aid, and 81 had their full need met. Average financial aid package met 61% of need; average scholarship/grant was $3,243; average loan was $3,245. For part-time students, average financial aid package was $7,383.

Students without need: 67 full-time freshmen who did not demonstrate need for aid received scholarships/grants; average award was $3,513. No-need awards available for academics, art, athletics, leadership, music/drama, ROTC.

Scholarships offered: 41 full-time freshmen received athletic scholarships; average amount $10,184.

Cumulative student debt: 53% of graduating class had student loans; average debt was $11,547.

FINANCIAL AID PROCEDURES
Forms required: FAFSA.

Dates and Deadlines: Priority date 3/1; no closing date. Applicants notified on a rolling basis starting 3/1; must reply within 2 week(s) of notification.

CONTACT
Jerry Donna, Director of Financial Aid
600 Lincoln Avenue, Charleston, IL 61920-3011
(217) 581-3713

Elgin Community College
Elgin, Illinois
www.elgin.edu   Federal Code: 001675

2-year public community college in small city.

Enrollment: 8,067 undergrads, 54% part-time. 955 full-time freshmen.

Selectivity: Open admission; but selective for some programs.

BASIC COSTS (2010-2011)
Tuition and fees: $2,740; out-of-district residents $10,752; out-of-state residents $13,290.
Per-credit charge: $91; out-of-district residents $358; out-of-state residents $443.

FINANCIAL AID PICTURE
Students with need: Need-based aid available for full-time and part-time students. Work study available nights, weekends, and for part-time students.

Students without need: No-need awards available for academics, alumni affiliation, art, athletics, job skills, leadership, minority status, music/drama, religious affiliation, ROTC, state/district residency.

FINANCIAL AID PROCEDURES
Forms required: FAFSA, institutional form.

Dates and Deadlines: Priority date 6/1; no closing date. Applicants notified on a rolling basis starting 4/6; must reply within 3 week(s) of notification.

CONTACT
Amy Perrin, Director of Student Financial Assistance
1700 Spartan Drive, Elgin, IL 60123-7193
(847) 214-7520

Elmhurst College
Elmhurst, Illinois
www.elmhurst.edu   Federal Code: 001676

4-year private liberal arts college in large town, affiliated with United Church of Christ.

Enrollment: 3,007 undergrads, 6% part-time. 561 full-time freshmen.

Selectivity: Admits 50 to 75% of applicants.

BASIC COSTS (2010-2011)
Tuition and fees: $28,600.
Per-credit charge: $814.
Room and board: $9,266.

FINANCIAL AID PICTURE (2008-2009)
Students with need: Out of 487 full-time freshmen who applied for aid, 409 were judged to have need. Of these, 409 received aid, and 71 had their full need met. Average financial aid package met 82% of need; average scholarship/grant was $15,062; average loan was $3,859. For part-time students, average financial aid package was $7,990.

Students without need: 124 full-time freshmen who did not demonstrate need for aid received scholarships/grants; average award was $11,491. No-need awards available for academics, alumni affiliation, art, minority status, music/drama, religious affiliation, ROTC, state/district residency.

Scholarships offered: Presidential Scholarship: $13,000-$18,000; 451 awarded. Dean's Scholarship: 9,000-$12,000; 458 awarded. Founder's Scholarship: $4,000-$8,000; 209 awarded. Combination of class rank, test scores, and GPA considered.

Cumulative student debt: 69% of graduating class had student loans; average debt was $20,675.

Additional info: Must apply for admission by 1/15 for priority consideration for scholarships.

FINANCIAL AID PROCEDURES
Forms required: FAFSA.

Dates and Deadlines: Priority date 4/15; no closing date. Applicants notified on a rolling basis starting 3/1; must reply within 3 week(s) of notification.

CONTACT
Ruth Pusich, Director of Financial Aid
190 South Prospect Avenue, Elmhurst, IL 60126-3296
(630) 617-3075

Eureka College
Eureka, Illinois
www.eureka.edu   Federal Code: 001678

4-year private liberal arts college in small town, affiliated with Christian Church (Disciples of Christ).

Enrollment: 716 undergrads.

BASIC COSTS (2009-2010)
Tuition and fees: $17,390.
Per-credit charge: $475.
Room and board: $7,440.

FINANCIAL AID PICTURE (2009-2010)
Students with need: Need-based aid available for full-time and part-time students. Work study available nights, weekends, and for part-time students.

Students without need: No-need awards available for academics, alumni affiliation, art, leadership, music/drama, religious affiliation.

Scholarships offered: Reagan Fellows Program: full tuition; 5 awarded. Sandifer Mentorships: fully paid mentorship anywhere in the world at end of sophomore year; all freshmen eligible. Eureka College Ministry Fellowship: full tuition scholarships; 2 available each year.

FINANCIAL AID PROCEDURES
Forms required: FAFSA.
Dates and Deadlines: Priority date 4/15; no closing date. Applicants notified on a rolling basis starting 2/15; must reply by 5/1 or within 3 week(s) of notification.
Transfers: No deadline. Applicants notified on a rolling basis; must reply within 2 week(s) of notification.

CONTACT
Ellen Rigsby, Director of Financial Aid
300 East College Avenue, Eureka, IL 61530-1500
(309) 467-6311

Governors State University
University Park, Illinois
www.govst.edu   Federal Code: 009145

Upper-division public university in large town.
Enrollment: 2,791 undergrads, 63% part-time.
Selectivity: Open admission; but selective for some programs.

BASIC COSTS (2009-2010)
Tuition and fees: $8,352; out-of-state residents $18,432.
Per-credit charge: $224; out-of-state residents $560.
Additional info: Tuition at time of enrollment locked for 2 years; tuition/fee waivers available for minority students.

FINANCIAL AID PICTURE (2008-2009)
Students with need: Need-based aid available for full-time and part-time students. Work study available nights, weekends, and for part-time students.
Students without need: No-need awards available for academics.

FINANCIAL AID PROCEDURES
Dates and Deadlines: Priority date 5/1; closing date 10/1. Applicants notified on a rolling basis.

CONTACT
Freda Whisenton-Comer, Office of Financial Aid
One University Parkway, University Park, IL 60484
(708) 534-4480

Greenville College
Greenville, Illinois
www.greenville.edu   Federal Code: 001684

4-year private liberal arts college in small town, affiliated with Free Methodist Church of North America.
Enrollment: 1,360 undergrads, 2% part-time. 320 full-time freshmen.
Selectivity: Admits over 75% of applicants.

BASIC COSTS (2010-2011)
Tuition and fees: $20,924.
Per-credit charge: $437.
Room and board: $7,034.

FINANCIAL AID PICTURE (2008-2009)
Students with need: Out of 279 full-time freshmen who applied for aid, 258 were judged to have need. Of these, 256 received aid, and 33 had their full need met. Average financial aid package met 83% of need; average scholarship/grant was $13,266; average loan was $3,767. For part-time students, average financial aid package was $6,408.

Students without need: 58 full-time freshmen who did not demonstrate need for aid received scholarships/grants; average award was $6,843. No-need awards available for academics, alumni affiliation, art, leadership, minority status, music/drama, religious affiliation, state/district residency.
Scholarships offered: President's Scholarships: $8,000; requiring cumulative GPA of 3.0, ACT of 27 or SAT of 1210, and leadership qualities. Dean's Scholarship: $6,000; for GPA of 3.0, ACT of 22 or SAT of 1020, and leadership qualities. Leadership Scholarships: $500-$4,000; for GPA of 2.5, ACT of 18 or SAT 860, and leadership qualities. (All SAT scores are exclusive of Writing.).
Cumulative student debt: 86% of graduating class had student loans; average debt was $25,268.

FINANCIAL AID PROCEDURES
Forms required: FAFSA.
Dates and Deadlines: Priority date 4/1; no closing date. Applicants notified on a rolling basis starting 3/1; must reply within 3 week(s) of notification.
Transfers: No deadline. Applicants notified on a rolling basis; must reply within 3 week(s) of notification.

CONTACT
Marilae Latham, Director of Financial Aid
315 East College Avenue, Greenville, IL 62246-0159
(618) 664-7111

Harper College
Palatine, Illinois
www.harpercollege.edu   Federal Code: 003961

2-year public community college in small city.
Enrollment: 8,044 undergrads, 42% part-time. 1,503 full-time freshmen.
Selectivity: Open admission; but selective for some programs.

BASIC COSTS (2009-2010)
Tuition and fees: $3,234; out-of-district residents $10,194; out-of-state residents $12,504.
Per-credit charge: $90; out-of-district residents $322; out-of-state residents $399.
Additional info: In-district tuition rates available to employees of in-district companies who reside outside college district.

FINANCIAL AID PICTURE (2008-2009)
Students with need: Need-based aid available for full-time and part-time students. Work study available nights, weekends, and for part-time students.
Students without need: No-need awards available for academics, art, leadership, minority status, music/drama, state/district residency.
Scholarships offered: Distinguished Scholar Award; full tuition and fees; available to full-time students during regular academic year who graduate in top 10% of class from district high school; renewable for second year.

FINANCIAL AID PROCEDURES
Forms required: FAFSA, institutional form.
Dates and Deadlines: Priority date 3/1; no closing date. Applicants notified on a rolling basis starting 3/1; must reply within 2 week(s) of notification.
Transfers: No deadline. Applicants notified on a rolling basis starting 3/1; must reply within 2 week(s) of notification.

CONTACT
Earl Dowling, Director, Scholarships and Financial Assistance
1200 West Algonquin Road, Palatine, IL 60067-7398
(847) 925-6248

Harrington College of Design
Chicago, Illinois
www.harringtoncollege.com   Federal Code: 013601

4-year for-profit visual arts college in very large city.
Enrollment: 1,084 undergrads.
Selectivity: Open admission; but selective for some programs.

BASIC COSTS (2009-2010)
Tuition and fees: $17,270.
Additional info: Required fees vary depending on program. Some programs require laptop computer purchase.

FINANCIAL AID PICTURE
Students with need: Need-based aid available for full-time and part-time students.
Students without need: This college awards aid only to students with need.

FINANCIAL AID PROCEDURES
Forms required: FAFSA.
Dates and Deadlines: Closing date 7/15. Applicants notified on a rolling basis; must reply within 2 week(s) of notification.
Transfers: No deadline.

CONTACT
Renee Darosky, Director of Financial Aid
200 West Madison Avenue, Chicago, IL 60606
(877) 939-4975

Harry S. Truman College
Chicago, Illinois
www.trumancollege.edu/   Federal Code: 001648

2-year public community college in very large city.
Enrollment: 6,240 undergrads.
Selectivity: Open admission; but selective for some programs.

BASIC COSTS (2009-2010)
Tuition and fees: $2,720; out-of-district residents $8,125; out-of-state residents $9,397.
Per-credit charge: $79; out-of-district residents $259; out-of-state residents $302.

FINANCIAL AID PICTURE
Students with need: Need-based aid available for full-time and part-time students. Work study available nights, weekends, and for part-time students.
Students without need: This college awards aid only to students with need.

FINANCIAL AID PROCEDURES
Forms required: FAFSA.
Dates and Deadlines: No deadline. Applicants notified on a rolling basis starting 7/1; must reply within 3 week(s) of notification.

CONTACT
Shirley Howell, Director of Financial Aid
1145 West Wilson Avenue, Chicago, IL 60640
(773) 907-4810

Heartland Community College
Normal, Illinois
www.heartland.edu   Federal Code: 030838

2-year public community college in small city.
Enrollment: 5,257 undergrads.

Selectivity: Open admission; but selective for some programs.

BASIC COSTS (2009-2010)
Tuition and fees: $2,850; out-of-district residents $5,490; out-of-state residents $8,130.
Per-credit charge: $88; out-of-district residents $176; out-of-state residents $264.

FINANCIAL AID PICTURE (2008-2009)
Students with need: Need-based aid available for full-time and part-time students. Work study available nights, weekends, and for part-time students.
Students without need: No-need awards available for academics, alumni affiliation, athletics, job skills, leadership, minority status, state/district residency.

FINANCIAL AID PROCEDURES
Forms required: FAFSA, institutional form.
Dates and Deadlines: Priority date 4/1; no closing date. Applicants notified on a rolling basis starting 5/15; must reply within 2 week(s) of notification.

CONTACT
Cheryl Schaffer, Director of Financial Aid
1500 West Raab Road, Normal, IL 61761
(309) 268-8020

Highland Community College
Freeport, Illinois
www.highland.edu   Federal Code: 001681

2-year public community college in large town.
Enrollment: 2,104 undergrads, 44% part-time. 317 full-time freshmen.
Selectivity: Open admission; but selective for some programs.

BASIC COSTS (2009-2010)
Tuition and fees: $2,730; out-of-district residents $4,230; out-of-state residents $4,410.
Per-credit charge: $84; out-of-district residents $134; out-of-state residents $140.

FINANCIAL AID PICTURE (2008-2009)
Students with need: Out of 234 full-time freshmen who applied for aid, 197 were judged to have need. Of these, 180 received aid. Average financial aid package met 32% of need; average scholarship/grant was $4,059; average loan was $2,509. For part-time students, average financial aid package was $2,333.
Students without need: 26 full-time freshmen who did not demonstrate need for aid received scholarships/grants; average award was $1,991. No-need awards available for academics, athletics.
Scholarships offered: 15 full-time freshmen received athletic scholarships; average amount $1,151.

FINANCIAL AID PROCEDURES
Forms required: FAFSA, institutional form.
Dates and Deadlines: No deadline. Applicants notified on a rolling basis starting 8/1; must reply within 2 week(s) of notification.
Transfers: No deadline. Applicants notified on a rolling basis starting 4/1.

CONTACT
Kathy Bangasser, Director of Financial Aid
2998 West Pearl City Road, Freeport, IL 61032-9341
(815) 599-3559

Illinois College

Jacksonville, Illinois
www.ic.edu   Federal Code: 001688

4-year private liberal arts college in large town, affiliated with United Church of Christ and Presbyterian Church (USA).

Enrollment: 854 undergrads. 218 full-time freshmen.

Selectivity: Admits 50 to 75% of applicants.

BASIC COSTS (2010-2011)

Tuition and fees: $21,300.

Room and board: $7,600.

FINANCIAL AID PICTURE (2009-2010)

Students with need: Out of 200 full-time freshmen who applied for aid, 174 were judged to have need. Of these, 174 received aid, and 52 had their full need met. Average financial aid package met 88% of need; average scholarship/grant was $14,346; average loan was $3,864. For part-time students, average financial aid package was $8,031.

Students without need: 41 full-time freshmen who did not demonstrate need for aid received scholarships/grants; average award was $9,852. No-need awards available for academics, art, minority status, music/drama.

Scholarships offered: College transfer scholarship; available with 12 transferable credit hours and minimum 3.0 GPA.

Cumulative student debt: 76% of graduating class had student loans; average debt was $21,258.

FINANCIAL AID PROCEDURES

Forms required: FAFSA.

Dates and Deadlines: Priority date 3/1; no closing date. Applicants notified on a rolling basis starting 3/1; must reply within 2 week(s) of notification.

Transfers: No deadline. Applicants notified on a rolling basis starting 6/1; must reply within 2 week(s) of notification.

CONTACT

Katherine Taylor, Director of Financial Aid
1101 West College Avenue, Jacksonville, IL 62650
(217) 245-3035

Illinois Eastern Community Colleges: Frontier Community College

Fairfield, Illinois
www.iecc.edu/fcc   Federal Code: 014090

2-year public community college in small town.

Enrollment: 556 undergrads, 46% part-time. 35 full-time freshmen.

Selectivity: Open admission; but selective for some programs.

BASIC COSTS (2009-2010)

Tuition and fees: $2,010; out-of-district residents $6,095; out-of-state residents $7,621.

Per-credit charge: $62; out-of-district residents $198; out-of-state residents $249.

FINANCIAL AID PICTURE

Students with need: Need-based aid available for full-time and part-time students.

Students without need: No-need awards available for academics, state/district residency.

FINANCIAL AID PROCEDURES

Forms required: FAFSA, institutional form.

Dates and Deadlines: No deadline. Applicants notified on a rolling basis starting 8/1; must reply within 2 week(s) of notification.

CONTACT

Adam Bowles, Financial Aid Coordinator
2 Frontier Drive, Fairfield, IL 62837-9801
(618) 842-3711

Illinois Eastern Community Colleges: Lincoln Trail College

Robinson, Illinois
www.iecc.edu/ltc   Federal Code: 009786

2-year public community college in small town.

Enrollment: 892 undergrads, 38% part-time. 119 full-time freshmen.

Selectivity: Open admission.

BASIC COSTS (2009-2010)

Tuition and fees: $2,010; out-of-district residents $6,095; out-of-state residents $7,621.

Per-credit charge: $62; out-of-district residents $198; out-of-state residents $249.

FINANCIAL AID PICTURE

Students with need: Need-based aid available for full-time and part-time students.

Students without need: No-need awards available for academics, athletics, state/district residency.

FINANCIAL AID PROCEDURES

Forms required: FAFSA, institutional form.

Dates and Deadlines: No deadline. Applicants notified on a rolling basis starting 8/1; must reply within 2 week(s) of notification.

CONTACT

Jennifer Barthelemy, Coordinator of Financial Aid
11220 State Highway 1, Robinson, IL 62454-5707
(618) 544-8657

Illinois Eastern Community Colleges: Olney Central College

Olney, Illinois
www.iecc.edu/occ   Federal Code: 001742

2-year public community college in small town.

Enrollment: 1,111 undergrads, 20% part-time. 102 full-time freshmen.

Selectivity: Open admission; but selective for some programs.

BASIC COSTS (2009-2010)

Tuition and fees: $2,010; out-of-district residents $6,095; out-of-state residents $7,621.

Per-credit charge: $62; out-of-district residents $198; out-of-state residents $249.

FINANCIAL AID PICTURE

Students with need: Need-based aid available for full-time and part-time students.

Students without need: No-need awards available for academics, athletics, state/district residency.

FINANCIAL AID PROCEDURES

Forms required: FAFSA, institutional form.

Dates and Deadlines: No deadline. Applicants notified on a rolling basis starting 8/1; must reply within 2 week(s) of notification.

CONTACT

Vicki Stuckey, Financial Aid Coordinator
305 North West Street, Olney, IL 62450
(618) 395-7777

Illinois Eastern Community Colleges: Wabash Valley College
Mount Carmel, Illinois
www.iecc.edu/wvc Federal Code: 001779

2-year public community college in small town.
Enrollment: 1,034 undergrads, 20% part-time. 117 full-time freshmen.
Selectivity: Open admission.

BASIC COSTS (2009-2010)
Tuition and fees: $2,010; out-of-district residents $6,095; out-of-state residents $7,621.
Per-credit charge: $62; out-of-district residents $198; out-of-state residents $249.

FINANCIAL AID PICTURE
Students with need: Need-based aid available for full-time and part-time students.
Students without need: No-need awards available for academics, athletics, state/district residency.

FINANCIAL AID PROCEDURES
Forms required: FAFSA, institutional form.
Dates and Deadlines: No deadline. Applicants notified on a rolling basis starting 8/1; must reply within 2 week(s) of notification.

CONTACT
Melinda Silvernale, Financial Aid Coordinator
2200 College Drive, Mount Carmel, IL 62863-2657
(618) 262-8641

Illinois Institute of Art: Schaumburg
Schaumburg, Illinois
www.artinstitutes.edu/schaumburg Federal Code: 012584

3-year for-profit visual arts and career college in small city.
Enrollment: 1,153 undergrads.
Selectivity: Open admission; but selective for some programs.

BASIC COSTS (2009-2010)
Tuition and fees: $21,600.
Per-credit charge: $450.
Room and board: $7,080.

FINANCIAL AID PICTURE
Students with need: Need-based aid available for full-time and part-time students. Work study available nights, weekends, and for part-time students.
Students without need: No-need awards available for academics, art.
Scholarships offered: Scholarships based on GPA and talent-based scholarships available.

FINANCIAL AID PROCEDURES
Forms required: FAFSA.
Dates and Deadlines: Priority date 3/1; no closing date.
Transfers: No deadline. Applicants notified on a rolling basis.

CONTACT
Joe Payne, Director of Student Financial Services
1000 North Plaza Drive, Schaumburg, IL 60173
(800) 314-3450

Illinois Institute of Technology
Chicago, Illinois
www.iit.edu Federal Code: 001691

4-year private university and engineering college in very large city.
Enrollment: 2,618 undergrads, 5% part-time. 521 full-time freshmen.
Selectivity: Admits 50 to 75% of applicants.

BASIC COSTS (2010-2011)
Tuition and fees: $32,393.
Per-credit charge: $945.
Room and board: $10,338.

FINANCIAL AID PICTURE (2008-2009)
Students with need: Out of 399 full-time freshmen who applied for aid, 344 were judged to have need. Of these, 342 received aid, and 71 had their full need met. Average financial aid package met 79% of need; average scholarship/grant was $19,900; average loan was $4,124. For part-time students, average financial aid package was $6,451.
Students without need: 173 full-time freshmen who did not demonstrate need for aid received scholarships/grants; average award was $13,672. No-need awards available for academics, alumni affiliation, athletics, leadership, ROTC.
Scholarships offered: *Merit:* Henry Heald Scholarship: up to $10,000; based on student application. University Scholarship: up to $10,000; based on student application. Crown Scholarship (College of Architecture): full-tuition; based on student application, on-campus interview and portfolio. Camras Scholarship: 3/4-tuition and full-tuition; based on student application, on-campus interview and essay. Leadership Edge Scholarship (Stuart School of Business): based on student application, on-campus interview and essay. *Athletic:* 19 full-time freshmen received athletic scholarships; average amount $8,905.

FINANCIAL AID PROCEDURES
Forms required: FAFSA.
Dates and Deadlines: Priority date 4/15; no closing date. Applicants notified on a rolling basis starting 3/5.
Transfers: No deadline. Applicants notified on a rolling basis starting 3/5.

CONTACT
Gerald Doyle, Vice Provost, Undergraduate Admission and Financial Aid
10 West 33rd Street, Chicago, IL 60616
(312) 567-7219

Illinois State University
Normal, Illinois
www.ilstu.edu Federal Code: 001692

4-year public university in small city.
Enrollment: 18,325 undergrads, 6% part-time. 3,030 full-time freshmen.
Selectivity: Admits 50 to 75% of applicants.

BASIC COSTS (2009-2010)
Tuition and fees: $10,531; out-of-state residents $16,561.
Per-credit charge: $276; out-of-state residents $477.
Room and board: $7,782.

FINANCIAL AID PICTURE (2009-2010)
Students with need: Out of 2,535 full-time freshmen who applied for aid, 1,727 were judged to have need. Of these, 1,602 received aid, and 654 had their full need met. Average financial aid package met 78% of need; average scholarship/grant was $9,134; average loan was $6,349. For part-time students, average financial aid package was $11,044.
Students without need: 48 full-time freshmen who did not demonstrate need for aid received scholarships/grants; average award was $2,062. No-need awards available for academics, art, athletics, music/drama.

Scholarships offered: *Merit:* Various non-need based merit scholarships available, including Presidential Scholars' Program, Provost's Scholarship, and Dean's Scholarship. ***Athletic:*** 26 full-time freshmen received athletic scholarships; average amount $11,593.
Cumulative student debt: 61% of graduating class had student loans; average debt was $20,105.

FINANCIAL AID PROCEDURES
Forms required: FAFSA.
Dates and Deadlines: Priority date 3/1; no closing date. Applicants notified on a rolling basis starting 5/1; must reply within 2 week(s) of notification.

CONTACT
Jana Albrecht, Director of Financial Aid
Campus Box 2200, Normal, IL 61790-2200
(309) 438-2231

Illinois Valley Community College
Oglesby, Illinois
www.ivcc.edu   Federal Code: 001705

2-year public community college in small town.
Enrollment: 3,291 undergrads, 42% part-time. 335 full-time freshmen.
Selectivity: Open admission; but selective for some programs.

BASIC COSTS (2009-2010)
Tuition and fees: $2,103; out-of-district residents $7,439; out-of-state residents $8,436.
Per-credit charge: $63; out-of-district residents $240; out-of-state residents $273.

FINANCIAL AID PICTURE (2008-2009)
Students with need: Need-based aid available for full-time and part-time students.

FINANCIAL AID PROCEDURES
Forms required: FAFSA.
Dates and Deadlines: Priority date 5/1; no closing date. Applicants notified on a rolling basis starting 5/1.

CONTACT
Steve Crick, Director, Financial Aid
815 North Orlando Smith Avenue, Oglesby, IL 61348-9693
(815) 224-0438

Illinois Wesleyan University
Bloomington, Illinois   Federal Code: 001696
www.iwu.edu   CSS Code: 1320

4-year private university and liberal arts college in small city.
Enrollment: 2,059 undergrads. 518 full-time freshmen.
Selectivity: Admits 50 to 75% of applicants.

BASIC COSTS (2010-2011)
Tuition and fees: $35,256.
Per-credit charge: $1,096.
Room and board: $8,106.

FINANCIAL AID PICTURE (2009-2010)
Students with need: Out of 417 full-time freshmen who applied for aid, 347 were judged to have need. Of these, 347 received aid, and 130 had their full need met. Average financial aid package met 92% of need; average scholarship/grant was $19,231; average loan was $3,951.
Students without need: 144 full-time freshmen who did not demonstrate need for aid received scholarships/grants; average award was $13,460. No-need awards available for academics, art, music/drama, ROTC.

Scholarships offered: Academic scholarships based on high school academic performance, recommendations, testing. Talent awards available in music, art, theater, and musical theater. Limited number of full-tuition awards in music.
Cumulative student debt: 56% of graduating class had student loans; average debt was $26,458.

FINANCIAL AID PROCEDURES
Forms required: FAFSA, institutional form. Institution's own financial aid form or CSS PROFILE required.
Dates and Deadlines: Closing date 3/1. Applicants notified on a rolling basis starting 2/15; must reply by 5/1 or within 3 week(s) of notification.
Transfers: No deadline. Applicants notified on a rolling basis; must reply by 5/1 or within 3 week(s) of notification.

CONTACT
Scott Seibring, Director of Financial Aid
PO Box 2900, Bloomington, IL 61702-2900
(309) 556-3096

International Academy of Design and Technology: Chicago
Chicago, Illinois
www.iadtchicago.edu   Federal Code: 021603

4-year for-profit visual arts and technical college in very large city.
Enrollment: 1,574 undergrads.
Selectivity: Open admission.

FINANCIAL AID PICTURE (2008-2009)
Students with need: Need-based aid available for full-time and part-time students.
Students without need: This college awards aid only to students with need.
Additional info: College work study programs available to day and evening students.

FINANCIAL AID PROCEDURES
Forms required: FAFSA.
Dates and Deadlines: No deadline. Applicants notified on a rolling basis.
Transfers: No deadline. Applicants notified on a rolling basis; must reply within 2 week(s) of notification.

CONTACT
Andrea Watkins, Associate Director of Financial Aid
One North State Street, Suite 500, Chicago, IL 60602
(312) 980-9200 ext. 9251

John A. Logan College
Carterville, Illinois
www.jalc.edu   Federal Code: 008076

2-year public community college in small town.
Enrollment: 2,608 undergrads, 25% part-time.
Selectivity: Open admission; but selective for some programs.

BASIC COSTS (2009-2010)
Tuition and fees: $2,280; out-of-district residents $5,874; out-of-state residents $7,877.
Per-credit charge: $71; out-of-district residents $196; out-of-state residents $263.

FINANCIAL AID PICTURE (2008-2009)
Students with need: Need-based aid available for full-time and part-time students.

Students without need: This college awards aid only to students with need.

FINANCIAL AID PROCEDURES

Forms required: FAFSA, institutional form.

Dates and Deadlines: Priority date 5/1; no closing date. Applicants notified on a rolling basis starting 5/1.

CONTACT

Sherry Summary, Director for Student Financial Assistance

700 Logan College Road, Carterville, IL 62918

(618) 985-3741 ext. 8308

John Wood Community College

Quincy, Illinois

www.jwcc.edu   Federal Code: 012813

2-year public community college in large town.

Enrollment: 2,115 undergrads.

Selectivity: Open admission; but selective for some programs.

BASIC COSTS (2009-2010)

Tuition and fees: $3,210; out-of-state residents $6,210.

Per-credit charge: $97; out-of-state residents $197.

FINANCIAL AID PICTURE

Students with need: Need-based aid available for full-time and part-time students. Work study available nights, weekends, and for part-time students.

FINANCIAL AID PROCEDURES

Forms required: FAFSA.

Dates and Deadlines: No deadline. Applicants notified on a rolling basis starting 3/1.

CONTACT

Melanie Lechtenberg, Director of Financial Aid

1301 South 48th Street, Quincy, IL 62305-8736

(217) 641-4336

Joliet Junior College

Joliet, Illinois

www.jjc.edu   Federal Code: 001699

2-year public community college in small city.

Enrollment: 12,694 undergrads.

Selectivity: Open admission; but selective for some programs and for out-of-state students.

BASIC COSTS (2009-2010)

Tuition and fees: $2,790; out-of-district residents $7,547; out-of-state residents $8,406.

Per-credit charge: $67; out-of-district residents $226; out-of-state residents $254.

Additional info: Additional course fees range from $3 to $90.

FINANCIAL AID PICTURE (2008-2009)

Students with need: Need-based aid available for full-time and part-time students. Work study available nights, weekends, and for part-time students.

Students without need: No-need awards available for academics.

FINANCIAL AID PROCEDURES

Forms required: FAFSA, institutional form.

Dates and Deadlines: Closing date 5/1. Applicants notified on a rolling basis starting 5/15.

CONTACT

David Seward, Director of Financial Aid

1215 Houbolt Road, Joliet, IL 60431-8938

(815) 729-9020 ext. 2701

Judson University

Elgin, Illinois

www.judsonu.edu   Federal Code: 001700

4-year private university and liberal arts college in small city, affiliated with American Baptist Churches in the USA.

Enrollment: 983 undergrads, 14% part-time. 179 full-time freshmen.

Selectivity: Admits 50 to 75% of applicants.

BASIC COSTS (2010-2011)

Tuition and fees: $24,780.

Room and board: $8,500.

Additional info: Tuition at time of enrollment locked for 4 years.

FINANCIAL AID PICTURE (2008-2009)

Students with need: Out of 150 full-time freshmen who applied for aid, 125 were judged to have need. Of these, 125 received aid. Average financial aid package met 40% of need; average scholarship/grant was $5,830; average loan was $2,897. For part-time students, average financial aid package was $2,877.

Students without need: 14 full-time freshmen who did not demonstrate need for aid received scholarships/grants; average award was $7,607. No-need awards available for academics, alumni affiliation, art, athletics, music/drama.

Scholarships offered: *Merit:* Academic Merit Award: 1 awarded; $7,000; incoming freshmen with ACT score of 25 (1140 SAT, exclusive of Writing) or higher with at least 3.33 GPA. Academic Merit Award: 2 awarded; $5,000; incoming freshmen with ACT score of 25 (1140 SAT, exclusive of Writing) or higher with a 3.32 GPA or less. Academic Merit Award: 3 awarded; $5,000; incoming freshmen with ACT score from 19-24 (910-1110 SAT, exclusive of Writing) with 3.3 GPA or higher. *Athletic:* 71 full-time freshmen received athletic scholarships; average amount $11,918.

Cumulative student debt: 100% of graduating class had student loans; average debt was $26,494.

FINANCIAL AID PROCEDURES

Forms required: FAFSA.

Dates and Deadlines: Priority date 3/15; closing date 5/1. Applicants notified on a rolling basis starting 3/1; must reply within 4 week(s) of notification.

Transfers: Priority date 3/1. Applicants notified on a rolling basis starting 3/1; must reply within 4 week(s) of notification.

CONTACT

Michael Davis, Director of Financial Aid

1151 North State Street, Elgin, IL 60123-1404

(800) 879-5376

Kankakee Community College

Kankakee, Illinois

www.kcc.edu   Federal Code: 007690

2-year public community college in large town.

Enrollment: 4,027 undergrads.

Selectivity: Open admission; but selective for some programs.

BASIC COSTS (2009-2010)

Tuition and fees: $2,520; out-of-district residents $5,400; out-of-state residents $9,360.

Per-credit charge: $76; out-of-district residents $172; out-of-state residents $304.

FINANCIAL AID PICTURE (2008-2009)

Students with need: Need-based aid available for full-time and part-time students.

Students without need: No-need awards available for athletics.

FINANCIAL AID PROCEDURES

Forms required: FAFSA.

Dates and Deadlines: Closing date 6/1. Applicants notified on a rolling basis; must reply within 4 week(s) of notification.

CONTACT

John Perry, Director of Financial Aid
100 College Drive, Kankakee, IL 60901-6505
(815) 802-8550

Kaskaskia College
Centralia, Illinois
www.kaskaskia.edu   Federal Code: 001701

2-year public community college in large town.

Enrollment: 3,795 undergrads, 47% part-time. 456 full-time freshmen.

Selectivity: Open admission; but selective for some programs.

BASIC COSTS (2009-2010)

Tuition and fees: $2,430; out-of-district residents $4,380; out-of-state residents $9,630.

Per-credit charge: $70; out-of-district residents $135; out-of-state residents $310.

FINANCIAL AID PICTURE (2009-2010)

Students with need: Out of 378 full-time freshmen who applied for aid, 378 were judged to have need. Of these, 351 received aid. Average financial aid package met 74% of need; average scholarship/grant was $635; average loan was $1,641. For part-time students, average financial aid package was $1,446.

Students without need: No-need awards available for academics, athletics, state/district residency.

Cumulative student debt: 29% of graduating class had student loans; average debt was $2,043.

FINANCIAL AID PROCEDURES

Forms required: FAFSA.

Dates and Deadlines: Priority date 5/15; no closing date. Applicants notified on a rolling basis starting 4/1; must reply within 2 week(s) of notification.

Transfers: No deadline. Applicants notified on a rolling basis.

CONTACT

Lisa Collier, Director of Financial Aid
27210 College Road, Centralia, IL 62801
(618) 545-3080

Kendall College
Chicago, Illinois
www.kendall.edu

4-year private culinary school and teachers college in very large city.

Enrollment: 2,159 undergrads, 35% part-time. 145 full-time freshmen.

Selectivity: Admits over 75% of applicants.

BASIC COSTS (2010-2011)

Per-credit charge: $350.

Room and board: $10,485.

Additional info: Tuition costs range from $7,200 to $21,450 per academic year. Required fees: $825. Tuition/fee waivers available for unemployed or children of unemployed.

FINANCIAL AID PICTURE (2008-2009)

Students with need: Out of 122 full-time freshmen who applied for aid, 101 were judged to have need. Of these, 101 received aid, and 66 had their full need met. Need-based aid available for part-time students.

Students without need: No-need awards available for academics, job skills.

FINANCIAL AID PROCEDURES

Forms required: FAFSA, state aid form, institutional form.

Dates and Deadlines: Priority date 4/15; no closing date. Applicants notified on a rolling basis starting 1/1; must reply within 2 week(s) of notification.

Transfers: No deadline. Applicants notified on a rolling basis.

CONTACT

900 N North Branch Street, Chicago, IL 60642-4278
(866) 952-3243

Kishwaukee College
Malta, Illinois
www.kishwaukeecollege.edu   Federal Code: 007684

2-year public community college in rural community.

Enrollment: 3,161 undergrads.

Selectivity: Open admission; but selective for some programs.

BASIC COSTS (2009-2010)

Tuition and fees: $2,500; out-of-district residents $8,440; out-of-state residents $9,580.

Per-credit charge: $75; out-of-district residents $273; out-of-state residents $311.

FINANCIAL AID PICTURE (2008-2009)

Students with need: Need-based aid available for full-time and part-time students. Work study available nights, weekends, and for part-time students.

Students without need: No-need awards available for academics, athletics, leadership, music/drama, state/district residency.

FINANCIAL AID PROCEDURES

Forms required: FAFSA, institutional form.

Dates and Deadlines: Priority date 5/1; no closing date. Applicants notified on a rolling basis starting 5/1; must reply within 2 week(s) of notification.

Transfers: Must reply within 2 week(s) of notification. Some state programs not available to sophomore status students.

CONTACT

Pamela Wagener, Director, Financial Aid/Veterans Affairs
21193 Malta Road, Malta, IL 60150-9699
(815) 825-2086 ext. 2240

Knox College
Galesburg, Illinois
www.knox.edu   Federal Code: 001704

4-year private liberal arts college in large town.

Enrollment: 1,384 undergrads. 359 full-time freshmen.

Selectivity: Admits 50 to 75% of applicants.

BASIC COSTS (2010-2011)

Tuition and fees: $33,024.

Room and board: $7,341.

FINANCIAL AID PICTURE (2009-2010)

Students with need: Out of 345 full-time freshmen who applied for aid, 293 were judged to have need. Of these, 293 received aid, and 94 had their full need met. Average financial aid package met 92% of need; average scholarship/grant was $21,625; average loan was $4,289. Need-based aid available for part-time students.

Students without need: 89 full-time freshmen who did not demonstrate need for aid received scholarships/grants; average award was $11,908. No-need awards available for academics, art, music/drama.

Scholarships offered: Academic scholarship: up to $15,000; based on high school academic performance and class rank. Visual and performing arts scholarships (in music, art, theater, dance, writing): up to $4,000; based on auditions or submission of portfolios. Social Concerns Scholarships: up to $4,000; based on community service activity.

Cumulative student debt: 73% of graduating class had student loans; average debt was $24,018.

FINANCIAL AID PROCEDURES

Forms required: FAFSA, institutional form.

Dates and Deadlines: Priority date 2/1; no closing date. Applicants notified on a rolling basis starting 3/15; must reply by 5/1 or within 2 week(s) of notification.

Transfers: Priority date 4/1. Applicants notified on a rolling basis starting 4/15; must reply by 6/1 or within 2 week(s) of notification.

CONTACT

Ann Brill, Director of Financial Aid
Knox College - Campus Box 148, Galesburg, IL 61401-4999
(309) 341-7149

Lake Forest College
Lake Forest, Illinois
www.lakeforest.edu   Federal Code: 001706

4-year private liberal arts college in large town.

Enrollment: 1,375 undergrads. 355 full-time freshmen.

Selectivity: Admits 50 to 75% of applicants.

BASIC COSTS (2010-2011)

Tuition and fees: $35,525.

Room and board: $8,327.

FINANCIAL AID PICTURE (2009-2010)

Students with need: Out of 282 full-time freshmen who applied for aid, 282 were judged to have need. Of these, 282 received aid, and 282 had their full need met.

Students without need: 57 full-time freshmen who did not demonstrate need for aid received scholarships/grants; average award was $13,800. No-need awards available for academics, alumni affiliation, leadership, music/drama, religious affiliation, state/district residency.

Cumulative student debt: 74% of graduating class had student loans; average debt was $29,279.

FINANCIAL AID PROCEDURES

Forms required: FAFSA, institutional form.

Dates and Deadlines: Priority date 2/15; closing date 5/1. Applicants notified on a rolling basis starting 3/1; must reply by 5/1 or within 2 week(s) of notification.

CONTACT

Gerard Cebrzynski, Financial Aid Director
555 North Sheridan Road, Lake Forest, IL 60045-2338
(847) 735-5015

Lake Land College
Mattoon, Illinois
www.lakelandcollege.edu   Federal Code: 007644

2-year public community college in large town.

Enrollment: 6,831 undergrads.

Selectivity: Open admission; but selective for some programs.

BASIC COSTS (2009-2010)

Tuition and fees: $2,544; out-of-district residents $5,409; out-of-state residents $9,819.

Per-credit charge: $68; out-of-district residents $163; out-of-state residents $310.

FINANCIAL AID PICTURE (2008-2009)

Students with need: Need-based aid available for full-time and part-time students. Work study available nights, weekends, and for part-time students.

Students without need: No-need awards available for academics, athletics.

FINANCIAL AID PROCEDURES

Forms required: FAFSA.

Dates and Deadlines: Priority date 5/1; no closing date. Applicants notified on a rolling basis starting 6/1.

Transfers: No deadline.

CONTACT

Paula Carpenter, Director of Financial Aid and Veteran Services
5001 Lake Land Boulevard, Mattoon, IL 61938-9366
(217) 234-5231

Lakeview College of Nursing
Danville, Illinois
www.lakeviewcol.edu   Federal Code: 010501

Upper-division private nursing college in large town.

Enrollment: 278 undergrads.

BASIC COSTS (2010-2011)

Tuition and fees: $12,900.

Per-credit charge: $430.

FINANCIAL AID PICTURE (2009-2010)

Students with need: Need-based aid available for full-time and part-time students.

Students without need: This college awards aid only to students with need.

FINANCIAL AID PROCEDURES

Forms required: FAFSA, institutional form.

Dates and Deadlines: Closing date 4/15.

Transfers: Priority date 4/15; no deadline.

CONTACT

Janet Ingargiola, Director of Financial Aid
903 North Logan Avenue, Danville, IL 61832
(217) 554-6887

Lewis and Clark Community College
Godfrey, Illinois
www.lc.edu   Federal Code: 010020

2-year public community college in large town.

Enrollment: 2,939 full-time undergrads.

Selectivity: Open admission; but selective for some programs.

BASIC COSTS (2009-2010)

Tuition and fees: $2,820; out-of-district residents $7,620; out-of-state residents $10,020.

Per-credit charge: $80; out-of-district residents $254; out-of-state residents $334.

FINANCIAL AID PICTURE (2009-2010)

Students with need: Need-based aid available for full-time and part-time students.

FINANCIAL AID PROCEDURES

Forms required: FAFSA.

Dates and Deadlines: Priority date 6/1; no closing date. Applicants notified on a rolling basis starting 8/1; must reply within 3 week(s) of notification.

Transfers: No deadline. Applicants notified on a rolling basis.

CONTACT

Angela Weaver, Director, Financial Aid
5800 Godfrey Road, Godfrey, IL 62035-2466
(618) 468-2223

Lewis University

Romeoville, Illinois
www.lewisu.edu   Federal Code: 001707

4-year private university in large town, affiliated with Roman Catholic Church.

Enrollment: 4,008 undergrads, 19% part-time. 654 full-time freshmen.

Selectivity: Admits 50 to 75% of applicants.

BASIC COSTS (2010-2011)

Tuition and fees: $23,780.

Per-credit charge: $730.

Room and board: $8,600.

Additional info: Tuition/fee waivers available for adults.

FINANCIAL AID PICTURE (2009-2010)

Students with need: Out of 602 full-time freshmen who applied for aid, 512 were judged to have need. Of these, 510 received aid, and 239 had their full need met. Average financial aid package met 81% of need; average scholarship/grant was $8,121; average loan was $3,378. For part-time students, average financial aid package was $10,274.

Students without need: 71 full-time freshmen who did not demonstrate need for aid received scholarships/grants; average award was $9,359. No-need awards available for academics, alumni affiliation, art, athletics, music/drama, religious affiliation, ROTC.

Scholarships offered: 59 full-time freshmen received athletic scholarships; average amount $9,005.

Cumulative student debt: 26% of graduating class had student loans; average debt was $20,413.

FINANCIAL AID PROCEDURES

Forms required: FAFSA.

Dates and Deadlines: Closing date 5/1. Applicants notified on a rolling basis starting 2/1; must reply by 5/1 or within 2 week(s) of notification.

Transfers: No deadline. Applicants notified on a rolling basis; must reply by 8/1 or within 2 week(s) of notification.

CONTACT

Janeen Decharinte, Director of Financial Aid
One University Parkway, Romeoville, IL 60446-2200
(815) 836-5262

Lexington College

Chicago, Illinois
www.lexingtoncollege.edu   Federal Code: 016942

4-year private hospitality management college for women in very large city, affiliated with Roman Catholic Church.

Enrollment: 60 full-time undergrads.

Selectivity: Admits less than 50% of applicants.

BASIC COSTS (2009-2010)

Tuition and fees: $23,800.

Per-credit charge: $760.

Room and board: $8,000.

FINANCIAL AID PICTURE (2009-2010)

Students with need: Need-based aid available for full-time and part-time students.

Students without need: This college awards aid only to students with need.

Additional info: Work-study is available.

FINANCIAL AID PROCEDURES

Forms required: FAFSA.

Dates and Deadlines: Closing date 5/15. Applicants notified on a rolling basis starting 7/1; must reply within 2 week(s) of notification.

Transfers: Students who enroll and then transfer to another college within a given term can only receive Illinois state aid at one institution per academic year.

CONTACT

Maria LeBron, Director of Financial Aid
310 South Peoria Street, Suite 512, Chicago, IL 60607-3534
(312) 226-6294 ext. 227

Lincoln Christian University

Lincoln, Illinois
www.lincolnchristian.edu   Federal Code: 001708

4-year private university and Bible college in large town, affiliated with Church of Christ.

Enrollment: 638 undergrads, 16% part-time. 88 full-time freshmen.

Selectivity: Admits 50 to 75% of applicants.

BASIC COSTS (2010-2011)

Tuition and fees: $13,680.

Per-credit charge: $456.

Room and board: $6,072.

FINANCIAL AID PICTURE (2008-2009)

Students with need: Out of 84 full-time freshmen who applied for aid, 64 were judged to have need. Of these, 63 received aid, and 28 had their full need met. Average financial aid package met 60% of need; average scholarship/grant was $6,000; average loan was $3,368. Need-based aid available for part-time students.

Students without need: 15 full-time freshmen who did not demonstrate need for aid received scholarships/grants; average award was $3,784. No-need awards available for academics.

Cumulative student debt: 75% of graduating class had student loans; average debt was $22,324.

FINANCIAL AID PROCEDURES

Forms required: FAFSA.

Dates and Deadlines: Priority date 3/1; no closing date. Applicants notified on a rolling basis starting 3/1; must reply within 2 week(s) of notification.

CONTACT

Nancy Siddens, Director of Student Financial Aid
100 Campus View Drive, Lincoln, IL 62656-2167
(217) 732-3168 ext. 2304

Lincoln College

Lincoln, Illinois
www.lincolncollege.edu   Federal Code: 001709

2-year private junior and liberal arts college in large town.

Enrollment: 1,276 undergrads, 25% part-time. 477 full-time freshmen.

Selectivity: Admits 50 to 75% of applicants.

BASIC COSTS (2010-2011)
Tuition and fees: $21,000.
Per-credit charge: $250.
Room and board: $6,700.

FINANCIAL AID PICTURE (2009-2010)
Students with need: Average financial aid package met 57% of need; average scholarship/grant was $15,522; average loan was $3,328. For part-time students, average financial aid package was $6,580.
Students without need: No-need awards available for academics, art, athletics, music/drama.
Additional info: Auditions recommended for music, speech, theater, broadcasting, and dance scholarship candidates, portfolios recommended for art and technical theater scholarship candidates.

FINANCIAL AID PROCEDURES
Forms required: FAFSA.
Dates and Deadlines: Priority date 4/1; closing date 6/1. Applicants notified on a rolling basis starting 6/1; must reply within 3 week(s) of notification.

CONTACT
Chris Steckmann, Director of Financial Aid
300 Keokuk Street, Lincoln, IL 62656
(217) 732-3155 ext. 231

Lincoln Land Community College
Springfield, Illinois
www.llcc.edu   Federal Code: 007170

2-year public community and junior college in small city.
Enrollment: 4,913 undergrads, 52% part-time. 559 full-time freshmen.
Selectivity: Open admission; but selective for some programs.

BASIC COSTS (2009-2010)
Tuition and fees: $2,700; out-of-district residents $5,070; out-of-state residents $7,440.
Per-credit charge: $79; out-of-district residents $158; out-of-state residents $237.
Additional info: Tuition/fee waivers available for minority students.

FINANCIAL AID PICTURE (2008-2009)
Students with need: Need-based aid available for full-time and part-time students. Work study available nights.
Students without need: No-need awards available for academics, athletics, minority status, state/district residency.

FINANCIAL AID PROCEDURES
Forms required: FAFSA, institutional form.
Dates and Deadlines: Priority date 5/1; no closing date. Applicants notified on a rolling basis starting 4/15; must reply within 2 week(s) of notification.

CONTACT
Lee Bursi, Associate Vice President, Financial Aid
5250 Shepherd Road, Springfield, IL 62794-9256
(217) 786-2237

Loyola University Chicago
Chicago, Illinois
www.luc.edu   Federal Code: 001710

4-year private university in very large city, affiliated with Roman Catholic Church.
Enrollment: 9,602 undergrads, 5% part-time. 2,074 full-time freshmen.
Selectivity: Admits over 75% of applicants.

BASIC COSTS (2010-2011)
Tuition and fees: $31,846.
Per-credit charge: $630.

Room and board: $11,220.

FINANCIAL AID PICTURE (2009-2010)
Students with need: Out of 1,833 full-time freshmen who applied for aid, 1,548 were judged to have need. Of these, 1,539 received aid, and 160 had their full need met. Average financial aid package met 84% of need; average scholarship/grant was $17,781; average loan was $3,810. For part-time students, average financial aid package was $15,005.
Students without need: 401 full-time freshmen who did not demonstrate need for aid received scholarships/grants; average award was $7,796. No-need awards available for academics, athletics, leadership, religious affiliation.
Scholarships offered: 11 full-time freshmen received athletic scholarships; average amount $22,254.
Cumulative student debt: 77% of graduating class had student loans; average debt was $35,526.

FINANCIAL AID PROCEDURES
Forms required: FAFSA.
Dates and Deadlines: Priority date 3/1; no closing date. Applicants notified on a rolling basis starting 2/15; must reply within 3 week(s) of notification.
Transfers: FAFSA must be filed by July 1 to receive Illinois map grant.

CONTACT
Eric Weems, Director, Student Financial Assistance
820 North Michigan Avenue, Chicago, IL 60611-9810
(773) 508-3155

MacMurray College
Jacksonville, Illinois
www.mac.edu   Federal Code: 001717

4-year private liberal arts college in large town, affiliated with United Methodist Church.
Enrollment: 507 undergrads, 7% part-time. 96 full-time freshmen.
Selectivity: Admits 50 to 75% of applicants.

BASIC COSTS (2009-2010)
Tuition and fees: $18,390.
Per-credit charge: $600.
Room and board: $7,278.

FINANCIAL AID PICTURE (2009-2010)
Students with need: Need-based aid available for full-time and part-time students. Work study available nights, weekends, and for part-time students.
Students without need: No-need awards available for academics, alumni affiliation, art, leadership, religious affiliation.
Scholarships offered: Academic scholarships: $500-$1,4000; based on merit. Music performance and art competition scholarships available. Transfer scholarships: to $10,000; based on academic merit. Leadership scholarships: available based on committee selection.
Additional info: Merit scholarships for accepted, enrolled freshman based on academic record. Need-based program meets 100% of direct tuition charges after family contribution and financial aid.

FINANCIAL AID PROCEDURES
Forms required: FAFSA.
Dates and Deadlines: Priority date 5/1; no closing date. Applicants notified on a rolling basis starting 2/1; must reply within 2 week(s) of notification.
Transfers: No deadline.

CONTACT
Charles Carothers, Director of Financial Aid
447 East College Avenue, Jacksonville, IL 62650-2590
(217) 479-7041

McHenry County College
Crystal Lake, Illinois
www.mchenry.edu   Federal Code: 007691

2-year public community college in large town.
Enrollment: 6,811 undergrads.
Selectivity: Open admission; but selective for some programs.

BASIC COSTS (2009-2010)
Tuition and fees: $2,684; out-of-district residents $8,806; out-of-state residents $9,942.
Per-credit charge: $80; out-of-district residents $284; out-of-state residents $322.

FINANCIAL AID PICTURE (2008-2009)
Students with need: Need-based aid available for full-time and part-time students. Work study available nights, weekends, and for part-time students.
Students without need: No-need awards available for academics, athletics, leadership, music/drama, state/district residency.
Scholarships offered: President's Scholarship: full tuition for two years; based on talent in academic areas; students must complete portfolio and have 3.0 GPA. Founding Faculty Scholarship: full tuition for 2 years; based on GPA and essay.
Additional info: Students can apply throughout the award year for federal and state aid. Students with physical handicaps or learning disabilities may apply for special needs scholarship.

FINANCIAL AID PROCEDURES
Forms required: FAFSA, institutional form.
Dates and Deadlines: Priority date 6/1; no closing date. Applicants notified on a rolling basis starting 5/1.

CONTACT
Marianne Devenny, Director, Office of Financial Aid and Records
8900 US Highway 14, Crystal Lake, IL 60012-2761
(815) 455-8761

McKendree University
Lebanon, Illinois
www.mckendree.edu   Federal Code: 001722

4-year private university and liberal arts college in small town, affiliated with United Methodist Church.
Enrollment: 2,194 undergrads, 30% part-time. 305 full-time freshmen.
Selectivity: Admits 50 to 75% of applicants.

BASIC COSTS (2010-2011)
Tuition and fees: $23,130.
Per-credit charge: $715.
Room and board: $8,240.

FINANCIAL AID PICTURE (2009-2010)
Students with need: Out of 289 full-time freshmen who applied for aid, 263 were judged to have need. Of these, 262 received aid, and 50 had their full need met. Average financial aid package met 84% of need; average scholarship/grant was $17,039; average loan was $3,196. For part-time students, average financial aid package was $5,689.
Students without need: 41 full-time freshmen who did not demonstrate need for aid received scholarships/grants; average award was $9,327. No-need awards available for academics, alumni affiliation, art, athletics, leadership, minority status, music/drama, religious affiliation.
Scholarships offered: *Merit:* Academic Scholarships; $4,000 to $17,000; 25 ACT or 3.4 GPA. *Athletic:* 28 full-time freshmen received athletic scholarships; average amount $7,956.
Cumulative student debt: 73% of graduating class had student loans; average debt was $19,445.

FINANCIAL AID PROCEDURES
Forms required: FAFSA.
Dates and Deadlines: Priority date 5/31; no closing date. Applicants notified on a rolling basis starting 3/1; must reply within 4 week(s) of notification.
Transfers: No deadline. Applicants notified on a rolling basis starting 3/1.

CONTACT
Chris Hall, Vice President for Admission and Financial Aid
701 College Road, Lebanon, IL 62254
(618) 537-6829

Midstate College
Peoria, Illinois
www.midstate.edu   Federal Code: 004568

4-year for-profit business college in small city.
Enrollment: 548 undergrads, 59% part-time. 15 full-time freshmen.
Selectivity: Admits over 75% of applicants.

BASIC COSTS (2009-2010)
Tuition and fees: $12,600.
Per-credit charge: $295.
Additional info: Fees vary according to program.

FINANCIAL AID PICTURE (2009-2010)
Students with need: Work study available nights, weekends, and for part-time students.

FINANCIAL AID PROCEDURES
Forms required: FAFSA, institutional form.
Dates and Deadlines: No deadline. Applicants notified on a rolling basis; must reply within 4 week(s) of notification.

CONTACT
Irene Bimrose, Director of Financial Assistance
411 West Northmoor Road, Peoria, IL 61614-3558
(800) 251-4299

Millikin University
Decatur, Illinois
www.millikin.edu   Federal Code: 001724

4-year private university in small city, affiliated with Presbyterian Church (USA).
Enrollment: 2,214 undergrads, 4% part-time. 484 full-time freshmen.
Selectivity: Admits 50 to 75% of applicants.

BASIC COSTS (2010-2011)
Tuition and fees: $27,425.
Per-credit charge: $895.
Room and board: $8,291.

FINANCIAL AID PICTURE (2008-2009)
Students with need: Out of 456 full-time freshmen who applied for aid, 388 were judged to have need. Of these, 387 received aid, and 210 had their full need met. Average financial aid package met 94% of need; average scholarship/grant was $10,361; average loan was $3,486. For part-time students, average financial aid package was $7,219.
Students without need: 68 full-time freshmen who did not demonstrate need for aid received scholarships/grants; average award was $9,364. No-need awards available for academics, alumni affiliation, art, leadership, minority status, music/drama.
Scholarships offered: Millikin University Merit Scholarships: $5,000 to $13,000, guaranteed for four years of attendance; for students who demonstrate potential for contributing to campus life.
Cumulative student debt: 82% of graduating class had student loans; average debt was $28,388.

FINANCIAL AID PROCEDURES
Forms required: FAFSA.
Dates and Deadlines: Priority date 3/15; no closing date. Applicants notified on a rolling basis starting 3/15; must reply by 5/1 or within 4 week(s) of notification.
Transfers: No deadline. Applicants notified on a rolling basis starting 3/15; must reply by 5/1 or within 4 week(s) of notification.

CONTACT
Cheryl Howerton, Director of Financial Aid
1184 West Main Street, Decatur, IL 62522-2084
(217) 424-6317

Monmouth College
Monmouth, Illinois
www.monm.edu   Federal Code: 001725

4-year private liberal arts college in large town, affiliated with Presbyterian Church (USA).
Enrollment: 1,362 undergrads. 380 full-time freshmen.
Selectivity: Admits 50 to 75% of applicants.

BASIC COSTS (2010-2011)
Tuition and fees: $26,900.
Per-credit charge: $895.
Room and board: $7,300.

FINANCIAL AID PICTURE (2009-2010)
Students with need: Out of 373 full-time freshmen who applied for aid, 337 were judged to have need. Of these, 337 received aid, and 73 had their full need met. Average financial aid package met 87% of need; average scholarship/grant was $18,189; average loan was $3,226. For part-time students, average financial aid package was $8,030.
Students without need: 43 full-time freshmen who did not demonstrate need for aid received scholarships/grants; average award was $12,081. No-need awards available for academics, art, leadership, music/drama, ROTC.
Cumulative student debt: 81% of graduating class had student loans; average debt was $24,476.

FINANCIAL AID PROCEDURES
Forms required: FAFSA.
Dates and Deadlines: Priority date 3/1; no closing date. Applicants notified on a rolling basis starting 3/1; must reply by 8/15 or within 2 week(s) of notification.
Transfers: No deadline. Applicants notified on a rolling basis; must reply by 8/15.

CONTACT
Jayne Schreck, Director of Financial Aid
700 East Broadway, Monmouth, IL 61462-1998
(309) 457-2129

Moody Bible Institute
Chicago, Illinois
www.moody.edu   Federal Code: 001727

4-year private Bible college in very large city, affiliated with interdenominational tradition.
Enrollment: 2,300 undergrads.
Selectivity: Admits over 75% of applicants.

BASIC COSTS (2009-2010)
Additional info: Undergraduate students in the BA and BMus programs on main campus are not charged tuition. Courses through distance learning programs (ABS, BSBS) and in BSMAT (Bachelor of Science in Missionary Aviation) program cost $230 per credit hour. Required fees of $1,880 and room/board of $8,250 per year for full-time students.

FINANCIAL AID PICTURE (2009-2010)
Students with need: For part-time students, average financial aid package was $999.28.
Students without need: This college awards aid only to students with need.
Additional info: Aid available to upperclassmen is based on private and not federal/state sources.

FINANCIAL AID PROCEDURES
Forms required: institutional form.
Dates and Deadlines: No deadline. Applicants notified on a rolling basis; must reply by 7/1.
Transfers: No deadline. Applicants notified on a rolling basis; must reply by 7/1.

CONTACT
Marc Hall, Financial Aid Coordinator
820 North La Salle Boulevard, Chicago, IL 60610
(312) 329-4178

Moraine Valley Community College
Palos Hills, Illinois
www.morainevalley.edu   Federal Code: 007692

2-year public community college in large town.
Enrollment: 11,929 undergrads, 46% part-time. 1,442 full-time freshmen.
Selectivity: Open admission; but selective for some programs.

BASIC COSTS (2010-2011)
Tuition and fees: $2,766; out-of-district residents $7,116; out-of-state residents $8,316.
Per-credit charge: $92; out-of-district residents $237; out-of-state residents $277.

FINANCIAL AID PICTURE (2008-2009)
Students with need: 88% of average financial aid package awarded as scholarships/grants, 12% awarded as loans/jobs. Need-based aid available for part-time students. Work study available nights.
Students without need: No-need awards available for academics, athletics, leadership.

FINANCIAL AID PROCEDURES
Forms required: FAFSA, institutional form.
Dates and Deadlines: Priority date 5/1; no closing date. Applicants notified on a rolling basis starting 3/1; must reply within 4 week(s) of notification.

CONTACT
Laurie Anema, Director of Financial Aid
9000 West College Parkway, Palos Hills, IL 60465-0937
(708) 974-5726

Morrison Institute of Technology
Morrison, Illinois
www.morrison.tech.edu   Federal Code: 008880

2-year private junior and technical college in small town.
Enrollment: 140 undergrads.
Selectivity: Open admission.

BASIC COSTS (2009-2010)

Tuition and fees: $14,560.
Per-credit charge: $579.
Room only: $2,800.

FINANCIAL AID PICTURE (2008-2009)

Students with need: Need-based aid available for full-time and part-time students. Work study available nights, weekends, and for part-time students.
Students without need: No-need awards available for academics.

FINANCIAL AID PROCEDURES

Forms required: FAFSA, institutional form.
Dates and Deadlines: No deadline. Applicants notified on a rolling basis; must reply within 2 week(s) of notification.

CONTACT

Julie Damhoff, Financial Aid Officer
701 Portland Avenue, Morrison, IL 61270-2959
(815) 772-7218

Morton College

Cicero, Illinois
www.morton.edu   Federal Code: 001728

2-year public community college in small city.
Enrollment: 2,555 undergrads, 58% part-time. 257 full-time freshmen.
Selectivity: Open admission; but selective for some programs and for out-of-state students.

BASIC COSTS (2009-2010)

Tuition and fees: $2,580; out-of-district residents $6,676; out-of-state residents $8,724.
Per-credit charge: $64; out-of-district residents $192; out-of-state residents $256.

FINANCIAL AID PICTURE (2008-2009)

Students with need: Need-based aid available for full-time and part-time students. Work study available nights, weekends, and for part-time students.

FINANCIAL AID PROCEDURES

Forms required: FAFSA, institutional form.
Dates and Deadlines: Priority date 6/1; no closing date. Applicants notified on a rolling basis starting 8/3.

CONTACT

Robert Tebbe, Director of Financial Aid
3801 South Central Avenue, Cicero, IL 60804-4398
(708) 656-8000 ext. 428

National University of Health Sciences

Lombard, Illinois
www.nuhs.edu   Federal Code: 001732

4-year private university and health science college in large town.
Enrollment: 74 undergrads.

BASIC COSTS (2009-2010)

Additional info: $18,352 represents average tuition cost for academic year, plus "room only" charge of $4,660 to $7,400.

FINANCIAL AID PICTURE (2008-2009)

Students with need: Average financial aid package for all full-time undergraduates was $11,618. 26% awarded as scholarships/grants, 74% awarded as loans/jobs. Need-based aid available for part-time students.
Additional info: Massage therapy certificate program is eligible for Title IV financial aid. Program is half-time and qualifies for half-time Pell grants, federal work-study and loan programs.

FINANCIAL AID PROCEDURES

Dates and Deadlines: No deadline.
Transfers: No deadline. Applicants notified on a rolling basis; must reply within 3 week(s) of notification.

CONTACT

Robert Dame, Director of Financial Aid
200 East Roosevelt Road, Lombard, IL 60148-4583
(630) 889-6700

North Central College

Naperville, Illinois
www.northcentralcollege.edu   Federal Code: 001734

4-year private liberal arts college in small city, affiliated with United Methodist Church.
Enrollment: 2,423 undergrads, 5% part-time. 542 full-time freshmen.
Selectivity: Admits 50 to 75% of applicants.

BASIC COSTS (2010-2011)

Tuition and fees: $28,224.
Per-credit charge: $676.
Room and board: $8,463.

FINANCIAL AID PICTURE (2009-2010)

Students with need: Out of 502 full-time freshmen who applied for aid, 440 were judged to have need. Of these, 439 received aid, and 139 had their full need met. Average financial aid package met 82% of need; average scholarship/grant was $17,228; average loan was $3,530. For part-time students, average financial aid package was $11,088.
Students without need: 98 full-time freshmen who did not demonstrate need for aid received scholarships/grants; average award was $12,081. No-need awards available for academics, art, leadership, minority status, music/drama, religious affiliation, ROTC, state/district residency.
Scholarships offered: Numerous merit and talent scholarship opportunities available.
Cumulative student debt: 72% of graduating class had student loans; average debt was $27,285.

FINANCIAL AID PROCEDURES

Forms required: FAFSA, institutional form.
Dates and Deadlines: No deadline. Applicants notified on a rolling basis starting 3/1; must reply within 4 week(s) of notification.

CONTACT

Marty Rossman, Director of Financial Aid
PO Box 3063, Naperville, IL 60566-7063
(630) 637-5600

North Park University

Chicago, Illinois
www.northpark.edu   Federal Code: 001735

4-year private university and liberal arts college in very large city, affiliated with Evangelical Covenant Church.
Enrollment: 2,131 undergrads, 18% part-time. 406 full-time freshmen.
Selectivity: Admits 50 to 75% of applicants.

BASIC COSTS (2010-2011)

Tuition and fees: $19,900.
Per-credit charge: $730.
Room and board: $8,410.

FINANCIAL AID PICTURE (2008-2009)

Students with need: Out of 348 full-time freshmen who applied for aid, 288 were judged to have need. Of these, 288 received aid, and 37 had their full need met. Average financial aid package met 69% of need; average scholarship/grant was $5,466; average loan was $3,875.

Students without need: 62 full-time freshmen who did not demonstrate need for aid received scholarships/grants; average award was $3,850. No-need awards available for academics, art, music/drama, religious affiliation.

Scholarships offered: North Park offers several competitive scholarships, including the Trustee Award for high achieving students, and talent based awards in music, art, theater and performance, journalism, and media studies. In addition, we have an exceptional scholarship program for students preparing to teach history, known as the Virginia E. Hahn Memorial Scholarship.

Cumulative student debt: 72% of graduating class had student loans; average debt was $23,343.

FINANCIAL AID PROCEDURES

Forms required: FAFSA.

Dates and Deadlines: Priority date 5/1; closing date 8/1. Applicants notified on a rolling basis starting 10/1; must reply by 5/1 or within 4 week(s) of notification.

Transfers: Priority date 6/1; closing date 8/1. Applicants notified on a rolling basis starting 10/1; must reply within 3 week(s) of notification.

CONTACT

Lucy Shaker, Director of Financial Aid
3225 West Foster Avenue Box 19, Chicago, IL 60625-4895
(773) 244-5506

Northeastern Illinois University
Chicago, Illinois
www.neiu.edu   Federal Code: 001693

4-year public university in very large city.

Enrollment: 9,025 undergrads, 42% part-time. 995 full-time freshmen.

Selectivity: Admits 50 to 75% of applicants.

BASIC COSTS (2009-2010)

Tuition and fees: $8,590; out-of-state residents $15,940.

Per-credit charge: $245; out-of-state residents $490.

FINANCIAL AID PICTURE (2009-2010)

Students with need: Need-based aid available for full-time and part-time students.

Students without need: No-need awards available for academics, art, leadership, music/drama.

FINANCIAL AID PROCEDURES

Forms required: FAFSA, institutional form.

Dates and Deadlines: Priority date 2/28; no closing date. Applicants notified on a rolling basis starting 4/1; must reply within 3 week(s) of notification.

CONTACT

J. Jennings, Director of Financial Aid
5500 North St. Louis Avenue, Chicago, IL 60625
(773) 442-5000

Northwestern College
Chicago, Illinois
www.northwesternbc.edu   Federal Code: 012362

2-year for-profit technical college in very large city.

Enrollment: 1,372 undergrads.

BASIC COSTS (2009-2010)

Tuition and fees: $18,790.

Per-credit charge: $410.

Additional info: Tuition may be higher for some classes.

FINANCIAL AID PICTURE (2009-2010)

Students with need: Need-based aid available for full-time and part-time students. Work study available nights.

Students without need: No-need awards available for academics.

Scholarships offered: President's Scholarship: $400 per quarter, up to $2,400. Vice-Presidential Scholarship: $300 per quarter, up to $1,800. Early bird scholarships: $750 first year, $1,500 sophomore year; must enroll by May 31 for fall quarter, must be full time.

Additional info: State grant programs for Illinois residents and alternative loans offered.

FINANCIAL AID PROCEDURES

Forms required: FAFSA, institutional form.

Dates and Deadlines: Priority date 6/30; no closing date. Applicants notified on a rolling basis starting 8/15; must reply within 4 week(s) of notification.

CONTACT

Mike Biel, Director of Financial Assistance
4839 North Milwaukee Avenue, Chicago, IL 60630
(708) 237-5050

Northwestern University
Evanston, Illinois   Federal Code: 001739
www.northwestern.edu   CSS Code: 1565

4-year private university in small city.

Enrollment: 8,908 undergrads, 5% part-time. 2,128 full-time freshmen.

Selectivity: Admits less than 50% of applicants.

BASIC COSTS (2009-2010)

Tuition and fees: $38,461.

Room and board: $11,703.

FINANCIAL AID PICTURE (2009-2010)

Students with need: Need-based aid available for full-time students.

Students without need: No-need awards available for academics, athletics, music/drama, ROTC.

FINANCIAL AID PROCEDURES

Forms required: FAFSA, CSS PROFILE.

Dates and Deadlines: Closing date 2/15. Applicants notified by 4/15; must reply by 5/1 or within 2 week(s) of notification.

Transfers: Closing date 6/1. Transfer student aid limited for first year.

CONTACT

Carolyn Lindley, Director of University Financial Aid
1801 Hinman Avenue, Evanston, IL 60204-3060
(847) 491-7400

Oakton Community College
Des Plaines, Illinois
www.oakton.edu   Federal Code: 009896

2-year public community college in small city.

Enrollment: 5,973 undergrads.

Selectivity: Open admission; but selective for some programs.

BASIC COSTS (2009-2010)

Tuition and fees: $2,738; out-of-district residents $8,318; out-of-state residents $10,028.

Per-credit charge: $86; out-of-district residents $272; out-of-state residents $329.

FINANCIAL AID PICTURE (2008-2009)

Students with need: 93% of average financial aid package awarded as scholarships/grants, 7% awarded as loans/jobs. Need-based aid available for part-time students. Work study available nights, weekends, and for part-time students.

Students without need: No-need awards available for academics, art, athletics, leadership, minority status, music/drama, state/district residency.

Scholarships offered: Oakton Merit Scholarship Program; tuition and related fees; first-time, in-district, freshmen in top 10% of high school class, U.S. citizens or permanent residents only.

FINANCIAL AID PROCEDURES

Forms required: FAFSA, institutional form.

Dates and Deadlines: Priority date 3/1; no closing date. Applicants notified on a rolling basis starting 3/1; must reply within 2 week(s) of notification.

Transfers: Applicants notified on a rolling basis starting 5/1.

CONTACT

Cheryl Warmann, Director of Financial Aid
1600 East Golf Road, Des Plaines, IL 60016
(847) 635-1708

Olivet Nazarene University
Bourbonnais, Illinois
www.olivet.edu   Federal Code: 001741

4-year private university and liberal arts college in small city, affiliated with Church of the Nazarene.

Enrollment: 3,175 undergrads.

Selectivity: Admits over 75% of applicants.

BASIC COSTS (2010-2011)

Tuition and fees: $25,590.

Per-credit charge: $1,032.

Room and board: $6,900.

FINANCIAL AID PICTURE (2008-2009)

Students with need: Need-based aid available for full-time and part-time students. Work study available nights, weekends, and for part-time students.

Students without need: No-need awards available for academics, art, athletics, leadership, music/drama, religious affiliation, ROTC, state/district residency.

FINANCIAL AID PROCEDURES

Forms required: FAFSA, institutional form.

Dates and Deadlines: Priority date 3/1; no closing date. Applicants notified on a rolling basis starting 1/15; must reply within 2 week(s) of notification.

Transfers: No deadline. Applicants notified on a rolling basis; must reply within 2 week(s) of notification.

CONTACT

Greg Bruner, Director of Financial Aid
One University Avenue, Bourbonnais, IL 60914
(815) 939-5249

Parkland College
Champaign, Illinois
www.parkland.edu   Federal Code: 007118

2-year public community college in small city.

Enrollment: 6,872 undergrads.

Selectivity: Open admission; but selective for some programs.

BASIC COSTS (2009-2010)

Tuition and fees: $2,760; out-of-district residents $7,290; out-of-state residents $11,340.

Per-credit charge: $92; out-of-district residents $243; out-of-state residents $378.

Additional info: For Internet classes, in-district students pay $87, all others pay $127 per credit hour.

FINANCIAL AID PICTURE (2008-2009)

Students with need: Need-based aid available for full-time students. Work study available nights.

Students without need: No-need awards available for academics, art, athletics, leadership, minority status, music/drama, state/district residency.

FINANCIAL AID PROCEDURES

Forms required: FAFSA, institutional form.

Dates and Deadlines: Closing date 3/1. Applicants notified on a rolling basis starting 6/1; must reply within 2 week(s) of notification.

CONTACT

Tim Wendt, Director of Financial Aid
2400 West Bradley Avenue, Champaign, IL 61821-1899
(217) 351-2276

Prairie State College
Chicago Heights, Illinois
www.prairiestate.edu   Federal Code: 001640

2-year public community college in large town.

Enrollment: 4,654 undergrads.

Selectivity: Open admission; but selective for some programs.

BASIC COSTS (2009-2010)

Tuition and fees: $2,760; out-of-district residents $7,470; out-of-state residents $10,110.

Per-credit charge: $92; out-of-district residents $249; out-of-state residents $337.

FINANCIAL AID PICTURE

Students with need: Need-based aid available for full-time and part-time students. Work study available nights, weekends, and for part-time students.

FINANCIAL AID PROCEDURES

Forms required: FAFSA, institutional form.

Dates and Deadlines: Closing date 7/1. Applicants notified on a rolling basis; must reply within 2 week(s) of notification.

CONTACT

Alice Garcia, Director of Financial Aid
202 South Halsted Street, Chicago Heights, IL 60411
(708) 709-3523

Principia College
Elsah, Illinois   Federal Code: 001744
www.principia.edu   CSS Code: 1630

4-year private liberal arts college in rural community, affiliated with First Church of Christ, Scientist (Christian Science).

Enrollment: 526 undergrads. 121 full-time freshmen.

Selectivity: Admits 50 to 75% of applicants.

BASIC COSTS (2010-2011)

Tuition and fees: $23,955.

Room and board: $9,000.

FINANCIAL AID PICTURE (2009-2010)

Students with need: Out of 100 full-time freshmen who applied for aid, 97 were judged to have need. Of these, 97 received aid, and 97 had their full need met. Average financial aid package met 100% of need; average scholarship/grant was $20,493; average loan was $4,922. Need-based aid available for part-time students.

Students without need: 27 full-time freshmen who did not demonstrate need for aid received scholarships/grants; average award was $14,952. No-need awards available for academics, alumni affiliation, leadership.

Scholarships offered: Trustee Scholarship: full tuition; Chairman's Scholarship: 3/4 tuition; Presidential Scholarship: 1/2 tuition; Dean's Scholarship: 1/4 tuition; Arthur Schulz, Jr. Alumni Scholarship: $4,500; 4-year scholarships based on high school GPA and test scores. Dean's and Arthur Schulz Scholarships available for transfer students who meet the above criteria with a minimum 3.5 GPA. Children and grandchildren of alumni eligible for 4-year scholarships based on high school or transfer GPA. Founders' Scholarships range from 1/4 to full tuition; awarded to students who demonstrate deep commitment to Christian Science, character, and citizenship as evidenced by active participation in these areas.

Additional info: Need-based tuition reduction work plan combines job with grant.

FINANCIAL AID PROCEDURES

Forms required: CSS PROFILE, institutional form.
Dates and Deadlines: Closing date 3/1. Applicants notified by 4/1.
Transfers: Priority date 3/1.

CONTACT

Tamara Gavaletz, Director of Financial Aid
One Maybeck Place, Elsah, IL 62028-9799
(800) 277-4648 ext. 2813

Quincy University

Quincy, Illinois
www.quincy.edu
Federal Code: 001745

4-year private university and liberal arts college in large town, affiliated with Roman Catholic Church.
Enrollment: 1,166 undergrads, 6% part-time. 249 full-time freshmen.
Selectivity: Admits over 75% of applicants.

BASIC COSTS (2010-2011)

Tuition and fees: $23,000.
Per-credit charge: $505.
Room and board: $8,960.
Additional info: Room and board charges vary according to board plan and housing facility selected.

FINANCIAL AID PICTURE (2009-2010)

Students with need: Out of 237 full-time freshmen who applied for aid, 221 were judged to have need. Of these, 221 received aid, and 54 had their full need met. Average financial aid package met 85% of need; average scholarship/grant was $17,950; average loan was $3,907. For part-time students, average financial aid package was $8,798.

Students without need: 8 full-time freshmen who did not demonstrate need for aid received scholarships/grants; average award was $11,875. No-need awards available for academics, alumni affiliation, art, athletics, music/drama.

Scholarships offered: *Merit:* Academic scholarships: $7,000-$12,000 per year; based on ACT and high school GPA; unlimited number awarded.
Athletic: 23 full-time freshmen received athletic scholarships; average amount $9,463.

Cumulative student debt: 77% of graduating class had student loans; average debt was $21,785.

FINANCIAL AID PROCEDURES

Forms required: FAFSA.

Dates and Deadlines: Priority date 3/1; no closing date. Applicants notified on a rolling basis starting 2/15.

CONTACT

Lisa Flack, Director of Financial Aid
1800 College Avenue, Quincy, IL 62301-2699
(217) 228-5260

Rend Lake College

Ina, Illinois
www.rlc.edu
Federal Code: 007119

2-year public community college in rural community.
Enrollment: 4,736 undergrads.
Selectivity: Open admission; but selective for some programs.

BASIC COSTS (2009-2010)

Tuition and fees: $2,370; out-of-district residents $3,645; out-of-state residents $4,500.
Per-credit charge: $79; out-of-district residents $122; out-of-state residents $150.

FINANCIAL AID PICTURE (2008-2009)

Students with need: Need-based aid available for full-time and part-time students.
Students without need: No-need awards available for academics, art, athletics, leadership, music/drama, state/district residency.

FINANCIAL AID PROCEDURES

Forms required: FAFSA.
Dates and Deadlines: No deadline. Applicants notified on a rolling basis starting 3/15; must reply within 4 week(s) of notification.

CONTACT

Douglas Carlson, Director of Financial Aid
468 North Ken Gray Parkway, Ina, IL 62846
(618) 437-5321 ext. 1385

Richard J. Daley College

Chicago, Illinois
www.daley.ccc.edu/
Federal Code: 001649

2-year public community college in very large city.
Enrollment: 4,292 undergrads.
Selectivity: Open admission; but selective for some programs.

BASIC COSTS (2009-2010)

Tuition and fees: $2,720; out-of-district residents $8,125; out-of-state residents $9,397.
Per-credit charge: $79; out-of-district residents $259; out-of-state residents $302.

FINANCIAL AID PICTURE

Students with need: Need-based aid available for full-time students.

FINANCIAL AID PROCEDURES

Forms required: FAFSA.
Dates and Deadlines: No deadline. Applicants notified on a rolling basis.
Transfers: College workstudy jobs and Federal Supplemental Educational Opportunity Grant (SEOG) may not be available to transfers.

CONTACT

Thelma Barnes, Dean of Student Services
7500 South Pulaski Road, Chicago, IL 60652
(773) 838-7579

Richland Community College
Decatur, Illinois
www.richland.edu   Federal Code: 010879

2-year public community college in small city.
Enrollment: 2,741 undergrads, 59% part-time. 223 full-time freshmen.
Selectivity: Open admission; but selective for some programs.

BASIC COSTS (2009-2010)
Tuition and fees: $2,490; out-of-district residents $11,731; out-of-state residents $15,191.
Per-credit charge: $79; out-of-district residents $387; out-of-state residents $502.

FINANCIAL AID PICTURE (2008-2009)
Students with need: Need-based aid available for full-time and part-time students. Work study available nights.
Students without need: No-need awards available for academics, art, leadership, music/drama.

FINANCIAL AID PROCEDURES
Forms required: FAFSA.
Dates and Deadlines: Closing date 6/30. Applicants notified on a rolling basis starting 3/20.
Transfers: No deadline. Applicants notified on a rolling basis.

CONTACT
Carmin Ross, Director of Financial Aid
One College Park, Decatur, IL 62521
(217) 875-7200 ext. 271

Robert Morris University: Chicago
Chicago, Illinois
www.robertmorris.edu   Federal Code: 001746

4-year private university in very large city.
Enrollment: 4,137 undergrads, 5% part-time. 1,340 full-time freshmen.
Selectivity: Admits over 75% of applicants.

BASIC COSTS (2010-2011)
Tuition and fees: $20,100.
Per-credit charge: $558.
Room and board: $10,272.
Additional info: Additional fees may apply, depending on program.

FINANCIAL AID PICTURE (2008-2009)
Students with need: Out of 1,245 full-time freshmen who applied for aid, 1,214 were judged to have need. Of these, 1,180 received aid, and 29 had their full need met. Average financial aid package met 41% of need; average scholarship/grant was $8,795; average loan was $4,606. For part-time students, average financial aid package was $7,627.
Students without need: 19 full-time freshmen who did not demonstrate need for aid received scholarships/grants; average award was $6,591. No-need awards available for academics, art, athletics, state/district residency.
Scholarships offered: 22 full-time freshmen received athletic scholarships; average amount $11,635.
Cumulative student debt: 92% of graduating class had student loans; average debt was $26,308.

FINANCIAL AID PROCEDURES
Forms required: FAFSA.
Dates and Deadlines: No deadline. Applicants notified on a rolling basis.
Transfers: No deadline. Applicants notified on a rolling basis.

CONTACT
Leigh Taylor, Vice President of Financial Aid
401 South State Street, Chicago, IL 60605
(312) 935-4075

Rock Valley College
Rockford, Illinois
www.rockvalleycollege.edu

2-year public community college in small city.
Enrollment: 8,502 undergrads.
Selectivity: Open admission; but selective for some programs.

BASIC COSTS (2009-2010)
Tuition and fees: $2,220; out-of-district residents $8,670; out-of-state residents $13,560.
Per-credit charge: $66; out-of-district residents $281; out-of-state residents $444.
Additional info: Costs vary by program.

FINANCIAL AID PICTURE (2008-2009)
Students with need: Need-based aid available for full-time and part-time students. Work study available nights.
Students without need: No-need awards available for academics, ROTC.

FINANCIAL AID PROCEDURES
Forms required: FAFSA.
Dates and Deadlines: Closing date 5/1. Applicants notified on a rolling basis starting 4/1; must reply within 2 week(s) of notification.

CONTACT
Cyndi Stonesifer, Director of Financial Aid
3301 North Mulford Road, Rockford, IL 61114-5699
(815) 921-4150

Rockford Career College
Rockford, Illinois
www.rockfordcareercollege.edu   Federal Code: 008545

2-year for-profit career college in small city.
Enrollment: 763 undergrads, 57% part-time. 162 full-time freshmen.
Selectivity: Open admission.

BASIC COSTS (2009-2010)
Tuition and fees: $7,560.
Per-credit charge: $210.

FINANCIAL AID PICTURE
Students with need: Need-based aid available for full-time and part-time students. Work study available nights.
Students without need: This college awards aid only to students with need.

FINANCIAL AID PROCEDURES
Forms required: FAFSA.
Dates and Deadlines: No deadline. Applicants notified on a rolling basis.

CONTACT
Garry Kirk, Director of Financial Aid
1130 South Alpine Road, Rockford, IL 61108
(815) 967-7311

Rockford College

Rockford, Illinois
www.rockford.edu   Federal Code: 001748

4-year private liberal arts college in small city.
Enrollment: 857 undergrads, 12% part-time. 89 full-time freshmen.
Selectivity: Admits less than 50% of applicants.

BASIC COSTS (2009-2010)
Tuition and fees: $24,250.
Per-credit charge: $650.
Room and board: $6,750.

FINANCIAL AID PICTURE (2008-2009)
Students with need: 56% of average financial aid package awarded as scholarships/grants, 44% awarded as loans/jobs. Need-based aid available for part-time students. Work study available nights, weekends, and for part-time students.
Students without need: No-need awards available for academics, alumni affiliation, leadership, minority status, music/drama, state/district residency.

FINANCIAL AID PROCEDURES
Forms required: FAFSA.
Dates and Deadlines: Priority date 3/1; no closing date. Applicants notified on a rolling basis starting 3/1; must reply within 4 week(s) of notification.

CONTACT
Todd Free, Assistant Vice President of Student Administrative Services
5050 East State Street, Rockford, IL 61108-2393
(815) 226-3383

Roosevelt University

Chicago, Illinois
www.roosevelt.edu   Federal Code: 001749

4-year private university in very large city.
Enrollment: 4,113 undergrads, 31% part-time. 575 full-time freshmen.
Selectivity: Admits less than 50% of applicants.

BASIC COSTS (2010-2011)
Tuition and fees: $23,000.
Room and board: $11,200.
Additional info: Full time tuition for undergraduate students in the College of Performing Arts is $29,900.

FINANCIAL AID PICTURE (2008-2009)
Students with need: Need-based aid available for full-time students.
Students without need: No-need awards available for academics, alumni affiliation, leadership, minority status, music/drama, state/district residency.

FINANCIAL AID PROCEDURES
Forms required: FAFSA.
Dates and Deadlines: Priority date 4/1; no closing date. Applicants notified on a rolling basis starting 3/15; must reply within 2 week(s) of notification.

CONTACT
Walter O'Neill, Assistant Vice President for Financial Aid
430 South Michigan Avenue, Chicago, IL 60605-1394
(866) 421-0935

Rush University

Chicago, Illinois
www.rushu.rush.edu   Federal Code: 009800

Upper-division private health science and nursing college in very large city.
Enrollment: 59 undergrads.

BASIC COSTS (2009-2010)
Tuition and fees: $23,022.
Room only: $9,000.
Additional info: Tuition costs vary by program.

FINANCIAL AID PICTURE (2008-2009)
Students with need: Need-based aid available for full-time and part-time students. Work study available nights, weekends, and for part-time students.

FINANCIAL AID PROCEDURES
Forms required: FAFSA, institutional form.
Dates and Deadlines: No deadline.
Transfers: Priority date 5/1; no deadline. Applicants notified on a rolling basis starting 4/1; must reply within 3 week(s) of notification.

CONTACT
David Nelson, Director of Student Financial Aid
College Admissions, Chicago, IL 60612
(312) 942-6256

Saint Anthony College of Nursing

Rockford, Illinois
www.sacn.edu   Federal Code: 009987

Upper-division private nursing college in small city, affiliated with Roman Catholic Church.
Enrollment: 163 undergrads, 19% part-time.

BASIC COSTS (2009-2010)
Tuition and fees: $19,086.
Per-credit charge: $590.
Additional info: Required fees may vary.

FINANCIAL AID PICTURE (2009-2010)
Students with need: Need-based aid available for full-time and part-time students.
Students without need: No-need awards available for academics, leadership, state/district residency.

FINANCIAL AID PROCEDURES
Forms required: FAFSA.
Dates and Deadlines: Priority date 4/15; no closing date.
Transfers: No deadline. Applicants notified on a rolling basis starting 8/18.

CONTACT
Serrita Woods, Financial Aid Officer
5658 East State Street, Rockford, IL 61108-2468
(815) 395-5089

St. Francis Medical Center College of Nursing

Peoria, Illinois
www.sfmccon.edu   Federal Code: 006240

Upper-division private nursing college in small city, affiliated with Roman Catholic Church.
Enrollment: 363 undergrads, 22% part-time.

BASIC COSTS (2010-2011)
Tuition and fees: $14,660.
Per-credit charge: $480.
Room only: $2,400.

FINANCIAL AID PICTURE (2008-2009)
Students with need: Average financial aid package for all full-time undergraduates was $11,324; for part-time $9,271. 38% awarded as scholarships/grants, 62% awarded as loans/jobs.

Students without need: No-need awards available for academics, alumni affiliation.

Additional info: OSF Saint Francis Medical Center Education student loan available to full-time students on a limited basis. Tuition waiver program for hospital employees available.

FINANCIAL AID PROCEDURES

Forms required: FAFSA, institutional form.

Dates and Deadlines: Priority date 6/1; no closing date. Applicants notified by 10/30; must reply within 4 week(s) of notification.

Transfers: No deadline. Applicants notified on a rolling basis starting 5/15; must reply within 2 week(s) of notification.

CONTACT

Nancy Perryman, Coordinator of Student Finance, Financial Assistance
511 NE Greenleaf Street, Peoria, IL 61603-3783
(309) 655-4119

St. John's College

Springfield, Illinois
www.stjohnscollegespringfield.edu/index.html
Federal Code: 030980

Upper-division private nursing college in small city, affiliated with Roman Catholic Church.

Enrollment: 79 undergrads.

BASIC COSTS (2010-2011)

Tuition and fees: $13,128.

Per-credit charge: $620.

FINANCIAL AID PICTURE (2009-2010)

Students with need: Average financial aid package for all full-time undergraduates was $11,506. 76% awarded as scholarships/grants, 24% awarded as loans/jobs. Work study available nights.

CONTACT

Mary Deatherage, Financial Aid Officer
729 East Carpenter Street, Springfield, IL 62702
(217) 544-6464 ext. 44705

Saint Xavier University

Chicago, Illinois
www.sxu.edu
Federal Code: 001768

4-year private university in very large city, affiliated with Roman Catholic Church.

Enrollment: 3,060 undergrads, 19% part-time. 545 full-time freshmen.

Selectivity: Admits less than 50% of applicants.

BASIC COSTS (2010-2011)

Tuition and fees: $25,520.

Per-credit charge: $830.

Room and board: $8,692.

FINANCIAL AID PICTURE (2008-2009)

Students with need: Out of 510 full-time freshmen who applied for aid, 470 were judged to have need. Of these, 470 received aid, and 94 had their full need met. Average financial aid package met 82% of need; average scholarship/grant was $14,870; average loan was $3,404. For part-time students, average financial aid package was $9,126.

Students without need: 58 full-time freshmen who did not demonstrate need for aid received scholarships/grants; average award was $9,694. No-need awards available for academics, athletics, music/drama.

Scholarships offered: 12 full-time freshmen received athletic scholarships; average amount $8,292.

Cumulative student debt: 63% of graduating class had student loans; average debt was $24,920.

FINANCIAL AID PROCEDURES

Forms required: FAFSA.

Dates and Deadlines: Priority date 3/1; no closing date. Applicants notified on a rolling basis starting 2/1; must reply by 5/1 or within 2 week(s) of notification.

Transfers: Priority date 3/1. Applicants notified on a rolling basis starting 2/15; must reply by 5/1 or within 2 week(s) of notification.

CONTACT

Susan Swisher, Assistant Vice President, Student Financial Services
3700 West 103rd Street, Chicago, IL 60655
(773) 298-3073

Sauk Valley Community College

Dixon, Illinois
www.svcc.edu
Federal Code: 001752

2-year public community college in large town.

Enrollment: 2,136 undergrads, 42% part-time. 187 full-time freshmen.

Selectivity: Open admission; but selective for some programs.

BASIC COSTS (2009-2010)

Tuition and fees: $2,670; out-of-district residents $7,500; out-of-state residents $8,520.

Per-credit charge: $89; out-of-district residents $250; out-of-state residents $284.

Room only: $4,131.

FINANCIAL AID PICTURE (2008-2009)

Students with need: Out of 136 full-time freshmen who applied for aid, 119 were judged to have need. Of these, 102 received aid. Average financial aid package met 43% of need; average scholarship/grant was $4,495; average loan was $2,330. For part-time students, average financial aid package was $3,187.

Students without need: 1 full-time freshmen who did not demonstrate need for aid received scholarships/grants; average award was $2,890. No-need awards available for academics, athletics, minority status, state/district residency.

Scholarships offered: 12 full-time freshmen received athletic scholarships; average amount $1,954.

FINANCIAL AID PROCEDURES

Forms required: FAFSA, institutional form.

Dates and Deadlines: Priority date 3/1; no closing date. Applicants notified on a rolling basis starting 5/1; must reply within 4 week(s) of notification.

Transfers: Priority date 3/9; no deadline. Applicants notified on a rolling basis starting 3/1; must reply within 4 week(s) of notification.

CONTACT

Debra Stiefel, Coordinator of Financial Aid
173 Illinois Route 2, Dixon, IL 61021-9110
(815) 288-5511 ext. 339

School of the Art Institute of Chicago

Chicago, Illinois
www.saic.edu
Federal Code: 001753

4-year private visual arts college in very large city.

Enrollment: 2,379 undergrads, 7% part-time. 449 full-time freshmen.

Selectivity: Admits over 75% of applicants.

BASIC COSTS (2009-2010)
Tuition and fees: $34,600.
Per-credit charge: $1,140.
Room only: $9,200.
Additional info: Students will be required to purchase a laptop through SAIC. Costs range from $2,000 to $2,200.

FINANCIAL AID PICTURE (2008-2009)
Students with need: Out of 281 full-time freshmen who applied for aid, 245 were judged to have need. Of these, 245 received aid, and 8 had their full need met. Average financial aid package met 73% of need; average scholarship/grant was $12,315; average loan was $3,740. For part-time students, average financial aid package was $14,041.
Students without need: 109 full-time freshmen who did not demonstrate need for aid received scholarships/grants; average award was $5,450. No-need awards available for academics, art.
Scholarships offered: Merit scholarships; $2,000 to full tuition; renewable.
Cumulative student debt: 61% of graduating class had student loans; average debt was $34,578.

FINANCIAL AID PROCEDURES
Forms required: FAFSA.
Dates and Deadlines: Priority date 3/15; no closing date. Applicants notified on a rolling basis starting 3/1.

CONTACT
Patrick James, Director of Financial Aid
36 South Wabash Avenue, Chicago, IL 60603
(312) 629-6600

Shawnee Community College
Ullin, Illinois
www.shawneecc.edu   Federal Code: 007693

2-year public community college in rural community.
Enrollment: 2,834 undergrads.
Selectivity: Open admission; but selective for some programs.

BASIC COSTS (2009-2010)
Tuition and fees: $2,310; out-of-district residents $3,480; out-of-state residents $3,870.
Per-credit charge: $77; out-of-district residents $116; out-of-state residents $129.

FINANCIAL AID PICTURE
Students with need: Need-based aid available for full-time and part-time students.
Students without need: This college awards aid only to students with need.

FINANCIAL AID PROCEDURES
Forms required: FAFSA.
Dates and Deadlines: Priority date 9/1; no closing date. Applicants notified on a rolling basis; must reply within 2 week(s) of notification.

CONTACT
Tammy Capps, Director of Financial Aid
8364 Shawnee College Road, Ullin, IL 62992
(618) 634-3280 ext. 3280

Shimer College
Chicago, Illinois
www.shimer.edu   Federal Code: 001756

4-year private liberal arts college in very large city.
Enrollment: 104 undergrads, 12% part-time. 29 full-time freshmen.

Selectivity: Admits less than 50% of applicants.

BASIC COSTS (2010-2011)
Tuition and fees: $28,110.
Per-credit charge: $900.
Room only: $7,526.
Additional info: Cost of 14 meal plan: $3,804. Tuition/fee waivers available for adults.

FINANCIAL AID PICTURE (2008-2009)
Students with need: Out of 29 full-time freshmen who applied for aid, 22 were judged to have need. Of these, 22 received aid. Average financial aid package met 64% of need; average scholarship/grant was $11,644; average loan was $3,545. For part-time students, average financial aid package was $7,570.
Students without need: 6 full-time freshmen who did not demonstrate need for aid received scholarships/grants; average award was $2,957. No-need awards available for alumni affiliation.
Scholarships offered: Michel de Montaigne Scholarship: half or full tuition; awarded to new students on the basis of merit in writing and discussion; 2 full and 2 half tuition scholarships awarded each year.
Cumulative student debt: 100% of graduating class had student loans; average debt was $35,000.

FINANCIAL AID PROCEDURES
Forms required: FAFSA, institutional form.
Dates and Deadlines: Priority date 3/1; no closing date. Applicants notified on a rolling basis starting 4/1; must reply by 5/1 or within 3 week(s) of notification.
Transfers: Closing date 8/1. Applicants notified on a rolling basis; must reply by 5/1 or within 3 week(s) of notification.

CONTACT
Janet Henthorn, Financial Aid Officer
3424 South State Street, Chicago, IL 60616
(312) 235-3507

South Suburban College of Cook County
South Holland, Illinois
www.ssc.edu   Federal Code: 001769

2-year public community college in large town.
Enrollment: 1,962 full-time undergrads.
Selectivity: Open admission; but selective for some programs.

BASIC COSTS (2009-2010)
Tuition and fees: $3,112; out-of-district residents $8,452; out-of-state residents $10,102.
Per-credit charge: $90; out-of-district residents $268; out-of-state residents $323.
Additional info: Some students may qualify for a tuition rate of $105 per credit hour for special programs in other in-state community college districts, in Lake County Illinois and in Chicago. Tuition/fee waivers available for adults.

FINANCIAL AID PICTURE (2008-2009)
Students with need: 99% of average financial aid package awarded as scholarships/grants, 1% awarded as loans/jobs. Need-based aid available for part-time students. Work study available nights.
Students without need: No-need awards available for academics, art, athletics, music/drama, state/district residency.

FINANCIAL AID PROCEDURES
Forms required: FAFSA.
Dates and Deadlines: Priority date 6/1; no closing date. Applicants notified on a rolling basis starting 7/1.
Transfers: No deadline. Applicants notified on a rolling basis.

CONTACT

John Semple, Director of Financial Aid
15800 South State Street, South Holland, IL 60473
(708) 596-2000 ext. 2321

Southeastern Illinois College

Harrisburg, Illinois
www.sic.edu   Federal Code: 001757

2-year public community college in small town.

Enrollment: 994 full-time undergrads.

Selectivity: Open admission; but selective for some programs.

BASIC COSTS (2009-2010)

Tuition and fees: $2,370; out-of-district residents $3,600; out-of-state residents $3,900.

Per-credit charge: $77; out-of-district residents $118; out-of-state residents $128.

FINANCIAL AID PICTURE (2008-2009)

Students with need: Need-based aid available for full-time and part-time students.

Students without need: No-need awards available for academics, alumni affiliation, art, athletics, music/drama.

FINANCIAL AID PROCEDURES

Forms required: FAFSA.

Dates and Deadlines: No deadline. Applicants notified on a rolling basis starting 4/15; must reply within 2 week(s) of notification.

CONTACT

Sarah Bond, Director of Financial Aid
3575 College Road, Harrisburg, IL 62946
(618) 252-5400 ext. 2450

Southern Illinois University Carbondale

Carbondale, Illinois
www.siuc.edu   Federal Code: 001758

4-year public university in large town.

Enrollment: 15,524 undergrads, 12% part-time. 2,660 full-time freshmen.

Selectivity: Admits 50 to 75% of applicants.

BASIC COSTS (2009-2010)

Tuition and fees: $10,411; out-of-state residents $21,346.

Per-credit charge: $243; out-of-state residents $608.

Room and board: $7,673.

FINANCIAL AID PICTURE (2008-2009)

Students with need: Out of 2,233 full-time freshmen who applied for aid, 1,785 were judged to have need. Of these, 1,738 received aid, and 1,536 had their full need met. Average financial aid package met 95% of need; average scholarship/grant was $7,406; average loan was $3,637. For part-time students, average financial aid package was $8,545.

Students without need: 154 full-time freshmen who did not demonstrate need for aid received scholarships/grants; average award was $6,718. No-need awards available for academics, alumni affiliation, athletics, leadership, minority status, ROTC.

Scholarships offered: 22 full-time freshmen received athletic scholarships; average amount $13,033.

Cumulative student debt: 50% of graduating class had student loans; average debt was $21,359.

Additional info: Need-based financial aid available to part-time students enrolled in minimum of 6 semester hours.

FINANCIAL AID PROCEDURES

Forms required: FAFSA.

Dates and Deadlines: Priority date 4/1; no closing date. Applicants notified on a rolling basis starting 5/1; must reply within 4 week(s) of notification.

Transfers: Must reply within 4 week(s) of notification.

CONTACT

Linda Clemons, Director, Financial Aid
Mailcode 4701, Carbondale, IL 62901-4701
(618) 453-4334

Southern Illinois University Edwardsville

Edwardsville, Illinois
www.siue.edu   Federal Code: 001759

4-year public university in very large city.

Enrollment: 11,055 undergrads, 14% part-time. 1,912 full-time freshmen.

Selectivity: Admits over 75% of applicants.

BASIC COSTS (2009-2010)

Tuition and fees: $8,336; out-of-state residents $17,638.

Per-credit charge: $207; out-of-state residents $517.

Room and board: $7,461.

Additional info: Required fees include book rental.

FINANCIAL AID PICTURE (2008-2009)

Students with need: Need-based aid available for full-time and part-time students. Work study available nights, weekends, and for part-time students.

Students without need: This college awards aid only to students with need.

FINANCIAL AID PROCEDURES

Forms required: FAFSA.

Dates and Deadlines: Priority date 3/1; closing date 6/1. Applicants notified on a rolling basis starting 3/15; must reply within 4 week(s) of notification.

CONTACT

Sharon Berry, Director of Student Financial Aid
Campus Box 1600, Rendleman Hall, Rm 2120, Edwardsville, IL 62026-1600
(618) 650-3880

Southwestern Illinois College

Belleville, Illinois
www.swic.edu   Federal Code: 001636

2-year public community college in small city.

Enrollment: 10,560 undergrads.

Selectivity: Open admission; but selective for some programs.

BASIC COSTS (2009-2010)

Tuition and fees: $2,550; out-of-district residents $5,790; out-of-state residents $8,790.

Per-credit charge: $85; out-of-district residents $193; out-of-state residents $293.

Additional info: Required fees vary by course taken. Those age 60 and over receive a $5 per-credit-hour tuition reduction.

FINANCIAL AID PICTURE

Students with need: Need-based aid available for full-time and part-time students.

Students without need: No-need awards available for academics, athletics.

FINANCIAL AID PROCEDURES

Forms required: FAFSA, institutional form.

Dates and Deadlines: Priority date 5/31; no closing date. Applicants notified on a rolling basis starting 7/1; must reply within 2 week(s) of notification.

CONTACT

Marsha Garner, Director of Financial Aid and Student Employment
2500 Carlyle Avenue, Belleville, IL 62221-5899
(618) 235-2700 ext. 5288

Spoon River College
Canton, Illinois
www.src.edu   Federal Code: 001643

2-year public community college in large town.
Enrollment: 1,458 undergrads.
Selectivity: Open admission; but selective for some programs.

BASIC COSTS (2009-2010)
Tuition and fees: $2,670; out-of-district residents $6,300; out-of-state residents $7,380.
Per-credit charge: $79; out-of-district residents $200; out-of-state residents $236.

FINANCIAL AID PICTURE (2008-2009)
Students with need: Need-based aid available for full-time and part-time students. Work study available nights.
Students without need: No-need awards available for academics, athletics.

FINANCIAL AID PROCEDURES
Forms required: FAFSA.
Dates and Deadlines: Closing date 7/1. Applicants notified on a rolling basis starting 3/15.

CONTACT
Jo Branson, Director of Financial Aid
23235 North County Road 22, Canton, IL 61520
(309) 649-7030

Taylor Business Institute
Chicago, Illinois
www.tbiil.edu   Federal Code: 011810

2-year for-profit business college in very large city.
Enrollment: 250 undergrads.
Selectivity: Admits over 75% of applicants.

FINANCIAL AID PICTURE
Students with need: Need-based aid available for full-time students. Work study available nights.

FINANCIAL AID PROCEDURES
Forms required: FAFSA, state aid form, institutional form.

CONTACT
Florence Davis, Financial Aid Director
318 West Adams Street, 5th Floor, Chicago, IL 60606
(312) 658-5100

Trinity Christian College
Palos Heights, Illinois
www.trnty.edu   Federal Code: 001771

4-year private liberal arts college in very large city, affiliated with Reformed (unaffiliated).
Enrollment: 1,345 undergrads, 22% part-time. 201 full-time freshmen.
Selectivity: Admits over 75% of applicants.

BASIC COSTS (2010-2011)
Tuition and fees: $21,733.
Per-credit charge: $715.
Room and board: $8,202.

FINANCIAL AID PICTURE (2009-2010)
Students with need: Out of 192 full-time freshmen who applied for aid, 153 were judged to have need. Of these, 153 received aid, and 10 had their full need met. Average financial aid package met 39% of need; average scholarship/grant was $4,287; average loan was $3,710. Need-based aid available for part-time students.
Students without need: 119 full-time freshmen who did not demonstrate need for aid received scholarships/grants; average award was $7,795. No-need awards available for academics, alumni affiliation, art, athletics, leadership, minority status, music/drama, religious affiliation.
Scholarships offered: 72 full-time freshmen received athletic scholarships; average amount $4,928.
Cumulative student debt: 82% of graduating class had student loans; average debt was $29,943.
Additional info: High school transcripts and ACT or SAT scores required for merit scholarships.

FINANCIAL AID PROCEDURES
Forms required: FAFSA, institutional form.
Dates and Deadlines: Priority date 2/15; closing date 4/15. Applicants notified on a rolling basis starting 4/1; must reply by 5/1 or within 2 week(s) of notification.
Transfers: Applicants notified by 3/15; must reply by 5/1 or within 2 week(s) of notification.

CONTACT
Denise Coleman, Director of Financial Aid
6601 West College Drive, Palos Heights, IL 60463
(708) 239-4706

Trinity College of Nursing and Health Sciences
Rock Island, Illinois
www.trinitycollegeqc.edu   Federal Code: 006225

4-year private nursing college in very large city.
Enrollment: 264 undergrads, 48% part-time. 4 full-time freshmen.
Selectivity: Admits 50 to 75% of applicants.

BASIC COSTS (2009-2010)
Tuition and fees: $12,227.
Per-credit charge: $403.
Additional info: Students are required to have a uniform and other health equipment.

FINANCIAL AID PICTURE (2009-2010)
Students with need: 45% of average financial aid package awarded as scholarships/grants, 55% awarded as loans/jobs.

CONTACT
Kris Hodgerson, Financial Aid Specialist
2122 25th Avenue, Rock Island, IL 61201
(309) 779-7740

Trinity International University
Deerfield, Illinois
www.tiu.edu   Federal Code: 001772

4-year private university and liberal arts college in large town, affiliated with Evangelical Free Church of America.
Enrollment: 987 undergrads.

left margin vertical text

Selectivity: Admits over 75% of applicants.

BASIC COSTS (2010-2011)
Tuition and fees: $23,370.
Per-credit charge: $957.
Room and board: $7,660.
Additional info: Tuition/fee waivers available for minority students.

FINANCIAL AID PICTURE (2009-2010)
Students with need: Need-based aid available for full-time and part-time students. Work study available nights, weekends, and for part-time students.
Students without need: No-need awards available for academics, alumni affiliation, athletics, minority status, music/drama, religious affiliation.

FINANCIAL AID PROCEDURES
Forms required: FAFSA.
Dates and Deadlines: Priority date 4/1; no closing date. Applicants notified on a rolling basis starting 2/15; must reply within 4 week(s) of notification.
Transfers: No deadline. Applicants notified on a rolling basis; must reply within 4 week(s) of notification.

CONTACT
Patricia Coles, Director of Financial Aid
2065 Half Day Road, Deerfield, IL 60015
(847) 317-8060

Triton College
River Grove, Illinois
www.triton.edu
Federal Code: 001773

2-year public community and junior college in large town.
Enrollment: 10,972 undergrads, 60% part-time. 1,257 full-time freshmen.
Selectivity: Open admission; but selective for some programs.

BASIC COSTS (2009-2010)
Tuition and fees: $2,410; out-of-district residents $5,974; out-of-state residents $7,400.
Per-credit charge: $72; out-of-district residents $191; out-of-state residents $238.

FINANCIAL AID PICTURE (2008-2009)
Students with need: Out of 531 full-time freshmen who applied for aid, 415 were judged to have need. Of these, 415 received aid, and 103 had their full need met. Average financial aid package met 66% of need; average scholarship/grant was $2,438. For part-time students, average financial aid package was $1,238.
Students without need: 7 full-time freshmen who did not demonstrate need for aid received scholarships/grants; average award was $1,141. No-need awards available for academics, athletics.
Scholarships offered: *Merit:* Board of Trustees Honor Scholarship; covers tuition and fees; for in-district high school students in top 10% of graduating class. *Athletic:* 3 full-time freshmen received athletic scholarships; average amount $740.

FINANCIAL AID PROCEDURES
Forms required: FAFSA, institutional form.
Dates and Deadlines: Priority date 4/15; no closing date. Applicants notified on a rolling basis starting 4/1; must reply within 2 week(s) of notification.

CONTACT
Pat Zinga, Director of Financial Aid
2000 North Fifth Avenue, River Grove, IL 60171
(708) 456-0300 ext. 3441

University of Chicago
Chicago, Illinois
www.uchicago.edu
Federal Code: 001774
CSS Code: 1832

4-year private university and liberal arts college in very large city.
Enrollment: 5,063 undergrads, 1% part-time. 1,336 full-time freshmen.
Selectivity: Admits less than 50% of applicants.

BASIC COSTS (2010-2011)
Tuition and fees: $41,091.
Room and board: $12,153.

FINANCIAL AID PICTURE (2009-2010)
Students with need: Need-based aid available for full-time students. Work study available nights, weekends, and for part-time students.
Students without need: No-need awards available for academics, leadership.

FINANCIAL AID PROCEDURES
Forms required: FAFSA, CSS PROFILE, institutional form.
Dates and Deadlines: Closing date 2/1. Applicants notified by 4/15; must reply by 5/1.
Transfers: Closing date 3/1. Applicants notified on a rolling basis starting 4/15; must reply by 6/1.

CONTACT
Alicia Reyes, Director of College Aid
1101 East 58th Street, Chicago, IL 60637
(773) 702-8666

University of Illinois at Chicago
Chicago, Illinois
www.uic.edu
Federal Code: 001776

4-year public university in very large city.
Enrollment: 15,986 undergrads, 7% part-time. 2,932 full-time freshmen.
Selectivity: Admits 50 to 75% of applicants.

BASIC COSTS (2009-2010)
Tuition and fees: $12,034; out-of-state residents $24,424.
Room and board: $9,435.
Additional info: Tuition at time of enrollment locked for 4 years; tuition/fee waivers available for minority students.

FINANCIAL AID PICTURE (2008-2009)
Students with need: Out of 2,467 full-time freshmen who applied for aid, 2,003 were judged to have need. Of these, 1,903 received aid, and 417 had their full need met. Average financial aid package met 73% of need; average scholarship/grant was $11,948; average loan was $3,277. For part-time students, average financial aid package was $10,254.
Students without need: 162 full-time freshmen who did not demonstrate need for aid received scholarships/grants; average award was $2,655. No-need awards available for academics, art, athletics, music/drama, ROTC.
Scholarships offered: 27 full-time freshmen received athletic scholarships; average amount $19,721.
Cumulative student debt: 57% of graduating class had student loans; average debt was $17,276.

FINANCIAL AID PROCEDURES
Forms required: FAFSA.
Dates and Deadlines: Priority date 3/1; no closing date. Applicants notified on a rolling basis starting 3/15; must reply by 5/1.

CONTACT
Timothy Opgenorth, Director of the Office of Student Financial Aid
PO Box 5220, Chicago, IL 60680-5220
(312) 996-3126

University of Illinois at Urbana-Champaign

Champaign, Illinois
www.illinois.edu
Federal Code: 001775

4-year public university in small city.
Enrollment: 30,694 undergrads.

BASIC COSTS (2009-2010)

Tuition and fees: $12,528; out-of-state residents $26,670.
Room and board: $9,284.

FINANCIAL AID PICTURE (2009-2010)

Students with need: Need-based aid available for full-time and part-time students. Work study available nights, weekends, and for part-time students.
Students without need: No-need awards available for academics, alumni affiliation, art, athletics, leadership, music/drama, ROTC, state/district residency.
Scholarships offered: President's Award Program: $1,000 - $4,000 for 4 years; for members of historically underrepresented group, with ACT score of 22-23 and in the top quarter of their class, or who have an ACT score of 24 or higher and are in the top half of their class. University Achievement Scholarship: $8,000; criteria set by each college, renewable with 3.0 GPA; 50 available. Matthews Scholars: $2,000 per year, renewable for 4 years if GPA of 3.3 is maintained; criteria includes academic achievement, leadership skills, commitment to campus and community efforts, good sponsor relations, diversity of college gender and ethnicity; approximately 150 available. FMC Award of Excellence: $1,000 a year, non-renewable; criteria set by individual colleges; 20 available. Provost Scholarship: full tuition, renewable with 3.0 GPA; National Achievement, National Hispanic Scholar finalists, or National Merit finalists who have indicated the University of Illinois at Urbana-Champaign as their top choice. Campus Merit: $3,000; students in historically under-represented groups who are in the top 10 percent of their graduating class. National Merit: $500; National Merit finalists who indicated the University of Illinois as their top choice, renewable with 3.0 GPA. James Hunter Anthony and Gerald Blackshear Scholarship: 1 year of tuition and fees, renewable with 3.0 GPA; incoming freshmen who are graduates of an Illinois high school, with superior academic and leadership qualities; need may be considered.

FINANCIAL AID PROCEDURES

Forms required: FAFSA.
Dates and Deadlines: Priority date 3/15; no closing date.

CONTACT

Daniel Mann, Director of Student Financial Aid
901 West Illinois, Urbana, IL 61801-3028
(217) 333-0100

University of Illinois: Springfield

Springfield, Illinois
www.uis.edu
Federal Code: 009333

4-year public university and liberal arts college in small city.
Enrollment: 2,920 undergrads, 34% part-time. 304 full-time freshmen.
Selectivity: Admits 50 to 75% of applicants.

BASIC COSTS (2009-2010)

Tuition and fees: $9,007; out-of-state residents $18,157.
Per-credit charge: $247; out-of-state residents $552.
Room and board: $9,200.
Additional info: Freshman costs reflect guaranteed tuition plan figures; tuition rate is fixed for 4 years. Tuition at time of enrollment locked for 4 years.

FINANCIAL AID PICTURE (2008-2009)

Students with need: Out of 289 full-time freshmen who applied for aid, 219 were judged to have need. Of these, 217 received aid, and 30 had their full need met. Average financial aid package met 76% of need; average scholarship/grant was $8,356; average loan was $3,172. For part-time students, average financial aid package was $6,971.
Students without need: 66 full-time freshmen who did not demonstrate need for aid received scholarships/grants; average award was $3,316. No-need awards available for academics, alumni affiliation, art, athletics, job skills, leadership, minority status, music/drama, state/district residency.
Scholarships offered: 12 full-time freshmen received athletic scholarships; average amount $5,738.
Cumulative student debt: 64% of graduating class had student loans; average debt was $14,717.

FINANCIAL AID PROCEDURES

Forms required: FAFSA.
Dates and Deadlines: Priority date 4/1; closing date 11/15. Applicants notified on a rolling basis starting 1/1; must reply within 3 week(s) of notification.
Transfers: No deadline. Applicants notified on a rolling basis.

CONTACT

Gerard Joseph, Director of Financial Aid
One University Plaza, MS UHB 1080, Springfield, IL 62703
(217) 206-6724

University of St. Francis

Joliet, Illinois
www.stfrancis.edu
Federal Code: 001664

4-year private university and liberal arts college in small city, affiliated with Roman Catholic Church.
Enrollment: 1,247 undergrads, 3% part-time. 223 full-time freshmen.
Selectivity: Admits less than 50% of applicants.

BASIC COSTS (2009-2010)

Tuition and fees: $22,698.
Per-credit charge: $743.
Room and board: $7,938.

FINANCIAL AID PICTURE (2009-2010)

Students with need: Out of 209 full-time freshmen who applied for aid, 178 were judged to have need. Of these, 178 received aid, and 113 had their full need met. Average financial aid package met 78% of need; average scholarship/grant was $7,734; average loan was $3,676. For part-time students, average financial aid package was $7,943.
Students without need: 44 full-time freshmen who did not demonstrate need for aid received scholarships/grants; average award was $9,040. No-need awards available for academics, alumni affiliation, art, athletics, leadership, music/drama, religious affiliation, state/district residency.
Scholarships offered: 22 full-time freshmen received athletic scholarships; average amount $7,434.
Cumulative student debt: 96% of graduating class had student loans; average debt was $21,594.

FINANCIAL AID PROCEDURES

Forms required: FAFSA, institutional form.
Dates and Deadlines: Priority date 3/15; no closing date. Applicants notified on a rolling basis starting 2/15.

CONTACT

Bruce Foote, Executive Director Financial Aid Services
500 Wilcox Street, Joliet, IL 60435
(866) 890-8331

Waubonsee Community College

Sugar Grove, Illinois
www.waubonsee.edu   Federal Code: 006931

2-year public community college in small town.
Enrollment: 7,861 undergrads, 53% part-time. 991 full-time freshmen.
Selectivity: Open admission; but selective for some programs.

BASIC COSTS (2010-2011)
Tuition and fees: $2,700; out-of-district residents $8,034; out-of-state residents $8,853.
Per-credit charge: $85; out-of-district residents $263; out-of-state residents $290.

FINANCIAL AID PICTURE (2008-2009)
Students with need: 71% of average financial aid package awarded as scholarships/grants, 29% awarded as loans/jobs. Need-based aid available for part-time students. Work study available nights.
Students without need: No-need awards available for academics, art, athletics, leadership, minority status, music/drama.
Scholarships offered: Gustafson Scholarship; provides tuition for 64 semester hours; selected graduates from each in-district school.

FINANCIAL AID PROCEDURES
Forms required: FAFSA.
Dates and Deadlines: Closing date 12/1. Applicants notified on a rolling basis.

CONTACT
Charles Boudreau, Director of Student Financial Aid Services
Route 47 at Waubonsee Drive, Sugar Grove, IL 60554-9454
(630) 466-7900 ext. 5774

West Suburban College of Nursing

Oak Park, Illinois
www.wscn.edu   Federal Code: 022141

Upper-division private nursing college in very large city, affiliated with Roman Catholic Church.
Enrollment: 236 undergrads.

BASIC COSTS (2009-2010)
Tuition and fees: $21,526.
Per-credit charge: $711.

FINANCIAL AID PICTURE (2008-2009)
Students with need: Need-based aid available for full-time and part-time students. Work study available nights, weekends, and for part-time students.
Students without need: No-need awards available for academics, alumni affiliation.

FINANCIAL AID PROCEDURES
Forms required: FAFSA.
Transfers: Priority date 4/15; no deadline. Applicants notified on a rolling basis; must reply within 3 week(s) of notification.

CONTACT
Shirley Howell, Financial Aid Officer
Three Erie Court, Oak Park, IL 60302
(708) 763-1426

Western Illinois University

Macomb, Illinois
www.wiu.edu   Federal Code: 001780

4-year public university in large town.
Enrollment: 10,553 undergrads, 9% part-time. 1,638 full-time freshmen.
Selectivity: Admits 50 to 75% of applicants.

BASIC COSTS (2009-2010)
Tuition and fees: $8,958; out-of-state residents $12,347.
Per-credit charge: $226; out-of-state residents $339.
Room and board: $7,642.
Additional info: Residents of nearby counties in Iowa and Missouri pay in-state tuition during first year. Tuition at time of enrollment locked for 4 years.

FINANCIAL AID PICTURE (2009-2010)
Students with need: Out of 1,370 full-time freshmen who applied for aid, 1,115 were judged to have need. Of these, 1,099 received aid, and 402 had their full need met. Average financial aid package met 58% of need; average scholarship/grant was $8,498; average loan was $3,333. For part-time students, average financial aid package was $6,393.
Students without need: 58 full-time freshmen who did not demonstrate need for aid received scholarships/grants; average award was $3,786. No-need awards available for academics, alumni affiliation, art, athletics, leadership, minority status, music/drama, ROTC.
Scholarships offered: 67 full-time freshmen received athletic scholarships; average amount $8,638.

FINANCIAL AID PROCEDURES
Forms required: FAFSA.
Dates and Deadlines: Priority date 2/15; no closing date. Applicants notified on a rolling basis starting 1/15.
Transfers: Priority date 1/31; no deadline. Applicants notified on a rolling basis.

CONTACT
William Bushaw, Director of Financial Aid
One University Circle, Macomb, IL 61455-1390
(309) 290-2440

Wheaton College

Wheaton, Illinois
www.wheaton.edu   Federal Code: 001781

4-year private liberal arts college in small city, affiliated with nondenominational tradition.
Enrollment: 2,369 undergrads, 2% part-time. 620 full-time freshmen.
Selectivity: Admits 50 to 75% of applicants.

BASIC COSTS (2010-2011)
Tuition and fees: $27,580.
Per-credit charge: $1,149.
Room and board: $8,050.

FINANCIAL AID PICTURE (2009-2010)
Students with need: Out of 486 full-time freshmen who applied for aid, 341 were judged to have need. Of these, 336 received aid, and 84 had their full need met. Average financial aid package met 86% of need; average scholarship/grant was $18,058; average loan was $4,460. For part-time students, average financial aid package was $6,078.
Students without need: 101 full-time freshmen who did not demonstrate need for aid received scholarships/grants; average award was $4,002. No-need awards available for academics, alumni affiliation, art, minority status, music/drama.

Scholarships offered: President's Award; $1,000 per year for 4 years; U.S. citizens with 3.6 GPA on 4.0 scale, plus minimum 1400 SAT or 32 ACT; unlimited number.
Cumulative student debt: 51% of graduating class had student loans; average debt was $20,455.
Additional info: First $500 to $2,000 of need awarded as grant instead of loan.

FINANCIAL AID PROCEDURES
Forms required: FAFSA, institutional form.
Dates and Deadlines: Priority date 2/15; no closing date. Applicants notified on a rolling basis starting 3/1.
Transfers: Priority date 3/1; no deadline. Applicants notified on a rolling basis.

CONTACT
Karen Belling, Director of Financial Aid
501 College Avenue, Wheaton, IL 60187-5593
(630) 752-5021

Wilbur Wright College
Chicago, Illinois
http://wright.ccc.edu/   Federal Code: 001655

2-year public community college in very large city.
Enrollment: 8,681 undergrads.
Selectivity: Open admission.

BASIC COSTS (2009-2010)
Tuition and fees: $2,720; out-of-district residents $8,125; out-of-state residents $9,397.
Per-credit charge: $79; out-of-district residents $259; out-of-state residents $302.

FINANCIAL AID PICTURE
Students with need: Need-based aid available for full-time and part-time students. Work study available nights, weekends, and for part-time students.

FINANCIAL AID PROCEDURES
Forms required: FAFSA, institutional form.
Dates and Deadlines: Priority date 6/1; no closing date. Applicants notified on a rolling basis starting 7/15.

CONTACT
Marco Sepulveda, Financial Aid Director
4300 North Narragansett Avenue, Chicago, IL 60634-4276
(773) 481-8100

Indiana

Ancilla College
Donaldson, Indiana
www.ancilla.edu   Federal Code: 001784

2-year private community and liberal arts college in rural community, affiliated with Roman Catholic Church.
Enrollment: 556 undergrads.
Selectivity: Open admission; but selective for some programs.

BASIC COSTS (2010-2011)
Tuition and fees: $13,165.
Per-credit charge: $435.

FINANCIAL AID PICTURE (2009-2010)
Students with need: Need-based aid available for full-time and part-time students.

Students without need: No-need awards available for academics, athletics, job skills, leadership.

FINANCIAL AID PROCEDURES
Forms required: FAFSA, institutional form.
Dates and Deadlines: Closing date 3/1. Applicants notified on a rolling basis starting 3/1; must reply within 2 week(s) of notification.

CONTACT
Katherine Mills, Director of Financial Aid
9001 Union Road, Donaldson, IN 46513
(574) 936-8898 ext. 307

Anderson University
Anderson, Indiana
www.anderson.edu   Federal Code: 001785

4-year private liberal arts college in small city, affiliated with Church of God.
Enrollment: 2,097 undergrads.
Selectivity: Admits 50 to 75% of applicants. GED not accepted.

BASIC COSTS (2010-2011)
Tuition and fees: $23,970.
Per-credit charge: $998.
Room and board: $8,350.
Additional info: Tuition/fee waivers available for adults.

FINANCIAL AID PICTURE (2009-2010)
Students with need: Need-based aid available for full-time and part-time students. Work study available nights, weekends, and for part-time students.
Students without need: No-need awards available for academics, alumni affiliation, art, leadership, minority status, music/drama, religious affiliation.

FINANCIAL AID PROCEDURES
Forms required: FAFSA.
Dates and Deadlines: Priority date 3/1; no closing date. Applicants notified on a rolling basis starting 3/1.

CONTACT
Kenneth Nieman, Director of Financial Aid
1100 East Fifth Street, Anderson, IN 46012-3495
(765) 641-4182

Ball State University
Muncie, Indiana
www.bsu.edu   Federal Code: 001786

4-year public university in small city.
Enrollment: 17,403 undergrads, 6% part-time. 4,157 full-time freshmen.
Selectivity: Admits 50 to 75% of applicants.

BASIC COSTS (2009-2010)
Tuition and fees: $7,830; out-of-state residents $20,398.
Room and board: $7,932.

FINANCIAL AID PICTURE (2009-2010)
Students with need: Out of 3,759 full-time freshmen who applied for aid, 2,747 were judged to have need. Of these, 2,725 received aid, and 701 had their full need met. Average financial aid package met 56% of need; average scholarship/grant was $7,145; average loan was $3,543. For part-time students, average financial aid package was $6,850.
Students without need: 402 full-time freshmen who did not demonstrate need for aid received scholarships/grants; average award was $4,226. No-need awards available for academics, athletics, leadership, minority status, music/drama, ROTC, state/district residency.
Scholarships offered: 68 full-time freshmen received athletic scholarships; average amount $13,821.

Cumulative student debt: 67% of graduating class had student loans; average debt was $22,598.

FINANCIAL AID PROCEDURES

Forms required: FAFSA.

Dates and Deadlines: Priority date 3/10; no closing date. Applicants notified on a rolling basis starting 4/1.

Transfers: No deadline. Applicants notified on a rolling basis starting 6/1.

CONTACT

Robert Zellers, Director of Scholarships/Financial Aid
2000 West University Avenue, Muncie, IN 47306-1022
(765) 285-5600

Bethel College
Mishawaka, Indiana
www.bethelcollege.edu   Federal Code: 001787

4-year private liberal arts college in small city, affiliated with Missionary Church.

Enrollment: 1,879 undergrads, 21% part-time. 295 full-time freshmen.

Selectivity: Admits over 75% of applicants.

BASIC COSTS (2010-2011)

Tuition and fees: $21,990.

Room and board: $6,670.

Additional info: Tuition/fee waivers available for adults, minority students.

FINANCIAL AID PICTURE (2009-2010)

Students with need: Need-based aid available for full-time and part-time students.

Students without need: No-need awards available for academics, art, athletics, job skills, leadership, minority status, music/drama, religious affiliation, ROTC, state/district residency.

FINANCIAL AID PROCEDURES

Forms required: FAFSA, institutional form.

Dates and Deadlines: Priority date 3/1; closing date 3/10. Applicants notified by 4/15; must reply within 3 week(s) of notification.

CONTACT

Guy Fisher, Director of Financial Aid
1001 Bethel Circle, Mishawaka, IN 46545-5591
(574) 807-7415

Brown Mackie College: South Bend
South Bend, Indiana
www.brownmackie.edu   Federal Code: 004583

2-year for-profit community and technical college in small city.

Enrollment: 910 undergrads.

Selectivity: Open admission.

BASIC COSTS (2009-2010)

Additional info: Tuition, which varies according to area of study, is $266 per credit hour for most programs. Practical Nursing program tuition is $325 per credit hour.

FINANCIAL AID PICTURE (2009-2010)

Students with need: Need-based aid available for full-time and part-time students.

Students without need: This college awards aid only to students with need.

FINANCIAL AID PROCEDURES

Forms required: FAFSA.

Dates and Deadlines: No deadline. Applicants notified on a rolling basis; must reply within 1 week(s) of notification.

CONTACT

Sue Kempt, Senior Financial Aid Officer
1030 East Jefferson Boulevard, South Bend, IN 46617

Butler University
Indianapolis, Indiana
www.butler.edu   Federal Code: 001788

4-year private university in very large city.

Enrollment: 3,715 undergrads, 2% part-time. 945 full-time freshmen.

Selectivity: Admits over 75% of applicants.

BASIC COSTS (2010-2011)

Tuition and fees: $30,558.

Per-credit charge: $1,250.

Room and board: $10,130.

FINANCIAL AID PICTURE (2009-2010)

Students with need: Out of 895 full-time freshmen who applied for aid, 664 were judged to have need. Of these, 664 received aid, and 135 had their full need met. For part-time students, average financial aid package was $10,841.

Students without need: 198 full-time freshmen who did not demonstrate need for aid received scholarships/grants; average award was $9,278. No-need awards available for academics, athletics, music/drama.

Scholarships offered: 19 full-time freshmen received athletic scholarships; average amount $21,007.

Cumulative student debt: 64% of graduating class had student loans; average debt was $30,470.

FINANCIAL AID PROCEDURES

Forms required: FAFSA.

Dates and Deadlines: Priority date 3/1; no closing date. Applicants notified on a rolling basis starting 3/15; must reply within 3 week(s) of notification.

Transfers: Priority date 3/15; no deadline.

CONTACT

Melissa Smurdon, Director of Financial Aid
4600 Sunset Avenue, Indianapolis, IN 46208
(317) 940-8200

Calumet College of St. Joseph
Whiting, Indiana
www.ccsj.edu   Federal Code: 001834

4-year private liberal arts college in small city, affiliated with Roman Catholic Church.

Enrollment: 1,088 undergrads, 49% part-time. 141 full-time freshmen.

Selectivity: Admits 50 to 75% of applicants.

BASIC COSTS (2010-2011)

Tuition and fees: $14,000.

Per-credit charge: $440.

FINANCIAL AID PICTURE (2008-2009)

Students with need: Need-based aid available for full-time and part-time students.

Students without need: No-need awards available for academics, alumni affiliation, athletics, religious affiliation.

Additional info: Immediate computerized estimate of financial aid eligibility available to students applying in person.

FINANCIAL AID PROCEDURES

Forms required: FAFSA.

Dates and Deadlines: Priority date 3/1; no closing date. Applicants notified on a rolling basis; must reply within 2 week(s) of notification.

CONTACT
Gina Pirtle, Director of Financial Aid
2400 New York Avenue, Whiting, IN 46394-2195
(219) 473-4296

DePauw University
Greencastle, Indiana
www.depauw.edu   Federal Code: 001792

4-year private music and liberal arts college in small town, affiliated with United Methodist Church.
Enrollment: 2,354 undergrads. 717 full-time freshmen.
Selectivity: Admits 50 to 75% of applicants.

BASIC COSTS (2010-2011)
Tuition and fees: $34,865.
Room and board: $9,180.
Additional info: Incoming freshman students pay additional fee for mandatory purchase of laptop computer; costs range from $1,435 to $2,004.

FINANCIAL AID PICTURE (2009-2010)
Students with need: Out of 518 full-time freshmen who applied for aid, 408 were judged to have need. Of these, 408 received aid, and 133 had their full need met. Average financial aid package met 90% of need; average scholarship/grant was $25,918; average loan was $2,905. For part-time students, average financial aid package was $5,500.
Students without need: 304 full-time freshmen who did not demonstrate need for aid received scholarships/grants; average award was $17,134. No-need awards available for academics, alumni affiliation, leadership, minority status, music/drama, ROTC.
Scholarships offered: Holton Scholarships; $1,000 to full tuition; based on exceptional leadership and/or service; 50 awarded.
Cumulative student debt: 48% of graduating class had student loans; average debt was $24,210.

FINANCIAL AID PROCEDURES
Forms required: FAFSA, institutional form.
Dates and Deadlines: Closing date 3/1. Applicants notified by 3/27; must reply by 5/1.
Transfers: Applicants notified by 3/27; must reply by 5/1.

CONTACT
Craig Slaughter, Director of Financial Aid
101 East Seminary Street, Greencastle, IN 46135-1611
(765) 658-4030

Earlham College
Richmond, Indiana
www.earlham.edu   Federal Code: 001793

4-year private liberal arts and seminary college in large town, affiliated with Society of Friends (Quaker).
Enrollment: 1,097 undergrads, 1% part-time. 328 full-time freshmen.
Selectivity: Admits over 75% of applicants.

BASIC COSTS (2010-2011)
Tuition and fees: $36,694.
Per-credit charge: $1,197.
Room and board: $7,400.

FINANCIAL AID PICTURE (2008-2009)
Students with need: Out of 222 full-time freshmen who applied for aid, 194 were judged to have need. Of these, 194 received aid, and 98 had their full need met. Average financial aid package met 91% of need; average scholarship/grant was $17,620; average loan was $4,662. Need-based aid available for part-time students.

Students without need: 53 full-time freshmen who did not demonstrate need for aid received scholarships/grants; average award was $8,981. No-need awards available for academics, minority status, religious affiliation.
Scholarships offered: Presidential Honors Scholarship; $9,000 per year; based on combination of grades and test scores; unlimited number. Cunningham Scholarship; $9,000 per year; based on combination of grades and test scores; unlimited number. C.B. Edwards Scholarship; up to $12,500 per year; for chemistry majors; 1-3 awarded per year. Wilkinson Award; $3,000 per year; must be Quaker; unlimited number awarded.

FINANCIAL AID PROCEDURES
Forms required: FAFSA.
Dates and Deadlines: Closing date 3/1. Applicants notified on a rolling basis starting 2/15; must reply by 5/1 or within 3 week(s) of notification.
Transfers: Priority date 3/1; no deadline. Deadline for State of Indiana Grants, 3/1 (FAFSA date).

CONTACT
Robert Arnold, Director of Financial Aid
801 National Road West, Richmond, IN 47374-4095
(765) 983-1217

Franklin College
Franklin, Indiana
www.franklincollege.edu   Federal Code: 001798

4-year private liberal arts college in large town, affiliated with American Baptist Churches in the USA.
Enrollment: 1,271 undergrads, 18% part-time. 341 full-time freshmen.
Selectivity: Admits 50 to 75% of applicants.

BASIC COSTS (2010-2011)
Tuition and fees: $24,655.
Room and board: $7,295.

FINANCIAL AID PICTURE (2008-2009)
Students with need: Out of 312 full-time freshmen who applied for aid, 265 were judged to have need. Of these, 265 received aid, and 49 had their full need met. Average financial aid package met 82% of need; average scholarship/grant was $14,379; average loan was $4,024. For part-time students, average financial aid package was $7,859.
Students without need: 76 full-time freshmen who did not demonstrate need for aid received scholarships/grants; average award was $6,537. No-need awards available for academics, alumni affiliation, art, leadership, minority status, religious affiliation, state/district residency.
Cumulative student debt: 85% of graduating class had student loans; average debt was $26,903.

FINANCIAL AID PROCEDURES
Forms required: FAFSA, institutional form.
Dates and Deadlines: Closing date 3/10. Applicants notified on a rolling basis; must reply by 5/1 or within 4 week(s) of notification.
Transfers: Must reply by 5/1 or within 2 week(s) of notification.

CONTACT
Elizabeth Sappenfield, Director of Financial Aid
101 Branigin Boulevard, Franklin, IN 46131-2623
(317) 738-8075

Goshen College
Goshen, Indiana
www.goshen.edu   Federal Code: 001799

4-year private liberal arts college in large town, affiliated with Mennonite Church.
Enrollment: 951 undergrads, 5% part-time. 238 full-time freshmen.
Selectivity: Admits 50 to 75% of applicants.

BASIC COSTS (2010-2011)
Tuition and fees: $24,500.
Per-credit charge: $1,020.
Room and board: $8,300.

FINANCIAL AID PICTURE (2009-2010)
Students with need: Out of 218 full-time freshmen who applied for aid, 201 were judged to have need. Of these, 199 received aid, and 33 had their full need met. Average financial aid package met 83% of need; average scholarship/grant was $17,214; average loan was $3,132. For part-time students, average financial aid package was $9,860.
Students without need: 48 full-time freshmen who did not demonstrate need for aid received scholarships/grants; average award was $12,785. No-need awards available for academics, art, athletics, leadership, music/drama.
Scholarships offered: *Merit:* President's Leadership Award; $15,000; must meet 2 of the following criteria: 3.8 GPA, 1270 SAT (exclusive of Writing) or 29 ACT, top 5% of class, National Merit semifinalist; 15 awards offered each year, renews annually with 3.20 GPA. Menno Simons Scholarships; $8,000; 3.75 GPA and 1200 SAT (exclusive of Writing) or 26 ACT required. Wens Honors Scholarship; $7,000; 3.50 GPA and 1100 SAT (exclusive of Writing) or ACT of 25. Yoder Honors Scholarship; $6,000; 3.30 GPA and 1050 SAT or 22 ACT. Kratz Honors Scholarship; $3,000; 3.0 GPA required. *Athletic:* 20 full-time freshmen received athletic scholarships; average amount $5,652.
Cumulative student debt: 77% of graduating class had student loans; average debt was $20,857.

FINANCIAL AID PROCEDURES
Forms required: FAFSA, institutional form.
Dates and Deadlines: Priority date 2/1; no closing date. Applicants notified on a rolling basis starting 3/1; must reply by 5/1 or within 2 week(s) of notification.
Transfers: Priority date 3/10; no deadline. Applicants notified on a rolling basis starting 3/1; must reply by 5/1 or within 2 week(s) of notification.

CONTACT
James Histand, Vice President for Finance
1700 South Main Street, Goshen, IN 46526-4724
(574) 535-7522

Grace College
Winona Lake, Indiana
www.grace.edu   Federal Code: 001800

4-year private liberal arts college in small town, affiliated with Brethren Church.
Enrollment: 1,384 undergrads, 6% part-time. 230 full-time freshmen.
Selectivity: Admits over 75% of applicants.

BASIC COSTS (2009-2010)
Tuition and fees: $21,100.
Per-credit charge: $466.
Room and board: $6,880.
Additional info: Tuition/fee waivers available for minority students.

FINANCIAL AID PICTURE (2008-2009)
Students with need: 74% of average financial aid package awarded as scholarships/grants, 26% awarded as loans/jobs. Need-based aid available for part-time students. Work study available nights, weekends, and for part-time students.
Students without need: No-need awards available for academics, art, athletics, leadership, minority status, music/drama, religious affiliation.

FINANCIAL AID PROCEDURES
Forms required: FAFSA.
Dates and Deadlines: Closing date 3/1. Applicants notified on a rolling basis starting 3/1; must reply by 5/1.

Transfers: Applicants notified by 3/15; must reply by 5/1. Applicants who miss dates for admission and financial aid are notified on rolling basis until class is full.

CONTACT
Charlette Sauders, Director of Financial Aid Services
200 Seminary Drive, Winona Lake, IN 46590
(574) 372-5100 ext. 6162

Hanover College
Hanover, Indiana
www.hanover.edu   Federal Code: 001801

4-year private liberal arts college in rural community, affiliated with Presbyterian Church (USA).
Enrollment: 932 undergrads. 328 full-time freshmen.
Selectivity: Admits 50 to 75% of applicants. GED not accepted.

BASIC COSTS (2010-2011)
Tuition and fees: $27,500.
Per-credit charge: $750.
Room and board: $8,300.

FINANCIAL AID PICTURE (2008-2009)
Students with need: Out of 322 full-time freshmen who applied for aid, 239 were judged to have need. Of these, 238 received aid, and 94 had their full need met. Average financial aid package met 85% of need; average scholarship/grant was $18,947; average loan was $2,654. For part-time students, average financial aid package was $14,143.
Students without need: 106 full-time freshmen who did not demonstrate need for aid received scholarships/grants; average award was $11,818. No-need awards available for academics, alumni affiliation, art, leadership, minority status, music/drama, religious affiliation, state/district residency.
Cumulative student debt: 60% of graduating class had student loans; average debt was $26,570.
Additional info: Academic Honors Diploma Scholarship is a grant program committed to meeting 100% of Indiana student's demonstrated need. Available to Indiana students who graduate with an Academic Honors Diploma (AHD), have completed their application for admission by January 15, and file a complete and valid FAFSA by March 10.

FINANCIAL AID PROCEDURES
Forms required: FAFSA.
Dates and Deadlines: Priority date 3/1; no closing date. Applicants notified on a rolling basis starting 3/31; must reply by 5/1 or within 2 week(s) of notification.
Transfers: No deadline. Applicants notified on a rolling basis starting 3/1; must reply by 5/1 or within 2 week(s) of notification.

CONTACT
Jon Riester, Associate Dean of Financial Assistance and Admission
PO Box 108, Hanover, IN 47243-0108
(812) 866-7030

Harrison College: Anderson
Anderson, Indiana
www.harrison.edu   Federal Code: 015227

2-year for-profit business and health science college in small city.
Enrollment: 225 undergrads.
Selectivity: Admits over 75% of applicants.

BASIC COSTS (2009-2010)
Additional info: Average cost of full-time tuition, which varies according to program, $11,423 for academic year; required fees, $330 to $555.

FINANCIAL AID PICTURE (2009-2010)

Students with need: Need-based aid available for full-time and part-time students.

Additional info: Work-study programs available.

FINANCIAL AID PROCEDURES

Forms required: FAFSA.

Dates and Deadlines: No deadline. Applicants notified on a rolling basis.

CONTACT

Billie Box, Financial Aid Director

140 East 53rd Street, Anderson, IN 46013

(800) 422-4723

Harrison College: Columbus

Columbus, Indiana

www.harrison.edu   Federal Code: 015226

2-year for-profit business and health science college in large town.

Enrollment: 270 undergrads.

Selectivity: Admits over 75% of applicants.

BASIC COSTS (2009-2010)

Additional info: Average cost of full-time tuition, which varies according to program, $11,423 for academic year; required fees, $330 to $555.

FINANCIAL AID PICTURE (2008-2009)

Students with need: Need-based aid available for full-time and part-time students.

Additional info: Work-study programs available.

FINANCIAL AID PROCEDURES

Forms required: FAFSA.

Dates and Deadlines: No deadline. Applicants notified on a rolling basis.

CONTACT

Kathy England, Financial Aid Director

2222 Poshard Drive, Columbus, IN 47203

(800) 422-4723

Harrison College: Evansville

Evansville, Indiana

www.harrison.edu   Federal Code: E00778

2-year for-profit business and health science college in small city.

Enrollment: 212 undergrads.

Selectivity: Admits 50 to 75% of applicants.

BASIC COSTS (2009-2010)

Additional info: Average cost of full-time tuition, which varies according to program, $11,423 for academic year; required fees, $330 to $555.

FINANCIAL AID PICTURE (2008-2009)

Students with need: Need-based aid available for full-time and part-time students.

Additional info: Work-study programs available.

FINANCIAL AID PROCEDURES

Forms required: FAFSA.

Dates and Deadlines: No deadline. Applicants notified on a rolling basis.

CONTACT

Jennifer Sermersheim, Financial Aid Director

4601 Theater Drive, Evansville, IN 47715

(800) 422-4723

Harrison College: Fort Wayne

Fort Wayne, Indiana

www.harrison.edu

2-year for-profit business and health science college in large city.

Enrollment: 561 undergrads.

Selectivity: Admits over 75% of applicants.

BASIC COSTS (2009-2010)

Additional info: Average cost of full-time tuition, which varies according to program, $12,053 for academic year; required fees, $330 to $615.

FINANCIAL AID PICTURE (2008-2009)

Students with need: Need-based aid available for full-time and part-time students.

Additional info: Work-study programs available.

FINANCIAL AID PROCEDURES

Forms required: FAFSA.

Transfers: Applicants notified on a rolling basis.

CONTACT

Jackie Edwards, Financial Aid Director

6413 North Clinton Street, Fort Wayne, IN 46825

(800) 422-4723

Harrison College: Indianapolis

Indianapolis, Indiana

www.harrison.edu   Federal Code: 075218

2-year for-profit business and health science college in very large city.

Enrollment: 2,196 undergrads.

Selectivity: Admits 50 to 75% of applicants.

BASIC COSTS (2009-2010)

Additional info: Average cost of full-time tuition, which varies according to program, $12,052 for academic year; required fees, $330 to $615.

FINANCIAL AID PICTURE

Students with need: Need-based aid available for full-time and part-time students.

Additional info: Work-study programs available.

FINANCIAL AID PROCEDURES

Forms required: FAFSA.

Dates and Deadlines: Applicants notified on a rolling basis.

CONTACT

550 East Washington Street, Indianapolis, IN 46204

(800) 422-4723

Harrison College: Indianapolis East

Indianapolis, Indiana

www.harrison.edu   Federal Code: E00777

2-year for-profit health science college in very large city.

Enrollment: 534 undergrads.

Selectivity: Admits 50 to 75% of applicants.

BASIC COSTS (2009-2010)

Additional info: Average cost of full-time tuition, which varies according to program, $12,000 for academic year; required fees, $555 to $900; per-credit-hour charge, $350.

FINANCIAL AID PICTURE (2008-2009)

Students with need: Need-based aid available for full-time and part-time students.

Additional info: Work-study programs available.

FINANCIAL AID PROCEDURES

Forms required: FAFSA.

Dates and Deadlines: No deadline. Applicants notified on a rolling basis.

Transfers: Applicants notified on a rolling basis.

CONTACT

Donald Ronan, Financial Aid Director

8150 Brookville Road, Indianapolis, IN 46239

(800) 422-4723

Harrison College: Indianapolis Northwest

Indianapolis, Indiana

www.harrison.edu   Federal Code: E01209

2-year for-profit health science college in very large city.

Enrollment: 290 undergrads.

BASIC COSTS (2009-2010)

Additional info: Tuition varies according to program; per-credit-hour charge, $320; required fees, $1,020.

FINANCIAL AID PICTURE (2008-2009)

Students with need: Need-based aid available for full-time students.

FINANCIAL AID PROCEDURES

Forms required: FAFSA.

Dates and Deadlines: No deadline.

CONTACT

John Egbert, Financial Aid Director

6300 Technology Center Drive, Indianapolis, IN 46278

Harrison College: Lafayette

Lafayette, Indiana

www.harrison.edu   Federal Code: 015224

2-year for-profit business and health science college in small city.

Enrollment: 279 undergrads.

Selectivity: Admits over 75% of applicants.

BASIC COSTS (2009-2010)

Additional info: Average cost of full-time tuition, which varies according to program, $11,423 for academic year; required fees, $330 to $555.

FINANCIAL AID PICTURE (2008-2009)

Students with need: Need-based aid available for full-time and part-time students.

Additional info: Work-study programs available.

FINANCIAL AID PROCEDURES

Forms required: FAFSA.

Dates and Deadlines: No deadline. Applicants notified on a rolling basis.

Transfers: Applicants notified on a rolling basis.

CONTACT

Mary Robinson, Financial Aid Director

4705 Meijer Court, Lafayette, IN 47905

(800) 422-4723

Harrison College: Muncie

Muncie, Indiana

www.harrison.edu   Federal Code: 015222

2-year for-profit business and health science college in small city.

Enrollment: 243 undergrads.

Selectivity: Admits over 75% of applicants.

BASIC COSTS (2009-2010)

Additional info: Average cost of full-time tuition, which varies according to program, $11,423 for academic year; required fees, $330 to $555.

FINANCIAL AID PICTURE (2008-2009)

Students with need: Need-based aid available for full-time and part-time students.

Additional info: Work-study programs available.

FINANCIAL AID PROCEDURES

Forms required: FAFSA.

Dates and Deadlines: Applicants notified on a rolling basis.

Transfers: Applicants notified on a rolling basis.

CONTACT

Kylee Burton, Director of Financial Aid

411 West Riggin Road, Muncie, IN 47303

(800) 422-4723

Harrison College: Terre Haute

Terre Haute, Indiana

www.harrison.edu   Federal Code: 015220

2-year for-profit business and health science college in small city.

Enrollment: 321 undergrads.

Selectivity: Admits over 75% of applicants.

BASIC COSTS (2009-2010)

Additional info: Average cost of full-time tuition, which varies according to program, $11,435 for academic year; required fees, $415.

FINANCIAL AID PICTURE

Students with need: Need-based aid available for full-time and part-time students.

Additional info: Work-study programs available.

FINANCIAL AID PROCEDURES

Forms required: FAFSA.

Dates and Deadlines: Applicants notified on a rolling basis.

Transfers: Applicants notified on a rolling basis.

CONTACT

David Marshall, Director of Financial Aid

1378 South State Road 46, Terre Haute, IN 47803

(812) 877-2100

Holy Cross College

Notre Dame, Indiana

www.hcc-nd.edu   Federal Code: 007263

4-year private liberal arts college in small city, affiliated with Roman Catholic Church.

Enrollment: 441 undergrads.

BASIC COSTS (2010-2011)

Tuition and fees: $20,700.

Room and board: $8,400.

FINANCIAL AID PICTURE (2008-2009)

Students with need: 55% of average financial aid package awarded as scholarships/grants, 45% awarded as loans/jobs. Need-based aid available for part-time students. Work study available nights, weekends, and for part-time students.

Students without need: No-need awards available for academics, leadership.

Cumulative student debt: 90% of graduating class had student loans; average debt was $19,000.

FINANCIAL AID PROCEDURES

Forms required: FAFSA.

Dates and Deadlines: Closing date 3/1. Applicants notified on a rolling basis starting 5/1; must reply within 2 week(s) of notification.

Transfers: Priority date 3/1; no deadline.

CONTACT

Robert Benjamin, Director of Financial Aid

54515 State Road 933 North, Notre Dame, IN 46556-0308

(574) 239-8400

Huntington University

Huntington, Indiana

www.huntington.edu   Federal Code: 001803

4-year private university and liberal arts college in large town, affiliated with United Brethren in Christ.

Enrollment: 949 undergrads.

Selectivity: Admits over 75% of applicants.

BASIC COSTS (2009-2010)

Tuition and fees: $21,290.

Room and board: $7,180.

FINANCIAL AID PICTURE (2009-2010)

Students with need: Need-based aid available for full-time and part-time students. Work study available nights, weekends, and for part-time students.

Students without need: No-need awards available for academics, alumni affiliation, art, athletics, leadership, music/drama, religious affiliation.

Scholarships offered: The Horizon Leader Scholarship covers all fees associated with tuition and housing costs for up to 10 semesters.

FINANCIAL AID PROCEDURES

Forms required: FAFSA.

Dates and Deadlines: Priority date 3/1; no closing date. Applicants notified on a rolling basis starting 3/1; must reply by 5/1 or within 2 week(s) of notification.

Transfers: No deadline. Applicants notified on a rolling basis; must reply by 5/1 or within 2 week(s) of notification.

CONTACT

Sharon Woods, Director of Financial Aid

2303 College Avenue, Huntington, IN 46750-1237

(260) 359-4015

Indiana Institute of Technology

Fort Wayne, Indiana

www.indianatech.edu   Federal Code: 001805

4-year private business and engineering college in large city.

Enrollment: 3,592 undergrads, 33% part-time. 475 full-time freshmen.

Selectivity: Admits 50 to 75% of applicants.

BASIC COSTS (2010-2011)

Tuition and fees: $22,420.

Per-credit charge: $860.

Room and board: $8,410.

Additional info: Books are included in the cost of tuition. Tuition/fee waivers available for adults.

FINANCIAL AID PICTURE (2009-2010)

Students with need: Need-based aid available for full-time and part-time students. Work study available nights, weekends, and for part-time students.

Students without need: No-need awards available for academics, alumni affiliation, athletics, leadership, minority status, music/drama, state/district residency.

FINANCIAL AID PROCEDURES

Forms required: FAFSA, institutional form.

Dates and Deadlines: Closing date 3/10. Applicants notified on a rolling basis starting 2/2; must reply within 2 week(s) of notification.

Transfers: Priority date 3/10; no deadline. Applicants notified on a rolling basis starting 2/2; must reply within 2 week(s) of notification.

CONTACT

Judy Roy, Vice President of Finance and Administration

1600 East Washington Boulevard, Fort Wayne, IN 46803-1297

(260) 422-5561 ext. 2208

Indiana State University

Terre Haute, Indiana

www.indstate.edu   Federal Code: 001807

4-year public university in small city.

Enrollment: 8,405 undergrads, 13% part-time. 1,912 full-time freshmen.

Selectivity: Admits 50 to 75% of applicants.

BASIC COSTS (2009-2010)

Tuition and fees: $7,426; out-of-state residents $16,002.

Per-credit charge: $262; out-of-state residents $558.

Room and board: $7,463.

FINANCIAL AID PICTURE (2008-2009)

Students with need: Out of 1,687 full-time freshmen who applied for aid, 1,344 were judged to have need. Of these, 1,312 received aid, and 242 had their full need met. Average financial aid package met 81% of need; average scholarship/grant was $6,322; average loan was $3,048. For part-time students, average financial aid package was $5,000.

Students without need: This college awards aid only to students with need.

Scholarships offered: 83 full-time freshmen received athletic scholarships; average amount $10,769.

Cumulative student debt: 66% of graduating class had student loans; average debt was $22,944.

Additional info: Financial aid application deadline March 1 for Indiana residents applying for state grant.

FINANCIAL AID PROCEDURES

Forms required: FAFSA.

Dates and Deadlines: Priority date 3/1; no closing date. Applicants notified on a rolling basis starting 4/15.

CONTACT

Kim Donat, Director of Student Financial Aid

Office of Admissions, Erickson 114, Terre Haute, IN 47809-9989

(800) 841-4744

Indiana University Bloomington

Bloomington, Indiana

www.iub.edu   Federal Code: 001809

4-year public university in small city.

Enrollment: 32,000 undergrads, 3% part-time. 7,553 full-time freshmen.

Selectivity: Admits 50 to 75% of applicants.

BASIC COSTS (2009-2010)

Tuition and fees: $8,613; out-of-state residents $26,160.

Per-credit charge: $241; out-of-state residents $790.

Room and board: $7,546.

FINANCIAL AID PICTURE (2008-2009)

Students with need: Out of 5,148 full-time freshmen who applied for aid, 3,222 were judged to have need. Of these, 3,121 received aid, and 537 had their full need met. Average financial aid package met 91% of need; average scholarship/grant was $8,980; average loan was $3,717. For part-time students, average financial aid package was $6,226.

Students without need: 1,907 full-time freshmen who did not demonstrate need for aid received scholarships/grants; average award was $5,823. No-need awards available for academics, art, athletics, leadership, minority status, music/drama, religious affiliation, ROTC.

Scholarships offered: *Merit:* Wells Scholarship; all costs for 4 years; individual schools nominate students; 25 students selected each year. Honors College Scholarship; $1,000-$6,000; 1300 SAT (30 ACT), top 10% class rank. Hudson & Holland; $4,000-$7,000; 1000 SAT (25 ACT), top 20% class rank, 3.0 GPA, based on African, Hispanic, Native American ethnicity. Mathematics and Science Scholarship; $5,000-$6,000; 1000 SAT (25 ACT), top 20% class rank, 3.0 GPA. E.W. Kelley Scholars Program; tuition, room and board, books (overseas study funding, if requested); business major, 1300 SAT (30 ACT), top 10% class rank. School of Music Dean's Award; amounts vary; exceptional talent displayed in audition. Residence Scholarship (via Honors College); $1,500; 1100 SAT (27 ACT), top 10% class rank. Faculty Scholarship; amounts vary; for out-of-state residents with superior test scores and class rank. Valedictorian Award; $1,000; for valedictorians from Indiana schools. 21st Century Scholars Award; in-state instructional fees; Indiana residence, fulfilled terms of pledged in eighth grade, filed FAFSA before March 1 of senior year. Army and Air Force ROTC Scholarships; tuition, fees, books, $200 monthly stipend. All SAT scores listed exclusive of the writing portion. *Athletic:* 69 full-time freshmen received athletic scholarships; average amount $18,114.

Cumulative student debt: 54% of graduating class had student loans; average debt was $25,522.

Additional info: Majority of institutional gift aid merit-based. Some need-based grants go to merit winners with financial need.

FINANCIAL AID PROCEDURES

Forms required: FAFSA.

Dates and Deadlines: Priority date 3/1; no closing date. Applicants notified on a rolling basis starting 4/1.

Transfers: Except for school of music, no merit-based aid for transfer students.

CONTACT

Susan Pugh, Director of Student Financial Assistance
300 North Jordan Avenue, Bloomington, IN 47405
(812) 855-0321

Indiana University East
Richmond, Indiana
www.iue.edu   Federal Code: 001811

4-year public university and branch campus college in large town.

Enrollment: 2,444 undergrads, 38% part-time. 291 full-time freshmen.

Selectivity: Admits 50 to 75% of applicants.

BASIC COSTS (2009-2010)

Tuition and fees: $5,801; out-of-state residents $14,957.

Per-credit charge: $181; out-of-state residents $486.

FINANCIAL AID PICTURE (2008-2009)

Students with need: Out of 273 full-time freshmen who applied for aid, 232 were judged to have need. Of these, 227 received aid, and 24 had their full need met. Average financial aid package met 95% of need; average scholarship/grant was $5,264; average loan was $2,797. For part-time students, average financial aid package was $5,113.

Students without need: 11 full-time freshmen who did not demonstrate need for aid received scholarships/grants; average award was $1,517. No-need awards available for academics, alumni affiliation, leadership.

Cumulative student debt: 78% of graduating class had student loans; average debt was $27,300.

FINANCIAL AID PROCEDURES

Forms required: FAFSA, institutional form.

Dates and Deadlines: Priority date 3/1; no closing date. Applicants notified on a rolling basis starting 5/1; must reply within 2 week(s) of notification.

CONTACT

William Gill, Director of Financial Aid
2325 Chester Boulevard, Richmond, IN 47374-1289
(765) 973-8288

Indiana University Kokomo
Kokomo, Indiana
www.iuk.edu   Federal Code: 001814

4-year public university in large town.

Enrollment: 2,350 undergrads, 34% part-time. 341 full-time freshmen.

Selectivity: Admits over 75% of applicants.

BASIC COSTS (2009-2010)

Tuition and fees: $5,838; out-of-state residents $14,527.

Per-credit charge: $180; out-of-state residents $470.

FINANCIAL AID PICTURE (2008-2009)

Students with need: Out of 311 full-time freshmen who applied for aid, 214 were judged to have need. Of these, 198 received aid, and 16 had their full need met. Average financial aid package met 93% of need; average scholarship/grant was $5,306; average loan was $2,875. For part-time students, average financial aid package was $5,448.

Students without need: 21 full-time freshmen who did not demonstrate need for aid received scholarships/grants; average award was $1,793. No-need awards available for academics.

Cumulative student debt: 65% of graduating class had student loans; average debt was $24,788.

FINANCIAL AID PROCEDURES

Forms required: FAFSA, institutional form.

Dates and Deadlines: Closing date 3/1. Applicants notified on a rolling basis starting 5/1; must reply within 4 week(s) of notification.

CONTACT

Karen Gallatin, Associate Director of Financial Aid
Box 9003, KC 230A, Kokomo, IN 46904-9003
(765) 455-9216

Indiana University Northwest
Gary, Indiana
www.iun.edu   Federal Code: 001815

4-year public university in small city.

Enrollment: 4,531 undergrads, 32% part-time. 598 full-time freshmen.

Selectivity: Admits over 75% of applicants.

BASIC COSTS (2009-2010)

Tuition and fees: $5,919; out-of-state residents $15,024.

Per-credit charge: $183; out-of-state residents $486.

FINANCIAL AID PICTURE (2008-2009)
Students with need: Out of 482 full-time freshmen who applied for aid, 375 were judged to have need. Of these, 357 received aid, and 19 had their full need met. Average financial aid package met 88% of need; average scholarship/grant was $5,047; average loan was $3,094. For part-time students, average financial aid package was $5,494.
Students without need: 44 full-time freshmen who did not demonstrate need for aid received scholarships/grants; average award was $2,843. No-need awards available for academics, athletics.
Scholarships offered: 3 full-time freshmen received athletic scholarships; average amount $1,267.
Cumulative student debt: 68% of graduating class had student loans; average debt was $28,403.

FINANCIAL AID PROCEDURES
Forms required: FAFSA, institutional form.
Dates and Deadlines: Priority date 3/1; no closing date. Applicants notified on a rolling basis starting 5/1; must reply within 2 week(s) of notification.

CONTACT
Harold Burtley, Financial Aid Director
3400 Broadway, Gary, IN 46408
(219) 980-6778

Indiana University South Bend
South Bend, Indiana
www.iusb.edu   Federal Code: 001816

4-year public university in small city.
Enrollment: 6,360 undergrads, 32% part-time. 948 full-time freshmen.
Selectivity: Admits over 75% of applicants.

BASIC COSTS (2009-2010)
Tuition and fees: $6,015; out-of-state residents $15,712.
Per-credit charge: $186; out-of-state residents $509.
Room only: $5,200.

FINANCIAL AID PICTURE (2008-2009)
Students with need: Out of 774 full-time freshmen who applied for aid, 581 were judged to have need. Of these, 558 received aid, and 21 had their full need met. Average financial aid package met 93% of need; average scholarship/grant was $5,679; average loan was $2,879. For part-time students, average financial aid package was $4,904.
Students without need: 55 full-time freshmen who did not demonstrate need for aid received scholarships/grants; average award was $1,655. No-need awards available for academics, athletics.
Scholarships offered: *Merit:* Honors Scholarship; $1,200 per academic year (full-time); based on 1200 SAT (exclusive of Writing) or 27 ACT, rank in top 10%, and 3.5 GPA; renewable up to 8 semesters. Alumni Scholarship; $3,500 freshman year; must be first-time freshman from Northern Indiana, meet Honors Scholarship criteria, submit essay and 3 letters of recommendation. *Athletic:* 2 full-time freshmen received athletic scholarships; average amount $9,700.
Cumulative student debt: 71% of graduating class had student loans; average debt was $25,384.

FINANCIAL AID PROCEDURES
Forms required: FAFSA, institutional form.
Dates and Deadlines: Closing date 3/1. Applicants notified on a rolling basis starting 5/1.
Transfers: No deadline.

CONTACT
Cyndi Lang, Director of Financial Aid
1700 Mishawaka Avenue, South Bend, IN 46634-7111
(574) 520-4357

Indiana University Southeast
New Albany, Indiana
www.ius.edu   Federal Code: 001817

4-year public university in large town.
Enrollment: 5,716 undergrads, 32% part-time. 970 full-time freshmen.
Selectivity: Admits over 75% of applicants.

BASIC COSTS (2009-2010)
Tuition and fees: $5,890; out-of-state residents $14,578.
Per-credit charge: $181; out-of-state residents $470.
Room and board: $6,230.

FINANCIAL AID PICTURE (2008-2009)
Students with need: Out of 810 full-time freshmen who applied for aid, 580 were judged to have need. Of these, 550 received aid, and 29 had their full need met. Average financial aid package met 91% of need; average scholarship/grant was $5,760; average loan was $2,918. For part-time students, average financial aid package was $4,813.
Students without need: 43 full-time freshmen who did not demonstrate need for aid received scholarships/grants; average award was $2,297. No-need awards available for academics, art, athletics, leadership, minority status, music/drama.
Scholarships offered: 5 full-time freshmen received athletic scholarships; average amount $1,040.
Cumulative student debt: 60% of graduating class had student loans; average debt was $22,649.

FINANCIAL AID PROCEDURES
Forms required: FAFSA.
Dates and Deadlines: Priority date 3/1; no closing date. Applicants notified on a rolling basis starting 5/1; must reply within 3 week(s) of notification.

CONTACT
Brittany Hubbard, Director of Financial Aid
4201 Grant Line Road, New Albany, IN 47150-6405
(812) 941-2246 ext. 2260

Indiana University-Purdue University Fort Wayne
Fort Wayne, Indiana
www.ipfw.edu   Federal Code: 001828

4-year public university and branch campus college in large city.
Enrollment: 11,483 undergrads, 27% part-time. 1,889 full-time freshmen.
Selectivity: Admits over 75% of applicants.

BASIC COSTS (2009-2010)
Tuition and fees: $6,926; out-of-state residents $16,478.
Per-credit charge: $202; out-of-state residents $520.
Room only: $5,620.

FINANCIAL AID PICTURE (2008-2009)
Students with need: Out of 1,671 full-time freshmen who applied for aid, 1,290 were judged to have need. Of these, 1,220 received aid, and 8 had their full need met. Average financial aid package met 52% of need; average scholarship/grant was $5,890; average loan was $3,104. For part-time students, average financial aid package was $6,154.
Students without need: 10 full-time freshmen who did not demonstrate need for aid received scholarships/grants; average award was $3,805. No-need awards available for academics, athletics, state/district residency.
Scholarships offered: 23 full-time freshmen received athletic scholarships; average amount $7,772.
Cumulative student debt: 34% of graduating class had student loans; average debt was $22,092.

FINANCIAL AID PROCEDURES

Forms required: FAFSA.

Dates and Deadlines: Priority date 3/10; no closing date. Applicants notified on a rolling basis starting 5/15; must reply within 3 week(s) of notification.

CONTACT

Judith Cramer, Director of Financial Aid

2101 East Coliseum Boulevard, Fort Wayne, IN 46805-1499

(260) 481-6820

Indiana University-Purdue University Indianapolis

Indianapolis, Indiana

www.iupui.edu   Federal Code: 001813

4-year public university in very large city.

Enrollment: 20,926 undergrads, 26% part-time. 2,808 full-time freshmen.

Selectivity: Admits 50 to 75% of applicants.

BASIC COSTS (2009-2010)

Tuition and fees: $7,523; out-of-state residents $22,420.

Per-credit charge: $231; out-of-state residents $727.

Room only: $3,320.

Additional info: Additional Residence Life Programming fee may be charged depending on dorm accommodations.

FINANCIAL AID PICTURE (2008-2009)

Students with need: Out of 2,354 full-time freshmen who applied for aid, 1,797 were judged to have need. Of these, 1,731 received aid, and 163 had their full need met. Average financial aid package met 89% of need; average scholarship/grant was $7,393; average loan was $2,987. For part-time students, average financial aid package was $5,422.

Students without need: 275 full-time freshmen who did not demonstrate need for aid received scholarships/grants; average award was $4,564. No-need awards available for academics, ROTC.

Scholarships offered: 29 full-time freshmen received athletic scholarships; average amount $7,241.

Cumulative student debt: 72% of graduating class had student loans; average debt was $27,062.

FINANCIAL AID PROCEDURES

Forms required: FAFSA.

Dates and Deadlines: Priority date 3/1; no closing date. Applicants notified on a rolling basis starting 4/1.

CONTACT

Kathy Purvis, Director of Scholarships and Financial Aid

420 North University Boulevard, Cavanaugh Hall R129, Indianapolis, IN 46202-5143

(317) 274-4162

Indiana Wesleyan University

Marion, Indiana

www.indwes.edu   Federal Code: 001822

4-year private university and liberal arts college in large town, affiliated with Wesleyan Church.

Enrollment: 3,400 undergrads.

BASIC COSTS (2009-2010)

Tuition and fees: $20,496.

Per-credit charge: $732.

Room and board: $6,770.

Additional info: Required fees vary by program.

FINANCIAL AID PICTURE (2009-2010)

Students with need: Need-based aid available for full-time and part-time students. Work study available nights, weekends, and for part-time students.

Students without need: No-need awards available for academics, alumni affiliation, art, athletics, music/drama, ROTC.

Scholarships offered: Academic Scholarships; $750-$6,000; 3.2 GPA and 1050 SAT (exclusive of Writing) or 23 ACT required.

FINANCIAL AID PROCEDURES

Forms required: FAFSA.

Dates and Deadlines: Closing date 3/1. Applicants notified by 4/1.

CONTACT

Thomas Ratliff, Associate Vice President for Financial Aid

4201 South Washington Street, Marion, IN 46953-4999

(765) 677-2116

Ivy Tech Community College: Bloomington

Bloomington, Indiana

www.ivytech.edu   Federal Code: 035213

2-year public community college in small city.

Enrollment: 5,670 undergrads, 49% part-time. 760 full-time freshmen.

Selectivity: Open admission; but selective for some programs.

BASIC COSTS (2009-2010)

Tuition and fees: $3,090; out-of-state residents $6,306.

Per-credit charge: $105; out-of-state residents $207.

Additional info: Out-of-state distance education tuition: $207 per credit hour ($6,205 for academic year).

FINANCIAL AID PICTURE (2008-2009)

Students with need: Need-based aid available for full-time and part-time students. Work study available nights.

FINANCIAL AID PROCEDURES

Forms required: FAFSA.

Dates and Deadlines: Priority date 3/1; no closing date. Applicants notified on a rolling basis starting 7/1.

CONTACT

Patt McCafferty, Director of Financial Aid

200 Daniels Way, Bloomington, IN 47404-1511

(812) 332-1559

Ivy Tech Community College: Central Indiana

Indianapolis, Indiana

www.ivytech.edu   Federal Code: 009917

2-year public community college in very large city.

Enrollment: 19,446 undergrads, 66% part-time. 1,913 full-time freshmen.

Selectivity: Open admission; but selective for some programs.

BASIC COSTS (2009-2010)

Tuition and fees: $3,090; out-of-state residents $6,306.

Per-credit charge: $105; out-of-state residents $207.

Additional info: Out-of-state distance education tuition: $207 per credit hour ($6,205 for academic year).

FINANCIAL AID PICTURE (2008-2009)

Students with need: Need-based aid available for full-time and part-time students. Work study available nights.

FINANCIAL AID PROCEDURES

Forms required: FAFSA.

Dates and Deadlines: Priority date 3/1; no closing date. Applicants notified on a rolling basis starting 7/1.

CONTACT

Lori Handy, Director of Financial Aid

50 West Fall Creek Parkway North Drive, Indianapolis, IN 46208-5752

(317) 921-4882

Ivy Tech Community College: Columbus

Columbus, Indiana

www.ivytech.edu   Federal Code: 010038

2-year public community college in large town.

Enrollment: 4,632 undergrads, 59% part-time. 576 full-time freshmen.

Selectivity: Open admission; but selective for some programs.

BASIC COSTS (2009-2010)

Tuition and fees: $3,090; out-of-state residents $6,306.

Per-credit charge: $105; out-of-state residents $207.

Additional info: Out-of-state distance education tuition: $207 per-credit-hour ($6,205 for academic year).

FINANCIAL AID PICTURE (2008-2009)

Students with need: Need-based aid available for full-time and part-time students. Work study available nights.

FINANCIAL AID PROCEDURES

Forms required: FAFSA.

Dates and Deadlines: Priority date 3/1; no closing date. Applicants notified on a rolling basis starting 7/1.

CONTACT

Paul Johnston, Director of Financial Aid

4475 Central Avenue, Columbus, IN 47203-1868

(812) 372-9925

Ivy Tech Community College: East Central

Muncie, Indiana

www.ivytech.edu   Federal Code: 009924

2-year public community college in small city.

Enrollment: 8,025 undergrads, 51% part-time. 1,289 full-time freshmen.

Selectivity: Open admission; but selective for some programs.

BASIC COSTS (2009-2010)

Tuition and fees: $3,090; out-of-state residents $6,306.

Per-credit charge: $105; out-of-state residents $207.

Additional info: Out-of-state distance education tuition: $207 per-credit-hour ($6,205 for academic year).

FINANCIAL AID PICTURE (2008-2009)

Students with need: Need-based aid available for full-time and part-time students. Work study available nights.

Additional info: Higher Education Aid (HEA), Child of Disabled/Deceased Veterans (CDV), Ivy Tech Scholarships (IVTC) and grants, vocational rehabilitation and veteran's assistance available. None require repayment.

FINANCIAL AID PROCEDURES

Forms required: FAFSA.

Dates and Deadlines: Priority date 3/1; no closing date. Applicants notified on a rolling basis starting 7/1.

CONTACT

Sylvia Bogle, Director of Financial Aid

4301 South Cowan Road, Muncie, IN 47302-9448

(765) 289-2291 ext. 1222

Ivy Tech Community College: Kokomo

Kokomo, Indiana

www.ivytech.edu   Federal Code: 010041

2-year public community college in large town.

Enrollment: 5,185 undergrads, 57% part-time. 485 full-time freshmen.

Selectivity: Open admission; but selective for some programs.

BASIC COSTS (2009-2010)

Tuition and fees: $3,090; out-of-state residents $6,306.

Per-credit charge: $105; out-of-state residents $207.

Additional info: Out-of-state distance education tuition: $207 per-credit-hour ($6,205 for academic year).

FINANCIAL AID PICTURE (2008-2009)

Students with need: Need-based aid available for full-time and part-time students. Work study available nights.

FINANCIAL AID PROCEDURES

Forms required: FAFSA.

Dates and Deadlines: Priority date 3/1; no closing date. Applicants notified on a rolling basis starting 7/1.

Transfers: Applicants notified on a rolling basis starting 7/1.

CONTACT

David Scheblo, Director of Financial Aid

1815 East Morgan Street, Kokomo, IN 46903-1373

(765) 459-0561

Ivy Tech Community College: Lafayette

Lafayette, Indiana

www.ivytech.edu   Federal Code: 010039

2-year public community college in large town.

Enrollment: 6,932 undergrads, 49% part-time. 1,051 full-time freshmen.

Selectivity: Open admission; but selective for some programs.

BASIC COSTS (2009-2010)

Tuition and fees: $3,090; out-of-state residents $6,306.

Per-credit charge: $105; out-of-state residents $207.

Additional info: Out-of-state distance education tuition: $207 per-credit-hour ($6,205 for academic year).

FINANCIAL AID PICTURE (2008-2009)

Students with need: Need-based aid available for full-time and part-time students. Work study available nights.

FINANCIAL AID PROCEDURES

Forms required: FAFSA.

Dates and Deadlines: Priority date 3/1; no closing date. Applicants notified on a rolling basis starting 7/1.

CONTACT

Beverly Cooper, Director of Financial Aid

3101 South Creasy Lane, Lafayette, IN 47905-6299

(765) 772-9100

Ivy Tech Community College: North Central

South Bend, Indiana

www.ivytech.edu   Federal Code: 008423

2-year public community college in small city.

Enrollment: 8,086 undergrads, 67% part-time. 637 full-time freshmen.

Selectivity: Open admission; but selective for some programs.

BASIC COSTS (2009-2010)

Tuition and fees: $3,090; out-of-state residents $6,306.

Per-credit charge: $105; out-of-state residents $207.

Additional info: Out-of-state distance education tuition: $207 per-credit-hour ($6,205 for academic year).

FINANCIAL AID PICTURE (2008-2009)

Students with need: Need-based aid available for full-time and part-time students. Work study available nights.

FINANCIAL AID PROCEDURES

Forms required: FAFSA.

Dates and Deadlines: Priority date 3/1; no closing date. Applicants notified on a rolling basis starting 7/1.

CONTACT

Jeff Fisher, Director of Financial Aid

220 Dean Johnson Boulevard, South Bend, IN 46601-3415

(219) 289-7001

Ivy Tech Community College: Northeast

Fort Wayne, Indiana

www.ivytech.edu   Federal Code: 009926

2-year public community college in small city.

Enrollment: 10,567 undergrads, 57% part-time. 1,260 full-time freshmen.

Selectivity: Open admission; but selective for some programs.

BASIC COSTS (2009-2010)

Tuition and fees: $3,090; out-of-state residents $6,306.

Per-credit charge: $105; out-of-state residents $207.

Additional info: Out-of-state distance education tuition: $207 per-credit-hour ($6,205 for academic year).

FINANCIAL AID PICTURE (2008-2009)

Students with need: Need-based aid available for full-time and part-time students. Work study available nights.

FINANCIAL AID PROCEDURES

Forms required: FAFSA.

Dates and Deadlines: Priority date 3/1; no closing date. Applicants notified on a rolling basis starting 7/1.

CONTACT

Teresa Sweazey, Director of Financial Aid

3800 North Anthony Boulevard, Fort Wayne, IN 46805-1489

(260) 482-9171

Ivy Tech Community College: Northwest

Gary, Indiana

www.ivytech.edu   Federal Code: 010040

2-year public community college in small city.

Enrollment: 8,349 undergrads, 59% part-time. 1,126 full-time freshmen.

Selectivity: Open admission; but selective for some programs.

BASIC COSTS (2009-2010)

Tuition and fees: $3,090; out-of-state residents $6,306.

Per-credit charge: $105; out-of-state residents $207.

Additional info: Out-of-state distance education tuition: $207 per-credit-hour ($6,205 for academic year).

FINANCIAL AID PICTURE (2008-2009)

Students with need: Need-based aid available for full-time and part-time students. Work study available nights.

FINANCIAL AID PROCEDURES

Forms required: FAFSA.

Dates and Deadlines: Priority date 3/1; no closing date. Applicants notified on a rolling basis starting 7/1.

CONTACT

Barb Jerzyk, Director of Financial Aid

1440 East 35th Avenue, Gary, IN 46409-1499

(219) 981-1111

Ivy Tech Community College: Richmond

Richmond, Indiana

www.ivytech.edu   Federal Code: 010037

2-year public community college in large town.

Enrollment: 3,418 undergrads, 61% part-time. 311 full-time freshmen.

Selectivity: Open admission; but selective for some programs.

BASIC COSTS (2009-2010)

Tuition and fees: $3,090; out-of-state residents $6,306.

Per-credit charge: $105; out-of-state residents $207.

Additional info: Out-of-state distance education tuition: $207 per-credit-hour ($6,205 for academic year).

FINANCIAL AID PICTURE (2008-2009)

Students with need: Need-based aid available for full-time and part-time students. Work study available nights.

FINANCIAL AID PROCEDURES

Forms required: FAFSA.

Dates and Deadlines: Priority date 3/1; no closing date. Applicants notified on a rolling basis starting 7/1.

CONTACT

Ann Franzen-Roha, Director of Financial Aid

2357 Chester Boulevard, Richmond, IN 47374-1298

(765) 966-2656

Ivy Tech Community College: South Central

Sellersburg, Indiana

www.ivytech.edu   Federal Code: 010109

2-year public community college in small town.

Enrollment: 4,548 undergrads, 59% part-time. 545 full-time freshmen.

Selectivity: Open admission; but selective for some programs.

BASIC COSTS (2009-2010)

Tuition and fees: $3,090; out-of-state residents $6,306.

Per-credit charge: $105; out-of-state residents $207.

Additional info: Out-of-state distance education tuition: $207 per-credit-hour ($6,205 for academic year).

FINANCIAL AID PICTURE (2008-2009)

Students with need: Need-based aid available for full-time and part-time students. Work study available nights.

FINANCIAL AID PROCEDURES

Forms required: FAFSA.

Dates and Deadlines: Priority date 3/1; no closing date. Applicants notified on a rolling basis starting 7/1.

CONTACT

Gary Cottrill, Director of Financial Aid

8204 Highway 311, Sellersburg, IN 47172-1897

(812) 246-3301

Ivy Tech Community College: Southeast

Madison, Indiana
www.ivytech.edu   Federal Code: 009923

2-year public community college in large town.
Enrollment: 2,608 undergrads, 54% part-time. 331 full-time freshmen.
Selectivity: Open admission; but selective for some programs.

BASIC COSTS (2009-2010)
Tuition and fees: $3,090; out-of-state residents $6,306.
Per-credit charge: $105; out-of-state residents $207.
Additional info: Out-of-state distance education tuition: $207 per-credit-hour ($6,205 for academic year).

FINANCIAL AID PICTURE (2008-2009)
Students with need: Need-based aid available for full-time and part-time students. Work study available nights.

FINANCIAL AID PROCEDURES
Forms required: FAFSA.
Dates and Deadlines: Priority date 3/1; no closing date. Applicants notified on a rolling basis starting 7/1.

CONTACT
Richard Hill, Director of Financial Aid
590 Ivy Tech Drive, Madison, IN 47250-1881
(812) 265-2580 ext. 4148

Ivy Tech Community College: Southwest

Evansville, Indiana
www.ivytech.edu   Federal Code: 009925

2-year public community college in small city.
Enrollment: 5,820 undergrads, 60% part-time. 670 full-time freshmen.
Selectivity: Open admission; but selective for some programs.

BASIC COSTS (2009-2010)
Tuition and fees: $3,090; out-of-state residents $6,306.
Per-credit charge: $105; out-of-state residents $207.
Additional info: Out-of-state distance education tuition: $207 per-credit-hour ($6,205 for academic year).

FINANCIAL AID PICTURE (2008-2009)
Students with need: Need-based aid available for full-time and part-time students. Work study available nights.

FINANCIAL AID PROCEDURES
Forms required: FAFSA.
Dates and Deadlines: Priority date 3/1; no closing date. Applicants notified on a rolling basis starting 7/1.

CONTACT
Kristi Eidson-Spahn, Director of Financial Aid
3501 First Avenue, Evansville, IN 47710-3398
(812) 426-2865

Ivy Tech Community College: Wabash Valley

Terre Haute, Indiana
www.ivytech.edu   Federal Code: 008547

2-year public community college in small city.
Enrollment: 5,688 undergrads, 52% part-time. 730 full-time freshmen.
Selectivity: Open admission; but selective for some programs.

BASIC COSTS (2009-2010)
Tuition and fees: $3,090; out-of-state residents $6,306.
Per-credit charge: $105; out-of-state residents $207.
Additional info: Out-of-state distance education tuition: $207 per-credit-hour ($6,205 for academic year).

FINANCIAL AID PICTURE (2008-2009)
Students with need: Need-based aid available for full-time and part-time students. Work study available nights.

FINANCIAL AID PROCEDURES
Forms required: FAFSA.
Dates and Deadlines: Priority date 3/1; no closing date. Applicants notified on a rolling basis starting 7/1.
Transfers: Applicants notified on a rolling basis starting 7/1.

CONTACT
Julie Wonderlin, Director of Financial Aid
8000 South Education Drive, Terre Haute, IN 47802-4898
(812) 299-1121

Kaplan College: Indianapolis

Indianapolis, Indiana
www.kcindy.com   Federal Code: 009777

2-year for-profit business and health science college in very large city.

FINANCIAL AID PICTURE
Students with need: Need-based aid available for full-time students.
Students without need: This college awards aid only to students with need.

CONTACT
Vincent O'Neal, Financial Aid Director
7302 Woodland Drive, Indianapolis, IN 46278-1736
(317) 293-6503

Kaplan College: Merrillville

Merrillville, Indiana
www.sawyercollege.edu   Federal Code: 022018

2-year for-profit technical college in large town.
Enrollment: 400 undergrads.
Selectivity: Open admission.

BASIC COSTS (2009-2010)
Tuition and fees: $13,480.

FINANCIAL AID PICTURE
Students with need: Need-based aid available for full-time and part-time students.

FINANCIAL AID PROCEDURES
Forms required: FAFSA.
Dates and Deadlines: No deadline. Applicants notified on a rolling basis.

CONTACT
Lisa Coff, Director of Financial Aid
3803 East Lincoln Highway, Merrillville, IN 46410
(219) 947-8400 ext. 8409

PART III: FINANCIAL AID COLLEGE BY COLLEGE

Manchester College
North Manchester, Indiana
www.manchester.edu
Federal Code: 001820

4-year private liberal arts college in small town, affiliated with Church of the Brethren.

Enrollment: 1,187 undergrads, 1% part-time. 426 full-time freshmen.
Selectivity: Admits over 75% of applicants.

BASIC COSTS (2010-2011)
Tuition and fees: $24,920.
Per-credit charge: $700.
Room and board: $8,860.

FINANCIAL AID PICTURE (2009-2010)
Students with need: Out of 404 full-time freshmen who applied for aid, 359 were judged to have need. Of these, 359 received aid, and 36 had their full need met. Average financial aid package met 87% of need; average scholarship/grant was $18,110; average loan was $3,775. For part-time students, average financial aid package was $17,499.
Students without need: 45 full-time freshmen who did not demonstrate need for aid received scholarships/grants; average award was $10,746. No-need awards available for academics, alumni affiliation, minority status, music/drama, religious affiliation.
Scholarships offered: Honors Fellowship; full tuition; based on academics; 2 awarded. Presidential Leadership Award; $2,500 travel grant; 3 awarded. Trustee Scholarships; $12,000; based on merit; 40 awarded to each incoming class. Presidential Scholarships; $9,000; based on merit. Arts, service, modern language scholarships; $9,000; based on merit/ability.
Cumulative student debt: 88% of graduating class had student loans; average debt was $16,333.
Additional info: Students automatically considered for all scholarship programs.

FINANCIAL AID PROCEDURES
Forms required: FAFSA.
Dates and Deadlines: Priority date 3/1; no closing date. Applicants notified on a rolling basis starting 2/15; must reply within 2 week(s) of notification.
Transfers: Aid eligibility remaining determined by reviewing total credit hours transferred and financial aid transcripts.

CONTACT
Gina Voelz, Director of Financial Aid
604 East College Avenue, North Manchester, IN 46962-0365
(260) 982-5066

Marian University
Indianapolis, Indiana
www.marian.edu
Federal Code: 001821

4-year private liberal arts college in very large city, affiliated with Roman Catholic Church.

Enrollment: 1,947 undergrads, 24% part-time. 320 full-time freshmen.
Selectivity: Admits 50 to 75% of applicants.

BASIC COSTS (2009-2010)
Tuition and fees: $24,000.
Per-credit charge: $1,050.
Room and board: $7,512.

FINANCIAL AID PICTURE (2009-2010)
Students with need: Need-based aid available for full-time and part-time students. Work study available nights, weekends, and for part-time students.
Students without need: No-need awards available for academics, alumni affiliation, art, athletics, leadership, music/drama, religious affiliation.

FINANCIAL AID PROCEDURES
Forms required: FAFSA, institutional form.
Dates and Deadlines: Priority date 3/15; no closing date. Applicants notified on a rolling basis starting 3/15; must reply within 2 week(s) of notification.
Transfers: No deadline. Applicants notified on a rolling basis starting 3/15; must reply within 2 week(s) of notification.

CONTACT
John Shelton, Dean for Financial Aid and Enrollment
3200 Cold Spring Road, Indianapolis, IN 46222-1997
(317) 955-6040

Oakland City University
Oakland City, Indiana
www.oak.edu
Federal Code: 001824

4-year private university and liberal arts college in small town, affiliated with Baptist General Conference.

Enrollment: 1,429 undergrads, 10% part-time. 217 full-time freshmen.

BASIC COSTS (2010-2011)
Tuition and fees: $15,600.
Per-credit charge: $520.
Room and board: $7,300.
Additional info: Tuition/fee waivers available for minority students, unemployed or children of unemployed.

FINANCIAL AID PICTURE (2009-2010)
Students with need: Need-based aid available for full-time and part-time students. Work study available nights, weekends, and for part-time students.
Students without need: No-need awards available for academics, alumni affiliation, art, athletics, minority status, music/drama, religious affiliation.

FINANCIAL AID PROCEDURES
Forms required: FAFSA.
Dates and Deadlines: Closing date 3/1. Applicants notified on a rolling basis starting 5/1.

CONTACT
Caren Richeson, Director of Financial Aid
138 North Lucretia Street, Oakland City, IN 47660
(812) 749-1224

Purdue University
West Lafayette, Indiana
www.purdue.edu
Federal Code: 001825

4-year public university in small city.

Enrollment: 30,932 undergrads, 4% part-time. 6,149 full-time freshmen.
Selectivity: Admits 50 to 75% of applicants.

BASIC COSTS (2009-2010)
Tuition and fees: $8,638; out-of-state residents $25,118.
Per-credit charge: $293; out-of-state residents $819.
Room and board: $8,710.
Additional info: Differential general service fees: Engineering students pay additional $1,000 per academic year. Management undergraduate students pay additional $1,274 per academic year. School of Technology students pay an additional $500 per academic year. Degree-seeking students who are continuously enrolled prior to the summer 2009 term are not charged the $500 per academic year Strategic Plan fee.

FINANCIAL AID PICTURE (2009-2010)

Students with need: Out of 4,620 full-time freshmen who applied for aid, 3,122 were judged to have need. Of these, 3,122 received aid, and 1,791 had their full need met. Average financial aid package met 96% of need; average scholarship/grant was $10,052; average loan was $10,052. Need-based aid available for part-time students.

Students without need: No-need awards available for academics, athletics, job skills, leadership, music/drama, ROTC.

Scholarships offered: Trustees Scholarship: $10,000 per year to non-Indiana residents; $8,000 per year to Indiana residents; renewable for up to four years; based on high school GPA of 3.8 on 4.0 scale plus SAT of 2000 or higher or a score of 30 or higher on both ACT composite and ACT writing. Presidential Scholarship: $7,000 per year to non-Indiana residents; $5,000 per year to Indiana residents; renewable for up to four years of continuous full-time enrollment with 3.0 GPA; based on high school GPA of 3.9 on 4.0 scale plus SAT of 1850-1990 or ACT composite of 27-29 and combined English/writing of 27-29.

Cumulative student debt: 54% of graduating class had student loans; average debt was $23,924.

Additional info: Cooperative work for credit available in many programs.

FINANCIAL AID PROCEDURES

Forms required: FAFSA.

Dates and Deadlines: Priority date 3/1; no closing date. Applicants notified by 4/15.

CONTACT

Joyce Hall, Director of Financial Aid
475 Stadium Mall Drive, West Lafayette, IN 47907-2050
(765) 494-0998

Purdue University Calumet
Hammond, Indiana
www.calumet.purdue.edu   Federal Code: 001827

4-year public university and branch campus college in small city.

Enrollment: 8,403 undergrads, 31% part-time. 1,271 full-time freshmen.

Selectivity: Admits 50 to 75% of applicants.

BASIC COSTS (2009-2010)

Tuition and fees: $6,308; out-of-state residents $14,116.

Per-credit charge: $190; out-of-state residents $450.

Room only: $4,680.

FINANCIAL AID PICTURE (2008-2009)

Students with need: Out of 967 full-time freshmen who applied for aid, 747 were judged to have need. Of these, 681 received aid, and 296 had their full need met. Average financial aid package met 12% of need; average scholarship/grant was $2,947; average loan was $1,908. For part-time students, average financial aid package was $3,877.

Students without need: 68 full-time freshmen who did not demonstrate need for aid received scholarships/grants; average award was $2,114. No-need awards available for academics, athletics, minority status, state/district residency.

Scholarships offered: 7 full-time freshmen received athletic scholarships; average amount $2,419.

Cumulative student debt: 62% of graduating class had student loans; average debt was $19,926.

FINANCIAL AID PROCEDURES

Forms required: FAFSA.

Dates and Deadlines: Priority date 3/10; closing date 6/30. Applicants notified on a rolling basis starting 4/15; must reply within 2 week(s) of notification.

CONTACT

Carol Zencka, Director of Financial Aid
2200 169th Street, Hammond, IN 46323-2094
(219) 989-2301

Purdue University North Central
Westville, Indiana
www.pnc.edu   Federal Code: 001826

4-year public branch campus college in rural community.

Enrollment: 3,814 undergrads, 28% part-time. 753 full-time freshmen.

Selectivity: Admits over 75% of applicants.

BASIC COSTS (2009-2010)

Tuition and fees: $6,384; out-of-state residents $15,057.

Per-credit charge: $195; out-of-state residents $484.

FINANCIAL AID PICTURE (2008-2009)

Students with need: Out of 565 full-time freshmen who applied for aid, 445 were judged to have need. Of these, 406 received aid, and 50 had their full need met. Average financial aid package met 35% of need; average scholarship/grant was $3,730; average loan was $3,014. For part-time students, average financial aid package was $5,291.

Students without need: 17 full-time freshmen who did not demonstrate need for aid received scholarships/grants; average award was $1,523. No-need awards available for academics, athletics, leadership, state/district residency.

Scholarships offered: 15 full-time freshmen received athletic scholarships; average amount $670.

Cumulative student debt: 75% of graduating class had student loans; average debt was $20,859.

FINANCIAL AID PROCEDURES

Forms required: FAFSA.

Dates and Deadlines: Priority date 3/10; closing date 6/30. Applicants notified on a rolling basis starting 4/1; must reply by 8/1 or within 2 week(s) of notification.

Transfers: No deadline. Transfer students not considered for campus-based financial aid.

CONTACT

Sandra Czekaj, Assistant Dean of Operations
1401 South US Highway 421, Westville, IN 46391-9542
(219) 785-55460

Rose-Hulman Institute of Technology
Terre Haute, Indiana
www.rose-hulman.edu   Federal Code: 001830

4-year private engineering college in small city.

Enrollment: 1,842 undergrads. 465 full-time freshmen.

Selectivity: Admits 50 to 75% of applicants. GED not accepted.

BASIC COSTS (2010-2011)

Tuition and fees: $36,270.

Per-credit charge: $1,038.

Room and board: $9,957.

Additional info: Incoming freshman students pay additional fee of $2,800 for mandatory purchase of laptop computer.

FINANCIAL AID PICTURE (2009-2010)

Students with need: Out of 391 full-time freshmen who applied for aid, 337 were judged to have need. Of these, 337 received aid, and 66 had their full need met. Average financial aid package met 88% of need; average scholarship/grant was $4,901; average loan was $3,580. For part-time students, average financial aid package was $7,928.

Students without need: 50 full-time freshmen who did not demonstrate need for aid received scholarships/grants; average award was $8,442. No-need awards available for academics, minority status, ROTC.

Cumulative student debt: 73% of graduating class had student loans; average debt was $35,261.

FINANCIAL AID PROCEDURES

Forms required: FAFSA.

Dates and Deadlines: Priority date 3/1; no closing date. Applicants notified on a rolling basis starting 3/10.

Transfers: No deadline. Applicants notified on a rolling basis; must reply by 6/1.

CONTACT

Melinda Middleton, Director of Financial Aid
Office of Admissions, Terre Haute, IN 47803-3999
(800) 248-7448

Saint Joseph's College

Rensselaer, Indiana
www.saintjoe.edu   Federal Code: 001833

4-year private liberal arts college in small town, affiliated with Roman Catholic Church.

Enrollment: 998 undergrads, 5% part-time. 272 full-time freshmen.

Selectivity: Admits 50 to 75% of applicants.

BASIC COSTS (2010-2011)

Tuition and fees: $25,260.

Per-credit charge: $840.

Room and board: $7,640.

FINANCIAL AID PICTURE (2008-2009)

Students with need: Out of 272 full-time freshmen who applied for aid, 229 were judged to have need. Of these, 229 received aid, and 80 had their full need met. Average financial aid package met 85% of need; average scholarship/grant was $15,789; average loan was $3,757. For part-time students, average financial aid package was $7,071.

Students without need: 39 full-time freshmen who did not demonstrate need for aid received scholarships/grants; average award was $11,943. No-need awards available for academics, alumni affiliation, athletics, minority status, music/drama.

Scholarships offered: 12 full-time freshmen received athletic scholarships; average amount $12,501.

Cumulative student debt: 77% of graduating class had student loans; average debt was $28,135.

FINANCIAL AID PROCEDURES

Forms required: FAFSA.

Dates and Deadlines: Priority date 3/1; no closing date. Applicants notified on a rolling basis starting 3/1; must reply by 5/1 or within 2 week(s) of notification.

Transfers: No deadline. Applicants notified on a rolling basis; must reply by 5/1 or within 2 week(s) of notification.

CONTACT

Debra Sizemore, Director of Student Financial Services
Box 890, Rensselaer, IN 47978
(219) 866-6163

St. Mary-of-the-Woods College

St. Mary-of-the-Woods, Indiana
www.smwc.edu   Federal Code: 001835

4-year private liberal arts college for women in rural community, affiliated with Roman Catholic Church.

Enrollment: 1,274 undergrads, 56% part-time. 140 full-time freshmen.

Selectivity: Admits over 75% of applicants.

BASIC COSTS (2010-2011)

Tuition and fees: $24,500.

Per-credit charge: $450.

Room and board: $8,890.

Additional info: Tuition/fee waivers available for minority students.

FINANCIAL AID PICTURE (2008-2009)

Students with need: 66% of average financial aid package awarded as scholarships/grants, 34% awarded as loans/jobs. Need-based aid available for part-time students. Work study available nights, weekends, and for part-time students.

Students without need: No-need awards available for academics, alumni affiliation, art, athletics, leadership, minority status, music/drama, state/district residency.

Scholarships offered: Saint Mother Theodore Guerin Scholarships; 2 per year at $20,000 a year for 4 years, 8 per year at $13,000 a year for 4 years; based on academics, service and leadership. Top Ten on 10 Scholarships; 2 per year at $20,000 a year for 4 years, 8 per year at $13,000 a year for four years; for local students based on academics, service and leadership. Trustees Scholarships; up to $11,000 a year for 4 years; based on academics. Presidential Scholarships; up to $9,000 a year for 4 years; based on academics. Dean's Scholarships; up to $6,000 a year for 4 years; based on academics. Woods Scholarships; up to $4,000 per year for 4 years; based on academics.

Additional info: Portfolio or audition required of applicants who wish to be considered for Creative Arts Scholarship.

FINANCIAL AID PROCEDURES

Forms required: FAFSA.

Dates and Deadlines: Priority date 3/1; no closing date. Applicants notified on a rolling basis starting 12/1; must reply within 6 week(s) of notification.

Transfers: Priority date 7/1; no deadline. Applicants notified on a rolling basis; must reply within 8 week(s) of notification. Transfer grants available for students graduating or transferring from Ivy Tech Community College.

CONTACT

Darla Hopper, Director of Financial Aid
Rooney Library, SMWC, St. Mary of the Woods, IN 47876
(812) 535-5110

Saint Mary's College

Notre Dame, Indiana   Federal Code: 001836
www.saintmarys.edu   CSS Code: 1702

4-year private liberal arts college for women in small city, affiliated with Roman Catholic Church.

Enrollment: 1,640 undergrads. 435 full-time freshmen.

Selectivity: Admits over 75% of applicants.

BASIC COSTS (2010-2011)

Tuition and fees: $31,020.

Per-credit charge: $1,200.

Room and board: $9,480.

FINANCIAL AID PICTURE (2009-2010)

Students with need: Out of 356 full-time freshmen who applied for aid, 312 were judged to have need. Of these, 311 received aid, and 71 had their full need met. Average financial aid package met 82% of need; average scholarship/grant was $20,093; average loan was $3,493. Need-based aid available for part-time students.

Students without need: 103 full-time freshmen who did not demonstrate need for aid received scholarships/grants; average award was $11,165. No-need awards available for academics, art.

Scholarships offered: Credentials of all admitted candidates automatically reviewed for merit scholarship consideration. Scholarship amounts vary depending on academic qualifications, renewable provided minimum GPA requirements are maintained.

Cumulative student debt: 72% of graduating class had student loans; average debt was $25,531.

FINANCIAL AID PROCEDURES

Forms required: FAFSA, CSS PROFILE.

Dates and Deadlines: Priority date 3/1; no closing date. Applicants notified on a rolling basis starting 12/15.

Transfers: Priority date 5/15; no deadline. Applicants notified on a rolling basis. To meet Indiana grant deadlines, Indiana residents must submit FAFSA by March 1.

CONTACT

Kathleen Brown, Director of Financial Aid Notre Dame, IN 46556-5001
(574) 284-4557

Taylor University
Upland, Indiana
www.taylor.edu   Federal Code: 001838

4-year private university and liberal arts college in small town, affiliated with interdenominational tradition.

Enrollment: 1,938 undergrads, 3% part-time. 486 full-time freshmen.

Selectivity: Admits over 75% of applicants.

BASIC COSTS (2010-2011)

Tuition and fees: $26,383.

Per-credit charge: $744.

Room and board: $6,972.

FINANCIAL AID PICTURE (2009-2010)

Students with need: Out of 400 full-time freshmen who applied for aid, 312 were judged to have need. Of these, 312 received aid, and 60 had their full need met. Average financial aid package met 75% of need; average scholarship/grant was $13,910; average loan was $4,429. For part-time students, average financial aid package was $8,891.

Students without need: 123 full-time freshmen who did not demonstrate need for aid received scholarships/grants; average award was $6,863. No-need awards available for academics, alumni affiliation, art, athletics, leadership, minority status, music/drama, religious affiliation, state/district residency.

Scholarships offered: 24 full-time freshmen received athletic scholarships; average amount $7,344.

Cumulative student debt: 53% of graduating class had student loans; average debt was $22,971.

FINANCIAL AID PROCEDURES

Forms required: FAFSA.

Dates and Deadlines: Closing date 3/10. Applicants notified on a rolling basis starting 3/1; must reply by 5/1.

Transfers: Applicants notified on a rolling basis starting 3/1; must reply by 5/1.

CONTACT

Tim Nace, Assistant Dean, Enrollment Management
236 West Reade Avenue, Upland, IN 46989-1001
(765) 998-5358

Trine University
Angola, Indiana
www.trine.edu   Federal Code: 001839

4-year private university and engineering college in small town.

Enrollment: 1,535 undergrads, 4% part-time. 457 full-time freshmen.

Selectivity: Admits over 75% of applicants.

BASIC COSTS (2010-2011)

Tuition and fees: $25,400.

Per-credit charge: $786.

Room and board: $8,300.

FINANCIAL AID PICTURE (2009-2010)

Students with need: Out of 439 full-time freshmen who applied for aid, 317 were judged to have need. Of these, 317 received aid, and 317 had their full need met. Average financial aid package met 95% of need; average scholarship/grant was $4,309; average loan was $3,048.

Students without need: 30 full-time freshmen who did not demonstrate need for aid received scholarships/grants; average award was $12,552. No-need awards available for academics, alumni affiliation, minority status, music/drama, ROTC.

Cumulative student debt: 81% of graduating class had student loans; average debt was $19,334.

FINANCIAL AID PROCEDURES

Forms required: FAFSA.

Dates and Deadlines: Priority date 3/10; no closing date. Applicants notified on a rolling basis starting 3/1; must reply by 5/1 or within 2 week(s) of notification.

Transfers: Applicants notified on a rolling basis starting 3/1; must reply by 5/1 or within 2 week(s) of notification.

CONTACT

Kim Bennett, Executive Director of Admission and Financial Aid
One University Avenue, Angola, IN 46703
(260) 665-4158

University of Evansville
Evansville, Indiana
www.evansville.edu   Federal Code: 001795

4-year private university and liberal arts college in small city, affiliated with United Methodist Church.

Enrollment: 2,549 undergrads, 3% part-time. 701 full-time freshmen.

Selectivity: Admits over 75% of applicants.

BASIC COSTS (2010-2011)

Tuition and fees: $28,076.

Per-credit charge: $760.

Room and board: $9,110.

FINANCIAL AID PICTURE (2009-2010)

Students with need: Out of 654 full-time freshmen who applied for aid, 553 were judged to have need. Of these, 550 received aid, and 163 had their full need met. Average financial aid package met 92% of need; average scholarship/grant was $22,648; average loan was $3,753. For part-time students, average financial aid package was $5,145.

Students without need: 126 full-time freshmen who did not demonstrate need for aid received scholarships/grants; average award was $15,676. No-need awards available for academics, alumni affiliation, art, athletics, leadership, minority status, music/drama, religious affiliation, ROTC, state/district residency.

Scholarships offered: 17 full-time freshmen received athletic scholarships; average amount $27,875.

Cumulative student debt: 72% of graduating class had student loans; average debt was $25,598.

Additional info: Early financial planning service allows prospective students to get free estimate of available aid.

FINANCIAL AID PROCEDURES

Forms required: FAFSA.

Dates and Deadlines: Priority date 3/10; no closing date. Applicants notified on a rolling basis starting 3/25; must reply by 5/1.

Transfers: Applicants notified on a rolling basis; must reply by 6/1. Indiana state aid is available for a total of 8 semesters.

CONTACT

JoAnn Laugel, Director of Financial Aid
1800 Lincoln Avenue, Evansville, IN 47722
(812) 488-2364

University of Indianapolis

Indianapolis, Indiana
www.uindy.edu   Federal Code: 001804

4-year private university and liberal arts college in very large city, affiliated with United Methodist Church.

Enrollment: 3,734 undergrads, 23% part-time. 737 full-time freshmen.

Selectivity: Admits over 75% of applicants.

BASIC COSTS (2010-2011)

Tuition and fees: $22,240.

Per-credit charge: $917.

Room and board: $7,990.

FINANCIAL AID PICTURE (2009-2010)

Students with need: Need-based aid available for full-time and part-time students. Work study available nights, weekends, and for part-time students.

Students without need: No-need awards available for academics, alumni affiliation, art, athletics, job skills, leadership, music/drama, religious affiliation, state/district residency.

Scholarships offered: Presidential Scholarship; full tuition; upper 5% of class, 1270 SAT/29 ACT, strong college prep required. Dean's Scholarship; 50% tuition; upper 7% of class, 1270 SAT/29 ACT, demonstrated leadership, strong college prep required. Alumni Scholarship; 30% tuition; upper 15% of class, 1100 SAT/24 ACT, alumnus connection to school required. Service Award; $2,500; based on demonstrated commitment to community volunteerism. United Methodist Award; $2,500; based on demonstrated commitment to church, activities. SAT scores listed are exclusive of writing portion.

FINANCIAL AID PROCEDURES

Forms required: FAFSA, institutional form.

Dates and Deadlines: Priority date 3/10; no closing date. Applicants notified on a rolling basis starting 3/1; must reply within 3 week(s) of notification.

Transfers: No deadline. Applicants notified on a rolling basis starting 3/1.

CONTACT

Linda Handy, Director of Financial Aid
1400 East Hanna Avenue, Indianapolis, IN 46227-3697
(317) 788-3217

University of Notre Dame

Notre Dame, Indiana   Federal Code: 001840
www.nd.edu   CSS Code: 1841

4-year private university in small city, affiliated with Roman Catholic Church.

Enrollment: 8,367 undergrads. 2,062 full-time freshmen.

Selectivity: Admits less than 50% of applicants. GED not accepted.

BASIC COSTS (2010-2011)

Tuition and fees: $39,919.

Per-credit charge: $1,642.

Room and board: $10,866.

FINANCIAL AID PICTURE (2009-2010)

Students with need: Need-based aid available for full-time and part-time students. Work study available nights, weekends, and for part-time students.

Students without need: No-need awards available for athletics, ROTC.

FINANCIAL AID PROCEDURES

Forms required: FAFSA, CSS PROFILE.

Dates and Deadlines: Closing date 2/15. Applicants notified by 4/1; must reply by 5/1.

Transfers: Closing date 3/31. Applicants notified on a rolling basis; must reply within 2 week(s) of notification. Require signed and completed federal tax returns, including all schedules and W-2 forms from both the applicant and the parents of the applicant.

CONTACT

Joseph Russo, Director of Student Financial Strategies
220 Main Building, Notre Dame, IN 46556
(574) 631-6436

University of St. Francis

Fort Wayne, Indiana
www.sf.edu   Federal Code: 001832

4-year private university and liberal arts college in small city, affiliated with Roman Catholic Church.

Enrollment: 1,780 undergrads. 305 full-time freshmen.

Selectivity: Admits 50 to 75% of applicants.

BASIC COSTS (2010-2011)

Tuition and fees: $22,810.

Per-credit charge: $695.

Room and board: $6,970.

Additional info: Tuition/fee waivers available for adults.

FINANCIAL AID PICTURE (2008-2009)

Students with need: Out of 301 full-time freshmen who applied for aid, 259 were judged to have need. Of these, 259 received aid, and 82 had their full need met. Average financial aid package met 80.72% of need; average scholarship/grant was $13,010; average loan was $3,181. For part-time students, average financial aid package was $7,392.

Students without need: 36 full-time freshmen who did not demonstrate need for aid received scholarships/grants; average award was $6,709. No-need awards available for academics, alumni affiliation, art, athletics, music/drama.

Scholarships offered: 41 full-time freshmen received athletic scholarships; average amount $7,565.

Cumulative student debt: 98% of graduating class had student loans; average debt was $26,670.

FINANCIAL AID PROCEDURES

Forms required: FAFSA.

Dates and Deadlines: Priority date 3/10; no closing date. Applicants notified on a rolling basis starting 3/1.

CONTACT
Jamie McGrath, Director of Financial Aid
2701 Spring Street, Fort Wayne, IN 46808
(260) 399-8003,

University of Southern Indiana
Evansville, Indiana
www.usi.edu   Federal Code: 001808

4-year public university and liberal arts college in small city.
Enrollment: 9,442 undergrads, 15% part-time. 2,052 full-time freshmen.
Selectivity: Admits over 75% of applicants.

BASIC COSTS (2009-2010)
Tuition and fees: $5,480; out-of-state residents $12,770.
Per-credit charge: $176; out-of-state residents $419.
Room and board: $6,750.

FINANCIAL AID PICTURE (2009-2010)
Students with need: Out of 1,876 full-time freshmen who applied for aid, 1,329 were judged to have need. Of these, 1,321 received aid, and 222 had their full need met. Average financial aid package met 80% of need; average scholarship/grant was $4,887; average loan was $2,886. For part-time students, average financial aid package was $6,088.
Students without need: 232 full-time freshmen who did not demonstrate need for aid received scholarships/grants; average award was $2,593. No-need awards available for academics, art, athletics, leadership, music/drama, state/district residency.
Scholarships offered: 20 full-time freshmen received athletic scholarships; average amount $5,031.

FINANCIAL AID PROCEDURES
Forms required: FAFSA, institutional form.
Dates and Deadlines: Closing date 3/1. Applicants notified on a rolling basis starting 3/15.

CONTACT
Mary Harper, Director of Student Financial Assistance
8600 University Boulevard, Evansville, IN 47712
(812) 464-1767

Valparaiso University
Valparaiso, Indiana
www.valpo.edu   Federal Code: 001842

4-year private university in large town, affiliated with Lutheran Church.
Enrollment: 2,823 undergrads, 4% part-time. 656 full-time freshmen.
Selectivity: Admits over 75% of applicants.

BASIC COSTS (2010-2011)
Tuition and fees: $29,582.
Per-credit charge: $1,295.
Room and board: $8,330.

FINANCIAL AID PICTURE (2008-2009)
Students with need: Out of 598 full-time freshmen who applied for aid, 494 were judged to have need. Of these, 494 received aid, and 118 had their full need met. Average financial aid package met 82% of need; average scholarship/grant was $18,200; average loan was $3,980. For part-time students, average financial aid package was $6,927.
Students without need: 142 full-time freshmen who did not demonstrate need for aid received scholarships/grants; average award was $9,268. No-need awards available for academics, alumni affiliation, art, athletics, leadership, music/drama, religious affiliation, ROTC, state/district residency.

Scholarships offered: *Merit:* Academic Scholarships; $7,500 to full tuition. Departmental and Lutheran Scholarships; amounts vary. *Athletic:* 17 full-time freshmen received athletic scholarships; average amount $20,076.
Cumulative student debt: 73% of graduating class had student loans; average debt was $31,783.
Additional info: Financial assistance based on need, academic record, talent available through university.

FINANCIAL AID PROCEDURES
Forms required: FAFSA.
Dates and Deadlines: Priority date 3/1; no closing date. Applicants notified on a rolling basis starting 3/1; must reply by 5/1.
Transfers: Transfer students eligible for scholarships based on previous college work. Scholarship amounts vary depending on the GPA at previous institutions.

CONTACT
Robert Helgeson, Director of Financial Aid
Kretzmann Hall, 1700 Chapel Drive, Valparaiso, IN 46383-6493
(219) 464-5015

Vincennes University
Vincennes, Indiana
www.vinu.edu   Federal Code: 001843

2-year public junior college in large town.
Enrollment: 9,107 undergrads, 33% part-time. 2,264 full-time freshmen.
Selectivity: Open admission; but selective for some programs.

BASIC COSTS (2009-2010)
Tuition and fees: $4,564; out-of-state residents $10,630.
Per-credit charge: $139; out-of-state residents $337.
Room and board: $7,316.
Additional info: Students from Crawford, Richland, Lawrence and Wabash counties in Illinois pay tuition of $217 per credit hour (including capital improvement and technology fees, not including student activity fee).

FINANCIAL AID PICTURE (2008-2009)
Students with need: Need-based aid available for full-time and part-time students. Work study available nights, weekends, and for part-time students.
Students without need: No-need awards available for academics, art, athletics, leadership, music/drama, state/district residency.
Scholarships offered: Presidential Scholarship; $2,000 annually; 1100 SAT and rank in upper 10% of class; 10 awarded. Blue & Gold Scholarship; $1,100 annually; 1010 SAT and rank in upper half of class; 40 awarded. Indiana Academic Honors Diploma; $900 annually. Walters Scholarship; tuition, room and board; for candidates in good standing. Education Scholarship; for education majors, based on SAT scores and rank in upper 10% of class; 1 awarded. Valedictorian/Salutatorian scholarship; covers full costs.

FINANCIAL AID PROCEDURES
Forms required: FAFSA.
Dates and Deadlines: Priority date 3/1; closing date 5/1. Applicants notified on a rolling basis starting 5/1; must reply by 8/24.
Transfers: No deadline. Applicants notified on a rolling basis starting 4/1. Transfer students must notify state student assistance commission within 30 days of start of term.

CONTACT
Stanley Werne, Director of Financial Aid
1002 North First Street, Vincennes, IN 47591
(812) 888-4361

Wabash College

Crawfordsville, Indiana
www.wabash.edu

Federal Code: 001844
CSS Code: 1895

4-year private liberal arts college for men in large town.
Enrollment: 874 undergrads, 1% part-time. 245 full-time freshmen.
Selectivity: Admits less than 50% of applicants.

BASIC COSTS (2010-2011)
Tuition and fees: $31,050.
Room and board: $8,300.

FINANCIAL AID PICTURE (2009-2010)
Students with need: Out of 233 full-time freshmen who applied for aid, 202 were judged to have need. Of these, 202 received aid, and 189 had their full need met. Average financial aid package met 98% of need; average scholarship/grant was $19,459; average loan was $5,674. Need-based aid available for part-time students.
Students without need: 30 full-time freshmen who did not demonstrate need for aid received scholarships/grants; average award was $14,262. No-need awards available for academics, art, leadership, music/drama, state/district residency.
Scholarships offered: Lilly Awards Program; full tuition, room, board, fees, and travel stipend; recognizes outstanding personal achievement and potential for leadership. Fine Arts Fellows; up to $15,000; based on creativity/ability; approximately 16 awarded. Honor Scholarships; up to $15,000; based on competitive exams; approximately 40 awarded. President's Scholarships; based on class rank, SAT scores; unlimited number awarded. Top-10 Scholarships; up to $17,500 per year; unlimited number awarded.
Cumulative student debt: 70% of graduating class had student loans; average debt was $28,383.

FINANCIAL AID PROCEDURES
Forms required: FAFSA, CSS PROFILE.
Dates and Deadlines: Priority date 2/15; closing date 3/1. Applicants notified by 3/31.
Transfers: Applicants notified by 4/1; must reply by 5/1 or within 2 week(s) of notification.

CONTACT
Clint Gasaway, Director of Financial Aid
PO Box 352, Crawfordsville, IN 47933
(800) 718-9746

Iowa

AIB College of Business

Des Moines, Iowa
www.aib.edu

Federal Code: 003963

2-year private business college in large city.
Enrollment: 936 undergrads, 36% part-time. 146 full-time freshmen.
Selectivity: Admits 50 to 75% of applicants.

BASIC COSTS (2010-2011)
Tuition and fees: $13,140.
Per-credit charge: $239.
Room only: $3,375.
Additional info: Tuition guarantee is only available to students who retain full-time status. Tuition at time of enrollment locked for 2 years; tuition/fee waivers available for minority students, unemployed or children of unemployed.

FINANCIAL AID PICTURE (2008-2009)
Students with need: 46% of average financial aid package awarded as scholarships/grants, 54% awarded as loans/jobs. Need-based aid available for part-time students. Work study available nights, weekends, and for part-time students.
Students without need: No-need awards available for academics, alumni affiliation, athletics, leadership, minority status.
Scholarships offered: Founder's Scholarship; full tuition; 3.75 GPA and upper 10% of high school graduating class or 3.75 GPA and 28 ACT required; up to 4 students per year.

FINANCIAL AID PROCEDURES
Forms required: FAFSA, institutional form.
Dates and Deadlines: Priority date 4/1; no closing date. Applicants notified on a rolling basis starting 3/1; must reply within 2 week(s) of notification.
Transfers: No deadline. Applicants notified on a rolling basis starting 3/1; must reply within 2 week(s) of notification. Prior aid from previous institutions considered.

CONTACT
Laurie Sanders, Financial Aid Director
2500 Fleur Drive, Des Moines, IA 50321-1799
(515) 244-4221

Allen College

Waterloo, Iowa
www.allencollege.edu

Federal Code: 030691

4-year private health science and nursing college in small city.
Enrollment: 314 undergrads, 21% part-time. 4 full-time freshmen.
Selectivity: Admits less than 50% of applicants.

BASIC COSTS (2010-2011)
Tuition and fees: $14,995.
Per-credit charge: $500.
Room and board: $7,157.

FINANCIAL AID PICTURE (2008-2009)
Students with need: Out of 4 full-time freshmen who applied for aid, 2 were judged to have need. Of these, 2 received aid. Average financial aid package met 32% of need; average scholarship/grant was $6,116; average loan was $3,375. For part-time students, average financial aid package was $7,092.
Students without need: 2 full-time freshmen who did not demonstrate need for aid received scholarships/grants; average award was $750. No-need awards available for academics, leadership, minority status, ROTC.
Cumulative student debt: 81% of graduating class had student loans; average debt was $27,568.

FINANCIAL AID PROCEDURES
Forms required: FAFSA, institutional form.
Dates and Deadlines: Priority date 6/1; no closing date. Applicants notified on a rolling basis starting 4/1; must reply within 2 week(s) of notification.
Transfers: No deadline. Applicants notified on a rolling basis starting 4/1; must reply within 2 week(s) of notification.

CONTACT
Kathie Walters, Financial Aid Director
1825 Logan Avenue, Waterloo, IA 50703
(319) 226-2003

Briar Cliff University

Sioux City, Iowa
www.briarcliff.edu   Federal Code: 001846

4-year private liberal arts college in small city, affiliated with Roman Catholic Church.

Enrollment: 1,018 undergrads, 12% part-time. 223 full-time freshmen.

Selectivity: Admits 50 to 75% of applicants.

BASIC COSTS (2009-2010)

Tuition and fees: $22,536.

Per-credit charge: $729.

Room and board: $6,978.

FINANCIAL AID PICTURE (2009-2010)

Students with need: Out of 220 full-time freshmen who applied for aid, 178 were judged to have need. Of these, 178 received aid, and 122 had their full need met. Average financial aid package met 87% of need; average scholarship/grant was $6,300; average loan was $3,900. Need-based aid available for part-time students.

Students without need: 45 full-time freshmen who did not demonstrate need for aid received scholarships/grants; average award was $12,250. No-need awards available for academics, alumni affiliation, art, athletics, leadership, music/drama, religious affiliation, state/district residency.

Scholarships offered: *Merit:* Presidential Scholarships; awarded each year for achievement and demonstrated leadership, based on application and on-campus interview; 2-5 awarded. *Athletic:* 137 full-time freshmen received athletic scholarships; average amount $5,109.

Cumulative student debt: 89% of graduating class had student loans; average debt was $30,862.

FINANCIAL AID PROCEDURES

Forms required: FAFSA.

Dates and Deadlines: Priority date 3/15; no closing date. Applicants notified on a rolling basis starting 3/15; must reply by 5/1 or within 2 week(s) of notification.

Transfers: Closing date 3/15.

CONTACT

Robert Piechota, Director of Financial Aid
3303 Rebecca Street, Sioux City, IA 51104-0100
(712) 279-5200

Buena Vista University

Storm Lake, Iowa
www.bvu.edu   Federal Code: 001847

4-year private liberal arts college in large town, affiliated with Presbyterian Church (USA).

Enrollment: 939 undergrads, 1% part-time. 273 full-time freshmen.

Selectivity: Admits 50 to 75% of applicants.

BASIC COSTS (2010-2011)

Tuition and fees: $26,306.

Per-credit charge: $884.

Room and board: $7,582.

FINANCIAL AID PICTURE (2009-2010)

Students with need: Need-based aid available for full-time and part-time students. Work study available nights, weekends, and for part-time students.

Students without need: No-need awards available for academics, art, minority status, music/drama, religious affiliation.

Cumulative student debt: 91% of graduating class had student loans; average debt was $40,569.

Additional info: Portfolio required of art scholarship applicants, audition required of music and drama scholarship applicants.

FINANCIAL AID PROCEDURES

Forms required: FAFSA.

Dates and Deadlines: Priority date 6/1; no closing date. Applicants notified on a rolling basis starting 2/15.

CONTACT

Leanne Valentine, Director of Financial Assistance
610 West Fourth Street, Storm Lake, IA 50588
(714) 749-2164

Central College

Pella, Iowa
www.central.edu   Federal Code: 001850

4-year private liberal arts college in large town, affiliated with Reformed Church in America.

Enrollment: 1,529 undergrads, 1% part-time. 443 full-time freshmen.

Selectivity: Admits 50 to 75% of applicants.

BASIC COSTS (2010-2011)

Tuition and fees: $26,242.

Per-credit charge: $898.

Room and board: $8,702.

FINANCIAL AID PICTURE (2009-2010)

Students with need: Out of 443 full-time freshmen who applied for aid, 394 were judged to have need. Of these, 394 received aid, and 104 had their full need met. Average financial aid package met 87% of need; average scholarship/grant was $17,824; average loan was $3,928. For part-time students, average financial aid package was $14,705.

Students without need: 49 full-time freshmen who did not demonstrate need for aid received scholarships/grants; average award was $12,169. No-need awards available for academics, alumni affiliation, art, minority status, music/drama, religious affiliation, state/district residency.

Cumulative student debt: 86% of graduating class had student loans; average debt was $34,885.

Additional info: Institutional parent loan program and interest-earning, tuition prepayment savings account available.

FINANCIAL AID PROCEDURES

Forms required: FAFSA.

Dates and Deadlines: Priority date 3/15; no closing date. Applicants notified on a rolling basis starting 3/15; must reply by 5/1 or within 2 week(s) of notification.

Transfers: Applicants notified on a rolling basis starting 3/15; must reply by 5/1 or within 2 week(s) of notification. Transfers only eligible for total of 4 years of state funds.

CONTACT

Jean Vander Wert, Financial Aid Director
812 University Street, Pella, IA 50219-1999
(641) 628-5336

Clarke College

Dubuque, Iowa
www.clarke.edu   Federal Code: 001852

4-year private liberal arts college in small city, affiliated with Roman Catholic Church.

Enrollment: 938 undergrads, 14% part-time. 148 full-time freshmen.

Selectivity: Admits over 75% of applicants.

BASIC COSTS (2010-2011)

Tuition and fees: $24,610.

Per-credit charge: $600.

Room and board: $7,080.

FINANCIAL AID PICTURE (2009-2010)

Students with need: Need-based aid available for full-time and part-time students. Work study available nights, weekends, and for part-time students.
Students without need: No-need awards available for academics, alumni affiliation, art, athletics, leadership, music/drama, religious affiliation, state/district residency.
Scholarships offered: Mary Frances Clarke Scholarship; full tuition; based on 3.8 GPA, 28 ACT, participation in campus competition. Trustee's Scholarship; 75% tuition; based on 3.8 GPA, 28 ACT, participation in campus competition; 4 awarded. View/Leadership Award; $1,000-$5,000; based on 2.9 GPA, participation in weekend competition, selected components of credentials and activities during the competition considered; up to 15 awarded.
Additional info: Reduced tuition for family members of BVMs.

FINANCIAL AID PROCEDURES

Dates and Deadlines: Priority date 4/15; no closing date. Applicants notified on a rolling basis starting 3/11; must reply by 5/1 or within 2 week(s) of notification.

CONTACT

Sharon Willenborg, Director of Financial Aid
1550 Clarke Drive, Dubuque, IA 52001-3198
(563) 588-6327

Coe College
Cedar Rapids, Iowa
www.coe.edu   Federal Code: 001854

4-year private nursing and liberal arts college in small city, affiliated with Presbyterian Church (USA).
Enrollment: 1,278 undergrads.
Selectivity: Admits 50 to 75% of applicants.

BASIC COSTS (2009-2010)

Tuition and fees: $29,270.
Room and board: $7,150.
Additional info: Cost per course for part-time students (fewer than 3 course credits) is $3,620. Tuition/fee waivers available for adults.

FINANCIAL AID PICTURE (2009-2010)

Students with need: Need-based aid available for full-time and part-time students. Work study available nights, weekends, and for part-time students.
Students without need: No-need awards available for academics, alumni affiliation, art, leadership, music/drama, ROTC.
Scholarships offered: Scholarships for business/economics, music, art, theater, writing, foreign language, science; based on portfolio or audition; available for non-majors except in science and business/economics. Academic Awards; $6,000-$19,000; based on high school achievement.

FINANCIAL AID PROCEDURES

Forms required: FAFSA.
Dates and Deadlines: Priority date 3/1; no closing date. Applicants notified on a rolling basis starting 3/15; must reply by 5/1 or within 2 week(s) of notification.

CONTACT

Barb Hoffman, Director of Financial Aid
1220 First Avenue NE, Cedar Rapids, IA 52402
(319) 399-8540

Cornell College
Mount Vernon, Iowa
www.cornellcollege.edu   Federal Code: 001856

4-year private liberal arts college in small town, affiliated with United Methodist Church.
Enrollment: 1,125 undergrads. 335 full-time freshmen.
Selectivity: Admits less than 50% of applicants.

BASIC COSTS (2010-2011)

Tuition and fees: $31,050.
Per-credit charge: $965.
Room and board: $7,660.
Additional info: Tuition/fee waivers available for adults, minority students.

FINANCIAL AID PICTURE (2009-2010)

Students with need: Out of 277 full-time freshmen who applied for aid, 242 were judged to have need. Of these, 242 received aid, and 107 had their full need met. Average financial aid package met 95% of need; average scholarship/grant was $22,730; average loan was $3,517. For part-time students, average financial aid package was $3,531.
Students without need: 74 full-time freshmen who did not demonstrate need for aid received scholarships/grants; average award was $13,570. No-need awards available for academics, art, leadership, minority status, music/drama, religious affiliation, state/district residency.
Scholarships offered: Portfolio required for art scholarship applicants. Audition required for music and theater scholarship applicants.
Cumulative student debt: 72% of graduating class had student loans; average debt was $27,990.

FINANCIAL AID PROCEDURES

Forms required: FAFSA, institutional form.
Dates and Deadlines: Closing date 3/1. Applicants notified on a rolling basis starting 3/1; must reply by 5/1 or within 2 week(s) of notification.
Transfers: Priority date 3/1; closing date 6/1. Applicants notified on a rolling basis starting 3/1; must reply by 5/1 or within 2 week(s) of notification.

CONTACT

Cindi Reints, Director of Financial Assistance
600 First Street SW, Mount Vernon, IA 52314-1098
(319) 895-4216

Des Moines Area Community College
Ankeny, Iowa
www.dmacc.edu   Federal Code: 004589

2-year public community college in large town.
Enrollment: 15,741 undergrads, 44% part-time. 3,436 full-time freshmen.
Selectivity: Open admission; but selective for some programs.

BASIC COSTS (2009-2010)

Tuition and fees: $3,450; out-of-state residents $6,900.
Per-credit charge: $115; out-of-state residents $230.

FINANCIAL AID PICTURE (2008-2009)

Students with need: Need-based aid available for full-time and part-time students. Work study available nights, weekends, and for part-time students.
Students without need: No-need awards available for academics, athletics, state/district residency.
Scholarships offered: Foundation Freshmen Scholar Award; full tuition, fees and books for maximum of 15 credit hours per semester based on available funds; open to all high school seniors in top 10% of graduating class.

FINANCIAL AID PROCEDURES

Forms required: FAFSA.
Dates and Deadlines: Priority date 4/1; no closing date. Applicants notified on a rolling basis starting 4/1; must reply within 2 week(s) of notification.

CONTACT

DeLores Hawkins, Director of Financial Aid
2006 South Ankeny Boulevard, Ankeny, IA 50023-3993
(515) 964-6282

Dordt College

Sioux Center, Iowa
www.dordt.edu   Federal Code: 001859

4-year private liberal arts college in small town, affiliated with Christian Reformed Church.

Enrollment: 1,274 undergrads, 1% part-time. 360 full-time freshmen.

Selectivity: Admits over 75% of applicants.

BASIC COSTS (2010-2011)

Tuition and fees: $23,180.

Per-credit charge: $880.

Room and board: $6,320.

Additional info: Tuition/fee waivers available for adults.

FINANCIAL AID PICTURE (2008-2009)

Students with need: Out of 317 full-time freshmen who applied for aid, 274 were judged to have need. Of these, 274 received aid, and 43 had their full need met. Average financial aid package met 90% of need; average scholarship/grant was $13,246; average loan was $5,266. For part-time students, average financial aid package was $10,897.

Students without need: 65 full-time freshmen who did not demonstrate need for aid received scholarships/grants; average award was $13,389. No-need awards available for academics, alumni affiliation, art, athletics, job skills, leadership, minority status, music/drama, religious affiliation, state/district residency.

Scholarships offered: 29 full-time freshmen received athletic scholarships; average amount $6,054.

Cumulative student debt: 87% of graduating class had student loans; average debt was $19,988.

FINANCIAL AID PROCEDURES

Forms required: FAFSA, institutional form.

Dates and Deadlines: Priority date 4/1; no closing date. Applicants notified on a rolling basis starting 3/1; must reply within 3 week(s) of notification.

Transfers: Closing date 6/1. Applicants notified on a rolling basis starting 10/1.

CONTACT

Michael Epema, Director of Financial Aid
498 Fourth Avenue, NE, Sioux Center, IA 51250
(712) 722-6087

Drake University

Des Moines, Iowa
www.drake.edu   Federal Code: 001860

4-year private university in large city.

Enrollment: 3,543 undergrads, 6% part-time. 860 full-time freshmen.

Selectivity: Admits 50 to 75% of applicants.

BASIC COSTS (2010-2011)

Tuition and fees: $26,960.

Room and board: $8,130.

FINANCIAL AID PICTURE (2009-2010)

Students with need: Out of 726 full-time freshmen who applied for aid, 546 were judged to have need. Of these, 546 received aid, and 186 had their full need met. Average financial aid package met 84% of need; average scholarship/grant was $14,496; average loan was $4,499. For part-time students, average financial aid package was $8,446.

Students without need: 274 full-time freshmen who did not demonstrate need for aid received scholarships/grants; average award was $11,324. No-need awards available for academics, alumni affiliation, art, athletics, music/drama, ROTC, state/district residency.

Scholarships offered: *Merit:* Drake University Presidential Scholarship; $7,000-$12,000; based on academic merit and awards; unlimited available. National Alumni Scholarship Competition; 6 full-time tuition with room and board and 10 full-time tuition; available to top students. *Athletic:* 19 full-time freshmen received athletic scholarships; average amount $21,057.

Cumulative student debt: 71% of graduating class had student loans; average debt was $34,919.

FINANCIAL AID PROCEDURES

Forms required: FAFSA.

Dates and Deadlines: Priority date 3/1; no closing date. Applicants notified on a rolling basis starting 3/1; must reply by 5/1 or within 3 week(s) of notification.

Transfers: No deadline. Applicants notified on a rolling basis starting 3/1; must reply by 5/1 or within 2 week(s) of notification. FAFSA must be filed by July 1 for Iowa Tuition Grant deadline.

CONTACT

Susan Ladd, Director of Student Financial Planning
2507 University Avenue, Des Moines, IA 50311-4505
(515) 271-2905

Ellsworth Community College

Iowa Falls, Iowa
www.iavalley.cc.ia.us/ecc   Federal Code: 001862

2-year public community college in small town.

Enrollment: 1,174 undergrads.

Selectivity: Open admission; but selective for some programs.

BASIC COSTS (2009-2010)

Tuition and fees: $4,590; out-of-state residents $5,550.

Per-credit charge: $127; out-of-state residents $159.

Room and board: $4,862.

Additional info: Tuition/fee waivers available for adults.

FINANCIAL AID PICTURE (2008-2009)

Students with need: Need-based aid available for full-time and part-time students. Work study available nights, weekends, and for part-time students.

Students without need: No-need awards available for academics, art, athletics, leadership, minority status, music/drama.

Scholarships offered: Academic scholarships; $500-$1,800; based on ACT and GPA; unlimited number offered. Directors Scholarship; $2,300; for those who are 1st or 2nd in class; unlimited number offered.

FINANCIAL AID PROCEDURES

Forms required: FAFSA, institutional form.

Dates and Deadlines: Closing date 4/1. Applicants notified on a rolling basis starting 2/15; must reply within 4 week(s) of notification.

Transfers: Priority date 4/15.

CONTACT

Tara Miller, Financial Aid Administrator
1100 College Avenue, Iowa Falls, IA 50126
(641) 648-4611 ext. 432

Emmaus Bible College

Dubuque, Iowa
www.emmaus.edu   Federal Code: 016487

4-year private Bible college in small city, affiliated with Brethren Church.

Enrollment: 245 undergrads.

Selectivity: Admits 50 to 75% of applicants.

BASIC COSTS (2009-2010)

Tuition and fees: $11,578.
Room and board: $5,396.

FINANCIAL AID PICTURE

Students with need: Need-based aid available for full-time and part-time students.
Students without need: No-need awards available for academics, music/drama.

FINANCIAL AID PROCEDURES

Forms required: FAFSA, institutional form.
Dates and Deadlines: Priority date 5/15; closing date 7/1. Applicants notified on a rolling basis starting 3/1; must reply within 2 week(s) of notification.

CONTACT

Steve Seeman, Financial Aid Director
2570 Asbury Road, Dubuque, IA 52001
(563) 588-8000 ext. 1309

Faith Baptist Bible College and Theological Seminary

Ankeny, Iowa
www.faith.edu   Federal Code: 007121

4-year private Bible and seminary college in large town, affiliated with General Association of Regular Baptist Churches.
Enrollment: 340 undergrads, 10% part-time. 90 full-time freshmen.
Selectivity: Admits 50 to 75% of applicants.

BASIC COSTS (2010-2011)

Tuition and fees: $13,814.
Per-credit charge: $490.
Room and board: $5,440.

FINANCIAL AID PICTURE (2008-2009)

Students with need: Need-based aid available for full-time and part-time students.
Students without need: No-need awards available for academics, leadership, music/drama.

FINANCIAL AID PROCEDURES

Forms required: FAFSA.
Dates and Deadlines: Priority date 4/1; no closing date. Applicants notified on a rolling basis starting 3/15.

CONTACT

Breck Appell, Financial Assistance Director
1900 NW Fourth Street, Ankeny, IA 50023
(515) 964-0601 ext. 216

Graceland University

Lamoni, Iowa
www.graceland.edu   Federal Code: 001866

4-year private university and liberal arts college in rural community, affiliated with Community of Christ.
Enrollment: 1,330 undergrads, 12% part-time. 228 full-time freshmen.
Selectivity: Admits over 75% of applicants.

BASIC COSTS (2010-2011)

Tuition and fees: $20,980.
Per-credit charge: $650.
Room and board: $7,040.

FINANCIAL AID PICTURE (2009-2010)

Students with need: Out of 202 full-time freshmen who applied for aid, 189 were judged to have need. Of these, 185 received aid, and 39 had their full need met. Average financial aid package met 86% of need; average scholarship/grant was $15,432; average loan was $4,790. For part-time students, average financial aid package was $6,532.
Students without need: 37 full-time freshmen who did not demonstrate need for aid received scholarships/grants; average award was $7,021. No-need awards available for academics, alumni affiliation, art, athletics, job skills, leadership, music/drama, religious affiliation.
Scholarships offered: *Merit:* Merit scholarships; up to $10,000; for incoming freshmen based on GPA and ACT/SAT. *Athletic:* 38 full-time freshmen received athletic scholarships; average amount $7,187.
Cumulative student debt: 89% of graduating class had student loans; average debt was $29,934.
Additional info: Founders Scholarship will supplement other gift aid until percentage of calculated need has been met.

FINANCIAL AID PROCEDURES

Forms required: FAFSA.
Dates and Deadlines: No deadline. Applicants notified on a rolling basis starting 3/1; must reply within 2 week(s) of notification.
Transfers: Must reply within 2 week(s) of notification.

CONTACT

Christine McGee, Director of Student Finance
One University Place, Lamoni, IA 50140
(641) 784-5140

Grand View University

Des Moines, Iowa
www.grandview.edu   Federal Code: 001867

4-year private liberal arts college in large city, affiliated with Evangelical Lutheran Church in America.
Enrollment: 1,921 undergrads, 17% part-time. 231 full-time freshmen.
Selectivity: Admits over 75% of applicants.

BASIC COSTS (2009-2010)

Tuition and fees: $19,274.
Per-credit charge: $485.
Room and board: $6,736.

FINANCIAL AID PICTURE (2009-2010)

Students with need: Out of 219 full-time freshmen who applied for aid, 191 were judged to have need. Of these, 191 received aid, and 49 had their full need met. Average financial aid package met 86% of need; average scholarship/grant was $14,884; average loan was $3,772. For part-time students, average financial aid package was $6,162.
Students without need: 39 full-time freshmen who did not demonstrate need for aid received scholarships/grants; average award was $6,975. No-need awards available for academics, alumni affiliation, art, athletics, leadership, music/drama, religious affiliation.
Scholarships offered: *Merit:* Presidential Scholarship; $8,000. Dean's Scholarship; $7,000. Director's Award; $6,500. *Athletic:* 84 full-time freshmen received athletic scholarships; average amount $3,147.

FINANCIAL AID PROCEDURES

Forms required: FAFSA.
Dates and Deadlines: Priority date 3/1; no closing date. Applicants notified on a rolling basis starting 3/1; must reply by 5/1 or within 4 week(s) of notification.

CONTACT

Michele Dunne, Director of Financial Aid
1200 Grandview Avenue, Des Moines, IA 50316-1599
(515) 263-2963

Grinnell College
Grinnell, Iowa
www.grinnell.edu   Federal Code: 001868

4-year private liberal arts college in small town.

Enrollment: 1,630 undergrads. 378 full-time freshmen.

Selectivity: Admits less than 50% of applicants.

BASIC COSTS (2010-2011)
Tuition and fees: $37,482.

Per-credit charge: $1,155.

Room and board: $8,880.

FINANCIAL AID PICTURE (2009-2010)
Students with need: Out of 321 full-time freshmen who applied for aid, 270 were judged to have need. Of these, 269 received aid, and 269 had their full need met. Average financial aid package met 100% of need; average scholarship/grant was $28,905; average loan was $2,854. For part-time students, average financial aid package was $7,830.

Students without need: 50 full-time freshmen who did not demonstrate need for aid received scholarships/grants; average award was $9,269. No-need awards available for academics.

Cumulative student debt: 54% of graduating class had student loans; average debt was $19,540.

Additional info: Need-blind admission policy, meets 100% of demonstrated institutional need for all domestic students, with loan cap programs. Students may apply financial aid to off-campus study programs.

FINANCIAL AID PROCEDURES
Forms required: FAFSA, institutional form.

Dates and Deadlines: Closing date 2/1. Applicants notified by 4/1; must reply by 5/1.

Transfers: Closing date 5/1. Applicants notified by 5/20; must reply by 6/1.

CONTACT
Arnold Woods, Director of Student Financial Aid
1103 Park Street, Grinnell, IA 50112-1690
(641) 269-3250

Hawkeye Community College
Waterloo, Iowa
www.hawkeyecollege.edu   Federal Code: 004595

2-year public community and technical college in small city.

Enrollment: 4,466 undergrads, 32% part-time. 1,020 full-time freshmen.

Selectivity: Open admission; but selective for some programs.

BASIC COSTS (2009-2010)
Tuition and fees: $3,840; out-of-state residents $4,590.

Per-credit charge: $121; out-of-state residents $146.

FINANCIAL AID PICTURE (2009-2010)
Students with need: Need-based aid available for full-time students. Work study available nights, weekends, and for part-time students.

Students without need: No-need awards available for academics, state/district residency.

FINANCIAL AID PROCEDURES
Forms required: FAFSA.

Dates and Deadlines: Priority date 7/1; no closing date. Applicants notified on a rolling basis starting 5/1; must reply within 2 week(s) of notification.

CONTACT
Lois Mulbrook, Director of Financial Aid
Box 8015, Waterloo, IA 50704-8015
(319) 296-4020

Indian Hills Community College
Ottumwa, Iowa
www.indianhills.edu   Federal Code: 008298

2-year public community and technical college in large town.

Enrollment: 3,815 undergrads, 39% part-time. 1,127 full-time freshmen.

Selectivity: Open admission; but selective for some programs.

BASIC COSTS (2009-2010)
Tuition and fees: $3,720; out-of-state residents $5,580.

Room and board: $5,610.

FINANCIAL AID PICTURE (2008-2009)
Students with need: Need-based aid available for full-time and part-time students. Work study available nights, weekends, and for part-time students.

Students without need: No-need awards available for academics, athletics, state/district residency.

FINANCIAL AID PROCEDURES
Forms required: FAFSA, institutional form.

Dates and Deadlines: Priority date 4/1; no closing date. Applicants notified on a rolling basis starting 6/1; must reply within 2 week(s) of notification.

CONTACT
Jo Altheide, Financial Aid
623 Indian Hills Drive, Building 12, Ottumwa, IA 52501

Iowa Central Community College
Fort Dodge, Iowa
www.iowacentral.edu   Federal Code: 004597

2-year public community college in large town.

Enrollment: 5,731 undergrads.

Selectivity: Open admission; but selective for some programs.

BASIC COSTS (2009-2010)
Tuition and fees: $3,840; out-of-state residents $5,580.

Per-credit charge: $116; out-of-state residents $174.

Room and board: $4,975.

FINANCIAL AID PICTURE
Students with need: Need-based aid available for full-time and part-time students. Work study available nights, weekends, and for part-time students.

Students without need: No-need awards available for academics, art, athletics, leadership, music/drama.

FINANCIAL AID PROCEDURES
Forms required: FAFSA.

Dates and Deadlines: Priority date 3/8; no closing date. Applicants notified on a rolling basis starting 4/15; must reply within 2 week(s) of notification.

CONTACT
Angie Martin, Director of Financial Aid
One Triton Circle, Fort Dodge, IA 50501

Iowa Lakes Community College-Estherville
Estherville, Iowa
www.iowalakes.edu   Federal Code: 001864

2-year public community college in small town.

Enrollment: 2,257 undergrads.

Selectivity: Open admission; but selective for some programs.

BASIC COSTS (2010-2011)

Tuition and fees: $4,652; out-of-state residents $4,716.

Per-credit charge: $128; out-of-state residents $130.

Room and board: $4,800.

FINANCIAL AID PICTURE (2009-2010)

Students with need: Need-based aid available for full-time and part-time students.

Students without need: This college awards aid only to students with need.

FINANCIAL AID PROCEDURES

Forms required: FAFSA, institutional form.

Dates and Deadlines: Priority date 4/22; no closing date. Applicants notified on a rolling basis starting 4/15.

CONTACT

John Beneke, Director of Financial Aid

300 South 18th Street, Estherville, IA 51334-2725

(712) 362-7917

Iowa State University

Ames, Iowa

www.iastate.edu　　　　　Federal Code: 001869

4-year public university in small city.

Enrollment: 21,959 undergrads, 4% part-time. 4,535 full-time freshmen.

Selectivity: Admits over 75% of applicants.

BASIC COSTS (2009-2010)

Tuition and fees: $6,651; out-of-state residents $17,871.

Per-credit charge: $240; out-of-state residents $708.

Room and board: $7,277.

Additional info: Additional tuition for junior and senior engineering students of $1,808 for residents and $1,792 for non-residents; additional tuition for junior and senior business students of $500. Additional fees of $216 for engineering and computer science programs; $40 for business students.

FINANCIAL AID PICTURE (2009-2010)

Students with need: Out of 3,623 full-time freshmen who applied for aid, 2,358 were judged to have need. Of these, 2,328 received aid, and 1,078 had their full need met. Average financial aid package met 83% of need; average scholarship/grant was $6,560; average loan was $3,780. For part-time students, average financial aid package was $9,536.

Students without need: 1,545 full-time freshmen who did not demonstrate need for aid received scholarships/grants; average award was $2,903. No-need awards available for academics, art, athletics, leadership, minority status, music/drama, ROTC, state/district residency.

Scholarships offered: 95 full-time freshmen received athletic scholarships; average amount $15,622.

Cumulative student debt: 71% of graduating class had student loans; average debt was $30,411.

Additional info: Short-term loan program available to meet unplanned needs. Financial counseling clinic provides budget and credit education assistance.

FINANCIAL AID PROCEDURES

Forms required: FAFSA.

Dates and Deadlines: Priority date 3/1; no closing date. Applicants notified on a rolling basis starting 4/1.

Transfers: Priority date 2/15.

CONTACT

Roberta Johnson, Director of Student Financial Aid

100 Enrollment Services Center, Ames, IA 50011-2011

(515) 294-0066

Iowa Wesleyan College

Mount Pleasant, Iowa

www.iwc.edu　　　　　Federal Code: 001871

4-year private liberal arts college in small town, affiliated with United Methodist Church.

Enrollment: 858 undergrads, 23% part-time. 154 full-time freshmen.

Selectivity: Admits 50 to 75% of applicants.

BASIC COSTS (2010-2011)

Tuition and fees: $22,050.

Per-credit charge: $550.

Room and board: $7,308.

FINANCIAL AID PICTURE (2009-2010)

Students with need: Out of 142 full-time freshmen who applied for aid, 142 were judged to have need. Of these, 142 received aid.

Students without need: No-need awards available for academics, art, athletics, music/drama.

Scholarships offered: Unlimited merit based scholarships; based on ACT/SAT and GPA.

FINANCIAL AID PROCEDURES

Forms required: FAFSA.

Dates and Deadlines: Priority date 4/1; no closing date. Applicants notified on a rolling basis starting 1/1; must reply within 2 week(s) of notification.

CONTACT

Phyllis Whitney, Chief Financial Officer

601 North Main Street, Mount Pleasant, IA 52641-1398

(319) 385-6242

Iowa Western Community College

Council Bluffs, Iowa

www.iwcc.edu　　　　　Federal Code: 004598

2-year public community and technical college in small city.

Enrollment: 4,535 undergrads.

Selectivity: Open admission; but selective for some programs.

BASIC COSTS (2009-2010)

Tuition and fees: $3,900; out-of-state residents $4,050.

Per-credit charge: $119; out-of-state residents $124.

Room and board: $7,100.

FINANCIAL AID PICTURE (2008-2009)

Students with need: Need-based aid available for full-time and part-time students.

Students without need: No-need awards available for athletics, music/drama.

FINANCIAL AID PROCEDURES

Forms required: FAFSA.

Dates and Deadlines: Closing date 7/1. Applicants notified on a rolling basis starting 3/1; must reply within 3 week(s) of notification.

CONTACT

Blaine Duistermars, Director of Financial Aid

2700 College Road, Council Bluffs, IA 51502-3004

(800) 432-5852 ext. 292

Kaplan University: Cedar Falls
Cedar Falls, Iowa
www.kucampus.edu   Federal Code: 004586

4-year for-profit university and branch campus college in small city.
Enrollment: 736 undergrads.
Selectivity: Open admission; but selective for some programs.

BASIC COSTS (2009-2010)
Tuition and fees: $15,985.
Per-credit charge: $353.
Additional info: Tuition may vary by program; includes books.

FINANCIAL AID PICTURE (2008-2009)
Students with need: Need-based aid available for full-time and part-time students. Work study available nights, weekends, and for part-time students.
Students without need: This college awards aid only to students with need.

FINANCIAL AID PROCEDURES
Forms required: FAFSA, institutional form.
Dates and Deadlines: No deadline. Applicants notified on a rolling basis.
Transfers: No deadline. Applicants notified on a rolling basis.

CONTACT
Brenda Biersner, Director of Financial Aid
7009 Nordic Drive, Cedar Falls, IA 50613

Kaplan University: Cedar Rapids
Cedar Rapids, Iowa
www.kucampus.edu   Federal Code: 004220

2-year for-profit liberal arts college in small city.
Enrollment: 855 undergrads.
Selectivity: Open admission; but selective for some programs.

BASIC COSTS (2009-2010)
Tuition and fees: $15,985.
Per-credit charge: $353.
Additional info: Tuition may vary by program; includes books.

FINANCIAL AID PICTURE (2008-2009)
Students with need: Need-based aid available for full-time and part-time students. Work study available nights, weekends, and for part-time students.
Students without need: No-need awards available for academics.

FINANCIAL AID PROCEDURES
Forms required: FAFSA, institutional form.
Dates and Deadlines: Priority date 6/30; no closing date. Applicants notified on a rolling basis.
Transfers: Priority date of 07/08 for filing Iowa Tuition Grant application.

CONTACT
Director of Financial Aid
3165 Edgewood Parkway, SW, Cedar Rapids, IA 52404

Kaplan University: Davenport
Davenport, Iowa
www.kucampus.edu   Federal Code: 004586

4-year for-profit university in large city.
Enrollment: 918 undergrads.
Selectivity: Open admission; but selective for some programs.

BASIC COSTS (2009-2010)
Tuition and fees: $15,985.
Per-credit charge: $353.
Additional info: Tuition may vary by program; includes books.

FINANCIAL AID PICTURE
Students with need: Need-based aid available for full-time and part-time students. Work study available nights.
Students without need: No-need awards available for academics.

FINANCIAL AID PROCEDURES
Forms required: FAFSA, institutional form.
Dates and Deadlines: No deadline. Applicants notified on a rolling basis starting 3/4; must reply by 6/15 or within 2 week(s) of notification.

CONTACT
1801 East Kimberly Road, Suite 1, Davenport, IA 52807-2095

Kaplan University: Des Moines
Urbandale, Iowa
www.kucampus.edu   Federal Code: 004220

4-year for-profit university in large city.
Enrollment: 1,135 undergrads.
Selectivity: Open admission; but selective for some programs.

BASIC COSTS (2009-2010)
Tuition and fees: $15,985.
Per-credit charge: $353.
Additional info: Tuition may vary by program; includes books.

FINANCIAL AID PICTURE
Students with need: Need-based aid available for full-time and part-time students. Work study available nights, weekends, and for part-time students.
Students without need: This college awards aid only to students with need.

FINANCIAL AID PROCEDURES
Forms required: FAFSA, institutional form.
Dates and Deadlines: Priority date 6/30; no closing date.

CONTACT
Brandy Sundt, Director of Financial Aid
4655 121st Street, Urbandale, IA 50323
(515) 727-2100

Kirkwood Community College
Cedar Rapids, Iowa
www.kirkwood.edu   Federal Code: 004076

2-year public community college in small city.
Enrollment: 14,037 undergrads, 33% part-time. 3,226 full-time freshmen.
Selectivity: Open admission; but selective for some programs.

BASIC COSTS (2009-2010)
Tuition and fees: $3,330; out-of-state residents $4,080.
Per-credit charge: $111; out-of-state residents $136.

FINANCIAL AID PICTURE
Students with need: Need-based aid available for full-time and part-time students. Work study available nights, weekends, and for part-time students.
Students without need: No-need awards available for art, athletics, leadership, music/drama.

FINANCIAL AID PROCEDURES
Forms required: FAFSA.
Dates and Deadlines: Priority date 7/1; no closing date. Applicants notified on a rolling basis starting 4/1.

CONTACT

Peg Julius, Director of Financial Aid
6301 Kirkwood Boulevard SW, Cedar Rapids, IA 52406
(319) 398-1274

Loras College

Dubuque, Iowa
www.loras.edu
Federal Code: 001873

4-year private liberal arts college in small city, affiliated with Roman Catholic Church.

Enrollment: 1,481 undergrads, 2% part-time. 408 full-time freshmen.
Selectivity: Admits 50 to 75% of applicants.

BASIC COSTS (2010-2011)

Tuition and fees: $26,288.
Per-credit charge: $490.
Room and board: $7,306.
Additional info: Tuition/fee waivers available for minority students.

FINANCIAL AID PICTURE (2008-2009)

Students with need: Average financial aid package met 87% of need; average scholarship/grant was $9,525; average loan was $3,175. For part-time students, average financial aid package was $5,620.
Students without need: No-need awards available for academics, alumni affiliation, leadership, minority status, music/drama.
Cumulative student debt: 80% of graduating class had student loans; average debt was $29,067.
Additional info: Audition or portfolio recommended for music and art financial aid applicants.

FINANCIAL AID PROCEDURES

Forms required: FAFSA.
Dates and Deadlines: Priority date 4/15; no closing date. Applicants notified on a rolling basis starting 3/1; must reply within 3 week(s) of notification.

CONTACT

Julie Dunn, Director of Financial Planning
1450 Alta Vista Street, Dubuque, IA 52004-0178
(563) 588-7136

Luther College

Decorah, Iowa
www.luther.edu
Federal Code: 001874

4-year private liberal arts college in small town, affiliated with Evangelical Lutheran Church in America.

Enrollment: 2,450 undergrads, 1% part-time. 657 full-time freshmen.
Selectivity: Admits 50 to 75% of applicants.

BASIC COSTS (2010-2011)

Tuition and fees: $33,480.
Per-credit charge: $1,190.
Room and board: $5,800.

FINANCIAL AID PICTURE (2009-2010)

Students with need: Out of 569 full-time freshmen who applied for aid, 478 were judged to have need. Of these, 478 received aid, and 175 had their full need met. Average financial aid package met 91% of need; average scholarship/grant was $18,292; average loan was $5,956. For part-time students, average financial aid package was $11,611.
Students without need: 90 full-time freshmen who did not demonstrate need for aid received scholarships/grants; average award was $13,347. No-need awards available for academics, alumni affiliation, art, minority status, music/drama.

Scholarships offered: Academic scholarship; $4,000-$17,000; based on class rank and SAT/ACT. National Merit Scholarship; $1,000-$2,000; depending on qualifications. Diversity Enrichment Scholarship; $3,000-$5,000 awarded to students with broadly diverse and distinctive backgrounds. Church Matching Scholarship; up to $750; for students from member churches. Music scholarship; $1,000-$4,000, plus one scholarship that covers one credit hour of private instruction. Legacy Award; $1,000 for children of Luther College alumni. Competitive Nursing scholarship; $1,000; determined by nursing faculty and strength of admission file. Art scholarship; $150-$500; determined by evaluation of portfolio.
Cumulative student debt: 82% of graduating class had student loans; average debt was $34,101.

FINANCIAL AID PROCEDURES

Forms required: FAFSA, institutional form.
Dates and Deadlines: Priority date 3/1; no closing date. Applicants notified on a rolling basis starting 3/15; must reply by 5/1 or within 4 week(s) of notification.

CONTACT

Janice Cordell, Director of Student Financial Planning
700 College Drive, Decorah, IA 52101-1042
(563) 387-1018

Maharishi University of Management

Fairfield, Iowa
www.mum.edu
Federal Code: 011113

4-year private university and liberal arts college in small town.

Enrollment: 271 undergrads, 7% part-time. 54 full-time freshmen.
Selectivity: Admits less than 50% of applicants.

BASIC COSTS (2010-2011)

Tuition and fees: $24,430.
Room and board: $6,000.

FINANCIAL AID PICTURE (2008-2009)

Students with need: Need-based aid available for full-time and part-time students. Work study available nights, weekends, and for part-time students.
Scholarships offered: Shelley Hoffman Scholarship; $500-$900; based on creative writing and/or cerebral palsy; 7 awarded. National Merit Scholarship; full tuition; for NMS finalists; 4 awarded. Ray Prat Scholarship; $500-$1,750; for musically-talented undergraduates; 4 awarded. Girl Scout Gold Award Scholarship; $1,500 renewable; for GS Gold Award recipients; 5 awarded. DeRoy D. Thomas Scholarship; $3,000 each; open to outstanding African American; 1 awarded.
Additional info: Students may earn scholarships through volunteer staff program.

FINANCIAL AID PROCEDURES

Forms required: FAFSA.
Dates and Deadlines: Priority date 7/15; closing date 7/30. Applicants notified on a rolling basis starting 3/1; must reply within 4 week(s) of notification.
Transfers: No deadline. Applicants notified on a rolling basis starting 3/15; must reply within 4 week(s) of notification.

CONTACT

Bill Christensen, Director of Financial Aid
Office of Admissions, Fairfield, IA 52557
(641) 472-1156

Mercy College of Health Sciences

Des Moines, Iowa
www.mchs.edu   Federal Code: 006273

4-year private health science college in large city, affiliated with Roman Catholic Church.

Enrollment: 778 undergrads. 31 full-time freshmen.

BASIC COSTS (2010-2011)

Tuition and fees: $13,500.
Per-credit charge: $460.

FINANCIAL AID PICTURE (2008-2009)

Students with need: Out of 30 full-time freshmen who applied for aid, 25 were judged to have need. Of these, 24 received aid, and 1 had their full need met. Average financial aid package met 40% of need; average scholarship/grant was $5,772; average loan was $3,284. For part-time students, average financial aid package was $8,261.

Students without need: 2 full-time freshmen who did not demonstrate need for aid received scholarships/grants; average award was $425. No-need awards available for academics, minority status.

FINANCIAL AID PROCEDURES

Forms required: FAFSA.
Dates and Deadlines: Closing date 7/1. Applicants notified on a rolling basis starting 3/1; must reply by 8/1 or within 3 week(s) of notification.
Transfers: Students must submit information by 7/1 to be eligible for Iowa Tuition Grant.

CONTACT

Wayne Dille, Financial Aid Director
921 Sixth Avenue, Des Moines, IA 50309
(515) 643-6611

Morningside College

Sioux City, Iowa
www.morningside.edu   Federal Code: 001879

4-year private liberal arts college in small city, affiliated with United Methodist Church.

Enrollment: 1,199 undergrads, 2% part-time. 325 full-time freshmen.
Selectivity: Admits 50 to 75% of applicants.

BASIC COSTS (2010-2011)

Tuition and fees: $22,980.
Per-credit charge: $700.
Room and board: $7,040.
Additional info: Required fees include cost of laptop computer. Tuition/fee waivers available for adults.

FINANCIAL AID PICTURE (2009-2010)

Students with need: Need-based aid available for full-time and part-time students. Work study available nights, weekends, and for part-time students.
Students without need: No-need awards available for academics, alumni affiliation, art, athletics, job skills, leadership, music/drama, religious affiliation, ROTC, state/district residency.
Scholarships offered: President's Scholarship; $6,000 to $10,000; based on 27 ACT and top 10% of class. Dean's Scholarship; $3,000 to $6,000; based on 23 ACT or top 20% of class. Mustang Co-Curricular Award; up to $3,000; based on leadership and involvement. National Merit; full tuition. Talent Awards; up to $4,000; based on talents in the areas of art, cheerleading, creative writing, computer technology, mass communications, music, and/or theater.

FINANCIAL AID PROCEDURES

Forms required: FAFSA.

Dates and Deadlines: Priority date 3/1; no closing date. Applicants notified on a rolling basis starting 3/31.

CONTACT

Karen Gagnon, Director Student Financial Planning
1501 Morningside Avenue, Sioux City, IA 51106
(712) 274-5159

Mount Mercy College

Cedar Rapids, Iowa
www.mtmercy.edu   Federal Code: 001880

4-year private liberal arts college in small city, affiliated with Roman Catholic Church.

Enrollment: 1,441 undergrads, 35% part-time. 150 full-time freshmen.
Selectivity: Admits over 75% of applicants.

BASIC COSTS (2009-2010)

Tuition and fees: $22,100.
Per-credit charge: $610.
Room and board: $6,980.

FINANCIAL AID PICTURE (2009-2010)

Students with need: Average financial aid package met 71% of need; average scholarship/grant was $11,381; average loan was $4,225. For part-time students, average financial aid package was $7,338.

Students without need: No-need awards available for academics, alumni affiliation, art, athletics, leadership, music/drama, religious affiliation.

Cumulative student debt: 93% of graduating class had student loans; average debt was $19,565.

FINANCIAL AID PROCEDURES

Forms required: FAFSA.
Dates and Deadlines: Priority date 3/1; no closing date. Applicants notified on a rolling basis starting 3/15; must reply by 5/1 or within 3 week(s) of notification.
Transfers: No deadline. Applicants notified on a rolling basis starting 3/1; must reply within 3 week(s) of notification.

CONTACT

Bethany Rinderknecht, Director of Financial Aid
1330 Elmhurst Drive NE, Cedar Rapids, IA 52402-4797
(319) 368-6467

North Iowa Area Community College

Mason City, Iowa
www.niacc.edu   Federal Code: 001877

2-year public community college in large town.

Enrollment: 3,600 undergrads, 45% part-time. 783 full-time freshmen.
Selectivity: Open admission; but selective for some programs.

BASIC COSTS (2009-2010)

Tuition and fees: $3,691; out-of-state residents $5,337.
Per-credit charge: $109; out-of-state residents $164.
Room and board: $4,806.

FINANCIAL AID PICTURE (2008-2009)

Students with need: Out of 695 full-time freshmen who applied for aid, 668 were judged to have need. Of these, 520 received aid, and 192 had their full need met. Average financial aid package met 28% of need; average scholarship/grant was $3,454; average loan was $2,179. For part-time students, average financial aid package was $3,739.

Students without need: No-need awards available for academics, alumni affiliation, art, athletics, leadership, music/drama.

FINANCIAL AID PROCEDURES

Forms required: FAFSA, institutional form.

Dates and Deadlines: Priority date 3/1; no closing date. Applicants notified on a rolling basis starting 4/1; must reply within 2 week(s) of notification.

CONTACT

Mary Bloomingdale, Director of Financial Aid
500 College Drive, Mason City, IA 50401
(641) 422-4351

Northeast Iowa Community College
Calmar, Iowa
www.nicc.edu
Federal Code: 004587

2-year public community college in rural community.

Enrollment: 3,568 undergrads, 30% part-time. 833 full-time freshmen.

Selectivity: Open admission; but selective for some programs.

BASIC COSTS (2009-2010)

Tuition and fees: $4,576; out-of-state residents $4,576.

Per-credit charge: $126.

FINANCIAL AID PICTURE (2008-2009)

Students with need: Need-based aid available for full-time and part-time students. Work study available nights.

Students without need: No-need awards available for academics, leadership.

FINANCIAL AID PROCEDURES

Forms required: FAFSA.

Dates and Deadlines: Priority date 7/1; no closing date. Applicants notified on a rolling basis starting 5/1.

CONTACT

Jeff Murphy, Director of Financial Aid
Box 400, Calmar, IA 52132
(563) 526-3263 ext. 447

Northwest Iowa Community College
Sheldon, Iowa
www.nwicc.edu
Federal Code: 004600

2-year public community college in small town.

Enrollment: 1,615 undergrads.

Selectivity: Open admission; but selective for some programs.

BASIC COSTS (2009-2010)

Tuition and fees: $4,200; out-of-state residents $5,250.

Per-credit charge: $119; out-of-state residents $154.

Room and board: $3,480.

FINANCIAL AID PICTURE

Students with need: Need-based aid available for full-time and part-time students.

FINANCIAL AID PROCEDURES

Forms required: FAFSA, institutional form.

Dates and Deadlines: Priority date 4/1; no closing date. Applicants notified on a rolling basis starting 5/1.

CONTACT

Karna Hofmeyer, Financial Aid Director
603 West Park Street, Sheldon, IA 51201
(712) 324-5061 ext. 138

Northwestern College
Orange City, Iowa
www.nwciowa.edu
Federal Code: 001883

4-year private liberal arts college in small town, affiliated with Reformed Church in America.

Enrollment: 1,163 undergrads, 1% part-time. 293 full-time freshmen.

Selectivity: Admits over 75% of applicants.

BASIC COSTS (2010-2011)

Tuition and fees: $23,330.

Room and board: $7,090.

Additional info: Tuition/fee waivers available for adults.

FINANCIAL AID PICTURE (2008-2009)

Students with need: Out of 243 full-time freshmen who applied for aid, 243 were judged to have need. Of these, 243 received aid, and 92 had their full need met. Average financial aid package met 90% of need; average scholarship/grant was $7,506; average loan was $3,808. For part-time students, average financial aid package was $7,706.

Students without need: 40 full-time freshmen who did not demonstrate need for aid received scholarships/grants; average award was $6,928. No-need awards available for academics, alumni affiliation, art, athletics, music/drama, religious affiliation, state/district residency.

Scholarships offered: 106 full-time freshmen received athletic scholarships; average amount $4,129.

Cumulative student debt: 87% of graduating class had student loans; average debt was $30,456.

FINANCIAL AID PROCEDURES

Forms required: FAFSA.

Dates and Deadlines: Priority date 4/1; closing date 6/30. Applicants notified on a rolling basis starting 3/15; must reply within 3 week(s) of notification.

Transfers: No deadline. Financial aid transcript required for aid.

CONTACT

Teresa Gunderson, Director of Financial Aid
101 Seventh Street, SW, Orange City, IA 51041
(712) 707-7131

St. Ambrose University
Davenport, Iowa
www.sau.edu
Federal Code: 001889

4-year private university and liberal arts college in small city, affiliated with Roman Catholic Church.

Enrollment: 2,821 undergrads, 15% part-time. 576 full-time freshmen.

Selectivity: Admits over 75% of applicants.

BASIC COSTS (2010-2011)

Tuition and fees: $23,910.

Per-credit charge: $735.

Room and board: $8,585.

Additional info: Tuition/fee waivers available for adults.

FINANCIAL AID PICTURE (2009-2010)

Students with need: Out of 576 full-time freshmen who applied for aid, 433 were judged to have need. Of these, 430 received aid, and 211 had their full need met. Average financial aid package met 24% of need; average scholarship/grant was $11,544; average loan was $3,896. For part-time students, average financial aid package was $5,804.

Students without need: 137 full-time freshmen who did not demonstrate need for aid received scholarships/grants; average award was $7,644. No-need awards available for academics, alumni affiliation, art, athletics, job skills, music/drama.

Scholarships offered: *Merit:* Ambrose Scholarship; 4.0 GPA and 30 ACT or 1320 SAT score required. Presidential Scholarship; 3.8 GPA and ACT 26-29 or SAT 1170-1319 required. SAT scores listed are exclusive of Writing. *Athletic:* 50 full-time freshmen received athletic scholarships; average amount $4,230.
Cumulative student debt: 77% of graduating class had student loans; average debt was $33,216.
Additional info: Iowa applicants must apply for financial aid by July 1. Audition required for music, drama scholarship applicants. .

FINANCIAL AID PROCEDURES

Forms required: FAFSA. ·

Dates and Deadlines: Priority date 3/15; no closing date. Applicants notified on a rolling basis starting 2/1; must reply within 2 week(s) of notification.

Transfers: No deadline. Must reply within 2 week(s) of notification.

CONTACT

Julie Haack, Director of Financial Aid
518 West Locust Street, Davenport, IA 52803-2898
(563) 333-6314

St. Luke's College
Sioux City, Iowa
www.stlukescollege.edu   Federal Code: 007291

2-year private health science college in small city, affiliated with Lutheran and Methodist churches.
Enrollment: 183 undergrads, 24% part-time. 3 full-time freshmen.
Selectivity: Admits less than 50% of applicants.

BASIC COSTS (2010-2011)

Tuition and fees: $15,500.
Per-credit charge: $405.
Additional info: Optional meal plan is $500.

FINANCIAL AID PICTURE (2009-2010)

Students with need: Out of 3 full-time freshmen who applied for aid, 3 were judged to have need. Of these, 3 received aid. Average financial aid package met 75% of need; average scholarship/grant was $10,540; average loan was $4,500. For part-time students, average financial aid package was $12,000.

Students without need: No-need awards available for academics, job skills, leadership.

Cumulative student debt: 90% of graduating class had student loans; average debt was $13,000.

FINANCIAL AID PROCEDURES

Forms required: FAFSA.

Dates and Deadlines: Priority date 3/1; no closing date. Applicants notified on a rolling basis starting 4/1; must reply within 2 week(s) of notification.

CONTACT

Danelle Johannsen, Department Chair, Student and Administrative Services
2720 Stone Park Boulevard, Sioux City, IA 51104
(712) 279-3377

Simpson College
Indianola, Iowa
www.simpson.edu   Federal Code: 001887

4-year private liberal arts college in large town, affiliated with United Methodist Church.
Enrollment: 1,919 undergrads, 23% part-time. 390 full-time freshmen.
Selectivity: Admits over 75% of applicants.

BASIC COSTS (2009-2010)

Tuition and fees: $25,733.
Per-credit charge: $290.
Room and board: $7,261.
Additional info: Tuition/fee waivers available for adults, minority students.

FINANCIAL AID PICTURE (2009-2010)

Students with need: Out of 390 full-time freshmen who applied for aid, 338 were judged to have need. Of these, 338 received aid, and 85 had their full need met. Average financial aid package met 92% of need; average scholarship/grant was $19,122; average loan was $2,597. For part-time students, average financial aid package was $9,910.

Students without need: 52 full-time freshmen who did not demonstrate need for aid received scholarships/grants; average award was $14,480. No-need awards available for academics, alumni affiliation, art, leadership, minority status, music/drama, religious affiliation, state/district residency.

Scholarships offered: Simpson College Sesquicentennial Scholarship Program: amount and criteria vary.

Cumulative student debt: 92% of graduating class had student loans; average debt was $34,354.

Additional info: Music and theater scholarships based on audition. Art scholarships based on portfolio.

FINANCIAL AID PROCEDURES

Forms required: FAFSA.

Dates and Deadlines: Priority date 4/1; no closing date. Applicants notified on a rolling basis starting 3/12; must reply by 5/1 or within 3 week(s) of notification.

CONTACT

Tracie Pavon, Assistant Vice President for Enrollment and Financial Assistance
701 North C Street, Indianola, IA 50125
(515) 961-1630

Southeastern Community College: North Campus
West Burlington, Iowa
www.scciowa.edu   Federal Code: 004603

2-year public community and junior college in large town.
Enrollment: 2,818 undergrads, 38% part-time. 311 full-time freshmen.
Selectivity: Open admission; but selective for some programs.

BASIC COSTS (2009-2010)

Tuition and fees: $3,600; out-of-state residents $3,750.
Per-credit charge: $120; out-of-state residents $125.
Room and board: $5,310.

FINANCIAL AID PICTURE (2008-2009)

Students with need: Out of 262 full-time freshmen who applied for aid, 232 were judged to have need. Of these, 232 received aid. For part-time students, average financial aid package was $5,115.

Students without need: 10 full-time freshmen who did not demonstrate need for aid received scholarships/grants; average award was $647. No-need awards available for academics, art, athletics, minority status.

Scholarships offered: 52 full-time freshmen received athletic scholarships; average amount $3,135.

FINANCIAL AID PROCEDURES

Forms required: FAFSA.

Dates and Deadlines: Priority date 7/1; no closing date. Applicants notified on a rolling basis starting 3/1; must reply within 4 week(s) of notification.

CONTACT
Gwen Scholer, Financial Aid Director
1500 West Agency Road, West Burlington, IA 52655-0605
(319) 752-2731 ext. 5014

Southwestern Community College
Creston, Iowa
www.swcciowa.edu   Federal Code: 001857

2-year public community college in small town.
Enrollment: 1,119 undergrads.
Selectivity: Open admission; but selective for some programs.

BASIC COSTS (2009-2010)
Tuition and fees: $4,096; out-of-state residents $4,944.
Per-credit charge: $116; out-of-state residents $143.
Room and board: $4,900.

FINANCIAL AID PICTURE (2008-2009)
Students with need: Need-based aid available for full-time and part-time students. Work study available nights, weekends, and for part-time students.
Students without need: No-need awards available for academics, athletics, leadership, music/drama, state/district residency.

FINANCIAL AID PROCEDURES
Forms required: FAFSA.
Dates and Deadlines: Closing date 7/1. Applicants notified on a rolling basis starting 6/1; must reply within 2 week(s) of notification.

CONTACT
Tracy Sleep, Financial Aid Officer
1501 West Townline Street, Creston, IA 50801
(641) 782-1333

University of Dubuque
Dubuque, Iowa
www.dbq.edu   Federal Code: 001891

4-year private university and seminary college in small city, affiliated with Presbyterian Church (USA).
Enrollment: 1,431 undergrads, 6% part-time. 353 full-time freshmen.
Selectivity: Admits 50 to 75% of applicants.

BASIC COSTS (2010-2011)
Tuition and fees: $21,590.
Per-credit charge: $460.
Room and board: $7,370.

FINANCIAL AID PICTURE (2009-2010)
Students with need: Out of 343 full-time freshmen who applied for aid, 322 were judged to have need. Of these, 322 received aid, and 104 had their full need met. Average financial aid package met 81% of need; average scholarship/grant was $13,616; average loan was $6,806. For part-time students, average financial aid package was $7,101.
Students without need: 28 full-time freshmen who did not demonstrate need for aid received scholarships/grants; average award was $7,307. No-need awards available for academics, alumni affiliation, leadership, music/drama, ROTC, state/district residency.
Scholarships offered: Presidential Scholarship; $6,000 for 4 years; top 20% of class and top 20% of ACT. Honors Scholarship; top 20% of class, or top 20% of ACT/SAT, or 3.5 GPA or greater.
Cumulative student debt: 97% of graduating class had student loans; average debt was $37,936.

FINANCIAL AID PROCEDURES
Forms required: FAFSA.

Dates and Deadlines: Priority date 4/1; no closing date. Applicants notified on a rolling basis starting 3/1; must reply within 3 week(s) of notification.
Transfers: No deadline. Applicants notified on a rolling basis starting 3/1; must reply within 3 week(s) of notification. Iowa Tuition Grant available to Iowa residents.

CONTACT
Timothy Kremer, Dean of Student Financial Planning and Scholarships
2000 University Avenue, Dubuque, IA 52001-5099
(563) 589-3396

University of Iowa
Iowa City, Iowa
www.uiowa.edu   Federal Code: 001892

4-year public university in small city.
Enrollment: 19,899 undergrads, 8% part-time. 4,182 full-time freshmen.
Selectivity: Admits over 75% of applicants.

BASIC COSTS (2010-2011)
Tuition and fees: $7,417; out-of-state residents $23,713.
Per-credit charge: $255; out-of-state residents $934.
Room and board: $8,331.

FINANCIAL AID PICTURE (2008-2009)
Students with need: Out of 3,420 full-time freshmen who applied for aid, 2,302 were judged to have need. Of these, 2,086 received aid, and 1,085 had their full need met. Average financial aid package met 52% of need; average scholarship/grant was $4,179; average loan was $2,904. Need-based aid available for part-time students.
Students without need: 911 full-time freshmen who did not demonstrate need for aid received scholarships/grants; average award was $2,313. No-need awards available for academics, alumni affiliation, art, athletics, leadership, music/drama.
Scholarships offered: *Merit:* Presidential Scholarship; $13,000 per year for 4 years; based on ACT/SAT, GPA, essay; 20 awarded. Old Gold Scholarship; $3,000 per year for 4 years; awarded to runners-up for Presidential Scholarship, 350 awarded. National Scholars Award; $4,240 for 4 years; for nonresidents who have a Regent Admission Index score of 290 or above. Iowa Heritage Award; $6,000, for nonresident students who have a parent, stepparent, legal guardian, or grandparent who graduated from UI. Advantage Iowa Award; $2,000 to full tuition; race/ethnic background, socioeconomic factors considered; other criteria include U.S. citizenship or permanent residency, whether student is a first-generation college student or participant in federal Upward Bound program. *Athletic:* 84 full-time freshmen received athletic scholarships; average amount $14,117.
Cumulative student debt: 61% of graduating class had student loans; average debt was $22,856.

FINANCIAL AID PROCEDURES
Forms required: FAFSA, institutional form.
Dates and Deadlines: Priority date 1/1; no closing date. Applicants notified on a rolling basis starting 3/15.
Transfers: No deadline. Applicants notified on a rolling basis starting 3/15.

CONTACT
Mark Warner, Assistant Provost for Enrollment Services
107 Calvin Hall, Iowa City, IA 52242-1396
(319) 335-1450

University of Northern Iowa
Cedar Falls, Iowa
www.uni.edu   Federal Code: 001890

4-year public university in small city.
Enrollment: 11,061 undergrads, 8% part-time. 1,921 full-time freshmen.
Selectivity: Admits over 75% of applicants.

BASIC COSTS (2009-2010)
Tuition and fees: $6,636; out-of-state residents $14,900.
Per-credit charge: $240; out-of-state residents $585.
Room and board: $6,960.

FINANCIAL AID PICTURE (2009-2010)
Students with need: Out of 1,686 full-time freshmen who applied for aid, 1,146 were judged to have need. Of these, 1,105 received aid, and 293 had their full need met. Average financial aid package met 72% of need; average scholarship/grant was $4,438; average loan was $3,233. For part-time students, average financial aid package was $7,324.
Students without need: 458 full-time freshmen who did not demonstrate need for aid received scholarships/grants; average award was $2,587. No-need awards available for academics, alumni affiliation, art, athletics, leadership, minority status, music/drama, ROTC, state/district residency.
Scholarships offered: *Merit:* Presidential Scholarship Award; $8,000/year for up to 4 years; must be in upper 10% of high school class with 29 ACT or Regent Admission Index of 335 and involved in leadership and service activities; 20 available. Distinguished Scholar Award for Iowans; $1,500/year, renewable for a 2nd year; Iowa residents in upper 20% of high school class or 26 ACT with college GPA of 3.0. *Athletic:* 66 full-time freshmen received athletic scholarships; average amount $11,278.
Cumulative student debt: 80% of graduating class had student loans; average debt was $24,123.

FINANCIAL AID PROCEDURES
Forms required: FAFSA.
Dates and Deadlines: No deadline. Applicants notified on a rolling basis starting 3/1.

CONTACT
Joyce Morrow, Director Financial Aid and Student Employment
1227 West 27th Street, Cedar Falls, IA 50614-0018
(319) 273-2700

Upper Iowa University
Fayette, Iowa
www.uiu.edu   Federal Code: 001893

4-year private university in rural community.
Enrollment: 5,811 undergrads, 47% part-time. 1,148 full-time freshmen.
Selectivity: Admits less than 50% of applicants.

BASIC COSTS (2009-2010)
Tuition and fees: $21,418.
Room and board: $6,578.

FINANCIAL AID PICTURE (2008-2009)
Students with need: Out of 816 full-time freshmen who applied for aid, 628 were judged to have need. Of these, 610 received aid, and 184 had their full need met. Average financial aid package met 64% of need; average scholarship/grant was $9,828; average loan was $3,218. For part-time students, average financial aid package was $9,116.
Students without need: 241 full-time freshmen who did not demonstrate need for aid received scholarships/grants; average award was $9,260. No-need awards available for academics, alumni affiliation, athletics.

FINANCIAL AID PROCEDURES
Forms required: FAFSA.

Dates and Deadlines: Priority date 3/1; no closing date. Applicants notified on a rolling basis starting 3/1; must reply within 9 week(s) of notification.

CONTACT
Jobyna Johnston, Director of Financial Aid
Parker Fox Hall, Fayette, IA 52142
(800) 553-4150 ext. 3

Vatterott College
Des Moines, Iowa
www.vatterott-college.edu   Federal Code: 026092

2-year for-profit health science and technical college in large city.
Enrollment: 430 undergrads.
Selectivity: Open admission.

BASIC COSTS (2009-2010)
Additional info: Program cost ranges: $14,900 to $22,300 (certificate/diploma); $23,200 to $31,500 (associate degree).

FINANCIAL AID PICTURE
Students with need: Need-based aid available for full-time students.
Students without need: This college awards aid only to students with need.
Scholarships offered: Make the Grade Scholarship; up to $1,000; based on final semester grades; available for 1 year after high school graduation.

FINANCIAL AID PROCEDURES
Forms required: FAFSA.
Dates and Deadlines: No deadline. Applicants notified on a rolling basis.

CONTACT
Afton McManaman, Financial Aid Administrator
7000 Fleur Drive, Des Moines, IA 50321
(515) 309-9000

Waldorf College
Forest City, Iowa
www.waldorf.edu   Federal Code: 001895

4-year private liberal arts college in small town, affiliated with Evangelical Lutheran Church in America.
Enrollment: 507 undergrads, 3% part-time. 139 full-time freshmen.
Selectivity: Admits 50 to 75% of applicants.

BASIC COSTS (2010-2011)
Tuition and fees: $18,760.
Per-credit charge: $464.
Room and board: $5,954.

FINANCIAL AID PICTURE (2008-2009)
Students with need: Out of 113 full-time freshmen who applied for aid, 96 were judged to have need. Of these, 96 received aid, and 18 had their full need met. Average financial aid package met 77% of need; average scholarship/grant was $12,191; average loan was $4,129. For part-time students, average financial aid package was $6,654.
Students without need: 36 full-time freshmen who did not demonstrate need for aid received scholarships/grants; average award was $5,364. No-need awards available for academics, alumni affiliation, athletics, job skills, leadership, music/drama, religious affiliation, state/district residency.
Scholarships offered: 23 full-time freshmen received athletic scholarships; average amount $3,703.
Cumulative student debt: 97% of graduating class had student loans; average debt was $28,836.

FINANCIAL AID PROCEDURES
Forms required: FAFSA, institutional form.

Dates and Deadlines: Priority date 3/1; no closing date. Applicants notified on a rolling basis starting 3/1; must reply within 2 week(s) of notification.
Transfers: Applicants notified on a rolling basis starting 3/1; must reply within 2 week(s) of notification.

CONTACT
Duane Polsdofer, Director of Student Financial Aid
106 South Sixth Street, Forest City, IA 50436-1713
(641) 585-8120

Wartburg College
Waverly, Iowa
www.wartburg.edu   Federal Code: 001896

4-year private liberal arts college in small town, affiliated with Evangelical Lutheran Church in America.
Enrollment: 1,755 undergrads, 1% part-time. 514 full-time freshmen.
Selectivity: Admits 50 to 75% of applicants.

BASIC COSTS (2010-2011)
Tuition and fees: $29,020.
Room and board: $7,975.

FINANCIAL AID PICTURE (2008-2009)
Students with need: Out of 474 full-time freshmen who applied for aid, 397 were judged to have need. Of these, 397 received aid, and 85 had their full need met. Average financial aid package met 85% of need; average scholarship/grant was $17,841; average loan was $3,411. For part-time students, average financial aid package was $3,364.
Students without need: 116 full-time freshmen who did not demonstrate need for aid received scholarships/grants; average award was $18,373. No-need awards available for academics, alumni affiliation, leadership, music/drama, religious affiliation.
Scholarships offered: Regents scholarship; up to full tuition, fees, room and board; based on 28 ACT (1240 SAT, exclusive of writing) or rank in top 10% of class; renewable for 4 years with 3.0 GPA. Presidential Scholarship; up to $6,000 per year; based on 25 ACT (1140 SAT, exclusive of writing) or rank in top 20% of class or 3.5 GPA; renewable for 4 years with 2.7 GPA. Students who participate in Regents Scholarship competition not eligible for Presidential Scholarship.
Cumulative student debt: 81% of graduating class had student loans; average debt was $27,225.

FINANCIAL AID PROCEDURES
Forms required: FAFSA.
Dates and Deadlines: Priority date 3/1; no closing date. Applicants notified on a rolling basis starting 3/1; must reply within 2 week(s) of notification.

CONTACT
Jennifer Sassman, Director of Financial Aid
100 Wartburg Boulevard, PO Box 1003, Waverly, IA 50677-0903
(319) 352-8262

Western Iowa Tech Community College
Sioux City, Iowa
www.witcc.com   Federal Code: 004590

2-year public community college in small city.
Enrollment: 2,842 undergrads, 34% part-time. 374 full-time freshmen.
Selectivity: Open admission; but selective for some programs.

BASIC COSTS (2009-2010)
Tuition and fees: $3,915; out-of-state residents $4,920.
Per-credit charge: $115; out-of-state residents $133.
Room and board: $4,887.

FINANCIAL AID PICTURE (2008-2009)
Students with need: Need-based aid available for full-time and part-time students. Work study available nights, weekends, and for part-time students.
Students without need: No-need awards available for academics, leadership, music/drama.

FINANCIAL AID PROCEDURES
Forms required: FAFSA.
Dates and Deadlines: No deadline. Applicants notified on a rolling basis starting 4/1.

CONTACT
Donald Duzik, Director of Financial Aid
Box 5199, Sioux City, IA 51102-5199
(712) 274-6402

William Penn University
Oskaloosa, Iowa
www.wmpenn.edu   Federal Code: 001900

4-year private liberal arts college in small town, affiliated with Society of Friends (Quaker).
Enrollment: 1,811 undergrads.
Selectivity: Admits 50 to 75% of applicants.

BASIC COSTS (2010-2011)
Tuition and fees: $20,234.
Per-credit charge: $450.
Room and board: $5,392.

FINANCIAL AID PICTURE (2008-2009)
Students with need: Need-based aid available for full-time and part-time students. Work study available nights, weekends, and for part-time students.
Students without need: No-need awards available for academics, alumni affiliation, athletics, leadership, music/drama, religious affiliation.
Scholarships offered: Participation awards; up to $3,000; for music, drama, media, cheerleading, dance, religious leadership. Academic scholarships; based on high school GPA, ACT/SAT, class rank.

FINANCIAL AID PROCEDURES
Forms required: FAFSA.
Dates and Deadlines: Priority date 4/15; no closing date. Applicants notified on a rolling basis starting 1/1; must reply within 3 week(s) of notification.
Transfers: No deadline. Applicants notified on a rolling basis starting 1/1.

CONTACT
Cyndi Peiffer, Director of Financial Aid
201 Trueblood Avenue, Oskaloosa, IA 52577
(641) 673-1060

Kansas

Allen County Community College
Iola, Kansas
www.allencc.edu   Federal Code: 001901

2-year public community college in small town.
Enrollment: 1,250 full-time undergrads.
Selectivity: Open admission.

BASIC COSTS (2009-2010)
Tuition and fees: $1,890; out-of-district residents $1,890; out-of-state residents $1,890.
Per-credit charge: $47; out-of-district residents $47; out-of-state residents $47.

Room and board: $4,250.

FINANCIAL AID PICTURE (2008-2009)
Students with need: Need-based aid available for full-time and part-time students. Work study available nights, weekends, and for part-time students.
Students without need: No-need awards available for academics, art, athletics, music/drama, state/district residency.
Additional info: Scholarships for livestock judging, cheerleading, choir, dance, drama, art, academic challenge, and student ambassadors.

FINANCIAL AID PROCEDURES
Forms required: FAFSA.
Dates and Deadlines: Closing date 6/1. Applicants notified on a rolling basis starting 6/1; must reply within 2 week(s) of notification.

CONTACT
Vicki Curry, Director of Financial Aid/Registrar
1801 North Cottonwood, Iola, KS 66749
(620) 365-5116 ext. 221

Baker University
Baldwin City, Kansas
www.bakeru.edu   Federal Code: 001903

4-year private liberal arts and teachers college in small town, affiliated with United Methodist Church.
Enrollment: 903 undergrads, 1% part-time. 257 full-time freshmen.
Selectivity: Admits 50 to 75% of applicants.

BASIC COSTS (2009-2010)
Tuition and fees: $21,130.
Per-credit charge: $640.
Room and board: $6,800.

FINANCIAL AID PICTURE (2009-2010)
Students with need: Out of 249 full-time freshmen who applied for aid, 172 were judged to have need. Of these, 172 received aid, and 59 had their full need met. Average financial aid package met 81% of need; average scholarship/grant was $5,340; average loan was $4,771. For part-time students, average financial aid package was $7,000.
Students without need: 42 full-time freshmen who did not demonstrate need for aid received scholarships/grants; average award was $13,273. No-need awards available for academics, alumni affiliation, art, athletics, leadership, music/drama, religious affiliation.
Scholarships offered: 21 full-time freshmen received athletic scholarships; average amount $4,408.

FINANCIAL AID PROCEDURES
Forms required: FAFSA, institutional form.
Dates and Deadlines: Priority date 3/1; no closing date. Applicants notified on a rolling basis starting 3/1; must reply by 5/1 or within 6 week(s) of notification.
Transfers: No deadline. Applicants notified on a rolling basis starting 3/1; must reply within 6 week(s) of notification.

CONTACT
Jeanne Mott, Director of Financial Aid
618 Eighth Street, Baldwin City, KS 66006-0065
(785) 594-4595

Barclay College
Haviland, Kansas
www.barclaycollege.edu   Federal Code: 001917

4-year private Bible college in rural community, affiliated with Evangelical Friends Alliance and Friends United Meeting.
Enrollment: 194 undergrads, 12% part-time. 51 full-time freshmen.
Selectivity: Admits over 75% of applicants.

BASIC COSTS (2010-2011)
Tuition and fees: $13,690.
Per-credit charge: $250.
Room and board: $6,600.

FINANCIAL AID PICTURE (2009-2010)
Students with need: 67% of average financial aid package awarded as scholarships/grants, 33% awarded as loans/jobs. Need-based aid available for part-time students. Work study available nights, weekends, and for part-time students.
Students without need: No-need awards available for academics, alumni affiliation, leadership, music/drama, state/district residency.

FINANCIAL AID PROCEDURES
Forms required: FAFSA, institutional form.
Dates and Deadlines: Priority date 5/31; closing date 7/15. Applicants notified on a rolling basis starting 1/1; must reply within 4 week(s) of notification.

CONTACT
Ryan Haase, Director of Student Financial Services
607 North Kingman, Haviland, KS 67059
(620) 862-5252 ext. 41

Barton County Community College
Great Bend, Kansas
www.bartonccc.edu   Federal Code: 004608

2-year public community college in large town.
Enrollment: 2,663 undergrads.
Selectivity: Open admission; but selective for some programs.

BASIC COSTS (2009-2010)
Tuition and fees: $2,220; out-of-state residents $2,850.
Per-credit charge: $49; out-of-state residents $70.
Room and board: $4,472.

FINANCIAL AID PICTURE (2008-2009)
Students with need: Need-based aid available for full-time and part-time students.
Students without need: No-need awards available for academics, athletics.

FINANCIAL AID PROCEDURES
Forms required: FAFSA, state aid form.
Dates and Deadlines: Priority date 3/1; no closing date. Applicants notified on a rolling basis starting 6/1; must reply within 4 week(s) of notification.

CONTACT
Myrna Perkins, Assistant Dean of Student Services/Director of Financial Aid
245 North East 30th Road, Great Bend, KS 67530-9283
(620) 792-2701

PART III: FINANCIAL AID COLLEGE BY COLLEGE

Benedictine College

Atchison, Kansas
www.benedictine.edu   Federal Code: 010256

4-year private liberal arts college in large town, affiliated with Roman Catholic Church.

Enrollment: 1,438 undergrads, 1% part-time. 428 full-time freshmen.

BASIC COSTS (2010-2011)
Tuition and fees: $20,700.
Per-credit charge: $600.
Room and board: $7,375.

FINANCIAL AID PICTURE (2009-2010)
Students with need: Out of 368 full-time freshmen who applied for aid, 299 were judged to have need. Of these, 299 received aid, and 72 had their full need met. Average financial aid package met 76% of need; average scholarship/grant was $13,106; average loan was $2,412. Need-based aid available for part-time students.
Students without need: 68 full-time freshmen who did not demonstrate need for aid received scholarships/grants; average award was $8,253. No-need awards available for academics, alumni affiliation, art, athletics, job skills, leadership, minority status, music/drama, religious affiliation, ROTC.
Scholarships offered: *Merit:* Presidential Scholarship; full tuition. Dean's Scholarship; partial tuition. Both renewable every year, 5 recipients each, must maintain 3.5 GPA. Students must be admitted by Jan. 31. Academic Scholarships; renewable every year; ranges from $2,500-$7,500 depending on ACT scores; unlimited number. ***Athletic:*** 37 full-time freshmen received athletic scholarships; average amount $4,672.
Cumulative student debt: 98% of graduating class had student loans; average debt was $9,801.

FINANCIAL AID PROCEDURES
Forms required: FAFSA.
Dates and Deadlines: Priority date 3/15; no closing date. Applicants notified on a rolling basis starting 2/1; must reply within 2 week(s) of notification.
Transfers: No deadline. Applicants notified on a rolling basis. Scholarship available for students transferring 2.0 cumulative GPA.

CONTACT
Tony Tanking, Director Financial Aid
1020 North Second Street, Atchison, KS 66002-1499
(913) 367-5340 ext. 2484

Bethany College

Lindsborg, Kansas
www.bethanylb.edu   Federal Code: 001904

4-year private liberal arts college in small town, affiliated with Evangelical Lutheran Church in America.

Enrollment: 571 undergrads.
Selectivity: Admits 50 to 75% of applicants.

BASIC COSTS (2009-2010)
Tuition and fees: $19,065.
Per-credit charge: $330.
Room and board: $5,876.

FINANCIAL AID PICTURE (2009-2010)
Students with need: Need-based aid available for full-time and part-time students.
Students without need: No-need awards available for academics, alumni affiliation, art, athletics, leadership, music/drama, religious affiliation.
Additional info: State financial aid deadline March 15.

FINANCIAL AID PROCEDURES
Forms required: FAFSA.

Dates and Deadlines: Priority date 3/15; no closing date. Applicants notified on a rolling basis starting 2/1; must reply within 3 week(s) of notification.

CONTACT
Amber Maneth, Director of Financial Aid
335 East Swensson, Lindsborg, KS 67456-1897
(785) 227-3311 ext. 8114

Bethel College

North Newton, Kansas
www.bethelks.edu   Federal Code: 001905

4-year private liberal arts college in large town, affiliated with Mennonite Church.
Enrollment: 437 undergrads, 5% part-time. 118 full-time freshmen.
Selectivity: Admits 50 to 75% of applicants.

BASIC COSTS (2010-2011)
Tuition and fees: $20,700.
Per-credit charge: $745.
Room and board: $6,980.

FINANCIAL AID PICTURE (2008-2009)
Students with need: Out of 108 full-time freshmen who applied for aid, 95 were judged to have need. Of these, 95 received aid, and 45 had their full need met. Average financial aid package met 96% of need; average scholarship/grant was $4,793; average loan was $5,079. For part-time students, average financial aid package was $15,662.
Students without need: 23 full-time freshmen who did not demonstrate need for aid received scholarships/grants; average award was $10,251. No-need awards available for academics, alumni affiliation, art, athletics, minority status, music/drama, religious affiliation, state/district residency.
Scholarships offered: *Merit:* Scholarships for academically talented students, ranging from 16% to 50% of tuition. ***Athletic:*** 63 full-time freshmen received athletic scholarships; average amount $3,405.
Cumulative student debt: 77% of graduating class had student loans; average debt was $24,241.

FINANCIAL AID PROCEDURES
Forms required: FAFSA.
Dates and Deadlines: Priority date 4/1; no closing date. Applicants notified on a rolling basis starting 2/1; must reply within 2 week(s) of notification.
Transfers: Applicants notified on a rolling basis starting 2/1; must reply within 2 week(s) of notification.

CONTACT
Tony Graber, Director of Financial Aid
300 E 27th Street, North Newton, KS 67117-8061
(800) 522-1887 ext. 232

Butler Community College

El Dorado, Kansas
www.butlercc.edu   Federal Code: 001906

2-year public community college in large town.
Enrollment: 7,973 undergrads.
Selectivity: Open admission; but selective for some programs.

BASIC COSTS (2009-2010)
Tuition and fees: $2,040; out-of-district residents $2,370; out-of-state residents $3,870.
Per-credit charge: $52; out-of-district residents $63; out-of-state residents $113.
Room and board: $5,000.
Additional info: Tuition/fee waivers available for unemployed or children of unemployed.

FINANCIAL AID PICTURE (2008-2009)
Students with need: Need-based aid available for full-time and part-time students. Work study available nights, weekends, and for part-time students.
Students without need: No-need awards available for academics, art, athletics, music/drama.

FINANCIAL AID PROCEDURES
Forms required: FAFSA, institutional form.
Dates and Deadlines: Priority date 4/1; no closing date. Applicants notified on a rolling basis starting 5/1; must reply within 2 week(s) of notification.
Transfers: Students with 90 hours or more must have classes validated by degree-granting 4-year institution.

CONTACT
Susie Edwards, Director of Financial Aid
901 South Haverhill Road, El Dorado, KS 67042-3280
(316) 322-3121

Central Christian College of Kansas
McPherson, Kansas
www.centralchristian.edu   Federal Code: 001908

4-year private liberal arts college in large town, affiliated with Free Methodist Church of North America.
Enrollment: 334 undergrads, 2% part-time. 98 full-time freshmen.
Selectivity: Admits 50 to 75% of applicants.

BASIC COSTS (2010-2011)
Tuition and fees: $18,200.
Per-credit charge: $500.
Room and board: $5,900.

FINANCIAL AID PICTURE (2008-2009)
Students with need: Need-based aid available for full-time and part-time students. Work study available nights, weekends, and for part-time students.
Students without need: No-need awards available for academics, alumni affiliation, athletics, leadership, music/drama, religious affiliation.
Scholarships offered: National Merit Scholarship: full tuition; National Merit semifinalists. Trustees Scholarship: 60% tuition; minimum score of 30 on ACT/1340 on SAT and minimum 3.5 high school GPA. Valedictorian Scholarship: half tuition; for students who are first in their class, with minimum 27 ACT/1220 SAT and 3.5 GPA. SAT scores listed are exclusive of the writing portion.

FINANCIAL AID PROCEDURES
Forms required: FAFSA.
Dates and Deadlines: Priority date 3/1; no closing date. Applicants notified on a rolling basis starting 3/1; must reply within 4 week(s) of notification.
Transfers: No deadline. Applicants notified on a rolling basis starting 3/1; must reply within 4 week(s) of notification.

CONTACT
Mike Reimer, Director of Financial Aid
1200 South Main, McPherson, KS 67460-5740
(620) 241-0723 ext. 333

Cloud County Community College
Concordia, Kansas
www.cloud.edu   Federal Code: 001909

2-year public community college in small town.
Enrollment: 971 undergrads, 24% part-time. 238 full-time freshmen.
Selectivity: Open admission.

BASIC COSTS (2009-2010)
Tuition and fees: $2,550; out-of-state residents $2,550.
Per-credit charge: $66.
Room and board: $4,700.

FINANCIAL AID PICTURE
Students with need: Need-based aid available for full-time and part-time students. Work study available nights, weekends, and for part-time students.

FINANCIAL AID PROCEDURES
Forms required: FAFSA.
Dates and Deadlines: Priority date 4/1; no closing date. Applicants notified on a rolling basis starting 5/1; must reply within 4 week(s) of notification.

CONTACT
Sherry Campbell, Director of Student Financial Aid
2221 Campus Drive, Concordia, KS 66901-1002
(785) 243-1435 ext. 280

Coffeyville Community College
Coffeyville, Kansas
www.coffeyville.edu   Federal Code: 001910

2-year public community and technical college in large town.
Enrollment: 1,475 undergrads, 17% part-time. 541 full-time freshmen.
Selectivity: Open admission.

BASIC COSTS (2009-2010)
Tuition and fees: $1,800; out-of-state residents $3,045.
Per-credit charge: $27; out-of-state residents $69.
Room and board: $4,796.
Additional info: Oklahoma border county resident tuition: $35 per-credit-hour.

FINANCIAL AID PICTURE (2008-2009)
Students with need: Need-based aid available for full-time and part-time students. Work study available nights, weekends, and for part-time students.
Students without need: No-need awards available for academics, alumni affiliation, art, athletics, leadership, music/drama, state/district residency.

FINANCIAL AID PROCEDURES
Forms required: FAFSA.
Dates and Deadlines: Priority date 8/1; no closing date. Applicants notified on a rolling basis starting 6/20.

CONTACT
Rhonda Baker, Director of Financial Aid
400 West 11th Street, Coffeyville, KS 67337-5064
(620) 252-7357

Colby Community College
Colby, Kansas
www.colbycc.edu   Federal Code: 001911

2-year public community college in small town.
Enrollment: 623 undergrads. 150 full-time freshmen.
Selectivity: Open admission; but selective for some programs.

BASIC COSTS (2009-2010)
Tuition and fees: $2,550; out-of-state residents $3,900.
Per-credit charge: $52; out-of-state residents $97.
Room and board: $4,200.
Additional info: Nebraska and Colorado border county residents pay $68 per credit hour for tuition.

FINANCIAL AID PICTURE (2008-2009)

Students with need: Out of 93 full-time freshmen who applied for aid, 93 were judged to have need. Of these, 93 received aid. For part-time students, average financial aid package was $4,980.

Students without need: 35 full-time freshmen who did not demonstrate need for aid received scholarships/grants; average award was $1,190. No-need awards available for academics, athletics, music/drama.

Scholarships offered: 38 full-time freshmen received athletic scholarships; average amount $2,709.

FINANCIAL AID PROCEDURES

Forms required: FAFSA, state aid form.

Dates and Deadlines: Priority date 6/1; no closing date. Applicants notified on a rolling basis starting 5/1.

CONTACT

Paula Halvorson, Director of Financial Aid
1255 South Range Avenue, Colby, KS 67701
(785) 460-4695

Cowley County Community College

Arkansas City, Kansas
www.cowley.edu   Federal Code: 001902

2-year public community and technical college in large town.

Enrollment: 3,576 undergrads, 49% part-time. 469 full-time freshmen.

Selectivity: Open admission; but selective for some programs.

BASIC COSTS (2009-2010)

Tuition and fees: $2,040; out-of-district residents $2,340; out-of-state residents $3,810.

Per-credit charge: $45; out-of-district residents $55; out-of-state residents $104.

Room and board: $4,300.

Additional info: Oklahoma border county resident tuition: $60 per-credit-hour.

FINANCIAL AID PICTURE (2009-2010)

Students with need: Out of 255 full-time freshmen who applied for aid, 255 were judged to have need. Of these, 255 received aid. For part-time students, average financial aid package was $6,090.

Students without need: 117 full-time freshmen who did not demonstrate need for aid received scholarships/grants; average award was $1,202. No-need awards available for academics, alumni affiliation, art, athletics, leadership, music/drama, state/district residency.

Scholarships offered: 31 full-time freshmen received athletic scholarships; average amount $1,122.

FINANCIAL AID PROCEDURES

Forms required: FAFSA.

Dates and Deadlines: Priority date 4/15; no closing date. Applicants notified on a rolling basis starting 1/15; must reply within 2 week(s) of notification.

CONTACT

Sally Palmer, Director of Financial Aid
PO Box 1147, Arkansas City, KS 67005-1147
(620) 442-0430 ext. 5248

Dodge City Community College

Dodge City, Kansas
www.dc3.edu   Federal Code: 001913

2-year public community and technical college in large town.

Enrollment: 1,706 undergrads.

Selectivity: Open admission; but selective for some programs.

BASIC COSTS (2009-2010)

Tuition and fees: $1,950; out-of-state residents $2,700.

Per-credit charge: $35; out-of-district residents $35; out-of-state residents $45.

Room and board: $4,502.

FINANCIAL AID PICTURE (2008-2009)

Students with need: Need-based aid available for full-time and part-time students. Work study available nights, weekends, and for part-time students.

Students without need: No-need awards available for academics, athletics, music/drama, state/district residency.

FINANCIAL AID PROCEDURES

Forms required: FAFSA, institutional form.

Dates and Deadlines: Priority date 3/15; no closing date. Applicants notified on a rolling basis; must reply within 2 week(s) of notification.

CONTACT

Russ McBee, Dean of Students
2501 North 14th Avenue, Dodge City, KS 67801-2399
(620) 227-9336

Donnelly College

Kansas City, Kansas
www.donnelly.edu   Federal Code: 001914

2-year private junior and liberal arts college in large city, affiliated with Roman Catholic Church.

Enrollment: 660 undergrads, 56% part-time. 48 full-time freshmen.

Selectivity: Open admission.

BASIC COSTS (2009-2010)

Tuition and fees: $5,610.

Per-credit charge: $187.

FINANCIAL AID PICTURE (2009-2010)

Students with need: 82% of average financial aid package awarded as scholarships/grants, 18% awarded as loans/jobs. Need-based aid available for part-time students.

Students without need: No-need awards available for academics, religious affiliation.

FINANCIAL AID PROCEDURES

Forms required: FAFSA, institutional form.

Dates and Deadlines: Priority date 4/1; no closing date. Applicants notified on a rolling basis starting 7/1.

Transfers: Applicants notified on a rolling basis starting 7/1.

CONTACT

Belinda Ogan, Director of Financial Aid
608 North 18th Street, Kansas City, KS 66102-4210
(913) 621-8740

Emporia State University

Emporia, Kansas
www.emporia.edu   Federal Code: 001927

4-year public university in large town.

Enrollment: 4,063 undergrads, 10% part-time. 655 full-time freshmen.

Selectivity: Admits over 75% of applicants.

BASIC COSTS (2009-2010)

Tuition and fees: $4,374; out-of-state residents $13,578.

Per-credit charge: $114; out-of-state residents $421.

Room and board: $6,146.

FINANCIAL AID PICTURE (2008-2009)

Students with need: Out of 642 full-time freshmen who applied for aid, 406 were judged to have need. Of these, 401 received aid, and 369 had their full need met. Average financial aid package met 49% of need; average scholarship/grant was $4,367; average loan was $3,314. For part-time students, average financial aid package was $5,040.

Students without need: 158 full-time freshmen who did not demonstrate need for aid received scholarships/grants; average award was $1,253. No-need awards available for academics, alumni affiliation, art, athletics, job skills, leadership, minority status, music/drama, religious affiliation, state/district residency.

Scholarships offered: *Merit:* Presidential Academic Awards; $1,000 to $1,200 (unlimited number) based on ACT. Challenge Awards; $500 (unlimited number) based on ACT/GPA. Transfer President's Academic Award; $500 to $1,000; based on cumulative GPA or Phi Theta Kappa membership. Guaranteed GPA Scholarship; $500 to $1,200; based on GPA for continuing full-time undergraduates. *Athletic:* 45 full-time freshmen received athletic scholarships; average amount $2,503.

Cumulative student debt: 70% of graduating class had student loans; average debt was $17,680.

Additional info: Institution's own payment plan is available.

FINANCIAL AID PROCEDURES

Forms required: FAFSA, state aid form.

Dates and Deadlines: Priority date 3/15; no closing date. Applicants notified on a rolling basis starting 2/2; must reply within 2 week(s) of notification.

CONTACT

M Henrie, Director of Financial Aid
1200 Commercial, Campus Box 4034, Emporia, KS 66801-5087
(620) 341-5457

Fort Hays State University
Hays, Kansas
www.fhsu.edu   Federal Code: 001915

4-year public university in large town.
Enrollment: 8,455 undergrads.
Selectivity: Admits over 75% of applicants.

BASIC COSTS (2009-2010)
Tuition and fees: $3,763; out-of-state residents $11,916.
Per-credit charge: $98; out-of-state residents $370.
Room and board: $6,560.

FINANCIAL AID PICTURE (2008-2009)
Students with need: Need-based aid available for full-time and part-time students. Work study available nights, weekends, and for part-time students.
Students without need: No-need awards available for academics, art, athletics, leadership, minority status, music/drama.

FINANCIAL AID PROCEDURES
Forms required: FAFSA.
Dates and Deadlines: Priority date 3/15; no closing date. Applicants notified on a rolling basis starting 3/15; must reply within 2 week(s) of notification.
Transfers: No deadline. Applicants notified on a rolling basis starting 3/15; must reply within 3 week(s) of notification.

CONTACT
Craig Karlin, Director of Student Financial Aid
600 Park Street, Hays, KS 67601
(785) 628-4408

Friends University
Wichita, Kansas
www.friends.edu   Federal Code: 001918

4-year private business and liberal arts college in large city, affiliated with non-denominational tradition.
Enrollment: 2,088 undergrads.
Selectivity: Admits 50 to 75% of applicants.

BASIC COSTS (2009-2010)
Tuition and fees: $19,080.
Per-credit charge: $631.
Room and board: $5,670.

FINANCIAL AID PICTURE (2009-2010)
Students with need: Need-based aid available for full-time and part-time students.
Students without need: No-need awards available for academics, alumni affiliation, art, athletics, leadership, music/drama.
Additional info: Scholarships for clergy/family of clergy available.

FINANCIAL AID PROCEDURES
Forms required: FAFSA, institutional form.
Dates and Deadlines: Priority date 3/15; no closing date. Applicants notified on a rolling basis; must reply within 3 week(s) of notification.

CONTACT
Brandon Pierce, Director of Financial Aid
2100 University, Wichita, KS 67213
(316) 295-5200

Garden City Community College
Garden City, Kansas
www.gcccks.edu   Federal Code: 001919

2-year public community college in large town.
Enrollment: 2,054 undergrads.
Selectivity: Open admission; but selective for some programs.

BASIC COSTS (2009-2010)
Tuition and fees: $1,920; out-of-state residents $2,580.
Per-credit charge: $41; out-of-state residents $65.
Room and board: $4,450.

FINANCIAL AID PICTURE (2008-2009)
Students with need: 73% of average financial aid package awarded as scholarships/grants, 27% awarded as loans/jobs. Need-based aid available for part-time students. Work study available nights, weekends, and for part-time students.
Students without need: No-need awards available for academics, art, athletics, job skills, leadership, minority status, music/drama, state/district residency.

FINANCIAL AID PROCEDURES
Forms required: FAFSA, institutional form.
Dates and Deadlines: Priority date 3/1; no closing date. Applicants notified on a rolling basis starting 4/15; must reply within 2 week(s) of notification.

CONTACT
Kathleen Blau, Director of Financial Aid
801 Campus Drive, Garden City, KS 67846-6333
(620) 276-9519

Hesston College
Hesston, Kansas
www.hesston.edu   Federal Code: 001920

2-year private junior college in small town, affiliated with Mennonite Church.
Enrollment: 439 undergrads, 15% part-time. 171 full-time freshmen.
Selectivity: Open admission; but selective for some programs.

BASIC COSTS (2010-2011)
Tuition and fees: $20,720.
Room and board: $6,856.

FINANCIAL AID PICTURE (2008-2009)
Students with need: Out of 162 full-time freshmen who applied for aid, 147 were judged to have need. Of these, 147 received aid, and 20 had their full need met. Average financial aid package met 80% of need; average scholarship/grant was $10,300; average loan was $5,500. Need-based aid available for part-time students.
Students without need: 15 full-time freshmen who did not demonstrate need for aid received scholarships/grants; average award was $2,800. No-need awards available for academics, alumni affiliation, art, athletics, job skills, music/drama.
Scholarships offered: 11 full-time freshmen received athletic scholarships; average amount $1,750.
Cumulative student debt: 89% of graduating class had student loans; average debt was $6,450.

FINANCIAL AID PROCEDURES
Forms required: FAFSA.
Dates and Deadlines: Priority date 4/1; no closing date. Applicants notified on a rolling basis starting 2/1; must reply within 4 week(s) of notification.
Transfers: No deadline. Applicants notified on a rolling basis starting 2/1.

CONTACT
Marcia Mendez, Financial Aid Director
Box 3000, Hesston, KS 67062-2093
(800) 995-2757

Highland Community College
Highland, Kansas
www.highlandcc.edu   Federal Code: 001921

2-year public community college in rural community.
Enrollment: 2,495 undergrads, 48% part-time. 710 full-time freshmen.
Selectivity: Open admission; but selective for out-of-state students.

BASIC COSTS (2009-2010)
Tuition and fees: $2,100; out-of-district residents $2,490; out-of-state residents $4,020.
Per-credit charge: $40; out-of-district residents $53; out-of-state residents $104.
Room and board: $4,980.
Additional info: Out-of-state within 150 miles: $66 per-credit-hour.

FINANCIAL AID PICTURE (2008-2009)
Students with need: 53% of average financial aid package awarded as scholarships/grants, 47% awarded as loans/jobs. Need-based aid available for part-time students. Work study available nights, weekends, and for part-time students.
Students without need: No-need awards available for academics, alumni affiliation, art, athletics, job skills, leadership, music/drama.
Additional info: Auditions and portfolios important for certain scholarship candidates.

FINANCIAL AID PROCEDURES
Forms required: FAFSA, institutional form.

Dates and Deadlines: Priority date 4/1; no closing date. Applicants notified on a rolling basis starting 4/15; must reply within 14 week(s) of notification.
Transfers: No deadline. Applicants notified on a rolling basis starting 4/1; must reply within 4 week(s) of notification.

CONTACT
Kelly Twombly, Director of Student Financial Aid
606 West Main Street, Highland, KS 66035
(785) 442-6023

Hutchinson Community College
Hutchinson, Kansas
www.hutchcc.edu   Federal Code: 001923

2-year public community college in large town.
Enrollment: 4,074 undergrads, 41% part-time. 971 full-time freshmen.
Selectivity: Open admission; but selective for some programs.

BASIC COSTS (2009-2010)
Tuition and fees: $2,280; out-of-state residents $3,300.
Per-credit charge: $60; out-of-state residents $94.
Room and board: $4,816.

FINANCIAL AID PICTURE
Students with need: Need-based aid available for full-time and part-time students.
Students without need: No-need awards available for academics, athletics, minority status, state/district residency.

FINANCIAL AID PROCEDURES
Forms required: FAFSA, institutional form.
Dates and Deadlines: Priority date 2/1; no closing date. Applicants notified on a rolling basis starting 4/1; must reply within 2 week(s) of notification.

CONTACT
Ron Menefee, Financial Aid Director
1300 North Plum, Hutchinson, KS 67501
(620) 665-3400

Johnson County Community College
Overland Park, Kansas
www.jccc.edu   Federal Code: 008244

2-year public community college in very large city.
Enrollment: 7,140 full-time undergrads.
Selectivity: Open admission; but selective for some programs.

BASIC COSTS (2009-2010)
Tuition and fees: $2,070; out-of-district residents $2,520; out-of-state residents $4,770.
Per-credit charge: $55; out-of-district residents $70; out-of-state residents $145.

FINANCIAL AID PICTURE (2009-2010)
Students with need: Need-based aid available for full-time and part-time students.
Students without need: No-need awards available for academics.

FINANCIAL AID PROCEDURES
Forms required: FAFSA, state aid form.
Dates and Deadlines: Priority date 4/1; no closing date. Applicants notified on a rolling basis starting 4/15; must reply within 2 week(s) of notification.

CONTACT
Chris Christensen, Program Director for Student Financial Aid
12345 College Boulevard, Overland Park, KS 66210-1299
(913) 469-3840

Kansas City Kansas Community College
Kansas City, Kansas
www.kckcc.edu   Federal Code: 001925

2-year public community and career college in very large city.
Enrollment: 6,492 undergrads, 64% part-time. 765 full-time freshmen.
Selectivity: Open admission; but selective for some programs.

BASIC COSTS (2009-2010)
Tuition and fees: $1,770; out-of-state residents $4,710.
Per-credit charge: $49; out-of-state residents $147.
Additional info: Fees vary by program.

FINANCIAL AID PICTURE (2008-2009)
Students with need: 41% of average financial aid package awarded as scholarships/grants, 59% awarded as loans/jobs. Need-based aid available for part-time students. Work study available nights, weekends, and for part-time students.
Students without need: No-need awards available for academics, art, athletics, music/drama.

FINANCIAL AID PROCEDURES
Forms required: FAFSA.
Dates and Deadlines: Priority date 4/15; no closing date. Applicants notified on a rolling basis starting 5/1; must reply within 4 week(s) of notification.

CONTACT
Mary Dorr, Director of Financial Aid
7250 State Avenue, Kansas City, KS 66112
(913) 288-7697

Kansas State University
Manhattan, Kansas
www.k-state.edu   Federal Code: 001928

4-year public university in large town.
Enrollment: 18,230 undergrads, 10% part-time. 3,541 full-time freshmen.
Selectivity: Admits 50 to 75% of applicants.

BASIC COSTS (2009-2010)
Tuition and fees: $6,870; out-of-state residents $17,577.
Per-credit charge: $206; out-of-state residents $563.
Room and board: $6,752.

FINANCIAL AID PICTURE (2008-2009)
Students with need: Out of 2,563 full-time freshmen who applied for aid, 1,706 were judged to have need. Of these, 1,663 received aid, and 385 had their full need met. Average financial aid package met 82% of need; average scholarship/grant was $3,822; average loan was $3,309. For part-time students, average financial aid package was $8,180.
Students without need: 544 full-time freshmen who did not demonstrate need for aid received scholarships/grants; average award was $3,490. No-need awards available for academics, alumni affiliation, art, athletics, leadership, music/drama, ROTC, state/district residency.
Scholarships offered: 19 full-time freshmen received athletic scholarships; average amount $2,728.
Cumulative student debt: 57% of graduating class had student loans; average debt was $19,281.

FINANCIAL AID PROCEDURES
Forms required: FAFSA.
Dates and Deadlines: Priority date 3/1; no closing date. Applicants notified on a rolling basis starting 4/1; must reply within 2 week(s) of notification.

CONTACT
Larry Moeder, Assistant Vice President for Student Financial Assistance and Admissions
119 Anderson Hall, Manhattan, KS 66506
(785) 532-6420

Kansas Wesleyan University
Salina, Kansas
www.kwu.edu   Federal Code: 001929

4-year private liberal arts college in large town, affiliated with United Methodist Church.
Enrollment: 783 undergrads.
Selectivity: Admits 50 to 75% of applicants.

BASIC COSTS (2009-2010)
Tuition and fees: $19,200.
Room and board: $6,600.
Additional info: $200 per-credit-hour charge for 1-5 credit hours; $1,800 per semester for 6-8 credit hours; $3,600 per semester for 9-11 credit hours. Tuition/fee waivers available for adults.

FINANCIAL AID PICTURE (2009-2010)
Students with need: Need-based aid available for full-time and part-time students.
Students without need: No-need awards available for academics, alumni affiliation, art, athletics, music/drama, state/district residency.
Additional info: Awards available for residence hall students: minimum $7,000 for 3.0 GPA plus ACT score of 22 or SAT of 950 (exclusive of Writing); minimum $8,000 for 3.5 GPA plus ACT score of 22 or SAT score of 1030 (exclusive of Writing); minimum $9,000 for 3.75 GPA plus ACT score of 25 or SAT score of 1140 (exclusive of Writing). Application deadline March 15.

FINANCIAL AID PROCEDURES
Forms required: FAFSA.
Dates and Deadlines: Closing date 3/15. Applicants notified on a rolling basis starting 1/1; must reply by 8/1 or within 3 week(s) of notification.
Transfers: Academic scholarships based upon cumulative GPA of transferring credit hours.

CONTACT
Glenna Alexander, Director of Enrollment & Financial Services
100 East Claflin Avenue, Salina, KS 67401-6196
(785) 827-5541 ext. 1130

Labette Community College
Parsons, Kansas
www.labette.edu   Federal Code: 001930

2-year public community college in large town.
Enrollment: 1,130 undergrads.
Selectivity: Open admission; but selective for some programs.

BASIC COSTS (2009-2010)
Tuition and fees: $2,160; out-of-state residents $3,000.
Per-credit charge: $41; out-of-state residents $69.
Additional info: Residents of neighboring states (AR, MO, OK) pay per-credit-hour tuition rate of $65. Tuition/fee waivers available for adults, minority students, unemployed or children of unemployed.

FINANCIAL AID PICTURE
Students with need: Need-based aid available for full-time and part-time students. Work study available nights.
Students without need: No-need awards available for academics, leadership.

Scholarships offered: Foundation Scholarships.

FINANCIAL AID PROCEDURES

Forms required: FAFSA.

Dates and Deadlines: No deadline. Applicants notified on a rolling basis starting 4/4; must reply within 2 week(s) of notification.

CONTACT

Kathy Johnston, Director of Financial Aid
200 South 14th Street, Parsons, KS 67357
(620) 820-1219

Manhattan Area Technical College

Manhattan, Kansas
www.matc.net   Federal Code: 005500

2-year public technical college in large town.

Enrollment: 494 undergrads.

Selectivity: Open admission; but selective for some programs.

FINANCIAL AID PICTURE (2008-2009)

Students with need: Need-based aid available for full-time and part-time students.

Students without need: No-need awards available for academics, leadership.

FINANCIAL AID PROCEDURES

Forms required: FAFSA, institutional form.

Dates and Deadlines: No deadline. Applicants notified on a rolling basis.

CONTACT

Kody Carlson, Director of Financial Aid/Registrar
3136 Dickens Avenue, Manhattan, KS 66503-2499
(785) 587-2800 ext. 105

McPherson College

McPherson, Kansas
www.mcpherson.edu   Federal Code: 001933

4-year private liberal arts college in large town, affiliated with Church of the Brethren.

Enrollment: 573 undergrads, 5% part-time. 137 full-time freshmen.

Selectivity: Admits over 75% of applicants.

BASIC COSTS (2009-2010)

Tuition and fees: $18,400.

Per-credit charge: $250.

Room and board: $6,910.

FINANCIAL AID PICTURE (2009-2010)

Students with need: 52% of average financial aid package awarded as scholarships/grants, 48% awarded as loans/jobs. Need-based aid available for part-time students. Work study available nights, weekends, and for part-time students.

Students without need: No-need awards available for academics, alumni affiliation, art, athletics, music/drama, religious affiliation, state/district residency.

Scholarships offered: Presidential Scholarship; $10,000 each year of attendance for four years; competition in fall and spring; 10 awards given per year.

FINANCIAL AID PROCEDURES

Forms required: FAFSA.

Dates and Deadlines: Priority date 3/1; no closing date. Applicants notified on a rolling basis starting 3/1; must reply within 3 week(s) of notification.

Transfers: No deadline. Applicants notified on a rolling basis; must reply within 3 week(s) of notification.

CONTACT

Steven Frick, Director of Financial Aid
1600 East Euclid Street, McPherson, KS 67460-1402
(620) 242-0400

MidAmerica Nazarene University

Olathe, Kansas
www.mnu.edu   Federal Code: 007032

4-year private university and liberal arts college in small city, affiliated with Church of the Nazarene.

Enrollment: 1,335 undergrads, 22% part-time. 195 full-time freshmen.

Selectivity: Admits 50 to 75% of applicants.

BASIC COSTS (2010-2011)

Tuition and fees: $20,250.

Per-credit charge: $645.

Room and board: $6,750.

FINANCIAL AID PICTURE (2009-2010)

Students with need: Out of 182 full-time freshmen who applied for aid, 156 were judged to have need. Of these, 156 received aid, and 35 had their full need met. Average financial aid package met 75% of need; average scholarship/grant was $12,739; average loan was $3,587. For part-time students, average financial aid package was $6,490.

Students without need: 38 full-time freshmen who did not demonstrate need for aid received scholarships/grants; average award was $7,244. No-need awards available for academics, athletics, leadership, music/drama, religious affiliation, ROTC.

Scholarships offered: 33 full-time freshmen received athletic scholarships; average amount $5,428.

Cumulative student debt: 85% of graduating class had student loans; average debt was $32,394.

FINANCIAL AID PROCEDURES

Forms required: FAFSA.

Dates and Deadlines: Priority date 3/1; no closing date. Applicants notified on a rolling basis starting 1/30; must reply within 2 week(s) of notification.

CONTACT

Rhonda Cole, Director of Student Financial Services
2030 East College Way, Olathe, KS 66062-1899
(913) 917-3298

Neosho County Community College

Chanute, Kansas
www.neosho.edu   Federal Code: 001936

2-year public community college in small town.

Enrollment: 2,275 undergrads.

Selectivity: Open admission; but selective for some programs.

BASIC COSTS (2009-2010)

Tuition and fees: $2,070; out-of-district residents $2,370; out-of-state residents $3,090.

Per-credit charge: $45.

Room and board: $4,400.

FINANCIAL AID PICTURE (2008-2009)

Students with need: Need-based aid available for full-time and part-time students. Work study available nights, weekends, and for part-time students.

Students without need: No-need awards available for academics, art, athletics, job skills, leadership, music/drama, state/district residency.

Scholarships offered: Visual and performing arts, Academic Challenge stipends, industrial engineering and business scholarship.

FINANCIAL AID PROCEDURES
Forms required: FAFSA.
Dates and Deadlines: Priority date 4/1; no closing date. Applicants notified on a rolling basis; must reply within 6 week(s) of notification.
Transfers: All academic transcripts and financial aid transcripts must be on file before aid will be awarded.

CONTACT
Kerrie Coomes, Director of Financial Aid
800 West 14th Street, Chanute, KS 66720
(620) 431-2820 ext. 278

Newman University
Wichita, Kansas
www.newmanu.edu   Federal Code: 001939

4-year private university and liberal arts college in large city, affiliated with Roman Catholic Church.
Enrollment: 1,133 undergrads, 14% part-time. 168 full-time freshmen.
Selectivity: Admits less than 50% of applicants.

BASIC COSTS (2010-2011)
Tuition and fees: $20,372.
Per-credit charge: $662.
Room and board: $6,656.
Additional info: Tuition/fee waivers available for adults.

FINANCIAL AID PICTURE (2009-2010)
Students with need: Average financial aid package met 73% of need; average scholarship/grant was $5,819; average loan was $2,948. For part-time students, average financial aid package was $5,649.
Students without need: No-need awards available for academics, alumni affiliation, art, athletics, leadership, music/drama.
Cumulative student debt: 65% of graduating class had student loans; average debt was $31,445.

FINANCIAL AID PROCEDURES
Forms required: FAFSA.
Dates and Deadlines: Priority date 3/1; no closing date. Applicants notified on a rolling basis starting 2/1.

CONTACT
Brenda Krehbiel, Director of Financial Aid
3100 McCormick, Wichita, KS 67213-2097
(316) 942-4291

North Central Kansas Technical College
Beloit, Kansas
www.ncktc.edu   Federal Code: 005265

2-year public technical college in small town.
Enrollment: 355 undergrads.
Selectivity: Open admission.

BASIC COSTS (2010-2011)
Tuition and fees: $4,270.
Room and board: $4,400.

FINANCIAL AID PICTURE (2009-2010)
Students with need: 37% of average financial aid package awarded as scholarships/grants, 63% awarded as loans/jobs. Need-based aid available for part-time students. Work study available nights.
Students without need: This college awards aid only to students with need.

FINANCIAL AID PROCEDURES
Forms required: FAFSA, state aid form.
Dates and Deadlines: No deadline.

CONTACT
Gary Odle, Financial Aid Director
P.O. Box 507, Beloit, KS 67420
(800) 658-4655

Ottawa University
Ottawa, Kansas
www.ottawa.edu   Federal Code: 001937

4-year private university and liberal arts college in large town, affiliated with American Baptist Churches in the USA.
Enrollment: 526 undergrads, 3% part-time. 150 full-time freshmen.
Selectivity: Admits 50 to 75% of applicants.

BASIC COSTS (2009-2010)
Tuition and fees: $19,360.
Per-credit charge: $796.
Room and board: $6,084.

FINANCIAL AID PICTURE (2008-2009)
Students with need: Need-based aid available for full-time and part-time students. Work study available nights, weekends, and for part-time students.
Students without need: No-need awards available for academics, alumni affiliation, athletics, music/drama, religious affiliation.

FINANCIAL AID PROCEDURES
Forms required: FAFSA.
Dates and Deadlines: Priority date 3/15; no closing date. Applicants notified on a rolling basis starting 2/1; must reply within 4 week(s) of notification.
Transfers: No deadline.

CONTACT
Gary Bateman, Financial Aid Director
1001 South Cedar Street, #17, Ottawa, KS 66067-3399
(785) 242-5200 ext. 5571

Pittsburg State University
Pittsburg, Kansas
www.pittstate.edu   Federal Code: 001926

4-year public university in large town.
Enrollment: 5,462 undergrads, 5% part-time. 974 full-time freshmen.
Selectivity: Admits over 75% of applicants.

BASIC COSTS (2009-2010)
Tuition and fees: $4,592; out-of-state residents $13,116.
Per-credit charge: $122; out-of-state residents $460.
Room and board: $5,744.

FINANCIAL AID PICTURE (2009-2010)
Students with need: Average financial aid package met 94% of need; average scholarship/grant was $5,375; average loan was $3,314. For part-time students, average financial aid package was $2,740.
Students without need: No-need awards available for academics, alumni affiliation, art, athletics, leadership, music/drama, ROTC.

FINANCIAL AID PROCEDURES
Forms required: FAFSA, state aid form, institutional form.
Dates and Deadlines: Priority date 3/1; no closing date. Applicants notified on a rolling basis; must reply within 2 week(s) of notification.
Transfers: No deadline. Applicants notified on a rolling basis. Transfer student scholarships available.

CONTACT

Tammy Higgins, Director of Student Financial Assistance
1701 South Broadway, Pittsburg, KS 66762
(620) 235-4240

Pratt Community College

Pratt, Kansas
www.prattcc.edu   Federal Code: 001938

2-year public community and technical college in small town.
Enrollment: 803 undergrads.
Selectivity: Open admission; but selective for some programs.

BASIC COSTS (2009-2010)

Tuition and fees: $2,280; out-of-state residents $2,400.
Per-credit charge: $47; out-of-state residents $51.
Room and board: $4,814.
Additional info: Out-of-district Kansas residents have additional fee of $100; out-of-state $200, and international students $300 for the year. Technology fee of $300 applicable for auto, ag power, and electrical power areas.

FINANCIAL AID PICTURE (2009-2010)

Students with need: Need-based aid available for full-time and part-time students.
Students without need: No-need awards available for academics, art, athletics, leadership, minority status, music/drama, state/district residency.

FINANCIAL AID PROCEDURES

Forms required: FAFSA, institutional form.
Dates and Deadlines: Priority date 5/1; closing date 8/1. Applicants notified on a rolling basis starting 2/1; must reply within 2 week(s) of notification.

CONTACT

Debbie Boley, Director of Financial Aid
348 Northeast State Road 61, Pratt, KS 67124-8317
(620) 672-9800 ext. 248

Seward County Community College

Liberal, Kansas
www.sccc.edu   Federal Code: 008228

2-year public community college in large town.
Enrollment: 1,483 undergrads, 50% part-time. 342 full-time freshmen.
Selectivity: Open admission.

BASIC COSTS (2009-2010)

Tuition and fees: $1,860; out-of-state residents $2,550.
Per-credit charge: $40; out-of-state residents $63.
Room and board: $4,200.
Additional info: Residents of neighboring counties in OK, TX and CO pay per-credit-hour rate of $50.

FINANCIAL AID PICTURE (2008-2009)

Students with need: Need-based aid available for full-time and part-time students.
Students without need: No-need awards available for academics, athletics.

FINANCIAL AID PROCEDURES

Forms required: FAFSA, institutional form.
Dates and Deadlines: Priority date 4/1; no closing date. Applicants notified on a rolling basis starting 6/15; must reply within 4 week(s) of notification.

CONTACT

Donna Fisher, Financial Aid Director
1801 North Kansas Avenue, Liberal, KS 67905-1137
(620) 417-1110

Southwestern College

Winfield, Kansas
www.sckans.edu   Federal Code: 001940

4-year private liberal arts college in large town, affiliated with United Methodist Church.
Enrollment: 1,471 undergrads, 61% part-time. 119 full-time freshmen.
Selectivity: Admits over 75% of applicants.

BASIC COSTS (2010-2011)

Tuition and fees: $20,776.
Per-credit charge: $954.
Room and board: $6,056.

FINANCIAL AID PICTURE (2009-2010)

Students with need: Out of 108 full-time freshmen who applied for aid, 99 were judged to have need. Of these, 99 received aid, and 20 had their full need met. Average financial aid package met 90% of need; average scholarship/grant was $13,182; average loan was $4,788. For part-time students, average financial aid package was $6,228.
Students without need: 18 full-time freshmen who did not demonstrate need for aid received scholarships/grants; average award was $7,978. No-need awards available for academics, athletics, leadership, minority status, music/drama, religious affiliation.
Scholarships offered: *Merit:* Presidential Scholarship based on GPA, SAT/ACT scores, essay, resume, leadership, community service. Scholarships for major based on GPA, SAT scores, essay, interview; 3 awarded. *Athletic:* 30 full-time freshmen received athletic scholarships; average amount $7,397.
Cumulative student debt: 86% of graduating class had student loans; average debt was $27,973.

FINANCIAL AID PROCEDURES

Forms required: FAFSA, institutional form.
Dates and Deadlines: Priority date 4/1; closing date 8/15. Applicants notified on a rolling basis starting 2/1; must reply within 2 week(s) of notification.
Transfers: Applicants notified on a rolling basis starting 2/1; must reply within 2 week(s) of notification. Activity grants and scholarships, except for presidential scholarship and premier scholarships, available to transfer students. Phi Theta Kappa scholarship available for transfer students who are members.

CONTACT

Brenda Hicks, Director of Financial Aid
100 College Street, Winfield, KS 67156
(620) 229-6215

Sterling College

Sterling, Kansas
www.sterling.edu   Federal Code: 001945

4-year private liberal arts college in rural community, affiliated with Presbyterian Church (USA).
Enrollment: 672 undergrads, 11% part-time. 186 full-time freshmen.
Selectivity: Admits 50 to 75% of applicants.

BASIC COSTS (2010-2011)

Tuition and fees: $19,100.
Room and board: $6,830.

FINANCIAL AID PICTURE (2008-2009)

Students with need: Need-based aid available for full-time and part-time students. Work study available nights, weekends, and for part-time students.
Students without need: No-need awards available for academics, athletics.

FINANCIAL AID PROCEDURES

Forms required: FAFSA.

Dates and Deadlines: Priority date 3/1; no closing date. Applicants notified on a rolling basis starting 2/1; must reply within 3 week(s) of notification.
Transfers: No deadline. Applicants notified on a rolling basis; must reply within 2 week(s) of notification.

CONTACT
Tricia Brothers, Financial Aid Coordinator
125 West Cooper, Sterling, KS 67579
(620) 278-4207

Tabor College
Hillsboro, Kansas
www.tabor.edu   Federal Code: 001946

4-year private liberal arts college in small town, affiliated with Mennonite Brethren Church.
Enrollment: 617 undergrads, 17% part-time. 140 full-time freshmen.
Selectivity: Admits over 75% of applicants.

BASIC COSTS (2010-2011)
Tuition and fees: $20,630.
Per-credit charge: $840.
Room and board: $7,160.
Additional info: Tuition/fee waivers available for adults.

FINANCIAL AID PICTURE (2009-2010)
Students with need: Out of 140 full-time freshmen who applied for aid, 124 were judged to have need. Of these, 124 received aid, and 26 had their full need met. Average financial aid package met 85% of need; average scholarship/grant was $5,330; average loan was $6,810. For part-time students, average financial aid package was $10,288.
Students without need: 16 full-time freshmen who did not demonstrate need for aid received scholarships/grants; average award was $9,071. No-need awards available for academics, alumni affiliation, athletics, music/drama, religious affiliation, state/district residency.
Scholarships offered: 96 full-time freshmen received athletic scholarships; average amount $3,673.
Cumulative student debt: 81% of graduating class had student loans; average debt was $30,155.

FINANCIAL AID PROCEDURES
Forms required: FAFSA, state aid form.
Dates and Deadlines: Priority date 3/1; no closing date. Applicants notified on a rolling basis starting 3/1; must reply within 3 week(s) of notification.
Transfers: No deadline. Applicants notified on a rolling basis starting 2/20; must reply within 4 week(s) of notification. Transfer students not eligible for Presidential, National Merit or Dean's scholarships.

CONTACT
Scott Franz, Director of Student Financial Assistance
400 South Jefferson, Hillsboro, KS 67063-1799
(620) 947-3121 ext. 1726

University of Kansas
Lawrence, Kansas
www.ku.edu   Federal Code: 001948

4-year public university in small city.
Enrollment: 20,240 undergrads, 9% part-time. 4,441 full-time freshmen.
Selectivity: Admits over 75% of applicants.

BASIC COSTS (2009-2010)
Tuition and fees: $8,206; out-of-state residents $20,174.
Per-credit charge: $245; out-of-state residents $644.
Room and board: $6,802.
Additional info: Tuition at time of enrollment locked for 4 years.

FINANCIAL AID PICTURE (2008-2009)
Students with need: Out of 3,503 full-time freshmen who applied for aid, 1,715 were judged to have need. Of these, 1,613 received aid, and 330 had their full need met. Average financial aid package met 44% of need; average scholarship/grant was $4,709; average loan was $2,873. For part-time students, average financial aid package was $6,687.
Students without need: 982 full-time freshmen who did not demonstrate need for aid received scholarships/grants; average award was $3,633. No-need awards available for academics, alumni affiliation, art, athletics, leadership, minority status, music/drama, ROTC, state/district residency.
Scholarships offered: 83 full-time freshmen received athletic scholarships; average amount $14,643.
Cumulative student debt: 45% of graduating class had student loans; average debt was $22,478.
Additional info: Students awarded federal work study are responsible for securing their own jobs on campus. There are positions on campus with a variety of schedules beyond 8-5.

FINANCIAL AID PROCEDURES
Forms required: FAFSA.
Dates and Deadlines: Priority date 3/1; no closing date. Applicants notified on a rolling basis starting 4/1; must reply within 2 week(s) of notification.

CONTACT
Brenda Maigaard, Director of Student Financial Aid
1502 Iowa Street, Lawrence, KS 66045-7576
(785) 864-4700

University of Kansas Medical Center
Kansas City, Kansas
www.kumc.edu   Federal Code: 001948

Upper-division public university and health science college in small city.
Enrollment: 510 undergrads, 20% part-time.
Selectivity: Open admission; but selective for some programs.

BASIC COSTS (2009-2010)
Tuition and fees: $7,057; out-of-state residents $17,740.
Per-credit charge: $219; out-of-state residents $575.

FINANCIAL AID PICTURE (2008-2009)
Students with need: Average financial aid package for all full-time undergraduates was $13,725; for part-time $8,520. 32% awarded as scholarships/grants, 68% awarded as loans/jobs. Work study available nights, weekends, and for part-time students.
Students without need: No-need awards available for academics, leadership, state/district residency.

FINANCIAL AID PROCEDURES
Dates and Deadlines: No deadline.
Transfers: Priority date 2/14; no deadline. Applicants notified on a rolling basis starting 4/1.

CONTACT
Sara Honeck, Director of Student Financial Aid
3901 Rainbow Boulevard, Kansas City, KS 66160-7116
(913) 588-5170

University of St. Mary
Leavenworth, Kansas
www.stmary.edu   Federal Code: 001943

4-year private university in large town, affiliated with Roman Catholic Church.
Enrollment: 684 undergrads, 25% part-time. 113 full-time freshmen.
Selectivity: Admits 50 to 75% of applicants.

BASIC COSTS (2010-2011)

Tuition and fees: $19,960.
Per-credit charge: $645.
Room and board: $6,350.

FINANCIAL AID PICTURE (2008-2009)

Students with need: Out of 105 full-time freshmen who applied for aid, 86 were judged to have need. Of these, 86 received aid, and 14 had their full need met. Average financial aid package met 71% of need; average scholarship/grant was $10,761; average loan was $3,583. For part-time students, average financial aid package was $5,525.
Students without need: 28 full-time freshmen who did not demonstrate need for aid received scholarships/grants; average award was $7,825. No-need awards available for academics, art, athletics, leadership, music/drama.
Scholarships offered: *Merit:* Essays may be required for scholarship applicants. Auditions recommended for music and drama scholarship applicants. Portfolio reviews for art award applicants. *Athletic:* 10 full-time freshmen received athletic scholarships; average amount $2,930.
Cumulative student debt: 96% of graduating class had student loans; average debt was $23,509.

FINANCIAL AID PROCEDURES

Forms required: FAFSA.
Dates and Deadlines: Priority date 4/1; no closing date. Applicants notified on a rolling basis starting 2/8; must reply within 2 week(s) of notification.
Transfers: No deadline. Applicants notified on a rolling basis; must reply within 2 week(s) of notification.

CONTACT

Judy Wiedower, Director of Financial Aid
4100 South Fourth Street Trafficway, Leavenworth, KS 66048
(913) 758-6314

Washburn University

Topeka, Kansas
www.washburn.edu   Federal Code: 001949

4-year public university in small city.
Enrollment: 5,448 undergrads, 30% part-time. 708 full-time freshmen.
Selectivity: Open admission; but selective for some programs.

BASIC COSTS (2009-2010)

Tuition and fees: $6,116; out-of-state residents $13,766.
Per-credit charge: $201; out-of-state residents $456.
Room and board: $5,792.

FINANCIAL AID PICTURE (2009-2010)

Students with need: Out of 655 full-time freshmen who applied for aid, 454 were judged to have need. Of these, 451 received aid, and 61 had their full need met. Average financial aid package met 35% of need; average scholarship/grant was $4,693; average loan was $3,331. For part-time students, average financial aid package was $7,225.
Students without need: 94 full-time freshmen who did not demonstrate need for aid received scholarships/grants; average award was $2,055. No-need awards available for academics, alumni affiliation, art, athletics, job skills, leadership, minority status, music/drama, religious affiliation, ROTC, state/district residency.
Scholarships offered: 26 full-time freshmen received athletic scholarships; average amount $4,851.
Cumulative student debt: 66% of graduating class had student loans; average debt was $17,031.

FINANCIAL AID PROCEDURES

Forms required: FAFSA.
Dates and Deadlines: Priority date 2/15; no closing date. Applicants notified on a rolling basis starting 3/15; must reply within 4 week(s) of notification.

Transfers: No deadline. Applicants notified on a rolling basis starting 3/15; must reply within 4 week(s) of notification.

CONTACT

Gail Palmer, Director of Financial Aid
1700 SW College Avenue, Morgan 114, Topeka, KS 66621
(785) 670-1151

Wichita State University

Wichita, Kansas
www.wichita.edu   Federal Code: 001950

4-year public university in large city.
Enrollment: 10,951 undergrads, 27% part-time. 1,186 full-time freshmen.
Selectivity: Admits over 75% of applicants.

BASIC COSTS (2009-2010)

Tuition and fees: $5,467; out-of-state residents $13,501.
Per-credit charge: $150; out-of-state residents $418.
Room and board: $6,060.

FINANCIAL AID PICTURE (2008-2009)

Students with need: Out of 1,062 full-time freshmen who applied for aid, 395 were judged to have need. Of these, 385 received aid, and 281 had their full need met. Average financial aid package met 49% of need; average scholarship/grant was $3,582; average loan was $3,201. For part-time students, average financial aid package was $5,886.
Students without need: 489 full-time freshmen who did not demonstrate need for aid received scholarships/grants; average award was $2,337. No-need awards available for academics, alumni affiliation, art, athletics, leadership, music/drama.
Scholarships offered: 40 full-time freshmen received athletic scholarships; average amount $8,759.
Additional info: Top freshman applicants admitted by October 1 invited to university scholarship competition.

FINANCIAL AID PROCEDURES

Forms required: FAFSA, state aid form.
Dates and Deadlines: Priority date 3/1; no closing date. Applicants notified on a rolling basis starting 3/1; must reply within 2 week(s) of notification.

CONTACT

Deborah Byers, Director of Financial Aid
1845 Fairmount Box 124, Wichita, KS 67260-0124
(316) 978-3430

Kentucky

Alice Lloyd College

Pippa Passes, Kentucky
www.alc.edu   Federal Code: 001951

4-year private liberal arts college in rural community.
Enrollment: 650 undergrads.
Selectivity: Admits less than 50% of applicants.

BASIC COSTS (2009-2010)

Tuition and fees: $7,600.
Room and board: $5,850.
Additional info: Guaranteed tuition for students from 108-county central Appalachian service area in Kentucky, West Virginia, Virginia, Tennessee, and Ohio. Tuition/fee waivers available for minority students.

FINANCIAL AID PICTURE (2008-2009)

Students with need: Need-based aid available for full-time and part-time students. Work study available nights, weekends, and for part-time students.

Students without need: No-need awards available for athletics, minority status, state/district residency.

Scholarships offered: Students meeting admissions criteria from one of 108 counties in West Virginia, Virginia, Tennessee, Ohio and Kentucky guaranteed free tuition of up to $3,180 per semester; based on admission application; no limit on awards given. Minority scholarships; tuition, room, and board; offered to students from 108 service areas. Alice Lloyd Scholars Program; tuition, room, board, fees, and books; awarded to up to 3 freshmen a year.

Additional info: All students receive financial aid through student work program. No student denied admission because of inability to pay. All full-time students required to work minimum of 10 hours per week.

FINANCIAL AID PROCEDURES

Forms required: FAFSA.

Dates and Deadlines: Priority date 3/15; no closing date. Applicants notified on a rolling basis starting 4/1; must reply within 6 week(s) of notification.

Transfers: Closing date 3/15. Tuition guarantee only for total of 10 semesters of course work from all schools attended.

CONTACT

Jacqueline Stewart, Director of Financial Aid

100 Purpose Road, Pippa Passes, KY 41844

(606) 368-6058

Asbury College

Wilmore, Kentucky

www.asbury.edu   Federal Code: 001952

4-year private university and liberal arts college in small town, affiliated with interdenominational tradition.

Enrollment: 1,371 undergrads, 2% part-time. 315 full-time freshmen.

Selectivity: Admits 50 to 75% of applicants.

BASIC COSTS (2010-2011)

Tuition and fees: $23,303.

Per-credit charge: $889.

Room and board: $5,566.

Additional info: Tuition/fee waivers available for minority students.

FINANCIAL AID PICTURE (2009-2010)

Students with need: Out of 289 full-time freshmen who applied for aid, 245 were judged to have need. Of these, 245 received aid, and 78 had their full need met. Average financial aid package met 89% of need; average scholarship/grant was $13,646; average loan was $3,226. For part-time students, average financial aid package was $9,050.

Students without need: 43 full-time freshmen who did not demonstrate need for aid received scholarships/grants; average award was $10,501. No-need awards available for academics, alumni affiliation, art, athletics, leadership, minority status, music/drama, religious affiliation, ROTC.

Scholarships offered: 20 full-time freshmen received athletic scholarships; average amount $4,571.

Cumulative student debt: 85% of graduating class had student loans; average debt was $26,150.

FINANCIAL AID PROCEDURES

Forms required: institutional form.

Dates and Deadlines: Priority date 3/1; no closing date. Applicants notified on a rolling basis starting 1/31; must reply within 4 week(s) of notification.

CONTACT

Ronald Anderson, Director of Financial Aid

One Macklem Drive, Wilmore, KY 40390-1198

(859) 858-3511 ext. 2195

Beckfield College

Florence, Kentucky

www.beckfield.edu   Federal Code: 016726

4-year for-profit business and health science and nursing college in large town.

Enrollment: 645 undergrads.

Selectivity: Open admission; but selective for some programs.

BASIC COSTS (2009-2010)

Tuition and fees: $13,353.

Per-credit charge: $286.

Additional info: Fees vary by program.

FINANCIAL AID PICTURE (2008-2009)

Students with need: Need-based aid available for full-time and part-time students.

Students without need: This college awards aid only to students with need.

Scholarships offered: High School scholarship; tuition for one course per quarter for maximum of 8 quarters; must achieve and maintain 3.0 GPA, be enrolled full-time, and enter college in July or October following graduation from high school. Merit scholarship; $100 per quarter; must maintain 4.0 GPA, perfect attendance, and carry at least 8 quarter credit hours.

Additional info: Deadline for filing of financial aid forms is end of first week of classes.

FINANCIAL AID PROCEDURES

Forms required: FAFSA.

Dates and Deadlines: Applicants notified on a rolling basis.

CONTACT

Pat Nettleton, Corporate Director of Student Financial

16 Spiral Drive, Florence, KY 41042

(859) 371-9393

Bellarmine University

Louisville, Kentucky

www.bellarmine.edu   Federal Code: 001954

4-year private university and liberal arts college in very large city, affiliated with Roman Catholic Church.

Enrollment: 2,139 undergrads, 5% part-time. 602 full-time freshmen.

Selectivity: Admits 50 to 75% of applicants.

BASIC COSTS (2010-2011)

Tuition and fees: $30,310.

Per-credit charge: $690.

Room and board: $8,550.

FINANCIAL AID PICTURE (2009-2010)

Students with need: Out of 536 full-time freshmen who applied for aid, 475 were judged to have need. Of these, 474 received aid, and 116 had their full need met. Average financial aid package met 79% of need; average scholarship/grant was $17,171; average loan was $3,303. For part-time students, average financial aid package was $10,168.

Students without need: 127 full-time freshmen who did not demonstrate need for aid received scholarships/grants; average award was $17,840. No-need awards available for academics, alumni affiliation, art, athletics, leadership, minority status, music/drama, religious affiliation, ROTC, state/district residency.

Scholarships offered: *Merit:* Academic awards range from $7,000 to full tuition. *Athletic:* 35 full-time freshmen received athletic scholarships; average amount $8,173.

Cumulative student debt: 69% of graduating class had student loans; average debt was $21,639.

FINANCIAL AID PROCEDURES
Forms required: FAFSA.
Dates and Deadlines: Priority date 3/1; no closing date. Applicants notified on a rolling basis starting 3/15.
Transfers: Applicants notified on a rolling basis starting 4/15; must reply within 3 week(s) of notification.

CONTACT
Heather Boutell, Director of Financial Aid
2001 Newburg Road, Louisville, KY 40205
(502) 452-8124

Berea College
Berea, Kentucky
www.berea.edu
Federal Code: 001955

4-year private liberal arts college in small town.
Enrollment: 1,496 undergrads. 392 full-time freshmen.
Selectivity: Admits less than 50% of applicants.

BASIC COSTS (2010-2011)
Additional info: Only those with financial need admitted. All students awarded 4-year tuition scholarship. Amount of scholarship varies depending on financial need and presence of any additional outside scholarships. Resources cover entire cost of tuition, which totals $24,100. Financial aid and scholarships available for meeting additional costs of room/board ($5,574) and fees ($910), depending on financial need.

FINANCIAL AID PICTURE (2009-2010)
Students with need: Out of 392 full-time freshmen who applied for aid, 392 were judged to have need. Of these, 392 received aid. Average financial aid package met 98% of need; average scholarship/grant was $31,341; average loan was $25. For part-time students, average financial aid package was $34,189.
Students without need: This college awards aid only to students with need.
Cumulative student debt: 79% of graduating class had student loans; average debt was $8,133.

FINANCIAL AID PROCEDURES
Forms required: FAFSA.
Dates and Deadlines: Priority date 3/15; no closing date. Applicants notified on a rolling basis starting 4/1.
Transfers: Financial aid transcript from previous school(s) must be received before awarding aid.

CONTACT
Nancy Melton, Director of Student Financial Aid Services
CPO 2220, Berea, KY 40404
(859) 985-3310

Big Sandy Community and Technical College
Prestonsburg, Kentucky
www.bigsandy.kctcs.edu
Federal Code: 001996

2-year public community and technical college in small town.
Enrollment: 1,900 full-time undergrads.
Selectivity: Open admission; but selective for some programs.

BASIC COSTS (2009-2010)
Tuition and fees: $3,750; out-of-state residents $12,750.
Per-credit charge: $125; out-of-state residents $425.
Additional info: Contiguous counties pay $250 per credit hour.

FINANCIAL AID PICTURE (2009-2010)
Students with need: Need-based aid available for full-time and part-time students.
Students without need: No-need awards available for academics.

FINANCIAL AID PROCEDURES
Forms required: FAFSA.
Dates and Deadlines: Priority date 4/1; no closing date. Applicants notified on a rolling basis; must reply within 2 week(s) of notification.
Transfers: Kentucky State Grant must be transferred by August 1 for fall semester, December 1 for spring semester.

CONTACT
Denise Trusty, Director of Financial Aid
One Bert T. Combs Drive, Prestonsburg, KY 41653
(606) 886-3863 ext. 67255

Bluegrass Community and Technical College
Lexington, Kentucky
www.bluegrass.kctcs.edu
Federal Code: 009707

2-year public community and technical college in large city.
Enrollment: 11,438 undergrads, 44% part-time. 1,697 full-time freshmen.
Selectivity: Open admission; but selective for some programs.

BASIC COSTS (2009-2010)
Tuition and fees: $3,750; out-of-state residents $12,750.
Per-credit charge: $125; out-of-state residents $425.
Room and board: $6,952.
Additional info: Contiguous counties pay $250 per credit hour.

FINANCIAL AID PICTURE (2008-2009)
Students with need: Need-based aid available for full-time and part-time students. Work study available nights, weekends, and for part-time students.
Students without need: No-need awards available for academics, minority status, state/district residency.

FINANCIAL AID PROCEDURES
Forms required: FAFSA, institutional form.
Dates and Deadlines: Priority date 4/15; no closing date. Applicants notified on a rolling basis starting 6/5; must reply within 3 week(s) of notification.

CONTACT
Runan Pendergrast, Director of Financial Aid
200 Oswald Building, Cooper Drive, Lexington, KY 40506-0235
(859) 246-6216

Brescia University
Owensboro, Kentucky
www.brescia.edu
Federal Code: 001958

4-year private university and liberal arts college in small city, affiliated with Roman Catholic Church.
Enrollment: 571 undergrads, 16% part-time. 115 full-time freshmen.
Selectivity: Admits 50 to 75% of applicants.

BASIC COSTS (2010-2011)
Tuition and fees: $17,390.
Per-credit charge: $510.
Room and board: $8,000.

FINANCIAL AID PICTURE (2009-2010)
Students with need: Need-based aid available for full-time and part-time students. Work study available nights, weekends, and for part-time students.

Students without need: No-need awards available for academics, alumni affiliation, art, athletics, minority status, music/drama, religious affiliation, state/district residency.

FINANCIAL AID PROCEDURES

Forms required: FAFSA.

Dates and Deadlines: Priority date 8/1; closing date 8/23. Applicants notified on a rolling basis starting 3/1; must reply within 3 week(s) of notification.

CONTACT

Marcie Tillett, Director of Financial Aid

717 Frederica Street, Owensboro, KY 42301-3023

(270) 685-3131 ext. 4216

Campbellsville University

Campbellsville, Kentucky

www.campbellsville.edu   Federal Code: 001959

4-year private university in large town, affiliated with Baptist faith.

Enrollment: 1,888 undergrads, 10% part-time. 374 full-time freshmen.

Selectivity: Admits 50 to 75% of applicants.

BASIC COSTS (2010-2011)

Tuition and fees: $19,710.

Per-credit charge: $805.

Room and board: $6,740.

Additional info: Tuition/fee waivers available for adults, minority students, unemployed or children of unemployed.

FINANCIAL AID PICTURE (2008-2009)

Students with need: Out of 371 full-time freshmen who applied for aid, 351 were judged to have need. Of these, 350 received aid, and 78 had their full need met. Average financial aid package met 78% of need; average scholarship/grant was $13,570; average loan was $2,859. For part-time students, average financial aid package was $7,196.

Students without need: 20 full-time freshmen who did not demonstrate need for aid received scholarships/grants; average award was $6,763. No-need awards available for academics, art, athletics, leadership, minority status, music/drama, religious affiliation, ROTC, state/district residency.

Scholarships offered: 19 full-time freshmen received athletic scholarships; average amount $8,347.

Cumulative student debt: 90% of graduating class had student loans; average debt was $21,500.

Additional info: Matching scholarships available for students whose church contributes $200 annually. Performance grants available to members of marching band.

FINANCIAL AID PROCEDURES

Forms required: FAFSA.

Dates and Deadlines: Priority date 4/1; no closing date. Applicants notified on a rolling basis starting 5/15.

CONTACT

Chris Tolson, Director of Financial Aid

One University Drive, Campbellsville, KY 42718-2799

(270) 789-5013

Centre College

Danville, Kentucky

www.centre.edu   Federal Code: 001961

4-year private liberal arts college in large town, affiliated with Presbyterian Church (USA).

Enrollment: 1,214 undergrads. 332 full-time freshmen.

Selectivity: Admits 50 to 75% of applicants.

BASIC COSTS (2009-2010)

Comprehensive fee: $39,000.

Additional info: Reduced comprehensive fee may be available if student is approved to live off-campus by dean of students.

FINANCIAL AID PICTURE (2009-2010)

Students with need: Out of 272 full-time freshmen who applied for aid, 214 were judged to have need. Of these, 214 received aid, and 98 had their full need met. Average financial aid package met 92% of need; average scholarship/grant was $23,827; average loan was $3,618.

Students without need: 110 full-time freshmen who did not demonstrate need for aid received scholarships/grants; average award was $17,038. No-need awards available for academics, alumni affiliation, music/drama, ROTC.

Scholarships offered: Institutional Merit Award: $9,500 to full tuition; applications must be on file by February 1; renewable. Music and Drama Scholarships: up to $7,500. Guaranteed minimum award available to admitted Centre Fellows and Kentucky Governor's Scholars.

Cumulative student debt: 53% of graduating class had student loans; average debt was $17,190.

FINANCIAL AID PROCEDURES

Forms required: FAFSA, institutional form.

Dates and Deadlines: Closing date 3/1. Applicants notified by 3/25; must reply by 5/1 or within 2 week(s) of notification.

Transfers: No deadline. Applicants notified on a rolling basis starting 3/1; must reply within 2 week(s) of notification. Financial aid transcript required.

CONTACT

Elaine Larson, Director of Student Financial Planning

600 West Walnut Street, Danville, KY 40422-1394

(859) 238-5365

Clear Creek Baptist Bible College

Pineville, Kentucky

www.ccbbc.edu   Federal Code: 017044

4-year private Bible college in small town, affiliated with Southern Baptist Convention.

Enrollment: 168 undergrads, 26% part-time. 13 full-time freshmen.

Selectivity: Open admission.

BASIC COSTS (2010-2011)

Tuition and fees: $5,570.

Per-credit charge: $238.

Room and board: $3,750.

FINANCIAL AID PICTURE (2008-2009)

Students with need: Need-based aid available for full-time and part-time students. Work study available nights, weekends, and for part-time students.

Students without need: No-need awards available for academics.

FINANCIAL AID PROCEDURES

Forms required: FAFSA, institutional form.

Dates and Deadlines: Priority date 6/30; no closing date. Applicants notified on a rolling basis.

Transfers: Priority date 5/5; no deadline. Applicants notified on a rolling basis starting 5/5; must reply by 8/1.

CONTACT

Sam Risner, Director of Financial Aid

300 Clear Creek Road, Pineville, KY 40977-9754

(606) 337-3196 ext. 142

Daymar College: Owensboro

Owensboro, Kentucky
www.daymarcollege.edu   Federal Code: 009313

2-year for-profit business and junior college in small city.
Enrollment: 300 undergrads.
Selectivity: Open admission.

BASIC COSTS (2009-2010)
Tuition and fees: $13,190.
Per-credit charge: $270.

FINANCIAL AID PICTURE
Students with need: Need-based aid available for full-time and part-time students.
Students without need: This college awards aid only to students with need.

FINANCIAL AID PROCEDURES
Forms required: FAFSA.
Dates and Deadlines: No deadline. Applicants notified on a rolling basis.

CONTACT
Denise Jernigan, Director of Financial Services
3361 Buckland Square, Owensboro, KY 42301
(270) 926-4040

Daymar College: Paducah

Paducah, Kentucky   Federal Code: 013661
www.daymarcollege.edu   CSS Code: 0669

2-year for-profit technical college in small city.
Enrollment: 410 undergrads.
Selectivity: Open admission.

BASIC COSTS (2009-2010)
Tuition and fees: $13,190.
Per-credit charge: $270.

FINANCIAL AID PICTURE
Students with need: Need-based aid available for full-time students.

FINANCIAL AID PROCEDURES
Forms required: FAFSA, CSS PROFILE.
Dates and Deadlines: No deadline. Applicants notified on a rolling basis; must reply within 3 week(s) of notification.

CONTACT
JoAnn Price, Financial Aid Officer
509 South 30th Street, Paducah, KY 42001

Draughons Junior College

Bowling Green, Kentucky
www.daymarcollege.edu   Federal Code: 004934

2-year for-profit branch campus and career college in large town.
Enrollment: 440 undergrads.
Selectivity: Open admission.

BASIC COSTS (2009-2010)
Tuition and fees: $12,870.
Per-credit charge: $270.

FINANCIAL AID PICTURE
Students with need: Need-based aid available for full-time and part-time students. Work study available nights.

Students without need: This college awards aid only to students with need.

FINANCIAL AID PROCEDURES
Forms required: FAFSA.
Dates and Deadlines: No deadline.

CONTACT
Janice Cutliff, Director of Financial Services
2421 Fitzgerald Industrial Drive, Bowling Green, KY 42101
(270) 843-6750

Eastern Kentucky University

Richmond, Kentucky
www.eku.edu   Federal Code: 001963

4-year public university in large town.
Enrollment: 13,151 undergrads, 12% part-time. 2,519 full-time freshmen.
Selectivity: Admits 50 to 75% of applicants.

BASIC COSTS (2009-2010)
Tuition and fees: $6,312; out-of-state residents $17,280.
Per-credit charge: $263; out-of-state residents $720.
Room and board: $6,480.

FINANCIAL AID PICTURE (2009-2010)
Students with need: Need-based aid available for full-time and part-time students. Work study available nights, weekends, and for part-time students.
Students without need: No-need awards available for academics, alumni affiliation, art, athletics, job skills, leadership, minority status, music/drama, ROTC.

FINANCIAL AID PROCEDURES
Forms required: FAFSA.
Dates and Deadlines: Priority date 3/15; no closing date. Applicants notified on a rolling basis starting 4/1.

CONTACT
Shelley Park, Director of Student Financial Assistance, Scholarship and Veteran Affairs
SSB CPO 54, 521 Lancaster Avenue, Richmond, KY 40475-3102

Elizabethtown Community and Technical College

Elizabethtown, Kentucky
www.elizabethtown.kctcs.edu   Federal Code: 001991

2-year public community and technical college in large town.
Enrollment: 4,438 undergrads.
Selectivity: Open admission; but selective for some programs.

BASIC COSTS (2009-2010)
Tuition and fees: $3,750; out-of-state residents $12,750.
Per-credit charge: $125; out-of-state residents $425.
Additional info: Contiguous counties pay $250 per credit hour.

FINANCIAL AID PICTURE
Students with need: Need-based aid available for full-time and part-time students. Work study available nights, weekends, and for part-time students.
Students without need: This college awards aid only to students with need.

FINANCIAL AID PROCEDURES
Forms required: FAFSA.
Dates and Deadlines: Priority date 4/1; no closing date. Applicants notified on a rolling basis starting 6/1; must reply within 2 week(s) of notification.
Transfers: Must reply within 2 week(s) of notification.

CONTACT

Michael Barlow, Director of Financial Aid
600 College Street Road, Elizabethtown, KY 42701
(270) 769-2371 ext. 68614

Georgetown College

Georgetown, Kentucky
www.georgetowncollege.edu   Federal Code: 001964

4-year private liberal arts college in large town, affiliated with Southern Baptist Convention.
Enrollment: 1,297 undergrads, 1% part-time. 378 full-time freshmen.
Selectivity: Admits over 75% of applicants.

BASIC COSTS (2010-2011)

Tuition and fees: $27,640.
Per-credit charge: $1,140.
Room and board: $7,320.
Additional info: Per-credit-hour charges: $800 for one course; $1,140 for more than one course or for credit hours over 18.

FINANCIAL AID PICTURE (2009-2010)

Students with need: Average financial aid package met 86.7% of need; average scholarship/grant was $21,622; average loan was $3,229.
Students without need: No-need awards available for academics, alumni affiliation, art, athletics, leadership, minority status, music/drama, religious affiliation, ROTC, state/district residency.
Cumulative student debt: 76% of graduating class had student loans; average debt was $24,462.

FINANCIAL AID PROCEDURES

Forms required: FAFSA, institutional form.
Dates and Deadlines: Priority date 2/15; closing date 3/15. Must reply by 5/1.

CONTACT

Rhyan Conyers, Director of Student Financial Planning
400 East College Street, Georgetown, KY 40324
(502) 863-8027

Hazard Community and Technical College

Hazard, Kentucky
www.hazard.kctcs.edu   Federal Code: 006962

2-year public community and technical college in small town.
Enrollment: 2,127 undergrads.
Selectivity: Open admission; but selective for some programs and for out-of-state students.

BASIC COSTS (2009-2010)

Tuition and fees: $3,750; out-of-state residents $12,750.
Per-credit charge: $125; out-of-state residents $425.
Additional info: Contiguous counties pay $250 per credit hour.

FINANCIAL AID PICTURE (2009-2010)

Students with need: Need-based aid available for full-time and part-time students.
Students without need: This college awards aid only to students with need.

FINANCIAL AID PROCEDURES

Forms required: FAFSA.
Dates and Deadlines: Priority date 4/1; no closing date. Applicants notified on a rolling basis starting 6/15; must reply within 2 week(s) of notification.

CONTACT

Chuck Anderson, Financial Aid Director
One Community College Drive, Hazard, KY 41701
(606) 487-3061

Hopkinsville Community College

Hopkinsville, Kentucky
www.hopkinsville.kctcs.edu   Federal Code: 001994

2-year public community college in small city.
Enrollment: 3,375 undergrads, 48% part-time. 398 full-time freshmen.
Selectivity: Open admission; but selective for some programs.

BASIC COSTS (2009-2010)

Tuition and fees: $3,750; out-of-state residents $12,750.
Per-credit charge: $125; out-of-state residents $425.
Additional info: Tuition reduction program available for qualified residents of contiguous states.

FINANCIAL AID PICTURE

Students with need: Need-based aid available for full-time and part-time students. Work study available nights.
Students without need: No-need awards available for academics, leadership, minority status, state/district residency.
Scholarships offered: The Rotary Scholars Program: two years of full-time study; any graduate of a Christian County high school (beginning with the Class of 2012); 2.5 high school GPA and 95% attendance required.
Additional info: ACT required for academic scholarships.

FINANCIAL AID PROCEDURES

Forms required: FAFSA.
Dates and Deadlines: No deadline. Applicants notified on a rolling basis starting 7/1.
Transfers: No deadline. Applicants notified on a rolling basis.

CONTACT

Janet Gunther, Director, Financial Aid
PO Box 2100, Hopkinsville, KY 42241-2100
(270) 707-3830

Kentucky Christian University

Grayson, Kentucky
www.kcu.edu   Federal Code: 001965

4-year private Bible and liberal arts college in small town, affiliated with Independent Christian Church/Church of Christ.
Enrollment: 675 undergrads.
Selectivity: Admits 50 to 75% of applicants.

BASIC COSTS (2009-2010)

Tuition and fees: $13,220.
Per-credit charge: $434.
Room and board: $5,800.

FINANCIAL AID PICTURE (2008-2009)

Students with need: Need-based aid available for full-time and part-time students. Work study available nights, weekends, and for part-time students.
Students without need: No-need awards available for academics, alumni affiliation, leadership, minority status, music/drama, religious affiliation.

FINANCIAL AID PROCEDURES

Forms required: FAFSA.
Dates and Deadlines: Priority date 3/1; no closing date. Applicants notified on a rolling basis starting 3/15; must reply within 2 week(s) of notification.

CONTACT

Jennie Bender, Director of Financial Aid

100 Academic Parkway, Grayson, KY 41143-2205

(606) 474-3226

Kentucky Mountain Bible College

Vancleve, Kentucky

www.kmbc.edu   Federal Code: 030021

4-year private Bible college in rural community, affiliated with Kentucky Mountain Holiness Association.

Enrollment: 60 undergrads.

Selectivity: Open admission; but selective for some programs and for out-of-state students.

BASIC COSTS (2010-2011)

Tuition and fees: $6,490.

Per-credit charge: $195.

Room and board: $4,000.

FINANCIAL AID PICTURE (2009-2010)

Students with need: 55% of average financial aid package awarded as scholarships/grants, 45% awarded as loans/jobs. Need-based aid available for part-time students. Work study available nights, weekends, and for part-time students.

Students without need: No-need awards available for academics, job skills, leadership, music/drama.

FINANCIAL AID PROCEDURES

Forms required: FAFSA, institutional form.

Dates and Deadlines: Priority date 4/1; closing date 6/30. Applicants notified on a rolling basis starting 3/15.

Transfers: No deadline. Applicants notified on a rolling basis starting 8/30; must reply within 6 week(s) of notification.

CONTACT

Jonette Englehardt, Director of Financial Aid

Box 10, Vancleve, KY 41385-0010

(606) 693-5000 ext. 175

Kentucky State University

Frankfort, Kentucky

www.kysu.edu   Federal Code: 001968

4-year public university and liberal arts college in large town.

Enrollment: 2,326 undergrads, 12% part-time. 526 full-time freshmen.

BASIC COSTS (2009-2010)

Tuition and fees: $5,920; out-of-state residents $14,208.

Per-credit charge: $197; out-of-state residents $474.

Room and board: $6,480.

Additional info: Tuition/fee waivers available for minority students, unemployed or children of unemployed.

FINANCIAL AID PICTURE (2009-2010)

Students with need: Out of 457 full-time freshmen who applied for aid, 455 were judged to have need. Of these, 414 received aid, and 77 had their full need met. Average financial aid package met 18% of need; average scholarship/grant was $5,739; average loan was $3,441. For part-time students, average financial aid package was $5,301.

Students without need: 19 full-time freshmen who did not demonstrate need for aid received scholarships/grants; average award was $5,246. No-need awards available for academics, alumni affiliation, art, athletics, minority status, music/drama.

Scholarships offered: 32 full-time freshmen received athletic scholarships; average amount $4,816.

Cumulative student debt: 76% of graduating class had student loans; average debt was $35,552.

FINANCIAL AID PROCEDURES

Forms required: FAFSA.

Dates and Deadlines: Priority date 4/15; no closing date. Applicants notified by 4/1; must reply within 2 week(s) of notification.

Transfers: No deadline. Applicants notified on a rolling basis; must reply within 2 week(s) of notification.

CONTACT

Carmella Conner, Director of Financial Aid

400 East Main Street, ASB 312, Frankfort, KY 40601

(502) 597-5960

Kentucky Wesleyan College

Owensboro, Kentucky

www.kwc.edu   Federal Code: 001969

4-year private liberal arts college in small city, affiliated with United Methodist Church.

Enrollment: 862 undergrads, 3% part-time. 222 full-time freshmen.

Selectivity: Admits 50 to 75% of applicants.

BASIC COSTS (2010-2011)

Tuition and fees: $18,180.

Per-credit charge: $515.

Room and board: $6,730.

FINANCIAL AID PICTURE (2009-2010)

Students with need: Out of 210 full-time freshmen who applied for aid, 200 were judged to have need. Of these, 197 received aid, and 49 had their full need met. Average financial aid package met 80% of need; average scholarship/grant was $14,085; average loan was $3,347. For part-time students, average financial aid package was $6,691.

Students without need: 21 full-time freshmen who did not demonstrate need for aid received scholarships/grants; average award was $10,678. No-need awards available for academics, alumni affiliation, art, athletics, leadership, music/drama, religious affiliation, state/district residency.

Scholarships offered: Scholarships range from $1,000 to full tuition. Students compete in on-campus scholarship competitions.

Cumulative student debt: 89% of graduating class had student loans; average debt was $20,906.

FINANCIAL AID PROCEDURES

Forms required: FAFSA.

Dates and Deadlines: Closing date 3/15. Applicants notified on a rolling basis starting 2/15; must reply within 2 week(s) of notification.

CONTACT

Samantha Hayes, Director of Financial Aid

3000 Frederica Street, Owensboro, KY 42301

(270) 852-3130

Lindsey Wilson College

Columbia, Kentucky

www.lindsey.edu   Federal Code: 001972

4-year private liberal arts college in small town, affiliated with United Methodist Church.

Enrollment: 1,700 undergrads.

Selectivity: Open admission; but selective for some programs.

BASIC COSTS (2009-2010)

Tuition and fees: $17,870.

Per-credit charge: $735.

Room and board: $7,280.

FINANCIAL AID PICTURE (2008-2009)
Students with need: Need-based aid available for full-time and part-time students.
Students without need: This college awards aid only to students with need.

FINANCIAL AID PROCEDURES
Forms required: FAFSA, institutional form.
Dates and Deadlines: Priority date 4/15; no closing date. Applicants notified on a rolling basis starting 5/1; must reply within 2 week(s) of notification.
Transfers: Applicants notified on a rolling basis.

CONTACT
Roger Drake, Vice President for Administration and Finance
210 Lindsey Wilson Street, Columbia, KY 42728
(270) 384-8022

Madisonville Community College
Madisonville, Kentucky
www.madisonville.kctcs.edu   Federal Code: 009010

2-year public community college in large town.
Enrollment: 4,100 undergrads.
Selectivity: Open admission; but selective for some programs.

BASIC COSTS (2009-2010)
Tuition and fees: $3,750; out-of-state residents $12,750.
Per-credit charge: $125; out-of-state residents $425.
Additional info: Tuition reduction program available for qualified residents of contiguous states. Tuition/fee waivers available for minority students, unemployed or children of unemployed.

FINANCIAL AID PICTURE (2008-2009)
Students with need: Need-based aid available for full-time and part-time students. Work study available nights, weekends, and for part-time students.
Students without need: No-need awards available for minority status.

FINANCIAL AID PROCEDURES
Forms required: FAFSA, institutional form.
Dates and Deadlines: Priority date 3/15; no closing date. Applicants notified on a rolling basis; must reply within 3 week(s) of notification.

CONTACT
Caroline Clayton, Director of Financial Aid
2000 College Drive, Madisonville, KY 42431
(270) 821-6514

Maysville Community and Technical College
Maysville, Kentucky
www.maysville.kctcs.edu   Federal Code: 006960

2-year public community and technical college in small town.
Enrollment: 4,128 undergrads.
Selectivity: Open admission; but selective for some programs.

BASIC COSTS (2009-2010)
Tuition and fees: $3,750; out-of-state residents $12,750.
Per-credit charge: $125; out-of-state residents $425.
Additional info: Contiguous counties pay $250 per credit hour.

FINANCIAL AID PICTURE (2008-2009)
Students with need: Need-based aid available for full-time and part-time students. Work study available nights.
Students without need: No-need awards available for academics.

FINANCIAL AID PROCEDURES
Forms required: FAFSA, institutional form.
Dates and Deadlines: Priority date 4/1; no closing date. Applicants notified on a rolling basis starting 3/1; must reply within 3 week(s) of notification.

CONTACT
Leslie Storie, Financial Aid Director
1755 US Highway 68, Maysville, KY 41056
(606) 759-7141 ext. 66207

Mid-Continent University
Mayfield, Kentucky
www.midcontinent.edu   Federal Code: 025762

4-year private Bible and liberal arts college in large town, affiliated with Southern Baptist Convention.
Enrollment: 1,822 undergrads, 13% part-time. 169 full-time freshmen.
Selectivity: Admits 50 to 75% of applicants.

BASIC COSTS (2010-2011)
Tuition and fees: $13,350.
Per-credit charge: $403.
Room and board: $6,600.

FINANCIAL AID PICTURE (2009-2010)
Students with need: Average financial aid package met 33% of need; average scholarship/grant was $5,479; average loan was $2,338. For part-time students, average financial aid package was $4,227.
Students without need: No-need awards available for academics.
Cumulative student debt: 82% of graduating class had student loans; average debt was $13,197.

FINANCIAL AID PROCEDURES
Forms required: FAFSA, institutional form.
Dates and Deadlines: Priority date 3/15; closing date 5/30. Applicants notified on a rolling basis starting 4/1; must reply within 2 week(s) of notification.
Transfers: No deadline. Must reply within 2 week(s) of notification.

CONTACT
Kent Youngblood, Director of Financial Aid
99 Powell Road East, Mayfield, KY 42066-0357
(270) 247-8521 ext. 260

Midway College
Midway, Kentucky
www.midway.edu   Federal Code: 001975

4-year private liberal arts college for women in small town, affiliated with Christian Church (Disciples of Christ).
Enrollment: 1,316 undergrads. 145 full-time freshmen.
Selectivity: Admits less than 50% of applicants.

BASIC COSTS (2009-2010)
Tuition and fees: $18,000.
Per-credit charge: $600.
Room and board: $6,800.

FINANCIAL AID PICTURE
Students with need: Need-based aid available for full-time and part-time students.
Students without need: No-need awards available for academics, alumni affiliation, art, athletics, leadership, minority status, religious affiliation.
Additional info: Audition required of applicants for music scholarships. Portfolio required for art scholarships.

FINANCIAL AID PROCEDURES
Forms required: FAFSA, institutional form.

Dates and Deadlines: Priority date 4/1; closing date 8/1. Applicants notified on a rolling basis; must reply within 4 week(s) of notification.

CONTACT
Katie Conrad, Director of Financial Aid
512 East Stephens Street, Midway, KY 40347-1120
(859) 846-5410

Morehead State University
Morehead, Kentucky
www.moreheadstate.edu   Federal Code: 001976

4-year public university in large town.
Enrollment: 6,725 undergrads, 17% part-time. 1,300 full-time freshmen.
Selectivity: Admits over 75% of applicants.

BASIC COSTS (2009-2010)
Tuition and fees: $6,036; out-of-state residents $15,096.
Per-credit charge: $234; out-of-state residents $585.
Room and board: $6,192.
Additional info: Tuition is based on enrollment of 15 credit hours.

FINANCIAL AID PICTURE (2008-2009)
Students with need: Out of 1,146 full-time freshmen who applied for aid, 891 were judged to have need. Of these, 881 received aid, and 357 had their full need met. Average financial aid package met 76% of need; average scholarship/grant was $5,126; average loan was $2,954. For part-time students, average financial aid package was $6,024.
Students without need: 218 full-time freshmen who did not demonstrate need for aid received scholarships/grants; average award was $6,588. No-need awards available for academics, alumni affiliation, art, athletics, leadership, minority status, music/drama, ROTC, state/district residency.
Scholarships offered: 81 full-time freshmen received athletic scholarships; average amount $4,599.
Cumulative student debt: 72% of graduating class had student loans; average debt was $20,404.

FINANCIAL AID PROCEDURES
Forms required: FAFSA, institutional form.
Dates and Deadlines: Priority date 3/15; no closing date. Applicants notified on a rolling basis.
Transfers: Transfer scholarships available.

CONTACT
Donna King, Director of Financial Aid
100 Admissions Center, Morehead, KY 40351
(606) 783-2011

Murray State University
Murray, Kentucky
www.murraystate.edu   Federal Code: 001977

4-year public university in large town.
Enrollment: 7,571 undergrads, 11% part-time. 1,376 full-time freshmen.

BASIC COSTS (2009-2010)
Tuition and fees: $5,976; out-of-district residents $8,852; out-of-state residents $16,236.
Per-credit charge: $249; out-of-state residents $677.
Room and board: $6,562.
Additional info: Tuition/fee waivers available for minority students.

FINANCIAL AID PICTURE (2009-2010)
Students with need: For part-time students, average financial aid package was $4,809.

Students without need: 624 full-time freshmen who did not demonstrate need for aid received scholarships/grants; average award was $2,275. No-need awards available for academics, alumni affiliation, art, athletics, job skills, leadership, minority status, music/drama, ROTC, state/district residency.
Scholarships offered: 60 full-time freshmen received athletic scholarships; average amount $8,884.
Additional info: Tuition discount for children and grandchildren of out-of-state alumni. Regional tuition for students from certain counties in Illinois, Tennessee, Missouri, and Indiana.

FINANCIAL AID PROCEDURES
Forms required: FAFSA, institutional form.
Dates and Deadlines: Priority date 4/1; no closing date. Applicants notified on a rolling basis starting 4/15.
Transfers: No deadline. Applicants notified on a rolling basis starting 4/15.

CONTACT
Lori Mitchum, Director of Financial Aid
102 Curris Center Murray State University, Murray, KY 42071
(270) 809-2546

National College: Danville
Danville, Kentucky
www.ncbt.edu   Federal Code: 010489

2-year for-profit business college in large town.
Enrollment: 474 undergrads.
Selectivity: Open admission.

BASIC COSTS (2009-2010)
Tuition and fees: $10,080.
Per-credit charge: $223.

FINANCIAL AID PICTURE
Students with need: Need-based aid available for full-time and part-time students.
Students without need: This college awards aid only to students with need.

FINANCIAL AID PROCEDURES
Forms required: FAFSA.
Dates and Deadlines: No deadline. Applicants notified on a rolling basis.

CONTACT
Pamela Cotton, Director of Financial Aid and Compliance Officer
PO Box 6400, Roanoke, VA 24017
(540) 986-1800

National College: Florence
Florence, Kentucky
www.ncbt.edu   Federal Code: 010489

2-year for-profit business college in large town.
Enrollment: 204 undergrads.
Selectivity: Open admission.

BASIC COSTS (2009-2010)
Tuition and fees: $10,080.
Per-credit charge: $223.

FINANCIAL AID PICTURE
Students with need: Need-based aid available for full-time and part-time students.
Students without need: This college awards aid only to students with need.

FINANCIAL AID PROCEDURES

Forms required: FAFSA.

Dates and Deadlines: No deadline. Applicants notified on a rolling basis.

CONTACT

Pamela Cotton, Director of Financial Aid and Compliance Officer
PO Box 6400, Roanoke, VA 24017
(540) 986-1800

National College: Lexington

Lexington, Kentucky
www.ncbt.edu   Federal Code: 010489

2-year for-profit business and junior college in small city.

Enrollment: 768 undergrads.

Selectivity: Open admission.

BASIC COSTS (2009-2010)

Tuition and fees: $10,080.

Per-credit charge: $223.

FINANCIAL AID PICTURE

Students with need: Need-based aid available for full-time and part-time students.

Students without need: This college awards aid only to students with need.

FINANCIAL AID PROCEDURES

Forms required: FAFSA.

Dates and Deadlines: No deadline. Applicants notified on a rolling basis.

CONTACT

Pamela Cotton, Director of Financial Aid and Compliance Officer
PO Box 6400, Roanoke, VA 24017
(859) 255-0621

National College: Louisville

Louisville, Kentucky
www.ncbt.edu   Federal Code: 010489

2-year for-profit business college in large city.

Enrollment: 926 undergrads.

Selectivity: Open admission.

BASIC COSTS (2009-2010)

Tuition and fees: $10,080.

Per-credit charge: $223.

FINANCIAL AID PICTURE

Students with need: Need-based aid available for full-time and part-time students.

Students without need: This college awards aid only to students with need.

FINANCIAL AID PROCEDURES

Forms required: FAFSA.

Dates and Deadlines: No deadline. Applicants notified on a rolling basis.

CONTACT

Pamela Cotton, Director of Financial Aid and Compliance Officer
PO Box 6400, Roanoke, VA 24017
(540) 986-1800

National College: Pikeville

Pikeville, Kentucky
www.ncbt.edu   Federal Code: 010489

2-year for-profit business college in large town.

Enrollment: 308 undergrads.

Selectivity: Open admission.

BASIC COSTS (2009-2010)

Tuition and fees: $10,080.

Per-credit charge: $223.

FINANCIAL AID PICTURE

Students with need: Need-based aid available for full-time and part-time students.

Students without need: This college awards aid only to students with need.

FINANCIAL AID PROCEDURES

Forms required: FAFSA.

Dates and Deadlines: No deadline.

CONTACT

Pamela Cotton, Director of Financial Aid and Compliance Officer
PO Box 6400, Roanoke, VA 24017
(540) 986-1800

National College: Richmond

Richmond, Kentucky
www.ncbt.edu   Federal Code: 010489

2-year for-profit business college in large town.

Enrollment: 453 undergrads.

Selectivity: Open admission.

BASIC COSTS (2009-2010)

Tuition and fees: $10,080.

Per-credit charge: $223.

FINANCIAL AID PICTURE

Students with need: Need-based aid available for full-time and part-time students.

Students without need: This college awards aid only to students with need.

FINANCIAL AID PROCEDURES

Forms required: FAFSA.

Dates and Deadlines: No deadline. Applicants notified on a rolling basis.

CONTACT

Pamela Cotton, Director of Financial Aid and Compliance Officer
PO Box 6400, Roanoke, VA 24017
(540) 986-1800

Northern Kentucky University

Highland Heights, Kentucky
www.nku.edu   Federal Code: 009275

4-year public university in small town.

Enrollment: 12,461 undergrads, 20% part-time. 2,001 full-time freshmen.

Selectivity: Admits 50 to 75% of applicants.

BASIC COSTS (2009-2010)

Tuition and fees: $6,792; out-of-state residents $12,792.

Per-credit charge: $283; out-of-state residents $533.

Room and board: $7,210.

FINANCIAL AID PICTURE (2008-2009)

Students with need: Out of 1,609 full-time freshmen who applied for aid, 1,178 were judged to have need. Of these, 1,167 received aid, and 213 had their full need met. Average financial aid package met 58% of need; average scholarship/grant was $5,379; average loan was $2,971. For part-time students, average financial aid package was $5,430.

Students without need: 206 full-time freshmen who did not demonstrate need for aid received scholarships/grants; average award was $3,531. No-need awards available for academics, alumni affiliation, art, athletics, leadership, music/drama, state/district residency.

Scholarships offered: 36 full-time freshmen received athletic scholarships; average amount $4,630.

Cumulative student debt: 40% of graduating class had student loans; average debt was $23,129.

FINANCIAL AID PROCEDURES

Forms required: FAFSA.

Dates and Deadlines: Priority date 3/1; no closing date. Applicants notified on a rolling basis starting 4/1.

Transfers: Applicants notified by 5/30.

CONTACT

Leah Stewart, Director of Financial Assistance
Administrative Center 401, Northern Kentucky University, Highland Heights, KY 41099
(859) 572-5143

Owensboro Community and Technical College

Owensboro, Kentucky
www.octc.kctcs.edu
Federal Code: 030345

2-year public community and technical college in small city.

Enrollment: 3,571 undergrads, 41% part-time. 186 full-time freshmen.

Selectivity: Open admission; but selective for some programs.

BASIC COSTS (2009-2010)

Tuition and fees: $3,750; out-of-state residents $12,750.

Per-credit charge: $125; out-of-state residents $425.

Additional info: Contiguous counties pay $250 per credit hour.

FINANCIAL AID PICTURE (2008-2009)

Students with need: Need-based aid available for full-time and part-time students.

Students without need: No-need awards available for academics, state/district residency.

FINANCIAL AID PROCEDURES

Forms required: FAFSA.

Dates and Deadlines: Priority date 3/16; no closing date. Must reply within 2 week(s) of notification.

Transfers: Must have financial aid transcripts from previous institutions.

CONTACT

Bernice Ayer, Financial Aid Officer
4800 New Hartford Road, Owensboro, KY 42303-1899
(270) 686-4655

Pikeville College

Pikeville, Kentucky
www.pc.edu
Federal Code: 001980

4-year private liberal arts college in small town, affiliated with Presbyterian Church (USA).

Enrollment: 673 undergrads, 7% part-time. 185 full-time freshmen.

Selectivity: Open admission; but selective for some programs.

BASIC COSTS (2010-2011)

Tuition and fees: $15,250.

Per-credit charge: $635.

Room and board: $6,300.

FINANCIAL AID PICTURE (2009-2010)

Students with need: Out of 185 full-time freshmen who applied for aid, 184 were judged to have need. Of these, 184 received aid, and 137 had their full need met. Average financial aid package met 93% of need; average scholarship/grant was $12,894; average loan was $3,457. For part-time students, average financial aid package was $7,554.

Students without need: This college awards aid only to students with need.

Cumulative student debt: 76% of graduating class had student loans; average debt was $18,103.

FINANCIAL AID PROCEDURES

Forms required: FAFSA, institutional form.

Dates and Deadlines: Priority date 3/15; no closing date. Applicants notified on a rolling basis starting 2/1; must reply by 5/1 or within 2 week(s) of notification.

Transfers: No deadline. Must reply by 5/1 or within 2 week(s) of notification.

CONTACT

Judy Bradley, Financial Aid Director
147 Sycamore Street, Pikeville, KY 41501-1194
(606) 218-5251

St. Catharine College

St. Catharine, Kentucky
www.sccky.edu
Federal Code: 001983

4-year private health science and liberal arts college in small town, affiliated with Roman Catholic Church.

Enrollment: 600 full-time undergrads.

Selectivity: Open admission.

BASIC COSTS (2009-2010)

Tuition and fees: $14,740.

Per-credit charge: $505.

Room and board: $7,210.

Additional info: Higher tuition applies for health science program.

FINANCIAL AID PICTURE

Students with need: Need-based aid available for full-time and part-time students.

Students without need: This college awards aid only to students with need.

FINANCIAL AID PROCEDURES

Forms required: FAFSA, institutional form.

Dates and Deadlines: Priority date 3/15; no closing date. Applicants notified on a rolling basis.

CONTACT

Laura Dean, Financial Aid Director
2735 Bardstown Road, St. Catharine, KY 40061
(502) 336-5082 ext. 1216

Somerset Community College

Somerset, Kentucky
www.somerset.kctcs.edu
Federal Code: 001997

2-year public community and technical college in large town.

Enrollment: 5,936 undergrads.

Selectivity: Open admission; but selective for some programs.

BASIC COSTS (2009-2010)

Tuition and fees: $3,750; out-of-state residents $12,750.
Per-credit charge: $125; out-of-state residents $425.
Additional info: Nonresident, Contiguous County: $250/credit hour or $7,500 per year.

FINANCIAL AID PICTURE (2008-2009)

Students with need: Need-based aid available for full-time and part-time students.
Students without need: This college awards aid only to students with need.

FINANCIAL AID PROCEDURES

Forms required: FAFSA.
Dates and Deadlines: Priority date 3/1; no closing date. Applicants notified on a rolling basis starting 5/1; must reply within 2 week(s) of notification.
Transfers: Priority date 3/15; closing date 8/15. Applicants notified on a rolling basis starting 5/1; must reply within 2 week(s) of notification.

CONTACT

Shawn Anderson, Chief Financial Aid Officer
808 Monticello Street, Somerset, KY 42501
(606) 679-8501 ext. 16640

Southeast Kentucky Community and Technical College

Cumberland, Kentucky
www.secc.kctcs.edu   Federal Code: 001998

2-year public community and technical college in small town.
Enrollment: 2,223 undergrads, 40% part-time. 648 full-time freshmen.
Selectivity: Open admission; but selective for some programs.

BASIC COSTS (2009-2010)

Tuition and fees: $3,750; out-of-state residents $12,750.
Per-credit charge: $125; out-of-state residents $425.
Additional info: Contiguous counties pay $250 per credit hour.

FINANCIAL AID PICTURE (2009-2010)

Students with need: Average financial aid package met 100% of need; average scholarship/grant was $3,200; average loan was $2,100. For part-time students, average financial aid package was $3,800.
Students without need: This college awards aid only to students with need.
Additional info: March 15 deadline for state financial aid.

FINANCIAL AID PROCEDURES

Forms required: FAFSA.
Dates and Deadlines: Priority date 3/15; no closing date. Must reply within 2 week(s) of notification.

CONTACT

Rebecca Robbins, Associate Dean of Student Affairs/Director Financial Aid
700 College Road, Cumberland, KY 40823
(606) 589-2145

Spalding University

Louisville, Kentucky
www.spalding.edu   Federal Code: 001960

4-year private university in large city, affiliated with Roman Catholic Church.
Enrollment: 1,180 undergrads, 27% part-time. 93 full-time freshmen.
Selectivity: Admits less than 50% of applicants.

BASIC COSTS (2009-2010)

Tuition and fees: $18,000.
Per-credit charge: $570.

Room only: $2,000.

FINANCIAL AID PICTURE (2008-2009)

Students with need: Need-based aid available for full-time and part-time students. Work study available nights, weekends, and for part-time students.
Students without need: No-need awards available for academics, religious affiliation.
Scholarships offered: Angela Garcia Residence Hall Scholarship: covers cost of a double room on campus; up to 12 awards per year; awarded to students who demonstrate leadership in campus activities, especially in residence halls.

FINANCIAL AID PROCEDURES

Forms required: FAFSA.
Dates and Deadlines: Priority date 3/1; no closing date. Applicants notified on a rolling basis starting 3/31; must reply within 2 week(s) of notification.

CONTACT

Gina Kuzuoka, Director of Financial Aid
845 South Third Street, Louisville, KY 40203
(502) 588-9911 ext. 2240

Spencerian College: Lexington

Lexington, Kentucky
www.spencerian.edu   Federal Code: 004618

2-year for-profit branch campus and technical college in small city.
Enrollment: 616 undergrads, 15% part-time. 401 full-time freshmen.
Selectivity: Open admission; but selective for some programs.

BASIC COSTS (2009-2010)

Tuition and fees: $11,040.
Per-credit charge: $315.
Additional info: Cost of programs ranges from $9,000 to $41,000; program-specific fees are additional. Cost of housing is $520 per month. Per-credit-hour charge ranges from $235 to $380 depending on program.

FINANCIAL AID PICTURE (2009-2010)

Students with need: Need-based aid available for full-time and part-time students.
Students without need: This college awards aid only to students with need.

FINANCIAL AID PROCEDURES

Forms required: FAFSA, state aid form, institutional form.
Dates and Deadlines: No deadline. Applicants notified on a rolling basis starting 1/1.
Transfers: No deadline. Applicants notified on a rolling basis.

CONTACT

Brian Highley, Director of Financial Planning
1575 Winchester Road, Lexington, KY 40505
(859) 223-9608 ext. 5441

Sullivan College of Technology and Design

Louisville, Kentucky
www.sctd.edu   Federal Code: 012088

2-year for-profit technical and career college in very large city.
Enrollment: 631 undergrads, 33% part-time. 138 full-time freshmen.
Selectivity: Admits over 75% of applicants.

BASIC COSTS (2009-2010)

Additional info: Tuition ranges from $15,570 to $18,165, depending upon program; average full-time tuition, approximately $16,425. Part-time students pay approximately $365 per-credit-hour. Required fees, $540; additional fee of $50 per-credit-hour for online courses. On-campus room $4,950 and board $1,800 for 3 quarters. Tuition at time of enrollment locked for 2 years; tuition/fee waivers available for adults.

FINANCIAL AID PICTURE (2008-2009)

Students with need: 24% of average financial aid package awarded as scholarships/grants, 76% awarded as loans/jobs. Need-based aid available for part-time students. Work study available nights.

Students without need: No-need awards available for academics, art, job skills.

Scholarships offered: Academic Scholarships; up to $3,000; based on class rank, GPA, essay. Scholarship Day Competition; up to $1,500 based upon testing scores. Scholarship Fair Competition; up to $3,000; based upon open competition in electronics, drafting, interior design, computer networking and art skills. Kentucky Skills USA Scholarships; up to $1,500; based upon state championship competitions in such fields as drafting, electronics, etc.

FINANCIAL AID PROCEDURES

Forms required: FAFSA.

Dates and Deadlines: No deadline. Applicants notified on a rolling basis; must reply within 2 week(s) of notification.

Transfers: No deadline. Applicants notified on a rolling basis.

CONTACT

Andre Downing, Financial Planning Director
3901 Atkinson Square Drive, Louisville, KY 40218-4524
(502) 456-6509

Sullivan University
Louisville, Kentucky
www.sullivan.edu   Federal Code: 004619

4-year for-profit university in large city.
Enrollment: 5,122 undergrads.

BASIC COSTS (2009-2010)

Room only: $4,950.
Additional info: Tuition, fees and per-credit-hour charges vary by program. Tuition costs range from $15,600 to $16,860 per academic year.

FINANCIAL AID PICTURE

Students with need: Need-based aid available for full-time and part-time students. Work study available nights.

Students without need: This college awards aid only to students with need.

FINANCIAL AID PROCEDURES

Forms required: FAFSA.

Dates and Deadlines: No deadline. Applicants notified on a rolling basis starting 1/2.

CONTACT

Lisa Wright, Financial Planning Director
3101 Bardstown Road, Louisville, KY 40205
(502) 456-6505

Thomas More College
Crestview Hills, Kentucky
www.thomasmore.edu   Federal Code: 002001

4-year private liberal arts college in small town, affiliated with Roman Catholic Church.
Enrollment: 1,415 undergrads, 7% part-time. 306 full-time freshmen.
Selectivity: Admits over 75% of applicants.

BASIC COSTS (2010-2011)

Tuition and fees: $24,720.
Per-credit charge: $545.
Room and board: $6,790.

FINANCIAL AID PICTURE (2009-2010)

Students with need: Out of 278 full-time freshmen who applied for aid, 241 were judged to have need. Of these, 240 received aid, and 77 had their full need met. Average financial aid package met 78% of need; average scholarship/grant was $11,950; average loan was $3,538. For part-time students, average financial aid package was $5,905.

Students without need: 50 full-time freshmen who did not demonstrate need for aid received scholarships/grants; average award was $13,224. No-need awards available for academics, alumni affiliation, art, job skills, leadership, minority status, music/drama, religious affiliation, ROTC, state/district residency.

Cumulative student debt: 75% of graduating class had student loans; average debt was $25,918.

FINANCIAL AID PROCEDURES

Forms required: FAFSA.

Dates and Deadlines: Priority date 3/15; no closing date. Applicants notified on a rolling basis starting 10/1.

Transfers: No deadline. Applicants notified on a rolling basis; must reply by 5/1.

CONTACT

Mary Givhan, Director of Financial Aid
333 Thomas More Parkway, Crestview Hills, KY 41017-3495
(859) 344-4043

Transylvania University
Lexington, Kentucky
www.transy.edu   Federal Code: 001987

4-year private liberal arts college in large city, affiliated with Christian Church (Disciples of Christ).
Enrollment: 1,088 undergrads. 283 full-time freshmen.
Selectivity: Admits over 75% of applicants.

BASIC COSTS (2009-2010)

Tuition and fees: $25,280.
Room and board: $7,770.
Additional info: Tuition/fee waivers available for minority students.

FINANCIAL AID PICTURE (2009-2010)

Students with need: 73% of average financial aid package awarded as scholarships/grants, 27% awarded as loans/jobs. Need-based aid available for part-time students. Work study available nights, weekends, and for part-time students.

Students without need: No-need awards available for academics, art, leadership, minority status, music/drama, religious affiliation, ROTC, state/district residency.

Scholarships offered: William T. Young Merit Scholarships: 25 awarded; tuition and fees.

Additional info: Auditions and portfolios required for music and art scholarships respectively. Essays required for other scholarship programs. Applications for William T. Young scholarships must be received by December 1.

FINANCIAL AID PROCEDURES

Forms required: FAFSA.

Dates and Deadlines: Priority date 3/1; no closing date. Applicants notified on a rolling basis starting 3/15; must reply by 5/1 or within 2 week(s) of notification.

Transfers: No deadline. Applicants notified on a rolling basis starting 3/15; must reply by 8/6.

CONTACT

David Cecil, Director of Financial Aid
300 North Broadway, Lexington, KY 40508-1797
(859) 233-8239

Union College

Barbourville, Kentucky
www.unionky.edu   Federal Code: 001988

4-year private liberal arts and teachers college in small town, affiliated with United Methodist Church.

Enrollment: 811 undergrads, 6% part-time. 190 full-time freshmen.

Selectivity: Admits less than 50% of applicants.

BASIC COSTS (2010-2011)

Tuition and fees: $18,860.

Per-credit charge: $305.

Room and board: $5,950.

FINANCIAL AID PICTURE (2009-2010)

Students with need: Out of 183 full-time freshmen who applied for aid, 183 were judged to have need. Of these, 170 received aid, and 36 had their full need met. Average financial aid package met 75% of need; average scholarship/grant was $12,644; average loan was $6,280. For part-time students, average financial aid package was $11,145.

Students without need: 18 full-time freshmen who did not demonstrate need for aid received scholarships/grants; average award was $10,522. No-need awards available for academics, athletics, leadership, music/drama, religious affiliation, state/district residency.

Cumulative student debt: 73% of graduating class had student loans; average debt was $22,388.

FINANCIAL AID PROCEDURES

Forms required: FAFSA.

Dates and Deadlines: Priority date 3/15; no closing date. Applicants notified on a rolling basis starting 3/1; must reply within 2 week(s) of notification.

CONTACT

Sue Buttery, Associate Dean for Financial Aid
310 College Street, Box 005, Barbourville, KY 40906
(606) 546-1618

University of Kentucky

Lexington, Kentucky
www.uky.edu   Federal Code: 001989

4-year public university in large city.

Enrollment: 18,806 undergrads, 7% part-time. 4,111 full-time freshmen.

Selectivity: Admits 50 to 75% of applicants.

BASIC COSTS (2009-2010)

Tuition and fees: $8,123; out-of-state residents $16,678.

Per-credit charge: $323; out-of-state residents $680.

Room and board: $9,125.

Additional info: Tuition/fee waivers available for adults, minority students.

FINANCIAL AID PICTURE (2009-2010)

Students with need: Need-based aid available for full-time and part-time students. Work study available weekends and for part-time students.

Students without need: No-need awards available for academics, alumni affiliation, art, athletics, job skills, leadership, minority status, music/drama, ROTC, state/district residency.

FINANCIAL AID PROCEDURES

Forms required: FAFSA.

Dates and Deadlines: Closing date 2/15. Applicants notified on a rolling basis starting 4/1; must reply within 3 week(s) of notification.

Transfers: Priority date 4/1.

CONTACT

Lynda George, Director of Student Financial Aid
100 W.D. Funkhouser Building, Lexington, KY 40506-0054
(859) 257-3172

University of Louisville

Louisville, Kentucky
www.louisville.edu   Federal Code: 001999

4-year public university in very large city.

Enrollment: 14,591 undergrads, 19% part-time. 2,442 full-time freshmen.

Selectivity: Admits 50 to 75% of applicants.

BASIC COSTS (2009-2010)

Tuition and fees: $7,944; out-of-state residents $19,272.

Per-credit charge: $331; out-of-state residents $803.

Room and board: $5,437.

Additional info: All full-time students not living on campus are required to purchase a $175 meal plan per semester.

FINANCIAL AID PICTURE (2009-2010)

Students with need: Need-based aid available for full-time and part-time students.

Students without need: No-need awards available for academics, art, athletics, leadership, minority status, music/drama, ROTC.

FINANCIAL AID PROCEDURES

Forms required: FAFSA.

Dates and Deadlines: Priority date 3/15; no closing date. Applicants notified on a rolling basis starting 4/1.

Transfers: Priority date 3/1.

CONTACT

Patricia Arauz, Director of Student Financial Aid
2211 South Brook Street, Louisville, KY 40292
(502) 852-5511

University of the Cumberlands

Williamsburg, Kentucky
www.ucumberlands.edu   Federal Code: 001962

4-year private university and liberal arts college in small town, affiliated with Baptist faith.

Enrollment: 1,461 undergrads, 3% part-time. 454 full-time freshmen.

Selectivity: Admits 50 to 75% of applicants.

BASIC COSTS (2010-2011)

Tuition and fees: $17,000.

Per-credit charge: $530.

Room and board: $6,826.

FINANCIAL AID PICTURE (2009-2010)

Students with need: Out of 438 full-time freshmen who applied for aid, 403 were judged to have need. Of these, 403 received aid, and 87 had their full need met. Average financial aid package met 81% of need; average scholarship/grant was $13,211; average loan was $3,239. For part-time students, average financial aid package was $6,068.

Students without need: 47 full-time freshmen who did not demonstrate need for aid received scholarships/grants; average award was $6,152. No-need awards available for academics, athletics.

Scholarships offered: 47 full-time freshmen received athletic scholarships; average amount $5,540.

Cumulative student debt: 79% of graduating class had student loans; average debt was $15,521.

FINANCIAL AID PROCEDURES

Forms required: FAFSA.

Dates and Deadlines: Priority date 3/1; no closing date. Applicants notified on a rolling basis starting 4/1; must reply within 2 week(s) of notification.

CONTACT

Steve Allen, Director of Financial Planning
6178 College Station Drive, Williamsburg, KY 40769
(800) 343-1609

West Kentucky Community and Technical College

Paducah, Kentucky
www.westkentucky.kctcs.edu　　Federal Code: 001979

2-year public community and technical college in large town.
Enrollment: 3,987 undergrads.
Selectivity: Open admission; but selective for some programs.

BASIC COSTS (2009-2010)

Tuition and fees: $3,750; out-of-state residents $12,750.
Per-credit charge: $125; out-of-state residents $425.
Additional info: Contiguous counties pay $250 pre credit hour.

FINANCIAL AID PICTURE

Students with need: Need-based aid available for full-time and part-time students.

FINANCIAL AID PROCEDURES

Forms required: FAFSA.
Dates and Deadlines: Priority date 4/1; no closing date. Applicants notified on a rolling basis starting 7/15; must reply within 4 week(s) of notification.

CONTACT

Sandy Barlow, Financial Aid Officer
4810 Alben Barkley Drive, Paducah, KY 42002-7380
(270) 534-3248

Western Kentucky University

Bowling Green, Kentucky
www.wku.edu　　Federal Code: 002002

4-year public university in small city.
Enrollment: 16,436 undergrads, 16% part-time. 3,211 full-time freshmen.
Selectivity: Open admission; but selective for some programs.

BASIC COSTS (2009-2010)

Tuition and fees: $7,200; out-of-state residents $17,784.
Per-credit charge: $300; out-of-state residents $741.
Room and board: $6,138.

FINANCIAL AID PICTURE (2008-2009)

Students with need: Out of 2,654 full-time freshmen who applied for aid, 1,943 were judged to have need. Of these, 1,924 received aid, and 611 had their full need met. Average financial aid package met 32% of need; average scholarship/grant was $5,247; average loan was $3,018. For part-time students, average financial aid package was $9,475.

Students without need: 321 full-time freshmen who did not demonstrate need for aid received scholarships/grants; average award was $5,226. No-need awards available for academics, alumni affiliation, art, athletics, job skills, leadership, minority status, music/drama, religious affiliation, ROTC, state/district residency.

Scholarships offered: *Merit:* Academic scholarships; $200 to full tuition; number awarded varies. *Athletic:* 97 full-time freshmen received athletic scholarships; average amount $10,058.

Cumulative student debt: 56% of graduating class had student loans; average debt was $17,436.

FINANCIAL AID PROCEDURES

Forms required: FAFSA.

Dates and Deadlines: Priority date 4/1; no closing date. Applicants notified on a rolling basis starting 3/1.

Transfers: Transfer students receiving CAP Grant must notify the state agency by December 1 of each year.

CONTACT

Cynthia Burnette, Director of Financial Assistance
1906 College Heights Boulevard, Bowling Green, KY 42101
(270) 745-2755

Louisiana

Baton Rouge Community College

Baton Rouge, Louisiana
www.mybrcc.edu　　Federal Code: 037303

2-year public community college in large city.
Enrollment: 7,248 undergrads, 42% part-time. 1,168 full-time freshmen.
Selectivity: Open admission; but selective for some programs.

BASIC COSTS (2009-2010)

Tuition and fees: $1,947; out-of-state residents $4,755.

FINANCIAL AID PICTURE (2008-2009)

Students with need: 98% of average financial aid package awarded as scholarships/grants, 2% awarded as loans/jobs. Need-based aid available for part-time students. Work study available weekends and for part-time students.

Students without need: No-need awards available for academics, athletics, leadership, minority status, state/district residency.

FINANCIAL AID PROCEDURES

Forms required: FAFSA, institutional form.
Dates and Deadlines: Priority date 4/15; closing date 6/30. Applicants notified on a rolling basis.
Transfers: No deadline. Applicants notified on a rolling basis.

CONTACT

Calaundra Brown, Director of Financial Aid
201 Community College Drive, Baton Rouge, LA 70806
(225) 216-8005

Bossier Parish Community College

Bossier City, Louisiana
www.bpcc.edu   Federal Code: 012033

2-year public community college in small city.
Enrollment: 4,597 undergrads, 34% part-time. 1,042 full-time freshmen.
Selectivity: Open admission; but selective for out-of-state students.

BASIC COSTS (2009-2010)
Tuition and fees: $1,940; out-of-state residents $4,080.

FINANCIAL AID PICTURE (2008-2009)
Students with need: Need-based aid available for full-time and part-time students. Work study available nights.
Students without need: No-need awards available for academics, alumni affiliation, athletics, minority status, music/drama.

FINANCIAL AID PROCEDURES
Forms required: FAFSA.
Dates and Deadlines: Closing date 7/1. Applicants notified on a rolling basis.
Transfers: Priority date 6/1; no deadline.

CONTACT
Vickie Temple, Financial Aid Director
6220 East Texas Street, Bossier City, LA 71111-6922
(318) 678-6026

Centenary College of Louisiana

Shreveport, Louisiana
www.centenary.edu   Federal Code: 002003

4-year private liberal arts college in small city, affiliated with United Methodist Church.
Enrollment: 879 undergrads, 1% part-time. 278 full-time freshmen.

BASIC COSTS (2009-2010)
Tuition and fees: $22,900.
Per-credit charge: $725.
Room and board: $7,940.

FINANCIAL AID PICTURE (2009-2010)
Students with need: Need-based aid available for full-time and part-time students. Work study available nights, weekends, and for part-time students.
Students without need: No-need awards available for academics, art, athletics, leadership, music/drama, religious affiliation, state/district residency.

FINANCIAL AID PROCEDURES
Forms required: FAFSA, institutional form.
Dates and Deadlines: Priority date 2/15; no closing date. Applicants notified on a rolling basis starting 2/15.

CONTACT
Mary Sue Rix, Director of Financial Aid
Box 41188, Shreveport, LA 71134-1188
(318) 869-5137

Delgado Community College

New Orleans, Louisiana
www.dcc.edu   Federal Code: 004626

2-year public community college in very large city.
Enrollment: 13,015 undergrads.
Selectivity: Open admission; but selective for some programs.

BASIC COSTS (2009-2010)
Tuition and fees: $2,012; out-of-state residents $4,992.

FINANCIAL AID PICTURE
Students with need: Need-based aid available for full-time and part-time students. Work study available nights, weekends, and for part-time students.
Students without need: No-need awards available for academics, athletics, leadership, music/drama, state/district residency.

FINANCIAL AID PROCEDURES
Forms required: FAFSA, institutional form.
Dates and Deadlines: Priority date 5/1; closing date 7/15. Applicants notified on a rolling basis starting 4/1; must reply within 2 week(s) of notification.

CONTACT
Germaine Edwards, Director of Student Financial Assistance
615 City Park Avenue, New Orleans, LA 70119
(504) 671-5037

Dillard University

New Orleans, Louisiana
www.dillard.edu   Federal Code: 002004

4-year private university and liberal arts college in large city, affiliated with United Church of Christ and United Methodist Church.
Enrollment: 1,011 undergrads, 6% part-time. 321 full-time freshmen.
Selectivity: Admits less than 50% of applicants.

BASIC COSTS (2009-2010)
Tuition and fees: $13,540.
Per-credit charge: $542.
Room and board: $8,210.

FINANCIAL AID PICTURE
Students with need: Need-based aid available for full-time and part-time students. Work study available nights, weekends, and for part-time students.
Students without need: This college awards aid only to students with need.

FINANCIAL AID PROCEDURES
Forms required: FAFSA, institutional form.
Dates and Deadlines: Priority date 12/1; closing date 5/1. Applicants notified on a rolling basis starting 3/1; must reply by 5/1 or within 2 week(s) of notification.

CONTACT
Shannon Neal, Director of Financial Aid
2601 Gentilly Boulevard, New Orleans, LA 70122-3097
(800) 216-8094

Grambling State University

Grambling, Louisiana
www.gram.edu   Federal Code: 002006

4-year public university in small town.
Enrollment: 4,534 undergrads, 7% part-time. 911 full-time freshmen.
Selectivity: GED not accepted.

BASIC COSTS (2009-2010)
Tuition and fees: $4,016; out-of-state residents $9,902.
Per-credit charge: $109.
Room and board: $5,468.

FINANCIAL AID PICTURE (2009-2010)
Students with need: For part-time students, average financial aid package was $1,900.
Students without need: No-need awards available for academics, alumni affiliation, art, athletics, job skills, leadership, minority status, music/drama, religious affiliation, ROTC, state/district residency.

Scholarships offered: 52 full-time freshmen received athletic scholarships; average amount $2,710.

FINANCIAL AID PROCEDURES

Forms required: FAFSA.

Dates and Deadlines: Priority date 4/1; closing date 6/1. Applicants notified on a rolling basis starting 3/1; must reply within 2 week(s) of notification.

Transfers: Applicants notified on a rolling basis starting 3/1; must reply within 2 week(s) of notification.

CONTACT

Jackie Greer, Director of Student Financial Aid

403 Main Street, GSU Box 4200, Grambling, LA 71245

(318) 274-6190

Herzing University

Kenner, Louisiana

www.herzing.edu   Federal Code: 020897

4-year for-profit branch campus and technical college in very large city.

Enrollment: 356 undergrads.

Selectivity: Admits over 75% of applicants.

BASIC COSTS (2009-2010)

Additional info: Tuition costs vary by program, $360-$390 per credit hour.

FINANCIAL AID PICTURE

Students with need: Work study available nights, weekends, and for part-time students.

CONTACT

Ava Gomez, Financial Aid Director

2400 Veterans Boulevard, Suite 410, Kenner, LA 70062

ITI Technical College

Baton Rouge, Louisiana

www.iticollege.edu   Federal Code: 015270

2-year for-profit technical college in large city.

Enrollment: 400 undergrads. 193 full-time freshmen.

Selectivity: Open admission.

BASIC COSTS (2009-2010)

Additional info: Full-time tuition varies by program from $13,350 to $26,650.

FINANCIAL AID PICTURE

Students with need: Need-based aid available for full-time and part-time students.

Students without need: This college awards aid only to students with need.

FINANCIAL AID PROCEDURES

Forms required: FAFSA.

Dates and Deadlines: No deadline.

CONTACT

Connie Roubique, Financial Aid Director

13944 Airline Highway, Baton Rouge, LA 70017

(225) 752-4233

Louisiana College

Pineville, Louisiana

www.lacollege.edu   Federal Code: 002007

4-year private liberal arts college in small city, affiliated with Southern Baptist Convention.

Enrollment: 1,037 undergrads, 7% part-time. 325 full-time freshmen.

Selectivity: Admits 50 to 75% of applicants.

BASIC COSTS (2010-2011)

Tuition and fees: $13,430.

Per-credit charge: $385.

Room and board: $4,560.

FINANCIAL AID PICTURE

Students with need: Need-based aid available for full-time and part-time students. Work study available nights, weekends, and for part-time students.

Students without need: No-need awards available for academics, art, leadership, music/drama, ROTC.

FINANCIAL AID PROCEDURES

Forms required: FAFSA, institutional form.

Dates and Deadlines: Priority date 3/31; no closing date. Applicants notified on a rolling basis starting 3/1; must reply by 5/1 or within 2 week(s) of notification.

Transfers: Scholarships available.

CONTACT

Ronnie LaLande, Director of Financial Aid

LC Box 566, Pineville, LA 71359

(318) 487-7386

Louisiana State University and Agricultural and Mechanical College

Baton Rouge, Louisiana

www.lsu.edu   Federal Code: 002010

4-year public university and agricultural college in large city.

Enrollment: 22,625 undergrads, 6% part-time. 5,135 full-time freshmen.

Selectivity: Admits 50 to 75% of applicants.

BASIC COSTS (2009-2010)

Tuition and fees: $5,233; out-of-state residents $14,383.

Room and board: $7,738.

FINANCIAL AID PICTURE (2008-2009)

Students with need: Out of 3,117 full-time freshmen who applied for aid, 1,750 were judged to have need. Of these, 1,750 received aid, and 436 had their full need met. Average financial aid package met 74% of need; average scholarship/grant was $8,549; average loan was $3,157. For part-time students, average financial aid package was $5,582.

Students without need: 1,472 full-time freshmen who did not demonstrate need for aid received scholarships/grants; average award was $3,830. No-need awards available for academics, alumni affiliation, athletics, leadership, music/drama, ROTC, state/district residency.

Scholarships offered: 106 full-time freshmen received athletic scholarships; average amount $15,115.

Cumulative student debt: 41% of graduating class had student loans; average debt was $18,118.

FINANCIAL AID PROCEDURES

Forms required: FAFSA.

Dates and Deadlines: Priority date 1/1; no closing date. Applicants notified on a rolling basis starting 4/1; must reply by 5/1 or within 3 week(s) of notification.

Transfers: No deadline. Applicants notified on a rolling basis.

CONTACT
Mary Parker, Executive Director of Undergraduate Admissions & Student Aid

1146 Pleasant Halll, Baton Rouge, LA 70803-2750

(225) 578-3103

Louisiana State University at Alexandria
Alexandria, Louisiana

www.lsua.edu   Federal Code: 002011

4-year public university in small city.

Enrollment: 1,287 full-time undergrads.

Selectivity: Admits over 75% of applicants.

BASIC COSTS (2009-2010)
Tuition and fees: $3,576; out-of-state residents $6,284.

Room and board: $6,234.

FINANCIAL AID PICTURE
Students with need: Need-based aid available for full-time and part-time students. Work study available nights.

Students without need: No-need awards available for academics, state/district residency.

FINANCIAL AID PROCEDURES
Forms required: FAFSA, institutional form.

Dates and Deadlines: Priority date 4/1; no closing date. Applicants notified on a rolling basis starting 4/20; must reply within 3 week(s) of notification.

CONTACT
Paul Monteleone, Director of Financial Aid & Scholarships

8100 Highway 71 South, Alexandria, LA 71302-9121

(318) 473-6423

Louisiana State University at Eunice
Eunice, Louisiana

www.lsue.edu   Federal Code: 002012

2-year public branch campus and community college in large town.

Enrollment: 3,332 undergrads.

Selectivity: Open admission; but selective for some programs.

BASIC COSTS (2009-2010)
Tuition and fees: $2,300; out-of-state residents $5,479.

Room and board: $8,236.

FINANCIAL AID PICTURE (2009-2010)
Students with need: Need-based aid available for full-time and part-time students.

FINANCIAL AID PROCEDURES
Forms required: FAFSA, institutional form.

Dates and Deadlines: Priority date 6/1; no closing date. Applicants notified on a rolling basis starting 4/1; must reply within 2 week(s) of notification.

CONTACT
Jacqueline LaChapelle, Director of Financial Aid

Box 1129, Eunice, LA 70535

(337) 550-1282

Louisiana State University Health Sciences Center
New Orleans, Louisiana

www.lsuhsc.edu   Federal Code: 002014

Upper-division public health science and nursing college in large city.

Enrollment: 836 undergrads.

BASIC COSTS (2009-2010)
Additional info: Allied Health Professions: $5,548 residents, $8,992 non-residents. Dental Hygiene: $3,314 residents, $4,856 non-residents. Dental Laboratory Technology: $3,039 residents, $4,581 non-residents. School of Nursing: $3,360 residents, $5,234 non-residents.

FINANCIAL AID PICTURE (2009-2010)
Students with need: Need-based aid available for full-time and part-time students. Work study available nights, weekends, and for part-time students.

Students without need: No-need awards available for academics.

FINANCIAL AID PROCEDURES
Forms required: FAFSA, institutional form.

Dates and Deadlines: Priority date 4/15; no closing date. Applicants notified on a rolling basis starting 7/1.

CONTACT
Patrick Gorman, Director of Financial Aid

433 Bolivar Street, New Orleans, LA 70112-2223

(504) 568-4820

Louisiana State University in Shreveport
Shreveport, Louisiana

www.lsus.edu   Federal Code: 002013

4-year public university and liberal arts college in large city.

Enrollment: 3,260 undergrads.

Selectivity: Admits over 75% of applicants.

BASIC COSTS (2009-2010)
Tuition and fees: $3,925; out-of-state residents $8,695.

FINANCIAL AID PICTURE
Students with need: Need-based aid available for full-time and part-time students. Work study available nights, weekends, and for part-time students.

FINANCIAL AID PROCEDURES
Dates and Deadlines: No deadline. Applicants notified on a rolling basis.

CONTACT
Betty McCrary, Director of Student Financial Aid

One University Place, Shreveport, LA 71115-2399

(318) 797-5363

Louisiana Tech University
Ruston, Louisiana

www.latech.edu   Federal Code: 002008

4-year public university in large town.

Enrollment: 7,101 undergrads.

Selectivity: Admits 50 to 75% of applicants.

BASIC COSTS (2009-2010)
Tuition and fees: $5,079; out-of-state residents $12,000.

Room and board: $5,055.

FINANCIAL AID PICTURE (2009-2010)
Students with need: Need-based aid available for full-time and part-time students.

Students without need: No-need awards available for academics, art, athletics, leadership, music/drama, ROTC.

FINANCIAL AID PROCEDURES

Forms required: FAFSA, institutional form.

Dates and Deadlines: Priority date 4/15; no closing date. Applicants notified on a rolling basis starting 3/18; must reply within 4 week(s) of notification.

Transfers: Priority date 8/1; no deadline. Applicants notified on a rolling basis starting 8/20; must reply within 2 week(s) of notification.

CONTACT

Roger Vick, Director of Student Financial Aid

Box 3178, Ruston, LA 71272

(318) 257-2641

Loyola University New Orleans

New Orleans, Louisiana

www.loyno.edu/   Federal Code: 002016

4-year private university and liberal arts college in large city, affiliated with Roman Catholic Church.

Enrollment: 2,721 undergrads, 10% part-time. 796 full-time freshmen.

Selectivity: Admits 50 to 75% of applicants.

BASIC COSTS (2010-2011)

Tuition and fees: $31,504.

Per-credit charge: $869.

Room and board: $10,388.

FINANCIAL AID PICTURE (2009-2010)

Students with need: Out of 627 full-time freshmen who applied for aid, 510 were judged to have need. Of these, 510 received aid, and 126 had their full need met. Average financial aid package met 88% of need; average scholarship/grant was $18,146; average loan was $3,562. For part-time students, average financial aid package was $12,470.

Students without need: 219 full-time freshmen who did not demonstrate need for aid received scholarships/grants; average award was $18,069. No-need awards available for academics, alumni affiliation, art, leadership, ROTC.

Scholarships offered: 9 full-time freshmen received athletic scholarships; average amount $11,401.

Cumulative student debt: 64% of graduating class had student loans; average debt was $22,320.

FINANCIAL AID PROCEDURES

Forms required: FAFSA.

Dates and Deadlines: Priority date 2/15; closing date 6/1. Applicants notified on a rolling basis starting 3/1; must reply by 5/1 or within 2 week(s) of notification.

Transfers: Priority date 3/1; closing date 5/1. Transfer scholarship deadline June 1.

CONTACT

Catherine Simoneaux, Director of Scholarships and Financial Aid

6363 St. Charles Avenue, New Orleans, LA 70118-6195

(504) 865-3231

McNeese State University

Lake Charles, Louisiana

www.mcneese.edu   Federal Code: 002017

4-year public university in small city.

Enrollment: 7,018 undergrads, 15% part-time. 1,235 full-time freshmen.

Selectivity: Admits 50 to 75% of applicants.

BASIC COSTS (2009-2010)

Tuition and fees: $3,588; out-of-state residents $10,260.

Room and board: $5,770.

FINANCIAL AID PICTURE (2008-2009)

Students with need: Need-based aid available for full-time and part-time students. Work study available nights, weekends, and for part-time students.

Students without need: No-need awards available for academics, alumni affiliation, art, athletics, leadership, minority status, music/drama, state/district residency.

Additional info: Books may be charged and paid in 2 installments during semester.

FINANCIAL AID PROCEDURES

Forms required: FAFSA, institutional form.

Dates and Deadlines: Priority date 5/1; no closing date. Applicants notified on a rolling basis starting 4/15; must reply within 2 week(s) of notification.

Transfers: Transfer students must exhibit satisfactory academic progress at school most recently attended to be eligible for financial aid.

CONTACT

Taina Savoit, Director of Financial Aid

Box 91740 MSU, Lake Charles, LA 70609-1740

(337) 475-5065

Nicholls State University

Thibodaux, Louisiana

www.nicholls.edu   Federal Code: 002005

4-year public university in large town.

Enrollment: 6,443 undergrads, 20% part-time. 1,219 full-time freshmen.

Selectivity: Admits over 75% of applicants.

BASIC COSTS (2009-2010)

Tuition and fees: $3,965; out-of-state residents $11,795.

Room and board: $7,310.

FINANCIAL AID PICTURE (2008-2009)

Students with need: Out of 1,108 full-time freshmen who applied for aid, 579 were judged to have need. Of these, 577 received aid, and 472 had their full need met. Average financial aid package met 95% of need; average scholarship/grant was $5,070; average loan was $2,743. For part-time students, average financial aid package was $4,974.

Students without need: 167 full-time freshmen who did not demonstrate need for aid received scholarships/grants; average award was $3,020. No-need awards available for academics, athletics, state/district residency.

Scholarships offered: 33 full-time freshmen received athletic scholarships; average amount $5,908.

Cumulative student debt: 56% of graduating class had student loans; average debt was $18,822.

FINANCIAL AID PROCEDURES

Forms required: FAFSA, state aid form, institutional form.

Dates and Deadlines: Priority date 4/15; closing date 6/30. Applicants notified on a rolling basis; must reply within 2 week(s) of notification.

Transfers: Priority date 5/1; no deadline. Applicants notified on a rolling basis.

CONTACT

Director of Financial Aid

PO Box 2004-NSU, Thibodaux, LA 70310

(985) 448-4048

Northwestern State University
Natchitoches, Louisiana
www.nsula.edu   Federal Code: 002021

4-year public university in large town.
Enrollment: 7,443 undergrads, 28% part-time. 1,181 full-time freshmen.
Selectivity: Admits over 75% of applicants.

BASIC COSTS (2009-2010)
Tuition and fees: $3,786; out-of-state residents $10,472.
Room and board: $6,680.

FINANCIAL AID PICTURE (2008-2009)
Students with need: Out of 986 full-time freshmen who applied for aid, 816 were judged to have need. Of these, 792 received aid, and 308 had their full need met. Average financial aid package met 61% of need; average scholarship/grant was $4,372; average loan was $5,064. For part-time students, average financial aid package was $4,805.
Students without need: 263 full-time freshmen who did not demonstrate need for aid received scholarships/grants; average award was $5,163. No-need awards available for academics, alumni affiliation, art, athletics, job skills, leadership, minority status, music/drama, religious affiliation, ROTC, state/district residency.
Scholarships offered: 50 full-time freshmen received athletic scholarships; average amount $10,062.
Cumulative student debt: 68% of graduating class had student loans; average debt was $21,773.

FINANCIAL AID PROCEDURES
Forms required: FAFSA, institutional form.
Dates and Deadlines: Priority date 5/1; no closing date. Applicants notified on a rolling basis starting 5/1; must reply within 4 week(s) of notification.
Transfers: No deadline. Applicants notified on a rolling basis starting 5/1; must reply within 4 week(s) of notification.

CONTACT
Misti Adams, Director of Financial Aid
Roy Hall, Room 209, Natchitoches, LA 71497
(800) 823-3008

Nunez Community College
Chalmette, Louisiana
www.nunez.edu   Federal Code: 015130

2-year public community and technical college in large town.
Enrollment: 1,158 undergrads, 39% part-time. 144 full-time freshmen.
Selectivity: Open admission; but selective for some programs.

BASIC COSTS (2009-2010)
Tuition and fees: $1,950; out-of-state residents $4,470.
Additional info: Tuition/fee waivers available for minority students.

FINANCIAL AID PICTURE (2008-2009)
Students with need: Need-based aid available for full-time and part-time students. Work study available nights.
Additional info: Pell Grants, Stafford Loans, campus workstudy, and tuition waiver scholarships available. Louisiana National Guard tuition exemption, teacher tuition exemption, dependents of injured fire-police tuition waivers.

FINANCIAL AID PROCEDURES
Forms required: FAFSA.
Dates and Deadlines: Priority date 6/1; closing date 8/1. Applicants notified by 9/1; must reply by 10/15.
Transfers: Applicant must supply academic transcripts from every postsecondary school attended before aid is awarded.

CONTACT
Glenda Despenza, Financial Aid Officer
3710 Paris Road, Chalmette, LA 70043
(504) 278-7487

Our Lady of Holy Cross College
New Orleans, Louisiana
www.olhcc.edu   Federal Code: 002023

4-year private liberal arts college in very large city, affiliated with Roman Catholic Church.
Enrollment: 535 full-time undergrads.

BASIC COSTS (2009-2010)
Tuition and fees: $10,320.
Per-credit charge: $310.

FINANCIAL AID PICTURE (2009-2010)
Students with need: Need-based aid available for full-time and part-time students. Work study available nights, weekends, and for part-time students.
Students without need: No-need awards available for academics, state/district residency.

FINANCIAL AID PROCEDURES
Forms required: FAFSA.
Dates and Deadlines: Priority date 7/1; no closing date. Applicants notified on a rolling basis starting 5/15; must reply within 4 week(s) of notification.
Transfers: Must reply within 2 week(s) of notification.

CONTACT
Kristine Hatfield, Vice President of Enrollment Management and Student Development
4123 Woodland Drive, New Orleans, LA 70131-7399
(504) 394-7744

Our Lady of the Lake College
Baton Rouge, Louisiana
www.ololcollege.edu   Federal Code: 031062

4-year private health science and nursing college in large city, affiliated with Roman Catholic Church.
Enrollment: 1,692 undergrads, 33% part-time. 95 full-time freshmen.
Selectivity: Admits over 75% of applicants.

BASIC COSTS (2010-2011)
Tuition and fees: $10,644.
Per-credit charge: $330.

FINANCIAL AID PICTURE (2008-2009)
Students with need: Out of 90 full-time freshmen who applied for aid, 69 were judged to have need. Of these, 68 received aid, and 2 had their full need met. For part-time students, average financial aid package was $4,713.

FINANCIAL AID PROCEDURES
Forms required: FAFSA.
Dates and Deadlines: Closing date 3/1.

CONTACT
Tiffany MaGee, Director of Financial Aid
7434 Perkins Road, Baton Rouge, LA 70808
(225) 768-1714

St. Joseph Seminary College

St. Benedict, Louisiana
www.sjasc.edu   Federal Code: 002027

4-year private liberal arts and seminary college for men in rural community, affiliated with Roman Catholic Church.
Enrollment: 83 undergrads. 10 full-time freshmen.

BASIC COSTS (2009-2010)
Tuition and fees: $13,082.
Per-credit charge: $175.
Room and board: $11,168.

FINANCIAL AID PICTURE (2009-2010)
Students with need: Out of 10 full-time freshmen who applied for aid, 5 were judged to have need. Of these, 5 received aid. Need-based aid available for part-time students.
Students without need: No-need awards available for academics, leadership.
Cumulative student debt: 1% of graduating class had student loans; average debt was $5,500.

FINANCIAL AID PROCEDURES
Forms required: FAFSA.
Dates and Deadlines: Priority date 3/15; no closing date. Applicants notified on a rolling basis starting 7/1; must reply within 4 week(s) of notification.
Transfers: Closing date 5/1. Applicants notified on a rolling basis starting 7/1; must reply within 4 week(s) of notification.

CONTACT
George Binder, Director of Student Financial Aid
75376 River Road, St. Benedict, LA 70457-9990
(985) 867-2248

South Louisiana Community College

Lafayette, Louisiana
www.southlouisiana.edu   Federal Code: 039563

2-year public community college in small city.
Enrollment: 3,243 undergrads, 46% part-time. 578 full-time freshmen.
Selectivity: Open admission; but selective for some programs.

BASIC COSTS (2009-2010)
Tuition and fees: $2,014; out-of-state residents $4,164.
Per-credit charge: $67.

FINANCIAL AID PICTURE
Students with need: Need-based aid available for full-time and part-time students.
Students without need: No-need awards available for academics, leadership, state/district residency.

FINANCIAL AID PROCEDURES
Forms required: FAFSA, institutional form.
Dates and Deadlines: Priority date 7/1; no closing date.

CONTACT
Shonda Rosinski, Director of Financial Aid
320 Devalcourt, Lafayette, LA 70506-4124
(337) 521-8910

Southeastern Louisiana University

Hammond, Louisiana
www.selu.edu   Federal Code: 002024

4-year public university in large town.
Enrollment: 13,086 undergrads, 15% part-time. 2,622 full-time freshmen.
Selectivity: Admits over 75% of applicants.

BASIC COSTS (2009-2010)
Tuition and fees: $3,655; out-of-state residents $10,910.
Per-credit charge: $122; out-of-state residents $364.
Room and board: $6,110.

FINANCIAL AID PICTURE (2008-2009)
Students with need: Out of 2,276 full-time freshmen who applied for aid, 1,420 were judged to have need. Of these, 1,345 received aid, and 486 had their full need met. For part-time students, average financial aid package was $3,224.
Students without need: 228 full-time freshmen who did not demonstrate need for aid received scholarships/grants; average award was $1,797. No-need awards available for academics, athletics, job skills, leadership, music/drama, state/district residency.
Scholarships offered: *Merit:* Various scholarships: $1,000-$3,500; any student admitted with 24 ACT and 3.0 GPA on a seven-semester transcript qualifies for scholarship. On-campus housing scholarships: range from half room award to full room award; based on ACT score and GPA. Presidential Honors Scholarship: $2,500-$3,500 plus on-campus housing and meals (full shared housing award and pack meal plan); 30 ACT, 3.0 GPA. *Athletic:* 42 full-time freshmen received athletic scholarships; average amount $5,497.
Cumulative student debt: 60% of graduating class had student loans; average debt was $18,947.

FINANCIAL AID PROCEDURES
Forms required: FAFSA.
Dates and Deadlines: Priority date 5/1; no closing date. Applicants notified on a rolling basis starting 3/1; must reply within 2 week(s) of notification.
Transfers: Applicants notified on a rolling basis starting 3/1; must reply within 2 week(s) of notification. Financial aid is available for transfer students, including those admitted on probation.

CONTACT
Sarah Schillage, Director of Financial Aid
SLU 10752, Hammond, LA 70402
(985) 549-2244

Southern University and Agricultural and Mechanical College

Baton Rouge, Louisiana
www.subr.edu   Federal Code: 002025

4-year public university in large city.
Enrollment: 6,280 undergrads, 8% part-time. 998 full-time freshmen.
Selectivity: Admits less than 50% of applicants.

BASIC COSTS (2009-2010)
Tuition and fees: $4,100; out-of-state residents $9,892.
Per-credit charge: $455.
Room and board: $5,666.
Additional info: Cable and internet, key deposit, and mail box rental $166.

FINANCIAL AID PICTURE (2008-2009)
Students with need: Need-based aid available for full-time students.
Students without need: No-need awards available for academics, athletics, ROTC, state/district residency.
Scholarships offered: College of Education Scholarship: full scholarship; 22 ACT (or comparable SAT), 3.2 GPA, evidence of community involvement/ex-

tracurricular activities, two letters of recommendation required. College of Education Scholarship: tuition only; 20 ACT (or comparable SAT), 3.0 GPA, evidence of community involvement/extracurricular activities, two letters of recommendation required.

FINANCIAL AID PROCEDURES

Forms required: FAFSA.

Dates and Deadlines: Priority date 1/31; closing date 3/30. Applicants notified on a rolling basis starting 5/1; must reply within 3 week(s) of notification. **Transfers:** Closing date 5/31. Applicants notified on a rolling basis starting 5/31; must reply within 3 week(s) of notification.

CONTACT

Ursula Shorty, Director of Financial Aid
T.H. Harris Hall, Baton Rouge, LA 70813
(225) 771-2790

Southern University at New Orleans
New Orleans, Louisiana
www.suno.edu   Federal Code: 002026

4-year public university in large city.
Enrollment: 2,600 undergrads.
Selectivity: Open admission.

BASIC COSTS (2009-2010)
Tuition and fees: $3,161; out-of-state residents $6,899.

FINANCIAL AID PICTURE
Students with need: Need-based aid available for full-time and part-time students.
Students without need: This college awards aid only to students with need.

FINANCIAL AID PROCEDURES
Forms required: FAFSA.
Dates and Deadlines: Closing date 4/1. Applicants notified by 5/15; must reply within 1 week(s) of notification.

CONTACT
Kathy Woods, Director of Financial Aid
6801 Press Drive, New Orleans, LA 70126
(504) 286-5263

Tulane University
New Orleans, Louisiana   Federal Code: 002029
www.tulane.edu   CSS Code: 6832

4-year private university in very large city.
Enrollment: 7,160 undergrads, 24% part-time. 1,502 full-time freshmen.
Selectivity: Admits less than 50% of applicants.

BASIC COSTS (2009-2010)
Tuition and fees: $40,584.
Per-credit charge: $1,750.
Room and board: $9,606.

FINANCIAL AID PICTURE (2008-2009)
Students with need: Out of 925 full-time freshmen who applied for aid, 598 were judged to have need. Of these, 598 received aid, and 451 had their full need met. Average financial aid package met 96% of need; average scholarship/grant was $22,910; average loan was $5,320. For part-time students, average financial aid package was $10,379.
Students without need: 733 full-time freshmen who did not demonstrate need for aid received scholarships/grants; average award was $22,972. No-need awards available for academics, athletics, leadership, music/drama, state/district residency.

Scholarships offered: *Merit:* Dean's Honor Scholarship; full-tuition. Distinguished Scholars Award; up to $18,000. Founders Scholarship; up to $16,000. Urban Scholars Award; full-tuition. *Athletic:* 28 full-time freshmen received athletic scholarships; average amount $38,236.
Cumulative student debt: 48% of graduating class had student loans; average debt was $25,284.
Additional info: Application deadline for merit scholarships December 1.

FINANCIAL AID PROCEDURES
Forms required: FAFSA, CSS PROFILE.
Dates and Deadlines: Closing date 2/15. Applicants notified on a rolling basis starting 3/15; must reply within 2 week(s) of notification.
Transfers: Applicants notified on a rolling basis starting 2/1; must reply by 5/1 or within 2 week(s) of notification.

CONTACT
Michael Goodman, Associate Vice President for Financial Aid
6823 St. Charles Avenue, New Orleans, LA 70118-5680
(504) 865-5723

University of Louisiana at Lafayette
Lafayette, Louisiana
www.louisiana.edu   Federal Code: 002031

4-year public university in small city.
Enrollment: 14,349 undergrads, 13% part-time. 2,569 full-time freshmen.

BASIC COSTS (2009-2010)
Tuition and fees: $4,046; out-of-state residents $12,618.
Per-credit charge: $108; out-of-state residents $357.
Room and board: $4,682.

FINANCIAL AID PICTURE (2008-2009)
Students with need: Need-based aid available for full-time and part-time students. Work study available nights, weekends, and for part-time students.
Students without need: This college awards aid only to students with need.

FINANCIAL AID PROCEDURES
Forms required: FAFSA.
Dates and Deadlines: Priority date 5/1; no closing date. Applicants notified on a rolling basis starting 4/1; must reply within 2 week(s) of notification.

CONTACT
Cindy Perez, Director, Student Financial Aid
Box 41210, Lafayette, LA 70504-1210
(337) 482-6506

University of Louisiana at Monroe
Monroe, Louisiana
www.ulm.edu   Federal Code: 002020

4-year public university in small city.
Enrollment: 7,793 undergrads, 23% part-time. 1,303 full-time freshmen.
Selectivity: Admits 50 to 75% of applicants.

BASIC COSTS (2009-2010)
Tuition and fees: $4,024; out-of-state residents $12,206.
Per-credit charge: $125.
Room and board: $5,790.

FINANCIAL AID PICTURE
Students with need: Need-based aid available for full-time and part-time students.
Students without need: No-need awards available for academics, alumni affiliation, art, athletics, job skills, leadership, minority status, music/drama, religious affiliation, ROTC, state/district residency.

FINANCIAL AID PROCEDURES

Forms required: FAFSA.

Dates and Deadlines: Priority date 4/1; no closing date. Applicants notified on a rolling basis starting 6/1; must reply within 2 week(s) of notification.

CONTACT

Teri Smith, Director of Financial Aid
700 University Avenue, Monroe, LA 71209-1160
(318) 342-5320

University of New Orleans
New Orleans, Louisiana
www.uno.edu   Federal Code: 002015

4-year public university in very large city.

Enrollment: 8,515 undergrads, 22% part-time. 1,221 full-time freshmen.

Selectivity: Admits 50 to 75% of applicants.

BASIC COSTS (2009-2010)

Tuition and fees: $4,372; out-of-state residents $12,528.

Per-credit charge: $123; out-of-state residents $395.

Room and board: $6,700.

FINANCIAL AID PICTURE (2009-2010)

Students with need: Out of 1,110 full-time freshmen who applied for aid, 833 were judged to have need. Of these, 799 received aid, and 171 had their full need met. Average financial aid package met 68% of need; average scholarship/grant was $6,780; average loan was $3,048. For part-time students, average financial aid package was $5,274.

Students without need: 100 full-time freshmen who did not demonstrate need for aid received scholarships/grants; average award was $1,666. No-need awards available for academics, athletics.

Scholarships offered: 22 full-time freshmen received athletic scholarships; average amount $9,240.

Cumulative student debt: 16% of graduating class had student loans; average debt was $13,623.

Additional info: Students in good academic and financial standing eligible to participate in Extended Payment Plan option.

FINANCIAL AID PROCEDURES

Forms required: FAFSA.

Dates and Deadlines: Priority date 5/15; no closing date. Applicants notified on a rolling basis starting 4/20; must reply within 4 week(s) of notification.

Transfers: Mid-year transfers must submit financial aid transcript from all post-secondary schools attended. Others submit NSLDS.

CONTACT

Emily London-Jones, Director of Student Financial Aid
Administration Building Room 103, New Orleans, LA 70148
(504) 280-6603

Xavier University of Louisiana
New Orleans, Louisiana
www.xula.edu   Federal Code: 002032

4-year private university in very large city, affiliated with Roman Catholic Church.

Enrollment: 2,644 undergrads, 3% part-time. 773 full-time freshmen.

Selectivity: Admits 50 to 75% of applicants.

BASIC COSTS (2010-2011)

Tuition and fees: $17,100.

Per-credit charge: $200.

Room and board: $7,200.

FINANCIAL AID PICTURE (2008-2009)

Students with need: Average financial aid package met 11% of need; average scholarship/grant was $5,137; average loan was $3,373. For part-time students, average financial aid package was $8,903.

Students without need: 49 full-time freshmen who did not demonstrate need for aid received scholarships/grants; average award was $8,341. No-need awards available for music/drama.

Scholarships offered: 21 full-time freshmen received athletic scholarships; average amount $17,591.

Cumulative student debt: 83% of graduating class had student loans; average debt was $23,067.

FINANCIAL AID PROCEDURES

Forms required: FAFSA.

Dates and Deadlines: Priority date 1/1; no closing date. Applicants notified on a rolling basis starting 4/1; must reply within 2 week(s) of notification.

CONTACT

Mildred Higgins, Director of Financial Aid
1 Drexel Drive, New Orleans, LA 70125-1098
(504) 520-7517

Maine

Bates College
Lewiston, Maine   Federal Code: 002036
www.bates.edu   CSS Code: 3076

4-year private liberal arts college in large town.

Enrollment: 1,738 undergrads. 469 full-time freshmen.

Selectivity: Admits less than 50% of applicants. GED not accepted.

BASIC COSTS (2009-2010)

Comprehensive fee: $51,300.

FINANCIAL AID PICTURE (2009-2010)

Students with need: Out of 229 full-time freshmen who applied for aid, 198 were judged to have need. Of these, 189 received aid, and 175 had their full need met. Average financial aid package met 100% of need; average scholarship/grant was $32,732; average loan was $3,555.

Students without need: This college awards aid only to students with need.

Cumulative student debt: 38% of graduating class had student loans; average debt was $17,945.

Additional info: Priority date for filing required financial aid forms for early decision students is 11/15.

FINANCIAL AID PROCEDURES

Forms required: FAFSA, CSS PROFILE.

Dates and Deadlines: Closing date 2/1. Applicants notified by 4/1; must reply by 5/1.

Transfers: Closing date 1/1. Applicants notified by 4/15; must reply by 5/15.

CONTACT

Wendy Glass, Director of Student Financial Services
23 Campus Avenue, Lindholm House, Lewiston, ME 04240-9917
(207) 786-6096

Bowdoin College
Brunswick, Maine   Federal Code: 002038
www.bowdoin.edu   CSS Code: 3089

4-year private liberal arts college in large town.

Enrollment: 1,772 undergrads. 488 full-time freshmen.

Selectivity: Admits less than 50% of applicants. GED not accepted.

BASIC COSTS (2009-2010)
Tuition and fees: $40,020.
Room and board: $10,880.

FINANCIAL AID PICTURE (2008-2009)
Students with need: Out of 273 full-time freshmen who applied for aid, 201 were judged to have need. Of these, 201 received aid, and 201 had their full need met. Average financial aid package met 100% of need; average scholarship/grant was $34,289.
Students without need: 19 full-time freshmen who did not demonstrate need for aid received scholarships/grants; average award was $1,000. No-need awards available for academics, leadership.
Cumulative student debt: 45% of graduating class had student loans; average debt was $18,135.
Additional info: Regardless of financial circumstances, students admitted will receive money they need to attend. International students for regular admission must submit their financial aid applications by January 1st.

FINANCIAL AID PROCEDURES
Forms required: FAFSA, CSS PROFILE.
Dates and Deadlines: Closing date 2/15. Applicants notified by 4/5; must reply by 5/1 or within 1 week(s) of notification.
Transfers: Closing date 3/1. Applicants notified by 5/1; must reply by 6/1 or within 1 week(s) of notification. Financial aid usually not available for transfer students. Early Decision applicants must submit financial aid applications by November 15 (ED I) and January 1 (ED II).

CONTACT
Stephen Joyce, Director of Student Aid
5000 College Station, Brunswick, ME 04011-8441
(207) 725-3273

Central Maine Community College
Auburn, Maine
www.cmcc.edu   Federal Code: 005276

2-year public community and technical college in small city.
Enrollment: 2,018 undergrads.
Selectivity: Open admission; but selective for some programs.

BASIC COSTS (2009-2010)
Tuition and fees: $3,516; out-of-state residents $6,036.
Per-credit charge: $84; out-of-state residents $168.
Room and board: $7,766.
Additional info: Additional lab and technology fees may apply to specific programs and courses. Tuition/fee waivers available for minority students.

FINANCIAL AID PICTURE (2009-2010)
Students with need: Need-based aid available for full-time and part-time students. Work study available nights, weekends, and for part-time students.
Students without need: This college awards aid only to students with need.
Additional info: Tuition and/or fee waivers may be available to orphans, Native Americans, fire fighters, police, disabled veterans, dependents or survivors of veterans killed in line of duty.

FINANCIAL AID PROCEDURES
Forms required: FAFSA, institutional form.
Dates and Deadlines: Priority date 5/8; no closing date. Applicants notified on a rolling basis starting 3/15; must reply within 2 week(s) of notification.
Transfers: Priority date 8/1; no deadline. Applicants notified on a rolling basis starting 1/15; must reply within 2 week(s) of notification.

CONTACT
Monique Schreiber, Financial Aid Director
1250 Turner Street, Auburn, ME 04210
(207) 755-5269

Central Maine Medical Center College of Nursing and Health Professions
Lewiston, Maine
www.cmmcson.edu   Federal Code: 006305

2-year private nursing college in large town.
Enrollment: 126 undergrads, 82% part-time. 7 full-time freshmen.
Selectivity: Admits 50 to 75% of applicants.

BASIC COSTS (2010-2011)
Tuition and fees: $7,930.
Per-credit charge: $210.
Room only: $1,960.

FINANCIAL AID PICTURE (2008-2009)
Students with need: Out of 7 full-time freshmen who applied for aid, 7 were judged to have need. Of these, 7 received aid, and 4 had their full need met. Average financial aid package met 26% of need; average scholarship/grant was $6,975; average loan was $4,947. For part-time students, average financial aid package was $8,400.
Students without need: This college awards aid only to students with need.

FINANCIAL AID PROCEDURES
Forms required: FAFSA, institutional form.
Dates and Deadlines: Priority date 5/1; closing date 7/1. Applicants notified on a rolling basis starting 4/1; must reply within 2 week(s) of notification.

CONTACT
Keith Bourgault, Controller
70 Middle Street, Lewiston, ME 04240
(207) 795-2270

Colby College
Waterville, Maine   Federal Code: 002039
www.colby.edu   CSS Code: 3280

4-year private liberal arts college in large town.
Enrollment: 1,838 undergrads. 480 full-time freshmen.
Selectivity: Admits less than 50% of applicants.

BASIC COSTS (2009-2010)
Comprehensive fee: $50,320.

FINANCIAL AID PICTURE (2009-2010)
Students with need: Need-based aid available for full-time students. Work study available nights, weekends, and for part-time students.
Students without need: This college awards aid only to students with need.
Additional info: Institutional loans have been replaced with institutional grants.

FINANCIAL AID PROCEDURES
Forms required: FAFSA, CSS PROFILE.
Dates and Deadlines: Closing date 2/1. Applicants notified by 4/1; must reply by 5/1.
Transfers: Priority date 2/1; closing date 3/1. Must reply within 2 week(s) of notification.

CONTACT

Lucia Whittelsey, Director of Financial Aid

4800 Mayflower Hill, Waterville, ME 04901-8848

(800) 723-3032

College of the Atlantic

Bar Harbor, Maine

www.coa.edu   Federal Code: 011385

4-year private liberal arts college in small town.

Enrollment: 321 undergrads, 5% part-time. 76 full-time freshmen.

Selectivity: Admits 50 to 75% of applicants.

BASIC COSTS (2009-2010)

Tuition and fees: $33,060.

Per-credit charge: $1,086.

Room and board: $8,490.

FINANCIAL AID PICTURE (2009-2010)

Students with need: Out of 69 full-time freshmen who applied for aid, 67 were judged to have need. Of these, 67 received aid, and 47 had their full need met. Average financial aid package met 96% of need; average scholarship/grant was $30,576; average loan was $4,132. For part-time students, average financial aid package was $20,887.

Students without need: This college awards aid only to students with need.

Cumulative student debt: 54% of graduating class had student loans; average debt was $20,170.

FINANCIAL AID PROCEDURES

Forms required: FAFSA, institutional form.

Dates and Deadlines: Closing date 2/15. Applicants notified by 4/1; must reply by 5/1.

Transfers: Priority date 2/15. Applicants notified by 4/1; must reply by 5/1. FAFSA must be filed by 5/1 for Maine residents to be eligible for Maine state grant.

CONTACT

Bruce Hazam, Director of Financial Aid

105 Eden Street, Bar Harbor, ME 04609

(207) 288-5015

Eastern Maine Community College

Bangor, Maine

www.emcc.edu   Federal Code: 005277

2-year public community and technical college in large town.

Enrollment: 1,734 undergrads.

Selectivity: Open admission; but selective for some programs.

BASIC COSTS (2009-2010)

Tuition and fees: $3,387; out-of-state residents $5,907.

Per-credit charge: $84; out-of-state residents $168.

Room and board: $6,490.

Additional info: Additional lab and technology fees may apply to specific programs and courses. Tuition/fee waivers available for minority students.

FINANCIAL AID PICTURE (2008-2009)

Students with need: Need based aid available for full-time and part-time students. Work study available nights, weekends, and for part-time students.

Students without need: This college awards aid only to students with need.

FINANCIAL AID PROCEDURES

Forms required: FAFSA, institutional form.

Dates and Deadlines: Priority date 5/1; no closing date. Applicants notified on a rolling basis starting 5/1; must reply within 3 week(s) of notification.

CONTACT

Candace Ward, Registrar/Financial Aid Director

354 Hogan Road, Bangor, ME 04401

(207) 974-4625

Husson University

Bangor, Maine

www.husson.edu   Federal Code: 002043

4-year private business and health science college in large town.

Enrollment: 2,383 undergrads, 20% part-time. 491 full-time freshmen.

Selectivity: Admits 50 to 75% of applicants.

BASIC COSTS (2010-2011)

Tuition and fees: $13,450.

Per-credit charge: $438.

Room and board: $7,239.

FINANCIAL AID PICTURE (2009-2010)

Students with need: Average financial aid package met 75% of need; average scholarship/grant was $8,979; average loan was $3,079. For part-time students, average financial aid package was $6,600.

Students without need: No-need awards available for academics, leadership.

Scholarships offered: Scholarships awarded based on academics and leadership, ranging from $1,000 to $4,000 renewable up to four years.

Cumulative student debt: 80% of graduating class had student loans; average debt was $33,010.

FINANCIAL AID PROCEDURES

Forms required: FAFSA.

Dates and Deadlines: Priority date 4/15; no closing date. Applicants notified on a rolling basis starting 4/1; must reply by 5/1 or within 2 week(s) of notification.

Transfers: No deadline. Applicants notified on a rolling basis starting 2/20.

CONTACT

Linda Conant, Director of Financial Aid

One College Circle, Bangor, ME 04401-2999

(207) 941-7156

Kennebec Valley Community College

Fairfield, Maine

www.kvcc.me.edu   Federal Code: 009826

2-year public community and technical college in small town.

Enrollment: 1,654 undergrads, 57% part-time. 282 full-time freshmen.

Selectivity: Open admission; but selective for some programs.

BASIC COSTS (2009-2010)

Tuition and fees: $3,121; out-of-state residents $5,641.

Per-credit charge: $84; out-of-state residents $168.

Additional info: Additional lab and technology fees apply to specific programs and courses.

FINANCIAL AID PICTURE (2008-2009)

Students with need: Out of 252 full-time freshmen who applied for aid, 223 were judged to have need. Of these, 207 received aid, and 19 had their full need met. Average financial aid package met 51% of need; average scholarship/grant was $3,853; average loan was $2,612. For part-time students, average financial aid package was $4,736.

FINANCIAL AID PROCEDURES

Forms required: FAFSA, institutional form.

Dates and Deadlines: Priority date 4/1; no closing date. Applicants notified on a rolling basis starting 5/1.

CONTACT

Anne Connors, Director of Financial Aid
92 Western Avenue, Fairfield, ME 04937-1367
(207) 453-5121

Maine College of Art

Portland, Maine
www.meca.edu   Federal Code: 011673

4-year private visual arts college in small city.
Enrollment: 304 undergrads, 3% part-time. 69 full-time freshmen.
Selectivity: Admits over 75% of applicants.

BASIC COSTS (2010-2011)

Tuition and fees: $29,130.
Per-credit charge: $1,165.
Room and board: $9,995.

FINANCIAL AID PICTURE (2009-2010)

Students with need: Need-based aid available for full-time and part-time students. Work study available nights, weekends, and for part-time students.
Students without need: No-need awards available for academics, art.

FINANCIAL AID PROCEDURES

Forms required: FAFSA.
Dates and Deadlines: Priority date 3/1; no closing date. Applicants notified on a rolling basis starting 2/15; must reply within 2 week(s) of notification.
Transfers: Closing date 4/15. Applicants notified on a rolling basis starting 2/15; must reply within 2 week(s) of notification.

CONTACT

Adrienne Amari, Director of Financial Aid
522 Congress Street, Portland, ME 04101
(207) 699-5073

Maine Maritime Academy

Castine, Maine
www.mainemaritime.edu   Federal Code: 002044

4-year public maritime college in rural community.
Enrollment: 921 undergrads, 1% part-time. 234 full-time freshmen.

BASIC COSTS (2009-2010)

Tuition and fees: $10,105; out-of-district residents $14,055; out-of-state residents $17,805.
Room and board: $8,450.
Additional info: Fee of $3,000 for U.S. Coast Guard licensing programs.

FINANCIAL AID PICTURE (2008-2009)

Students with need: Out of 174 full-time freshmen who applied for aid, 130 were judged to have need. Of these, 129 received aid, and 17 had their full need met. Average financial aid package met 51% of need; average scholarship/grant was $5,606; average loan was $4,227. Need-based aid available for part-time students.
Students without need: 22 full-time freshmen who did not demonstrate need for aid received scholarships/grants; average award was $3,636. No-need awards available for academics, leadership, state/district residency.
Cumulative student debt: 82% of graduating class had student loans; average debt was $35,968.

FINANCIAL AID PROCEDURES

Forms required: FAFSA.
Dates and Deadlines: Priority date 4/15; no closing date. Applicants notified on a rolling basis starting 4/1; must reply within 4 week(s) of notification.

CONTACT

Kathy Heath, Director of Financial Aid
Pleasant Street, Castine, ME 04420
(207) 326-2339

New England School of Communications

Bangor, Maine
www.nescom.edu   Federal Code: 023471

4-year private college of communications in small city.
Enrollment: 496 undergrads, 5% part-time. 139 full-time freshmen.
Selectivity: Admits 50 to 75% of applicants.

BASIC COSTS (2009-2010)

Tuition and fees: $11,200.
Per-credit charge: $360.
Room and board: $6,994.
Additional info: Additional cost of $160 for FireWire hard drive. Tuition/fee waivers available for unemployed or children of unemployed.

FINANCIAL AID PICTURE (2008-2009)

Students with need: Average financial aid package met 16% of need; average scholarship/grant was $4,559; average loan was $3,430. For part-time students, average financial aid package was $5,512.
Students without need: No-need awards available for academics, leadership.
Scholarships offered: Scholarships are merit based for second semester.
Cumulative student debt: 87% of graduating class had student loans; average debt was $26,000.

FINANCIAL AID PROCEDURES

Forms required: FAFSA, institutional form.
Dates and Deadlines: Priority date 4/15; no closing date. Applicants notified on a rolling basis starting 2/1; must reply by 8/15.
Transfers: No deadline. Applicants notified on a rolling basis starting 2/15; must reply within 4 week(s) of notification.

CONTACT

Nicole Rediker, Director of Financial Aid
One College Circle, Bangor, ME 04401
(207) 941-7176

Northern Maine Community College

Presque Isle, Maine
www.nmcc.edu   Federal Code: 005760

2-year public community and career college in small town.
Enrollment: 941 undergrads.
Selectivity: Admits 50 to 75% of applicants.

BASIC COSTS (2009-2010)

Tuition and fees: $3,188; out-of-state residents $5,708.
Per-credit charge: $84; out-of-state residents $168.
Room and board: $5,780.
Additional info: Additional lab and technology fees may apply to specific programs and courses. Tuition/fee waivers available for minority students.

FINANCIAL AID PICTURE

Students with need: Need-based aid available for full-time and part-time students.

FINANCIAL AID PROCEDURES

Forms required: FAFSA, institutional form.
Dates and Deadlines: Closing date 5/1. Applicants notified on a rolling basis starting 4/15; must reply within 2 week(s) of notification.

CONTACT
Norma Smith, Financial Aid Coordinator
33 Edgemont Drive, Presque Isle, ME 04769
(207) 768-2790

Saint Joseph's College of Maine
Standish, Maine
www.sjcme.edu   Federal Code: 002051

4-year private liberal arts college in small town, affiliated with Roman Catholic Church.
Enrollment: 1,039 undergrads.
Selectivity: Admits over 75% of applicants.

BASIC COSTS (2009-2010)
Tuition and fees: $26,050.
Per-credit charge: $835.
Room and board: $10,350.

FINANCIAL AID PICTURE (2009-2010)
Students with need: Need-based aid available for full-time and part-time students. Work study available nights, weekends, and for part-time students.
Students without need: No-need awards available for academics, leadership.

FINANCIAL AID PROCEDURES
Forms required: FAFSA, institutional form.
Dates and Deadlines: Priority date 3/1; no closing date. Applicants notified on a rolling basis starting 3/1; must reply within 3 week(s) of notification.

CONTACT
Andrea Cross, Associate Dean for Financial Aid
278 Whites Bridge Road, Standish, ME 04084-5263
(800) 752-1266

Southern Maine Community College
South Portland, Maine
www.smccme.edu   Federal Code: 005525

2-year public community and technical college in large town.
Enrollment: 5,722 undergrads, 46% part-time.
Selectivity: Open admission; but selective for some programs.

BASIC COSTS (2009-2010)
Tuition and fees: $3,239; out-of-state residents $5,759.
Per-credit charge: $84; out-of-state residents $168.
Room and board: $8,212.
Additional info: Additional lab and technology fees may apply to specific programs and courses.

FINANCIAL AID PICTURE
Students with need: Need-based aid available for full-time and part-time students. Work study available nights, weekends, and for part-time students.
Students without need: This college awards aid only to students with need.

FINANCIAL AID PROCEDURES
Forms required: FAFSA.
Dates and Deadlines: Priority date 3/30; no closing date. Applicants notified on a rolling basis; must reply by 5/1 or within 2 week(s) of notification.

CONTACT
Michel Lussier, Director of Financial Aid
2 Fort Road, South Portland, ME 04106
(207) 741-5518

Thomas College
Waterville, Maine
www.thomas.edu   Federal Code: 002052

4-year private business and liberal arts college in large town.
Enrollment: 740 undergrads, 12% part-time. 210 full-time freshmen.
Selectivity: Admits over 75% of applicants.

BASIC COSTS (2009-2010)
Tuition and fees: $20,440.
Per-credit charge: $830.
Room and board: $8,410.

FINANCIAL AID PICTURE (2009-2010)
Students with need: Out of 210 full-time freshmen who applied for aid, 206 were judged to have need. Of these, 206 received aid, and 15 had their full need met. Average financial aid package met 85% of need; average scholarship/grant was $13,611; average loan was $4,005. For part-time students, average financial aid package was $12,854.
Students without need: 10 full-time freshmen who did not demonstrate need for aid received scholarships/grants; average award was $4,940. No-need awards available for academics, leadership, state/district residency.
Cumulative student debt: 93% of graduating class had student loans; average debt was $30,928.

FINANCIAL AID PROCEDURES
Forms required: FAFSA.
Dates and Deadlines: Priority date 2/15; no closing date. Applicants notified on a rolling basis starting 3/15; must reply within 2 week(s) of notification.

CONTACT
Jeannine Bosse, Director of Student Financial Services
180 West River Road, Waterville, ME 04901
(207) 859-1105

Unity College
Unity, Maine
www.unity.edu   Federal Code: 006858

4-year private liberal arts college in rural community.
Enrollment: 558 undergrads, 1% part-time. 169 full-time freshmen.
Selectivity: Admits over 75% of applicants.

BASIC COSTS (2010-2011)
Tuition and fees: $22,200.
Room and board: $8,220.

FINANCIAL AID PICTURE (2009-2010)
Students with need: Out of 161 full-time freshmen who applied for aid, 150 were judged to have need. Of these, 150 received aid, and 5 had their full need met. Average financial aid package met 73% of need; average scholarship/grant was $12,395; average loan was $4,720. For part-time students, average financial aid package was $7,030.
Students without need: 13 full-time freshmen who did not demonstrate need for aid received scholarships/grants; average award was $3,623. No-need awards available for academics, leadership, minority status.

FINANCIAL AID PROCEDURES
Forms required: FAFSA.
Dates and Deadlines: Priority date 3/1; no closing date. Applicants notified on a rolling basis starting 3/10; must reply within 2 week(s) of notification.

CONTACT
Rand Newell, Director of Financial Aid
P.O. 532, Unity, ME 04988-0532
(207) 948-3131 ext. 235

University of Maine
Orono, Maine
www.umaine.edu   Federal Code: 002053

4-year public university in large town.
Enrollment: 8,759 undergrads, 9% part-time. 1,701 full-time freshmen.
Selectivity: Admits over 75% of applicants.

BASIC COSTS (2009-2010)
Tuition and fees: $9,626; out-of-state residents $23,876.
Per-credit charge: $253; out-of-state residents $728.
Room and board: $8,348.
Additional info: New England Regional Student Program tuition is $11,400.

FINANCIAL AID PICTURE (2008-2009)
Students with need: Average financial aid package met 76% of need; average scholarship/grant was $6,608; average loan was $4,312. For part-time students, average financial aid package was $9,205.
Students without need: No-need awards available for academics, alumni affiliation, art, athletics, job skills, leadership, minority status, music/drama, religious affiliation, ROTC, state/district residency.
Scholarships offered: Academic merit scholarships range in value from $1,000 to full tuition. All awards are renewable for up to eight (8) consecutive semesters, based upon academic performance. Top Scholar Awards and Tuition Scholarships pay full resident tuition or full nonresident differential per semester each academic year.
Cumulative student debt: 73% of graduating class had student loans; average debt was $24,330.
Additional info: Financial aid is available for students entering in the spring.

FINANCIAL AID PROCEDURES
Forms required: FAFSA.
Dates and Deadlines: Priority date 3/1; no closing date. Applicants notified on a rolling basis starting 3/15; must reply by 5/1 or within 2 week(s) of notification.

CONTACT
Peggy Crawford, Director of Student Financial Aid
5713 Chadbourne Hall, Orono, ME 04469-5713
(207) 581-1324

University of Maine at Augusta
Augusta, Maine
www.uma.edu   Federal Code: 006760

4-year public university in large town.
Enrollment: 4,370 undergrads, 62% part-time. 308 full-time freshmen.
Selectivity: Open admission; but selective for some programs.

BASIC COSTS (2009-2010)
Tuition and fees: $6,855; out-of-state residents $15,375.
Per-credit charge: $200; out-of-state residents $484.
Additional info: New England Regional Student Program tuition is $9,000.

FINANCIAL AID PICTURE (2009-2010)
Students with need: Average financial aid package met 63% of need; average scholarship/grant was $4,628; average loan was $3,087. For part-time students, average financial aid package was $4,723.
Students without need: No-need awards available for academics, athletics, leadership, music/drama, state/district residency.

FINANCIAL AID PROCEDURES
Forms required: FAFSA.
Dates and Deadlines: Priority date 3/1; no closing date. Applicants notified on a rolling basis starting 3/15; must reply within 2 week(s) of notification.

CONTACT
Sherry McCollett, Director of Financial Aid
46 University Drive, Augusta, ME 04330
(207) 621-3455

University of Maine at Farmington
Farmington, Maine
www.farmington.edu   Federal Code: 002040

4-year public liberal arts and teachers college in small town.
Enrollment: 2,046 undergrads, 4% part-time. 492 full-time freshmen.
Selectivity: Admits over 75% of applicants.

BASIC COSTS (2009-2010)
Tuition and fees: $8,446; out-of-state residents $16,862.
Per-credit charge: $241; out-of-state residents $504.
Room and board: $7,552.
Additional info: New England Regional Student Program tuition and fees: $11,616. Tuition/fee waivers available for minority students.

FINANCIAL AID PICTURE (2008-2009)
Students with need: Need-based aid available for full-time and part-time students. Work study available nights, weekends, and for part-time students.
Students without need: No-need awards available for academics, leadership, minority status, state/district residency.
Scholarships offered: Presidential Scholarships; $2,000 renewable annually; for non-residents graduating in top half of high school class.
Additional info: FAFSA must arrive at Federal processor by 3/1.

FINANCIAL AID PROCEDURES
Forms required: FAFSA.
Dates and Deadlines: Priority date 3/1; no closing date. Applicants notified on a rolling basis starting 3/15; must reply within 2 week(s) of notification.

CONTACT
Ronald Milliken, Director of Financial Aid
246 Main Street, Farmington, ME 04938
(207) 778-7100

University of Maine at Fort Kent
Fort Kent, Maine
www.umfk.maine.edu   Federal Code: 002041

4-year public university and branch campus college in small town.
Enrollment: 1,063 undergrads, 46% part-time. 118 full-time freshmen.
Selectivity: Admits over 75% of applicants.

BASIC COSTS (2009-2010)
Tuition and fees: $6,803; out-of-state residents $15,953.
Per-credit charge: $201; out-of-state residents $506.
Room and board: $7,080.
Additional info: New England Regional Student Program tuition is $9,060.

FINANCIAL AID PICTURE (2009-2010)
Students with need: Need-based aid available for full-time and part-time students. Work study available nights, weekends, and for part-time students.
Students without need: No-need awards available for academics, leadership, state/district residency.

FINANCIAL AID PROCEDURES
Forms required: FAFSA, state aid form, institutional form.
Dates and Deadlines: Priority date 3/1; closing date 2/1. Applicants notified on a rolling basis starting 3/15; must reply within 2 week(s) of notification.

CONTACT

Ellen Cost, Director of Financial Aid
23 University Drive, Fort Kent, ME 04743
(207) 834-7607

University of Maine at Machias

Machias, Maine
www.umm.maine.edu   Federal Code: 002055

4-year public university and liberal arts college in rural community.

Enrollment: 573 undergrads, 21% part-time. 99 full-time freshmen.

Selectivity: Admits 50 to 75% of applicants.

BASIC COSTS (2009-2010)

Tuition and fees: $6,775; out-of-state residents $17,515.

Per-credit charge: $201; out-of-state residents $559.

Room and board: $6,936.

Additional info: New England Regional Student Program tuition is $9,060. Tuition/fee waivers available for minority students.

FINANCIAL AID PICTURE

Students with need: Need-based aid available for full-time and part-time students.

Students without need: No-need awards available for academics, alumni affiliation, art, job skills, leadership, minority status, music/drama, state/district residency.

FINANCIAL AID PROCEDURES

Forms required: FAFSA.

Dates and Deadlines: Priority date 3/1; no closing date. Applicants notified on a rolling basis starting 2/15; must reply within 2 week(s) of notification.

CONTACT

Stephanie Larrabee, Director of Financial Aid
9 O'Brien Avenue, Machias, ME 04654
(207) 255-1203

University of Maine at Presque Isle

Presque Isle, Maine
www.umpi.edu   Federal Code: 002033

4-year public university in small town.

Enrollment: 1,243 undergrads, 26% part-time. 181 full-time freshmen.

BASIC COSTS (2009-2010)

Tuition and fees: $6,670; out-of-state residents $15,820.

Per-credit charge: $201; out-of-state residents $506.

Room and board: $6,192.

Additional info: Tuition/fee waivers available for minority students.

FINANCIAL AID PICTURE (2009-2010)

Students with need: Need-based aid available for full-time and part-time students. Work study available nights, weekends, and for part-time students.

Students without need: No-need awards available for academics, alumni affiliation, art, job skills, leadership, minority status, music/drama, state/district residency.

FINANCIAL AID PROCEDURES

Forms required: FAFSA.

Dates and Deadlines: Priority date 4/1; no closing date. Applicants notified on a rolling basis starting 3/1; must reply within 2 week(s) of notification.

CONTACT

Christopher Bell, Director of Financial Aid
181 Main Street, Presque Isle, ME 04769
(207) 768-9510

University of New England

Biddeford, Maine
www.une.edu   Federal Code: 002050

4-year private university in small city.

Enrollment: 2,149 undergrads, 5% part-time. 607 full-time freshmen.

Selectivity: Admits over 75% of applicants.

BASIC COSTS (2010-2011)

Tuition and fees: $29,330.

Per-credit charge: $1,020.

Room and board: $11,410.

FINANCIAL AID PICTURE (2008-2009)

Students with need: Need-based aid available for full-time and part-time students. Work study available nights, weekends, and for part-time students.

Students without need: No-need awards available for academics, alumni affiliation, leadership.

Scholarships offered: UNE Scholarships and UNE Departmental Award; award amounts range from $1,000 to $12,000; non-need, based on academic qualifications as determined from GPA and SAT/ACT scores, must be a full-time undergraduate student and maintain a 2.5 GPA.

FINANCIAL AID PROCEDURES

Forms required: FAFSA.

Dates and Deadlines: Priority date 5/1; no closing date. Applicants notified on a rolling basis starting 2/1.

CONTACT

Kathryn Blair-Enman, Associate Director of Financial Aid
Hills Beach Road, Biddeford, ME 04005
(207) 602-2404

University of Southern Maine

Portland, Maine
www.usm.maine.edu   Federal Code: 009762

4-year public university and liberal arts college in small city.

Enrollment: 6,548 undergrads, 27% part-time. 963 full-time freshmen.

Selectivity: Admits over 75% of applicants.

BASIC COSTS (2009-2010)

Tuition and fees: $7,814; out-of-state residents $20,024.

Per-credit charge: $231; out-of-state residents $638.

Room and board: $8,762.

Additional info: New England Regional Student Program tuition is $10,410.

FINANCIAL AID PICTURE (2009-2010)

Students with need: Need-based aid available for full-time and part-time students. Work study available nights, weekends, and for part-time students.

Students without need: No-need awards available for academics, music/drama.

Scholarships offered: Range from $1,000 to $5,500 based on academic record, school/community leadership, and potential for intellectual/social contribution.

FINANCIAL AID PROCEDURES

Forms required: FAFSA.

Dates and Deadlines: Priority date 2/15; no closing date. Applicants notified on a rolling basis starting 3/15; must reply by 5/1 or within 2 week(s) of notification.

Transfers: Applicants notified on a rolling basis; must reply by 5/1 or within 2 week(s) of notification.

Maryland

CONTACT
Keith Dubois, Director of Financial Aid Office
PO Box 9300, Portland, ME 04104
(207) 780-5250

Washington County Community College
Calais, Maine
www.wccc.me.edu   Federal Code: 009231

2-year public community and technical college in small town.
Enrollment: 388 undergrads.
Selectivity: Open admission; but selective for some programs.

BASIC COSTS (2009-2010)
Tuition and fees: $3,134; out-of-state residents $5,654.
Per-credit charge: $84; out-of-state residents $168.
Room only: $3,002.
Additional info: Additional lab and technology fees may apply to specific programs and courses.

FINANCIAL AID PICTURE
Students with need: Need-based aid available for full-time and part-time students.
Students without need: No-need awards available for academics.

FINANCIAL AID PROCEDURES
Forms required: FAFSA, institutional form.
Dates and Deadlines: Priority date 5/1; no closing date. Applicants notified on a rolling basis starting 6/1; must reply within 2 week(s) of notification.

CONTACT
Eric MacDonald, Financial Aid Coordinator
One College Drive, Calais, ME 04619
(207) 454-1033

York County Community College
Wells, Maine
www.yccc.edu   Federal Code: 031229

2-year public community and technical college in small town.
Enrollment: 1,139 undergrads, 55% part-time. 138 full-time freshmen.
Selectivity: Open admission.

BASIC COSTS (2009-2010)
Tuition and fees: $3,102; out-of-state residents $5,622.
Per-credit charge: $84; out-of-state residents $168.
Additional info: Additional lab and technology fees may apply to specific programs and courses. Tuition/fee waivers available for minority students.

FINANCIAL AID PICTURE (2008-2009)
Students with need: Need-based aid available for full-time and part-time students. Work study available nights, weekends, and for part-time students.
Students without need: No-need awards available for academics, art, leadership.

FINANCIAL AID PROCEDURES
Forms required: FAFSA.
Dates and Deadlines: Priority date 5/1; no closing date. Applicants notified by 3/1; must reply within 2 week(s) of notification.

CONTACT
David Daigle, Director of Financial Aid
112 College Drive, Wells, ME 04090
(207) 646-9282 ext. 312

Allegany College of Maryland
Cumberland, Maryland
www.allegany.edu   Federal Code: 002057

2-year public community college in large town.
Enrollment: 3,238 undergrads, 29% part-time. 797 full-time freshmen.
Selectivity: Open admission; but selective for some programs.

BASIC COSTS (2009-2010)
Tuition and fees: $3,164; out-of-district residents $5,714; out-of-state residents $6,824.
Per-credit charge: $99; out-of-district residents $184; out-of-state residents $221.

FINANCIAL AID PICTURE (2008-2009)
Students with need: Need-based aid available for full-time and part-time students. Work study available nights.
Students without need: No-need awards available for academics, athletics, leadership, state/district residency.

FINANCIAL AID PROCEDURES
Forms required: FAFSA, institutional form.
Dates and Deadlines: Priority date 3/1; no closing date. Applicants notified on a rolling basis starting 4/15; must reply within 2 week(s) of notification.

CONTACT
Vicki Smith, Director of Financial Aid
12401 Willowbrook Road, SE, Cumberland, MD 21502
(301) 784-5213

Anne Arundel Community College
Arnold, Maryland
www.aacc.edu   Federal Code: 002058

2-year public community college in large town.
Enrollment: 13,997 undergrads, 58% part-time. 2,093 full-time freshmen.
Selectivity: Open admission; but selective for some programs.

BASIC COSTS (2009-2010)
Tuition and fees: $2,920; out-of-district residents $5,350; out-of-state residents $9,250.
Per-credit charge: $88; out-of-district residents $169; out-of-state residents $299.

FINANCIAL AID PICTURE (2008-2009)
Students with need: 38% of average financial aid package awarded as scholarships/grants, 62% awarded as loans/jobs. Need-based aid available for part-time students. Work study available nights, weekends, and for part-time students.

FINANCIAL AID PROCEDURES
Forms required: FAFSA, institutional form.
Dates and Deadlines: Priority date 5/15; no closing date. Applicants notified on a rolling basis starting 7/1; must reply within 2 week(s) of notification.

CONTACT
Richard Heath, Director of Student Financial Services
101 College Parkway, Arnold, MD 21012-1895
(410) 777-2240

Baltimore City Community College
Baltimore, Maryland
www.bccc.edu   Federal Code: 002061

2-year public community college in very large city.
Enrollment: 6,554 undergrads, 59% part-time. 712 full-time freshmen.
Selectivity: Open admission; but selective for some programs.

BASIC COSTS (2009-2010)
Tuition and fees: $3,062; out-of-state residents $6,722.

FINANCIAL AID PICTURE (2009-2010)
Students with need: Need-based aid available for full-time and part-time students. Work study available nights, weekends, and for part-time students.
Students without need: This college awards aid only to students with need.

FINANCIAL AID PROCEDURES
Forms required: FAFSA, state aid form, institutional form.
Dates and Deadlines: Priority date 6/1; no closing date. Applicants notified on a rolling basis starting 7/1; must reply within 2 week(s) of notification.

CONTACT
Donald Smith, Director of Financial Aid
2901 Liberty Heights Avenue, Baltimore, MD 21215-7893
(410) 462-8348

Baltimore International College
Baltimore, Maryland
www.bic.edu   Federal Code: 016376

4-year private culinary school and business college in very large city.
Enrollment: 482 undergrads.

BASIC COSTS (2010-2011)
Tuition and fees: $27,390.
Room and board: $8,542.

FINANCIAL AID PICTURE (2008-2009)
Students with need: Need-based aid available for full-time students. Work study available nights, weekends, and for part-time students.
Students without need: No-need awards available for academics, alumni affiliation, job skills, leadership, state/district residency.

FINANCIAL AID PROCEDURES
Forms required: FAFSA, institutional form.
Dates and Deadlines: Applicants notified on a rolling basis; must reply within 2 week(s) of notification.
Transfers: No deadline. Applicants notified on a rolling basis; must reply within 2 week(s) of notification.

CONTACT
Kim Wittler, Director of Student Financial Planning
17 Commerce Street, Baltimore, MD 21202-3230
(410) 752-4710

Bowie State University
Bowie, Maryland
www.bowiestate.edu   Federal Code: 002062

4-year public university in small city.
Enrollment: 4,244 undergrads, 16% part-time. 618 full-time freshmen.
Selectivity: Admits less than 50% of applicants.

BASIC COSTS (2009-2010)
Tuition and fees: $6,040; out-of-state residents $16,479.
Per-credit charge: $189; out-of-state residents $620.
Room and board: $7,536.
Additional info: Tuition at time of enrollment locked for 4 years.

FINANCIAL AID PICTURE (2009-2010)
Students with need: Out of 496 full-time freshmen who applied for aid, 494 were judged to have need. Of these, 494 received aid, and 280 had their full need met. Average financial aid package met 47% of need; average scholarship/grant was $6,730; average loan was $3,413. For part-time students, average financial aid package was $6,106.
Students without need: 12 full-time freshmen who did not demonstrate need for aid received scholarships/grants; average award was $162. No-need awards available for academics, alumni affiliation, art, athletics, leadership, music/drama, ROTC, state/district residency.
Scholarships offered: 23 full-time freshmen received athletic scholarships; average amount $4,354.
Cumulative student debt: 66% of graduating class had student loans; average debt was $17,108.

FINANCIAL AID PROCEDURES
Forms required: FAFSA.
Dates and Deadlines: Closing date 3/1. Applicants notified on a rolling basis starting 4/1; must reply within 2 week(s) of notification.
Transfers: Applicants notified on a rolling basis starting 4/1; must reply within 2 week(s) of notification.

CONTACT
Deborah Stanley, Director of Financial Aid
14000 Jericho Park Road, Bowie, MD 20715
(301) 860-3540

Carroll Community College
Westminster, Maryland
www.carrollcc.edu   Federal Code: 031007

2-year public community college in large town.
Enrollment: 3,913 undergrads, 56% part-time. 745 full-time freshmen.
Selectivity: Open admission; but selective for some programs.

BASIC COSTS (2010-2011)
Tuition and fees: $3,565; out-of-district residents $5,158; out-of-state residents $7,246.
Per-credit charge: $119; out-of-district residents $172; out-of-state residents $242.

FINANCIAL AID PICTURE (2008-2009)
Students with need: 95% of average financial aid package awarded as scholarships/grants, 5% awarded as loans/jobs. Need-based aid available for part-time students. Work study available nights, weekends, and for part-time students.
Students without need: No-need awards available for academics, art, job skills, leadership, state/district residency.

FINANCIAL AID PROCEDURES
Forms required: FAFSA.
Dates and Deadlines: Priority date 3/1; no closing date. Applicants notified by 6/1; must reply within 2 week(s) of notification.

CONTACT
Peter D'Annibale, Director of Financial Aid
1601 Washington Road, Westminster, MD 21157
(410) 386-8435

Cecil College
North East, Maryland
www.my.cecil.edu   Federal Code: 008308

2-year public community college in large town.
Enrollment: 2,270 undergrads, 62% part-time. 198 full-time freshmen.
Selectivity: Open admission; but selective for some programs.

BASIC COSTS (2009-2010)
Tuition and fees: $2,912; out-of-district residents $5,612; out-of-state residents $6,962.
Per-credit charge: $85; out-of-district residents $175; out-of-state residents $220.
Additional info: Tuition at time of enrollment locked for 2 years.

FINANCIAL AID PICTURE (2008-2009)
Students with need: 45% of average financial aid package awarded as scholarships/grants, 55% awarded as loans/jobs. Work study available nights, weekends, and for part-time students.
Students without need: No-need awards available for academics, alumni affiliation, athletics, job skills, state/district residency.

FINANCIAL AID PROCEDURES
Forms required: FAFSA.
Dates and Deadlines: Priority date 8/1; no closing date. Applicants notified on a rolling basis; must reply within 2 week(s) of notification.

CONTACT
Kate Lockhart, Director of Financial Aid
One Seahawk Drive, North East, MD 21901
(410) 287-1003

Chesapeake College
Wye Mills, Maryland
www.chesapeake.edu   Federal Code: 004650

2-year public community college in rural community.
Enrollment: 2,417 undergrads, 56% part-time. 449 full-time freshmen.
Selectivity: Open admission; but selective for some programs.

BASIC COSTS (2009-2010)
Tuition and fees: $3,304; out-of-district residents $5,374; out-of-state residents $7,684.
Per-credit charge: $91; out-of-district residents $159; out-of-state residents $236.

FINANCIAL AID PICTURE
Students with need: Need-based aid available for full-time and part-time students.
Students without need: No-need awards available for academics, art, athletics, state/district residency.

FINANCIAL AID PROCEDURES
Forms required: FAFSA, institutional form.
Dates and Deadlines: Priority date 5/1; no closing date. Applicants notified on a rolling basis starting 5/1; must reply within 2 week(s) of notification.

CONTACT
Mindy Schaffer, Director of Financial Aid
Box 8, Wye Mills, MD 21679-0008
(410) 822-5400 ext. 252

College of Notre Dame of Maryland
Baltimore, Maryland
www.ndm.edu   Federal Code: 002065

4-year private liberal arts college for women in very large city, affiliated with Roman Catholic Church.
Enrollment: 1,254 undergrads.
Selectivity: Admits over 75% of applicants.

BASIC COSTS (2009-2010)
Tuition and fees: $27,250.
Per-credit charge: $410.
Room and board: $9,100.

FINANCIAL AID PICTURE (2009-2010)
Students with need: Need-based aid available for full-time and part-time students.
Students without need: No-need awards available for academics, alumni affiliation, art, leadership, music/drama, ROTC.
Scholarships offered: Academic/achievement awards; $6,000 to full tuition. Endowed scholarships; $1,000 to $8,000; variable criteria; usually 20-35 awards.
Additional info: Maximum consideration for financial aid if application received by February 15. Auditions and portfolios in areas of art, music and writing considered for scholarships.

FINANCIAL AID PROCEDURES
Forms required: FAFSA.
Dates and Deadlines: Priority date 2/15; no closing date. Applicants notified on a rolling basis starting 3/15; must reply by 5/1 or within 2 week(s) of notification.
Transfers: Applicants notified by 3/15; must reply by 5/1 or within 2 week(s) of notification. Specific non-need based merit scholarships available for transfer students. Transfer scholarships; range from $7000 to full tuition.

CONTACT
Zhana Goltser, Director of Financial Aid
4701 North Charles Street, Baltimore, MD 21210
(410) 532-5369

College of Southern Maryland
La Plata, Maryland
www.csmd.edu   Federal Code: 002064

2-year public community college in large town.
Enrollment: 7,346 undergrads, 59% part-time. 959 full-time freshmen.
Selectivity: Open admission; but selective for some programs.

BASIC COSTS (2009-2010)
Tuition and fees: $3,690; out-of-district residents $4,110; out-of-state residents $8,303.
Per-credit charge: $100; out-of-district residents $174; out-of-state residents $225.

FINANCIAL AID PICTURE (2008-2009)
Students with need: 83% of average financial aid package awarded as scholarships/grants, 17% awarded as loans/jobs. Need-based aid available for part-time students. Work study available nights, weekends, and for part-time students.
Students without need: No-need awards available for academics, athletics, state/district residency.

FINANCIAL AID PROCEDURES
Forms required: FAFSA.
Dates and Deadlines: Priority date 3/1; no closing date. Applicants notified on a rolling basis starting 5/15; must reply within 2 week(s) of notification.

CONTACT
Joan Middleton, Director of Financial Assistance
College of Southern Maryland-AOD, La Plata, MD 20646-0910
(301) 934-7531

Community College of Baltimore County
Baltimore, Maryland
www.ccbcmd.edu   Federal Code: 002063

2-year public community college in very large city.
Enrollment: 20,959 undergrads, 62% part-time. 2,663 full-time freshmen.
Selectivity: Open admission; but selective for some programs.

BASIC COSTS (2009-2010)
Tuition and fees: $3,102; out-of-district residents $5,892; out-of-state residents $8,622.
Per-credit charge: $90; out-of-district residents $183; out-of-state residents $274.

FINANCIAL AID PICTURE (2008-2009)
Students with need: Need-based aid available for full-time and part-time students. Work study available nights, weekends, and for part-time students.
Students without need: No-need awards available for academics, athletics, state/district residency.
Additional info: On-campus employment typically available.

FINANCIAL AID PROCEDURES
Forms required: FAFSA.
Dates and Deadlines: Closing date 3/1. Applicants notified on a rolling basis starting 5/1; must reply within 2 week(s) of notification.

CONTACT
Jerome Lovick, Director of Financial Aid
800 South Rolling Road, Baltimore, MD 21228
(443) 840-4706

Coppin State University
Baltimore, Maryland
www.coppin.edu   Federal Code: 002068

4-year public liberal arts college in very large city.
Enrollment: 3,227 undergrads, 21% part-time. 541 full-time freshmen.
Selectivity: Admits 50 to 75% of applicants.

BASIC COSTS (2009-2010)
Tuition and fees: $5,276; out-of-state residents $13,971.
Per-credit charge: $151; out-of-state residents $420.
Room and board: $7,496.

FINANCIAL AID PICTURE (2009-2010)
Students with need: Need-based aid available for full-time and part-time students.
Students without need: No-need awards available for academics, alumni affiliation, athletics, ROTC, state/district residency.
Scholarships offered: Gold Freshman Merit Award; $1,200 per year; awarded to freshmen with 950 combined SAT and 2.5 high school GPA. Gold Transfer Merit Award; $1,200 per year; awarded to Maryland Community College transfer students with 2.8 GPA and successful completion of 56 credits. Blue Freshman Merit Award; $800 per year; awarded to freshman with 900 combined SAT and 2.5 GPA. Blue Transfer Merit Award; $600 per year; awarded to Maryland Community College transfer students with 2.5 GPA and successful completion of 25 credits. SAT scores exclusive of Writing.
Additional info: Funds allocated by State of Maryland for minority students enrolled for at least 6 credits who are Maryland residents and U.S. citizens (Other Race Grant).

FINANCIAL AID PROCEDURES
Forms required: FAFSA.
Dates and Deadlines: Priority date 3/1; no closing date. Applicants notified on a rolling basis starting 4/15; must reply within 2 week(s) of notification.

CONTACT
Lady Jenkins, Director of Financial Aid
2500 West North Avenue, Baltimore, MD 21216
(410) 951-3636

Frederick Community College
Frederick, Maryland
www.frederick.edu   Federal Code: 002071

2-year public community college in small city.
Enrollment: 5,518 undergrads, 58% part-time. 970 full-time freshmen.
Selectivity: Open admission; but selective for some programs.

BASIC COSTS (2009-2010)
Tuition and fees: $3,267; out-of-district residents $6,627; out-of-state residents $8,877.
Per-credit charge: $96; out-of-district residents $208; out-of-state residents $283.

FINANCIAL AID PICTURE (2008-2009)
Students with need: 64% of average financial aid package awarded as scholarships/grants, 36% awarded as loans/jobs. Need-based aid available for part-time students.
Students without need: No-need awards available for academics, athletics, state/district residency.
Scholarships offered: Scholarships available for Frederick County Public Schools students with high gpas to participate in student ambassador program; other general scholarships available for prospective students.

FINANCIAL AID PROCEDURES
Forms required: FAFSA, institutional form.
Dates and Deadlines: Priority date 6/1; no closing date. Applicants notified on a rolling basis starting 5/15; must reply within 2 week(s) of notification.
Transfers: Applicants notified on a rolling basis starting 6/1. Financial aid transcripts from prior institutions must be submitted before awards are made.

CONTACT
Brenda Dayhoff, Executive Director, Financial Aid
7932 Opossumtown Pike, Frederick, MD 21702
(301) 846-2480

Frostburg State University
Frostburg, Maryland
www.frostburg.edu   Federal Code: 002072

4-year public university and teachers college in small town.
Enrollment: 4,634 undergrads, 5% part-time. 1,027 full-time freshmen.
Selectivity: Admits 50 to 75% of applicants.

BASIC COSTS (2009-2010)
Tuition and fees: $6,684; out-of-state residents $16,880.
Per-credit charge: $207; out-of-state residents $427.
Room and board: $7,304.

FINANCIAL AID PICTURE (2009-2010)
Students with need: Need-based aid available for full-time and part-time students.
Students without need: No-need awards available for academics, leadership, minority status.

FINANCIAL AID PROCEDURES
Forms required: FAFSA.

Dates and Deadlines: Priority date 3/1; no closing date. Applicants notified on a rolling basis starting 3/15; must reply within 3 week(s) of notification.

CONTACT
Angela Hovatter, Director of Financial Aid
101 Braddock Road, Frostburg, MD 21532-1099
(301) 687-4201

Garrett College
McHenry, Maryland
www.garrettcollege.edu   Federal Code: 010014

2-year public community college in rural community.
Enrollment: 684 undergrads.
Selectivity: Open admission.

BASIC COSTS (2009-2010)
Tuition and fees: $3,210; out-of-district residents $7,110; out-of-state residents $8,280.
Per-credit charge: $86; out-of-district residents $216; out-of-state residents $255.
Room and board: $5,590.

FINANCIAL AID PICTURE
Students with need: Need-based aid available for full-time and part-time students.
Students without need: No-need awards available for academics, athletics, leadership.
Additional info: Many local scholarships both merit and need based.

FINANCIAL AID PROCEDURES
Forms required: FAFSA.
Dates and Deadlines: Closing date 3/1. Applicants notified on a rolling basis starting 5/15; must reply within 2 week(s) of notification.

CONTACT
Cissy Vansickle, Director of Financial Aid
687 Mosser Road, McHenry, MD 21541
(301) 387-3057

Goucher College
Baltimore, Maryland   Federal Code: 002073
www.goucher.edu   CSS Code: 5257

4-year private liberal arts college in small city.
Enrollment: 1,464 undergrads, 2% part-time. 363 full-time freshmen.
Selectivity: Admits less than 50% of applicants.

BASIC COSTS (2010-2011)
Tuition and fees: $35,142.
Per-credit charge: $1,154.
Room and board: $10,283.

FINANCIAL AID PICTURE (2008-2009)
Students with need: Out of 242 full-time freshmen who applied for aid, 192 were judged to have need. Of these, 190 received aid, and 47 had their full need met. Average financial aid package met 81% of need; average scholarship/grant was $22,609; average loan was $3,394. For part-time students, average financial aid package was $9,703.
Students without need: 66 full-time freshmen who did not demonstrate need for aid received scholarships/grants; average award was $12,670. No-need awards available for academics, art, leadership, music/drama.
Cumulative student debt: 65% of graduating class had student loans; average debt was $14,783.

FINANCIAL AID PROCEDURES
Forms required: FAFSA, CSS PROFILE.

Dates and Deadlines: Closing date 2/1. Applicants notified on a rolling basis starting 4/1; must reply by 5/1 or within 2 week(s) of notification.
Transfers: Must reply within 2 week(s) of notification.

CONTACT
Sharon Hassan, Director of Financial Aid
1021 Dulaney Valley Road, Baltimore, MD 21204-2753
(410) 337-6141

Hagerstown Community College
Hagerstown, Maryland
www.hagerstowncc.edu   Federal Code: 002074

2-year public community college in small city.
Enrollment: 3,877 undergrads, 62% part-time. 488 full-time freshmen.
Selectivity: Open admission; but selective for some programs.

BASIC COSTS (2009-2010)
Tuition and fees: $3,270; out-of-district residents $4,920; out-of-state residents $6,330.
Per-credit charge: $98; out-of-district residents $153; out-of-state residents $200.

FINANCIAL AID PICTURE (2008-2009)
Students with need: Need-based aid available for full-time and part-time students. Work study available nights, weekends, and for part-time students.
Students without need: This college awards aid only to students with need.

FINANCIAL AID PROCEDURES
Forms required: FAFSA.
Dates and Deadlines: Priority date 3/1; no closing date. Applicants notified on a rolling basis starting 5/1.
Transfers: No deadline.

CONTACT
Carolyn Cox, Director of Financial Aid
11400 Robinwood Drive, Hagerstown, MD 21742
(301) 790-2800 ext. 473

Hood College
Frederick, Maryland
www.hood.edu   Federal Code: 002076

4-year private liberal arts college in small city.
Enrollment: 1,363 undergrads, 9% part-time. 251 full-time freshmen.
Selectivity: Admits 50 to 75% of applicants.

BASIC COSTS (2010-2011)
Tuition and fees: $29,860.
Per-credit charge: $850.
Room and board: $9,901.

FINANCIAL AID PICTURE (2009-2010)
Students with need: Out of 231 full-time freshmen who applied for aid, 202 were judged to have need. Of these, 194 received aid, and 50 had their full need met. Average financial aid package met 80% of need; average scholarship/grant was $20,993; average loan was $3,153. For part-time students, average financial aid package was $7,200.
Students without need: 51 full-time freshmen who did not demonstrate need for aid received scholarships/grants; average award was $21,810. No-need awards available for academics, alumni affiliation, music/drama, ROTC.
Scholarships offered: Hood Trust Academic Scholarship: amount varies. Hodson Scholarship: amount varies. Project Excellence Scholarship: up to full tuition. Presidential Scholarship: $10,000-$14,000. Trustee Scholarship: $8,000-$10,000.

Cumulative student debt: 64% of graduating class had student loans; average debt was $17,382.

FINANCIAL AID PROCEDURES
Forms required: FAFSA.
Dates and Deadlines: Priority date 2/15; no closing date. Applicants notified on a rolling basis starting 3/1; must reply by 5/1 or within 3 week(s) of notification.

CONTACT
Margherite Powell, Director of Financial Aid
401 Rosemont Avenue, Frederick, MD 21701-8575
(301) 696-3411

Howard Community College
Columbia, Maryland
www.howardcc.edu   Federal Code: 008175

2-year public community college in small city.
Enrollment: 8,036 undergrads, 58% part-time. 1,157 full-time freshmen.
Selectivity: Open admission; but selective for some programs.

BASIC COSTS (2009-2010)
Tuition and fees: $3,993; out-of-district residents $6,483; out-of-state residents $8,193.

FINANCIAL AID PICTURE (2008-2009)
Students with need: 74% of average financial aid package awarded as scholarships/grants, 26% awarded as loans/jobs. Need-based aid available for part-time students. Work study available nights, weekends, and for part-time students.

FINANCIAL AID PROCEDURES
Forms required: FAFSA.
Dates and Deadlines: Priority date 3/1; no closing date. Applicants notified on a rolling basis starting 5/1.

CONTACT
Katherine Allen, Director of Financial Aid
10901 Little Patuxent Parkway, Columbia, MD 21044-3197
(410) 772-4898

Johns Hopkins University
Baltimore, Maryland   Federal Code: 002077
www.jhu.edu   CSS Code: 5332

4-year private university in very large city.
Enrollment: 4,970 undergrads. 1,349 full-time freshmen.
Selectivity: Admits less than 50% of applicants.

BASIC COSTS (2010-2011)
Tuition and fees: $41,180.
Per-credit charge: $1,355.
Room and board: $12,510.

FINANCIAL AID PICTURE (2009-2010)
Students with need: Out of 801 full-time freshmen who applied for aid, 577 were judged to have need. Of these, 560 received aid, and 527 had their full need met. Average financial aid package met 94% of need; average scholarship/grant was $27,706; average loan was $3,364.
Students without need: 11 full-time freshmen who did not demonstrate need for aid received scholarships/grants; average award was $31,100. No-need awards available for academics, athletics, leadership, ROTC, state/district residency.
Scholarships offered: Merit: Hodson Trust Scholarship; $27,500 annually for 4 years; 20 awards. Westgate Scholarship for engineering freshmen; tuition plus $1,000 for 4 years: academic excellence, leadership, demonstrated re-

search experience required, 2 offered per year per class. Wilson Research grants; $10,000. Baltimore Scholars Program; full tuition scholarship for US citizens or permanent residents who have attended a Baltimore City public school for at least 10th, 11th, and 12th grades and meet a residency requirement. **Athletic:** 8 full-time freshmen received athletic scholarships; average amount $30,856.
Cumulative student debt: 46% of graduating class had student loans; average debt was $21,859.
Additional info: Selected students receive aid packages without loan expectation, grants to full need. Private merit aid does not reduce Hopkins grant.

FINANCIAL AID PROCEDURES
Forms required: FAFSA, CSS PROFILE.
Dates and Deadlines: Closing date 3/1. Applicants notified by 4/1; must reply by 5/1 or within 2 week(s) of notification.
Transfers: Closing date 3/15. Must reply within 2 week(s) of notification. Aid on funds-available basis.

CONTACT
Vincent Amoroso, Director of Student Financial Services
3400 North Charles Street, Mason Hall, Baltimore, MD 21218
(410) 516-8028

Johns Hopkins University: Peabody Conservatory of Music
Baltimore, Maryland
www.peabody.jhu.edu   Federal Code: E00233

4-year private music college in very large city.
Enrollment: 340 undergrads, 2% part-time. 83 full-time freshmen.
Selectivity: Admits less than 50% of applicants.

BASIC COSTS (2010-2011)
Tuition and fees: $36,725.
Per-credit charge: $1,015.
Room and board: $11,700.

FINANCIAL AID PICTURE (2008-2009)
Students with need: Out of 73 full-time freshmen who applied for aid, 64 were judged to have need. Of these, 64 received aid, and 21 had their full need met. Average financial aid package met 73% of need; average scholarship/grant was $14,130; average loan was $3,027. Need-based aid available for part-time students.
Students without need: 14 full-time freshmen who did not demonstrate need for aid received scholarships/grants; average award was $10,338. No-need awards available for academics, music/drama.
Cumulative student debt: 44% of graduating class had student loans; average debt was $34,442.

FINANCIAL AID PROCEDURES
Forms required: FAFSA, institutional form.
Dates and Deadlines: Priority date 2/1; closing date 2/1. Applicants notified by 4/1; must reply by 5/1.

CONTACT
Thomas McDermott, Director of Financial Aid
One East Mount Vernon Place, Baltimore, MD 21202
(410) 234-4900

Kaplan College: Hagerstown
Hagerstown, Maryland
www.Hagerstown.KaplanUniversity.edu   Federal Code: 007946

2-year for-profit business and junior college in large town.
Enrollment: 611 undergrads.

Selectivity: Open admission; but selective for some programs.

FINANCIAL AID PICTURE (2008-2009)

Students with need: Need-based aid available for full-time and part-time students.

FINANCIAL AID PROCEDURES

Forms required: FAFSA, institutional form.

Dates and Deadlines: No deadline. Applicants notified on a rolling basis starting 6/1; must reply within 2 week(s) of notification.

CONTACT

Kristen Brezler, Director of Financial Aid
18618 Crestwood Drive, Hagerstown, MD 21742
(301) 739-2670

Loyola University Maryland

Baltimore, Maryland
www.loyola.edu
Federal Code: 002078
CSS Code: 5370

4-year private business and liberal arts college in very large city, affiliated with Roman Catholic Church.

Enrollment: 3,757 undergrads, 1% part-time. 968 full-time freshmen.

Selectivity: Admits 50 to 75% of applicants.

BASIC COSTS (2010-2011)

Tuition and fees: $39,350.

Per-credit charge: $615.

Room and board: $10,650.

FINANCIAL AID PICTURE (2009-2010)

Students with need: Out of 705 full-time freshmen who applied for aid, 548 were judged to have need. Of these, 548 received aid, and 548 had their full need met. Average financial aid package met 100% of need; average scholarship/grant was $18,750; average loan was $5,445. For part-time students, average financial aid package was $3,500.

Students without need: 75 full-time freshmen who did not demonstrate need for aid received scholarships/grants; average award was $12,530. No-need awards available for academics, athletics, ROTC.

Scholarships offered: 26 full-time freshmen received athletic scholarships; average amount $32,280.

Cumulative student debt: 72% of graduating class had student loans; average debt was $26,855.

FINANCIAL AID PROCEDURES

Forms required: FAFSA, CSS PROFILE.

Dates and Deadlines: Priority date 2/15; closing date 2/15. Applicants notified by 4/1; must reply by 5/1.

Transfers: No deadline. Academic (merit-based) scholarships not available to transfer students.

CONTACT

Mark Lindenmeyer, Director of Financial Aid
4501 North Charles Street, Baltimore, MD 21210-2699
(410) 617-2576

Maryland Institute College of Art

Baltimore, Maryland
www.mica.edu
Federal Code: 002080

4-year private visual arts college in very large city.

Enrollment: 1,699 undergrads, 1% part-time. 458 full-time freshmen.

Selectivity: Admits less than 50% of applicants.

BASIC COSTS (2010-2011)

Tuition and fees: $35,690.

Per-credit charge: $1,440.

Room and board: $9,850.

FINANCIAL AID PICTURE

Students with need: Need-based aid available for full-time and part-time students. Work study available nights, weekends, and for part-time students.

Students without need: No-need awards available for academics, art.

FINANCIAL AID PROCEDURES

Forms required: FAFSA, institutional form.

Dates and Deadlines: Closing date 3/1. Applicants notified by 4/10; must reply by 5/1.

Transfers: Priority date 3/2. Applicants notified by 4/20; must reply by 5/21.

CONTACT

Diane Prengaman, Associate Vice President for Financial Aid
1300 Mount Royal Avenue, Baltimore, MD 21217-4134
(410) 225-2285

McDaniel College

Westminster, Maryland
www.mcdaniel.edu
Federal Code: 002109

4-year private liberal arts college in large town.

Enrollment: 1,666 undergrads, 1% part-time. 423 full-time freshmen.

Selectivity: Admits over 75% of applicants.

BASIC COSTS (2010-2011)

Tuition and fees: $33,280.

Per-credit charge: $1,040.

Room and board: $7,020.

FINANCIAL AID PICTURE (2009-2010)

Students with need: Out of 354 full-time freshmen who applied for aid, 301 were judged to have need. Of these, 301 received aid, and 90 had their full need met. Average financial aid package met 95% of need; average scholarship/grant was $21,937; average loan was $4,393. For part-time students, average financial aid package was $3,272.

Students without need: 86 full-time freshmen who did not demonstrate need for aid received scholarships/grants; average award was $13,692. No-need awards available for academics, ROTC, state/district residency.

Cumulative student debt: 63% of graduating class had student loans; average debt was $25,325.

FINANCIAL AID PROCEDURES

Forms required: FAFSA, institutional form.

Dates and Deadlines: Priority date 3/1; no closing date. Applicants notified on a rolling basis starting 2/15; must reply by 5/1 or within 2 week(s) of notification.

Transfers: No deadline. Applicants notified on a rolling basis starting 2/15; must reply by 8/1 or within 2 week(s) of notification.

CONTACT

Patricia Williams, Director of Financial Aid
Two College Hill, Westminster, MD 21157-4390
(410) 857-2233

Montgomery College

Rockville, Maryland
www.montgomerycollege.edu
Federal Code: 006911

2-year public community college in very large city.

Enrollment: 21,786 undergrads.

Selectivity: Open admission; but selective for some programs.

BASIC COSTS (2009-2010)

Tuition and fees: $4,092; out-of-district residents $7,944; out-of-state residents $10,644.

FINANCIAL AID PICTURE (2008-2009)

Students with need: Need-based aid available for full-time and part-time students. Work study available nights, weekends, and for part-time students.

Students without need: No-need awards available for academics, alumni affiliation, art, music/drama, state/district residency.

Scholarships offered: Board of Trustees Academic Potential Scholarship; first year of tuition; based on GPA and high school nominations; 125 awards available.

FINANCIAL AID PROCEDURES

Forms required: FAFSA, institutional form.

Dates and Deadlines: Priority date 5/15; no closing date. Applicants notified on a rolling basis starting 5/30.

Transfers: Priority date 5/15; no deadline. Applicants notified on a rolling basis starting 1/1; must reply within 4 week(s) of notification.

CONTACT

Melissa Gregory, Director of Financial Aid

51 Mannakee Street, Rockville, MD 20850

(240) 567-5100

Morgan State University

Baltimore, Maryland

www.morgan.edu   Federal Code: 002083

4-year public university and liberal arts college in large city.

Enrollment: 6,171 undergrads, 10% part-time. 1,256 full-time freshmen.

Selectivity: Admits less than 50% of applicants.

BASIC COSTS (2010-2011)

Tuition and fees: $6,548; out-of-state residents $15,418.

Per-credit charge: $194; out-of-state residents $520.

Room and board: $8,340.

Additional info: Tuition/fee waivers available for minority students.

FINANCIAL AID PICTURE

Students with need: Need-based aid available for full-time and part-time students.

FINANCIAL AID PROCEDURES

Forms required: FAFSA.

Dates and Deadlines: Priority date 4/1; no closing date. Applicants notified on a rolling basis starting 6/1; must reply within 2 week(s) of notification.

CONTACT

Abraham Moore, Vice President

1700 East Cold Spring Lane, Baltimore, MD 21251

(443) 885-3000

Mount St. Mary's University

Emmitsburg, Maryland

www.msmary.edu   Federal Code: 002086

4-year private university and liberal arts college in rural community, affiliated with Roman Catholic Church.

Enrollment: 1,609 undergrads, 7% part-time. 400 full-time freshmen.

Selectivity: Admits over 75% of applicants.

BASIC COSTS (2010-2011)

Tuition and fees: $30,350.

Per-credit charge: $990.

Room and board: $10,308.

Additional info: Tuition/fee waivers available for minority students.

FINANCIAL AID PICTURE (2009-2010)

Students with need: Out of 400 full-time freshmen who applied for aid, 343 were judged to have need. Of these, 343 received aid, and 88 had their full need met. Average financial aid package met 76% of need; average scholarship/grant was $16,102; average loan was $4,150. For part-time students, average financial aid package was $7,773.

Students without need: 113 full-time freshmen who did not demonstrate need for aid received scholarships/grants; average award was $11,744. No-need awards available for academics, art, athletics, leadership, minority status, music/drama, ROTC.

Scholarships offered: *Merit:* Founder's Scholarship; full-tuition scholarship for 4 years; based on competitive examinations, strong academic records and SAT scores of 1200 or higher (exclusive of writing); 3 awards. *Athletic:* 37 full-time freshmen received athletic scholarships; average amount $11,496.

Cumulative student debt: 67% of graduating class had student loans; average debt was $26,160.

FINANCIAL AID PROCEDURES

Forms required: FAFSA, institutional form.

Dates and Deadlines: Closing date 3/1. Applicants notified on a rolling basis starting 2/15; must reply by 5/1.

Transfers: Scholarships available based on GPA at previous institution.

CONTACT

David Reeder, Director of Financial Aid

16300 Old Emmitsburg Road, Emmitsburg, MD 21727

(800) 448-4347

Prince George's Community College

Largo, Maryland

www.pgcc.edu   Federal Code: 002089

2-year public community college in very large city.

Enrollment: 8,439 undergrads, 65% part-time. 1,410 full-time freshmen.

Selectivity: Open admission; but selective for some programs.

BASIC COSTS (2009-2010)

Tuition and fees: $3,920; out-of-district residents $6,050; out-of-state residents $8,690.

Per-credit charge: $96; out-of-district residents $167; out-of-state residents $255.

Additional info: Instructional services fees range from $27 to $37 per credit depending on course.

FINANCIAL AID PICTURE (2008-2009)

Students with need: Need-based aid available for full-time and part-time students.

Students without need: This college awards aid only to students with need.

FINANCIAL AID PROCEDURES

Forms required: FAFSA, institutional form.

Dates and Deadlines: Priority date 6/1; no closing date. Applicants notified on a rolling basis starting 6/1; must reply within 2 week(s) of notification.

CONTACT

Jane Hickey, Director of Financial Aid

301 Largo Road, Largo, MD 20774

(301) 322-0866

St. John's College

Annapolis, Maryland
www.stjohnscollege.edu

Federal Code: 002092
CSS Code: 5598

4-year private liberal arts college in large town.
Enrollment: 464 undergrads. 133 full-time freshmen.
Selectivity: Admits over 75% of applicants.

BASIC COSTS (2010-2011)

Tuition and fees: $42,192.
Room and board: $9,984.

FINANCIAL AID PICTURE (2009-2010)

Students with need: 70% of average financial aid package awarded as scholarships/grants, 30% awarded as loans/jobs. Need-based aid available for part-time students. Work study available nights, weekends, and for part-time students.
Students without need: This college awards aid only to students with need.

FINANCIAL AID PROCEDURES

Forms required: FAFSA, CSS PROFILE.
Dates and Deadlines: Priority date 2/15; no closing date. Applicants notified on a rolling basis starting 1/15; must reply by 5/1.

CONTACT

Robyn Fisher, Director of Financial Aid
PO Box 2800, Annapolis, MD 21404
(410) 626-2502

St. Mary's College of Maryland

St. Mary's City, Maryland
www.smcm.edu

Federal Code: 002095

4-year public liberal arts college in large town.
Enrollment: 1,978 undergrads, 2% part-time. 456 full-time freshmen.
Selectivity: Admits 50 to 75% of applicants.

BASIC COSTS (2010-2011)

Tuition and fees: $13,630; out-of-state residents $25,023.
Per-credit charge: $185.
Room and board: $10,235.

FINANCIAL AID PICTURE (2008-2009)

Students with need: Out of 320 full-time freshmen who applied for aid, 205 were judged to have need. Of these, 205 received aid. Average financial aid package met 59% of need; average scholarship/grant was $3,000; average loan was $3,500. For part-time students, average financial aid package was $3,500.
Students without need: 145 full-time freshmen who did not demonstrate need for aid received scholarships/grants; average award was $3,000. No-need awards available for academics, alumni affiliation.
Cumulative student debt: 70% of graduating class had student loans; average debt was $17,125.

FINANCIAL AID PROCEDURES

Forms required: FAFSA.
Dates and Deadlines: Priority date 2/15; closing date 3/1. Applicants notified by 4/1; must reply by 5/1.
Transfers: Priority date 3/1; closing date 6/1. Must reply by 8/1 or within 2 week(s) of notification. All financial aid recipients must have GED or high school diploma. Financial aid transcript required from previous colleges attended.

CONTACT

Timothy Wolfe, Director of Financial Aid
18952 East Fisher Road, St. Mary's City, MD 20686-3001
(240) 895-3000

Salisbury University

Salisbury, Maryland
www.salisbury.edu

Federal Code: 002091

4-year public university and liberal arts college in large town.
Enrollment: 7,285 undergrads, 5% part-time. 1,199 full-time freshmen.
Selectivity: Admits 50 to 75% of applicants.

BASIC COSTS (2009-2010)

Tuition and fees: $6,618; out-of-state residents $15,114.
Per-credit charge: $200; out-of-state residents $553.
Room and board: $7,810.

FINANCIAL AID PICTURE (2008-2009)

Students with need: Out of 961 full-time freshmen who applied for aid, 490 were judged to have need. Of these, 478 received aid, and 108 had their full need met. Average financial aid package met 63% of need; average scholarship/grant was $5,398; average loan was $3,002. For part-time students, average financial aid package was $4,717.
Students without need: 270 full-time freshmen who did not demonstrate need for aid received scholarships/grants; average award was $1,730. No-need awards available for academics, alumni affiliation, art, leadership, music/drama, state/district residency.
Cumulative student debt: 56% of graduating class had student loans; average debt was $17,521.

FINANCIAL AID PROCEDURES

Forms required: FAFSA.
Dates and Deadlines: Closing date 3/1. Applicants notified on a rolling basis starting 3/15; must reply by 5/1 or within 2 week(s) of notification.
Transfers: No deadline. Financial aid transcripts from previous schools required.

CONTACT

Elizabeth Zimmerman, Director of Financial Aid
1200 Camden Avenue, Salisbury, MD 21801-6862
(410) 543-6165

Sojourner-Douglass College

Baltimore, Maryland
www.sdc.edu

Federal Code: 021279

4-year private liberal arts college in very large city.
Enrollment: 1,250 undergrads.
Selectivity: Open admission.

BASIC COSTS (2009-2010)

Tuition and fees: $8,360.

FINANCIAL AID PICTURE (2008-2009)

Students with need: Need-based aid available for full-time and part-time students.

FINANCIAL AID PROCEDURES

Forms required: FAFSA, institutional form.
Dates and Deadlines: Priority date 3/1; no closing date. Applicants notified on a rolling basis; must reply within 2 week(s) of notification.

CONTACT

Rebecca Chalk, Financial Aid Administrator
500 North Caroline Street, Baltimore, MD 21205
(410) 276-0306 ext. 260

Stevenson University

Stevenson, Maryland
www.stevenson.edu   Federal Code: 002107

4-year private university and career college in very large city.
Enrollment: 3,133 undergrads, 16% part-time. 630 full-time freshmen.
Selectivity: Admits 50 to 75% of applicants.

BASIC COSTS (2009-2010)
Tuition and fees: $20,644.
Per-credit charge: $487.
Room and board: $10,296.
Additional info: Room and board fees includes laundry.

FINANCIAL AID PICTURE (2008-2009)
Students with need: Out of 545 full-time freshmen who applied for aid, 437 were judged to have need. Of these, 436 received aid, and 91 had their full need met. Average financial aid package met 59% of need; average scholarship/grant was $11,823; average loan was $4,616. For part-time students, average financial aid package was $7,033.
Students without need: 135 full-time freshmen who did not demonstrate need for aid received scholarships/grants; average award was $6,865. No-need awards available for academics, art, leadership, music/drama, ROTC.
Cumulative student debt: 62% of graduating class had student loans; average debt was $17,896.
Additional info: Cooperative Education Program allows students to work in their field of study with area corporations.

FINANCIAL AID PROCEDURES
Forms required: FAFSA.
Dates and Deadlines: Priority date 2/15; no closing date. Applicants notified on a rolling basis starting 3/15; must reply by 5/1 or within 2 week(s) of notification.

CONTACT
Barbara Miller, Director of Financial Aid
1525 Greenspring Valley Road, Stevenson, MD 21153-0641
(443) 334-3500

Towson University

Towson, Maryland
www.towson.edu   Federal Code: 002099

4-year public university in large city.
Enrollment: 16,598 undergrads, 9% part-time. 2,398 full-time freshmen.
Selectivity: Admits 50 to 75% of applicants.

BASIC COSTS (2009-2010)
Tuition and fees: $7,418; out-of-state residents $18,232.
Per-credit charge: $225; out-of-state residents $611.
Room and board: $8,670.

FINANCIAL AID PICTURE (2009-2010)
Students with need: Out of 1,941 full-time freshmen who applied for aid, 1,275 were judged to have need. Of these, 1,202 received aid, and 213 had their full need met. Average financial aid package met 67% of need; average scholarship/grant was $8,753; average loan was $3,237. For part-time students, average financial aid package was $5,770.
Students without need: 235 full-time freshmen who did not demonstrate need for aid received scholarships/grants; average award was $4,740. No-need awards available for academics, art, athletics, music/drama, ROTC.
Scholarships offered: *Merit:* Towson Scholar Award: full tuition, fees, room and board. Presidential Scholarship: full tuition and fees. University Scholarship: full tuition. Provost Scholarship: $1,000-$6,000. Selection based on GPA and combined SAT score. *Athletic:* 1 full-time freshmen received athletic scholarships; average amount $3,500.

Cumulative student debt: 23% of graduating class had student loans; average debt was $13,245.

FINANCIAL AID PROCEDURES
Forms required: FAFSA.
Dates and Deadlines: Closing date 2/10. Applicants notified on a rolling basis starting 3/21; must reply by 5/1 or within 2 week(s) of notification.
Transfers: Priority date 3/1.

CONTACT
Vincent Pecora, Director of Financial Aid
8000 York Road, Towson, MD 21252-0001
(410) 704-4236

United States Naval Academy

Annapolis, Maryland
www.usna.edu   Federal Code: 002101

4-year public military college in large town.
Enrollment: 4,552 undergrads. 1,228 full-time freshmen.
Selectivity: Admits less than 50% of applicants.

BASIC COSTS (2010-2011)
Additional info: Tuition, room and board, and medical and dental care provided by United States government. Each midshipman receives monthly salary of about $929 to cover costs of books, supplies, uniforms, laundry, and equipment, including microcomputer.

CONTACT
117 Decatur Road, Annapolis, MD 21402-5018

University of Baltimore

Baltimore, Maryland
www.ubalt.edu   Federal Code: 002102

4-year public business and liberal arts college in very large city.
Enrollment: 2,967 undergrads, 41% part-time. 175 full-time freshmen.
Selectivity: Admits 50 to 75% of applicants.

BASIC COSTS (2009-2010)
Tuition and fees: $7,171; out-of-state residents $20,678.
Per-credit charge: $243; out-of-state residents $784.

FINANCIAL AID PICTURE
Students with need: Need-based aid available for full-time and part-time students.

FINANCIAL AID PROCEDURES
Forms required: FAFSA, institutional form.
Dates and Deadlines: No deadline. Applicants notified on a rolling basis.
Transfers: Closing date 5/1. Applicants notified on a rolling basis; must reply within 2 week(s) of notification. Scholarship application deadline, March 1.

CONTACT
Anne Hamill, Director, Financial Aid
1420 North Charles Street, Baltimore, MD 21201-5779
(410) 837-4763

University of Maryland: Baltimore

Baltimore, Maryland
www.umaryland.edu   Federal Code: 002104

Upper-division public university and health science college in very large city.
Enrollment: 840 undergrads, 35% part-time.
Selectivity: Admits 50 to 75% of applicants.

BASIC COSTS (2009-2010)

Tuition and fees: $7,941; out-of-state residents $23,650.
Per-credit charge: $301; out-of-state residents $583.

FINANCIAL AID PICTURE (2008-2009)

Students with need: Need-based aid available for full-time and part-time students. Work study available nights, weekends, and for part-time students.
Additional info: Maryland state deadline 3/1.

FINANCIAL AID PROCEDURES

Forms required: FAFSA, state aid form.
Dates and Deadlines: Priority date 3/15; no closing date. Applicants notified on a rolling basis starting 4/15; must reply within 2 week(s) of notification.

CONTACT

Patricia Scott, Associate Director of Financial Aid
620 West Lexington Street, Baltimore, MD 21201
(410) 706-7347

University of Maryland: Baltimore County
Baltimore, Maryland
www.umbc.edu   Federal Code: 002105

4-year public university in large city.
Enrollment: 9,815 undergrads, 12% part-time. 1,557 full-time freshmen.
Selectivity: Admits 50 to 75% of applicants.

BASIC COSTS (2009-2010)

Tuition and fees: $8,872; out-of-state residents $18,213.
Per-credit charge: $270; out-of-state residents $658.
Room and board: $9,303.

FINANCIAL AID PICTURE (2008-2009)

Students with need: Out of 1,102 full-time freshmen who applied for aid, 675 were judged to have need. Of these, 675 received aid, and 222 had their full need met. Average financial aid package met 88% of need; average scholarship/grant was $9,612; average loan was $3,574. For part-time students, average financial aid package was $8,235.
Students without need: 528 full-time freshmen who did not demonstrate need for aid received scholarships/grants; average award was $3,811. No-need awards available for academics, alumni affiliation, art, athletics, music/drama.
Scholarships offered: *Merit:* UMBC General Merit Awards, range from $500-$22,000 per year. Scholars Programs, awards range from $5,000-$22,000 per year. These programs include Center for Women and Information Technology (CWIT) Scholars Program, Humanities Scholars Program, Linehan Artist Scholars Program, Meyerhoff Scholars Program (Sciences and Engineering), and Sondheim Public Affairs Scholars Program Scholars Programs; tuition, fees, room and board. *Athletic:* 73 full-time freshmen received athletic scholarships; average amount $3,855.
Cumulative student debt: 51% of graduating class had student loans; average debt was $19,353.

FINANCIAL AID PROCEDURES

Forms required: FAFSA.
Dates and Deadlines: Priority date 2/14; no closing date. Applicants notified on a rolling basis starting 3/15; must reply within 2 week(s) of notification.
Transfers: 2-year merit scholarships available for transfer students from community colleges.

CONTACT

Stephanie Johnson, Director of Financial Aid
1000 Hilltop Circle, Baltimore, MD 21250
(410) 455-2387

University of Maryland: College Park
College Park, Maryland
www.maryland.edu   Federal Code: 002103

4-year public university in large town.
Enrollment: 25,898 undergrads, 5% part-time. 4,193 full-time freshmen.
Selectivity: Admits less than 50% of applicants.

BASIC COSTS (2009-2010)

Tuition and fees: $8,053; out-of-state residents $23,990.
Per-credit charge: $273; out-of-state residents $938.
Room and board: $9,377.

FINANCIAL AID PICTURE (2008-2009)

Students with need: Need-based aid available for full-time and part-time students. Work study available nights, weekends, and for part-time students.
Students without need: No-need awards available for academics, art, athletics, music/drama.
Additional info: Prepaid tuition plans available through state.

FINANCIAL AID PROCEDURES

Forms required: FAFSA.
Dates and Deadlines: Priority date 2/15; no closing date. Applicants notified on a rolling basis starting 4/1.

CONTACT

Sarah Bauder, Director of Student Financial Aid
Mitchell Building, College Park, MD 20742-5235
(301) 314-9000

University of Maryland: Eastern Shore
Princess Anne, Maryland
www.umes.edu   Federal Code: 002106

4-year public university in rural community.
Enrollment: 3,827 undergrads, 6% part-time. 876 full-time freshmen.
Selectivity: Admits 50 to 75% of applicants.

BASIC COSTS (2009-2010)

Tuition and fees: $6,082; out-of-state residents $13,306.
Per-credit charge: $171; out-of-state residents $417.
Room and board: $7,230.

FINANCIAL AID PICTURE (2008-2009)

Students with need: Out of 789 full-time freshmen who applied for aid, 710 were judged to have need. Of these, 710 received aid, and 427 had their full need met. For part-time students, average financial aid package was $2,270.
Students without need: 79 full-time freshmen who did not demonstrate need for aid received scholarships/grants; average award was $3,219. No-need awards available for academics, alumni affiliation, art, athletics, leadership, music/drama, ROTC, state/district residency.
Scholarships offered: 10 full-time freshmen received athletic scholarships; average amount $15,380.
Cumulative student debt: 89% of graduating class had student loans; average debt was $9,789.

FINANCIAL AID PROCEDURES

Forms required: FAFSA.
Dates and Deadlines: Priority date 3/1; closing date 4/1. Applicants notified on a rolling basis starting 4/15.

CONTACT

James Kellam, Director of Financial Aid
Student Development Center, Suite 1140, Princess Anne, MD 21853
(410) 651-6172

University of Maryland: University College
Adelphi, Maryland
www.umuc.edu   Federal Code: 011644

4-year public university in large town.

Enrollment: 23,168 undergrads, 85% part-time. 108 full-time freshmen.

Selectivity: Open admission.

BASIC COSTS (2009-2010)
Tuition and fees: $5,820; out-of-state residents $12,276.

Per-credit charge: $230; out-of-state residents $490.

FINANCIAL AID PICTURE (2008-2009)
Students with need: Out of 81 full-time freshmen who applied for aid, 74 were judged to have need. Of these, 68 received aid. Average financial aid package met 17% of need; average scholarship/grant was $3,447; average loan was $2,594. For part-time students, average financial aid package was $4,939.

Students without need: No-need awards available for academics, leadership.

FINANCIAL AID PROCEDURES
Forms required: FAFSA.

Dates and Deadlines: Priority date 6/1; no closing date. Applicants notified on a rolling basis starting 5/1; must reply within 2 week(s) of notification.

CONTACT
Cheryl Storie, Associate Vice President, Financial Aid

3501 University Boulevard East, Adelphi, MD 20783

Washington Adventist University
Takoma Park, Maryland
www.cuc.edu   Federal Code: 002067

4-year private liberal arts college in large town, affiliated with Seventh-day Adventists.

Enrollment: 986 undergrads, 22% part-time. 144 full-time freshmen.

Selectivity: Admits less than 50% of applicants.

BASIC COSTS (2010-2011)
Tuition and fees: $19,480.

Room and board: $7,200.

FINANCIAL AID PICTURE (2008-2009)
Students with need: Need-based aid available for full-time and part-time students.

Students without need: No-need awards available for academics, athletics, leadership, music/drama, state/district residency.

FINANCIAL AID PROCEDURES
Forms required: FAFSA.

Dates and Deadlines: Closing date 3/31. Applicants notified on a rolling basis starting 5/31; must reply within 4 week(s) of notification.

CONTACT
Sharon Conway, Director of Financial Aid

7600 Flower Avenue, Takoma Park, MD 20912

(301) 891-4005

Washington Bible College
Lanham, Maryland
www.bible.edu   Federal Code: 001462

4-year private Bible and seminary college in large town, affiliated with nondenominational tradition.

Enrollment: 300 undergrads.

BASIC COSTS (2009-2010)
Tuition and fees: $13,230.

Per-credit charge: $420.

Room and board: $6,770.

FINANCIAL AID PICTURE (2008-2009)
Students with need: Need-based aid available for full-time and part-time students. Work study available nights, weekends, and for part-time students.

Students without need: No-need awards available for academics, leadership, music/drama, state/district residency.

FINANCIAL AID PROCEDURES
Forms required: FAFSA, institutional form.

Dates and Deadlines: Closing date 3/1. Applicants notified on a rolling basis starting 7/1; must reply within 2 week(s) of notification.

Transfers: Priority date 7/1; no deadline. Applicants notified on a rolling basis; must reply within 2 week(s) of notification.

CONTACT
Nichole Sefiane, Director of Financial Aid

6511 Princess Garden Parkway, Lanham, MD 20706-3599

(877) 793-7227

Washington College
Chestertown, Maryland
www.washcoll.edu   Federal Code: 002108

4-year private liberal arts college in small town.

Enrollment: 1,268 undergrads. 378 full-time freshmen.

Selectivity: Admits 50 to 75% of applicants.

BASIC COSTS (2010-2011)
Tuition and fees: $36,738.

Room and board: $7,834.

FINANCIAL AID PICTURE (2009-2010)
Students with need: Out of 300 full-time freshmen who applied for aid, 219 were judged to have need. Of these, 219 received aid, and 48 had their full need met. Average financial aid package met 81% of need; average scholarship/grant was $21,904; average loan was $4,087. For part-time students, average financial aid package was $25,795.

Students without need: 113 full-time freshmen who did not demonstrate need for aid received scholarships/grants; average award was $14,932. No-need awards available for academics.

Scholarships offered: National Honor Society Scholarship; $40,000 over 4 years; applicant must be member of National Honor Society.

Cumulative student debt: 58% of graduating class had student loans; average debt was $28,727.

FINANCIAL AID PROCEDURES
Forms required: FAFSA, institutional form.

Dates and Deadlines: Priority date 2/15; no closing date. Applicants notified on a rolling basis starting 2/1; must reply by 5/1.

CONTACT
Jean Narcum, Director of Financial Aid

300 Washington Avenue, Chestertown, MD 21620-1197

(410) 778-7214

Wor-Wic Community College
Salisbury, Maryland
www.worwic.edu   Federal Code: 013842

2-year public community college in large town.
Enrollment: 3,628 undergrads, 66% part-time. 431 full-time freshmen.
Selectivity: Open admission; but selective for some programs.

BASIC COSTS (2010-2011)
Tuition and fees: $2,898; out-of-district residents $6,138; out-of-state residents $7,518.
Per-credit charge: $89; out-of-district residents $197; out-of-state residents $243.

FINANCIAL AID PICTURE (2009-2010)
Students with need: Need-based aid available for full-time and part-time students. Work study available nights, weekends, and for part-time students.
Students without need: No-need awards available for academics, state/district residency.

FINANCIAL AID PROCEDURES
Forms required: FAFSA, institutional form.
Dates and Deadlines: Priority date 6/1; no closing date. Applicants notified on a rolling basis starting 4/1.

CONTACT
Deborah Jenkins, Director of Financial Aid
32000 Campus Drive, Salisbury, MD 21804
(410) 334-2905

Massachusetts

American International College
Springfield, Massachusetts
www.aic.edu   Federal Code: 002114

4-year private liberal arts college in small city.
Enrollment: 1,729 undergrads, 9% part-time. 392 full-time freshmen.
Selectivity: Admits over 75% of applicants.

BASIC COSTS (2010-2011)
Tuition and fees: $26,700.
Per-credit charge: $550.
Room and board: $10,930.

FINANCIAL AID PICTURE (2008-2009)
Students with need: Out of 339 full-time freshmen who applied for aid, 320 were judged to have need. Of these, 320 received aid, and 35 had their full need met. Average financial aid package met 70% of need; average scholarship/grant was $16,590; average loan was $3,100. For part-time students, average financial aid package was $12,888.
Students without need: 64 full-time freshmen who did not demonstrate need for aid received scholarships/grants; average award was $9,062. No-need awards available for academics, alumni affiliation, athletics, leadership.
Scholarships offered: Merit: Presidential, Provost, Opportunity Scholarships; $5,000 to $11,000; based on class rank, SAT, GPA. **Athletic:** 48 full-time freshmen received athletic scholarships; average amount $13,694.

FINANCIAL AID PROCEDURES
Forms required: FAFSA, state aid form.
Dates and Deadlines: Priority date 5/1; no closing date. Applicants notified on a rolling basis starting 3/15; must reply by 5/1 or within 2 week(s) of notification.

CONTACT
Douglas Fish, Director of Financial Aid
1000 State Street, Springfield, MA 01109
(413) 205-3259

Amherst College
Amherst, Massachusetts   Federal Code: 002115
www.amherst.edu   CSS Code: 3003

4-year private liberal arts college in large town.
Enrollment: 1,744 undergrads. 438 full-time freshmen.
Selectivity: Admits less than 50% of applicants.

BASIC COSTS (2009-2010)
Tuition and fees: $38,928.
Room and board: $10,150.
Additional info: Health Insurance (waivable): $950.

FINANCIAL AID PICTURE (2008-2009)
Students with need: Out of 249 full-time freshmen who applied for aid, 224 were judged to have need. Of these, 224 received aid, and 224 had their full need met. Average financial aid package met 100% of need; average scholarship/grant was $36,075; average loan was $2,375.
Students without need: This college awards aid only to students with need.
Cumulative student debt: 46% of graduating class had student loans; average debt was $12,603.

FINANCIAL AID PROCEDURES
Forms required: FAFSA, CSS PROFILE.
Dates and Deadlines: Priority date 2/15; no closing date. Applicants notified by 4/1; must reply by 5/1.

CONTACT
Joe Case, Dean of Financial Aid
PO Box 5000, Amherst, MA 01002-5000
(413) 542-2296

Anna Maria College
Paxton, Massachusetts
www.annamaria.edu   Federal Code: 002117

4-year private liberal arts college in small town, affiliated with Roman Catholic Church.
Enrollment: 1,168 undergrads, 18% part-time. 373 full-time freshmen.
Selectivity: Admits 50 to 75% of applicants.

BASIC COSTS (2009-2010)
Tuition and fees: $26,620.
Per-credit charge: $806.
Room and board: $9,730.
Additional info: Annual tuition for music program: $27,588.

FINANCIAL AID PICTURE (2009-2010)
Students with need: Need-based aid available for full-time and part-time students. Work study available nights, weekends, and for part-time students.
Students without need: No-need awards available for academics, alumni affiliation, music/drama, religious affiliation, state/district residency.

FINANCIAL AID PROCEDURES
Forms required: FAFSA, state aid form.
Dates and Deadlines: Priority date 3/1; no closing date. Applicants notified on a rolling basis starting 4/1; must reply within 4 week(s) of notification.
Transfers: No deadline. Applicants notified on a rolling basis starting 4/1; must reply within 4 week(s) of notification. Deadline May 1 for state aid.

CONTACT

Diane Gillespie, Director of Financial Aid

50 Sunset Lane, Box O, Paxton, MA 01612-1198

(508) 849-3363

Art Institute of Boston at Lesley University

Boston, Massachusetts

www.aiboston.edu   Federal Code: 002160

4-year private visual arts college in very large city.

Enrollment: 517 undergrads.

BASIC COSTS (2010-2011)

Tuition and fees: $27,600.

Room and board: $12,800.

FINANCIAL AID PICTURE (2009-2010)

Students with need: Average financial aid package met 74% of need; average scholarship/grant was $15,193; average loan was $3,715. For part-time students, average financial aid package was $7,727.

Students without need: No-need awards available for academics, art, leadership, minority status.

Scholarships offered: Freshmen academic scholarships; $7,500 annually; 1100 SAT (exclusive of Writing) and 2.8 GPA required. Freshmen academic scholarships; $5,500 annually; 3.0 GPA required. Portfolio scholarships; top portfolios awarded $7,500 annually; other qualified portfolios awarded $5,500 annually. Presidential Scholarship; full tuition; based on portfolio, academic grades, SAT/ACT, interview, cocurricular activity; renewed annually. Access Scholarships; half tuition; awarded for portfolio, academics, interview, cocurricular activity, ethnic, geographic or economic diversity.

Cumulative student debt: 90% of graduating class had student loans; average debt was $18,000.

FINANCIAL AID PROCEDURES

Forms required: FAFSA.

Dates and Deadlines: Priority date 2/15; no closing date. Applicants notified on a rolling basis starting 2/15.

Transfers: Priority date 3/15; no deadline. Applicants notified on a rolling basis starting 3/15. AIB transfers students scholarship; $4,000 annually; based on college grades, portfolio, interview.

CONTACT

Scott Jewell, Director of Student Financial Services

700 Beacon Street, Boston, MA 02215-2598

(617) 349-8581

Assumption College

Worcester, Massachusetts

www.assumption.edu   Federal Code: 002118

4-year private liberal arts college in small city, affiliated with Roman Catholic Church.

Enrollment: 2,114 undergrads. 515 full-time freshmen.

Selectivity: Admits over 75% of applicants.

BASIC COSTS (2010-2011)

Tuition and fees: $31,305.

Per-credit charge: $1,031.

Room and board: $10,260.

FINANCIAL AID PICTURE (2009-2010)

Students with need: Out of 468 full-time freshmen who applied for aid, 400 were judged to have need. Of these, 400 received aid, and 74 had their full need met. Average financial aid package met 70% of need; average scholarship/grant was $16,000; average loan was $3,430. For part-time students, average financial aid package was $14,227.

Students without need: 82 full-time freshmen who did not demonstrate need for aid received scholarships/grants; average award was $9,064. No-need awards available for academics, athletics.

Scholarships offered: *Merit:* Academic scholarships; $2,500-$20,000 per year; based on academic achievement and leadership talents. *Athletic:* 15 full-time freshmen received athletic scholarships; average amount $18,779.

Cumulative student debt: 83% of graduating class had student loans; average debt was $24,382.

FINANCIAL AID PROCEDURES

Forms required: FAFSA.

Dates and Deadlines: Closing date 2/15. Applicants notified on a rolling basis starting 2/16; must reply by 5/1.

Transfers: Closing date 3/1. Applicants notified on a rolling basis starting 5/1.

CONTACT

Linda Mularczyk, Director of Financial Aid

500 Salisbury Street, Worcester, MA 01609-1296

(508) 767-7158

Atlantic Union College

South Lancaster, Massachusetts

www.auc.edu   Federal Code: 002119

4-year private professional school in small town, affiliated with Seventh-day Adventists.

Enrollment: 431 undergrads, 16% part-time. 87 full-time freshmen.

Selectivity: Admits 50 to 75% of applicants.

BASIC COSTS (2010-2011)

Tuition and fees: $17,066.

Room and board: $5,150.

Additional info: Tuition/fee waivers available for adults.

FINANCIAL AID PICTURE (2009-2010)

Students with need: Average financial aid package met 67% of need; average scholarship/grant was $6,325; average loan was $3,695. For part-time students, average financial aid package was $6,913.

Students without need: No-need awards available for academics, art, leadership, music/drama.

Cumulative student debt: 67% of graduating class had student loans; average debt was $32,254.

FINANCIAL AID PROCEDURES

Forms required: FAFSA, institutional form.

Dates and Deadlines: Priority date 3/1; closing date 9/16. Applicants notified on a rolling basis starting 3/1; must reply by 9/12 or within 2 week(s) of notification.

Transfers: Applicants notified on a rolling basis starting 3/1; must reply within 2 week(s) of notification.

CONTACT

Sandra Pereira, Financial Aid Director

Main Street, South Lancaster, MA 01561

(978) 368-2275

Babson College

Babson Park, Massachusetts   Federal Code: 002121
www.babson.edu   CSS Code: 3075

4-year private business college in large town.
Enrollment: 1,898 undergrads. 471 full-time freshmen.
Selectivity: Admits less than 50% of applicants.

BASIC COSTS (2009-2010)
Tuition and fees: $37,824.
Room and board: $12,500.

FINANCIAL AID PICTURE (2009-2010)
Students with need: Out of 265 full-time freshmen who applied for aid, 213 were judged to have need. Of these, 213 received aid, and 51 had their full need met. Average financial aid package met 92% of need; average scholarship/grant was $24,739; average loan was $2,862.
Students without need: This college awards aid only to students with need.
Scholarships offered: Presidential Scholarship; half tuition; based on high school record, co-curricular achievements, demonstrated leadership, writing skills, standardized test scores; approximately 40 awarded each year. Woman's Leadership Award; one quarter tuition; based on demonstrated leadership experience, future leadership potential, and academic achievement. Diversity Leadership Award; either full or half tuition; awarded to students with the greatest potential for leadership in creating a diverse Babson community.
Cumulative student debt: 49% of graduating class had student loans; average debt was $28,164.

FINANCIAL AID PROCEDURES
Forms required: FAFSA, CSS PROFILE.
Dates and Deadlines: Closing date 2/15. Applicants notified by 4/1; must reply by 5/1.
Transfers: Priority date 2/15; closing date 4/15. Applicants notified by 5/1; must reply by 6/1.

CONTACT
Melissa Shaak, Director, Student Financial Services
231 Forest Street, Babson Park, MA 02457-0310
(781) 239-4219

Bard College at Simon's Rock

Great Barrington, Massachusetts   Federal Code: 009645
www.simons-rock.edu   CSS Code: 3795

4-year private liberal arts college in small town.
Enrollment: 421 undergrads. 179 full-time freshmen.
Selectivity: Admits over 75% of applicants.

BASIC COSTS (2009-2010)
Tuition and fees: $39,380.
Per-credit charge: $1,490.
Room and board: $10,960.
Additional info: Annual health services fee of $640. Student activity fee $150.

FINANCIAL AID PICTURE (2009-2010)
Students with need: Out of 139 full-time freshmen who applied for aid, 118 were judged to have need. Of these, 112 received aid, and 37 had their full need met. Average financial aid package met 77% of need; average scholarship/grant was $19,325.
Students without need: 39 full-time freshmen who did not demonstrate need for aid received scholarships/grants; average award was $18,036. No-need awards available for academics, alumni affiliation, minority status, state/district residency.

Scholarships offered: Acceleration to Excellence Program; 2 years full tuition; based on excellent grades, community service, maturity; special application process required.

FINANCIAL AID PROCEDURES
Forms required: FAFSA, CSS PROFILE.
Dates and Deadlines: Priority date 4/15; no closing date. Applicants notified on a rolling basis starting 4/15; must reply within 2 week(s) of notification.

CONTACT
Ann Gitto, Director of Financial Aid
Office of Admission, Great Barrington, MA 01230-1990
(413) 528-7297

Bay Path College

Longmeadow, Massachusetts
www.baypath.edu   Federal Code: 002122

4-year private liberal arts college for women in large town.
Enrollment: 1,481 undergrads, 19% part-time. 192 full-time freshmen.
Selectivity: Admits 50 to 75% of applicants.

BASIC COSTS (2010-2011)
Tuition and fees: $25,515.
Per-credit charge: $470.
Room and board: $11,653.

FINANCIAL AID PICTURE (2009-2010)
Students with need: Out of 187 full-time freshmen who applied for aid, 177 were judged to have need. Of these, 168 received aid, and 17 had their full need met. Average financial aid package met 76% of need; average scholarship/grant was $15,286; average loan was $4,821. For part-time students, average financial aid package was $2,216.
Students without need: 19 full-time freshmen who did not demonstrate need for aid received scholarships/grants; average award was $10,028. No-need awards available for academics, music/drama.
Additional info: Opportunity Grant program for students whose family may be facing financial difficulties paying tuition resulting from economic conditions. Additional funding available in an endowment program to assist students who qualify.

FINANCIAL AID PROCEDURES
Forms required: FAFSA.
Dates and Deadlines: Priority date 3/1; no closing date. Applicants notified on a rolling basis starting 3/1; must reply within 2 week(s) of notification.

CONTACT
Stephanie King, Director of Student Financial Services
588 Longmeadow Street, Longmeadow, MA 01106
(413) 565-1000 ext. 1345

Bay State College

Boston, Massachusetts
www.baystate.edu   Federal Code: 003965

2-year private career college in very large city.
Enrollment: 1,114 undergrads, 34% part-time. 330 full-time freshmen.
Selectivity: Admits 50 to 75% of applicants.

BASIC COSTS (2010-2011)
Tuition and fees: $21,305.
Per-credit charge: $696.
Room and board: $11,800.

FINANCIAL AID PICTURE (2008-2009)

Students with need: Out of 300 full-time freshmen who applied for aid, 268 were judged to have need. Of these, 268 received aid, and 12 had their full need met. Average financial aid package met 76% of need; average scholarship/grant was $7,000; average loan was $3,500. For part-time students, average financial aid package was $7,000.

Students without need: 330 full-time freshmen who did not demonstrate need for aid received scholarships/grants; average award was $3,000. No-need awards available for academics, art, job skills, leadership.

Scholarships offered: Community Service Scholarship; $1,000-$2,500; based on essay and community service involvement. Presidential and Honors Scholarship; $1,500-$2,500; based on essay and academic acheivement.

FINANCIAL AID PROCEDURES

Forms required: FAFSA, institutional form.

Dates and Deadlines: Priority date 3/15; no closing date. Applicants notified on a rolling basis starting 3/15; must reply within 3 week(s) of notification.

CONTACT

Jeanie Stella-Devani, Director of Financial Aid
122 Commonwealth Avenue, Boston, MA 02116
(617) 217-9000

Becker College

Worcester, Massachusetts
www.becker.edu   Federal Code: 002123

4-year private liberal arts college in small city.

Enrollment: 1,742 undergrads, 18% part-time. 488 full-time freshmen.

Selectivity: Admits over 75% of applicants.

BASIC COSTS (2010-2011)

Tuition and fees: $26,880.
Per-credit charge: $1,075.
Room and board: $10,020.

FINANCIAL AID PICTURE (2009-2010)

Students with need: Need-based aid available for full-time and part-time students. Work study available nights, weekends, and for part-time students.

Students without need: No-need awards available for academics.

FINANCIAL AID PROCEDURES

Forms required: FAFSA.

Dates and Deadlines: Priority date 3/1; no closing date. Applicants notified on a rolling basis starting 2/1; must reply within 2 week(s) of notification.

CONTACT

61 Sever Street, Worcester, MA 01609
(508) 791-9241 ext. 242

Benjamin Franklin Institute of Technology

Boston, Massachusetts
www.bfit.edu   Federal Code: 002151

2-year private technical college in very large city.

Enrollment: 579 undergrads, 13% part-time. 281 full-time freshmen.

Selectivity: Admits 50 to 75% of applicants.

BASIC COSTS (2009-2010)

Tuition and fees: $13,950.
Per-credit charge: $581.
Additional info: Cost shown is for certificate program.

FINANCIAL AID PICTURE (2008-2009)

Students with need: Need-based aid available for full-time and part-time students.

Students without need: No-need awards available for academics.

FINANCIAL AID PROCEDURES

Forms required: FAFSA.

Dates and Deadlines: Priority date 4/1; no closing date. Applicants notified on a rolling basis starting 3/1; must reply within 4 week(s) of notification.

CONTACT

Katie Fleuriel, Director of Financial Aid
41 Berkeley Street, Boston, MA 02116
(617) 423-4630

Bentley University

Waltham, Massachusetts   Federal Code: 002124
www.bentley.edu   CSS Code: 3096

4-year private business college in small city.

Enrollment: 4,179 undergrads, 5% part-time. 1,012 full-time freshmen.

Selectivity: Admits less than 50% of applicants.

BASIC COSTS (2010-2011)

Tuition and fees: $37,058.
Room and board: $12,180.

FINANCIAL AID PICTURE (2008-2009)

Students with need: Out of 752 full-time freshmen who applied for aid, 479 were judged to have need. Of these, 477 received aid, and 205 had their full need met. Average financial aid package met 94% of need; average scholarship/grant was $20,801; average loan was $4,498. For part-time students, average financial aid package was $5,516.

Students without need: 178 full-time freshmen who did not demonstrate need for aid received scholarships/grants; average award was $17,052. No-need awards available for academics, athletics, leadership, minority status.

Scholarships offered: *Merit:* Trustee Scholarships; full tuition; based on superior record of academic accomplishment. President's Scholarships; half or one-third tuition; based on excellent academic record. Service Learning Scholarships; $7,500; for students with excellent academic records who have demonstrated commitment to community service. *Athletic:* 9 full-time freshmen received athletic scholarships; average amount $31,526.

Cumulative student debt: 64% of graduating class had student loans; average debt was $33,073.

Additional info: Deadlines for receipt of CSS PROFILE: early decision 12/1, early action and regular decision 2/1.

FINANCIAL AID PROCEDURES

Forms required: FAFSA. CSS PROFILE required if student is applying for institutional grants.

Dates and Deadlines: Closing date 2/1. Applicants notified on a rolling basis starting 3/25.

Transfers: Closing date 3/1. Applicants notified on a rolling basis.

CONTACT

Donna Kendall, Director of Financial Assistance
175 Forest Street, Waltham, MA 02452-4705
(781) 891-3441

Berklee College of Music

Boston, Massachusetts
www.berklee.edu   Federal Code: 002126

4-year private music college in very large city.

Enrollment: 3,531 undergrads, 8% part-time. 675 full-time freshmen.

Selectivity: Admits less than 50% of applicants.

BASIC COSTS (2009-2010)
Tuition and fees: $33,653.
Per-credit charge: $1,053.
Room and board: $15,080.
Additional info: Required fees include one-time charge $2,950 for purchase of laptop, which all freshmen must purchase.

FINANCIAL AID PICTURE (2009-2010)
Students with need: Average financial aid package met 31% of need; average scholarship/grant was $5,979; average loan was $4,647. For part-time students, average financial aid package was $10,455.

FINANCIAL AID PROCEDURES
Dates and Deadlines: Closing date 5/1. Applicants notified on a rolling basis starting 3/7; must reply within 2 week(s) of notification.

CONTACT
Julie Poorman, Director of Financial Aid
1140 Boylston Street, Boston, MA 02215
(800) 538-3844

Berkshire Community College
Pittsfield, Massachusetts
www.berkshirecc.edu   Federal Code: 002167

2-year public community college in large town.
Enrollment: 2,060 undergrads, 49% part-time. 339 full-time freshmen.
Selectivity: Open admission; but selective for some programs.

BASIC COSTS (2009-2010)
Tuition and fees: $4,680; out-of-state residents $12,300.
Per-credit charge: $26; out-of-state residents $280.

FINANCIAL AID PICTURE (2008-2009)
Students with need: 73% of average financial aid package awarded as scholarships/grants, 27% awarded as loans/jobs. Need-based aid available for part-time students. Work study available nights, weekends, and for part-time students.
Students without need: No-need awards available for academics, job skills, leadership, state/district residency.
Additional info: Tuition waivers available to Massachusetts residents who fall into one of the following categories: Department of Social Services adopted or foster children, Massachusetts Rehabilitation Commission clients, high-scoring MCAS students, National Guard members, Native Americans, state employees and their dependents, veterans.

FINANCIAL AID PROCEDURES
Forms required: FAFSA.
Dates and Deadlines: Priority date 5/1; no closing date. Applicants notified on a rolling basis starting 5/10; must reply within 2 week(s) of notification.
Transfers: No deadline. Applicants notified on a rolling basis.

CONTACT
Anne Moore, Director of Financial Aid
1350 West Street, Pittsfield, MA 01201-5786
(413) 236-1644

Boston Architectural College
Boston, Massachusetts
www.the-bac.edu   Federal Code: 003966

6-year private architecture and design college in very large city.
Enrollment: 636 undergrads, 3% part-time.
Selectivity: Open admission.

BASIC COSTS (2009-2010)
Tuition and fees: $11,468.
Per-credit charge: $954.
Additional info: Academic Only program tuition is $15,340 plus $20 required fees.

FINANCIAL AID PICTURE (2009-2010)
Students with need: Average financial aid package met 32% of need; average scholarship/grant was $5,765; average loan was $4,941. Need-based aid available for part-time students.
Students without need: No-need awards available for academics, art, leadership.
Scholarships offered: Creative Exercise Scholarship; 20% of semester's tuition; based on completion of creative exercise on admission application; 6 issued annually.
Cumulative student debt: 60% of graduating class had student loans; average debt was $46,875.

FINANCIAL AID PROCEDURES
Forms required: FAFSA.
Dates and Deadlines: Priority date 4/15; no closing date. Applicants notified on a rolling basis starting 3/30; must reply within 2 week(s) of notification.
Transfers: No deadline. Applicants notified on a rolling basis starting 3/1; must reply within 2 week(s) of notification.

CONTACT
Anne Downey, Director of Financial Aid
320 Newbury Street, Boston, MA 02115-2795
(617) 585-0125

Boston College
Chestnut Hill, Massachusetts   Federal Code: 002128
www.bc.edu   CSS Code: 3083

4-year private university in small city, affiliated with Roman Catholic Church.
Enrollment: 9,171 undergrads. 2,181 full-time freshmen.
Selectivity: Admits less than 50% of applicants.

BASIC COSTS (2009-2010)
Tuition and fees: $39,130.
Room and board: $11,840.

FINANCIAL AID PICTURE (2009-2010)
Students with need: Out of 1,198 full-time freshmen who applied for aid, 957 were judged to have need. Of these, 957 received aid, and 957 had their full need met. Average financial aid package met 100% of need; average scholarship/grant was $27,618; average loan was $3,521. Need-based aid available for part-time students.
Students without need: 25 full-time freshmen who did not demonstrate need for aid received scholarships/grants; average award was $20,992. No-need awards available for academics, athletics, leadership, ROTC.
Scholarships offered: 84 full-time freshmen received athletic scholarships; average amount $38,323.
Cumulative student debt: 52% of graduating class had student loans; average debt was $19,358.

FINANCIAL AID PROCEDURES
Forms required: FAFSA, CSS PROFILE.
Dates and Deadlines: Priority date 2/1; no closing date. Applicants notified on a rolling basis starting 4/1.
Transfers: Priority date 3/15. Must reply within 2 week(s) of notification.

CONTACT
Mary McGranahan, Director of Financial Aid
140 Commonwealth Avenue, Devlin Hall 208, Chestnut Hill, MA 02467-3809
(617) 552-3300

Boston Conservatory

Boston, Massachusetts
www.bostonconservatory.edu   Federal Code: 002129

4-year private music and performing arts college in very large city.

Enrollment: 489 undergrads. 145 full-time freshmen.

Selectivity: Admits less than 50% of applicants.

BASIC COSTS (2009-2010)

Tuition and fees: $33,976.

Per-credit charge: $1,320.

Room and board: $15,880.

FINANCIAL AID PICTURE (2009-2010)

Students with need: Average financial aid package met 40% of need; average scholarship/grant was $15,215; average loan was $3,546. For part-time students, average financial aid package was $3,500.

Students without need: No-need awards available for music/drama.

Cumulative student debt: 54% of graduating class had student loans; average debt was $49,608.

FINANCIAL AID PROCEDURES

Forms required: FAFSA.

Dates and Deadlines: Priority date 3/1; no closing date. Applicants notified on a rolling basis.

Transfers: Applicants notified on a rolling basis starting 4/1; must reply within 4 week(s) of notification.

CONTACT

Nicole Brennan, Director of Financial Aid
8 The Fenway, Boston, MA 02215

Boston University

Boston, Massachusetts   Federal Code: 002130
www.bu.edu   CSS Code: 3087

4-year private university in very large city.

Enrollment: 16,295 undergrads, 3% part-time. 4,130 full-time freshmen.

Selectivity: Admits 50 to 75% of applicants.

BASIC COSTS (2009-2010)

Tuition and fees: $38,440.

Per-credit charge: $1,184.

Room and board: $11,848.

FINANCIAL AID PICTURE (2009-2010)

Students with need: Out of 2,497 full-time freshmen who applied for aid, 2,065 were judged to have need. Of these, 2,063 received aid, and 1,171 had their full need met. Average financial aid package met 91% of need; average scholarship/grant was $24,183; average loan was $6,331. For part-time students, average financial aid package was $14,439.

Students without need: 290 full-time freshmen who did not demonstrate need for aid received scholarships/grants; average award was $18,862. No-need awards available for academics, alumni affiliation, art, athletics, leadership, music/drama, religious affiliation, ROTC, state/district residency.

Scholarships offered: *Merit:* Trustee Scholar Program: full tuition and fees (renewable); candidates nominated by high school principals, headmasters, or students. University Scholarships: half tuition (renewable); based on exceptionally strong high school academic record. Dean's Scholarships: $10,000 (renewable); based on strong academic credentials, for students who have applied for need-based financial aid but have financial resources that exceed cost of attendance. Dr. Martin Luther King, Jr. Scholarship: full tuition; for academically gifted students with proven leadership abilities and strong commitment to social justice and community involvement. *Athletic:* 66 full-time freshmen received athletic scholarships; average amount $37,607.

Cumulative student debt: 57% of graduating class had student loans; average debt was $30,998.

Additional info: Financial aid deadline for early decision applicants: 11/01; notification date: 2/15. Graduates of Boston's public high schools who complete their financial aid application and demonstrate need will be awarded financial aid packages that contain no loans and meet their full demonstrated need.

FINANCIAL AID PROCEDURES

Forms required: FAFSA, CSS PROFILE, state aid form.

Dates and Deadlines: Closing date 2/15. Applicants notified on a rolling basis starting 3/15; must reply by 5/1 or within 2 week(s) of notification.

Transfers: Priority date 4/1. Transfer students cannot receive duplicate disbursements simultaneously from different institutions.

CONTACT

Christine McGuire, Director of Financial Assistance
121 Bay State Road, Boston, MA 02215
(617) 353-2965

Brandeis University

Waltham, Massachusetts   Federal Code: 002133
www.brandeis.edu   CSS Code: 3092

4-year private university in small city.

Enrollment: 3,299 undergrads. 781 full-time freshmen.

Selectivity: Admits less than 50% of applicants.

BASIC COSTS (2009-2010)

Tuition and fees: $38,762.

Room and board: $10,800.

FINANCIAL AID PICTURE (2009-2010)

Students with need: Out of 546 full-time freshmen who applied for aid, 451 were judged to have need. Of these, 446 received aid, and 57 had their full need met. Average financial aid package met 82% of need; average scholarship/grant was $27,392; average loan was $3,696. For part-time students, average financial aid package was $5,248.

Students without need: 38 full-time freshmen who did not demonstrate need for aid received scholarships/grants; average award was $23,479. No-need awards available for academics.

Scholarships offered: Justice Brandeis Scholarships; full tuition. Martin Luther King scholarships; tuition and room and board. Presidential scholarships; $25,000. Dean's Awards; $15,000. Waltham High School scholarships; full tuition.

Cumulative student debt: 58% of graduating class had student loans; average debt was $26,078.

FINANCIAL AID PROCEDURES

Forms required: FAFSA, CSS PROFILE.

Dates and Deadlines: Priority date 2/1; no closing date. Applicants notified on a rolling basis starting 4/1.

Transfers: Priority date 4/1. International transfer students seeking scholarship or need-based financial assistance must apply by 2/1.

CONTACT

Peter Giumette, Dean of Student Financial Services
Box 549110, Waltham, MA 02454-9110
(781) 736-3700

Bridgewater State College

Bridgewater, Massachusetts
www.bridgew.edu   Federal Code: 002183

4-year public liberal arts and teachers college in large town.

Enrollment: 8,725 undergrads, 14% part-time. 1,453 full-time freshmen.

Selectivity: Admits 50 to 75% of applicants.

BASIC COSTS (2009-2010)

Tuition and fees: $6,473; out-of-state residents $12,613.
Per-credit charge: $38; out-of-state residents $294.
Room and board: $8,116.
Additional info: Tuition/fee waivers available for unemployed or children of unemployed.

FINANCIAL AID PICTURE (2008-2009)

Students with need: Out of 1,251 full-time freshmen who applied for aid, 871 were judged to have need. Of these, 866 received aid. Need-based aid available for part-time students.
Students without need: 7 full-time freshmen who did not demonstrate need for aid received scholarships/grants; average award was $6,230. No-need awards available for academics, leadership, minority status, state/district residency.
Cumulative student debt: 80% of graduating class had student loans; average debt was $22,093.

FINANCIAL AID PROCEDURES

Forms required: FAFSA.
Dates and Deadlines: Priority date 3/1; no closing date.

CONTACT

Janet Gumbris, Director of Financial Aid
Gates House, Bridgewater, MA 02325
(508) 531-1341

Bristol Community College

Fall River, Massachusetts
www.bristolcc.edu   Federal Code: 002176

2-year public community college in small city.
Enrollment: 7,180 undergrads, 45% part-time. 1,399 full-time freshmen.
Selectivity: Open admission; but selective for some programs.

BASIC COSTS (2009-2010)

Tuition and fees: $4,454; out-of-state residents $10,634.
Per-credit charge: $24; out-of-state residents $230.
Additional info: Tuition/fee waivers available for unemployed or children of unemployed.

FINANCIAL AID PICTURE (2008-2009)

Students with need: Need-based aid available for full-time and part-time students. Work study available nights, weekends, and for part-time students.
Students without need: No-need awards available for academics, art, leadership, minority status, music/drama.

FINANCIAL AID PROCEDURES

Forms required: FAFSA, institutional form.
Dates and Deadlines: Priority date 5/1; no closing date. Applicants notified on a rolling basis starting 5/1; must reply within 2 week(s) of notification.
Transfers: No deadline. Applicants notified on a rolling basis starting 3/1.

CONTACT

David Allen, Director of Financial Aid
777 Elsbree Street, Fall River, MA 02720-7395
(508) 678-2811 ext. 2513

Bunker Hill Community College

Boston, Massachusetts
www.bhcc.mass.edu   Federal Code: 011210

2-year public community college in very large city.
Enrollment: 8,867 undergrads, 60% part-time. 1,572 full-time freshmen.
Selectivity: Open admission; but selective for some programs.

BASIC COSTS (2009-2010)

Tuition and fees: $3,780; out-of-state residents $9,960.
Per-credit charge: $24; out-of-state residents $230.
Additional info: New England Regional Tuition: $112 per-credit-hour. Tuition/fee waivers available for minority students.

FINANCIAL AID PICTURE (2008-2009)

Students with need: Need-based aid available for full-time and part-time students.
Students without need: No-need awards available for academics.

FINANCIAL AID PROCEDURES

Forms required: FAFSA.
Dates and Deadlines: Priority date 4/15; no closing date. Applicants notified on a rolling basis starting 6/1; must reply within 2 week(s) of notification.
Transfers: No deadline. Applicants notified on a rolling basis; must reply within 2 week(s) of notification.

CONTACT

Melissa Holster, Director of Financial Aid
250 New Rutherford Avenue, Boston, MA 02129-2925
(617) 228-2275

Cambridge College

Cambridge, Massachusetts
www.cambridgecollege.edu   Federal Code: 021829

4-year private liberal arts and teachers college in small city.
Enrollment: 1,287 undergrads.
Selectivity: Open admission.

BASIC COSTS (2009-2010)

Tuition and fees: $10,950.
Per-credit charge: $365.

FINANCIAL AID PICTURE (2009-2010)

Students with need: Average financial aid package met 26% of need; average scholarship/grant was $5,092; average loan was $3,478. For part-time students, average financial aid package was $6,904.
Students without need: This college awards aid only to students with need.

FINANCIAL AID PROCEDURES

Forms required: FAFSA, institutional form.
Dates and Deadlines: Priority date 9/1; no closing date. Applicants notified on a rolling basis starting 6/1.
Transfers: No deadline. Applicants notified on a rolling basis.

CONTACT

Francis Lauder, Director of Financial Aid
1000 Massachusetts Avenue, Cambridge, MA 02138-5304
(617) 868-1000 ext. 1440

Cape Cod Community College

West Barnstable, Massachusetts
www.capecod.edu   Federal Code: 002168

2-year public community college in small town.
Enrollment: 3,799 undergrads, 53% part-time. 805 full-time freshmen.
Selectivity: Open admission; but selective for some programs.

BASIC COSTS (2009-2010)

Tuition and fees: $4,320; out-of-state residents $10,500.
Per-credit charge: $24; out-of-state residents $230.
Additional info: Tuition/fee waivers available for minority students.

FINANCIAL AID PICTURE (2008-2009)

Students with need: Out of 464 full-time freshmen who applied for aid, 359 were judged to have need. Of these, 342 received aid, and 26 had their full need met. Average financial aid package met 52% of need; average scholarship/grant was $3,354; average loan was $1,547. For part-time students, average financial aid package was $2,821.

Students without need: 33 full-time freshmen who did not demonstrate need for aid received scholarships/grants; average award was $1,413. No-need awards available for academics, art, job skills, leadership, music/drama, state/district residency.

FINANCIAL AID PROCEDURES

Forms required: FAFSA.

Dates and Deadlines: Priority date 5/1; no closing date. Applicants notified on a rolling basis starting 5/1.

Transfers: No deadline. Applicants notified on a rolling basis starting 6/1.

CONTACT

Sherry Andersen, Director of Financial Aid
2240 Iyannough Road, West Barnstable, MA 02668-1599
(508) 362-2131 ext. 4393

Clark University

Worcester, Massachusetts   Federal Code: 002139
www.clarku.edu   CSS Code: 3279

4-year private university and liberal arts college in small city.

Enrollment: 2,243 undergrads, 2% part-time. 548 full-time freshmen.

Selectivity: Admits 50 to 75% of applicants.

BASIC COSTS (2010-2011)

Tuition and fees: $36,420.

Per-credit charge: $1,128.

Room and board: $6,950.

Additional info: New student contingency fee: $50. Fifth-year tuition waived for eligible undergraduates admitted to accelerated bachelor's/master's.

FINANCIAL AID PICTURE (2009-2010)

Students with need: Out of 404 full-time freshmen who applied for aid, 306 were judged to have need. Of these, 303 received aid, and 192 had their full need met. Average financial aid package met 94% of need; average scholarship/grant was $20,705; average loan was $3,288. Need-based aid available for part-time students.

Students without need: 188 full-time freshmen who did not demonstrate need for aid received scholarships/grants; average award was $13,013. No-need awards available for academics, leadership.

Scholarships offered: Scholarships; $12,000-$18,000 per year; based on superior academic achievement or community service involvement.

Cumulative student debt: 86% of graduating class had student loans; average debt was $21,925.

FINANCIAL AID PROCEDURES

Forms required: FAFSA, CSS PROFILE.

Dates and Deadlines: Closing date 2/1. Applicants notified by 3/31; must reply by 5/1.

Transfers: Closing date 4/1. Applicants notified on a rolling basis. Financial aid transcript from previous institution(s) attended required.

CONTACT

Mary Ellen Severance, Director of Financial Aid and Student Employment
950 Main Street, Worcester, MA 01610-1477
(508) 793-7478

College of the Holy Cross

Worcester, Massachusetts   Federal Code: 002141
www.holycross.edu   CSS Code: 3282

4-year private liberal arts college in small city, affiliated with Roman Catholic Church.

Enrollment: 2,897 undergrads. 746 full-time freshmen.

Selectivity: Admits less than 50% of applicants.

BASIC COSTS (2010-2011)

Tuition and fees: $39,892.

Room and board: $10,940.

FINANCIAL AID PICTURE (2009-2010)

Students with need: Out of 522 full-time freshmen who applied for aid, 438 were judged to have need. Of these, 411 received aid, and 411 had their full need met. Average financial aid package met 100% of need; average scholarship/grant was $26,977; average loan was $5,262.

Students without need: 3 full-time freshmen who did not demonstrate need for aid received scholarships/grants; average award was $21,207. No-need awards available for academics, athletics, ROTC.

Scholarships offered: 27 full-time freshmen received athletic scholarships; average amount $28,320.

Cumulative student debt: 57% of graduating class had student loans; average debt was $23,785.

Additional info: Cost of tuition waived above the amount of the Pell Grant award for Worcester residents whose families earn less than $50,000.

FINANCIAL AID PROCEDURES

Forms required: FAFSA. CSS PROFILE required of all students applying for institutional aid.

Dates and Deadlines: Closing date 2/1. Applicants notified by 3/30; must reply by 5/1.

Transfers: Financial aid generally not available to transfer students.

CONTACT

Lynne Myers, Director of Financial Aid
One College Street, Worcester, MA 01610-2395
(508) 793-2265

Curry College

Milton, Massachusetts
www.curry.edu   Federal Code: 002143

4-year private nursing and liberal arts college in large town.

Enrollment: 2,703 undergrads, 27% part-time. 573 full-time freshmen.

Selectivity: Admits over 75% of applicants.

BASIC COSTS (2009-2010)

Tuition and fees: $29,370.

Room and board: $11,110.

Additional info: PAL (Program for Advancement of Learning) students pay additional program participation fee of up to $6,250.

FINANCIAL AID PICTURE (2008-2009)

Students with need: Out of 382 full-time freshmen who applied for aid, 382 were judged to have need. Of these, 382 received aid, and 8 had their full need met. Average financial aid package met 61% of need; average scholarship/grant was $11,768; average loan was $3,422. For part-time students, average financial aid package was $4,830.

Students without need: 29 full-time freshmen who did not demonstrate need for aid received scholarships/grants; average award was $4,503. No-need awards available for academics, leadership.

Scholarships offered: Presidential Scholarship; $12,000 per year. Dean's Scholarship; $6,500 per year. Leadership Scholarship; $3,000 per year.

Cumulative student debt: 78% of graduating class had student loans; average debt was $38,374.

FINANCIAL AID PROCEDURES

Forms required: FAFSA.

Dates and Deadlines: Priority date 3/1; no closing date. Applicants notified on a rolling basis starting 3/1; must reply by 5/1 or within 2 week(s) of notification.

CONTACT

Stephanny Elias, Director, Student Financial Services

1071 Blue Hill Avenue, Milton, MA 02186-9984

(617) 333-2354

Dean College

Franklin, Massachusetts

www.dean.edu   Federal Code: 002144

2-year private junior and liberal arts college in large town.

Enrollment: 1,090 undergrads.

BASIC COSTS (2009-2010)

Tuition and fees: $28,020.

Room and board: $11,964.

FINANCIAL AID PICTURE (2008-2009)

Students with need: Need-based aid available for full-time and part-time students. Work study available nights, weekends, and for part-time students.

Students without need: No-need awards available for academics, athletics, leadership, music/drama, state/district residency.

Scholarships offered: Trustee's Scholarship; $10,000 - $12,000 per year; based on outstanding academic accomplishments or potential. President's Leadership Scholarship; $8,000 - $12,000 per year; given to students with leadership positions during their high school careers. Performing Arts Scholarship; $5,000 - $11,000 per year; based on achievement in dance or theater.

FINANCIAL AID PROCEDURES

Forms required: FAFSA.

Dates and Deadlines: Priority date 3/15; no closing date. Applicants notified on a rolling basis starting 3/6; must reply by 5/1 or within 2 week(s) of notification.

Transfers: No deadline. Applicants notified on a rolling basis starting 3/1.

CONTACT

Jenny Aguiar, Director of Financial Aid

99 Main Street, Franklin, MA 02038-1994

(508) 541-1518

Eastern Nazarene College

Quincy, Massachusetts

www.enc.edu   Federal Code: 002145

4-year private liberal arts college in small city, affiliated with Church of the Nazarene.

Enrollment: 833 undergrads, 2% part-time. 173 full-time freshmen.

Selectivity: Admits 50 to 75% of applicants.

BASIC COSTS (2010-2011)

Tuition and fees: $23,772.

Per-credit charge: $901.

Room and board: $7,250.

Additional info: Tuition/fee waivers available for minority students.

FINANCIAL AID PICTURE (2008-2009)

Students with need: Out of 164 full-time freshmen who applied for aid, 147 were judged to have need. Of these, 147 received aid, and 48 had their full need met. Average financial aid package met 71% of need; average scholarship/grant was $9,499; average loan was $8,298. For part-time students, average financial aid package was $12,696.

Students without need: 23 full-time freshmen who did not demonstrate need for aid received scholarships/grants; average award was $9,707. No-need awards available for academics, alumni affiliation, leadership, religious affiliation, ROTC.

Scholarships offered: Academic scholarships: amounts vary based on test scores; minimum 1500 SAT or 21 ACT. Honors Scholar: based on 1800 SAT or 27 ACT. Dean's Scholar: based on 2100 SAT or 32 ACT. Munro Scholar: full-tuition; based on interview and 2100 SAT or 32 ACT. President's Scholar: full-tuition plus room and board; based on interview and 2250 SAT or 34 ACT.

Additional info: Participant in Massachusetts University pre-payment plan.

FINANCIAL AID PROCEDURES

Forms required: FAFSA, institutional form.

Dates and Deadlines: Priority date 3/1; closing date 8/1. Applicants notified on a rolling basis starting 3/14; must reply by 8/1 or within 2 week(s) of notification.

CONTACT

Dana Parker, Director of Financial Aid

23 East Elm Avenue, Quincy, MA 02170

(617) 745-3712

Elms College

Chicopee, Massachusetts

www.elms.edu   Federal Code: 002140

4-year private liberal arts college in small city, affiliated with Roman Catholic Church.

Enrollment: 1,010 undergrads.

Selectivity: Admits over 75% of applicants.

BASIC COSTS (2010-2011)

Tuition and fees: $27,045.

Per-credit charge: $524.

Room and board: $9,810.

FINANCIAL AID PICTURE (2009-2010)

Students with need: Need-based aid available for full-time and part-time students. Work study available nights, weekends, and for part-time students.

Students without need: No-need awards available for academics, alumni affiliation, leadership, religious affiliation, state/district residency.

Scholarships offered: Elms Scholarship; $1,000-$6,000 per year; based on academic transcript, standardized test scores and class rank. Presidential Scholarship; $7,000-$14,000 per year; awarded to most competitive applicants based on academic transcript, standardized test scores and class rank.

FINANCIAL AID PROCEDURES

Forms required: FAFSA.

Dates and Deadlines: Priority date 3/1; no closing date. Applicants notified on a rolling basis starting 3/10; must reply by 5/1 or within 2 week(s) of notification.

Transfers: No deadline. Applicants notified on a rolling basis starting 5/1; must reply by 9/6.

CONTACT

Troy Davis, Director of Student Financial Aid Services

291 Springfield Street, Chicopee, MA 01013-2839

(413) 265-2249

Emerson College

Boston, Massachusetts — Federal Code: 002146
www.emerson.edu — CSS Code: 3367

4-year private college of communication and the arts in very large city.
Enrollment: 3,454 undergrads, 1% part-time. 766 full-time freshmen.
Selectivity: Admits less than 50% of applicants.

BASIC COSTS (2009-2010)
Tuition and fees: $29,928.
Per-credit charge: $919.
Room and board: $12,280.

FINANCIAL AID PICTURE (2008-2009)
Students with need: Out of 644 full-time freshmen who applied for aid, 486 were judged to have need. Of these, 486 received aid, and 267 had their full need met. Average financial aid package met 89% of need; average scholarship/grant was $14,243; average loan was $3,865. For part-time students, average financial aid package was $6,004.
Students without need: 40 full-time freshmen who did not demonstrate need for aid received scholarships/grants; average award was $12,396. No-need awards available for academics, leadership, music/drama, state/district residency.
Scholarships offered: Trustees Scholarships: half-tuition; Honors Program students may apply. Dean's Scholarships: $14,000. Emerson Stage Scholarships: amounts vary; based on performing arts audition and academic merit.
Cumulative student debt: 59% of graduating class had student loans; average debt was $15,262.
Additional info: Massachusetts Loan Plan available for parents of dependent undergraduates.

FINANCIAL AID PROCEDURES
Forms required: FAFSA, CSS PROFILE.
Dates and Deadlines: Priority date 3/1; no closing date. Applicants notified by 4/1; must reply by 5/1 or within 3 week(s) of notification.
Transfers: Priority date 4/1.

CONTACT
Michelle Smith, Director of Student Financial Services
120 Boylston Street, Boston, MA 02116-4624
(617) 824-8655

Emmanuel College

Boston, Massachusetts
www.emmanuel.edu — Federal Code: 002147

4-year private liberal arts college in very large city, affiliated with Roman Catholic Church.
Enrollment: 1,997 undergrads, 18% part-time. 424 full-time freshmen.
Selectivity: Admits 50 to 75% of applicants.

BASIC COSTS (2010-2011)
Tuition and fees: $30,765.
Per-credit charge: $956.
Room and board: $12,300.

FINANCIAL AID PICTURE (2009-2010)
Students with need: Out of 385 full-time freshmen who applied for aid, 344 were judged to have need. Of these, 344 received aid, and 154 had their full need met. Average financial aid package met 75% of need; average scholarship/grant was $20,527; average loan was $3,688. For part-time students, average financial aid package was $15,428.
Students without need: 53 full-time freshmen who did not demonstrate need for aid received scholarships/grants; average award was $9,890. No-need awards available for academics, alumni affiliation, leadership.

FINANCIAL AID PROCEDURES
Forms required: FAFSA, institutional form.
Dates and Deadlines: Priority date 4/1; no closing date. Applicants notified on a rolling basis starting 3/15.

CONTACT
Jennifer Porter, Assistant Vice President for Student Financial Services
400 The Fenway, Boston, MA 02115
(617) 735-9938

Endicott College

Beverly, Massachusetts
www.endicott.edu — Federal Code: 002148

4-year private liberal arts college in large town.
Enrollment: 2,273 undergrads, 7% part-time. 561 full-time freshmen.
Selectivity: Admits 50 to 75% of applicants.

BASIC COSTS (2010-2011)
Tuition and fees: $26,248.
Per-credit charge: $793.
Room and board: $12,310.

FINANCIAL AID PICTURE (2009-2010)
Students with need: Out of 503 full-time freshmen who applied for aid, 371 were judged to have need. Of these, 367 received aid, and 44 had their full need met. Average financial aid package met 60% of need; average scholarship/grant was $9,439; average loan was $3,803. For part-time students, average financial aid package was $5,755.
Students without need: 91 full-time freshmen who did not demonstrate need for aid received scholarships/grants; average award was $6,306. No-need awards available for academics, alumni affiliation, art, job skills, leadership, music/drama, religious affiliation, ROTC, state/district residency.
Cumulative student debt: 69% of graduating class had student loans; average debt was $33,783.

FINANCIAL AID PROCEDURES
Forms required: FAFSA, institutional form.
Dates and Deadlines: Priority date 3/15; no closing date. Applicants notified on a rolling basis starting 3/15; must reply within 2 week(s) of notification.

CONTACT
Marcia Toomey, Director of Financial Aid
376 Hale Street, Beverly, MA 01915-9985
(978) 232-2060

Fisher College

Boston, Massachusetts
www.fisher.edu — Federal Code: 002150

2-year private liberal arts college in very large city.
Enrollment: 1,311 undergrads, 32% part-time. 293 full-time freshmen.
Selectivity: Admits 50 to 75% of applicants.

BASIC COSTS (2010-2011)
Tuition and fees: $24,400.
Per-credit charge: $788.
Room and board: $12,600.

FINANCIAL AID PICTURE (2009-2010)
Students with need: 59% of average financial aid package awarded as scholarships/grants, 41% awarded as loans/jobs. Need-based aid available for part-time students. Work study available nights, weekends, and for part-time students.
Students without need: No-need awards available for academics, alumni affiliation, state/district residency.

Scholarships offered: Fisher Honor Scholarship; $2,500; based on outstanding academic and personal achievement, contribution to school and community; renewable with 3.0 GPA. Business Administration and Computer Technology Scholarship; $1,500 for 2.5-2.99 GPA, $3,000 for 3.0 GPA; for students enrolling in associate programs in business administration or computer technology; renewable.

FINANCIAL AID PROCEDURES
Forms required: FAFSA.
Dates and Deadlines: Priority date 3/1; no closing date. Applicants notified on a rolling basis starting 3/1; must reply within 2 week(s) of notification.

CONTACT
Anne Sylvain, Director of Financial Aid
118 Beacon Street, Boston, MA 02116
(617) 236-8821

Fitchburg State College
Fitchburg, Massachusetts
www.fsc.edu   Federal Code: 002184

4-year public liberal arts and teachers college in small city.
Enrollment: 3,987 undergrads, 13% part-time. 783 full-time freshmen.
Selectivity: Admits 50 to 75% of applicants.

BASIC COSTS (2009-2010)
Tuition and fees: $6,900; out-of-state residents $12,980.
Per-credit charge: $40; out-of-state residents $294.
Room and board: $7,632.

FINANCIAL AID PICTURE (2008-2009)
Students with need: Out of 727 full-time freshmen who applied for aid, 443 were judged to have need. Of these, 432 received aid, and 402 had their full need met. Average financial aid package met 93% of need; average scholarship/grant was $4,391; average loan was $2,463. For part-time students, average financial aid package was $5,029.
Students without need: 58 full-time freshmen who did not demonstrate need for aid received scholarships/grants; average award was $1,431. No-need awards available for academics, alumni affiliation, leadership, ROTC, state/district residency.
Scholarships offered: Renewable scholarships awarded on basis of high school record and test scores.
Cumulative student debt: 68% of graduating class had student loans; average debt was $18,177.

FINANCIAL AID PROCEDURES
Forms required: FAFSA.
Dates and Deadlines: Priority date 3/1; no closing date. Applicants notified on a rolling basis starting 3/15.

CONTACT
Lynn Beauregard, Director of Financial Aid
160 Pearl Street, Fitchburg, MA 01420-2697
(978) 665-3156

Framingham State College
Framingham, Massachusetts
www.framingham.edu   Federal Code: 002185

4-year public liberal arts and teachers college in small city.
Enrollment: 3,485 undergrads, 12% part-time. 653 full-time freshmen.
Selectivity: Admits 50 to 75% of applicants.

BASIC COSTS (2009-2010)
Tuition and fees: $6,540; out-of-state residents $12,620.
Per-credit charge: $40; out-of-state residents $294.

Room and board: $8,148.
Additional info: Fees include mandatory laptop purchase by new students. New England Regional tuition rate $1,455.

FINANCIAL AID PICTURE (2008-2009)
Students with need: Out of 526 full-time freshmen who applied for aid, 367 were judged to have need. Of these, 367 received aid, and 268 had their full need met. Average financial aid package met 76% of need; average scholarship/grant was $4,060; average loan was $4,525. For part-time students, average financial aid package was $5,725.
Students without need: 20 full-time freshmen who did not demonstrate need for aid received scholarships/grants; average award was $2,174. No-need awards available for academics.
Scholarships offered: Senator Paul E. Tsongas Scholarship; full-tuition and fees; available to Massachusetts residents based on 3.75 GPA and test scores; 5 awarded. Merit scholarships; available to students majoring in education, natural or physical sciences based on GPA and test scores.
Cumulative student debt: 65% of graduating class had student loans; average debt was $19,000.

FINANCIAL AID PROCEDURES
Forms required: FAFSA.
Dates and Deadlines: Priority date 3/1; no closing date. Applicants notified on a rolling basis starting 3/15; must reply by 5/1 or within 2 week(s) of notification.
Transfers: Priority date 11/1; no deadline. Applicants notified on a rolling basis starting 11/1; must reply within 2 week(s) of notification.

CONTACT
Susan Lanzillo, Director of Financial Aid
PO Box 9101, Framingham, MA 01701-9101
(508) 626-4534

Franklin W. Olin College of Engineering
Needham, Massachusetts
www.olin.edu   Federal Code: 039463

4-year private engineering college in large town.
Enrollment: 330 undergrads. 85 full-time freshmen.
Selectivity: Admits less than 50% of applicants.

BASIC COSTS (2009-2010)
Tuition and fees: $36,795.
Per-credit charge: $1,213.
Room and board: $13,230.
Additional info: All incoming students will receive Olin Scholarship, currently valued at one-half tuition. Additional need-based aid available to cover other costs.

FINANCIAL AID PICTURE (2009-2010)
Students with need: 89% of average financial aid package awarded as scholarships/grants, 11% awarded as loans/jobs.
Students without need: No-need awards available for academics, leadership.
Additional info: Financial aid forms not needed for one-half tuition scholarship which all students receive; FAFSA forms required for need-based aid considerations.

FINANCIAL AID PROCEDURES
Forms required: FAFSA.
Dates and Deadlines: Priority date 2/15; no closing date. Applicants notified on a rolling basis starting 3/31; must reply by 5/1.

CONTACT
Jean Ricker, Manager, Financial Aid
Olin Way, Needham, MA 02492-1245
(781) 292-2343

Gordon College
Wenham, Massachusetts
www.gordon.edu   Federal Code: 002153

4-year private liberal arts college in small town, affiliated with nondenominational tradition.

Enrollment: 1,572 undergrads, 2% part-time. 381 full-time freshmen.

Selectivity: Admits 50 to 75% of applicants.

BASIC COSTS (2010-2011)
Tuition and fees: $29,458.

Room and board: $8,100.

FINANCIAL AID PICTURE (2009-2010)
Students with need: Average financial aid package met 73% of need; average scholarship/grant was $12,753; average loan was $4,995. For part-time students, average financial aid package was $9,948.

Students without need: No-need awards available for academics, alumni affiliation, art, leadership, minority status, music/drama, religious affiliation.

Scholarships offered: A.J. Gordon Scholarship; $12,000; based on academic achievement and leadership. Dean's Scholarships; $9,000; based on academic record. Challenge Scholarships; $7,000; based on academic record. Discipleship Scholarships; $6,000; based on academic record. Choral Scholars Program; $5,000; for students with excellent ability/academic performance seeking career in vocal music field. National Merit Finalists; 75% off tuition. All scholarships renewable annually.

Cumulative student debt: 81% of graduating class had student loans; average debt was $33,332.

FINANCIAL AID PROCEDURES
Forms required: FAFSA.

Dates and Deadlines: Closing date 3/1. Applicants notified on a rolling basis starting 4/15; must reply by 5/1 or within 2 week(s) of notification.

Transfers: Priority date 3/15. Applicants notified on a rolling basis starting 4/1; must reply by 5/1 or within 2 week(s) of notification.

CONTACT
Brook Berry, Vice President for Enrollment and Marketing
255 Grapevine Road, Wenham, MA 01984
(800) 343-1379

Greenfield Community College
Greenfield, Massachusetts
www.gcc.mass.edu   Federal Code: 002169

2-year public community college in large town.

Enrollment: 2,203 undergrads, 55% part-time. 333 full-time freshmen.

Selectivity: Open admission; but selective for some programs.

BASIC COSTS (2009-2010)
Tuition and fees: $4,817; out-of-state residents $12,467.

Per-credit charge: $26; out-of-state residents $281.

Additional info: Tuition/fee waivers available for adults.

FINANCIAL AID PICTURE
Students with need: Need-based aid available for full-time and part-time students. Work study available nights, weekends, and for part-time students.

Students without need: This college awards aid only to students with need.

FINANCIAL AID PROCEDURES
Forms required: FAFSA, institutional form.

Dates and Deadlines: Priority date 4/15; no closing date. Applicants notified on a rolling basis starting 5/1; must reply within 2 week(s) of notification.

CONTACT
Linda Dejardins, Director of Financial Aid
One College Drive, Greenfield, MA 01301
(413) 775-1109

Hampshire College
Amherst, Massachusetts   Federal Code: 004661
www.hampshire.edu   CSS Code: 3447

4-year private liberal arts college in large town.

Enrollment: 1,438 undergrads. 363 full-time freshmen.

Selectivity: Admits 50 to 75% of applicants.

BASIC COSTS (2010-2011)
Tuition and fees: $41,404.

Room and board: $10,798.

FINANCIAL AID PICTURE (2009-2010)
Students with need: Average financial aid package met 98% of need; average scholarship/grant was $30,240; average loan was $3,500.

Students without need: No-need awards available for academics, leadership.

Cumulative student debt: 51% of graduating class had student loans; average debt was $20,669.

FINANCIAL AID PROCEDURES
Forms required: FAFSA, CSS PROFILE.

Dates and Deadlines: Closing date 2/1. Applicants notified by 4/1; must reply by 5/1.

Transfers: Applicants notified by 4/1; must reply by 5/1.

CONTACT
Kathleen Methot, Director of Financial Aid
893 West Street, Amherst, MA 01002-9988
(413) 559-5484

Harvard College
Cambridge, Massachusetts   Federal Code: 002155
www.college.harvard.edu   CSS Code: 3434

4-year private university and liberal arts college in large city.

Enrollment: 6,655 undergrads. 1,663 full-time freshmen.

Selectivity: Admits less than 50% of applicants.

BASIC COSTS (2009-2010)
Tuition and fees: $36,828.

Room and board: $11,856.

FINANCIAL AID PICTURE (2009-2010)
Students with need: Out of 1,202 full-time freshmen who applied for aid, 1,060 were judged to have need. Of these, 1,060 received aid, and 1,060 had their full need met. Average financial aid package met 100% of need; average scholarship/grant was $39,803; average loan was $2,948. Need-based aid available for part-time students.

Students without need: This college awards aid only to students with need.

Cumulative student debt: 38% of graduating class had student loans; average debt was $11,059.

Additional info: Institution meets full need of all admitted students. Aid includes no loans; home equity and retirement excluded from need analysis; families with incomes below $60,000 have zero parent contribution; $60,000 to $180,000 and standard assets have parent contributions from 0-10% of income.

FINANCIAL AID PROCEDURES
Forms required: FAFSA, CSS PROFILE.

Dates and Deadlines: Closing date 2/1. Applicants notified by 4/1; must reply by 5/1 or within 2 week(s) of notification.
Transfers: Closing date 2/15. Applicants notified by 5/30; must reply within 2 week(s) of notification.

CONTACT
Janet Irons, Senior Associate Director of Financial Aid
86 Brattle Street, Cambridge, MA 02138
(617) 495-1581

Hellenic College/Holy Cross
Brookline, Massachusetts
www.hchc.edu   Federal Code: 002154

4-year private liberal arts and seminary college in large town, affiliated with Eastern Orthodox Church.
Enrollment: 69 undergrads.

BASIC COSTS (2009-2010)
Tuition and fees: $18,850.
Per-credit charge: $767.
Room and board: $11,780.

FINANCIAL AID PICTURE (2008-2009)
Students with need: Need-based aid available for full-time students. Work study available nights, weekends, and for part-time students.
Students without need: This college awards aid only to students with need.

FINANCIAL AID PROCEDURES
Forms required: FAFSA, institutional form.
Dates and Deadlines: Closing date 4/1. Applicants notified on a rolling basis starting 10/1; must reply within 2 week(s) of notification.
Transfers: No deadline. Applicants notified on a rolling basis; must reply within 2 week(s) of notification.

CONTACT
Director of Financial Aid
50 Goddard Avenue, Brookline, MA 02445
(617) 850-1297

Holyoke Community College
Holyoke, Massachusetts
www.hcc.edu   Federal Code: 002170

2-year public community college in large town.
Enrollment: 6,956 undergrads, 44% part-time. 1,430 full-time freshmen.
Selectivity: Open admission; but selective for some programs.

BASIC COSTS (2009-2010)
Tuition and fees: $3,798; out-of-state residents $9,978.
Per-credit charge: $24; out-of-state residents $230.

FINANCIAL AID PICTURE (2008-2009)
Students with need: 77% of average financial aid package awarded as scholarships/grants, 23% awarded as loans/jobs. Need-based aid available for part-time students. Work study available nights.
Students without need: No-need awards available for academics, art, leadership, music/drama.

FINANCIAL AID PROCEDURES
Forms required: FAFSA.
Dates and Deadlines: Priority date 5/1; no closing date. Applicants notified on a rolling basis starting 5/1; must reply within 2 week(s) of notification.

CONTACT
Karen Derouin, Director of Financial Aid
303 Homestead Avenue, Holyoke, MA 01040
(413) 552-2150

Laboure College
Boston, Massachusetts
www.laboure.edu   Federal Code: 006324

2-year private health science and junior college in very large city, affiliated with Roman Catholic Church.
Enrollment: 612 undergrads.
Selectivity: Admits 50 to 75% of applicants.

BASIC COSTS (2010-2011)
Additional info: Cost of full-time, 4-term academic year is $25,008, inclusive of fees.

FINANCIAL AID PICTURE (2009-2010)
Students with need: For part-time students, average financial aid package was $5,066.
Students without need: No-need awards available for academics, alumni affiliation, leadership, religious affiliation.
Scholarships offered: Caritas Christi Scholarship; 25% of tuition for all professional courses for those who work 16 plus hours per week, 10% for all professional courses for those who work 10-15 hours a week. Nursing scholarship; 25% of cost of nursing courses for students with LPN credential. First year scholarship; 50% of tuition; for graduates of Catholic high schools; 2 awarded annually.

FINANCIAL AID PROCEDURES
Forms required: FAFSA.
Dates and Deadlines: Priority date 4/1; no closing date. Applicants notified on a rolling basis starting 6/15; must reply within 2 week(s) of notification.
Transfers: Priority date 12/1. Applicants notified on a rolling basis starting 12/1; must reply within 2 week(s) of notification.

CONTACT
Erin Hanlon, Director of Financial Aid
2120 Dorchester Avenue, Boston, MA 02124-5698
(617) 296-8300 ext. 4054

Lasell College
Newton, Massachusetts
www.lasell.edu   Federal Code: 002158

4-year private liberal arts college in small city.
Enrollment: 1,520 undergrads, 1% part-time. 521 full-time freshmen.
Selectivity: Admits 50 to 75% of applicants.

BASIC COSTS (2010-2011)
Tuition and fees: $26,000.
Per-credit charge: $825.
Room and board: $11,800.

FINANCIAL AID PICTURE (2009-2010)
Students with need: Out of 480 full-time freshmen who applied for aid, 431 were judged to have need. Of these, 431 received aid, and 60 had their full need met. Average financial aid package met 89% of need; average scholarship/grant was $16,546; average loan was $2,075. For part-time students, average financial aid package was $9,113.
Students without need: 48 full-time freshmen who did not demonstrate need for aid received scholarships/grants; average award was $8,488. No-need awards available for academics, alumni affiliation.
Cumulative student debt: 64% of graduating class had student loans; average debt was $38,428.

FINANCIAL AID PROCEDURES

Forms required: FAFSA, institutional form.

Dates and Deadlines: Priority date 3/1; no closing date. Applicants notified on a rolling basis starting 2/15; must reply by 5/1 or within 2 week(s) of notification.

CONTACT

Michele Kosboth, Director of Student Financial Planning

1844 Commonwealth Avenue, Newton, MA 02466-2709

(617) 243-2227

Lesley University

Cambridge, Massachusetts

www.lesley.edu   Federal Code: 002160

4-year private liberal arts and teachers college in very large city.

Enrollment: 1,369 undergrads, 3% part-time. 376 full-time freshmen.

Selectivity: Admits 50 to 75% of applicants.

BASIC COSTS (2010-2011)

Tuition and fees: $29,400.

Room and board: $12,800.

FINANCIAL AID PICTURE (2009-2010)

Students with need: Out of 326 full-time freshmen who applied for aid, 294 were judged to have need. Of these, 294 received aid, and 37 had their full need met. Average financial aid package met 74% of need; average scholarship/grant was $15,193; average loan was $3,715. For part-time students, average financial aid package was $7,727.

Students without need: 6 full-time freshmen who did not demonstrate need for aid received scholarships/grants; average award was $11,272. No-need awards available for academics, art, leadership, minority status, state/district residency.

Scholarships offered: Freshmen scholarships; $5,000-full tuition; for students with strong academic backgrounds who have shown a commitment to community service and making a difference in the lives of others.

FINANCIAL AID PROCEDURES

Forms required: FAFSA.

Dates and Deadlines: Priority date 2/15; no closing date. Applicants notified on a rolling basis starting 2/15.

Transfers: Priority date 3/15.

CONTACT

Scott Jewell, Director of Financial Aid

29 Everett Street, Cambridge, MA 02140-2790

(617) 349-8667

Marian Court College

Swampscott, Massachusetts

www.mariancourt.edu   Federal Code: 006873

2-year private junior college in large town, affiliated with Roman Catholic Church.

Enrollment: 220 full-time undergrads.

BASIC COSTS (2009-2010)

Tuition and fees: $15,400.

Additional info: Evening program: $800 for 3 credit course.

FINANCIAL AID PICTURE (2008-2009)

Students with need: Need-based aid available for full-time and part-time students.

Students without need: No-need awards available for academics.

Scholarships offered: Merit Scholarships; $5,000 for recent high school graduates with a GPA of 3.5 or higher, $4,000 for recent high school graduates with a GPA of 3.0-3.49, $3,000 for recent high school graduates with a

GPA of 2.5 to 2.99, $2,000 for recent high school graduates with a GPA of 2.0 to 2.49.

FINANCIAL AID PROCEDURES

Forms required: FAFSA, institutional form.

Dates and Deadlines: Priority date 4/1; no closing date. Applicants notified on a rolling basis starting 4/15.

CONTACT

Kathy Angle, Director of Financial Aid

35 Little's Point Road, Swampscott, MA 01907-2896

(781) 309-5200

Massachusetts Bay Community College

Wellesley Hills, Massachusetts

www.massbay.edu   Federal Code: 002171

2-year public community college in large town.

Enrollment: 2,150 full-time undergrads.

Selectivity: Open admission; but selective for some programs.

BASIC COSTS (2009-2010)

Tuition and fees: $4,530; out-of-state residents $10,710.

Per-credit charge: $24; out-of-state residents $230.

Additional info: NEBHE tuition rate is 150% of in-state cost and fees are approximately the same. Tuition/fee waivers available for unemployed or children of unemployed.

FINANCIAL AID PICTURE (2008-2009)

Students with need: Need-based aid available for full-time and part-time students.

FINANCIAL AID PROCEDURES

Forms required: FAFSA, institutional form.

Dates and Deadlines: Priority date 8/30; no closing date. Applicants notified on a rolling basis starting 4/1.

CONTACT

Todd Hughes, Director of Financial Aid

50 Oakland Street, Wellesley Hills, MA 02481

(781) 239-2600

Massachusetts College of Art and Design

Boston, Massachusetts

www.massart.edu   Federal Code: 002180

4-year public visual arts college in very large city.

Enrollment: 1,772 undergrads, 10% part-time. 275 full-time freshmen.

Selectivity: Admits 50 to 75% of applicants.

BASIC COSTS (2009-2010)

Tuition and fees: $8,400; out-of-state residents $24,400.

Room and board: $11,288.

Additional info: Tuition for New England resident students $14,900. Tuition/fee waivers available for unemployed or children of unemployed.

FINANCIAL AID PICTURE (2008-2009)

Students with need: Out of 227 full-time freshmen who applied for aid, 176 were judged to have need. Of these, 176 received aid. For part-time students, average financial aid package was $7,008.

Students without need: No-need awards available for academics, art, leadership, state/district residency.

Additional info: Tuition waiver available to Vietnam veterans.

FINANCIAL AID PROCEDURES

Forms required: FAFSA.

Dates and Deadlines: Priority date 3/1; no closing date. Applicants notified on a rolling basis starting 3/15; must reply within 3 week(s) of notification.
Transfers: Priority date 5/1. Financial aid transcripts required.

CONTACT
Aurelio Ramirez, Director of Financial Aid
621 Huntington Avenue, Boston, MA 02115-5882
(617) 879-7850

Massachusetts College of Liberal Arts
North Adams, Massachusetts
www.mcla.edu   Federal Code: 002187

4-year public liberal arts college in large town.
Enrollment: 1,625 undergrads, 10% part-time. 348 full-time freshmen.
Selectivity: Admits 50 to 75% of applicants.

BASIC COSTS (2009-2010)
Tuition and fees: $7,015; out-of-state residents $15,960.
Per-credit charge: $43; out-of-state residents $416.
Room and board: $7,868.
Additional info: Tuition/fee waivers available for unemployed or children of unemployed.

FINANCIAL AID PICTURE (2009-2010)
Students with need: Out of 332 full-time freshmen who applied for aid, 259 were judged to have need. Of these, 258 received aid. For part-time students, average financial aid package was $6,359.
Students without need: 19 full-time freshmen who did not demonstrate need for aid received scholarships/grants; average award was $1,914. No-need awards available for academics, alumni affiliation, art, leadership, minority status, music/drama.
Cumulative student debt: 51% of graduating class had student loans; average debt was $22,168.

FINANCIAL AID PROCEDURES
Forms required: FAFSA, institutional form.
Dates and Deadlines: Priority date 3/1; no closing date. Applicants notified on a rolling basis starting 3/1; must reply by 5/1 or within 2 week(s) of notification.

CONTACT
Elizabeth Petri, Director of Financial Aid
375 Church Street, North Adams, MA 01247
(413) 662-5219

Massachusetts College of Pharmacy and Health Sciences
Boston, Massachusetts
www.mcphs.edu   Federal Code: 002165

4-year private health science and pharmacy college in very large city.
Enrollment: 2,883 undergrads, 4% part-time. 685 full-time freshmen.
Selectivity: Admits 50 to 75% of applicants.

BASIC COSTS (2010-2011)
Tuition and fees: $25,480.
Per-credit charge: $910.
Room and board: $12,290.

FINANCIAL AID PICTURE (2009-2010)
Students with need: Average financial aid package met 48% of need; average scholarship/grant was $10,934; average loan was $5,165. For part-time students, average financial aid package was $8,406.
Students without need: No-need awards available for academics.

FINANCIAL AID PROCEDURES
Forms required: FAFSA.
Dates and Deadlines: Priority date 3/15; no closing date. Applicants notified on a rolling basis.
Transfers: Massachusetts State Grant deadline May 1.

CONTACT
Carrie Glass, Executive Director of Enrollment Services
179 Longwood Avenue, Boston, MA 02115-5896
(617) 732-2864

Massachusetts Institute of Technology
Cambridge, Massachusetts   Federal Code: 002178
web.mit.edu   CSS Code: 3514

4-year private university in small city.
Enrollment: 4,218 undergrads, 1% part-time. 1,051 full-time freshmen.
Selectivity: Admits less than 50% of applicants.

BASIC COSTS (2009-2010)
Tuition and fees: $37,782.
Per-credit charge: $585.
Room and board: $11,360.

FINANCIAL AID PICTURE (2008-2009)
Students with need: Out of 834 full-time freshmen who applied for aid, 673 were judged to have need. Of these, 673 received aid, and 673 had their full need met. Average financial aid package met 100% of need; average scholarship/grant was $34,136; average loan was $2,127. For part-time students, average financial aid package was $23,870.
Students without need: This college awards aid only to students with need.
Cumulative student debt: 45% of graduating class had student loans; average debt was $15,043.
Additional info: Filing deadline 2/15 for CSS PROFILE.

FINANCIAL AID PROCEDURES
Forms required: FAFSA, CSS PROFILE.
Dates and Deadlines: Closing date 2/15. Applicants notified by 4/1; must reply by 5/1.
Transfers: Closing date 3/1. Applicants notified by 4/15; must reply by 5/1. Access to MIT funds may be limited to fewer than 8 terms.

CONTACT
Elizabeth Hicks, Executive Director of Student Financial Services
77 Massachusetts Avenue, Room 3-108, Cambridge, MA 02139-4307
(617) 253-4971

Massachusetts Maritime Academy
Buzzards Bay, Massachusetts
www.maritime.edu   Federal Code: 002181

4-year public maritime college in large town.
Enrollment: 1,097 undergrads, 3% part-time. 296 full-time freshmen.

BASIC COSTS (2009-2010)
Tuition and fees: $6,119; out-of-state residents $18,758.
Room and board: $8,917.
Additional info: Semester at Sea cost: $3,499.

FINANCIAL AID PICTURE (2008-2009)
Students with need: Need-based aid available for full-time and part-time students. Work study available nights, weekends, and for part-time students.
Students without need: No-need awards available for academics, leadership, music/drama.

FINANCIAL AID PROCEDURES

Forms required: FAFSA, institutional form.
Dates and Deadlines: Priority date 4/30; no closing date. Applicants notified on a rolling basis starting 3/1.

CONTACT

Elizabeth Benway, Financial Aid Director
101 Academy Drive, Buzzards Bay, MA 02532-1803
(508) 830-5086

Massasoit Community College

Brockton, Massachusetts
www.massasoit.mass.edu   Federal Code: 002177

2-year public community college in small city.
Enrollment: 5,914 undergrads, 45% part-time. 1,252 full-time freshmen.
Selectivity: Open admission; but selective for some programs.

BASIC COSTS (2009-2010)

Tuition and fees: $4,110; out-of-state residents $10,290.
Per-credit charge: $24; out-of-state residents $230.
Additional info: Tuition/fee waivers available for unemployed or children of unemployed.

FINANCIAL AID PICTURE

Students with need: Need-based aid available for full-time students.
Students without need: This college awards aid only to students with need.

FINANCIAL AID PROCEDURES

Forms required: FAFSA.
Dates and Deadlines: Priority date 4/15; no closing date. Applicants notified on a rolling basis starting 6/1.

CONTACT

Mary Courtright, Director of Financial Aid
One Massasoit Boulevard, Brockton, MA 02302-3996
(508) 588-9100

Merrimack College

North Andover, Massachusetts
www.merrimack.edu   Federal Code: 002120

4-year private business and liberal arts college in large town, affiliated with Roman Catholic Church.
Enrollment: 1,927 undergrads.
Selectivity: Admits over 75% of applicants.

BASIC COSTS (2009-2010)

Tuition and fees: $29,810.
Per-credit charge: $1,085.
Room and board: $10,190.

FINANCIAL AID PICTURE (2008-2009)

Students with need: Need-based aid available for full-time students. Work study available nights, weekends, and for part-time students.
Students without need: No-need awards available for academics, athletics, leadership, minority status, religious affiliation.
Additional info: Accept the Challenge program provides tuition for students from Lawrence who meet program criteria.

FINANCIAL AID PROCEDURES

Forms required: FAFSA.
Dates and Deadlines: Closing date 2/1. Applicants notified by 3/15; must reply by 5/1 or within 2 week(s) of notification.
Transfers: Priority date 3/1; closing date 4/30. Must reply within 2 week(s) of notification.

CONTACT

Christine Mordach, Director of Financial Aid
315 Turnpike Street, North Andover, MA 01845
(978) 837-5186

Middlesex Community College

Bedford, Massachusetts
www.middlesex.mass.edu   Federal Code: 009936

2-year public community college in small city.
Enrollment: 8,632 undergrads.
Selectivity: Open admission; but selective for some programs.

BASIC COSTS (2009-2010)

Tuition and fees: $4,550; out-of-state residents $10,730.
Per-credit charge: $150; out-of-state residents $356.
Additional info: Tuition/fee waivers available for adults.

FINANCIAL AID PICTURE (2008-2009)

Students with need: Need-based aid available for full-time and part-time students. Work study available nights, weekends, and for part-time students.
Students without need: This college awards aid only to students with need.
Additional info: Application priority date 5/1 for Massachusetts state funds.

FINANCIAL AID PROCEDURES

Forms required: FAFSA, institutional form.
Dates and Deadlines: Priority date 5/1; no closing date. Applicants notified on a rolling basis starting 6/1; must reply within 2 week(s) of notification.

CONTACT

Robert Baumel, Financial Aid Director
33 Kearney Square, Lowell, MA 01852-1987
(978) 656-3242

Montserrat College of Art

Beverly, Massachusetts
www.montserrat.edu   Federal Code: 013774

4-year private visual arts college in large town.
Enrollment: 339 undergrads, 1% part-time. 128 full-time freshmen.
Selectivity: Admits over 75% of applicants.

BASIC COSTS (2010-2011)

Tuition and fees: $24,790.
Per-credit charge: $993.
Room and board: $6,370.

FINANCIAL AID PICTURE (2009-2010)

Students with need: Out of 122 full-time freshmen who applied for aid, 105 were judged to have need. Of these, 104 received aid, and 9 had their full need met. Average financial aid package met 58% of need; average scholarship/grant was $12,132; average loan was $4,017. For part-time students, average financial aid package was $8,483.
Students without need: 24 full-time freshmen who did not demonstrate need for aid received scholarships/grants; average award was $6,708. No-need awards available for academics, art.
Scholarships offered: Talent Awards; $5,000-$10,000; based on artistic and academic ability.
Cumulative student debt: 100% of graduating class had student loans; average debt was $41,937.

FINANCIAL AID PROCEDURES

Forms required: FAFSA, institutional form.
Dates and Deadlines: Priority date 3/1; no closing date. Applicants notified on a rolling basis starting 12/20; must reply within 2 week(s) of notification.

PART III: FINANCIAL AID COLLEGE BY COLLEGE

Transfers: No deadline. Applicants notified on a rolling basis starting 12/20; must reply within 2 week(s) of notification.

CONTACT

Creda Camacho, Director of Financial Aid
23 Essex Street, Beverly, MA 01915
(978) 922-8222

Mount Holyoke College

South Hadley, Massachusetts
www.mtholyoke.edu

Federal Code: 002192
CSS Code: 3529

4-year private liberal arts college for women in large town.
Enrollment: 2,247 undergrads, 2% part-time. 560 full-time freshmen.
Selectivity: Admits 50 to 75% of applicants.

BASIC COSTS (2010-2011)

Tuition and fees: $40,256.
Per-credit charge: $1,255.
Room and board: $11,780.

FINANCIAL AID PICTURE (2009-2010)

Students with need: Out of 469 full-time freshmen who applied for aid, 401 were judged to have need. Of these, 401 received aid, and 401 had their full need met. Average financial aid package met 100% of need; average scholarship/grant was $31,435; average loan was $3,250. For part-time students, average financial aid package was $23,731.
Students without need: 67 full-time freshmen who did not demonstrate need for aid received scholarships/grants; average award was $16,858. No-need awards available for academics, leadership.
Scholarships offered: Academic scholarships; awarded competitively to first-year candidates who have outstanding record of scholarship and co-curricular achievement in high school and who demonstrate noteworthy leadership skills; renewable for up to 8 semesters with full-time status and good academic standing.
Cumulative student debt: 61% of graduating class had student loans; average debt was $23,008.

FINANCIAL AID PROCEDURES

Forms required: FAFSA, CSS PROFILE.
Dates and Deadlines: Priority date 2/15; closing date 3/1. Applicants notified by 4/1; must reply by 5/1.
Transfers: Closing date 5/15. Applicants notified on a rolling basis; must reply within 4 week(s) of notification. Financial aid transcripts from all schools previously attended required.

CONTACT

Kathy Blaisdell, Director of Student Financial Services
Newhall Center, South Hadley, MA 01075-1488
(413) 538-2291

Mount Ida College

Newton, Massachusetts
www.mountida.edu

Federal Code: 002193

4-year private business and liberal arts college in small city.
Enrollment: 1,479 undergrads, 5% part-time. 430 full-time freshmen.
Selectivity: Admits 50 to 75% of applicants.

BASIC COSTS (2009-2010)

Tuition and fees: $23,100.
Per-credit charge: $625.
Room and board: $11,450.

FINANCIAL AID PICTURE (2009-2010)

Students with need: Need-based aid available for full-time and part-time students. Work study available nights.

FINANCIAL AID PROCEDURES

Forms required: FAFSA, institutional form.
Dates and Deadlines: Priority date 4/15; no closing date. Applicants notified on a rolling basis starting 3/1; must reply within 3 week(s) of notification.

CONTACT

David Goldman, Director of Financial Aid
777 Dedham Street, Newton, MA 02459
(617) 928-4785

Mount Wachusett Community College

Gardner, Massachusetts
www.mwcc.edu

Federal Code: 002172

2-year public community college in large town.
Enrollment: 4,151 undergrads, 55% part-time. 729 full-time freshmen.
Selectivity: Open admission; but selective for some programs.

BASIC COSTS (2009-2010)

Tuition and fees: $5,025; out-of-state residents $11,175.
Per-credit charge: $25; out-of-state residents $230.
Additional info: New England resident tuition is $1,125.

FINANCIAL AID PICTURE (2008-2009)

Students with need: Out of 584 full-time freshmen who applied for aid, 403 were judged to have need. Of these, 377 received aid, and 46 had their full need met. Average financial aid package met 93% of need; average scholarship/grant was $4,207; average loan was $1,076. For part-time students, average financial aid package was $3,357.
Students without need: This college awards aid only to students with need.

FINANCIAL AID PROCEDURES

Forms required: FAFSA, institutional form.
Dates and Deadlines: Priority date 4/15; no closing date. Applicants notified on a rolling basis starting 5/1.

CONTACT

JoEllen Soucier, Director of Financial Aid
444 Green Street, Gardner, MA 01440-1000
(978) 632-6600 ext. 524

New England Conservatory of Music

Boston, Massachusetts
www.necmusic.edu

Federal Code: 002194

4-year private music college in very large city.
Enrollment: 405 undergrads, 8% part-time. 102 full-time freshmen.
Selectivity: Admits less than 50% of applicants.

BASIC COSTS (2009-2010)

Tuition and fees: $33,325.
Per-credit charge: $1,050.
Room and board: $11,600.
Additional info: On-campus residents and all incoming students pay $440 health center fee.

FINANCIAL AID PICTURE (2009-2010)

Students with need: Out of 65 full-time freshmen who applied for aid, 58 were judged to have need. Of these, 58 received aid, and 12 had their full need met. Average financial aid package met 59% of need; average scholarship/grant was $16,675; average loan was $2,938. Need-based aid available for part-time students.

Students without need: 30 full-time freshmen who did not demonstrate need for aid received scholarships/grants; average award was $15,446. No-need awards available for academics, music/drama.
Cumulative student debt: 69% of graduating class had student loans; average debt was $48,013.

FINANCIAL AID PROCEDURES
Forms required: FAFSA, institutional form.
Dates and Deadlines: Closing date 12/1. Applicants notified by 4/1; must reply by 5/1 or within 2 week(s) of notification.

CONTACT
Lauren Urbanek, Director of Financial Aid
290 Huntington Avenue, Boston, MA 02115
(617) 585-1110

New England Institute of Art
Brookline, Massachusetts
www.artinstitutes.edu/boston   Federal Code: 007486

4-year for-profit visual arts and technical college in very large city.
Enrollment: 1,700 undergrads.
Selectivity: Admits less than 50% of applicants.

FINANCIAL AID PICTURE
Students with need: Need-based aid available for full-time and part-time students. Work study available nights, weekends, and for part-time students.
Students without need: No-need awards available for academics.

FINANCIAL AID PROCEDURES
Forms required: FAFSA, institutional form.
Dates and Deadlines: Priority date 5/1; no closing date. Applicants notified on a rolling basis starting 3/1.

CONTACT
Anna Kelly, Director of Student Financial Services
10 Brookline Place West, Brookline, MA 02445-7295
(617) 739-1700

Newbury College
Brookline, Massachusetts
www.newbury.edu   Federal Code: 007484

4-year private business and liberal arts college in large city.
Enrollment: 887 undergrads, 3% part-time. 333 full-time freshmen.
Selectivity: Admits 50 to 75% of applicants.

BASIC COSTS (2010-2011)
Tuition and fees: $25,100.
Room and board: $11,750.

FINANCIAL AID PICTURE
Students with need: Need-based aid available for full-time and part-time students.
Students without need: This college awards aid only to students with need.

FINANCIAL AID PROCEDURES
Forms required: FAFSA.
Dates and Deadlines: Closing date 5/1. Applicants notified on a rolling basis starting 3/1; must reply by 5/1 or within 2 week(s) of notification.
Transfers: No deadline. Applicants notified on a rolling basis.

CONTACT
Kim Tibbets, Executive Director of Financial Assistance
129 Fisher Avenue, Brookline, MA 02445
(617) 730-7196

Nichols College
Dudley, Massachusetts
www.nichols.edu   Federal Code: 002197

4-year private business and liberal arts college in small town.
Enrollment: 1,319 undergrads, 12% part-time. 250 full-time freshmen.
Selectivity: Admits 50 to 75% of applicants.

BASIC COSTS (2009-2010)
Tuition and fees: $28,040.
Per-credit charge: $925.
Room and board: $9,200.

FINANCIAL AID PICTURE (2009-2010)
Students with need: Average financial aid package met 77% of need; average scholarship/grant was $18,579; average loan was $3,028. For part-time students, average financial aid package was $5,832.
Students without need: No-need awards available for academics, alumni affiliation, ROTC.
Cumulative student debt: 89% of graduating class had student loans; average debt was $27,112.

FINANCIAL AID PROCEDURES
Forms required: FAFSA.
Dates and Deadlines: Priority date 3/1; closing date 6/1. Applicants notified on a rolling basis starting 2/26; must reply within 4 week(s) of notification.
Transfers: Applicants notified by 3/1; must reply within 4 week(s) of notification.

CONTACT
Denise Brindle, Director of Financial Aid
PO Box 5000, Dudley, MA 01571-5000
(508) 213-2372

North Shore Community College
Danvers, Massachusetts
www.northshore.edu   Federal Code: 002173

2-year public community college in small city.
Enrollment: 7,088 undergrads, 50% part-time. 1,251 full-time freshmen.
Selectivity: Open admission; but selective for some programs.

BASIC COSTS (2009-2010)
Tuition and fees: $4,110; out-of-state residents $11,070.
Per-credit charge: $25; out-of-state residents $257.
Additional info: New England regional tuition: $133.50 per credit hour.

FINANCIAL AID PICTURE (2008-2009)
Students with need: Out of 965 full-time freshmen who applied for aid, 611 were judged to have need. Of these, 611 received aid, and 53 had their full need met. Average financial aid package met 16% of need; average scholarship/grant was $2,516; average loan was $1,537. For part-time students, average financial aid package was $9,646.
Students without need: This college awards aid only to students with need.

FINANCIAL AID PROCEDURES
Forms required: FAFSA.
Dates and Deadlines: Priority date 4/15; no closing date. Applicants notified on a rolling basis starting 4/1; must reply within 2 week(s) of notification.

CONTACT
Susan Sullivan, Director of Student Financial Services
One Ferncroft Road, Danvers, MA 01923-0840
(978) 762-4000

Northeastern University

Boston, Massachusetts
www.northeastern.edu
Federal Code: 002199
CSS Code: 3667

4-year private university in very large city.
Enrollment: 15,699 undergrads. 2,833 full-time freshmen.
Selectivity: Admits less than 50% of applicants.

BASIC COSTS (2009-2010)
Tuition and fees: $35,362.
Room and board: $12,350.

FINANCIAL AID PICTURE (2009-2010)
Students with need: Need-based aid available for full-time students. Work study available nights, weekends, and for part-time students.
Students without need: No-need awards available for academics, athletics, minority status.

FINANCIAL AID PROCEDURES
Forms required: FAFSA, CSS PROFILE.
Dates and Deadlines: Closing date 2/15. Applicants notified on a rolling basis starting 3/15; must reply by 5/1.
Transfers: Institutional application and financial aid transcript from all previously attended colleges required.

CONTACT
M. Seamus Harreys, Dean and Director of Student Financial Services
360 Huntington Avenue, 150 Richards Hall, Boston, MA 02115-9959
(617) 373-3190

Northern Essex Community College

Haverhill, Massachusetts
www.necc.mass.edu
Federal Code: 002174

2-year public community and junior college in small city.
Enrollment: 6,585 undergrads, 57% part-time. 988 full-time freshmen.
Selectivity: Open admission; but selective for some programs.

BASIC COSTS (2009-2010)
Tuition and fees: $3,870; out-of-state residents $11,100.
Per-credit charge: $25; out-of-state residents $266.
Additional info: New England residents pay $142 per credit hour.

FINANCIAL AID PICTURE
Students with need: Need-based aid available for full-time and part-time students.
Students without need: No-need awards available for academics.

FINANCIAL AID PROCEDURES
Forms required: FAFSA.
Dates and Deadlines: Priority date 5/1; no closing date. Applicants notified on a rolling basis starting 3/1; must reply within 2 week(s) of notification.

CONTACT
Teresa Jardon, Assistant Dean for Financial Aid
100 Elliott Street, Haverhill, MA 01830-2399
(978) 556-3600

Pine Manor College

Chestnut Hill, Massachusetts
www.pmc.edu
Federal Code: 002201

4-year private liberal arts college for women in very large city.
Enrollment: 161 undergrads, 1% part-time. 158 full-time freshmen.
Selectivity: Admits 50 to 75% of applicants.

BASIC COSTS (2009-2010)
Tuition and fees: $20,189.
Per-credit charge: $650.
Room and board: $11,670.

FINANCIAL AID PICTURE (2008-2009)
Students with need: Need-based aid available for full-time and part-time students. Work study available nights.
Students without need: No-need awards available for academics, alumni affiliation, leadership.

FINANCIAL AID PROCEDURES
Forms required: FAFSA.
Dates and Deadlines: Priority date 5/1; no closing date. Applicants notified on a rolling basis starting 3/1; must reply by 5/1 or within 2 week(s) of notification.
Transfers: No deadline. Applicants notified on a rolling basis starting 3/1; must reply by 5/1 or within 2 week(s) of notification.

CONTACT
Sophia Henderson, Assistant Dean for Student Recruitment and Retention
400 Heath Street, Chestnut Hill, MA 02467
(617) 731-7104

Quinsigamond Community College

Worcester, Massachusetts
www.qcc.edu
Federal Code: 002175

2-year public community college in small city.
Enrollment: 7,160 undergrads, 46% part-time. 1,467 full-time freshmen.
Selectivity: Open admission; but selective for some programs.

BASIC COSTS (2009-2010)
Tuition and fees: $5,040; out-of-state residents $11,220.
Per-credit charge: $24; out-of-state residents $230.

FINANCIAL AID PICTURE (2008-2009)
Students with need: Need-based aid available for full-time and part-time students. Work study available nights, weekends, and for part-time students.
Students without need: No-need awards available for academics, leadership, minority status.

FINANCIAL AID PROCEDURES
Forms required: FAFSA.
Dates and Deadlines: Priority date 4/1; no closing date. Applicants notified on a rolling basis starting 4/1.

CONTACT
Paula Ogden, Director of Financial Aid
670 West Boylston Street, Worcester, MA 01606
(508) 854-4261

Regis College

Weston, Massachusetts
www.regiscollege.edu
Federal Code: 002206

4-year private nursing and liberal arts college in large town, affiliated with Roman Catholic Church.
Enrollment: 972 undergrads, 23% part-time. 241 full-time freshmen.
Selectivity: Admits 50 to 75% of applicants.

BASIC COSTS (2010-2011)
Tuition and fees: $30,300.
Room and board: $12,190.
Additional info: Tuition/fee waivers available for adults.

FINANCIAL AID PICTURE (2009-2010)

Students with need: Need-based aid available for full-time and part-time students. Work study available nights, weekends, and for part-time students.
Students without need: No-need awards available for academics, alumni affiliation, leadership, ROTC.
Additional info: Family tuition discount scholarship; offered during any semester in which 2 or more unmarried, dependent siblings attend full-time.

FINANCIAL AID PROCEDURES

Forms required: FAFSA, institutional form.
Dates and Deadlines: Priority date 2/15; no closing date. Applicants notified on a rolling basis starting 3/15; must reply by 5/1 or within 2 week(s) of notification.
Transfers: No deadline. Applicants notified on a rolling basis.

CONTACT

Dolores Ludwick, Director of Financial Aid
235 Wellesley Street, Weston, MA 02493-1571
(781) 768-7180

Roxbury Community College
Roxbury Crossing, Massachusetts
www.rcc.mass.edu   Federal Code: 011930

2-year public community college in very large city.
Enrollment: 2,447 undergrads.
Selectivity: Open admission; but selective for some programs.

BASIC COSTS (2009-2010)

Tuition and fees: $3,990; out-of-state residents $11,640.
Per-credit charge: $26; out-of-state residents $247.

FINANCIAL AID PICTURE

Students with need: Need-based aid available for full-time and part-time students.
Students without need: This college awards aid only to students with need.

FINANCIAL AID PROCEDURES

Forms required: FAFSA, institutional form.
Dates and Deadlines: Closing date 5/1. Applicants notified on a rolling basis starting 6/15; must reply within 2 week(s) of notification.

CONTACT

Ray O'Rourke, Director of Financial Aid
1234 Columbus Avenue, Roxbury Crossing, MA 02120-3400
(617) 541-5322

School of the Museum of Fine Arts
Boston, Massachusetts
www.smfa.edu   Federal Code: 004667

4-year private visual arts college in very large city.
Enrollment: 564 undergrads, 5% part-time. 102 full-time freshmen.
Selectivity: Admits over 75% of applicants.

BASIC COSTS (2009-2010)

Tuition and fees: $30,660.
Room only: $13,046.

FINANCIAL AID PICTURE (2009-2010)

Students with need: Out of 81 full-time freshmen who applied for aid, 70 were judged to have need. Of these, 70 received aid, and 13 had their full need met. Average financial aid package met 58% of need; average scholarship/grant was $14,944; average loan was $3,441. For part-time students, average financial aid package was $11,109.

Students without need: 10 full-time freshmen who did not demonstrate need for aid received scholarships/grants; average award was $5,708. No-need awards available for art.

FINANCIAL AID PROCEDURES

Forms required: FAFSA, institutional form.
Dates and Deadlines: Closing date 3/15. Applicants notified by 4/15; must reply by 5/1 or within 2 week(s) of notification.
Transfers: Applicants notified on a rolling basis starting 4/15; must reply by 5/1 or within 2 week(s) of notification.

CONTACT

Elizabeth Goreham, Director of Financial Aid
230 The Fenway, Boston, MA 02115
(800) 776-0135

Simmons College
Boston, Massachusetts
www.simmons.edu   Federal Code: 002208

4-year private health science and liberal arts college for women in very large city.
Enrollment: 1,933 undergrads, 10% part-time. 354 full-time freshmen.
Selectivity: Admits 50 to 75% of applicants.

BASIC COSTS (2009-2010)

Tuition and fees: $31,220.
Per-credit charge: $910.
Room and board: $12,050.

FINANCIAL AID PICTURE (2009-2010)

Students with need: Out of 344 full-time freshmen who applied for aid, 276 were judged to have need. Of these, 276 received aid, and 20 had their full need met. Average financial aid package met 65% of need; average scholarship/grant was $15,937; average loan was $4,126. For part-time students, average financial aid package was $14,070.
Students without need: 57 full-time freshmen who did not demonstrate need for aid received scholarships/grants; average award was $7,825. No-need awards available for academics, alumni affiliation, leadership, minority status.
Cumulative student debt: 78% of graduating class had student loans; average debt was $45,237.

FINANCIAL AID PROCEDURES

Forms required: FAFSA, institutional form.
Dates and Deadlines: Priority date 2/15; closing date 3/1. Applicants notified on a rolling basis starting 3/15; must reply by 5/1 or within 4 week(s) of notification.
Transfers: Applicants notified on a rolling basis starting 3/15; must reply by 5/1 or within 4 week(s) of notification. Combination of grants, loans, employment opportunities available.

CONTACT

Diane Hallisey, Director of Student Financial Services
300 The Fenway, Boston, MA 02115-5898
(617) 521-2004

Smith College
Northampton, Massachusetts   Federal Code: 002209
www.smith.edu   CSS Code: 3762

4-year private liberal arts college for women in large town.
Enrollment: 2,614 undergrads, 1% part-time. 665 full-time freshmen.
Selectivity: Admits less than 50% of applicants.

BASIC COSTS (2010-2011)

Tuition and fees: $38,898.

Per-credit charge: $1,210.

Room and board: $13,000.

FINANCIAL AID PICTURE (2008-2009)

Students with need: Out of 526 full-time freshmen who applied for aid, 406 were judged to have need. Of these, 406 received aid, and 406 had their full need met. Average financial aid package met 100% of need; average scholarship/grant was $31,980; average loan was $3,198. For part-time students, average financial aid package was $28,323.

Students without need: 31 full-time freshmen who did not demonstrate need for aid received scholarships/grants; average award was $17,985. No-need awards available for academics, state/district residency.

Scholarships offered: Zollman Scholarships; $20,000; for academic excellence; about 15 awarded. STRIDE scholarship; $15,000; about 50 awarded. Springfield Partnership; full-tuition; for academic excellence in Springfield public high schools; up to 3 awarded.

Cumulative student debt: 62% of graduating class had student loans; average debt was $21,573.

Additional info: Financial aid policy guarantees to meet full financial need, as calculated by college, of all admitted students who have met application deadlines.

FINANCIAL AID PROCEDURES

Forms required: FAFSA, CSS PROFILE.

Dates and Deadlines: Closing date 2/15. Applicants notified by 4/1; must reply by 5/1.

Transfers: Priority date 2/15; closing date 4/1. Must reply by 5/1. Applicants who apply after admission decision is made cannot receive college aid until they complete at least 32 credits at Smith.

CONTACT

David Belanger, Director of Student Financial Services

7 College Lane, Northampton, MA 01063

(413) 585-2530

Springfield College

Springfield, Massachusetts

www.springfieldcollege.edu

Federal Code: 002211

CSS Code: 3763

4-year private health science and liberal arts college in small city.

Enrollment: 2,292 undergrads.

Selectivity: Admits 50 to 75% of applicants.

BASIC COSTS (2009-2010)

Tuition and fees: $26,480.

Per-credit charge: $790.

Room and board: $11,050.

FINANCIAL AID PICTURE (2008-2009)

Students with need: Need-based aid available for full-time students.

Additional info: Co-operative education program available to students after freshman year.

FINANCIAL AID PROCEDURES

Forms required: FAFSA, CSS PROFILE, institutional form.

Dates and Deadlines: Priority date 3/15; no closing date. Applicants notified on a rolling basis starting 3/15; must reply by 5/1 or within 2 week(s) of notification.

Transfers: Priority date 4/15.

CONTACT

Edward Ciosek, Director of Financial Aid

263 Alden Street, Springfield, MA 01109

(413) 748-3000

Springfield Technical Community College

Springfield, Massachusetts

www.stcc.edu

Federal Code: 005549

2-year public community and technical college in small city.

Enrollment: 5,728 undergrads, 50% part-time. 1,036 full-time freshmen.

Selectivity: Open admission; but selective for some programs.

BASIC COSTS (2009-2010)

Tuition and fees: $3,936; out-of-state residents $10,446.

Per-credit charge: $25; out-of-state residents $242.

Additional info: New England reciprocal rate $237 per credit hour, including fees.

FINANCIAL AID PICTURE (2008-2009)

Students with need: 78% of average financial aid package awarded as scholarships/grants, 22% awarded as loans/jobs. Need-based aid available for part-time students.

Students without need: This college awards aid only to students with need.

FINANCIAL AID PROCEDURES

Forms required: FAFSA, institutional form.

Dates and Deadlines: Priority date 5/1; no closing date. Applicants notified on a rolling basis starting 7/1.

CONTACT

Mary Forni, Coordinator of Financial Aid Services

One Armory Square, Springfield, MA 01102-9000

(413) 755-4214

Stonehill College

Easton, Massachusetts

www.stonehill.edu

Federal Code: 002217

CSS Code: 3770

4-year private liberal arts college in large town, affiliated with Roman Catholic Church.

Enrollment: 2,448 undergrads, 1% part-time. 683 full-time freshmen.

Selectivity: Admits 50 to 75% of applicants.

BASIC COSTS (2009-2010)

Tuition and fees: $31,210.

Per-credit charge: $1,040.

Room and board: $12,240.

Additional info: Tuition/fee waivers available for minority students, unemployed or children of unemployed.

FINANCIAL AID PICTURE (2009-2010)

Students with need: Out of 617 full-time freshmen who applied for aid, 485 were judged to have need. Of these, 485 received aid, and 100 had their full need met. Average financial aid package met 76% of need; average scholarship/grant was $18,707; average loan was $3,430. For part-time students, average financial aid package was $3,048.

Students without need: 159 full-time freshmen who did not demonstrate need for aid received scholarships/grants; average award was $9,153. No-need awards available for academics, art, athletics, leadership, minority status, music/drama, ROTC.

Scholarships offered: 21 full-time freshmen received athletic scholarships; average amount $10,794.

Cumulative student debt: 73% of graduating class had student loans; average debt was $29,163.

FINANCIAL AID PROCEDURES

Forms required: FAFSA, CSS PROFILE.

Dates and Deadlines: Priority date 2/1; no closing date. Applicants notified by 4/1; must reply by 5/1.

Transfers: Closing date 4/1. Applicants notified by 6/1; must reply by 6/30.

CONTACT

Eileen O'Leary, Assistant Vice President for Finance/Director of Student Aid and Finance

320 Washington Street, Easton, MA 02357-0100

(508) 565-1088

Suffolk University

Boston, Massachusetts

www.suffolk.edu   Federal Code: 002218

4-year private university in very large city.

Enrollment: 5,617 undergrads, 6% part-time. 1,249 full-time freshmen.

Selectivity: Admits over 75% of applicants.

BASIC COSTS (2009-2010)

Tuition and fees: $27,208.

Per-credit charge: $665.

Room and board: $14,544.

FINANCIAL AID PICTURE (2009-2010)

Students with need: Out of 1,016 full-time freshmen who applied for aid, 873 were judged to have need. Of these, 868 received aid, and 95 had their full need met. Average financial aid package met 72% of need; average scholarship/grant was $13,201; average loan was $3,466. For part-time students, average financial aid package was $10,384.

Students without need: 75 full-time freshmen who did not demonstrate need for aid received scholarships/grants; average award was $7,047. No-need awards available for academics, alumni affiliation.

Scholarships offered: Various scholarships; amounts vary; based on academic achievement, talent, and contribution to applicant's school and community.

Additional info: Foreign students may apply for institutional employment awards.

FINANCIAL AID PROCEDURES

Forms required: FAFSA, institutional form.

Dates and Deadlines: Closing date 3/1. Applicants notified on a rolling basis starting 2/5.

CONTACT

Christine Perry, Director of Financial Aid

8 Ashburton Place, Boston, MA 02108

(617) 573-8470

Tufts University

Medford, Massachusetts   Federal Code: 002219

www.tufts.edu   CSS Code: 3901

4-year private university in small city.

Enrollment: 5,146 undergrads, 1% part-time. 1,309 full-time freshmen.

Selectivity: Admits less than 50% of applicants.

BASIC COSTS (2009-2010)

Tuition and fees: $40,342.

Room and board: $10,746.

FINANCIAL AID PICTURE (2009-2010)

Students with need: Need-based aid available for full-time and part-time students.

Students without need: This college awards aid only to students with need.

Scholarships offered: National Merit Scholarships; $500 for non-need; $2,000 for need.

FINANCIAL AID PROCEDURES

Forms required: FAFSA, CSS PROFILE.

Dates and Deadlines: Closing date 2/15. Applicants notified by 4/1; must reply by 5/1.

Transfers: Closing date 3/1. Applicants notified by 5/1; must reply within 2 week(s) of notification.

CONTACT

Patricia Reilly, Director of Financial Aid

Bendetson Hall, Medford, MA 02155

(617) 627-2000

University of Massachusetts Amherst

Amherst, Massachusetts

www.umass.edu   Federal Code: 002221

4-year public university in large town.

Enrollment: 20,287 undergrads, 5% part-time. 4,136 full-time freshmen.

Selectivity: Admits 50 to 75% of applicants.

BASIC COSTS (2009-2010)

Tuition and fees: $11,917; out-of-state residents $23,414.

Room and board: $8,276.

FINANCIAL AID PICTURE (2008-2009)

Students with need: Out of 3,646 full-time freshmen who applied for aid, 2,203 were judged to have need. Of these, 2,136 received aid, and 451 had their full need met. Average financial aid package met 84% of need; average scholarship/grant was $7,952; average loan was $3,463. For part-time students, average financial aid package was $10,583.

Students without need: 238 full-time freshmen who did not demonstrate need for aid received scholarships/grants; average award was $3,689. No-need awards available for academics, art, athletics, music/drama, ROTC, state/district residency.

Scholarships offered: *Merit:* Merit scholarships; all applicants automatically considered. *Athletic:* 48 full-time freshmen received athletic scholarships; average amount $16,070.

Cumulative student debt: 66% of graduating class had student loans; average debt was $23,614.

FINANCIAL AID PROCEDURES

Forms required: FAFSA.

Dates and Deadlines: Priority date 2/14; no closing date. Applicants notified on a rolling basis starting 3/1.

Transfers: Financial aid transcripts required.

CONTACT

Suzanne Peters, Director of Financial Aid

University Admissions Center, Amherst, MA 01003-9291

(413) 545-0801

University of Massachusetts Boston

Boston, Massachusetts

www.umb.edu   Federal Code: 002222

4-year public university in very large city.

Enrollment: 10,130 undergrads, 26% part-time. 949 full-time freshmen.

Selectivity: Admits 50 to 75% of applicants.

BASIC COSTS (2009-2010)

Tuition and fees: $10,611; out-of-state residents $22,797.

Per-credit charge: $72; out-of-state residents $406.

FINANCIAL AID PICTURE (2008-2009)

Students with need: Out of 737 full-time freshmen who applied for aid, 616 were judged to have need. Of these, 616 received aid, and 287 had their full need met. Average financial aid package met 90% of need; average scholarship/grant was $6,757; average loan was $3,730. For part-time students, average financial aid package was $8,791.

Students without need: 72 full-time freshmen who did not demonstrate need for aid received scholarships/grants; average award was $3,618. No-need awards available for academics, leadership, state/district residency.

Cumulative student debt: 60% of graduating class had student loans; average debt was $17,486.

Additional info: Some Massachusetts state employees and Massachusetts Vietnam veterans eligible for tuition waiver. Some waivers available based on talent and academic excellence.

FINANCIAL AID PROCEDURES

Forms required: FAFSA.

Dates and Deadlines: Priority date 3/1; no closing date. Applicants notified on a rolling basis starting 3/21.

CONTACT

Judy Keyes, Director of Financial Aid Services
100 Morrissey Boulevard, Boston, MA 02125-3393
(617) 287-6300

University of Massachusetts Dartmouth
North Dartmouth, Massachusetts
www.umassd.edu   Federal Code: 002210

4-year public university in large town.
Enrollment: 7,775 undergrads, 9% part-time. 1,782 full-time freshmen.
Selectivity: Admits 50 to 75% of applicants.

BASIC COSTS (2009-2010)
Tuition and fees: $10,358; out-of-state residents $20,061.
Room and board: $9,699.

FINANCIAL AID PICTURE (2008-2009)

Students with need: Out of 1,454 full-time freshmen who applied for aid, 1,101 were judged to have need. Of these, 1,101 received aid, and 533 had their full need met. Average financial aid package met 91% of need; average scholarship/grant was $6,186; average loan was $5,631. For part-time students, average financial aid package was $10,629.

Students without need: 181 full-time freshmen who did not demonstrate need for aid received scholarships/grants; average award was $2,311. No-need awards available for academics, minority status, ROTC, state/district residency.

Scholarships offered: Chancellor's Merit Scholarship; approximately $2,000; for Massachusetts high school seniors with 1250 SAT (exclusive of Writing) and in top 25% of class; 50 awarded. Solveig E.J. Balestracci Scholarship; $1,000; for academic achievement in marine-related area for residents of New Bedford, Dartmouth, Acushnet, Westport, Mattapoisett, Marion, Rochester or Lakeville; 1 awarded. Boivon Scholarship; $1,000; based on academic involvement in French language and culture. A.J. Carvalho Memorial Scholarship; approximately $5,000; for New Bedford graduates of Portuguese descent with 3.0 GPA. Cranston Foundation Scholarship; $500; for students in the Textile Science Department.

Cumulative student debt: 73% of graduating class had student loans; average debt was $21,905.

FINANCIAL AID PROCEDURES

Forms required: FAFSA.

Dates and Deadlines: Priority date 3/1; no closing date. Applicants notified on a rolling basis starting 3/25; must reply within 3 week(s) of notification.

CONTACT

Bruce Palmer, Director of Financial Aid
285 Old Westport Road, North Dartmouth, MA 02747-2300
(508) 999-8632

University of Massachusetts Lowell
Lowell, Massachusetts
www.uml.edu   Federal Code: 002161

4-year public university in small city.
Enrollment: 9,615 undergrads, 22% part-time. 1,504 full-time freshmen.
Selectivity: Admits 50 to 75% of applicants.

BASIC COSTS (2009-2010)
Tuition and fees: $10,422; out-of-state residents $22,843.
Per-credit charge: $61; out-of-state residents $357.
Room and board: $8,635.

FINANCIAL AID PICTURE (2009-2010)

Students with need: Out of 1,362 full-time freshmen who applied for aid, 926 were judged to have need. Of these, 926 received aid, and 620 had their full need met. Average financial aid package met 94% of need; average scholarship/grant was $6,805; average loan was $5,359. For part-time students, average financial aid package was $8,897.

Students without need: 422 full-time freshmen who did not demonstrate need for aid received scholarships/grants; average award was $2,435. No-need awards available for academics, alumni affiliation, art, athletics, job skills, leadership, minority status, music/drama, ROTC, state/district residency.

Scholarships offered: 21 full-time freshmen received athletic scholarships; average amount $4,834.

Cumulative student debt: 73% of graduating class had student loans; average debt was $21,542.

FINANCIAL AID PROCEDURES

Forms required: FAFSA.

Dates and Deadlines: Priority date 3/1; no closing date. Applicants notified on a rolling basis starting 3/20.

CONTACT

Joyce McLaughlin, Director of Financial Aid
883 Broadway Street, Room 110, Lowell, MA 01854-5104
(978) 934-4220

Urban College of Boston
Boston, Massachusetts
www.urbancollege.edu   Federal Code: 031305

2-year private community college in very large city.
Enrollment: 378 undergrads.
Selectivity: Open admission.

BASIC COSTS (2009-2010)
Tuition and fees: $5,000.
Per-credit charge: $166.

FINANCIAL AID PICTURE (2008-2009)

Students with need: Need-based aid available for full-time and part-time students.

Students without need: This college awards aid only to students with need.

FINANCIAL AID PROCEDURES

Forms required: FAFSA.

Dates and Deadlines: Priority date 12/10; no closing date. Applicants notified on a rolling basis starting 4/15.

CONTACT
Sandra Coswatte, Director of Financial Aid
178 Tremont Street, Seventh Floor, Boston, MA 02111
(617) 348-6220

Wellesley College
Wellesley, Massachusetts
www.wellesley.edu

Federal Code: 002224
CSS Code: 3957

4-year private liberal arts college for women in large town.
Enrollment: 2,193 undergrads, 1% part-time. 589 full-time freshmen.
Selectivity: Admits less than 50% of applicants.

BASIC COSTS (2010-2011)
Tuition and fees: $39,666.
Room and board: $12,284.

FINANCIAL AID PICTURE (2009-2010)
Students with need: Out of 413 full-time freshmen who applied for aid, 341 were judged to have need. Of these, 341 received aid, and 341 had their full need met. Average financial aid package met 100% of need; average scholarship/grant was $34,246; average loan was $2,601. Need-based aid available for part-time students.
Students without need: This college awards aid only to students with need.
Cumulative student debt: 56% of graduating class had student loans; average debt was $13,324.
Additional info: No student will graduate with more than $12,825 in packaged student loans. Students from families with a calculated income between $60,000 and $100,000 will graduate with no more than $8,600 in packaged student loans. Students from families with the greatest need ($60,000 income or less) will graduate with $0 in packaged student loans; their packages will consist of scholarship and work-study money.

FINANCIAL AID PROCEDURES
Forms required: FAFSA, CSS PROFILE.
Dates and Deadlines: Closing date 1/15. Applicants notified by 4/1; must reply by 5/1.
Transfers: Closing date 3/1.

CONTACT
Kathryn Osmond, Director of Student Financial Services
106 Central Street, Wellesley, MA 02481
(781) 283-2360

Wentworth Institute of Technology
Boston, Massachusetts
www.wit.edu

Federal Code: 002225

4-year private engineering and technical college in very large city.
Enrollment: 3,781 undergrads, 11% part-time. 852 full-time freshmen.
Selectivity: Admits 50 to 75% of applicants.

BASIC COSTS (2010-2011)
Tuition and fees: $22,870.
Room and board: $11,000.
Additional info: Tuition includes cost of laptop computer; students in architecture and design programs pay $2,000 in required fees for academic year.

FINANCIAL AID PICTURE (2009-2010)
Students with need: Out of 751 full-time freshmen who applied for aid, 660 were judged to have need. Of these, 660 received aid, and 4 had their full need met. Average financial aid package met 52% of need; average scholarship/grant was $6,402; average loan was $3,460. For part-time students, average financial aid package was $3,930.

Students without need: 152 full-time freshmen who did not demonstrate need for aid received scholarships/grants; average award was $5,910. No-need awards available for academics, leadership, ROTC, state/district residency.
Scholarships offered: Applicants for admission automatically considered for merit scholarships.
Cumulative student debt: 83% of graduating class had student loans; average debt was $22,000.

FINANCIAL AID PROCEDURES
Forms required: FAFSA.
Dates and Deadlines: Priority date 3/1; no closing date. Applicants notified on a rolling basis starting 3/15; must reply within 2 week(s) of notification.
Transfers: Review of NSLDS history within 30 days of beginning of enrollment required.

CONTACT
Anne-Marie Caruso, Director of Financial Aid
550 Huntington Avenue, Boston, MA 02115
(617) 989-4020

Western New England College
Springfield, Massachusetts
www.wnec.edu

Federal Code: 002226

4-year private university in small city.
Enrollment: 2,716 undergrads, 9% part-time. 679 full-time freshmen.
Selectivity: Admits over 75% of applicants.

BASIC COSTS (2010-2011)
Tuition and fees: $29,812.
Per-credit charge: $523.
Room and board: $11,336.

FINANCIAL AID PICTURE (2009-2010)
Students with need: Out of 612 full-time freshmen who applied for aid, 535 were judged to have need. Of these, 535 received aid, and 67 had their full need met. Average financial aid package met 70% of need; average scholarship/grant was $15,024; average loan was $4,122. For part-time students, average financial aid package was $7,162.
Students without need: 95 full-time freshmen who did not demonstrate need for aid received scholarships/grants; average award was $9,767. No-need awards available for academics, music/drama, ROTC.

FINANCIAL AID PROCEDURES
Forms required: FAFSA.
Dates and Deadlines: Priority date 4/15; closing date 5/1. Applicants notified on a rolling basis starting 3/15; must reply by 5/1 or within 2 week(s) of notification.

CONTACT
Kathy Chambers, Associate Director of Financial Aid
1215 Wilbraham Road, Springfield, MA 01119-2684
(800) 325-1122 ext. 2080

Westfield State College
Westfield, Massachusetts
www.wsc.ma.edu

Federal Code: 002189

4-year public liberal arts and teachers college in large town.
Enrollment: 4,925 undergrads, 8% part-time. 1,078 full-time freshmen.
Selectivity: Admits 50 to 75% of applicants.

BASIC COSTS (2009-2010)
Tuition and fees: $7,016; out-of-state residents $13,096.
Per-credit charge: $85; out-of-state residents $95.

Room and board: $7,728.

FINANCIAL AID PICTURE (2008-2009)

Students with need: Out of 948 full-time freshmen who applied for aid, 572 were judged to have need. Of these, 556 received aid, and 78 had their full need met. Average financial aid package met 70% of need; average scholarship/grant was $4,634; average loan was $3,151. Need-based aid available for part-time students.

Students without need: 15 full-time freshmen who did not demonstrate need for aid received scholarships/grants; average award was $4,079.

Cumulative student debt: 73% of graduating class had student loans; average debt was $18,648.

FINANCIAL AID PROCEDURES

Forms required: FAFSA.

Dates and Deadlines: Priority date 3/1; no closing date. Applicants notified on a rolling basis starting 4/1.

CONTACT

Catherine Ryan, Director of Financial Aid
577 Western Avenue, Westfield, MA 01086-1630
(413) 572-5218

Wheaton College

Norton, Massachusetts   Federal Code: 002227
www.wheatoncollege.edu/   CSS Code: 3963

4-year private liberal arts college in large town.
Enrollment: 1,632 undergrads. 424 full-time freshmen.
Selectivity: Admits 50 to 75% of applicants.

BASIC COSTS (2010-2011)

Tuition and fees: $41,084.
Room and board: $10,180.
Additional info: Freshmen pay one-time $50 general fee (non-refundable).

FINANCIAL AID PICTURE (2009-2010)

Students with need: Out of 289 full-time freshmen who applied for aid, 257 were judged to have need. Of these, 257 received aid, and 130 had their full need met. Average financial aid package met 96% of need; average scholarship/grant was $25,818; average loan was $3,897. Need-based aid available for part-time students.

Students without need: 66 full-time freshmen who did not demonstrate need for aid received scholarships/grants; average award was $11,250. No-need awards available for academics.

Scholarships offered: Balfour Scholarship; $15,000 annually plus $3,000 total in research/internship/community service stipends. Trustee Scholarship; $10,000 annually plus $3,000 total in research/internship/community service stipends. Community Scholarship; $7,500 annually plus $3,000 total in research/internship/community service stipends. Regional Scholarship; $7,500 annually plus $3,000 total in research/internship/community service stipends. All selected from top 20% of applicant pool.

Cumulative student debt: 53% of graduating class had student loans; average debt was $25,540.

FINANCIAL AID PROCEDURES

Forms required: FAFSA, CSS PROFILE.

Dates and Deadlines: Closing date 2/1. Applicants notified by 4/1; must reply by 5/1.

Transfers: Closing date 3/15. Applicants notified on a rolling basis; must reply by 6/1. Limited funds available for transfer applicants.

CONTACT

Robin Randall, Assistant Vice President for Enrollment and Student Financial Services
26 East Main Street, Norton, MA 02766
(508) 286-8232

Wheelock College

Boston, Massachusetts
www.wheelock.edu   Federal Code: 002228

4-year private liberal arts and teachers college in very large city.
Enrollment: 746 undergrads, 3% part-time. 180 full-time freshmen.
Selectivity: Admits over 75% of applicants.

BASIC COSTS (2010-2011)

Tuition and fees: $28,940.
Per-credit charge: $875.
Room and board: $11,900.

FINANCIAL AID PICTURE (2009-2010)

Students with need: Out of 177 full-time freshmen who applied for aid, 170 were judged to have need. Of these, 170 received aid, and 31 had their full need met. Average financial aid package met 74% of need; average scholarship/grant was $18,775; average loan was $3,815. For part-time students, average financial aid package was $7,887.

Students without need: 9 full-time freshmen who did not demonstrate need for aid received scholarships/grants; average award was $10,095. No-need awards available for academics, job skills, leadership.

Scholarships offered: Wheelock College Grants; based on 1050 SAT (exclusive of writing) plus 3.0 GPA; renewable if 3.0 GPA maintained.

Cumulative student debt: 96% of graduating class had student loans; average debt was $43,318.

FINANCIAL AID PROCEDURES

Forms required: FAFSA.

Dates and Deadlines: Closing date 2/15. Applicants notified on a rolling basis starting 3/1; must reply by 5/1.

Transfers: Priority date 4/15. Applicants notified by 5/1; must reply by 6/1.

CONTACT

Roxanne Dumas, Director of Financial Aid
200 The Riverway, Boston, MA 02215-4176
(617) 879-2443

Williams College

Williamstown, Massachusetts   Federal Code: 002229
www.williams.edu   CSS Code: 3965

4-year private liberal arts college in small town, affiliated with United Church of Christ.
Enrollment: 2,032 undergrads. 546 full-time freshmen.
Selectivity: Admits less than 50% of applicants.

BASIC COSTS (2010-2011)

Tuition and fees: $41,434.
Room and board: $10,906.

FINANCIAL AID PICTURE (2009-2010)

Students with need: Out of 346 full-time freshmen who applied for aid, 289 were judged to have need. Of these, 289 received aid, and 289 had their full need met. Average financial aid package met 100% of need; average scholarship/grant was $37,175. Need-based aid available for part-time students.

Students without need: This college awards aid only to students with need.

Cumulative student debt: 43% of graduating class had student loans; average debt was $8,103.

FINANCIAL AID PROCEDURES

Forms required: FAFSA, CSS PROFILE.

Dates and Deadlines: Closing date 2/1. Applicants notified by 4/1; must reply by 5/1.

Transfers: Closing date 4/1. Applicants notified by 5/15; must reply within 2 week(s) of notification.

CONTACT

Paul Boyer, Director of Financial Aid
33 Stetson Court, Williamstown, MA 01267
(413) 597-3131

Worcester Polytechnic Institute

Worcester, Massachusetts   Federal Code: 002233
www.wpi.edu   CSS Code: 3969

4-year private university in small city.
Enrollment: 3,391 undergrads, 3% part-time. 918 full-time freshmen.
Selectivity: Admits 50 to 75% of applicants.

BASIC COSTS (2010-2011)

Tuition and fees: $38,920.
Room and board: $11,610.

FINANCIAL AID PICTURE (2008-2009)

Students with need: Need-based aid available for full-time and part-time students. Work study available nights, weekends, and for part-time students.
Students without need: No-need awards available for academics, leadership, minority status, ROTC.
Scholarships offered: Merit scholarships; typically $12,500-$25,000; renewable for 4 years.

FINANCIAL AID PROCEDURES

Forms required: FAFSA, CSS PROFILE.
Dates and Deadlines: Closing date 2/1. Applicants notified by 4/1; must reply by 5/1.
Transfers: Priority date 2/1; closing date 3/1. Applicants notified by 4/15; must reply by 5/1.

CONTACT

Monica Blondin, Director, Financial Aid
100 Institute Road, Worcester, MA 01609-2280
(508) 831-5469

Worcester State College

Worcester, Massachusetts
www.worcester.edu   Federal Code: 002190

4-year public liberal arts and teachers college in small city.
Enrollment: 4,211 undergrads, 17% part-time. 654 full-time freshmen.
Selectivity: Admits 50 to 75% of applicants.

BASIC COSTS (2009-2010)

Tuition and fees: $6,605; out-of-state residents $12,685.
Per-credit charge: $40; out-of-state residents $294.
Room and board: $9,067.

FINANCIAL AID PICTURE (2008-2009)

Students with need: Out of 598 full-time freshmen who applied for aid, 378 were judged to have need. Of these, 372 received aid, and 165 had their full need met. Average financial aid package met 82% of need; average scholarship/grant was $4,643; average loan was $1,876. For part-time students, average financial aid package was $7,081.
Students without need: 21 full-time freshmen who did not demonstrate need for aid received scholarships/grants; average award was $3,029. No-need awards available for academics, ROTC.
Scholarships offered: Presidential Scholarship; full in state tuition and fees; 3.5 GPA and 1150 SAT required; 15 awarded. Tsongas Scholarship; full in-state tuition and fees to Massachusetts residents; 3.75 GPA and 1200 SAT required; 5 awarded. Access Scholarship; $1,000 per year; for underserved groups with 2.5 GPA and 920 SAT; 15 awarded. Teacher Education Scholarship; full in-state tuition and fees; for future teachers with 3.2 GPA and 1100

SAT; 15 awarded. Honors Scholarship; $1,500 per year; 3.2 GPA and 1100 SAT equired; 25 awarded. All SAT scores exclusive of writing.
Cumulative student debt: 42% of graduating class had student loans; average debt was $17,819.
Additional info: Veterans, Native Americans and those certified by Massachusetts Rehabilitation Commission and Massachusetts Commission for the Blind considered for tuition waivers while funds available. Tuition also waived for needy Massachusetts residents and in-state National Guard members.

FINANCIAL AID PROCEDURES

Forms required: FAFSA.
Dates and Deadlines: Priority date 3/1; closing date 5/1. Applicants notified on a rolling basis starting 3/1; must reply within 2 week(s) of notification.

CONTACT

Jayne McGinn, Director of Financial Aid
Office of Undergraduate Admission, Worcester, MA 01602-2597
(508) 929-8056

Zion Bible College

Haverhill, Massachusetts
www.zbc.edu   Federal Code: 035705

4-year private Bible college in small city, affiliated with Assemblies of God.
Enrollment: 258 undergrads, 14% part-time. 42 full-time freshmen.
Selectivity: Open admission.

BASIC COSTS (2009-2010)

Tuition and fees: $8,470.
Per-credit charge: $260.
Room and board: $6,200.

FINANCIAL AID PICTURE (2009-2010)

Students with need: Need-based aid available for full-time and part-time students.
Students without need: No-need awards available for academics, leadership, minority status, state/district residency.

FINANCIAL AID PROCEDURES

Forms required: FAFSA.
Dates and Deadlines: Priority date 6/1; no closing date. Applicants notified on a rolling basis; must reply within 4 week(s) of notification.

CONTACT

Patricia Stauffer, Financial Aid Director
320 South Main Street, Haverhill, MA 01835

Michigan

Adrian College

Adrian, Michigan
www.adrian.edu   Federal Code: 002234

4-year private liberal arts college in large town, affiliated with United Methodist Church.
Enrollment: 1,500 undergrads.
Selectivity: Admits 50 to 75% of applicants.

BASIC COSTS (2009-2010)

Tuition and fees: $24,440.
Per-credit charge: $685.
Room and board: $7,660.

FINANCIAL AID PICTURE (2008-2009)

Students with need: Need-based aid available for full-time and part-time students. Work study available nights, weekends, and for part-time students.

Students without need: No-need awards available for academics, alumni affiliation, art, leadership, music/drama, religious affiliation, state/district residency.

Scholarships offered: Academic scholarships; based on ACT score of 20 and GPA of 3.0.

FINANCIAL AID PROCEDURES
Forms required: FAFSA.

Dates and Deadlines: Priority date 3/1; no closing date. Applicants notified on a rolling basis starting 3/15; must reply by 5/1 or within 2 week(s) of notification.

CONTACT
Andrew Spohn, Director of Financial Services
110 South Madison Street, Adrian, MI 49221-2575
(517) 265-5161 ext. 4306

Albion College
Albion, Michigan
www.albion.edu   Federal Code: 002235

4-year private liberal arts college in small town, affiliated with United Methodist Church.

Enrollment: 1,722 undergrads, 1% part-time. 437 full-time freshmen.
Selectivity: Admits over 75% of applicants.

BASIC COSTS (2010-2011)
Tuition and fees: $31,497.
Per-credit charge: $1,303.
Room and board: $8,842.

FINANCIAL AID PICTURE (2009-2010)
Students with need: Out of 362 full-time freshmen who applied for aid, 312 were judged to have need. Of these, 312 received aid, and 94 had their full need met. Average financial aid package met 89% of need; average scholarship/grant was $21,528; average loan was $4,429.

Students without need: 124 full-time freshmen who did not demonstrate need for aid received scholarships/grants; average award was $14,655. No-need awards available for academics, alumni affiliation, art, music/drama, state/district residency.

Scholarships offered: Distinguished Albion Scholarships: full tuition for 4 years; awarded to students who present original research during on-campus competition; up to 10 awarded. Trustee Scholarships: $15,500; based on GPA and SAT or ACT. Presidential Scholarships: $14,000; based on GPA and SAT or ACT. Performing and Fine Arts Scholarships: up to $3,000. Speech Communication Scholarships: up to $8,000. Diversity Awards: $4,000 renewable annually; awarded to students involved with promoting and enhancing multicultural on-campus relations.

Cumulative student debt: 55% of graduating class had student loans; average debt was $30,149.

FINANCIAL AID PROCEDURES
Forms required: FAFSA.

Dates and Deadlines: Priority date 3/1; no closing date. Applicants notified on a rolling basis starting 3/15; must reply by 5/1 or within 2 week(s) of notification.

Transfers: Applicants notified on a rolling basis.

CONTACT
Doug Kellar, Associate Vice President for Enrollment and Financial Aid
611 East Porter Street, Albion, MI 49224-1831
(517) 629-0440

Alma College
Alma, Michigan
www.alma.edu   Federal Code: 002236

4-year private liberal arts college in small town, affiliated with Presbyterian Church (USA).

Enrollment: 1,394 undergrads, 2% part-time. 396 full-time freshmen.
Selectivity: Admits over 75% of applicants.

BASIC COSTS (2010-2011)
Tuition and fees: $27,580.
Per-credit charge: $1,000.
Room and board: $8,700.

FINANCIAL AID PICTURE (2009-2010)
Students with need: Out of 386 full-time freshmen who applied for aid, 338 were judged to have need. Of these, 338 received aid, and 81 had their full need met. Average financial aid package met 87% of need; average scholarship/grant was $19,894; average loan was $4,156. For part-time students, average financial aid package was $16,377.

Students without need: 60 full-time freshmen who did not demonstrate need for aid received scholarships/grants; average award was $14,565. No-need awards available for academics, alumni affiliation, art, minority status, music/drama.

Scholarships offered: Distinguished Scholar Award; up to full tuition; awarded to designated National Merit Scholarship Finalist. Trustee Honors Scholarship; $14,000; awarded on basis of superior academic achievement, national test scores. Presidential Scholarships; $13,000; awarded on basis of outstanding scholarship and high national test scores. Dean's Scholarship; $12,000; awarded on basis on academic achievement and high national test scores. Tartan Scholars Award ($10,000) and Achievement Awards ($8,000); both awards based on academic achievement or high national test scores. Performance Scholarships; up to $1,000; awarded to students with a demonstrated high level of accomplishment in the fine or performing arts.

Cumulative student debt: 74% of graduating class had student loans; average debt was $31,476.

Additional info: Auditions required for music, drama, dance scholarship candidates. Portfolios required for art scholarship candidates.

FINANCIAL AID PROCEDURES
Forms required: FAFSA.

Dates and Deadlines: Priority date 3/1; no closing date. Applicants notified on a rolling basis starting 3/1; must reply within 3 week(s) of notification.

Transfers: No deadline. Applicants notified on a rolling basis starting 3/1; must reply within 3 week(s) of notification.

CONTACT
Christopher Brown, Director of Financial Assistance
614 West Superior Street, Alma, MI 48801-1599
(989) 463-7347

Alpena Community College
Alpena, Michigan
www.alpenacc.edu   Federal Code: 002237

2-year public community college in large town.
Enrollment: 2,100 undergrads.
Selectivity: Open admission; but selective for some programs.

BASIC COSTS (2009-2010)
Tuition and fees: $3,040; out-of-district residents $4,300; out-of-state residents $5,560.
Per-credit charge: $84; out-of-district residents $126; out-of-state residents $168.

FINANCIAL AID PICTURE (2009-2010)

Students with need: 97% of average financial aid package awarded as scholarships/grants, 3% awarded as loans/jobs. Need-based aid available for part-time students.

Students without need: No-need awards available for academics, art, athletics, job skills, leadership, music/drama.

FINANCIAL AID PROCEDURES

Forms required: FAFSA.

Dates and Deadlines: Priority date 8/1; no closing date. Applicants notified on a rolling basis starting 5/15; must reply within 3 week(s) of notification.

CONTACT

Max Lindsay, Dean of Students
665 Johnson Street, Alpena, MI 49707
(989) 358-7205

Andrews University
Berrien Springs, Michigan
www.andrews.edu   Federal Code: 002238

4-year private university in small town, affiliated with Seventh-day Adventists.

Enrollment: 1,817 undergrads, 7% part-time. 375 full-time freshmen.

Selectivity: Admits less than 50% of applicants.

BASIC COSTS (2010-2011)

Tuition and fees: $22,242.

Per-credit charge: $900.

Room and board: $7,140.

FINANCIAL AID PICTURE (2008-2009)

Students with need: Need-based aid available for full-time and part-time students. Work study available nights, weekends, and for part-time students.

Students without need: No-need awards available for academics, alumni affiliation, leadership, music/drama, religious affiliation.

FINANCIAL AID PROCEDURES

Forms required: FAFSA, institutional form.

Dates and Deadlines: Priority date 3/31; no closing date. Applicants notified on a rolling basis starting 3/15.

CONTACT

Elynda Bedney, Director of Student Financial Services
100 US Highway 31, Berrien Springs, MI 49104

Aquinas College
Grand Rapids, Michigan
www.aquinas.edu   Federal Code: 002239

4-year private liberal arts college in small city, affiliated with Roman Catholic Church.

Enrollment: 1,879 undergrads, 13% part-time. 402 full-time freshmen.

Selectivity: Admits over 75% of applicants. GED not accepted.

BASIC COSTS (2010-2011)

Tuition and fees: $23,206.

Per-credit charge: $726.

Room and board: $7,226.

Additional info: Tuition/fee waivers available for adults.

FINANCIAL AID PICTURE (2009-2010)

Students with need: Out of 381 full-time freshmen who applied for aid, 347 were judged to have need. Of these, 347 received aid, and 123 had their full need met. Average financial aid package met 90% of need; average scholarship/grant was $18,803; average loan was $2,750. For part-time students, average financial aid package was $9,492.

Students without need: 53 full-time freshmen who did not demonstrate need for aid received scholarships/grants; average award was $9,058. No-need awards available for academics, alumni affiliation, art, athletics, leadership, music/drama.

Scholarships offered: *Merit:* Spectrum Scholarship; $3,000 to full tuition; awarded to students who have excelled in academics, leadership or community service; renewable. *Athletic:* 69 full-time freshmen received athletic scholarships; average amount $2,200.

Cumulative student debt: 66% of graduating class had student loans; average debt was $14,983.

FINANCIAL AID PROCEDURES

Forms required: FAFSA.

Dates and Deadlines: Priority date 3/1; no closing date. Applicants notified on a rolling basis starting 2/15; must reply within 2 week(s) of notification.

Transfers: Priority date 4/15; closing date 7/1. Must reply within 2 week(s) of notification.

CONTACT

David Steffee, Director of Financial Aid
1607 Robinson Road Southeast, Grand Rapids, MI 49506-1799
(616) 632-2893

Baker College of Auburn Hills
Auburn Hills, Michigan
www.baker.edu   Federal Code: E00466

4-year private business and technical college in small city.

Enrollment: 4,285 undergrads.

Selectivity: Open admission.

BASIC COSTS (2009-2010)

Tuition and fees: $8,775.

Per-credit charge: $195.

FINANCIAL AID PICTURE

Students with need: Work study available nights, weekends, and for part-time students.

Students without need: No-need awards available for academics, alumni affiliation.

FINANCIAL AID PROCEDURES

Forms required: FAFSA, institutional form.

Dates and Deadlines: Priority date 2/21; closing date 9/1. Applicants notified on a rolling basis starting 4/1.

Transfers: Must have been deemed financial aid-eligible at previous school.

CONTACT

Greg Little, Financial Aid Director
1500 University Drive, Auburn Hills, MI 48326
(248) 340-0600

Baker College of Cadillac
Cadillac, Michigan
www.baker.edu   Federal Code: E00461

4-year private business and health science college in large town.

Enrollment: 2,070 undergrads.

Selectivity: Open admission.

BASIC COSTS (2009-2010)

Tuition and fees: $8,775.

Per-credit charge: $195.

FINANCIAL AID PICTURE

Students with need: Need-based aid available for full-time and part-time students. Work study available nights, weekends, and for part-time students.

Students without need: No-need awards available for academics.
Scholarships offered: Baker College Career Scholarships; $400 per term for 4 years; based on 2.5 GPA after junior year of high school. Board of Regents Scholarships; half tuition for 4 years; based on 3.5 GPA through grade 11.

FINANCIAL AID PROCEDURES
Forms required: FAFSA, institutional form.
Dates and Deadlines: Priority date 2/21; no closing date. Applicants notified on a rolling basis starting 5/1.
Transfers: Priority date 3/20; closing date 9/1.

CONTACT
Kristin Bonney, Financial Aid Officer
9600 East 13th Street, Cadillac, MI 49601
(231) 876-3118

Baker College of Clinton Township
Clinton Township, Michigan
www.baker.edu   Federal Code: E00462

4-year private business and technical college in very large city.
Enrollment: 6,455 undergrads.
Selectivity: Open admission; but selective for some programs.

BASIC COSTS (2009-2010)
Tuition and fees: $8,775.
Per-credit charge: $195.

FINANCIAL AID PICTURE
Students with need: Need-based aid available for full-time and part-time students. Work study available nights, weekends, and for part-time students.
Students without need: No-need awards available for academics, minority status.

FINANCIAL AID PROCEDURES
Forms required: FAFSA, institutional form.
Dates and Deadlines: Priority date 2/21; closing date 9/1. Applicants notified on a rolling basis starting 4/1.

CONTACT
Lisa Harvener, Vice President of Student Services
34950 Little Mack Avenue, Clinton Township, MI 48035
(586) 790-9589

Baker College of Muskegon
Muskegon, Michigan
www.baker.edu   Federal Code: E00463

4-year private business and technical college in small city.
Enrollment: 6,132 undergrads.
Selectivity: Open admission; but selective for some programs.

BASIC COSTS (2009-2010)
Tuition and fees: $8,775.
Per-credit charge: $195.
Room only: $2,965.

FINANCIAL AID PICTURE
Students with need: Need-based aid available for full-time and part-time students. Work study available nights, weekends, and for part-time students.
Students without need: No-need awards available for academics, minority status.
Scholarships offered: Career Scholarship; $4,800 over 4 years; based on GPA over 3.0. Board Regents Scholarship; one-half tuition for 4 years; based on GPA over 3.5. Alternative Scholarship; one-half tuition for 2 years; based on academic success in alternative high school education program.

FINANCIAL AID PROCEDURES
Forms required: FAFSA, institutional form.
Dates and Deadlines: Priority date 2/21; no closing date. Applicants notified on a rolling basis starting 4/1.
Transfers: Priority date 3/21.

CONTACT
Jody Zerlant, Director of Financial Aid
1903 Marquette Avenue, Muskegon, MI 49442
(231) 777-5231

Baker College of Owosso
Owosso, Michigan
www.baker.edu   Federal Code: E00464

4-year private business and technical college in large town.
Enrollment: 3,637 undergrads.
Selectivity: Open admission.

BASIC COSTS (2009-2010)
Tuition and fees: $8,775.
Per-credit charge: $195.
Room only: $2,700.

FINANCIAL AID PICTURE
Students with need: Need-based aid available for full-time and part-time students. Work study available nights, weekends, and for part-time students.
Students without need: No-need awards available for academics, minority status.

FINANCIAL AID PROCEDURES
Forms required: FAFSA, institutional form.
Dates and Deadlines: Priority date 2/21; closing date 9/1. Applicants notified on a rolling basis starting 4/1.
Transfers: Priority date 3/21.

CONTACT
Nicole Patterson, Financial Aid Director
1020 South Washington Street, Owosso, MI 48867
(989) 720-3430

Baker College of Port Huron
Port Huron, Michigan
www.baker.edu   Federal Code: E00465

4-year private business and technical college in large town.
Enrollment: 1,984 undergrads.
Selectivity: Open admission; but selective for some programs.

BASIC COSTS (2009-2010)
Tuition and fees: $8,775.
Per-credit charge: $195.

FINANCIAL AID PICTURE
Students with need: Need-based aid available for full-time and part-time students. Work study available nights.
Students without need: This college awards aid only to students with need.

FINANCIAL AID PROCEDURES
Forms required: FAFSA, institutional form.
Dates and Deadlines: Priority date 2/21; no closing date. Applicants notified on a rolling basis starting 4/1.
Transfers: Priority date 3/21; closing date 9/1.

CONTACT
Barbara Fosgard, Financial Aid Director
3403 Lapeer Road, Port Huron, MI 48060-2597
(810) 985-7000

Bay de Noc Community College
Escanaba, Michigan
www.baycollege.edu   Federal Code: 002240

2-year public community college in large town.
Enrollment: 2,507 undergrads, 36% part-time. 495 full-time freshmen.
Selectivity: Open admission; but selective for some programs.

BASIC COSTS (2009-2010)
Tuition and fees: $2,805; out-of-district residents $4,455; out-of-state residents $5,565.
Per-credit charge: $83; out-of-district residents $138; out-of-state residents $175.
Room and board: $2,800.
Additional info: Tuition and instructional fees based on contact hours.

FINANCIAL AID PICTURE (2009-2010)
Students with need: Need-based aid available for full-time and part-time students. Work study available nights, weekends, and for part-time students.
Students without need: No-need awards available for academics.

FINANCIAL AID PROCEDURES
Forms required: FAFSA.
Dates and Deadlines: Priority date 4/1; no closing date. Applicants notified on a rolling basis starting 2/1; must reply within 2 week(s) of notification.

CONTACT
Sue Hebert, Financial Aid Director
2001 North Lincoln Road, Escanaba, MI 49829-2511
(906) 786-5802 ext. 1215

Bay Mills Community College
Brimley, Michigan
www.bmcc.edu   Federal Code: 030666

2-year public community college in rural community.
Enrollment: 547 undergrads.
Selectivity: Open admission.

BASIC COSTS (2009-2010)
Tuition and fees: $2,910.
Per-credit charge: $85.

FINANCIAL AID PICTURE
Students with need: Work study available nights.

FINANCIAL AID PROCEDURES
Forms required: FAFSA.
Dates and Deadlines: Priority date 6/30; no closing date.

CONTACT
Tina Miller, Financial Aid Director
12214 West Lakeshore Drive, Brimley, MI 49715
(906) 248-3354 ext. 8437

Calvin College
Grand Rapids, Michigan
www.calvin.edu   Federal Code: 002241

4-year private liberal arts college in large city, affiliated with Christian Reformed Church.
Enrollment: 3,939 undergrads, 2% part-time. 936 full-time freshmen.
Selectivity: Admits over 75% of applicants.

BASIC COSTS (2010-2011)
Tuition and fees: $24,870.
Per-credit charge: $590.
Room and board: $8,525.

FINANCIAL AID PICTURE (2008-2009)
Students with need: Out of 778 full-time freshmen who applied for aid, 599 were judged to have need. Of these, 598 received aid, and 197 had their full need met. Average financial aid package met 84% of need; average scholarship/grant was $10,791; average loan was $4,625. For part-time students, average financial aid package was $9,801.
Students without need: 292 full-time freshmen who did not demonstrate need for aid received scholarships/grants; average award was $4,037. No-need awards available for academics, alumni affiliation, art, leadership, minority status, music/drama, religious affiliation, state/district residency.
Cumulative student debt: 68% of graduating class had student loans; average debt was $28,500.

FINANCIAL AID PROCEDURES
Forms required: FAFSA.
Dates and Deadlines: Priority date 2/15; no closing date. Applicants notified on a rolling basis starting 3/15.
Transfers: Priority date 3/15; closing date 8/15. Applicants notified on a rolling basis starting 3/15.

CONTACT
Dale Kuiper, Director of Admissions and Financial Aid
3201 Burton Street Southeast, Grand Rapids, MI 49546
(616) 526-6134

Central Michigan University
Mount Pleasant, Michigan
www.cmich.edu   Federal Code: 002243

4-year public university in large town.
Enrollment: 20,141 undergrads, 10% part-time. 3,862 full-time freshmen.
Selectivity: Admits 50 to 75% of applicants.

BASIC COSTS (2009-2010)
Tuition and fees: $10,170; out-of-state residents $23,670.
Per-credit charge: $339; out-of-state residents $789.
Room and board: $7,896.

FINANCIAL AID PICTURE (2008-2009)
Students with need: Out of 3,139 full-time freshmen who applied for aid, 2,198 were judged to have need. Of these, 2,150 received aid, and 1,217 had their full need met. Average financial aid package met 83% of need; average scholarship/grant was $5,822; average loan was $5,410. For part-time students, average financial aid package was $9,927.
Students without need: 476 full-time freshmen who did not demonstrate need for aid received scholarships/grants; average award was $3,160. No-need awards available for academics, alumni affiliation, art, athletics, leadership, minority status, music/drama, ROTC, state/district residency.
Scholarships offered: 39 full-time freshmen received athletic scholarships; average amount $1,629.
Cumulative student debt: 71% of graduating class had student loans; average debt was $26,615.

Additional info: Tuition waiver for Native American students qualifying under state program criteria.

FINANCIAL AID PROCEDURES

Forms required: FAFSA.

Dates and Deadlines: Priority date 3/1; no closing date. Applicants notified on a rolling basis starting 4/1.

CONTACT

Kirk Yats, Interim Director, Scholarships and Financial Aid
Admissions Office, Mount Pleasant, MI 48859
(989) 774-3674

Cleary University
Howell, Michigan
www.cleary.edu   Federal Code: 002246

4-year private university and business college in small city.

Enrollment: 626 undergrads, 34% part-time.

Selectivity: Open admission; but selective for some programs.

BASIC COSTS (2010-2011)

Tuition and fees: $16,560.

Per-credit charge: $345.

Additional info: Tuition prices guaranteed if student enrolled continuously. Tuition includes all books and fees. Tuition at time of enrollment locked for 4 years.

FINANCIAL AID PICTURE (2009-2010)

Students with need: Average financial aid package met 14% of need; average scholarship/grant was $1,322; average loan was $1,323. For part-time students, average financial aid package was $14,265.

Students without need: No-need awards available for academics.

Scholarships offered: Oren Beutler Endowed Scholarship: $750; new or continuing full-time student maintaining 3.0 GPA, demonstrated leadership and service to community; one awarded annually, renewable for 4 years.

Additional info: Filing electronically preferred; paper applications available. Tuition guarantee based on continuous enrollment. Essay and recommendations required for scholarship consideration.

FINANCIAL AID PROCEDURES

Forms required: FAFSA.

Dates and Deadlines: Priority date 3/15; closing date 8/15. Applicants notified on a rolling basis; must reply within 2 week(s) of notification.

CONTACT

Vesta Smith-Campbell, Director of Financial Aid
3750 Cleary Drive, Howell, MI 48843
(517) 548-3670 ext. 2222

College for Creative Studies
Detroit, Michigan
www.collegeforcreativestudies.edu Federal Code: 006771

4-year private visual arts college in very large city.

Enrollment: 1,382 undergrads, 14% part-time. 221 full-time freshmen.

Selectivity: Admits less than 50% of applicants.

BASIC COSTS (2010-2011)

Tuition and fees: $31,275.

Per-credit charge: $998.

Room and board: $8,500.

FINANCIAL AID PICTURE (2008-2009)

Students with need: 52% of average financial aid package awarded as scholarships/grants, 48% awarded as loans/jobs. Need-based aid available for part-time students. Work study available nights, weekends, and for part-time students.

Students without need: No-need awards available for academics, art.

Cumulative student debt: 79% of graduating class had student loans; average debt was $47,604.

FINANCIAL AID PROCEDURES

Forms required: FAFSA.

Dates and Deadlines: Priority date 7/1; no closing date. Applicants notified on a rolling basis starting 3/15; must reply within 3 week(s) of notification.

Transfers: Priority date 3/21.

CONTACT

Kristin Moskovitz, Director of Financial Aid
201 East Kirby, Detroit, MI 48202-4034
(313) 664-7495

Cornerstone University
Grand Rapids, Michigan
www.cornerstone.edu   Federal Code: 002266

4-year private university and liberal arts college in small city, affiliated with interdenominational tradition.

Enrollment: 1,833 undergrads, 22% part-time. 331 full-time freshmen.

Selectivity: Admits over 75% of applicants.

BASIC COSTS (2010-2011)

Tuition and fees: $21,378.

Per-credit charge: $798.

Room and board: $6,910.

Additional info: Tuition includes laptop computer.

FINANCIAL AID PICTURE (2009-2010)

Students with need: Average financial aid package met 89% of need; average scholarship/grant was $15,398; average loan was $3,394. For part-time students, average financial aid package was $11,776.

Students without need: No-need awards available for academics, athletics, leadership, music/drama, state/district residency.

Scholarships offered: Academic scholarships; based on high school GPA and ACT scores.

Cumulative student debt: 83% of graduating class had student loans; average debt was $26,025.

Additional info: Audition required for music scholarship applicants.

FINANCIAL AID PROCEDURES

Forms required: FAFSA.

Dates and Deadlines: Priority date 3/1; no closing date. Applicants notified on a rolling basis starting 3/15; must reply within 2 week(s) of notification.

Transfers: No deadline.

CONTACT

Scott Stewart, Student Financial Services
1001 East Beltline NE, Grand Rapids, MI 49525-5897
(616) 222-1424

Davenport University
Grand Rapids, Michigan
www.davenport.edu   Federal Code: 015260

4-year private university and business college in small city.

Enrollment: 9,951 undergrads, 66% part-time. 497 full-time freshmen.

Selectivity: Admits over 75% of applicants.

BASIC COSTS (2010-2011)
Tuition and fees: $14,661.
Per-credit charge: $481.

FINANCIAL AID PICTURE (2008-2009)
Students with need: Need-based aid available for full-time and part-time students. Work study available nights, weekends, and for part-time students.
Students without need: No-need awards available for academics, alumni affiliation, athletics, leadership.

FINANCIAL AID PROCEDURES
Forms required: FAFSA.
Dates and Deadlines: Priority date 3/1; no closing date. Applicants notified on a rolling basis starting 3/1; must reply within 2 week(s) of notification.
Transfers: No deadline. Applicants notified on a rolling basis.

CONTACT
David De Boer, Executive Director of Financial Aid
6191 Kraft Avenue SE, Grand Rapids, MI 49512-5926
(866) 925-3884

Delta College
University Center, Michigan
www.delta.edu
Federal Code: 002251

2-year public community college in small city.
Enrollment: 9,620 undergrads, 54% part-time. 1,100 full-time freshmen.
Selectivity: Open admission.

BASIC COSTS (2009-2010)
Tuition and fees: $2,922; out-of-district residents $4,122; out-of-state residents $5,712.
Per-credit charge: $79; out-of-district residents $119; out-of-state residents $172.

FINANCIAL AID PICTURE (2008-2009)
Students with need: 60% of average financial aid package awarded as scholarships/grants, 40% awarded as loans/jobs. Need-based aid available for part-time students. Work study available nights.
Students without need: No-need awards available for academics, athletics.

FINANCIAL AID PROCEDURES
Forms required: FAFSA.
Dates and Deadlines: Priority date 8/1; no closing date. Applicants notified on a rolling basis; must reply within 2 week(s) of notification.
Transfers: No deadline. Applicants notified on a rolling basis.

CONTACT
David Urbaniak, Financial Aid Director
1961 Delta Road D101, University Center, MI 48710
(989) 686-9080

Eastern Michigan University
Ypsilanti, Michigan
www.emich.edu
Federal Code: 002259

4-year public university in small city.
Enrollment: 17,399 undergrads, 27% part-time. 2,167 full-time freshmen.
Selectivity: Admits 50 to 75% of applicants.

BASIC COSTS (2009-2010)
Tuition and fees: $8,378; out-of-state residents $22,283.
Per-credit charge: $238; out-of-state residents $702.
Room and board: $7,785.

FINANCIAL AID PICTURE (2008-2009)
Students with need: Out of 1,839 full-time freshmen who applied for aid, 1,485 were judged to have need. Of these, 1,453 received aid, and 220 had their full need met. Average financial aid package met 62% of need; average scholarship/grant was $4,231; average loan was $3,700. For part-time students, average financial aid package was $5,326.
Students without need: 410 full-time freshmen who did not demonstrate need for aid received scholarships/grants; average award was $3,943. No-need awards available for academics, alumni affiliation, art, athletics, leadership, minority status, music/drama, ROTC, state/district residency.
Scholarships offered: 89 full-time freshmen received athletic scholarships; average amount $15,406.
Cumulative student debt: 63% of graduating class had student loans; average debt was $22,370.

FINANCIAL AID PROCEDURES
Forms required: FAFSA.
Dates and Deadlines: Priority date 3/15; no closing date. Applicants notified on a rolling basis starting 3/1.
Transfers: No deadline. Applicants notified on a rolling basis.

CONTACT
Bernice Lindke, Vice President
400 Pierce Hall, Ypsilanti, MI 48197
(734) 487-0455

Ferris State University
Big Rapids, Michigan
www.ferris.edu
Federal Code: 002260

4-year public university in large town.
Enrollment: 12,208 undergrads, 25% part-time. 1,954 full-time freshmen.
Selectivity: Admits 50 to 75% of applicants.

BASIC COSTS (2009-2010)
Tuition and fees: $9,480; out-of-state residents $16,770.
Per-credit charge: $316; out-of-state residents $559.
Room and board: $8,940.
Additional info: Midwest Compact states of Illinois, Indiana, Kansas, Minnesota, Missouri, Nebraska, Ohio, and Wisconsin tuition is $14,220.

FINANCIAL AID PICTURE (2009-2010)
Students with need: Average financial aid package met 88% of need; average scholarship/grant was $5,154; average loan was $3,313. For part-time students, average financial aid package was $10,669.
Students without need: No-need awards available for academics, alumni affiliation, art, athletics, leadership, minority status, music/drama, religious affiliation, ROTC.
Cumulative student debt: 76% of graduating class had student loans; average debt was $34,767.

FINANCIAL AID PROCEDURES
Forms required: FAFSA.
Dates and Deadlines: Priority date 3/1; no closing date. Applicants notified on a rolling basis starting 3/1; must reply within 3 week(s) of notification.
Transfers: Applicants notified on a rolling basis.

CONTACT
Robin Wirt, Director of Financial Aid
1201 South State Street, CSS 201, Big Rapids, MI 49307-2714
(231) 591-2110

Finlandia University

Hancock, Michigan
www.finlandia.edu   Federal Code: 002322

4-year private university and liberal arts college in small town, affiliated with Evangelical Lutheran Church in America.
Enrollment: 559 undergrads, 10% part-time. 126 full-time freshmen.
Selectivity: Admits over 75% of applicants.

BASIC COSTS (2009-2010)
Tuition and fees: $18,436.
Per-credit charge: $598.
Room and board: $5,974.

FINANCIAL AID PICTURE (2009-2010)
Students with need: Need-based aid available for full-time and part-time students. Work study available nights, weekends, and for part-time students.
Students without need: No-need awards available for academics, leadership, religious affiliation, state/district residency.
Additional info: Work/study program; up to $2,800 per year.

FINANCIAL AID PROCEDURES
Forms required: FAFSA, institutional form.
Dates and Deadlines: Priority date 3/1; no closing date. Applicants notified on a rolling basis starting 3/1; must reply within 2 week(s) of notification.
Transfers: Priority date 3/10; no deadline. Applicants notified on a rolling basis starting 2/1; must reply within 2 week(s) of notification.

CONTACT
Sandra Turnquist, Director of Financial Aid
601 Quincy Street, Hancock, MI 49930-1882
(906) 487-7261

Glen Oaks Community College

Centreville, Michigan
www.glenoaks.edu   Federal Code: 002263

2-year public community college in rural community.
Enrollment: 1,847 undergrads.
Selectivity: Open admission; but selective for some programs.

BASIC COSTS (2009-2010)
Tuition and fees: $3,140.
Per-credit charge: $77.
Additional info: In-county residents pay $77 per contact hour. Students from service area counties (Branch and Cass counties in Michigan and LaGrange, Elkhart, Steuben counties in Indiana) pay $115 per contact hour. All others pay $144 per contact hour.

FINANCIAL AID PICTURE
Students with need: Need-based aid available for full-time and part-time students. Work study available nights.
Students without need: No-need awards available for academics, art, athletics, leadership, music/drama.

FINANCIAL AID PROCEDURES
Forms required: FAFSA, institutional form.
Dates and Deadlines: No deadline. Applicants notified on a rolling basis.

CONTACT
Jean Zimmerman, Director of Financial Aid and Scholarship
62249 Shimmel Road, Centreville, MI 49032-9719
(269) 467-9945 ext. 250

Gogebic Community College

Ironwood, Michigan
www.gogebic.edu   Federal Code: 002264

2-year public community college in small town.
Enrollment: 925 undergrads.
Selectivity: Open admission; but selective for some programs.

BASIC COSTS (2009-2010)
Tuition and fees: $3,124; out-of-district residents $3,814; out-of-state residents $4,594.
Per-credit charge: $86; out-of-district residents $109; out-of-state residents $135.
Room only: $3,790.

FINANCIAL AID PICTURE
Students with need: Need-based aid available for full-time and part-time students. Work study available nights, weekends, and for part-time students.
Students without need: No-need awards available for academics, art, athletics, job skills, leadership, music/drama, state/district residency.

FINANCIAL AID PROCEDURES
Forms required: FAFSA.
Dates and Deadlines: Priority date 5/1; no closing date. Applicants notified on a rolling basis starting 3/15; must reply within 2 week(s) of notification.

CONTACT
Sue Forbes, Director of Financial Aid
E4946 Jackson Road, Ironwood, MI 49938
(906) 932-4231 ext. 206

Grace Bible College

Grand Rapids, Michigan
www.gbcol.edu   Federal Code: 002265

4-year private Bible and liberal arts college in small city, affiliated with Grace Gospel Fellowship.
Enrollment: 192 undergrads, 6% part-time. 48 full-time freshmen.
Selectivity: Admits 50 to 75% of applicants.

BASIC COSTS (2010-2011)
Tuition and fees: $14,770.
Per-credit charge: $475.
Room and board: $6,850.

FINANCIAL AID PICTURE (2008-2009)
Students with need: Need-based aid available for full-time and part-time students.
Students without need: No-need awards available for academics, music/drama, religious affiliation.

FINANCIAL AID PROCEDURES
Forms required: FAFSA.
Dates and Deadlines: Priority date 3/1; no closing date. Applicants notified on a rolling basis starting 5/15; must reply within 2 week(s) of notification.
Transfers: No deadline. Applicants notified on a rolling basis; must reply within 2 week(s) of notification.

CONTACT
Kurt Postma, Director of Financial Aid
1011 Aldon Street SW, PO Box 910, Grand Rapids, MI 49509
(616) 261-8557

Grand Rapids Community College

Grand Rapids, Michigan
www.grcc.edu   Federal Code: 002267

2-year public community college in small city.

Enrollment: 16,194 undergrads, 54% part-time. 2,653 full-time freshmen.

Selectivity: Open admission; but selective for some programs.

BASIC COSTS (2009-2010)

Tuition and fees: $2,615; out-of-district residents $5,510; out-of-state residents $8,120.

Per-credit charge: $85; out-of-district residents $181; out-of-state residents $268.

FINANCIAL AID PICTURE (2009-2010)

Students with need: Out of 2,274 full-time freshmen who applied for aid, 1,794 were judged to have need. Of these, 1,552 received aid, and 296 had their full need met. For part-time students, average financial aid package was $3,509.

Students without need: 44 full-time freshmen who did not demonstrate need for aid received scholarships/grants; average award was $1,200. No-need awards available for academics, alumni affiliation, art, athletics, leadership, minority status, music/drama, state/district residency.

Scholarships offered: *Merit:* Michigan Merit Award; $2,500; based on Michigan Educational Assessment Program scores. *Athletic:* 39 full-time freshmen received athletic scholarships; average amount $35,358.

Additional info: Tuition reimbursement and/or child-care services for single parents and displaced homemakers who meet Perkins guidelines.

FINANCIAL AID PROCEDURES

Forms required: FAFSA.

Dates and Deadlines: Priority date 4/1; no closing date. Applicants notified on a rolling basis starting 5/1; must reply within 3 week(s) of notification.

CONTACT

Jill Nutt, Executive Director of Student Financial Services
143 Bostwick Avenue NE, Grand Rapids, MI 49503-3295
(616) 234-4030

Grand Valley State University

Allendale, Michigan
www.gvsu.edu   Federal Code: 002268

4-year public university in large town.

Enrollment: 20,731 undergrads, 11% part-time. 3,884 full-time freshmen.

Selectivity: Admits over 75% of applicants.

BASIC COSTS (2009-2010)

Tuition and fees: $8,630; out-of-state residents $12,944.

Per-credit charge: $375; out-of-state residents $393.

Room and board: $7,448.

FINANCIAL AID PICTURE (2008-2009)

Students with need: Out of 3,279 full-time freshmen who applied for aid, 2,097 were judged to have need. Of these, 2,087 received aid, and 613 had their full need met. Average financial aid package met 83% of need; average scholarship/grant was $5,721; average loan was $4,169. For part-time students, average financial aid package was $5,553.

Students without need: 493 full-time freshmen who did not demonstrate need for aid received scholarships/grants; average award was $2,321. No-need awards available for academics, alumni affiliation, art, athletics, music/drama, state/district residency.

Scholarships offered: 39 full-time freshmen received athletic scholarships; average amount $6,666.

Cumulative student debt: 70% of graduating class had student loans; average debt was $21,475.

FINANCIAL AID PROCEDURES

Forms required: FAFSA.

Dates and Deadlines: Priority date 3/1; no closing date. Applicants notified on a rolling basis starting 4/1; must reply by 5/1 or within 4 week(s) of notification.

Transfers: No deadline. Applicants notified on a rolling basis starting 3/20; must reply within 4 week(s) of notification.

CONTACT

Ed Kerestly, Director of Financial Aid
1 Campus Drive, Allendale, MI 49401-9403
(616) 331-3234

Great Lakes Christian College

Lansing, Michigan
www.glcc.edu   Federal Code: 002269

4-year private Bible college in small city, affiliated with Church of Christ / Christian Church.

Enrollment: 232 undergrads.

BASIC COSTS (2010-2011)

Tuition and fees: $12,460.

Per-credit charge: $376.

Room and board: $7,800.

FINANCIAL AID PICTURE (2009-2010)

Students with need: Need-based aid available for full-time and part-time students. Work study available nights, weekends, and for part-time students.

Students without need: No-need awards available for academics, alumni affiliation, music/drama.

FINANCIAL AID PROCEDURES

Forms required: FAFSA, state aid form, institutional form.

Dates and Deadlines: Priority date 8/1; no closing date. Applicants notified on a rolling basis starting 5/1; must reply within 3 week(s) of notification.

Transfers: Priority date 3/31; closing date 8/31. Applicants notified on a rolling basis; must reply within 3 week(s) of notification. FAFSA due by 6/30.

CONTACT

Tedd Kees, Financial Aid Director
6211 West Willow Highway, Lansing, MI 48917-1231
(517) 321-0242 ext. 227

Henry Ford Community College

Dearborn, Michigan
www.hfcc.edu

2-year public community college in small city.

Enrollment: 16,309 undergrads, 58% part-time. 2,402 full-time freshmen.

Selectivity: Open admission; but selective for some programs.

BASIC COSTS (2009-2010)

Tuition and fees: $2,602; out-of-district residents $4,402; out-of-state residents $4,552.

Per-credit charge: $70; out-of-district residents $130; out-of-state residents $135.

FINANCIAL AID PICTURE

Students with need: Work study available nights, weekends, and for part-time students.

FINANCIAL AID PROCEDURES

Forms required: FAFSA.

Dates and Deadlines: Priority date 4/1; no closing date. Applicants notified on a rolling basis starting 3/1.

CONTACT

Kevin Culler, Director, Financial Aid
5101 Evergreen Road, Dearborn, MI 48128
(313) 845-9616

Hillsdale College

Hillsdale, Michigan
www.hillsdale.edu   Federal Code: 002272

4-year private liberal arts college in large town.
Enrollment: 1,378 undergrads.
Selectivity: Admits 50 to 75% of applicants.

BASIC COSTS (2009-2010)

Tuition and fees: $19,920.
Per-credit charge: $760.
Room and board: $7,750.

FINANCIAL AID PICTURE (2009-2010)

Students with need: 50% of average financial aid package awarded as scholarships/grants, 50% awarded as loans/jobs.
Students without need: No-need awards available for academics, alumni affiliation, art, athletics, leadership, music/drama, state/district residency.
Scholarships offered: Distinct Honor Scholarship: full tuition; 5 awarded. Presidential Scholarship: half tuition; 35 awarded. Trustee Scholarship: up to $8,000; 40 awarded.
Cumulative student debt: 62% of graduating class had student loans; average debt was $17,000.
Additional info: Campus employment available.

FINANCIAL AID PROCEDURES

Forms required: institutional form. CSS PROFILE required for returning students only.
Dates and Deadlines: Priority date 3/1; closing date 3/15. Applicants notified on a rolling basis starting 2/1; must reply by 5/1 or within 4 week(s) of notification.
Transfers: Priority date 2/1. Applicants notified on a rolling basis starting 2/1; must reply by 5/1 or within 4 week(s) of notification.

CONTACT

Richard Moeggenberg, Director of Financial Aid
33 East College Street, Hillsdale, MI 49242
(517) 607-2350

Hope College

Holland, Michigan
www.hope.edu   Federal Code: 002273

4-year private liberal arts college in small city, affiliated with Reformed Church in America.
Enrollment: 3,153 undergrads, 2% part-time. 796 full-time freshmen.
Selectivity: Admits over 75% of applicants.

BASIC COSTS (2010-2011)

Tuition and fees: $26,510.
Room and board: $8,110.
Additional info: Tuition/fee waivers available for minority students.

FINANCIAL AID PICTURE (2009-2010)

Students with need: Out of 673 full-time freshmen who applied for aid, 533 were judged to have need. Of these, 533 received aid, and 188 had their full need met. Average financial aid package met 84% of need; average scholarship/grant was $18,368; average loan was $3,733. For part-time students, average financial aid package was $9,705.
Students without need: 198 full-time freshmen who did not demonstrate need for aid received scholarships/grants; average award was $7,579. No-

need awards available for academics, art, minority status, music/drama, religious affiliation.
Scholarships offered: Merit Scholarships: $3,000-$17,000 per year. Talent Awards: $2,500; for music, art, theater, creative writing.
Cumulative student debt: 64% of graduating class had student loans; average debt was $22,682.

FINANCIAL AID PROCEDURES

Forms required: FAFSA, institutional form.
Dates and Deadlines: Priority date 3/1; no closing date. Applicants notified on a rolling basis starting 3/15.
Transfers: No deadline. Applicants notified on a rolling basis starting 3/25.

CONTACT

Phyllis Hooyman, Director of Financial Aid
69 East 10th Street, Holland, MI 49422-9000
(888) 439-8907

Jackson Community College

Jackson, Michigan
www.jccmi.edu   Federal Code: 002274

2-year public community college in small city.
Enrollment: 7,307 undergrads, 49% part-time. 1,286 full-time freshmen.
Selectivity: Open admission; but selective for some programs.

BASIC COSTS (2009-2010)

Tuition and fees: $3,480; out-of-district residents $4,575; out-of-state residents $6,225.
Per-credit charge: $91; out-of-district residents $127; out-of-state residents $182.

FINANCIAL AID PICTURE (2009-2010)

Students with need: 36% of average financial aid package awarded as scholarships/grants, 64% awarded as loans/jobs. Need-based aid available for part-time students. Work study available nights, weekends, and for part-time students.
Students without need: No-need awards available for academics, art, leadership, music/drama, state/district residency.

FINANCIAL AID PROCEDURES

Forms required: FAFSA, institutional form.
Dates and Deadlines: Priority date 6/15; no closing date. Applicants notified on a rolling basis starting 3/1.

CONTACT

Anthony Rana
2111 Emmons Road, Jackson, MI 49201-8399
(517) 796-8436

Kalamazoo College

Kalamazoo, Michigan
www.kzoo.edu   Federal Code: 002275

4-year private liberal arts college in small city.
Enrollment: 1,356 undergrads. 391 full-time freshmen.
Selectivity: Admits less than 50% of applicants.

BASIC COSTS (2010-2011)

Tuition and fees: $34,417.
Room and board: $7,893.

FINANCIAL AID PICTURE (2008-2009)

Students with need: Need-based aid available for full-time students. Work study available nights, weekends, and for part-time students.
Students without need: No-need awards available for academics, alumni affiliation, art, leadership, minority status, music/drama.

Scholarships offered: Honors Scholarship: $5,000 - $18,000; based on academic and co-curricular record and accomplishments; varied number awarded. Enlightened Leadership Awards: $5,000; based on written application and/or creative expression portfolio.

Additional info: Paid career development internship and senior project experiences available on campus.

FINANCIAL AID PROCEDURES

Forms required: FAFSA, institutional form. CSS PROFILE required for Early Decision applicants requesting need-based financial aid.

Dates and Deadlines: Priority date 2/15; no closing date. Applicants notified on a rolling basis starting 3/21; must reply by 5/1.

Transfers: Closing date 3/1. Must reply by 5/1.

CONTACT

Marian Stowers, Director of Financial Aid
1200 Academy Street, Kalamazoo, MI 49006
(269) 337-7192

Kalamazoo Valley Community College

Kalamazoo, Michigan
www.kvcc.edu   Federal Code: 006949

2-year public community college in small city.

Enrollment: 11,052 undergrads, 54% part-time. 1,584 full-time freshmen.

Selectivity: Open admission.

BASIC COSTS (2009-2010)

Tuition and fees: $2,130; out-of-district residents $3,390; out-of-state residents $4,560.

Per-credit charge: $71; out-of-district residents $113; out-of-state residents $152.

FINANCIAL AID PICTURE

Students with need: Need-based aid available for full-time and part-time students. Work study available nights, weekends, and for part-time students.

Students without need: No-need awards available for academics, athletics.

FINANCIAL AID PROCEDURES

Forms required: FAFSA, institutional form.

Dates and Deadlines: Priority date 6/1; no closing date. Applicants notified on a rolling basis starting 5/1; must reply within 2 week(s) of notification.

CONTACT

Roger Miller, Director of Financial Aid
6767 West O Avenue, Kalamazoo, MI 49003-4070
(269) 488-4340

Kellogg Community College

Battle Creek, Michigan
www.kellogg.edu   Federal Code: 002276

2-year public community college in small city.

Enrollment: 5,026 undergrads, 61% part-time. 581 full-time freshmen.

Selectivity: Open admission; but selective for some programs.

BASIC COSTS (2009-2010)

Tuition and fees: $2,325; out-of-district residents $3,638; out-of-state residents $5,123.

FINANCIAL AID PICTURE (2009-2010)

Students with need: 61% of average financial aid package awarded as scholarships/grants, 39% awarded as loans/jobs. Need-based aid available for part-time students. Work study available nights.

Students without need: No-need awards available for academics, alumni affiliation, athletics.

FINANCIAL AID PROCEDURES

Forms required: FAFSA, institutional form.

Dates and Deadlines: Priority date 4/1; no closing date. Applicants notified on a rolling basis starting 4/1.

Transfers: No deadline. Applicants notified on a rolling basis.

CONTACT

Barbara Sudeikis, Director, Financial Aid
450 North Avenue, Battle Creek, MI 49017-3397
(269) 965-4123

Kendall College of Art and Design of Ferris State University

Grand Rapids, Michigan
www.kcad.edu   Federal Code: 002260

4-year public visual arts college in large city.

Enrollment: 1,149 undergrads.

BASIC COSTS (2009-2010)

Tuition and fees: $15,642; out-of-state residents $23,322.

Additional info: Studio art courses: $613 per credit hour in-state and $920 out-of-state. General education courses: $316 per credit hour in-state and $474 out-of-state.

FINANCIAL AID PICTURE (2009-2010)

Students with need: Need-based aid available for full-time and part-time students. Work study available nights, weekends, and for part-time students.

Students without need: This college awards aid only to students with need.

FINANCIAL AID PROCEDURES

Forms required: FAFSA.

Dates and Deadlines: Priority date 2/15; no closing date. Applicants notified on a rolling basis starting 4/15.

CONTACT

Lori Deforest, Financial Aid Officer
17 Fountain Street NW, Grand Rapids, MI 49503-3002
(616) 451-2787

Kettering University

Flint, Michigan
www.kettering.edu   Federal Code: 002262

4-year private university and engineering college in small city.

Enrollment: 2,009 undergrads, 1% part-time. 439 full-time freshmen.

Selectivity: Admits 50 to 75% of applicants. GED not accepted.

BASIC COSTS (2010-2011)

Tuition and fees: $29,270.

Per-credit charge: $896.

Room and board: $6,390.

FINANCIAL AID PICTURE (2009-2010)

Students with need: Out of 406 full-time freshmen who applied for aid, 363 were judged to have need. Of these, 363 received aid, and 70 had their full need met. Average financial aid package met 91% of need; average scholarship/grant was $17,135; average loan was $3,402. Need-based aid available for part-time students.

Students without need: 76 full-time freshmen who did not demonstrate need for aid received scholarships/grants; average award was $13,130. No-need awards available for academics, leadership, minority status, state/district residency.

Scholarships offered: Various scholarships; $20,000-$40,000 for 4 years; based on merit. Renewable scholarships; $250-$5,000 per year.

Cumulative student debt: 84% of graduating class had student loans; average debt was $41,485.

FINANCIAL AID PROCEDURES
Forms required: FAFSA.
Dates and Deadlines: Priority date 2/14; no closing date. Applicants notified on a rolling basis starting 1/31.
Transfers: No deadline. Applicants notified on a rolling basis starting 2/8; must reply within 2 week(s) of notification.

CONTACT
Diane Bice, Director of Financial Aid
1700 University Avenue, Flint, MI 48504-6214
(810) 762-7859

Kirtland Community College
Roscommon, Michigan
www.kirtland.edu   Federal Code: 007171

2-year public community college in rural community.
Enrollment: 1,858 undergrads, 51% part-time. 240 full-time freshmen.
Selectivity: Open admission; but selective for some programs.

BASIC COSTS (2009-2010)
Tuition and fees: $2,672; out-of-district residents $4,672; out-of-state residents $5,710.
Per-credit charge: $78; out-of-district residents $142; out-of-state residents $176.
Additional info: Tuition/fee waivers available for minority students.

FINANCIAL AID PICTURE (2009-2010)
Students with need: Average financial aid package met 55.15% of need; average scholarship/grant was $5,213; average loan was $2,173. For part-time students, average financial aid package was $5,085.
Students without need: No-need awards available for academics, athletics, minority status.
Cumulative student debt: 75% of graduating class had student loans; average debt was $7,133.
Additional info: Federal, state, and institutional work-study programs available.

FINANCIAL AID PROCEDURES
Forms required: FAFSA.
Dates and Deadlines: Priority date 5/1; no closing date. Applicants notified on a rolling basis.
Transfers: No deadline.

CONTACT
Christin Horndt, Director of Financial Aid
10775 North Saint Helen Road, Roscommon, MI 48653
(989) 275-5000 ext. 257

Kuyper College
Grand Rapids, Michigan
www.kuyper.edu   Federal Code: 002311

4-year private Bible college in large city, affiliated with Reformed.
Enrollment: 341 undergrads, 11% part-time. 76 full-time freshmen.

BASIC COSTS (2010-2011)
Tuition and fees: $16,396.
Room and board: $6,720.

FINANCIAL AID PICTURE (2009-2010)
Students with need: Out of 73 full-time freshmen who applied for aid, 67 were judged to have need. Of these, 67 received aid, and 6 had their full need met. Average financial aid package met 67% of need; average scholarship/grant was $7,565; average loan was $4,336. For part-time students, average financial aid package was $11,517.
Students without need: No-need awards available for academics, leadership, minority status.
Scholarships offered: Kuyper Achievement Awards: $1,000-$6,000; GPA of 3.0-4.0, ACT of 21 and above. Christian Leadership Scholarship: $1,500 renewable annually; based on Christian service activities, 3.2 cumulative GPA. Christian Ministry Scholarship: up to $2,000; renewable annually; based on family's primary source of income. Multicultural Scholarships: $500-$5,000; based on academic record, leadership involvement, essays, cross-cultural experiences, and student's ethnic, cultural and socioeconomic background; 2.5 cumulative GPA.
Cumulative student debt: 67% of graduating class had student loans; average debt was $21,618.

FINANCIAL AID PROCEDURES
Forms required: FAFSA.
Dates and Deadlines: Priority date 3/1; no closing date. Applicants notified on a rolling basis starting 3/15; must reply within 2 week(s) of notification.
Transfers: No deadline. Applicants notified on a rolling basis; must reply within 2 week(s) of notification.

CONTACT
Agnes Russell, Director of Financial Aid
3333 East Beltline Avenue Northeast, Grand Rapids, MI 49525-9749
(616) 988-3656

Lake Michigan College
Benton Harbor, Michigan
www.lakemichigancollege.edu   Federal Code: 002277

2-year public community college in large town.
Enrollment: 4,631 undergrads, 65% part-time. 457 full-time freshmen.
Selectivity: Open admission; but selective for some programs.

BASIC COSTS (2009-2010)
Tuition and fees: $3,105; out-of-district residents $4,170; out-of-state residents $5,190.
Per-credit charge: $73; out-of-district residents $108; out-of-state residents $142.
Additional info: Tuition/fee waivers available for adults.

FINANCIAL AID PICTURE (2008-2009)
Students with need: Out of 359 full-time freshmen who applied for aid, 287 were judged to have need. Of these, 274 received aid, and 19 had their full need met. Average financial aid package met 51% of need; average scholarship/grant was $4,457; average loan was $2,769. For part-time students, average financial aid package was $4,274.
Students without need: 29 full-time freshmen who did not demonstrate need for aid received scholarships/grants; average award was $1,371.
Scholarships offered: *Merit:* Presidential Scholarship, full tuition, fees and books. At least 10 scholarships available to new high school graduates each year. *Athletic:* 11 full-time freshmen received athletic scholarships; average amount $2,240.

FINANCIAL AID PROCEDURES
Forms required: FAFSA.
Dates and Deadlines: Priority date 3/1; no closing date. Applicants notified on a rolling basis; must reply within 2 week(s) of notification.
Transfers: No deadline. Must reply within 2 week(s) of notification.

CONTACT

Anne Tews, Director of Financial Aid
2755 East Napier Avenue, Benton Harbor, MI 49022-1899
(269) 927-8100 ext. 5200

Lake Superior State University
Sault Ste. Marie, Michigan
www.lssu.edu   Federal Code: 002293

4-year public university and engineering college in large town.
Enrollment: 2,528 undergrads, 14% part-time. 482 full-time freshmen.
Selectivity: Admits over 75% of applicants.

BASIC COSTS (2009-2010)
Tuition and fees: $8,284; out-of-state residents $16,468.
Per-credit charge: $341; out-of-state residents $682.
Room and board: $7,923.
Additional info: Residents of Ontario pay in-state tuition. Residents of Kansas, Minnesota, Missouri, Nebraska, and North Dakota eligible for Midwest Consortium agreement rate of $512 per credit.

FINANCIAL AID PICTURE (2008-2009)
Students with need: 27% of average financial aid package awarded as scholarships/grants, 73% awarded as loans/jobs. Need-based aid available for part-time students. Work study available nights, weekends, and for part-time students.
Students without need: No-need awards available for academics, alumni affiliation, athletics, state/district residency.

FINANCIAL AID PROCEDURES
Forms required: FAFSA.
Dates and Deadlines: Priority date 3/1; no closing date. Applicants notified on a rolling basis starting 11/1; must reply within 3 week(s) of notification.
Transfers: Closing date 3/1. Applicants notified on a rolling basis starting 3/1.

CONTACT
Deborah Faust, Director of Financial Aid
650 West Easterday Avenue, Sault Ste. Marie, MI 49783-1699
(906) 635-2678

Lansing Community College
Lansing, Michigan
www.lansing.cc.mi.us   Federal Code: 002278

2-year public community college in small city.
Enrollment: 17,225 undergrads, 58% part-time. 2,014 full-time freshmen.
Selectivity: Open admission; but selective for some programs.

BASIC COSTS (2009-2010)
Tuition and fees: $2,240; out-of-district residents $4,070; out-of-state residents $6,080.
Per-credit charge: $73; out-of-district residents $134; out-of-state residents $201.
Additional info: There is a $10 online course fee applied to all online courses, and separate course fees may be assessed for courses required special supplies, equipment, or travel. A $5 per billable hour facility fee is charged to students on all credit classes.

FINANCIAL AID PICTURE (2008-2009)
Students with need: 30% of average financial aid package awarded as scholarships/grants, 70% awarded as loans/jobs. Need-based aid available for part-time students. Work study available nights, weekends, and for part-time students.
Students without need: No-need awards available for academics, athletics.

FINANCIAL AID PROCEDURES
Forms required: FAFSA.
Dates and Deadlines: Priority date 7/5; no closing date. Applicants notified on a rolling basis starting 4/3.
Transfers: Priority date 7/15.

CONTACT
Stephanie Bogard, Director of Financial Aid
422 North Washington Square, Lansing, MI 48901
(517) 483-1200

Lawrence Technological University
Southfield, Michigan
www.ltu.edu   Federal Code: 002279

4-year private university in small city.
Enrollment: 2,257 undergrads, 28% part-time. 278 full-time freshmen.
Selectivity: Admits less than 50% of applicants.

BASIC COSTS (2010-2011)
Tuition and fees: $24,633.
Per-credit charge: $809.
Room and board: $9,147.
Additional info: Tuition/fee waivers available for unemployed or children of unemployed.

FINANCIAL AID PICTURE (2008-2009)
Students with need: Out of 262 full-time freshmen who applied for aid, 210 were judged to have need. Of these, 208 received aid, and 48 had their full need met. Average financial aid package met 69% of need; average scholarship/grant was $11,703; average loan was $6,079. For part-time students, average financial aid package was $11,762.
Students without need: 36 full-time freshmen who did not demonstrate need for aid received scholarships/grants; average award was $8,788. No-need awards available for academics, alumni affiliation, art, job skills, leadership, minority status, ROTC, state/district residency.
Cumulative student debt: 73% of graduating class had student loans; average debt was $42,723.
Additional info: March 1 state deadline for Michigan Competitive Scholarship and Michigan Tuition Grant.

FINANCIAL AID PROCEDURES
Forms required: FAFSA.
Dates and Deadlines: Priority date 4/1; no closing date. Applicants notified on a rolling basis starting 3/1; must reply within 2 week(s) of notification.
Transfers: Applicants notified on a rolling basis starting 4/1; must reply within 2 week(s) of notification.

CONTACT
Mark Martin, Director of Student Financial Aid
21000 West Ten Mile Road, Southfield, MI 48075-1058
(248) 204-2121

Macomb Community College
Warren, Michigan
www.macomb.edu   Federal Code: 008906

2-year public community college in small city.
Enrollment: 14,454 undergrads, 61% part-time. 845 full-time freshmen.
Selectivity: Open admission; but selective for some programs.

BASIC COSTS (2009-2010)
Tuition and fees: $2,200; out-of-district residents $3,340; out-of-state residents $4,330.
Per-credit charge: $72; out-of-district residents $110; out-of-state residents $142.

FINANCIAL AID PICTURE (2008-2009)
Students with need: Need-based aid available for full-time and part-time students. Work study available nights, weekends, and for part-time students.
Students without need: No-need awards available for academics, athletics, leadership, music/drama, state/district residency.

FINANCIAL AID PROCEDURES
Forms required: FAFSA, institutional form.
Dates and Deadlines: Priority date 4/15; no closing date. Applicants notified on a rolling basis starting 5/15; must reply within 2 week(s) of notification.
Transfers: Must submit financial aid transcripts from all institutions attended.

CONTACT
Judy Florian, Director of Financial Aid
14500 East Twelve Mile Road, Warren, MI 48088-3896
(586) 445-7228

Madonna University
Livonia, Michigan
www.madonna.edu
Federal Code: 002282

4-year private university and liberal arts college in small city, affiliated with Roman Catholic Church.
Enrollment: 2,854 undergrads, 42% part-time. 204 full-time freshmen.
Selectivity: Admits 50 to 75% of applicants.

BASIC COSTS (2010-2011)
Tuition and fees: $13,840.
Per-credit charge: $458.
Room and board: $7,120.

FINANCIAL AID PICTURE (2008-2009)
Students with need: Out of 126 full-time freshmen who applied for aid, 93 were judged to have need. Of these, 93 received aid, and 22 had their full need met. Average financial aid package met 49% of need; average scholarship/grant was $5,825; average loan was $2,970. For part-time students, average financial aid package was $6,352.
Students without need: 62 full-time freshmen who did not demonstrate need for aid received scholarships/grants; average award was $3,761. No-need awards available for academics, alumni affiliation, art, athletics, leadership, minority status, music/drama, religious affiliation, state/district residency.
Scholarships offered: 37 full-time freshmen received athletic scholarships; average amount $3,148.
Cumulative student debt: 59% of graduating class had student loans; average debt was $23,323.

FINANCIAL AID PROCEDURES
Forms required: FAFSA.
Dates and Deadlines: Priority date 2/21; no closing date. Applicants notified on a rolling basis starting 3/15; must reply by 9/1 or within 2 week(s) of notification.
Transfers: No deadline. Applicants notified on a rolling basis starting 4/15; must reply by 9/1 or within 2 week(s) of notification. Deadline for state aid is May 15.

CONTACT
Chris Ziegler, Director of Financial Aid
36600 Schoolcraft Road, Livonia, MI 48150-1176
(734) 432-5664

Marygrove College
Detroit, Michigan
www.marygrove.edu
Federal Code: 002284

4-year private liberal arts college in very large city, affiliated with Roman Catholic Church.
Enrollment: 911 undergrads.
Selectivity: Admits less than 50% of applicants.

BASIC COSTS (2009-2010)
Tuition and fees: $16,280.
Per-credit charge: $565.
Room and board: $7,000.

FINANCIAL AID PICTURE (2009-2010)
Students with need: Need-based aid available for full-time and part-time students.
Students without need: This college awards aid only to students with need.

FINANCIAL AID PROCEDURES
Forms required: FAFSA, institutional form.
Dates and Deadlines: Priority date 3/15; no closing date. Applicants notified on a rolling basis starting 5/15; must reply within 2 week(s) of notification.

CONTACT
Patricia Chaplin, Director of Financial Aid
8425 West McNichols Road, Detroit, MI 48221
(313) 927-1245

Michigan Jewish Institute
West Bloomfield, Michigan
www.mji.edu
Federal Code: 032843

4-year private business and liberal arts college in very large city, affiliated with Jewish faith.
Enrollment: 75 undergrads.
Selectivity: Open admission; but selective for some programs.

BASIC COSTS (2009-2010)
Tuition and fees: $10,500.
Per-credit charge: $350.

FINANCIAL AID PICTURE
Students with need: Work study available nights, weekends, and for part-time students.
Students without need: No-need awards available for academics.
Scholarships offered: Cooperative Computing program scholarships. Partial scholarships available for some programs.

FINANCIAL AID PROCEDURES
Transfers: Priority date 3/1; no deadline. Applicants notified on a rolling basis; must reply within 5 week(s) of notification.

CONTACT
Fran Herman, Registrar/Financial Aid Administrator
6890 West Maple Road, West Bloomfield, MI 48322
(248) 414-6900 ext. 102

Michigan State University
East Lansing, Michigan
www.msu.edu
Federal Code: 002290

4-year public university in small city.
Enrollment: 36,224 undergrads, 8% part-time. 7,280 full-time freshmen.
Selectivity: Admits 50 to 75% of applicants.

BASIC COSTS (2009-2010)

Tuition and fees: $10,880; out-of-state residents $27,343.

Per-credit charge: $347; out-of-state residents $896.

Room and board: $7,394.

FINANCIAL AID PICTURE (2009-2010)

Students with need: Out of 5,427 full-time freshmen who applied for aid, 3,700 were judged to have need. Of these, 3,675 received aid, and 878 had their full need met. Average financial aid package met 70% of need; average scholarship/grant was $9,119; average loan was $3,464. For part-time students, average financial aid package was $8,618.

Students without need: This college awards aid only to students with need.

Scholarships offered: 57 full-time freshmen received athletic scholarships; average amount $18,681.

Cumulative student debt: 44% of graduating class had student loans; average debt was $19,696.

FINANCIAL AID PROCEDURES

Forms required: FAFSA.

Dates and Deadlines: No deadline. Applicants notified on a rolling basis starting 3/15; must reply within 4 week(s) of notification.

CONTACT

Richard Shipman, Director of Financial Aid

250 Administration Building, East Lansing, MI 48824

(517) 353-5940

Michigan Technological University

Houghton, Michigan

www.mtu.edu

Federal Code: 002292

4-year public university in small town.

Enrollment: 5,835 undergrads, 5% part-time. 1,157 full-time freshmen.

Selectivity: Admits 50 to 75% of applicants.

BASIC COSTS (2009-2010)

Tuition and fees: $11,348; out-of-state residents $23,618.

Per-credit charge: $350; out-of-state residents $759.

Room and board: $8,121.

FINANCIAL AID PICTURE (2009-2010)

Students with need: Average financial aid package met 74% of need; average scholarship/grant was $6,037; average loan was $3,366. For part-time students, average financial aid package was $6,364.

Students without need: No-need awards available for academics, alumni affiliation, art, athletics, job skills, leadership, music/drama, ROTC, state/district residency.

Cumulative student debt: 68% of graduating class had student loans; average debt was $26,764.

FINANCIAL AID PROCEDURES

Forms required: FAFSA.

Dates and Deadlines: No deadline. Applicants notified on a rolling basis.

CONTACT

Timothy Malette, Director of Financial Aid

1400 Townsend Drive, Houghton, MI 49931-1295

(906) 487-2622

Mid Michigan Community College

Harrison, Michigan

www.midmich.edu

Federal Code: 006768

2-year public community college in small town.

Enrollment: 4,814 undergrads.

Selectivity: Open admission; but selective for some programs.

BASIC COSTS (2009-2010)

Tuition and fees: $2,520; out-of-district residents $4,590; out-of-state residents $8,280.

Per-credit charge: $80; out-of-district residents $149; out-of-state residents $272.

Additional info: Tuition/fee waivers available for adults.

FINANCIAL AID PICTURE (2008-2009)

Students with need: Need-based aid available for full-time and part-time students.

Students without need: No-need awards available for academics.

Scholarships offered: Scholastic Incentive Scholarships; $350 per semester; for any student who completes full-time semester, is enrolled full-time for next regular semester, maintains 3.5-3.89 GPA. $500 per semester for students meeting above criteria, maintaining 3.9-4.0 GPA.

FINANCIAL AID PROCEDURES

Forms required: FAFSA, institutional form.

Dates and Deadlines: Priority date 5/1; no closing date. Applicants notified on a rolling basis starting 4/1; must reply within 2 week(s) of notification.

CONTACT

Gale Crandell, Financial Aid Director

1375 South Clare Avenue, Harrison, MI 48625

(989) 386-6622

Monroe County Community College

Monroe, Michigan

www.monroeccc.edu

Federal Code: 002294

2-year public community college in large town.

Enrollment: 4,624 undergrads.

Selectivity: Open admission; but selective for some programs.

BASIC COSTS (2009-2010)

Additional info: Tuition/fee waivers available for minority students.

FINANCIAL AID PICTURE

Students with need: Need-based aid available for full-time and part-time students. Work study available nights, weekends, and for part-time students.

Students without need: No-need awards available for academics, alumni affiliation, art, leadership, music/drama, state/district residency.

FINANCIAL AID PROCEDURES

Forms required: FAFSA, institutional form.

Dates and Deadlines: Priority date 4/1; no closing date. Applicants notified on a rolling basis starting 4/1; must reply within 2 week(s) of notification.

CONTACT

Tracy Vogt, Director of Financial Aid/Placement

1555 South Raisinville Road, Monroe, MI 48161-9746

(734) 384-4135

Montcalm Community College

Sidney, Michigan

www.montcalm.edu

Federal Code: 002295

2-year public community and liberal arts college in rural community.

Enrollment: 2,005 undergrads, 55% part-time. 179 full-time freshmen.

Selectivity: Open admission; but selective for some programs.

BASIC COSTS (2009-2010)

Tuition and fees: $2,505; out-of-district residents $4,185; out-of-state residents $6,105.

Per-credit charge: $77; out-of-district residents $133; out-of-state residents $197.

FINANCIAL AID PICTURE

Students with need: Need-based aid available for full-time and part-time students.

Students without need: No-need awards available for academics, state/district residency.

FINANCIAL AID PROCEDURES

Forms required: FAFSA, institutional form.

Dates and Deadlines: Priority date 2/15; no closing date. Applicants notified on a rolling basis starting 6/15; must reply within 2 week(s) of notification.

Transfers: Priority date 4/1.

CONTACT

Rebecca Powell, Director of Financial Aid
2800 College Drive, Sidney, MI 48885
(989) 328-1228

Mott Community College
Flint, Michigan
www.mcc.edu   Federal Code: 002261

2-year public community college in large city.

Enrollment: 7,570 undergrads.

Selectivity: Open admission; but selective for some programs.

BASIC COSTS (2009-2010)

Tuition and fees: $3,060; out-of-district residents $4,324; out-of-state residents $5,596.

FINANCIAL AID PICTURE (2009-2010)

Students with need: Need-based aid available for full-time and part-time students. Work study available nights.

Students without need: No-need awards available for academics, alumni affiliation, art, athletics, leadership, minority status, music/drama, state/district residency.

FINANCIAL AID PROCEDURES

Forms required: FAFSA.

Dates and Deadlines: No deadline. Applicants notified on a rolling basis starting 5/1.

Transfers: Pell Grants adjusted for amount used at another institution.

CONTACT

Jennifer Dow-McDonald, Interim Executive Director of Student Financial Services
1401 East Court Street, Flint, MI 48503-2089
(810) 762-0144

Muskegon Community College
Muskegon, Michigan
www.muskegoncc.edu   Federal Code: 002297

2-year public community college in small city.

Enrollment: 3,664 undergrads, 57% part-time. 462 full-time freshmen.

Selectivity: Open admission; but selective for some programs.

BASIC COSTS (2009-2010)

Tuition and fees: $2,448; out-of-district residents $3,850; out-of-state residents $5,125.

Per-credit charge: $72; out-of-district residents $119; out-of-state residents $162.

Additional info: Students also assessed contact hour fees, which vary according to residency status, and course fees, which vary.

FINANCIAL AID PICTURE

Students with need: Work study available nights, weekends, and for part-time students.

FINANCIAL AID PROCEDURES

Forms required: FAFSA, institutional form.

Dates and Deadlines: Priority date 5/1; no closing date. Applicants notified on a rolling basis starting 6/1; must reply within 2 week(s) of notification.

CONTACT

Bruce Wierda, Director of Financial Aid
221 South Quarterline Road, Muskegon, MI 49442
(231) 777-0221

North Central Michigan College
Petoskey, Michigan
www.ncmich.edu   Federal Code: 002299

2-year public community college in small town.

Enrollment: 3,123 undergrads.

Selectivity: Open admission; but selective for some programs.

BASIC COSTS (2009-2010)

Tuition and fees: $2,528; out-of-district residents $3,923; out-of-state residents $4,958.

Per-credit charge: $72; out-of-district residents $119; out-of-state residents $153.

Room and board: $5,400.

FINANCIAL AID PICTURE

Students with need: Need-based aid available for full-time and part-time students. Work study available nights, weekends, and for part-time students.

FINANCIAL AID PROCEDURES

Forms required: FAFSA, institutional form.

Dates and Deadlines: Closing date 4/1. Applicants notified on a rolling basis starting 4/30.

CONTACT

Virginia Panoff, Director of Financial Aid
1515 Howard Street, Petoskey, MI 49770
(231) 348-6627

Northern Michigan University
Marquette, Michigan
www.nmu.edu   Federal Code: 002301

4-year public university in large town.

Enrollment: 8,386 undergrads, 7% part-time. 1,785 full-time freshmen.

Selectivity: Admits 50 to 75% of applicants.

BASIC COSTS (2009-2010)

Tuition and fees: $7,454; out-of-state residents $11,828.

Per-credit charge: $285; out-of-state residents $467.

Room and board: $7,646.

Additional info: Excludes one-time $200 athletic fee for first time freshmen. All full-time students provided with ThinkPad or MacBook computer as part of tuition and fees. Tuition/fee waivers available for minority students.

FINANCIAL AID PICTURE (2008-2009)

Students with need: Out of 1,681 full-time freshmen who applied for aid, 1,144 were judged to have need. Of these, 1,112 received aid, and 243 had their full need met. Average financial aid package met 60% of need; average scholarship/grant was $4,544; average loan was $2,921. For part-time students, average financial aid package was $7,230.

Students without need: 149 full-time freshmen who did not demonstrate need for aid received scholarships/grants; average award was $2,937. No-

need awards available for academics, art, athletics, leadership, minority status, music/drama, religious affiliation, ROTC, state/district residency.

Scholarships offered: _Merit:_ Talent recognition awards: available in art and design, music, theater. Freshman Fellowship: $1,000 in student employment; 3.5+ GPA and ACT 24+. Dr. Edgar L. Harden Scholarship: "full ride"; 3.5+ GPA and ACT 24+. National Academic Award: $3,500; minimum 3.0+ GPA and ACT 19+; awarded to non-Michigan residents. NMU Merit Excellence Award: $2,750-$3,500; based on 3.0+ GPA and 33+ ACT. NMU Merit Award: $2,250-$3,000; 3.0+ GPA and 30-32 ACT. NMU Scholars Award: $1,250-$2,000; 3.0+ GPA and ACT 27-29. NMU Outstanding Achievement: $750-$1,500; 3.0+ GPA and 25-26 ACT. **_Athletic:_** 6 full-time freshmen received athletic scholarships; average amount $4,573.

Cumulative student debt: 67% of graduating class had student loans; average debt was $24,074.

Additional Info: Audition or portfolio required for music, drama, and art scholarship applicants. Alumni Dependent Tuition Program gives resident tuition rates to nonresident dependents of NMU alumni who received master's, baccalaureate, or associate degree; renewable.

FINANCIAL AID PROCEDURES

Forms required: FAFSA.

Dates and Deadlines: Priority date 3/1; no closing date. Applicants notified on a rolling basis starting 4/1; must reply within 2 week(s) of notification.

Transfers: No deadline. Applicants notified on a rolling basis starting 4/1; must reply within 2 week(s) of notification. Merit-based transfer scholarships available.

CONTACT

Michael Rotundo, Director of Financial Aid
1401 Presque Isle Avenue, Marquette, MI 49855
(906) 227-2327

Northwestern Michigan College

Traverse City, Michigan
www.nmc.edu   Federal Code: 002302

2-year public community and maritime college in large town.

Enrollment: 4,100 undergrads.

Selectivity: Open admission; but selective for some programs.

BASIC COSTS (2009-2010)

Tuition and fees: $2,692; out-of-district residents $4,750; out-of-state residents $5,990.

Per-credit charge: $77; out-of-district residents $146; out-of-state residents $187.

Room and board: $8,448.

Additional info: Tuition/fee waivers available for adults, minority students, unemployed or children of unemployed.

FINANCIAL AID PICTURE (2008-2009)

Students with need: 31% of average financial aid package awarded as scholarships/grants, 69% awarded as loans/jobs. Need-based aid available for part-time students. Work study available nights, weekends, and for part-time students.

Students without need: No-need awards available for academics, art, job skills, leadership, minority status, music/drama, ROTC, state/district residency.

FINANCIAL AID PROCEDURES

Forms required: FAFSA.

Dates and Deadlines: Priority date 4/1; no closing date. Applicants notified on a rolling basis starting 5/1; must reply within 2 week(s) of notification.

CONTACT

Pam Palermo, Director for Financial Aid
1701 East Front Street, Traverse City, MI 49686
(231) 995-1035

Northwood University: Michigan

Midland, Michigan
www.northwood.edu   Federal Code: 004072

4-year private university and business college in large town.

Enrollment: 1,814 undergrads, 3% part-time. 340 full-time freshmen.

Selectivity: Admits 50 to 75% of applicants.

BASIC COSTS (2010-2011)

Tuition and fees: $19,272.

Per-credit charge: $715.

Room and board: $8,160.

FINANCIAL AID PICTURE (2009-2010)

Students with need: Out of 283 full-time freshmen who applied for aid, 256 were judged to have need. Of these, 256 received aid, and 53 had their full need met. Average financial aid package met 58% of need; average scholarship/grant was $5,766; average loan was $3,307. For part-time students, average financial aid package was $7,612.

Students without need: 47 full-time freshmen who did not demonstrate need for aid received scholarships/grants; average award was $7,594. No-need awards available for academics, athletics, leadership, minority status, ROTC.

Scholarships offered: _Merit:_ Academic scholarships based on test scores and GPA; unlimited number awarded. **_Athletic:_** 22 full-time freshmen received athletic scholarships; average amount $9,899.

Cumulative student debt: 72% of graduating class had student loans; average debt was $28,634.

FINANCIAL AID PROCEDURES

Forms required: FAFSA.

Dates and Deadlines: No deadline. Applicants notified on a rolling basis starting 3/1.

Transfers: No deadline. Applicants notified on a rolling basis.

CONTACT

Theresa Mieler, Financial Aid Director
4000 Whiting Drive, Midland, MI 48640
(989) 837-4230

Oakland Community College

Bloomfield Hills, Michigan
www.oaklandcc.edu   Federal Code: 002303

2-year public community college in very large city.

Enrollment: 20,073 undergrads, 63% part-time. 2,472 full-time freshmen.

Selectivity: Open admission.

BASIC COSTS (2009-2010)

Tuition and fees: $1,873; out-of-district residents $3,121; out-of-state residents $4,351.

Per-credit charge: $60; out-of-district residents $102; out-of-state residents $143.

FINANCIAL AID PICTURE (2009-2010)

Students with need: Out of 1,642 full-time freshmen who applied for aid, 1,244 were judged to have need. Of these, 1,180 received aid, and 20 had their full need met. Average financial aid package met 54% of need; average scholarship/grant was $4,786; average loan was $1,281. For part-time students, average financial aid package was $7,518.

Students without need: 19 full-time freshmen who did not demonstrate need for aid received scholarships/grants; average award was $1,964. No-need awards available for academics, athletics.

Scholarships offered: 43 full-time freshmen received athletic scholarships; average amount $1,737.

FINANCIAL AID PROCEDURES

Forms required: FAFSA.

Dates and Deadlines: Priority date 4/15; no closing date. Applicants notified on a rolling basis starting 4/15.

Transfers: Closing date 6/30. Michigan residency required for aid to transfer students.

CONTACT

Wilma Porter, Director of Financial Assistance and Scholarships
2480 Opdyke Road, Bloomfield Hills, MI 48304-2266
(248) 341-2000

Oakland University
Rochester, Michigan
www.oakland.edu   Federal Code: 002307

4-year public university in small city.

Enrollment: 14,728 undergrads, 24% part-time. 2,331 full-time freshmen.

Selectivity: Admits 50 to 75% of applicants.

BASIC COSTS (2009-2010)

Tuition and fees: $8,783; out-of-state residents $20,498.

Room and board: $7,350.

FINANCIAL AID PICTURE (2009-2010)

Students with need: Need-based aid available for full-time and part-time students.

Students without need: No-need awards available for academics, art, athletics, leadership, music/drama, state/district residency.

Scholarships offered: Wide range of scholarships awarded on the basis of accomplishment.

FINANCIAL AID PROCEDURES

Forms required: FAFSA.

Dates and Deadlines: Priority date 2/15; no closing date. Applicants notified on a rolling basis starting 3/15.

Transfers: Closing date 4/1.

CONTACT

Cindy Hermsen, Director of Financial Aid
101 North Foundation Hall, Rochester, MI 48309-4401
(248) 370-2550

Rochester College
Rochester Hills, Michigan
www.rc.edu   Federal Code: 002288

4-year private liberal arts college in small city, affiliated with Church of Christ.

Enrollment: 950 undergrads.

BASIC COSTS (2010-2011)

Tuition and fees: $18,056.

Per-credit charge: $533.

Room and board: $6,046.

Additional info: Tuition/fee waivers available for minority students.

FINANCIAL AID PICTURE

Students with need: Need-based aid available for full-time and part-time students. Work study available nights, weekends, and for part-time students.

Students without need: No-need awards available for academics, alumni affiliation, athletics, leadership, music/drama, state/district residency.

FINANCIAL AID PROCEDURES

Forms required: FAFSA.

Dates and Deadlines: Priority date 8/1; no closing date. Applicants notified on a rolling basis starting 6/1; must reply within 2 week(s) of notification.

CONTACT

Kara Miller, Director of Financial Aid
800 West Avon Road, Rochester Hills, MI 48307
(248) 218-2029

Sacred Heart Major Seminary
Detroit, Michigan
www.shms.org   Federal Code: 002313

4-year private seminary college in very large city, affiliated with Roman Catholic Church.

Enrollment: 88 undergrads, 43% part-time. 1 full-time freshmen.

Selectivity: Admits over 75% of applicants.

BASIC COSTS (2009-2010)

Tuition and fees: $14,390.

Per-credit charge: $335.

Room and board: $7,800.

Additional info: Tuition/fee waivers available for adults.

FINANCIAL AID PICTURE (2008-2009)

Students with need: Average financial aid package for all full-time undergraduates was $16,277; for part-time $3,511. 92% awarded as scholarships/grants, 8% awarded as loans/jobs. Work study available nights, weekends, and for part-time students.

Students without need: No-need awards available for academics, religious affiliation.

Cumulative student debt: 50% of graduating class had student loans; average debt was $5,474.

FINANCIAL AID PROCEDURES

Forms required: FAFSA, institutional form.

Dates and Deadlines: No deadline. Applicants notified on a rolling basis; must reply within 2 week(s) of notification.

Transfers: No deadline. Applicants notified on a rolling basis. Must submit certified high school transcript, copy of high school diploma, copy of GED certificate showing passing score, or college transcript showing associate degree as certification of eligibility; must submit financial aid transcripts from all previous post-secondary institutions attended.

CONTACT

Jeannette Murrell, Director of Financial Aid
2701 Chicago Boulevard, Detroit, MI 48206-1799
(313) 883-8781

Saginaw Valley State University
University Center, Michigan
www.svsu.edu   Federal Code: 002314

4-year public university in small city.

Enrollment: 8,609 undergrads, 15% part-time. 1,646 full-time freshmen.

Selectivity: Admits over 75% of applicants.

BASIC COSTS (2009-2010)

Tuition and fees: $6,900; out-of-state residents $16,200.

Per-credit charge: $215; out-of-state residents $525.

Room and board: $7,270.

FINANCIAL AID PICTURE (2008-2009)

Students with need: Out of 1,596 full-time freshmen who applied for aid, 1,141 were judged to have need. Of these, 1,120 received aid, and 246 had their full need met. Average financial aid package met 65% of need; average scholarship/grant was $3,542; average loan was $2,986. For part-time students, average financial aid package was $5,097.

Students without need: 213 full-time freshmen who did not demonstrate need for aid received scholarships/grants; average award was $3,276. No-

need awards available for academics, art, athletics, leadership, minority status, music/drama.

Scholarships offered: *Merit:* Presidential Scholarships; tuition and selective fees up to 136 credit hours; granted to students who are first or second in high school class with minimum 24 ACT or 3.7 GPA and 28 ACT. Dean's Scholarship; $3,000 per year for four years; 3.0 GPA and 24 ACT. University Foundation Scholarship; tuition and selective fees for four courses and $1,000 to apply toward study abroad or a research project; 3.5 GPA and 24 ACT. University Scholarship; $1,000 per year for four years; 3.5 GPA. Various private scholarships also available. *Athletic:* 89 full-time freshmen received athletic scholarships; average amount $4,001.

Cumulative student debt: 57% of graduating class had student loans; average debt was $23,555.

FINANCIAL AID PROCEDURES
Forms required: FAFSA.
Dates and Deadlines: Priority date 2/14; no closing date. Applicants notified on a rolling basis starting 3/20; must reply within 10 week(s) of notification.
Transfers: No deadline. Applicants notified on a rolling basis; must reply within 10 week(s) of notification. Community college scholarship, private scholarships, and Transfer Dean's scholarships available.

CONTACT
Robert Lemuel, Director of Scholarships and Financial Aid
7400 Bay Road, University Center, MI 48710
(989) 964-4103

Schoolcraft College
Livonia, Michigan
www.schoolcraft.edu   Federal Code: 002315

2-year public community college in small city.
Enrollment: 9,800 undergrads.
Selectivity: Open admission; but selective for some programs.

BASIC COSTS (2009-2010)
Tuition and fees: $2,510; out-of-district residents $3,590; out-of-state residents $5,270.
Per-credit charge: $77; out-of-district residents $113; out-of-state residents $169.

FINANCIAL AID PICTURE (2008-2009)
Students with need: Need-based aid available for full-time and part-time students. Work study available nights, weekends, and for part-time students.
Students without need: No-need awards available for academics, athletics, leadership, music/drama, state/district residency.
Scholarships offered: Trustee Scholarships; $1,000-$1,200; renewable for 2nd year; based on essay, placement test, trustee application, graduation from local high school; 80 awarded.

FINANCIAL AID PROCEDURES
Forms required: FAFSA.
Dates and Deadlines: No deadline. Applicants notified on a rolling basis starting 6/1.

CONTACT
Regina Mosley, Director of Financial Aid
18600 Haggerty Road, Livonia, MI 48152-2696
(734) 462-4433

Siena Heights University
Adrian, Michigan   Federal Code: 002316
www.sienaheights.edu   CSS Code: 1719

4-year private university and liberal arts college in large town, affiliated with Roman Catholic Church.
Enrollment: 1,938 undergrads, 49% part-time. 205 full-time freshmen.
Selectivity: Admits 50 to 75% of applicants.

BASIC COSTS (2010-2011)
Tuition and fees: $19,790.
Room and board: $7,170.

FINANCIAL AID PICTURE (2008-2009)
Students with need: Work study available nights, weekends, and for part-time students.
Students without need: No-need awards available for academics, alumni affiliation, art, athletics, music/drama, religious affiliation.
Scholarships offered: Merit scholarships for first time freshmen range from $4000 up to $10,000 per academic year.

FINANCIAL AID PROCEDURES
Forms required: FAFSA, CSS PROFILE, institutional form.
Dates and Deadlines: Priority date 3/15; closing date 8/15. Applicants notified on a rolling basis starting 2/15.
Transfers: Priority date 3/1; no deadline. Applicants notified on a rolling basis starting 3/1. Transfer scholarship available.

CONTACT
Christian Howard, Director of Financial Aid
1247 East Siena Heights Drive, Adrian, MI 49221-1796
(517) 264-7130

Southwestern Michigan College
Dowagiac, Michigan
www.swmich.edu   Federal Code: 002317

2-year public community college in small town.
Enrollment: 2,553 undergrads, 44% part-time. 499 full-time freshmen.
Selectivity: Open admission; but selective for some programs.

BASIC COSTS (2009-2010)
Tuition and fees: $3,458; out-of-district residents $4,193; out-of-state residents $4,478.
Per-credit charge: $88; out-of-district residents $113; out-of-state residents $122.

FINANCIAL AID PICTURE (2008-2009)
Students with need: Need-based aid available for full-time and part-time students. Work study available nights, weekends, and for part-time students.
Students without need: No-need awards available for academics, art, leadership, music/drama.

FINANCIAL AID PROCEDURES
Forms required: FAFSA, institutional form.
Dates and Deadlines: Priority date 7/1; no closing date. Applicants notified on a rolling basis starting 4/1; must reply within 2 week(s) of notification.

CONTACT
Susan Fintze, Director of Financial Aid
58900 Cherry Grove Road, Dowagiac, MI 49047-9793
(269) 782-1313

Spring Arbor University
Spring Arbor, Michigan
www.arbor.edu   Federal Code: 002318

4-year private university and liberal arts college in rural community, affiliated with Free Methodist Church of North America.
Enrollment: 2,710 undergrads, 27% part-time. 381 full-time freshmen.
Selectivity: Admits over 75% of applicants.

BASIC COSTS (2010-2011)
Tuition and fees: $20,536.
Per-credit charge: $504.
Room and board: $7,254.

FINANCIAL AID PICTURE (2009-2010)
Students with need: Out of 371 full-time freshmen who applied for aid, 333 were judged to have need. Of these, 333 received aid, and 160 had their full need met. Average financial aid package met 92% of need; average scholarship/grant was $12,493; average loan was $3,674. For part-time students, average financial aid package was $10,212.
Students without need: 1 full-time freshmen who did not demonstrate need for aid received scholarships/grants; average award was $2,800. No-need awards available for academics, art, athletics, minority status, music/drama, religious affiliation.
Scholarships offered: *Merit:* President Scholarship: $5,000; Provost Scholarship: $3,000; Faculty Scholarship: $2,000; Partnership Scholarship: $1,000; based on GPA, rank in class, and ACT scores. National Merit Finalist: full tuition; National Merit Semifinalist: half-tuition. Trustee scholarship: $7,500; based on 29 ACT/1280 SAT. ***Athletic:*** 58 full-time freshmen received athletic scholarships; average amount $6,157.
Cumulative student debt: 86% of graduating class had student loans; average debt was $26,077.

FINANCIAL AID PROCEDURES
Forms required: FAFSA.
Dates and Deadlines: Priority date 3/1; no closing date. Applicants notified on a rolling basis starting 3/1; must reply within 2 week(s) of notification.
Transfers: No deadline. Applicants notified on a rolling basis starting 5/1; must reply within 2 week(s) of notification. A financial aid transcript is required from each college previously attended.

CONTACT
Geoff Marsh, Director of Financial Aid
106 East Main Street, Spring Arbor, MI 49283-9799
(517) 750-6468

University of Detroit Mercy
Detroit, Michigan
www.udmercy.edu   Federal Code: 002323

4-year private university in very large city, affiliated with Roman Catholic Church.
Enrollment: 3,149 undergrads.
Selectivity: Admits 50 to 75% of applicants.

BASIC COSTS (2010-2011)
Tuition and fees: $30,660.
Per-credit charge: $780.
Room and board: $8,930.

FINANCIAL AID PICTURE
Students with need: Need-based aid available for full-time and part-time students.
Students without need: No-need awards available for academics, alumni affiliation, athletics, leadership, minority status, music/drama, religious affiliation.

FINANCIAL AID PROCEDURES
Forms required: FAFSA.
Dates and Deadlines: Priority date 3/1; no closing date. Applicants notified on a rolling basis starting 3/1; must reply within 3 week(s) of notification.

CONTACT
Jenny McAlonan, Director of Scholarship and Financial Aid
4001 West McNichols Road, Detroit, MI 48221-3038
(313) 993-3350

University of Michigan
Ann Arbor, Michigan   Federal Code: 002325
www.umich.edu   CSS Code: 1839

4-year public university in small city.
Enrollment: 26,033 undergrads, 3% part-time. 5,739 full-time freshmen.
Selectivity: Admits less than 50% of applicants.

BASIC COSTS (2009-2010)
Tuition and fees: $11,659; out-of-state residents $34,937.
Per-credit charge: $423; out-of-state residents $1,341.
Room and board: $8,924.

FINANCIAL AID PICTURE (2008-2009)
Students with need: Out of 3,788 full-time freshmen who applied for aid, 2,622 were judged to have need. Of these, 2,622 received aid, and 2,360 had their full need met. Average financial aid package met 90% of need; average scholarship/grant was $8,375; average loan was $4,340. Need-based aid available for part-time students.
Students without need: 2,526 full-time freshmen who did not demonstrate need for aid received scholarships/grants; average award was $5,808. No-need awards available for academics, alumni affiliation, art, athletics, leadership, music/drama, religious affiliation, ROTC, state/district residency.
Scholarships offered: 136 full-time freshmen received athletic scholarships; average amount $27,230.
Cumulative student debt: 46% of graduating class had student loans; average debt was $26,819.

FINANCIAL AID PROCEDURES
Forms required: FAFSA, CSS PROFILE.
Dates and Deadlines: Priority date 4/29; closing date 5/29. Applicants notified on a rolling basis starting 3/15.
Transfers: Applicants notified on a rolling basis starting 3/9. Community College Scholarship available for qualified students.

CONTACT
Pamela Fowler, Executive Director, Office of Financial Aid
1220 Student Activities Building, Ann Arbor, MI 48109-1316
(734) 763-6600

University of Michigan: Dearborn
Dearborn, Michigan
www.umd.umich.edu   Federal Code: 002326

4-year public university in small city.
Enrollment: 6,509 undergrads, 28% part-time. 886 full-time freshmen.
Selectivity: Admits 50 to 75% of applicants.

BASIC COSTS (2009-2010)
Tuition and fees: $9,100; out-of-state residents $19,883.

FINANCIAL AID PICTURE (2008-2009)
Students with need: Need-based aid available for full-time and part-time students. Work study available nights, weekends, and for part-time students.
Students without need: No-need awards available for academics, alumni affiliation, athletics, job skills, leadership, minority status, ROTC.

FINANCIAL AID PROCEDURES

Forms required: FAFSA.

Dates and Deadlines: Priority date 2/15; no closing date. Applicants notified on a rolling basis starting 3/10; must reply within 3 week(s) of notification.

Transfers: Applicants notified on a rolling basis starting 4/1; must reply within 3 week(s) of notification.

CONTACT

Judy Tatum, Director of Financial Aid

4901 Evergreen Road, 1145 UC, Dearborn, MI 48128-1491

(313) 593-5000

University of Michigan: Flint

Flint, Michigan

www.umflint.edu   Federal Code: 002327

4-year public university and branch campus college in small city.

Enrollment: 6,280 undergrads, 31% part-time. 835 full-time freshmen.

Selectivity: Admits over 75% of applicants.

BASIC COSTS (2009-2010)

Tuition and fees: $8,279; out-of-state residents $15,793.

Per-credit charge: $311; out-of-state residents $623.

Room and board: $6,874.

FINANCIAL AID PICTURE (2008-2009)

Students with need: Out of 721 full-time freshmen who applied for aid, 558 were judged to have need. Of these, 552 received aid, and 41 had their full need met. Average financial aid package met 78% of need; average scholarship/grant was $6,159; average loan was $3,346. For part-time students, average financial aid package was $9,035.

Students without need: 46 full-time freshmen who did not demonstrate need for aid received scholarships/grants; average award was $1,810. No-need awards available for academics, art, leadership, minority status, music/drama.

Additional info: SAT/ACT scores must be submitted for scholarship consideration.

FINANCIAL AID PROCEDURES

Forms required: FAFSA.

Dates and Deadlines: Priority date 3/1; no closing date. Applicants notified on a rolling basis starting 3/15.

Transfers: Must not be in default or owe refunds for Title IV aid.

CONTACT

Lori Vedder, Director of Financial Aid

303 East Kearsley Street, Flint, MI 48502-1950

(810) 762-3444

Walsh College of Accountancy and Business Administration

Troy, Michigan

www.walshcollege.edu   Federal Code: 004071

Upper-division private business college in large city.

Enrollment: 1,076 undergrads, 86% part-time.

BASIC COSTS (2010-2011)

Tuition and fees: $11,355.

Per-credit charge: $305.

FINANCIAL AID PICTURE (2008-2009)

Students with need: Average financial aid package for all full-time undergraduates was $15,307; for part-time $14,963. 17% awarded as scholarships/grants, 83% awarded as loans/jobs.

Students without need: No-need awards available for academics.

Cumulative student debt: 61% of graduating class had student loans; average debt was $13,077.

FINANCIAL AID PROCEDURES

Forms required: FAFSA.

Dates and Deadlines: Priority date 3/23; no closing date.

Transfers: Priority date 3/1; no deadline. Applicants notified on a rolling basis.

CONTACT

Howard Thomas, Director, Financial Aid

PO Box 7006, Troy, MI 48007-7006

(248) 823-1285

Wayne County Community College

Detroit, Michigan

www.wcccd.edu   Federal Code: 009230

2-year public community and liberal arts college in very large city.

Enrollment: 20,770 undergrads, 77% part-time. 1,361 full-time freshmen.

Selectivity: Open admission.

BASIC COSTS (2010-2011)

Tuition and fees: $2,330; out-of-district residents $3,300; out-of-state residents $4,200.

Per-credit charge: $68; out-of-district residents $100; out-of-state residents $130.

FINANCIAL AID PICTURE (2008-2009)

Students with need: 58% of average financial aid package awarded as scholarships/grants, 42% awarded as loans/jobs. Need-based aid available for part-time students. Work study available nights, weekends, and for part-time students.

Additional info: High school diploma, GED, or passing grade on ABT required for financial aid.

FINANCIAL AID PROCEDURES

Forms required: FAFSA.

Dates and Deadlines: Priority date 5/1; no closing date. Applicants notified on a rolling basis starting 5/1.

CONTACT

Myra Hawkins, Executive District Director of Financial Aid

801 West Fort Street, Detroit, MI 48226

(313) 496-2614

Wayne State University

Detroit, Michigan

www.wayne.edu   Federal Code: 002329

4-year public university in very large city.

Enrollment: 19,650 undergrads, 34% part-time. 2,625 full-time freshmen.

Selectivity: Admits over 75% of applicants.

BASIC COSTS (2009-2010)

Tuition and fees: $8,599; out-of-state residents $18,412.

Room and board: $7,210.

FINANCIAL AID PICTURE (2008-2009)

Students with need: Out of 2,241 full-time freshmen who applied for aid, 1,800 were judged to have need. Of these, 1,764 received aid, and 395 had their full need met. Average financial aid package met 72% of need; average scholarship/grant was $5,546; average loan was $3,549. For part-time students, average financial aid package was $9,835.

Students without need: 294 full-time freshmen who did not demonstrate need for aid received scholarships/grants; average award was $4,720. No-need awards available for academics, art, athletics, leadership, music/drama.

Scholarships offered: *Merit:* Presidential Scholarships; full tuition and fees; offered to top academic students; more than 350 available. *Athletic:* 31 full-time freshmen received athletic scholarships; average amount $7,957.

Cumulative student debt: 56% of graduating class had student loans; average debt was $19,781.

Additional info: Need-based institutional grants cover tuition and fees with grants and EFC (no loans).

FINANCIAL AID PROCEDURES

Forms required: FAFSA.

Dates and Deadlines: Priority date 2/15; closing date 4/30. Applicants notified on a rolling basis starting 3/1; must reply within 2 week(s) of notification.

Transfers: No deadline. Applicants notified on a rolling basis starting 3/1; must reply within 2 week(s) of notification.

CONTACT

Al Hermsen, Director of Student Financial Aid

42 West Warren, Detroit, MI 48201

(313) 577-3378

West Shore Community College
Scottville, Michigan
www.westshore.edu   Federal Code: 007950

2-year public community college in rural community.

Enrollment: 1,254 undergrads.

Selectivity: Open admission; but selective for some programs.

BASIC COSTS (2009-2010)

Tuition and fees: $2,370; out-of-district residents $3,990; out-of-state residents $5,070.

Per-credit charge: $72; out-of-district residents $126; out-of-state residents $162.

FINANCIAL AID PICTURE (2009-2010)

Students with need: 79% of average financial aid package awarded as scholarships/grants, 21% awarded as loans/jobs. Need-based aid available for part-time students. Work study available nights, weekends, and for part-time students.

FINANCIAL AID PROCEDURES

Forms required: FAFSA.

Dates and Deadlines: Priority date 3/15; no closing date. Applicants notified on a rolling basis starting 5/15; must reply within 2 week(s) of notification.

CONTACT

Victoria Oddo, Director of Student Services

3000 North Stiles Road, Scottville, MI 49454-0277

(231) 845-6211

Western Michigan University
Kalamazoo, Michigan
www.wmich.edu   Federal Code: 002330

4-year public university in small city.

Enrollment: 19,302 undergrads, 12% part-time. 3,870 full-time freshmen.

Selectivity: Admits over 75% of applicants.

BASIC COSTS (2009-2010)

Tuition and fees: $8,382; out-of-state residents $19,502.

Per-credit charge: $265; out-of-state residents $649.

Room and board: $7,784.

FINANCIAL AID PICTURE (2008-2009)

Students with need: Out of 3,800 full-time freshmen who applied for aid, 3,468 were judged to have need. Of these, 3,468 received aid, and 1,042 had their full need met. Average financial aid package met 85% of need; average scholarship/grant was $4,566; average loan was $3,422. Need-based aid available for part-time students.

Students without need: 368 full-time freshmen who did not demonstrate need for aid received scholarships/grants; average award was $3,400. No-need awards available for academics, alumni affiliation, art, athletics, minority status, music/drama, ROTC, state/district residency.

Scholarships offered: *Merit:* Medallion Scholarship; $3,000-$10,000 annually; based on academic performance in high school (3.8 GPA, 25 ACT or 1130 SAT, exclusive of writing); renewable for students maintaining full-time enrollment and 3.25 GPA. *Athletic:* 74 full-time freshmen received athletic scholarships; average amount $16,323.

Cumulative student debt: 64% of graduating class had student loans; average debt was $20,415.

FINANCIAL AID PROCEDURES

Forms required: FAFSA.

Dates and Deadlines: Priority date 3/15; no closing date. Applicants notified on a rolling basis starting 3/15.

Transfers: No deadline. Applicants notified on a rolling basis starting 3/15.

CONTACT

Mark Delorey, Director of Financial Aid

1903 West Michigan Avenue, Kalamazoo, MI 49008-5211

(269) 387-6000

Minnesota

Academy College
Bloomington, Minnesota
www.academycollege.edu   Federal Code: 013505

2-year for-profit junior and career college in large city.

Enrollment: 199 undergrads.

Selectivity: Open admission.

BASIC COSTS (2009-2010)

Additional info: Tuition ranges from $335 to $399 per credit hour depending on program.

FINANCIAL AID PICTURE (2008-2009)

Students with need: Need-based aid available for full-time and part-time students. Work study available nights, weekends, and for part-time students.

FINANCIAL AID PROCEDURES

Forms required: FAFSA, institutional form.

Dates and Deadlines: No deadline. Applicants notified on a rolling basis.

CONTACT

Mary Erickson, Director of Administration

1101 East 78th Street, Bloomington, MN 55420

(952) 851-0066

Alexandria Technical College
Alexandria, Minnesota
www.alextech.edu   Federal Code: 005544

2-year public technical college in large town.

Enrollment: 1,770 undergrads.

Selectivity: Open admission; but selective for some programs.

BASIC COSTS (2009-2010)
Tuition and fees: $4,627.
Per-credit charge: $139.
Additional info: In-state and out-of-state tuition rates are the same.

FINANCIAL AID PICTURE
Students with need: Need-based aid available for full-time and part-time students.
Students without need: This college awards aid only to students with need.

FINANCIAL AID PROCEDURES
Forms required: FAFSA, institutional form.
Dates and Deadlines: Priority date 5/1; no closing date. Applicants notified on a rolling basis starting 6/30; must reply within 2 week(s) of notification.
Transfers: No deadline. Applicants notified on a rolling basis; must reply within 2 week(s) of notification.

CONTACT
Steve Richards, Financial Aid Coordinator
1601 Jefferson Street, Alexandria, MN 56308-3799
(320) 762-4540

Anoka Technical College
Anoka, Minnesota
www.anokatech.edu   Federal Code: 007350

2-year public technical college in large town.
Enrollment: 2,260 undergrads.
Selectivity: Open admission.

BASIC COSTS (2009-2010)
Tuition and fees: $4,719.
Per-credit charge: $144.
Additional info: In-state and out-of-state tuition rates are the same.

FINANCIAL AID PICTURE
Students with need: Need-based aid available for full-time and part-time students. Work study available nights.
Students without need: This college awards aid only to students with need.

FINANCIAL AID PROCEDURES
Forms required: FAFSA, institutional form.
Dates and Deadlines: No deadline. Applicants notified on a rolling basis starting 5/1.

CONTACT
Susan Rumpca, Director of Financial Aid
1355 West Highway 10, Anoka, MN 55303
(763) 576-4760

Anoka-Ramsey Community College
Coon Rapids, Minnesota
www.anokaramsey.edu   Federal Code: 002332

2-year public community college in small city.
Enrollment: 7,440 undergrads.
Selectivity: Open admission; but selective for some programs.

BASIC COSTS (2009-2010)
Tuition and fees: $4,208.
Per-credit charge: $123.
Additional info: In-state and out-of-state tuition rates are the same.

FINANCIAL AID PICTURE
Students with need: Work study available nights, weekends, and for part-time students.
Students without need: This college awards aid only to students with need.

FINANCIAL AID PROCEDURES
Forms required: FAFSA, institutional form.
Dates and Deadlines: Priority date 4/1; no closing date. Applicants notified on a rolling basis; must reply within 2 week(s) of notification.

CONTACT
Karla Seymour, Financial Aid Officer
11200 Mississippi Boulevard NW, Coon Rapids, MN 55433
(763) 433-1500

Art Institutes International Minnesota
Minneapolis, Minnesota
www.artinstitutes.edu/minneapolis Federal Code: 010248

4-year for-profit culinary school and visual arts college in large city.
Enrollment: 1,974 undergrads.
Selectivity: Open admission.

BASIC COSTS (2009-2010)
Tuition and fees: $22,416.
Per-credit charge: $467.
Additional info: Typical full-time credit load 16 credits/quarter. Starter kits for most programs $350 to $1,300.

FINANCIAL AID PICTURE
Students with need: Need-based aid available for full-time students.

FINANCIAL AID PROCEDURES
Forms required: FAFSA.

CONTACT
Dave Aune, Director of Administrative and Financial Services
15 South Ninth Street, Minneapolis, MN 55402
(612) 332-3361

Augsburg College
Minneapolis, Minnesota
www.augsburg.edu   Federal Code: 002334

4-year private liberal arts college in large city, affiliated with Evangelical Lutheran Church in America.
Enrollment: 2,979 undergrads, 16% part-time. 459 full-time freshmen.
Selectivity: Admits 50 to 75% of applicants.

BASIC COSTS (2010-2011)
Tuition and fees: $29,488.
Per-credit charge: $865.
Room and board: $7,760.

FINANCIAL AID PICTURE (2008-2009)
Students with need: Need-based aid available for full-time and part-time students.
Students without need: No-need awards available for academics, alumni affiliation, leadership, minority status, music/drama, religious affiliation.
Scholarships offered: President's Scholarships: up to full tuition annually; 3.7 GPA and ACT/SAT score 27 or higher; number awarded determined annually. Regents Scholarships: $4,000-$10,000; top 30% of class rank or test scores. Must apply before 5/1 for both scholarships.

FINANCIAL AID PROCEDURES
Forms required: FAFSA.

Dates and Deadlines: Priority date 4/15; closing date 8/1. Applicants notified on a rolling basis starting 3/1; must reply within 3 week(s) of notification.

Transfers: Priority date 7/1; closing date 8/15. Applicants notified on a rolling basis starting 3/1; must reply by 9/1.

CONTACT

Paul Terrio, Director of Enrollment Services
2211 Riverside Avenue, Minneapolis, MN 55454
(612) 330-1046

Bemidji State University

Bemidji, Minnesota
www.bemidjistate.edu   Federal Code: 002336

4-year public university in large town.

Enrollment: 4,235 undergrads, 16% part-time. 787 full-time freshmen.

Selectivity: Admits over 75% of applicants.

BASIC COSTS (2010-2011)

Tuition and fees: $7,510; out-of-state residents $7,510.

Per-credit charge: $230.

Room and board: $6,425.

Additional info: Tuition/fee waivers available for minority students.

FINANCIAL AID PICTURE (2009-2010)

Students with need: Out of 662 full-time freshmen who applied for aid, 471 were judged to have need. Of these, 470 received aid, and 156 had their full need met. Average financial aid package met 76% of need; average scholarship/grant was $5,877; average loan was $336. For part-time students, average financial aid package was $6,481.

Students without need: 176 full-time freshmen who did not demonstrate need for aid received scholarships/grants; average award was $9,050. No-need awards available for academics, alumni affiliation, art, athletics, music/drama.

Scholarships offered: 63 full-time freshmen received athletic scholarships; average amount $4,422.

Cumulative student debt: 68% of graduating class had student loans; average debt was $25,089.

FINANCIAL AID PROCEDURES

Forms required: FAFSA, institutional form.

Dates and Deadlines: Priority date 5/15; no closing date. Applicants notified on a rolling basis starting 5/15.

CONTACT

Paul Lindseth, Director of Financial Aid
1500 Birchmont Drive NE, #13, Bemidji, MN 56601
(218) 755-2034

Bethany Lutheran College

Mankato, Minnesota
www.blc.edu   Federal Code: 002337

4-year private liberal arts college in large town, affiliated with Evangelical Lutheran Synod.

Enrollment: 615 undergrads. 181 full-time freshmen.

Selectivity: Admits over 75% of applicants.

BASIC COSTS (2009-2010)

Tuition and fees: $19,650.

Per-credit charge: $810.

Room and board: $6,200.

FINANCIAL AID PICTURE (2008-2009)

Students with need: Out of 167 full-time freshmen who applied for aid, 152 were judged to have need. Of these, 151 received aid, and 31 had their full need met. Average financial aid package met 86% of need; average scholarship/grant was $11,909; average loan was $3,952. For part-time students, average financial aid package was $10,965.

Students without need: 23 full-time freshmen who did not demonstrate need for aid received scholarships/grants; average award was $5,350. No-need awards available for academics, art, music/drama.

Cumulative student debt: 79% of graduating class had student loans; average debt was $22,410.

FINANCIAL AID PROCEDURES

Forms required: FAFSA, institutional form.

Dates and Deadlines: Priority date 4/15; no closing date. Applicants notified on a rolling basis starting 3/1; must reply within 2 week(s) of notification.

Transfers: No deadline. Applicants notified on a rolling basis starting 3/1; must reply within 2 week(s) of notification.

CONTACT

Jeffrey Younge, Financial Aid Director
700 Luther Drive, Mankato, MN 56001-4490
(507) 344-7328

Bethel University

Saint Paul, Minnesota
www.bethel.edu   Federal Code: 002338

4-year private university and liberal arts college in large city, affiliated with Baptist General Conference.

Enrollment: 3,335 undergrads, 19% part-time. 599 full-time freshmen.

Selectivity: Admits over 75% of applicants.

BASIC COSTS (2010-2011)

Tuition and fees: $28,080.

Per-credit charge: $1,165.

Room and board: $8,220.

Additional info: Housing rate frozen as long as student continues to reside in campus housing. Tuition/fee waivers available for minority students.

FINANCIAL AID PICTURE (2008-2009)

Students with need: Out of 517 full-time freshmen who applied for aid, 442 were judged to have need. Of these, 442 received aid, and 82 had their full need met. Average financial aid package met 78% of need; average scholarship/grant was $15,158; average loan was $4,132. For part-time students, average financial aid package was $8,334.

Students without need: 139 full-time freshmen who did not demonstrate need for aid received scholarships/grants; average award was $4,602. No-need awards available for academics, alumni affiliation, art, leadership, music/drama, state/district residency.

Scholarships offered: Faculty Scholarship: $2,000-$4,900 per year. Dean's Scholarship: $5,000-$9,900 per year. President's Scholarship: $10,000-$15,000 per year; based on academic merit or potential as signified by high school GPA, high school class rank, ACT or SAT score, and/or evidence of potential to make a significant contribution to the spiritual and social atmosphere at Bethel. Royal Scholarship: $2,000; awarded to students with family members who have previously attended Bethel University. Ministerial Scholarship: $1,000; dependent children of full-time ordained ministers or missionaries of Converge Worldwide (formerly the BGC) qualify for $1,200; those of other denominations qualify for $1,000 (both are contingent on good standing).

Cumulative student debt: 80% of graduating class had student loans; average debt was $30,496.

FINANCIAL AID PROCEDURES

Forms required: FAFSA, institutional form.

Dates and Deadlines: Priority date 4/15; no closing date. Applicants notified on a rolling basis starting 3/1.

Transfers: Phi Theta Kappa Scholarship ($1,000 per year) awarded to transfer students with a minimum cumulative college GPA of 3.00 and previous membership in Phi Theta Kappa academic honor society for at least one term.

CONTACT

Jeffrey Olson, Director of Financial Aid
3900 Bethel Drive, Saint Paul, MN 55112
(651) 638-6241

Capella University

Minneapolis, Minnesota
www.capella.edu   Federal Code: 032673

4-year for-profit virtual university in very large city.

Enrollment: 5,619 undergrads.

Selectivity: Open admission; but selective for some programs.

BASIC COSTS (2009-2010)

Tuition and fees: $13,275.

Per-credit charge: $295.

FINANCIAL AID PICTURE

Students with need: Need-based aid available for full-time and part-time students.

CONTACT

Michael Nylund, Director of Financial Aid
225 South Sixth Street, 9th Floor, Minneapolis, MN 55402
(888) 227-3552

Carleton College

Northfield, Minnesota   Federal Code: 002340
www.carleton.edu   CSS Code: 6081

4-year private liberal arts college in large town.

Enrollment: 1,986 undergrads. 528 full-time freshmen.

Selectivity: Admits less than 50% of applicants.

BASIC COSTS (2010-2011)

Tuition and fees: $41,304.

Room and board: $10,806.

FINANCIAL AID PICTURE (2008-2009)

Students with need: Out of 406 full-time freshmen who applied for aid, 311 were judged to have need. Of these, 311 received aid, and 311 had their full need met. Average financial aid package met 100% of need; average scholarship/grant was $28,868; average loan was $3,979.

Students without need: 26 full-time freshmen who did not demonstrate need for aid received scholarships/grants; average award was $1,962. No-need awards available for academics.

Scholarships offered: National Merit, National Achievement, National Hispanic Scholars Awards: $2,000 per year; based on outstanding academic achievement and promise.

Cumulative student debt: 54% of graduating class had student loans; average debt was $18,601.

Additional info: Full financial need of all admitted applicants met through combination of work, loans, grants. Carleton Access Scholarship reduces loans for entering students whose family income is below $75,000.

FINANCIAL AID PROCEDURES

Forms required: FAFSA, CSS PROFILE.

Dates and Deadlines: Closing date 2/15. Applicants notified by 4/1; must reply by 5/1 or within 2 week(s) of notification.

Transfers: Closing date 3/15. Applicants notified by 5/15; must reply by 6/1 or within 2 week(s) of notification.

CONTACT

Rodney Oto, Director of Student Financial Services
100 South College Street, Northfield, MN 55057
(507) 222-4138

Central Lakes College

Brainerd, Minnesota
www.clcmn.edu   Federal Code: 002339

2-year public community and technical college in large town.

Enrollment: 3,008 undergrads.

Selectivity: Open admission; but selective for some programs.

BASIC COSTS (2009-2010)

Tuition and fees: $4,705.

Per-credit charge: $137.

Additional info: In-state and out-of-state tuition rates same.

FINANCIAL AID PICTURE (2008-2009)

Students with need: 39% of average financial aid package awarded as scholarships/grants, 61% awarded as loans/jobs. Need-based aid available for part-time students.

FINANCIAL AID PROCEDURES

Forms required: FAFSA, institutional form.

Dates and Deadlines: Priority date 6/1; no closing date. Applicants notified on a rolling basis starting 6/10; must reply within 2 week(s) of notification.

CONTACT

Mike Barnaby, Director of Financial Aid
501 West College Drive, Brainerd, MN 56401
(218) 855-8025

Century Community and Technical College

White Bear Lake, Minnesota
www.century.edu   Federal Code: 010546

2-year public community and technical college in large town.

Enrollment: 9,801 undergrads, 52% part-time. 1,281 full-time freshmen.

Selectivity: Open admission; but selective for some programs.

BASIC COSTS (2009-2010)

Tuition and fees: $4,780.

Per-credit charge: $142.

Additional info: In-state and out-of-state tuition rates are the same.

FINANCIAL AID PICTURE (2008-2009)

Students with need: 31% of average financial aid package awarded as scholarships/grants, 69% awarded as loans/jobs. Need-based aid available for part-time students.

Students without need: This college awards aid only to students with need.

Additional info: Minnesota resident out of high school or not enrolled in college for 7 years without bachelor's or other higher degree offered cost of tuition and books for 1 course in 1 semester up to maximum of 5 credits.

FINANCIAL AID PROCEDURES

Forms required: FAFSA.

Dates and Deadlines: No deadline. Applicants notified on a rolling basis starting 5/15.

CONTACT

Lois Larson, Financial Aid Director
3300 Century Avenue North, White Bear Lake, MN 55110
(651) 779-3305

College of St. Benedict

St. Joseph, Minnesota
www.csbsju.edu   Federal Code: 002341

4-year private liberal arts college for women in small town, affiliated with Roman Catholic Church.

Enrollment: 2,106 undergrads, 2% part-time. 551 full-time freshmen.

Selectivity: Admits over 75% of applicants.

BASIC COSTS (2010-2011)

Tuition and fees: $32,246.

Per-credit charge: $1,309.

Room and board: $8,652.

FINANCIAL AID PICTURE (2009-2010)

Students with need: Out of 447 full-time freshmen who applied for aid, 375 were judged to have need. Of these, 375 received aid, and 207 had their full need met. Average financial aid package met 94% of need; average scholarship/grant was $20,316; average loan was $3,422. For part-time students, average financial aid package was $1,780.

Students without need: 142 full-time freshmen who did not demonstrate need for aid received scholarships/grants; average award was $11,985. No-need awards available for academics, art, leadership, music/drama, ROTC.

Scholarships offered: Regents/Trustees Scholarships: $16,000; minimum 3.6 GPA, 30 ACT, 1980 SAT, demonstrated leadership and service, faculty interview. President's Scholarships: $10,500-$13,500; and Dean's Scholarships: $3,000-$9,500; GPA, high school rank, ACT/SAT scores, leadership and service considered. Art, music and theater scholarships: up to $4,000. Diversity Leadership Scholarships: up to $5,000; demonstrated diversity leadership and service in the area of cultural and ethnic diversity, personal statement on topic. Army ROTC and ROTC Nursing Scholarships: demonstrated leadership potential, high school GPA, class standing, ACT/SAT scores, high achievement with broad interests and willingness to take on challenges. Catholic High School Scholarship: $3,000; students attending Catholic high schools outside Minnesota. Saints Scholarship: $1,000- $3,000; students attending public high schools outside Minnesota. Phi Theta Kappa Scholarship: $1,000; member of Phi Theta Kappa (transfer students only).

Additional info: Scholarship letters will be mailed on a rolling basis approximately two weeks from the time the admission acceptance letter is sent.

FINANCIAL AID PROCEDURES

Forms required: FAFSA, institutional form.

Dates and Deadlines: Priority date 3/15; no closing date. Applicants notified on a rolling basis starting 3/15; must reply by 5/1.

CONTACT

Jane Haugen, Executive Director of Financial Aid
College of St Benedict/St John's University, Collegeville, MN 56321-7155
(320) 363-5388

College of St. Scholastica

Duluth, Minnesota
www.css.edu   Federal Code: 002343

4-year private liberal arts college in small city, affiliated with Roman Catholic Church.

Enrollment: 2,144 undergrads, 2% part-time. 479 full-time freshmen.

Selectivity: Admits over 75% of applicants.

BASIC COSTS (2010-2011)

Tuition and fees: $28,370.

Per-credit charge: $881.

Room and board: $7,498.

Additional info: Tuition/fee waivers available for minority students.

FINANCIAL AID PICTURE (2009-2010)

Students with need: Average financial aid package met 82% of need; average scholarship/grant was $8,043; average loan was $3,434. For part-time students, average financial aid package was $12,560.

Students without need: No-need awards available for academics, alumni affiliation, music/drama, religious affiliation, ROTC, state/district residency.

Scholarships offered: Benedictine Scholarship: $5,000-$13,500 per year for up to 4 years. Access Scholarship: $7,500. Both based on GPA, SAT/ACT score; unlimited number awarded. Summit Scholarship: an additional $1,500 for those who qualify for the Benedictine Scholarship and who graduate at the top of their high school class. Divisional Merit Awards: $4,000; available to transfer students; based on major; unlimited number awarded.

Cumulative student debt: 81% of graduating class had student loans; average debt was $40,401.

FINANCIAL AID PROCEDURES

Forms required: FAFSA.

Dates and Deadlines: Priority date 3/1; no closing date. Applicants notified on a rolling basis starting 3/1; must reply by 5/1 or within 2 week(s) of notification.

CONTACT

Jon Erickson, Director of Financial Aid
1200 Kenwood Avenue, Duluth, MN 55811-4199
(218) 723-6047

College of Visual Arts

Saint Paul, Minnesota
www.cva.edu   Federal Code: 007462

4-year private visual arts college in large city.

Enrollment: 180 undergrads, 2% part-time. 36 full-time freshmen.

Selectivity: Admits 50 to 75% of applicants.

BASIC COSTS (2010-2011)

Tuition and fees: $23,988.

Per-credit charge: $1,175.

FINANCIAL AID PICTURE (2009-2010)

Students with need: Out of 36 full-time freshmen who applied for aid, 34 were judged to have need. Of these, 34 received aid, and 1 had their full need met. Average financial aid package met 58% of need; average scholarship/grant was $12,407; average loan was $3,328. For part-time students, average financial aid package was $5,670.

Students without need: 2 full-time freshmen who did not demonstrate need for aid received scholarships/grants; average award was $5,000. No-need awards available for academics, art.

Scholarships offered: Merit scholarship program provides annual awards ranging from $2,000 to $8,500; stipends are based on artistic and academic merit.

Cumulative student debt: 86% of graduating class had student loans; average debt was $41,776.

FINANCIAL AID PROCEDURES

Forms required: FAFSA, institutional form.

Dates and Deadlines: Priority date 3/1; no closing date. Applicants notified on a rolling basis starting 2/15; must reply within 2 week(s) of notification.

Transfers: Priority date 4/15. Applicants notified on a rolling basis starting 3/1; must reply within 2 week(s) of notification.

CONTACT
Susan Ant, Executive Director of Enrollment
344 Summit Avenue, Saint Paul, MN 55102-2199
(651) 757-4020

Concordia College: Moorhead
Moorhead, Minnesota
www.concordiacollege.edu   Federal Code: 002346

4-year private liberal arts college in small city, affiliated with Evangelical Lutheran Church in America.
Enrollment: 2,744 undergrads, 1% part-time. 765 full-time freshmen.
Selectivity: Admits over 75% of applicants.

BASIC COSTS (2010-2011)
Tuition and fees: $27,160.
Per-credit charge: $1,004.
Room and board: $6,510.
Additional info: Tuition/fee waivers available for minority students, unemployed or children of unemployed.

FINANCIAL AID PICTURE (2008-2009)
Students with need: Out of 674 full-time freshmen who applied for aid, 558 were judged to have need. Of these, 558 received aid, and 158 had their full need met. Average financial aid package met 88% of need; average scholarship/grant was $14,140; average loan was $3,791. For part-time students, average financial aid package was $12,854.
Students without need: 201 full-time freshmen who did not demonstrate need for aid received scholarships/grants; average award was $9,075. No-need awards available for academics, art, leadership, minority status, music/drama.
Scholarships offered: Concordia College Regents Scholarship: covers tuition for 4 years; based on a cumulative GPA of at least 3.90 and score of 30 or higher on the ACT, or a score of 1980 or above on the SAT; 5 awarded annually. Presidential Distinction Awards: approximately 75 incoming first-year students selected as Presidential Scholars receive $14,000 per year up to 4 years; students eligible to compete for the scholarship with a GPA of 3.80 and a score of 26 or higher on the ACT or 1760 or above on the SAT. Faculty Scholarships: approximately 150 incoming first-year students receive $13,000 per year up to 4 years; eligibility based on the same criteria as the Presidential Distinction Award. National Merit Scholars: National Merit finalists who name Concordia as their first choice receive a minimum of $14,000 per year. Excellence Scholarships: based on academic achievement; $9,000 to $12,000 per year; admitted students notified of their eligibility automatically; no separate application required. Concordia College Renewable Grants: $5,000 to $7,000 per year; given to students who show strong potential for success and contribution to the Concordia community; no separate application required. Performance Scholarships: $2,500 per year for up to 4 years; awarded to incoming first-year students in recognition of excellence in music performance, theater performance, speech and debate, and visual arts.
Cumulative student debt: 87% of graduating class had student loans; average debt was $29,885.

FINANCIAL AID PROCEDURES
Forms required: FAFSA.
Dates and Deadlines: No deadline. Applicants notified on a rolling basis starting 3/15.
Transfers: No deadline. Applicants notified on a rolling basis. Concordia College offers a $1,000 Honor Scholarship for transfer students.

CONTACT
Jane Williams, Director of Financial Aid
901 Eighth Street South, Moorhead, MN 56562
(218) 299-3010

Concordia University: St. Paul
St. Paul, Minnesota
www.csp.edu   Federal Code: 002347

4-year private university in large city, affiliated with Lutheran Church - Missouri Synod.
Enrollment: 1,471 undergrads, 9% part-time. 183 full-time freshmen.
Selectivity: Admits 50 to 75% of applicants.

BASIC COSTS (2010-2011)
Tuition and fees: $27,400.
Per-credit charge: $575.
Room and board: $7,500.

FINANCIAL AID PICTURE (2009-2010)
Students with need: Out of 183 full-time freshmen who applied for aid, 162 were judged to have need. Of these, 162 received aid, and 29 had their full need met. Average financial aid package met 80% of need; average scholarship/grant was $16,705; average loan was $4,320. For part-time students, average financial aid package was $7,360.
Students without need: 21 full-time freshmen who did not demonstrate need for aid received scholarships/grants; average award was $8,462. No-need awards available for academics, art, athletics, minority status, music/drama, religious affiliation.
Scholarships offered: 5 full-time freshmen received athletic scholarships; average amount $7,300.
Cumulative student debt: 85% of graduating class had student loans; average debt was $32,444.
Additional info: Church districts and local congregations are major sources of aid for church-vocation students.

FINANCIAL AID PROCEDURES
Forms required: FAFSA, institutional form.
Dates and Deadlines: Priority date 5/1; no closing date. Applicants notified on a rolling basis starting 3/1.
Transfers: Adult learners in degree completion programs typically not eligible for most types of institutional scholarships/grants because of discounted tuition rates.

CONTACT
Carolyn Chesebrough, Director of Financial Aid
275 Syndicate Street North, St. Paul, MN 55104-5494
(651) 603-6300

Crossroads College
Rochester, Minnesota
www.crossroadscollege.edu   Federal Code: 002366

4-year private Bible college in small city, affiliated with Christian Church.
Enrollment: 170 undergrads.

BASIC COSTS (2010-2011)
Tuition and fees: $14,780.
Per-credit charge: $410.
Room only: $3,950.

FINANCIAL AID PICTURE (2009-2010)
Students with need: Need-based aid available for full-time and part-time students. Work study available nights.
Students without need: No-need awards available for academics, leadership, music/drama, religious affiliation.
Scholarships offered: Home-Educated Grant: $500 per semester if home-schooled for two years during high school. Travel Grant: $500 per semester for student who resides in states other than Minnesota, Iowa, Wisconsin. Crossroads Matching Grant: church funds matched up to $500 per semester; awarded to first year students.

FINANCIAL AID PROCEDURES

Forms required: FAFSA, institutional form.

Dates and Deadlines: Priority date 4/1; no closing date. Applicants notified on a rolling basis starting 2/1; must reply within 4 week(s) of notification.

Transfers: Mid-year transfer students will have financial aid calculated with the prior school term award in mind.

CONTACT

Polly Kellogg-Bradley, Director of Financial Aid
920 Mayowood Road, SW, Rochester, MN 55902
(507) 288-4563

Crown College
St. Bonifacius, Minnesota
www.crown.edu   Federal Code: 002383

4-year private liberal arts college in small town, affiliated with Christian and Missionary Alliance.

Enrollment: 936 undergrads, 17% part-time. 149 full-time freshmen.

Selectivity: Admits 50 to 75% of applicants.

BASIC COSTS (2010-2011)

Tuition and fees: $20,870.

Per-credit charge: $870.

Room and board: $7,580.

Additional info: Tuition/fee waivers available for minority students.

FINANCIAL AID PICTURE (2009-2010)

Students with need: Average financial aid package met 66% of need; average scholarship/grant was $6,547; average loan was $3,693. For part-time students, average financial aid package was $3,854.

Students without need: No-need awards available for academics, alumni affiliation, leadership, minority status, music/drama, religious affiliation.

Cumulative student debt: 88% of graduating class had student loans; average debt was $31,804.

FINANCIAL AID PROCEDURES

Forms required: FAFSA, institutional form.

Dates and Deadlines: Priority date 4/1; closing date 8/1. Applicants notified on a rolling basis starting 4/1; must reply within 3 week(s) of notification.

Transfers: No deadline. Applicants notified on a rolling basis; must reply within 3 week(s) of notification. Cannot have attended more than 4 years of college to receive state grant.

CONTACT

Judy Bedford, Director of Financial Aid
8700 College View Drive, St. Bonifacius, MN 55375-9001
(952) 446-4177

Dakota County Technical College
Rosemount, Minnesota
www.dctc.edu   Federal Code: 010402

2-year public technical college in large town.

Enrollment: 2,429 undergrads, 34% part-time. 579 full-time freshmen.

Selectivity: Open admission; but selective for some programs.

BASIC COSTS (2009-2010)

Tuition and fees: $5,084; out-of-state residents $9,544.

Per-credit charge: $149; out-of-state residents $297.

FINANCIAL AID PICTURE

Students with need: Need-based aid available for full-time and part-time students. Work study available nights, weekends, and for part-time students.

Students without need: No-need awards available for academics, leadership.

FINANCIAL AID PROCEDURES

Forms required: FAFSA.

Dates and Deadlines: No deadline. Applicants notified on a rolling basis starting 3/15.

Transfers: No deadline. FAFSA must be processed within 14 days of the first day of the semester to be considered for Minnesota State Grant for the semester.

CONTACT

Scott Roelke, Director of Scholarships and Financial Aid
1300 145th Street East, Rosemount, MN 55068
(651) 423-8299

Dunwoody College of Technology
Minneapolis, Minnesota
www.dunwoody.edu   Federal Code: 004641

2-year private technical college in very large city.

Enrollment: 1,352 undergrads, 11% part-time. 464 full-time freshmen.

Selectivity: Admits 50 to 75% of applicants.

BASIC COSTS (2009-2010)

Tuition and fees: $15,765.

Per-credit charge: $200.

FINANCIAL AID PICTURE (2008-2009)

Students with need: Out of 450 full-time freshmen who applied for aid, 396 were judged to have need. Of these, 365 received aid, and 41 had their full need met. Average financial aid package met 42% of need; average scholarship/grant was $5,239; average loan was $4,273. For part-time students, average financial aid package was $5,828.

Students without need: 14 full-time freshmen who did not demonstrate need for aid received scholarships/grants; average award was $6,435. No-need awards available for academics.

Cumulative student debt: 91% of graduating class had student loans; average debt was $21,363.

FINANCIAL AID PROCEDURES

Forms required: FAFSA, state aid form.

Dates and Deadlines: Priority date 6/1; no closing date. Applicants notified on a rolling basis starting 2/1; must reply within 4 week(s) of notification.

Transfers: No deadline. Applicants notified on a rolling basis starting 7/1.

CONTACT

Barb Charboneau, Director of Financial Aid
818 Dunwoody Boulevard, Minneapolis, MN 55403-1192
(612) 374-5800 ext. 3346

Fond du Lac Tribal and Community College
Cloquet, Minnesota
www.fdltcc.edu   Federal Code: E00482

2-year public community college in large town.

Enrollment: 1,121 full-time undergrads.

Selectivity: Open admission.

BASIC COSTS (2009-2010)

Tuition and fees: $4,560; out-of-state residents $8,668.

Per-credit charge: $137; out-of-state residents $274.

Room only: $3,536.

FINANCIAL AID PICTURE (2009-2010)

Students with need: Need-based aid available for full-time and part-time students.

Students without need: No-need awards available for academics.

FINANCIAL AID PROCEDURES
Forms required: FAFSA, institutional form.
Dates and Deadlines: Priority date 3/15; no closing date. Applicants notified on a rolling basis starting 4/15.

CONTACT
David Sutherland, Director of Financial Aid
2101 14th Street, Cloquet, MN 55720
(218) 879-0816

Globe University
Woodbury, Minnesota
www.globeuniversity.edu   Federal Code: 004642

4-year for-profit business and health science college in small city.
Enrollment: 890 undergrads, 12% part-time. 232 full-time freshmen.
Selectivity: Open admission.

BASIC COSTS (2009-2010)
Tuition and fees: $18,675.
Per-credit charge: $415.

FINANCIAL AID PICTURE (2009-2010)
Students with need: Need-based aid available for full-time and part-time students.

FINANCIAL AID PROCEDURES
Forms required: FAFSA, institutional form.
Dates and Deadlines: No deadline. Applicants notified on a rolling basis starting 5/1.

CONTACT
Ben Flikeid, Director of Financial Aid
8089 Globe Drive, Woodbury, MN 55125
(651) 730-5100 ext. 13336

Gustavus Adolphus College
St. Peter, Minnesota   Federal Code: 002353
www.gustavus.edu   CSS Code: 6253

4-year private liberal arts college in small town, affiliated with Evangelical Lutheran Church in America.
Enrollment: 2,462 undergrads, 1% part-time. 630 full-time freshmen.
Selectivity: Admits 50 to 75% of applicants.

BASIC COSTS (2009-2010)
Tuition and fees: $32,110.
Room and board: $7,900.

FINANCIAL AID PICTURE (2009-2010)
Students with need: Need-based aid available for full-time students. Work study available nights, weekends, and for part-time students.
Students without need: No-need awards available for academics, alumni affiliation, art, music/drama, religious affiliation, ROTC.
Scholarships offered: Presidential Scholarship: $10,000-$14,000. National Merit finalist: $7,500; academic. Legacy Scholarship: $2,500; academic for children or siblings of alumni. Jussi Bjorling Scholarship: $1,000-$4,000; for music; 40 awarded. Anderson Theatre and Dance Scholarship: $2,000; 15 awarded. Dean's Scholarship: $1,000-$10,000; Forensic $500 - $2,000.

FINANCIAL AID PROCEDURES
Forms required: FAFSA. CSS PROFILE required of students applying for need-based assistance.
Dates and Deadlines: Priority date 2/15; closing date 4/15. Applicants notified on a rolling basis starting 12/20; must reply by 5/1 or within 2 week(s) of notification.

Transfers: Applicants notified on a rolling basis starting 12/20; must reply by 5/1 or within 2 week(s) of notification.

CONTACT
Doug Minter, Director of Student Financial Assistance
800 West College Avenue, St. Peter, MN 56082
(507) 933-7527

Hamline University
St. Paul, Minnesota
www.hamline.edu   Federal Code: 002354

4-year private university and liberal arts college in very large city, affiliated with United Methodist Church.
Enrollment: 1,826 undergrads, 3% part-time. 451 full-time freshmen.
Selectivity: Admits over 75% of applicants.

BASIC COSTS (2010-2011)
Tuition and fees: $30,503.
Per-credit charge: $938.
Room and board: $9,014.

FINANCIAL AID PICTURE (2008-2009)
Students with need: Out of 410 full-time freshmen who applied for aid, 358 were judged to have need. Of these, 358 received aid, and 89 had their full need met. Average financial aid package met 85% of need; average scholarship/grant was $15,448; average loan was $4,856. For part-time students, average financial aid package was $7,821.
Students without need: 60 full-time freshmen who did not demonstrate need for aid received scholarships/grants; average award was $12,695. No-need awards available for academics, alumni affiliation, art, leadership, minority status, music/drama, religious affiliation.
Scholarships offered: Academic scholarships ranging from $7,500 to $18,000. Departmental scholarships in biology, chemistry, French, German, music, physics, theater, creative writing: $3,000-$5,000 depending on department. National Merit Finalist Scholarship: $20,000. Bishop Hamline Scholarship - Participation in College Preparedness Program: $6,000. Eagle Scout or Gold Award Scholarships: $3,000. Hamline Heritage Award (legacy scholarship): $2,000. All scholarships renewable for a total of four years.
Cumulative student debt: 79% of graduating class had student loans; average debt was $34,688.

FINANCIAL AID PROCEDURES
Forms required: FAFSA.
Dates and Deadlines: Priority date 3/1; no closing date. Applicants notified on a rolling basis starting 3/1; must reply within 2 week(s) of notification.
Transfers: Priority date 4/1; no deadline. Applicants notified on a rolling basis starting 4/1; must reply within 2 week(s) of notification. Students who qualify for Minnesota State Grant must carry 15 semester credits to qualify for full grant each semester. If less credit is carried, grant prorated.

CONTACT
Lynette Wahl, Director of Financial Aid
1536 Hewitt Avenue, St. Paul, MN 55104-1284
(651) 523-3000

Inver Hills Community College
Inver Grove Heights, Minnesota
www.inverhills.edu   Federal Code: 006935

2-year public community college in large town.
Enrollment: 5,175 undergrads, 55% part-time. 674 full-time freshmen.
Selectivity: Open admission; but selective for some programs.

BASIC COSTS (2009-2010)
Tuition and fees: $4,811.
Per-credit charge: $144.
Additional info: In-state and out-of-state tuition rates are the same.

FINANCIAL AID PICTURE (2008-2009)
Students with need: Average financial aid package met 60% of need; average scholarship/grant was $4,500; average loan was $3,000. For part-time students, average financial aid package was $6,175.
Students without need: This college awards aid only to students with need.

FINANCIAL AID PROCEDURES
Forms required: FAFSA.
Dates and Deadlines: No deadline. Applicants notified on a rolling basis starting 6/1.
Transfers: No deadline. Applicants notified on a rolling basis.

CONTACT
John Pogue, Director
2500 80th Street East, Inver Grove Heights, MN 55076-3224
(651) 450-3518

Itasca Community College
Grand Rapids, Minnesota
www.itascacc.edu   Federal Code: 002356

2-year public junior and liberal arts college in large town.
Enrollment: 1,067 undergrads, 18% part-time. 322 full-time freshmen.
Selectivity: Open admission.

BASIC COSTS (2009-2010)
Tuition and fees: $4,638; out-of-state residents $5,769.
Per-credit charge: $136; out-of-state residents $173.

FINANCIAL AID PICTURE (2008-2009)
Students with need: 59% of average financial aid package awarded as scholarships/grants, 41% awarded as loans/jobs. Need-based aid available for part-time students. Work study available nights, weekends, and for part-time students.
Students without need: No-need awards available for academics, leadership, music/drama, state/district residency.

FINANCIAL AID PROCEDURES
Forms required: FAFSA.
Dates and Deadlines: Priority date 5/1; no closing date. Applicants notified on a rolling basis starting 4/1.
Transfers: No deadline. Applicants notified on a rolling basis starting 4/1.

CONTACT
Nathan Wright, Director of Financial Aid
1851 Highway 169 East, Grand Rapids, MN 55744
(218) 322-2320

Lake Superior College
Duluth, Minnesota
www.lsc.edu   Federal Code: 005757

2-year public community and technical college in small city.
Enrollment: 3,879 undergrads, 40% part-time. 558 full-time freshmen.
Selectivity: Open admission; but selective for some programs.

BASIC COSTS (2009-2010)
Tuition and fees: $1,101, out-of-state residents $8,374.
Per-credit charge: $126; out-of-state residents $258.

FINANCIAL AID PICTURE (2008-2009)
Students with need: Need-based aid available for full-time and part-time students. Work study available nights, weekends, and for part-time students.
Students without need: No-need awards available for academics, leadership.

FINANCIAL AID PROCEDURES
Forms required: FAFSA.
Dates and Deadlines: Priority date 5/1; no closing date. Applicants notified on a rolling basis starting 5/1.
Transfers: No deadline.

CONTACT
LaNita Robinson, Director of Financial Aid
2101 Trinity Road, Duluth, MN 55811
(218) 733-7616

Leech Lake Tribal College
Cass Lake, Minnesota
www.lltc.edu   Federal Code: 030964

2-year public Tribal College grounded in Anishinaabe values. in small town.
Enrollment: 217 undergrads, 24% part-time. 41 full-time freshmen.
Selectivity: Open admission.

BASIC COSTS (2009-2010)
Tuition and fees: $4,432.
Per-credit charge: $140.

FINANCIAL AID PICTURE
Students with need: Need-based aid available for full-time and part-time students.
Students without need: This college awards aid only to students with need.

FINANCIAL AID PROCEDURES
Forms required: FAFSA.
Dates and Deadlines: Closing date 6/30.

CONTACT
Barbara Carlson, Director of Financial Aid
PO Box 180, Cass Lake, MN 56633
(218) 335-4224

Macalester College
St. Paul, Minnesota   Federal Code: 002358
www.macalester.edu/admissions   CSS Code: 6390

4-year private liberal arts college in very large city, affiliated with Presbyterian Church (USA).
Enrollment: 1,965 undergrads. 565 full-time freshmen.
Selectivity: Admits less than 50% of applicants.

BASIC COSTS (2010-2011)
Tuition and fees: $40,046.
Per-credit charge: $1,245.
Room and board: $9,078.

FINANCIAL AID PICTURE (2009-2010)
Students with need: Out of 454 full-time freshmen who applied for aid, 400 were judged to have need. Of these, 400 received aid, and 400 had their full need met. Average financial aid package met 100% of need; average scholarship/grant was $28,280; average loan was $2,909. For part-time students, average financial aid package was $13,574.
Students without need: 29 full-time freshmen who did not demonstrate need for aid received scholarships/grants; average award was $10,000. No-need awards available for academics, minority status.

Scholarships offered: National Merit Scholarships: $5,000; to National Merit Finalists whose first choice college is Macalester. DeWitt Wallace Distinguished Scholarships: minimum $3,000; open to National Merit semifinalists, commended students, and finalists not awarded National Merit Scholarship. DeWitt Wallace Scholarships: minimum $3,000; to selected middle-income students with need and academic records worthy of recognition. Catherine Lealtad Scholarships: minimum $3,000; to African American, Latino, and Native American students with strong high school records. Students who are National Achievement or National Hispanic Scholarship finalists with strong high school record will receive a minimum annual award of $5,000.

Cumulative student debt: 76% of graduating class had student loans; average debt was $17,275.

Additional info: College meets full need for all admitted students. Minnesota Self Loan available to qualified students.

FINANCIAL AID PROCEDURES

Forms required: FAFSA, CSS PROFILE.

Dates and Deadlines: Priority date 2/8; closing date 3/1. Applicants notified by 4/1; must reply by 5/1 or within 1 week(s) of notification.

Transfers: Applicants notified by 5/15; must reply within 2 week(s) of notification.

CONTACT

Brian Lindeman, Director of Financial Aid

1600 Grand Avenue, St. Paul, MN 55105-1899

(651) 696-6214

Martin Luther College

New Ulm, Minnesota

www.mlc-wels.edu   Federal Code: 002361

4-year private college of theology and education in large town, affiliated with Wisconsin Evangelical Lutheran Synod.

Enrollment: 722 undergrads, 3% part-time. 175 full-time freshmen.

Selectivity: Admits over 75% of applicants.

BASIC COSTS (2009-2010)

Tuition and fees: $10,660.

Per-credit charge: $230.

Room and board: $4,140.

FINANCIAL AID PICTURE (2008-2009)

Students with need: Out of 165 full-time freshmen who applied for aid, 130 were judged to have need. Of these, 130 received aid, and 40 had their full need met. Average financial aid package met 60% of need; average scholarship/grant was $4,150; average loan was $3,847. Need-based aid available for part-time students.

Students without need: 25 full-time freshmen who did not demonstrate need for aid received scholarships/grants; average award was $1,570. No-need awards available for academics, music/drama.

Scholarships offered: Academic Scholarship: $500; 3.75 GPA after 6 semesters of high school or 27 ACT. Presidential Scholarship: $1,000; to student selected as high school valedictorian or ranked first in class after 7 semesters.

Cumulative student debt: 47% of graduating class had student loans; average debt was $15,600.

FINANCIAL AID PROCEDURES

Forms required: FAFSA, institutional form.

Dates and Deadlines: Priority date 4/15; closing date 9/30. Applicants notified on a rolling basis starting 3/15.

CONTACT

Gene Slettedahl, Director of Financial Aid

1995 Luther Court, New Ulm, MN 56073-3965

(507) 354-8221

Mesabi Range Community and Technical College

Virginia, Minnesota

www.mr.mnscu.edu   Federal Code: 004009

2-year public community and technical college in large town.

Enrollment: 913 full-time undergrads. 913 full-time freshmen.

Selectivity: Open admission.

BASIC COSTS (2009-2010)

Tuition and fees: $4,644; out-of-state residents $5,761.

Per-credit charge: $136; out-of-state residents $173.

FINANCIAL AID PICTURE (2009-2010)

Students with need: Need-based aid available for full-time and part-time students. Work study available nights, weekends, and for part-time students.

Students without need: No-need awards available for state/district residency.

FINANCIAL AID PROCEDURES

Forms required: FAFSA, institutional form.

Dates and Deadlines: Priority date 4/22; no closing date. Applicants notified on a rolling basis starting 5/1; must reply within 2 week(s) of notification.

CONTACT

George Walters, Director of Financial Aid

1001 Chestnut Street West, Virginia, MN 55792-3448

(218) 741-3095

Metropolitan State University

St. Paul, Minnesota

www.metrostate.edu   Federal Code: 010374

4-year public university in very large city.

Enrollment: 6,178 undergrads, 62% part-time. 66 full-time freshmen.

Selectivity: Admits over 75% of applicants.

BASIC COSTS (2009-2010)

Tuition and fees: $5,627; out-of-state residents $11,173.

Per-credit charge: $177; out-of-state residents $362.

FINANCIAL AID PICTURE (2009-2010)

Students with need: Need-based aid available for full-time and part-time students. Work study available nights, weekends, and for part-time students.

Students without need: No-need awards available for academics, leadership, minority status, state/district residency.

FINANCIAL AID PROCEDURES

Forms required: FAFSA.

Dates and Deadlines: Priority date 5/1; no closing date. Applicants notified on a rolling basis starting 5/1; must reply within 2 week(s) of notification.

CONTACT

Robert Bode, Director of Financial Aid

700 East Seventh Street, St. Paul, MN 55106-5000

(651) 793-1414

Minneapolis College of Art and Design

Minneapolis, Minnesota

www.mcad.edu   Federal Code: 002365

4-year private visual arts college in very large city.

Enrollment: 655 undergrads, 4% part-time. 108 full-time freshmen.

Selectivity: Admits 50 to 75% of applicants.

BASIC COSTS (2010-2011)
Tuition and fees: $29,700.
Per-credit charge: $985.
Room only: $5,115.
Additional info: Purchase of laptop computer ($1,400) required of all new students; laptop requirement may be waived if student has comparable machine with required software.

FINANCIAL AID PICTURE (2009-2010)
Students with need: Need-based aid available for full-time and part-time students.
Students without need: No-need awards available for academics, alumni affiliation, art.
Scholarships offered: Admissions Merit Scholarships: $6,000-$14,000; based on admissions file. Students admitted to the college by February 15 automatically entered into scholarship competition.

FINANCIAL AID PROCEDURES
Forms required: FAFSA.
Dates and Deadlines: Priority date 3/15; closing date 3/15. Applicants notified on a rolling basis starting 4/1; must reply by 5/1 or within 2 week(s) of notification.
Transfers: Applicants notified by 4/1; must reply by 5/1 or within 2 week(s) of notification. Transfer students apply for admission by Feb. 15 (the scholarship priority deadline). Only students accepted will receive an award letter. Complete the FAFSA by March 15. Be sure to include MCAD on the list of schools to receive your FAFSA analysis (Code: 002365).

CONTACT
Laura Link, Director, Financial Aid Office
2501 Stevens Avenue, Minneapolis, MN 55404
(612) 874-8782

Minneapolis Community and Technical College
Minneapolis, Minnesota
www.minneapolis.edu   Federal Code: 002362

2-year public community and technical college in large city.
Enrollment: 9,533 undergrads.
Selectivity: Open admission; but selective for some programs.

BASIC COSTS (2009-2010)
Tuition and fees: $4,885.
Per-credit charge: $141.
Additional info: In-state and out-of-state tuition rates are the same.

FINANCIAL AID PICTURE (2008-2009)
Students with need: Need-based aid available for full-time and part-time students. Work study available nights, weekends, and for part-time students.
Students without need: This college awards aid only to students with need.

FINANCIAL AID PROCEDURES
Forms required: FAFSA.
Dates and Deadlines: Priority date 6/1; no closing date. Applicants notified on a rolling basis starting 7/15; must reply within 2 week(s) of notification.

CONTACT
Angela Christensen, Director of Financial Aid
1501 Hennepin Avenue, Minneapolis, MN 55403-1779
(612) 659-6240

Minnesota School of Business
Minneapolis, Minnesota
www.msbcollege.edu   Federal Code: 017145

4-year for-profit business and technical college in very large city.
Enrollment: 402 full-time undergrads.

BASIC COSTS (2009-2010)
Tuition and fees: $18,675.
Per-credit charge: $415.

FINANCIAL AID PICTURE (2009-2010)
Students with need: Need-based aid available for full-time and part-time students.

FINANCIAL AID PROCEDURES
Forms required: FAFSA, state aid form, institutional form.
Dates and Deadlines: No deadline. Applicants notified on a rolling basis starting 7/1; must reply within 2 week(s) of notification.

CONTACT
Tim Jacobson, Corporate Director of Financial Aid
1401 West 76 Street, Suite 500, Richfield, MN 55423
(612) 861-2000

Minnesota School of Business: Brooklyn Center
Brooklyn Center, Minnesota
www.msbcollege.edu   Federal Code: 004646

2-year for-profit career college in large town.
Enrollment: 688 undergrads.
Selectivity: Admits over 75% of applicants.

BASIC COSTS (2009-2010)
Tuition and fees: $18,675.
Per-credit charge: $415.

FINANCIAL AID PICTURE (2009-2010)
Students with need: Need-based aid available for full-time and part-time students.
Students without need: This college awards aid only to students with need.

FINANCIAL AID PROCEDURES
Forms required: FAFSA.

CONTACT
Kari Martin, Director of Financial Aid
5910 Shingle Creek Parkway, Brooklyn Center, MN 55430
(763) 566-7777

Minnesota School of Business: St. Cloud
Waite Park, Minnesota
www.msbcollege.edu

4-year for-profit virtual university in small city.
Enrollment: 1,003 undergrads.
Selectivity: Admits over 75% of applicants.

BASIC COSTS (2009-2010)
Tuition and fees: $18,675.
Per-credit charge: $415.

FINANCIAL AID PICTURE (2009-2010)
Students with need: Need-based aid available for full-time and part-time students.

CONTACT
Renee Cannon, Director of Financial Aid
1201 Second Street South, Waite Park, MN 55387

Minnesota State College - Southeast Technical
Winona, Minnesota
www.southeastmn.edu   Federal Code: 002393

2-year public technical college in large town.
Enrollment: 2,198 undergrads, 33% part-time. 606 full-time freshmen.
Selectivity: Open admission; but selective for some programs.

BASIC COSTS (2009-2010)
Tuition and fees: $4,711; out-of-state residents $4,711.
Per-credit charge: $145; out-of-state residents $145.
Additional info: In-state and out-of-state tuition rates are the same.

FINANCIAL AID PICTURE (2008-2009)
Students with need: Need-based aid available for full-time and part-time students.
Students without need: No-need awards available for academics, leadership.

FINANCIAL AID PROCEDURES
Forms required: FAFSA, state aid form, institutional form.
Dates and Deadlines: Priority date 5/15; closing date 6/30. Applicants notified on a rolling basis; must reply within 3 week(s) of notification.
Transfers: Applicants notified on a rolling basis; must reply within 3 week(s) of notification. Mid-year transfer application forms must be accompanied by financial aid transcript.

CONTACT
Anne Dahlen, Director of Financial Aid
1250 Homer Road, Winona, MN 55987-0409
(507) 453-2710

Minnesota State Community and Technical College
Fergus Falls, Minnesota
www.minnesota.edu   Federal Code: 002352

2-year public community and technical college in large town.
Enrollment: 3,447 full-time undergrads.
Selectivity: Open admission.

BASIC COSTS (2009-2010)
Tuition and fees: $4,970.
Per-credit charge: $144.
Room only: $2,450.
Additional info: Tuition/fee waivers available for adults.

FINANCIAL AID PICTURE
Students with need: Need-based aid available for full-time and part-time students. Work study available nights, weekends, and for part-time students.
Students without need: No-need awards available for academics, art, leadership, minority status, music/drama, state/district residency.
Scholarships offered: Academic and leadership scholarships: $400-$1,000 each; available to 1st and 2nd year students; over 150 awarded annually.

FINANCIAL AID PROCEDURES
Forms required: FAFSA, institutional form.
Dates and Deadlines: Priority date 6/1; no closing date. Applicants notified on a rolling basis starting 7/1.
Transfers: No deadline. Applicants notified on a rolling basis.

CONTACT
Tom Whelihan, Director of Financial Aid
1414 College Way, Fergus Falls, MN 56537-1000
(218) 736-1534

Minnesota State University Mankato
Mankato, Minnesota
www.mnsu.edu   Federal Code: 002360

4-year public university in large town.
Enrollment: 12,825 undergrads. 2,370 full-time freshmen.
Selectivity: Admits over 75% of applicants.

BASIC COSTS (2009-2010)
Tuition and fees: $6,429; out-of-state residents $12,861.
Per-credit charge: $225; out-of-state residents $481.
Room and board: $6,019.

FINANCIAL AID PICTURE (2008-2009)
Students with need: Out of 1,968 full-time freshmen who applied for aid, 1,206 were judged to have need. Of these, 1,206 received aid, and 464 had their full need met. Average financial aid package met 80% of need; average scholarship/grant was $4,528; average loan was $2,963. For part-time students, average financial aid package was $5,166.
Students without need: 156 full-time freshmen who did not demonstrate need for aid received scholarships/grants; average award was $1,813. No-need awards available for academics, art, athletics, leadership, minority status, music/drama.
Scholarships offered: 54 full-time freshmen received athletic scholarships; average amount $4,168.
Cumulative student debt: 82% of graduating class had student loans; average debt was $22,962.

FINANCIAL AID PROCEDURES
Forms required: FAFSA.
Dates and Deadlines: Priority date 3/15; no closing date. Applicants notified on a rolling basis starting 3/30; must reply within 2 week(s) of notification.

CONTACT
Sandra Loerts, Director of Financial Aid
122 Taylor Center, Mankato, MN 56001
(507) 389-1185

Minnesota State University Moorhead
Moorhead, Minnesota
www.mnstate.edu   Federal Code: 002367

4-year public university in small city.
Enrollment: 6,567 undergrads, 13% part-time. 1,017 full-time freshmen.
Selectivity: Admits over 75% of applicants.

BASIC COSTS (2009-2010)
Tuition and fees: $6,598.
Per-credit charge: $188.
Room and board: $6,242.
Additional info: Out-of-state students pay same rate as in-state.

FINANCIAL AID PICTURE (2009-2010)
Students with need: Need-based aid available for full-time and part-time students.
Students without need: No-need awards available for academics, art, athletics, leadership, minority status, music/drama, state/district residency.

FINANCIAL AID PROCEDURES
Forms required: FAFSA.

Dates and Deadlines: Priority date 2/15; no closing date. Applicants notified on a rolling basis starting 6/1; must reply within 2 week(s) of notification.

CONTACT

Carolyn Zehren, Director of Financial Aid and Scholarships
Owens Hall, Moorhead, MN 56563
(218) 236-2251

Minnesota West Community and Technical College

Pipestone, Minnesota
www.mnwest.edu   Federal Code: 005263

2-year public community and technical college in large town.
Enrollment: 2,588 undergrads, 39% part-time. 440 full-time freshmen.
Selectivity: Open admission; but selective for some programs.

BASIC COSTS (2009-2010)
Tuition and fees: $4,937.
Per-credit charge: $149.
Additional info: In-state and out-of-state tuition rates are the same.

FINANCIAL AID PICTURE (2009-2010)
Students with need: Need-based aid available for full-time and part-time students. Work study available nights, weekends, and for part-time students.

FINANCIAL AID PROCEDURES
Forms required: FAFSA.
Dates and Deadlines: Priority date 6/9; no closing date. Applicants notified on a rolling basis starting 4/9; must reply within 2 week(s) of notification.

CONTACT

Jodi Landgaard, Financial Aid Director
1314 North Hiawatha Avenue, Pipestone, MN 56164
(800) 657-3966 ext. 3403

National American University: Bloomington

Bloomington, Minnesota
www.national.edu   Federal Code: E00640

4-year for-profit branch campus and business college in very large city.
Enrollment: 400 undergrads.
Selectivity: Open admission.

BASIC COSTS (2009-2010)
Tuition and fees: $14,975.
Additional info: Required fees include a one-time matriculation fee ($50) and one-time assessment fee ($75).

FINANCIAL AID PICTURE
Students with need: Need-based aid available for full-time and part-time students. Work study available nights, weekends, and for part-time students.
Students without need: No-need awards available for academics.

FINANCIAL AID PROCEDURES
Forms required: FAFSA.
Dates and Deadlines: Priority date 8/21; no closing date. Applicants notified on a rolling basis.

CONTACT

Auriel Collins, Financial Aid Coordinator
Mall of America West 112 West Market, Bloomington, MN 55425

Normandale Community College

Bloomington, Minnesota
www.normandale.edu   Federal Code: 007954

2-year public community college in very large city.
Enrollment: 10,094 undergrads.
Selectivity: Open admission; but selective for some programs.

BASIC COSTS (2009-2010)
Tuition and fees: $4,888.
Per-credit charge: $141.
Additional info: In-state and out-of-state tuition rates are the same.

FINANCIAL AID PICTURE (2008-2009)
Students with need: 56% of average financial aid package awarded as scholarships/grants, 44% awarded as loans/jobs. Need-based aid available for part-time students. Work study available nights, weekends, and for part-time students.
Students without need: No-need awards available for academics, leadership, music/drama, state/district residency.

FINANCIAL AID PROCEDURES
Forms required: FAFSA.
Dates and Deadlines: Priority date 4/1; no closing date. Applicants notified on a rolling basis starting 4/15.

CONTACT

Catherine Breuer, Associate Dean of Students
9700 France Avenue South, Bloomington, MN 55431
(952) 487-8202

North Central University

Minneapolis, Minnesota
www.northcentral.edu   Federal Code: 002369

4-year private university and Bible college in large city, affiliated with Assemblies of God.
Enrollment: 1,050 undergrads, 16% part-time. 271 full-time freshmen.
Selectivity: Admits over 75% of applicants.

BASIC COSTS (2010-2011)
Tuition and fees: $15,995.
Per-credit charge: $522.
Room and board: $5,360.

FINANCIAL AID PICTURE (2008-2009)
Students with need: Need-based aid available for full-time and part-time students. Work study available nights, weekends, and for part-time students.
Students without need: No-need awards available for academics, leadership, music/drama.
Scholarships offered: President's Scholarship: $2,500 per year; renewable; based on academic performance. Dean's Scholarship: $1,500 per year; renewable; based on academic performance. First Choice Scholarship awarded to those who submit their application early and meet academic criteria.

FINANCIAL AID PROCEDURES
Forms required: FAFSA.
Dates and Deadlines: No deadline. Applicants notified on a rolling basis starting 3/1; must reply within 2 week(s) of notification.
Transfers: Priority date 4/15; no deadline. Applicants notified on a rolling basis starting 3/1.

CONTACT

Donna Jager, Director of Financial Aid
910 Elliot Avenue, Minneapolis, MN 55404
(800) 289-4488 ext. 289

North Hennepin Community College

Brooklyn Park, Minnesota
www.nhcc.edu   Federal Code: 002370

2-year public community college in small city.
Enrollment: 7,188 undergrads, 59% part-time. 900 full-time freshmen.
Selectivity: Open admission; but selective for some programs.

BASIC COSTS (2009-2010)
Tuition and fees: $4,749.
Per-credit charge: $144.
Additional info: In-state and out-of-state tuition rates are the same.

FINANCIAL AID PICTURE (2008-2009)
Students with need: Need-based aid available for full-time and part-time students. Work study available nights, weekends, and for part-time students.
Students without need: No-need awards available for academics, art, leadership.
Additional info: Computerized financial aid application.

FINANCIAL AID PROCEDURES
Forms required: FAFSA.
Dates and Deadlines: Priority date 4/15; no closing date. Applicants notified on a rolling basis starting 6/1.
Transfers: No deadline. Applicants notified on a rolling basis.

CONTACT
Jackie Olsson, Director of Financial Aid
7411 85th Avenue North, Brooklyn Park, MN 55445
(763) 424-0702

Northland Community & Technical College

Thief River Falls, Minnesota
www.northlandcollege.edu   Federal Code: 002385

2-year public community and technical college in small town.
Enrollment: 575 full-time undergrads.
Selectivity: Open admission.

BASIC COSTS (2009-2010)
Tuition and fees: $4,899.
Per-credit charge: $147.
Additional info: In-state and out-of-state tuition rates are the same.

FINANCIAL AID PICTURE (2008-2009)
Students with need: Need-based aid available for full-time and part-time students. Work study available nights.
Students without need: No-need awards available for academics.

FINANCIAL AID PROCEDURES
Forms required: FAFSA.
Dates and Deadlines: Priority date 5/1; no closing date. Applicants notified on a rolling basis starting 5/15.

CONTACT
Gerald Schulte, Financial Aid Director
1101 Highway One East, Thief River Falls, MN 56701
(218) 681-0946

Northwest Technical College

Bemidji, Minnesota
www.ntcmn.edu   Federal Code: 005759

2-year public technical college in large town.
Enrollment: 1,031 undergrads, 44% part-time. 172 full-time freshmen.

Selectivity: Open admission.

BASIC COSTS (2009-2010)
Tuition and fees: $4,955.
Per-credit charge: $154.

FINANCIAL AID PICTURE (2009-2010)
Students with need: 59% of average financial aid package awarded as scholarships/grants, 41% awarded as loans/jobs. Need-based aid available for part-time students. Work study available nights.
Students without need: This college awards aid only to students with need.

FINANCIAL AID PROCEDURES
Forms required: FAFSA, institutional form.
Dates and Deadlines: Priority date 7/1; no closing date. Applicants notified on a rolling basis.

CONTACT
Paul Lindseth, Director of Financial Aid
905 Grant Avenue Southeast, Bemidji, MN 56601-4907
(218) 333-6648

Northwest Technical Institute

Eagan, Minnesota
www.nti.edu   Federal Code: 008267

2-year for-profit technical college in small city.
Enrollment: 126 undergrads.
Selectivity: Open admission.

BASIC COSTS (2009-2010)
Tuition and fees: $16,975.
Per-credit charge: $529.

FINANCIAL AID PICTURE
Students with need: Need-based aid available for full-time and part-time students.

FINANCIAL AID PROCEDURES
Forms required: FAFSA, institutional form.
Dates and Deadlines: No deadline. Applicants notified on a rolling basis; must reply within 2 week(s) of notification.

CONTACT
Katherine Spear, Director of Financial Aid
950 Blue Gentian Road, Eagan, MN 55121
(952) 944-0080 ext. 101

Northwestern College

Saint Paul, Minnesota
www.nwc.edu   Federal Code: 002371

4-year private liberal arts college in very large city, affiliated with nondenominational tradition.
Enrollment: 1,852 undergrads, 3% part-time. 435 full-time freshmen.
Selectivity: Admits over 75% of applicants.

BASIC COSTS (2010-2011)
Tuition and fees: $24,570.
Per-credit charge: $1,040.
Room and board: $7,720.
Additional info: Tuition/fee waivers available for minority students.

FINANCIAL AID PICTURE (2008-2009)

Students with need: Out of 408 full-time freshmen who applied for aid, 348 were judged to have need. Of these, 348 received aid, and 30 had their full need met. Average financial aid package met 70% of need; average scholarship/grant was $11,949; average loan was $3,830. For part-time students, average financial aid package was $8,768.

Students without need: 77 full-time freshmen who did not demonstrate need for aid received scholarships/grants; average award was $6,150. No-need awards available for academics, alumni affiliation, leadership, music/drama.

Scholarships offered: Eagle Scholars Program: $12,000-$15,000 per year; ACT score of 30 or SAT score of 1320; up to 15 awarded yearly to incoming freshmen; renewable annually with successful involvement in program, including a cumulative GPA of 3.65 or higher.

Cumulative student debt: 84% of graduating class had student loans; average debt was $26,259.

Additional info: Students enrolled at least half-time in the FOCUS or Distance Education degree programs may apply for financial aid from the same Federal and state sources as traditional undergraduates. However, their expense budgets and aid are less due to lower tuition: FOCUS, $345/credit; Center for Distance Education, $260/credit.

FINANCIAL AID PROCEDURES

Forms required: FAFSA, institutional form.

Dates and Deadlines: Priority date 3/1; closing date 8/1. Applicants notified on a rolling basis starting 3/1; must reply within 2 week(s) of notification.

CONTACT

Richard Blatchley, Director of Financial Aid
3003 Snelling Avenue North, Saint Paul, MN 55113-1598
(651) 631-5212

Oak Hills Christian College

Bemidji, Minnesota
www.oakhills.edu   Federal Code: 016116

4-year private Bible college in large town, affiliated with interdenominational tradition.

Enrollment: 149 undergrads, 17% part-time. 33 full-time freshmen.

Selectivity: Admits 50 to 75% of applicants.

BASIC COSTS (2010-2011)

Tuition and fees: $14,110.
Per-credit charge: $580.
Room and board: $9,960.

FINANCIAL AID PICTURE (2008-2009)

Students with need: Need-based aid available for full-time and part-time students. Work study available nights, weekends, and for part-time students.

Students without need: No-need awards available for academics, alumni affiliation.

FINANCIAL AID PROCEDURES

Forms required: FAFSA, institutional form.

Dates and Deadlines: No deadline. Applicants notified on a rolling basis starting 3/1.

Transfers: No deadline. Applicants notified on a rolling basis starting 3/1.

CONTACT

Dan Hovestol, Financial Aid Director
1600 Oak Hills Road SW, Bemidji, MN 56601-8826
(218) 751-8671 ext. 1220

Pine Technical College

Pine City, Minnesota
www.pinetech.edu   Federal Code: 005535

2-year public technical college in small town.

Enrollment: 387 full-time undergrads.

Selectivity: Open admission; but selective for some programs.

BASIC COSTS (2009-2010)

Tuition and fees: $4,457; out-of-state residents $8,427.
Per-credit charge: $132; out-of-state residents $265.

FINANCIAL AID PICTURE

Students with need: Need-based aid available for full-time and part-time students.

Students without need: No-need awards available for academics, state/district residency.

FINANCIAL AID PROCEDURES

Forms required: FAFSA, institutional form.

Dates and Deadlines: Priority date 5/5; no closing date. Applicants notified on a rolling basis starting 6/5.

CONTACT

Susan Pixley, Financial Aid Director
900 Fourth Street, SE, Pine City, MN 55063
(320) 629-5100 ext. 161

Rainy River Community College

International Falls, Minnesota
www.rrcc.mnscu.edu   Federal Code: 006775

2-year public community and technical college in small town.

Enrollment: 322 undergrads, 18% part-time.

Selectivity: Open admission.

BASIC COSTS (2009-2010)

Tuition and fees: $4,660; out-of-state residents $5,791.
Per-credit charge: $136; out-of-state residents $173.
Room and board: $3,280.

Additional info: Tuition/fee waivers available for unemployed or children of unemployed.

FINANCIAL AID PICTURE (2009-2010)

Students with need: 58% of average financial aid package awarded as scholarships/grants, 42% awarded as loans/jobs. Need-based aid available for part-time students. Work study available nights, weekends, and for part-time students.

Students without need: No-need awards available for academics, alumni affiliation, minority status, state/district residency.

Additional info: Many scholarship and employment opportunities for applicants showing little or no need.

FINANCIAL AID PROCEDURES

Forms required: FAFSA, institutional form.

Dates and Deadlines: Priority date 6/1; no closing date. Applicants notified on a rolling basis starting 5/1; must reply within 3 week(s) of notification.

CONTACT

Scott Riley, Director of Financial Aid
1501 Highway 71, International Falls, MN 56649
(218) 285-7722

Rasmussen College: Brooklyn Park
Brooklyn Park, Minnesota
www.rasmussen.edu

2-year for-profit career college in small city.
Enrollment: 1,118 undergrads.
Selectivity: Open admission; but selective for some programs.

BASIC COSTS (2009-2010)
Additional info: Regular courses are $420 per credit hour; networking classes: $535/credit; child care classes: $295/credit; practical nursing classes: $515/credit.

FINANCIAL AID PICTURE
Students with need: Need-based aid available for full-time and part-time students.

FINANCIAL AID PROCEDURES
Forms required: FAFSA, institutional form.
Dates and Deadlines: No deadline. Applicants notified on a rolling basis.

CONTACT
Steve Yang, Director of Student Financial Services
8301 93rd Avenue North, Brooklyn Park, MN 55445

Rasmussen College: Eagan
Eagan, Minnesota
www.rasmussen.edu   Federal Code: 004648

2-year for-profit career college in small city.
Enrollment: 888 undergrads.
Selectivity: Open admission; but selective for some programs.

BASIC COSTS (2009-2010)
Additional info: Regular courses are $420 per credit hour; networking classes: $535/credit; child care classes: $295/credit; practical nursing classes: $515/credit.

FINANCIAL AID PICTURE (2008-2009)
Students with need: Need-based aid available for full-time and part-time students.

FINANCIAL AID PROCEDURES
Forms required: FAFSA, institutional form.
Dates and Deadlines: No deadline. Applicants notified on a rolling basis.

CONTACT
Lindsay Kagol, Director of Student Financial Services
3500 Federal Drive, Eagan, MN 55122
(651) 687-9000

Rasmussen College: Eden Prairie
Eden Prairie, Minnesota
www.rasmussen.edu   Federal Code: 011686

2-year for-profit career college in small city.
Enrollment: 1,366 undergrads.
Selectivity: Open admission; but selective for some programs.

BASIC COSTS (2009-2010)
Additional info: Regular courses are $420 per credit hour; networking classes: $535/credit; child care classes: $295/credit.

FINANCIAL AID PICTURE
Students with need: Need-based aid available for full-time and part-time students.

FINANCIAL AID PROCEDURES
Forms required: FAFSA, institutional form.
Dates and Deadlines: No deadline. Applicants notified on a rolling basis.

CONTACT
Alan Grueneich, Director of Student Financial Services
7905 Golden Triangle Drive, Suite 100, Eden Prairie, MN 55344
(952) 545-2000

Rasmussen College: Mankato
Mankato, Minnesota
www.rasmussen.edu   Federal Code: 016845

2-year for-profit career college in large town.
Enrollment: 858 undergrads.
Selectivity: Open admission; but selective for some programs.

BASIC COSTS (2009-2010)
Additional info: Regular courses are $420 per credit hour; networking classes: $535/credit; child care classes: $295/credit; practical nursing classes: $515/credit.

FINANCIAL AID PICTURE
Students with need: Need-based aid available for full-time and part-time students.

FINANCIAL AID PROCEDURES
Forms required: FAFSA, institutional form.
Dates and Deadlines: No deadline. Applicants notified on a rolling basis.

CONTACT
Michelle Ahrendt, Director of Financial Aid
130 Saint Andrews Drive, Mankato, MN 56001
(507) 625-6556

Rasmussen College: St. Cloud
St. Cloud, Minnesota
www.rasmussen.edu   Federal Code: 008694

2-year for-profit community and career college in small city.
Enrollment: 1,116 undergrads.
Selectivity: Open admission; but selective for some programs.

BASIC COSTS (2009-2010)
Additional info: Regular courses are $420 per credit hour; networking classes: $535/credit; child care classes: $295/credit; practical nursing classes: $515/credit.

FINANCIAL AID PICTURE (2009-2010)
Students with need: Need-based aid available for full-time and part-time students.

FINANCIAL AID PROCEDURES
Forms required: FAFSA, institutional form.
Dates and Deadlines: No deadline. Applicants notified on a rolling basis.

CONTACT
Carole Inderrieden, Director of Student Financial Services
226 Park Avenue South, St. Cloud, MN 56301-3713
(320) 251-5600

Ridgewater College

Willmar, Minnesota
www.ridgewater.edu   Federal Code: 005252

2-year public community and technical college in large town.
Enrollment: 3,633 undergrads.
Selectivity: Open admission; but selective for some programs.

BASIC COSTS (2009-2010)

Tuition and fees: $4,729.
Per-credit charge: $141.
Additional info: In-state and out-of-state tuition rates are the same. Tuition/fee waivers available for adults.

FINANCIAL AID PICTURE (2009-2010)

Students with need: Need-based aid available for full-time and part-time students. Work study available nights, weekends, and for part-time students.
Additional info: Special funds are available for adult transfer students returning or continuing education after a 7-year absence from academic training. ALLISS grants provide reimbursement for one class, up to five credits for one semester.

FINANCIAL AID PROCEDURES

Forms required: FAFSA, institutional form.
Dates and Deadlines: No deadline. Applicants notified on a rolling basis.

CONTACT

Jim Rice, Director of Financial Aid
2101 15th Avenue Northwest, Willmar, MN 56201
(320) 222-7474

Riverland Community College

Austin, Minnesota
www.riverland.edu   Federal Code: 002335

2-year public community and technical college in large town.
Enrollment: 3,230 undergrads, 58% part-time. 407 full-time freshmen.
Selectivity: Open admission; but selective for some programs.

BASIC COSTS (2009-2010)

Tuition and fees: $4,841.
Per-credit charge: $143.
Room only: $2,640.
Additional info: In-state and out-of-state tuition rates are the same.

FINANCIAL AID PICTURE (2008-2009)

Students with need: Need-based aid available for full-time and part-time students.
Students without need: No-need awards available for alumni affiliation, art, job skills, leadership, music/drama, state/district residency.
Additional info: One class tuition-free for Minnesota residents over 25 who have not attended college for at least 7 years.

FINANCIAL AID PROCEDURES

Forms required: FAFSA.
Dates and Deadlines: Priority date 5/15; no closing date. Applicants notified on a rolling basis; must reply within 5 week(s) of notification.
Transfers: No deadline. Applicants notified on a rolling basis.

CONTACT

Judy Robeck, Financial Aid Director
1900 Eighth Avenue, NW, Austin, MN 55912-1407
(507) 433-0511

Rochester Community and Technical College

Rochester, Minnesota
www.roch.edu   Federal Code: 002373

2-year public community and technical college in small city.
Enrollment: 6,266 undergrads. 1,758 full-time freshmen.
Selectivity: Open admission; but selective for some programs.

BASIC COSTS (2009-2010)

Tuition and fees: $5,028.
Per-credit charge: $145.

FINANCIAL AID PICTURE

Students with need: Need-based aid available for full-time and part-time students. Work study available nights, weekends, and for part-time students.

FINANCIAL AID PROCEDURES

Forms required: FAFSA.
Dates and Deadlines: Priority date 4/15; no closing date. Applicants notified on a rolling basis.

CONTACT

Rosemary Hicks, Director of Financial Aid
851 30th Avenue SE, Rochester, MN 55904-4999
(507) 285-7271

St. Catherine University

Saint Paul, Minnesota
www.stkate.edu   Federal Code: 002342

4-year private health science and liberal arts college for women in large city, affiliated with Roman Catholic Church.
Enrollment: 3,689 undergrads, 33% part-time. 359 full-time freshmen.
Selectivity: Admits 50 to 75% of applicants.

BASIC COSTS (2010-2011)

Tuition and fees: $28,400.
Per-credit charge: $934.
Room and board: $7,658.

FINANCIAL AID PICTURE (2008-2009)

Students with need: Out of 340 full-time freshmen who applied for aid, 305 were judged to have need. Of these, 305 received aid, and 30 had their full need met. Average financial aid package met 86% of need; average scholarship/grant was $11,400; average loan was $6,250. For part-time students, average financial aid package was $21,000.
Students without need: 34 full-time freshmen who did not demonstrate need for aid received scholarships/grants; average award was $7,500. No-need awards available for academics, alumni affiliation, leadership, state/district residency.
Scholarships offered: St. Catherine of Alexandria Merit Scholarships: $2,000-$6,000; high school seniors in top 15% of class, evidence of academic preparation, outstanding leadership abilities, involvement in extracurricular activities and community service; renewable for 3 years.
Cumulative student debt: 96% of graduating class had student loans; average debt was $24,400.
Additional info: Audition required for music scholarships.

FINANCIAL AID PROCEDURES

Forms required: FAFSA, institutional form.
Dates and Deadlines: Priority date 4/15; no closing date. Applicants notified on a rolling basis starting 3/30; must reply within 2 week(s) of notification.

CONTACT

Elizabeth Stevens, Director of Financial Aid
2004 Randolph Avenue #4-02, St. Paul, MN 55105
(651) 690-6540

Saint Cloud State University
St. Cloud, Minnesota
www.stcloudstate.edu   Federal Code: 002377

4-year public university in small city.
Enrollment: 13,718 undergrads, 12% part-time. 2,332 full-time freshmen.
Selectivity: Admits over 75% of applicants.

BASIC COSTS (2009-2010)
Tuition and fees: $6,330; out-of-state residents $13,844.
Per-credit charge: $186; out-of-state residents $411.
Room and board: $6,016.

FINANCIAL AID PICTURE (2009-2010)
Students with need: Work study available nights, weekends, and for part-time students.
Students without need: No-need awards available for academics, art, athletics, leadership, music/drama.

FINANCIAL AID PROCEDURES
Forms required: FAFSA, institutional form.
Dates and Deadlines: No deadline. Applicants notified on a rolling basis starting 6/15.
Transfers: No deadline. Applicants notified on a rolling basis starting 6/15.

CONTACT
Michael Uran, Financial Aid Director
720 Fourth Avenue South, St. Cloud, MN 56301
(320) 308-2047

St. Cloud Technical College
St. Cloud, Minnesota
www.sctc.edu   Federal Code: 005534

2-year public technical college in small city.
Enrollment: 4,016 undergrads, 33% part-time. 810 full-time freshmen.
Selectivity: Open admission; but selective for some programs.

BASIC COSTS (2009-2010)
Tuition and fees: $4,737.
Per-credit charge: $141.
Additional info: In-state and out-of-state tuition rates are the same.

FINANCIAL AID PICTURE (2008-2009)
Students with need: 54% of average financial aid package awarded as scholarships/grants, 46% awarded as loans/jobs. Need-based aid available for part-time students. Work study available nights, weekends, and for part-time students.
Students without need: No-need awards available for academics, leadership, state/district residency.

FINANCIAL AID PROCEDURES
Forms required: FAFSA, institutional form.
Dates and Deadlines: No deadline. Applicants notified on a rolling basis starting 6/1.

CONTACT
Anita Baugh, Financial Aid Director
1540 Northway Drive, St. Cloud, MN 56303
(320) 308-5961

St. John's University
Collegeville, Minnesota
www.csbsju.edu   Federal Code: 002379

4-year private university and liberal arts college for men in rural community, affiliated with Roman Catholic Church.
Enrollment: 1,915 undergrads, 3% part-time. 461 full-time freshmen.
Selectivity: Admits over 75% of applicants.

BASIC COSTS (2010-2011)
Tuition and fees: $31,576.
Per-credit charge: $1,292.
Room and board: $8,044.

FINANCIAL AID PICTURE (2009-2010)
Students with need: Out of 361 full-time freshmen who applied for aid, 275 were judged to have need. Of these, 275 received aid, and 166 had their full need met. Average financial aid package met 96% of need; average scholarship/grant was $20,744; average loan was $4,234. For part-time students, average financial aid package was $11,335.
Students without need: 144 full-time freshmen who did not demonstrate need for aid received scholarships/grants; average award was $12,148. No-need awards available for academics, art, leadership, music/drama, ROTC.
Scholarships offered: Regents/Trustees Scholarships: $16,000; minimum 3.6 GPA, 30 ACT, 1980 SAT, demonstrated leadership and service, faculty interview. President's Scholarships: $10,500-$13,500; and Dean's Scholarships: $3,000-$9,500; GPA, high school rank, ACT/SAT scores, leadership and service considered. Art, music and theater scholarships: up to $4,000. Diversity Leadership Scholarships: up to $5,000; demonstrated diversity leadership and service in the area of cultural and ethnic diversity, personal statement on topic. Army ROTC and ROTC Nursing Scholarships: tuition and fees; demonstrated leadership potential, high school GPA, class standing, ACT/SAT scores, high achievement with broad interests and willingness to take on challenges. Catholic High School Scholarship: $3,000; Students attending Catholic high schools outside Minnesota. Saints Scholarship: $1,000- $3,000 ; students attending public high schools outside Minnesota. Phi Theta Kappa Scholarship: $1,000; member of Phi Theta Kappa (transfer students only).

FINANCIAL AID PROCEDURES
Forms required: FAFSA, institutional form.
Dates and Deadlines: Priority date 3/15; no closing date. Applicants notified on a rolling basis starting 3/15; must reply by 5/1.

CONTACT
Stuart Perry, Director of Financial Aid
College of St Benedict/St John's University, Collegeville, MN 56321-7155
(320) 363-3664

St. Mary's University of Minnesota
Winona, Minnesota
www.smumn.edu   Federal Code: 002380

4-year private university in large town, affiliated with Roman Catholic Church.
Enrollment: 2,046 undergrads, 30% part-time. 330 full-time freshmen.
Selectivity: Admits 50 to 75% of applicants.

BASIC COSTS (2010-2011)
Tuition and fees: $26,090.
Per-credit charge: $850.
Room and board: $6,940.

FINANCIAL AID PICTURE (2009-2010)

Students with need: Out of 300 full-time freshmen who applied for aid, 269 were judged to have need. Of these, 269 received aid, and 52 had their full need met. Average financial aid package met 82% of need; average scholarship/grant was $16,374; average loan was $4,091. Need-based aid available for part-time students.

Students without need: 58 full-time freshmen who did not demonstrate need for aid received scholarships/grants; average award was $8,672. No-need awards available for academics, alumni affiliation, art, leadership, minority status, music/drama.

Cumulative student debt: 77% of graduating class had student loans; average debt was $32,166.

FINANCIAL AID PROCEDURES

Forms required: FAFSA.

Dates and Deadlines: Priority date 3/15; no closing date. Applicants notified on a rolling basis starting 2/1; must reply within 3 week(s) of notification.

Transfers: No deadline. Applicants notified on a rolling basis starting 2/1.

CONTACT

Jayne Wobig, Director of Financial Aid
700 Terrace Heights #2, Winona, MN 55987-1399
(507) 457-1437

St. Olaf College

Northfield, Minnesota — Federal Code: 002382
www.stolaf.edu — CSS Code: 6638

4-year private liberal arts college in large town, affiliated with Evangelical Lutheran Church in America.

Enrollment: 3,033 undergrads. 778 full-time freshmen.

Selectivity: Admits 50 to 75% of applicants.

BASIC COSTS (2010-2011)

Tuition and fees: $36,800.

Per-credit charge: $1,150.

Room and board: $8,500.

Additional info: Tuition/fee waivers available for adults.

FINANCIAL AID PICTURE (2009-2010)

Students with need: Need-based aid available for full-time students. Work study available nights, weekends, and for part-time students.

Students without need: No-need awards available for academics, leadership, music/drama.

Scholarships offered: Buntrock Scholarship: $14,000. Presidential Scholarship: $8,500. National Hispanic Scholar/National Achievement: $7,500. National Merit Scholarship: $7,500; TRiO Scholarships: $6,000. Music scholarships: $4,000 - $10,000. Service leadership awards: $6,000. All are 4-year renewable; number awarded varies yearly.

Additional info: Limited number of music lesson fee waivers available for music majors, awarded on audition basis only.

FINANCIAL AID PROCEDURES

Forms required: FAFSA, CSS PROFILE.

Dates and Deadlines: Priority date 1/15; closing date 2/1. Applicants notified on a rolling basis starting 3/1; must reply by 5/1 or within 2 week(s) of notification.

Transfers: Closing date 3/1. Must reply by 5/1 or within 2 week(s) of notification.

CONTACT

Katharine Ruby, Assistant Vice President for Enrollment and Dean of Student Financial Aid
1520 St. Olaf Avenue, Northfield, MN 55057
(507) 786-3019

St. Paul College

Saint Paul, Minnesota
www.saintpaul.edu — Federal Code: 005533

2-year public community and technical college in large city.

Enrollment: 5,456 undergrads, 56% part-time. 5,376 full-time freshmen.

Selectivity: Open admission; but selective for some programs.

BASIC COSTS (2009-2010)

Tuition and fees: $4,642.

Per-credit charge: $143.

Additional info: In-state and out-of-state tuition rates are the same.

FINANCIAL AID PICTURE (2009-2010)

Students with need: Out of 3,225 full-time freshmen who applied for aid, 2,857 were judged to have need. Of these, 2,599 received aid. Need-based aid available for part-time students.

Students without need: No-need awards available for leadership.

FINANCIAL AID PROCEDURES

Forms required: FAFSA.

Dates and Deadlines: No deadline. Applicants notified on a rolling basis starting 6/1.

Transfers: Priority date 5/1; no deadline. Applicants notified on a rolling basis starting 6/1.

CONTACT

Susan Pixley, Financial Aid Director
235 Marshall Avenue, Saint Paul, MN 55102-1800
(651) 846-1386

South Central College

North Mankato, Minnesota
www.southcentral.edu — Federal Code: 005537

2-year public community and technical college in large town.

Enrollment: 3,662 undergrads.

Selectivity: Open admission.

BASIC COSTS (2009-2010)

Tuition and fees: $4,697.

Per-credit charge: $139.

FINANCIAL AID PICTURE (2008-2009)

Students with need: Need-based aid available for full-time and part-time students. Work study available nights.

FINANCIAL AID PROCEDURES

Forms required: FAFSA, institutional form.

Dates and Deadlines: Priority date 5/1; no closing date. Applicants notified on a rolling basis starting 6/1.

Transfers: No deadline. Applicants notified on a rolling basis starting 6/1.

CONTACT

Jayne Dinse, Financial Aid Director
1920 Lee Boulevard, North Mankato, MN 56003
(507) 389-7220

Southwest Minnesota State University

Marshall, Minnesota
www.smsu.edu — Federal Code: 002375

4-year public university and liberal arts college in large town.

Enrollment: 2,584 undergrads, 13% part-time. 456 full-time freshmen.

Selectivity: Admits 50 to 75% of applicants.

BASIC COSTS (2009-2010)

Tuition and fees: $6,932.

Per-credit charge: $192.

Room and board: $6,520.

Additional info: Out-of-state students pay same rate as in-state.

FINANCIAL AID PICTURE (2009-2010)

Students with need: Out of 394 full-time freshmen who applied for aid, 295 were judged to have need. Of these, 291 received aid, and 50 had their full need met. Average financial aid package met 61% of need; average scholarship/grant was $5,598; average loan was $3,438. For part-time students, average financial aid package was $5,357.

Students without need: 95 full-time freshmen who did not demonstrate need for aid received scholarships/grants; average award was $3,036. No-need awards available for academics, alumni affiliation, art, athletics, leadership, minority status, music/drama, state/district residency.

Scholarships offered: 52 full-time freshmen received athletic scholarships; average amount $3,994.

Cumulative student debt: 82% of graduating class had student loans; average debt was $24,431.

FINANCIAL AID PROCEDURES

Forms required: FAFSA, institutional form.

Dates and Deadlines: Priority date 3/1; no closing date. Applicants notified on a rolling basis starting 6/1.

CONTACT

David Vikander, Director of Financial Aid

1501 State Street, Marshall, MN 56258-1598

(507) 537-6281

University of Minnesota: Crookston

Crookston, Minnesota

www.UMCrookston.edu   Federal Code: 004069

4-year public branch campus college in small town.

Enrollment: 1,310 undergrads, 18% part-time. 274 full-time freshmen.

Selectivity: Admits over 75% of applicants.

BASIC COSTS (2009-2010)

Tuition and fees: $9,988.

Per-credit charge: $284.

Room and board: $6,254.

Additional info: In-state and out-of-state tuition rates are the same. Tuition/fee waivers available for minority students.

FINANCIAL AID PICTURE (2009-2010)

Students with need: Need-based aid available for full-time and part-time students. Work study available nights, weekends, and for part-time students.

Students without need: No-need awards available for academics, alumni affiliation, athletics, leadership, minority status, music/drama, ROTC, state/district residency.

Scholarships offered: Merit Scholarship: based on a minimum GPA of 3.25 and a minimum ACT score of 21. Presidential Scholarship: $20,000 total ($5,000 annually for four years); based on ACT score of 30 and GPA of 3.25. Chancellor Scholarship: $8,000 total ($4,000 annually for two years); based on ACT score of 27-29 and GPA of 3.25. Distinguished Scholarship: $6,000 total ($3,000 annually for two years); based on ACT score of 25-26 and 3.25 GPA. Merriam Legacy Scholarship: $4,000 total ($2,000 annually for two years); based on ACT score of 23-24 and a 3.25 GPA. Achievement Scholarship: $2,000; based on ACT score of 21-22 and 3.25 GPA.

FINANCIAL AID PROCEDURES

Forms required: FAFSA.

Dates and Deadlines: Priority date 2/15; no closing date. Applicants notified on a rolling basis starting 3/15.

CONTACT

Melissa Dingmann, Director of Financial Aid

2900 University Avenue, Crookston, MN 56716-5001

(218) 281-8563

University of Minnesota: Duluth

Duluth, Minnesota

www.d.umn.edu   Federal Code: 002388

4-year public university in small city.

Enrollment: 9,422 undergrads, 4% part-time. 2,111 full-time freshmen.

Selectivity: Admits 50 to 75% of applicants.

BASIC COSTS (2009-2010)

Tuition and fees: $11,004; out-of-state residents $13,004.

Per-credit charge: $340; out-of-state residents $417.

Room and board: $6,176.

FINANCIAL AID PICTURE (2008-2009)

Students with need: Out of 1,782 full-time freshmen who applied for aid, 1,229 were judged to have need. Of these, 1,228 received aid, and 437 had their full need met. Average financial aid package met 81% of need; average scholarship/grant was $7,967; average loan was $4,220. For part-time students, average financial aid package was $6,694.

Students without need: 386 full-time freshmen who did not demonstrate need for aid received scholarships/grants; average award was $2,262. No-need awards available for academics, athletics, ROTC.

Cumulative student debt: 72% of graduating class had student loans; average debt was $27,931.

FINANCIAL AID PROCEDURES

Forms required: FAFSA.

Dates and Deadlines: Priority date 3/1; no closing date. Applicants notified on a rolling basis starting 3/1; must reply within 2 week(s) of notification.

CONTACT

Brenda Herzig, Director of Financial Aid

25 Solon Campus Center, Duluth, MN 55812-3000

(218) 726-8000

University of Minnesota: Morris

Morris, Minnesota

www.morris.umn.edu   Federal Code: 002389

4-year public university and liberal arts college in small town.

Enrollment: 1,599 undergrads.

Selectivity: Admits 50 to 75% of applicants.

BASIC COSTS (2009-2010)

Tuition and fees: $10,716.

Per-credit charge: $340.

Room and board: $7,056.

Additional info: In-state and out-of-state tuition rates are the same.

FINANCIAL AID PICTURE (2009-2010)

Students with need: Need-based aid available for full-time and part-time students. Work study available nights, weekends, and for part-time students.

Students without need: No-need awards available for academics, alumni affiliation, leadership, minority status, music/drama.

Scholarships offered: Chancellor's Scholarship: $3,500/year for 4 years; top 5%. Dean's Scholarship: $2,500/year for 4 years; top 10%. Founder's Scholarship: $1,000/year for 4 years; top 20%. National Merit Scholarship: full tuition scholarship for 4 years. Prairie Scholars Award: full tuition/year for 4 years; Morris Scholars Award: $5,000/year for 4 years plus one-time $2,500 research or creative project stipend. President's Distinguished Scholar Award: $1,000 to $3,000/year for four years.

Additional info: Land-grant program waiving tuition for Native Americans.

FINANCIAL AID PROCEDURES

Forms required: FAFSA.

Dates and Deadlines: Priority date 3/1; no closing date. Applicants notified on a rolling basis starting 3/1; must reply within 3 week(s) of notification.

CONTACT

Jill Beauregard, Director of Financial Aid
600 East 4th Street, Morris, MN 56267
(800) 992-8863

University of Minnesota: Twin Cities
Minneapolis, Minnesota
www.umn.edu/tc   Federal Code: 003969

4-year public university in very large city.

Enrollment: 29,921 undergrads, 8% part-time. 5,385 full-time freshmen.

Selectivity: Admits 50 to 75% of applicants.

BASIC COSTS (2009-2010)

Tuition and fees: $11,287; out-of-state residents $15,287.

Per-credit charge: $351; out-of-state residents $799.

Room and board: $7,392.

FINANCIAL AID PICTURE (2009-2010)

Students with need: Out of 4,292 full-time freshmen who applied for aid, 2,786 were judged to have need. Of these, 2,783 received aid, and 1,451 had their full need met. Average financial aid package met 87% of need; average scholarship/grant was $8,703; average loan was $4,532. For part-time students, average financial aid package was $7,365.

Students without need: This college awards aid only to students with need.

Cumulative student debt: 63% of graduating class had student loans; average debt was $26,516.

FINANCIAL AID PROCEDURES

Forms required: FAFSA, institutional form.

Dates and Deadlines: Priority date 3/1; no closing date. Applicants notified on a rolling basis starting 2/15.

CONTACT

Kris Wright, Director of Financial Aid
240 Williamson Hall, 231 Pillsbury Drive SE, Minneapolis, MN 55455-0115
(612) 624-1111

University of St. Thomas
St. Paul, Minnesota
www.stthomas.edu   Federal Code: 002345

4-year private university and liberal arts college in very large city, affiliated with Roman Catholic Church.

Enrollment: 5,992 undergrads, 4% part-time. 1,352 full-time freshmen.

Selectivity: Admits over 75% of applicants.

BASIC COSTS (2010-2011)

Tuition and fees: $33,477.

Per-credit charge: $936.

Room and board: $8,320.

FINANCIAL AID PICTURE (2009-2010)

Students with need: Out of 1,109 full-time freshmen who applied for aid, 841 were judged to have need. Of these, 841 received aid, and 687 had their full need met. Average financial aid package met 94% of need; average scholarship/grant was $19,162; average loan was $5,981. For part-time students, average financial aid package was $15,599.

Students without need: 245 full-time freshmen who did not demonstrate need for aid received scholarships/grants; average award was $13,206. No-need awards available for academics, music/drama, ROTC.

Cumulative student debt: 67% of graduating class had student loans; average debt was $32,132.

FINANCIAL AID PROCEDURES

Forms required: FAFSA.

Dates and Deadlines: Priority date 4/1; no closing date. Applicants notified on a rolling basis starting 3/1; must reply within 3 week(s) of notification.

Transfers: Recognition scholarship available for Minnesota community college transfer students.

CONTACT

Kris Roach, Director of Admissions and Financial Aid
2115 Summit Avenue, 32F, St. Paul, MN 55105-1096
(651) 962-6550

Vermilion Community College
Ely, Minnesota
www.vcc.edu   Federal Code: 002350

2-year public community and technical college in small town.

Enrollment: 605 undergrads.

Selectivity: Open admission.

BASIC COSTS (2009-2010)

Tuition and fees: $4,660; out-of-state residents $5,791.

Per-credit charge: $136; out-of-state residents $173.

Room and board: $4,860.

FINANCIAL AID PICTURE

Students with need: Need-based aid available for full-time and part-time students. Work study available nights, weekends, and for part-time students.

FINANCIAL AID PROCEDURES

Forms required: FAFSA, institutional form.

Dates and Deadlines: No deadline. Applicants notified on a rolling basis starting 4/1.

CONTACT

Kristi L'Allier, Financial Aid Director
1900 East Camp Street, Ely, MN 55731-9989
(218) 235-2153

Walden University
Minneapolis, Minnesota
www.waldenu.edu   Federal Code: 025402

4-year for-profit virtual university in large city.

Enrollment: 5,227 undergrads, 88% part-time. 17 full-time freshmen.

Selectivity: Open admission; but selective for some programs.

BASIC COSTS (2009-2010)

Tuition and fees: $11,790.

Per-credit charge: $260.

FINANCIAL AID PICTURE (2008-2009)

Students with need: Average financial aid package for all full-time undergraduates was $6,860; for part-time $6,392. 15% awarded as scholarships/grants, 85% awarded as loans/jobs.

Students without need: This college awards aid only to students with need.

FINANCIAL AID PROCEDURES

Forms required: FAFSA.

Dates and Deadlines: No deadline. Applicants notified on a rolling basis.

Transfers: No deadline. Applicants notified on a rolling basis.

CONTACT

Ernestine Whiting, National Director of Financial Aid

650 South Exeter Street, 8th Floor, Baltimore, MD 21202

(800) 492-5336

Winona State University

Winona, Minnesota

www.winona.edu   Federal Code: 002394

4-year public university in large town.

Enrollment: 7,872 undergrads, 6% part-time. 1,808 full-time freshmen.

Selectivity: Admits 50 to 75% of applicants.

BASIC COSTS (2009-2010)

Tuition and fees: $7,809; out-of-state residents $12,639.

Per-credit charge: $196; out-of-state residents $356.

Room and board: $6,680.

Additional info: Fees include mandatory laptop lease for full-time students.

FINANCIAL AID PICTURE (2008-2009)

Students with need: Need-based aid available for full-time and part-time students. Work study available nights, weekends, and for part-time students.

Students without need: No-need awards available for academics, alumni affiliation, art, athletics, leadership, minority status, music/drama, ROTC, state/district residency.

Scholarships offered: Outstanding Academics Honors Award: $2,500, renewable, top 5% of class, ACT 32 or above. WSU Foundation Board Scholarship: $2,000 renewable, top 15% of class, ACT 28-31, essay/interview. Presidential Honor Scholarships: $1,500 renewable; top 15% of class, ACT 28-31; $1,000, renewable, top 10% of class, ACT 27; $750, renewable, top 15% of class, ACT 26. Resident Tuition Scholarships: $3,400, renewable, to out-of-state students, top 15% of class or ACT 25.

FINANCIAL AID PROCEDURES

Forms required: FAFSA.

Dates and Deadlines: No deadline. Applicants notified on a rolling basis starting 5/1; must reply within 3 week(s) of notification.

CONTACT

Greg Peterson, Director of Financial Aid

Office of Admissions, Winona, MN 55987

(800) 342-5978

Mississippi

Alcorn State University

Alcorn State, Mississippi

www.alcorn.edu   Federal Code: 002396

4-year public university and agricultural college in rural community.

Enrollment: 2,700 undergrads, 10% part-time. 462 full-time freshmen.

Selectivity: Admits less than 50% of applicants.

BASIC COSTS (2009-2010)

Tuition and fees: $4,498; out-of-state residents $11,064.

Per-credit charge: $150; out-of-state residents $369.

Room and board: $5,384.

FINANCIAL AID PICTURE (2009-2010)

Students with need: Out of 462 full-time freshmen who applied for aid, 431 were judged to have need. Of these, 431 received aid, and 360 had their full need met. Average financial aid package met 77% of need; average scholarship/grant was $5,400; average loan was $3,370. For part-time students, average financial aid package was $6,888.

Students without need: 145 full-time freshmen who did not demonstrate need for aid received scholarships/grants; average award was $2,406. No-need awards available for academics, athletics, ROTC.

Scholarships offered: 32 full-time freshmen received athletic scholarships; average amount $7,549.

FINANCIAL AID PROCEDURES

Forms required: FAFSA, institutional form.

Dates and Deadlines: Priority date 4/1; no closing date. Applicants notified on a rolling basis starting 4/1; must reply within 4 week(s) of notification.

CONTACT

Juanita Russell, Director of Financial Aid

1000 ASU Drive #300, Alcorn State, MS 39096-7500

(601) 877-6190

Belhaven University

Jackson, Mississippi

www.belhaven.edu   Federal Code: 002397

4-year private liberal arts college in large city, affiliated with Presbyterian Church (USA).

Enrollment: 2,298 undergrads, 5% part-time. 191 full-time freshmen.

Selectivity: Admits 50 to 75% of applicants.

BASIC COSTS (2010-2011)

Tuition and fees: $17,700.

Per-credit charge: $350.

Room and board: $6,500.

FINANCIAL AID PICTURE (2009-2010)

Students with need: Out of 165 full-time freshmen who applied for aid, 139 were judged to have need. Of these, 138 received aid, and 16 had their full need met. Average financial aid package met 62% of need; average scholarship/grant was $11,499; average loan was $3,260. For part-time students, average financial aid package was $6,445.

Students without need: 26 full-time freshmen who did not demonstrate need for aid received scholarships/grants; average award was $7,162. No-need awards available for academics, alumni affiliation, art, athletics, job skills, leadership, music/drama.

Scholarships offered: 28 full-time freshmen received athletic scholarships; average amount $6,010.

FINANCIAL AID PROCEDURES

Forms required: FAFSA.

Dates and Deadlines: Priority date 1/31; no closing date. Applicants notified on a rolling basis starting 2/1.

Transfers: No deadline. Applicants notified on a rolling basis.

CONTACT

Linda Phillips, Assistant Vice President for Institutional Advancement

1500 Peachtree Street, Jackson, MS 39202

(601) 968-5933

Blue Cliff College: Gulfport

Gulfport, Mississippi

www.bluecliffcollege.com   Federal Code: 035253

2-year for-profit career college in small city.

Enrollment: 260 undergrads.

Selectivity: Admits over 75% of applicants.

FINANCIAL AID PICTURE (2009-2010)
Students with need: Need-based aid available for full-time and part-time students.
Students without need: This college awards aid only to students with need.

FINANCIAL AID PROCEDURES
Forms required: FAFSA.

CONTACT
Judy May, Financial Planner
12251 Bernard Parkway, Gulfport, MS 39503

Blue Mountain College
Blue Mountain, Mississippi
www.bmc.edu   Federal Code: 002398

4-year private liberal arts college in rural community, affiliated with Southern Baptist Convention.
Enrollment: 479 undergrads, 12% part-time. 73 full-time freshmen.
Selectivity: Admits less than 50% of applicants.

BASIC COSTS (2010-2011)
Tuition and fees: $9,020.
Per-credit charge: $265.
Room and board: $3,900.

FINANCIAL AID PICTURE (2008-2009)
Students with need: Need-based aid available for full-time and part-time students. Work study available nights, weekends, and for part-time students.
Students without need: No-need awards available for academics, alumni affiliation, art, athletics, leadership, music/drama, religious affiliation, state/district residency.
Scholarships offered: ACT/SAT Scholarships: varies from $1,000 to $7,000 per year; based on ACT/SAT score; number varies depending on number of applicants. Valedictorian/Salutatorian Scholarships: $1,000 to $5,000 first year; based on rank in class; unlimited number available. Child of Alumnae/Alumni: $500 first year; must be dependent of graduate; unlimited number available.

FINANCIAL AID PROCEDURES
Forms required: FAFSA, institutional form.
Dates and Deadlines: Priority date 3/1; closing date 7/31. Applicants notified on a rolling basis starting 4/1; must reply within 2 week(s) of notification.
Transfers: No deadline.

CONTACT
Michelle Hall, Director of Financial Aid
201 West Main Street, PO Box 160, Blue Mountain, MS 38610-0160
(662) 685-4771 ext. 145

Copiah-Lincoln Community College
Wesson, Mississippi
www.colin.edu   Federal Code: 002402

2-year public community college in small town.
Enrollment: 3,754 undergrads. 3,077 full-time freshmen.
Selectivity: Open admission; but selective for some programs.

BASIC COSTS (2009-2010)
Tuition and fees: $1,800; out-of-state residents $3,600.
Per-credit charge: $105; out-of-state residents $180.
Room and board: $2,600.

FINANCIAL AID PICTURE (2008-2009)
Students with need: Need-based aid available for full-time and part-time students. Work study available nights, weekends, and for part-time students.
Students without need: No-need awards available for academics, art, athletics, job skills, leadership, music/drama, state/district residency.

FINANCIAL AID PROCEDURES
Forms required: FAFSA.
Dates and Deadlines: Priority date 4/1; no closing date. Applicants notified on a rolling basis starting 4/1; must reply within 2 week(s) of notification.

CONTACT
Leslie Smith, Director of Financial Aid
PO Box 649, Wesson, MS 39191
(601) 643-8340

Delta State University
Cleveland, Mississippi
www.deltastate.edu   Federal Code: 002403

4-year public university in large town.
Enrollment: 3,115 undergrads, 20% part-time. 392 full-time freshmen.
Selectivity: Admits less than 50% of applicants.

BASIC COSTS (2009-2010)
Tuition and fees: $4,449; out-of-state residents $11,519.
Per-credit charge: $148; out-of-state residents $384.
Room and board: $5,705.

FINANCIAL AID PICTURE (2008-2009)
Students with need: Out of 295 full-time freshmen who applied for aid, 249 were judged to have need. Of these, 249 received aid. For part-time students, average financial aid package was $4,832.
Students without need: No-need awards available for academics, alumni affiliation, art, athletics, leadership, music/drama, state/district residency.
Scholarships offered: 45 full-time freshmen received athletic scholarships; average amount $4,624.

FINANCIAL AID PROCEDURES
Forms required: FAFSA.
Dates and Deadlines: Priority date 3/1; no closing date. Applicants notified on a rolling basis starting 5/1.

CONTACT
Ann Mullins, Director of Student Financial Assistance
117 Kent Wyatt Hall, Cleveland, MS 38733
(662) 846-4670

East Mississippi Community College
Scooba, Mississippi
www.eastms.edu   Federal Code: 002405

2-year public community college in rural community.
Enrollment: 4,962 undergrads, 41% part-time. 771 full-time freshmen.
Selectivity: Open admission; but selective for some programs.

BASIC COSTS (2009-2010)
Tuition and fees: $2,000; out-of-state residents $3,800.
Room and board: $3,300.
Additional info: $50 health fee for on-campus residents.

FINANCIAL AID PICTURE
Students with need: Need-based aid available for full-time and part-time students.
Students without need: No-need awards available for academics, art, athletics, leadership, music/drama, state/district residency.

FINANCIAL AID PROCEDURES

Forms required: FAFSA, state aid form, institutional form.
Dates and Deadlines: Priority date 4/1; no closing date. Applicants notified on a rolling basis starting 4/1; must reply within 2 week(s) of notification.

CONTACT

Jim Gibson, Vice President for Student services
Admissions Office, Scooba, MS 39358
(662) 476-5079

Hinds Community College

Raymond, Mississippi
www.hindscc.edu   Federal Code: 002407

2-year public branch campus and community college in small town.
Enrollment: 11,751 undergrads.
Selectivity: Open admission; but selective for some programs.

BASIC COSTS (2009-2010)

Tuition and fees: $1,760; out-of-state residents $3,966.
Per-credit charge: $85; out-of-state residents $170.
Room and board: $3,240.

FINANCIAL AID PICTURE (2008-2009)

Students with need: Need-based aid available for full-time and part-time students.
Students without need: No-need awards available for academics, art, athletics, job skills, leadership, minority status, music/drama, state/district residency.

FINANCIAL AID PROCEDURES

Forms required: FAFSA.
Dates and Deadlines: Priority date 4/1; no closing date. Applicants notified on a rolling basis starting 5/15; must reply within 2 week(s) of notification.
Transfers: Financial aid transcripts from all previous colleges must be on file prior to award letter being released.

CONTACT

Carrie Cooper, Director of Financial Aid
505 East Main Street, Raymond, MS 39154-1100
(601) 857-3223

Holmes Community College

Goodman, Mississippi
www.holmescc.edu   Federal Code: 002408

2-year public community college in rural community.
Enrollment: 5,720 undergrads.
Selectivity: Open admission; but selective for some programs.

BASIC COSTS (2009-2010)

Tuition and fees: $1,630; out-of-state residents $3,580.
Per-credit charge: $75.
Room and board: $1,980.

FINANCIAL AID PICTURE (2008-2009)

Students with need: 65% of average financial aid package awarded as scholarships/grants, 35% awarded as loans/jobs.
Students without need: No-need awards available for academics, athletics.
Scholarships offered: President's Scholarship for full-time students provides full tuition, requires ACT of 20 or higher. Board of Trustees Scholarship for full-time students provides tuition, room and board, requires ACT of 28 or higher.

FINANCIAL AID PROCEDURES

Forms required: FAFSA, state aid form, institutional form.

Dates and Deadlines: Priority date 6/1; no closing date. Applicants notified on a rolling basis.

CONTACT

Jim Haffey, Director of Financial Aid
Box 398, Goodman, MS 39079
(662) 472-2312

Jackson State University

Jackson, Mississippi
www.jsums.edu   Federal Code: 002410

4-year public university in small city.
Enrollment: 6,810 undergrads, 19% part-time. 839 full-time freshmen.
Selectivity: Admits 50 to 75% of applicants.

BASIC COSTS (2009-2010)

Tuition and fees: $4,634; out-of-state residents $11,359.
Per-credit charge: $154; out-of-state residents $379.
Room and board: $6,254.

FINANCIAL AID PICTURE (2008-2009)

Students with need: Need-based aid available for full-time and part-time students.
Students without need: This college awards aid only to students with need.

FINANCIAL AID PROCEDURES

Forms required: FAFSA.
Dates and Deadlines: Priority date 4/1; closing date 5/1. Applicants notified on a rolling basis starting 5/1.

CONTACT

Betty Moncure, Director, Financial Aid
1400 JR Lynch Street, Jackson, MS 39217
(601) 979-2227

Jones County Junior College

Ellisville, Mississippi
www.jcjc.edu   Federal Code: 002411

2-year public community and junior college in small town.
Enrollment: 4,821 full-time undergrads.
Selectivity: Open admission; but selective for some programs.

BASIC COSTS (2009-2010)

Tuition and fees: $2,160; out-of-state residents $4,160.
Room and board: $3,120.

FINANCIAL AID PICTURE

Students with need: Need-based aid available for full-time and part-time students. Work study available nights, weekends, and for part-time students.
Students without need: No-need awards available for academics, athletics, state/district residency.

FINANCIAL AID PROCEDURES

Forms required: FAFSA, state aid form, institutional form.
Dates and Deadlines: Priority date 5/1; no closing date. Applicants notified on a rolling basis starting 6/1; must reply within 2 week(s) of notification.

CONTACT

Jennifer Suber, Director of Student Financial Aid
900 South Court Street, Ellisville, MS 39437
(601) 477-4040

Meridian Community College

Meridian, Mississippi
www.meridiancc.edu Federal Code: 002413

2-year public community college in large town.
Enrollment: 4,097 undergrads.
Selectivity: Open admission; but selective for some programs.

BASIC COSTS (2009-2010)

Tuition and fees: $1,810; out-of-state residents $3,190.
Per-credit charge: $90; out-of-state residents $147.
Room and board: $3,250.

FINANCIAL AID PICTURE

Students with need: Need-based aid available for full-time and part-time students.
Students without need: No-need awards available for academics, art, athletics, leadership, music/drama, state/district residency.

FINANCIAL AID PROCEDURES

Forms required: FAFSA, institutional form.
Dates and Deadlines: Priority date 6/1; no closing date. Applicants notified on a rolling basis starting 5/15; must reply within 2 week(s) of notification.

CONTACT

Nedra Bradley, Director of Financial Aid
910 Highway 19 North, Meridian, MS 39307-5890
(601) 484-8628

Millsaps College

Jackson, Mississippi
www.millsaps.edu Federal Code: 002414

4-year private business and liberal arts college in large city, affiliated with United Methodist Church.
Enrollment: 1,002 undergrads, 1% part-time. 282 full-time freshmen.
Selectivity: Admits 50 to 75% of applicants.

BASIC COSTS (2010-2011)

Tuition and fees: $27,812.
Per-credit charge: $808.
Room and board: $9,728.

FINANCIAL AID PICTURE (2009-2010)

Students with need: Out of 245 full-time freshmen who applied for aid, 186 were judged to have need. Of these, 186 received aid, and 90 had their full need met. Average financial aid package met 92% of need; average scholarship/grant was $22,158; average loan was $3,071. For part-time students, average financial aid package was $3,264.
Students without need: 94 full-time freshmen who did not demonstrate need for aid received scholarships/grants; average award was $17,910. No-need awards available for academics, art, leadership, music/drama, religious affiliation.
Cumulative student debt: 59% of graduating class had student loans; average debt was $31,304.

FINANCIAL AID PROCEDURES

Forms required: FAFSA.
Dates and Deadlines: Priority date 3/1; no closing date. Applicants notified on a rolling basis starting 3/15; must reply by 5/1 or within 2 week(s) of notification.

CONTACT

Patrick James, Director of Financial Aid
1701 North State Street, Jackson, MS 39210-0001
(601) 974-1220

Mississippi College

Clinton, Mississippi
www.mc.edu Federal Code: 002415

4-year private university in large city, affiliated with Southern Baptist Convention.
Enrollment: 3,084 undergrads, 13% part-time. 452 full-time freshmen.
Selectivity: Admits 50 to 75% of applicants.

BASIC COSTS (2010-2011)

Tuition and fees: $13,550.
Per-credit charge: $405.
Room and board: $6,150.

FINANCIAL AID PICTURE (2009-2010)

Students with need: Out of 452 full-time freshmen who applied for aid, 284 were judged to have need. Of these, 283 received aid, and 106 had their full need met. Average financial aid package met 80% of need; average scholarship/grant was $10,549; average loan was $5,685. For part-time students, average financial aid package was $13,339.
Students without need: 168 full-time freshmen who did not demonstrate need for aid received scholarships/grants; average award was $11,181. No-need awards available for academics, alumni affiliation, art, leadership, music/drama, religious affiliation.
Scholarships offered: Merit Scholarships: up to $15,000; based on various criteria including leadership, academics, church and community involvement; extensive number awarded.
Cumulative student debt: 72% of graduating class had student loans; average debt was $26,323.
Additional info: Student reply date for institutional scholarships: May 1.

FINANCIAL AID PROCEDURES

Forms required: FAFSA, state aid form.
Dates and Deadlines: Priority date 3/1; no closing date. Applicants notified on a rolling basis starting 3/1; must reply by 5/1.
Transfers: No deadline. Applicants notified on a rolling basis; must reply by 5/1.

CONTACT

Karon McMillan, Director of Financial Aid
PO Box 4026, Clinton, MS 39058
(601) 925-3212

Mississippi Delta Community College

Moorhead, Mississippi
www.msdelta.edu Federal Code: 002416

2-year public community college in rural community.
Enrollment: 3,218 undergrads.
Selectivity: Open admission; but selective for some programs.

BASIC COSTS (2009-2010)

Tuition and fees: $1,920; out-of-state residents $3,528.
Room and board: $4,390.

FINANCIAL AID PICTURE

Students with need: Need-based aid available for full-time students.
Students without need: No-need awards available for academics, athletics, state/district residency.

FINANCIAL AID PROCEDURES

Forms required: FAFSA, institutional form.
Dates and Deadlines: Closing date 8/1. Applicants notified on a rolling basis; must reply within 2 week(s) of notification.

CONTACT

Mary Rodgers, Director of Financial Aid
Box 668, Moorhead, MS 38761
(662) 246-6263

Mississippi Gulf Coast Community College

Perkinston, Mississippi
www.mgccc.edu   Federal Code: 002419

2-year public community college in large city.
Enrollment: 10,013 undergrads, 32% part-time. 1,964 full-time freshmen.
Selectivity: Open admission; but selective for some programs.

BASIC COSTS (2010-2011)

Tuition and fees: $2,212; out-of-state residents $4,058.
Per-credit charge: $90; out-of-state residents $167.
Additional info: $30 rental fee required per book.

FINANCIAL AID PICTURE (2008-2009)

Students with need: 75% of average financial aid package awarded as scholarships/grants, 25% awarded as loans/jobs.
Students without need: This college awards aid only to students with need.

FINANCIAL AID PROCEDURES

Forms required: institutional form.
Dates and Deadlines: Priority date 6/1; no closing date. Applicants notified on a rolling basis starting 7/1.

CONTACT

Searcy Taylor, Financial Aid
PO Box 548, Perkinston, MS 39573
(228) 896-2511

Mississippi State University

Mississippi State, Mississippi
www.msstate.edu   Federal Code: 002423

4-year public university and agricultural college in large town.
Enrollment: 13,730 undergrads, 9% part-time. 2,489 full-time freshmen.
Selectivity: Admits 50 to 75% of applicants.

BASIC COSTS (2009-2010)

Tuition and fees: $5,151; out-of-state residents $13,021.
Per-credit charge: $215; out-of-state residents $543.
Room and board: $7,520.

FINANCIAL AID PICTURE (2008-2009)

Students with need: Out of 1,714 full-time freshmen who applied for aid, 1,402 were judged to have need. Of these, 1,385 received aid, and 391 had their full need met. Average financial aid package met 68% of need; average scholarship/grant was $5,170; average loan was $3,246. For part-time students, average financial aid package was $9,588.
Students without need: 722 full-time freshmen who did not demonstrate need for aid received scholarships/grants; average award was $2,950. No-need awards available for academics, alumni affiliation, art, athletics, job skills, leadership, minority status, music/drama, ROTC, state/district residency.
Scholarships offered: *Merit:* Entering Freshman Scholarships: starting at $1,000 per year; based on minimum 24 ACT and 3.0 core GPA. Competitive Freshman Scholarship: covers cost of tuition, fees, room and board, books; based on a minimum 29 ACT and 3.5 core GPA. *Athletic:* 81 full-time freshmen received athletic scholarships; average amount $15,461.
Cumulative student debt: 51% of graduating class had student loans; average debt was $23,413.

Additional info: No institutional closing date for FAFSA.

FINANCIAL AID PROCEDURES

Forms required: FAFSA.
Dates and Deadlines: Priority date 4/1; no closing date. Applicants notified on a rolling basis starting 12/1; must reply by 5/1.
Transfers: No deadline. Applicants notified on a rolling basis.

CONTACT

Bruce Crain, Director
Box 6334, Mississippi State, MS 39762
(662) 325-2450

Mississippi University for Women

Columbus, Mississippi
www.muw.edu   Federal Code: 002422

4-year public university and liberal arts college in large town.
Enrollment: 2,069 undergrads, 15% part-time. 220 full-time freshmen.
Selectivity: Admits less than 50% of applicants.

BASIC COSTS (2009-2010)

Tuition and fees: $4,423; out-of-state residents $12,051.
Per-credit charge: $147; out-of-state residents $402.
Room and board: $5,249.
Additional info: Tuition/fee waivers available for adults, minority students.

FINANCIAL AID PICTURE (2009-2010)

Students with need: Need-based aid available for full-time and part-time students. Work study available nights, weekends, and for part-time students.
Students without need: No-need awards available for academics, alumni affiliation, leadership, minority status, music/drama, ROTC, state/district residency.

FINANCIAL AID PROCEDURES

Forms required: FAFSA, state aid form.
Dates and Deadlines: Priority date 3/1; no closing date. Applicants notified on a rolling basis starting 3/15; must reply within 2 week(s) of notification.
Transfers: Closing date 4/1.

CONTACT

Dan Miller, Director of Financial Aid
1100 College St. MUW-1613, Columbus, MS 39701
(662) 329-7114

Northwest Mississippi Community College

Senatobia, Mississippi
www.northwestms.edu   Federal Code: 002427

2-year public community college in small town.
Enrollment: 8,364 undergrads.
Selectivity: Open admission; but selective for some programs.

BASIC COSTS (2010-2011)

Tuition and fees: $1,700; out-of-state residents $3,700.
Room and board: $2,700.

FINANCIAL AID PICTURE (2008-2009)

Students with need: Need-based aid available for full-time students.

FINANCIAL AID PROCEDURES

Forms required: FAFSA.
Dates and Deadlines: Priority date 4/1; no closing date. Applicants notified by 8/16.

CONTACT

Joe Boyles, Director of Financial Aid

4975 Highway 51 North, Senatobia, MS 38668 .

(662) 562-3271

Pearl River Community College

Poplarville, Mississippi

www.prcc.edu   Federal Code: 002430

2-year public community college in small town.

Enrollment: 3,790 undergrads.

Selectivity: Open admission; but selective for some programs.

BASIC COSTS (2009-2010)

Tuition and fees: $1,806; out-of-state residents $4,204.

Per-credit charge: $90; out-of-state residents $190.

Room and board: $3,400.

FINANCIAL AID PICTURE (2008-2009)

Students with need: Need-based aid available for full-time and part-time students.

Students without need: No-need awards available for academics, alumni affiliation, athletics, leadership, music/drama, state/district residency.

FINANCIAL AID PROCEDURES

Forms required: FAFSA, institutional form.

Dates and Deadlines: Priority date 4/17; no closing date. Applicants notified on a rolling basis.

CONTACT

Valerie Horne, Director of Financial Aid

101 Highway 11 North, Poplarville, MS 39470

(601) 403-1212

Rust College

Holly Springs, Mississippi

www.rustcollege.edu   Federal Code: 002433

4-year private liberal arts college in small town, affiliated with United Methodist Church.

Enrollment: 1,200 undergrads.

Selectivity: Admits 50 to 75% of applicants.

BASIC COSTS (2010-2011)

Tuition and fees: $7,610.

Per-credit charge: $330.

Room and board: $3,320.

Additional info: Tuition/fee waivers available for adults.

FINANCIAL AID PICTURE (2008-2009)

Students with need: Average financial aid package met 92% of need; average scholarship/grant was $4,314; average loan was $2,945. For part-time students, average financial aid package was $4,271.

Students without need: No-need awards available for academics, leadership, music/drama, religious affiliation, state/district residency.

Scholarships offered: Honor Track: full tuition; based on top 10% of high school graduating class, GPA 3.5 and above, ACT 22 or above, SAT 1030 or above, 3 letters of recommendation, essay; 17 awarded. Presidential Scholarship: $2,000; for top 10% of high school graduating class, GPA 3.25 and above, ACT 19 and above, SAT 910 and above; 17 awarded. Academic Dean's Scholarship: for top 10% of high school graduating class, GPA 3.0 or above, ACT 17 and above, SAT 830 and above; 17 awarded. SAT scores exclusive of Writing.

Cumulative student debt: 71% of graduating class had student loans; average debt was $13,055.

FINANCIAL AID PROCEDURES

Forms required: FAFSA, state aid form, institutional form.

Dates and Deadlines: Closing date 5/1. Applicants notified on a rolling basis starting 5/1; must reply within 2 week(s) of notification.

Transfers: No deadline. Financial aid transcripts from previous schools required.

CONTACT

Helen Street, Director of Financial Aid

150 Rust Avenue, Holly Springs, MS 38635-2328

(662) 252-8000 ext. 4062

Southwest Mississippi Community College

Summit, Mississippi

www.smcc.edu   Federal Code: 002436

2-year public community college in rural community.

Enrollment: 1,740 undergrads, 7% part-time. 552 full-time freshmen.

Selectivity: Open admission; but selective for some programs.

BASIC COSTS (2009-2010)

Tuition and fees: $1,800; out-of-state residents $4,500.

Per-credit charge: $75; out-of-state residents $190.

Room and board: $2,530.

FINANCIAL AID PICTURE (2009-2010)

Students with need: 99% of average financial aid package awarded as scholarships/grants, 1% awarded as loans/jobs. Need-based aid available for part-time students.

FINANCIAL AID PROCEDURES

Dates and Deadlines: No deadline. Applicants notified on a rolling basis.

CONTACT

Stacey Hodges, Director of Financial Aid

1156 College Drive, Summit, MS 39666

(601) 276-3707

Tougaloo College

Tougaloo, Mississippi

www.tougaloo.edu   Federal Code: 002439

4-year private liberal arts college in large city, affiliated with United Christian Mission Society and United Church of Christ.

Enrollment: 930 undergrads, 3% part-time. 234 full-time freshmen.

Selectivity: Admits over 75% of applicants.

BASIC COSTS (2010-2011)

Tuition and fees: $9,718.

Per-credit charge: $385.

Room and board: $6,330.

Additional info: Tuition/fee waivers available for adults.

FINANCIAL AID PICTURE (2009-2010)

Students with need: Out of 210 full-time freshmen who applied for aid, 200 were judged to have need. Of these, 195 received aid, and 20 had their full need met. Average financial aid package met 60% of need; average scholarship/grant was $7,350; average loan was $3,500. For part-time students, average financial aid package was $8,800.

Students without need: 10 full-time freshmen who did not demonstrate need for aid received scholarships/grants; average award was $14,000. No-need awards available for academics, athletics, ROTC.

Scholarships offered: 1 full-time freshmen received athletic scholarships; average amount $14,000.

FINANCIAL AID PROCEDURES

Forms required: FAFSA, state aid form, institutional form.
Dates and Deadlines: Priority date 4/15; no closing date. Applicants notified on a rolling basis starting 5/1; must reply within 2 week(s) of notification.

CONTACT

Maria Thomas, Director of Financial Aid
500 West County Line Road, Tougaloo, MS 39174
(601) 977-7766

University of Mississippi

University, Mississippi
www.olemiss.edu   Federal Code: 002440

4-year public university in large town.
Enrollment: 13,024 undergrads, 8% part-time. 2,317 full-time freshmen.
Selectivity: Admits over 75% of applicants.

BASIC COSTS (2009-2010)

Tuition and fees: $5,106; out-of-state residents $13,046.
Room and board: $6,190.
Additional info: Tuition/fee waivers available for minority students.

FINANCIAL AID PICTURE (2008-2009)

Students with need: Out of 1,507 full-time freshmen who applied for aid, 976 were judged to have need. Of these, 949 received aid, and 160 had their full need met. Average financial aid package met 77% of need; average scholarship/grant was $7,169; average loan was $3,513. For part-time students, average financial aid package was $2,198.
Students without need: 623 full-time freshmen who did not demonstrate need for aid received scholarships/grants; average award was $4,465. No-need awards available for academics, alumni affiliation, art, athletics, leadership, minority status, music/drama, ROTC, state/district residency.
Scholarships offered: 68 full-time freshmen received athletic scholarships; average amount $16,344.
Cumulative student debt: 39% of graduating class had student loans; average debt was $22,866.

FINANCIAL AID PROCEDURES

Forms required: FAFSA.
Dates and Deadlines: Priority date 3/15; no closing date. Applicants notified on a rolling basis starting 4/1; must reply within 3 week(s) of notification.
Transfers: Priority date 3/1; no deadline. Applicants notified on a rolling basis starting 4/1; must reply within 3 week(s) of notification.

CONTACT

Laura Diven-Brown, Director of Financial Aid
145 Martindale, University, MS 38677-1848
(800) 891-4596

University of Southern Mississippi

Hattiesburg, Mississippi
www.usm.edu   Federal Code: 002441

4-year public university in small city.
Enrollment: 12,383 undergrads, 14% part-time. 1,738 full-time freshmen.
Selectivity: Admits 50 to 75% of applicants.

BASIC COSTS (2009-2010)

Tuition and fees: $5,096; out-of-state residents $13,051.
Per-credit charge: $170; out-of-state residents $435.
Room and board: $5,972.

FINANCIAL AID PICTURE (2008-2009)

Students with need: Out of 1,433 full-time freshmen who applied for aid, 1,172 were judged to have need. Of these, 1,143 received aid, and 309 had their full need met. Average financial aid package met 84% of need; average scholarship/grant was $4,771; average loan was $4,057. For part-time students, average financial aid package was $5,909.
Students without need: 214 full-time freshmen who did not demonstrate need for aid received scholarships/grants; average award was $4,310.
Scholarships offered: 78 full-time freshmen received athletic scholarships; average amount $5,759.
Cumulative student debt: 63% of graduating class had student loans; average debt was $19,915.

FINANCIAL AID PROCEDURES

Forms required: FAFSA, institutional form.
Dates and Deadlines: Priority date 3/15; no closing date.
Transfers: Merit scholarships available to community college transfer students based on college GPA.

CONTACT

David Williamson, Director of Financial Aid
118 College Drive #5166, Hattiesburg, MS 39406-0001
(601) 266-4111

Wesley College

Florence, Mississippi
www.wesleycollege.edu   Federal Code: 011461

4-year private Bible college in small town, affiliated with Congregational Methodist Church.
Enrollment: 143 undergrads.
Selectivity: Admits over 75% of applicants.

BASIC COSTS (2009-2010)

Tuition and fees: $9,084.
Per-credit charge: $278.
Room and board: $4,800.

FINANCIAL AID PICTURE (2008-2009)

Students with need: Need-based aid available for full-time and part-time students. Work study available nights, weekends, and for part-time students.
Students without need: No-need awards available for academics, alumni affiliation, leadership, religious affiliation.

FINANCIAL AID PROCEDURES

Forms required: FAFSA.
Dates and Deadlines: Closing date 5/14. Applicants notified on a rolling basis starting 7/1; must reply within 2 week(s) of notification.

CONTACT

William Devore, Director of Financial Aid
PO Box 1070, Florence, MS 39073-0070
(601) 845-2265

Missouri

Avila University

Kansas City, Missouri
www.avila.edu   Federal Code: 002449

4-year private university and liberal arts college in very large city, affiliated with Roman Catholic Church.
Enrollment: 1,120 undergrads, 18% part-time. 183 full-time freshmen.
Selectivity: Admits less than 50% of applicants.

BASIC COSTS (2010-2011)
Tuition and fees: $21,800.
Per-credit charge: $535.
Room and board: $6,350.

FINANCIAL AID PICTURE (2008-2009)
Students with need: Out of 114 full-time freshmen who applied for aid, 114 were judged to have need. Of these, 114 received aid, and 24 had their full need met. Average financial aid package met 65% of need; average scholarship/grant was $6,600; average loan was $2,970. For part-time students, average financial aid package was $3,600.
Students without need: 69 full-time freshmen who did not demonstrate need for aid received scholarships/grants; average award was $4,200. No-need awards available for academics, alumni affiliation, art, athletics, music/drama, religious affiliation.
Scholarships offered: 102 full-time freshmen received athletic scholarships; average amount $6,812.
Cumulative student debt: 83% of graduating class had student loans; average debt was $5,831.
Additional info: Financial aid adjusted for increases in tuition based on need.

FINANCIAL AID PROCEDURES
Forms required: FAFSA, institutional form.
Dates and Deadlines: Priority date 3/1; closing date 4/1. Applicants notified on a rolling basis starting 2/1; must reply within 2 week(s) of notification.
Transfers: No deadline. Applicants notified on a rolling basis; must reply within 2 week(s) of notification. Non-need-based academic scholarship available for transfer students.

CONTACT
Nancy Merz, Director of Financial Aid
11901 Wornall Road, Kansas City, MO 64145-1007
(816) 501-3600

Baptist Bible College
Springfield, Missouri
www.gobbc.edu   Federal Code: 013208

4-year private Bible and seminary college in small city, affiliated with Baptist faith.
Enrollment: 481 undergrads.
Selectivity: Open admission.

BASIC COSTS (2009-2010)
Tuition and fees: $13,610.
Per-credit charge: $206.
Room and board: $5,400.

FINANCIAL AID PICTURE (2008-2009)
Students with need: Need-based aid available for full-time and part-time students.
Students without need: No-need awards available for academics.
Scholarships offered: Founder's Scholarship: $5,500-$9,500. Bible Scholarships: $800 per year.

FINANCIAL AID PROCEDURES
Forms required: FAFSA, institutional form.
Dates and Deadlines: Closing date 5/1. Applicants notified on a rolling basis; must reply within 2 week(s) of notification.

CONTACT
Bob Kotulski, Financial Aid Director
628 East Kearney Street, Springfield, MO 65803
(417) 268-6036

Bolivar Technical College
Bolivar, Missouri
www.bolivarcollege.org   Federal Code: 035793

2-year private branch campus and technical college in small town.
Enrollment: 125 undergrads.
Selectivity: Open admission; but selective for some programs.

BASIC COSTS (2010-2011)
Tuition and fees: $11,940.
Per-credit charge: $340.
Additional info: Tution varies by program, $158-$340 per credit hour.

FINANCIAL AID PICTURE (2008-2009)
Students with need: 65% of average financial aid package awarded as scholarships/grants, 35% awarded as loans/jobs.

FINANCIAL AID PROCEDURES
Dates and Deadlines: Priority date 4/1; no closing date.

CONTACT
Holly Wheelbarger, Director of Financial Aid
PO Box 592, Bolivar, MO 65613
(417) 777-5062

Calvary Bible College and Theological Seminary
Kansas City, Missouri
www.calvary.edu   Federal Code: 002450

4-year private Bible and seminary college in large city, affiliated with nondenominational tradition.
Enrollment: 214 undergrads, 33% part-time. 26 full-time freshmen.
Selectivity: Open admission; but selective for some programs.

BASIC COSTS (2010-2011)
Tuition and fees: $9,192.
Per-credit charge: $280.
Room and board: $4,400.
Additional info: Tuition/fee waivers available for minority students.

FINANCIAL AID PICTURE (2009-2010)
Students with need: Need-based aid available for full-time and part-time students.
Students without need: No-need awards available for academics, alumni affiliation, job skills, music/drama, religious affiliation, ROTC.

FINANCIAL AID PROCEDURES
Forms required: FAFSA, institutional form.
Dates and Deadlines: Priority date 3/1; closing date 4/1. Applicants notified on a rolling basis starting 5/1.
Transfers: Applicants notified on a rolling basis.

CONTACT
Ryan Lowe, Financial Aid Counselor
15800 Calvary Road, Kansas City, MO 64147-1341
(816) 322-5152 ext. 1323

Central Christian College of the Bible
Moberly, Missouri
www.cccb.edu   Federal Code: 014619

4-year private Bible college in large town, affiliated with Christian Church.
Enrollment: 391 undergrads.
Selectivity: Admits 50 to 75% of applicants.

BASIC COSTS (2010-2011)

Additional info: Full-time students receive full scholarship for tuition only, $9,000. Room and board: $4,000; required fees: $3,600.

FINANCIAL AID PICTURE (2009-2010)

Students with need: Need-based aid available for full-time and part-time students.

FINANCIAL AID PROCEDURES

Forms required: FAFSA.

Dates and Deadlines: Priority date 3/15; closing date 4/1. Applicants notified by 5/15; must reply within 2 week(s) of notification.

CONTACT

Rhonda Dunham, Financial Aid Director
911 East Urbandale Drive, Moberly, MO 65270-1997
(888) 263-3900

Central Methodist University

Fayette, Missouri
www.centralmethodist.edu   Federal Code: E00605

4-year private university and liberal arts college in small town, affiliated with United Methodist Church.

Enrollment: 1,022 undergrads, 2% part-time. 260 full-time freshmen.
Selectivity: Admits 50 to 75% of applicants.

BASIC COSTS (2009-2010)

Tuition and fees: $18,670.
Per-credit charge: $180.
Room and board: $6,240.

FINANCIAL AID PICTURE (2009-2010)

Students with need: Need-based aid available for full-time and part-time students. Work study available nights, weekends, and for part-time students.
Students without need: No-need awards available for academics, alumni affiliation, athletics, leadership, music/drama, religious affiliation, ROTC.

FINANCIAL AID PROCEDURES

Forms required: FAFSA.

Dates and Deadlines: Priority date 3/15; no closing date. Applicants notified on a rolling basis starting 1/30; must reply within 2 week(s) of notification.
Transfers: Merit based institutional financial aid is determined by college transfer GPA.

CONTACT

Linda Mackey, Director of Financial Aid
411 Central Methodist Square, Fayette, MO 65248-1198
(660) 248-6245

College of the Ozarks

Point Lookout, Missouri
www.cofo.edu   Federal Code: 002500

4-year private liberal arts college in small town, affiliated with interdenominational tradition.

Enrollment: 1,350 undergrads, 1% part-time. 244 full-time freshmen.
Selectivity: Admits less than 50% of applicants.

BASIC COSTS (2010-2011)

Room and board: $5,300.
Additional info: Cost of full-time tuition met through combination of institutional work program and federal, state, and institutional funding. Full-time students work 15 hours per week for 16 weeks and one 40-hour work week per semester. Part-time students (commuters only) pay $295 per credit hour for tuition. Required fees for academic year, $410.

FINANCIAL AID PICTURE (2009-2010)

Students with need: Average financial aid package met 80% of need; average scholarship/grant was $11,067. For part-time students, average financial aid package was $4,297.
Students without need: No-need awards available for academics, art, athletics, leadership, music/drama, ROTC, state/district residency.
Cumulative student debt: 7% of graduating class had student loans; average debt was $6,029.

FINANCIAL AID PROCEDURES

Forms required: FAFSA.

Dates and Deadlines: Priority date 2/15; no closing date. Applicants notified by 7/1.
Transfers: No deadline. Applicants notified on a rolling basis starting 2/15.

CONTACT

Kyla McCarty, Financial Aid Director
PO Box 17, Point Lookout, MO 65726-0017
(417) 690-3290

Columbia College

Columbia, Missouri
www.ccis.edu   Federal Code: 002456

4-year private liberal arts college in small city, affiliated with Christian Church (Disciples of Christ).

Enrollment: 1,038 undergrads, 18% part-time. 165 full-time freshmen.
Selectivity: Admits less than 50% of applicants.

BASIC COSTS (2010-2011)

Tuition and fees: $15,596.
Per-credit charge: $411.
Room and board: $6,074.

FINANCIAL AID PICTURE (2008-2009)

Students with need: 51% of average financial aid package awarded as scholarships/grants, 49% awarded as loans/jobs. Need-based aid available for part-time students. Work study available nights, weekends, and for part-time students.
Students without need: No-need awards available for academics, alumni affiliation, art, athletics, job skills, leadership, music/drama, religious affiliation, ROTC, state/district residency.
Scholarships offered: Columbia College Scholarship: full tuition, room/board; requires 3.5 GPA, 25 ACT or 1140 SAT, campus visit, interview, essay, letter of recommendation; renewable with 30 semester hours and 3.5 GPA. Half-tuition scholarship: minimum 3.4 GPA or GED of 2900, 24 ACT or 1110 SAT; renewable with 24 semester hours per year and 3.2 GPA for up to 3 years.

FINANCIAL AID PROCEDURES

Forms required: FAFSA.

Dates and Deadlines: No deadline. Applicants notified on a rolling basis starting 3/1.

CONTACT

Sharon Abernathy, Director of Financial Aid
1001 Rogers Street, Columbia, MO 65216
(573) 875-7390

Conception Seminary College

Conception, Missouri
www.conception.edu   Federal Code: 002467

4-year private seminary college for men in rural community, affiliated with Roman Catholic Church.

Enrollment: 112 undergrads. 12 full-time freshmen.

BASIC COSTS (2009-2010)
Tuition and fees: $15,786.
Per-credit charge: $180.
Room and board: $9,362.

FINANCIAL AID PICTURE
Students with need: Need-based aid available for full-time and part-time students. Work study available nights, weekends, and for part-time students.
Students without need: No-need awards available for academics.

FINANCIAL AID PROCEDURES
Forms required: FAFSA.
Dates and Deadlines: No deadline. Applicants notified on a rolling basis starting 8/1; must reply by 8/20.

CONTACT
Justin Hernandez, Financial Aid Officer
Box 502, Conception, MO 64433-0502
(660) 944-2851

Cottey College
Nevada, Missouri
www.cottey.edu   Federal Code: 002458

2-year private junior and liberal arts college for women in small town.
Enrollment: 330 undergrads.
Selectivity: Admits 50 to 75% of applicants.

BASIC COSTS (2010-2011)
Tuition and fees: $15,100.
Per-credit charge: $150.
Room and board: $6,000.

FINANCIAL AID PICTURE (2009-2010)
Students with need: Need-based aid available for full-time and part-time students. Work study available nights, weekends, and for part-time students.
Students without need: No-need awards available for academics, alumni affiliation, art, athletics, leadership, music/drama.

FINANCIAL AID PROCEDURES
Forms required: FAFSA.
Dates and Deadlines: Priority date 3/1; no closing date. Applicants notified on a rolling basis starting 3/15; must reply by 5/1 or within 4 week(s) of notification.
Transfers: Applicants notified on a rolling basis starting 3/15; must reply within 4 week(s) of notification.

CONTACT
Sherry Pennington, Coordinator of Financial Aid
1000 West Austin Boulevard, Nevada, MO 64772
(417) 667-8181 ext. 2190

Crowder College
Neosho, Missouri
www.crowder.edu   Federal Code: 002459

2-year public community and liberal arts college in small town.
Enrollment: 3,416 undergrads, 41% part-time. 259 full-time freshmen.
Selectivity: Open admission; but selective for some programs.

BASIC COSTS (2009-2010)
Tuition and fees: $2,400; out-of-district residents $3,210; out-of-state residents $4,050.
Per-credit charge: $68; out-of-district residents $95; out-of-state residents $123.
Room and board: $3,870.

FINANCIAL AID PICTURE (2008-2009)
Students with need: 56% of average financial aid package awarded as scholarships/grants, 44% awarded as loans/jobs. Need-based aid available for part-time students. Work study available nights, weekends, and for part-time students.
Students without need: This college awards aid only to students with need.

FINANCIAL AID PROCEDURES
Forms required: FAFSA, institutional form.
Dates and Deadlines: Priority date 7/1; no closing date. Applicants notified on a rolling basis starting 5/15.

CONTACT
Michelle Paul, Director of Financial Aid
601 LaClede Avenue, Neosho, MO 64850
(417) 451-3223 ext. 5434

Culver-Stockton College
Canton, Missouri
www.culver.edu   Federal Code: 002460

4-year private liberal arts college in small town, affiliated with Christian Church (Disciples of Christ).
Enrollment: 723 undergrads, 3% part-time. 148 full-time freshmen.
Selectivity: Admits 50 to 75% of applicants.

BASIC COSTS (2010-2011)
Tuition and fees: $22,550.
Per-credit charge: $515.
Room and board: $7,400.

FINANCIAL AID PICTURE (2009-2010)
Students with need: Out of 141 full-time freshmen who applied for aid, 132 were judged to have need. Of these, 132 received aid, and 27 had their full need met. Average financial aid package met 78% of need; average scholarship/grant was $17,385; average loan was $3,916. For part-time students, average financial aid package was $7,504.
Students without need: 16 full-time freshmen who did not demonstrate need for aid received scholarships/grants; average award was $13,953. No-need awards available for academics, alumni affiliation, art, athletics, job skills, leadership, music/drama, religious affiliation, state/district residency.
Scholarships offered: 10 full-time freshmen received athletic scholarships; average amount $2,195.
Cumulative student debt: 90% of graduating class had student loans; average debt was $23,761.

FINANCIAL AID PROCEDURES
Forms required: FAFSA.
Dates and Deadlines: Priority date 3/1; closing date 6/1. Applicants notified on a rolling basis starting 2/15; must reply within 2 week(s) of notification.
Transfers: Must reply within 2 week(s) of notification.

CONTACT
Tina Wiseman, Director of Financial Aid
One College Hill, Canton, MO 63435-1299
(573) 288-6307

DeVry University: Kansas City
Kansas City, Missouri
www.devry.edu

4-year for-profit university in large city.
Enrollment: 1,052 undergrads, 46% part-time. 126 full-time freshmen.

BASIC COSTS (2009-2010)
Tuition and fees: $14,160.
Per-credit charge: $550.

FINANCIAL AID PICTURE (2008-2009)
Students with need: Need-based aid available for full-time and part-time students.
Students without need: This college awards aid only to students with need.

FINANCIAL AID PROCEDURES
Forms required: FAFSA.
Dates and Deadlines: No deadline. Applicants notified on a rolling basis.

CONTACT
Maureen Kelly, Senior Associate Director of Financial Aid
11224 Holmes Street, Kansas City, MO 64131-3626
(816) 941-0439

Drury University
Springfield, Missouri
www.drury.edu   Federal Code: 002461

4-year private university and liberal arts college in large city, affiliated with United Church of Christ and Christian Church (Disciples of Christ).
Enrollment: 1,538 undergrads, 2% part-time. 359 full-time freshmen.
Selectivity: Admits 50 to 75% of applicants.

BASIC COSTS (2010-2011)
Tuition and fees: $19,944.
Per-credit charge: $645.
Room and board: $6,971.

FINANCIAL AID PICTURE (2009-2010)
Students with need: Out of 338 full-time freshmen who applied for aid, 309 were judged to have need. Of these, 309 received aid, and 268 had their full need met. Average financial aid package met 84% of need; average scholarship/grant was $5,680; average loan was $4,500. Need-based aid available for part-time students.
Students without need: 57 full-time freshmen who did not demonstrate need for aid received scholarships/grants; average award was $425. No-need awards available for academics, alumni affiliation, art, athletics, job skills, leadership, minority status, music/drama, religious affiliation.
Scholarships offered: *Merit:* Trustee Scholarship: $10,000 up to tuition, room and board; 30 awarded. Presidential Scholarship: up to $12,000 per year; 10 awarded. Dean's Scholarship: up to $8,000 a year; top 2% of high school class awarded. Leadership Scholarship: $1,000 a year. Clergy-dependent scholarship: $7,000. Edward Jones Minority Scholarship: $10,000; 10 awarded. Missouri A+ Scholarship: $1,000. International Baccalaureate Award: $7,000 a year. *Athletic:* 23 full-time freshmen received athletic scholarships; average amount $5,000.
Cumulative student debt: 67% of graduating class had student loans; average debt was $20,500.

FINANCIAL AID PROCEDURES
Forms required: FAFSA, institutional form.
Dates and Deadlines: Closing date 3/1. Applicants notified on a rolling basis starting 3/30; must reply within 2 week(s) of notification.
Transfers: No deadline. Phi Theta Kappa Scholarship of $1,000 available.

CONTACT
Annette Avery, Director of Financial Aid
900 North Benton Avenue, Springfield, MO 65802-3712
(417) 873-7312

East Central College
Union, Missouri
www.eastcentral.edu   Federal Code: 008862

2-year public community college in small town.
Enrollment: 2,982 undergrads, 33% part-time. 782 full-time freshmen.
Selectivity: Open admission; but selective for some programs.

BASIC COSTS (2009-2010)
Tuition and fees: $2,130; out-of-district residents $2,910; out-of-state residents $4,230.
Per-credit charge: $61; out-of-district residents $87; out-of-state residents $131.

FINANCIAL AID PICTURE (2008-2009)
Students with need: Need-based aid available for full-time and part-time students.
Students without need: No-need awards available for academics, alumni affiliation, art, athletics, music/drama, state/district residency.

FINANCIAL AID PROCEDURES
Forms required: FAFSA.
Dates and Deadlines: Priority date 3/1; no closing date. Applicants notified on a rolling basis starting 3/15.
Transfers: No deadline. Applicants notified on a rolling basis starting 3/15.

CONTACT
Karen Koenig-Griffin, Director of Financial Aid
1964 Prairie Dell Road, Union, MO 63084-0529
(636) 584-6570

Evangel University
Springfield, Missouri
www.evangel.edu   Federal Code: 002463

4-year private liberal arts college in small city, affiliated with Assemblies of God.
Enrollment: 1,735 undergrads.
Selectivity: Admits 50 to 75% of applicants.

BASIC COSTS (2010-2011)
Tuition and fees: $16,900.
Room and board: $6,000.

FINANCIAL AID PICTURE (2008-2009)
Students with need: Need-based aid available for full-time and part-time students. Work study available nights, weekends, and for part-time students.
Students without need: This college awards aid only to students with need.

FINANCIAL AID PROCEDURES
Forms required: FAFSA.
Dates and Deadlines: Priority date 4/1; closing date 6/30. Applicants notified on a rolling basis starting 4/1; must reply within 3 week(s) of notification.

CONTACT
Dorynda Carpenter, Director of Student Financial Services
1111 North Glenstone, Springfield, MO 65802
(417) 865-2811 ext. 7300

Fontbonne University
St. Louis, Missouri
www.fontbonne.edu   Federal Code: 002464

4-year private university and liberal arts college in large city, affiliated with Roman Catholic Church.
Enrollment: 1,972 undergrads, 26% part-time. 174 full-time freshmen.
Selectivity: Admits over 75% of applicants.

BASIC COSTS (2010-2011)
Tuition and fees: $20,380.
Per-credit charge: $537.
Room and board: $7,600.

FINANCIAL AID PICTURE (2008-2009)
Students with need: Out of 141 full-time freshmen who applied for aid, 117 were judged to have need. Of these, 117 received aid. Need-based aid available for part-time students.
Students without need: 2 full-time freshmen who did not demonstrate need for aid received scholarships/grants. No-need awards available for academics, alumni affiliation, art, leadership, minority status, music/drama, religious affiliation, state/district residency.
Scholarships offered: Dean's Scholarship: $6,000-$8,000; GPA, ACT, rank criteria. Alumni Scholarship: $1,000-$6,000; GPA, ACT and class rank criteria. Presidential Scholarship: up to full tuition. Campus Service Scholarship: $500-$3,000; activities, leadership. Art, theater, English, writing and computer science scholarships also available.

FINANCIAL AID PROCEDURES
Forms required: FAFSA, institutional form.
Dates and Deadlines: Closing date 4/1. Applicants notified on a rolling basis starting 2/1; must reply within 2 week(s) of notification.
Transfers: Applicants notified on a rolling basis starting 2/1; must reply within 2 week(s) of notification.

CONTACT
Nicole Moore, Director of Financial Aid
6800 Wydown Boulevard, St. Louis, MO 63105
(314) 889-1414

Goldfarb School of Nursing at Barnes-Jewish College
St. Louis, Missouri
www.barnesjewishcollege.edu   Federal Code: 003689

Upper-division private nursing college in very large city.
Enrollment: 517 undergrads, 29% part-time.

BASIC COSTS (2010-2011)
Tuition and fees: $14,953.
Per-credit charge: $548.

FINANCIAL AID PICTURE (2008-2009)
Students with need: Need-based aid available for full-time and part-time students.
Students without need: No-need awards available for academics, leadership.

FINANCIAL AID PROCEDURES
Forms required: FAFSA.
Dates and Deadlines: Priority date 4/1; no closing date. Applicants notified on a rolling basis.
Transfers: No deadline. Applicants notified on a rolling basis.

CONTACT
Jason Crowe, Financial Aid Director
4483 Duncan Avenue, St. Louis, MO 63110-1091
(314) 362-9250

Hannibal-LaGrange College
Hannibal, Missouri
www.hlg.edu   Federal Code: 009089

4-year private liberal arts college in large town, affiliated with Southern Baptist Convention.
Enrollment: 902 undergrads, 6% part-time. 184 full-time freshmen.
Selectivity: Admits over 75% of applicants.

BASIC COSTS (2010-2011)
Tuition and fees: $15,842.
Room and board: $6,180.

FINANCIAL AID PICTURE (2009-2010)
Students with need: For part-time students, average financial aid package was $4,326.
Students without need: 25 full-time freshmen who did not demonstrate need for aid received scholarships/grants. No-need awards available for academics, art, athletics, music/drama, religious affiliation.
Scholarships offered: 64 full-time freshmen received athletic scholarships; average amount $7,813.
Additional info: Work-study opportunities vary according to on- and off-campus needs.

FINANCIAL AID PROCEDURES
Forms required: FAFSA, institutional form.
Dates and Deadlines: Closing date 7/1. Applicants notified on a rolling basis; must reply by 8/31.
Transfers: No deadline.

CONTACT
Brice Baumgardner, Director of Financial Aid
2800 Palmyra Road, Hannibal, MO 63401
(573) 629-3267

Harris-Stowe State University
St. Louis, Missouri
www.hssu.edu   Federal Code: 002466

4-year public university in large city.
Enrollment: 1,844 undergrads, 24% part-time. 414 full-time freshmen.
Selectivity: Admits over 75% of applicants.

BASIC COSTS (2009-2010)
Tuition and fees: $5,340; out-of-state residents $10,092.
Per-credit charge: $164; out-of-state residents $323.

FINANCIAL AID PICTURE (2009-2010)
Students with need: Out of 414 full-time freshmen who applied for aid, 400 were judged to have need. Of these, 400 received aid, and 8 had their full need met. Average financial aid package met 98% of need; average scholarship/grant was $1,375; average loan was $3,500. For part-time students, average financial aid package was $3,750.
Students without need: No-need awards available for academics, athletics, music/drama, state/district residency.
Scholarships offered: 2 full-time freshmen received athletic scholarships; average amount $984.

FINANCIAL AID PROCEDURES
Forms required: FAFSA, institutional form.

Dates and Deadlines: Priority date 4/1; no closing date. Applicants notified on a rolling basis starting 4/1; must reply within 3 week(s) of notification.

CONTACT

Regina Blackshear, Director of Financial Assistance
3026 Laclede Avenue, St. Louis, MO 63103-2199
(314) 340-3500

Hickey College

St. Louis, Missouri
www.hickeycollege.edu   Federal Code: 014209

4-year for-profit business and technical college in very large city.
Enrollment: 444 undergrads.
Selectivity: Open admission; but selective for some programs.

FINANCIAL AID PICTURE

Students with need: Need-based aid available for full-time students.

FINANCIAL AID PROCEDURES

Forms required: FAFSA.
Dates and Deadlines: No deadline. Applicants notified on a rolling basis.

CONTACT

Deana Pecoroni, Director, Student Services
940 West Port Plaza, St. Louis, MO 63146
(314) 434-2212 ext. 128

Jefferson College

Hillsboro, Missouri
www.jeffco.edu   Federal Code: 002468

2-year public community and technical college in rural community.
Enrollment: 5,375 undergrads, 43% part-time. 972 full-time freshmen.
Selectivity: Open admission; but selective for some programs.

BASIC COSTS (2010-2011)

Tuition and fees: $2,550; out-of-district residents $3,840; out-of-state residents $5,100.
Per-credit charge: $85; out-of-district residents $128; out-of-state residents $170.
Room and board: $5,794.

FINANCIAL AID PICTURE (2008-2009)

Students with need: Out of 821 full-time freshmen who applied for aid, 545 were judged to have need. Of these, 518 received aid, and 15 had their full need met. Average financial aid package met 52% of need; average scholarship/grant was $2,012; average loan was $2,487. For part-time students, average financial aid package was $3,072.
Students without need: 15 full-time freshmen who did not demonstrate need for aid received scholarships/grants; average award was $1,390. No-need awards available for academics, art, athletics, leadership, music/drama, state/district residency.
Scholarships offered: 36 full-time freshmen received athletic scholarships; average amount $6,372.
Cumulative student debt: 36% of graduating class had student loans; average debt was $10,917.

FINANCIAL AID PROCEDURES

Forms required: FAFSA.
Dates and Deadlines: Priority date 4/1; no closing date. Applicants notified on a rolling basis starting 4/15.

CONTACT

Julie Fraser, Director of Admissions and Financial Aid
1000 Viking Drive, Hillsboro, MO 63050-2441
(636) 797-3000 ext. 212

Kansas City Art Institute

Kansas City, Missouri
www.kcai.edu   Federal Code: 002473

4-year private visual arts college in large city.
Enrollment: 679 undergrads, 2% part-time. 180 full-time freshmen.
Selectivity: Admits 50 to 75% of applicants.

BASIC COSTS (2010-2011)

Tuition and fees: $29,866.
Room and board: $9,100.

FINANCIAL AID PICTURE (2009-2010)

Students with need: Out of 166 full-time freshmen who applied for aid, 152 were judged to have need. Of these, 152 received aid, and 19 had their full need met. Average financial aid package met 70% of need; average scholarship/grant was $18,537; average loan was $4,459. For part-time students, average financial aid package was $20,381.
Students without need: 18 full-time freshmen who did not demonstrate need for aid received scholarships/grants; average award was $13,752. No-need awards available for academics, art.
Scholarships offered: February 1, March 1 and April 1 priority application dates for merit scholarships; deadline August 1.
Cumulative student debt: 100% of graduating class had student loans; average debt was $26,000.

FINANCIAL AID PROCEDURES

Forms required: FAFSA.
Dates and Deadlines: Priority date 3/15; closing date 4/1. Applicants notified on a rolling basis starting 4/1; must reply within 2 week(s) of notification.
Transfers: Priority date 3/1; no deadline. Applicants notified on a rolling basis starting 4/1; must reply within 2 week(s) of notification.

CONTACT

Kim Warren, Director of Financial Aid
4415 Warwick Boulevard, Kansas City, MO 64111
(816) 802-3337

Lincoln University

Jefferson City, Missouri
www.lincolnu.edu   Federal Code: 002479

4-year public university and liberal arts college in large town.
Enrollment: 2,650 undergrads, 21% part-time. 706 full-time freshmen.
Selectivity: Open admission; but selective for some programs and for out-of-state students.

BASIC COSTS (2010-2011)

Tuition and fees: $6,175; out-of-state residents $10,885.
Room and board: $4,660.
Additional info: Students enrolled full-time must pay $233 per fall/spring semester or $96 per summer semester for health insurance if they do not provide proof of other coverage. Enrollment in the student health insurance program is required for international students.

FINANCIAL AID PICTURE (2009-2010)

Students with need: Need-based aid available for full-time students. Work study available nights, weekends, and for part-time students.
Students without need: No-need awards available for academics, art, athletics, job skills, leadership, minority status, music/drama, ROTC, state/district residency.

FINANCIAL AID PROCEDURES

Forms required: FAFSA, institutional form.
Dates and Deadlines: Priority date 3/1; no closing date. Applicants notified on a rolling basis starting 3/15; must reply within 2 week(s) of notification.

Transfers: Applicants notified on a rolling basis starting 3/15; must reply within 2 week(s) of notification.

CONTACT

Alfred Robinson, Director of Financial Aid and Student Employment
820 Chestnut Stree, B7 Young Hall, Jefferson City, MO 65102-0029
(573) 681-5363

Lindenwood University

Saint Charles, Missouri
www.lindenwood.edu/ · Federal Code: 002480

4-year private university and liberal arts college in very large city, affiliated with Presbyterian Church (USA).

Enrollment: 6,384 undergrads, 4% part-time. 1,056 full-time freshmen.
Selectivity: Admits 50 to 75% of applicants.

BASIC COSTS (2010-2011)

Tuition and fees: $13,600.
Per-credit charge: $380.
Room and board: $7,120.

FINANCIAL AID PICTURE (2009-2010)

Students with need: Out of 744 full-time freshmen who applied for aid, 637 were judged to have need. Of these, 637 received aid, and 223 had their full need met. Average financial aid package met 90% of need; average scholarship/grant was $3,274; average loan was $2,472. For part-time students, average financial aid package was $2,587.
Students without need: 293 full-time freshmen who did not demonstrate need for aid received scholarships/grants; average award was $4,431. No-need awards available for academics, alumni affiliation, art, job skills, leadership, music/drama, ROTC.

FINANCIAL AID PROCEDURES

Forms required: FAFSA.
Dates and Deadlines: Priority date 4/1; no closing date. Applicants notified on a rolling basis.

CONTACT

Lori Bode, Director of Financial Aid
209 South Kingshighway, St. Charles, MO 63301
(636) 949-4923

Linn State Technical College

Linn, Missouri
www.linnstate.edu · Federal Code: 004711

2-year public community and technical college in rural community.

Enrollment: 1,081 undergrads, 11% part-time. 478 full-time freshmen.
Selectivity: Open admission; but selective for some programs.

BASIC COSTS (2009-2010)

Tuition and fees: $4,950; out-of-state residents $9,330.
Per-credit charge: $146; out-of-state residents $292.
Room and board: $4,980.

FINANCIAL AID PICTURE (2008-2009)

Students with need: Out of 419 full-time freshmen who applied for aid, 419 were judged to have need. Of these, 321 received aid, and 154 had their full need met. Average financial aid package met 18% of need; average scholarship/grant was $3,577; average loan was $2,990. Need-based aid available for part-time students.
Students without need: 3 full-time freshmen who did not demonstrate need for aid received scholarships/grants; average award was $1,100. No-need awards available for academics, alumni affiliation, state/district residency.

Cumulative student debt: 59% of graduating class had student loans; average debt was $7,444.

FINANCIAL AID PROCEDURES

Forms required: FAFSA.
Dates and Deadlines: Priority date 4/1; no closing date. Applicants notified on a rolling basis starting 4/1; must reply within 3 week(s) of notification.

CONTACT

Becky Whithaus, Director of Financial Aid
One Technology Drive, Linn, MO 65051
(573) 897-5143

Maryville University of Saint Louis

St. Louis, Missouri
www.maryville.edu · Federal Code: 002482

4-year private university in very large city.

Enrollment: 2,826 undergrads, 41% part-time. 340 full-time freshmen.
Selectivity: Admits 50 to 75% of applicants.

BASIC COSTS (2010-2011)

Tuition and fees: $21,910.
Per-credit charge: $634.
Room and board: $8,500.

FINANCIAL AID PICTURE (2009-2010)

Students with need: Out of 292 full-time freshmen who applied for aid, 254 were judged to have need. Of these, 254 received aid, and 51 had their full need met. Average financial aid package met 79% of need; average scholarship/grant was $13,040; average loan was $3,010. For part-time students, average financial aid package was $8,132.
Students without need: 69 full-time freshmen who did not demonstrate need for aid received scholarships/grants; average award was $10,718. No-need awards available for academics, alumni affiliation, art, athletics, leadership, minority status, ROTC.
Scholarships offered: *Merit:* University Scholars Program: awarded to full-time freshmen with 28 ACT or 1170 SAT (exclusive of writing), high school GPA 3.5-4.0; interview required. M-PACT Award: awarded to full-time freshmen based on campus activity and impact on student life. *Athletic:* 6 full-time freshmen received athletic scholarships; average amount $11,797.
Cumulative student debt: 73% of graduating class had student loans; average debt was $18,341.

FINANCIAL AID PROCEDURES

Forms required: FAFSA.
Dates and Deadlines: Priority date 3/1; no closing date. Applicants notified on a rolling basis starting 3/1; must reply by 5/1 or within 2 week(s) of notification.
Transfers: No deadline. Applicants notified on a rolling basis starting 2/1. Outstanding Transfer Student Award, PTK Award, Art & Design Award scholarships available.

CONTACT

Martha Harbaugh, Director of Financial Aid
650 Maryville University Drive, St. Louis, MO 63141-7299
(314) 529-9360

Metro Business College: Jefferson City

Jefferson City, Missouri
www.metrobusinesscollege.edu · Federal Code: 014710

2-year for-profit business and health science college in large town.
Enrollment: 178 undergrads.
Selectivity: Open admission; but selective for some programs.

BASIC COSTS (2009-2010)
Tuition and fees: $9,375.

FINANCIAL AID PICTURE
Students with need: Need-based aid available for full-time and part-time students.

FINANCIAL AID PROCEDURES
Forms required: FAFSA, institutional form.
Dates and Deadlines: No deadline. Applicants notified on a rolling basis.

CONTACT
Debbie Jenkins, Financial Aid Coordinator
1407 Southwest Boulevard, Jefferson City, MO 65109
(573) 635-6600

Metropolitan Community College: Blue River
Independence, Missouri
www.mcckc.edu   Federal Code: 009140

2-year public community college in small city.
Enrollment: 2,502 undergrads, 45% part-time. 536 full-time freshmen.
Selectivity: Open admission.

BASIC COSTS (2009-2010)
Tuition and fees: $2,460; out-of-district residents $4,380; out-of-state residents $5,850.
Per-credit charge: $82; out-of-district residents $146; out-of-state residents $195.

FINANCIAL AID PICTURE (2008-2009)
Students with need: Need-based aid available for full-time and part-time students. Work study available nights.
Students without need: No-need awards available for academics, athletics, leadership.

FINANCIAL AID PROCEDURES
Forms required: FAFSA, institutional form.
Dates and Deadlines: Priority date 5/30; closing date 8/20. Applicants notified on a rolling basis starting 4/8.
Transfers: No deadline.

CONTACT
Cindy Butler, District Director, Student Financial Aid
3200 Broadway, Kansas City, MO 64111-2429
(816) 604-1527

Metropolitan Community College: Longview
Lee's Summit, Missouri
www.mcckc.edu   Federal Code: 009140

2-year public community college in small city.
Enrollment: 4,793 undergrads, 45% part-time. 1,001 full-time freshmen.
Selectivity: Open admission.

BASIC COSTS (2009-2010)
Tuition and fees: $2,460; out-of-district residents $4,380; out-of-state residents $5,850.
Per-credit charge: $82; out-of-district residents $146; out-of-state residents $195.

FINANCIAL AID PICTURE (2008-2009)
Students with need: Need-based aid available for full-time students. Work study available nights.

Students without need: No-need awards available for academics, athletics, leadership.

FINANCIAL AID PROCEDURES
Forms required: FAFSA, institutional form.
Dates and Deadlines: Priority date 5/30; closing date 8/20. Applicants notified on a rolling basis starting 4/8.
Transfers: No deadline.

CONTACT
Cindy Butler, District Director, Student Financial Aid
500 Longview Road, Lee's Summit, MO 64081-2105
(816) 604-1527

Metropolitan Community College: Maple Woods
Kansas City, Missouri
www.mcckc.edu   Federal Code: 004432

2-year public community college in large city.
Enrollment: 3,602 undergrads, 46% part-time. 760 full-time freshmen.
Selectivity: Open admission; but selective for some programs.

BASIC COSTS (2009-2010)
Tuition and fees: $2,480; out-of-district residents $4,380; out-of-state residents $5,850.
Per-credit charge: $82; out-of-district residents $146; out-of-state residents $195.

FINANCIAL AID PICTURE (2008-2009)
Students with need: Need-based aid available for full-time and part-time students. Work study available nights.
Students without need: No-need awards available for academics, athletics, leadership.

FINANCIAL AID PROCEDURES
Forms required: FAFSA, institutional form.
Dates and Deadlines: Priority date 5/30; no closing date. Applicants notified on a rolling basis.

CONTACT
Cindy Butler, District Director, Student Financial Aid
2601 NE Barry Road, Kansas City, MO 64156-1299
(816) 604-1527

Metropolitan Community College: Penn Valley
Kansas City, Missouri
www.mcckc.edu   Federal Code: 002484

2-year public community college in large city.
Enrollment: 3,889 undergrads, 63% part-time. 359 full-time freshmen.
Selectivity: Open admission; but selective for some programs.

BASIC COSTS (2009-2010)
Tuition and fees: $2,480; out-of-district residents $4,380; out-of-state residents $5,850.
Per-credit charge: $82; out-of-district residents $146; out-of-state residents $195.

FINANCIAL AID PICTURE (2008-2009)
Students with need: Need-based aid available for full-time students. Work study available nights.
Students without need: 359 full-time freshmen who did not demonstrate need for aid received scholarships/grants. No-need awards available for academics, athletics, leadership.

FINANCIAL AID PROCEDURES
Forms required: FAFSA, institutional form.
Dates and Deadlines: Priority date 5/30; no closing date. Applicants notified on a rolling basis starting 4/8.

CONTACT
Cindy Butler, District Director, Student Financial Aid
3201 Southwest Trafficway, Kansas City, MO 64111-2429
(816) 604-1527

Mineral Area College
Park Hills, Missouri
www.mineralarea.edu   Federal Code: 002486

2-year public community college in small town.
Enrollment: 3,145 undergrads.
Selectivity: Open admission; but selective for some programs.

BASIC COSTS (2009-2010)
Tuition and fees: $2,490; out-of-district residents $3,240; out-of-state residents $3,960.
Per-credit charge: $83; out-of-district residents $108; out-of-state residents $132.
Room and board: $2,925.

FINANCIAL AID PICTURE (2008-2009)
Students with need: Need-based aid available for full-time and part-time students.
Students without need: No-need awards available for academics, alumni affiliation, art, athletics, leadership, music/drama, state/district residency.

FINANCIAL AID PROCEDURES
Forms required: FAFSA.
Dates and Deadlines: Closing date 4/1. Applicants notified on a rolling basis starting 2/15; must reply within 4 week(s) of notification.

CONTACT
Denise Sebastian, Financial Aid Director
PO Box 1000, Park Hills, MO 63601-1000
(573) 518-2133

Missouri Baptist University
St. Louis, Missouri
www.mobap.edu   Federal Code: 007540

4-year private university and liberal arts college in very large city, affiliated with Baptist faith.
Enrollment: 1,541 undergrads, 18% part-time. 218 full-time freshmen.
Selectivity: Admits 50 to 75% of applicants.

BASIC COSTS (2009-2010)
Tuition and fees: $17,860.
Per-credit charge: $590.
Room and board: $7,090.

FINANCIAL AID PICTURE (2008-2009)
Students with need: Need-based aid available for full-time and part-time students.
Students without need: No-need awards available for academics, alumni affiliation, athletics, leadership, music/drama, religious affiliation.

FINANCIAL AID PROCEDURES
Forms required: FAFSA, institutional form.
Dates and Deadlines: Priority date 4/1; no closing date. Applicants notified on a rolling basis starting 4/15; must reply within 2 week(s) of notification.
Transfers: Institutional academic scholarships available.

CONTACT
Laurie Wallace, Director of Financial Services
One College Park Drive, St. Louis, MO 63141-8698
(314) 392-2366

Missouri College
St. Louis, Missouri
www.missouricollege.com   Federal Code: 009795

2-year for-profit technical college in large city.
Enrollment: 508 undergrads.
Selectivity: Open admission; but selective for some programs.

BASIC COSTS (2009-2010)
Additional info: Diploma programs are $345 per semester credit hour, degree programs are $365 per semester credit hour.

FINANCIAL AID PICTURE
Students with need: Need-based aid available for full-time and part-time students. Work study available nights.

FINANCIAL AID PROCEDURES
Forms required: FAFSA.
Dates and Deadlines: No deadline.

CONTACT
Jennifer Malotte, Director of Student Finance
10121 Manchester Road, St. Louis, MO 63122-1583
(314) 821-7700

Missouri Southern State University
Joplin, Missouri
www.mssu.edu   Federal Code: 002488

4-year public university and liberal arts college in large town.
Enrollment: 5,195 undergrads, 21% part-time. 681 full-time freshmen.
Selectivity: Admits over 75% of applicants.

BASIC COSTS (2009-2010)
Tuition and fees: $4,816; out-of-state residents $9,106.
Per-credit charge: $143; out-of-state residents $286.
Room and board: $5,382.

FINANCIAL AID PICTURE (2008-2009)
Students with need: Out of 671 full-time freshmen who applied for aid, 468 were judged to have need. Of these, 463 received aid, and 40 had their full need met. Average financial aid package met 65% of need; average scholarship/grant was $3,607; average loan was $2,671. For part-time students, average financial aid package was $5,376.
Students without need: 179 full-time freshmen who did not demonstrate need for aid received scholarships/grants; average award was $4,254. No-need awards available for academics, alumni affiliation, art, minority status, music/drama.
Scholarships offered: 79 full-time freshmen received athletic scholarships; average amount $3,495.
Cumulative student debt: 64% of graduating class had student loans; average debt was $16,737.

FINANCIAL AID PROCEDURES
Forms required: FAFSA, institutional form.
Dates and Deadlines: Priority date 5/1; no closing date. Applicants notified by 3/1.

CONTACT
Kathy Feith, Director of Student Financial Aid
3950 East Newman Road, Joplin, MO 64801-1595
(417) 625-9325

Missouri State University

Springfield, Missouri
www.missouristate.edu   Federal Code: 002503

4-year public university in small city.
Enrollment: 14,974 undergrads, 11% part-time. 2,285 full-time freshmen.
Selectivity: Admits 50 to 75% of applicants.

BASIC COSTS (2009-2010)
Tuition and fees: $6,276; out-of-state residents $11,556.
Per-credit charge: $186; out-of-state residents $362.
Room and board: $5,836.

FINANCIAL AID PICTURE (2008-2009)
Students with need: Out of 1,945 full-time freshmen who applied for aid, 1,311 were judged to have need. Of these, 1,289 received aid, and 360 had their full need met. Average financial aid package met 71% of need; average scholarship/grant was $5,897; average loan was $3,122. For part-time students, average financial aid package was $5,178.
Students without need: No-need awards available for academics, alumni affiliation, art, athletics, job skills, leadership, minority status, music/drama, ROTC, state/district residency.
Scholarships offered: Presidential Scholarships: full tuition, room, and board; based on 30 ACT and rank in top 10% of class; 40 awarded, application deadline January 15. Board of Governors Scholarships: cover basic fees for 32 credit hours per year (plus two thirds of out of state fees for non-residents); based on 28 ACT and either top 10% class rank or 3.85 GPA; unlimited number of awards. Freshman Academic Scholarships: $2,000 per year (plus two thirds of out of state fees for non-residents); based on 26 ACT and either top 20% class rank or 3.7 GPA; unlimited number of awards. Freshman Recognition Scholarships: $1,000 per year (plus two thirds of out of state fees for non-residents); based on 24 ACT and either top 10% class rank or 3.85 GPA; unlimited number of awards. Multicultural Leadership Scholarships: cover required student fees (in-state); for students in top half of class who have demonstrated leadership in the minority community; 50 awarded; February 1 deadline. Applications must be received by March 1 to be considered for scholarships, unless otherwise noted.
Cumulative student debt: 85% of graduating class had student loans; average debt was $19,813.
Additional info: Extensive scholarship program offered to freshmen and transfer students. Out-of-state fee stipends available. Student employment service available to assist students in securing employment on campus and in community.

FINANCIAL AID PROCEDURES
Forms required: FAFSA.
Dates and Deadlines: Priority date 3/31; no closing date. Applicants notified on a rolling basis starting 4/30; must reply within 4 week(s) of notification.
Transfers: No deadline. Applicants notified on a rolling basis.

CONTACT
Vicki Mattocks, Director of Financial Aid
901 South National Avenue, Springfield, MO 65897
(417) 836-5262

Missouri State University: West Plains

West Plains, Missouri
www.wp.missouristate.edu   Federal Code: 031060

2-year public branch campus college in large town.
Enrollment: 1,708 undergrads, 26% part-time. 440 full-time freshmen.
Selectivity: Open admission; but selective for some programs.

BASIC COSTS (2010-2011)
Tuition and fees: $3,304; out-of-state residents $6,364.
Per-credit charge: $102; out-of-state residents $204.

Room and board: $5,116.

FINANCIAL AID PICTURE (2008-2009)
Students with need: 54% of average financial aid package awarded as scholarships/grants, 46% awarded as loans/jobs. Need-based aid available for part-time students. Work study available nights, weekends, and for part-time students.
Students without need: No-need awards available for academics, athletics, state/district residency.

FINANCIAL AID PROCEDURES
Forms required: FAFSA, institutional form.
Dates and Deadlines: Priority date 3/31; no closing date. Applicants notified on a rolling basis; must reply by 4/15.

CONTACT
Donna Bassham, Coordinator of Financial Aid
128 Garfield Avenue, West Plains, MO 65775-2715
(417) 255-7243

Missouri Technical School

St. Charles, Missouri
www.motech.edu   Federal Code: 016272

4-year for-profit engineering and technical college in very large city.
Enrollment: 130 undergrads.

BASIC COSTS (2009-2010)
Additional info: Tuition is $500 per credit hour. Fees are $95 per 2-month term.

FINANCIAL AID PICTURE
Students with need: Need-based aid available for full-time and part-time students.
Students without need: This college awards aid only to students with need.

FINANCIAL AID PROCEDURES
Forms required: FAFSA, institutional form.
Dates and Deadlines: No deadline. Applicants notified on a rolling basis.

CONTACT
Cindy Ann Sinnott, Financial Aid Director
1690 Country Club Plaza Drive, St. Charles, MO 63303
(314) 569-3600 ext. 316

Missouri University of Science and Technology

Rolla, Missouri
www.mst.edu   Federal Code: 002517

4-year public university in large town.
Enrollment: 5,145 undergrads, 5% part-time. 1,011 full-time freshmen.
Selectivity: Admits over 75% of applicants.

BASIC COSTS (2009-2010)
Tuition and fees: $8,488; out-of-state residents $19,579.
Per-credit charge: $246; out-of-state residents $615.
Room and board: $7,545.
Additional info: Tuition/fee waivers available for minority students.

FINANCIAL AID PICTURE (2008-2009)
Students with need: Out of 905 full-time freshmen who applied for aid, 587 were judged to have need. Of these, 587 received aid, and 353 had their full need met. Average financial aid package met 46% of need; average scholarship/grant was $8,616; average loan was $4,088. For part-time students, average financial aid package was $8,892.

Students without need: 402 full-time freshmen who did not demonstrate need for aid received scholarships/grants. No-need awards available for academics, alumni affiliation, athletics, job skills, leadership, minority status, music/drama, religious affiliation, ROTC, state/district residency.

Scholarships offered: 30 full-time freshmen received athletic scholarships.

Cumulative student debt: 81% of graduating class had student loans; average debt was $23,760.

FINANCIAL AID PROCEDURES

Forms required: FAFSA.

Dates and Deadlines: Priority date 3/1; no closing date. Applicants notified on a rolling basis; must reply within 3 week(s) of notification.

Transfers: Special scholarships available to transfer students.

CONTACT

Lynn Stichnote, Director of Financial Assistance
106 Parker Hall, Rolla, MO 65409-1060
(573) 341-4282

Missouri Valley College
Marshall, Missouri
www.moval.edu   Federal Code: 002489

4-year private liberal arts college in large town, affiliated with Presbyterian Church (USA).

Enrollment: 1,450 undergrads.

BASIC COSTS (2010-2011)

Tuition and fees: $17,170.
Per-credit charge: $350.
Room and board: $6,450.

FINANCIAL AID PICTURE

Students with need: Need-based aid available for full-time and part-time students. Work study available nights, weekends, and for part-time students.

Students without need: No-need awards available for academics, state/district residency.

Scholarships offered: Talent scholarships: $1,000 to $13,000; 100 awarded for general achievement.

FINANCIAL AID PROCEDURES

Forms required: FAFSA, state aid form.

Dates and Deadlines: Priority date 3/1; no closing date. Applicants notified on a rolling basis starting 2/1; must reply within 6 week(s) of notification.

Transfers: Closing date 3/1.

CONTACT

Charles Mayfield, Director of Financial Aid
500 East College Street, Marshall, MO 65340
(660) 831-4176

Missouri Western State University
St. Joseph, Missouri
www.missouriwestern.edu   Federal Code: 002490

4-year public business and liberal arts college in small city.

Enrollment: 5,071 undergrads, 20% part-time. 1,004 full-time freshmen.

Selectivity: Open admission; but selective for some programs.

BASIC COSTS (2010-2011)

Tuition and fees: $5,460; out-of-state residents $9,818.
Per-credit charge: $166; out-of-state residents $310.
Room and board: $6,500.

FINANCIAL AID PICTURE (2008-2009)

Students with need: Need-based aid available for full-time and part-time students.

Students without need: No-need awards available for academics, alumni affiliation, art, athletics, job skills, leadership, minority status, music/drama, state/district residency.

Scholarships offered: Golden Griffon Scholarship: up to $10,000 per year for 4 years; 27 ACT, top 10% of class or 3.5 GPA, evidence of involvement in extracurricular activities and community service; 2 essays and personal interview required; application deadline 2/1. President's Academic Scholarship: up to $4,000 per year; 25 ACT and either rank in the top 15% of class or 3.25 GPA required; application deadline 3/1.

FINANCIAL AID PROCEDURES

Forms required: FAFSA, institutional form.

Dates and Deadlines: Closing date 3/1. Applicants notified on a rolling basis starting 4/5; must reply within 3 week(s) of notification.

Transfers: Priority date 3/1; no deadline. Applicants notified on a rolling basis starting 4/15; must reply within 2 week(s) of notification.

CONTACT

Angela Beam, Director of Student Financial Aid
4525 Downs Drive, St. Joseph, MO 64507
(816) 271-4361

North Central Missouri College
Trenton, Missouri
www.ncmissouri.edu   Federal Code: 002514

2-year public community college in small town.

Enrollment: 859 full-time undergrads.

Selectivity: Open admission; but selective for some programs.

BASIC COSTS (2009-2010)

Tuition and fees: $2,550; out-of-district residents $3,510; out-of-state residents $4,650.
Per-credit charge: $65; out-of-district residents $97; out-of-state residents $135.
Room and board: $5,090.
Additional info: Tuition/fee waivers available for adults, minority students.

FINANCIAL AID PICTURE (2008-2009)

Students with need: Need-based aid available for full-time and part-time students.

Students without need: No-need awards available for academics, athletics, minority status, music/drama.

FINANCIAL AID PROCEDURES

Forms required: FAFSA, institutional form.

Dates and Deadlines: Closing date 3/15. Applicants notified on a rolling basis starting 3/15.

Transfers: No deadline. Applicants notified on a rolling basis starting 4/1. Transfer students may not receive same awards after transferring since some funds campus-based.

CONTACT

Melissa Guess, Financial Aid Director
1301 Main Street, Trenton, MO 64683
(660) 359-3948 ext. 402

Northwest Missouri State University
Maryville, Missouri
www.nwmissouri.edu   Federal Code: 002496

4-year public university in large town.

Enrollment: 5,740 undergrads, 5% part-time. 1,535 full-time freshmen.

Selectivity: Admits 50 to 75% of applicants.

BASIC COSTS (2009-2010)

Tuition and fees: $7,032; out-of-state residents $11,753.
Per-credit charge: $234; out-of-state residents $392.
Room and board: $6,790.
Additional info: Tuition/fees includes free laptop for full-time students and textbook rental for primary textbooks. Tuition/fee waivers available for minority students.

FINANCIAL AID PICTURE (2008-2009)

Students with need: Out of 1,348 full-time freshmen who applied for aid, 966 were judged to have need. Of these, 966 received aid, and 346 had their full need met. Average financial aid package met 65% of need; average scholarship/grant was $4,678; average loan was $3,243. For part-time students, average financial aid package was $6,015.
Students without need: 399 full-time freshmen who did not demonstrate need for aid received scholarships/grants; average award was $1,554. No-need awards available for academics, alumni affiliation, art, athletics, job skills, leadership, minority status, music/drama, ROTC, state/district residency.
Scholarships offered: 31 full-time freshmen received athletic scholarships; average amount $4,419.
Cumulative student debt: 70% of graduating class had student loans; average debt was $19,861.

FINANCIAL AID PROCEDURES

Forms required: FAFSA.
Dates and Deadlines: Priority date 4/1; no closing date. Applicants notified on a rolling basis starting 3/15; must reply within 4 week(s) of notification.
Transfers: No deadline. Applicants notified on a rolling basis starting 5/10; must reply within 4 week(s) of notification. Transfer scholarship based on academic record.

CONTACT

Del Morley, Director of Financial Assistance
800 University Drive, Maryville, MO 64468-6001
(660) 562-1363

Ozark Christian College

Joplin, Missouri
www.occ.edu   Federal Code: 015569

4-year private Bible college in large town, affiliated with nondenominational tradition.
Enrollment: 616 undergrads, 14% part-time. 142 full-time freshmen.
Selectivity: Admits 50 to 75% of applicants.

BASIC COSTS (2010-2011)

Tuition and fees: $8,900.
Per-credit charge: $280.
Room and board: $4,290.

FINANCIAL AID PICTURE (2008-2009)

Students with need: 44% of average financial aid package awarded as scholarships/grants, 56% awarded as loans/jobs. Need-based aid available for part-time students.
Students without need: No-need awards available for academics, leadership.

FINANCIAL AID PROCEDURES

Forms required: FAFSA.
Dates and Deadlines: Priority date 4/1; no closing date. Applicants notified on a rolling basis starting 4/15; must reply within 4 week(s) of notification.
Transfers: Academic transcripts required. ACT scores may qualify student for grants or scholarships.

CONTACT

Kim Balentine, Director of Financial Aid
1111 North Main Street, Joplin, MO 64801
(417) 624-2518

Ozarks Technical Community College

Springfield, Missouri
www.otc.edu   Federal Code: 030830

2-year public community and technical college in small city.
Enrollment: 11,500 undergrads. 2,418 full-time freshmen.
Selectivity: Open admission; but selective for some programs.

BASIC COSTS (2009-2010)

Tuition and fees: $2,940; out-of-district residents $3,870; out-of-state residents $4,905.
Per-credit charge: $81; out-of-district residents $112; out-of-state residents $147.

FINANCIAL AID PICTURE (2008-2009)

Students with need: Need-based aid available for full-time and part-time students.
Students without need: This college awards aid only to students with need.

FINANCIAL AID PROCEDURES

Forms required: FAFSA, institutional form.
Dates and Deadlines: Closing date 3/31. Applicants notified on a rolling basis starting 5/16.

CONTACT

Jeff Ford, Director of Financial Aid
1001 East Chestnut Expressway, Springfield, MO 65802
(417) 447-6930

Park University

Parkville, Missouri
www.park.edu   Federal Code: 002498

4-year private university in small town.
Enrollment: 11,135 undergrads, 88% part-time. 202 full-time freshmen.
Selectivity: Admits 50 to 75% of applicants.

BASIC COSTS (2009-2010)

Tuition and fees: $8,820.
Per-credit charge: $294.
Room and board: $5,850.
Additional info: Tuition varies by program.

FINANCIAL AID PICTURE (2008-2009)

Students with need: Need-based aid available for full-time and part-time students.
Students without need: No-need awards available for academics, alumni affiliation, art, athletics, job skills, leadership, minority status, music/drama, religious affiliation, ROTC.

FINANCIAL AID PROCEDURES

Forms required: FAFSA, institutional form.
Dates and Deadlines: Priority date 4/1; closing date 8/1. Applicants notified on a rolling basis starting 4/1.
Transfers: No deadline. Applicants notified by 11/1.

CONTACT

Cathy Colapietro, Associate Director of Admissions and Student Financial Services
8700 NW River Park Drive, Parkville, MO 64152
(816) 584-6290

Patricia Stevens College

St. Louis, Missouri
www.patriciastevenscollege.edu   Federal Code: 008552

2-year for-profit junior and liberal arts college in very large city.
Enrollment: 253 undergrads.
Selectivity: Open admission; but selective for some programs.

BASIC COSTS (2009-2010)
Tuition and fees: $9,450.
Additional info: Use of textbooks included in tuition.

FINANCIAL AID PICTURE
Students with need: Need-based aid available for full-time and part-time students.
Students without need: This college awards aid only to students with need.

FINANCIAL AID PROCEDURES
Forms required: FAFSA.
Dates and Deadlines: No deadline. Applicants notified on a rolling basis.

CONTACT
Greg Elsenrath, Financial Aid Director
330 North Fourth Street, Suite 306, St. Louis, MO 63102
(314) 421-0949 ext. 17

Ranken Technical College

St. Louis, Missouri
www.ranken.edu   Federal Code: 012500

2-year private technical college in very large city.
Enrollment: 1,939 undergrads.
Selectivity: Open admission.

BASIC COSTS (2009-2010)
Tuition and fees: $12,498.
Per-credit charge: $515.
Additional info: Book and tool costs vary by program.

FINANCIAL AID PICTURE (2008-2009)
Students with need: Need-based aid available for full-time and part-time students. Work study available nights.

FINANCIAL AID PROCEDURES
Forms required: FAFSA.
Dates and Deadlines: No deadline. Applicants notified on a rolling basis starting 4/1.

CONTACT
Peter Murtaugh, Vice President for Finance and Administration
4431 Finney Avenue, St. Louis, MO 63113
(314) 286-4863

Research College of Nursing

Kansas City, Missouri
www.researchcollege.edu   Federal Code: 006392

4-year for-profit nursing college in very large city.
Enrollment: 328 undergrads.
Selectivity: Admits 50 to 75% of applicants.

BASIC COSTS (2009-2010)
Tuition and fees: $25,690.
Per-credit charge: $832.
Room and board: $7,480.

FINANCIAL AID PICTURE (2009-2010)
Students with need: Need-based aid available for full-time and part-time students.
Students without need: No-need awards available for academics, alumni affiliation, leadership.
Additional info: Financial aid handled by Rockhurst University for freshmen and sophomores.

FINANCIAL AID PROCEDURES
Forms required: FAFSA, institutional form.
Dates and Deadlines: Priority date 3/15; no closing date. Applicants notified on a rolling basis starting 3/15.
Transfers: No deadline.

CONTACT
Angela Karlin, Director of Financial Aid
2525 East Meyer Boulevard, Kansas City, MO 64132-1199
(816) 995-2814

Rockhurst University

Kansas City, Missouri
www.rockhurst.edu   Federal Code: 002499

4-year private business and liberal arts college in very large city, affiliated with Roman Catholic Church.
Enrollment: 1,541 undergrads, 9% part-time. 417 full-time freshmen.
Selectivity: Admits over 75% of applicants.

BASIC COSTS (2010-2011)
Tuition and fees: $27,390.
Per-credit charge: $882.
Room and board: $7,490.

FINANCIAL AID PICTURE (2009-2010)
Students with need: Out of 417 full-time freshmen who applied for aid, 380 were judged to have need. Of these, 379 received aid, and 78 had their full need met. Average financial aid package met 100% of need; average scholarship/grant was $7,413; average loan was $2,988. For part-time students, average financial aid package was $12,126.
Students without need: 28 full-time freshmen who did not demonstrate need for aid received scholarships/grants; average award was $13,266. No-need awards available for academics, alumni affiliation, athletics, leadership, music/drama.
Scholarships offered: 42 full-time freshmen received athletic scholarships; average amount $13,986.
Cumulative student debt: 79% of graduating class had student loans; average debt was $21,950.
Additional info: Auditions, portfolios required for some scholarships.

FINANCIAL AID PROCEDURES
Forms required: FAFSA.
Dates and Deadlines: Priority date 3/1; no closing date. Applicants notified on a rolling basis starting 3/1; must reply within 4 week(s) of notification.
Transfers: No deadline. Applicants notified on a rolling basis starting 1/30; must reply within 4 week(s) of notification. Scholarships awarded to qualified first-time transfers.

CONTACT
Angela Karlin, Director of Financial Aid
1100 Rockhurst Road, Kansas City, MO 64110-2561
(816) 405-4600

St. Charles Community College

Cottleville, Missouri
www.stchas.edu   Federal Code: 025306

2-year public community college in small city.
Enrollment: 7,155 undergrads, 45% part-time. 1,467 full-time freshmen.
Selectivity: Open admission; but selective for some programs.

BASIC COSTS (2009-2010)

Tuition and fees: $2,400; out-of-district residents $3,540; out-of-state residents $5,250.
Per-credit charge: $80; out-of-district residents $118; out-of-state residents $175.

FINANCIAL AID PICTURE (2008-2009)

Students with need: 67% of average financial aid package awarded as scholarships/grants, 33% awarded as loans/jobs. Need-based aid available for part-time students.
Students without need: No-need awards available for academics, art, athletics, leadership, music/drama.

FINANCIAL AID PROCEDURES

Forms required: FAFSA, institutional form.
Dates and Deadlines: Priority date 7/1; no closing date. Applicants notified on a rolling basis starting 3/1.

CONTACT

Kathy Brockgreitens-Gober, Dean of Enrollment Services
4601 Mid Rivers Mall Drive, Cottleville, MO 63376
(636) 922-8270

St. Louis Christian College

Florissant, Missouri
www.slcconline.edu   Federal Code: 012580

4-year private Bible college in small city, affiliated with Church of Christ.
Enrollment: 333 undergrads, 12% part-time. 103 full-time freshmen.
Selectivity: Admits less than 50% of applicants.

BASIC COSTS (2010-2011)

Tuition and fees: $14,200.
Per-credit charge: $430.
Room and board: $8,200.
Additional info: Full tuition scholarship available to students enrolled full-time who live on campus.

FINANCIAL AID PICTURE (2009-2010)

Students with need: Need-based aid available for full-time and part-time students.
Students without need: No-need awards available for academics, alumni affiliation, leadership, music/drama, religious affiliation.
Scholarships offered: President's Scholarship: full tuition; ACT score 30+; 1 available. Chancellor's Scholarships: two-thirds tuition; ACT 28+; 2 available. Dean's Scholarships: half tuition; ACT 28+; unlimited number available.

FINANCIAL AID PROCEDURES

Forms required: FAFSA, institutional form.
Dates and Deadlines: Closing date 8/1. Applicants notified on a rolling basis starting 7/20; must reply within 2 week(s) of notification.

CONTACT

Cathi Wilhoit, Financial Aid Director
1360 Grandview Drive, Florissant, MO 63033
(314) 837-6777 ext. 1101

St. Louis Community College at Meramec

St. Louis, Missouri
www.stlcc.edu   Federal Code: 002471

2-year public community college in large city.
Enrollment: 10,217 undergrads.
Selectivity: Open admission; but selective for some programs.

BASIC COSTS (2009-2010)

Tuition and fees: $2,490; out-of-district residents $3,690; out-of-state residents $4,740.
Per-credit charge: $83; out-of-district residents $123; out-of-state residents $158.
Additional info: Tuition at time of enrollment locked for 2 years.

FINANCIAL AID PICTURE

Students with need: Need-based aid available for full-time and part-time students.

FINANCIAL AID PROCEDURES

Forms required: FAFSA, institutional form.
Dates and Deadlines: Closing date 6/30. Applicants notified on a rolling basis starting 2/1.

CONTACT

Michael Smith, Manager of Student Aid
11333 Big Bend Boulevard, Kirkwood, MO 63122-5799
(314) 984-7500

Saint Louis University

Saint Louis, Missouri
www.slu.edu   Federal Code: 002506

4-year private university in very large city, affiliated with Roman Catholic Church.
Enrollment: 7,945 undergrads, 10% part-time. 1,593 full-time freshmen.
Selectivity: Admits 50 to 75% of applicants.

BASIC COSTS (2010-2011)

Tuition and fees: $32,656.
Per-credit charge: $1,125.
Room and board: $9,170.
Additional info: Tuition/fee waivers available for unemployed or children of unemployed.

FINANCIAL AID PICTURE (2008-2009)

Students with need: Out of 1,260 full-time freshmen who applied for aid, 1,043 were judged to have need. Of these, 1,043 received aid, and 209 had their full need met. Average financial aid package met 73% of need; average scholarship/grant was $19,795; average loan was $3,973. For part-time students, average financial aid package was $8,562.
Students without need: 461 full-time freshmen who did not demonstrate need for aid received scholarships/grants; average award was $12,372. No-need awards available for academics, art, athletics, leadership, music/drama, religious affiliation, ROTC.
Scholarships offered: *Merit:* $3,000 to $15,000 scholarship based on applicants' high school academic achievements, test scores, leadership and community service. *Athletic:* 34 full-time freshmen received athletic scholarships; average amount $14,196.
Cumulative student debt: 64% of graduating class had student loans; average debt was $33,747.
Additional info: Presidential scholarship applications are due by December 1. Martin Luther King Jr. (MLK) scholarship applications have a priority date of February 1.

FINANCIAL AID PROCEDURES

Forms required: FAFSA.

Dates and Deadlines: Priority date 3/1; no closing date. Applicants notified on a rolling basis starting 3/1; must reply by 5/1 or within 4 week(s) of notification.
Transfers: No deadline. Applicants notified on a rolling basis starting 3/1; must reply by 5/1 or within 4 week(s) of notification. Students should file FAFSA by March 1 for Missouri State Funds.

CONTACT

Cari Wickliffe, Assistant Vice Provost, Student Financial Services
221 North Grand Boulevard, St. Louis, MO 63103
(314) 977-2350

St. Luke's College

Kansas City, Missouri
www.saintlukescollege.edu   Federal Code: 009782

Upper-division private nursing college in large city, affiliated with Episcopal Church.
Enrollment: 123 undergrads, 2% part-time.

BASIC COSTS (2010-2011)
Tuition and fees: $12,373.
Per-credit charge: $369.

FINANCIAL AID PICTURE (2009-2010)
Students with need: Average financial aid package for all full-time undergraduates was $12,000. 30% awarded as scholarships/grants, 70% awarded as loans/jobs. Need-based aid available for part-time students.

FINANCIAL AID PROCEDURES
Dates and Deadlines: No deadline. Applicants notified by 5/1.

CONTACT
Marcia Shaw, Executive Director, Business Operations and Student Services
8320 Ward Parkway, Suite 300, Kansas City, MO 64114
(816) 932-2194

Southeast Missouri State University

Cape Girardeau, Missouri
www.semo.edu   Federal Code: 002501

4-year public university in large town.
Enrollment: 8,882 undergrads, 19% part-time. 1,635 full-time freshmen.
Selectivity: Admits over 75% of applicants.

BASIC COSTS (2009-2010)
Tuition and fees: $6,255; out-of-state residents $10,890.
Per-credit charge: $185; out-of-state residents $339.
Room and board: $6,358.
Additional info: Tuition at time of enrollment locked for 4 years.

FINANCIAL AID PICTURE (2008-2009)
Students with need: Out of 1,318 full-time freshmen who applied for aid, 901 were judged to have need. Of these, 900 received aid, and 225 had their full need met. Average financial aid package met 77% of need; average scholarship/grant was $5,718; average loan was $3,054. For part-time students, average financial aid package was $5,395.
Students without need: 506 full-time freshmen who did not demonstrate need for aid received scholarships/grants; average award was $3,593. No-need awards available for academics, alumni affiliation, art, athletics, job skills, leadership, minority status, music/drama, ROTC, state/district residency.
Scholarships offered: 19 full-time freshmen received athletic scholarships; average amount $10,831.
Cumulative student debt: 63% of graduating class had student loans; average debt was $19,613.

FINANCIAL AID PROCEDURES
Forms required: FAFSA.
Dates and Deadlines: Priority date 3/1; no closing date. Applicants notified on a rolling basis starting 4/1; must reply within 3 week(s) of notification.
Transfers: Applicants notified on a rolling basis starting 4/1; must reply by 8/15 or within 3 week(s) of notification.

CONTACT
Karen Walker, Director of Financial Aid Services
One University Plaza, Cape Girardeau, MO 63701
(573) 651-2253

Southwest Baptist University

Bolivar, Missouri
www.sbuniv.edu   Federal Code: 002502

4-year private university in small town, affiliated with Southern Baptist Convention.
Enrollment: 2,646 undergrads, 24% part-time. 465 full-time freshmen.
Selectivity: Admits over 75% of applicants.

BASIC COSTS (2010-2011)
Tuition and fees: $17,280.
Room and board: $5,720.

FINANCIAL AID PICTURE (2009-2010)
Students with need: Out of 437 full-time freshmen who applied for aid, 381 were judged to have need. Of these, 380 received aid, and 107 had their full need met. Average financial aid package met 84% of need; average scholarship/grant was $4,023; average loan was $3,092. For part-time students, average financial aid package was $4,917.
Students without need: 80 full-time freshmen who did not demonstrate need for aid received scholarships/grants; average award was $8,332. No-need awards available for academics, art, athletics, minority status, music/drama, state/district residency.
Scholarships offered: 73 full-time freshmen received athletic scholarships; average amount $7,908.
Cumulative student debt: 69% of graduating class had student loans; average debt was $22,913.

FINANCIAL AID PROCEDURES
Forms required: FAFSA, institutional form.
Dates and Deadlines: Priority date 3/15; no closing date. Applicants notified on a rolling basis starting 3/1; must reply within 2 week(s) of notification.

CONTACT
Brad Gamble, Director of Financial Aid
1600 University Avenue, Bolivar, MO 65613-2597
(417) 328-1822

State Fair Community College

Sedalia, Missouri
www.sfccmo.edu   Federal Code: 007628

2-year public community college in large town.
Enrollment: 3,862 undergrads, 37% part-time. 902 full-time freshmen.
Selectivity: Open admission; but selective for some programs.

BASIC COSTS (2009-2010)
Tuition and fees: $2,460; out-of-district residents $3,300; out-of-state residents $4,980.
Per-credit charge: $68; out-of-district residents $96; out-of-state residents $152.

FINANCIAL AID PICTURE (2008-2009)

Students with need: Need-based aid available for full-time and part-time students. Work study available nights, weekends, and for part-time students.
Students without need: No-need awards available for academics, art, athletics, music/drama, state/district residency.

FINANCIAL AID PROCEDURES

Forms required: FAFSA.
Dates and Deadlines: Priority date 7/1; no closing date. Applicants notified on a rolling basis starting 7/15; must reply within 3 week(s) of notification.
Transfers: No deadline. Applicants notified on a rolling basis starting 7/15; must reply within 3 week(s) of notification.

CONTACT

John Matthews, Director of Financial Aid
3201 West 16th Street, Sedalia, MO 65301-2199
(660) 596-7295

Stephens College
Columbia, Missouri
www.stephens.edu   Federal Code: 002512

4-year private liberal arts college in small city.
Enrollment: 948 undergrads, 17% part-time. 238 full-time freshmen.
Selectivity: Admits 50 to 75% of applicants.

BASIC COSTS (2010-2011)

Tuition and fees: $25,400.
Per-credit charge: $700.
Room and board: $8,070.

FINANCIAL AID PICTURE (2009-2010)

Students with need: Need-based aid available for full-time students. Work study available nights, weekends, and for part-time students.
Students without need: No-need awards available for academics, alumni affiliation, athletics, leadership, music/drama, state/district residency.

FINANCIAL AID PROCEDURES

Forms required: FAFSA.
Dates and Deadlines: Priority date 3/15; no closing date. Applicants notified on a rolling basis starting 3/1.
Transfers: Phi Theta Kappa students transferring from 2-year institutions eligible for Phi Theta Kappa scholarship.

CONTACT

Rachel Touchatt, Director of Financial Aid
1200 East Broadway, Columbia, MO 65215
(800) 876-7106

Texas County Technical Institute
Houston, Missouri
www.texascountytech.edu   Federal Code: 035793

2-year private nursing and technical college in small town.
Enrollment: 165 undergrads.

BASIC COSTS (2010-2011)

Tuition and fees: $12,612.
Per-credit charge: $345.
Additional info: Required fees include: clinical tuition, student fees, liability insurance, achievement and diagnostic testing, and supplies.

FINANCIAL AID PICTURE (2009-2010)

Students with need: Need-based aid available for full-time and part-time students.
Students without need: This college awards aid only to students with need.

FINANCIAL AID PROCEDURES

Forms required: FAFSA, institutional form.
Dates and Deadlines: No deadline.

CONTACT

Clarice Casebeer, Director of Financial Aid
6915 South Highway 63, Houston, MO 65483
(417) 967-5466

Three Rivers Community College
Poplar Bluff, Missouri
www.trcc.edu   Federal Code: 004713

2-year public community college in large town.
Enrollment: 2,877 undergrads, 34% part-time. 739 full-time freshmen.
Selectivity: Open admission; but selective for some programs.

BASIC COSTS (2009-2010)

Tuition and fees: $2,505; out-of-district residents $3,765; out-of-state residents $4,605.
Per-credit charge: $70; out-of-district residents $112; out-of-state residents $140.
Room only: $3,114.
Additional info: Book rental $20 per book. Lab fees vary per course.

FINANCIAL AID PICTURE (2008-2009)

Students with need: 74% of average financial aid package awarded as scholarships/grants, 26% awarded as loans/jobs. Need-based aid available for part-time students.
Students without need: No-need awards available for academics, athletics, state/district residency.

FINANCIAL AID PROCEDURES

Forms required: FAFSA, institutional form.
Dates and Deadlines: Priority date 5/1; no closing date. Applicants notified on a rolling basis starting 6/1; must reply within 2 week(s) of notification.

CONTACT

Charlotte Eubank, Chief Financial Officer
2080 Three Rivers Boulevard, Poplar Bluff, MO 63901-1308
(573) 840-9607

Truman State University
Kirksville, Missouri
www.truman.edu   Federal Code: 002495

4-year public university and liberal arts college in large town.
Enrollment: 5,381 undergrads, 2% part-time. 1,334 full-time freshmen.
Selectivity: Admits 50 to 75% of applicants.

BASIC COSTS (2009-2010)

Tuition and fees: $6,692; out-of-state residents $11,543.
Room and board: $6,854.
Additional info: Tuition/fee waivers available for adults.

FINANCIAL AID PICTURE (2008-2009)

Students with need: Out of 1,064 full-time freshmen who applied for aid, 634 were judged to have need. Of these, 634 received aid, and 444 had their full need met. Average financial aid package met 85% of need; average scholarship/grant was $3,821; average loan was $3,556. Need-based aid available for part-time students.
Students without need: 771 full-time freshmen who did not demonstrate need for aid received scholarships/grants; average award was $4,926. No-need awards available for academics, alumni affiliation, art, athletics, leadership, minority status, music/drama, ROTC, state/district residency.

Scholarships offered: *Merit:* Pershing Scholarship: up to full tuition, room and board and up to $4,000 for study-abroad; awarded to outstanding scholars and leaders; 12 awarded. Truman Leadership Award: up to full tuition, room and board for Missouri residents; awarded for demonstrated leadership and academic achievement. International Baccalaureate Scholarship: $2,000 per academic year; awarded to students who complete the IB Diploma Programme. President's Combined Ability: $2,000-$3,000; A 170 combined ability or higher; calculated by adding high school rank percent or GPA percent (whichever is higher) to national percentile on the ACT or SAT; unlimited number available. *Athletic:* 78 full-time freshmen received athletic scholarships; average amount $2,585.

Cumulative student debt: 53% of graduating class had student loans; average debt was $21,858.

Additional info: Out-of-state students whose parents work in Missouri may deduct $1 for every dollar paid in Missouri income taxes from out-of-state tuition.

FINANCIAL AID PROCEDURES

Forms required: FAFSA, institutional form.

Dates and Deadlines: Priority date 4/1; no closing date. Applicants notified on a rolling basis starting 3/1; must reply within 4 week(s) of notification.

Transfers: Applicants notified on a rolling basis starting 3/1; must reply within 4 week(s) of notification. Limited number of automatic and competitive awards offered to transfer students.

CONTACT

Kathy Elsea, Financial Aid Director
100 East Normal Street, Kirksville, MO 63501-9980
(660) 785-4130

University of Central Missouri
Warrensburg, Missouri
www.ucmo.edu   Federal Code: 02454

4-year public university in large town.

Enrollment: 8,401 undergrads, 11% part-time. 1,427 full-time freshmen.

Selectivity: Admits over 75% of applicants.

BASIC COSTS (2009-2010)

Tuition and fees: $6,885; out-of-state residents $12,444.

Per-credit charge: $195; out-of-state residents $391.

Room and board: $6,320.

FINANCIAL AID PICTURE (2008-2009)

Students with need: Out of 1,193 full-time freshmen who applied for aid, 499 were judged to have need. Of these, 499 received aid, and 103 had their full need met. Average financial aid package met 88% of need; average scholarship/grant was $3,406; average loan was $4,084. For part-time students, average financial aid package was $8,475.

Students without need: 233 full-time freshmen who did not demonstrate need for aid received scholarships/grants; average award was $8,049. No-need awards available for academics, alumni affiliation, art, athletics, leadership, minority status, music/drama, ROTC, state/district residency.

Scholarships offered: 52 full-time freshmen received athletic scholarships; average amount $4,713.

Cumulative student debt: 69% of graduating class had student loans; average debt was $18,272.

FINANCIAL AID PROCEDURES

Forms required: FAFSA.

Dates and Deadlines: Priority date 3/1; no closing date. Applicants notified on a rolling basis starting 3/1; must reply within 2 week(s) of notification.

Transfers: No deadline. Must reply within 2 week(s) of notification.

CONTACT

Phil Shreves, Director, Student Financial Assistance
WDE 1400, Warrensburg, MO 64093
(660) 543-8080

University of Missouri: Columbia
Columbia, Missouri
www.missouri.edu   Federal Code: 002516

4-year public university in small city.

Enrollment: 23,529 undergrads, 5% part-time. 5,702 full-time freshmen.

Selectivity: Admits over 75% of applicants.

BASIC COSTS (2009-2010)

Tuition and fees: $8,501; out-of-state residents $19,682.

Per-credit charge: $246; out-of-state residents $615.

Room and board: $8,285.

FINANCIAL AID PICTURE (2008-2009)

Students with need: Out of 4,201 full-time freshmen who applied for aid, 2,722 were judged to have need. Of these, 2,654 received aid, and 546 had their full need met. Average financial aid package met 87% of need; average scholarship/grant was $7,660; average loan was $3,515. For part-time students, average financial aid package was $10,026.

Students without need: 1,310 full-time freshmen who did not demonstrate need for aid received scholarships/grants; average award was $3,617. No-need awards available for academics, alumni affiliation, art, athletics, leadership, minority status, music/drama, ROTC, state/district residency.

Scholarships offered: 210 full-time freshmen received athletic scholarships; average amount $9,342.

Cumulative student debt: 61% of graduating class had student loans; average debt was $20,814.

Additional info: Scholarship available for international students based on success during 1st semester.

FINANCIAL AID PROCEDURES

Forms required: FAFSA.

Dates and Deadlines: No deadline. Applicants notified on a rolling basis.

Transfers: No deadline. Applicants notified on a rolling basis starting 4/1; must reply within 4 week(s) of notification.

CONTACT

James Brooks, Director of Student Financial Aid
230 Jesse Hall, Columbia, MO 65211
(573) 882-7506

University of Missouri: Kansas City
Kansas City, Missouri
www.umkc.edu   Federal Code: 002518

4-year public university in large city.

Enrollment: 7,721 undergrads, 20% part-time. 979 full-time freshmen.

Selectivity: Admits 50 to 75% of applicants.

BASIC COSTS (2009-2010)

Tuition and fees: $8,272; out-of-state residents $19,363.

Per-credit charge: $246; out-of-state residents $614.

Room and board: $8,773.

FINANCIAL AID PICTURE (2009-2010)

Students with need: Out of 814 full-time freshmen who applied for aid, 659 were judged to have need. Of these, 643 received aid, and 65 had their full need met. Average financial aid package met 56% of need; average scholarship/grant was $7,882; average loan was $6,358. For part-time students, average financial aid package was $5,909.

Students without need: 209 full-time freshmen who did not demonstrate need for aid received scholarships/grants; average award was $4,053. No-need awards available for academics, alumni affiliation, art, athletics, leadership, minority status, music/drama, state/district residency.

Scholarships offered: *Merit:* Many automatic scholarships and non-resident fee waivers are available for students who apply for admission by February 1. Automatic awards range from $1000 to a complete non-resident fee differential. A competitive Trustees Scholarship is available that covers most educational expenses. ***Athletic:*** 27 full-time freshmen received athletic scholarships; average amount $13,682.

Cumulative student debt: 65% of graduating class had student loans; average debt was $20,512.

FINANCIAL AID PROCEDURES

Forms required: FAFSA.

Dates and Deadlines: Priority date 3/1; no closing date. Applicants notified on a rolling basis starting 4/15; must reply within 2 week(s) of notification.

CONTACT

Jan Brandow, Director of Student Financial Aid
5100 Rockhill Road, AC120, Kansas City, MO 64110-2499
(816) 235-1154

University of Missouri: St. Louis

St. Louis, Missouri
www.umsl.edu   Federal Code: 002519

4-year public university in very large city.

Enrollment: 8,933 undergrads, 34% part-time. 494 full-time freshmen.

Selectivity: Admits over 75% of applicants.

BASIC COSTS (2009-2010)

Tuition and fees: $8,595; out-of-state residents $19,686.

Per-credit charge: $246; out-of-state residents $615.

Room and board: $8,164.

FINANCIAL AID PICTURE (2009-2010)

Students with need: Out of 410 full-time freshmen who applied for aid, 355 were judged to have need. Of these, 348 received aid, and 38 had their full need met. Average financial aid package met 54% of need; average scholarship/grant was $6,842; average loan was $3,368. For part-time students, average financial aid package was $6,309.

Students without need: 75 full-time freshmen who did not demonstrate need for aid received scholarships/grants; average award was $4,028. No-need awards available for academics, alumni affiliation, art, athletics, music/drama, ROTC, state/district residency.

Scholarships offered: *Merit:* Curators? Scholarship: $7,000 per year, renewable; for Missouri freshmen with 28 ACT and top 5% of class; unlimited number awarded. Chancellor?s Scholarship: $5,000 per year, renewable; 26 ACT and top 10% of class; unlimited awarded. University Scholarship: $2,000 per year, renewable; 25 ACT and top 25% of class; unlimited awarded. Academic Scholarship: $1,500 per year, renewable; 24 ACT and top 25% of class; unlimited awarded. Mark Twain Scholarship: $1,000 per year, renewable; 23 ACT and top 35% of class; unlimited awarded. National Access Award (Full): Pays full non-resident fees, renewable; 28 ACT; unlimited awarded. National Access Award (Partial): Pays $5,000 annually toward non-resident fees, renewable; 24 ACT; unlimited awarded. Pierre Laclede Honors College Merit Scholarships: for freshmen in the Honors College; amounts based on test scores, class rank, writing sample, interview. ***Athletic:*** 9 full-time freshmen received athletic scholarships; average amount $13,827.

Cumulative student debt: 65% of graduating class had student loans; average debt was $25,776.

FINANCIAL AID PROCEDURES

Forms required: FAFSA.

Dates and Deadlines: Priority date 4/1; no closing date. Applicants notified on a rolling basis starting 4/1; must reply within 2 week(s) of notification.

Transfers: Transfer scholarships awarded on merit basis to students entering in both Fall and Spring semesters. Priority consideration given to students admitted by March 15th for Fall semester and by October 15th for the Spring semester. Students must transfer at least 45 credit hours and have minimum GPA of 3.25 to be eligible. Amounts vary, and additional criteria apply.

CONTACT

Tony Georges, Director of Student Financial Aid
One University Boulevard, St. Louis, MO 63121-4400
(314) 516-5526

Washington University in St. Louis

St. Louis, Missouri   Federal Code: 002520
www.wustl.edu   CSS Code: 6929

4-year private university in large city.

Enrollment: 6,436 undergrads, 5% part-time. 1,501 full-time freshmen.

Selectivity: Admits less than 50% of applicants.

BASIC COSTS (2010-2011)

Tuition and fees: $40,374.

Room and board: $12,941.

FINANCIAL AID PICTURE (2009-2010)

Students with need: Out of 996 full-time freshmen who applied for aid, 566 were judged to have need. Of these, 556 received aid, and 556 had their full need met. Average financial aid package met 100% of need; average scholarship/grant was $27,699; average loan was $5,275. Need-based aid available for part-time students.

Students without need: 270 full-time freshmen who did not demonstrate need for aid received scholarships/grants; average award was $9,195. No-need awards available for academics, ROTC.

Scholarships offered: Numerous merit scholarships available ranging up to full tuition plus stipend, renewable for 4 years, based upon academic merit.

FINANCIAL AID PROCEDURES

Forms required: FAFSA, CSS PROFILE.

Dates and Deadlines: Closing date 2/15. Applicants notified by 4/1; must reply by 5/1.

CONTACT

William Witbrodt, Director of Student Financial Services
Campus Box 1089, One Brookings Drive, St. Louis, MO 63130-4899
(314) 935-5900

Webster University

St. Louis, Missouri
www.webster.edu   Federal Code: 002521

4-year private university in large city.

Enrollment: 3,411 undergrads, 23% part-time. 491 full-time freshmen.

Selectivity: Admits 50 to 75% of applicants.

BASIC COSTS (2010-2011)

Tuition and fees: $21,688.

Per-credit charge: $570.

Room and board: $9,290.

Additional info: Tuition is $25,294 for theatre conservatory students.

FINANCIAL AID PICTURE (2008-2009)

Students with need: Need-based aid available for full-time and part-time students. Work study available nights.

Students without need: No-need awards available for academics, art, music/drama, state/district residency.

Scholarships offered: Daniel Webster Scholarships: full tuition; 3.8 GPA, top 10% class rank, 29 ACT and interview; 5 awarded. Webster Academic Scholarships: from $2,000-$10,000; minimum 3.0 GPA and 23 ACT; unlimited awarded. Leadership Scholarships: $1,500; minimum 3.3 GPA and 24 ACT, resume of activities; 15 awarded.

FINANCIAL AID PROCEDURES

Forms required: FAFSA, institutional form.

Dates and Deadlines: Priority date 4/1; no closing date. Applicants notified on a rolling basis starting 2/9; must reply within 2 week(s) of notification.

CONTACT

David Garafola, Vice President, Financial
470 East Lockwood Avenue, St. Louis, MO 63119-3194
(314) 968-6992

Westminster College
Fulton, Missouri
www.westminster-mo.edu   Federal Code: 002523

4-year private liberal arts college in large town, affiliated with Presbyterian Church (USA).

Enrollment: 1,067 undergrads, 1% part-time. 311 full-time freshmen.
Selectivity: Admits over 75% of applicants.

BASIC COSTS (2010-2011)

Tuition and fees: $19,740.
Per-credit charge: $750.
Room and board: $7,610.
Additional info: Tuition/fee waivers available for minority students.

FINANCIAL AID PICTURE (2009-2010)

Students with need: Out of 249 full-time freshmen who applied for aid, 186 were judged to have need. Of these, 186 received aid, and 109 had their full need met. Average financial aid package met 82% of need; average scholarship/grant was $14,707; average loan was $3,403. For part-time students, average financial aid package was $10,875.

Students without need: 122 full-time freshmen who did not demonstrate need for aid received scholarships/grants; average award was $9,098. No-need awards available for academics, alumni affiliation, leadership, minority status, music/drama, religious affiliation, ROTC, state/district residency.

FINANCIAL AID PROCEDURES

Forms required: FAFSA.

Dates and Deadlines: Priority date 2/15; no closing date. Applicants notified on a rolling basis starting 3/1; must reply within 3 week(s) of notification.

Transfers: Applicants notified on a rolling basis starting 3/1; must reply within 3 week(s) of notification.

CONTACT

Aimee Bristow, Director of Financial Aid
501 Westminster Avenue, Fulton, MO 65251-1299
(573) 592-5365

William Jewell College
Liberty, Missouri
www.jewell.edu   Federal Code: 002524

4-year private liberal arts college in large town.

Enrollment: 1,083 undergrads, 5% part-time. 282 full-time freshmen.
Selectivity: Admits 50 to 75% of applicants.

BASIC COSTS (2010-2011)

Tuition and fees: $28,450.
Per-credit charge: $825.
Room and board: $7,200.

FINANCIAL AID PICTURE (2009-2010)

Students with need: Out of 258 full-time freshmen who applied for aid, 217 were judged to have need. Of these, 217 received aid, and 61 had their full need met. Average financial aid package met 89% of need; average loan was $5,205. Need-based aid available for part-time students.

Students without need: No-need awards available for academics, alumni affiliation, art, athletics, music/drama, ROTC.

Scholarships offered: *Merit:* Jewell Scholarship: $15,000 to full tuition; competitive academic scholarship offered annually by invitation only to qualified high school seniors; 4 full-tuition scholarships awarded annually. Oxbridge Honors Scholarship: $15,000; for students accepted into Oxbridge Honors Program. *Athletic:* 27 full-time freshmen received athletic scholarships; average amount $6,543.

Cumulative student debt: 75% of graduating class had student loans; average debt was $24,102.

FINANCIAL AID PROCEDURES

Forms required: FAFSA.

Dates and Deadlines: Priority date 3/1; no closing date. Applicants notified on a rolling basis starting 2/15; must reply within 1.5 week(s) of notification.

Transfers: Transfer students evaluated individually by financial aid staff to determine number of semesters of aid available.

CONTACT

Susan Karnes, Director, Financial Aid and Scholarship Services
500 College Hill, Liberty, MO 64068
(816) 415-5977

William Woods University
Fulton, Missouri
www.williamwoods.edu   Federal Code: 002525

4-year private university and liberal arts college in large town, affiliated with Christian Church (Disciples of Christ).

Enrollment: 1,068 undergrads, 19% part-time. 242 full-time freshmen.
Selectivity: Admits over 75% of applicants.

BASIC COSTS (2010-2011)

Tuition and fees: $18,000.
Per-credit charge: $540.
Room and board: $7,200.

FINANCIAL AID PICTURE (2009-2010)

Students with need: Out of 236 full-time freshmen who applied for aid, 176 were judged to have need. Of these, 169 received aid, and 37 had their full need met. Average financial aid package met 73% of need; average scholarship/grant was $12,823; average loan was $3,219. For part-time students, average financial aid package was $4,391.

Students without need: 76 full-time freshmen who did not demonstrate need for aid received scholarships/grants; average award was $7,658. No-need awards available for academics, alumni affiliation, art, athletics, leadership, music/drama, religious affiliation.

Scholarships offered: *Merit:* LEAD (Leading, Educating, Achieving and Developing) Award; $5,000 for campus residents, $2,500 for commuters; based on commitment to campus and community involvement; renewable each year if commitment has been met in previous year. *Athletic:* 9 full-time freshmen received athletic scholarships; average amount $6,415.

Cumulative student debt: 75% of graduating class had student loans; average debt was $18,997.

FINANCIAL AID PROCEDURES

Forms required: FAFSA, institutional form.

Dates and Deadlines: Priority date 3/1; no closing date. Applicants notified on a rolling basis starting 3/15; must reply within 2 week(s) of notification.

Transfers: No deadline. Applicants notified on a rolling basis; must reply within 2 week(s) of notification. Transfer students eligible for scholarship.

CONTACT

Deana Ready, Director of Financial Aid
One University Avenue, Fulton, MO 65251-2388
(573) 592-4232

Montana

Blackfeet Community College

Browning, Montana
www.bfcc.org   Federal Code: 014902

2-year public community college in small town.
Enrollment: 522 undergrads.
Selectivity: Open admission.

BASIC COSTS (2009-2010)

Tuition and fees: $2,190; out-of-state residents $2,190.
Per-credit charge: $75.

FINANCIAL AID PICTURE (2008-2009)

Students with need: Need-based aid available for full-time and part-time students.

FINANCIAL AID PROCEDURES

Forms required: FAFSA, institutional form.
Dates and Deadlines: No deadline.

CONTACT

Margaret Bird, Director of Financial Aid
Highway 2 & 89, Browning, MT 59417
(406) 338-5421 ext. 245

Chief Dull Knife College

Lame Deer, Montana
www.cdkc.edu   Federal Code: 014878

2-year public junior college in rural community.
Enrollment: 127 full-time undergrads.
Selectivity: Open admission.

BASIC COSTS (2009-2010)

Tuition and fees: $2,260.
Per-credit charge: $70.

FINANCIAL AID PICTURE (2009-2010)

Students with need: Need-based aid available for full-time and part-time students. Work study available nights.

FINANCIAL AID PROCEDURES

Forms required: FAFSA, institutional form.
Dates and Deadlines: Priority date 3/1; no closing date. Applicants notified on a rolling basis; must reply within 2 week(s) of notification.

CONTACT

Michelle Three Fingers, Financial Aid Director
Box 98, Lame Deer, MT 59043
(406) 477-6215

Dawson Community College

Glendive, Montana
www.dawson.edu   Federal Code: 002529

2-year public community college in small town.
Enrollment: 367 undergrads, 19% part-time. 126 full-time freshmen.

Selectivity: Open admission.

BASIC COSTS (2009-2010)

Tuition and fees: $2,736; out-of-district residents $3,843; out-of-state residents $8,499.
Per-credit charge: $52; out-of-district residents $89; out-of-state residents $244.
Room only: $2,100.
Additional info: Mandatory $600-per-semester a la carte meal plan for on-campus residents. Full-time tuition for Western Undergraduate Exchange students: $4,020 ($134 per credit hour).

FINANCIAL AID PICTURE (2008-2009)

Students with need: Work study available nights, weekends, and for part-time students.
Students without need: No-need awards available for academics, art, athletics, music/drama.

FINANCIAL AID PROCEDURES

Forms required: FAFSA.
Dates and Deadlines: Priority date 3/1; no closing date. Applicants notified on a rolling basis starting 5/15; must reply within 2 week(s) of notification.

CONTACT

Jolene Myers, Director of Admissions
300 College Drive, Glendive, MT 59330
(406) 377-9410

Flathead Valley Community College

Kalispell, Montana
www.fvcc.edu   Federal Code: 006777

2-year public community college in large town.
Enrollment: 1,954 undergrads, 31% part-time. 356 full-time freshmen.
Selectivity: Open admission; but selective for some programs.

BASIC COSTS (2009-2010)

Tuition and fees: $3,497; out-of-district residents $4,869; out-of-state residents $10,637.
Per-credit charge: $93; out-of-district residents $142; out-of-state residents $348.

FINANCIAL AID PICTURE (2009-2010)

Students with need: Out of 329 full-time freshmen who applied for aid, 281 were judged to have need. Of these, 268 received aid. Need-based aid available for part-time students.
Students without need: No-need awards available for academics, athletics.

FINANCIAL AID PROCEDURES

Forms required: FAFSA.
Dates and Deadlines: Priority date 3/1; no closing date. Applicants notified by 4/15; must reply within 2 week(s) of notification.

CONTACT

Cynthia Kiefer, Director of Financial Aid
777 Grandview Drive, Kalispell, MT 59901
(406) 756-3849

Fort Peck Community College

Poplar, Montana
www.fpcc.edu   Federal Code: 016616

2-year public community college in small town.
Enrollment: 356 full-time undergrads.
Selectivity: Open admission.

BASIC COSTS (2009-2010)

Tuition and fees: $2,250.

Per-credit charge: $70.

Additional info: Tuition/fee waivers available for adults, minority students.

FINANCIAL AID PICTURE

Students with need: Need-based aid available for full-time and part-time students. Work study available nights.

FINANCIAL AID PROCEDURES

Forms required: FAFSA, institutional form.

Dates and Deadlines: No deadline. Applicants notified on a rolling basis; must reply within 2 week(s) of notification.

CONTACT

Lanette Clark, Financial Aid Officer

Box 398 605 Indian, Poplar, MT 59255-0398

(406) 768-6328

Helena College of Technology of the University of Montana

Helena, Montana

www.umhelena.edu   Federal Code: 007570

2-year public community and technical college in large town.

Enrollment: 1,118 undergrads.

Selectivity: Open admission.

BASIC COSTS (2009-2010)

Tuition and fees: $3,072; out-of-state residents $8,068.

Additional info: Tuition/fee waivers available for minority students.

FINANCIAL AID PICTURE (2008-2009)

Students with need: Need-based aid available for full-time and part-time students.

FINANCIAL AID PROCEDURES

Forms required: FAFSA, institutional form.

Dates and Deadlines: Priority date 3/1; no closing date. Applicants notified on a rolling basis starting 5/1.

CONTACT

Valerie Lambert, Director of Financial Aid

1115 North Roberts Street, Helena, MT 59601-3098

(406) 444-6879

Little Big Horn College

Crow Agency, Montana

www.lbhc.cc.mt.us   Federal Code: 016135

2-year private community college in rural community.

Enrollment: 410 undergrads.

Selectivity: Open admission.

BASIC COSTS (2009-2010)

Tuition and fees: $2,760.

Per-credit charge: $75.

Additional info: Tuition/fee waivers available for minority students.

FINANCIAL AID PICTURE (2009-2010)

Students with need: Need-based aid available for full-time and part-time students.

FINANCIAL AID PROCEDURES

Dates and Deadlines: No deadline. Applicants notified on a rolling basis.

CONTACT

Beverly Snell, Financial Aid Assistant

Box 370, Crow Agency, MT 59022

(406) 638-3140

Miles Community College

Miles City, Montana

www.milescc.edu   Federal Code: 002528

2-year public community college in small town.

Enrollment: 500 undergrads, 25% part-time. 132 full-time freshmen.

Selectivity: Open admission; but selective for some programs.

BASIC COSTS (2009-2010)

Tuition and fees: $3,420; out-of-district residents $4,290; out-of-state residents $7,080.

Per-credit charge: $71; out-of-district residents $100; out-of-state residents $193.

Room and board: $4,800.

FINANCIAL AID PICTURE

Students with need: Need-based aid available for full-time and part-time students. Work study available nights, weekends, and for part-time students.

Students without need: No-need awards available for academics, athletics, leadership.

FINANCIAL AID PROCEDURES

Forms required: FAFSA.

Dates and Deadlines: Priority date 3/1; no closing date. Applicants notified on a rolling basis starting 4/15; must reply within 4 week(s) of notification.

CONTACT

Loren Lancaster, Financial Aid Officer

2715 Dickinson Street, Miles City, MT 59301

(406) 874-6208

Montana State University College of Technology: Great Falls

Great Falls, Montana

www.msugf.edu   Federal Code: 009314

2-year public community and technical college in small city.

Enrollment: 1,583 undergrads, 43% part-time. 169 full-time freshmen.

Selectivity: Open admission; but selective for some programs.

BASIC COSTS (2009-2010)

Tuition and fees: $3,012; out-of-state residents $9,081.

Additional info: Tuition/fee waivers available for minority students, unemployed or children of unemployed.

FINANCIAL AID PICTURE (2008-2009)

Students with need: Out of 139 full-time freshmen who applied for aid, 119 were judged to have need. Of these, 115 received aid, and 7 had their full need met. Average financial aid package met 61% of need; average scholarship/grant was $3,897; average loan was $2,621. For part-time students, average financial aid package was $5,125.

Cumulative student debt: 81% of graduating class had student loans; average debt was $10,025.

FINANCIAL AID PROCEDURES

Forms required: FAFSA, institutional form.

Dates and Deadlines: Priority date 3/1; no closing date. Applicants notified on a rolling basis starting 4/1; must reply within 3 week(s) of notification.

Transfers: No deadline. Applicants notified on a rolling basis; must reply within 3 week(s) of notification.

CONTACT

Leah Habel, Director of Financial Aid
2100 16th Avenue South, Great Falls, MT 59405
(800) 446-2698 ext. 4334

Montana State University: Billings

Billings, Montana
www.msubillings.edu   Federal Code: 002530

4-year public university and technical college in small city.
Enrollment: 4,425 undergrads, 28% part-time. 676 full-time freshmen.
Selectivity: Admits over 75% of applicants.

BASIC COSTS (2009-2010)

Tuition and fees: $5,207; out-of-state residents $14,543.
Room and board: $5,460.

FINANCIAL AID PICTURE (2008-2009)

Students with need: Out of 533 full-time freshmen who applied for aid, 419 were judged to have need. Of these, 403 received aid, and 18 had their full need met. Average financial aid package met 67% of need; average scholarship/grant was $4,044; average loan was $2,850. For part-time students, average financial aid package was $6,965.
Students without need: 22 full-time freshmen who did not demonstrate need for aid received scholarships/grants; average award was $2,069. No-need awards available for academics, alumni affiliation, art, athletics, job skills, leadership, minority status, music/drama, state/district residency.
Scholarships offered: 12 full-time freshmen received athletic scholarships; average amount $4,185.
Cumulative student debt: 73% of graduating class had student loans; average debt was $23,189.
Additional info: Veterans and honors fee waivers offered.

FINANCIAL AID PROCEDURES

Forms required: FAFSA.
Dates and Deadlines: Priority date 3/1; no closing date. Applicants notified on a rolling basis starting 4/1; must reply within 3 week(s) of notification.

CONTACT

Judy Chapman, Director of Financial Aid
1500 University Drive, Billings, MT 59101-0298
(406) 657-2188

Montana State University: Bozeman

Bozeman, Montana
www.montana.edu   Federal Code: 002532

4-year public university in large town.
Enrollment: 10,754 undergrads, 17% part-time. 1,801 full-time freshmen.
Selectivity: Admits 50 to 75% of applicants.

BASIC COSTS (2009-2010)

Tuition and fees: $5,988; out-of-state residents $17,651.
Room and board: $7,578.
Additional info: Non-resident alien fees: $1,379 in required fees, in addition to $150 administrative fee. Tuition/fee waivers available for minority students.

FINANCIAL AID PICTURE (2008-2009)

Students with need: 35% of average financial aid package awarded as scholarships/grants, 65% awarded as loans/jobs. Need-based aid available for part-time students.
Students without need: No-need awards available for academics, alumni affiliation, art, athletics, job skills, leadership, minority status, music/drama, ROTC, state/district residency.

FINANCIAL AID PROCEDURES

Forms required: FAFSA.
Dates and Deadlines: Priority date 3/1; no closing date. Applicants notified on a rolling basis starting 4/1; must reply within 3 week(s) of notification.
Transfers: Priority date 7/1; no deadline.

CONTACT

Brandi Payne, Director of Financial Aid Services
PO Box 172190, Bozeman, MT 59717-2190
(406) 994-2845

Montana Tech of the University of Montana

Butte, Montana
www.mtech.edu   Federal Code: 002531

4-year public engineering and technical college in large town.
Enrollment: 2,345 undergrads, 8% part-time. 492 full-time freshmen.
Selectivity: Admits over 75% of applicants.

BASIC COSTS (2009-2010)

Tuition and fees: $5,872; out-of-state residents $16,149.
Room and board: $6,602.
Additional info: Tuition/fee waivers available for adults, minority students.

FINANCIAL AID PICTURE (2008-2009)

Students with need: Need-based aid available for full-time and part-time students. Work study available nights, weekends, and for part-time students.
Students without need: No-need awards available for academics, alumni affiliation, athletics, minority status, state/district residency.

FINANCIAL AID PROCEDURES

Forms required: FAFSA, institutional form.
Dates and Deadlines: Priority date 3/1; no closing date. Applicants notified on a rolling basis starting 4/1; must reply within 2 week(s) of notification.

CONTACT

Mike Richardson, Director of Enrollment Processing
1300 West Park Street, Butte, MT 59701-8997
(406) 496-4212

Rocky Mountain College

Billings, Montana
www.rocky.edu   Federal Code: 002534

4-year private liberal arts college in small city, affiliated with United Church of Christ, United Methodist Church, United Presbyterian Church.
Enrollment: 811 undergrads, 4% part-time. 233 full-time freshmen.
Selectivity: Admits 50 to 75% of applicants.

BASIC COSTS (2010-2011)

Tuition and fees: $21,100.
Per-credit charge: $860.
Room and board: $6,678.

FINANCIAL AID PICTURE (2008-2009)

Students with need: Need-based aid available for full-time and part-time students. Work study available nights, weekends, and for part-time students.
Students without need: No-need awards available for academics, alumni affiliation, art, athletics, leadership, minority status, music/drama, religious affiliation, state/district residency.

FINANCIAL AID PROCEDURES

Forms required: FAFSA, institutional form.
Dates and Deadlines: Priority date 3/1; no closing date. Applicants notified on a rolling basis starting 2/1; must reply within 4 week(s) of notification.

Transfers: No deadline. Applicants notified on a rolling basis starting 2/1; must reply within 4 week(s) of notification.

CONTACT
Lisa Browning, Vice President of Enrollment Services
1511 Poly Drive, Billings, MT 59102-1796
(406) 657-1032

Salish Kootenai College
Pablo, Montana
www.skc.edu   Federal Code: 015023

4-year private liberal arts college in rural community.
Enrollment: 1,090 undergrads.
Selectivity: Open admission; but selective for some programs.

BASIC COSTS (2010-2011)
Additional info: Full-time tuition for Native American students, $2,880 ($80 per-credit-hour); full-time tuition for students of Native American descent, $3,528. Full-time tuition for Montana Residents, $4,932; Out-of-State, $9,900. Academic year required fees, $1,122. Tuition/fee waivers available for minority students.

FINANCIAL AID PICTURE (2008-2009)
Students with need: Need-based aid available for full-time and part-time students. Work study available nights, weekends, and for part-time students.

FINANCIAL AID PROCEDURES
Forms required: FAFSA.
Dates and Deadlines: Priority date 3/31; no closing date. Applicants notified on a rolling basis starting 7/15; must reply within 6 week(s) of notification.

CONTACT
Jackie Swain, Financial Aid Director
PO Box 70, Pablo, MT 59855
(406) 275-4855

Stone Child College
Box Elder, Montana
www.stonechild.edu   Federal Code: 026109

2-year public community and junior college in rural community.
Enrollment: 194 undergrads. 23 full-time freshmen.
Selectivity: Open admission.

BASIC COSTS (2009-2010)
Tuition and fees: $2,350.
Per-credit charge: $60.
Additional info: Students not members of Federally-recognized Native American tribe pay additional $420 in fees/year. Tuition/fee waivers available for unemployed or children of unemployed.

FINANCIAL AID PICTURE (2008-2009)
Students with need: Out of 23 full-time freshmen who applied for aid, 23 were judged to have need. Of these, 23 received aid, and 3 had their full need met. Average financial aid package met 70% of need; average scholarship/grant was $550. For part-time students, average financial aid package was $1,800.
Students without need: No-need awards available for academics.
Additional info: Scholarships available to high school and GED graduates who apply for college admission during the first term after graduation.

FINANCIAL AID PROCEDURES
Forms required: FAFSA, institutional form.
Dates and Deadlines: Priority date 3/1; closing date 6/30. Applicants notified on a rolling basis.

CONTACT
Tiffany Galbavy, Financial Aid Director
8294 Upper Box Elder Road, Box Elder, MT 59521-9796
(406) 395-4313 ext. 220

University of Great Falls
Great Falls, Montana
www.ugf.edu   Federal Code: 002527

4-year private university and liberal arts college in small city, affiliated with Roman Catholic Church.
Enrollment: 775 undergrads, 24% part-time. 148 full-time freshmen.
Selectivity: Admits less than 50% of applicants.

BASIC COSTS (2009-2010)
Tuition and fees: $18,212.
Per-credit charge: $545.
Room and board: $6,610.

FINANCIAL AID PICTURE (2009-2010)
Students with need: Average financial aid package met 64% of need; average scholarship/grant was $4,919; average loan was $3,405. For part-time students, average financial aid package was $8,437.
Students without need: No-need awards available for academics, art, athletics, religious affiliation.
Scholarships offered: Freshmen scholarships: $1,000-$6,000; based on high school GPA; renewable.

FINANCIAL AID PROCEDURES
Forms required: FAFSA.
Dates and Deadlines: Priority date 5/1; no closing date. Applicants notified on a rolling basis starting 3/1; must reply within 2 week(s) of notification.
Transfers: Transfer student scholarships; $2,500-$4,000; based on college GPA; renewable.

CONTACT
Peggy Boord, Director of Financial Aid
1301 20th Street South, Great Falls, MT 59405
(406) 791-5235

University of Montana
Missoula, Montana   Federal Code: 002536
www.umt.edu   CSS Code: 4489

4-year public university and liberal arts college in small city.
Enrollment: 12,673 undergrads.
Selectivity: Admits over 75% of applicants.

BASIC COSTS (2009-2010)
Tuition and fees: $5,330; out-of-state residents $17,763.
Room and board: $6,611.
Additional info: Tuition/fee waivers available for minority students.

FINANCIAL AID PICTURE (2009-2010)
Students with need: Need-based aid available for full-time and part-time students. Work study available nights, weekends, and for part-time students.
Students without need: No-need awards available for academics, art, athletics, leadership, music/drama, ROTC, state/district residency.

FINANCIAL AID PROCEDURES
Forms required: FAFSA, CSS PROFILE, institutional form.
Dates and Deadlines: Priority date 2/15; no closing date. Applicants notified on a rolling basis starting 4/1; must reply by 8/1 or within 4 week(s) of notification.

CONTACT

Myron Hanson, Director of Financial Aid
Lommasson Center 103, Missoula, MT 59812
(406) 243-5373

University of Montana: Western

Dillon, Montana
www.umwestern.edu   Federal Code: 002537

4-year public liberal arts and teachers college in small town.

Enrollment: 1,207 undergrads, 15% part-time. 341 full-time freshmen.

Selectivity: Open admission; but selective for some programs.

BASIC COSTS (2009-2010)

Tuition and fees: $3,689; out-of-state residents $12,745.

Room and board: $5,510.

Additional info: Tuition/fee waivers available for minority students.

FINANCIAL AID PICTURE (2008-2009)

Students with need: Average financial aid package met 16% of need; average scholarship/grant was $2,494; average loan was $3,589. For part-time students, average financial aid package was $2,692.

Students without need: 2 full-time freshmen who did not demonstrate need for aid received scholarships/grants; average award was $1,000. No-need awards available for academics, alumni affiliation, art, athletics, leadership, minority status, state/district residency.

Scholarships offered: 199 full-time freshmen received athletic scholarships; average amount $1,860.

Cumulative student debt: 71% of graduating class had student loans; average debt was $21,969.

Additional info: Tuition and/or fee waivers for veterans, American Indian, senior citizens, and dependents of Montana University System employees.

FINANCIAL AID PROCEDURES

Forms required: FAFSA, institutional form.

Dates and Deadlines: Priority date 3/1; no closing date. Applicants notified on a rolling basis starting 4/1; must reply within 4 week(s) of notification.

Transfers: No deadline. Applicants notified on a rolling basis starting 4/1; must reply within 4 week(s) of notification. Transfer students must have a cumulative G.P.A of 2.0 or greater for good academic progress status. Students with transfer GPA below 2.0 must appeal to have Financial Aid at Montana Western.

CONTACT

Erica Jones, Director of Financial Aid
710 South Atlantic Street, Dillon, MT 59725
(406) 683-7511

Nebraska

Bellevue University

Bellevue, Nebraska
www.bellevue.edu   Federal Code: 002538

4-year private university and business college in large city.

Enrollment: 6,194 undergrads, 42% part-time. 14 full-time freshmen.

Selectivity: Open admission; but selective for some programs.

BASIC COSTS (2010-2011)

Tuition and fees: $7,050.

Per-credit charge: $230.

FINANCIAL AID PICTURE (2008-2009)

Students with need: For part-time students, average financial aid package was $3,254.

Students without need: No-need awards available for academics, athletics, leadership.

FINANCIAL AID PROCEDURES

Forms required: FAFSA, institutional form.

Dates and Deadlines: Priority date 4/15; no closing date. Applicants notified on a rolling basis starting 4/15; must reply within 2 week(s) of notification.

Transfers: No deadline. Applicants notified on a rolling basis starting 4/15; must reply within 2 week(s) of notification.

CONTACT

Jon Dotterer, Director of Financial Aid
1000 Galvin Road South, Bellevue, NE 68005-3098
(402) 557-7326

BryanLGH College of Health Sciences

Lincoln, Nebraska
www.bryanlghcollege.edu   Federal Code: 006399

4-year private health science college in large city.

Enrollment: 449 undergrads, 43% part-time. 28 full-time freshmen.

Selectivity: Admits over 75% of applicants.

BASIC COSTS (2010-2011)

Tuition and fees: $12,300.

Per-credit charge: $410.

Additional info: Clinical Fees Nursing: $175/course; Clinical Fees Allied Health: $250/semester; Board Registry Fee estimated: $90/semester (Allied Health); ATI Testing Fee (Nursing): $60/semester.

FINANCIAL AID PICTURE (2008-2009)

Students with need: Out of 28 full-time freshmen who applied for aid, 28 were judged to have need. Of these, 28 received aid. Average financial aid package met 17% of need; average scholarship/grant was $2,160; average loan was $3,500. For part-time students, average financial aid package was $2,750.

Students without need: No-need awards available for academics, leadership.

FINANCIAL AID PROCEDURES

Forms required: FAFSA, institutional form.

Dates and Deadlines: Closing date 5/1. Applicants notified on a rolling basis starting 5/1; must reply within 3 week(s) of notification.

CONTACT

Deborah Wilke, Financial Aid Coordinator
5035 Everett Street, Lincoln, NE 68506

Central Community College

Grand Island, Nebraska
www.cccneb.edu   Federal Code: 014468

2-year public community and technical college in large town.

Enrollment: 4,659 undergrads, 45% part-time. 890 full-time freshmen.

Selectivity: Open admission; but selective for some programs and for out-of-state students.

BASIC COSTS (2009-2010)

Tuition and fees: $2,190; out-of-state residents $3,045.

Per-credit charge: $73; out-of-state residents $106.

Room and board: $4,080.

FINANCIAL AID PICTURE

Students with need: Need-based aid available for full-time and part-time students. Work study available nights.
Students without need: No-need awards available for academics, art, athletics, job skills, leadership, music/drama.
Additional info: All students are eligible to apply for a Pell Grant. Students enrolled for at least six semester hours (half-time) are eligible to apply for grants, loans, work study, and scholarships. To be considered for full-time benefits, students must be enrolled for at least 12 credit hours during the semester.

FINANCIAL AID PROCEDURES

Forms required: FAFSA, institutional form.
Dates and Deadlines: Priority date 3/1; no closing date. Applicants notified on a rolling basis starting 2/1; must reply within 2 week(s) of notification.

CONTACT

Steve Millnitz, Financial Aid Officer
3134 West Highway 34, Grand Island, NE 68802-4903
(308) 398-7407

Chadron State College
Chadron, Nebraska
www.csc.edu   Federal Code: 002539

4-year public business and liberal arts and teachers college in small town.
Enrollment: 2,100 undergrads.
Selectivity: Open admission; but selective for some programs.

BASIC COSTS (2009-2010)
Tuition and fees: $4,831; out-of-state residents $8,506.
Per-credit charge: $123; out-of-state residents $245.
Room and board: $4,888.

FINANCIAL AID PICTURE
Students with need: Need-based aid available for full-time and part-time students. Work study available nights, weekends, and for part-time students.
Students without need: No-need awards available for academics, alumni affiliation, art, athletics, leadership, minority status, music/drama, state/district residency.

FINANCIAL AID PROCEDURES
Forms required: FAFSA, institutional form.
Dates and Deadlines: Priority date 6/1; no closing date. Applicants notified on a rolling basis starting 4/1; must reply within 2 week(s) of notification.

CONTACT
Sherry Douglas, Director of Financial Aid
1000 Main Street, Chadron, NE 69337
(308) 432-6230

Clarkson College
Omaha, Nebraska
www.clarksoncollege.edu   Federal Code: 009862

4-year private health science college in large city, affiliated with Episcopal Church.
Enrollment: 750 undergrads.
Selectivity: Open admission; but selective for some programs.

BASIC COSTS (2009-2010)
Tuition and fees: $13,530.
Per-credit charge: $410.
Room and board: $6,400.

FINANCIAL AID PICTURE (2008-2009)
Students with need: Need-based aid available for full-time and part-time students. Work study available nights, weekends, and for part-time students.

Students without need: No-need awards available for academics, alumni affiliation, minority status, religious affiliation.

FINANCIAL AID PROCEDURES
Forms required: FAFSA, institutional form.
Dates and Deadlines: Priority date 4/1; no closing date. Applicants notified on a rolling basis starting 4/13; must reply within 3 week(s) of notification.
Transfers: Priority date 3/1; no deadline. Applicants notified on a rolling basis starting 3/30.

CONTACT
Margie Harris, Director of Student Financial Services
101 South 42nd Street, Omaha, NE 68131-2739
(402) 552-2749

College of Saint Mary
Omaha, Nebraska
www.csm.edu   Federal Code: 002540

4-year private nursing and liberal arts and teachers college for women in large city, affiliated with Roman Catholic Church.
Enrollment: 816 undergrads, 16% part-time. 103 full-time freshmen.
Selectivity: Admits less than 50% of applicants.

BASIC COSTS (2010-2011)
Tuition and fees: $23,230.
Per-credit charge: $750.
Room and board: $6,400.

FINANCIAL AID PICTURE (2009-2010)
Students with need: Average financial aid package met 76% of need; average scholarship/grant was $17,861; average loan was $3,730. For part-time students, average financial aid package was $5,700.
Students without need: No-need awards available for academics, athletics, music/drama.
Cumulative student debt: 75% of graduating class had student loans; average debt was $37,408.

FINANCIAL AID PROCEDURES
Forms required: FAFSA.
Dates and Deadlines: Priority date 3/1; no closing date. Applicants notified on a rolling basis starting 3/1; must reply within 2 week(s) of notification.
Transfers: No deadline. Applicants notified on a rolling basis starting 3/1; must reply within 2 week(s) of notification. Scholarships and need based grants available for full-time transfer students.

CONTACT
Beth Sisk, Director of Financial Aid
7000 Mercy Road, Omaha, NE 68106
(402) 399-2362

Concordia University
Seward, Nebraska
www.cune.edu   Federal Code: 002541

4-year private university in small town, affiliated with Lutheran Church - Missouri Synod.
Enrollment: 1,129 undergrads, 6% part-time. 288 full-time freshmen.
Selectivity: Admits over 75% of applicants.

BASIC COSTS (2009-2010)
Tuition and fees: $21,250.
Room and board: $5,520.

FINANCIAL AID PICTURE (2009-2010)
Students with need: Need-based aid available for full-time and part-time students. Work study available nights, weekends, and for part-time students.

Students without need: No-need awards available for academics, alumni affiliation, art, athletics, leadership, music/drama, religious affiliation.

Scholarships offered: President's scholarship: $15,000 per year; based on academic achievement. Regent's scholarship: $8,000-$11,000 per year; based on high school GPA and SAT/ACT scores. Achievement award: $3,500-$6,500 per year; based on high school GPA and SAT/ACT scores.

FINANCIAL AID PROCEDURES

Forms required: FAFSA.

Dates and Deadlines: Priority date 3/1; no closing date. Applicants notified on a rolling basis starting 3/1; must reply within 4 week(s) of notification.

Transfers: Applicants notified on a rolling basis starting 3/1; must reply within 4 week(s) of notification.

CONTACT

Gloria Hennig, Director of Financial Aid
800 North Columbia Avenue, Seward, NE 68434-1556
(800) 535-5494 ext. 7270

Creative Center
Omaha, Nebraska
www.creativecenter.edu   Federal Code: 031643

4-year for-profit visual arts and career college in large city.

Enrollment: 125 undergrads, 2% part-time. 47 full-time freshmen.

Selectivity: Admits over 75% of applicants.

BASIC COSTS (2010-2011)

Tuition and fees: $21,600.

Additional info: Tuition/fees may vary by program.

FINANCIAL AID PICTURE

Students with need: Need-based aid available for full-time and part-time students.

Students without need: No-need awards available for academics, art.

Scholarships offered: President's Award: $500. Founder's Award: $1,000. Both awards based on portfolio and high school academics. Andy Arrants Memorial Scholarship: supply kit (approx. $500); based on submitted artwork and essay.

FINANCIAL AID PROCEDURES

Forms required: FAFSA.

Dates and Deadlines: No deadline. Applicants notified on a rolling basis starting 1/1.

Transfers: No deadline. Applicants notified on a rolling basis.

CONTACT

Sandy LaRocca, Director of Financial Aid
10850 Emmet Street, Omaha, NE 68164
(402) 898-1000 ext. 203

Creighton University
Omaha, Nebraska
www.creighton.edu   Federal Code: 002542

4-year private university in very large city, affiliated with Roman Catholic Church.

Enrollment: 4,133 undergrads, 6% part-time. 1,054 full-time freshmen.

Selectivity: Admits over 75% of applicants.

BASIC COSTS (2010-2011)

Tuition and fees: $30,578.

Per-credit charge: $912.

Room and board: $9,164.

Additional info: Tuition/fee waivers available for minority students.

FINANCIAL AID PICTURE (2009-2010)

Students with need: Out of 840 full-time freshmen who applied for aid, 651 were judged to have need. Of these, 651 received aid, and 375 had their full need met. Average financial aid package met 93% of need; average scholarship/grant was $20,675; average loan was $5,755. Need-based aid available for part-time students.

Students without need: 336 full-time freshmen who did not demonstrate need for aid received scholarships/grants; average award was $13,614. No-need awards available for academics, alumni affiliation, art, athletics, leadership, minority status, music/drama, ROTC.

Scholarships offered: *Merit:* William Jennings Bryan Debate and Speech Scholarship: $4,000. Diversity Scholarship & Native American Merit Scholarship: three-quarter tuition scholarships; awarded to students who show commitment to diversity; 3.3 GPA or higher on a 4.0 scale required; applicants evaluated on academic merit, community service, school activities, leadership, and financial need. First-generation college bound students and families that earn under $60,000 encouraged to apply. Ron Hansen Scholarship in Creative Writing: $4,000. Grace Keenan Scholarship for Excellence in the Arts: $3,000; awarded to students who intend to major in visual or performing arts. Christina M. Hixson Scholarship in Business Administration: $4,500; awarded to freshman business students from high schools in CO, IA, IL, KA, MN, MO, NE, ND, SD, WI or WY with a minimum of 3.0 GPA. College of Business Administration Ethics and Social Responsibility Scholarship: $4,500; awarded to students with exceptional service accomplishments and leadership potential; 3.8 GPA and a minimum 26 ACT or 1200 SAT. Presidential Scholarship: three-quarter tuition scholarship awarded to selected applicants in the top 10% of applicant pool, based upon academics. Scott Scholarship: full tuition scholarship in the College of Business Administration; awarded to selected students in the top 10% of applicant pool; based on academics. G. Robert Muchemore Foundation Undergraduate Scholarship: full tuition scholarship; awarded to graduates of Nebraska high schools entering as freshmen; based upon academics. *Athletic:* 35 full-time freshmen received athletic scholarships; average amount $19,648.

Cumulative student debt: 70% of graduating class had student loans; average debt was $32,888.

FINANCIAL AID PROCEDURES

Forms required: FAFSA, institutional form.

Dates and Deadlines: Priority date 3/1; no closing date. Applicants notified on a rolling basis starting 3/15; must reply by 5/1 or within 4 week(s) of notification.

Transfers: If transferring 24 or more hours of credit, student not eligible for academic, non-need scholarships.

CONTACT

Robert Walker, Director of Financial Aid
2500 California Plaza, Omaha, NE 68178-0001
(402) 280-2731

Dana College
Blair, Nebraska
www.dana.edu   Federal Code: 002543

4-year private liberal arts college in small town, affiliated with Evangelical Lutheran Church in America.

Enrollment: 590 undergrads, 2% part-time. 174 full-time freshmen.

Selectivity: Admits 50 to 75% of applicants.

BASIC COSTS (2010-2011)

Tuition and fees: $21,800.

Per-credit charge: $580.

Room and board: $7,050.

FINANCIAL AID PICTURE (2009-2010)

Students with need: Out of 172 full-time freshmen who applied for aid, 151 were judged to have need. Of these, 151 received aid, and 44 had their full need met. Average financial aid package met 86% of need; average scholarship/grant was $5,604; average loan was $3,398. Need-based aid available for part-time students.

Students without need: 21 full-time freshmen who did not demonstrate need for aid received scholarships/grants; average award was $5,929. No-need awards available for academics, alumni affiliation, art, athletics, music/drama, religious affiliation, ROTC, state/district residency.

Scholarships offered: *Merit:* Departmental scholarships, Presidential scholarships, All-American Scholarship, athletic and performing arts scholarships available. *Athletic:* 127 full-time freshmen received athletic scholarships; average amount $6,743.

Cumulative student debt: 88% of graduating class had student loans; average debt was $19,971.

Additional info: Auditions recommended for music and drama scholarship applicants. Portfolios recommended for art, graphic design, and cheerleading/dance scholarship applicants.

FINANCIAL AID PROCEDURES

Forms required: FAFSA, institutional form.

Dates and Deadlines: Priority date 4/9; no closing date. Applicants notified on a rolling basis starting 3/9; must reply within 3 week(s) of notification.

Transfers: Must reply within 3 week(s) of notification. Academic scholarships awarded on basis of high school GPA, rank, and test scores for students with 1 year or less as full time college student. Awards for transfers with 27 credits or more will be based on college GPA.

CONTACT

Rita McManigal, Director of Financial Services
2848 College Drive, Blair, NE 68008-1099
(402) 426-7226

Doane College
Crete, Nebraska
www.doane.edu   Federal Code: 002544

4-year private liberal arts college in small town, affiliated with United Church of Christ.

Enrollment: 966 undergrads. 312 full-time freshmen.

Selectivity: Admits over 75% of applicants.

BASIC COSTS (2010-2011)

Tuition and fees: $22,170.

Per-credit charge: $720.

Room and board: $6,460.

FINANCIAL AID PICTURE (2009-2010)

Students with need: Out of 305 full-time freshmen who applied for aid, 265 were judged to have need. Of these, 265 received aid, and 110 had their full need met. Average financial aid package met 96% of need; average scholarship/grant was $14,148; average loan was $3,920. Need-based aid available for part-time students.

Students without need: 48 full-time freshmen who did not demonstrate need for aid received scholarships/grants; average award was $14,141. No-need awards available for academics, art, athletics, music/drama.

Cumulative student debt: 81% of graduating class had student loans; average debt was $19,196.

FINANCIAL AID PROCEDURES

Forms required: FAFSA.

Dates and Deadlines: Priority date 3/1; no closing date. Applicants notified on a rolling basis starting 3/1; must reply within 2 week(s) of notification.

CONTACT

Peggy Tvrdy, Director of Financial Aid
1014 Boswell Avenue, Crete, NE 68333
(402) 826-8260

Grace University
Omaha, Nebraska
www.graceuniversity.edu   Federal Code: 002547

4-year private university and Bible college in very large city, affiliated with interdenominational tradition.

Enrollment: 399 undergrads.

Selectivity: Admits 50 to 75% of applicants.

BASIC COSTS (2010-2011)

Tuition and fees: $15,728.

Per-credit charge: $430.

Room and board: $5,886.

Additional info: Tuition/fee waivers available for minority students.

FINANCIAL AID PICTURE (2009-2010)

Students with need: 55% of average financial aid package awarded as scholarships/grants, 45% awarded as loans/jobs. Need-based aid available for part-time students.

Students without need: No-need awards available for academics, alumni affiliation, leadership, minority status, music/drama.

FINANCIAL AID PROCEDURES

Forms required: FAFSA, institutional form.

Dates and Deadlines: Priority date 3/1; closing date 4/1. Applicants notified on a rolling basis starting 3/1; must reply within 2 week(s) of notification.

Transfers: No deadline. Applicants notified on a rolling basis starting 3/1; must reply within 2 week(s) of notification.

CONTACT

Dale Brown, Director of Revenue
1311 South Ninth Street, Omaha, NE 68108-3629
(402) 449-2810

Kaplan University: Lincoln
Lincoln, Nebraska
www.kucampus.edu   Federal Code: 004721

2-year for-profit branch campus college in small city.

Enrollment: 500 undergrads.

Selectivity: Open admission; but selective for some programs.

BASIC COSTS (2009-2010)

Tuition and fees: $14,560.

FINANCIAL AID PICTURE (2008-2009)

Students with need: Need-based aid available for full-time and part-time students. Work study available nights, weekends, and for part-time students.

Students without need: This college awards aid only to students with need.

FINANCIAL AID PROCEDURES

Forms required: FAFSA, institutional form.

Dates and Deadlines: No deadline. Applicants notified on a rolling basis starting 2/1.

Transfers: No deadline.

CONTACT

Sara Christensen, Associate Director of Financial Aid
1821 K Street, Lincoln, NE 68508
(402) 474-5315

Kaplan University: Omaha
Omaha, Nebraska
www.omaha.kaplanuniversity.edu   Federal Code: 008491

2-year for-profit career college in large city.
Enrollment: 613 undergrads, 37% part-time. 136 full-time freshmen.
Selectivity: Open admission; but selective for some programs.

FINANCIAL AID PICTURE
Students with need: Need-based aid available for full-time and part-time students. Work study available nights, weekends, and for part-time students.
Students without need: This college awards aid only to students with need.

FINANCIAL AID PROCEDURES
Forms required: FAFSA, institutional form.
Dates and Deadlines: No deadline. Applicants notified on a rolling basis.

CONTACT
Crystal Faxon, Director Of Financial Aid
5425 North 103rd Street, Omaha, NE 68134
(402) 431-6100

Little Priest Tribal College
Winnebago, Nebraska
www.lptc.bia.edu   Federal Code: 033233

2-year private community college in rural community.
Enrollment: 120 undergrads.
Selectivity: Open admission.

BASIC COSTS (2009-2010)
Tuition and fees: $2,985.
Per-credit charge: $80.

FINANCIAL AID PICTURE
Students with need: Need-based aid available for full-time and part-time students.

FINANCIAL AID PROCEDURES
Forms required: FAFSA, institutional form.
Dates and Deadlines: No deadline.

CONTACT
Billie Kitcheyan, Director of Financial Aid
PO Box 270, Winnebago, NE 68071
(402) 878-2380 ext. 125

Metropolitan Community College
Omaha, Nebraska
www.mccneb.edu   Federal Code: 004432

2-year public community and technical college in large city.
Enrollment: 7,461 undergrads, 55% part-time. 953 full-time freshmen.
Selectivity: Open admission; but selective for some programs.

BASIC COSTS (2009-2010)
Tuition and fees: $2,160; out-of-state residents $3,128.
Per-credit charge: $43; out-of-state residents $65.
Room and board: $3,555.

FINANCIAL AID PICTURE (2009-2010)
Students with need: Need-based aid available for full-time and part-time students.
Students without need: No-need awards available for academics.

FINANCIAL AID PROCEDURES
Forms required: FAFSA, institutional form.
Dates and Deadlines: Priority date 3/15; no closing date. Applicants notified on a rolling basis starting 4/15.

CONTACT
Wilma Hjelum, Director of Financial Aid & Veteran Services
Box 3777, Omaha, NE 68103-0777
(402) 457-2330

Mid-Plains Community College Area
North Platte, Nebraska
www.mpcc.edu   Federal Code: 002557

2-year public community and technical college in large town.
Enrollment: 1,385 undergrads, 28% part-time. 356 full-time freshmen.
Selectivity: Open admission; but selective for some programs.

BASIC COSTS (2009-2010)
Tuition and fees: $2,430; out-of-state residents $3,030.
Per-credit charge: $67; out-of-state residents $87.
Room and board: $4,900.

FINANCIAL AID PICTURE (2008-2009)
Students with need: Need-based aid available for full-time and part-time students. Work study available nights.
Students without need: No-need awards available for academics, art, athletics, music/drama.

FINANCIAL AID PROCEDURES
Forms required: FAFSA, institutional form.
Dates and Deadlines: Priority date 5/1; no closing date. Applicants notified on a rolling basis starting 5/1; must reply within 3 week(s) of notification.

CONTACT
Ted Fellers, Director of Financial Aid
1101 Halligan Drive, North Platte, NE 69101
(800) 658-4348

Nebraska Christian College
Papillion, Nebraska
www.nechristian.edu   Federal Code: 012976

4-year private Bible college in large town, affiliated with Christian Church/Churches of Christ.
Enrollment: 142 undergrads.

BASIC COSTS (2009-2010)
Tuition and fees: $10,500.
Per-credit charge: $325.
Room and board: $4,800.
Additional info: Tuition at time of enrollment locked for 4 years.

FINANCIAL AID PICTURE (2008-2009)
Students with need: Need-based aid available for full-time and part-time students. Work study available nights.
Students without need: No-need awards available for academics, leadership.

FINANCIAL AID PROCEDURES
Forms required: FAFSA, institutional form.
Dates and Deadlines: Priority date 6/1; no closing date. Applicants notified on a rolling basis starting 5/5.

CONTACT
Tina Larsen, Financial Aid Officer
12550 South 114th Street, Papillion, NE 68046

Nebraska College of Technical Agriculture

Curtis, Nebraska
www.ncta.unl.edu   Federal Code: 007358

2-year public agricultural college in rural community.
Enrollment: 246 full-time undergrads.
Selectivity: Open admission.

BASIC COSTS (2009-2010)

Tuition and fees: $3,724; out-of-state residents $6,732.
Per-credit charge: $150; out-of-state residents $275.
Room and board: $4,309.

FINANCIAL AID PICTURE (2008-2009)

Students with need: 51% of average financial aid package awarded as scholarships/grants, 49% awarded as loans/jobs. Need-based aid available for part-time students.
Students without need: This college awards aid only to students with need.

FINANCIAL AID PROCEDURES

Forms required: FAFSA.
Dates and Deadlines: Priority date 4/1; no closing date. Applicants notified on a rolling basis starting 5/1; must reply within 2 week(s) of notification.
Transfers: Must reply within 2 week(s) of notification.

CONTACT

Mary Ann Mercer, Financial Aid Coordinator
404 East 7th Street, Curtis, NE 69025-0069
(308) 367-5207

Nebraska Indian Community College

Macy, Nebraska
www.thenicc.edu   Federal Code: 015339

2-year public Tribal college in rural community.
Enrollment: 100 undergrads.
Selectivity: Open admission.

BASIC COSTS (2010-2011)

Tuition and fees: $5,100.

FINANCIAL AID PICTURE

Students with need: Need-based aid available for full-time and part-time students.
Students without need: This college awards aid only to students with need.

FINANCIAL AID PROCEDURES

Forms required: FAFSA, state aid form, institutional form.
Dates and Deadlines: Priority date 7/15; no closing date. Applicants notified on a rolling basis starting 8/30; must reply within 2 week(s) of notification.

CONTACT

Annette Loche, Financial Aid Director
PO Box 428, Macy, NE 68039

Nebraska Methodist College of Nursing and Allied Health

Omaha, Nebraska
www.methodistcollege.edu   Federal Code: 009937

4-year private health science and nursing college in large city, affiliated with United Methodist Church.
Enrollment: 568 undergrads, 28% part-time. 46 full-time freshmen.
Selectivity: Admits less than 50% of applicants.

BASIC COSTS (2010-2011)

Tuition and fees: $14,550.
Per-credit charge: $465.
Room and board: $5,770.

FINANCIAL AID PICTURE (2009-2010)

Students with need: Average financial aid package met 77% of need; average scholarship/grant was $7,211; average loan was $2,852. For part-time students, average financial aid package was $6,149.
Students without need: No-need awards available for academics, leadership, religious affiliation, ROTC.
Scholarships offered: President's Leadership Scholarship: $8,000 per year for 4 years; 4 awarded. Dean's Scholarship: $5,000 for 4 years; 3 awarded. Excellence in Allied Health Scholarship: $5,000 per year for 2 years; 3 awarded. Horizon Scholarship: $3,000 per year; based on academic and personal merit; 45 awarded.
Cumulative student debt: 87% of graduating class had student loans; average debt was $28,799.

FINANCIAL AID PROCEDURES

Forms required: FAFSA, institutional form.
Dates and Deadlines: Priority date 5/1; no closing date. Applicants notified on a rolling basis starting 3/1; must reply within 3 week(s) of notification.
Transfers: Priority date 4/1; no deadline. Applicants notified on a rolling basis.

CONTACT

Brenda Boyd, Director of Financial Aid
720 North 87th Street, Omaha, NE 68114
(402) 354-7225

Nebraska Wesleyan University

Lincoln, Nebraska
www.nebrwesleyan.edu   Federal Code: 002555

4-year private liberal arts college in small city, affiliated with United Methodist Church.
Enrollment: 1,790 undergrads, 11% part-time. 393 full-time freshmen.
Selectivity: Admits over 75% of applicants.

BASIC COSTS (2009-2010)

Tuition and fees: $22,312.
Per-credit charge: $828.
Room and board: $6,230.
Additional info: Tuition/fee waivers available for adults.

FINANCIAL AID PICTURE (2009-2010)

Students with need: Out of 345 full-time freshmen who applied for aid, 298 were judged to have need. Of these, 297 received aid, and 50 had their full need met. Average financial aid package met 74% of need; average scholarship/grant was $12,819; average loan was $4,335. For part-time students, average financial aid package was $10,512.
Students without need: 95 full-time freshmen who did not demonstrate need for aid received scholarships/grants; average award was $7,669. No-need awards available for academics, alumni affiliation, art, minority status, music/drama.

Scholarships offered: Huge-NWU Scholarship: tuition, books, fees, and room and board up to $27,000; competitive; 2 awards per year. Board of Governors Scholar Award: $11,500; ACT 32 or SAT 1410. Wesleyan Scholar Award: $10,000; ACT 29-31 or SAT 1280-1400. Fredstrom Scholarship: $8,500; ACT 27-28 or SAT 1200-1270, or top 10% class rank. President's Scholarship: $7,000; ACT 24-26 or SAT 1090-1190 or top 25% class rank. Recognition Scholarship: $5,500; ACT 22-23 or SAT 1010-1080 or top 33% class rank.

Cumulative student debt: 78% of graduating class had student loans; average debt was $21,931.

FINANCIAL AID PROCEDURES
Forms required: FAFSA.
Dates and Deadlines: No deadline. Applicants notified on a rolling basis starting 3/1; must reply within 4 week(s) of notification.
Transfers: No deadline. Applicants notified on a rolling basis starting 3/1; must reply within 4 week(s) of notification.

CONTACT
Thomas Ochsner, Director of Scholarships and Financial Aid
5000 St. Paul Avenue, Lincoln, NE 68504
(402) 465-2212

means that every student, regardless of your residency status, has the opportunity to pay the in-state tuition rate. Since we already offer a single tuition rate for online courses, the program applies only to those students pursuing their degrees on-site.

FINANCIAL AID PICTURE (2008-2009)
Students with need: Need-based aid available for full-time and part-time students.
Students without need: This college awards aid only to students with need.

FINANCIAL AID PROCEDURES
Forms required: FAFSA, institutional form.
Dates and Deadlines: Priority date 3/1; no closing date. Applicants notified on a rolling basis starting 3/1; must reply within 2 week(s) of notification.
Transfers: Must have financial aid transcripts from all previous schools sent to college.

CONTACT
Janice Volker, Director of Financial Aid
Box 10, Peru, NE 68421-0010
(402) 872-2228

Northeast Community College
Norfolk, Nebraska
www.northeast.edu　　　　Federal Code: 002556

2-year public community college in large town.
Enrollment: 2,788 undergrads, 20% part-time. 881 full-time freshmen.
Selectivity: Open admission; but selective for some programs.

BASIC COSTS (2009-2010)
Tuition and fees: $2,430; out-of-state residents $2,933.
Per-credit charge: $67; out-of-state residents $84.
Room and board: $4,656.

FINANCIAL AID PICTURE (2008-2009)
Students with need: Need-based aid available for full-time and part-time students. Work study available nights, weekends, and for part-time students.
Students without need: No-need awards available for academics, athletics, music/drama.

FINANCIAL AID PROCEDURES
Forms required: FAFSA, institutional form.
Dates and Deadlines: No deadline. Applicants notified on a rolling basis; must reply within 2 week(s) of notification.

CONTACT
Stacy Dieckman, Director of Financial Aid
801 East Benjamin Avenue, Norfolk, NE 68702-0469
(402) 844-7280

Peru State College
Peru, Nebraska
www.peru.edu　　　　Federal Code: 002559

4-year public liberal arts and teachers college in rural community.
Enrollment: 1,997 undergrads.
Selectivity: Open admission; but selective for out-of-state students.

BASIC COSTS (2009-2010)
Tuition and fees: $4,581; out-of-state residents $4,581.
Per-credit charge: $123.
Room and board: $4,962.
Additional info: Peru State College has eliminated out-of-state (non-resident) tuition beginning in 2009 fall as part of a three-year pilot program. That

Southeast Community College
Lincoln, Nebraska
www.southeast.edu　　　　Federal Code: 007591

2-year public community college in small city.
Enrollment: 9,069 undergrads, 32% part-time. 1,640 full-time freshmen.
Selectivity: Open admission.

BASIC COSTS (2009-2010)
Tuition and fees: $2,207; out-of-state residents $2,680.
Per-credit charge: $48; out-of-state residents $59.

FINANCIAL AID PICTURE
Students with need: Need-based aid available for full-time and part-time students. Work study available nights, weekends, and for part-time students.
Students without need: No-need awards available for academics.

FINANCIAL AID PROCEDURES
Forms required: FAFSA, institutional form.
Dates and Deadlines: No deadline. Applicants notified on a rolling basis; must reply within 2 week(s) of notification.

CONTACT
Dave Sonenberg, Dean of Financial Aid
8800 O Street, Lincoln, NE 68520
(402) 437-2619

Union College
Lincoln, Nebraska
www.ucollege.edu　　　　Federal Code: 002563

4-year private liberal arts college in small city, affiliated with Seventh-day Adventists.
Enrollment: 736 undergrads, 10% part-time. 117 full-time freshmen.
Selectivity: Admits less than 50% of applicants.

BASIC COSTS (2010-2011)
Tuition and fees: $18,150.
Per-credit charge: $735.
Room and board: $5,900.

FINANCIAL AID PICTURE (2008-2009)
Students with need: Need-based aid available for full-time and part-time students.

Students without need: No-need awards available for academics.
Additional info: Special institutional grants offered to all freshmen and sophomores demonstrating exceptional financial need.

FINANCIAL AID PROCEDURES
Forms required: FAFSA.
Dates and Deadlines: Priority date 5/1; no closing date. Applicants notified on a rolling basis starting 4/15; must reply by 5/1 or within 3 week(s) of notification.

CONTACT
Elaina Camarena, Director of Financial Aid
3800 South 48th Street, Lincoln, NE 68506-4300
(402) 486-2505

University of Nebraska - Kearney
Kearney, Nebraska
www.unk.edu   Federal Code: 002551

4-year public university in large town.
Enrollment: 4,904 undergrads, 8% part-time. 969 full-time freshmen.
Selectivity: Admits over 75% of applicants.

BASIC COSTS (2009-2010)
Tuition and fees: $5,635; out-of-state residents $10,397.
Per-credit charge: $151; out-of-state residents $310.
Room and board: $6,830.

FINANCIAL AID PICTURE (2009-2010)
Students with need: Out of 820 full-time freshmen who applied for aid, 657 were judged to have need. Of these, 649 received aid, and 215 had their full need met. Average financial aid package met 83% of need; average scholarship/grant was $6,283; average loan was $2,573. For part-time students, average financial aid package was $6,884.
Students without need: 5 full-time freshmen who did not demonstrate need for aid received scholarships/grants; average award was $3,185. No-need awards available for academics, alumni affiliation, art, athletics, leadership, minority status, music/drama, ROTC, state/district residency.
Scholarships offered: 1 full-time freshmen received athletic scholarships; average amount $443.
Cumulative student debt: 73% of graduating class had student loans; average debt was $19,160.

FINANCIAL AID PROCEDURES
Forms required: FAFSA, institutional form.
Dates and Deadlines: Priority date 4/1; no closing date. Applicants notified on a rolling basis starting 3/15; must reply within 2 week(s) of notification.

CONTACT
Mary Sommers, Director of Financial Aid
905 West 25th, Kearney, NE 68849
(308) 865-8520

University of Nebraska - Lincoln
Lincoln, Nebraska
www.unl.edu   Federal Code: 002565

4-year public university in small city.
Enrollment: 18,955 undergrads, 6% part-time. 3,986 full-time freshmen.
Selectivity: Admits 50 to 75% of applicants.

BASIC COSTS (2009-2010)
Tuition and fees: $6,857; out-of-state residents $17,897.
Per-credit charge: $187; out-of-state residents $555.
Room and board: $7,260.

FINANCIAL AID PICTURE (2008-2009)
Students with need: Out of 2,956 full-time freshmen who applied for aid, 1,917 were judged to have need. Of these, 1,884 received aid, and 566 had their full need met. Average financial aid package met 89% of need; average scholarship/grant was $7,585; average loan was $3,198. For part-time students, average financial aid package was $6,648.
Students without need: 673 full-time freshmen who did not demonstrate need for aid received scholarships/grants; average award was $4,778. No-need awards available for academics, alumni affiliation, art, athletics, leadership, minority status, music/drama, state/district residency.
Scholarships offered: 138 full-time freshmen received athletic scholarships; average amount $9,152.
Cumulative student debt: 61% of graduating class had student loans; average debt was $19,128.

FINANCIAL AID PROCEDURES
Forms required: FAFSA.
Dates and Deadlines: Priority date 4/15; no closing date. Applicants notified on a rolling basis starting 4/1.
Transfers: Priority application date of April 1 for scholarship consideration.

CONTACT
Craig Munier, Director of Scholarships and Financial Aid
1410 Q Street, Lincoln, NE 68588-0417
(402) 472-2030

University of Nebraska - Omaha
Omaha, Nebraska
www.unomaha.edu   Federal Code: 002554

4-year public university in large city.
Enrollment: 11,323 undergrads, 20% part-time. 1,764 full-time freshmen.
Selectivity: Admits over 75% of applicants.

BASIC COSTS (2009-2010)
Tuition and fees: $6,229; out-of-state residents $16,189.
Per-credit charge: $171; out-of-state residents $503.
Room and board: $7,230.

FINANCIAL AID PICTURE (2008-2009)
Students with need: Out of 1,304 full-time freshmen who applied for aid, 869 were judged to have need. Of these, 841 received aid. For part-time students, average financial aid package was $2,130.
Students without need: 184 full-time freshmen who did not demonstrate need for aid received scholarships/grants; average award was $2,236. No-need awards available for academics, alumni affiliation, art, athletics, leadership, minority status, music/drama, ROTC, state/district residency.
Scholarships offered: 11 full-time freshmen received athletic scholarships; average amount $3,014.
Cumulative student debt: 49% of graduating class had student loans; average debt was $19,500.

FINANCIAL AID PROCEDURES
Forms required: FAFSA.
Dates and Deadlines: Priority date 3/1; no closing date. Applicants notified on a rolling basis starting 4/15; must reply within 2 week(s) of notification.

CONTACT
Randall Sell, Director of Financial Aid
6001 Dodge Street, Omaha, NE 68182-0005
(402) 554-2327

University of Nebraska Medical Center
Omaha, Nebraska
www.unmc.edu • Federal Code: 006895

Upper-division public health science college in very large city.
Enrollment: 790 undergrads, 9% part-time.

BASIC COSTS (2009-2010)
Tuition and fees: $5,990; out-of-state residents $17,030.
Per-credit charge: $187; out-of-state residents $555.
Additional info: Tuition varies by program. Tuition/fee waivers available for minority students.

FINANCIAL AID PICTURE (2008-2009)
Students with need: Average financial aid package for all full-time undergraduates was $8,600; for part-time $4,857. 38% awarded as scholarships/grants, 62% awarded as loans/jobs. Work study available nights, weekends, and for part-time students.
Cumulative student debt: 82% of graduating class had student loans; average debt was $29,589.

FINANCIAL AID PROCEDURES
Forms required: FAFSA, institutional form.
Dates and Deadlines: Priority date 4/1; no closing date. Applicants notified by 7/1; must reply by 7/30 or within 2 week(s) of notification.
Transfers: No deadline. Applicants notified on a rolling basis starting 5/1; must reply within 2 week(s) of notification.

CONTACT
Judith Walker, Director of Financial Aid
984230 Nebraska Medical Center, Omaha, NE 68198-4230
(402) 559-4199

Wayne State College
Wayne, Nebraska
www.wsc.edu Federal Code: 002566

4-year public liberal arts and teachers college in small town.
Selectivity: Open admission.

BASIC COSTS (2009-2010)
Tuition and fees: $4,805; out-of-state residents $8,480.
Per-credit charge: $123; out-of-state residents $245.
Room and board: $5,280.

FINANCIAL AID PICTURE (2009-2010)
Students with need: Out of 596 full-time freshmen who applied for aid, 476 were judged to have need. Of these, 461 received aid, and 226 had their full need met. Average financial aid package met 60% of need; average scholarship/grant was $3,916; average loan was $3,329. For part-time students, average financial aid package was $5,516.
Students without need: 32 full-time freshmen who did not demonstrate need for aid received scholarships/grants; average award was $1,486. No-need awards available for academics, art, athletics, leadership, minority status, music/drama, religious affiliation, state/district residency.
Scholarships offered: 21 full-time freshmen received athletic scholarships; average amount $2,391.

FINANCIAL AID PROCEDURES
Forms required: FAFSA.
Dates and Deadlines: Priority date 4/1; no closing date. Applicants notified on a rolling basis starting 3/1; must reply within 4 week(s) of notification.

CONTACT
Kyle Rose, Director of Financial Aid
1111 Main Street, Wayne, NE 68787
(402) 375-7230

Western Nebraska Community College
Scottsbluff, Nebraska
www.wncc.edu Federal Code: 002560

2-year public community college in large town.
Enrollment: 1,738 undergrads, 36% part-time. 380 full-time freshmen.
Selectivity: Open admission; but selective for some programs.

BASIC COSTS (2009-2010)
Tuition and fees: $2,430; out-of-state residents $2,790.
Per-credit charge: $68; out-of-state residents $80.
Room and board: $5,700.
Additional info: For 2009/2010, students from border states of Wyoming, Colorado, and South Dakota will receive in-state, out-of-district tuition and fee rates. There are two residence halls with a difference in cost of at Pioneer Hall which is $4700.

FINANCIAL AID PICTURE (2009-2010)
Students with need: Out of 308 full-time freshmen who applied for aid, 243 were judged to have need. Of these, 238 received aid. Average financial aid package met 91% of need; average scholarship/grant was $5,051; average loan was $2,598. For part-time students, average financial aid package was $6,678.
Students without need: 43 full-time freshmen who did not demonstrate need for aid received scholarships/grants; average award was $672. No-need awards available for academics, art, athletics, leadership, music/drama, state/district residency.
Scholarships offered: 61 full-time freshmen received athletic scholarships; average amount $7,796.
Cumulative student debt: 33% of graduating class had student loans; average debt was $4,968.

FINANCIAL AID PROCEDURES
Forms required: FAFSA.
Dates and Deadlines: Priority date 3/1; no closing date. Applicants notified on a rolling basis starting 4/1.
Transfers: State of Nebraska limits the amount of Nebraska State Grant funds a student receives in any one year.

CONTACT
Sheila Johns, Director of Financial Aid
1601 East 27th Street, Scottsbluff, NE 69361
(308) 635-6011

York College
York, Nebraska
www.york.edu Federal Code: 002567

4-year private liberal arts and teachers college in small town, affiliated with Church of Christ.
Enrollment: 410 undergrads.
Selectivity: Admits 50 to 75% of applicants.

BASIC COSTS (2010-2011)
Tuition and fees: $14,998.
Per-credit charge: $400.
Room and board: $5,780.

FINANCIAL AID PICTURE (2008-2009)
Students with need: Need-based aid available for full-time and part-time students. Work study available nights, weekends, and for part-time students.

Students without need: No-need awards available for academics, alumni affiliation, athletics, leadership, music/drama.

FINANCIAL AID PROCEDURES

Forms required: FAFSA.

Dates and Deadlines: Priority date 4/1; no closing date. Applicants notified on a rolling basis starting 3/1; must reply within 4 week(s) of notification.

Transfers: No deadline. Applicants notified on a rolling basis starting 3/1; must reply within 4 week(s) of notification.

CONTACT

Brien Alley, Director of Financial Aid
1125 East 8th Street, York, NE 68467
(402) 363-5624

Nevada

Art Institute of Las Vegas

Henderson, Nevada
www.artinstitutes.edu/lasvegas/   Federal Code: 030846

3-year for-profit culinary school and visual arts college in very large city.

Enrollment: 1,182 undergrads.

Selectivity: Open admission; but selective for some programs.

BASIC COSTS (2009-2010)

Tuition and fees: $22,002.

Per-credit charge: $449.

FINANCIAL AID PICTURE (2009-2010)

Students with need: Need-based aid available for full-time and part-time students. Work study available nights, weekends, and for part-time students.

Students without need: No-need awards available for academics, state/district residency.

Scholarships offered: Academic Competitiveness Grant: up to $750 the first year and up to $1,300 the second year; available to students who are receiving a Pell Grant, are full time in their first or second year of college in a degree program, who graduated from high school in 2005 or later, and who took a program of study in high school that was considered to be rigorous; each eligible student may receive 2 years of ACG; must have a 3.0 GPA at the end of the first year to receive a second year grant. C-CAP Careers Through Culinary Arts Program: approximately $36,000 - $72,000; available to students who are enrolled in a C-CAP program. CKYBER National Kitchen and Bath Association VNU Scholarship: provided for students enrolled in a NKBA (National Kitchen and Bath Association) endorsed program; GPA of 2.7 or higher; must be attending full time for the full academic year; Interior Design program students are eligible to apply. Evelyn Keedy Memorial Scholarship: $30,000 tuition; available to high school seniors who show dedication to their education and a desire for a creative career. National Art Honor Society Scholarship: first Place $20,000, second place $10,000, third place $5,000, fourth place $3,000, fifth place $2,000; high school seniors who also belong to the National Art Honor Society may apply; senior class members of the National Art Honor Society are eligible to compete.

FINANCIAL AID PROCEDURES

Dates and Deadlines: No deadline. Applicants notified on a rolling basis.

Transfers: No deadline. Applicants notified on a rolling basis.

CONTACT

Dana Sirolli, Director of Student Financial Services
2350 Corporate Circle, Henderson, NV 89074-7737
(702) 369-9944

Career College of Northern Nevada

Reno, Nevada
www.ccnn.edu   Federal Code: 026215

2-year for-profit career college in large city.

Enrollment: 462 undergrads.

Selectivity: Open admission.

BASIC COSTS (2009-2010)

Per-credit charge: $205.

Additional info: Tuition for associate programs ranges from $20,055 to $26,250; diploma programs, $11,655 to $15,960. Fees are $210 to $672; books range from $650 to $2,650.

FINANCIAL AID PICTURE

Students with need: Need-based aid available for full-time students.

Students without need: This college awards aid only to students with need.

FINANCIAL AID PROCEDURES

Forms required: FAFSA.

Dates and Deadlines: Closing date 5/30. Applicants notified on a rolling basis.

CONTACT

Andrea Wiggins
1195 A Corporate Boulevard, Reno, NV 89502-2331
(775) 856-2266

College of Southern Nevada

Las Vegas, Nevada
www.csn.edu   Federal Code: 010362

2-year public community college in very large city.

Enrollment: 34,546 undergrads, 74% part-time. 2,498 full-time freshmen.

Selectivity: Open admission; but selective for some programs.

BASIC COSTS (2009-2010)

Tuition and fees: $2,010; out-of-state residents $8,198.

Per-credit charge: $60; out-of-state residents $266.

Additional info: Discounted tuition for residents of western states participating in Western Undergraduate Exchange: Alaska, Arizona, California, Colorado, Hawaii, Idaho, Montana, Nevada, New Mexico, North Dakota, Oregon, South Dakota, Utah, Washington, Wyoming.

FINANCIAL AID PICTURE (2008-2009)

Students with need: Work study available nights, weekends, and for part-time students.

Students without need: No-need awards available for state/district residency.

FINANCIAL AID PROCEDURES

Forms required: FAFSA.

Dates and Deadlines: Priority date 5/1; closing date 6/30. Applicants notified on a rolling basis starting 7/15; must reply within 2 week(s) of notification.

CONTACT

Peter Hurley, Director, Student Financial Services
6375 West Charleston Boulevard, Las Vegas, NV 89146-1164
(702) 651-4047

Everest College: Las Vegas

Henderson, Nevada
www.lasvegas-college.com   Federal Code: 015804

2-year for-profit business and health science college in very large city.
Enrollment: 758 undergrads.
Selectivity: Open admission.

BASIC COSTS (2009-2010)
Tuition and fees: $16,425.
Per-credit charge: $365.

FINANCIAL AID PICTURE (2009-2010)
Students with need: Need-based aid available for full-time and part-time students. Work study available nights, weekends, and for part-time students.
Students without need: This college awards aid only to students with need.

FINANCIAL AID PROCEDURES
Forms required: FAFSA.
Dates and Deadlines: Applicants notified on a rolling basis; must reply within 2 week(s) of notification.

CONTACT
RoseMarie Young, Director of Financial Aid
170 North Stephanie Street, Henderson, NV 89074

Great Basin College

Elko, Nevada
www.gbcnv.edu   Federal Code: 006977

4-year public community and teachers college in large town.
Enrollment: 2,389 undergrads.
Selectivity: Open admission; but selective for some programs.

BASIC COSTS (2009-2010)
Tuition and fees: $2,130; out-of-state residents $8,318.
Per-credit charge: $60; out-of-state residents $126.
Room only: $3,300.
Additional info: Discounted tuition (Good Neighbor rates) available for non-resident students residing in certain counties bordering Nevada. On-campus room only $2,090-$3,300 (extended semester has additional costs).

FINANCIAL AID PICTURE
Students with need: Need-based aid available for full-time and part-time students. Work study available nights, weekends, and for part-time students.

FINANCIAL AID PROCEDURES
Forms required: FAFSA.
Dates and Deadlines: Priority date 6/1; no closing date. Applicants notified on a rolling basis starting 7/1.
Transfers: Priority date 4/1.

CONTACT
Scott Neilsen, Director of Financial Aid
1500 College Parkway, Elko, NV 89801
(775) 753-2267

Kaplan College: Las Vegas

Las Vegas, Nevada
www.kaplancollege.com   Federal Code: 030432

2-year for-profit career college in very large city.
Enrollment: 426 undergrads.
Selectivity: Open admission; but selective for some programs.

BASIC COSTS (2009-2010)
Additional info: Cost of full programs: associate degree programs $28,250, diploma programs $14,320, including fees and books.

FINANCIAL AID PICTURE (2009-2010)
Students with need: 43% of average financial aid package awarded as scholarships/grants, 57% awarded as loans/jobs. Need-based aid available for part-time students. Work study available nights.

FINANCIAL AID PROCEDURES
Forms required: FAFSA, institutional form.
Dates and Deadlines: No deadline.
Transfers: No deadline. Applicants notified on a rolling basis.

CONTACT
Carmen Torres, Director of Finance
3535 West Sahara Avenue, Las Vegas, NV 89102
(702) 368-2338

Morrison University

Reno, Nevada
www.morrisonuniversity.com   Federal Code: 008441

4-year for-profit university and business college in small city.
Enrollment: 164 undergrads.
Selectivity: Open admission.

BASIC COSTS (2009-2010)
Tuition and fees: $9,025.
Per-credit charge: $200.

FINANCIAL AID PICTURE
Students with need: Need-based aid available for full-time students. Work study available nights.

FINANCIAL AID PROCEDURES
Forms required: FAFSA.
Dates and Deadlines: No deadline. Applicants notified on a rolling basis starting 7/1.

CONTACT
Jim Hadwick, Financial Aid Manager
10315 Professional Circle, #201, Reno, NV 89521
(775) 850-0700 ext. 110

Nevada State College

Henderson, Nevada
www.nsc.nevada.edu   Federal Code: 041143

4-year public nursing and liberal arts and teachers college in large city.
Enrollment: 1,990 undergrads, 49% part-time. 142 full-time freshmen.
Selectivity: Admits 50 to 75% of applicants.

BASIC COSTS (2009-2010)
Tuition and fees: $3,260; out-of-state residents $12,524.
Per-credit charge: $108.

FINANCIAL AID PICTURE (2008-2009)
Students with need: Out of 68 full-time freshmen who applied for aid, 62 were judged to have need. Of these, 61 received aid, and 15 had their full need met. Average financial aid package met 62% of need; average scholarship/grant was $4,300; average loan was $3,200. For part-time students, average financial aid package was $7,200.

FINANCIAL AID PROCEDURES
Forms required: FAFSA, institutional form.
Dates and Deadlines: Priority date 3/1; closing date 6/1. Applicants notified on a rolling basis starting 5/1.

Transfers: Applicants notified on a rolling basis starting 5/1.

CONTACT

Neil Woolf, Director, Student Financial Services & Scholarships

1125 Nevada State Drive, Henderson, NV 89002

(702) 992-2150

Sierra Nevada College

Incline Village, Nevada

www.sierranevada.edu   Federal Code: 009192

4-year private liberal arts college in small town.

Enrollment: 379 undergrads.

Selectivity: Admits 50 to 75% of applicants.

BASIC COSTS (2009-2010)

Tuition and fees: $22,978.

Per-credit charge: $971.

Room and board: $8,824.

FINANCIAL AID PICTURE (2009-2010)

Students with need: Need-based aid available for full-time and part-time students.

Students without need: No-need awards available for academics, art, athletics.

Scholarships offered: Academic scholarships; $2,000-$13,000 per year; renewable.

FINANCIAL AID PROCEDURES

Forms required: FAFSA, institutional form.

Dates and Deadlines: Priority date 4/1; no closing date. Applicants notified on a rolling basis; must reply by 5/1 or within 4 week(s) of notification.

Transfers: Priority date 3/15; no deadline.

CONTACT

Nicole Ferguson, Director of Financial Aid

999 Tahoe Boulevard, Incline Village, NV 89451-4269

(775) 831-1314 ext. 7440

Truckee Meadows Community College

Reno, Nevada

www.tmcc.edu   Federal Code: 010363

2-year public community and technical college in large city.

Enrollment: 10,599 undergrads, 67% part-time. 852 full-time freshmen.

Selectivity: Open admission.

BASIC COSTS (2009-2010)

Tuition and fees: $1,965; out-of-state residents $8,153.

Per-credit charge: $60; out-of-state residents $266.

Additional info: Discounted tuition (Good Neighbor rates) available for non-resident students residing in certain counties bordering Nevada.

FINANCIAL AID PICTURE (2008-2009)

Students with need: Work study available nights, weekends, and for part-time students.

Students without need: No-need awards available for academics, art, leadership, minority status, music/drama, state/district residency.

Additional info: Institutional grants to state residents, short-term emergency loans available. Work-study applications must reply within 10 days of notification.

FINANCIAL AID PROCEDURES

Forms required: FAFSA, institutional form.

Dates and Deadlines: Priority date 1/15; no closing date. Applicants notified by 5/15.

Transfers: Priority date 3/9; no deadline. Must provide academic transcript from previous institution.

CONTACT

John Gottardy, Director of Financial Aid, Scholarships and Student Employment

7000 Dandini Boulevard, Reno, NV 89512

(775) 673-7072

University of Nevada: Las Vegas

Las Vegas, Nevada

www.unlv.edu   Federal Code: 002569

4-year public university in very large city.

Enrollment: 22,708 undergrads.

Selectivity: GED not accepted.

BASIC COSTS (2009-2010)

Tuition and fees: $4,527; out-of-state residents $16,867.

Per-credit charge: $136; out-of-state residents $1,095.

Room and board: $10,456.

Additional info: Discounted tuition (Good Neighbor rates) available for non-resident students residing in certain counties bordering Nevada.

FINANCIAL AID PICTURE (2008-2009)

Students with need: Need-based aid available for full-time and part-time students.

Students without need: No-need awards available for academics, alumni affiliation, art, athletics, job skills, leadership, minority status, music/drama, ROTC, state/district residency.

Additional info: Tuition reduction for state residents through consortium programs and for out-of-state students graduating from high schools in designated counties bordering Nevada, for military dependents residing in-state, and for dependents of children of alumni not residing in-state.

FINANCIAL AID PROCEDURES

Forms required: FAFSA, institutional form.

Dates and Deadlines: Priority date 2/1; no closing date. Applicants notified on a rolling basis starting 3/20; must reply within 2 week(s) of notification.

CONTACT

Norm Bedford, Director of Financial Aid & Scholarships

4505 Maryland Parkway Box 451021, Las Vegas, NV 89154-1021

(702) 895-3424

University of Nevada: Reno

Reno, Nevada

www.unr.edu   Federal Code: 002568

4-year public university in small city.

Enrollment: 12,878 undergrads, 17% part-time. 2,259 full-time freshmen.

Selectivity: Admits over 75% of applicants. GED not accepted.

BASIC COSTS (2009-2010)

Tuition and fees: $4,901; out-of-state residents $17,241.

Per-credit charge: $136; out-of-state residents $547.

Room and board: $10,595.

Additional info: Discounted tuition (Good Neighbor rates) available for non-resident students residing in certain counties bordering Nevada. Discounted tuition also available for Western Undergraduate Exchange students.

FINANCIAL AID PICTURE (2008-2009)

Students with need: Out of 1,363 full-time freshmen who applied for aid, 855 were judged to have need. Of these, 831 received aid, and 124 had their full need met. Average financial aid package met 55% of need; average scholarship/grant was $5,605; average loan was $3,182. For part-time students, average financial aid package was $5,183.

Students without need: 1,158 full-time freshmen who did not demonstrate need for aid received scholarships/grants; average award was $2,662. No-need awards available for academics, alumni affiliation, art, athletics, music/drama.

Scholarships offered: *Merit:* Presidential scholarship awards: $5,000 per year; must have 3.5 unweighted GPA and 1380 SAT (exclusive of writing) or 31 ACT; must be admitted by 2/1 of year prior to enrollment and meet Nevada residency requirements. Additional scholarships: ranging from $2,500 to $5,000; based on combination of test scores and unweighted GPA. *Athletic:* 60 full-time freshmen received athletic scholarships; average amount $15,550.

Cumulative student debt: 35% of graduating class had student loans; average debt was $15,854.

Additional info: Reduced out-of-state tuition available for children of alumni and for non-residents from some neighboring counties in California and participants in WUE program.

FINANCIAL AID PROCEDURES

Forms required: FAFSA.

Dates and Deadlines: Priority date 3/1; no closing date. Applicants notified on a rolling basis starting 4/1; must reply within 2 week(s) of notification.

Transfers: No deadline. Applicants notified on a rolling basis; must reply within 2 week(s) of notification. Transfer GPA must be 2.0 or higher to be eligible for aid.

CONTACT

Sandy Guidry, Director, Student Financial Services
Mail Stop 120, Reno, NV 89557
(775) 784-4666

University of Southern Nevada

Henderson, Nevada
www.usn.edu   Federal Code: 040653

Upper-division private university in very large city.

Enrollment: 142 undergrads.

BASIC COSTS (2010-2011)

Tuition and fees: $30,565.

Per-credit charge: $517.

Additional info: Required fees include a laptop fee of $1,300.00. Tuition and fees reported cover the first 12 months of study within an 18 month expedited BSN program. University of Southern Nevada operates under a block system of curriculum. University of Southern Nevada does not offer on-site housing; however, the figure shown above for room and board reflects the approximate cost of living for a student for one year.

FINANCIAL AID PICTURE (2009-2010)

Students with need: Average financial aid package for all full-time undergraduates was $10,350. 40% awarded as scholarships/grants, 60% awarded as loans/jobs. Need-based aid available for part-time students.

Cumulative student debt: 84% of graduating class had student loans; average debt was $21,087.

FINANCIAL AID PROCEDURES

Dates and Deadlines: Priority date 1/1; closing date 4/1.

Transfers: Priority date 1/1; closing date 4/1. Applicants notified on a rolling basis starting 7/1; must reply within 2 week(s) of notification.

CONTACT

Jesse Stasher, Director of Financial Aid
11 Sunset Way, Henderson, NV 89014-2333
(702) 968-2026

Western Nevada College

Carson City, Nevada
www.wnc.edu   Federal Code: 013896

2-year public community college in small city.

Enrollment: 3,939 undergrads.

Selectivity: Open admission; but selective for some programs.

BASIC COSTS (2009-2010)

Tuition and fees: $2,010; out-of-state residents $8,198.

Per-credit charge: $60.

Additional info: Discounted tuition (Good Neighbor rates) available for non-resident students residing in certain counties bordering Nevada.

FINANCIAL AID PICTURE (2008-2009)

Students with need: Need-based aid available for full-time and part-time students. Work study available nights, weekends, and for part-time students.

Students without need: No-need awards available for academics, state/district residency.

FINANCIAL AID PROCEDURES

Forms required: FAFSA.

Dates and Deadlines: Priority date 4/1; no closing date. Applicants notified on a rolling basis.

Transfers: Maximum loan debt of $14,125 allowed. Loans received at other schools counted toward limit.

CONTACT

Lori Tiede, Director of Financial Assistance
2201 West College Parkway, Carson City, NV 89703-7399
(775) 445-3264

New Hampshire

Chester College of New England

Chester, New Hampshire
www.chestercollege.edu   Federal Code: 004733

4-year private visual arts and liberal arts college in rural community.

Enrollment: 187 undergrads, 9% part-time. 60 full-time freshmen.

Selectivity: Admits 50 to 75% of applicants.

BASIC COSTS (2010-2011)

Tuition and fees: $18,525.

Room and board: $8,360.

FINANCIAL AID PICTURE (2008-2009)

Students with need: Out of 56 full-time freshmen who applied for aid, 51 were judged to have need. Of these, 51 received aid. Average financial aid package met 20% of need; average scholarship/grant was $2,800; average loan was $3,500. For part-time students, average financial aid package was $3,150.

Students without need: 4 full-time freshmen who did not demonstrate need for aid received scholarships/grants; average award was $3,500. No-need awards available for academics, art, state/district residency.

Cumulative student debt: 95% of graduating class had student loans; average debt was $32,500.

FINANCIAL AID PROCEDURES

Forms required: FAFSA, state aid form.

Dates and Deadlines: Priority date 3/15; no closing date. Applicants notified on a rolling basis starting 12/1; must reply within 2 week(s) of notification. **Transfers:** Closing date 8/1. Applicants notified on a rolling basis starting 4/1; must reply by 8/1.

CONTACT
Roger Illescas, Director of Financial Aid
40 Chester Street, Chester, NH 03036
(603) 887-7404

Colby-Sawyer College
New London, New Hampshire
www.colby-sawyer.edu   Federal Code: 002572

4-year private liberal arts college in small town.
Enrollment: 1,100 undergrads.
Selectivity: Admits over 75% of applicants.

BASIC COSTS (2009-2010)
Tuition and fees: $31,090.
Per-credit charge: $990.
Room and board: $10,860.

FINANCIAL AID PICTURE (2009-2010)
Students with need: Need-based aid available for full-time and part-time students. Work study available nights, weekends, and for part-time students.
Students without need: No-need awards available for academics, alumni affiliation, art, leadership, minority status, music/drama.

FINANCIAL AID PROCEDURES
Forms required: FAFSA.
Dates and Deadlines: Priority date 2/15; closing date 3/1. Applicants notified on a rolling basis starting 1/1; must reply by 5/1 or within 2 week(s) of notification.
Transfers: Priority date 3/1; closing date 4/15. Applicants notified on a rolling basis starting 12/15; must reply within 2 week(s) of notification.

CONTACT
Ted Craigie, Director of Financial Aid
541 Main Street, New London, NH 03257-7835
(603) 526-3717

Daniel Webster College
Nashua, New Hampshire
www.dwc.edu   Federal Code: 004731

4-year private business and engineering and liberal arts college in small city.
Enrollment: 730 undergrads.
Selectivity: Admits 50 to 75% of applicants.

BASIC COSTS (2009-2010)
Tuition and fees: $28,614.
Per-credit charge: $1,098.
Room and board: $9,698.

FINANCIAL AID PICTURE (2008-2009)
Students with need: Need-based aid available for full-time and part-time students. Work study available nights, weekends, and for part-time students.
Students without need: No-need awards available for academics, alumni affiliation, leadership.
Scholarships offered: Scholarships based on GPA and test scores, leadership, guidance counselor recommendation, awarded in amounts ranging from $500 to $7,500. Alumni and other scholarships range from $500 to full tuition.

FINANCIAL AID PROCEDURES
Forms required: FAFSA, institutional form.

Dates and Deadlines: Priority date 3/1; no closing date. Applicants notified on a rolling basis starting 3/15; must reply within 2 week(s) of notification.

CONTACT
Rebecca MacLennan, Director of Finance
20 University Drive, Nashua, NH 03063
(603) 577-6590

Dartmouth College
Hanover, New Hampshire   Federal Code: 002573
www.dartmouth.edu   CSS Code: 3351

4-year private university and liberal arts college in large town.
Enrollment: 4,090 undergrads. 1,096 full-time freshmen.
Selectivity: Admits less than 50% of applicants.

BASIC COSTS (2009-2010)
Tuition and fees: $38,789.
Room and board: $11,295.

FINANCIAL AID PICTURE (2008-2009)
Students with need: Out of 678 full-time freshmen who applied for aid, 535 were judged to have need. Of these, 535 received aid, and 535 had their full need met. Average financial aid package met 100% of need; average scholarship/grant was $34,939; average loan was $2,401. Need-based aid available for part-time students.
Students without need: This college awards aid only to students with need.
Cumulative student debt: 48% of graduating class had student loans; average debt was $19,051.

FINANCIAL AID PROCEDURES
Forms required: FAFSA, CSS PROFILE.
Dates and Deadlines: Closing date 2/1. Applicants notified by 4/10; must reply by 5/1.
Transfers: Closing date 3/15. Applicants notified by 4/2; must reply by 5/1. Grant budget for transfer students is limited. Some admitted transfer students may not have their full needs met.

CONTACT
Virginia Hazen, Director of Financial Aid
6016 McNutt Hall, Hanover, NH 03755
(603) 646-2451

Franklin Pierce University
Rindge, New Hampshire
www.franklinpierce.edu   Federal Code: 002575

4-year private university and liberal arts college in small town.
Enrollment: 1,846 undergrads, 14% part-time. 495 full-time freshmen.
Selectivity: Admits over 75% of applicants.

BASIC COSTS (2010-2011)
Tuition and fees: $28,800.
Per-credit charge: $923.
Room and board: $10,100.
Additional info: Additional $100 contingency deposit required of new students; refundable when student leaves institution.

FINANCIAL AID PICTURE (2008-2009)
Students with need: Out of 406 full-time freshmen who applied for aid, 357 were judged to have need. Of these, 353 received aid, and 53 had their full need met. Average financial aid package met 71% of need; average scholarship/grant was $15,681. Need-based aid available for part-time students.
Students without need: 87 full-time freshmen who did not demonstrate need for aid received scholarships/grants; average award was $9,681. No-

need awards available for academics, alumni affiliation, art, athletics, leadership.

Scholarships offered: *Merit:* Marlin Fitzwater Mass Communication: $2,000; 6 awarded. Robert Alvin Performing Arts-Theater, Music, Dance; $2,000; 2 awarded in each category. Leadership Scholarship: $2,000; 10 awarded. *Athletic:* 24 full-time freshmen received athletic scholarships; average amount $10,647.

Cumulative student debt: 83% of graduating class had student loans; average debt was $38,148.

FINANCIAL AID PROCEDURES

Forms required: FAFSA.

Dates and Deadlines: Closing date 3/1. Applicants notified on a rolling basis starting 3/1; must reply within 2 week(s) of notification.

Transfers: No deadline. Applicants notified on a rolling basis starting 3/1; must reply within 2 week(s) of notification.

CONTACT

Ken Ferreria, Director of Student Financial Services
40 University Drive, Rindge, NH 03461-0060
(603) 899-4180

Granite State College
Concord, New Hampshire
www.granite.edu   Federal Code: 031013

4-year public liberal arts college in large town.

Enrollment: 1,338 undergrads, 50% part-time. 34 full-time freshmen.

Selectivity: Open admission.

BASIC COSTS (2009-2010)

Tuition and fees: $7,695; out-of-state residents $8,145.

Per-credit charge: $250; out-of-state residents $265.

FINANCIAL AID PICTURE (2008-2009)

Students with need: 97% of average financial aid package awarded as scholarships/grants, 3% awarded as loans/jobs. Need-based aid available for part-time students. Work study available nights.

Students without need: This college awards aid only to students with need.

FINANCIAL AID PROCEDURES

Forms required: FAFSA, institutional form.

Dates and Deadlines: No deadline. Applicants notified on a rolling basis starting 4/15.

Transfers: No deadline. Applicants notified on a rolling basis starting 4/15.

CONTACT

Kevin Piotrowski, Director of Financial Aid
8 Old Suncook Road, Concord, NH 03301-7317
(603) 228-3000 ext. 324

Keene State College
Keene, New Hampshire
www.keene.edu   Federal Code: 002590

4-year public liberal arts and teachers college in large town.

Enrollment: 4,990 undergrads, 3% part-time. 1,298 full-time freshmen.

Selectivity: Admits 50 to 75% of applicants.

BASIC COSTS (2009-2010)

Tuition and fees: $9,334; out-of-state residents $17,504.

Per-credit charge: $292; out-of-state residents $632.

Room and board: $8,444.

Additional info: New England Regional tuition is 175% of in-state public institution tuition.

FINANCIAL AID PICTURE (2008-2009)

Students with need: Out of 1,103 full-time freshmen who applied for aid, 746 were judged to have need. Of these, 728 received aid, and 117 had their full need met. Average financial aid package met 65% of need; average scholarship/grant was $5,512; average loan was $3,386. For part-time students, average financial aid package was $6,328.

Students without need: No-need awards available for academics, alumni affiliation, art, music/drama.

FINANCIAL AID PROCEDURES

Forms required: FAFSA.

Dates and Deadlines: Closing date 3/1. Applicants notified on a rolling basis; must reply within 4 week(s) of notification.

Transfers: Applicants notified on a rolling basis; must reply within 4 week(s) of notification.

CONTACT

Patricia Blodgett, Director of Financial Aid
229 Main Street, Keene, NH 03435-2604
(603) 358-2280

Lakes Region Community College
Laconia, New Hampshire
www.lrcc.edu   Federal Code: 007555

2-year public community and technical college in small city.

Enrollment: 950 undergrads.

Selectivity: Open admission; but selective for some programs.

BASIC COSTS (2009-2010)

Tuition and fees: $5,640; out-of-state residents $12,690.

Per-credit charge: $183; out-of-state residents $418.

Additional info: New England regional tuition per-credit-hour charge: $274.

FINANCIAL AID PICTURE (2009-2010)

Students with need: Need-based aid available for full-time and part-time students.

FINANCIAL AID PROCEDURES

Forms required: FAFSA, institutional form.

Dates and Deadlines: Priority date 5/1; no closing date.

CONTACT

Kristen Purrington, Financial Aid Officer
379 Belmont Road, Laconia, NH 03246-9204
(603) 524-3207

Lebanon College
Lebanon, New Hampshire
www.lebanoncollege.edu   Federal Code: 007025

2-year private health science and community college in large town.

Enrollment: 167 undergrads, 38% part-time. 33 full-time freshmen.

Selectivity: Open admission; but selective for some programs.

BASIC COSTS (2009-2010)

Tuition and fees: $4,725.

Per-credit charge: $145.

FINANCIAL AID PICTURE (2008-2009)

Students with need: 40% of average financial aid package awarded as scholarships/grants, 60% awarded as loans/jobs.

FINANCIAL AID PROCEDURES

Forms required: FAFSA, institutional form.

Dates and Deadlines: No deadline. Applicants notified on a rolling basis.

Transfers: No deadline. Applicants notified on a rolling basis.

CONTACT
Rebecca Timmins, Financial Aid Director
15 Hanover Street, Lebanon, NH 03766
(603) 448-2445 ext. 121

Magdalen College
Warner, New Hampshire
www.magdalen.edu   Federal Code: 022233

4-year private liberal arts college in small town, affiliated with Roman Catholic Church.
Enrollment: 68 undergrads.
Selectivity: Admits 50 to 75% of applicants.

BASIC COSTS (2009-2010)
Tuition and fees: $14,200.
Room and board: $6,750.

FINANCIAL AID PICTURE (2008-2009)
Students with need: Need-based aid available for full-time and part-time students.
Students without need: This college awards aid only to students with need.

FINANCIAL AID PROCEDURES
Forms required: institutional form.
Dates and Deadlines: Closing date 6/30. Applicants notified by 7/1; must reply by 7/1 or within 4 week(s) of notification.

CONTACT
Donald Regan, VP of Finance and Operations
511 Kearsarge Mountain Road, Warner, NH 03278
(603) 456-2656

Manchester Community College
Manchester, New Hampshire
www.manchestercommunitycollege.edu   Federal Code: 002582

2-year public community and technical college in small city.
Enrollment: 2,180 undergrads.
Selectivity: Open admission; but selective for some programs.

BASIC COSTS (2009-2010)
Tuition and fees: $5,670; out-of-state residents $12,720.
Per-credit charge: $183; out-of-state residents $418.
Additional info: New England Regional tuition: $274 per credit hour.

FINANCIAL AID PICTURE
Students with need: Need-based aid available for full-time and part-time students. Work study available nights, weekends, and for part-time students.
Students without need: This college awards aid only to students with need.
Scholarships offered: NH high school valedictorians receive 100% tuition scholarship.

FINANCIAL AID PROCEDURES
Forms required: FAFSA, institutional form.
Dates and Deadlines: Priority date 5/1; no closing date. Applicants notified on a rolling basis starting 4/15; must reply within 2 week(s) of notification.

CONTACT
Stephanie Weldon, Financial Aid Officer
1066 Front Street, Manchester, NH 03102-8518
(603) 668-6706 ext. 352

Nashua Community College
Nashua, New Hampshire
www.nashuacc.edu   Federal Code: 009236

2-year public community and technical college in small city.
Enrollment: 2,038 undergrads, 59% part-time.
Selectivity: Open admission; but selective for some programs.

BASIC COSTS (2009-2010)
Tuition and fees: $5,970; out-of-state residents $13,020.
Per-credit charge: $183; out-of-state residents $418.
Additional info: New England regional tuition: $274 per credit hour.

FINANCIAL AID PICTURE (2008-2009)
Students with need: Need-based aid available for full-time and part-time students. Work study available nights.
Students without need: This college awards aid only to students with need.

FINANCIAL AID PROCEDURES
Forms required: FAFSA.
Dates and Deadlines: Priority date 5/1; no closing date. Applicants notified on a rolling basis starting 3/1; must reply within 2 week(s) of notification.

CONTACT
Lisbeth Gonzalez, Director of Financial Aid
505 Amherst Street, Nashua, NH 03063-1026
(603) 882-6923 ext. 1528

New England College
Henniker, New Hampshire
www.nec.edu   Federal Code: 002579

4-year private business and liberal arts and teachers college in small town.
Enrollment: 997 undergrads, 6% part-time. 256 full-time freshmen.
Selectivity: Admits over 75% of applicants.

BASIC COSTS (2010-2011)
Tuition and fees: $29,054.
Per-credit charge: $1,377.
Room and board: $10,170.
Additional info: Tuition/fee waivers available for adults.

FINANCIAL AID PICTURE (2009-2010)
Students with need: Out of 223 full-time freshmen who applied for aid, 209 were judged to have need. Of these, 209 received aid, and 30 had their full need met. Average financial aid package met 81% of need; average scholarship/grant was $16,469; average loan was $8,098. For part-time students, average financial aid package was $18,729.
Students without need: 46 full-time freshmen who did not demonstrate need for aid received scholarships/grants; average award was $10,387. No-need awards available for academics, alumni affiliation, art, job skills, leadership, music/drama, state/district residency.
Cumulative student debt: 77% of graduating class had student loans; average debt was $33,466.

FINANCIAL AID PROCEDURES
Forms required: FAFSA, institutional form.
Dates and Deadlines: Priority date 4/1; no closing date. Applicants notified on a rolling basis starting 1/12; must reply within 2 week(s) of notification.
Transfers: No deadline. Applicants notified on a rolling basis starting 1/1; must reply within 2 week(s) of notification. May 1 deadline for state grant consideration.

CONTACT
Russell Romandini, Director of Admission and Financial Aid
102 Bridge Street, Henniker, NH 03242
(603) 428-2226

NHTI-Concord's Community College
Concord, New Hampshire
www.nhti.edu   Federal Code: 002581

2-year public community and technical college in large town.
Enrollment: 3,050 undergrads.
Selectivity: Open admission; but selective for some programs.

BASIC COSTS (2009-2010)
Tuition and fees: $6,090; out-of-state residents $13,140.
Per-credit charge: $183; out-of-state residents $418.
Room and board: $7,924.
Additional info: New England Regional tuition: $274 per credit hour.

FINANCIAL AID PICTURE (2009-2010)
Students with need: Need-based aid available for full-time and part-time students. Work study available nights, weekends, and for part-time students.
Students without need: This college awards aid only to students with need.
Additional info: 60% of students who apply receive some form of financial aid. State school; all financial aid need-based, primarily from federal sources. No scholarships awarded.

FINANCIAL AID PROCEDURES
Forms required: FAFSA, institutional form.
Dates and Deadlines: Priority date 5/1; no closing date. Applicants notified on a rolling basis starting 6/1; must reply within 2 week(s) of notification.
Transfers: No deadline. Applicants notified on a rolling basis.

CONTACT
Sheri Gonthier, Financial Aid Director
31 College Drive, Concord, NH 03301
(603) 271-7136

Plymouth State University
Plymouth, New Hampshire
www.plymouth.edu   Federal Code: 002591

4-year public university and teachers college in small town.
Enrollment: 4,155 undergrads, 3% part-time. 961 full-time freshmen.
Selectivity: Admits 50 to 75% of applicants.

BASIC COSTS (2009-2010)
Tuition and fees: $8,944; out-of-state residents $17,114.
Per-credit charge: $292; out-of-state residents $632.
Room and board: $9,134.
Additional info: New England Regional tuition: 175% of in-state tuition.

FINANCIAL AID PICTURE (2008-2009)
Students with need: Need-based aid available for full-time and part-time students. Work study available nights, weekends, and for part-time students.
Students without need: No-need awards available for academics, minority status, music/drama.
Scholarships offered: Presidential Scholars: $3,500; based on outstanding academic performance and overall achievement. PSU Scholars: $2,500; based on overall merit and past achievement. New Hampshire Top Scholars: $2,500; for New Hampshire residents in top 15%. Music/Theater Talent Grants: $2,500; based on talent and audition. ALANA; $2,000; for minority students based on student's admission application.

FINANCIAL AID PROCEDURES
Forms required: FAFSA.
Dates and Deadlines: Priority date 3/1; no closing date. Applicants notified on a rolling basis starting 2/15; must reply by 5/1.
Transfers: Applicants notified by 5/1.

CONTACT
June Schlabach, Director of Financial Aid
17 High Street MSC 52, Plymouth, NH 03264-1595
(603) 535-2338

River Valley Community College
Claremont, New Hampshire
www.rivervalley.edu   Federal Code: 007560

2-year public community college in large town.
Enrollment: 900 undergrads.
Selectivity: Open admission; but selective for some programs.

BASIC COSTS (2009-2010)
Tuition and fees: $5,640; out-of-state residents $12,690.
Per-credit charge: $183; out-of-state residents $418.
Additional info: New England Regional tuition: $274 per credit hour.

FINANCIAL AID PICTURE
Students with need: Need-based aid available for full-time and part-time students.
Students without need: This college awards aid only to students with need.

FINANCIAL AID PROCEDURES
Forms required: FAFSA.
Dates and Deadlines: Closing date 4/1. Applicants notified on a rolling basis; must reply within 2 week(s) of notification.

CONTACT
Julia Dower, Director of Financial Aid
One College Drive, Claremont, NH 03743-9707
(603) 542-7744

Rivier College
Nashua, New Hampshire
www.rivier.edu   Federal Code: 002586

4-year private liberal arts and teachers college in small city, affiliated with Roman Catholic Church.
Enrollment: 1,406 undergrads, 31% part-time. 236 full-time freshmen.
Selectivity: Open admission; but selective for some programs.

BASIC COSTS (2010-2011)
Tuition and fees: $25,050.
Per-credit charge: $815.
Room and board: $9,428.
Additional info: Tuition/fee waivers available for unemployed or children of unemployed.

FINANCIAL AID PICTURE (2009-2010)
Students with need: Out of 229 full-time freshmen who applied for aid, 203 were judged to have need. Of these, 202 received aid, and 13 had their full need met. Average financial aid package met 64% of need; average scholarship/grant was $13,076; average loan was $3,457. For part-time students, average financial aid package was $5,402.
Students without need: 36 full-time freshmen who did not demonstrate need for aid received scholarships/grants; average award was $5,527. No-need awards available for academics, alumni affiliation.

Scholarships offered: Dean's Scholarship: $6,000 for residents, $5,000 for commuters, high school seniors with minimum 1000 SAT (exclusive of writing) and 3.0 GPA; renewable annually with minimum 2.67 GPA. Presidential Scholarship: $7,000 for residents, $6,000 for commuters, high school seniors with minimum 1150 SAT (exclusive of writing) and 3.4 GPA; renewable annually with minimum 3.0 GPA. Catholic High School Grant: $4,000 for residents, $3,000 for commuters, for students graduating from Catholic high school; renewable annually with 2.5 GPA. Honors Scholarship for honors program participants: $10,000 for residents, $2,000 for commuters. Alumni Scholarship: $2,000, for children of Rivier alumni; renewable annually with minimum 2.0 GPA. Trustee Scholarship: $8,000 for residents, $7,000 for commuters, high school seniors with minimum 1200 SAT (exclusive of writing) and 3.4 GPA; renewable annually with minimum 3.0 GPA. Founders Scholarship for National Merit Finalists: full tuition; renewable with minimum 3.0 GPA.

FINANCIAL AID PROCEDURES

Forms required: FAFSA.

Dates and Deadlines: Priority date 3/1; no closing date. Applicants notified on a rolling basis starting 3/1; must reply by 5/1 or within 2 week(s) of notification.

Transfers: Applicants notified on a rolling basis starting 3/1; must reply by 5/1 or within 2 week(s) of notification. Scholarship for transfer students with minimum 2.5 GPA and 12 transferable credits.

CONTACT

Valerie Patnaude, Director of Financial Aid
420 South Main Street, Nashua, NH 03060-5086
(603) 897-8510

Saint Anselm College

Manchester, New Hampshire   Federal Code: 002587
www.anselm.edu   CSS Code: 3748

4-year private nursing and liberal arts college in small city, affiliated with Roman Catholic Church.

Enrollment: 1,889 undergrads, 1% part-time. 528 full-time freshmen.
Selectivity: Admits over 75% of applicants.

BASIC COSTS (2009-2010)

Tuition and fees: $30,470.
Room and board: $11,240.
Additional info: Tuition/fee waivers available for minority students.

FINANCIAL AID PICTURE (2009-2010)

Students with need: Out of 475 full-time freshmen who applied for aid, 390 were judged to have need. Of these, 390 received aid, and 66 had their full need met. Average financial aid package met 83% of need; average scholarship/grant was $19,133; average loan was $4,584. For part-time students, average financial aid package was $15,640.
Students without need: 111 full-time freshmen who did not demonstrate need for aid received scholarships/grants; average award was $8,384. No-need awards available for academics, alumni affiliation, athletics, state/district residency.
Scholarships offered: *Merit:* Presidential Scholarships: $4,000 to $16,000; based on grades, class rank, SAT results and extracurricular experience.
Athletic: 6 full-time freshmen received athletic scholarships; average amount $17,671.
Cumulative student debt: 75% of graduating class had student loans; average debt was $36,823.

FINANCIAL AID PROCEDURES

Forms required: FAFSA, CSS PROFILE.
Dates and Deadlines: Closing date 3/15. Applicants notified on a rolling basis starting 3/1; must reply by 5/1 or within 2 week(s) of notification.
Transfers: Merit scholarships not available for transfer students.

CONTACT

Elizabeth Keuffel, Director of Financial Aid
100 Saint Anselm Drive, Manchester, NH 03102-1310
(603) 641-7110

Southern New Hampshire University

Manchester, New Hampshire
www.snhu.edu   Federal Code: 002580

4-year private university in small city.
Enrollment: 1,929 undergrads, 2% part-time. 471 full-time freshmen.
Selectivity: Admits over 75% of applicants.

BASIC COSTS (2009-2010)

Tuition and fees: $26,442.
Room and board: $10,176.

FINANCIAL AID PICTURE (2009-2010)

Students with need: Need-based aid available for full-time and part-time students. Work study available nights, weekends, and for part-time students.
Students without need: No-need awards available for academics, alumni affiliation, athletics, leadership, state/district residency.
Scholarships offered: Academic scholarship: $3000-$8000; awarded to new students based on 3.0 GPA and 1000 SAT (exclusive of writing); unlimited number awarded. Presidential scholarship: 3.5 GPA and 1100 SAT (exclusive of writing).

FINANCIAL AID PROCEDURES

Forms required: FAFSA.
Dates and Deadlines: Priority date 3/15; no closing date. Applicants notified on a rolling basis starting 3/1; must reply within 3 week(s) of notification.

CONTACT

Robin Gagnon, Interim Director of Financial Aid
2500 North River Road, Manchester, NH 03106-1045
(603) 668-2211

Thomas More College of Liberal Arts

Merrimack, New Hampshire
www.thomasmorecollege.edu   Federal Code: 030431

4-year private liberal arts college in large town, affiliated with Roman Catholic Church.
Enrollment: 80 undergrads. 25 full-time freshmen.

BASIC COSTS (2009-2010)

Tuition and fees: $14,500.
Per-credit charge: $650.
Room and board: $9,100.

FINANCIAL AID PICTURE (2009-2010)

Students with need: Need-based aid available for full-time and part-time students.
Students without need: No-need awards available for academics.
Scholarships offered: Thomas More Scholarship: full or partial tuition; based on superior academic achievement, exceptional promise or potential; several awarded. Commuter Grants: offered to full-time students within commuting distance of the college. Faith and Reason Essay Contest: half tuition for 4 years; based on essay. Summer Program Scholarship: $1,000; for students who have attended the Thomas More College Summer Program for high school students.

FINANCIAL AID PROCEDURES

Forms required: FAFSA.
Dates and Deadlines: Priority date 5/1; no closing date. Applicants notified on a rolling basis starting 5/15; must reply within 2 week(s) of notification.

CONTACT
Clint Hanson, Director of Financial Aid
Six Manchester Street, Merrimack, NH 03054-4818
(603) 880-8308 ext. 23

University of New Hampshire
Durham, New Hampshire
www.unh.edu   Federal Code: 002589

4-year public university in small town.
Enrollment: 12,226 undergrads, 2% part-time. 2,506 full-time freshmen.
Selectivity: Admits 50 to 75% of applicants.

BASIC COSTS (2009-2010)
Tuition and fees: $12,743; out-of-state residents $26,713.
Per-credit charge: $420; out-of-state residents $1,002.
Room and board: $9,674.
Additional info: New England Regional Student Program tuition 175% of in-state tuition. College of Earth and Physical Science charges additional $793 per year. Whittemore School of Business charges additional $777 per year. Music majors pay additional $800 per year. Tuition/fee waivers available for minority students.

FINANCIAL AID PICTURE (2008-2009)
Students with need: Out of 2,101 full-time freshmen who applied for aid, 1,542 were judged to have need. Of these, 1,519 received aid, and 374 had their full need met. Average financial aid package met 84% of need; average scholarship/grant was $4,283; average loan was $2,658. For part-time students, average financial aid package was $14,784.
Students without need: 526 full-time freshmen who did not demonstrate need for aid received scholarships/grants; average award was $7,368. No-need awards available for academics, art, athletics, leadership, music/drama, religious affiliation, ROTC.
Scholarships offered: *Merit:* Presidential Scholarship: half tuition. Various other awards recognizing outstanding high school achievement determined during freshmen candidate application review process; no additional application materials required. *Athletic:* 43 full-time freshmen received athletic scholarships; average amount $28,230.
Cumulative student debt: 74% of graduating class had student loans; average debt was $30,760.

FINANCIAL AID PROCEDURES
Forms required: FAFSA.
Dates and Deadlines: Closing date 3/1. Applicants notified on a rolling basis starting 3/1; must reply by 5/1.
Transfers: Closing date 5/1. Applicants notified on a rolling basis starting 5/1.

CONTACT
Susan Allen, Director of Financial Aid
Grant House, Durham, NH 03824
(603) 862-3600

University of New Hampshire at Manchester
Manchester, New Hampshire
www.unhm.unh.edu   Federal Code: 002589

4-year public university and liberal arts college in small city.
Enrollment: 844 undergrads, 20% part-time. 145 full-time freshmen.
Selectivity: Admits over 75% of applicants.

BASIC COSTS (2009-2010)
Tuition and fees: $10,136; out-of-state residents $24,406.
Per-credit charge: $408; out-of-state residents $1,002.

Additional info: New England Regional Student tuition 175% of in-state public institution tuition.

FINANCIAL AID PICTURE (2009-2010)
Students with need: Work study available nights, weekends, and for part-time students.
Students without need: No-need awards available for academics, state/district residency.

FINANCIAL AID PROCEDURES
Forms required: FAFSA.
Dates and Deadlines: Closing date 3/1. Applicants notified on a rolling basis starting 4/1; must reply within 2 week(s) of notification.

CONTACT
Jodi Abad, Director of Financial Aid
400 Commercial Street, Manchester, NH 03101-1113
(603) 641-4189

White Mountains Community College
Berlin, New Hampshire
www.wmcc.edu   Federal Code: 005291

2-year public community and technical college in large town.
Enrollment: 731 undergrads.

BASIC COSTS (2009-2010)
Tuition and fees: $6,000; out-of-state residents $13,050.
Per-credit charge: $183; out-of-state residents $418.
Additional info: New England Regional tuition: $274 per credit hour.

FINANCIAL AID PICTURE
Students with need: Need-based aid available for full-time and part-time students.
Students without need: This college awards aid only to students with need.

FINANCIAL AID PROCEDURES
Forms required: FAFSA, institutional form.
Dates and Deadlines: Priority date 5/1; no closing date. Applicants notified on a rolling basis starting 5/1; must reply within 2 week(s) of notification.

CONTACT
Jacqueline Catello, Director of Financial Aid
2020 Riverside Drive, Berlin, NH 03570
(603) 752-1113

New Jersey

Atlantic Cape Community College
Mays Landing, New Jersey
www.atlantic.edu   Federal Code: 002596

2-year public culinary school and community college in small town.
Enrollment: 7,080 undergrads, 46% part-time. 1,349 full-time freshmen.
Selectivity: Open admission; but selective for some programs.

BASIC COSTS (2009-2010)
Tuition and fees: $3,350; out-of-district residents $6,200; out-of-state residents $11,780.
Per-credit charge: $93; out-of-district residents $186; out-of-state residents $372.
Additional info: Tuition/fee waivers available for unemployed or children of unemployed.

FINANCIAL AID PICTURE (2008-2009)

Students with need: Need-based aid available for full-time and part-time students.

Additional info: Installment plan available for culinary arts majors. Employees of Atlantic City casinos may attend ACCC at in-county rates regardless of residence.

FINANCIAL AID PROCEDURES

Forms required: FAFSA, institutional form.

Dates and Deadlines: Priority date 5/1; no closing date. Applicants notified on a rolling basis starting 5/1.

CONTACT

Linda Desantis, Director of Financial Aid and Veterans' Affairs
5100 Black Horse Pike, Mays Landing, NJ 08330-2699
(609) 343-5082

Berkeley College- Garret Mountain Campus

Woodland Park, New Jersey
http://berkeleycollege.edu/campuses/GarretMountain.htm
Federal Code: 007502

4-year for-profit business and career college in large town.

Enrollment: 3,688 undergrads, 15% part-time. 672 full-time freshmen.

BASIC COSTS (2010-2011)

Tuition and fees: $20,700.

Per-credit charge: $465.

Room and board: $10,812.

FINANCIAL AID PICTURE

Students with need: Need-based aid available for full-time students.

Students without need: No-need awards available for academics, alumni affiliation.

Additional info: Alumni scholarship examination given in November and December. Full and partial scholarships awarded.

FINANCIAL AID PROCEDURES

Forms required: FAFSA.

Dates and Deadlines: No deadline. Applicants notified on a rolling basis starting 3/1; must reply within 6 week(s) of notification.

CONTACT

Howard Leslie, Vice President Financial Aid
44 Rifle Camp Road, Woodland Park, NJ 07424-0440
(973) 278-5400

Bloomfield College

Bloomfield, New Jersey
www.bloomfield.edu
Federal Code: 002597

4-year private liberal arts and teachers college in large town, affiliated with Presbyterian Church (USA).

Enrollment: 2,131 undergrads, 19% part-time. 456 full-time freshmen.

Selectivity: Admits 50 to 75% of applicants.

BASIC COSTS (2010-2011)

Tuition and fees: $22,400.

Room and board: $10,600.

FINANCIAL AID PICTURE (2009-2010)

Students with need: Out of 451 full-time freshmen who applied for aid, 437 were judged to have need. Of these, 435 received aid, and 64 had their full need met. Average financial aid package met 62% of need; average scholarship/grant was $16,016; average loan was $7,409. For part-time students, average financial aid package was $14,398.

Students without need: 12 full-time freshmen who did not demonstrate need for aid received scholarships/grants; average award was $12,158. No-need awards available for academics, alumni affiliation, athletics, music/drama, religious affiliation.

Scholarships offered: *Merit:* Trustee Scholar Award: up to $10,000; 3.2 GPA, 1100 SAT required. Presidential Scholarship: up to $8,000; 3.0 GPA and 950 SAT required. Transfer Scholarship: up to $5,000; for transfer students from 2-year colleges with 3.0 GPA. Community Service Scholarships: up to $5,000; for students with commitment to community service. Phi Theta Kappa Transfer Scholarships: $6,000; for day transfer students from 2-year colleges with 3.5 GPA who are members of Phi Theta Kappa. All required SAT scores are exclusive of Writing. *Athletic:* 1 full-time freshmen received athletic scholarships; average amount $27,000.

Cumulative student debt: 87% of graduating class had student loans; average debt was $28,310.

FINANCIAL AID PROCEDURES

Forms required: FAFSA.

Dates and Deadlines: Priority date 3/15; closing date 6/1. Applicants notified on a rolling basis starting 3/15; must reply within 2 week(s) of notification.

Transfers: Applicants notified on a rolling basis starting 3/15; must reply within 2 week(s) of notification.

CONTACT

Stacy Salinas, Director of Financial Aid
One Park Place, Bloomfield, NJ 07003
(973) 748-9000 ext. 212

Brookdale Community College

Lincroft, New Jersey
www.brookdalecc.edu
Federal Code: 008404

2-year public community college in small city.

Enrollment: 13,786 undergrads, 35% part-time.

Selectivity: Open admission; but selective for some programs.

BASIC COSTS (2010-2011)

Tuition and fees: $4,408; out-of-district residents $7,963; out-of-state residents $8,713.

Per-credit charge: $119; out-of-district residents $237; out-of-state residents $262.

Additional info: Tuition/fee waivers available for unemployed or children of unemployed.

FINANCIAL AID PICTURE

Students with need: Need-based aid available for full-time and part-time students.

Students without need: No-need awards available for academics, athletics.

FINANCIAL AID PROCEDURES

Forms required: FAFSA, institutional form.

Dates and Deadlines: Priority date 5/1; no closing date. Applicants notified on a rolling basis starting 5/1; must reply within 2 week(s) of notification.

CONTACT

Stephanie Fitzsimmons, Director of Financial Aid
765 Newman Springs Road, Lincroft, NJ 07738
(732) 224-2362

Burlington County College

Pemberton, New Jersey
www.bcc.edu   Federal Code: 007730

2-year public community college in small town.
Enrollment: 8,438 undergrads, 40% part-time. 1,950 full-time freshmen.
Selectivity: Open admission; but selective for some programs.

BASIC COSTS (2009-2010)
Tuition and fees: $3,315; out-of-district residents $3,795; out-of-state residents $5,745.
Per-credit charge: $86; out-of-district residents $102; out-of-state residents $167.
Additional info: Tuition/fee waivers available for unemployed or children of unemployed.

FINANCIAL AID PICTURE
Students with need: Need-based aid available for full-time and part-time students. Work study available nights, weekends, and for part-time students.
Students without need: This college awards aid only to students with need.

FINANCIAL AID PROCEDURES
Forms required: FAFSA.
Dates and Deadlines: No deadline. Applicants notified on a rolling basis.

CONTACT
Ronald Brand, Vice President of Finance and Administration
601 Pemberton-Browns Mills Road, Pemberton, NJ 08068-1599
(609) 894-9311 ext. 1575

Caldwell College

Caldwell, New Jersey
www.caldwell.edu   Federal Code: 002598

4-year private liberal arts college in large town, affiliated with Roman Catholic Church.
Enrollment: 1,548 undergrads.
Selectivity: Admits 50 to 75% of applicants.

BASIC COSTS (2009-2010)
Tuition and fees: $24,600.
Per-credit charge: $665.
Room and board: $10,000.

FINANCIAL AID PICTURE (2009-2010)
Students with need: Need-based aid available for full-time and part-time students. Work study available nights, weekends, and for part-time students.
Students without need: No-need awards available for academics, alumni affiliation, art, athletics, leadership, music/drama, religious affiliation.

FINANCIAL AID PROCEDURES
Forms required: FAFSA, state aid form, institutional form.
Dates and Deadlines: Priority date 4/1; no closing date. Applicants notified on a rolling basis starting 3/1; must reply within 4 week(s) of notification.
Transfers: No deadline. Applicants notified on a rolling basis; must reply within 4 week(s) of notification. Students who have filed for aid through the state previously must file FAFSA by June 1 for succeeding year.

CONTACT
Shawn O'Neil, Financial Aid Director
9 Ryerson Avenue, Caldwell, NJ 07006-6195
(973) 618-3221

Camden County College

Blackwood, New Jersey
www.camdencc.edu   Federal Code: 006865

2-year public community college in large town.
Enrollment: 13,115 undergrads.
Selectivity: Open admission; but selective for some programs.

BASIC COSTS (2009-2010)
Tuition and fees: $3,612; out-of-district residents $3,732; out-of-state residents $5,832.
Per-credit charge: $93; out-of-district residents $97; out-of-state residents $167.
Additional info: Tuition/fee waivers available for unemployed or children of unemployed.

FINANCIAL AID PICTURE (2009-2010)
Students with need: Need-based aid available for full-time and part-time students.

FINANCIAL AID PROCEDURES
Forms required: FAFSA, institutional form.
Dates and Deadlines: Priority date 5/1; closing date 7/1. Applicants notified on a rolling basis starting 7/1.
Transfers: Must submit financial aid transcripts from all previously attended institutions.

CONTACT
Aquila Wedington, Director of Financial Aid
Box 200, Blackwood, NJ 08012
(856) 227-7200

Centenary College

Hackettstown, New Jersey
www.centenarycollege.edu   Federal Code: 002599

4-year private liberal arts college in large town, affiliated with United Methodist Church.
Enrollment: 2,140 undergrads, 8% part-time. 310 full-time freshmen.
Selectivity: Admits over 75% of applicants.

BASIC COSTS (2009-2010)
Tuition and fees: $26,534.
Per-credit charge: $490.
Room and board: $9,434.
Additional info: Additional fees required for equine majors and for comprehensive learning support program.

FINANCIAL AID PICTURE (2008-2009)
Students with need: Out of 265 full-time freshmen who applied for aid, 224 were judged to have need. Of these, 224 received aid, and 50 had their full need met. Average financial aid package met 75% of need; average scholarship/grant was $14,806; average loan was $5,143. For part-time students, average financial aid package was $11,469.
Students without need: 42 full-time freshmen who did not demonstrate need for aid received scholarships/grants; average award was $7,700. No-need awards available for academics, alumni affiliation, art, leadership, minority status, music/drama, religious affiliation, state/district residency.
Scholarships offered: Academic awards; based on 2.5 GPA, 800 SAT (exclusive of Writing) or 16 ACT. Leadership awards; based on demonstrated leadership ability and potential. Equine Award. Centenary Resident Grant. Out-of-State Centenary Grant. Skylands Centenary Grant. Centenary United Methodist Scholarship.
Cumulative student debt: 83% of graduating class had student loans; average debt was $28,104.

FINANCIAL AID PROCEDURES
Forms required: FAFSA.
Dates and Deadlines: Priority date 4/1; closing date 6/1. Applicants notified on a rolling basis starting 3/1.
Transfers: Students from New Jersey colleges who have received tuition aid grants (TAG) must apply by state deadline. Students must submit financial aid transcripts from all previous institutions attended.

CONTACT
Mike Corso, Director of Financial Aid
400 Jefferson Street, Hackettstown, NJ 07840-9989
(908) 852-1400 ext. 2350

The College of New Jersey
Ewing, New Jersey
www.tcnj.edu   Federal Code: 002642

4-year public liberal arts college in large town.
Enrollment: 6,197 undergrads, 2% part-time. 1,289 full-time freshmen.
Selectivity: Admits less than 50% of applicants.

BASIC COSTS (2009-2010)
Tuition and fees: $12,722; out-of-state residents $21,408.
Per-credit charge: $318; out-of-state residents $625.
Room and board: $9,996.
Additional info: Tuition/fee waivers available for unemployed or children of unemployed.

FINANCIAL AID PICTURE (2008-2009)
Students with need: Out of 1,124 full-time freshmen who applied for aid, 633 were judged to have need. Of these, 596 received aid, and 138 had their full need met. Average financial aid package met 47% of need; average scholarship/grant was $14,125; average loan was $3,285. For part-time students, average financial aid package was $3,836.
Students without need: 266 full-time freshmen who did not demonstrate need for aid received scholarships/grants; average award was $6,111. No-need awards available for academics.
Additional info: Merit scholarships available to New Jersey high school graduates based on academic distinction. Limited number of scholarships available to out-of-state students who demonstrate exceptional academic achievement in high school and on SAT. The EOF Promise Award meets the direct cost of attendance freshman and sophomore years, with merit scholarship awards available in junior and senior years.

FINANCIAL AID PROCEDURES
Forms required: FAFSA.
Dates and Deadlines: Priority date 3/1; closing date 10/1. Applicants notified on a rolling basis starting 6/1; must reply within 2 week(s) of notification.
Transfers: No deadline. Applicants notified on a rolling basis; must reply within 2 week(s) of notification.

CONTACT
Jamie Hightower, Executive Director of Student Financial Services
Box 7718, Ewing, NJ 08628
(609) 771-2211

College of St. Elizabeth
Morristown, New Jersey
www.cse.edu   Federal Code: 002600

4-year private liberal arts college for women in large town, affiliated with Roman Catholic Church.
Enrollment: 1,216 undergrads, 45% part-time. 178 full-time freshmen.
Selectivity: Admits over 75% of applicants.

BASIC COSTS (2009-2010)
Tuition and fees: $25,058.
Room and board: $10,904.
Additional info: Tuition/fee waivers available for adults.

FINANCIAL AID PICTURE (2008-2009)
Students with need: Need-based aid available for full-time and part-time students. Work study available nights, weekends, and for part-time students.
Students without need: No-need awards available for academics, alumni affiliation, art, leadership, state/district residency.
Scholarships offered: Presidential Scholarship for campus residents; full tuition. Elizabethan Scholarship; $8,000-$10,000. Seton Scholarship; $3,000-$7,000. Awards guaranteed to eligible students who apply by March 1 and enroll by May 1 for fall semester. International scholarships; tuition, room and board; awarded annually for fall semester only to first year students enrolled in Women's College; based on academic record, SAT scores (if submitted) and TOEFL score.

FINANCIAL AID PROCEDURES
Forms required: FAFSA.
Dates and Deadlines: Closing date 10/1. Applicants notified on a rolling basis starting 11/15; must reply by 5/1 or within 2 week(s) of notification.
Transfers: Priority date 4/15; closing date 8/20. Scholarships available for full-time students who enroll immediately following full-time enrollment at another college. Applicants must have completed 32 credits and have 3.0 GPA. Awards range from $3,500 to half tuition. Minimum of 5 awarded annually. Preference given to applications received by June 1 for fall semester and by December 1 for spring semester. Limited number of partial scholarships awarded to international students.

CONTACT
Debra Wolff, Director of Financial Aid
2 Convent Road, Morristown, NJ 07960-6989
(973) 290-4445

County College of Morris
Randolph, New Jersey
www.ccm.edu   Federal Code: 007106

2-year public community college in small city.
Enrollment: 7,223 undergrads, 38% part-time. 1,443 full-time freshmen.
Selectivity: Open admission; but selective for some programs.

BASIC COSTS (2009-2010)
Tuition and fees: $3,750; out-of-district residents $6,900; out-of-state residents $9,480.
Per-credit charge: $105; out-of-district residents $210; out-of-state residents $296.
Additional info: Tuition reciprocity agreements with neighboring counties allow some out-of-county residents to pay in-county rates. Tuition/fee waivers available for unemployed or children of unemployed.

FINANCIAL AID PICTURE
Students with need: Need-based aid available for full-time and part-time students.
Students without need: No-need awards available for athletics.

FINANCIAL AID PROCEDURES
Forms required: FAFSA.
Dates and Deadlines: Priority date 3/1; no closing date. Applicants notified on a rolling basis starting 5/1.

CONTACT
Harvey Willis, Director, Financial Aid
214 Center Grove Road, Randolph, NJ 07869-2086
(973) 328-5230

Cumberland County College
Vineland, New Jersey
www.cccnj.edu   Federal Code: 002601

2-year public community college in small city.
Enrollment: 3,843 undergrads.
Selectivity: Open admission; but selective for some programs.

BASIC COSTS (2010-2011)
Tuition and fees: $3,840; out-of-district residents $6,810; out-of-state residents $12,750.
Per-credit charge: $99; out-of-district residents $198; out-of-state residents $396.
Additional info: Tuition/fee waivers available for unemployed or children of unemployed.

FINANCIAL AID PICTURE (2008-2009)
Students with need: Need-based aid available for full-time and part-time students.
Students without need: No-need awards available for academics.

FINANCIAL AID PROCEDURES
Forms required: FAFSA.
Dates and Deadlines: No deadline. Applicants notified on a rolling basis; must reply within 3 week(s) of notification.

CONTACT
Kimberly Mitchell, Director, Financial Aid
PO Box 1500, Vineland, NJ 08362-9912
(609) 691-8600

DeVry University: North Brunswick
North Brunswick, New Jersey
www.devry.edu   Federal Code: 009228

4-year for-profit university in small city.
Enrollment: 1,432 undergrads, 42% part-time. 197 full-time freshmen.

BASIC COSTS (2009-2010)
Tuition and fees: $14,800.
Per-credit charge: $550.

FINANCIAL AID PICTURE (2008-2009)
Students with need: Need-based aid available for full-time and part-time students.
Students without need: This college awards aid only to students with need.

FINANCIAL AID PROCEDURES
Forms required: FAFSA.
Dates and Deadlines: No deadline. Applicants notified on a rolling basis.

CONTACT
Albert Cama, Director of Financial Aid
630 US Highway One, North Brunswick, NJ 08902-3362
(800) 333-3879

Drew University
Madison, New Jersey   Federal Code: 002603
www.drew.edu   CSS Code: 2193

4-year private university and liberal arts college in large town, affiliated with United Methodist Church.
Enrollment: 1,684 undergrads, 1% part-time. 505 full-time freshmen.
Selectivity: Admits 50 to 75% of applicants.

BASIC COSTS (2009-2010)
Tuition and fees: $38,017.
Per-credit charge: $1,554.
Room and board: $10,368.

FINANCIAL AID PICTURE (2008-2009)
Students with need: Average financial aid package for all full-time undergraduates was $29,480. 83% awarded as scholarships/grants, 17% awarded as loans/jobs.
Students without need: No-need awards available for academics, art, minority status, music/drama.
Cumulative student debt: 61% of graduating class had student loans; average debt was $17,444.

FINANCIAL AID PROCEDURES
Forms required: FAFSA, CSS PROFILE.
Dates and Deadlines: Closing date 2/15. Must reply by 5/1.

CONTACT
Alyssa McCloud, Vice President for Enrollment Management
36 Madison Avenue, Madison, NJ 07940-4063
(973) 408-3112

Essex County College
Newark, New Jersey
www.essex.edu   Federal Code: 007107

2-year public community college in large city.
Enrollment: 11,962 undergrads, 36% part-time. 2,671 full-time freshmen.
Selectivity: Open admission; but selective for some programs.

BASIC COSTS (2009-2010)
Tuition and fees: $3,901; out-of-district residents $7,005; out-of-state residents $7,005.
Additional info: Tuition/fee waivers available for unemployed or children of unemployed.

FINANCIAL AID PICTURE
Students with need: Need-based aid available for full-time and part-time students.

FINANCIAL AID PROCEDURES
Forms required: FAFSA, institutional form.
Dates and Deadlines: Priority date 6/30; no closing date. Applicants notified on a rolling basis starting 6/15; must reply within 3 week(s) of notification.

CONTACT
Mildred Cofer, Director of Financial Aid
303 University Avenue, Newark, NJ 07102
(973) 877-3000

Felician College
Lodi, New Jersey
www.felician.edu   Federal Code: 002610

4-year private liberal arts college in large town, affiliated with Roman Catholic Church.
Enrollment: 1,675 undergrads, 20% part-time. 251 full-time freshmen.
Selectivity: Admits over 75% of applicants.

BASIC COSTS (2009-2010)
Tuition and fees: $25,050.
Per-credit charge: $780.
Room and board: $9,700.
Additional info: Tuition/fee waivers available for adults.

FINANCIAL AID PICTURE (2008-2009)

Students with need: Need-based aid available for full-time and part-time students. Work study available nights, weekends, and for part-time students.

Students without need: No-need awards available for academics, alumni affiliation, athletics, religious affiliation.

FINANCIAL AID PROCEDURES

Forms required: FAFSA.

Dates and Deadlines: Priority date 6/1; no closing date. Applicants notified on a rolling basis starting 4/1; must reply within 2 week(s) of notification.

CONTACT

Marc Chalfin, Executive Vice President for Business and Finance
262 South Main Street, Lodi, NJ 07644-2198
(201) 559-6000 ext. 6010

Georgian Court University

Lakewood, New Jersey
www.georgian.edu   Federal Code: 002608

4-year private university and liberal arts college for women in large town, affiliated with Roman Catholic Church.

Enrollment: 1,736 undergrads, 13% part-time. 251 full-time freshmen.

Selectivity: Admits 50 to 75% of applicants.

BASIC COSTS (2010-2011)

Tuition and fees: $26,176.

Per-credit charge: $570.

Room and board: $9,856.

FINANCIAL AID PICTURE (2009-2010)

Students with need: Out of 250 full-time freshmen who applied for aid, 224 were judged to have need. Of these, 224 received aid, and 25 had their full need met. Average financial aid package met 73% of need; average scholarship/grant was $18,731; average loan was $3,656. For part-time students, average financial aid package was $5,138.

Students without need: 27 full-time freshmen who did not demonstrate need for aid received scholarships/grants; average award was $9,538. No-need awards available for academics, alumni affiliation, art, athletics, leadership, minority status, music/drama, religious affiliation.

Scholarships offered: 8 full-time freshmen received athletic scholarships; average amount $8,919.

Cumulative student debt: 85% of graduating class had student loans; average debt was $33,729.

FINANCIAL AID PROCEDURES

Forms required: FAFSA, institutional form.

Dates and Deadlines: Priority date 3/1; no closing date. Applicants notified on a rolling basis starting 2/1; must reply within 2 week(s) of notification.

Transfers: Transfer students who have outstanding financial obligations to previous college or who are in default are not admitted before being cleared by previous college or following federal guidelines concerning defaults.

CONTACT

Larry Sharp, Director of Financial Aid
900 Lakewood Avenue, Lakewood, NJ 08701-2697
(732) 987-2258

Gloucester County College

Sewell, New Jersey
www.gccnj.edu   Federal Code: 006901

2-year public community and liberal arts college in large town.

Enrollment: 6,045 undergrads.

Selectivity: Open admission; but selective for some programs.

BASIC COSTS (2010-2011)

Tuition and fees: $3,120; out-of-district residents $3,330; out-of-state residents $6,030.

Per-credit charge: $83; out-of-district residents $90; out-of-state residents $180.

FINANCIAL AID PICTURE (2008-2009)

Students with need: Need-based aid available for full-time and part-time students. Work study available nights.

Students without need: This college awards aid only to students with need.

FINANCIAL AID PROCEDURES

Forms required: FAFSA, institutional form.

Dates and Deadlines: Priority date 5/1; no closing date. Applicants notified on a rolling basis starting 3/20.

CONTACT

Jeffrey Williams, Financial Aid Director
1400 Tanyard Road, Sewell, NJ 08080
(856) 415-2210

Hudson County Community College

Jersey City, New Jersey
www.hccc.edu   Federal Code: 012954

2-year public community college in large city.

Enrollment: 8,437 undergrads, 35% part-time. 1,849 full-time freshmen.

Selectivity: Open admission.

BASIC COSTS (2009-2010)

Tuition and fees: $4,091; out-of-district residents $6,978; out-of-state residents $9,866.

Per-credit charge: $96; out-of-district residents $193; out-of-state residents $289.

FINANCIAL AID PICTURE (2008-2009)

Students with need: Need-based aid available for full-time and part-time students.

Students without need: This college awards aid only to students with need.

FINANCIAL AID PROCEDURES

Forms required: FAFSA.

Dates and Deadlines: Priority date 7/15; no closing date. Applicants notified on a rolling basis starting 6/1; must reply within 1 week(s) of notification.

Transfers: No deadline.

CONTACT

Pamela Littles, Associate Dean of Student Financial Assistance
70 Sip Avenue, 1st Floor, Jersey City, NJ 07306
(201) 360-4200

Kean University

Union, New Jersey
www.kean.edu   Federal Code: 002622

4-year public university and liberal arts college in small city.

Enrollment: 11,730 undergrads, 21% part-time. 1,518 full-time freshmen.

Selectivity: Admits 50 to 75% of applicants.

BASIC COSTS (2009-2010)

Tuition and fees: $9,446; out-of-state residents $14,081.

Per-credit charge: $206; out-of-state residents $360.

Room and board: $12,264.

Additional info: Tuition/fee waivers available for unemployed or children of unemployed.

FINANCIAL AID PICTURE (2009-2010)

Students with need: Out of 1,331 full-time freshmen who applied for aid, 1,095 were judged to have need. Of these, 1,009 received aid, and 86 had their full need met. Average financial aid package met 58% of need; average scholarship/grant was $8,414; average loan was $3,550. For part-time students, average financial aid package was $6,155.

Students without need: 15 full-time freshmen who did not demonstrate need for aid received scholarships/grants; average award was $5,400. No-need awards available for academics, alumni affiliation, art, leadership, music/drama.

Scholarships offered: Academic Merit Scholarship: $2,000; 3.25 GPA and 1200 SAT required. William Livingston Scholarship: full in-state tuition; 3.90 GPA and 1400 SAT required. Kean Scholarship: $4,000; 3.80 GPA and 1350 SAT required. Presidential Scholarship: $2,500; 3.50 GPA and 1250 SAT required. Trustee Scholarship: $3,000; 3.70 GPA and 1300 SAT required. New Jersey Center for Science and Technology Education (NJCSTE) Scholarship: full-tuition; 3.0 GPA and 1100 SAT required for students who are interested in pursuing BS/MS or BS/MA degree programs in science and technology; all applicants must be interviewed by the NJCSTE. Visual and Performing Arts Scholarship: full tuition; 3.0 GPA and portfolio review or audition required.

Cumulative student debt: 68% of graduating class had student loans; average debt was $19,698.

FINANCIAL AID PROCEDURES

Forms required: FAFSA.

Dates and Deadlines: Priority date 3/15; no closing date. Applicants notified on a rolling basis starting 3/15; must reply by 5/1.

Transfers: No deadline. Applicants notified on a rolling basis; must reply by 5/1.

CONTACT

Sharon Audet, Associate Director
1000 Morris Avenue, Union, NJ 07083-0411
(908) 737-3190

Mercer County Community College

Trenton, New Jersey
www.mccc.edu   Federal Code: 002641

2-year public community college in small city.

Enrollment: 8,648 undergrads, 51% part-time. 1,623 full-time freshmen.

Selectivity: Open admission.

BASIC COSTS (2009-2010)

Tuition and fees: $3,570; out-of-district residents $4,770; out-of-state residents $7,170.

Additional info: Tuition/fee waivers available for unemployed or children of unemployed.

FINANCIAL AID PICTURE (2008-2009)

Students with need: Need-based aid available for full-time and part-time students. Work study available nights.

Students without need: No-need awards available for academics, athletics, state/district residency.

Scholarships offered: MCCC Foundation Scholarship; $2,500; top 25% of high school class; 15 total awards. NJ STARS program; for top 20% of high school class.

FINANCIAL AID PROCEDURES

Forms required: FAFSA.

Dates and Deadlines: No deadline. Applicants notified on a rolling basis.

CONTACT

Reginald Page, Director of Financial Aid
Box B, Trenton, NJ 08690-1099
(609) 570-3210

Middlesex County College

Edison, New Jersey
www.middlesexcc.edu   Federal Code: 002615

2-year public community college in small city.

Enrollment: 11,485 undergrads, 25% part-time. 2,489 full-time freshmen.

Selectivity: Open admission; but selective for some programs.

BASIC COSTS (2010-2011)

Tuition and fees: $3,888; out-of-state residents $6,996.

Per-credit charge: $97; out-of-state residents $194.

FINANCIAL AID PICTURE

Students with need: Need-based aid available for full-time and part-time students.

FINANCIAL AID PROCEDURES

Forms required: FAFSA, institutional form.

Dates and Deadlines: Priority date 4/1; no closing date. Applicants notified on a rolling basis starting 5/4.

CONTACT

Gail Scott Bey, Director of Financial Aid
2600 Woodbridge Avenue, Edison, NJ 08818-3050
(732) 906-2520 ext. 4157

Monmouth University

West Long Branch, New Jersey
www.monmouth.edu   Federal Code: 002616

4-year private university in small town.

Enrollment: 4,633 undergrads, 7% part-time. 996 full-time freshmen.

Selectivity: Admits 50 to 75% of applicants.

BASIC COSTS (2010-2011)

Tuition and fees: $26,356.

Per-credit charge: $745.

Room and board: $9,936.

FINANCIAL AID PICTURE (2009-2010)

Students with need: Out of 878 full-time freshmen who applied for aid, 706 were judged to have need. Of these, 706 received aid, and 38 had their full need met. Average financial aid package met 74% of need; average scholarship/grant was $12,972; average loan was $3,444. For part-time students, average financial aid package was $6,706.

Students without need: 269 full-time freshmen who did not demonstrate need for aid received scholarships/grants; average award was $8,269. No-need awards available for academics, alumni affiliation, art, athletics, leadership.

Scholarships offered: *Merit:* Academic Excellence Awards; $3,000-$16,000; based on SAT scores and high school GPA; renewable annually as long as required GPA is maintained. *Athletic:* 27 full-time freshmen received athletic scholarships; average amount $12,837.

Cumulative student debt: 73% of graduating class had student loans; average debt was $25,000.

FINANCIAL AID PROCEDURES

Forms required: FAFSA.

Dates and Deadlines: Priority date 2/15; no closing date. Applicants notified on a rolling basis starting 2/15; must reply within 2 week(s) of notification.

Transfers: No deadline. Applicants notified on a rolling basis; must reply within 2 week(s) of notification.

CONTACT

Claire Alasio, Associate Vice President for Enrollment Management
400 Cedar Avenue, West Long Branch, NJ 07764-1898
(732) 571-3463

Montclair State University
Upper Montclair, New Jersey
www.montclair.edu   Federal Code: 002617

4-year public university in large town.
Enrollment: 13,542 undergrads, 14% part-time. 2,098 full-time freshmen.
Selectivity: Admits less than 50% of applicants.

BASIC COSTS (2009-2010)
Tuition and fees: $9,771; out-of-state residents $17,783.
Per-credit charge: $238; out-of-state residents $502.
Room and board: $10,208.
Additional info: Tuition/fee waivers available for unemployed or children of unemployed.

FINANCIAL AID PICTURE (2009-2010)
Students with need: Out of 1,440 full-time freshmen who applied for aid, 1,156 were judged to have need. Of these, 1,114 received aid, and 195 had their full need met. Average financial aid package met 63% of need; average scholarship/grant was $8,932; average loan was $3,444. For part-time students, average financial aid package was $6,677.
Students without need: 40 full-time freshmen who did not demonstrate need for aid received scholarships/grants; average award was $8,022. No-need awards available for academics, alumni affiliation, art, leadership, minority status, music/drama, ROTC, state/district residency.

FINANCIAL AID PROCEDURES
Forms required: FAFSA.
Dates and Deadlines: Priority date 3/1; no closing date. Applicants notified on a rolling basis starting 4/1; must reply within 2 week(s) of notification.
Transfers: Students will be eligible for financial aid beginning fall semester of the academic year for which they are admitted.

CONTACT
Pat Gully, Director of Financial Aid
One Normal Avenue, Upper Montclair, NJ 07043-1624
(973) 655-4461

New Jersey City University
Jersey City, New Jersey
www.njcu.edu   Federal Code: 002613

4-year public university in small city.
Enrollment: 6,325 undergrads, 26% part-time. 649 full-time freshmen.
Selectivity: Admits less than 50% of applicants.

BASIC COSTS (2009-2010)
Tuition and fees: $8,990; out-of-state residents $16,268.
Per-credit charge: $218; out-of-state residents $461.
Room and board: $9,043.

FINANCIAL AID PICTURE (2008-2009)
Students with need: Out of 572 full-time freshmen who applied for aid, 517 were judged to have need. Of these, 480 received aid, and 18 had their full need met. Average financial aid package met 58% of need; average scholarship/grant was $7,661; average loan was $3,417. For part-time students, average financial aid package was $4,417.
Students without need: 17 full-time freshmen who did not demonstrate need for aid received scholarships/grants; average award was $6,052.

FINANCIAL AID PROCEDURES
Forms required: FAFSA.
Dates and Deadlines: Priority date 4/15; no closing date. Applicants notified by 5/5.

CONTACT
Carmen Panlilio, Assistant Vice President for Admissions and Financial Aid
2039 Kennedy Boulevard, Jersey City, NJ 07305-1597
(201) 200-3173

New Jersey Institute of Technology
Newark, New Jersey
www.njit.edu   Federal Code: 002621

4-year public university in large city.
Enrollment: 5,528 undergrads, 14% part-time. 905 full-time freshmen.
Selectivity: Admits 50 to 75% of applicants.

BASIC COSTS (2009-2010)
Tuition and fees: $12,860; out-of-state residents $22,604.
Per-credit charge: $412; out-of-state residents $879.
Room and board: $9,504.

FINANCIAL AID PICTURE (2009-2010)
Students with need: Out of 809 full-time freshmen who applied for aid, 691 were judged to have need. Of these, 691 received aid, and 116 had their full need met. Average financial aid package met 63% of need; average scholarship/grant was $15,000; average loan was $3,100. For part-time students, average financial aid package was $7,200.
Students without need: 160 full-time freshmen who did not demonstrate need for aid received scholarships/grants; average award was $14,200. No-need awards available for academics, athletics, job skills, leadership, minority status, ROTC, state/district residency.
Scholarships offered: 55 full-time freshmen received athletic scholarships; average amount $15,500.
Cumulative student debt: 40% of graduating class had student loans; average debt was $20,000.
Additional info: Extensive co-op program for all majors.

FINANCIAL AID PROCEDURES
Forms required: FAFSA.
Dates and Deadlines: Priority date 3/15; closing date 5/15. Applicants notified on a rolling basis starting 3/1; must reply within 2 week(s) of notification.

CONTACT
Ivon Nunez, Director of Financial Aid
University Heights, Newark, NJ 07102
(973) 596-3479

Ocean County College
Toms River, New Jersey
www.ocean.edu   Federal Code: 002624

2-year public community college in small city.
Enrollment: 10,415 undergrads.
Selectivity: Open admission; but selective for some programs.

BASIC COSTS (2009-2010)
Tuition and fees: $3,600; out-of-district residents $4,620; out-of-state residents $7,020.
Per-credit charge: $92; out-of-district residents $126; out-of-state residents $206.
Additional info: Tuition/fee waivers available for unemployed or children of unemployed.

FINANCIAL AID PICTURE (2008-2009)
Students with need: 65% of average financial aid package awarded as scholarships/grants, 35% awarded as loans/jobs. Need-based aid available for part-time students.
Students without need: This college awards aid only to students with need.

FINANCIAL AID PROCEDURES

Forms required: FAFSA.

Dates and Deadlines: Priority date 5/31; no closing date. Applicants notified on a rolling basis starting 7/15; must reply within 1 week(s) of notification.

CONTACT

Norma Betz, Director of Financial Aid

College Drive, Toms River, NJ 08754-2001

(732) 255-0400 ext. 2020

Passaic County Community College

Paterson, New Jersey   Federal Code: 009994

www.pccc.edu   CSS Code: 2694

2-year public community college in small city.

Enrollment: 8,467 undergrads, 66% part-time. 734 full-time freshmen.

Selectivity: Open admission; but selective for some programs.

BASIC COSTS (2009-2010)

Tuition and fees: $3,584; out-of-state residents $6,374.

Per-credit charge: $93; out-of-state residents $186.

Additional info: Additional course fees up to maximum of $790 per year (excluding nursing and radiography). Tuition/fee waivers available for unemployed or children of unemployed.

FINANCIAL AID PICTURE (2008-2009)

Students with need: Need-based aid available for full-time and part-time students.

Students without need: No-need awards available for academics.

Additional info: Limited scholarship funds available for low income students eligible for federal or state aid.

FINANCIAL AID PROCEDURES

Forms required: FAFSA, CSS PROFILE.

Dates and Deadlines: Priority date 8/1; no closing date. Applicants notified on a rolling basis starting 8/1; must reply within 2 week(s) of notification.

Transfers: Priority date 5/15; closing date 6/30.

CONTACT

Linda Gaten, Director of Financial Aid

One College Boulevard, Paterson, NJ 07505-1179

(973) 684-6100

Princeton University

Princeton, New Jersey

www.princeton.edu   Federal Code: 002627

4-year private university in large town.

Enrollment: 5,029 undergrads. 1,245 full-time freshmen.

Selectivity: Admits less than 50% of applicants.

BASIC COSTS (2010-2011)

Tuition and fees: $36,640.

Room and board: $11,940.

FINANCIAL AID PICTURE (2008-2009)

Students with need: Out of 816 full-time freshmen who applied for aid, 697 were judged to have need. Of these, 697 received aid, and 697 had their full need met. Average financial aid package met 100% of need; average scholarship/grant was $33,671.

Students without need: This college awards aid only to students with need.

Cumulative student debt: 21% of graduating class had student loans; average debt was $4,957.

Additional info: All aid need-based; all aid grant money (no loans); institution meets full demonstrated need.

FINANCIAL AID PROCEDURES

Forms required: FAFSA, institutional form.

Dates and Deadlines: Priority date 2/1; no closing date. Applicants notified by 4/1; must reply by 5/1.

CONTACT

Robin Moscato, Director of Financial Aid

Box 430, Princeton, NJ 08542-0430

(609) 258-3330

Ramapo College of New Jersey

Mahwah, New Jersey

www.ramapo.edu   Federal Code: 009344

4-year public liberal arts college in large town.

Enrollment: 5,529 undergrads, 7% part-time. 879 full-time freshmen.

Selectivity: Admits 50 to 75% of applicants.

BASIC COSTS (2009-2010)

Tuition and fees: $11,416; out-of-state residents $19,099.

Per-credit charge: $240; out-of-state residents $480.

Room and board: $11,290.

Additional info: Tuition/fee waivers available for unemployed or children of unemployed.

FINANCIAL AID PICTURE (2008-2009)

Students with need: Out of 697 full-time freshmen who applied for aid, 479 were judged to have need. Of these, 448 received aid, and 86 had their full need met. Average financial aid package met 69% of need; average scholarship/grant was $11,114; average loan was $3,349. For part-time students, average financial aid package was $3,682.

Students without need: 47 full-time freshmen who did not demonstrate need for aid received scholarships/grants; average award was $13,539. No-need awards available for academics, state/district residency.

Cumulative student debt: 55% of graduating class had student loans; average debt was $19,789.

FINANCIAL AID PROCEDURES

Forms required: FAFSA.

Dates and Deadlines: Priority date 3/1; no closing date. Applicants notified on a rolling basis starting 4/1; must reply by 5/1 or within 2 week(s) of notification.

Transfers: No deadline. Applicants notified on a rolling basis.

CONTACT

Mark Singer, Director of Financial Aid

505 Ramapo Valley Road, Mahwah, NJ 07430-1680

(201) 684-7549

Raritan Valley Community College

Somerville, New Jersey

www.raritanval.edu   Federal Code: 007731

2-year public community college in large town.

Enrollment: 6,729 undergrads, 41% part-time. 1,311 full-time freshmen.

Selectivity: Open admission; but selective for some programs.

BASIC COSTS (2009-2010)

Tuition and fees: $3,750; out-of-state residents $4,050.

Per-credit charge: $96; out-of-state residents $106.

Additional info: Tuition/fee waivers available for unemployed or children of unemployed.

FINANCIAL AID PICTURE (2009-2010)

Students with need: Need-based aid available for full-time and part-time students.

Students without need: No-need awards available for academics.

FINANCIAL AID PROCEDURES

Forms required: FAFSA.

Dates and Deadlines: No deadline. Applicants notified on a rolling basis starting 4/1.

CONTACT

Leonard Mesonas, Director of Financial Aid
PO Box 3300, Somerville, NJ 08876-1265
(908) 526-1200 ext. 8273

Richard Stockton College of New Jersey
Pomona, New Jersey
www.stockton.edu   Federal Code: 009345

4-year public liberal arts college in large town.

Enrollment: 6,717 undergrads, 10% part-time. 867 full-time freshmen.

Selectivity: Admits 50 to 75% of applicants.

BASIC COSTS (2009-2010)

Tuition and fees: $10,940; out-of-state residents $16,624.

Per-credit charge: $236; out-of-state residents $425.

Room and board: $10,286.

Additional info: Tuition/fee waivers available for unemployed or children of unemployed.

FINANCIAL AID PICTURE (2009-2010)

Students with need: Need-based aid available for full-time and part-time students. Work study available nights, weekends, and for part-time students.

Students without need: No-need awards available for academics, art, leadership, minority status, music/drama, state/district residency.

Scholarships offered: Freshman Scholarship Program: up to full tuition, fees, and housing for 4 years; based on class rank in top 15% and 1150 SAT (exclusive of Writing).

Additional info: Institutional grants provided for majority of neediest incoming students.

FINANCIAL AID PROCEDURES

Forms required: FAFSA.

Dates and Deadlines: Priority date 3/1; no closing date. Applicants notified on a rolling basis starting 4/1; must reply within 2 week(s) of notification.

Transfers: No deadline. Applicants notified on a rolling basis starting 4/1; must reply within 2 week(s) of notification.

CONTACT

Jeanne Lewis, Director of Financial Aid
Jim Leeds Road, Pomona, NJ 08240-0195
(609) 652-4201

Rider University
Lawrenceville, New Jersey
www.rider.edu   Federal Code: 002628

4-year private university in small town.

Enrollment: 4,712 undergrads, 14% part-time. 1,027 full-time freshmen.

Selectivity: Admits over 75% of applicants.

BASIC COSTS (2010-2011)

Tuition and fees: $30,470.

Per-credit charge: $910.

Room and board: $11,200.

FINANCIAL AID PICTURE (2009-2010)

Students with need: Out of 938 full-time freshmen who applied for aid, 789 were judged to have need. Of these, 789 received aid, and 174 had their full need met. Average financial aid package met 75% of need; average scholarship/grant was $17,170; average loan was $3,590. For part-time students, average financial aid package was $7,116.

Students without need: 183 full-time freshmen who did not demonstrate need for aid received scholarships/grants; average award was $10,965. No-need awards available for academics, alumni affiliation, athletics, leadership, minority status, music/drama.

Scholarships offered: 77 full-time freshmen received athletic scholarships; average amount $12,749.

Cumulative student debt: 72% of graduating class had student loans; average debt was $35,042.

FINANCIAL AID PROCEDURES

Forms required: FAFSA.

Dates and Deadlines: Priority date 3/1; no closing date. Applicants notified on a rolling basis starting 2/20.

Transfers: No deadline.

CONTACT

Drew Aromando, Director of Student Financial Services
2083 Lawrenceville Road, Lawrenceville, NJ 08648-3099
(609) 896-5360

Rowan University
Glassboro, New Jersey
www.rowan.edu   Federal Code: 002609

4-year public university in large town.

Enrollment: 9,292 undergrads, 11% part-time. 1,182 full-time freshmen.

Selectivity: Admits 50 to 75% of applicants.

BASIC COSTS (2009-2010)

Tuition and fees: $11,234; out-of-state residents $18,308.

Per-credit charge: $311; out-of-state residents $584.

Room and board: $9,958.

FINANCIAL AID PICTURE (2008-2009)

Students with need: Out of 979 full-time freshmen who applied for aid, 620 were judged to have need. Of these, 573 received aid, and 31 had their full need met. Average financial aid package met 81% of need; average scholarship/grant was $7,589; average loan was $3,128. For part-time students, average financial aid package was $5,469.

Students without need: No-need awards available for academics, art, music/drama.

Cumulative student debt: 73% of graduating class had student loans; average debt was $26,092.

FINANCIAL AID PROCEDURES

Forms required: FAFSA.

Dates and Deadlines: Priority date 3/15; no closing date. Applicants notified on a rolling basis starting 3/15.

CONTACT

Luis Taverez, Director of Financial Aid
Savitz Hall, 201 Mullica Hill Road, Glassboro, NJ 08028
(856) 256-4250

Saint Peter's College
Jersey City, New Jersey
www.spc.edu   Federal Code: 002638

4-year private liberal arts college in small city, affiliated with Roman Catholic Church.
Enrollment: 2,322 undergrads, 10% part-time. 581 full-time freshmen.
Selectivity: Admits less than 50% of applicants.

BASIC COSTS (2009-2010)
Tuition and fees: $26,870.
Per-credit charge: $873.
Room and board: $10,854.

FINANCIAL AID PICTURE (2008-2009)
Students with need: Out of 575 full-time freshmen who applied for aid, 480 were judged to have need. Of these, 480 received aid, and 68 had their full need met. Average financial aid package met 80% of need; average scholarship/grant was $18,601; average loan was $3,251. For part-time students, average financial aid package was $7,505.
Students without need: 92 full-time freshmen who did not demonstrate need for aid received scholarships/grants; average award was $13,608. No-need awards available for academics, athletics.
Scholarships offered: Merit: Academic Awards: full tuition; based on 1100 SAT (exclusive of Writing), 3.0 GPA, and top 20% of class; 50 awarded. Incentive Awards: $500-$4,000; for selected applicants with some qualities necessary for academic awards but who are otherwise ineligible. Residential Grants: $500-$2,500 toward housing; based on academics and extracurricular activities. **Athletic:** 19 full-time freshmen received athletic scholarships; average amount $13,086.
Cumulative student debt: 70% of graduating class had student loans; average debt was $19,553.
Additional info: Cooperative education internships available in all majors, with average salaries exceeding $5,200.

FINANCIAL AID PROCEDURES
Forms required: FAFSA.
Dates and Deadlines: Priority date 3/15; no closing date. Applicants notified on a rolling basis starting 2/15; must reply by 5/1 or within 2 week(s) of notification.
Transfers: Student and parents (if dependent students) must be New Jersey residents for at least 1 year prior to start date. Students must complete renewal application before June 1.

CONTACT
Steve Smith, Registrar
2641 Kennedy Boulevard, Jersey City, NJ 07306
(201) 761-6060

Salem Community College
Carneys Point, New Jersey
www.salemcc.edu   Federal Code: 005461

2-year public community college in small town.
Enrollment: 898 undergrads.
Selectivity: Open admission; but selective for some programs.

BASIC COSTS (2009-2010)
Tuition and fees: $3,774; out-of-state residents $4,074.
Per-credit charge: $93; out-of-state residents $103.
Additional info: Tuition/fee waivers available for unemployed or children of unemployed.

FINANCIAL AID PICTURE (2008-2009)
Students with need: Need-based aid available for full-time and part-time students.

Students without need: No-need awards available for academics, athletics, state/district residency.

FINANCIAL AID PROCEDURES
Forms required: FAFSA, institutional form.
Dates and Deadlines: Priority date 6/1; no closing date. Applicants notified on a rolling basis starting 4/1; must reply within 2 week(s) of notification.

CONTACT
Sharon Eastlack, Director of Financial Aid
460 Hollywood Avenue, Carneys Point, NJ 08069-2799
(856) 351-2699

Seton Hall University
South Orange, New Jersey
www.shu.edu   Federal Code: 002632

4-year private university in large town, affiliated with Roman Catholic Church.
Enrollment: 4,972 undergrads, 6% part-time. 1,135 full-time freshmen.
Selectivity: Admits over 75% of applicants.

BASIC COSTS (2010-2011)
Tuition and fees: $31,890.
Per-credit charge: $912.
Room and board: $12,050.

FINANCIAL AID PICTURE (2008-2009)
Students with need: Need-based aid available for full-time and part-time students.
Students without need: No-need awards available for academics, alumni affiliation, athletics, minority status, ROTC, state/district residency.

FINANCIAL AID PROCEDURES
Forms required: FAFSA.
Dates and Deadlines: Priority date 2/15; no closing date. Applicants notified on a rolling basis starting 3/1; must reply by 5/1 or within 4 week(s) of notification.
Transfers: Transfer academic scholarships available.

CONTACT
Lasaundra Floyd, Director of Financial Aid
400 South Orange Avenue, South Orange, NJ 07079-2680
(973) 761-9350

Somerset Christian College
Zarephath, New Jersey
www.somerset.edu   Federal Code: 036663

4-year private Bible and liberal arts college in small town, affiliated with Pillar of Fire International.
Enrollment: 242 undergrads.
Selectivity: Admits less than 50% of applicants.

BASIC COSTS (2009-2010)
Tuition and fees: $11,294.
Per-credit charge: $456.

FINANCIAL AID PICTURE
Students with need: Need-based aid available for full-time and part-time students. Work study available nights.
Students without need: This college awards aid only to students with need.

FINANCIAL AID PROCEDURES
Forms required: FAFSA, state aid form.
Dates and Deadlines: No deadline. Applicants notified on a rolling basis starting 1/31.

CONTACT

Marsha Griffin, Financial Aid Administrator
10 College Way, Zarephath, NJ 08890
(800) 234-9305 ext. 1101

Stevens Institute of Technology

Hoboken, New Jersey
www.stevens.edu   Federal Code: 002639

4-year private university and engineering college in small city.
Enrollment: 2,234 undergrads. 561 full-time freshmen.
Selectivity: Admits 50 to 75% of applicants. GED not accepted.

BASIC COSTS (2009-2010)

Tuition and fees: $38,600.
Per-credit charge: $1,220.
Room and board: $12,150.

FINANCIAL AID PICTURE (2009-2010)

Students with need: Need-based aid available for full-time and part-time students. Work study available nights, weekends, and for part-time students.
Students without need: No-need awards available for academics, leadership, music/drama, ROTC.
Scholarships offered: Neupauer Scholarship; full tuition; for top candidates in freshman class. Edwin A. Stevens Scholarship; $3,000-$20,000; for top candidates in freshman class. Becton Dickinson Scholarship; full tuition; for top student pursuing engineering degree. DeBaun Performing Arts Scholarship; $1,000-$5,000.

FINANCIAL AID PROCEDURES

Forms required: FAFSA.
Dates and Deadlines: Priority date 2/15; no closing date. Applicants notified on a rolling basis starting 3/30; must reply by 5/1 or within 2 week(s) of notification.
Transfers: Transfer merit scholarships, Phi Theta Kappa awards.

CONTACT

Maureen Weatherall, Vice President for University Enrollment and Academic Services
1 Castle Point on Hudson, Hoboken, NJ 07030
(201) 216-5555

Sussex County Community College

Newton, New Jersey
www.sussex.edu   Federal Code: 025688

2-year public community college in small town.
Enrollment: 3,493 undergrads, 34% part-time. 821 full-time freshmen.
Selectivity: Open admission; but selective for some programs.

BASIC COSTS (2009-2010)

Tuition and fees: $3,570; out-of-district residents $6,600; out-of-state residents $6,600.
Per-credit charge: $101; out-of-district residents $202; out-of-state residents $202.
Additional info: Residents of Wayne, Monroe and Pike County (PA): $152 per credit hour. Tuition/fee waivers available for unemployed or children of unemployed.

FINANCIAL AID PICTURE

Students with need: Need-based aid available for full-time and part-time students.
Students without need: This college awards aid only to students with need.

FINANCIAL AID PROCEDURES

Forms required: FAFSA, institutional form.
Dates and Deadlines: Closing date 6/1. Applicants notified on a rolling basis; must reply within 2 week(s) of notification.

CONTACT

James Pegg, Director, Financial Aid
One College Hill Road, Newton, NJ 07860
(973) 300-2225

Thomas Edison State College

Trenton, New Jersey
www.tesc.edu   Federal Code: 011648

4-year public liberal arts college in small city.
Enrollment: 17,320 undergrads, 100% part-time.
Selectivity: Open admission; but selective for some programs.

BASIC COSTS (2009-2010)

Tuition and fees: $4,695; out-of-state residents $6,720.
Per-credit charge: $136; out-of-state residents $180.
Additional info: Two tuition plans available. Comprehensive Tuition Plan: covers up to 36 credits per year for all credit-earning options, at $4,695 per year for in-state students and military personnel, $6,720 for out-of-state students; Enrolled Options Plan: $1,390 per year (state residents and military personnel), $2,520 (out-of-state), and $3,440 (international) for annual enrollment tuition and a technology services fee ($103); tests, portfolios, courses and other fees at additional cost.

FINANCIAL AID PICTURE (2008-2009)

Students with need: 20% of average financial aid package awarded as scholarships/grants, 80% awarded as loans/jobs.
Additional info: Financial aid applications should be received two months before each new term begins.

FINANCIAL AID PROCEDURES

Forms required: FAFSA, institutional form.
Dates and Deadlines: No deadline. Applicants notified on a rolling basis; must reply within 4 week(s) of notification.
Transfers: No deadline. Applicants notified on a rolling basis; must reply within 4 week(s) of notification.

CONTACT

James Owens, Director of Financial Aid
101 West State Street, Trenton, NJ 08608-1176
(609) 633-9658

Union County College

Cranford, New Jersey
www.ucc.edu   Federal Code: 002643

2-year public community college in large town.
Enrollment: 11,303 undergrads, 46% part-time. 2,104 full-time freshmen.
Selectivity: Open admission; but selective for some programs.

BASIC COSTS (2009-2010)

Tuition and fees: $3,630; out-of-state residents $6,450.
Per-credit charge: $94; out-of-state residents $188.
Additional info: Tuition/fee waivers available for unemployed or children of unemployed.

FINANCIAL AID PICTURE (2008-2009)

Students with need: 77% of average financial aid package awarded as scholarships/grants, 23% awarded as loans/jobs. Need-based aid available for part-time students. Work study available nights, weekends, and for part-time students.

PART III: FINANCIAL AID COLLEGE BY COLLEGE

Students without need: This college awards aid only to students with need.

FINANCIAL AID PROCEDURES

Forms required: FAFSA, institutional form.

Dates and Deadlines: Priority date 5/1; no closing date. Must reply within 2 week(s) of notification.

CONTACT

Evelynn Blatt, Director of Financial Aid
1033 Springfield Avenue, Cranford, NJ 07016-1599
(908) 709-7018

University of Medicine and Dentistry of New Jersey: School of Health Related Professions
Newark, New Jersey
www.shrp.umdnj.edu

Upper-division public health science college in large city.

Enrollment: 525 undergrads.

FINANCIAL AID PICTURE

Students with need: Need-based aid available for full-time and part-time students.

FINANCIAL AID PROCEDURES

Forms required: FAFSA, institutional form.

CONTACT

Cheryl White, Senior Financial Aid Analyst
65 Bergen Street, Newark, NJ 07101-1709
(973) 972-4376

University of Medicine and Dentistry of New Jersey: School of Nursing
Newark, New Jersey
www.sn.umdnj.edu

4-year public nursing college in large city.

Enrollment: 390 undergrads.

BASIC COSTS (2009-2010)

Tuition and fees: $13,302; out-of-state residents $17,652.

Per-credit charge: $345; out-of-state residents $490.

Additional info: Costs vary by program; costs cited are for BSN program. Additional insurance fee ($2,065) for students not covered by equivalent plan.

FINANCIAL AID PICTURE

Students with need: Need-based aid available for full-time and part-time students.

FINANCIAL AID PROCEDURES

Dates and Deadlines: Priority date 3/1; no closing date. Applicants notified on a rolling basis.

CONTACT

Elaine Varas, University Director of Financial Aid
65 Bergen Street Room 149, Newark, NJ 07101-1709
(973) 972-4376

Warren County Community College
Washington, New Jersey
www.warren.edu   Federal Code: 016857

2-year public community college in small town.

Enrollment: 2,189 undergrads.

Selectivity: Open admission; but selective for some programs.

BASIC COSTS (2009-2010)

Tuition and fees: $3,631; out-of-district residents $3,931; out-of-state residents $4,531.

Per-credit charge: $97; out-of-district residents $107; out-of-state residents $127.

Additional info: Tuition/fee waivers available for unemployed or children of unemployed.

FINANCIAL AID PICTURE (2009-2010)

Students with need: 66% of average financial aid package awarded as scholarships/grants, 34% awarded as loans/jobs. Need-based aid available for part-time students. Work study available nights, weekends, and for part-time students.

Students without need: This college awards aid only to students with need.

FINANCIAL AID PROCEDURES

Forms required: FAFSA, institutional form.

Dates and Deadlines: Closing date 7/1. Applicants notified on a rolling basis; must reply within 2 week(s) of notification.

Transfers: No deadline. Applicants notified on a rolling basis.

CONTACT

Jessica Leeper, Director of Financial Aid
Route 57 West, Washington, NJ 07882-4343
(908) 835-2309

William Paterson University of New Jersey
Wayne, New Jersey
www.wpunj.edu   Federal Code: 002625

4-year public university and liberal arts college in large town.

Enrollment: 9,055 undergrads, 15% part-time. 1,435 full-time freshmen.

Selectivity: Admits 50 to 75% of applicants.

BASIC COSTS (2009-2010)

Tuition and fees: $10,838; out-of-state residents $17,592.

Per-credit charge: $210; out-of-state residents $431.

Room and board: $9,480.

Additional info: Tuition/fee waivers available for unemployed or children of unemployed.

FINANCIAL AID PICTURE (2009-2010)

Students with need: Need-based aid available for full-time and part-time students.

Students without need: No-need awards available for academics, alumni affiliation, music/drama.

Scholarships offered: Trustee Scholarship; full tuition for freshmen. Residential Scholarships; full tuition for freshmen and transfer. Distinguished, Academic Excellence, African American and Hispanic Students scholarships; $1,000 annually for 4 years.

FINANCIAL AID PROCEDURES

Forms required: FAFSA.

Dates and Deadlines: Priority date 4/1; no closing date. Applicants notified on a rolling basis starting 3/15.

Transfers: Must reply within 2 week(s) of notification.

CONTACT

Elizabeth Riquez, Director of Financial Aid

300 Pompton Road, Wayne, NJ 07470

(973) 720-2202

New Mexico

Art Center Design College

Albuquerque, New Mexico

www.theartcenter.edu   Federal Code: 024915

4-year for-profit visual arts college in very large city.

Enrollment: 274 undergrads, 53% part-time. 31 full-time freshmen.

Selectivity: Admits over 75% of applicants.

BASIC COSTS (2009-2010)

Tuition and fees: $16,680.

Per-credit charge: $695.

FINANCIAL AID PICTURE (2009-2010)

Students with need: Work study available nights, weekends, and for part-time students.

Students without need: No-need awards available for academics.

Scholarships offered: Board of Trustees Scholarship, Transfer Student Scholarship, Scholarship for Continuing Students.

FINANCIAL AID PROCEDURES

Forms required: FAFSA.

Transfers: No deadline. Applicants notified on a rolling basis.

CONTACT

Amy Woods, Director of Student Services

5000 Marble Avenue NE, Albuquerque, NM 87119

(520) 325-0123

Brookline College: Albuquerque

Albuquerque, New Mexico

www.brooklinecollege.edu   Federal Code: 022188

2-year for-profit branch campus and career college in large city.

Enrollment: 472 undergrads.

Selectivity: Open admission; but selective for some programs.

BASIC COSTS (2009-2010)

Tuition and fees: $12,850.

Additional info: Tuition shown is an average, actual tuition and fees may vary by program.

FINANCIAL AID PICTURE

Students with need: Need-based aid available for full-time students.

Students without need: This college awards aid only to students with need.

FINANCIAL AID PROCEDURES

Forms required: FAFSA, institutional form.

Dates and Deadlines: No deadline.

CONTACT

Genna Gillary, Corporate Director of Financial Aid

4201 Central Avenue NW, Suite J, Albuquerque, NM 87105-1649

(505) 880-2877

Central New Mexico Community College

Albuquerque, New Mexico

www.cnm.edu   Federal Code: 004742

2-year public community and technical college in very large city.

Enrollment: 24,148 undergrads, 64% part-time. 2,285 full-time freshmen.

Selectivity: Open admission.

BASIC COSTS (2009-2010)

Tuition and fees: $1,064; out-of-district residents $1,304; out-of-state residents $4,880.

Per-credit charge: $41; out-of-district residents $51; out-of-state residents $200.

Additional info: Non-residents pay $51 per credit hour for 1-6 hours and $200 per credit hour for 7-12 hours; during summer trimester, they pay $51 per credit hour for 1-12 hours and $612 + $51 per hour for more than 18 hours. Out-of district resident students who are within the college's Geographic Area of Responsibility (GAR) pay $51 per credit hour for academic courses and $10 per credit for occupational and developmental courses.

FINANCIAL AID PICTURE (2008-2009)

Students with need: Need-based aid available for full-time and part-time students.

Students without need: No-need awards available for academics, state/district residency.

FINANCIAL AID PROCEDURES

Forms required: FAFSA.

Dates and Deadlines: Priority date 5/1; no closing date. Applicants notified on a rolling basis starting 5/1.

CONTACT

Lee Carrillo, Director of Financial Aid

525 Buena Vista SE, Albuquerque, NM 87106

(505) 224-3090

Clovis Community College

Clovis, New Mexico

www.clovis.edu   Federal Code: 004743

2-year public community and junior college in large town.

Enrollment: 1,700 undergrads.

Selectivity: Open admission; but selective for some programs.

BASIC COSTS (2009-2010)

Tuition and fees: $832; out-of-district residents $880; out-of-state residents $1,672.

Per-credit charge: $30; out-of-district residents $32; out-of-state residents $65.

FINANCIAL AID PICTURE (2008-2009)

Students with need: 70% of average financial aid package awarded as scholarships/grants, 30% awarded as loans/jobs. Need-based aid available for part-time students. Work study available nights, weekends, and for part-time students.

Students without need: No-need awards available for academics, state/district residency.

Additional info: Endowment of over $1,000,000 to assist nursing students.

FINANCIAL AID PROCEDURES

Forms required: FAFSA.

Dates and Deadlines: Priority date 9/1; no closing date. Applicants notified on a rolling basis starting 4/15.

CONTACT

April Chavez, Director of Financial Aid
417 Schepps Boulevard, Clovis, NM 88101-8381
(575) 769-4060

College of Santa Fe

Santa Fe, New Mexico
www.csf.edu   Federal Code: 002649

4-year private visual arts college in small city.
Enrollment: 650 undergrads.
Selectivity: Admits over 75% of applicants.

FINANCIAL AID PICTURE (2008-2009)

Students with need: Need-based aid available for full-time and part-time students. Work study available nights, weekends, and for part-time students.
Students without need: No-need awards available for academics, alumni affiliation, art, athletics, leadership, minority status, music/drama.

FINANCIAL AID PROCEDURES

Forms required: FAFSA.
Dates and Deadlines: Priority date 3/15; no closing date. Applicants notified on a rolling basis starting 3/1; must reply by 5/1 or within 2 week(s) of notification.
Transfers: No deadline. Applicants notified on a rolling basis starting 3/1; must reply by 5/1 or within 2 week(s) of notification. No financial aid credited to student accounts until all financial aid transcripts received.

CONTACT

Darlene Sandoval, Associate Director of Student Financial Services
1600 Saint Michael's Drive, Santa Fe, NM 87505-7634
(505) 473-6454

Dona Ana Community College of New Mexico State University

Las Cruces, New Mexico
www.dacc.nmsu.edu   Federal Code: 002657

2-year public branch campus and community college in small city.
Enrollment: 8,998 undergrads, 65% part-time. 1,004 full-time freshmen.
Selectivity: Open admission; but selective for some programs.

BASIC COSTS (2009-2010)

Tuition and fees: $1,272; out-of-district residents $1,512; out-of-state residents $3,984.
Per-credit charge: $53; out-of-district residents $63; out-of-state residents $166.
Room and board: $6,086.

FINANCIAL AID PICTURE

Students with need: Need-based aid available for full-time and part-time students.

FINANCIAL AID PROCEDURES

Forms required: FAFSA.
Dates and Deadlines: Priority date 3/1; no closing date. Applicants notified on a rolling basis starting 5/1.

CONTACT

Gladys Chairez, Financial Aid Director
MSC-3DA, Las Cruces, NM 88003-8001
(505) 527-7510

Eastern New Mexico University

Portales, New Mexico
www.enmu.edu   Federal Code: 002651

4-year public university in large town.
Enrollment: 3,442 undergrads, 27% part-time. 622 full-time freshmen.
Selectivity: Admits 50 to 75% of applicants.

BASIC COSTS (2009-2010)

Tuition and fees: $3,552; out-of-state residents $9,102.
Per-credit charge: $105; out-of-state residents $335.
Room and board: $5,374.

FINANCIAL AID PICTURE (2009-2010)

Students with need: Out of 390 full-time freshmen who applied for aid, 390 were judged to have need. Of these, 390 received aid, and 390 had their full need met. Average financial aid package met 40% of need; average scholarship/grant was $4,191; average loan was $3,243. For part-time students, average financial aid package was $6,821.
Students without need: 5 full-time freshmen who did not demonstrate need for aid received scholarships/grants; average award was $2,589. No-need awards available for academics, alumni affiliation, art, athletics, leadership, music/drama, state/district residency.
Scholarships offered: 92 full-time freshmen received athletic scholarships; average amount $3,172.

FINANCIAL AID PROCEDURES

Forms required: FAFSA.
Dates and Deadlines: Priority date 3/1; no closing date. Applicants notified by 4/1.
Transfers: Priority date 2/14. Child care grants and non-need-based college work study limited to New Mexico residents.

CONTACT

Brent Small, Director of Financial Aid
Station Seven, Portales, NM 88130
(575) 562-2194

Eastern New Mexico University: Roswell

Roswell, New Mexico
www.roswell.enmu.edu   Federal Code: 002651

2-year public branch campus and community college in large town.
Enrollment: 2,562 undergrads, 57% part-time. 415 full-time freshmen.
Selectivity: Open admission; but selective for some programs.

BASIC COSTS (2009-2010)

Tuition and fees: $1,239; out-of-state residents $4,212.
Per-credit charge: $46; out-of-state residents $170.
Room and board: $7,951.

FINANCIAL AID PICTURE (2008-2009)

Students with need: Need-based aid available for full-time and part-time students. Work study available nights, weekends, and for part-time students.
Scholarships offered: New Mexico Lottery Scholarship; tuition for New Mexico residents; must attend school full-time the semester following high school graduation or GED and maintain 12 credit hours and 2.5 GPA.

FINANCIAL AID PROCEDURES

Forms required: FAFSA.
Dates and Deadlines: Priority date 4/1; no closing date. Applicants notified on a rolling basis starting 7/1; must reply within 3 week(s) of notification.
Transfers: All students receiving state aid must be New Mexico residents and enrolled in at least 6 credit hours.

CONTACT

Jessie Sjue, Director of Financial Aid
Box 6000, Roswell, NM 88202-6000
(575) 624-7152

Institute of American Indian Arts

Santa Fe, New Mexico
www.iaia.edu   Federal Code: 014152

4-year public visual arts and liberal arts college in small city.
Enrollment: 250 undergrads.

BASIC COSTS (2009-2010)
Tuition and fees: $3,156.
Room and board: $4,900.

FINANCIAL AID PICTURE (2008-2009)
Students with need: Need-based aid available for full-time and part-time students. Work study available nights.
Students without need: No-need awards available for academics, art.
Scholarships offered: IAIA merit scholarships; $1,000 for all students with 3.0 GPA, $1,500 for 3.5 GPA, $2,000 for 4.0 GPA.
Additional info: For American Indian and Alaskan natives, financial aid available through Tribe or Native Corporation in which student is enrolled.

FINANCIAL AID PROCEDURES
Forms required: FAFSA, institutional form.
Dates and Deadlines: Priority date 3/15; no closing date. Applicants notified on a rolling basis starting 5/1.

CONTACT
LaLa Gallegos, Financial Aid Manager
83 Avan Nu Po Road, Santa Fe, NM 87508-1300
(505) 424-4500

Mesalands Community College

Tucumcari, New Mexico
www.mesalands.edu   Federal Code: 032063

2-year public community and technical college in small town.
Enrollment: 489 undergrads, 31% part-time. 145 full-time freshmen.
Selectivity: Open admission.

BASIC COSTS (2009-2010)
Tuition and fees: $1,525; out-of-state residents $2,561.
Per-credit charge: $40; out-of-state residents $75.

FINANCIAL AID PICTURE (2008-2009)
Students with need: Need-based aid available for full-time and part-time students. Work study available nights.
Students without need: No-need awards available for academics, athletics, leadership, minority status, state/district residency.

FINANCIAL AID PROCEDURES
Forms required: FAFSA.
Dates and Deadlines: Priority date 4/1; no closing date. Applicants notified on a rolling basis starting 4/1; must reply within 3 week(s) of notification.

CONTACT
Amanda Hammer, Director of Financial Aid
911 South Tenth Street, Tucumcari, NM 88401
(575) 461-4413 ext. 136

Navajo Technical College

Crownpoint, New Mexico
www.navajotech.edu

2-year public community and technical college in rural community.
Enrollment: 153 undergrads, 24% part-time. 33 full-time freshmen.
Selectivity: Open admission.

BASIC COSTS (2009-2010)
Tuition and fees: $960.
Per-credit charge: $35.
Room and board: $4,056.
Additional info: Figures quoted are for members of federally recognized tribes. Non-members pay $1800 in tuition.

FINANCIAL AID PICTURE (2008-2009)
Students with need: Need-based aid available for full-time and part-time students.
Students without need: No-need awards available for academics.

FINANCIAL AID PROCEDURES
Forms required: FAFSA, institutional form.
Dates and Deadlines: No deadline. Applicants notified on a rolling basis starting 8/5; must reply by 11/30 or within 4 week(s) of notification.
Transfers: Priority date 8/30; closing date 11/30. Applicants notified by 9/30; must reply within 4 week(s) of notification.

CONTACT
Tyrell Hardy, Financial Aid Officer
PO Box 849, Crownpoint, NM 87313
(505) 786-4309

New Mexico Highlands University

Las Vegas, New Mexico
www.nmhu.edu   Federal Code: 002653

4-year public university in large town.
Enrollment: 2,107 undergrads, 23% part-time. 381 full-time freshmen.
Selectivity: Admits 50 to 75% of applicants.

BASIC COSTS (2009-2010)
Tuition and fees: $2,755; out-of-state residents $4,323.
Room and board: $5,650.

FINANCIAL AID PICTURE (2008-2009)
Students with need: Need-based aid available for full-time and part-time students. Work study available nights, weekends, and for part-time students.
Students without need: No-need awards available for academics, athletics, leadership, minority status, music/drama, state/district residency.
Additional info: Work study funds available on no-need basis to state residents.

FINANCIAL AID PROCEDURES
Forms required: FAFSA, institutional form.
Dates and Deadlines: Priority date 3/1; closing date 5/1. Applicants notified on a rolling basis starting 5/15; must reply within 2 week(s) of notification.
Transfers: Closing date 6/30.

CONTACT
Eileen Sedillo, Director of Financial Aid
Box 9000, Las Vegas, NM 87701
(505) 454-3318

New Mexico Institute of Mining and Technology

Socorro, New Mexico
www.nmt.edu   Federal Code: 002654

4-year public engineering and liberal arts college in small town.
Enrollment: 1,151 undergrads, 5% part-time. 359 full-time freshmen.
Selectivity: Admits over 75% of applicants.

BASIC COSTS (2009-2010)
Tuition and fees: $4,607; out-of-state residents $13,568.
Per-credit charge: $166; out-of-state residents $539.
Room and board: $5,702.

FINANCIAL AID PICTURE (2008-2009)
Students with need: Out of 280 full-time freshmen who applied for aid, 124 were judged to have need. Of these, 122 received aid, and 57 had their full need met. Average financial aid package met 94% of need; average scholarship/grant was $4,567; average loan was $3,819. For part-time students, average financial aid package was $10,051.
Students without need: 127 full-time freshmen who did not demonstrate need for aid received scholarships/grants; average award was $4,028. No-need awards available for academics, alumni affiliation, minority status, state/district residency.
Cumulative student debt: 92% of graduating class had student loans; average debt was $8,129.
Additional info: Campus research projects offer student employment based on merit.

FINANCIAL AID PROCEDURES
Forms required: FAFSA, institutional form.
Dates and Deadlines: Priority date 6/1; no closing date. Applicants notified on a rolling basis starting 4/1; must reply within 2 week(s) of notification.
Transfers: Priority date 3/1; no deadline. Applicants notified on a rolling basis starting 4/1; must reply within 2 week(s) of notification. Financial aid transcripts required from all colleges attended.

CONTACT
Annette Kaus, Director of Financial Aid
801 Leroy Place, Socorro, NM 87801
(575) 835-5333

New Mexico Junior College

Hobbs, New Mexico
www.nmjc.edu   Federal Code: 002655

2-year public community and technical college in large town.
Enrollment: 3,438 undergrads.
Selectivity: Open admission; but selective for some programs.

BASIC COSTS (2009-2010)
Tuition and fees: $1,146; out-of-district residents $1,578; out-of-state residents $1,698.
Per-credit charge: $29; out-of-district residents $47; out-of-state residents $52.
Room and board: $4,050.

FINANCIAL AID PICTURE
Students with need: Need-based aid available for full-time and part-time students. Work study available nights, weekends, and for part-time students.
Students without need: No-need awards available for academics, art, athletics, leadership, music/drama.

FINANCIAL AID PROCEDURES
Forms required: FAFSA.

Dates and Deadlines: Priority date 6/1; no closing date. Applicants notified on a rolling basis; must reply within 2 week(s) of notification.

CONTACT
Laura Marquez, Director of Financial Aid
5317 Lovington Highway, Hobbs, NM 88240
(575) 392-4510

New Mexico Military Institute

Roswell, New Mexico
www.nmmi.edu   Federal Code: 002656

2-year public junior and military college in large town.
Enrollment: 450 undergrads.

BASIC COSTS (2009-2010)
Tuition and fees: $4,916; out-of-state residents $8,466.
Room and board: $3,830.

FINANCIAL AID PICTURE (2008-2009)
Students with need: Need-based aid available for full-time students.
Students without need: No-need awards available for academics, alumni affiliation, athletics, leadership, minority status, ROTC, state/district residency.

FINANCIAL AID PROCEDURES
Forms required: FAFSA.
Dates and Deadlines: Priority date 4/1; no closing date. Applicants notified on a rolling basis starting 5/1; must reply within 3 week(s) of notification.
Transfers: New Mexico Scholars Program, New Mexico Success Scholarship programs available.

CONTACT
Sonya Rodriguez, Director of Admissions & Financial Aid
101 West College Boulevard, Roswell, NM 88201-5173
(575) 624-8066

New Mexico State University

Las Cruces, New Mexico
www.nmsu.edu   Federal Code: 002657

4-year public university in small city.
Enrollment: 14,536 undergrads, 14% part-time. 1,785 full-time freshmen.
Selectivity: Admits over 75% of applicants.

BASIC COSTS (2009-2010)
Tuition and fees: $4,998; out-of-state residents $15,150.
Per-credit charge: $208; out-of-state residents $631.
Room and board: $6,338.

FINANCIAL AID PICTURE (2008-2009)
Students with need: Out of 1,470 full-time freshmen who applied for aid, 1,142 were judged to have need. Of these, 929 received aid, and 73 had their full need met. Average financial aid package met 52% of need; average scholarship/grant was $5,455; average loan was $3,261. For part-time students, average financial aid package was $5,420.
Students without need: 26 full-time freshmen who did not demonstrate need for aid received scholarships/grants; average award was $424. No-need awards available for academics, alumni affiliation, athletics, leadership, minority status, state/district residency.
Scholarships offered: 17 full-time freshmen received athletic scholarships; average amount $8,219.
Cumulative student debt: 51% of graduating class had student loans; average debt was $23,262.

FINANCIAL AID PROCEDURES
Forms required: FAFSA, institutional form.

Dates and Deadlines: Priority date 3/1; no closing date. Applicants notified on a rolling basis starting 3/1.

CONTACT

Michael Zimmerman, Interim Director of Financial Aid
Box 30001, MSC 3A, Las Cruces, NM 88003-8001
(575) 646-4105

New Mexico State University at Alamogordo

Alamogordo, New Mexico
www.nmsua.edu/   Federal Code: 002658

2-year public branch campus college in large town.
Enrollment: 3,643 undergrads, 41% part-time. 297 full-time freshmen.
Selectivity: Open admission; but selective for some programs.

BASIC COSTS (2009-2010)
Tuition and fees: $1,512; out-of-district residents $1,728; out-of-state residents $4,176.
Per-credit charge: $61; out-of-district residents $70; out-of-state residents $172.

FINANCIAL AID PICTURE (2009-2010)
Students with need: Need-based aid available for full-time and part-time students.
Students without need: No-need awards available for academics, state/district residency.

FINANCIAL AID PROCEDURES
Forms required: FAFSA, institutional form.
Dates and Deadlines: Priority date 3/1; no closing date. Applicants notified by 6/1.

CONTACT
Darlene Ellinger, Financial Aid Coordinator
2400 North Scenic Drive, Alamogordo, NM 88310
(575) 439-3600

New Mexico State University at Carlsbad

Carlsbad, New Mexico
www.cavern.nmsu.edu   Federal Code: 002657

2-year public branch campus and community college in large town.
Enrollment: 1,398 undergrads, 59% part-time. 236 full-time freshmen.
Selectivity: Open admission; but selective for some programs.

BASIC COSTS (2009-2010)
Tuition and fees: $964; out-of-district residents $1,420; out-of-state residents $2,812.
Per-credit charge: $36; out-of-district residents $55; out-of-state residents $113.

FINANCIAL AID PICTURE (2008-2009)
Students with need: Need-based aid available for full-time and part-time students.
Students without need: No-need awards available for academics, state/district residency.

FINANCIAL AID PROCEDURES
Forms required: FAFSA.
Dates and Deadlines: Priority date 3/1; no closing date. Applicants notified on a rolling basis starting 5/1; must reply within 4 week(s) of notification.

CONTACT
Judith Sears, Financial Aid Coordinator
1500 University Drive, Carlsbad, NM 88220
(575) 234-9226

New Mexico State University at Grants

Grants, New Mexico
www.grants.nmsu.edu   Federal Code: 008854

2-year public branch campus and community college in small town.
Enrollment: 1,300 undergrads.
Selectivity: Open admission.

BASIC COSTS (2009-2010)
Tuition and fees: $1,392; out-of-district residents $1,512; out-of-state residents $2,976.
Per-credit charge: $58; out-of-district residents $63; out-of-state residents $124.

FINANCIAL AID PICTURE
Students with need: Need-based aid available for full-time and part-time students. Work study available nights, weekends, and for part-time students.

FINANCIAL AID PROCEDURES
Forms required: FAFSA, institutional form.
Dates and Deadlines: Priority date 3/5; no closing date. Applicants notified on a rolling basis starting 6/15; must reply by 8/28.

CONTACT
Beth Armstead, Vice President for Student Services
1500 North Third Street, Grants, NM 87020
(505) 287-6678

Northern New Mexico College

Espanola, New Mexico
www.nnmc.edu   Federal Code: 005286

2-year public community college in small town.
Enrollment: 2,066 undergrads.
Selectivity: Open admission; but selective for some programs and for out-of-state students.

BASIC COSTS (2009-2010)
Tuition and fees: $1,303; out-of-state residents $2,604.
Per-credit charge: $41; out-of-state residents $95.
Room and board: $5,432.
Additional info: Upper division courses $95 per credit hour for in-state students, $404 per credit hour for out-of-state students.

FINANCIAL AID PICTURE (2008-2009)
Students with need: Need-based aid available for full-time students.
Students without need: This college awards aid only to students with need.

FINANCIAL AID PROCEDURES
Forms required: FAFSA.
Dates and Deadlines: Priority date 3/1; no closing date. Applicants notified on a rolling basis starting 6/1; must reply within 2 week(s) of notification.

CONTACT
Alfredo Montoya, Director of Financial Aid
921 Paseo de Onate, Espanola, NM 87532
(505) 747-2128 ext. 128

St. John's College
Santa Fe, New Mexico
www.sjcsf.edu

Federal Code: 002093
CSS Code: 4737

4-year private liberal arts college in small city.
Enrollment: 414 undergrads. 119 full-time freshmen.
Selectivity: Admits over 75% of applicants.

BASIC COSTS (2010-2011)
Tuition and fees: $40,392.
Per-credit charge: $1,176.
Room and board: $9,600.

FINANCIAL AID PICTURE (2008-2009)
Students with need: Out of 91 full-time freshmen who applied for aid, 88 were judged to have need. Of these, 88 received aid, and 83 had their full need met. Average financial aid package met 97% of need; average scholarship/grant was $24,521; average loan was $3,875. For part-time students, average financial aid package was $14,664.
Students without need: This college awards aid only to students with need.
Cumulative student debt: 65% of graduating class had student loans; average debt was $27,235.
Additional info: Families receive individual attention in determining need. Independent students must submit parental data. Financial aid information also required of noncustodial parent in cases of separation or divorce. Aid is awarded on a first-come, first-served basis until institutional money is exhausted. Apply by February 15; after April 1 aid is difficult to obtain.

FINANCIAL AID PROCEDURES
Forms required: FAFSA, CSS PROFILE.
Dates and Deadlines: Priority date 2/15; no closing date. Applicants notified on a rolling basis starting 12/10; must reply by 5/1 or within 2 week(s) of notification.

CONTACT
Michael Rodriguez, Director of Financial Aid
1160 Camino Cruz Blanca, Santa Fe, NM 87505
(505) 984-6058

San Juan College
Farmington, New Mexico
www.sanjuancollege.edu

Federal Code: 002660

2-year public community college in large town.
Enrollment: 5,839 undergrads, 55% part-time. 800 full-time freshmen.
Selectivity: Open admission.

BASIC COSTS (2009-2010)
Tuition and fees: $960; out-of-state residents $2,100.
Per-credit charge: $32; out-of-state residents $70.

FINANCIAL AID PICTURE (2008-2009)
Students with need: 55% of average financial aid package awarded as scholarships/grants, 45% awarded as loans/jobs. Need-based aid available for part-time students. Work study available nights, weekends, and for part-time students.
Students without need: No-need awards available for academics, state/district residency.

FINANCIAL AID PROCEDURES
Forms required: FAFSA.
Dates and Deadlines: No deadline. Applicants notified on a rolling basis starting 7/1; must reply within 2 week(s) of notification.

CONTACT
Jerry McKeen, Director for Financial Aid
4601 College Boulevard, Farmington, NM 87402-4699
(505) 566-3323

Santa Fe Community College
Santa Fe, New Mexico
www.sfccnm.edu

Federal Code: 016065

2-year public community college in small city.
Enrollment: 3,151 undergrads, 59% part-time. 511 full-time freshmen.
Selectivity: Open admission.

BASIC COSTS (2009-2010)
Tuition and fees: $1,113; out-of-district residents $1,434; out-of-state residents $2,469.
Per-credit charge: $32; out-of-district residents $43; out-of-state residents $78.

FINANCIAL AID PICTURE (2008-2009)
Students with need: Need-based aid available for full-time and part-time students. Work study available nights, weekends, and for part-time students.
Students without need: No-need awards available for academics, state/district residency.

FINANCIAL AID PROCEDURES
Forms required: FAFSA, institutional form.
Dates and Deadlines: Priority date 5/1; no closing date. Applicants notified on a rolling basis starting 7/15; must reply within 4 week(s) of notification.

CONTACT
Scott Whitaker, Financial Aid Director
6401 Richards Avenue, Santa Fe, NM 87508-4887
(505) 428-1268

Southwestern Indian Polytechnic Institute
Albuquerque, New Mexico
www.sipi.bia.edu

Federal Code: 011185

2-year public community and technical college in large city.
Enrollment: 400 undergrads, 30% part-time. 69 full-time freshmen.
Selectivity: Open admission.

BASIC COSTS (2010-2011)
Additional info: Tuition-free to Native Americans of Federally-recognized tribes. Required fees: full-time Lodge student $280, full-time commuter $225, part-time $150. Tuition/fee waivers available for minority students.

FINANCIAL AID PICTURE (2008-2009)
Students with need: Out of 69 full-time freshmen who applied for aid, 41 were judged to have need. Of these, 41 received aid, and 12 had their full need met. Average financial aid package met 59% of need; average scholarship/grant was $2,012. Need-based aid available for part-time students.
Students without need: No-need awards available for academics, leadership, minority status.
Additional info: Students with valid membership in recognized Indian tribe attend tuition-free.

FINANCIAL AID PROCEDURES
Forms required: FAFSA.
Dates and Deadlines: Closing date 3/1. Applicants notified on a rolling basis starting 9/30.
Transfers: No deadline.

CONTACT

Joseph Carpio, Director Admissions/Financial Aid
9169 Coors Road NW, Albuquerque, NM 87184
(505) 346-2344

University of New Mexico
Albuquerque, New Mexico
www.unm.edu   Federal Code: 002663

4-year public university in very large city.
Enrollment: 19,613 undergrads, 19% part-time. 3,342 full-time freshmen.
Selectivity: Admits 50 to 75% of applicants.

BASIC COSTS (2009-2010)
Tuition and fees: $5,101; out-of-state residents $17,234.
Per-credit charge: $213.
Room and board: $7,746.

FINANCIAL AID PICTURE
Students with need: Need-based aid available for full-time and part-time students. Work study available nights, weekends, and for part-time students.
Students without need: No-need awards available for academics, alumni affiliation, art, athletics, job skills, leadership, minority status, music/drama, religious affiliation, ROTC, state/district residency.
Scholarships offered: Bridge to Success Scholarship: for first semester only while awaiting other scholarship aid; requires New Mexico residency, full-time status in degree-granting program, and acceptable GED test score and/or requisite high school GPA per sponsor. NM Legislature Lottery Scholarship: for second and subsequent semesters;requires New Mexico residency, full-time status in degree-granting program, and acceptable GED test score and/or requisite high school GPA, and 12 or more credit hours with a 2.5 GPA in the first semester.

FINANCIAL AID PROCEDURES
Forms required: FAFSA.
Dates and Deadlines: Priority date 3/1; no closing date. Applicants notified on a rolling basis.

CONTACT
Brian Malone, Director of Student Financial Aid
Office of Admissions, Albuquerque, NM 87196-4895
(505) 277-8900

University of the Southwest
Hobbs, New Mexico
www.usw.edu   Federal Code: 013935

4-year private liberal arts and teachers college in large town.
Enrollment: 267 undergrads. 59 full-time freshmen.
Selectivity: Open admission; but selective for some programs.

BASIC COSTS (2010-2011)
Tuition and fees: $13,633.
Per-credit charge: $486.
Room and board: $6,590.

FINANCIAL AID PICTURE (2008-2009)
Students with need: Out of 59 full-time freshmen who applied for aid, 50 were judged to have need. Of these, 50 received aid, and 5 had their full need met. Average financial aid package met 70% of need; average scholarship/grant was $3,051; average loan was $2,481. Need-based aid available for part-time students.
Students without need: 6 full-time freshmen who did not demonstrate need for aid received scholarships/grants; average award was $1,333. No-need awards available for academics, alumni affiliation, athletics, leadership, religious affiliation, state/district residency.

Scholarships offered: 51 full-time freshmen received athletic scholarships; average amount $1,418.
Cumulative student debt: 94% of graduating class had student loans; average debt was $24,274.

FINANCIAL AID PROCEDURES
Forms required: FAFSA, institutional form.
Dates and Deadlines: Priority date 4/1; closing date 6/1. Applicants notified on a rolling basis starting 4/1; must reply within 2 week(s) of notification.
Transfers: Priority date 3/1; closing date 6/15.

CONTACT
Kerrie Mitchell, Director of Financial Aid
6610 Lovington Highway #506, Hobbs, NM 88240
(575) 392-6561 ext. 1003

Western New Mexico University
Silver City, New Mexico
www.wnmu.edu   Federal Code: 002664

4-year public university in large town.
Enrollment: 1,113 undergrads.
Selectivity: Open admission.

BASIC COSTS (2009-2010)
Tuition and fees: $3,589; out-of-state residents $12,805.
Room and board: $5,560.

FINANCIAL AID PICTURE (2008-2009)
Students with need: Need-based aid available for full-time and part-time students.
Students without need: No-need awards available for academics, athletics, state/district residency.

FINANCIAL AID PROCEDURES
Forms required: FAFSA, institutional form.
Dates and Deadlines: Closing date 4/1. Applicants notified on a rolling basis starting 4/1; must reply within 2 week(s) of notification.

CONTACT
Charles Kelly, Director of Financial Aid
Castorena 106, Silver City, NM 88062
(505) 538-6173

New York

Adelphi University
Garden City, New York
www.adelphi.edu   Federal Code: 002666

4-year private university in large town.
Enrollment: 4,923 undergrads, 13% part-time. 985 full-time freshmen.
Selectivity: Admits 50 to 75% of applicants.

BASIC COSTS (2010-2011)
Tuition and fees: $27,900.
Per-credit charge: $820.
Room and board: $11,000.

FINANCIAL AID PICTURE (2009-2010)
Students with need: Out of 864 full-time freshmen who applied for aid, 718 were judged to have need. Of these, 696 received aid, and 14 had their full need met. Average financial aid package met 38% of need; average scholarship/grant was $6,340; average loan was $3,979. Need-based aid available for part-time students.

Students without need: 569 full-time freshmen who did not demonstrate need for aid received scholarships/grants; average award was $8,994. No-need awards available for academics, alumni affiliation, art, athletics, leadership, minority status, music/drama, religious affiliation.

Scholarships offered: *Merit:* Trustee Scholarships: for full-time freshmen with the most outstanding academic achievement and co-curricular activities, minimum 2020 score on SAT and rank in top 10% of high school class; 12 available. Presidential Scholarship: typically have minimum SAT of 1950 and rank in top 10% of high school class; $15,000-$16,000 depending upon the individual's academic profile; 25 available. Provost Scholarship: minimum SAT of 1800 and rank in the top 15% of high school class or have minimum transfer GPA of 3.5; $12,000 to $14,500; 55 available. Dean's Scholarship: for full-time freshmen with very good academic performances. Generally minimum SAT scores 1580 to 1790 and rank in top 25% of high school class. *Athletic:* 22 full-time freshmen received athletic scholarships; average amount $7,663.

Cumulative student debt: 69% of graduating class had student loans; average debt was $28,307.

FINANCIAL AID PROCEDURES

Forms required: FAFSA, state aid form.

Dates and Deadlines: Priority date 3/1; no closing date. Applicants notified on a rolling basis starting 2/15.

Transfers: No deadline. Applicants notified on a rolling basis.

CONTACT

Sheryl Mihopulos, Director of Financial Aid

One South Avenue, Levermore 110, Garden City, NY 11530-0701

(516) 877-3080

Adirondack Community College

Queensbury, New York

www.sunyacc.edu   Federal Code: 002860

2-year public community college in large town.

Enrollment: 3,244 undergrads, 30% part-time. 820 full-time freshmen.

Selectivity: Open admission; but selective for some programs.

BASIC COSTS (2009-2010)

Tuition and fees: $3,528; out-of-state residents $6,784.

Per-credit charge: $136; out-of-state residents $272.

FINANCIAL AID PICTURE

Students with need: Need-based aid available for full-time and part-time students.

Students without need: This college awards aid only to students with need.

Scholarships offered: Academic Excellence Scholarship: $750 per semester for up to 4 semesters; for local high school graduates who are 1st or 2nd in class, GPA 3.5. Hill Scholarship: $500 per semester for 4 semesters; for Fort Edward High School graduate.

FINANCIAL AID PROCEDURES

Forms required: FAFSA, state aid form, institutional form.

Dates and Deadlines: Priority date 4/15; no closing date. Applicants notified on a rolling basis starting 5/1.

CONTACT

Maureen Reilly, Director of Financial Aid

640 Bay Road, Queensbury, NY 12804

(518) 743-2223

Albany College of Pharmacy and Health Sciences

Albany, New York   Federal Code: 002885
www.acphs.edu   CSS Code: 2013

4-year private health science and pharmacy college in small city.

Enrollment: 1,112 undergrads, 1% part-time. 196 full-time freshmen.

Selectivity: Admits 50 to 75% of applicants.

BASIC COSTS (2009-2010)

Tuition and fees: $26,410.

Per-credit charge: $775.

Room and board: $8,300.

Additional info: Required fees includes cost of laptop ($2,000).

FINANCIAL AID PICTURE (2009-2010)

Students with need: Out of 195 full-time freshmen who applied for aid, 177 were judged to have need. Of these, 146 received aid, and 15 had their full need met. Average financial aid package met 51% of need; average scholarship/grant was $9,280; average loan was $3,618. For part-time students, average financial aid package was $4,359.

Students without need: 30 full-time freshmen who did not demonstrate need for aid received scholarships/grants; average award was $4,566. No-need awards available for academics, alumni affiliation.

Cumulative student debt: 100% of graduating class had student loans; average debt was $15,943.

FINANCIAL AID PROCEDURES

Forms required: FAFSA, CSS PROFILE.

Dates and Deadlines: Priority date 2/1; closing date 5/1. Applicants notified by 3/25; must reply within 2 week(s) of notification.

Transfers: Applicants notified by 3/25; must reply within 2 week(s) of notification.

CONTACT

Kathleen Montague, Director of Financial Aid

106 New Scotland Avenue, Albany, NY 12208-3492

(518) 694-7256

Alfred University

Alfred, New York
www.alfred.edu   Federal Code: 002668

4-year private university in rural community.

Enrollment: 1,846 undergrads, 1% part-time. 465 full-time freshmen.

Selectivity: Admits 50 to 75% of applicants.

BASIC COSTS (2010-2011)

Tuition and fees: $25,976.

Per-credit charge: $814.

Room and board: $11,364.

Additional info: Tuition info provided is for students enrolling in the College of Business or the College of Liberal Arts and Sciences. Costs for students enrolling in the School of Engineering vary by program and/or residency. Costs for students enrolling in the School of Art and Design vary by residency.

FINANCIAL AID PICTURE (2008-2009)

Students with need: Need-based aid available for full-time students. Work study available nights, weekends, and for part-time students.

Students without need: No-need awards available for academics, art, leadership, music/drama.

FINANCIAL AID PROCEDURES

Forms required: FAFSA, state aid form, institutional form.

Dates and Deadlines: Closing date 3/15. Applicants notified on a rolling basis starting 2/15; must reply by 5/1 or within 2 week(s) of notification.
Transfers: Closing date 5/15. Applicants notified on a rolling basis starting 2/15; must reply by 5/1 or within 2 week(s) of notification.

CONTACT
Earl Pierce, Director of Student Financial Aid
Alumni Hall, Alfred, NY 14802-1205
(607) 871-2159

American Academy McAllister Institute of Funeral Service
New York, New York
www.funeraleducation.org   Federal Code: 010813

2-year private school of mortuary science in very large city.
Enrollment: 314 undergrads.
Selectivity: Open admission.

BASIC COSTS (2009-2010)
Tuition and fees: $11,370.

FINANCIAL AID PICTURE
Students with need: Need-based aid available for full-time students.
Students without need: This college awards aid only to students with need.

FINANCIAL AID PROCEDURES
Forms required: FAFSA, state aid form.
Dates and Deadlines: Applicants notified on a rolling basis starting 7/1; must reply by 9/1 or within 3 week(s) of notification.
Transfers: Priority date 6/1.

CONTACT
Jaway Tso, Financial Aid Administrator
619 West 54th Street, New York, NY 10019-3602
(212) 220-4275

American Academy of Dramatic Arts
New York, New York
www.aada.org   Federal Code: 007465

2-year private junior and performing arts college in very large city.
Enrollment: 184 undergrads. 59 full-time freshmen.
Selectivity: Admits 50 to 75% of applicants.

BASIC COSTS (2010-2011)
Tuition and fees: $29,220.

FINANCIAL AID PICTURE (2008-2009)
Students with need: Out of 42 full-time freshmen who applied for aid, 39 were judged to have need. Of these, 39 received aid. Average financial aid package met 40% of need; average scholarship/grant was $11,500; average loan was $2,500.
Students without need: This college awards aid only to students with need.
Scholarships offered: Merit awards of $1,000-$6,000 for first-year students. Scholarships of $500-$4,000 available for second year. Scholarships of $500-$6,000 available for post-degree third year.
Cumulative student debt: 59% of graduating class had student loans; average debt was $6,400.
Additional info: Need-based incentive grants of $200-$2,000 for first-year students.

FINANCIAL AID PROCEDURES
Forms required: FAFSA, institutional form.
Dates and Deadlines: No deadline. Applicants notified on a rolling basis.

CONTACT
Roberto Lopez, Financial Aid Director
120 Madison Avenue, New York, NY 10016
(212) 686-9244 ext. 342

ASA Institute of Business and Computer Technology
Brooklyn, New York
www.asa.edu   Federal Code: 030955

2-year for-profit career college in very large city.
Enrollment: 4,575 undergrads, 3% part-time. 1,710 full-time freshmen.
Selectivity: Open admission.

BASIC COSTS (2009-2010)
Tuition and fees: $12,099.
Per-credit charge: $495.

FINANCIAL AID PICTURE (2008-2009)
Students with need: Need-based aid available for full-time and part-time students. Work study available nights, weekends, and for part-time students.
Students without need: No-need awards available for academics, alumni affiliation, leadership, state/district residency.

FINANCIAL AID PROCEDURES
Forms required: FAFSA, state aid form.
Dates and Deadlines: No deadline. Applicants notified on a rolling basis starting 7/6; must reply by 10/6.
Transfers: No deadline. Applicants notified on a rolling basis starting 7/6; must reply by 10/6.

CONTACT
Victoria Shtamler, Assistant Vice President of Financial Aid
151 Lawrence Street, Brooklyn, NY 11201
(718) 532-1431

Bard College
Annandale-on-Hudson, New York   Federal Code: 002671
www.bard.edu   CSS Code: 2037

4-year private liberal arts college in small town, affiliated with Episcopal Church.
Enrollment: 1,900 undergrads, 2% part-time. 505 full-time freshmen.
Selectivity: Admits less than 50% of applicants.

BASIC COSTS (2010-2011)
Tuition and fees: $41,670.
Per-credit charge: $1,277.
Room and board: $11,810.

FINANCIAL AID PICTURE (2009-2010)
Students with need: Out of 362 full-time freshmen who applied for aid, 336 were judged to have need. Of these, 336 received aid, and 201 had their full need met. Average financial aid package met 90% of need; average scholarship/grant was $31,540; average loan was $3,547. For part-time students, average financial aid package was $11,980.
Students without need: 7 full-time freshmen who did not demonstrate need for aid received scholarships/grants; average award was $20,594. No-need awards available for academics.
Scholarships offered: Distinguished Scientist Scholarship: full tuition; for students intending to major in math or sciences; 10-20 awarded annually.
Cumulative student debt: 52% of graduating class had student loans; average debt was $26,131.
Additional info: Excellence and Equal Cost Program for students who graduate in top 10 of public high school class lowers fees to levels equivalent to those at home state university or college.

FINANCIAL AID PROCEDURES

Forms required: FAFSA, CSS PROFILE, state aid form.
Dates and Deadlines: Priority date 2/1; closing date 2/15. Applicants notified by 4/1; must reply by 5/1.
Transfers: Applicants notified by 4/1; must reply by 5/1.

CONTACT

Denise Ackerman, Director of Financial Aid
30 Campus Road, Annandale-on-Hudson, NY 12504-5000
(845) 758-7526

Barnard College

New York, New York
www.barnard.edu

Federal Code: 002708
CSS Code: 2038

4-year private liberal arts college for women in very large city.
Enrollment: 2,417 undergrads, 3% part-time. 583 full-time freshmen.
Selectivity: Admits less than 50% of applicants.

BASIC COSTS (2009-2010)

Tuition and fees: $38,650.
Per-credit charge: $1,235.
Room and board: $12,319.

FINANCIAL AID PICTURE (2009-2010)

Students with need: Out of 308 full-time freshmen who applied for aid, 231 were judged to have need. Of these, 231 received aid, and 231 had their full need met. Average financial aid package met 100% of need; average scholarship/grant was $33,153; average loan was $3,257. Need-based aid available for part-time students.
Students without need: This college awards aid only to students with need.
Cumulative student debt: 44% of graduating class had student loans; average debt was $14,706.
Additional info: HEOP for NY residents only; no loan. Pell eligible students: no loan for first-year students, loan reduced to $2,000 for sophomores, juniors and seniors.

FINANCIAL AID PROCEDURES

Forms required: FAFSA, CSS PROFILE, state aid form, institutional form.
Dates and Deadlines: Closing date 2/1. Applicants notified by 3/31; must reply by 5/1.
Transfers: Closing date 4/1. Transfers admitted in the spring are not eligible for institutional grant aid.

CONTACT

Gregory Brown, Vice President for Finance & Planning
3009 Broadway, New York, NY 10027-6598
(212) 854-2154

Berkeley College

White Plains, New York
www.berkeleycollege.edu

Federal Code: 007421

4-year for-profit business college in small city.
Enrollment: 718 undergrads, 4% part-time. 138 full-time freshmen.

BASIC COSTS (2010-2011)

Tuition and fees: $20,700.
Per-credit charge: $465.
Room only: $8,300.

FINANCIAL AID PICTURE

Students with need: Need-based aid available for full-time students.
Students without need: No-need awards available for academics, alumni affiliation.

Additional info: Alumni scholarship examination given in November and December. Full and partial scholarships awarded.

FINANCIAL AID PROCEDURES

Forms required: FAFSA, state aid form.
Dates and Deadlines: No deadline. Applicants notified on a rolling basis starting 3/1; must reply within 6 week(s) of notification.

CONTACT

Cheryll Hope, Director, Financial Aid
99 Church Street, White Plains, NY 10601
(914) 694-1122

Berkeley College of New York City

New York, New York
www.berkeleycollege.edu

Federal Code: 007502

4-year for-profit business college in very large city.
Enrollment: 3,672 undergrads, 13% part-time. 570 full-time freshmen.

BASIC COSTS (2010-2011)

Tuition and fees: $20,700.
Per-credit charge: $465.

FINANCIAL AID PICTURE

Students with need: Need-based aid available for full-time students.
Students without need: No-need awards available for academics, alumni affiliation.
Additional info: Alumni scholarship examination given in November and December. Full and partial scholarships awarded.

FINANCIAL AID PROCEDURES

Forms required: FAFSA.
Dates and Deadlines: No deadline. Applicants notified on a rolling basis starting 3/1; must reply within 6 week(s) of notification.
Transfers: New York State TAP Grant eligibility may be affected.

CONTACT

Howard Leslie, Vice President Financial Aid
3 East 43rd Street, New York, NY 10017
(212) 986-4343

Boricua College

New York, New York
www.boricuacollege.edu

Federal Code: 013029

4-year private liberal arts college in very large city.
Enrollment: 993 undergrads.
Selectivity: Admits 50 to 75% of applicants.

BASIC COSTS (2009-2010)

Tuition and fees: $9,500.

FINANCIAL AID PICTURE (2008-2009)

Students with need: Need-based aid available for full-time students.

FINANCIAL AID PROCEDURES

Forms required: FAFSA, state aid form.
Dates and Deadlines: Priority date 4/30; no closing date. Applicants notified on a rolling basis; must reply within 3 week(s) of notification.

CONTACT

Rosalia Cruz, Director of Financial Aid
3755 Broadway, New York, NY 10032
(212) 694-1000 ext. 611

Briarcliffe College

Bethpage, New York
www.briarcliffe.edu   Federal Code: 020757

4-year for-profit business and technical college in large town.
Enrollment: 1,503 undergrads.

BASIC COSTS (2009-2010)
Tuition and fees: $18,592.
Per-credit charge: $683.

FINANCIAL AID PICTURE
Students with need: Need-based aid available for full-time and part-time students.
Students without need: No-need awards available for academics.

FINANCIAL AID PROCEDURES
Forms required: FAFSA, state aid form, institutional form.
Dates and Deadlines: No deadline. Applicants notified on a rolling basis.

CONTACT
Cindy Roys, Director of Financial Aid
1055 Stewart Avenue, Bethpage, NY 11714
(516) 918-3600

Broome Community College

Binghamton, New York
www.sunybroome.edu   Federal Code: 002862

2-year public community college in small city.
Enrollment: 5,783 undergrads, 21% part-time. 1,386 full-time freshmen.
Selectivity: Open admission; but selective for some programs.

BASIC COSTS (2009-2010)
Tuition and fees: $3,671; out-of-state residents $6,947.
Per-credit charge: $137; out-of-state residents $274.

FINANCIAL AID PICTURE (2009-2010)
Students with need: Need-based aid available for full-time and part-time students. Work study available nights.

FINANCIAL AID PROCEDURES
Forms required: FAFSA.
Dates and Deadlines: Priority date 3/1; no closing date. Applicants notified on a rolling basis starting 3/15; must reply within 2 week(s) of notification.

CONTACT
Doug Lukasik, Director of Financial Aid
Box 1017, Binghamton, NY 13902
(607) 778-5028

Bryant & Stratton College: Albany

Albany, New York
www.bryantstratton.edu   Federal Code: 004749

2-year for-profit business college in small city.
Enrollment: 771 undergrads, 30% part-time. 157 full-time freshmen.
Selectivity: Admits over 75% of applicants.

BASIC COSTS (2010-2011)
Tuition and fees: $14,850.

FINANCIAL AID PICTURE (2008-2009)
Students with need: Need-based aid available for full-time and part-time students. Work study available nights, weekends, and for part-time students.
Students without need: This college awards aid only to students with need.

FINANCIAL AID PROCEDURES
Forms required: FAFSA, state aid form.
Dates and Deadlines: No deadline. Applicants notified on a rolling basis.

CONTACT
Jackie Rivers, FA Coordinator
1259 Central Avenue, Albany, NY 12205
(518) 437-1802

Bryant & Stratton College: Syracuse

Syracuse, New York
www.bryantstratton.edu   Federal Code: 008276

2-year for-profit business and junior college in small city.
Enrollment: 785 undergrads, 28% part-time. 312 full-time freshmen.
Selectivity: Open admission.

BASIC COSTS (2009-2010)
Tuition and fees: $14,805.
Per-credit charge: $489.
Additional info: Total room and board is $7,600 for triple-occupancy residence.

FINANCIAL AID PICTURE (2009-2010)
Students with need: Work study available nights, weekends, and for part-time students.
Students without need: This college awards aid only to students with need.

FINANCIAL AID PROCEDURES
Forms required: FAFSA.
Dates and Deadlines: No deadline. Applicants notified on a rolling basis starting 10/1.
Transfers: Priority date 5/1.

CONTACT
Mary Clifton, Financial Services Manager
953 James Street, Syracuse, NY 13203
(315) 472-6603

Bryant & Stratton College: Syracuse North

Liverpool, New York
www.bryantstratton.edu

2-year for-profit career college in small city.
Enrollment: 553 undergrads, 32% part-time. 98 full-time freshmen.
Selectivity: Open admission.

BASIC COSTS (2009-2010)
Tuition and fees: $14,670.
Per-credit charge: $489.

FINANCIAL AID PICTURE (2008-2009)
Students with need: Need-based aid available for full-time and part-time students. Work study available nights.
Students without need: This college awards aid only to students with need.

FINANCIAL AID PROCEDURES
Forms required: FAFSA, state aid form, institutional form.
Dates and Deadlines: No deadline.
Transfers: No deadline.

PART III: FINANCIAL AID COLLEGE BY COLLEGE

CONTACT

Michelle Lee, Financial Services Manager
8687 Carling Road, Liverpool, NY 13090
(315) 652-6500

Canisius College

Buffalo, New York
www.canisius.edu   Federal Code: 002681

4-year private liberal arts and teachers college in large city, affiliated with Roman Catholic Church.

Enrollment: 3,105 undergrads, 3% part-time. 707 full-time freshmen.
Selectivity: Admits over 75% of applicants.

BASIC COSTS (2010-2011)

Tuition and fees: $30,077.
Per-credit charge: $828.
Room and board: $10,980.
Additional info: Tuition/fee waivers available for minority students.

FINANCIAL AID PICTURE (2009-2010)

Students with need: Out of 641 full-time freshmen who applied for aid, 584 were judged to have need. Of these, 579 received aid, and 214 had their full need met. Average financial aid package met 86% of need; average scholarship/grant was $20,026; average loan was $3,294. Need-based aid available for part-time students.
Students without need: 146 full-time freshmen who did not demonstrate need for aid received scholarships/grants; average award was $11,145. No-need awards available for academics, alumni affiliation, art, athletics, job skills, music/drama, religious affiliation, ROTC.
Scholarships offered: *Merit:* Presidential Scholarship: $20,000 per year for four years. Ignatian Scholarship: $15,000 per year for four years; applicants who apply by Nov. 15 given priority consideration. Trustee's Scholarship: $12,000 per year for on-campus student, $10,000 per year for off-campus student; based on high school GPA, test scores. Dean's Scholarship: $10,000 per year for on-campus student, $8,000 per year for off-campus student; based on high school GPA, test scores. Benefactor's Scholarship: $7,000 per year for on-campus student, $5,000 per year for off-campus student; based on high school GPA, test scores. International Scholarships: international students, including Canadian students, may be eligible for academic scholarships based on academic records. *Athletic:* 15 full-time freshmen received athletic scholarships; average amount $26,613.
Cumulative student debt: 77% of graduating class had student loans; average debt was $33,645.

FINANCIAL AID PROCEDURES

Forms required: FAFSA, state aid form.
Dates and Deadlines: Priority date 2/15; no closing date. Applicants notified on a rolling basis starting 3/1; must reply within 2 week(s) of notification.

CONTACT

Curtis Gaume, Director of Student Financial Aid
2001 Main Street, Buffalo, NY 14208-1098
(800) 541-6348

Cayuga Community College

Auburn, New York
www.cayuga-cc.edu   Federal Code: 002861

2-year public community college in large town.
Enrollment: 3,574 undergrads.
Selectivity: Open admission; but selective for some programs.

BASIC COSTS (2009-2010)

Tuition and fees: $4,031; out-of-state residents $7,591.
Per-credit charge: $140; out-of-state residents $280.

FINANCIAL AID PICTURE (2008-2009)

Students with need: Need-based aid available for full-time and part-time students. Work study available nights, weekends, and for part-time students.
Students without need: This college awards aid only to students with need.

FINANCIAL AID PROCEDURES

Forms required: FAFSA, state aid form.
Dates and Deadlines: Closing date 5/1. Applicants notified on a rolling basis starting 3/15.

CONTACT

Judi Miladin, Director of Financial Aid
197 Franklin Street, Auburn, NY 13021-3099
(315) 255-1743 ext. 2470

Cazenovia College

Cazenovia, New York
www.cazenovia.edu   Federal Code: 002685

4-year private liberal arts college in small town.
Enrollment: 1,073 undergrads, 10% part-time. 272 full-time freshmen.
Selectivity: Admits 50 to 75% of applicants.

BASIC COSTS (2009-2010)

Tuition and fees: $24,152.
Room and board: $10,476.

FINANCIAL AID PICTURE (2009-2010)

Students with need: Out of 265 full-time freshmen who applied for aid, 234 were judged to have need. Of these, 234 received aid, and 50 had their full need met. Average financial aid package met 77% of need; average scholarship/grant was $14,711; average loan was $3,067. For part-time students, average financial aid package was $4,090.
Students without need: 29 full-time freshmen who did not demonstrate need for aid received scholarships/grants; average award was $9,034. No-need awards available for academics.

FINANCIAL AID PROCEDURES

Forms required: FAFSA, state aid form.
Dates and Deadlines: Priority date 3/1; no closing date. Applicants notified on a rolling basis starting 11/1; must reply by 5/1 or within 2 week(s) of notification.
Transfers: No deadline. Applicants notified on a rolling basis starting 11/1; must reply by 5/1 or within 2 week(s) of notification.

CONTACT

Christine Mandel, Director of Financial Aid
3 Sullivan Street, Cazenovia, NY 13035
(315) 655-7887

City University of New York: Baruch College

New York, New York
www.baruch.cuny.edu   Federal Code: 007273

4-year public business and liberal arts college in very large city.
Enrollment: 12,080 undergrads, 22% part-time. 1,430 full-time freshmen.
Selectivity: Admits less than 50% of applicants.

BASIC COSTS (2009-2010)

Tuition and fees: $4,970; out-of-state residents $12,820.
Per-credit charge: $195; out-of-state residents $415.

FINANCIAL AID PICTURE (2009-2010)

Students with need: 82% of average financial aid package awarded as scholarships/grants, 18% awarded as loans/jobs. Need-based aid available for part-time students.

Students without need: No-need awards available for academics, state/district residency.

Scholarships offered: Honors college scholarships based on SAT scores and high school GPA.

FINANCIAL AID PROCEDURES

Forms required: FAFSA, state aid form.

Dates and Deadlines: Priority date 3/15; closing date 4/30. Applicants notified on a rolling basis starting 4/1; must reply by 6/1 or within 6 week(s) of notification.

Transfers: Priority date 4/1; no deadline. Applicants notified on a rolling basis; must reply within 4 week(s) of notification.

CONTACT

Nancy West, Director of Financial Aid
One Bernard Baruch Way, Box H-0720, New York, NY 10010-5585
(646) 312-1360

City University of New York: Borough of Manhattan Community College
New York, New York
www.bmcc.cuny.edu   Federal Code: 002691

2-year public community college in very large city.

Enrollment: 20,942 undergrads, 33% part-time. 3,694 full-time freshmen.

Selectivity: Open admission; but selective for some programs.

BASIC COSTS (2009-2010)

Tuition and fees: $3,468; out-of-state residents $6,618.

Per-credit charge: $135; out-of-state residents $210.

Additional info: Tuition/fee waivers available for unemployed or children of unemployed.

FINANCIAL AID PICTURE (2009-2010)

Students with need: Out of 3,341 full-time freshmen who applied for aid, 3,192 were judged to have need. Of these, 3,040 received aid. Need-based aid available for part-time students.

Students without need: This college awards aid only to students with need.

Cumulative student debt: 7% of graduating class had student loans; average debt was $3,158.

FINANCIAL AID PROCEDURES

Forms required: FAFSA, state aid form, institutional form.

Dates and Deadlines: Priority date 4/15; closing date 5/1. Applicants notified on a rolling basis starting 8/1; must reply within 2 week(s) of notification.

Transfers: No deadline. Applicants notified on a rolling basis starting 6/1; must reply within 2 week(s) of notification.

CONTACT

Howard Entin, Director of Financial Aid
199 Chambers Street, New York, NY 10007-1097
(212) 220-1430

City University of New York: Bronx Community College
Bronx, New York
www.bcc.cuny.edu   Federal Code: 002692

2-year public community college in very large city.

Enrollment: 10,131 undergrads.

Selectivity: Open admission.

BASIC COSTS (2009-2010)

Tuition and fees: $3,504; out-of-state residents $6,654.

Per-credit charge: $135; out-of-state residents $210.

FINANCIAL AID PICTURE

Students with need: Need-based aid available for full-time and part-time students. Work study available nights, weekends, and for part-time students.

Students without need: This college awards aid only to students with need.

FINANCIAL AID PROCEDURES

Forms required: FAFSA.

Dates and Deadlines: Closing date 7/15. Applicants notified on a rolling basis starting 8/1.

CONTACT

Wilma Rosario, Assistant Financial Aid Officer
2155 University Avenue, Bronx, NY 10453
(718) 289-5700

City University of New York: Brooklyn College
Brooklyn, New York
www.brooklyn.cuny.edu   Federal Code: 002687

4-year public liberal arts college in very large city.

Enrollment: 12,021 undergrads, 23% part-time. 952 full-time freshmen.

Selectivity: Admits less than 50% of applicants.

BASIC COSTS (2009-2010)

Tuition and fees: $5,051; out-of-state residents $12,901.

Per-credit charge: $195; out-of-state residents $415.

FINANCIAL AID PICTURE (2009-2010)

Students with need: Out of 852 full-time freshmen who applied for aid, 754 were judged to have need. Of these, 750 received aid, and 738 had their full need met. Average financial aid package met 99% of need; average scholarship/grant was $3,600; average loan was $3,500. For part-time students, average financial aid package was $3,150.

Students without need: 200 full-time freshmen who did not demonstrate need for aid received scholarships/grants; average award was $1,700. No-need awards available for academics, art, leadership, music/drama, state/district residency.

Scholarships offered: Presidential Scholarship Program: for 25 freshman students for 8 tuition payments totaling $13,000. Brooklyn College Freshman Scholarships: $1,000 per year of study at Brooklyn College. Many scholarships for freshman students based on degree of study, academic merit, and community service.

FINANCIAL AID PROCEDURES

Forms required: FAFSA, state aid form.

Dates and Deadlines: Priority date 4/1; no closing date. Applicants notified on a rolling basis starting 5/1.

CONTACT

Sherwood Johnson, Director of Financial Aid
2900 Bedford Avenue, Brooklyn, NY 11210
(718) 951-5051

City University of New York: City College
New York, New York
www.ccny.cuny.edu   Federal Code: 002688

4-year public university in very large city.

Enrollment: 12,340 undergrads, 22% part-time. 1,750 full-time freshmen.

Selectivity: Admits less than 50% of applicants.

BASIC COSTS (2009-2010)

Tuition and fees: $4,929; out-of-state residents $12,779.

Per-credit charge: $195; out-of-state residents $415.

Additional info: Some student housing available, rates vary by apartment size. Tuition/fee waivers available for minority students.

FINANCIAL AID PICTURE (2008-2009)

Students with need: Out of 1,596 full-time freshmen who applied for aid, 1,560 were judged to have need. Of these, 1,535 received aid, and 1,145 had their full need met. Average financial aid package met 80% of need; average scholarship/grant was $6,103; average loan was $1,859. Need-based aid available for part-time students.

Students without need: 381 full-time freshmen who did not demonstrate need for aid received scholarships/grants; average award was $2,098. No-need awards available for academics, alumni affiliation, leadership.

FINANCIAL AID PROCEDURES

Forms required: FAFSA.

Dates and Deadlines: Priority date 4/15; no closing date. Applicants notified on a rolling basis starting 4/15.

Transfers: Priority date 3/31; no deadline. Applicants notified on a rolling basis starting 3/31.

CONTACT

Thelma Mason, Director of Financial Aid

160 Convent Avenue, New York, NY 10031

(212) 650-7000

City University of New York: College of Staten Island

Staten Island, New York

www.csi.cuny.edu   Federal Code: 002698

4-year public liberal arts college in very large city.

Enrollment: 12,578 undergrads, 27% part-time. 2,404 full-time freshmen.

Selectivity: Admits over 75% of applicants.

BASIC COSTS (2009-2010)

Tuition and fees: $4,978; out-of-state residents $12,828.

Per-credit charge: $195; out-of-state residents $415.

FINANCIAL AID PICTURE (2009-2010)

Students with need: Need-based aid available for full-time and part-time students. Work study available nights, weekends, and for part-time students.

Students without need: No-need awards available for academics, art, leadership, minority status, music/drama.

Scholarships offered: CSI Scholarship Program offers a number of non-need-based scholarships.

FINANCIAL AID PROCEDURES

Forms required: FAFSA, state aid form.

Dates and Deadlines: Priority date 3/31; no closing date. Applicants notified on a rolling basis starting 6/1.

Transfers: Applicants notified on a rolling basis starting 5/10.

CONTACT

Philippe Marius, Director of Financial Aid

2800 Victory Boulevard 2A-104, Staten Island, NY 10314

(718) 982-2030

City University of New York: Hostos Community College

Bronx, New York

www.hostos.cuny.edu   Federal Code: 008611

2-year public community college in very large city.

Enrollment: 5,502 undergrads, 36% part-time. 1,102 full-time freshmen.

Selectivity: Open admission; but selective for some programs.

BASIC COSTS (2009-2010)

Tuition and fees: $3,505; out-of-state residents $6,655.

Per-credit charge: $135; out-of-state residents $210.

FINANCIAL AID PICTURE

Students with need: Need-based aid available for full-time and part-time students.

FINANCIAL AID PROCEDURES

Forms required: FAFSA.

Dates and Deadlines: Priority date 7/1; no closing date. Applicants notified on a rolling basis; must reply within 3 week(s) of notification.

CONTACT

Joseph Alicea, Director of Financial Aid

500 Grand Concourse, Bronx, NY 10451

(718) 518-6555

City University of New York: Hunter College

New York, New York

www.hunter.cuny.edu/   Federal Code: 002689

4-year public liberal arts college in very large city.

Enrollment: 14,806 undergrads, 25% part-time. 1,854 full-time freshmen.

Selectivity: Admits less than 50% of applicants.

BASIC COSTS (2009-2010)

Tuition and fees: $4,999; out-of-state residents $12,849.

Per-credit charge: $195; out-of-state residents $415.

Room only: $3,726.

Additional info: Room-only rates by room size and semester.

FINANCIAL AID PICTURE (2008-2009)

Students with need: Out of 1,563 full-time freshmen who applied for aid, 1,436 were judged to have need. Of these, 1,216 received aid, and 279 had their full need met. Average financial aid package met 77% of need; average scholarship/grant was $5,571; average loan was $2,732. For part-time students, average financial aid package was $3,302.

Students without need: 324 full-time freshmen who did not demonstrate need for aid received scholarships/grants; average award was $2,100. No-need awards available for academics.

Cumulative student debt: 48% of graduating class had student loans; average debt was $6,801.

FINANCIAL AID PROCEDURES

Forms required: FAFSA, state aid form.

Dates and Deadlines: Priority date 5/1; no closing date. Applicants notified on a rolling basis starting 5/15.

CONTACT

Aristalia Cortorreal Diaz, Director of Financial Aid

695 Park Avenue, New York, NY 10065

(212) 772-4820

City University of New York: John Jay College of Criminal Justice

New York, New York
www.jjay.cuny.edu/

4-year public College of criminal justice and public safety. in very large city.
Enrollment: 13,170 undergrads, 21% part-time. 2,414 full-time freshmen.
Selectivity: Admits 50 to 75% of applicants.

BASIC COSTS (2009-2010)

Tuition and fees: $4,929; out-of-state residents $12,779.
Per-credit charge: $195; out-of-state residents $415.

FINANCIAL AID PICTURE (2008-2009)

Students with need: Out of 2,099 full-time freshmen who applied for aid, 1,784 were judged to have need. Of these, 1,469 received aid. Average financial aid package met 85% of need; average scholarship/grant was $2,926; average loan was $2,331. For part-time students, average financial aid package was $5,004.
Students without need: No-need awards available for academics, leadership, minority status.
Cumulative student debt: 46% of graduating class had student loans; average debt was $45,000.

FINANCIAL AID PROCEDURES

Forms required: FAFSA, state aid form.
Dates and Deadlines: Priority date 4/30; no closing date. Applicants notified on a rolling basis starting 4/1; must reply within 2 week(s) of notification.
Transfers: Closing date 4/30.

CONTACT

Sylvia Lopez-Crespo, Director of Financial Aid
445 West 59th Street, New York, NY 10019
(212) 237-8149

City University of New York: Kingsborough Community College

Brooklyn, New York
www.kbcc.cuny.edu   Federal Code: 002694

2-year public community college in very large city.
Enrollment: 13,836 undergrads, 25% part-time. 2,698 full-time freshmen.
Selectivity: Open admission.

BASIC COSTS (2009-2010)

Tuition and fees: $3,500; out-of-state residents $6,650.
Per-credit charge: $135; out-of-state residents $210.

FINANCIAL AID PICTURE

Students with need: Need-based aid available for full-time and part-time students.
Students without need: This college awards aid only to students with need.

FINANCIAL AID PROCEDURES

Forms required: FAFSA.
Dates and Deadlines: Closing date 4/30. Applicants notified on a rolling basis; must reply within 2 week(s) of notification.

CONTACT

Wayne Harewood, Director of Financial Aid
2001 Oriental Boulevard, Brooklyn, NY 11235
(718) 368-4644

City University of New York: LaGuardia Community College

Long Island City, New York
www.lagcc.cuny.edu   Federal Code: 010051

2-year public community college in very large city.
Enrollment: 14,933 undergrads, 38% part-time. 3,571 full-time freshmen.
Selectivity: Open admission.

BASIC COSTS (2009-2010)

Tuition and fees: $3,492; out-of-state residents $6,642.
Per-credit charge: $135; out-of-state residents $210.

FINANCIAL AID PICTURE (2008-2009)

Students with need: Out of 2,788 full-time freshmen who applied for aid, 2,648 were judged to have need. Of these, 2,502 received aid. Average financial aid package met 45% of need; average scholarship/grant was $3,757. For part-time students, average financial aid package was $1,938.
Students without need: This college awards aid only to students with need.

FINANCIAL AID PROCEDURES

Forms required: FAFSA, state aid form, institutional form.
Dates and Deadlines: Priority date 4/15; no closing date. Applicants notified on a rolling basis starting 3/1; must reply within 4 week(s) of notification.

CONTACT

Gail Baksh-Jarrett, Director of Financial Aid
31-10 Thomson Avenue, Long Island City, NY 11101
(718) 482-7200

City University of New York: Lehman College

Bronx, New York
www.lehman.cuny.edu   Federal Code: 007022

4-year public liberal arts college in very large city.
Enrollment: 8,819 undergrads, 33% part-time. 754 full-time freshmen.
Selectivity: Admits less than 50% of applicants.

BASIC COSTS (2009-2010)

Tuition and fees: $4,940; out-of-state residents $12,790.
Per-credit charge: $195; out-of-state residents $415.

FINANCIAL AID PICTURE (2008-2009)

Students with need: Need-based aid available for full-time and part-time students.
Students without need: This college awards aid only to students with need.

FINANCIAL AID PROCEDURES

Forms required: FAFSA, state aid form.
Dates and Deadlines: No deadline. Applicants notified on a rolling basis starting 3/1.
Transfers: Applicants notified on a rolling basis starting 3/1.

CONTACT

David Martinez, Director of Financial Aid
250 Bedford Park Boulevard West, Bronx, NY 10468
(718) 960-8545

City University of New York: Medgar Evers College

Brooklyn, New York
www.mec.cuny.edu   Federal Code: 010097

4-year public liberal arts college in very large city.
Enrollment: 6,757 undergrads, 31% part-time. 1,285 full-time freshmen.
Selectivity: Open admission; but selective for some programs.

BASIC COSTS (2009-2010)
Tuition and fees: $4,902; out-of-state residents $12,752.
Per-credit charge: $195; out-of-state residents $415.

FINANCIAL AID PICTURE (2009-2010)
Students with need: 92% of average financial aid package awarded as scholarships/grants, 8% awarded as loans/jobs. Need-based aid available for part-time students. Work study available weekends and for part-time students.
Students without need: No-need awards available for academics, leadership.

FINANCIAL AID PROCEDURES
Forms required: FAFSA, state aid form.
Dates and Deadlines: Priority date 1/2; closing date 6/1. Applicants notified on a rolling basis; must reply within 3 week(s) of notification.
Transfers: Priority date 3/1. Must reply within 2 week(s) of notification.

CONTACT
Conley James, Director of Financial Aid
1665 Bedford Avenue, Brooklyn, NY 11225-2201
(718) 270-6194

City University of New York: New York City College of Technology

Brooklyn, New York
www.citytech.cuny.edu   Federal Code: 002696

4-year public technical college in very large city.
Enrollment: 14,366 undergrads, 37% part-time. 2,967 full-time freshmen.
Selectivity: Open admission; but selective for some programs.

BASIC COSTS (2009-2010)
Tuition and fees: $4,939; out-of-state residents $12,789.
Per-credit charge: $195; out-of-state residents $415.

FINANCIAL AID PICTURE (2009-2010)
Students with need: Out of 2,530 full-time freshmen who applied for aid, 2,241 were judged to have need. Of these, 2,165 received aid, and 105 had their full need met. Average financial aid package met 59% of need; average scholarship/grant was $6,442; average loan was $564. For part-time students, average financial aid package was $3,500.
Students without need: 56 full-time freshmen who did not demonstrate need for aid received scholarships/grants; average award was $536. No-need awards available for state/district residency.
Additional info: Foreign students applying for aid must have resided in New York for at least 1 year.

FINANCIAL AID PROCEDURES
Forms required: FAFSA.
Dates and Deadlines: Priority date 5/15; no closing date.

CONTACT
Sandra Higgins, Director of Financial Aid
300 Jay Street Namm G17, Brooklyn, NY 11201
(718) 260-5700

City University of New York: Queens College

Flushing, New York
www.qc.cuny.edu   Federal Code: 002690

4-year public liberal arts college in very large city.
Enrollment: 15,270 undergrads, 23% part-time. 1,684 full-time freshmen.
Selectivity: Admits less than 50% of applicants.

BASIC COSTS (2009-2010)
Tuition and fees: $5,047; out-of-state residents $12,897.
Per-credit charge: $195; out-of-state residents $415.

FINANCIAL AID PICTURE (2008-2009)
Students with need: Need-based aid available for full-time and part-time students.
Students without need: No-need awards available for academics, athletics, music/drama, state/district residency.
Scholarships offered: CUNY Honors College; full tuition. Regents Award for Deceased or Disabled Veterans; $450 per year. Vietnam Veteran Tuition Aid Program; cost of tuition per semester. Regents Award for children of deceased police officers, firefighters, or corrections officers; $450 per year. Paul Douglas Teacher Scholarship Program; up to $5,000 per year. State Aid to Native Americans; $1,100 per year. SEEK Presidential Scholarship; Beinstock Memorial Scholarship for students with disabilities; CMP Publications Scholarship in Journalism or English; Daly Scholarship in the Physical Sciences; Foster Scholarship for women and minorities; Kupferberg Memorial Scholarship; Linakis Scholarship; Mitsui USA Scholarships; Nagdimon Scholarship; Queens College Scholarships; Weprin Memorial Scholarship in the Public Interest.

FINANCIAL AID PROCEDURES
Forms required: FAFSA, state aid form, institutional form.
Dates and Deadlines: Priority date 2/1; no closing date. Applicants notified on a rolling basis starting 3/1; must reply within 3 week(s) of notification.
Transfers: Priority date 5/1; no deadline. Applicants notified on a rolling basis.

CONTACT
Rena Smith-Kiawu, Director of Financial Aid
6530 Kissena Boulevard, Jefferson 117, Flushing, NY 11367-1597
(718) 997-5123

City University of New York: Queensborough Community College

Bayside, New York
www.qcc.cuny.edu   Federal Code: 002697

2-year public community college in very large city.
Enrollment: 13,776 undergrads.
Selectivity: Open admission.

BASIC COSTS (2009-2010)
Tuition and fees: $3,490; out-of-state residents $6,640.
Per-credit charge: $135; out-of-state residents $210.

FINANCIAL AID PICTURE (2008-2009)
Students with need: Need-based aid available for full-time students.

FINANCIAL AID PROCEDURES
Forms required: FAFSA, institutional form.
Dates and Deadlines: No deadline. Applicants notified on a rolling basis starting 7/15.

CONTACT
Veronica Lukas, Director of Financial Aid
Springfield Boulevard & 56th Avenue, Bayside, NY 11364-1497
(718) 631-6262

City University of New York: York College

Jamaica, New York
www.york.cuny.edu   Federal Code: 004759

4-year public liberal arts college in very large city.
Enrollment: 6,915 undergrads, 30% part-time. 1,045 full-time freshmen.

BASIC COSTS (2009-2010)

Tuition and fees: $4,912; out-of-state residents $12,762.
Per-credit charge: $195; out-of-state residents $415.

FINANCIAL AID PICTURE (2009-2010)

Students with need: Out of 888 full-time freshmen who applied for aid, 837 were judged to have need. Of these, 756 received aid. Average financial aid package met 69% of need; average scholarship/grant was $2,595; average loan was $2,686. For part-time students, average financial aid package was $2,978.
Students without need: 43 full-time freshmen who did not demonstrate need for aid received scholarships/grants; average award was $814. No-need awards available for academics.
Cumulative student debt: 12% of graduating class had student loans; average debt was $10,183.

FINANCIAL AID PROCEDURES

Forms required: FAFSA.
Dates and Deadlines: Priority date 5/1; no closing date. Applicants notified on a rolling basis starting 3/1.
Transfers: No deadline. Applicants notified on a rolling basis starting 3/1.

CONTACT

Cathy Tsiapanos, Director of Financial Aid
94-20 Guy R. Brewer Boulevard, Jamaica, NY 11451-9989
(718) 262-2000 ext. 2230

Clarkson University

Potsdam, New York
www.clarkson.edu   Federal Code: 002699

4-year private university in small town.
Enrollment: 2,717 undergrads. 777 full-time freshmen.
Selectivity: Admits 50 to 75% of applicants.

BASIC COSTS (2010-2011)

Tuition and fees: $34,760.
Per-credit charge: $1,136.
Room and board: $11,564.
Additional info: Tuition/fee waivers available for minority students.

FINANCIAL AID PICTURE (2009-2010)

Students with need: Out of 733 full-time freshmen who applied for aid, 641 were judged to have need. Of these, 641 received aid, and 173 had their full need met. Average financial aid package met 85% of need; average scholarship/grant was $24,862; average loan was $4,066. Need-based aid available for part-time students.
Students without need: 92 full-time freshmen who did not demonstrate need for aid received scholarships/grants; average award was $16,595. No-need awards available for academics, alumni affiliation, leadership, minority status, ROTC.
Scholarships offered: 9 full-time freshmen received athletic scholarships; average amount $27,218.
Cumulative student debt: 85% of graduating class had student loans; average debt was $32,125.

FINANCIAL AID PROCEDURES

Forms required: FAFSA, state aid form.

Dates and Deadlines: Priority date 2/15; no closing date. Applicants notified on a rolling basis starting 3/19; must reply by 5/1 or within 2 week(s) of notification.
Transfers: Closing date 4/15. Applicants notified on a rolling basis. Presidential scholarships, Phi Theta Kappa scholarships and Alpha Beta Gamma awards available in addition to state and federal programs.

CONTACT

Jennifer Wick, Director of New Student Financial Aid
Holcroft House, Potsdam, NY 13699-5605
(800) 527-6577

Clinton Community College

Plattsburgh, New York
www.clinton.edu   Federal Code: 006787

2-year public community college in large town.
Enrollment: 1,567 undergrads. 441 full-time freshmen.
Selectivity: Open admission; but selective for some programs.

BASIC COSTS (2009-2010)

Tuition and fees: $3,842; out-of-state residents $8,802.
Per-credit charge: $148; out-of-state residents $350.

FINANCIAL AID PICTURE (2008-2009)

Students with need: 46% of average financial aid package awarded as scholarships/grants, 54% awarded as loans/jobs. Need-based aid available for part-time students.
Students without need: This college awards aid only to students with need.

FINANCIAL AID PROCEDURES

Forms required: FAFSA, state aid form.
Dates and Deadlines: Priority date 6/9; no closing date. Applicants notified on a rolling basis starting 5/9; must reply within 2 week(s) of notification.

CONTACT

Karen Burnam, Director of Financial Aid
136 Clinton Point Drive, Plattsburgh, NY 12901-4297
(518) 562-4125

Cochran School of Nursing

Yonkers, New York
www.cochranschoolofnursing.us   Federal Code: 006443

2-year private nursing college in small city.
Enrollment: 295 undergrads, 80% part-time.

BASIC COSTS (2009-2010)

Additional info: Tuition and required fees for full 2-year AAS program is $25,111.

FINANCIAL AID PICTURE (2009-2010)

Students with need: 16% of average financial aid package awarded as scholarships/grants, 84% awarded as loans/jobs. Need-based aid available for part-time students.
Students without need: This college awards aid only to students with need.

FINANCIAL AID PROCEDURES

Forms required: FAFSA.
Dates and Deadlines: No deadline. Applicants notified on a rolling basis.

CONTACT

Geraldine Owens, Financial Aid Officer
967 North Broadway, Yonkers, NY 10701
(914) 964-4265

Colgate University

Hamilton, New York
www.colgate.edu

Federal Code: 002701
CSS Code: 2086

4-year private liberal arts college in small town.
Enrollment: 2,799 undergrads. 750 full-time freshmen.
Selectivity: Admits less than 50% of applicants.

BASIC COSTS (2009-2010)

Tuition and fees: $40,970.
Room and board: $9,970.

FINANCIAL AID PICTURE (2009-2010)

Students with need: Out of 318 full-time freshmen who applied for aid, 252 were judged to have need. Of these, 252 received aid, and 252 had their full need met. Average financial aid package met 100% of need; average scholarship/grant was $35,526; average loan was $2,107.
Students without need: No-need awards available for athletics.
Scholarships offered: 47 full-time freshmen received athletic scholarships; average amount $33,771.
Cumulative student debt: 30% of graduating class had student loans; average debt was $19,202.

FINANCIAL AID PROCEDURES

Forms required: CSS PROFILE.
Dates and Deadlines: Closing date 1/15. Applicants notified by 4/1; must reply by 5/1 or within 2 week(s) of notification.
Transfers: Closing date 3/15. Applicants notified by 4/30; must reply by 5/15 or within 2 week(s) of notification. Financial aid for transfer students extremely limited.

CONTACT

Marcelle Tyburski, Director of Financial Aid
13 Oak Drive, Hamilton, NY 13346-1383
(315) 228-7431

College of Mount St. Vincent

Riverdale, New York
www.mountsaintvincent.edu

Federal Code: 002703

4-year private liberal arts college in very large city, affiliated with Roman Catholic Church.
Enrollment: 1,504 undergrads, 10% part-time. 391 full-time freshmen.
Selectivity: Admits 50 to 75% of applicants.

BASIC COSTS (2009-2010)

Tuition and fees: $25,710.
Per-credit charge: $750.
Room and board: $9,900.

FINANCIAL AID PICTURE (2008-2009)

Students with need: Need-based aid available for full-time students.
Students without need: No-need awards available for academics, alumni affiliation, leadership.

FINANCIAL AID PROCEDURES

Forms required: FAFSA, state aid form.
Dates and Deadlines: Priority date 3/1; no closing date. Applicants notified on a rolling basis starting 3/1; must reply by 5/1 or within 3 week(s) of notification.
Transfers: Priority date 5/15. Applicants notified on a rolling basis starting 3/1; must reply by 5/1 or within 3 week(s) of notification.

CONTACT

Monica Simotas, Director of Financial Aid
6301 Riverdale Avenue, Riverdale, NY 10471-1093
(718) 405-3289

College of New Rochelle

New Rochelle, New York
www.cnr.edu

Federal Code: 002704

4-year private nursing and liberal arts college for women in small city, affiliated with Roman Catholic Church.
Enrollment: 811 undergrads.
Selectivity: Admits less than 50% of applicants.

BASIC COSTS (2010-2011)

Tuition and fees: $28,010.
Per-credit charge: $861.
Room and board: $10,176.
Additional info: All incoming freshmen given laptop at no additional cost.

FINANCIAL AID PICTURE (2008-2009)

Students with need: Need-based aid available for full-time and part-time students. Work study available nights, weekends, and for part-time students.
Students without need: No-need awards available for academics, art, leadership.

FINANCIAL AID PROCEDURES

Forms required: FAFSA, institutional form.
Dates and Deadlines: Priority date 3/1; no closing date. Applicants notified on a rolling basis starting 1/1; must reply within 2 week(s) of notification.

CONTACT

Ann Pelak, Director of Financial Aid
29 Castle Place, New Rochelle, NY 10805-2339
(914) 654-5225

College of Saint Rose

Albany, New York
www.strose.edu

Federal Code: 002705

4-year private liberal arts and teachers college in small city.
Enrollment: 2,993 undergrads, 5% part-time. 587 full-time freshmen.
Selectivity: Admits 50 to 75% of applicants.

BASIC COSTS (2010-2011)

Tuition and fees: $24,138.
Per-credit charge: $776.
Room and board: $9,880.

FINANCIAL AID PICTURE (2008-2009)

Students with need: Out of 540 full-time freshmen who applied for aid, 537 were judged to have need. Of these, 536 received aid, and 14 had their full need met. Average financial aid package met 11% of need; average scholarship/grant was $4,098; average loan was $1,638. For part-time students, average financial aid package was $5,360.
Students without need: 60 full-time freshmen who did not demonstrate need for aid received scholarships/grants; average award was $2,451. No-need awards available for academics, alumni affiliation, art, athletics, minority status, music/drama, state/district residency.
Scholarships offered: 9 full-time freshmen received athletic scholarships; average amount $9,408.
Cumulative student debt: 84% of graduating class had student loans; average debt was $29,391.

FINANCIAL AID PROCEDURES

Forms required: FAFSA.
Dates and Deadlines: Priority date 3/1; no closing date. Applicants notified on a rolling basis starting 2/15; must reply by 5/1 or within 2 week(s) of notification.

CONTACT

Steve Dwire, Director of Financial Aid
432 Western Avenue, Albany, NY 12203
(518) 458-5424

College of Westchester

White Plains, New York
www.cw.edu
Federal Code: 005208

2-year for-profit business and career college in large town.
Enrollment: 1,295 undergrads, 14% part-time. 361 full-time freshmen.
Selectivity: Admits 50 to 75% of applicants.

BASIC COSTS (2009-2010)

Tuition and fees: $21,100.
Additional info: Tuition/fee waivers available for unemployed or children of unemployed.

FINANCIAL AID PICTURE (2008-2009)

Students with need: Need-based aid available for full-time and part-time students. Work study available nights, weekends, and for part-time students.
Students without need: No-need awards available for academics, alumni affiliation.

FINANCIAL AID PROCEDURES

Forms required: FAFSA, state aid form, institutional form.
Dates and Deadlines: No deadline. Applicants notified on a rolling basis starting 1/7; must reply within 2 week(s) of notification.

CONTACT

Dianne Pepitone, Director, Student Financial Services
325 Central Park Avenue, White Plains, NY 10602
(914) 948-4442 ext. 473

Columbia University

New York, New York
www.columbia.edu
Federal Code: E00485
CSS Code: 2116

4-year private university in very large city.
Enrollment: 5,766 undergrads. 1,419 full-time freshmen.
Selectivity: Admits less than 50% of applicants.

BASIC COSTS (2009-2010)

Tuition and fees: $41,316.
Room and board: $10,228.

FINANCIAL AID PICTURE (2009-2010)

Students with need: Out of 908 full-time freshmen who applied for aid, 774 were judged to have need. Of these, 774 received aid, and 744 had their full need met. Average financial aid package met 100% of need; average scholarship/grant was $36,464; average loan was $2,698.
Students without need: This college awards aid only to students with need.
Additional info: We have eliminated student loans for those receiving Columbia need-based aid and replaced them with additional University grants, and significantly reduced the parent contribution for families making less than $100,000 per year.

FINANCIAL AID PROCEDURES

Forms required: FAFSA, CSS PROFILE.
Dates and Deadlines: Closing date 3/2. Applicants notified by 4/1; must reply by 5/1.
Transfers: Closing date 4/20. Must reply within 3 week(s) of notification.

CONTACT

Daniel Barkowitz, Dean of Financial Aid/Associate Dean of Student Affairs
1130 Amsterdam Avenue, New York, NY 10027
(212) 854-6452

Columbia University: School of General Studies

New York, New York
www.gs.columbia.edu
Federal Code: E00487

4-year private university and liberal arts college in very large city.
Enrollment: 1,351 undergrads, 40% part-time.
Selectivity: Admits less than 50% of applicants.

BASIC COSTS (2009-2010)

Tuition and fees: $39,910.
Per-credit charge: $1,270.
Room and board: $12,020.
Additional info: First-year students also pay a one-time transcript fee of $95.

FINANCIAL AID PICTURE (2009-2010)

Students with need: 63% of average financial aid package awarded as scholarships/grants, 37% awarded as loans/jobs. Need-based aid available for part-time students.
Students without need: This college awards aid only to students with need.
Scholarships offered: All applicants should submit General Studies Application for Financial Aid.

FINANCIAL AID PROCEDURES

Forms required: FAFSA, institutional form.
Dates and Deadlines: Priority date 4/15; closing date 6/1. Applicants notified on a rolling basis; must reply within 3 week(s) of notification.
Transfers: Applicants notified on a rolling basis starting 4/1; must reply within 2 week(s) of notification.

CONTACT

William Bailey, Director of Educational Financing
408 Lewisohn Hall, Mail Code 4101, New York, NY 10027
(212) 854-5410

Columbia-Greene Community College

Hudson, New York
www.sunycgcc.edu
Federal Code: 006789

2-year public community college in small town.
Enrollment: 1,640 undergrads, 30% part-time. 426 full-time freshmen.
Selectivity: Open admission; but selective for some programs.

BASIC COSTS (2009-2010)

Tuition and fees: $3,620; out-of-state residents $6,932.
Per-credit charge: $138; out-of-state residents $276.

FINANCIAL AID PICTURE (2008-2009)

Students with need: 57% of average financial aid package awarded as scholarships/grants, 43% awarded as loans/jobs. Need-based aid available for part-time students. Work study available nights, weekends, and for part-time students.
Students without need: No-need awards available for academics, state/district residency.

FINANCIAL AID PROCEDURES

Forms required: FAFSA, institutional form.
Dates and Deadlines: Priority date 5/1; no closing date. Applicants notified on a rolling basis starting 7/1; must reply within 2 week(s) of notification.

CONTACT

Earl Tretheway, Director of Financial Aid

4400 Route 23, Hudson, NY 12534

Concordia College

Bronxville, New York

www.concordia-ny.edu

Federal Code: 002709

4-year private liberal arts college in small town, affiliated with Lutheran Church - Missouri Synod.

Enrollment: 734 undergrads, 13% part-time. 101 full-time freshmen.

Selectivity: Admits 50 to 75% of applicants.

BASIC COSTS (2009-2010)

Tuition and fees: $24,700.

Room and board: $9,125.

FINANCIAL AID PICTURE

Students with need: Need-based aid available for full-time and part-time students. Work study available nights, weekends, and for part-time students.

Students without need: No-need awards available for academics, athletics, leadership, music/drama.

Scholarships offered: Fellows Scholarship: $15,000 a year; for 1800 SAT (exclusive of Writing) and 95 average. Merit Scholarships: $6,000-$9,000 for 80 average and above. Lutheran students grants available.

FINANCIAL AID PROCEDURES

Forms required: FAFSA, state aid form.

Dates and Deadlines: Priority date 4/1; no closing date. Applicants notified on a rolling basis starting 4/1; must reply by 5/1 or within 3 week(s) of notification.

CONTACT

Janice Spikereit, Director of Financial Aid

171 White Plains Road, Bronxville, NY 10708

(914) 337-9300 ext. 2146

Cooper Union for the Advancement of Science and Art

New York, New York

www.cooper.edu

Federal Code: 002710

CSS Code: 2097

4-year private visual arts and engineering college in very large city.

Enrollment: 880 undergrads. 238 full-time freshmen.

Selectivity: Admits less than 50% of applicants.

BASIC COSTS (2009-2010)

Tuition and fees: $36,650.

Room only: $9,900.

Additional info: All students receive a full-tuition scholarship (covering tuition only) for the duration of their enrollment.

FINANCIAL AID PICTURE (2008-2009)

Students with need: Out of 117 full-time freshmen who applied for aid, 88 were judged to have need. Of these, 88 received aid, and 36 had their full need met. Average financial aid package met 92% of need; average scholarship/grant was $3,309; average loan was $2,972.

Students without need: 164 full-time freshmen who did not demonstrate need for aid received scholarships/grants; average award was $35,000. No-need awards available for academics.

Cumulative student debt: 27% of graduating class had student loans; average debt was $12,717.

Additional info: All students receive full-tuition scholarships. Students able to document need receive financial aid package that may include combination of grants, loans, work-study, internships. Late financial aid applications processed on rolling basis.

FINANCIAL AID PROCEDURES

Forms required: FAFSA, CSS PROFILE.

Dates and Deadlines: Priority date 4/15; closing date 6/1. Applicants notified by 6/1; must reply by 6/30 or within 2 week(s) of notification.

Transfers: Priority date 4/1; closing date 5/1. Applicants notified by 6/1; must reply by 6/30 or within 2 week(s) of notification.

CONTACT

Mary Ruokonen, Director of Financial Aid

30 Cooper Square, Suite 300, New York, NY 10003-7183

(212) 353-4130

Cornell University

Ithaca, New York

www.cornell.edu

Federal Code: 002711

CSS Code: 2098

4-year private university in large town.

Enrollment: 13,882 undergrads. 3,181 full-time freshmen.

Selectivity: Admits less than 50% of applicants.

BASIC COSTS (2010-2011)

Tuition and fees: $39,666.

Room and board: $12,650.

FINANCIAL AID PICTURE (2009-2010)

Students with need: Out of 2,223 full-time freshmen who applied for aid, 1,647 were judged to have need. Of these, 1,647 received aid, and 1,647 had their full need met. Average financial aid package met 100% of need; average scholarship/grant was $32,614; average loan was $2,944.

Students without need: This college awards aid only to students with need.

Cumulative student debt: 53% of graduating class had student loans; average debt was $21,549.

Additional info: No parental contribution for students from families with incomes below $60,000 and assets below $100,000; need-based student loans capped at $7,500 annually whose families have annual incomes above $120,000; parental contribution reduced for selected students who have financial need and whose families have annual incomes above $60,000.

FINANCIAL AID PROCEDURES

Forms required: FAFSA, CSS PROFILE, institutional form.

Dates and Deadlines: Closing date 1/2. Applicants notified by 4/1; must reply by 5/1.

Transfers: Priority date 2/15; closing date 3/15. Applicants notified on a rolling basis starting 3/15; must reply by 6/1 or within 2 week(s) of notification. Submit Cornell aid application forms in addition to regular required forms.

CONTACT

Thomas Keane, Director, Financial Aid and Student Employment

410 Thurston Avenue, Ithaca, NY 14850-2488

(607) 255-2000

Corning Community College

Corning, New York

www.corning-cc.edu

Federal Code: 002863

2-year public community college in large town.

Enrollment: 3,696 undergrads, 34% part-time. 879 full-time freshmen.

Selectivity: Open admission; but selective for some programs.

BASIC COSTS (2009-2010)

Tuition and fees: $3,980; out-of-state residents $7,550.

Per-credit charge: $149; out-of-state residents $298.

FINANCIAL AID PICTURE

Students with need: Need-based aid available for full-time and part-time students. Work study available weekends and for part-time students.
Students without need: This college awards aid only to students with need.

FINANCIAL AID PROCEDURES

Forms required: FAFSA.
Dates and Deadlines: Priority date 4/1; no closing date. Applicants notified on a rolling basis starting 4/15; must reply within 2 week(s) of notification.

CONTACT

Barbara Snow, Director of Financial Aid
One Academic Drive, Corning, NY 14830
(607) 962-9011

Culinary Institute of America

Hyde Park, New York
www.ciachef.edu   Federal Code: 007304

4-year private culinary school in large town.
Enrollment: 2,824 undergrads. 566 full-time freshmen.
Selectivity: Admits over 75% of applicants.

BASIC COSTS (2009-2010)

Tuition and fees: $24,630.
Room and board: $8,110.
Additional info: Room and board costs shown for typical undergraduate; costs may vary.

FINANCIAL AID PICTURE (2008-2009)

Students with need: Average financial aid package for all full-time undergraduates was $14,916. 31% awarded as scholarships/grants, 69% awarded as loans/jobs. Work study available nights, weekends, and for part-time students.
Students without need: No-need awards available for academics, alumni affiliation, job skills, leadership, minority status.
Scholarships offered: Cream of the Crop Scholarship: up to $20,000; 10 per year; for prospective students with outstanding academic and leadership skills.

FINANCIAL AID PROCEDURES

Forms required: FAFSA.
Dates and Deadlines: Priority date 12/15; no closing date. Applicants notified by 4/1; must reply by 5/1 or within 4 week(s) of notification.

CONTACT

Carol Mulqueen, Director of Financial Aid
1946 Campus Drive, Hyde Park, NY 12538-1499
(845) 451-1243

Daemen College

Amherst, New York
www.daemen.edu   Federal Code: 002808

4-year private liberal arts college in small city.
Enrollment: 1,750 undergrads, 14% part-time. 406 full-time freshmen.
Selectivity: Admits 50 to 75% of applicants.

BASIC COSTS (2009-2010)

Tuition and fees: $20,720.
Per-credit charge: $675.
Room and board: $9,450.

FINANCIAL AID PICTURE (2008-2009)

Students with need: Out of 367 full-time freshmen who applied for aid, 358 were judged to have need. Of these, 358 received aid. For part-time students, average financial aid package was $12,429.
Students without need: 60 full-time freshmen who did not demonstrate need for aid received scholarships/grants; average award was $6,290. No-need awards available for academics, art, athletics, leadership.
Scholarships offered: *Merit:* President's Scholarship, Dean's Scholarship, and Alumni Grant: $2,500-$10,000; renewable awards to freshmen and transfers, based on high school GPA & SAT scores. Competitive and renewable Trustee Scholarship: $17,000 (2 awards) and $14,000 (4 awards). Renewable visual arts scholarships: $5,000; 2 awards. *Athletic:* 18 full-time freshmen received athletic scholarships; average amount $5,055.

FINANCIAL AID PROCEDURES

Forms required: FAFSA, state aid form.
Dates and Deadlines: Priority date 2/15; no closing date. Applicants notified on a rolling basis starting 2/1; must reply within 2 week(s) of notification.

CONTACT

Jeffrey Pagano, Director of Financial Aid
4380 Main Street, Amherst, NY 14226-3592
(716) 839-8254

DeVry College of New York

Long Island City, New York
www.devry.edu   Federal Code: 003099

4-year for-profit business and technical college in very large city.
Enrollment: 1,166 undergrads, 22% part-time. 241 full-time freshmen.

BASIC COSTS (2009-2010)

Tuition and fees: $14,800.
Per-credit charge: $575.

FINANCIAL AID PICTURE (2008-2009)

Students with need: Need-based aid available for full-time and part-time students.
Students without need: This college awards aid only to students with need.

FINANCIAL AID PROCEDURES

Dates and Deadlines: No deadline. Applicants notified on a rolling basis.

CONTACT

Elvira Senese, Director, Student Finance
3020 Thomson Avenue, Long Island City, NY 11101-3051
(718) 472-2728

Dominican College of Blauvelt

Orangeburg, New York
www.dc.edu   Federal Code: 002713

4-year private The College has six divisions: Allied Health, Arts & Sciences, Business, Nursing, Social Sciences, and Teacher Education. in small town.
Enrollment: 1,637 undergrads, 17% part-time. 374 full-time freshmen.
Selectivity: Admits 50 to 75% of applicants.

BASIC COSTS (2010-2011)

Tuition and fees: $21,990.
Per-credit charge: $640.
Room and board: $10,560.

FINANCIAL AID PICTURE (2009-2010)

Students with need: Out of 350 full-time freshmen who applied for aid, 335 were judged to have need. Of these, 335 received aid, and 64 had their full need met. Average financial aid package met 78% of need; average scholarship/grant was $11,829; average loan was $3,270. For part-time students, average financial aid package was $8,355.

Students without need: 45 full-time freshmen who did not demonstrate need for aid received scholarships/grants; average award was $8,050. No-need awards available for academics, athletics.

Scholarships offered: *Merit:* All applicants considered for non-need based scholarships or grants based on high school GPA and SAT/ACT scores. *Athletic:* 29 full-time freshmen received athletic scholarships; average amount $9,223.

Cumulative student debt: 97% of graduating class had student loans; average debt was $18,398.

Additional info: Individual financial aid counseling available.

FINANCIAL AID PROCEDURES

Forms required: FAFSA, state aid form.

Dates and Deadlines: Priority date 2/15; no closing date. Applicants notified on a rolling basis starting 2/1; must reply within 2 week(s) of notification.

CONTACT

Eileen Felske, Director of Financial Aid
470 Western Highway, Orangeburg, NY 10962-1210
(845) 848-7821

Dowling College

Oakdale, New York
www.dowling.edu   Federal Code: 002667

4-year private business and liberal arts college in large town.

Enrollment: 2,681 undergrads, 21% part-time. 527 full-time freshmen.

Selectivity: Admits over 75% of applicants.

BASIC COSTS (2009-2010)

Tuition and fees: $22,850.

Per-credit charge: $698.

Room and board: $10,200.

FINANCIAL AID PICTURE (2009-2010)

Students with need: Need-based aid available for full-time and part-time students. Work study available weekends and for part-time students.

Students without need: No-need awards available for academics, alumni affiliation, athletics.

FINANCIAL AID PROCEDURES

Forms required: FAFSA, state aid form.

Dates and Deadlines: Priority date 4/30; no closing date. Applicants notified on a rolling basis starting 3/1.

Transfers: No deadline. Applicants notified on a rolling basis. Academic scholarships available for transfers with associate degrees.

CONTACT

Patricia Noren, Director of Student Financial Services & Bursar
150 Idle Hour Boulevard, Oakdale, NY 11769-1999
(631) 244-3368

Dutchess Community College

Poughkeepsie, New York
www.sunydutchess.edu   Federal Code: 002864

2-year public community college in large town.

Enrollment: 6,973 undergrads. 1,957 full-time freshmen.

Selectivity: Open admission; but selective for some programs.

BASIC COSTS (2009-2010)

Tuition and fees: $3,320; out-of-state residents $6,220.

Per-credit charge: $125; out-of-state residents $250.

FINANCIAL AID PICTURE (2008-2009)

Students with need: 76% of average financial aid package awarded as scholarships/grants, 24% awarded as loans/jobs. Need-based aid available for part-time students.

Students without need: No-need awards available for academics.

FINANCIAL AID PROCEDURES

Forms required: FAFSA, state aid form, institutional form.

Dates and Deadlines: Priority date 5/1; no closing date. Applicants notified on a rolling basis starting 5/15; must reply within 2 week(s) of notification.

CONTACT

Susan Mead, Director of Financial Aid
53 Pendell Road, Poughkeepsie, NY 12601-1595
(845) 431-8030

D'Youville College

Buffalo, New York
www.dyc.edu   Federal Code: 002712

4-year private health science and liberal arts college in large city.

Enrollment: 1,709 undergrads, 14% part-time. 214 full-time freshmen.

Selectivity: Admits over 75% of applicants.

BASIC COSTS (2009-2010)

Tuition and fees: $20,030.

Per-credit charge: $545.

Room and board: $9,800.

Additional info: Substantial scholarships available depending on SAT/ACT scores.

FINANCIAL AID PICTURE (2008-2009)

Students with need: Out of 207 full-time freshmen who applied for aid, 183 were judged to have need. Of these, 183 received aid, and 52 had their full need met. Average financial aid package met 80% of need; average scholarship/grant was $13,679; average loan was $3,993. For part-time students, average financial aid package was $8,671.

Students without need: 21 full-time freshmen who did not demonstrate need for aid received scholarships/grants; average award was $8,267. No-need awards available for academics, leadership, religious affiliation, ROTC.

Scholarships offered: Presidential Honors Scholarship: for students with 1100 SAT (Math and Verbal) or 24 ACT Composite; covers 50% tuition and 25% of standard double room rate.Academic Initiative Scholarship: For students with 1000-1090 SAT (math & verbal scores only) or 21-23 ACT score and an 85 high school average. The award is for 25% of tuition and 50% of the standard double room rate in Marguerite Hall or 50% of the standard room rate in the apartments for full-time students.Achievement Scholarship: For students with 900-1090 SAT score or 19-23 ACT and an 80-84 high school average, demonstrated leadership and community service. The awards range from $1,000- $4,000.Transfer Achievement Scholarship: For students with a G.P.A. of 2.75-4.0 from previously attended institution(s). The award amounts range from $2,500-$5,000.All awards are renewable for the standard duration of the specific academic program and have GPA and other requirements.

FINANCIAL AID PROCEDURES

Forms required: FAFSA, state aid form.

Dates and Deadlines: Priority date 3/1; no closing date. Applicants notified on a rolling basis starting 4/1; must reply within 2 week(s) of notification.

Transfers: Applicants notified on a rolling basis starting 4/1; must reply within 2 week(s) of notification.

CONTACT
Lorraine Metz, Director of Financial Aid
320 Porter Avenue, Buffalo, NY 14201-1084
(716) 829-7500

Eastman School of Music of the University of Rochester
Rochester, New York
www.esm.rochester.edu   Federal Code: 008124

4-year private music and performing arts college in large city.
Enrollment: 500 undergrads.
Selectivity: Admits less than 50% of applicants.

BASIC COSTS (2009-2010)
Tuition and fees: $38,936.
Per-credit charge: $1,100.
Room and board: $11,920.

FINANCIAL AID PICTURE (2008-2009)
Students with need: Need-based aid available for full-time and part-time students.
Students without need: No-need awards available for academics, alumni affiliation, job skills, leadership, minority status, music/drama, state/district residency.
Scholarships offered: All merit scholarships awarded based on admission criteria, and do not require separate application, audition, or interview.

FINANCIAL AID PROCEDURES
Forms required: FAFSA, state aid form, institutional form.
Dates and Deadlines: Closing date 2/28. Applicants notified on a rolling basis starting 3/15; must reply by 5/1 or within 2 week(s) of notification.
Transfers: No deadline. Applicants notified on a rolling basis starting 3/15; must reply by 5/1 or within 2 week(s) of notification.

CONTACT
Mary Ellen Nugent, Director of Financial Aid
26 Gibbs Street, Rochester, NY 14604-2599
(585) 274-1070

Elmira Business Institute
Elmira, New York
www.ebi-college.com   Federal Code: 009043

2-year for-profit business and technical college in large town.
Enrollment: 164 undergrads, 21% part-time. 51 full-time freshmen.
Selectivity: Open admission.

BASIC COSTS (2009-2010)
Tuition and fees: $10,100.
Per-credit charge: $330.
Additional info: Tuition varies by program.

FINANCIAL AID PICTURE (2008-2009)
Students with need: Need-based aid available for full-time and part-time students.
Students without need: This college awards aid only to students with need.

FINANCIAL AID PROCEDURES
Forms required: FAFSA, state aid form, institutional form.
Dates and Deadlines: Closing date 5/1.

CONTACT
Sue Reinbold, Financial Aid Director
303 North Main Street, Elmira, NY 14901
(607) 729-8915

Elmira Business Institute: Vestal
Vestal, New York
www.ebi-college.com   Federal Code: 009043

2-year for-profit business and technical college in small city.
Enrollment: 141 undergrads, 19% part-time. 31 full-time freshmen.
Selectivity: Open admission.

BASIC COSTS (2009-2010)
Tuition and fees: $10,100.
Per-credit charge: $330.
Additional info: Tuition varies by program. Tuition at time of enrollment locked for 2 years.

FINANCIAL AID PICTURE (2008-2009)
Students with need: Need-based aid available for full-time and part-time students.
Students without need: This college awards aid only to students with need.

FINANCIAL AID PROCEDURES
Forms required: FAFSA, state aid form, institutional form.
Dates and Deadlines: No deadline. Applicants notified on a rolling basis.

CONTACT
Susan Reinbold, Director of Finaical Services
4100 Vestal Road, Vestal, NY 13850

Elmira College
Elmira, New York
www.elmira.edu   Federal Code: 002718

4-year private liberal arts college in large town.
Enrollment: 1,277 undergrads, 18% part-time. 305 full-time freshmen.
Selectivity: Admits over 75% of applicants. GED not accepted.

BASIC COSTS (2010-2011)
Tuition and fees: $35,900.
Room and board: $11,150.

FINANCIAL AID PICTURE (2009-2010)
Students with need: Out of 277 full-time freshmen who applied for aid, 252 were judged to have need. Of these, 252 received aid, and 49 had their full need met. Average financial aid package met 80% of need; average scholarship/grant was $23,653; average loan was $3,266. Need-based aid available for part-time students.
Students without need: 49 full-time freshmen who did not demonstrate need for aid received scholarships/grants; average award was $19,134. No-need awards available for academics, leadership, ROTC, state/district residency.
Scholarships offered: Valedictorian and salutatorian: 20 anticipated awards; full tuition; renewable for four years. Additional scholarships: $23,000, $20,000, $18,000, $12,000 or $10,000; based on GPA, test scores, class rank, leadership; renewable for four years.
Cumulative student debt: 81% of graduating class had student loans; average debt was $26,874.
Additional info: Sibling Scholarship program provides 50% discounts on second immediate family member's room and board, regardless of need.

FINANCIAL AID PROCEDURES
Forms required: FAFSA, state aid form.
Dates and Deadlines: Priority date 2/1; no closing date. Applicants notified on a rolling basis starting 2/1; must reply by 5/1 or within 2 week(s) of notification.
Transfers: No deadline. Applicants notified on a rolling basis starting 2/1; must reply by 5/1 or within 2 week(s) of notification. Award for enrolled U.S.

citizens from outside New York State. New merit scholarship for transfer students.

CONTACT

Kathleen Cohen, Dean of Financial Aid
One Park Place, Elmira, NY 14901
(607) 735-1728

Erie Community College: City Campus

Buffalo, New York
www.ecc.edu   Federal Code: 010684

2-year public community college in large city.
Enrollment: 3,193 undergrads, 19% part-time. 754 full-time freshmen.
Selectivity: Open admission; but selective for some programs.

BASIC COSTS (2009-2010)
Tuition and fees: $3,640; out-of-state residents $6,940.
Per-credit charge: $138; out-of-state residents $276.

FINANCIAL AID PICTURE
Students with need: Need-based aid available for full-time and part-time students. Work study available weekends and for part-time students.
Students without need: This college awards aid only to students with need.

FINANCIAL AID PROCEDURES
Forms required: FAFSA, state aid form.
Dates and Deadlines: Priority date 6/1; no closing date. Applicants notified on a rolling basis starting 4/1; must reply within 2 week(s) of notification.

CONTACT
Scott Weltjen, Director of Financial Aid
121 Ellicott Street, Buffalo, NY 14203-2698
(716) 851-1177

Erie Community College: North

Williamsville, New York
www.ecc.edu   Federal Code: 010684

2-year public community college in small city.
Enrollment: 5,753 undergrads, 23% part-time. 1,191 full-time freshmen.
Selectivity: Open admission; but selective for some programs.

BASIC COSTS (2009-2010)
Tuition and fees: $3,640; out-of-state residents $6,940.
Per-credit charge: $138; out-of-state residents $276.

FINANCIAL AID PICTURE (2008-2009)
Students with need: Need-based aid available for full-time and part-time students. Work study available weekends and for part-time students.
Students without need: This college awards aid only to students with need.

FINANCIAL AID PROCEDURES
Forms required: FAFSA, state aid form.
Dates and Deadlines: Priority date 6/1; no closing date. Applicants notified on a rolling basis starting 4/1; must reply within 2 week(s) of notification.

CONTACT
Scott Weltjen, Director of Financial Aid
6205 Main Street, Williamsville, NY 14221-7095
(716) 851-1477

Erie Community College: South Campus

Orchard Park, New York
www.ecc.edu   Federal Code: 010684

2-year public community college in large town.
Enrollment: 3,447 undergrads, 19% part-time. 896 full-time freshmen.
Selectivity: Open admission; but selective for some programs.

BASIC COSTS (2009-2010)
Tuition and fees: $3,670; out-of-state residents $6,940.
Per-credit charge: $138; out-of-state residents $276.

FINANCIAL AID PICTURE
Students with need: Need-based aid available for full-time and part-time students. Work study available weekends and for part-time students.
Students without need: This college awards aid only to students with need.

FINANCIAL AID PROCEDURES
Forms required: FAFSA, state aid form.
Dates and Deadlines: Priority date 6/1; no closing date. Applicants notified on a rolling basis starting 4/1; must reply within 2 week(s) of notification.

CONTACT
Scott Weltjen, Director of Financial Aid
4041 Southwestern Boulevard, Orchard Park, NY 14127-2199
(716) 851-1677

Eugene Lang College The New School for Liberal Arts

New York, New York
www.lang.edu   Federal Code: 002780

4-year private liberal arts college in very large city.
Enrollment: 1,439 undergrads, 6% part-time. 293 full-time freshmen.
Selectivity: Admits 50 to 75% of applicants.

BASIC COSTS (2010-2011)
Tuition and fees: $36,090.
Per-credit charge: $1,200.
Room and board: $15,260.

FINANCIAL AID PICTURE (2009-2010)
Students with need: Out of 201 full-time freshmen who applied for aid, 173 were judged to have need. Of these, 173 received aid, and 6 had their full need met. Average financial aid package met 75% of need; average scholarship/grant was $23,130; average loan was $9,913.
Students without need: 22 full-time freshmen who did not demonstrate need for aid received scholarships/grants; average award was $2,600. No-need awards available for academics, leadership, music/drama.
Cumulative student debt: 62% of graduating class had student loans; average debt was $25,348.

FINANCIAL AID PROCEDURES
Forms required: FAFSA, state aid form.
Dates and Deadlines: Priority date 3/1; no closing date. Applicants notified on a rolling basis starting 3/1; must reply within 4 week(s) of notification.
Transfers: Must reply within 4 week(s) of notification.

CONTACT
Eileen Doyle, Assistant Vice President for Financial Aid
72 Fifth Avenue, New York, NY 10011
(212) 229-8930

Excelsior College

Albany, New York
www.excelsior.edu   Federal Code: 014251

4-year private virtual liberal arts college in small city.
Enrollment: 30,780 undergrads, 100% part-time.
Selectivity: Open admission; but selective for some programs.

BASIC COSTS (2009-2010)

Additional info: Students charged $895 enrollment fee and $315 per credit hour. Because of nontraditional pricing, school does not charge set tuition based on 15 credit hours per semester.

FINANCIAL AID PICTURE (2008-2009)

Students with need: 45% of average financial aid package awarded as scholarships/grants, 55% awarded as loans/jobs.
Students without need: This college awards aid only to students with need.
Additional info: Excelsior College is Title IV eligible for certain degree programs. College approved·for all veterans educational benefit programs.

FINANCIAL AID PROCEDURES

Forms required: FAFSA, institutional form.
Dates and Deadlines: Priority date 7/1; no closing date. Applicants notified on a rolling basis starting 8/1; must reply within 2 week(s) of notification.

CONTACT

Thomas Dalton, Assistant Vice President for Enrollment Management, Financial Aid
7 Columbia Circle, Albany, NY 12203-5159
(518) 464-8500

Fashion Institute of Technology

New York, New York
www.fitnyc.edu   Federal Code: 002866

4-year public visual arts and business college in very large city.
Enrollment: 7,989 undergrads, 12% part-time. 1,055 full-time freshmen.
Selectivity: Admits less than 50% of applicants.

BASIC COSTS (2009-2010)

Tuition and fees: $4,164; out-of-state residents $11,592.
Per-credit charge: $155; out-of-state residents $464.
Room and board: $11,248.

FINANCIAL AID PICTURE (2009-2010)

Students with need: Need-based aid available for full-time and part-time students.
Students without need: This college awards aid only to students with need.

FINANCIAL AID PROCEDURES

Forms required: FAFSA, state aid form, institutional form.
Dates and Deadlines: Priority date 2/1; no closing date. Applicants notified on a rolling basis starting 4/15; must reply within 2 week(s) of notification.

CONTACT

Mina Friedmann, Director of Financial Aid
Seventh Avenue at 27th Street, New York, NY 10001-5992
(212) 217-7999

Finger Lakes Community College

Canandaigua, New York
www.flcc.edu   Federal Code: 007532

2-year public community college in small town.
Enrollment: 4,692 undergrads, 21% part-time. 1,286 full-time freshmen.
Selectivity: Open admission; but selective for some programs.

BASIC COSTS (2009-2010)

Tuition and fees: $3,706; out-of-state residents $7,002.
Per-credit charge: $126; out-of-state residents $252.

FINANCIAL AID PICTURE (2008-2009)

Students with need: Out of 1,117 full-time freshmen who applied for aid, 994 were judged to have need. Of these, 980 received aid. Need-based aid available for part-time students.
Students without need: This college awards aid only to students with need.

FINANCIAL AID PROCEDURES

Forms required: FAFSA, state aid form.
Dates and Deadlines: Priority date 4/1; no closing date. Applicants notified on a rolling basis starting 3/1; must reply within 2 week(s) of notification.

CONTACT

Susan Romano, Director, Financial Aid
3325 Marvin Sands Drive, Canandaigua, NY 14424-8395
(585) 394-3500 ext. 7275

Five Towns College

Dix Hills, New York
www.ftc.edu   Federal Code: 012561

4-year for-profit music and liberal arts college in large town.
Enrollment: 997 undergrads.
Selectivity: Admits 50 to 75% of applicants.

BASIC COSTS (2009-2010)

Tuition and fees: $17,750.
Per-credit charge: $725.
Room and board: $12,650.

FINANCIAL AID PICTURE (2009-2010)

Students with need: Average financial aid package met 48% of need; average scholarship/grant was $7,800; average loan was $3,500. For part-time students, average financial aid package was $4,500.
Students without need: No-need awards available for academics, music/drama.
Cumulative student debt: 80% of graduating class had student loans; average debt was $19,000.

FINANCIAL AID PROCEDURES

Forms required: FAFSA, state aid form, institutional form.
Dates and Deadlines: Priority date 3/31; no closing date. Applicants notified on a rolling basis; must reply within 4 week(s) of notification.
Transfers: No deadline. Applicants notified on a rolling basis starting 1/1; must reply within 4 week(s) of notification.

CONTACT

Mary Venezia, Director of Financial Aid
305 North Service Road, Dix Hills, NY 11746-6055
(631) 424-7000 ext. 2113

Fordham University

Bronx, New York
www.fordham.edu

Federal Code: 002722
CSS Code: 2259

4-year private university in very large city, affiliated with Roman Catholic Church.
Enrollment: 7,873 undergrads, 7% part-time. 1,812 full-time freshmen.
Selectivity: Admits less than 50% of applicants.

BASIC COSTS (2009-2010)
Tuition and fees: $36,882.
Per-credit charge: $744.
Room and board: $13,716.

FINANCIAL AID PICTURE (2008-2009)
Students with need: Need-based aid available for full-time and part-time students.
Students without need: No-need awards available for academics, athletics, ROTC.

FINANCIAL AID PROCEDURES
Forms required: FAFSA, CSS PROFILE.
Dates and Deadlines: Closing date 2/1. Applicants notified by 3/31; must reply by 5/1 or within 2 week(s) of notification.
Transfers: Priority date 2/1; closing date 5/1.

CONTACT
Angela Van Dekker, Assistant Vice President of Student Financial Services
East 441 Fordham Road, Bronx, NY 10458-9993
(718) 817-3800

Fulton-Montgomery Community College

Johnstown, New York
www.fmcc.suny.edu

Federal Code: 002867

2-year public community college in large town.
Enrollment: 2,149 undergrads, 20% part-time. 713 full-time freshmen.
Selectivity: Open admission; but selective for some programs.

BASIC COSTS (2009-2010)
Tuition and fees: $3,738; out-of-state residents $6,932.
Per-credit charge: $133; out-of-state residents $266.

FINANCIAL AID PICTURE (2008-2009)
Students with need: Need-based aid available for full-time and part-time students. Work study available nights, weekends, and for part-time students.
Students without need: No-need awards available for academics.
Scholarships offered: Academic Excellence Scholarship: $1,000 a year with limit of 2 years for residents of Fulton, Montgomery, or Hamilton or Galway Central School District. Applicants must have 3.5 cumulative GPA, submit an essay and list of extracurricular activities, and be enrolled full-time at college. Must maintain 3.3 cumulative GPA. CTW Scholarship: $1,000 a year with limit of 2 years, for Montgomery residents or applicants who attend high school in Montgomery County. Applicants must have B average. Must maintain 3.3 cumulative GPA at end of first year.

FINANCIAL AID PROCEDURES
Forms required: FAFSA, state aid form.
Dates and Deadlines: Priority date 6/1; no closing date. Applicants notified on a rolling basis starting 6/15; must reply within 2 week(s) of notification.

CONTACT
Rebecca Cozzocrea, Coordinator of Financial Aid
2805 State Highway 67, Johnstown, NY 12095
(518) 762-4651 ext. 8201

Genesee Community College

Batavia, New York
www.genesee.edu

Federal Code: 006782

2-year public community college in large town.
Enrollment: 4,213 undergrads, 22% part-time. 1,084 full-time freshmen.
Selectivity: Open admission; but selective for some programs.

BASIC COSTS (2009-2010)
Tuition and fees: $3,720; out-of-state residents $4,610.
Per-credit charge: $140; out-of-state residents $160.

FINANCIAL AID PICTURE (2008-2009)
Students with need: 55% of average financial aid package awarded as scholarships/grants, 45% awarded as loans/jobs. Need-based aid available for part-time students. Work study available nights, weekends, and for part-time students.

FINANCIAL AID PROCEDURES
Forms required: FAFSA, state aid form.
Dates and Deadlines: Priority date 3/1; closing date 5/1. Applicants notified on a rolling basis starting 4/15; must reply within 2 week(s) of notification.
Transfers: No deadline.

CONTACT
Joseph Bailey, Director of Student Financial Services
One College Road, Batavia, NY 14020-9704
(585) 345-6900

Globe Institute of Technology

New York, New York
www.globe.edu

Federal Code: 025408

4-year for-profit university and business college in very large city.
Enrollment: 542 undergrads.
Selectivity: Open admission; but selective for some programs.

BASIC COSTS (2009-2010)
Tuition and fees: $11,040.
Per-credit charge: $450.
Room and board: $4,500.
Additional info: Tuition/fee waivers available for adults, minority students, unemployed or children of unemployed.

FINANCIAL AID PICTURE (2009-2010)
Students with need: Need-based aid available for full-time and part-time students. Work study available nights, weekends, and for part-time students.
Students without need: No-need awards available for academics, athletics.

FINANCIAL AID PROCEDURES
Forms required: FAFSA, state aid form, institutional form.
Dates and Deadlines: No deadline. Applicants notified on a rolling basis.
Transfers: No deadline. Applicants notified on a rolling basis.

CONTACT
Tatyana Nusenbaum, Director of Financial Aid
500 Seventh Ave, 2nd Floor, New York, NY 10018
(212) 349-4330

Hamilton College

Clinton, New York
www.hamilton.edu

Federal Code: 002728
CSS Code: 2286

4-year private liberal arts college in rural community.
Enrollment: 1,851 undergrads. 466 full-time freshmen.
Selectivity: Admits less than 50% of applicants.

BASIC COSTS (2010-2011)
Tuition and fees: $41,280.
Room and board: $10,480.

FINANCIAL AID PICTURE (2009-2010)
Students with need: Out of 269 full-time freshmen who applied for aid, 207 were judged to have need. Of these, 207 received aid, and 207 had their full need met. Average financial aid package met 100% of need; average scholarship/grant was $34,004; average loan was $2,914.
Students without need: This college awards aid only to students with need.
Cumulative student debt: 46% of graduating class had student loans; average debt was $19,466.
Additional info: Will meet demonstrated need of all aided applicants. Incoming students no longer awarded merit scholarships.

FINANCIAL AID PROCEDURES
Forms required: FAFSA, CSS PROFILE, state aid form, institutional form.
Dates and Deadlines: Closing date 2/8. Applicants notified by 4/1; must reply by 5/1.

CONTACT
Melissa Rose, Director of Financial Aid
198 College Hill Road, Clinton, NY 13323-1293
(315) 859-4413

Hartwick College
Oneonta, New York
www.hartwick.edu   Federal Code: 002729

4-year private liberal arts college in large town.
Enrollment: 1,455 undergrads, 2% part-time. 402 full-time freshmen.
Selectivity: Admits over 75% of applicants.

BASIC COSTS (2010-2011)
Tuition and fees: $35,030.
Per-credit charge: $1,070.
Room and board: $9,345.
Additional info: Reported mandatory fees include $400 matriculation fee for new students.

FINANCIAL AID PICTURE (2008-2009)
Students with need: Need-based aid available for full-time and part-time students. Work study available nights, weekends, and for part-time students.
Students without need: No-need awards available for academics, alumni affiliation, athletics, leadership, state/district residency.

FINANCIAL AID PROCEDURES
Forms required: FAFSA.
Dates and Deadlines: Priority date 2/15; no closing date. Applicants notified by 3/15; must reply within 2 week(s) of notification.
Transfers: Priority date 8/1; no deadline. Applicants notified on a rolling basis starting 3/15; must reply within 2 week(s) of notification.

CONTACT
Melissa Allen, Director of Financial Aid
Box 4022, Oneonta, NY 13820-4022
(607) 431-4130

Helene Fuld College of Nursing
New York, New York
www.helenefuld.edu   Federal Code: 015395

2-year private nursing and junior college in very large city.
Enrollment: 431 undergrads, 66% part-time. 20 full-time freshmen.

BASIC COSTS (2009-2010)
Tuition and fees: $15,526.

FINANCIAL AID PICTURE (2008-2009)
Students with need: Need-based aid available for full-time and part-time students.
Students without need: This college awards aid only to students with need.

FINANCIAL AID PROCEDURES
Forms required: FAFSA, state aid form.
Dates and Deadlines: No deadline. Applicants notified on a rolling basis.

CONTACT
Andrine Thomas, Financial Aid Counselor and Loan Coordinator
24 East 120th Street, New York, NY 10035
(212) 616-7253

Herkimer County Community College
Herkimer, New York
www.herkimer.edu   Federal Code: 004788

2-year public community college in small town.
Enrollment: 2,869 undergrads.
Selectivity: Open admission; but selective for some programs.

BASIC COSTS (2009-2010)
Tuition and fees: $3,760; out-of-state residents $6,120.
Per-credit charge: $120; out-of-state residents $233.
Additional info: Apartment-style dorms with a la carte meal service available. Tuition/fee waivers available for unemployed or children of unemployed.

FINANCIAL AID PICTURE
Students with need: Need-based aid available for full-time and part-time students. Work study available nights, weekends, and for part-time students.

FINANCIAL AID PROCEDURES
Forms required: FAFSA, state aid form.
Dates and Deadlines: Closing date 4/1. Applicants notified on a rolling basis starting 4/1; must reply within 2 week(s) of notification.

CONTACT
Susan Tripp, Director of Financial Aid
100 Reservoir Road, Herkimer, NY 13350-1598
(315) 866-0300 ext. 8282

Hilbert College
Hamburg, New York
www.hilbert.edu   Federal Code: 002735

4-year private liberal arts college in large town, affiliated with Roman Catholic Church.
Enrollment: 959 undergrads, 19% part-time. 229 full-time freshmen.
Selectivity: Admits over 75% of applicants.

BASIC COSTS (2009-2010)
Tuition and fees: $17,950.
Per-credit charge: $410.
Room and board: $7,700.
Additional info: Tuition/fee waivers available for minority students.

FINANCIAL AID PICTURE (2008-2009)
Students with need: Out of 225 full-time freshmen who applied for aid, 208 were judged to have need. Of these, 208 received aid, and 32 had their full need met. Average financial aid package met 69% of need; average scholarship/grant was $8,520; average loan was $3,994. For part-time students, average financial aid package was $7,121.

Students without need: 16 full-time freshmen who did not demonstrate need for aid received scholarships/grants; average award was $3,468. No-need awards available for academics, alumni affiliation, leadership, minority status, state/district residency.

Cumulative student debt: 100% of graduating class had student loans; average debt was $20,193.

FINANCIAL AID PROCEDURES

Forms required: FAFSA, state aid form.

Dates and Deadlines: Priority date 3/1; no closing date. Applicants notified on a rolling basis starting 3/1; must reply within 2 week(s) of notification.

CONTACT

Beverly Chudy, Director of Student Financial Aid
5200 South Park Avenue, Hamburg, NY 14075-1597
(716) 649-7900

Hobart and William Smith Colleges

Geneva, New York   Federal Code: 002731
www.hws.edu   CSS Code: 2294

4-year private liberal arts college in large town.
Enrollment: 2,093 undergrads. 448 full-time freshmen.
Selectivity: Admits 50 to 75% of applicants.

BASIC COSTS (2009-2010)

Tuition and fees: $40,221.
Room and board: $10,024.

FINANCIAL AID PICTURE (2008-2009)

Students with need: Out of 400 full-time freshmen who applied for aid, 328 were judged to have need. Of these, 323 received aid, and 71 had their full need met. Average financial aid package met 81% of need; average scholarship/grant was $25,109; average loan was $3,043.

Students without need: 113 full-time freshmen who did not demonstrate need for aid received scholarships/grants; average award was $13,046. No-need awards available for academics, art, leadership, music/drama.

Scholarships offered: Cornelius and Muriel P. Wood Scholarship and Richard Hersh Scholarship: full tuition for 4 years. Trustee Scholarship for Academic Excellence: $20,000 annually, for 4 years; based on GPA, test scores, class standing. Faculty Scholarships: $3,000-$15,000. Phi Theta Kappa Trustee Scholarship: $2,500-$20,000 annually; for academically qualified transfer students with 2-year degree from junior or community college. Presidential Leaders and Service Scholarships: $3,000-$12,000; based on academic excellence, leadership, service, personal qualities. Arts Scholarships: $3,000-$15,000; for special talent in visual and performing arts; 20 awarded. Blackwell Medical Scholarships: full tuition for 4 years; MCAT waived, guaranteed seat at Upstate Medical Center at Syracuse University.

Cumulative student debt: 85% of graduating class had student loans; average debt was $31,567.

FINANCIAL AID PROCEDURES

Forms required: FAFSA, CSS PROFILE, state aid form.

Dates and Deadlines: Closing date 2/15. Applicants notified by 4/1; must reply by 5/1 or within 2 week(s) of notification.

Transfers: No deadline. Applicants notified on a rolling basis; must reply within 2 week(s) of notification.

CONTACT

Beth Turner, Director of Financial Aid Services
629 South Main Street, Geneva, NY 14456
(315) 781-3315

Hofstra University

Hempstead, New York
www.hofstra.edu   Federal Code: 002732

4-year private university in large city.
Enrollment: 7,756 undergrads, 6% part-time. 1,650 full-time freshmen.
Selectivity: Admits 50 to 75% of applicants.

BASIC COSTS (2009-2010)

Tuition and fees: $30,130.
Per-credit charge: $890.
Room and board: $11,330.

FINANCIAL AID PICTURE (2008-2009)

Students with need: Out of 1,338 full-time freshmen who applied for aid, 1,048 were judged to have need. Of these, 1,037 received aid, and 198 had their full need met. Average financial aid package met 55% of need; average scholarship/grant was $11,578; average loan was $3,393. For part-time students, average financial aid package was $8,301.

Students without need: 351 full-time freshmen who did not demonstrate need for aid received scholarships/grants; average award was $11,152. No-need awards available for academics, art, athletics, leadership, music/drama, ROTC, state/district residency.

Scholarships offered: *Merit:* Distinguished Academic Scholar Program; full tuition; number awarded varies. Presidential Scholarship; partial tuition; number awarded varies; for students with high academic achievement. *Athletic:* 12 full-time freshmen received athletic scholarships; average amount $25,075.

FINANCIAL AID PROCEDURES

Forms required: FAFSA, state aid form.

Dates and Deadlines: Priority date 2/15; no closing date. Applicants notified on a rolling basis starting 3/1; must reply by 5/1 or within 2 week(s) of notification.

CONTACT

Sandra Filbry, Director of Financial Aid
Admissions Center, 100 Hofstra University, Hempstead, NY 11549
(516) 463-8000

Houghton College

Houghton, New York
www.houghton.edu   Federal Code: 002734

4-year private liberal arts college in rural community, affiliated with Wesleyan Church.
Enrollment: 1,270 undergrads, 2% part-time. 284 full-time freshmen.
Selectivity: Admits over 75% of applicants.

BASIC COSTS (2010-2011)

Tuition and fees: $25,360.
Per-credit charge: $1,065.
Room and board: $7,330.
Additional info: Tuition/fee waivers available for minority students.

FINANCIAL AID PICTURE (2009-2010)

Students with need: Out of 259 full-time freshmen who applied for aid, 230 were judged to have need. Of these, 230 received aid, and 46 had their full need met. Average financial aid package met 79% of need; average scholarship/grant was $15,549; average loan was $4,482. For part-time students, average financial aid package was $5,793.

Students without need: 54 full-time freshmen who did not demonstrate need for aid received scholarships/grants; average award was $9,091. No-need awards available for academics, alumni affiliation, art, athletics, music/drama, religious affiliation, ROTC, state/district residency.

Scholarships offered: *Merit:* Excellence Scholarships: $1,250-$7,500; Chamberlain Scholarships: $10,000; Heritage Scholarships: $15,000; 6 awarded each year. Phi Theta Kappa Transfer Scholarship: $2,000; Art Scholarships: $1,000-$5,000 (based on art portfolio); Music Scholarships: $1,000-$12,500 (based on audition). *Athletic:* 3 full-time freshmen received athletic scholarships; average amount $5,948.

Additional info: Wesley Full Tuition Grant offered to 25 new students each year. Covers the balance of tuition after all state and federal aid is awarded.

FINANCIAL AID PROCEDURES

Forms required: FAFSA.

Dates and Deadlines: Priority date 3/1; no closing date. Applicants notified on a rolling basis starting 3/15; must reply by 5/1.

Transfers: No deadline. Applicants notified on a rolling basis starting 3/1; must reply by 5/1 or within 4 week(s) of notification.

CONTACT

Troy Martin, Director of Student Financial Services
1 Willard Avenue/PO Box 128, Houghton, NY 14744-0128
(585) 567-9328

Institute of Design and Construction
Brooklyn, New York
www.idc.edu   Federal Code: 012107

2-year private junior and technical college in very large city.

Enrollment: 141 undergrads. 33 full-time freshmen.

Selectivity: Open admission.

BASIC COSTS (2010-2011)

Tuition and fees: $9,040.

Per-credit charge: $300.

FINANCIAL AID PICTURE (2008-2009)

Students with need: Out of 28 full-time freshmen who applied for aid, 22 were judged to have need. Of these, 22 received aid. Average financial aid package met 35% of need.

FINANCIAL AID PROCEDURES

Forms required: FAFSA, state aid form, institutional form.

Dates and Deadlines: No deadline. Applicants notified on a rolling basis starting 3/1; must reply within 4 week(s) of notification.

Transfers: No deadline.

CONTACT

John Anselmo, Director of Financial Aid
141 Willoughby Street, Brooklyn, NY 11201-5380
(718) 855-3661

Iona College
New Rochelle, New York
www.iona.edu   Federal Code: 002737

4-year private business and liberal arts college in small city, affiliated with Roman Catholic Church.

Enrollment: 3,314 undergrads, 2% part-time. 792 full-time freshmen.

Selectivity: Admits 50 to 75% of applicants.

BASIC COSTS (2010-2011)

Tuition and fees: $28,850.

Per-credit charge: $892.

Room and board: $11,800.

FINANCIAL AID PICTURE (2009-2010)

Students with need: Out of 783 full-time freshmen who applied for aid, 630 were judged to have need. Of these, 630 received aid, and 129 had their full need met. Average financial aid package met 31% of need; average scholarship/grant was $6,039; average loan was $3,077. For part-time students, average financial aid package was $3,739.

Students without need: 144 full-time freshmen who did not demonstrate need for aid received scholarships/grants; average award was $10,964. No-need awards available for academics, alumni affiliation, athletics, ROTC.

Scholarships offered: 64 full-time freshmen received athletic scholarships; average amount $13,800.

Cumulative student debt: 68% of graduating class had student loans; average debt was $24,213.

FINANCIAL AID PROCEDURES

Forms required: FAFSA, state aid form, institutional form.

Dates and Deadlines: Closing date 4/15. Applicants notified on a rolling basis starting 12/20; must reply by 5/1 or within 2 week(s) of notification.

Transfers: No deadline. Applicants notified on a rolling basis; must reply within 2 week(s) of notification.

CONTACT

Mary Grant, Director of Financial Aid
715 North Avenue, New Rochelle, NY 10801-1890
(914) 633-2497

Island Drafting and Technical Institute
Amityville, New York
www.idti.edu   Federal Code: 007375

2-year for-profit technical and career college in large town.

Enrollment: 137 undergrads.

Selectivity: Open admission.

BASIC COSTS (2009-2010)

Tuition and fees: $14,600.

Per-credit charge: $475.

FINANCIAL AID PICTURE

Students with need: Need-based aid available for full-time students.

Students without need: This college awards aid only to students with need.

FINANCIAL AID PROCEDURES

Dates and Deadlines: No deadline. Applicants notified on a rolling basis.

CONTACT

Daniel Greener, Financial Aid Office
128 Broadway, Amityville, NY 11701-2704
(631) 691-8733

Ithaca College
Ithaca, New York   Federal Code: 002739
www.ithaca.edu   CSS Code: 2325

4-year private health science and liberal arts college in large town.

Enrollment: 6,400 undergrads, 1% part-time. 2,027 full-time freshmen.

Selectivity: Admits over 75% of applicants.

BASIC COSTS (2010-2011)

Tuition and fees: $33,630.

Per-credit charge: $1,121.

Room and board: $12,314.

Additional info: Tuition/fee waivers available for minority students.

FINANCIAL AID PICTURE (2009-2010)

Students with need: Out of 1,777 full-time freshmen who applied for aid, 1,497 were judged to have need. Of these, 1,497 received aid, and 939 had their full need met. Average financial aid package met 93% of need; average scholarship/grant was $19,799; average loan was $5,746. For part-time students, average financial aid package was $11,219.

Students without need: 389 full-time freshmen who did not demonstrate need for aid received scholarships/grants; average award was $8,718. No-need awards available for academics, alumni affiliation, leadership, minority status, music/drama, ROTC.

Scholarships offered: President's Scholarship: $12,500-$15,000; approximately top 10% of applicants. Dean's Scholarship: $7,500-$10,000; approximately top 11% to 35% of applicants. ALANA Scholarship: $2,500-$5,000; for representatives of minority groups who show excellent academic achievement. Flora Brown Award: $5,000; given to those who deserve recognition. MLK Scholarship: $18,000; academic excellence and community service involvement; approximately 15. Ithaca Leadership Scholarship: $7,000; demonstrated record of leadership and above average academic performance; approximately 80. Ithaca Premier Talent Scholarship: maximum $16,000; for music and theater majors; approximately 10. Park Scholar Achievement award: full cost of attendance; outstanding achievement in communications; approximately 20. Ithaca College Merit Scholarship and Ithaca College National Merit Recognition Award: $2,000 plus Ithaca College President's Scholarship of $16,000; for students who designate Ithaca their first-choice institution.

FINANCIAL AID PROCEDURES

Forms required: FAFSA, CSS PROFILE.

Dates and Deadlines: Priority date 2/1; no closing date. Applicants notified on a rolling basis starting 2/15.

Transfers: No deadline. Applicants notified on a rolling basis starting 2/15; must reply by 5/1. All need-based and merit awards available for freshmen are also available for transfers.

CONTACT

Larry Chambers, Director of Student Financial Services
953 Danby Road, Ithaca, NY 14850-7000
(607) 274-3131

Jamestown Business College

Jamestown, New York
www.jamestownbusinesscollege.edu Federal Code: 008495

2-year for-profit business and junior college in large town.

Enrollment: 329 undergrads. 90 full-time freshmen.

Selectivity: Admits over 75% of applicants.

BASIC COSTS (2009-2010)

Tuition and fees: $10,800.

FINANCIAL AID PICTURE (2008-2009)

Students with need: 59% of average financial aid package awarded as scholarships/grants, 41% awarded as loans/jobs. Need-based aid available for part-time students.

Students without need: No-need awards available for academics.

FINANCIAL AID PROCEDURES

Forms required: FAFSA, state aid form.

Dates and Deadlines: No deadline. Applicants notified on a rolling basis starting 2/15.

Transfers: Priority date 3/1; no deadline. Applicants notified on a rolling basis starting 5/1.

CONTACT

Diane Sturzenbecker, Financial Aid Officer
7 Fairmount Avenue, Jamestown, NY 14702-0429
(716) 664-5100

Jamestown Community College

Jamestown, New York
www.sunyjcc.edu   Federal Code: 002869

2-year public community college in large town.

Enrollment: 3,661 undergrads, 23% part-time. 1,146 full-time freshmen.

Selectivity: Open admission; but selective for some programs.

BASIC COSTS (2009-2010)

Tuition and fees: $4,115; out-of-state residents $7,755.

Per-credit charge: $151; out-of-state residents $272.

FINANCIAL AID PICTURE (2009-2010)

Students with need: Out of 1,081 full-time freshmen who applied for aid, 895 were judged to have need. Of these, 895 received aid. Need-based aid available for part-time students.

Students without need: 39 full-time freshmen who did not demonstrate need for aid received scholarships/grants; average award was $3,400. No-need awards available for academics, alumni affiliation, art, athletics, music/drama, state/district residency.

Scholarships offered: 100% resident tuition scholarship (less federal and state grants) for students who apply for admissions by 3/1 and are in the top 20% of their high school graduating class with Regents diploma if residents of Chautauqua, Cattaraugus, or Allegany counties. Guaranteed in-state tuition rate for students in Warren, Potter, McKean, Forest, Elk and Cameron counties in Pennsylvania, in top 20% of graduating class with an academic diploma.

FINANCIAL AID PROCEDURES

Forms required: FAFSA, state aid form.

Dates and Deadlines: Priority date 3/1; no closing date. Applicants notified on a rolling basis starting 4/15.

CONTACT

Laurie Vorp, Director of Financial Aid
525 Falconer Street, Jamestown, NY 14702-0020
(800) 388-8557

Jefferson Community College

Watertown, New York
www.sunyjefferson.edu   Federal Code: 002870

2-year public community college in large town.

Enrollment: 2,627 undergrads, 24% part-time. 773 full-time freshmen.

Selectivity: Open admission; but selective for some programs.

BASIC COSTS (2009-2010)

Tuition and fees: $3,780; out-of-state residents $5,628.

Per-credit charge: $138; out-of-state residents $215.

FINANCIAL AID PICTURE (2009-2010)

Students with need: Need-based aid available for full-time and part-time students.

Students without need: This college awards aid only to students with need.

FINANCIAL AID PROCEDURES

Forms required: FAFSA, state aid form, institutional form.

Dates and Deadlines: Priority date 4/1; closing date 8/15. Applicants notified on a rolling basis starting 4/15; must reply within 2 week(s) of notification.

Transfers: No deadline.

CONTACT

James Ambrose, Director of Financial Aid
1220 Coffeen Street, Watertown, NY 13601
(315) 786-2355

Jewish Theological Seminary of America
New York, New York
www.jtsa.edu   CSS Code: 2339

4-year private rabbinical and seminary college in very large city, affiliated with Jewish faith.

Enrollment: 177 undergrads, 6% part-time. 40 full-time freshmen.
Selectivity: Admits 50 to 75% of applicants. GED not accepted.

BASIC COSTS (2009-2010)
Tuition and fees: $15,000.
Per-credit charge: $750.
Room only: $9,200.
Additional info: Costs quoted paid to school only; separate costs assessed for dual-degree enrollment at Columbia University/Barnard College.

FINANCIAL AID PICTURE (2009-2010)
Students with need: Need-based aid available for full-time students.
Students without need: No-need awards available for academics, alumni affiliation, leadership.

FINANCIAL AID PROCEDURES
Forms required: FAFSA, CSS PROFILE, state aid form, institutional form.
Dates and Deadlines: Priority date 2/1; closing date 3/1. Applicants notified on a rolling basis starting 4/1; must reply within 4 week(s) of notification.

CONTACT
Linda Levine, Registrar/Director of Financial Aid
3080 Broadway, New York, NY 10027
(212) 678-8007

Juilliard School
New York, New York
www.juilliard.edu   Federal Code: 002742

4-year private music and performing arts college in very large city.
Enrollment: 489 undergrads. 102 full-time freshmen.
Selectivity: Admits less than 50% of applicants.

BASIC COSTS (2009-2010)
Tuition and fees: $30,500.
Room and board: $11,810.

FINANCIAL AID PICTURE (2009-2010)
Students with need: Out of 101 full-time freshmen who applied for aid, 80 were judged to have need. Of these, 80 received aid, and 19 had their full need met. Average financial aid package met 75% of need; average scholarship/grant was $22,359; average loan was $3,333. Need-based aid available for part-time students.
Students without need: 5 full-time freshmen who did not demonstrate need for aid received scholarships/grants; average award was $15,600. No-need awards available for music/drama.
Cumulative student debt: 64% of graduating class had student loans; average debt was $26,780.

FINANCIAL AID PROCEDURES
Forms required: FAFSA, institutional form.
Dates and Deadlines: Closing date 3/1. Applicants notified by 4/1; must reply by 5/1.
Transfers: Applicants notified by 4/1; must reply by 5/1 or within 2 week(s) of notification.

CONTACT
Tina Gonzalez, Director of Financial Aid
60 Lincoln Center Plaza, New York, NY 10023-6588
(212) 799-5000 ext. 211

Keuka College
Keuka Park, New York
www.keuka.edu   Federal Code: 002744

4-year private liberal arts college in rural community, affiliated with American Baptist Churches in the USA.

Enrollment: 1,522 undergrads, 20% part-time. 247 full-time freshmen.
Selectivity: Admits over 75% of applicants.

BASIC COSTS (2010-2011)
Tuition and fees: $23,920.
Per-credit charge: $770.
Room and board: $9,500.

FINANCIAL AID PICTURE (2009-2010)
Students with need: Out of 240 full-time freshmen who applied for aid, 225 were judged to have need. Of these, 225 received aid, and 18 had their full need met. Average financial aid package met 70% of need; average scholarship/grant was $14,052; average loan was $5,087. For part-time students, average financial aid package was $5,034.
Students without need: 17 full-time freshmen who did not demonstrate need for aid received scholarships/grants; average award was $8,039. No-need awards available for academics, alumni affiliation, leadership, minority status, religious affiliation.
Scholarships offered: Goals Scholarship: 1/2 tuition; 82 average and 1000 SAT or 22 ACT required. Dean's Scholarship: 1/2-full tuition; 82 average and 1000 SAT or 22 ACT required. Presidential Scholarship: full tuition; based on GPA, SAT scores, class rank. SAT scores listed are exclusive of Writing portion.
Cumulative student debt: 95% of graduating class had student loans; average debt was $16,119.

FINANCIAL AID PROCEDURES
Forms required: FAFSA.
Dates and Deadlines: Priority date 3/15; no closing date. Applicants notified on a rolling basis starting 3/1; must reply by 5/1 or within 2 week(s) of notification.

CONTACT
Jerry Hiller, Vice President of Finance and Administration
141 Cental Avenue, Keuka Park, NY 14478-0098
(315) 279-5232

King's College
New York, New York
www.tkc.edu   Federal Code: 040953

4-year private liberal arts college in very large city, affiliated with nondenominational tradition.

Enrollment: 298 undergrads, 3% part-time. 103 full-time freshmen.
Selectivity: Admits 50 to 75% of applicants.

BASIC COSTS (2010-2011)
Tuition and fees: $27,350.
Per-credit charge: $1,125.
Room only: $10,500.

FINANCIAL AID PICTURE (2009-2010)
Students with need: Out of 91 full-time freshmen who applied for aid, 78 were judged to have need. Of these, 78 received aid, and 10 had their full need met. Average financial aid package met 63% of need; average scholarship/grant was $17,776; average loan was $3,500. For part-time students, average financial aid package was $9,780.
Students without need: 25 full-time freshmen who did not demonstrate need for aid received scholarships/grants; average award was $15,457. No-need awards available for academics, leadership.

Scholarships offered: Presidential Scholarships: unlimited number; based on SAT/ACT and National Merit; $1,500 to $8,000. Founders Scholarships: 4 awards; $10,000 each; based on essay and presentation; competition held in February.

Cumulative student debt: 79% of graduating class had student loans; average debt was $15,434.

FINANCIAL AID PROCEDURES

Forms required: FAFSA.

Dates and Deadlines: No deadline. Applicants notified on a rolling basis starting 2/15.

CONTACT

Anna Peters, Director of Financial Aid

350 Fifth Avenue, Lower Lobby, New York, NY 10118

(212) 659-7281

Laboratory Institute of Merchandising

New York, New York

www.limcollege.edu   Federal Code: 007466

4-year for-profit college of fashion business in very large city.

Enrollment: 1,357 undergrads.

Selectivity: Admits 50 to 75% of applicants.

BASIC COSTS (2009-2010)

Tuition and fees: $20,425.

Per-credit charge: $665.

Room and board: $19,400.

FINANCIAL AID PICTURE (2008-2009)

Students with need: Need-based aid available for full-time and part-time students.

Students without need: This college awards aid only to students with need.

FINANCIAL AID PROCEDURES

Forms required: FAFSA, state aid form, institutional form.

Dates and Deadlines: Priority date 4/1; no closing date. Applicants notified on a rolling basis starting 2/15; must reply within 2 week(s) of notification.

CONTACT

Christopher Barto, Dean of Student Financial Services

12 East 53rd Street, New York, NY 10022

(212) 752-1530

Le Moyne College

Syracuse, New York

www.lemoyne.edu   Federal Code: 002748

4-year private liberal arts college in small city, affiliated with Roman Catholic Church.

Enrollment: 2,465 undergrads, 6% part-time. 544 full-time freshmen.

Selectivity: Admits 50 to 75% of applicants.

BASIC COSTS (2010-2011)

Tuition and fees: $27,340.

Per-credit charge: $552.

Room and board: $10,480.

FINANCIAL AID PICTURE (2008-2009)

Students with need: Out of 511 full-time freshmen who applied for aid, 451 were judged to have need. Of these, 451 received aid, and 133 had their full need met. Average financial aid package met 81% of need; average scholarship/grant was $11,013; average loan was $3,588. For part-time students, average financial aid package was $5,742.

Students without need: 54 full-time freshmen who did not demonstrate need for aid received scholarships/grants; average award was $10,399. No-need awards available for academics, alumni affiliation, athletics, leadership, minority status, ROTC.

Scholarships offered: *Merit:* Presidential Scholarships: $20,000. Dean Scholarships: $15,000. Ignation Scholarships (Jesuit High Schools): $15,000. Leadership Scholarships: $11,000; all based on academic criteria (GPA, rank, test scores). Loyola Scholarships: $15,000; for students of color; based on academic criteria. Phi Theta Kappa members receive an additional $2,500 per academic year. *Athletic:* 45 full-time freshmen received athletic scholarships; average amount $6,652.

Cumulative student debt: 84% of graduating class had student loans; average debt was $27,483.

Additional info: Parent loan program at low interest, monthly payment plans and alternative loans for students.

FINANCIAL AID PROCEDURES

Forms required: FAFSA, state aid form, institutional form.

Dates and Deadlines: Priority date 2/1; no closing date. Applicants notified by 3/15; must reply by 5/1 or within 2 week(s) of notification.

Transfers: Priority date 6/1; no deadline. Must reply by 5/1 or within 2 week(s) of notification.

CONTACT

William Cheetham, Director of Financial Aid

1419 Salt Springs Road, Syracuse, NY 13214-1301

(315) 445-4400

Long Island Business Institute

Commack, New York

www.libi.edu   Federal Code: 014514

2-year for-profit business college in large town.

Enrollment: 628 undergrads, 34% part-time. 147 full-time freshmen.

Selectivity: Admits over 75% of applicants.

BASIC COSTS (2009-2010)

Tuition and fees: $10,350.

FINANCIAL AID PICTURE (2009-2010)

Students with need: Need-based aid available for full-time and part-time students. Work study available nights.

Students without need: No-need awards available for academics.

FINANCIAL AID PROCEDURES

Forms required: FAFSA, state aid form.

Dates and Deadlines: No deadline. Must reply within 2 week(s) of notification.

Transfers: No deadline.

CONTACT

Nazaret Kiregian, Director of Financial Aid

6500 Jericho Turnpike, Commack, NY 11725

(631) 499-7100 ext. 13

Long Island University: Brooklyn Campus

Brooklyn, New York

www.liu.edu   Federal Code: 004779

4-year private university and liberal arts college in very large city.

Enrollment: 4,873 undergrads, 14% part-time. 1,027 full-time freshmen.

Selectivity: Admits 50 to 75% of applicants.

BASIC COSTS (2009-2010)

Tuition and fees: $28,730.

Per-credit charge: $854.

Room and board: $10,450.

FINANCIAL AID PICTURE (2009-2010)

Students with need: Need-based aid available for full-time and part-time students.

FINANCIAL AID PROCEDURES

Forms required: FAFSA.

Dates and Deadlines: Priority date 3/15; closing date 5/1. Applicants notified on a rolling basis.

CONTACT

Rose Iannicelli, Dean of Student Financial Services
1 University Plaza, Brooklyn, NY 11201-8423
(718) 488-1037

Long Island University: C. W. Post Campus

Brookville, New York
www.liu.edu   Federal Code: 002751

4-year private university and liberal arts college in small town.
Enrollment: 4,558 undergrads, 11% part-time. 835 full-time freshmen.
Selectivity: Admits over 75% of applicants.

BASIC COSTS (2009-2010)

Tuition and fees: $28,768.
Per-credit charge: $854.
Room and board: $10,942.

FINANCIAL AID PICTURE (2009-2010)

Students with need: Need-based aid available for full-time and part-time students. Work study available nights, weekends, and for part-time students.

FINANCIAL AID PROCEDURES

Forms required: FAFSA.

Dates and Deadlines: Priority date 3/1; no closing date. Applicants notified on a rolling basis starting 3/1; must reply by 5/1.

Transfers: Applicants notified on a rolling basis starting 3/1; must reply by 5/1.

CONTACT

Karen Urdahl, Director of Financial Assistance
720 Northern Boulevard, Brookville, NY 11548-1300
(516) 299-2338

Manhattan College

Riverdale, New York
www.manhattan.edu   Federal Code: 002758

4-year private engineering and liberal arts college in very large city, affiliated with Roman Catholic Church.
Enrollment: 3,049 undergrads, 3% part-time. 773 full-time freshmen.
Selectivity: Admits 50 to 75% of applicants.

BASIC COSTS (2009-2010)

Tuition and fees: $26,000.
Room and board: $10,160.
Additional info: Program fees range from $1,700 to $2,700 depending on program.

FINANCIAL AID PICTURE (2009-2010)

Students with need: Need-based aid available for full-time students. Work study available nights, weekends, and for part-time students.
Students without need: This college awards aid only to students with need.

FINANCIAL AID PROCEDURES

Forms required: FAFSA.

Dates and Deadlines: Priority date 3/1; closing date 4/1. Applicants notified on a rolling basis starting 2/15; must reply by 5/1.

Transfers: Priority date 4/1; no deadline.

CONTACT

Ed Keough, Director of Student Financial Services
4513 Manhattan College Parkway, Riverdale, NY 10471
(718) 862-7100

Manhattan School of Music

New York, New York   Federal Code: 002759
www.msmnyc.edu   CSS Code: 2396

4-year private music college in very large city.
Enrollment: 392 undergrads, 1% part-time. 104 full-time freshmen.
Selectivity: Admits less than 50% of applicants.

BASIC COSTS (2010-2011)

Tuition and fees: $32,815.
Per-credit charge: $1,300.
Room and board: $11,480.
Additional info: Health fees approximately $2,200 additional unless already insured.

FINANCIAL AID PICTURE (2008-2009)

Students with need: Out of 64 full-time freshmen who applied for aid, 51 were judged to have need. Of these, 51 received aid, and 5 had their full need met. Average financial aid package met 36% of need; average scholarship/grant was $12,572; average loan was $3,873. For part-time students, average financial aid package was $8,047.
Students without need: 31 full-time freshmen who did not demonstrate need for aid received scholarships/grants; average award was $14,469. No-need awards available for academics, alumni affiliation, leadership, music/drama.
Cumulative student debt: 54% of graduating class had student loans; average debt was $16,715.

FINANCIAL AID PROCEDURES

Forms required: FAFSA, CSS PROFILE, institutional form.

Dates and Deadlines: Closing date 3/1. Applicants notified by 4/1; must reply by 5/1 or within 2 week(s) of notification.

Transfers: Applicants notified by 4/1; must reply by 5/1 or within 2 week(s) of notification. CSS PROFILE required for transfer students.

CONTACT

Patricia Zumaran, Associate Dean for Enrollment Management
120 Claremont Avenue, New York, NY 10027-4698
(212) 749-2802 ext. 4463

Manhattanville College

Purchase, New York
www.manhattanville.edu   Federal Code: 002760

4-year private liberal arts and teachers college in small town.
Enrollment: 1,781 undergrads, 4% part-time. 489 full-time freshmen.
Selectivity: Admits 50 to 75% of applicants.

BASIC COSTS (2010-2011)

Tuition and fees: $34,350.
Per-credit charge: $765.
Room and board: $13,920.

FINANCIAL AID PICTURE (2008-2009)

Students with need: Out of 377 full-time freshmen who applied for aid, 346 were judged to have need. Of these, 346 received aid, and 33 had their full need met. Average financial aid package met 99% of need; average scholarship/grant was $18,740; average loan was $3,927. For part-time students, average financial aid package was $4,084.

Students without need: 117 full-time freshmen who did not demonstrate need for aid received scholarships/grants; average award was $20,812. No-need awards available for academics, alumni affiliation, art, leadership, music/drama.

Cumulative student debt: 53% of graduating class had student loans; average debt was $23,138.

Additional info: Upper level students may earn additional money and academic credit through internship program.

FINANCIAL AID PROCEDURES

Forms required: FAFSA, state aid form.

Dates and Deadlines: Closing date 3/1. Applicants notified on a rolling basis starting 2/1; must reply by 5/1 or within 2 week(s) of notification.

Transfers: No deadline.

CONTACT

Maria Barlaam, Director of Financial Aid
2900 Purchase Street, Purchase, NY 10577
(914) 323-5357

Mannes College The New School for Music
New York, New York
www.mannes.edu   Federal Code: 002780

4-year private music college in very large city.

Enrollment: 207 undergrads, 8% part-time. 47 full-time freshmen.

Selectivity: Admits less than 50% of applicants.

BASIC COSTS (2010-2011)

Tuition and fees: $35,100.

Per-credit charge: $1,125.

Room and board: $15,260.

FINANCIAL AID PICTURE (2009-2010)

Students with need: Out of 13 full-time freshmen who applied for aid, 11 were judged to have need. Of these, 11 received aid. Average financial aid package met 54% of need; average scholarship/grant was $12,079; average loan was $10,636.

Students without need: 2 full-time freshmen who did not demonstrate need for aid received scholarships/grants; average award was $22,585. No-need awards available for music/drama.

Cumulative student debt: 71% of graduating class had student loans; average debt was $30,942.

Additional info: Closing date for scholarship applications 2 weeks prior to audition date.

FINANCIAL AID PROCEDURES

Forms required: FAFSA, state aid form.

Dates and Deadlines: Priority date 3/1; no closing date. Applicants notified on a rolling basis starting 3/1; must reply within 4 week(s) of notification.

CONTACT

Eileen Doyle, Executive Director of Undergraduate Financial Aid
150 West 85th Street, New York, NY 10024
(212) 229-8930

Maria College
Albany, New York
www.mariacollege.edu   Federal Code: 002763

2-year private junior college in small city.

Enrollment: 793 undergrads, 68% part-time. 41 full-time freshmen.

Selectivity: Admits less than 50% of applicants.

BASIC COSTS (2009-2010)

Tuition and fees: $9,500.

Per-credit charge: $375.

FINANCIAL AID PICTURE (2009-2010)

Students with need: Need-based aid available for full-time and part-time students. Work study available nights, weekends, and for part-time students.

Students without need: This college awards aid only to students with need.

FINANCIAL AID PROCEDURES

Forms required: FAFSA, state aid form.

Dates and Deadlines: No deadline. Applicants notified on a rolling basis starting 2/1; must reply within 2 week(s) of notification.

Transfers: No deadline. Applicants notified on a rolling basis; must reply within 2 week(s) of notification.

CONTACT

Christina Roarke, Director of Financial Aid
700 New Scotland Avenue, Albany, NY 12208
(518) 438-3111 ext. 229

Marist College
Poughkeepsie, New York
www.marist.edu   Federal Code: 002765

4-year private liberal arts college in small city.

Enrollment: 4,837 undergrads, 6% part-time. 1,041 full-time freshmen.

Selectivity: Admits less than 50% of applicants.

BASIC COSTS (2009-2010)

Tuition and fees: $26,605.

Per-credit charge: $610.

Room and board: $11,225.

Additional info: Tuition/fee waivers available for minority students.

FINANCIAL AID PICTURE (2009-2010)

Students with need: Out of 865 full-time freshmen who applied for aid, 632 were judged to have need. Of these, 632 received aid, and 129 had their full need met. Average financial aid package met 67% of need; average scholarship/grant was $12,758; average loan was $5,049. For part-time students, average financial aid package was $4,975.

Students without need: 313 full-time freshmen who did not demonstrate need for aid received scholarships/grants; average award was $7,116. No-need awards available for academics, athletics, music/drama, ROTC, state/district residency.

Scholarships offered: *Merit:* Awards vary, as much as $12,000 per recipient. *Athletic:* 85 full-time freshmen received athletic scholarships; average amount $10,804.

Cumulative student debt: 76% of graduating class had student loans; average debt was $35,993.

FINANCIAL AID PROCEDURES

Forms required: FAFSA, institutional form.

Dates and Deadlines: Priority date 2/15; closing date 5/1. Applicants notified on a rolling basis starting 3/15; must reply by 5/1 or within 2 week(s) of notification.

Transfers: No deadline. Applicants notified on a rolling basis. FAFSA should be filed as soon as possible after January 1.

CONTACT

Joseph Weglarz, Executive Director, Student Financial Services

3399 North Road, Poughkeepsie, NY 12601-1387

(845) 575-3230

Marymount Manhattan College

New York, New York

www.mmm.edu   Federal Code: 002769

4-year private liberal arts college in very large city.

Enrollment: 1,979 undergrads, 13% part-time. 487 full-time freshmen.

Selectivity: Admits 50 to 75% of applicants.

BASIC COSTS (2010-2011)

Tuition and fees: $23,536.

Per-credit charge: $716.

Room and board: $13,416.

FINANCIAL AID PICTURE (2009-2010)

Students with need: Out of 411 full-time freshmen who applied for aid, 343 were judged to have need. Of these, 343 received aid, and 23 had their full need met. Average financial aid package met 50% of need; average scholarship/grant was $11,158; average loan was $3,388. For part-time students, average financial aid package was $6,444.

Students without need: 72 full-time freshmen who did not demonstrate need for aid received scholarships/grants; average award was $5,674. No-need awards available for academics, art, leadership, state/district residency.

Cumulative student debt: 84% of graduating class had student loans; average debt was $15,988.

Additional info: Limited international scholarships for top applicants.

FINANCIAL AID PROCEDURES

Forms required: FAFSA.

Dates and Deadlines: Priority date 3/15; no closing date. Applicants notified on a rolling basis starting 3/15; must reply by 5/1 or within 2 week(s) of notification.

Transfers: Applicants notified by 3/1. Must submit academic and financial transcripts from previous institutions.

CONTACT

Paul Ciraulo, Executive VP for Administration and Finance

221 East 71st Street, New York, NY 10021-4597

(212) 517-0500

Medaille College

Buffalo, New York

www.medaille.edu   Federal Code: 002777

4-year private liberal arts college in large city.

Enrollment: 1,750 undergrads, 2% part-time. 411 full-time freshmen.

Selectivity: Admits 50 to 75% of applicants.

BASIC COSTS (2009-2010)

Tuition and fees: $19,590.

Per-credit charge: $690.

Room and board: $9,288.

Additional info: Tuition for students admitted in Fall 2008 is $19,140; tuition for students admitted before Fall 2008 is $18,290. Tuition/fee waivers available for adults.

FINANCIAL AID PICTURE (2008-2009)

Students with need: Out of 360 full-time freshmen who applied for aid, 360 were judged to have need. Of these, 360 received aid, and 10 had their full need met. Average financial aid package met 70% of need; average scholarship/grant was $8,000; average loan was $5,000. Need-based aid available for part-time students.

Students without need: 8 full-time freshmen who did not demonstrate need for aid received scholarships/grants; average award was $7,000. No-need awards available for academics, leadership.

Scholarships offered: Available from $1,000 to $10,500.

Cumulative student debt: 93% of graduating class had student loans; average debt was $22,000.

FINANCIAL AID PROCEDURES

Forms required: FAFSA, state aid form.

Dates and Deadlines: Priority date 3/1; no closing date. Applicants notified on a rolling basis starting 3/1; must reply within 2 week(s) of notification.

Transfers: Applicants notified on a rolling basis starting 3/1.

CONTACT

Catherine Buzanski, Director of Financial Aid

18 Agassiz Circle, Buffalo, NY 14214

(716) 880-2256

Mercy College

Dobbs Ferry, New York

www.mercy.edu   Federal Code: 002772

4-year private liberal arts college in large town.

Enrollment: 5,516 undergrads, 26% part-time. 702 full-time freshmen.

Selectivity: Admits 50 to 75% of applicants.

BASIC COSTS (2009-2010)

Tuition and fees: $16,490.

Per-credit charge: $672.

Room and board: $10,812.

FINANCIAL AID PICTURE (2008-2009)

Students with need: Out of 647 full-time freshmen who applied for aid, 604 were judged to have need. Of these, 582 received aid, and 22 had their full need met. Average financial aid package met 53% of need; average scholarship/grant was $8,713; average loan was $3,125. For part-time students, average financial aid package was $4,498.

Students without need: 12 full-time freshmen who did not demonstrate need for aid received scholarships/grants; average award was $4,375. No-need awards available for academics, athletics.

Scholarships offered: 2 full-time freshmen received athletic scholarships; average amount $3,582.

Cumulative student debt: 68% of graduating class had student loans; average debt was $15,481.

FINANCIAL AID PROCEDURES

Forms required: FAFSA, state aid form.

Dates and Deadlines: Priority date 2/15; no closing date. Applicants notified on a rolling basis starting 4/1; must reply within 2 week(s) of notification.

Transfers: No deadline. Applicants notified on a rolling basis starting 4/1; must reply within 2 week(s) of notification.

CONTACT

Margaret McGrail, Vice President for Student Services

555 Broadway, Dobbs Ferry, NY 10522

(888) 464-6737

Metropolitan College of New York

New York, New York

www.metropolitan.edu   Federal Code: 009769

4-year private business and liberal arts college in very large city.

Enrollment: 676 undergrads.

Selectivity: Admits 50 to 75% of applicants.

BASIC COSTS (2010-2011)

Tuition and fees: $16,750.

Additional info: Tuition reported is for undergraduate business program; costs for other programs may vary.

FINANCIAL AID PICTURE (2008-2009)

Students with need: Need-based aid available for full-time and part-time students.

Students without need: No-need awards available for academics.

Scholarships offered: Presidential scholarships: up to $1,300 per semester; based on academic merit; given to top 10% of accepted students each semester.

Additional info: Limited merit scholarships.

FINANCIAL AID PROCEDURES

Forms required: FAFSA, state aid form.

Dates and Deadlines: Priority date 3/15; no closing date. Applicants notified on a rolling basis.

CONTACT

Timothy James, Director of Financial Aid

431 Canal Street, New York, NY 10013-1919

(212) 343-1234 ext. 3500

Mildred Elley

Albany, New York

www.mildred-elley.edu   Federal Code: 022195

2-year for-profit career college in very large city.

Enrollment: 724 undergrads.

Selectivity: Open admission; but selective for some programs.

BASIC COSTS (2009-2010)

Tuition and fees: $11,100.

Per-credit charge: $354.

FINANCIAL AID PICTURE

Students with need: Need-based aid available for full-time and part-time students. Work study available nights.

Students without need: This college awards aid only to students with need.

FINANCIAL AID PROCEDURES

Forms required: FAFSA, state aid form.

Dates and Deadlines: No deadline.

CONTACT

Chris Arnold, Director of Financial Aid

855 Central Avenue, Albany, NY 12206-1513

(518) 786-0855 ext. 228

Mohawk Valley Community College

Utica, New York

www.mvcc.edu   Federal Code: 002871

2-year public community college in small city.

Enrollment: 5,422 undergrads, 20% part-time. 1,576 full-time freshmen.

Selectivity: Open admission; but selective for some programs.

BASIC COSTS (2009-2010)

Tuition and fees: $3,774; out-of-state residents $7,124.

Per-credit charge: $120; out-of-state residents $240.

Room and board: $7,940.

FINANCIAL AID PICTURE (2009-2010)

Students with need: Out of 1,446 full-time freshmen who applied for aid, 1,067 were judged to have need. Of these, 1,059 received aid, and 933 had their full need met. Average financial aid package met 88% of need; average scholarship/grant was $5,804; average loan was $3,448. For part-time students, average financial aid package was $7,195.

Students without need: No-need awards available for academics, alumni affiliation, art, leadership, state/district residency.

FINANCIAL AID PROCEDURES

Forms required: FAFSA, institutional form.

Dates and Deadlines: Priority date 4/15; no closing date. Applicants notified on a rolling basis starting 3/1; must reply within 2 week(s) of notification.

Transfers: Applicants notified on a rolling basis.

CONTACT

Annette Broski, Director, Financial Aid

1101 Sherman Drive, Utica, NY 13501-5394

(315) 792-5415

Molloy College

Rockville Centre, New York

www.molloy.edu   Federal Code: 002775

4-year private liberal arts college in large town, affiliated with Roman Catholic Church.

Enrollment: 2,969 undergrads, 23% part-time. 445 full-time freshmen.

Selectivity: Admits 50 to 75% of applicants.

BASIC COSTS (2009-2010)

Tuition and fees: $21,070.

Per-credit charge: $660.

Additional info: Tuition/fee waivers available for unemployed or children of unemployed.

FINANCIAL AID PICTURE (2008-2009)

Students with need: Out of 389 full-time freshmen who applied for aid, 324 were judged to have need. Of these, 323 received aid, and 65 had their full need met. Average financial aid package met 61% of need; average scholarship/grant was $10,102; average loan was $4,308. For part-time students, average financial aid package was $7,049.

Students without need: 52 full-time freshmen who did not demonstrate need for aid received scholarships/grants; average award was $5,757. No-need awards available for academics, alumni affiliation, art, athletics, leadership, music/drama, religious affiliation.

Scholarships offered: *Merit:* Molloy Scholar Scholarship: full tuition; minimum 95 high school average and minimum 1250 SAT (exclusive of Writing) or 28 ACT; 10 awarded annually; renewable for 3.5 GPA. Dominican Academic Scholarship: $1,000 to $8,500; minimum 88 high school average and minimum 1000 SAT (exclusive of Writing); 50 awarded annually, renewable with 3.0 GPA. Community Service Awards: $1,000 to $3,000; awarded to incoming freshmen demonstrating commitment to community and school; 10 awarded annually; renewable for 2.5 GPA. *Athletic:* 20 full-time freshmen received athletic scholarships; average amount $8,725.

Cumulative student debt: 77% of graduating class had student loans; average debt was $29,823.

FINANCIAL AID PROCEDURES

Forms required: FAFSA, state aid form.

Dates and Deadlines: Priority date 4/15; closing date 5/1. Applicants notified on a rolling basis starting 3/1; must reply within 5 week(s) of notification.

Transfers: All transfer applicants with a minimum of 30 credits and 3.0 GPA automatically considered for transfer scholarships ranging from $1,500-$3,000.

CONTACT

Ana Lockward, Director of Financial Aid
PO Box 5002, Rockville Centre, NY 11570
(516) 678-5000 ext. 6249

Monroe College

Bronx, New York
www.monroecollege.edu   Federal Code: 004799

4-year for-profit business and health science college in very large city.
Enrollment: 6,674 undergrads, 22% part-time. 1,167 full-time freshmen.
Selectivity: Admits 50 to 75% of applicants.

BASIC COSTS (2009-2010)

Tuition and fees: $11,744.
Per-credit charge: $456.
Room and board: $7,540.

FINANCIAL AID PICTURE (2008-2009)

Students with need: Need-based aid available for full-time and part-time students. Work study available nights, weekends, and for part-time students.
Students without need: This college awards aid only to students with need.

FINANCIAL AID PROCEDURES

Forms required: FAFSA.
Dates and Deadlines: Closing date 3/31. Applicants notified on a rolling basis starting 7/1.
Transfers: No deadline. Applicants notified on a rolling basis.

CONTACT

Alex Ephrem, Senior Vice President
Monroe College Way, Bronx, NY 10468
(718) 933-6700

Monroe Community College

Rochester, New York
www.monroecc.edu   Federal Code: 002872

2-year public community college in large city.
Enrollment: 17,366 undergrads, 30% part-time. 4,097 full-time freshmen.
Selectivity: Open admission; but selective for some programs.

BASIC COSTS (2009-2010)

Tuition and fees: $3,278; out-of-state residents $6,178.
Per-credit charge: $121; out-of-state residents $242.
Room only: $5,600.

FINANCIAL AID PICTURE (2008-2009)

Students with need: Need-based aid available for full-time and part-time students. Work study available nights, weekends, and for part-time students.
Students without need: This college awards aid only to students with need.

FINANCIAL AID PROCEDURES

Forms required: FAFSA, state aid form.
Dates and Deadlines: Priority date 3/30; no closing date. Applicants notified on a rolling basis starting 3/15; must reply within 2 week(s) of notification.
Transfers: No deadline. Applicants notified on a rolling basis starting 3/15; must reply within 2 week(s) of notification.

CONTACT

Jerome St. Croix, Director of Financial Aid
Office of Admissions-Monroe Community College, Rochester, NY 14692-8908
(585) 292-2050

Mount Saint Mary College

Newburgh, New York
www.msmc.edu   Federal Code: 002778

4-year private liberal arts college in large town, affiliated with Roman Catholic Church.
Enrollment: 2,214 undergrads, 16% part-time. 474 full-time freshmen.
Selectivity: Admits 50 to 75% of applicants.

BASIC COSTS (2010-2011)

Tuition and fees: $23,300.
Per-credit charge: $745.
Room and board: $11,900.
Additional info: Tuition/fee waivers available for adults.

FINANCIAL AID PICTURE (2009-2010)

Students with need: Out of 443 full-time freshmen who applied for aid, 364 were judged to have need. Of these, 364 received aid, and 82 had their full need met. Average financial aid package met 66% of need; average scholarship/grant was $11,818; average loan was $3,144. For part-time students, average financial aid package was $7,374.
Students without need: 82 full-time freshmen who did not demonstrate need for aid received scholarships/grants; average award was $7,774. No-need awards available for academics, ROTC.
Scholarships offered: Presidential Scholarship: approximately 65% of tuition in the year of enrollment, renewable for three years with minimum 3.0 GPA. Merit Awards: $3,000-$7,500; renewable each year with 2.5 GPA. Based on combined SAT/ACT test scores, GPA, and class rank.
Cumulative student debt: 94% of graduating class had student loans; average debt was $32,729.

FINANCIAL AID PROCEDURES

Forms required: FAFSA.
Dates and Deadlines: Priority date 2/15; closing date 3/1. Applicants notified on a rolling basis starting 3/15; must reply by 5/1.
Transfers: Applicants notified on a rolling basis starting 3/15; must reply by 5/1.

CONTACT

Michelle Taylor, Director of Financial Aid
330 Powell Avenue, Newburgh, NY 12550
(845) 569-3194

Nassau Community College

Garden City, New York
www.ncc.edu   Federal Code: 002873

2-year public community college in large town.
Enrollment: 20,228 undergrads, 28% part-time. 4,664 full-time freshmen.
Selectivity: Open admission; but selective for some programs.

BASIC COSTS (2009-2010)

Tuition and fees: $3,902; out-of-state residents $7,524.
Per-credit charge: $151; out-of-state residents $302.

FINANCIAL AID PICTURE (2008-2009)

Students with need: Need-based aid available for full-time and part-time students. Work study available nights, weekends, and for part-time students.
Students without need: No-need awards available for academics, minority status.

FINANCIAL AID PROCEDURES

Forms required: FAFSA, state aid form.
Dates and Deadlines: Priority date 6/7; no closing date. Applicants notified on a rolling basis; must reply within 1 week(s) of notification.

CONTACT

Evangeline Manjares, Dean, Financial Student Services
One Education Drive, Garden City, NY 11530
(516) 572-7396

Nazareth College

Rochester, New York
www.naz.edu   Federal Code: 002779

4-year private liberal arts college in large city.
Enrollment: 2,189 undergrads, 6% part-time. 471 full-time freshmen.
Selectivity: Admits over 75% of applicants.

BASIC COSTS (2009-2010)

Tuition and fees: $25,186.
Per-credit charge: $574.
Room and board: $10,304.

FINANCIAL AID PICTURE (2008-2009)

Students with need: Out of 430 full-time freshmen who applied for aid, 365 were judged to have need. Of these, 365 received aid, and 73 had their full need met. Average financial aid package met 77% of need; average scholarship/grant was $13,635; average loan was $3,629. For part-time students, average financial aid package was $7,061.
Students without need: 106 full-time freshmen who did not demonstrate need for aid received scholarships/grants; average award was $13,991. No-need awards available for academics, alumni affiliation, art, leadership, minority status, music/drama, ROTC, state/district residency.
Scholarships offered: Presidential Scholarship: $14,500 to full tuition. Dean's Scholarship: $11,500-$14,000. Founders Scholarship: $9,500-$11,000. Trustee Scholarship: $7,500-$9,000. Class of 1928 Scholarship: $1,000-$7,500. All awarded based on grades, test scores, class rank, and course load. Campus diversity, regional, art, music, and theater scholarships also available.
Cumulative student debt: 86% of graduating class had student loans; average debt was $36,911.

FINANCIAL AID PROCEDURES

Forms required: FAFSA, state aid form. CSS PROFILE required of early decision applicants only.
Dates and Deadlines: Priority date 2/15; no closing date. Applicants notified on a rolling basis starting 2/1; must reply by 5/1.
Transfers: No deadline.

CONTACT

Samantha Veeder, Director of Financial Aid
4245 East Avenue, Rochester, NY 14618-3790
(585) 389-2310

New York Career Institute

New York, New York
www.nyci.edu   Federal Code: 014576

2-year for-profit junior college in very large city.
Enrollment: 720 undergrads, 45% part-time. 56 full-time freshmen.
Selectivity: Open admission.

BASIC COSTS (2009-2010)

Additional info: Full-time tuition and fees for Court Reporting, Paralegal, and Medical daytime programs $11,550; for court reporting night program $10,950. Tuition for paralegal and medical evening programs $370 per credit hour.

FINANCIAL AID PICTURE

Students with need: Need-based aid available for full-time and part-time students. Work study available nights.

Students without need: This college awards aid only to students with need.

FINANCIAL AID PROCEDURES

Dates and Deadlines: No deadline. Applicants notified on a rolling basis.

CONTACT

Dennis Byrns, Director of Student Financial Services
11 Park Place, New York, NY 10007

New York Institute of Technology

Old Westbury, New York
www.nyit.edu   Federal Code: 002782

4-year private university and health science college in large town.
Enrollment: 4,927 undergrads, 14% part-time. 1,617 full-time freshmen.
Selectivity: Admits 50 to 75% of applicants.

BASIC COSTS (2010-2011)

Tuition and fees: $25,470.
Per-credit charge: $835.
Room only: $11,100.
Additional info: Room and board charges apply to Old Westbury campus; board charges vary on other campuses. Tuition/fee costs reported for non-technology majors, vary for other programs. Tuition/fee waivers available for unemployed or children of unemployed.

FINANCIAL AID PICTURE (2008-2009)

Students with need: Out of 1,103 full-time freshmen who applied for aid, 965 were judged to have need. Of these, 960 received aid. For part-time students, average financial aid package was $6,611.
Students without need: 217 full-time freshmen who did not demonstrate need for aid received scholarships/grants; average award was $9,212. No-need awards available for academics, athletics.

FINANCIAL AID PROCEDURES

Forms required: FAFSA.
Dates and Deadlines: Priority date 3/1; no closing date. Applicants notified on a rolling basis starting 3/15; must reply by 5/1 or within 2 week(s) of notification.

CONTACT

Rosemary Ferrucci, Associate Dean of Financial Aid
Box 8000, Old Westbury, NY 11568
(516) 686-3835

New York School of Interior Design

New York, New York
www.nysid.edu   Federal Code: 013606

4-year private visual arts college in very large city.
Enrollment: 533 undergrads, 63% part-time. 28 full-time freshmen.
Selectivity: Admits 50 to 75% of applicants.

BASIC COSTS (2010-2011)

Tuition and fees: $22,895.
Per-credit charge: $685.

FINANCIAL AID PICTURE (2009-2010)

Students with need: Out of 9 full-time freshmen who applied for aid, 9 were judged to have need. Of these, 9 received aid. Average financial aid package met 30% of need; average scholarship/grant was $2,500; average loan was $3,500. For part-time students, average financial aid package was $3,500.
Students without need: This college awards aid only to students with need.

Cumulative student debt: 60% of graduating class had student loans; average debt was $20,000.

FINANCIAL AID PROCEDURES

Forms required: FAFSA, state aid form.

Dates and Deadlines: Priority date 5/1; no closing date. Applicants notified on a rolling basis starting 2/1; must reply within 2 week(s) of notification.

Transfers: No deadline. Applicants notified on a rolling basis.

CONTACT

Rashmi Wadhvani, Financial Aid Officer

170 East 70th Street, New York, NY 10021-5110

(212) 472-1500 ext. 212

New York University

New York, New York

www.nyu.edu　　　　　　　　　　Federal Code: 002785

4-year private university in very large city.

Enrollment: 21,227 undergrads, 6% part-time. 4,467 full-time freshmen.

Selectivity: Admits less than 50% of applicants.

BASIC COSTS (2009-2010)

Tuition and fees: $38,765.

Per-credit charge: $1,078.

Room and board: $13,228.

FINANCIAL AID PICTURE (2008-2009)

Students with need: Out of 3,004 full-time freshmen who applied for aid, 2,390 were judged to have need. Of these, 2,342 received aid. Average financial aid package met 71% of need; average scholarship/grant was $19,120; average loan was $4,947. For part-time students, average financial aid package was $8,350.

Students without need: 244 full-time freshmen who did not demonstrate need for aid received scholarships/grants; average award was $6,683. No-need awards available for academics.

Cumulative student debt: 59% of graduating class had student loans; average debt was $33,487.

FINANCIAL AID PROCEDURES

Forms required: FAFSA, state aid form.

Dates and Deadlines: Closing date 2/15. Applicants notified on a rolling basis starting 4/1; must reply by 5/1.

Transfers: Priority date 2/15; no deadline.

CONTACT

Randall Deike, Vice President for Enrollment Management and University Institutional Research

665 Broadway, 11th floor, New York, NY 10012-2339

(212) 998-4444

Niagara County Community College

Sanborn, New York

www.niagaracc.suny.edu　　　　　Federal Code: 002874

2-year public community college in rural community.

Enrollment: 5,983 undergrads, 23% part-time. 1,766 full-time freshmen.

Selectivity: Open admission; but selective for some programs.

BASIC COSTS (2009-2010)

Tuition and fees: $3,750; out-of-state residents $7,158.

Per-credit charge: $142; out-of-state residents $284.

FINANCIAL AID PICTURE (2008-2009)

Students with need: 52% of average financial aid package awarded as scholarships/grants, 48% awarded as loans/jobs. Need-based aid available for part-time students. Work study available nights.

Students without need: This college awards aid only to students with need.

Additional info: Assistance offered placing students in part-time employment. Students can charge books, food coupons, or $100 advance against anticipated financial aid.

FINANCIAL AID PROCEDURES

Forms required: FAFSA, state aid form.

Dates and Deadlines: Priority date 4/1; no closing date. Applicants notified on a rolling basis starting 5/1; must reply within 2 week(s) of notification.

Transfers: Must file appropriate state and federal change forms at least 4 weeks before registration date.

CONTACT

James Trimboli, Director of Financial Aid

3111 Saunders Settlement Road, Sanborn, NY 14132-9460

(716) 614-6266

Niagara University

Niagara University, New York

www.niagara.edu　　　　　　　　Federal Code: 002788

4-year private university in small city, affiliated with Roman Catholic Church.

Enrollment: 3,224 undergrads, 8% part-time. 676 full-time freshmen.

Selectivity: Admits over 75% of applicants.

BASIC COSTS (2010-2011)

Tuition and fees: $25,775.

Per-credit charge: $820.

Room and board: $10,650.

Additional info: Tuition at time of enrollment locked for 4 years.

FINANCIAL AID PICTURE (2009-2010)

Students with need: Out of 644 full-time freshmen who applied for aid, 573 were judged to have need. Of these, 573 received aid, and 315 had their full need met. Average financial aid package met 85% of need; average scholarship/grant was $16,843; average loan was $4,116. For part-time students, average financial aid package was $11,561.

Students without need: 14 full-time freshmen who did not demonstrate need for aid received scholarships/grants; average award was $9,495. No-need awards available for academics, athletics, music/drama, ROTC.

Scholarships offered: *Merit:* Honors Scholarship: full tuition; minimum 97 average; 1340 SAT or 30 ACT; limited number. Trustee Scholarship: $15,000; minimum 95 average, 1150 SAT or 26 ACT; or 91 average, 1210 SAT or 27 ACT; unlimited number. Presidential Scholarship: $13,500; minimum 90 average, 1050 SAT or 23 ACT; or 85 average, 1120 SAT or 24 ACT; unlimited. Achievement Grant: $12,000; mid to upper 80 average; 950-1050 SAT or 20-22 ACT; unlimited. Niagara University Grant: $7,500; mid 80 average; SAT above 950 or ACT above 20; unlimited. *Athletic:* 25 full-time freshmen received athletic scholarships; average amount $21,263.

Cumulative student debt: 78% of graduating class had student loans; average debt was $27,215.

Additional info: Opportunity program available for academically and economically disadvantaged students.

FINANCIAL AID PROCEDURES

Forms required: FAFSA, state aid form.

Dates and Deadlines: Priority date 2/15; no closing date. Applicants notified on a rolling basis starting 3/1; must reply within 3 week(s) of notification.

Transfers: Must reply within 3 week(s) of notification. Academic scholarship available: $11000 per year based on minimum 3.34 GPA from transfer institution; $10,000 per year for 3.0 to 3.33 GPA; $7500 per year for 2.5 to 2.99 GPA.

CONTACT

Maureen Salfi, Director of Financial Aid Niagara University, NY 14109

(716) 286-8686

North Country Community College
Saranac Lake, New York
www.nccc.edu   Federal Code: 007111

2-year public community college in small town.
Enrollment: 1,202 undergrads.
Selectivity: Open admission; but selective for some programs.

BASIC COSTS (2009-2010)
Tuition and fees: $4,660; out-of-state residents $10,100.
Per-credit charge: $160; out-of-state residents $390.
Room and board: $8,700.
Additional info: Annual room rate based on single-occupancy bedroom; no double-occupancy rooms available.

FINANCIAL AID PICTURE (2008-2009)
Students with need: Need-based aid available for full-time and part-time students. Work study available nights, weekends, and for part-time students.
Students without need: This college awards aid only to students with need.

FINANCIAL AID PROCEDURES
Forms required: FAFSA, state aid form.
Dates and Deadlines: Priority date 4/1; no closing date. Applicants notified on a rolling basis starting 4/1; must reply within 3 week(s) of notification.

CONTACT
Edwin Trathen, Vice President for Enrollment and Student Services
23 Santanoni Avenue, Saranac Lake, NY 12983
(518) 891-2915 ext. 229

Nyack College
Nyack, New York
www.nyack.edu   Federal Code: 002790

4-year private liberal arts college in large town, affiliated with Christian and Missionary Alliance.
Enrollment: 1,994 undergrads, 18% part-time. 277 full-time freshmen.
Selectivity: Admits over 75% of applicants.

BASIC COSTS (2010-2011)
Tuition and fees: $20,500.
Per-credit charge: $812.
Room and board: $8,200.

FINANCIAL AID PICTURE (2008-2009)
Students with need: Out of 246 full-time freshmen who applied for aid, 228 were judged to have need. Of these, 228 received aid, and 34 had their full need met. Average financial aid package met 71% of need; average scholarship/grant was $12,464; average loan was $4,225. For part-time students, average financial aid package was $6,624.
Students without need: 49 full-time freshmen who did not demonstrate need for aid received scholarships/grants; average award was $6,678. No-need awards available for academics, alumni affiliation, art, athletics, leadership, minority status, music/drama, religious affiliation, state/district residency.
Scholarships offered: 9 full-time freshmen received athletic scholarships; average amount $8,628.
Cumulative student debt: 89% of graduating class had student loans; average debt was $19,532.

FINANCIAL AID PROCEDURES
Forms required: FAFSA, state aid form.
Dates and Deadlines: Priority date 3/1; no closing date. Applicants notified on a rolling basis starting 3/1; must reply by 4/1 or within 4 week(s) of notification.
Transfers: Applicants notified on a rolling basis.

CONTACT
Steve Phillips, Director of Student Financial Services
1 South Boulevard, Nyack, NY 10960-3698
(845) 675-4737

Onondaga Community College
Syracuse, New York
www.sunyocc.edu   Federal Code: 002875

2-year public community college in small city.
Enrollment: 8,520 undergrads, 24% part-time. 1,859 full-time freshmen.
Selectivity: Open admission; but selective for some programs.

BASIC COSTS (2009-2010)
Tuition and fees: $3,922; out-of-state residents $7,446.
Per-credit charge: $140; out-of-state residents $280.

FINANCIAL AID PICTURE (2008-2009)
Students with need: Need-based aid available for full-time and part-time students.
Students without need: This college awards aid only to students with need.

FINANCIAL AID PROCEDURES
Forms required: FAFSA, state aid form.
Dates and Deadlines: Priority date 2/15; no closing date. Applicants notified on a rolling basis starting 4/15; must reply within 4 week(s) of notification.

CONTACT
Lorna Roberts, Director of Financial Aid
4585 West Seneca Turnpike, Syracuse, NY 13215-4585
(315) 498-2291

Orange County Community College
Middletown, New York
www.orange.cc.ny.us   Federal Code: 002876

2-year public community college in large town.
Enrollment: 5,672 undergrads.
Selectivity: Open admission; but selective for some programs.

BASIC COSTS (2009-2010)
Tuition and fees: $3,894; out-of-state residents $7,394.
Per-credit charge: $146; out-of-state residents $292.
Additional info: Tuition/fee waivers available for unemployed or children of unemployed.

FINANCIAL AID PICTURE (2009-2010)
Students with need: Need-based aid available for full-time and part-time students.

FINANCIAL AID PROCEDURES
Forms required: FAFSA, state aid form, institutional form.
Dates and Deadlines: Priority date 5/1; closing date 7/1. Applicants notified on a rolling basis starting 5/1; must reply within 4 week(s) of notification.

CONTACT
John Ivankovic, Director of Finacial Aid
115 South Street, Middletown, NY 10940-0115
(845) 341-4190

Pace University
New York, New York
www.pace.edu   Federal Code: 002791

4-year private university in very large city.
Enrollment: 7,411 undergrads, 13% part-time. 1,637 full-time freshmen.
Selectivity: Admits over 75% of applicants.

BASIC COSTS (2009-2010)
Tuition and fees: $32,926.
Per-credit charge: $914.
Room and board: $11,560.

FINANCIAL AID PICTURE (2009-2010)
Students with need: Out of 1,446 full-time freshmen who applied for aid, 1,310 were judged to have need. Of these, 1,309 received aid, and 156 had their full need met. Average financial aid package met 76% of need; average scholarship/grant was $22,683; average loan was $3,923. For part-time students, average financial aid package was $5,482.
Students without need: 316 full-time freshmen who did not demonstrate need for aid received scholarships/grants; average award was $12,252. No-need awards available for academics, athletics, leadership, music/drama.
Scholarships offered: 7 full-time freshmen received athletic scholarships; average amount $27,627.
Cumulative student debt: 58% of graduating class had student loans; average debt was $34,115.

FINANCIAL AID PROCEDURES
Forms required: FAFSA, state aid form.
Dates and Deadlines: Priority date 2/15; no closing date. Applicants notified on a rolling basis starting 3/1; must reply by 5/1 or within 2 week(s) of notification.

CONTACT
Mark Stephens, University Director, Financial Aid
1 Pace Plaza, New York, NY 10038-1598
(212) 346-1300

Parsons The New School for Design
New York, New York
www.parsons.edu   Federal Code: 002780

4-year private visual arts college in very large city.
Enrollment: 4,107 undergrads, 10% part-time. 747 full-time freshmen.
Selectivity: Admits 50 to 75% of applicants.

BASIC COSTS (2010-2011)
Tuition and fees: $37,610.
Per-credit charge: $1,255.
Room and board: $15,260.

FINANCIAL AID PICTURE (2009-2010)
Students with need: Out of 513 full-time freshmen who applied for aid, 470 were judged to have need. Of these, 452 received aid, and 22 had their full need met. Average financial aid package met 71% of need; average scholarship/grant was $16,029; average loan was $11,300. Need-based aid available for part-time students.
Students without need: 39 full-time freshmen who did not demonstrate need for aid received scholarships/grants; average award was $4,800. No-need awards available for academics, art.

FINANCIAL AID PROCEDURES
Forms required: FAFSA, state aid form.
Dates and Deadlines: Priority date 3/1; no closing date. Applicants notified on a rolling basis starting 3/1; must reply within 4 week(s) of notification.

CONTACT
Eileen Doyle, Assistant Provost for University Financial Aid and Enrollment Management
72 Fifth Avenue, New York, NY 10011
(212) 229-8930

Paul Smith's College
Paul Smiths, New York
www.paulsmiths.edu   Federal Code: 002795

4-year private liberal arts college in rural community.
Enrollment: 915 undergrads. 313 full-time freshmen.

BASIC COSTS (2010-2011)
Tuition and fees: $20,865.
Per-credit charge: $560.
Room and board: $9,350.
Additional info: Program fees range from $660 to $2,120 depending on program.

FINANCIAL AID PICTURE (2008-2009)
Students with need: Out of 290 full-time freshmen who applied for aid, 273 were judged to have need. Of these, 273 received aid, and 11 had their full need met. Average financial aid package met 73% of need; average scholarship/grant was $11,113; average loan was $4,447.
Students without need: 23 full-time freshmen who did not demonstrate need for aid received scholarships/grants; average award was $5,267. No-need awards available for academics.
Cumulative student debt: 98% of graduating class had student loans; average debt was $20,093.
Additional info: Merit aid only for international students; no financial aid application required.

FINANCIAL AID PROCEDURES
Forms required: FAFSA.
Dates and Deadlines: Priority date 3/31; no closing date. Applicants notified on a rolling basis starting 3/5; must reply within 4 week(s) of notification.
Transfers: No deadline. Applicants notified by 2/5; must reply within 4 week(s) of notification.

CONTACT
Mary Ellen Chamberlain, Director of Financial Aid
PO Box 265, Routes 30 & 86, Paul Smiths, NY 12970-0265
(518) 327-6220

Phillips Beth Israel School of Nursing
New York, New York
www.futurenursebi.org   Federal Code: 006438

2-year private nursing college in very large city.
Enrollment: 242 undergrads, 90% part-time. 2 full-time freshmen.
Selectivity: Admits less than 50% of applicants.

BASIC COSTS (2010-2011)
Tuition and fees: $18,190.
Per-credit charge: $380.

FINANCIAL AID PICTURE (2009-2010)
Students with need: Out of 2 full-time freshmen who applied for aid, 2 were judged to have need. Of these, 2 received aid. Average financial aid package met 65% of need; average scholarship/grant was $1,000; average loan was $2,750. For part-time students, average financial aid package was $8,500.
Scholarships offered: Hillman Scholarship Program: full tuition, books, and uniforms; variable number awarded each year; based on academic achieve-

ment. Karpas Scholarship Program: $3,000 a year awarded to senior students; 15 awarded; based on academic achievement.

FINANCIAL AID PROCEDURES

Forms required: FAFSA, state aid form, institutional form.

Dates and Deadlines: Closing date 6/1. Applicants notified by 8/1; must reply within 3 week(s) of notification.

Transfers: Applicants notified by 8/1; must reply within 3 week(s) of notification.

CONTACT

Wendy Chan, Financial Aid Director

776 Sixth Avenue, Fourth Floor, New York, NY 10001

(212) 614-6104

Polytechnic Institute of New York University

Brooklyn, New York   Federal Code: 002796
www.poly.edu   CSS Code: 2668

4-year private university in very large city.

Enrollment: 1,632 undergrads, 4% part-time. 292 full-time freshmen.

Selectivity: Admits 50 to 75% of applicants.

BASIC COSTS (2009-2010)

Tuition and fees: $34,420.

Per-credit charge: $1,058.

Room and board: $9,000.

FINANCIAL AID PICTURE (2008-2009)

Students with need: Out of 288 full-time freshmen who applied for aid, 217 were judged to have need. Of these, 217 received aid, and 151 had their full need met. Average financial aid package met 95% of need; average scholarship/grant was $12,293; average loan was $4,729. For part-time students, average financial aid package was $8,607.

Students without need: 69 full-time freshmen who did not demonstrate need for aid received scholarships/grants; average award was $17,434. No-need awards available for academics.

Scholarships offered: Board of Trustees Scholarships: full tuition, less any outside aid for which students are eligible; awarded to academically superior freshmen. Geiger/Fialkov Scholarships: full tuition less any outside aid for which students are eligible; awarded to superior freshmen majoring in engineering or computer science. High School Principal's Scholarship: for students nominated by high school principals in New York metropolitan region; $10,000 per year; Scholarship Committee selects recipients. Students must file FAFSA to be eligible for merit scholarships.

Cumulative student debt: 67% of graduating class had student loans; average debt was $26,619.

FINANCIAL AID PROCEDURES

Forms required: FAFSA, CSS PROFILE, state aid form, institutional form.

Dates and Deadlines: Priority date 3/1; no closing date. Applicants notified on a rolling basis starting 3/15; must reply within 2 week(s) of notification.

Transfers: Priority date 5/5; no deadline. Applicants notified on a rolling basis; must reply within 2 week(s) of notification.

CONTACT

Christine Falzerano, Director of Financial Aid

6 Metrotech Center, Brooklyn, NY 11201-2999

(718) 260-3300

Pratt Institute

Brooklyn, New York
www.pratt.edu   Federal Code: 002798

4-year private university and visual arts college in very large city.

Enrollment: 2,973 undergrads, 5% part-time. 630 full-time freshmen.

Selectivity: Admits less than 50% of applicants.

BASIC COSTS (2010-2011)

Tuition and fees: $36,790.

Per-credit charge: $1,142.

Room and board: $10,020.

FINANCIAL AID PICTURE (2009-2010)

Students with need: Out of 507 full-time freshmen who applied for aid, 434 were judged to have need. Of these, 434 received aid. Average financial aid package met 71% of need; average scholarship/grant was $9,674; average loan was $5,140. For part-time students, average financial aid package was $7,943.

Students without need: 186 full-time freshmen who did not demonstrate need for aid received scholarships/grants; average award was $8,674. No-need awards available for academics.

FINANCIAL AID PROCEDURES

Forms required: FAFSA.

Dates and Deadlines: Closing date 2/1. Applicants notified on a rolling basis starting 3/10; must reply within 2 week(s) of notification.

Transfers: Must reply by 5/1 or within 2 week(s) of notification.

CONTACT

Fiona Approo, Director of Financial Aid

200 Willoughby Avenue, Brooklyn, NY 11205-3817

(718) 636-3519

Rensselaer Polytechnic Institute

Troy, New York   Federal Code: 002803
www.rpi.edu   CSS Code: 2757

4-year private university in small city.

Enrollment: 5,539 undergrads. 1,337 full-time freshmen.

Selectivity: Admits less than 50% of applicants.

BASIC COSTS (2010-2011)

Tuition and fees: $40,680.

Per-credit charge: $1,238.

Room and board: $11,465.

Additional info: Students required to purchase a university-subsidized Lenovo laptop costing approximately $1,800 or an equivalent laptop that meets RPI's technology and software requirements.

FINANCIAL AID PICTURE (2008-2009)

Students with need: Out of 1,097 full-time freshmen who applied for aid, 877 were judged to have need. Of these, 877 received aid, and 384 had their full need met. Average financial aid package met 88% of need; average scholarship/grant was $22,418; average loan was $5,741.

Students without need: 454 full-time freshmen who did not demonstrate need for aid received scholarships/grants; average award was $13,043. No-need awards available for academics, alumni affiliation, art, athletics, leadership, minority status, music/drama, ROTC.

Scholarships offered: *Merit:* Rensselaer Medals: $15,000; awarded by participating high schools for excellence in science and mathematics. *Athletic:* 10 full-time freshmen received athletic scholarships; average amount $43,106.

Cumulative student debt: 71% of graduating class had student loans; average debt was $30,838.

FINANCIAL AID PROCEDURES

Forms required: FAFSA, CSS PROFILE.

Dates and Deadlines: Closing date 2/15. Applicants notified by 3/25.

Transfers: No deadline. Applicants notified on a rolling basis starting 3/31. Entering transfer students must complete two applications to apply for institutional and federal need-based aid: FAFSA and Transfer Financial Aid Application/Verification Worksheet (available upon acceptance). A number of special transfer scholarships available each year.

CONTACT

Lynnette Koch, Director of Financial Aid
110 Eighth Street, Troy, NY 12180-3590
(518) 276-6813

Roberts Wesleyan College
Rochester, New York
www.roberts.edu   Federal Code: 002805

4-year private liberal arts college in large city, affiliated with Free Methodist Church of North America.

Enrollment: 1,388 undergrads, 9% part-time. 227 full-time freshmen.

BASIC COSTS (2009-2010)

Tuition and fees: $23,780.
Per-credit charge: $940.
Room and board: $8,520.

FINANCIAL AID PICTURE (2008-2009)

Students with need: Out of 210 full-time freshmen who applied for aid, 199 were judged to have need. Of these, 199 received aid, and 29 had their full need met. Average financial aid package met 79% of need; average scholarship/grant was $14,411; average loan was $5,149. For part-time students, average financial aid package was $11,150.

Students without need: 23 full-time freshmen who did not demonstrate need for aid received scholarships/grants; average award was $6,060. No-need awards available for academics, alumni affiliation, art, athletics, music/drama, religious affiliation, ROTC, state/district residency.

Scholarships offered: 12 full-time freshmen received athletic scholarships; average amount $7,029.

Cumulative student debt: 99% of graduating class had student loans; average debt was $30,329.

Additional info: Dollars for Scholars offer matching grants of up to $750.

FINANCIAL AID PROCEDURES

Forms required: FAFSA, state aid form.

Dates and Deadlines: Priority date 3/15; no closing date. Applicants notified on a rolling basis starting 3/15; must reply by 5/1 or within 2 week(s) of notification.

Transfers: Applicants notified on a rolling basis starting 3/15.

CONTACT

Stephen Field, Director of Student Financial Services
2301 Westside Drive, Rochester, NY 14624-1997
(585) 594-6150

Rochester Institute of Technology
Rochester, New York
www.rit.edu   Federal Code: 002806

4-year private university in large city.

Enrollment: 13,260 undergrads, 7% part-time. 2,625 full-time freshmen.

Selectivity: Admits 50 to 75% of applicants.

BASIC COSTS (2010-2011)

Tuition and fees: $30,717.
Per-credit charge: $673.

Room and board: $10,044.

Additional info: Tuition for students matriculated full-time at the National Technical Institute for the Deaf (NTID) is $10,719. Tuition/fee waivers available for unemployed or children of unemployed.

FINANCIAL AID PICTURE (2008-2009)

Students with need: Out of 2,305 full-time freshmen who applied for aid, 1,945 were judged to have need. Of these, 1,945 received aid, and 1,595 had their full need met. Average financial aid package met 88% of need; average scholarship/grant was $15,000; average loan was $5,100. For part-time students, average financial aid package was $7,500.

Students without need: 337 full-time freshmen who did not demonstrate need for aid received scholarships/grants; average award was $8,700. No-need awards available for academics, art, leadership, ROTC.

Scholarships offered: Presidential Scholarships: $7,500 to $13,000 per year; top 10% of high school class with minimum SAT of 1860 on the three combined sections (or ACT Composite 27) or top 20% of high school class with SAT of 1950 on the three combined sections (or ACT 28).

Additional info: Most juniors and seniors participate in cooperative education program, earning an average $4,500-$6,500 per 3-month employment period through paid employment in jobs related to major.

FINANCIAL AID PROCEDURES

Forms required: FAFSA, state aid form.

Dates and Deadlines: Priority date 3/1; no closing date. Applicants notified on a rolling basis starting 3/15; must reply by 5/1.

Transfers: Priority date 3/15. Applicants notified on a rolling basis starting 4/1; must reply by 5/1. Special merit scholarship programs available specifically for transfers with high GPA.

CONTACT

Verna Hazen, Assistant Vice President and Director of Financial Aid
60 Lomb Memorial Drive, Rochester, NY 14623-5604
(585) 475-2186

Rockland Community College
Suffern, New York
www.sunyrockland.edu   Federal Code: 002877

2-year public community college in large town.

Enrollment: 6,661 undergrads.

Selectivity: Open admission.

BASIC COSTS (2009-2010)

Tuition and fees: $3,718; out-of-state residents $7,143.
Per-credit charge: $142; out-of-state residents $284.

FINANCIAL AID PICTURE (2009-2010)

Students with need: Need-based aid available for full-time and part-time students. Work study available nights, weekends, and for part-time students.

Scholarships offered: SUNY Empire State Honors Minority Scholarships: available to African American, Latino, and Native American students; 8 awarded; $1,000 per semester for 4 semesters. Jack Watson Scholarships: minimum 3.5 high school GPA or 94 average in Regents; 5 awarded; $1,163 per semester, renewable for 2nd year. Alumni Scholarships for children of alumni with 75 average; varying amounts.

FINANCIAL AID PROCEDURES

Forms required: FAFSA, institutional form.

Dates and Deadlines: Priority date 5/31; no closing date. Applicants notified on a rolling basis starting 6/1; must reply within 3 week(s) of notification.

CONTACT

Debra Brouabidi, Director of Financial Aid
145 College Road, Suffern, NY 10901
(845) 574-4000

Russell Sage College

Troy, New York
www.sage.edu/rsc Federal Code: 002810

4-year private liberal arts college for women in small city.
Enrollment: 704 undergrads, 3% part-time. 128 full-time freshmen.
Selectivity: Admits over 75% of applicants.

BASIC COSTS (2010-2011)

Tuition and fees: $27,850.
Per-credit charge: $900.
Room and board: $10,150.

FINANCIAL AID PICTURE (2009-2010)

Students with need: Out of 128 full-time freshmen who applied for aid, 123 were judged to have need. Of these, 123 received aid, and 82 had their full need met. For part-time students, average financial aid package was $13,305.
Students without need: 5 full-time freshmen who did not demonstrate need for aid received scholarships/grants; average award was $10,200. No-need awards available for academics, alumni affiliation, leadership, music/drama.
Scholarships offered: Multiple awards to qualified students: Presidential and Dean's scholarship, Girl Scout scholarship, first-generation scholarship, valedictorian-salutatorian scholarship, student Sage scholarship, endowed scholarships for minority students and specific majors.
Cumulative student debt: 96% of graduating class had student loans; average debt was $29,000.

FINANCIAL AID PROCEDURES

Forms required: FAFSA, state aid form.
Dates and Deadlines: Priority date 3/1; no closing date. Applicants notified on a rolling basis starting 3/1; must reply by 5/1 or within 2 week(s) of notification.
Transfers: Phi Theta Kappa Transfer Scholarship available.

CONTACT

James Dease, Associate Vice President for Student Services
45 Ferry Street, Troy, NY 12180-4115
(518) 244-4525

Sage College of Albany

Albany, New York
www.sage.edu Federal Code: 002811

4-year private business and liberal arts college in small city.
Enrollment: 806 undergrads, 31% part-time. 105 full-time freshmen.
Selectivity: Admits 50 to 75% of applicants.

BASIC COSTS (2010-2011)

Tuition and fees: $27,850.
Per-credit charge: $900.
Room and board: $10,150.

FINANCIAL AID PICTURE (2009-2010)

Students with need: Out of 104 full-time freshmen who applied for aid, 104 were judged to have need. Of these, 104 received aid, and 76 had their full need met. For part-time students, average financial aid package was $9,290.
Students without need: 5 full-time freshmen who did not demonstrate need for aid received scholarships/grants; average award was $10,000. No-need awards available for academics, art, leadership.
Scholarships offered: Multiple awards to qualified students: Presidential and Dean's scholarships, first-generation scholarship, art scholarship, valedictorian-salutatorian scholarship, diversity leadership scholarship. Endowed scholarships available for minority students and specific majors.

Cumulative student debt: 96% of graduating class had student loans; average debt was $24,000.

FINANCIAL AID PROCEDURES

Forms required: FAFSA, state aid form.
Dates and Deadlines: Priority date 3/1; no closing date. Applicants notified on a rolling basis starting 3/1; must reply by 5/1 or within 2 week(s) of notification.
Transfers: Phi Theta Kappa transfer scholarship available.

CONTACT

James Dease, Associate Vice President for Student Services
140 New Scotland Avenue, Albany, NY 12208
(518) 292-1783

Saint Bonaventure University

St. Bonaventure, New York
www.sbu.edu Federal Code: 002817

4-year private university in large town, affiliated with Roman Catholic Church.
Enrollment: 1,878 undergrads, 1% part-time. 466 full-time freshmen.
Selectivity: Admits over 75% of applicants.

BASIC COSTS (2009-2010)

Tuition and fees: $25,885.
Per-credit charge: $745.
Room and board: $9,015.
Additional info: Tuition/fee waivers available for minority students.

FINANCIAL AID PICTURE

Students with need: Need-based aid available for full-time and part-time students. Work study available nights, weekends, and for part-time students.
Students without need: No-need awards available for academics, art, athletics, leadership, minority status, music/drama, religious affiliation, ROTC, state/district residency.

FINANCIAL AID PROCEDURES

Forms required: FAFSA, state aid form, institutional form.
Dates and Deadlines: Priority date 2/1; no closing date. Applicants notified on a rolling basis starting 4/1; must reply by 5/1 or within 3 week(s) of notification.
Transfers: Closing date 5/1.

CONTACT

Elisabeth Rankin, Director of Financial Aid
Route 417, St. Bonaventure, NY 14778-2284
(716) 375-2400

St. Elizabeth College of Nursing

Utica, New York
www.secon.edu Federal Code: 006461

2-year private nursing college in small city, affiliated with Roman Catholic Church.
Enrollment: 239 undergrads.
Selectivity: Admits less than 50% of applicants.

BASIC COSTS (2010-2011)

Tuition and fees: $12,700.
Per-credit charge: $325.

FINANCIAL AID PICTURE (2009-2010)

Students with need: Need-based aid available for full-time and part-time students.

FINANCIAL AID PROCEDURES

Forms required: FAFSA, state aid form.

Dates and Deadlines: No deadline. Applicants notified on a rolling basis starting 1/1; must reply within 2 week(s) of notification.

CONTACT

Sherry Wojnas, Director, Financial Aid
2215 Genesee Street, Utica, NY 13501
(315) 798-8206

St. Francis College
Brooklyn Heights, New York
www.stfranciscollege.edu   Federal Code: 002820

4-year private liberal arts college in very large city, affiliated with Roman Catholic Church.

Enrollment: 2,451 undergrads, 10% part-time. 571 full-time freshmen.
Selectivity: Admits over 75% of applicants.

BASIC COSTS (2009-2010)

Tuition and fees: $16,480.
Additional info: Tuition/fee waivers available for unemployed or children of unemployed.

FINANCIAL AID PICTURE (2009-2010)

Students with need: Need-based aid available for full-time and part-time students.
Students without need: No-need awards available for academics, athletics.
Scholarships offered: Presidential Scholarship: full tuition; minimum 90 high school GPA, 1150 SAT. St. Francis Scholarship: $7,500; minimum 85 high school GPA, 1100 SAT. St. Clare Scholarship: $6,500; minimum 85 high school GPA, 1100 SAT. Dean's Scholarship: $3,500; minimum 1000 SAT. All scholarships renewable annually for 4 years provided student maintains full-time status and minimum 3.0 cumulative GPA. SAT scores are exclusive of Writing.

FINANCIAL AID PROCEDURES

Forms required: FAFSA, state aid form.
Dates and Deadlines: Priority date 2/15; no closing date. Applicants notified on a rolling basis starting 3/15; must reply within 2 week(s) of notification.

CONTACT

Joseph Cummings, Director, Student Financial Services
180 Remsen Street, Brooklyn Heights, NY 11201-9902
(718) 489-5255

St. John Fisher College
Rochester, New York
www.sjfc.edu   Federal Code: 002821

4-year private liberal arts college in large town, affiliated with Roman Catholic Church.

Enrollment: 2,810 undergrads, 7% part-time. 569 full-time freshmen.
Selectivity: Admits 50 to 75% of applicants. GED not accepted.

BASIC COSTS (2010-2011)

Tuition and fees: $25,270.
Per-credit charge: $675.
Room and board: $10,290.

FINANCIAL AID PICTURE (2008-2009)

Students with need: Out of 543 full-time freshmen who applied for aid, 457 were judged to have need. Of these, 457 received aid, and 179 had their full need met. Average financial aid package met 84% of need; average scholarship/grant was $14,893; average loan was $4,030.
Students without need: 105 full-time freshmen who did not demonstrate need for aid received scholarships/grants; average award was $8,447. No-need awards available for academics, leadership.

Scholarships offered: Merit based scholarships, $9,500 to $12,500; Honors and Science Scholars programs, $3,000 annually; Fisher Service Scholars Program, one-third cost of education; First Generation Scholars Program, $5,000 up to one-half of cost of education.
Cumulative student debt: 84% of graduating class had student loans; average debt was $30,281.

FINANCIAL AID PROCEDURES

Forms required: FAFSA, state aid form.
Dates and Deadlines: Priority date 2/15; no closing date. Applicants notified on a rolling basis starting 3/22; must reply by 5/1 or within 3 week(s) of notification.
Transfers: No deadline. Applicants notified on a rolling basis starting 3/22; must reply within 3 week(s) of notification.

CONTACT

Angela Monnat, Director of Financial Aid
3690 East Avenue, Rochester, NY 14618-3597
(585) 385-8042

St. John's University
Queens, New York
www.stjohns.edu   Federal Code: 002823

4-year private university in very large city, affiliated with Roman Catholic Church.

Enrollment: 12,115 undergrads, 3% part-time. 3,261 full-time freshmen.
Selectivity: Admits less than 50% of applicants.

BASIC COSTS (2009-2010)

Tuition and fees: $30,040.
Per-credit charge: $978.
Room and board: $13,140.
Additional info: Tuition may vary by program and class year. Four-year fixed rate tuition plan available for incoming freshmen. Tuition at time of enrollment locked for 4 years.

FINANCIAL AID PICTURE (2008-2009)

Students with need: Out of 2,866 full-time freshmen who applied for aid, 2,634 were judged to have need. Of these, 2,622 received aid, and 8 had their full need met. Average financial aid package met 71% of need; average scholarship/grant was $13,428; average loan was $4,190. For part-time students, average financial aid package was $9,536.
Students without need: 194 full-time freshmen who did not demonstrate need for aid received scholarships/grants; average award was $12,274. No-need awards available for academics, alumni affiliation, art, athletics, leadership, music/drama, religious affiliation, ROTC.
Scholarships offered: 46 full-time freshmen received athletic scholarships; average amount $28,362.
Cumulative student debt: 70% of graduating class had student loans; average debt was $30,692.

FINANCIAL AID PROCEDURES

Forms required: FAFSA.
Dates and Deadlines: Priority date 2/1; no closing date. Applicants notified on a rolling basis starting 3/15; must reply within 2 week(s) of notification.
Transfers: Must reply within 2 week(s) of notification. Scholarships available if 24 credits college study completed with a minimum GPA of 3.0.

CONTACT

Jorge Rodriguez, Associate Vice President and Executive Director, Financial Aid
8000 Utopia Parkway, Queens, NY 11439
(718) 990-2000

St. Joseph's College

Brooklyn, New York
www.sjcny.edu   Federal Code: 002825

4-year private liberal arts and teachers college in very large city.
Enrollment: 1,133 undergrads, 27% part-time. 211 full-time freshmen.
Selectivity: Admits 50 to 75% of applicants.

BASIC COSTS (2009-2010)
Tuition and fees: $16,763.
Per-credit charge: $530.

FINANCIAL AID PICTURE (2009-2010)
Students with need: Out of 198 full-time freshmen who applied for aid, 163 were judged to have need. Of these, 163 received aid, and 44 had their full need met. Average financial aid package met 76% of need; average scholarship/grant was $11,009; average loan was $3,147. Need-based aid available for part-time students.
Students without need: 32 full-time freshmen who did not demonstrate need for aid received scholarships/grants; average award was $8,545. No-need awards available for academics, alumni affiliation, leadership, minority status.
Cumulative student debt: 55% of graduating class had student loans; average debt was $20,616.

FINANCIAL AID PROCEDURES
Forms required: FAFSA, state aid form.
Dates and Deadlines: Priority date 2/25; no closing date. Applicants notified on a rolling basis starting 3/15; must reply by 5/1 or within 2 week(s) of notification.
Transfers: Priority date 3/15; no deadline.

CONTACT
Amy Thompson, Director of Financial Aid
245 Clinton Avenue, Brooklyn, NY 11205-3688
(718) 636-6808

St. Joseph's College of Nursing

Syracuse, New York
www.sjhsyr.org/nursing   Federal Code: 006467

2-year private nursing college in small city, affiliated with Roman Catholic Church.
Enrollment: 289 undergrads, 43% part-time.
Selectivity: Admits less than 50% of applicants.

BASIC COSTS (2009-2010)
Tuition and fees: $12,160.
Per-credit charge: $330.
Room only: $3,900.
Additional info: Tuition includes liberal arts component of degree taken at other institution.

FINANCIAL AID PICTURE (2008-2009)
Students with need: 21% of average financial aid package awarded as scholarships/grants; 79% awarded as loans/jobs. Need-based aid available for part-time students.
Students without need: This college awards aid only to students with need.

FINANCIAL AID PROCEDURES
Forms required: FAFSA, state aid form.
Dates and Deadlines: Priority date 3/1; no closing date. Applicants notified on a rolling basis starting 6/15.

CONTACT
Theresa Moser, Director of Financial Aid
206 Prospect Avenue, Syracuse, NY 13203
(315) 448-5040

St. Joseph's College: Suffolk Campus

Patchogue, New York
www.sjcny.edu   Federal Code: E00505

4-year private branch campus and liberal arts college in large town.
Enrollment: 3,828 undergrads, 19% part-time. 489 full-time freshmen.
Selectivity: Admits 50 to 75% of applicants.

BASIC COSTS (2009-2010)
Tuition and fees: $16,763.
Per-credit charge: $530.

FINANCIAL AID PICTURE (2009-2010)
Students with need: Out of 477 full-time freshmen who applied for aid, 330 were judged to have need. Of these, 325 received aid, and 107 had their full need met. Average financial aid package met 83% of need; average scholarship/grant was $9,477; average loan was $3,109. Need-based aid available for part-time students.
Students without need: 119 full-time freshmen who did not demonstrate need for aid received scholarships/grants; average award was $7,906. No-need awards available for academics, alumni affiliation, leadership, minority status.
Scholarships offered: Board of Trustees Scholarship: full tuition less outside aid; entering freshmen with a 92 high school average and 1200 SAT. Alumni Scholarship: variable award on yearly basis to children of alumni based on need and merit. Scholastic Achievement Award: up to $8,000 per year for entering freshmen. Academic Achievement Scholarship: automatically awards up to $4,500 for 3.6 GPA or better and $3,000 for 3.3 GPA or better; to entering transfer students with 3.3 GPA or better and associate degree. SAT scores listed exclusive of Writing.
Cumulative student debt: 64% of graduating class had student loans; average debt was $21,023.

FINANCIAL AID PROCEDURES
Forms required: FAFSA, state aid form.
Dates and Deadlines: Priority date 2/25; no closing date. Applicants notified on a rolling basis starting 3/15; must reply by 5/1 or within 2 week(s) of notification.
Transfers: Priority date 3/15; no deadline. Applicants notified on a rolling basis starting 3/15; must reply within 2 week(s) of notification.

CONTACT
Amy Thompson, Director of Financial Aid
155 West Roe Boulevard, Patchogue, NY 11772-2603
(631) 447-3214

St. Lawrence University

Canton, New York
www.stlawu.edu   Federal Code: 002829

4-year private liberal arts college in small town.
Enrollment: 2,271 undergrads. 580 full-time freshmen.
Selectivity: Admits less than 50% of applicants.

BASIC COSTS (2009-2010)
Tuition and fees: $39,765.
Room and board: $10,160.

FINANCIAL AID PICTURE (2009-2010)

Students with need: Out of 446 full-time freshmen who applied for aid, 384 were judged to have need. Of these, 384 received aid, and 159 had their full need met. Average financial aid package met 92% of need; average scholarship/grant was $27,822; average loan was $3,223.

Students without need: 88 full-time freshmen who did not demonstrate need for aid received scholarships/grants; average award was $11,344. No-need awards available for academics, alumni affiliation, athletics, minority status, ROTC, state/district residency.

Scholarships offered: *Merit:* Merit scholarships: $10,000 to $30,000 annually. Augsbury/North Country Scholarship: for students in some schools in northern New York and southern Ontario; nomination by counselor required. Community Service Scholarship: based on past and current service. Presidential Diversity Scholarship: for students of African American, Asian American, Hispanic American and Native American heritage and those who support multiculturalism. Sesquicentennial and University Scholarship: based on academic excellence, character and leadership. Vilas Scholarship: for students interested in business. *Athletic:* 6 full-time freshmen received athletic scholarships; average amount $49,925.

Cumulative student debt: 74% of graduating class had student loans; average debt was $31,653.

FINANCIAL AID PROCEDURES

Forms required: FAFSA.

Dates and Deadlines: Closing date 2/1. Applicants notified by 3/31; must reply by 5/1 or within 2 week(s) of notification.

Transfers: Priority date 4/1; closing date 5/1. Applicants notified on a rolling basis starting 6/1; must reply within 2 week(s) of notification.

CONTACT

Patricia Farmer, Director of Financial Aid
Payson Hall, Canton, NY 13617
(315) 229-5265

St. Thomas Aquinas College

Sparkill, New York
www.stac.edu
Federal Code: 002832

4-year private liberal arts college in large town.

Enrollment: 1,414 undergrads, 6% part-time. 352 full-time freshmen.

Selectivity: Admits over 75% of applicants.

BASIC COSTS (2010-2011)

Tuition and fees: $22,410.

Per-credit charge: $705.

Room and board: $10,300.

FINANCIAL AID PICTURE (2008-2009)

Students with need: Out of 316 full-time freshmen who applied for aid, 227 were judged to have need. Of these, 220 received aid, and 32 had their full need met. Average financial aid package met 58% of need; average scholarship/grant was $10,809; average loan was $3,544. For part-time students, average financial aid package was $4,750.

Students without need: 45 full-time freshmen who did not demonstrate need for aid received scholarships/grants; average award was $5,054. No-need awards available for academics, athletics.

Scholarships offered: 4 full-time freshmen received athletic scholarships; average amount $14,740.

FINANCIAL AID PROCEDURES

Forms required: FAFSA, state aid form.

Dates and Deadlines: Priority date 2/15; no closing date. Applicants notified on a rolling basis starting 3/1; must reply by 5/1 or within 4 week(s) of notification.

Transfers: Closing date 5/1. Applicants notified on a rolling basis; must reply within 4 week(s) of notification.

CONTACT

Anna Chrissotimos, Director of Financial Aid
125 Route 340, Sparkill, NY 10976
(845) 398-4097

Sarah Lawrence College

Bronxville, New York
www.slc.edu
Federal Code: 002813
CSS Code: 2810

4-year private liberal arts college in small city.

Enrollment: 1,295 undergrads, 3% part-time. 364 full-time freshmen.

Selectivity: Admits 50 to 75% of applicants.

BASIC COSTS (2009-2010)

Tuition and fees: $41,968.

Room and board: $13,820.

FINANCIAL AID PICTURE (2009-2010)

Students with need: Out of 261 full-time freshmen who applied for aid, 235 were judged to have need. Of these, 235 received aid, and 93 had their full need met. Average financial aid package met 96% of need; average scholarship/grant was $32,318; average loan was $2,590. For part-time students, average financial aid package was $18,079.

Students without need: This college awards aid only to students with need.

Cumulative student debt: 52% of graduating class had student loans; average debt was $17,246.

FINANCIAL AID PROCEDURES

Forms required: FAFSA, CSS PROFILE, state aid form.

Dates and Deadlines: Closing date 2/1. Applicants notified by 4/1; must reply by 5/1.

Transfers: Closing date 3/15. Applicants notified by 5/15. Maximum institutional grant to transfer students is $27,000 a year. Loans and work study available above and beyond this grant.

CONTACT

Heather McDonnell, Director of Financial Aid
1 Mead Way, Bronxville, NY 10708-5999
(914) 395-2570

Schenectady County Community College

Schenectady, New York
www.sunysccc.edu
Federal Code: 006785

2-year public community college in small city.

Enrollment: 3,424 undergrads, 28% part-time. 772 full-time freshmen.

Selectivity: Open admission; but selective for some programs.

BASIC COSTS (2009-2010)

Tuition and fees: $3,402; out-of-state residents $6,552.

Per-credit charge: $141; out-of-state residents $272.

FINANCIAL AID PICTURE (2008-2009)

Students with need: Need-based aid available for full-time and part-time students.

Students without need: This college awards aid only to students with need.

FINANCIAL AID PROCEDURES

Forms required: FAFSA.

Dates and Deadlines: Priority date 5/1; no closing date. Applicants notified on a rolling basis starting 4/15; must reply by 8/31.

CONTACT

Brian McGarvey, Director of Financial Aid
78 Washington Avenue, Schenectady, NY 12305
(518) 381-1352

School of Visual Arts

New York, New York
www.sva.edu   Federal Code: 007468

4-year for-profit visual arts college in very large city.
Enrollment: 3,379 undergrads, 4% part-time. 653 full-time freshmen.
Selectivity: Admits 50 to 75% of applicants.

BASIC COSTS (2009-2010)

Tuition and fees: $26,800.
Per-credit charge: $895.
Room only: $12,700.
Additional info: Additional fees vary by department.

FINANCIAL AID PICTURE (2009-2010)

Students with need: Out of 452 full-time freshmen who applied for aid, 396 were judged to have need. Of these, 386 received aid, and 2 had their full need met. Average financial aid package met 41% of need; average scholarship/grant was $9,473; average loan was $3,581. For part-time students, average financial aid package was $8,268.
Students without need: 30 full-time freshmen who did not demonstrate need for aid received scholarships/grants; average award was $8,600. No-need awards available for art.
Scholarships offered: SVA matching scholarship available to full- and part-time undergraduate and graduate students. SVA will match 25% of any outside scholarship, up to $2,500, that a student obtains.
Cumulative student debt: 75% of graduating class had student loans; average debt was $37,699.

FINANCIAL AID PROCEDURES

Forms required: FAFSA, state aid form.
Dates and Deadlines: Priority date 2/1; closing date 3/1. Applicants notified on a rolling basis starting 2/15; must reply within 4 week(s) of notification.
Transfers: No deadline. Applicants notified on a rolling basis; must reply within 4 week(s) of notification.

CONTACT

William Berrios, Director of Financial Aid
209 East 23rd Street, New York, NY 10010-3994
(212) 592-2030

Siena College

Loudonville, New York
www.siena.edu   Federal Code: 002816

4-year private liberal arts college in large town, affiliated with Roman Catholic Church.
Enrollment: 3,220 undergrads, 4% part-time. 824 full-time freshmen.
Selectivity: Admits 50 to 75% of applicants.

BASIC COSTS (2010-2011)

Tuition and fees: $26,495.
Per-credit charge: $500.
Room and board: $10,375.

FINANCIAL AID PICTURE (2008-2009)

Students with need: Out of 737 full-time freshmen who applied for aid, 583 were judged to have need. Of these, 581 received aid, and 73 had their full need met. Average financial aid package met 77% of need; average scholarship/grant was $14,505; average loan was $3,307. For part-time students, average financial aid package was $12,326.

Students without need: 138 full-time freshmen who did not demonstrate need for aid received scholarships/grants; average award was $8,059. No-need awards available for academics, athletics, leadership, minority status, ROTC, state/district residency.
Scholarships offered: 73 full-time freshmen received athletic scholarships; average amount $11,785.

FINANCIAL AID PROCEDURES

Forms required: FAFSA, state aid form.
Dates and Deadlines: Priority date 2/15; closing date 5/1. Applicants notified by 4/1; must reply by 5/1.
Transfers: Priority date 3/1.

CONTACT

Mary Lawyer, Associate Vice President for Enrollment Management
515 Loudon Road, Loudonville, NY 12211-1462
(518) 783-2427

Skidmore College

Saratoga Springs, New York   Federal Code: 002814
www.skidmore.edu   CSS Code: 2815

4-year private liberal arts college in large town.
Enrollment: 2,630 undergrads.
Selectivity: Admits less than 50% of applicants.

BASIC COSTS (2009-2010)

Tuition and fees: $40,420.
Per-credit charge: $1,320.
Room and board: $10,776.

FINANCIAL AID PICTURE (2009-2010)

Students with need: Need-based aid available for full-time students. Work study available nights, weekends, and for part-time students.
Students without need: No-need awards available for music/drama.
Scholarships offered: Porter Presidential Scholarships in Science and Mathematics: $10,000 annually; based on outstanding ability and achievement in math, science, or computer science. Filene Undergraduate Music Scholarships: $10,000 annually; based on music ability. No drama scholarships.

FINANCIAL AID PROCEDURES

Forms required: FAFSA, CSS PROFILE.
Dates and Deadlines: Closing date 1/15. Applicants notified by 4/1; must reply by 5/1.
Transfers: Priority date 4/1. Applicants notified on a rolling basis starting 4/15; must reply within 3 week(s) of notification. Some transfer students eligible for need-based grant assistance. Other transfer students eligible for grant assistance after 1 full year of enrollment or at beginning of junior year, whichever comes first.

CONTACT

Robert Shorb, Associate Dean, Director of Student Aid and Family Finance
815 North Broadway, Saratoga Springs, NY 12866
(518) 580-5750

State University of New York at Albany

Albany, New York
www.albany.edu   Federal Code: 002835

4-year public university in small city.
Enrollment: 12,797 undergrads, 4% part-time. 2,398 full-time freshmen.
Selectivity: Admits less than 50% of applicants.

BASIC COSTS (2009-2010)

Tuition and fees: $6,748; out-of-state residents $14,648.
Per-credit charge: $207; out-of-state residents $536.

Room and board: $10,238.

FINANCIAL AID PICTURE (2008-2009)

Students with need: Out of 2,012 full-time freshmen who applied for aid, 1,338 were judged to have need. Of these, 1,303 received aid, and 146 had their full need met. Average financial aid package met 71% of need; average scholarship/grant was $6,331; average loan was $3,878. For part-time students, average financial aid package was $5,170.

Students without need: 210 full-time freshmen who did not demonstrate need for aid received scholarships/grants; average award was $3,445. No-need awards available for academics, athletics, state/district residency.

Scholarships offered: *Merit:* Presidential Scholarship: up to $4,000 per year for NY residents and $5,000 per year for out-of-state students; renewable; requires minimum 90 high school average and combined SAT Critical Reading and Math scores in the upper 1200s or higher. *Athletic:* 55 full-time freshmen received athletic scholarships; average amount $9,764.

Cumulative student debt: 71% of graduating class had student loans; average debt was $22,092.

FINANCIAL AID PROCEDURES

Forms required: FAFSA, state aid form.

Dates and Deadlines: Priority date 3/15; no closing date. Applicants notified on a rolling basis starting 3/20; must reply by 5/1.

CONTACT

Diane Corbett, Director of Financial Aid
Office of Undergraduate Admissions, University Hall 112, Albany, NY 12222
(518) 442-3202

State University of New York at Binghamton
Binghamton, New York
www.binghamton.edu   Federal Code: 002836

4-year public university in small city.
Enrollment: 11,646 undergrads, 3% part-time. 2,026 full-time freshmen.
Selectivity: Admits less than 50% of applicants.

BASIC COSTS (2009-2010)
Tuition and fees: $6,761; out-of-state residents $14,661.
Per-credit charge: $207; out-of-state residents $536.
Room and board: $10,614.

FINANCIAL AID PICTURE (2009-2010)

Students with need: Out of 1,626 full-time freshmen who applied for aid, 902 were judged to have need. Of these, 902 received aid, and 158 had their full need met. Average financial aid package met 79% of need; average scholarship/grant was $7,395; average loan was $3,791. For part-time students, average financial aid package was $10,977.

Students without need: 9 full-time freshmen who did not demonstrate need for aid received scholarships/grants; average award was $2,133. No-need awards available for academics, art, athletics, leadership, minority status, music/drama, state/district residency.

Scholarships offered: 74 full-time freshmen received athletic scholarships; average amount $9,469.

Cumulative student debt: 49% of graduating class had student loans; average debt was $14,560.

FINANCIAL AID PROCEDURES

Forms required: FAFSA, state aid form.

Dates and Deadlines: Priority date 2/1; no closing date. Applicants notified on a rolling basis starting 4/1; must reply within 2 week(s) of notification.

Transfers: No deadline. Applicants notified on a rolling basis starting 4/1; must reply within 2 week(s) of notification. Awards based on self-reported grade level until an official transfer credit evaluation is completed.

CONTACT

Dennis Chavez, Director of Financial Aid Services
Box 6001, Binghamton, NY 13902-6001
(607) 777-2428

State University of New York at Buffalo
Buffalo, New York
www.buffalo.edu   Federal Code: 002837

4-year public university in large city.
Enrollment: 19,149 undergrads, 6% part-time. 3,378 full-time freshmen.
Selectivity: Admits 50 to 75% of applicants.

BASIC COSTS (2009-2010)
Tuition and fees: $7,013; out-of-state residents $14,913.
Per-credit charge: $207; out-of-state residents $536.
Room and board: $9,648.
Additional info: Tuition/fee waivers available for adults.

FINANCIAL AID PICTURE (2008-2009)

Students with need: Out of 2,588 full-time freshmen who applied for aid, 1,692 were judged to have need. Of these, 1,687 received aid, and 414 had their full need met. Average financial aid package met 64% of need; average scholarship/grant was $1,014; average loan was $2,715. For part-time students, average financial aid package was $3,850.

Students without need: 174 full-time freshmen who did not demonstrate need for aid received scholarships/grants; average award was $4,171. No-need awards available for academics, athletics, minority status, music/drama, state/district residency.

Scholarships offered: *Merit:* Honors program includes scholarships for high academic achievement, high SAT scores. *Athletic:* 75 full-time freshmen received athletic scholarships; average amount $12,259.

Cumulative student debt: 44% of graduating class had student loans; average debt was $15,911.

FINANCIAL AID PROCEDURES

Forms required: FAFSA.

Dates and Deadlines: Priority date 3/1; no closing date. Applicants notified on a rolling basis starting 2/1; must reply by 5/1.

CONTACT

Cindy Kohlman, Director of Financial Aid
12 Capen Hall, Buffalo, NY 14260-1660
(716) 645-2450

State University of New York at Farmingdale
Farmingdale, New York
www.farmingdale.edu   Federal Code: 002858

4-year public technical college in large town.
Enrollment: 6,147 undergrads, 21% part-time. 888 full-time freshmen.
Selectivity: Admits less than 50% of applicants.

BASIC COSTS (2009-2010)
Tuition and fees: $6,030; out-of-state residents $13,930.
Per-credit charge: $207; out-of-state residents $536.
Room and board: $11,618.

FINANCIAL AID PICTURE

Students with need: Need-based aid available for full-time and part-time students.

Students without need: No-need awards available for academics.

FINANCIAL AID PROCEDURES

Forms required: FAFSA, state aid form, institutional form.

Dates and Deadlines: Priority date 4/1; no closing date. Applicants notified on a rolling basis starting 4/1.

CONTACT

Catherine Malnichuck, Director of Financial Services
2350 Broadhollow Road, Farmingdale, NY 11735-1021
(631) 420-2578

State University of New York at New Paltz

New Paltz, New York
www.newpaltz.edu   Federal Code: 002846

4-year public liberal arts college in large town.

Enrollment: 6,308 undergrads, 8% part-time. 1,055 full-time freshmen.

Selectivity: Admits less than 50% of applicants.

BASIC COSTS (2009-2010)

Tuition and fees: $6,081; out-of-state residents $13,981.

Per-credit charge: $207; out-of-state residents $536.

Room and board: $9,242.

FINANCIAL AID PICTURE (2009-2010)

Students with need: Out of 928 full-time freshmen who applied for aid, 554 were judged to have need. Of these, 552 received aid, and 85 had their full need met. Average financial aid package met 57% of need; average scholarship/grant was $5,214; average loan was $3,546. For part-time students, average financial aid package was $5,071.

Students without need: This college awards aid only to students with need.

Cumulative student debt: 66% of graduating class had student loans; average debt was $16,823.

FINANCIAL AID PROCEDURES

Forms required: FAFSA, state aid form.

Dates and Deadlines: Priority date 3/15; no closing date. Applicants notified on a rolling basis starting 4/1; must reply within 6 week(s) of notification.

Transfers: No deadline. Applicants notified on a rolling basis starting 4/1; must reply within 4 week(s) of notification.

CONTACT

Daniel Sistarenik, Director of Financial Aid
100 Hawk Drive, New Paltz, NY 12561-2443
(845) 257-3250

State University of New York at Oswego

Oswego, New York
www.oswego.edu   Federal Code: 002848

4-year public university in large town.

Enrollment: 7,145 undergrads, 5% part-time. 1,383 full-time freshmen.

Selectivity: Admits less than 50% of applicants.

BASIC COSTS (2009-2010)

Tuition and fees: $6,256; out-of-state residents $14,156.

Per-credit charge: $207; out-of-state residents $536.

Room and board: $10,870.

FINANCIAL AID PICTURE (2009-2010)

Students with need: Out of 1,264 full-time freshmen who applied for aid, 912 were judged to have need. Of these, 873 received aid, and 441 had their full need met. Average financial aid package met 84% of need; average scholarship/grant was $5,263; average loan was $5,812. For part-time students, average financial aid package was $8,278.

Students without need: 242 full-time freshmen who did not demonstrate need for aid received scholarships/grants; average award was $5,812. No-need awards available for academics, state/district residency.

Scholarships offered: Annual scholarships: $500 to $4,400 annually; based on class rank in top 15%. Additional residential scholarships for out-of-state students: $4,490 annually; requires on-campus housing.

Cumulative student debt: 86% of graduating class had student loans; average debt was $25,488.

FINANCIAL AID PROCEDURES

Forms required: FAFSA.

Dates and Deadlines: Priority date 3/1; no closing date. Applicants notified on a rolling basis starting 3/1; must reply by 5/1 or within 3 week(s) of notification.

Transfers: No deadline. Applicants notified on a rolling basis starting 4/1; must reply by 5/1 or within 21 week(s) of notification.

CONTACT

Mark Humbert, Director of Financial Aid
229 Sheldon Hall, Oswego, NY 13126-3599
(315) 312-2248

State University of New York at Purchase

Purchase, New York
www.purchase.edu   Federal Code: 006791

4-year public university in large town.

Enrollment: 3,830 undergrads, 6% part-time. 694 full-time freshmen.

Selectivity: Admits less than 50% of applicants.

BASIC COSTS (2009-2010)

Tuition and fees: $6,475; out-of-state residents $14,375.

Per-credit charge: $207; out-of-state residents $536.

Room and board: $10,270.

FINANCIAL AID PICTURE (2009-2010)

Students with need: Out of 567 full-time freshmen who applied for aid, 378 were judged to have need. Of these, 378 received aid, and 25 had their full need met. Average financial aid package met 53% of need; average scholarship/grant was $6,067; average loan was $3,586. For part-time students, average financial aid package was $4,464.

Students without need: 27 full-time freshmen who did not demonstrate need for aid received scholarships/grants; average award was $2,175. No-need awards available for academics, art, minority status, music/drama.

Cumulative student debt: 58% of graduating class had student loans; average debt was $26,275.

Additional info: All applicants automatically considered for scholarship upon review of applications, essays, auditions, and/or portfolio.

FINANCIAL AID PROCEDURES

Forms required: FAFSA, state aid form.

Dates and Deadlines: Priority date 2/1; no closing date. Applicants notified on a rolling basis starting 3/1; must reply within 2 week(s) of notification.

Transfers: Financial aid transcripts required from all previously attended institutions.

CONTACT

Corey York, Director of Financial Aid
735 Anderson Hill Road, Purchase, NY 10577-1400
(914) 251-6350

State University of New York at Stony Brook

Stony Brook, New York
www.stonybrook.edu   Federal Code: 002838

4-year public university in large town.
Enrollment: 16,034 undergrads, 6% part-time. 2,876 full-time freshmen.
Selectivity: Admits less than 50% of applicants.

BASIC COSTS (2009-2010)

Tuition and fees: $6,489; out-of-state residents $14,389.
Per-credit charge: $207; out-of-state residents $536.
Room and board: $10,018.

FINANCIAL AID PICTURE (2008-2009)

Students with need: Out of 2,318 full-time freshmen who applied for aid, 1,521 were judged to have need. Of these, 1,468 received aid, and 438 had their full need met. Average financial aid package met 67% of need; average scholarship/grant was $6,849; average loan was $4,557. For part-time students, average financial aid package was $4,922.
Students without need: 451 full-time freshmen who did not demonstrate need for aid received scholarships/grants; average award was $2,982. No-need awards available for academics, alumni affiliation, art, athletics, job skills, leadership, music/drama.
Scholarships offered: 32 full-time freshmen received athletic scholarships; average amount $13,652.
Cumulative student debt: 63% of graduating class had student loans; average debt was $17,487.

FINANCIAL AID PROCEDURES

Forms required: FAFSA.
Dates and Deadlines: Priority date 3/1; no closing date. Applicants notified on a rolling basis starting 3/1; must reply by 5/1 or within 2 week(s) of notification.

CONTACT

Jacqueline Pascariello, Director Financial Aid
118 Administration Building, Stony Brook, NY 11794-1901
(631) 689-6840

State University of New York College at Brockport

Brockport, New York
www.brockport.edu   Federal Code: 002841

4-year public liberal arts college in small town.
Enrollment: 7,052 undergrads.

BASIC COSTS (2009-2010)

Tuition and fees: $6,108; out-of-state residents $14,008.
Per-credit charge: $207; out-of-state residents $536.
Room and board: $9,200.

FINANCIAL AID PICTURE (2008-2009)

Students with need: Need-based aid available for full-time and part-time students. Work study available nights, weekends, and for part-time students.
Students without need: No-need awards available for academics, alumni affiliation, art, leadership, minority status, ROTC, state/district residency.
Scholarships offered: Extraordinary Academic Scholarships: $2,250 to $12,100 per year; minimum qualifications include SAT scores of 1100 (24 ACT), rank in top 25% of class, 90 average or higher. SAT score exclusive of Writing portion.

FINANCIAL AID PROCEDURES

Forms required: FAFSA.

Dates and Deadlines: Priority date 2/15; no closing date. Applicants notified on a rolling basis starting 3/15; must reply by 5/1 or within 4 week(s) of notification.

CONTACT

J. Atkinson, Assistant Vice President for Enrollment Management and Student Affairs
350 New Campus Drive, Brockport, NY 14420-2915
(585) 395-2501

State University of New York College at Buffalo

Buffalo, New York
www.buffalostate.edu   Federal Code: 002842

4-year public liberal arts and teachers college in large city.
Enrollment: 9,626 undergrads.
Selectivity: Admits less than 50% of applicants.

BASIC COSTS (2009-2010)

Tuition and fees: $6,007; out-of-state residents $13,907.
Per-credit charge: $207; out-of-state residents $536.
Room and board: $9,186.
Additional info: Tuition/fee waivers available for minority students.

FINANCIAL AID PICTURE (2008-2009)

Students with need: Need-based aid available for full-time and part-time students.
Students without need: This college awards aid only to students with need.
Scholarships offered: Empire Minority Scholarships; $1,000 annually for 4 years. Honors Program; $2,000 for 2 years and $1,000 for remaining 2 years.

FINANCIAL AID PROCEDURES

Forms required: FAFSA.
Dates and Deadlines: Priority date 3/15; closing date 5/1. Applicants notified on a rolling basis starting 5/1; must reply within 4 week(s) of notification.
Transfers: No deadline.

CONTACT

Kent McGowan, Director of Financial Aid
1300 Elmwood Avenue, Moot Hall, Buffalo, NY 14222-1095
(716) 878-4902

State University of New York College at Cortland

Cortland, New York
www.cortland.edu   Federal Code: 002843

4-year public liberal arts and teachers college in large town.
Enrollment: 6,131 undergrads, 1% part-time. 1,167 full-time freshmen.
Selectivity: Admits less than 50% of applicants.

BASIC COSTS (2009-2010)

Tuition and fees: $6,145; out-of-state residents $14,045.
Per-credit charge: $207; out-of-state residents $536.
Room and board: $9,790.

FINANCIAL AID PICTURE (2008-2009)

Students with need: Need-based aid available for full-time and part-time students. Work study available nights, weekends, and for part-time students.
Students without need: No-need awards available for academics, art, leadership, minority status, music/drama, state/district residency.

FINANCIAL AID PROCEDURES

Forms required: FAFSA, state aid form.

Dates and Deadlines: Priority date 3/1; no closing date. Applicants notified on a rolling basis starting 3/15; must reply by 5/1 or within 4 week(s) of notification.

CONTACT

Karen Gallagher, Director of Financial Aid
PO Box 2000, Cortland, NY 13045-0900
(607) 753-4717

State University of New York College at Fredonia

Fredonia, New York
www.fredonia.edu   Federal Code: 002844

4-year public liberal arts college in large town.
Enrollment: 5,321 undergrads, 2% part-time. 1,085 full-time freshmen.
Selectivity: Admits less than 50% of applicants.

BASIC COSTS (2009-2010)

Tuition and fees: $6,259; out-of-state residents $14,159.
Per-credit charge: $207; out-of-state residents $536.
Room and board: $9,630.

FINANCIAL AID PICTURE (2009-2010)

Students with need: Out of 989 full-time freshmen who applied for aid, 690 were judged to have need. Of these, 684 received aid, and 160 had their full need met. Average financial aid package met 68% of need; average scholarship/grant was $4,047; average loan was $3,717. For part-time students, average financial aid package was $6,964.
Students without need: 111 full-time freshmen who did not demonstrate need for aid received scholarships/grants; average award was $1,912. No-need awards available for academics, alumni affiliation, art, athletics, leadership, minority status, music/drama.
Scholarships offered: Dean's Scholar Award: $1,000; minimum 90 high school average, 1150 SAT or 25 ACT; 100 awards. Foundation Academic Scholarship: $1,000; minimum 90 high school average, 1100 SAT or 24 ACT; 50 awards. President's Award of Excellence: $3,000, renewable; minimum 94 high school average, 1250 SAT or 28 ACT; 12 awards. President's Out-of-State Scholar Award: $5,000, renewable; approximately 50 awards.
Cumulative student debt: 86% of graduating class had student loans; average debt was $23,915.

FINANCIAL AID PROCEDURES

Forms required: FAFSA, state aid form.
Dates and Deadlines: Priority date 2/1; closing date 5/15. Applicants notified on a rolling basis starting 3/10; must reply within 4 week(s) of notification.
Transfers: Priority date 1/31. Applicants notified on a rolling basis starting 10/15. Financial aid transcripts required from prior institutions attended.

CONTACT

Daniel Tramuta, Director of Financial Aid
178 Central Avenue, Fredonia, NY 14063-1136
(716) 673-3253

State University of New York College at Geneseo

Geneseo, New York
www.geneseo.edu   Federal Code: 002845

4-year public liberal arts college in small town.
Enrollment: 5,488 undergrads, 2% part-time. 948 full-time freshmen.
Selectivity: Admits less than 50% of applicants.

BASIC COSTS (2009-2010)

Tuition and fees: $6,326; out-of-state residents $14,226.
Per-credit charge: $207; out-of-state residents $536.
Room and board: $9,550.

FINANCIAL AID PICTURE (2009-2010)

Students with need: Out of 798 full-time freshmen who applied for aid, 394 were judged to have need. Of these, 394 received aid, and 276 had their full need met. Average financial aid package met 70% of need; average scholarship/grant was $3,846; average loan was $3,870. Need-based aid available for part-time students.
Students without need: 5 full-time freshmen who did not demonstrate need for aid received scholarships/grants; average award was $2,297. No-need awards available for academics, art, leadership, minority status, music/drama, religious affiliation, ROTC, state/district residency.
Cumulative student debt: 63% of graduating class had student loans; average debt was $21,000.

FINANCIAL AID PROCEDURES

Forms required: FAFSA, state aid form.
Dates and Deadlines: Closing date 2/15. Applicants notified on a rolling basis starting 3/15; must reply by 5/1.

CONTACT

Archie Cureton, Director of Financial Aid
1 College Circle, Geneseo, NY 14454-1471
(585) 245-5731

State University of New York College at Old Westbury

Old Westbury, New York
www.oldwestbury.edu   Federal Code: 007109

4-year public business and liberal arts college in small city.
Enrollment: 3,696 undergrads, 14% part-time. 341 full-time freshmen.
Selectivity: Admits 50 to 75% of applicants.

BASIC COSTS (2009-2010)

Tuition and fees: $5,797; out-of-state residents $13,697.
Per-credit charge: $207; out-of-state residents $536.
Room and board: $9,032.

FINANCIAL AID PICTURE (2008-2009)

Students with need: Out of 283 full-time freshmen who applied for aid, 281 were judged to have need. Of these, 239 received aid, and 239 had their full need met. Average financial aid package met 44% of need; average scholarship/grant was $5,909; average loan was $1,845. For part-time students, average financial aid package was $2,614.
Students without need: No-need awards available for academics, alumni affiliation, state/district residency.
Cumulative student debt: 51% of graduating class had student loans; average debt was $15,901.

FINANCIAL AID PROCEDURES

Forms required: FAFSA, state aid form, institutional form.
Dates and Deadlines: Priority date 4/1; no closing date. Applicants notified on a rolling basis starting 4/15; must reply within 2 week(s) of notification.
Transfers: No deadline. Applicants notified on a rolling basis starting 4/15; must reply within 2 week(s) of notification. Financial aid transcript required.

CONTACT

Mildred O'Keefe, Director of Financial Aid
Box 307, Old Westbury, NY 11568-0307
(516) 876-3222

State University of New York College at Oneonta

Oneonta, New York
www.oneonta.edu   Federal Code: 002847

4-year public liberal arts college in large town.
Enrollment: 5,650 undergrads, 2% part-time. 1,131 full-time freshmen.
Selectivity: Admits less than 50% of applicants.

BASIC COSTS (2009-2010)

Tuition and fees: $6,185; out-of-state residents $14,085.
Per-credit charge: $207; out-of-state residents $536.
Room and board: $8,900.

FINANCIAL AID PICTURE (2009-2010)

Students with need: Out of 996 full-time freshmen who applied for aid, 629 were judged to have need. Of these, 605 received aid, and 93 had their full need met. Average financial aid package met 60% of need; average scholarship/grant was $5,131; average loan was $3,685. For part-time students, average financial aid package was $5,942.
Students without need: 263 full-time freshmen who did not demonstrate need for aid received scholarships/grants; average award was $2,200. No-need awards available for academics, alumni affiliation, leadership, minority status, music/drama, state/district residency.
Scholarships offered: Presidential Scholarships: $4,000, awarded to approximately 150 applicants for academics, service, extracurricular activities. Deans' Scholarships: $2,000, awarded to 50 applicants based on academics. Oneonta Auxiliary Services Scholarships: $1,000, awarded to 150 applicants for academics, service, extracurricular activities. Alumni Association Board of Directors Scholarships: $1,000, awarded to 15 applicants for academics, service, extracurricular activities. Mildred Haight Memorial Scholarships: $1,000, awarded to 20 applicants for academics. All scholarships are renewable.
Cumulative student debt: 75% of graduating class had student loans; average debt was $16,490.

FINANCIAL AID PROCEDURES

Forms required: FAFSA, state aid form.
Dates and Deadlines: Priority date 3/15; no closing date. Applicants notified on a rolling basis starting 3/1; must reply by 5/1 or within 4 week(s) of notification.
Transfers: No deadline. Applicants notified on a rolling basis starting 3/1.

CONTACT

C. Goodhue, Director of Student Financial Aid
Admissions Office, 116 Alumni Hall, Oneonta, NY 13820-4016
(607) 436-2532

State University of New York College at Plattsburgh

Plattsburgh, New York
www.plattsburgh.edu   Federal Code: 002849

4-year public liberal arts and teachers college in large town.
Enrollment: 5,810 undergrads, 5% part-time. 1,024 full-time freshmen.
Selectivity: Admits less than 50% of applicants.

BASIC COSTS (2009-2010)

Tuition and fees: $6,100; out-of-state residents $14,000.
Per-credit charge: $207; out-of-state residents $536.
Room and board: $8,600.

FINANCIAL AID PICTURE (2008-2009)

Students with need: Out of 891 full-time freshmen who applied for aid, 609 were judged to have need. Of these, 604 received aid, and 186 had their full need met. Average financial aid package met 92% of need; average scholarship/grant was $5,811; average loan was $5,375. For part-time students, average financial aid package was $6,577.
Students without need: 322 full-time freshmen who did not demonstrate need for aid received scholarships/grants; average award was $4,827. No-need awards available for academics, alumni affiliation, art, leadership, minority status, music/drama, ROTC, state/district residency.
Cumulative student debt: 72% of graduating class had student loans; average debt was $21,010.

FINANCIAL AID PROCEDURES

Forms required: FAFSA, state aid form.
Dates and Deadlines: Priority date 2/15; no closing date. Applicants notified on a rolling basis starting 3/1; must reply by 5/1.
Transfers: Closing date 2/15. Applicants notified by 3/1.

CONTACT

Todd Moravec, Director of Financial Aid
Kehoe Administration Building, Plattsburgh, NY 12901
(518) 564-4076

State University of New York College at Potsdam

Potsdam, New York
www.potsdam.edu   Federal Code: 002850

4-year public liberal arts and teachers college in large town.
Enrollment: 3,691 undergrads, 2% part-time. 826 full-time freshmen.
Selectivity: Admits 50 to 75% of applicants.

BASIC COSTS (2009-2010)

Tuition and fees: $6,124; out-of-state residents $14,024.
Per-credit charge: $207; out-of-state residents $536.
Room and board: $9,270.

FINANCIAL AID PICTURE (2009-2010)

Students with need: Out of 766 full-time freshmen who applied for aid, 584 were judged to have need. Of these, 579 received aid, and 504 had their full need met. Average financial aid package met 87% of need; average scholarship/grant was $6,536; average loan was $3,843. For part-time students, average financial aid package was $8,733.
Students without need: 79 full-time freshmen who did not demonstrate need for aid received scholarships/grants; average award was $7,542. No-need awards available for academics, art, leadership, minority status, music/drama, ROTC.
Scholarships offered: Mt. Emmons Scholarship: covers balance of in-state tuition and mandatory fees after TAP awards, $500 book stipend, residence hall fee waiver and board; renewable with minimum 3.25 GPA; 5 awarded. Freshman Scholars Program: $1,000-$4,600; for students who show academic promise and potential for leadership; 1100 or higher SAT (exclusive of Writing), ACT composite of 23, or minimum 90 high school average and history of participation, leadership in extracurricular activities and community service.
Cumulative student debt: 80% of graduating class had student loans; average debt was $19,220.
Additional info: Apply early to access limited, need-based awards.

FINANCIAL AID PROCEDURES

Forms required: FAFSA, state aid form.
Dates and Deadlines: Priority date 3/1; no closing date. Applicants notified on a rolling basis starting 2/1; must reply by 5/1 or within 4 week(s) of notification.

Transfers: Transfer Scholars Program for incoming transfer students based upon outstanding academic achievement as measured by previous college GPA. $1,000-$3,000 to students with minimum cumulative GPA of 3.25 and higher. Renewable for 1 year with cumulative 3.25 GPA.

CONTACT

Susan Aldrich, Director of Financial Aid
44 Pierrepont Avenue, Potsdam, NY 13676
(315) 267-2162

State University of New York College of Agriculture and Technology at Cobleskill

Cobleskill, New York
www.cobleskill.edu   Federal Code: 002856

2-year public agricultural and technical college in small town.

Enrollment: 2,661 undergrads, 4% part-time. 1,049 full-time freshmen.

Selectivity: Admits 50 to 75% of applicants.

BASIC COSTS (2009-2010)

Tuition and fees: $6,226; out-of-state residents $10,006.

Per-credit charge: $207; out-of-state residents $365.

Room and board: $9,430.

Additional info: Out-of-state tuition for bachelor's program: $12,870; per-credit-hour $536.

FINANCIAL AID PICTURE (2008-2009)

Students with need: Out of 948 full-time freshmen who applied for aid, 772 were judged to have need. Of these, 761 received aid, and 10 had their full need met. Average financial aid package met 85% of need; average scholarship/grant was $5,135; average loan was $2,992. For part-time students, average financial aid package was $2,896.

Students without need: 176 full-time freshmen who did not demonstrate need for aid received scholarships/grants; average award was $374. No-need awards available for academics, alumni affiliation, state/district residency.

Cumulative student debt: 66% of graduating class had student loans; average debt was $19,627.

Additional info: Application deadline for scholarships March 15. Separate application required, available through admissions office.

FINANCIAL AID PROCEDURES

Forms required: FAFSA, state aid form, institutional form.

Dates and Deadlines: Closing date 2/15. Applicants notified on a rolling basis starting 3/20; must reply within 2 week(s) of notification.

Transfers: Priority date 2/15; no deadline. Applicants notified on a rolling basis; must reply within 3 week(s) of notification.

CONTACT

Brian Smith, Director of Financial Aid
Knapp Hall, Cobleskill, NY 12043
(800) 295-8998

State University of New York College of Agriculture and Technology at Morrisville

Morrisville, New York
www.morrisville.edu   Federal Code: 002859

2-year public agricultural and technical college in small town.

Enrollment: 3,338 undergrads.

BASIC COSTS (2009-2010)

Tuition and fees: $6,055; out-of-state residents $9,835.

Per-credit charge: $207; out-of-state residents $365.

Room and board: $8,510.

Additional info: Out-of-state tuition for bachelor's program: $12,870; per-credit-hour $536. Tuition/fee waivers available for unemployed or children of unemployed.

FINANCIAL AID PICTURE (2008-2009)

Students with need: Need-based aid available for full-time and part-time students. Work study available nights, weekends, and for part-time students.

Students without need: No-need awards available for academics.

FINANCIAL AID PROCEDURES

Forms required: FAFSA, state aid form.

Dates and Deadlines: Priority date 2/1; no closing date. Applicants notified on a rolling basis starting 3/1; must reply within 3 week(s) of notification.

Transfers: No deadline. Applicants notified on a rolling basis; must reply within 3 week(s) of notification.

CONTACT

Dacia Banks, Director of Financial Aid
PO Box 901, Morrisville, NY 13408-0901
(800) 626-5844

State University of New York College of Environmental Science and Forestry

Syracuse, New York
www.esf.edu   Federal Code: 002851

4-year public university in small city.

Enrollment: 1,561 undergrads, 2% part-time. 283 full-time freshmen.

Selectivity: Admits less than 50% of applicants.

BASIC COSTS (2009-2010)

Tuition and fees: $5,829; out-of-state residents $13,729.

Per-credit charge: $207; out-of-state residents $536.

Additional info: Room and board available through Syracuse University at $11,920 per year. Tuition/fee waivers available for minority students.

FINANCIAL AID PICTURE (2009-2010)

Students with need: Out of 260 full-time freshmen who applied for aid, 166 were judged to have need. Of these, 166 received aid, and 166 had their full need met. Average financial aid package met 100% of need; average scholarship/grant was $4,000; average loan was $5,500. For part-time students, average financial aid package was $8,000.

Students without need: 50 full-time freshmen who did not demonstrate need for aid received scholarships/grants; average award was $2,500. No-need awards available for academics, alumni affiliation, leadership, minority status, ROTC, state/district residency.

Cumulative student debt: 80% of graduating class had student loans; average debt was $27,000.

FINANCIAL AID PROCEDURES

Forms required: FAFSA.

Dates and Deadlines: Priority date 3/1; no closing date. Applicants notified on a rolling basis starting 3/15; must reply within 2 week(s) of notification.

Transfers: Applicants notified on a rolling basis starting 3/15; must reply within 2 week(s) of notification.

CONTACT

John View, Director of Financial Aid
106 Bray Hall, Syracuse, NY 13210
(315) 470-6670

State University of New York College of Technology at Alfred
Alfred, New York
www.alfredstate.edu Federal Code: 002854

2-year public liberal arts and technical college in rural community.
Enrollment: 3,481 undergrads, 9% part-time. 1,036 full-time freshmen.
Selectivity: Admits 50 to 75% of applicants.

BASIC COSTS (2009-2010)
Tuition and fees: $6,162; out-of-state residents $9,942.
Per-credit charge: $207; out-of-state residents $365.
Room and board: $9,190.
Additional info: Tuition for bachelor's degree: full-time out-of-state, $12,870; per-credit-hour $536.

FINANCIAL AID PICTURE (2008-2009)
Students with need: Out of 1,006 full-time freshmen who applied for aid, 854 were judged to have need. Of these, 849 received aid, and 86 had their full need met. Average financial aid package met 73% of need; average scholarship/grant was $3,978; average loan was $3,143. For part-time students, average financial aid package was $6,806.
Students without need: 41 full-time freshmen who did not demonstrate need for aid received scholarships/grants; average award was $3,817. No-need awards available for academics, alumni affiliation, job skills, minority status.
Scholarships offered: 216 full-time freshmen received athletic scholarships; average amount $1,978.
Cumulative student debt: 80% of graduating class had student loans; average debt was $24,567.

FINANCIAL AID PROCEDURES
Forms required: FAFSA, state aid form.
Dates and Deadlines: No deadline. Applicants notified on a rolling basis starting 3/1; must reply within 4 week(s) of notification.
Transfers: No deadline. Applicants notified on a rolling basis starting 3/1; must reply within 4 week(s) of notification.

CONTACT
Jane Gilliland, Senior Director of Student Financial Services
Huntington Administration Building, Alfred, NY 14802-1196
(607) 587-4253

State University of New York College of Technology at Canton
Canton, New York
www.canton.edu Federal Code: 002855

2-year public technical college in small town.
Enrollment: 2,988 undergrads, 14% part-time. 962 full-time freshmen.
Selectivity: Admits over 75% of applicants.

BASIC COSTS (2009-2010)
Tuition and fees: $6,269; out-of-state residents $10,049.
Per-credit charge: $207; out-of-state residents $365.
Room and board: $9,320.
Additional info: Laundry fee of $90 annually added to the bill for room and board. Out-of-state tuition for bachelor's degree program: $12,870; $536 per credit hour.

FINANCIAL AID PICTURE (2008-2009)
Students with need: Need-based aid available for full-time and part-time students. Work study available nights, weekends, and for part-time students.
Students without need: No-need awards available for academics, alumni affiliation, leadership, minority status, state/district residency.

FINANCIAL AID PROCEDURES
Forms required: FAFSA, state aid form.
Dates and Deadlines: Priority date 3/15; no closing date. Applicants notified on a rolling basis starting 2/15; must reply within 4 week(s) of notification.
Transfers: Financial aid transcripts required from all previously attended schools for mid-year transfers.

CONTACT
Kerrie Cooper, Director of Financial Aid
34 Cornell Drive, Canton, NY 13617-1098
(315) 386-7616

State University of New York College of Technology at Delhi
Delhi, New York
www.delhi.edu Federal Code: 002857

2-year public liberal arts and technical college in rural community.
Enrollment: 2,956 undergrads, 12% part-time. 957 full-time freshmen.
Selectivity: Admits less than 50% of applicants.

BASIC COSTS (2009-2010)
Tuition and fees: $6,360; out-of-state residents $10,140.
Per-credit charge: $207; out-of-state residents $365.
Room and board: $9,380.
Additional info: Out-of-state tuition for bachelor's program: $12,870; per-credit-hour $536.

FINANCIAL AID PICTURE (2008-2009)
Students with need: Need-based aid available for full-time and part-time students.

FINANCIAL AID PROCEDURES
Forms required: FAFSA, state aid form.
Dates and Deadlines: Priority date 2/15; no closing date. Applicants notified on a rolling basis starting 3/1; must reply within 2 week(s) of notification.

CONTACT
Nancy Hughes, Financial Aid Director
2 Main Street, Delhi, NY 13753-1190
(607) 746-4000

State University of New York Empire State College
Saratoga Springs, New York
www.esc.edu Federal Code: 010286

4-year public liberal arts college in large town.
Enrollment: 11,893 undergrads, 60% part-time. 266 full-time freshmen.
Selectivity: Admits over 75% of applicants.

BASIC COSTS (2009-2010)
Tuition and fees: $5,195; out-of-state residents $13,095.
Per-credit charge: $207; out-of-state residents $536.

FINANCIAL AID PICTURE (2008-2009)
Students with need: 36% of average financial aid package awarded as scholarships/grants, 64% awarded as loans/jobs. Need-based aid available for part-time students.
Students without need: This college awards aid only to students with need.

FINANCIAL AID PROCEDURES
Forms required: FAFSA, state aid form.
Dates and Deadlines: Priority date 4/1; no closing date. Applicants notified on a rolling basis; must reply within 3 week(s) of notification.

Transfers: No deadline. Applicants notified on a rolling basis.

CONTACT
Kristina Delbridge, Director of Business Services
Two Union Avenue, Saratoga Springs, NY 12866
(518) 587-2100 ext. 2311

State University of New York Institute of Technology at Utica/Rome

Utica, New York
www.sunyit.edu　　　　Federal Code: 011678

4-year public business and engineering and nursing and liberal arts college in small city.
Enrollment: 2,003 undergrads, 24% part-time. 203 full-time freshmen.
Selectivity: Admits less than 50% of applicants.

BASIC COSTS (2009-2010)
Tuition and fees: $6,090; out-of-state residents $13,990.
Per-credit charge: $207; out-of-state residents $536.
Room and board: $8,750.

FINANCIAL AID PICTURE (2009-2010)
Students with need: Out of 179 full-time freshmen who applied for aid, 146 were judged to have need. Of these, 145 received aid. Need-based aid available for part-time students.
Students without need: 15 full-time freshmen who did not demonstrate need for aid received scholarships/grants; average award was $1,767. No-need awards available for academics.

FINANCIAL AID PROCEDURES
Forms required: FAFSA, state aid form.
Dates and Deadlines: Priority date 3/15; no closing date. Applicants notified on a rolling basis starting 3/17; must reply within 2 week(s) of notification.
Transfers: No deadline. Applicants notified on a rolling basis starting 3/17; must reply within 2 week(s) of notification.

CONTACT
Lisa Hoskey, Director of Financial Aid
100 Seymour Road, Utica, NY 13502
(315) 792-7210

State University of New York Maritime College

Throggs Neck, New York
www.sunymaritime.edu　　　Federal Code: 002853

4-year public maritime college in very large city.
Enrollment: 1,562 undergrads, 6% part-time. 395 full-time freshmen.
Selectivity: Admits 50 to 75% of applicants.

BASIC COSTS (2009-2010)
Tuition and fees: $6,090; out-of-state residents $13,990.
Per-credit charge: $207; out-of-state residents $536.
Room and board: $9,930.
Additional info: Additional fees required for students in the regiment.

FINANCIAL AID PICTURE (2008-2009)
Students with need: Out of 212 full-time freshmen who applied for aid, 198 were judged to have need. Of these, 187 received aid, and 31 had their full need met. Average financial aid package met 58% of need; average scholarship/grant was $4,344; average loan was $3,155. For part-time students, average financial aid package was $8,684.
Students without need: 42 full-time freshmen who did not demonstrate need for aid received scholarships/grants; average award was $2,298. No-

need awards available for academics, leadership, ROTC, state/district residency.
Scholarships offered: NROTC Scholarships: tuition and full room for 4 years.
Cumulative student debt: 73% of graduating class had student loans; average debt was $30,244.
Additional info: All cadets who are United States citizens, physically qualified for Merchant Marine license, and not yet 25 at time of enrollment eligible to apply for Student Incentive Payment (SIP) of $3,000 per year from Maritime Administration of the Department of Transportation. Out-of-state students who elect to participate in SIP pay in-state tuition fees.

FINANCIAL AID PROCEDURES
Forms required: FAFSA, institutional form.
Dates and Deadlines: Priority date 3/15; closing date 7/15. Applicants notified on a rolling basis starting 3/15.
Transfers: Must have minimum 2.0 cumulative GPA if degree has not yet been earned.

CONTACT
Paul Bamonte, Director of Financial Aid
6 Pennyfield Avenue, Throggs Neck, NY 10465-4198
(718) 409-7267

State University of New York Upstate Medical University

Syracuse, New York
www.upstate.edu　　　　Federal Code: 002840

Upper-division public health science and nursing college in small city.
Enrollment: 277 undergrads, 46% part-time.

BASIC COSTS (2009-2010)
Tuition and fees: $5,522; out-of-state residents $13,422.
Per-credit charge: $207; out-of-state residents $536.
Room only: $4,127.

FINANCIAL AID PICTURE (2009-2010)
Students with need: Average financial aid package for all full-time undergraduates was $12,039. 35% awarded as scholarships/grants, 65% awarded as loans/jobs. Need-based aid available for part-time students. Work study available nights, weekends, and for part-time students.
Students without need: This college awards aid only to students with need.
Cumulative student debt: 60% of graduating class had student loans; average debt was $10,825.

FINANCIAL AID PROCEDURES
Forms required: FAFSA.
Dates and Deadlines: Priority date 3/1; no closing date. Applicants notified on a rolling basis starting 6/1; must reply within 2 week(s) of notification.
Transfers: Applicants notified on a rolling basis; must reply within 2 week(s) of notification.

CONTACT
Mike Pede, Director of Financial Aid
766 Irving Avenue, Syracuse, NY 13210
(315) 464-4329

Suffolk County Community College

Selden, New York
www.sunysuffolk.edu　　　Federal Code: 002878

2-year public community college in large town.
Enrollment: 22,341 undergrads.
Selectivity: Open admission; but selective for some programs.

BASIC COSTS (2009-2010)

Tuition and fees: $3,996; out-of-state residents $7,572.

FINANCIAL AID PICTURE (2008-2009)

Students with need: Need-based aid available for full-time and part-time students. Work study available nights, weekends, and for part-time students.

Students without need: No-need awards available for academics, art, leadership, minority status, music/drama, state/district residency.

FINANCIAL AID PROCEDURES

Forms required: FAFSA, state aid form.

Dates and Deadlines: Priority date 4/15; closing date 6/1. Applicants notified on a rolling basis starting 4/15; must reply within 2 week(s) of notification.

Transfers: No deadline. Applicants notified on a rolling basis starting 4/15.

CONTACT

Nancy Dunnagan, Director of Financial Aid

533 College Road, Selden, NY 11784

(631) 451-4110

Sullivan County Community College

Loch Sheldrake, New York

www.sullivan.suny.edu   Federal Code: 002879

2-year public community college in small town.

Enrollment: 1,418 undergrads.

Selectivity: Open admission; but selective for some programs.

BASIC COSTS (2009-2010)

Tuition and fees: $4,192; out-of-state residents $7,896.

Per-credit charge: $145; out-of-state residents $190.

FINANCIAL AID PICTURE

Students with need: Need-based aid available for full-time and part-time students.

Additional info: 60% of students hold part-time jobs locally.

FINANCIAL AID PROCEDURES

Forms required: FAFSA.

Dates and Deadlines: Priority date 4/15; no closing date. Applicants notified on a rolling basis starting 5/15; must reply within 2 week(s) of notification.

CONTACT

James Winderl, Director of Financial Aid

112 College Road, Loch Sheldrake, NY 12759-5151

(845) 434-5750 ext. 4231

Swedish Institute

New York, New York

www.swedishinstitute.edu   Federal Code: 021700

2-year for-profit health science college in very large city.

Enrollment: 494 undergrads.

BASIC COSTS (2009-2010)

Tuition and fees: $9,500.

Additional info: Students generally attend 3 semesters/year.

FINANCIAL AID PICTURE

Students with need: Need-based aid available for full-time and part-time students.

Students without need: This college awards aid only to students with need.

FINANCIAL AID PROCEDURES

Forms required: FAFSA, institutional form.

Dates and Deadlines: No deadline.

CONTACT

Martha Padilla, Financial Aid Director

226 West 26th Street, 5th Floor, New York, NY 10001-6700

(212) 924-5900 ext. 124

Syracuse University

Syracuse, New York   Federal Code: 002882

www.syr.edu   CSS Code: 2823

4-year private university in small city.

Enrollment: 13,243 undergrads, 4% part-time. 3,248 full-time freshmen.

Selectivity: Admits 50 to 75% of applicants.

BASIC COSTS (2010-2011)

Tuition and fees: $36,302.

Per-credit charge: $1,522.

Room and board: $12,850.

FINANCIAL AID PICTURE (2009-2010)

Students with need: Out of 2,524 full-time freshmen who applied for aid, 1,983 were judged to have need. Of these, 1,983 received aid, and 1,668 had their full need met. Average financial aid package met 95% of need; average scholarship/grant was $24,300; average loan was $6,280. Need-based aid available for part-time students.

Students without need: 336 full-time freshmen who did not demonstrate need for aid received scholarships/grants; average award was $8,840. No-need awards available for academics, art, athletics, music/drama, ROTC, state/district residency.

Scholarships offered: 66 full-time freshmen received athletic scholarships; average amount $40,600.

Cumulative student debt: 65% of graduating class had student loans; average debt was $28,358.

FINANCIAL AID PROCEDURES

Forms required: FAFSA, CSS PROFILE.

Dates and Deadlines: Closing date 2/2. Applicants notified by 3/15; must reply by 5/1.

Transfers: Closing date 3/1. Applicants notified on a rolling basis starting 3/20; must reply by 5/1 or within 2 week(s) of notification.

CONTACT

Youlonda Copeland-Morgan, Director of Scholarship and Student Aid

100 Crouse-Hinds Hall, Syracuse, NY 13244-2130

(315) 443-1513

Tompkins Cortland Community College

Dryden, New York

www.TC3.edu   Federal Code: 006788

2-year public community college in small town.

Enrollment: 3,383 undergrads, 16% part-time. 1,030 full-time freshmen.

Selectivity: Open admission; but selective for some programs.

BASIC COSTS (2009-2010)

Tuition and fees: $4,206; out-of-state residents $8,086.

Per-credit charge: $135; out-of-state residents $280.

FINANCIAL AID PICTURE (2008-2009)

Students with need: Need-based aid available for full-time and part-time students. Work study available nights, weekends, and for part-time students.

Students without need: No-need awards available for academics.

FINANCIAL AID PROCEDURES

Forms required: FAFSA, state aid form, institutional form.

Dates and Deadlines: Priority date 4/15; no closing date. Applicants notified on a rolling basis starting 3/15; must reply within 4 week(s) of notification.

CONTACT
Sharon Karwowski, Director of Financial Aid
170 North Street, Dryden, NY 13053-0139
(607) 844-6581

Trocaire College
Buffalo, New York
www.trocaire.edu   Federal Code: 002812

2-year private junior college in large city, affiliated with Roman Catholic Church.
Enrollment: 1,150 undergrads.
Selectivity: Open admission; but selective for some programs.

BASIC COSTS (2009-2010)
Tuition and fees: $12,292.
Per-credit charge: $484.

FINANCIAL AID PICTURE
Students with need: Need-based aid available for full-time and part-time students.
Students without need: No-need awards available for academics, alumni affiliation.

FINANCIAL AID PROCEDURES
Forms required: FAFSA, state aid form.
Dates and Deadlines: No deadline. Applicants notified on a rolling basis starting 3/1; must reply within 2 week(s) of notification.

CONTACT
Janet McGrath, Director of Financial Aid
360 Choate Avenue, Buffalo, NY 14220
(716) 826-1200

Ulster County Community College
Stone Ridge, New York
www.sunyulster.edu   Federal Code: 002880

2-year public community college in small town.
Enrollment: 2,379 undergrads, 28% part-time. 570 full-time freshmen.
Selectivity: Open admission; but selective for some programs.

BASIC COSTS (2009-2010)
Tuition and fees: $4,156; out-of-state residents $7,776.
Per-credit charge: $135; out-of-state residents $270.

FINANCIAL AID PICTURE (2009-2010)
Students with need: Need-based aid available for full-time and part-time students.

FINANCIAL AID PROCEDURES
Forms required: FAFSA.
Dates and Deadlines: Priority date 6/1; no closing date. Applicants notified on a rolling basis starting 6/1; must reply within 2 week(s) of notification.

CONTACT
Christopher Chang, Director of Financial Aid
Cottekill Road, Stone Ridge, NY 12484
(845) 687-5058

Union College
Schenectady, New York   Federal Code: 002889
www.union.edu   CSS Code: 2920

4-year private engineering and liberal arts college in small city.
Enrollment: 2,141 undergrads. 520 full-time freshmen.

Selectivity: Admits less than 50% of applicants. GED not accepted.

BASIC COSTS (2009-2010)
Comprehensive fee: $50,439.
Additional info: Rebates offered to students living off-campus and/or not using a meal plan.

FINANCIAL AID PICTURE (2009-2010)
Students with need: Out of 342 full-time freshmen who applied for aid, 279 were judged to have need. Of these, 277 received aid, and 273 had their full need met. Average financial aid package met 99% of need; average scholarship/grant was $32,597; average loan was $2,670. Need-based aid available for part-time students.
Students without need: 72 full-time freshmen who did not demonstrate need for aid received scholarships/grants; average award was $10,016. No-need awards available for academics, ROTC.
Cumulative student debt: 61% of graduating class had student loans; average debt was $24,739.
Additional info: Cancellable loans given to eligible students who engage in public service work after graduation. Loans cancellable at rate of 20% for each year of service.

FINANCIAL AID PROCEDURES
Forms required: FAFSA, CSS PROFILE, state aid form.
Dates and Deadlines: Closing date 2/1. Applicants notified by 4/1; must reply by 5/1.
Transfers: Closing date 3/1. Financial aid applicants must submit the CSS PROFILE form and FAFSA to their respective processing agencies at least two months prior to application deadline.

CONTACT
Linda Parker, Director of Financial Aid
Grant Hall, Schenectady, NY 12308-3107
(518) 388-6123

United States Merchant Marine Academy
Kings Point, New York
www.usmma.edu   Federal Code: 002892

4-year public military and maritime college in large town.
Enrollment: 975 undergrads.
Selectivity: Admits less than 50% of applicants.

BASIC COSTS (2009-2010)
Additional info: All midshipmen receive full tuition, room, board, and medical and dental expenses from the federal government. Total required freshman fees ($2,828) include purchase of laptop computer, color printer, and PDA. International freshman students pay required fees plus additional international student fee ($13,003 total).

FINANCIAL AID PICTURE (2008-2009)
Students with need: Need-based aid available for full-time students.
Additional info: Students paid by steamship companies while at sea.

FINANCIAL AID PROCEDURES
Forms required: FAFSA, institutional form.
Dates and Deadlines: Closing date 5/1. Applicants notified on a rolling basis starting 1/31.

CONTACT
Robert Johnson, Director of Admissions and Financial Aid
300 Steamboat Road, Admissions Center, Kings Point, NY 11024-1699
(516) 773-5295

United States Military Academy
West Point, New York
www.westpoint.edu

4-year public military college in small town.
Enrollment: 4,621 undergrads. 1,262 full-time freshmen.
Selectivity: Admits less than 50% of applicants.

BASIC COSTS (2010-2011)
Additional info: Tuition is covered by a full scholarship. All students are on Active Duty as members of the U.S. Army and receive an annual salary of approximately $10,150. Room and board, medical and dental care are provided by the U.S. Army; however, a one-time deposit of $2,000 is required upon admission to defray the initial cost of uniforms, books, supplies, equipment and fees. If needed, loans of $100 to $2,000 are available for the deposit.

FINANCIAL AID PICTURE (2008-2009)
Additional info: Cadets permitted to receive scholarships, but since there are no tuition, room or board charges, scholarships stipulated for tuition, room or board that are based only on need rather than merit cannot be accepted. Scholarships may be used for textbooks, uniforms and other expenses, or used dollar for dollar to offset initial $2,000 deposit.

CONTACT
646 Swift Road, West Point, NY 10996-1905

University of Rochester
Rochester, New York — Federal Code: 002894
www.rochester.edu — CSS Code: 2928

4-year private university in large city.
Enrollment: 5,291 undergrads, 2% part-time. 1,200 full-time freshmen.
Selectivity: Admits less than 50% of applicants.

BASIC COSTS (2010-2011)
Tuition and fees: $40,282.
Per-credit charge: $1,234.
Room and board: $11,640.

FINANCIAL AID PICTURE (2009-2010)
Students with need: Need-based aid available for full-time and part-time students. Work study available nights, weekends, and for part-time students.
Students without need: No-need awards available for academics, alumni affiliation, leadership, music/drama, ROTC, state/district residency.
Additional info: Alternative loans and financing information available.

FINANCIAL AID PROCEDURES
Forms required: FAFSA, CSS PROFILE, state aid form.
Dates and Deadlines: Closing date 2/1. Applicants notified by 4/1; must reply by 5/1.
Transfers: Priority date 2/1. Must reply by 8/1.

CONTACT
Charles Puls, Associate Dean and Director of Financial Aid
300 Wilson Boulevard, Rochester, NY 14627-0251
(585) 275-3226

Utica College
Utica, New York
www.utica.edu — Federal Code: 002883

4-year private liberal arts college in small city.
Enrollment: 2,478 undergrads, 17% part-time. 544 full-time freshmen.
Selectivity: Admits over 75% of applicants.

BASIC COSTS (2010-2011)
Tuition and fees: $28,620.
Per-credit charge: $950.
Room and board: $11,590.

FINANCIAL AID PICTURE (2009-2010)
Students with need: Out of 535 full-time freshmen who applied for aid, 504 were judged to have need. Of these, 504 received aid, and 38 had their full need met. Average financial aid package met 70% of need; average scholarship/grant was $8,635; average loan was $3,444. For part-time students, average financial aid package was $5,632.
Students without need: 27 full-time freshmen who did not demonstrate need for aid received scholarships/grants; average award was $13,203. No-need awards available for academics.

FINANCIAL AID PROCEDURES
Forms required: FAFSA, state aid form.
Dates and Deadlines: Priority date 2/15; no closing date. Applicants notified on a rolling basis starting 2/1; must reply by 5/1 or within 4 week(s) of notification.
Transfers: Applicants notified on a rolling basis.

CONTACT
Laura Bedford, Executive Director of Student Financial Services
1600 Burrstone Road, Utica, NY 13502-4892
(315) 792-3179

Vassar College
Poughkeepsie, New York — Federal Code: 002895
www.vassar.edu — CSS Code: 2956

4-year private liberal arts college in small city.
Enrollment: 2,394 undergrads. 658 full-time freshmen.
Selectivity: Admits less than 50% of applicants.

BASIC COSTS (2010-2011)
Tuition and fees: $43,190.
Per-credit charge: $1,440.
Room and board: $9,900.

FINANCIAL AID PICTURE (2009-2010)
Students with need: Out of 478 full-time freshmen who applied for aid, 399 were judged to have need. Of these, 399 received aid, and 399 had their full need met. Average financial aid package met 100% of need; average scholarship/grant was $35,696; average loan was $1,754.
Students without need: This college awards aid only to students with need.
Cumulative student debt: 49% of graduating class had student loans; average debt was $18,876.
Additional info: No loans in the initial financial aid packages for students from families with total income used in need analysis of $60,000 or less.

FINANCIAL AID PROCEDURES
Forms required: FAFSA, CSS PROFILE.
Dates and Deadlines: Closing date 2/1. Applicants notified by 3/30; must reply by 5/1.
Transfers: Closing date 4/1. Limited number of need-based award packages offered to transfers.

CONTACT
Michael Fraher, Director of Financial Aid
Box 10, 124 Raymond Avenue, Poughkeepsie, NY 12604-0077
(845) 437-5320

Vaughn College of Aeronautics and Technology

Flushing, New York
www.vaughn.edu   Federal Code: 002665

4-year private engineering college in very large city.

Enrollment: 1,283 undergrads, 27% part-time. 239 full-time freshmen.

Selectivity: Admits over 75% of applicants.

BASIC COSTS (2010-2011)

Tuition and fees: $17,515.

Per-credit charge: $580.

Room and board: $11,025.

FINANCIAL AID PICTURE (2009-2010)

Students with need: Out of 239 full-time freshmen who applied for aid, 239 were judged to have need. Of these, 239 received aid, and 33 had their full need met. Average financial aid package met 85% of need; average scholarship/grant was $1,100; average loan was $1,750. For part-time students, average financial aid package was $6,506.

Students without need: 57 full-time freshmen who did not demonstrate need for aid received scholarships/grants; average award was $2,200. No-need awards available for academics, alumni affiliation, job skills, leadership, ROTC, state/district residency.

FINANCIAL AID PROCEDURES

Forms required: FAFSA, state aid form.

Dates and Deadlines: Priority date 3/1; no closing date. Applicants notified by 4/15; must reply within 2 week(s) of notification.

Transfers: No deadline. Applicants notified on a rolling basis; must reply within 2 week(s) of notification.

CONTACT

Dorothy Martin, Director of Financial Aid
86-01 23rd Avenue, Flushing, NY 11369
(718) 429-6600

Villa Maria College of Buffalo

Buffalo, New York
www.villa.edu   Federal Code: 002896

2-year private visual arts and liberal arts college in large city, affiliated with Roman Catholic Church.

Enrollment: 497 undergrads, 16% part-time. 127 full-time freshmen.

Selectivity: Admits 50 to 75% of applicants.

BASIC COSTS (2010-2011)

Tuition and fees: $15,590.

Per-credit charge: $500.

Additional info: Tuition/fee waivers available for unemployed or children of unemployed.

FINANCIAL AID PICTURE (2008-2009)

Students with need: Out of 119 full-time freshmen who applied for aid, 103 were judged to have need. Of these, 103 received aid, and 11 had their full need met. Average financial aid package met 10% of need; average scholarship/grant was $5,560; average loan was $2,625. For part-time students, average financial aid package was $5,655.

Students without need: 7 full-time freshmen who did not demonstrate need for aid received scholarships/grants; average award was $3,286. No-need awards available for academics, alumni affiliation, art, leadership, minority status, music/drama.

FINANCIAL AID PROCEDURES

Forms required: FAFSA.

Dates and Deadlines: No deadline. Applicants notified on a rolling basis starting 2/15; must reply within 2 week(s) of notification.

Transfers: No deadline. Applicants notified on a rolling basis starting 2/15; must reply within 2 week(s) of notification.

CONTACT

Christina Horner, Director of Financial Aid and Veterans Affairs
240 Pine Ridge Road, Buffalo, NY 14225-3999
(716) 896-0700 ext. 1850

Wagner College

Staten Island, New York
www.wagner.edu   Federal Code: 002899

4-year private liberal arts college in very large city, affiliated with Lutheran Church in America.

Enrollment: 1,861 undergrads, 3% part-time. 519 full-time freshmen.

Selectivity: Admits 50 to 75% of applicants.

BASIC COSTS (2010-2011)

Tuition and fees: $34,190.

Room and board: $10,170.

Additional info: Tuition/fee waivers available for unemployed or children of unemployed.

FINANCIAL AID PICTURE (2009-2010)

Students with need: Out of 430 full-time freshmen who applied for aid, 356 were judged to have need. Of these, 356 received aid, and 88 had their full need met. Average financial aid package met 74% of need; average scholarship/grant was $12,489; average loan was $3,808.

Students without need: 123 full-time freshmen who did not demonstrate need for aid received scholarships/grants; average award was $11,473. No-need awards available for academics, athletics, music/drama.

Scholarships offered: 27 full-time freshmen received athletic scholarships; average amount $19,987.

Cumulative student debt: 61% of graduating class had student loans; average debt was $36,988.

FINANCIAL AID PROCEDURES

Forms required: FAFSA, state aid form, institutional form.

Dates and Deadlines: Priority date 2/15; no closing date. Applicants notified on a rolling basis starting 3/1; must reply within 3 week(s) of notification.

Transfers: No deadline. Applicants notified on a rolling basis starting 3/1; must reply within 3 week(s) of notification.

CONTACT

Theresa Weimer, Director of Financial Aid
One Campus Road, Staten Island, NY 10301-4495
(718) 390-3183

Webb Institute

Glen Cove, New York
www.webb-institute.edu   Federal Code: 002900

4-year private engineering and maritime college in large town.

Enrollment: 89 undergrads. 19 full-time freshmen.

Selectivity: Admits less than 50% of applicants. GED not accepted.

BASIC COSTS (2010-2011)

Room and board: $12,000.

Additional info: All students receive 4-year, full-tuition scholarships.

FINANCIAL AID PICTURE (2008-2009)

Students with need: Need-based aid available for full-time students.

Students without need: This college awards aid only to students with need.

FINANCIAL AID PROCEDURES

Forms required: FAFSA.

Dates and Deadlines: Closing date 7/1. Applicants notified by 8/1; must reply within 2 week(s) of notification.

CONTACT

William Murray, Director of Financial Aid

298 Crescent Beach Road, Glen Cove, NY 11542-1398

(516) 671-2213 ext. 104

Wells College

Aurora, New York

www.wells.edu   Federal Code: 002901

4-year private liberal arts college in rural community.

Enrollment: 552 undergrads, 1% part-time. 145 full-time freshmen.

Selectivity: Admits 50 to 75% of applicants.

BASIC COSTS (2010-2011)

Tuition and fees: $32,180.

Per-credit charge: $790.

Room and board: $11,000.

FINANCIAL AID PICTURE (2009-2010)

Students with need: Out of 136 full-time freshmen who applied for aid, 125 were judged to have need. Of these, 125 received aid, and 16 had their full need met. Average financial aid package met 79% of need; average scholarship/grant was $21,320; average loan was $3,680. For part-time students, average financial aid package was $3,212.

Students without need: 16 full-time freshmen who did not demonstrate need for aid received scholarships/grants; average award was $11,656. No-need awards available for academics, alumni affiliation, leadership.

Scholarships offered: Henry Wells Scholarship: guaranteed first-year internship or related experience and paid $3,000 internship or experiential learning program in student's upper-class years; tuition-based scholarship valued at $18,000 a year for four years. Scholarship for Leaders: $8,000 to $60,000 over 4 years, based on academic and leadership abilities.

Cumulative student debt: 82% of graduating class had student loans; average debt was $24,182.

FINANCIAL AID PROCEDURES

Forms required: FAFSA. CSS PROFILE required of early decision candidates only.

Dates and Deadlines: Priority date 2/15; no closing date. Applicants notified on a rolling basis starting 3/1; must reply by 5/1.

Transfers: Priority date 3/1; no deadline. Applicants notified on a rolling basis starting 3/1; must reply by 8/1.

CONTACT

Cathleen Patella, Director of Financial Aid

170 Main Street, Aurora, NY 13026

(315) 364-3289

Westchester Community College

Valhalla, New York

www.sunywcc.edu   Federal Code: 002881

2-year public community college in large town.

Enrollment: 12,566 undergrads, 40% part-time. 2,360 full-time freshmen.

Selectivity: Open admission; but selective for some programs.

BASIC COSTS (2009-2010)

Tuition and fees: $4,013; out-of-state residents $9,489.

Per-credit charge: $153; out-of-state residents $383.

FINANCIAL AID PICTURE (2008-2009)

Students with need: 88% of average financial aid package awarded as scholarships/grants, 12% awarded as loans/jobs. Need-based aid available for part-time students. Work study available nights, weekends, and for part-time students.

Students without need: No-need awards available for academics.

Cumulative student debt: 13% of graduating class had student loans; average debt was $7,554.

FINANCIAL AID PROCEDURES

Forms required: FAFSA, state aid form, institutional form.

Dates and Deadlines: No deadline. Applicants notified on a rolling basis; must reply within 4 week(s) of notification.

Transfers: No deadline.

CONTACT

Eleanor Hackett, Director of Financial Aid

75 Grasslands Road, Valhalla, NY 10595

(914) 606-6773

Yeshivat Mikdash Melech

Brooklyn, New York

www.mikdashmelech.net   Federal Code: 014615

5-year private rabbinical college for men in very large city, affiliated with Jewish faith.

Enrollment: 93 undergrads.

Selectivity: Open admission; but selective for some programs.

BASIC COSTS (2010-2011)

Tuition and fees: $6,500.

Room and board: $3,800.

Additional info: Tuition/fee waivers available for adults.

FINANCIAL AID PICTURE (2008-2009)

Students with need: 98% of average financial aid package awarded as scholarships/grants, 2% awarded as loans/jobs. Need-based aid available for part-time students. Work study available nights.

Students without need: No-need awards available for academics, leadership, religious affiliation.

FINANCIAL AID PROCEDURES

Forms required: FAFSA, institutional form.

Dates and Deadlines: No deadline. Applicants notified on a rolling basis starting 5/1.

Transfers: No deadline. Applicants notified on a rolling basis starting 5/1.

CONTACT

Samuel Ani, Financial Aid Administrator

1326 Ocean Parkway, Brooklyn, NY 11230

(718) 339-1090

North Carolina

Alamance Community College

Graham, North Carolina

www.alamancecc.edu   Federal Code: 005463

2-year public community college in large town.

Enrollment: 4,596 undergrads, 44% part-time. 533 full-time freshmen.

Selectivity: Open admission; but selective for some programs.

BASIC COSTS (2009-2010)

Tuition and fees: $1,530; out-of-state residents $7,269.

Per-credit charge: $50; out-of-state residents $241.

FINANCIAL AID PICTURE (2008-2009)

Students with need: Out of 260 full-time freshmen who applied for aid, 252 were judged to have need. Of these, 250 received aid, and 100 had their full need met. Average financial aid package met 30% of need; average scholarship/grant was $4,000. For part-time students, average financial aid package was $2,000.

Students without need: 50 full-time freshmen who did not demonstrate need for aid received scholarships/grants; average award was $1,000. No-need awards available for academics, state/district residency.

FINANCIAL AID PROCEDURES

Forms required: FAFSA.

Dates and Deadlines: Priority date 5/15; no closing date. Applicants notified on a rolling basis starting 3/15; must reply within 2 week(s) of notification.

Transfers: Supplemental educational opportunity grants limited.

CONTACT

Liz Solazzo, Director of Financial Aid
Box 8000, Graham, NC 27253
(336) 506-4109

Appalachian State University

Boone, North Carolina
www.appstate.edu   Federal Code: 002906

4-year public university in large town.

Enrollment: 14,698 undergrads, 4% part-time. 2,733 full-time freshmen.

Selectivity: Admits 50 to 75% of applicants. GED not accepted.

BASIC COSTS (2009-2010)

Tuition and fees: $4,425; out-of-state residents $15,046.

Room and board: $6,240.

FINANCIAL AID PICTURE (2009-2010)

Students with need: Out of 2,046 full-time freshmen who applied for aid, 1,116 were judged to have need. Of these, 1,067 received aid, and 157 had their full need met. Average financial aid package met 82% of need; average scholarship/grant was $6,194; average loan was $3,666. For part-time students, average financial aid package was $6,190.

Students without need: 76 full-time freshmen who did not demonstrate need for aid received scholarships/grants; average award was $2,281. No-need awards available for academics, alumni affiliation, art, athletics, job skills, leadership, minority status, music/drama, religious affiliation, ROTC, state/district residency.

Scholarships offered: 78 full-time freshmen received athletic scholarships; average amount $10,415.

Cumulative student debt: 55% of graduating class had student loans; average debt was $16,153.

FINANCIAL AID PROCEDURES

Forms required: FAFSA.

Dates and Deadlines: Priority date 3/15; no closing date. Applicants notified on a rolling basis starting 4/1; must reply within 3 week(s) of notification.

Transfers: No deadline. Applicants notified on a rolling basis starting 4/1; must reply within 3 week(s) of notification.

CONTACT

Esther Manogin, Director of Financial Aid
ASU Box 32004, Boone, NC 28608
(828) 262-2190

Art Institute of Charlotte

Charlotte, North Carolina
www.artinstitutes.edu/charlotte   Federal Code: 014578

4-year for-profit visual arts and career college in very large city.

Enrollment: 1,024 undergrads, 24% part-time. 323 full-time freshmen.

Selectivity: Open admission; but selective for some programs.

BASIC COSTS (2009-2010)

Tuition and fees: $22,188.

Per-credit charge: $456.

Room only: $4,950.

Additional info: Fees for culinary students $300; fees for all other students $150. Housing cost is for four-person, furnished apartment and includes utilities (elect/water), washer/dryer, and free transportation between housing and campus.

FINANCIAL AID PICTURE (2009-2010)

Students with need: 21% of average financial aid package awarded as scholarships/grants, 79% awarded as loans/jobs. Need-based aid available for part-time students. Work study available nights, weekends, and for part-time students.

FINANCIAL AID PROCEDURES

Forms required: FAFSA.

Dates and Deadlines: No deadline. Applicants notified on a rolling basis starting 7/1; must reply within 1 week(s) of notification.

Transfers: No deadline. Applicants notified on a rolling basis starting 7/1; must reply within 1 week(s) of notification.

CONTACT

Barbara Grimm, Director of Financial Aid
Three LakePointe Plaza, Charlotte, NC 28217-4536
(704) 357-8020 ext. 4681

Barton College

Wilson, North Carolina
www.barton.edu   Federal Code: 002908

4-year private liberal arts college in large town, affiliated with Christian Church (Disciples of Christ).

Enrollment: 1,126 undergrads, 22% part-time. 230 full-time freshmen.

Selectivity: Admits 50 to 75% of applicants.

BASIC COSTS (2010-2011)

Tuition and fees: $21,734.

Per-credit charge: $850.

Room and board: $7,316.

Additional info: Tuition/fee waivers available for adults.

FINANCIAL AID PICTURE (2009-2010)

Students with need: Out of 217 full-time freshmen who applied for aid, 204 were judged to have need. Of these, 204 received aid, and 30 had their full need met. Average financial aid package met 76% of need; average scholarship/grant was $6,347; average loan was $4,927. For part-time students, average financial aid package was $5,192.

Students without need: 23 full-time freshmen who did not demonstrate need for aid received scholarships/grants; average award was $4,510. No-need awards available for academics, alumni affiliation, art, athletics, leadership, minority status, music/drama, religious affiliation, state/district residency.

Scholarships offered: 12 full-time freshmen received athletic scholarships; average amount $7,125.

Cumulative student debt: 72% of graduating class had student loans; average debt was $35,553.

FINANCIAL AID PROCEDURES

Forms required: FAFSA.

Dates and Deadlines: Priority date 4/1; no closing date. Applicants notified on a rolling basis starting 5/1; must reply within 2 week(s) of notification.

CONTACT

Shakeena White, Director of Enrollment Management

Box 5000, Wilson, NC 27893-7000

(252) 399-6323

Beaufort County Community College
Washington, North Carolina
www.beaufortccc.edu   Federal Code: 008558

2-year public community college in small town.

Enrollment: 1,122 full-time undergrads.

Selectivity: Open admission; but selective for some programs.

BASIC COSTS (2009-2010)

Tuition and fees: $1,560; out-of-state residents $7,299.

Per-credit charge: $50; out-of-state residents $241.

Additional info: Some programs require insurance and uniforms.

FINANCIAL AID PICTURE (2009-2010)

Students with need: Need-based aid available for full-time and part-time students.

Students without need: No-need awards available for academics.

FINANCIAL AID PROCEDURES

Forms required: FAFSA, institutional form.

Dates and Deadlines: Priority date 6/1; no closing date. Applicants notified on a rolling basis starting 5/1; must reply within 2 week(s) of notification.

CONTACT

Harold Smith, Director of Financial Aid

Box 1069, Washington, NC 27889

(252) 940-6222

Belmont Abbey College
Belmont, North Carolina
www.belmontabbeycollege.edu   Federal Code: 002910

4-year private liberal arts college in small town, affiliated with Roman Catholic Church.

Enrollment: 1,625 undergrads, 6% part-time. 346 full-time freshmen.

Selectivity: Admits 50 to 75% of applicants.

BASIC COSTS (2010-2011)

Tuition and fees: $24,584.

Per-credit charge: $819.

Room and board: $10,094.

Additional info: Room rates vary depending on the dormitory, the rates provided represent the least expensive dorm option. Housing costs for a double-occupancy room ranges from $5828 to $6508 for the full academic year with 19 meal plan at $4266 for the full year.

FINANCIAL AID PICTURE (2009-2010)

Students with need: Need-based aid available for full-time and part-time students. Work study available nights, weekends, and for part-time students.

Students without need: No-need awards available for academics, athletics, leadership, religious affiliation, state/district residency.

Scholarships offered: Many merit scholarships offered; ranging from $500 to $20,000; based solely on academic achievement.

FINANCIAL AID PROCEDURES

Forms required: FAFSA, state aid form.

Dates and Deadlines: Priority date 4/1; no closing date. Applicants notified on a rolling basis starting 3/1; must reply within 2 week(s) of notification.

CONTACT

Anne Stevens, Director of Enrollment Management

100 Belmont - Mt. Holly Road, Belmont, NC 28012-2795

(704) 825-6665

Bennett College for Women
Greensboro, North Carolina
www.bennett.edu   Federal Code: 002911

4-year private liberal arts college for women in small city, affiliated with United Methodist Church.

Enrollment: 711 undergrads, 1% part-time. 226 full-time freshmen.

Selectivity: Admits 50 to 75% of applicants.

BASIC COSTS (2009-2010)

Tuition and fees: $15,234.

Per-credit charge: $552.

Room and board: $6,736.

FINANCIAL AID PICTURE (2009-2010)

Students with need: Out of 221 full-time freshmen who applied for aid, 214 were judged to have need. Of these, 214 received aid, and 2 had their full need met. Average financial aid package met 49% of need; average scholarship/grant was $10,070; average loan was $3,468. For part-time students, average financial aid package was $8,404.

Students without need: 2 full-time freshmen who did not demonstrate need for aid received scholarships/grants; average award was $3,000. No-need awards available for state/district residency.

Cumulative student debt: 98% of graduating class had student loans; average debt was $37,667.

FINANCIAL AID PROCEDURES

Forms required: FAFSA, institutional form.

Dates and Deadlines: Closing date 4/15. Applicants notified by 7/15.

CONTACT

Keisha Ragsdale, Director of Financial Aid

900 East Washington Street, Greensboro, NC 27401-3239

(336) 517-2204

Bladen Community College
Dublin, North Carolina
www.bladencc.edu   Federal Code: 007987

2-year public community college in rural community.

Enrollment: 1,699 undergrads.

Selectivity: Open admission; but selective for some programs.

BASIC COSTS (2009-2010)

Tuition and fees: $1,580; out-of-state residents $7,319.

Per-credit charge: $50; out-of-state residents $241.

FINANCIAL AID PICTURE

Students with need: Need-based aid available for full-time and part-time students. Work study available nights.

FINANCIAL AID PROCEDURES

Forms required: FAFSA.

Dates and Deadlines: Priority date 6/1; no closing date. Applicants notified on a rolling basis starting 8/1; must reply within 2 week(s) of notification.

CONTACT

Marva Dinkins, Financial Aid Director
Box 266, Dublin, NC 28332-0266
(910) 879-5562

Blue Ridge Community College

Flat Rock, North Carolina
www.blueridge.edu   Federal Code: 009684

2-year public community and technical college in large town.
Enrollment: 1,668 undergrads.
Selectivity: Open admission.

BASIC COSTS (2009-2010)

Tuition and fees: $1,595; out-of-state residents $7,334.
Per-credit charge: $50; out-of-state residents $241.

FINANCIAL AID PICTURE (2009-2010)

Students with need: Need-based aid available for full-time and part-time students. Work study available nights.
Students without need: No-need awards available for academics, athletics, leadership, minority status, state/district residency.

FINANCIAL AID PROCEDURES

Forms required: FAFSA, institutional form.
Dates and Deadlines: Priority date 6/30; no closing date. Applicants notified on a rolling basis starting 2/1; must reply within 4 week(s) of notification.

CONTACT

Rita Blythe, Financial Aid Officer
180 West Campus Drive, Flat Rock, NC 28731-9624
(828) 694-1815

Brevard College

Brevard, North Carolina
www.brevard.edu   Federal Code: 002912

4-year private liberal arts college in small town, affiliated with United Methodist Church.
Enrollment: 651 undergrads, 1% part-time. 191 full-time freshmen.
Selectivity: Admits 50 to 75% of applicants.

BASIC COSTS (2010-2011)

Tuition and fees: $22,900.
Per-credit charge: $445.
Room and board: $7,850.

FINANCIAL AID PICTURE (2009-2010)

Students with need: Out of 150 full-time freshmen who applied for aid, 132 were judged to have need. Of these, 132 received aid, and 36 had their full need met. Average financial aid package met 81% of need; average scholarship/grant was $13,500; average loan was $3,850. For part-time students, average financial aid package was $9,400.
Students without need: 35 full-time freshmen who did not demonstrate need for aid received scholarships/grants; average award was $3,500. No-need awards available for academics, art, athletics, leadership, music/drama, religious affiliation, state/district residency.
Scholarships offered: 14 full-time freshmen received athletic scholarships; average amount $12,100.
Cumulative student debt: 59% of graduating class had student loans; average debt was $20,770.

FINANCIAL AID PROCEDURES

Forms required: FAFSA, state aid form.
Dates and Deadlines: Priority date 4/15; no closing date. Applicants notified on a rolling basis starting 2/1; must reply within 4 week(s) of notification.

CONTACT

Lisanne Masterson, Director of Financial Aid
One Brevard College Drive, Brevard, NC 28712
(828) 884-8287

Brunswick Community College

Supply, North Carolina
www.brunswickcc.edu   Federal Code: 015285

2-year public community college in small town.
Enrollment: 736 undergrads. 222 full-time freshmen.
Selectivity: Open admission; but selective for some programs.

BASIC COSTS (2009-2010)

Tuition and fees: $1,600; out-of-state residents $7,339.
Per-credit charge: $50; out-of-state residents $241.

FINANCIAL AID PICTURE (2009-2010)

Students with need: Need-based aid available for full-time and part-time students. Work study available nights, weekends, and for part-time students.
Students without need: No-need awards available for academics, state/district residency.
Scholarships offered: La Dane Williamson Universal Scholarship: $1,200 per year for 2 years; must be a resident of Brunswick County for 5 years prior to application, must be a high school graduate of Brunswick County or complete GED or adult high school diploma program at Brunswick Community College, must not be eligible for Pell. Brunswick Family Scholarship: may cover total amount of tuition and fees; for Brunswick County residents of 3 years prior to application with GED or high school graduate, must not be eligible for Pell.
Additional info: Attendance required at financial aid orientation session for those receiving federal student aid.

FINANCIAL AID PROCEDURES

Forms required: FAFSA, institutional form.
Dates and Deadlines: Priority date 6/1; closing date 6/15. Applicants notified on a rolling basis starting 3/1; must reply by 6/15 or within 2 week(s) of notification.
Transfers: Priority date 6/30; no deadline.

CONTACT

Paula Almond, Coordinator of Financial Aid and Veterans Affairs
Box 30, Supply, NC 28462
(910) 755-7422

Caldwell Community College and Technical Institute

Hudson, North Carolina
www.cccti.edu   Federal Code: 004835

2-year public community and technical college in small town.
Enrollment: 3,970 undergrads.
Selectivity: Open admission; but selective for some programs.

BASIC COSTS (2009-2010)

Tuition and fees: $1,556; out-of-state residents $7,295.
Per-credit charge: $50; out-of-state residents $241.

FINANCIAL AID PICTURE (2009-2010)

Students with need: Need-based aid available for full-time and part-time students.
Students without need: This college awards aid only to students with need.

FINANCIAL AID PROCEDURES

Forms required: FAFSA.

Dates and Deadlines: Closing date 5/1. Applicants notified on a rolling basis starting 6/30.

CONTACT
Eva Rader-Harmon, Director of Financial Aid
2855 Hickory Boulevard, Hudson, NC 28638-2672
(828) 726-2714

Campbell University
Buies Creek, North Carolina
www.campbell.edu   Federal Code: 002913

4-year private university and liberal arts college in small town.
Enrollment: 2,755 undergrads.
Selectivity: Admits less than 50% of applicants.

BASIC COSTS (2010-2011)
Tuition and fees: $22,520.
Per-credit charge: $360.
Room and board: $7,800.

FINANCIAL AID PICTURE (2009-2010)
Students with need: Need-based aid available for full-time students. Work study available nights, weekends, and for part-time students.
Students without need: No-need awards available for academics, athletics, music/drama, ROTC, state/district residency.
Scholarships offered: Presidential Scholarship: $13,000-$15,000. Campbell Scholarship: $7,000-$12,000.

FINANCIAL AID PROCEDURES
Forms required: FAFSA.
Dates and Deadlines: Priority date 3/15; no closing date. Applicants notified on a rolling basis.
Transfers: Applicants notified on a rolling basis.

CONTACT
Michelle Day, Director of Financial Aid
PO Box 546, Buies Creek, NC 27506
(800) 334-4111 ext. 1310

Cape Fear Community College
Wilmington, North Carolina
www.cfcc.edu   Federal Code: 005320

2-year public community college in small city.
Enrollment: 8,159 undergrads, 45% part-time. 271 full-time freshmen.
Selectivity: Open admission; but selective for some programs.

BASIC COSTS (2009-2010)
Tuition and fees: $1,635; out-of-state residents $7,374.
Per-credit charge: $50; out-of-state residents $241.

FINANCIAL AID PICTURE (2009-2010)
Students with need: 49% of average financial aid package awarded as scholarships/grants, 51% awarded as loans/jobs. Need-based aid available for part-time students. Work study available nights.
Students without need: No-need awards available for academics, athletics, job skills, leadership, music/drama, religious affiliation.

FINANCIAL AID PROCEDURES
Forms required: FAFSA.
Dates and Deadlines: Priority date 6/1; no closing date. Applicants notified on a rolling basis starting 4/1; must reply within 2 week(s) of notification.

CONTACT
Jo-Ann Craig, Director of Financial Aid
411 North Front Street, Wilmington, NC 28401-3910
(910) 362-7055

Carolina Christian College
Winston-Salem, North Carolina
www.carolina.edu

4-year private Bible college in large city, affiliated with Church of Christ.
Enrollment: 41 undergrads.
Selectivity: Open admission.

BASIC COSTS (2009-2010)
Tuition and fees: $4,700.
Per-credit charge: $125.

FINANCIAL AID PICTURE (2009-2010)
Students with need: Need-based aid available for full-time and part-time students.

FINANCIAL AID PROCEDURES
Forms required: FAFSA.
Dates and Deadlines: No deadline. Applicants notified on a rolling basis.
Transfers: No deadline. Applicants notified on a rolling basis.

CONTACT
LaTanya Lucas, Director of Financial Aid
Box 777, Winston-Salem, NC 27102
(336) 744-0900 ext. 103

Carolinas College of Health Sciences
Charlotte, North Carolina
www.carolinascollege.edu   Federal Code: 031042

2-year public health science and junior college in very large city.
Enrollment: 506 undergrads.
Selectivity: Open admission; but selective for some programs.

BASIC COSTS (2009-2010)
Tuition and fees: $7,651.
Per-credit charge: $218.
Additional info: Tuition and fees vary by program. Commuter college with no on-campus room and board.

FINANCIAL AID PICTURE (2008-2009)
Students with need: Need-based aid available for full-time and part-time students.
Students without need: No-need awards available for academics.

FINANCIAL AID PROCEDURES
Forms required: FAFSA, institutional form.
Dates and Deadlines: Priority date 5/1; no closing date. Applicants notified on a rolling basis starting 5/1.

CONTACT
Jill Powell, Financial Aid Officer
PO Box 32861, Charlotte, NC 28232
(704) 355-8894

Carteret Community College
Morehead City, North Carolina
www.carteret.edu   Federal Code: 008081

2-year public community and technical college in small town.
Enrollment: 1,419 undergrads.

Selectivity: Open admission; but selective for some programs.

BASIC COSTS (2009-2010)

Tuition and fees: $1,563; out-of-state residents $7,293.
Per-credit charge: $50; out-of-state residents $241.

FINANCIAL AID PICTURE (2008-2009)

Students with need: Need-based aid available for full-time and part-time students.
Students without need: No-need awards available for academics, leadership, minority status, state/district residency.
Additional info: Institutional student loan program administered by college. Student may charge up to $600 for books, supplies and tuition per quarter. Repayment due by 11th week of semester.

FINANCIAL AID PROCEDURES

Forms required: FAFSA, institutional form.
Dates and Deadlines: No deadline. Applicants notified on a rolling basis starting 7/1; must reply within 2 week(s) of notification.

CONTACT

Brenda Long, Financial Aid Officer
3505 Arendell Street, Morehead City, NC 28557-2989
(252) 222-6297

Catawba College

Salisbury, North Carolina
www.catawba.edu   Federal Code: 002914

4-year private liberal arts college in large town, affiliated with United Church of Christ.
Enrollment: 1,324 undergrads, 4% part-time. 248 full-time freshmen.
Selectivity: Admits 50 to 75% of applicants.

BASIC COSTS (2010-2011)

Tuition and fees: $25,160.
Per-credit charge: $655.
Room and board: $8,700.

FINANCIAL AID PICTURE (2008-2009)

Students with need: Out of 207 full-time freshmen who applied for aid, 171 were judged to have need. Of these, 171 received aid, and 53 had their full need met. Average financial aid package met 96% of need; average scholarship/grant was $5,629; average loan was $4,336. For part-time students, average financial aid package was $7,246.
Students without need: 39 full-time freshmen who did not demonstrate need for aid received scholarships/grants; average award was $12,403. No-need awards available for academics, athletics, music/drama, state/district residency.
Scholarships offered: 82 full-time freshmen received athletic scholarships; average amount $6,956.
Cumulative student debt: 77% of graduating class had student loans; average debt was $21,891.

FINANCIAL AID PROCEDURES

Forms required: FAFSA, state aid form.
Dates and Deadlines: Priority date 3/15; no closing date. Applicants notified on a rolling basis starting 11/1; must reply within 2 week(s) of notification.

CONTACT

Melanie McCulloh, Director of Scholarships and Financial Assistance
2300 West Innes Street, Salisbury, NC 28144-2488
(704) 637-4416

Catawba Valley Community College

Hickory, North Carolina
www.cvcc.edu   Federal Code: 005318

2-year public community college in large town.
Enrollment: 4,630 undergrads, 53% part-time. 716 full-time freshmen.
Selectivity: Open admission; but selective for some programs.

BASIC COSTS (2009-2010)

Tuition and fees: $1,687; out-of-state residents $7,809.
Per-credit charge: $50; out-of-state residents $241.
Additional info: Tuition/fee waivers available for unemployed or children of unemployed.

FINANCIAL AID PICTURE (2008-2009)

Students with need: Out of 501 full-time freshmen who applied for aid, 460 were judged to have need. Of these, 306 received aid. Need-based aid available for part-time students.
Students without need: No-need awards available for academics, leadership, music/drama.

FINANCIAL AID PROCEDURES

Forms required: FAFSA.
Dates and Deadlines: Closing date 3/15. Applicants notified on a rolling basis starting 5/15.

CONTACT

Debbie Barger, Director of Scholarships and Financial Aid
2550 Highway 70 SE, Hickory, NC 28602
(828) 327-7000 ext. 4214

Central Carolina Community College

Sanford, North Carolina
www.cccc.edu   Federal Code: 005449

2-year public community college in large town.
Enrollment: 3,296 undergrads.
Selectivity: Open admission; but selective for some programs.

BASIC COSTS (2009-2010)

Tuition and fees: $1,588; out-of-state residents $7,327.
Per-credit charge: $50; out-of-state residents $241.

FINANCIAL AID PICTURE (2008-2009)

Students with need: 99% of average financial aid package awarded as scholarships/grants, 1% awarded as loans/jobs. Need-based aid available for part-time students. Work study available nights.
Students without need: No-need awards available for academics.

FINANCIAL AID PROCEDURES

Forms required: FAFSA, institutional form.
Dates and Deadlines: Priority date 3/16; closing date 5/3. Applicants notified on a rolling basis starting 7/1; must reply within 2 week(s) of notification.
Transfers: No deadline.

CONTACT

David Bowman, Director of Financial Aid
1105 Kelly Drive, Sanford, NC 27330
(919) 718-7229

Central Piedmont Community College

Charlotte, North Carolina
www.cpcc.edu   Federal Code: 002915

2-year public community college in very large city.
Enrollment: 16,722 undergrads, 61% part-time. 1,610 full-time freshmen.

PART III: FINANCIAL AID COLLEGE BY COLLEGE

Selectivity: Open admission; but selective for some programs.

BASIC COSTS (2009-2010)

Tuition and fees: $1,688; out-of-state residents $7,420.
Per-credit charge: $50; out-of-state residents $241.

FINANCIAL AID PICTURE

Students with need: Need-based aid available for full-time and part-time students.
Students without need: No-need awards available for academics, minority status.

FINANCIAL AID PROCEDURES

Forms required: FAFSA.
Dates and Deadlines: Priority date 4/1; closing date 6/1. Applicants notified on a rolling basis.

CONTACT

Debbie Brooks, Director, Student Financial Aid
Box 35009, Charlotte, NC 28235-5009
(704) 330-6942

Chowan University
Murfreesboro, North Carolina
www.chowan.edu   Federal Code: 002916

4-year private university and liberal arts college in rural community, affiliated with Southern Baptist Convention.
Enrollment: 1,080 undergrads.
Selectivity: Admits 50 to 75% of applicants.

BASIC COSTS (2009-2010)

Tuition and fees: $19,065.
Per-credit charge: $325.
Room and board: $7,310.

FINANCIAL AID PICTURE (2009-2010)

Students with need: Need-based aid available for full-time and part-time students. Work study available nights, weekends, and for part-time students.
Students without need: No-need awards available for academics, athletics, leadership, music/drama, religious affiliation, state/district residency.
Scholarships offered: Scholarship program for students serving as student body president who qualify for admission; full tuition.

FINANCIAL AID PROCEDURES

Forms required: FAFSA.
Dates and Deadlines: Priority date 3/1; no closing date. Applicants notified on a rolling basis starting 3/1; must reply within 2 week(s) of notification.

CONTACT

Sharon Rose, Director of Financial Aid
One University Place, Murfreesboro, NC 27855-9901
(252) 398-1229

Cleveland Community College
Shelby, North Carolina
www.clevelandcommunitycollege.edu Federal Code: 008082

2-year public community college in large town.
Enrollment: 4,166 undergrads. 394 full-time freshmen.
Selectivity: Open admission; but selective for some programs.

BASIC COSTS (2009-2010)

Tuition and fees: $1,565; out-of-state residents $7,304.
Per-credit charge: $50; out-of-state residents $241.

FINANCIAL AID PICTURE (2008-2009)

Students with need: Need-based aid available for full-time and part-time students. Work study available nights.

FINANCIAL AID PROCEDURES

Forms required: FAFSA.
Dates and Deadlines: Priority date 7/1; no closing date. Applicants notified on a rolling basis.

CONTACT

Andy Gardner, Director of Financial Aid
137 South Post Road, Shelby, NC 28152
(704) 484-4096

Coastal Carolina Community College
Jacksonville, North Carolina
www.coastalcarolina.edu   Federal Code: 005316

2-year public community college in large town.
Enrollment: 3,667 undergrads, 51% part-time. 502 full-time freshmen.
Selectivity: Open admission; but selective for some programs.

BASIC COSTS (2009-2010)

Tuition and fees: $1,530; out-of-state residents $7,269.
Per-credit charge: $50; out-of-state residents $241.

FINANCIAL AID PICTURE (2008-2009)

Students with need: 99% of average financial aid package awarded as scholarships/grants, 1% awarded as loans/jobs. Need-based aid available for part-time students. Work study available nights, weekends, and for part-time students.
Students without need: No-need awards available for academics, state/district residency.

FINANCIAL AID PROCEDURES

Forms required: FAFSA, institutional form.
Dates and Deadlines: Priority date 5/15; no closing date. Applicants notified on a rolling basis starting 5/15; must reply within 2 week(s) of notification.

CONTACT

Lyon Tammy, Director for Financial Aid Services
444 Western Boulevard, Jacksonville, NC 28546-6877

College of the Albemarle
Elizabeth City, North Carolina
www.albemarle.cc.nc.us   Federal Code: 002917

2-year public branch campus and community college in large town.
Enrollment: 2,224 undergrads.
Selectivity: Open admission; but selective for some programs.

BASIC COSTS (2009-2010)

Tuition and fees: $1,590; out-of-state residents $7,329.
Per-credit charge: $50; out-of-state residents $241.

FINANCIAL AID PICTURE (2008-2009)

Students with need: Need-based aid available for full-time and part-time students.
Students without need: No-need awards available for academics, art, leadership, minority status, music/drama, state/district residency.
Additional info: Separate application must be submitted for COA Private Scholarships.

FINANCIAL AID PROCEDURES

Forms required: FAFSA.
Dates and Deadlines: Priority date 3/15; no closing date. Applicants notified on a rolling basis starting 5/1; must reply within 2 week(s) of notification.

CONTACT

Angie Dawson, Director of Scholarships and Student Aid
1208 North Road Street, Elizabeth City, NC 27906-2327
(252) 335-0821 ext. 2355

Davidson College

Davidson, North Carolina   Federal Code: 002918
www.davidson.edu   CSS Code: 5150

4-year private liberal arts college in small town, affiliated with Presbyterian Church (USA).

Enrollment: 1,739 undergrads. 480 full-time freshmen.

Selectivity: Admits less than 50% of applicants. GED not accepted.

BASIC COSTS (2009-2010)

Tuition and fees: $35,124.
Room and board: $9,906.

FINANCIAL AID PICTURE (2008-2009)

Students with need: Out of 306 full-time freshmen who applied for aid, 211 were judged to have need. Of these, 203 received aid, and 203 had their full need met. Average financial aid package met 100% of need; average scholarship/grant was $23,853; average loan was $2,313. Need-based aid available for part-time students.

Students without need: 57 full-time freshmen who did not demonstrate need for aid received scholarships/grants; average award was $19,079. No-need awards available for academics, art, athletics, leadership, minority status, music/drama, ROTC.

Scholarships offered: *Merit:* Thompson S./Sarah S. Baker Scholarships: comprehensive fees; for first-time students with highest achievements; 3 awarded. John Montgomery Belk Scholarship: comprehensive fees; for Southeast applicants with highest achievements; 6 awarded. Amos Norris Scholarship: full cost; for first-time student athlete; 1 awarded. William Holt Terry Scholarships: full tuition; for first-year students with leadership skills and personal qualities, 2 awarded. John I. Smith Scholars Programs: full tuition; for first-year students with leadership, academic excellence, and commitment to community service; 2 awarded. *Athletic:* 41 full-time freshmen received athletic scholarships; average amount $15,173.

Cumulative student debt: 38% of graduating class had student loans; average debt was $20,858.

Additional info: The college has increased the money it provides for grants in financial aid packages and eliminated mandatory loans.

FINANCIAL AID PROCEDURES

Forms required: FAFSA, CSS PROFILE.
Dates and Deadlines: Closing date 2/15. Applicants notified by 4/1; must reply by 5/1.
Transfers: Priority date 2/15; closing date 3/15. Applicants notified by 5/15.

CONTACT

David Gelinas, Director of Financial Aid
Box 7156, Davidson, NC 28035-7156
(704) 894-2232

Davidson County Community College

Lexington, North Carolina
www.davidsonccc.edu   Federal Code: 002919

2-year public community college in large town.

Enrollment: 3,568 undergrads.

Selectivity: Open admission; but selective for some programs.

BASIC COSTS (2009-2010)

Tuition and fees: $1,610; out-of-state residents $7,349.
Per-credit charge: $50; out-of-state residents $241.

FINANCIAL AID PICTURE (2008-2009)

Students with need: Need-based aid available for full-time and part-time students.

Students without need: No-need awards available for academics, leadership.

FINANCIAL AID PROCEDURES

Forms required: FAFSA, institutional form.
Dates and Deadlines: Closing date 3/31. Applicants notified on a rolling basis starting 7/1; must reply within 2 week(s) of notification.

CONTACT

Anita Pennix, Director, Financial Aid
PO Box 1287, Lexington, NC 27293-1287
(336) 249-8186 ext. 237

Duke University

Durham, North Carolina   Federal Code: 002920
www.duke.edu   CSS Code: 5156

4-year private university in small city, affiliated with United Methodist Church.

Enrollment: 6,416 undergrads. 1,724 full-time freshmen.

Selectivity: Admits less than 50% of applicants. GED not accepted.

BASIC COSTS (2010-2011)

Tuition and fees: $40,243.
Per-credit charge: $1,218.
Room and board: $11,622.

FINANCIAL AID PICTURE

Students with need: Need-based aid available for full-time students.

Students without need: No-need awards available for academics, alumni affiliation, art, athletics, leadership, minority status, religious affiliation, ROTC, state/district residency.

FINANCIAL AID PROCEDURES

Forms required: FAFSA, CSS PROFILE.
Dates and Deadlines: Closing date 3/1. Applicants notified by 4/1; must reply by 5/1 or within 4 week(s) of notification.

CONTACT

Alison Rabil, Director of Financial Aid
2138 Campus Drive, Durham, NC 27708
(919) 684-6225

Durham Technical Community College

Durham, North Carolina
www.durhamtech.edu   Federal Code: 005448

2-year public community and technical college in small city.

Enrollment: 5,474 undergrads.

Selectivity: Open admission; but selective for some programs.

BASIC COSTS (2009-2010)

Tuition and fees: $1,580; out-of-state residents $7,319.
Per-credit charge: $50; out-of-state residents $241.

FINANCIAL AID PICTURE

Students with need: Need-based aid available for full-time and part-time students. Work study available nights.

Students without need: No-need awards available for academics, minority status, state/district residency.

Additional info: Special funds available to single parents for tuition, fees, books, supplies and child care expenses.

FINANCIAL AID PROCEDURES

Forms required: FAFSA.

Dates and Deadlines: Applicants notified on a rolling basis starting 1/31; must reply within 3 week(s) of notification.

CONTACT

Cameron Murray, Director of Financial Aid
1637 Lawson Street, Durham, NC 27703
(919) 686-3661

East Carolina University
Greenville, North Carolina
www.ecu.edu   Federal Code: 002923

4-year public university in small city.
Enrollment: 20,571 undergrads, 11% part-time. 3,849 full-time freshmen.
Selectivity: Admits 50 to 75% of applicants.

BASIC COSTS (2009-2010)
Tuition and fees: $4,271; out-of-state residents $15,105.
Room and board: $7,490.

FINANCIAL AID PICTURE (2009-2010)
Students with need: Out of 3,008 full-time freshmen who applied for aid, 1,919 were judged to have need. Of these, 1,855 received aid, and 545 had their full need met. Average financial aid package met 78% of need; average scholarship/grant was $7,943; average loan was $2,833. For part-time students, average financial aid package was $6,685.
Students without need: 55 full-time freshmen who did not demonstrate need for aid received scholarships/grants; average award was $2,155. No-need awards available for academics, alumni affiliation, art, athletics, music/drama, ROTC.
Scholarships offered: 58 full-time freshmen received athletic scholarships; average amount $11,929.

FINANCIAL AID PROCEDURES
Forms required: FAFSA.
Dates and Deadlines: Priority date 3/1; no closing date. Applicants notified on a rolling basis starting 4/1; must reply within 3 week(s) of notification.

CONTACT

Julie Poorman, Director of Student Financial Aid
Office of Undergraduate Admissions, Greenville, NC 27858-4353
(252) 328-6610

Edgecombe Community College
Tarboro, North Carolina
www.edgecombe.edu   Federal Code: 008855

2-year public community college in large town.
Enrollment: 2,841 undergrads, 53% part-time. 403 full-time freshmen.
Selectivity: Open admission; but selective for some programs.

BASIC COSTS (2009-2010)
Tuition and fees: $1,568; out-of-state residents $7,307.
Per-credit charge: $50; out-of-state residents $241.

FINANCIAL AID PICTURE (2009-2010)
Students with need: 68% of average financial aid package awarded as scholarships/grants, 32% awarded as loans/jobs. Need-based aid available for part-time students.
Students without need: This college awards aid only to students with need.

FINANCIAL AID PROCEDURES
Forms required: FAFSA, institutional form.
Dates and Deadlines: No deadline. Applicants notified on a rolling basis starting 8/15; must reply within 3 week(s) of notification.
Transfers: No deadline.

CONTACT

Henry Anderson, Director of Financial Aid
2009 West Wilson Street, Tarboro, NC 27886
(252) 823-5166 ext. 258

Elizabeth City State University
Elizabeth City, North Carolina
www.ecsu.edu   Federal Code: 002926

4-year public liberal arts college in large town.
Enrollment: 3,045 undergrads, 7% part-time. 662 full-time freshmen.
Selectivity: Admits 50 to 75% of applicants.

BASIC COSTS (2009-2010)
Tuition and fees: $3,031; out-of-state residents $12,080.
Room and board: $5,495.

FINANCIAL AID PICTURE
Students with need: Need-based aid available for full-time students. Work study available nights, weekends, and for part-time students.
Students without need: No-need awards available for academics, athletics, minority status, ROTC, state/district residency.

FINANCIAL AID PROCEDURES
Forms required: FAFSA.
Dates and Deadlines: Closing date 3/15. Applicants notified on a rolling basis starting 6/1; must reply within 3 week(s) of notification.
Transfers: Closing date 3/15. Applicants notified on a rolling basis starting 6/1; must reply within 3 week(s) of notification.

CONTACT

Kenneth Wilson, Associate Director of Financial Aid
1704 Weeksville Road, Campus Box 901, Elizabeth City, NC 27909
(252) 335-3283

Elon University
Elon, North Carolina   Federal Code: 002927
www.elon.edu   CSS Code: 5183

4-year private university and liberal arts college in large town, affiliated with United Church of Christ.
Enrollment: 4,995 undergrads, 2% part-time. 1,291 full-time freshmen.
Selectivity: Admits less than 50% of applicants.

BASIC COSTS (2010-2011)
Tuition and fees: $26,827.
Per-credit charge: $831.
Room and board: $8,648.

FINANCIAL AID PICTURE (2009-2010)
Students with need: Out of 776 full-time freshmen who applied for aid, 456 were judged to have need. Of these, 453 received aid. Average financial aid package met 86% of need; average scholarship/grant was $13,887; average loan was $4,100. Need-based aid available for part-time students.
Students without need: 282 full-time freshmen who did not demonstrate need for aid received scholarships/grants; average award was $5,670. No-need awards available for academics, art, athletics, leadership, music/drama, ROTC, state/district residency.
Scholarships offered: *Merit:* Presidential Scholarships: $2,000-$4,500 annually; based on academic credentials. Fellows Programs (Communications, Science, Jefferson-Pilot Business, Honors, Isabella Cannon Leadership): $2,500-$10,000 annually; based on merit. North Carolina Teaching Fellows: $15,000 annually. Engineering Scholarships: $7,000 annually. Performing Arts Scholarships: $500-$6,000; talent-based. Music Scholarships: $500-$5,000; talent and need-based. *Athletic:* 66 full-time freshmen received athletic scholarships; average amount $21,349.

Cumulative student debt: 45% of graduating class had student loans; average debt was $22,939.

FINANCIAL AID PROCEDURES

Forms required: FAFSA, CSS PROFILE, institutional form.

Dates and Deadlines: Priority date 2/15; no closing date. Applicants notified on a rolling basis starting 3/30.

CONTACT

Pat Murphy, Director of Financial Planning
2700 Campus Box, Elon, NC 27244-2010
(336) 278-7640

Fayetteville State University
Fayetteville, North Carolina
www.uncfsu.edu   Federal Code: 002928

4-year public university in small city.

Enrollment: 5,259 undergrads, 21% part-time. 566 full-time freshmen.

BASIC COSTS (2009-2010)

Tuition and fees: $3,177; out-of-state residents $13,520.

Room and board: $5,421.

Additional info: Car registration $45, insurance $378, room breakage deposit $125, late registration $20.

FINANCIAL AID PICTURE

Students with need: Out of 553 full-time freshmen who applied for aid, 509 were judged to have need. Of these, 506 received aid, and 38 had their full need met. Average financial aid package met 86% of need; average scholarship/grant was $8,691; average loan was $2,914. For part-time students, average financial aid package was $6,746.

Students without need: 30 full-time freshmen who did not demonstrate need for aid received scholarships/grants; average award was $1,065. No-need awards available for academics, alumni affiliation, athletics, music/drama, ROTC, state/district residency.

Scholarships offered: 13 full-time freshmen received athletic scholarships; average amount $11,919.

FINANCIAL AID PROCEDURES

Forms required: FAFSA.

Dates and Deadlines: Priority date 3/1; closing date 4/1. Applicants notified on a rolling basis starting 4/15; must reply within 2 week(s) of notification.

CONTACT

Kamesia Ewing, Director of Financial Aid
1200 Murchison Road, Fayetteville, NC 28301-4298
(910) 672-1325

Fayetteville Technical Community College
Fayetteville, North Carolina
www.faytechcc.edu   Federal Code: 007640

2-year public community and technical college in large city.

Enrollment: 8,247 undergrads, 66% part-time. 767 full-time freshmen.

Selectivity: Open admission; but selective for some programs.

BASIC COSTS (2010-2011)

Tuition and fees: $1,660; out-of-state residents $7,782.

Per-credit charge: $50; out-of-state residents $241.

FINANCIAL AID PICTURE (2008-2009)

Students with need: Out of 624 full-time freshmen who applied for aid, 596 were judged to have need. Of these, 547 received aid, and 526 had their full need met. Average financial aid package met 95% of need; average scholarship/grant was $421; average loan was $3,500. For part-time students, average financial aid package was $6,125.

Cumulative student debt: 82% of graduating class had student loans; average debt was $26,000.

FINANCIAL AID PROCEDURES

Forms required: FAFSA.

Dates and Deadlines: Priority date 6/1; closing date 7/15. Applicants notified on a rolling basis starting 4/1; must reply by 6/1.

Transfers: Priority date 3/1; closing date 6/1. Applicants notified by 1/1; must reply within 2 week(s) of notification.

CONTACT

Christine Porchia, Director of Financial Aid
PO Box 35236, Fayetteville, NC 28303-0236
(910) 678-0040

Forsyth Technical Community College
Winston-Salem, North Carolina
www.forsythtech.edu   Federal Code: 005317

2-year public community and technical college in small city.

Enrollment: 8,002 undergrads, 46% part-time. 1,040 full-time freshmen.

Selectivity: Open admission; but selective for some programs.

BASIC COSTS (2009-2010)

Tuition and fees: $1,562; out-of-state residents $7,301.

Per-credit charge: $50; out-of-state residents $241.

FINANCIAL AID PICTURE (2008-2009)

Students with need: Need-based aid available for full-time and part-time students. Work study available nights.

Students without need: No-need awards available for academics, state/district residency.

Additional info: Apply for aid as close to January 1 as possible for best consideration.

FINANCIAL AID PROCEDURES

Forms required: FAFSA, institutional form.

Dates and Deadlines: Priority date 6/1; no closing date. Applicants notified on a rolling basis starting 7/1; must reply within 2 week(s) of notification.

Transfers: No deadline. Mid-year transfer students must submit a financial aid transcript from previous college in order for financial aid office to award any Federal Pell Grant funds to eligible students.

CONTACT

Ricky Hodges, Director of Student Financial Services
2100 Silas Creek Parkway, Winston-Salem, NC 27103

Gardner-Webb University
Boiling Springs, North Carolina
www.gardner-webb.edu   Federal Code: 002929

4-year private university and liberal arts college in small town, affiliated with Southern Baptist Convention.

Enrollment: 2,640 undergrads, 15% part-time. 448 full-time freshmen.

Selectivity: Admits 50 to 75% of applicants.

BASIC COSTS (2010-2011)

Tuition and fees: $22,410.

Per-credit charge: $357.

Room and board: $7,220.

FINANCIAL AID PICTURE (2008-2009)

Students with need: Out of 419 full-time freshmen who applied for aid, 339 were judged to have need. Of these, 339 received aid, and 108 had their full need met. Average financial aid package met 76% of need; average scholarship/grant was $9,624; average loan was $3,463.

Students without need: 85 full-time freshmen who did not demonstrate need for aid received scholarships/grants; average award was $7,149. No-need awards available for academics, athletics, leadership, music/drama, religious affiliation, ROTC, state/district residency.

Scholarships offered: 28 full-time freshmen received athletic scholarships; average amount $10,083.

FINANCIAL AID PROCEDURES

Forms required: FAFSA, state aid form.

Dates and Deadlines: Priority date 3/15; no closing date. Applicants notified on a rolling basis starting 3/1; must reply within 2 week(s) of notification.

Transfers: No deadline. Applicants notified on a rolling basis.

CONTACT

Summer Robertson, Director of Financial Planning
P.O. Box 817, Boiling Springs, NC 28017
(704) 406-4243

Gaston College
Dallas, North Carolina
www.gaston.edu   Federal Code: 002973

2-year public community college in small town.

Enrollment: 5,892 undergrads, 40% part-time. 1,017 full-time freshmen.

Selectivity: Open admission; but selective for some programs.

BASIC COSTS (2009-2010)

Tuition and fees: $1,578; out-of-state residents $7,317.

Per-credit charge: $50; out-of-state residents $241.

FINANCIAL AID PICTURE

Students with need: Need-based aid available for full-time students.

Students without need: No-need awards available for academics, state/district residency.

Scholarships offered: Academic Scholarship: over 30 available, $1,100, GPA of 3.0 or better. Careers Scholarship: 10 available, $1,100 each, must pursue career in specified engineering technologies or industrial technologies major and have GPA of 3.0 or better.

Additional info: Grants/scholarships available for women pursuing nontraditional roles.

FINANCIAL AID PROCEDURES

Forms required: FAFSA, institutional form.

Dates and Deadlines: Priority date 3/15; no closing date. Applicants notified on a rolling basis.

CONTACT

Peggy Oates, Director of Financial Aid and Veterans Affairs
201 Highway 321 South, Dallas, NC 28034-1499
(704) 922-6227

Greensboro College
Greensboro, North Carolina
www.greensborocollege.edu   Federal Code: 002930

4-year private liberal arts college in large city, affiliated with United Methodist Church.

Enrollment: 931 undergrads, 4% part-time. 241 full-time freshmen.

Selectivity: Admits 50 to 75% of applicants.

BASIC COSTS (2010-2011)

Tuition and fees: $23,350.

Per-credit charge: $635.

Room and board: $8,720.

FINANCIAL AID PICTURE (2009-2010)

Students with need: Need-based aid available for full-time and part-time students. Work study available nights, weekends, and for part-time students.

Students without need: No-need awards available for academics, alumni affiliation, art, leadership, music/drama, religious affiliation, state/district residency.

Scholarships offered: Presidential Scholarships: full tuition, fees, room, and board; number of awards vary.

FINANCIAL AID PROCEDURES

Forms required: FAFSA, state aid form, institutional form.

Dates and Deadlines: Priority date 4/15; no closing date. Applicants notified on a rolling basis starting 2/1; must reply within 2 week(s) of notification.

Transfers: Closing date 4/15. Must reply within 4 week(s) of notification.

CONTACT

Ron Elmore, Executive Director of Financial Aid
815 West Market Street, Greensboro, NC 27401-1875
(336) 272-7102 ext. 217

Guilford College
Greensboro, North Carolina
www.guilford.edu   Federal Code: 002931

4-year private liberal arts college in small city, affiliated with Society of Friends (Quaker).

Enrollment: 2,681 undergrads, 18% part-time. 449 full-time freshmen.

Selectivity: Admits 50 to 75% of applicants.

BASIC COSTS (2010-2011)

Tuition and fees: $28,800.

Per-credit charge: $885.

Room and board: $7,950.

Additional info: Tuition/fee waivers available for adults.

FINANCIAL AID PICTURE (2009-2010)

Students with need: Out of 398 full-time freshmen who applied for aid, 343 were judged to have need. Of these, 343 received aid, and 151 had their full need met. For part-time students, average financial aid package was $7,397.

Students without need: 121 full-time freshmen who did not demonstrate need for aid received scholarships/grants; average award was $7,558. No-need awards available for academics.

Scholarships offered: Honors Scholarship: $7,500 to full tuition. Presidential Scholarship: $5,000. Incentive grants: $3,000; based on participation or leadership in school or community activities. Quaker Leadership Scholarships: $3,000; candidates must be active members of the Religious Society of Friends.

Cumulative student debt: 69% of graduating class had student loans; average debt was $24,500.

FINANCIAL AID PROCEDURES

Forms required: FAFSA.

Dates and Deadlines: Priority date 3/1; no closing date. Applicants notified on a rolling basis starting 2/15; must reply within 2 week(s) of notification.

CONTACT

Dianne Harrison, Director of Financial Aid
Admissions, New Garden Hall, Greensboro, NC 27410-4108
(336) 316-2354

Guilford Technical Community College

Jamestown, North Carolina
www.gtcc.edu   Federal Code: 004838

2-year public community college in small city.
Enrollment: 12,747 undergrads, 38% part-time. 2,485 full-time freshmen.
Selectivity: Open admission; but selective for some programs.

BASIC COSTS (2009-2010)

Tuition and fees: $1,672; out-of-state residents $7,411.
Per-credit charge: $50; out-of-state residents $241.

FINANCIAL AID PICTURE (2008-2009)

Students with need: 65% of average financial aid package awarded as scholarships/grants, 35% awarded as loans/jobs. Need-based aid available for part-time students.

FINANCIAL AID PROCEDURES

Forms required: FAFSA.
Dates and Deadlines: Priority date 3/15; closing date 8/1. Applicants notified on a rolling basis starting 7/1; must reply within 2 week(s) of notification.

CONTACT

Lisa Koretoff, Director of Financial Aid
PO Box 309, Jamestown, NC 27282
(336) 334-4822 ext. 5352

Halifax Community College

Weldon, North Carolina
www.halifaxcc.edu/   Federal Code: 007986

2-year public community college in small town.
Enrollment: 1,545 undergrads, 46% part-time. 245 full-time freshmen.
Selectivity: Open admission; but selective for some programs.

BASIC COSTS (2009-2010)

Tuition and fees: $1,618; out-of-state residents $7,357.
Per-credit charge: $50; out-of-state residents $241.

FINANCIAL AID PICTURE (2008-2009)

Students with need: Need-based aid available for full-time students.

FINANCIAL AID PROCEDURES

Dates and Deadlines: Priority date 6/1; no closing date. Applicants notified on a rolling basis starting 8/1; must reply within 2 week(s) of notification.

CONTACT

Tara Keeter, Director, Financial Aid
Drawer 809, Weldon, NC 27890
(252) 536-7223

Haywood Community College

Clyde, North Carolina
www.haywood.edu   Federal Code: 008083

2-year public community and technical college in rural community.
Enrollment: 1,636 undergrads.
Selectivity: Open admission; but selective for some programs.

BASIC COSTS (2009-2010)

Tuition and fees: $1,600; out-of-state residents $7,339.
Per-credit charge: $50; out-of-state residents $241.

FINANCIAL AID PICTURE (2008-2009)

Students with need: Need-based aid available for full-time and part-time students.
Students without need: No-need awards available for academics.

Additional info: Complete FAFSA by priority filing date for consideration for institutional scholarships.

FINANCIAL AID PROCEDURES

Forms required: FAFSA, institutional form.
Dates and Deadlines: Priority date 4/1; no closing date. Applicants notified on a rolling basis starting 4/15; must reply within 2 week(s) of notification.

CONTACT

Misty Guge, Director of Financial Aid
185 Freelander Drive, Clyde, NC 28721-9454
(828) 627-4506

High Point University

High Point, North Carolina
www.highpoint.edu   Federal Code: 002933

4-year private university and liberal arts college in small city, affiliated with United Methodist Church.
Enrollment: 3,248 undergrads, 3% part-time. 1,045 full-time freshmen.
Selectivity: Admits 50 to 75% of applicants.

BASIC COSTS (2010-2011)

Per-credit charge: $700.
Comprehensive fee: $35,400.

FINANCIAL AID PICTURE (2008-2009)

Students with need: Need-based aid available for full-time and part-time students. Work study available nights, weekends, and for part-time students.
Students without need: No-need awards available for academics, alumni affiliation, art, athletics, leadership, music/drama, religious affiliation, state/district residency.
Scholarships offered: Awarded annually to qualified freshmen: Keller Scholarship: $24,000. University Fellowship: $20,000. Presidential Fellowship: $15,000. Presidential Scholarship: $9,000. Leadership Fellowship: $7,000. Leadership Scholarship: $5,000. All scholarships based on merit. Application and interview required.

FINANCIAL AID PROCEDURES

Forms required: FAFSA, state aid form.
Dates and Deadlines: Priority date 3/1; no closing date. Applicants notified on a rolling basis starting 4/1; must reply within 3 week(s) of notification.
Transfers: No deadline. Applicants notified on a rolling basis starting 5/1; must reply within 3 week(s) of notification.

CONTACT

Julie Setzer, Director of Student Financial Services
833 Montlieu Avenue, High Point, NC 27262-3598
(336) 841-9166

Isothermal Community College

Spindale, North Carolina
www.isothermal.edu   Federal Code: 002934

2-year public community college in small town.
Enrollment: 2,092 undergrads, 35% part-time. 311 full-time freshmen.
Selectivity: Open admission.

BASIC COSTS (2009-2010)

Tuition and fees: $1,538; out-of-state residents $7,277.
Per-credit charge: $50; out-of-state residents $241.

FINANCIAL AID PICTURE (2008-2009)

Students with need: 99% of average financial aid package awarded as scholarships/grants, 1% awarded as loans/jobs. Need-based aid available for part-time students. Work study available nights.

Students without need: No-need awards available for academics, job skills, leadership, minority status, music/drama, state/district residency.

FINANCIAL AID PROCEDURES

Forms required: FAFSA, institutional form.

Dates and Deadlines: Priority date 5/31; no closing date. Applicants notified on a rolling basis starting 4/30; must reply within 4 week(s) of notification.

CONTACT

Jeffery Boyle, Director of Financial Aid
PO Box 804, Spindale, NC 28160-0804
(828) 286-3636 ext. 468

James Sprunt Community College

Kenansville, North Carolina
www.jamessprunt.edu   Federal Code: 007687

2-year public community college in rural community.

Enrollment: 1,147 undergrads, 38% part-time. 198 full-time freshmen.

Selectivity: Open admission; but selective for some programs.

BASIC COSTS (2009-2010)

Tuition and fees: $1,670; out-of-state residents $7,792.

Per-credit charge: $50; out-of-state residents $241.

FINANCIAL AID PICTURE (2009-2010)

Students with need: Out of 198 full-time freshmen who applied for aid, 192 were judged to have need. Of these, 192 received aid. Average financial aid package met 75% of need; average scholarship/grant was $1,551. For part-time students, average financial aid package was $4,415.

Students without need: This college awards aid only to students with need.

Cumulative student debt: 75% of graduating class had student loans; average debt was $3,800.

FINANCIAL AID PROCEDURES

Forms required: FAFSA, state aid form, institutional form.

Dates and Deadlines: Priority date 6/1; no closing date. Applicants notified on a rolling basis starting 7/15; must reply within 2 week(s) of notification.

CONTACT

Connie Taylor, Financial Aid Officer
PO Box 398, Kenansville, NC 28349-0398
(910) 296-2503

John Wesley College

High Point, North Carolina
www.johnwesley.edu   Federal Code: 013819

4-year private Bible college in small city, affiliated with interdenominational tradition.

Enrollment: 93 undergrads, 28% part-time. 7 full-time freshmen.

Selectivity: Admits 50 to 75% of applicants.

BASIC COSTS (2009-2010)

Tuition and fees: $10,730.

Per-credit charge: $375.

Room only: $2,344.

FINANCIAL AID PICTURE (2008-2009)

Students with need: Need-based aid available for full-time and part-time students. Work study available nights, weekends, and for part-time students.

Scholarships offered: Early Acceptance; $100. Academic Honor; 10% of tuition.

Additional info: Early Acceptance Scholarships, Academic Honor Scholarships, Married Student Credit and Minister/Missionary Dependent Scholarship available.

FINANCIAL AID PROCEDURES

Forms required: FAFSA.

Dates and Deadlines: Priority date 3/15; no closing date. Applicants notified on a rolling basis starting 6/1; must reply within 3 week(s) of notification.

Transfers: Closing date 3/15.

CONTACT

Shirley Carter, Director of Financial Aid
2314 North Centennial, High Point, NC 27265-3197
(336) 889-2262 ext. 129

Johnson C. Smith University

Charlotte, North Carolina
www.jcsu.edu   Federal Code: 002936

4-year private university and liberal arts college in very large city.

Enrollment: 1,466 undergrads, 3% part-time. 282 full-time freshmen.

Selectivity: Admits less than 50% of applicants.

BASIC COSTS (2009-2010)

Tuition and fees: $15,754.

Per-credit charge: $361.

Room and board: $6,132.

FINANCIAL AID PICTURE (2009-2010)

Students with need: Out of 269 full-time freshmen who applied for aid, 259 were judged to have need. Of these, 259 received aid, and 10 had their full need met. Average financial aid package met 51% of need; average scholarship/grant was $10,086; average loan was $3,676. Need-based aid available for part-time students.

Students without need: 5 full-time freshmen who did not demonstrate need for aid received scholarships/grants; average award was $7,891. No-need awards available for academics, athletics, ROTC, state/district residency.

Scholarships offered: 8 full-time freshmen received athletic scholarships; average amount $9,810.

Cumulative student debt: 93% of graduating class had student loans; average debt was $19,000.

FINANCIAL AID PROCEDURES

Forms required: FAFSA.

Dates and Deadlines: Priority date 3/1; no closing date. Applicants notified on a rolling basis starting 3/1; must reply within 2 week(s) of notification.

Transfers: No deadline. Applicants notified on a rolling basis starting 4/1; must reply within 2 week(s) of notification.

CONTACT

Keisha Ramey, Interim Director
100 Beatties Ford Road, Charlotte, NC 28216-5398
(704) 378-1035

Johnston Community College

Smithfield, North Carolina
www.johnstoncc.edu   Federal Code: 009336

2-year public community and technical college in large town.

Enrollment: 4,410 undergrads. 710 full-time freshmen.

Selectivity: Open admission; but selective for some programs.

BASIC COSTS (2009-2010)

Tuition and fees: $1,595; out-of-state residents $7,334.

Per-credit charge: $50; out-of-state residents $241.

FINANCIAL AID PICTURE (2008-2009)

Students with need: 78% of average financial aid package awarded as scholarships/grants, 22% awarded as loans/jobs. Need-based aid available for part-time students.

Students without need: This college awards aid only to students with need.

FINANCIAL AID PROCEDURES

Forms required: FAFSA, institutional form.

Dates and Deadlines: Priority date 5/31; no closing date. Applicants notified on a rolling basis starting 6/1; must reply within 2 week(s) of notification.

CONTACT

Betty Woodall, Financial Aid Director
PO Box 2350, Smithfield, NC 27577
(919) 209-2036

Lees-McRae College

Banner Elk, North Carolina
www.lmc.edu   Federal Code: 002923

4-year private liberal arts college in rural community, affiliated with Presbyterian Church (USA).

Enrollment: 906 undergrads, 1% part-time. 163 full-time freshmen.

Selectivity: Admits 50 to 75% of applicants.

BASIC COSTS (2009-2010)

Tuition and fees: $21,625.

Per-credit charge: $600.

Room and board: $7,400.

FINANCIAL AID PICTURE (2008-2009)

Students with need: Out of 136 full-time freshmen who applied for aid, 115 were judged to have need. Of these, 115 received aid, and 6 had their full need met. Average financial aid package met 73% of need; average scholarship/grant was $9,500; average loan was $3,500. Need-based aid available for part-time students.

Students without need: 18 full-time freshmen who did not demonstrate need for aid received scholarships/grants; average award was $5,200. No-need awards available for academics, athletics, music/drama, religious affiliation, state/district residency.

Scholarships offered: 65 full-time freshmen received athletic scholarships; average amount $6,171.

FINANCIAL AID PROCEDURES

Forms required: FAFSA, state aid form.

Dates and Deadlines: Priority date 4/15; no closing date. Applicants notified on a rolling basis starting 3/1; must reply within 2 week(s) of notification.

CONTACT

Cathy Shell, Director of Financial Aid
Box 128, Banner Elk, NC 28604
(828) 898-8740

Lenoir Community College

Kinston, North Carolina
www.lenoircc.edu   Federal Code: 002940

2-year public community college in large town.

Enrollment: 3,514 undergrads.

Selectivity: Open admission; but selective for some programs.

BASIC COSTS (2009-2010)

Tuition and fees: $1,603; out-of-state residents $7,342.

Per-credit charge: $50; out-of-state residents $241.

FINANCIAL AID PICTURE

Students with need: Need-based aid available for full-time and part-time students. Work study available nights.

Students without need: No-need awards available for academics, athletics, leadership, state/district residency.

FINANCIAL AID PROCEDURES

Forms required: institutional form.

Dates and Deadlines: Priority date 7/1; closing date 8/15. Applicants notified on a rolling basis starting 8/1; must reply within 2 week(s) of notification.

CONTACT

Reekita Brunton, Director of Student Financial Aid
Box 188, Kinston, NC 28502-0188
(252) 527-6223

Lenoir-Rhyne University

Hickory, North Carolina
www.lr.edu   Federal Code: 002941

4-year private liberal arts college in large town, affiliated with Evangelical Lutheran Church in America.

Enrollment: 1,387 undergrads.

Selectivity: Admits over 75% of applicants.

BASIC COSTS (2010-2011)

Tuition and fees: $25,290.

Per-credit charge: $1,045.

Room and board: $8,930.

Additional info: Tuition/fee waivers available for minority students.

FINANCIAL AID PICTURE (2008-2009)

Students with need: Need-based aid available for full-time and part-time students. Work study available nights, weekends, and for part-time students.

Students without need: No-need awards available for academics, athletics, job skills, leadership, minority status, music/drama, ROTC, state/district residency.

FINANCIAL AID PROCEDURES

Forms required: FAFSA, state aid form.

Dates and Deadlines: Priority date 3/1; closing date 8/1. Applicants notified on a rolling basis starting 3/1; must reply within 2 week(s) of notification.

CONTACT

Division of Enrollment Management
PO Box 7227, Hickory, NC 28603
(800) 277-05721

Livingstone College

Salisbury, North Carolina
www.livingstone.edu   Federal Code: 002942

4-year private liberal arts college in large town, affiliated with African Methodist Episcopal Zion Church.

Enrollment: 1,082 undergrads.

BASIC COSTS (2009-2010)

Tuition and fees: $13,358.

Room and board: $6,342.

FINANCIAL AID PICTURE (2008-2009)

Students with need: Need-based aid available for full-time and part-time students. Work study available nights, weekends, and for part-time students.

Students without need: No-need awards available for academics, alumni affiliation, athletics, leadership, music/drama, religious affiliation, ROTC, state/district residency.

FINANCIAL AID PROCEDURES

Forms required: FAFSA, state aid form.
Dates and Deadlines: Priority date 3/15; closing date 6/30. Applicants notified by 5/1; must reply within 4 week(s) of notification.

CONTACT

Sherri Jefferson, Director of Financial Aid
701 West Monroe Street, Salisbury, NC 28144-5213
(704) 216-6273

Louisburg College
Louisburg, North Carolina
www.louisburg.edu   Federal Code: 002943

2-year private junior college in small town, affiliated with United Methodist Church.
Enrollment: 725 undergrads, 2% part-time. 361 full-time freshmen.
Selectivity: Admits over 75% of applicants.

BASIC COSTS (2010-2011)

Tuition and fees: $14,336.
Per-credit charge: $1,195.
Room and board: $8,752.
Additional info: Tuition at time of enrollment locked for 2 years.

FINANCIAL AID PICTURE (2008-2009)

Students with need: Need-based aid available for full-time students. Work study available nights, weekends, and for part-time students.
Students without need: No-need awards available for academics, athletics, leadership, religious affiliation, state/district residency.
Scholarships offered: Academic Merit Scholarships: $2,000-$6,000. Leadership Scholarship: $1,000. Robbins Scholarship: $1,000.
Additional info: Job location and development program helps students obtain work in the community.

FINANCIAL AID PROCEDURES

Forms required: FAFSA, institutional form.
Dates and Deadlines: Priority date 3/1; no closing date. Applicants notified on a rolling basis starting 3/15.

CONTACT

Mike Abernathy, Director of Financial Aid
501 North Main Street, Louisburg, NC 27549
(919) 497-3203

Mars Hill College
Mars Hill, North Carolina
www.mhc.edu   Federal Code: 002944

4-year private liberal arts college in small town, affiliated with Baptist faith.
Enrollment: 1,213 undergrads, 6% part-time. 293 full-time freshmen.
Selectivity: Admits 50 to 75% of applicants.

BASIC COSTS (2010-2011)

Tuition and fees: $21,997.
Room and board: $7,632.

FINANCIAL AID PICTURE (2008-2009)

Students with need: Out of 293 full-time freshmen who applied for aid, 265 were judged to have need. Of these, 265 received aid, and 63 had their full need met. Average financial aid package met 79% of need; average scholarship/grant was $14,116; average loan was $2,827. For part-time students, average financial aid package was $5,497.
Students without need: 25 full-time freshmen who did not demonstrate need for aid received scholarships/grants; average award was $7,581. No-

need awards available for academics, alumni affiliation, art, athletics, leadership, music/drama, religious affiliation, state/district residency.
Scholarships offered: *Merit:* Academic scholarships available to students based on merit: SAT/ACT scores and GPA. Scholarships available for four years, requiring minimum GPA. Talent based scholarships available in numerous areas such as: clogging, theatre, band, and art. ***Athletic:*** 23 full-time freshmen received athletic scholarships; average amount $5,280.
Cumulative student debt: 100% of graduating class had student loans; average debt was $16,025.

FINANCIAL AID PROCEDURES

Forms required: FAFSA, state aid form.
Dates and Deadlines: Priority date 3/15; no closing date. Applicants notified on a rolling basis; must reply within 2 week(s) of notification.

CONTACT

Amanda Willis, Director of Financial Aid
Blackwell Hall, Box 370, Mars Hill, NC 28754
(828) 689-1123

Martin Community College
Williamston, North Carolina
www.martincc.edu   Federal Code: 007988

2-year public community and technical college in small town.
Enrollment: 716 undergrads, 42% part-time. 140 full-time freshmen.
Selectivity: Open admission; but selective for some programs.

BASIC COSTS (2009-2010)

Tuition and fees: $1,538; out-of-state residents $7,277.
Per-credit charge: $50; out-of-state residents $241.

FINANCIAL AID PICTURE

Students with need: Need-based aid available for full-time and part-time students. Work study available nights.
Students without need: No-need awards available for academics.

FINANCIAL AID PROCEDURES

Forms required: FAFSA.
Dates and Deadlines: No deadline. Applicants notified on a rolling basis starting 5/1.

CONTACT

Michelle Cobb, Director of Financial Aid
1161 Kehukee Park Road, Williamston, NC 27892-9988
(252) 792-1521 ext. 244

Mayland Community College
Spruce Pine, North Carolina
www.mayland.edu   Federal Code: 011197

2-year public community college in rural community.
Enrollment: 1,641 undergrads.
Selectivity: Open admission; but selective for some programs.

BASIC COSTS (2009-2010)

Tuition and fees: $1,608; out-of-state residents $7,347.
Per-credit charge: $50; out-of-state residents $241.

FINANCIAL AID PICTURE (2009-2010)

Students with need: Need-based aid available for full-time and part-time students.

FINANCIAL AID PROCEDURES

Forms required: FAFSA, institutional form.
Dates and Deadlines: Priority date 3/15; no closing date. Applicants notified on a rolling basis starting 6/15.

CONTACT

Pamela Ellis, Director of Financial Aid
Box 547, Spruce Pine, NC 28777
(828) 765-7351

McDowell Technical Community College

Marion, North Carolina
www.mcdowelltech.edu　　　　　Federal Code: 008085

2-year public community and technical college in small town.
Enrollment: 1,556 undergrads.
Selectivity: Open admission; but selective for some programs.

BASIC COSTS (2009-2010)

Tuition and fees: $1,570; out-of-state residents $7,309.
Per-credit charge: $50; out-of-state residents $241.

FINANCIAL AID PICTURE (2008-2009)

Students with need: Need-based aid available for full-time and part-time students. Work study available nights.
Students without need: This college awards aid only to students with need.

FINANCIAL AID PROCEDURES

Forms required: FAFSA, institutional form.
Dates and Deadlines: Priority date 3/15; no closing date. Applicants notified on a rolling basis starting 7/1.

CONTACT

Kim Shuford, Director of Financial Aid
54 College Drive, Marion, NC 28752
(828) 652-0602

Meredith College

Raleigh, North Carolina
www.meredith.edu　　　　　Federal Code: 002945

4-year private liberal arts college for women in large city.
Enrollment: 1,889 undergrads, 7% part-time. 476 full-time freshmen.
Selectivity: Admits 50 to 75% of applicants. GED not accepted.

BASIC COSTS (2009-2010)

Tuition and fees: $24,490.
Per-credit charge: $640.
Room and board: $7,020.
Additional info: Tuition includes a new laptop computer for each full-time freshman, which will be replaced with a new laptop during her junior year. Upon graduation from Meredith, the laptop remains the property of the student.

FINANCIAL AID PICTURE (2009-2010)

Students with need: Need-based aid available for full-time and part-time students.
Students without need: No-need awards available for academics, art, leadership, minority status, music/drama, religious affiliation, state/district residency.
Scholarships offered: Presidential Scholarships: tuition plus a stipend for study abroad; based on superior academic ability and achievement; 3-5 awarded. Talent Scholarships: varying amounts; available for students planning to major in art, music, interior design and computer science/mathematics/pre-engineering and based on on-campus competition. Teaching Fellows Scholarship: $6,500 per year to match a similar stipend from the State; study abroad opportunity, based on state-wide competition; approximately 25 awarded.

FINANCIAL AID PROCEDURES

Forms required: FAFSA.
Dates and Deadlines: Priority date 2/15; no closing date. Applicants notified on a rolling basis starting 3/15; must reply by 5/1 or within 2 week(s) of notification.

CONTACT

Kevin Michaelsen, Director of Financial Assistance
3800 Hillsborough Street, Raleigh, NC 27607-5298
(919) 760-8565

Methodist University

Fayetteville, North Carolina
www.methodist.edu　　　　　Federal Code: 002946

4-year private liberal arts college in small city, affiliated with United Methodist Church.
Enrollment: 1,965 undergrads.
Selectivity: Admits less than 50% of applicants.

BASIC COSTS (2010-2011)

Tuition and fees: $24,220.
Room and board: $8,899.
Additional info: Professional golf management, professional tennis management, and music students have additional fees.

FINANCIAL AID PICTURE (2008-2009)

Students with need: Need-based aid available for full-time and part-time students. Work study available nights, weekends, and for part-time students.
Students without need: No-need awards available for academics, alumni affiliation, leadership, music/drama, religious affiliation, ROTC, state/district residency.
Scholarships offered: Presidential Scholarship: $5,250-$17,000/yr; 3.1+ GPA, 1000+ SAT or 22+ ACT. Merit scholarship: $3,250-$4,250; residential freshmen; 2.9+ GPA, 900+ SAT or 19+ ACT; leadership. SAT scores exclusive of Writing.

FINANCIAL AID PROCEDURES

Forms required: FAFSA.
Dates and Deadlines: Priority date 5/1; closing date 7/1. Applicants notified on a rolling basis starting 3/1; must reply within 2 week(s) of notification.
Transfers: No deadline. Applicants notified on a rolling basis; must reply within 2 week(s) of notification.

CONTACT

Bonnie Adamson, Director of Financial Aid
5400 Ramsey Street, Fayetteville, NC 28311-1498
(910) 630-7192

Mid-Atlantic Christian University

Elizabeth City, North Carolina
www.macuniversity.edu　　　　　Federal Code: 014101

4-year private university and Bible college in large town, affiliated with Church of Christ.
Enrollment: 159 undergrads, 18% part-time. 38 full-time freshmen.
Selectivity: Admits less than 50% of applicants.

BASIC COSTS (2010-2011)

Tuition and fees: $10,120.
Per-credit charge: $324.
Room and board: $7,094.

FINANCIAL AID PICTURE (2008-2009)

Students with need: Out of 37 full-time freshmen who applied for aid, 37 were judged to have need. Of these, 37 received aid, and 11 had their full need met. Average financial aid package met 80% of need; average scholarship/grant was $3,895; average loan was $6,326. For part-time students, average financial aid package was $4,116.

Students without need: 1 full-time freshmen who did not demonstrate need for aid received scholarships/grants; average award was $750. No-need awards available for academics, alumni affiliation, leadership, music/drama, religious affiliation.

Scholarships offered: Full tuition and half tuition available, based on demonstration of exceptional academic ability.

Cumulative student debt: 81% of graduating class had student loans; average debt was $14,476.

FINANCIAL AID PROCEDURES

Forms required: FAFSA, institutional form.

Dates and Deadlines: Priority date 2/1; no closing date. Applicants notified on a rolling basis starting 5/1; must reply within 2 week(s) of notification.

Transfers: Priority date 3/1; no deadline. Must reply within 2 week(s) of notification.

CONTACT

Lisa Pipkin, Financial Aid Administrator
715 North Poindexter Street, Elizabeth City, NC 27909
(252) 334-2020

Miller-Motte Technical College
Wilmington, North Carolina
www.miller-motte.edu   Federal Code: E00896

4-year for-profit business and technical college in small city.

Enrollment: 842 undergrads.

Selectivity: Open admission; but selective for some programs.

BASIC COSTS (2010-2011)

Tuition and fees: $13,650.

Per-credit charge: $255.

FINANCIAL AID PICTURE (2009-2010)

Students with need: Need-based aid available for full-time and part-time students. Work study available nights, weekends, and for part-time students.

Students without need: This college awards aid only to students with need.

FINANCIAL AID PROCEDURES

Forms required: FAFSA, institutional form.

Dates and Deadlines: No deadline.

CONTACT

Michele Carroll, Financial Services Manager
5000 Market Street, Wilmington, NC 28405
(910) 392-4660

Mitchell Community College
Statesville, North Carolina
www.mitchellcc.edu   Federal Code: 002947

2-year public community college in large town.

Enrollment: 2,792 undergrads.

Selectivity: Open admission; but selective for some programs.

BASIC COSTS (2009-2010)

Tuition and fees: $1,570; out-of-state residents $7,309.

Per-credit charge: $50; out-of-state residents $241.

FINANCIAL AID PICTURE

Students with need: Need-based aid available for full-time and part-time students.

FINANCIAL AID PROCEDURES

Forms required: FAFSA, institutional form.

Dates and Deadlines: No deadline. Applicants notified on a rolling basis starting 3/1; must reply within 2 week(s) of notification.

Transfers: Students are monitored through NSLDS's Transfer Monitoring List.

CONTACT

Candace Cooper, Financial Aid Officer
500 West Broad Street, Statesville, NC 28677
(704) 878-3256

Montgomery Community College
Troy, North Carolina
www.montgomery.edu   Federal Code: 008087

2-year public community college in small town.

Enrollment: 802 undergrads, 57% part-time. 92 full-time freshmen.

Selectivity: Open admission; but selective for some programs.

BASIC COSTS (2009-2010)

Tuition and fees: $1,566; out-of-state residents $7,305.

Per-credit charge: $50; out-of-state residents $241.

FINANCIAL AID PICTURE

Students with need: Need-based aid available for full-time and part-time students. Work study available nights.

Students without need: No-need awards available for academics, minority status, state/district residency.

FINANCIAL AID PROCEDURES

Forms required: FAFSA, institutional form.

Dates and Deadlines: Priority date 7/15; no closing date. Applicants notified on a rolling basis starting 6/1.

CONTACT

Doni Cody, Director of Financial Aid
1011 Page Street, Troy, NC 27371-0787
(910) 576-6222 ext. 519

Montreat College
Montreat, North Carolina
www.montreat.edu   Federal Code: 002948

4-year private liberal arts college in small town, affiliated with Presbyterian Church Reformed and Independent.

Enrollment: 934 undergrads.

Selectivity: Open admission; but selective for some programs.

BASIC COSTS (2009-2010)

Tuition and fees: $20,576.

Room and board: $6,541.

FINANCIAL AID PICTURE (2008-2009)

Students with need: Need-based aid available for full-time and part-time students. Work study available nights, weekends, and for part-time students.

Students without need: No-need awards available for academics, alumni affiliation, athletics, leadership, music/drama, religious affiliation, state/district residency.

FINANCIAL AID PROCEDURES

Forms required: FAFSA, state aid form, institutional form.

Dates and Deadlines: Priority date 3/15; no closing date. Applicants notified on a rolling basis starting 1/15; must reply within 2 week(s) of notification.
Transfers: Priority date 4/1; no deadline. Applicants notified on a rolling basis starting 1/15; must reply within 2 week(s) of notification.

CONTACT
Beth Pocock, Director of Financial Aid
Box 1267, Montreat, NC 28757-1267
(800) 545-4656

Mount Olive College
Mount Olive, North Carolina
www.moc.edu   Federal Code: 002949

4-year private liberal arts college in small town, affiliated with Free Will Baptists.
Enrollment: 3,305 undergrads, 17% part-time. 332 full-time freshmen.
Selectivity: Admits less than 50% of applicants.

BASIC COSTS (2010-2011)
Tuition and fees: $14,446.
Per-credit charge: $350.
Room and board: $5,550.

FINANCIAL AID PICTURE (2008-2009)
Students with need: Out of 331 full-time freshmen who applied for aid, 281 were judged to have need. Of these, 273 received aid, and 42 had their full need met. Average financial aid package met 72% of need; average scholarship/grant was $8,806; average loan was $2,846. For part-time students, average financial aid package was $5,299.
Students without need: 4 full-time freshmen who did not demonstrate need for aid received scholarships/grants; average award was $2,187. No-need awards available for academics, art, athletics, leadership, music/drama, religious affiliation.
Scholarships offered: 24 full-time freshmen received athletic scholarships; average amount $3,432.
Cumulative student debt: 93% of graduating class had student loans; average debt was $16,117.

FINANCIAL AID PROCEDURES
Forms required: FAFSA, state aid form.
Dates and Deadlines: No deadline. Applicants notified on a rolling basis starting 2/14; must reply within 2 week(s) of notification.
Transfers: Special scholarship program available for transfers from North Carolina community colleges.

CONTACT
Karen Statler, Director of Financial Aid
634 Henderson Street, Mount Olive, NC 28365
(919) 658-7164

Nash Community College
Rocky Mount, North Carolina
www.nashcc.edu   Federal Code: 008557

2-year public community college in small city.
Enrollment: 3,112 undergrads. 330 full-time freshmen.
Selectivity: Open admission; but selective for some programs.

BASIC COSTS (2009-2010)
Tuition and fees: $1,620; out-of-state residents $7,359.
Per-credit charge: $50; out-of-state residents $241.

FINANCIAL AID PICTURE
Students with need: Need-based aid available for full-time and part-time students.

Students without need: No-need awards available for academics.

FINANCIAL AID PROCEDURES
Forms required: FAFSA, institutional form.
Dates and Deadlines: Priority date 6/30; no closing date. Applicants notified on a rolling basis starting 7/15.

CONTACT
Tammy Lester, Financial Aid Officer
Box 7488, Rocky Mount, NC 27804-0488
(252) 451-8371

North Carolina Agricultural and Technical State University
Greensboro, North Carolina
www.ncat.edu   Federal Code: 002905

4-year public university in small city.
Enrollment: 8,669 undergrads, 9% part-time. 1,879 full-time freshmen.
Selectivity: Admits 50 to 75% of applicants.

BASIC COSTS (2009-2010)
Tuition and fees: $3,696; out-of-state residents $13,138.
Room and board: $5,659.

FINANCIAL AID PICTURE (2009-2010)
Students with need: Need-based aid available for full-time and part-time students.
Students without need: No-need awards available for academics, athletics, music/drama, ROTC.

FINANCIAL AID PROCEDURES
Forms required: FAFSA.
Dates and Deadlines: Priority date 3/15; no closing date. Applicants notified on a rolling basis starting 4/1; must reply within 2 week(s) of notification.

CONTACT
Sherri Avent, Director of Student Financial Aid
Webb Hall, Greensboro, NC 27411-0001
(800) 443-0835

North Carolina Central University
Durham, North Carolina
www.nccu.edu   Federal Code: 002950

4-year public university in small city.
Enrollment: 5,885 undergrads.
Selectivity: Admits over 75% of applicants.

BASIC COSTS (2009-2010)
Tuition and fees: $3,862; out-of-state residents $13,931.
Room and board: $6,540.

FINANCIAL AID PICTURE
Students with need: Need-based aid available for full-time and part-time students.
Students without need: No-need awards available for academics, alumni affiliation, athletics, minority status, music/drama, state/district residency.
Additional info: Departmental grants based on need plus other available criteria

FINANCIAL AID PROCEDURES
Forms required: FAFSA.
Dates and Deadlines: Priority date 4/1; no closing date. Applicants notified by 5/1; must reply within 2 week(s) of notification.

CONTACT

Sharon Oliver, Director of Student Financial Aid
PO Box 19717, Durham, NC 27707
(919) 530-6180

North Carolina State University
Raleigh, North Carolina
www.ncsu.edu   Federal Code: 002972

4-year public university in large city.
Enrollment: 23,361 undergrads, 7% part-time. 4,718 full-time freshmen.
Selectivity: Admits 50 to 75% of applicants. GED not accepted.

BASIC COSTS (2009-2010)
Tuition and fees: $5,474; out-of-state residents $17,959.
Room and board: $7,966.

FINANCIAL AID PICTURE (2009-2010)
Students with need: Out of 3,529 full-time freshmen who applied for aid, 2,190 were judged to have need. Of these, 2,167 received aid, and 1,232 had their full need met. Average financial aid package met 89% of need; average scholarship/grant was $9,356; average loan was $2,174. For part-time students, average financial aid package was $6,703.
Students without need: 135 full-time freshmen who did not demonstrate need for aid received scholarships/grants; average award was $6,402. No-need awards available for academics, alumni affiliation, athletics, leadership, ROTC, state/district residency.
Scholarships offered: *Merit:* Park Scholarships: 4 year scholarship that covers almost all expenses; approximately 50 awarded each year. Caldwell scholarships: awarded at end of freshmen year for 3 years covering most expenses. *Athletic:* 81 full-time freshmen received athletic scholarships; average amount $8,842.
Cumulative student debt: 48% of graduating class had student loans; average debt was $19,011.
Additional info: Freshman Merit Scholarships; students submitting complete admissions application by the November 1 Early Action deadline automatically considered, additional information may be required after initial review.

FINANCIAL AID PROCEDURES
Forms required: FAFSA, institutional form. CSS PROFILE recommended for early scholarship consideration.
Dates and Deadlines: Priority date 3/1; no closing date. Applicants notified on a rolling basis starting 4/1.

CONTACT
Julia Mallette, Associate Vice Provost and Director of Scholarships and Financial Aid
203 Peele Hall, Box 7103, Raleigh, NC 27695-7103
(919) 515-2421

North Carolina Wesleyan College
Rocky Mount, North Carolina
www.ncwc.edu   Federal Code: 002951

4-year private liberal arts college in small city, affiliated with United Methodist Church.
Enrollment: 1,577 undergrads.

BASIC COSTS (2009-2010)
Tuition and fees: $20,790.
Per-credit charge: $300.
Room and board: $7,380.

FINANCIAL AID PICTURE (2009-2010)
Students with need: Need-based aid available for full-time and part-time students.

Students without need: This college awards aid only to students with need.
Additional info: Scholarships based on GPA. Various scholarship and leadership awards available.

FINANCIAL AID PROCEDURES
Forms required: FAFSA.
Dates and Deadlines: Priority date 3/1; no closing date. Applicants notified on a rolling basis starting 1/1; must reply within 2 week(s) of notification.
Transfers: No deadline. Applicants notified on a rolling basis; must reply within 2 week(s) of notification.

CONTACT
Deana Summerlin, Director of Financial Aid
3400 North Wesleyan Boulevard, Rocky Mount, NC 27804
(252) 985-5295

Peace College
Raleigh, North Carolina
www.peace.edu   Federal Code: 002953

4-year private liberal arts college for women in large city, affiliated with Presbyterian Church (USA).
Enrollment: 692 undergrads, 5% part-time. 151 full-time freshmen.
Selectivity: Admits 50 to 75% of applicants.

BASIC COSTS (2010-2011)
Tuition and fees: $25,282.
Per-credit charge: $640.
Room and board: $8,662.

FINANCIAL AID PICTURE (2009-2010)
Students with need: Out of 140 full-time freshmen who applied for aid, 129 were judged to have need. Of these, 129 received aid, and 9 had their full need met. Average financial aid package met 77% of need; average scholarship/grant was $20,112; average loan was $3,290. For part-time students, average financial aid package was $8,978.
Students without need: 23 full-time freshmen who did not demonstrate need for aid received scholarships/grants; average award was $8,695. No-need awards available for academics, art, leadership, music/drama, state/district residency.
Cumulative student debt: 79% of graduating class had student loans; average debt was $23,428.

FINANCIAL AID PROCEDURES
Forms required: FAFSA.
Dates and Deadlines: Priority date 3/15; no closing date. Applicants notified on a rolling basis starting 3/1; must reply within 4 week(s) of notification.
Transfers: Priority date 3/1; no deadline. Applicants notified on a rolling basis starting 2/28; must reply within 4 week(s) of notification. Transfer merit scholarships available.

CONTACT
Angela Kirkley, Director of Financial Aid
15 East Peace Street, Raleigh, NC 27604-1194
(919) 508-2249

Pfeiffer University
Misenheimer, North Carolina
www.pfeiffer.edu   Federal Code: 002955

4-year private university and liberal arts college in rural community, affiliated with United Methodist Church.
Enrollment: 1,066 undergrads, 12% part-time. 196 full-time freshmen.

BASIC COSTS (2009-2010)

Tuition and fees: $19,215.
Per-credit charge: $435.
Room and board: $7,928.

FINANCIAL AID PICTURE (2008-2009)

Students with need: Out of 181 full-time freshmen who applied for aid, 152 were judged to have need. Of these, 152 received aid, and 28 had their full need met. Average financial aid package met 81% of need; average scholarship/grant was $14,860; average loan was $2,868. For part-time students, average financial aid package was $8,769.
Students without need: 40 full-time freshmen who did not demonstrate need for aid received scholarships/grants; average award was $6,374. No-need awards available for academics, alumni affiliation, athletics, leadership, music/drama, religious affiliation, state/district residency.
Scholarships offered: *Merit:* Honor, Presidential, University, and Legacy Scholarships - from $3,500 to full tuition per year. *Athletic:* 19 full-time freshmen received athletic scholarships; average amount $7,407.
Cumulative student debt: 87% of graduating class had student loans; average debt was $20,500.

FINANCIAL AID PROCEDURES

Forms required: FAFSA, state aid form.
Dates and Deadlines: Priority date 5/1; no closing date. Applicants notified on a rolling basis starting 3/1; must reply within 2 week(s) of notification.
Transfers: Priority date 3/15.

CONTACT

Amy Brown, Director of Financial Aid
Box 960, Misenheimer, NC 28109
(704) 463-1360 ext. 2074

Piedmont Baptist College

Winston-Salem, North Carolina
www.pbc.edu   Federal Code: 002956

4-year private Bible and seminary college in small city, affiliated with Baptist faith.
Enrollment: 262 undergrads.

BASIC COSTS (2010-2011)

Tuition and fees: $11,170.
Per-credit charge: $346.
Room and board: $5,760.

FINANCIAL AID PICTURE

Students with need: Need-based aid available for full-time and part-time students. Work study available nights, weekends, and for part-time students.

FINANCIAL AID PROCEDURES

Forms required: institutional form.
Dates and Deadlines: No deadline. Applicants notified on a rolling basis starting 3/1.

CONTACT

Ronnie Mathis, Financial Aid Officer
420 South Boad Street, Winston-Salem, NC 27101-5133
(336) 714-7987

Pitt Community College

Greenville, North Carolina
www.pittcc.edu   Federal Code: 004062

2-year public community and technical college in small city.
Enrollment: 6,395 undergrads.
Selectivity: Open admission; but selective for some programs.

BASIC COSTS (2009-2010)

Tuition and fees: $1,586; out-of-state residents $7,325.
Per-credit charge: $50; out-of-state residents $241.

FINANCIAL AID PICTURE (2008-2009)

Students with need: Need-based aid available for full-time and part-time students. Work study available nights.
Students without need: No-need awards available for academics, athletics, ROTC.

FINANCIAL AID PROCEDURES

Forms required: FAFSA.
Dates and Deadlines: Priority date 3/15; no closing date. Applicants notified on a rolling basis starting 2/1.

CONTACT

Lisa Reichstein, Financial Aid Director
PO Drawer 7007, Greenville, NC 27835-7007
(252) 493-7264

Queens University of Charlotte

Charlotte, North Carolina
www.queens.edu   Federal Code: 002957

4-year private university in very large city, affiliated with Presbyterian Church (USA).
Enrollment: 1,880 undergrads, 30% part-time. 314 full-time freshmen.
Selectivity: Admits over 75% of applicants.

BASIC COSTS (2010-2011)

Tuition and fees: $23,752.
Per-credit charge: $395.
Room and board: $8,608.

FINANCIAL AID PICTURE (2009-2010)

Students with need: Out of 263 full-time freshmen who applied for aid, 225 were judged to have need. Of these, 225 received aid, and 54 had their full need met. Average financial aid package met 76% of need; average scholarship/grant was $15,556; average loan was $3,287. For part-time students, average financial aid package was $3,355.
Students without need: 62 full-time freshmen who did not demonstrate need for aid received scholarships/grants; average award was $9,336. No-need awards available for academics, art, athletics, leadership, minority status, music/drama, religious affiliation.
Scholarships offered: *Merit:* Presidential Scholarships: full tuition; based on special application/recommendations; deadline 12/15; up to 12 awarded. University Scholars (Trustee, Deans' & Alumni): range from $8,000 - $12,000 in Fall 2010 (based on admitted student's academic profile). *Athletic:* 37 full-time freshmen received athletic scholarships; average amount $5,789.
Cumulative student debt: 79% of graduating class had student loans; average debt was $20,108.

FINANCIAL AID PROCEDURES

Forms required: FAFSA, state aid form.
Dates and Deadlines: Priority date 3/1; no closing date. Applicants notified on a rolling basis starting 3/15; must reply by 5/1 or within 3 week(s) of notification.
Transfers: No deadline. Applicants notified on a rolling basis starting 3/15; must reply by 5/1 or within 3 week(s) of notification.

CONTACT

Anita Elliott, Assistant Vice President of Student Financial Services
1900 Selwyn Ave, Charlotte, NC 28274
(704) 337-2225

Randolph Community College

Asheboro, North Carolina
www.randolph.edu   Federal Code: 005447

2-year public community and technical college in large town.
Enrollment: 2,138 undergrads, 43% part-time. 322 full-time freshmen.
Selectivity: Open admission; but selective for some programs.

BASIC COSTS (2009-2010)
Tuition and fees: $1,583; out-of-state residents $7,322.
Per-credit charge: $50; out-of-state residents $241.

FINANCIAL AID PICTURE (2008-2009)
Students with need: Need-based aid available for full-time and part-time students. Work study available nights.
Students without need: No-need awards available for academics, leadership, minority status, state/district residency.

FINANCIAL AID PROCEDURES
Forms required: FAFSA.
Dates and Deadlines: No deadline. Applicants notified on a rolling basis starting 3/1.
Transfers: No deadline. Applicants notified on a rolling basis starting 3/1.

CONTACT
Chad Williams, Director of Financial Aid
PO Box 1009, Asheboro, NC 27204
(336) 633-0222

Richmond Community College

Hamlet, North Carolina
www.richmondcc.edu   Federal Code: 005464

2-year public community college in small town.
Enrollment: 1,978 undergrads.
Selectivity: Open admission; but selective for some programs.

BASIC COSTS (2009-2010)
Tuition and fees: $1,558; out-of-state residents $7,297.
Per-credit charge: $50; out-of-state residents $241.

FINANCIAL AID PICTURE
Students with need: Need-based aid available for full-time and part-time students. Work study available nights.
Students without need: No-need awards available for academics, leadership.

FINANCIAL AID PROCEDURES
Forms required: FAFSA, institutional form.
Dates and Deadlines: Closing date 7/25. Applicants notified on a rolling basis starting 7/8; must reply within 2 week(s) of notification.

CONTACT
Beth McQueen, Director of Financial Aid
Box 1189, Hamlet, NC 28345
(910) 410-1726

Roanoke-Chowan Community College

Ahoskie, North Carolina
www.roanokechowan.edu   Federal Code: 008613

2-year public community college in small town.
Enrollment: 749 undergrads.
Selectivity: Open admission; but selective for some programs.

BASIC COSTS (2009-2010)
Tuition and fees: $1,601; out-of-state residents $7,340.
Per-credit charge: $50; out-of-state residents $241.

FINANCIAL AID PICTURE (2008-2009)
Students with need: Need-based aid available for full-time and part-time students.
Students without need: No-need awards available for academics.

FINANCIAL AID PROCEDURES
Forms required: FAFSA.
Dates and Deadlines: Priority date 3/15; no closing date. Applicants notified on a rolling basis starting 7/1.

CONTACT
Tricia Sawyer, Financial Aid Director
109 Community College Road, Ahoskie, NC 27910-9522
(252) 862-1320

Robeson Community College

Lumberton, North Carolina
www.robeson.edu   Federal Code: 008612

2-year public community college in large town.
Enrollment: 2,358 undergrads.
Selectivity: Open admission; but selective for some programs.

BASIC COSTS (2009-2010)
Tuition and fees: $1,568; out-of-state residents $7,307.
Per-credit charge: $50; out-of-state residents $241.

FINANCIAL AID PICTURE (2008-2009)
Students with need: Need-based aid available for full-time and part-time students.

FINANCIAL AID PROCEDURES
Forms required: FAFSA.
Dates and Deadlines: Priority date 5/15; no closing date. Applicants notified on a rolling basis starting 7/31.

CONTACT
Ronnie Locklear, Director of Financial Aid
PO Box 1420, Lumberton, NC 28359
(910) 272-3352

Rockingham Community College

Wentworth, North Carolina
www.rockinghamcc.edu   Federal Code: 002958

2-year public community college in rural community.
Enrollment: 2,259 undergrads, 50% part-time. 340 full-time freshmen.
Selectivity: Open admission; but selective for some programs.

BASIC COSTS (2009-2010)
Tuition and fees: $1,596; out-of-state residents $7,335.
Per-credit charge: $50; out-of-state residents $241.

FINANCIAL AID PICTURE (2008-2009)
Students with need: Need-based aid available for full-time and part-time students.
Students without need: No-need awards available for academics, art, job skills, leadership, minority status, state/district residency.

FINANCIAL AID PROCEDURES
Forms required: FAFSA, institutional form.
Dates and Deadlines: Priority date 3/15; no closing date. Applicants notified on a rolling basis starting 5/30; must reply within 2 week(s) of notification.

CONTACT
Coe Trent, Director of Financial Aid
Box 38, Wentworth, NC 27375-0038
(336) 342-4261 ext. 2204

Rowan-Cabarrus Community College
Salisbury, North Carolina
www.rowancabarrus.edu   Federal Code: 005754

2-year public community and technical college in large town.
Enrollment: 6,993 undergrads.
Selectivity: Open admission; but selective for some programs.

BASIC COSTS (2009-2010)
Tuition and fees: $1,602; out-of-state residents $7,341.
Per-credit charge: $50; out-of-state residents $241.

FINANCIAL AID PICTURE (2009-2010)
Students with need: Need-based aid available for full-time and part-time students. Work study available nights.
Students without need: No-need awards available for academics, job skills, state/district residency.

FINANCIAL AID PROCEDURES
Forms required: FAFSA.
Dates and Deadlines: Priority date 3/15; no closing date. Applicants notified on a rolling basis starting 5/1; must reply within 3 week(s) of notification.
Transfers: No deadline.

CONTACT
Lisa Ledbetter, Director, Financial Aid
Box 1595, Salisbury, NC 28145
(704) 637-0760 ext. 273

St. Andrews Presbyterian College
Laurinburg, North Carolina
www.sapc.edu   Federal Code: 002967

4-year private liberal arts college in large town, affiliated with Presbyterian Church (USA).
Enrollment: 579 undergrads, 4% part-time. 147 full-time freshmen.
Selectivity: Admits over 75% of applicants.

BASIC COSTS (2010-2011)
Tuition and fees: $21,614.
Per-credit charge: $450.
Room and board: $8,938.

FINANCIAL AID PICTURE (2008-2009)
Students with need: Out of 120 full-time freshmen who applied for aid, 106 were judged to have need. Of these, 106 received aid, and 29 had their full need met. Average financial aid package met 74% of need; average scholarship/grant was $11,798; average loan was $3,621. For part-time students, average financial aid package was $7,167.
Students without need: 24 full-time freshmen who did not demonstrate need for aid received scholarships/grants; average award was $3,950. No-need awards available for academics, alumni affiliation, art, athletics, leadership, music/drama.
Scholarships offered: 22 full-time freshmen received athletic scholarships; average amount $3,479.
Cumulative student debt: 57% of graduating class had student loans; average debt was $15,076.

FINANCIAL AID PROCEDURES
Forms required: FAFSA, state aid form.

Dates and Deadlines: Priority date 5/1; no closing date. Applicants notified on a rolling basis starting 10/1; must reply within 2 week(s) of notification.
Transfers: No deadline. Applicants notified on a rolling basis starting 10/1; must reply within 2 week(s) of notification.

CONTACT
Kimberly Driggers, Director of Student Financial Planning
1700 Dogwood Mile, Laurinburg, NC 28352
(910) 277-5560

St. Augustine's College
Raleigh, North Carolina
www.st-aug.edu   Federal Code: 002968

4-year private liberal arts college in large city, affiliated with Episcopal Church.
Enrollment: 1,527 undergrads.

BASIC COSTS (2010-2011)
Tuition and fees: $17,160.
Per-credit charge: $515.
Room and board: $7,126.

FINANCIAL AID PICTURE (2009-2010)
Students with need: Need-based aid available for full-time and part-time students.
Students without need: No-need awards available for academics, art, athletics, leadership, minority status, music/drama, religious affiliation, ROTC, state/district residency.
Scholarships offered: Institutional Merit Scholarships based on high school record, evidence of leadership, and SAT score.

FINANCIAL AID PROCEDURES
Forms required: FAFSA, institutional form.
Dates and Deadlines: Closing date 3/15. Applicants notified on a rolling basis starting 5/1; must reply within 2 week(s) of notification.
Transfers: All transfer students must submit a financial aid transcript.

CONTACT
Nadine Ford, Director of Financial Aid
1315 Oakwood Avenue, Raleigh, NC 27610-2298
(919) 516-4131

Salem College
Winston-Salem, North Carolina
www.salem.edu   Federal Code: 002960

4-year private liberal arts college for women in small city, affiliated with Moravian Church in America.
Enrollment: 729 undergrads, 16% part-time. 142 full-time freshmen.
Selectivity: Admits 50 to 75% of applicants.

BASIC COSTS (2010-2011)
Tuition and fees: $21,948.
Room and board: $11,520.
Additional info: Traditional-age students must enroll full-time. Students registering through the Fleer Center for Adult Education pay $1,074 tuition per course. Graduate students pay $302 per credit hour. Tuition/fee waivers available for adults.

FINANCIAL AID PICTURE (2008-2009)
Students with need: 71% of average financial aid package awarded as scholarships/grants, 29% awarded as loans/jobs. Need-based aid available for part-time students. Work study available nights, weekends, and for part-time students.
Students without need: No-need awards available for academics, alumni affiliation, leadership, minority status, music/drama, state/district residency.

FINANCIAL AID PROCEDURES

Forms required: FAFSA.

Dates and Deadlines: Priority date 3/1; no closing date. Applicants notified on a rolling basis starting 3/1; must reply by 5/1 or within 2 week(s) of notification.

CONTACT

Lori Lewis, Director of Financial Aid
601 South Church Street, Winston-Salem, NC 27108
(336) 721-2808

Sampson Community College
Clinton, North Carolina
www.sampsoncc.edu   Federal Code: 007892

2-year public community college in small town.

Enrollment: 1,471 undergrads.

Selectivity: Open admission; but selective for some programs.

BASIC COSTS (2009-2010)

Tuition and fees: $1,577; out-of-state residents $7,316.

Per-credit charge: $50; out-of-state residents $241.

FINANCIAL AID PICTURE

Students with need: Need-based aid available for full-time and part-time students.

Students without need: No-need awards available for academics, state/district residency.

FINANCIAL AID PROCEDURES

Forms required: FAFSA.

Dates and Deadlines: Priority date 7/1; no closing date. Applicants notified on a rolling basis starting 7/15; must reply within 2 week(s) of notification.

CONTACT

Judye Tart, Director of Financial Aid
PO Box 318, Clinton, NC 28329
(910) 592-8084 ext. 2024

Sandhills Community College
Pinehurst, North Carolina
www.sandhills.edu   Federal Code: 002961

2-year public community college in large town.

Enrollment: 4,249 undergrads.

Selectivity: Open admission; but selective for some programs.

BASIC COSTS (2009-2010)

Tuition and fees: $1,597; out-of-state residents $7,336.

Per-credit charge: $50; out-of-state residents $241.

FINANCIAL AID PICTURE (2008-2009)

Students with need: Need-based aid available for full-time and part-time students.

Students without need: No-need awards available for academics.

Scholarships offered: Sandhills Scholars; upper 15% of graduating class; 11 awarded.

Additional info: Scholarships available, limited loan capability.

FINANCIAL AID PROCEDURES

Forms required: FAFSA.

Dates and Deadlines: Priority date 6/1; no closing date. Applicants notified on a rolling basis starting 3/1; must reply by 8/1 or within 4 week(s) of notification.

CONTACT

Heather Willett, Director of Financial Aid
3395 Airport Road, Pinehurst, NC 28374
(910) 695-3743

Shaw University
Raleigh, North Carolina
www.shawuniversity.edu   Federal Code: 002962

4-year private university and liberal arts college in large city, affiliated with Baptist faith.

Enrollment: 2,331 undergrads, 8% part-time. 581 full-time freshmen.

Selectivity: Admits less than 50% of applicants.

BASIC COSTS (2009-2010)

Tuition and fees: $11,696.

Per-credit charge: $389.

Room and board: $7,200.

FINANCIAL AID PICTURE (2008-2009)

Students with need: Need-based aid available for full-time and part-time students. Work study available nights, weekends, and for part-time students.

Students without need: No-need awards available for academics, alumni affiliation, art, athletics, music/drama, religious affiliation.

Scholarships offered: Presidential Scholarship, based on GPA and SAT.

FINANCIAL AID PROCEDURES

Forms required: FAFSA.

Dates and Deadlines: Priority date 3/1; no closing date. Applicants notified on a rolling basis starting 3/15; must reply within 2 week(s) of notification.

CONTACT

Rochelle King, Director of Financial Aid
118 East South Street, Raleigh, NC 27601
(919) 546-8240

South College
Asheville, North Carolina
www.southcollegenc.edu   Federal Code: 010264

2-year for-profit health science and technical college in small city.

Enrollment: 264 undergrads.

Selectivity: Open admission; but selective for some programs.

BASIC COSTS (2009-2010)

Tuition and fees: $14,100.

Per-credit charge: $430.

FINANCIAL AID PICTURE (2008-2009)

Students with need: Need-based aid available for full-time and part-time students.

FINANCIAL AID PROCEDURES

Forms required: FAFSA.

Dates and Deadlines: No deadline. Applicants notified on a rolling basis.

CONTACT

Julia Dennis, Financial Aid Director
29 Turtle Creek Drive, Asheville, NC 28803
(828) 277-5521

South Piedmont Community College

Polkton, North Carolina
www.spcc.edu   Federal Code: 007985

2-year public community college in small city.
Enrollment: 2,521 undergrads.
Selectivity: Open admission; but selective for some programs.

BASIC COSTS (2009-2010)
Tuition and fees: $1,610; out-of-state residents $7,349.
Per-credit charge: $50; out-of-state residents $241.

FINANCIAL AID PICTURE (2009-2010)
Students with need: 98% of average financial aid package awarded as scholarships/grants, 2% awarded as loans/jobs. Need-based aid available for part-time students. Work study available nights.
Additional info: Small amount of non-federal scholarship aid available. FAFSA applications received before June 1 will receive first priority.

FINANCIAL AID PROCEDURES
Forms required: FAFSA.
Dates and Deadlines: No deadline. Applicants notified on a rolling basis.

CONTACT
John Ratliff, Director of Financial Aid
PO Box 126, Polkton, NC 28135
(704) 272-5325

Southeastern Community College

Whiteville, North Carolina
www.sccnc.edu   Federal Code: 002964

2-year public community college in small town.
Enrollment: 1,695 undergrads.
Selectivity: Open admission; but selective for some programs.

BASIC COSTS (2009-2010)
Tuition and fees: $1,599; out-of-state residents $7,338.
Per-credit charge: $50; out-of-state residents $241.

FINANCIAL AID PICTURE (2008-2009)
Students with need: Need-based aid available for full-time and part-time students.
Students without need: No-need awards available for academics, athletics, leadership, music/drama, state/district residency.

FINANCIAL AID PROCEDURES
Forms required: FAFSA.
Dates and Deadlines: Priority date 4/1; no closing date. Applicants notified on a rolling basis starting 6/1; must reply within 2 week(s) of notification.

CONTACT
Glenn Hanson, Director of Financial Aid
4564 Chadbourn Highway, Whiteville, NC 28472-0151
(910) 642-7141 ext. 214

Southwestern Community College

Sylva, North Carolina
www.southwesterncc.edu   Federal Code: 008466

2-year public community college in rural community.
Enrollment: 950 full-time undergrads.
Selectivity: Open admission; but selective for some programs.

BASIC COSTS (2009-2010)
Tuition and fees: $1,561; out-of-state residents $7,300.
Per-credit charge: $50; out-of-state residents $241.

FINANCIAL AID PICTURE
Students with need: Need-based aid available for full-time and part-time students.

FINANCIAL AID PROCEDURES
Forms required: FAFSA.
Dates and Deadlines: Priority date 4/30; no closing date. Applicants notified on a rolling basis starting 5/1; must reply within 2 week(s) of notification.

CONTACT
Melody Lawrence, Director of Financial Aid
447 College Drive, Sylva, NC 28779
(828) 586-4091 ext. 224

Stanly Community College

Albemarle, North Carolina
www.stanly.edu   Federal Code: 011194

2-year public community college in large town.
Enrollment: 3,183 undergrads.
Selectivity: Open admission; but selective for some programs.

BASIC COSTS (2009-2010)
Tuition and fees: $1,621; out-of-state residents $7,360.
Per-credit charge: $50; out-of-state residents $241.

FINANCIAL AID PICTURE (2008-2009)
Students with need: Need-based aid available for full-time and part-time students.
Students without need: This college awards aid only to students with need.

FINANCIAL AID PROCEDURES
Forms required: FAFSA, institutional form.
Dates and Deadlines: No deadline. Applicants notified on a rolling basis starting 6/1; must reply within 2 week(s) of notification.
Transfers: No deadline. Applicants notified on a rolling basis.

CONTACT
Petra Fields, Director of Financial Aid
141 College Drive, Albemarle, NC 28001
(704) 991-0231

Surry Community College

Dobson, North Carolina
www.surry.edu   Federal Code: 002970

2-year public community college in rural community.
Enrollment: 1,580 full-time undergrads.
Selectivity: Open admission; but selective for some programs.

BASIC COSTS (2009-2010)
Tuition and fees: $1,603; out-of-state residents $7,342.
Per-credit charge: $50; out-of-state residents $241.

FINANCIAL AID PICTURE (2008-2009)
Students with need: Need-based aid available for full-time and part-time students. Work study available nights.
Students without need: No-need awards available for academics.

FINANCIAL AID PROCEDURES
Forms required: FAFSA, institutional form.
Dates and Deadlines: Priority date 5/1; no closing date. Applicants notified on a rolling basis starting 6/1; must reply within 2 week(s) of notification.

Transfers: Priority date 6/1.

CONTACT

Andrea Simpson, Financial Aid Director
630 South Main Street, Dobson, NC 27017
(336) 386-3263

Tri-County Community College
Murphy, North Carolina
www.tricountycc.edu   Federal Code: 009430

2-year public community college in rural community.
Enrollment: 900 undergrads.
Selectivity: Open admission.

BASIC COSTS (2009-2010)
Tuition and fees: $1,559; out-of-state residents $7,298.
Per-credit charge: $50; out-of-state residents $241.

FINANCIAL AID PICTURE (2008-2009)
Students with need: Need-based aid available for full-time and part-time students.
Students without need: This college awards aid only to students with need.

FINANCIAL AID PROCEDURES
Forms required: FAFSA.
Dates and Deadlines: Priority date 6/30; no closing date. Applicants notified on a rolling basis starting 6/1; must reply within 4 week(s) of notification.

CONTACT

Diane Owl, Financial Aid Officer
21 Campus Circle, Murphy, NC 28906
(828) 837-6810

University of North Carolina at Asheville
Asheville, North Carolina
www.unca.edu   Federal Code: 002907

4-year public university and liberal arts college in small city.
Enrollment: 3,320 undergrads, 9% part-time. 586 full-time freshmen.
Selectivity: Admits over 75% of applicants. GED not accepted.

BASIC COSTS (2009-2010)
Tuition and fees: $4,411; out-of-state residents $16,128.
Room and board: $6,890.

FINANCIAL AID PICTURE (2008-2009)
Students with need: Out of 457 full-time freshmen who applied for aid, 264 were judged to have need. Of these, 262 received aid, and 182 had their full need met. Average financial aid package met 91% of need; average scholarship/grant was $6,339; average loan was $4,957. For part-time students, average financial aid package was $7,792.
Students without need: 40 full-time freshmen who did not demonstrate need for aid received scholarships/grants; average award was $2,405. No-need awards available for academics, alumni affiliation, art, athletics, job skills, leadership, minority status, music/drama, state/district residency.
Scholarships offered: *Merit:* North Carolina Teaching Fellows program: for outstanding North Carolina students with desire and talent to become teachers. University Laurels Program: $500 to full in-state tuition and fees; essay, list of co-curricular activities and participation in Laurels Interview Day. Leadership Scholarship: $1,000, renewable; solid academic record and leadership ability. *Athletic:* 18 full-time freshmen received athletic scholarships; average amount $7,535.
Cumulative student debt: 50% of graduating class had student loans; average debt was $14,596.

FINANCIAL AID PROCEDURES
Forms required: FAFSA.
Dates and Deadlines: Priority date 3/1; no closing date. Applicants notified on a rolling basis starting 3/15.

CONTACT

Patrice Mitchell, Dean of Admissions and Financial Aid
CPO#1320, UNCA, Asheville, NC 28804-8502
(828) 251-6535

University of North Carolina at Chapel Hill
Chapel Hill, North Carolina   Federal Code: 002974
www.unc.edu   CSS Code: 5816

4-year public university in large town.
Enrollment: 17,565 undergrads, 2% part-time. 3,852 full-time freshmen.
Selectivity: Admits less than 50% of applicants. GED not accepted.

BASIC COSTS (2009-2010)
Tuition and fees: $5,625; out-of-state residents $23,513.
Room and board: $8,671.
Additional info: Fees may be higher for dental programs.

FINANCIAL AID PICTURE (2008-2009)
Students with need: Out of 2,878 full-time freshmen who applied for aid, 1,218 were judged to have need. Of these, 1,208 received aid, and 1,184 had their full need met. Average financial aid package met 100% of need; average scholarship/grant was $10,996; average loan was $3,065. For part-time students, average financial aid package was $8,727.
Students without need: 820 full-time freshmen who did not demonstrate need for aid received scholarships/grants; average award was $4,646. No-need awards available for academics, alumni affiliation, art, athletics, leadership, music/drama, religious affiliation, state/district residency.
Scholarships offered: *Merit:* Morehead Scholarships: full tuition and expenses; based on academic merit, leadership, athletics, moral character; approximately 50 awarded, in-state and out-of-state. Robertson Scholarships: full tuition and expenses; based on academic merit, leadership, community service; 15 to 18 awarded to both in-state and out-of-state residents. Carolina Scholars: $7,500 for in-state residents; cost of tuition, fees, room and board for non-NC residents; based on academic merit, leadership, residency specifications; 30-40 awarded with majority going to in-state residents. Pogue Scholarships: $7,500 for NC residents; cost of tuition, fees, room and board * for non-NC residents; based on academic merit, leadership, involvement and interest in issues of diversity; 22 in-state, 5 out-of-state scholarships awarded. College Fellows Awards: $2,500; based on academic merit, leadership; North Carolina residency; 15-200 awarded. Other academic scholarships: $2,500, full cost; based on academic merit, leadership, North Carolina residency; approximately 75 awarded. As a result of legislation passed in 2005, non-residents receiving "full" academic scholarships are eligible for North Carolina residency status for tuition purposes. *Athletic:* 81 full-time freshmen received athletic scholarships; average amount $10,706.
Additional info: Carolina meets 100% of all need documented for both resident and non-resident undergraduates who quality for need based aid, with a favorable mix of approximately 2/3 grants and scholarships and 1/3 loans and work study.

FINANCIAL AID PROCEDURES
Forms required: FAFSA, CSS PROFILE.
Dates and Deadlines: Priority date 3/1; no closing date. Applicants notified on a rolling basis starting 3/15; must reply by 5/1.

CONTACT

Shirley Ort, Director for Office of Student Aid/Associate Provost
Jackson Hall, Chapel Hill, NC 27599-2200
(919) 962-8396

University of North Carolina at Charlotte

Charlotte, North Carolina
www.uncc.edu   Federal Code: 002975

4-year public university in very large city.
Enrollment: 19,263 undergrads, 14% part-time. 3,056 full-time freshmen.
Selectivity: Admits over 75% of applicants.

BASIC COSTS (2009-2010)

Tuition and fees: $4,427; out-of-state residents $15,039.
Room and board: $6,796.

FINANCIAL AID PICTURE (2008-2009)

Students with need: Out of 2,283 full-time freshmen who applied for aid, 1,504 were judged to have need. Of these, 1,463 received aid, and 159 had their full need met. Average financial aid package met 78% of need; average scholarship/grant was $6,911; average loan was $2,969. For part-time students, average financial aid package was $5,735.
Students without need: 46 full-time freshmen who did not demonstrate need for aid received scholarships/grants; average award was $3,046. No-need awards available for academics, athletics, leadership, music/drama.
Scholarships offered: 55 full-time freshmen received athletic scholarships; average amount $13,315.

FINANCIAL AID PROCEDURES

Forms required: FAFSA.
Dates and Deadlines: Priority date 4/1; no closing date. Applicants notified on a rolling basis starting 4/1; must reply within 3 week(s) of notification.

CONTACT

Anthony Carter, Director of Student Financial Aid
Undergraduate Admissions- Cato Hall, Charlotte, NC 28223-0001
(704) 687-2461

University of North Carolina at Greensboro

Greensboro, North Carolina
www.uncg.edu   Federal Code: 002976

4-year public university in small city.
Enrollment: 14,275 undergrads, 11% part-time. 2,497 full-time freshmen.
Selectivity: Admits 50 to 75% of applicants. GED not accepted.

BASIC COSTS (2009-2010)

Tuition and fees: $4,234; out-of-state residents $15,995.
Room and board: $6,507.

FINANCIAL AID PICTURE (2009-2010)

Students with need: Out of 2,144 full-time freshmen who applied for aid, 1,936 were judged to have need. Of these, 1,935 received aid, and 617 had their full need met. Average financial aid package met 62% of need; average scholarship/grant was $7,805; average loan was $2,625. For part-time students, average financial aid package was $5,849.
Students without need: 97 full-time freshmen who did not demonstrate need for aid received scholarships/grants; average award was $1,941. No-need awards available for academics, alumni affiliation, art, athletics, leadership, music/drama, state/district residency.
Scholarships offered: 26 full-time freshmen received athletic scholarships; average amount $10,032.
Cumulative student debt: 67% of graduating class had student loans; average debt was $18,604.

FINANCIAL AID PROCEDURES

Forms required: FAFSA.
Dates and Deadlines: Priority date 3/1; no closing date. Applicants notified on a rolling basis starting 3/15; must reply within 3 week(s) of notification.

CONTACT

Deborah Tollefson, Director of Financial Aid
1400 Spring Garden Street, Greensboro, NC 27402-6170
(336) 334-5702

University of North Carolina at Pembroke

Pembroke, North Carolina
www.uncp.edu   Federal Code: 002954

4-year public university and liberal arts college in small town.
Enrollment: 5,631 undergrads, 17% part-time. 1,202 full-time freshmen.
Selectivity: Admits over 75% of applicants.

BASIC COSTS (2009-2010)

Tuition and fees: $3,737; out-of-state residents $12,944.
Room and board: $6,490.

FINANCIAL AID PICTURE (2009-2010)

Students with need: Need-based aid available for full-time and part-time students.
Students without need: No-need awards available for academics, alumni affiliation, art, athletics, music/drama, state/district residency.
Scholarships offered: Academic Scholarships, Endowed Scholarship, University Incentive Scholarship, University Scholarships for Native Americans, Epsilon Sigma Alpha Scholarship.

FINANCIAL AID PROCEDURES

Forms required: FAFSA.
Dates and Deadlines: Priority date 3/15; no closing date. Applicants notified on a rolling basis starting 4/15; must reply within 2 week(s) of notification.

CONTACT

Alvin Blackmon, Director of Financial Aid
Box 1510, Pembroke, NC 28372
(910) 521-6255

University of North Carolina at Wilmington

Wilmington, North Carolina
www.uncw.edu   Federal Code: 002984

4-year public university in small city.
Enrollment: 10,761 undergrads, 7% part-time. 1,946 full-time freshmen.
Selectivity: Admits 50 to 75% of applicants.

BASIC COSTS (2009-2010)

Tuition and fees: $4,874; out-of-state residents $15,756.
Room and board: $7,620.

FINANCIAL AID PICTURE (2009-2010)

Students with need: Out of 1,476 full-time freshmen who applied for aid, 838 were judged to have need. Of these, 831 received aid, and 381 had their full need met. Average financial aid package met 85% of need; average scholarship/grant was $6,208; average loan was $2,688. For part-time students, average financial aid package was $6,507.
Students without need: 31 full-time freshmen who did not demonstrate need for aid received scholarships/grants; average award was $3,168. No-need awards available for academics, alumni affiliation, art, athletics, leadership, music/drama, state/district residency.
Scholarships offered: 40 full-time freshmen received athletic scholarships; average amount $10,761.
Cumulative student debt: 54% of graduating class had student loans; average debt was $16,115.

FINANCIAL AID PROCEDURES

Forms required: FAFSA, institutional form.

Dates and Deadlines: Priority date 4/1; no closing date. Applicants notified on a rolling basis starting 4/1; must reply within 3 week(s) of notification.

CONTACT

Emily Bliss, Director of Financial Aid and Veteran Services

601 South College Road, Wilmington, NC 28403-5904

(910) 962-3177

University of North Carolina School of the Arts

Winston-Salem, North Carolina

www.uncsa.edu   Federal Code: 003981

4-year public visual arts and performing arts college in small city.

Enrollment: 736 undergrads. 179 full-time freshmen.

Selectivity: Admits less than 50% of applicants.

BASIC COSTS (2009-2010)

Tuition and fees: $5,278; out-of-state residents $17,224.

Room and board: $7,256.

Additional info: Required fees may vary by program.

FINANCIAL AID PICTURE (2008-2009)

Students with need: Need-based aid available for full-time and part-time students. Work study available nights, weekends, and for part-time students.

Students without need: No-need awards available for academics, art, leadership, music/drama, state/district residency.

FINANCIAL AID PROCEDURES

Forms required: FAFSA.

Dates and Deadlines: Priority date 3/1; no closing date. Applicants notified on a rolling basis starting 4/1; must reply within 2 week(s) of notification.

CONTACT

Jane Kamiab, Director of Financial Aid

1533 South Main Street, Winston-Salem, NC 27127-2188

(336) 770-3297

Vance-Granville Community College

Henderson, North Carolina

www.vgcc.edu   Federal Code: 009903

2-year public community college in large town.

Enrollment: 3,817 undergrads.

Selectivity: Open admission; but selective for some programs.

BASIC COSTS (2009-2010)

Tuition and fees: $1,591; out-of-state residents $7,330.

Per-credit charge: $50; out-of-state residents $241.

FINANCIAL AID PICTURE (2008-2009)

Students with need: Need-based aid available for full-time and part-time students.

Students without need: No-need awards available for academics.

FINANCIAL AID PROCEDURES

Forms required: FAFSA.

Dates and Deadlines: Closing date 3/15. Applicants notified on a rolling basis starting 5/1; must reply within 2 week(s) of notification.

CONTACT

Frank Clark, Financial Aid Officer

Box 917, Henderson, NC 27536

(252) 492-2061

Wake Forest University

Winston-Salem, North Carolina   Federal Code: 002978

www.wfu.edu   CSS Code: 5885

4-year private university in small city.

Enrollment: 4,560 undergrads, 1% part-time. 1,201 full-time freshmen.

Selectivity: Admits less than 50% of applicants.

BASIC COSTS (2010-2011)

Tuition and fees: $39,970.

Per-credit charge: $1,640.

Room and board: $11,010.

FINANCIAL AID PICTURE (2009-2010)

Students with need: Out of 432 full-time freshmen who applied for aid, 354 were judged to have need. Of these, 349 received aid, and 326 had their full need met. Average financial aid package met 100% of need; average scholarship/grant was $28,085; average loan was $8,028. For part-time students, average financial aid package was $27,652.

Students without need: 69 full-time freshmen who did not demonstrate need for aid received scholarships/grants; average award was $16,327. No-need awards available for academics, alumni affiliation, art, athletics, leadership, music/drama, religious affiliation, ROTC, state/district residency.

Scholarships offered: *Merit:* Reynolds Scholarship: full tuition, room and board, books, fees for 4 years, also provides for summer study; 6 awarded. Joseph G. Gordon Scholarship: full tuition for 4 years; for underrepresented students with exceptional promise and leadership; 7 awarded. Carswell Scholarship: based on intellect and leadership; between 3/4 and full tuition for 4 years, including summer grant for travel and study projects; 10-12 awarded. Presidential Scholarship: for students gifted in areas such as writing, studio art, music theater, debate, leadership, dance, entrepreneurship, and community service; 20 awarded. Poteat Scholarship: $12,100; for North Carolina residents who are active members of a Baptist Church in North Carolina, must make an active contribution to church and society; 18 awarded. *Athletic:* 60 full-time freshmen received athletic scholarships; average amount $36,849.

Cumulative student debt: 38% of graduating class had student loans; average debt was $24,561.

Additional info: In fall 2008, freshmen with an annual family income of less than $40,000 will have their student loans capped at $4,000 per year during their college years. Other financial aid to the students will come from grant and scholarship increases and work-study opportunities.

FINANCIAL AID PROCEDURES

Forms required: FAFSA, CSS PROFILE, state aid form.

Dates and Deadlines: Priority date 2/15; closing date 3/1. Applicants notified on a rolling basis starting 4/1; must reply by 5/1 or within 4 week(s) of notification.

CONTACT

William Wells, Director of Financial Aid

PO Box 7305, Winston-Salem, NC 27109-7305

(336) 758-5154

Wake Technical Community College

Raleigh, North Carolina

www.waketech.edu   Federal Code: 004844

2-year public community and technical college in large city.

Enrollment: 15,214 undergrads, 56% part-time.

Selectivity: Open admission; but selective for some programs.

BASIC COSTS (2009-2010)

Tuition and fees: $1,580; out-of-state residents $7,319.

Per-credit charge: $50; out-of-state residents $241.

FINANCIAL AID PICTURE

Students with need: Need-based aid available for full-time and part-time students.

Students without need: No-need awards available for academics, job skills, leadership, ROTC, state/district residency.

FINANCIAL AID PROCEDURES

Forms required: FAFSA, institutional form.

Dates and Deadlines: Priority date 3/15; no closing date. Applicants notified on a rolling basis starting 4/1; must reply within 2 week(s) of notification.

Transfers: Child care grant and NCCCS Grant and Loan Program available.

CONTACT

Regina Huggins, Dean, Student Support Services
9101 Fayetteville Road, Raleigh, NC 27603
(919) 866-5410

Warren Wilson College

Asheville, North Carolina
www.warren-wilson.edu   Federal Code: 002979

4-year private liberal arts college in small city, affiliated with Presbyterian Church (USA).

Enrollment: 941 undergrads.

Selectivity: Admits over 75% of applicants.

BASIC COSTS (2009-2010)

Tuition and fees: $24,196.

Per-credit charge: $996.

Room and board: $7,770.

Additional info: All resident students required to work 15 hours per week in college's work program. $3,480 earnings credited toward tuition costs.

FINANCIAL AID PICTURE (2009-2010)

Students with need: Need-based aid available for full-time and part-time students.

Students without need: No-need awards available for academics, art, job skills, leadership, religious affiliation, state/district residency.

Scholarships offered: Wilson Honor: 1 awarded; $5,000 annually. Warner Honor: 2 awarded; $4,000 annually. Transfer Honor: 2 awarded; $2,000 annually. Sutton Honor: 20 awarded; $1,000 annually. Work Scholarship: 2 awarded; $1,500 annually. Service Scholarship: 2 awarded; $1,500 annually. National Merit: unlimited numbers awarded; $4,000 annually. Valedictorian/Salutatorian Scholarship: 10 awarded; $2,000 annually. North Carolina Presidential Scholarship: 30 awarded; $1,000 annually. All renewable with 3.0 cumulative GPA and successful completion of a minimum of 12 credit hours each semester.

FINANCIAL AID PROCEDURES

Forms required: FAFSA, state aid form, institutional form.

Dates and Deadlines: Priority date 4/1; no closing date. Applicants notified on a rolling basis starting 3/1; must reply within 3 week(s) of notification.

Transfers: No deadline. Applicants notified on a rolling basis starting 3/1; must reply within 3 week(s) of notification.

CONTACT

Kathy Pack, Director of Financial Aid
Office of Admission, Asheville, NC 28815-9000
(828) 771-2082

Wayne Community College

Goldsboro, North Carolina
www.waynecc.edu   Federal Code: 008216

2-year public community college in large town.

Enrollment: 3,110 undergrads, 36% part-time. 606 full-time freshmen.

Selectivity: Open admission; but selective for some programs.

BASIC COSTS (2009-2010)

Tuition and fees: $1,672; out-of-state residents $7,794.

Per-credit charge: $50; out-of-state residents $241.

FINANCIAL AID PICTURE (2008-2009)

Students with need: 97% of average financial aid package awarded as scholarships/grants, 3% awarded as loans/jobs. Need-based aid available for part-time students. Work study available nights.

Students without need: No-need awards available for academics, job skills.

FINANCIAL AID PROCEDURES

Forms required: FAFSA, institutional form.

Dates and Deadlines: Priority date 3/15; no closing date. Applicants notified on a rolling basis starting 6/1; must reply within 2 week(s) of notification.

CONTACT

Brenda Mercer, Financial Aid Director
PO Box 8002, Goldsboro, NC 27533-8002
(919) 735-5151 ext. 6735

Western Carolina University

Cullowhee, North Carolina
www.wcu.edu   Federal Code: 002981

4-year public university in small town.

Enrollment: 7,205 undergrads, 14% part-time. 1,551 full-time freshmen.

Selectivity: Admits less than 50% of applicants.

BASIC COSTS (2009-2010)

Tuition and fees: $4,330; out-of-state residents $13,927.

Room and board: $5,912.

FINANCIAL AID PICTURE (2009-2010)

Students with need: Out of 1,341 full-time freshmen who applied for aid, 926 were judged to have need. Of these, 921 received aid, and 304 had their full need met. Average financial aid package met 81% of need; average scholarship/grant was $7,351; average loan was $3,963. For part-time students, average financial aid package was $4,442.

Students without need: 66 full-time freshmen who did not demonstrate need for aid received scholarships/grants; average award was $2,157. No-need awards available for academics, art, athletics, leadership, music/drama, state/district residency.

Scholarships offered: *Merit:* WCU awards merit-based scholarships each year to students that demonstrate excellent academic, athletic, artistic, professional, cultural and/or civic achievement. The number and amount of awards vary. *Athletic:* 67 full-time freshmen received athletic scholarships; average amount $7,949.

FINANCIAL AID PROCEDURES

Forms required: FAFSA, institutional form.

Dates and Deadlines: Priority date 3/15; no closing date. Applicants notified on a rolling basis starting 4/1.

CONTACT

Trina Orr, Director of Student Financial Aid
102 Camp Building, Cullowhee, NC 28723
(828) 227-7290

Western Piedmont Community College

Morganton, North Carolina
www.wpcc.edu   Federal Code: 002982

2-year public community college in large town.

Enrollment: 2,735 undergrads.

Selectivity: Open admission; but selective for some programs.

BASIC COSTS (2009-2010)
Tuition and fees: $1,527; out-of-state residents $7,266.
Per-credit charge: $50; out-of-state residents $241.

FINANCIAL AID PICTURE (2008-2009)
Students with need: Need-based aid available for full-time and part-time students.
Students without need: No-need awards available for academics.

FINANCIAL AID PROCEDURES
Forms required: FAFSA.
Dates and Deadlines: Closing date 6/1. Applicants notified on a rolling basis starting 6/15; must reply within 2 week(s) of notification.

CONTACT
Keith Conley, Director of Financial Aid
1001 Burkemont Avenue, Morganton, NC 28655-4504
(828) 448-6042

Wilkes Community College
Wilkesboro, North Carolina
www.wilkescc.edu   Federal Code: 002983

2-year public community college in small town.
Enrollment: 2,430 undergrads.
Selectivity: Open admission; but selective for some programs.

BASIC COSTS (2009-2010)
Tuition and fees: $1,620; out-of-state residents $7,359.
Per-credit charge: $50; out-of-state residents $241.

FINANCIAL AID PICTURE (2008-2009)
Students with need: Need-based aid available for full-time and part-time students. Work study available nights.
Students without need: No-need awards available for academics, art, job skills, leadership, minority status, music/drama, state/district residency.

FINANCIAL AID PROCEDURES
Forms required: FAFSA.
Dates and Deadlines: Priority date 6/1; no closing date. Applicants notified on a rolling basis starting 4/1; must reply by 8/1.
Transfers: No deadline.

CONTACT
Vickie Call, Director of Financial Aid
1328 South Collegiate Drive, Wilkesboro, NC 28697-0120
(336) 838-6146

Wilson Community College
Wilson, North Carolina
www.wilsoncc.edu   Federal Code: 004845

2-year public community college in large town.
Enrollment: 1,700 undergrads, 44% part-time. 258 full-time freshmen.
Selectivity: Open admission; but selective for some programs.

BASIC COSTS (2009-2010)
Tuition and fees: $1,585; out-of-state residents $7,324.
Per-credit charge: $50; out-of-state residents $241.

FINANCIAL AID PICTURE
Students with need: Need-based aid available for full-time and part-time students.
Students without need: No-need awards available for academics.

FINANCIAL AID PROCEDURES
Forms required: FAFSA, institutional form.

Dates and Deadlines: Priority date 3/15; no closing date. Applicants notified on a rolling basis.

CONTACT
Rex Bissette, Director of Financial Aid and Veterans Affairs
Box 4305, Wilson, NC 27893-0305
(252) 246-1274

Wingate University
Wingate, North Carolina
www.wingate.edu   Federal Code: 002985

4-year private university in small town, affiliated with Baptist faith.
Enrollment: 1,409 undergrads, 3% part-time. 375 full-time freshmen.
Selectivity: Admits 50 to 75% of applicants.

BASIC COSTS (2010-2011)
Tuition and fees: $21,140.
Per-credit charge: $666.
Room and board: $8,350.

FINANCIAL AID PICTURE (2009-2010)
Students with need: Out of 342 full-time freshmen who applied for aid, 301 were judged to have need. Of these, 301 received aid, and 67 had their full need met. Average financial aid package met 86% of need; average scholarship/grant was $9,405; average loan was $2,948. For part-time students, average financial aid package was $3,785.
Students without need: 71 full-time freshmen who did not demonstrate need for aid received scholarships/grants; average award was $8,550. No-need awards available for academics, alumni affiliation, art, athletics, music/drama, religious affiliation, state/district residency.
Scholarships offered: 70 full-time freshmen received athletic scholarships; average amount $6,832.
Cumulative student debt: 75% of graduating class had student loans; average debt was $27,616.
Additional info: Institutional aid may not be available after June 1.

FINANCIAL AID PROCEDURES
Forms required: FAFSA, state aid form.
Dates and Deadlines: Priority date 5/1; no closing date. Applicants notified on a rolling basis starting 3/15; must reply within 2 week(s) of notification.
Transfers: Priority date 3/1; no deadline. Applicants notified on a rolling basis; must reply within 2 week(s) of notification. Must submit financial aid transcripts from previous colleges attended.

CONTACT
Teresa Williams, Director of Financial Planning
Campus Box 3059, Wingate, NC 28174-0157
(704) 233-8209

Winston-Salem State University
Winston-Salem, North Carolina
www.wssu.edu   Federal Code: 002986

4-year public university and health science college in small city.
Enrollment: 5,914 undergrads, 10% part-time. 1,357 full-time freshmen.
Selectivity: Admits 50 to 75% of applicants.

BASIC COSTS (2009-2010)
Tuition and fees: $3,522; out-of-state residents $12,508.
Room and board: $6,362.

PART III: FINANCIAL AID COLLEGE BY COLLEGE

FINANCIAL AID PICTURE (2008-2009)

Students with need: Out of 1,312 full-time freshmen who applied for aid, 1,145 were judged to have need. Of these, 1,143 received aid, and 215 had their full need met. Average financial aid package met 79% of need; average scholarship/grant was $3,211; average loan was $1,474. For part-time students, average financial aid package was $1,970.

Students without need: 20 full-time freshmen who did not demonstrate need for aid received scholarships/grants; average award was $2,842. No-need awards available for academics, athletics, ROTC, state/district residency.

Scholarships offered: 40 full-time freshmen received athletic scholarships; average amount $5,635.

Cumulative student debt: 85% of graduating class had student loans; average debt was $10,419.

FINANCIAL AID PROCEDURES

Forms required: FAFSA.

Dates and Deadlines: Priority date 5/1; no closing date. Applicants notified by 5/15; must reply within 2 week(s) of notification.

Transfers: Closing date 3/15. Applicants notified on a rolling basis.

CONTACT

Sheryl Spivey, Director of Financial Aid
601 Martin Luther King Jr Drive, Winston-Salem, NC 27110
(336) 750-3280

North Dakota

Bismarck State College

Bismarck, North Dakota
www.bismarckstate.edu   Federal Code: 002988

2-year public community college in small city.
Enrollment: 4,020 undergrads, 33% part-time. 892 full-time freshmen.
Selectivity: Open admission; but selective for some programs.

BASIC COSTS (2009-2010)
Tuition and fees: $4,029; out-of-state residents $9,647.
Per-credit charge: $112; out-of-state residents $299.
Room and board: $4,738.
Additional info: Full-time annual tuition for residents of South Dakota, Montana, Manitoba, Saskatchewan: $4,205. Tuition/fee waivers available for minority students.

FINANCIAL AID PICTURE
Students with need: Need-based aid available for full-time and part-time students. Work study available nights, weekends, and for part-time students.
Students without need: This college awards aid only to students with need.

FINANCIAL AID PROCEDURES
Forms required: FAFSA.
Dates and Deadlines: Priority date 3/15; no closing date. Applicants notified on a rolling basis starting 6/1; must reply within 3 week(s) of notification.
Transfers: Financial aid based on funds available.

CONTACT
Jeffrey Jacobs, Director of Financial Aid
PO Box 5587, Bismarck, ND 58506-5587
(701) 224-5494

Cankdeska Cikana Community College

Fort Totten, North Dakota
www.littlehoop.edu   Federal Code: 015793

2-year public community college in rural community.
Enrollment: 222 undergrads.
Selectivity: Open admission.

FINANCIAL AID PICTURE (2008-2009)
Students with need: Need-based aid available for full-time and part-time students.
Students without need: This college awards aid only to students with need.

FINANCIAL AID PROCEDURES
Forms required: FAFSA, institutional form.
Dates and Deadlines: Closing date 8/20. Applicants notified on a rolling basis.

CONTACT
Phillip Longie, Director of Financial Aid
Box 269, Fort Totten, ND 58335
(701) 766-1341

Dakota College at Bottineau

Bottineau, North Dakota
www.dakotacollege.edu   Federal Code: 002995

2-year public nursing and junior college in small town.
Enrollment: 335 full-time undergrads.
Selectivity: Open admission.

BASIC COSTS (2009-2010)
Tuition and fees: $3,837; out-of-state residents $5,397.
Per-credit charge: $130; out-of-state residents $195.
Room and board: $4,308.
Additional info: Tuition/fee waivers available for minority students.

FINANCIAL AID PICTURE
Students with need: Need-based aid available for full-time and part-time students. Work study available nights, weekends, and for part-time students.
Students without need: No-need awards available for academics, alumni affiliation, athletics, minority status, music/drama, state/district residency.

FINANCIAL AID PROCEDURES
Forms required: FAFSA.
Dates and Deadlines: Priority date 4/15; no closing date. Applicants notified on a rolling basis starting 6/1; must reply within 2 week(s) of notification.

CONTACT
Kim Gourneau, Financial Aid Officer
105 Simrall Boulevard, Bottineau, ND 58318-1198
(701) 228-5437

Dickinson State University

Dickinson, North Dakota
www.dsu.nodak.edu   Federal Code: 002989

4-year public university in large town.
Enrollment: 2,767 undergrads, 35% part-time. 310 full-time freshmen.
Selectivity: Open admission; but selective for some programs.

BASIC COSTS (2009-2010)
Tuition and fees: $5,249; out-of-state residents $12,195.
Per-credit charge: $173; out-of-state residents $463.
Room and board: $4,494.

Additional info: Tuition for South Dakota, Montana, Manitoba, Saskatchewan residents: $5,024. Tuition/fee waivers available for minority students.

FINANCIAL AID PICTURE (2008-2009)

Students with need: Need-based aid available for full-time and part-time students. Work study available nights, weekends, and for part-time students.
Students without need: No-need awards available for academics, alumni affiliation, art, athletics, job skills, leadership, minority status, music/drama, religious affiliation, state/district residency.
Additional info: Scholarships available to new students, priority deadline December 1.

FINANCIAL AID PROCEDURES

Forms required: FAFSA.
Dates and Deadlines: Priority date 3/15; no closing date. Must reply within 2 week(s) of notification.

CONTACT

Sandy Klein, Director of Financial Aid
291 Campus Drive, Dickinson, ND 58601-4896
(701) 483-2371

Jamestown College

Jamestown, North Dakota
www.jc.edu   Federal Code: 002990

4-year private liberal arts college in large town, affiliated with Presbyterian Church (USA).

Enrollment: 965 undergrads, 4% part-time. 233 full-time freshmen.
Selectivity: Admits 50 to 75% of applicants.

BASIC COSTS (2010-2011)

Tuition and fees: $16,780.
Per-credit charge: $400.
Room and board: $5,536.

FINANCIAL AID PICTURE (2009-2010)

Students with need: Out of 208 full-time freshmen who applied for aid, 164 were judged to have need. Of these, 164 received aid, and 39 had their full need met. Average financial aid package met 77% of need; average scholarship/grant was $9,709; average loan was $3,566. For part-time students, average financial aid package was $3,209.
Students without need: 80 full-time freshmen who did not demonstrate need for aid received scholarships/grants; average award was $5,746. No-need awards available for academics, alumni affiliation, art, athletics, job skills, leadership, music/drama, religious affiliation.
Scholarships offered: *Merit:* Wilson Scholarships: full tuition; for academic merit and leadership. Presidential Scholarships: $9,000 annually; for academic merit and leadership. Arnold Chemistry Scholarships: $2,500 annually; for chemistry majors. *Athletic:* 69 full-time freshmen received athletic scholarships; average amount $329.
Cumulative student debt: 82% of graduating class had student loans; average debt was $25,818.
Additional info: FAFSA must be received by March 15th for North Dakota residents to be considered for North Dakota state grants.

FINANCIAL AID PROCEDURES

Forms required: FAFSA.
Dates and Deadlines: Priority date 3/15; no closing date. Applicants notified on a rolling basis starting 2/1; must reply within 2 week(s) of notification.
Transfers: No deadline. Applicants notified on a rolling basis starting 2/1; must reply within 2 week(s) of notification.

CONTACT

Margery Michael, Director of Financial Aid
6081 College Lane, Jamestown, ND 58405
(701) 252-3467 ext. 5556

Lake Region State College

Devils Lake, North Dakota
www.lrsc.edu   Federal Code: 002991

2-year public community and technical college in small town.
Enrollment: 696 undergrads, 31% part-time. 183 full-time freshmen.
Selectivity: Open admission; but selective for some programs.

BASIC COSTS (2009-2010)

Tuition and fees: $3,908; out-of-state residents $3,908.
Per-credit charge: $128; out-of-state residents $122.
Room and board: $4,780.
Additional info: Tuition/fee waivers available for minority students.

FINANCIAL AID PICTURE (2009-2010)

Students with need: Average financial aid package met 93% of need; average scholarship/grant was $3,725; average loan was $2,977. For part-time students, average financial aid package was $4,960.
Students without need: No-need awards available for academics, athletics, leadership, minority status, music/drama.
Cumulative student debt: 71% of graduating class had student loans; average debt was $9,392.

FINANCIAL AID PROCEDURES

Forms required: FAFSA.
Dates and Deadlines: Priority date 3/15; no closing date. Applicants notified on a rolling basis starting 5/15; must reply within 2 week(s) of notification.
Transfers: No deadline. Applicants notified on a rolling basis starting 5/1; must reply within 4 week(s) of notification.

CONTACT

Katie Nettell, Director of Financial Aid
1801 College Drive North, Devils Lake, ND 58301-1598
(701) 662-1516

Mayville State University

Mayville, North Dakota
www.mayvillestate.edu   Federal Code: 002993

4-year public business and teachers college in small town.
Enrollment: 887 undergrads, 39% part-time. 147 full-time freshmen.
Selectivity: Open admission; but selective for some programs.

BASIC COSTS (2009-2010)

Tuition and fees: $5,793; out-of-state residents $7,849.
Per-credit charge: $172; out-of-state residents $258.
Room and board: $4,488.
Additional info: Full-time tuition for South Dakota, Montana, Kansas, Michigan, Missouri, Nebraska, Manitoba, and Saskatchewan residents: $5,156. Full-time tuition for Minnesota residents: $4,307. All other states and Canadian provinces: $6,180. Tuition/fee waivers available for minority students.

FINANCIAL AID PICTURE (2009-2010)

Students with need: Average financial aid package met 91% of need; average scholarship/grant was $5,015; average loan was $3,310. For part-time students, average financial aid package was $7,294.
Students without need: No-need awards available for academics, athletics, leadership, minority status, music/drama, state/district residency.
Scholarships offered: Non-resident academic scholarship; $500-2,000 per year; based on academic criteria of students from select states.
Cumulative student debt: 90% of graduating class had student loans; average debt was $25,931.

FINANCIAL AID PROCEDURES

Forms required: FAFSA.
Dates and Deadlines: Priority date 2/15; no closing date. Applicants notified on a rolling basis starting 5/1; must reply within 2 week(s) of notification.

Transfers: No deadline. Applicants notified on a rolling basis starting 5/1; must reply within 2 week(s) of notification.

CONTACT

Shirley Hanson, Director of Financial Aid
330 Third Street, NE, Mayville, ND 58257-1299
(701) 788-4767

Medcenter One College of Nursing

Bismarck, North Dakota
www.medcenterone.com/collegeofnursing
Federal Code: 009354

Upper-division private nursing college in small city.
Enrollment: 89 undergrads.

BASIC COSTS (2009-2010)
Tuition and fees: $10,294.
Per-credit charge: $405.

FINANCIAL AID PICTURE (2008-2009)
Students with need: Average financial aid package for all full-time undergraduates was $12,368; for part-time $5,447. 40% awarded as scholarships/grants, 60% awarded as loans/jobs. Work study available weekends and for part-time students.

FINANCIAL AID PROCEDURES
Dates and Deadlines: Priority date 3/1; no closing date. Must reply within 2 week(s) of notification.
Transfers: No deadline. Applicants notified on a rolling basis starting 6/1; must reply within 2 week(s) of notification.

CONTACT
Janell Thomas, Director/Registrar
512 North 7th Street, Bismarck, ND 58501-4425
(701) 323-6270

Minot State University

Minot, North Dakota
www.minotstateu.edu
Federal Code: 002994

4-year public university and liberal arts college in large town.
Enrollment: 3,345 undergrads, 31% part-time. 419 full-time freshmen.
Selectivity: Admits over 75% of applicants.

BASIC COSTS (2009-2010)
Tuition and fees: $5,389; out-of-state residents $5,389.
Per-credit charge: $180; out-of-state residents $180.
Room and board: $4,602.
Additional info: Tuition/fee waivers available for minority students.

FINANCIAL AID PICTURE (2008-2009)
Students with need: Need-based aid available for full-time and part-time students. Work study available nights.
Students without need: No-need awards available for academics, alumni affiliation, art, athletics, minority status, music/drama, state/district residency.
Additional info: Scholarship application deadline is 2/15.

FINANCIAL AID PROCEDURES
Forms required: FAFSA, institutional form.
Dates and Deadlines: Priority date 3/15; no closing date. Applicants notified on a rolling basis starting 5/1; must reply within 2 week(s) of notification.
Transfers: No deadline. Applicants notified by 5/1; must reply within 2 week(s) of notification.

CONTACT
Dale Gehring, Director of Financial Aid
500 University Avenue West, Minot, ND 58707-5002
(701) 858-3375

North Dakota State College of Science

Wahpeton, North Dakota
www.ndscs.nodak.edu
Federal Code: 002996

2-year public junior and technical college in small town.
Enrollment: 2,650 undergrads, 40% part-time. 630 full-time freshmen.
Selectivity: Open admission; but selective for some programs.

BASIC COSTS (2009-2010)
Tuition and fees: $3,890; out-of-state residents $9,512.
Per-credit charge: $112; out-of-state residents $300.
Room and board: $4,796.
Additional info: Full-time tuition for South Dakota, Montana, Saskatchewan, Manitoba residents: $4,209. Tuition/fee waivers available for minority students.

FINANCIAL AID PICTURE (2008-2009)
Students with need: 21% of average financial aid package awarded as scholarships/grants, 79% awarded as loans/jobs. Need-based aid available for part-time students. Work study available nights, weekends, and for part-time students.
Students without need: No-need awards available for academics, athletics, job skills, music/drama, state/district residency.

FINANCIAL AID PROCEDURES
Forms required: FAFSA, institutional form.
Dates and Deadlines: Priority date 4/15; no closing date. Applicants notified on a rolling basis starting 6/1; must reply within 2 week(s) of notification.
Transfers: Priority date 3/15; no deadline. Must reply within 2 week(s) of notification.

CONTACT
Shelly Blome, Director of Financial Aid
800 North 6th Street, Wahpeton, ND 58076
(701) 671-2207

North Dakota State University

Fargo, North Dakota
www.ndsu.edu
Federal Code: 002997

4-year public university in small city.
Enrollment: 11,733 undergrads, 9% part-time. 2,688 full-time freshmen.
Selectivity: Admits over 75% of applicants.

BASIC COSTS (2009-2010)
Tuition and fees: $6,455; out-of-state residents $15,554.
Per-credit charge: $227; out-of-state residents $606.
Room and board: $6,568.
Additional info: Tuition for South Dakota, Montana, Manitoba, Saskatchewan residents: $8,172. Tuition/fee waivers available for minority students.

FINANCIAL AID PICTURE (2008-2009)
Students with need: Out of 2,086 full-time freshmen who applied for aid, 1,343 were judged to have need. Of these, 1,297 received aid, and 398 had their full need met. Average financial aid package met 66% of need; average scholarship/grant was $3,636; average loan was $3,639. For part-time students, average financial aid package was $6,111.
Students without need: 922 full-time freshmen who did not demonstrate need for aid received scholarships/grants; average award was $2,037. No-

need awards available for academics, alumni affiliation, art, athletics, leadership, minority status, music/drama, ROTC, state/district residency.
Scholarships offered: *Merit:* New Student Scholarships: vary in amount awarded; based on 25 ACT or 1200 SAT (exclusive of writing) and 3.5 GPA. *Athletic:* 89 full-time freshmen received athletic scholarships; average amount $7,582.
Cumulative student debt: 79% of graduating class had student loans; average debt was $26,916.

FINANCIAL AID PROCEDURES

Forms required: FAFSA.
Dates and Deadlines: Closing date 3/15. Applicants notified on a rolling basis starting 3/15.
Transfers: Priority date 3/15.

CONTACT

Jeanne Enebo, Director of Student Financial Services
Ceres Hall 114, Fargo, ND 58108-6050
(701) 231-7533

Rasmussen College: Bismarck

Bismarck, North Dakota
www.rasmussen.edu

2-year for-profit career college in small city.
Enrollment: 560 undergrads.
Selectivity: Open admission; but selective for some programs.

BASIC COSTS (2009-2010)

Tuition and fees: $16,425.
Per-credit charge: $365.

FINANCIAL AID PICTURE

Students with need: Need-based aid available for full-time and part-time students.

FINANCIAL AID PROCEDURES

Forms required: FAFSA, institutional form.
Dates and Deadlines: No deadline. Applicants notified on a rolling basis.

CONTACT.

Tina Fisher, Director of Student Financial Services
1701 East Century Avenue, Bismarck, ND 58503
(701) 530-9600

Rasmussen College: Fargo

Fargo, North Dakota
www.rasmussen.edu   Federal Code: 004846

4-year for-profit career college in small city.
Enrollment: 510 full-time undergrads.
Selectivity: Open admission; but selective for some programs.

BASIC COSTS (2009-2010)

Additional info: Per-credit tuition ranges from $365 to $450 depending on course level.

FINANCIAL AID PICTURE (2008-2009)

Students with need: Need-based aid available for full-time and part-time students.

FINANCIAL AID PROCEDURES

Forms required: FAFSA, institutional form.
Dates and Deadlines: No deadline. Applicants notified on a rolling basis.

CONTACT

Crystal Vold, Director of Student Financial Services
4012 19th Avenue SW, Fargo, ND 58103
(701) 277-3889

Sitting Bull College

Fort Yates, North Dakota
www.sittingbull.edu   Federal Code: 014993

2-year public community college in small town.
Enrollment: 264 undergrads, 6% part-time. 39 full-time freshmen.
Selectivity: Open admission.

BASIC COSTS (2010-2011)

Tuition and fees: $3,810.
Per-credit charge: $125.

FINANCIAL AID PICTURE (2008-2009)

Students with need: Need-based aid available for full-time and part-time students.

FINANCIAL AID PROCEDURES

Forms required: FAFSA, institutional form.
Dates and Deadlines: Priority date 5/1; no closing date. Applicants notified on a rolling basis starting 7/15; must reply within 6 week(s) of notification.
Transfers: No deadline. Applicants notified on a rolling basis.

CONTACT

Donna Seaboy, Financial Aid Director
1341 92nd Street, Fort Yates, ND 58538
(701) 854-8013

Trinity Bible College

Ellendale, North Dakota
www.trinitybiblecollege.edu   Federal Code: 012059

4-year private Bible college in rural community, affiliated with Assemblies of God.
Enrollment: 296 undergrads.

BASIC COSTS (2009-2010)

Tuition and fees: $13,000.
Per-credit charge: $385.
Room and board: $4,900.

FINANCIAL AID PICTURE (2009-2010)

Students with need: Need-based aid available for full-time and part-time students. Work study available nights, weekends, and for part-time students.
Students without need: No-need awards available for academics, alumni affiliation, art, leadership, music/drama, religious affiliation.

FINANCIAL AID PROCEDURES

Forms required: FAFSA.
Dates and Deadlines: Priority date 3/1; closing date 9/1. Applicants notified on a rolling basis starting 3/1; must reply within 3 week(s) of notification.

CONTACT

Don Flaherty, Financial Aid Director
50 6th Avenue South, Ellendale, ND 58436-7150
(888) 822-2329

United Tribes Technical College
Bismarck, North Dakota
www.uttc.edu   Federal Code: 014470

2-year private technical college in small city.
Enrollment: 365 undergrads.
Selectivity: Open admission; but selective for some programs.

BASIC COSTS (2009-2010)
Additional info: Tuition/fee waivers available for adults, minority students.

FINANCIAL AID PICTURE (2009-2010)
Students with need: Need-based aid available for full-time and part-time students. Work study available nights, weekends, and for part-time students.

FINANCIAL AID PROCEDURES
Forms required: FAFSA.
Dates and Deadlines: Priority date 5/29; no closing date. Applicants notified on a rolling basis starting 5/29; must reply within 2 week(s) of notification.

CONTACT
Nathan Stratton, Financial Aid Director
3315 University Drive, Bismarck, ND 58504
(701) 255-3285 ext. 1211

University of Mary
Bismarck, North Dakota
www.umary.edu   Federal Code: 002992

4-year private university in small city, affiliated with Roman Catholic Church.
Enrollment: 1,994 undergrads, 20% part-time. 312 full-time freshmen.
Selectivity: Admits over 75% of applicants.

BASIC COSTS (2010-2011)
Tuition and fees: $13,050.
Per-credit charge: $420.
Room and board: $5,180.

FINANCIAL AID PICTURE (2009-2010)
Students with need: 38% of average financial aid package awarded as scholarships/grants, 62% awarded as loans/jobs. Need-based aid available for part-time students. Work study available nights, weekends, and for part-time students.
Students without need: No-need awards available for academics, athletics, leadership, music/drama, religious affiliation, state/district residency.
Scholarships offered: 100% of 2009-2010 freshmen received a University of Mary scholarship; Scholarship competition days held annually with awards ranging from $3,500 to 100% of tuition; athletic, music, speech, drama and leadership scholarships also offered.

FINANCIAL AID PROCEDURES
Forms required: FAFSA.
Dates and Deadlines: Priority date 3/15; no closing date. Applicants notified on a rolling basis starting 2/1; must reply within 2 week(s) of notification.
Transfers: No deadline. Applicants notified on a rolling basis starting 2/1; must reply within 2 week(s) of notification.

CONTACT
Brenda Zastoupil, Director of Student Financial Aid
7500 University Drive, Bismarck, ND 58504-9652
(701) 355-8244

University of North Dakota
Grand Forks, North Dakota
www.und.edu   Federal Code: 003005

4-year public university in small city.
Enrollment: 10,440 undergrads, 16% part-time. 2,040 full-time freshmen.
Selectivity: Admits 50 to 75% of applicants.

BASIC COSTS (2009-2010)
Tuition and fees: $6,726; out-of-state residents $15,845.
Per-credit charge: $227; out-of-state residents $607.
Room and board: $5,978.
Additional info: Tuition for South Dakota, Montana, Saskatchewan, Manitoba residents: $8,191. Tuition/fee waivers available for minority students.

FINANCIAL AID PICTURE (2009-2010)
Students with need: Out of 1,616 full-time freshmen who applied for aid, 997 were judged to have need. Of these, 991 received aid, and 351 had their full need met. Average financial aid package met 69% of need; average scholarship/grant was $4,159; average loan was $3,507. For part-time students, average financial aid package was $7,687.
Students without need: 786 full-time freshmen who did not demonstrate need for aid received scholarships/grants; average award was $1,482. No-need awards available for academics, alumni affiliation, art, athletics, job skills, leadership, music/drama, religious affiliation, ROTC.
Scholarships offered: *Merit:* 15 freshmen will receive $2,500 a year for 4 years; they are either National Merit Finalists listing UND as first choice and in top 10% of graduating class, or in top 10% and have minimum composite of 32 on the ACT. 55 scholarships of $2,000/yr for 4 years provided to students in top 10% of graduating class who are National Merit Semifinalists or have ACT composite of 29-31. 40 students with ACT of 27-28 and in upper 10% of graduating class will receive $1,000 for their freshman year. *Athletic:* 74 full-time freshmen received athletic scholarships; average amount $9,603.
Cumulative student debt: 85% of graduating class had student loans; average debt was $38,804.

FINANCIAL AID PROCEDURES
Forms required: FAFSA.
Dates and Deadlines: Priority date 3/15; no closing date. Applicants notified on a rolling basis starting 5/15; must reply within 4 week(s) of notification.

CONTACT
Robin Holden, Director of Student Financial Aid
Twamley Hall Room 205 264 Centennial Drive Stop 8357, Grand Forks, ND 58202-8357
(701) 777-3121

Williston State College
Williston, North Dakota
www.wsc.nodak.edu   Federal Code: 003007

2-year public junior college in large town.
Enrollment: 567 undergrads, 28% part-time. 127 full-time freshmen.
Selectivity: Open admission; but selective for some programs.

BASIC COSTS (2009-2010)
Tuition and fees: $3,378; out-of-state residents $4,687.
Per-credit charge: $101; out-of-state residents $151.
Room and board: $3,378.
Additional info: Tuition for South Dakota, Montana, and Canadian residents: $2,618. Tuition/fee waivers available for minority students.

FINANCIAL AID PICTURE (2008-2009)

Students with need: Out of 90 full-time freshmen who applied for aid, 69 were judged to have need. Of these, 68 received aid, and 67 had their full need met. Average financial aid package met 52% of need; average scholarship/grant was $4,032; average loan was $3,004. For part-time students, average financial aid package was $5,287.

Students without need: 84 full-time freshmen who did not demonstrate need for aid received scholarships/grants; average award was $1,314. No-need awards available for academics, athletics, music/drama.

Scholarships offered: 36 full-time freshmen received athletic scholarships; average amount $3,278.

FINANCIAL AID PROCEDURES

Forms required: FAFSA.

Dates and Deadlines: Priority date 3/15; no closing date. Applicants notified on a rolling basis starting 5/15.

CONTACT

Lynn Hagen-Aaberg, Financial Aid Director
1410 University Avenue, Williston, ND 58801
(701) 774-4244

Ohio

Antioch University McGregor

Yellow Springs, Ohio
www.mcgregor.edu   Federal Code: E00553

4-year private university and branch campus college in small town.
Enrollment: 176 undergrads, 50% part-time.

BASIC COSTS (2010-2011)

Tuition and fees: $15,810.
Per-credit charge: $320.

FINANCIAL AID PICTURE (2008-2009)

Students with need: Need-based aid available for full-time and part-time students.

FINANCIAL AID PROCEDURES

Dates and Deadlines: No deadline. Applicants notified on a rolling basis.

CONTACT

Kathy John, Director of Financial Aid
900 Dayton Street, Yellow Springs, OH 45387
(937) 769-1840

Art Academy of Cincinnati

Cincinnati, Ohio
www.artacademy.edu   Federal Code: 003011

4-year private visual arts college in large city.
Enrollment: 183 undergrads.
Selectivity: Admits less than 50% of applicants.

BASIC COSTS (2009-2010)

Tuition and fees: $21,880.
Per-credit charge: $900.
Room only: $6,000.

FINANCIAL AID PICTURE

Students with need: Need-based aid available for full-time and part-time students.

Students without need: No-need awards available for academics, art.

Scholarships offered: Annual scholarships awarded to entering and transfer students and to continuing students based on portfolio competition.

FINANCIAL AID PROCEDURES

Forms required: FAFSA.

Dates and Deadlines: Priority date 4/1; no closing date. Applicants notified on a rolling basis starting 3/1.

CONTACT

Karen Geiger, Financial Aid Director
1212 Jackson Street, Cincinnati, OH 45202
(513) 562-8751

Art Institute of Cincinnati

Cincinnati, Ohio
www.aic-arts.edu   Federal Code: 014804

2-year for-profit visual arts college in large city.
Enrollment: 70 undergrads.
Selectivity: Admits over 75% of applicants.

BASIC COSTS (2009-2010)

Additional info: Total program cost $40,221 (8 quarters).

FINANCIAL AID PICTURE (2008-2009)

Students with need: Need-based aid available for full-time students.
Students without need: No-need awards available for academics, art.

FINANCIAL AID PROCEDURES

Forms required: FAFSA.

Dates and Deadlines: No deadline. Applicants notified on a rolling basis starting 9/1; must reply within 1 week(s) of notification.

Transfers: No deadline. Applicants notified on a rolling basis; must reply within 4 week(s) of notification.

CONTACT

Gary Lay, Financial Aid Director
1171 East Kemper Road, Cincinnati, OH 45246
(513) 751-1206

Ashland University

Ashland, Ohio
www.ashland.edu   Federal Code: 003012

4-year private university and liberal arts college in large town, affiliated with Brethren Church.
Enrollment: 2,612 undergrads, 15% part-time. 605 full-time freshmen.
Selectivity: Admits over 75% of applicants.

BASIC COSTS (2010-2011)

Tuition and fees: $27,404.
Room and board: $9,352.
Additional info: Tuition/fee waivers available for minority students.

FINANCIAL AID PICTURE (2009-2010)

Students with need: Out of 605 full-time freshmen who applied for aid, 521 were judged to have need. Of these, 521 received aid, and 90 had their full need met. Average financial aid package met 90% of need; average scholarship/grant was $16,963; average loan was $4,044. For part-time students, average financial aid package was $13,641.

Students without need: 56 full-time freshmen who did not demonstrate need for aid received scholarships/grants; average award was $10,490. No-need awards available for academics, alumni affiliation, art, athletics, job skills, leadership, minority status, music/drama, religious affiliation.

Scholarships offered: *Merit:* Presidential Scholarships; $10,000 based on 3.75 GPA and 27 ACT or 1200 SAT; $9,000 based on 3.5-3.74 GPA and 25-26 ACT or 1130-1190 SAT; $8,000 based on 3.25-3.49 GPA and 23-24 ACT or

1050-1120 SAT. Director's Scholarships; $6,000; based on 3.0 GPA, 21 ACT or 970 SAT. SAT scores exclusive of Writing. **Athletic:** 21 full-time freshmen received athletic scholarships; average amount $11,166.

Cumulative student debt: 82% of graduating class had student loans; average debt was $36,545.

FINANCIAL AID PROCEDURES

Forms required: FAFSA, institutional form.

Dates and Deadlines: Priority date 3/15; no closing date. Applicants notified on a rolling basis starting 3/15; must reply within 3 week(s) of notification.

Transfers: Applicants notified on a rolling basis starting 3/1; must reply within 3 week(s) of notification. Awards for students transferring in 15 credits or more will be based on the student's college transfer GPA while awards for students transferring fewer than 15 credits will be based on the student's high school GPA and ACT/SAT score.

CONTACT

Stephen Howell, Director of Financial Aid
401 College Avenue, Ashland, OH 44805-9981
(419) 289-5002

Aultman College of Nursing and Health Sciences
Canton, Ohio
www.aultmancollege.org

2-year private health science and nursing college in small city.
Enrollment: 268 undergrads, 68% part-time. 15 full-time freshmen.
Selectivity: Admits less than 50% of applicants.

BASIC COSTS (2010-2011)
Tuition and fees: $13,530.

FINANCIAL AID PICTURE (2008-2009)
Students with need: 17% of average financial aid package awarded as scholarships/grants, 83% awarded as loans/jobs.

FINANCIAL AID PROCEDURES
Dates and Deadlines: Priority date 5/1; closing date 10/1.

CONTACT
Jennie Carlson, Financial Aid Administrator
2600 Sixth Street SW, Canton, OH 44710-1799

Baldwin-Wallace College
Berea, Ohio
www.bw.edu   Federal Code: 003014

4-year private liberal arts college in large town, affiliated with United Methodist Church.
Enrollment: 3,561 undergrads, 11% part-time. 754 full-time freshmen.
Selectivity: Admits 50 to 75% of applicants.

BASIC COSTS (2010-2011)
Tuition and fees: $25,260.
Per-credit charge: $785.
Room and board: $7,020.
Additional info: Tuition/fee waivers available for minority students.

FINANCIAL AID PICTURE (2009-2010)
Students with need: Out of 681 full-time freshmen who applied for aid, 603 were judged to have need. Of these, 603 received aid, and 210 had their full need met. Average financial aid package met 86% of need; average scholarship/grant was $14,542; average loan was $3,891. For part-time students, average financial aid package was $8,586.
Students without need: 129 full-time freshmen who did not demonstrate need for aid received scholarships/grants; average award was $8,454. No-

need awards available for academics, alumni affiliation, minority status, music/drama, religious affiliation, state/district residency.

Scholarships offered: Academic scholarships; $5,000 to $13,000; for students enrolled full-time; typically based on class rank in top 25% and 3.4 GPA; SAT/ACT scores also considered if submitted. Alumni Award; $2,000; provided to children and grandchildren of alumni who are attending full-time. Sibling scholarship; $2,000; provided to student siblings who reside in same household and are enrolled full-time. Heritage Award; $1,000-$4,000; awarded to under-represented, under-served students who enrich the College's cultural diversity; students must be enrolled full-time and be in top 25% of high school class with 3.4 GPA. Ministerial Award; up to 50% of tuition; awarded to dependent students (ages 17 to 23) of ordained United Methodist ministers who are full members of an annual conference. Griffiths Award; $1,000-$8,000; awarded to full-time students of the Conservatory who demonstrate outstanding musicianship and talent in audition process.
Cumulative student debt: 67% of graduating class had student loans; average debt was $17,716.

FINANCIAL AID PROCEDURES
Forms required: FAFSA.
Dates and Deadlines: Priority date 5/1; closing date 9/1. Applicants notified on a rolling basis starting 2/14.
Transfers: Priority date 7/1; closing date 9/15. Applicants notified on a rolling basis starting 3/1.

CONTACT
George Rolleston, Director of Financial Aid
275 Eastland Road, Berea, OH 44017-2088
(440) 826-2108

Belmont Technical College
St. Clairsville, Ohio
www.btc.edu   Federal Code: 009941

2-year public community and technical college in small town.
Enrollment: 1,798 undergrads.
Selectivity: Open admission; but selective for some programs.

BASIC COSTS (2009-2010)
Tuition and fees: $3,787; out-of-state residents $6,588.
Per-credit charge: $61; out-of-state residents $123.
Additional info: Tuition/fee waivers available for unemployed or children of unemployed.

FINANCIAL AID PICTURE (2008-2009)
Students with need: Need-based aid available for full-time and part-time students.
Students without need: No-need awards available for state/district residency.

FINANCIAL AID PROCEDURES
Forms required: FAFSA.
Dates and Deadlines: No deadline. Applicants notified on a rolling basis starting 6/1; must reply within 2 week(s) of notification.

CONTACT
Jody Peeler, Associate Dean of Financial Aid
120 Fox Shannon Place, St. Clairsville, OH 43950
(740) 695-9500 ext. 1029

Bowling Green State University
Bowling Green, Ohio
www.bgsu.edu   Federal Code: 003018

4-year public university in large town.
Enrollment: 14,023 undergrads, 7% part-time. 3,079 full-time freshmen.

Selectivity: Admits over 75% of applicants.

BASIC COSTS (2009-2010)

Tuition and fees: $9,060; out-of-state residents $16,368.
Per-credit charge: $380; out-of-state residents $729.
Room and board: $7,670.

FINANCIAL AID PICTURE (2008-2009)

Students with need: Out of 2,659 full-time freshmen who applied for aid, 2,098 were judged to have need. Of these, 2,087 received aid, and 319 had their full need met. Average financial aid package met 77% of need; average scholarship/grant was $6,058; average loan was $5,924. For part-time students, average financial aid package was $10,069.
Students without need: 586 full-time freshmen who did not demonstrate need for aid received scholarships/grants; average award was $2,712. No-need awards available for academics, alumni affiliation, art, athletics, leadership, minority status, music/drama, ROTC, state/district residency.
Scholarships offered: 63 full-time freshmen received athletic scholarships; average amount $15,814.
Cumulative student debt: 72% of graduating class had student loans; average debt was $28,542.

FINANCIAL AID PROCEDURES

Forms required: FAFSA.
Dates and Deadlines: No deadline. Applicants notified on a rolling basis starting 4/15; must reply within 3 week(s) of notification.

CONTACT

Gregory Guzman, Director, Financial Aid
110 McFall Center, Bowling Green, OH 43403-0085
(419) 372-2651

Bowling Green State University: Firelands College

Huron, Ohio
www.firelands.bgsu.edu   Federal Code: 003018

2-year public branch campus college in small town.
Enrollment: 1,917 undergrads.
Selectivity: Open admission.

BASIC COSTS (2009-2010)

Tuition and fees: $4,228; out-of-state residents $11,506.
Per-credit charge: $196; out-of-state residents $501.

FINANCIAL AID PICTURE (2008-2009)

Students with need: Need-based aid available for full-time and part-time students.
Students without need: This college awards aid only to students with need.
Scholarships offered: FOCUS Scholarship (Firelands Opportunities in College for Under-represented Students); full tuition; for historically under-represented students in all Firelands majors; 4-6 awards annually.
Additional info: Scholarship application deadline May 1. Technology computer loan program available. Based on need, students may receive computer on semester by semester loan basis.

FINANCIAL AID PROCEDURES

Forms required: FAFSA.
Dates and Deadlines: Priority date 3/1; no closing date. Applicants notified on a rolling basis starting 4/15; must reply within 2 week(s) of notification.

CONTACT

Debralee Divers, Director of Admissions and Financial Aid
One University Drive, Huron, OH 44839
(419) 433-5560

Bryant & Stratton College: Cleveland

Cleveland, Ohio
www.bryantstratton.edu   Federal Code: 022744

2-year for-profit technical and career college in very large city.
Enrollment: 848 undergrads.
Selectivity: Open admission; but selective for some programs.

BASIC COSTS (2009-2010)

Tuition and fees: $14,670.
Per-credit charge: $489.

FINANCIAL AID PICTURE (2008-2009)

Students with need: Need-based aid available for full-time and part-time students. Work study available nights.
Students without need: No-need awards available for academics.

FINANCIAL AID PROCEDURES

Forms required: FAFSA, institutional form.
Dates and Deadlines: No deadline. Applicants notified on a rolling basis starting 5/1; must reply within 2 week(s) of notification.
Transfers: No deadline. By state regulation, Ohio Institutional Grant can be awarded only 3 times a fiscal year.

CONTACT

Donna McCullough, Director of Financial Services
1700 East 13th Street, Cleveland, OH 44114-3203
(216) 771-1700

Bryant & Stratton College: Eastlake

Eastlake, Ohio
www.bryantstratton.edu   Federal Code: 022744

4-year for-profit business college in small town.
Enrollment: 806 undergrads.
Selectivity: Open admission.

FINANCIAL AID PICTURE (2008-2009)

Students with need: Need-based aid available for full-time and part-time students.
Students without need: No-need awards available for academics.

FINANCIAL AID PROCEDURES

Forms required: FAFSA.
Dates and Deadlines: No deadline. Applicants notified on a rolling basis.

CONTACT

Lisa Patterson, Financial Aid Manager
35350 Curtis Boulevard, Eastlake, OH 44095
(440) 510-1112

Bryant & Stratton College: Parma

Parma, Ohio
www.bryantstratton.edu   Federal Code: 015298

4-year for-profit nursing and junior college in small city.
Enrollment: 662 undergrads, 39% part-time. 177 full-time freshmen.
Selectivity: Open admission; but selective for some programs.

FINANCIAL AID PICTURE (2008-2009)

Students with need: Need-based aid available for full-time and part-time students. Work study available nights.
Students without need: This college awards aid only to students with need.

FINANCIAL AID PROCEDURES

Forms required: FAFSA.

Dates and Deadlines: No deadline. Applicants notified on a rolling basis starting 6/1.

Transfers: Transfer form must be completed for state grant.

CONTACT

Robert Eden, Financial Services Manager
12955 Snow Road, Parma, OH 44130-1013
(216) 265-3151 ext. 223

Capital University
Columbus, Ohio
www.capital.edu   Federal Code: 003023

4-year private university in very large city, affiliated with Evangelical Lutheran Church in America.

Enrollment: 2,519 undergrads, 8% part-time. 610 full-time freshmen.

Selectivity: Admits 50 to 75% of applicants.

BASIC COSTS (2009-2010)

Tuition and fees: $28,480.

Per-credit charge: $950.

Room and board: $7,510.

FINANCIAL AID PICTURE (2008-2009)

Students with need: Need-based aid available for full-time and part-time students. Work study available nights, weekends, and for part-time students.

Students without need: No-need awards available for academics, alumni affiliation, art, minority status, music/drama, religious affiliation, ROTC, state/district residency.

Scholarships offered: Scholarships and grants from $1,000 to full tuition available.

FINANCIAL AID PROCEDURES

Forms required: FAFSA.

Dates and Deadlines: Priority date 2/28; no closing date. Applicants notified on a rolling basis starting 3/1; must reply by 5/1.

Transfers: Priority date 7/15.

CONTACT

Pamela Varda, Director of Financial Aid
1 College and Main, Columbus, OH 43209-2394
(614) 236-6511

Case Western Reserve University
Cleveland, Ohio
www.case.edu   Federal Code: E00077

4-year private university in very large city.

Enrollment: 4,145 undergrads, 2% part-time. 966 full-time freshmen.

Selectivity: Admits 50 to 75% of applicants.

BASIC COSTS (2010-2011)

Tuition and fees: $37,648.

Per-credit charge: $1,554.

Room and board: $11,400.

FINANCIAL AID PICTURE (2009-2010)

Students with need: Out of 749 full-time freshmen who applied for aid, 617 were judged to have need. Of these, 617 received aid, and 563 had their full need met. Average financial aid package met 80% of need; average scholarship/grant was $25,196; average loan was $6,869. Need-based aid available for part-time students.

Students without need: 187 full-time freshmen who did not demonstrate need for aid received scholarships/grants; average award was $18,985. No-need awards available for academics, art, leadership, music/drama.

Cumulative student debt: 61% of graduating class had student loans; average debt was $37,394.

FINANCIAL AID PROCEDURES

Forms required: FAFSA, institutional form.

Dates and Deadlines: Priority date 2/15; no closing date. Applicants notified on a rolling basis starting 3/15; must reply by 5/1 or within 2 week(s) of notification.

Transfers: Priority date 5/15.

CONTACT

Venus Puliafico, Director of University Financial Aid
Wolstein Hall, Cleveland, OH 44106-7055
(216) 368-4530

Cedarville University
Cedarville, Ohio
www.cedarville.edu   Federal Code: 003025

4-year private university and liberal arts college in small town, affiliated with Baptist faith.

Enrollment: 2,926 undergrads, 3% part-time. 849 full-time freshmen.

Selectivity: Admits over 75% of applicants.

BASIC COSTS (2010-2011)

Tuition and fees: $23,500.

Room and board: $5,086.

FINANCIAL AID PICTURE (2008-2009)

Students with need: Out of 685 full-time freshmen who applied for aid, 549 were judged to have need. Of these, 548 received aid, and 101 had their full need met. Average financial aid package met 38% of need; average scholarship/grant was $3,316; average loan was $4,761. For part-time students, average financial aid package was $12,142.

Students without need: 170 full-time freshmen who did not demonstrate need for aid received scholarships/grants; average award was $14,083. No-need awards available for academics, alumni affiliation, athletics, leadership, minority status, music/drama, ROTC, state/district residency.

Scholarships offered: 47 full-time freshmen received athletic scholarships; average amount $3,977.

Cumulative student debt: 67% of graduating class had student loans; average debt was $26,647.

FINANCIAL AID PROCEDURES

Forms required: FAFSA.

Dates and Deadlines: Priority date 3/1; no closing date. Applicants notified on a rolling basis starting 3/1; must reply within 4 week(s) of notification.

Transfers: No deadline. Applicants notified on a rolling basis starting 2/1.

CONTACT

Roscoe Smith, Director of Financial Aid
251 North Main Street, Cedarville, OH 45314-0601
(937) 766-7866

Central Ohio Technical College
Newark, Ohio
www.cotc.edu   Federal Code: 011046

2-year public technical college in large town.

Enrollment: 4,062 undergrads, 46% part-time. 653 full-time freshmen.

Selectivity: Open admission; but selective for some programs.

BASIC COSTS (2009-2010)

Tuition and fees: $3,600; out-of-state residents $6,300.
Per-credit charge: $100; out-of-state residents $175.

FINANCIAL AID PICTURE (2008-2009)

Students with need: 50% of average financial aid package awarded as scholarships/grants, 50% awarded as loans/jobs. Need-based aid available for part-time students. Work study available nights, weekends, and for part-time students.
Students without need: No-need awards available for academics, state/district residency.
Scholarships offered: Presidential Achievement Award; $1,800 annually; based on 3.0 GPA; 5 awarded. Minority Achievement Award; $850 annually; based on 2.5 GPA; 2 awarded.

FINANCIAL AID PROCEDURES

Forms required: FAFSA.
Dates and Deadlines: Priority date 3/1; no closing date. Applicants notified on a rolling basis starting 5/1; must reply within 3 week(s) of notification.

CONTACT

Faith Phillips, Director of Financial Aid
1179 University Drive, Newark, OH 43055
(740) 366-9435

Central State University

Wilberforce, Ohio
www.centralstate.edu   Federal Code: 003026

4-year public university and liberal arts college in rural community.
Enrollment: 2,362 undergrads, 6% part-time. 703 full-time freshmen.
Selectivity: Admits less than 50% of applicants.

BASIC COSTS (2009-2010)

Tuition and fees: $5,294; out-of-state residents $11,806.
Room and board: $7,920.

FINANCIAL AID PICTURE (2009-2010)

Students with need: Need-based aid available for full-time and part-time students. Work study available nights, weekends, and for part-time students.
Students without need: No-need awards available for academics, alumni affiliation, art, athletics, leadership, music/drama, religious affiliation, ROTC.

FINANCIAL AID PROCEDURES

Forms required: FAFSA, institutional form.
Dates and Deadlines: Priority date 2/15; no closing date. Applicants notified on a rolling basis starting 5/1.
Transfers: No deadline.

CONTACT

Sonia Slomba, Director, Student Financial Aid Office
PO Box 1004, Wilberforce, OH 45384-1004
(937) 376-6519

Chatfield College

St. Martin, Ohio
www.chatfield.edu   Federal Code: 010880

2-year private liberal arts college in rural community, affiliated with Roman Catholic Church.
Enrollment: 251 undergrads, 38% part-time. 55 full-time freshmen.
Selectivity: Open admission.

BASIC COSTS (2009-2010)

Tuition and fees: $9,640.
Per-credit charge: $310.

FINANCIAL AID PICTURE

Students with need: Need-based aid available for full-time and part-time students.
Students without need: No-need awards available for academics, leadership.
Additional info: Institutional grants/scholarships given primarily to first-year students to reduce debt load during initial year.

FINANCIAL AID PROCEDURES

Forms required: FAFSA, institutional form.
Dates and Deadlines: Priority date 5/1; closing date 8/3. Applicants notified on a rolling basis starting 4/1; must reply within 2 week(s) of notification.

CONTACT

Zana Smith, Student Financial Services Officer
20918 State Route 251, St. Martin, OH 45118
(513) 875-3344

Cincinnati Christian University

Cincinnati, Ohio
www.ccuniversity.edu   Federal Code: 003029

4-year private university in very large city, affiliated with Church of Christ/Christian Church.
Enrollment: 779 undergrads, 12% part-time. 142 full-time freshmen.
Selectivity: Admits over 75% of applicants.

BASIC COSTS (2010-2011)

Tuition and fees: $13,780.
Per-credit charge: $425.
Room and board: $6,710.

FINANCIAL AID PICTURE (2008-2009)

Students with need: Need-based aid available for full-time and part-time students. Work study available nights, weekends, and for part-time students.
Students without need: No-need awards available for academics, athletics, leadership, music/drama, religious affiliation, state/district residency.

FINANCIAL AID PROCEDURES

Forms required: FAFSA.
Dates and Deadlines: Priority date 3/1; no closing date. Applicants notified on a rolling basis starting 4/1; must reply within 2 week(s) of notification.
Transfers: No deadline.

CONTACT

Michael Gibboney, Financial Aid Director
2700 Glenway Avenue, Cincinnati, OH 45204-3200
(513) 244-8100 ext. 8450

Cincinnati College of Mortuary Science

Cincinnati, Ohio
www.ccms.edu   Federal Code: 010906

4-year private school of mortuary science in large city.
Enrollment: 77 undergrads. 11 full-time freshmen.
Selectivity: Admits over 75% of applicants.

BASIC COSTS (2009-2010)

Per-credit charge: $225.
Additional info: Tuition for 4-qtr. A.A.S. $16,875; 5-qtr. B.M.S. $20,250; 6-qtr. A.A.S. $22,275. Books and supplies for 4 quarter students $1,400; 6 quarter students $1,800; 5th quarter only $100.

FINANCIAL AID PICTURE (2009-2010)

Students with need: Need-based aid available for full-time and part-time students.

Students without need: This college awards aid only to students with need.

FINANCIAL AID PROCEDURES

Forms required: FAFSA.

Dates and Deadlines: Priority date 7/1; no closing date. Applicants notified on a rolling basis starting 3/1; must reply within 2 week(s) of notification.

CONTACT

Gail Warnemunde, Financial Aid Director
645 West North Bend Road, Cincinnati, OH 45224-1428
(513) 618-1926

Cincinnati State Technical and Community College

Cincinnati, Ohio
www.cincinnatistate.edu   Federal Code: 010345

2-year public community and technical college in large city.
Enrollment: 9,289 undergrads, 57% part-time. 1,143 full-time freshmen.
Selectivity: Open admission; but selective for some programs.

BASIC COSTS (2009-2010)

Tuition and fees: $3,867; out-of-state residents $7,476.
Per-credit charge: $80; out-of-state residents $160.

FINANCIAL AID PICTURE (2008-2009)

Students with need: 54% of average financial aid package awarded as scholarships/grants, 46% awarded as loans/jobs. Need-based aid available for part-time students. Work study available nights, weekends, and for part-time students.
Students without need: No-need awards available for academics, athletics, state/district residency.

FINANCIAL AID PROCEDURES

Forms required: FAFSA.

Dates and Deadlines: Priority date 2/15; no closing date. Applicants notified on a rolling basis starting 3/15; must reply within 4 week(s) of notification.

CONTACT

Dawn Smith, Director of Student Financial Aid/Scholarships
3520 Central Parkway, Cincinnati, OH 45223-2690
(513) 569-1530

Clark State Community College

Springfield, Ohio
www.clarkstate.edu   Federal Code: 004852

2-year public community college in small city.
Enrollment: 3,912 undergrads, 53% part-time. 587 full-time freshmen.
Selectivity: Open admission; but selective for some programs.

BASIC COSTS (2009-2010)

Tuition and fees: $3,770; out-of-state residents $7,000.
Per-credit charge: $66; out-of-state residents $131.

FINANCIAL AID PICTURE

Students with need: Work study available nights, weekends, and for part-time students.

FINANCIAL AID PROCEDURES

Forms required: FAFSA.

Dates and Deadlines: Priority date 6/15; no closing date. Applicants notified on a rolling basis.
Transfers: No deadline. Applicants notified on a rolling basis.

CONTACT

Kathy Klay, Director of Financial Aid
Box 570, Springfield, OH 45501-0570
(937) 328-6034

Cleveland Institute of Art

Cleveland, Ohio
www.cia.edu   Federal Code: 003982

4-year private visual arts college in very large city.
Enrollment: 495 undergrads, 1% part-time. 110 full-time freshmen.
Selectivity: Admits over 75% of applicants.

BASIC COSTS (2009-2010)

Tuition and fees: $31,904.
Per-credit charge: $1,250.
Room and board: $10,536.

FINANCIAL AID PICTURE (2009-2010)

Students with need: Average financial aid package met 41% of need; average scholarship/grant was $13,447; average loan was $3,860. For part-time students, average financial aid package was $3,701.
Students without need: No-need awards available for academics, art.

FINANCIAL AID PROCEDURES

Forms required: FAFSA, institutional form.

Dates and Deadlines: Priority date 3/15; no closing date. Applicants notified on a rolling basis starting 3/16; must reply within 4 week(s) of notification.
Transfers: Applicants notified on a rolling basis.

CONTACT

Karen Kopp, Director of Admissions and Financial Aid
11141 East Boulevard, Cleveland, OH 44106-1710
(216) 421-7425

Cleveland Institute of Electronics

Cleveland, Ohio
www.cie-wc.edu   Federal Code: 015382

2-year for-profit technical college in very large city.
Enrollment: 1,738 undergrads.
Selectivity: Open admission.

BASIC COSTS (2010-2011)

Tuition and fees: $3,770.
Additional info: Associate degree tuition $1,885 per 6 month term.

FINANCIAL AID PICTURE (2009-2010)

Students with need: Need-based aid available for full-time students.
Students without need: This college awards aid only to students with need.

FINANCIAL AID PROCEDURES

Forms required: FAFSA.

Dates and Deadlines: No deadline.

CONTACT

Scott Meyer, Director of Financial Aid
1776 East 17th Street, Cleveland, OH 44114-3679
(216) 781-9400

Cleveland Institute of Music
Cleveland, Ohio
www.cim.edu   Federal Code: 003031

4-year private music college in very large city.
Enrollment: 253 undergrads. 45 full-time freshmen.
Selectivity: Admits less than 50% of applicants.

BASIC COSTS (2009-2010)
Tuition and fees: $36,590.
Per-credit charge: $1,406.
Room and board: $10,567.

FINANCIAL AID PICTURE (2008-2009)
Students with need: Out of 31 full-time freshmen who applied for aid, 27 were judged to have need. Of these, 27 received aid, and 14 had their full need met. Average financial aid package met 81% of need; average scholarship/grant was $16,870; average loan was $5,126. For part-time students, average financial aid package was $25,000.
Students without need: 15 full-time freshmen who did not demonstrate need for aid received scholarships/grants; average award was $12,833. No-need awards available for academics, music/drama.
Cumulative student debt: 68% of graduating class had student loans; average debt was $26,355.

FINANCIAL AID PROCEDURES
Forms required: FAFSA.
Dates and Deadlines: Priority date 2/15; no closing date. Applicants notified on a rolling basis starting 4/1; must reply by 5/1 or within 2 week(s) of notification.
Transfers: Applicants notified on a rolling basis starting 4/1; must reply by 5/1 or within 2 week(s) of notification.

CONTACT
Kristie Gripp, Director of Financial Aid
11021 East Boulevard, Cleveland, OH 44106
(216) 795-3192

Cleveland State University
Cleveland, Ohio
www.csuohio.edu   Federal Code: 003032

4-year public university in large city.
Enrollment: 9,805 undergrads, 24% part-time. 1,137 full-time freshmen.
Selectivity: Admits 50 to 75% of applicants.

BASIC COSTS (2010-2011)
Tuition and fees: $8,196; out-of-state residents $11,026.
Per-credit charge: $342; out-of-state residents $459.
Room and board: $10,250.

FINANCIAL AID PICTURE (2009-2010)
Students with need: Out of 811 full-time freshmen who applied for aid, 746 were judged to have need. Of these, 728 received aid, and 45 had their full need met. Average financial aid package met 52% of need; average scholarship/grant was $7,106; average loan was $3,286. For part-time students, average financial aid package was $6,528.
Students without need: 44 full-time freshmen who did not demonstrate need for aid received scholarships/grants; average award was $2,036. No-need awards available for academics, alumni affiliation, art, athletics, leadership, minority status, music/drama, religious affiliation, ROTC.
Scholarships offered: 23 full-time freshmen received athletic scholarships; average amount $9,731.

FINANCIAL AID PROCEDURES
Forms required: FAFSA.

Dates and Deadlines: Priority date 2/15; no closing date. Applicants notified on a rolling basis starting 3/15; must reply within 4 week(s) of notification.

CONTACT
Rachel Schmidt, Director of Financial Aid
2121 Euclid Avenue, Cleveland, OH 44115-2214
(888) 278-6446

College of Mount St. Joseph
Cincinnati, Ohio
www.msj.edu   Federal Code: 003033

4-year private liberal arts college in very large city, affiliated with Roman Catholic Church.
Enrollment: 1,860 undergrads, 28% part-time. 357 full-time freshmen.
Selectivity: Admits 50 to 75% of applicants.

BASIC COSTS (2010-2011)
Tuition and fees: $23,550.
Per-credit charge: $475.
Room and board: $7,392.

FINANCIAL AID PICTURE (2009-2010)
Students with need: Out of 343 full-time freshmen who applied for aid, 307 were judged to have need. Of these, 307 received aid, and 61 had their full need met. Average financial aid package met 81% of need; average scholarship/grant was $14,456; average loan was $4,035. For part-time students, average financial aid package was $7,940.
Students without need: 46 full-time freshmen who did not demonstrate need for aid received scholarships/grants; average award was $10,361. No-need awards available for academics, alumni affiliation, art, leadership, music/drama, ROTC, state/district residency.
Scholarships offered: Presidential Scholarship; $11,000; 26-36 ACT or 1170 SAT. Trustee Scholarship; $10,000; 24-25 ACT or 1090 SAT. Dean's Scholarship; $9,000; 22-23 ACT or 1020 SAT. Merit Award; $7,500; 20-21 ACT or 940 SAT. Challenge Award; $3,500 per semester; 18-19 ACT or 860 SAT. Director's Award; $3,500 per semester; 21 ACT or 990 SAT and 2.75 high school GPA. Transfer Scholarship; $5,000; 3.0 college GPA with at least 24 hours earned. All SAT scores exclusive of Writing.
Cumulative student debt: 86% of graduating class had student loans; average debt was $33,646.

FINANCIAL AID PROCEDURES
Forms required: FAFSA.
Dates and Deadlines: Priority date 3/1; no closing date. Applicants notified on a rolling basis starting 1/31; must reply by 5/1 or within 4 week(s) of notification.
Transfers: Applicants notified on a rolling basis starting 2/15; must reply within 4 week(s) of notification.

CONTACT
Kathryn Kelly, Director of Student Administrative Services
5701 Delhi Road, Cincinnati, OH 45233-1670
(513) 244-4418

College of Wooster
Wooster, Ohio   Federal Code: 003037
www.wooster.edu   CSS Code: 1134

4-year private liberal arts college in large town.
Enrollment: 1,815 undergrads, 1% part-time. 480 full-time freshmen.
Selectivity: Admits 50 to 75% of applicants.

BASIC COSTS (2010-2011)
Tuition and fees: $36,598.
Room and board: $9,070.

FINANCIAL AID PICTURE (2009-2010)

Students with need: Out of 385 full-time freshmen who applied for aid, 313 were judged to have need. Of these, 313 received aid, and 143 had their full need met. Average financial aid package met 89% of need; average scholarship/grant was $23,066; average loan was $3,511. Need-based aid available for part-time students.

Students without need: 136 full-time freshmen who did not demonstrate need for aid received scholarships/grants; average award was $15,650. No-need awards available for academics, minority status, music/drama, religious affiliation, state/district residency.

Cumulative student debt: 58% of graduating class had student loans; average debt was $25,140.

FINANCIAL AID PROCEDURES

Forms required: FAFSA, institutional form. Either CSS PROFILE or institution application from prospective students.

Dates and Deadlines: Priority date 2/15; no closing date. Applicants notified by 4/1; must reply by 5/1.

CONTACT

David Miller, Director of Financial Aid
847 College Avenue, Wooster, OH 44691-2363
(330) 263-2317

Columbus College of Art and Design

Columbus, Ohio
www.ccad.edu
Federal Code: 003039

4-year private visual arts college in very large city.

Enrollment: 1,302 undergrads, 5% part-time. 155 full-time freshmen.

Selectivity: Admits 50 to 75% of applicants.

BASIC COSTS (2010-2011)

Tuition and fees: $24,864.

Per-credit charge: $1,036.

Room and board: $9,410.

FINANCIAL AID PICTURE (2009-2010)

Students with need: Average financial aid package met 56% of need; average scholarship/grant was $13,293; average loan was $3,792. For part-time students, average financial aid package was $14,106.

Students without need: No-need awards available for academics, art, ROTC, state/district residency.

Cumulative student debt: 72% of graduating class had student loans; average debt was $38,196.

FINANCIAL AID PROCEDURES

Forms required: FAFSA.

Dates and Deadlines: Closing date 2/15. Applicants notified on a rolling basis starting 3/15; must reply within 2 week(s) of notification.

CONTACT

Anna Marie Schofield, Director of Financial Aid
60 Cleveland Avenue, Columbus, OH 43215-3875
(614) 222-3274

Columbus State Community College

Columbus, Ohio
www.cscc.edu
Federal Code: 006867

2-year public community and technical college in very large city.

Enrollment: 12,444 undergrads.

Selectivity: Open admission; but selective for some programs.

BASIC COSTS (2009-2010)

Tuition and fees: $3,605; out-of-state residents $7,925.

Per-credit charge: $79; out-of-state residents $175.

FINANCIAL AID PICTURE

Students with need: Need-based aid available for full-time and part-time students. Work study available nights, weekends, and for part-time students.

Students without need: No-need awards available for athletics, state/district residency.

FINANCIAL AID PROCEDURES

Forms required: FAFSA.

Dates and Deadlines: Priority date 7/24; no closing date. Applicants notified on a rolling basis starting 4/1.

CONTACT

David Metz, Director of Financial Aid
550 East Spring Street, Columbus, OH 43216-1609
(614) 287-2648

Cuyahoga Community College: Metropolitan Campus

Cleveland, Ohio
www.tri-c.edu
Federal Code: 003040

2-year public community college in very large city.

Enrollment: 13,820 undergrads, 55% part-time. 2,117 full-time freshmen.

Selectivity: Open admission; but selective for some programs.

BASIC COSTS (2009-2010)

Tuition and fees: $2,416; out-of-district residents $3,194; out-of-state residents $6,541.

Per-credit charge: $73; out-of-district residents $99; out-of-state residents $210.

FINANCIAL AID PICTURE (2009-2010)

Students with need: Average financial aid package met 100% of need; average scholarship/grant was $4,893; average loan was $3,031. For part-time students, average financial aid package was $5,906.

Students without need: No-need awards available for academics, art, athletics, leadership, minority status, music/drama.

Cumulative student debt: 17% of graduating class had student loans; average debt was $8,937.

FINANCIAL AID PROCEDURES

Forms required: FAFSA, institutional form.

Dates and Deadlines: No deadline. Applicants notified on a rolling basis starting 5/8.

Transfers: Priority date 5/10.

CONTACT

Angela Johnson, Campus Director
2900 Community College Avenue, Cleveland, OH 44115-2878
(216) 987-4100

Davis College

Toledo, Ohio
www.daviscollege.edu
Federal Code: 004855

2-year for-profit junior college in large city.

Enrollment: 524 undergrads, 60% part-time. 28 full-time freshmen.

Selectivity: Admits over 75% of applicants.

BASIC COSTS (2009-2010)

Tuition and fees: $11,415.

Per-credit charge: $243.

FINANCIAL AID PICTURE (2008-2009)

Students with need: Need-based aid available for full-time and part-time students. Work study available nights, weekends, and for part-time students.
Students without need: This college awards aid only to students with need.

FINANCIAL AID PROCEDURES

Forms required: FAFSA.
Dates and Deadlines: No deadline. Applicants notified on a rolling basis.

CONTACT

Kelly Parker, Director of Financial Aid
4747 Monroe Street, Toledo, OH 43623
(419) 473-2700

Defiance College

Defiance, Ohio
www.defiance.edu   Federal Code: 003041

4-year private liberal arts college in large town, affiliated with United Church of Christ.
Enrollment: 944 undergrads, 20% part-time. 215 full-time freshmen.
Selectivity: Admits 50 to 75% of applicants.

BASIC COSTS (2010-2011)

Tuition and fees: $24,320.
Per-credit charge: $360.
Room and board: $8,120.
Additional info: Tuition/fee waivers available for adults.

FINANCIAL AID PICTURE (2008-2009)

Students with need: Need-based aid available for full-time and part-time students. Work study available nights, weekends, and for part-time students.
Students without need: No-need awards available for academics, leadership.
Scholarships offered: Presidential Scholar Program; $11,000 to full tuition; based on 3.5 GPA, 27 ACT or 1210 SAT, and interview. Pilgrim Scholar Program; $10,000-$16,000; based on 3.2 GPA, 24 ACT or 1090 SAT, and interview. Achievement Scholar Program; $9,000-$13,000; based on 2.8 GPA, 21 ACT or 980 SAT, and interview. Defiance College Scholarship; $4,000-$10,000; based on 2.5-4.0 GPA and 18-36 ACT or 850-1600 SAT. Citizen Leader Award; $2,000; awarded to students with demonstrated record of service in their communities; application and interview required. Lillian Rae Dunlap Award; $1,000; minimum 2.25 GPA; rewards achievements of underrepresented students.

FINANCIAL AID PROCEDURES

Forms required: FAFSA.
Dates and Deadlines: Priority date 3/1; no closing date. Applicants notified on a rolling basis starting 3/15; must reply within 3 week(s) of notification.

CONTACT

Amy Francis, Director of Financial Aid
701 North Clinton Street, Defiance, OH 43512-1695
(419) 782-458

Denison University

Granville, Ohio
www.denison.edu   Federal Code: 003042

4-year private liberal arts college in small town.
Enrollment: 2,240 undergrads. 649 full-time freshmen.
Selectivity: Admits 50 to 75% of applicants.

BASIC COSTS (2010-2011)

Tuition and fees: $38,220.
Per-credit charge: $1,165.
Room and board: $9,580.
Additional info: Tuition/fee waivers available for adults.

FINANCIAL AID PICTURE (2009-2010)

Students with need: Out of 434 full-time freshmen who applied for aid, 344 were judged to have need. Of these, 344 received aid, and 135 had their full need met. Average financial aid package met 94% of need; average scholarship/grant was $27,128; average loan was $3,954. Need-based aid available for part-time students.
Students without need: 256 full-time freshmen who did not demonstrate need for aid received scholarships/grants; average award was $16,959. No-need awards available for academics, alumni affiliation, art, leadership, minority status, music/drama, state/district residency.

FINANCIAL AID PROCEDURES

Dates and Deadlines: No deadline. Applicants notified on a rolling basis starting 3/28.

CONTACT

Nancy Hoover, Director of Financial Aid and Student Employment
100 West College PO Box B, Granville, OH 43023
(740) 587-6279

DeVry University: Columbus

Columbus, Ohio
www.devry.edu   Federal Code: 003099

4-year for-profit university in very large city.
Enrollment: 2,697 undergrads, 47% part-time. 341 full-time freshmen.

BASIC COSTS (2009-2010)

Tuition and fees: $14,160.
Per-credit charge: $550.

FINANCIAL AID PICTURE (2008-2009)

Students with need: Need-based aid available for full-time and part-time students.
Students without need: This college awards aid only to students with need.

FINANCIAL AID PROCEDURES

Forms required: FAFSA.
Dates and Deadlines: No deadline. Applicants notified on a rolling basis.

CONTACT

Cynthia Price, Director of Financial Aid
1350 Alum Creek Drive, Columbus, OH 43209-2705
(614) 253-7291

Eastern Gateway Community College

Steubenville, Ohio
www.egcc.edu   Federal Code: 007275

2-year public community and technical college in large town.
Enrollment: 2,053 undergrads.
Selectivity: Open admission; but selective for some programs.

BASIC COSTS (2009-2010)

Tuition and fees: $2,790; out-of-district residents $2,970; out-of-state residents $3,780.
Per-credit charge: $90; out-of-district residents $96; out-of-state residents $123.
Additional info: Residents of 5 neighboring West Virginia counties eligible for in-state, out-of-district tuition rates.

FINANCIAL AID PICTURE

Students with need: Need-based aid available for full-time and part-time students. Work study available nights, weekends, and for part-time students.
Students without need: This college awards aid only to students with need.
Scholarships offered: Horizon Grant; two-year tuition scholarship; awarded to all students graduating from a Jefferson County high school with 2.5 GPA; student must enroll full-time for fall semester immediately following high school graduation.

FINANCIAL AID PROCEDURES

Forms required: FAFSA, institutional form.
Dates and Deadlines: Priority date 4/1; no closing date. Applicants notified on a rolling basis starting 6/15.

CONTACT

Kelly Wilson, Director of Student Information and Financial Aid
Jefferson County Campus, Steubenville, OH 43952
(740) 264-5591 ext. 135

Edison State Community College
Piqua, Ohio
www.edisonohio.edu   Federal Code: 012750

2-year public community college in large town.
Enrollment: 2,516 undergrads, 53% part-time. 409 full-time freshmen.
Selectivity: Open admission; but selective for some programs.

BASIC COSTS (2009-2010)
Tuition and fees: $3,570; out-of-state residents $6,660.
Per-credit charge: $119; out-of-state residents $222.

FINANCIAL AID PICTURE
Students with need: Need-based aid available for full-time and part-time students. Work study available nights, weekends, and for part-time students.
Students without need: No-need awards available for academics, athletics, job skills, minority status, state/district residency.

FINANCIAL AID PROCEDURES
Forms required: FAFSA, institutional form.
Dates and Deadlines: Priority date 5/2; no closing date. Applicants notified on a rolling basis starting 5/15.

CONTACT
Kathi Richards, Director of Student Financial Aid
1973 Edison Drive, Piqua, OH 45356-9253
(937) 778-7910

ETI Technical College of Niles
Niles, Ohio
www.eticollege.edu   Federal Code: 030790

2-year for-profit technical college in large city.
Enrollment: 273 undergrads, 33% part-time. 35 full-time freshmen.
Selectivity: Open admission; but selective for some programs.

BASIC COSTS (2009-2010)
Tuition and fees: $7,865.
Per-credit charge: $256.
Additional info: Full-time tuition varies by program. Tuition at time of enrollment locked for 2 years.

FINANCIAL AID PICTURE (2009-2010)

Students with need: Out of 35 full-time freshmen who applied for aid, 35 were judged to have need. Of these, 35 received aid. Average financial aid package met 95% of need; average scholarship/grant was $5,350; average loan was $3,500. For part-time students, average financial aid package was $7,712.
Students without need: No-need awards available for academics.
Cumulative student debt: 75% of graduating class had student loans; average debt was $20,000.

FINANCIAL AID PROCEDURES

Forms required: FAFSA.
Dates and Deadlines: No deadline. Applicants notified on a rolling basis; must reply within 4 week(s) of notification.
Transfers: No deadline. Applicants notified on a rolling basis; must reply within 4 week(s) of notification.

CONTACT

Kay Madigan, Financial Aid Director
2076 Youngstown Warren Road, Niles, OH 44446-4398
(330) 652-9919

Franciscan University of Steubenville
Steubenville, Ohio
www.franciscan.edu   Federal Code: 003036

4-year private university in large town, affiliated with Roman Catholic Church.
Enrollment: 2,034 undergrads.
Selectivity: Admits 50 to 75% of applicants.

BASIC COSTS (2009-2010)
Tuition and fees: $19,650.
Per-credit charge: $645.
Room and board: $6,750.

FINANCIAL AID PICTURE (2008-2009)
Students with need: Need-based aid available for full-time and part-time students. Work study available nights, weekends, and for part-time students.
Students without need: No-need awards available for academics, leadership, religious affiliation.

FINANCIAL AID PROCEDURES
Forms required: FAFSA.
Dates and Deadlines: No deadline. Applicants notified on a rolling basis starting 3/15; must reply within 3 week(s) of notification.
Transfers: Closing date 8/1.

CONTACT
John Herrmann, Director of Student Financial Services
1235 University Boulevard, Steubenville, OH 43952-1763
(740) 283-6211

Franklin University
Columbus, Ohio
www.franklin.edu   Federal Code: 003046

4-year private university and business college in very large city.
Enrollment: 7,014 undergrads, 63% part-time. 253 full-time freshmen.
Selectivity: Open admission; but selective for some programs.

BASIC COSTS (2009-2010)
Tuition and fees: $8,940.
Per-credit charge: $298.

FINANCIAL AID PICTURE (2008-2009)
Students with need: Need-based aid available for full-time and part-time students.

Students without need: No-need awards available for academics, leadership, minority status.

FINANCIAL AID PROCEDURES

Forms required: FAFSA.

Dates and Deadlines: Priority date 6/15; no closing date. Applicants notified on a rolling basis; must reply within 2 week(s) of notification.

Transfers: One scholarship specifically for transfer students: Transfer Achievement.

CONTACT

Goldie Langley, Director of Financial Aid

201 South Grant Avenue, Columbus, OH 43215-5399

(614) 797-4700

Gallipolis Career College

Gallipolis, Ohio

www.gallipoliscareercollege.com   Federal Code: 030079

2-year for-profit business and technical college in small town.

Enrollment: 162 undergrads, 9% part-time. 41 full-time freshmen.

Selectivity: Open admission.

BASIC COSTS (2010-2011)

Tuition and fees: $9,650.

Per-credit charge: $200.

Additional info: Tuition at time of enrollment locked for 2 years.

FINANCIAL AID PICTURE (2008-2009)

Students with need: 57% of average financial aid package awarded as scholarships/grants, 43% awarded as loans/jobs. Need-based aid available for part-time students.

Students without need: This college awards aid only to students with need.

FINANCIAL AID PROCEDURES

Forms required: FAFSA, institutional form.

Dates and Deadlines: No deadline.

CONTACT

Jeanette Shirey, Financial Aid Administrator

1176 Jackson Pike, Suite 312, Gallipolis, OH 45631

(740) 446-4367

God's Bible School and College

Cincinnati, Ohio

www.gbs.edu   Federal Code: 015691

4-year private Bible college in large city, affiliated with interdenominational tradition.

Enrollment: 264 undergrads.

BASIC COSTS (2009-2010)

Tuition and fees: $5,580.

Per-credit charge: $185.

Room and board: $3,450.

FINANCIAL AID PICTURE (2009-2010)

Students with need: Need-based aid available for full-time and part-time students.

Students without need: No-need awards available for academics, leadership, music/drama, religious affiliation.

Additional info: Institutional work scholarships available.

FINANCIAL AID PROCEDURES

Forms required: FAFSA.

Dates and Deadlines: Priority date 4/30; no closing date. Applicants notified on a rolling basis.

CONTACT

Stephen Buckland, Director of Financial Aid

1810 Young Street, Cincinnati, OH 45202-6838

(513) 721-7944 ext. 205

Heidelberg University

Tiffin, Ohio

www.heidelberg.edu   Federal Code: 003048

4-year private liberal arts college in large town, affiliated with United Church of Christ.

Enrollment: 1,271 undergrads, 7% part-time. 364 full-time freshmen.

Selectivity: Admits 50 to 75% of applicants.

BASIC COSTS (2010-2011)

Tuition and fees: $22,780.

Room and board: $8,636.

FINANCIAL AID PICTURE (2009-2010)

Students with need: Out of 356 full-time freshmen who applied for aid, 327 were judged to have need. Of these, 327 received aid, and 47 had their full need met. Average financial aid package met 80% of need; average scholarship/grant was $14,695; average loan was $4,143. Need-based aid available for part-time students.

Students without need: 42 full-time freshmen who did not demonstrate need for aid received scholarships/grants; average award was $9,660. No-need awards available for academics, music/drama, religious affiliation, state/district residency.

Cumulative student debt: 90% of graduating class had student loans; average debt was $35,397.

FINANCIAL AID PROCEDURES

Forms required: FAFSA.

Dates and Deadlines: Priority date 3/1; no closing date. Applicants notified on a rolling basis starting 3/1; must reply by 5/1 or within 2 week(s) of notification.

Transfers: No deadline. Applicants notified on a rolling basis starting 3/1; must reply by 5/1 or within 2 week(s) of notification.

CONTACT

Juli Weininger, Director of Financial Aid

310 East Market Street, Tiffin, OH 44883-2462

(419) 448-2293

Hiram College

Hiram, Ohio

www.hiram.edu   Federal Code: 003049

4-year private liberal arts college in rural community, affiliated with Christian Church (Disciples of Christ).

Enrollment: 1,339 undergrads, 11% part-time. 296 full-time freshmen.

Selectivity: Admits over 75% of applicants.

BASIC COSTS (2009-2010)

Tuition and fees: $27,135.

Room and board: $9,010.

FINANCIAL AID PICTURE (2009-2010)

Students with need: Need-based aid available for full-time and part-time students. Work study available nights, weekends, and for part-time students.

Students without need: No-need awards available for academics, alumni affiliation, music/drama, religious affiliation, state/district residency.

FINANCIAL AID PROCEDURES

Forms required: FAFSA.

Dates and Deadlines: Priority date 2/15; no closing date. Applicants notified on a rolling basis starting 2/15; must reply by 5/1 or within 2 week(s) of notification.

Transfers: Transfer merit scholarships available. Phi Theta Kappa scholarships available.

CONTACT

Andrea Caputo, Director of Student Financial Aid
Teachout Price Hall, Hiram, OH 44234
(330) 569-5107

Hocking College

Nelsonville, Ohio
www.hocking.edu   Federal Code: 007598

2-year public technical college in small town.

Enrollment: 4,504 undergrads, 22% part-time. 1,017 full-time freshmen.

Selectivity: Open admission; but selective for some programs.

BASIC COSTS (2009-2010)

Tuition and fees: $3,672; out-of-state residents $6,192.

Per-credit charge: $98; out-of-state residents $197.

FINANCIAL AID PICTURE (2008-2009)

Students with need: Need-based aid available for full-time and part-time students. Work study available nights, weekends, and for part-time students.

Students without need: No-need awards available for academics, minority status, state/district residency.

FINANCIAL AID PROCEDURES

Forms required: FAFSA, institutional form.

Dates and Deadlines: Priority date 2/28; no closing date. Applicants notified on a rolling basis starting 4/15.

Transfers: Non-entitlement aid awarded on first-come, first-served basis.

CONTACT

Roger Springer, Financial Services Director
3301 Hocking Parkway, Nelsonville, OH 45764-9704
(740) 753-7080

Hondros College

Westerville, Ohio
www.hondros.edu   Federal Code: 040743

2-year for-profit nursing college in very large city.

Enrollment: 860 undergrads.

Selectivity: Open admission; but selective for some programs.

BASIC COSTS (2009-2010)

Tuition and fees: $9,550.

Per-credit charge: $210.

FINANCIAL AID PICTURE (2008-2009)

Students with need: 37% of average financial aid package awarded as scholarships/grants, 63% awarded as loans/jobs.

FINANCIAL AID PROCEDURES

Transfers: No deadline. Applicants notified on a rolling basis.

CONTACT

Christopher Harris, Director of Financial Aid
4140 Executive Parkway, Westerville, OH 43081-3855
(614) 508-7200

International College of Broadcasting

Dayton, Ohio
www.icbcollege.com   Federal Code: 013132

2-year for-profit technical college in small city.

Enrollment: 110 undergrads.

Selectivity: Open admission.

BASIC COSTS (2009-2010)

Tuition and fees: $11,200.

FINANCIAL AID PICTURE

Students with need: Need-based aid available for full-time and part-time students.

FINANCIAL AID PROCEDURES

Forms required: FAFSA.

Dates and Deadlines: No deadline. Applicants notified on a rolling basis starting 11/1.

CONTACT

Zena Williams, Financial Aid Director
6 South Smithville Road, Dayton, OH 45431
(937) 258-8251 ext. 203

James A. Rhodes State College

Lima, Ohio
www.rhodesstate.edu   Federal Code: 010027

2-year public nursing and technical college in large town.

Enrollment: 3,930 undergrads, 41% part-time.

Selectivity: Open admission; but selective for some programs.

BASIC COSTS (2010-2011)

Tuition and fees: $4,253; out-of-state residents $8,407.

Per-credit charge: $92; out-of-state residents $185.

FINANCIAL AID PICTURE (2008-2009)

Students with need: Need-based aid available for full-time and part-time students. Work study available nights, weekends, and for part-time students.

Students without need: No-need awards available for academics.

FINANCIAL AID PROCEDURES

Forms required: FAFSA.

Dates and Deadlines: Priority date 2/15; no closing date. Applicants notified on a rolling basis starting 5/1; must reply within 2 week(s) of notification.

CONTACT

Cathy Kohli, Director of Financial Aid
4240 Campus Drive, PS 148, Lima, OH 45804-3597
(419) 995-8800

John Carroll University

University Heights, Ohio
www.jcu.edu   Federal Code: 003050

4-year private university in large town, affiliated with Roman Catholic Church.

Enrollment: 2,957 undergrads, 2% part-time. 661 full-time freshmen.

Selectivity: Admits over 75% of applicants.

BASIC COSTS (2009-2010)

Tuition and fees: $28,840.

Per-credit charge: $846.

Room and board: $8,330.

FINANCIAL AID PICTURE (2009-2010)

Students with need: Out of 563 full-time freshmen who applied for aid, 491 were judged to have need. Of these, 491 received aid, and 110 had their full need met. Average financial aid package met 85% of need; average scholarship/grant was $17,877; average loan was $3,975. For part-time students, average financial aid package was $10,083.

Students without need: 145 full-time freshmen who did not demonstrate need for aid received scholarships/grants; average award was $10,462. No-need awards available for academics, alumni affiliation, leadership, minority status, ROTC, state/district residency.

Cumulative student debt: 74% of graduating class had student loans; average debt was $28,830.

Additional info: Institutional form for need analysis required from upperclassmen and transfer students only.

FINANCIAL AID PROCEDURES

Forms required: FAFSA.

Dates and Deadlines: Priority date 2/15; closing date 3/15. Applicants notified on a rolling basis starting 2/1; must reply by 5/1 or within 4 week(s) of notification.

Transfers: Renewable scholarships for students transferring from local community colleges.

CONTACT

Claudia Wenzel, Director of Financial Aid
20700 North Park Boulevard, University Heights, OH 44118-4581
(216) 397-4248

Kaplan College: Columbus

Columbus, Ohio
www.kc-columbus.com   Federal Code: 011005

2-year for-profit health science and technical and career college in very large city.

Enrollment: 500 undergrads. 150 full-time freshmen.

Selectivity: Open admission.

BASIC COSTS (2009-2010)

Additional info: Tuition varies per program, but averages $11,952 per academic year.

FINANCIAL AID PICTURE

Students with need: Need-based aid available for full-time and part-time students. Work study available nights.

Students without need: This college awards aid only to students with need.

FINANCIAL AID PROCEDURES

Forms required: FAFSA, institutional form.

Dates and Deadlines: No deadline. Applicants notified on a rolling basis.

CONTACT

Nicole Morgan, Director of Financial Aid
2745 Winchester Pike, Columbus, OH 43232
(614) 456-4600

Kaplan College: Dayton

Dayton, Ohio
www.kc_dayton.com   Federal Code: 020520

2-year for-profit technical college in very large city.

Enrollment: 654 undergrads.

Selectivity: Open admission; but selective for some programs.

BASIC COSTS (2009-2010)

Additional info: Tuition varies by program.

FINANCIAL AID PICTURE

Students with need: Need-based aid available for full-time and part-time students.

FINANCIAL AID PROCEDURES

Forms required: FAFSA, institutional form.

Dates and Deadlines: No deadline. Applicants notified on a rolling basis starting 3/1.

CONTACT

Deidre Vance, Director of Financial Aid
2800 East River Road, Dayton, OH 45439
(937) 294-6155

Kent State University

Kent, Ohio
www.kent.edu   Federal Code: 003051

4-year public university in large town.

Enrollment: 19,337 undergrads, 10% part-time. 4,029 full-time freshmen.

Selectivity: Admits 50 to 75% of applicants.

BASIC COSTS (2009-2010)

Tuition and fees: $8,726; out-of-state residents $16,418.

Per-credit charge: $397; out-of-state residents $747.

Room and board: $7,940.

FINANCIAL AID PICTURE (2009-2010)

Students with need: Out of 3,347 full-time freshmen who applied for aid, 2,648 were judged to have need. Of these, 2,642 received aid, and 1,150 had their full need met. Average financial aid package met 56% of need; average scholarship/grant was $6,248; average loan was $3,217. For part-time students, average financial aid package was $6,740.

Students without need: 681 full-time freshmen who did not demonstrate need for aid received scholarships/grants; average award was $3,609. No-need awards available for academics, alumni affiliation, art, athletics, leadership, minority status, music/drama, ROTC, state/district residency.

Scholarships offered: *Merit:* Trustee Scholarship; $1,000-$2,500 annually; based on 3.25 GPA, ACT scores, leadership activities; 500 available. *Athletic:* 34 full-time freshmen received athletic scholarships; average amount $13,586.

Cumulative student debt: 75% of graduating class had student loans; average debt was $26,698.

Additional info: Participant in US Department of Education's Quality Assurance Program and Experimental Sites Program.

FINANCIAL AID PROCEDURES

Forms required: FAFSA.

Dates and Deadlines: Priority date 3/1; no closing date. Applicants notified on a rolling basis starting 3/15; must reply within 2 week(s) of notification.

CONTACT

Mark Evans, Director of Student Financial Aid
PO Box 5190, Kent, OH 44242-0001
(330) 672-2972

Kent State University: Ashtabula

Ashtabula, Ohio
www.ashtabula.kent.edu   Federal Code: 003051

2-year public branch campus college in large town.

Enrollment: 2,076 undergrads, 45% part-time. 289 full-time freshmen.

Selectivity: Open admission; but selective for some programs.

BASIC COSTS (2009-2010)

Tuition and fees: $4,938; out-of-state residents $12,630.
Per-credit charge: $225; out-of-state residents $575.

FINANCIAL AID PICTURE (2009-2010)

Students with need: Out of 262 full-time freshmen who applied for aid, 240 were judged to have need. Of these, 239 received aid, and 50 had their full need met. Average financial aid package met 51% of need; average scholarship/grant was $5,084; average loan was $3,322. For part-time students, average financial aid package was $6,539.

Students without need: 7 full-time freshmen who did not demonstrate need for aid received scholarships/grants; average award was $1,971. No-need awards available for academics, alumni affiliation, art, athletics, job skills, leadership, minority status, music/drama, ROTC, state/district residency.

FINANCIAL AID PROCEDURES

Forms required: FAFSA.
Dates and Deadlines: Priority date 3/1; no closing date. Applicants notified on a rolling basis starting 3/15; must reply within 2 week(s) of notification.

CONTACT

Robyn Gifford, Academic Advisor
3300 Lake Road West, Ashtabula, OH 44004
(440) 964-3322

Kent State University: East Liverpool

East Liverpool, Ohio
www.kenteliv.kent.edu   Federal Code: 003051

2-year public branch campus college in large town.
Enrollment: 1,073 undergrads, 35% part-time. 134 full-time freshmen.
Selectivity: Open admission; but selective for some programs.

BASIC COSTS (2009-2010)

Tuition and fees: $4,938; out-of-state residents $12,630.
Per-credit charge: $225; out-of-state residents $575.

FINANCIAL AID PICTURE (2009-2010)

Students with need: Out of 126 full-time freshmen who applied for aid, 115 were judged to have need. Of these, 115 received aid, and 26 had their full need met. Average financial aid package met 47% of need; average scholarship/grant was $4,753; average loan was $2,920. For part-time students, average financial aid package was $6,673.

Students without need: 2 full-time freshmen who did not demonstrate need for aid received scholarships/grants; average award was $2,423. No-need awards available for academics, alumni affiliation, art, athletics, leadership, minority status, music/drama, ROTC, state/district residency.

FINANCIAL AID PROCEDURES

Forms required: FAFSA.
Dates and Deadlines: Priority date 3/1; no closing date. Applicants notified on a rolling basis starting 3/15; must reply within 2 week(s) of notification.

CONTACT

Beth Allison-Christy, Administrative Assistant
400 East Fourth Street, East Liverpool, OH 43920
(330) 385-3805

Kent State University: Geauga

Burton, Ohio
www.geauga.kent.edu   Federal Code: 003059

2-year public branch campus college in rural community.
Enrollment: 1,763 undergrads, 37% part-time. 170 full-time freshmen.
Selectivity: Open admission; but selective for some programs.

BASIC COSTS (2009-2010)

Tuition and fees: $4,938; out-of-state residents $12,630.
Per-credit charge: $225; out-of-state residents $575.

FINANCIAL AID PICTURE (2009-2010)

Students with need: Out of 121 full-time freshmen who applied for aid, 105 were judged to have need. Of these, 104 received aid, and 42 had their full need met. Average financial aid package met 47% of need; average scholarship/grant was $4,053; average loan was $3,019. For part-time students, average financial aid package was $5,839.

Students without need: 3 full-time freshmen who did not demonstrate need for aid received scholarships/grants; average award was $167. No-need awards available for academics, alumni affiliation, art, athletics, leadership, minority status, music/drama, ROTC, state/district residency.

FINANCIAL AID PROCEDURES

Forms required: FAFSA.
Dates and Deadlines: Priority date 3/1; no closing date. Must reply within 2 week(s) of notification.

CONTACT

Donna Holcomb, Financial Aid Advisor
Office of Admissions, Burton, OH 44021
(440) 834-8846

Kent State University: Salem

Salem, Ohio
www.salem.kent.edu   Federal Code: 003061

2-year public branch campus college in large town.
Enrollment: 1,475 undergrads, 25% part-time. 265 full-time freshmen.
Selectivity: Open admission; but selective for some programs.

BASIC COSTS (2009-2010)

Tuition and fees: $4,938; out-of-state residents $12,630.
Per-credit charge: $225; out-of-state residents $575.

FINANCIAL AID PICTURE (2009-2010)

Students with need: Out of 236 full-time freshmen who applied for aid, 215 were judged to have need. Of these, 213 received aid, and 62 had their full need met. Average financial aid package met 49% of need; average scholarship/grant was $4,766; average loan was $3,078. For part-time students, average financial aid package was $6,036.

Students without need: No-need awards available for academics, alumni affiliation, art, athletics, leadership, minority status, music/drama, ROTC.

Cumulative student debt: 78% of graduating class had student loans; average debt was $23,058.

FINANCIAL AID PROCEDURES

Forms required: FAFSA.
Dates and Deadlines: Priority date 3/1; no closing date. Applicants notified on a rolling basis starting 3/15; must reply within 2 week(s) of notification.
Transfers: Priority date 2/15.

CONTACT

Judy Heisler, Administrative Clerk
2491 State Route 45 South, Salem, OH 44460
(330) 332-0361

Kent State University: Stark

Canton, Ohio
www.stark.kent.edu   Federal Code: 003054

2-year public branch campus college in small city.
Enrollment: 4,082 undergrads, 29% part-time. 663 full-time freshmen.
Selectivity: Open admission; but selective for some programs.

BASIC COSTS (2009-2010)
Tuition and fees: $4,938; out-of-state residents $12,630.
Per-credit charge: $225; out-of-state residents $575.

FINANCIAL AID PICTURE (2009-2010)
Students with need: Out of 530 full-time freshmen who applied for aid, 457 were judged to have need. Of these, 456 received aid, and 158 had their full need met. Average financial aid package met 56% of need; average scholarship/grant was $4,401; average loan was $2,913. For part-time students, average financial aid package was $6,022.
Students without need: 22 full-time freshmen who did not demonstrate need for aid received scholarships/grants; average award was $2,080. No-need awards available for academics, alumni affiliation, art, athletics, leadership, minority status, music/drama, ROTC, state/district residency.

FINANCIAL AID PROCEDURES
Forms required: FAFSA.
Dates and Deadlines: Priority date 3/1; no closing date. Applicants notified on a rolling basis starting 3/15; must reply within 2 week(s) of notification.

CONTACT
Nina Antram, Financial Aid Officer
6000 Frank Avenue NW, Canton, OH 44720-7599
(330) 535-3377

Kent State University: Trumbull
Warren, Ohio
www.trumbull.kent.edu   Federal Code: 003051

2-year public branch campus college in small city.
Enrollment: 2,500 undergrads, 35% part-time. 352 full-time freshmen.
Selectivity: Open admission; but selective for some programs.

BASIC COSTS (2009-2010)
Tuition and fees: $4,938; out-of-state residents $12,630.
Per-credit charge: $225; out-of-state residents $575.

FINANCIAL AID PICTURE (2009-2010)
Students with need: Out of 304 full-time freshmen who applied for aid, 277 were judged to have need. Of these, 275 received aid, and 85 had their full need met. Average financial aid package met 50% of need; average scholarship/grant was $5,192; average loan was $2,932. For part-time students, average financial aid package was $6,502.
Students without need: 2 full-time freshmen who did not demonstrate need for aid received scholarships/grants; average award was $2,000. No-need awards available for academics, alumni affiliation, art, athletics, leadership, minority status, music/drama, ROTC, state/district residency.

FINANCIAL AID PROCEDURES
Forms required: FAFSA.
Dates and Deadlines: Priority date 3/1; no closing date. Applicants notified on a rolling basis starting 3/15; must reply within 2 week(s) of notification.

CONTACT
Sarah Helmick, Financial Aid Advisor
4314 Mahoning Avenue, NW, Warren, OH 44483-1998
(330) 847-0571

Kent State University: Tuscarawas
New Philadelphia, Ohio
www.tusc.kent.edu   Federal Code: 003051

2-year public branch campus college in large town.
Enrollment: 2,126 undergrads, 36% part-time. 384 full-time freshmen.
Selectivity: Open admission; but selective for some programs and for out-of-state students.

BASIC COSTS (2009-2010)
Tuition and fees: $4,938; out-of-state residents $12,630.
Per-credit charge: $225; out-of-state residents $575.

FINANCIAL AID PICTURE (2009-2010)
Students with need: Out of 336 full-time freshmen who applied for aid, 304 were judged to have need. Of these, 301 received aid, and 43 had their full need met. Average financial aid package met 51% of need; average scholarship/grant was $4,973; average loan was $3,080. For part-time students, average financial aid package was $6,338.
Students without need: 4 full-time freshmen who did not demonstrate need for aid received scholarships/grants; average award was $1,125. No-need awards available for academics, alumni affiliation, art, athletics, leadership, minority status, music/drama, ROTC.

FINANCIAL AID PROCEDURES
Forms required: FAFSA.
Dates and Deadlines: Closing date 3/1. Applicants notified on a rolling basis starting 3/15; must reply within 2 week(s) of notification.
Transfers: Financial aid transcripts from all previous institutions required.

CONTACT
Dawn Plug, Financial Aid Coordinator
330 University Drive Northeast, New Philadelphia, OH 44663-9403
(330) 339-3391 ext. 47474

Kenyon College
Gambier, Ohio   Federal Code: 003065
www.kenyon.edu   CSS Code: 1370

4-year private liberal arts college in rural community.
Enrollment: 1,616 undergrads. 470 full-time freshmen.
Selectivity: Admits less than 50% of applicants.

BASIC COSTS (2010-2011)
Tuition and fees: $40,900.
Room and board: $9,500.

FINANCIAL AID PICTURE (2009-2010)
Students with need: Out of 281 full-time freshmen who applied for aid, 212 were judged to have need. Of these, 212 received aid, and 108 had their full need met. Average financial aid package met 98% of need; average scholarship/grant was $28,858; average loan was $3,389.
Students without need: 45 full-time freshmen who did not demonstrate need for aid received scholarships/grants; average award was $10,403. No-need awards available for academics, leadership, minority status.
Scholarships offered: Honor Scholarships, Science Scholarships, Trustee Opportunity Scholarships; averages around $16,000 a year; competitively based on excellence in academic achievement, extracurricular leadership, and community involvement. Distinguished Academic Scholarships; $2,000-$10,000; based on academic accomplishment, standardized test results, and extracurricular achievement. Scholarships for National Merit finalists available.
Cumulative student debt: 58% of graduating class had student loans; average debt was $19,934.

FINANCIAL AID PROCEDURES
Forms required: FAFSA, CSS PROFILE.
Dates and Deadlines: Closing date 2/15. Applicants notified by 4/1; must reply by 5/1.
Transfers: Closing date 4/15. Applicants notified by 5/15; must reply by 6/1.

CONTACT
Craig Daugherty, Director of Financial Aid
Ransom Hall, Gambier, OH 43022-9623
(740) 427-5430

PART III: FINANCIAL AID COLLEGE BY COLLEGE

Kettering College of Medical Arts
Kettering, Ohio
www.kcma.edu   Federal Code: 007035

4-year private health science and nursing college in large city, affiliated with Seventh-day Adventists.

Enrollment: 785 undergrads, 40% part-time. 76 full-time freshmen.

Selectivity: Admits 50 to 75% of applicants.

BASIC COSTS (2010-2011)
Tuition and fees: $10,980.

Per-credit charge: $366.

Room only: $3,140.

Additional info: $175 program fee per semester for areas of study with clinical requirements.

FINANCIAL AID PICTURE
Students with need: Need-based aid available for full-time and part-time students.

Students without need: No-need awards available for academics.

FINANCIAL AID PROCEDURES
Forms required: FAFSA, institutional form.

Dates and Deadlines: Priority date 3/31; no closing date. Applicants notified on a rolling basis starting 5/15; must reply within 3 week(s) of notification.

CONTACT
Kim Snell, Director of Student Finance

3737 Southern Boulevard, Kettering, OH 45429-1299

(937) 296-7210

Lourdes College
Sylvania, Ohio
www.lourdes.edu   Federal Code: 003069

4-year private liberal arts college in large town, affiliated with Roman Catholic Church.

Enrollment: 1,789 undergrads, 44% part-time. 114 full-time freshmen.

Selectivity: Admits over 75% of applicants.

BASIC COSTS (2010-2011)
Tuition and fees: $15,870.

Per-credit charge: $466.

FINANCIAL AID PICTURE (2009-2010)
Students with need: Out of 109 full-time freshmen who applied for aid, 92 were judged to have need. Of these, 92 received aid. For part-time students, average financial aid package was $6,700.

Students without need: No-need awards available for academics, art, minority status, state/district residency.

FINANCIAL AID PROCEDURES
Forms required: FAFSA.

Dates and Deadlines: Priority date 3/1; no closing date. Applicants notified on a rolling basis starting 3/1; must reply within 4 week(s) of notification.

CONTACT
Denise McCluskey, Director of Financial Aid

6832 Convent Boulevard, Sylvania, OH 43560-2898

(419) 824-3732

Malone University
Canton, Ohio
www.malone.edu   Federal Code: 003072

4-year private university in small city, affiliated with Evangelical Friends Church-Eastern Region.

Enrollment: 2,097 undergrads, 12% part-time. 478 full-time freshmen.

Selectivity: Admits 50 to 75% of applicants.

BASIC COSTS (2010-2011)
Tuition and fees: $22,444.

Per-credit charge: $425.

Room and board: $7,548.

FINANCIAL AID PICTURE (2009-2010)
Students with need: Out of 445 full-time freshmen who applied for aid, 414 were judged to have need. Of these, 414 received aid, and 75 had their full need met. Average financial aid package met 78% of need; average scholarship/grant was $15,254; average loan was $3,701. For part-time students, average financial aid package was $7,000.

Students without need: 53 full-time freshmen who did not demonstrate need for aid received scholarships/grants; average award was $8,561. No-need awards available for academics, alumni affiliation, athletics, leadership, music/drama, religious affiliation.

Scholarships offered: 21 full-time freshmen received athletic scholarships; average amount $4,200.

Cumulative student debt: 81% of graduating class had student loans; average debt was $25,655.

Additional info: Prepayment discounts and employer deferred payments available for students in adult degree-completion programs. Employer deferred payment plan is available for traditional undergraduate students.

FINANCIAL AID PROCEDURES
Forms required: FAFSA.

Dates and Deadlines: Priority date 3/1; closing date 7/31. Applicants notified on a rolling basis starting 3/1; must reply within 2 week(s) of notification.

CONTACT
Pamela Pustay, Director of Financial Aid

2600 Cleveland Avenue NW, Canton, OH 44709-3897

(330) 471-8100 ext. 8159

Marietta College
Marietta, Ohio
www.marietta.edu   Federal Code: 003073

4-year private liberal arts college in large town.

Enrollment: 1,470 undergrads, 3% part-time. 386 full-time freshmen.

Selectivity: Admits over 75% of applicants.

BASIC COSTS (2009-2010)
Tuition and fees: $27,066.

Room and board: $8,046.

FINANCIAL AID PICTURE (2009-2010)
Students with need: Out of 371 full-time freshmen who applied for aid, 320 were judged to have need. Of these, 320 received aid, and 168 had their full need met. Average financial aid package met 94% of need; average scholarship/grant was $14,468; average loan was $2,705. For part-time students, average financial aid package was $13,412.

Students without need: 51 full-time freshmen who did not demonstrate need for aid received scholarships/grants; average award was $10,231. No-need awards available for academics, alumni affiliation, art, leadership, minority status, music/drama, state/district residency.

Scholarships offered: McCoy Scholarship; full tuition, room/board. Trustees' Scholarships; full tuition; up to 10 awarded. President's Scholarship; half tuition; up to 20 awarded. Dean's Awards; $6,000-$10,000. Rickey Physics Scholarships; $18,000. Charles Sumner Harrison Awards; $5,000; for multicultural students and leaders. Fine Arts Awards; $1,000-$3,000; audition/portfolio required. All scholarships renewable for four years.

Additional info: Auditions/portfolios for art, creative writing, music and theater required for competitive fine art scholarships.

FINANCIAL AID PROCEDURES

Forms required: FAFSA, institutional form.

Dates and Deadlines: Priority date 3/1; closing date 4/15. Applicants notified on a rolling basis starting 3/15; must reply by 5/1 or within 2 week(s) of notification.

Transfers: Priority date 4/15; closing date 6/15. Applicants notified on a rolling basis starting 4/1; must reply by 6/30 or within 2 week(s) of notification.

CONTACT

Kevin Lamb, Director of Student Financial Services
215 Fifth Street, Marietta, OH 45750-4005
(740) 376-4712

Marion Technical College
Marion, Ohio
www.mtc.edu   Federal Code: 010736

2-year public community and technical college in large town.
Enrollment: 2,210 undergrads.
Selectivity: Open admission; but selective for some programs.

BASIC COSTS (2009-2010)
Tuition and fees: $3,636; out-of-state residents $5,568.
Per-credit charge: $83; out-of-state residents $237.

FINANCIAL AID PICTURE (2009-2010)
Students with need: Need-based aid available for full-time and part-time students.
Students without need: No-need awards available for academics, leadership, minority status.
Scholarships offered: Foundation Scholarship; first year full tuition; for applicants in top 5% of class. President's Scholarship; $1,200; for applicants in top 50% of class. Tech Prep Scholarship; $1,200; for graduates of Tech Prep program. All scholarships require 2.5 GPA and successful completion of proficiency exams.

FINANCIAL AID PROCEDURES
Forms required: FAFSA, institutional form.
Dates and Deadlines: Closing date 5/1. Applicants notified on a rolling basis.
Transfers: No deadline. Applicants notified on a rolling basis.

CONTACT
Deb Langdon, Coordinator of Financial Aid
1467 Mt. Vernon Avenue, Marion, OH 43302-5694
(740) 389-4636 ext. 334

MedCentral College of Nursing
Mansfield, Ohio
www.medcentral.edu   Federal Code: 035864

4-year private nursing college in small city.
Enrollment: 373 undergrads, 4% part-time. 83 full-time freshmen.

BASIC COSTS (2009-2010)
Tuition and fees: $13,765.
Per-credit charge: $450.
Room only: $5,385.

FINANCIAL AID PICTURE (2008-2009)
Students with need: 29% of average financial aid package awarded as scholarships/grants, 71% awarded as loans/jobs. Need-based aid available for part-time students. Work study available nights, weekends, and for part-time students.
Students without need: No-need awards available for academics, leadership.

FINANCIAL AID PROCEDURES
Forms required: FAFSA, institutional form.
Dates and Deadlines: Priority date 4/2; closing date 9/15. Applicants notified on a rolling basis starting 4/1; must reply by 5/1 or within 2 week(s) of notification.
Transfers: Closing date 4/1. Applicants notified on a rolling basis starting 3/15; must reply by 5/1 or within 2 week(s) of notification.

CONTACT
Allen Wright, Director of Financial Aid
335 Glessner Avenue, Mansfield, OH 44903-2265
(419) 520-2600

Mercy College of Northwest Ohio
Toledo, Ohio
www.mercycollege.edu   Federal Code: 030970

4-year private health science and nursing college in large city, affiliated with Roman Catholic Church.
Enrollment: 1,042 undergrads, 48% part-time. 56 full-time freshmen.
Selectivity: Admits less than 50% of applicants:

BASIC COSTS (2009-2010)
Tuition and fees: $9,500.
Per-credit charge: $295.

FINANCIAL AID PICTURE (2008-2009)
Students with need: Out of 54 full-time freshmen who applied for aid, 47 were judged to have need. Of these, 44 received aid, and 2 had their full need met. Average financial aid package met 53% of need; average scholarship/grant was $5,739; average loan was $3,310. For part-time students, average financial aid package was $6,796.
Students without need: 2 full-time freshmen who did not demonstrate need for aid received scholarships/grants; average award was $3,698. No-need awards available for academics, alumni affiliation, leadership, religious affiliation, state/district residency.
Cumulative student debt: 77% of graduating class had student loans; average debt was $19,620.

FINANCIAL AID PROCEDURES
Forms required: FAFSA.
Dates and Deadlines: Priority date 3/1; no closing date. Applicants notified on a rolling basis starting 3/1; must reply within 2 week(s) of notification.

CONTACT
Julie Leslie, Financial Aid Director
2221 Madison Avenue, Toledo, OH 43604
(419) 251-1598

Miami University: Hamilton Campus
Hamilton, Ohio
www.ham.muohio.edu   Federal Code: 003077

2-year public branch campus college in small city.
Enrollment: 3,549 undergrads, 18% part-time. 770 full-time freshmen.
Selectivity: Open admission; but selective for some programs.

PART III: FINANCIAL AID COLLEGE BY COLLEGE

BASIC COSTS (2009-2010)
Tuition and fees: $4,550; out-of-state residents $16,952.

FINANCIAL AID PICTURE (2009-2010)
Students with need: Need-based aid available for full-time and part-time students. Work study available nights, weekends, and for part-time students.
Students without need: No-need awards available for academics, athletics, leadership, minority status, state/district residency.
Additional info: Special gift funds for needy, multicultural students who enter with appropriate academic record. Separate application required for scholarships; closing date January 31.

FINANCIAL AID PROCEDURES
Forms required: FAFSA.
Dates and Deadlines: Priority date 2/15; no closing date. Applicants notified on a rolling basis starting 4/1.
Transfers: Transfer students must complete one semester at Miami University to be considered for scholarships.

CONTACT
Ann Alfers, Financial Aid Coordinator
1601 University Boulevard, Hamilton, OH 45011-3399
(513) 785-3123

Miami University: Oxford Campus
Oxford, Ohio
www.muohio.edu   Federal Code: 003077

4-year public university in large town.
Enrollment: 14,553 undergrads, 1% part-time. 3,571 full-time freshmen.
Selectivity: Admits over 75% of applicants.

BASIC COSTS (2009-2010)
Tuition and fees: $11,910; out-of-state residents $26,670.
Room and board: $9,458.
Additional info: Reported in-state tuition represents maximum range that freshmen will be charged.

FINANCIAL AID PICTURE (2008-2009)
Students with need: Out of 2,538 full-time freshmen who applied for aid, 1,505 were judged to have need. Of these, 1,492 received aid, and 603 had their full need met. Average financial aid package met 72% of need; average scholarship/grant was $6,716; average loan was $5,571. For part-time students, average financial aid package was $8,170.
Students without need: 697 full-time freshmen who did not demonstrate need for aid received scholarships/grants; average award was $3,785. No-need awards available for academics, art, athletics, leadership, minority status, music/drama, ROTC, state/district residency.
Scholarships offered: Merit: Ohio Resident Scholarship; approximately $4,700; all full-time students who are Ohio residents are eligible. Ohio Leader Scholarship; $9,150-$11,900 depending on need; all full-time students who are Ohio residents are eligible. **Athletic:** 72 full-time freshmen received athletic scholarships; average amount $23,384.
Cumulative student debt: 51% of graduating class had student loans; average debt was $26,798.

FINANCIAL AID PROCEDURES
Forms required: FAFSA.
Dates and Deadlines: Priority date 2/15; no closing date. Applicants notified on a rolling basis starting 3/20; must reply by 5/1 or within 3 week(s) of notification.
Transfers: Institutional merit scholarships not available to transfer students during first year of enrollment.

CONTACT
Chuck Knepfle, Director of Student Financial Assistance
301 South Campus Avenue, Oxford, OH 45056
(513) 529-8734

Mount Union College
Alliance, Ohio
www.muc.edu   Federal Code: 003083

4-year private liberal arts college in large town, affiliated with United Methodist Church.
Enrollment: 2,187 undergrads, 2% part-time. 727 full-time freshmen.
Selectivity: Admits over 75% of applicants.

BASIC COSTS (2010-2011)
Tuition and fees: $24,800.
Per-credit charge: $1,030.
Room and board: $7,780.
Additional info: Tuition/fee waivers available for minority students.

FINANCIAL AID PICTURE (2008-2009)
Students with need: Out of 547 full-time freshmen who applied for aid, 480 were judged to have need. Of these, 479 received aid, and 107 had their full need met. Average financial aid package met 83% of need; average scholarship/grant was $13,776; average loan was $5,071. For part-time students, average financial aid package was $17,503.
Students without need: 102 full-time freshmen who did not demonstrate need for aid received scholarships/grants; average award was $6,372. No-need awards available for academics, alumni affiliation, art, job skills, leadership, music/drama, religious affiliation, ROTC, state/district residency.
Cumulative student debt: 86% of graduating class had student loans; average debt was $29,348.

FINANCIAL AID PROCEDURES
Forms required: FAFSA.
Dates and Deadlines: Priority date 4/1; no closing date. Applicants notified on a rolling basis starting 3/15; must reply within 4 week(s) of notification.
Transfers: No deadline. Applicants notified on a rolling basis; must reply within 4 week(s) of notification.

CONTACT
Emily Swain, Director of Student Financial Services
1972 Clark Avenue, Alliance, OH 44601-3993
(330) 823-2674

Mount Vernon Nazarene University
Mount Vernon, Ohio
www.mvnu.edu   Federal Code: 007085

4-year private university in large town, affiliated with Church of the Nazarene.
Enrollment: 1,939 undergrads, 11% part-time. 302 full-time freshmen.
Selectivity: Admits 50 to 75% of applicants.

BASIC COSTS (2010-2011)
Tuition and fees: $21,330.
Per-credit charge: $739.
Room and board: $6,180.
Additional info: Tuition/fee waivers available for minority students.

FINANCIAL AID PICTURE (2009-2010)
Students with need: Out of 302 full-time freshmen who applied for aid, 277 were judged to have need. Of these, 277 received aid, and 32 had their full need met. Average financial aid package met 70% of need; average scholarship/grant was $11,360; average loan was $3,703. For part-time students, average financial aid package was $9,019.
Students without need: 20 full-time freshmen who did not demonstrate need for aid received scholarships/grants; average award was $5,565. No-need awards available for academics, athletics, minority status, music/drama, religious affiliation, state/district residency.

Scholarships offered: *Merit:* Academic scholarships; $5,000-$15,000; for first time students based on ACT/SAT and GPA. *Athletic:* 11 full-time freshmen received athletic scholarships; average amount $4,617.
Cumulative student debt: 85% of graduating class had student loans; average debt was $29,761.

FINANCIAL AID PROCEDURES
Forms required: FAFSA, institutional form.
Dates and Deadlines: Priority date 3/15; no closing date. Applicants notified on a rolling basis starting 3/15; must reply within 2 week(s) of notification.
Transfers: No deadline. Applicants notified on a rolling basis starting 3/15; must reply within 2 week(s) of notification. Filing deadline for Ohio financial aid is October 1st.

CONTACT
Michelle Saigh, Director of Financial Aid
800 Martinsburg Road, Mount Vernon, OH 43050
(740) 397-9000 ext. 4520

Muskingum University
New Concord, Ohio
www.muskingum.edu   Federal Code: 003084

4-year private liberal arts college in small town, affiliated with Presbyterian Church (USA).
Enrollment: 1,661 undergrads, 6% part-time. 473 full-time freshmen.
Selectivity: Admits over 75% of applicants.

BASIC COSTS (2010-2011)
Tuition and fees: $20,946.
Per-credit charge: $425.
Room and board: $8,170.
Additional info: Tuition/fee waivers available for minority students.

FINANCIAL AID PICTURE (2009-2010)
Students with need: Need-based aid available for full-time and part-time students.
Students without need: No-need awards available for academics, alumni affiliation, art, leadership, minority status, music/drama, religious affiliation, state/district residency.
Additional info: Scholarship priority date February 1.

FINANCIAL AID PROCEDURES
Forms required: FAFSA.
Dates and Deadlines: Priority date 3/15; closing date 8/1. Applicants notified on a rolling basis starting 3/1; must reply by 5/1 or within 2 week(s) of notification.

CONTACT
Jeff Zellers, Vice President of Enrollment
163 Stormont Street, New Concord, OH 43762-1199
(740) 826-8139

North Central State College
Mansfield, Ohio
www.ncstatecollege.edu   Federal Code: 005313

2-year public technical college in small city.
Enrollment: 3,595 undergrads.
Selectivity: Open admission; but selective for some programs.

BASIC COSTS (2009-2010)
Tuition and fees: $3,634; out-of-state residents $7,267.
Per-credit charge: $81; out-of-state residents $161.

FINANCIAL AID PICTURE
Students with need: Need-based aid available for full-time and part-time students.
Students without need: This college awards aid only to students with need.

FINANCIAL AID PROCEDURES
Forms required: FAFSA.
Dates and Deadlines: Priority date 4/1; no closing date. Applicants notified on a rolling basis starting 5/30; must reply within 1 week(s) of notification.

CONTACT
Doris Smith, Assistant Dean of Financial Aid
2441 Kenwood Circle, PO Box 698, Mansfield, OH 44901-0698
(419) 755-4899

Northwest State Community College
Archbold, Ohio
www.northweststate.edu   Federal Code: 008677

2-year public community and technical college in small town.
Enrollment: 2,982 full-time undergrads.
Selectivity: Open admission; but selective for some programs.

BASIC COSTS (2009-2010)
Tuition and fees: $3,930; out-of-state residents $7,680.
Per-credit charge: $125; out-of-state residents $250.

FINANCIAL AID PICTURE
Students with need: Need-based aid available for full-time and part-time students.
Students without need: No-need awards available for academics.

FINANCIAL AID PROCEDURES
Forms required: FAFSA, institutional form.
Dates and Deadlines: Priority date 6/1; no closing date. Applicants notified on a rolling basis starting 4/1.

CONTACT
Charlotte Sorg, Director of Financial Aid
22600 State Route 34, Archbold, OH 43502
(419) 267-5511 ext. 326

Notre Dame College
Cleveland, Ohio
www.notredamecollege.edu   Federal Code: 003085

4-year private liberal arts college in very large city, affiliated with Roman Catholic Church.
Enrollment: 1,584 undergrads.
Selectivity: Admits 50 to 75% of applicants.

BASIC COSTS (2010-2011)
Tuition and fees: $23,630.
Per-credit charge: $475.
Room and board: $7,820.

FINANCIAL AID PICTURE
Students with need: Need-based aid available for full-time students.
Students without need: No-need awards available for academics, state/district residency.
Scholarships offered: Merit Scholarships; $2,500-$7,500; based on GPA and ACT or SAT scores. Presidential Scholarships; $3,000 awarded in addition to Merit Scholarships; based on 3.9 GPA and 27 ACT or 1210 SAT (exclusive of Writing).

FINANCIAL AID PROCEDURES
Forms required: FAFSA.
Dates and Deadlines: Closing date 5/1. Applicants notified on a rolling basis starting 1/1; must reply within 2 week(s) of notification.

CONTACT
Mary McCrystal, Director of Student Financial Assistance
4545 College Road, Cleveland, OH 44121-4293
(216) 373-5263

Oberlin College
Oberlin, Ohio
www.oberlin.edu

Federal Code: 003086
CSS Code: 1587

4-year private music and liberal arts college in small town.
Enrollment: 2,888 undergrads, 2% part-time. 806 full-time freshmen.
Selectivity: Admits less than 50% of applicants. GED not accepted.

BASIC COSTS (2009-2010)
Tuition and fees: $40,004.
Per-credit charge: $1,650.
Room and board: $10,480.

FINANCIAL AID PICTURE (2009-2010)
Students with need: Out of 544 full-time freshmen who applied for aid, 472 were judged to have need. Of these, 472 received aid, and 472 had their full need met. Average financial aid package met 100% of need; average scholarship/grant was $27,888; average loan was $4,448. Need-based aid available for part-time students.
Students without need: 240 full-time freshmen who did not demonstrate need for aid received scholarships/grants; average award was $11,275. No-need awards available for academics, music/drama.
Scholarships offered: Bonner Scholarship; based on community service. John Frederick Oberlin Scholarship; based on academic merit. Stern Scholarship; based on excellence in sciences. Mary Elizabeth Johnston Scholarship; based on academic merit; available to Ohio residents only. Dean's Scholarship; available to Conservatory of Music students.

FINANCIAL AID PROCEDURES
Forms required: FAFSA, CSS PROFILE, state aid form, institutional form.
Dates and Deadlines: Priority date 1/15; closing date 2/1. Applicants notified by 4/1; must reply by 5/1 or within 2 week(s) of notification.
Transfers: Closing date 3/1. Limited scholarship funding available for transfer students.

CONTACT
Robert Reddy, Director of Financial Aid
Carnegie Building, 101 North Professor Street, Oberlin, OH 44074
(440) 775-8142

Ohio Business College: Sandusky
Sandusky, Ohio
www.ohiobusinesscollege.edu

Federal Code: 021585

2-year for-profit business college in small city.
Enrollment: 321 undergrads.
Selectivity: Open admission.

BASIC COSTS (2009-2010)
Tuition and fees: $10,035.
Per-credit charge: $215.

FINANCIAL AID PICTURE
Students with need: Need-based aid available for full-time and part-time students.

FINANCIAL AID PROCEDURES
Forms required: FAFSA.
Dates and Deadlines: No deadline.

CONTACT
Gerilyn Wilson, Lead Financial Aid Administrator
5202 Timber Commons Drive, Sandusky, OH 44870
(419) 627-8345 ext. 14

Ohio Christian University
Circleville, Ohio
www.ohiochristian.edu

Federal Code: 003030

4-year private university and Bible and teachers college in large town, affiliated with Churches of Christ in Christian Union.
Enrollment: 846 undergrads.
Selectivity: Admits less than 50% of applicants.

BASIC COSTS (2009-2010)
Tuition and fees: $14,650.
Per-credit charge: $550.
Room and board: $5,990.
Additional info: Tuition/fee waivers available for minority students.

FINANCIAL AID PICTURE (2008-2009)
Students with need: Need-based aid available for full-time and part-time students.
Students without need: This college awards aid only to students with need.
Additional info: Religious affiliation tuition discount.

FINANCIAL AID PROCEDURES
Forms required: FAFSA, institutional form.
Dates and Deadlines: Priority date 5/7; no closing date. Applicants notified on a rolling basis starting 5/1; must reply within 2 week(s) of notification.
Transfers: Closing date 3/1. Applicants notified on a rolling basis; must reply within 2 week(s) of notification.

CONTACT
Mike Fracassa, Director of Financial Aid
1476 Lancaster Pike, Circleville, OH 43113
(800) 701-0222

Ohio Dominican University
Columbus, Ohio
www.ohiodominican.edu

Federal Code: 003035

4-year private university and liberal arts college in very large city, affiliated with Roman Catholic Church.
Enrollment: 1,882 undergrads, 20% part-time. 274 full-time freshmen.
Selectivity: Admits 50 to 75% of applicants.

BASIC COSTS (2009-2010)
Tuition and fees: $24,558.
Per-credit charge: $488.
Room and board: $7,900.

FINANCIAL AID PICTURE
Students with need: Need-based aid available for full-time and part-time students. Work study available nights, weekends, and for part-time students.
Students without need: No-need awards available for academics, athletics, state/district residency.

FINANCIAL AID PROCEDURES
Forms required: FAFSA.
Dates and Deadlines: Priority date 4/1; no closing date. Applicants notified on a rolling basis starting 3/1; must reply within 2 week(s) of notification.

CONTACT

Laura Meek, Director of Financial Aid
1216 Sunbury Road, Columbus, OH 43219
(614) 251-4778

Ohio Northern University
Ada, Ohio
www.onu.edu   Federal Code: 003089

4-year private university in small town, affiliated with United Methodist Church.
Enrollment: 2,445 undergrads, 2% part-time. 641 full-time freshmen.
Selectivity: Admits over 75% of applicants.

BASIC COSTS (2009-2010)
Tuition and fees: $31,866.
Room and board: $8,280.
Additional info: Tuition/fee waivers available for minority students.

FINANCIAL AID PICTURE (2009-2010)
Students with need: Need-based aid available for full-time and part-time students. Work study available nights, weekends, and for part-time students.
Students without need: No-need awards available for academics, alumni affiliation, art, leadership, minority status, music/drama, ROTC, state/district residency.
Scholarships offered: Presidential Scholarship: up to $27,000; based on 3.5 GPA, 30 ACT or 1330 SAT (Pharmacy - 3.8, 31 ACT or 1360 SAT), and on-campus competition. Trustees Scholarship: up to $24,000; based on 3.5 GPA, 28 ACT or 1250 SAT (Pharmacy - 3.7 GPA, 29 ACT or 1290 SAT), and on-campus competition. Academic Honors Scholarship: up to $21,000; based on 3.3 GPA, 26 ACT or 1170 SAT (Pharmacy - 3.5 GPA, 27 ACT or 1210 SAT), and on-campus competition. Distinguished Achievement Scholarship: up to $18,000; based on 3.2 GPA, 24 ACT or 1090 SAT, on-campus competition, and leadership activities. Deans Scholarship: $9,000 to $13,000; based on 3.3 GPA and 25 ACT or 1130 SAT (Pharmacy - 3.5 GPA, 27 ACT or 1210 SAT). SAT scores exclusive of Writing.

FINANCIAL AID PROCEDURES
Forms required: FAFSA, institutional form.
Dates and Deadlines: Priority date 4/15; no closing date. Applicants notified on a rolling basis starting 2/15; must reply within 2 week(s) of notification.

CONTACT
Melanie Weaver, Director of Financial Aid
525 South Main Street, Ada, OH 45810
(419) 772-2272

Ohio State University Agricultural Technical Institute
Wooster, Ohio
www.ati.osu.edu   Federal Code: 003090

2-year public agricultural and branch campus college in large town.
Enrollment: 702 undergrads, 10% part-time. 284 full-time freshmen.
Selectivity: Open admission; but selective for out-of-state students.

BASIC COSTS (2009-2010)
Tuition and fees: $5,859; out-of-state residents $19,098.

FINANCIAL AID PICTURE (2009-2010)
Students with need: Out of 246 full-time freshmen who applied for aid, 212 were judged to have need. Of these, 205 received aid, and 19 had their full need met. Average financial aid package met 52% of need; average scholarship/grant was $5,412; average loan was $3,447. For part-time students, average financial aid package was $7,344.
Students without need: This college awards aid only to students with need.

FINANCIAL AID PROCEDURES
Forms required: FAFSA.
Dates and Deadlines: Priority date 3/1; no closing date. Applicants notified on a rolling basis starting 5/1; must reply within 4 week(s) of notification.
Transfers: Priority date 6/25. Applicants notified on a rolling basis starting 6/1; must reply within 4 week(s) of notification.

CONTACT
Barbara LaMoreaux, Coordinator, Financial Aid
1328 Dover Road, Wooster, OH 44691

Ohio State University: Columbus Campus
Columbus, Ohio
www.osu.edu   Federal Code: 003090

4-year public university in very large city.
Enrollment: 40,178 undergrads, 6% part-time. 6,596 full-time freshmen.
Selectivity: Admits over 75% of applicants.

BASIC COSTS (2009-2010)
Tuition and fees: $8,706; out-of-state residents $22,278.
Room and board: $8,409.

FINANCIAL AID PICTURE (2009-2010)
Students with need: Out of 5,464 full-time freshmen who applied for aid, 3,619 were judged to have need. Of these, 3,603 received aid, and 933 had their full need met. Average financial aid package met 58% of need; average scholarship/grant was $8,430; average loan was $3,445. For part-time students, average financial aid package was $8,829.
Students without need: 1,968 full-time freshmen who did not demonstrate need for aid received scholarships/grants; average award was $4,491. No-need awards available for academics, alumni affiliation, art, athletics, job skills, leadership, minority status, music/drama, ROTC, state/district residency.
Scholarships offered: 72 full-time freshmen received athletic scholarships; average amount $14,318.
Cumulative student debt: 54% of graduating class had student loans; average debt was $18,426.

FINANCIAL AID PROCEDURES
Forms required: FAFSA.
Dates and Deadlines: Priority date 2/15; no closing date. Applicants notified by 4/15; must reply by 5/1 or within 4 week(s) of notification.
Transfers: Priority date 6/25. Applicants notified on a rolling basis starting 6/1; must reply within 4 week(s) of notification.

CONTACT
110 Enarson Hall, Columbus, OH 43210
(614) 292-0300

Ohio State University: Lima Campus
Lima, Ohio
www.lima.ohio-state.edu   Federal Code: 003090

4-year public branch campus college in large town.
Enrollment: 1,342 undergrads, 11% part-time. 452 full-time freshmen.
Selectivity: Open admission; but selective for out-of-state students.

BASIC COSTS (2009-2010)
Tuition and fees: $5,664; out-of-state residents $19,233.

FINANCIAL AID PICTURE (2009-2010)

Students with need: Out of 428 full-time freshmen who applied for aid, 346 were judged to have need. Of these, 343 received aid, and 31 had their full need met. Average financial aid package met 50% of need; average scholarship/grant was $3,710; average loan was $3,334. For part-time students, average financial aid package was $7,468.

Students without need: 74 full-time freshmen who did not demonstrate need for aid received scholarships/grants; average award was $770. No-need awards available for academics, alumni affiliation, art, athletics, job skills, leadership, minority status, music/drama, ROTC, state/district residency.

FINANCIAL AID PROCEDURES

Forms required: FAFSA.

Dates and Deadlines: Priority date 3/1; no closing date. Applicants notified on a rolling basis starting 4/1; must reply within 4 week(s) of notification.

Transfers: Priority date 6/25. Applicants notified on a rolling basis starting 6/1; must reply within 4 week(s) of notification.

CONTACT

Bryan Albright, Coordinator, Financial Aid
4240 Campus Drive, Lima, OH 45804-3596
(419) 995-8147

Ohio State University: Mansfield Campus
Mansfield, Ohio
www.mansfield.ohio-state.edu   Federal Code: 003090

4-year public branch campus college in large town.

Enrollment: 1,274 undergrads, 13% part-time. 474 full-time freshmen.

Selectivity: Open admission; but selective for out-of-state students.

BASIC COSTS (2009-2010)

Tuition and fees: $5,664; out-of-state residents $19,233.

Room and board: $4,440.

FINANCIAL AID PICTURE (2009-2010)

Students with need: Out of 412 full-time freshmen who applied for aid, 338 were judged to have need. Of these, 335 received aid, and 26 had their full need met. Average financial aid package met 52% of need; average scholarship/grant was $4,681; average loan was $3,496. For part-time students, average financial aid package was $8,228.

Students without need: 35 full-time freshmen who did not demonstrate need for aid received scholarships/grants; average award was $1,931. No-need awards available for academics, alumni affiliation, art, athletics, job skills, leadership, minority status, music/drama, ROTC, state/district residency.

FINANCIAL AID PROCEDURES

Forms required: FAFSA.

Dates and Deadlines: Priority date 3/1; no closing date. Applicants notified on a rolling basis starting 4/5; must reply within 4 week(s) of notification.

Transfers: Priority date 6/25. Applicants notified on a rolling basis starting 6/1; must reply within 4 week(s) of notification.

CONTACT

Director, Student Financial Aid
1680 University Drive, Mansfield, OH 44906
(419) 755-4011

Ohio State University: Marion Campus
Marion, Ohio
www.marion.ohio-state.edu   Federal Code: 003090

4-year public branch campus college in large town.

Enrollment: 1,681 undergrads, 12% part-time. 557 full-time freshmen.

Selectivity: Open admission; but selective for out-of-state students.

BASIC COSTS (2009-2010)

Tuition and fees: $5,664; out-of-state residents $19,233.

FINANCIAL AID PICTURE (2009-2010)

Students with need: Out of 465 full-time freshmen who applied for aid, 368 were judged to have need. Of these, 363 received aid, and 33 had their full need met. Average financial aid package met 54% of need; average scholarship/grant was $5,102; average loan was $3,385. For part-time students, average financial aid package was $9,006.

Students without need: 52 full-time freshmen who did not demonstrate need for aid received scholarships/grants; average award was $2,163. No-need awards available for academics, alumni affiliation, art, athletics, job skills, leadership, minority status, music/drama, ROTC, state/district residency.

FINANCIAL AID PROCEDURES

Forms required: FAFSA.

Dates and Deadlines: Priority date 3/1; no closing date. Applicants notified on a rolling basis starting 5/1; must reply within 4 week(s) of notification.

Transfers: Priority date 6/25. Applicants notified on a rolling basis starting 6/1; must reply within 4 week(s) of notification.

CONTACT

Matt Moreau, Coordinator of Admissions
1465 Mount Vernon Avenue, Marion, OH 43302
(740) 389-6786 ext. 6273

Ohio State University: Newark Campus
Newark, Ohio
www.newark.osu.edu   Federal Code: 003095

4-year public branch campus college in large town.

Enrollment: 2,321 undergrads, 11% part-time. 1,057 full-time freshmen.

Selectivity: Open admission; but selective for out-of-state students.

BASIC COSTS (2009-2010)

Tuition and fees: $5,664; out-of-state residents $19,233.

Room only: $6,105.

FINANCIAL AID PICTURE (2009-2010)

Students with need: Out of 909 full-time freshmen who applied for aid, 716 were judged to have need. Of these, 701 received aid, and 70 had their full need met. Average financial aid package met 52% of need; average scholarship/grant was $4,976; average loan was $3,361. For part-time students, average financial aid package was $7,859.

Students without need: 16 full-time freshmen who did not demonstrate need for aid received scholarships/grants; average award was $2,126. No-need awards available for academics, alumni affiliation, art, athletics, job skills, leadership, minority status, music/drama, ROTC, state/district residency.

FINANCIAL AID PROCEDURES

Forms required: FAFSA.

Dates and Deadlines: Priority date 3/1; no closing date. Applicants notified on a rolling basis starting 5/1; must reply within 4 week(s) of notification.

Transfers: Priority date 6/25. Applicants notified on a rolling basis starting 6/1; must reply within 4 week(s) of notification.

CONTACT

1179 University Drive, Newark, OH 43055
(740) 366-9435

Ohio University
Athens, Ohio
www.ohio.edu   Federal Code: 003100

4-year public university in large town.
Enrollment: 18,005 undergrads, 9% part-time. 4,054 full-time freshmen.
Selectivity: Admits over 75% of applicants.

BASIC COSTS (2009-2010)
Tuition and fees: $8,973; out-of-state residents $17,937.
Per-credit charge: $285; out-of-state residents $580.
Room and board: $9,408.

FINANCIAL AID PICTURE (2009-2010)
Students with need: Out of 3,685 full-time freshmen who applied for aid, 2,453 were judged to have need. Of these, 2,411 received aid, and 372 had their full need met. Average financial aid package met 58% of need; average scholarship/grant was $6,589; average loan was $3,457. For part-time students, average financial aid package was $5,743.
Students without need: 610 full-time freshmen who did not demonstrate need for aid received scholarships/grants; average award was $2,123. No-need awards available for academics, art, athletics, minority status, music/drama, religious affiliation, ROTC.
Scholarships offered: 84 full-time freshmen received athletic scholarships; average amount $16,520.
Cumulative student debt: 66% of graduating class had student loans; average debt was $22,095.

FINANCIAL AID PROCEDURES
Forms required: FAFSA.
Dates and Deadlines: Priority date 3/15; closing date 4/1. Applicants notified on a rolling basis starting 4/1; must reply within 3 week(s) of notification.
Transfers: Priority date 5/15; no deadline. Applicants notified on a rolling basis starting 5/15.

CONTACT
Sondra Williams, Director, Student Financial Aid and Scholarships
120 Chubb Hall, Athens, OH 45701-2979
(740) 593-4141

Ohio University: Southern Campus at Ironton
Ironton, Ohio
www.southern.ohiou.edu   Federal Code: 003103

4-year public branch campus college in large town.
Enrollment: 2,138 undergrads.
Selectivity: Open admission.

BASIC COSTS (2009-2010)
Tuition and fees: $4,461; out-of-state residents $5,781.
Per-credit charge: $156; out-of-state residents $196.

FINANCIAL AID PICTURE
Students with need: Need-based aid available for full-time and part-time students.
Students without need: No-need awards available for academics, state/district residency.

FINANCIAL AID PROCEDURES
Forms required: FAFSA.
Dates and Deadlines: Priority date 3/15; no closing date. Applicants notified on a rolling basis starting 4/1.

CONTACT
Jacki Adkins, Coordinator of Financial Aid and Scholarships
1804 Liberty Avenue, Ironton, OH 45638
(740) 533-4600

Ohio Valley College of Technology
East Liverpool, Ohio
www.ovct.edu   Federal Code: 016261

2-year for-profit business and technical college in large town.
Enrollment: 183 undergrads, 4% part-time. 62 full-time freshmen.
Selectivity: Admits over 75% of applicants.

BASIC COSTS (2010-2011)
Tuition and fees: $9,590.

FINANCIAL AID PICTURE
Students with need: Need-based aid available for full-time and part-time students.
Students without need: This college awards aid only to students with need.

FINANCIAL AID PROCEDURES
Forms required: FAFSA.
Dates and Deadlines: No deadline. Applicants notified on a rolling basis; must reply within 6 week(s) of notification.

CONTACT
Mary Galeno, Financial Aid Officer
16808 St. Clair Avenue, PO Box 7000, East Liverpool, OH 43920
(330) 385-1070

Ohio Wesleyan University
Delaware, Ohio
www.owu.edu   Federal Code: 003109

4-year private liberal arts college in large town, affiliated with United Methodist Church.
Enrollment: 1,880 undergrads, 1% part-time. 498 full-time freshmen.
Selectivity: Admits 50 to 75% of applicants.

BASIC COSTS (2010-2011)
Tuition and fees: $36,398.
Room and board: $9,700.

FINANCIAL AID PICTURE (2009-2010)
Students with need: Need-based aid available for full-time students. Work study available nights, weekends, and for part-time students.
Students without need: No-need awards available for academics, alumni affiliation, art, leadership, minority status, music/drama, religious affiliation, state/district residency.
Scholarships offered: Presidential scholarships; full tuition; 25 awarded. Trustee scholarships; 75% of tuition; 40 awarded. Faculty scholarships; 50% of tuition; 140 awarded.

FINANCIAL AID PROCEDURES
Forms required: FAFSA, institutional form.
Dates and Deadlines: Priority date 3/1; closing date 5/1. Applicants notified on a rolling basis starting 2/15; must reply by 5/1 or within 2 week(s) of notification.
Transfers: Must reply within 2 week(s) of notification.

CONTACT
Lee Harrell, Assistant Vice President of Admission and Financial Aid
75 South Sandusky Street, Delaware, OH 43015-2398
(740) 368-3050

Otterbein College
Westerville, Ohio
www.otterbein.edu Federal Code: 003110

4-year private liberal arts college in large town, affiliated with United Methodist Church.

Enrollment: 2,616 undergrads, 13% part-time. 635 full-time freshmen.
Selectivity: Admits over 75% of applicants.

BASIC COSTS (2009-2010)
Tuition and fees: $27,321.
Room and board: $7,605.
Additional info: Tuition/fee waivers available for adults, minority students.

FINANCIAL AID PICTURE (2009-2010)
Students with need: Work study available nights, weekends, and for part-time students.
Students without need: No-need awards available for academics, alumni affiliation, art, leadership, minority status, music/drama, state/district residency.

FINANCIAL AID PROCEDURES
Forms required: FAFSA.
Dates and Deadlines: Priority date 4/1; no closing date. Applicants notified on a rolling basis starting 2/15.
Transfers: Transfer students must complete appropriate state grant transfer paperwork.

CONTACT
Thomas Yarnell, Director of Financial Aid
One Otterbein College, Westerville, OH 43081
(614) 823-1502

Owens Community College: Toledo
Toledo, Ohio
www.owens.edu Federal Code: 005753

2-year public community college in large city.
Enrollment: 11,390 undergrads, 47% part-time. 2,034 full-time freshmen.
Selectivity: Open admission; but selective for some programs.

BASIC COSTS (2009-2010)
Tuition and fees: $3,012; out-of-state residents $5,592.
Per-credit charge: $123; out-of-state residents $230.

FINANCIAL AID PICTURE (2009-2010)
Students with need: Average financial aid package met 67% of need; average scholarship/grant was $4,986; average loan was $7,013. For part-time students, average financial aid package was $4,610.
Students without need: No-need awards available for academics, alumni affiliation, athletics, leadership, state/district residency.
Additional info: Other types of financial aid available: federal family education loan program, private foundation loan (SCHELL).

FINANCIAL AID PROCEDURES
Forms required: FAFSA.
Dates and Deadlines: Priority date 3/31; no closing date.

CONTACT
Betsy Johnson, Director of Financial Aid
30335 Oregon Road, Toledo, OH 43699-1947
(567) 661-7343

Pontifical College Josephinum
Columbus, Ohio
www.pcj.edu Federal Code: 003113

4-year private liberal arts and seminary college for men in very large city, affiliated with Roman Catholic Church.

Enrollment: 78 undergrads. 6 full-time freshmen.
Selectivity: Admits over 75% of applicants.

BASIC COSTS (2009-2010)
Tuition and fees: $17,417.
Per-credit charge: $650.
Room and board: $7,908.

FINANCIAL AID PICTURE (2009-2010)
Students with need: Need-based aid available for full-time and part-time students. Work study available nights, weekends, and for part-time students.
Students without need: This college awards aid only to students with need.

FINANCIAL AID PROCEDURES
Forms required: FAFSA, institutional form.
Dates and Deadlines: Priority date 9/2; no closing date. Applicants notified on a rolling basis starting 8/15; must reply within 2 week(s) of notification.

CONTACT
Marky Leichtnam, Director of Financial Aid
7625 North High Street, Columbus, OH 43235-1499
(614) 985-2212

RETS College
Centerville, Ohio
www.retstechcenter.com Federal Code: 012267

2-year for-profit junior and technical college in large town.
Enrollment: 1,225 undergrads.
Selectivity: Open admission.

BASIC COSTS (2009-2010)
Additional Info: Costs are charged per entire associate degree or diploma program and vary with specific program. Associate programs range from $17,015 to $24,785. Diploma programs range from $8,400 to $17,085.

FINANCIAL AID PICTURE
Students with need: Need-based aid available for full-time and part-time students.
Students without need: This college awards aid only to students with need.

FINANCIAL AID PROCEDURES
Forms required: FAFSA, institutional form.
Dates and Deadlines: No deadline. Applicants notified on a rolling basis.

CONTACT
Tom Barker, Director of Financial Aid
555 East Alex Bell Road, Centerville, OH 45459-9627

Rosedale Bible College
Irwin, Ohio
www.rosedale.edu Federal Code: 034253

2-year private Bible and junior college in rural community, affiliated with Mennonite Church.
Enrollment: 61 undergrads.
Selectivity: Open admission.

BASIC COSTS (2010-2011)
Tuition and fees: $7,755.
Per-credit charge: $249.
Room and board: $5,350.

FINANCIAL AID PICTURE
Students with need: Need-based aid available for full-time and part-time students.

FINANCIAL AID PROCEDURES
Forms required: FAFSA, institutional form.
Dates and Deadlines: No deadline. Applicants notified on a rolling basis.
Transfers: Priority date 5/1. Applicants notified on a rolling basis.

CONTACT
Chris Jones
2270 Rosedale Road, Irwin, OH 43029
(740) 857-1311

School of Advertising Art
Kettering, Ohio
www.saa.edu   Federal Code: 017160

2-year for-profit visual arts and technical college in small city.
Enrollment: 64 undergrads. 62 full-time freshmen.

BASIC COSTS (2010-2011)
Tuition and fees: $24,742.
Per-credit charge: $350.
Additional info: Tuition/fee waivers available for minority students.

FINANCIAL AID PICTURE (2009-2010)
Students with need: Out of 62 full-time freshmen who applied for aid, 60 were judged to have need. Of these, 60 received aid. Average financial aid package met 16% of need; average scholarship/grant was $3,000; average loan was $3,500.
Students without need: No-need awards available for academics, art, leadership.
Cumulative student debt: 97% of graduating class had student loans; average debt was $18,000.

FINANCIAL AID PROCEDURES
Forms required: FAFSA.
Dates and Deadlines: No deadline. Applicants notified on a rolling basis starting 4/1; must reply by 7/1 or within 1 week(s) of notification.
Transfers: No deadline. Applicants notified on a rolling basis starting 4/1; must reply by 7/1 or within 1 week(s) of notification.

CONTACT
Tamara Arment, Financial Aid Director
1725 East David Road, Kettering, OH 45440-1612
(937) 294-0592 ext. 104

Shawnee State University
Portsmouth, Ohio
www.shawnee.edu   Federal Code: 009942

4-year public university in large town.
Enrollment: 4,027 undergrads, 14% part-time. 1,093 full-time freshmen.
Selectivity: Open admission; but selective for some programs.

BASIC COSTS (2009-2010)
Tuition and fees: $5,832; out-of-state residents $10,176.
Per-credit charge: $216; out-of-state residents $397.
Room and board: $8,046.

FINANCIAL AID PICTURE
Students with need: Need-based aid available for full-time and part-time students.
Students without need: No-need awards available for academics.
Additional info: ACT recommended for scholarship applicants.

FINANCIAL AID PROCEDURES
Forms required: FAFSA, institutional form.
Dates and Deadlines: Priority date 6/15; no closing date. Applicants notified on a rolling basis starting 5/1; must reply within 4 week(s) of notification.

CONTACT
Barbara Bradbury, Financial Aid Director
940 Second Street, Portsmouth, OH 45662
(740) 351-4243

Southern State Community College
Hillsboro, Ohio
www.sscc.edu   Federal Code: 012870

2-year public community college in small town.
Enrollment: 3,027 undergrads, 36% part-time. 583 full-time freshmen.
Selectivity: Open admission; but selective for some programs.

BASIC COSTS (2009-2010)
Tuition and fees: $3,390; out-of-state residents $6,528.
Per-credit charge: $81; out-of-state residents $162.

FINANCIAL AID PICTURE (2008-2009)
Students with need: 51% of average financial aid package awarded as scholarships/grants, 49% awarded as loans/jobs. Need-based aid available for part-time students. Work study available nights.
Students without need: No-need awards available for academics, art, athletics, music/drama.

FINANCIAL AID PROCEDURES
Forms required: FAFSA, institutional form.
Dates and Deadlines: Priority date 7/1; closing date 9/1. Applicants notified by 4/15; must reply within 2 week(s) of notification.
Transfers: No deadline.

CONTACT
Janeen Deatley, Financial Aid Director
100 Hobart Drive, Hillsboro, OH 45133
(937) 393-3431 ext. 2610

Southwestern College: Dayton
Dayton, Ohio
www.swcollege.net   Federal Code: 030161

2-year for-profit business college in small city.
Enrollment: 848 undergrads.
Selectivity: Open admission.

BASIC COSTS (2009-2010)
Tuition and fees: $10,600.

FINANCIAL AID PICTURE
Students with need: Need-based aid available for full-time and part-time students.
Students without need: This college awards aid only to students with need.

FINANCIAL AID PROCEDURES
Forms required: FAFSA.
Dates and Deadlines: No deadline.

CONTACT

Abby Wilkins, Director of Financial Aid

111 West 1st Street, Dayton, OH 45402

Southwestern College: Tri-County

Cincinnati, Ohio

www.swcollege.net   Federal Code: 012128

2-year for-profit career college in small city.

Enrollment: 670 undergrads.

Selectivity: Open admission.

BASIC COSTS (2009-2010)

Tuition and fees: $11,400.

FINANCIAL AID PICTURE (2008-2009)

Students with need: Need-based aid available for full-time students.

Students without need: This college awards aid only to students with need.

FINANCIAL AID PROCEDURES

Forms required: FAFSA, state aid form.

Dates and Deadlines: No deadline.

CONTACT

Jill Matosky, Financial Aid Director

149 Northland Boulevard, Cincinnati, OH 45246

(513) 874-0432

Stark State College of Technology

North Canton, Ohio

www.starkstate.edu   Federal Code: 011141

2-year public technical college in small city.

Enrollment: 10,023 undergrads.

Selectivity: Open admission; but selective for some programs.

BASIC COSTS (2009-2010)

Tuition and fees: $3,810; out-of-state residents $5,610.

Per-credit charge: $103; out-of-state residents $163.

FINANCIAL AID PICTURE

Students with need: Need-based aid available for full-time and part-time students. Work study available nights, weekends, and for part-time students.

Students without need: This college awards aid only to students with need.

FINANCIAL AID PROCEDURES

Forms required: FAFSA, institutional form.

Dates and Deadlines: Priority date 5/1; no closing date. Applicants notified on a rolling basis starting 4/1; must reply within 4 week(s) of notification.

CONTACT

Amy Baker, Director of Financial Aid

6200 Frank Avenue NW, North Canton, OH 44720

(330) 494-6170

Stautzenberger College: Brecksville

Brecksville, Ohio

www.LearnWhatYouLove.com

2-year for-profit career college in large town.

Enrollment: 503 undergrads.

Selectivity: Open admission.

BASIC COSTS (2010-2011)

Tuition and fees: $10,440.

Per-credit charge: $230.

FINANCIAL AID PICTURE (2008-2009)

Students with need: Need-based aid available for full-time and part-time students.

Students without need: This college awards aid only to students with need.

FINANCIAL AID PROCEDURES

Forms required: FAFSA.

Dates and Deadlines: No deadline. Applicants notified on a rolling basis.

Transfers: No deadline. Applicants notified on a rolling basis.

CONTACT

Mari Huffman, Director of Financial Aid

8001 Katherine Boulevard, Brecksville, OH 44141

Terra State Community College

Fremont, Ohio

www.terra.edu   Federal Code: 008278

2-year public community and technical college in large town.

Enrollment: 2,981 undergrads.

Selectivity: Open admission.

BASIC COSTS (2009-2010)

Tuition and fees: $3,735; out-of-state residents $5,854.

Per-credit charge: $112; out-of-state residents $182.

FINANCIAL AID PICTURE

Students with need: Need-based aid available for full-time and part-time students.

Students without need: No-need awards available for academics.

FINANCIAL AID PROCEDURES

Forms required: FAFSA, institutional form.

Dates and Deadlines: Priority date 5/1; no closing date. Applicants notified on a rolling basis starting 5/15.

CONTACT

Ed Recker, Director of Financial Aid

2830 Napoleon Road, Fremont, OH 43420-9600

(419) 559-2344

Tiffin University

Tiffin, Ohio

www.tiffin.edu   Federal Code: 003121

4-year private university and business and liberal arts college in large town.

Enrollment: 2,277 undergrads, 19% part-time. 501 full-time freshmen.

Selectivity: Admits 50 to 75% of applicants.

BASIC COSTS (2010-2011)

Tuition and fees: $18,390.

Per-credit charge: $613.

Room and board: $8,340.

FINANCIAL AID PICTURE (2009-2010)

Students with need: Out of 501 full-time freshmen who applied for aid, 496 were judged to have need. Of these, 496 received aid, and 38 had their full need met. Average financial aid package met 8% of need; average scholarship/grant was $5,647; average loan was $3,209. For part-time students, average financial aid package was $7,537.

Students without need: 17 full-time freshmen who did not demonstrate need for aid received scholarships/grants; average award was $7,882. No-

need awards available for academics, alumni affiliation, athletics, leadership, music/drama, state/district residency.

Scholarships offered: 8 full-time freshmen received athletic scholarships; average amount $9,767.

Cumulative student debt: 82% of graduating class had student loans; average debt was $26,345.

FINANCIAL AID PROCEDURES

Forms required: FAFSA.

Dates and Deadlines: No deadline. Applicants notified on a rolling basis starting 1/15; must reply within 2 week(s) of notification.

Transfers: No deadline.

CONTACT

Cindy Little, Director of Financial Aid

155 Miami Street, Tiffin, OH 44883

(800) 968-6446 ext. 3415

Trumbull Business College

Warren, Ohio

www.tbc-trumbullbusiness.com   Federal Code: 013585

2-year for-profit business college in large town.

Enrollment: 430 undergrads.

Selectivity: Open admission.

BASIC COSTS (2009-2010)

Tuition and fees: $12,171.

Per-credit charge: $252.

FINANCIAL AID PICTURE

Students with need: Need-based aid available for full-time and part-time students.

FINANCIAL AID PROCEDURES

Forms required: FAFSA.

CONTACT

Florence Henning, Financial Assistance Director

3200 Ridge Road, Warren, OH 44484

(330) 369-3200 ext. 12

Union Institute & University

Cincinnati, Ohio

www.myunion.edu   Federal Code: 010923

4-year private university in very large city.

Enrollment: 920 undergrads.

BASIC COSTS (2009-2010)

Tuition and fees: $11,012.

Per-credit charge: $454.

FINANCIAL AID PICTURE (2008-2009)

Students with need: Need-based aid available for full-time and part-time students.

Students without need: No-need awards available for academics, state/district residency.

FINANCIAL AID PROCEDURES

Forms required: FAFSA.

Dates and Deadlines: No deadline. Must reply within 4 week(s) of notification.

CONTACT

Dawnia Smith, Director of Financial Aid

440 East McMillan Street, Cincinnati, OH 45206

(800) 486-3116

University of Akron

Akron, Ohio

www.uakron.edu   Federal Code: 003123

4-year public university in small city.

Enrollment: 19,864 undergrads, 18% part-time. 3,931 full-time freshmen.

Selectivity: Admits over 75% of applicants.

BASIC COSTS (2009-2010)

Tuition and fees: $8,752; out-of-state residents $18,000.

Per-credit charge: $306; out-of-state residents $614.

Room and board: $8,697.

FINANCIAL AID PICTURE (2008-2009)

Students with need: Out of 3,458 full-time freshmen who applied for aid, 2,713 were judged to have need. Of these, 2,713 received aid, and 231 had their full need met. Average financial aid package met 53% of need; average scholarship/grant was $5,471; average loan was $3,488. For part-time students, average financial aid package was $4,879.

Students without need: 450 full-time freshmen who did not demonstrate need for aid received scholarships/grants; average award was $3,498. No-need awards available for academics, art, athletics, leadership, music/drama, ROTC, state/district residency.

Scholarships offered: *Merit:* Scholarships for Excellence; $6,000 per year; based on 3.8 GPA, 30 ACT, 1320 SAT (exclusive of Writing); deadline February 1. Presidential Scholarships; $3,000 per year; based on 3.8 GPA, 27 ACT, 1200 SAT. Honors Scholarships; $1,500-$3,000 per year; based on top 10% of class, 3.5 GPA; deadline December 31. Jim and Vanita Oeschlager Leadership Award; $1,000-$17,000 per year; based on leadership and service. Academic Scholarship; $500-$1,500 per year; based on upper 30% of high school class, 21 ACT, 3.0 GPA. Akron Advantage Award; non-resident surcharge reduction of 60% or 100%; for students who meet academic criteria from 49 states outside of Ohio plus U.S. territories. *Athletic:* 42 full-time freshmen received athletic scholarships; average amount $11,804.

Cumulative student debt: 65% of graduating class had student loans; average debt was $19,000.

FINANCIAL AID PROCEDURES

Forms required: FAFSA, institutional form.

Dates and Deadlines: Priority date 2/1; no closing date. Applicants notified on a rolling basis starting 4/1; must reply within 2 week(s) of notification.

Transfers: Priority date 3/1; no deadline. Applicants notified on a rolling basis starting 6/15; must reply within 2 week(s) of notification.

CONTACT

Douglas McNutt, Director, Student Financial Aid

Simmons Hall, Akron, OH 44325-2001

(330) 972-7032

University of Akron: Wayne College

Orrville, Ohio

www.wayne.uakron.edu   Federal Code: 003123

2-year public branch campus and junior college in small town.

Enrollment: 1,514 undergrads.

Selectivity: Open admission.

BASIC COSTS (2009-2010)

Tuition and fees: $5,424; out-of-state residents $12,948.

Per-credit charge: $219; out-of-state residents $614.

FINANCIAL AID PICTURE

Students with need: Need-based aid available for full-time and part-time students. Work study available nights, weekends, and for part-time students.

Students without need: No-need awards available for academics, art, athletics, leadership, minority status, music/drama, state/district residency.

Additional info: All financial aid processed through University of Akron.

FINANCIAL AID PROCEDURES
Forms required: FAFSA, institutional form.
Dates and Deadlines: Closing date 3/15. Applicants notified on a rolling basis starting 4/15.

CONTACT
Theresa Mountel, Financial Aid Counselor
1901 Smucker Road, Orrville, OH 44667-9758
(330) 684-8900

University of Cincinnati
Cincinnati, Ohio
www.uc.edu   Federal Code: 003125

4-year public university in large city.
Enrollment: 21,339 undergrads, 15% part-time. 4,240 full-time freshmen.
Selectivity: Admits 50 to 75% of applicants.

BASIC COSTS (2009-2010)
Tuition and fees: $9,399; out-of-state residents $23,922.
Per-credit charge: $262; out-of-state residents $665.
Room and board: $9,702.

FINANCIAL AID PICTURE (2009-2010)
Students with need: Out of 3,566 full-time freshmen who applied for aid, 2,680 were judged to have need. Of these, 2,653 received aid, and 115 had their full need met. Average financial aid package met 64% of need; average scholarship/grant was $6,342; average loan was $3,365. For part-time students, average financial aid package was $6,498.
Students without need: 644 full-time freshmen who did not demonstrate need for aid received scholarships/grants; average award was $4,589. No-need awards available for academics, alumni affiliation, art, athletics, leadership, minority status, music/drama, ROTC, state/district residency.
Scholarships offered: 29 full-time freshmen received athletic scholarships; average amount $15,305.
Cumulative student debt: 69% of graduating class had student loans; average debt was $25,878.

FINANCIAL AID PROCEDURES
Forms required: FAFSA.
Dates and Deadlines: No deadline. Applicants notified on a rolling basis starting 3/12; must reply within 2 week(s) of notification.

CONTACT
Connie Williams, Director, Financial Aid
PO Box 210091, Cincinnati, OH 45221-0091
(513) 556-6982

University of Cincinnati: Clermont College
Batavia, Ohio
www.ucclermont.edu   Federal Code: 003125

2-year public branch campus college in small town.
Enrollment: 3,273 undergrads, 30% part-time. 760 full-time freshmen.
Selectivity: Open admission; but selective for some programs.

BASIC COSTS (2009-2010)
Tuition and fees: $4,542; out-of-state residents $11,394.
Per-credit charge: $127; out-of-state residents $317.

FINANCIAL AID PICTURE (2009-2010)
Students with need: Need-based aid available for full-time and part-time students. Work study available nights, weekends, and for part-time students.

Students without need: No-need awards available for academics, state/district residency.
Additional info: All financial aid applications and awards administered through Uptown campus except in-house loans and scholarships.

FINANCIAL AID PROCEDURES
Forms required: FAFSA.
Dates and Deadlines: No deadline. Applicants notified on a rolling basis.

CONTACT
Jessica Max, University Services Associate
4200 Clermont College Drive, Batavia, OH 45103
(513) 732-5202

University of Cincinnati: Raymond Walters College
Cincinnati, Ohio
www.rwc.uc.edu   Federal Code: 003125

2-year public branch campus college in large city.
Enrollment: 4,477 undergrads.
Selectivity: Open admission; but selective for some programs.

BASIC COSTS (2009-2010)
Tuition and fees: $5,232; out-of-state residents $13,566.
Per-credit charge: $146; out-of-state residents $377.

FINANCIAL AID PICTURE
Students with need: Need-based aid available for full-time and part-time students.
Students without need: This college awards aid only to students with need.
Scholarships offered: Dean's scholarships: $1,500; based on 2.5 GPA, tech prep program participation, 2-page essay; 10 available. Cincinnatus Scholarship Competition: $1,500 to full tuition, room, board and books; must have 26 ACT or be in top 5% of high school class to qualify.
Additional info: All financial aid applications and awards administered through main campus.

FINANCIAL AID PROCEDURES
Forms required: FAFSA.
Dates and Deadlines: Priority date 3/15; no closing date. Applicants notified on a rolling basis starting 3/15; must reply within 2 week(s) of notification.

CONTACT
Chris Powers, Director of Enrollment Management
9555 Plainfield Road, Cincinnati, OH 45236-1096
(513) 745-5740

University of Dayton
Dayton, Ohio
www.udayton.edu   Federal Code: 003127

4-year private university in small city, affiliated with Roman Catholic Church.
Enrollment: 7,183 undergrads, 4% part-time. 1,995 full-time freshmen.
Selectivity: Admits 50 to 75% of applicants.

BASIC COSTS (2010-2011)
Tuition and fees: $29,930.
Per-credit charge: $957.
Room and board: $9,500.
Additional info: Tuition/fee waivers available for adults.

FINANCIAL AID PICTURE (2008-2009)

Students with need: Out of 1,540 full-time freshmen who applied for aid, 1,116 were judged to have need. Of these, 1,112 received aid, and 519 had their full need met. Average financial aid package met 98% of need; average scholarship/grant was $18,956; average loan was $6,962. For part-time students, average financial aid package was $3,577.

Students without need: 870 full-time freshmen who did not demonstrate need for aid received scholarships/grants; average award was $8,913. No-need awards available for academics, alumni affiliation, art, leadership, music/drama, ROTC, state/district residency.

Scholarships offered: *Merit:* Berry Scholarships; up to full tuition; based on GPA, ACT/SAT scores, service and leadership. Marianist Heritage Awards; $1,000 to full tuition; available to all graduates of Marianist high schools who meet academic criteria. Music talent awards; $1,000 to $5,000; based on auditions. President's Scholarship; $1,000 to $10,000; based on GPA, ACT/SAT scores, service and leadership. Visual arts awards; amounts vary; based on student portfolios. Chaminade Scholarships; $2,500; for students accepted to the Chaminade Scholars Program. National Merit Scholarships; $1,000 to $2,000; available to all students who are selected by the National Merit Scholarship Corporation and select UD as their first choice. Army ROTC awards; supplements U.S. Army ROTC awards with scholarship incentives. *Athletic:* 21 full-time freshmen received athletic scholarships; average amount $22,162.

Cumulative student debt: 87% of graduating class had student loans; average debt was $32,862.

FINANCIAL AID PROCEDURES

Forms required: FAFSA.

Dates and Deadlines: Priority date 3/31; no closing date. Applicants notified on a rolling basis starting 3/15; must reply by 5/1 or within 3 week(s) of notification.

Transfers: Priority date 6/1; no deadline. Applicants notified on a rolling basis starting 2/25; must reply within 2 week(s) of notification. Students must submit FAFSA prior to October 1 each year for consideration for state funds.

CONTACT

Kathy Harmon, Director of Financial Aid
300 College Park, Dayton, OH 45469-1300
(937) 229-4311

University of Findlay
Findlay, Ohio
www.findlay.edu   Federal Code: 003045

4-year private university and health science college in large town, affiliated with Church of God.

Enrollment: 2,944 undergrads, 11% part-time. 645 full-time freshmen.

Selectivity: Admits 50 to 75% of applicants.

BASIC COSTS (2009-2010)

Tuition and fees: $25,774.

Per-credit charge: $552.

Room and board: $8,554.

Additional info: Pre-veterinary and equestrian students pay higher tuition in years one and two; pharmacy students pay higher tuition throughout the program.

FINANCIAL AID PICTURE (2008-2009)

Students with need: Out of 585 full-time freshmen who applied for aid, 462 were judged to have need. Of these, 462 received aid, and 59 had their full need met. Average financial aid package met 71% of need; average scholarship/grant was $12,371; average loan was $2,828.

Students without need: 97 full-time freshmen who did not demonstrate need for aid received scholarships/grants; average award was $11,464. No-need awards available for academics, alumni affiliation, athletics, music/drama, state/district residency.

Scholarships offered: *Merit:* Full tuition available to select valedictorian/salutatorians. Automatic academic awards available based on GPA, test scores. *Athletic:* 62 full-time freshmen received athletic scholarships; average amount $8,921.

Cumulative student debt: 89% of graduating class had student loans; average debt was $37,267.

FINANCIAL AID PROCEDURES

Forms required: FAFSA.

Dates and Deadlines: Priority date 8/1; closing date 9/1. Applicants notified on a rolling basis starting 3/1; must reply within 2 week(s) of notification.

CONTACT

Arman Habegger, Director of Financial Aid
1000 North Main Street, Findlay, OH 45840-3653
(419) 434-4791

University of Northwestern Ohio
Lima, Ohio
www.unoh.edu   Federal Code: 004861

2-year private business and technical college in large town.

Enrollment: 3,873 undergrads.

BASIC COSTS (2009-2010)

Tuition and fees: $9,075.

Per-credit charge: $195.

Room only: $2,700.

Additional info: $250 per credit hour charge for virtual classes. Tuition/fee waivers available for minority students.

FINANCIAL AID PICTURE (2008-2009)

Students with need: Need-based aid available for full-time and part-time students. Work study available nights.

Students without need: No-need awards available for academics, job skills, minority status.

FINANCIAL AID PROCEDURES

Forms required: FAFSA.

Dates and Deadlines: Priority date 4/1; no closing date. Applicants notified on a rolling basis starting 4/30; must reply within 2 week(s) of notification.

Transfers: No deadline. Applicants notified on a rolling basis.

CONTACT

Wendell Schick, Director of Financial Aid
1441 North Cable Road, Lima, OH 45805
(419) 227-3141

University of Rio Grande
Rio Grande, Ohio
www.rio.edu   Federal Code: 003116

4-year private community and liberal arts college in rural community.

Enrollment: 1,534 undergrads, 20% part-time. 310 full-time freshmen.

Selectivity: Open admission; but selective for some programs.

BASIC COSTS (2009-2010)

Tuition and fees: $18,260.

Room and board: $7,600.

Additional info: Tuition reported is for private university sector of institution. Public community college in-state in-district tuition: $2,970 ($96 per credit hour); in-state out-of-district, $3,450 ($115 per credit hour). All public community college undergraduates pay $632 in required fees. Out-of-state community college students charged private tuition rate.

FINANCIAL AID PICTURE (2008-2009)

Students with need: Out of 296 full-time freshmen who applied for aid, 225 were judged to have need. Of these, 225 received aid. Need-based aid available for part-time students.

Students without need: No-need awards available for academics, alumni affiliation, athletics, leadership, music/drama, state/district residency.

Scholarships offered: 8 full-time freshmen received athletic scholarships; average amount $8,246.

Cumulative student debt: 75% of graduating class had student loans; average debt was $17,862.

FINANCIAL AID PROCEDURES

Forms required: FAFSA, institutional form.

Dates and Deadlines: Priority date 3/15; no closing date. Applicants notified on a rolling basis starting 1/15; must reply within 3 week(s) of notification.

CONTACT

Dawn Knepper, Financial Aid Director
218 North College Avenue, Rio Grande, OH 45674
(740) 245-7218

University of Toledo
Toledo, Ohio
www.utoledo.edu   Federal Code: 003131

4-year public university in large city.

Enrollment: 17,545 undergrads, 15% part-time. 4,178 full-time freshmen.

Selectivity: Open admission, but selective for some programs and for out-of-state students.

BASIC COSTS (2009-2010)

Tuition and fees: $7,926; out-of-state residents $16,738.

Per-credit charge: $284; out-of-state residents $651.

Room and board: $8,814.

FINANCIAL AID PICTURE (2009-2010)

Students with need: Out of 3,826 full-time freshmen who applied for aid, 3,139 were judged to have need. Of these, 3,132 received aid, and 30 had their full need met. Average financial aid package met 60% of need; average scholarship/grant was $7,294; average loan was $3,585. For part-time students, average financial aid package was $8,127.

Students without need: 971 full-time freshmen who did not demonstrate need for aid received scholarships/grants; average award was $4,346. No-need awards available for academics, alumni affiliation, art, athletics, leadership, minority status, music/drama, ROTC, state/district residency.

Scholarships offered: *Merit:* Freshman merit scholarships; $100 to $4,500; 400 awarded. *Athletic:* 28 full-time freshmen received athletic scholarships; average amount $13,267.

Cumulative student debt: 41% of graduating class had student loans; average debt was $36,116.

Additional info: March priority date for federal aid. Students encouraged to apply as early as December for priority consideration for institutional aid.

FINANCIAL AID PROCEDURES

Forms required: FAFSA.

Dates and Deadlines: Priority date 4/1; no closing date. Applicants notified on a rolling basis starting 4/1.

CONTACT

Carolyn Baumgartner, Director of Financial Aid
2801 West Bancroft Street, Toledo, OH 43606-3398
(419) 530-2800

Urbana University
Urbana, Ohio
www.urbana.edu   Federal Code: 003133

4-year private liberal arts college in large town.

Enrollment: 787 full-time undergrads. 177 full-time freshmen.

Selectivity: Admits 50 to 75% of applicants.

BASIC COSTS (2009-2010)

Tuition and fees: $20,410.

Per-credit charge: $415.

Room and board: $8,000.

FINANCIAL AID PICTURE (2008-2009)

Students with need: Out of 174 full-time freshmen who applied for aid, 161 were judged to have need. Of these, 161 received aid, and 26 had their full need met. Average financial aid package met 73% of need; average scholarship/grant was $2,547; average loan was $3,695. For part-time students, average financial aid package was $5,187.

Students without need: 1 full-time freshmen who did not demonstrate need for aid received scholarships/grants; average award was $14,000. No-need awards available for academics, alumni affiliation, athletics, music/drama.

Scholarships offered: 19 full-time freshmen received athletic scholarships; average amount $6,618.

Cumulative student debt: 100% of graduating class had student loans; average debt was $31,149.

FINANCIAL AID PROCEDURES

Forms required: FAFSA.

Dates and Deadlines: Closing date 4/15. Applicants notified on a rolling basis starting 3/1; must reply within 4 week(s) of notification.

Transfers: No deadline. Applicants notified on a rolling basis starting 3/1; must reply within 4 week(s) of notification.

CONTACT

Amy Barnhart, Director of Financial Aid
579 College Way, Urbana, OH 43078
(937) 484-1355

Ursuline College
Pepper Pike, Ohio
www.ursuline.edu   Federal Code: 003134

4-year private liberal arts college for women in small town, affiliated with Roman Catholic Church.

Enrollment: 1,062 undergrads, 35% part-time. 110 full-time freshmen.

Selectivity: Admits over 75% of applicants.

BASIC COSTS (2010-2011)

Tuition and fees: $23,940.

Per-credit charge: $790.

Room and board: $7,970.

FINANCIAL AID PICTURE (2008-2009)

Students with need: Out of 109 full-time freshmen who applied for aid, 104 were judged to have need. Of these, 104 received aid, and 25 had their full need met. Average financial aid package met 86% of need; average scholarship/grant was $15,692; average loan was $4,416. For part-time students, average financial aid package was $8,439.

Students without need: 5 full-time freshmen who did not demonstrate need for aid received scholarships/grants; average award was $5,822. No-need awards available for academics, art, athletics, leadership, religious affiliation, ROTC.

Scholarships offered: *Merit:* Ursuline Scholarship; $5,000 to $7,000 renewable. Ursuline Award; $1,500 to $3,500 renewable. Presidential Scholarship;

$11,000 renewable. Dean's Scholarship; $9,000 renewable. Unlimited number available for each. *Athletic:* 3 full-time freshmen received athletic scholarships; average amount $4,132.
Cumulative student debt: 84% of graduating class had student loans; average debt was $22,723.

FINANCIAL AID PROCEDURES
Forms required: FAFSA.
Dates and Deadlines: Priority date 3/15; no closing date. Applicants notified on a rolling basis starting 3/1; must reply within 2 week(s) of notification.
Transfers: No deadline. Applicants notified on a rolling basis; must reply within 4 week(s) of notification.

CONTACT
Mary Lynn Perri, Director of Financial Aid
2550 Lander Road, Pepper Pike, OH 44124-4398
(440) 684-6114

Virginia Marti College of Art and Design
Lakewood, Ohio
www.vmcad.edu   Federal Code: 012896

2-year for-profit visual arts and business college in large city.
Enrollment: 279 undergrads.

BASIC COSTS (2009-2010)
Tuition and fees: $20,040.
Per-credit charge: $360.

FINANCIAL AID PICTURE
Students with need: Need-based aid available for full-time students.
Students without need: This college awards aid only to students with need.

FINANCIAL AID PROCEDURES
Forms required: FAFSA.
Dates and Deadlines: No deadline. Applicants notified on a rolling basis.

CONTACT
Jennifer Minkiewicz, Financial Aid Officer
11724 Detroit Avenue, Lakewood, OH 44107

Walsh University
North Canton, Ohio
www.walsh.edu   Federal Code: 003135

4-year private university and liberal arts college in small city, affiliated with Roman Catholic Church.
Enrollment: 2,278 undergrads, 17% part-time. 490 full-time freshmen.
Selectivity: Admits over 75% of applicants.

BASIC COSTS (2010-2011)
Tuition and fees: $22,280.
Per-credit charge: $710.
Room and board: $8,360.

FINANCIAL AID PICTURE (2009-2010)
Students with need: Out of 471 full-time freshmen who applied for aid, 409 were judged to have need. Of these, 409 received aid, and 209 had their full need met. Average financial aid package met 77% of need; average scholarship/grant was $5,918; average loan was $3,960. For part-time students, average financial aid package was $7,066.
Students without need. 81 full-time freshmen who did not demonstrate need for aid received scholarships/grants; average award was $8,200. No-need awards available for academics, alumni affiliation, athletics, music/drama, religious affiliation, state/district residency.

Scholarships offered: *Merit:* $1,000 for incoming freshmen who have graduated from Catholic high school. *Athletic:* 123 full-time freshmen received athletic scholarships; average amount $4,338.
Cumulative student debt: 92% of graduating class had student loans; average debt was $23,446.

FINANCIAL AID PROCEDURES
Forms required: FAFSA, institutional form.
Dates and Deadlines: Priority date 2/14; no closing date. Applicants notified on a rolling basis starting 2/15.
Transfers: No deadline. Applicants notified on a rolling basis starting 3/15.

CONTACT
Holly Van Gilder, Financial Aid Director
2020 East Maple Street NW, North Canton, OH 44720-3396
(330) 490-7146

Wilberforce University
Wilberforce, Ohio
www.wilberforce.edu   Federal Code: 003141

4-year private liberal arts college in rural community, affiliated with African Methodist Episcopal Church.
Enrollment: 733 undergrads.

BASIC COSTS (2010-2011)
Tuition and fees: $12,470.
Per-credit charge: $469.
Room and board: $5,700.

FINANCIAL AID PICTURE
Students with need: Need-based aid available for full-time and part-time students.

FINANCIAL AID PROCEDURES
Forms required: FAFSA, institutional form.
Dates and Deadlines: Priority date 3/15; closing date 6/1. Applicants notified on a rolling basis starting 3/15; must reply within 2 week(s) of notification.

CONTACT
Shelline Warren, Director for Financial Aid
1055 North Bickett Road, Wilberforce, OH 45384-1001
(937) 708-5727

Wilmington College
Wilmington, Ohio
www.wilmington.edu   Federal Code: 003142

4-year private liberal arts college in large town, affiliated with Society of Friends (Quaker).
Enrollment: 1,395 undergrads, 17% part-time. 335 full-time freshmen.
Selectivity: Admits over 75% of applicants.

BASIC COSTS (2009-2010)
Tuition and fees: $24,286.
Room and board: $8,272.

FINANCIAL AID PICTURE
Students with need: Need-based aid available for full-time and part-time students.
Students without need: No-need awards available for academics, alumni affiliation, religious affiliation, state/district residency.

FINANCIAL AID PROCEDURES
Forms required: FAFSA.

Dates and Deadlines: Priority date 3/31; closing date 6/1. Applicants notified on a rolling basis starting 3/1; must reply by 5/1 or within 2 week(s) of notification.

CONTACT
Cheryl Louallen, Director of Financial Aid
Box 1325 Pyle Center, Wilmington, OH 45177
(937) 382-6661 ext. 249

Wittenberg University
Springfield, Ohio
www.wittenberg.edu   Federal Code: 003143

4-year private liberal arts college in small city, affiliated with Evangelical Lutheran Church in America.

Enrollment: 1,745 undergrads. 490 full-time freshmen.
Selectivity: Admits 50 to 75% of applicants.

BASIC COSTS (2010-2011)
Tuition and fees: $35,424.
Per-credit charge: $1,162.
Room and board: $9,032.
Additional info: Tuition/fee waivers available for adults.

FINANCIAL AID PICTURE (2009-2010)
Students with need: Out of 432 full-time freshmen who applied for aid, 376 were judged to have need. Of these, 376 received aid, and 120 had their full need met. Average financial aid package met 88% of need; average scholarship/grant was $24,377; average loan was $4,147. For part-time students, average financial aid package was $8,573.
Students without need: This college awards aid only to students with need.
Scholarships offered: Smith Family Scholar Award; full tuition; renewable; based on academic achievement and other qualities. University Scholar Award; half tuition; renewable; based on academic achievement and other qualities. Broadwell Chinn Scholarship; half tuition; renewable; based on minority status, academic achievement, and other qualities.
Cumulative student debt: 68% of graduating class had student loans; average debt was $29,332.
Additional info: Auditions required from applicants for music, theater, and dance scholarships. Portfolio required of applicants for art scholarships.

FINANCIAL AID PROCEDURES
Forms required: FAFSA.
Dates and Deadlines: Priority date 3/1; no closing date. Applicants notified on a rolling basis starting 3/1; must reply by 5/1 or within 2 week(s) of notification.
Transfers: Priority date 5/15; no deadline. Applicants notified on a rolling basis; must reply within 2 week(s) of notification.

CONTACT
Jonathan Green, Director of Financial Aid
Ward Street and North Wittenberg, Springfield, OH 45501-0720
(937) 327-7321

Wright State University
Dayton, Ohio
www.wright.edu   Federal Code: 003078

4-year public university in small city.

Enrollment: 13,024 undergrads, 14% part-time. 2,508 full-time freshmen.
Selectivity: Admits over 75% of applicants.

BASIC COSTS (2009-2010)
Tuition and fees: $7,533; out-of-state residents $14,595.
Per-credit charge: $227; out-of-state residents $443.

Room and board: $7,829.

FINANCIAL AID PICTURE (2009-2010)
Students with need: Out of 2,248 full-time freshmen who applied for aid, 1,849 were judged to have need. Of these, 1,833 received aid, and 209 had their full need met. Average financial aid package met 56% of need; average scholarship/grant was $6,099; average loan was $3,288. For part-time students, average financial aid package was $8,145.
Students without need: 248 full-time freshmen who did not demonstrate need for aid received scholarships/grants; average award was $3,249. No-need awards available for academics, alumni affiliation, art, athletics, leadership, minority status, music/drama, ROTC.
Scholarships offered: 24 full-time freshmen received athletic scholarships; average amount $14,242.
Cumulative student debt: 73% of graduating class had student loans; average debt was $25,357.

FINANCIAL AID PROCEDURES
Forms required: FAFSA.
Dates and Deadlines: Priority date 2/15; no closing date. Applicants notified on a rolling basis starting 3/15.

CONTACT
Willie Boyd, Director of Financial Aid
3640 Colonel Glenn Highway, Dayton, OH 45435
(937) 775-5721

Wright State University: Lake Campus
Celina, Ohio
www.wright.edu/lake   Federal Code: 003078

2-year public branch campus college in small town.

Enrollment: 840 undergrads, 17% part-time. 191 full-time freshmen.
Selectivity: Open admission; but selective for some programs.

BASIC COSTS (2009-2010)
Tuition and fees: $5,064; out-of-state residents $12,126.
Per-credit charge: $153; out-of-state residents $369.

FINANCIAL AID PICTURE (2009-2010)
Students with need: Average financial aid package met 58% of need; average scholarship/grant was $5,791; average loan was $3,260. For part-time students, average financial aid package was $8,339.
Students without need: No-need awards available for academics, alumni affiliation, art, athletics, leadership, minority status, music/drama, ROTC.
Cumulative student debt: 73% of graduating class had student loans; average debt was $25,357.

FINANCIAL AID PROCEDURES
Forms required: FAFSA.
Dates and Deadlines: Priority date 2/15; no closing date. Applicants notified on a rolling basis starting 3/15.

CONTACT
Willie Boyd, Director of Financial Aid
7600 State Route 703, Celina, OH 45822-2952
(937) 775-5721

Xavier University
Cincinnati, Ohio
www.xavier.edu   Federal Code: 003144

4-year private university in large city, affiliated with Roman Catholic Church.

Enrollment: 4,083 undergrads, 9% part-time. 1,178 full-time freshmen.
Selectivity: Admits 50 to 75% of applicants.

BASIC COSTS (2010-2011)

Tuition and fees: $29,970.
Per-credit charge: $575.
Room and board: $9,900.

FINANCIAL AID PICTURE (2009-2010)

Students with need: Out of 977 full-time freshmen who applied for aid, 776 were judged to have need. Of these, 775 received aid, and 176 had their full need met. Average financial aid package met 80% of need; average scholarship/grant was $14,659; average loan was $4,165. For part-time students, average financial aid package was $6,928.
Students without need: 372 full-time freshmen who did not demonstrate need for aid received scholarships/grants; average award was $12,034. No-need awards available for academics, alumni affiliation, art, athletics, leadership, music/drama, religious affiliation.
Scholarships offered: *Merit:* Saint Francis Xavier Scholarship; full tuition; based on leadership, talent and highest academic achievement, competitive; 10 awarded. Community Engaged Fellowship; $18,000; 10 awarded. Chancellor Scholarship; $17,000; based on leadership, talent, and highest academic achievement; number of award varies. Trustee Scholarship; $15,000; based on academic achievement; number of award varies. Schawe Scholarship; $15,000; based on academic achievement; number of award varies. Presidential Scholarship; $13,000; based on academic achievement; number of award varies. Honor Award; $10,000; based on academic achievement; number of award varies. Buschmann Award; $8,000; based on academic leadership and service records; number of award varies. Leadership Award; $5,000; number of award varies. *Athletic:* 43 full-time freshmen received athletic scholarships; average amount $12,032.
Cumulative student debt: 69% of graduating class had student loans; average debt was $22,769.

FINANCIAL AID PROCEDURES

Forms required: FAFSA.
Dates and Deadlines: Priority date 2/15; no closing date. Applicants notified on a rolling basis starting 2/15; must reply by 5/1.
Transfers: No deadline. Applicants notified on a rolling basis starting 3/1; must reply by 5/1.

CONTACT

Paul Calme, Director of Financial Aid
3800 Victory Parkway, Cincinnati, OH 45207-5311
(513) 745-3142

Youngstown State University

Youngstown, Ohio
www.ysu.edu   Federal Code: 003145

4-year public university in small city.
Enrollment: 13,035 undergrads, 20% part-time. 2,082 full-time freshmen.
Selectivity: Open admission; but selective for some programs and for out-of-state students.

BASIC COSTS (2009-2010)

Tuition and fees: $6,721; out-of-state residents $12,394.
Room and board: $7,400.
Additional info: Residents of any out-of-state area within 100 miles of campus are charged $9,414 yearly tuition. Per credit hour charge is $392.

FINANCIAL AID PICTURE (2008-2009)

Students with need: Out of 1,839 full-time freshmen who applied for aid, 1,528 were judged to have need. Of these, 1,528 received aid, and 148 had their full need met. For part-time students, average financial aid package was $1,551.
Students without need: 158 full-time freshmen who did not demonstrate need for aid received scholarships/grants. No-need awards available for academics, alumni affiliation, athletics, ROTC, state/district residency.
Scholarships offered: 56 full-time freshmen received athletic scholarships.

FINANCIAL AID PROCEDURES

Forms required: FAFSA, institutional form.
Dates and Deadlines: Priority date 2/15; no closing date. Applicants notified on a rolling basis starting 5/30; must reply within 2 week(s) of notification.

CONTACT

Elaine Ruse, Director of Scholarships and Financial Aid
One University Plaza, Youngstown, OH 44555-0001
(330) 941-3505

Zane State College

Zanesville, Ohio
www.zanestate.edu   Federal Code: 008133

2-year public technical college in large town.
Enrollment: 2,173 undergrads.
Selectivity: Open admission; but selective for some programs.

BASIC COSTS (2009-2010)

Tuition and fees: $3,875; out-of-state residents $7,700.
Per-credit charge: $85; out-of-state residents $170.

FINANCIAL AID PICTURE

Students with need: Need-based aid available for full-time and part-time students.

FINANCIAL AID PROCEDURES

Forms required: FAFSA.
Dates and Deadlines: Priority date 5/1; closing date 6/30. Must reply by 9/1.

CONTACT

Amanda Reisinger, Financial Aid Director
1555 Newark Road, Zanesville, OH 43701-2626
(740) 454-2501 ext. 1275

Oklahoma

Bacone College

Muskogee, Oklahoma
www.bacone.edu   Federal Code: 003147

4-year private liberal arts college in large town, affiliated with American Baptist Churches in the USA.
Enrollment: 1,021 undergrads.
Selectivity: Admits over 75% of applicants.

BASIC COSTS (2010-2011)

Tuition and fees: $12,300.
Per-credit charge: $450.
Room and board: $7,700.

FINANCIAL AID PICTURE (2009-2010)

Students with need: Need-based aid available for full-time and part-time students. Work study available nights, weekends, and for part-time students.
Students without need: This college awards aid only to students with need.

FINANCIAL AID PROCEDURES

Forms required: FAFSA.
Dates and Deadlines: Priority date 3/31; no closing date. Applicants notified on a rolling basis starting 4/1; must reply within 2 week(s) of notification.
Transfers: No deadline. Applicants notified on a rolling basis.

CONTACT

Kathye Watson, Director of Financial Aid
2299 Old Bacone Road, Muskogee, OK 74403
(918) 781-7340

Cameron University

Lawton, Oklahoma
www.cameron.edu   Federal Code: 003150

4-year public university in small city.
Enrollment: 5,222 undergrads, 29% part-time. 969 full-time freshmen.
Selectivity: Open admission.

BASIC COSTS (2009-2010)

Tuition and fees: $4,110; out-of-state residents $9,975.
Per-credit charge: $94; out-of-state residents $289.
Room and board: $3,576.

FINANCIAL AID PICTURE (2008-2009)

Students with need: Out of 688 full-time freshmen who applied for aid, 605 were judged to have need. Of these, 532 received aid, and 441 had their full need met. Average financial aid package met 91% of need; average scholarship/grant was $4,000; average loan was $1,200. For part-time students, average financial aid package was $8,200.
Students without need: 364 full-time freshmen who did not demonstrate need for aid received scholarships/grants; average award was $750. No-need awards available for academics, alumni affiliation, art, athletics, leadership, music/drama, ROTC.
Scholarships offered: 24 full-time freshmen received athletic scholarships; average amount $1,000.
Cumulative student debt: 30% of graduating class had student loans; average debt was $7,000.

FINANCIAL AID PROCEDURES

Forms required: FAFSA.
Dates and Deadlines: Priority date 5/1; no closing date. Applicants notified on a rolling basis starting 4/1; must reply by 8/7 or within 2 week(s) of notification.
Transfers: Priority date 6/1; no deadline. Applicants notified on a rolling basis starting 6/1. Academic transcripts required.

CONTACT

Carol Claiborne, Director of Financial Assistance
2800 West Gore Boulevard, Lawton, OK 73505-6377
(580) 581-2293

Carl Albert State College

Poteau, Oklahoma
www.carlalbert.edu   Federal Code: 003176

2-year public community and junior college in large town.
Enrollment: 2,496 undergrads.
Selectivity: Open admission; but selective for some programs.

BASIC COSTS (2009-2010)

Tuition and fees: $2,250; out-of-state residents $5,220.
Per-credit charge: $50; out-of-state residents $150.
Room and board: $3,584.
Additional info: Tuition/fee waivers available for minority students.

FINANCIAL AID PICTURE

Students with need: Need-based aid available for full-time and part-time students. Work study available nights.
Students without need: This college awards aid only to students with need.

FINANCIAL AID PROCEDURES

Forms required: FAFSA, institutional form.
Dates and Deadlines: No deadline. Applicants notified on a rolling basis.

CONTACT

Robin Benson, Director of Financial Aid
1507 South McKenna, Poteau, OK 74953-5208
(918) 647-1343

Connors State College

Warner, Oklahoma
www.connorsstate.edu   Federal Code: 003153

2-year public community and junior college in rural community.
Enrollment: 1,809 undergrads, 29% part-time. 513 full-time freshmen.
Selectivity: Open admission; but selective for some programs.

BASIC COSTS (2009-2010)

Tuition and fees: $2,648; out-of-state residents $6,275.
Per-credit charge: $66; out-of-state residents $187.
Room and board: $6,976.
Additional info: Apartment-style housing.

FINANCIAL AID PICTURE (2009-2010)

Students with need: Need-based aid available for full-time and part-time students.
Students without need: No-need awards available for academics, alumni affiliation, athletics, leadership, state/district residency.

FINANCIAL AID PROCEDURES

Forms required: FAFSA, institutional form.
Dates and Deadlines: Priority date 2/28; closing date 5/1. Applicants notified on a rolling basis starting 4/1; must reply within 2 week(s) of notification.

CONTACT

Jennifer Watkins, Director of Financial Aid
RR 1, Box 1000, Warner, OK 74469-9700
(918) 463-6220

East Central University

Ada, Oklahoma
www.ecok.edu   Federal Code: 003154

4-year public university in large town.
Enrollment: 3,730 undergrads, 19% part-time. 516 full-time freshmen.
Selectivity: Admits over 75% of applicants.

BASIC COSTS (2009-2010)

Tuition and fees: $4,221; out-of-state residents $10,236.
Per-credit charge: $100; out-of-state residents $301.
Room and board: $4,324.

FINANCIAL AID PICTURE (2008-2009)

Students with need: Out of 429 full-time freshmen who applied for aid, 341 were judged to have need. Of these, 327 received aid, and 94 had their full need met. Average financial aid package met 56% of need; average scholarship/grant was $5,297; average loan was $3,705. For part-time students, average financial aid package was $646.
Students without need: No-need awards available for academics, athletics.
Scholarships offered: 74 full-time freshmen received athletic scholarships; average amount $4,269.
Cumulative student debt: 37% of graduating class had student loans; average debt was $20,965.

FINANCIAL AID PROCEDURES

Forms required: FAFSA.

Dates and Deadlines: Closing date 3/1. Applicants notified on a rolling basis starting 4/15; must reply within 2 week(s) of notification.

CONTACT

Marilyn Schwarz, Director of Student Financial Aid
PMBJ8, 1100 East 14th Street, Ada, OK 74820
(580) 559-5243

Eastern Oklahoma State College
Wilburton, Oklahoma
www.eosc.edu   Federal Code: 003155

2-year public community college in small town.
Enrollment: 1,909 undergrads.
Selectivity: Open admission; but selective for some programs.

BASIC COSTS (2009-2010)
Tuition and fees: $2,835; out-of-state residents $6,451.
Per-credit charge: $68; out-of-state residents $189.
Room and board: $4,668.
Additional info: Tuition/fee waivers available for minority students, unemployed or children of unemployed.

FINANCIAL AID PICTURE (2008-2009)
Students with need: Need-based aid available for full-time and part-time students.
Students without need: This college awards aid only to students with need.

FINANCIAL AID PROCEDURES
Forms required: FAFSA, institutional form.
Dates and Deadlines: Priority date 3/1; closing date 6/30. Applicants notified on a rolling basis starting 5/1; must reply within 2 week(s) of notification.
Transfers: Priority date 4/30.

CONTACT
Mimi Kelley, Director of Financial Aid
1301 West Main Street, Wilburton, OK 74578-4999
(918) 465-2361 ext. 207

Langston University
Langston, Oklahoma   Federal Code: 003157
www.lunet.edu   CSS Code: 6361

4-year public university and liberal arts college in rural community.
Enrollment: 2,390 undergrads, 13% part-time. 536 full-time freshmen.
Selectivity: Admits less than 50% of applicants.

BASIC COSTS (2009-2010)
Tuition and fees: $3,827; out-of-state residents $9,407.
Per-credit charge: $88; out-of-state residents $274.
Room and board: $7,120.
Additional info: Housing is apartment-style.

FINANCIAL AID PICTURE (2009-2010)
Students with need: Need-based aid available for full-time and part-time students.
Students without need: This college awards aid only to students with need.

FINANCIAL AID PROCEDURES
Forms required: CSS PROFILE, state aid form.
Dates and Deadlines: Priority date 3/1; closing date 5/1. Applicants notified on a rolling basis starting 7/15; must reply within 2 week(s) of notification.

CONTACT
Linda Morris, Financial Aid Director
Box 728, Langston, OK 73050

Mid-America Christian University
Oklahoma City, Oklahoma
www.macu.edu   Federal Code: 006942

4-year private university and liberal arts college in very large city, affiliated with Church of God.
Enrollment: 1,181 undergrads.
Selectivity: Open admission.

BASIC COSTS (2009-2010)
Tuition and fees: $13,480.
Per-credit charge: $520.
Room and board: $5,560.

FINANCIAL AID PICTURE (2009-2010)
Students with need: Need-based aid available for full-time and part-time students.
Students without need: No-need awards available for academics, leadership, minority status, music/drama.

FINANCIAL AID PROCEDURES
Forms required: FAFSA.
Dates and Deadlines: Priority date 5/1; no closing date. Applicants notified on a rolling basis starting 5/1.

CONTACT
James Menefee, Director of Student Financial Services
3500 SW 119th Street, Oklahoma City, OK 73170
(405) 692-3182

Northeastern Oklahoma Agricultural and Mechanical College
Miami, Oklahoma
www.neo.edu   Federal Code: 316000

2-year public community and junior college in large town.
Enrollment: 1,698 undergrads.
Selectivity: Open admission.

BASIC COSTS (2009-2010)
Tuition and fees: $2,637; out-of-state residents $6,458.
Per-credit charge: $58; out-of-state residents $185.
Room and board: $4,006.

FINANCIAL AID PICTURE (2008-2009)
Students with need: 66% of average financial aid package awarded as scholarships/grants, 34% awarded as loans/jobs. Need-based aid available for part-time students. Work study available nights, weekends, and for part-time students.
Students without need: No-need awards available for academics, art, athletics, leadership, music/drama, state/district residency.

FINANCIAL AID PROCEDURES
Forms required: FAFSA.
Dates and Deadlines: Priority date 4/1; no closing date. Applicants notified on a rolling basis starting 4/1; must reply by 8/30 or within 2 week(s) of notification.
Transfers: No deadline. Applicants notified on a rolling basis starting 4/1; must reply within 2 week(s) of notification.

CONTACT
David Fisher, Director of Financial Aid
200 I Street Northeast, Miami, OK 74354-6497
(918) 540-6235

Northeastern State University
Tahlequah, Oklahoma
www.nsuok.edu   Federal Code: 003161

4-year public university in large town.
Enrollment: 8,092 undergrads, 27% part-time. 1,056 full-time freshmen.
Selectivity: Admits 50 to 75% of applicants.

BASIC COSTS (2009-2010)
Tuition and fees: $4,180; out-of-state residents $10,270.
Per-credit charge: $107; out-of-state residents $310.
Room and board: $4,966.
Additional info: Tuition/fee waivers available for adults, minority students.

FINANCIAL AID PICTURE (2009-2010)
Students with need: Out of 917 full-time freshmen who applied for aid, 744 were judged to have need. Of these, 637 received aid, and 436 had their full need met. Average financial aid package met 72% of need; average scholarship/grant was $5,207; average loan was $2,391. For part-time students, average financial aid package was $6,175.
Students without need: 56 full-time freshmen who did not demonstrate need for aid received scholarships/grants; average award was $2,603. No-need awards available for academics, alumni affiliation, art, athletics, leadership, minority status, music/drama, religious affiliation, ROTC, state/district residency.
Scholarships offered: *Merit:* Honors Program; $3,000 per year with 28 ACT or up to $7,844 per year with 30 ACT; 3.8 high school GPA required.
Athletic: 48 full-time freshmen received athletic scholarships; average amount $5,174.
Cumulative student debt: 68% of graduating class had student loans; average debt was $24,143.

FINANCIAL AID PROCEDURES
Forms required: FAFSA, institutional form.
Dates and Deadlines: Priority date 3/15; no closing date. Applicants notified on a rolling basis starting 3/15.
Transfers: Priority date 12/15; no deadline. State grant deadline is April 15.

CONTACT
Teri Cochran, Director of Student Financial Services
600 North Grand Avenue, Tahlequah, OK 74464-2399
(918) 444-3456

Northern Oklahoma College
Tonkawa, Oklahoma
www.north-ok.edu   Federal Code: 003162

2-year public community college in small town.
Enrollment: 5,003 undergrads.
Selectivity: Open admission; but selective for out-of-state students.

BASIC COSTS (2009-2010)
Tuition and fees: $2,303; out-of-state residents $5,813.
Per-credit charge: $53; out-of-state residents $170.
Room and board: $3,980.
Additional info: Tuition/fee waivers available for adults, minority students, unemployed or children of unemployed.

FINANCIAL AID PICTURE
Students with need: Need-based aid available for full-time and part-time students.

FINANCIAL AID PROCEDURES
Forms required: FAFSA, institutional form.
Dates and Deadlines: Priority date 6/1; no closing date. Applicants notified on a rolling basis starting 4/1.

CONTACT
Linda Brown, Director of Financial Aid
Box 310, Tonkawa, OK 74653-0310
(580) 628-6240

Northwestern Oklahoma State University
Alva, Oklahoma
www.nwosu.edu   Federal Code: 003163

4-year public university and teachers college in small town.
Enrollment: 1,906 undergrads, 28% part-time. 337 full-time freshmen.
Selectivity: Admits over 75% of applicants.

BASIC COSTS (2009-2010)
Tuition and fees: $4,111; out-of-state residents $10,141.
Per-credit charge: $116; out-of-state residents $317.
Room and board: $3,700.

FINANCIAL AID PICTURE (2009-2010)
Students with need: Need-based aid available for full-time and part-time students. Work study available nights, weekends, and for part-time students.
Students without need: No-need awards available for academics, alumni affiliation, art, athletics, leadership, music/drama.

FINANCIAL AID PROCEDURES
Forms required: FAFSA.
Dates and Deadlines: No deadline. Applicants notified on a rolling basis starting 5/1.

CONTACT
Caleb Mosburg, Director of Financial Aid
709 Oklahoma Boulevard, Alva, OK 73717-2799
(580) 327-8542

Oklahoma Baptist University
Shawnee, Oklahoma
www.okbu.edu   Federal Code: 003164

4-year private university and liberal arts college in large town, affiliated with Southern Baptist Convention.
Enrollment: 1,520 undergrads, 5% part-time. 338 full-time freshmen.
Selectivity: Admits 50 to 75% of applicants.

BASIC COSTS (2010-2011)
Tuition and fees: $18,670.
Per-credit charge: $474.
Room and board: $5,630.

FINANCIAL AID PICTURE (2008-2009)
Students with need: Out of 280 full-time freshmen who applied for aid, 243 were judged to have need. Of these, 243 received aid, and 170 had their full need met. Average financial aid package met 70% of need; average scholarship/grant was $5,222; average loan was $2,370. For part-time students, average financial aid package was $6,448.
Students without need: 34 full-time freshmen who did not demonstrate need for aid received scholarships/grants; average award was $4,885. No-need awards available for academics, alumni affiliation, art, athletics, job skills, leadership, music/drama, religious affiliation, ROTC, state/district residency.
Scholarships offered: *Merit:* Prichard Church Vocation Scholarship; $1,800; offered to all students preparing for vocational ministry associated with

Southern Baptist Convention. Missionary Kid (MK) Scholarship; minimum $5,000 per year; for children of Southern Baptist missionaries. OBU Bison Grants; amount varies; based on award package and need. *Athletic:* 104 full-time freshmen received athletic scholarships; average amount $9,835.
Cumulative student debt: 65% of graduating class had student loans; average debt was $17,859.

FINANCIAL AID PROCEDURES

Forms required: FAFSA, institutional form.
Dates and Deadlines: Priority date 4/1; no closing date. Applicants notified on a rolling basis starting 2/1; must reply by 5/1 or within 2 week(s) of notification.
Transfers: No deadline. Applicants notified on a rolling basis starting 3/1; must reply within 2 week(s) of notification. Transfers receive 1 semester of financial aid on probationary basis. During probation semester, must complete 12 hours with at least 2.0 GPA in order to receive financial aid in subsequent semesters.

CONTACT

Jonna Raney, Director of Student Financial Services
500 West University, Shawnee, OK 74804
(405) 878-2016

Oklahoma Christian University
Oklahoma City, Oklahoma
www.oc.edu   Federal Code: 003165

4-year private liberal arts college in very large city, affiliated with Church of Christ.
Enrollment: 1,918 undergrads.
Selectivity: Admits 50 to 75% of applicants.

BASIC COSTS (2009-2010)

Tuition and fees: $16,366.
Per-credit charge: $612.
Room and board: $6,630.

FINANCIAL AID PICTURE (2009-2010)

Students with need: Need-based aid available for full-time and part-time students. Work study available nights, weekends, and for part-time students.
Students without need: No-need awards available for academics, art, athletics, leadership, music/drama, religious affiliation, ROTC.
Scholarships offered: Academic merit scholarships available.

FINANCIAL AID PROCEDURES

Forms required: FAFSA.
Dates and Deadlines: Priority date 3/15; closing date 8/31. Applicants notified on a rolling basis starting 1/15; must reply within 4 week(s) of notification.
Transfers: Applicants notified on a rolling basis starting 1/15; must reply within 4 week(s) of notification. Will award based on unofficial transcript. Must have all official transcripts before awards will be disbursed.

CONTACT

Clint LaRue, Director, Student Financial Services
Box 11000, Oklahoma City, OK 73136-1100
(405) 425-5190

Oklahoma City Community College
Oklahoma City, Oklahoma
www.occc.edu   Federal Code: 010391

2-year public community college in large city.
Enrollment: 13,831 undergrads, 60% part-time. 1,571 full-time freshmen.
Selectivity: Open admission; but selective for some programs.

BASIC COSTS (2009-2010)

Tuition and fees: $2,521; out-of-state residents $6,721.
Per-credit charge: $61; out-of-state residents $201.
Additional info: Tuition/fee waivers available for adults.

FINANCIAL AID PICTURE (2008-2009)

Students with need: Out of 1,099 full-time freshmen who applied for aid, 440 were judged to have need. Of these, 440 received aid. Average financial aid package met 60% of need; average scholarship/grant was $1,368; average loan was $2,444. For part-time students, average financial aid package was $3,187.
Students without need: 122 full-time freshmen who did not demonstrate need for aid received scholarships/grants; average award was $563. No-need awards available for academics, alumni affiliation, art, leadership, music/drama, state/district residency.

FINANCIAL AID PROCEDURES

Forms required: FAFSA.
Dates and Deadlines: Priority date 4/15; no closing date. Applicants notified on a rolling basis starting 2/15.
Transfers: Applicants notified on a rolling basis starting 2/15. Those with previous degrees or over 90 credit hours attempted must appeal for eligibility for federally funded financial assistance.

CONTACT

Harold Case, Director of Financial Aid
7777 South May Avenue, Oklahoma City, OK 73159
(405) 682-7525

Oklahoma City University
Oklahoma City, Oklahoma
www.okcu.edu   Federal Code: 003166

4-year private university and liberal arts college in very large city, affiliated with United Methodist Church.
Enrollment: 2,283 undergrads, 17% part-time. 424 full-time freshmen.
Selectivity: Admits over 75% of applicants.

BASIC COSTS (2009-2010)

Tuition and fees: $24,350.
Per-credit charge: $760.
Room and board: $7,160.

FINANCIAL AID PICTURE (2009-2010)

Students with need: Average financial aid package met 91% of need; average scholarship/grant was $17,731; average loan was $3,826. For part-time students, average financial aid package was $7,783.
Students without need: No-need awards available for academics, alumni affiliation, art, athletics, leadership, music/drama, religious affiliation, ROTC, state/district residency.
Cumulative student debt: 48% of graduating class had student loans; average debt was $18,532.

FINANCIAL AID PROCEDURES

Forms required: FAFSA, institutional form.
Dates and Deadlines: Priority date 3/1; closing date 6/30. Applicants notified on a rolling basis starting 2/20; must reply within 2 week(s) of notification.
Transfers: Applicants notified on a rolling basis starting 3/10; must reply within 2 week(s) of notification. Financial aid transcripts required from all previously attended institutions whether or not financial aid was received.

CONTACT

Denise Flis, Director of Financial Aid
2501 North Blackwelder Avenue, Oklahoma City, OK 73106-1493
(405) 208-5211

Oklahoma Panhandle State University
Goodwell, Oklahoma
www.opsu.edu   Federal Code: 003174

4-year public university and liberal arts college in rural community.
Enrollment: 1,177 undergrads, 12% part-time. 293 full-time freshmen.
Selectivity: Admits over 75% of applicants.

BASIC COSTS (2009-2010)
Tuition and fees: $5,102; out-of-state residents $10,442.
Per-credit charge: $91; out-of-state residents $269.
Room and board: $3,370.

FINANCIAL AID PICTURE (2008-2009)
Students with need: Need-based aid available for full-time and part-time students.
Students without need: This college awards aid only to students with need.

FINANCIAL AID PROCEDURES
Forms required: FAFSA, institutional form.
Dates and Deadlines: Priority date 3/15; no closing date. Applicants notified by 5/1.
Transfers: No deadline. Applicants notified on a rolling basis.

CONTACT
Mel Riley, Director of Financial Aid
OPSU Admissions, Goodwell, OK 73939-0430
(580) 349-1582

Oklahoma State University
Stillwater, Oklahoma
http://osu.okstate.edu   Federal Code: 003170

4-year public university in small city.
Enrollment: 17,606 undergrads, 13% part-time. 2,928 full-time freshmen.
Selectivity: Admits over 75% of applicants.

BASIC COSTS (2009-2010)
Tuition and fees: $6,887; out-of-state residents $17,241.
Per-credit charge: $131; out-of-state residents $477.
Room and board: $6,258.

FINANCIAL AID PICTURE (2008-2009)
Students with need: Out of 2,018 full-time freshmen who applied for aid, 1,484 were judged to have need. Of these, 1,444 received aid, and 261 had their full need met. Average financial aid package met 72% of need; average scholarship/grant was $5,866; average loan was $3,145. For part-time students, average financial aid package was $7,182.
Students without need: 746 full-time freshmen who did not demonstrate need for aid received scholarships/grants; average award was $4,422. No-need awards available for academics, alumni affiliation, art, athletics, leadership, minority status, music/drama, ROTC, state/district residency.
Scholarships offered: 38 full-time freshmen received athletic scholarships; average amount $12,597.
Cumulative student debt: 56% of graduating class had student loans; average debt was $19,458.

FINANCIAL AID PROCEDURES
Forms required: FAFSA.
Dates and Deadlines: Priority date 2/1; no closing date. Applicants notified on a rolling basis starting 10/1; must reply within 4 week(s) of notification.

CONTACT
Charles Bruce, Senior Director of Scholarships & Financial Aid
219 Student Union, Stillwater, OK 74078
(405) 744-6604

Oklahoma State University Institute of Technology: Okmulgee
Okmulgee, Oklahoma
www.osuit.edu   Federal Code: 003172

2-year public branch campus and technical college in large town.
Enrollment: 3,018 undergrads.
Selectivity: Open admission; but selective for some programs.

BASIC COSTS (2009-2010)
Tuition and fees: $3,705; out-of-state residents $9,015.
Per-credit charge: $92; out-of-state residents $269.
Room and board: $5,180.

FINANCIAL AID PICTURE (2008-2009)
Students with need: Need-based aid available for full-time and part-time students. Work study available nights, weekends, and for part-time students.

FINANCIAL AID PROCEDURES
Forms required: FAFSA, institutional form.
Dates and Deadlines: Priority date 4/1; no closing date. Applicants notified on a rolling basis.
Transfers: Requirement of financial aid transcript from any institution(s) attended during transferring academic year.

CONTACT
Mary Bledsoe, Director of Student Financial Services
1801 East Fourth Street, Okmulgee, OK 74447-3901
(918) 293-5290

Oklahoma State University: Oklahoma City
Oklahoma City, Oklahoma
www.osuokc.edu   Federal Code: 009647

2-year public branch campus and technical college in very large city.
Enrollment: 7,179 undergrads.
Selectivity: Open admission; but selective for some programs.

BASIC COSTS (2009-2010)
Tuition and fees: $2,930; out-of-state residents $7,790.
Per-credit charge: $76; out-of-state residents $238.
Additional info: Tuition/fee waivers available for adults, minority students.

FINANCIAL AID PICTURE (2008-2009)
Students with need: Need-based aid available for full-time and part-time students.
Students without need: This college awards aid only to students with need.

FINANCIAL AID PROCEDURES
Forms required: FAFSA.
Dates and Deadlines: Priority date 7/15; no closing date. Applicants notified on a rolling basis starting 8/1; must reply within 2 week(s) of notification.

CONTACT
Bessie Carter, Director of Financial Aid
900 North Portland, Oklahoma City, OK 73107-6195
(405) 945-8646

Oklahoma Wesleyan University
Bartlesville, Oklahoma
www.okwu.edu   Federal Code: 003151

4-year private university and liberal arts college in large town, affiliated with Wesleyan Church.
Enrollment: 1,031 undergrads, 56% part-time. 118 full-time freshmen.

BASIC COSTS (2009-2010)
Tuition and fees: $17,770.
Per-credit charge: $700.
Room and board: $6,288.

FINANCIAL AID PICTURE (2009-2010)
Students with need: Out of 118 full-time freshmen who applied for aid, 118 were judged to have need. Of these, 118 received aid. Average financial aid package met 53% of need; average scholarship/grant was $3,300; average loan was $2,731. For part-time students, average financial aid package was $5,281.
Students without need: No-need awards available for academics, alumni affiliation, athletics, leadership, music/drama, religious affiliation, state/district residency.

FINANCIAL AID PROCEDURES
Forms required: FAFSA, institutional form.
Dates and Deadlines: Priority date 4/1; no closing date. Applicants notified on a rolling basis starting 4/1; must reply by 5/1 or within 2 week(s) of notification.
Transfers: Priority date 3/1; closing date 8/1. Applicants notified on a rolling basis; must reply within 2 week(s) of notification.

CONTACT
Lee Kanakis, Director of Student Financial Services
2201 Silver Lake Road, Bartlesville, OK 74006
(918) 335-6282

Oral Roberts University
Tulsa, Oklahoma
www.oru.edu   Federal Code: 003985

4-year private university and liberal arts college in large city, affiliated with non-denominational tradition.
Enrollment: 2,558 undergrads, 9% part-time. 598 full-time freshmen.
Selectivity: Admits 50 to 75% of applicants.

BASIC COSTS (2009-2010)
Tuition and fees: $19,106.
Per-credit charge: $772.
Room and board: $7,916.

FINANCIAL AID PICTURE (2008-2009)
Students with need: Average financial aid package met 86% of need; average scholarship/grant was $9,759; average loan was $6,534. For part-time students, average financial aid package was $6,289.
Students without need: 152 full-time freshmen who did not demonstrate need for aid received scholarships/grants; average award was $6,871. No-need awards available for academics, alumni affiliation, art, athletics, leadership, music/drama.
Scholarships offered: 16 full-time freshmen received athletic scholarships; average amount $19,354.
Cumulative student debt: 67% of graduating class had student loans; average debt was $34,555.

FINANCIAL AID PROCEDURES
Forms required: FAFSA.
Dates and Deadlines: Priority date 3/15; no closing date. Must reply by 7/15.

Transfers: Priority date 3/30. Applicants notified on a rolling basis starting 4/1. Transfer applicants eligible for some scholarships.

CONTACT
Shannon Panthin, Director of Financial Aid
7777 South Lewis Avenue, Tulsa, OK 74171
(918) 495-6510

Platt College: Oklahoma City Central
Oklahoma City, Oklahoma
www.plattcollege.org   Federal Code: 023068

2-year for-profit branch campus and health science college in small city.
Enrollment: 238 undergrads.
Selectivity: Open admission; but selective for some programs.

BASIC COSTS (2009-2010)
Additional info: Tuition varies by program. Full-time tuition ranges from $10,200 to $23,600. Required fees $100.

FINANCIAL AID PICTURE
Students with need: Need-based aid available for full-time students.

FINANCIAL AID PROCEDURES
Forms required: FAFSA.
Dates and Deadlines: No deadline.

CONTACT
Amy Hocker, Financial Aid Director
309 South Ann Arbor, Oklahoma City, OK 73128
(405) 946-7799

Platt College: Tulsa
Tulsa, Oklahoma
www.plattcollege.org   Federal Code: 016312

2-year for-profit culinary school and health science college in large city.
Enrollment: 353 undergrads.
Selectivity: Open admission; but selective for some programs.

BASIC COSTS (2009-2010)
Additional info: Tuition varies by program. Full-time tuition ranges from $10,300 to $23,600, depending on program. Required fees $100.

FINANCIAL AID PICTURE
Students with need: Need-based aid available for full-time and part-time students.
Students without need: This college awards aid only to students with need.

FINANCIAL AID PROCEDURES
Forms required: FAFSA.
Dates and Deadlines: No deadline.

CONTACT
Linda Bates, Director of Compliance-Financial Services
3801 South Sheridan, Tulsa, OK 74145-1132
(918) 663-9000

Redlands Community College
El Reno, Oklahoma
www.redlandscc.edu   Federal Code: 003156

2-year public community college in large town.
Enrollment: 2,474 undergrads.
Selectivity: Open admission; but selective for some programs.

BASIC COSTS (2009-2010)

Tuition and fees: $2,903; out-of-state residents $5,153.

Per-credit charge: $97; out-of-state residents $172.

Room only: $3,870.

Additional info: Tuition/fee waivers available for adults.

FINANCIAL AID PICTURE (2008-2009)

Students with need: Need-based aid available for full-time and part-time students. Work study available nights, weekends, and for part-time students.

Students without need: No-need awards available for academics, athletics, leadership.

FINANCIAL AID PROCEDURES

Forms required: FAFSA.

Dates and Deadlines: Priority date 7/1; no closing date. Applicants notified on a rolling basis starting 6/1; must reply within 6 week(s) of notification.

Transfers: No deadline. Applicants notified on a rolling basis; must reply within 6 week(s) of notification.

CONTACT

Karen Jeffers, Director of Financial Aid

1300 South Country Club Road, El Reno, OK 73036

(866) 415-6367 ext. 1442

Rogers State University

Claremore, Oklahoma

www.rsu.edu   Federal Code: 003168

4-year public university in large town.

Enrollment: 4,115 undergrads, 37% part-time. 747 full-time freshmen.

Selectivity: Admits 50 to 75% of applicants.

BASIC COSTS (2009-2010)

Tuition and fees: $4,277; out-of-state residents $9,734.

Per-credit charge: $91; out-of-state residents $273.

Room and board: $7,095.

Additional info: Apartment-style housing.

FINANCIAL AID PICTURE (2009-2010)

Students with need: Out of 677 full-time freshmen who applied for aid, 472 were judged to have need. Of these, 470 received aid, and 14 had their full need met. Average financial aid package met 27% of need; average scholarship/grant was $5,049; average loan was $2,962. For part-time students, average financial aid package was $5,342.

Students without need: 22 full-time freshmen who did not demonstrate need for aid received scholarships/grants; average award was $901. No-need awards available for academics, art, athletics, leadership, music/drama, state/district residency.

Scholarships offered: 4 full-time freshmen received athletic scholarships; average amount $1,144.

FINANCIAL AID PROCEDURES

Forms required: FAFSA, institutional form.

Dates and Deadlines: Priority date 6/1; no closing date. Applicants notified on a rolling basis starting 4/1; must reply within 1 week(s) of notification.

Transfers: No deadline. Applicants notified on a rolling basis starting 4/1; must reply within 3 week(s) of notification.

CONTACT

David Barron, Director, Financial Aid

1701 West Will Rogers Boulevard, Claremore, OK 74017

(918) 343-7553

Rose State College

Midwest City, Oklahoma

www.rose.edu   Federal Code: 009185

2-year public community college in small city.

Enrollment: 7,811 undergrads, 59% part-time. 1,036 full-time freshmen.

Selectivity: Open admission; but selective for some programs.

BASIC COSTS (2009-2010)

Tuition and fees: $2,534; out-of-state residents $7,394.

Per-credit charge: $65; out-of-state residents $227.

FINANCIAL AID PICTURE (2008-2009)

Students with need: 45% of average financial aid package awarded as scholarships/grants, 55% awarded as loans/jobs. Need-based aid available for part-time students. Work study available nights, weekends, and for part-time students.

Students without need: No-need awards available for academics, athletics.

FINANCIAL AID PROCEDURES

Forms required: FAFSA.

Dates and Deadlines: Priority date 6/1; no closing date. Applicants notified on a rolling basis starting 3/1; must reply within 4 week(s) of notification.

CONTACT

Steven Daffer, Director of Financial Aid

6420 SE 15th Street, Midwest City, OK 73110-2799

(405) 733-7424

St. Gregory's University

Shawnee, Oklahoma

www.stgregorys.edu   Federal Code: 003183

4-year private university and liberal arts college in large town, affiliated with Roman Catholic Church.

Enrollment: 649 undergrads, 49% part-time. 69 full-time freshmen.

Selectivity: Admits 50 to 75% of applicants.

BASIC COSTS (2009-2010)

Tuition and fees: $16,294.

Per-credit charge: $515.

Room and board: $6,404.

Additional info: Tuition/fee waivers available for adults.

FINANCIAL AID PICTURE (2008-2009)

Students with need: Need-based aid available for full-time and part-time students. Work study available nights, weekends, and for part-time students.

Students without need: No-need awards available for academics, alumni affiliation, art, athletics, job skills, leadership, music/drama, religious affiliation.

Scholarships offered: Leadership Scholarship; $500-$2,000. Academic Scholarship; $500-$5,100. Need-based scholarship; $500-$1,500.

FINANCIAL AID PROCEDURES

Forms required: FAFSA, institutional form.

Dates and Deadlines: Priority date 4/1; no closing date. Applicants notified on a rolling basis starting 2/15; must reply within 3 week(s) of notification.

Transfers: No deadline. Applicants notified on a rolling basis.

CONTACT

Debra Gambill, Director of Financial Aid

1900 West MacArthur Drive, Shawnee, OK 74804

(405) 878-5412

Seminole State College
Seminole, Oklahoma
www.ssc.cc.ok.us   Federal Code: 003178

2-year public community and junior college in small town.
Enrollment: 2,400 undergrads.
Selectivity: Open admission; but selective for some programs.

BASIC COSTS (2009-2010)
Tuition and fees: $2,849; out-of-state residents $6,665.
Per-credit charge: $58; out-of-state residents $185.
Room and board: $6,150.

FINANCIAL AID PICTURE (2009-2010)
Students with need: Need-based aid available for full-time students.
Students without need: No-need awards available for academics, athletics, state/district residency.

FINANCIAL AID PROCEDURES
Forms required: FAFSA, institutional form.
Dates and Deadlines: Closing date 6/30. Applicants notified on a rolling basis starting 3/1; must reply within 4 week(s) of notification.

CONTACT
Chris Lindley, Director of Enrollment Management
2701 Boren Boulevard, Seminole, OK 74868
(405) 382-9247

Southeastern Oklahoma State University
Durant, Oklahoma
www.sosu.edu   Federal Code: 003179

4-year public liberal arts and teachers college in large town.
Enrollment: 3,730 undergrads, 21% part-time. 534 full-time freshmen.
Selectivity: Admits over 75% of applicants.

BASIC COSTS (2009-2010)
Tuition and fees: $4,416; out-of-state residents $10,887.
Per-credit charge: $121; out-of-state residents $334.
Room and board: $4,900.
Additional info: Tuition/fee waivers available for minority students.

FINANCIAL AID PICTURE (2008-2009)
Students with need: Out of 449 full-time freshmen who applied for aid, 384 were judged to have need. Of these, 378 received aid, and 46 had their full need met. Average financial aid package met 11% of need; average scholarship/grant was $1,225; average loan was $1,321. For part-time students, average financial aid package was $1,412.
Students without need: 4 full-time freshmen who did not demonstrate need for aid received scholarships/grants; average award was $667. No-need awards available for academics, alumni affiliation, art, athletics, job skills, leadership, minority status, music/drama, state/district residency.
Scholarships offered: 50 full-time freshmen received athletic scholarships; average amount $1,761.
Cumulative student debt: 36% of graduating class had student loans; average debt was $2,374.

FINANCIAL AID PROCEDURES
Forms required: FAFSA, institutional form.
Dates and Deadlines: Priority date 3/1; no closing date. Applicants notified on a rolling basis starting 4/15; must reply within 2 week(s) of notification.

CONTACT
Sherry Hudson, Director of Student Financial Aid
1405 North Fourth Avenue, PMB 4225, Durant, OK 74701-0607
(580) 745-2186

Southwestern Christian University
Bethany, Oklahoma
www.swcu.edu   Federal Code: 003180

4-year private liberal arts college in large town, affiliated with Pentecostal Holiness Church.
Enrollment: 230 undergrads, 5% part-time. 48 full-time freshmen.
Selectivity: Admits 50 to 75% of applicants.

BASIC COSTS (2009-2010)
Tuition and fees: $10,700.
Per-credit charge: $325.
Room and board: $4,800.
Additional info: Adult education program $350 per credit hour.

FINANCIAL AID PICTURE (2009-2010)
Students with need: Out of 48 full-time freshmen who applied for aid, 48 were judged to have need. Of these, 48 received aid, and 1 had their full need met. Average financial aid package met 95% of need. For part-time students, average financial aid package was $3,500.
Students without need: No-need awards available for academics, alumni affiliation, leadership, music/drama, religious affiliation.

FINANCIAL AID PROCEDURES
Forms required: FAFSA.
Dates and Deadlines: Priority date 8/1; no closing date. Applicants notified on a rolling basis starting 5/1; must reply within 2 week(s) of notification.

CONTACT
Daniel Watkins, Director of Financial Aid
Box 340, Bethany, OK 73008
(405) 789-7661 ext. 3456

Southwestern Oklahoma State University
Weatherford, Oklahoma
www.swosu.edu   Federal Code: 003181

4-year public university in large town.
Enrollment: 4,194 undergrads, 13% part-time. 885 full-time freshmen.
Selectivity: Admits over 75% of applicants.

BASIC COSTS (2009-2010)
Tuition and fees: $4,530; out-of-state residents $9,870.
Per-credit charge: $112; out-of-state residents $290.
Room and board: $4,400.

FINANCIAL AID PICTURE (2009-2010)
Students with need: Out of 679 full-time freshmen who applied for aid, 513 were judged to have need. Of these, 505 received aid, and 222 had their full need met. Average financial aid package met 87% of need; average scholarship/grant was $1,282; average loan was $1,397. For part-time students, average financial aid package was $3,418.
Students without need: 117 full-time freshmen who did not demonstrate need for aid received scholarships/grants; average award was $431. No-need awards available for academics, alumni affiliation, art, athletics, leadership, music/drama, state/district residency.
Scholarships offered: 63 full-time freshmen received athletic scholarships; average amount $807.

FINANCIAL AID PROCEDURES
Forms required: FAFSA, institutional form.
Dates and Deadlines: Closing date 3/1. Applicants notified by 3/15.

CONTACT
Jerome Wichert, Director of Student Financial Services
100 Campus Drive, Weatherford, OK 73096
(508) 774-3786

Spartan College of Aeronautics and Technology

Tulsa, Oklahoma
www.spartan.edu   Federal Code: 007678

4-year for-profit technical college in large city.
Enrollment: 1,084 undergrads.

BASIC COSTS (2010-2011)
Tuition and fees: $15,000.
Room only: $4,680.
Additional info: Tuition at time of enrollment locked for 4 years.

FINANCIAL AID PICTURE (2008-2009)
Students with need: Need-based aid available for full-time and part-time students. Work study available nights, weekends, and for part-time students.

FINANCIAL AID PROCEDURES
Forms required: FAFSA, institutional form.
Dates and Deadlines: No deadline. Applicants notified on a rolling basis starting 2/1; must reply within 2 week(s) of notification.
Transfers: No deadline. Applicants notified on a rolling basis; must reply within 2 week(s) of notification.

CONTACT
Christina Foster, Director of Financial Aid
Box 582833, Tulsa, OK 74158-2833
(918) 836-6886

Tulsa Community College

Tulsa, Oklahoma
www.tulsacc.edu   Federal Code: 009763

2-year public community college in large city.
Enrollment: 17,829 undergrads, 66% part-time. 1,872 full-time freshmen.
Selectivity: Open admission; but selective for some programs.

BASIC COSTS (2009-2010)
Tuition and fees: $2,709; out-of-state residents $7,376.
Per-credit charge: $62; out-of-state residents $218.
Additional info: Tuition/fee waivers available for minority students.

FINANCIAL AID PICTURE
Students with need: Need-based aid available for full-time and part-time students. Work study available nights, weekends, and for part-time students.
Students without need: No-need awards available for academics, art, leadership, music/drama, state/district residency.

FINANCIAL AID PROCEDURES
Forms required: FAFSA, institutional form.
Dates and Deadlines: Priority date 8/1; no closing date. Applicants notified on a rolling basis starting 4/1; must reply within 2 week(s) of notification.

CONTACT
Matt Short, Director of Student Financial Services
6111 East Skelly Drive, Tulsa, OK 74135
(918) 595-7155

Tulsa Welding School

Tulsa, Oklahoma
www.weldingschool.com   Federal Code: 015733

2-year for-profit technical college in very large city.
Enrollment: 795 undergrads.
Selectivity: Open admission.

BASIC COSTS (2009-2010)
Additional info: Tuition and fees vary by program from $8,773 to $15,425.

FINANCIAL AID PICTURE (2009-2010)
Students with need: 26% of average financial aid package awarded as scholarships/grants, 74% awarded as loans/jobs.
Students without need: This college awards aid only to students with need.

FINANCIAL AID PROCEDURES
Forms required: FAFSA.

CONTACT
Teresa Franklin, Financial Aid Director
2545 East 11th Street, Tulsa, OK 74104-3909
(918) 587-6789

University of Central Oklahoma

Edmond, Oklahoma
www.uco.edu   Federal Code: 003152

4-year public university in small city.
Enrollment: 14,246 undergrads, 31% part-time. 1,532 full-time freshmen.
Selectivity: Admits over 75% of applicants.

BASIC COSTS (2009-2010)
Tuition and fees: $4,223; out-of-state residents $10,652.
Per-credit charge: $123; out-of-state residents $337.
Room and board: $5,942.
Additional info: Tuition/fee waivers available for minority students.

FINANCIAL AID PICTURE (2008-2009)
Students with need: Out of 1,083 full-time freshmen who applied for aid, 804 were judged to have need. Of these, 727 received aid, and 66 had their full need met. Average financial aid package met 66% of need; average scholarship/grant was $6,995; average loan was $3,127. For part-time students, average financial aid package was $5,479.
Students without need: 117 full-time freshmen who did not demonstrate need for aid received scholarships/grants; average award was $2,628. No-need awards available for academics, alumni affiliation, art, athletics, leadership, minority status, music/drama, ROTC, state/district residency.
Scholarships offered: 67 full-time freshmen received athletic scholarships; average amount $3,994.

FINANCIAL AID PROCEDURES
Forms required: FAFSA, institutional form.
Dates and Deadlines: Priority date 5/31; no closing date. Applicants notified on a rolling basis starting 5/1; must reply by 6/30 or within 4 week(s) of notification.
Transfers: No deadline. Applicants notified on a rolling basis starting 5/1; must reply by 6/30 or within 4 week(s) of notification.

CONTACT
Susan Prater, Director of Financial Aid
100 North University Drive, Edmond, OK 73034-0151
(405) 974-3334

University of Oklahoma

Norman, Oklahoma
www.ou.edu   Federal Code: 003184

4-year public university in small city.
Enrollment: 20,685 undergrads, 13% part-time. 3,762 full-time freshmen.
Selectivity: Admits over 75% of applicants.

BASIC COSTS (2009-2010)
Tuition and fees: $7,483; out-of-state residents $17,464.
Per-credit charge: $118; out-of-state residents $451.
Room and board: $7,598.
Additional info: Computer course fees and other college level fees vary by college. Tuition/fee waivers available for adults, minority students.

FINANCIAL AID PICTURE (2008-2009)
Students with need: Out of 2,406 full-time freshmen who applied for aid, 2,305 were judged to have need. Of these, 2,305 received aid, and 1,222 had their full need met. Average financial aid package met 95% of need; average scholarship/grant was $5,978; average loan was $3,648. For part-time students, average financial aid package was $8,472.
Students without need: 511 full-time freshmen who did not demonstrate need for aid received scholarships/grants; average award was $1,161. No-need awards available for academics, alumni affiliation, art, athletics, leadership, minority status, music/drama, religious affiliation, ROTC.
Scholarships offered: 45 full-time freshmen received athletic scholarships; average amount $17,358.
Cumulative student debt: 53% of graduating class had student loans; average debt was $15,190.

FINANCIAL AID PROCEDURES
Forms required: FAFSA.
Dates and Deadlines: Priority date 3/1; no closing date. Applicants notified on a rolling basis starting 3/15; must reply within 6 week(s) of notification.
Transfers: No deadline. Applicants notified on a rolling basis starting 4/1.

CONTACT
Caryn Pacheco, Director of Financial Aid
550 Parrington Oval, L-1, Norman, OK 73019-3032
(405) 325-5505

University of Science and Arts of Oklahoma
Chickasha, Oklahoma
www.usao.edu   Federal Code: 003167

4-year public university and liberal arts college in large town.
Enrollment: 1,013 undergrads, 9% part-time. 184 full-time freshmen.
Selectivity: Admits 50 to 75% of applicants.

BASIC COSTS (2009-2010)
Tuition and fees: $4,440; out-of-state residents $10,560.
Per-credit charge: $109; out-of-state residents $313.
Room and board: $5,000.
Additional info: Tuition at time of enrollment locked for 4 years.

FINANCIAL AID PICTURE (2009-2010)
Students with need: Out of 154 full-time freshmen who applied for aid, 134 were judged to have need. Of these, 134 received aid, and 30 had their full need met. Average financial aid package met 77% of need; average scholarship/grant was $7,559; average loan was $2,390. For part-time students, average financial aid package was $4,747.
Students without need: 14 full-time freshmen who did not demonstrate need for aid received scholarships/grants; average award was $2,103. No-need awards available for academics, art, athletics, leadership, music/drama, state/district residency.
Scholarships offered: 12 full-time freshmen received athletic scholarships; average amount $6,643.
Cumulative student debt: 58% of graduating class had student loans; average debt was $15,598.

FINANCIAL AID PROCEDURES
Forms required: FAFSA, institutional form.
Dates and Deadlines: Priority date 3/15; no closing date. Applicants notified on a rolling basis starting 3/15.

Transfers: No deadline. Applicants notified on a rolling basis starting 3/15; must reply within 4 week(s) of notification.

CONTACT
Nancy Moats, Director of Financial Aid
1727 West Alabama, Chickasha, OK 73018-5322
(405) 574-1240

University of Tulsa
Tulsa, Oklahoma
www.utulsa.edu   Federal Code: 003185

4-year private university in large city, affiliated with Presbyterian Church (USA).
Enrollment: 3,027 undergrads, 4% part-time. 692 full-time freshmen.
Selectivity: Admits less than 50% of applicants.

BASIC COSTS (2010-2011)
Tuition and fees: $28,310.
Per-credit charge: $1,007.
Room and board: $9,018.

FINANCIAL AID PICTURE (2008-2009)
Students with need: Out of 649 full-time freshmen who applied for aid, 355 were judged to have need. Of these, 355 received aid, and 185 had their full need met. Average financial aid package met 88% of need; average scholarship/grant was $6,056; average loan was $5,033. For part-time students, average financial aid package was $13,332.
Students without need: 251 full-time freshmen who did not demonstrate need for aid received scholarships/grants; average award was $13,746. No-need awards available for academics, alumni affiliation, art, athletics, leadership, minority status, music/drama, religious affiliation.
Scholarships offered: 88 full-time freshmen received athletic scholarships; average amount $19,571.
Cumulative student debt: 36% of graduating class had student loans; average debt was $28,364.

FINANCIAL AID PROCEDURES
Forms required: FAFSA, institutional form.
Dates and Deadlines: Priority date 4/1; no closing date. Applicants notified on a rolling basis starting 3/1; must reply by 5/1 or within 2 week(s) of notification.
Transfers: Priority date 5/1. Applicants notified on a rolling basis starting 3/1; must reply by 5/1 or within 2 week(s) of notification.

CONTACT
Vicki Hendrickson, Director of Student Financial Services
800 South Tucker Drive, Tulsa, OK 74104-3189
(918) 631-2526

Vatterott College
Oklahoma City, Oklahoma
www.vatterott-college.com   Federal Code: 020693

2-year for-profit technical and career college in very large city.
Enrollment: 300 undergrads.
Selectivity: Open admission.

BASIC COSTS (2009-2010)
Additional info: Program cost ranges: $19,000 to $23,750 (certificate/diploma); $26,450 to $35,375 (associate degree).

FINANCIAL AID PICTURE (2008-2009)
Students with need: Need-based aid available for full-time students.
Students without need: This college awards aid only to students with need.

FINANCIAL AID PROCEDURES

Forms required: FAFSA.

Dates and Deadlines: No deadline.

CONTACT

Janice Stepp, Director of Financial Aid
4621 NW 23rd Street, Oklahoma City, OK 73127
(405) 945-0088

Western Oklahoma State College

Altus, Oklahoma
www.wosc.edu   Federal Code: 003146

2-year public community college in large town.

Enrollment: 750 full-time undergrads.

Selectivity: Open admission; but selective for some programs.

BASIC COSTS (2009-2010)

Tuition and fees: $2,684; out-of-state residents $6,164.

Per-credit charge: $57; out-of-state residents $173.

Room and board: $3,750.

FINANCIAL AID PICTURE (2008-2009)

Students with need: Need-based aid available for full-time and part-time students. Work study available nights, weekends, and for part-time students.

Students without need: No-need awards available for academics, alumni affiliation, art, athletics, leadership, music/drama, state/district residency.

FINANCIAL AID PROCEDURES

Forms required: FAFSA, institutional form.

Dates and Deadlines: Priority date 3/1; no closing date. Applicants notified on a rolling basis; must reply within 3 week(s) of notification.

CONTACT

Myrna Cross, Director of Financial Aid/Veterans' Affairs
2801 North Main Street, Altus, OK 73521
(580) 477-7709

Oregon

Art Institute of Portland

Portland, Oregon
www.aipd.artinstitutes.edu   Federal Code: 007819

4-year for-profit visual arts and liberal arts college in large city.

Enrollment: 1,896 undergrads.

Selectivity: Admits 50 to 75% of applicants.

BASIC COSTS (2009-2010)

Tuition and fees: $21,195.

Per-credit charge: $471.

Room only: $8,415.

FINANCIAL AID PICTURE (2009-2010)

Students with need: Need-based aid available for full-time and part-time students. Work study available nights, weekends, and for part-time students.

Students without need: No-need awards available for art.

Additional info: Applicants encouraged to apply early for financial aid. Scholarship deadlines range from January 1 to March 1.

FINANCIAL AID PROCEDURES

Forms required: FAFSA.

Dates and Deadlines: Priority date 3/1; no closing date. Applicants notified on a rolling basis starting 1/1; must reply within 5 week(s) of notification.

Transfers: No deadline. Applicants notified on a rolling basis starting 1/1.

CONTACT

Mickey Jacobson, Director of Student Financial Services
1122 Northwest Davis Street, Portland, OR 97209-2911
(503) 382-4784

Blue Mountain Community College

Pendleton, Oregon
www.bluecc.edu   Federal Code: 003186

2-year public community college in large town.

Enrollment: 1,025 full-time undergrads.

Selectivity: Open admission; but selective for some programs.

BASIC COSTS (2009-2010)

Tuition and fees: $3,610; out-of-state residents $9,730.

Per-credit charge: $68; out-of-state residents $204.

Additional info: Students in limited entry programs such as dental and nursing pay additional program fees. Washington state, Idaho, Nevada, California and Montana residents all pay in-state rates.

FINANCIAL AID PICTURE

Students with need: Need-based aid available for full-time and part-time students. Work study available nights, weekends, and for part-time students.

Students without need: No-need awards available for athletics, music/drama.

FINANCIAL AID PROCEDURES

Forms required: FAFSA.

Dates and Deadlines: Priority date 3/30; no closing date. Applicants notified on a rolling basis starting 4/1; must reply within 2 week(s) of notification.

CONTACT

Karen Graybeal, Director of Financial Aid
2411 NW Carden Avenue, Pendleton, OR 97801
(541) 278-5790

Central Oregon Community College

Bend, Oregon
www.cocc.edu   Federal Code: 003188

2-year public community college in small city.

Enrollment: 5,644 undergrads, 50% part-time. 527 full-time freshmen.

Selectivity: Open admission; but selective for some programs.

BASIC COSTS (2009-2010)

Tuition and fees: $3,093; out-of-district residents $4,218; out-of-state residents $8,493.

Per-credit charge: $66; out-of-district residents $91; out-of-state residents $186.

Room and board: $7,626.

Additional info: Residents of WA, ID, NV and CA pay the in-state, out-of-district tuition. Emergency Medical Services, Aviation, Nursing, Culinary and Massage Therapy programs carry additional fees.

FINANCIAL AID PICTURE (2009-2010)

Students with need: Out of 437 full-time freshmen who applied for aid, 387 were judged to have need. Of these, 379 received aid, and 32 had their full need met. Average financial aid package met 76% of need; average scholarship/grant was $6,278; average loan was $3,198. For part-time students, average financial aid package was $9,000.

Students without need: 11 full-time freshmen who did not demonstrate need for aid received scholarships/grants; average award was $3,000. No-need awards available for academics, state/district residency.

Additional info: Institution-sponsored short-term loans. Extensive part-time student employment.

FINANCIAL AID PROCEDURES

Forms required: FAFSA.

Dates and Deadlines: No deadline. Applicants notified on a rolling basis starting 3/30; must reply within 4 week(s) of notification.

CONTACT

Kevin Multop, Director of Financial Aid
2600 Northwest College Way, Bend, OR 97701-5998
(541) 383-7260

Chemeketa Community College
Salem, Oregon
www.chemeketa.edu   Federal Code: 003218

2-year public community and junior college in small city.

Enrollment: 4,947 undergrads.

Selectivity: Open admission; but selective for some programs.

BASIC COSTS (2009-2010)

Tuition and fees: $3,510; out-of-state residents $10,935.

Per-credit charge: $70; out-of-state residents $235.

Additional info: International students have additional required fees. Individual courses may have extra fees.

FINANCIAL AID PICTURE (2008-2009)

Students with need: Need-based aid available for full-time and part-time students. Work study available nights, weekends, and for part-time students.

Students without need: This college awards aid only to students with need.

FINANCIAL AID PROCEDURES

Forms required: FAFSA.

Dates and Deadlines: Priority date 4/1; no closing date. Applicants notified on a rolling basis starting 6/30; must reply within 2 week(s) of notification.

Transfers: Priority date 6/30; no deadline. Applicants notified on a rolling basis; must reply within 4 week(s) of notification.

CONTACT

Kathy Campbell, Financial Aid Director
Admissions Office, Salem, OR 97309-7070
(503) 399-5018

Clackamas Community College
Oregon City, Oregon
www.clackamas.edu   Federal Code: 004878

2-year public community college in small city.

Enrollment: 2,400 full-time undergrads.

Selectivity: Open admission; but selective for some programs.

BASIC COSTS (2009-2010)

Tuition and fees: $3,465; out-of-state residents $9,810.

Per-credit charge: $72; out-of-state residents $213.

Additional info: In-state tuition applies to residents of Oregon, Washington, Idaho, Nevada and California.

FINANCIAL AID PICTURE (2008-2009)

Students with need: Need-based aid available for full-time and part-time students. Work study available nights, weekends, and for part-time students.

Students without need: No-need awards available for academics, art, athletics, leadership, music/drama.

Additional info: Institutional tuition rebate guarantee. Frozen tuition rates for new fall students who graduate within 3 years. Any tuition increase levied by college during those 3 years will be refunded to student upon graduation.

FINANCIAL AID PROCEDURES

Forms required: FAFSA, institutional form.

Dates and Deadlines: Priority date 4/10; no closing date. Applicants notified on a rolling basis starting 3/15; must reply within 3 week(s) of notification.

Transfers: No deadline. Applicants notified on a rolling basis.

CONTACT

Fayne Griffiths, Director, Student Financial Services
19600 Molalla Avenue, Oregon City, OR 97045
(503) 657-6958 ext. 2745

Clatsop Community College
Astoria, Oregon
www.clatsopcollege.com   Federal Code: 003189

2-year public community college in large town.

Enrollment: 788 undergrads.

Selectivity: Open admission; but selective for some programs.

BASIC COSTS (2009-2010)

Tuition and fees: $3,510; out-of-state residents $6,750.

Per-credit charge: $72; out-of-state residents $144.

FINANCIAL AID PICTURE (2008-2009)

Students with need: Need-based aid available for full-time and part-time students.

Students without need: No-need awards available for academics.

Scholarships offered: Rochester scholarships; $3,000-$5,000; awarded to math or science majors with 3.0 GPA; 3 reference letters required; number awarded varies yearly.

FINANCIAL AID PROCEDURES

Forms required: FAFSA, institutional form.

Dates and Deadlines: Priority date 5/1; no closing date. Applicants notified on a rolling basis starting 2/1.

Transfers: Students who apply after July 1 may only be eligible for Pell Grants and loans depending on availability of funds. Reply deadline 1 week before start of classes.

CONTACT

Sharon Boring, Director of Financial Aid
1653 Jerome Avenue, Astoria, OR 97103
(503) 338-2412

Concordia University
Portland, Oregon
www.cu-portland.edu   Federal Code: 003191

4-year private liberal arts and teachers college in very large city, affiliated with Lutheran Church - Missouri Synod.

Enrollment: 1,073 undergrads, 12% part-time. 186 full-time freshmen.

Selectivity: Admits 50 to 75% of applicants.

BASIC COSTS (2009-2010)

Tuition and fees: $23,400.

Per-credit charge: $715.

Room and board: $6,800.

Additional info: Tuition/fee waivers available for adults.

FINANCIAL AID PICTURE (2009-2010)

Students with need: Need-based aid available for full-time and part-time students. Work study available nights, weekends, and for part-time students.

Students without need: No-need awards available for academics, athletics, leadership, music/drama, religious affiliation.

Scholarships offered: President's Scholarship; $8,000; based on academic index. Regent's Scholarship; $6,000; calculated from GPA and ACT/SAT score. University Award; $4,500; calculated from GPA and ACT/SAT score.

Dean's Award; $5,000; based on academic index. Honors Scholarship; 50% tuition.

FINANCIAL AID PROCEDURES

Forms required: FAFSA.

Dates and Deadlines: No deadline. Applicants notified on a rolling basis starting 3/15; must reply by 5/1 or within 3 week(s) of notification.

Transfers: No deadline. Applicants notified on a rolling basis.

CONTACT

Rhoda Reseburg, Financial Aid Director
2811 Northeast Holman Street, Portland, OR 97211-6099
(503) 280-8514

Corban College

Salem, Oregon
www.corban.edu
Federal Code: 001339

4-year private liberal arts college in small city, affiliated with Baptist faith.

Enrollment: 820 undergrads, 8% part-time. 211 full-time freshmen.

Selectivity: Admits 50 to 75% of applicants.

BASIC COSTS (2009-2010)

Tuition and fees: $23,220.

Per-credit charge: $956.

Room and board: $7,520.

FINANCIAL AID PICTURE (2009-2010)

Students with need: Out of 187 full-time freshmen who applied for aid, 175 were judged to have need. Of these, 175 received aid, and 22 had their full need met. Average financial aid package met 72% of need; average scholarship/grant was $17,115; average loan was $3,881. For part-time students, average financial aid package was $9,154.

Students without need: 33 full-time freshmen who did not demonstrate need for aid received scholarships/grants; average award was $6,327. No-need awards available for academics, alumni affiliation, athletics, leadership, music/drama, ROTC.

Scholarships offered: 17 full-time freshmen received athletic scholarships; average amount $5,410.

Cumulative student debt: 91% of graduating class had student loans; average debt was $28,537.

FINANCIAL AID PROCEDURES

Forms required: FAFSA.

Dates and Deadlines: Priority date 2/15; no closing date. Applicants notified on a rolling basis starting 3/1.

CONTACT

Nathan Warthan, Director of Financial Aid
5000 Deer Park Drive SE, Salem, OR 97317-9392
(503) 375-7006

Eastern Oregon University

La Grande, Oregon
www.eou.edu
Federal Code: 003193

4-year public university and liberal arts college in large town.

Enrollment: 3,160 undergrads, 34% part-time. 436 full-time freshmen.

Selectivity: Admits over 75% of applicants.

BASIC COSTS (2009-2010)

Tuition and fees: $6,456; out-of-state residents $6,456.

Room and board: $7,750.

Additional info: Per Oregon statute, nonresident tuition rates same as resident rates.

FINANCIAL AID PICTURE (2009-2010)

Students with need: Out of 406 full-time freshmen who applied for aid, 326 were judged to have need. Of these, 326 received aid, and 131 had their full need met. Average financial aid package met 53% of need; average scholarship/grant was $5,901; average loan was $2,570. For part-time students, average financial aid package was $8,061.

Students without need: 4 full-time freshmen who did not demonstrate need for aid received scholarships/grants; average award was $875. No-need awards available for academics, art, leadership, minority status, music/drama, state/district residency.

Scholarships offered: *Merit:* University Scholars Scholarships; full-tuition; based on personal essay, recommendations, GPA, activities and awards. *Athletic:* 51 full-time freshmen received athletic scholarships; average amount $2,159.

Cumulative student debt: 77% of graduating class had student loans; average debt was $19,881.

FINANCIAL AID PROCEDURES

Forms required: FAFSA.

Dates and Deadlines: Priority date 3/1; no closing date. Applicants notified on a rolling basis starting 4/1; must reply within 4 week(s) of notification.

Transfers: No deadline. Applicants notified on a rolling basis.

CONTACT

Sam Collie, Director of Financial Aid
One University Boulevard, La Grande, OR 97850
(541) 962-3550

Eugene Bible College

Eugene, Oregon
www.ebc.edu
Federal Code: 015167

4-year private Bible college in small city, affiliated with Open Bible Standard Churches.

Enrollment: 107 undergrads.

Selectivity: Admits less than 50% of applicants.

BASIC COSTS (2009-2010)

Tuition and fees: $10,923.

Per-credit charge: $275.

Room and board: $6,027.

FINANCIAL AID PICTURE (2008-2009)

Students with need: Need-based aid available for full-time and part-time students. Work study available nights, weekends, and for part-time students.

Students without need: No-need awards available for academics, athletics, leadership, religious affiliation.

Scholarships offered: Honors award; $300; 3.7 GPA required.

Additional info: Some early acceptance awards possible for those admitted by May 15. Distance awards to those coming from over 1,000 miles away. Some awards for husbands and wives enrolled at same time.

FINANCIAL AID PROCEDURES

Forms required: FAFSA.

Dates and Deadlines: Priority date 5/1; closing date 9/1. Applicants notified on a rolling basis starting 7/15; must reply within 4 week(s) of notification.

Transfers: No deadline.

CONTACT

Aaron Denbo, Director of Financial Aid
2155 Bailey Hill Road, Eugene, OR 97405
(800) 322-2638

George Fox University
Newberg, Oregon
www.georgefox.edu   Federal Code: 003194

4-year private university and seminary college in large town, affiliated with Society of Friends (Quaker).
Enrollment: 1,949 undergrads, 14% part-time. 407 full-time freshmen.
Selectivity: Admits 50 to 75% of applicants.

BASIC COSTS (2010-2011)
Tuition and fees: $27,970.
Per-credit charge: $840.
Room and board: $8,630.
Additional info: Tuition/fee waivers available for minority students.

FINANCIAL AID PICTURE (2009-2010)
Students with need: Out of 360 full-time freshmen who applied for aid, 319 were judged to have need. Of these, 319 received aid, and 138 had their full need met. Average financial aid package met 90% of need; average scholarship/grant was $10,215; average loan was $3,155. For part-time students, average financial aid package was $10,833.
Students without need: 31 full-time freshmen who did not demonstrate need for aid received scholarships/grants; average award was $6,740. No-need awards available for academics, alumni affiliation, art, job skills, leadership, minority status, music/drama, religious affiliation.
Scholarships offered: Academic merit awards; $2,500-$10,000 per year; based on GPA, SAT/ACT scores and rigor of high school curriculum; renewable based on academic performance.
Additional info: Audition required for music and drama scholarships.

FINANCIAL AID PROCEDURES
Forms required: FAFSA, state aid form.
Dates and Deadlines: Priority date 2/1; no closing date. Applicants notified on a rolling basis starting 3/1; must reply within 6 week(s) of notification.

CONTACT
Rob Clarke, Executive Director of Student Financial Services
414 North Meridian Street #6089, Newberg, OR 97132-2697
(503) 554-2290

Lane Community College
Eugene, Oregon
www.lanecc.edu   Federal Code: 003196

2-year public community college in small city.
Enrollment: 9,142 undergrads, 43% part-time. 1,175 full-time freshmen.
Selectivity: Open admission; but selective for some programs.

BASIC COSTS (2009-2010)
Tuition and fees: $4,110; out-of-state residents $10,050.
Per-credit charge: $81; out-of-state residents $213.

FINANCIAL AID PICTURE (2008-2009)
Students with need: Need-based aid available for full-time and part-time students. Work study available nights, weekends, and for part-time students.
Students without need: No-need awards available for art, athletics, minority status, music/drama.

FINANCIAL AID PROCEDURES
Forms required: FAFSA.
Dates and Deadlines: Closing date 2/15. Applicants notified on a rolling basis starting 6/1; must reply within 2 week(s) of notification.

CONTACT
Burt Logan, Director of Financial Aid
4000 East 30th Avenue, Eugene, OR 97405
(541) 463-3100

Lewis & Clark College
Portland, Oregon
www.lclark.edu   Federal Code: 003197
                                  CSS Code: 4384

4-year private liberal arts college in very large city.
Enrollment: 1,905 undergrads, 1% part-time. 498 full-time freshmen.
Selectivity: Admits 50 to 75% of applicants.

BASIC COSTS (2010-2011)
Tuition and fees: $36,632.
Per-credit charge: $1,832.
Room and board: $9,648.

FINANCIAL AID PICTURE (2009-2010)
Students with need: Average financial aid package met 83% of need; average scholarship/grant was $21,303; average loan was $3,414. Need-based aid available for part-time students.
Students without need: 56 full-time freshmen who did not demonstrate need for aid received scholarships/grants; average award was $11,010. No-need awards available for academics.
Scholarships offered: Neely Scholarship; full tuition; up to 10 awards. Trustee Scholarship; half tuition; up to 15 awards. Dean's Scholarships; one quarter tuition. Leadership and service awards; one quarter tuition. Music scholarships; $2,525-$8,425; by audition. Forensic scholarships; $2,525-$8,425; separate application required.
Cumulative student debt: 58% of graduating class had student loans; average debt was $17,084.

FINANCIAL AID PROCEDURES
Forms required: FAFSA, CSS PROFILE.
Dates and Deadlines: Priority date 2/15; no closing date. Applicants notified on a rolling basis starting 3/1.
Transfers: Transfers eligible for merit-based Dean's scholarships of up to $10,000, not eligible for Neely or Trustee scholarships. Financial aid transcript form from previous institutions required.

CONTACT
Glendi Gaddis, Director of Student Financial Services
0615 SW Palatine Hill Road, Portland, OR 97219-7899
(503) 768-7090

Linfield College
McMinnville, Oregon
www.linfield.edu   Federal Code: 003198

4-year private liberal arts college in large town, affiliated with American Baptist Churches in the USA.
Enrollment: 1,625 undergrads, 2% part-time. 422 full-time freshmen.
Selectivity: Admits over 75% of applicants.

BASIC COSTS (2010-2011)
Tuition and fees: $30,604.
Per-credit charge: $945.
Room and board: $8,650.

FINANCIAL AID PICTURE (2009-2010)
Students with need: Out of 299 full-time freshmen who applied for aid, 299 were judged to have need. Of these, 266 received aid, and 105 had their full need met. Average financial aid package met 84% of need; average scholarship/grant was $13,361; average loan was $3,320. For part-time students, average financial aid package was $8,598.
Students without need: 123 full-time freshmen who did not demonstrate need for aid received scholarships/grants; average award was $13,155. No-need awards available for academics, minority status, music/drama.
Scholarships offered: National Merit Scholarship; half- to full-tuition; for National Merit Finalists who list Linfield as first choice. Trustee Scholarships;

$11,300-$16,900; based on academic record and 3.75 GPA. Faculty Scholarships; $7,700-$11,000; based on academic record and 3.4 GPA. Linfield Competitive Scholarships; $10,000-$16,000; separate application required. Music Achievement Awards; $1,500-$2,500; audition or recorded performance required, must intend to major or minor in music. Leadership/ Service Scholarship; up to $3,000; based on high levels of leadership, initiative, and service to others through student government, school activities, community organizations, and church or social service agencies; separate application required; up to 5 awarded. Academic All-Star Scholarships; $2,500 for 1st place, $1,500 for 2nd or 3rd place; supplements other competition-based scholarships. **Cumulative student debt:** 72% of graduating class had student loans; average debt was $27,750.

FINANCIAL AID PROCEDURES

Forms required: FAFSA.

Dates and Deadlines: Priority date 2/1; no closing date. Must reply by 5/1 or within 2 week(s) of notification.

Transfers: Priority date 2/15. Transfer Scholarships; $5,000-$10,000; for students who have attended 2- or 4-year accredited colleges full-time and have 3.25 GPA. Phi Theta Kappa Scholarships; $2,000; up to 10 awarded each year to members of Phi Theta Kappa; 3.25 GPA in transferable courses required.

CONTACT

Crisanne Werner, Director of Financial Aid
900 Southeast Baker Street, McMinnville, OR 97218-6894
(503) 883-2225

Linn-Benton Community College
Albany, Oregon
www.linnbenton.edu   Federal Code: 006938

2-year public community college in large town.

Enrollment: 6,369 undergrads, 45% part-time. 1,566 full-time freshmen.

Selectivity: Open admission; but selective for some programs.

BASIC COSTS (2009-2010)

Tuition and fees: $3,330; out-of-state residents $7,875.

Per-credit charge: $74; out-of-state residents $175.

Additional info: Tuition/fee waivers available for unemployed or children of unemployed.

FINANCIAL AID PICTURE (2009-2010)

Students with need: Average financial aid package met 65% of need; average scholarship/grant was $5,197; average loan was $2,847. For part-time students, average financial aid package was $5,364.

Students without need: No-need awards available for academics, alumni affiliation, art, athletics, leadership, music/drama.

Cumulative student debt: 40% of graduating class had student loans; average debt was $10,260.

FINANCIAL AID PROCEDURES

Forms required: FAFSA.

Dates and Deadlines: Priority date 4/1; no closing date. Applicants notified on a rolling basis starting 4/15; must reply within 2 week(s) of notification.

CONTACT

Danny Aynes
6500 SW Pacific Boulevard, Albany, OR 97321-3779
(541) 917-4850

Marylhurst University
Marylhurst, Oregon
www.marylhurst.edu   Federal Code: 003199

4-year private university and liberal arts college in large town, affiliated with Roman Catholic Church.

Enrollment: 911 undergrads, 70% part-time. 13 full-time freshmen.

Selectivity: Open admission; but selective for some programs.

BASIC COSTS (2009-2010)

Tuition and fees: $16,920.

Per-credit charge: $376.

FINANCIAL AID PICTURE (2008-2009)

Students with need: Out of 7 full-time freshmen who applied for aid, 5 were judged to have need. Of these, 4 received aid. Average financial aid package met 35% of need; average scholarship/grant was $5,804; average loan was $2,896. For part-time students, average financial aid package was $7,459.

Students without need: 6 full-time freshmen who did not demonstrate need for aid received scholarships/grants; average award was $5,405. No-need awards available for academics.

Cumulative student debt: 80% of graduating class had student loans; average debt was $27,927.

FINANCIAL AID PROCEDURES

Forms required: FAFSA, institutional form.

Dates and Deadlines: Priority date 3/1; no closing date. Applicants notified on a rolling basis starting 5/1.

Transfers: No deadline. Applicants notified on a rolling basis starting 5/1.

CONTACT

Tracy Reisinger, Director of Financial Aid
PO Box 261, Marylhurst, OR 97036-0261
(503) 699-6253

Mt. Hood Community College
Gresham, Oregon
www.mhcc.cc.or.us   Federal Code: 003204

2-year public community college in small city.

Enrollment: 8,578 undergrads.

Selectivity: Open admission; but selective for some programs.

BASIC COSTS (2009-2010)

Tuition and fees: $3,522; out-of-state residents $9,732.

Per-credit charge: $71; out-of-state residents $209.

FINANCIAL AID PICTURE (2008-2009)

Students with need: Need-based aid available for full-time and part-time students.

Students without need: No-need awards available for academics.

FINANCIAL AID PROCEDURES

Forms required: FAFSA, institutional form.

Dates and Deadlines: No deadline. Applicants notified on a rolling basis starting 2/15; must reply within 4 week(s) of notification.

CONTACT

Christi Hart, Financial Aid Director
26000 SE Stark Street, Gresham, OR 97030
(503) 491-7265

Multnomah University
Portland, Oregon
www.multnomah.edu   Federal Code: 003206

4-year private Bible and seminary college in very large city, affiliated with interdenominational tradition.
Enrollment: 578 undergrads, 17% part-time. 72 full-time freshmen.
Selectivity: Admits over 75% of applicants.

BASIC COSTS (2009-2010)
Tuition and fees: $14,520.
Per-credit charge: $484.
Room and board: $6,150.
Additional info: Cost of health insurance if student is not covered is approximately $1,200.

FINANCIAL AID PICTURE (2008-2009)
Students with need: Out of 69 full-time freshmen who applied for aid, 57 were judged to have need. Of these, 56 received aid, and 3 had their full need met. Average financial aid package met 44% of need; average scholarship/grant was $4,971; average loan was $2,718. For part-time students, average financial aid package was $4,997.
Students without need: 3 full-time freshmen who did not demonstrate need for aid received scholarships/grants; average award was $1,842. No-need awards available for academics, leadership, music/drama, religious affiliation.

FINANCIAL AID PROCEDURES
Forms required: FAFSA, institutional form.
Dates and Deadlines: Priority date 3/1; closing date 7/1. Applicants notified on a rolling basis starting 4/1; must reply within 2 week(s) of notification.
Transfers: Priority date 4/1. Must reply within 2 week(s) of notification.

CONTACT
Mary McGlothlan, Director of Financial Aid
8435 Northeast Glisan Street, Portland, OR 97220-5898
(503) 251-5336

Northwest Christian University
Eugene, Oregon
www.northwestchristian.edu   Federal Code: 003208

4-year private university in small city, affiliated with Christian Church (Disciples of Christ).
Enrollment: 443 undergrads, 17% part-time. 78 full-time freshmen.
Selectivity: Admits over 75% of applicants.

BASIC COSTS (2010-2011)
Tuition and fees: $22,900.
Per-credit charge: $770.
Room and board: $7,100.

FINANCIAL AID PICTURE (2009-2010)
Students with need: Need-based aid available for full-time and part-time students. Work study available nights, weekends, and for part-time students.
Students without need: No-need awards available for academics, athletics, leadership, music/drama, religious affiliation.
Scholarships offered: Academic scholarships; $2,000-$12,000; GPA/SAT or ACT scores; not limited. Leadership bonuses; $500-$3,000; school, community, church leadership roles; not limited.

FINANCIAL AID PROCEDURES
Forms required: FAFSA.
Dates and Deadlines: Priority date 3/1; no closing date. Applicants notified on a rolling basis starting 3/1; must reply within 2 week(s) of notification.
Transfers: No deadline. Applicants notified on a rolling basis.

CONTACT
David Haggard, Director of Financial Aid
828 East 11th Avenue, Eugene, OR 97401-3745
(541) 684-7211

Oregon College of Art & Craft
Portland, Oregon
www.ocac.edu   Federal Code: 030073

4-year private visual arts college in very large city.
Enrollment: 124 undergrads, 29% part-time. 10 full-time freshmen.
Selectivity: Admits over 75% of applicants.

BASIC COSTS (2009-2010)
Tuition and fees: $21,610.
Per-credit charge: $871.
Room and board: $9,500.
Additional info: Fees vary by area of concentration.

FINANCIAL AID PICTURE (2009-2010)
Students with need: Average financial aid package met 36% of need; average scholarship/grant was $7,111; average loan was $3,500. For part-time students, average financial aid package was $10,227.
Students without need: No-need awards available for academics, art.
Cumulative student debt: 71% of graduating class had student loans; average debt was $33,627.

FINANCIAL AID PROCEDURES
Forms required: FAFSA.
Dates and Deadlines: Priority date 3/1; no closing date. Applicants notified on a rolling basis starting 3/15.

CONTACT
Jessica Wright, Financial Aid Officer
8245 SW Barnes Road, Portland, OR 97225-6349
(971) 255-4224

Oregon Health & Science University
Portland, Oregon
www.ohsu.edu   Federal Code: 004883

3-year public university and health science college in very large city.
Enrollment: 728 undergrads, 73% part-time.

BASIC COSTS (2009-2010)
Tuition and fees: $18,724; out-of-state residents $29,974.
Per-credit charge: $297; out-of-state residents $547.
Additional info: Tuition shown is for undergraduate nursing program; costs for other programs vary.

FINANCIAL AID PICTURE (2009-2010)
Students with need: Average financial aid package for all full-time undergraduates was $10,096; for part-time $9,116. 99% awarded as scholarships/grants, 1% awarded as loans/jobs. Work study available nights, weekends, and for part-time students.
Students without need: No-need awards available for academics, minority status, state/district residency.

FINANCIAL AID PROCEDURES
Dates and Deadlines: Priority date 3/1; no closing date.
Transfers: Must reply within 4 week(s) of notification.

CONTACT
Cherie Honnell, Director of Financial Aid/Registrar
3181 SW Sam Jackson Park Road, Portland, OR 97239-3098
(503) 494-7800

Oregon Institute of Technology
Klamath Falls, Oregon
www.oit.edu   Federal Code: 003211

4-year public career college in small city.
Enrollment: 3,036 undergrads, 32% part-time. 269 full-time freshmen.
Selectivity: Admits over 75% of applicants.

BASIC COSTS (2009-2010)
Tuition and fees: $6,570; out-of-state residents $18,090.
Room and board: $8,245.
Additional info: Tuition/fee waivers available for minority students.

FINANCIAL AID PICTURE (2008-2009)
Students with need: Out of 269 full-time freshmen who applied for aid, 237 were judged to have need. Of these, 233 received aid, and 64 had their full need met. Average financial aid package met 20% of need; average scholarship/grant was $5,049; average loan was $2,746. For part-time students, average financial aid package was $4,764.
Students without need: No-need awards available for academics, athletics, leadership, minority status.
Scholarships offered: 2 full-time freshmen received athletic scholarships; average amount $770.
Cumulative student debt: 64% of graduating class had student loans; average debt was $27,266.

FINANCIAL AID PROCEDURES
Forms required: FAFSA.
Dates and Deadlines: Priority date 2/1; no closing date. Applicants notified on a rolling basis starting 4/1; must reply within 3 week(s) of notification.
Transfers: Closing date 2/1.

CONTACT
Tracey Lehman, Director of Financial Aid
3201 Campus Drive, Klamath Falls, OR 97601
(541) 885-1280

Oregon State University
Corvallis, Oregon
www.oregonstate.edu   Federal Code: 003210

4-year public university in small city.
Enrollment: 17,139 undergrads, 13% part-time. 3,209 full-time freshmen.
Selectivity: Admits over 75% of applicants.

BASIC COSTS (2009-2010)
Tuition and fees: $6,727; out-of-state residents $19,651.
Room and board: $9,920.

FINANCIAL AID PICTURE (2009-2010)
Students with need: Out of 2,565 full-time freshmen who applied for aid, 1,740 were judged to have need. Of these, 1,698 received aid, and 331 had their full need met. Average financial aid package met 65% of need; average scholarship/grant was $2,669; average loan was $3,207. For part-time students, average financial aid package was $8,136.
Students without need: 19 full-time freshmen who did not demonstrate need for aid received scholarships/grants; average award was $4,068. No-need awards available for academics, athletics, job skills, leadership, minority status, ROTC, state/district residency.
Scholarships offered: 51 full-time freshmen received athletic scholarships; average amount $11,863.

FINANCIAL AID PROCEDURES
Forms required: FAFSA.
Dates and Deadlines: Priority date 2/1; closing date 5/1. Applicants notified on a rolling basis starting 4/1; must reply within 4 week(s) of notification.
Transfers: Priority date 3/1; no deadline.

CONTACT
Doug Severs, Director of Financial Aid
104 Kerr Administration Building, Corvallis, OR 97331-2130
(541) 731-2241

Pacific Northwest College of Art
Portland, Oregon
www.pnca.edu   Federal Code: 003207

4-year private visual arts college in large city.
Enrollment: 554 undergrads, 7% part-time. 105 full-time freshmen.
Selectivity: Admits 50 to 75% of applicants.

BASIC COSTS (2009-2010)
Tuition and fees: $23,304.
Per-credit charge: $930.
Additional info: Off-campus housing available, approximately one mile from campus. Cost is $4,090.

FINANCIAL AID PICTURE (2009-2010)
Students with need: Need-based aid available for full-time and part-time students. Work study available nights, weekends, and for part-time students.
Students without need: No-need awards available for academics, art.
Scholarships offered: Leta Kennedy Student Scholarships; $10,000; based on artistic merit. Dorothy Lemelson Scholarship; cost of attendance; based on artistic and academic merit; renewable up to 4 years; 1 awarded. Other renewable scholarships available.

FINANCIAL AID PROCEDURES
Forms required: FAFSA.
Dates and Deadlines: Priority date 3/1; no closing date. Applicants notified on a rolling basis starting 4/1; must reply by 5/1 or within 4 week(s) of notification.
Transfers: No deadline. Applicants notified on a rolling basis starting 4/1; must reply by 5/1 or within 4 week(s) of notification.

CONTACT
Heidi Locke, Director of Financial Aid
1241 NW Johnson Street, Portland, OR 97209
(503) 821-8972

Pacific University
Forest Grove, Oregon
www.pacificu.edu   Federal Code: 003212

4-year private university in large town, affiliated with United Church of Christ.
Enrollment: 1,445 undergrads, 4% part-time. 332 full-time freshmen.
Selectivity: Admits over 75% of applicants.

BASIC COSTS (2009-2010)
Tuition and fees: $29,966.
Per-credit charge: $1,219.
Room and board: $8,118.

FINANCIAL AID PICTURE (2009-2010)
Students with need: Out of 316 full-time freshmen who applied for aid, 272 were judged to have need. Of these, 272 received aid, and 87 had their full need met. Average financial aid package met 88% of need; average scholarship/grant was $16,292; average loan was $3,344. For part-time students, average financial aid package was $8,021.
Students without need: 60 full-time freshmen who did not demonstrate need for aid received scholarships/grants; average award was $12,170. No-need awards available for academics, alumni affiliation, art, music/drama.
Scholarships offered: Honors Scholarship; $9,000. Presidential Scholarship; $8,000. Trustee Scholarship; $7,500. University Scholarship; $6,500. Paceset-

ters Scholarship; $1,000 to $3,000. Music and Forensics Talent Awards; $1,000 to $3,000. Number of awards varies.

Cumulative student debt: 85% of graduating class had student loans; average debt was $27,770.

FINANCIAL AID PROCEDURES

Forms required: FAFSA.

Dates and Deadlines: Priority date 3/1; no closing date. Applicants notified on a rolling basis starting 3/1.

CONTACT

Michael Johnson, Director of Financial Aid

2043 College Way, Forest Grove, OR 97116-1797

(503) 352-2222

Portland Community College

Portland, Oregon

www.pcc.edu   Federal Code: 003213

2-year public community college in very large city.

Enrollment: 12,092 full-time undergrads.

Selectivity: Open admission; but selective for some programs.

BASIC COSTS (2009-2010)

Tuition and fees: $3,666; out-of-state residents $9,426.

Per-credit charge: $74; out-of-state residents $202.

FINANCIAL AID PICTURE (2008-2009)

Students with need: 35% of average financial aid package awarded as scholarships/grants, 65% awarded as loans/jobs. Need-based aid available for part-time students. Work study available nights, weekends, and for part-time students.

Students without need: This college awards aid only to students with need.

FINANCIAL AID PROCEDURES

Forms required: FAFSA.

Dates and Deadlines: Priority date 3/1; no closing date. Applicants notified on a rolling basis starting 6/1; must reply within 3 week(s) of notification.

CONTACT

Corbett Gottfried, Director of Financial Aid

Box 19000, Portland, OR 97280-0990

(503) 977-4934

Portland State University

Portland, Oregon

www.pdx.edu   Federal Code: 003216

4-year public university in very large city.

Enrollment: 19,267 undergrads.

Selectivity: Admits over 75% of applicants.

BASIC COSTS (2009-2010)

Tuition and fees: $6,764; out-of-state residents $21,198.

Per-credit charge: $118; out-of-state residents $439.

Room and board: $9,135.

FINANCIAL AID PICTURE (2009-2010)

Students with need: Need-based aid available for full-time and part-time students. Work study available nights, weekends, and for part-time students.

Students without need: No-need awards available for academics, art, athletics, music/drama, state/district residency.

FINANCIAL AID PROCEDURES

Forms required: FAFSA.

Dates and Deadlines: Priority date 2/28; no closing date. Applicants notified on a rolling basis; must reply within 4 week(s) of notification.

CONTACT

Phillip Rodgers, Director of Financial Aid

PO Box 751-ADM, Portland, OR 97207-0751

(800) 547-8887

Reed College

Portland, Oregon   Federal Code: 003217

www.reed.edu   CSS Code: 4654

4-year private liberal arts college in very large city.

Enrollment: 1,440 undergrads, 2% part-time. 367 full-time freshmen.

Selectivity: Admits less than 50% of applicants.

BASIC COSTS (2010-2011)

Tuition and fees: $41,200.

Per-credit charge: $1,750.

Room and board: $10,650.

FINANCIAL AID PICTURE (2009-2010)

Students with need: Out of 241 full-time freshmen who applied for aid, 183 were judged to have need. Of these, 183 received aid, and 177 had their full need met. Average financial aid package met 100% of need; average scholarship/grant was $33,181; average loan was $3,004.

Students without need: This college awards aid only to students with need.

Cumulative student debt: 53% of graduating class had student loans; average debt was $20,750.

Additional info: College meets demonstrated need of continuing students who have attended Reed minimum of 2 semesters, who file financial aid applications on time, and who maintain satisfactory academic progress. Institutional aid consideration is for total of 8 semesters.

FINANCIAL AID PROCEDURES

Forms required: FAFSA, CSS PROFILE, institutional form.

Dates and Deadlines: Closing date 2/1. Applicants notified by 4/1; must reply by 5/1 or within 2 week(s) of notification.

Transfers: Must reply by 6/1.

CONTACT

Leslie Limper, Director of Financial Aid

3203 SE Woodstock Boulevard, Portland, OR 97202-8199

(800) 547-4750

Rogue Community College

Grants Pass, Oregon

www.roguecc.edu   Federal Code: 010071

2-year public community college in large town.

Enrollment: 4,189 undergrads, 48% part-time. 419 full-time freshmen.

Selectivity: Open admission; but selective for some programs.

BASIC COSTS (2009-2010)

Tuition and fees: $3,615; out-of-state residents $4,335.

Per-credit charge: $73; out-of-state residents $89.

Additional info: Washington, Idaho, Nevada, and California residents pay in-state tuition. Tuition/fee waivers available for unemployed or children of unemployed.

FINANCIAL AID PICTURE (2008-2009)

Students with need: Out of 356 full-time freshmen who applied for aid, 267 were judged to have need. Of these, 267 received aid, and 52 had their full need met. Average financial aid package met 57% of need; average scholarship/grant was $1,215; average loan was $1,236. For part-time students, average financial aid package was $5,013.

Students without need: 32 full-time freshmen who did not demonstrate need for aid received scholarships/grants; average award was $511.

FINANCIAL AID PROCEDURES

Forms required: FAFSA, institutional form.

Dates and Deadlines: Priority date 5/1; no closing date. Applicants notified on a rolling basis; must reply within 2 week(s) of notification.

CONTACT

Anna Manley, Director of Financial Aid

3345 Redwood Highway, Grants Pass, OR 97527

(541) 956-7501 ext. 1

Southern Oregon University
Ashland, Oregon
www.sou.edu   Federal Code: 003219

4-year public university and liberal arts college in large town.

Enrollment: 4,132 undergrads, 19% part-time. 624 full-time freshmen.

BASIC COSTS (2009-2010)

Tuition and fees: $6,252; out-of-state residents $19,914.

Room and board: $9,174.

Additional info: Tuition/fee waivers available for minority students.

FINANCIAL AID PICTURE (2009-2010)

Students with need: Need-based aid available for full-time and part-time students. Work study available nights, weekends, and for part-time students.

Students without need: No-need awards available for academics, alumni affiliation, art, athletics, leadership, minority status, music/drama, religious affiliation, state/district residency.

FINANCIAL AID PROCEDURES

Forms required: FAFSA.

Dates and Deadlines: No deadline. Applicants notified on a rolling basis starting 3/1; must reply within 2 week(s) of notification.

CONTACT

Diana Watson-Paul, Associate Director of Financial Aid

1250 Siskiyou Boulevard, Ashland, OR 97520-5032

(541) 552-6600

Southwestern Oregon Community College
Coos Bay, Oregon
www.socc.edu   Federal Code: 003220

2-year public culinary school and community college in large town.

Enrollment: 1,132 full-time undergrads.

Selectivity: Open admission; but selective for some programs.

BASIC COSTS (2009-2010)

Tuition and fees: $4,245.

Room and board: $6,605.

Additional info: Tuition/fee waivers available for adults, unemployed or children of unemployed.

FINANCIAL AID PICTURE (2009-2010)

Students with need: Need-based aid available for full-time and part-time students.

Students without need: No-need awards available for art, athletics, leadership, music/drama.

FINANCIAL AID PROCEDURES

Forms required: FAFSA.

Dates and Deadlines: Priority date 2/28; closing date 6/30. Applicants notified on a rolling basis starting 5/1; must reply within 3 week(s) of notification.

CONTACT

Avena Singh, Director of Financial Aid

1988 Newmark Avenue, Coos Bay, OR 97420-2956

(541) 888-7337

Treasure Valley Community College
Ontario, Oregon
www.tvcc.cc   Federal Code: 003221

2-year public community college in small town.

Enrollment: 2,475 undergrads, 43% part-time. 1,279 full-time freshmen.

Selectivity: Open admission; but selective for some programs.

BASIC COSTS (2009-2010)

Tuition and fees: $3,825; out-of-state residents $4,275.

Per-credit charge: $73; out-of-state residents $83.

Room and board: $6,660.

FINANCIAL AID PICTURE (2008-2009)

Students with need: Out of 1,249 full-time freshmen who applied for aid, 1,074 were judged to have need. Of these, 902 received aid, and 39 had their full need met. Average financial aid package met 35% of need; average scholarship/grant was $3,925; average loan was $2,466. For part-time students, average financial aid package was $4,715.

Students without need: 2 full-time freshmen who did not demonstrate need for aid received scholarships/grants; average award was $699. No-need awards available for academics, athletics, leadership, music/drama, state/district residency.

Scholarships offered: 29 full-time freshmen received athletic scholarships; average amount $1,454.

Cumulative student debt: 82% of graduating class had student loans; average debt was $11,074.

FINANCIAL AID PROCEDURES

Forms required: FAFSA.

Dates and Deadlines: Priority date 4/1; no closing date. Applicants notified on a rolling basis starting 5/1.

Transfers: No deadline. Applicants notified on a rolling basis.

CONTACT

Jonathan Gillen, Comptroller

650 College Boulevard, Ontario, OR 97914

(541) 881-8822 ext. 233

Umpqua Community College
Roseburg, Oregon
www.umpqua.edu   Federal Code: 003222

2-year public community college in large town.

Enrollment: 2,190 undergrads, 37% part-time. 352 full-time freshmen.

Selectivity: Open admission; but selective for some programs.

BASIC COSTS (2010-2011)

Tuition and fees: $3,585; out-of-state residents $9,075.

Per-credit charge: $70; out-of-state residents $191.

FINANCIAL AID PICTURE (2008-2009)

Students with need: 47% of average financial aid package awarded as scholarships/grants, 53% awarded as loans/jobs. Need-based aid available for part-time students. Work study available nights, weekends, and for part-time students.

Students without need: No-need awards available for academics, athletics.

FINANCIAL AID PROCEDURES

Forms required: FAFSA, institutional form.

Dates and Deadlines: Priority date 3/10; no closing date. Applicants notified on a rolling basis starting 2/9; must reply within 2 week(s) of notification.

CONTACT

Laurie Spangenberg, Director of Financial Aid
1140 College Road, Roseburg, OR 97470-0226
(541) 440-4602

University of Oregon

Eugene, Oregon
www.uoregon.edu   Federal Code: 003223

4-year public university in small city.

Enrollment: 18,213 undergrads, 7% part-time. 3,792 full-time freshmen.

Selectivity: Admits over 75% of applicants.

BASIC COSTS (2009-2010)

Tuition and fees: $7,428; out-of-state residents $23,718.

Room and board: $10,645.

Additional info: Additional program-specific fees may apply.

FINANCIAL AID PICTURE (2009-2010)

Students with need: Out of 2,559 full-time freshmen who applied for aid, 1,596 were judged to have need. Of these, 1,493 received aid, and 222 had their full need met. Average financial aid package met 53% of need; average scholarship/grant was $6,794; average loan was $3,529. For part-time students, average financial aid package was $7,827.

Students without need: 461 full-time freshmen who did not demonstrate need for aid received scholarships/grants; average award was $2,812. No-need awards available for academics, athletics, leadership, minority status, music/drama, ROTC, state/district residency.

Scholarships offered: Presidential Scholarship; approximately $7,800 per year for up to 4 years; based on merit and Oregon residency. National Merit Scholarship; $2,000 per year for up to 4 years; based on test scores. Laurel Award; $1,000-$3,000; based on merit; must apply annually. General University Scholarship; $1,000-$3,000; based on merit; must apply annually. Dean's Scholarship; $1,000-$7,000 per year for up to 12 terms; based on merit.

Cumulative student debt: 55% of graduating class had student loans; average debt was $19,336.

FINANCIAL AID PROCEDURES

Forms required: FAFSA.

Dates and Deadlines: Priority date 3/1; no closing date. Applicants notified on a rolling basis starting 4/15; must reply within 4 week(s) of notification.

CONTACT

Elizabeth Bickford, Director, Financial Aid and Scholarships
1217 University of Oregon, Eugene, OR 97403-1217
(541) 346-3221

University of Portland

Portland, Oregon
www.up.edu   Federal Code: 003224

4-year private university in large city, affiliated with Roman Catholic Church.

Enrollment: 3,077 undergrads, 1% part-time. 816 full-time freshmen.

Selectivity: Admits 50 to 75% of applicants.

BASIC COSTS (2010-2011)

Tuition and fees: $32,330.

Per-credit charge: $1,010.

Room and board: $9,540.

FINANCIAL AID PICTURE (2009-2010)

Students with need: Out of 676 full-time freshmen who applied for aid, 549 were judged to have need. Of these, 548 received aid, and 54 had their full need met. Average financial aid package met 77% of need; average scholarship/grant was $8,897; average loan was $3,436. For part-time students, average financial aid package was $12,393.

Students without need: 215 full-time freshmen who did not demonstrate need for aid received scholarships/grants; average award was $11,423. No-need awards available for academics, alumni affiliation, athletics, music/drama, religious affiliation, ROTC.

Scholarships offered: *Merit:* President's Scholarship; up to $10,000; based on academic excellence, school and community involvement, and other factors. Holy Cross Scholarship; up to $6,000; based on academic excellence, school and community involvement, and other factors. Arthur A. Schulte Scholarship; up to $6,000. *Athletic:* 33 full-time freshmen received athletic scholarships; average amount $23,010.

Cumulative student debt: 62% of graduating class had student loans; average debt was $23,955.

FINANCIAL AID PROCEDURES

Forms required: FAFSA.

Dates and Deadlines: Priority date 3/1; no closing date. Applicants notified on a rolling basis starting 3/15; must reply within 3 week(s) of notification.

CONTACT

Janet Turner, Director of Financial Aid
5000 North Willamette Boulevard, Portland, OR 97203-5798
(503) 943-7311

Warner Pacific College

Portland, Oregon
www.warnerpacific.edu   Federal Code: 003225

4-year private liberal arts college in very large city, affiliated with Church of God.

Enrollment: 1,181 undergrads, 1% part-time. 91 full-time freshmen.

Selectivity: Admits 50 to 75% of applicants.

BASIC COSTS (2010-2011)

Tuition and fees: $17,604.

Room and board: $6,980.

Additional info: Per-credit-hour charge: 1-5 credits, $490; 6-11 credits, $775.

FINANCIAL AID PICTURE (2008-2009)

Students with need: Out of 90 full-time freshmen who applied for aid, 79 were judged to have need. Of these, 79 received aid, and 9 had their full need met. Average financial aid package met 71% of need; average scholarship/grant was $5,130; average loan was $3,462. For part-time students, average financial aid package was $12,786.

Students without need: 12 full-time freshmen who did not demonstrate need for aid received scholarships/grants; average award was $2,750. No-need awards available for academics, alumni affiliation, athletics, leadership, minority status, music/drama, religious affiliation.

Scholarships offered: 2 full-time freshmen received athletic scholarships; average amount $5,000.

Cumulative student debt: 93% of graduating class had student loans; average debt was $22,433.

FINANCIAL AID PROCEDURES

Forms required: FAFSA.

Dates and Deadlines: Priority date 3/1; closing date 8/30. Applicants notified on a rolling basis starting 3/1; must reply within 2 week(s) of notification.

Transfers: No deadline. Applicants notified on a rolling basis starting 3/1; must reply within 2 week(s) of notification.

CONTACT

Bryan Cook, Director of Student Financial Services
2219 SE 68th Avenue, Portland, OR 97215-4026
(503) 517-1352

Western Oregon University

Monmouth, Oregon
www.wou.edu   Federal Code: 003209

4-year public liberal arts and teachers college in small town.
Enrollment: 4,731 undergrads, 11% part-time. 940 full-time freshmen.
Selectivity: Admits over 75% of applicants.

BASIC COSTS (2009-2010)

Tuition and fees: $6,813; out-of-state residents $17,868.
Per-credit charge: $125; out-of-state residents $371.
Room and board: $8,040.
Additional info: Resident tuition reflects WOU "Promise 2009" which is a four-year tuition commitment for resident UG students. Nonresident rate shown is for non-Promise students. Tuition at time of enrollment locked for 4 years; tuition/fee waivers available for minority students.

FINANCIAL AID PICTURE (2009-2010)

Students with need: Average financial aid package met 68% of need; average scholarship/grant was $7,040; average loan was $3,309. For part-time students, average financial aid package was $5,891.
Students without need: No-need awards available for academics, alumni affiliation, art, athletics, leadership, music/drama.

FINANCIAL AID PROCEDURES

Forms required: FAFSA.
Dates and Deadlines: Priority date 3/1; no closing date. Applicants notified on a rolling basis starting 2/28; must reply within 3 week(s) of notification.

CONTACT

Donna Fossum, Director of Financial Aid
345 North Monmouth Avenue, Monmouth, OR 97361
(503) 838-8475

Willamette University

Salem, Oregon
www.willamette.edu   Federal Code: 003227

4-year private university and liberal arts college in small city, affiliated with United Methodist Church.
Enrollment: 1,853 undergrads, 1% part-time. 541 full-time freshmen.
Selectivity: Admits 50 to 75% of applicants.

BASIC COSTS (2010-2011)

Tuition and fees: $37,361.
Room and board: $8,900.

FINANCIAL AID PICTURE (2009-2010)

Students with need: Out of 459 full-time freshmen who applied for aid, 357 were judged to have need. Of these, 357 received aid, and 53 had their full need met. Average financial aid package met 89% of need; average scholarship/grant was $24,061; average loan was $3,426. For part-time students, average financial aid package was $9,936.
Students without need: 167 full-time freshmen who did not demonstrate need for aid received scholarships/grants; average award was $13,072. No-need awards available for academics, alumni affiliation, leadership, minority status, music/drama, religious affiliation.

Scholarships offered: Academic merit awards; $5,000-$15,000; based on superior academic achievement and promise. Music, forensics, theater scholarships; average $3,000-$5,000; based on talent. Mark O. Hatfield Scholarship; full tuition; based on excellent academic record and demonstrated commitment to service leadership.
Cumulative student debt: 63% of graduating class had student loans; average debt was $23,643.

FINANCIAL AID PROCEDURES

Forms required: FAFSA. CSS PROFILE recommended of early action applicants.
Dates and Deadlines: Priority date 2/1; no closing date. Applicants notified on a rolling basis starting 4/1; must reply by 5/1 or within 2 week(s) of notification.
Transfers: Applicants notified by 4/15.

CONTACT

Patricia Hoban, Director of Financial Aid
900 State Street, Salem, OR 97301-3922
(503) 370-6273

Pennsylvania

Albright College

Reading, Pennsylvania
www.albright.edu   Federal Code: 003229

4-year private liberal arts college in small city, affiliated with United Methodist Church.
Enrollment: 2,259 undergrads. 515 full-time freshmen.
Selectivity: Admits 50 to 75% of applicants.

BASIC COSTS (2010-2011)

Tuition and fees: $32,740.
Per-credit charge: $998.
Room and board: $8,858.
Additional info: Tuition/fee waivers available for minority students.

FINANCIAL AID PICTURE (2009-2010)

Students with need: Out of 490 full-time freshmen who applied for aid, 455 were judged to have need. Of these, 451 received aid, and 63 had their full need met. Average financial aid package met 81% of need; average scholarship/grant was $21,335; average loan was $4,849. For part-time students, average financial aid package was $5,764.
Students without need: 44 full-time freshmen who did not demonstrate need for aid received scholarships/grants; average award was $11,748. No-need awards available for academics, alumni affiliation, art, leadership, minority status, music/drama, religious affiliation.
Cumulative student debt: 83% of graduating class had student loans; average debt was $31,845.

FINANCIAL AID PROCEDURES

Forms required: FAFSA.
Dates and Deadlines: Priority date 3/1; no closing date. Applicants notified on a rolling basis starting 2/15; must reply by 5/1 or within 2 week(s) of notification.
Transfers: Priority date 6/1; no deadline. Applicants notified on a rolling basis starting 2/15; must reply within 2 week(s) of notification.

CONTACT

Mary Duffy, Director of Financial Aid
13th & Bern Streets, Reading, PA 19612-5234
(610) 921-7515

Allegheny College
Meadville, Pennsylvania
www.allegheny.edu   Federal Code: 003230

4-year private liberal arts college in large town, affiliated with United Methodist Church.
Enrollment: 2,099 undergrads, 1% part-time. 580 full-time freshmen.
Selectivity: Admits 50 to 75% of applicants.

BASIC COSTS (2010-2011)
Tuition and fees: $34,810.
Per-credit charge: $1,437.
Room and board: $8,790.

FINANCIAL AID PICTURE (2009-2010)
Students with need: Out of 498 full-time freshmen who applied for aid, 402 were judged to have need. Of these, 402 received aid, and 159 had their full need met. Average financial aid package met 92% of need; average scholarship/grant was $21,029; average loan was $4,761. For part-time students, average financial aid package was $8,793.
Students without need: 172 full-time freshmen who did not demonstrate need for aid received scholarships/grants; average award was $13,523. No-need awards available for academics, leadership, minority status, state/district residency.
Scholarships offered: Trustee Scholarships; up to $20,000 per year.

FINANCIAL AID PROCEDURES
Forms required: FAFSA.
Dates and Deadlines: Priority date 2/15; no closing date. Applicants notified on a rolling basis starting 3/1; must reply by 5/1 or within 4 week(s) of notification.
Transfers: Priority date 6/1; no deadline. Applicants notified on a rolling basis; must reply within 3 week(s) of notification. Trustee Scholarships; up to $15,000; available for entering transfer students.

CONTACT
Sheryle Proper, Director of Financial Aid
Box 5, 520 North Main Street, Meadville, PA 16335
(800) 835-7780

Alvernia University
Reading, Pennsylvania
www.alvernia.edu   Federal Code: 003233

4-year private university and liberal arts college in small city, affiliated with Roman Catholic Church.
Enrollment: 1,990 undergrads, 19% part-time. 383 full-time freshmen.
Selectivity: Admits over 75% of applicants.

BASIC COSTS (2009-2010)
Tuition and fees: $24,350.
Per-credit charge: $660.
Room and board: $9,212.
Additional info: Tuition/fee waivers available for minority students.

FINANCIAL AID PICTURE (2008-2009)
Students with need: Out of 364 full-time freshmen who applied for aid, 323 were judged to have need. Of these, 323 received aid, and 58 had their full need met. Average financial aid package met 75% of need; average scholarship/grant was $11,728; average loan was $5,698. For part-time students, average financial aid package was $17,685.
Students without need: 43 full-time freshmen who did not demonstrate need for aid received scholarships/grants; average award was $5,660. No-need awards available for academics, state/district residency.
Cumulative student debt: 96% of graduating class had student loans; average debt was $31,075.

FINANCIAL AID PROCEDURES
Forms required: FAFSA, state aid form.
Dates and Deadlines: Priority date 5/1; no closing date. Applicants notified on a rolling basis starting 2/20; must reply within 2 week(s) of notification.
Transfers: Priority date 5/8; no deadline. Applicants notified on a rolling basis starting 2/20; must reply within 2 week(s) of notification.

CONTACT
Christine Saadi, Associate Director of Financial Aid
400 St. Bernardine Street, Reading, PA 19607-1799
(610) 796-8356

Antonelli Institute of Art and Photography
Erdenheim, Pennsylvania
www.antonelli.edu   Federal Code: 007430

2-year for-profit visual arts and junior college in large town.
Enrollment: 223 undergrads. 131 full-time freshmen.

BASIC COSTS (2009-2010)
Additional info: Annual tuition for graphic design/commercial art students is $18,200; for photography students $20,200. Required fees, $125; on-campus room, $7,800.

FINANCIAL AID PICTURE (2008-2009)
Students with need: Need-based aid available for full-time and part-time students. Work study available nights.
Students without need: This college awards aid only to students with need.

FINANCIAL AID PROCEDURES
Forms required: FAFSA.
Dates and Deadlines: No deadline. Applicants notified on a rolling basis; must reply within 2 week(s) of notification.
Transfers: Priority date 3/15; closing date 8/1. Applicants notified on a rolling basis.

CONTACT
Eugene Awot, Director of Financial Aid
300 Montgomery Avenue, Erdenheim, PA 19038-8242
(215) 836-2222

Arcadia University
Glenside, Pennsylvania
www.arcadia.edu   Federal Code: 003235

4-year private university in large town, affiliated with Presbyterian Church (USA).
Enrollment: 2,174 undergrads, 7% part-time. 529 full-time freshmen.
Selectivity: Admits 50 to 75% of applicants.

BASIC COSTS (2009-2010)
Tuition and fees: $31,260.
Per-credit charge: $515.
Room and board: $10,680.

FINANCIAL AID PICTURE (2009-2010)
Students with need: Out of 508 full-time freshmen who applied for aid, 485 were judged to have need. Of these, 485 received aid, and 128 had their full need met. Average financial aid package met 75% of need; average scholarship/grant was $19,403; average loan was $3,834. For part-time students, average financial aid package was $11,795.
Students without need: 36 full-time freshmen who did not demonstrate need for aid received scholarships/grants; average award was $14,761. No-need awards available for academics, alumni affiliation, art, leadership, music/drama.

Scholarships offered: Distinguished Scholarships: $16,000-$22,000; granted to full-time students based on grades, test scores, coursework taken, high school rank and involvement. Arcadia University Achievement Awards: $1,000-$15,500; granted to full-time students who have demonstrated outstanding leadership, exceptional community and/or volunteer service or special talents. President's Scholarship: full tuition; based on academic excellence, outstanding leadership, and community and volunteer service. Writing Achievement Awards: offered to those who score among the highest in the applicant pool annually on SAT or ACT writing sections.
Cumulative student debt: 88% of graduating class had student loans; average debt was $35,975.

FINANCIAL AID PROCEDURES

Forms required: FAFSA, institutional form.
Dates and Deadlines: Priority date 3/1; no closing date. Applicants notified on a rolling basis starting 2/15; must reply by 5/1.
Transfers: Applicants notified on a rolling basis starting 2/15; must reply by 5/1.

CONTACT

Holly Kirkpatrick, Director of Enrollment Management and Director of Financial Aid
450 South Easton Road, Glenside, PA 19038-3295
(215) 572-2980

Art Institute of Philadelphia
Philadelphia, Pennsylvania
www.artinstitutes.edu/Philadelphia   Federal Code: 008350

4-year for-profit visual arts college in very large city.
Enrollment: 3,500 undergrads.

BASIC COSTS (2010-2011)

Tuition and fees: $22,614.
Per-credit charge: $500.

FINANCIAL AID PICTURE

Students with need: Need-based aid available for full-time and part-time students. Work study available nights, weekends, and for part-time students.
Additional info: Institute-sponsored scholarships available.

FINANCIAL AID PROCEDURES

Forms required: FAFSA, institutional form.
Dates and Deadlines: No deadline. Applicants notified on a rolling basis starting 3/1; must reply within 2 week(s) of notification.
Transfers: No deadline. Transfer students applying for financial aid must meet standards for satisfactory academic progress as defined by State Grant Program.

CONTACT

Felicia Bryant, Director of Student Financial Services
1622 Chestnut Street, Philadelphia, PA 19103-5198
(215) 567-7080 ext. 6392

Baptist Bible College of Pennsylvania
Clarks Summit, Pennsylvania
www.bbc.edu   Federal Code: 002670

4-year private Bible and seminary college in small city, affiliated with Baptist faith.
Enrollment: 566 undergrads.
Selectivity: Admits 50 to 75% of applicants.

BASIC COSTS (2010-2011)

Tuition and fees: $17,340.
Per-credit charge: $540.

Room and board: $6,350.

FINANCIAL AID PICTURE (2008-2009)

Students with need: 55% of average financial aid package awarded as scholarships/grants, 45% awarded as loans/jobs. Need-based aid available for part-time students. Work study available nights, weekends, and for part-time students.
Students without need: No-need awards available for academics, leadership, music/drama, religious affiliation.

FINANCIAL AID PROCEDURES

Forms required: FAFSA, institutional form.
Dates and Deadlines: Closing date 5/1. Applicants notified on a rolling basis starting 4/1.

CONTACT

Steve Brown, Director of Student Financial Services
538 Venard Road, Clarks Summit, PA 18411-1297
(570) 585-9215

Bloomsburg University of Pennsylvania
Bloomsburg, Pennsylvania
www.bloomu.edu   Federal Code: 003315

4-year public university and liberal arts college in large town.
Enrollment: 8,377 undergrads, 4% part-time. 2,033 full-time freshmen.
Selectivity: Admits 50 to 75% of applicants.

BASIC COSTS (2009-2010)

Tuition and fees: $7,110; out-of-state residents $15,442.
Per-credit charge: $231; out-of-state residents $579.
Room and board: $6,488.
Additional info: Tuition/fee waivers available for minority students.

FINANCIAL AID PICTURE (2009-2010)

Students with need: Out of 1,882 full-time freshmen who applied for aid, 1,788 were judged to have need. Of these, 1,667 received aid, and 1,500 had their full need met. Average financial aid package met 74% of need; average scholarship/grant was $6,609; average loan was $3,395. For part-time students, average financial aid package was $7,862.
Students without need: 48 full-time freshmen who did not demonstrate need for aid received scholarships/grants; average award was $2,025. No-need awards available for academics, art, athletics, job skills, leadership, minority status, music/drama, ROTC, state/district residency.
Scholarships offered: 63 full-time freshmen received athletic scholarships; average amount $2,867.
Cumulative student debt: 71% of graduating class had student loans; average debt was $21,322.

FINANCIAL AID PROCEDURES

Forms required: FAFSA.
Dates and Deadlines: Priority date 3/15; no closing date. Applicants notified on a rolling basis starting 4/1.
Transfers: Evaluation of transfer credits must be completed before financial aid can be finalized.

CONTACT

Thomas Lyons, Director of Financial Aid
104 Student Service Center, Bloomsburg, PA 17815
(570) 389-4297

Bryn Athyn College of the New Church

Bryn Athyn, Pennsylvania
www.brynathyn.edu   Federal Code: 003228

4-year private liberal arts college in small town, affiliated with General Church of the New Jerusalem (Swedenborgian).

Enrollment: 184 undergrads; 4% part-time. 70 full-time freshmen.

Selectivity: Admits over 75% of applicants.

BASIC COSTS (2010-2011)

Tuition and fees: $15,540.

Per-credit charge: $507.

Room and board: $8,540.

FINANCIAL AID PICTURE (2009-2010)

Students with need: Average financial aid package met 94% of need; average scholarship/grant was $10,645; average loan was $1,974. For part-time students, average financial aid package was $2,683.

Students without need: No-need awards available for academics, leadership, religious affiliation.

Cumulative student debt: 57% of graduating class had student loans; average debt was $12,729.

FINANCIAL AID PROCEDURES

Forms required: FAFSA, institutional form.

Dates and Deadlines: Closing date 6/1. Applicants notified on a rolling basis starting 4/30; must reply by 9/30.

Transfers: No deadline. Applicants notified on a rolling basis starting 7/1; must reply within 6 week(s) of notification.

CONTACT

Matthew Posey, Associate Director of Financial Aid
PO Box 462, Bryn Athyn, PA 19009-0462
(267) 502-2493

Bryn Mawr College

Bryn Mawr, Pennsylvania   Federal Code: 003237
www.brynmawr.edu   CSS Code: 2049

4-year private liberal arts college for women in very large city.

Enrollment: 1,289 undergrads, 1% part-time. 362 full-time freshmen.

Selectivity: Admits less than 50% of applicants.

BASIC COSTS (2010-2011)

Tuition and fees: $39,360.

Room and board: $12,420.

FINANCIAL AID PICTURE (2009-2010)

Students with need: Out of 278 full-time freshmen who applied for aid, 249 were judged to have need. Of these, 249 received aid, and 249 had their full need met. Average financial aid package met 100% of need; average scholarship/grant was $33,108; average loan was $3,330. Need-based aid available for part-time students.

Students without need: This college awards aid only to students with need.

Cumulative student debt: 52% of graduating class had student loans; average debt was $20,156.

FINANCIAL AID PROCEDURES

Forms required: FAFSA, CSS PROFILE.

Dates and Deadlines: Priority date 2/5; closing date 3/1. Applicants notified by 3/23; must reply by 5/1.

Transfers: Closing date 3/15. Must reply by 5/1.

CONTACT

Ethel Desmarais, Director of Financial Aid
101 North Merion Avenue, Bryn Mawr, PA 19010-2899
(610) 526-5245

Bucknell University

Lewisburg, Pennsylvania   Federal Code: 003238
www.bucknell.edu   CSS Code: 2050

4-year private university in small town.

Enrollment: 3,523 undergrads. 920 full-time freshmen.

Selectivity: Admits less than 50% of applicants.

BASIC COSTS (2010-2011)

Tuition and fees: $42,342.

Room and board: $9,938.

FINANCIAL AID PICTURE (2009-2010)

Students with need: Out of 527 full-time freshmen who applied for aid, 434 were judged to have need. Of these, 434 received aid, and 410 had their full need met. Average financial aid package met 95% of need; average scholarship/grant was $22,500; average loan was $4,400.

Students without need: 45 full-time freshmen who did not demonstrate need for aid received scholarships/grants; average award was $10,325. No-need awards available for academics, art, athletics, leadership, music/drama, ROTC.

Scholarships offered: *Merit:* Scholarships available to a limited number of students who have demonstrated exceptional achievements in academics, art and performing arts, music, and athletics. ***Athletic:*** 23 full-time freshmen received athletic scholarships; average amount $9,104.

Cumulative student debt: 61% of graduating class had student loans; average debt was $18,800.

FINANCIAL AID PROCEDURES

Forms required: FAFSA, CSS PROFILE.

Dates and Deadlines: Closing date 1/1. Applicants notified by 4/1; must reply by 5/1.

Transfers: Closing date 3/15. Applicants notified by 5/1; must reply by 6/1. Aid restricted to 2-year college graduates.

CONTACT

Andrea Stauffer, Director of Financial Aid
Freas Hall, Lewisburg, PA 17837-9988
(570) 577-1331

Bucks County Community College

Newtown, Pennsylvania
www.bucks.edu   Federal Code: 003239

2-year public community college in large town.

Enrollment: 9,980 undergrads.

Selectivity: Open admission; but selective for some programs.

BASIC COSTS (2009-2010)

Tuition and fees: $3,794; out-of-district residents $6,764; out-of-state residents $9,734.

Per-credit charge: $99; out-of-district residents $198; out-of-state residents $297.

Additional info: Additional per-credit-hour capital fee: $10 for out-of-county residents, $20 for out-of-state residents.

FINANCIAL AID PICTURE (2009-2010)

Students with need: Need-based aid available for full-time and part-time students. Work study available nights, weekends, and for part-time students.

Students without need: No-need awards available for academics.

FINANCIAL AID PROCEDURES

Forms required: FAFSA.

Dates and Deadlines: Closing date 5/1. Applicants notified on a rolling basis starting 6/1; must reply within 2 week(s) of notification.

Transfers: Applicants notified on a rolling basis starting 6/1; must reply within 2 week(s) of notification.

CONTACT

Donna Wilkoski, Director of Financial Aid

275 Swamp Road, Newtown, PA 18940

(215) 968-8200

Butler County Community College

Butler, Pennsylvania

www.bc3.edu   Federal Code: 003240

2-year public community college in small city.

Enrollment: 4,238 undergrads, 45% part-time.

Selectivity: Open admission; but selective for some programs.

BASIC COSTS (2009-2010)

Tuition and fees: $2,970; out-of-district residents $5,340; out-of-state residents $7,710.

Per-credit charge: $79; out-of-district residents $158; out-of-state residents $237.

FINANCIAL AID PICTURE (2008-2009)

Students with need: 49% of average financial aid package awarded as scholarships/grants, 51% awarded as loans/jobs. Need-based aid available for part-time students.

Students without need: No-need awards available for academics, state/district residency.

FINANCIAL AID PROCEDURES

Forms required: FAFSA.

Dates and Deadlines: Priority date 4/15; no closing date. Applicants notified on a rolling basis starting 5/1; must reply within 2 week(s) of notification.

CONTACT

Julianne Louttit, Director of Financial Aid

PO Box 1203, Butler, PA 16003-1203

(724) 287-8711 ext. 8329

Cabrini College

Radnor, Pennsylvania

www.cabrini.edu   Federal Code: 003241

4-year private liberal arts college in large town, affiliated with Roman Catholic Church.

Enrollment: 1,538 undergrads, 6% part-time. 357 full-time freshmen.

Selectivity: Admits 50 to 75% of applicants.

BASIC COSTS (2009-2010)

Tuition and fees: $31,030.

Room and board: $11,400.

FINANCIAL AID PICTURE (2009-2010)

Students with need: Out of 315 full-time freshmen who applied for aid, 280 were judged to have need. Of these, 280 received aid, and 40 had their full need met. Average financial aid package met 71% of need; average scholarship/grant was $9,890; average loan was $3,696. For part-time students, average financial aid package was $5,446.

Students without need: 69 full-time freshmen who did not demonstrate need for aid received scholarships/grants; average award was $10,079. No-need awards available for academics.

Cumulative student debt: 81% of graduating class had student loans; average debt was $30,633.

FINANCIAL AID PROCEDURES

Forms required: FAFSA.

Dates and Deadlines: Closing date 4/1. Applicants notified on a rolling basis starting 2/15.

Transfers: Achievement scholarships available.

CONTACT

Michael Colahan, Financial Aid Director

610 King of Prussia Road, Radnor, PA 19087-3698

(610) 902-8420

California University of Pennsylvania

California, Pennsylvania

www.cup.edu   Federal Code: 003316

4-year public university in small town.

Enrollment: 7,151 undergrads.

Selectivity: Admits 50 to 75% of applicants.

BASIC COSTS (2009-2010)

Tuition and fees: $7,676; out-of-state residents $11,010.

Per-credit charge: $231; out-of-state residents $370.

Room and board: $9,320.

Additional info: Tuition/fee waivers available for adults, minority students.

FINANCIAL AID PICTURE (2009-2010)

Students with need: Need-based aid available for full-time and part-time students. Work study available nights, weekends, and for part-time students.

Students without need: No-need awards available for academics, alumni affiliation, art, athletics, leadership, minority status, music/drama, religious affiliation, ROTC, state/district residency.

FINANCIAL AID PROCEDURES

Forms required: FAFSA, state aid form.

Dates and Deadlines: Priority date 5/1; no closing date. Applicants notified on a rolling basis starting 4/1; must reply within 3 week(s) of notification.

CONTACT

Robert Thorn, Director of Financial Aid

250 University Avenue, California, PA 15419-1394

(724) 938-4415

Cambria-Rowe Business College: Indiana

Indiana, Pennsylvania

www.crbc.net   Federal Code: 004889

2-year for-profit business and technical college in small town.

Enrollment: 128 undergrads, 7% part-time. 38 full-time freshmen.

Selectivity: Admits over 75% of applicants.

BASIC COSTS (2010-2011)

Tuition and fees: $10,590.

Per-credit charge: $270.

FINANCIAL AID PICTURE

Students with need: Need-based aid available for full-time and part-time students.

FINANCIAL AID PROCEDURES

Forms required: FAFSA.

Dates and Deadlines: No deadline. Applicants notified on a rolling basis.

CONTACT

Judy Miller, Financial Aid Officer
422 South 13th Street, Indiana, PA 15701
(814) 536-5168

Career Training Academy

New Kensington, Pennsylvania
www.careerta.edu   Federal Code: 026095

2-year for-profit career college in small town.
Enrollment: 52 full-time undergrads.
Selectivity: Open admission; but selective for some programs.

BASIC COSTS (2009-2010)

Additional info: Tuition ranges from $7,750 to $19,750 depending on program; required fees range from $253 to $1,378. Books and supplies range from $458 to $3,295.

FINANCIAL AID PICTURE

Students with need: Need-based aid available for full-time students.
Students without need: This college awards aid only to students with need.
Additional info: Work study available after class day.

FINANCIAL AID PROCEDURES

Forms required: FAFSA, institutional form.
Dates and Deadlines: No deadline.

CONTACT

Karen Schonbachler, Financial Services Coordinator
950 Fifth Avenue, New Kensington, PA 15068

Carlow University

Pittsburgh, Pennsylvania
www.carlow.edu   Federal Code: 003303

4-year private university and liberal arts college in large city, affiliated with Roman Catholic Church.
Enrollment: 1,520 undergrads, 27% part-time. 250 full-time freshmen.
Selectivity: Admits 50 to 75% of applicants.

BASIC COSTS (2010-2011)

Tuition and fees: $22,600.
Per-credit charge: $710.
Room and board: $8,900.
Additional info: Undergraduate adult students pay $540 per-credit-hour.

FINANCIAL AID PICTURE (2008-2009)

Students with need: 46% of average financial aid package awarded as scholarships/grants, 54% awarded as loans/jobs. Need-based aid available for part-time students. Work study available nights, weekends, and for part-time students.
Scholarships offered: Full tuition scholarship: 3.75 GPA, 1300 SAT required. Half tuition scholarship: 3.5 GPA, 1200 SAT required. Presidential scholarship: $5,000 to $10,000; 3.25 GPA, 1000 SAT required. Valedictorian scholarship: $10,000. McAuley scholarship: $2,500; 3.25 GPA, 930 SAT required; one per Catholic high school in diocese of Pittsburgh, Johnston/Altoona and Greensburg. Legacy scholarship: $2,500; to children or grandchildren of alumnae. Dean's Recognition scholarship: $4,000; 3.00 GPA and 930 SAT required. Sister Maurice Whalen scholarship: to those who submit projects to Pittsburgh Regional Science and Engineering Fair, also requires 3.25 GPA and 1000 SAT. Rose Marie Beard Women of Spirit Honors Scholarship: $4,000 for first year; 3.5 GPA, 1100 SAT, rank in top 15% of high school class, evidence of significant leadership required. All SAT scores exclusive of Writing.

FINANCIAL AID PROCEDURES

Forms required: FAFSA.
Dates and Deadlines: Priority date 4/1; no closing date. Applicants notified on a rolling basis starting 2/15; must reply within 4 week(s) of notification.
Transfers: No deadline. Applicants notified on a rolling basis; must reply within 4 week(s) of notification.

CONTACT

Natalie Wilson, Director of Financial Aid
3333 Fifth Avenue, Pittsburgh, PA 15213-3165
(412) 578-6058

Carnegie Mellon University

Pittsburgh, Pennsylvania
www.cmu.edu   Federal Code: 003242

4-year private university in large city.
Enrollment: 5,951 undergrads, 1% part-time. 1,423 full-time freshmen.
Selectivity: Admits less than 50% of applicants.

BASIC COSTS (2010-2011)

Tuition and fees: $41,940.
Per-credit charge: $576.
Room and board: $10,750.

FINANCIAL AID PICTURE (2009-2010)

Students with need: Out of 1,014 full-time freshmen who applied for aid, 792 were judged to have need. Of these, 783 received aid, and 241 had their full need met. Average financial aid package met 82% of need; average scholarship/grant was $24,707; average loan was $3,657. For part-time students, average financial aid package was $18,548.
Students without need: 121 full-time freshmen who did not demonstrate need for aid received scholarships/grants; average award was $10,643. No-need awards available for academics, art, leadership, minority status, music/drama, state/district residency.
Cumulative student debt: 50% of graduating class had student loans; average debt was $29,546.
Additional info: Early need analysis offered; merit awards available. Students notified within week to 10 days of receipt of financial aid application.

FINANCIAL AID PROCEDURES

Forms required: FAFSA, institutional form.
Dates and Deadlines: Priority date 2/15; closing date 5/1. Applicants notified by 3/15.
Transfers: Students applying for spring transfer must file FAFSA by 11/1 and are notified of award 12/15 or soon after. College of Fine Arts applicants applying for fall transfer must file FAFSA by 2/15 and are notified of award by 4/15. All other applicants for fall transfer must submit FAFSA by 5/1 and are notified of award during the month of June.

CONTACT

Linda Anderson, Director of Student Financial Aid
5000 Forbes Avenue, Pittsburgh, PA 15213-3890
(412) 268-8186

Cedar Crest College

Allentown, Pennsylvania
www.cedarcrest.edu   Federal Code: 003243

4-year private liberal arts college for women in small city.
Enrollment: 1,653 undergrads, 42% part-time. 196 full-time freshmen.
Selectivity: Admits 50 to 75% of applicants.

BASIC COSTS (2010-2011)

Tuition and fees: $28,967.
Per-credit charge: $952.

Room and board: $9,540.

FINANCIAL AID PICTURE (2009-2010)

Students with need: Out of 194 full-time freshmen who applied for aid, 183 were judged to have need. Of these, 183 received aid, and 21 had their full need met. Average financial aid package met 79% of need; average scholarship/grant was $19,347; average loan was $3,552. For part-time students, average financial aid package was $7,920.

Students without need: 15 full-time freshmen who did not demonstrate need for aid received scholarships/grants; average award was $6,915. No-need awards available for academics, alumni affiliation, art, leadership, music/drama.

Scholarships offered: Presidential Scholarship; up to half tuition; for freshmen with SAT scores over 1150 and in top 10% of class; renewable for four years with GPA of 3.0. 1867 Award; one-third of tuition; renewable for four years with GPA of 3.0; for freshmen with SAT of 1100 and in top 25% of class. Girl Scout Gold Awards; $1,000 per year; for recipients of the Girl Scout Gold Award. Art, Dance, and Performing Arts Scholarships; $1,500 per year; based on portfolio review, audition, and commitment to the creative process. Governor's School of Excellence Award; $1,000 per year; for graduates of Governor's Schools of Excellence. Hugh O'Brian Youth (HOBY) Awards; $1,000 per year; for freshmen who are HOBY alumnae. SAT scores exclusive of Writing portion.

Cumulative student debt: 92% of graduating class had student loans; average debt was $24,641.

FINANCIAL AID PROCEDURES

Forms required: FAFSA.

Dates and Deadlines: Priority date 5/1; no closing date. Applicants notified on a rolling basis starting 1/1; must reply by 5/15.

Transfers: Must reply by 5/15. Certain academic scholarships are available for transfers only, such as the Phi Theta Kappa Scholarship, Lifelong Learning Transfer Scholarship and Traditional Transfer Scholarship.

CONTACT

Lori Williams, Director of Student Financial Services
100 College Drive, Allentown, PA 18104-6196
(610) 606-4653

Central Pennsylvania College
Summerdale, Pennsylvania
www.centralpenn.edu   Federal Code: 004890

4-year for-profit business and technical college in rural community.
Enrollment: 1,213 undergrads, 44% part-time. 171 full-time freshmen.
Selectivity: Open admission; but selective for some programs.

BASIC COSTS (2009-2010)

Tuition and fees: $17,130.
Per-credit charge: $365.
Room and board: $6,285.

FINANCIAL AID PICTURE

Students with need: Need-based aid available for full-time and part-time students.
Students without need: No-need awards available for academics, alumni affiliation, job skills, leadership, minority status, state/district residency.

FINANCIAL AID PROCEDURES

Forms required: FAFSA, state aid form, institutional form.
Dates and Deadlines: Priority date 3/15; no closing date. Applicants notified on a rolling basis starting 2/1; must reply within 2 week(s) of notification.

CONTACT

Kathy Shepard, Financial Aid Director
College Hill & Valley Roads, Summerdale, PA 17093-0309
(717) 728-2261

Chatham University
Pittsburgh, Pennsylvania
www.chatham.edu   Federal Code: 003244

4-year private university and liberal arts college for women in large city.
Enrollment: 771 undergrads, 12% part-time. 131 full-time freshmen.
Selectivity: Admits 50 to 75% of applicants.

BASIC COSTS (2009-2010)

Tuition and fees: $28,290.
Per-credit charge: $662.
Room and board: $8,700.
Additional info: Required fees ($1,020) cover technology fee, which includes cost of HP tablet computer (required for all first-time first-year students) and the campus fee.

FINANCIAL AID PICTURE (2009-2010)

Students with need: Average financial aid package met 78% of need; average scholarship/grant was $8,021; average loan was $4,586. For part-time students, average financial aid package was $4,085.

Students without need: No-need awards available for academics, alumni affiliation, leadership, minority status.

Scholarships offered: Presidential Scholarship; up to $12,000. Trustee Scholarship; up to $9,000. Founders' Scholarship; up to $7,000. All based on academic excellence and renewable annually based on GPA of 2.8 or higher.

Cumulative student debt: 85% of graduating class had student loans; average debt was $39,404.

FINANCIAL AID PROCEDURES

Forms required: FAFSA.

Dates and Deadlines: Priority date 5/1; no closing date. Applicants notified on a rolling basis starting 2/15; must reply by 5/1 or within 2 week(s) of notification.

Transfers: Special scholarships are available for transfer students.

CONTACT

Jennifer Burns, Director of Financial Aid
Woodland Road, Pittsburgh, PA 15232
(412) 365-1777

Chestnut Hill College
Philadelphia, Pennsylvania
www.chc.edu   Federal Code: 003245

4-year private liberal arts college in very large city, affiliated with Roman Catholic Church.
Enrollment: 1,431 undergrads, 20% part-time. 273 full-time freshmen.
Selectivity: Admits 50 to 75% of applicants.

BASIC COSTS (2010-2011)

Tuition and fees: $28,100.
Per-credit charge: $600.
Room and board: $9,065.

FINANCIAL AID PICTURE (2009-2010)

Students with need: Out of 268 full-time freshmen who applied for aid, 225 were judged to have need. Of these, 223 received aid, and 49 had their full need met. Average financial aid package met 75% of need; average scholarship/grant was $15,577; average loan was $3,836. For part-time students, average financial aid package was $8,925.

Students without need: 1 full-time freshmen who did not demonstrate need for aid received scholarships/grants; average award was $1,000. No-need awards available for academics, alumni affiliation, athletics, leadership, religious affiliation.

Scholarships offered: *Merit:* Full-tuition and partial-tuition awards; based on academics. ***Athletic:*** 33 full-time freshmen received athletic scholarships; average amount $4,311.
Additional info: Application priority date 1/15 for merit-based scholarships.

FINANCIAL AID PROCEDURES
Forms required: FAFSA.
Dates and Deadlines: Closing date 4/15. Applicants notified on a rolling basis starting 1/31; must reply by 5/1 or within 3 week(s) of notification.
Transfers: Priority date 4/16; no deadline. Applicants notified on a rolling basis starting 2/15.

CONTACT
Nicholas Flocco, Director of Financial Aid
9601 Germantown Avenue, Philadelphia, PA 19118-2693
(215) 248-7182

Cheyney University of Pennsylvania
Cheyney, Pennsylvania
www.cheyney.edu Federal Code: 003317

4-year public university in small town.
Enrollment: 1,339 undergrads, 6% part-time. 382 full-time freshmen.
Selectivity: Admits less than 50% of applicants.

BASIC COSTS (2009-2010)
Tuition and fees: $7,360; out-of-state residents $15,692.
Per-credit charge: $231; out-of-state residents $579.
Room and board: $7,746.
Additional info: Tuition for residents of MD, NY, NJ and DE is $11,108. Tuition/fee waivers available for minority students.

FINANCIAL AID PICTURE
Students with need: Need-based aid available for full-time and part-time students.
Students without need: No-need awards available for academics, athletics.

FINANCIAL AID PROCEDURES
Forms required: FAFSA.
Dates and Deadlines: Priority date 3/15; no closing date. Applicants notified on a rolling basis starting 4/1; must reply within 2 week(s) of notification.

CONTACT
Harold Johnson, Director of Financial Aid
1837 University Circle, Cheyney, PA 19319-0019
(610) 399-2302

CHI Institute: Broomall
Broomall, Pennsylvania
www.chitraining.com Federal Code: 007781

2-year for-profit career college in large town.
Enrollment: 697 undergrads.
Selectivity: Open admission.

BASIC COSTS (2009-2010)
Additional info: Tuition ranges from $14,440 to $22,640 per 18-month diploma and associate degree program, inclusive of books and fees.

FINANCIAL AID PICTURE
Students with need: Need-based aid available for full-time and part-time students.

FINANCIAL AID PROCEDURES
Forms required: FAFSA.
Dates and Deadlines: No deadline. Applicants notified on a rolling basis.

CONTACT
Director of Financial Aid
1991 Sproul Road, Suite 42, Broomall, PA 19008
(610) 355-3300

Clarion University of Pennsylvania
Clarion, Pennsylvania
www.clarion.edu Federal Code: 003318

4-year public business and teachers college in small town.
Enrollment: 5,929 undergrads, 11% part-time. 1,309 full-time freshmen.
Selectivity: Admits 50 to 75% of applicants.

BASIC COSTS (2009-2010)
Tuition and fees: $7,380; out-of-state residents $12,934.
Per-credit charge: $231; out-of-state residents $463.
Room and board: $6,390.
Additional info: Tuition for incoming out-of-state residents with SAT of 1000 or higher and at least a 3.0 GPA or the top 30% of their graduating class is $8,331.

FINANCIAL AID PICTURE (2008-2009)
Students with need: Out of 1,209 full-time freshmen who applied for aid, 960 were judged to have need. Of these, 918 received aid, and 162 had their full need met. Average financial aid package met 69% of need; average scholarship/grant was $5,735; average loan was $3,164. For part-time students, average financial aid package was $4,385.
Students without need: 102 full-time freshmen who did not demonstrate need for aid received scholarships/grants; average award was $2,571. No-need awards available for academics, art, athletics, leadership, minority status, music/drama, state/district residency.
Scholarships offered: 86 full-time freshmen received athletic scholarships; average amount $2,276.

FINANCIAL AID PROCEDURES
Forms required: FAFSA.
Dates and Deadlines: Closing date 4/15. Applicants notified on a rolling basis starting 3/1.

CONTACT
Kenneth Grugel, Director of Financial Aid
840 Wood Street, Clarion, PA 16214
(814) 226-2315

Commonwealth Technical Institute
Johnstown, Pennsylvania
www.hgac.org

2-year private technical college in small city.
Enrollment: 135 undergrads. 33 full-time freshmen.
Selectivity: Open admission.

BASIC COSTS (2009-2010)
Tuition and fees: $11,224.
Room and board: $9,516.

FINANCIAL AID PICTURE (2008-2009)
Students with need: Out of 23 full-time freshmen who applied for aid, 16 were judged to have need. Of these, 15 received aid. Average financial aid package met 75% of need; average scholarship/grant was $2,000. Need-based aid available for part-time students.
Students without need: This college awards aid only to students with need.

FINANCIAL AID PROCEDURES

Forms required: FAFSA.

Dates and Deadlines: No deadline. Applicants notified on a rolling basis.

Transfers: No deadline. Applicants notified on a rolling basis.

CONTACT

Ann Yurcisin, Financial Aid Director
727 Goucher Street, Johnstown, PA 15905-3902
(814) 255-8351

Community College of Allegheny County-Allegheny

Pittsburgh, Pennsylvania
www.ccac.edu

2-year public community college in very large city.

Enrollment: 19,036 undergrads, 56% part-time. 3,107 full-time freshmen.

Selectivity: Open admission; but selective for some programs.

BASIC COSTS (2009-2010)

Tuition and fees: $2,905; out-of-district residents $5,455; out-of-state residents $8,005.

Per-credit charge: $86; out-of-district residents $171; out-of-state residents $256.

Additional info: If county does not have community college, tuition is $3,584 per year. Nursing and allied health courses subject to additional fees.

FINANCIAL AID PICTURE (2008-2009)

Students with need: Need-based aid available for full-time and part-time students. Work study available nights, weekends, and for part-time students.

Students without need: No-need awards available for academics, minority status.

FINANCIAL AID PROCEDURES

Forms required: FAFSA.

Dates and Deadlines: Priority date 5/1; no closing date. Applicants notified on a rolling basis starting 5/1.

CONTACT

Margaret Barton, Director of Financial Aid
800 Allegheny Avenue, Pittsburgh, PA 15233
(412) 323-2323

Community College of Beaver County

Monaca, Pennsylvania
www.ccbc.edu   Federal Code: 006807

2-year public community college in small town.

Enrollment: 1,859 undergrads.

Selectivity: Open admission; but selective for some programs.

BASIC COSTS (2009-2010)

Tuition and fees: $3,420; out-of-district residents $6,090; out-of-state residents $8,790.

Per-credit charge: $90; out-of-district residents $179; out-of-state residents $269.

Additional info: Academic enhancement fees, ranging from $25 to $900 per course, apply in programs requiring specialized technology and equipment; $10 per-credit-hour fee for courses that include a lab. Additional per-credit-hour capital fee: $10 for out-of-county residents, $20 for out-of-state residents.

FINANCIAL AID PICTURE (2008-2009)

Students with need: Need-based aid available for full-time and part-time students. Work study available nights, weekends, and for part-time students.

Students without need: No-need awards available for academics, athletics, state/district residency.

Scholarships offered: Academic Excellence Scholarship; full tuition.

FINANCIAL AID PROCEDURES

Forms required: FAFSA, state aid form, institutional form.

Dates and Deadlines: Priority date 5/1; closing date 7/1. Applicants notified on a rolling basis starting 8/5; must reply within 2 week(s) of notification.

Transfers: Priority date 5/6.

CONTACT

Doug Mailer, Director of Financial Aid
One Campus Drive, Monaca, PA 15061-2588
(724) 480-3501

Community College of Philadelphia

Philadelphia, Pennsylvania
www.ccp.edu   Federal Code: 003249

2-year public community college in very large city.

Enrollment: 19,051 undergrads, 66% part-time. 1,864 full-time freshmen.

Selectivity: Open admission; but selective for some programs.

BASIC COSTS (2009-2010)

Tuition and fees: $4,620; out-of-district residents $8,280; out-of-state residents $11,940.

Per-credit charge: $122; out-of-district residents $244; out-of-state residents $366.

FINANCIAL AID PICTURE (2008-2009)

Students with need: 53% of average financial aid package awarded as scholarships/grants, 47% awarded as loans/jobs. Need-based aid available for part-time students. Work study available nights, weekends, and for part-time students.

Students without need: This college awards aid only to students with need.

FINANCIAL AID PROCEDURES

Forms required: FAFSA, institutional form.

Dates and Deadlines: Closing date 5/1. Applicants notified on a rolling basis.

Transfers: No deadline.

CONTACT

Gim Lim, Director of Financial Aid
1700 Spring Garden Street, Philadelphia, PA 19130-3991
(215) 751-8270

Consolidated School of Business: Lancaster

Lancaster, Pennsylvania
www.csb.edu   Federal Code: 030299

2-year for-profit business college in small city.

Enrollment: 120 undergrads.

Selectivity: Open admission.

BASIC COSTS (2009-2010)

Tuition and fees: $11,500.

FINANCIAL AID PICTURE

Students with need: Need-based aid available for full-time and part-time students.

FINANCIAL AID PROCEDURES

Forms required: FAFSA, state aid form.

Dates and Deadlines: No deadline. Applicants notified on a rolling basis.

CONTACT
William Hoyt, Director of Financial Aid
2124 Ambassador Circle, Lancaster, PA 17603
(717) 394-6211

Consolidated School of Business: York
York, Pennsylvania
www.csb.edu   Federal Code: 022896

2-year for-profit business college in small city.
Enrollment: 132 undergrads.
Selectivity: Open admission.

BASIC COSTS (2009-2010)
Tuition and fees: $11,850.

FINANCIAL AID PICTURE
Students with need: Need-based aid available for full-time and part-time students.

FINANCIAL AID PROCEDURES
Forms required: FAFSA, state aid form.
Dates and Deadlines: No deadline. Applicants notified on a rolling basis.

CONTACT
William Hoyt, Director of Financial Aid
York City Business and Industry Park, York, PA 17404
(717) 764-9550

Curtis Institute of Music
Philadelphia, Pennsylvania
www.curtis.edu   Federal Code: 003251

4-year private music college in very large city.
Enrollment: 127 undergrads. 11 full-time freshmen.
Selectivity: Admits less than 50% of applicants.

BASIC COSTS (2009-2010)
Additional info: All students awarded a full-tuition scholarship. Bachelor of Music students pay $2,290 (required fees) and $17,910 (additional expenses), which covers supplies, off-campus room/board, and miscellaneous expenses for the academic year. Students required to have adequate health insurance coverage.

FINANCIAL AID PICTURE (2009-2010)
Students with need: Out of 9 full-time freshmen who applied for aid, 7 were judged to have need. Of these, 5 received aid, and 2 had their full need met. Average financial aid package met 91% of need; average scholarship/grant was $4,187; average loan was $3,500. Need-based aid available for part-time students.
Students without need: This college awards aid only to students with need.
Cumulative student debt: 60% of graduating class had student loans; average debt was $12,765.
Additional info: All admitted students receive a full tuition scholarship. The estimated value of this scholarship is $33,500.

FINANCIAL AID PROCEDURES
Forms required: FAFSA, institutional form.
Dates and Deadlines: Priority date 3/1; no closing date. Applicants notified by 4/1; must reply by 5/1 or within 2 week(s) of notification.

CONTACT
Richard Woodland, Associate Dean of Student Services and Financial Assistance
1726 Locust Street, Philadelphia, PA 19103-6187
(215) 717-3188

Delaware Valley College
Doylestown, Pennsylvania
www.delval.edu   Federal Code: 003252

4-year private agricultural and liberal arts college in large town.
Enrollment: 1,877 undergrads, 12% part-time. 452 full-time freshmen.
Selectivity: Admits 50 to 75% of applicants.

BASIC COSTS (2009-2010)
Tuition and fees: $27,742.
Per-credit charge: $708.
Room and board: $9,836.
Additional info: Tuition/fee waivers available for adults.

FINANCIAL AID PICTURE (2009-2010)
Students with need: Out of 416 full-time freshmen who applied for aid, 373 were judged to have need. Of these, 373 received aid, and 52 had their full need met. Average financial aid package met 70% of need; average scholarship/grant was $15,780; average loan was $3,570. For part-time students, average financial aid package was $3,750.
Students without need: 77 full-time freshmen who did not demonstrate need for aid received scholarships/grants; average award was $11,847. No-need awards available for academics, alumni affiliation, music/drama.
Cumulative student debt: 63% of graduating class had student loans; average debt was $26,350.

FINANCIAL AID PROCEDURES
Forms required: FAFSA, state aid form.
Dates and Deadlines: Priority date 4/1; no closing date. Applicants notified on a rolling basis starting 2/1; must reply by 5/1 or within 2 week(s) of notification.
Transfers: No deadline. Applicants notified on a rolling basis; must reply by 4/1.

CONTACT
Robert Sauer, Director of Financial Aid
700 East Butler Avenue, Doylestown, PA 18901-2697
(215) 489-2272

DeSales University
Center Valley, Pennsylvania
www.desales.edu   Federal Code: 003986

4-year private university in small town, affiliated with Roman Catholic Church.
Enrollment: 2,333 undergrads, 26% part-time. 378 full-time freshmen.
Selectivity: Admits 50 to 75% of applicants.

BASIC COSTS (2010-2011)
Tuition and fees: $28,000.
Per-credit charge: $1,125.
Room and board: $10,140.

FINANCIAL AID PICTURE (2009-2010)
Students with need: Out of 347 full-time freshmen who applied for aid, 294 were judged to have need. Of these, 294 received aid, and 51 had their full need met. Average financial aid package met 70% of need; average scholarship/grant was $15,482; average loan was $3,352. For part-time students, average financial aid package was $1,551.
Students without need: 70 full-time freshmen who did not demonstrate need for aid received scholarships/grants; average award was $8,464. No-need awards available for academics, leadership, music/drama.
Scholarships offered: Presidential Scholarships; full tuition; top 5% of class and 1300 SAT. Trustee Scholarships; from $6,000; top 15% of class, minimum 1200 SAT. DeSales Scholarships; $4,000; top 25% of class, minimum 1100 SAT. All SAT scores exclusive of writing.

Cumulative student debt: 76% of graduating class had student loans; average debt was $31,077.

FINANCIAL AID PROCEDURES

Forms required: FAFSA, state aid form.

Dates and Deadlines: Priority date 2/1; closing date 5/1. Applicants notified on a rolling basis starting 2/15; must reply by 5/1 or within 2 week(s) of notification.

Transfers: No deadline. Transfer scholarships require 3.0 GPA, 8 completed courses. Transfer Opportunity Program (TOP), a grant equal to tuition at participating community college, requires associate degree to qualify.

CONTACT

Joyce Farmer, Director of Financial Aid
2755 Station Avenue, Center Valley, PA 18034-9568
(610) 282-1100 ext. 1287

DeVry University: Fort Washington

Fort Washington, Pennsylvania
www.devry.edu

4-year for-profit university in large town.

Enrollment: 891 undergrads, 51% part-time. 126 full-time freshmen.

BASIC COSTS (2009-2010)

Tuition and fees: $14,800.
Per-credit charge: $575.

FINANCIAL AID PICTURE (2008-2009)

Students with need: Need-based aid available for full-time and part-time students.

Students without need: This college awards aid only to students with need.

FINANCIAL AID PROCEDURES

Forms required: FAFSA.

Dates and Deadlines: No deadline. Applicants notified on a rolling basis.

CONTACT

Citristal Claiborne, Director of Financial Aid
1140 Virginia Drive, Fort Washington, PA 19034-3204
(215) 591-5724

Dickinson College

Carlisle, Pennsylvania   Federal Code: 003253
www.dickinson.edu   CSS Code: 2186

4-year private liberal arts college in large town.

Enrollment: 2,330 undergrads. 581 full-time freshmen.

Selectivity: Admits less than 50% of applicants.

BASIC COSTS (2010-2011)

Tuition and fees: $41,545.
Per-credit charge: $1,286.
Room and board: $10,430.

FINANCIAL AID PICTURE (2009-2010)

Students with need: Out of 393 full-time freshmen who applied for aid, 323 were judged to have need. Of these, 320 received aid, and 251 had their full need met. Average financial aid package met 97% of need; average scholarship/grant was $28,583; average loan was $4,026. For part-time students, average financial aid package was $11,795.

Students without need: 38 full-time freshmen who did not demonstrate need for aid received scholarships/grants; average award was $10,177. No-need awards available for academics, leadership, ROTC.

Scholarships offered: John Dickinson and Benjamin Rush Scholarships; awarded to most academically competitive students. Additional Engage the

World Fellowship for selected John Dickinson Scholarship winners. John Montgomery Scholarship; awarded to first-year students who possess strong credentials, talent in the arts, or competency in 2 foreign languages in addition to English. Scholars must also demonstrate strong leadership in high school and community.

Cumulative student debt: 55% of graduating class had student loans; average debt was $23,224.

FINANCIAL AID PROCEDURES

Forms required: FAFSA, CSS PROFILE, state aid form.

Dates and Deadlines: Priority date 11/15; closing date 2/1. Applicants notified by 3/20; must reply by 5/1 or within 2 week(s) of notification.

Transfers: Closing date 4/1. Applicants notified by 5/1; must reply within 2 week(s) of notification.

CONTACT

Judith Carter, Director of Financial Aid
PO Box 1773, Carlisle, PA 17013-2896
(717) 245-1308

Douglas Education Center

Monessen, Pennsylvania
www.dec.edu   Federal Code: 013957

2-year for-profit visual arts and business college in small town.

Enrollment: 338 undergrads.

BASIC COSTS (2009-2010)

Additional info: All-inclusive associate, certificate and diploma programs in art, business, cosmetology and medical fields available from $3,290 to $39,825. Books and supplies range from $190 to $2,240.

FINANCIAL AID PICTURE (2009-2010)

Students with need: Need-based aid available for full-time and part-time students.

Students without need: This college awards aid only to students with need.

FINANCIAL AID PROCEDURES

Forms required: FAFSA.

Dates and Deadlines: No deadline. Applicants notified on a rolling basis.

CONTACT

Alison Pfender, Director of Financial Aid
130 Seventh Street, Monessen, PA 15062
(724) 684-3684 ext. 129

Drexel University

Philadelphia, Pennsylvania
www.drexel.edu   Federal Code: 003256

5-year private university in very large city.

Enrollment: 13,069 undergrads, 18% part-time. 2,285 full-time freshmen.

Selectivity: Admits 50 to 75% of applicants.

BASIC COSTS (2010-2011)

Tuition and fees: $33,005.
Per-credit charge: $850.
Room and board: $13,125.

FINANCIAL AID PICTURE (2009-2010)

Students with need: Need-based aid available for full-time students.

Students without need: No-need awards available for academics, alumni affiliation, art, athletics, leadership, music/drama, ROTC.

FINANCIAL AID PROCEDURES

Forms required: FAFSA.

Dates and Deadlines: Closing date 3/1. Applicants notified on a rolling basis starting 3/15.
Transfers: Priority date 3/2. Scholarships available in amounts up to $8,000. 3.2 GPA and 30 credit hours at time of application required for eligibility.

CONTACT

Helen Gourousis, Director of Financial Aid
3141 Chestnut Street, Philadelphia, PA 19104-2875
(215) 895-2537

Duquesne University

Pittsburgh, Pennsylvania
www.duq.edu   Federal Code: 003258

4-year private university in large city, affiliated with Roman Catholic Church.
Enrollment: 5,735 undergrads, 3% part-time. 1,354 full-time freshmen.
Selectivity: Admits over 75% of applicants.

BASIC COSTS (2010-2011)

Tuition and fees: $27,502.
Per-credit charge: $826.
Room and board: $9,476.

FINANCIAL AID PICTURE (2008-2009)

Students with need: Out of 1,278 full-time freshmen who applied for aid, 976 were judged to have need. Of these, 976 received aid, and 292 had their full need met. Average financial aid package met 91% of need; average scholarship/grant was $14,011; average loan was $4,160. For part-time students, average financial aid package was $11,064.
Students without need: 434 full-time freshmen who did not demonstrate need for aid received scholarships/grants; average award was $8,228. No-need awards available for academics, athletics, music/drama, ROTC.
Scholarships offered: *Merit:* Competitive scholarships available for academically and/or artistically talented students. *Athletic:* 100 full-time freshmen received athletic scholarships; average amount $14,055.

FINANCIAL AID PROCEDURES

Forms required: FAFSA, institutional form.
Dates and Deadlines: Closing date 5/1. Applicants notified on a rolling basis starting 3/1; must reply by 5/1 or within 3 week(s) of notification.
Transfers: No deadline. Must reply within 3 week(s) of notification.

CONTACT

Richard Esposito, Director of Financial Aid
600 Forbes Avenue, Administration Building, Pittsburgh, PA 15282-0201
(412) 396-6607

East Stroudsburg University of Pennsylvania

East Stroudsburg, Pennsylvania
www4.esu.edu   Federal Code: 003320

4-year public university in large town.
Enrollment: 6,288 undergrads, 8% part-time. 1,358 full-time freshmen.

BASIC COSTS (2009-2010)

Tuition and fees: $7,394; out-of-state residents $15,726.
Per-credit charge: $231; out-of-state residents $579.
Room and board: $6,418.
Additional info: Tuition for incoming out of state residents who are high achieving science and technology majors (biology, chemistry, computer science, mathematics, and physics) is $8,332.

FINANCIAL AID PICTURE (2008-2009)

Students with need: Out of 1,045 full-time freshmen who applied for aid, 725 were judged to have need. Of these, 599 received aid, and 422 had their full need met. Average financial aid package met 80% of need; average scholarship/grant was $4,497; average loan was $3,334. For part-time students, average financial aid package was $4,673.
Students without need: 307 full-time freshmen who did not demonstrate need for aid received scholarships/grants; average award was $9,613. No-need awards available for academics, alumni affiliation, art, athletics, leadership, minority status, music/drama, religious affiliation, state/district residency.
Scholarships offered: 41 full-time freshmen received athletic scholarships; average amount $2,179.
Cumulative student debt: 73% of graduating class had student loans; average debt was $25,887.

FINANCIAL AID PROCEDURES

Forms required: FAFSA.
Dates and Deadlines: Closing date 3/1. Applicants notified by 4/1; must reply by 5/1.

CONTACT

Phyllis Swinson, Associate Director of Financial Aid
200 Prospect Street, East Stroudsburg, PA 18301-2999
(570) 422-2800

Edinboro University of Pennsylvania

Edinboro, Pennsylvania
www.edinboro.edu   Federal Code: 003321

4-year public university in small town.
Enrollment: 6,301 undergrads, 10% part-time. 1,229 full-time freshmen.
Selectivity: Admits 50 to 75% of applicants.

BASIC COSTS (2009-2010)

Tuition and fees: $7,316; out-of-state residents $10,094.
Per-credit charge: $231; out-of-state residents $347.
Room and board: $7,430.

FINANCIAL AID PICTURE (2008-2009)

Students with need: Out of 1,174 full-time freshmen who applied for aid, 965 were judged to have need. Of these, 936 received aid, and 51 had their full need met. Average financial aid package met 59% of need; average scholarship/grant was $2,586; average loan was $2,924. For part-time students, average financial aid package was $5,982.
Students without need: 64 full-time freshmen who did not demonstrate need for aid received scholarships/grants; average award was $3,000. No-need awards available for academics, alumni affiliation, art, athletics, job skills, leadership, minority status, music/drama, religious affiliation, ROTC, state/district residency.
Scholarships offered: 43 full-time freshmen received athletic scholarships; average amount $1,600.
Cumulative student debt: 46% of graduating class had student loans; average debt was $21,518.

FINANCIAL AID PROCEDURES

Forms required: FAFSA.
Dates and Deadlines: Priority date 3/15; closing date 5/1. Applicants notified on a rolling basis starting 3/22; must reply within 2 week(s) of notification.

CONTACT

Dorothy Body, Assistant Vice President for Student Financial Support and Services
200 East Normal Street, Edinboro, PA 16444
(888) 611-2680

Elizabethtown College

Elizabethtown, Pennsylvania
www.etown.edu   Federal Code: 003262

4-year private liberal arts college in large town, affiliated with Church of the Brethren.

Enrollment: 2,243 undergrads, 17% part-time. 554 full-time freshmen.

Selectivity: Admits 50 to 75% of applicants.

BASIC COSTS (2010-2011)

Tuition and fees: $33,250.

Per-credit charge: $805.

Room and board: $8,500.

FINANCIAL AID PICTURE (2009-2010)

Students with need: Out of 479 full-time freshmen who applied for aid, 409 were judged to have need. Of these, 409 received aid, and 91 had their full need met. Average financial aid package met 84% of need; average scholarship/grant was $19,243; average loan was $3,733. Need-based aid available for part-time students.

Students without need: 132 full-time freshmen who did not demonstrate need for aid received scholarships/grants; average award was $14,357. No-need awards available for academics, art, music/drama, religious affiliation.

Scholarships offered: Presidential Scholarships; up to $16,000 annually; top 2% of class and minimum 1300 SAT score. Provost Scholarships; up to $13,500 annually; top 10% of class with minimum 1150 SAT; unlimited number awarded. Dean's Scholarships; up to $11,000 annually; for students with very strong academic achievement who do not qualify for other merit awards; unlimited number awarded. Music scholarships; $1,000-$4,000; based on audition. SAT scores exclusive of Writing portion.

FINANCIAL AID PROCEDURES

Forms required: FAFSA, institutional form.

Dates and Deadlines: Priority date 3/15; no closing date. Applicants notified on a rolling basis starting 3/1; must reply by 5/1 or within 2 week(s) of notification.

CONTACT

Elizabeth McCloud, Director of Financial Aid
One Alpha Drive, Elizabethtown, PA 17022-2298
(717) 361-1404

Erie Business Center

Erie, Pennsylvania
www.eriebc.edu   Federal Code: 004894

2-year for-profit business college in small city.

Enrollment: 390 undergrads.

Selectivity: Open admission.

BASIC COSTS (2009-2010)

Tuition and fees: $11,290.

Per-credit charge: $340.

FINANCIAL AID PICTURE

Students with need: Need-based aid available for full-time and part-time students.

FINANCIAL AID PROCEDURES

Forms required: FAFSA.

Dates and Deadlines: No deadline.

Transfers: Applicants notified on a rolling basis.

CONTACT

Heidi Salusky, Financial Aid Administrator
246 West Ninth Street, Erie, PA 16501
(814) 456-7504 ext. 115

Erie Business Center South

New Castle, Pennsylvania
www.eriebc.edu/newcastle   Federal Code: 004894

2-year for-profit branch campus and business college in small city.

Enrollment: 80 undergrads.

Selectivity: Open admission.

BASIC COSTS (2009-2010)

Tuition and fees: $5,820.

Per-credit charge: $184.

FINANCIAL AID PICTURE (2008-2009)

Students with need: 54% of average financial aid package awarded as scholarships/grants, 46% awarded as loans/jobs.

FINANCIAL AID PROCEDURES

Dates and Deadlines: Closing date 8/1.

CONTACT

Rhonda Antonelli, Director of Financial Aid
170 Cascade Galleria, New Castle, PA 16101
(724) 658-9066

Franklin & Marshall College

Lancaster, Pennsylvania   Federal Code: 003265
www.fandm.edu   CSS Code: 2261

4-year private liberal arts college in small city.

Enrollment: 2,137 undergrads. 633 full-time freshmen.

Selectivity: Admits less than 50% of applicants.

BASIC COSTS (2010-2011)

Tuition and fees: $41,190.

Room and board: $10,920.

FINANCIAL AID PICTURE (2009-2010)

Students with need: Out of 407 full-time freshmen who applied for aid, 291 were judged to have need. Of these, 291 received aid, and 291 had their full need met. Average financial aid package met 100% of need; average scholarship/grant was $28,914; average loan was $3,554.

Students without need: 61 full-time freshmen who did not demonstrate need for aid received scholarships/grants; average award was $11,437. No-need awards available for academics, art, leadership, minority status, music/drama.

Scholarships offered: John Marshall Scholarships; $12,500 awarded annually; independent initiative in intellectual or service areas considered. National Merit Recognition; $18,000 renewable annually. Presidential Scholarships; $7,500 annually. All based on academic performance, class rank. Klein Scholarship; $5,000; awarded based on academic and community achievement. Gray Scholarship; awarded to outstanding applicants of African-, Latino-, and Asian-American descent; minimizes loans.

Cumulative student debt: 52% of graduating class had student loans; average debt was $27,162.

FINANCIAL AID PROCEDURES

Forms required: FAFSA, CSS PROFILE.

Dates and Deadlines: Priority date 2/1; closing date 3/1. Applicants notified by 4/1; must reply by 5/1.

Transfers: Closing date 2/1.

CONTACT

Clarke Paine, Director of Student Aid
PO Box 3003, Lancaster, PA 17604-3003
(717) 291-3991

Gannon University

Erie, Pennsylvania
www.gannon.edu   Federal Code: 003266

4-year private university in small city, affiliated with Roman Catholic Church.
Enrollment: 2,593 undergrads, 6% part-time. 649 full-time freshmen.
Selectivity: Admits over 75% of applicants.

BASIC COSTS (2010-2011)

Tuition and fees: $24,582.
Per-credit charge: $745.
Room and board: $9,720.
Additional info: Tuition/fee waivers available for adults, unemployed or children of unemployed.

FINANCIAL AID PICTURE (2009-2010)

Students with need: Out of 620 full-time freshmen who applied for aid, 573 were judged to have need. Of these, 573 received aid, and 142 had their full need met. Average financial aid package met 83% of need; average scholarship/grant was $17,012; average loan was $3,390. For part-time students, average financial aid package was $5,699.
Students without need: 46 full-time freshmen who did not demonstrate need for aid received scholarships/grants; average award was $10,158. No-need awards available for academics, athletics, leadership, music/drama, religious affiliation, ROTC.
Scholarships offered: *Merit:* Academic Awards; $1,000 to full tuition; based on high school rank, GPA, and test scores. Leadership Awards; $1,000-$1,500; based on leadership and activities. Diocesan Scholarship; $1,000 Parish Grant; for students that belong to a parish within the Diocese of Erie. Diocesan High School Grant; $1,500; for students who attended a Catholic high school within the Diocese of Erie. Catholic High School Grant; $1,000; for any student who attended a Catholic high school outside of the Diocese of Erie. Athletic scholarships; $1,000 to full tuition, room and board. *Athletic:* 20 full-time freshmen received athletic scholarships; average amount $20,050.
Cumulative student debt: 86% of graduating class had student loans; average debt was $31,234.

FINANCIAL AID PROCEDURES

Forms required: FAFSA, institutional form.
Dates and Deadlines: Priority date 3/15; no closing date. Applicants notified on a rolling basis starting 11/1; must reply by 5/1 or within 4 week(s) of notification.
Transfers: No deadline. Applicants notified on a rolling basis starting 11/1; must reply by 5/1 or within 4 week(s) of notification.

CONTACT

Sharon Krahe, Director of Financial Aid
109 University Square, Erie, PA 16541-0001
(814) 871-7337

Geneva College

Beaver Falls, Pennsylvania
www.geneva.edu   Federal Code: 003267

4-year private liberal arts college in large town, affiliated with Reformed Presbyterian Church of North America.
Enrollment: 1,306 undergrads, 1% part-time. 332 full-time freshmen.
Selectivity: Admits over 75% of applicants.

BASIC COSTS (2010-2011)

Tuition and fees: $22,236.
Per-credit charge: $745.
Room and board: $8,000.
Additional info: Tuition/fee waivers available for minority students, unemployed or children of unemployed.

FINANCIAL AID PICTURE (2009-2010)

Students with need: Out of 301 full-time freshmen who applied for aid, 278 were judged to have need. Of these, 278 received aid, and 50 had their full need met. Average financial aid package met 85% of need; average scholarship/grant was $15,253; average loan was $3,954. For part-time students, average financial aid package was $9,825.
Students without need: 39 full-time freshmen who did not demonstrate need for aid received scholarships/grants; average award was $7,448. No-need awards available for academics, alumni affiliation, music/drama, religious affiliation.
Scholarships offered: Academic scholarships, scholarships for National Merit finalists and semifinalists, grants for members of controlling church and other denominations identified by the college.
Cumulative student debt: 94% of graduating class had student loans; average debt was $24,507.

FINANCIAL AID PROCEDURES

Forms required: FAFSA.
Dates and Deadlines: Priority date 3/15; no closing date. Applicants notified on a rolling basis starting 3/1; must reply by 5/1 or within 4 week(s) of notification.
Transfers: Applicants notified on a rolling basis starting 3/1; must reply within 4 week(s) of notification.

CONTACT

Steven Bell, Director of Financial Aid
3200 College Avenue, Beaver Falls, PA 15010
(724) 847-6530

Gettysburg College

Gettysburg, Pennsylvania   Federal Code: 003268
www.gettysburg.edu   CSS Code: 2275

4-year private liberal arts college in large town.
Enrollment: 2,692 undergrads. 739 full-time freshmen.
Selectivity: Admits less than 50% of applicants.

BASIC COSTS (2010-2011)

Tuition and fees: $41,580.
Room and board: $9,810.

FINANCIAL AID PICTURE (2009-2010)

Students with need: Out of 574 full-time freshmen who applied for aid, 438 were judged to have need. Of these, 433 received aid, and 425 had their full need met. Average financial aid package met 100% of need; average scholarship/grant was $24,791; average loan was $3,701.
Students without need: 125 full-time freshmen who did not demonstrate need for aid received scholarships/grants; average award was $9,983. No-need awards available for academics, music/drama, religious affiliation.
Scholarships offered: Presidential, Dean's, and Founders Scholarships; based on high school class rank and standardized test scores; number awarded varies. Wagnild Scholarship and Sunderman Scholarships for music talent; audition required.
Cumulative student debt: 61% of graduating class had student loans; average debt was $23,258.

FINANCIAL AID PROCEDURES

Forms required: FAFSA, CSS PROFILE.
Dates and Deadlines: Closing date 2/15. Applicants notified by 3/26; must reply by 5/1.
Transfers: Priority date 4/15. Must reply within 2 week(s) of notification.

CONTACT

Christina Gormley, Director of Financial Aid
300 North Washington Street, Gettysburg, PA 17325-1484
(717) 337-6611

Grove City College
Grove City, Pennsylvania
www.gcc.edu
Federal Code: G03269

4-year private liberal arts college in small town, affiliated with Presbyterian Church (USA).

Enrollment: 2,504 undergrads, 1% part-time. 650 full-time freshmen.

Selectivity: Admits 50 to 75% of applicants.

BASIC COSTS (2010-2011)
Tuition and fees: $13,088.
Room and board: $7,132.

FINANCIAL AID PICTURE (2009-2010)
Students with need: Out of 373 full-time freshmen who applied for aid, 285 were judged to have need. Of these, 275 received aid, and 34 had their full need met. Average financial aid package met 53% of need; average scholarship/grant was $6,024.

Students without need: 54 full-time freshmen who did not demonstrate need for aid received scholarships/grants; average award was $2,188. No-need awards available for academics, leadership, minority status.

Scholarships offered: Trustee Scholarships; $5,000; issued to a select group of accepted students who meet academic requirements; 24 awarded. Presidential Scholarships; $500; for all valedictorians in class of 30 or more, salutatorians in class of 100 or more, and National Merit Finalists. Engineering Scholarships; $2,500; 4 awarded.

Cumulative student debt: 45% of graduating class had student loans; average debt was $24,895.

Additional info: Institutional aid applications required for institutional scholarships, loans, and student employment.

FINANCIAL AID PROCEDURES
Forms required: institutional form.
Dates and Deadlines: Closing date 4/15. Applicants notified on a rolling basis starting 3/15; must reply by 5/1.
Transfers: Closing date 8/15. Applicants notified on a rolling basis; must reply within 2 week(s) of notification. Financial aid form must be submitted with transfer enrollment application.

CONTACT
Thomas Ball, Director of Financial Aid
100 Campus Drive, Grove City, PA 16127-2104
(724) 458-3300

Gwynedd-Mercy College
Gwynedd Valley, Pennsylvania
www.gmc.edu
Federal Code: 003270

4-year private nursing and liberal arts college in large town, affiliated with Roman Catholic Church.

Enrollment: 2,130 undergrads, 30% part-time. 350 full-time freshmen.

Selectivity: Admits 50 to 75% of applicants.

BASIC COSTS (2009-2010)
Tuition and fees: $24,180.
Per-credit charge: $500.
Room and board: $9,330.
Additional info: Tuition and fees for nursing and allied health programs $25,230 for full-time, and $600 per credit hour for part-time.

FINANCIAL AID PICTURE (2008-2009)
Students with need: Out of 318 full-time freshmen who applied for aid, 257 were judged to have need. Of these, 257 received aid, and 64 had their full need met. Average financial aid package met 75% of need; average scholarship/grant was $12,479; average loan was $4,210. Need-based aid available for part-time students.

Students without need: 70 full-time freshmen who did not demonstrate need for aid received scholarships/grants; average award was $14,710. No-need awards available for academics, leadership.

Scholarships offered: Presidential scholarship; $10,000; must have 1200 SAT and be in top 30% of class, essay required; 2/15 deadline. Connelly Scholarship; $6,000-$7,000; must have 1100 SAT and be in top 50% of class. Mother Mary Bernard Scholarship; $4,500-$5,000; must have 1000 SAT, be in top 50% of class, and have documented leadership experience. Yearly scholarship for Catholic school graduates; $2,000 (tuition incentive grant). All SAT scores exclusive of Writing.

Cumulative student debt: 90% of graduating class had student loans; average debt was $36,255.

FINANCIAL AID PROCEDURES
Forms required: FAFSA, institutional form.
Dates and Deadlines: Priority date 3/15; closing date 7/15. Applicants notified on a rolling basis starting 3/1; must reply by 5/1 or within 2 week(s) of notification.

CONTACT
Barbara Kaufmann, Director of Student Financial Aid
1325 Sumneytown Pike, Gwynedd Valley, PA 19437-0901
(215) 646-7300 ext. 483

Harcum College
Bryn Mawr, Pennsylvania
www.harcum.edu
Federal Code: 003272

2-year private junior college in large town.

Enrollment: 1,099 undergrads.

Selectivity: Admits less than 50% of applicants.

BASIC COSTS (2009-2010)
Tuition and fees: $18,210.
Per-credit charge: $575.
Room and board: $7,990.

FINANCIAL AID PICTURE (2009-2010)
Students with need: Need-based aid available for full-time and part-time students. Work study available nights, weekends, and for part-time students.

Students without need: No-need awards available for academics, leadership.

Scholarships offered: Scholarships available based on academic achievement.

FINANCIAL AID PROCEDURES
Forms required: FAFSA, institutional form.
Dates and Deadlines: Priority date 4/15; closing date 5/1. Applicants notified on a rolling basis starting 3/1; must reply within 3 week(s) of notification.
Transfers: Priority date 3/15.

CONTACT
Eli Moinester, Director of Financial Aid
750 Montgomery Avenue, Bryn Mawr, PA 19010-3476
(610) 526-6098

Harrisburg Area Community College
Harrisburg, Pennsylvania
www.hacc.edu
Federal Code: 003273

2-year public community college in small city.

Enrollment: 13,547 undergrads, 63% part-time. 1,927 full-time freshmen.

Selectivity: Open admission; but selective for some programs.

BASIC COSTS (2009-2010)

Tuition and fees: $3,480; out-of-district residents $5,985; out-of-state residents $8,790.

Per-credit charge: $99; out-of-district residents $182; out-of-state residents $275.

FINANCIAL AID PICTURE (2008-2009)

Students with need: Out of 1,517 full-time freshmen who applied for aid, 1,037 were judged to have need. Of these, 966 received aid, and 48 had their full need met. Average financial aid package met 52% of need; average scholarship/grant was $1,818; average loan was $2,948. For part-time students, average financial aid package was $4,544.

Students without need: 3 full-time freshmen who did not demonstrate need for aid received scholarships/grants; average award was $1,282. No-need awards available for academics.

Additional info: Federal work study community service positions available.

FINANCIAL AID PROCEDURES

Forms required: FAFSA, institutional form.

Dates and Deadlines: Priority date 3/15; no closing date. Applicants notified on a rolling basis starting 6/1.

Transfers: PHEAA state grants require separate academic progress review by financial aid staff.

CONTACT

James Carideo, Director of Financial Aid

One HACC Drive, Cooper 206, Harrisburg, PA 17110-2999

(717) 780-2330

Harrisburg University of Science and Technology

Harrisburg, Pennsylvania
www.HarrisburgU.edu   Federal Code: 039483

4-year private university in small city.

Enrollment: 146 undergrads, 16% part-time. 39 full-time freshmen.

Selectivity: Admits 50 to 75% of applicants.

BASIC COSTS (2010-2011)

Tuition and fees: $19,500.

Per-credit charge: $800.

FINANCIAL AID PICTURE (2009-2010)

Students with need: Average financial aid package met 52% of need; average scholarship/grant was $10,938; average loan was $3,791. For part-time students, average financial aid package was $7,194.

Students without need: No-need awards available for academics, leadership, state/district residency.

Scholarships offered: Various scholarships; $1,000-$18,000, depending on specific criteria.

FINANCIAL AID PROCEDURES

Forms required: FAFSA.

Dates and Deadlines: No deadline. Applicants notified on a rolling basis; must reply within 2 week(s) of notification.

Transfers: Priority date 5/1; no deadline. Applicants notified on a rolling basis; must reply within 4 week(s) of notification.

CONTACT

Vincent Frank, Director of Financial Aid

326 Market Street, Harrisburg, PA 17101-2208

(717) 901-5115

Haverford College

Haverford, Pennsylvania   Federal Code: 003274
www.haverford.edu   CSS Code: 2289

4-year private liberal arts college in large town.

Enrollment: 1,190 undergrads. 323 full-time freshmen.

Selectivity: Admits less than 50% of applicants.

BASIC COSTS (2010-2011)

Tuition and fees: $40,624.

Room and board: $12,346.

FINANCIAL AID PICTURE (2009-2010)

Students with need: Out of 206 full-time freshmen who applied for aid, 156 were judged to have need. Of these, 156 received aid, and 156 had their full need met. Average financial aid package met 100% of need; average scholarship/grant was $33,575; average loan was $625.

Students without need: This college awards aid only to students with need.

Cumulative student debt: 38% of graduating class had student loans; average debt was $16,500.

FINANCIAL AID PROCEDURES

Forms required: FAFSA, CSS PROFILE.

Dates and Deadlines: Closing date 2/1. Applicants notified by 4/1; must reply by 5/1.

Transfers: Closing date 3/1.

CONTACT

David Hoy, Director of Financial Aid

370 Lancaster Avenue, Haverford, PA 19041-1392

(610) 896-1350

Holy Family University

Philadelphia, Pennsylvania
www.holyfamily.edu   Federal Code: 003275

4-year private university and liberal arts college in very large city, affiliated with Roman Catholic Church.

Enrollment: 2,084 undergrads, 25% part-time. 378 full-time freshmen.

Selectivity: Admits 50 to 75% of applicants.

BASIC COSTS (2010-2011)

Tuition and fees: $23,520.

Per-credit charge: $490.

Room and board: $10,400.

FINANCIAL AID PICTURE (2009-2010)

Students with need: Out of 363 full-time freshmen who applied for aid, 318 were judged to have need. Of these, 318 received aid. Average financial aid package met 89% of need; average scholarship/grant was $14,220; average loan was $3,468. For part-time students, average financial aid package was $12,188.

Students without need: 43 full-time freshmen who did not demonstrate need for aid received scholarships/grants; average award was $9,626. No-need awards available for academics, alumni affiliation, athletics.

Scholarships offered: 7 full-time freshmen received athletic scholarships; average amount $11,000.

Cumulative student debt: 84% of graduating class had student loans; average debt was $31,459.

FINANCIAL AID PROCEDURES

Forms required: FAFSA, institutional form.

Dates and Deadlines: Priority date 3/1; no closing date. Applicants notified on a rolling basis starting 3/15; must reply within 2 week(s) of notification.

Transfers: Priority date 4/1; closing date 5/1. Applicants notified on a rolling basis starting 5/1; must reply within 3 week(s) of notification.

CONTACT

Janice Hetrick, Director of Financial Aid
9801 Frankford Avenue, Philadelphia, PA 19114-2009
(215) 637-5538

Hussian School of Art

Philadelphia, Pennsylvania
www.hussianart.edu   Federal Code: 007469

2-year for-profit visual arts and technical college in very large city.
Enrollment: 130 undergrads.
Selectivity: Admits over 75% of applicants.

BASIC COSTS (2010-2011)

Tuition and fees: $13,550.

FINANCIAL AID PICTURE (2008-2009)

Students with need: Need-based aid available for full-time students.

FINANCIAL AID PROCEDURES

Forms required: FAFSA, state aid form, institutional form.
Dates and Deadlines: No deadline. Applicants notified on a rolling basis starting 2/15; must reply within 3 week(s) of notification.
Transfers: Priority date 3/15; no deadline. Applicants notified on a rolling basis starting 4/1.

CONTACT

Susan Cohen, Financial Aid Director
The Bourse, Suite 300, 111 South Independence Mall East, Philadelphia, PA 19106
(215) 574-9600 ext. 206

Immaculata University

Immaculata, Pennsylvania
www.immaculata.edu   Federal Code: 003276

4-year private university and liberal arts college in large town, affiliated with Roman Catholic Church.
Enrollment: 2,950 undergrads, 64% part-time. 196 full-time freshmen.
Selectivity: Admits over 75% of applicants.

BASIC COSTS (2010-2011)

Tuition and fees: $27,870.
Per-credit charge: $440.
Room and board: $11,460.

FINANCIAL AID PICTURE (2009-2010)

Students with need: Need-based aid available for full-time and part-time students. Work study available nights, weekends, and for part-time students.
Students without need: No-need awards available for academics, alumni affiliation, art, job skills, leadership, minority status, music/drama, religious affiliation, state/district residency.

FINANCIAL AID PROCEDURES

Forms required: FAFSA.
Dates and Deadlines: Priority date 2/15; closing date 4/15. Applicants notified on a rolling basis starting 2/1; must reply within 2 week(s) of notification.
Transfers: No deadline. Applicants notified on a rolling basis starting 1/1; must reply within 2 week(s) of notification.

CONTACT

Robert Forest, Director of Financial Aid
PO Box 642, Immaculata, PA 19345-0642
(610) 647-4400 ext. 3026

Indiana University of Pennsylvania

Indiana, Pennsylvania
www.iup.edu   Federal Code: 003277

4-year public university in large town.
Enrollment: 11,821 undergrads, 5% part-time. 3,076 full-time freshmen.
Selectivity: Admits 50 to 75% of applicants.

BASIC COSTS (2009-2010)

Tuition and fees: $7,209; out-of-state residents $15,541.
Per-credit charge: $231; out-of-state residents $579.
Room and board: $6,278.
Additional info: Additional fees of $104 for out-of-state students. Tuition is $8,332 for students in any of these categories: OH, VA, WV, IN and MI residents; branch campus students from any state; out-of-state students with high school GPA of at least 3.0; any transfer student with GPA of at least 3.0.

FINANCIAL AID PICTURE (2008-2009)

Students with need: Out of 2,787 full-time freshmen who applied for aid, 2,097 were judged to have need. Of these, 2,081 received aid, and 256 had their full need met. Average financial aid package met 77% of need; average scholarship/grant was $5,387; average loan was $3,650. For part-time students, average financial aid package was $6,114.
Students without need: 160 full-time freshmen who did not demonstrate need for aid received scholarships/grants; average award was $2,346. No-need awards available for academics, alumni affiliation, art, athletics, job skills, leadership, music/drama, ROTC, state/district residency.
Scholarships offered: 60 full-time freshmen received athletic scholarships; average amount $2,967.
Cumulative student debt: 84% of graduating class had student loans; average debt was $25,224.

FINANCIAL AID PROCEDURES

Forms required: FAFSA.
Dates and Deadlines: Priority date 4/15; no closing date. Applicants notified on a rolling basis starting 3/15.
Transfers: Must reply within 2 week(s) of notification.

CONTACT

Patricia McCarthy, Director of Financial Aid
117 John Sutton Hall, 1011 South Drive, Indiana, PA 15705-1088
(724) 357-2218

JNA Institute of Culinary Arts

Philadelphia, Pennsylvania
www.culinaryarts.com   Federal Code: 031033

2-year for-profit technical college in very large city.
Enrollment: 58 undergrads.
Selectivity: Open admission.

BASIC COSTS (2009-2010)

Additional info: Tuition for 15-month associate program, $20,000; 6-month professional cooking diploma program, $10,000. Required fees $75 for both programs. Books and supplies are $325 for the diploma program and $1,050 for the associate program.

FINANCIAL AID PICTURE

Students with need: Need-based aid available for full-time students.

FINANCIAL AID PROCEDURES

Forms required: FAFSA.
Dates and Deadlines: No deadline.

CONTACT

J Partyka, Financial Aid Director

1212 South Broad Street, Philadelphia, PA 19146

(215) 468-8800

Johnson College

Scranton, Pennsylvania

www.johnson.edu   Federal Code: 014734

2-year private technical college in small city.

Enrollment: 410 undergrads, 2% part-time. 181 full-time freshmen.

Selectivity: Open admission; but selective for some programs.

BASIC COSTS (2010-2011)

Tuition and fees: $15,772.

Room only: $5,233.

FINANCIAL AID PICTURE

Students with need: Need-based aid available for full-time and part-time students. Work study available nights, weekends, and for part-time students.

Students without need: No-need awards available for academics.

FINANCIAL AID PROCEDURES

Forms required: FAFSA, institutional form.

Dates and Deadlines: Priority date 4/28; no closing date. Applicants notified on a rolling basis starting 4/15; must reply within 2 week(s) of notification.

Transfers: Priority date 5/1.

CONTACT

Ed Moyer, Director of Financial Aid

3427 North Main Avenue, Scranton, PA 18508

(570) 702-8914

Juniata College

Huntingdon, Pennsylvania

www.juniata.edu   Federal Code: 003279

4-year private liberal arts college in small town.

Enrollment: 1,360 undergrads. 364 full-time freshmen.

Selectivity: Admits 50 to 75% of applicants.

BASIC COSTS (2010-2011)

Tuition and fees: $32,820.

Per-credit charge: $1,335.

Room and board: $8,980.

Additional info: Tuition/fee waivers available for adults.

FINANCIAL AID PICTURE (2009-2010)

Students with need: Out of 305 full-time freshmen who applied for aid, 262 were judged to have need. Of these, 262 received aid, and 52 had their full need met. Average financial aid package met 86% of need; average scholarship/grant was $21,571; average loan was $3,847. Need-based aid available for part-time students.

Students without need: 101 full-time freshmen who did not demonstrate need for aid received scholarships/grants; average award was $13,609. No-need awards available for academics, art, leadership.

Scholarships offered: Ron & Ann Wertz Arts Scholarship, Richard M. Simpson Leadership Scholarship, J. Omar Good Service & Peacemaking Scholarship; full tuition; nominated by alumni, 1 awarded for each. Burkholder Scholarship; full tuition, room and board; 1 awarded. Friendship Scholarship; $2,000; awarded to international student. Calvert Ellis Scholarships; $16,000; based on high school GPA or SAT scores. Area Residents Scholarships; half tuition. Ray Day Scholarship; up to $5,000; for a minority student. John & Irene Dale Scholarship; $3,000; for information technology student. Heritage Scholarships; up to $8,000; for minority students with demonstrated commitment to leadership, community service and diversity. John Stauffer Scholar-

ships; 4 full tuition for National Merit or National Achievement finalist status. James Quinter Scholarships; $18,000; based upon GPA and SAT. M. G. Brumbaugh Scholarships; $14,000; based upon GPA and SAT. Transfer Scholarships; up to $16,000; based upon credits completed and GPA. Eagles Abroad Scholarships; international experience plus $3,000, based upon commitment to international experience in France, Germany, Mexico, Spain, or Russia.

Cumulative student debt: 89% of graduating class had student loans; average debt was $23,618.

FINANCIAL AID PROCEDURES

Forms required: FAFSA.

Dates and Deadlines: Closing date 3/1. Applicants notified on a rolling basis starting 2/28; must reply by 5/1.

Transfers: Applicants notified on a rolling basis starting 2/28; must reply by 5/1.

CONTACT

Valerie Rennell, Director of Student Financial Planning

1700 Moore Street, Huntingdon, PA 16652-2196

(814) 641-3142

Kaplan Career Institute: Harrisburg

Harrisburg, Pennsylvania

www.kci-harrisburg.com   Federal Code: 004910

2-year for-profit health science and technical college in small city.

Enrollment: 600 full-time undergrads.

FINANCIAL AID PICTURE

Students with need: Need-based aid available for full-time and part-time students. Work study available nights.

FINANCIAL AID PROCEDURES

Forms required: FAFSA, institutional form.

Dates and Deadlines: No deadline.

CONTACT

Sarah Brooker, Financial Aid Director

5650 Derry Street, Harrisburg, PA 17111-4112

Kaplan Career Institute: Pittsburgh

Pittsburgh, Pennsylvania

www.icmschool.com   Federal Code: 007436

2-year for-profit business and health science college in large city.

Enrollment: 1,192 undergrads.

BASIC COSTS (2009-2010)

Additional info: Tuition costs include books and supplies.

FINANCIAL AID PICTURE

Students with need: Need-based aid available for full-time and part-time students. Work study available nights.

Students without need: This college awards aid only to students with need.

FINANCIAL AID PROCEDURES

Forms required: FAFSA, state aid form, institutional form.

Dates and Deadlines: Closing date 4/30. Applicants notified on a rolling basis.

CONTACT

Denise Ringer-Fisher, Director of Financial Aid

10 Wood Street, Pittsburgh, PA 15222

(412) 261-2647 ext. 265

Keystone College
La Plume, Pennsylvania
www.keystone.edu Federal Code: 003280

4-year private liberal arts college in small town.
Enrollment: 1,612 undergrads, 21% part-time. 348 full-time freshmen.
Selectivity: Admits over 75% of applicants.

BASIC COSTS (2010-2011)
Tuition and fees: $19,020.
Per-credit charge: $400.
Room and board: $8,950.

FINANCIAL AID PICTURE (2008-2009)
Students with need: Average financial aid package met 72% of need; average scholarship/grant was $19,907; average loan was $3,500. For part-time students, average financial aid package was $3,174.
Students without need: 17 full-time freshmen who did not demonstrate need for aid received scholarships/grants; average award was $8,000. No-need awards available for academics, leadership.
Scholarships offered: Academic Excellence Scholarship: one-half up to full tuition; for full-time, first-time students in the top 5% of their class with SAT scores of 1100 or above (exclusive of Writing). Presidential Scholarship: up to $9,000 each year; based on class rank and SAT/ACT scores. Trustee Scholarship: up to $8,000 each year; based on class rank and SAT/ACT scores. Leadership Award: up to $5,000 each year; for students demonstrating non-athletic leadership skills.
Cumulative student debt: 84% of graduating class had student loans; average debt was $23,479.

FINANCIAL AID PROCEDURES
Forms required: FAFSA, state aid form.
Dates and Deadlines: Priority date 5/1; no closing date. Applicants notified on a rolling basis starting 2/1; must reply within 2 week(s) of notification.
Transfers: Applicants notified on a rolling basis starting 2/1; must reply within 2 week(s) of notification.

CONTACT
Ginger Kline, Director of Financial Assistance & Planning
One College Green, La Plume, PA 18440-1099
(570) 945-8967

Keystone Technical Institute
Harrisburg, Pennsylvania
www.kti.edu Federal Code: 022342

2-year for-profit health science and technical college in small city.
Enrollment: 121 undergrads.
Selectivity: Open admission.

BASIC COSTS (2009-2010)
Additional info: Tuition and fees vary by program.

FINANCIAL AID PICTURE
Students with need: Need-based aid available for full-time and part-time students. Work study available nights.
Students without need: This college awards aid only to students with need.
Scholarships offered: Half-tuition scholarships; 13 available to degree-seeking students.

FINANCIAL AID PROCEDURES
Forms required: FAFSA, state aid form.
Dates and Deadlines: Priority date 8/1; no closing date. Applicants notified on a rolling basis.
Transfers: State grant deadline for first-time recipients August 1. Renewal application deadline May 1.

CONTACT
Tracy Stewart, Financial Aid Coordinator
2301 Academy Drive, Harrisburg, PA 17112-1012
(717) 545-4747

King's College
Wilkes-Barre, Pennsylvania
www.kings.edu Federal Code: 003282

4-year private business and liberal arts college in small city, affiliated with Roman Catholic Church.
Enrollment: 2,042 undergrads, 4% part-time. 496 full-time freshmen.
Selectivity: Admits over 75% of applicants.

BASIC COSTS (2010-2011)
Tuition and fees: $26,644.
Per-credit charge: $495.
Room and board: $10,068.

FINANCIAL AID PICTURE (2009-2010)
Students with need: Out of 474 full-time freshmen who applied for aid, 427 were judged to have need. Of these, 427 received aid, and 81 had their full need met. Average financial aid package met 73% of need; average scholarship/grant was $16,246; average loan was $4,129. For part-time students, average financial aid package was $10,383.
Students without need: 68 full-time freshmen who did not demonstrate need for aid received scholarships/grants; average award was $12,165. No-need awards available for academics, leadership, ROTC.
Additional info: Any minority student with financial need may receive some aid in the form of a diversity scholarship.

FINANCIAL AID PROCEDURES
Forms required: FAFSA, institutional form.
Dates and Deadlines: Priority date 2/15; no closing date. Applicants notified on a rolling basis starting 3/1; must reply within 2 week(s) of notification.
Transfers: Priority date 2/1; no deadline. Applicants notified on a rolling basis; must reply by 5/1 or within 2 week(s) of notification.

CONTACT
Ellen McGuire, Director of Financial Aid
133 North River Street, Wilkes-Barre, PA 18711
(570) 208-5868

Kutztown University of Pennsylvania
Kutztown, Pennsylvania
www.kutztown.edu Federal Code: 003322

4-year public university in small town.
Enrollment: 9,181 undergrads, 5% part-time. 1,847 full-time freshmen.
Selectivity: Admits 50 to 75% of applicants.

BASIC COSTS (2009-2010)
Tuition and fees: $7,398; out-of-state residents $15,730.
Per-credit charge: $231; out-of-state residents $579.
Room and board: $7,698.

FINANCIAL AID PICTURE (2008-2009)
Students with need: Out of 1,653 full-time freshmen who applied for aid, 1,129 were judged to have need. Of these, 1,093 received aid, and 846 had their full need met. Average financial aid package met 54% of need; average scholarship/grant was $4,766; average loan was $3,269. For part-time students, average financial aid package was $5,352.
Students without need: 77 full-time freshmen who did not demonstrate need for aid received scholarships/grants; average award was $1,872. No-need awards available for academics, art, athletics, leadership, minority status, music/drama.

Scholarships offered: 29 full-time freshmen received athletic scholarships; average amount $2,133.

Cumulative student debt: 86% of graduating class had student loans; average debt was $20,707.

FINANCIAL AID PROCEDURES

Forms required: FAFSA.

Dates and Deadlines: Priority date 3/1; no closing date. Applicants notified on a rolling basis starting 3/30; must reply by 5/1 or within 4 week(s) of notification.

CONTACT

Bernard McCree, Director of Financial Aid
Admissions Office, Kutztown, PA 19530-0730
(610) 683-4077

La Roche College
Pittsburgh, Pennsylvania
www.laroche.edu   Federal Code: 003987

4-year private liberal arts college in large city, affiliated with Roman Catholic Church.

Enrollment: 1,181 undergrads, 17% part-time. 187 full-time freshmen.

Selectivity: Admits 50 to 75% of applicants.

BASIC COSTS (2010-2011)

Tuition and fees: $22,476.

Per-credit charge: $550.

Room and board: $8,916.

FINANCIAL AID PICTURE (2009-2010)

Students with need: Out of 164 full-time freshmen who applied for aid, 155 were judged to have need. Of these, 150 received aid, and 50 had their full need met. Average financial aid package met 93% of need; average scholarship/grant was $3,586; average loan was $4,955. For part-time students, average financial aid package was $10,118.

Students without need: 12 full-time freshmen who did not demonstrate need for aid received scholarships/grants; average award was $4,951. No-need awards available for academics.

Cumulative student debt: 78% of graduating class had student loans; average debt was $69,494.

FINANCIAL AID PROCEDURES

Forms required: FAFSA.

Dates and Deadlines: Priority date 2/15; closing date 5/1. Applicants notified on a rolling basis starting 3/1; must reply within 2 week(s) of notification.

CONTACT

Sharon Platt, Director of Financial Aid
9000 Babcock Boulevard, Pittsburgh, PA 15237
(412) 536-1120

La Salle University
Philadelphia, Pennsylvania
www.lasalle.edu   Federal Code: 003287

4-year private university and liberal arts college in very large city, affiliated with Roman Catholic Church.

Enrollment: 4,206 undergrads, 23% part-time. 948 full-time freshmen.

Selectivity: Admits 50 to 75% of applicants.

BASIC COSTS (2010-2011)

Tuition and fees: $33,700.

Room and board: $11,230.

FINANCIAL AID PICTURE (2009-2010)

Students with need: Out of 860 full-time freshmen who applied for aid, 761 were judged to have need. Of these, 761 received aid, and 175 had their full need met. Average financial aid package met 75% of need; average scholarship/grant was $19,406; average loan was $3,594. For part-time students, average financial aid package was $7,492.

Students without need: 167 full-time freshmen who did not demonstrate need for aid received scholarships/grants; average award was $14,147. No-need awards available for academics, athletics, ROTC.

Scholarships offered: *Merit:* Christian Brothers Scholarship; full tuition; based on academics and extracurricular leadership. Community Service Scholarship; half tuition; based on involvement in community service and academics. *Athletic:* 54 full-time freshmen received athletic scholarships; average amount $10,287.

Cumulative student debt: 85% of graduating class had student loans; average debt was $32,757.

FINANCIAL AID PROCEDURES

Forms required: FAFSA.

Dates and Deadlines: Priority date 2/15; no closing date. Applicants notified on a rolling basis starting 3/15; must reply by 5/1 or within 2 week(s) of notification.

Transfers: Applicants notified on a rolling basis starting 3/15; must reply by 5/1 or within 2 week(s) of notification.

CONTACT

Michael Wisnieski, Director of Financial Aid
1900 West Olney Avenue, Philadelphia, PA 19141-1199
(215) 951-1070

Lackawanna College
Scranton, Pennsylvania
www.lackawanna.edu   Federal Code: 003283

2-year private junior college in small city.

Enrollment: 1,294 undergrads, 23% part-time. 355 full-time freshmen.

Selectivity: Open admission.

BASIC COSTS (2009-2010)

Tuition and fees: $11,160.

Per-credit charge: $370.

Room and board: $7,000.

FINANCIAL AID PICTURE (2009-2010)

Students with need: Average financial aid package met 57% of need; average scholarship/grant was $6,825; average loan was $3,476. For part-time students, average financial aid package was $6,212.

Students without need: No-need awards available for academics, athletics, leadership.

Cumulative student debt: 92% of graduating class had student loans; average debt was $14,342.

FINANCIAL AID PROCEDURES

Forms required: FAFSA, state aid form, institutional form.

Dates and Deadlines: Priority date 5/1; no closing date. Applicants notified on a rolling basis starting 5/1.

Transfers: No deadline. Applicants notified on a rolling basis starting 5/1.

CONTACT

Babara Hapeman, Director of Financial Aid
501 Vine Street, Scranton, PA 18509
(570) 961-7859

Lafayette College

Easton, Pennsylvania
www.lafayette.edu

Federal Code: 003284
CSS Code: 2361

4-year private engineering and liberal arts college in large town, affiliated with Presbyterian Church (USA).

Enrollment: 2,378 undergrads, 1% part-time. 616 full-time freshmen.

Selectivity: Admits less than 50% of applicants.

BASIC COSTS (2010-2011)

Tuition and fees: $39,815.

Per-credit charge: $433.75.

Room and board: $11,959.

FINANCIAL AID PICTURE (2008-2009)

Students with need: Out of 395 full-time freshmen who applied for aid, 260 were judged to have need. Of these, 258 received aid, and 126 had their full need met. Average financial aid package met 98% of need; average scholarship/grant was $31,097; average loan was $3,579. Need-based aid available for part-time students.

Students without need: 29 full-time freshmen who did not demonstrate need for aid received scholarships/grants; average award was $18,968. No-need awards available for academics, athletics, leadership, ROTC.

Scholarships offered: *Merit:* Marquis Scholarships: $20,000; based on academic merit, awarded to 10% of each entering class. *Athletic:* 13 full-time freshmen received athletic scholarships; average amount $31,617.

Cumulative student debt: 47% of graduating class had student loans; average debt was $20,745.

Additional info: Parent loans, up to $7,500 annually, available with college absorbing interest while student is enrolled. Family has 8 years after graduation to repay. Not limited to those demonstrating need.

FINANCIAL AID PROCEDURES

Forms required: FAFSA, CSS PROFILE.

Dates and Deadlines: Priority date 2/15; closing date 3/15. Applicants notified by 4/1; must reply by 5/1.

Transfers: Closing date 5/1.

CONTACT

Arlina DeNardo, Director of Student Financial Aid
118 Markle Hall, Easton, PA 18042
(610) 330-5055

Lancaster Bible College

Lancaster, Pennsylvania
www.lbc.edu

Federal Code: 003285

4-year private Bible college in small city, affiliated with nondenominational tradition.

Enrollment: 702 undergrads, 16% part-time. 118 full-time freshmen.

Selectivity: Admits over 75% of applicants.

BASIC COSTS (2009-2010)

Tuition and fees: $15,840.

Per-credit charge: $513.

Room and board: $6,780.

FINANCIAL AID PICTURE (2008-2009)

Students with need: Out of 109 full-time freshmen who applied for aid, 93 were judged to have need. Of these, 92 received aid, and 13 had their full need met. Average financial aid package met 44% of need; average scholarship/grant was $8,518; average loan was $3,288. Need-based aid available for part-time students.

Students without need: 23 full-time freshmen who did not demonstrate need for aid received scholarships/grants; average award was $4,140. No-need awards available for academics, alumni affiliation, leadership, music/drama.

Cumulative student debt: 27% of graduating class had student loans; average debt was $19,579.

FINANCIAL AID PROCEDURES

Forms required: FAFSA, state aid form.

Dates and Deadlines: Priority date 5/1; no closing date. Applicants notified on a rolling basis starting 3/1; must reply within 3 week(s) of notification.

CONTACT

Karen Fox, Director of Financial Aid
901 Eden Road, Lancaster, PA 17601-5036
(717) 560-8254

Laurel Business Institute

Uniontown, Pennsylvania
www.laurel.edu

Federal Code: 017118

2-year for-profit technical and career college in large town.

Enrollment: 315 undergrads.

Selectivity: Admits over 75% of applicants.

BASIC COSTS (2009-2010)

Tuition and fees: $8,500.

Per-credit charge: $250.

FINANCIAL AID PICTURE (2009-2010)

Students with need: Need-based aid available for full-time and part-time students.

Students without need: This college awards aid only to students with need.

Scholarships offered: One full tuition, several half tuition (including GED scholarships); based on high school transcripts or GED scores, letters of reference, and personal interview.

FINANCIAL AID PROCEDURES

Forms required: FAFSA, institutional form.

Dates and Deadlines: Closing date 8/1. Applicants notified on a rolling basis; must reply within 4 week(s) of notification.

Transfers: No deadline. Must reply within 4 week(s) of notification.

CONTACT

Stephanie Migyanko, Director of Financial Aid
11 East Penn Street, Uniontown, PA 15401
(724) 439-4900

Lebanon Valley College

Annville, Pennsylvania
www.lvc.edu

Federal Code: 003288

4-year private liberal arts college in small town, affiliated with United Methodist Church.

Enrollment: 1,650 undergrads, 5% part-time. 378 full-time freshmen.

Selectivity: Admits over 75% of applicants.

BASIC COSTS (2009-2010)

Tuition and fees: $30,490.

Per-credit charge: $500.

Room and board: $8,080.

Additional info: Tuition/fee waivers available for minority students.

FINANCIAL AID PICTURE (2009-2010)

Students with need: Out of 364 full-time freshmen who applied for aid, 321 were judged to have need. Of these, 321 received aid, and 78 had their full need met. Average financial aid package met 85% of need; average scholarship/grant was $20,015; average loan was $4,318. For part-time students, average financial aid package was $3,911.

Students without need: 49 full-time freshmen who did not demonstrate need for aid received scholarships/grants; average award was $12,684. No-need awards available for academics, alumni affiliation, music/drama.

Scholarships offered: Vickroy Scholarship; half tuition; automatic for admitted applicants in top 10% of graduating class. Leadership scholarship; one-third tuition; automatic for admitted applicants in top 20% of graduating class. Achievement Scholarship; one-quarter tuition; automatic for admitted applicants in top 30% of graduating class.

Cumulative student debt: 82% of graduating class had student loans; average debt was $33,348.

FINANCIAL AID PROCEDURES

Forms required: FAFSA, institutional form.

Dates and Deadlines: Priority date 3/1; no closing date. Applicants notified on a rolling basis starting 3/1; must reply by 5/1 or within 2 week(s) of notification.

Transfers: Must reply by 5/1 or within 2 week(s) of notification. Students transferring 15 or fewer credits are considered for scholarships on the same basis as high school seniors. Students transferring 16 or more credits are considered for scholarships based on their college academic performance and program.

CONTACT

Kendra Feigert, Director of Financial Aid
101 North College Avenue, Annville, PA 17003-1400
(717) 867-6181

Lehigh Carbon Community College

Schnecksville, Pennsylvania
www.lccc.edu   Federal Code: 006810

2-year public community college in small town.

Enrollment: 6,876 undergrads, 51% part-time. 1,209 full-time freshmen.

Selectivity: Open admission; but selective for some programs.

BASIC COSTS (2009-2010)

Tuition and fees: $3,030; out-of-district residents $5,850; out-of-state residents $8,670.

Per-credit charge: $85; out-of-district residents $179; out-of-state residents $273.

Additional info: Tuition/fee waivers available for unemployed or children of unemployed.

FINANCIAL AID PICTURE (2008-2009)

Students with need: Out of 917 full-time freshmen who applied for aid, 581 were judged to have need. Of these, 549 received aid, and 51 had their full need met. For part-time students, average financial aid package was $3,484.

Students without need: No-need awards available for academics, job skills.

FINANCIAL AID PROCEDURES

Forms required: FAFSA.

Dates and Deadlines: Priority date 5/1; no closing date. Applicants notified on a rolling basis starting 1/1; must reply within 2 week(s) of notification.

Transfers: No deadline. Applicants notified on a rolling basis.

CONTACT

Marian Snyder, Director of Financial Aid
4525 Education Park Drive, Schnecksville, PA 18078
(610) 799-1133

Lehigh University

Bethlehem, Pennsylvania   Federal Code: 003289
www.lehigh.edu   CSS Code: 2365

4-year private university in small city.

Enrollment: 4,792 undergrads, 1% part-time. 1,193 full-time freshmen.

Selectivity: Admits less than 50% of applicants.

BASIC COSTS (2010-2011)

Tuition and fees: $39,780.

Per-credit charge: $1,650.

Room and board: $10,520.

FINANCIAL AID PICTURE (2009-2010)

Students with need: Out of 777 full-time freshmen who applied for aid, 554 were judged to have need. Of these, 554 received aid, and 313 had their full need met. Average financial aid package met 97% of need; average scholarship/grant was $27,887; average loan was $3,388. For part-time students, average financial aid package was $19,996.

Students without need: 70 full-time freshmen who did not demonstrate need for aid received scholarships/grants; average award was $10,139. No-need awards available for academics, art, athletics, leadership, music/drama, ROTC.

Scholarships offered: *Merit:* Dean's Scholarships; $10,000; for academic excellence and leadership skills. Baker Scholarship; $3,000; for excellence in music or theater and superior academic record. Choral Arts Scholarships; $2,500; for singing talent. Performing Arts Scholarship; $3,000; for those who display exceptional theatrical talent (including performance, design, technical, and playwriting). Snyder Family Marching 97 Scholarships; $1,000-$2,500; for those who demonstrate musical talent and leadership and who fully participate in the marching band. Athletic Awards/Scholarships. *Athletic:* 17 full-time freshmen received athletic scholarships; average amount $30,506.

Cumulative student debt: 54% of graduating class had student loans; average debt was $31,123.

Additional info: Loans eliminated for students eligible for financial aid and whose family income is less than $50,000.

FINANCIAL AID PROCEDURES

Forms required: FAFSA, CSS PROFILE.

Dates and Deadlines: Closing date 2/15. Applicants notified by 3/30; must reply by 5/1 or within 3 week(s) of notification.

Transfers: Closing date 4/1. Applicants notified on a rolling basis starting 5/15; must reply within 3 week(s) of notification.

CONTACT

Linda Bell, Director of Financial Aid
27 Memorial Drive West, Bethlehem, PA 18015-3094
(610) 758-3181

Lincoln University

Lincoln University, Pennsylvania
www.lincoln.edu   Federal Code: 003290

4-year public university and liberal arts college in small town.

Enrollment: 2,030 undergrads, 1% part-time. 579 full-time freshmen.

Selectivity: Admits less than 50% of applicants.

BASIC COSTS (2009-2010)

Tuition and fees: $8,718; out-of-state residents $12,832.

Per-credit charge: $246; out-of-state residents $417.

Room and board: $7,890.

Additional info: Out-of-state students pay additional $630 in fees, which are included in out-of-state tuition figure.

FINANCIAL AID PICTURE (2009-2010)

Students with need: Need-based aid available for full-time and part-time students. Work study available nights, weekends, and for part-time students.
Students without need: No-need awards available for academics, alumni affiliation, leadership, music/drama.

FINANCIAL AID PROCEDURES

Forms required: FAFSA.
Dates and Deadlines: Closing date 5/1. Applicants notified on a rolling basis starting 4/1; must reply within 3 week(s) of notification.

CONTACT

Thelma Ross, Director of Financial Aid
1570 Baltimore Pike, Lincoln University, PA 19352-0999
(800) 561-2606

Lock Haven University of Pennsylvania
Lock Haven, Pennsylvania
www.lhup.edu   Federal Code: 003323

4-year public university and liberal arts college in small town.
Enrollment: 4,874 undergrads, 5% part-time. 1,185 full-time freshmen.
Selectivity: Admits over 75% of applicants.

BASIC COSTS (2009-2010)

Tuition and fees: $7,201; out-of-state residents $13,533.
Per-credit charge: $231; out-of-state residents $495.
Room and board: $6,736.
Additional info: All freshman students are required to have a laptop computer for use in the classroom. Computers can be purchased through the university; cost of computer is not included in mandatory fees. The university has a small number of laptops available to students who cannot afford to make such a purchase. Tuition/fee waivers available for minority students.

FINANCIAL AID PICTURE (2009-2010)

Students with need: Out of 1,149 full-time freshmen who applied for aid, 885 were judged to have need. Of these, 885 received aid, and 398 had their full need met. Average financial aid package met 75% of need; average scholarship/grant was $6,304; average loan was $3,233. For part-time students, average financial aid package was $5,294.
Students without need: 20 full-time freshmen who did not demonstrate need for aid received scholarships/grants; average award was $1,835. No-need awards available for academics, art, athletics, leadership, minority status, music/drama, ROTC, state/district residency.
Scholarships offered: 46 full-time freshmen received athletic scholarships; average amount $2,087.
Cumulative student debt: 85% of graduating class had student loans; average debt was $22,585.

FINANCIAL AID PROCEDURES

Forms required: FAFSA.
Dates and Deadlines: Closing date 3/15. Applicants notified on a rolling basis starting 4/1; must reply within 2 week(s) of notification.
Transfers: Priority date 4/1.

CONTACT

James Theeuwes, Director of Student Financial Services
LHU Office of Admissions, Lock Haven, PA 17745
(877) 405-3057

Luzerne County Community College
Nanticoke, Pennsylvania
www.luzerne.edu   Federal Code: 006811

2-year public community college in large town.
Enrollment: 6,796 undergrads, 45% part-time. 1,362 full-time freshmen.

Selectivity: Open admission; but selective for some programs.

BASIC COSTS (2009-2010)

Tuition and fees: $3,090; out-of-district residents $5,910; out-of-state residents $8,730.
Per-credit charge: $84; out-of-district residents $168; out-of-state residents $252.

FINANCIAL AID PICTURE (2008-2009)

Students with need: 48% of average financial aid package awarded as scholarships/grants, 52% awarded as loans/jobs. Need-based aid available for part-time students.

FINANCIAL AID PROCEDURES

Forms required: FAFSA, institutional form.
Dates and Deadlines: Priority date 4/15; no closing date. Applicants notified on a rolling basis starting 7/1.

CONTACT

Mary Kosin, Director of Financial Aid
1333 South Prospect Street, Nanticoke, PA 18634-3899
(570) 740-0395

Lycoming College
Williamsport, Pennsylvania
www.lycoming.edu   Federal Code: 003293

4-year private liberal arts college in small city, affiliated with United Methodist Church.
Enrollment: 1,347 undergrads, 1% part-time. 386 full-time freshmen.
Selectivity: Admits 50 to 75% of applicants.

BASIC COSTS (2010-2011)

Tuition and fees: $30,800.
Per-credit charge: $945.
Room and board: $8,542.
Additional info: Tuition/fee waivers available for minority students.

FINANCIAL AID PICTURE (2009-2010)

Students with need: Out of 368 full-time freshmen who applied for aid, 347 were judged to have need. Of these, 347 received aid, and 53 had their full need met. Average financial aid package met 81% of need; average scholarship/grant was $20,267; average loan was $4,044. For part-time students, average financial aid package was $10,049.
Students without need: 35 full-time freshmen who did not demonstrate need for aid received scholarships/grants; average award was $12,406. No-need awards available for academics, art, leadership, minority status, music/drama, religious affiliation, ROTC.
Cumulative student debt: 85% of graduating class had student loans; average debt was $29,478.

FINANCIAL AID PROCEDURES

Forms required: FAFSA, institutional form.
Dates and Deadlines: Priority date 3/1; no closing date. Applicants notified on a rolling basis starting 3/1; must reply by 5/1.
Transfers: No deadline.

CONTACT

James Spencer, Dean of Admissions and Financial Aid
700 College Place, Williamsport, PA 17701
(570) 321-4026

Manor College
Jenkintown, Pennsylvania
www.manor.edu   Federal Code: 003294

2-year private junior college in small town, affiliated with Ukrainian Catholic Church.

Enrollment: 778 undergrads, 43% part-time. 148 full-time freshmen.

Selectivity: Admits less than 50% of applicants.

BASIC COSTS (2010-2011)
Tuition and fees: $13,238.

Per-credit charge: $277.

Room and board: $5,972.

Additional info: Tuition for allied health program: $13,464; $378 per-credit-hour. Tuition/fee waivers available for minority students, unemployed or children of unemployed.

FINANCIAL AID PICTURE (2009-2010)
Students with need: Average financial aid package met 32% of need; average scholarship/grant was $4,850; average loan was $3,520. For part-time students, average financial aid package was $4,680.

Students without need: No-need awards available for academics, alumni affiliation, art.

Scholarships offered: Basilian Scholarship; for every freshman with A or B high school average and minimum 900 SAT (exclusive of Writing).

Cumulative student debt: 97% of graduating class had student loans; average debt was $8,000.

FINANCIAL AID PROCEDURES
Forms required: FAFSA.

Dates and Deadlines: Priority date 4/1; no closing date. Applicants notified on a rolling basis starting 3/1; must reply within 2 week(s) of notification.

Transfers: No deadline. Applicants notified on a rolling basis starting 12/1; must reply within 2 week(s) of notification.

CONTACT
Peter Lysionek, Director of Financial Aid
700 Fox Chase Road, Jenkintown, PA 19046-3319
(215) 884-6051

Mansfield University of Pennsylvania
Mansfield, Pennsylvania
www.mansfield.edu   Federal Code: 003324

4-year public university in small town.

Enrollment: 2,999 undergrads, 6% part-time. 884 full-time freshmen.

Selectivity: Admits over 75% of applicants.

BASIC COSTS (2009-2010)
Tuition and fees: $7,756; out-of-state residents $16,088.

Per-credit charge: $231; out-of-state residents $579.

Room and board: $7,016.

Additional info: Tuition for NY residents is $9,166; per-credit-hour charge for NY residents is $382.

FINANCIAL AID PICTURE (2008-2009)
Students with need: Average financial aid package met 81% of need; average scholarship/grant was $2,200; average loan was $2,664. For part-time students, average financial aid package was $2,351.

Students without need: No-need awards available for academics, art, athletics, leadership, music/drama, state/district residency.

Scholarships offered: 17 full-time freshmen received athletic scholarships; average amount $1,221.

Cumulative student debt: 81% of graduating class had student loans; average debt was $28,937.

FINANCIAL AID PROCEDURES
Forms required: FAFSA, institutional form.

Dates and Deadlines: Priority date 3/15; no closing date. Applicants notified on a rolling basis starting 3/15; must reply within 2 week(s) of notification.

CONTACT
Barbara Schmitt, Director of Financial Aid
South Hall, Mansfield, PA 16933
(570) 662-4129

Marywood University
Scranton, Pennsylvania
www.marywood.edu   Federal Code: 003296

4-year private university in small city, affiliated with Roman Catholic Church.

Enrollment: 2,147 undergrads, 5% part-time. 422 full-time freshmen.

Selectivity: Admits 50 to 75% of applicants.

BASIC COSTS (2010-2011)
Tuition and fees: $27,150.

Room and board: $12,172.

FINANCIAL AID PICTURE (2008-2009)
Students with need: Out of 395 full-time freshmen who applied for aid, 350 were judged to have need. Of these, 349 received aid, and 87 had their full need met. Average financial aid package met 81% of need; average scholarship/grant was $6,308; average loan was $3,705. For part-time students, average financial aid package was $8,692.

Students without need: 68 full-time freshmen who did not demonstrate need for aid received scholarships/grants; average award was $11,044. No-need awards available for academics, alumni affiliation, art, leadership, music/drama, ROTC.

FINANCIAL AID PROCEDURES
Forms required: FAFSA.

Dates and Deadlines: Priority date 2/15; no closing date. Applicants notified on a rolling basis starting 2/15; must reply by 5/1 or within 3 week(s) of notification.

Transfers: No deadline. Applicants notified on a rolling basis starting 3/1; must reply by 5/1 or within 3 week(s) of notification.

CONTACT
Stanley Skrutski, Director of Financial Aid
2300 Adams Avenue, Scranton, PA 18509-1598
(570) 348-6225

Mercyhurst College
Erie, Pennsylvania
www.mercyhurst.edu   Federal Code: 003297

4-year private liberal arts college in small city, affiliated with Roman Catholic Church.

Enrollment: 3,941 undergrads, 12% part-time. 667 full-time freshmen.

Selectivity: Admits 50 to 75% of applicants.

BASIC COSTS (2010-2011)
Tuition and fees: $26,346.

Per-credit charge: $822.

Room and board: $9,195.

Additional info: Tuition/fee waivers available for adults, minority students, unemployed or children of unemployed.

FINANCIAL AID PICTURE (2009-2010)
Students with need: Need-based aid available for full-time and part-time students. Work study available nights, weekends, and for part-time students.

Students without need: No-need awards available for academics, alumni affiliation, art, athletics, leadership, minority status, music/drama, religious affiliation, ROTC.

FINANCIAL AID PROCEDURES

Forms required: FAFSA.

Dates and Deadlines: Priority date 3/1; no closing date. Applicants notified on a rolling basis starting 2/15; must reply by 5/1 or within 2 week(s) of notification.

Transfers: No deadline. Applicants notified on a rolling basis; must reply within 2 week(s) of notification.

CONTACT

Carrie Newman, Director of Student Financial Services
501 East 38th Street, Erie, PA 16546-0001
(814) 824-2288

Messiah College

Grantham, Pennsylvania
www.messiah.edu   Federal Code: 003298

4-year private liberal arts college in small town, affiliated with interdenominational tradition.

Enrollment: 2,728 undergrads, 1% part-time. 698 full-time freshmen.

Selectivity: Admits 50 to 75% of applicants.

BASIC COSTS (2010-2011)

Tuition and fees: $27,480.

Per-credit charge: $1,112.

Room and board: $8,160.

Additional info: Tuition/fee waivers available for adults.

FINANCIAL AID PICTURE (2009-2010)

Students with need: Out of 609 full-time freshmen who applied for aid, 527 were judged to have need. Of these, 527 received aid, and 111 had their full need met. Average financial aid package met 72% of need; average scholarship/grant was $13,875; average loan was $3,719. For part-time students, average financial aid package was $7,829.

Students without need: 168 full-time freshmen who did not demonstrate need for aid received scholarships/grants; average award was $10,237. No-need awards available for academics, art, leadership, music/drama, religious affiliation.

Cumulative student debt: 76% of graduating class had student loans; average debt was $33,867.

FINANCIAL AID PROCEDURES

Forms required: FAFSA.

Dates and Deadlines: Priority date 4/1; no closing date. Applicants notified on a rolling basis starting 3/15; must reply by 5/1 or within 4 week(s) of notification.

CONTACT

Greg Gearhart, Director of Financial Aid
PO Box 3005, Grantham, PA 17027-0800
(717) 691-6007

Millersville University of Pennsylvania

Millersville, Pennsylvania
www.millersville.edu   Federal Code: 003325

4-year public university and liberal arts college in small town.

Enrollment: 7,242 undergrads, 8% part-time. 1,311 full-time freshmen.

Selectivity: Admits 50 to 75% of applicants.

BASIC COSTS (2009-2010)

Tuition and fees: $7,147; out-of-state residents $15,479.

Per-credit charge: $231; out-of-state residents $579.

Room and board: $7,766.

FINANCIAL AID PICTURE (2008-2009)

Students with need: Out of 1,152 full-time freshmen who applied for aid, 753 were judged to have need. Of these, 735 received aid, and 94 had their full need met. Average financial aid package met 78% of need; average scholarship/grant was $5,130; average loan was $3,232. For part-time students, average financial aid package was $5,282.

Students without need: 29 full-time freshmen who did not demonstrate need for aid received scholarships/grants; average award was $2,027. No-need awards available for academics, athletics, minority status.

Scholarships offered: 15 full-time freshmen received athletic scholarships; average amount $1,377.

Cumulative student debt: 64% of graduating class had student loans; average debt was $22,408.

FINANCIAL AID PROCEDURES

Forms required: FAFSA.

Dates and Deadlines: Closing date 3/15. Applicants notified on a rolling basis starting 3/19; must reply within 2 week(s) of notification.

Transfers: No deadline. Applicants notified on a rolling basis.

CONTACT

Dwight Horsey, Assistant Vice President for Student Affairs
PO Box 1002, Millersville, PA 17551-0302
(717) 872-3026

Misericordia University

Dallas, Pennsylvania
www.misericordia.edu   Federal Code: 003247

4-year private health science and liberal arts college in large town, affiliated with Roman Catholic Church.

Enrollment: 2,315 undergrads, 28% part-time. 371 full-time freshmen.

Selectivity: Admits 50 to 75% of applicants.

BASIC COSTS (2010-2011)

Tuition and fees: $24,990.

Per-credit charge: $450.

Room and board: $10,410.

Additional info: Tuition/fee waivers available for adults.

FINANCIAL AID PICTURE (2009-2010)

Students with need: Out of 357 full-time freshmen who applied for aid, 308 were judged to have need. Of these, 308 received aid, and 45 had their full need met. Average financial aid package met 73% of need; average scholarship/grant was $13,218; average loan was $6,800. For part-time students, average financial aid package was $3,932.

Students without need: 48 full-time freshmen who did not demonstrate need for aid received scholarships/grants; average award was $7,646. No-need awards available for academics, alumni affiliation, leadership, minority status, state/district residency.

Scholarships offered: McAuley Award; $1,000-$5,000 per year; based on out-of-classroom activities. Academic Scholarship; $2,000-$15,000 per year; based on academic abilities.

Cumulative student debt: 78% of graduating class had student loans; average debt was $33,641.

FINANCIAL AID PROCEDURES

Forms required: FAFSA, institutional form.

Dates and Deadlines: Priority date 3/1; closing date 5/1. Applicants notified on a rolling basis starting 3/15; must reply by 5/1.

Transfers: No deadline. Applicants notified on a rolling basis starting 3/15.

CONTACT

Jane Dessoye, Executive Director of Enrollment Management
301 Lake Street, Dallas, PA 18612-1098
(570) 674-6280

Montgomery County Community College
Blue Bell, Pennsylvania
www.mc3.edu   Federal Code: 004452

2-year public community college in large town.
Enrollment: 13,310 undergrads, 53% part-time. 2,481 full-time freshmen.
Selectivity: Open admission; but selective for some programs.

BASIC COSTS (2009-2010)
Tuition and fees: $3,270; out-of-district residents $6,270; out-of-state residents $9,270.
Per-credit charge: $90; out-of-district residents $180; out-of-state residents $270.

FINANCIAL AID PICTURE (2008-2009)
Students with need: Out of 1,213 full-time freshmen who applied for aid, 987 were judged to have need. Of these, 870 received aid, and 30 had their full need met. Average financial aid package met 17% of need; average scholarship/grant was $2,315; average loan was $1,660. For part-time students, average financial aid package was $3,443.
Students without need: 199 full-time freshmen who did not demonstrate need for aid received scholarships/grants; average award was $2,609. No-need awards available for academics.

FINANCIAL AID PROCEDURES
Forms required: FAFSA.
Dates and Deadlines: Priority date 5/1; no closing date. Applicants notified on a rolling basis starting 2/1.
Transfers: No deadline.

CONTACT
Cindy Haney, Executive Director of Enrollment Services
340 DeKalb Pike, Blue Bell, PA 19422
(215) 641-6566

Moore College of Art and Design
Philadelphia, Pennsylvania
www.moore.edu   Federal Code: 003300

4-year private visual arts college for women in very large city.
Enrollment: 527 undergrads, 6% part-time. 100 full-time freshmen.
Selectivity: Admits 50 to 75% of applicants.

BASIC COSTS (2009-2010)
Tuition and fees: $29,240.
Room and board: $11,026.

FINANCIAL AID PICTURE (2009-2010)
Students with need: Need-based aid available for full-time and part-time students.
Students without need: No-need awards available for academics, art, leadership.

FINANCIAL AID PROCEDURES
Forms required: FAFSA.
Dates and Deadlines: Priority date 3/1; closing date 5/1. Applicants notified on a rolling basis starting 2/15; must reply within 2 week(s) of notification.
Transfers: Priority date 5/1; no deadline.

CONTACT

Kristina Fripps, Director of Financial Aid
The Parkway at 20th Street, Philadelphia, PA 19103-1179
(215) 568-4515

Moravian College
Bethlehem, Pennsylvania
www.moravian.edu   Federal Code: 003301

4-year private liberal arts college in small city, affiliated with Moravian Church in America.
Enrollment: 1,618 undergrads, 5% part-time. 381 full-time freshmen.
Selectivity: Admits over 75% of applicants.

BASIC COSTS (2010-2011)
Tuition and fees: $32,317.
Per-credit charge: $880.
Room and board: $9,164.

FINANCIAL AID PICTURE (2009-2010)
Students with need: Out of 355 full-time freshmen who applied for aid, 320 were judged to have need. Of these, 320 received aid, and 38 had their full need met. Average financial aid package met 80% of need; average scholarship/grant was $20,141; average loan was $4,148. For part-time students, average financial aid package was $11,550.
Students without need: 53 full-time freshmen who did not demonstrate need for aid received scholarships/grants; average award was $10,194. No-need awards available for academics, alumni affiliation, leadership, minority status, music/drama, religious affiliation, ROTC.
Scholarships offered: Comenius Scholarship; $10,000 to full tuition; top 10% of high school class and minimum 1850 SAT required. Founders Scholarship; $4,000-$8,000; for top 25% or 1700 SAT. Trustee Scholarship; $6,000-$10,000; must be National Honor Society member, in top 20% of class. All scholarships require at least 500 on each section of SAT. Other scholarships available based on interest in the sciences, leadership and interest in promoting diversity and/or challenging circumstances in attending college.

FINANCIAL AID PROCEDURES
Forms required: FAFSA.
Dates and Deadlines: Priority date 2/14; closing date 3/15. Applicants notified on a rolling basis starting 4/1; must reply by 5/1 or within 2 week(s) of notification.
Transfers: Priority date 3/15; closing date 5/1. Applicants notified on a rolling basis starting 4/1.

CONTACT
Stephen Cassel, Director of Financial Aid
1200 Main Street, Bethlehem, PA 18018
(610) 861-1330

Mount Aloysius College
Cresson, Pennsylvania
www.mtaloy.edu   Federal Code: 003302

4-year private liberal arts college in small town, affiliated with Roman Catholic Church.
Enrollment: 1,482 undergrads, 21% part-time. 349 full-time freshmen.
Selectivity: Admits over 75% of applicants.

BASIC COSTS (2010-2011)
Tuition and fees: $18,000.
Per-credit charge: $520.
Room and board: $7,660.
Additional info: Tuition/fee waivers available for unemployed or children of unemployed.

FINANCIAL AID PICTURE (2009-2010)

Students with need: Out of 349 full-time freshmen who applied for aid, 328 were judged to have need. Of these, 328 received aid. Average financial aid package met 30% of need; average scholarship/grant was $2,890; average loan was $3,470. For part-time students, average financial aid package was $5,000.

Students without need: 21 full-time freshmen who did not demonstrate need for aid received scholarships/grants; average award was $3,860. No-need awards available for academics, art, leadership, music/drama, religious affiliation.

Cumulative student debt: 80% of graduating class had student loans; average debt was $29,802.

FINANCIAL AID PROCEDURES

Forms required: FAFSA.

Dates and Deadlines: Priority date 4/1; no closing date. Applicants notified on a rolling basis starting 3/15; must reply within 2 week(s) of notification.

Transfers: No deadline.

CONTACT

Stacy Schenk, Director of Financial Aid
7373 Admiral Peary Highway, Cresson, PA 16630
(814) 886-6357

Muhlenberg College

Allentown, Pennsylvania
www.muhlenberg.edu

Federal Code: 003304
CSS Code: 2424

4-year private liberal arts college in small city, affiliated with Evangelical Lutheran Church in America.

Enrollment: 2,411 undergrads, 4% part-time, 577 full-time freshmen.

Selectivity: Admits less than 50% of applicants.

BASIC COSTS (2009-2010)

Tuition and fees: $36,990.

Room and board: $8,440.

FINANCIAL AID PICTURE (2009-2010)

Students with need: 80% of average financial aid package awarded as scholarships/grants, 20% awarded as loans/jobs. Need-based aid available for part-time students.

Students without need: No-need awards available for academics, art, leadership, music/drama.

FINANCIAL AID PROCEDURES

Forms required: FAFSA, CSS PROFILE, institutional form.

Dates and Deadlines: Closing date 2/15. Applicants notified by 4/1; must reply by 5/1.

Transfers: Closing date 4/15. Transfers awarded aid on a funds-available basis after returning students and freshmen have been served.

CONTACT

Gregory Mitton, Director of Financial Aid
2400 Chew Street, Allentown, PA 18104
(484) 664-3175

Neumann University

Aston, Pennsylvania
www.neumann.edu

Federal Code: 003988

4-year private university in large town, affiliated with Roman Catholic Church.

Enrollment: 2,501 undergrads, 20% part-time. 539 full-time freshmen.

Selectivity: Admits over 75% of applicants.

BASIC COSTS (2009-2010)

Tuition and fees: $21,360.

Per-credit charge: $470.

Room and board: $9,718.

FINANCIAL AID PICTURE (2008-2009)

Students with need: Out of 512 full-time freshmen who applied for aid, 485 were judged to have need. Of these, 485 received aid, and 315 had their full need met. Average financial aid package met 65% of need; average scholarship/grant was $12,000; average loan was $3,000.

Students without need: This college awards aid only to students with need.

Cumulative student debt: 70% of graduating class had student loans; average debt was $25,000.

FINANCIAL AID PROCEDURES

Forms required: FAFSA.

Dates and Deadlines: No deadline. Applicants notified on a rolling basis; must reply within 2 week(s) of notification.

Transfers: Priority date 3/7; closing date 6/1. Must reply within 2 week(s) of notification.

CONTACT

Katharine Markert, Director of Financial Aid
One Neumann Drive, Aston, PA 19014-1298
(610) 558-5520

Newport Business Institute: Lower Burrell

Lower Burrell, Pennsylvania
www.nbi.edu

Federal Code: 004901

2-year for-profit business college in small town.

Enrollment: 60 undergrads.

Selectivity: Open admission.

BASIC COSTS (2009-2010)

Tuition and fees: $11,325.

FINANCIAL AID PICTURE

Students with need: Need-based aid available for full-time and part-time students.

Students without need: No-need awards available for academics, leadership.

FINANCIAL AID PROCEDURES

Forms required: FAFSA, state aid form.

Dates and Deadlines: No deadline. Applicants notified on a rolling basis starting 5/1.

CONTACT

Rosemary Leipertz, Director of Financial Aid
945 Greensburg Road, Lower Burrell, PA 15068
(724) 339-7542

Northampton Community College

Bethlehem, Pennsylvania
www.northampton.edu

Federal Code: 007191

2-year public community college in small city.

Enrollment: 10,909 undergrads, 50% part-time. 1,923 full-time freshmen.

Selectivity: Open admission; but selective for some programs.

BASIC COSTS (2009-2010)

Tuition and fees: $3,180; out-of-district residents $5,490; out-of-state residents $10,290.

Per-credit charge: $77; out-of-district residents $154; out-of-state residents $231.

Room and board: $6,862.

Additional info: Tuition/fee waivers available for unemployed or children of unemployed.

FINANCIAL AID PICTURE (2009-2010)

Students with need: Average financial aid package for all full-time undergraduates was $3,744; for part-time $1,944. 75% awarded as scholarships/grants, 25% awarded as loans/jobs. Work study available nights, weekends, and for part-time students.

Students without need: No-need awards available for academics, alumni affiliation, art, leadership, minority status, music/drama.

FINANCIAL AID PROCEDURES

Forms required: FAFSA, institutional form.

Dates and Deadlines: Priority date 3/31; no closing date. Applicants notified on a rolling basis starting 6/1.

CONTACT

Cindy King, Director of Financial Aid

3835 Green Pond Road, Bethlehem, PA 18020

(610) 861-5510

Oakbridge Academy of Arts
Lower Burrell, Pennsylvania
www.oaa.edu   Federal Code: 015063

2-year for-profit visual arts college in large town.

Enrollment: 61 undergrads.

Selectivity: Open admission.

BASIC COSTS (2009-2010)

Tuition and fees: $11,025.

FINANCIAL AID PICTURE

Students with need: Need-based aid available for full-time and part-time students.

Students without need: This college awards aid only to students with need.

Scholarships offered: Jeanne H. Mullen art scholarship; half tuition; based on portfolio; 2 awarded per year.

FINANCIAL AID PROCEDURES

Forms required: FAFSA, state aid form.

Dates and Deadlines: Closing date 5/1. Applicants notified on a rolling basis; must reply by 5/1.

CONTACT

Rosemary Leipertz, Financial Aid Director

1250 Greensburg Road, Lower Burrell, PA 15068

(724) 335-5336

Orleans Technical Institute
Philadelphia, Pennsylvania
www.orleanstech.edu

2-year private technical and career college in very large city.

Enrollment: 94 undergrads.

Selectivity: Open admission.

BASIC COSTS (2009-2010)

Additional info: Tuition for full associate program (3 years, including internship) is $34,550.

FINANCIAL AID PICTURE

Students with need: Need-based aid available for full-time and part-time students.

FINANCIAL AID PROCEDURES

Forms required: FAFSA, institutional form.

Dates and Deadlines: No deadline. Applicants notified on a rolling basis.

CONTACT

Latanya Byrd, Financial Aid Director

2770 Red Lion Road, Philadelphia, PA 19114

(215) 728-4702

Peirce College
Philadelphia, Pennsylvania
www.peirce.edu   Federal Code: 003309

4-year private business and technical college in very large city.

Enrollment: 2,067 undergrads, 60% part-time. 20 full-time freshmen.

Selectivity: Open admission.

BASIC COSTS (2010-2011)

Tuition and fees: $15,300.

Per-credit charge: $475.

FINANCIAL AID PICTURE (2008-2009)

Students with need: Out of 15 full-time freshmen who applied for aid, 14 were judged to have need. Of these, 14 received aid. Average financial aid package met 47% of need; average scholarship/grant was $4,699; average loan was $4,107. For part-time students, average financial aid package was $6,124.

Students without need: No-need awards available for academics, alumni affiliation, leadership.

Cumulative student debt: 87% of graduating class had student loans; average debt was $19,748.

Additional info: Tuition discounts available for US students serving in US military and in protect-and-serve fields.

FINANCIAL AID PROCEDURES

Forms required: FAFSA.

Dates and Deadlines: Priority date 5/1; no closing date. Applicants notified on a rolling basis starting 5/1.

Transfers: No deadline. Applicants notified on a rolling basis.

CONTACT

Lisa Gargiulo, Manager, Student Financial Services

1420 Pine Street, Philadelphia, PA 19102-4699

(888) 467-3472 ext. 9370

Penn State Abington
Abington, Pennsylvania
www.abington.psu.edu   Federal Code: 003329

4-year public branch campus college in small city.

Enrollment: 2,907 undergrads, 10% part-time. 805 full-time freshmen.

Selectivity: Admits over 75% of applicants.

BASIC COSTS (2009-2010)

Tuition and fees: $12,250; out-of-state residents $18,268.

Per-credit charge: $463; out-of-state residents $728.

FINANCIAL AID PICTURE (2008-2009)

Students with need: Out of 705 full-time freshmen who applied for aid, 539 were judged to have need. Of these, 519 received aid, and 22 had their full need met. Average financial aid package met 66% of need; average scholarship/grant was $6,764; average loan was $3,287. For part-time students, average financial aid package was $6,022.

Students without need: 50 full-time freshmen who did not demonstrate need for aid received scholarships/grants; average award was $1,612. No-need awards available for academics, alumni affiliation, athletics, ROTC.
Cumulative student debt: 68% of graduating class had student loans; average debt was $28,680.

FINANCIAL AID PROCEDURES
Forms required: FAFSA.
Dates and Deadlines: Priority date 2/15; no closing date. Applicants notified on a rolling basis starting 3/1.
Transfers: Closing date 5/1. Schools required to obtain student aid information through National Student Loan Data System (NSLDS).

CONTACT
Anna Griswold, Assistant Vice Provost for Student Aid
201 Shields Building, University Park, PA 16802-1294
(814) 865-6301

Penn State Altoona
Altoona, Pennsylvania
www.aa.psu.edu   Federal Code: 003329

4-year public branch campus college in small city.
Enrollment: 4,017 undergrads, 4% part-time. 1,467 full-time freshmen.
Selectivity: Admits over 75% of applicants.

BASIC COSTS (2009-2010)
Tuition and fees: $12,750; out-of-state residents $19,078.
Per-credit charge: $498; out-of-state residents $761.
Room and board: $8,790.

FINANCIAL AID PICTURE (2008-2009)
Students with need: Out of 1,238 full-time freshmen who applied for aid, 967 were judged to have need. Of these, 923 received aid, and 57 had their full need met. Average financial aid package met 61% of need; average scholarship/grant was $5,588; average loan was $3,387. For part-time students, average financial aid package was $6,372.
Students without need: 35 full-time freshmen who did not demonstrate need for aid received scholarships/grants; average award was $1,100. No-need awards available for academics, alumni affiliation, athletics, ROTC.
Cumulative student debt: 68% of graduating class had student loans; average debt was $28,680.

FINANCIAL AID PROCEDURES
Forms required: FAFSA.
Dates and Deadlines: Priority date 2/15; no closing date. Applicants notified on a rolling basis starting 3/1.
Transfers: Closing date 5/1. Schools required to obtain student aid information through National Student Loan Data System (NSLDS).

CONTACT
Anna Griswold, Assistant Vice Provost for Student Aid
201 Shields Building, University Park, PA 16802-1294
(814) 865-6301

Penn State Beaver
Monaca, Pennsylvania
www.br.psu.edu   Federal Code: 003329

4-year public branch campus college in small town.
Enrollment: 671 undergrads, 5% part-time. 293 full-time freshmen.
Selectivity: Admits over 75% of applicants.

BASIC COSTS (2009-2010)
Tuition and fees: $12,250; out-of-state residents $18,268.
Per-credit charge: $463; out-of-state residents $728.

Room and board: $8,790.

FINANCIAL AID PICTURE (2008-2009)
Students with need: Out of 269 full-time freshmen who applied for aid, 210 were judged to have need. Of these, 207 received aid, and 18 had their full need met. Average financial aid package met 67% of need; average scholarship/grant was $5,591; average loan was $3,231. For part-time students, average financial aid package was $7,071.
Students without need: 31 full-time freshmen who did not demonstrate need for aid received scholarships/grants; average award was $1,945. No-need awards available for academics, alumni affiliation, athletics, ROTC.
Cumulative student debt: 68% of graduating class had student loans; average debt was $28,680.

FINANCIAL AID PROCEDURES
Forms required: FAFSA.
Dates and Deadlines: Priority date 2/15; no closing date. Applicants notified on a rolling basis starting 3/1.
Transfers: Closing date 5/1. Schools required to obtain student aid information through National Student Loan Data System (NSLDS).

CONTACT
Anna Griswold, Assistant Vice Provost for Student Aid
201 Shields Building, University Park, PA 16802-1294
(814) 865-6301

Penn State Berks
Reading, Pennsylvania
www.bk.psu.edu   Federal Code: 003329

4-year public branch campus college in small city.
Enrollment: 2,501 undergrads, 8% part-time. 988 full-time freshmen.
Selectivity: Admits over 75% of applicants.

BASIC COSTS (2009-2010)
Tuition and fees: $12,750; out-of-state residents $19,078.
Per-credit charge: $498; out-of-state residents $761.
Room and board: $9,560.

FINANCIAL AID PICTURE (2008-2009)
Students with need: Out of 840 full-time freshmen who applied for aid, 621 were judged to have need. Of these, 594 received aid, and 24 had their full need met. Average financial aid package met 58% of need; average scholarship/grant was $5,799; average loan was $3,389. For part-time students, average financial aid package was $5,746.
Students without need: 15 full-time freshmen who did not demonstrate need for aid received scholarships/grants; average award was $1,811. No-need awards available for academics, alumni affiliation, athletics, ROTC.
Cumulative student debt: 68% of graduating class had student loans; average debt was $28,680.

FINANCIAL AID PROCEDURES
Forms required: FAFSA.
Dates and Deadlines: Priority date 2/15; no closing date. Applicants notified on a rolling basis starting 3/1.
Transfers: Closing date 5/1. Schools required to obtain student aid information through National Student Loan Data System (NSLDS).

CONTACT
Anna Griswold, Assistant Vice Provost for Student Aid
201 Shields Building, University Park, PA 16802-1294
(814) 865-6301

Penn State Brandywine
Media, Pennsylvania
www.brandywine.psu.edu   Federal Code: 006922

4-year public branch campus college in small town.
Enrollment: 1,411 undergrads, 10% part-time. 394 full-time freshmen.
Selectivity: Admits over 75% of applicants.

BASIC COSTS (2009-2010)
Tuition and fees: $12,150; out-of-state residents $18,168.
Per-credit charge: $463; out-of-state residents $728.

FINANCIAL AID PICTURE (2008-2009)
Students with need: Out of 324 full-time freshmen who applied for aid, 232 were judged to have need. Of these, 225 received aid, and 18 had their full need met. Average financial aid package met 65% of need; average scholarship/grant was $5,605; average loan was $3,008. For part-time students, average financial aid package was $5,245.
Students without need: 65 full-time freshmen who did not demonstrate need for aid received scholarships/grants; average award was $2,642. No-need awards available for academics, alumni affiliation, athletics, ROTC.
Cumulative student debt: 68% of graduating class had student loans; average debt was $28,680.

FINANCIAL AID PROCEDURES
Forms required: FAFSA.
Dates and Deadlines: Priority date 2/15; no closing date. Applicants notified on a rolling basis starting 3/1.
Transfers: Closing date 5/1. Schools required to obtain student aid information through National Student Loan Data System (NSLDS).

CONTACT
Anna Griswold, Assistant Vice Provost for Student Aid
201 Shields Building, University Park, PA 16802-1294
(814) 865-6301

Penn State DuBois
DuBois, Pennsylvania
www.ds.psu.edu   Federal Code: 003335

4-year public branch campus college in small town.
Enrollment: 774 undergrads, 11% part-time. 233 full-time freshmen.
Selectivity: Admits over 75% of applicants.

BASIC COSTS (2009-2010)
Tuition and fees: $12,130; out-of-state residents $18,148.
Per-credit charge: $463; out-of-state residents $728.

FINANCIAL AID PICTURE (2008-2009)
Students with need: Out of 220 full-time freshmen who applied for aid, 182 were judged to have need. Of these, 181 received aid, and 14 had their full need met. Average financial aid package met 70% of need; average scholarship/grant was $6,046; average loan was $3,283. For part-time students, average financial aid package was $6,362.
Students without need: 11 full-time freshmen who did not demonstrate need for aid received scholarships/grants; average award was $1,693. No-need awards available for academics, alumni affiliation, athletics, ROTC.
Cumulative student debt: 68% of graduating class had student loans; average debt was $28,680.

FINANCIAL AID PROCEDURES
Forms required: FAFSA.
Dates and Deadlines: Priority date 2/15; no closing date. Applicants notified on a rolling basis starting 3/1.
Transfers: Closing date 5/1. Schools required to obtain student aid information through National Student Loan Data System (NSLDS).

CONTACT
Anna Griswold, Assistant Vice Provost for Student Aid
201 Shields Building, University Park, PA 16802-1294
(814) 865-6301

Penn State Erie, The Behrend College
Erie, Pennsylvania
www.erie.psu.edu   Federal Code: 003329

4-year public branch campus college in small city.
Enrollment: 4,099 undergrads, 5% part-time. 1,074 full-time freshmen.
Selectivity: Admits over 75% of applicants.

BASIC COSTS (2009-2010)
Tuition and fees: $12,750; out-of-state residents $19,078.
Per-credit charge: $498; out-of-state residents $761.
Room and board: $8,790.

FINANCIAL AID PICTURE (2008-2009)
Students with need: Out of 975 full-time freshmen who applied for aid, 787 were judged to have need. Of these, 766 received aid, and 37 had their full need met. Average financial aid package met 63% of need; average scholarship/grant was $5,483; average loan was $3,493. For part-time students, average financial aid package was $6,015.
Students without need: 25 full-time freshmen who did not demonstrate need for aid received scholarships/grants; average award was $2,079. No-need awards available for academics, alumni affiliation, athletics, ROTC.
Cumulative student debt: 68% of graduating class had student loans; average debt was $28,680.

FINANCIAL AID PROCEDURES
Forms required: FAFSA.
Dates and Deadlines: Priority date 2/15; no closing date. Applicants notified on a rolling basis starting 3/1.
Transfers: Closing date 5/1. Schools required to obtain student aid information through National Student Loan Data System (NSLDS).

CONTACT
Anna Griswold, Assistant Vice Provost for Student Aid
201 Shields Building, University Park, PA 16801-1294
(814) 865-6301

Penn State Fayette, The Eberly Campus
Uniontown, Pennsylvania
www.fe.psu.edu   Federal Code: 003329

4-year public branch campus college in large town.
Enrollment: 895 undergrads, 19% part-time. 204 full-time freshmen.
Selectivity: Admits over 75% of applicants.

BASIC COSTS (2009-2010)
Tuition and fees: $12,150; out-of-state residents $18,168.
Per-credit charge: $463; out-of-state residents $728.

FINANCIAL AID PICTURE (2008-2009)
Students with need: Out of 197 full-time freshmen who applied for aid, 177 were judged to have need. Of these, 176 received aid, and 15 had their full need met. Average financial aid package met 67% of need; average scholarship/grant was $5,579; average loan was $3,297. For part-time students, average financial aid package was $6,657.
Students without need: 12 full-time freshmen who did not demonstrate need for aid received scholarships/grants; average award was $1,910. No-need awards available for academics, alumni affiliation, athletics, ROTC.
Cumulative student debt: 68% of graduating class had student loans; average debt was $28,680.

CONTACT
Anna Griswold, Assistant Vice Provost for Student Aid
201 Shields Building, University Park, PA 16802-1294
(814) 865-6301

FINANCIAL AID PROCEDURES

Forms required: FAFSA.

Dates and Deadlines: Priority date 2/15; no closing date. Applicants notified on a rolling basis starting 3/1.

Transfers: Closing date 5/1. Schools required to obtain student aid information through National Student Loan Data System (NSLDS).

CONTACT

Anna Griswold, Assistant Vice Provost for Student Aid
201 Shields Building, University Park, PA 16802-1294
(814) 865-6301

Penn State Greater Allegheny

McKeesport, Pennsylvania
www.ga.psu.edu   Federal Code: 003329

4-year public branch campus college in large town.

Enrollment: 648 undergrads, 5% part-time. 233 full-time freshmen.

Selectivity: Admits over 75% of applicants.

BASIC COSTS (2009-2010)

Tuition and fees: $12,250; out-of-state residents $18,268.

Per-credit charge: $463; out-of-state residents $728.

Room and board: $8,790.

FINANCIAL AID PICTURE (2008-2009)

Students with need: Out of 212 full-time freshmen who applied for aid, 186 were judged to have need. Of these, 185 received aid, and 6 had their full need met. Average financial aid package met 70% of need; average scholarship/grant was $6,374; average loan was $3,361. For part-time students, average financial aid package was $6,368.

Students without need: 23 full-time freshmen who did not demonstrate need for aid received scholarships/grants; average award was $3,663. No-need awards available for academics, alumni affiliation, athletics, ROTC.

Cumulative student debt: 68% of graduating class had student loans; average debt was $28,680.

FINANCIAL AID PROCEDURES

Forms required: FAFSA.

Dates and Deadlines: Priority date 2/15; no closing date. Applicants notified on a rolling basis starting 3/1.

Transfers: Closing date 5/1. Schools required to obtain student aid information through National Student Loan Data System (NSLDS).

CONTACT

Anna Griswold, Assistant Vice Provost for Student Aid
101 Frable Building, McKeesport, PA 15132-7698
(814) 865-6301

Penn State Harrisburg

Middletown, Pennsylvania
www.hbg.psu.edu   Federal Code: 003329

4-year public branch campus college in small town.

Enrollment: 2,567 undergrads, 15% part-time. 444 full-time freshmen.

Selectivity: Admits over 75% of applicants.

BASIC COSTS (2009-2010)

Tuition and fees: $12,750; out-of-state residents $19,078.

Per-credit charge: $498; out-of-state residents $761.

Room and board: $9,080.

FINANCIAL AID PICTURE (2008-2009)

Students with need: Out of 353 full-time freshmen who applied for aid, 273 were judged to have need. Of these, 262 received aid, and 20 had their full need met. Average financial aid package met 60% of need; average scholarship/grant was $5,420; average loan was $3,409. For part-time students, average financial aid package was $6,464.

Students without need: 6 full-time freshmen who did not demonstrate need for aid received scholarships/grants; average award was $2,392. No-need awards available for academics, alumni affiliation, athletics, ROTC.

Cumulative student debt: 68% of graduating class had student loans; average debt was $28,680.

FINANCIAL AID PROCEDURES

Forms required: FAFSA.

Dates and Deadlines: Priority date 2/15; no closing date. Applicants notified on a rolling basis starting 3/1.

Transfers: Closing date 5/1. Schools required to obtain student aid information through National Student Loan Data System (NSLDS).

CONTACT

Anna Griswold, Assistant Vice Provost for Student Aid
201 Shields Building, University Park, PA 16802-1294
(814) 865-6301

Penn State Hazleton

Hazleton, Pennsylvania
www.hn.psu.edu   Federal Code: 003338

4-year public branch campus college in large town.

Enrollment: 1,207 undergrads, 3% part-time. 540 full-time freshmen.

Selectivity: Admits over 75% of applicants.

BASIC COSTS (2009-2010)

Tuition and fees: $12,200; out-of-state residents $18,218.

Per-credit charge: $463; out-of-state residents $728.

Room and board: $8,790.

FINANCIAL AID PICTURE (2008-2009)

Students with need: Out of 482 full-time freshmen who applied for aid, 388 were judged to have need. Of these, 382 received aid, and 18 had their full need met. Average financial aid package met 62% of need; average scholarship/grant was $5,754; average loan was $3,411. For part-time students, average financial aid package was $7,696.

Students without need: 50 full-time freshmen who did not demonstrate need for aid received scholarships/grants; average award was $2,493. No-need awards available for academics, alumni affiliation, athletics, ROTC.

Cumulative student debt: 68% of graduating class had student loans; average debt was $26,680.

FINANCIAL AID PROCEDURES

Forms required: FAFSA.

Dates and Deadlines: Priority date 2/15; no closing date. Applicants notified on a rolling basis starting 3/1.

Transfers: Closing date 5/1. Schools required to obtain student aid information through National Student Loan Data System (NSLDS).

CONTACT

Anna Griswold, Assistant Vice Provost for Student Aid
201 Shields Building, University Park, PA 16802-1294
(814) 865-6301

Penn State Lehigh Valley
Center Valley, Pennsylvania
www.lv.psu.edu   Federal Code: 003329

4-year public branch campus college in rural community.
Enrollment: 649 undergrads, 12% part-time. 211 full-time freshmen.
Selectivity: Admits over 75% of applicants.

BASIC COSTS (2009-2010)
Tuition and fees: $12,250; out-of-state residents $18,268.
Per-credit charge: $463; out-of-state residents $728.

FINANCIAL AID PICTURE (2008-2009)
Students with need: Out of 176 full-time freshmen who applied for aid, 125 were judged to have need. Of these, 121 received aid, and 5 had their full need met. Average financial aid package met 59% of need; average scholarship/grant was $6,036; average loan was $3,270. For part-time students, average financial aid package was $6,812.
Students without need: 15 full-time freshmen who did not demonstrate need for aid received scholarships/grants; average award was $2,305. No-need awards available for academics, alumni affiliation, athletics, ROTC.
Cumulative student debt: 68% of graduating class had student loans; average debt was $28,680.

FINANCIAL AID PROCEDURES
Forms required: FAFSA.
Dates and Deadlines: Priority date 2/15; no closing date. Applicants notified on a rolling basis starting 3/1.
Transfers: Closing date 5/1. Schools required to obtain student aid information through National Student Loan Data System (NSLDS).

CONTACT
Anna Griswold, Assistant Vice Provost for Student Aid
2809 Saucon Valley Road, Center Vally, PA 18034-8447
(814) 865-6301

Penn State Mont Alto
Mont Alto, Pennsylvania
www.ma.psu.edu   Federal Code: 003329

4-year public branch campus college in rural community.
Enrollment: 1,069 undergrads, 20% part-time. 363 full-time freshmen.
Selectivity: Admits over 75% of applicants.

BASIC COSTS (2009-2010)
Tuition and fees: $12,250; out-of-state residents $18,268.
Per-credit charge: $463; out-of-state residents $728.
Room and board: $8,790.

FINANCIAL AID PICTURE (2008-2009)
Students with need: Out of 334 full-time freshmen who applied for aid, 261 were judged to have need. Of these, 258 received aid, and 14 had their full need met. Average financial aid package met 66% of need; average scholarship/grant was $5,325; average loan was $3,324. For part-time students, average financial aid package was $6,618.
Students without need: 24 full-time freshmen who did not demonstrate need for aid received scholarships/grants; average award was $2,414. No-need awards available for academics, alumni affiliation, athletics, ROTC.
Cumulative student debt: 68% of graduating class had student loans; average debt was $28,680.

FINANCIAL AID PROCEDURES
Forms required: FAFSA.
Dates and Deadlines: Priority date 2/15; no closing date. Applicants notified on a rolling basis starting 3/1.
Transfers: Closing date 5/1. Schools required to obtain student aid information through National Student Loan Data System (NSLDS).

CONTACT
Anna Griswold, Assistant Vice Provost for Student Aid
201 Shields Building, University Park, PA 16802-1294
(814) 865-6301

Penn State New Kensington
New Kensington, Pennsylvania
www.nk.psu.edu   Federal Code: 003329

4-year public branch campus college in large town.
Enrollment: 711 undergrads, 16% part-time. 188 full-time freshmen.
Selectivity: Admits over 75% of applicants.

BASIC COSTS (2009-2010)
Tuition and fees: $12,200; out-of-state residents $18,218.
Per-credit charge: $463; out-of-state residents $728.

FINANCIAL AID PICTURE (2008-2009)
Students with need: Out of 172 full-time freshmen who applied for aid, 137 were judged to have need. Of these, 137 received aid, and 11 had their full need met. Average financial aid package met 70% of need; average scholarship/grant was $5,394; average loan was $3,313. For part-time students, average financial aid package was $5,292.
Students without need: 26 full-time freshmen who did not demonstrate need for aid received scholarships/grants; average award was $2,433. No-need awards available for academics, alumni affiliation, athletics, ROTC.
Cumulative student debt: 68% of graduating class had student loans; average debt was $28,680.

FINANCIAL AID PROCEDURES
Forms required: FAFSA.
Dates and Deadlines: Priority date 2/15; no closing date. Applicants notified on a rolling basis starting 3/1.
Transfers: Closing date 5/1. Schools required to obtain student aid information through National Student Loan Data System (NSLDS).

CONTACT
Anna Griswold, Assistant Vice Provost for Student Aid
201 Shields Building, University Park, PA 16802-1294
(814) 865-6301

Penn State Schuylkill
Schuylkill Haven, Pennsylvania
www.sl.psu.edu   Federal Code: 003329

4-year public branch campus college in small town.
Enrollment: 908 undergrads, 10% part-time. 369 full-time freshmen.
Selectivity: Admits over 75% of applicants.

BASIC COSTS (2009-2010)
Tuition and fees: $12,150; out-of-state residents $18,168.
Per-credit charge: $463; out-of-state residents $728.

FINANCIAL AID PICTURE (2008-2009)
Students with need: Out of 356 full-time freshmen who applied for aid, 317 were judged to have need. Of these, 313 received aid, and 12 had their full need met. Average financial aid package met 71% of need; average scholarship/grant was $6,638; average loan was $3,407. For part-time students, average financial aid package was $6,095.
Students without need: 9 full-time freshmen who did not demonstrate need for aid received scholarships/grants; average award was $2,870. No-need awards available for academics, alumni affiliation, athletics, ROTC.
Cumulative student debt: 68% of graduating class had student loans; average debt was $28,680.

FINANCIAL AID PROCEDURES

Forms required: FAFSA.

Dates and Deadlines: Priority date 2/15; no closing date. Applicants notified on a rolling basis starting 3/1.

Transfers: Closing date 5/1. Schools required to obtain student aid information through National Student Loan Data System (NSLDS).

CONTACT

Anna Griswold, Assistant Vice Provost for Student Aid

200 University Drive, Schuylkill Haven, PA 17972-2208

(814) 865-6301

Penn State Shenango

Sharon, Pennsylvania

www.shenango.psu.edu   Federal Code: 003329

4-year public branch campus college in large town.

Enrollment: 661 undergrads, 31% part-time. 128 full-time freshmen.

Selectivity: Admits over 75% of applicants.

BASIC COSTS (2009-2010)

Tuition and fees: $12,050; out-of-state residents $18,068.

Per-credit charge: $463; out-of-state residents $728.

FINANCIAL AID PICTURE (2008-2009)

Students with need: Out of 120 full-time freshmen who applied for aid, 105 were judged to have need. Of these, 105 received aid, and 3 had their full need met. Average financial aid package met 67% of need; average scholarship/grant was $5,556; average loan was $3,299. For part-time students, average financial aid package was $6,491.

Students without need: 14 full-time freshmen who did not demonstrate need for aid received scholarships/grants; average award was $2,134. No-need awards available for academics, alumni affiliation, athletics, ROTC.

Cumulative student debt: 68% of graduating class had student loans; average debt was $28,680.

FINANCIAL AID PROCEDURES

Forms required: FAFSA.

Dates and Deadlines: Priority date 2/15; no closing date. Applicants notified on a rolling basis starting 3/1.

Transfers: Closing date 5/1. Schools required to obtain student aid information through National Student Loan Data System (NSLDS).

CONTACT

Anna Griswold, Assistant Vice Provost for Student Aid

201 Shields Building, University Park, PA 16802-1294

(814) 865-6301

Penn State University Park

University Park, Pennsylvania

www.psu.edu   Federal Code: 003329

4-year public university in large town.

Enrollment: 37,855 undergrads, 2% part-time. 7,234 full-time freshmen.

Selectivity: Admits 50 to 75% of applicants.

BASIC COSTS (2009-2010)

Tuition and fees: $14,416; out-of-state residents $25,946.

Per-credit charge: $567; out-of-state residents $1,047.

Room and board: $8,790.

FINANCIAL AID PICTURE (2008-2009)

Students with need: Out of 5,327 full-time freshmen who applied for aid, 3,414 were judged to have need. Of these, 3,209 received aid, and 272 had their full need met. Average financial aid package met 63% of need; average scholarship/grant was $6,122; average loan was $3,414. For part-time students, average financial aid package was $7,271.

Students without need: 476 full-time freshmen who did not demonstrate need for aid received scholarships/grants; average award was $3,571. No-need awards available for academics, alumni affiliation, athletics, ROTC.

Scholarships offered: 115 full-time freshmen received athletic scholarships; average amount $17,834.

Cumulative student debt: 68% of graduating class had student loans; average debt was $28,680.

FINANCIAL AID PROCEDURES

Forms required: FAFSA.

Dates and Deadlines: Priority date 2/15; no closing date. Applicants notified on a rolling basis starting 3/1.

Transfers: Closing date 5/1. Schools required to obtain student aid information through National Student Loan Data System (NSLDS).

CONTACT

Anna Griswold, Assistant Vice Provost for Student Aid

201 Shields Building, University Park, PA 16802-1294

(814) 865-6301

Penn State Wilkes-Barre

Lehman, Pennsylvania

www.wb.psu.edu   Federal Code: 003329

4-year public branch campus college in small city.

Enrollment: 594 undergrads, 7% part-time. 178 full-time freshmen.

Selectivity: Admits over 75% of applicants.

BASIC COSTS (2009-2010)

Tuition and fees: $12,150; out-of-state residents $18,168.

Per-credit charge: $463; out-of-state residents $728.

FINANCIAL AID PICTURE (2008-2009)

Students with need: Out of 161 full-time freshmen who applied for aid, 116 were judged to have need. Of these, 115 received aid, and 6 had their full need met. Average financial aid package met 67% of need; average scholarship/grant was $5,794; average loan was $3,179. For part-time students, average financial aid package was $5,858.

Students without need: 19 full-time freshmen who did not demonstrate need for aid received scholarships/grants; average award was $3,368. No-need awards available for academics, alumni affiliation, athletics, ROTC.

Cumulative student debt: 68% of graduating class had student loans; average debt was $28,680.

FINANCIAL AID PROCEDURES

Forms required: FAFSA.

Dates and Deadlines: Priority date 2/15; no closing date. Applicants notified on a rolling basis starting 3/1.

Transfers: Closing date 5/1. Schools required to obtain student aid information through National Student Loan Data System (NSLDS).

CONTACT

Anna Griswold, Assistant Vice Provost for Student Aid

201 Shields Building, University Park, PA 16802-1294

(814) 865-6301

Penn State Worthington Scranton

Dunmore, Pennsylvania
www.sn.psu.edu   Federal Code: 003344

4-year public branch campus college in large town.
Enrollment: 1,224 undergrads, 17% part-time. 326 full-time freshmen.
Selectivity: Admits over 75% of applicants.

BASIC COSTS (2009-2010)

Tuition and fees: $12,110; out-of-state residents $18,128.
Per-credit charge: $463; out-of-state residents $728.

FINANCIAL AID PICTURE (2008-2009)

Students with need: Out of 306 full-time freshmen who applied for aid, 241 were judged to have need. Of these, 238 received aid, and 24 had their full need met. Average financial aid package met 66% of need; average scholarship/grant was $4,796; average loan was $3,244. For part-time students, average financial aid package was $5,875.
Students without need: 39 full-time freshmen who did not demonstrate need for aid received scholarships/grants; average award was $2,434. No-need awards available for academics, alumni affiliation, athletics, ROTC.
Cumulative student debt: 68% of graduating class had student loans; average debt was $28,680.

FINANCIAL AID PROCEDURES

Forms required: FAFSA.
Dates and Deadlines: Priority date 2/15; no closing date. Applicants notified on a rolling basis starting 3/1.
Transfers: Closing date 5/1. Schools required to obtain student aid information through National Student Loan Data System (NSLDS).

CONTACT

Anna Griswold, Assistant Vice Provost for Student Aid
201 Shields Building, University Park, PA 16802-1294
(814) 865-6301

Penn State York

York, Pennsylvania
www.yk.psu.edu   Federal Code: 003329

4-year public branch campus college in large town.
Enrollment: 1,157 undergrads, 21% part-time. 329 full-time freshmen.
Selectivity: Admits over 75% of applicants.

BASIC COSTS (2009-2010)

Tuition and fees: $12,110; out-of-state residents $18,128.
Per-credit charge: $463; out-of-state residents $728.

FINANCIAL AID PICTURE (2008-2009)

Students with need: Out of 291 full-time freshmen who applied for aid, 208 were judged to have need. Of these, 200 received aid, and 18 had their full need met. Average financial aid package met 63% of need; average scholarship/grant was $5,730; average loan was $3,093. For part-time students, average financial aid package was $5,917.
Students without need: 36 full-time freshmen who did not demonstrate need for aid received scholarships/grants; average award was $3,098. No-need awards available for academics, alumni affiliation, athletics, ROTC.
Cumulative student debt: 68% of graduating class had student loans; average debt was $28,680.

FINANCIAL AID PROCEDURES

Forms required: FAFSA.
Dates and Deadlines: Priority date 2/15; no closing date. Applicants notified on a rolling basis starting 3/1.
Transfers: Closing date 5/1. Schools required to obtain student aid information through National Student Loan Data System (NSLDS).

CONTACT

Anna Griswold, Assistant Vice Provost for Student Aid
201 Shields Building, University Park, PA 16802-1294
(814) 865-6301

Pennsylvania College of Art and Design

Lancaster, Pennsylvania
www.pcad.edu

4-year private visual arts college in small city.
Enrollment: 273 undergrads, 8% part-time. 68 full-time freshmen.
Selectivity: Admits less than 50% of applicants.

BASIC COSTS (2010-2011)

Tuition and fees: $18,180.
Per-credit charge: $717.
Additional info: Estimated cost for laptop computer and software, $2,865; estimated cost for camera, $440.

FINANCIAL AID PICTURE (2009-2010)

Students with need: 35% of average financial aid package awarded as scholarships/grants, 65% awarded as loans/jobs.

CONTACT

David Hershey, Director of Financial Aid
PO Box 59, Lancaster, PA 17608-0059

Pennsylvania College of Technology

Williamsport, Pennsylvania
www.pct.edu   Federal Code: 003395

4-year public technical college in small city.
Enrollment: 6,324 undergrads, 14% part-time. 1,335 full-time freshmen.
Selectivity: Open admission; but selective for some programs.

BASIC COSTS (2009-2010)

Tuition and fees: $12,480; out-of-state residents $15,630.
Per-credit charge: $350; out-of-state residents $455.
Room and board: $8,350.

FINANCIAL AID PICTURE (2008-2009)

Students with need: Need-based aid available for full-time and part-time students. Work study available nights, weekends, and for part-time students.
Students without need: No-need awards available for academics, alumni affiliation.

FINANCIAL AID PROCEDURES

Forms required: FAFSA, institutional form.
Dates and Deadlines: Priority date 4/1; no closing date. Applicants notified on a rolling basis starting 6/1; must reply by 7/1 or within 4 week(s) of notification.

CONTACT

Candace Baran, Director of Financial Aid
One College Avenue, Williamsport, PA 17701
(570) 327-4766

Pennsylvania Highlands Community College

Johnstown, Pennsylvania
www.pennhighlands.edu   Federal Code: 031804

2-year public community college in large town.
Enrollment: 871 full-time undergrads.
Selectivity: Open admission.

BASIC COSTS (2009-2010)

Tuition and fees: $3,640; out-of-district residents $6,280; out-of-state residents $8,920.
Per-credit charge: $88; out-of-district residents $176; out-of-state residents $263.
Additional info: Students in Blair, Bedford, Fulton, Huntingdon, and Somerset counties pay tuition of $3,960 per year. Students outside Cambria County pay additional fee of $210 per year.

FINANCIAL AID PICTURE

Students with need: Need-based aid available for full-time and part-time students. Work study available nights.
Students without need: No-need awards available for academics, state/district residency.

FINANCIAL AID PROCEDURES

Forms required: FAFSA.
Dates and Deadlines: Closing date 4/1. Applicants notified on a rolling basis; must reply by 8/1.

CONTACT

Brenda Coughenour, Director of Financial Aid
101 Community College Way, Johnstown, PA 15904
(814) 262-6454

Pennsylvania Institute of Technology
Media, Pennsylvania
www.pit.edu   Federal Code: 010998

2-year private technical college in small town.
Enrollment: 1,037 undergrads, 11% part-time. 499 full-time freshmen.
Selectivity: Open admission; but selective for some programs.

BASIC COSTS (2009-2010)

Tuition and fees: $10,350.
Per-credit charge: $315.

FINANCIAL AID PICTURE

Students with need: Need-based aid available for full-time and part-time students. Work study available nights, weekends, and for part-time students.
Students without need: No-need awards available for academics, leadership.
Scholarships offered: Presidential Scholarship; half tuition; for current high school graduates; SAT scores required.

FINANCIAL AID PROCEDURES

Forms required: FAFSA, institutional form.
Dates and Deadlines: Closing date 8/1. Applicants notified on a rolling basis starting 7/1.
Transfers: No deadline.

CONTACT

Crystal Donnelly, Director of Financial Aid
800 Manchester Avenue, Media, PA 19063-4098
(610) 892-1536

Pennsylvania School of Business
Allentown, Pennsylvania
www.pennschoolofbusiness.edu-search.com
Federal Code: 022552

2-year for-profit business and technical college in small city.
Enrollment: 164 undergrads.
Selectivity: Open admission.

BASIC COSTS (2009-2010)

Additional info: Tuition for associate-degree programs: network technician (6 semesters): $25,800; personal computer administration (5 semesters): $21,500.

FINANCIAL AID PICTURE

Students with need: Need-based aid available for full-time and part-time students.

FINANCIAL AID PROCEDURES

Forms required: FAFSA.
Dates and Deadlines: No deadline. Applicants notified on a rolling basis.

CONTACT

Stephanie Azar, Director of Financial Aid
406 West Hamilton Street, Allentown, PA 18101
(610) 264-8029

Philadelphia Biblical University
Langhorne, Pennsylvania
www.pbu.edu   Federal Code: 003351

4-year private university and Bible college in small town, affiliated with Protestant Evangelical tradition.
Enrollment: 1,044 undergrads, 6% part-time. 191 full-time freshmen.
Selectivity: Admits over 75% of applicants.

BASIC COSTS (2010-2011)

Tuition and fees: $19,997.
Per-credit charge: $587.
Room and board: $8,050.

FINANCIAL AID PICTURE (2009-2010)

Students with need: Need-based aid available for full-time and part-time students. Work study available nights, weekends, and for part-time students.
Students without need: No-need awards available for academics, leadership, minority status.
Scholarships offered: PBU Merit Scholarship: $500-$9,500; based on high school GPA.

FINANCIAL AID PROCEDURES

Forms required: FAFSA.
Dates and Deadlines: Priority date 3/1; no closing date. Applicants notified on a rolling basis starting 2/15.
Transfers: No deadline. Applicants notified on a rolling basis.

CONTACT

Raye Thompson, Director of Financial Aid
200 Manor Avenue, Langhorne, PA 19047-2990
(215) 702-4246

Philadelphia University
Philadelphia, Pennsylvania
www.philau.edu   Federal Code: 003354

4-year private university in very large city.
Enrollment: 2,880 undergrads, 7% part-time. 717 full-time freshmen.
Selectivity: Admits 50 to 75% of applicants.

BASIC COSTS (2010-2011)

Tuition and fees: $28,800.
Per-credit charge: $510.
Room and board: $9,502.

FINANCIAL AID PICTURE (2009-2010)

Students with need: Out of 653 full-time freshmen who applied for aid, 561 were judged to have need. Of these, 561 received aid, and 65 had their full need met. Average financial aid package met 76% of need; average scholarship/grant was $16,233; average loan was $4,011. For part-time students, average financial aid package was $7,611.

Students without need: 156 full-time freshmen who did not demonstrate need for aid received scholarships/grants; average award was $6,542. No-need awards available for academics, athletics.

Scholarships offered: 11 full-time freshmen received athletic scholarships; average amount $16,730.

Cumulative student debt: 81% of graduating class had student loans; average debt was $32,037.

FINANCIAL AID PROCEDURES

Forms required: FAFSA.

Dates and Deadlines: Closing date 4/15. Applicants notified on a rolling basis starting 2/10; must reply by 5/1.

CONTACT

Lisa Cooper, Director of Financial Aid
School House Lane and Henry Avenue, Philadelphia, PA 19144-5497
(215) 951-2940

Pittsburgh Institute of Aeronautics
Pittsburgh, Pennsylvania
www.pia.edu   Federal Code: 005310

2-year private technical college in large city.

Enrollment: 249 undergrads.

Selectivity: Open admission.

BASIC COSTS (2010-2011)

Tuition and fees: $14,355.

FINANCIAL AID PICTURE

Students with need: Need-based aid available for full-time students.

FINANCIAL AID PROCEDURES

Forms required: FAFSA.

Dates and Deadlines: Priority date 5/1; no closing date. Applicants notified on a rolling basis.

Transfers: No deadline. Applicants notified on a rolling basis.

CONTACT

Donata Clark, Financial Aid Officer
Box 10897, Pittsburgh, PA 15236-0897
(412) 346-2100

Pittsburgh Institute of Mortuary Science
Pittsburgh, Pennsylvania
www.pims.edu   Federal Code: 010814

2-year private technical college in large city.

Enrollment: 90 full-time undergrads.

Selectivity: Open admission.

BASIC COSTS (2009-2010)

Tuition and fees: $15,500.

FINANCIAL AID PICTURE (2008-2009)

Students with need: Need-based aid available for full-time and part-time students.

FINANCIAL AID PROCEDURES

Forms required: FAFSA.

Dates and Deadlines: No deadline. Applicants notified on a rolling basis.

CONTACT

Karen Rocco, Financial Aid Officer
5808 Baum Boulevard, Pittsburgh, PA 15206-3706
(412) 362-8500

PJA School
Upper Darby, Pennsylvania
www.pjaschool.com   Federal Code: 023013

2-year for-profit business and career college in very large city.

Enrollment: 206 undergrads.

BASIC COSTS (2009-2010)

Additional info: Costs for degree programs: Paralegal $30,225; Legal accounting, $30,325; Business accounting specialist, $30,090. Costs for diploma programs: Computer office specialist, $12,195; Legal secretary, $12,350. Registration fee of $50 required for all programs. Books and materials included in cost of tuition.

FINANCIAL AID PICTURE

Students with need: Need-based aid available for full-time and part-time students.

Students without need: This college awards aid only to students with need.

Additional info: Interest-free payment plan available.

FINANCIAL AID PROCEDURES

Forms required: FAFSA, institutional form.

Dates and Deadlines: No deadline. Applicants notified on a rolling basis.

CONTACT

Nyeima Rohn, Director of Financial Aid
7900 West Chester Pike, Upper Darby, PA 19082
(610) 789-6700

Point Park University
Pittsburgh, Pennsylvania
www.pointpark.edu   Federal Code: 003357

4-year private university in large city.

Enrollment: 3,355 undergrads, 22% part-time. 712 full-time freshmen.

Selectivity: Admits 50 to 75% of applicants.

BASIC COSTS (2009-2010)

Tuition and fees: $21,334.

Per-credit charge: $574.

Room and board: $9,020.

Additional info: Tuition/fee waivers available for adults.

FINANCIAL AID PICTURE (2009-2010)

Students with need: Out of 489 full-time freshmen who applied for aid, 433 were judged to have need. Of these, 433 received aid, and 71 had their full need met. Average financial aid package met 74% of need; average scholarship/grant was $13,547; average loan was $4,605. For part-time students, average financial aid package was $9,473.

Students without need: 227 full-time freshmen who did not demonstrate need for aid received scholarships/grants; average award was $6,310. No-need awards available for academics, alumni affiliation, art, athletics, leadership, music/drama.

Scholarships offered: 20 full-time freshmen received athletic scholarships; average amount $9,734.

Cumulative student debt: 83% of graduating class had student loans; average debt was $31,656.

FINANCIAL AID PROCEDURES

Forms required: FAFSA.

Dates and Deadlines: Priority date 4/15; no closing date. Applicants notified on a rolling basis starting 2/15; must reply by 8/30 or within 2 week(s) of notification.

Transfers: No deadline. Applicants notified on a rolling basis starting 2/15.

CONTACT

Sandra Cronin, Director of Financial Aid
201 Wood Street, Pittsburgh, PA 15222-1984
(412) 392-3935

Robert Morris University

Moon Township, Pennsylvania
www.rmu.edu   Federal Code: 001746

4-year private university in large town.

Enrollment: 3,587 undergrads, 14% part-time. 718 full-time freshmen.

Selectivity: Admits over 75% of applicants.

BASIC COSTS (2010-2011)

Tuition and fees: $21,550.
Per-credit charge: $695.
Room and board: $10,660.

FINANCIAL AID PICTURE (2009-2010)

Students with need: Out of 647 full-time freshmen who applied for aid, 577 were judged to have need. Of these, 577 received aid, and 77 had their full need met. Average financial aid package met 75% of need; average scholarship/grant was $13,211; average loan was $3,960. For part-time students, average financial aid package was $5,651.

Students without need: 130 full-time freshmen who did not demonstrate need for aid received scholarships/grants; average award was $8,728. No-need awards available for academics, athletics.

Scholarships offered: 28 full-time freshmen received athletic scholarships; average amount $14,950.

Cumulative student debt: 84% of graduating class had student loans; average debt was $35,055.

FINANCIAL AID PROCEDURES

Forms required: FAFSA.
Dates and Deadlines: No deadline. Applicants notified on a rolling basis starting 3/15.

CONTACT

Stephanie Hendershot, Director of Financial Aid
6001 University Boulevard, Moon Township, PA 15108-1189
(412) 397-6250

Rosedale Technical Institute

Pittsburgh, Pennsylvania
www.rosedaletech.org   Federal Code: 012050

2-year private technical and career college in large city.

Enrollment: 241 undergrads.

BASIC COSTS (2009-2010)

Tuition and fees: $11,610.

FINANCIAL AID PICTURE

Students with need: Need-based aid available for full-time students.

FINANCIAL AID PROCEDURES

Forms required: FAFSA.
Dates and Deadlines: Closing date 8/1.

CONTACT

Kathleen Stein, Director of Financial Aid
215 Beecham Drive, Pittsburgh, PA 15205-9791
(412) 521-6200

Rosemont College

Rosemont, Pennsylvania
www.rosemont.edu   Federal Code: 003360

4-year private liberal arts college in small town, affiliated with Roman Catholic Church.

Enrollment: 543 undergrads, 20% part-time. 175 full-time freshmen.

Selectivity: Admits 50 to 75% of applicants.

BASIC COSTS (2010-2011)

Tuition and fees: $27,450.
Per-credit charge: $1,010.
Room and board: $11,000.

FINANCIAL AID PICTURE (2009-2010)

Students with need: Out of 168 full-time freshmen who applied for aid, 165 were judged to have need. Of these, 165 received aid, and 11 had their full need met. Average financial aid package met 75% of need; average scholarship/grant was $22,462; average loan was $3,323. For part-time students, average financial aid package was $17,985.

Students without need: 8 full-time freshmen who did not demonstrate need for aid received scholarships/grants; average award was $16,500. No-need awards available for academics, art, religious affiliation.

Cumulative student debt: 87% of graduating class had student loans; average debt was $21,338.

FINANCIAL AID PROCEDURES

Forms required: FAFSA.
Dates and Deadlines: Priority date 2/15; no closing date. Applicants notified on a rolling basis starting 2/15; must reply within 4 week(s) of notification.
Transfers: No deadline. Applicants notified on a rolling basis starting 2/15; must reply within 4 week(s) of notification.

CONTACT

Melissa Walsh, Director of Financial Aid
1400 Montgomery Avenue, Rosemont, PA 19010-1699
(610) 527-0200 ext. 2220

St. Charles Borromeo Seminary - Overbrook

Wynnewood, Pennsylvania
www.scs.edu   Federal Code: 016229

4-year private seminary college for men in large town, affiliated with Roman Catholic Church.

Enrollment: 57 undergrads. 13 full-time freshmen.

Selectivity: Admits over 75% of applicants.

BASIC COSTS (2009-2010)

Tuition and fees: $15,190.
Room and board: $9,560.

FINANCIAL AID PICTURE (2009-2010)

Students with need: Average financial aid package met 81% of need; average scholarship/grant was $16,517; average loan was $2,990. Need-based aid available for part-time students.

Students without need: No-need awards available for religious affiliation.

FINANCIAL AID PROCEDURES

Forms required: FAFSA, institutional form.

Dates and Deadlines: No deadline. Applicants notified on a rolling basis starting 6/1; must reply within 4 week(s) of notification.

CONTACT

Bonnie Behm, Financial Aid Coordinator
100 East Wynnewood Road, Wynnewood, PA 19096
(610) 785-6582

St. Francis University

Loretto, Pennsylvania
www.francis.edu   Federal Code: 003366

4-year private university and liberal arts college in rural community, affiliated with Roman Catholic Church.
Enrollment: 1,643 undergrads, 5% part-time. 429 full-time freshmen.
Selectivity: Admits over 75% of applicants.

BASIC COSTS (2010-2011)

Tuition and fees: $25,484.
Per-credit charge: $795.
Room and board: $9,066.
Additional info: Additional mandatory laptop fee of $1,050 per academic year for all undergraduate students. Tuition/fee waivers available for adults.

FINANCIAL AID PICTURE (2008-2009)

Students with need: Out of 415 full-time freshmen who applied for aid, 368 were judged to have need. Of these, 365 received aid, and 70 had their full need met. Average financial aid package met 67% of need; average scholarship/grant was $15,254; average loan was $2,732. For part-time students, average financial aid package was $4,852.
Students without need: 55 full-time freshmen who did not demonstrate need for aid received scholarships/grants; average award was $9,861. No-need awards available for academics, alumni affiliation, athletics, music/drama, religious affiliation.
Scholarships offered: *Merit:* Red Flash Co-Curricular Award: $1,000-$5,000; 2.5 GPA minimum. Assisi Scholarship: $3,000-$6,500; 3.2 GPA,1020 SAT, 22 ACT minimum. Presidential Scholarship: $4,500-$9,500; 3.5 GPA, 1100 SAT, 24 ACT minimum. Founders Award: $10,000-$15,500; 3.7 GPA, 1250 SAT, 28 ACT minimum. Franciscan Scholarship: $1,000 over four years awarded to graduates of a Catholic high school. Athletic Scholarships: amounts vary, awarded at the discretion of head coach. *Athletic:* 44 full-time freshmen received athletic scholarships; average amount $10,478.
Cumulative student debt: 81% of graduating class had student loans; average debt was $11,689.

FINANCIAL AID PROCEDURES

Forms required: FAFSA.
Dates and Deadlines: Priority date 5/1; no closing date. Applicants notified on a rolling basis starting 3/1.
Transfers: No deadline. Applicants notified on a rolling basis. Associate degree transfer scholarship based on academic achievement. Returning adult student scholarships available to qualifying transfers after one semester.

CONTACT

Jamie Kosh, Director of Financial Aid
Box 600, Loretto, PA 15940

Saint Joseph's University

Philadelphia, Pennsylvania
www.sju.edu   Federal Code: 003367

4-year private university in very large city, affiliated with Roman Catholic Church.
Enrollment: 5,188 undergrads, 13% part-time. 1,188 full-time freshmen.
Selectivity: Admits over 75% of applicants. GED not accepted.

BASIC COSTS (2010-2011)

Tuition and fees: $35,230.
Room and board: $11,925.
Additional info: Traditional day students taking additional credits over 5 courses pay an additional per-credit-hour fee of $1,113. Part-time, evening division per-credit-hour fee is $466 (non-traditional, adult continuing education).

FINANCIAL AID PICTURE (2009-2010)

Students with need: Out of 888 full-time freshmen who applied for aid, 650 were judged to have need. Of these, 650 received aid, and 161 had their full need met. Average financial aid package met 83% of need; average scholarship/grant was $16,206; average loan was $4,063. Need-based aid available for part-time students.
Students without need: 455 full-time freshmen who did not demonstrate need for aid received scholarships/grants; average award was $10,125. No-need awards available for academics, alumni affiliation, art, athletics, minority status, music/drama, ROTC.
Scholarships offered: 27 full-time freshmen received athletic scholarships; average amount $16,413.

FINANCIAL AID PROCEDURES

Forms required: FAFSA.
Dates and Deadlines: Priority date 2/15; no closing date. Applicants notified on a rolling basis starting 3/1; must reply by 5/1.
Transfers: Financial aid for transfers subject to availability of funds.

CONTACT

Eileen Tucker, Director of Financial Aid
5600 City Avenue, Philadelphia, PA 19131
(610) 660-1556

St. Vincent College

Latrobe, Pennsylvania
www.stvincent.edu   Federal Code: 003368

4-year private liberal arts college in large town, affiliated with Roman Catholic Church.
Enrollment: 1,653 undergrads, 2% part-time. 438 full-time freshmen.
Selectivity: Admits 50 to 75% of applicants.

BASIC COSTS (2009-2010)

Tuition and fees: $26,146.
Per-credit charge: $793.
Room and board: $8,184.

FINANCIAL AID PICTURE (2009-2010)

Students with need: Need-based aid available for full-time and part-time students. Work study available nights, weekends, and for part-time students.
Students without need: No-need awards available for academics, alumni affiliation, leadership, minority status, religious affiliation.
Scholarships offered: Academic Merit Scholarship: $5,000 to $14,000, based on high school GPA, class rank, and SAT scores. Leadership Merit Grant: $500 to $3,000, based on extracurricular activities and recommendations. Competitive scholarships from $4,000 to full tuition.

FINANCIAL AID PROCEDURES

Forms required: FAFSA, state aid form.
Dates and Deadlines: Priority date 3/1; closing date 5/1. Applicants notified on a rolling basis starting 3/1; must reply within 2 week(s) of notification.
Transfers: Applicants notified on a rolling basis starting 3/1; must reply within 2 week(s) of notification.

CONTACT

Kimberly Woodley, Director of Financial Aid
300 Fraser Purchase Road, Latrobe, PA 15650-2690
(800) 782-5549

Seton Hill University
Greensburg, Pennsylvania
www.setonhill.edu   Federal Code: 003362

4-year private university and liberal arts college in large town, affiliated with Roman Catholic Church.

Enrollment: 1,483 undergrads, 9% part-time. 299 full-time freshmen.

Selectivity: Admits 50 to 75% of applicants.

BASIC COSTS (2010-2011)

Tuition and fees: $27,948.

Per-credit charge: $720.

Room and board: $8,810.

Additional info: Required fees covers mandatory MacBook and iPad along with other services. Tuition/fee waivers available for adults.

FINANCIAL AID PICTURE (2009-2010)

Students with need: Out of 260 full-time freshmen who applied for aid, 239 were judged to have need. Of these, 238 received aid, and 45 had their full need met. Average financial aid package met 80% of need; average scholarship/grant was $19,367; average loan was $4,672. For part-time students, average financial aid package was $12,965.

Students without need: 35 full-time freshmen who did not demonstrate need for aid received scholarships/grants; average award was $10,662. No-need awards available for academics, alumni affiliation, art, athletics, job skills, music/drama, religious affiliation, ROTC.

Scholarships offered: *Merit:* Presidential Scholarships; up to one-half of tuition per academic year; given to top students. *Athletic:* 30 full-time freshmen received athletic scholarships; average amount $10,859.

Cumulative student debt: 91% of graduating class had student loans; average debt was $25,807.

FINANCIAL AID PROCEDURES

Forms required: FAFSA, institutional form.

Dates and Deadlines: Priority date 5/1; no closing date. Applicants notified on a rolling basis starting 11/15; must reply by 5/1 or within 2 week(s) of notification.

Transfers: Priority date 8/1; closing date 8/15. Applicants notified on a rolling basis starting 1/1; must reply within 2 week(s) of notification. Scholarship available for full-time transfer students with 3.5 GPA.

CONTACT

Maryann Dudas, Director of Financial Aid

1 Seton Hill Drive, Greensburg, PA 15601

(724) 838-4293

Shippensburg University of Pennsylvania
Shippensburg, Pennsylvania
www.ship.edu   Federal Code: 003326

4-year public university in small town.

Enrollment: 6,861 undergrads, 4% part-time. 1,675 full-time freshmen.

Selectivity: Admits 50 to 75% of applicants.

BASIC COSTS (2009-2010)

Tuition and fees: $7,444; out-of-state residents $15,776.

Per-credit charge: $231; out-of-state residents $579.

Room and board: $7,086.

Additional info: Tuition for transfer students from five neighboring MD community colleges with dual admission agreements is $8,332. Tuition for all MD residents not covered by the aforementioned differential for transfer students is $12,498.

FINANCIAL AID PICTURE (2009-2010)

Students with need: Out of 1,508 full-time freshmen who applied for aid, 1,065 were judged to have need. Of these, 1,023 received aid, and 163 had their full need met. Average financial aid package met 67% of need; average scholarship/grant was $6,298; average loan was $3,217. For part-time students, average financial aid package was $6,320.

Students without need: 149 full-time freshmen who did not demonstrate need for aid received scholarships/grants; average award was $3,978. No-need awards available for academics, athletics.

Scholarships offered: 73 full-time freshmen received athletic scholarships; average amount $2,210.

Cumulative student debt: 74% of graduating class had student loans; average debt was $21,163.

FINANCIAL AID PROCEDURES

Forms required: FAFSA.

Dates and Deadlines: Priority date 3/15; no closing date. Applicants notified on a rolling basis; must reply within 2 week(s) of notification.

Transfers: No deadline. Applicants notified on a rolling basis; must reply within 2 week(s) of notification.

CONTACT

Peter D'Annibale, Director of Financial Aid

1871 Old Main Drive, Shippensburg, PA 17257-2299

(717) 477-1131

Slippery Rock University of Pennsylvania
Slippery Rock, Pennsylvania
www.sru.edu   Federal Code: 003327

4-year public university in rural community.

Enrollment: 7,703 undergrads, 6% part-time. 1,545 full-time freshmen.

Selectivity: Admits 50 to 75% of applicants.

BASIC COSTS (2009-2010)

Tuition and fees: $7,235; out-of-state residents $10,012.

Per-credit charge: $231; out-of-state residents $463.

Room and board: $8,332.

Additional info: Tuition for out-of-state students with at least 3.0 GPA is $8,331; all out-of-state undergraduates pay an additional $104 in required fees.

FINANCIAL AID PICTURE (2009-2010)

Students with need: Out of 1,474 full-time freshmen who applied for aid, 1,103 were judged to have need. Of these, 1,096 received aid, and 455 had their full need met. Average financial aid package met 65% of need; average scholarship/grant was $3,865; average loan was $3,247. For part-time students, average financial aid package was $5,989.

Students without need: 345 full-time freshmen who did not demonstrate need for aid received scholarships/grants; average award was $6,712. No-need awards available for academics, alumni affiliation, art, athletics, job skills, leadership, minority status, music/drama, ROTC, state/district residency.

Scholarships offered: 61 full-time freshmen received athletic scholarships; average amount $3,456.

Cumulative student debt: 81% of graduating class had student loans; average debt was $23,879.

Additional info: May 1 closing date for Pennsylvania state grants.

FINANCIAL AID PROCEDURES

Forms required: FAFSA.

Dates and Deadlines: Priority date 5/1; no closing date. Applicants notified on a rolling basis starting 3/15.

CONTACT

Patricia Hladio, Director of Financial Aid
1 Morrow Way, Slippery Rock, PA 16057-1383
(724) 738-2044

South Hills School of Business & Technology

State College, Pennsylvania
www.southhills.edu   Federal Code: 013263

2-year for-profit business and technical college in large town.
Enrollment: 706 undergrads, 8% part-time. 293 full-time freshmen.
Selectivity: Open admission; but selective for some programs.

BASIC COSTS (2010-2011)
Tuition and fees: $14,925.
Per-credit charge: $374.

FINANCIAL AID PICTURE (2009-2010)
Students with need: For part-time students, average financial aid package was $2,393.
Students without need: This college awards aid only to students with need.
Cumulative student debt: 89% of graduating class had student loans; average debt was $10,500.

FINANCIAL AID PROCEDURES
Forms required: FAFSA.
Dates and Deadlines: Closing date 6/30. Applicants notified on a rolling basis starting 7/5.
Transfers: No deadline.

CONTACT
Harriet Arndt, Financial Aid Director
480 Waupelani Drive, State College, PA 16801-4516
(814) 234-7755

South Hills School of Business & Technology: Altoona

Altoona, Pennsylvania
www.southhills.edu   Federal Code: 010281

2-year for-profit business and technical college in small city.
Enrollment: 125 undergrads.
Selectivity: Open admission; but selective for some programs.

BASIC COSTS (2010-2011)
Tuition and fees: $14,148.
Per-credit charge: $393.
Additional info: Diagnostic medical sonography (tuition), $16,935 per year; engineering technology (tuition), $14,748 per year. Activity fee of $35 per term charged each student.

FINANCIAL AID PICTURE
Students with need: Need-based aid available for full-time and part-time students.
Students without need: This college awards aid only to students with need.

FINANCIAL AID PROCEDURES
Forms required: FAFSA.
Dates and Deadlines: Closing date 6/30. Applicants notified on a rolling basis starting 7/1.
Transfers: No deadline.

CONTACT

Joan Grassi, Financial Aid Counselor
508 58th Street, Altoona, PA 16602
(814) 944-6134 ext. 3026

Susquehanna University

Selinsgrove, Pennsylvania   Federal Code: 003369
www.susqu.edu   CSS Code: 2820

4-year private university and liberal arts college in small town, affiliated with Evangelical Lutheran Church in America.
Enrollment: 2,170 undergrads, 1% part-time. 624 full-time freshmen.
Selectivity: Admits 50 to 75% of applicants.

BASIC COSTS (2010-2011)
Tuition and fees: $34,070.
Per-credit charge: $1,065.
Room and board: $9,230.

FINANCIAL AID PICTURE (2009-2010)
Students with need: Average financial aid package met 82% of need; average scholarship/grant was $19,942; average loan was $3,545. For part-time students, average financial aid package was $5,730.
Students without need: No-need awards available for academics, alumni affiliation, leadership, minority status, music/drama, ROTC.
Scholarships offered: Scholarships; $1,000 to $16,000; renewable annually; based on outstanding academic achievement, personal accomplishment, and/or musical talent. Alumni scholarships; $2,500; for 5 new legacy students with best academic records. Annual scholarships; $2,000; to dependent children of ordained Lutheran clergy.
Additional info: Graduated pay scale for federal work-study program.

FINANCIAL AID PROCEDURES
Forms required: FAFSA, CSS PROFILE.
Dates and Deadlines: Priority date 3/1; closing date 5/1. Applicants notified on a rolling basis starting 3/15.
Transfers: Priority date 5/1; closing date 7/1. Transfer students eligible for financial aid and scholarship consideration.

CONTACT
Helen Nunn, Director of Financial Aid
514 University Avenue, Selinsgrove, PA 17870-1164
(570) 372-4450

Swarthmore College

Swarthmore, Pennsylvania   Federal Code: 003370
www.swarthmore.edu   CSS Code: 2821

4-year private liberal arts college in small town.
Enrollment: 1,505 undergrads. 394 full-time freshmen.
Selectivity: Admits less than 50% of applicants.

BASIC COSTS (2010-2011)
Tuition and fees: $39,600.
Room and board: $11,900.

FINANCIAL AID PICTURE (2009-2010)
Students with need: Out of 277 full-time freshmen who applied for aid, 216 were judged to have need. Of these, 216 received aid, and 216 had their full need met. Average financial aid package met 100% of need; average scholarship/grant was $34,615.
Students without need: 4 full-time freshmen who did not demonstrate need for aid received scholarships/grants; average award was $37,510. No-need awards available for academics, leadership, state/district residency.
Additional info: Swarthmore maintains need-blind admissions policy for U.S. citizens and permanent residents, wherein admission and financial aid deci-

sions are made independently. All Swarthmore aid awards are loan-free and are packaged to meet the full demonstrated need for admitted students.

FINANCIAL AID PROCEDURES

Forms required: FAFSA, CSS PROFILE, state aid form, institutional form.
Dates and Deadlines: Closing date 2/15. Applicants notified by 4/1; must reply by 5/1.
Transfers: Closing date 4/1. Applicants notified by 5/15. No aid consideration is presently possible for foreign national transfer applicants.

CONTACT

Laura Talbot, Director of Financial Aid
500 College Avenue, Swarthmore, PA 19081
(610) 328-8358

Talmudical Yeshiva of Philadelphia
Philadelphia, Pennsylvania   Federal Code: 012523

4-year private rabbinical college for men in very large city, affiliated with Jewish faith.
Enrollment: 116 undergrads. 34 full-time freshmen.
Selectivity: Admits over 75% of applicants.

BASIC COSTS (2009-2010)

Tuition and fees: $7,600.
Room and board: $6,300.

FINANCIAL AID PICTURE (2008-2009)

Students with need: Out of 21 full-time freshmen who applied for aid, 21 were judged to have need. Of these, 21 received aid.
Students without need: This college awards aid only to students with need.

FINANCIAL AID PROCEDURES

Forms required: FAFSA, institutional form.
Dates and Deadlines: Priority date 8/1; closing date 5/1. Applicants notified on a rolling basis starting 3/15; must reply within 2 week(s) of notification.

CONTACT

Chaya Hoberman, Financial Aid Officer
6063 Drexel Road, Philadelphia, PA 19131
(215) 477-1000

Temple University
Philadelphia, Pennsylvania
www.temple.edu   Federal Code: 003371

4-year public university in very large city.
Enrollment: 26,469 undergrads, 9% part-time. 4,136 full-time freshmen.
Selectivity: Admits 50 to 75% of applicants.

BASIC COSTS (2009-2010)

Tuition and fees: $11,764; out-of-state residents $21,044.
Per-credit charge: $432; out-of-state residents $728.
Room and board: $9,198.

FINANCIAL AID PICTURE (2008-2009)

Students with need: Out of 3,746 full-time freshmen who applied for aid, 2,749 were judged to have need. Of these, 2,685 received aid, and 971 had their full need met. Average financial aid package met 91% of need; average scholarship/grant was $5,804; average loan was $3,427. For part-time students, average financial aid package was $9,782.
Students without need: 632 full-time freshmen who did not demonstrate need for aid received scholarships/grants; average award was $8,437. No-need awards available for academics, art, athletics, music/drama, ROTC.
Scholarships offered: 30 full-time freshmen received athletic scholarships; average amount $14,356.

Cumulative student debt: 75% of graduating class had student loans; average debt was $29,886.

FINANCIAL AID PROCEDURES

Forms required: FAFSA.
Dates and Deadlines: Closing date 3/1. Applicants notified on a rolling basis starting 2/15; must reply by 5/1 or within 3 week(s) of notification.
Transfers: Priority date 3/1; no deadline. Must reply within 2 week(s) of notification.

CONTACT

John Morris, Director, Student Financial Services
103 Conwell Hall, Philadelphia, PA 19122-6096
(215) 204-2244

Thiel College
Greenville, Pennsylvania
www.thiel.edu   Federal Code: 003376

4-year private liberal arts college in small town, affiliated with Evangelical Lutheran Church in America.
Enrollment: 962 undergrads, 2% part-time. 271 full-time freshmen.
Selectivity: Admits 50 to 75% of applicants.

BASIC COSTS (2010-2011)

Tuition and fees: $23,828.
Per-credit charge: $732.
Room and board: $9,200.
Additional info: Required fees include cost of laptop computer, $900, which is a mandatory expense for incoming freshman students.

FINANCIAL AID PICTURE (2009-2010)

Students with need: Average financial aid package met 71% of need; average scholarship/grant was $15,767; average loan was $4,631. For part-time students, average financial aid package was $16,764.
Students without need: No-need awards available for academics, alumni affiliation, leadership, music/drama, religious affiliation.
Cumulative student debt: 92% of graduating class had student loans; average debt was $37,783.

FINANCIAL AID PROCEDURES

Forms required: FAFSA, state aid form.
Dates and Deadlines: Priority date 3/15; no closing date. Applicants notified on a rolling basis starting 2/15; must reply within 2 week(s) of notification.
Transfers: Priority date 6/1. Applicants notified on a rolling basis starting 2/1; must reply within 2 week(s) of notification.

CONTACT

Scott Hartle, Vice President Financial Services
75 College Avenue, Greenville, PA 16125-2181
(724) 589-2250

Thomas Jefferson University: College of Health Professions
Philadelphia, Pennsylvania
www.jefferson.edu   Federal Code: 012393

Upper-division private health science and nursing college in very large city.
Enrollment: 841 undergrads.

BASIC COSTS (2009-2010)

Tuition and fees: $25,939.
Per-credit charge: $797.

FINANCIAL AID PICTURE (2009-2010)

Students with need: Need-based aid available for full-time students.

Students without need: No-need awards available for academics, leadership, state/district residency.
Scholarships offered: Range of merit-based scholarships available for selected applicants.

FINANCIAL AID PROCEDURES
Forms required: FAFSA, institutional form.
Dates and Deadlines: Priority date 5/1; no closing date. Applicants notified on a rolling basis starting 4/1; must reply within 2 week(s) of notification.
Transfers: Applicants notified on a rolling basis starting 11/15; must reply within 2 week(s) of notification.

CONTACT
Susan McFadden, University Director of Financial Aid
130 South Ninth Street, Edison Building, Suite 100, Philadelphia, PA 19107
(215) 955-2867

Triangle Tech: Bethlehem
Bethlehem, Pennsylvania
www.triangle-tech.edu   Federal Code: 014895

2-year for-profit branch campus and technical college in small city.
Enrollment: 123 undergrads. 48 full-time freshmen.
Selectivity: Open admission.

BASIC COSTS (2009-2010)
Tuition and fees: $14,207.
Per-credit charge: $385.

FINANCIAL AID PICTURE (2008-2009)
Students with need: Average financial aid package met 35% of need; average scholarship/grant was $2,207; average loan was $3,227. Need-based aid available for part-time students.
Cumulative student debt: 72% of graduating class had student loans; average debt was $7,024.

FINANCIAL AID PROCEDURES
Forms required: FAFSA.
Dates and Deadlines: No deadline. Applicants notified on a rolling basis.

CONTACT
Catherine Waxter, Director of Financial Aid
31 South Commerce Way, Lehigh Valley Industrial Park IV, Bethlehem, PA 18017
(610) 691-1300

Triangle Tech: DuBois
DuBois, Pennsylvania
www.triangle-tech.edu   Federal Code: 021744

2-year for-profit technical college in large town.
Enrollment: 329 undergrads. 216 full-time freshmen.
Selectivity: Open admission.

BASIC COSTS (2009-2010)
Tuition and fees: $14,265.
Per-credit charge: $385.

FINANCIAL AID PICTURE (2008-2009)
Students with need: Out of 194 full-time freshmen who applied for aid, 194 were judged to have need. Of these, 194 received aid. Average financial aid package met 100% of need; average scholarship/grant was $3,375; average loan was $2,950. Need-based aid available for part-time students.
Students without need: This college awards aid only to students with need.

FINANCIAL AID PROCEDURES
Forms required: FAFSA, state aid form, institutional form.
Dates and Deadlines: No deadline. Applicants notified on a rolling basis.

CONTACT
Catherine Waxter, Corporate Director of Financial Aid
PO Box 551, DuBois, PA 15801-0551
(724) 832-1050

Triangle Tech: Erie
Erie, Pennsylvania
www.triangle-tech.edu   Federal Code: 014417

2-year for-profit technical college in small city.
Enrollment: 165 undergrads. 74 full-time freshmen.
Selectivity: Open admission.

BASIC COSTS (2009-2010)
Tuition and fees: $14,157.
Per-credit charge: $385.

FINANCIAL AID PICTURE (2008-2009)
Students with need: 55% of average financial aid package awarded as scholarships/grants, 45% awarded as loans/jobs. Need-based aid available for part-time students.

FINANCIAL AID PROCEDURES
Forms required: FAFSA.
Dates and Deadlines: Applicants notified on a rolling basis.

CONTACT
Cathy Waxter, Corporate Director of Financial Aid
2000 Liberty Street, Erie, PA 16502-2594
(724) 832-1050

Triangle Tech: Greensburg
Greensburg, Pennsylvania
www.triangle-tech.edu   Federal Code: 014895

2-year for-profit technical college in large town.
Enrollment: 262 undergrads. 116 full-time freshmen.
Selectivity: Open admission.

BASIC COSTS (2009-2010)
Tuition and fees: $14,138.
Per-credit charge: $385.

FINANCIAL AID PICTURE (2008-2009)
Students with need: Out of 116 full-time freshmen who applied for aid, 116 were judged to have need. Of these, 115 received aid, and 31 had their full need met. Average financial aid package met 27% of need; average scholarship/grant was $7,345; average loan was $3,398. Need-based aid available for part-time students.
Cumulative student debt: 77% of graduating class had student loans; average debt was $6,679.

FINANCIAL AID PROCEDURES
Forms required: FAFSA, institutional form.
Dates and Deadlines: No deadline. Applicants notified on a rolling basis starting 1/1.
Transfers: No deadline.

CONTACT
Catherine Waxter, Director of Financial Aid
222 East Pittsburgh Street, Suite A, Greensburg, PA 15601-3304
(724) 832-1050

Triangle Tech: Pittsburgh
Pittsburgh, Pennsylvania
www.triangle-tech.edu   Federal Code: 007839

2-year for-profit technical college in large city.
Enrollment: 265 undergrads. 63 full-time freshmen.
Selectivity: Open admission; but selective for some programs.

BASIC COSTS (2009-2010)
Tuition and fees: $14,218.
Per-credit charge: $385.

FINANCIAL AID PICTURE (2008-2009)
Students with need: Out of 61 full-time freshmen who applied for aid, 61 were judged to have need. Of these, 60 received aid, and 5 had their full need met. Average financial aid package met 8% of need; average scholarship/grant was $4,062; average loan was $1,724. Need-based aid available for part-time students.
Students without need: No-need awards available for academics, state/district residency.

FINANCIAL AID PROCEDURES
Forms required: FAFSA, institutional form.
Dates and Deadlines: No deadline. Applicants notified on a rolling basis.
Transfers: No deadline.

CONTACT
Cathy Waxter, Corporate Director of Financial Aid
1940 Perrysville Avenue, Pittsburgh, PA 15214-3897
(412) 359-1000

Triangle Tech: Sunbury
Sunbury, Pennsylvania
www.triangle-tech.edu

2-year for-profit technical college in large town.
Enrollment: 170 undergrads. 72 full-time freshmen.
Selectivity: Open admission.

BASIC COSTS (2009-2010)
Tuition and fees: $14,330.
Per-credit charge: $385.

FINANCIAL AID PICTURE (2008-2009)
Students with need: Out of 67 full-time freshmen who applied for aid, 67 were judged to have need. Of these, 67 received aid, and 58 had their full need met. Average financial aid package met 93% of need; average scholarship/grant was $4,768; average loan was $2,994.

FINANCIAL AID PROCEDURES
Forms required: FAFSA, institutional form.
Dates and Deadlines: No deadline.

CONTACT
Cathy Waxter, Director of Financial Aid
191 Performance Road, Sunbury, PA 17801

University of Pennsylvania
Philadelphia, Pennsylvania   Federal Code: 003378
www.upenn.edu   CSS Code: 2926

4-year private university in very large city.
Enrollment: 9,768 undergrads, 3% part-time. 2,400 full-time freshmen.
Selectivity: Admits less than 50% of applicants.

BASIC COSTS (2010-2011)
Tuition and fees: $40,514.
Room and board: $11,430.

FINANCIAL AID PICTURE (2008-2009)
Students with need: Out of 1,322 full-time freshmen who applied for aid, 1,031 were judged to have need. Of these, 1,031 received aid, and 1,031 had their full need met. Average financial aid package met 100% of need; average scholarship/grant was $34,724; average loan was $965. Need-based aid available for part-time students.
Students without need: This college awards aid only to students with need.
Cumulative student debt: 41% of graduating class had student loans; average debt was $17,787.

FINANCIAL AID PROCEDURES
Forms required: FAFSA, CSS PROFILE, institutional form.
Dates and Deadlines: Priority date 2/15; no closing date. Applicants notified by 4/1; must reply by 5/1.
Transfers: Priority date 3/15. Applicants notified on a rolling basis starting 5/15; must reply within 4 week(s) of notification.

CONTACT
William Schilling, Director of Financial Aid
1 College Hall, Philadelphia, PA 19104
(215) 898-1988

University of Pittsburgh
Pittsburgh, Pennsylvania
www.pitt.edu   Federal Code: 008815

4-year public university in large city.
Enrollment: 17,682 undergrads, 6% part-time. 3,642 full-time freshmen.
Selectivity: Admits 50 to 75% of applicants. GED not accepted.

BASIC COSTS (2009-2010)
Tuition and fees: $14,154; out-of-state residents $23,852.
Per-credit charge: $556; out-of-state residents $960.
Room and board: $8,900.

FINANCIAL AID PICTURE (2009-2010)
Students with need: Out of 3,007 full-time freshmen who applied for aid, 2,059 were judged to have need. Of these, 2,020 received aid, and 794 had their full need met. Average financial aid package met 81% of need; average scholarship/grant was $9,623; average loan was $4,318. Need-based aid available for part-time students.
Students without need: 274 full-time freshmen who did not demonstrate need for aid received scholarships/grants; average award was $14,678. No-need awards available for academics, athletics.
Scholarships offered: *Merit:* Academic Scholarships; $1,000 to full tuition, room and board; renewable up to 4 years with 3.0 GPA. *Athletic:* 30 full-time freshmen received athletic scholarships; average amount $20,538.

FINANCIAL AID PROCEDURES
Forms required: FAFSA.
Dates and Deadlines: Priority date 3/1; no closing date. Applicants notified on a rolling basis starting 3/15.
Transfers: Priority date 5/1; no deadline. Applicants notified on a rolling basis. Transfer students not eligible for freshman scholarships.

CONTACT
Betsy Porter, Director, Office of Admissions and Financial Aid
4227 Fifth Avenue, 1st Floor, Alumni Hall, Pittsburgh, PA 15260
(412) 624-7488

University of Pittsburgh at Bradford

Bradford, Pennsylvania
www.upb.pitt.edu   Federal Code: 003380

4-year public university in large town.
Enrollment: 1,600 undergrads, 9% part-time. 415 full-time freshmen.
Selectivity: Admits over 75% of applicants.

BASIC COSTS (2009-2010)
Tuition and fees: $11,722; out-of-state residents $21,282.
Per-credit charge: $458; out-of-state residents $857.
Room and board: $7,480.

FINANCIAL AID PICTURE (2009-2010)
Students with need: Out of 412 full-time freshmen who applied for aid, 358 were judged to have need. Of these, 358 received aid, and 350 had their full need met. Average financial aid package met 95% of need; average scholarship/grant was $5,482; average loan was $3,408. For part-time students, average financial aid package was $6,284.
Students without need: 119 full-time freshmen who did not demonstrate need for aid received scholarships/grants; average award was $5,942. No-need awards available for academics, alumni affiliation, ROTC, state/district residency.
Scholarships offered: Panther Scholarship; for full-time on-campus residents or students who commute from Cameron, Elk, Forest, McKean, Potter, or Warren counties. Valedictorian/Salutatorian Scholarship; for Pennsylvania students. International Student Scholarship; for international students who plan to enroll full-time and reside on campus.
Cumulative student debt: 82% of graduating class had student loans; average debt was $21,683.

FINANCIAL AID PROCEDURES
Forms required: FAFSA.
Dates and Deadlines: Priority date 3/1; no closing date. Applicants notified on a rolling basis starting 4/1; must reply within 2 week(s) of notification.
Transfers: No deadline. Applicants notified on a rolling basis starting 4/1; must reply within 2 week(s) of notification. Transfers must meet academic policy guidelines.

CONTACT
Melissa Ibanez, Director of Financial Aid
300 Campus Drive, Bradford, PA 16701
(814) 362-7550

University of Pittsburgh at Greensburg

Greensburg, Pennsylvania
www.upg.pitt.edu   Federal Code: 003381

4-year public branch campus and liberal arts college in large town.
Enrollment: 1,785 undergrads, 6% part-time. 410 full-time freshmen.
Selectivity: Admits 50 to 75% of applicants.

BASIC COSTS (2009-2010)
Tuition and fees: $11,852; out-of-state residents $21,412.
Per-credit charge: $458; out-of-state residents $857.
Room and board: $7,840.

FINANCIAL AID PICTURE (2009-2010)
Students with need: Out of 383 full-time freshmen who applied for aid, 324 were judged to have need. Of these, 320 received aid, and 67 had their full need met. Average financial aid package met 48% of need; average scholarship/grant was $4,601; average loan was $3,606. For part-time students, average financial aid package was $5,794.
Students without need: 4 full-time freshmen who did not demonstrate need for aid received scholarships/grants; average award was $3,750. No-need awards available for academics, leadership, minority status.

Cumulative student debt: 82% of graduating class had student loans; average debt was $24,707.

FINANCIAL AID PROCEDURES
Forms required: FAFSA, state aid form.
Dates and Deadlines: Priority date 2/15; no closing date. Applicants notified on a rolling basis starting 3/15; must reply within 3 week(s) of notification.
Transfers: No deadline.

CONTACT
Brandi Darr, Director of Financial Aid
150 Finoli Drive, Greensburg, PA 15601
(724) 836-9881

University of Pittsburgh at Johnstown

Johnstown, Pennsylvania
www.upj.pitt.edu   Federal Code: 008815

4-year public engineering and liberal arts college in small city.
Enrollment: 3,043 undergrads, 4% part-time. 785 full-time freshmen.
Selectivity: Admits over 75% of applicants.

BASIC COSTS (2009-2010)
Tuition and fees: $11,754; out-of-state residents $21,314.
Per-credit charge: $458; out-of-state residents $857.
Room and board: $7,370.

FINANCIAL AID PICTURE (2009-2010)
Students with need: Out of 733 full-time freshmen who applied for aid, 589 were judged to have need. Of these, 584 received aid, and 27 had their full need met. Average financial aid package met 57% of need; average scholarship/grant was $5,736; average loan was $3,611. For part-time students, average financial aid package was $5,721.
Students without need: 30 full-time freshmen who did not demonstrate need for aid received scholarships/grants; average award was $2,300. No-need awards available for academics, athletics, leadership, minority status, state/district residency.
Scholarships offered: *Merit:* President's Scholarships and Leadership Scholarships; $1,500 to full tuition yearly; renewable; 1220 SAT (exclusive of Writing), 3.8 GPA, and top 10% of graduating class required; priority given to those who apply by 12/1. *Athletic:* 40 full-time freshmen received athletic scholarships; average amount $3,053.
Cumulative student debt: 85% of graduating class had student loans; average debt was $23,243.

FINANCIAL AID PROCEDURES
Forms required: FAFSA, state aid form.
Dates and Deadlines: Priority date 4/1; no closing date. Applicants notified on a rolling basis starting 3/15; must reply within 2 week(s) of notification.

CONTACT
Jeanine Lawn, Director of Financial Aid
450 Schoolhouse Road, 157 Blackington Hall, Johnstown, PA 15904-1200
(800) 881-5544

University of Pittsburgh at Titusville

Titusville, Pennsylvania
www.upt.pitt.edu   Federal Code: 008815

2-year public branch campus and liberal arts college in small town.
Enrollment: 539 undergrads, 14% part-time. 203 full-time freshmen.

BASIC COSTS (2009-2010)
Tuition and fees: $10,430; out-of-state residents $19,050.
Per-credit charge: $404; out-of-state residents $763.
Room and board: $8,256.

FINANCIAL AID PICTURE (2009-2010)

Students with need: Average financial aid package met 86% of need; average scholarship/grant was $8,927; average loan was $7,076. For part-time students, average financial aid package was $12,465.

Students without need: No-need awards available for academics, athletics, state/district residency.

Scholarships offered: Rees scholarships; $2,000; awarded to top 5 students with science as a major; renewable with 3.0 GPA and continued science major. Presidential scholarships; $2,500; based on high school academic record; 10 awarded.

FINANCIAL AID PROCEDURES

Forms required: FAFSA.

Dates and Deadlines: Priority date 3/1; no closing date. Applicants notified on a rolling basis; must reply within 2 week(s) of notification.

Transfers: No deadline. Applicants notified on a rolling basis starting 4/1; must reply within 2 week(s) of notification. Pennsylvania residents must apply by 5/1 for PHEAA. Transfer students must have completed 24 credits to renew. Information retrieved from NSLDS is utilized to determine transfer student eligibility for financial aid.

CONTACT

Sue Bloom, Director of Financial Aid
UPT Admissions Office, Titusville, PA 16354-0287
(814) 827-4495

University of Scranton

Scranton, Pennsylvania
www.scranton.edu
Federal Code: 003384

4-year private university and liberal arts college in small city, affiliated with Roman Catholic Church.

Enrollment: 4,067 undergrads, 3% part-time. 1,028 full-time freshmen.

Selectivity: Admits 50 to 75% of applicants.

BASIC COSTS (2010-2011)

Tuition and fees: $34,626.

Per-credit charge: $882.

Room and board: $11,862.

FINANCIAL AID PICTURE (2009-2010)

Students with need: Need-based aid available for full-time and part-time students. Work study available nights, weekends, and for part-time students.

Students without need: No-need awards available for academics, minority status, ROTC.

FINANCIAL AID PROCEDURES

Forms required: FAFSA.

Dates and Deadlines: Priority date 2/15; no closing date. Applicants notified on a rolling basis starting 3/1; must reply by 5/1 or within 2 week(s) of notification.

Transfers: Institutional grants available based on financial need.

CONTACT

William Burke, Director of Financial Aid
800 Linden Street, Scranton, PA 18510-4699
(570) 941-7700

University of the Arts

Philadelphia, Pennsylvania
www.uarts.edu
Federal Code: 003350

4-year private visual arts and performing arts college in very large city.

Enrollment: 2,139 undergrads, 1% part-time. 473 full-time freshmen.

Selectivity: Admits less than 50% of applicants.

BASIC COSTS (2009-2010)

Tuition and fees: $31,000.

Per-credit charge: $1,280.

Room only: $7,200.

FINANCIAL AID PICTURE

Students with need: Need-based aid available for full-time and part-time students. Work study available nights, weekends, and for part-time students.

Students without need: No-need awards available for academics, art, music/drama.

Scholarships offered: Merit awards; available to students who demonstrate exceptional talent and academic abilities.

FINANCIAL AID PROCEDURES

Forms required: FAFSA.

Dates and Deadlines: Priority date 3/1; no closing date. Applicants notified on a rolling basis starting 3/15; must reply within 2 week(s) of notification.

Transfers: Undergraduate transfers not eligible for federal, state, or university aid if 4-year degree previously conferred.

CONTACT

Chris Pesotski, Director, Financial Aid
320 South Broad Street, Philadelphia, PA 19102
(215) 717-6170

University of the Sciences in Philadelphia

Philadelphia, Pennsylvania
www.usp.edu
Federal Code: 003353

4-year private health science and pharmacy college in very large city.

Enrollment: 2,602 undergrads, 1% part-time. 513 full-time freshmen.

Selectivity: Admits 50 to 75% of applicants.

BASIC COSTS (2009-2010)

Tuition and fees: $29,630.

Per-credit charge: $1,175.

Room and board: $11,582.

FINANCIAL AID PICTURE (2008-2009)

Students with need: Out of 495 full-time freshmen who applied for aid, 432 were judged to have need. Of these, 432 received aid, and 247 had their full need met. Average financial aid package met 72% of need; average scholarship/grant was $7,799; average loan was $3,457. For part-time students, average financial aid package was $19,220.

Students without need: 39 full-time freshmen who did not demonstrate need for aid received scholarships/grants; average award was $9,989. No-need awards available for academics, athletics.

Scholarships offered: 2 full-time freshmen received athletic scholarships; average amount $2,500.

FINANCIAL AID PROCEDURES

Forms required: FAFSA.

Dates and Deadlines: Closing date 3/15. Applicants notified on a rolling basis starting 1/15; must reply by 5/1 or within 2 week(s) of notification.

CONTACT

Paula Lehrberger, Director of Financial Aid
600 South 43rd Street, Philadelphia, PA 19104-4495
(215) 596-8894

Ursinus College

Collegeville, Pennsylvania
www.ursinus.edu
Federal Code: 003385
CSS Code: 2931

4-year private liberal arts college in small town.

Enrollment: 1,716 undergrads. 504 full-time freshmen.

Selectivity: Admits 50 to 75% of applicants.

BASIC COSTS (2010-2011)
Tuition and fees: $39,950.
Per-credit charge: $1,249.
Room and board: $9,750.
Additional info: Required $170 insurance fee for laptop computer students are given.

FINANCIAL AID PICTURE (2009-2010)
Students with need: Out of 452 full-time freshmen who applied for aid, 359 were judged to have need. Of these, 359 received aid, and 84 had their full need met. Average financial aid package met 85% of need; average scholarship/grant was $25,580; average loan was $3,661.
Students without need: 118 full-time freshmen who did not demonstrate need for aid received scholarships/grants; average award was $15,000. No-need awards available for academics, alumni affiliation, art, leadership, music/drama.
Cumulative student debt: 80% of graduating class had student loans; average debt was $31,125.

FINANCIAL AID PROCEDURES
Forms required: FAFSA, CSS PROFILE, institutional form.
Dates and Deadlines: Closing date 2/15. Applicants notified by 4/1; must reply by 5/1 or within 2 week(s) of notification.
Transfers: Closing date 8/1.

CONTACT
Suzanne Sparrow, Director of Student Financial Services
PO Box 1000, Collegeville, PA 19426-1000
(610) 409-3600

Valley Forge Christian College
Phoenixville, Pennsylvania
www.vfcc.edu   Federal Code: 003306

4-year private liberal arts college in large town, affiliated with Assemblies of God.
Enrollment: 927 undergrads, 10% part-time. 346 full-time freshmen.
Selectivity: Admits 50 to 75% of applicants.

BASIC COSTS (2010-2011)
Tuition and fees: $16,250.
Per-credit charge: $564.
Room and board: $7,096.

FINANCIAL AID PICTURE (2008-2009)
Students with need: Out of 183 full-time freshmen who applied for aid, 158 were judged to have need. Of these, 157 received aid, and 22 had their full need met. Average financial aid package met 51% of need; average scholarship/grant was $5,543; average loan was $3,095. For part-time students, average financial aid package was $6,079.
Students without need: 176 full-time freshmen who did not demonstrate need for aid received scholarships/grants; average award was $1,834. No-need awards available for academics, leadership, music/drama, religious affiliation, state/district residency.
Scholarships offered: Trustee's Scholarship, President's Scholarship, Dean's Scholarship, Professor's Scholarship; ranging from full tuition (minimum 3.5 GPA, 1300 SAT or 29 ACT, and upper 10% class rank) to $1,000-$5,000 (minimum 3.3 GPA and 1030 SAT or 22 ACT); application required for awards; renewable with 3.5 GPA. SAT scores exclusive of Writing.
Cumulative student debt: 96% of graduating class had student loans; average debt was $35,973.

FINANCIAL AID PROCEDURES
Forms required: FAFSA.
Dates and Deadlines: Priority date 5/1; no closing date. Applicants notified on a rolling basis starting 3/15; must reply within 3 week(s) of notification.

CONTACT
Linda Stein, Director of Financial Aid
1401 Charlestown Road, Phoenixville, PA 19460
(610) 917-1475

Valley Forge Military Academy & College
Wayne, Pennsylvania
www.vfmac.edu   Federal Code: 003386

2-year private junior and military college in small city.
Enrollment: 217 undergrads.

BASIC COSTS (2009-2010)
Tuition and fees: $28,790.
Room and board: $9,415.

FINANCIAL AID PICTURE (2008-2009)
Students with need: Need-based aid available for full-time students. Work study available nights, weekends, and for part-time students.
Students without need: No-need awards available for academics, alumni affiliation, athletics, music/drama, ROTC, state/district residency.
Additional info: Students enrolled in advanced military science program can receive up to $5,000 from the Army. In addition, competitively awarded ROTC scholarships pay average of another $14,100 per school year for direct educational expenses.

FINANCIAL AID PROCEDURES
Forms required: FAFSA, institutional form.
Dates and Deadlines: Closing date 5/1. Applicants notified on a rolling basis starting 5/15; must reply within 2 week(s) of notification.
Transfers: Must submit financial aid transcripts from all previously attended colleges, even if aid was not received.

CONTACT
Donna Speranza, Financial Aid Director
1001 Eagle Road, Wayne, PA 19087
(610) 989-1300 ext. 1306

Vet Tech Institute
Pittsburgh, Pennsylvania
www.vettechinstitute.edu   Federal Code: 008568

2-year for-profit health science and technical college in large city.
Enrollment: 345 undergrads.

BASIC COSTS (2009-2010)
Tuition and fees: $13,200.

FINANCIAL AID PICTURE
Students with need: Work study available nights.
Students without need: No-need awards available for academics.
Scholarships offered: $1,000 scholarships; 5 offered to commuters. $2,000 scholarships; 2 offered to students not living at home. Awarded based on results of examination given at school in November and March.

FINANCIAL AID PROCEDURES
Forms required: FAFSA, state aid form.
Dates and Deadlines: No deadline. Applicants notified on a rolling basis.

CONTACT
Donna Durr, Financial Aid Director
125 Seventh Street, Pittsburgh, PA 15222-3400
(800) 570-0693

Villanova University

Villanova, Pennsylvania
www.villanova.edu

Federal Code: 003388
CSS Code: 2959

4-year private university in large town, affiliated with Roman Catholic Church.
Enrollment: 6,897 undergrads, 4% part-time. 1,643 full-time freshmen.
Selectivity: Admits less than 50% of applicants.

BASIC COSTS (2010-2011)
Tuition and fees: $39,930.
Per-credit charge: $1,640.
Room and board: $10,620.
Additional info: Full-time tuition includes laptop for all students.

FINANCIAL AID PICTURE (2009-2010)
Students with need: Out of 1,187 full-time freshmen who applied for aid, 870 were judged to have need. Of these, 869 received aid, and 233 had their full need met. Average financial aid package met 87% of need; average scholarship/grant was $25,493; average loan was $3,462. For part-time students, average financial aid package was $8,657.
Students without need: 125 full-time freshmen who did not demonstrate need for aid received scholarships/grants; average award was $8,492. No-need awards available for academics, alumni affiliation, athletics, leadership, minority status, religious affiliation, ROTC.
Scholarships offered: 29 full-time freshmen received athletic scholarships; average amount $40,023.
Cumulative student debt: 55% of graduating class had student loans; average debt was $31,048.

FINANCIAL AID PROCEDURES
Forms required: FAFSA, CSS PROFILE, institutional form.
Dates and Deadlines: Closing date 2/7. Applicants notified by 4/1; must reply by 5/1 or within 2 week(s) of notification.
Transfers: Closing date 7/15. Applicants notified on a rolling basis starting 5/1; must reply within 2 week(s) of notification.

CONTACT
Bonnie Lee Behm, Director of Financial Assistance
800 Lancaster Avenue, Villanova, PA 19085-1672
(610) 519-4010

Washington & Jefferson College

Washington, Pennsylvania
www.washjeff.edu

Federal Code: 003389

4-year private liberal arts college in large town.
Enrollment: 1,479 undergrads, 1% part-time. 393 full-time freshmen.
Selectivity: Admits less than 50% of applicants.

BASIC COSTS (2010-2011)
Tuition and fees: $34,610.
Per-credit charge: $856.
Room and board: $9,470.

FINANCIAL AID PICTURE (2009-2010)
Students with need: Out of 359 full-time freshmen who applied for aid, 310 were judged to have need. Of these, 310 received aid, and 62 had their full need met. Average financial aid package met 82% of need; average scholarship/grant was $9,524; average loan was $3,730. For part-time students, average financial aid package was $29,253.
Students without need: 81 full-time freshmen who did not demonstrate need for aid received scholarships/grants; average award was $11,851. No-need awards available for academics, alumni affiliation.
Scholarships offered: Presidential Scholarship; based on distinguished academic performance. Scholars Award; based on distinguished academic performance. Joseph Hardy Sr. Scholarship; for students in entrepreneurial stud-

ies program. Dean's Award; based on academic performance in high school, distinguished achievement outside the classroom, and good citizenship. Challenge Grant; for students who show academic promise. Alumni Scholarship; for students whose father and/or mother are alumni.
Cumulative student debt: 75% of graduating class had student loans; average debt was $23,000.

FINANCIAL AID PROCEDURES
Forms required: FAFSA.
Dates and Deadlines: Priority date 2/15; no closing date. Applicants notified on a rolling basis starting 3/1; must reply by 5/1.
Transfers: Must reply within 2 week(s) of notification. Students should complete the FAFSA as soon as possible. Financial aid awards will be made when FAFSA has been received and the student has been accepted for admission. For students selected for verification, these awards are estimated until the required tax documentation has been received and reviewed.

CONTACT
Michelle Vettorel, Director of Financial Aid
60 South Lincoln Street, Washington, PA 15301
(724) 223-6019

Waynesburg University

Waynesburg, Pennsylvania
www.waynesburg.edu

Federal Code: 003391

4-year private liberal arts college in small town, affiliated with Presbyterian Church (USA).
Enrollment: 1,533 undergrads, 2% part-time. 385 full-time freshmen.
Selectivity: Admits 50 to 75% of applicants.

BASIC COSTS (2010-2011)
Tuition and fees: $18,410.
Per-credit charge: $760.
Room and board: $7,580.

FINANCIAL AID PICTURE (2009-2010)
Students with need: Average financial aid package met 81% of need; average scholarship/grant was $12,105; average loan was $3,286. For part-time students, average financial aid package was $7,568.
Students without need: No-need awards available for academics, alumni affiliation, job skills, leadership, religious affiliation, state/district residency.
Scholarships offered: A.B. Miller Scholarship; $8,000. Presidential Honor Scholarship; $6,000. Honor Scholarship; $4,000. College Leadership Program; $1,000-$1,900.
Cumulative student debt: 86% of graduating class had student loans; average debt was $5,500.

FINANCIAL AID PROCEDURES
Forms required: FAFSA, state aid form.
Dates and Deadlines: Priority date 3/15; no closing date. Applicants notified on a rolling basis starting 2/15; must reply within 2 week(s) of notification.
Transfers: No deadline. Applicants notified on a rolling basis; must reply within 2 week(s) of notification.

CONTACT
Matthew Stokan, Director of Financial Aid
51 West College Street, Waynesburg, PA 15370-1222
(724) 852-3269

West Chester University of Pennsylvania

West Chester, Pennsylvania
www.wcupa.edu

Federal Code: 003328

4-year public university in large town.
Enrollment: 11,561 undergrads, 7% part-time. 2,241 full-time freshmen.

Selectivity: Admits less than 50% of applicants.

BASIC COSTS (2009-2010)

Tuition and fees: $7,211; out-of-state residents $15,543.
Per-credit charge: $231; out-of-state residents $579.
Room and board: $7,214.

FINANCIAL AID PICTURE (2008-2009)

Students with need: Need-based aid available for full-time and part-time students. Work study available nights, weekends, and for part-time students.

FINANCIAL AID PROCEDURES

Forms required: FAFSA.
Dates and Deadlines: Priority date 3/1; no closing date. Must reply within 4 week(s) of notification.

CONTACT

Dana Parker, Director of Financial Aid
Messikomer Hall, West Chester, PA 19383
(610) 436-2627

Westminster College
New Wilmington, Pennsylvania
www.westminster.edu   Federal Code: 003392

4-year private liberal arts college in small town, affiliated with Presbyterian Church (USA).
Enrollment: 1,469 undergrads.
Selectivity: Admits 50 to 75% of applicants.

BASIC COSTS (2010-2011)

Tuition and fees: $29,150.
Per-credit charge: $890.
Room and board: $8,840.
Additional info: Tuition/fee waivers available for adults.

FINANCIAL AID PICTURE (2009-2010)

Students with need: Need-based aid available for full-time and part-time students.
Students without need: No-need awards available for academics, athletics.

FINANCIAL AID PROCEDURES

Forms required: FAFSA, institutional form.
Dates and Deadlines: Closing date 5/1. Applicants notified on a rolling basis starting 11/1; must reply by 5/1 or within 3 week(s) of notification.

CONTACT

Cheryl Gerber, Director of Financial Aid
Admissions, Westminster College, New Wilmington, PA 16172-0001
(724) 946-7102

Westmoreland County Community College
Youngwood, Pennsylvania
www.wccc.edu   Federal Code: 010176

2-year public community college in small town.
Enrollment: 6,323 undergrads, 45% part-time. 1,426 full-time freshmen.
Selectivity: Open admission; but selective for some programs.

BASIC COSTS (2009-2010)

Tuition and fees: $2,580; out-of-district residents $4,860; out-of-state residents $7,140.
Per-credit charge: $76; out-of-district residents $152; out-of-state residents $228.

FINANCIAL AID PICTURE

Students with need: Need-based aid available for full-time and part-time students. Work study available nights.
Students without need: No-need awards available for academics.

FINANCIAL AID PROCEDURES

Forms required: FAFSA, institutional form.
Dates and Deadlines: No deadline. Applicants notified on a rolling basis starting 5/1.

CONTACT

Gary Means, Director of Financial Aid
145 Pavilion Lane, Youngwood, PA 15697
(724) 925-4063

Widener University
Chester, Pennsylvania
www.widener.edu   Federal Code: 003313

4-year private university in large town.
Enrollment: 3,247 undergrads, 17% part-time. 714 full-time freshmen.
Selectivity: Admits 50 to 75% of applicants.

BASIC COSTS (2010-2011)

Tuition and fees: $33,270.
Per-credit charge: $1,090.
Room and board: $11,720.

FINANCIAL AID PICTURE (2009-2010)

Students with need: Out of 667 full-time freshmen who applied for aid, 622 were judged to have need. Of these, 621 received aid, and 86 had their full need met. Average financial aid package met 77% of need; average scholarship/grant was $9,460; average loan was $4,130. For part-time students, average financial aid package was $8,082.
Students without need: 68 full-time freshmen who did not demonstrate need for aid received scholarships/grants; average award was $14,600. No-need awards available for academics, leadership, music/drama, ROTC.
Scholarships offered: Academic Scholarships; $4,000 to full tuition; based on SAT and GPA; renewable. Music, leadership, and community service scholarships; based on performance evaluations.
Cumulative student debt: 87% of graduating class had student loans; average debt was $38,372.

FINANCIAL AID PROCEDURES

Forms required: FAFSA.
Dates and Deadlines: Priority date 2/15; no closing date. Applicants notified on a rolling basis starting 3/15; must reply within 4 week(s) of notification.
Transfers: Transfer scholarships; $2,500 to $10,000; based on GPA and minimum of 24 transferable credits.

CONTACT

Thomas Malloy, Director of Financial Aid
One University Place, Chester, PA 19013
(610) 499-4174

Wilkes University
Wilkes-Barre, Pennsylvania
www.wilkes.edu   Federal Code: 003394

4-year private university in small city.
Enrollment: 2,133 undergrads, 6% part-time. 561 full-time freshmen.
Selectivity: Admits over 75% of applicants.

BASIC COSTS (2010-2011)

Tuition and fees: $27,178.
Per-credit charge: $715.

Room and board: $11,470.

FINANCIAL AID PICTURE (2008-2009)

Students with need: Out of 534 full-time freshmen who applied for aid, 474 were judged to have need. Of these, 471 received aid, and 81 had their full need met. Average financial aid package met 78% of need; average scholarship/grant was $9,136; average loan was $2,835. For part-time students, average financial aid package was $6,951.

Students without need: 63 full-time freshmen who did not demonstrate need for aid received scholarships/grants; average award was $11,397. No-need awards available for academics, leadership, minority status, music/drama.

Cumulative student debt: 88% of graduating class had student loans; average debt was $31,935.

FINANCIAL AID PROCEDURES

Forms required: FAFSA.

Dates and Deadlines: Priority date 3/1; no closing date. Applicants notified on a rolling basis starting 3/1.

CONTACT

Melanie Mickelson, Vice President of Enrollment Services
84 West South Street, Wilkes-Barre, PA 18766
(570) 408-2000

Wilson College
Chambersburg, Pennsylvania
www.wilson.edu   Federal Code: 003396

4-year private liberal arts college for women in large town, affiliated with Presbyterian Church (USA).

Enrollment: 525 undergrads, 34% part-time. 104 full-time freshmen.

Selectivity: Admits 50 to 75% of applicants.

BASIC COSTS (2010-2011)

Tuition and fees: $28,220.
Per-credit charge: $2,765.
Room and board: $9,434.

FINANCIAL AID PICTURE (2009-2010)

Students with need: Out of 98 full-time freshmen who applied for aid, 92 were judged to have need. Of these, 92 received aid, and 18 had their full need met. Average financial aid package met 82% of need; average scholarship/grant was $20,354; average loan was $3,323. For part-time students, average financial aid package was $5,978.

Students without need: 11 full-time freshmen who did not demonstrate need for aid received scholarships/grants; average award was $13,783. No-need awards available for academics, alumni affiliation, religious affiliation, state/district residency.

Scholarships offered: Presidential Merit Scholarships: half tuition, cumulative GPA 3.75 or higher, top 15% of class. Dean's Merit Scholarship: 35% tuition, 3.40 to 3.74 cum GPA, top 25% of class. Faculty Merit Scholarship: 25% tuition, 3.0-3.39 cumulative GPA, rank top 50% of class. Scholarships for full-time students who are members of Presbyterian Church, USA. Curran Scholarships: awarded to incoming students with significant community service.

Cumulative student debt: 87% of graduating class had student loans; average debt was $33,673.

FINANCIAL AID PROCEDURES

Forms required: FAFSA, state aid form, institutional form.

Dates and Deadlines: Priority date 4/30; no closing date. Applicants notified on a rolling basis starting 2/15.

Transfers: Applicants notified on a rolling basis starting 2/15. Tuition scholarships available to transfer articulation students who hold associate degrees from Harrisburg Area Community College, Hagerstown Community College, Central Penn College, Luzerne County Community College, Lehigh Carbon Community College, Harcum College, Cottey College, Frederick Community College, Howard Community College; transfer merit scholarships for students with 3.0 GPA from 25% to 50% tuition, Phi Theta Kappa scholarship.

CONTACT

Linda Brittain, Dean of Financial Aid
1015 Philadelphia Avenue, Chambersburg, PA 17201-1285
(717) 262-2016

York College of Pennsylvania
York, Pennsylvania
www.ycp.edu   Federal Code: 003399

4-year private liberal arts college in small city.

Enrollment: 5,086 undergrads, 10% part-time. 1,092 full-time freshmen.

Selectivity: Admits 50 to 75% of applicants.

BASIC COSTS (2010-2011)

Tuition and fees: $15,140.
Per-credit charge: $425.
Room and board: $8,530.

FINANCIAL AID PICTURE (2009-2010)

Students with need: Out of 996 full-time freshmen who applied for aid, 703 were judged to have need. Of these, 698 received aid, and 167 had their full need met. Average financial aid package met 74% of need; average scholarship/grant was $5,659; average loan was $4,822. For part-time students, average financial aid package was $6,553.

Students without need: 179 full-time freshmen who did not demonstrate need for aid received scholarships/grants; average award was $4,133. No-need awards available for academics, alumni affiliation, music/drama.

Scholarships offered: All accepted freshman applicants considered for merit scholarships, including Presidential and Dean's Scholarships, based on academic criteria (GPA, rank, test scores). Scholarship awards reduce tuition to approximately $7,000 - $11,500 annually for many students, not including additional eligibility for need-based financial aid.

Cumulative student debt: 75% of graduating class had student loans; average debt was $27,583.

FINANCIAL AID PROCEDURES

Forms required: FAFSA.

Dates and Deadlines: No deadline. Applicants notified on a rolling basis starting 3/1; must reply within 4 week(s) of notification.

Transfers: No deadline. Applicants notified on a rolling basis starting 3/9. Transfer Merit Scholarship; $2,000 ($1,000 per semester) for entering transfer students with minimum 3.5 GPA.

CONTACT

Calvin Williams, Director of Financial Aid
441 Country Club Road, York, PA 17403-3651
(717) 849-1682

Puerto Rico

Bayamon Central University
Bayamon, Puerto Rico
www.ucb.edu.pr   Federal Code: 010015

4-year private university in large city, affiliated with Roman Catholic Church.

Enrollment: 1,832 undergrads, 19% part-time. 270 full-time freshmen.

Selectivity: Admits less than 50% of applicants.

BASIC COSTS (2009-2010)

Tuition and fees: $7,250.

Additional info: Tuition/fee waivers available for unemployed or children of unemployed.

FINANCIAL AID PICTURE (2009-2010)

Students with need: Need-based aid available for full-time and part-time students. Work study available nights.

Students without need: This college awards aid only to students with need.

FINANCIAL AID PROCEDURES

Forms required: FAFSA, institutional form.

Dates and Deadlines: Priority date 5/31; closing date 7/2.

Transfers: Closing date 5/30.

CONTACT

Edna Ortiz, Director of Financial Aid Office
PO Box 1725, Bayamon, PR 00960-1725
(787) 786-3030 ext. 2116

Caribbean University

Bayamon, Puerto Rico
www.caribbean.edu   Federal Code: 012525

4-year private health science and liberal arts college in large city.

Selectivity: Open admission.

BASIC COSTS (2009-2010)

Tuition and fees: $4,520.

Additional info: Annual full-time tuition for engineering program: $3,960; per-credit-hour charge: $165.

FINANCIAL AID PICTURE (2008-2009)

Students with need: Need-based aid available for full-time and part-time students. Work study available nights, weekends, and for part-time students.

Students without need: This college awards aid only to students with need.

FINANCIAL AID PROCEDURES

Forms required: FAFSA.

Dates and Deadlines: Priority date 5/80; no closing date. Applicants notified on a rolling basis starting 7/30; must reply within 2 week(s) of notification.

Transfers: Closing date 5/30. Applicants notified on a rolling basis.

CONTACT

Edwin Sanchez, Financial Aid Director
PO Box 493, Bayamon, PR 00960-0493
(787) 780-0070 ext. 1125

Columbia Centro Universitario: Caguas

Caguas, Puerto Rico
www.columbiaco.edu   Federal Code: 013517

4-year for-profit business and technical college in small city.

Enrollment: 1,270 undergrads, 44% part-time. 202 full-time freshmen.

Selectivity: Open admission; but selective for some programs.

BASIC COSTS (2009-2010)

Tuition and fees: $5,380.

FINANCIAL AID PICTURE (2008-2009)

Students with need: Need-based aid available for full-time and part-time students.

Students without need: This college awards aid only to students with need.

CONTACT

Virginia Guang, Financial Aid Administrator
PO Box 8517, Caguas, PR 00726
(787) 743-4041 ext. 223

Columbia Centro Universitario: Yauco

Yauco, Puerto Rico
www.columbiaco.edu   Federal Code: 008902

2-year for-profit business and nursing college in large town.

Enrollment: 1,341 undergrads, 35% part-time. 199 full-time freshmen.

Selectivity: Open admission; but selective for some programs.

BASIC COSTS (2009-2010)

Tuition and fees: $5,380.

Per-credit charge: $160.

FINANCIAL AID PICTURE (2008-2009)

Students with need: 53% of average financial aid package awarded as scholarships/grants, 47% awarded as loans/jobs. Need-based aid available for part-time students. Work study available weekends and for part-time students.

Students without need: This college awards aid only to students with need.

FINANCIAL AID PROCEDURES

Forms required: FAFSA, institutional form.

CONTACT

Edwin Vargas, Director of Financial Aid
Box 3062, Yauco, PR 00698-3062

Conservatory of Music of Puerto Rico

San Juan, Puerto Rico
www.cmpr.edu   Federal Code: 010819

4-year public music college in large city.

Enrollment: 368 undergrads, 22% part-time. 110 full-time freshmen.

Selectivity: Admits 50 to 75% of applicants.

BASIC COSTS (2009-2010)

Tuition and fees: $2,750; out-of-state residents $2,750.

Per-credit charge: $75; out-of-state residents $75.

Additional info: Education or instrument seminar, $150; piano accompanist (only for voice students in all four years of studies and performance students in their third and fourth year of studies), $150 for academic year.

FINANCIAL AID PICTURE (2008-2009)

Students with need: Out of 50 full-time freshmen who applied for aid, 50 were judged to have need. Of these, 50 received aid, and 5 had their full need met. Average financial aid package met 40% of need; average scholarship/grant was $4,500; average loan was $2,342. Need-based aid available for part-time students.

Students without need: This college awards aid only to students with need.

FINANCIAL AID PROCEDURES

Forms required: FAFSA.

Dates and Deadlines: Priority date 12/15; no closing date. Applicants notified on a rolling basis starting 4/30.

Transfers: Closing date 4/15.

CONTACT

Jorge Medina, Financial Aid Officer
951 Ave. Ponce de Leon, San Juan, PR 00907-3373
(787) 751-0160 ext. 231

PART III: FINANCIAL AID COLLEGE BY COLLEGE

Escuela de Artes Plasticas de Puerto Rico
San Juan, Puerto Rico
www.eap.edu   Federal Code: 017345

4-year public visual arts college in large city.
Enrollment: 530 undergrads, 31% part-time. 67 full-time freshmen.
Selectivity: Admits less than 50% of applicants.

BASIC COSTS (2009-2010)
Tuition and fees: $2,950; out-of-state residents $5,650.
Per-credit charge: $90; out-of-state residents $180.

FINANCIAL AID PICTURE (2008-2009)
Students with need: 99% of average financial aid package awarded as scholarships/grants, 1% awarded as loans/jobs. Need-based aid available for part-time students.
Students without need: This college awards aid only to students with need.

FINANCIAL AID PROCEDURES
Forms required: FAFSA.
Dates and Deadlines: Priority date 4/25; closing date 5/23. Applicants notified by 7/11.

CONTACT
Alfred Melendez, Director of Financial Aid
PO Box 9021112, San Juan, PR 00902-1112

Huertas Junior College
Caguas, Puerto Rico
www.huertas.edu   Federal Code: 014105

2-year for-profit junior and technical college in small city.
Enrollment: 1,853 undergrads, 16% part-time. 362 full-time freshmen.
Selectivity: Open admission.

FINANCIAL AID PICTURE (2009-2010)
Students with need: Out of 362 full-time freshmen who applied for aid, 348 were judged to have need. Of these, 348 received aid. Average financial aid package met 96% of need; average scholarship/grant was $96; average loan was $13. Need-based aid available for part-time students.
Students without need: This college awards aid only to students with need.

FINANCIAL AID PROCEDURES
Forms required: FAFSA, institutional form.
Dates and Deadlines: No deadline. Applicants notified on a rolling basis.

CONTACT
Wanda Ortiz, Financial Aid Director
PO Box 8429, Caguas, PR 00726
(787) 746-1400

Humacao Community College
Humacao, Puerto Rico
www.humacaocommunitycollege.com Federal Code: 014952

2-year private business and community college in small city.
Enrollment: 768 undergrads, 12% part-time. 219 full-time freshmen.
Selectivity: Open admission.

BASIC COSTS (2009-2010)
Tuition and fees: $5,328.

FINANCIAL AID PICTURE (2008-2009)
Students with need: Need-based aid available for full-time and part-time students. Work study available nights.
Students without need: This college awards aid only to students with need.

FINANCIAL AID PROCEDURES
Forms required: FAFSA, state aid form, institutional form.
Dates and Deadlines: Priority date 1/1; closing date 6/30. Applicants notified on a rolling basis starting 3/4.
Transfers: No deadline.

CONTACT
Cheryle Perez, Financial Aid Director
PO Box 9139, Humacao, PR 00792-9139
(787) 852-1430 ext. 28

Inter American University of Puerto Rico: Aguadilla Campus
Aguadilla, Puerto Rico
www.aguadilla.inter.edu   Federal Code: 003939

4-year private university and liberal arts college in small city.
Enrollment: 4,188 undergrads, 16% part-time. 887 full-time freshmen.
Selectivity: Open admission; but selective for some programs.

BASIC COSTS (2009-2010)
Tuition and fees: $5,368.
Per-credit charge: $163.
Additional info: Students without health insurance coverage must pay an additional $1,395 in fees for the academic year. Tuition at time of enrollment locked for 4 years.

FINANCIAL AID PICTURE (2009-2010)
Students with need: 64% of average financial aid package awarded as scholarships/grants, 36% awarded as loans/jobs. Need-based aid available for part-time students. Work study available nights, weekends, and for part-time students.
Students without need: No-need awards available for academics.

FINANCIAL AID PROCEDURES
Forms required: FAFSA.
Dates and Deadlines: Closing date 4/30. Applicants notified by 6/15; must reply by 8/8.
Transfers: No deadline.

CONTACT
Gloria Cortes, Director of Financial Aid
Box 20000, Aguadilla, PR 00605
(787) 891-0925 ext. 2110

Inter American University of Puerto Rico: Arecibo Campus
Arecibo, Puerto Rico
www.arecibo.inter.edu   Federal Code: 005026

4-year private liberal arts college in small city.
Enrollment: 4,528 undergrads.

BASIC COSTS (2009-2010)
Tuition and fees: $5,406.
Per-credit charge: $163.
Additional info: Students without health insurance coverage must pay an additional $1,395 in fees for the academic year.

FINANCIAL AID PICTURE (2008-2009)

Students with need: Need-based aid available for full-time and part-time students. Work study available nights, weekends, and for part-time students.
Students without need: No-need awards available for academics, athletics.

FINANCIAL AID PROCEDURES

Forms required: FAFSA, institutional form.
Dates and Deadlines: Priority date 5/1; no closing date. Applicants notified on a rolling basis.

CONTACT

Ramon de Jesus, Director of Financial Aid
PO Box 4050, Arecibo, PR 00614-4050
(787) 878-5475 ext. 2275

Inter American University of Puerto Rico: Bayamon Campus

Bayamon, Puerto Rico
www.bc.inter.edu   Federal Code: 003938

4-year private university and engineering college in small city.
Enrollment: 5,075 undergrads, 14% part-time. 1,125 full-time freshmen.
Selectivity: Admits less than 50% of applicants.

BASIC COSTS (2009-2010)

Tuition and fees: $5,406.
Per-credit charge: $163.
Additional info: Students without health insurance coverage must pay an additional $1,395 in fees for the academic year.

FINANCIAL AID PICTURE (2009-2010)

Students with need: Out of 1,111 full-time freshmen who applied for aid, 1,064 were judged to have need. Of these, 647 received aid, and 1 had their full need met. Average financial aid package met 1% of need; average scholarship/grant was $105; average loan was $140. For part-time students, average financial aid package was $154.
Students without need: This college awards aid only to students with need.
Scholarships offered: 11 full-time freshmen received athletic scholarships; average amount $309.

FINANCIAL AID PROCEDURES

Forms required: FAFSA.
Dates and Deadlines: Priority date 6/30; no closing date. Applicants notified on a rolling basis starting 5/10.

CONTACT

Carlos Alicea, Director of Student Services
500 Dr. John Will Harris Road, Bayamon, PR 00957
(787) 279-1912 ext. 2025

Inter American University of Puerto Rico: Guayama Campus

Guayama, Puerto Rico
www.guayama.inter.edu   Federal Code: 010764

4-year private university in large town.
Enrollment: 2,289 undergrads, 18% part-time. 311 full-time freshmen.
Selectivity: Admits less than 50% of applicants.

BASIC COSTS (2009-2010)

Tuition and fees: $5,368.
Per-credit charge: $163.
Additional info: Students without health insurance coverage must pay an additional $1,395 in fees for the academic year.

FINANCIAL AID PICTURE (2009-2010)

Students with need: Average financial aid package met 1% of need; average scholarship/grant was $58; average loan was $149. For part-time students, average financial aid package was $289.
Students without need: This college awards aid only to students with need.

FINANCIAL AID PROCEDURES

Forms required: FAFSA, institutional form.
Dates and Deadlines: Closing date 4/29. Applicants notified by 6/15; must reply by 7/30.
Transfers: No deadline.

CONTACT

Jose Vechini-Rodriguez, Director of Financial Aid
PO Box 10004, Guayama, PR 00785
(787) 864-2222 ext. 2206

Inter American University of Puerto Rico: Metropolitan Campus

San Juan, Puerto Rico
www.metro.inter.edu   Federal Code: 003938

4-year private branch campus college in large city.
Enrollment: 6,518 undergrads, 29% part-time. 956 full-time freshmen.
Selectivity: Admits less than 50% of applicants.

BASIC COSTS (2009-2010)

Tuition and fees: $5,406.
Per-credit charge: $163.
Additional info: Students without health insurance coverage must pay an additional $1,395 in fees for the academic year.

FINANCIAL AID PICTURE (2009-2010)

Students with need: For part-time students, average financial aid package was $511.

FINANCIAL AID PROCEDURES

Forms required: FAFSA.
Dates and Deadlines: Closing date 4/30. Applicants notified on a rolling basis.

CONTACT

Glenda Diaz, Director of Financial Aid
Box 191293, San Juan, PR 00919-1293
(787) 250-1912 ext. 2185

Inter American University of Puerto Rico: Ponce Campus

Mercedita, Puerto Rico
www.ponce.inter.edu   Federal Code: 005029

4-year private university in large town.
Enrollment: 5,703 undergrads, 14% part-time. 1,092 full-time freshmen.
Selectivity: Admits 50 to 75% of applicants.

BASIC COSTS (2009-2010)

Tuition and fees: $5,406.
Per-credit charge: $163.
Additional info: Students without health insurance coverage must pay an additional $1,395 in fees for the academic year.

FINANCIAL AID PICTURE (2009-2010)

Students with need: Average financial aid package met 2% of need; average scholarship/grant was $172; average loan was $239. For part-time students, average financial aid package was $154.

Students without need: This college awards aid only to students with need.

Scholarships offered: Scholarship program for first-time freshmen with a high school academic index of 3.0 or higher.

FINANCIAL AID PROCEDURES

Forms required: FAFSA.

Dates and Deadlines: No deadline.

CONTACT

Juan Portalatin, Director of Financial Aid

104 Turpo Industrial Park Road #1, Mercedita, PR 00715-1602

(787) 841-0102

Inter American University of Puerto Rico: San German Campus

San German, Puerto Rico

www.sg.inter.edu   Federal Code: 00714

4-year private university in large town.

Enrollment: 4,800 undergrads. 1,124 full-time freshmen.

Selectivity: Admits over 75% of applicants.

BASIC COSTS (2009-2010)

Tuition and fees: $5,406.

Per-credit charge: $163.

Room and board: $2,500.

Additional info: Students without health insurance coverage must pay an additional $1,395 in fees for the academic year.

FINANCIAL AID PICTURE (2008-2009)

Students with need: Out of 1,092 full-time freshmen who applied for aid, 1,065 were judged to have need. Of these, 751 received aid, and 3 had their full need met. Average financial aid package met 2% of need; average scholarship/grant was $293; average loan was $258. For part-time students, average financial aid package was $222.

Students without need: No-need awards available for academics, athletics.

Scholarships offered: 26 full-time freshmen received athletic scholarships; average amount $586.

FINANCIAL AID PROCEDURES

Forms required: FAFSA, institutional form.

Dates and Deadlines: Closing date 5/14. Applicants notified on a rolling basis; must reply by 8/1.

CONTACT

Maria Lugo, Director of Financial Aid

Box 5100, San German, PR 00683-9801

(787) 264-1912

National College of Business and Technology: Arecibo

Arecibo, Puerto Rico

www.nationalcollegepr.edu   Federal Code: 015953

3-year for-profit business and technical college in small city.

Enrollment: 2,015 undergrads. 919 full-time freshmen.

Selectivity: Admits over 75% of applicants.

BASIC COSTS (2009-2010)

Tuition and fees: $7,260.

Per-credit charge: $165.

FINANCIAL AID PICTURE (2008-2009)

Students with need: Out of 904 full-time freshmen who applied for aid, 904 were judged to have need. Of these, 883 received aid, and 2 had their full need met. Average financial aid package met 3% of need; average scholarship/grant was $3,195; average loan was $684. For part-time students, average financial aid package was $2,366.

Students without need: This college awards aid only to students with need.

FINANCIAL AID PROCEDURES

Forms required: FAFSA.

Dates and Deadlines: Priority date 12/31; closing date 4/29. Applicants notified on a rolling basis starting 5/2; must reply by 5/15 or within 2 week(s) of notification.

CONTACT

Desi Lopez-Padilla, Vice President of Compliance

PO Box 4035, MSC 452, Arecibo, PR 00614

(787) 780-5134 ext. 4020

National College of Business and Technology: Bayamon

Bayamon, Puerto Rico

www.nationalcollegepr.edu   Federal Code: 015953

3-year for-profit business and technical college in small city.

Enrollment: 2,500 undergrads. 1,043 full-time freshmen.

Selectivity: Admits over 75% of applicants.

BASIC COSTS (2009-2010)

Tuition and fees: $7,260.

Per-credit charge: $165.

FINANCIAL AID PICTURE (2008-2009)

Students with need: Out of 1,012 full-time freshmen who applied for aid, 1,012 were judged to have need. Of these, 975 received aid, and 6 had their full need met. Average financial aid package met 2% of need; average scholarship/grant was $3,195; average loan was $684. For part-time students, average financial aid package was $2,366.

Students without need: This college awards aid only to students with need.

FINANCIAL AID PROCEDURES

Forms required: FAFSA.

Dates and Deadlines: Priority date 12/31; closing date 4/29. Applicants notified on a rolling basis starting 5/2; must reply by 5/15 or within 2 week(s) of notification.

Transfers: No deadline.

CONTACT

Desi Lopez, Vice President of Compliance

PO Box 2036, Bayamon, PR 00960

(787) 780-5134 ext. 4134

National College of Business and Technology: Rio Grande

Rio Grande, Puerto Rico

www.nationalcollegepr.edu   Federal Code: E01213

3-year for-profit business and technical college in small town.

Enrollment: 1,550 undergrads. 739 full-time freshmen.

Selectivity: Admits over 75% of applicants.

BASIC COSTS (2009-2010)

Tuition and fees: $7,260.

Per-credit charge: $165.

FINANCIAL AID PICTURE (2008-2009)

Students with need: Out of 695 full-time freshmen who applied for aid, 695 were judged to have need. Of these, 670 received aid, and 2 had their full need met. Average financial aid package met 2% of need; average scholarship/grant was $3,195; average loan was $684. For part-time students, average financial aid package was $2,366.

Students without need: This college awards aid only to students with need.

FINANCIAL AID PROCEDURES

Forms required: FAFSA.

Dates and Deadlines: Must reply by 5/15 or within 2 week(s) of notification.

Transfers: No deadline.

CONTACT

Desi Lopez, Vice President of Compliance
PO Box 3064, Rio Grande, PR 00745
(787) 780-5134 ext. 4134

Pontifical Catholic University of Puerto Rico

Ponce, Puerto Rico
www.pucpr.edu   Federal Code: 003936

4-year private university in small city, affiliated with Roman Catholic Church.

Enrollment: 5,371 undergrads.

Selectivity: Admits over 75% of applicants.

BASIC COSTS (2009-2010)

Tuition and fees: $5,318.

Per-credit charge: $160.

Room only: $1,300.

FINANCIAL AID PICTURE (2009-2010)

Students with need: Need-based aid available for full-time and part-time students. Work study available nights, weekends, and for part-time students.

Students without need: No-need awards available for academics, athletics.

FINANCIAL AID PROCEDURES

Forms required: FAFSA, institutional form.

Dates and Deadlines: Closing date 5/30. Applicants notified by 6/15; must reply within 4 week(s) of notification.

Transfers: Priority date 5/8. Distribution of awards based on availability of funds when application received.

CONTACT

Rosalia Martinez, Director of Financial Aid
2250 Las Americas Avenue, Suite 284, Ponce, PR 00717-9777
(787) 651-2000 ext. 1054

Turabo University

Gurabo, Puerto Rico
www.suagm.edu/ut   Federal Code: 011719

4-year private university in small city.

Enrollment: 13,098 undergrads, 21% part-time. 2,025 full-time freshmen.

Selectivity: Open admission; but selective for some programs.

BASIC COSTS (2009-2010)

Tuition and fees: $4,924.

Per-credit charge: $171.

FINANCIAL AID PICTURE (2009-2010)

Students with need: Need-based aid available for full-time and part-time students.

Students without need: This college awards aid only to students with need.

FINANCIAL AID PROCEDURES

Forms required: FAFSA.

Dates and Deadlines: Priority date 5/30; no closing date. Applicants notified by 8/30.

CONTACT

Carmen Rivera-Lopez, Admissions and Financial Aid Director
PO Box 3030, Gurabo, PR 00778
(787) 743-797 ext. 4350

Universidad Adventista de las Antillas

Mayaguez, Puerto Rico
www.uaa.edu   Federal Code: 005019

4-year private university and liberal arts college in small city, affiliated with Seventh-day Adventists.

Enrollment: 927 undergrads, 6% part-time.

Selectivity: Open admission; but selective for some programs.

BASIC COSTS (2009-2010)

Tuition and fees: $10,320.

Room and board: $3,800.

Additional info: On-campus room/board figure ($3,800) includes most expensive meal plan ($1,200); less expensive meal plans are available for $300 or $600 for the academic year. Tuition for nonresident aliens is the sum of private tuition ($4,535 per semester) and the Form I-20 deposit ($4,000 only in the first year); after the first year, these students receive credit refund at registration ($500 per semester).

FINANCIAL AID PICTURE (2009-2010)

Students with need: Average financial aid package met 100% of need; average scholarship/grant was $3,375; average loan was $2,250. Need-based aid available for part-time students.

FINANCIAL AID PROCEDURES

Forms required: FAFSA, institutional form.

Dates and Deadlines: No deadline. Applicants notified on a rolling basis starting 8/15; must reply within 3 week(s) of notification.

CONTACT

Awilda Matos, Director of Financial Aid
PO Box 118, Mayaguez, PR 00681-0118
(787) 834-9595 ext. 2200

Universidad del Este

Carolina, Puerto Rico
www.suagm.edu/une   Federal Code: 011718

4-year private university and liberal arts college in small city.

Enrollment: 12,075 undergrads, 26% part-time. 2,082 full-time freshmen.

Selectivity: Open admission; but selective for some programs.

BASIC COSTS (2009-2010)

Tuition and fees: $4,924.

Per-credit charge: $171.

FINANCIAL AID PICTURE (2009-2010)

Students with need: 76% of average financial aid package awarded as scholarships/grants, 24% awarded as loans/jobs. Need-based aid available for part-time students.

Students without need: No-need awards available for academics, athletics.

FINANCIAL AID PROCEDURES

Forms required: FAFSA, state aid form, institutional form.

Dates and Deadlines: Priority date 5/30; no closing date. Applicants notified by 7/30.

CONTACT

Clotilde Santiago, Admissions and Financial Aid Director
PO Box 2010, Carolina, PR 00984-2010
(787) 257-7373 ext. 3401

Universidad Metropolitana
Rio Piedras, Puerto Rico
www.suagm.edu/umet   Federal Code: 025875

4-year private university and liberal arts college in large city.
Enrollment: 10,316 undergrads, 20% part-time. 1,792 full-time freshmen.
Selectivity: Admits 50 to 75% of applicants.

BASIC COSTS (2009-2010)
Tuition and fees: $4,924.
Per-credit charge: $171.

FINANCIAL AID PICTURE
Students with need: Need-based aid available for full-time and part-time students. Work study available nights.
Students without need: This college awards aid only to students with need.

FINANCIAL AID PROCEDURES
Forms required: FAFSA.
Dates and Deadlines: Priority date 5/30; no closing date. Applicants notified by 7/30.

CONTACT
Julio Rodriguez, Admissions and Financial Aid Director
Apartado 21150, San Juan, PR 00928
(787) 766-1717 ext. 6587

Universidad Pentecostal Mizpa
San Juan, Puerto Rico
www.colmizpa.edu   Federal Code: 035313

4-year private university and Bible college in very large city, affiliated with Pentecostal Holiness Church.
Enrollment: 255 undergrads, 56% part-time. 9 full-time freshmen.
Selectivity: Admits over 75% of applicants.

BASIC COSTS (2009-2010)
Tuition and fees: $3,530.
Per-credit charge: $105.
Room only: $1,400.

FINANCIAL AID PICTURE (2009-2010)
Students with need: Out of 9 full-time freshmen who applied for aid, 9 were judged to have need. Of these, 9 received aid. Need-based aid available for part-time students.
Students without need: This college awards aid only to students with need.

FINANCIAL AID PROCEDURES
Forms required: FAFSA.
Dates and Deadlines: No deadline.
Transfers: Applicants notified by 8/30.

CONTACT
Elisamuel Rodriguez, Administrative Dean
PO Box 20966, San Juan, PR 00928-0966

Universidad Politecnica de Puerto Rico
Hato Rey, Puerto Rico
www.pupr.edu   Federal Code: 014055

5-year private university and engineering college in large city.
Enrollment: 4,853 undergrads, 47% part-time. 534 full-time freshmen.
Selectivity: Admits over 75% of applicants.

FINANCIAL AID PICTURE (2008-2009)
Students with need: Need-based aid available for full-time and part-time students.
Students without need: No-need awards available for academics, music/drama.

FINANCIAL AID PROCEDURES
Forms required: FAFSA.
Dates and Deadlines: Priority date 5/15; closing date 6/30. Applicants notified by 7/15.

CONTACT
Sergio Villoldo, Director of Financial Aid
PO Box 192017, San Juan, PR 00919-2017
(787) 622-8000 ext. 249

University College of San Juan
San Juan, Puerto Rico
www.cunisanjuan.edu   Federal Code: 010567

4-year public community and technical college in very large city.
Selectivity: Admits over 75% of applicants.

BASIC COSTS (2009-2010)
Tuition and fees: $3,150.
Per-credit charge: $85.

FINANCIAL AID PICTURE (2008-2009)
Students with need: Need-based aid available for full-time and part-time students.
Students without need: This college awards aid only to students with need.

FINANCIAL AID PROCEDURES
Forms required: FAFSA, institutional form.
Dates and Deadlines: Closing date 9/30. Applicants notified by 10/30.
Transfers: Financial aid transcripts.

CONTACT
Gloria Mirabal, Director of Financial Aid
180 Jose R. Oliver Avenue, San Juan, PR 00918
(787) 250-7111 ext. 2287

University of Puerto Rico: Aguadilla
Aguadilla, Puerto Rico
www.uprag.edu   Federal Code: 012123

4-year public liberal arts and technical college in small city.
Enrollment: 2,997 undergrads, 8% part-time. 749 full-time freshmen.
Selectivity: Admits over 75% of applicants.

BASIC COSTS (2009-2010)
Tuition and fees: $1,812; out-of-state residents $4,226.
Per-credit charge: $49.

FINANCIAL AID PICTURE (2008-2009)
Students with need: 84% of average financial aid package awarded as scholarships/grants, 16% awarded as loans/jobs. Need-based aid available for part-time students.
Students without need: This college awards aid only to students with need.

FINANCIAL AID PROCEDURES
Forms required: FAFSA, institutional form.
Dates and Deadlines: Closing date 5/6. Applicants notified on a rolling basis starting 4/1; must reply within 1 week(s) of notification.
Transfers: No deadline.

CONTACT
Doris Roman, Financial Aid Director
Box 6150, Aguadilla, PR 00604-6150
(787) 890-0109

University of Puerto Rico: Arecibo
Arecibo, Puerto Rico
www.upra.edu   Federal Code: 007228

4-year public university in small city.
Enrollment: 3,563 full-time undergrads.

BASIC COSTS (2009-2010)
Tuition and fees: $1,812; out-of-state residents $4,226.
Per-credit charge: $49.

FINANCIAL AID PICTURE (2008-2009)
Students with need: Need-based aid available for full-time and part-time students.
Students without need: This college awards aid only to students with need.

FINANCIAL AID PROCEDURES
Forms required: FAFSA, institutional form.
Dates and Deadlines: Closing date 4/27.
Transfers: Closing date 5/25.

CONTACT
Myrta Ortiz, Financial Aid Officer
PO Box 4010, Arecibo, PR 00614-4010
(787) 815-0000 ext. 4501

University of Puerto Rico: Carolina Regional College
Carolina, Puerto Rico
www.uprc.edu   Federal Code: 003942

4-year public university in small city.
Enrollment: 4,293 undergrads, 24% part-time. 1,137 full-time freshmen.
Selectivity: Admits over 75% of applicants.

BASIC COSTS (2009-2010)
Tuition and fees: $3,012; out-of-state residents $4,397.
Per-credit charge: $49.

FINANCIAL AID PICTURE (2008-2009)
Students with need: Need-based aid available for full-time and part-time students.
Students without need: This college awards aid only to students with need.

FINANCIAL AID PROCEDURES
Forms required: FAFSA, state aid form, institutional form.

Dates and Deadlines: Closing date 6/30. Applicants notified on a rolling basis starting 6/10.

CONTACT
Santa Castro, Financial Aid Officer/Director
PO Box 4800, Carolina, PR 00984-4800
(787) 769-0188

University of Puerto Rico: Cayey University College
Cayey, Puerto Rico
www.cayey.upr.edu   Federal Code: 007206

4-year public liberal arts and teachers college in large town.
Enrollment: 3,735 undergrads, 9% part-time. 871 full-time freshmen.

BASIC COSTS (2009-2010)
Tuition and fees: $1,812; out-of-state residents $4,226.
Per-credit charge: $49.

FINANCIAL AID PICTURE (2009-2010)
Students with need: Need-based aid available for full-time and part-time students. Work study available nights, weekends, and for part-time students.
Students without need: This college awards aid only to students with need.

FINANCIAL AID PROCEDURES
Forms required: FAFSA.
Dates and Deadlines: Closing date 6/30. Applicants notified by 7/30.
Transfers: Priority date 1/30; closing date 2/28.

CONTACT
James Rivera, Director of Financial Aid
Oficina de Admisiones UPR- Cayey, Cayey, PR 00736
(787) 738-2161 ext. 2061

University of Puerto Rico: Humacao
Humacao, Puerto Rico
www.uprh.edu   Federal Code: 003942

4-year public university and liberal arts college in small city.
Enrollment: 4,510 undergrads, 8% part-time. 943 full-time freshmen.
Selectivity: Admits less than 50% of applicants.

BASIC COSTS (2009-2010)
Tuition and fees: $1,812; out-of-state residents $4,226.
Per-credit charge: $49.

FINANCIAL AID PICTURE (2008-2009)
Students with need: 89% of average financial aid package awarded as scholarships/grants, 11% awarded as loans/jobs. Need-based aid available for part-time students.
Students without need: No-need awards available for academics, athletics, music/drama.

FINANCIAL AID PROCEDURES
Forms required: FAFSA, institutional form.
Dates and Deadlines: Priority date 3/1; closing date 6/30. Applicants notified on a rolling basis starting 4/30; must reply by 7/31.

CONTACT
Larry Cruz, Acvting Director of Financial Aid
100 Road 908 CUH Station, Humacao, PR 00791
(787) 850-9342

University of Puerto Rico: Medical Sciences

San Juan, Puerto Rico
www.rcm.upr.edu   Federal Code: 003945

4-year public university in large city.
Enrollment: 535 undergrads, 8% part-time.

BASIC COSTS (2009-2010)
Tuition and fees: $1,812; out-of-state residents $4,226.
Per-credit charge: $49.

FINANCIAL AID PICTURE (2009-2010)
Students with need: Need-based aid available for full-time and part-time students. Work study available nights, weekends, and for part-time students.
Students without need: This college awards aid only to students with need.

FINANCIAL AID PROCEDURES
Forms required: FAFSA, institutional form.
Dates and Deadlines: Priority date 4/30; closing date 6/15. Applicants notified on a rolling basis starting 8/1; must reply within 2 week(s) of notification.

CONTACT
Cruz Figueroa, Director of Financial Aid
PO Box 365067, San Juan, PR 00936-5067
(787) 758-2525 ext. 3205

University of Puerto Rico: Ponce

Ponce, Puerto Rico
www.uprp.edu   Federal Code: 009652

4-year public university and branch campus college in small city.
Enrollment: 3,438 undergrads, 11% part-time. 862 full-time freshmen.
Selectivity: Admits less than 50% of applicants.

BASIC COSTS (2009-2010)
Tuition and fees: $1,812; out-of-state residents $4,226.
Per-credit charge: $49.

FINANCIAL AID PICTURE (2008-2009)
Students with need: 85% of average financial aid package awarded as scholarships/grants, 15% awarded as loans/jobs.
Students without need: This college awards aid only to students with need.

FINANCIAL AID PROCEDURES
Forms required: FAFSA, institutional form.
Dates and Deadlines: Closing date 5/30.

CONTACT
Carmelo Vega, Financial Aid Officer
Box 7186, Ponce, PR 00732
(787) 844-8181 ext. 2555

University of Puerto Rico: Rio Piedras

San Juan, Puerto Rico
www.uprrp.edu   Federal Code: 007108

4-year public university in large city.
Enrollment: 15,344 undergrads, 13% part-time. 2,814 full-time freshmen.
Selectivity: Admits less than 50% of applicants.

BASIC COSTS (2009-2010)
Tuition and fees: $1,812; out-of-state residents $4,226.
Per-credit charge: $49.

Room and board: $8,280.

FINANCIAL AID PICTURE (2009-2010)
Students with need: Need-based aid available for full-time and part-time students.
Students without need: This college awards aid only to students with need.
Additional info: Tuition waived for honor students, athletes, members of chorus, and others with special talents.

FINANCIAL AID PROCEDURES
Forms required: FAFSA.

CONTACT
Luz Santiago, Director of Financial Aid
Box 23344, San Juan, PR 00931-3344

University of Puerto Rico: Utuado

Utuado, Puerto Rico
www.uprutuado.edu   Federal Code: 010922

4-year public agricultural college in large town.
Enrollment: 1,544 undergrads, 7% part-time. 557 full-time freshmen.
Selectivity: Admits less than 50% of applicants. GED not accepted.

BASIC COSTS (2009-2010)
Tuition and fees: $1,812; out-of-state residents $4,226.
Per-credit charge: $49.

FINANCIAL AID PICTURE
Students with need: Need-based aid available for full-time and part-time students. Work study available nights.
Students without need: This college awards aid only to students with need.

FINANCIAL AID PROCEDURES
Forms required: FAFSA.
Dates and Deadlines: Priority date 5/31; no closing date. Applicants notified on a rolling basis starting 9/30; must reply within 4 week(s) of notification.
Transfers: Priority date 5/30; closing date 6/15. Closing date for Pell Grant applicants March 31.

CONTACT
Edgar Salva, Financial Assistance Officer
PO Box 2500, Utuado, PR 00641
(787) 894-2828 ext. 2603

University of the Sacred Heart

Santurce, Puerto Rico
www.sagrado.edu   Federal Code: 003937

4-year private university and liberal arts college in large city, affiliated with Roman Catholic Church.
Enrollment: 4,518 undergrads, 14% part-time. 726 full-time freshmen.

BASIC COSTS (2009-2010)
Tuition and fees: $5,870.
Per-credit charge: $170.
Room only: $2,500.

FINANCIAL AID PICTURE
Students with need: Need-based aid available for full-time and part-time students.
Students without need: No-need awards available for academics, athletics.

FINANCIAL AID PROCEDURES
Forms required: FAFSA, institutional form.

Dates and Deadlines: Priority date 4/30; closing date 5/30. Applicants notified on a rolling basis starting 6/15; must reply by 8/30.
Transfers: No deadline.

CONTACT
Luis Diaz, Director of Financial Aid
Universidad del Sagrado Corazon Oficina de Nuevo Ingreso, San Juan, PR 00914-0383

Rhode Island

Brown University
Providence, Rhode Island
www.brown.edu

Federal Code: 003401
CSS Code: 3094

4-year private university and liberal arts college in small city.
Enrollment: 6,013 undergrads. 1,493 full-time freshmen.
Selectivity: Admits less than 50% of applicants. GED not accepted.

BASIC COSTS (2010-2011)
Tuition and fees: $40,820.
Room and board: $10,540.
Additional info: Part-time students pay $4,991 per course in tuition; most undergraduates take eight courses per academic year.

FINANCIAL AID PICTURE (2009-2010)
Students with need: Out of 880 full-time freshmen who applied for aid, 637 were judged to have need. Of these, 637 received aid, and 637 had their full need met. Average financial aid package met 100% of need; average scholarship/grant was $32,100; average loan was $4,659. For part-time students, average financial aid package was $20,985.
Students without need: This college awards aid only to students with need.
Cumulative student debt: 41% of graduating class had student loans; average debt was $21,858.

FINANCIAL AID PROCEDURES
Forms required: FAFSA, CSS PROFILE.
Dates and Deadlines: Closing date 2/1. Applicants notified by 4/1; must reply by 5/1.
Transfers: Closing date 4/15.

CONTACT
James Tilton, Director of Financial Aid
45 Prospect Street, Providence, RI 02912
(401) 863-2721

Bryant University
Smithfield, Rhode Island
www.bryant.edu

Federal Code: 003402

4-year private business and liberal arts college in large town.
Enrollment: 3,367 undergrads, 3% part-time. 750 full-time freshmen.
Selectivity: Admits 50 to 75% of applicants.

BASIC COSTS (2010-2011)
Tuition and fees: $33,357.
Per-credit charge: $584.
Room and board: $12,458.

FINANCIAL AID PICTURE (2008-2009)
Students with need: Out of 573 full-time freshmen who applied for aid, 478 were judged to have need. Of these, 478 received aid, and 320 had their full need met. Average financial aid package met 67% of need; average scholarship/grant was $13,850; average loan was $3,360. For part-time students, average financial aid package was $6,609.
Students without need: 92 full-time freshmen who did not demonstrate need for aid received scholarships/grants; average award was $13,174. No-need awards available for academics, athletics, minority status, ROTC.
Scholarships offered: 30 full-time freshmen received athletic scholarships; average amount $21,387.
Cumulative student debt: 75% of graduating class had student loans; average debt was $38,270.

FINANCIAL AID PROCEDURES
Forms required: FAFSA.
Dates and Deadlines: Closing date 2/15. Applicants notified by 3/24; must reply by 5/1.
Transfers: Closing date 4/1.

CONTACT
John Canning, Director of Financial Aid
1150 Douglas Pike, Smithfield, RI 02917
(401) 232-6020

Community College of Rhode Island
Warwick, Rhode Island
www.ccri.edu

Federal Code: 004916

2-year public community college in small city.
Enrollment: 16,264 undergrads, 60% part-time. 2,164 full-time freshmen.
Selectivity: Open admission; but selective for some programs.

BASIC COSTS (2009-2010)
Tuition and fees: $3,376; out-of-state residents $9,008.
Per-credit charge: $140; out-of-state residents $416.
Additional info: Tuition/fee waivers available for unemployed or children of unemployed.

FINANCIAL AID PICTURE
Students with need: Need-based aid available for full-time and part-time students. Work study available nights, weekends, and for part-time students.
Students without need: No-need awards available for athletics.

FINANCIAL AID PROCEDURES
Forms required: FAFSA, institutional form.
Dates and Deadlines: Priority date 3/1; no closing date. Applicants notified on a rolling basis starting 5/1; must reply within 2 week(s) of notification.

CONTACT
Christine Jenkins, Associate Dean of Enrollment Services
400 East Avenue, Warwick, RI 02886-1807
(401) 455-6006

Johnson & Wales University: Providence
Providence, Rhode Island
www.jwu.edu

Federal Code: 003404

4-year private university in small city.
Enrollment: 9,495 undergrads, 8% part-time. 2,262 full-time freshmen.
Selectivity: Admits 50 to 75% of applicants.

BASIC COSTS (2010-2011)
Tuition and fees: $24,429.
Per-credit charge: $152.
Room and board: $8,904.

FINANCIAL AID PICTURE (2009-2010)

Students with need: Need-based aid available for full-time and part-time students.

Students without need: No-need awards available for academics, alumni affiliation, job skills, leadership, state/district residency.

FINANCIAL AID PROCEDURES

Forms required: FAFSA.

Dates and Deadlines: No deadline. Applicants notified on a rolling basis starting 3/1; must reply within 2 week(s) of notification.

Transfers: Transfer scholarships available.

CONTACT

Lynn Robinson, Director of Financial Aid
8 Abbott Park Place, Providence, RI 02903-3703
(800) 342-5598 ext. 4648

New England Institute of Technology
Warwick, Rhode Island
www.neit.edu   Federal Code: 007845

4-year private technical college in small city.

Enrollment: 3,341 undergrads, 11% part-time. 766 full-time freshmen.

Selectivity: Open admission.

BASIC COSTS (2009-2010)

Tuition and fees: $18,140.

Per-credit charge: $400.

FINANCIAL AID PICTURE

Students with need: Need-based aid available for full-time and part-time students. Work study available nights, weekends, and for part-time students.

Students without need: No-need awards available for academics.

Additional info: Tuition at time of first enrollment guaranteed all students for 2 years.

FINANCIAL AID PROCEDURES

Forms required: FAFSA, institutional form.

Dates and Deadlines: Priority date 6/1; no closing date. Applicants notified on a rolling basis starting 6/15.

CONTACT

Larry Blair, Director of Financial Aid
2500 Post Road, Warwick, RI 02886-2286
(401) 467-7744

Providence College
Providence, Rhode Island   Federal Code: 003406
www.providence.edu   CSS Code: 3693

4-year private liberal arts college in small city, affiliated with Roman Catholic Church.

Enrollment: 3,829 undergrads. 955 full-time freshmen.

Selectivity: Admits 50 to 75% of applicants. GED not accepted.

BASIC COSTS (2010-2011)

Tuition and fees: $39,435.

Per-credit charge: $1,120.

Room and board: $11,690.

Additional info: Tuition/fee waivers available for minority students.

FINANCIAL AID PICTURE (2009-2010)

Students with need: Out of 754 full-time freshmen who applied for aid, 579 were judged to have need. Of these, 579 received aid, and 318 had their full need met. Average financial aid package met 76% of need; average scholarship/grant was $17,180; average loan was $4,413. For part-time students, average financial aid package was $5,624.

Students without need: 75 full-time freshmen who did not demonstrate need for aid received scholarships/grants; average award was $21,598. No-need awards available for academics, athletics, minority status, ROTC.

Scholarships offered: 42 full-time freshmen received athletic scholarships; average amount $16,646.

Cumulative student debt: 63% of graduating class had student loans; average debt was $34,927.

FINANCIAL AID PROCEDURES

Forms required: FAFSA, CSS PROFILE.

Dates and Deadlines: Closing date 2/1. Applicants notified by 4/1; must reply by 5/1.

Transfers: Closing date 4/15. Applicants notified by 6/30.

CONTACT

Sandra Oliveira, Director of Financial Aid
Harkins Hall 222, 1 Cunningham Square, Providence, RI 02918-0001
(401) 865-2286

Rhode Island College
Providence, Rhode Island
www.ric.edu   Federal Code: 003407

4-year public liberal arts college in small city.

Enrollment: 7,500 undergrads, 24% part-time. 1,218 full-time freshmen.

Selectivity: Admits over 75% of applicants.

BASIC COSTS (2009-2010)

Tuition and fees: $6,408; out-of-state residents $15,488.

Per-credit charge: $226; out-of-state residents $604.

Room and board: $8,818.

Additional info: Permanent residents of Massachusetts and Connecticut communities within a 50-mile radius of Providence are eligible for Rhode Island's in-state tuition plus 50% of the in-state rate. Tuition/fee waivers available for unemployed or children of unemployed.

FINANCIAL AID PICTURE (2009-2010)

Students with need: Out of 1,085 full-time freshmen who applied for aid, 805 were judged to have need. Of these, 782 received aid, and 194 had their full need met. Average financial aid package met 77% of need; average scholarship/grant was $6,160; average loan was $3,265. For part-time students, average financial aid package was $6,079.

Students without need: 51 full-time freshmen who did not demonstrate need for aid received scholarships/grants; average award was $1,592. No-need awards available for academics, alumni affiliation, art, music/drama.

Scholarships offered: Presidential Scholarships ($2,000 per year) for entering freshmen in the top 30% of class with minimum combined SAT score of 1100 (exclusive of Writing) who apply for admission by Dec 15; approximately 100 awards available to each entering class.

Cumulative student debt: 71% of graduating class had student loans; average debt was $18,352.

FINANCIAL AID PROCEDURES

Forms required: FAFSA, institutional form.

Dates and Deadlines: Priority date 3/1; no closing date. Applicants notified on a rolling basis starting 3/15; must reply within 3 week(s) of notification.

Transfers: Priority date 5/15. Applicants notified on a rolling basis starting 3/15; must reply by 5/1 or within 3 week(s) of notification.

CONTACT

James Hanbury, Director of Financial Aid
600 Mount Pleasant Avenue, Providence, RI 02908
(401) 456-8033

Rhode Island School of Design
Providence, Rhode Island Federal Code: 003409
www.risd.edu CSS Code: 3726

4-year private visual arts college in small city.
Enrollment: 1,940 undergrads.
Selectivity: Admits less than 50% of applicants.

BASIC COSTS (2009-2010)
Tuition and fees: $36,659.
Per-credit charge: $1,205.
Room and board: $10,846.

FINANCIAL AID PICTURE (2008-2009)
Students with need: Need-based aid available for full-time students. Work study available nights, weekends, and for part-time students.

FINANCIAL AID PROCEDURES
Forms required: FAFSA, CSS PROFILE.
Dates and Deadlines: Closing date 2/15. Applicants notified by 4/1; must reply by 5/1.
Transfers: Closing date 3/15. Applicants notified by 4/25; must reply by 5/22. Transfer students with previous undergraduate degree not eligible for scholarship aid.

CONTACT
Edward Newhall, Director of Financial Aid
Two College Street, Providence, RI 02903-2791
(401) 454-6661

Roger Williams University
Bristol, Rhode Island Federal Code: 003410
www.rwu.edu CSS Code: 3729

4-year private university and liberal arts college in large town.
Enrollment: 4,267 undergrads.
Selectivity: Admits 50 to 75% of applicants.

BASIC COSTS (2009-2010)
Tuition and fees: $28,700.
Per-credit charge: $1,120.
Room and board: $12,290.
Additional info: Tuition differential for architecture program.

FINANCIAL AID PICTURE (2009-2010)
Students with need: Need-based aid available for full-time and part-time students. Work study available nights, weekends, and for part-time students.
Students without need: No-need awards available for academics, ROTC.

FINANCIAL AID PROCEDURES
Forms required: FAFSA, CSS PROFILE.
Dates and Deadlines: Priority date 1/1; closing date 2/1. Applicants notified on a rolling basis starting 3/20; must reply by 5/1.
Transfers: Must reply by 5/1.

CONTACT
Tracy DaCosta, Assistant Vice President of Enrollment Management & Retention
1 Old Ferry Road, Bristol, RI 02809-2921
(401) 254-3100

Salve Regina University
Newport, Rhode Island Federal Code: 003411
www.salve.edu CSS Code: 3759

4-year private university and liberal arts college in large town, affiliated with Roman Catholic Church.
Enrollment: 1,976 undergrads, 4% part-time. 501 full-time freshmen.
Selectivity: Admits 50 to 75% of applicants.

BASIC COSTS (2009-2010)
Tuition and fees: $32,350.
Per-credit charge: $993.
Room and board: $10,950.
Additional info: Required fees include a one-time laptop fee of $2,350 for all first-year students.

FINANCIAL AID PICTURE (2009-2010)
Students with need: Need-based aid available for full-time and part-time students. Work study available nights, weekends, and for part-time students.
Students without need: No-need awards available for academics, ROTC.

FINANCIAL AID PROCEDURES
Forms required: FAFSA, CSS PROFILE.
Dates and Deadlines: Priority date 3/1; no closing date. Applicants notified by 4/1; must reply by 4/15 or within 2 week(s) of notification.
Transfers: Closing date 2/1. Applicants notified by 3/1; must reply by 5/1 or within 2 week(s) of notification. Must provide financial aid transcripts from previous institutions attended.

CONTACT
Aida Mirante, Director of Financial Aid
100 Ochre Point Avenue, Newport, RI 02840-4192
(401) 341-2901

University of Rhode Island
Kingston, Rhode Island
www.uri.edu Federal Code: 003414

4-year public university in small town.
Enrollment: 12,972 undergrads, 10% part-time. 2,919 full-time freshmen.
Selectivity: Admits over 75% of applicants.

BASIC COSTS (2009-2010)
Tuition and fees: $9,528; out-of-state residents $26,026.
Per-credit charge: $343; out-of-state residents $1,031.
Room and board: $9,892.
Additional info: Tuition/fee waivers available for unemployed or children of unemployed.

FINANCIAL AID PICTURE (2009-2010)
Students with need: Out of 2,577 full-time freshmen who applied for aid, 2,033 were judged to have need. Of these, 1,754 received aid, and 1,709 had their full need met. Average financial aid package met 59% of need; average scholarship/grant was $7,501; average loan was $4,191. For part-time students, average financial aid package was $7,731.
Students without need: 143 full-time freshmen who did not demonstrate need for aid received scholarships/grants; average award was $3,992. No-need awards available for academics, alumni affiliation, art, athletics, music/drama, ROTC.
Scholarships offered: 10 full-time freshmen received athletic scholarships; average amount $2,950.
Cumulative student debt: 72% of graduating class had student loans; average debt was $22,500.

FINANCIAL AID PROCEDURES
Forms required: FAFSA.

Dates and Deadlines: Priority date 3/1; no closing date. Applicants notified on a rolling basis starting 3/31; must reply by 5/1.
Transfers: No deadline. Applicants notified on a rolling basis starting 4/1; must reply within 2 week(s) of notification.

CONTACT

Bonnie Saccucci, Senior Associate Director of Enrollment Services
14 Upper College Road, Kingston, RI 02881-1322
(401) 874-9500

South Carolina

Aiken Technical College
Aiken, South Carolina
www.atc.edu   Federal Code: 010056

2-year public community and technical college in small city.
Enrollment: 3,225 undergrads, 64% part-time.
Selectivity: Open admission; but selective for some programs.

BASIC COSTS (2009-2010)
Tuition and fees: $3,626; out-of-district residents $3,986; out-of-state residents $10,130.

FINANCIAL AID PICTURE (2008-2009)
Students with need: Need-based aid available for full-time and part-time students. Work study available nights, weekends, and for part-time students.
Students without need: No-need awards available for academics, athletics, leadership, minority status, state/district residency.
Scholarships offered: Vernon Ford Scholarships: $1,000 annually; for candidates with minimum GPA of 3.0; 8 awarded annually. N. Augusta 2000: $2,000 annually; 2 awarded. Wackenhut Criminal Justice Scholarship: $1,000; 1 awarded. Presidential Scholarship: $10,000 annually; 10 awarded.

FINANCIAL AID PROCEDURES
Forms required: FAFSA.
Dates and Deadlines: Priority date 5/1; closing date 6/30. Applicants notified on a rolling basis starting 4/1; must reply within 2 week(s) of notification.
Transfers: Applicants notified on a rolling basis; must reply within 2 week(s) of notification.

CONTACT

Amanda Chittum, Director of Financial Aid
PO Drawer 696, Aiken, SC 29802
(803) 593-9954 ext. 1261

Allen University
Columbia, South Carolina
www.allenuniversity.edu   Federal Code: 003417

4-year private university and liberal arts college in large city, affiliated with African Methodist Episcopal Church.
Enrollment: 827 undergrads, 3% part-time. 241 full-time freshmen.
Selectivity: Admits 50 to 75% of applicants.

BASIC COSTS (2010-2011)
Tuition and fees: $10,884.
Room and board: $5,240.

FINANCIAL AID PICTURE (2009-2010)
Students with need: Average financial aid package met 62% of need; average scholarship/grant was $7,346; average loan was $3,238. For part-time students, average financial aid package was $6,831.
Students without need: No-need awards available for academics, athletics, music/drama, ROTC.

FINANCIAL AID PROCEDURES
Forms required: FAFSA.
Dates and Deadlines: Priority date 4/15; closing date 7/20. Applicants notified on a rolling basis starting 4/1; must reply within 2 week(s) of notification.
Transfers: No deadline.

CONTACT

Melvin Miller, Vice President for Business and Finance
1530 Harden Street, Columbia, SC 29204

Anderson University
Anderson, South Carolina
www.andersonuniversity.edu   Federal Code: 003418

4-year private liberal arts and teachers college in large town, affiliated with Southern Baptist Convention.
Enrollment: 2,127 undergrads, 21% part-time. 450 full-time freshmen.
Selectivity: Admits 50 to 75% of applicants.

BASIC COSTS (2009-2010)
Tuition and fees: $19,212.
Per-credit charge: $500.
Room and board: $7,600.
Additional info: Tuition/fee waivers available for adults.

FINANCIAL AID PICTURE
Students with need: Need-based aid available for full-time and part-time students. Work study available nights, weekends, and for part-time students.
Students without need: No-need awards available for academics, alumni affiliation, art, athletics, leadership, minority status, music/drama, religious affiliation, state/district residency.

FINANCIAL AID PROCEDURES
Forms required: FAFSA.
Dates and Deadlines: Priority date 3/1; closing date 6/30. Applicants notified on a rolling basis starting 3/15; must reply within 2 week(s) of notification.

CONTACT

Becky Pressley, Director of Financial Aid
316 Boulevard, Anderson, SC 29621-4002
(864) 231-2070

Benedict College
Columbia, South Carolina
www.benedict.edu   Federal Code: 003420

4-year private liberal arts college in very large city, affiliated with American Baptist Churches in the USA.
Enrollment: 2,984 undergrads, 1% part-time. 837 full-time freshmen.
Selectivity: Admits over 75% of applicants.

BASIC COSTS (2009-2010)
Tuition and fees: $15,590.
Per-credit charge: $467.
Room and board: $7,172.

FINANCIAL AID PICTURE
Students with need: Need-based aid available for full-time and part-time students.

FINANCIAL AID PROCEDURES
Forms required: FAFSA.
Dates and Deadlines: Priority date 4/15; no closing date. Applicants notified on a rolling basis starting 4/15.

CONTACT

Sul Black, Director of Financial Aid
1600 Harden Street, Columbia, SC 29204
(803) 253-5105

Bob Jones University

Greenville, South Carolina
www.bju.edu   Federal Code: 003421

4-year private Bible and liberal arts college in small city, affiliated with Non-demoninational.

Enrollment: 3,432 undergrads, 2% part-time. 806 full-time freshmen.

Selectivity: Admits over 75% of applicants.

BASIC COSTS (2009-2010)

Tuition and fees: $11,825.

FINANCIAL AID PICTURE (2009-2010)

Students with need: 38% of average financial aid package awarded as scholarships/grants, 62% awarded as loans/jobs. Need-based aid available for part-time students.

FINANCIAL AID PROCEDURES

Forms required: FAFSA, state aid form, institutional form.

Dates and Deadlines: No deadline. Applicants notified on a rolling basis.

CONTACT

Chris Baker, Director of Financial Aid
1700 Wade Hampton Boulevard, Greenville, SC 29614
(864) 242-5100 ext. 3040

Central Carolina Technical College

Sumter, South Carolina
www.cctech.edu   Federal Code: 003995

2-year public community and technical college in large town.

Enrollment: 3,815 undergrads, 63% part-time. 472 full-time freshmen.

Selectivity: Open admission; but selective for some programs.

BASIC COSTS (2009-2010)

Tuition and fees: $3,308; out-of-district residents $3,856; out-of-state residents $5,744.

FINANCIAL AID PICTURE (2008-2009)

Students with need: Need-based aid available for full-time and part-time students. Work study available nights.

Students without need: This college awards aid only to students with need.

FINANCIAL AID PROCEDURES

Forms required: FAFSA.

Dates and Deadlines: No deadline. Applicants notified on a rolling basis starting 4/10; must reply within 2 week(s) of notification.

CONTACT

Sarah Dowd, Director of Financial Aid
506 North Guignard Drive, Sumter, SC 29150-2499
(803) 778-7831

Charleston Southern University

Charleston, South Carolina
www.csuniv.edu   Federal Code: 003419

4-year private university and liberal arts college in large city, affiliated with Southern Baptist Convention.

Enrollment: 2,757 undergrads, 14% part-time. 658 full-time freshmen.

BASIC COSTS (2009-2010)

Tuition and fees: $19,238.

Per-credit charge: $400.

Room and board: $7,394.

FINANCIAL AID PICTURE (2008-2009)

Students with need: Need-based aid available for full-time and part-time students. Work study available nights, weekends, and for part-time students.

Students without need: No-need awards available for academics, athletics, religious affiliation, ROTC.

FINANCIAL AID PROCEDURES

Forms required: FAFSA, state aid form.

Dates and Deadlines: Priority date 4/15; no closing date. Applicants notified on a rolling basis starting 3/1; must reply within 2 week(s) of notification.

CONTACT

Jenna Parish, Director of Financial Aid
9200 University Boulevard, Charleston, SC 29423-8087
(843) 863-7050

The Citadel

Charleston, South Carolina
www.citadel.edu   Federal Code: 003423

4-year public military college in large city.

Enrollment: 2,311 undergrads, 3% part-time. 591 full-time freshmen.

Selectivity: Admits over 75% of applicants.

BASIC COSTS (2009-2010)

Tuition and fees: $8,735; out-of-state residents $22,545.

Per-credit charge: $341; out-of-state residents $598.

Room and board: $7,054.

Additional info: Freshmen also pay $5,940 deposit and upperclassmen pay $1,874 deposit for uniforms, laundry, dry cleaning charges, infirmary fees, books, and supplies.

FINANCIAL AID PICTURE (2009-2010)

Students with need: Out of 497 full-time freshmen who applied for aid, 371 were judged to have need. Of these, 359 received aid, and 132 had their full need met. Average financial aid package met 69% of need; average scholarship/grant was $12,229; average loan was $3,537. For part-time students, average financial aid package was $5,349.

Students without need: 38 full-time freshmen who did not demonstrate need for aid received scholarships/grants; average award was $11,857. No-need awards available for academics, alumni affiliation, athletics, leadership, ROTC, state/district residency.

Scholarships offered: 21 full-time freshmen received athletic scholarships; average amount $23,858.

Cumulative student debt: 73% of graduating class had student loans; average debt was $25,817.

FINANCIAL AID PROCEDURES

Forms required: FAFSA, institutional form.

Dates and Deadlines: Priority date 3/1; no closing date. Applicants notified on a rolling basis starting 4/1; must reply by 4/1 or within 2 week(s) of notification.

Transfers: No deadline. Applicants notified on a rolling basis starting 4/1; must reply within 2 week(s) of notification.

CONTACT

Henry Fuller, Director of Financial Aid
171 Moultrie Street, Charleston, SC 29409
(843) 953-5187

Claflin University
Orangeburg, South Carolina
www.claflin.edu   Federal Code: 003424

4-year private liberal arts college in large town, affiliated with United Methodist Church.
Enrollment: 1,735 undergrads, 1% part-time. 466 full-time freshmen.
Selectivity: Admits less than 50% of applicants.

BASIC COSTS (2009-2010)
Tuition and fees: $12,768.
Room and board: $6,806.

FINANCIAL AID PICTURE (2009-2010)
Students with need: Need-based aid available for full-time students. Work study available nights.

FINANCIAL AID PROCEDURES
Forms required: FAFSA, institutional form.
Dates and Deadlines: Priority date 4/15; no closing date. Applicants notified on a rolling basis starting 5/15; must reply within 2 week(s) of notification.
Transfers: No deadline. Applicants notified on a rolling basis.

CONTACT
Terria Williams, Director of Financial Aid
400 Magnolia Street, Orangeburg, SC 29115
(803) 535-5334

Clemson University
Clemson, South Carolina
www.clemson.edu   Federal Code: 003425

4-year public university and engineering college in large town.
Enrollment: 15,247 undergrads, 6% part-time. 3,339 full-time freshmen.
Selectivity: Admits 50 to 75% of applicants.

BASIC COSTS (2009-2010)
Tuition and fees: $11,478; out-of-state residents $25,388.
Room and board: $6,980.
Additional info: Laptop computer required of all entering new students. This cost has been estimated at $1600.

FINANCIAL AID PICTURE (2008-2009)
Students with need: Need-based aid available for full-time and part-time students. Work study available nights, weekends, and for part-time students.
Students without need: No-need awards available for academics, art, athletics, leadership, minority status, music/drama, ROTC, state/district residency.

FINANCIAL AID PROCEDURES
Forms required: FAFSA.
Dates and Deadlines: Priority date 4/1; no closing date. Applicants notified on a rolling basis starting 4/1; must reply within 3 week(s) of notification.
Transfers: Transfer students must earn 12 semester hours before being considered for institutional scholarship.

CONTACT
Marvin Carmichael, Director of Student Financial Aid
105 Sikes Hall, Clemson, SC 29634-5124
(864) 656-2280

Coastal Carolina University
Conway, South Carolina
www.coastal.edu   Federal Code: 003451

4-year public university in small city.
Enrollment: 7,544 undergrads, 6% part-time. 1,643 full-time freshmen.
Selectivity: Admits 50 to 75% of applicants.

BASIC COSTS (2009-2010)
Tuition and fees: $8,950; out-of-state residents $18,470.
Per-credit charge: $373; out-of-state residents $782.
Room and board: $7,200.

FINANCIAL AID PICTURE (2008-2009)
Students with need: Out of 1,419 full-time freshmen who applied for aid, 1,037 were judged to have need. Of these, 1,001 received aid, and 122 had their full need met. Average financial aid package met 53% of need; average scholarship/grant was $4,664; average loan was $7,279. For part-time students, average financial aid package was $4,885.
Students without need: 347 full-time freshmen who did not demonstrate need for aid received scholarships/grants; average award was $9,526. No-need awards available for academics, art, athletics, leadership, music/drama, ROTC, state/district residency.
Scholarships offered: 70 full-time freshmen received athletic scholarships; average amount $8,810.
Cumulative student debt: 71% of graduating class had student loans; average debt was $26,646.

FINANCIAL AID PROCEDURES
Forms required: FAFSA.
Dates and Deadlines: Priority date 3/1; no closing date. Applicants notified on a rolling basis starting 3/1; must reply by 5/15.
Transfers: No deadline. Applicants notified on a rolling basis starting 3/1; must reply within 4 week(s) of notification.

CONTACT
Dawn Hitchcock, Director of Financial Aid
PO Box 261954, Conway, SC 29528-6054
(843) 349-2313

Coker College
Hartsville, South Carolina
www.coker.edu   Federal Code: 003427

4-year private liberal arts college in large town.
Enrollment: 653 undergrads, 2% part-time. 191 full-time freshmen.
Selectivity: Admits 50 to 75% of applicants.

BASIC COSTS (2009-2010)
Tuition and fees: $19,723.
Room and board: $6,240.
Additional info: Tuition/fee waivers available for adults.

FINANCIAL AID PICTURE (2009-2010)
Students with need: Need-based aid available for full-time and part-time students. Work study available nights, weekends, and for part-time students.
Students without need: No-need awards available for academics, alumni affiliation, art, athletics, job skills, leadership, minority status, music/drama, religious affiliation, ROTC, state/district residency.
Scholarships offered: Scholarships for Excellence: awarded on a competitive basis to students showing potential for continued high performance and leadership; up to $17,000 per year; candidates may be invited to campus for interviews. President's Scholarships: based on SAT or ACT score and GPA; up to $7,500 per year. Dean's Scholarships: based on SAT or ACT score and GPA; up to $7,000 per year. Departmental Scholarships: art, dance, music, theater, biology, and chemistry scholarships to talented students; language

and literature/ creative writing scholarship; range from $500 to $4,000 per year; art, dance, music, and theater scholarships require an audition or portfolio; some departments require an interview. Valedictorian Scholarships: $500 per year to students ranked number one in their class at the end of their junior year or first semester of their senior year.

Additional info: Endowed scholarship program for qualified applicants. June 1 deadline for filing South Carolina Tuition Grant forms.

FINANCIAL AID PROCEDURES

Forms required: FAFSA.

Dates and Deadlines: Priority date 4/1; closing date 6/1. Applicants notified on a rolling basis starting 3/1; must reply by 5/1 or within 3 week(s) of notification.

Transfers: No deadline.

CONTACT

Betty Williams, Director of Financial Aid
300 East College Avenue, Hartsville, SC 29550
(843) 383-8055

College of Charleston
Charleston, South Carolina
www.cofc.edu   Federal Code: 003428

4-year public liberal arts college in large city.

Enrollment: 9,736 undergrads, 5% part-time. 1,955 full-time freshmen.

Selectivity: Admits 50 to 75% of applicants.

BASIC COSTS (2009-2010)

Tuition and fees: $8,988; out-of-state residents $21,846.

Per-credit charge: $375; out-of-state residents $910.

Room and board: $9,411.

FINANCIAL AID PICTURE (2008-2009)

Students with need: Out of 1,192 full-time freshmen who applied for aid, 763 were judged to have need. Of these, 733 received aid, and 270 had their full need met. Average financial aid package met 66% of need; average scholarship/grant was $3,052; average loan was $3,336. For part-time students, average financial aid package was $9,581.

Students without need: 211 full-time freshmen who did not demonstrate need for aid received scholarships/grants; average award was $11,279. No-need awards available for academics, alumni affiliation, art, athletics, music/drama.

Scholarships offered: _Merit:_ Foundation Scholarships: from $1,000-$4,000 annually for up to 4 years; based on high school performance, test scores, and leadership qualities, no additional application required. **_Athletic:_** 34 full-time freshmen received athletic scholarships; average amount $16,963.

Cumulative student debt: 42% of graduating class had student loans; average debt was $17,139.

FINANCIAL AID PROCEDURES

Forms required: FAFSA.

Dates and Deadlines: Priority date 3/15; no closing date. Applicants notified on a rolling basis starting 4/10; must reply within 8 week(s) of notification.

Transfers: No aid available to transfer students who enroll for first time in summer school.

CONTACT

Donald Griggs, Director of Financial Assistance and Veterans Affairs
Office of Admissions and Adult Student Services, Charleston, SC 29424-0001
(843) 953-5540

Columbia College
Columbia, South Carolina
www.columbiasc.edu   Federal Code: 003430

4-year private liberal arts college for women in large city, affiliated with United Methodist Church.

Enrollment: 1,185 undergrads, 19% part-time. 285 full-time freshmen.

Selectivity: Admits 50 to 75% of applicants.

BASIC COSTS (2010-2011)

Tuition and fees: $24,060.

Per-credit charge: $635.

Room and board: $6,574.

FINANCIAL AID PICTURE (2008-2009)

Students with need: Out of 269 full-time freshmen who applied for aid, 250 were judged to have need. Of these, 250 received aid, and 60 had their full need met. Average financial aid package met 78% of need; average scholarship/grant was $18,434; average loan was $3,040. For part-time students, average financial aid package was $7,674.

Students without need: 32 full-time freshmen who did not demonstrate need for aid received scholarships/grants; average award was $13,005. No-need awards available for academics, alumni affiliation, art, athletics, leadership, music/drama.

Scholarships offered: _Merit:_ Founders Scholarship: full tuition. Presidential Scholarships: $10,000 annually. Trustees Scholarships: $8,000 annually. **_Athletic:_** 9 full-time freshmen received athletic scholarships; average amount $5,910.

Cumulative student debt: 95% of graduating class had student loans; average debt was $15,364.

FINANCIAL AID PROCEDURES

Forms required: FAFSA.

Dates and Deadlines: Priority date 4/1; no closing date. Applicants notified on a rolling basis starting 3/15; must reply within 2 week(s) of notification.

Transfers: Priority date 4/15. Must meet institutional standards of satisfactory academic progress.

CONTACT

Donna Quick, Director of Financial Aid
1301 Columbia College Drive, Columbia, SC 29203
(803) 786-3612

Columbia International University
Columbia, South Carolina
www.ciu.edu   Federal Code: 003429

4-year private university and Bible college in small city, affiliated with multidenominational/evangelical churches.

Enrollment: 505 undergrads, 6% part-time. 87 full-time freshmen.

Selectivity: Admits 50 to 75% of applicants.

BASIC COSTS (2010-2011)

Tuition and fees: $17,395.

Per-credit charge: $695.

Room and board: $6,410.

Additional info: Tuition/fee waivers available for minority students.

FINANCIAL AID PICTURE (2009-2010)

Students with need: Out of 63 full-time freshmen who applied for aid, 52 were judged to have need. Of these, 48 received aid. Average financial aid package met 49% of need; average scholarship/grant was $1,200; average loan was $1,900. For part-time students, average financial aid package was $1,000.

Students without need: 22 full-time freshmen who did not demonstrate need for aid received scholarships/grants; average award was $1,000. No-need awards available for academics, leadership, state/district residency.

Cumulative student debt: 52% of graduating class had student loans; average debt was $11,200.

Additional info: Spouse scholarship program; special short quarter scholarships for missionaries on furlough.

FINANCIAL AID PROCEDURES

Forms required: FAFSA, institutional form.

Dates and Deadlines: Priority date 1/31; no closing date. Applicants notified on a rolling basis starting 12/18; must reply within 4 week(s) of notification.

Transfers: FAFSA must be processed by June 30 for state need-based aid. State aid requires 1-year residency prior to award in most cases. Non-need-based state aid requires graduation from state high school.

CONTACT

Dan Griffin, Director of Student Financial Services
PO Box 3122, Columbia, SC 29230-3122
(803) 777-2227 ext. 5036

Converse College
Spartanburg, South Carolina
www.converse.edu   Federal Code: 003431

4-year private music and liberal arts and performing arts college for women in small city.

Enrollment: 720 undergrads, 18% part-time. 156 full-time freshmen.

Selectivity: Admits 50 to 75% of applicants.

BASIC COSTS (2010-2011)

Tuition and fees: $26,138.

Per-credit charge: $800.

Room and board: $8,032.

FINANCIAL AID PICTURE (2009-2010)

Students with need: Out of 156 full-time freshmen who applied for aid, 142 were judged to have need. Of these, 142 received aid, and 43 had their full need met. Average financial aid package met 86% of need; average scholarship/grant was $19,848; average loan was $4,526. For part-time students, average financial aid package was $6,289.

Students without need: 19 full-time freshmen who did not demonstrate need for aid received scholarships/grants; average award was $14,313. No-need awards available for academics, alumni affiliation, art, athletics, leadership, music/drama, ROTC, state/district residency.

Scholarships offered: 19 full-time freshmen received athletic scholarships; average amount $5,729.

Cumulative student debt: 61% of graduating class had student loans; average debt was $20,739.

FINANCIAL AID PROCEDURES

Forms required: FAFSA.

Dates and Deadlines: Closing date 3/15. Applicants notified on a rolling basis starting 3/1; must reply by 5/1 or within 2 week(s) of notification.

CONTACT

Margaret Collins, Director of Scholarships and Financial Assistance
580 East Main Street, Spartanburg, SC 29302-0006
(864) 596-9019

Denmark Technical College
Denmark, South Carolina
www.denmarktech.edu   Federal Code: 005363

2-year public technical college in small town.

Enrollment: 1,500 undergrads.

Selectivity: Open admission.

BASIC COSTS (2009-2010)

Tuition and fees: $2,484; out-of-state residents $5,130.

Room and board: $3,532.

FINANCIAL AID PICTURE

Students with need: Need-based aid available for full-time and part-time students.

FINANCIAL AID PROCEDURES

Forms required: FAFSA.

Dates and Deadlines: No deadline. Applicants notified on a rolling basis starting 6/1; must reply within 2 week(s) of notification.

CONTACT

Kelvin Bonnett, Assistant Director of Financial Aid
1126 Solomon Blatt Boulevard, Denmark, SC 29042
(803) 793-5161

Erskine College
Due West, South Carolina
www.erskine.edu   Federal Code: 003432

4-year private liberal arts and seminary college in rural community, affiliated with Associate Reformed Presbyterian Church.

Enrollment: 578 undergrads, 2% part-time. 182 full-time freshmen.

Selectivity: Admits 50 to 75% of applicants.

BASIC COSTS (2010-2011)

Tuition and fees: $26,475.

Per-credit charge: $917.

Room and board: $8,775.

FINANCIAL AID PICTURE (2008-2009)

Students with need: Need-based aid available for full-time and part-time students. Work study available nights, weekends, and for part-time students.

Students without need: No-need awards available for academics, alumni affiliation, art, athletics, leadership, minority status, music/drama, religious affiliation, state/district residency.

Additional info: Filing deadline 5/1 for institutional form, 6/30 for state form.

FINANCIAL AID PROCEDURES

Forms required: FAFSA, state aid form, institutional form.

Dates and Deadlines: Priority date 4/1; no closing date. Applicants notified on a rolling basis starting 12/15; must reply within 2 week(s) of notification.

Transfers: Closing date 5/1. South Carolina residents must have earned 24 hours in previous year to receive SC tuition grant and 30 hours plus 3.0 GPA to receive the Life Scholarship.

CONTACT

Allison Sullivan, Director of Financial Aid
PO Box 176, Due West, SC 29639-0176
(864) 379-8832

Florence-Darlington Technical College
Florence, South Carolina
www.fdtc.edu   Federal Code: 003990

2-year public community and technical college in small city.

Enrollment: 4,561 undergrads.

Selectivity: Open admission; but selective for some programs.

BASIC COSTS (2009-2010)

Tuition and fees: $3,267; out-of-district residents $3,529; out-of-state residents $5,363.

FINANCIAL AID PICTURE (2008-2009)
Students with need: Need-based aid available for full-time and part-time students.
Students without need: No-need awards available for academics.

FINANCIAL AID PROCEDURES
Forms required: FAFSA.
Dates and Deadlines: Priority date 5/1; no closing date. Applicants notified on a rolling basis starting 7/1; must reply within 2 week(s) of notification.

CONTACT
Joseph Durant, Director of Financial Assistance
PO Box 100548, Florence, SC 29501-0548
(843) 661-8085

Forrest Junior College
Anderson, South Carolina
www.forrestcollege.edu   Federal Code: 004924

2-year for-profit business and junior college in large town.
Enrollment: 93 undergrads, 39% part-time. 42 full-time freshmen.
Selectivity: Open admission; but selective for some programs.

BASIC COSTS (2009-2010)
Tuition and fees: $9,290.
Per-credit charge: $197.

FINANCIAL AID PICTURE (2009-2010)
Students with need: Need-based aid available for full-time and part-time students. Work study available nights, weekends, and for part-time students.
Students without need: This college awards aid only to students with need.

FINANCIAL AID PROCEDURES
Forms required: FAFSA.
Dates and Deadlines: No deadline. Applicants notified on a rolling basis starting 4/30; must reply by 5/31 or within 4 week(s) of notification.

CONTACT
Kathy Montgomery, Director of Financial Aid
601 East River Street, Anderson, SC 29624
(864) 225-7653

Francis Marion University
Florence, South Carolina
www.fmarion.edu   Federal Code: 009226

4-year public university and liberal arts college in small city.
Enrollment: 3,381 undergrads, 4% part-time. 791 full-time freshmen.
Selectivity: Admits 50 to 75% of applicants.

BASIC COSTS (2009-2010)
Tuition and fees: $7,960; out-of-state residents $15,585.
Per-credit charge: $381; out-of-state residents $763.
Room and board: $6,024.

FINANCIAL AID PICTURE (2009-2010)
Students with need: Need-based aid available for full-time and part-time students. Work study available nights, weekends, and for part-time students.
Students without need: No-need awards available for academics, music/drama.

FINANCIAL AID PROCEDURES
Forms required: FAFSA.
Dates and Deadlines: Priority date 3/1; no closing date. Applicants notified on a rolling basis starting 4/15.

Transfers: Institutional scholarships available after 1 semester completed in residence.

CONTACT
Kim Ellisor, Director of Financial Assistance
PO Box 100547, Florence, SC 29502-0547
(843) 661-1190

Furman University
Greenville, South Carolina   Federal Code: 003434
www.furman.edu   CSS Code: 5222

4-year private liberal arts college in small city.
Enrollment: 2,724 undergrads, 4% part-time. 655 full-time freshmen.
Selectivity: Admits 50 to 75% of applicants.

BASIC COSTS (2010-2011)
Tuition and fees: $38,088.
Per-credit charge: $1,179.
Room and board: $9,572.

FINANCIAL AID PICTURE (2009-2010)
Students with need: Out of 447 full-time freshmen who applied for aid, 348 were judged to have need. Of these, 348 received aid, and 150 had their full need met. Average financial aid package met 85% of need; average scholarship/grant was $26,737; average loan was $3,297. Need-based aid available for part-time students.
Students without need: 154 full-time freshmen who did not demonstrate need for aid received scholarships/grants; average award was $16,230. No-need awards available for academics, alumni affiliation, art, athletics, leadership, music/drama, religious affiliation, ROTC, state/district residency.
Scholarships offered: 69 full-time freshmen received athletic scholarships; average amount $33,011.
Cumulative student debt: 40% of graduating class had student loans; average debt was $27,373.
Additional info: 5-point comprehensive education financing plan includes financial aid packaging, money management counseling, debt management counseling, outside scholarship coordination, summer job-match program.

FINANCIAL AID PROCEDURES
Forms required: FAFSA, CSS PROFILE, state aid form, institutional form.
Dates and Deadlines: Closing date 1/15. Applicants notified by 3/15; must reply by 5/1.
Transfers: Closing date 6/1. For South Carolina Tuition Grant, must have earned 24 credits in previous year. For Life Scholarship, must have 3.0 cumulative GPA and 30 credits earned.

CONTACT
Forrest Stuart, Director of Financial Aid
3300 Poinsett Highway, Greenville, SC 29613
(864) 294-2204

Greenville Technical College
Greenville, South Carolina
www.gvltec.edu   Federal Code: 003991

2-year public community and technical college in large city.
Enrollment: 13,726 undergrads, 50% part-time. 642 full-time freshmen.
Selectivity: Open admission; but selective for some programs.

BASIC COSTS (2009-2010)
Tuition and fees: $3,492; out-of-district residents $3,780; out-of-state residents $7,116.

FINANCIAL AID PICTURE (2008-2009)
Students with need: 46% of average financial aid package awarded as scholarships/grants, 54% awarded as loans/jobs. Need-based aid available for part-time students. Work study available nights, weekends, and for part-time students.
Students without need: No-need awards available for academics, state/district residency.

FINANCIAL AID PROCEDURES
Forms required: FAFSA.
Dates and Deadlines: Priority date 5/1; no closing date. Applicants notified on a rolling basis starting 6/15; must reply within 2 week(s) of notification.
Transfers: No deadline. Applicants notified on a rolling basis starting 12/1; must reply within 2 week(s) of notification.

CONTACT
Janie Reid, Financial Aid Director
P.O. Box 5616, Greenville, SC 29606-5616
(864) 250-8128

Horry-Georgetown Technical College
Conway, South Carolina
www.hgtc.edu   Federal Code: 004925

2-year public community and technical college in large town.
Enrollment: 4,359 undergrads, 51% part-time. 457 full-time freshmen.
Selectivity: Open admission; but selective for some programs.

BASIC COSTS (2009-2010)
Tuition and fees: $3,206; out-of-district residents $4,038; out-of-state residents $5,046.

FINANCIAL AID PICTURE (2009-2010)
Students with need: 59% of average financial aid package awarded as scholarships/grants, 41% awarded as loans/jobs. Need-based aid available for part-time students.
Students without need: No-need awards available for academics, state/district residency.
Additional info: Participates in South Carolina lottery tuition assistance program. Full-time technical college students who are state residents receive assistance for tuition not covered by federal or need-based grants.

FINANCIAL AID PROCEDURES
Forms required: FAFSA.
Dates and Deadlines: Priority date 4/1; closing date 6/30. Applicants notified on a rolling basis starting 4/1.

CONTACT
Susan Thompson, Director of Financial Aid and Veterans Affairs
PO Box 261966, Conway, SC 29528-6066
(843) 349-5251

Lander University
Greenwood, South Carolina
www.lander.edu   Federal Code: 003435

4-year public liberal arts and teachers college in large town.
Enrollment: 2,760 undergrads, 6% part-time. 581 full-time freshmen.
Selectivity: Admits less than 50% of applicants.

BASIC COSTS (2009-2010)
Tuition and fees: $8,920; out-of-state residents $16,720.
Per-credit charge: $365; out-of-state residents $690.
Room and board: $6,842.

FINANCIAL AID PICTURE (2008-2009)
Students with need: Need-based aid available for full-time and part-time students. Work study available weekends and for part-time students.
Students without need: No-need awards available for academics, art, athletics, leadership, music/drama.

FINANCIAL AID PROCEDURES
Forms required: FAFSA.
Dates and Deadlines: Priority date 4/15; no closing date. Applicants notified on a rolling basis starting 4/15; must reply within 4 week(s) of notification.

CONTACT
Fred Hardin, Director of Financial Aid
Stanley Avenue, Greenwood, SC 29649-2099
(864) 388-8340

Limestone College
Gaffney, South Carolina
www.limestone.edu   Federal Code: 003436

4-year private liberal arts college in large town.
Enrollment: 805 undergrads, 1% part-time. 328 full-time freshmen.
Selectivity: Admits 50 to 75% of applicants.

BASIC COSTS (2010-2011)
Tuition and fees: $19,200.
Per-credit charge: $800.
Room and board: $7,000.

FINANCIAL AID PICTURE (2008-2009)
Students with need: Out of 328 full-time freshmen who applied for aid, 298 were judged to have need. Of these, 298 received aid, and 33 had their full need met. Average financial aid package met 52% of need; average scholarship/grant was $7,806; average loan was $2,773. For part-time students, average financial aid package was $15,336.
Students without need: 21 full-time freshmen who did not demonstrate need for aid received scholarships/grants; average award was $4,233. No-need awards available for academics, art, athletics, job skills, leadership, music/drama, religious affiliation, ROTC, state/district residency.
Scholarships offered: *Merit:* Presidential Scholarship: full tuition; SAT above 1300, GPA 3.5 or above; 1 available. Academic Dean Scholarships: partial tuition; based on academic achievement (GPA 3.0 or above). Founders Scholarships: partial tuition; GPA 2.75 or above. R.S. Campbell Scholarship: SAT above 1100, GPA 3.25 or above; 1 available. Leadership Scholarship: partial tuition; based on evidence of student leadership. Drada Hoover Scholarship: SAT 1200 or higher; GPA 3.5; top 10% of graduating class. SAT scores exclusive of Writing. *Athletic:* 23 full-time freshmen received athletic scholarships; average amount $4,561.
Cumulative student debt: 69% of graduating class had student loans; average debt was $20,701.

FINANCIAL AID PROCEDURES
Forms required: FAFSA.
Dates and Deadlines: Priority date 2/1; no closing date. Applicants notified on a rolling basis starting 1/15; must reply within 3 week(s) of notification.
Transfers: Priority date 5/1; no deadline. Applicants notified on a rolling basis; must reply within 3 week(s) of notification.

CONTACT
Bobby Greer, Director of Financial Aid
1115 College Drive, Gaffney, SC 29340-3799
(800) 795-7151 ext. 8231

Medical University of South Carolina
Charleston, South Carolina
www.musc.edu   Federal Code: 003438

Upper-division public university in large city.
Enrollment: 267 undergrads, 18% part-time.

BASIC COSTS (2009-2010)
Additional info: Tuition and fees for BS in nursing for in-state $13,168 out-of-state $22,776; BS in cardiovascular perfusion for in-state is $13,496 out-of-state $34,240; BS in health professions, in-state $13,526, out-of-state $35,258. Tuition/fee waivers available for adults, minority students.

FINANCIAL AID PICTURE (2008-2009)
Students with need: Average financial aid package for all full-time undergraduates was $15,109; for part-time $7,317. 27% awarded as scholarships/grants, 73% awarded as loans/jobs.
Students without need: No-need awards available for academics, alumni affiliation, minority status, state/district residency.

FINANCIAL AID PROCEDURES
Forms required: FAFSA, institutional form.
Dates and Deadlines: Priority date 3/10; no closing date. Applicants notified on a rolling basis starting 4/21.

CONTACT
Cecile Kamath, Director, Student Financial Aid
41 Bee Street, Charleston, SC 29425
(843) 792-2536

Midlands Technical College
Columbia, South Carolina
www.midlandstech.edu   Federal Code: 003993

2-year public technical college in large city.
Enrollment: 11,589 undergrads, 52% part-time. 1,674 full-time freshmen.
Selectivity: Open admission; but selective for some programs.

BASIC COSTS (2009-2010)
Tuition and fees: $3,608; out-of-district residents $4,472; out-of-state residents $10,424.

FINANCIAL AID PICTURE (2008-2009)
Students with need: Average financial aid package met 51% of need; average scholarship/grant was $3,582; average loan was $2,922. For part-time students, average financial aid package was $3,987.

FINANCIAL AID PROCEDURES
Forms required: FAFSA.
Dates and Deadlines: Priority date 4/15; no closing date. Applicants notified on a rolling basis; must reply within 2 week(s) of notification.

CONTACT
Michele Bowles, Director of Student Financial Services
PO Box 2408, Columbia, SC 29202
(803) 738-7792

Morris College
Sumter, South Carolina
www.morris.edu   Federal Code: 003439

4-year private liberal arts college in large town, affiliated with Baptist faith.
Enrollment: 966 undergrads, 1% part-time. 312 full-time freshmen.
Selectivity: Admits over 75% of applicants.

BASIC COSTS (2010-2011)
Tuition and fees: $10,140.
Per-credit charge: $417.
Room and board: $4,497.

FINANCIAL AID PICTURE (2008-2009)
Students with need: Out of 306 full-time freshmen who applied for aid, 306 were judged to have need. Of these, 306 received aid, and 15 had their full need met. Average financial aid package met 85% of need; average scholarship/grant was $9,500; average loan was $4,500. For part-time students, average financial aid package was $7,500.
Students without need: This college awards aid only to students with need.
Scholarships offered: Presidential Scholarship: $750-$2,500; rank in the first quarter of high school graduating class; larger awards available to salutatorians ($2,000) and valedictorians ($2,500); awards renewable up to 4 years if student maintains B average and excellent citizenship record. Luns C. Richardson Endowed Scholarship: $4,500; freshman student who has completed college prep curriculum with GPA of 3.5 or better, has exceptional letters of recommendation from at least 2 classroom teachers and one guidance counselor, principal, or assistant principal, and plans to enroll as full-time student for 4 consecutive years.
Cumulative student debt: 99% of graduating class had student loans; average debt was $20,000.

FINANCIAL AID PROCEDURES
Forms required: FAFSA, institutional form.
Dates and Deadlines: Priority date 3/30; no closing date. Applicants notified on a rolling basis starting 6/1; must reply within 2 week(s) of notification.
Transfers: Must reply within 2 week(s) of notification.

CONTACT
Sandra Gibson, Financial Aid Officer
100 West College Street, Sumter, SC 29150-3599
(803) 934-3238

Newberry College
Newberry, South Carolina
www.newberry.edu   Federal Code: 003440

4-year private liberal arts college in small city, affiliated with Evangelical Lutheran Church in America.
Enrollment: 1,098 undergrads, 1% part-time. 344 full-time freshmen.
Selectivity: Admits 50 to 75% of applicants.

BASIC COSTS (2009-2010)
Tuition and fees: $21,470.
Per-credit charge: $500.
Room and board: $7,750.

FINANCIAL AID PICTURE (2009-2010)
Students with need: Out of 318 full-time freshmen who applied for aid, 300 were judged to have need. Of these, 300 received aid, and 60 had their full need met. Average financial aid package met 75% of need; average scholarship/grant was $18,600; average loan was $3,468. For part-time students, average financial aid package was $7,699.
Students without need: 36 full-time freshmen who did not demonstrate need for aid received scholarships/grants; average award was $10,958. No-need awards available for academics, alumni affiliation, athletics, leadership, music/drama, religious affiliation, ROTC, state/district residency.
Scholarships offered: 15 full-time freshmen received athletic scholarships; average amount $6,890.
Cumulative student debt: 86% of graduating class had student loans; average debt was $30,693.

FINANCIAL AID PROCEDURES
Forms required: FAFSA, state aid form, institutional form.

Dates and Deadlines: Priority date 3/15; no closing date. Applicants notified on a rolling basis starting 3/1; must reply by 5/1 or within 2 week(s) of notification.
Transfers: No deadline. Applicants notified on a rolling basis.

CONTACT
Missy Lutz, Director of Financial Aid
2100 College Street, Newberry, SC 29108
(803) 321-5128

North Greenville University
Tigerville, South Carolina
www.ngu.edu   Federal Code: 003441

4-year private liberal arts college in rural community, affiliated with Southern Baptist Convention.
Enrollment: 1,953 undergrads, 3% part-time. 493 full-time freshmen.
Selectivity: Admits 50 to 75% of applicants.

BASIC COSTS (2010-2011)
Tuition and fees: $12,820.
Per-credit charge: $220.
Room and board: $7,510.

FINANCIAL AID PICTURE (2008-2009)
Students with need: 76% of average financial aid package awarded as scholarships/grants, 24% awarded as loans/jobs. Need-based aid available for part-time students.
Students without need: No-need awards available for academics, athletics, leadership, music/drama, religious affiliation, state/district residency.

FINANCIAL AID PROCEDURES
Forms required: FAFSA.
Dates and Deadlines: Priority date 6/1; closing date 6/30. Applicants notified on a rolling basis starting 8/1; must reply within 2 week(s) of notification.
Transfers: No deadline.

CONTACT
Mike Jordan, Director of Financial Aid
PO Box 1892, Tigerville, SC 29688-1892
(864) 977-7050

Orangeburg-Calhoun Technical College
Orangeburg, South Carolina
www.octech.edu   Federal Code: 006815

2-year public community and technical college in large town.
Enrollment: 2,300 undergrads.
Selectivity: Open admission; but selective for some programs.

BASIC COSTS (2009-2010)
Tuition and fees: $3,218; out-of-district residents $3,986; out-of-state residents $6,218.

FINANCIAL AID PICTURE
Students with need: Need-based aid available for full-time and part-time students.
Students without need: This college awards aid only to students with need.
Scholarships offered: College Foundation Scholarship: full academic tuition; for high school valedictorians and salutatorians.

FINANCIAL AID PROCEDURES
Forms required: FAFSA, institutional form.
Dates and Deadlines: Priority date 6/4; no closing date. Applicants notified on a rolling basis starting 5/1; must reply within 2 week(s) of notification.

Transfers: Priority date 6/1. Financial aid transcripts required of mid-year transfers prior to disbursement of aid.

CONTACT
Bobbie Felder, Director of Institutional Research
3250 St. Matthews Road, Orangeburg, SC 29118-8222
(803) 535-1249

Presbyterian College
Clinton, South Carolina
www.presby.edu   Federal Code: 003445

4-year private liberal arts college in small town, affiliated with Presbyterian Church (USA).
Enrollment: 1,200 undergrads, 1% part-time. 364 full-time freshmen.
Selectivity: Admits 50 to 75% of applicants.

BASIC COSTS (2010-2011)
Tuition and fees: $30,450.
Per-credit charge: $1,150.
Room and board: $8,670.

FINANCIAL AID PICTURE (2009-2010)
Students with need: Out of 314 full-time freshmen who applied for aid, 264 were judged to have need. Of these, 264 received aid, and 139 had their full need met. Average financial aid package met 91% of need; average scholarship/grant was $29,691; average loan was $3,384. For part-time students, average financial aid package was $7,159.
Students without need: 83 full-time freshmen who did not demonstrate need for aid received scholarships/grants; average award was $14,937. No-need awards available for academics, alumni affiliation, athletics, job skills, leadership, minority status, music/drama, religious affiliation, ROTC.
Scholarships offered: *Merit:* Academic and leadership scholarships, applications by December 5; number and amounts awarded vary; music awards based on audition. *Athletic:* 40 full-time freshmen received athletic scholarships; average amount $20,353.
Cumulative student debt: 56% of graduating class had student loans; average debt was $23,391.

FINANCIAL AID PROCEDURES
Forms required: FAFSA.
Dates and Deadlines: Priority date 3/15; closing date 6/30. Applicants notified by 3/1; must reply by 5/1.
Transfers: No deadline. Applicants notified on a rolling basis; must reply within 1 week(s) of notification.

CONTACT
Jeffrey Holliday, Director of Financial Aid
503 South Broad Street, Clinton, SC 29325
(864) 833-8290

South Carolina State University
Orangeburg, South Carolina
www.scsu.edu   Federal Code: 003446

4-year public university in large town.
Enrollment: 3,831 undergrads, 7% part-time. 713 full-time freshmen.
Selectivity: Admits over 75% of applicants.

BASIC COSTS (2009-2010)
Tuition and fees: $8,462; out-of-state residents $16,626.
Per-credit charge: $353; out-of-state residents $693.
Room and board: $8,662.

FINANCIAL AID PICTURE (2008-2009)
Students with need: Need-based aid available for full-time students.

Students without need: No-need awards available for academics, athletics, ROTC.

FINANCIAL AID PROCEDURES

Forms required: FAFSA.

Dates and Deadlines: Closing date 5/1. Applicants notified on a rolling basis starting 4/15; must reply by 7/1 or within 2 week(s) of notification.

Transfers: Must reply by 7/1 or within 2 week(s) of notification. Must provide documentation on amount of state aid received, and which semesters it was received, prior to transfer.

CONTACT

Sandra Davis, Director of Financial Aid
300 College Street NE, Orangeburg, SC 29117
(803) 536-7067

South University: Columbia

Columbia, South Carolina
www.southuniversity.edu   Federal Code: 004922

4-year for-profit university in small city.

Enrollment: 1,006 undergrads, 37% part-time. 65 full-time freshmen.

Selectivity: Open admission; but selective for some programs.

BASIC COSTS (2009-2010)

Tuition and fees: $14,985.

FINANCIAL AID PICTURE

Students with need: Need-based aid available for full-time and part-time students.

Students without need: This college awards aid only to students with need.

FINANCIAL AID PROCEDURES

Forms required: FAFSA.

Dates and Deadlines: Priority date 5/30; no closing date. Applicants notified on a rolling basis starting 5/30.

CONTACT

Walter Haversat, Financial Aid Director
9 Science Court, Columbia, SC 29203
(803) 799-9082

Southern Wesleyan University

Central, South Carolina
www.swu.edu   Federal Code: 003422

4-year private university and liberal arts college in small town, affiliated with Wesleyan Church.

Enrollment: 1,692 undergrads, 1% part-time. 163 full-time freshmen.

BASIC COSTS (2010-2011)

Tuition and fees: $19,500.
Per-credit charge: $755.
Room and board: $8,150.

FINANCIAL AID PICTURE (2009-2010)

Students with need: Out of 162 full-time freshmen who applied for aid, 154 were judged to have need. Of these, 153 received aid, and 32 had their full need met. Average financial aid package met 81% of need; average scholarship/grant was $15,065; average loan was $3,106. For part-time students, average financial aid package was $6,935.

Students without need: 9 full-time freshmen who did not demonstrate need for aid received scholarships/grants; average award was $6,833. No-need awards available for academics, athletics, music/drama.

Scholarships offered: 8 full-time freshmen received athletic scholarships; average amount $5,375.

FINANCIAL AID PROCEDURES

Forms required: FAFSA, institutional form.

Dates and Deadlines: Priority date 3/31; closing date 6/30. Applicants notified on a rolling basis starting 2/1; must reply within 2 week(s) of notification.

Transfers: Priority date 4/1. Applicants notified on a rolling basis starting 2/1; must reply within 2 week(s) of notification.

CONTACT

Kim Jenerette, Financial Aid Director
PO Box 1020, Central, SC 29630-1020
(800) 289-1292

Spartanburg Community College

Spartanburg, South Carolina
www.sccsc.edu   Federal Code: 003994

2-year public community and technical college in small city.

Enrollment: 5,226 undergrads.

Selectivity: Open admission; but selective for some programs.

BASIC COSTS (2009-2010)

Tuition and fees: $3,434; out-of-district residents $4,282; out-of-state residents $7,196.

Per-credit charge: $142; out-of-district residents $177; out-of-state residents $299.

FINANCIAL AID PICTURE (2008-2009)

Students with need: 75% of average financial aid package awarded as scholarships/grants, 25% awarded as loans/jobs. Need-based aid available for part-time students.

Additional info: Participates in South Carolina lottery tuition assistance program. Full-time technical college students who are state residents receive assistance for tuition not covered by federal or need-based grants.

FINANCIAL AID PROCEDURES

Forms required: FAFSA.

Dates and Deadlines: Priority date 2/28; closing date 5/1. Applicants notified on a rolling basis starting 5/1.

Transfers: No deadline. Applicants notified on a rolling basis starting 8/15.

CONTACT

Nancy Garmroth, Director of Financial Aid
Box 4386, Spartanburg, SC 29305-4386
(864) 592-4810

Spartanburg Methodist College

Spartanburg, South Carolina
www.smcsc.edu   Federal Code: 003447

2-year private junior and liberal arts college in small city, affiliated with United Methodist Church.

Enrollment: 788 undergrads, 2% part-time. 451 full-time freshmen.

Selectivity: Admits 50 to 75% of applicants.

BASIC COSTS (2009-2010)

Tuition and fees: $12,888.
Per-credit charge: $344.
Room and board: $7,048.

Additional info: Tuition/fee waivers available for adults, unemployed or children of unemployed.

FINANCIAL AID PICTURE (2009-2010)

Students with need: Out of 451 full-time freshmen who applied for aid, 433 were judged to have need. Of these, 433 received aid, and 194 had their full need met. Average financial aid package met 73% of need; average scholarship/grant was $1,236; average loan was $3,318. For part-time students, average financial aid package was $644.

Students without need: 225 full-time freshmen who did not demonstrate need for aid received scholarships/grants; average award was $1,522. No-need awards available for academics, athletics, job skills, leadership, music/drama, religious affiliation, state/district residency.

Scholarships offered: *Merit:* Milliken Scholars: $4,100. Camak Scholars: $3,500. Trustee Scholars: $3,000. Presidential Scholars: $2,400. *Athletic:* 90 full-time freshmen received athletic scholarships; average amount $818.

Cumulative student debt: 71% of graduating class had student loans; average debt was $8,312.

FINANCIAL AID PROCEDURES

Forms required: FAFSA.

Dates and Deadlines: Priority date 6/30; closing date 8/22. Applicants notified on a rolling basis starting 3/1; must reply within 2 week(s) of notification.

Transfers: No deadline. Applicants notified on a rolling basis starting 3/1; must reply within 2 week(s) of notification. To be eligible for financial aid, full time students must pass the equivalent of 12 hours.

CONTACT

Kendra Burnette, Director of Financial Aid
1000 Powell Mill Road, Spartanburg, SC 29301-5899
(864) 587-4298

Technical College of the Lowcountry
Beaufort, South Carolina
www.tcl.edu   Federal Code: 009910

2-year public community and technical college in small town.

Enrollment: 1,610 undergrads.

Selectivity: Open admission; but selective for some programs.

BASIC COSTS (2009-2010)

Tuition and fees: $3,382; out-of-state residents $7,436.

FINANCIAL AID PICTURE

Students with need: Need-based aid available for full-time and part-time students.

Students without need: This college awards aid only to students with need.

Additional info: State lottery aid may be available to South Carolina residents who take 6 credit hours or more.

FINANCIAL AID PROCEDURES

Forms required: FAFSA.

Dates and Deadlines: No deadline.

CONTACT

Cleo Martin, Coordinator of Financial Aid
921 South Ribaut Road, Beaufort, SC 29901-1288
(843) 525-8337

Tri-County Technical College
Pendleton, South Carolina
www.tctc.edu   Federal Code: 004926

2-year public community and technical college in small town.

Enrollment: 6,758 undergrads.

Selectivity: Open admission; but selective for some programs.

BASIC COSTS (2009-2010)

Tuition and fees: $3,168; out-of-district residents $3,504; out-of-state residents $7,032.

FINANCIAL AID PICTURE

Students with need: Need-based aid available for full-time and part-time students. Work study available nights.

Students without need: No-need awards available for academics, state/district residency.

Scholarships offered: General and departmental scholarships: more than 125 awarded; some with special qualification criteria, such as student's career field or place of residency.

Additional info: Deadline for application to institutional scholarships April 2.

FINANCIAL AID PROCEDURES

Forms required: FAFSA.

Dates and Deadlines: Priority date 3/31; closing date 8/2. Applicants notified on a rolling basis starting 6/15; must reply within 2 week(s) of notification.

Transfers: Priority date 5/1; no deadline. Applicants notified on a rolling basis starting 6/1.

CONTACT

Bill Whitlock, Director of Financial Aid
Box 587, Pendleton, SC 29670
(864) 646-1650

Trident Technical College
Charleston, South Carolina
www.tridenttech.edu   Federal Code: 004920

2-year public community and technical college in large city.

Enrollment: 13,519 undergrads, 50% part-time. 2,030 full-time freshmen.

Selectivity: Open admission; but selective for some programs.

BASIC COSTS (2009-2010)

Tuition and fees: $3,450; out-of-district residents $3,828; out-of-state residents $6,532.

FINANCIAL AID PICTURE (2009-2010)

Students with need: Need-based aid available for full-time and part-time students. Work study available nights, weekends, and for part-time students.

FINANCIAL AID PROCEDURES

Forms required: FAFSA.

Dates and Deadlines: No deadline. Applicants notified on a rolling basis; must reply within 6 week(s) of notification.

Transfers: No deadline. Applicants notified on a rolling basis; must reply within 6 week(s) of notification.

CONTACT

Ellen Green, Director of Financial Aid/Veterans Assistance
Box 118067, AM-M, Charleston, SC 29423-8067
(843) 574-6147

University of South Carolina
Columbia, South Carolina
www.sc.edu   Federal Code: 003448

4-year public university in small city.

Enrollment: 20,135 undergrads, 6% part-time. 3,797 full-time freshmen.

Selectivity: Admits 50 to 75% of applicants.

BASIC COSTS (2009-2010)

Tuition and fees: $9,156; out-of-state residents $23,732.

Per-credit charge: $410; out-of-state residents $1,065.

Room and board: $6,986.

Additional info: Health professions (pharmacy, health, nursing), law and medical professions have higher undergraduate and graduate fees.

FINANCIAL AID PICTURE (2009-2010)

Students with need: Out of 2,699 full-time freshmen who applied for aid, 1,560 were judged to have need. Of these, 1,539 received aid, and 449 had their full need met. Average financial aid package met 75% of need; average scholarship/grant was $4,650; average loan was $2,703. For part-time students, average financial aid package was $8,329.

Students without need: 1,729 full-time freshmen who did not demonstrate need for aid received scholarships/grants; average award was $6,382. No-need awards available for academics, alumni affiliation, art, athletics, job skills, leadership, minority status, music/drama, religious affiliation, ROTC, state/district residency.

Scholarships offered: 122 full-time freshmen received athletic scholarships; average amount $9,423.

Cumulative student debt: 46% of graduating class had student loans; average debt was $21,755.

FINANCIAL AID PROCEDURES

Forms required: FAFSA.

Dates and Deadlines: Priority date 4/1; no closing date. Applicants notified on a rolling basis starting 4/1.

Transfers: Applicants notified on a rolling basis starting 4/1.

CONTACT

Edgar Miller, Director of Financial Aid and Scholarships
Office of Undergraduate Admissions, Columbia, SC 29208
(803) 777-8134

University of South Carolina at Aiken

Aiken, South Carolina
web.usca.edu   Federal Code: 003449

4-year public university and liberal arts college in large town.
Enrollment: 2,919 undergrads, 16% part-time. 559 full-time freshmen.
Selectivity: Admits less than 50% of applicants.

BASIC COSTS (2009-2010)

Tuition and fees: $7,950; out-of-state residents $15,682.
Per-credit charge: $334; out-of-state residents $663.
Room and board: $6,400.

FINANCIAL AID PICTURE (2008-2009)

Students with need: Out of 540 full-time freshmen who applied for aid, 352 were judged to have need. Of these, 352 received aid, and 71 had their full need met. Average financial aid package met 74% of need; average scholarship/grant was $7,871; average loan was $3,170. For part-time students, average financial aid package was $5,838.

Students without need: 162 full-time freshmen who did not demonstrate need for aid received scholarships/grants; average award was $5,035. No-need awards available for academics, alumni affiliation, art, athletics, leadership, minority status, music/drama, state/district residency.

Scholarships offered: 18 full-time freshmen received athletic scholarships; average amount $2,041.

FINANCIAL AID PROCEDURES

Forms required: FAFSA.
Dates and Deadlines: Priority date 3/15; no closing date. Applicants notified on a rolling basis starting 11/1; must reply within 2 week(s) of notification.
Transfers: Financial aid transcripts from previous institutions required.

CONTACT

Glenn Shumpert, Director of Financial Aid
471 University Parkway, Aiken, SC 29801-6399
(803) 641-3476

University of South Carolina at Beaufort

Bluffton, South Carolina
www.uscb.edu   Federal Code: 003450

4-year public university and liberal arts college in large town.
Enrollment: 1,319 undergrads, 23% part-time. 360 full-time freshmen.

BASIC COSTS (2009-2010)

Tuition and fees: $7,330; out-of-state residents $15,180.
Per-credit charge: $288; out-of-state residents $615.
Room and board: $6,100.

FINANCIAL AID PICTURE (2009-2010)

Students with need: Need-based aid available for full-time and part-time students. Work study available nights, weekends, and for part-time students.
Students without need: No-need awards available for academics, state/district residency.

FINANCIAL AID PROCEDURES

Forms required: FAFSA.
Dates and Deadlines: Priority date 4/15; no closing date. Applicants notified on a rolling basis starting 5/31; must reply within 2 week(s) of notification.

CONTACT

Patricia Greene, Director and VA Coordinator of Financial Aid
One University Boulevard, Bluffton, SC 29909
(843) 521-3104

University of South Carolina at Sumter

Sumter, South Carolina
www.uscsumter.edu   Federal Code: 003426

2-year public branch campus college in small city.
Enrollment: 872 undergrads.

BASIC COSTS (2009-2010)

Tuition and fees: $5,528; out-of-state residents $13,304.
Per-credit charge: $214; out-of-state residents $538.

FINANCIAL AID PICTURE (2009-2010)

Students with need: Need-based aid available for full-time and part-time students. Work study available nights, weekends, and for part-time students.
Students without need: This college awards aid only to students with need.

FINANCIAL AID PROCEDURES

Forms required: FAFSA.
Dates and Deadlines: Priority date 4/15; no closing date. Applicants notified on a rolling basis starting 4/16; must reply within 2 week(s) of notification.

CONTACT

Sue Sims, Financial Aid Director
200 Miller Road, Sumter, SC 29150-2498
(803) 938-3766

University of South Carolina at Union

Union, South Carolina
uscunion.sc.edu   Federal Code: 004927

2-year public branch campus and liberal arts college in small town.
Enrollment: 350 undergrads.

BASIC COSTS (2009-2010)

Tuition and fees: $5,528; out-of-state residents $13,304.
Per-credit charge: $214; out-of-state residents $538.

FINANCIAL AID PICTURE

Students with need: Work study available nights, weekends, and for part-time students.

Students without need: This college awards aid only to students with need.

FINANCIAL AID PROCEDURES

Forms required: FAFSA.

Dates and Deadlines: Priority date 4/15; no closing date. Applicants notified on a rolling basis starting 7/15; must reply within 2 week(s) of notification.

CONTACT

Bobby Holcombe, Financial Aid Director
PO Drawer 729, Union, SC 29379
(864) 429-8728

University of South Carolina Upstate

Spartanburg, South Carolina
www.uscupstate.edu   Federal Code: 006951

4-year public university in small city.

Enrollment: 5,001 undergrads, 11% part-time. 708 full-time freshmen.

Selectivity: Admits over 75% of applicants.

BASIC COSTS (2009-2010)

Tuition and fees: $8,812; out-of-state residents $17,454.

Per-credit charge: $357; out-of-state residents $723.

Room and board: $6,580.

FINANCIAL AID PICTURE (2008-2009)

Students with need: Out of 571 full-time freshmen who applied for aid, 449 were judged to have need. Of these, 446 received aid, and 89 had their full need met. Average financial aid package met 65% of need; average scholarship/grant was $4,475; average loan was $3,049. For part-time students, average financial aid package was $5,339.

Students without need: 16 full-time freshmen who did not demonstrate need for aid received scholarships/grants; average award was $2,023. No-need awards available for academics, athletics, minority status, ROTC, state/district residency.

Scholarships offered: 40 full-time freshmen received athletic scholarships; average amount $9,928.

Cumulative student debt: 67% of graduating class had student loans; average debt was $21,699.

Additional info: Out-of-state students who are recipients of financial aid may qualify for out-of-state fee waiver. Educational benefits available to veterans and children of deceased/disabled veterans.

FINANCIAL AID PROCEDURES

Forms required: FAFSA, institutional form.

Dates and Deadlines: Priority date 3/1; closing date 7/15. Applicants notified on a rolling basis starting 5/1; must reply within 2 week(s) of notification.

Transfers: Students eligible for financial assistance for total of 5 years or 10 full-time semesters at all post-secondary institutions attended for the bachelor's degree, and 5 full-time semesters of enrollment for associate's degree in nursing.

CONTACT

Kim Jenerette, Director of Financial Aid and Scholarships
800 University Way, Spartanburg, SC 29303
(864) 503-5340

University of South Carolina: Salkehatchie Regional Campus

Allendale, South Carolina
uscsalkehatchie.sc.edu   Federal Code: 003454

2-year public branch campus college in rural community.

Enrollment: 800 undergrads.

BASIC COSTS (2009-2010)

Tuition and fees: $5,528; out-of-state residents $13,304.

Per-credit charge: $214; out-of-state residents $538.

FINANCIAL AID PICTURE (2008-2009)

Students with need: Need-based aid available for full-time and part-time students. Work study available nights, weekends, and for part-time students.

Students without need: No-need awards available for academics.

FINANCIAL AID PROCEDURES

Forms required: FAFSA.

Dates and Deadlines: Priority date 4/30; no closing date. Applicants notified on a rolling basis starting 6/1.

CONTACT

Julie Hadwin, Director of Financial Aid
PO Box 617, Allendale, SC 29810
(803) 584-3446

Williamsburg Technical College

Kingstree, South Carolina
www.wiltech.edu   Federal Code: 009322

2-year public community and technical college in small town.

Enrollment: 683 undergrads, 47% part-time. 144 full-time freshmen.

Selectivity: Open admission.

BASIC COSTS (2009-2010)

Tuition and fees: $3,042; out-of-district residents $3,162; out-of-state residents $5,850.

FINANCIAL AID PICTURE

Students with need: Need-based aid available for full-time and part-time students. Work study available nights, weekends, and for part-time students.

Students without need: No-need awards available for academics, leadership, minority status, state/district residency.

Additional info: Tuition waivers for children of war veterans.

FINANCIAL AID PROCEDURES

Forms required: FAFSA.

Dates and Deadlines: Priority date 4/15; no closing date. Applicants notified on a rolling basis starting 7/1; must reply within 4 week(s) of notification.

CONTACT

Jean Boos, Director of Financial Aid
601 Martin Luther King Jr. Avenue, Kingstree, SC 29556-4197
(843) 355-4166

Winthrop University

Rock Hill, South Carolina
www.winthrop.edu   Federal Code: 003456

4-year public university in small city.

Enrollment: 4,770 undergrads, 7% part-time. 1,075 full-time freshmen.

Selectivity: Admits 50 to 75% of applicants.

BASIC COSTS (2009-2010)
Tuition and fees: $11,586; out-of-state residents $21,576.
Per-credit charge: $484; out-of-state residents $900.
Room and board: $6,530.

FINANCIAL AID PICTURE (2008-2009)
Students with need: Out of 897 full-time freshmen who applied for aid, 683 were judged to have need. Of these, 680 received aid, and 182 had their full need met. Average financial aid package met 72% of need; average scholarship/grant was $8,347; average loan was $3,391. For part-time students, average financial aid package was $4,956.
Students without need: 64 full-time freshmen who did not demonstrate need for aid received scholarships/grants; average award was $5,460. No-need awards available for academics, art, athletics, leadership, music/drama.
Scholarships offered: 40 full-time freshmen received athletic scholarships; average amount $7,381.
Cumulative student debt: 70% of graduating class had student loans; average debt was $21,600.
Additional info: Academic scholarships from $1,500 to full tuition and board awarded to approximately one-third of entering freshman class each year.

FINANCIAL AID PROCEDURES
Forms required: FAFSA.
Dates and Deadlines: Priority date 3/1; no closing date. Applicants notified on a rolling basis starting 3/15; must reply within 4 week(s) of notification.
Transfers: Transfer students are not eligible for academic scholarship their first year.

CONTACT
Betty Whalen, Director, Office of Financial Aid
701 Oakland Avenue, Rock Hill, SC 29733
(803) 323-2189

Wofford College
Spartanburg, South Carolina
www.wofford.edu   Federal Code: 003457

4-year private liberal arts college in small city, affiliated with United Methodist Church.
Enrollment: 1,429 undergrads, 1% part-time. 392 full-time freshmen.
Selectivity: Admits 50 to 75% of applicants.

BASIC COSTS (2010-2011)
Tuition and fees: $31,710.
Room and board: $8,870.

FINANCIAL AID PICTURE (2009-2010)
Students with need: Out of 300 full-time freshmen who applied for aid, 223 were judged to have need. Of these, 222 received aid, and 108 had their full need met. Average financial aid package met 88% of need; average scholarship/grant was $26,184; average loan was $3,016. For part-time students, average financial aid package was $9,828.
Students without need: 99 full-time freshmen who did not demonstrate need for aid received scholarships/grants; average award was $14,219. No-need awards available for academics, athletics, leadership, music/drama, religious affiliation, ROTC, state/district residency.
Scholarships offered: 37 full-time freshmen received athletic scholarships; average amount $14,478.
Cumulative student debt: 45% of graduating class had student loans; average debt was $22,199.

FINANCIAL AID PROCEDURES
Forms required: FAFSA.
Dates and Deadlines: Closing date 3/15. Applicants notified on a rolling basis starting 4/1; must reply by 5/1.

CONTACT
Kay Walton, Director of Financial Aid
429 North Church Street, Spartanburg, SC 29303-3663
(864) 597-4149

York Technical College
Rock Hill, South Carolina
www.yorktech.com   Federal Code: 003996

2-year public community and technical college in large town.
Enrollment: 5,093 undergrads.
Selectivity: Open admission; but selective for some programs.

BASIC COSTS (2009-2010)
Tuition and fees: $3,352; out-of-district residents $3,664; out-of-state residents $7,528.

FINANCIAL AID PICTURE (2008-2009)
Students with need: Need-based aid available for full-time and part-time students. Work study available nights.
Students without need: No-need awards available for academics, leadership, state/district residency.

FINANCIAL AID PROCEDURES
Forms required: FAFSA.
Dates and Deadlines: Closing date 6/1. Applicants notified on a rolling basis starting 3/1.
Transfers: No deadline. Applicants notified on a rolling basis starting 3/1.

CONTACT
Angela Fowler, Financial Aid Department Manager
452 South Anderson Road, Rock Hill, SC 29730
(803) 327-8005

South Dakota

Augustana College
Sioux Falls, South Dakota
www.augie.edu   Federal Code: 003458

4-year private liberal arts college in small city, affiliated with Evangelical Lutheran Church in America.
Enrollment: 1,771 undergrads, 6% part-time. 431 full-time freshmen.
Selectivity: Admits over 75% of applicants.

BASIC COSTS (2010-2011)
Tuition and fees: $25,104.
Per-credit charge: $375.
Room and board: $6,260.
Additional info: Tuition/fee waivers available for minority students.

FINANCIAL AID PICTURE (2009-2010)
Students with need: Need-based aid available for full-time and part-time students. Work study available nights, weekends, and for part-time students.
Students without need: No-need awards available for academics, alumni affiliation, art, athletics, leadership, minority status, music/drama, religious affiliation, state/district residency.
Scholarships offered: Distinguished Scholars Scholarships: Trustees and Presidential Scholarships for students with a 27 ACT or above and 3.5 GPA and above; ProMusica scholarships, ProDramatis scholarships, ProArtis Scholarships; Fryxell Scholarships for journalism/English majors;.

FINANCIAL AID PROCEDURES
Forms required: FAFSA.

Dates and Deadlines: Priority date 3/1; no closing date. Applicants notified on a rolling basis starting 3/15; must reply within 3 week(s) of notification.
Transfers: No deadline. Applicants notified on a rolling basis starting 4/1; must reply within 3 week(s) of notification.

CONTACT
Brenda Murtha, Director of Financial Aid
2001 South Summit Avenue, Sioux Falls, SD 57197-9990
(605) 274-5216

Black Hills State University
Spearfish, South Dakota
www.bhsu.edu   Federal Code: 003459

4-year public liberal arts and teachers college in large town.
Enrollment: 3,225 undergrads, 22% part-time. 551 full-time freshmen.
Selectivity: Admits over 75% of applicants.

BASIC COSTS (2009-2010)
Tuition and fees: $6,227; out-of-state residents $7,600.
Per-credit charge: $92; out-of-state residents $137.
Room and board: $5,524.
Additional info: Reciprocity agreements reduce tuition for some out-of-state students .

FINANCIAL AID PICTURE (2008-2009)
Students with need: Need-based aid available for full-time and part-time students.
Students without need: This college awards aid only to students with need.

FINANCIAL AID PROCEDURES
Forms required: FAFSA.
Dates and Deadlines: Closing date 2/15. Applicants notified on a rolling basis starting 5/15; must reply within 3 week(s) of notification.

CONTACT
Deb Henriksen, Director of Financial Aid
1200 University Street Box 9502, Spearfish, SD 57799-9502
(605) 642-6581

Dakota State University
Madison, South Dakota
www.dsu.edu   Federal Code: 003463

4-year public university in small town.
Enrollment: 1,450 undergrads. 258 full-time freshmen.
Selectivity: Admits over 75% of applicants.

BASIC COSTS (2009-2010)
Tuition and fees: $6,872; out-of-state residents $8,245.
Per-credit charge: $92; out-of-state residents $137.
Room and board: $4,890.
Additional info: Reciprocity agreements reduce tuition for some out-of-state students.

FINANCIAL AID PICTURE (2008-2009)
Students with need: Out of 228 full-time freshmen who applied for aid, 168 were judged to have need. Of these, 168 received aid, and 22 had their full need met. Average financial aid package met 80% of need; average scholarship/grant was $3,957; average loan was $3,283. For part-time students, average financial aid package was $5,678.
Students without need: 29 full-time freshmen who did not demonstrate need for aid received scholarships/grants; average award was $3,268. No-need awards available for academics, alumni affiliation, art, athletics, leadership, minority status, music/drama, state/district residency.

Scholarships offered: 35 full-time freshmen received athletic scholarships; average amount $1,411.
Cumulative student debt: 92% of graduating class had student loans; average debt was $21,189.
Additional info: Application deadline for grants and scholarships March 1. No deadline for loan and job applications.

FINANCIAL AID PROCEDURES
Forms required: FAFSA.
Dates and Deadlines: Priority date 3/1; no closing date. Applicants notified on a rolling basis starting 4/1; must reply within 2 week(s) of notification.
Transfers: No deadline. Applicants notified on a rolling basis starting 4/1; must reply within 2 week(s) of notification.

CONTACT
Denise Grayson, Financial Aid Director
820 North Washington Avenue, Madison, SD 57042
(605) 256-5152

Dakota Wesleyan University
Mitchell, South Dakota
www.dwu.edu   Federal Code: 003461

4-year private university and liberal arts college in large town, affiliated with United Methodist Church.
Enrollment: 724 undergrads, 6% part-time. 168 full-time freshmen.
Selectivity: Admits over 75% of applicants.

BASIC COSTS (2009-2010)
Tuition and fees: $19,000.
Per-credit charge: $410.
Room and board: $5,870.

FINANCIAL AID PICTURE (2009-2010)
Students with need: Out of 159 full-time freshmen who applied for aid, 141 were judged to have need. Of these, 141 received aid, and 28 had their full need met. Average financial aid package met 66% of need; average scholarship/grant was $10,600; average loan was $3,300. For part-time students, average financial aid package was $8,600.
Students without need: 12 full-time freshmen who did not demonstrate need for aid received scholarships/grants; average award was $8,200. No-need awards available for academics, alumni affiliation, art, athletics, leadership, minority status, music/drama, religious affiliation.
Scholarships offered: 3 full-time freshmen received athletic scholarships; average amount $3,500.
Cumulative student debt: 67% of graduating class had student loans; average debt was $30,000.

FINANCIAL AID PROCEDURES
Forms required: FAFSA.
Dates and Deadlines: Priority date 4/15; no closing date. Applicants notified on a rolling basis starting 3/1; must reply within 2 week(s) of notification.
Transfers: No deadline. Applicants notified on a rolling basis; must reply within 2 week(s) of notification.

CONTACT
Kristy O'Kief, Director of Financial Aid
1200 West University Avenue, Mitchell, SD 57301-4398
(605) 995-2650

Kilian Community College
Sioux Falls, South Dakota
www.kilian.edu   Federal Code: 015000

2-year private community college in small city.
Enrollment: 304 undergrads, 79% part-time. 25 full-time freshmen.

Selectivity: Open admission.

BASIC COSTS (2010-2011)
Tuition and fees: $7,960.
Per-credit charge: $252.

FINANCIAL AID PICTURE (2008-2009)
Students with need: Out of 21 full-time freshmen who applied for aid, 21 were judged to have need. Of these, 21 received aid. Need-based aid available for part-time students.
Students without need: No-need awards available for academics, leadership, minority status.
Cumulative student debt: 90% of graduating class had student loans; average debt was $2,517.

FINANCIAL AID PROCEDURES
Forms required: FAFSA, institutional form.
Dates and Deadlines: No deadline. Applicants notified on a rolling basis starting 7/1; must reply within 2 week(s) of notification.
Transfers: No deadline. Applicants notified on a rolling basis starting 7/1; must reply within 2 week(s) of notification.

CONTACT
Patti Klinkhammer, Director of Financial Aid
300 East 6th Street, Sioux Falls, SD 57103-7020
(605) 221-3100

Lake Area Technical Institute
Watertown, South Dakota
www.lakeareatech.edu   Federal Code: 005309

2-year public technical college in large town.
Enrollment: 1,300 undergrads.
Selectivity: Open admission; but selective for some programs.

BASIC COSTS (2009-2010)
Additional info: Approximate program costs $4,000 - $7,000 per year, depending on course of study; includes tuition, books and supplies.

FINANCIAL AID PICTURE
Students with need: Need-based aid available for full-time and part-time students.
Students without need: This college awards aid only to students with need.

FINANCIAL AID PROCEDURES
Forms required: FAFSA.
Dates and Deadlines: Priority date 4/15; no closing date. Applicants notified on a rolling basis starting 5/1.

CONTACT
Marlene Seeklander, Financial Aid Director
PO Box 730, Watertown, SD 57201
(605) 882-5284

Mitchell Technical Institute
Mitchell, South Dakota
www.mitchelltech.edu   Federal Code: 008284

2-year public culinary school and technical college in large town.
Enrollment: 876 undergrads, 4% part-time. 418 full-time freshmen.
Selectivity: Admits 50 to 75% of applicants.

BASIC COSTS (2010-2011)
Tuition and fees: $4,900.

FINANCIAL AID PICTURE (2008-2009)
Students with need: Need-based aid available for full-time and part-time students.

FINANCIAL AID PROCEDURES
Forms required: FAFSA.
Dates and Deadlines: No deadline. Applicants notified on a rolling basis; must reply within 3 week(s) of notification.

CONTACT
Grant Uecker, Financial Aid Coordinator
821 North Capital Street, Mitchell, SD 57301
(605) 995-3052

Mount Marty College
Yankton, South Dakota
www.mtmc.edu   Federal Code: 003465

4-year private liberal arts college in large town, affiliated with Roman Catholic Church.
Enrollment: 833 undergrads, 26% part-time. 148 full-time freshmen.
Selectivity: Admits over 75% of applicants.

BASIC COSTS (2010-2011)
Tuition and fees: $19,932.
Per-credit charge: $6,557.
Room and board: $5,636.

FINANCIAL AID PICTURE (2009-2010)
Students with need: Need-based aid available for full-time and part-time students. Work study available nights, weekends, and for part-time students.
Students without need: No-need awards available for academics, art, athletics, leadership, music/drama, religious affiliation.
Additional info: Prestige scholarships application deadline 2/1.

FINANCIAL AID PROCEDURES
Forms required: FAFSA, institutional form.
Dates and Deadlines: Priority date 3/1; no closing date. Applicants notified on a rolling basis starting 3/15; must reply within 2 week(s) of notification.
Transfers: No deadline. Applicants notified on a rolling basis; must reply within 2 week(s) of notification.

CONTACT
Kenneth Kocer, Director of Financial Assistance
1105 West Eighth Street, Yankton, SD 57078
(605) 668-1589

National American University: Rapid City
Rapid City, South Dakota
www.national.edu   Federal Code: 004057

4-year for-profit business and technical college in small city.
Enrollment: 1,413 undergrads.
Selectivity: Open admission; but selective for some programs.

BASIC COSTS (2009-2010)
Additional info: Tuition/fee waivers available for unemployed or children of unemployed.

FINANCIAL AID PICTURE
Students with need: Need-based aid available for full-time and part-time students. Work study available nights, weekends, and for part-time students.
Students without need: This college awards aid only to students with need.

FINANCIAL AID PROCEDURES
Forms required: FAFSA, institutional form.

Dates and Deadlines: No deadline. Applicants notified on a rolling basis; must reply within 4 week(s) of notification.

CONTACT

Cheryl Bullinger, Director of Financial Aid
321 Kansas City Street, Rapid City, SD 57701

Northern State University
Aberdeen, South Dakota
www.northern.edu   Federal Code: 003466

4-year public university and liberal arts college in large town.
Enrollment: 1,667 undergrads, 16% part-time. 318 full-time freshmen.
Selectivity: Admits over 75% of applicants.

BASIC COSTS (2009-2010)
Tuition and fees: $6,063; out-of-state residents $7,436.
Per-credit charge: $92; out-of-state residents $137.
Room and board: $4,875.
Additional info: Reciprocity agreements reduce tuition for some out-of-state students.

FINANCIAL AID PICTURE (2008-2009)
Students with need: 32% of average financial aid package awarded as scholarships/grants, 68% awarded as loans/jobs. Need-based aid available for part-time students. Work study available nights, weekends, and for part-time students.
Students without need: No-need awards available for academics, art, athletics, leadership, minority status, music/drama, state/district residency.

FINANCIAL AID PROCEDURES
Forms required: FAFSA.
Dates and Deadlines: Priority date 3/1; no closing date. Applicants notified on a rolling basis starting 5/1; must reply within 2 week(s) of notification.
Transfers: Applicants notified by 4/15; must reply within 2 week(s) of notification. Financial aid transcript(s) required from all schools previously attended.

CONTACT

Sharon Kienow, Director of Student Financial Assistance
1200 South Jay Street, Aberdeen, SD 57401-7198
(605) 626-2640

Presentation College
Aberdeen, South Dakota
www.presentation.edu   Federal Code: 003467

4-year private business and health science college in large town, affiliated with Roman Catholic Church.
Enrollment: 614 undergrads.

BASIC COSTS (2009-2010)
Tuition and fees: $14,250.
Per-credit charge: $525.
Room and board: $5,500.

FINANCIAL AID PICTURE (2009-2010)
Students with need: Need-based aid available for full-time and part-time students. Work study available nights, weekends, and for part-time students.

FINANCIAL AID PROCEDURES
Forms required: FAFSA.
Dates and Deadlines: Priority date 4/1; no closing date. Applicants notified on a rolling basis starting 5/1; must reply within 2 week(s) of notification.

CONTACT

Val Weisser, Financial Aid Director
1500 North Main Street, Aberdeen, SD 57401
(605) 229-8429

Sinte Gleska University
Mission, South Dakota
www.sintegleska.edu   Federal Code: 014303

4-year public university and liberal arts college in rural community.
Enrollment: 848 undergrads.
Selectivity: Open admission.

BASIC COSTS (2009-2010)
Tuition and fees: $3,590.
Per-credit charge: $110.

FINANCIAL AID PICTURE
Students with need: Need-based aid available for full-time and part-time students.

FINANCIAL AID PROCEDURES
Forms required: FAFSA.
Dates and Deadlines: No deadline.

CONTACT

William Hay, Director of Financial Aid
Box 105, Mission, SD 57555

South Dakota School of Mines and Technology
Rapid City, South Dakota
www.sdsmt.edu   Federal Code: 003470

4-year public university in small city.
Enrollment: 1,632 undergrads, 9% part-time. 361 full-time freshmen.
Selectivity: Admits over 75% of applicants.

BASIC COSTS (2009-2010)
Tuition and fees: $6,830; out-of-state residents $8,210.
Per-credit charge: $92; out-of-state residents $137.
Room and board: $4,602.
Additional info: Reciprocity agreements reduce tuition for some out-of-state students.

FINANCIAL AID PICTURE (2009-2010)
Students with need: Out of 348 full-time freshmen who applied for aid, 207 were judged to have need. Of these, 207 received aid, and 40 had their full need met. Average financial aid package met 70% of need; average scholarship/grant was $4,290; average loan was $3,018. For part-time students, average financial aid package was $7,097.
Students without need: 106 full-time freshmen who did not demonstrate need for aid received scholarships/grants; average award was $2,675. No-need awards available for academics, athletics, leadership, ROTC.
Scholarships offered: *Merit:* Presidential Scholarship: $1,000 to $4,000; 5 awarded. Surbeck Scholars: $7,000; 2 awarded. All based on ACT/SAT scores, high school GPA, and class rank. Number of awards may vary from year to year depending on availability of funding. *Athletic:* 15 full-time freshmen received athletic scholarships; average amount $3,467.
Additional info: Closing date for scholarship applications February 1.

FINANCIAL AID PROCEDURES
Forms required: FAFSA.
Dates and Deadlines: Priority date 3/15; no closing date. Applicants notified on a rolling basis starting 5/1; must reply within 3 week(s) of notification.

CONTACT
David Martin, Director of Financial Aid
501 East St. Joseph Street, Rapid City, SD 57701
(605) 394-2274

South Dakota State University
Brookings, South Dakota
www.sdstate.edu   Federal Code: 003471

4-year public university in large town.
Enrollment: 9,786 undergrads, 13% part-time. 2,048 full-time freshmen.
Selectivity: Admits over 75% of applicants.

BASIC COSTS (2009-2010)
Tuition and fees: $6,155; out-of-state residents $7,528.
Per-credit charge: $92; out-of-state residents $137.
Room and board: $5,668.
Additional info: Reduced out-of-state tuition for Minnesota students.

FINANCIAL AID PICTURE (2009-2010)
Students with need: Need-based aid available for full-time and part-time students. Work study available nights, weekends, and for part-time students.
Students without need: No-need awards available for academics, art, athletics, job skills, leadership, minority status, music/drama, ROTC, state/district residency.
Scholarships offered: Academic scholarships for first-year freshmen: $500-$7,000; based on academic performance in high school; 1,420 awarded. Minimum academic scholarship for new first-year students: $1,000; based on ACT 24+; renewable.

FINANCIAL AID PROCEDURES
Forms required: FAFSA.
Dates and Deadlines: Priority date 3/11; no closing date. Applicants notified on a rolling basis starting 4/1; must reply within 3 week(s) of notification.
Transfers: No deadline. Applicants notified on a rolling basis starting 4/1; must reply within 3 week(s) of notification.

CONTACT
Jay Larsen, Director of Financial Aid
Box 2201 SAD 200, Brookings, SD 57007-0649
(605) 688-4695

Southeast Technical Institute
Sioux Falls, South Dakota
www.southeasttech.edu   Federal Code: 008285

2-year public technical college in small city.
Enrollment: 2,464 undergrads, 20% part-time. 670 full-time freshmen.
Selectivity: Open admission; but selective for some programs.

BASIC COSTS (2009-2010)
Tuition and fees: $4,237.
Per-credit charge: $84.
Additional info: $1,380 laptop fee required for some students.

FINANCIAL AID PICTURE
Students with need: Need-based aid available for full-time and part-time students.
Students without need: This college awards aid only to students with need.

FINANCIAL AID PROCEDURES
Forms required: FAFSA.
Dates and Deadlines: Priority date 5/1; no closing date. Applicants notified on a rolling basis starting 5/1; must reply within 3 week(s) of notification.

CONTACT
Lynette Grabowska, Financial Aid Officer
2320 North Career Avenue, Sioux Falls, SD 57107
(605) 367-7867

University of Sioux Falls
Sioux Falls, South Dakota
www.usiouxfalls.edu   Federal Code: 003469

4-year private university and liberal arts college in small city, affiliated with American Baptist Churches in the USA.
Enrollment: 1,197 undergrads, 15% part-time. 272 full-time freshmen.
Selectivity: Admits over 75% of applicants.

BASIC COSTS (2010-2011)
Tuition and fees: $21,895.
Per-credit charge: $280.
Room and board: $6,330.
Additional info: Tuition/fee waivers available for adults.

FINANCIAL AID PICTURE (2008-2009)
Students with need: Need-based aid available for full-time and part-time students. Work study available nights, weekends, and for part-time students.
Students without need: No-need awards available for academics, alumni affiliation, art, athletics, job skills, leadership, music/drama, religious affiliation, state/district residency.

FINANCIAL AID PROCEDURES
Forms required: FAFSA.
Dates and Deadlines: Priority date 3/1; no closing date. Applicants notified on a rolling basis starting 3/1; must reply within 2 week(s) of notification.

CONTACT
Laura Olson, Director of Financial Aid
1101 West 22nd Street, Sioux Falls, SD 57105-1699
(605) 331-6623

University of South Dakota
Vermillion, South Dakota
www.usd.edu   Federal Code: 003474

4-year public university in large town.
Enrollment: 6,043 undergrads, 28% part-time. 964 full-time freshmen.
Selectivity: Admits over 75% of applicants.

BASIC COSTS (2009-2010)
Tuition and fees: $6,468; out-of-state residents $7,841.
Per-credit charge: $92; out-of-state residents $137.
Room and board: $5,787.
Additional info: Reciprocity agreement in place for Minnesota residents. Reduced tuition for Iowa residents.

FINANCIAL AID PICTURE (2008-2009)
Students with need: Average financial aid package met 75% of need; average scholarship/grant was $4,176; average loan was $3,360. For part-time students, average financial aid package was $6,236.
Students without need: No-need awards available for academics, art, athletics, leadership, minority status, music/drama, ROTC.

FINANCIAL AID PROCEDURES
Forms required: FAFSA.
Dates and Deadlines: Priority date 3/15; no closing date. Applicants notified on a rolling basis starting 5/5.

CONTACT

Julie Pier, Director of Student Financial Aid
414 East Clark Street, Vermillion, SD 57069-2390
(605) 677-5446

Western Dakota Technical Institute

Rapid City, South Dakota
www.wdt.edu   Federal Code: 010170

2-year public technical college in small city.
Enrollment: 1,139 undergrads.
Selectivity: Open admission; but selective for some programs.

BASIC COSTS (2009-2010)

Tuition and fees: $4,320.
Per-credit charge: $84.
Additional info: Total program cost ranges from $5,766 - $21,838 depending on course of study.

FINANCIAL AID PICTURE

Students with need: Need-based aid available for full-time and part-time students. Work study available nights, weekends, and for part-time students.

FINANCIAL AID PROCEDURES

Forms required: FAFSA.
Dates and Deadlines: Priority date 4/20; no closing date. Applicants notified on a rolling basis starting 6/30; must reply within 2 week(s) of notification.

CONTACT

Starla Russell, Manager of Financial Aid
800 Mickelson Drive, Rapid City, SD 57703
(605) 394-4034

Tennessee

Aquinas College

Nashville, Tennessee
www.aquinascollege.edu   Federal Code: 003477

4-year private nursing and liberal arts college in very large city, affiliated with Roman Catholic Church.
Enrollment: 858 undergrads. 29 full-time freshmen.
Selectivity: Admits less than 50% of applicants.

BASIC COSTS (2010-2011)

Tuition and fees: $18,330.
Per-credit charge: $591.

FINANCIAL AID PICTURE (2008-2009)

Students with need: Need-based aid available for full-time and part-time students. Work study available nights.
Students without need: No-need awards available for academics, alumni affiliation, leadership, religious affiliation.

FINANCIAL AID PROCEDURES

Forms required: FAFSA.
Dates and Deadlines: Priority date 3/1; no closing date. Applicants notified on a rolling basis starting 3/1; must reply within 2 week(s) of notification.
Transfers: No deadline. Applicants notified on a rolling basis; must reply within 2 week(s) of notification.

CONTACT

Kylie Pruitt, Director of Financial Aid
4210 Harding Road, Nashville, TN 37205-2086
(615) 297-7545 ext. 442

Austin Peay State University

Clarksville, Tennessee
www.apsu.edu   Federal Code: 003478

4-year public university and liberal arts college in small city.
Enrollment: 9,084 undergrads, 23% part-time. 1,326 full-time freshmen.
Selectivity: Admits over 75% of applicants.

BASIC COSTS (2009-2010)

Tuition and fees: $5,868; out-of-state residents $17,946.
Per-credit charge: $191; out-of-state residents $688.
Room and board: $6,120.

FINANCIAL AID PICTURE (2008-2009)

Students with need: Out of 1,254 full-time freshmen who applied for aid, 974 were judged to have need. Of these, 971 received aid. For part-time students, average financial aid package was $6,411.
Students without need: 236 full-time freshmen who did not demonstrate need for aid received scholarships/grants; average award was $4,694. No-need awards available for academics, art, athletics, leadership, music/drama, ROTC, state/district residency.
Scholarships offered: 37 full-time freshmen received athletic scholarships; average amount $8,152.
Cumulative student debt: 56% of graduating class had student loans; average debt was $20,158.

FINANCIAL AID PROCEDURES

Forms required: FAFSA.
Dates and Deadlines: Priority date 4/1; no closing date. Applicants notified on a rolling basis starting 5/1.

CONTACT

Donna Price, Director of Financial Aid
PO Box 4548, Clarksville, TN 37044
(931) 221-7907

Baptist College of Health Sciences

Memphis, Tennessee
www.bchs.edu   Federal Code: 034403

4-year private health science and nursing college in very large city, affiliated with Baptist faith.
Enrollment: 1,018 undergrads, 45% part-time. 55 full-time freshmen.
Selectivity: Admits less than 50% of applicants. GED not accepted.

BASIC COSTS (2009-2010)

Tuition and fees: $9,730.
Per-credit charge: $296.

FINANCIAL AID PICTURE (2008-2009)

Students with need: 41% of average financial aid package awarded as scholarships/grants, 59% awarded as loans/jobs.

CONTACT

Leanne Smith, Vice President of Business and Financial Services
1003 Monroe Avenue, Memphis, TN 38104
(901) 572-2446

Belmont University

Nashville, Tennessee
www.belmont.edu   Federal Code: 003479

4-year private university in very large city.
Enrollment: 4,339 undergrads, 7% part-time. 932 full-time freshmen.
Selectivity: Admits over 75% of applicants.

BASIC COSTS (2010-2011)
Tuition and fees: $23,680.
Per-credit charge: $865.
Room and board: $9,030.

FINANCIAL AID PICTURE (2008-2009)
Students with need: Out of 859 full-time freshmen who applied for aid, 464 were judged to have need. Of these, 450 received aid, and 112 had their full need met. Average financial aid package met 89% of need; average scholarship/grant was $5,175; average loan was $3,524. For part-time students, average financial aid package was $4,770.
Students without need: 242 full-time freshmen who did not demonstrate need for aid received scholarships/grants; average award was $5,839. No-need awards available for academics, art, athletics, leadership, music/drama, religious affiliation, state/district residency.
Scholarships offered: 46 full-time freshmen received athletic scholarships; average amount $17,204.
Cumulative student debt: 57% of graduating class had student loans; average debt was $29,268.

FINANCIAL AID PROCEDURES
Forms required: FAFSA.
Dates and Deadlines: Priority date 3/1; no closing date. Applicants notified on a rolling basis starting 3/15; must reply by 5/1 or within 2 week(s) of notification.
Transfers: Applicants notified on a rolling basis starting 3/1; must reply by 5/1 or within 2 week(s) of notification. Scholarships available.

CONTACT
Paula Gill, Director of Student Financial Services
1900 Belmont Boulevard, Nashville, TN 37212-3757
(615) 460-6403

Bethel University
McKenzie, Tennessee
www.bethelu.edu
Federal Code: 003480

4-year private university and liberal arts college in small town, affiliated with Presbyterian Church (USA).
Enrollment: 2,550 undergrads, 1% part-time. 352 full-time freshmen.
Selectivity: Admits 50 to 75% of applicants.

BASIC COSTS (2010-2011)
Tuition and fees: $12,938.
Per-credit charge: $393.
Room and board: $7,272.

FINANCIAL AID PICTURE (2009-2010)
Students with need: 55% of average financial aid package awarded as scholarships/grants, 45% awarded as loans/jobs. Need-based aid available for part-time students. Work study available nights, weekends, and for part-time students.
Students without need: No-need awards available for academics, athletics, music/drama, religious affiliation, state/district residency.

FINANCIAL AID PROCEDURES
Forms required: FAFSA, institutional form.
Dates and Deadlines: Priority date 3/3; closing date 6/30. Applicants notified on a rolling basis starting 3/1.
Transfers: Financial aid transcripts from previously attended institutions required.

CONTACT
Laura Bateman, Director of Financial Aid
325 Cherry Avenue, McKenzie, TN 38201
(731) 352-4021

Bryan College
Dayton, Tennessee
www.bryan.edu
Federal Code: 003536

4-year private liberal arts college in small town, affiliated with interdenominational tradition.
Enrollment: 1,011 undergrads, 4% part-time. 190 full-time freshmen.
Selectivity: Admits 50 to 75% of applicants.

BASIC COSTS (2010-2011)
Tuition and fees: $18,620.
Per-credit charge: $775.
Room and board: $5,454.
Additional info: Tuition/fee waivers available for adults, minority students, unemployed or children of unemployed.

FINANCIAL AID PICTURE (2009-2010)
Students with need: Out of 174 full-time freshmen who applied for aid, 151 were judged to have need. Of these, 150 received aid, and 99 had their full need met. Average financial aid package met 81% of need; average scholarship/grant was $11,374; average loan was $2,919. For part-time students, average financial aid package was $7,410.
Students without need: 35 full-time freshmen who did not demonstrate need for aid received scholarships/grants; average award was $5,307. No-need awards available for academics, alumni affiliation, art, athletics, job skills, leadership, music/drama.
Scholarships offered: 13 full-time freshmen received athletic scholarships; average amount $6,699.
Cumulative student debt: 74% of graduating class had student loans; average debt was $14,976.

FINANCIAL AID PROCEDURES
Forms required: FAFSA.
Dates and Deadlines: Priority date 2/15; no closing date. Applicants notified on a rolling basis starting 1/1; must reply within 2 week(s) of notification.

CONTACT
Rick Taphorn, Director of Financial Aid
PO Box 7000, Dayton, TN 37321-7000
(423) 775-7339

Carson-Newman College
Jefferson City, Tennessee
www.cn.edu
Federal Code: 003481

4-year private liberal arts college in small town, affiliated with Southern Baptist Convention.
Enrollment: 1,887 undergrads, 7% part-time. 513 full-time freshmen.
Selectivity: Admits 50 to 75% of applicants.

BASIC COSTS (2010-2011)
Tuition and fees: $20,562.
Per-credit charge: $818.
Room and board: $5,918.
Additional info: Tuition/fee waivers available for adults, minority students.

FINANCIAL AID PICTURE (2009-2010)
Students with need: Need-based aid available for full-time and part-time students. Work study available nights, weekends, and for part-time students.
Students without need: No-need awards available for academics, art, athletics, leadership, minority status, music/drama, religious affiliation, ROTC.

FINANCIAL AID PROCEDURES
Forms required: FAFSA, institutional form.
Dates and Deadlines: Priority date 4/1; no closing date. Applicants notified on a rolling basis starting 2/1; must reply within 2 week(s) of notification.

CONTACT

Danette Seale, Director of Financial Aid

1646 Russell Avenue, Jefferson City, TN 37760

(865) 471-3247

Chattanooga State Community College

Chattanooga, Tennessee

www.chattanoogastate.edu   Federal Code: 003998

2-year public community and technical college in small city.

Enrollment: 7,717 undergrads.

Selectivity: Open admission; but selective for some programs.

BASIC COSTS (2009-2010)

Tuition and fees: $2,991; out-of-state residents $11,475.

Per-credit charge: $111; out-of-state residents $460.

FINANCIAL AID PICTURE (2009-2010)

Students with need: Need-based aid available for full-time and part-time students. Work study available nights, weekends, and for part-time students.

Students without need: No-need awards available for state/district residency.

FINANCIAL AID PROCEDURES

Forms required: FAFSA.

Dates and Deadlines: Priority date 4/1; no closing date. Applicants notified on a rolling basis starting 4/1; must reply within 2 week(s) of notification.

CONTACT

Jeanne Hinchee, Director of Financial Aid

4501 Amnicola Highway, Chattanooga, TN 37406

(423) 697-4402

Christian Brothers University

Memphis, Tennessee

www.cbu.edu   Federal Code: 003482

4-year private university in very large city, affiliated with Roman Catholic Church.

Enrollment: 1,413 undergrads, 11% part-time. 297 full-time freshmen.

Selectivity: Admits less than 50% of applicants.

BASIC COSTS (2010-2011)

Tuition and fees: $24,870.

Per-credit charge: $870.

Room and board: $6,490.

Additional info: Tuition/fee waivers available for adults.

FINANCIAL AID PICTURE (2009-2010)

Students with need: Out of 280 full-time freshmen who applied for aid, 235 were judged to have need. Of these, 235 received aid, and 67 had their full need met. Average financial aid package met 89% of need; average scholarship/grant was $7,388; average loan was $3,285. For part-time students, average financial aid package was $7,146.

Students without need: 45 full-time freshmen who did not demonstrate need for aid received scholarships/grants; average award was $10,162. No-need awards available for academics, alumni affiliation, athletics, music/drama, state/district residency.

Scholarships offered: 47 full-time freshmen received athletic scholarships; average amount $8,835.

Additional info: ROTC scholarships available to qualified applicants.

FINANCIAL AID PROCEDURES

Forms required: FAFSA.

Dates and Deadlines: Priority date 2/15; no closing date. Applicants notified on a rolling basis starting 3/1; must reply within 2 week(s) of notification.

CONTACT

Jim Shannon, Director of Student Financial Resources

650 East Parkway South, Memphis, TN 38104-5519

(901) 321-3305

Cleveland State Community College

Cleveland, Tennessee

www.clevelandstatecc.edu   Federal Code: 003999

2-year public community college in small city.

Enrollment: 2,357 undergrads, 34% part-time. 632 full-time freshmen.

Selectivity: Open admission; but selective for some programs.

BASIC COSTS (2009-2010)

Tuition and fees: $2,969; out-of-state residents $11,453.

Per-credit charge: $111; out-of-state residents $460.

FINANCIAL AID PICTURE (2009-2010)

Students with need: Average financial aid package met 77% of need; average scholarship/grant was $4,247; average loan was $2,679. For part-time students, average financial aid package was $3,640.

Students without need: No-need awards available for athletics, minority status.

FINANCIAL AID PROCEDURES

Forms required: FAFSA, institutional form.

Dates and Deadlines: Priority date 6/15; no closing date. Applicants notified on a rolling basis starting 7/1; must reply within 2 week(s) of notification.

Transfers: Priority date 5/15.

CONTACT

Geraldine Parks, Director of Financial Aid

3535 Adkisson Drive, Cleveland, TN 37320-3570

(423) 478-6215

Columbia State Community College

Columbia, Tennessee

www.columbiastate.edu   Federal Code: 003483

2-year public community college in large town.

Enrollment: 4,893 undergrads.

Selectivity: Open admission; but selective for some programs.

BASIC COSTS (2009-2010)

Tuition and fees: $2,947; out-of-state residents $11,431.

Per-credit charge: $111; out-of-state residents $460.

FINANCIAL AID PICTURE

Students with need: Need-based aid available for full-time and part-time students.

Students without need: No-need awards available for academics, athletics, state/district residency.

FINANCIAL AID PROCEDURES

Forms required: FAFSA, institutional form.

Dates and Deadlines: Closing date 8/1. Applicants notified on a rolling basis starting 5/15; must reply within 2 week(s) of notification.

CONTACT

Pauletta Burns, Director of Financial Assistance

1665 Hampshire Pike, Columbia, TN 38401

(931) 540-2583

Crichton College
Memphis, Tennessee
www.crichton.edu   Federal Code: 009982

4-year private liberal arts college in very large city, affiliated with nondenominational tradition.
Enrollment: 673 undergrads, 28% part-time. 10 full-time freshmen.

BASIC COSTS (2010-2011)
Tuition and fees: $10,620.
Per-credit charge: $335.

FINANCIAL AID PICTURE (2009-2010)
Students with need: For part-time students, average financial aid package was $7,520.

FINANCIAL AID PROCEDURES
Forms required: FAFSA.
Dates and Deadlines: Priority date 2/15; no closing date. Applicants notified on a rolling basis starting 3/1; must reply within 2 week(s) of notification.
Transfers: No deadline. Applicants notified on a rolling basis; must reply within 2 week(s) of notification.

CONTACT
LaTonya Branch, Director of Student Finance
255 North Highland, Memphis, TN 38111-1375
(901) 320-9787

Cumberland University
Lebanon, Tennessee
www.cumberland.edu   Federal Code: 003485

4-year private university and liberal arts college in large town.
Enrollment: 990 undergrads, 9% part-time. 200 full-time freshmen.
Selectivity: Admits 50 to 75% of applicants.

BASIC COSTS (2009-2010)
Tuition and fees: $17,430.
Per-credit charge: $690.
Room and board: $6,350.

FINANCIAL AID PICTURE (2009-2010)
Students with need: Need-based aid available for full-time and part-time students.
Students without need: No-need awards available for academics, art, athletics, music/drama.

FINANCIAL AID PROCEDURES
Forms required: FAFSA, institutional form.
Dates and Deadlines: Priority date 2/1; no closing date. Applicants notified on a rolling basis starting 5/1; must reply within 2 week(s) of notification.
Transfers: Priority date 2/15. Applicants notified on a rolling basis starting 5/1.

CONTACT
Judy Jordan, Vice President of Fiscal Affairs
One Cumberland Square, Lebanon, TN 37087
(615) 444-2562 ext. 1222

Draughons Junior College: Nashville
Nashville, Tennessee
www.daymarinstitute.edu   Federal Code: 004934

2-year for-profit career college in very large city.
Enrollment: 216 undergrads.
Selectivity: Open admission; but selective for some programs.

BASIC COSTS (2010-2011)
Tuition and fees: $12,960.

FINANCIAL AID PICTURE
Students with need: Need-based aid available for full-time and part-time students. Work study available nights.
Students without need: This college awards aid only to students with need.
Additional info: Financial aid form for in-state applicants must be filed before 5/1.

FINANCIAL AID PROCEDURES
Forms required: FAFSA.
Dates and Deadlines: No deadline. Applicants notified on a rolling basis.
Transfers: Students must notify Tennessee Student Assistance Corporation of institutional change before appropriate deadlines.

CONTACT
Janie Rager, Director of Financial Services
340 & 283 Plus Park at Pavilion Boulevard, Nashville, TN 37217
(615) 361-7555

Dyersburg State Community College
Dyersburg, Tennessee
www.dscc.edu   Federal Code: 006835

2-year public community college in large town.
Enrollment: 2,800 undergrads, 45% part-time. 487 full-time freshmen.
Selectivity: Open admission; but selective for some programs.

BASIC COSTS (2009-2010)
Tuition and fees: $2,971; out-of-state residents $11,455.
Per-credit charge: $111; out-of-state residents $460.

FINANCIAL AID PICTURE (2008-2009)
Students with need: Need-based aid available for full-time and part-time students. Work study available nights.
Students without need: No-need awards available for academics, alumni affiliation, athletics, job skills, leadership, minority status, music/drama, state/district residency.

FINANCIAL AID PROCEDURES
Forms required: FAFSA.
Dates and Deadlines: Priority date 3/1; no closing date. Applicants notified on a rolling basis starting 3/1; must reply within 2 week(s) of notification.

CONTACT
Sandra Rockett, Director of Financial Aid
1510 Lake Road, Dyersburg, TN 38024
(731) 286-3238

East Tennessee State University
Johnson City, Tennessee
www.etsu.edu   Federal Code: 003487

4-year public university in small city.
Enrollment: 11,286 undergrads, 13% part-time. 2,068 full-time freshmen.
Selectivity: Admits over 75% of applicants.

BASIC COSTS (2009-2010)
Tuition and fees: $5,588; out-of-state residents $17,666.
Per-credit charge: $191; out-of-state residents $688.
Room and board: $5,500.

FINANCIAL AiD PICTURE (2008-2009)

Students with need: 54% of average financial aid package awarded as scholarships/grants, 46% awarded as loans/jobs. Need-based aid available for part-time students. Work study available nights, weekends, and for part-time students.

Students without need: No-need awards available for academics, alumni affiliation, art, athletics, job skills, leadership, minority status, music/drama, religious affiliation, ROTC, state/district residency.

Additional info: Housing costs payable by installment.

FINANCIAL AID PROCEDURES

Forms required: FAFSA.

Dates and Deadlines: Priority date 4/15; no closing date. Applicants notified on a rolling basis starting 4/15; must reply within 3 week(s) of notification.

CONTACT

Margaret Miller, Director of Financial Aid
ETSU Box 70731, Johnson City, TN 37614
(423) 439-4300

Fisk University
Nashville, Tennessee
www.fisk.edu   Federal Code: 003490

4-year private liberal arts college in very large city, affiliated with United Church of Christ.

Enrollment: 593 undergrads, 5% part-time. 95 full-time freshmen.

Selectivity: Admits 50 to 75% of applicants.

BASIC COSTS (2010-2011)

Tuition and fees: $18,358.

Per-credit charge: $702.

Room and board: $8,586.

FINANCIAL AID PICTURE (2009-2010)

Students with need: Out of 95 full-time freshmen who applied for aid, 95 were judged to have need. Of these, 86 received aid, and 13 had their full need met. Average financial aid package met 54% of need; average scholarship/grant was $13,688; average loan was $2,310. For part-time students, average financial aid package was $8,716.

Students without need: This college awards aid only to students with need.

Cumulative student debt: 54% of graduating class had student loans; average debt was $19,370.

FINANCIAL AID PROCEDURES

Forms required: FAFSA.

Dates and Deadlines: Priority date 3/1; closing date 7/1. Applicants notified on a rolling basis starting 4/1; must reply within 2 week(s) of notification.

CONTACT

Russelle Keese, Director of Financial Aid
1000 17th Avenue North, Nashville, TN 37208-3051
(615) 329-8585

Free Will Baptist Bible College
Nashville, Tennessee
www.fwbbc.edu   Federal Code: 030018

4-year private Bible and teachers college in very large city, affiliated with Free Will Baptists.

Enrollment: 283 undergrads, 19% part-time. 53 full-time freshmen.

Selectivity: Open admission.

BASIC COSTS (2009-2010)

Tuition and fees: $13,534.

Per-credit charge: $423.

Room and board: $5,700.

FINANCIAL AID PICTURE (2008-2009)

Students with need: 47% of average financial aid package awarded as scholarships/grants, 53% awarded as loans/jobs. Need-based aid available for part-time students. Work study available nights, weekends, and for part-time students.

Students without need: No-need awards available for academics, art, music/drama.

Scholarships offered: Presidential Honors Scholarship: $1,000 per semester, renewable for 8 semesters; high school GPA 3.5+, and ACT 29+, must maintain college GPA 3.25; awarded to four students yearly.

FINANCIAL AID PROCEDURES

Forms required: FAFSA, institutional form.

Dates and Deadlines: Priority date 4/15; no closing date. Applicants notified on a rolling basis starting 7/1; must reply within 2 week(s) of notification.

Transfers: No deadline.

CONTACT

Jeff Caudill, Director of Enrollment Services
3606 West End Avenue, Nashville, TN 37205-2403
(615) 844-5000 ext. 5249

Freed-Hardeman University
Henderson, Tennessee
www.fhu.edu   Federal Code: 003492

4-year private university and liberal arts college in small town, affiliated with Church of Christ.

Enrollment: 1,461 undergrads, 4% part-time. 408 full-time freshmen.

Selectivity: Admits over 75% of applicants.

BASIC COSTS (2009-2010)

Tuition and fees: $14,300.

Per-credit charge: $402.

Room and board: $7,090.

Additional info: Tuition/fee waivers available for minority students.

FINANCIAL AID PICTURE (2009-2010)

Students with need: Out of 383 full-time freshmen who applied for aid, 319 were judged to have need. Of these, 318 received aid, and 75 had their full need met. Average financial aid package met 72% of need; average scholarship/grant was $11,779; average loan was $3,395. For part-time students, average financial aid package was $9,176.

Students without need: 77 full-time freshmen who did not demonstrate need for aid received scholarships/grants; average award was $5,685. No-need awards available for academics, art, athletics, leadership, minority status, music/drama.

Scholarships offered: 25 full-time freshmen received athletic scholarships; average amount $8,909.

Cumulative student debt: 67% of graduating class had student loans; average debt was $33,659.

FINANCIAL AID PROCEDURES

Forms required: FAFSA.

Dates and Deadlines: Priority date 2/1; no closing date. Applicants notified on a rolling basis starting 3/10; must reply within 4 week(s) of notification.

CONTACT

Larry Cyr, Director of Financial Aid
158 East Main Street, Henderson, TN 38340
(731) 989-6662

Jackson State Community College
Jackson, Tennessee
www.jscc.edu   Federal Code: 004937

2-year public community college in small city.
Enrollment: 5,109 undergrads.
Selectivity: Open admission; but selective for some programs.

BASIC COSTS (2009-2010)
Tuition and fees: $2,953; out-of-state residents $11,437.
Per-credit charge: $111; out-of-state residents $460.
Additional info: Tuition/fee waivers available for adults, minority students.

FINANCIAL AID PICTURE (2008-2009)
Students with need: Need-based aid available for full-time and part-time students. Work study available nights, weekends, and for part-time students.
Students without need: No-need awards available for academics, art, athletics, job skills, leadership, minority status, music/drama.

FINANCIAL AID PROCEDURES
Forms required: FAFSA, institutional form.
Dates and Deadlines: Priority date 3/15; no closing date. Applicants notified on a rolling basis starting 6/1; must reply within 2 week(s) of notification.

CONTACT
Dewana Latimer, Director of Financial Aid
2046 North Parkway, Jackson, TN 38301-3797
(731) 425-2605

John A. Gupton College
Nashville, Tennessee
www.guptoncollege.com   Federal Code: 008859

2-year private school of mortuary science in large city.
Enrollment: 101 undergrads.
Selectivity: Open admission; but selective for some programs.

BASIC COSTS (2010-2011)
Tuition and fees: $8,640.
Per-credit charge: $270.
Room only: $3,600.

FINANCIAL AID PICTURE
Students with need: Need-based aid available for full-time and part-time students.
Students without need: This college awards aid only to students with need.

FINANCIAL AID PROCEDURES
Forms required: FAFSA.
Dates and Deadlines: No deadline. Applicants notified on a rolling basis.

CONTACT
B. Steven Spann, President/CFO
1616 Church Street, Nashville, TN 37203-2920
(615) 327-3927

Johnson Bible College
Knoxville, Tennessee
www.jbc.edu   Federal Code: 003495

4-year private Bible college in large city, affiliated with Christian Church.
Enrollment: 672 undergrads, 4% part-time. 127 full-time freshmen.
Selectivity: Admits over 75% of applicants.

BASIC COSTS (2009-2010)
Tuition and fees: $8,610.
Room and board: $5,350.
Additional info: Part-time students pay mandatory fee of $35 per-credit-hour. Tuition/fee waivers available for minority students.

FINANCIAL AID PICTURE (2009-2010)
Students with need: Need-based aid available for full-time and part-time students. Work study available nights, weekends, and for part-time students.
Students without need: No-need awards available for academics, leadership, minority status, music/drama, religious affiliation, state/district residency.

FINANCIAL AID PROCEDURES
Forms required: FAFSA, institutional form.
Dates and Deadlines: Priority date 5/1; closing date 8/1. Applicants notified on a rolling basis starting 4/30; must reply within 2 week(s) of notification.
Transfers: No deadline.

CONTACT
Janette Overton, Financial Aid Director
7900 Johnson Drive, Knoxville, TN 37998-0001
(865) 251-2303

King College
Bristol, Tennessee
www.king.edu   Federal Code: 003496

4-year private nursing and liberal arts college in large town, affiliated with Presbyterian Church (USA).
Enrollment: 1,365 undergrads, 2% part-time. 207 full-time freshmen.
Selectivity: Admits 50 to 75% of applicants.

BASIC COSTS (2010-2011)
Tuition and fees: $22,908.
Room and board: $7,790.

FINANCIAL AID PICTURE (2009-2010)
Students with need: Average financial aid package met 78% of need; average scholarship/grant was $17,190; average loan was $3,690. For part-time students, average financial aid package was $11,843.
Students without need: No-need awards available for academics, athletics, music/drama.
Cumulative student debt: 100% of graduating class had student loans; average debt was $15,757.

FINANCIAL AID PROCEDURES
Forms required: FAFSA.
Dates and Deadlines: Priority date 3/1; no closing date. Applicants notified on a rolling basis starting 3/1; must reply within 2 week(s) of notification.

CONTACT
Brenda Clark, Financial Aid Director
1350 King College Road, Bristol, TN 37620-2699
(423) 652-4725

Lambuth University
Jackson, Tennessee
www.lambuth.edu   Federal Code: 003498

4-year private university and liberal arts college in small city, affiliated with United Methodist Church.
Enrollment: 573 undergrads, 3% part-time. 155 full-time freshmen.
Selectivity: Admits 50 to 75% of applicants.

BASIC COSTS (2009-2010)
Tuition and fees: $18,570.
Per-credit charge: $750.
Room and board: $8,015.
Additional info: Tuition/fee waivers available for adults.

FINANCIAL AID PICTURE (2009-2010)
Students with need: Need-based aid available for full-time students. Work study available nights, weekends, and for part-time students.
Students without need: No-need awards available for academics, alumni affiliation, art, athletics, job skills, leadership, music/drama, religious affiliation, state/district residency.
Scholarships offered: Hyde Scholarships; full tuition, require admission acceptance deadline of February 1, ACT of 30 or higher, GPA, of 3.5 or higher, 2 awarded.
Additional info: Part-time students eligible for federal and state aid, but not institutional aid.

FINANCIAL AID PROCEDURES
Forms required: FAFSA.
Dates and Deadlines: Priority date 2/15; no closing date. Applicants notified on a rolling basis starting 3/1; must reply by 5/1 or within 2 week(s) of notification.
Transfers: Applicants notified on a rolling basis starting 3/1; must reply by 5/1 or within 2 week(s) of notification.

CONTACT
Gregory Thornburg, Director of Financial Aid
705 Lambuth Boulevard, Jackson, TN 38301-5296
(731) 425-3332

Lane College
Jackson, Tennessee
www.lanecollege.edu   Federal Code: 003499

4-year private liberal arts college in small city, affiliated with Christian Methodist Episcopal Church.
Enrollment: 2,146 undergrads, 1% part-time. 686 full-time freshmen.
Selectivity: Admits less than 50% of applicants.

BASIC COSTS (2009-2010)
Tuition and fees: $8,000.
Per-credit charge: $310.
Room and board: $5,520.

FINANCIAL AID PICTURE (2008-2009)
Students with need: Out of 672 full-time freshmen who applied for aid, 659 were judged to have need. Of these, 646 received aid, and 7 had their full need met. For part-time students, average financial aid package was $3,676.
Students without need: 23 full-time freshmen who did not demonstrate need for aid received scholarships/grants; average award was $6,992. No-need awards available for academics, athletics, religious affiliation.
Scholarships offered: 3 full-time freshmen received athletic scholarships; average amount $4,000.

FINANCIAL AID PROCEDURES
Forms required: FAFSA.
Dates and Deadlines: Priority date 3/1; no closing date. Applicants notified on a rolling basis starting 3/31; must reply within 2 week(s) of notification.
Transfers: No deadline. Applicants notified on a rolling basis; must reply within 2 week(s) of notification.

CONTACT
Tony Calhoun, Director of Financial Aid
545 Lane Avenue, Jackson, TN 38301-4598
(731) 426-7537

Lee University
Cleveland, Tennessee
www.leeuniversity.edu   Federal Code: 003500

4-year private university and liberal arts college in large town, affiliated with Church of God.
Enrollment: 3,602 undergrads, 5% part-time. 829 full-time freshmen.
Selectivity: Admits 50 to 75% of applicants.

BASIC COSTS (2009-2010)
Tuition and fees: $11,660.
Per-credit charge: $463.
Room and board: $5,650.

FINANCIAL AID PICTURE (2009-2010)
Students with need: Out of 724 full-time freshmen who applied for aid, 542 were judged to have need. Of these, 534 received aid, and 165 had their full need met. Average financial aid package met 69% of need; average scholarship/grant was $9,509; average loan was $3,307. For part-time students, average financial aid package was $6,363.
Students without need: 181 full-time freshmen who did not demonstrate need for aid received scholarships/grants; average award was $8,634. No-need awards available for academics, alumni affiliation, athletics, leadership, minority status, music/drama, religious affiliation, state/district residency.
Scholarships offered: 31 full-time freshmen received athletic scholarships; average amount $6,616.
Cumulative student debt: 64% of graduating class had student loans; average debt was $27,549.

FINANCIAL AID PROCEDURES
Forms required: FAFSA.
Dates and Deadlines: Priority date 3/15; no closing date. Applicants notified on a rolling basis starting 2/1; must reply within 3 week(s) of notification.

CONTACT
Michael Ellis, Director of Student Financial Aid
1120 North Ocoee Street, Cleveland, TN 37320-3450
(423) 614-8304

LeMoyne-Owen College
Memphis, Tennessee
www.loc.edu   Federal Code: 003501

4-year private liberal arts college in very large city, affiliated with United Church of Christ and Tennessee Baptist Convention.
Enrollment: 890 undergrads.
Selectivity: Admits less than 50% of applicants.

BASIC COSTS (2009-2010)
Tuition and fees: $10,318.
Per-credit charge: $421.
Room and board: $4,852.

FINANCIAL AID PICTURE (2008-2009)
Students with need: Need-based aid available for full-time and part-time students.
Students without need: No-need awards available for academics, athletics, music/drama.

FINANCIAL AID PROCEDURES
Forms required: FAFSA.
Dates and Deadlines: Priority date 4/15; no closing date. Applicants notified on a rolling basis starting 4/1.
Transfers: No deadline. Applicants notified on a rolling basis starting 4/1.

CONTACT

Phyllis Torry, Financial Aid Director
807 Walker Avenue, Memphis, TN 38126
(901) 435-1550

Lincoln Memorial University
Harrogate, Tennessee
www.lmunet.edu Federal Code: 003502

4-year private university and liberal arts college in small town.
Enrollment: 1,464 undergrads, 13% part-time. 314 full-time freshmen.
Selectivity: Admits 50 to 75% of applicants.

BASIC COSTS (2009-2010)
Tuition and fees: $15,120.
Per-credit charge: $630.
Room and board: $5,680.

FINANCIAL AID PICTURE (2009-2010)
Students with need: Out of 306 full-time freshmen who applied for aid, 285 were judged to have need. Of these, 285 received aid, and 35 had their full need met. Average financial aid package met 78% of need; average scholarship/grant was $14,047; average loan was $3,487. For part-time students, average financial aid package was $7,315.
Students without need: 13 full-time freshmen who did not demonstrate need for aid received scholarships/grants; average award was $4,077. No-need awards available for academics, alumni affiliation, athletics, music/drama, ROTC.
Scholarships offered: 40 full-time freshmen received athletic scholarships; average amount $4,023.

FINANCIAL AID PROCEDURES
Forms required: FAFSA.
Dates and Deadlines: Priority date 4/1; no closing date. Applicants notified on a rolling basis starting 4/15; must reply within 3 week(s) of notification.

CONTACT
Bryan Erslan, Director of Financial Aid
6965 Cumberland Gap Parkway, Harrogate, TN 37752-1901
(423) 869-6336

Lipscomb University
Nashville, Tennessee
www.lipscomb.edu Federal Code: 003486

4-year private university and liberal arts college in very large city, affiliated with Church of Christ.
Enrollment: 2,467 undergrads, 6% part-time. 601 full-time freshmen.
Selectivity: Admits 50 to 75% of applicants.

BASIC COSTS (2009-2010)
Tuition and fees: $20,390.
Per-credit charge: $775.
Room and board: $7,850.

FINANCIAL AID PICTURE (2009-2010)
Students with need: Need-based aid available for full-time and part-time students. Work study available nights, weekends, and for part-time students.
Students without need: No-need awards available for academics, alumni affiliation, art, athletics, leadership, minority status, music/drama, religious affiliation, state/district residency.

FINANCIAL AID PROCEDURES
Forms required: FAFSA.
Dates and Deadlines: Priority date 3/1; no closing date. Applicants notified on a rolling basis starting 2/15.

CONTACT

Karita Waters, Director of Financial Aid
One University Park Drive, Nashville, TN 37204-3951
(615) 966-1791

Martin Methodist College
Pulaski, Tennessee
www.martinmethodist.edu Federal Code: 003504

4-year private liberal arts college in small town, affiliated with United Methodist Church.
Enrollment: 940 undergrads.
Selectivity: Admits over 75% of applicants.

BASIC COSTS (2009-2010)
Tuition and fees: $18,638.
Per-credit charge: $760.
Room and board: $6,400.

FINANCIAL AID PICTURE (2008-2009)
Students with need: Need-based aid available for full-time and part-time students. Work study available nights, weekends, and for part-time students.
Students without need: No-need awards available for academics, art, athletics, leadership, music/drama, religious affiliation, state/district residency.
Scholarships offered: Two full academic scholarships per year awarded through interview and essay competition.

FINANCIAL AID PROCEDURES
Forms required: FAFSA, institutional form.
Dates and Deadlines: No deadline. Applicants notified on a rolling basis starting 3/1; must reply within 2 week(s) of notification.
Transfers: Closing date 9/13.

CONTACT
Emma Hiubb, Director of Financial Aid
433 West Madison, Pulaski, TN 38478-2799
(931) 363-9804

Maryville College
Maryville, Tennessee
www.maryvillecollege.edu Federal Code: 003505

4-year private liberal arts college in small city, affiliated with Presbyterian Church (USA).
Enrollment: 1,103 undergrads.
Selectivity: Admits 50 to 75% of applicants.

BASIC COSTS (2010-2011)
Tuition and fees: $29,473.
Per-credit charge: $1,200.
Room and board: $9,032.

FINANCIAL AID PICTURE (2009-2010)
Students with need: Need-based aid available for full-time and part-time students. Work study available nights, weekends, and for part-time students.
Students without need: No-need awards available for academics, art, leadership, minority status, music/drama, religious affiliation, state/district residency.
Scholarships offered: Presidential Scholarship: full tuition; awarded for leadership and academic ability. Dean's Scholarship: covers a large portion of tuition; awarded to selected entering freshmen with 3.5 GPA.

FINANCIAL AID PROCEDURES
Forms required: FAFSA.
Dates and Deadlines: Priority date 3/1; no closing date. Applicants notified on a rolling basis starting 3/15; must reply within 4 week(s) of notification.

CONTACT

Richard Brand, Director of Financial Aid
502 East Lamar Alexander Parkway, Maryville, TN 37804-5907
(865) 981-8100

Memphis College of Art

Memphis, Tennessee
www.mca.edu   Federal Code: 003507

4-year private visual arts college in very large city.
Enrollment: 356 undergrads, 5% part-time. 100 full-time freshmen.
Selectivity: Admits less than 50% of applicants.

BASIC COSTS (2010-2011)

Tuition and fees: $23,950.
Per-credit charge: $1,012.
Room and board: $8,000.

FINANCIAL AID PICTURE (2009-2010)

Students with need: Out of 92 full-time freshmen who applied for aid, 86 were judged to have need. Of these, 86 received aid, and 20 had their full need met. Average financial aid package met 80% of need; average scholarship/grant was $6,252; average loan was $3,500. For part-time students, average financial aid package was $8,734.
Students without need: 15 full-time freshmen who did not demonstrate need for aid received scholarships/grants; average award was $12,900. No-need awards available for academics, art.
Additional info: Students considered for institutional resources through admissions application process.

FINANCIAL AID PROCEDURES

Forms required: FAFSA.
Dates and Deadlines: Priority date 2/15; no closing date. Applicants notified on a rolling basis starting 3/15; must reply within 3 week(s) of notification.
Transfers: Applicants notified on a rolling basis; must reply within 3 week(s) of notification. Grants of $1,000 awarded to students who attended accredited junior or community college earning at least 60 credit hours.

CONTACT

Lynn Holladay, Director of Financial Aid
1930 Poplar Avenue, Memphis, TN 38104-2764
(901) 272-5136

Middle Tennessee State University

Murfreesboro, Tennessee
www.mtsu.edu   Federal Code: 003510

4-year public university in small city.
Enrollment: 22,125 undergrads, 15% part-time. 3,528 full-time freshmen.
Selectivity: Admits 50 to 75% of applicants.

BASIC COSTS (2009-2010)

Tuition and fees: $6,048; out-of-state residents $18,126.
Per-credit charge: $191; out-of-state residents $688.
Room and board: $6,453.

FINANCIAL AID PICTURE (2009-2010)

Students with need: Need-based aid available for full-time and part-time students. Work study available nights, weekends, and for part-time students.
Students without need: No-need awards available for academics, alumni affiliation, art, athletics, job skills, leadership, minority status, music/drama, religious affiliation, ROTC, state/district residency.
Additional info: Application filing deadline for scholarships February 15.

FINANCIAL AID PROCEDURES

Forms required: FAFSA.

Dates and Deadlines: Priority date 5/1; no closing date. Applicants notified on a rolling basis starting 4/15; must reply within 2 week(s) of notification.

CONTACT

David Hutton, Director of Student Financial Aid
1301 East Main Street, Murfreesboro, TN 37132
(615) 898-2830

Milligan College

Milligan College, Tennessee
www.milligan.edu   Federal Code: 003511

4-year private liberal arts college in small city, affiliated with Christian Churches/Churches of Christ.
Enrollment: 859 undergrads, 6% part-time. 209 full-time freshmen.
Selectivity: Admits 50 to 75% of applicants.

BASIC COSTS (2010-2011)

Tuition and fees: $23,520.
Per-credit charge: $630.
Room and board: $5,850.

FINANCIAL AID PICTURE (2009-2010)

Students with need: Average financial aid package met 83% of need; average scholarship/grant was $15,919; average loan was $3,525. For part-time students, average financial aid package was $6,166.
Students without need: No-need awards available for academics, alumni affiliation, art, athletics, job skills, minority status, music/drama, religious affiliation, state/district residency.
Cumulative student debt: 75% of graduating class had student loans; average debt was $19,803.

FINANCIAL AID PROCEDURES

Forms required: FAFSA.
Dates and Deadlines: Priority date 3/1; no closing date. Applicants notified on a rolling basis starting 3/15; must reply within 2 week(s) of notification.

CONTACT

Diane Keasling, Coordinator of Financial Aid
Box 210, Milligan College, TN 37682
(800) 447-4880

Motlow State Community College

Lynchburg, Tennessee
www.mscc.edu   Federal Code: 006836

2-year public community college in rural community.
Enrollment: 4,968 undergrads, 45% part-time. 1,069 full-time freshmen.
Selectivity: Open admission; but selective for some programs.

BASIC COSTS (2009-2010)

Tuition and fees: $2,959; out-of-state residents $11,443.
Per-credit charge: $111; out-of-state residents $460.

FINANCIAL AID PICTURE (2008-2009)

Students with need: 76% of average financial aid package awarded as scholarships/grants, 24% awarded as loans/jobs. Need-based aid available for part-time students.
Students without need: No-need awards available for academics, alumni affiliation, art, athletics, leadership, music/drama.

FINANCIAL AID PROCEDURES

Forms required: FAFSA, institutional form.
Dates and Deadlines: Priority date 2/15; no closing date. Applicants notified on a rolling basis starting 3/15.
Transfers: No deadline. Applicants notified on a rolling basis starting 3/15.

CONTACT

Joe Myers, Director of Financial Aid and Scholarships
Box 8500, Lynchburg, TN 37352-8500
(931) 393-1553

Nashville State Community College

Nashville, Tennessee
www.nscc.edu   Federal Code: 007534

2-year public community and technical college in very large city.
Enrollment: 3,260 full-time undergrads.
Selectivity: Open admission; but selective for some programs.

BASIC COSTS (2009-2010)

Tuition and fees: $2,925; out-of-state residents $11,409.
Per-credit charge: $111; out-of-state residents $460.

FINANCIAL AID PICTURE (2009-2010)

Students with need: Need-based aid available for full-time and part-time
students. Work study available nights, weekends, and for part-time students.
Students without need: No-need awards available for academics, minority
status.

FINANCIAL AID PROCEDURES

Forms required: FAFSA, institutional form.
Dates and Deadlines: Priority date 3/1; no closing date. Applicants notified
on a rolling basis starting 6/1; must reply within 2 week(s) of notification.

CONTACT

Stephen White, Director of Financial Aid
120 White Bridge Road, Nashville, TN 37209-4515
(615) 353-3250

National College: Bristol

Bristol, Tennessee
www.ncbt.edu   Federal Code: 003726

2-year for-profit business college in large town.
Enrollment: 399 undergrads.
Selectivity: Open admission.

BASIC COSTS (2009-2010)

Tuition and fees: $10,080.
Per-credit charge: $223.

FINANCIAL AID PICTURE

Students with need: Need-based aid available for full-time and part-time
students.
Students without need: This college awards aid only to students with
need.

FINANCIAL AID PROCEDURES

Forms required: FAFSA.
Dates and Deadlines: No deadline. Applicants notified on a rolling basis
starting 9/1.

CONTACT

Pamela Cotton, Director of Financial Aid and Compliance Officer
1328 Highway 11W, Bristol, TN 37620

National College: Nashville

Nashville, Tennessee
www.ncbt.edu   Federal Code: 003726

2-year for-profit business and technical college in large city.
Enrollment: 513 undergrads.

Selectivity: Open admission.

BASIC COSTS (2009-2010)

Tuition and fees: $10,080.
Per-credit charge: $223.

FINANCIAL AID PICTURE

Students with need: Need-based aid available for full-time and part-time
students.
Students without need: This college awards aid only to students with
need.

FINANCIAL AID PROCEDURES

Forms required: FAFSA.
Dates and Deadlines: No deadline.

CONTACT

Pamela Cotton, Director of Financial Aid and Compliance Officer
PO Box 6400, Roanoke, VA 24017
(615) 333-3344

Northeast State Community College

Blountville, Tennessee
www.NortheastState.edu   Federal Code: 005378

2-year public community and technical college in small city.
Enrollment: 6,245 undergrads.
Selectivity: Open admission; but selective for some programs.

BASIC COSTS (2009-2010)

Tuition and fees: $2,981; out-of-state residents $11,465.
Per-credit charge: $111; out-of-state residents $460.

FINANCIAL AID PICTURE

Students with need: Need-based aid available for full-time and part-time
students. Work study available nights.
Students without need: No-need awards available for academics, alumni
affiliation, art, job skills, leadership, minority status, music/drama, religious
affiliation.

FINANCIAL AID PROCEDURES

Forms required: FAFSA.
Dates and Deadlines: Priority date 3/31; no closing date. Applicants notified
on a rolling basis starting 3/1; must reply within 3 week(s) of notification.

CONTACT

Cruzita Lucero, Director of Financial Aid
Box 246, Blountville, TN 37617-0246
(423) 323-0252

Nossi College of Art

Goodlettsville, Tennessee
www.nossi.com   Federal Code: 017347

2-year private visual arts and technical college in large town.
Enrollment: 445 undergrads.

BASIC COSTS (2010-2011)

Additional info: Tuition for first year (3 semesters) $12,900; required fees
$700.

FINANCIAL AID PICTURE

Students with need: Need-based aid available for full-time and part-time
students.

CONTACT

Mary Kidd, Financial Aid Director

907 Rivergate Parkway, Building E-6, Goodlettsville, TN 37072

(615) 851-1088

O'More College of Design

Franklin, Tennessee

www.omorecollege.edu   Federal Code: 014663

4-year private visual arts college in large town.

Enrollment: 200 undergrads.

BASIC COSTS (2009-2010)

Tuition and fees: $19,735.

FINANCIAL AID PICTURE (2009-2010)

Students with need: Need-based aid available for full-time and part-time students.

Students without need: This college awards aid only to students with need.

Scholarships offered: Academic scholarships available.

FINANCIAL AID PROCEDURES

Forms required: FAFSA.

Dates and Deadlines: Priority date 4/1; no closing date. Applicants notified on a rolling basis starting 8/1.

Transfers: Priority date 5/5; no deadline.

CONTACT

Jerry Masterson, Financial Aid Director

423 South Margin Street, Franklin, TN 37064-0908

(615) 794-4254 ext. 238

Pellissippi State Community College

Knoxville, Tennessee

www.pstcc.edu   Federal Code: 012693

2-year public community and technical college in small city.

Enrollment: 10,297 undergrads.

Selectivity: Open admission.

BASIC COSTS (2009-2010)

Tuition and fees: $2,993; out-of-state residents $11,477.

Per-credit charge: $111; out-of-state residents $460.

FINANCIAL AID PICTURE (2009-2010)

Students with need: Need-based aid available for full-time and part-time students. Work study available nights, weekends, and for part-time students.

Students without need: No-need awards available for academics, art, minority status, music/drama.

FINANCIAL AID PROCEDURES

Forms required: FAFSA.

Dates and Deadlines: Priority date 5/1; no closing date. Applicants notified on a rolling basis starting 7/15; must reply within 2 week(s) of notification.

CONTACT

Paul McKinney, Director of Financial Aid

Box 22990, Knoxville, TN 37933-0990

(423) 694-6565

Remington College: Memphis

Memphis, Tennessee

www.remingtoncollege.edu

2-year for-profit business and technical college in very large city.

Enrollment: 450 undergrads.

Selectivity: Admits 50 to 75% of applicants.

BASIC COSTS (2009-2010)

Additional info: Costs of entire programs leading to diploma, associate degree, and bachelor's degree range from $13,950 to $39,950; include books and supplies.

FINANCIAL AID PICTURE

Students with need: Need-based aid available for full-time and part-time students.

Students without need: This college awards aid only to students with need.

FINANCIAL AID PROCEDURES

Forms required: FAFSA, institutional form.

Dates and Deadlines: No deadline. Applicants notified on a rolling basis; must reply within 2 week(s) of notification.

CONTACT

Jimmy Bessinger, Director of Financial Services

2710 Nonconnah Boulevard, Memphis, TN 38132

Rhodes College

Memphis, Tennessee   Federal Code: 003519

www.rhodes.edu   CSS Code: 1730

4-year private liberal arts college in very large city, affiliated with Presbyterian Church (USA).

Enrollment: 1,659 undergrads. 431 full-time freshmen.

Selectivity: Admits less than 50% of applicants.

BASIC COSTS (2010-2011)

Tuition and fees: $34,580.

Room and board: $8,480.

FINANCIAL AID PICTURE (2009-2010)

Students with need: Average financial aid package met 87% of need; average scholarship/grant was $21,487; average loan was $4,510.

Students without need: No-need awards available for academics, art, minority status, music/drama, religious affiliation.

Cumulative student debt: 47% of graduating class had student loans; average debt was $26,071.

Additional info: Auditions required for theater and music achievement awards and art achievement awards. Interviews recommended for merit scholarships. Notification of admissions decision for Bellingrath Scholarship applicants by 3/15; must reply by 5/01.

FINANCIAL AID PROCEDURES

Forms required: FAFSA, CSS PROFILE.

Dates and Deadlines: Closing date 3/1. Must reply by 5/1.

CONTACT

Ashley Bianchi, Director of Financial Aid

2000 North Parkway, Memphis, TN 38112

(901) 843-3810

Roane State Community College
Harriman, Tennessee
www.roanestate.edu   Federal Code: 009914

2-year public community and junior college in small town.
Enrollment: 5,014 undergrads, 35% part-time. 1,234 full-time freshmen.
Selectivity: Open admission; but selective for some programs.

BASIC COSTS (2009-2010)
Tuition and fees: $2,982; out-of-state residents $11,466.
Per-credit charge: $111; out-of-state residents $460.

FINANCIAL AID PICTURE (2008-2009)
Students with need: Need-based aid available for full-time and part-time students. Work study available nights, weekends, and for part-time students.
Students without need: No-need awards available for academics, art, athletics, leadership, music/drama, state/district residency.

FINANCIAL AID PROCEDURES
Forms required: FAFSA, institutional form.
Dates and Deadlines: Priority date 4/1; no closing date. Applicants notified on a rolling basis starting 5/1.

CONTACT
Tina Long, Director, Financial Aid
276 Patton Lane, Harriman, TN 37748
(865) 882-4545

South College
Knoxville, Tennessee
www.southcollegetn.edu   Federal Code: 004938

4-year for-profit liberal arts college in small city.
Enrollment: 1,033 undergrads.

BASIC COSTS (2009-2010)
Tuition and fees: $15,825.
Additional info: Reported annual costs are for programs in physical therapy assistance, radiography, health science. Costs of other programs vary by program.

FINANCIAL AID PICTURE (2008-2009)
Students with need: Need-based aid available for full-time and part-time students.
Students without need: This college awards aid only to students with need.

FINANCIAL AID PROCEDURES
Forms required: FAFSA, institutional form.
Dates and Deadlines: No deadline. Applicants notified on a rolling basis.

CONTACT
Larry Broadwater, Financial Aid Director
3904 Lonas Drive, Knoxville, TN 37909
(865) 251-1800

Southern Adventist University
Collegedale, Tennessee
www.southern.edu   Federal Code: 003518

4-year private university and liberal arts college in small town, affiliated with Seventh-day Adventists.
Enrollment: 2,647 undergrads. 595 full-time freshmen.
Selectivity: Admits 50 to 75% of applicants.

BASIC COSTS (2010-2011)
Tuition and fees: $17,712.
Per-credit charge: $716.
Room and board: $5,174.

FINANCIAL AID PICTURE (2009-2010)
Students with need: Out of 476 full-time freshmen who applied for aid, 282 were judged to have need. Of these, 280 received aid, and 271 had their full need met. Average financial aid package met 82% of need; average scholarship/grant was $1,272; average loan was $3,963. For part-time students, average financial aid package was $16,595.
Students without need: 189 full-time freshmen who did not demonstrate need for aid received scholarships/grants; average award was $6,990. No-need awards available for academics, alumni affiliation, art, leadership, music/drama.
Scholarships offered: Freshman scholarship based on combination of high school GPA, ACT/SAT scores, leadership positions held.
Cumulative student debt: 58% of graduating class had student loans; average debt was $22,977.

FINANCIAL AID PROCEDURES
Forms required: FAFSA.
Dates and Deadlines: Priority date 3/1; no closing date. Applicants notified on a rolling basis starting 2/15; must reply within 2 week(s) of notification.
Transfers: No deadline. Applicants notified on a rolling basis.

CONTACT
Marc Grundy, Associate VP for Enrollment Services
Box 370, Collegedale, TN 37315-0370
(423) 236-2835

Southwest Tennessee Community College
Memphis, Tennessee
www.southwest.tn.edu   Federal Code: 010439

2-year public community college in very large city.
Enrollment: 12,052 undergrads, 47% part-time. 1,948 full-time freshmen.
Selectivity: Open admission; but selective for some programs.

BASIC COSTS (2009-2010)
Tuition and fees: $2,985; out-of-state residents $11,469.
Per-credit charge: $111; out-of-state residents $460.
Additional info: Tuition/fee waivers available for minority students.

FINANCIAL AID PICTURE
Students with need: Need-based aid available for full-time and part-time students. Work study available nights, weekends, and for part-time students.
Students without need: This college awards aid only to students with need.
Additional info: State grants available to eligible students who apply by 4/1.

FINANCIAL AID PROCEDURES
Forms required: FAFSA.
Dates and Deadlines: Priority date 3/15; no closing date. Applicants notified on a rolling basis starting 6/1; must reply within 4 week(s) of notification.
Transfers: Priority date 4/15.

CONTACT
Tina Studaway, Director Financial Aid
PO Box 780, Memphis, TN 38101-0780
(901) 333-5956

Tennessee State University
Nashville, Tennessee
www.tnstate.edu   Federal Code: 003522

4-year public university in very large city.
Enrollment: 6,660 undergrads, 18% part-time. 1,302 full-time freshmen.
Selectivity: Admits 50 to 75% of applicants.

BASIC COSTS (2009-2010)
Tuition and fees: $5,444; out-of-state residents $17,522.
Per-credit charge: $191; out-of-state residents $688.
Room and board: $5,610.
Additional info: Tuition/fee waivers available for minority students.

FINANCIAL AID PICTURE (2008-2009)
Students with need: Need-based aid available for full-time students.
Students without need: No-need awards available for academics.

FINANCIAL AID PROCEDURES
Forms required: FAFSA.
Dates and Deadlines: Priority date 4/1; no closing date. Applicants notified on a rolling basis starting 4/15; must reply within 3 week(s) of notification.

CONTACT
Cynthia Brooks, Vice President of Finance/Accounting
3500 John A. Merritt Boulevard, Nashville, TN 37209-1561
(615) 963-5701

Tennessee Technological University
Cookeville, Tennessee
www.tntech.edu   Federal Code: 003523

4-year public university in large town.
Enrollment: 8,676 undergrads, 8% part-time. 1,882 full-time freshmen.
Selectivity: Admits over 75% of applicants.

BASIC COSTS (2009-2010)
Tuition and fees: $5,586; out-of-state residents $17,664.
Per-credit charge: $191; out-of-state residents $688.
Room and board: $6,634.
Additional info: Tuition/fee waivers available for minority students.

FINANCIAL AID PICTURE (2008-2009)
Students with need: Need-based aid available for full-time and part-time students. Work study available nights, weekends, and for part-time students.
Students without need: No-need awards available for academics, alumni affiliation, art, athletics, leadership, minority status, music/drama, ROTC, state/district residency.
Scholarships offered: Presidential Scholarship; $4,000 renewable annually. Awarded to National Merit Finalists.
Additional info: Tuition and/or fee waivers available for children of Tennessee public school teachers.

FINANCIAL AID PROCEDURES
Forms required: FAFSA.
Dates and Deadlines: Priority date 3/15; no closing date. Applicants notified on a rolling basis starting 3/15; must reply within 2 week(s) of notification.
Transfers: No deadline. Applicants notified on a rolling basis starting 6/1; must reply within 2 week(s) of notification.

CONTACT
Lester McKenzie, Director of Student Financial Aid
Office of Admissions, Cookeville, TN 38505-0001
(931) 372-3073

Tennessee Temple University
Chattanooga, Tennessee
www.tntemple.edu   Federal Code: 003524

4-year private university and seminary college in small city, affiliated with Baptist faith.
Enrollment: 677 undergrads.
Selectivity: Admits less than 50% of applicants.

BASIC COSTS (2009-2010)
Tuition and fees: $11,250.
Per-credit charge: $375.
Room and board: $6,030.

FINANCIAL AID PICTURE
Students with need: Need-based aid available for full-time and part-time students. Work study available nights, weekends, and for part-time students.
Students without need: No-need awards available for academics, alumni affiliation, athletics, leadership, music/drama, state/district residency.

FINANCIAL AID PROCEDURES
Forms required: FAFSA.
Dates and Deadlines: Priority date 3/31; no closing date. Applicants notified on a rolling basis starting 2/15; must reply within 2 week(s) of notification.

CONTACT
Jennifer Buckley, Assistant Director of Financial Aid
1815 Union Avenue, Chattanooga, TN 37404
(423) 493-4207

Tennessee Wesleyan College
Athens, Tennessee
www.twcnet.edu   Federal Code: 003525

4-year private liberal arts and teachers college in large town, affiliated with United Methodist Church.
Enrollment: 1,060 undergrads, 12% part-time. 264 full-time freshmen.
Selectivity: Admits over 75% of applicants.

BASIC COSTS (2009-2010)
Tuition and fees: $18,600.
Room and board: $6,100.
Additional info: Tuition/fee waivers available for minority students.

FINANCIAL AID PICTURE (2008-2009)
Students with need: Out of 250 full-time freshmen who applied for aid, 207 were judged to have need. Of these, 204 received aid, and 62 had their full need met. Average financial aid package met 77% of need; average scholarship/grant was $13,070; average loan was $2,731. For part-time students, average financial aid package was $5,930.
Students without need: 22 full-time freshmen who did not demonstrate need for aid received scholarships/grants; average award was $7,652. No-need awards available for academics, alumni affiliation, athletics, minority status, music/drama, religious affiliation.
Scholarships offered: 47 full-time freshmen received athletic scholarships; average amount $6,533.
Cumulative student debt: 45% of graduating class had student loans; average debt was $16,304.

FINANCIAL AID PROCEDURES
Forms required: FAFSA, institutional form.
Dates and Deadlines: No deadline. Applicants notified on a rolling basis starting 2/15; must reply within 2 week(s) of notification.

CONTACT

Bob Perry, Director of Financial Aid
204 East College Street, Athens, TN 37371-0040
(423) 746-5215

Trevecca Nazarene University

Nashville, Tennessee
www.trevecca.edu   Federal Code: 003526

4-year private university and liberal arts college in very large city, affiliated with Church of the Nazarene.

Enrollment: 1,234 undergrads, 8% part-time. 240 full-time freshmen.
Selectivity: Admits 50 to 75% of applicants.

BASIC COSTS (2010-2011)

Tuition and fees: $18,318.
Room and board: $7,734.

FINANCIAL AID PICTURE (2008-2009)

Students with need: 23% of average financial aid package awarded as scholarships/grants, 77% awarded as loans/jobs.
Students without need: No-need awards available for academics, alumni affiliation, art, athletics, leadership, minority status, music/drama, religious affiliation.

FINANCIAL AID PROCEDURES

Forms required: FAFSA.
Dates and Deadlines: Priority date 2/25; closing date 7/30. Applicants notified on a rolling basis starting 3/1.

CONTACT

Eddie White, Director of Financial Aid
333 Murfreesboro Road, Nashville, TN 37210
(615) 248-1242

Tusculum College

Greeneville, Tennessee
www.tusculum.edu   Federal Code: 003527

4-year private liberal arts college in large town, affiliated with Presbyterian Church (USA).

Enrollment: 2,019 undergrads, 3% part-time. 373 full-time freshmen.
Selectivity: Admits over 75% of applicants.

BASIC COSTS (2010-2011)

Tuition and fees: $19,920.
Room and board: $8,000.

FINANCIAL AID PICTURE

Students with need: Need-based aid available for full-time and part-time students. Work study available nights, weekends, and for part-time students.
Students without need: No-need awards available for academics, athletics, leadership, religious affiliation, state/district residency.

FINANCIAL AID PROCEDURES

Forms required: FAFSA.
Dates and Deadlines: Closing date 2/15. Applicants notified on a rolling basis starting 3/1; must reply within 3 week(s) of notification.

CONTACT

Karen Chapman, Director of Financial Aid
60 Shiloh Road, Greeneville, TN 37743
(423) 636-7376

Union University

Jackson, Tennessee
www.uu.edu   Federal Code: 003528

4-year private university and liberal arts college in small city, affiliated with Southern Baptist Convention.

Enrollment: 2,439 undergrads, 10% part-time. 496 full-time freshmen.
Selectivity: Admits over 75% of applicants.

BASIC COSTS (2010-2011)

Tuition and fees: $22,390.
Per-credit charge: $735.
Room and board: $7,460.
Additional info: Tuition/fee waivers available for minority students.

FINANCIAL AID PICTURE (2009-2010)

Students with need: Need-based aid available for full-time and part-time students. Work study available nights, weekends, and for part-time students.
Students without need: No-need awards available for academics, alumni affiliation, art, athletics, leadership, minority status, music/drama, religious affiliation, state/district residency.

FINANCIAL AID PROCEDURES

Forms required: FAFSA, institutional form.
Dates and Deadlines: Priority date 2/15; closing date 3/1. Applicants notified on a rolling basis starting 2/15; must reply by 5/1 or within 2 week(s) of notification.

CONTACT

John Brandt, Director of Student Financial Planning
1050 Union University Drive, Jackson, TN 38305-3697
(731) 661-5015

University of Memphis

Memphis, Tennessee
www.memphis.edu   Federal Code: 003509

4-year public university in very large city.

Enrollment: 16,011 undergrads, 22% part-time. 2,207 full-time freshmen.
Selectivity: Admits 50 to 75% of applicants.

BASIC COSTS (2009-2010)

Tuition and fees: $6,524; out-of-state residents $19,406.
Per-credit charge: $221; out-of-state residents $530.
Room and board: $5,870.
Additional info: Tuition/fee waivers available for adults, minority students.

FINANCIAL AID PICTURE (2009-2010)

Students with need: Out of 2,076 full-time freshmen who applied for aid, 1,578 were judged to have need. Of these, 1,339 received aid, and 230 had their full need met. Average financial aid package met 82% of need; average scholarship/grant was $6,987; average loan was $3,382. For part-time students, average financial aid package was $6,236.
Students without need: 482 full-time freshmen who did not demonstrate need for aid received scholarships/grants; average award was $7,937. No-need awards available for academics, alumni affiliation, art, athletics, leadership, minority status, music/drama, ROTC, state/district residency.
Scholarships offered: 55 full-time freshmen received athletic scholarships; average amount $13,159.
Cumulative student debt: 32% of graduating class had student loans; average debt was $23,342.

FINANCIAL AID PROCEDURES

Forms required: FAFSA.
Dates and Deadlines: Priority date 3/1; closing date 6/1. Applicants notified on a rolling basis starting 3/1; must reply within 2 week(s) of notification.

CONTACT

Richard Ritzman, Director of Student Financial Aid
101 Wilder Tower, Memphis, TN 38152
(901) 678-4825

University of Tennessee Health Science Center
Memphis, Tennessee
www.uthsc.edu   Federal Code: 353006

Upper-division public university and health science college in very large city.
Enrollment: 174 undergrads.

BASIC COSTS (2009-2010)
Tuition and fees: $6,186; out-of-state residents $14,166.
Additional info: Above cost are for bachelor's program in nursing. Other programs vary by cost. Tuition/fee waivers available for minority students.

FINANCIAL AID PICTURE (2008-2009)
Students with need: Average financial aid package for all full-time undergraduates was $10,750; for part-time $19,995. 7% awarded as scholarships/grants, 93% awarded as loans/jobs. Work study available nights, weekends, and for part-time students.
Students without need: No-need awards available for academics, leadership, minority status, state/district residency.
Cumulative student debt: 98% of graduating class had student loans; average debt was $20,000.
Additional info: Scholarships available to defray out-of-state portion of fees charged to out-of-state minority students.

FINANCIAL AID PROCEDURES
Forms required: FAFSA.
Dates and Deadlines: Priority date 2/28; no closing date. Applicants notified on a rolling basis starting 5/1; must reply within 2 week(s) of notification.
Transfers: No deadline. Applicants notified on a rolling basis starting 5/1; must reply within 2 week(s) of notification.

CONTACT
John Lewis, Director of Financial Aid
910 Madison Avenue, Memphis, TN 38163
(901) 448-5568

University of Tennessee: Chattanooga
Chattanooga, Tennessee
www.utc.edu   Federal Code: 003529

4-year public university in large city.
Enrollment: 8,855 undergrads, 10% part-time. 2,193 full-time freshmen.
Selectivity: Admits over 75% of applicants.

BASIC COSTS (2009-2010)
Tuition and fees: $5,710; out-of-state residents $16,954.
Per-credit charge: $188; out-of-state residents $659.
Room and board: $8,056.

FINANCIAL AID PICTURE (2009-2010)
Students with need: Out of 2,103 full-time freshmen who applied for aid, 1,351 were judged to have need. Of these, 1,347 received aid, and 871 had their full need met. Average financial aid package met 87% of need; average scholarship/grant was $4,480; average loan was $3,904. For part-time students, average financial aid package was $4,236.
Students without need: 403 full-time freshmen who did not demonstrate need for aid received scholarships/grants; average award was $3,015. No-need awards available for academics, alumni affiliation, art, athletics, job skills, leadership, minority status, music/drama, religious affiliation, ROTC, state/district residency.

Scholarships offered: 44 full-time freshmen received athletic scholarships; average amount $10,336.
Cumulative student debt: 65% of graduating class had student loans; average debt was $19,456.

FINANCIAL AID PROCEDURES
Forms required: FAFSA, institutional form.
Dates and Deadlines: Priority date 4/1; no closing date. Applicants notified on a rolling basis starting 3/1.
Transfers: Applicants notified on a rolling basis starting 3/1; must reply within 6 week(s) of notification.

CONTACT
Dianne Cox, Director of Financial Aid
615 McCallie Avenue, Chattanooga, TN 37403
(423) 425-4677

University of Tennessee: Knoxville
Knoxville, Tennessee
www.utk.edu   Federal Code: 003530

4-year public university in large city.
Enrollment: 20,849 undergrads, 6% part-time. 3,698 full-time freshmen.
Selectivity: Admits 50 to 75% of applicants.

BASIC COSTS (2009-2010)
Tuition and fees: $6,855; out-of-state residents $20,651.
Per-credit charge: $248; out-of-state residents $823.
Room and board: $7,254.
Additional info: Out-of-state students pay additional required fees of $300.

FINANCIAL AID PICTURE (2009-2010)
Students with need: Need-based aid available for full-time and part-time students. Work study available nights, weekends, and for part-time students.
Students without need: This college awards aid only to students with need.
Scholarships offered: Academic College Scholarship Application part of financial aid forms, must be completed by all students.
Additional info: Application priority date for scholarships 2/1.

FINANCIAL AID PROCEDURES
Forms required: FAFSA.
Dates and Deadlines: Priority date 3/1; no closing date. Applicants notified on a rolling basis starting 3/15; must reply within 3 week(s) of notification.
Transfers: Transfer students must provide financial aid transcripts from all colleges previously attended regardless of whether any aid was received.

CONTACT
Jeff Gerkin, Director of Financial Aid
320 Student Services Building, Circle Park, Knoxville, TN 37996-0230
(865) 974-3131

University of the South
Sewanee, Tennessee
www.sewanee.edu   Federal Code: 003534

4-year private university in rural community, affiliated with Episcopal Church.
Enrollment: 1,450 undergrads. 402 full-time freshmen.
Selectivity: Admits 50 to 75% of applicants. GED not accepted.

BASIC COSTS (2010-2011)
Tuition and fees: $35,862.
Per-credit charge: $1,290.
Room and board: $10,250.

FINANCIAL AID PICTURE (2009-2010)

Students with need: Out of 272 full-time freshmen who applied for aid, 182 were judged to have need. Of these, 182 received aid, and 136 had their full need met. Average financial aid package met 95% of need; average scholarship/grant was $25,561; average loan was $3,959.

Students without need: 117 full-time freshmen who did not demonstrate need for aid received scholarships/grants; average award was $13,735. No-need awards available for academics, minority status, religious affiliation.

Scholarships offered: Benedict Scholars Program for exceptional freshmen; 3 full cost scholarships. Wilkins Scholarships for outstanding incoming freshmen; half tuition, 25 awarded.

Cumulative student debt: 38% of graduating class had student loans; average debt was $18,717.

FINANCIAL AID PROCEDURES

Forms required: FAFSA, institutional form.

Dates and Deadlines: Priority date 3/1; no closing date. Must reply within 4 week(s) of notification.

CONTACT

Beth Crager, Associate Dean of Admission for Financial Aid
Office of Admission, Sewanee, TN 37383-1000
(931) 598-1312

Vanderbilt University
Nashville, Tennessee
www.vanderbilt.edu
Federal Code: 003535
CSS Code: 1871

4-year private university in very large city.

Enrollment: 6,764 undergrads, 1% part-time. 1,599 full-time freshmen.

Selectivity: Admits less than 50% of applicants.

BASIC COSTS (2010-2011)

Tuition and fees: $39,932.

Room and board: $13,068.

FINANCIAL AID PICTURE (2009-2010)

Students with need: Out of 860 full-time freshmen who applied for aid, 743 were judged to have need. Of these, 740 received aid, and 740 had their full need met. Average financial aid package met 100% of need; average scholarship/grant was $34,489; average loan was $238.

Students without need: 127 full-time freshmen who did not demonstrate need for aid received scholarships/grants; average award was $20,488. No-need awards available for academics, athletics, leadership, minority status, music/drama, ROTC, state/district residency.

Scholarships offered: 59 full-time freshmen received athletic scholarships; average amount $34,726.

Cumulative student debt: 40% of graduating class had student loans; average debt was $19,563.

Additional info: Financial aid packages for incoming students do not include need-based loans. Need-based loans replaced with increased amounts of scholarship and/or grant assistance.

FINANCIAL AID PROCEDURES

Forms required: FAFSA, CSS PROFILE.

Dates and Deadlines: Priority date 2/1; no closing date. Applicants notified on a rolling basis starting 4/1.

Transfers: Priority date 4/15.

CONTACT

David Mohning, Director of Student Financial Aid
2305 West End Avenue, Nashville, TN 37203-1727
(615) 322-3591

Volunteer State Community College
Gallatin, Tennessee
www.volstate.edu
Federal Code: 009912

2-year public community and junior college in small city.

Enrollment: 7,029 undergrads, 39% part-time. 1,427 full-time freshmen.

Selectivity: Open admission; but selective for some programs.

BASIC COSTS (2009-2010)

Tuition and fees: $2,965; out-of-state residents $11,449.

Per-credit charge: $111; out-of-state residents $460.

Additional info: Tuition/fee waivers available for minority students.

FINANCIAL AID PICTURE (2008-2009)

Students with need: Need-based aid available for full-time and part-time students.

Students without need: No-need awards available for academics, art, athletics, leadership, minority status, music/drama, religious affiliation, state/district residency.

FINANCIAL AID PROCEDURES

Forms required: FAFSA, institutional form.

Dates and Deadlines: Priority date 4/15; no closing date. Applicants notified on a rolling basis; must reply within 2 week(s) of notification.

Transfers: No deadline. Applicants notified on a rolling basis; must reply within 2 week(s) of notification.

CONTACT

Sue Pedigo, Director of Financial Aid
1480 Nashville Pike, Gallatin, TN 37066
(615) 452-8600 ext. 3456

Walters State Community College
Morristown, Tennessee
www.ws.edu
Federal Code: 008863

2-year public culinary school and community college in small city.

Enrollment: 5,037 undergrads, 37% part-time. 1,144 full-time freshmen.

Selectivity: Open admission; but selective for some programs.

BASIC COSTS (2009-2010)

Tuition and fees: $2,969; out-of-state residents $11,453.

Per-credit charge: $111; out-of-state residents $460.

Additional info: Tuition/fee waivers available for minority students.

FINANCIAL AID PICTURE (2008-2009)

Students with need: 81% of average financial aid package awarded as scholarships/grants, 19% awarded as loans/jobs. Need-based aid available for part-time students.

Students without need: No-need awards available for academics, athletics, minority status, music/drama, state/district residency.

FINANCIAL AID PROCEDURES

Forms required: FAFSA.

Dates and Deadlines: Priority date 5/1; no closing date. Applicants notified on a rolling basis.

Transfers: No deadline. Applicants notified on a rolling basis.

CONTACT

Linda Mason, Director of Financial Aid
500 South Davy Crockett Parkway, Morristown, TN 37813-6899
(423) 585-6811

Williamson Christian College
Franklin, Tennessee
www.williamsoncc.edu   Federal Code: 035315

4-year private liberal arts college in small city, affiliated with interdenominational tradition.
Enrollment: 70 undergrads, 26% part-time. 3 full-time freshmen.
Selectivity: Open admission; but selective for some programs.

BASIC COSTS (2010-2011)
Tuition and fees: $9,600.
Per-credit charge: $315.

FINANCIAL AID PICTURE (2009-2010)
Students with need: Out of 2 full-time freshmen who applied for aid, 2 were judged to have need. Of these, 2 received aid, and 1 had their full need met. Average financial aid package met 75% of need; average scholarship/grant was $2,719; average loan was $2,748. For part-time students, average financial aid package was $4,151.

FINANCIAL AID PROCEDURES
Forms required: FAFSA.
Dates and Deadlines: No deadline. Applicants notified on a rolling basis starting 7/1; must reply within 2 week(s) of notification.
Transfers: No deadline. Applicants notified on a rolling basis starting 7/1; must reply within 2 week(s) of notification.

CONTACT
Zelena O'Sullivan, Director of Financial Aid
200 Seaboard Lane, Franklin, TN 37067
(615) 771-7821

Texas

Abilene Christian University
Abilene, Texas
www.acu.edu   Federal Code: 003537

4-year private university in small city, affiliated with Church of Christ.
Enrollment: 3,787 undergrads, 6% part-time. 971 full-time freshmen.
Selectivity: Admits less than 50% of applicants.

BASIC COSTS (2010-2011)
Tuition and fees: $22,760.
Per-credit charge: $717.
Room and board: $7,884.

FINANCIAL AID PICTURE (2008-2009)
Students with need: Out of 832 full-time freshmen who applied for aid, 630 were judged to have need. Of these, 629 received aid, and 145 had their full need met. Average financial aid package met 73% of need; average scholarship/grant was $10,654; average loan was $3,287. For part-time students, average financial aid package was $5,843.
Students without need: 200 full-time freshmen who did not demonstrate need for aid received scholarships/grants; average award was $6,566. No-need awards available for academics, art, athletics, leadership, minority status, music/drama, religious affiliation, state/district residency.
Scholarships offered: *Merit:* Presidential Scholarship: half or full tuition; based on interview, ACT or SAT scores. Heritage Award: $1,000 per year; based on Church of Christ, ACT or SAT scores. Transfer Scholarship: $1,000-$2,000; based on GPA. *Athletic:* 31 full-time freshmen received athletic scholarships; average amount $8,221.
Cumulative student debt: 71% of graduating class had student loans; average debt was $35,453.
Additional info: Early estimate service available.

FINANCIAL AID PROCEDURES
Forms required: FAFSA, institutional form.
Dates and Deadlines: Priority date 3/1; no closing date. Applicants notified on a rolling basis starting 4/1.

CONTACT
Michael Lewis, Director of Student Financial Services
ACU Box 29000, Abilene, TX 79699
(325) 674-6850

Alvin Community College
Alvin, Texas
www.alvincollege.edu   Federal Code: 003539

2-year public community and liberal arts college in large town.
Enrollment: 5,038 undergrads.
Selectivity: Open admission; but selective for some programs.

BASIC COSTS (2009-2010)
Tuition and fees: $1,336; out-of-district residents $2,326; out-of-state residents $3,676.
Per-credit charge: $32; out-of-district residents $65; out-of-state residents $110.

FINANCIAL AID PICTURE
Students with need: Need-based aid available for full-time and part-time students. Work study available nights, weekends, and for part-time students.
Students without need: This college awards aid only to students with need.

FINANCIAL AID PROCEDURES
Forms required: FAFSA.
Dates and Deadlines: Closing date 6/30. Applicants notified on a rolling basis; must reply within 2 week(s) of notification.

CONTACT
Dora Sims, Director of Student Financial Aid and Placement
3110 Mustang Road, Alvin, TX 77511-4898
(281) 756-3524

Angelina College
Lufkin, Texas
www.angelina.edu   Federal Code: 006661

2-year public community college in large town.
Enrollment: 5,424 undergrads, 59% part-time. 1,040 full-time freshmen.
Selectivity: Open admission; but selective for some programs.

BASIC COSTS (2009-2010)
Tuition and fees: $1,320; out-of-district residents $1,980; out-of-state residents $2,790.
Per-credit charge: $35; out-of-district residents $57; out-of-state residents $84.
Room and board: $3,300.

FINANCIAL AID PICTURE (2008-2009)
Students with need: Out of 548 full-time freshmen who applied for aid, 534 were judged to have need. Of these, 523 received aid, and 74 had their full need met. Average financial aid package met 71% of need; average scholarship/grant was $3,665. For part-time students, average financial aid package was $2,004.
Students without need: This college awards aid only to students with need.
Scholarships offered: *Merit:* Angelina Challenge Award: $500 per semester; available to graduating seniors from the six Angelina County high schools;

students must receive less than $1,000 in other need-based aid. *Athletic:* 29 full-time freshmen received athletic scholarships; average amount $6,233.

FINANCIAL AID PROCEDURES
Forms required: FAFSA, institutional form.
Dates and Deadlines: Priority date 7/15; no closing date. Applicants notified on a rolling basis starting 7/15.

CONTACT
Susan Jones, Director of Financial Aid
PO Box 1768, Lufkin, TX 75902-1768
(936) 633-5291

Angelo State University
San Angelo, Texas
www.angelo.edu   Federal Code: 003541

4-year public university in small city.
Enrollment: 5,725 undergrads, 15% part-time. 1,418 full-time freshmen.
Selectivity: Admits over 75% of applicants.

BASIC COSTS (2010-2011)
Tuition and fees: $6,138; out-of-state residents $14,568.
Per-credit charge: $142; out-of-state residents $423.
Room and board: $7,256.

FINANCIAL AID PICTURE (2008-2009)
Students with need: Out of 1,209 full-time freshmen who applied for aid, 925 were judged to have need. Of these, 912 received aid, and 304 had their full need met. Average financial aid package met 46% of need; average scholarship/grant was $4,966; average loan was $2,891. For part-time students, average financial aid package was $4,925.
Students without need: 236 full-time freshmen who did not demonstrate need for aid received scholarships/grants; average award was $2,958. No-need awards available for academics, art, athletics, leadership, music/drama, ROTC, state/district residency.
Scholarships offered: 19 full-time freshmen received athletic scholarships; average amount $3,589.
Cumulative student debt: 37% of graduating class had student loans; average debt was $16,372.

FINANCIAL AID PROCEDURES
Forms required: FAFSA.
Dates and Deadlines: Priority date 4/1; no closing date. Applicants notified on a rolling basis starting 4/1; must reply within 4 week(s) of notification.
Transfers: Must reply within 4 week(s) of notification.

CONTACT
Steven Klein, Associate Vice President for Enrollment Management
ASU Station #11014, San Angelo, TX 76909-1014
(800) 946-8627

Arlington Baptist College
Arlington, Texas
www.abconline.edu   Federal Code: 014305

4-year private Bible and teachers college in very large city, affiliated with Baptist faith.
Enrollment: 153 undergrads, 21% part-time. 22 full-time freshmen.
Selectivity: Open admission.

BASIC COSTS (2009-2010)
Tuition and fees: $7,340.
Per-credit charge: $220.
Room and board: $4,200.

FINANCIAL AID PICTURE (2008-2009)
Students with need: Need-based aid available for full-time and part-time students.
Students without need: This college awards aid only to students with need.

FINANCIAL AID PROCEDURES
Forms required: FAFSA.
Dates and Deadlines: Closing date 8/15. Applicants notified on a rolling basis.

CONTACT
Alan Van Zandt, Business Manager
3001 West Division, Arlington, TX 76012
(817) 461-8741 ext. 114

Austin College
Sherman, Texas
www.austincollege.edu   Federal Code: 003543

4-year private liberal arts and teachers college in small city, affiliated with Presbyterian Church (USA).
Enrollment: 1,328 undergrads. 413 full-time freshmen.
Selectivity: Admits over 75% of applicants.

BASIC COSTS (2010-2011)
Tuition and fees: $29,235.
Per-credit charge: $1,054.
Room and board: $9,549.

FINANCIAL AID PICTURE (2009-2010)
Students with need: Out of 341 full-time freshmen who applied for aid, 282 were judged to have need. Of these, 282 received aid, and 268 had their full need met. Average financial aid package met 95% of need; average scholarship/grant was $21,036; average loan was $4,074. For part-time students, average financial aid package was $7,392.
Students without need: 62 full-time freshmen who did not demonstrate need for aid received scholarships/grants; average award was $16,020. No-need awards available for academics, alumni affiliation, art, leadership, music/drama, religious affiliation, state/district residency.

FINANCIAL AID PROCEDURES
Forms required: FAFSA.
Dates and Deadlines: Priority date 4/1; no closing date. Applicants notified on a rolling basis starting 3/1; must reply by 5/1.
Transfers: Applicants notified on a rolling basis starting 3/1; must reply by 5/1.

CONTACT
Laurie Coulter, Executive Director of Financial Aid
900 North Grand Avenue, Suite 6N, Sherman, TX 75090-4400
(903) 813-2900

Austin Community College
Austin, Texas
www.austincc.edu   Federal Code: 012015

2-year public community college in very large city.
Enrollment: 40,248 undergrads. 1,598 full-time freshmen.
Selectivity: Open admission; but selective for some programs.

BASIC COSTS (2009-2010)
Tuition and fees: $1,608; out-of-district residents $4,548; out-of-state residents $8,988.
Per-credit charge: $39; out-of-district residents $137; out-of-state residents $285.

FINANCIAL AID PICTURE (2008-2009)

Students with need: Out of 585 full-time freshmen who applied for aid, 484 were judged to have need. Of these, 484 received aid. Need-based aid available for part-time students.

FINANCIAL AID PROCEDURES

Forms required: FAFSA, institutional form.

Dates and Deadlines: Closing date 4/1. Applicants notified on a rolling basis starting 6/1; must reply within 2 week(s) of notification.

CONTACT

Terry Bazan, Director, Financial Assistance
PO Box 15306, Austin, TX 78761-5306
(512) 223-7550

Austin Graduate School of Theology

Austin, Texas
www.austingrad.edu   Federal Code: 017322

Upper-division private Bible and seminary college in very large city, affiliated with Church of Christ.

Enrollment: 26 undergrads, 85% part-time.

BASIC COSTS (2009-2010)

Tuition and fees: $8,250.

Per-credit charge: $275.

FINANCIAL AID PICTURE (2008-2009)

Students with need: Need-based aid available for full-time and part-time students. Work study available nights.

Students without need: No-need awards available for academics, leadership.

Additional info: Generous scholarships for students taking at least 12 hours. Federal work study program available. Institutional work study program (need-based) available.

FINANCIAL AID PROCEDURES

Forms required: FAFSA, institutional form.

Dates and Deadlines: Priority date 7/1; closing date 8/1.

Transfers: No deadline.

CONTACT

Dave Arthur, Vice President
7640 Guadalupe Street, Austin, TX 78752-1333
(512) 476-2772

Baylor University

Waco, Texas
www.baylor.edu   Federal Code: 003545

4-year private university in small city, affiliated with Baptist faith.

Enrollment: 12,101 undergrads, 2% part-time. 3,098 full-time freshmen.

Selectivity: Admits less than 50% of applicants.

BASIC COSTS (2010-2011)

Tuition and fees: $29,724.

Per-credit charge: $1,124.

Room and board: $8,331.

Additional info: Cited cost includes room rate for community bath and 16-meal plan. Other room types are higher.

FINANCIAL AID PICTURE (2009-2010)

Students with need: Out of 2,410 full-time freshmen who applied for aid, 1,990 were judged to have need. Of these, 1,988 received aid, and 260 had their full need met. Average financial aid package met 69% of need; average scholarship/grant was $16,768; average loan was $2,753. For part-time students, average financial aid package was $10,585.

Students without need: 886 full-time freshmen who did not demonstrate need for aid received scholarships/grants; average award was $9,270. No-need awards available for academics, art, athletics, job skills, leadership, music/drama, ROTC.

Scholarships offered: *Merit:* Regent's Scholarship: full tuition, limited to National Merit finalists who list Baylor as first choice, unlimited number. President's Scholarship, Provost's Scholarship, Dean's Scholarship also available. ***Athletic:*** 79 full-time freshmen received athletic scholarships; average amount $25,500.

FINANCIAL AID PROCEDURES

Forms required: FAFSA.

Dates and Deadlines: Priority date 1/15; closing date 8/15. Applicants notified on a rolling basis starting 3/1; must reply by 5/1 or within 2 week(s) of notification.

Transfers: Must reply by 5/1 or within 2 week(s) of notification. To be eligible for State Tuition Remission, transfers must meet program guidelines, including overall 2.5 GPA and must have passed minimum of 12 hours in each semester attempted in the past year.

CONTACT

Jackie Diaz, Assistant Vice President
One Bear Place #97056, Waco, TX 76798-7056
(800) 229-5678

Blinn College

Brenham, Texas
www.blinn.edu   Federal Code: 003549

2-year public community college in large town.

Enrollment: 14,961 undergrads.

Selectivity: Open admission; but selective for some programs.

BASIC COSTS (2009-2010)

Tuition and fees: $1,890; out-of-district residents $2,760; out-of-state residents $5,040.

Per-credit charge: $35; out-of-district residents $64; out-of-state residents $140.

Room and board: $4,940.

FINANCIAL AID PICTURE (2009-2010)

Students with need: Need-based aid available for full-time and part-time students.

FINANCIAL AID PROCEDURES

Forms required: FAFSA, institutional form.

Dates and Deadlines: Priority date 6/1; no closing date. Applicants notified on a rolling basis starting 7/1.

CONTACT

Tracy Lutkenhaus, Director of Financial Aid
902 College Avenue, Brenham, TX 77833
(979) 830-4144

Brazosport College

Lake Jackson, Texas
www.brazosport.edu   Federal Code: 007287

2-year public community college in large town.

Enrollment: 3,866 undergrads.

Selectivity: Open admission; but selective for some programs.

BASIC COSTS (2009-2010)

Tuition and fees: $1,542; out-of-district residents $2,172; out-of-state residents $3,582.

Per-credit charge: $36; out-of-district residents $57; out-of-state residents $104.

FINANCIAL AID PICTURE (2008-2009)

Students with need: 45% of average financial aid package awarded as scholarships/grants, 55% awarded as loans/jobs. Need-based aid available for part-time students.

Students without need: No-need awards available for academics, art, job skills, leadership, music/drama, state/district residency.

FINANCIAL AID PROCEDURES

Forms required: FAFSA, institutional form.

Dates and Deadlines: Priority date 7/1; no closing date. Applicants notified on a rolling basis starting 5/1.

CONTACT

Kay Wright, Director of Financial Aid

500 College Drive, Lake Jackson, TX 77566

(979) 230-3377

Cedar Valley College

Lancaster, Texas

www.cedarvalleycollege.edu   Federal Code: 014035

2-year public community college in large town.

Enrollment: 5,886 undergrads.

Selectivity: Open admission.

BASIC COSTS (2009-2010)

Tuition and fees: $1,230; out-of-district residents $2,280; out-of-state residents $3,630.

Per-credit charge: $41; out-of-district residents $76; out-of-state residents $121.

FINANCIAL AID PICTURE

Students with need: Need-based aid available for full-time students.

FINANCIAL AID PROCEDURES

Forms required: FAFSA.

Dates and Deadlines: Priority date 5/1; no closing date. Applicants notified on a rolling basis.

CONTACT

DeCha Reid, Director of Financial Aid

3030 North Dallas Avenue, Lancaster, TX 75134

(972) 860-8280

Central Texas College

Killeen, Texas

www.ctcd.edu   Federal Code: 004003

2-year public community and technical college in small city.

Enrollment: 21,863 undergrads, 88% part-time. 685 full-time freshmen.

Selectivity: Open admission; but selective for some programs.

BASIC COSTS (2009-2010)

Tuition and fees: $1,530; out-of-district residents $1,860; out-of-state residents $4,440.

Per-credit charge: $43; out-of-district residents $54; out-of-state residents $140.

Room and board: $3,500.

FINANCIAL AID PICTURE

Students with need: Need-based aid available for full-time and part-time students. Work study available nights, weekends, and for part-time students.

Students without need: This college awards aid only to students with need.

FINANCIAL AID PROCEDURES

Forms required: FAFSA, institutional form.

Dates and Deadlines: Closing date 7/1. Applicants notified on a rolling basis starting 3/1; must reply within 4 week(s) of notification.

CONTACT

Annabelle Smith, Director of Student Financial Aid

Box 1800, Killeen, TX 76540

(254) 526-1508

Clarendon College

Clarendon, Texas

www.clarendoncollege.edu   Federal Code: 003554

2-year public community college in rural community.

Enrollment: 1,328 undergrads.

Selectivity: Open admission; but selective for some programs.

BASIC COSTS (2009-2010)

Tuition and fees: $2,370; out-of-district residents $2,940; out-of-state residents $3,510.

Room and board: $3,450.

FINANCIAL AID PICTURE (2008-2009)

Students with need: Need-based aid available for full-time and part-time students. Work study available nights, weekends, and for part-time students.

Students without need: No-need awards available for academics, art, athletics, leadership, music/drama, state/district residency.

Scholarships offered: Named and endowed scholarships available based on academic achievement, need, and/or other requirements as stipulated by the scholarship donor.

FINANCIAL AID PROCEDURES

Forms required: FAFSA, institutional form.

Dates and Deadlines: Priority date 8/1; no closing date. Applicants notified on a rolling basis starting 5/15; must reply by 8/15 or within 2 week(s) of notification.

Transfers: No deadline. Applicants notified on a rolling basis starting 11/15; must reply within 4 week(s) of notification.

CONTACT

Michele Copelin, Director of Financial Aid

PO Box 968, Clarendon, TX 79226

(806) 874-3571 ext. 112

Coastal Bend College

Beeville, Texas

www.coastalbend.edu   Federal Code: 003546

2-year public community college in large town.

Enrollment: 4,196 undergrads.

Selectivity: Open admission; but selective for some programs.

BASIC COSTS (2009-2010)

Tuition and fees: $1,910; out-of-district residents $3,680; out-of-state residents $4,130.

Room only: $1,700.

Additional info: Meal ticket (a la carte) food service available.

FINANCIAL AID PICTURE (2008-2009)

Students with need: Need-based aid available for full-time and part-time students.

Students without need: No-need awards available for academics, leadership.

FINANCIAL AID PROCEDURES

Forms required: FAFSA, institutional form.

Dates and Deadlines: Priority date 4/1; no closing date. Applicants notified on a rolling basis starting 5/1; must reply within 2 week(s) of notification.

Transfers: No deadline. Applicants notified on a rolling basis.

CONTACT

Nora Morales, Director of Financial Aid
3800 Charco Road, Beeville, TX 78102
(361) 354-2238

College of Saint Thomas More

Fort Worth, Texas
www.cstm.edu   Federal Code: 031894

4-year private liberal arts college in very large city, affiliated with Roman Catholic Church.

Enrollment: 30 undergrads.

Selectivity: Admits 50 to 75% of applicants.

BASIC COSTS (2009-2010)

Tuition and fees: $12,550.

Per-credit charge: $400.

Room only: $4,050.

Additional info: Student housing includes use of private kitchen.

FINANCIAL AID PICTURE (2008-2009)

Students with need: Need-based aid available for full-time and part-time students. Work study available nights, weekends, and for part-time students.

Students without need: No-need awards available for academics.

FINANCIAL AID PROCEDURES

Forms required: FAFSA.

Dates and Deadlines: Closing date 7/1. Applicants notified on a rolling basis starting 1/1.

CONTACT

Corky Swanson, Financial Aid Department
3020 Lubbock Avenue, Fort Worth, TX 76109
(817) 673-1934

College of the Mainland

Texas City, Texas
www.com.edu   Federal Code: 007096

2-year public community and technical college in large town.

Enrollment: 3,916 undergrads.

Selectivity: Open admission; but selective for some programs.

BASIC COSTS (2009-2010)

Tuition and fees: $1,166; out-of-district residents $2,126; out-of-state residents $3,356.

Per-credit charge: $33; out-of-district residents $65; out-of-state residents $106.

FINANCIAL AID PICTURE

Students with need: Need-based aid available for full-time and part-time students. Work study available nights, weekends, and for part-time students.

Students without need: This college awards aid only to students with need.

FINANCIAL AID PROCEDURES

Forms required: FAFSA, institutional form.

Dates and Deadlines: No deadline. Applicants notified on a rolling basis.

Transfers: Priority date 8/1.

CONTACT

Becky Miles, Director, Student Financial Services
1200 Amburn Road, Texas City, TX 77591
(409) 938-1211 ext. 274

Collin County Community College District

McKinney, Texas
www.collin.edu   Federal Code: 016792

2-year public community college in large city.

Enrollment: 23,952 undergrads, 60% part-time. 2,756 full-time freshmen.

Selectivity: Open admission; but selective for some programs.

BASIC COSTS (2009-2010)

Tuition and fees: $1,020; out-of-district residents $1,785; out-of-state residents $3,435.

FINANCIAL AID PICTURE (2008-2009)

Students with need: Out of 876 full-time freshmen who applied for aid, 657 were judged to have need. Of these, 516 received aid, and 11 had their full need met. Average financial aid package met 49% of need; average scholarship/grant was $4,023; average loan was $2,904. For part-time students, average financial aid package was $3,490.

Students without need: 54 full-time freshmen who did not demonstrate need for aid received scholarships/grants; average award was $589. No-need awards available for academics, art, athletics, job skills, leadership, minority status, music/drama, state/district residency.

Scholarships offered: 16 full-time freshmen received athletic scholarships; average amount $4,662.

Cumulative student debt: 11% of graduating class had student loans; average debt was $4,497.

FINANCIAL AID PROCEDURES

Forms required: FAFSA, institutional form.

Dates and Deadlines: Priority date 6/1; closing date 6/30. Applicants notified on a rolling basis starting 5/1; must reply within 2 week(s) of notification.

Transfers: Applicants must have cumulative GPA of 2.0 and less than 90 transferable credit hours.

CONTACT

Debra Wilkison, Director of Financial Aid
2800 East Spring Creek Parkway, Plano, TX 75074
(972) 881-5760

Commonwealth Institute of Funeral Service

Houston, Texas
www.commonwealthinst.org   Federal Code: 003556

2-year private school of mortuary science in very large city.

Enrollment: 143 undergrads.

BASIC COSTS (2009-2010)

Tuition and fees: $7,715.

Per-credit charge: $198.

Additional info: Tuition includes cost of textbooks and clinical supplies.

FINANCIAL AID PICTURE

Students with need: Need-based aid available for full-time and part-time students.

Students without need: This college awards aid only to students with need.

Scholarships offered: Scholarship awards: $250-$500 based on funds available; recipients selected on academic achievement, leadership and professional promise, as well as any stipulations by the donor, by a committee of Commonwealth Institute graduate employers, alumni, and benefactors.

FINANCIAL AID PROCEDURES

Forms required: FAFSA.

Dates and Deadlines: Priority date 8/31; no closing date. Applicants notified on a rolling basis starting 7/12.

CONTACT

Jessika Jenkins, Director of Financial Aid
415 Barren Springs Drive, Houston, TX 77090-5913
(281) 873-0262

Concordia University Texas
Austin, Texas
www.concordia.edu   Federal Code: 003557

4-year private university and liberal arts college in very large city, affiliated with Lutheran Church - Missouri Synod.

Enrollment: 1,110 undergrads, 22% part-time. 138 full-time freshmen.

Selectivity: Admits 50 to 75% of applicants.

BASIC COSTS (2009-2010)

Tuition and fees: $21,200.

Per-credit charge: $700.

Room and board: $8,000.

Additional info: Tuition/fee waivers available for adults.

FINANCIAL AID PICTURE (2008-2009)

Students with need: Out of 60 full-time freshmen who applied for aid, 47 were judged to have need. Of these, 45 received aid, and 25 had their full need met. Average financial aid package met 89% of need; average scholarship/grant was $11,481; average loan was $8,926. For part-time students, average financial aid package was $11,658.

Students without need: 12 full-time freshmen who did not demonstrate need for aid received scholarships/grants; average award was $7,512. No-need awards available for academics, alumni affiliation, leadership, music/drama, religious affiliation.

Cumulative student debt: 66% of graduating class had student loans; average debt was $22,095.

FINANCIAL AID PROCEDURES

Forms required: FAFSA.

Dates and Deadlines: No deadline. Applicants notified on a rolling basis starting 2/15; must reply within 2 week(s) of notification.

Transfers: Financial aid transcripts from all previously attended trade/technical schools and colleges/universities required.

CONTACT

Cathy Schryer, Director of Financial Assistance
11400 Concordia University Drive, Austin, TX 78726
(512) 486-1283

Dallas Baptist University
Dallas, Texas
www.dbu.edu   Federal Code: 003560

4-year private university in very large city, affiliated with Baptist faith.

Enrollment: 3,533 undergrads, 37% part-time. 350 full-time freshmen.

Selectivity: Admits less than 50% of applicants.

BASIC COSTS (2009-2010)

Tuition and fees: $17,490.

Per-credit charge: $583.

Room and board: $5,636.

FINANCIAL AID PICTURE (2009-2010)

Students with need: Out of 335 full-time freshmen who applied for aid, 239 were judged to have need. Of these, 238 received aid, and 157 had their full need met. Average financial aid package met 75% of need; average scholarship/grant was $3,384; average loan was $3,247. For part-time students, average financial aid package was $6,682.

Students without need: 77 full-time freshmen who did not demonstrate need for aid received scholarships/grants; average award was $7,739. No-need awards available for academics, athletics, job skills, leadership, music/drama, religious affiliation.

Scholarships offered: 22 full-time freshmen received athletic scholarships; average amount $12,741.

Cumulative student debt: 79% of graduating class had student loans; average debt was $17,214.

FINANCIAL AID PROCEDURES

Forms required: FAFSA, institutional form.

Dates and Deadlines: Priority date 3/6; closing date 5/1. Applicants notified on a rolling basis starting 2/1.

Transfers: Priority date 3/17; no deadline. Applicants notified on a rolling basis.

CONTACT

Donald Zackary, Director of Financial Aid
3000 Mountain Creek Parkway, Dallas, TX 75211-9299
(214) 333-5363

Dallas Christian College
Dallas, Texas
www.dallas.edu   Federal Code: 006941

4-year private Bible college in very large city, affiliated with nondenominational tradition.

Enrollment: 315 undergrads.

BASIC COSTS (2009-2010)

Tuition and fees: $10,770.

Per-credit charge: $339.

Room and board: $6,500.

FINANCIAL AID PICTURE (2009-2010)

Students with need: Need-based aid available for full-time and part-time students.

Students without need: No-need awards available for leadership, music/drama.

FINANCIAL AID PROCEDURES

Forms required: FAFSA, institutional form.

Dates and Deadlines: Closing date 4/15. Applicants notified on a rolling basis; must reply within 2 week(s) of notification.

CONTACT

Mark Stanley, Executive Vice President
2700 Christian Parkway, Dallas, TX 75234-7299
(972) 241-3371 ext. 158

Del Mar College
Corpus Christi, Texas
www.delmar.edu   Federal Code: 003563

2-year public community college in large city.

Enrollment: 12,069 undergrads, 70% part-time. 882 full-time freshmen.

Selectivity: Open admission; but selective for some programs.

BASIC COSTS (2009-2010)

Tuition and fees: $2,154; out-of-district residents $3,654; out-of-state residents $4,764.

Per-credit charge: $38; out-of-district residents $88; out-of-state residents $125.

FINANCIAL AID PICTURE (2008-2009)

Students with need: 69% of average financial aid package awarded as scholarships/grants, 31% awarded as loans/jobs. Need-based aid available for part-time students. Work study available nights, weekends, and for part-time students.

Students without need: This college awards aid only to students with need.

FINANCIAL AID PROCEDURES

Forms required: FAFSA.

Dates and Deadlines: Priority date 5/1; no closing date. Applicants notified on a rolling basis starting 7/1; must reply within 2 week(s) of notification.

CONTACT

Enrique Garcia, Assistant Dean of Financial Aid and Retention Services
101 Baldwin Boulevard, Corpus Christi, TX 78404-3897
(361) 698-1293

DeVry University: Irving
Dallas, Texas
www.devry.edu   Federal Code: 010139

4-year for-profit university in small city.
Enrollment: 1,712 undergrads, 52% part-time. 210 full-time freshmen.

BASIC COSTS (2009-2010)

Tuition and fees: $14,160.
Per-credit charge: $550.

FINANCIAL AID PICTURE (2008-2009)

Students with need: Need-based aid available for full-time and part-time students.
Students without need: This college awards aid only to students with need.

FINANCIAL AID PROCEDURES

Dates and Deadlines: No deadline. Applicants notified on a rolling basis.

CONTACT

Nga Phan, Director, Financial Aid
4800 Regent Boulevard, Dallas, TX 75063-2439
(972) 929-9740

East Texas Baptist University
Marshall, Texas
www.etbu.edu   Federal Code: 003564

4-year private university and liberal arts college in large town, affiliated with Baptist faith.
Enrollment: 1,116 undergrads, 3% part-time. 295 full-time freshmen.
Selectivity: Admits 50 to 75% of applicants.

BASIC COSTS (2010-2011)

Tuition and fees: $19,550.
Per-credit charge: $625.
Room and board: $5,436.
Additional info: Tuition at time of enrollment locked for 4 years.

FINANCIAL AID PICTURE (2008-2009)

Students with need: Out of 282 full-time freshmen who applied for aid, 247 were judged to have need. Of these, 247 received aid, and 53 had their full need met. Average financial aid package met 46% of need; average scholarship/grant was $6,538; average loan was $3,044. For part-time students, average financial aid package was $5,954.

Students without need: 48 full-time freshmen who did not demonstrate need for aid received scholarships/grants; average award was $8,412. No-need awards available for academics, alumni affiliation, leadership, music/drama, religious affiliation.

Scholarships offered: For freshmen or students transferring less than 24 hours, based on ACT/SAT (Critical Reading and Math) and recalculated high school GPA: Presidential Scholarship; $7,500. Honor Scholarship; $6,500. Dean Scholarship; $5,500. Achievement Grant; $2,700. For transfer students: Transfer Honor Scholarship; $6,500. Transfer Dean Scholarship; $5,500. Transfer Achievement Grant; $2,700. All amounts are per academic year.

Cumulative student debt: 77% of graduating class had student loans; average debt was $21,380.

FINANCIAL AID PROCEDURES

Forms required: FAFSA, institutional form.

Dates and Deadlines: Priority date 6/1; no closing date. Applicants notified on a rolling basis starting 1/1.

Transfers: No deadline. Applicants notified on a rolling basis starting 2/1.

CONTACT

Tommy Young, Director of Financial Aid
1209 North Grove, Marshall, TX 75670-1498
(903) 923-2138

Eastfield College
Mesquite, Texas
www.efc.dcccd.edu   Federal Code: 008510

2-year public community and liberal arts college in small city.
Enrollment: 9,554 undergrads, 73% part-time. 709 full-time freshmen.
Selectivity: Open admission.

BASIC COSTS (2009-2010)

Tuition and fees: $1,230; out-of-district residents $2,280; out-of-state residents $3,630.

Per-credit charge: $41; out-of-district residents $76; out-of-state residents $121.

FINANCIAL AID PICTURE

Students with need: Need-based aid available for full-time and part-time students. Work study available nights, weekends, and for part-time students.

Scholarships offered: Lecroy Scholars Program: $600 per semester; based on demonstrated church, community, or academic leadership and 3.0 GPA; requires enrollment in at least 12 credit hours; 5-10 awarded. Erin Tierney Kramp Encouragement Program: $600 per semester; based on demonstrated courage in the face of adversity, moral character, leadership, and high academic standards; requires enrollment in 8 hours for awarding semester, and maintenance of high academic standards; 2 awarded.

FINANCIAL AID PROCEDURES

Forms required: FAFSA, institutional form.
Dates and Deadlines: Priority date 5/1; no closing date. Applicants notified on a rolling basis starting 4/15.

CONTACT

Dana Mingo, Dean of Financial Aid
3737 Motley Drive, Mesquite, TX 75150
(972) 860-8385

El Centro College
Dallas, Texas
www.elcentrocollege.edu   Federal Code: 004453

2-year public community college in very large city.
Enrollment: 7,257 undergrads, 78% part-time. 310 full-time freshmen.
Selectivity: Open admission; but selective for some programs.

BASIC COSTS (2009-2010)
Tuition and fees: $1,230; out-of-district residents $2,280; out-of-state residents $3,630.
Per-credit charge: $41; out-of-district residents $76; out-of-state residents $121.
Additional info: Tuition/fee waivers available for minority students, unemployed or children of unemployed.

FINANCIAL AID PICTURE
Students with need: Need-based aid available for full-time and part-time students.
Additional info: Interview required for financial aid applicants.

FINANCIAL AID PROCEDURES
Forms required: FAFSA.
Dates and Deadlines: Priority date 5/1; no closing date. Applicants notified on a rolling basis; must reply within 2 week(s) of notification.
Transfers: Financial aid transcript may be required from previous institutions attended.

CONTACT
John Wells, Director of Financial Aid
801 Main Street, Dallas, TX 75202
(214) 860-2099

El Paso Community College
El Paso, Texas
www.epcc.edu   Federal Code: 010387

2-year public community college in very large city.
Enrollment: 26,274 undergrads.
Selectivity: Open admission; but selective for some programs.

BASIC COSTS (2009-2010)
Tuition and fees: $2,085; out-of-state residents $2,774.
Per-credit charge: $59; out-of-state residents $82.
Additional info: Per-credit-hour costs listed are for each additional credit-hour beyond one credit-hour for in-state students, and beyond six credit-hours for out-of-state students.

FINANCIAL AID PICTURE (2008-2009)
Students with need: Work study available nights, weekends, and for part-time students.
Students without need: No-need awards available for academics, athletics.

FINANCIAL AID PROCEDURES
Forms required: FAFSA, institutional form.
Dates and Deadlines: Priority date 5/1; no closing date. Applicants notified on a rolling basis starting 7/1; must reply within 2 week(s) of notification.

CONTACT
Linda Gonzalez-Hensgen, Director of Student Financial Services
Box 20500, El Paso, TX 79998
(915) 831-2566

Frank Phillips College
Borger, Texas
www.fpctx.edu   Federal Code: 003568

2-year public community and junior college in large town.
Enrollment: 701 undergrads, 28% part-time. 191 full-time freshmen.
Selectivity: Open admission.

BASIC COSTS (2009-2010)
Tuition and fees: $2,333; out-of-district residents $2,963; out-of-state residents $3,173.
Per-credit charge: $64; out-of-district residents $106; out-of-state residents $120.
Room and board: $4,150.

FINANCIAL AID PICTURE (2008-2009)
Students with need: Need-based aid available for full-time and part-time students. Work study available nights, weekends, and for part-time students.
Students without need: No-need awards available for academics, athletics, music/drama, state/district residency.
Scholarships offered: Various scholarships available including BEDC, Presidential, Dean's, Access, Opportunity, and Re-entering Adult Learner.
Additional info: Some Texas fire department and police department personnel, active duty military personnel, children of military missing in action may qualify for reduced or waived tuition. Out-of-state tuition waived for students living in Oklahoma counties adjacent to Texas.

FINANCIAL AID PROCEDURES
Forms required: FAFSA, institutional form.
Dates and Deadlines: Closing date 7/1. Applicants notified on a rolling basis; must reply within 2 week(s) of notification.
Transfers: No deadline. Applicants notified on a rolling basis.

CONTACT
Beverly Fields, Director of Financial Services
Box 5118, Borger, TX 79008-5118
(806) 457-4200 ext. 796

Galveston College
Galveston, Texas
www.gc.edu   Federal Code: 004972

2-year public community college in small city.
Enrollment: 2,166 undergrads, 70% part-time. 180 full-time freshmen.
Selectivity: Open admission; but selective for some programs.

BASIC COSTS (2009-2010)
Tuition and fees: $1,414; out-of-state residents $2,314.
Per-credit charge: $30; out-of-state residents $60.

FINANCIAL AID PICTURE (2008-2009)
Students with need: Need-based aid available for full-time and part-time students.
Students without need: This college awards aid only to students with need.

FINANCIAL AID PROCEDURES
Forms required: FAFSA.
Dates and Deadlines: Priority date 6/9; no closing date. Applicants notified on a rolling basis starting 6/1.

CONTACT
Ron Crumedy, Financial Aid Manager
4015 Avenue Q, Galveston, TX 77550-7447
(409) 944-1235

Grayson County College
Denison, Texas
www.grayson.edu   Federal Code: 003570

2-year public community and technical college in large town.
Enrollment: 4,216 undergrads.
Selectivity: Open admission; but selective for some programs.

BASIC COSTS (2009-2010)
Tuition and fees: $1,350; out-of-district residents $1,920; out-of-state residents $3,390.
Per-credit charge: $45; out-of-district residents $64; out-of-state residents $113.
Room and board: $3,650.

FINANCIAL AID PICTURE (2008-2009)
Students with need: Need-based aid available for full-time and part-time students.
Additional info: Short term loans available.

FINANCIAL AID PROCEDURES
Forms required: FAFSA.
Dates and Deadlines: Priority date 6/1; no closing date. Applicants notified on a rolling basis; must reply within 5 week(s) of notification.

CONTACT
Donna King, Director of Financial Aid
6101 Grayson Drive, Denison, TX 75020
(903) 463-8642

Hallmark College of Aeronautics
San Antonio, Texas
www.hallmarkcollege.edu   Federal Code: 010509

2-year for-profit technical and career college in very large city.
Enrollment: 204 undergrads.

BASIC COSTS (2010-2011)
Additional info: Combined AAS Airframe Technology/AAS Powerplant Technology, $29,400; AAS Airframe Technology, $18,711; AAS Powerplant Technology, $19,602; Aviation Technician Diploma, $26,727; Airframe Technician Diploma, $16,929; Powerplant Technician Diploma, $16,038. Cost includes books, equipment and supplies. Additional fees include registration, $110; security, $95. International student tuition and fees is the tuition plus 8%.

FINANCIAL AID PICTURE
Students with need: Need-based aid available for full-time students.

FINANCIAL AID PROCEDURES
Forms required: FAFSA.
Dates and Deadlines: No deadline. Applicants notified on a rolling basis.

CONTACT
Grace Calixto, Director of Financial Planning
8901 Wetmore Road, San Antonio, TX 78230-4229
(210) 690-9000

Hallmark College of Technology
San Antonio, Texas
www.hallmarkcollege.edu   Federal Code: 010509

2-year for-profit technical and career college in very large city.
Enrollment: 351 undergrads. 351 full-time freshmen.

BASIC COSTS (2010-2011)
Additional info: Tuition varies by program and includes books, equipment and supplies. Accounting certificate, Medical Assistant certificate, and Healthcare Information Specialist (Billing/Coding) certificate: $12,600; Associate of Applied Science Medical Assistant, $19,850; Associate of Applied Science Computer Network Systems Technology, $30,800; Bachelor of Science in Business Management, $55,000. Registration fee, $110. All medical programs have a $100 lab fee. International student tuition and fees is the tuition plus 8%.

FINANCIAL AID PICTURE
Students with need: Need-based aid available for full-time students.

FINANCIAL AID PROCEDURES
Forms required: FAFSA.
Dates and Deadlines: No deadline. Applicants notified on a rolling basis.

CONTACT
Grace Calixto, Director of Financial Planning
Hallmark College, San Antonio, TX 78230-1737
(210) 690-9000 ext. 212

Hardin-Simmons University
Abilene, Texas
www.hsutx.edu   Federal Code: 003571

4-year private university in small city, affiliated with Baptist faith.
Enrollment: 1,882 undergrads, 8% part-time. 409 full-time freshmen.
Selectivity: Admits less than 50% of applicants.

BASIC COSTS (2010-2011)
Tuition and fees: $20,990.
Per-credit charge: $665.
Room and board: $6,282.
Additional info: Tuition guarantee is only for students enrolled full-time. Tuition at time of enrollment locked for 4 years.

FINANCIAL AID PICTURE (2009-2010)
Students with need: Out of 401 full-time freshmen who applied for aid, 306 were judged to have need. Of these, 306 received aid, and 98 had their full need met. Average financial aid package met 81% of need; average scholarship/grant was $7,301; average loan was $2,889. For part-time students, average financial aid package was $8,740.
Students without need: 100 full-time freshmen who did not demonstrate need for aid received scholarships/grants; average award was $9,970. No-need awards available for academics, art, job skills, leadership, music/drama, religious affiliation.
Cumulative student debt: 73% of graduating class had student loans; average debt was $35,429.

FINANCIAL AID PROCEDURES
Forms required: FAFSA.
Dates and Deadlines: Priority date 3/15; no closing date. Applicants notified on a rolling basis starting 2/1; must reply within 2 week(s) of notification.
Transfers: No deadline. Applicants notified on a rolling basis starting 2/1; must reply within 2 week(s) of notification.

CONTACT
Jim Jones, Director of Financial Aid and Scholarships
PO Box 16050, Abilene, TX 79698-0001
(325) 670-1206

Hill College
Hillsboro, Texas
www.hillcollege.edu   Federal Code: 003573

2-year public community college in small town.
Enrollment: 4,298 undergrads, 61% part-time.
Selectivity: Open admission; but selective for some programs.

BASIC COSTS (2009-2010)
Tuition and fees: $1,680; out-of-district residents $2,310; out-of-state residents $2,710.
Room and board: $3,150.

FINANCIAL AID PICTURE (2009-2010)
Students with need: Need-based aid available for full-time and part-time students.
Students without need: No-need awards available for academics, athletics, music/drama.

FINANCIAL AID PROCEDURES
Forms required: FAFSA, institutional form.
Dates and Deadlines: Closing date 7/1. Applicants notified on a rolling basis.

CONTACT
Susan Russell, Director of Student Financial Aid
112 Lamar Drive, Hillsboro, TX 76645
(254) 659-7600

Houston Baptist University
Houston, Texas
www.hbu.edu   Federal Code: 003576

4-year private university and liberal arts college in very large city, affiliated with Baptist faith.
Enrollment: 2,322 undergrads, 14% part-time. 537 full-time freshmen.
Selectivity: Admits less than 50% of applicants.

BASIC COSTS (2010-2011)
Tuition and fees: $23,160.
Room and board: $6,830.

FINANCIAL AID PICTURE (2009-2010)
Students with need: Out of 464 full-time freshmen who applied for aid, 412 were judged to have need. Of these, 410 received aid, and 141 had their full need met. Average financial aid package met 85% of need; average scholarship/grant was $6,228; average loan was $2,703. For part-time students, average financial aid package was $12,932.
Students without need: 78 full-time freshmen who did not demonstrate need for aid received scholarships/grants; average award was $3,758. No-need awards available for academics, alumni affiliation, art, athletics, music/drama, religious affiliation, ROTC.
Scholarships offered: *Merit:* Endowed Academic Scholarship: full or three-quarters tuition for four years; limited number available; for new freshmen with 1300 SAT or 30 ACT. Founders Academic Scholarship: minimum 1250 SAT or 28 ACT required for freshmen, 3.75 GPA on 30 or more semester hours required for transfers. Presidential Academic Scholarship: $4,300 per year, renewable; 1175 SAT or 26 ACT required for freshmen, 3.5 GPA required for transfers. Legacy Grant: $2,700 per year; renewable; 1100 SAT or 24 ACT required for freshmen, 3.25 GPA required for transfers. All SAT scores are exclusive of Writing. Valedictorian Scholarship: $1,500 per year; renewable; for valedictorians from Texas high schools. Ministerial Dependents Grant: $4,300 per year; for dependent children of ordained/licensed Southern Baptist ministers and missionaries. Grants-In-Aid: awards vary; for students who contribute special abilities or services to the University; awarded in music, art, athletics and nursing. Church Matching Award: awards vary. *Athletic:* 47 full-time freshmen received athletic scholarships; average amount $7,877.

FINANCIAL AID PROCEDURES
Forms required: FAFSA.
Dates and Deadlines: Priority date 3/1; closing date 4/15. Applicants notified on a rolling basis starting 3/10.

CONTACT
Barrett Bell, Executive Director of Financial Services
7502 Fondren Road, Houston, TX 77074-3298
(281) 649-3471

Houston Community College System
Houston, Texas
www.hccs.edu   Federal Code: 010422

2-year public community college in very large city.
Enrollment: 43,171 undergrads, 67% part-time. 3,824 full-time freshmen.
Selectivity: Open admission; but selective for some programs.

BASIC COSTS (2009-2010)
Tuition and fees: $1,701; out-of-district residents $3,321; out-of-state residents $3,921.

FINANCIAL AID PICTURE (2008-2009)
Students with need: Need-based aid available for full-time and part-time students. Work study available nights, weekends, and for part-time students.

FINANCIAL AID PROCEDURES
Dates and Deadlines: No deadline. Applicants notified on a rolling basis starting 6/1; must reply within 2 week(s) of notification.

CONTACT
Avis Horde, Director of Financial Aid
3100 Main, Houston, TX 77266-7517
(713) 718-8550

Howard College
Big Spring, Texas
www.howardcollege.edu   Federal Code: 003574

2-year public community college in large town.
Enrollment: 3,900 undergrads.
Selectivity: Open admission; but selective for some programs.

BASIC COSTS (2009-2010)
Tuition and fees: $1,712; out-of-district residents $2,132; out-of-state residents $2,832.
Room and board: $3,667.

FINANCIAL AID PICTURE
Students with need: Need-based aid available for full-time and part-time students.
Students without need: No-need awards available for academics, art, athletics, leadership, music/drama.

FINANCIAL AID PROCEDURES
Forms required: FAFSA, institutional form.
Dates and Deadlines: Priority date 4/1; no closing date. Applicants notified on a rolling basis starting 7/15; must reply within 2 week(s) of notification.

CONTACT
Rebecca Villanueva, Director of Financial Aid
1001 Birdwell Lane, Big Spring, TX 79720
(432) 264-5083

Howard Payne University

Brownwood, Texas
www.hputx.edu   Federal Code: 003575

4-year private liberal arts and teachers college in large town, affiliated with Baptist faith.

Enrollment: 1,130 undergrads, 17% part-time. 304 full-time freshmen.

Selectivity: Admits 50 to 75% of applicants.

BASIC COSTS (2010-2011)

Tuition and fees: $19,950.

Per-credit charge: $625.

Room and board: $5,640.

FINANCIAL AID PICTURE (2008-2009)

Students with need: Out of 286 full-time freshmen who applied for aid, 249 were judged to have need. Of these, 249 received aid, and 66 had their full need met. Average financial aid package met 84% of need; average scholarship/grant was $10,608; average loan was $3,212. For part-time students, average financial aid package was $6,225.

Students without need: 53 full-time freshmen who did not demonstrate need for aid received scholarships/grants; average award was $6,405. No-need awards available for academics, alumni affiliation, art, music/drama.

Scholarships offered: Merit-based scholarship available to all approved home school applicants, $5,000 annually ($20,000 over 4 years).

Cumulative student debt: 69% of graduating class had student loans; average debt was $21,700.

FINANCIAL AID PROCEDURES

Forms required: FAFSA, state aid form, institutional form.

Dates and Deadlines: Priority date 3/15; no closing date. Applicants notified on a rolling basis starting 2/1; must reply within 2 week(s) of notification.

CONTACT

Glenda Huff, Director of Student Financial Aid
1000 Fisk Street, Brownwood, TX 76801-2794
(325) 649-8015

Huston-Tillotson University

Austin, Texas
www.htu.edu   Federal Code: 003577

4-year private business and liberal arts college in very large city, affiliated with United Church of Christ and United Methodist Church.

Enrollment: 843 undergrads, 4% part-time. 179 full-time freshmen.

Selectivity: Admits less than 50% of applicants.

BASIC COSTS (2009-2010)

Tuition and fees: $11,434.

Per-credit charge: $315.

Room and board: $6,690.

FINANCIAL AID PICTURE (2008-2009)

Students with need: Out of 159 full-time freshmen who applied for aid, 159 were judged to have need. Of these, 159 received aid, and 124 had their full need met. Average financial aid package met 72% of need; average scholarship/grant was $9,802; average loan was $3,500. For part-time students, average financial aid package was $9,500.

Students without need: 4 full-time freshmen who did not demonstrate need for aid received scholarships/grants; average award was $4,630. No-need awards available for academics, alumni affiliation, art, athletics, job skills, leadership, minority status, music/drama, religious affiliation, state/district residency.

Cumulative student debt: 93% of graduating class had student loans; average debt was $23,343.

FINANCIAL AID PROCEDURES

Forms required: FAFSA, institutional form.

Dates and Deadlines: Priority date 3/15; no closing date. Applicants notified on a rolling basis starting 4/1; must reply within 4 week(s) of notification.

Transfers: No deadline.

CONTACT

Antonio Holloway, Director of Financial Aid
900 Chicon Street, Austin, TX 78702-2795
(512) 505-3031

Jacksonville College

Jacksonville, Texas
www.jacksonville-college.edu   Federal Code: 003579

2-year private junior and liberal arts college in large town, affiliated with Baptist faith.

Enrollment: 327 undergrads.

Selectivity: Open admission.

BASIC COSTS (2010-2011)

Tuition and fees: $6,920.

Per-credit charge: $210.

Room and board: $3,258.

FINANCIAL AID PICTURE (2009-2010)

Students with need: Need-based aid available for full-time and part-time students.

Students without need: No-need awards available for academics, athletics, leadership, music/drama, religious affiliation, state/district residency.

FINANCIAL AID PROCEDURES

Forms required: FAFSA, state aid form, institutional form.

Dates and Deadlines: Priority date 8/1; no closing date. Applicants notified on a rolling basis.

Transfers: No deadline. Applicants notified on a rolling basis.

CONTACT

Don Compton, Financial Aid Officer
105 B.J. Albritton Drive, Jacksonville, TX 75766-4759
(903) 586-2518 ext. 7135

Jarvis Christian College

Hawkins, Texas
www.jarvis.edu   Federal Code: 003637

4-year private liberal arts and teachers college in rural community, affiliated with Christian Church (Disciples of Christ).

Enrollment: 608 undergrads, 1% part-time. 119 full-time freshmen.

Selectivity: Open admission.

BASIC COSTS (2009-2010)

Tuition and fees: $8,208.

Room and board: $5,078.

FINANCIAL AID PICTURE (2008-2009)

Students with need: Need-based aid available for full-time and part-time students. Work study available nights, weekends, and for part-time students.

Students without need: This college awards aid only to students with need.

Additional info: High school transcript required for scholarship consideration.

FINANCIAL AID PROCEDURES

Forms required: FAFSA, state aid form.

Dates and Deadlines: Priority date 6/30; closing date 1/3. Applicants notified on a rolling basis starting 5/1; must reply within 2 week(s) of notification.

Transfers: Priority date 4/15; no deadline. Applicants notified on a rolling basis starting 7/1; must reply within 2 week(s) of notification.

CONTACT
Reginald Dickens, Director of Admission and Financial Aid
PO Box 1470, Hawkins, TX 75765-1470
(903) 769-5740

Kilgore College
Kilgore, Texas
www.kilgore.edu   Federal Code: 003580

2-year public community college in large town.
Enrollment: 6,375 undergrads, 53% part-time. 1,065 full-time freshmen.
Selectivity: Open admission; but selective for some programs.

BASIC COSTS (2009-2010)
Tuition and fees: $1,350; out-of-district residents $2,880; out-of-state residents $3,960.
Per-credit charge: $23; out-of-district residents $74; out-of-state residents $110.
Room and board: $3,980.
Additional info: Tuition/fee waivers available for unemployed or children of unemployed.

FINANCIAL AID PICTURE (2008-2009)
Students with need: Need-based aid available for full-time and part-time students.
Students without need: No-need awards available for academics, alumni affiliation, art, athletics, job skills, leadership, music/drama, state/district residency.
Scholarships offered: Presidential Scholarships: tuition, fees and books for 4 semesters; ACT 25 or top 10% of senior class; 20 available; renewable at 2.5 GPA.
Additional info: State of Texas grants and loans available for honor graduates with unmet needs and for non-traditional students.

FINANCIAL AID PROCEDURES
Forms required: FAFSA, state aid form, institutional form.
Dates and Deadlines: Priority date 6/1; closing date 7/15. Applicants notified on a rolling basis starting 3/1; must reply within 2 week(s) of notification.
Transfers: No deadline. Transfer students must submit financial aid transcript from previous school plus all appropriate internal aid forms and show proof of high school graduation or GED.

CONTACT
Annette Morgan, Director of Financial Aid
1100 Broadway, Kilgore, TX 75662-3299
(903) 983-8183

Lamar State College at Orange
Orange, Texas
www.lsco.edu   Federal Code: 016748

2-year public junior and liberal arts college in small city.
Enrollment: 1,970 undergrads, 44% part-time. 383 full-time freshmen.
Selectivity: Open admission; but selective for some programs.

BASIC COSTS (2009-2010)
Tuition and fees: $3,460; out-of-state residents $11,770.
Per-credit charge: $84; out-of-state residents $362.

FINANCIAL AID PICTURE (2008-2009)
Students with need: Need-based aid available for full-time and part-time students.

Students without need: This college awards aid only to students with need.

FINANCIAL AID PROCEDURES
Forms required: FAFSA, institutional form.
Dates and Deadlines: Priority date 4/1; no closing date. Applicants notified on a rolling basis starting 5/15; must reply within 2 week(s) of notification.

CONTACT
Kerry Olson, Director of Financial Aid
410 Front Street, Orange, TX 77630
(409) 882-3317

Lamar State College at Port Arthur
Port Arthur, Texas
www.lamarpa.edu   Federal Code: 016666

2-year public community and technical college in small city.
Enrollment: 2,162 undergrads.
Selectivity: Open admission; but selective for some programs.

BASIC COSTS (2009-2010)
Tuition and fees: $4,117; out-of-state residents $12,427.

FINANCIAL AID PICTURE
Students with need: Need-based aid available for full-time and part-time students. Work study available nights, weekends, and for part-time students.
Students without need: This college awards aid only to students with need.

FINANCIAL AID PROCEDURES
Forms required: FAFSA, institutional form.
Dates and Deadlines: Priority date 4/1; no closing date. Applicants notified on a rolling basis starting 4/15; must reply within 2 week(s) of notification.

CONTACT
Diane Hargett, Director of Financial Aid
Box 310, Port Arthur, TX 77641-0310
(409) 984-6203

Lamar University
Beaumont, Texas
www.lamar.edu   Federal Code: 003581

4-year public university in small city.
Enrollment: 9,127 undergrads, 25% part-time. 1,427 full-time freshmen.
Selectivity: Admits over 75% of applicants.

BASIC COSTS (2009-2010)
Tuition and fees: $6,607; out-of-state residents $14,917.
Per-credit charge: $150; out-of-state residents $427.
Room and board: $6,290.

FINANCIAL AID PICTURE (2009-2010)
Students with need: Out of 1,042 full-time freshmen who applied for aid, 656 were judged to have need. Of these, 656 received aid, and 120 had their full need met. Average financial aid package met 58% of need. For part-time students, average financial aid package was $10,850.
Students without need: This college awards aid only to students with need.

FINANCIAL AID PROCEDURES
Forms required: FAFSA, institutional form.
Dates and Deadlines: Priority date 4/1; no closing date. Applicants notified on a rolling basis starting 4/1; must reply within 2 week(s) of notification.

CONTACT

Jill Rowley, Director of Financial Aid
Box 10009, Beaumont, TX 77705
(409) 880-8450

Lee College

Baytown, Texas
www.lee.edu   Federal Code: 003583

2-year public community college in small city.
Enrollment: 5,968 undergrads.
Selectivity: Open admission; but selective for some programs.

BASIC COSTS (2009-2010)

Tuition and fees: $1,302; out-of-district residents $2,052; out-of-state residents $3,102.
Per-credit charge: $25; out-of-district residents $50; out-of-state residents $85.

FINANCIAL AID PICTURE

Students with need: Need-based aid available for full-time and part-time students.
Students without need: No-need awards available for academics, art, athletics, job skills, music/drama.

FINANCIAL AID PROCEDURES

Forms required: FAFSA.
Dates and Deadlines: Priority date 4/1; no closing date. Applicants notified on a rolling basis starting 6/1.

CONTACT

Sharon Mullins, Financial Aid Officer
Box 818, Baytown, TX 77522
(281) 425-6362

LeTourneau University

Longview, Texas
www.letu.edu   Federal Code: 003584

4-year private university in small city, affiliated with nondenominational tradition.
Enrollment: 3,040 undergrads, 5% part-time. 342 full-time freshmen.
Selectivity: Admits 50 to 75% of applicants.

BASIC COSTS (2009-2010)

Tuition and fees: $20,400.
Per-credit charge: $802.
Room and board: $7,960.

FINANCIAL AID PICTURE (2009-2010)

Students with need: Need-based aid available for full-time and part-time students. Work study available nights, weekends, and for part-time students.
Students without need: No-need awards available for academics, alumni affiliation, leadership.
Scholarships offered: Freshmen scholarships: Honors Scholarship, $6,000 per year; Dean's Scholarship: $8,000 per year; Presidential: $9,000 per year; based on SAT and/or ACT scores and cumulative high school GPA.

FINANCIAL AID PROCEDURES

Forms required: FAFSA.
Dates and Deadlines: Priority date 2/1; no closing date. Applicants notified on a rolling basis starting 3/1; must reply within 3 week(s) of notification.

CONTACT

Delinda Hall, Senior Director of Enrollment Services and Financial Aid
PO Box 7001, Longview, TX 75607-7001
(903) 233-4350

Lon Morris College

Jacksonville, Texas
www.lonmorris.edu   Federal Code: 003585

2-year private junior and liberal arts college in large town, affiliated with United Methodist Church.
Enrollment: 816 undergrads.
Selectivity: Admits 50 to 75% of applicants.

BASIC COSTS (2009-2010)

Tuition and fees: $13,500.
Room and board: $6,130.

FINANCIAL AID PICTURE (2008-2009)

Students with need: Need-based aid available for full-time and part-time students. Work study available nights, weekends, and for part-time students.
Students without need: This college awards aid only to students with need.

FINANCIAL AID PROCEDURES

Forms required: FAFSA, state aid form, institutional form.
Dates and Deadlines: Priority date 5/1; no closing date. Applicants notified on a rolling basis starting 2/15; must reply within 2 week(s) of notification.

CONTACT

Kris Marquis, Director of Admissions/Student Financial Aid
800 College Avenue, Jacksonville, TX 75766
(903) 589-4061

Lone Star College System

The Woodlands, Texas
www.nhmccd.edu   Federal Code: 011145

2-year public community college in very large city.
Enrollment: 58,844 undergrads, 75% part-time. 7,733 full-time freshmen.
Selectivity: Open admission; but selective for some programs.

BASIC COSTS (2010-2011)

Tuition and fees: $1,494; out-of-district residents $3,594; out-of-state residents $4,044.

FINANCIAL AID PICTURE (2008-2009)

Students with need: Need-based aid available for part-time students.
Students without need: No-need awards available for academics.

FINANCIAL AID PROCEDURES

Forms required: FAFSA, institutional form.
Dates and Deadlines: Priority date 4/1; no closing date. Applicants notified on a rolling basis starting 4/1.

CONTACT

Reggie Brazzle, Director, Student Financial Aid
5000 Research Forest Drive, The Woodlands, TX 77381-4356

Lubbock Christian University

Lubbock, Texas
www.lcu.edu   Federal Code: 003586

4-year private university and liberal arts college in small city, affiliated with Church of Christ.
Enrollment: 1,541 undergrads, 17% part-time. 250 full-time freshmen.
Selectivity: Admits 50 to 75% of applicants.

BASIC COSTS (2010-2011)

Tuition and fees: $16,180.
Per-credit charge: $497.

Room and board: $5,146.

FINANCIAL AID PICTURE (2008-2009)

Students with need: Out of 187 full-time freshmen who applied for aid, 162 were judged to have need. Of these, 162 received aid, and 16 had their full need met. Average financial aid package met 71% of need; average scholarship/grant was $9,859; average loan was $3,527. For part-time students, average financial aid package was $7,044.

Students without need: 34 full-time freshmen who did not demonstrate need for aid received scholarships/grants; average award was $4,157. No-need awards available for academics, athletics, job skills, leadership, music/drama.

Scholarships offered: 21 full-time freshmen received athletic scholarships; average amount $7,594.

Cumulative student debt: 79% of graduating class had student loans; average debt was $26,321.

FINANCIAL AID PROCEDURES

Forms required: FAFSA, institutional form.

Dates and Deadlines: Priority date 6/1; no closing date. Applicants notified on a rolling basis starting 3/1.

Transfers: No deadline. Applicants notified on a rolling basis.

CONTACT

Amy Hardesty, Director, Financial Assistance
5601 19th Street, Lubbock, TX 79407
(806) 720-7176

McLennan Community College
Waco, Texas
www.mclennan.edu   Federal Code: 003590

2-year public community and junior college in small city.

Enrollment: 7,321 undergrads.

Selectivity: Open admission; but selective for some programs.

BASIC COSTS (2009-2010)

Tuition and fees: $2,190; out-of-district residents $2,550; out-of-state residents $3,990.

Per-credit charge: $64; out-of-district residents $76; out-of-state residents $124.

FINANCIAL AID PICTURE (2008-2009)

Students with need: Need-based aid available for full-time and part-time students.

Students without need: No-need awards available for athletics.

Scholarships offered: Academic scholarship: awarded to individuals selected for Tartan scholar's program.

FINANCIAL AID PROCEDURES

Forms required: FAFSA.

Dates and Deadlines: Priority date 6/1; no closing date. Applicants notified on a rolling basis starting 5/1.

CONTACT

James Kubacak, Director of Financial Aid
1400 College Drive, Waco, TX 76708
(254) 299-8698

McMurry University
Abilene, Texas
www.mcm.edu   Federal Code: 003591

4-year private university and liberal arts college in small city, affiliated with United Methodist Church.

Enrollment: 1,396 undergrads, 13% part-time. 320 full-time freshmen.

Selectivity: Admits 50 to 75% of applicants.

BASIC COSTS (2010-2011)

Tuition and fees: $20,680.

Per-credit charge: $620.

Room and board: $6,976.

Additional info: Block tuition rate for 12-18 hours per semester allows students to earn additional credits at no extra cost.

FINANCIAL AID PICTURE (2009-2010)

Students with need: Out of 304 full-time freshmen who applied for aid, 272 were judged to have need. Of these, 270 received aid, and 45 had their full need met. Average financial aid package met 86% of need; average scholarship/grant was $11,759; average loan was $3,390. For part-time students, average financial aid package was $6,589.

Students without need: 23 full-time freshmen who did not demonstrate need for aid received scholarships/grants; average award was $5,889. No-need awards available for academics, alumni affiliation, art, music/drama, religious affiliation.

Cumulative student debt: 77% of graduating class had student loans; average debt was $27,935.

FINANCIAL AID PROCEDURES

Forms required: FAFSA.

Dates and Deadlines: Priority date 3/15; no closing date. Applicants notified on a rolling basis starting 2/1; must reply within 3 week(s) of notification.

Transfers: No deadline. Applicants notified on a rolling basis starting 2/1; must reply by 6/30.

CONTACT

Rachel Atkins, Director of Financial Aid
South 14th and Sayles Boulevard, Abilene, TX 79697-0001
(325) 793-4713

Midland College
Midland, Texas
www.midland.edu   Federal Code: 009797

2-year public community college in small city.

Enrollment: 3,730 undergrads.

Selectivity: Open admission; but selective for some programs.

BASIC COSTS (2009-2010)

Tuition and fees: $1,800; out-of-district residents $2,460; out-of-state residents $3,450.

Room and board: $3,900.

FINANCIAL AID PICTURE (2008-2009)

Students with need: 81% of average financial aid package awarded as scholarships/grants, 19% awarded as loans/jobs. Need-based aid available for part-time students.

Students without need: No-need awards available for academics, athletics, minority status, music/drama, state/district residency.

Scholarships offered: Abell-Hangar Foundations Scholarships: varying amounts; renewable; available for full-time or part-time study to any Midland High, Midland Lee, or Greenwood High School graduate.

FINANCIAL AID PROCEDURES

Forms required: FAFSA.

Dates and Deadlines: Priority date 4/2; closing date 6/1. Applicants notified on a rolling basis starting 5/15; must reply within 2 week(s) of notification.

Transfers: No deadline.

CONTACT

Latisha Williams, Director of Financial Aid
3600 North Garfield, Midland, TX 79705
(432) 685-4733

Midwestern State University

Wichita Falls, Texas
www.mwsu.edu   Federal Code: 003592

4-year public university and liberal arts college in small city.
Enrollment: 5,606 undergrads, 26% part-time. 701 full-time freshmen.
Selectivity: Admits over 75% of applicants.

BASIC COSTS (2009-2010)

Tuition and fees: $6,226; out-of-state residents $7,126.
Per-credit charge: $50; out-of-state residents $80.
Room and board: $5,770.

FINANCIAL AID PICTURE (2009-2010)

Students with need: Out of 563 full-time freshmen who applied for aid, 378 were judged to have need. Of these, 375 received aid, and 108 had their full need met. Average financial aid package met 79% of need; average scholarship/grant was $7,448; average loan was $5,757. For part-time students, average financial aid package was $5,555.
Students without need: 116 full-time freshmen who did not demonstrate need for aid received scholarships/grants; average award was $2,339. No-need awards available for academics, alumni affiliation, art, athletics, leadership, music/drama.
Scholarships offered: 2 full-time freshmen received athletic scholarships; average amount $5,100.
Cumulative student debt: 59% of graduating class had student loans; average debt was $19,645.
Additional info: Employees offered tuition reimbursement provided they meet stated criteria. Dependents and children of faculty and staff may receive scholarship to defer local tuition and fees.

FINANCIAL AID PROCEDURES

Forms required: FAFSA, institutional form.
Dates and Deadlines: Priority date 3/1; no closing date. Applicants notified on a rolling basis starting 4/15; must reply within 4 week(s) of notification.
Transfers: No deadline. Applicants notified on a rolling basis starting 4/15; must reply within 4 week(s) of notification.

CONTACT

Kathy Pennartz, Director of Financial Aid
3410 Taft Boulevard, Wichita Falls, TX 76308-2099
(940) 397-4119

Mountain View College

Dallas, Texas
www.mvc.dcccd.edu   Federal Code: 008503

2-year public community college in very large city.
Enrollment: 8,200 undergrads.
Selectivity: Open admission.

BASIC COSTS (2009-2010)

Tuition and fees: $1,230; out-of-district residents $2,280; out-of-state residents $3,630.
Per-credit charge: $41; out-of-district residents $76; out-of-state residents $121.
Additional info: Tuition/fee waivers available for adults.

FINANCIAL AID PICTURE (2009-2010)

Students with need: Need-based aid available for full-time and part-time students. Work study available nights, weekends, and for part-time students.
Students without need: No-need awards available for academics.

FINANCIAL AID PROCEDURES

Forms required: FAFSA, institutional form.
Dates and Deadlines: Priority date 5/1; no closing date. Applicants notified on a rolling basis starting 6/1.

CONTACT

Pam Shuttlesworth, Director of Financial Aid
4849 West Illinois Avenue, Dallas, TX 75211-6599
(214) 860-8688

North Central Texas College

Gainesville, Texas
www.nctc.edu   Federal Code: 003558

2-year public community college in small city.
Enrollment: 4,186 undergrads, 58% part-time. 712 full-time freshmen.
Selectivity: Open admission; but selective for some programs.

BASIC COSTS (2009-2010)

Tuition and fees: $1,350; out-of-district residents $2,310; out-of-state residents $3,450.
Per-credit charge: $35; out-of-district residents $67; out-of-state residents $105.
Room and board: $3,528.

FINANCIAL AID PICTURE

Students with need: Need-based aid available for full-time and part-time students. Work study available nights.
Students without need: This college awards aid only to students with need.

FINANCIAL AID PROCEDURES

Forms required: FAFSA.
Dates and Deadlines: Priority date 5/1; no closing date. Applicants notified on a rolling basis starting 6/1; must reply within 4 week(s) of notification.

CONTACT

Ashley Tatum, Director of Financial Aid
1525 West California Street, Gainesville, TX 76240

North Lake College

Irving, Texas
www.northlakecollege.edu   Federal Code: 014036

2-year public community and liberal arts college in large city.
Enrollment: 7,756 undergrads, 66% part-time. 559 full-time freshmen.
Selectivity: Open admission.

BASIC COSTS (2009-2010)

Tuition and fees: $1,230; out-of-district residents $2,280; out-of-state residents $3,630.
Per-credit charge: $41; out-of-district residents $76; out-of-state residents $121.

FINANCIAL AID PICTURE (2008-2009)

Students with need: Need-based aid available for part-time students. Work study available nights, weekends, and for part-time students.
Students without need: No-need awards available for academics, minority status, state/district residency.

FINANCIAL AID PROCEDURES

Forms required: FAFSA, state aid form.
Dates and Deadlines: Priority date 3/1; closing date 5/1. Applicants notified on a rolling basis starting 7/1.
Transfers: Priority date 2/1. Applicants notified on a rolling basis starting 8/1.

CONTACT

Paul Felix, Director of Financial Aid
5001 North MacArthur Boulevard, Irving, TX 75038-3899
(972) 273-3321

Northeast Texas Community College
Mount Pleasant, Texas
www.ntcc.edu   Federal Code: 016396

2-year public community college in large town.
Enrollment: 2,740 undergrads, 51% part-time. 411 full-time freshmen.
Selectivity: Open admission; but selective for some programs.

BASIC COSTS (2009-2010)
Tuition and fees: $1,950; out-of-district residents $2,940; out-of-state residents $4,074.
Per-credit charge: $30; out-of-district residents $63; out-of-state residents $108.
Room and board: $4,000.

FINANCIAL AID PICTURE (2008-2009)
Students with need: Need-based aid available for full-time and part-time students.

FINANCIAL AID PROCEDURES
Forms required: FAFSA, institutional form.
Dates and Deadlines: Priority date 6/1; no closing date. Applicants notified on a rolling basis starting 6/1.

CONTACT
Patricia Durst, Director of Financial Aid & Veterans Affairs
PO Box 1307, Mount Pleasant, TX 75456-1307
(903) 434-8132

Northwest Vista College
San Antonio, Texas
www.accd.edu/nvc   Federal Code: 033723

2-year public community college in very large city.
Enrollment: 3,516 full-time undergrads.
Selectivity: Open admission.

BASIC COSTS (2009-2010)
Tuition and fees: $1,859; out-of-district residents $3,359; out-of-state residents $6,344.

FINANCIAL AID PICTURE
Students with need: Need-based aid available for full-time and part-time students. Work study available nights, weekends, and for part-time students.
Students without need: No-need awards available for academics, leadership.

FINANCIAL AID PROCEDURES
Forms required: FAFSA.
Dates and Deadlines: Priority date 4/1; no closing date. Applicants notified on a rolling basis starting 5/15; must reply within 2 week(s) of notification.

CONTACT
Noe Ortiz, Financial Aid Director
3535 North Ellison Drive, San Antonio, TX 78251-4217
(210) 486-4168

Northwood University: Texas
Cedar Hill, Texas
www.northwood.edu   Federal Code: 013040

4-year private university and business college in large town.
Enrollment: 514 undergrads, 2% part-time. 139 full-time freshmen.
Selectivity: Admits 50 to 75% of applicants.

BASIC COSTS (2009-2010)
Tuition and fees: $18,408.
Per-credit charge: $363.
Room and board: $7,590.

FINANCIAL AID PICTURE (2009-2010)
Students with need: Out of 118 full-time freshmen who applied for aid, 108 were judged to have need. Of these, 108 received aid, and 15 had their full need met. Average financial aid package met 64% of need; average scholarship/grant was $5,088; average loan was $3,401. For part-time students, average financial aid package was $7,994.
Students without need: 16 full-time freshmen who did not demonstrate need for aid received scholarships/grants; average award was $8,625. No-need awards available for academics, athletics, leadership, minority status, state/district residency.
Scholarships offered: *Merit:* Academic Scholarships: $4,000-$10,000; based on test scores and GPA; unlimited number awarded. *Athletic:* 13 full-time freshmen received athletic scholarships; average amount $4,692.
Cumulative student debt: 86% of graduating class had student loans; average debt was $23,182.

FINANCIAL AID PROCEDURES
Forms required: FAFSA.
Dates and Deadlines: No deadline. Applicants notified on a rolling basis starting 3/1.
Transfers: No deadline. Applicants notified on a rolling basis.

CONTACT
Lisa Seals, Director of Financial Aid
1114 West FM 1382, Cedar Hill, TX 75104
(972) 293-5430

Odessa College
Odessa, Texas
www.odessa.edu   Federal Code: 003596

2-year public community college in small city.
Enrollment: 3,678 undergrads, 61% part-time. 472 full-time freshmen.
Selectivity: Open admission; but selective for some programs.

BASIC COSTS (2009-2010)
Tuition and fees: $1,740; out-of-district residents $2,340; out-of-state residents $3,240.
Room and board: $4,687.

FINANCIAL AID PICTURE (2008-2009)
Students with need: Need-based aid available for full-time and part-time students. Work study available nights.
Students without need: No-need awards available for academics, athletics, music/drama.

FINANCIAL AID PROCEDURES
Forms required: FAFSA.
Dates and Deadlines: Priority date 5/1; no closing date. Applicants notified on a rolling basis starting 6/15.

CONTACT
Dee Nesmith, Director of Student Financial Aid
201 West University, Odessa, TX 79764-7127
(432) 335-6429

Our Lady of the Lake University of San Antonio

San Antonio, Texas
www.ollusa.edu   Federal Code: 003598

4-year private university in very large city, affiliated with Roman Catholic Church.
Enrollment: 1,564 undergrads, 26% part-time. 247 full-time freshmen.
Selectivity: Admits 50 to 75% of applicants.

BASIC COSTS (2010-2011)
Tuition and fees: $21,948.
Per-credit charge: $690.
Room and board: $6,838.

FINANCIAL AID PICTURE (2009-2010)
Students with need: 51% of average financial aid package awarded as scholarships/grants, 49% awarded as loans/jobs. Need-based aid available for part-time students. Work study available nights, weekends, and for part-time students.
Students without need: No-need awards available for academics, religious affiliation.
Scholarships offered: General academic scholarship: $1,205 awarded yearly, renewable. Art/fine arts and music: 4 awarded yearly, renewable. Children of faculty/staff: 60 awarded yearly, renewable. All based on GPA scores and high school record.

FINANCIAL AID PROCEDURES
Forms required: FAFSA, institutional form.
Dates and Deadlines: Priority date 5/1; no closing date.

CONTACT
Michael Fuller, Director of Financial Aid
411 Southwest 24th Street, San Antonio, TX 78207-4689
(210) 434-6711 ext. 2541

Palo Alto College

San Antonio, Texas
www.accd.edu/pac   Federal Code: 016615

2-year public community college in very large city.
Enrollment: 8,335 undergrads.
Selectivity: Open admission.

BASIC COSTS (2009-2010)
Tuition and fees: $1,802; out-of-district residents $3,122; out-of-state residents $5,762.

FINANCIAL AID PICTURE (2008-2009)
Students with need: Need-based aid available for full-time and part-time students.
Students without need: This college awards aid only to students with need.
Scholarships offered: Alamo Community College District Scholarship: $1,000; 50 awarded.

FINANCIAL AID PROCEDURES
Forms required: FAFSA, state aid form.
Dates and Deadlines: Priority date 4/1; closing date 6/1. Applicants notified on a rolling basis starting 5/31.

CONTACT
Lamar Duarte, Director of Financial Aid
1400 West Villaret Boulevard, San Antonio, TX 78224-2499
(210) 921-5316

Panola College

Carthage, Texas
www.panola.edu   Federal Code: 003600

2-year public community and junior college in small town.
Enrollment: 2,079 undergrads, 55% part-time. 313 full-time freshmen.
Selectivity: Open admission; but selective for some programs.

BASIC COSTS (2009-2010)
Tuition and fees: $1,680; out-of-district residents $2,610; out-of-state residents $3,390.
Room and board: $4,374.

FINANCIAL AID PICTURE (2008-2009)
Students with need: Need-based aid available for full-time and part-time students. Work study available nights, weekends, and for part-time students.
Students without need: No-need awards available for academics, alumni affiliation, art, athletics, leadership, music/drama.
Scholarships offered: Several departmental and organization-sponsored scholarships, Presidential scholarship, Dean's scholarship.

FINANCIAL AID PROCEDURES
Forms required: FAFSA, institutional form.
Dates and Deadlines: Priority date 6/1; no closing date. Applicants notified on a rolling basis starting 6/1.
Transfers: No deadline. Applicants notified on a rolling basis.

CONTACT
Denise Welch, Director of Financial Aid
1109 West Panola Street, Carthage, TX 75633
(903) 693-2039

Paris Junior College

Paris, Texas
www.parisjc.edu   Federal Code: 003601

2-year public community and junior college in large town.
Enrollment: 5,570 undergrads. 1,179 full-time freshmen.
Selectivity: Open admission; but selective for some programs.

BASIC COSTS (2009-2010)
Tuition and fees: $1,380; out-of-district residents $2,280; out-of-state residents $3,480.
Per-credit charge: $123; out-of-district residents $183; out-of-state residents $263.
Room and board: $4,170.

FINANCIAL AID PICTURE (2008-2009)
Students with need: Need-based aid available for full-time and part-time students.
Students without need: No-need awards available for athletics, music/drama.

FINANCIAL AID PROCEDURES
Forms required: FAFSA.
Dates and Deadlines: No deadline. Applicants notified on a rolling basis starting 6/1.

CONTACT
Linda Slawson, Director of Financial Aid
2400 Clarksville Street, Paris, TX 75460
(903) 782-0256

Prairie View A&M University
Prairie View, Texas
www.pvamu.edu   Federal Code: 003630

4-year public university in small town.
Enrollment: 6,712 undergrads, 9% part-time. 1,584 full-time freshmen.
Selectivity: Admits less than 50% of applicants.

BASIC COSTS (2009-2010)
Tuition and fees: $7,199; out-of-state residents $15,689.
Room and board: $7,445.

FINANCIAL AID PICTURE (2009-2010)
Students with need: Need-based aid available for full-time and part-time students. Work study available nights, weekends, and for part-time students.
Students without need: No-need awards available for academics, athletics, ROTC.

FINANCIAL AID PROCEDURES
Forms required: FAFSA, institutional form.
Dates and Deadlines: Closing date 3/15. Applicants notified by 6/1; must reply by 8/1.
Transfers: Closing date 3/1. Minimum 2.0 GPA from all colleges attended required to be considered for financial aid.

CONTACT
Carlos Clark, Director of Financial Aid
PO Box 519, MS 1009, Prairie View, TX 77446-0519

Ranger College
Ranger, Texas
www.rangercollege.edu   Federal Code: 003603

2-year public junior college in rural community.
Enrollment: 377 undergrads.
Selectivity: Open admission; but selective for some programs.

BASIC COSTS (2009-2010)
Tuition and fees: $2,110; out-of-district residents $2,230; out-of-state residents $2,410.
Room and board: $3,590.

FINANCIAL AID PICTURE (2008-2009)
Students with need: Need-based aid available for full-time and part-time students.
Students without need: This college awards aid only to students with need.

FINANCIAL AID PROCEDURES
Forms required: FAFSA.
Dates and Deadlines: Priority date 6/1; closing date 7/24. Applicants notified on a rolling basis; must reply within 2 week(s) of notification.
Transfers: Applicants notified on a rolling basis; must reply within 2 week(s) of notification.

CONTACT
Don Hilton, Financial Aid Director
1100 College Circle, Ranger, TX 76470
(254) 647-3234 ext. 117

Rice University
Houston, Texas   Federal Code: 003604
www.rice.edu   CSS Code: 6609

4-year private university in very large city.
Enrollment: 3,279 undergrads, 1% part-time. 894 full-time freshmen.

Selectivity: Admits less than 50% of applicants.

BASIC COSTS (2009-2010)
Tuition and fees: $32,057.
Per-credit charge: $1,310.
Room and board: $11,230.

FINANCIAL AID PICTURE (2009-2010)
Students with need: Out of 606 full-time freshmen who applied for aid, 370 were judged to have need. Of these, 370 received aid, and 370 had their full need met. Average financial aid package met 100% of need; average scholarship/grant was $26,850; average loan was $1,333. Need-based aid available for part-time students.
Students without need: 102 full-time freshmen who did not demonstrate need for aid received scholarships/grants; average award was $17,340. No-need awards available for academics, art, athletics, leadership, minority status, music/drama, ROTC, state/district residency.
Scholarships offered: 65 full-time freshmen received athletic scholarships; average amount $30,534.
Cumulative student debt: 31% of graduating class had student loans; average debt was $18,166.

FINANCIAL AID PROCEDURES
Forms required: FAFSA, CSS PROFILE.
Dates and Deadlines: Priority date 3/1; no closing date. Applicants notified by 4/1; must reply by 5/1.
Transfers: Priority date 4/1.

CONTACT
Anne Walker, Director of Student Financial Services
6100 Main Street, Houston, TX 77251-1892
(713) 348-4958

Richland College
Dallas, Texas
www.rlc.dcccd.edu   Federal Code: 008504

2-year public community college in very large city.
Enrollment: 14,843 undergrads.
Selectivity: Open admission.

BASIC COSTS (2009-2010)
Tuition and fees: $1,230; out-of-district residents $2,280; out-of-state residents $3,630.
Per-credit charge: $41; out-of-district residents $76; out-of-state residents $121.

FINANCIAL AID PICTURE (2009-2010)
Students with need: Need-based aid available for full-time and part-time students. Work study available nights.
Students without need: No-need awards available for art, leadership, music/drama.

FINANCIAL AID PROCEDURES
Forms required: FAFSA.
Dates and Deadlines: Priority date 5/2; no closing date. Applicants notified on a rolling basis starting 6/1; must reply within 2 week(s) of notification.

CONTACT
Michael Williams, Director of Financial Aid
12800 Abrams Road, Dallas, TX 75243-2199
(972) 238-6188

St. Edward's University
Austin, Texas
www.gotostedwards.com   Federal Code: 003621

4-year private university and liberal arts college in very large city, affiliated with Roman Catholic Church.

Enrollment: 4,339 undergrads, 20% part-time. 757 full-time freshmen.

Selectivity: Admits 50 to 75% of applicants.

BASIC COSTS (2010-2011)
Tuition and fees: $26,484.

Per-credit charge: $870.

Room and board: $9,036.

FINANCIAL AID PICTURE (2009-2010)
Students with need: Out of 643 full-time freshmen who applied for aid, 547 were judged to have need. Of these, 546 received aid, and 66 had their full need met. Average financial aid package met 74% of need; average scholarship/grant was $13,705; average loan was $3,323. For part-time students, average financial aid package was $6,804.

Students without need: 65 full-time freshmen who did not demonstrate need for aid received scholarships/grants; average award was $8,405. No-need awards available for academics, art, athletics, leadership, music/drama, state/district residency.

Scholarships offered: *Merit:* Trustees' Scholar Award: $10,000 per year; minimum 1200 SAT; top 20% of class. Holy Cross Scholar Award: full tuition; minimum 1250 SAT; top 10% of class; demonstrate academic excellence, leadership ability and commitment to community service. Academic Scholar Award: $5,000-$14,000 per year; minimum 1100 SAT; top 25% of class. All SAT scores exclusive of Writing. *Athletic:* 30 full-time freshmen received athletic scholarships; average amount $15,578.

Cumulative student debt: 79% of graduating class had student loans; average debt was $29,810.

FINANCIAL AID PROCEDURES
Forms required: FAFSA.

Dates and Deadlines: Priority date 3/1; closing date 4/15. Applicants notified on a rolling basis starting 1/15; must reply by 5/1 or within 2 week(s) of notification.

Transfers: Must reply by 5/1 or within 2 week(s) of notification.

CONTACT
Doris Constantine, Associate VP and Director of Student Financial Services
3001 South Congress Avenue, Austin, TX 78704-6489
(512) 448-8520

St. Mary's University
San Antonio, Texas
www.stmarytx.edu   Federal Code: 003623

4-year private university in very large city, affiliated with Roman Catholic Church.

Enrollment: 2,369 undergrads, 7% part-time. 535 full-time freshmen.

Selectivity: Admits over 75% of applicants.

BASIC COSTS (2009-2010)
Tuition and fees: $21,876.

Per-credit charge: $640.

Room and board: $7,090.

FINANCIAL AID PICTURE (2008-2009)
Students with need: Out of 470 full-time freshmen who applied for aid, 429 were judged to have need. Of these, 428 received aid, and 94 had their full need met. Average financial aid package met 78% of need; average scholarship/grant was $13,542; average loan was $6,317. For part-time students, average financial aid package was $7,369.

Students without need: 85 full-time freshmen who did not demonstrate need for aid received scholarships/grants; average award was $11,165. No-need awards available for academics, alumni affiliation, athletics, leadership, minority status, music/drama, ROTC, state/district residency.

Scholarships offered: 41 full-time freshmen received athletic scholarships; average amount $13,979.

Cumulative student debt: 79% of graduating class had student loans; average debt was $27,416.

FINANCIAL AID PROCEDURES
Forms required: FAFSA.

Dates and Deadlines: Priority date 3/31; no closing date. Applicants notified on a rolling basis starting 3/1; must reply by 5/1 or within 2 week(s) of notification.

CONTACT
David Krause, Director of Financial Assistance
One Camino Santa Maria, San Antonio, TX 78228-8503
(210) 436-3141

St. Philip's College
San Antonio, Texas
www.alamo.edu/spc   Federal Code: 003608

2-year public community college in very large city.

Enrollment: 7,953 undergrads, 62% part-time. 919 full-time freshmen.

Selectivity: Open admission; but selective for some programs.

BASIC COSTS (2009-2010)
Tuition and fees: $1,889; out-of-district residents $3,389; out-of-state residents $6,374.

Per-credit charge: $53; out-of-district residents $103; out-of-state residents $203.

FINANCIAL AID PICTURE (2008-2009)
Students with need: 72% of average financial aid package awarded as scholarships/grants, 28% awarded as loans/jobs. Need-based aid available for part-time students. Work study available nights, weekends, and for part-time students.

Students without need: This college awards aid only to students with need.

FINANCIAL AID PROCEDURES
Forms required: FAFSA.

Dates and Deadlines: No deadline.

CONTACT
Diego Bernal, Director of Financial Aid
1801 Martin Luther King Drive, San Antonio, TX 78203
(210) 486-2275

Sam Houston State University
Huntsville, Texas
www.shsu.edu   Federal Code: 003606

4-year public university in large town.

Enrollment: 14,569 undergrads, 16% part-time. 2,090 full-time freshmen.

Selectivity: Admits 50 to 75% of applicants.

BASIC COSTS (2009-2010)
Tuition and fees: $6,515; out-of-state residents $14,825.

Per-credit charge: $155; out-of-state residents $432.

Room and board: $6,744.

FINANCIAL AID PICTURE (2008-2009)

Students with need: Out of 1,529 full-time freshmen who applied for aid, 1,083 were judged to have need. Of these, 968 received aid, and 3 had their full need met. Average financial aid package met 36% of need; average scholarship/grant was $1,205; average loan was $215. For part-time students, average financial aid package was $821.

Students without need: 114 full-time freshmen who did not demonstrate need for aid received scholarships/grants; average award was $508. No-need awards available for academics, alumni affiliation, art, athletics, job skills, leadership, music/drama, religious affiliation, ROTC, state/district residency.

Cumulative student debt: 55% of graduating class had student loans; average debt was $6,196.

FINANCIAL AID PROCEDURES

Forms required: FAFSA, institutional form.

Dates and Deadlines: Priority date 4/1; no closing date. Applicants notified on a rolling basis starting 3/1; must reply within 4 week(s) of notification.

CONTACT

Randal Lewis, Vice President for Finance & Operations
Box 2418, Huntsville, TX 77341-2418
(936) 294-1774

San Antonio College

San Antonio, Texas
www.accd.edu/sac   Federal Code: 009163

2-year public community college in very large city.

Enrollment: 18,278 undergrads.

Selectivity: Open admission; but selective for some programs.

BASIC COSTS (2009-2010)

Tuition and fees: $1,747; out-of-district residents $3,247; out-of-state residents $6,232.

Per-credit charge: $54; out-of-district residents $104; out-of-state residents $203.

FINANCIAL AID PICTURE (2008-2009)

Students with need: Need-based aid available for full-time and part-time students. Work study available nights, weekends, and for part-time students.

Students without need: This college awards aid only to students with need.

Additional info: Leveraging Educational Assistance Partnership (LEAP), public student incentive grant, towards excellence access and success grants (Texas and Texas II grants) available.

FINANCIAL AID PROCEDURES

Forms required: FAFSA.

Dates and Deadlines: Priority date 3/1; no closing date. Applicants notified by 7/1.

CONTACT

Tom Campos, Director of Student Financial Services
1300 San Pedro Avenue, San Antonio, TX 78212-4299
(210) 486-0600

San Jacinto College

Pasadena, Texas
www.sanjac.edu

2-year public community and technical college in very large city.

Enrollment: 27,047 undergrads, 64% part-time. 4,373 full-time freshmen.

Selectivity: Open admission; but selective for some programs.

BASIC COSTS (2009-2010)

Tuition and fees: $1,250; out-of-district residents $2,000; out-of-state residents $3,500.

Per-credit charge: $33; out-of-district residents $58; out-of-state residents $108.

FINANCIAL AID PICTURE (2008-2009)

Students with need: Out of 2,139 full-time freshmen who applied for aid, 1,876 were judged to have need. Of these, 1,491 received aid, and 1 had their full need met. For part-time students, average financial aid package was $2,249.

Students without need: This college awards aid only to students with need.

Scholarships offered: 58 full-time freshmen received athletic scholarships; average amount $2,126.

FINANCIAL AID PROCEDURES

Forms required: FAFSA, institutional form.

Dates and Deadlines: Priority date 7/1; no closing date. Applicants notified on a rolling basis starting 4/1; must reply within 4 week(s) of notification.

Transfers: Applicants notified on a rolling basis starting 4/1; must reply within 4 week(s) of notification.

CONTACT

Robert Merino, Director of Financial Aid
8060 Spencer Highway, Pasadena, TX 77505-5999
(281) 998-6150

Schreiner University

Kerrville, Texas
www.schreiner.edu   Federal Code: 003610

4-year private liberal arts college in large town, affiliated with Presbyterian Church (USA).

Enrollment: 1,013 undergrads, 4% part-time. 271 full-time freshmen.

Selectivity: Admits 50 to 75% of applicants.

BASIC COSTS (2010-2011)

Tuition and fees: $19,547.

Per-credit charge: $809.

Room and board: $9,390.

FINANCIAL AID PICTURE (2008-2009)

Students with need: Out of 242 full-time freshmen who applied for aid, 191 were judged to have need. Of these, 191 received aid, and 37 had their full need met. Average financial aid package met 75% of need; average scholarship/grant was $11,815; average loan was $2,978. For part-time students, average financial aid package was $7,777.

Students without need: 70 full-time freshmen who did not demonstrate need for aid received scholarships/grants; average award was $6,654. No-need awards available for academics, art, leadership, music/drama, religious affiliation.

Scholarships offered: Awards for students with exceptional academic achievement and leadership abilities; partial and full tuition; 3.5 GPA and 1100 SAT (exclusive of Writing) or 24 ACT; 66 awarded after participation in the Schreiner Scholars program.

Cumulative student debt: 97% of graduating class had student loans; average debt was $27,986.

FINANCIAL AID PROCEDURES

Forms required: FAFSA.

Dates and Deadlines: No deadline. Applicants notified on a rolling basis starting 2/15; must reply within 2 week(s) of notification.

Transfers: Priority date 4/15; no deadline.

PART III: FINANCIAL AID COLLEGE BY COLLEGE

CONTACT

Toni Bryant, Director of Financial Aid
2100 Memorial Boulevard, Kerrville, TX 78028-5697
(830) 896-5411

South Plains College
Levelland, Texas
www.southplainscollege.edu   Federal Code: 003611

2-year public community and junior college in large town.
Enrollment: 8,546 undergrads, 46% part-time. 1,149 full-time freshmen.
Selectivity: Open admission; but selective for some programs.

BASIC COSTS (2009-2010)
Tuition and fees: $1,892; out-of-district residents $2,552; out-of-state residents $3,032.
Room and board: $3,200.

FINANCIAL AID PICTURE
Students with need: Need-based aid available for full-time and part-time students.
Students without need: No-need awards available for academics, art, athletics, leadership, music/drama, state/district residency.

FINANCIAL AID PROCEDURES
Forms required: FAFSA.
Dates and Deadlines: Priority date 6/1; no closing date. Applicants notified on a rolling basis starting 6/30; must reply within 2 week(s) of notification.

CONTACT
Jim Ann Batenhorst, Director of Financial Aid
1401 South College Avenue, Levelland, TX 79336
(806) 894-9611

South Texas College
McAllen, Texas
www.southtexascollege.edu   Federal Code: 031034

2-year public community and technical college in small city.
Enrollment: 17,555 undergrads, 51% part-time. 2,459 full-time freshmen.
Selectivity: Open admission; but selective for some programs.

BASIC COSTS (2009-2010)
Tuition and fees: $2,785; out-of-district residents $3,298; out-of-state residents $7,075.

FINANCIAL AID PICTURE (2008-2009)
Students with need: Out of 542 full-time freshmen who applied for aid, 470 were judged to have need. Of these, 315 received aid. Need-based aid available for part-time students.
Students without need: This college awards aid only to students with need.

FINANCIAL AID PROCEDURES
Forms required: FAFSA.
Dates and Deadlines: Priority date 3/1; no closing date. Applicants notified on a rolling basis starting 4/15.

CONTACT
Miguel Carranza, Director of Financial Aid
3201 West Pecan Boulevard, McAllen, TX 78502
(956) 872-8375

Southern Methodist University
Dallas, Texas   Federal Code: 003613
www.smu.edu   CSS Code: 6660

4-year private university in large town, affiliated with United Methodist Church.
Enrollment: 6,150 undergrads, 4% part-time. 1,329 full-time freshmen.
Selectivity: Admits 50 to 75% of applicants. GED not accepted.

BASIC COSTS (2010-2011)
Tuition and fees: $37,230.
Per-credit charge: $1,381.
Room and board: $12,735.

FINANCIAL AID PICTURE (2009-2010)
Students with need: Out of 726 full-time freshmen who applied for aid, 538 were judged to have need. Of these, 537 received aid, and 237 had their full need met. Average financial aid package met 90% of need; average scholarship/grant was $20,259; average loan was $2,454. For part-time students, average financial aid package was $8,327.
Students without need: 440 full-time freshmen who did not demonstrate need for aid received scholarships/grants; average award was $15,539. No-need awards available for academics, art, athletics, leadership, music/drama, religious affiliation, ROTC, state/district residency.
Scholarships offered: 57 full-time freshmen received athletic scholarships; average amount $39,091.
Cumulative student debt: 32% of graduating class had student loans; average debt was $20,146.

FINANCIAL AID PROCEDURES
Forms required: FAFSA, CSS PROFILE.
Dates and Deadlines: Priority date 2/15; no closing date. Applicants notified on a rolling basis starting 3/15.
Transfers: Priority date 4/1. Merit scholarships available for community college and senior institution honor transfers. Students entering without scholarship aid will receive need-based aid up to cost of tuition.

CONTACT
Marc Peterson, Executive Director of Enrollment Services
PO Box 750181, Dallas, TX 75275-0181
(214) 768-2068

Southwest Texas Junior College
Uvalde, Texas
www.swtjc.edu   Federal Code: 003614

2-year public community and junior college in large town.
Enrollment: 5,767 undergrads.
Selectivity: Open admission.

BASIC COSTS (2009-2010)
Tuition and fees: $2,021; out-of-district residents $2,951; out-of-state residents $3,341.
Per-credit charge: $46; out-of-district residents $77; out-of-state residents $90.
Room and board: $3,600.
Additional info: Additional fees for off-campus classes may apply.

FINANCIAL AID PICTURE
Students with need: Need-based aid available for full-time and part-time students.

FINANCIAL AID PROCEDURES
Forms required: FAFSA.
Dates and Deadlines: Priority date 6/15; no closing date. Applicants notified on a rolling basis starting 5/1; must reply within 2 week(s) of notification.

CONTACT
Ana Almaraz, Director of Financial Aid
2401 Garner Field Road, Uvalde, TX 78801
(830) 278-4401

Southwestern Adventist University
Keene, Texas
www.swau.edu — Federal Code: 003619

4-year private university and liberal arts college in small town, affiliated with Seventh-day Adventists.
Enrollment: 735 undergrads, 10% part-time. 129 full-time freshmen.
Selectivity: Admits 50 to 75% of applicants.

BASIC COSTS (2010-2011)
Tuition and fees: $16,216.
Per-credit charge: $644.
Room and board: $7,148.

FINANCIAL AID PICTURE
Students with need: Need-based aid available for full-time and part-time students.
Students without need: No-need awards available for academics, leadership, music/drama.

FINANCIAL AID PROCEDURES
Forms required: FAFSA, institutional form.
Dates and Deadlines: Priority date 3/15; no closing date. Applicants notified on a rolling basis starting 4/15.
Transfers: No deadline. Applicants notified on a rolling basis.

CONTACT
Patricia Norwood, Assistant Vice President for Financial Administration, Student Finance
Box 567, Keene, TX 76059
(817) 202-6262

Southwestern Assemblies of God University
Waxahachie, Texas
www.sagu.edu — Federal Code: 003616

4-year private university and Bible college in large town, affiliated with Assemblies of God.
Enrollment: 1,708 undergrads.
Selectivity: Admits less than 50% of applicants.

BASIC COSTS (2009-2010)
Tuition and fees: $13,780.
Per-credit charge: $430.
Room and board: $4,880.

FINANCIAL AID PICTURE (2008-2009)
Students with need: Need-based aid available for full-time and part-time students.

FINANCIAL AID PROCEDURES
Forms required: FAFSA.
Dates and Deadlines: Priority date 3/1; closing date 6/1. Applicants notified on a rolling basis starting 6/1; must reply within 2 week(s) of notification.

CONTACT
Karen Lazarz, Director of Financial Aid
1200 Sycamore Street, Waxahachie, TX 75165
(972) 825-4730

Southwestern University
Georgetown, Texas
www.southwestern.edu — Federal Code: 003620

4-year private liberal arts college in large town, affiliated with United Methodist Church.
Enrollment: 1,291 undergrads, 1% part-time. 374 full-time freshmen.
Selectivity: Admits 50 to 75% of applicants.

BASIC COSTS (2010-2011)
Tuition and fees: $31,360.
Per-credit charge: $1,320.
Room and board: $9,230.

FINANCIAL AID PICTURE (2009-2010)
Students with need: Need-based aid available for full-time students. Work study available nights, weekends, and for part-time students.
Students without need: No-need awards available for academics, art, minority status, music/drama, religious affiliation.
Scholarships offered: Academic Merit Scholarships: $2,000 to $19,000 per year. Brown Scholarships: full tuition, room and board. National Merit Finalist Awards: $2,000 per year. Fine Arts Scholarships: $3,500 to $10,000 per year; for students majoring in art, music or theater; based on talent, auditions or portfolio review. Music Performance Awards: up to $2,500; based on talent and awarded to non-fine arts majors who wish to participate in university ensemble. Dixon Scholarship: $5,000 per year or full tuition; awarded to high-achieving African-American, Hispanic, and Native American students. Beneficiary Grants: $6,000 per year; awarded to dependents of United Methodist clergy. Preministerial Scholarships: $3,000 per year; to students interested in full-time ministry careers.

FINANCIAL AID PROCEDURES
Forms required: FAFSA.
Dates and Deadlines: Priority date 3/1; no closing date. Applicants notified on a rolling basis starting 3/1; must reply by 5/1 or within 2 week(s) of notification.
Transfers: Closing date 5/15.

CONTACT
James Gaeta, Director of Financial Aid
1001 East University Avenue, Georgetown, TX 78626
(512) 863-1259

Stephen F. Austin State University
Nacogdoches, Texas
www.sfasu.edu — Federal Code: 003624

4-year public university in large town.
Enrollment: 11,144 undergrads, 13% part-time. 2,290 full-time freshmen.
Selectivity: Admits 50 to 75% of applicants.

BASIC COSTS (2009-2010)
Tuition and fees: $6,732; out-of-state residents $15,042.
Per-credit charge: $161; out-of-state residents $438.
Room and board: $7,377.

FINANCIAL AID PICTURE (2008-2009)
Students with need: Out of 1,806 full-time freshmen who applied for aid, 1,409 were judged to have need. Of these, 1,382 received aid, and 892 had their full need met. Average financial aid package met 84% of need; average scholarship/grant was $3,535; average loan was $3,138. For part-time students, average financial aid package was $8,883.
Students without need: 130 full-time freshmen who did not demonstrate need for aid received scholarships/grants; average award was $2,286. No-need awards available for academics, alumni affiliation, athletics, leadership, music/drama, state/district residency.

Scholarships offered: *Merit:* Academic Excellence Scholarship Program: $3,000 per year; rank in top 10% of high school class or top quartile class with 1100 SAT (exclusive of Writing) or 24 ACT; renewable with 3.5 GPA. Dugas Honors Scholarship: $2,500 per semester; active member of School of Honors. University Scholars Program: $2,000 per semester; minimum 1220 SAT, 27 ACT, 3.0 GPA maintenance; up to 11 awarded. Student Foundation Association Leadership Scholarship: amounts vary; demonstrated leadership capabilities and academic achievement throughout high school career; 1 awarded. *Athletic:* 75 full-time freshmen received athletic scholarships; average amount $9,219.

Cumulative student debt: 68% of graduating class had student loans; average debt was $20,547.

FINANCIAL AID PROCEDURES

Forms required: FAFSA.

Dates and Deadlines: Priority date 4/1; no closing date. Applicants notified on a rolling basis starting 4/1.

CONTACT

Mike O'Rear, Director of Financial Aid
Box 13051, SFA Station, Nacogdoches, TX 75962-3051
(936) 468-2403

Sul Ross State University
Alpine, Texas
www.sulross.edu   Federal Code: 003625

4-year public university in small town.

Enrollment: 2,167 undergrads, 35% part-time. 369 full-time freshmen.

Selectivity: Admits over 75% of applicants.

BASIC COSTS (2009-2010)

Tuition and fees: $5,302; out-of-state residents $13,612.

Per-credit charge: $122; out-of-state residents $399.

Room and board: $6,370.

FINANCIAL AID PICTURE (2008-2009)

Students with need: Average financial aid package met 22% of need; average scholarship/grant was $5,960; average loan was $4,993. For part-time students, average financial aid package was $7,945.

Students without need: No-need awards available for academics, art, athletics, job skills, leadership, music/drama, state/district residency.

FINANCIAL AID PROCEDURES

Forms required: FAFSA, institutional form.

Dates and Deadlines: Priority date 3/1; closing date 4/1. Applicants notified on a rolling basis starting 5/1; must reply within 2 week(s) of notification.

CONTACT

Rowena Gallego, Director Student Financial Assistance
Box C-2, Alpine, TX 79832
(432) 837-8055

Tarleton State University
Stephenville, Texas
www.tarleton.edu   Federal Code: 003631

4-year public university in large town.

Enrollment: 7,239 undergrads, 19% part-time. 2,519 full-time freshmen.

Selectivity: Admits 50 to 75% of applicants.

BASIC COSTS (2009-2010)

Tuition and fees: $5,565; out-of-state residents $13,995.

Per-credit charge: $139; out-of-state residents $420.

Room and board: $7,046.

Additional info: Freshmen pay additional $100 first-year experience fee, first semester only. Distance learning fee is additional $40 per credit hour.

FINANCIAL AID PICTURE (2008-2009)

Students with need: Out of 1,942 full-time freshmen who applied for aid, 1,897 were judged to have need. Of these, 1,819 received aid, and 723 had their full need met. Average financial aid package met 49% of need; average scholarship/grant was $2,248; average loan was $1,867. For part-time students, average financial aid package was $4,620.

Students without need: 529 full-time freshmen who did not demonstrate need for aid received scholarships/grants; average award was $3,231. No-need awards available for academics, alumni affiliation, art, athletics, leadership, music/drama, ROTC.

Scholarships offered: 120 full-time freshmen received athletic scholarships; average amount $2,115.

Cumulative student debt: 52% of graduating class had student loans; average debt was $14,685.

FINANCIAL AID PROCEDURES

Forms required: FAFSA.

Dates and Deadlines: Priority date 4/1; no closing date. Applicants notified on a rolling basis starting 2/1.

Transfers: No deadline.

CONTACT

Betty Murray, Director, Student Financial Aid
Box T-0030, Stephenville, TX 76402
(254) 968-9070

Tarrant County College
Fort Worth, Texas
www.tccd.edu   Federal Code: 003626

2-year public community and liberal arts college in very large city.

Enrollment: 44,786 undergrads.

Selectivity: Open admission; but selective for some programs.

BASIC COSTS (2009-2010)

Tuition and fees: $1,500; out-of-district residents $2,190; out-of-state residents $4,950.

Per-credit charge: $50; out-of-district residents $73; out-of-state residents $165.

FINANCIAL AID PICTURE (2008-2009)

Students with need: Need-based aid available for full-time and part-time students.

Students without need: No-need awards available for academics.

FINANCIAL AID PROCEDURES

Forms required: FAFSA, institutional form.

Dates and Deadlines: Priority date 5/1; no closing date. Applicants notified on a rolling basis starting 5/1; must reply within 2 week(s) of notification.

CONTACT

David Ximenez, District Director of Financial Aid
1500 Houston Street, Fort Worth, TX 76102-6599
(817) 515-4243

Temple College
Temple, Texas
www.templejc.edu   Federal Code: 003627

2-year public community college in small city.

Enrollment: 5,445 undergrads, 60% part-time. 482 full-time freshmen.

Selectivity: Open admission; but selective for some programs.

BASIC COSTS (2009-2010)

Tuition and fees: $2,250; out-of-district residents $3,600; out-of-state residents $5,700.

Per-credit charge: $75; out-of-district residents $120; out-of-state residents $190.

FINANCIAL AID PICTURE (2008-2009)

Students with need: Need-based aid available for full-time and part-time students. Work study available nights.

Students without need: This college awards aid only to students with need.

FINANCIAL AID PROCEDURES

Forms required: FAFSA.

Dates and Deadlines: Priority date 6/1; no closing date. Applicants notified on a rolling basis starting 5/1; must reply within 4 week(s) of notification.

Transfers: No deadline. Applicants notified on a rolling basis starting 5/1; must reply within 4 week(s) of notification.

CONTACT

Federico Pena, Director of Financial Aid

2600 South First Street, Temple, TX 76504-7435

(254) 298-8321

Texarkana College

Texarkana, Texas

www.texarkanacollege.edu   Federal Code: 003628

2-year public community college in small city.

Enrollment: 4,654 undergrads.

Selectivity: Open admission.

BASIC COSTS (2009-2010)

Tuition and fees: $1,170; out-of-district residents $1,890; out-of-state residents $2,390.

Per-credit charge: $36; out-of-district residents $60; out-of-state residents $77.

Additional info: Arkansas and Oklahoma residents pay out-of-district rates.

FINANCIAL AID PICTURE

Students with need: Need-based aid available for full-time and part-time students. Work study available nights, weekends, and for part-time students.

Students without need: No-need awards available for academics, athletics.

FINANCIAL AID PROCEDURES

Forms required: FAFSA, institutional form.

Dates and Deadlines: Priority date 6/1; no closing date. Applicants notified on a rolling basis starting 3/1.

CONTACT

Robin Thomas, Director of Financial Aid

2500 North Robison Road, Texarkana, TX 75599

(903) 832-5565 ext. 3214

Texas A&M International University

Laredo, Texas

www.tamiu.edu   Federal Code: 009651

4-year public university in small city.

Enrollment: 5,281 undergrads, 37% part-time. 663 full-time freshmen.

Selectivity: Admits 50 to 75% of applicants.

BASIC COSTS (2009-2010)

Tuition and fees: $5,717; out-of-state residents $14,027.

Per-credit charge: $135; out-of-state residents $412.

Room and board: $6,918.

FINANCIAL AID PICTURE (2008-2009)

Students with need: Out of 612 full-time freshmen who applied for aid, 545 were judged to have need. Of these, 543 received aid, and 36 had their full need met. Average financial aid package met 55% of need; average scholarship/grant was $5,890; average loan was $2,927. For part-time students, average financial aid package was $5,640.

Students without need: 56 full-time freshmen who did not demonstrate need for aid received scholarships/grants; average award was $1,685. No-need awards available for academics.

Scholarships offered: 10 full-time freshmen received athletic scholarships; average amount $2,790.

FINANCIAL AID PROCEDURES

Forms required: FAFSA, institutional form.

Dates and Deadlines: Priority date 3/15; no closing date. Applicants notified on a rolling basis starting 4/15; must reply within 2 week(s) of notification.

Transfers: No deadline. Applicants notified on a rolling basis starting 11/30; must reply within 2 week(s) of notification.

CONTACT

Laura Elizondo, Director of Financial Aid

5201 University Boulevard, Laredo, TX 78041-1900

(956) 326-2225

Texas A&M University

College Station, Texas

www.tamu.edu   Federal Code: 003632

4-year public university in small city.

Enrollment: 38,718 undergrads, 9% part-time. 7,466 full-time freshmen.

Selectivity: Admits 50 to 75% of applicants.

BASIC COSTS (2009-2010)

Tuition and fees: $8,176; out-of-state residents $22,609.

Per-credit charge: $172; out-of-state residents $653.

Room and board: $8,039.

FINANCIAL AID PICTURE (2008-2009)

Students with need: Out of 4,954 full-time freshmen who applied for aid, 2,968 were judged to have need. Of these, 2,913 received aid, and 1,771 had their full need met. Average financial aid package met 92% of need; average scholarship/grant was $10,946; average loan was $4,018. For part-time students, average financial aid package was $9,781.

Students without need: 1,141 full-time freshmen who did not demonstrate need for aid received scholarships/grants; average award was $4,320. No-need awards available for academics, alumni affiliation, art, athletics, job skills, leadership, music/drama, religious affiliation, ROTC, state/district residency.

Scholarships offered: 66 full-time freshmen received athletic scholarships; average amount $11,098.

Cumulative student debt: 51% of graduating class had student loans; average debt was $21,182.

Additional info: Short-term loans available. Out-of-state students awarded academic scholarships of $1,000 or more are eligible for waiver of out-of-state tuition.

FINANCIAL AID PROCEDURES

Forms required: FAFSA.

Dates and Deadlines: Priority date 3/31; no closing date. Applicants notified on a rolling basis starting 3/15; must reply within 4 week(s) of notification.

Transfers: Must provide previous financial aid transcript.

CONTACT

Joseph Pettibon, Assistant Provost - Student Financial Aid

PO Box 30014, College Station, TX 77842-3014

(979) 845-3236

Texas A&M University-Baylor College of Dentistry
Dallas, Texas
www.bcd.tamhsc.edu   Federal Code: 004948

Upper-division public health science college in very large city.
Enrollment: 61 undergrads.

FINANCIAL AID PICTURE (2009-2010)
Students with need: Average financial aid package for all full-time under-graduates was $8,233. 50% awarded as scholarships/grants, 50% awarded as loans/jobs. Need-based aid available for part-time students.
Students without need: No-need awards available for academics.

FINANCIAL AID PROCEDURES
Forms required: FAFSA, institutional form.
Dates and Deadlines: Priority date 3/15; no closing date. Applicants notified on a rolling basis starting 6/1; must reply within 2 week(s) of notification.

CONTACT
Kay Egbert, Director of Student Aid
PO Box 660677, Dallas, TX 75266-0677

Texas A&M University-Commerce
Commerce, Texas
www.tamu-commerce.edu   Federal Code: 003565

4-year public university in small town.
Enrollment: 5,194 undergrads, 23% part-time. 619 full-time freshmen.
Selectivity: Admits over 75% of applicants.

BASIC COSTS (2009-2010)
Tuition and fees: $5,500; out-of-state residents $13,840.
Room and board: $7,090.

FINANCIAL AID PICTURE (2008-2009)
Students with need: Need-based aid available for full-time and part-time students.
Students without need: No-need awards available for academics, art, athletics, leadership, music/drama.
Additional info: Work-study also available for full-time students.

FINANCIAL AID PROCEDURES
Forms required: FAFSA.
Dates and Deadlines: Priority date 4/1; no closing date. Applicants notified on a rolling basis starting 4/1; must reply within 2 week(s) of notification.

CONTACT
Dolly Lasater, Director of Financial Aid
Box 3011, Commerce, TX 75429-3011
(903) 886-5091

Texas A&M University-Corpus Christi
Corpus Christi, Texas
www.tamucc.edu   Federal Code: 011161

4-year public university in large city.
Enrollment: 7,591 undergrads, 23% part-time. 1,270 full-time freshmen.
Selectivity: Admits over 75% of applicants.

BASIC COSTS (2009-2010)
Tuition and fees: $6,098; out-of-state residents $14,408.
Per-credit charge: $153; out-of-state residents $430.
Room and board: $9,250.

FINANCIAL AID PICTURE (2009-2010)
Students with need: 57% of average financial aid package awarded as scholarships/grants, 43% awarded as loans/jobs. Need-based aid available for part-time students.
Students without need: No-need awards available for academics, art, athletics, music/drama.

FINANCIAL AID PROCEDURES
Forms required: FAFSA, institutional form.
Dates and Deadlines: Closing date 4/1. Applicants notified on a rolling basis starting 5/1; must reply within 2 week(s) of notification.

CONTACT
Jeannie Gage, Director, Financial Assistance
6300 Ocean Drive, Unit 5774, Corpus Christi, TX 78412-5774
(361) 825-2338

Texas A&M University-Galveston
Galveston, Texas
www.tamug.edu   Federal Code: 003632

4-year public university and branch campus college in small city.
Enrollment: 1,718 undergrads.
Selectivity: Admits 50 to 75% of applicants.

BASIC COSTS (2009-2010)
Tuition and fees: $6,818; out-of-state residents $15,128.
Per-credit charge: $175; out-of-state residents $452.
Room and board: $5,676.

FINANCIAL AID PICTURE (2008-2009)
Students with need: Need-based aid available for full-time and part-time students.
Students without need: No-need awards available for academics, state/district residency.

FINANCIAL AID PROCEDURES
Forms required: FAFSA.
Dates and Deadlines: Priority date 4/1; no closing date. Applicants notified on a rolling basis starting 3/15; must reply within 3 week(s) of notification.

CONTACT
Dennis Carlton, Director of Financial Aid
PO Box 1675, Galveston, TX 77553-1675
(409) 740-4500

Texas A&M University-Kingsville
Kingsville, Texas
www.tamuk.edu   Federal Code: 003639

4-year public university in large town.
Enrollment: 6,289 undergrads.
Selectivity: Open admission; but selective for some programs.

BASIC COSTS (2009-2010)
Tuition and fees: $5,982; out-of-state residents $14,292.
Room and board: $5,130.

FINANCIAL AID PICTURE
Students with need: Need-based aid available for full-time students.
Students without need: No-need awards available for academics, leadership.

FINANCIAL AID PROCEDURES
Forms required: FAFSA.
Dates and Deadlines: Applicants notified on a rolling basis.

CONTACT

William Saenz, Financial Aid Officer

MSC 105, Kingsville, TX 78363-8201

(361) 593-3911

Texas A&M University-Texarkana

Texarkana, Texas

www.tamut.edu   Federal Code: 031703

Upper-division public university in small city.

Enrollment: 1,010 undergrads.

BASIC COSTS (2009-2010)

Tuition and fees: $4,538; out-of-state residents $13,448.

FINANCIAL AID PICTURE (2009-2010)

Students with need: Need-based aid available for full-time and part-time students. Work study available nights, weekends, and for part-time students.

Students without need: No-need awards available for academics, leadership, state/district residency.

FINANCIAL AID PROCEDURES

Dates and Deadlines: Priority date 5/1; closing date 11/1.

Transfers: Applicants notified on a rolling basis; must reply within 10 week(s) of notification. Transfer students must have completed minimum of 54 semester hours of transferable college credit to apply for financial aid and notified applicants must reply within 45 days from date of award letter. Exceptions made on individual basis. April 1 financial aid deadline for scholarships.

CONTACT

Becky Hejduk, Director of Financial Aid

2600 North Robinson Road, Texarkana, TX 75505-5518

(903) 233-3060

Texas Christian University

Fort Worth, Texas

www.tcu.edu   Federal Code: 003636

4-year private university in very large city, affiliated with Christian Church (Disciples of Christ).

Enrollment: 7,580 undergrads, 4% part-time. 1,818 full-time freshmen.

Selectivity: Admits 50 to 75% of applicants. GED not accepted.

BASIC COSTS (2010-2011)

Tuition and fees: $30,048.

Per-credit charge: $1,265.

Room and board: $10,010.

Additional info: Tuition is a flat rate for 12-18 hours per semester. Tuition/fee waivers available for adults, minority students.

FINANCIAL AID PICTURE (2009-2010)

Students with need: Out of 1,000 full-time freshmen who applied for aid, 728 were judged to have need. Of these, 724 received aid, and 220 had their full need met. Average financial aid package met 71% of need; average scholarship/grant was $16,220; average loan was $3,358. For part-time students, average financial aid package was $15,993.

Students without need: 475 full-time freshmen who did not demonstrate need for aid received scholarships/grants; average award was $10,055. No-need awards available for academics, alumni affiliation, art, minority status, music/drama, religious affiliation, ROTC, state/district residency.

Scholarships offered: 57 full-time freshmen received athletic scholarships; average amount $16,043.

Cumulative student debt: 43% of graduating class had student loans; average debt was $32,357.

FINANCIAL AID PROCEDURES

Forms required: FAFSA.

Dates and Deadlines: Closing date 5/1. Applicants notified on a rolling basis starting 3/15; must reply by 5/1 or within 2 week(s) of notification.

Transfers: Priority date 6/1. Applicants notified on a rolling basis starting 6/15; must reply by 5/1.

CONTACT

Michael Scott, Director of Scholarships and Student Financial Aid

TCU Box 297013, Fort Worth, TX 76129

(817) 257-7858

Texas College

Tyler, Texas

www.texascollege.edu   Federal Code: 003638

4-year private liberal arts college in small city, affiliated with Christian Methodist Episcopal Church.

Enrollment: 936 undergrads, 3% part-time. 213 full-time freshmen.

Selectivity: Open admission.

BASIC COSTS (2009-2010)

Tuition and fees: $9,490.

Per-credit charge: $333.

Room and board: $6,600.

FINANCIAL AID PICTURE (2008-2009)

Students with need: Out of 202 full-time freshmen who applied for aid, 199 were judged to have need. Of these, 195 received aid, and 56 had their full need met. Average financial aid package met 93% of need; average scholarship/grant was $6,931; average loan was $2,763. For part-time students, average financial aid package was $7,875.

Students without need: No-need awards available for academics, athletics, leadership, music/drama.

Scholarships offered: 26 full-time freshmen received athletic scholarships; average amount $3,040.

Cumulative student debt: 96% of graduating class had student loans; average debt was $23,554.

FINANCIAL AID PROCEDURES

Forms required: FAFSA, institutional form.

Dates and Deadlines: Priority date 6/1; no closing date. Applicants notified on a rolling basis starting 4/15.

CONTACT

Cecelia Jones, Director of Financial Aid

2404 North Grand Avenue, Tyler, TX 75712-4500

(903) 593-8311 ext. 2208

Texas Lutheran University

Seguin, Texas

www.tlu.edu   Federal Code: 003641

4-year private university and liberal arts college in large town, affiliated with Evangelical Lutheran Church in America.

Enrollment: 1,350 undergrads, 3% part-time. 345 full-time freshmen.

Selectivity: Admits 50 to 75% of applicants.

BASIC COSTS (2010-2011)

Tuition and fees: $22,890.

Per-credit charge: $760.

Room and board: $7,200.

FINANCIAL AID PICTURE (2009-2010)
Students with need: Out of 316 full-time freshmen who applied for aid, 284 were judged to have need. Of these, 284 received aid, and 120 had their full need met. Average financial aid package met 42% of need; average scholarship/grant was $15,693; average loan was $4,122. For part-time students, average financial aid package was $8,057.
Students without need: 52 full-time freshmen who did not demonstrate need for aid received scholarships/grants; average award was $10,909. No-need awards available for academics, alumni affiliation, leadership, music/drama, religious affiliation.
Scholarships offered: National Merit Finalist Scholarship: full tuition; Pacesetter Award for College Excellence: up to $18,000 a year; Locus Aduro Award in Dramatic Media: up to $18,000 a year; Da capo Award in Music: up to $18,000 a year; TLU CHOICE Scholarship: difference between cost at TLU and University of Texas-Austin or Texas AM?College Station; Presidential Scholarship: up to $11,000 a year; Academic Excellence Award: up to $9,000 a year.
Cumulative student debt: 63% of graduating class had student loans; average debt was $29,200.

FINANCIAL AID PROCEDURES
Forms required: FAFSA.
Dates and Deadlines: Priority date 3/1; no closing date. Applicants notified on a rolling basis starting 3/1; must reply within 6 week(s) of notification.
Transfers: No deadline. Applicants notified on a rolling basis starting 3/1; must reply within 6 week(s) of notification.

CONTACT
Cathleen Wright, Director Financial Aid
1000 West Court Street, Seguin, TX 78155-5999
(830) 372-8075

Texas Southern University
Houston, Texas
www.tsu.edu   Federal Code: 003642

4-year public university in very large city.
Enrollment: 7,258 undergrads, 19% part-time. 1,091 full-time freshmen.
Selectivity: Admits less than 50% of applicants.

BASIC COSTS (2009-2010)
Tuition and fees: $7,080; out-of-state residents $15,390.
Per-credit charge: $100; out-of-state residents $331.
Additional info: Tuition/fee waivers available for minority students.

FINANCIAL AID PICTURE (2008-2009)
Students with need: Need-based aid available for full-time and part-time students. Work study available nights, weekends, and for part-time students.
Students without need: This college awards aid only to students with need.

FINANCIAL AID PROCEDURES
Forms required: FAFSA.
Dates and Deadlines: Priority date 5/1; no closing date. Applicants notified on a rolling basis starting 6/1.
Transfers: Priority date 4/1; closing date 8/30.

CONTACT
Hasan Jamil, Director of Financial Aid
3100 Cleburne Street, Houston, TX 77004
(713) 313-7071

Texas State Technical College: Harlingen
Harlingen, Texas
www.harlingen.tstc.edu   Federal Code: 009225

2-year public technical college in small city.
Enrollment: 2,545 undergrads, 50% part-time. 403 full-time freshmen.
Selectivity: Open admission; but selective for some programs.

BASIC COSTS (2009-2010)
Tuition and fees: $3,030; out-of-state residents $6,660.
Per-credit charge: $67; out-of-state residents $188.
Room and board: $3,160.

FINANCIAL AID PICTURE (2008-2009)
Students with need: Need-based aid available for full-time and part-time students.

FINANCIAL AID PROCEDURES
Forms required: FAFSA, institutional form.
Dates and Deadlines: Applicants notified on a rolling basis starting 6/30; must reply within 2 week(s) of notification.

CONTACT
Mary Gallegos-Adams, Director of Financial Aid
1902 North Loop 499, Harlingen, TX 78550-3697
(956) 364-4337

Texas State Technical College: Waco
Waco, Texas
www.waco.tstc.edu   Federal Code: 003634

2-year public technical college in small city.
Enrollment: 4,685 undergrads.
Selectivity: Open admission.

BASIC COSTS (2009-2010)
Tuition and fees: $3,030; out-of-state residents $6,660.
Per-credit charge: $67; out-of-state residents $188.
Room and board: $4,970.

FINANCIAL AID PICTURE (2008-2009)
Students with need: Need-based aid available for full-time and part-time students.
Students without need: This college awards aid only to students with need.

FINANCIAL AID PROCEDURES
Forms required: FAFSA.
Dates and Deadlines: Priority date 6/1; no closing date. Applicants notified on a rolling basis starting 5/15.
Transfers: No deadline. Applicants notified on a rolling basis.

CONTACT
Jackie Adler, Director, Financial Aid
3801 Campus Drive, Waco, TX 76705
(254) 867-4814

Texas State Technical College: West Texas
Sweetwater, Texas
www.westtexas.tstc.edu   Federal Code: 009932

2-year public technical college in large town.
Enrollment: 1,152 undergrads.
Selectivity: Open admission; but selective for some programs.

BASIC COSTS (2009-2010)

Tuition and fees: $3,030; out-of-state residents $6,660.
Per-credit charge: $67; out-of-state residents $188.
Room and board: $4,450.

FINANCIAL AID PICTURE (2008-2009)

Students with need: Need-based aid available for full-time and part-time students. Work study available nights, weekends, and for part-time students.
Students without need: No-need awards available for academics, leadership.

FINANCIAL AID PROCEDURES

Forms required: FAFSA, institutional form.
Dates and Deadlines: Priority date 5/1; no closing date. Applicants notified on a rolling basis starting 7/1.
Transfers: No deadline. Applicants notified on a rolling basis starting 7/1; must reply by 8/20.

CONTACT

Connie Chance, Director of Financial Aid
300 Homer K Taylor Drive, Sweetwater, TX 79556
(325) 235-7378

Texas State University: San Marcos

San Marcos, Texas
www.txstate.edu   Federal Code: 003615

4-year public university in large town.
Enrollment: 26,002 undergrads, 18% part-time. 3,612 full-time freshmen.
Selectivity: Admits over 75% of applicants.

BASIC COSTS (2009-2010)

Tuition and fees: $7,482; out-of-state residents $15,792.
Per-credit charge: $182; out-of-state residents $459.
Room and board: $6,392.

FINANCIAL AID PICTURE (2009-2010)

Students with need: Out of 2,745 full-time freshmen who applied for aid, 1,910 were judged to have need. Of these, 1,835 received aid, and 172 had their full need met. Average financial aid package met 71% of need; average scholarship/grant was $7,663; average loan was $3,573. For part-time students, average financial aid package was $11,659.
Students without need: 181 full-time freshmen who did not demonstrate need for aid received scholarships/grants; average award was $2,296. No-need awards available for academics, art, athletics, leadership, music/drama, ROTC, state/district residency.
Scholarships offered: *Merit:* Terry Foundation Scholarship: $12,500; 16 awarded. McCoy Scholarship of Excellence: $8,000; number awarded varies. McCoy Scholarship of Distinction: $5,000; number varies. University Scholars: $3,000; 8 awarded. Lone Star Scholarship: $2,500; 10 awarded. *Athletic:* 61 full-time freshmen received athletic scholarships; average amount $6,724.
Cumulative student debt: 58% of graduating class had student loans; average debt was $19,691.
Additional info: To be eligible for the Bobcat Promise program you must be an entering first-time freshmen (transfer students are not eligible), be a Texas resident, have a family adjusted gross income of $25,000 or less, be enrolled full-time and complete at least 30 credit hours during each academic year (fall and spring semester), and submit a completed FAFSA no later than April 1.

FINANCIAL AID PROCEDURES

Forms required: FAFSA.
Dates and Deadlines: Priority date 4/1; no closing date. Applicants notified on a rolling basis starting 5/1; must reply within 3 week(s) of notification.

CONTACT

Christopher Murr, Director of Financial Aid & Scholarship Office
429 North Guadalupe Street, San Marcos, TX 78666-5709
(512) 245-2315

Texas Tech University

Lubbock, Texas
www.ttu.edu   Federal Code: 003644

4-year public university in small city.
Enrollment: 24,236 undergrads, 9% part-time. 4,338 full-time freshmen.
Selectivity: Admits 50 to 75% of applicants.

BASIC COSTS (2009-2010)

Tuition and fees: $7,485; out-of-state residents $15,795.
Per-credit charge: $163; out-of-state residents $440.
Room and board: $7,527.
Additional info: Students from adjacent counties in New Mexico and Oklahoma pay in-state tuition rates; students from all other counties in New Mexico and Oklahoma pay reduced out-of-state tuition rates.

FINANCIAL AID PICTURE (2008-2009)

Students with need: Out of 3,117 full-time freshmen who applied for aid, 1,802 were judged to have need. Of these, 1,779 received aid, and 147 had their full need met. Average financial aid package met 49% of need; average scholarship/grant was $6,984; average loan was $3,144. For part-time students, average financial aid package was $5,970.
Students without need: 281 full-time freshmen who did not demonstrate need for aid received scholarships/grants; average award was $3,637. No-need awards available for academics, art, athletics, job skills, leadership, music/drama, ROTC.
Scholarships offered: *Merit:* Presidential Plus Scholarship: $12,700 per year for up to 5 years; awarded to National Merit Finalists who select Texas Tech as school of choice. Presidential Endowed Scholarship: $6,000 per year for up to 5 years; top 10% of high school graduating class and SAT 1400 or ACT 31. Honors Endowed Scholarship: $4,000 per year up to 5 years; top 10% of high school graduating class and SAT 1300 or ACT 29. University Scholars Scholarship: $2,500 per year up to 4 years; top 10% of high school graduating class and SAT 1250 or ACT 28. *Athletic:* 69 full-time freshmen received athletic scholarships; average amount $11,215.

FINANCIAL AID PROCEDURES

Forms required: FAFSA.
Dates and Deadlines: Priority date 4/15; no closing date. Applicants notified on a rolling basis; must reply within 2 week(s) of notification.

CONTACT

Becky Wilson, Director of Financial Aid
Box 45005, Lubbock, TX 79409-5005
(806) 742-3681

Texas Tech University Health Sciences Center

Lubbock, Texas
www.ttuhsc.edu   Federal Code: 010674

Upper-division public university in small city.
Enrollment: 682 undergrads, 10% part-time.

BASIC COSTS (2009-2010)

Tuition and fees: $4,500; out-of-state residents $12,810.
Per-credit charge: $150; out-of-state residents $427.
Additional info: Reported costs are for Allied Health Sciences and School of Nursing.

FINANCIAL AID PICTURE (2008-2009)

Students with need: Need-based aid available for full-time and part-time students.

Students without need: No-need awards available for academics.

FINANCIAL AID PROCEDURES

Transfers: No deadline. Applicants notified on a rolling basis.

CONTACT

Marcus Wilson, Director, Financial Aid
3601 Fourth Street, Lubbock, TX 79430

Texas Wesleyan University
Fort Worth, Texas
www.txwes.edu   Federal Code: 003645

4-year private university in large city, affiliated with United Methodist Church.

Enrollment: 1,509 undergrads, 23% part-time. 183 full-time freshmen.

Selectivity: Admits 50 to 75% of applicants.

BASIC COSTS (2009-2010)

Tuition and fees: $17,760.

Per-credit charge: $546.

Room and board: $6,656.

FINANCIAL AID PICTURE (2008-2009)

Students with need: Need-based aid available for full-time and part-time students. Work study available nights, weekends, and for part-time students.

Students without need: This college awards aid only to students with need.

FINANCIAL AID PROCEDURES

Forms required: FAFSA.

Dates and Deadlines: Priority date 3/15; no closing date. Applicants notified on a rolling basis starting 3/15.

CONTACT

Shanna Hollis, Financial Aid Director
1201 Wesleyan Street, Fort Worth, TX 76105-1536
(817) 531-4420

Texas Woman's University
Denton, Texas
www.twu.edu   Federal Code: 003646

4-year public university in small city.

Enrollment: 7,685 undergrads, 31% part-time. 737 full-time freshmen.

Selectivity: Admits over 75% of applicants.

BASIC COSTS (2009-2010)

Tuition and fees: $6,660; out-of-state residents $15,000.

Per-credit charge: $143; out-of-state residents $421.

Room and board: $5,932.

FINANCIAL AID PICTURE (2009-2010)

Students with need: Need-based aid available for full-time and part-time students. Work study available nights, weekends, and for part-time students.

Scholarships offered: Chancellor's Endowed Scholarship: full tuition and fees, room and board; based on high school valedictorian status, extracurricular activities, SAT score; 2 awarded. Presidential Scholarship: full tuition and fees; awarded to valedictorian or salutatorian. Honors Scholarship: $1,500 annually up to 4 years; based on admission to honors program and SAT score. New Freshman Scholarship: $1,500 annually up to 4 years; based on SAT/ACT score, class rank and GPA. Transfer Student Scholarship: $1,500 annually up to 4 years; based on GPA, must have completed at least 12 credit hours. New Student Scholarship: $1,800 annually up to 4 years; based on high school rank, ACT/SAT score; 150 awarded.

FINANCIAL AID PROCEDURES

Forms required: FAFSA, institutional form.

Dates and Deadlines: Priority date 4/1; no closing date. Applicants notified on a rolling basis starting 3/1; must reply within 2 week(s) of notification.

CONTACT

Governor Jackson, Director of Financial Aid
Box 425589, Denton, TX 76204-5589
(940) 898-3064

Trinity University
San Antonio, Texas
www.trinity.edu   Federal Code: 003647

4-year private liberal arts college in very large city, affiliated with Presbyterian Church (USA).

Enrollment: 2,458 undergrads, 1% part-time. 642 full-time freshmen.

Selectivity: Admits 50 to 75% of applicants.

BASIC COSTS (2010-2011)

Tuition and fees: $30,877.

Per-credit charge: $1,243.

Room and board: $9,190.

FINANCIAL AID PICTURE (2009-2010)

Students with need: Out of 407 full-time freshmen who applied for aid, 285 were judged to have need. Of these, 285 received aid, and 146 had their full need met. Average financial aid package met 94% of need; average scholarship/grant was $19,259; average loan was $5,491. For part-time students, average financial aid package was $5,521.

Students without need: 281 full-time freshmen who did not demonstrate need for aid received scholarships/grants; average award was $14,865. No-need awards available for academics, leadership, music/drama.

FINANCIAL AID PROCEDURES

Forms required: FAFSA.

Dates and Deadlines: Priority date 2/15; closing date 4/1. Applicants notified by 4/1; must reply by 5/1 or within 3 week(s) of notification.

Transfers: Priority date 5/1; no deadline.

CONTACT

Sean Smith, Director of Financial Aid
One Trinity Place, San Antonio, TX 78212-7200
(210) 999-8315

Trinity Valley Community College
Athens, Texas
www.tvcc.edu   Federal Code: 003572

2-year public community college in large town.

Enrollment: 5,439 undergrads.

Selectivity: Open admission; but selective for some programs.

BASIC COSTS (2009-2010)

Tuition and fees: $1,260; out-of-district residents $1,890; out-of-state residents $2,670.

Per-credit charge: $21; out-of-district residents $42; out-of-state residents $68.

Room and board: $3,870.

Additional info: Tuition/fee waivers available for adults.

FINANCIAL AID PICTURE

Students with need: Need-based aid available for full-time and part-time students. Work study available nights, weekends, and for part-time students.

Students without need: No-need awards available for academics, athletics.

FINANCIAL AID PROCEDURES

Forms required: FAFSA, institutional form.

Dates and Deadlines: Priority date 7/1; no closing date. Applicants notified on a rolling basis starting 7/1; must reply within 2 week(s) of notification.

Transfers: Students on suspension at previous institution ineligible to receive aid.

CONTACT

Julie Lively, Director of Financial Aid
100 Cardinal Drive, Athens, TX 75751
(903) 675-6233

Tyler Junior College

Tyler, Texas
www.tjc.edu   Federal Code: 003648

2-year public junior college in small city.

Enrollment: 9,866 undergrads.

Selectivity: Open admission; but selective for some programs.

BASIC COSTS (2009-2010)

Tuition and fees: $2,072; out-of-district residents $3,272; out-of-state residents $3,872.

Per-credit charge: $28; out-of-district residents $68; out-of-state residents $98.

Room and board: $4,150.

FINANCIAL AID PICTURE (2009-2010)

Students with need: Need-based aid available for full-time and part-time students.

Students without need: No-need awards available for academics, alumni affiliation, art, athletics, leadership, music/drama.

FINANCIAL AID PROCEDURES

Forms required: FAFSA, institutional form.

Dates and Deadlines: Priority date 6/1; no closing date. Applicants notified on a rolling basis starting 3/1; must reply within 2 week(s) of notification.

Transfers: Financial aid transcript required if student enrolled same year elsewhere.

CONTACT

Devon Wiggins, Director of Student Financial Aid and Scholarship
Box 9020, Tyler, TX 77711-9020
(903) 510-2385

University of Dallas

Irving, Texas
www.udallas.edu   Federal Code: 003651

4-year private university and liberal arts college in small city, affiliated with Roman Catholic Church.

Enrollment: 1,297 undergrads, 1% part-time. 342 full-time freshmen.

Selectivity: Admits over 75% of applicants.

BASIC COSTS (2010-2011)

Tuition and fees: $27,815.

Per-credit charge: $1,090.

Room and board: $8,650.

FINANCIAL AID PICTURE (2008-2009)

Students with need: Out of 256 full-time freshmen who applied for aid, 209 were judged to have need. Of these, 209 received aid, and 59 had their full need met. Average financial aid package met 79% of need; average scholarship/grant was $16,393; average loan was $3,865. For part-time students, average financial aid package was $6,752.

Students without need: 119 full-time freshmen who did not demonstrate need for aid received scholarships/grants; average award was $11,500. No-need awards available for academics, alumni affiliation, art, leadership, music/drama.

Cumulative student debt: 57% of graduating class had student loans; average debt was $24,650.

FINANCIAL AID PROCEDURES

Forms required: FAFSA.

Dates and Deadlines: Priority date 3/1; closing date 7/1. Applicants notified on a rolling basis starting 3/1; must reply by 5/1 or within 2 week(s) of notification.

Transfers: Priority date 4/1; closing date 7/15. Must reply by 5/1 or within 2 week(s) of notification.

CONTACT

Laurie Rosenkrantz, Assistant Dean of Financial Aid and Enrollment
1845 East Northgate Drive, Irving, TX 75062-4736
(972) 721-5266

University of Houston

Houston, Texas
www.uh.edu   Federal Code: 003652

4-year public university in very large city.

Enrollment: 28,056 undergrads, 26% part-time. 3,100 full-time freshmen.

Selectivity: Admits 50 to 75% of applicants.

BASIC COSTS (2009-2010)

Tuition and fees: $8,496; out-of-state residents $16,806.

Per-credit charge: $185; out-of-state residents $462.

Room and board: $7,164.

FINANCIAL AID PICTURE (2009-2010)

Students with need: Out of 2,364 full-time freshmen who applied for aid, 1,913 were judged to have need. Of these, 1,857 received aid, and 722 had their full need met. Average financial aid package met 83% of need; average scholarship/grant was $9,424; average loan was $4,870. For part-time students, average financial aid package was $9,096.

Students without need: 176 full-time freshmen who did not demonstrate need for aid received scholarships/grants; average award was $5,419. No-need awards available for academics, alumni affiliation, art, athletics, job skills, leadership, music/drama, ROTC, state/district residency.

Scholarships offered: 40 full-time freshmen received athletic scholarships; average amount $4,202.

FINANCIAL AID PROCEDURES

Forms required: FAFSA.

Dates and Deadlines: Priority date 4/1; no closing date. Applicants notified on a rolling basis starting 5/1.

Transfers: Applicants notified on a rolling basis starting 4/1; must reply by 7/1.

CONTACT

Sal Loria, Executive Director
Welcome Center, Houston, TX 77204-2023
(713) 743-1010

University of Houston-Clear Lake

Houston, Texas
www.uhcl.edu   Federal Code: 011711

Upper-division public university in very large city.

Enrollment: 4,104 undergrads, 51% part-time.

BASIC COSTS (2009-2010)
Tuition and fees: $5,798; out-of-state residents $15,038.
Room only: $10,828.

FINANCIAL AID PICTURE (2008-2009)
Students with need: Need-based aid available for full-time and part-time students. Work study available nights, weekends, and for part-time students.
Students without need: No-need awards available for state/district residency.

FINANCIAL AID PROCEDURES
Forms required: FAFSA, institutional form.
Dates and Deadlines: Priority date 4/1; no closing date. Applicants notified on a rolling basis starting 6/4; must reply within 4 week(s) of notification.
Transfers: Applicants notified on a rolling basis starting 5/15; must reply within 4 week(s) of notification.

CONTACT
Billy Satterfield, Director of Student Financial Aid
2700 Bay Area Boulevard, Houston, TX 77058-1098
(281) 283-2481.

University of Houston-Downtown
Houston, Texas
www.uhd.edu   Federal Code: 003612

4-year public university in very large city.
Enrollment: 12,517 undergrads, 51% part-time. 722 full-time freshmen.
Selectivity: Open admission.

BASIC COSTS (2009-2010)
Tuition and fees: $5,232; out-of-state residents $13,542.
Per-credit charge: $140; out-of-state residents $417.

FINANCIAL AID PICTURE (2009-2010)
Students with need: Out of 570 full-time freshmen who applied for aid, 563 were judged to have need. Of these, 563 received aid, and 28 had their full need met. Average financial aid package met 65% of need; average scholarship/grant was $8,153; average loan was $3,203. For part-time students, average financial aid package was $7,805.
Students without need: 78 full-time freshmen who did not demonstrate need for aid received scholarships/grants; average award was $2,000. No-need awards available for academics, leadership.
Cumulative student debt: 61% of graduating class had student loans; average debt was $18,041.

FINANCIAL AID PROCEDURES
Forms required: FAFSA.
Dates and Deadlines: Priority date 4/1; no closing date. Applicants notified on a rolling basis starting 4/15; must reply within 4 week(s) of notification.
Transfers: No deadline. Applicants notified on a rolling basis starting 4/15; must reply within 4 week(s) of notification.

CONTACT
LaTasha Goudeau, Director of Scholarships and Financial Aid
One Main Street, Suite 350-S, Houston, TX 77002
(713) 221-8041

University of Houston-Victoria
Victoria, Texas
www.uhv.edu   Federal Code: 013231

Upper-division public university in small city.
Enrollment: 1,779 undergrads, 62% part-time.

BASIC COSTS (2009-2010)
Tuition and fees: $5,400; out-of-state residents $13,710.
Per-credit charge: $143; out-of-state residents $420.

FINANCIAL AID PICTURE (2008-2009)
Students with need: Need-based aid available for full-time and part-time students. Work study available weekends and for part-time students.
Students without need: No-need awards available for academics, athletics, leadership, state/district residency.
Additional info: Short-term loans available at registration.

FINANCIAL AID PROCEDURES
Forms required: FAFSA.
Dates and Deadlines: No deadline. Applicants notified on a rolling basis; must reply within 3 week(s) of notification.
Transfers: No deadline. Applicants notified on a rolling basis; must reply within 3 week(s) of notification.

CONTACT
Carolyn Mallory, Financial Aid Director
3007 North Ben Wilson, Victoria, TX 77901-4450
(361) 570-4131

University of Mary Hardin-Baylor
Belton, Texas
www.umhb.edu   Federal Code: 003588

4-year private university in large town, affiliated with Baptist faith.
Enrollment: 2,547 undergrads, 10% part-time. 603 full-time freshmen.
Selectivity: Admits less than 50% of applicants.

BASIC COSTS (2010-2011)
Tuition and fees: $21,700.
Per-credit charge: $645.
Room and board: $5,570.
Additional info: Tuition/fee waivers available for minority students.

FINANCIAL AID PICTURE (2009-2010)
Students with need: Out of 602 full-time freshmen who applied for aid, 522 were judged to have need. Of these, 522 received aid, and 79 had their full need met. Average financial aid package met 67% of need; average scholarship/grant was $8,932; average loan was $3,315. For part-time students, average financial aid package was $7,632.
Students without need: 79 full-time freshmen who did not demonstrate need for aid received scholarships/grants; average award was $7,500. No-need awards available for academics, art, leadership, music/drama, religious affiliation, ROTC.

FINANCIAL AID PROCEDURES
Forms required: FAFSA.
Dates and Deadlines: Priority date 3/1; no closing date. Applicants notified on a rolling basis starting 2/1; must reply within 2 week(s) of notification.
Transfers: No deadline. Applicants notified on a rolling basis starting 11/1; must reply within 2 week(s) of notification.

CONTACT
Ron Brown, Associate VP for Enrollment Management/Director of Financial Aid
900 College Street, Belton, TX 76513
(254) 295-4517

University of North Texas
Denton, Texas
www.unt.edu   Federal Code: 003594

4-year public university in small city.
Enrollment: 28,474 undergrads, 22% part-time. 3,223 full-time freshmen.
Selectivity: Admits 50 to 75% of applicants.

BASIC COSTS (2009-2010)
Tuition and fees: $7,301; out-of-state residents $15,611.
Per-credit charge: $178; out-of-state residents $455.
Room and board: $6,535.

FINANCIAL AID PICTURE (2009-2010)
Students with need: Out of 2,534 full-time freshmen who applied for aid, 1,777 were judged to have need. Of these, 1,751 received aid, and 778 had their full need met. Average financial aid package met 85% of need; average scholarship/grant was $7,243; average loan was $3,475. Need-based aid available for part-time students.
Students without need: 415 full-time freshmen who did not demonstrate need for aid received scholarships/grants; average award was $4,231.
Scholarships offered: 25 full-time freshmen received athletic scholarships; average amount $12,927.

FINANCIAL AID PROCEDURES
Forms required: FAFSA.
Dates and Deadlines: Priority date 4/15; no closing date. Applicants notified on a rolling basis starting 4/1.

CONTACT
Carolyn Cunningham, Director of Financial Aid
1401 West Prairie, Suite 309, Denton, TX 76203-5017
(940) 565-2302

University of St. Thomas
Houston, Texas
www.stthom.edu   Federal Code: 003654

4-year private university and liberal arts college in very large city, affiliated with Roman Catholic Church.
Enrollment: 1,668 undergrads, 22% part-time. 284 full-time freshmen.
Selectivity: Admits over 75% of applicants.

BASIC COSTS (2010-2011)
Tuition and fees: $23,500.
Per-credit charge: $772.
Room and board: $7,900.

FINANCIAL AID PICTURE (2009-2010)
Students with need: Out of 228 full-time freshmen who applied for aid, 185 were judged to have need. Of these, 184 received aid, and 23 had their full need met. Average financial aid package met 71% of need; average scholarship/grant was $13,259; average loan was $3,478. For part-time students, average financial aid package was $7,022.
Students without need: 82 full-time freshmen who did not demonstrate need for aid received scholarships/grants; average award was $8,587. No-need awards available for academics, athletics.
Scholarships offered: 7 full-time freshmen received athletic scholarships; average amount $2,136.
Cumulative student debt: 71% of graduating class had student loans; average debt was $22,857.

FINANCIAL AID PROCEDURES
Forms required: FAFSA.
Dates and Deadlines: No deadline. Applicants notified on a rolling basis starting 3/22; must reply within 2 week(s) of notification.

CONTACT
Lynda McKendree, Dean of Scholarships and Financial Aid
3800 Montrose Boulevard, Houston, TX 77006-4626
(713) 942-3465

University of Texas at Arlington
Arlington, Texas
www.uta.edu   Federal Code: 003656

4-year public university in large city.
Enrollment: 20,885 undergrads, 33% part-time. 2,127 full-time freshmen.
Selectivity: Admits 50 to 75% of applicants. GED not accepted.

BASIC COSTS (2009-2010)
Tuition and fees: $8,186; out-of-state residents $16,496.
Room and board: $6,147.

FINANCIAL AID PICTURE (2009-2010)
Students with need: Out of 1,891 full-time freshmen who applied for aid, 1,563 were judged to have need. Of these, 1,563 received aid, and 345 had their full need met. Average financial aid package met 73% of need; average scholarship/grant was $8,077; average loan was $3,248. For part-time students, average financial aid package was $7,190.
Students without need: 180 full-time freshmen who did not demonstrate need for aid received scholarships/grants; average award was $5,750. No-need awards available for academics, art, athletics, leadership, music/drama, ROTC.
Scholarships offered: *Merit:* Academic Scholarships: $1,000-$4,000 per year, renewable; based on minimum SAT 1050 (exclusive of Writing) or ACT 22, top 25% of high school class. *Athletic:* 6 full-time freshmen received athletic scholarships; average amount $4,055.
Additional info: Free tuition to eligible students whose household income is $65,000 or less through the Maverick Promise program.

FINANCIAL AID PROCEDURES
Forms required: FAFSA.
Dates and Deadlines: Priority date 5/15; no closing date. Applicants notified on a rolling basis starting 4/1; must reply within 3 week(s) of notification.
Transfers: Must reply within 3 week(s) of notification. To receive Texas grant or Texas B on Time loan, student must have either received Texas grant or completed associates degree at prior school.

CONTACT
Karen Krause, Director of Financial Aid
Box 19111, Arlington, TX 76019
(817) 272-3561

University of Texas at Austin
Austin, Texas
www.utexas.edu   Federal Code: 003658

4-year public university in very large city.
Enrollment: 37,464 undergrads, 6% part-time. 7,199 full-time freshmen.
Selectivity: Admits less than 50% of applicants.

BASIC COSTS (2009-2010)
Tuition and fees: $8,930; out-of-state residents $30,006.
Room and board: $9,602.

FINANCIAL AID PICTURE (2009-2010)
Students with need: Out of 5,477 full-time freshmen who applied for aid, 3,475 were judged to have need. Of these, 3,474 received aid, and 1,195 had their full need met. Average financial aid package met 85% of need; average scholarship/grant was $9,453; average loan was $3,001. Need-based aid available for part-time students.

Students without need: 909 full-time freshmen who did not demonstrate need for aid received scholarships/grants. No-need awards available for academics, art, athletics, leadership, music/drama, ROTC, state/district residency.

Cumulative student debt: 50% of graduating class had student loans; average debt was $22,102.

Additional info: In general, Texas resident students from families earning less than $40,000 will be awarded grant/scholarship aid (from federal, state, institutional and private sources) to cover tuition costs.

FINANCIAL AID PROCEDURES

Forms required: FAFSA.

Dates and Deadlines: Priority date 3/31; no closing date. Applicants notified on a rolling basis starting 3/15.

CONTACT

Thomas Melecki, Director of Student Financial Services
PO Box 8058, Austin, TX 78713-8058
(512) 475-6282

University of Texas at Brownsville - Texas Southmost College

Brownsville, Texas
www.utb.edu   Federal Code: 030646

4-year public university and community college in small city.

Enrollment: 10,145 undergrads. 1,378 full-time freshmen.

Selectivity: Open admission; but selective for some programs.

BASIC COSTS (2009-2010)

Tuition and fees: $5,498; out-of-state residents $13,808.

Per-credit charge: $133; out-of-state residents $410.

FINANCIAL AID PICTURE (2008-2009)

Students with need: Out of 1,191 full-time freshmen who applied for aid, 1,118 were judged to have need. Of these, 1,117 received aid. Average financial aid package met 64% of need; average scholarship/grant was $6,259; average loan was $2,991. For part-time students, average financial aid package was $5,419.

Students without need: 39 full-time freshmen who did not demonstrate need for aid received scholarships/grants; average award was $4,106. No-need awards available for academics, alumni affiliation, art, athletics, minority status, music/drama, state/district residency.

Scholarships offered: 21 full-time freshmen received athletic scholarships; average amount $4,157.

FINANCIAL AID PROCEDURES

Forms required: FAFSA.

Dates and Deadlines: Priority date 3/1; closing date 8/15. Applicants notified on a rolling basis; must reply by 7/1 or within 12 week(s) of notification.

CONTACT

Mari Chapa, Director of Financial Aid
80 Fort Brown, Brownsville, TX 78520
(956) 882-8277

University of Texas at Dallas

Richardson, Texas
www.utdallas.edu   Federal Code: 009741

4-year public university in very large city.

Enrollment: 9,634 undergrads, 25% part-time. 1,091 full-time freshmen.

Selectivity: Admits 50 to 75% of applicants.

BASIC COSTS (2009-2010)

Tuition and fees: $10,340; out-of-state residents $23,730.

Per-credit charge: $345; out-of-state residents $791.

Room and board: $7,733.

Additional info: Tuition costs reflect guaranteed tuition rate for 2009-2010 incoming class.

FINANCIAL AID PICTURE (2008-2009)

Students with need: Out of 712 full-time freshmen who applied for aid, 496 were judged to have need. Of these, 478 received aid, and 37 had their full need met. Average financial aid package met 68% of need; average scholarship/grant was $8,016; average loan was $3,208. For part-time students, average financial aid package was $12,099.

Students without need: 316 full-time freshmen who did not demonstrate need for aid received scholarships/grants; average award was $10,245. No-need awards available for academics.

Scholarships offered: Eugene McDermott Scholars Program Awards: full tuition and fees plus domestic and international travel costs for enhancement of scholar's education; based on being in top 10% of high school class, high scores on entrance exams, evidence of leadership abilities; 20 awarded.

Cumulative student debt: 42% of graduating class had student loans; average debt was $7,343.

FINANCIAL AID PROCEDURES

Forms required: FAFSA.

Dates and Deadlines: Priority date 3/31; closing date 4/12. Applicants notified on a rolling basis starting 3/1; must reply within 2 week(s) of notification.

Transfers: Priority date 4/1.

CONTACT

Karen Jarrell, Assistant VP of Financial Aid
Office of Enrollment Services, Richardson, TX 75083-0688
(972) 883-2941

University of Texas at El Paso

El Paso, Texas
www.utep.edu   Federal Code: 003661

4-year public university in very large city.

Enrollment: 17,110 undergrads, 33% part-time. 2,250 full-time freshmen.

Selectivity: Admits over 75% of applicants.

BASIC COSTS (2009-2010)

Tuition and fees: $6,224; out-of-state residents $14,534.

Per-credit charge: $160; out-of-state residents $437.

Room only: $4,500.

Additional info: Mexican citizens who show need may qualify for in-state tuition. Reported room-only cost based on double-occupancy apartment at $500 per month for nine months. Optional a la carte meal plan.

FINANCIAL AID PICTURE (2008-2009)

Students with need: Out of 1,641 full-time freshmen who applied for aid, 1,338 were judged to have need. Of these, 1,324 received aid, and 430 had their full need met. Average financial aid package met 81% of need; average scholarship/grant was $8,218; average loan was $4,033. For part-time students, average financial aid package was $10,815.

Students without need: 227 full-time freshmen who did not demonstrate need for aid received scholarships/grants; average award was $1,086. No-need awards available for academics, alumni affiliation, art, athletics, job skills, leadership, minority status, music/drama, religious affiliation, ROTC, state/district residency.

Scholarships offered: 22 full-time freshmen received athletic scholarships; average amount $6,841.

Cumulative student debt: 60% of graduating class had student loans; average debt was $19,862.

Additional info: Emergency loans available.

FINANCIAL AID PROCEDURES
Forms required: FAFSA, institutional form.
Dates and Deadlines: Closing date 3/15. Applicants notified by 6/30; must reply within 2 week(s) of notification.
Transfers: No deadline.

CONTACT
Raul Lerma, Director of Financial Aid
500 West University Avenue, El Paso, TX 79968-0510
(915) 747-5204

University of Texas at San Antonio
San Antonio, Texas
www.utsa.edu   Federal Code: 010115

4-year public university in very large city.
Enrollment: 24,883 undergrads, 21% part-time. 4,763 full-time freshmen.
Selectivity: Admits over 75% of applicants.

BASIC COSTS (2009-2010)
Tuition and fees: $7,527; out-of-state residents $15,837.
Per-credit charge: $171; out-of-state residents $448.
Room and board: $8,937.

FINANCIAL AID PICTURE (2008-2009)
Students with need: Out of 3,699 full-time freshmen who applied for aid, 2,496 were judged to have need. Of these, 2,381 received aid, and 618 had their full need met. Average financial aid package met 61% of need; average scholarship/grant was $7,089; average loan was $3,187. For part-time students, average financial aid package was $5,168.
Students without need: 313 full-time freshmen who did not demonstrate need for aid received scholarships/grants; average award was $1,432. No-need awards available for academics, alumni affiliation, art, athletics, job skills, leadership, music/drama, ROTC, state/district residency.
Scholarships offered: 80 full-time freshmen received athletic scholarships; average amount $6,626.
Cumulative student debt: 65% of graduating class had student loans; average debt was $22,118.

FINANCIAL AID PROCEDURES
Forms required: FAFSA, institutional form.
Dates and Deadlines: Priority date 3/31; no closing date. Applicants notified on a rolling basis starting 4/1; must reply within 4 week(s) of notification.
Transfers: No deadline. Applicants notified on a rolling basis starting 4/1; must reply within 4 week(s) of notification.

CONTACT
Lisa Blazer, Assistant Vice President of Financial Aid
One UTSA Circle, San Antonio, TX 78249-0617
(210) 458-7828

University of Texas at Tyler
Tyler, Texas
www.uttyler.edu   Federal Code: 011163

4-year public university in small city.
Enrollment: 5,035 undergrads, 23% part-time. 585 full-time freshmen.
Selectivity: Admits over 75% of applicants.

BASIC COSTS (2009-2010)
Tuition and fees: $6,042; out-of-state residents $14,472.
Per-credit charge: $50; out-of-state residents $131.
Room and board: $8,016.

FINANCIAL AID PICTURE (2008-2009)
Students with need: Out of 414 full-time freshmen who applied for aid, 287 were judged to have need. Of these, 282 received aid, and 67 had their full need met. Average financial aid package met 58% of need; average scholarship/grant was $7,496; average loan was $2,256. For part-time students, average financial aid package was $6,554.
Students without need: 109 full-time freshmen who did not demonstrate need for aid received scholarships/grants; average award was $3,228. No-need awards available for academics, art, music/drama.
Cumulative student debt: 51% of graduating class had student loans; average debt was $18,041.
Additional info: Apply early for all programs.

FINANCIAL AID PROCEDURES
Forms required: FAFSA, institutional form.
Dates and Deadlines: Priority date 4/1; no closing date. Applicants notified on a rolling basis starting 4/15; must reply within 2 week(s) of notification.

CONTACT
Candice Lindsey, Associate Dean for Enrollment Management and Financial Aid
3900 University Boulevard, Tyler, TX 75799
(903) 566-7180

University of Texas Health Science Center at Houston
Houston, Texas
www.uth.tmc.edu   Federal Code: 013956

Upper-division public university and health science college in very large city.
Enrollment: 462 undergrads.

BASIC COSTS (2009-2010)
Tuition and fees: $6,222; out-of-state residents $23,286.
Additional info: Costs may vary by program.

FINANCIAL AID PICTURE (2008-2009)
Students with need: Need-based aid available for full-time and part-time students.
Students without need: This college awards aid only to students with need.

FINANCIAL AID PROCEDURES
Forms required: FAFSA, institutional form.
Dates and Deadlines: No deadline. Applicants notified on a rolling basis starting 6/1.

CONTACT
Carl Gordon, Director of Student Financial Aid
Box 20036, Houston, TX 77225
(713) 500-3860

University of Texas Medical Branch at Galveston
Galveston, Texas
www.utmb.edu   Federal Code: 013976

Upper-division public health science and nursing college in small city.
Enrollment: 492 undergrads, 36% part-time.

BASIC COSTS (2009-2010)
Tuition and fees: $5,652; out-of-state residents $14,082.
Per-credit charge: $162; out-of-state residents $443.
Additional info: Costs reported are for Allied Health Sciences program. Tuition and fees vary for other programs.

FINANCIAL AID PICTURE (2008-2009)

Students with need: Need-based aid available for full-time and part-time students. Work study available nights, weekends, and for part-time students.
Students without need: No-need awards available for academics, minority status, state/district residency.

FINANCIAL AID PROCEDURES

Forms required: FAFSA.
Dates and Deadlines: No deadline. Applicants notified on a rolling basis; must reply within 4 week(s) of notification.

CONTACT

Carol Cromie, Assistant Director of Enrollment Services for Financial Aid
301 University Boulevard, Galveston, TX 77555-1305
(409) 772-1215

University of Texas of the Permian Basin
Odessa, Texas
www.utpb.edu   Federal Code: 009930

4-year public university in small city.
Enrollment: 2,600 undergrads, 26% part-time. 316 full-time freshmen.
Selectivity: Admits over 75% of applicants.

BASIC COSTS (2009-2010)

Tuition and fees: $5,599; out-of-state residents $13,909.
Per-credit charge: $146; out-of-state residents $423.
Additional info: New Mexico residents living in areas contiguous to Texas border pay in-district rate.

FINANCIAL AID PICTURE (2008-2009)

Students with need: Out of 231 full-time freshmen who applied for aid, 157 were judged to have need. Of these, 157 received aid, and 35 had their full need met. Average financial aid package met 24% of need; average scholarship/grant was $6,516; average loan was $1,979. For part-time students, average financial aid package was $3,751.
Students without need: 138 full-time freshmen who did not demonstrate need for aid received scholarships/grants; average award was $3,278. No-need awards available for academics, alumni affiliation, art, athletics, leadership, music/drama.
Scholarships offered: 28 full-time freshmen received athletic scholarships; average amount $2,449.
Cumulative student debt: 5% of graduating class had student loans; average debt was $14,477.

FINANCIAL AID PROCEDURES

Forms required: FAFSA.
Dates and Deadlines: Priority date 3/1; no closing date. Applicants notified on a rolling basis starting 3/15.

CONTACT

Robert Vasquez, Director of Financial Aid
4901 East University, Odessa, TX 79762
(432) 552-2620

University of Texas Southwestern Medical Center at Dallas
Dallas, Texas
www.utsouthwestern.edu   Federal Code: 010019

Upper-division public university and health science college in very large city.
Enrollment: 90 undergrads, 14% part-time.

BASIC COSTS (2009-2010)

Tuition and fees: $4,408; out-of-state residents $12,838.
Per-credit charge: $118; out-of-state residents $399.

Additional info: Tuition and fees are based on UT Southwestern School of Health Professions.

FINANCIAL AID PICTURE (2009-2010)

Students with need: Need-based aid available for full-time and part-time students. Work study available nights, weekends, and for part-time students.

FINANCIAL AID PROCEDURES

Dates and Deadlines: No deadline. Must reply within 2 week(s) of notification.
Transfers: Priority date 3/1. Applicants notified on a rolling basis starting 4/1; must reply within 3 week(s) of notification.

CONTACT

Charles Kettlewell, Registrar and Director of Financial Aid
5323 Harry Hines Boulevard, Dallas, TX 75390-9162
(214) 648-3611

University of Texas: Pan American
Edinburg, Texas
www.utpa.edu   Federal Code: 003599

4-year public university in small city.
Enrollment: 15,705 undergrads, 25% part-time. 2,524 full-time freshmen.
Selectivity: Admits 50 to 75% of applicants.

BASIC COSTS (2009-2010)

Tuition and fees: $5,425; out-of-state residents $13,735.
Per-credit charge: $147; out-of-state residents $424.
Room and board: $5,294.
Additional info: Mexican citizens may be eligible for in-state tuition rates.

FINANCIAL AID PICTURE (2008-2009)

Students with need: Out of 2,148 full-time freshmen who applied for aid, 2,064 were judged to have need. Of these, 2,064 received aid, and 129 had their full need met. Average financial aid package met 76% of need; average scholarship/grant was $9,769; average loan was $2,295. For part-time students, average financial aid package was $6,192.
Students without need: 71 full-time freshmen who did not demonstrate need for aid received scholarships/grants; average award was $4,606. No-need awards available for academics, alumni affiliation, art, athletics, leadership.
Scholarships offered: 15 full-time freshmen received athletic scholarships; average amount $8,234.
Cumulative student debt: 64% of graduating class had student loans; average debt was $13,087.

FINANCIAL AID PROCEDURES

Forms required: FAFSA.
Dates and Deadlines: Priority date 4/1; no closing date. Applicants notified on a rolling basis starting 3/15; must reply within 2 week(s) of notification.
Transfers: Priority date 3/1; no deadline. Applicants notified on a rolling basis; must reply within 2 week(s) of notification.

CONTACT

Elaine Rivera, Executive Director of Student Financial Services
1201 West University Drive, Edinburg, TX 78539-2999
(956) 381-2501

University of the Incarnate Word
San Antonio, Texas
www.uiw.edu   Federal Code: 003578

4-year private university and liberal arts college in very large city, affiliated with Roman Catholic Church.
Enrollment: 5,197 undergrads, 35% part-time. 721 full-time freshmen.

Selectivity: Admits 50 to 75% of applicants.

BASIC COSTS (2010-2011)

Tuition and fees: $21,890.
Per-credit charge: $675.
Room and board: $9,220.

FINANCIAL AID PICTURE (2009-2010)

Students with need: Out of 637 full-time freshmen who applied for aid, 574 were judged to have need. Of these, 574 received aid, and 167 had their full need met. Average financial aid package met 66% of need; average scholarship/grant was $13,345; average loan was $3,372. For part-time students, average financial aid package was $7,805.
Students without need: 66 full-time freshmen who did not demonstrate need for aid received scholarships/grants; average award was $8,416. No-need awards available for academics, alumni affiliation, art, athletics, leadership, music/drama, religious affiliation, ROTC, state/district residency.
Scholarships offered: 4 full-time freshmen received athletic scholarships; average amount $10,850.
Additional info: Students encouraged to pursue outside scholarship programs.

FINANCIAL AID PROCEDURES

Forms required: FAFSA, institutional form.
Dates and Deadlines: Priority date 4/1; no closing date. Applicants notified on a rolling basis starting 2/15; must reply within 2 week(s) of notification.

CONTACT

Amy Carcanagues, Director, Financial Assistance
4301 Broadway, San Antonio, TX 78209-6397
(210) 829-6008

Vernon College

Vernon, Texas
www.vernoncollege.edu   Federal Code: 010060

2-year public community and junior college in large town.
Enrollment: 2,451 undergrads.
Selectivity: Open admission; but selective for some programs.

BASIC COSTS (2009-2010)

Tuition and fees: $2,490; out-of-district residents $3,330; out-of-state residents $4,830.
Room and board: $3,380.

FINANCIAL AID PICTURE (2009-2010)

Students with need: Need-based aid available for full-time and part-time students. Work study available nights, weekends, and for part-time students.
Students without need: This college awards aid only to students with need.

FINANCIAL AID PROCEDURES

Forms required: FAFSA.
Dates and Deadlines: Priority date 7/1; no closing date. Applicants notified on a rolling basis starting 4/1.
Transfers: No deadline. Applicants notified on a rolling basis.

CONTACT

Melissa Elliott, Director of Financial Aid
4400 College Drive, Vernon, TX 76384-4092
(940) 552-6291

Wade College

Dallas, Texas
www.wadecollege.edu   Federal Code: 010130

2-year for-profit junior and career college in very large city.
Enrollment: 245 undergrads.
Selectivity: Open admission.

BASIC COSTS (2009-2010)

Tuition and fees: $10,295.
Room only: $4,000.

FINANCIAL AID PICTURE (2008-2009)

Students with need: Need-based aid available for full-time and part-time students. Work study available nights, weekends, and for part-time students.
Students without need: This college awards aid only to students with need.

FINANCIAL AID PROCEDURES

Forms required: FAFSA.
Dates and Deadlines: No deadline. Applicants notified on a rolling basis; must reply within 4 week(s) of notification.

CONTACT

Lisa Hoover, Director of Financial Aid
Dallas Market Center, PO Box 421149, Dallas, TX 75342
(214) 637-3530

Wayland Baptist University

Plainview, Texas
www.wbu.edu   Federal Code: 003663

4-year private university and liberal arts college in large town, affiliated with Southern Baptist Convention.
Enrollment: 862 undergrads, 13% part-time. 215 full-time freshmen.
Selectivity: Admits over 75% of applicants.

BASIC COSTS (2009-2010)

Tuition and fees: $12,740.
Per-credit charge: $395.
Room and board: $3,864.

FINANCIAL AID PICTURE (2009-2010)

Students with need: Average financial aid package met 74% of need; average scholarship/grant was $9,472; average loan was $3,038. For part-time students, average financial aid package was $7,337.
Students without need: No-need awards available for academics, alumni affiliation, art, athletics, job skills, leadership, minority status, music/drama, religious affiliation, state/district residency.
Cumulative student debt: 78% of graduating class had student loans; average debt was $25,387.

FINANCIAL AID PROCEDURES

Forms required: FAFSA, institutional form.
Dates and Deadlines: Priority date 5/1; no closing date. Applicants notified on a rolling basis starting 2/15; must reply within 3 week(s) of notification.
Transfers: No deadline. Applicants notified on a rolling basis.

CONTACT

Karen LaQuey, Director of Financial Aid
1900 West Seventh Street, CMB #712, Plainview, TX 79072
(806) 291-3520

Weatherford College
Weatherford, Texas
www.wc.edu   Federal Code: 003664

2-year public community college in large town.
Enrollment: 5,027 undergrads, 50% part-time. 820 full-time freshmen.
Selectivity: Open admission; but selective for some programs.

BASIC COSTS (2009-2010)
Tuition and fees: $1,830; out-of-district residents $2,760; out-of-state residents $4,140.
Per-credit charge: $61; out-of-district residents $92; out-of-state residents $138.
Room and board: $7,380.

FINANCIAL AID PICTURE
Students with need: Work study available nights, weekends, and for part-time students.
Students without need: This college awards aid only to students with need.

FINANCIAL AID PROCEDURES
Forms required: FAFSA.
Dates and Deadlines: Priority date 7/3; no closing date. Applicants notified on a rolling basis; must reply within 2 week(s) of notification.

CONTACT
Donnie Purvis, Director, Financial Aid
225 College Park Drive, Weatherford, TX 76086
(817) 598-6295

West Texas A&M University
Canyon, Texas
www.wtamu.edu   Federal Code: 003665

4-year public university in large town.
Enrollment: 6,214 undergrads, 22% part-time. 1,144 full-time freshmen.
Selectivity: Admits 50 to 75% of applicants.

BASIC COSTS (2009-2010)
Tuition and fees: $5,732; out-of-state residents $14,042.
Per-credit charge: $140; out-of-state residents $417.
Room and board: $5,898.
Additional info: Out-of-district students from border counties pay in-state tuition. Tuition reduction plan available to students from border states.

FINANCIAL AID PICTURE (2008-2009)
Students with need: 49% of average financial aid package awarded as scholarships/grants, 51% awarded as loans/jobs. Need-based aid available for part-time students. Work study available nights, weekends, and for part-time students.
Students without need: No-need awards available for academics, art, athletics, leadership, music/drama, state/district residency.
Additional info: Scholarship deadline February 1.

FINANCIAL AID PROCEDURES
Forms required: FAFSA.
Dates and Deadlines: Priority date 4/15; no closing date. Applicants notified on a rolling basis starting 3/1; must reply within 2 week(s) of notification.
Transfers: No deadline. Applicants notified on a rolling basis; must reply within 2 week(s) of notification. Must provide financial aid transcripts through last semester of attendance. All academic transcripts must be on file.

CONTACT
Jim Reed, Director of Financial Aid
2501 Fourth Avenue, WTAMU Box 60907, Canyon, TX 79016-0001
(806) 651-2055

Western Technical College
El Paso, Texas
www.westerntech.edu   Federal Code: 014535

2-year for-profit technical college in very large city.
Enrollment: 775 undergrads.
Selectivity: Open admission; but selective for some programs.

BASIC COSTS (2009-2010)
Additional info: Tuition varies by program: Automotive Technology, $22,065; Refrigeration/HVAC Technology, $22,065; Diesel Technology, $20,594; Advanced Welding Technology, $24,810; Medical/Clinical Assistant, $11,640. Registration fee, $100.

FINANCIAL AID PICTURE
Students with need: Need-based aid available for full-time and part-time students.
Students without need: This college awards aid only to students with need.

FINANCIAL AID PROCEDURES
Forms required: FAFSA.
Dates and Deadlines: No deadline. Applicants notified on a rolling basis.

CONTACT
Jennifer Phillips, Financial Aid Director
9624 Plaza Circle, El Paso, TX 79927
(915) 532-3737 ext. 8105

Western Texas College
Snyder, Texas
www.wtc.edu   Federal Code: 009549

2-year public community and junior college in large town.
Enrollment: 2,235 undergrads. 641 full-time freshmen.
Selectivity: Open admission; but selective for some programs.

BASIC COSTS (2009-2010)
Tuition and fees: $2,070; out-of-district residents $2,490; out-of-state residents $3,240.
Per-credit charge: $47; out-of-district residents $61; out-of-state residents $86.
Room and board: $5,077.

FINANCIAL AID PICTURE (2009-2010)
Students with need: Average financial aid package met 60% of need; average loan was $1,750. For part-time students, average financial aid package was $1,500.
Students without need: No-need awards available for academics, art, athletics, leadership, music/drama, state/district residency.

FINANCIAL AID PROCEDURES
Forms required: FAFSA, institutional form.
Dates and Deadlines: Priority date 8/1; no closing date. Applicants notified on a rolling basis starting 5/1; must reply within 2 week(s) of notification.
Transfers: No deadline. Applicants notified on a rolling basis.

CONTACT
Kathy Hall, Director of Student Financial Aid
6200 College Avenue, Snyder, TX 79549
(866) 270-6184

Westwood College: Houston South

Houston, Texas
www.westwood.edu   Federal Code: 007548

2-year for-profit technical college in very large city.
Enrollment: 517 undergrads.

BASIC COSTS (2009-2010)
Additional info: Cost per term differs by program and ranges from $3,088-$4,805. One-time cost of toolkits $110-$595.

FINANCIAL AID PICTURE (2008-2009)
Students with need: Need-based aid available for full-time and part-time students.

FINANCIAL AID PROCEDURES
Forms required: FAFSA, institutional form.
Dates and Deadlines: No deadline.

CONTACT
Teresa Washburn-Grant, Director of Student Finance
7322 Southwest Freeway, Houston, TX 77074
(713) 777-4779 ext. 13131

Wharton County Junior College

Wharton, Texas
www.wcjc.edu   Federal Code: 003668

2-year public community and junior college in small town.
Enrollment: 6,622 undergrads, 55% part-time. 1,092 full-time freshmen.
Selectivity: Open admission; but selective for some programs.

BASIC COSTS (2010-2011)
Tuition and fees: $1,940; out-of-state residents $2,900.
Per-credit charge: $32; out-of-state residents $64.
Room and board: $2,800.

FINANCIAL AID PICTURE
Students with need: Need-based aid available for full-time and part-time students.
Students without need: No-need awards available for academics, athletics, music/drama.

FINANCIAL AID PROCEDURES
Forms required: FAFSA.
Dates and Deadlines: Closing date 6/1. Applicants notified on a rolling basis starting 8/1; must reply by 8/15.

CONTACT
Richard Hyde, Director of Financial Aid
911 Boling Highway, Wharton, TX 77488-0080
(979) 532-4560 ext. 6345

Wiley College

Marshall, Texas
www.wileyc.edu   Federal Code: 003669

4-year private liberal arts college in large town, affiliated with United Methodist Church.
Enrollment: 1,237 undergrads.
Selectivity: Open admission; but selective for some programs.

BASIC COSTS (2009-2010)
Tuition and fees: $9,970.
Per-credit charge: $269.
Room and board: $5,620.

Additional info: Reported tuition includes cost of books.

FINANCIAL AID PICTURE
Students with need: Need-based aid available for full-time and part-time students.
Students without need: This college awards aid only to students with need.

FINANCIAL AID PROCEDURES
Forms required: FAFSA, institutional form.
Dates and Deadlines: No deadline. Applicants notified on a rolling basis.

CONTACT
Eric King, Director of Financial Aid
711 Wiley Avenue, Marshall, TX 75670
(903) 927-3217

Utah

Brigham Young University

Provo, Utah
www.byu.edu   Federal Code: 003670

4-year private university in small city, affiliated with Church of Jesus Christ of Latter-day Saints.
Enrollment: 30,745 undergrads, 9% part-time. 5,072 full-time freshmen.
Selectivity: Admits 50 to 75% of applicants.

BASIC COSTS (2010-2011)
Tuition and fees: $4,420.
Per-credit charge: $227.
Room and board: $7,120.
Additional info: Tuition is $8,840 for nonmembers of The Church of Jesus Christ of Latter-day Saints. Undergraduate per-credit-hour charge $454 for nonmembers.

FINANCIAL AID PICTURE (2008-2009)
Students with need: Out of 1,988 full-time freshmen who applied for aid, 1,212 were judged to have need. Of these, 1,057 received aid, and 30 had their full need met. Average financial aid package met 40% of need; average scholarship/grant was $3,922; average loan was $3,269. For part-time students, average financial aid package was $4,160.
Students without need: 1,919 full-time freshmen who did not demonstrate need for aid received scholarships/grants; average award was $3,326. No-need awards available for academics, art, athletics, leadership, minority status, music/drama, religious affiliation, ROTC, state/district residency.
Scholarships offered: 149 full-time freshmen received athletic scholarships; average amount $4,944.
Cumulative student debt: 24% of graduating class had student loans; average debt was $10,730.
Additional info: Students notified of scholarships on or about April 20.

FINANCIAL AID PROCEDURES
Forms required: FAFSA.
Dates and Deadlines: Priority date 4/15; no closing date. Applicants notified on a rolling basis starting 5/1.
Transfers: Must provide financial aid transcript.

CONTACT
Paul Conrad, Director of Financial Aid
A-41ASB, BYU, Provo, UT 84602
(801) 422-4104

College of Eastern Utah
Price, Utah
www.ceu.edu   Federal Code: 003676

2-year public community and junior college in small town.
Enrollment: 2,173 undergrads.
Selectivity: Open admission; but selective for some programs.

BASIC COSTS (2009-2010)
Tuition and fees: $2,470; out-of-state residents $4,540.
Room and board: $3,458.

FINANCIAL AID PICTURE
Students with need: Need-based aid available for full-time and part-time students. Work study available nights, weekends, and for part-time students.
Students without need: No-need awards available for academics, art, athletics, leadership, minority status, music/drama, religious affiliation, state/district residency.

FINANCIAL AID PROCEDURES
Forms required: FAFSA, institutional form.
Dates and Deadlines: Priority date 2/1; no closing date. Applicants notified on a rolling basis starting 3/15; must reply within 2 week(s) of notification.

CONTACT
Kim Booth, Financial Aid Director
451 East 400 North, Price, UT 84501
(435) 613-5207

Dixie State College of Utah
St. George, Utah
new.dixie.edu   Federal Code: 003671

4-year public liberal arts college in small city.
Enrollment: 6,484 undergrads, 32% part-time. 1,400 full-time freshmen.
Selectivity: Open admission; but selective for some programs.

BASIC COSTS (2009-2010)
Tuition and fees: $3,145; out-of-state residents $10,897.
Room and board: $3,548.

FINANCIAL AID PICTURE (2008-2009)
Students with need: 67% of average financial aid package awarded as scholarships/grants, 33% awarded as loans/jobs. Work study available nights, weekends, and for part-time students.
Students without need: No-need awards available for academics, alumni affiliation, art, athletics, leadership, minority status, music/drama, religious affiliation.
Additional info: SunFirst Bank Scholarship for communications students; Daniels Fund Scholarship for non-traditional students based on need.

FINANCIAL AID PROCEDURES
Forms required: FAFSA.
Dates and Deadlines: Priority date 3/1; closing date 5/1. Applicants notified on a rolling basis starting 3/1; must reply within 2 week(s) of notification.

CONTACT
JD Robertson, Director of Financial Aid
225 South 700 East, St. George, UT 84770-3876
(435) 652-7575

LDS Business College
Salt Lake City, Utah
www.ldsbc.edu   Federal Code: 003672

2-year private business and junior college in small city, affiliated with Church of Jesus Christ of Latter-day Saints.
Enrollment: 1,588 undergrads, 23% part-time. 379 full-time freshmen.
Selectivity: Open admission; but selective for some programs.

BASIC COSTS (2010-2011)
Tuition and fees: $2,900.
Per-credit charge: $120.

FINANCIAL AID PICTURE (2008-2009)
Students with need: Need-based aid available for full-time and part-time students.
Students without need: No-need awards available for academics, leadership.
Scholarships offered: Service scholarships; half-tuition for one semester; for Church of Jesus Christ of Latter-day Saints missionaries who have returned from mission within past year.

FINANCIAL AID PROCEDURES
Forms required: FAFSA.
Dates and Deadlines: Priority date 7/1; no closing date. Applicants notified on a rolling basis starting 3/1; must reply within 3 week(s) of notification.
Transfers: No deadline. Applicants notified on a rolling basis starting 1/1.

CONTACT
Doug Horne, Financial Aid Administrator
95 North 300 West, Salt Lake City, UT 84101-3500
(801) 524-8110

Salt Lake Community College
Salt Lake City, Utah
www.slcc.edu   Federal Code: 005220

2-year public community and technical college in very large city.
Enrollment: 25,678 undergrads, 64% part-time. 2,036 full-time freshmen.
Selectivity: Open admission; but selective for some programs.

BASIC COSTS (2009-2010)
Tuition and fees: $2,790; out-of-state residents $8,730.
Per-credit charge: $132; out-of-state residents $473.
Additional info: Tuition/fee waivers available for adults, minority students.

FINANCIAL AID PICTURE (2008-2009)
Students with need: Need-based aid available for full-time and part-time students. Work study available nights, weekends, and for part-time students.
Students without need: No-need awards available for academics, alumni affiliation, art, athletics, leadership, minority status, music/drama.

FINANCIAL AID PROCEDURES
Forms required: FAFSA, institutional form.
Dates and Deadlines: Priority date 5/1; no closing date. Applicants notified on a rolling basis starting 5/1; must reply within 4 week(s) of notification.

CONTACT
Cristi Millard, Director of Financial Aid
4600 South Redwood Road, Salt Lake City, UT 84130-0808
(801) 957-4410

Snow College
Ephraim, Utah
www.snow.edu   Federal Code: 003679

2-year public community and junior college in small town.
Enrollment: 4,368 undergrads, 39% part-time. 1,147 full-time freshmen.
Selectivity: Open admission.

BASIC COSTS (2009-2010)
Tuition and fees: $2,542; out-of-state residents $8,238.
Room and board: $2,620.
Additional info: Tuition/fee waivers available for unemployed or children of unemployed.

FINANCIAL AID PICTURE (2008-2009)
Students with need: Out of 895 full-time freshmen who applied for aid, 865 were judged to have need. Of these, 865 received aid, and 82 had their full need met. Average financial aid package met 18% of need; average scholarship/grant was $1,800; average loan was $1,560. For part-time students, average financial aid package was $2,150.
Students without need: 13 full-time freshmen who did not demonstrate need for aid received scholarships/grants; average award was $600. No-need awards available for academics, alumni affiliation, athletics, leadership, music/drama, state/district residency.
Scholarships offered: 81 full-time freshmen received athletic scholarships; average amount $1,390.

FINANCIAL AID PROCEDURES
Forms required: FAFSA, institutional form.
Dates and Deadlines: Priority date 3/1; closing date 7/15. Applicants notified on a rolling basis starting 8/1; must reply within 1 week(s) of notification.
Transfers: Priority date 3/15; closing date 6/15. Applicants notified on a rolling basis. F.A.T. required for mid-year transfers.

CONTACT
Jack Dalene, Director of Financial Aid
150 East College Avenue, Ephraim, UT 84627
(435) 283-7132

Southern Utah University
Cedar City, Utah
www.suu.edu   Federal Code: 003678

4-year public university in large town.
Enrollment: 5,797 undergrads, 12% part-time. 1,198 full-time freshmen.
Selectivity: Admits over 75% of applicants.

BASIC COSTS (2009-2010)
Tuition and fees: $4,269; out-of-state residents $12,847.
Room and board: $5,300.

FINANCIAL AID PICTURE (2008-2009)
Students with need: Out of 795 full-time freshmen who applied for aid, 615 were judged to have need. Of these, 614 received aid, and 89 had their full need met. Average financial aid package met 63% of need; average scholarship/grant was $4,922; average loan was $3,015. For part-time students, average financial aid package was $4,562.
Students without need: 614 full-time freshmen who did not demonstrate need for aid received scholarships/grants; average award was $5,507. No-need awards available for academics, alumni affiliation, art, athletics, job skills, leadership, minority status, music/drama, state/district residency.
Scholarships offered: 69 full-time freshmen received athletic scholarships; average amount $5,198.
Cumulative student debt: 51% of graduating class had student loans; average debt was $10,485.

FINANCIAL AID PROCEDURES
Forms required: FAFSA.
Dates and Deadlines: No deadline. Applicants notified on a rolling basis starting 11/1.

CONTACT
Paul Morris, Director of Financial Aid
351 West Center Street, Cedar City, UT 84720
(435) 586-7735

University of Utah
Salt Lake City, Utah
www.utah.edu   Federal Code: 003675

4-year public university in very large city.
Enrollment: 20,983 undergrads, 29% part-time. 2,551 full-time freshmen.
Selectivity: Admits over 75% of applicants.

BASIC COSTS (2009-2010)
Tuition and fees: $5,746; out-of-state residents $18,136.
Room and board: $6,240.

FINANCIAL AID PICTURE (2009-2010)
Students with need: Out of 1,345 full-time freshmen who applied for aid, 980 were judged to have need. Of these, 966 received aid, and 189 had their full need met. Average financial aid package met 55% of need; average scholarship/grant was $6,070; average loan was $4,261. For part-time students, average financial aid package was $9,768.
Students without need: 232 full-time freshmen who did not demonstrate need for aid received scholarships/grants; average award was $6,275. No-need awards available for academics, alumni affiliation, art, athletics, leadership, minority status, music/drama, ROTC, state/district residency.
Scholarships offered: 4 full-time freshmen received athletic scholarships; average amount $18,241.
Cumulative student debt: 40% of graduating class had student loans; average debt was $15,201.

FINANCIAL AID PROCEDURES
Forms required: FAFSA, institutional form.
Dates and Deadlines: Priority date 4/1; no closing date. Applicants notified on a rolling basis starting 4/15; must reply within 6 week(s) of notification.
Transfers: No deadline. Applicants notified on a rolling basis starting 4/15; must reply within 6 week(s) of notification.

CONTACT
John Curl, Director of Financial Aid and Scholarship
201 South 1460 East, Room 250 S, Salt Lake City, UT 84112-9057
(801) 581-6211

Utah Career College
West Jordan, Utah
www.utahcollege.edu   Federal Code: 011166

2-year for-profit technical and career college in small city.
Enrollment: 700 undergrads, 77% part-time. 21 full-time freshmen.
Selectivity: Open admission; but selective for some programs.

BASIC COSTS (2009-2010)
Tuition and fees: $17,325.
Per-credit charge: $385.
Additional info: Nursing program courses $458 per-credit-hour.

FINANCIAL AID PICTURE (2009-2010)
Students with need: Need-based aid available for full-time and part-time students.

Students without need: This college awards aid only to students with need.

FINANCIAL AID PROCEDURES

Forms required: FAFSA, institutional form.

Dates and Deadlines: No deadline. Applicants notified on a rolling basis starting 7/1; must reply within 2 week(s) of notification.

CONTACT

Nicole Whitesides, Director of Financial Aid
1902 West 7800 South, West Jordan, UT 84088
(801) 304-4224

Utah State University

Logan, Utah
www.usu.edu   Federal Code: 003677

4-year public university in small city.

Enrollment: 13,652 undergrads, 16% part-time. 2,639 full-time freshmen.

Selectivity: Admits over 75% of applicants.

BASIC COSTS (2009-2010)

Tuition and fees: $4,828; out-of-state residents $13,802.

Room and board: $4,900.

FINANCIAL AID PICTURE (2009-2010)

Students with need: Need-based aid available for full-time and part-time students. Work study available nights, weekends, and for part-time students.

Students without need: No-need awards available for academics, alumni affiliation, art, athletics, leadership, minority status, music/drama, religious affiliation, ROTC.

FINANCIAL AID PROCEDURES

Forms required: FAFSA.

Dates and Deadlines: No deadline. Applicants notified on a rolling basis starting 4/1; must reply within 4 week(s) of notification.

CONTACT

Steve Sharp, Director of Financial Aid
0160 Old Main Hill, Logan, UT 84322-0160
(435) 797-0173

Utah Valley University

Orem, Utah
www.uvu.edu   Federal Code: 004027

4-year public university and technical college in small city.

Enrollment: 24,061 undergrads, 40% part-time. 2,686 full-time freshmen.

Selectivity: Open admission.

BASIC COSTS (2009-2010)

Tuition and fees: $4,048; out-of-state residents $11,888.

FINANCIAL AID PICTURE (2009-2010)

Students with need: Out of 1,561 full-time freshmen who applied for aid, 1,397 were judged to have need. Of these, 1,321 received aid, and 78 had their full need met. Average financial aid package met 46% of need; average scholarship/grant was $4,532; average loan was $3,263. For part-time students, average financial aid package was $5,788.

Students without need: 407 full-time freshmen who did not demonstrate need for aid received scholarships/grants; average award was $3,233. No-need awards available for academics, alumni affiliation, art, athletics, job skills, leadership, minority status, music/drama, religious affiliation, ROTC, state/district residency.

Scholarships offered: 31 full-time freshmen received athletic scholarships; average amount $6,135.

Cumulative student debt: 63% of graduating class had student loans; average debt was $17,274.

FINANCIAL AID PROCEDURES

Forms required: FAFSA, institutional form.

Dates and Deadlines: Priority date 5/1; no closing date. Applicants notified on a rolling basis starting 5/15; must reply within 2 week(s) of notification.

Transfers: No deadline.

CONTACT

Michael Francis, Assistant Vice President for Finance and Controller
800 West University Parkway, Orem, UT 84058-5999
(801) 863-8442

Weber State University

Ogden, Utah
www.weber.edu   Federal Code: 003680

4-year public university in small city.

Enrollment: 17,342 undergrads.

Selectivity: Open admission; but selective for some programs.

BASIC COSTS (2009-2010)

Tuition and fees: $4,088; out-of-state residents $11,555.

Room and board: $6,634.

FINANCIAL AID PICTURE (2008-2009)

Students with need: Need-based aid available for full-time and part-time students. Work study available nights, weekends, and for part-time students.

Students without need: This college awards aid only to students with need.

FINANCIAL AID PROCEDURES

Forms required: FAFSA, institutional form.

Dates and Deadlines: Priority date 3/1; no closing date. Applicants notified on a rolling basis starting 3/15; must reply within 2 week(s) of notification.

CONTACT

Jeb Spencer, Director of Financial Aid
1137 University Circle, Ogden, UT 84408-1137
(801) 626-7569

Western Governors University

Salt Lake City, Utah
www.wgu.edu   Federal Code: 033394

4-year private virtual university in very large city.

Enrollment: 12,025 undergrads. 1,116 full-time freshmen.

Selectivity: Open admission.

BASIC COSTS (2010-2011)

Tuition and fees: $5,870.

Additional info: Two six-month terms at $2,890 per term. Students may complete an unlimited number of credit equivalency units in any term. Tuition/fee waivers available for adults.

FINANCIAL AID PICTURE

Students with need: Need-based aid available for full-time students.

Students without need: This college awards aid only to students with need.

FINANCIAL AID PROCEDURES

Forms required: FAFSA.

Transfers: No deadline.

CONTACT

David Grow, Chief Financial Officer/Director of Financial Aid
4001 South 700 East, Suite 700, Salt Lake City, UT 84107
(877) 435-7948 ext. 3104

Westminster College

Salt Lake City, Utah
www.westminstercollege.edu   Federal Code: 003681

4-year private liberal arts college in very large city.
Enrollment: 2,141 undergrads, 6% part-time. 466 full-time freshmen.
Selectivity: Admits over 75% of applicants.

BASIC COSTS (2010-2011)

Tuition and fees: $25,980.
Per-credit charge: $1,065.
Room and board: $7,274.

FINANCIAL AID PICTURE (2009-2010)

Students with need: Out of 343 full-time freshmen who applied for aid, 278 were judged to have need. Of these, 278 received aid, and 97 had their full need met. Average financial aid package met 89% of need; average scholarship/grant was $15,732; average loan was $4,171. For part-time students, average financial aid package was $11,063.
Students without need: 167 full-time freshmen who did not demonstrate need for aid received scholarships/grants; average award was $12,341. No-need awards available for academics, alumni affiliation, art, athletics, leadership, minority status, music/drama, religious affiliation.
Scholarships offered: 7 full-time freshmen received athletic scholarships; average amount $3,357.
Cumulative student debt: 54% of graduating class had student loans; average debt was $20,251.

FINANCIAL AID PROCEDURES

Forms required: FAFSA.
Dates and Deadlines: Priority date 4/15; no closing date. Applicants notified on a rolling basis starting 3/1; must reply within 3 week(s) of notification.
Transfers: Full-time transfer students with 3.0 GPA eligible for work study, loans, scholarships and grants which range from $5,000-$10,000 per year.

CONTACT

Elizabeth Key, Director of Financial Aid
1840 South 1300 East, Salt Lake City, UT 84105
(801) 832-2500

Vermont

Bennington College

Bennington, Vermont   Federal Code: 003682
www.bennington.edu   CSS Code: 3080

4-year private liberal arts college in large town.
Enrollment: 664 undergrads, 1% part-time. 197 full-time freshmen.
Selectivity: Admits 50 to 75% of applicants.

BASIC COSTS (2010-2011)

Tuition and fees: $41,350.
Per-credit charge: $1,340.
Room and board: $11,550.

FINANCIAL AID PICTURE (2009-2010)

Students with need: Out of 154 full-time freshmen who applied for aid, 142 were judged to have need. Of these, 139 received aid, and 24 had their full need met. Average financial aid package met 81% of need; average scholarship/grant was $29,549; average loan was $2,797. For part-time students, average financial aid package was $14,984.
Students without need: 21 full-time freshmen who did not demonstrate need for aid received scholarships/grants; average award was $10,166. No-need awards available for academics.
Additional info: All applicants for undergraduate admission considered for scholarships based on quality of overall application.

FINANCIAL AID PROCEDURES

Forms required: FAFSA, institutional form. CSS PROFILE required of early decision applicants only.
Dates and Deadlines: Priority date 2/1; closing date 2/15. Applicants notified by 4/1; must reply by 5/1 or within 2 week(s) of notification.
Transfers: Priority date 3/15; closing date 8/1. Applicants notified on a rolling basis starting 5/1; must reply by 6/1 or within 2 week(s) of notification.

CONTACT

One College Drive, Bennington, VT 05201-6003

Burlington College

Burlington, Vermont
www.burlington.edu   Federal Code: 012183

4-year private visual arts and liberal arts college in small city.
Enrollment: 169 undergrads, 29% part-time. 19 full-time freshmen.
Selectivity: Admits over 75% of applicants.

BASIC COSTS (2010-2011)

Tuition and fees: $21,340.
Room only: $6,750.

FINANCIAL AID PICTURE (2009-2010)

Students with need: Average financial aid package met 49% of need; average scholarship/grant was $9,321; average loan was $3,730. For part-time students, average financial aid package was $6,771.
Students without need: No-need awards available for academics, leadership.
Cumulative student debt: 80% of graduating class had student loans; average debt was $38,198.

FINANCIAL AID PROCEDURES

Forms required: FAFSA, state aid form.
Dates and Deadlines: No deadline. Applicants notified on a rolling basis starting 3/15.
Transfers: No deadline. Applicants notified on a rolling basis.

CONTACT

Lindy Walsh, Director of Financial Aid
95 North Avenue, Burlington, VT 05401
(802) 862-9616 ext. 110

Castleton State College

Castleton, Vermont
www.castleton.edu   Federal Code: 003683

4-year public liberal arts college in small town.
Enrollment: 1,965 undergrads, 8% part-time. 506 full-time freshmen.
Selectivity: Admits 50 to 75% of applicants.

BASIC COSTS (2009-2010)

Tuition and fees: $8,820; out-of-state residents $18,060.
Per-credit charge: $333; out-of-state residents $718.

Room and board: $7,808.

Additional info: New England Board of Higher Education rate for students from other New England states: 150% of Vermont resident tuition. Available to degree candidates in academic areas not offered by educational institutions in their home states.

FINANCIAL AID PICTURE (2008-2009)

Students with need: Need-based aid available for full-time and part-time students.

Students without need: No-need awards available for academics, alumni affiliation, art, leadership, music/drama, state/district residency.

FINANCIAL AID PROCEDURES

Forms required: FAFSA.

Dates and Deadlines: Priority date 2/15; no closing date. Applicants notified on a rolling basis starting 1/1; must reply by 5/1 or within 2 week(s) of notification.

CONTACT

Kathy O'Meara, Financial Aid Director
Seminary Street, Castleton, VT 05735
(802) 468-1286

Champlain College

Burlington, Vermont
www.champlain.edu   Federal Code: 003684

4-year private liberal arts and career college in small city.

Enrollment: 1,993 undergrads, 3% part-time. 545 full-time freshmen.

Selectivity: Admits over 75% of applicants.

BASIC COSTS (2010-2011)

Tuition and fees: $27,180.

Per-credit charge: $1,130.

Room and board: $12,130.

FINANCIAL AID PICTURE (2009-2010)

Students with need: Out of 435 full-time freshmen who applied for aid, 353 were judged to have need. Of these, 353 received aid, and 71 had their full need met. Average financial aid package met 76% of need; average scholarship/grant was $8,197; average loan was $4,178. For part-time students, average financial aid package was $8,727.

Students without need: 77 full-time freshmen who did not demonstrate need for aid received scholarships/grants; average award was $3,266. No-need awards available for academics, leadership.

FINANCIAL AID PROCEDURES

Forms required: FAFSA.

Dates and Deadlines: Closing date 3/1. Applicants notified by 3/19; must reply by 5/1.

Transfers: Closing date 5/1. Applicants notified on a rolling basis starting 5/1; must reply within 2 week(s) of notification.

CONTACT

Donna Stevens, Director of Financial Aid
163 South Willard Street, Burlington, VT 05402-0670
(802) 860-2730

College of St. Joseph in Vermont

Rutland, Vermont
www.csj.edu   Federal Code: 003685

4-year private liberal arts and teachers college in large town, affiliated with Roman Catholic Church.

Enrollment: 211 undergrads, 17% part-time. 44 full-time freshmen.

Selectivity: Admits over 75% of applicants.

BASIC COSTS (2009-2010)

Tuition and fees: $17,550.

Per-credit charge: $250.

Room and board: $8,350.

FINANCIAL AID PICTURE (2009-2010)

Students with need: Out of 44 full-time freshmen who applied for aid, 42 were judged to have need. Of these, 42 received aid, and 2 had their full need met. Average financial aid package met 75% of need; average scholarship/grant was $14,111; average loan was $3,900. For part-time students, average financial aid package was $6,647.

Students without need: 2 full-time freshmen who did not demonstrate need for aid received scholarships/grants; average award was $4,500. No-need awards available for academics, alumni affiliation.

Cumulative student debt: 100% of graduating class had student loans; average debt was $34,459.

FINANCIAL AID PROCEDURES

Forms required: FAFSA.

Dates and Deadlines: Priority date 3/1; no closing date. Applicants notified on a rolling basis starting 3/15.

Transfers: No deadline. Applicants notified on a rolling basis.

CONTACT

Julie Rosmus, Financial Aid Director
71 Clement Road, Rutland, VT 05701-3899
(802) 773-5900 ext. 3274

Community College of Vermont

Montpelier, Vermont
www.ccv.edu   Federal Code: 011167

2-year public community and liberal arts college in small town.

Enrollment: 4,590 undergrads.

Selectivity: Open admission.

BASIC COSTS (2009-2010)

Tuition and fees: $6,070; out-of-state residents $12,040.

Per-credit charge: $199; out-of-state residents $398.

Additional info: New England Board of Higher Education rate for students from other New England states: 150% of Vermont resident tuition. Available to degree candidates in academic areas not offered by educational institutions in their home states.

FINANCIAL AID PICTURE (2009-2010)

Students with need: For part-time students, average financial aid package was $3,664.

Students without need: This college awards aid only to students with need.

FINANCIAL AID PROCEDURES

Forms required: FAFSA, state aid form, institutional form.

Dates and Deadlines: No deadline. Applicants notified on a rolling basis starting 9/1; must reply within 3 week(s) of notification.

CONTACT

Pam Chisholm, Director for Financial Aid
PO Box 489, Montpelier, VT 05601
(802) 828-2800

Goddard College

Plainfield, Vermont
www.goddard.edu   Federal Code: 003686

4-year private liberal arts college in rural community.

Enrollment: 275 undergrads.

Selectivity: Admits 50 to 75% of applicants.

BASIC COSTS (2010-2011)
Additional info: Annualized tuition for Individualized Bachelor of Arts is $12,854, for Health Arts & Sciences BA $12,854, for Education BA with licensure $13,356, for Creative Writing BFA $13,956. In all programs, students spend one week on campus at the start of each semester and study from home or elsewhere the rest of the term. Room and board fee is $1,152 per year. Required fees $168 per year.

FINANCIAL AID PICTURE (2008-2009)
Students with need: Need-based aid available for full-time students.
Students without need: No-need awards available for academics, art, job skills, leadership, music/drama, state/district residency.

FINANCIAL AID PROCEDURES
Forms required: FAFSA.
Dates and Deadlines: No deadline. Applicants notified on a rolling basis starting 4/15; must reply within 4 week(s) of notification.
Transfers: No deadline. Applicants notified on a rolling basis.

CONTACT
Beverly Jene, Director of Financial Aid
Goddard College Admissions, Plainfield, VT 05667
(800) 468-4888

Green Mountain College
Poultney, Vermont
www.greenmtn.edu   Federal Code: 003687

4-year private liberal arts college in small town, affiliated with United Methodist Church.
Enrollment: 746 undergrads, 2% part-time. 217 full-time freshmen.
Selectivity: Admits 50 to 75% of applicants.

BASIC COSTS (2009-2010)
Tuition and fees: $26,900.
Per-credit charge: $864.
Room and board: $9,670.

FINANCIAL AID PICTURE (2009-2010)
Students with need: Out of 191 full-time freshmen who applied for aid, 168 were judged to have need. Of these, 168 received aid, and 17 had their full need met. Average financial aid package met 67% of need; average scholarship/grant was $16,516; average loan was $3,110. For part-time students, average financial aid package was $10,385.
Students without need: 42 full-time freshmen who did not demonstrate need for aid received scholarships/grants; average award was $12,061. No-need awards available for academics, alumni affiliation, art, leadership, minority status, music/drama, religious affiliation.
Scholarships offered: Scholarships for art, performing arts, environmental service, leadership, service: range from $1,000 to $7,000; renewable annually. Make A Difference Scholarship: full tuition; room and board fees; based on merit.
Cumulative student debt: 76% of graduating class had student loans; average debt was $35,245.
Additional info: Service/recognition awards available to all students.

FINANCIAL AID PROCEDURES
Forms required: FAFSA. CSS PROFILE is recommended to receive an earlier financial aid package.
Dates and Deadlines: Priority date 3/1; no closing date. Applicants notified on a rolling basis starting 11/1; must reply by 5/1 or within 3 week(s) of notification.
Transfers: No deadline. Applicants notified on a rolling basis; must reply by 5/1 or within 3 week(s) of notification.

CONTACT
Wendy Ellis, Director of Financial Aid
One Brennan Circle, Poultney, VT 05764
(802) 287-8210

Johnson State College
Johnson, Vermont
www.jsc.edu   Federal Code: 003688

4-year public liberal arts college in small town.
Enrollment: 1,672 undergrads, 28% part-time. 300 full-time freshmen.

BASIC COSTS (2009-2010)
Tuition and fees: $8,716; out-of-state residents $17,956.
Per-credit charge: $333; out-of-state residents $718.
Room and board: $7,809.
Additional info: New England Board of Higher Education rate for students from other New England states: 150% of Vermont resident tuition. Available to degree candidates in academic areas not offered by educational institutions in their home states.

FINANCIAL AID PICTURE (2009-2010)
Students with need: Out of 277 full-time freshmen who applied for aid, 232 were judged to have need. Of these, 232 received aid, and 33 had their full need met. Average financial aid package met 88% of need; average scholarship/grant was $6,151; average loan was $3,583. For part-time students, average financial aid package was $10,649.
Students without need: 16 full-time freshmen who did not demonstrate need for aid received scholarships/grants; average award was $2,949. No-need awards available for academics, alumni affiliation, art, leadership, music/drama, state/district residency.

FINANCIAL AID PROCEDURES
Forms required: FAFSA, state aid form.
Dates and Deadlines: Priority date 3/1; no closing date. Applicants notified on a rolling basis starting 4/1; must reply within 3 week(s) of notification.
Transfers: Financial aid transcripts from previously attended colleges required.

CONTACT
Lisa Cummings, Director of Financial Aid
337 College Hill, Johnson, VT 05656
(800) 635-2356

Landmark College
Putney, Vermont
www.landmark.edu   Federal Code: 017157

2-year private liberal arts college in small town.
Enrollment: 498 undergrads. 183 full-time freshmen.
Selectivity: Admits 50 to 75% of applicants.

BASIC COSTS (2010-2011)
Tuition and fees: $48,000.
Room and board: $8,500.

FINANCIAL AID PICTURE (2009-2010)
Students with need: Out of 166 full-time freshmen who applied for aid, 166 were judged to have need. Of these, 166 received aid, and 5 had their full need met. Average financial aid package met 35% of need; average scholarship/grant was $18,500; average loan was $5,500. Need-based aid available for part-time students.
Students without need: 17 full-time freshmen who did not demonstrate need for aid received scholarships/grants; average award was $6,000. No-need awards available for academics, art, leadership, minority status, music/drama.

Cumulative student debt: 45% of graduating class had student loans; average debt was $17,000.

Additional info: Students encouraged to apply to their state departments of vocational rehabilitation for additional financial assistance.

FINANCIAL AID PROCEDURES

Forms required: FAFSA.

Dates and Deadlines: Priority date 3/15; no closing date. Applicants notified on a rolling basis starting 3/15; must reply within 2 week(s) of notification.

Transfers: No deadline. Applicants notified on a rolling basis; must reply within 2 week(s) of notification.

CONTACT

Cathy Mullins, Director of Financial Aid
River Road South, Putney, VT 05346
(802) 387-6736

Lyndon State College
Lyndonville, Vermont
www.lyndonstate.edu   Federal Code: 003689

4-year public liberal arts and teachers college in small town.

Enrollment: 1,500 undergrads.

Selectivity: Admits over 75% of applicants.

BASIC COSTS (2009-2010)

Tuition and fees: $8,820; out-of-state residents $18,060.

Per-credit charge: $415; out-of-state residents $792.

Room and board: $7,808.

Additional info: New England Board of Higher Education rate for students from other New England states: 150% of Vermont resident tuition. Available to degree candidates in academic areas not offered by educational institutions in their home states. Tuition/fee waivers available for unemployed or children of unemployed.

FINANCIAL AID PICTURE (2008-2009)

Students with need: Need-based aid available for full-time and part-time students. Work study available nights, weekends, and for part-time students.

Students without need: No-need awards available for academics, leadership.

FINANCIAL AID PROCEDURES

Forms required: FAFSA.

Dates and Deadlines: Priority date 2/1; no closing date. Applicants notified on a rolling basis starting 4/1; must reply within 2 week(s) of notification.

CONTACT

Tanya Bradley, Director of Financial Aid
1001 College Road, Lyndonville, VT 05851
(802) 626-6218

Marlboro College
Marlboro, Vermont
www.marlboro.edu   Federal Code: 003690

4-year private liberal arts college in rural community.

Enrollment: 311 undergrads, 1% part-time. 63 full-time freshmen.

Selectivity: Admits 50 to 75% of applicants.

BASIC COSTS (2010-2011)

Tuition and fees: $35,120.

Room and board: $9,420.

FINANCIAL AID PICTURE (2009-2010)

Students with need: Average financial aid package met 88% of need; average scholarship/grant was $14,746; average loan was $3,500. Need-based aid available for part-time students.

Students without need: No-need awards available for academics, leadership.

Cumulative student debt: 94% of graduating class had student loans; average debt was $6,631.

FINANCIAL AID PROCEDURES

Forms required: FAFSA.

Dates and Deadlines: Closing date 3/1. Applicants notified on a rolling basis starting 3/15; must reply by 5/1 or within 2 week(s) of notification.

CONTACT

Cathy Fuller, Associate Director of Financial Aid
PO Box A, Marlboro, VT 05344-0300
(802) 258-9237

Middlebury College
Middlebury, Vermont   Federal Code: 003691
www.middlebury.edu   CSS Code: 3526

4-year private liberal arts college in small town.

Enrollment: 2,455 undergrads, 1% part-time. 576 full-time freshmen.

Selectivity: Admits less than 50% of applicants.

BASIC COSTS (2010-2011)

Comprehensive fee: $52,500.

FINANCIAL AID PICTURE (2008-2009)

Students with need: Out of 336 full-time freshmen who applied for aid, 249 were judged to have need. Of these, 249 received aid, and 249 had their full need met. Average financial aid package met 100% of need; average scholarship/grant was $34,362; average loan was $2,782. For part-time students, average financial aid package was $4,558.

Students without need: This college awards aid only to students with need.

Cumulative student debt: 44% of graduating class had student loans; average debt was $21,458.

Additional info: College maintains need-blind admissions policy and meets full demonstrated financial need of students who qualify for admission, to degree resources permit.

FINANCIAL AID PROCEDURES

Forms required: FAFSA, CSS PROFILE.

Dates and Deadlines: Priority date 11/1; closing date 2/1. Applicants notified by 4/1; must reply by 5/1.

Transfers: Closing date 3/1. Applicants notified by 4/10; must reply by 5/1.

CONTACT

Kim Downs, Director of Student Financial Services
The Emma Willard House, Middlebury, VT 05753-6002
(802) 443-5158

New England Culinary Institute: Essex Junction
Montpelier, Vermont
www.neci.edu   Federal Code: 022540

2-year for-profit culinary school and business college in small city.

Enrollment: 516 full-time undergrads.

BASIC COSTS (2009-2010)

Tuition and fees: $25,900.

Room and board: $6,776.

Additional info: Costs will vary by program.

FINANCIAL AID PICTURE

Students with need: Need-based aid available for full-time students. Work study available nights.

Scholarships offered: Second Generation Scholarship: $1,000 awarded to students recommended by alumni. James Beard Foundation: $1,000 - $2,000 awarded. Massachusetts Restaurant Association: up to $2,500 awarded. National Restaurant Association: up to $2,000 awarded.

FINANCIAL AID PROCEDURES

Forms required: FAFSA.

Dates and Deadlines: No deadline. Applicants notified on a rolling basis.

CONTACT

Rich Goodwin, Chief Financial Officer
56 College Street, Montpelier, VT 05602
(802) 223-6324

Norwich University

Northfield, Vermont
www.norwich.edu

Federal Code: 003692
CSS Code: 3669

4-year private university and military college in small town.

Enrollment: 2,120 undergrads, 2% part-time. 653 full-time freshmen.

Selectivity: Admits 50 to 75% of applicants.

BASIC COSTS (2010-2011)

Tuition and fees: $28,738.

Per-credit charge: $799.

Room and board: $9,958.

FINANCIAL AID PICTURE

Students with need: Need-based aid available for full-time and part-time students.

Students without need: No-need awards available for academics, leadership, music/drama, ROTC.

Additional info: Winners of ROTC scholarships receive full room and board; must maintain 2.75 GPA. Renewable up to 4 years.

FINANCIAL AID PROCEDURES

Forms required: FAFSA, CSS PROFILE, institutional form.

Dates and Deadlines: Priority date 3/1; no closing date. Applicants notified on a rolling basis starting 12/15.

CONTACT

Tracey Mingo, Director of Financial Aid
158 Harmon Drive, Northfield, VT 05663
(802) 485-2015

St. Michael's College

Colchester, Vermont
www.smcvt.edu

Federal Code: 003694

4-year private liberal arts college in small city, affiliated with Roman Catholic Church.

Enrollment: 1,915 undergrads, 1% part-time. 470 full-time freshmen.

Selectivity: Admits over 75% of applicants.

BASIC COSTS (2010-2011)

Tuition and fees: $34,845.

Per-credit charge: $1,155.

Room and board: $8,685.

FINANCIAL AID PICTURE (2009-2010)

Students with need: Out of 388 full-time freshmen who applied for aid, 317 were judged to have need. Of these, 317 received aid, and 86 had their full need met. Average financial aid package met 81% of need; average scholarship/grant was $17,779; average loan was $4,846. Need-based aid available for part-time students.

Students without need: 137 full-time freshmen who did not demonstrate need for aid received scholarships/grants; average award was $9,195. No-need awards available for academics, athletics, ROTC.

Scholarships offered: 2 full-time freshmen received athletic scholarships; average amount $41,495.

Cumulative student debt: 76% of graduating class had student loans; average debt was $30,742.

FINANCIAL AID PROCEDURES

Forms required: FAFSA.

Dates and Deadlines: Priority date 2/15; no closing date. Applicants notified on a rolling basis starting 2/1; must reply by 5/1 or within 2 week(s) of notification.

CONTACT

Daniel Couture, Director of Student Financial Services
One Winooski Park, Colchester, VT 05439
(802) 654-3244

Southern Vermont College

Bennington, Vermont
www.svc.edu

Federal Code: 003693

4-year private liberal arts college in large town.

Enrollment: 477 undergrads, 10% part-time. 105 full-time freshmen.

Selectivity: Admits over 75% of applicants.

BASIC COSTS (2009-2010)

Tuition and fees: $18,880.

Room and board: $8,840.

Additional info: Health insurance, if applicable, $650 per year.

FINANCIAL AID PICTURE (2009-2010)

Students with need: Need-based aid available for full-time and part-time students. Work study available nights, weekends, and for part-time students.

Students without need: No-need awards available for academics, leadership.

FINANCIAL AID PROCEDURES

Forms required: FAFSA, state aid form.

Dates and Deadlines: No deadline. Applicants notified on a rolling basis.

CONTACT

Joel Phelps, Director of Financial Aid Services
982 Mansion Drive, Bennington, VT 05201-6002
(802) 447-6306

Sterling College

Craftsbury Common, Vermont
www.sterlingcollege.edu

Federal Code: 014991

4-year private liberal arts college in rural community.

Enrollment: 108 undergrads, 7% part-time. 25 full-time freshmen.

Selectivity: Admits over 75% of applicants.

BASIC COSTS (2009-2010)

Tuition and fees: $23,621.

Per-credit charge: $690.

Room and board: $7,554.

Additional info: Students receive $1,600 tuition and book credit in exchange for work done on campus.

FINANCIAL AID PICTURE (2008-2009)

Students with need: Out of 24 full-time freshmen who applied for aid, 22 were judged to have need. Of these, 22 received aid, and 1 had their full need met. Average financial aid package met 65% of need; average scholarship/grant was $15,694; average loan was $3,000. Need-based aid available for part-time students.

Students without need: 1 full-time freshmen who did not demonstrate need for aid received scholarships/grants; average award was $4,000. No-need awards available for academics, leadership, state/district residency.

Scholarships offered: Gladys Brooks: up to $6,000; academic merit, resident of Northeast Kingdom of Vermont, leadership. Presidential Scholarship: up to $5,000, significant academic merit and achievement. Achievement Scholarships: up to $5,000; demonstration of a significant life achievement. Vermont Scholarship: up to $2,000 for Vermont residents. Service Scholarship: up to $5,000; significant service. Bounder Scholarship: $500; applicants who live west of the Mississippi or in the Deep South. SCA Award: $1,000; alumni of Student Conservation Association. Transfer Award: $1,000. Vermont Youth Conservation Corps Award: $1,000; awarded to alumni of VYCC. Scholarships also offered for service and volunteer commitments and experience.

Cumulative student debt: 100% of graduating class had student loans; average debt was $31,867.

FINANCIAL AID PROCEDURES

Forms required: FAFSA, institutional form.

Dates and Deadlines: Priority date 3/15; no closing date. Applicants notified on a rolling basis starting 2/1; must reply by 5/1 or within 2 week(s) of notification.

CONTACT

Edward Houston, Director of Financial Aid
PO Box 72, Craftsbury Common, VT 05827-0072
(800) 648-3591 ext. 3

University of Vermont
Burlington, Vermont
www.uvm.edu   Federal Code: 003696

4-year public university in large town.

Enrollment: 10,371 undergrads, 3% part-time. 2,454 full-time freshmen.
Selectivity: Admits 50 to 75% of applicants.

BASIC COSTS (2009-2010)

Tuition and fees: $13,554; out-of-state residents $31,410.
Per-credit charge: $488; out-of-state residents $1,232.
Room and board: $8,996.

FINANCIAL AID PICTURE (2008-2009)

Students with need: Out of 1,834 full-time freshmen who applied for aid, 1,401 were judged to have need. Of these, 1,399 received aid, and 288 had their full need met. Average financial aid package met 82% of need; average scholarship/grant was $14,108; average loan was $5,696. For part-time students, average financial aid package was $11,647.

Students without need: 797 full-time freshmen who did not demonstrate need for aid received scholarships/grants; average award was $2,199. No-need awards available for academics, art, athletics, ROTC.

Scholarships offered: 51 full-time freshmen received athletic scholarships; average amount $19,626.

Cumulative student debt: 63% of graduating class had student loans; average debt was $27,682.

FINANCIAL AID PROCEDURES

Forms required: FAFSA.

Dates and Deadlines: Priority date 2/10; no closing date. Applicants notified on a rolling basis starting 3/15; must reply within 4 week(s) of notification.

Transfers: No deadline. Applicants notified on a rolling basis starting 3/15; must reply within 4 week(s) of notification. Merit-based scholarships not available to transfer students.

CONTACT

Marie Johnson, Director Student Financial Services
194 South Prospect Street, Burlington, VT 05401-3596
(802) 656-5700

Vermont Technical College
Randolph Center, Vermont
www.vtc.edu   Federal Code: 003698

4-year public technical college in small town.

Enrollment: 1,515 undergrads, 17% part-time. 291 full-time freshmen.
Selectivity: Admits 50 to 75% of applicants.

BASIC COSTS (2009-2010)

Tuition and fees: $10,684; out-of-state residents $19,743.
Per-credit charge: $415; out-of-state residents $792.
Room and board: $7,809.
Additional info: New England Board of Higher Education rate for students from other New England states: 150% of Vermont resident tuition. Available to degree candidates in academic areas not offered by educational institutions in their home states.

FINANCIAL AID PICTURE (2008-2009)

Students with need: Out of 260 full-time freshmen who applied for aid, 222 were judged to have need. Of these, 220 received aid, and 32 had their full need met. Average financial aid package met 68% of need; average scholarship/grant was $5,420; average loan was $3,310. For part-time students, average financial aid package was $5,850.

Students without need: 26 full-time freshmen who did not demonstrate need for aid received scholarships/grants; average award was $4,184. No-need awards available for academics.

Scholarships offered: Presidential Scholarship: $5,000; awarded to 5 non-residents. Scholars program: full tuition for 2 years (excluding room and board); awarded to 4 Vermont students.

Cumulative student debt: 80% of graduating class had student loans; average debt was $26,000.

FINANCIAL AID PROCEDURES

Forms required: FAFSA.

Dates and Deadlines: Priority date 3/1; no closing date. Applicants notified on a rolling basis starting 3/15; must reply within 2 week(s) of notification.

CONTACT

Cathy McCullough, Director of Financial Aid
PO Box 500, Randolph Center, VT 05061-0500
(800) 965-8790

Virginia

Averett University
Danville, Virginia
www.averett.edu   Federal Code: 003702

4-year private university and liberal arts college in small city.

Enrollment: 846 undergrads, 6% part-time. 244 full-time freshmen.
Selectivity: Admits over 75% of applicants.

BASIC COSTS (2010-2011)

Tuition and fees: $22,956.
Per-credit charge: $375.

Room and board: $8,138.

FINANCIAL AID PICTURE (2008-2009)
Students with need: Out of 217 full-time freshmen who applied for aid, 194 were judged to have need. Of these, 192 received aid, and 30 had their full need met. Average financial aid package met 70% of need; average scholarship/grant was $10,545; average loan was $3,926. For part-time students, average financial aid package was $6,593.
Students without need: 50 full-time freshmen who did not demonstrate need for aid received scholarships/grants; average award was $7,444. No-need awards available for academics, alumni affiliation, art, leadership, minority status, music/drama, state/district residency.
Cumulative student debt: 67% of graduating class had student loans; average debt was $30,943.

FINANCIAL AID PROCEDURES
Forms required: FAFSA, state aid form.
Dates and Deadlines: Priority date 4/1; no closing date. Applicants notified on a rolling basis starting 2/15; must reply within 2 week(s) of notification.
Transfers: No deadline. Applicants notified on a rolling basis starting 2/15; must reply within 2 week(s) of notification.

CONTACT
Carl Bradsher, Dean of Financial Assistance
420 West Main Street, Danville, VA 24541
(434) 791-5890

Aviation Institute of Maintenance: Virginia Beach
Chesapeake, Virginia
www.aviationmaintenance.edu   Federal Code: 031263

2-year for-profit technical college in large city.
Enrollment: 59 undergrads. 46 full-time freshmen.
Selectivity: Open admission.

BASIC COSTS (2009-2010)
Per-credit charge: $320.
Additional info: $320 per-credit-hour and $14,400 for the academic year (3 quarters). Tuition at time of enrollment locked for 2 years.

FINANCIAL AID PICTURE (2008-2009)
Students with need: 21% of average financial aid package awarded as scholarships/grants, 79% awarded as loans/jobs.

FINANCIAL AID PROCEDURES
Dates and Deadlines: No deadline.
Transfers: No deadline.

CONTACT
Tracy Asper, Financial Aid Officer
2211 South Military Highway, Chesapeake, VA 23320
(757) 363-2121

Blue Ridge Community College
Weyers Cave, Virginia
www.brcc.edu   Federal Code: 006819

2-year public community college in large town.
Enrollment: 4,779 undergrads.
Selectivity: Open admission; but selective for some programs.

BASIC COSTS (2009-2010)
Tuition and fees: $3,024; out-of-state residents $8,187.
Per-credit charge: $87; out-of-state residents $259.
Additional info: Out-of-state students pay an additional $300 capital outlay fee.

FINANCIAL AID PICTURE (2008-2009)
Students with need: Need-based aid available for full-time and part-time students.
Students without need: No-need awards available for academics, job skills, leadership, minority status.

FINANCIAL AID PROCEDURES
Forms required: FAFSA, institutional form.
Dates and Deadlines: Priority date 5/1; no closing date. Applicants notified on a rolling basis starting 5/30; must reply within 2 week(s) of notification.

CONTACT
Robert Clemmer, Financial Aid Director
Box 80, Weyers Cave, VA 24486-9989
(540) 234-9261 ext. 2223

Bluefield College
Bluefield, Virginia
www.bluefield.edu   Federal Code: 003703

4-year private liberal arts and teachers college in small town, affiliated with Baptist faith.
Enrollment: 722 undergrads, 11% part-time. 121 full-time freshmen.
Selectivity: Admits less than 50% of applicants.

BASIC COSTS (2010-2011)
Tuition and fees: $18,800.
Per-credit charge: $750.
Room and board: $7,150.
Additional info: Tuition/fee waivers available for adults.

FINANCIAL AID PICTURE (2009-2010)
Students with need: Average financial aid package met 79% of need; average scholarship/grant was $13,663; average loan was $3,855. For part-time students, average financial aid package was $5,285.
Students without need: No-need awards available for academics, alumni affiliation, art, athletics, music/drama, religious affiliation, state/district residency.
Cumulative student debt: 86% of graduating class had student loans; average debt was $18,185.

FINANCIAL AID PROCEDURES
Forms required: FAFSA, state aid form.
Dates and Deadlines: Priority date 3/15; no closing date. Applicants notified on a rolling basis starting 3/1; must reply within 3 week(s) of notification.
Transfers: No deadline. Applicants notified on a rolling basis starting 3/1; must reply within 3 week(s) of notification.

CONTACT
Sheila Nelson-Hensley, Director of Financial Aid
3000 College Drive, Bluefield, VA 24605
(276) 326-4215

Bridgewater College
Bridgewater, Virginia
www.bridgewater.edu   Federal Code: 003704

4-year private liberal arts college in small town, affiliated with Church of the Brethren.
Enrollment: 1,575 undergrads, 1% part-time. 497 full-time freshmen.
Selectivity: Admits over 75% of applicants.

BASIC COSTS (2010-2011)
Tuition and fees: $25,500.
Per-credit charge: $850.
Room and board: $10,350.

PART III: FINANCIAL AID COLLEGE BY COLLEGE

FINANCIAL AID PICTURE (2009-2010)

Students with need: Out of 461 full-time freshmen who applied for aid, 408 were judged to have need. Of these, 408 received aid, and 79 had their full need met. Average financial aid package met 79% of need; average scholarship/grant was $17,512; average loan was $4,315. For part-time students, average financial aid package was $4,016.

Students without need: 89 full-time freshmen who did not demonstrate need for aid received scholarships/grants; average award was $10,876. No-need awards available for academics, music/drama, religious affiliation.

Scholarships offered: Renewable academic scholarships are provided to freshmen based on high school grade point average and other criteria from the applicant's record.

Cumulative student debt: 74% of graduating class had student loans; average debt was $29,331.

FINANCIAL AID PROCEDURES

Forms required: FAFSA, state aid form.

Dates and Deadlines: Priority date 3/1; no closing date. Applicants notified on a rolling basis starting 3/16; must reply within 2 week(s) of notification.

CONTACT

Scott Morrison, Director of Financial Aid
402 East College Street, Bridgewater, VA 22812-1599
(540) 828-5377

Bryant & Stratton College: Richmond
Richmond, Virginia
www.bryantstratton.edu   Federal Code: 010061

2-year for-profit career college in small city.

Enrollment: 730 undergrads, 50% part-time.

Selectivity: Open admission; but selective for some programs.

BASIC COSTS (2009-2010)

Additional info: Annual tuition for bachelor's degree may vary by program.

FINANCIAL AID PICTURE (2008-2009)

Students with need: 100% of average financial aid package awarded as scholarships/grants, 0% awarded as loans/jobs. Need-based aid available for part-time students. Work study available nights.

Students without need: This college awards aid only to students with need.

FINANCIAL AID PROCEDURES

Forms required: FAFSA.

Dates and Deadlines: No deadline.

Transfers: No deadline.

CONTACT

Dita Terry, Business Office Director
8141 Hull Street Road, Richmond, VA 23235
(804) 745-2444

Bryant & Stratton College: Virginia Beach
Virginia Beach, Virginia
www.bryantstratton.edu   Federal Code: 002678

2-year for-profit business and junior college in large city.

Enrollment: 737 undergrads, 55% part-time. 144 full-time freshmen.

Selectivity: Open admission; but selective for some programs.

FINANCIAL AID PICTURE (2009-2010)

Students with need: Need-based aid available for full-time and part-time students. Work study available nights.

FINANCIAL AID PROCEDURES

Forms required: FAFSA.

Dates and Deadlines: No deadline. Applicants notified on a rolling basis.

CONTACT

Bethann Verbal, Director of Financial Aid
301 Centre Pointe Drive, Virginia Beach, VA 23462-4417
(757) 499-7900

Christendom College
Front Royal, Virginia
www.christendom.edu

4-year private liberal arts college in large town, affiliated with Roman Catholic Church.

Enrollment: 390 undergrads, 1% part-time. 91 full-time freshmen.

Selectivity: Admits over 75% of applicants.

BASIC COSTS (2010-2011)

Tuition and fees: $19,668.

Room and board: $7,506.

FINANCIAL AID PICTURE (2009-2010)

Students with need: Out of 49 full-time freshmen who applied for aid, 40 were judged to have need. Of these, 40 received aid, and 40 had their full need met. Average financial aid package met 90% of need; average scholarship/grant was $5,770; average loan was $5,500.

Students without need: 22 full-time freshmen who did not demonstrate need for aid received scholarships/grants; average award was $6,540. No-need awards available for academics, alumni affiliation.

Additional info: Christendom accepts no direct federal aid, nor does it participate in indirect programs of federal aid.

FINANCIAL AID PROCEDURES

Forms required: institutional form.

Dates and Deadlines: Priority date 4/1; closing date 6/1. Applicants notified on a rolling basis starting 2/1; must reply within 4 week(s) of notification.

CONTACT

Alisa Polk, Financial Aid Officer
134 Christendom Drive, Front Royal, VA 22630
(800) 877-5456

Christopher Newport University
Newport News, Virginia
www.cnu.edu   Federal Code: 003706

4-year public university and liberal arts college in small city.

Enrollment: 4,771 undergrads, 3% part-time. 1,213 full-time freshmen.

Selectivity: Admits 50 to 75% of applicants.

BASIC COSTS (2009-2010)

Tuition and fees: $8,050; out-of-state residents $15,992.

Per-credit charge: $335; out-of-state residents $665.

Room and board: $9,040.

FINANCIAL AID PICTURE (2009-2010)

Students with need: Out of 893 full-time freshmen who applied for aid, 492 were judged to have need. Of these, 483 received aid, and 105 had their full need met. Average financial aid package met 75% of need; average scholarship/grant was $5,779; average loan was $3,242. For part-time students, average financial aid package was $6,108.

Students without need: 221 full-time freshmen who did not demonstrate need for aid received scholarships/grants; average award was $1,787. No-need awards available for academics, art, leadership, music/drama, ROTC, state/district residency.

Cumulative student debt: 53% of graduating class had student loans; average debt was $19,103.

FINANCIAL AID PROCEDURES

Forms required: FAFSA.

Dates and Deadlines: Priority date 3/1; no closing date. Applicants notified on a rolling basis starting 2/21; must reply within 3 week(s) of notification.

Transfers: No deadline. Applicants notified on a rolling basis starting 3/1; must reply within 2 week(s) of notification.

CONTACT

Mary Wigginton, Director of Financial Aid

1 University Place, Newport News, VA 23606-2998

(757) 594-7170

College of William and Mary

Williamsburg, Virginia

www.wm.edu   Federal Code: 003705

4-year public university in large town.

Enrollment: 5,790 undergrads, 1% part-time. 1,391 full-time freshmen.

Selectivity: Admits less than 50% of applicants.

BASIC COSTS (2009-2010)

Tuition and fees: $10,800; out-of-state residents $30,592.

Per-credit charge: $240; out-of-state residents $880.

Room and board: $8,382.

FINANCIAL AID PICTURE (2008-2009)

Students with need: Need-based aid available for full-time and part-time students.

CONTACT

Edward Irish, Director of Student Financial Aid

PO Box 8795, Williamsburg, VA 23187-8795

(757) 221-2420

Dabney S. Lancaster Community College

Clifton Forge, Virginia

www.dslcc.edu   Federal Code: 004996

2-year public community college in small town.

Enrollment: 551 undergrads, 44% part-time. 107 full-time freshmen.

Selectivity: Open admission; but selective for some programs.

BASIC COSTS (2009-2010)

Tuition and fees: $2,832; out-of-state residents $7,995.

Per-credit charge: $87; out-of-state residents $259.

Additional info: Out-of-state students pay an additional $300 capital outlay fee.

FINANCIAL AID PICTURE

Students with need: Need-based aid available for full-time and part-time students.

Students without need: This college awards aid only to students with need.

FINANCIAL AID PROCEDURES

Forms required: FAFSA, institutional form.

Dates and Deadlines: Priority date 3/15; no closing date. Applicants notified on a rolling basis starting 4/15; must reply within 2 week(s) of notification.

CONTACT

Sandra Haverlack, Coordinator of Financial Aid and Veterans Affairs

Box 1000, Clifton Forge, VA 24422

(540) 863-2822

Danville Community College

Danville, Virginia

www.dcc.vccs.edu   Federal Code: 003758

2-year public community college in small city.

Enrollment: 4,380 undergrads.

Selectivity: Open admission; but selective for some programs.

BASIC COSTS (2009-2010)

Tuition and fees: $2,811; out-of-state residents $7,974.

Per-credit charge: $87; out-of-state residents $259.

Additional info: Out-of-state students pay an additional $300 capital outlay fee.

FINANCIAL AID PICTURE (2009-2010)

Students with need: Need-based aid available for full-time and part-time students.

Students without need: This college awards aid only to students with need.

Scholarships offered: Educational Foundation Scholarship: $250 to $1,500; based on separate application; deadline mid-March prior to award year.

FINANCIAL AID PROCEDURES

Forms required: FAFSA.

Dates and Deadlines: Priority date 6/1; no closing date. Applicants notified on a rolling basis starting 5/1; must reply within 2 week(s) of notification.

Transfers: Limited aid available to transfer students admitted in spring semester.

CONTACT

Mary Gore, Assistant Coordinator of Financial Aid

1008 South Main Street, Danville, VA 24541

(434) 797-8439

DeVry University: Arlington

Arlington, Virginia

www.devry.edu

4-year for-profit university in very large city.

Enrollment: 698 undergrads, 41% part-time. 97 full-time freshmen.

BASIC COSTS (2009-2010)

Tuition and fees: $14,160.

Per-credit charge: $550.

FINANCIAL AID PICTURE (2008-2009)

Students with need: Need-based aid available for full-time and part-time students.

Students without need: This college awards aid only to students with need.

FINANCIAL AID PROCEDURES

Forms required: FAFSA.

Dates and Deadlines: No deadline. Applicants notified on a rolling basis.

CONTACT

Roberta McDevitt, Director of Student Finance

2450 Crystal Drive, Arlington, VA 22202

(703) 414-4000

Eastern Mennonite University
Harrisonburg, Virginia
www.emu.edu   Federal Code: 003708

4-year private university and liberal arts college in large town, affiliated with Mennonite Church.
Enrollment: 1,028 undergrads, 18% part-time. 218 full-time freshmen.
Selectivity: Admits less than 50% of applicants.

BASIC COSTS (2010-2011)
Tuition and fees: $24,320.
Room and board: $7,650.

FINANCIAL AID PICTURE (2009-2010)
Students with need: Need-based aid available for full-time and part-time students. Work study available nights, weekends, and for part-time students.
Students without need: No-need awards available for academics, alumni affiliation, art, leadership, religious affiliation, state/district residency.
Scholarships offered: President's Scholarship: GPA of 3.9 or higher. Academic Achievement Scholarship: minimum 3.2 GPA. University Grant: minimum 2.5 GPA; minimum SAT score of 920 (exclusive of Writing) or ACT score of 20 required for all scholarships. Amounts based on GPA and test scores; no limit on number of awards. Full-tuition scholarships available for 2 honors program applicants with highest test scores and GPA; half tuition scholarships available for next 10 candidates.

FINANCIAL AID PROCEDURES
Forms required: FAFSA, state aid form.
Dates and Deadlines: Priority date 3/1; no closing date. Applicants notified on a rolling basis starting 3/1; must reply within 4 week(s) of notification.
Transfers: No deadline. Applicants notified on a rolling basis starting 3/1; must reply within 4 week(s) of notification.

CONTACT
Michele Hensley, Director of Financial Assistance
1200 Park Road, Harrisonburg, VA 22802-2462
(540) 432-4137

Eastern Shore Community College
Melfa, Virginia
www.es.vccs.edu   Federal Code: 003748

2-year public community college in rural community.
Enrollment: 868 undergrads.
Selectivity: Open admission.

BASIC COSTS (2009-2010)
Tuition and fees: $2,841; out-of-state residents $8,004.
Per-credit charge: $87; out-of-state residents $259.
Additional info: Out-of-state students pay an additional $300 capital outlay fee.

FINANCIAL AID PICTURE
Students with need: Need-based aid available for full-time and part-time students.
Students without need: This college awards aid only to students with need.
Additional info: ESCC is a member of the Servicemembers Opportunity Colleges program.

FINANCIAL AID PROCEDURES
Forms required: FAFSA.
Dates and Deadlines: Priority date 5/1; no closing date. Applicants notified on a rolling basis starting 6/1; must reply within 2 week(s) of notification.

CONTACT
P Smith, Chief Financial Aid Officer
29300 Lankford Highway, Melfa, VA 23410-9755
(757) 789-1732

ECPI College of Technology: Virginia Beach
Virginia Beach, Virginia
www.ecpi.edu   Federal Code: 010198

4-year for-profit health science and technical college in very large city.
Enrollment: 6,200 undergrads.

BASIC COSTS (2009-2010)
Tuition and fees: $12,500.

FINANCIAL AID PICTURE
Students with need: Need-based aid available for full-time and part-time students. Work study available nights.
Students without need: No-need awards available for academics.

FINANCIAL AID PROCEDURES
Forms required: institutional form.
Dates and Deadlines: No deadline. Applicants notified on a rolling basis.

CONTACT
Kathi Turner, Director of Financial Aid
5555 Greenwich Road, Suite 300, Virginia Beach, VA 23462-6542
(757) 671-7171 ext. 311

ECPI Technical College: Roanoke
Roanoke, Virginia
www.ecpitech.edu   Federal Code: 017205

2-year for-profit technical college in small city.
Enrollment: 351 undergrads.

BASIC COSTS (2009-2010)
Tuition and fees: $12,500.

FINANCIAL AID PICTURE
Students with need: Need-based aid available for full-time and part-time students.

FINANCIAL AID PROCEDURES
Forms required: FAFSA.
Dates and Deadlines: No deadline. Applicants notified on a rolling basis.

CONTACT
Carol Rouch, Director of Financial Aid
5234 Airport Road, Roanoke, VA 24012
(540) 563-8080

Emory & Henry College
Emory, Virginia
www.ehc.edu   Federal Code: 003709

4-year private liberal arts college in rural community, affiliated with United Methodist Church.
Enrollment: 918 undergrads, 2% part-time. 291 full-time freshmen.
Selectivity: Admits 50 to 75% of applicants.

BASIC COSTS (2010-2011)
Tuition and fees: $26,000.
Per-credit charge: $1,040.
Room and board: $8,560.

FINANCIAL AID PICTURE (2009-2010)

Students with need: Out of 265 full-time freshmen who applied for aid, 231 were judged to have need. Of these, 230 received aid, and 72 had their full need met. Average financial aid package met 90% of need; average scholarship/grant was $22,287; average loan was $3,375. For part-time students, average financial aid package was $20,260.

Students without need: 59 full-time freshmen who did not demonstrate need for aid received scholarships/grants; average award was $12,813. No-need awards available for academics, art, music/drama, religious affiliation, state/district residency.

Cumulative student debt: 65% of graduating class had student loans; average debt was $19,168.

Additional info: Virginia residents eligible for additional in-state tuition grants.

FINANCIAL AID PROCEDURES

Forms required: FAFSA, state aid form.

Dates and Deadlines: Priority date 4/15; no closing date. Applicants notified on a rolling basis starting 3/1; must reply by 6/15.

Transfers: Priority date 4/1; closing date 5/15. Applicants notified on a rolling basis starting 2/15; must reply by 6/15 or within 4 week(s) of notification. Financial aid based on academic credits accepted for transfer.

CONTACT

Margaret Murphy, Director of Financial Aid and Student Services
Box 10, Emory, VA 24327
(276) 944-6115

Ferrum College
Ferrum, Virginia
www.ferrum.edu

4-year private liberal arts college in rural community, affiliated with United Methodist Church.

Enrollment: 1,424 undergrads, 3% part-time. 596 full-time freshmen.

Selectivity: Admits over 75% of applicants.

BASIC COSTS (2010-2011)

Tuition and fees: $24,945.

Per-credit charge: $500.

Room and board: $8,080.

FINANCIAL AID PICTURE (2008-2009)

Students with need: Out of 575 full-time freshmen who applied for aid, 517 were judged to have need. Of these, 517 received aid, and 2 had their full need met. Average financial aid package met 74% of need; average scholarship/grant was $6,191; average loan was $3,204. For part-time students, average financial aid package was $4,140.

Students without need: 79 full-time freshmen who did not demonstrate need for aid received scholarships/grants; average award was $4,826. No-need awards available for academics, leadership, religious affiliation, state/district residency.

Scholarships offered: Ferrum Scholarship: $5,000-$10,000; high school GPA must be 3.0 or higher and SAT score must be 1500 or higher. Ferrum Merit Grant: $1,000-$7,000; high school GPA must be 2.0 or higher and SAT score must be in the range of 1050.

Cumulative student debt: 86% of graduating class had student loans; average debt was $24,680.

FINANCIAL AID PROCEDURES

Forms required: FAFSA, state aid form.

Dates and Deadlines: Priority date 3/1; no closing date. Applicants notified on a rolling basis starting 1/10.

CONTACT

Heather Hollandsworth, Director of Financial Aid
Spilman-Daniel House, Ferrum, VA 24088
(540) 365-4282

George Mason University
Fairfax, Virginia
www.gmu.edu   Federal Code: 003749

4-year public university in large town.

Enrollment: 19,130 undergrads, 21% part-time. 2,628 full-time freshmen.

Selectivity: Admits 50 to 75% of applicants.

BASIC COSTS (2009-2010)

Tuition and fees: $8,024; out-of-state residents $24,008.

Per-credit charge: $235; out-of-state residents $901.

Room and board: $7,700.

FINANCIAL AID PICTURE (2009-2010)

Students with need: Out of 1,948 full-time freshmen who applied for aid, 1,224 were judged to have need. Of these, 1,191 received aid, and 142 had their full need met. Average financial aid package met 74% of need; average scholarship/grant was $7,157; average loan was $3,528. For part-time students, average financial aid package was $7,768.

Students without need: 109 full-time freshmen who did not demonstrate need for aid received scholarships/grants; average award was $7,329. No-need awards available for academics, athletics, minority status, music/drama, ROTC, state/district residency.

Scholarships offered: 64 full-time freshmen received athletic scholarships; average amount $16,167.

Cumulative student debt: 52% of graduating class had student loans; average debt was $19,528.

FINANCIAL AID PROCEDURES

Forms required: FAFSA.

Dates and Deadlines: Priority date 3/1; no closing date. Applicants notified on a rolling basis starting 4/1; must reply within 3 week(s) of notification.

CONTACT

Jevita Rogers, Director, Student Financial Aid
4400 University Drive, MSN 3A4, Fairfax, VA 22030-4444
(703) 993-2353

Germanna Community College
Locust Grove, Virginia
www.germanna.edu   Federal Code: 008660

2-year public community college in rural community.

Enrollment: 5,185 undergrads.

Selectivity: Open admission; but selective for some programs.

BASIC COSTS (2009-2010)

Tuition and fees: $2,871; out-of-state residents $8,034.

Per-credit charge: $87; out-of-state residents $259.

Additional info: Out-of-state students pay additional $300 capital outlay fee.

FINANCIAL AID PICTURE (2008-2009)

Students with need: Need-based aid available for full-time and part-time students.

Students without need: No-need awards available for academics.

FINANCIAL AID PROCEDURES

Forms required: FAFSA.

Dates and Deadlines: Priority date 4/1; no closing date. Applicants notified on a rolling basis starting 5/15; must reply within 2 week(s) of notification.

CONTACT

Michael Farris, Financial Aid Coordinator
2130 Germanna Highway, Locust Grove, VA 22508-2102
(540) 423-9124

Hampden-Sydney College

Hampden-Sydney, Virginia
www.hsc.edu

Federal Code: 003713
CSS Code: 5291

4-year private liberal arts college for men in rural community, affiliated with Presbyterian Church (USA).
Enrollment: 1,068 undergrads. 295 full-time freshmen.
Selectivity: Admits 50 to 75% of applicants.

BASIC COSTS (2009-2010)

Tuition and fees: $30,688.
Room and board: $9,690.

FINANCIAL AID PICTURE (2009-2010)

Students with need: Out of 232 full-time freshmen who applied for aid, 171 were judged to have need. Of these, 171 received aid, and 45 had their full need met. Average financial aid package met 81% of need; average scholarship/grant was $19,751; average loan was $3,876. Need-based aid available for part-time students.
Students without need: 121 full-time freshmen who did not demonstrate need for aid received scholarships/grants; average award was $9,033. No-need awards available for academics, leadership, minority status, religious affiliation, ROTC, state/district residency.
Scholarships offered: Allan Scholarship: $20,000 annually. Venable Scholarship: $16,000 annually. Patrick Henry Scholarship: $12,000 annually. Achievement Awards: range from $2,000-$10,000 annually. All merit based.
Cumulative student debt: 54% of graduating class had student loans; average debt was $23,822.

FINANCIAL AID PROCEDURES

Forms required: FAFSA, CSS PROFILE, state aid form.
Dates and Deadlines: Priority date 11/15; closing date 5/1. Applicants notified by 3/15; must reply by 5/1 or within 2 week(s) of notification.
Transfers: No deadline. Applicants notified on a rolling basis; must reply within 2 week(s) of notification.

CONTACT

Zita Barree, Director of Financial Aid
Box 667, Hampden-Sydney, VA 23943
(434) 223-6119

Hampton University

Hampton, Virginia
www.hamptonu.edu

Federal Code: 003714

4-year private university in small city.
Enrollment: 4,495 undergrads, 6% part-time. 1,036 full-time freshmen.
Selectivity: Admits 50 to 75% of applicants.

BASIC COSTS (2010-2011)

Tuition and fees: $18,074.
Per-credit charge: $390.
Room and board: $7,724.

FINANCIAL AID PICTURE (2009-2010)

Students with need: Out of 701 full-time freshmen who applied for aid, 604 were judged to have need. Of these, 535 received aid, and 230 had their full need met. Average financial aid package met 43% of need; average scholarship/grant was $1,992; average loan was $1,500. For part-time students, average financial aid package was $2,395.

Students without need: 43 full-time freshmen who did not demonstrate need for aid received scholarships/grants; average award was $5,729. No-need awards available for academics, athletics, leadership, music/drama, ROTC.
Scholarships offered: 5 full-time freshmen received athletic scholarships; average amount $10,150.
Cumulative student debt: 96% of graduating class had student loans; average debt was $9,477.

FINANCIAL AID PROCEDURES

Forms required: FAFSA.
Dates and Deadlines: Priority date 3/1; no closing date. Applicants notified on a rolling basis starting 3/1; must reply within 2 week(s) of notification.

CONTACT

Martin Miles, Financial Aid Director
Office of Admissions, Hampton, VA 23668
(757) 727-5635

Hollins University

Roanoke, Virginia
www.hollins.edu

Federal Code: 003715

4-year private university and liberal arts college for women in small city.
Enrollment: 775 undergrads, 3% part-time. 204 full-time freshmen.
Selectivity: Admits over 75% of applicants.

BASIC COSTS (2010-2011)

Tuition and fees: $29,485.
Room and board: $10,200.

FINANCIAL AID PICTURE (2009-2010)

Students with need: Out of 179 full-time freshmen who applied for aid, 156 were judged to have need. Of these, 156 received aid, and 21 had their full need met. Average financial aid package met 90% of need; average scholarship/grant was $17,236; average loan was $6,768. For part-time students, average financial aid package was $14,828.
Students without need: 48 full-time freshmen who did not demonstrate need for aid received scholarships/grants; average award was $12,749. No-need awards available for academics, alumni affiliation, art, leadership, music/drama, state/district residency.
Scholarships offered: Scholar Awards: $5,000 full tuition; academic merit. Founder's Awards: $1,500-$7,000; organizational involvement. Creative Talent Awards: $1,500-$7,000; distinguished achievement or outstanding involvement in art, photography/film, creative writing, music, dance or theater.
Cumulative student debt: 83% of graduating class had student loans; average debt was $24,002.

FINANCIAL AID PROCEDURES

Forms required: FAFSA, state aid form.
Dates and Deadlines: Priority date 2/15; no closing date. Applicants notified on a rolling basis starting 3/1; must reply by 5/1.
Transfers: Priority date 7/1; closing date 7/15.

CONTACT

Ken Flick, Director of Scholarships and Financial Assistance
PO Box 9707, Roanoke, VA 24020-1707
(540) 362-6332

J. Sargeant Reynolds Community College- Parham Road

Richmond, Virginia
www.reynolds.edu

Federal Code: 003759

2-year public community college in very large city.
Enrollment: 9,890 undergrads.

Selectivity: Open admission; but selective for some programs.

BASIC COSTS (2009-2010)

Tuition and fees: $3,006; out-of-state residents $8,169.

Per-credit charge: $87; out-of-state residents $259.

Additional info: Out-of-state students pay additional $300 capital outlay fee.

FINANCIAL AID PICTURE

Students with need: Need-based aid available for full-time and part-time students. Work study available nights, weekends, and for part-time students.

Students without need: No-need awards available for academics.

Scholarships offered: Local Board Scholarship: full tuition; high school students with minimum 3.0 GPA; 23 awarded. Eric and Jeanette Lipman Endowed Scholarship: based on academic excellence; number and amount awarded varies. Central Fidelity Bank Scholarship: $1,500; first-year students; minimum 2.5 cumulative GPA; 2 awarded.

FINANCIAL AID PROCEDURES

Forms required: FAFSA.

Dates and Deadlines: Priority date 6/30; no closing date. Applicants notified on a rolling basis starting 7/15; must reply within 2 week(s) of notification.

CONTACT

Keisha Pope, Director of Financial Aid

Box 85622, Richmond, VA 23285-5622

(804) 523-5137

James Madison University

Harrisonburg, Virginia

www.jmu.edu   Federal Code: 003721

4-year public university in large town.

Enrollment: 16,979 undergrads, 3% part-time. 3,950 full-time freshmen.

Selectivity: Admits 50 to 75% of applicants.

BASIC COSTS (2009-2010)

Tuition and fees: $7,244; out-of-state residents $19,376.

Per-credit charge: $124; out-of-state residents $517.

Room and board: $7,690.

FINANCIAL AID PICTURE (2009-2010)

Students with need: Out of 3,106 full-time freshmen who applied for aid, 1,562 were judged to have need. Of these, 1,292 received aid, and 1,213 had their full need met. Average financial aid package met 44% of need; average scholarship/grant was $7,029; average loan was $3,673. For part-time students, average financial aid package was $7,144.

Students without need: 59 full-time freshmen who did not demonstrate need for aid received scholarships/grants; average award was $3,614. No-need awards available for academics, alumni affiliation, art, athletics, leadership, minority status, music/drama, state/district residency.

Scholarships offered: 80 full-time freshmen received athletic scholarships; average amount $14,858.

Cumulative student debt: 51% of graduating class had student loans; average debt was $18,183.

FINANCIAL AID PROCEDURES

Forms required: FAFSA.

Dates and Deadlines: Priority date 3/1; no closing date. Applicants notified on a rolling basis starting 4/1; must reply within 4 week(s) of notification.

Transfers: Closing date 3/1. Applicants notified on a rolling basis starting 4/1; must reply within 4 week(s) of notification.

CONTACT

Lisa Tumer, Director of Financial Aid and Scholarships

Sonner Hall, MSC 0101, Harrisonburg, VA 22807

(540) 568-7820

Jefferson College of Health Sciences

Roanoke, Virginia

www.jchs.edu   Federal Code: 009893

4-year private health science and nursing college in large city.

Enrollment: 880 undergrads, 29% part-time. 91 full-time freshmen.

Selectivity: Admits less than 50% of applicants.

BASIC COSTS (2010-2011)

Tuition and fees: $18,810.

Per-credit charge: $545.

Room only: $4,700.

FINANCIAL AID PICTURE (2008-2009)

Students with need: Average financial aid package met 43% of need; average scholarship/grant was $4,033; average loan was $7,171. For part-time students, average financial aid package was $5,803.

Students without need: No-need awards available for academics.

FINANCIAL AID PROCEDURES

Forms required: FAFSA, institutional form.

Dates and Deadlines: No deadline. Applicants notified on a rolling basis; must reply within 2 week(s) of notification.

CONTACT

Deborah Johnson, Financial Aid Officer

Box 13186, Roanoke, VA 24031-3186

(540) 985-8483

John Tyler Community College

Chester, Virginia

www.jtcc.edu   Federal Code: 004004

2-year public community college in small city.

Enrollment: 5,434 undergrads, 60% part-time. 439 full-time freshmen.

Selectivity: Open admission; but selective for some programs.

BASIC COSTS (2009-2010)

Tuition and fees: $2,831; out-of-state residents $7,994.

Per-credit charge: $87; out-of-state residents $259.

Additional info: Out-of-state students pay additional $300 capital outlay fee.

FINANCIAL AID PICTURE (2008-2009)

Students with need: Need-based aid available for full-time and part-time students. Work study available nights, weekends, and for part-time students.

Students without need: No-need awards available for academics, state/district residency.

FINANCIAL AID PROCEDURES

Forms required: FAFSA.

Dates and Deadlines: Priority date 5/15; closing date 7/15. Applicants notified on a rolling basis starting 6/15.

CONTACT

Fred Taylor, Vice President for Finance and Administration

13101 Jefferson Davis Highway, Chester, VA 23831-5316

(804) 706-5016

Liberty University

Lynchburg, Virginia

www.liberty.edu   Federal Code: 010392

4-year private university in small city, affiliated with Baptist faith.

Enrollment: 28,243 undergrads, 35% part-time. 3,860 full-time freshmen.

BASIC COSTS (2010-2011)
Tuition and fees: $17,202.
Per-credit charge: $550.
Room and board: $5,996.

FINANCIAL AID PICTURE (2009-2010)
Students with need: Need-based aid available for full-time and part-time students.
Students without need: No-need awards available for academics, alumni affiliation, athletics, leadership, music/drama, religious affiliation, ROTC, state/district residency.
Scholarships offered: Liberty Academic Achievement Scholarship: based on combination of high school grades and standardized test scores. Students may qualify for up to $6,000. Additional $3,500 could be applied if student is also accepted into the Honors Program.

FINANCIAL AID PROCEDURES
Forms required: FAFSA, state aid form.
Dates and Deadlines: Closing date 3/1. Applicants notified on a rolling basis starting 3/15; must reply within 3 week(s) of notification.
Transfers: Applicants notified on a rolling basis starting 3/15; must reply within 3 week(s) of notification.

CONTACT
Robert Ritz, Director of Student Financial Aid
1971 University Boulevard, Lynchburg, VA 24502
(434) 582-2270

Longwood University
Farmville, Virginia
www.longwood.edu   Federal Code: 003719

4-year public university in small town.
Enrollment: 4,021 undergrads, 5% part-time. 1,031 full-time freshmen.
Selectivity: Admits 50 to 75% of applicants.

BASIC COSTS (2009-2010)
Tuition and fees: $8,925; out-of-state residents $17,835.
Per-credit charge: $156; out-of-state residents $453.
Room and board: $7,596.
Additional info: Required laptop computer for first-year students $1,700. Out-of-state students pay an additional $390 capital outlay fee.

FINANCIAL AID PICTURE (2008-2009)
Students with need: Out of 755 full-time freshmen who applied for aid, 440 were judged to have need. Of these, 435 received aid, and 347 had their full need met. Average financial aid package met 80% of need; average scholarship/grant was $5,580; average loan was $727. For part-time students, average financial aid package was $8,421.
Students without need: 47 full-time freshmen who did not demonstrate need for aid received scholarships/grants; average award was $3,339. No-need awards available for academics, alumni affiliation, art, athletics, leadership, music/drama, ROTC, state/district residency.
Scholarships offered: *Merit:* Longwood Scholars: $2,200. Hull Scholarship: $5,000. Citizen Scholars: $5,500. All awards based on high school GPA and test scores. *Athletic:* 36 full-time freshmen received athletic scholarships; average amount $8,676.
Cumulative student debt: 62% of graduating class had student loans; average debt was $20,855.

FINANCIAL AID PROCEDURES
Forms required: FAFSA.
Dates and Deadlines: Priority date 3/1; no closing date. Applicants notified on a rolling basis starting 4/1; must reply within 4 week(s) of notification.
Transfers: Applicants notified by 4/1; must reply by 5/1.

CONTACT
Karen Schinabeck, Director of Financial Aid
201 High Street, Farmville, VA 23909-1898
(434) 395-2077

Lord Fairfax Community College
Middletown, Virginia
www.lfcc.edu   Federal Code: 008659

2-year public community college in small town.
Enrollment: 4,000 undergrads.
Selectivity: Open admission.

BASIC COSTS (2009-2010)
Tuition and fees: $2,843; out-of-state residents $8,006.
Per-credit charge: $87; out-of-state residents $299.
Additional info: Out-of-state students pay an additional $300 capital outlay fee.

FINANCIAL AID PICTURE (2008-2009)
Students with need: Need-based aid available for full-time and part-time students.
Students without need: This college awards aid only to students with need.

FINANCIAL AID PROCEDURES
Forms required: FAFSA.
Dates and Deadlines: Priority date 5/1; no closing date. Applicants notified on a rolling basis starting 6/1.

CONTACT
Aaron Whitacre, Coordinator of Financial Aid and Veterans Affairs
173 Skirmisher Lane, Middletown, VA 22645
(540) 868-7274

Lynchburg College
Lynchburg, Virginia
www.lynchburg.edu   Federal Code: 003720

4-year private liberal arts college in small city, affiliated with Christian Church (Disciples of Christ).
Enrollment: 2,165 undergrads, 3% part-time. 578 full-time freshmen.
Selectivity: Admits 50 to 75% of applicants.

BASIC COSTS (2010-2011)
Tuition and fees: $29,905.
Per-credit charge: $400.
Room and board: $8,020.
Additional info: Tuition/fee waivers available for adults.

FINANCIAL AID PICTURE (2009-2010)
Students with need: Out of 512 full-time freshmen who applied for aid, 420 were judged to have need. Of these, 420 received aid, and 83 had their full need met. Average financial aid package met 83% of need; average scholarship/grant was $18,465; average loan was $3,126. For part-time students, average financial aid package was $6,764.
Students without need: 149 full-time freshmen who did not demonstrate need for aid received scholarships/grants; average award was $9,987. No-need awards available for academics, leadership, music/drama, religious affiliation.
Cumulative student debt: 67% of graduating class had student loans; average debt was $30,954.

FINANCIAL AID PROCEDURES
Forms required: FAFSA, state aid form.

Dates and Deadlines: Priority date 3/1; no closing date. Applicants notified on a rolling basis starting 3/5; must reply by 5/1 or within 2 week(s) of notification.
Transfers: Priority date 7/1; no deadline. Applicants notified on a rolling basis starting 3/5; must reply within 2 week(s) of notification.

CONTACT
Michelle Davis, Director of Financial Aid
1501 Lakeside Drive, Lynchburg, VA 24501-3199
(434) 544-8228

Mary Baldwin College
Staunton, Virginia
www.mbc.edu   Federal Code: 003723

4-year private liberal arts college for women in large town, affiliated with Presbyterian Church (USA).
Enrollment: 1,363 undergrads, 27% part-time. 293 full-time freshmen.
Selectivity: Admits 50 to 75% of applicants.

BASIC COSTS (2010-2011)
Tuition and fees: $25,655.
Room and board: $7,420.

FINANCIAL AID PICTURE (2009-2010)
Students with need: Out of 268 full-time freshmen who applied for aid, 213 were judged to have need. Of these, 213 received aid, and 127 had their full need met. Average financial aid package met 83% of need; average scholarship/grant was $16,053; average loan was $4,242. For part-time students, average financial aid package was $7,636.
Students without need: 15 full-time freshmen who did not demonstrate need for aid received scholarships/grants; average award was $9,128. No-need awards available for academics, leadership, state/district residency.
Cumulative student debt: 74% of graduating class had student loans; average debt was $25,665.

FINANCIAL AID PROCEDURES
Forms required: FAFSA, state aid form.
Dates and Deadlines: Priority date 3/1; no closing date. Applicants notified on a rolling basis starting 2/27; must reply by 5/1.
Transfers: No deadline. Applicants notified on a rolling basis starting 2/1; must reply by 5/1.

CONTACT
Andrew Modlin, Executive Director of Enrollment Management
Office of Admissions, Staunton, VA 24401
(540) 887-7022

Marymount University
Arlington, Virginia
www.marymount.edu   Federal Code: 003724

4-year private university in small city, affiliated with Roman Catholic Church.
Enrollment: 2,194 undergrads, 14% part-time. 384 full-time freshmen.
Selectivity: Admits over 75% of applicants.

BASIC COSTS (2010-2011)
Tuition and fees: $23,426.
Per-credit charge: $750.
Room and board: $10,325.

FINANCIAL AID PICTURE (2009-2010)
Students with need: Out of 322 full-time freshmen who applied for aid, 260 were judged to have need. Of these, 258 received aid, and 54 had their full need met. Average financial aid package met 73% of need; average scholarship/grant was $5,295; average loan was $3,525. For part-time students, average financial aid package was $7,669.
Students without need: 105 full-time freshmen who did not demonstrate need for aid received scholarships/grants; average award was $8,558. No-need awards available for academics, alumni affiliation, leadership, ROTC, state/district residency.
Scholarships offered: Freshman Academic Scholarship: Guaranteed for full-time freshman with cumulative high school GPA of 3.3 or better and combined SAT score (exclusive of Writing) of 1100 or higher; renewable for four years for students who maintain academic eligibility.
Cumulative student debt: 76% of graduating class had student loans; average debt was $22,946.

FINANCIAL AID PROCEDURES
Forms required: FAFSA.
Dates and Deadlines: Priority date 3/1; no closing date. Applicants notified on a rolling basis starting 3/15; must reply within 2 week(s) of notification.
Transfers: No deadline. Applicants notified on a rolling basis starting 3/15; must reply within 2 week(s) of notification. Academic scholarships available; apply by May 1.

CONTACT
Debbie Raines, Director of Financial Aid
2807 North Glebe Road, Arlington, VA 22207-4299
(703) 284-1530

Mountain Empire Community College
Big Stone Gap, Virginia
www.mecc.edu   Federal Code: 009629

2-year public community college in small town.
Enrollment: 2,266 undergrads.
Selectivity: Open admission; but selective for some programs.

BASIC COSTS (2009-2010)
Tuition and fees: $2,849; out-of-state residents $8,012.
Per-credit charge: $87; out-of-state residents $259.
Additional info: Out-of-state students pay additional $300 capital outlay fee.

FINANCIAL AID PICTURE (2008-2009)
Students with need: Need-based aid available for full-time and part-time students.
Students without need: No-need awards available for academics, state/district residency.
Scholarships offered: Presidential Honor Scholarship: full tuition; for valedictorian or salutatorian. Dean's Academic Honor Award: $500-$1,000; for top 10 in graduating class.
Additional info: The college does not participate in loan programs. All financial aid is in form of grants, scholarships, or work study.

FINANCIAL AID PROCEDURES
Forms required: FAFSA.
Dates and Deadlines: Priority date 5/1; no closing date. Applicants notified on a rolling basis starting 1/1.

CONTACT
Director of Enrollment Services
3441 Mountain Empire Road, Big Stone Gap, VA 24219
(276) 523-2400 ext. 470

National College: Bluefield

Bluefield, Virginia
www.ncbt.edu   Federal Code: 003726

2-year for-profit business college in small city.
Enrollment: 195 undergrads.
Selectivity: Open admission.

BASIC COSTS (2009-2010)
Tuition and fees: $10,080.

FINANCIAL AID PICTURE
Students with need: Need-based aid available for full-time and part-time students.
Students without need: This college awards aid only to students with need.

FINANCIAL AID PROCEDURES
Forms required: FAFSA.
Dates and Deadlines: No deadline. Applicants notified on a rolling basis starting 9/1.

CONTACT
Pamela Cotton, Director of Financial Aid and Compliance Officer
PO Box 6400, Roanoke, VA 24017
(540) 986-1800

National College: Charlottesville

Charlottesville, Virginia
www.ncbt.edu   Federal Code: 003726

2-year for-profit business college in small city.
Enrollment: 250 undergrads.
Selectivity: Open admission.

BASIC COSTS (2009-2010)
Tuition and fees: $10,080.

FINANCIAL AID PICTURE
Students with need: Need-based aid available for full-time and part-time students.
Students without need: This college awards aid only to students with need.

FINANCIAL AID PROCEDURES
Forms required: FAFSA.
Dates and Deadlines: No deadline. Applicants notified on a rolling basis.

CONTACT
Pamela Cotton, Director of Financial Aid and Compliance Officer
PO Box 6400, Roanoke, VA 24017
(540) 986-1800

National College: Danville

Danville, Virginia
www.ncbt.edu   Federal Code: 003726

2-year for-profit branch campus and business college in small city.
Enrollment: 454 undergrads.
Selectivity: Open admission.

BASIC COSTS (2009-2010)
Tuition and fees: $10,080.

FINANCIAL AID PICTURE
Students with need: Need-based aid available for full-time and part-time students.

Students without need: This college awards aid only to students with need.

FINANCIAL AID PROCEDURES
Forms required: FAFSA.
Dates and Deadlines: No deadline. Applicants notified on a rolling basis starting 9/1.

CONTACT
Pamela Cotton, Director of Financial Aid and Compliance Officer
PO Box 6400, Roanoke, VA 24017
(540) 986-1800

National College: Harrisonburg

Harrisonburg, Virginia
www.national-college.edu   Federal Code: 003726

2-year for-profit business college in large town.
Enrollment: 489 undergrads.
Selectivity: Open admission.

BASIC COSTS (2009-2010)
Tuition and fees: $10,080.

FINANCIAL AID PICTURE
Students with need: Need-based aid available for full-time and part-time students.
Students without need: This college awards aid only to students with need.

FINANCIAL AID PROCEDURES
Forms required: FAFSA.
Dates and Deadlines: No deadline. Applicants notified on a rolling basis starting 9/1.

CONTACT
Pamela Cotton, Director of Financial Aid and Compliance Officer
PO Box 6400, Roanoke, VA 24017
(540) 986-1800

National College: Lynchburg

Lynchburg, Virginia
www.national-college.edu   Federal Code: 010489

2-year for-profit business college in small city.
Enrollment: 459 undergrads.
Selectivity: Open admission.

BASIC COSTS (2009-2010)
Tuition and fees: $10,080.

FINANCIAL AID PICTURE
Students with need: Need-based aid available for full-time and part-time students.
Students without need: This college awards aid only to students with need.

FINANCIAL AID PROCEDURES
Forms required: FAFSA.
Dates and Deadlines: No deadline. Applicants notified on a rolling basis starting 9/1.

CONTACT
Pamela Cotton, Director of Financial Aid and Compliance Officer
PO Box 6400, Roanoke, VA 24017
(540) 986-1000

National College: Martinsville
Martinsville, Virginia
www.national-college.edu   Federal Code: 003726

2-year for-profit business and junior college in small city.
Enrollment: 589 undergrads.
Selectivity: Open admission.

BASIC COSTS (2009-2010)
Tuition and fees: $10,080.

FINANCIAL AID PICTURE
Students with need: Need-based aid available for full-time and part-time students.
Students without need: This college awards aid only to students with need.

FINANCIAL AID PROCEDURES
Forms required: FAFSA.
Dates and Deadlines: No deadline. Applicants notified on a rolling basis.

CONTACT
Pamela Cotton, Director of Financial Aid and Compliance Officer
PO Box 6400, Roanoke, VA 24017
(540) 986-1800

National College: Roanoke Valley
Roanoke, Virginia
www.national-college.edu   Federal Code: 003726

4-year for-profit business college in large city.
Enrollment: 805 undergrads.
Selectivity: Open admission.

BASIC COSTS (2009-2010)
Tuition and fees: $10,080.

FINANCIAL AID PICTURE
Students with need: Need-based aid available for full-time and part-time students.
Students without need: This college awards aid only to students with need.

FINANCIAL AID PROCEDURES
Forms required: FAFSA.
Dates and Deadlines: No deadline. Applicants notified on a rolling basis.

CONTACT
Pamela Cotton, Director of Financial Aid and Compliance Officer
PO Box 6400, Roanoke, VA 24017-0400
(540) 986-1800

New River Community College
Dublin, Virginia
www.nr.edu   Federal Code: 005223

2-year public community college in rural community.
Enrollment: 3,114 undergrads.
Selectivity: Open admission.

BASIC COSTS (2009-2010)
Tuition and fees: $2,843; out-of-state residents $8,006.
Per-credit charge: $87; out-of-state residents $259.
Additional info: Out-of-state students pay additional $300 capital outlay fee.

FINANCIAL AID PICTURE (2008-2009)
Students with need: Need-based aid available for full-time and part-time students.

FINANCIAL AID PROCEDURES
Forms required: FAFSA, institutional form.
Dates and Deadlines: Priority date 4/15; no closing date. Applicants notified on a rolling basis starting 6/1.

CONTACT
Joseph Sheffey, Coordinator of Financial Aid
Drawer 1127, Dublin, VA 24084
(540) 674-3615

Norfolk State University
Norfolk, Virginia
www.nsu.edu   Federal Code: 003765

4-year public university in small city.
Enrollment: 6,102 undergrads, 15% part-time. 1,160 full-time freshmen.
Selectivity: Admits 50 to 75% of applicants.

BASIC COSTS (2009-2010)
Tuition and fees: $5,872; out-of-state residents $17,931.
Per-credit charge: $260; out-of-state residents $662.
Room and board: $7,329.

FINANCIAL AID PICTURE (2009-2010)
Students with need: Need-based aid available for full-time and part-time students.
Students without need: No-need awards available for academics, alumni affiliation, athletics, leadership, music/drama, ROTC, state/district residency.

FINANCIAL AID PROCEDURES
Forms required: FAFSA.
Dates and Deadlines: Priority date 5/31; no closing date. Applicants notified on a rolling basis starting 4/1; must reply within 2 week(s) of notification.

CONTACT
Kevin Burns, Director of Student Financial Services
700 Park Avenue, Norfolk, VA 23504
(757) 823-8381

Old Dominion University
Norfolk, Virginia
www.odu.edu   Federal Code: 003728

4-year public university in small city.
Enrollment: 17,819 undergrads, 23% part-time. 2,707 full-time freshmen.
Selectivity: Admits 50 to 75% of applicants.

BASIC COSTS (2009-2010)
Tuition and fees: $7,318; out-of-state residents $19,768.
Per-credit charge: $236; out-of-state residents $651.
Room and board: $7,868.

FINANCIAL AID PICTURE (2009-2010)
Students with need: Out of 2,186 full-time freshmen who applied for aid, 1,819 were judged to have need. Of these, 1,659 received aid, and 964 had their full need met. Average financial aid package met 78% of need; average scholarship/grant was $5,103; average loan was $3,220. For part-time students, average financial aid package was $4,971.
Students without need: 69 full-time freshmen who did not demonstrate need for aid received scholarships/grants; average award was $3,233. No-need awards available for academics, alumni affiliation, art, athletics, leadership, music/drama, ROTC, state/district residency.

Scholarships offered: 69 full-time freshmen received athletic scholarships; average amount $14,054.

Cumulative student debt: 81% of graduating class had student loans; average debt was $17,250.

FINANCIAL AID PROCEDURES

Forms required: FAFSA.

Dates and Deadlines: Priority date 2/15; closing date 3/15. Applicants notified on a rolling basis starting 2/1; must reply within 2 week(s) of notification.

Transfers: Applicants notified on a rolling basis starting 2/1; must reply within 2 week(s) of notification.

CONTACT

Veronica Finch, Director of Financial Aid
108 Rollins Hall, 5215 Hampton Boulevard, Norfolk, VA 23529
(757) 683-3683

Patrick Henry Community College

Martinsville, Virginia
www.ph.vccs.edu   Federal Code: 003751

2-year public community college in large town.

Enrollment: 3,000 undergrads.

Selectivity: Open admission.

BASIC COSTS (2009-2010)

Tuition and fees: $2,836; out-of-state residents $7,999.

Per-credit charge: $87; out-of-state residents $259.

Additional info: Out-of-state students pay additional $300 capital outlay fee.

FINANCIAL AID PICTURE

Students with need: Need-based aid available for full-time and part-time students.

FINANCIAL AID PROCEDURES

Forms required: FAFSA.

Dates and Deadlines: Priority date 6/1; no closing date. Applicants notified on a rolling basis starting 6/15.

CONTACT

Cindy Keller, Financial Aid
Box 5311, Martinsville, VA 24115-5311
(276) 656-0317

Paul D. Camp Community College

Franklin, Virginia
www.pc.vccs.edu   Federal Code: 009159

2-year public community college in small town.

Enrollment: 750 undergrads.

Selectivity: Open admission; but selective for some programs.

BASIC COSTS (2009-2010)

Tuition and fees: $2,811; out-of-state residents $7,974.

Per-credit charge: $87; out-of-state residents $259.

Additional info: Out-of-state students pay additional $300 capital outlay fee.

FINANCIAL AID PICTURE

Students with need: Need-based aid available for full-time and part-time students. Work study available nights.

FINANCIAL AID PROCEDURES

Forms required: FAFSA.

Dates and Deadlines: Priority date 6/1; no closing date. Applicants notified on a rolling basis starting 8/1; must reply within 2 week(s) of notification.

CONTACT

Teresa King, Financial Aid Coordinator
100 North College Drive, Franklin, VA 23851-0737
(757) 925-6307

Piedmont Virginia Community College

Charlottesville, Virginia
www.pvcc.edu   Federal Code: 009928

2-year public community college in large town.

Enrollment: 3,539 undergrads, 68% part-time. 297 full-time freshmen.

Selectivity: Open admission; but selective for some programs.

BASIC COSTS (2009-2010)

Tuition and fees: $2,861; out-of-state residents $8,024.

Per-credit charge: $87; out-of-state residents $259.

Additional info: Out-of-state students pay additional $300 capital outlay fee.

FINANCIAL AID PICTURE (2008-2009)

Students with need: Need-based aid available for full-time and part-time students. Work study available nights, weekends, and for part-time students.

Students without need: No-need awards available for academics.

FINANCIAL AID PROCEDURES

Forms required: FAFSA.

Dates and Deadlines: No deadline. Applicants notified on a rolling basis starting 4/1.

Transfers: Must meet Satisfactory Academic Progress standards.

CONTACT

Carol Larson, Director of Financial Aid
501 College Drive, Charlottesville, VA 22902-7589
(434) 961-6545

Radford University

Radford, Virginia
www.radford.edu   Federal Code: 003732

4-year public university in large town.

Enrollment: 7,736 undergrads, 4% part-time. 1,872 full-time freshmen.

Selectivity: Admits 50 to 75% of applicants.

BASIC COSTS (2009-2010)

Tuition and fees: $6,904; out-of-state residents $16,568.

Per-credit charge: $183; out-of-state residents $586.

Room and board: $6,970.

FINANCIAL AID PICTURE (2008-2009)

Students with need: Out of 1,217 full-time freshmen who applied for aid, 689 were judged to have need. Of these, 649 received aid, and 203 had their full need met. Average financial aid package met 79% of need; average scholarship/grant was $7,635; average loan was $2,733. For part-time students, average financial aid package was $6,577.

Students without need: 29 full-time freshmen who did not demonstrate need for aid received scholarships/grants; average award was $4,810. No-need awards available for academics, alumni affiliation, art, athletics, leadership, music/drama, ROTC.

Scholarships offered: 34 full-time freshmen received athletic scholarships; average amount $6,690.

Cumulative student debt: 51% of graduating class had student loans; average debt was $19,465.

Additional info: Student's need and grades considered. Top consideration given to those with greatest need and who apply by deadline.

FINANCIAL AID PROCEDURES

Forms required: FAFSA.

Dates and Deadlines: Priority date 3/1; no closing date. Applicants notified on a rolling basis starting 4/15; must reply within 4 week(s) of notification.

CONTACT
Barbara Porter, Director of Financial Aid
115 Martin Hall, Radford, VA 24142
(540) 831-5408

Randolph College
Lynchburg, Virginia
www.randolphcollege.edu   Federal Code: 003734

4-year private liberal arts college in small city, affiliated with United Methodist Church.
Enrollment: 470 undergrads, 1% part-time. 135 full-time freshmen.
Selectivity: Admits over 75% of applicants.

BASIC COSTS (2010-2011)
Tuition and fees: $29,254.
Per-credit charge: $1,200.
Room and board: $9,995.
Additional info: Tuition/fee waivers available for adults.

FINANCIAL AID PICTURE (2009-2010)
Students with need: Out of 118 full-time freshmen who applied for aid, 102 were judged to have need. Of these, 102 received aid, and 26 had their full need met. Average financial aid package met 77% of need; average scholarship/grant was $17,863; average loan was $4,461. For part-time students, average financial aid package was $14,665.
Students without need: 33 full-time freshmen who did not demonstrate need for aid received scholarships/grants; average award was $15,094. No-need awards available for academics, alumni affiliation, art, leadership, minority status, music/drama, religious affiliation, state/district residency.
Scholarships offered: Gottwald Scholarship: full tuition plus travel stipend; based on academic profile; approximately 3 awarded in each class. Presidential Scholars: $17,500; renewable annually; based on academic profile.
Cumulative student debt: 78% of graduating class had student loans; average debt was $9,904.

FINANCIAL AID PROCEDURES
Forms required: FAFSA.
Dates and Deadlines: Priority date 3/1; no closing date. Applicants notified on a rolling basis starting 3/1; must reply by 5/1 or within 2 week(s) of notification.
Transfers: Applicants notified on a rolling basis starting 3/1; must reply by 5/1 or within 2 week(s) of notification.

CONTACT
Kay Mattox, Director of Student Financial Services
2500 Rivermont Avenue, Lynchburg, VA 24503-1555
(434) 947-8128

Randolph-Macon College
Ashland, Virginia
www.rmc.edu   Federal Code: 003733

4-year private liberal arts college in small town, affiliated with United Methodist Church.
Enrollment: 1,227 undergrads, 1% part-time. 362 full-time freshmen.
Selectivity: Admits 50 to 75% of applicants.

BASIC COSTS (2010-2011)
Tuition and fees: $30,608.
Room and board: $9,326.

FINANCIAL AID PICTURE (2009-2010)
Students with need: Out of 301 full-time freshmen who applied for aid, 246 were judged to have need. Of these, 246 received aid, and 54 had their full need met. Average financial aid package met 80% of need; average scholarship/grant was $18,530; average loan was $4,573. For part-time students, average financial aid package was $5,725.
Students without need: 115 full-time freshmen who did not demonstrate need for aid received scholarships/grants; average award was $11,533. No-need awards available for academics, alumni affiliation, minority status, religious affiliation, state/district residency.
Scholarships offered: Randolph-Macon College's academic scholarship; range from $12,500 to $20,000 per year based solely on the student's academic record and extra-curricular activities, renewable.
Cumulative student debt: 72% of graduating class had student loans; average debt was $26,763.

FINANCIAL AID PROCEDURES
Forms required: FAFSA, state aid form.
Dates and Deadlines: Priority date 3/1; closing date 2/15. Applicants notified by 3/15; must reply by 5/1 or within 2 week(s) of notification.
Transfers: Applicants notified by 3/15; must reply by 5/1 or within 2 week(s) of notification.

CONTACT
Mary Neal, Director of Financial Aid
PO Box 5005, Ashland, VA 23005-5505
(804) 752-7529

Rappahannock Community College
Glenns, Virginia
www.rappahannock.edu   Federal Code: 009160

2-year public community college in rural community.
Enrollment: 1,761 undergrads.
Selectivity: Open admission.

BASIC COSTS (2009-2010)
Tuition and fees: $2,811; out-of-state residents $7,974.
Per-credit charge: $87; out-of-state residents $259.
Additional info: Out-of-state students pay additional $300 capital outlay fee.

FINANCIAL AID PICTURE
Students with need: Need-based aid available for full-time and part-time students.

FINANCIAL AID PROCEDURES
Forms required: FAFSA, institutional form.
Dates and Deadlines: Priority date 5/15; no closing date. Applicants notified on a rolling basis starting 6/30.

CONTACT
Carolyn Ward, Director of Financial Aid
12745 College Drive, Glenns, VA 23149-2616
(804) 758-6737

Regent University
Virginia Beach, Virginia
www.regent.edu   Federal Code: 030913

4-year private university in large city, affiliated with interdenominational tradition.
Enrollment: 1,874 undergrads, 44% part-time. 72 full-time freshmen.
Selectivity: Admits 50 to 75% of applicants.

BASIC COSTS (2010-2011)

Tuition and fees: $15,100.
Per-credit charge: $495.
Room only: $5,900.

FINANCIAL AID PICTURE (2009-2010)

Students with need: Average financial aid package met 26% of need; average scholarship/grant was $6,013; average loan was $3,461. For part-time students, average financial aid package was $7,745.
Students without need: No-need awards available for academics, alumni affiliation, leadership.
Cumulative student debt: 69% of graduating class had student loans; average debt was $33,451.

FINANCIAL AID PROCEDURES

Forms required: FAFSA, state aid form, institutional form.
Dates and Deadlines: Priority date 3/15; no closing date. Applicants notified on a rolling basis starting 3/1; must reply within 2 week(s) of notification.
Transfers: Priority date 7/1; no deadline. Applicants notified on a rolling basis starting 3/15; must reply within 2 week(s) of notification. Must be able to determine number of transfer credits before full award package is offered. Student should submit all academic transcripts in a timely manner to ensure transfer articulation occurs in a timely manner.

CONTACT

Joe Dobrota, Director of Central Financial Aid
1000 Regent University Drive, Virginia Beach, VA 23464-9800
(757) 352-4125

Richard Bland College
Petersburg, Virginia
www.rbc.edu   Federal Code: 003707

2-year public junior and liberal arts college in small city.
Enrollment: 1,282 undergrads, 18% part-time. 491 full-time freshmen.
Selectivity: Admits over 75% of applicants.

BASIC COSTS (2009-2010)

Tuition and fees: $3,002; out-of-state residents $11,490.
Per-credit charge: $102; out-of-state residents $465.
Room only: $8,400.
Additional info: Fees for full-time out-of-state students are an additional $189.

FINANCIAL AID PICTURE (2008-2009)

Students with need: Need-based aid available for full-time and part-time students.
Students without need: No-need awards available for academics.
Scholarships offered: Presidential Scholarships: average $1,000; for full-time first-time Virginia residents; based on minimum 3.5 high school GPA.

FINANCIAL AID PROCEDURES

Forms required: FAFSA, institutional form.
Dates and Deadlines: Priority date 5/1; no closing date. Applicants notified by 6/1; must reply within 2 week(s) of notification.

CONTACT

J. Tyler Hart, Coordinator of Financial Aid
11301 Johnson Road, Petersburg, VA 23805
(804) 862-6223

Roanoke College
Salem, Virginia
www.roanoke.edu   Federal Code: 003736

4-year private liberal arts college in large town, affiliated with Evangelical Lutheran Church in America.
Enrollment: 1,978 undergrads, 3% part-time. 560 full-time freshmen.
Selectivity: Admits 50 to 75% of applicants.

BASIC COSTS (2010-2011)

Tuition and fees: $31,214.
Room and board: $10,308.
Additional info: Tuition/fee waivers available for adults.

FINANCIAL AID PICTURE (2009-2010)

Students with need: Out of 482 full-time freshmen who applied for aid, 410 were judged to have need. Of these, 410 received aid, and 143 had their full need met. Average financial aid package met 86% of need; average scholarship/grant was $20,634; average loan was $3,941. For part-time students, average financial aid package was $5,151.
Students without need: 142 full-time freshmen who did not demonstrate need for aid received scholarships/grants; average award was $10,357. No-need awards available for academics, minority status, music/drama, religious affiliation.
Scholarships offered: William Beard Scholarship: up to 3 awarded; full tuition, room and board. David Bittle Scholarship: up to 12 awarded; full tuition. Christopher Baughman Scholarship: up to 50 awarded; $4,500 per year; added to previously awarded college scholarships. Julius Dreher Scholarship: up to 75 awarded; $1,500 per year added to previously awarded college scholarships. John Morehead Scholarship; $1,000 per year; added to previously awarded college scholarships.
Cumulative student debt: 66% of graduating class had student loans; average debt was $25,932.

FINANCIAL AID PROCEDURES

Forms required: FAFSA, state aid form.
Dates and Deadlines: Priority date 3/1; no closing date. Applicants notified on a rolling basis starting 11/1; must reply within 2 week(s) of notification.

CONTACT

Thomas Blair, Director of Financial Aid
221 College Lane, Salem, VA 24153-3794
(540) 375-2235

St. Paul's College
Lawrenceville, Virginia
www.saintpauls.edu   Federal Code: 003739

4-year private liberal arts college in small town, affiliated with Episcopal Church.
Enrollment: 584 undergrads, 3% part-time. 201 full-time freshmen.
Selectivity: Admits over 75% of applicants.

BASIC COSTS (2009-2010)

Tuition and fees: $13,210.
Per-credit charge: $495.
Room and board: $6,640.
Additional info: Tuition/fee waivers available for minority students.

FINANCIAL AID PICTURE (2008-2009)

Students with need: Out of 201 full-time freshmen who applied for aid, 196 were judged to have need. Of these, 186 received aid, and 6 had their full need met. Average financial aid package met 55% of need; average scholarship/grant was $4,009; average loan was $997. For part-time students, average financial aid package was $5,276.
Students without need: No-need awards available for academics, alumni affiliation, athletics.

Scholarships offered: 28 full-time freshmen received athletic scholarships; average amount $10,984.

Cumulative student debt: 19% of graduating class had student loans; average debt was $21,917.

FINANCIAL AID PROCEDURES

Forms required: FAFSA, state aid form.

Dates and Deadlines: No deadline. Applicants notified on a rolling basis starting 1/15; must reply by 7/1 or within 4 week(s) of notification.

Transfers: No deadline. Applicants notified on a rolling basis; must reply within 2 week(s) of notification.

CONTACT

Karen Lyons, Assistant Director of Financial Aid

115 College Drive, Lawrenceville, VA 23868

(434) 848-6496

Shenandoah University

Winchester, Virginia

www.su.edu   Federal Code: 003737

4-year private university in small city, affiliated with United Methodist Church.

Enrollment: 1,717 undergrads, 3% part-time. 407 full-time freshmen.

Selectivity: Admits over 75% of applicants.

BASIC COSTS (2010-2011)

Tuition and fees: $25,080.

Per-credit charge: $723.

Room and board: $8,870.

FINANCIAL AID PICTURE (2009-2010)

Students with need: Out of 345 full-time freshmen who applied for aid, 345 were judged to have need. Of these, 345 received aid, and 53 had their full need met. Average financial aid package met 85% of need; average scholarship/grant was $8,500; average loan was $3,500. Need-based aid available for part-time students.

Students without need: 52 full-time freshmen who did not demonstrate need for aid received scholarships/grants; average award was $6,000. No-need awards available for academics, job skills, leadership, music/drama, religious affiliation, state/district residency.

Additional info: Emergency Grant Fund available for books, meals, tuition and fees.

FINANCIAL AID PROCEDURES

Forms required: FAFSA, state aid form.

Dates and Deadlines: Closing date 3/15. Applicants notified on a rolling basis starting 3/15; must reply within 2 week(s) of notification.

Transfers: Priority date 3/15; closing date 4/15. Applicants notified on a rolling basis starting 3/15; must reply within 2 week(s) of notification.

CONTACT

Nancy Bragg, Director of Financial Aid

1460 University Drive, Winchester, VA 22601-5195

(540) 665-4538

Southern Virginia University

Buena Vista, Virginia

www.svu.edu   Federal Code: 003738

4-year private liberal arts college in small town, affiliated with Church of Jesus Christ of Latter-day Saints.

Enrollment: 638 undergrads. 250 full-time freshmen.

Selectivity: Admits over 75% of applicants.

BASIC COSTS (2010-2011)

Tuition and fees: $17,800.

Per-credit charge: $630.

Room and board: $6,100.

FINANCIAL AID PICTURE (2008-2009)

Students with need: Out of 192 full-time freshmen who applied for aid, 157 were judged to have need. Of these, 157 received aid, and 30 had their full need met. Average financial aid package met 61% of need; average scholarship/grant was $8,151; average loan was $2,852. For part-time students, average financial aid package was $5,255.

Students without need: 91 full-time freshmen who did not demonstrate need for aid received scholarships/grants; average award was $5,659. No-need awards available for academics, art, athletics, leadership, music/drama, ROTC.

Scholarships offered: 23 full-time freshmen received athletic scholarships; average amount $1,045.

Cumulative student debt: 92% of graduating class had student loans; average debt was $23,625.

FINANCIAL AID PROCEDURES

Forms required: FAFSA, state aid form.

Dates and Deadlines: Priority date 5/1; no closing date. Applicants notified on a rolling basis starting 3/1; must reply by 5/1 or within 3 week(s) of notification.

Transfers: No deadline. Applicants notified on a rolling basis starting 3/1.

CONTACT

John Brandt, Director of Financial Aid

One University Hill Drive, Buena Vista, VA 24416-3097

(540) 261-4351

Southside Virginia Community College-Alberta

Alberta, Virginia

www.sv.vccs.edu   Federal Code: 008661

2-year public community college in rural community.

Enrollment: 3,275 undergrads.

Selectivity: Open admission; but selective for some programs.

BASIC COSTS (2009-2010)

Tuition and fees: $2,856; out-of-state residents $8,019.

Per-credit charge: $87; out-of-state residents $259.

Additional info: Out-of-state students pay additional $300 capital outlay fee.

FINANCIAL AID PICTURE (2008-2009)

Students with need: Need-based aid available for full-time and part-time students. Work study available nights.

Students without need: No-need awards available for academics.

Scholarships offered: Guaranteed Academic Merit Award: $1,500, for high school graduates within college's service area with 3.0 GPA who do not receive at least $1,500 in need-based aid.

FINANCIAL AID PROCEDURES

Forms required: FAFSA.

Dates and Deadlines: Priority date 6/1; closing date 8/1. Applicants notified on a rolling basis starting 6/15.

Transfers: State aid limited to in-state residents.

CONTACT

Sally Tharrington, Director of Financial Aid

109 Campus Drive, Alberta, VA 23821

(434) 736-2026

Southwest Virginia Community College
Richlands, Virginia
www.sw.edu   Federal Code: 007260

2-year public community college in small town.
Enrollment: 2,696 undergrads.
Selectivity: Open admission; but selective for some programs.

BASIC COSTS (2009-2010)
Tuition and fees: $2,826; out-of-state residents $7,989.
Per-credit charge: $87; out-of-state residents $259.
Additional info: Out-of-state students pay an additional $300 capital outlay fee.

FINANCIAL AID PICTURE (2009-2010)
Students with need: Need-based aid available for part-time students.
Students without need: This college awards aid only to students with need.

FINANCIAL AID PROCEDURES
Forms required: FAFSA, institutional form.
Dates and Deadlines: Priority date 5/30; no closing date. Applicants notified on a rolling basis starting 7/1.

CONTACT
Virginia Stevens, Administrative &Office Specialist III, Financial Aid
PO Box SVCC, Richlands, VA 24641-1101
(276) 964-7290

Sweet Briar College
Sweet Briar, Virginia
www.sbc.edu   Federal Code: 003742

4-year private liberal arts college for women in rural community.
Enrollment: 611 undergrads, 1% part-time. 194 full-time freshmen.
Selectivity: Admits over 75% of applicants.

BASIC COSTS (2010-2011)
Tuition and fees: $30,195.
Per-credit charge: $760.
Room and board: $10,780.
Additional info: Tuition/fee waivers available for adults.

FINANCIAL AID PICTURE (2008-2009)
Students with need: Out of 146 full-time freshmen who applied for aid, 146 were judged to have need. Of these, 144 received aid, and 103 had their full need met. Average financial aid package met 31% of need; average scholarship/grant was $17,084; average loan was $4,179. For part-time students, average financial aid package was $8,683.
Students without need: 64 full-time freshmen who did not demonstrate need for aid received scholarships/grants; average award was $11,817. No-need awards available for academics, art, leadership, music/drama, state/district residency.
Scholarships offered: Founders and Prothro Scholarships: up to $15,000. Commonwealth Scholarships: up to $13,000. Betty Bean Black Scholarships: up to $12,000. Sweet Briar Scholarships: up to $9,000; for students with special talents in specific area. All awards based on academic qualifications; renewable annually with specified GPA.
Cumulative student debt: 52% of graduating class had student loans; average debt was $25,372.

FINANCIAL AID PROCEDURES
Forms required: FAFSA.
Dates and Deadlines: Priority date 2/15; no closing date. Applicants notified on a rolling basis starting 3/1; must reply by 5/1.
Transfers: Closing date 7/15.

CONTACT
Bobbi Carpenter, Director of Financial Aid
PO Box 1052, Sweet Briar, VA 24595-1502

Thomas Nelson Community College
Hampton, Virginia
www.tncc.edu   Federal Code: 006871

2-year public community college in small city.
Enrollment: 8,190 undergrads.
Selectivity: Open admission; but selective for some programs.

BASIC COSTS (2009-2010)
Tuition and fees: $2,822; out-of-state residents $7,985.
Per-credit charge: $87; out-of-state residents $259.
Additional info: Out-of-state students pay additional $300 capital outlay fee.

FINANCIAL AID PICTURE (2009-2010)
Students with need: Need-based aid available for full-time and part-time students. Work study available nights.

FINANCIAL AID PROCEDURES
Forms required: FAFSA, institutional form.
Dates and Deadlines: Priority date 5/1; no closing date. Applicants notified on a rolling basis starting 6/1; must reply within 2 week(s) of notification.
Transfers: Priority date 5/8; no deadline. Applicants notified on a rolling basis; must reply within 2 week(s) of notification.

CONTACT
Kathryn Anderson, Director of Financial Aid, Veterans Affairs, and Scholarships
Box 9407, Hampton, VA 23670
(757) 825-2848

Tidewater Community College
Norfolk, Virginia
www.tcc.vccs.edu   Federal Code: 003712

2-year public community college in large city.
Enrollment: 30,447 undergrads.
Selectivity: Open admission; but selective for some programs.

BASIC COSTS (2009-2010)
Tuition and fees: $3,406; out-of-state residents $8,569.
Per-credit charge: $87; out-of-state residents $259.
Additional info: Out-of-state students pay additional $300 capital outlay fee.

FINANCIAL AID PICTURE (2008-2009)
Students with need: Need-based aid available for full-time and part-time students.
Students without need: This college awards aid only to students with need.

FINANCIAL AID PROCEDURES
Forms required: FAFSA.
Dates and Deadlines: Priority date 4/1; no closing date. Applicants notified on a rolling basis starting 4/1.

CONTACT
Norma Ferki, Director of Financial Aid
7000 College Drive/Portsmouth Campus, Portsmouth, VA 23703
(757) 822-1360

University of Mary Washington
Fredericksburg, Virginia
www.umw.edu   Federal Code: 003746

4-year public university and liberal arts college in small city.
Enrollment: 4,258 undergrads, 12% part-time. 848 full-time freshmen.
Selectivity: Admits 50 to 75% of applicants.

BASIC COSTS (2009-2010)
Tuition and fees: $7,112; out-of-state residents $18,840.
Per-credit charge: $249; out-of-state residents $737.
Room and board: $8,316.

FINANCIAL AID PICTURE (2008-2009)
Students with need: Out of 576 full-time freshmen who applied for aid, 221 were judged to have need. Of these, 221 received aid, and 41 had their full need met. Average financial aid package met 53% of need; average scholarship/grant was $6,360; average loan was $3,170. For part-time students, average financial aid package was $5,440.
Students without need: 116 full-time freshmen who did not demonstrate need for aid received scholarships/grants; average award was $2,300. No-need awards available for academics, alumni affiliation, art, leadership, music/drama, state/district residency.
Scholarships offered: Scholastic Excellence Award: from $500 to $6,000; honors admissions automatically considered. Two Virginia residents will receive tuition, fees, room and board up to $10,000. One non-Virginia award for tuition, fees, room and board. All scholarships renewable.
Cumulative student debt: 44% of graduating class had student loans; average debt was $15,630.

FINANCIAL AID PROCEDURES
Forms required: FAFSA, institutional form.
Dates and Deadlines: Priority date 3/1; closing date 5/31. Applicants notified by 4/15; must reply by 5/1 or within 2 week(s) of notification.

CONTACT
Debra Harber, Director of Financial Aid
1301 College Avenue, Fredericksburg, VA 22401-5300
(540) 654-2468

University of Richmond
University of Richmond, Virginia
www.richmond.edu   Federal Code: 003744

4-year private university and liberal arts college in very large city.
Enrollment: 2,826 undergrads, 1% part-time. 917 full-time freshmen.
Selectivity: Admits less than 50% of applicants.

BASIC COSTS (2010-2011)
Tuition and fees: $41,610.
Room and board: $8,810.

FINANCIAL AID PICTURE (2009-2010)
Students with need: Out of 603 full-time freshmen who applied for aid, 486 were judged to have need. Of these, 486 received aid, and 441 had their full need met. Average financial aid package met 100% of need; average scholarship/grant was $33,712; average loan was $2,930. For part-time students, average financial aid package was $24,599.
Students without need: 46 full-time freshmen who did not demonstrate need for aid received scholarships/grants; average award was $37,783. No-need awards available for academics, art, athletics, leadership, minority status, music/drama, ROTC.
Scholarships offered: *Merit:* Richmond Scholars program: full tuition scholarships; up to 50 entering freshmen. Presidential Scholarships: up to $15,000. *Athletic:* 53 full-time freshmen received athletic scholarships; average amount $31,734.

Cumulative student debt: 42% of graduating class had student loans; average debt was $21,555.
Additional info: VA residents whose family income is $40,000 or less and who qualify for need-based aid will receive grant assistance equal to full tuition, room and board. Early decision: Financial aid package estimated using historical data; applicant still required to submit all financial aid forms.

FINANCIAL AID PROCEDURES
Forms required: FAFSA, institutional form. Prior year federal tax return.
Dates and Deadlines: Closing date 2/15. Applicants notified by 4/1; must reply within 4 week(s) of notification.

CONTACT
Cindy Deffenbaugh, Director of Student Financial Aid
28 Westhampton Way, University of Richmond, VA 23173
(804) 289-8438

University of Virginia
Charlottesville, Virginia
www.virginia.edu   Federal Code: 003745

4-year public university in small city.
Enrollment: 14,225 undergrads, 3% part-time. 3,239 full-time freshmen.
Selectivity: Admits less than 50% of applicants.

BASIC COSTS (2009-2010)
Tuition and fees: $9,672; out-of-state residents $31,230.
Per-credit charge: $250; out-of-state residents $968.
Room and board: $8,290.

FINANCIAL AID PICTURE (2009-2010)
Students with need: Need-based aid available for full-time and part-time students. Work study available nights, weekends, and for part-time students.
Students without need: No-need awards available for academics, athletics, leadership, minority status, music/drama, state/district residency.

FINANCIAL AID PROCEDURES
Forms required: FAFSA, institutional form.
Dates and Deadlines: Priority date 3/1; no closing date. Applicants notified by 4/1; must reply by 5/1.

CONTACT
Yvonne Hubbard, Director Student Financial Services
Box 400160, Charlottesville, VA 22904-4160
(434) 982-6000

University of Virginia's College at Wise
Wise, Virginia
www.uvawise.edu   Federal Code: 003747

4-year public liberal arts college in small town.
Enrollment: 1,627 undergrads, 9% part-time. 425 full-time freshmen.
Selectivity: Admits over 75% of applicants.

BASIC COSTS (2010-2011)
Tuition and fees: $6,748; out-of-state residents $18,876.
Per-credit charge: $153; out-of-state residents $666.
Room and board: $7,323.

FINANCIAL AID PICTURE (2008-2009)
Students with need: Out of 349 full-time freshmen who applied for aid, 272 were judged to have need. Of these, 272 received aid, and 258 had their full need met. Average financial aid package met 94% of need; average scholarship/grant was $5,837; average loan was $2,180. For part-time students, average financial aid package was $4,845.
Students without need: 128 full-time freshmen who did not demonstrate need for aid received scholarships/grants; average award was $2,505. No-

need awards available for academics, alumni affiliation, art, athletics, job skills, leadership, music/drama, religious affiliation, state/district residency.

Scholarships offered: 43 full-time freshmen received athletic scholarships; average amount $1,593.

Cumulative student debt: 59% of graduating class had student loans; average debt was $10,252.

FINANCIAL AID PROCEDURES

Forms required: FAFSA.

Dates and Deadlines: Priority date 4/1; no closing date. Applicants notified on a rolling basis starting 2/15; must reply within 4 week(s) of notification.

CONTACT

Bill Wendle, Director of Financial Aid
1 College Avenue, Wise, VA 24293-4412
(276) 328-0139

Virginia Commonwealth University
Richmond, Virginia
www.vcu.edu   Federal Code: 003735

4-year public university in small city.

Enrollment: 21,500 undergrads, 12% part-time. 3,855 full-time freshmen.

Selectivity: Admits 50 to 75% of applicants.

BASIC COSTS (2009-2010)

Tuition and fees: $7,117; out-of-state residents $20,341.

Per-credit charge: $221; out-of-state residents $772.

Room and board: $8,335.

FINANCIAL AID PICTURE (2008-2009)

Students with need: Out of 2,274 full-time freshmen who applied for aid, 1,723 were judged to have need. Of these, 1,723 received aid, and 198 had their full need met. Average financial aid package met 58% of need; average scholarship/grant was $5,344; average loan was $3,427. For part-time students, average financial aid package was $5,419.

Students without need: 426 full-time freshmen who did not demonstrate need for aid received scholarships/grants; average award was $2,854. No-need awards available for academics, alumni affiliation, art, athletics, leadership, music/drama.

Scholarships offered: *Merit:* Academic Achievement scholarship: $1,500 grants awarded based on demonstrated need and merit to non-scholarship continuing Virginia residents at the sophomore or junior level. Access Grant: $1,500 grants to freshman or sophomore Virginia Residents with household income at federal poverty level. Transfer Achievement scholarship: $1,000 awarded based on demonstrated need and merit to Virginia residents transferring to VCU from a Virginia community college. *Athletic:* 24 full-time freshmen received athletic scholarships; average amount $15,451.

Cumulative student debt: 61% of graduating class had student loans; average debt was $22,864.

FINANCIAL AID PROCEDURES

Forms required: FAFSA.

Dates and Deadlines: Priority date 3/1; no closing date. Applicants notified on a rolling basis starting 4/1; must reply within 2 week(s) of notification.

Transfers: Applicants notified by 4/1; must reply within 2 week(s) of notification.

CONTACT

Susan Kadir, Director of Financial Aid
Box 842526, Richmond, VA 23284-2526
(804) 828-6669

Virginia Intermont College
Bristol, Virginia
www.vic.edu   Federal Code: 003752

4-year private liberal arts and teachers college in small city, affiliated with Baptist faith.

Enrollment: 577 undergrads. 98 full-time freshmen.

Selectivity: Admits less than 50% of applicants.

BASIC COSTS (2010-2011)

Tuition and fees: $24,542.

Per-credit charge: $225.

Room and board: $7,690.

FINANCIAL AID PICTURE (2008-2009)

Students with need: Out of 82 full-time freshmen who applied for aid, 74 were judged to have need. Of these, 74 received aid, and 10 had their full need met. Average financial aid package met 67% of need; average scholarship/grant was $12,818; average loan was $3,791. For part-time students, average financial aid package was $6,248.

Students without need: 17 full-time freshmen who did not demonstrate need for aid received scholarships/grants; average award was $7,630. No-need awards available for art, athletics, music/drama, religious affiliation, state/district residency.

Scholarships offered: 3 full-time freshmen received athletic scholarships; average amount $6,067.

Cumulative student debt: 76% of graduating class had student loans; average debt was $16,338.

FINANCIAL AID PROCEDURES

Forms required: FAFSA, state aid form.

Dates and Deadlines: Priority date 3/1; closing date 6/1. Applicants notified on a rolling basis starting 2/15; must reply within 3 week(s) of notification.

Transfers: Priority date 2/15; no deadline. Applicants notified on a rolling basis starting 1/1; must reply within 3 week(s) of notification. Limited to certain number of units of state aid.

CONTACT

Denise Posey, Financial Aid Director
1013 Moore Street, Bristol, VA 24201
(276) 466-7871

Virginia Military Institute
Lexington, Virginia
www.vmi.edu   Federal Code: 003753

4-year public liberal arts and military college in small town.

Enrollment: 1,500 undergrads. 412 full-time freshmen.

Selectivity: Admits 50 to 75% of applicants. GED not accepted.

BASIC COSTS (2010-2011)

Tuition and fees: $11,190; out-of-state residents $28,738.

Per-credit charge: $216; out-of-state residents $675.

Room and board: $6,792.

FINANCIAL AID PICTURE (2008-2009)

Students with need: Out of 297 full-time freshmen who applied for aid, 198 were judged to have need. Of these, 192 received aid, and 123 had their full need met. Average financial aid package met 89.5% of need; average scholarship/grant was $9,600; average loan was $4,130.

Students without need: 65 full-time freshmen who did not demonstrate need for aid received scholarships/grants; average award was $2,707. No-need awards available for academics, alumni affiliation, athletics, leadership.

Scholarships offered: *Merit:* Institute Scholarship: up to $19,830; 10-12 awarded; for superior academic performance, demonstrated character and leadership, extracurricular activities, 3.7 high school GPA, minimum 1250 SAT

(exclusive of Writing) or 27 ACT, rank in top 5% of class. *Athletic:* 22 full-time freshmen received athletic scholarships; average amount $11,417.
Cumulative student debt: 34% of graduating class had student loans; average debt was $19,046.

FINANCIAL AID PROCEDURES

Forms required: FAFSA, institutional form.
Dates and Deadlines: Priority date 3/1; closing date 3/1. Applicants notified on a rolling basis starting 3/1; must reply by 5/1.

CONTACT

Timothy Golden, Director of Financial Aid
VMI Office of Admissions, Lexington, VA 24450-9967
(540) 464-7208

Virginia Polytechnic Institute and State University

Blacksburg, Virginia
www.vt.edu   Federal Code: 003754

4-year public university in large town.
Enrollment: 23,461 undergrads, 2% part-time. 5,456 full-time freshmen.
Selectivity: Admits 50 to 75% of applicants.

BASIC COSTS (2009-2010)

Tuition and fees: $8,605; out-of-state residents $21,488.
Per-credit charge: $282; out-of-state residents $814.
Room and board: $5,824.
Additional info: Tuition/fee waivers available for unemployed or children of unemployed.

FINANCIAL AID PICTURE (2008-2009)

Students with need: Out of 3,837 full-time freshmen who applied for aid, 2,245 were judged to have need. Of these, 1,992 received aid, and 353 had their full need met. Average financial aid package met 63% of need; average scholarship/grant was $6,653; average loan was $3,837. Need-based aid available for part-time students.
Students without need: 662 full-time freshmen who did not demonstrate need for aid received scholarships/grants; average award was $2,853. No-need awards available for academics, art, athletics, leadership, minority status, music/drama, ROTC, state/district residency.
Scholarships offered: 99 full-time freshmen received athletic scholarships; average amount $10,677.
Cumulative student debt: 52% of graduating class had student loans; average debt was $22,070.

FINANCIAL AID PROCEDURES

Forms required: FAFSA.
Dates and Deadlines: Priority date 3/1; no closing date. Must reply by 5/1 or within 4 week(s) of notification.
Transfers: Based on family EFC per FAFSA and available resources. Significant academic scholarships for graduates of Virginia Community College System.

CONTACT

Barry Simmons, Director of Financial Aid
201 Burruss Hall, Blacksburg, VA 24061-0202
(540) 231-5179

Virginia State University

Petersburg, Virginia
www.vsu.edu   Federal Code: 003764

4-year public university in large town.
Enrollment: 4,775 undergrads, 5% part-time. 1,202 full-time freshmen.
Selectivity: Admits 50 to 75% of applicants.

BASIC COSTS (2009-2010)

Tuition and fees: $6,174; out-of-state residents $14,236.
Per-credit charge: $208; out-of-state residents $482.
Room and board: $8,050.
Additional info: Out-of-state students pay an additional fee.

FINANCIAL AID PICTURE (2008-2009)

Students with need: Need-based aid available for full-time and part-time students. Work study available nights, weekends, and for part-time students.
Students without need: No-need awards available for academics, alumni affiliation, art, athletics, job skills, leadership, music/drama, religious affiliation, ROTC.
Scholarships offered: Presidential Scholarships: 3.2 GPA, SAT 1100 or ACT 24; $7,000. Provost's Scholarships: 3.0 GPA, SAT 1000 or ACT 21; $3,500. SAT exclusive of Writing. Fine and Performing Arts Scholarships: outstanding talent in music or fine arts, audition or portfolio may be required, recommendation required; $1,500. Math, Science, and Technology Scholarships: 3.0 GPA, above average ability in math, science, or technology, recommendation and essay required; $1,500.
Additional info: Strongly recommend that students apply for scholarship assistance through federal, state, local and private agencies.

FINANCIAL AID PROCEDURES

Forms required: FAFSA, institutional form.
Dates and Deadlines: Priority date 3/31; closing date 5/1. Applicants notified on a rolling basis starting 5/1; must reply within 2 week(s) of notification.
Transfers: Priority date 3/1.

CONTACT

Henry Debose, Director of Financial Aid
One Hayden Drive, Petersburg, VA 23806
(804) 524-5990

Virginia Union University

Richmond, Virginia
www.vuu.edu   Federal Code: 003766

4-year private university and liberal arts college in small city, affiliated with Baptist faith.
Enrollment: 1,210 undergrads.
Selectivity: Admits over 75% of applicants.

BASIC COSTS (2009-2010)

Tuition and fees: $13,934.
Room and board: $6,506.

FINANCIAL AID PICTURE (2009-2010)

Students with need: Need-based aid available for full-time and part-time students. Work study available nights, weekends, and for part-time students.
Students without need: No-need awards available for academics, athletics, ROTC, state/district residency.

FINANCIAL AID PROCEDURES

Forms required: FAFSA.
Dates and Deadlines: Priority date 4/27; no closing date. Applicants notified on a rolling basis starting 5/1; must reply within 2 week(s) of notification.
Transfers: No deadline. Student must submit a financial aid transcript from all prior schools attended before receiving aid.

CONTACT

Donna Mack-Tatum, Director of Financial Aid
1500 North Lombardy Street, Richmond, VA 23220
(804) 257-5882

Virginia Wesleyan College
Norfolk, Virginia
www.vwc.edu   Federal Code: 003767

4-year private liberal arts college in large city, affiliated with United Methodist Church.
Enrollment: 1,300 undergrads, 12% part-time. 329 full-time freshmen.
Selectivity: Admits over 75% of applicants.

BASIC COSTS (2010-2011)
Tuition and fees: $28,556.
Per-credit charge: $1,169.
Room and board: $7,680.
Additional info: Tuition/fee waivers available for adults.

FINANCIAL AID PICTURE (2008-2009)
Students with need: Out of 308 full-time freshmen who applied for aid, 256 were judged to have need. Of these, 252 received aid, and 93 had their full need met. Average financial aid package met 86% of need; average scholarship/grant was $15,330; average loan was $5,828. For part-time students, average financial aid package was $7,359.
Students without need: 64 full-time freshmen who did not demonstrate need for aid received scholarships/grants; average award was $7,634. No-need awards available for academics, alumni affiliation, leadership, religious affiliation, ROTC, state/district residency.
Cumulative student debt: 80% of graduating class had student loans; average debt was $27,658.

FINANCIAL AID PROCEDURES
Forms required: FAFSA, state aid form.
Dates and Deadlines: Priority date 3/1; no closing date. Applicants notified on a rolling basis starting 2/15; must reply by 5/1 or within 2 week(s) of notification.
Transfers: No deadline. Applicants notified on a rolling basis starting 2/15; must reply by 5/1 or within 2 week(s) of notification. 4-semester maximum of special aid available for students who graduated with 3.0 GPA and earned an associate degree from local community college. Must enroll full time and maintain 2.5 GPA minimum.

CONTACT
Angie Hawkins, Director of Financial Aid
1584 Wesleyan Drive, Norfolk, VA 23502-5599
(757) 455-3345

Virginia Western Community College
Roanoke, Virginia
www.virginiawestern.edu   Federal Code: 003760

2-year public community college in small city.
Enrollment: 8,931 undergrads.
Selectivity: Open admission; but selective for some programs.

BASIC COSTS (2009-2010)
Tuition and fees: $2,874; out-of-state residents $8,037.
Per-credit charge: $87; out-of-state residents $259.
Additional info: Out-of-state students pay additional $300 capital outlay fee.

FINANCIAL AID PICTURE
Students with need: Need-based aid available for full-time and part-time students.
Students without need: No-need awards available for academics, state/district residency.

FINANCIAL AID PROCEDURES
Forms required: FAFSA.
Dates and Deadlines: No deadline. Applicants notified on a rolling basis starting 4/1.

Transfers: No deadline. Applicants notified on a rolling basis.

CONTACT
Shawn Thomas, Financial Aid Officer
Box 14007, Roanoke, VA 24038
(540) 857-7331

Washington and Lee University
Lexington, Virginia   Federal Code: 003768
www.wlu.edu   CSS Code: 5887

4-year private university and liberal arts college in small town.
Enrollment: 1,757 undergrads. 472 full-time freshmen.
Selectivity: Admits less than 50% of applicants.

BASIC COSTS (2010-2011)
Tuition and fees: $40,387.
Per-credit charge: $1,411.
Room and board: $10,243.

FINANCIAL AID PICTURE (2009-2010)
Students with need: Out of 282 full-time freshmen who applied for aid, 220 were judged to have need. Of these, 220 received aid, and 196 had their full need met. Average financial aid package met 99% of need; average scholarship/grant was $30,451; average loan was $2,948. Need-based aid available for part-time students.
Students without need: 29 full-time freshmen who did not demonstrate need for aid received scholarships/grants; average award was $30,405. No-need awards available for academics.
Scholarships offered: Various memorial and endowed scholarships available.
Cumulative student debt: 31% of graduating class had student loans; average debt was $23,615.

FINANCIAL AID PROCEDURES
Forms required: FAFSA, CSS PROFILE, state aid form.
Dates and Deadlines: Priority date 2/1; closing date 3/1. Applicants notified by 4/1; must reply by 5/1.
Transfers: Transfer students are awarded institutional funds only after commitments to enrolled students are met. Notification usually in late summer.

CONTACT
John DeCourcy, Director of Student Financial Aid
204 West Washington Street, Lexington, VA 24450-2116
(540) 458-8715

Wytheville Community College
Wytheville, Virginia
www.wcc.vccs.edu   Federal Code: 003761

2-year public community college in small town.
Enrollment: 2,310 undergrads.
Selectivity: Open admission; but selective for some programs.

BASIC COSTS (2009-2010)
Tuition and fees: $2,811; out-of-state residents $7,974.
Per-credit charge: $87; out-of-state residents $259.
Additional info: Out-of-state students pay additional $90 capital outlay fee.

FINANCIAL AID PICTURE (2008-2009)
Students with need: Need-based aid available for full-time and part-time students.
Students without need: This college awards aid only to students with need.

FINANCIAL AID PROCEDURES
Forms required: FAFSA, institutional form.

Dates and Deadlines: Priority date 4/1; no closing date. Applicants notified on a rolling basis starting 5/1; must reply within 4 week(s) of notification.

CONTACT
Mary Gallagher, Financial Aid Coordinator
1000 East Main Street, Wytheville, VA 24382
(540) 223-4703

Washington

Antioch University Seattle
Seattle, Washington
www.antiochsea.edu   Federal Code: 003010

Upper-division private university and liberal arts college in very large city.
Enrollment: 238 undergrads. 40 full-time freshmen.
Selectivity: Admits over 75% of applicants.

BASIC COSTS (2009-2010)
Tuition and fees: $22,440.
Per-credit charge: $490.
Additional info: For BA with Teacher Prep program, $20,925 per year, $465 per-credit-hour.

FINANCIAL AID PICTURE (2008-2009)
Students with need: For part-time students, average financial aid package was $4,851.
Students without need: 5 full-time freshmen who did not demonstrate need for aid received scholarships/grants; average award was $2,000.
Cumulative student debt: 76% of graduating class had student loans; average debt was $22,000.

FINANCIAL AID PROCEDURES
Forms required: FAFSA, state aid form.
Dates and Deadlines: Priority date 4/15; no closing date. Applicants notified on a rolling basis starting 3/15; must reply within 2 week(s) of notification.
Transfers: Applicants notified on a rolling basis starting 3/15; must reply within 2 week(s) of notification.

CONTACT
Katy Stahl, Director of Financial Aid
2326 Sixth Avenue, Seattle, WA 98121-1814
(206) 268-4010

Art Institute of Seattle
Seattle, Washington
www.ais.edu   Federal Code: 016210

4-year for-profit visual arts and technical college in very large city.
Enrollment: 2,202 undergrads, 32% part-time. 556 full-time freshmen.
Selectivity: Open admission; but selective for some programs.

BASIC COSTS (2009-2010)
Tuition and fees: $21,195.
Per-credit charge: $471.
Room only: $11,136.

FINANCIAL AID PICTURE (2009-2010)
Students with need: Need-based aid available for full-time and part-time students. Work study available nights, weekends, and for part-time students.
Students without need: No-need awards available for academics, art.

FINANCIAL AID PROCEDURES
Forms required: FAFSA, state aid form.

Dates and Deadlines: Priority date 4/15; no closing date. Applicants notified on a rolling basis; must reply within 4 week(s) of notification.

CONTACT
Angela Hedwall, Director of Student Financial Services
2323 Elliott Avenue, Seattle, WA 98121-1622
(206) 239-2261

Bastyr University
Kenmore, Washington
www.bastyr.edu   Federal Code: 016059

Upper-division private university and health science college in small city.
Enrollment: 173 undergrads, 17% part-time.

BASIC COSTS (2009-2010)
Tuition and fees: $20,790.
Per-credit charge: $505.
Room only: $4,100.

FINANCIAL AID PICTURE (2008-2009)
Students with need: Average financial aid package for all full-time undergraduates was $15,150. 10% awarded as scholarships/grants, 90% awarded as loans/jobs. Need-based aid available for part-time students. Work study available nights, weekends, and for part-time students.
Students without need: No-need awards available for academics.
Cumulative student debt: 85% of graduating class had student loans; average debt was $32,500.

FINANCIAL AID PROCEDURES
Forms required: FAFSA, institutional form.
Dates and Deadlines: Priority date 5/1; no closing date. Applicants notified on a rolling basis starting 5/15; must reply within 2 week(s) of notification.
Transfers: No deadline. Applicants notified on a rolling basis; must reply within 3 week(s) of notification.

CONTACT
Carol Duke, Director of Financial Aid
14500 Juanita Drive, NE, Kenmore, WA 98028
(425) 602-3080

Bates Technical College
Tacoma, Washington
www.bates.ctc.edu   Federal Code: 012259

2-year public technical college in small city.
Enrollment: 1,486 undergrads.
Selectivity: Open admission.

BASIC COSTS (2009-2010)
Additional info: Programs costs range from $4,317 to $5,696; includes tuition and fees.

FINANCIAL AID PICTURE (2008-2009)
Students with need: Need-based aid available for full-time and part-time students. Work study available nights.
Students without need: This college awards aid only to students with need.

FINANCIAL AID PROCEDURES
Forms required: FAFSA, institutional form.
Dates and Deadlines: No deadline. Applicants notified on a rolling basis starting 9/7.
Transfers: No deadline. Applicants notified on a rolling basis.

CONTACT

Susan Neese, Financial Aid Officer
1101 South Yakima Avenue, Tacoma, WA 98405
(253) 680-7025

Bellevue College

Bellevue, Washington
www.bcc.ctc.edu   Federal Code: 003769

2-year public community college in small city.
Enrollment: 4,834 undergrads.
Selectivity: Open admission; but selective for some programs.

BASIC COSTS (2009-2010)

Tuition and fees: $3,165; out-of-state residents $8,385.
Per-credit charge: $89; out-of-state residents $261.

FINANCIAL AID PICTURE (2008-2009)

Students with need: Need-based aid available for full-time and part-time students. Work study available nights, weekends, and for part-time students.
Students without need: No-need awards available for academics, athletics.

FINANCIAL AID PROCEDURES

Forms required: FAFSA, institutional form.
Dates and Deadlines: Priority date 4/16; no closing date. Applicants notified on a rolling basis starting 8/1.

CONTACT

Sherri Ballantyne, Assistant Dean, Financial Aid
3000 Landerholm Circle SE, Bellevue, WA 98007-6484
(425) 564-2227

Bellingham Technical College

Bellingham, Washington
www.btc.ctc.edu   Federal Code: 016227

2-year public technical college in small city.
Enrollment: 1,966 undergrads.
Selectivity: Open admission; but selective for some programs.

BASIC COSTS (2009-2010)

Tuition and fees: $3,660.

FINANCIAL AID PICTURE

Students with need: Need-based aid available for full-time and part-time students.
Students without need: This college awards aid only to students with need.

FINANCIAL AID PROCEDURES

Forms required: FAFSA.
Dates and Deadlines: Priority date 4/30; no closing date. Applicants notified on a rolling basis starting 7/1; must reply within 2 week(s) of notification.

CONTACT

Jack Wollens, Director of Financial Aid
3028 Lindbergh Avenue, Bellingham, WA 98225-1599
(360) 752-8351

Big Bend Community College

Moses Lake, Washington
www.bigbend.edu   Federal Code: 003770

2-year public community college in large town.
Enrollment: 1,255 undergrads, 23% part-time. 294 full-time freshmen.

Selectivity: Open admission; but selective for some programs.

BASIC COSTS (2009-2010)

Tuition and fees: $3,015; out-of-state residents $3,405.
Per-credit charge: $81; out-of-state residents $94.
Room only: $2,925.
Additional info: Tuition/fee waivers available for unemployed or children of unemployed.

FINANCIAL AID PICTURE (2008-2009)

Students with need: Need-based aid available for full-time and part-time students. Work study available nights, weekends, and for part-time students.
Students without need: This college awards aid only to students with need.

FINANCIAL AID PROCEDURES

Forms required: FAFSA, institutional form.
Dates and Deadlines: Priority date 4/15; no closing date. Applicants notified on a rolling basis starting 5/15; must reply within 2 week(s) of notification.

CONTACT

Andre Guzman, Director of Financial Aid
7662 Chanute Street, Moses Lake, WA 98837-3299
(509) 793-2034

Cascadia Community College

Bothell, Washington
www.cascadia.edu   Federal Code: 034835

2-year public community college in large town.
Enrollment: 1,971 undergrads, 57% part-time.
Selectivity: Open admission.

BASIC COSTS (2009-2010)

Tuition and fees: $3,052; out-of-state residents $8,272.

FINANCIAL AID PICTURE (2008-2009)

Students with need: Work study available nights, weekends, and for part-time students.

FINANCIAL AID PROCEDURES

Forms required: FAFSA, institutional form.
Dates and Deadlines: Priority date 4/16; no closing date.

CONTACT

Sybil Smith, Director of Student Financial Services
18345 Campus Way, NE, Bothell, WA 98011
(425) 352-8860

Centralia College

Centralia, Washington
www.centralia.edu   Federal Code: 003772

2-year public community college in large town.
Enrollment: 1,325 undergrads.
Selectivity: Open admission; but selective for some programs.

BASIC COSTS (2009-2010)

Tuition and fees: $3,206; out-of-state residents $3,596.
Per-credit charge: $81; out-of-state residents $94.
Additional info: Tuition/fee waivers available for unemployed or children of unemployed.

FINANCIAL AID PICTURE (2008-2009)

Students with need: Need-based aid available for full-time and part-time students.
Students without need: No-need awards available for academics, alumni affiliation, art, athletics, leadership, minority status, music/drama.

FINANCIAL AID PROCEDURES

Forms required: FAFSA, institutional form.
Dates and Deadlines: Priority date 5/1; closing date 9/1. Applicants notified on a rolling basis starting 7/10; must reply within 2 week(s) of notification.

CONTACT

Tracy Dahl, Director of Financial Aid
600 Centralia College Boulevard, Centralia, WA 98531
(360) 736-9391 ext. 234

City University of Seattle

Bellevue, Washington
www.cityu.edu   Federal Code: 013022

Upper-division private university in very large city.
Enrollment: 1,180 undergrads, 41% part-time. 8 full-time freshmen.
Selectivity: Open admission; but selective for some programs.

BASIC COSTS (2009-2010)

Tuition and fees: $15,615.
Per-credit charge: $347.

FINANCIAL AID PICTURE

Students with need: Need-based aid available for full-time and part-time students.
Students without need: No-need awards available for academics.
Additional info: All degree programs approved for veteran's administration education benefits.

FINANCIAL AID PROCEDURES

Forms required: FAFSA, institutional form.
Dates and Deadlines: No deadline. Applicants notified on a rolling basis.

CONTACT

Jean Roberts, Director of Financial Aid
11900 NE First Street, Bellevue, WA 98005
(800) 426-5596

Clark College

Vancouver, Washington
www.clark.edu   Federal Code: 003773

2-year public community college in small city.
Enrollment: 8,024 undergrads, 43% part-time. 936 full-time freshmen.
Selectivity: Open admission; but selective for some programs.

BASIC COSTS (2009-2010)

Tuition and fees: $3,175; out-of-state residents $3,564.
Per-credit charge: $80; out-of-state residents $93.
Additional info: Tuition/fee waivers available for unemployed or children of unemployed.

FINANCIAL AID PICTURE (2008-2009)

Students with need: 55% of average financial aid package awarded as scholarships/grants, 45% awarded as loans/jobs. Need-based aid available for part-time students. Work study available nights, weekends, and for part-time students.
Students without need: No-need awards available for academics, alumni affiliation, art, athletics, job skills, leadership, minority status, music/drama, religious affiliation, ROTC, state/district residency.
Scholarships offered: Clark College Foundation Scholarships; range from $500 to full tuition; recipients selected from those completing Clark's Foundation Standard Scholarship application form.

FINANCIAL AID PROCEDURES

Forms required: FAFSA, institutional form.

Dates and Deadlines: Priority date 5/1; no closing date. Applicants notified on a rolling basis starting 5/1; must reply within 2 week(s) of notification.

CONTACT

Karen Driscoll, Director of Financial Aid
1933 Fort Vancouver Way, Vancouver, WA 98663
(360) 992-2153

Clover Park Technical College

Lakewood, Washington
www.cptc.edu   Federal Code: 015984

2-year public technical college in small city.
Enrollment: 1,413 undergrads.
Selectivity: Open admission; but selective for some programs.

BASIC COSTS (2009-2010)

Tuition and fees: $4,084.
Per-credit charge: $74.
Additional info: Students in programs with high computer usage pay $51 per quarter computer use fee. Online students pay $25 per class course management fee.

FINANCIAL AID PICTURE (2008-2009)

Students with need: Need-based aid available for full-time and part-time students. Work study available nights, weekends, and for part-time students.
Students without need: This college awards aid only to students with need.

FINANCIAL AID PROCEDURES

Forms required: FAFSA, institutional form.
Dates and Deadlines: Priority date 6/15; closing date 8/25. Applicants notified on a rolling basis.

CONTACT

Cheryl Reid, Financial Aid Director
4500 Steilacoom Boulevard, SW, Lakewood, WA 98499-4098
(253) 589-5660

Cornish College of the Arts

Seattle, Washington
www.cornish.edu   Federal Code: 012315

4-year private visual arts and performing arts college in very large city.
Enrollment: 775 undergrads.
Selectivity: Admits 50 to 75% of applicants.

BASIC COSTS (2009-2010)

Tuition and fees: $27,400.
Per-credit charge: $1,125.
Room and board: $9,500.
Additional info: Design majors required to have laptop computer and Adobe software, estimated cost $3,000.

FINANCIAL AID PICTURE (2009-2010)

Students with need: Need-based aid available for full-time and part-time students. Work study available nights, weekends, and for part-time students.
Students without need: No-need awards available for academics.

FINANCIAL AID PROCEDURES

Forms required: FAFSA, institutional form.
Dates and Deadlines: Priority date 3/1; no closing date. Applicants notified on a rolling basis starting 4/15; must reply by 5/1 or within 2 week(s) of notification.
Transfers: No deadline. Applicants notified on a rolling basis; must reply by 2/15.

CONTACT

Monique Theriault, Director for Financial Aid
1000 Lenora Street, Seattle, WA 98121
(206) 726-5014

DeVry University: Federal Way

Federal Way, Washington
www.devry.edu

4-year for-profit university in large city.
Enrollment: 672 undergrads, 37% part-time. 95 full-time freshmen.

BASIC COSTS (2009-2010)

Tuition and fees: $14,800.
Per-credit charge: $575.

FINANCIAL AID PICTURE (2008-2009)

Students with need: Need-based aid available for full-time and part-time students.
Students without need: This college awards aid only to students with need.

FINANCIAL AID PROCEDURES

Forms required: FAFSA.
Dates and Deadlines: No deadline. Applicants notified on a rolling basis.

CONTACT

Scott Sand, Director of Financial Aid
3600 South 344th Way, Federal Way, WA 98001-9558
(253) 943-3060

DigiPen Institute of Technology

Redmond, Washington
www.digipen.edu   Federal Code: 037243

4-year for-profit visual arts and engineering college in large town.
Enrollment: 839 undergrads.
Selectivity: Admits less than 50% of applicants.

BASIC COSTS (2009-2010)

Additional info: Full-time tuition for academic year (based on 20 hours per term), $19,040; required fees, $160; per-credit-hour charge, $476. Full-time tuition for non-resident aliens for academic year (based on 20 hours per term), $24,840; per-credit-hour charge, $621.

FINANCIAL AID PICTURE (2008-2009)

Students with need: Need-based aid available for full-time and part-time students.
Students without need: No-need awards available for job skills, leadership, minority status.
Scholarships offered: Imagine America Scholarship Program: $1,000; based on financial need, grade point average of 2.5 or greater, voluntary community service during the senior year; 10 awarded annually. Women's Scholarship: $1,000; based on gender and academic performance; 10 awarded annually. Military Award Program: $1,000; based on service in the military; 10 awarded annually. First Scholarship: $2,500; based on essay and academic record; 2 awarded annually. First Scholarship: $1,000; based on essay and academic record; 5 awarded annually.
Additional info: Many aid programs are on a first-come, first-served basis.

FINANCIAL AID PROCEDURES

Forms required: FAFSA, institutional form.
Dates and Deadlines: Priority date 4/15; no closing date. Applicants notified on a rolling basis starting 1/1; must reply within 4 week(s) of notification.
Transfers: No deadline. Applicants notified on a rolling basis starting 1/1; must reply within 4 week(s) of notification. Transfer student should meet

with financial aid administrator as soon as they are accepted. Need prior financial aid history to determine eligibility.

CONTACT

Kim King, Director of Financial Aid
5001-150th Avenue Northeast, Redmond, WA 98052
(425) 895-4446

Eastern Washington University

Cheney, Washington
www.ewu.edu   Federal Code: 003775

4-year public university in large town.
Enrollment: 9,919 undergrads, 13% part-time. 1,484 full-time freshmen.
Selectivity: Admits over 75% of applicants.

BASIC COSTS (2009-2010)

Tuition and fees: $5,872; out-of-state residents $14,599.
Room and board: $7,073.

FINANCIAL AID PICTURE (2008-2009)

Students with need: Out of 1,203 full-time freshmen who applied for aid, 831 were judged to have need. Of these, 814 received aid, and 296 had their full need met. Average financial aid package met 91% of need; average scholarship/grant was $6,041; average loan was $2,266. For part-time students, average financial aid package was $7,944.
Students without need: 119 full-time freshmen who did not demonstrate need for aid received scholarships/grants; average award was $2,864. No-need awards available for academics, alumni affiliation, athletics, ROTC, state/district residency.
Scholarships offered: *Merit:* Killin Scholarship; $3,500; three awards; for academic excellence, must have 3.7 GPA and 1100 SAT score (exclusive of Writing). Honors Scholarship; $2,500; 38 awards; for academic excellence. Presidential Scholarship; $2,000; 75 awards; based on GPA, SAT, early admission. *Athletic:* 40 full-time freshmen received athletic scholarships; average amount $6,171.
Cumulative student debt: 68% of graduating class had student loans; average debt was $18,435.
Additional info: The High Demand Scholarship program helps low income students pursue "high demand" careers.

FINANCIAL AID PROCEDURES

Forms required: FAFSA.
Dates and Deadlines: Priority date 2/15; no closing date. Applicants notified on a rolling basis starting 4/1; must reply within 4 week(s) of notification.
Transfers: Educational Opportunity Grant (EOG); financially needy, placebound students with AA or junior status, $2,500 renewable, rolling priority, first-come, first-served at end of each month beginning April 1, ending September 30.

CONTACT

Bruce Defrates, Director of Financial Aid
101 Sutton Hall, Cheney, WA 99004-2447
(509) 359-2314

Everett Community College

Everett, Washington
www.everettcc.edu   Federal Code: 003776

2-year public community college in small city.
Enrollment: 4,282 undergrads, 44% part-time. 453 full-time freshmen.
Selectivity: Open admission; but selective for some programs.

BASIC COSTS (2009-2010)

Tuition and fees: $3,030; out-of-state residents $8,250.
Per-credit charge: $81; out-of-state residents $253.

FINANCIAL AID PICTURE (2008-2009)

Students with need: Need-based aid available for full-time and part-time students. Work study available nights, weekends, and for part-time students. **Students without need:** No-need awards available for academics, alumni affiliation, art, athletics, job skills, leadership, minority status, music/drama, state/district residency.

FINANCIAL AID PROCEDURES

Forms required: FAFSA, institutional form.

Dates and Deadlines: Priority date 5/5; no closing date. Applicants notified on a rolling basis starting 4/15; must reply within 4 week(s) of notification. **Transfers:** No deadline. Applicants notified on a rolling basis starting 6/15; must reply within 4 week(s) of notification.

CONTACT

Laurie Franklin, Director of Student Financial Services
2000 Tower Street, Everett, WA 98201-1352
(425) 388-9280

Evergreen State College
Olympia, Washington
www.evergreen.edu   Federal Code: 008155

4-year public liberal arts college in small city.
Enrollment: 4,385 undergrads, 6% part-time. 659 full-time freshmen.
Selectivity: Admits over 75% of applicants.

BASIC COSTS (2009-2010)

Tuition and fees: $5,959; out-of-state residents $16,987.
Per-credit charge: $180; out-of-state residents $567.
Room and board: $8,052.
Additional info: Tuition/fee waivers available for minority students.

FINANCIAL AID PICTURE (2008-2009)

Students with need: Out of 449 full-time freshmen who applied for aid, 324 were judged to have need. Of these, 311 received aid, and 51 had their full need met. Average financial aid package met 83% of need; average scholarship/grant was $6,783; average loan was $3,280. For part-time students, average financial aid package was $2,921.
Students without need: 70 full-time freshmen who did not demonstrate need for aid received scholarships/grants; average award was $2,906. No-need awards available for academics, art, athletics, state/district residency.
Scholarships offered: 5 full-time freshmen received athletic scholarships; average amount $1,009.
Cumulative student debt: 51% of graduating class had student loans; average debt was $14,310.
Additional info: Application deadline for merit and cultural diversity scholarships February 1. Minority students may apply for tuition and fee waiver scholarships; amount of award equal to in-state tuition and fees. Discount waiver for employees. To meet priority deadline for required financial aid forms, official results of FAFSA must be received by March 15.

FINANCIAL AID PROCEDURES

Forms required: FAFSA, institutional form.
Dates and Deadlines: Priority date 3/15; no closing date. Applicants notified on a rolling basis starting 4/1; must reply within 8 week(s) of notification. **Transfers:** No deadline. Applicants notified on a rolling basis; must reply within 8 week(s) of notification.

CONTACT

Tracy Hall, Director of Financial Aid
2700 Evergreen Parkway NW, Olympia, WA 98505
(360) 867-6205

Gonzaga University
Spokane, Washington
www.gonzaga.edu   Federal Code: 003778

4-year private university and liberal arts college in large city, affiliated with Roman Catholic Church.
Enrollment: 4,655 undergrads, 2% part-time. 1,104 full-time freshmen.
Selectivity: Admits over 75% of applicants. GED not accepted.

BASIC COSTS (2009-2010)

Tuition and fees: $29,675.
Per-credit charge: $850.
Room and board: $7,976.
Additional info: Tuition/fee waivers available for adults.

FINANCIAL AID PICTURE (2008-2009)

Students with need: Out of 869 full-time freshmen who applied for aid, 596 were judged to have need. Of these, 596 received aid, and 180 had their full need met. Average financial aid package met 87% of need; average scholarship/grant was $13,457; average loan was $4,305. For part-time students, average financial aid package was $6,109.
Students without need: 451 full-time freshmen who did not demonstrate need for aid received scholarships/grants; average award was $8,857. No-need awards available for academics, alumni affiliation, athletics, leadership, minority status, music/drama, ROTC.
Scholarships offered: *Merit:* All freshmen are considered for Academic Merit Scholarships: awards range from $3,000 to $10,000. *Athletic:* 38 full-time freshmen received athletic scholarships; average amount $22,913.
Cumulative student debt: 64% of graduating class had student loans; average debt was $19,735.

FINANCIAL AID PROCEDURES

Forms required: FAFSA.
Dates and Deadlines: Priority date 2/1; closing date 6/30. Applicants notified on a rolling basis starting 3/1; must reply by 5/1 or within 3 week(s) of notification.
Transfers: No deadline. Applicants notified on a rolling basis; must reply by 4/15 or within 3 week(s) of notification.

CONTACT

Joan Allbery, Vice President for Administration and Planning
502 East Boone Avenue, Spokane, WA 99258-0001
(509) 313-5816

Grays Harbor College
Aberdeen, Washington
www.ghc.edu   Federal Code: 003779

2-year public community college in large town.
Enrollment: 709 undergrads.
Selectivity: Open admission; but selective for some programs.

BASIC COSTS (2009-2010)

Tuition and fees: $3,296; out-of-state residents $8,516.
Additional info: Tuition/fee waivers available for adults, unemployed or children of unemployed.

FINANCIAL AID PICTURE (2008-2009)

Students with need: Need-based aid available for full-time and part-time students. Work study available nights.
Students without need: No-need awards available for academics, art, athletics, music/drama.

FINANCIAL AID PROCEDURES

Forms required: FAFSA, institutional form.
Dates and Deadlines: Closing date 5/1. Applicants notified on a rolling basis starting 5/15.

CONTACT

Ben Beus, Director of Financial Aid

1620 Edward P Smith Drive, Aberdeen, WA 98520

(360) 538-4081

Green River Community College

Auburn, Washington

www.greenriver.edu   Federal Code: 003780

2-year public community college in large town.

Enrollment: 5,378 undergrads.

Selectivity: Open admission; but selective for some programs.

BASIC COSTS (2009-2010)

Tuition and fees: $3,323; out-of-state residents $3,743.

FINANCIAL AID PICTURE (2008-2009)

Students with need: Need-based aid available for full-time and part-time students.

Students without need: This college awards aid only to students with need.

FINANCIAL AID PROCEDURES

Forms required: FAFSA, institutional form.

Dates and Deadlines: Priority date 4/15; no closing date. Applicants notified on a rolling basis starting 6/30; must reply within 2 week(s) of notification.

CONTACT

Mary Edington, Director of Financial Aid

12401 SE 320th Street, Auburn, WA 98092

(253) 833-9111 ext. 2440

Highline Community College

Des Moines, Washington

www.highline.edu   Federal Code: 003781

2-year public community college in small city.

Enrollment: 4,424 undergrads, 42% part-time. 437 full-time freshmen.

Selectivity: Open admission; but selective for some programs.

BASIC COSTS (2009-2010)

Tuition and fees: $3,000; out-of-state residents $3,390.

Per-credit charge: $81; out-of-state residents $94.

FINANCIAL AID PICTURE (2008-2009)

Students with need: Need-based aid available for full-time and part-time students.

FINANCIAL AID PROCEDURES

Forms required: FAFSA.

Dates and Deadlines: Priority date 5/31; no closing date. Applicants notified on a rolling basis starting 6/1.

CONTACT

Lorraine Odom, Director of Financial Aid

2400 South 240th Street, Des Moines, WA 98198-9800

(206) 878-3710

Lake Washington Technical College

Kirkland, Washington

www.lwtc.edu   Federal Code: 005373

2-year public technical college in large town.

Enrollment: 2,341 undergrads.

Selectivity: Open admission; but selective for some programs.

BASIC COSTS (2009-2010)

Tuition and fees: $1,791; out-of-state residents $1,971.

FINANCIAL AID PICTURE (2008-2009)

Students with need: Need-based aid available for full-time and part-time students.

FINANCIAL AID PROCEDURES

Forms required: FAFSA, institutional form.

Dates and Deadlines: Closing date 4/15. Applicants notified on a rolling basis.

CONTACT

Bill Chaney, Director of Financial Aid

11605 132nd Avenue, NE, Kirkland, WA 98034

Lower Columbia College

Longview, Washington   Federal Code: 003782

www.lowercolumbia.edu   CSS Code: 4402

2-year public community college in small city.

Enrollment: 1,574 undergrads, 35% part-time. 199 full-time freshmen.

Selectivity: Open admission; but selective for some programs.

BASIC COSTS (2009-2010)

Tuition and fees: $3,389; out-of-state residents $4,112.

Per-credit charge: $88; out-of-state residents $111.

Additional info: Full-time "border county" tuition for students in Oregon's Clatsop, Multnomah, Washington, and Columbia counties: $3,352. Tuition/fee waivers available for adults, unemployed or children of unemployed.

FINANCIAL AID PICTURE (2008-2009)

Students with need: 61% of average financial aid package awarded as scholarships/grants, 39% awarded as loans/jobs. Need-based aid available for part-time students.

FINANCIAL AID PROCEDURES

Forms required: CSS PROFILE, institutional form.

Dates and Deadlines: Priority date 5/1; no closing date. Applicants notified on a rolling basis starting 4/21; must reply within 2 week(s) of notification.

Transfers: State-need grant awards transfer with students if previously awarded at another WA institution; SEOG usually not available to transfer students. Student employment, loans, Pell Grant available.

CONTACT

Marisa Greear, Director of Financial Aid

1600 Maple Street, Longview, WA 98632-0310

(360) 442-2311

North Seattle Community College

Seattle, Washington

www.northseattle.edu   Federal Code: 009704

2-year public community college in very large city.

Enrollment: 2,147 undergrads, 52% part-time. 304 full-time freshmen.

Selectivity: Open admission.

BASIC COSTS (2009-2010)

Tuition and fees: $3,210; out-of-state residents $8,430.

Per-credit charge: $81; out-of-state residents $253.

Additional info: Tuition/fee waivers available for adults, unemployed or children of unemployed.

FINANCIAL AID PICTURE (2008-2009)

Students with need: Need-based aid available for full-time and part-time students. Work study available weekends and for part-time students.

FINANCIAL AID PROCEDURES

Forms required: FAFSA, institutional form.

Dates and Deadlines: Priority date 4/30; closing date 8/31. Applicants notified on a rolling basis starting 7/1; must reply within 2 week(s) of notification.

CONTACT

Suzanne Scheldt, Director of Financial Aid

9600 College Way North, Seattle, WA 98103-3599

(206) 528-4700

Northwest College of Art

Poulsbo, Washington

www.nca.edu   Federal Code: 026021

4-year for-profit visual arts college in large town.

Enrollment: 108 full-time undergrads.

BASIC COSTS (2010-2011)

Tuition and fees: $17,350.

Per-credit charge: $1,140.

FINANCIAL AID PICTURE

Students with need: Need-based aid available for full-time and part-time students.

Students without need: No-need awards available for academics, art, state/district residency.

FINANCIAL AID PROCEDURES

Forms required: FAFSA.

Dates and Deadlines: Priority date 3/1; closing date 6/1. Applicants notified on a rolling basis.

CONTACT

Heidi Townsend, Financial Aid Officer

16301 Creative Drive NE, Poulsbo, WA 98370-8651

(360) 697-8136

Northwest Indian College

Bellingham, Washington

www.nwic.edu   Federal Code: 021800

2-year public community college in small town.

Enrollment: 429 undergrads.

Selectivity: Open admission.

BASIC COSTS (2010-2011)

Tuition and fees: $3,720; out-of-state residents $9,588.

Per-credit charge: $95; out-of-state residents $258.

Additional info: Tuition/fee waivers available for minority students.

FINANCIAL AID PICTURE (2008-2009)

Students with need: 98% of average financial aid package awarded as scholarships/grants, 2% awarded as loans/jobs. Need-based aid available for part-time students.

Students without need: No-need awards available for academics.

FINANCIAL AID PROCEDURES

Forms required: FAFSA, institutional form.

Dates and Deadlines: No deadline. Applicants notified on a rolling basis.

Transfers: No deadline. Applicants notified on a rolling basis.

CONTACT

Crystal Bagby, Associate Dean of Student Services

2522 Kwina Road, Bellingham, WA 98226-9217

(360) 676-2772 ext. 4206

Northwest University

Kirkland, Washington

www.northwestu.edu   Federal Code: 003783

4-year private university and liberal arts college in small city, affiliated with Assemblies of God.

Enrollment: 1,046 undergrads, 7% part-time. 188 full-time freshmen.

Selectivity: Admits 50 to 75% of applicants.

BASIC COSTS (2009-2010)

Tuition and fees: $21,994.

Per-credit charge: $905.

Room and board: $6,724.

FINANCIAL AID PICTURE (2008-2009)

Students with need: Out of 164 full-time freshmen who applied for aid, 135 were judged to have need. Of these, 135 received aid, and 27 had their full need met. Average financial aid package met 74% of need; average scholarship/grant was $12,453; average loan was $3,252. For part-time students, average financial aid package was $9,256.

Students without need: 38 full-time freshmen who did not demonstrate need for aid received scholarships/grants; average award was $4,772. No-need awards available for academics, art, athletics, leadership, music/drama, religious affiliation.

Scholarships offered: 10 full-time freshmen received athletic scholarships; average amount $8,507.

Cumulative student debt: 96% of graduating class had student loans; average debt was $27,570.

FINANCIAL AID PROCEDURES

Forms required: FAFSA, institutional form.

Dates and Deadlines: Priority date 3/1; closing date 8/1. Applicants notified on a rolling basis starting 3/3; must reply within 4 week(s) of notification.

CONTACT

Lana Walter, Director of Financial Aid

5520 108th Avenue, NE, Kirkland, WA 98083-0579

(425) 889-5210

Olympic College

Bremerton, Washington

www.olympic.edu   Federal Code: 003784

2-year public community and liberal arts college in large town.

Enrollment: 3,422 undergrads.

Selectivity: Open admission; but selective for some programs.

BASIC COSTS (2009-2010)

Tuition and fees: $3,315; out-of-state residents $3,705.

Per-credit charge: $81; out-of-state residents $94.

FINANCIAL AID PICTURE (2008-2009)

Students with need: 76% of average financial aid package awarded as scholarships/grants, 24% awarded as loans/jobs. Need-based aid available for part-time students. Work study available nights.

Students without need: No-need awards available for academics, state/district residency.

FINANCIAL AID PROCEDURES

Forms required: FAFSA, institutional form.

Dates and Deadlines: Priority date 3/1; no closing date. Applicants notified on a rolling basis starting 6/1; must reply within 2 week(s) of notification.

Transfers: No deadline. Applicants notified on a rolling basis starting 1/2.

CONTACT

Joseph Koroma, Associate Dean, Student Financial Services
1600 Chester Avenue, Bremerton, WA 98337-1699
(360) 475-7163

Pacific Lutheran University

Tacoma, Washington
www.plu.edu   Federal Code: 003785

4-year private university in large city, affiliated with Evangelical Lutheran Church in America.
Enrollment: 3,305 undergrads.
Selectivity: Admits over 75% of applicants.

BASIC COSTS (2010-2011)
Tuition and fees: $29,200.
Per-credit charge: $915.
Room and board: $8,801.

FINANCIAL AID PICTURE (2009-2010)
Students with need: Need-based aid available for full-time and part-time students.
Students without need: No-need awards available for academics, alumni affiliation, art, leadership, music/drama, religious affiliation, ROTC.

FINANCIAL AID PROCEDURES
Forms required: FAFSA.
Dates and Deadlines: Priority date 1/31; no closing date. Applicants notified on a rolling basis starting 3/15; must reply by 5/1 or within 4 week(s) of notification.

CONTACT
Kay Soltis, Director of Financial Aid
Office of Admissions, Tacoma, WA 98447-0003
(253) 535-7134

Peninsula College

Port Angeles, Washington
www.pencol.edu   Federal Code: 003786

2-year public community college in large town.
Enrollment: 1,232 undergrads.
Selectivity: Open admission; but selective for some programs.

BASIC COSTS (2009-2010)
Tuition and fees: $3,012; out-of-state residents $3,402.
Per-credit charge: $81; out-of-state residents $94.
Additional info: Tuition/fee waivers available for unemployed or children of unemployed.

FINANCIAL AID PICTURE (2008-2009)
Students with need: Need-based aid available for full-time and part-time students.
Students without need: No-need awards available for academics, athletics, job skills.

FINANCIAL AID PROCEDURES
Forms required: FAFSA, institutional form.
Dates and Deadlines: Closing date 4/1. Applicants notified on a rolling basis starting 6/1; must reply within 2 week(s) of notification.

CONTACT
Krista Francis, Director of Financial Aid
1502 East Lauridsen Boulevard, Port Angeles, WA 98362
(360) 417-6390

Pierce College

Lakewood, Washington
www.pierce.ctc.edu   Federal Code: 005000

2-year public community college in small city.
Enrollment: 10,205 undergrads.
Selectivity: Open admission; but selective for some programs.

BASIC COSTS (2009-2010)
Tuition and fees: $3,266; out-of-state residents $3,716.
Per-credit charge: $81; out-of-state residents $94.
Additional info: Tuition/fee waivers available for unemployed or children of unemployed.

FINANCIAL AID PICTURE
Students with need: Need-based aid available for full-time and part-time students.
Students without need: No-need awards available for academics, athletics, music/drama.

FINANCIAL AID PROCEDURES
Forms required: FAFSA, institutional form.
Dates and Deadlines: Closing date 5/1. Applicants notified on a rolling basis starting 4/15.

CONTACT
Martin Daniels, Director of Financial Aid
9401 Farwest Drive SW, Lakewood, WA 98498-1999
(253) 964-6544

Renton Technical College

Renton, Washington
www.RTC.edu   Federal Code: 014001

2-year public technical college in large town.
Enrollment: 900 undergrads.
Selectivity: Open admission.

BASIC COSTS (2009-2010)
Tuition and fees: $3,288.

FINANCIAL AID PICTURE (2008-2009)
Students with need: Need-based aid available for full-time and part-time students.
Students without need: This college awards aid only to students with need.

FINANCIAL AID PROCEDURES
Forms required: FAFSA, institutional form.
Dates and Deadlines: Priority date 5/1; no closing date. Applicants notified on a rolling basis.

CONTACT
Debbie Solomon, Director of Financial Aid
3000 NE Fourth Street, Renton, WA 98056-4195
(425) 235-5841

Saint Martin's University

Lacey, Washington
www.stmartin.edu   Federal Code: 003794

4-year private university in large town, affiliated with Roman Catholic Church.
Enrollment: 1,298 undergrads, 19% part-time. 182 full-time freshmen.
Selectivity: Admits over 75% of applicants.

BASIC COSTS (2010-2011)
Tuition and fees: $26,402.
Per-credit charge: $870.
Room and board: $8,660.

FINANCIAL AID PICTURE (2008-2009)
Students with need: Out of 164 full-time freshmen who applied for aid, 148 were judged to have need. Of these, 148 received aid, and 43 had their full need met. Average financial aid package met 81% of need; average scholarship/grant was $16,664; average loan was $2,746. For part-time students, average financial aid package was $13,994.
Students without need: 31 full-time freshmen who did not demonstrate need for aid received scholarships/grants; average award was $9,483. No-need awards available for academics, alumni affiliation, art, athletics, leadership, minority status, music/drama, religious affiliation, ROTC, state/district residency.
Scholarships offered: 22 full-time freshmen received athletic scholarships; average amount $6,982.
Cumulative student debt: 79% of graduating class had student loans; average debt was $27,807.

FINANCIAL AID PROCEDURES
Forms required: FAFSA.
Dates and Deadlines: Priority date 3/1; no closing date. Applicants notified on a rolling basis starting 2/15.

CONTACT
Shelle Riehl, Director, Office of Financial Aid
5300 Pacific Avenue SE, Lacey, WA 98503-7500
(360) 438-4397

Seattle Pacific University
Seattle, Washington
www.spu.edu   Federal Code: 003788

4-year private university in very large city, affiliated with Free Methodist Church of North America.
Enrollment: 3,001 undergrads, 4% part-time. 681 full-time freshmen.
Selectivity: Admits over 75% of applicants.

BASIC COSTS (2010-2011)
Tuition and fees: $28,965.
Per-credit charge: $795.
Room and board: $8,817.

FINANCIAL AID PICTURE (2009-2010)
Students with need: Out of 596 full-time freshmen who applied for aid, 505 were judged to have need. Of these, 505 received aid, and 41 had their full need met. Average financial aid package met 83% of need; average scholarship/grant was $23,290; average loan was $5,033. For part-time students, average financial aid package was $23,002.
Students without need: 147 full-time freshmen who did not demonstrate need for aid received scholarships/grants; average award was $13,632. No-need awards available for academics, alumni affiliation, art, athletics, leadership, minority status, music/drama, religious affiliation, ROTC.
Scholarships offered: 9 full-time freshmen received athletic scholarships; average amount $9,722.
Cumulative student debt: 70% of graduating class had student loans; average debt was $25,799.

FINANCIAL AID PROCEDURES
Forms required: FAFSA.
Dates and Deadlines: Priority date 2/1; no closing date. Applicants notified on a rolling basis starting 3/11; must reply by 5/1 or within 30 week(s) of notification.
Transfers: No deadline. Applicants notified on a rolling basis starting 3/13; must reply by 5/1 or within 4 week(s) of notification.

CONTACT
Jordan Grant, Director of Financial Aid
3307 Third Avenue West, Suite 115, Seattle, WA 98119-1997
(206) 281-2061

Seattle University
Seattle, Washington
www.seattleu.edu   Federal Code: 003790

4-year private university in very large city, affiliated with Roman Catholic Church.
Enrollment: 4,267 undergrads, 5% part-time. 730 full-time freshmen.
Selectivity: Admits 50 to 75% of applicants.

BASIC COSTS (2010-2011)
Tuition and fees: $30,825.
Per-credit charge: $685.
Room and board: $9,315.
Additional info: $200 enrollment deposit, $95 matriculation fee required, $95 per-credit-hour charge for credit by examination. $95 per-credit-hour charge for validation of field experience.

FINANCIAL AID PICTURE (2009-2010)
Students with need: Out of 662 full-time freshmen who applied for aid, 500 were judged to have need. Of these, 498 received aid, and 89 had their full need met. Average financial aid package met 77% of need; average scholarship/grant was $16,022; average loan was $4,363. For part-time students, average financial aid package was $20,705.
Students without need: 2 full-time freshmen who did not demonstrate need for aid received scholarships/grants; average award was $4,935. No-need awards available for academics, alumni affiliation, athletics, leadership, minority status, music/drama, ROTC, state/district residency.
Scholarships offered: *Merit:* Sullivan Leadership Award: full tuition, room and board for 4 years, for entering freshmen of Oregon, Washington, or Idaho residency; service, leadership, strong academics (3.5 GPA) important, 6 awarded. Presidential Scholarship: $11,000 annually for 4 years. Trustee Scholarship: $8,000 annually for 4 years. Campion Scholarship: $5,000 annually for 4 years; for first-time freshmen of U.S. citizenship or permanent resident status, strong academic and extracurricular records important. *Athletic:* 5 full-time freshmen received athletic scholarships; average amount $10,838.
Cumulative student debt: 79% of graduating class had student loans; average debt was $26,665.

FINANCIAL AID PROCEDURES
Forms required: FAFSA.
Dates and Deadlines: Priority date 2/1; no closing date. Applicants notified on a rolling basis starting 3/21; must reply by 5/1 or within 2 week(s) of notification.
Transfers: Closing date 3/1.

CONTACT
Janet Cantelon, Director of Student Financial Aid
901 12th Avenue, Seattle, WA 98122-4340
(206) 296-2000

Shoreline Community College
Shoreline, Washington
www.shoreline.edu   Federal Code: 003791

2-year public community college in small city.
Enrollment: 5,988 undergrads.
Selectivity: Open admission; but selective for some programs.

BASIC COSTS (2009-2010)
Tuition and fees: $3,152, out-of-state residents $5,811.

FINANCIAL AID PICTURE (2008-2009)

Students with need: Work study available nights, weekends, and for part-time students.

Additional info: Tuition and/or fee waiver for students with need on space-available basis.

FINANCIAL AID PROCEDURES

Forms required: FAFSA, institutional form.

Dates and Deadlines: Closing date 3/31. Applicants notified on a rolling basis starting 8/1; must reply within 3 week(s) of notification.

CONTACT

Ted Haase, Director of Financial Services
16101 Greenwood Avenue North, Seattle, WA 98133
(206) 546-4762

Skagit Valley College
Mount Vernon, Washington
www.skagit.edu   Federal Code: 003792

2-year public community college in large town.

Enrollment: 5,078 full-time undergrads.

Selectivity: Open admission.

BASIC COSTS (2009-2010)

Tuition and fees: $3,077; out-of-state residents $4,052.

Per-credit charge: $80; out-of-state residents $93.

Room only: $3,420.

Additional info: Tuition/fee waivers available for unemployed or children of unemployed.

FINANCIAL AID PICTURE (2009-2010)

Students with need: Need-based aid available for full-time and part-time students. Work study available nights, weekends, and for part-time students.

Students without need: This college awards aid only to students with need.

FINANCIAL AID PROCEDURES

Forms required: FAFSA, institutional form.

Dates and Deadlines: Priority date 5/1; no closing date. Applicants notified on a rolling basis starting 7/1; must reply within 2 week(s) of notification.

CONTACT

Steve Epperson, Financial Aid Director
2405 East College Way, Mount Vernon, WA 98273
(360) 416-7666

South Puget Sound Community College
Olympia, Washington
www.spscc.ctc.edu   Federal Code: 005372

2-year public community college in small city.

Enrollment: 3,240 undergrads, 41% part-time. 303 full-time freshmen.

Selectivity: Open admission; but selective for some programs.

BASIC COSTS (2010-2011)

Tuition and fees: $3,026; out-of-state residents $3,503.

Per-credit charge: $84; out-of-state residents $102.

FINANCIAL AID PICTURE (2008-2009)

Students with need: Need-based aid available for full-time and part-time students.

Students without need: No-need awards available for academics, athletics.

FINANCIAL AID PROCEDURES

Forms required: FAFSA, institutional form.

Dates and Deadlines: Priority date 5/1; closing date 6/27. Applicants notified on a rolling basis starting 7/10; must reply within 2 week(s) of notification.

CONTACT

Carla Idohl-Corwin, Dean of Student Financial Services
2011 Mottman Road, SW, Olympia, WA 98512-6218
(360) 596-5232

South Seattle Community College
Seattle, Washington
www.southseattle.edu   Federal Code: 009706

2-year public community college in very large city.

Enrollment: 3,715 undergrads.

Selectivity: Open admission; but selective for some programs.

BASIC COSTS (2009-2010)

Tuition and fees: $3,045; out-of-state residents $8,265.

Additional info: Tuition/fee waivers available for unemployed or children of unemployed.

FINANCIAL AID PICTURE (2008-2009)

Students with need: Need-based aid available for full-time and part-time students.

Students without need: No-need awards available for academics, state/district residency.

FINANCIAL AID PROCEDURES

Forms required: FAFSA, institutional form.

Dates and Deadlines: Priority date 4/16; no closing date. Applicants notified on a rolling basis starting 7/1.

CONTACT

Patricia Billings, Financial Aid Director
6000 16th Avenue, SW, Seattle, WA 98106-1499
(206) 764-5317

Spokane Falls Community College
Spokane, Washington
www.spokanefalls.edu   Federal Code: 009544

2-year public community college in small city.

Enrollment: 5,850 undergrads.

Selectivity: Open admission; but selective for some programs.

BASIC COSTS (2009-2010)

Tuition and fees: $3,040; out-of-state residents $3,623.

Per-credit charge: $81; out-of-state residents $109.

Additional info: Tuition/fee waivers available for unemployed or children of unemployed.

FINANCIAL AID PICTURE

Students with need: Need-based aid available for full-time and part-time students.

Students without need: This college awards aid only to students with need.

FINANCIAL AID PROCEDURES

Forms required: FAFSA, institutional form.

Dates and Deadlines: Priority date 4/1; no closing date. Applicants notified on a rolling basis starting 5/15; must reply within 2 week(s) of notification.

CONTACT

Assistant Dean of Student Services for Financial Aid
3410 West Fort George Wright Drive, Spokane, WA 99224
(509) 533-3550

Trinity Lutheran College
Everett, Washington
www.tlc.edu   Federal Code: 013525

4-year private Bible and liberal arts college in small city, affiliated with Lutheran Church.
Enrollment: 119 undergrads.

BASIC COSTS (2009-2010)
Tuition and fees: $19,425.
Per-credit charge: $790.
Room only: $6,570.
Additional info: Lunch-only meal plan (5 days per week) for academic year, $900.

FINANCIAL AID PICTURE (2009-2010)
Students with need: Need-based aid available for full-time and part-time students. Work study available nights, weekends, and for part-time students.
Students without need: No-need awards available for academics, alumni affiliation, art, leadership, music/drama.

FINANCIAL AID PROCEDURES
Forms required: FAFSA, institutional form.
Dates and Deadlines: Priority date 3/1; no closing date. Applicants notified on a rolling basis starting 3/15; must reply within 2 week(s) of notification.
Transfers: No deadline. Applicants notified on a rolling basis starting 3/15; must reply within 2 week(s) of notification.

CONTACT
Susan Dalgleish, Director of Financial Aid
2802 Wetmore Avenue, Everett, WA 98201
(425) 961-5514

University of Puget Sound
Tacoma, Washington
www.pugetsound.edu   Federal Code: 003797

4-year private liberal arts college in small city.
Enrollment: 2,596 undergrads, 1% part-time. 721 full-time freshmen.
Selectivity: Admits 50 to 75% of applicants.

BASIC COSTS (2010-2011)
Tuition and fees: $37,225.
Per-credit charge: $1,168.
Room and board: $9,650.

FINANCIAL AID PICTURE (2009-2010)
Students with need: Out of 551 full-time freshmen who applied for aid, 465 were judged to have need. Of these, 465 received aid, and 136 had their full need met. Average financial aid package met 85% of need; average scholarship/grant was $23,361; average loan was $4,785. Need-based aid available for part-time students.
Students without need: 172 full-time freshmen who did not demonstrate need for aid received scholarships/grants; average award was $10,172. No-need awards available for academics, alumni affiliation, art, leadership, music/drama, religious affiliation.
Scholarships offered: Trustee Scholarships: $12,000 annually; President's Scholarships: $9,000 annually; Dean's Scholarships: $7,000 annually. Incoming students eligible based on admission application, academic performance in high school, and standardized test scores; renewable for 3 additional years.
Cumulative student debt: 63% of graduating class had student loans; average debt was $29,514.
Additional info: Cooperative education allows qualified upperclassmen to alternate semesters of full-time study and full-time work.

FINANCIAL AID PROCEDURES
Forms required: FAFSA. Students applying for Early Decision must complete the CSS PROFILE for notification of need-based financial aid eligibility.
Dates and Deadlines: Priority date 2/1; no closing date. Applicants notified on a rolling basis starting 3/15; must reply by 5/1 or within 2 week(s) of notification.
Transfers: Priority date 3/1; no deadline. Applicants notified on a rolling basis starting 3/15.

CONTACT
Maggie Mittuch, Associate Vice President of Student Financial Services
1500 North Warner Street, Tacoma, WA 98416-1062
(253) 879-3214

University of Washington
Seattle, Washington
www.washington.edu   Federal Code: 003798

4-year public university in very large city.
Enrollment: 30,554 undergrads, 8% part-time. 6,115 full-time freshmen.
Selectivity: Admits 50 to 75% of applicants.

BASIC COSTS (2009-2010)
Tuition and fees: $7,692; out-of-state residents $24,367.
Room and board: $8,949.
Additional info: Required fees include mandatory intramural bond fee of $105.

FINANCIAL AID PICTURE (2009-2010)
Students with need: Need-based aid available for full-time and part-time students. Work study available nights, weekends, and for part-time students.
Students without need: No-need awards available for academics, alumni affiliation, art, athletics, leadership, music/drama, ROTC.
Additional info: Tuition not due until third week of term.

FINANCIAL AID PROCEDURES
Forms required: FAFSA.
Dates and Deadlines: Priority date 2/28; no closing date. Applicants notified by 3/31; must reply within 3 week(s) of notification.

CONTACT
Kay Lewis, Director of Student Financial Aid
1410 Northeast Campus Parkway, Box 355852, Seattle, WA 98195-5852
(206) 543-6101

University of Washington Bothell
Bothell, Washington
www.uwb.edu

4-year public university in large town.
Enrollment: 2,329 undergrads, 33% part-time. 283 full-time freshmen.
Selectivity: Admits over 75% of applicants.

BASIC COSTS (2009-2010)
Tuition and fees: $7,575; out-of-state residents $24,250.

FINANCIAL AID PICTURE (2009-2010)
Students with need: Out of 195 full-time freshmen who applied for aid, 135 were judged to have need. Of these, 126 received aid, and 22 had their full need met. Average financial aid package met 78% of need; average scholarship/grant was $9,900; average loan was $4,300. For part-time students, average financial aid package was $8,000.
Cumulative student debt: 47% of graduating class had student loans; average debt was $16,560.

FINANCIAL AID PROCEDURES
Forms required: FAFSA.

Dates and Deadlines: Priority date 2/28; no closing date. Applicants notified by 4/1; must reply within 3 week(s) of notification.

CONTACT

Dannett Iyall, Assistant Director, Financial Aid
18115 Campus Way NE, Bothell, WA 98011-8246
(425) 352-5326

University of Washington Tacoma

Tacoma, Washington
www.tacoma.washington.edu   Federal Code: 003798

4-year public university and branch campus college in small city.
Enrollment: 2,530 undergrads, 21% part-time. 200 full-time freshmen.
Selectivity: Admits over 75% of applicants.

BASIC COSTS (2009-2010)
Tuition and fees: $7,575; out-of-state residents $24,250.

FINANCIAL AID PICTURE
Students with need: Need-based aid available for full-time and part-time students.
Students without need: No-need awards available for academics.

CONTACT

Shari King, Associate Director of Financial Aid and Veterans Affairs
Campus Box 358400, Tacoma, WA 98402-3100
(253) 692-4400

Walla Walla University

College Place, Washington
www.wallawalla.edu   Federal Code: 003799

4-year private university and liberal arts college in large town, affiliated with Seventh-day Adventists.
Enrollment: 1,570 undergrads, 7% part-time. 313 full-time freshmen.
Selectivity: Admits over 75% of applicants.

BASIC COSTS (2009-2010)
Tuition and fees: $22,794.
Per-credit charge: $590.
Room and board: $4,710.

FINANCIAL AID PICTURE (2008-2009)
Students with need: Need-based aid available for full-time and part-time students.
Students without need: No-need awards available for academics, leadership, music/drama.

FINANCIAL AID PROCEDURES
Forms required: FAFSA, institutional form.
Dates and Deadlines: Priority date 4/30; no closing date. Applicants notified on a rolling basis starting 3/15.

CONTACT

Cassie Ragenovich, Director of Student Financial Services
204 South College Avenue, College Place, WA 99324-3000
(509) 527-2815

Washington State University

Pullman, Washington
www.wsu.edu   Federal Code: 003800

4-year public university in large town.
Enrollment: 21,312 undergrads, 13% part-time. 3,677 full-time freshmen.
Selectivity: Admits over 75% of applicants.

BASIC COSTS (2009-2010)
Tuition and fees: $8,489; out-of-state residents $19,565.
Room and board: $9,330.

FINANCIAL AID PICTURE (2008-2009)
Students with need: Out of 2,642 full-time freshmen who applied for aid, 1,624 were judged to have need. Of these, 1,619 received aid, and 512 had their full need met. Average financial aid package met 77% of need; average scholarship/grant was $6,890; average loan was $3,268. For part-time students, average financial aid package was $8,789.
Students without need: 713 full-time freshmen who did not demonstrate need for aid received scholarships/grants; average award was $3,751. No-need awards available for academics, alumni affiliation, art, athletics, job skills, leadership, minority status, music/drama, religious affiliation, ROTC, state/district residency.
Scholarships offered: *Merit:* Regents Scholars Program: $10,000 per academic year for four years. Regents Semifinalists: $6,000 per academic year for four years; based on entering freshmen who are Washington residents or meet Native American tribal affiliation criteria and who apply for admission and scholarships by the University?s priority deadline will be considered for the awards; based on high school academic achievement and standardized test scores; community, civic, and co-curricular involvement and educator or tribal council recommendations; number of awards varies annually. Lighty Leadership Award: A full tuition scholarship for out-of-state students. Selection is based on academic achievement and community involvement, and preference is given to applicants from Northern California. Number of awards varies annually. University Achievement Award: Awards generally range from $2,000 to $4,000 and are granted to Washington high school students who meet certain GPA and SAT/ACT requirements and apply for freshman admission to the Pullman campus by the January 31 priority application date. Awards are renewable for one year, contingent upon academic performance. Number of awards varies annually. Cougar Academic Award: Top students from out of state may be eligible for two levels of scholarships: $4,000 or $9,000 per academic year, renewable for three years, contingent upon academic performance. Selection is based on high school grades, standardized test scores, and admission to the University as a freshman. Number of awards varies annually. *Athletic:* 94 full-time freshmen received athletic scholarships; average amount $17,026.

FINANCIAL AID PROCEDURES
Forms required: FAFSA.
Dates and Deadlines: Priority date 2/15; no closing date. Applicants notified on a rolling basis starting 4/15.
Transfers: No deadline. Applicants notified on a rolling basis starting 3/15. The Transfer Achievement Award is offered to entering transfer students who have already earned their associate degree and are attending the Pullman campus. Must be residents of Washington, have a minimum grade point average of 3.0, and demonstrate financial need through the FAFSA. Award is valued at $2,500 and renewable for a second year.

CONTACT

Chio Flores, Director of Student Financial Aid and Scholarships
370 Lighty Student Services Bldg, Pullman, WA 99164-1067
(509) 335-9711

Wenatchee Valley College

Wenatchee, Washington
www.wvc.edu   Federal Code: 003801

2-year public community college in large town.
Enrollment: 3,175 undergrads, 17% part-time. 515 full-time freshmen.
Selectivity: Open admission; but selective for some programs.

BASIC COSTS (2009-2010)
Tuition and fees: $3,021; out-of-state residents $3,419.
Per-credit charge: $81; out-of-state residents $94.

Additional info: Tuition/fee waivers available for adults, unemployed or children of unemployed.

FINANCIAL AID PICTURE

Students with need: Need-based aid available for full-time and part-time students.

Students without need: No-need awards available for academics, athletics.

FINANCIAL AID PROCEDURES

Forms required: FAFSA.

Dates and Deadlines: Closing date 3/1. Applicants notified by 7/2; must reply within 3 week(s) of notification.

Transfers: Priority date 3/1. Applicants notified on a rolling basis.

CONTACT

Kevin Berg, Financial Aid Director
1300 Fifth Street, Wenatchee, WA 98801-1799
(509) 682-6845

Western Washington University

Bellingham, Washington
www.wwu.edu   Federal Code: 003802

4-year public university in small city.

Enrollment: 13,249 undergrads, 7% part-time. 2,666 full-time freshmen.

Selectivity: Admits 50 to 75% of applicants.

BASIC COSTS (2009-2010)

Tuition and fees: $6,159; out-of-state residents $17,190.

Room and board: $8,394.

Additional info: Tuition/fee waivers available for adults, minority students.

FINANCIAL AID PICTURE (2009-2010)

Students with need: Out of 2,032 full-time freshmen who applied for aid, 1,151 were judged to have need. Of these, 1,106 received aid, and 280 had their full need met. Average financial aid package met 88% of need; average scholarship/grant was $7,779; average loan was $3,521. For part-time students, average financial aid package was $10,074.

Students without need: 37 full-time freshmen who did not demonstrate need for aid received scholarships/grants; average award was $1,365. No-need awards available for academics, alumni affiliation, art, athletics, job skills, leadership, minority status, music/drama, state/district residency.

Scholarships offered: 16 full-time freshmen received athletic scholarships; average amount $5,871.

Cumulative student debt: 50% of graduating class had student loans; average debt was $15,929.

Additional info: Short-term student loans ranging from $100 to $1,000 available on a quarterly basis.

FINANCIAL AID PROCEDURES

Forms required: FAFSA.

Dates and Deadlines: Priority date 2/15; no closing date. Applicants notified on a rolling basis starting 3/20; must reply within 3 week(s) of notification.

Transfers: No deadline. Applicants notified on a rolling basis starting 3/20; must reply within 3 week(s) of notification. Some state aid not available for out-of-state transfer students.

CONTACT

Clara Capron, Director of Financial Aid
516 High Street, Bellingham, WA 98225-9009
(360) 650-3470

Whatcom Community College

Bellingham, Washington
www.whatcom.ctc.edu   Federal Code: 010364

2-year public community college in small city.

Enrollment: 4,690 undergrads.

Selectivity: Open admission.

BASIC COSTS (2009-2010)

Tuition and fees: $3,105; out-of-state residents $8,325.

Per-credit charge: $87; out-of-state residents $259.

FINANCIAL AID PICTURE (2008-2009)

Students with need: Need-based aid available for full-time and part-time students. Work study available nights.

Students without need: No-need awards available for academics, athletics, state/district residency.

FINANCIAL AID PROCEDURES

Forms required: FAFSA, institutional form.

Dates and Deadlines: Priority date 3/1; no closing date. Applicants notified on a rolling basis starting 7/1; must reply within 3 week(s) of notification.

CONTACT

Jack Wollens, Director of Financial Aid
237 West Kellogg Road, Bellingham, WA 98226
(360) 383-3010

Whitman College

Walla Walla, Washington
www.whitman.edu   Federal Code: 003803
                                CSS Code: 4951

4-year private liberal arts college in large town.

Enrollment: 1,491 undergrads, 1% part-time. 396 full-time freshmen.

Selectivity: Admits less than 50% of applicants.

BASIC COSTS (2010-2011)

Tuition and fees: $38,770.

Per-credit charge: $1,602.

Room and board: $9,720.

FINANCIAL AID PICTURE (2009-2010)

Students with need: Out of 282 full-time freshmen who applied for aid, 194 were judged to have need. Of these, 194 received aid, and 163 had their full need met. Average financial aid package met 94% of need; average scholarship/grant was $24,003; average loan was $4,145. For part-time students, average financial aid package was $24,404.

Students without need: 122 full-time freshmen who did not demonstrate need for aid received scholarships/grants; average award was $9,775. No-need awards available for academics, art, leadership, minority status, music/drama, religious affiliation, state/district residency.

Cumulative student debt: 49% of graduating class had student loans; average debt was $17,955.

FINANCIAL AID PROCEDURES

Forms required: FAFSA, CSS PROFILE.

Dates and Deadlines: Priority date 11/15; closing date 2/1. Applicants notified on a rolling basis starting 12/22; must reply within 2 week(s) of notification.

Transfers: Closing date 3/1. Applicants notified by 4/22; must reply by 5/15.

CONTACT

Tony Cabasco, Dean of Admission and Financial Aid
345 Boyer Avenue, Walla Walla, WA 99362-2046
(509) 527-5178

Whitworth University

Spokane, Washington
www.whitworth.edu   Federal Code: 003804

4-year private liberal arts college in large city, affiliated with Presbyterian Church (USA).

Enrollment: 2,413 undergrads, 5% part-time. 555 full-time freshmen.
Selectivity: Admits 50 to 75% of applicants.

BASIC COSTS (2010-2011)
Tuition and fees: $30,204.
Per-credit charge: $1,245.
Room and board: $8,450.
Additional info: Tuition/fee waivers available for minority students.

FINANCIAL AID PICTURE (2009-2010)
Students with need: Out of 484 full-time freshmen who applied for aid, 427 were judged to have need. Of these, 426 received aid, and 99 had their full need met. Average financial aid package met 86% of need; average scholarship/grant was $19,575; average loan was $4,243. For part-time students, average financial aid package was $8,907.
Students without need: 106 full-time freshmen who did not demonstrate need for aid received scholarships/grants; average award was $10,706. No-need awards available for academics, art, music/drama, ROTC.
Scholarships offered: $4,000 to $8,500; based on GPA, SAT/ACT scores, class rank.
Cumulative student debt: 68% of graduating class had student loans; average debt was $18,801.

FINANCIAL AID PROCEDURES
Forms required: FAFSA.
Dates and Deadlines: Priority date 3/1; no closing date. Applicants notified on a rolling basis starting 3/1; must reply by 5/1 or within 4 week(s) of notification.
Transfers: Priority date 4/1; no deadline. Applicants notified on a rolling basis starting 3/1; must reply by 5/1.

CONTACT
Wendy Olson, Director of Financial Aid
300 West Hawthorne Road, Spokane, WA 99251-0002
(509) 777-3215

Yakima Valley Community College

Yakima, Washington
www.yvcc.edu   Federal Code: 003805

2-year public community college in small city.
Enrollment: 2,675 undergrads.
Selectivity: Open admission; but selective for some programs.

BASIC COSTS (2009-2010)
Tuition and fees: $3,233; out-of-state residents $3,623.
Per-credit charge: $81; out-of-state residents $94.
Additional info: Tuition/fee waivers available for unemployed or children of unemployed.

FINANCIAL AID PICTURE (2009-2010)
Students with need: Need-based aid available for full-time and part-time students. Work study available nights, weekends, and for part-time students.
Students without need: No-need awards available for academics, athletics.

FINANCIAL AID PROCEDURES
Forms required: FAFSA.
Dates and Deadlines: Priority date 5/1; no closing date. Applicants notified on a rolling basis starting 8/1; must reply within 2 week(s) of notification.
Transfers: No deadline. Applicants notified on a rolling basis starting 8/1; must reply within 2 week(s) of notification.

CONTACT
Denise Anderson, Registrar and Director for Enrollment Services
PO Box 22520, Yakima, WA 98907-2520
(509) 574-6855

West Virginia

Alderson-Broaddus College

Philippi, West Virginia
www.ab.edu   Federal Code: 003806

4-year private liberal arts college in small town, affiliated with American Baptist Churches in the USA.

Enrollment: 582 undergrads, 3% part-time. 162 full-time freshmen.
Selectivity: Admits 50 to 75% of applicants.

BASIC COSTS (2010-2011)
Tuition and fees: $22,204.
Per-credit charge: $733.
Room and board: $7,222.

FINANCIAL AID PICTURE (2009-2010)
Students with need: Out of 161 full-time freshmen who applied for aid, 153 were judged to have need. Of these, 152 received aid, and 50 had their full need met. Average financial aid package met 85% of need; average scholarship/grant was $17,914; average loan was $4,450. For part-time students, average financial aid package was $9,464.
Students without need: 9 full-time freshmen who did not demonstrate need for aid received scholarships/grants; average award was $11,039. No-need awards available for academics, athletics, music/drama.
Scholarships offered: *Merit:* IMPACT Scholarship; $15,000; 25 ACT or 1150 SAT and 3.5 GPA required for consideration; 5 awards. *Athletic:* 5 full-time freshmen received athletic scholarships; average amount $6,200.
Cumulative student debt: 98% of graduating class had student loans; average debt was $29,613.

FINANCIAL AID PROCEDURES
Forms required: FAFSA, state aid form.
Dates and Deadlines: Priority date 3/1; no closing date. Applicants notified on a rolling basis starting 2/15; must reply within 2 week(s) of notification.

CONTACT
Brian Weingart, Director of Financial Aid
101 College Hill Drive, Philippi, WV 26416
(304) 457-6354

American Public University System

Charles Town, West Virginia
www.apus.edu   Federal Code: 038193

4-year for-profit virtual university in small town.
Enrollment: 47,258 undergrads.
Selectivity: Open admission.

BASIC COSTS (2009-2010)
Tuition and fees: $7,500.
Per-credit charge: $250.
Additional info: Distance learning only.

FINANCIAL AID PICTURE
Students with need: Need-based aid available for full-time and part-time students.

Additional info: Students should complete a Federal Student Aid Intent Form and register for classes at least 37 days prior to start to allow sufficient time for financial aid process.

FINANCIAL AID PROCEDURES
Forms required: FAFSA, institutional form.
Dates and Deadlines: No deadline. Applicants notified on a rolling basis; must reply within 14 week(s) of notification.
Transfers: Must reply within 14 week(s) of notification. Students should ensure that financial aid is processed and confirmed at least 10-14 days prior to beginning a semester.

CONTACT
Gary Spoales, Associate Vice President, Financial Services
111 West Congress Street, Charles Town, WV 25414
(877) 777-9081

Appalachian Bible College
Bradley, West Virginia
www.abc.edu   Federal Code: 007544

4-year private Bible college in rural community, affiliated with nondenominational tradition.
Enrollment: 258 undergrads.
Selectivity: Admits over 75% of applicants.

BASIC COSTS (2009-2010)
Tuition and fees: $10,390.
Per-credit charge: $365.
Room and board: $5,400.

FINANCIAL AID PICTURE (2008-2009)
Students with need: Need-based aid available for full-time and part-time students.
Students without need: This college awards aid only to students with need.
Scholarships offered: Scholastic Achievement Scholarship; $1,500 per year; based on 26 ACT or 1180 SAT (exclusive of Writing).

FINANCIAL AID PROCEDURES
Forms required: FAFSA, state aid form, institutional form.
Dates and Deadlines: Closing date 6/15. Applicants notified on a rolling basis starting 6/15; must reply by 8/1 or within 4 week(s) of notification.

CONTACT
Cindi Turner, Director of Financial Aid
PO Box ABC, Bradley, WV 25818-1353
(304) 877-6428 ext. 3247

Bethany College
Bethany, West Virginia
www.bethanywv.edu   Federal Code: 003808

4-year private liberal arts college in rural community, affiliated with Christian Church (Disciples of Christ).
Enrollment: 822 undergrads, 1% part-time. 263 full-time freshmen.
Selectivity: Admits over 75% of applicants.

BASIC COSTS (2009-2010)
Tuition and fees: $21,465.
Room and board: $8,700.

FINANCIAL AID PICTURE (2008-2009)
Students with need: Out of 261 full-time freshmen who applied for aid, 237 were judged to have need. Of these, 237 received aid, and 8 had their full need met. Average financial aid package met 81% of need; average scholarship/grant was $14,960; average loan was $5,108.

Students without need: 30 full-time freshmen who did not demonstrate need for aid received scholarships/grants; average award was $6,075.
Additional info: Scholarships available for travel program.

FINANCIAL AID PROCEDURES
Forms required: FAFSA, state aid form.
Dates and Deadlines: Priority date 3/1; no closing date. Applicants notified on a rolling basis starting 3/1; must reply within 2 week(s) of notification.
Transfers: No deadline.

CONTACT
Karina Dayich, Director of Admission and Student Financial Planning
Office of Admission, Bethany, WV 26032-0428
(304) 829-7611

Bluefield State College
Bluefield, West Virginia
www.bluefieldstate.edu   Federal Code: 003809

4-year public liberal arts and technical college in large town.
Enrollment: 1,868 undergrads, 15% part-time. 315 full-time freshmen.
Selectivity: Admits over 75% of applicants.

BASIC COSTS (2009-2010)
Tuition and fees: $4,596; out-of-state residents $9,000.
Per-credit charge: $192; out-of-state residents $375.
Additional info: Tuition for students residing in border counties is $6,288.

FINANCIAL AID PICTURE (2009-2010)
Students with need: Out of 265 full-time freshmen who applied for aid, 230 were judged to have need. Of these, 230 received aid, and 130 had their full need met. Average financial aid package met 70% of need; average scholarship/grant was $3,500; average loan was $3,600. For part-time students, average financial aid package was $3,100.
Students without need: 57 full-time freshmen who did not demonstrate need for aid received scholarships/grants; average award was $1,400. No-need awards available for academics, alumni affiliation, art, athletics, job skills, leadership, minority status, state/district residency.
Scholarships offered: 22 full-time freshmen received athletic scholarships; average amount $3,100.
Cumulative student debt: 49% of graduating class had student loans; average debt was $18,000.

FINANCIAL AID PROCEDURES
Forms required: FAFSA, institutional form.
Dates and Deadlines: Priority date 3/1; no closing date. Applicants notified on a rolling basis starting 5/1.
Transfers: No deadline.

CONTACT
Tom Ilse, Director of Financial Aid
219 Rock Street, Bluefield, WV 24701
(304) 327-4020

Concord University
Athens, West Virginia
www.concord.edu   Federal Code: 003810

4-year public university and liberal arts college in small town.
Enrollment: 2,634 undergrads, 11% part-time. 608 full-time freshmen.
Selectivity: Admits 50 to 75% of applicants.

BASIC COSTS (2009-2010)
Tuition and fees: $4,974; out-of-state residents $11,050.
Per-credit charge: $207; out-of-state residents $460.
Room and board: $6,766.

FINANCIAL AID PICTURE (2008-2009)

Students with need: 43% of average financial aid package awarded as scholarships/grants, 57% awarded as loans/jobs. Need-based aid available for part-time students.

Students without need: No-need awards available for academics, alumni affiliation, art, athletics, job skills, leadership, minority status, music/drama, state/district residency.

Additional info: March 1 priority deadline for state forms. April 15 priority deadline for FAFSA.

FINANCIAL AID PROCEDURES

Forms required: FAFSA, state aid form, institutional form.

Dates and Deadlines: Applicants notified on a rolling basis starting 3/1; must reply within 2 week(s) of notification.

CONTACT

Director of Financial Aid
PO Box 1000, Athens, WV 24712-1000
(304) 384-6069

Davis and Elkins College

Elkins, West Virginia
www.davisandelkins.edu   Federal Code: 003811

4-year private liberal arts college in small town, affiliated with Presbyterian Church (USA).

Enrollment: 648 undergrads, 4% part-time. 234 full-time freshmen.

Selectivity: Admits 50 to 75% of applicants.

BASIC COSTS (2010-2011)

Tuition and fees: $21,120.

Per-credit charge: $700.

Room and board: $7,750.

Additional info: Reduced tuition for qualified students in 7 surrounding counties through Highland Scholars Program.

FINANCIAL AID PICTURE (2009-2010)

Students with need: Average financial aid package met 85% of need; average scholarship/grant was $4,406; average loan was $3,289. For part-time students, average financial aid package was $13,856.

Students without need: No-need awards available for academics, alumni affiliation, art, athletics, leadership, minority status, music/drama, religious affiliation.

Cumulative student debt: 83% of graduating class had student loans; average debt was $17,650.

FINANCIAL AID PROCEDURES

Forms required: FAFSA.

Dates and Deadlines: Priority date 3/1; no closing date. Applicants notified on a rolling basis starting 5/1; must reply within 2 week(s) of notification.

Transfers: No deadline. Applicants notified on a rolling basis starting 5/1; must reply within 2 week(s) of notification.

CONTACT

Matthew Summers
100 Campus Drive, Elkins, WV 26241-3996
(304) 637-1373

Eastern West Virginia Community and Technical College

Moorefield, West Virginia
www.eastern.wvnet.edu

2-year public community and technical college in rural community.

Enrollment: 624 undergrads, 75% part-time. 85 full-time freshmen.

Selectivity: Open admission.

BASIC COSTS (2009-2010)

Tuition and fees: $2,064; out-of-state residents $6,816.

Per-credit charge: $86; out-of-state residents $284.

FINANCIAL AID PICTURE

Students with need: Need-based aid available for full-time and part-time students.

FINANCIAL AID PROCEDURES

Forms required: FAFSA, institutional form.

Dates and Deadlines: Priority date 6/1; no closing date. Applicants notified on a rolling basis; must reply within 2 week(s) of notification.

CONTACT

Amanda Sites, Director of Financial Aid
316 Eastern Drive, PO Box 59, Moorefield, WV 26836
(304) 434-8000

Fairmont State University

Fairmont, West Virginia
www.fairmontstate.edu   Federal Code: 003812

4-year public university in large town.

Enrollment: 4,170 undergrads, 12% part-time. 800 full-time freshmen.

Selectivity: Admits over 75% of applicants.

BASIC COSTS (2009-2010)

Tuition and fees: $4,952; out-of-state residents $10,684.

Per-credit charge: $206; out-of-state residents $445.

Room and board: $6,683.

Additional info: Tuition/fee waivers available for adults, minority students.

FINANCIAL AID PICTURE (2008-2009)

Students with need: Need-based aid available for full-time and part-time students. Work study available nights, weekends, and for part-time students.

Students without need: This college awards aid only to students with need.

FINANCIAL AID PROCEDURES

Forms required: FAFSA.

Dates and Deadlines: Closing date 3/1. Applicants notified on a rolling basis starting 4/1; must reply within 2 week(s) of notification.

Transfers: Academic transcripts required.

CONTACT

Cynthia Hudok, Director of Financial Aid and Scholarships
1201 Locust Avenue, Fairmont, WV 26554-2470
(304) 367-4213

Glenville State College

Glenville, West Virginia
www.glenville.edu   Federal Code: 003813

4-year public liberal arts and teachers college in rural community.

Enrollment: 1,191 undergrads, 4% part-time. 302 full-time freshmen.

Selectivity: Admits over 75% of applicants.

BASIC COSTS (2009-2010)

Tuition and fees: $4,888; out-of-state residents $11,702.

Per-credit charge: $204; out-of-state residents $488.

Room and board: $6,660.

Additional info: Tuition for students residing in border counties is $8,064.

FINANCIAL AID PICTURE (2008-2009)

Students with need: Out of 288 full-time freshmen who applied for aid, 252 were judged to have need. Of these, 251 received aid, and 40 had their full need met. Average financial aid package met 72% of need; average scholarship/grant was $4,859; average loan was $3,096. Need-based aid available for part-time students.

Students without need: 26 full-time freshmen who did not demonstrate need for aid received scholarships/grants; average award was $2,179. No-need awards available for academics, athletics, music/drama, state/district residency.

Cumulative student debt: 71% of graduating class had student loans; average debt was $17,545.

FINANCIAL AID PROCEDURES

Forms required: FAFSA.

Dates and Deadlines: Priority date 2/1; no closing date. Applicants notified on a rolling basis starting 3/1; must reply within 3 week(s) of notification.

CONTACT

Karen Lay, Director of Financial Aid
Office of Enrollment Services, Glenville, WV 26351-1292
(304) 462-4103

Marshall University

Huntington, West Virginia
www.marshall.edu   Federal Code: 003815

4-year public university in small city.
Enrollment: 9,051 undergrads, 12% part-time. 1,857 full-time freshmen.
Selectivity: Admits over 75% of applicants.

BASIC COSTS (2009-2010)

Tuition and fees: $5,236; out-of-state residents $12,482.
Per-credit charge: $219; out-of-state residents $521.
Room and board: $7,556.
Additional info: Tuition for students residing in border counties is $8,668.

FINANCIAL AID PICTURE (2009-2010)

Students with need: Out of 1,207 full-time freshmen who applied for aid, 898 were judged to have need. Of these, 887 received aid, and 263 had their full need met. Average financial aid package met 55% of need; average scholarship/grant was $6,635; average loan was $5,651. For part-time students, average financial aid package was $6,850.

Students without need: 275 full-time freshmen who did not demonstrate need for aid received scholarships/grants; average award was $6,193. No-need awards available for academics, art, athletics, minority status, music/drama, ROTC, state/district residency.

Scholarships offered: *Merit:* Michael Perry Scholarship; $500 based on 3.2 GPA and 20 ACT score; $750 based on 3.5 GPA and 23 ACT, or 3.2 GPA and 25 ACT; one-year only. Presidential Scholarship; $1,250; 3.5 GPA and 25 ACT; renewable with 3.5 GPA. John Marshall Scholarship; tuition waiver plus $1,250 stipend; 3.5 GPA and 30 ACT; renewable yearly with 3.5 GPA. Yeager scholarship; full tuition and fees, full room and board, book allowance, stipend, personal computer for use during program, and $4,000 toward study abroad; 28 ACT/1260 SAT (exclusive of Writing). ***Athletic:*** 60 full-time freshmen received athletic scholarships; average amount $8,290.

Cumulative student debt: 62% of graduating class had student loans; average debt was $19,562.

FINANCIAL AID PROCEDURES

Forms required: FAFSA, state aid form.
Dates and Deadlines: Priority date 3/1; no closing date. Applicants notified on a rolling basis starting 5/1; must reply within 2 week(s) of notification.
Transfers: Priority date 1/1.

CONTACT

Kathy Bialk, Director of Financial Aid
One John Marshall Drive, Huntington, WV 25755
(304) 696-3162

Mountain State College

Parkersburg, West Virginia
www.msc.edu   Federal Code: 005008

2-year for-profit junior college in large town.
Enrollment: 144 undergrads. 6 full-time freshmen.
Selectivity: Open admission.

BASIC COSTS (2009-2010)

Tuition and fees: $7,165.

FINANCIAL AID PICTURE

Students with need: Work study available nights, weekends, and for part-time students.

FINANCIAL AID PROCEDURES

Forms required: FAFSA.
Dates and Deadlines: No deadline. Applicants notified on a rolling basis.

CONTACT

Faye Wagoner, Director of Student Financial Plan
Spring at 16th Street, Parkersburg, WV 26101-3993
(304) 485-5487

Mountain State University

Beckley, West Virginia
www.mountainstate.edu   Federal Code: 003807

4-year private university and health science college in large town.
Enrollment: 5,137 undergrads, 28% part-time. 571 full-time freshmen.
Selectivity: Open admission; but selective for some programs.

BASIC COSTS (2010-2011)

Tuition and fees: $8,700.
Per-credit charge: $215.
Room and board: $6,116.
Additional info: Certain undergraduate programs require additional costs. Per-credit-hour costs vary: $300 for Organizational Leadership; $310 for Medical Assisting, Online Criminal Justice, Online Business and Accounting, and Online General Education; $320 for Online Administration of Criminal Justice, Online Medical Assisting, and Online Organizational Leadership; $330 for Culinary Arts, Diagnostic Medical Sonography, Engineering, Occupational Therapy Assistant, Physical Therapy Assistant, and Radiologic Technology; $350 for Nursing; $430 for Online Diagnostic Medical Sonography.

FINANCIAL AID PICTURE (2008-2009)

Students with need: Out of 210 full-time freshmen who applied for aid, 195 were judged to have need. Of these, 195 received aid, and 23 had their full need met. Average financial aid package met 39% of need; average scholarship/grant was $3,916; average loan was $2,982. For part-time students, average financial aid package was $5,160.

Students without need: No-need awards available for academics, alumni affiliation, athletics, leadership, minority status, state/district residency.

Scholarships offered: 10 full-time freshmen received athletic scholarships; average amount $4,780.

Cumulative student debt: 81% of graduating class had student loans; average debt was $33,218.

FINANCIAL AID PROCEDURES

Forms required: FAFSA.

Dates and Deadlines: Priority date 3/1; no closing date. Applicants notified on a rolling basis starting 4/1.

CONTACT
Michelle Sarrett, Vice President of Finance and Chief Financial Officer
609 South Kanawha Street, Beckley, WV 25802-9003
(304) 929-1517

Ohio Valley University
Vienna, West Virginia
www.ovu.edu   Federal Code: 003819

4-year private university and liberal arts college in small city, affiliated with Church of Christ.
Enrollment: 444 undergrads, 7% part-time. 88 full-time freshmen.
Selectivity: Admits 50 to 75% of applicants.

BASIC COSTS (2009-2010)
Tuition and fees: $17,200.
Per-credit charge: $525.
Room and board: $6,676.

FINANCIAL AID PICTURE (2009-2010)
Students with need: Out of 80 full-time freshmen who applied for aid, 67 were judged to have need. Of these, 67 received aid, and 19 had their full need met. Average financial aid package met 69% of need; average scholarship/grant was $10,326; average loan was $3,281. For part-time students, average financial aid package was $5,527.
Students without need: 11 full-time freshmen who did not demonstrate need for aid received scholarships/grants; average award was $4,181. No-need awards available for academics, alumni affiliation, athletics, job skills, leadership, music/drama.
Scholarships offered: 20 full-time freshmen received athletic scholarships; average amount $7,220.
Cumulative student debt: 93% of graduating class had student loans; average debt was $14,976.

FINANCIAL AID PROCEDURES
Forms required: FAFSA.
Dates and Deadlines: Priority date 2/15; no closing date. Applicants notified on a rolling basis starting 3/15; must reply within 4 week(s) of notification.
Transfers: No deadline. Applicants notified on a rolling basis starting 3/15; must reply within 4 week(s) of notification.

CONTACT
Dennis Cox, Director of Student Financial Services
One Campus View Drive, Vienna, WV 26105
(304) 865-6081

Potomac State College of West Virginia University
Keyser, West Virginia
www.potomacstatecollege.edu   Federal Code: 003829

2-year public branch campus and junior college in small town.
Enrollment: 1,435 undergrads, 6% part-time. 716 full-time freshmen.
Selectivity: Open admission; but selective for out-of-state students.

BASIC COSTS (2009-2010)
Tuition and fees: $2,886; out-of-state residents $8,746.
Per-credit charge: $121; out-of-state residents $366.
Room and board: $7,156.
Additional info: Tuition for students residing in border counties is $5,074.

FINANCIAL AID PICTURE (2008-2009)
Students with need: Need-based aid available for full-time and part-time students. Work study available nights, weekends, and for part-time students.
Students without need: No-need awards available for academics, athletics, leadership.

FINANCIAL AID PROCEDURES
Forms required: FAFSA.
Dates and Deadlines: Priority date 3/1; no closing date. Applicants notified on a rolling basis starting 3/15; must reply within 2 week(s) of notification.
Transfers: Applicants notified on a rolling basis starting 3/15; must reply within 2 week(s) of notification.

CONTACT
Beth Little, Director of Enrollment Services
75 Arnold Street, Keyser, WV 26726
(304) 788-6820

Salem International University
Salem, West Virginia
www.salemu.edu   Federal Code: 003820

4-year for-profit university and liberal arts college in rural community.
Enrollment: 442 undergrads.
Selectivity: Open admission.

FINANCIAL AID PICTURE (2008-2009)
Students with need: Need-based aid available for full-time and part-time students. Work study available nights, weekends, and for part-time students.
Students without need: No-need awards available for academics.
Scholarships offered: Scholarships; extensive amount awarded; based on high school GPA, standardized test scores. Breed-related awards; for students in equine career and industry management program. Awards for GED diploma recipients; based on academic excellence.

FINANCIAL AID PROCEDURES
Forms required: FAFSA.
Dates and Deadlines: Priority date 4/15; no closing date. Applicants notified on a rolling basis starting 2/15; must reply within 4 week(s) of notification.
Transfers: Priority date 3/1; closing date 4/15. Applicants notified on a rolling basis starting 3/1.

CONTACT
Patricia Zinsmeister, Vice President for Financial Aid and Compliance
223 West Main Street, Salem, WV 26426
(304) 326-1303

Shepherd University
Shepherdstown, West Virginia
www.shepherd.edu   Federal Code: 003822

4-year public university in small town.
Enrollment: 3,676 undergrads, 10% part-time. 699 full-time freshmen.
Selectivity: Admits over 75% of applicants.

BASIC COSTS (2009-2010)
Tuition and fees: $5,234; out-of-state residents $13,574.
Per-credit charge: $218; out-of-state residents $566.
Room and board: $7,228.
Additional info: Tuition/fee waivers available for minority students.

FINANCIAL AID PICTURE (2008-2009)

Students with need: Out of 621 full-time freshmen who applied for aid, 364 were judged to have need. Of these, 352 received aid, and 98 had their full need met. Average financial aid package met 91% of need; average scholarship/grant was $4,306; average loan was $3,383. For part-time students, average financial aid package was $8,680.

Students without need: 177 full-time freshmen who did not demonstrate need for aid received scholarships/grants; average award was $8,197. No-need awards available for academics, art, athletics, job skills, leadership, minority status, music/drama, state/district residency.

Scholarships offered: *Merit:* Presidential scholarship; up to $5,000; requires 3.5 GPA, 26 ACT or 1200 SAT; renewable with 3.5 GPA. Academic scholarship; up to $1,500; requires 3.2 GPA, 21 ACT or 1000 SAT; renewable with 3.0 GPA. Leadership scholarship; up to $3,000; requires 3.0 GPA, 21 ACT, or 1000 SAT; nonrenewable. *Athletic:* 39 full-time freshmen received athletic scholarships; average amount $6,036.

Cumulative student debt: 65% of graduating class had student loans; average debt was $18,271.

FINANCIAL AID PROCEDURES

Forms required: FAFSA, state aid form.

Dates and Deadlines: Priority date 3/1; no closing date. Applicants notified on a rolling basis starting 3/15; must reply within 3 week(s) of notification.

Transfers: No deadline. Applicants notified on a rolling basis starting 11/1; must reply within 3 week(s) of notification.

CONTACT

Sandra Oerly-Bennett, Director of Financial Aid
PO Box 5000, Shepherdstown, WV 25443-5000
(304) 876-5470

Southern West Virginia Community and Technical College

Mount Gay, West Virginia
www.southernwv.edu   Federal Code: 003816

2-year public community college in small town.

Enrollment: 2,192 undergrads.

Selectivity: Open admission; but selective for some programs.

BASIC COSTS (2009-2010)

Tuition and fees: $2,102; out-of-state residents $6,916.

Per-credit charge: $88; out-of-state residents $288.

FINANCIAL AID PICTURE (2008-2009)

Students with need: Need-based aid available for full-time and part-time students.

FINANCIAL AID PROCEDURES

Forms required: FAFSA.

Dates and Deadlines: No deadline. Applicants notified on a rolling basis.

CONTACT

Cindy Whitlock, Financial Aid Director
PO Box 2900, Mount Gay, WV 25637
(304) 896-7382

University of Charleston

Charleston, West Virginia
www.ucwv.edu   Federal Code: 003818

4-year private university and liberal arts college in small city.

Enrollment: 1,006 undergrads, 2% part-time. 311 full-time freshmen.

Selectivity: Admits over 75% of applicants.

BASIC COSTS (2010-2011)

Tuition and fees: $24,700.

Per-credit charge: $900.

Room and board: $8,700.

Additional info: Tuition for pharmacy students $25,750, plus $1,200 in fees.

FINANCIAL AID PICTURE (2008-2009)

Students with need: Out of 292 full-time freshmen who applied for aid, 256 were judged to have need. Of these, 256 received aid, and 74 had their full need met. Average financial aid package met 84% of need; average scholarship/grant was $5,310; average loan was $7,110. For part-time students, average financial aid package was $5,175.

Students without need: 18 full-time freshmen who did not demonstrate need for aid received scholarships/grants; average award was $21,320. No-need awards available for academics, alumni affiliation, athletics, leadership, music/drama, ROTC.

Scholarships offered: 4 full-time freshmen received athletic scholarships; average amount $21,980.

Cumulative student debt: 91% of graduating class had student loans; average debt was $23,250.

FINANCIAL AID PROCEDURES

Forms required: FAFSA.

Dates and Deadlines: Priority date 3/1; no closing date. Applicants notified on a rolling basis starting 3/1.

Transfers: Applicants notified on a rolling basis starting 4/1; must reply by 5/1 or within 4 week(s) of notification.

CONTACT

Janet Ruge, Director of Financial Aid
2300 MacCorkle Avenue, SE, Charleston, WV 25304
(304) 357-4759

Valley College

Martinsburg, West Virginia
www.vct.edu   Federal Code: G26094

2-year for-profit business and career college in large town.

Enrollment: 65 undergrads.

Selectivity: Open admission.

BASIC COSTS (2010-2011)

Tuition and fees: $8,100.

Per-credit charge: $250.

FINANCIAL AID PICTURE (2008-2009)

Students with need: Need-based aid available for full-time and part-time students.

FINANCIAL AID PROCEDURES

Forms required: FAFSA, institutional form.

Dates and Deadlines: No deadline. Applicants notified on a rolling basis.

Transfers: No deadline. Applicants notified on a rolling basis.

CONTACT

Kathy Gundling, Financial Aid Director
287 Aikens Center, Martinsburg, WV 25404
(304) 263-0979

West Liberty University

West Liberty, West Virginia
www.westliberty.edu   Federal Code: 003823

4-year public university in rural community.

Enrollment: 2,399 undergrads, 6% part-time. 575 full-time freshmen.

Selectivity: Admits over 75% of applicants.

BASIC COSTS (2009-2010)

Tuition and fees: $4,880; out-of-state residents $11,950.
Per-credit charge: $203; out-of-state residents $498.
Room and board: $6,870.
Additional info: Tuition for students residing in border counties is $9,560.

FINANCIAL AID PICTURE (2009-2010)

Students with need: For part-time students, average financial aid package was $6,502.
Students without need: No-need awards available for academics, alumni affiliation, art, athletics, music/drama, state/district residency.
Cumulative student debt: 82% of graduating class had student loans; average debt was $18,910.
Additional info: Non-need based student employment available at food service, college union, bookstore, and tutoring office. Resident assistant and campus security jobs also available.

FINANCIAL AID PROCEDURES

Forms required: FAFSA.
Dates and Deadlines: Priority date 3/1; no closing date. Applicants notified on a rolling basis starting 3/1; must reply within 2 week(s) of notification.
Transfers: Financial aid transcript required from all previous colleges attended regardless of whether aid was received.

CONTACT

Scott Cook, Financial Aid Director
PO Box 295, West Liberty, WV 26074-0295
(304) 336-8016

West Virginia Business College: Nutter Fort

Wheeling, West Virginia
www.wvbc.edu   Federal Code: 010861

2-year for-profit business college in small city.
Enrollment: 55 undergrads.
Selectivity: Open admission; but selective for some programs.

BASIC COSTS (2009-2010)

Additional info: Associate degree program costs $18,000 for entire 2-year program.

FINANCIAL AID PICTURE (2009-2010)

Students with need: Average financial aid package met 100% of need; average scholarship/grant was $5,000; average loan was $9,500. Need-based aid available for part-time students.
Students without need: This college awards aid only to students with need.

FINANCIAL AID PROCEDURES

Forms required: FAFSA, institutional form.
Dates and Deadlines: No deadline.

CONTACT

James Weir, Financial Aid Manager
1052 Main Street, Wheeling, WV 26003
(304) 232-0361

West Virginia Business College: Wheeling

Wheeling, West Virginia
www.wvbc.edu   Federal Code: 010861

2-year for-profit business and career college in small city.
Enrollment: 80 undergrads. 80 full-time freshmen.
Selectivity: Open admission.

BASIC COSTS (2009-2010)

Additional info: Associate degree program costs $18,000 for entire 2-year program. Tuition at time of enrollment locked for 2 years.

FINANCIAL AID PICTURE (2008-2009)

Students with need: Out of 80 full-time freshmen who applied for aid, 80 were judged to have need. Of these, 80 received aid, and 60 had their full need met. Average financial aid package met 70% of need; average scholarship/grant was $5,000; average loan was $4,000.

CONTACT

James Weir, Financial Aid Administraor
1052 Main Street, Wheeling, WV 26003
(304) 232-0361 ext. 14

West Virginia Junior College

Morgantown, West Virginia
www.wvjc.edu   Federal Code: 005007

2-year for-profit junior college in large town.
Enrollment: 150 undergrads.
Selectivity: Open admission.

FINANCIAL AID PICTURE

Students with need: Need-based aid available for full-time and part-time students.

FINANCIAL AID PROCEDURES

Forms required: FAFSA.
Dates and Deadlines: No deadline. Applicants notified on a rolling basis.

CONTACT

Patricia Callen, Executive Director
148 Willey Street, Morgantown, WV 26505

West Virginia Northern Community College

Wheeling, West Virginia
www.wvncc.edu   Federal Code: 010920

2-year public community and technical college in large town.
Enrollment: 2,526 undergrads.
Selectivity: Open admission; but selective for some programs.

BASIC COSTS (2009-2010)

Tuition and fees: $2,358; out-of-state residents $6,816.
Additional info: Tuition for students residing in bordering counties is $4,750. Tuition/fee waivers available for adults.

FINANCIAL AID PICTURE

Students with need: Need-based aid available for full-time and part-time students.

FINANCIAL AID PROCEDURES

Forms required: FAFSA, institutional form.
Dates and Deadlines: Priority date 3/15; no closing date. Applicants notified on a rolling basis starting 3/10.

CONTACT

Janet Fike, Director, Financial Aid
1704 Market Street, Wheeling, WV 26003
(304) 233-5900 ext. 4363

West Virginia State Community and Technical College

Institute, West Virginia
www.wvsctc.edu   Federal Code: 040386

2-year public community and technical college in small town.
Enrollment: 1,745 undergrads.
Selectivity: Open admission; but selective for some programs.

BASIC COSTS (2009-2010)
Tuition and fees: $2,956; out-of-state residents $8,638.
Per-credit charge: $123; out-of-state residents $360.
Room and board: $6,070.

FINANCIAL AID PICTURE (2008-2009)
Students with need: Work study available nights, weekends, and for part-time students.
Students without need: No-need awards available for academics, state/district residency.
Additional info: All students may apply for tuition waivers. Financial aid deadline enforced only if Federal financial aid is the only source of payment.

FINANCIAL AID PROCEDURES
Dates and Deadlines: Closing date 6/30.

CONTACT
Mary Blizzard, Director, Office of Student Financial Assistance
PO Box 1000, Institute, WV 25112-1000
(304) 766-3131

West Virginia State University

Institute, West Virginia
www.wvstateu.edu   Federal Code: 003826

4-year public liberal arts and teachers college in small town.
Enrollment: 2,525 undergrads, 31% part-time. 222 full-time freshmen.
Selectivity: Admits over 75% of applicants.

BASIC COSTS (2009-2010)
Tuition and fees: $4,644; out-of-state residents $10,884.
Per-credit charge: $194; out-of-state residents $454.
Room and board: $6,070.

FINANCIAL AID PICTURE
Students with need: Need-based aid available for full-time and part-time students. Work study available nights, weekends, and for part-time students.
Students without need: No-need awards available for academics, athletics, ROTC, state/district residency.

FINANCIAL AID PROCEDURES
Forms required: FAFSA.
Dates and Deadlines: Priority date 3/1; closing date 6/15. Applicants notified on a rolling basis starting 2/15; must reply within 2 week(s) of notification.

CONTACT
Sally Marcus, Director of Financial Aid
Campus Box 197, Institute, WV 25112-1000
(304) 766-3131

West Virginia University

Morgantown, West Virginia
www.wvu.edu   Federal Code: 003827

4-year public university in small city.
Enrollment: 21,720 undergrads, 7% part-time. 4,558 full-time freshmen.

Selectivity: Admits over 75% of applicants.

BASIC COSTS (2009-2010)
Tuition and fees: $5,304; out-of-state residents $16,402.
Per-credit charge: $221; out-of-state residents $683.
Room and board: $7,770.
Additional info: Tuition/fee waivers available for minority students.

FINANCIAL AID PICTURE (2009-2010)
Students with need: Out of 3,765 full-time freshmen who applied for aid, 2,937 were judged to have need. Of these, 2,052 received aid, and 616 had their full need met. Average financial aid package met 72% of need; average scholarship/grant was $5,384; average loan was $3,804. For part-time students, average financial aid package was $4,935.
Students without need: 1,325 full-time freshmen who did not demonstrate need for aid received scholarships/grants; average award was $1,601. No-need awards available for academics, alumni affiliation, art, athletics, job skills, leadership, minority status, music/drama, state/district residency.
Scholarships offered: *Merit:* Promise Scholarships; full tuition. *Athletic:* 62 full-time freshmen received athletic scholarships; average amount $18,125.
Additional info: February 1 closing date for freshman scholarships.

FINANCIAL AID PROCEDURES
Forms required: FAFSA, state aid form.
Dates and Deadlines: Closing date 3/1. Applicants notified on a rolling basis starting 3/15; must reply within 4 week(s) of notification.

CONTACT
Kaye Widney, Director of Financial Aid
Admissions and Records Office, Morgantown, WV 26506-6009
(800) 344-9881

West Virginia University at Parkersburg

Parkersburg, West Virginia
www.wvup.edu   Federal Code: 003828

4-year public community college in large town.
Enrollment: 3,649 undergrads.
Selectivity: Open admission; but selective for some programs.

BASIC COSTS (2009-2010)
Tuition and fees: $2,076; out-of-state residents $7,347.
Per-credit charge: $87; out-of-state residents $306.

FINANCIAL AID PICTURE (2009-2010)
Students with need: Need-based aid available for full-time and part-time students. Work study available nights, weekends, and for part-time students.
Students without need: No-need awards available for academics, leadership, state/district residency.

FINANCIAL AID PROCEDURES
Forms required: FAFSA.
Dates and Deadlines: Priority date 3/1; no closing date. Applicants notified on a rolling basis; must reply within 2 week(s) of notification.

CONTACT
August Kafer, Director of Financial Aid
300 Campus Drive, Parkersburg, WV 26104-8647
(304) 424-8210

West Virginia University Institute of Technology

Montgomery, West Virginia
www.wvutech.edu   Federal Code: 003825

4-year public engineering college in small town.
Enrollment: 1,244 undergrads.

Selectivity: Admits 50 to 75% of applicants.

BASIC COSTS (2009-2010)

Tuition and fees: $5,164; out-of-state residents $13,264.
Per-credit charge: $217; out-of-state residents $555.
Room and board: $7,607.

FINANCIAL AID PICTURE

Students with need: Need-based aid available for full-time students. Work study available nights, weekends, and for part-time students.
Additional info: Room and board may be deferred for up to 60 days. First 50% due in 30 days.

FINANCIAL AID PROCEDURES

Forms required: FAFSA.
Dates and Deadlines: Closing date 3/1. Applicants notified on a rolling basis; must reply within 3 week(s) of notification.

CONTACT

Sue Beaver, Director of Financial Aid
405 Fayette Pike, Montgomery, WV 25136-2436
(304) 442-3140

West Virginia Wesleyan College

Buckhannon, West Virginia
www.wvwc.edu   Federal Code: 003830

4-year private liberal arts college in small town, affiliated with United Methodist Church.
Enrollment: 1,341 undergrads, 2% part-time. 399 full-time freshmen.
Selectivity: Admits over 75% of applicants.

BASIC COSTS (2009-2010)

Tuition and fees: $22,880.
Room and board: $6,800.

FINANCIAL AID PICTURE (2009-2010)

Students with need: Need-based aid available for full-time and part-time students. Work study available nights, weekends, and for part-time students.
Students without need: No-need awards available for academics, alumni affiliation, art, athletics, leadership, music/drama, religious affiliation, state/district residency.
Cumulative student debt: 71% of graduating class had student loans; average debt was $21,502.

FINANCIAL AID PROCEDURES

Forms required: FAFSA.
Dates and Deadlines: Priority date 3/1; no closing date. Applicants notified on a rolling basis starting 3/15; must reply within 4 week(s) of notification.
Transfers: No deadline. Applicants notified on a rolling basis starting 3/15; must reply within 4 week(s) of notification. Financial aid transcripts required from all institutions previously attended.

CONTACT

Susan George, Director of Financial Aid
59 College Avenue, Buckhannon, WV 26201-2998
(304) 473-8080

Wheeling Jesuit University

Wheeling, West Virginia
www.wju.edu   Federal Code: 003831

4-year private university and liberal arts college in small city, affiliated with Roman Catholic Church.
Enrollment: 1,001 undergrads, 10% part-time. 264 full-time freshmen.
Selectivity: Admits 50 to 75% of applicants.

BASIC COSTS (2010-2011)

Tuition and fees: $25,010.
Room and board: $8,828.

FINANCIAL AID PICTURE (2009-2010)

Students with need: Out of 256 full-time freshmen who applied for aid, 221 were judged to have need. Of these, 221 received aid, and 77 had their full need met. Average financial aid package met 89% of need; average scholarship/grant was $7,436; average loan was $4,401. For part-time students, average financial aid package was $5,050.
Students without need: 43 full-time freshmen who did not demonstrate need for aid received scholarships/grants; average award was $11,094. No-need awards available for academics, alumni affiliation, athletics, leadership, music/drama.
Scholarships offered: 16 full-time freshmen received athletic scholarships; average amount $5,190.
Cumulative student debt: 89% of graduating class had student loans; average debt was $26,334.

FINANCIAL AID PROCEDURES

Forms required: FAFSA.
Dates and Deadlines: Priority date 2/15; no closing date. Applicants notified on a rolling basis starting 3/15; must reply within 2 week(s) of notification.
Transfers: No deadline. Applicants notified on a rolling basis starting 3/15; must reply within 2 week(s) of notification. Academic scholarships available to qualified transfer students.

CONTACT

Christie Tomczyk, Director of Financial Aid
316 Washington Avenue, Wheeling, WV 26003-6295
(304) 243-2304

Wisconsin

Alverno College

Milwaukee, Wisconsin
www.alverno.edu   Federal Code: 003832

4-year private liberal arts college for women in very large city, affiliated with Roman Catholic Church.
Enrollment: 2,307 undergrads, 26% part-time. 231 full-time freshmen.
Selectivity: Admits over 75% of applicants.

BASIC COSTS (2010-2011)

Tuition and fees: $20,060.
Per-credit charge: $815.
Room and board: $6,780.

FINANCIAL AID PICTURE (2009-2010)

Students with need: Out of 224 full-time freshmen who applied for aid, 202 were judged to have need. Of these, 202 received aid. For part-time students, average financial aid package was $7,035.
Students without need: 21 full-time freshmen who did not demonstrate need for aid received scholarships/grants; average award was $7,664. No-need awards available for academics, alumni affiliation, leadership.
Scholarships offered: Four-year academic scholarships range from $16,000 to $35,600. Alverno Scholars of Wisconsin: $42,000 scholarship, one available for each Wisconsin county.
Cumulative student debt: 83% of graduating class had student loans; average debt was $32,142.

FINANCIAL AID PROCEDURES

Forms required: FAFSA, institutional form.
Dates and Deadlines: Priority date 3/15; no closing date. Applicants notified on a rolling basis starting 3/15; must reply within 2 week(s) of notification.

Transfers: No deadline. Applicants notified on a rolling basis; must reply within 2 week(s) of notification. Transfer students are eligible for academic scholarships.

CONTACT
Dan Goyette, Director of Financial Aid
3400 South 43rd Street, Milwaukee, WI 53234-3922
(414) 382-6046

Beloit College
Beloit, Wisconsin
www.beloit.edu   Federal Code: 003835

4-year private liberal arts college in large town.
Enrollment: 1,323 undergrads, 1% part-time. 332 full-time freshmen.
Selectivity: Admits 50 to 75% of applicants.

BASIC COSTS (2010-2011)
Tuition and fees: $35,038.
Per-credit charge: $1,088.
Room and board: $7,164.
Additional info: Tuition/fee waivers available for adults.

FINANCIAL AID PICTURE (2009-2010)
Students with need: Out of 258 full-time freshmen who applied for aid, 215 were judged to have need. Of these, 215 received aid, and 103 had their full need met. Average financial aid package met 95% of need; average scholarship/grant was $23,727; average loan was $2,833.
Students without need: 98 full-time freshmen who did not demonstrate need for aid received scholarships/grants; average award was $14,291. No-need awards available for academics, leadership, minority status, music/drama.
Scholarships offered: Presidential Scholarships: $13,000-$15,000 per year; campus interview required.
Cumulative student debt: 68% of graduating class had student loans; average debt was $17,909.

FINANCIAL AID PROCEDURES
Forms required: FAFSA, state aid form, institutional form.
Dates and Deadlines: Closing date 3/1. Applicants notified on a rolling basis starting 4/1; must reply by 5/1 or within 2 week(s) of notification.
Transfers: No deadline. Applicants notified on a rolling basis starting 4/1; must reply by 5/1 or within 2 week(s) of notification.

CONTACT
Jane Hessian, Director of Financial Aid
700 College Street, Beloit, WI 53511-5595
(608) 363-2663

Blackhawk Technical College
Janesville, Wisconsin
www.blackhawk.edu   Federal Code: 005390

2-year public technical college in small city.
Enrollment: 3,380 undergrads, 48% part-time. 520 full-time freshmen.
Selectivity: Open admission; but selective for some programs.

BASIC COSTS (2009-2010)
Tuition and fees: $3,194; out-of-state residents $4,715.
Per-credit charge: $101; out-of-state residents $152.
Additional info: Material fees vary by program; minimum $4 per course. $10 per credit fee for online courses.

FINANCIAL AID PICTURE (2008-2009)
Students with need: 60% of average financial aid package awarded as scholarships/grants, 40% awarded as loans/jobs. Need-based aid available for part-time students. Work study available nights.

FINANCIAL AID PROCEDURES
Forms required: FAFSA.
Dates and Deadlines: Priority date 4/30; no closing date. Applicants notified on a rolling basis starting 3/15.

CONTACT
Sue Ullrick, Financial Aid Officer
Box 5009, Janesville, WI 53547-5009
(608) 757-7664

Cardinal Stritch University
Milwaukee, Wisconsin
www.stritch.edu   Federal Code: 003837

4-year private university in very large city, affiliated with Roman Catholic Church.
Enrollment: 3,046 undergrads.
Selectivity: Admits less than 50% of applicants.

BASIC COSTS (2009-2010)
Tuition and fees: $21,790.
Per-credit charge: $665.
Room and board: $6,500.

FINANCIAL AID PICTURE
Students with need: Need-based aid available for full-time and part-time students.
Students without need: No-need awards available for academics, art, athletics, music/drama.

FINANCIAL AID PROCEDURES
Forms required: FAFSA, institutional form.
Dates and Deadlines: Priority date 4/15; no closing date. Applicants notified on a rolling basis starting 3/1; must reply within 3 week(s) of notification.

CONTACT
Amy Hoss, Director of Financial Aid
6801 North Yates Road, Box 516, Milwaukee, WI 53217-7516
(414) 410-4048

Carroll University
Waukesha, Wisconsin
www.carrollu.edu   Federal Code: 003838

4-year private liberal arts college in small city, affiliated with Presbyterian Church (USA).
Enrollment: 3,050 undergrads, 15% part-time. 730 full-time freshmen.
Selectivity: Admits 50 to 75% of applicants.

BASIC COSTS (2009-2010)
Tuition and fees: $22,937.
Per-credit charge: $270.
Room and board: $7,023.

FINANCIAL AID PICTURE (2009-2010)
Students with need: Out of 650 full-time freshmen who applied for aid, 517 were judged to have need. Of these, 517 received aid, and 342 had their full need met. Average financial aid package met 100% of need; average scholarship/grant was $14,644; average loan was $2,122. Need-based aid available for part-time students.
Students without need: 153 full-time freshmen who did not demonstrate need for aid received scholarships/grants; average award was $10,956. No-

need awards available for academics, alumni affiliation, art, leadership, music/drama, ROTC.

Scholarships offered: Trustee Scholarship; $12,000 per year. Voorhees Scholarship; $11,000 per year. Charles Caroll Scholarship; $10,000 per year.

Cumulative student debt: 77% of graduating class had student loans; average debt was $30,678.

FINANCIAL AID PROCEDURES

Forms required: FAFSA.

Dates and Deadlines: No deadline. Applicants notified on a rolling basis starting 2/15; must reply by 5/1 or within 2 week(s) of notification.

Transfers: No deadline. Applicants notified on a rolling basis.

CONTACT

Dawn Scott, Director of Student Financial Services
100 North East Avenue, Waukesha, WI 53186-9988
(262) 524-7296

Carthage College

Kenosha, Wisconsin
www.carthage.edu   Federal Code: 003839

4-year private liberal arts college in small city, affiliated with Evangelical Lutheran Church in America.

Enrollment: 2,648 undergrads.

Selectivity: Admits over 75% of applicants.

BASIC COSTS (2010-2011)

Tuition and fees: $29,750.

Per-credit charge: $400.

Room and board: $8,150.

Additional info: Tuition/fee waivers available for minority students.

FINANCIAL AID PICTURE (2009-2010)

Students with need: Need-based aid available for full-time and part-time students.

Students without need: No-need awards available for academics, alumni affiliation, art, leadership, minority status, music/drama, religious affiliation.

Scholarships offered: Lincoln Scholarship Program: range from 75% tuition to full tuition, room and board, renewable; separate scholarship application; 17 awarded. Math/Science Scholarship: three awarded; range from $17,000/year to full tuition, renewable; requires separate scholarship application, restricted to math and natural science majors. French/German Scholarship: four awarded; $17,000/year, renewable; requires separate scholarship application, restricted to French and German majors. Fine Arts Scholarships: $500-$10,000/year, renewable; requires separate audition/portfolio showing, open to majors and non majors in music and theater, and majors in studio art or graphic design. Tarble Scholarships: number awarded variable; up to $17,000 year, renewable; requires separate scholarship application, restricted to California residents.

FINANCIAL AID PROCEDURES

Forms required: FAFSA.

Dates and Deadlines: Priority date 2/15; no closing date. Applicants notified on a rolling basis starting 3/1.

Transfers: Priority date 3/1; no deadline. Applicants notified on a rolling basis starting 3/1.

CONTACT

Vatistas Vatistas, Director of Financial Aid
2001 Alford Park Drive, Kenosha, WI 53140-1994
(262) 551-6001

Chippewa Valley Technical College

Eau Claire, Wisconsin
www.cvtc.edu   Federal Code: 005304

2-year public technical college in small city.

Enrollment: 5,966 undergrads.

Selectivity: Open admission; but selective for some programs.

BASIC COSTS (2009-2010)

Tuition and fees: $3,224; out-of-state residents $4,745.

Per-credit charge: $101; out-of-state residents $152.

Additional info: Material fees vary by program; minimum $4 per course. $10 per credit fee for online courses.

FINANCIAL AID PICTURE (2008-2009)

Students with need: Need-based aid available for full-time and part-time students. Work study available nights, weekends, and for part-time students.

FINANCIAL AID PROCEDURES

Forms required: FAFSA.

Dates and Deadlines: Priority date 3/15; no closing date. Applicants notified on a rolling basis starting 6/1; must reply within 2 week(s) of notification.

CONTACT

Mary Gorud, Financial Aid Manager
620 West Clairemont Avenue, Eau Claire, WI 54701-6162
(715) 833-6252

College of Menominee Nation

Keshena, Wisconsin
www.menominee.edu   Federal Code: 031251

2-year private community college in rural community.

Enrollment: 575 undergrads. 119 full-time freshmen.

Selectivity: Open admission; but selective for some programs.

BASIC COSTS (2009-2010)

Tuition and fees: $7,080.

Per-credit charge: $230.

FINANCIAL AID PICTURE (2008-2009)

Students with need: Need-based aid available for full-time and part-time students. Work study available nights.

Students without need: This college awards aid only to students with need.

FINANCIAL AID PROCEDURES

Forms required: FAFSA.

Dates and Deadlines: Applicants notified on a rolling basis.

Transfers: No deadline. Applicants notified on a rolling basis.

CONTACT

Nicole Fish, Financial Aid Director
N 172 State Highway 47/55, Keshena, WI 54135
(715) 799-5600 ext. 3039

Concordia University Wisconsin

Mequon, Wisconsin
www.cuw.edu   Federal Code: 003842

4-year private university and liberal arts college in large town, affiliated with Lutheran Church - Missouri Synod.

Enrollment: 3,790 undergrads, 39% part-time. 462 full-time freshmen.

Selectivity: Admits 50 to 75% of applicants.

BASIC COSTS (2009-2010)

Tuition and fees: $20,990.
Room and board: $7,990.

FINANCIAL AID PICTURE (2009-2010)

Students with need: Out of 444 full-time freshmen who applied for aid, 376 were judged to have need. Of these, 376 received aid, and 118 had their full need met. Average financial aid package met 80% of need; average scholarship/grant was $13,226; average loan was $4,972. For part-time students, average financial aid package was $12,733.

Students without need: 81 full-time freshmen who did not demonstrate need for aid received scholarships/grants; average award was $10,008. No-need awards available for academics, minority status, music/drama, religious affiliation.

Cumulative student debt: 75% of graduating class had student loans; average debt was $25,179.

FINANCIAL AID PROCEDURES

Forms required: FAFSA.

Dates and Deadlines: Priority date 4/1; no closing date. Applicants notified on a rolling basis starting 2/15; must reply within 3 week(s) of notification.

CONTACT

Steve Taylor, Director of Financial Aid
12800 North Lake Shore Drive, Mequon, WI 53097
(262) 243-4392

Edgewood College

Madison, Wisconsin
www.edgewood.edu   Federal Code: 003848

4-year private liberal arts college in small city, affiliated with Roman Catholic Church.
Enrollment: 1,779 undergrads, 16% part-time. 302 full-time freshmen.
Selectivity: Admits 50 to 75% of applicants.

BASIC COSTS (2010-2011)

Tuition and fees: $21,988.
Per-credit charge: $692.
Room and board: $7,384.

FINANCIAL AID PICTURE (2008-2009)

Students with need: Out of 263 full-time freshmen who applied for aid, 226 were judged to have need. Of these, 226 received aid, and 51 had their full need met. Average financial aid package met 81% of need; average scholarship/grant was $12,232; average loan was $3,774. For part-time students, average financial aid package was $9,860.

Students without need: 66 full-time freshmen who did not demonstrate need for aid received scholarships/grants; average award was $4,666. No-need awards available for academics, alumni affiliation, art, leadership, music/drama, religious affiliation.

Cumulative student debt: 76% of graduating class had student loans; average debt was $28,982.

Additional info: Auditions required for music scholarships; portfolios required for fine arts scholarships; essays required for many institutional scholarships.

FINANCIAL AID PROCEDURES

Forms required: FAFSA, institutional form.

Dates and Deadlines: Priority date 3/1; no closing date. Applicants notified on a rolling basis starting 3/15.

CONTACT

Kari Gribble, Director of Financial Aid
1000 Edgewood College Drive, Madison, WI 53711-1997
(608) 663-2206

Fox Valley Technical College

Appleton, Wisconsin
www.fvtc.edu   Federal Code: 009744

2-year public technical college in small city.
Enrollment: 7,359 undergrads.
Selectivity: Open admission; but selective for some programs.

BASIC COSTS (2009-2010)

Tuition and fees: $3,381; out-of-state residents $4,902.
Per-credit charge: $101; out-of-state residents $152.
Additional info: Material fees vary by program; minimum $4 per course. $10 per credit fee for online courses.

FINANCIAL AID PICTURE (2008-2009)

Students with need: 41% of average financial aid package awarded as scholarships/grants, 59% awarded as loans/jobs. Need-based aid available for part-time students. Work study available weekends and for part-time students.

Students without need: This college awards aid only to students with need.

FINANCIAL AID PROCEDURES

Forms required: FAFSA.

Dates and Deadlines: Priority date 4/15; no closing date. Applicants notified on a rolling basis.

CONTACT

Mary Moede, Financial Aid Director
1825 North Bluemound Drive, Appleton, WI 54912-2277
(920) 735-5645

Gateway Technical College

Kenosha, Wisconsin
www.gtc.edu   Federal Code: 005389

2-year public technical college in small city.
Enrollment: 5,049 undergrads.
Selectivity: Open admission; but selective for some programs.

BASIC COSTS (2009-2010)

Tuition and fees: $3,285; out-of-state residents $4,806.
Per-credit charge: $101; out-of-state residents $152.
Additional info: Materials fees vary by program; minimum $4 per course.

FINANCIAL AID PICTURE (2008-2009)

Students with need: Need-based aid available for full-time and part-time students.

Students without need: No-need awards available for state/district residency.

FINANCIAL AID PROCEDURES

Forms required: FAFSA, institutional form.

Dates and Deadlines: Priority date 7/1; no closing date. Applicants notified on a rolling basis starting 5/1; must reply within 2 week(s) of notification.

CONTACT

Janice Riutta, Director of Student Financial Aid
3520 30th Avenue, Kenosha, WI 53144-1690
(262) 564-3072

Herzing University
Madison, Wisconsin
www.herzing.edu/madison   Federal Code: 009621

3-year for-profit business and career college in small city.
Enrollment: 964 undergrads.
Selectivity: Open admission; but selective for some programs.

BASIC COSTS (2009-2010)
Tuition and fees: $11,300.
Per-credit charge: $365.
Additional info: Tuition is $365 per-credit-hour for most on-campus courses; $405 for on-line courses. Book use included in tuition.

FINANCIAL AID PICTURE (2009-2010)
Students with need: Need-based aid available for full-time and part-time students.

FINANCIAL AID PROCEDURES
Forms required: FAFSA, institutional form.
Dates and Deadlines: No deadline. Applicants notified on a rolling basis.

CONTACT
Beverly Faga, Director of Financial Services
5218 East Terrace Drive, Madison, WI 53718
(608) 249-6611

Lac Courte Oreilles Ojibwa Community College
Hayward, Wisconsin
www.lco.edu   Federal Code: 017199

2-year public community college in small town.
Enrollment: 613 undergrads.
Selectivity: Open admission.

BASIC COSTS (2009-2010)
Tuition and fees: $4,075.
Per-credit charge: $140.

FINANCIAL AID PICTURE
Students with need: Need-based aid available for full-time students.

FINANCIAL AID PROCEDURES
Forms required: FAFSA.
Dates and Deadlines: No deadline. Applicants notified on a rolling basis.

CONTACT
Diane McKnight, Financial Aid Director
13466 West Trepania Road, Hayward, WI 54843

Lakeland College
Sheboygan, Wisconsin
www.lakeland.edu   Federal Code: 003854

4-year private liberal arts college in small city, affiliated with United Church of Christ.
Enrollment: 2,790 undergrads.
Selectivity: Admits over 75% of applicants.

BASIC COSTS (2009-2010)
Tuition and fees: $18,970.
Per-credit charge: $635.
Room and board: $6,588.

FINANCIAL AID PICTURE (2009-2010)
Students with need: Need-based aid available for full-time and part-time students. Work study available nights, weekends, and for part-time students.
Students without need: No-need awards available for academics.

FINANCIAL AID PROCEDURES
Forms required: FAFSA, institutional form.
Dates and Deadlines: Priority date 3/31; closing date 7/1. Applicants notified on a rolling basis starting 2/1; must reply within 2 week(s) of notification.

CONTACT
Patty Taylor, Director of Financial Aid
Box 359, Sheboygan, WI 53082-0359
(920) 565-1297

Lakeshore Technical College
Cleveland, Wisconsin
www.gotoltc.edu   Federal Code: 009194

2-year public technical college in rural community.
Enrollment: 2,526 undergrads, 56% part-time. 193 full-time freshmen.
Selectivity: Open admission.

BASIC COSTS (2009-2010)
Tuition and fees: $3,214; out-of-state residents $4,735.
Per-credit charge: $101; out-of-state residents $152.
Additional info: Materials fees vary by program; minimum $4 per course. $10 per credit fee for online courses.

FINANCIAL AID PICTURE (2009-2010)
Students with need: Need-based aid available for full-time and part-time students. Work study available nights.
Students without need: This college awards aid only to students with need.

FINANCIAL AID PROCEDURES
Forms required: FAFSA, institutional form.
Dates and Deadlines: Priority date 6/1; no closing date. Applicants notified on a rolling basis starting 6/1; must reply within 3 week(s) of notification.

CONTACT
Corey Givens-Novak, Financial Aid Manager
1290 North Avenue, Cleveland, WI 53015-9761
(920) 693-1118

Lawrence University
Appleton, Wisconsin
www.lawrence.edu   Federal Code: 003856

4-year private music and liberal arts college in small city.
Enrollment: 1,433 undergrads, 2% part-time. 348 full-time freshmen.
Selectivity: Admits 50 to 75% of applicants. GED not accepted.

BASIC COSTS (2009-2010)
Tuition and fees: $34,596.
Room and board: $7,053.

FINANCIAL AID PICTURE (2009-2010)
Students with need: Out of 286 full-time freshmen who applied for aid, 230 were judged to have need. Of these, 230 received aid, and 174 had their full need met. Average financial aid package met 95% of need; average scholarship/grant was $20,960; average loan was $4,460. Need-based aid available for part-time students.
Students without need: 104 full-time freshmen who did not demonstrate need for aid received scholarships/grants; average award was $11,850. No-need awards available for academics, alumni affiliation, minority status, music/drama.

Scholarships offered: Warch Scholarships: $15,000 per year. Trustee Scholarships: $12,000 per year. Presidential Scholarships: $9,000 per year. Alumni Scholarships: $7,000 per year. Conservatory Scholarships: $2,000-$12,000 per year.

Cumulative student debt: 72% of graduating class had student loans; average debt was $25,049.

Additional info: The first $1,000 (aggregate) of independently-sponsored scholarships received by a needy student will reduce student's loan or work-study commitment. Half of scholarships in excess of $1,000 will offset loan or work-study and the other half will reduce institutional need-based grant funding.

FINANCIAL AID PROCEDURES

Forms required: FAFSA, institutional form.

Dates and Deadlines: Priority date 3/1; no closing date. Applicants notified on a rolling basis starting 3/1; must reply by 5/1 or within 2 week(s) of notification.

Transfers: Priority date 4/1. Applicants notified on a rolling basis starting 5/23.

CONTACT

Steven Syverson, Vice President for Enrollment Management
Box 599, Appleton, WI 54912-0599
(920) 832-6583

Maranatha Baptist Bible College
Watertown, Wisconsin
www.mbbc.edu   Federal Code: 016394

4-year private Bible college in large town, affiliated with Baptist faith.

Enrollment: 773 undergrads, 5% part-time. 194 full-time freshmen.

Selectivity: Admits 50 to 75% of applicants.

BASIC COSTS (2010-2011)

Tuition and fees: $11,550.

Per-credit charge: $437.

Room and board: $6,290.

FINANCIAL AID PICTURE (2009-2010)

Students with need: Need-based aid available for full-time and part-time students.

Students without need: No-need awards available for academics.

FINANCIAL AID PROCEDURES

Forms required: FAFSA.

Dates and Deadlines: Priority date 3/1; no closing date. Applicants notified on a rolling basis starting 2/1; must reply within 2 week(s) of notification.

Transfers: Financial aid transcript or equivalent required.

CONTACT

Randy Hibbs, Financial Aid Director
745 West Main Street, Watertown, WI 53094
(920) 206-2318

Marian University
Fond du Lac, Wisconsin
www.marianuniversity.edu   Federal Code: 003861

4-year private university and liberal arts college in large town, affiliated with Roman Catholic Church.

Enrollment: 1,935 undergrads, 23% part-time. 284 full-time freshmen.

Selectivity: Admits over 75% of applicants.

BASIC COSTS (2009-2010)

Tuition and fees: $20,900.

Per-credit charge: $315.

Room and board: $5,640.

FINANCIAL AID PICTURE (2008-2009)

Students with need: Out of 283 full-time freshmen who applied for aid, 260 were judged to have need. Of these, 260 received aid, and 104 had their full need met. Average financial aid package met 89% of need; average scholarship/grant was $11,291; average loan was $5,264. For part-time students, average financial aid package was $11,075.

Students without need: 23 full-time freshmen who did not demonstrate need for aid received scholarships/grants; average award was $5,964. No-need awards available for academics, ROTC, state/district residency.

Scholarships offered: Academic Achievement Award: $7,500; based on 3.5 GPA, 25 ACT, top 15% of class; 7 awarded. Presidential Scholarship: $5,000; based on 3.1 GPA, top 20% of class. Naber Leadership Scholarship: $3,000; based on 2.5 GPA, top 50% of class.

FINANCIAL AID PROCEDURES

Forms required: FAFSA, institutional form.

Dates and Deadlines: Priority date 3/1; no closing date. Applicants notified on a rolling basis starting 3/1; must reply within 4 week(s) of notification.

CONTACT

Pam Warren, Associate Director of Financial Aid
45 South National Avenue, Fond du Lac, WI 54935-4699
(920) 923-7614

Marquette University
Milwaukee, Wisconsin
www.marquette.edu   Federal Code: 003863

4-year private university in very large city, affiliated with Roman Catholic Church.

Enrollment: 7,857 undergrads, 3% part-time. 1,947 full-time freshmen.

Selectivity: Admits 50 to 75% of applicants.

BASIC COSTS (2009-2010)

Tuition and fees: $29,096.

Per-credit charge: $835.

Room and board: $9,680.

Additional info: Required fees include cost of UPASS, which allows unlimited use of Milwaukee County Bus System.

FINANCIAL AID PICTURE (2009-2010)

Students with need: Need-based aid available for full-time and part-time students. Work study available nights, weekends, and for part-time students.

Students without need: No-need awards available for academics, athletics, leadership, music/drama, ROTC.

Scholarships offered: Ignatius Scholarships: $6,000-$11,000. College Scholarships: $5,000. Raynor Scholarships: full tuition; 3 awarded. National Merit Scholarships: $2,000.

FINANCIAL AID PROCEDURES

Forms required: FAFSA.

Dates and Deadlines: Priority date 2/1; no closing date. Applicants notified on a rolling basis starting 3/20; must reply by 5/1 or within 3 week(s) of notification.

Transfers: No deadline. Applicants notified on a rolling basis starting 3/15; must reply by 5/1 or within 3 week(s) of notification. Transfer scholarships available.

CONTACT

Susan Teerink, Director of Student Financial Aid
PO Box 1881, Milwaukee, WI 53201-1881
(414) 288-0200

Mid-State Technical College

Wisconsin Rapids, Wisconsin
www.mstc.edu   Federal Code: 005380

2-year public technical college in large town.
Enrollment: 4,070 undergrads.
Selectivity: Open admission; but selective for some programs.

BASIC COSTS (2009-2010)
Tuition and fees: $3,194; out-of-state residents $4,715.
Per-credit charge: $101; out-of-state residents $152.
Additional info: Material fees vary by program; minimum $4 per course.

FINANCIAL AID PICTURE (2008-2009)
Students with need: Need-based aid available for full-time and part-time students. Work study available nights, weekends, and for part-time students.
Students without need: No-need awards available for academics, leadership.

FINANCIAL AID PROCEDURES
Forms required: FAFSA.
Dates and Deadlines: No deadline. Applicants notified on a rolling basis starting 5/30; must reply within 2 week(s) of notification.

CONTACT
MaryJo Green, Financial Aid Supervisor
500 32nd Street North, Wisconsin Rapids, WI 54494
(715) 422-5501

Milwaukee Area Technical College

Milwaukee, Wisconsin
www.matc.edu   Federal Code: 003866

2-year public junior and technical college in very large city.
Enrollment: 17,473 undergrads.
Selectivity: Open admission; but selective for some programs.

BASIC COSTS (2009-2010)
Tuition and fees: $3,438; out-of-state residents $4,959.
Per-credit charge: $101; out-of-state residents $152.
Additional info: Material fees vary by program; minimum $4 per course. $10 per credit fee for online courses. Tuition/fee waivers available for minority students.

FINANCIAL AID PICTURE (2008-2009)
Students with need: Need-based aid available for full-time and part-time students.
Students without need: No-need awards available for academics.

FINANCIAL AID PROCEDURES
Forms required: FAFSA.
Dates and Deadlines: Priority date 3/15; no closing date. Applicants notified on a rolling basis starting 4/15.
Transfers: No deadline. Applicants notified on a rolling basis starting 4/15.

CONTACT
Camille Nicolai, Director of Financial Aid
700 West State Street, Milwaukee, WI 53233-1443
(414) 297-8875

Milwaukee School of Engineering

Milwaukee, Wisconsin
www.msoe.edu   Federal Code: 003868

4-year private university in very large city.
Enrollment: 2,438 undergrads, 8% part-time. 625 full-time freshmen.

Selectivity: Admits 50 to 75% of applicants.

BASIC COSTS (2010-2011)
Tuition and fees: $29,520.
Per-credit charge: $513.
Room and board: $7,431.

FINANCIAL AID PICTURE (2008-2009)
Students with need: Out of 581 full-time freshmen who applied for aid, 509 were judged to have need. Of these, 506 received aid, and 70 had their full need met. Average financial aid package met 70% of need; average scholarship/grant was $15,572; average loan was $2,473. For part-time students, average financial aid package was $6,687.
Students without need: 104 full-time freshmen who did not demonstrate need for aid received scholarships/grants; average award was $9,824. No-need awards available for academics, ROTC.
Scholarships offered: President Scholarship; full tuition; awarded to students with high academic standing; 8 awarded each year to first-time, full-time students.
Cumulative student debt: 94% of graduating class had student loans; average debt was $35,722.

FINANCIAL AID PROCEDURES
Forms required: FAFSA.
Dates and Deadlines: Priority date 3/15; no closing date. Applicants notified on a rolling basis starting 3/1; must reply within 2 week(s) of notification.

CONTACT
Steven Midthun, Director, Financial Aid
1025 North Broadway, Milwaukee, WI 53202-3109
(414) 277-7223

Moraine Park Technical College

Fond du Lac, Wisconsin
www.morainepark.edu   Federal Code: 005303

2-year public technical college in large town.
Enrollment: 3,711 undergrads.
Selectivity: Open admission; but selective for some programs.

BASIC COSTS (2009-2010)
Tuition and fees: $3,209; out-of-state residents $4,730.
Per-credit charge: $101; out-of-state residents $152.
Additional info: Material fees vary by program; minimum $4 per course. $10 per credit fee for online courses.

FINANCIAL AID PICTURE (2009-2010)
Students with need: Need-based aid available for full-time and part-time students. Work study available nights.
Students without need: No-need awards available for academics, job skills, leadership, minority status, state/district residency.

FINANCIAL AID PROCEDURES
Forms required: FAFSA, institutional form.
Dates and Deadlines: Priority date 5/1; no closing date. Applicants notified on a rolling basis starting 6/15; must reply within 2 week(s) of notification.

CONTACT
Tanya Wasmer, Enrollment Management Partner
235 North National Avenue, Fond du Lac, WI 54935-1940

Mount Mary College
Milwaukee, Wisconsin
www.mtmary.edu Federal Code: 003869

4-year private liberal arts college for women in very large city, affiliated with Roman Catholic Church.
Enrollment: 1,253 undergrads, 27% part-time. 157 full-time freshmen.
Selectivity: Admits 50 to 75% of applicants.

BASIC COSTS (2010-2011)
Tuition and fees: $21,668.
Per-credit charge: $648.
Room and board: $7,498.

FINANCIAL AID PICTURE (2009-2010)
Students with need: Out of 150 full-time freshmen who applied for aid, 145 were judged to have need. Of these, 145 received aid, and 7 had their full need met. Average financial aid package met 78% of need; average scholarship/grant was $16,781; average loan was $3,451. For part-time students, average financial aid package was $6,670.
Students without need: 23 full-time freshmen who did not demonstrate need for aid received scholarships/grants; average award was $8,767. No-need awards available for academics, alumni affiliation, art, leadership, music/drama.
Cumulative student debt: 86% of graduating class had student loans; average debt was $20,729.

FINANCIAL AID PROCEDURES
Forms required: FAFSA.
Dates and Deadlines: Priority date 3/1; no closing date. Applicants notified on a rolling basis starting 3/1; must reply within 2 week(s) of notification.
Transfers: No deadline. Applicants notified on a rolling basis; must reply within 2 week(s) of notification.

CONTACT
Debra Duff, Director of Financial Aid
2900 North Menomonee River Parkway, Milwaukee, WI 53222-4597
(414) 256-1258

Nicolet Area Technical College
Rhinelander, Wisconsin
www.nicoletcollege.edu Federal Code: 008919

2-year public community and technical college in small town.
Enrollment: 1,439 undergrads.
Selectivity: Open admission; but selective for some programs.

BASIC COSTS (2009-2010)
Tuition and fees: $3,163; out-of-state residents $4,684.
Per-credit charge: $101; out-of-state residents $152.
Additional info: Material fees vary by program; minimum $4 per course. $10 per credit fee for online courses.

FINANCIAL AID PICTURE (2008-2009)
Students with need: Work study available nights, weekends, and for part-time students.

FINANCIAL AID PROCEDURES
Forms required: FAFSA, institutional form.
Dates and Deadlines: Priority date 4/15; no closing date. Applicants notified on a rolling basis starting 6/1; must reply within 2 week(s) of notification.

CONTACT
William Peshel, Director of Financial Aid
Box 518, Rhinelander, WI 54501
(715) 365-4423

Northcentral Technical College
Wausau, Wisconsin
www.ntc.edu Federal Code: 005387

2-year public community and technical college in small city.
Enrollment: 3,161 undergrads.
Selectivity: Open admission; but selective for some programs.

BASIC COSTS (2009-2010)
Tuition and fees: $3,285; out-of-state residents $4,806.
Per-credit charge: $101; out-of-state residents $152.
Additional info: Materials fees vary by program; minimum $4 per course.

FINANCIAL AID PICTURE (2008-2009)
Students with need: Need-based aid available for full-time and part-time students. Work study available nights.

FINANCIAL AID PROCEDURES
Forms required: FAFSA.
Dates and Deadlines: No deadline. Applicants notified on a rolling basis.
Transfers: No deadline.

CONTACT
1000 West Campus Drive, Wausau, WI 54401
(715) 675-3331

Northeast Wisconsin Technical College
Green Bay, Wisconsin
www.nwtc.edu Federal Code: 005301

2-year public community and technical college in small city.
Enrollment: 5,374 undergrads, 59% part-time. 785 full-time freshmen.
Selectivity: Open admission; but selective for some programs.

BASIC COSTS (2009-2010)
Tuition and fees: $3,245; out-of-state residents $4,766.
Per-credit charge: $101; out-of-state residents $152.
Additional info: Material fees vary by program; minimum $4 per course.

FINANCIAL AID PICTURE (2008-2009)
Students with need: 51% of average financial aid package awarded as scholarships/grants, 49% awarded as loans/jobs. Need-based aid available for part-time students. Work study available nights, weekends, and for part-time students.

FINANCIAL AID PROCEDURES
Forms required: FAFSA.
Dates and Deadlines: Priority date 4/1; no closing date. Applicants notified on a rolling basis starting 5/1; must reply within 2 week(s) of notification.

CONTACT
Emily Ysebaert, Financial Aid Director
2740 West Mason Street, Green Bay, WI 54307-9042
(920) 498-5444

Northland College
Ashland, Wisconsin
www.northland.edu Federal Code: 003875

4-year private liberal arts college in small town, affiliated with United Church of Christ.
Enrollment: 587 undergrads, 4% part-time. 135 full-time freshmen.
Selectivity: Admits over 75% of applicants.

BASIC COSTS (2009-2010)

Tuition and fees: $24,021.
Per-credit charge: $450.
Room and board: $6,765.

FINANCIAL AID PICTURE (2009-2010)

Students with need: Out of 126 full-time freshmen who applied for aid, 118 were judged to have need. Of these, 118 received aid, and 33 had their full need met. Average financial aid package met 92% of need; average scholarship/grant was $15,867; average loan was $4,028. Need-based aid available for part-time students.
Students without need: 17 full-time freshmen who did not demonstrate need for aid received scholarships/grants; average award was $10,792. No-need awards available for academics, alumni affiliation, art, job skills, leadership, minority status, music/drama, religious affiliation, state/district residency.
Cumulative student debt: 81% of graduating class had student loans; average debt was $24,237.
Additional info: $500 grant available to students to help offset travel costs.

FINANCIAL AID PROCEDURES

Forms required: FAFSA.
Dates and Deadlines: Priority date 3/15; no closing date. Applicants notified on a rolling basis starting 3/1; must reply by 5/1 or within 4 week(s) of notification.

CONTACT

Paul Borens, Dean of Admissions and Financial Aid
1411 Ellis Avenue, Ashland, WI 54806-3999
(715) 682-1255

Ripon College

Ripon, Wisconsin
www.ripon.edu   Federal Code: 003884

4-year private liberal arts college in small town.
Enrollment: 1,038 undergrads, 1% part-time. 249 full-time freshmen.
Selectivity: Admits over 75% of applicants.

BASIC COSTS (2010-2011)

Tuition and fees: $27,080.
Per-credit charge: $900.
Room and board: $7,770.

FINANCIAL AID PICTURE (2009-2010)

Students with need: Out of 228 full-time freshmen who applied for aid, 202 were judged to have need. Of these, 202 received aid, and 42 had their full need met. Average financial aid package met 92% of need; average scholarship/grant was $19,198; average loan was $4,002. Need-based aid available for part-time students.
Students without need: 40 full-time freshmen who did not demonstrate need for aid received scholarships/grants; average award was $10,996. No-need awards available for academics, alumni affiliation, art, leadership, minority status, music/drama, religious affiliation, ROTC, state/district residency.
Scholarships offered: Pickard Scholarships: one full tuition and ten $60,000; both by invitation only. Gleason Presidential Scholarships: $52,000; minimum 3.8 GPA, top 5% of class, ACT 30, SAT 1340; by invitation only. Knop Scholars Program: one full tuition; natural science or math major, 3.8 GPA, top 5% of class, interview, by invitation only; one awarded. Faculty Scholarships: $44,000; 3.76 GPA, ACT 29, SAT 1300. Dean's Scholarships: $36,000; 3.51 GPA, ACT 27, SAT 1220. Founder's Scholarships: $32,000; 3.36 GPA, ACT 25, SAT 1140. Honor Scholarships: $24,000; 3.2 GPA, ACT 24, SAT 1110. U.S. All SAT scores exclusive of Writing. Army ROTC Scholarships: starting at $80,000. Diversity Scholarships: $20,000; application required. Forensics Scholarships: $20,000; interview. Valedictorian Scholarships: $24,000. Art Scholarships: $20,000 maximum award; portfolio. Theater Scholarships: $20,000 maximum; interview. Music Scholarships: $20,000; audition. Service

Awards: $20,000; not available to academic scholarship recipients. Boy/Girl State Scholarships: $16,000 maximum award. Legacy Awards: $8,000. United Church of Christ Scholarships: $8,000; application required. National Latin Exam: $8,000.
Cumulative student debt: 76% of graduating class had student loans; average debt was $26,073.

FINANCIAL AID PROCEDURES

Forms required: FAFSA.
Dates and Deadlines: Priority date 3/1; no closing date. Applicants notified on a rolling basis starting 3/1; must reply within 2 week(s) of notification.
Transfers: No deadline. Applicants notified on a rolling basis starting 3/1; must reply within 2 week(s) of notification.

CONTACT

Steven Schuetz, Director of Financial Aid
300 Seward Street, Ripon, WI 54971-0248
(920) 748-8301

St. Norbert College

De Pere, Wisconsin
www.snc.edu   Federal Code: 003892

4-year private liberal arts college in large town, affiliated with Roman Catholic Church.
Enrollment: 2,060 undergrads, 2% part-time. 531 full-time freshmen.
Selectivity: Admits over 75% of applicants.

BASIC COSTS (2009-2010)

Tuition and fees: $26,972.
Per-credit charge: $828.
Room and board: $7,052.

FINANCIAL AID PICTURE (2008-2009)

Students with need: Out of 449 full-time freshmen who applied for aid, 366 were judged to have need. Of these, 366 received aid, and 108 had their full need met. Average financial aid package met 98% of need; average scholarship/grant was $18,460; average loan was $3,440. For part-time students, average financial aid package was $8,854.
Students without need: 146 full-time freshmen who did not demonstrate need for aid received scholarships/grants; average award was $8,326. No-need awards available for academics, art, leadership, minority status, music/drama, ROTC, state/district residency.
Cumulative student debt: 76% of graduating class had student loans; average debt was $28,113.

FINANCIAL AID PROCEDURES

Forms required: FAFSA.
Dates and Deadlines: Priority date 3/1; no closing date. Applicants notified on a rolling basis starting 3/15; must reply within 2 week(s) of notification.

CONTACT

Jeff Zahn, Director of Financial Aid
100 Grant Street, De Pere, WI 54115-2099
(920) 403-3071

Silver Lake College

Manitowoc, Wisconsin
www.sl.edu   Federal Code: 003850

4-year private business and liberal arts college in large town, affiliated with Roman Catholic Church.
Enrollment: 339 undergrads, 48% part-time. 30 full-time freshmen.
Selectivity: Admits 50 to 75% of applicants.

BASIC COSTS (2010-2011)
Tuition and fees: $21,180.
Per-credit charge: $625.
Room and board: $8,224.

FINANCIAL AID PICTURE (2009-2010)
Students with need: Out of 30 full-time freshmen who applied for aid, 29 were judged to have need. Of these, 29 received aid, and 8 had their full need met. Average financial aid package met 77% of need; average scholarship/grant was $8,835; average loan was $3,478. For part-time students, average financial aid package was $6,567.
Students without need: 1 full-time freshmen who did not demonstrate need for aid received scholarships/grants; average award was $1,000. No-need awards available for academics, art, athletics, leadership, music/drama, religious affiliation, state/district residency.
Scholarships offered: 1 full-time freshmen received athletic scholarships; average amount $3,000.
Cumulative student debt: 88% of graduating class had student loans; average debt was $18,706.

FINANCIAL AID PROCEDURES
Forms required: FAFSA.
Dates and Deadlines: Priority date 3/15; no closing date. Applicants notified on a rolling basis starting 3/15.
Transfers: No deadline. Applicants notified on a rolling basis starting 3/15. Transfer Merit Scholarships and Phi Theta Kappa Scholarships available, as well as other institutional scholarship and grant assistance.

CONTACT
Michelle Krajnik, Director of Student Financial Aid
2406 South Alverno Road, Manitowoc, WI 54220-9319
(920) 686-6122

Southwest Wisconsin Technical College
Fennimore, Wisconsin
www.swtc.edu   Federal Code: 007699

2-year public technical college in rural community.
Enrollment: 1,753 undergrads, 51% part-time. 336 full-time freshmen.
Selectivity: Open admission; but selective for some programs.

BASIC COSTS (2009-2010)
Tuition and fees: $3,214; out-of-state residents $4,735.
Per-credit charge: $101; out-of-state residents $152.
Additional info: Materials fees vary by program; minimum $4 per course. $10 per credit fee for online courses.

FINANCIAL AID PICTURE (2008-2009)
Students with need: 55% of average financial aid package awarded as scholarships/grants, 45% awarded as loans/jobs. Work study available nights.

FINANCIAL AID PROCEDURES
Forms required: FAFSA, institutional form.
Dates and Deadlines: Priority date 4/15; no closing date. Applicants notified on a rolling basis starting 5/15; must reply within 4 week(s) of notification.

CONTACT
Joy Kite, Director of Financial Aid
1800 Bronson Boulevard, Fennimore, WI 53809
(608) 822-2319

University of Wisconsin-Baraboo/Sauk County
Baraboo, Wisconsin
www.baraboo.uwc.edu   Federal Code: 003897

2-year public branch campus and liberal arts college in large town.
Enrollment: 593 undergrads.

BASIC COSTS (2009-2010)
Tuition and fees: $4,653; out-of-state residents $11,637.
Per-credit charge: $178; out-of-state residents $469.
Additional info: Minnesota reciprocity tuition: $178 per-credit-hour.

FINANCIAL AID PICTURE (2008-2009)
Students with need: Need-based aid available for full-time and part-time students. Work study available nights.
Students without need: This college awards aid only to students with need.
Scholarships offered: Campus scholarships; $250 to full tuition.

FINANCIAL AID PROCEDURES
Forms required: FAFSA, institutional form.
Dates and Deadlines: Priority date 4/15; no closing date. Applicants notified on a rolling basis starting 4/15; must reply within 3 week(s) of notification.
Transfers: Must reply within 3 week(s) of notification.

CONTACT
Marilyn Krump, Director of Student Financial Aid
1006 Connie Road, Baraboo, WI 53913-1098
(608) 263-7727

University of Wisconsin-Barron County
Rice Lake, Wisconsin
www.barron.uwc.edu   Federal Code: 003897

2-year public branch campus and junior college in small town.
Enrollment: 446 undergrads.

BASIC COSTS (2009-2010)
Tuition and fees: $4,718; out-of-state residents $11,702.
Per-credit charge: $178; out-of-state residents $469.
Additional info: Minnesota reciprocity tuition: $178 per-credit-hour.

FINANCIAL AID PICTURE (2008-2009)
Students with need: Need-based aid available for full-time and part-time students.

FINANCIAL AID PROCEDURES
Forms required: FAFSA.
Dates and Deadlines: Priority date 4/15; no closing date. Applicants notified on a rolling basis starting 6/1.

CONTACT
Marilyn Krump, Director of Student Financial Aid
1800 College Drive, Rice Lake, WI 54868

University of Wisconsin-Eau Claire
Eau Claire, Wisconsin
www.uwec.edu   Federal Code: 003917

4-year public university in small city.
Enrollment: 10,384 undergrads, 6% part-time. 2,051 full-time freshmen.
Selectivity: Admits 50 to 75% of applicants.

BASIC COSTS (2009-2010)

Tuition and fees: $6,633; out-of-state residents $14,206.

Per-credit charge: $230; out-of-state residents $546.

Room and board: $5,630.

Additional info: Minnesota reciprocity tuition: $239 per-credit-hour.

FINANCIAL AID PICTURE (2008-2009)

Students with need: Out of 1,574 full-time freshmen who applied for aid, 840 were judged to have need. Of these, 834 received aid, and 532 had their full need met. Average financial aid package met 92% of need; average scholarship/grant was $5,603; average loan was $3,881. For part-time students, average financial aid package was $6,022.

Students without need: 353 full-time freshmen who did not demonstrate need for aid received scholarships/grants; average award was $1,894. No-need awards available for academics, art, leadership, minority status, music/drama, state/district residency.

Scholarships offered: Wisconsin Academic Excellence Scholars: $2,250; selected valedictorians; renewable; National Merit Scholarship finalists: full in-state tuition/fees. Have at least a 25 ACT; top 25% of class. Mark of Excellence Award: $2,000; 25 awards. Chancellor's Award: $1,000; 35 awards. Diversity Scholar: up to $6,000 a year for 4 years; 5 awards. Blugold Fellowship: $1,000 scholarship and $1,200 research stipend; renewable; 20 awards. Freshman honor scholarship: ACT 28; top 5% of class; $1,000; 40-50 awards.

Cumulative student debt: 68% of graduating class had student loans; average debt was $19,687.

FINANCIAL AID PROCEDURES

Forms required: FAFSA.

Dates and Deadlines: Priority date 4/15; no closing date. Applicants notified on a rolling basis starting 4/15.

CONTACT

Kathleen Sahlhoff, Director of Financial Aid

112 Schofield Hall, Eau Claire, WI 54701

(715) 836-3373

University of Wisconsin-Fond du Lac

Fond du Lac, Wisconsin

www.fdl.uwc.edu   Federal Code: 003897

2-year public junior college in large town.

Enrollment: 734 undergrads. 187 full-time freshmen.

Selectivity: Admits over 75% of applicants.

BASIC COSTS (2009-2010)

Tuition and fees: $4,594; out-of-state residents $11,578.

Per-credit charge: $178; out-of-state residents $469.

Additional info: Minnesota reciprocity tuition: $178 per-credit-hour.

FINANCIAL AID PICTURE (2008-2009)

Students with need: 41% of average financial aid package awarded as scholarships/grants, 59% awarded as loans/jobs. Need-based aid available for part-time students.

Students without need: No-need awards available for academics, leadership, music/drama.

FINANCIAL AID PROCEDURES

Forms required: FAFSA.

Dates and Deadlines: Priority date 4/15; no closing date. Applicants notified on a rolling basis starting 6/1; must reply within 2 week(s) of notification.

CONTACT

Marilyn Krump, Director of Student Financial Aid

400 University Drive, Fond du Lac, WI 54935-2950

(608) 262-5928

University of Wisconsin-Fox Valley

Menasha, Wisconsin

www.uwfox.uwc.edu   Federal Code: 011459

2-year public liberal arts college in small city.

Enrollment: 1,710 undergrads.

Selectivity: Admits less than 50% of applicants.

BASIC COSTS (2009-2010)

Tuition and fees: $4,506; out-of-state residents $11,728.

Per-credit charge: $178; out-of-state residents $469.

Additional info: Minnesota reciprocity tuition: $178 per-credit-hour.

FINANCIAL AID PICTURE (2008-2009)

Students with need: Need-based aid available for full-time and part-time students. Work study available nights, weekends, and for part-time students.

FINANCIAL AID PROCEDURES

Forms required: FAFSA.

Dates and Deadlines: Priority date 4/15; no closing date. Applicants notified on a rolling basis starting 6/1; must reply within 3 week(s) of notification.

CONTACT

Marilyn Krump, Director of Student Financial Aid

1478 Midway Road, Menasha, WI 54952-2850

University of Wisconsin-Green Bay

Green Bay, Wisconsin

www.uwgb.edu   Federal Code: 003899

4-year public university and liberal arts college in small city.

Enrollment: 6,068 undergrads, 18% part-time. 1,035 full-time freshmen.

Selectivity: Admits 50 to 75% of applicants.

BASIC COSTS (2009-2010)

Tuition and fees: $6,814; out-of-state residents $14,387.

Per-credit charge: $223; out-of-state residents $539.

Room and board: $5,300.

Additional info: Minnesota reciprocity tuition: $239 per-credit-hour.

FINANCIAL AID PICTURE (2009-2010)

Students with need: Out of 917 full-time freshmen who applied for aid, 672 were judged to have need. Of these, 642 received aid, and 276 had their full need met. Average financial aid package met 85% of need; average scholarship/grant was $6,046; average loan was $4,302. For part-time students, average financial aid package was $9,205.

Students without need: 14 full-time freshmen who did not demonstrate need for aid received scholarships/grants; average award was $2,043. No-need awards available for academics, art, athletics, leadership, minority status, music/drama.

Scholarships offered: 28 full-time freshmen received athletic scholarships; average amount $7,791.

Cumulative student debt: 71% of graduating class had student loans; average debt was $19,636.

Additional info: Auditions required for music and theater scholarships. Tuition is waived for children of Wisconsin soldiers and policemen who were slain in the line of duty. Tuition is also waived for all veterans.

FINANCIAL AID PROCEDURES

Forms required: FAFSA.

Dates and Deadlines: Priority date 4/1; no closing date. Applicants notified on a rolling basis starting 1/1; must reply within 3 week(s) of notification.

CONTACT

Ron Ronnenberg, Director of Financial Aid and Student Employment

2420 Nicolet Drive, Green Bay, WI 54311-7001

(920) 465-2075

University of Wisconsin-La Crosse

La Crosse, Wisconsin
www.uwlax.edu   Federal Code: 003919

4-year public university in small city.

Enrollment: 8,493 undergrads, 4% part-time. 1,729 full-time freshmen.

Selectivity: Admits 50 to 75% of applicants.

BASIC COSTS (2009-2010)

Tuition and fees: $7,509; out-of-state residents $15,082.

Per-credit charge: $268; out-of-state residents $583.

Room and board: $5,630.

Additional info: Minnesota reciprocity tuition: $268 per-credit-hour.

FINANCIAL AID PICTURE (2008-2009)

Students with need: Out of 1,331 full-time freshmen who applied for aid, 736 were judged to have need. Of these, 695 received aid, and 203 had their full need met. Average financial aid package met 76% of need; average scholarship/grant was $5,784; average loan was $3,048. For part-time students, average financial aid package was $6,799.

Students without need: 53 full-time freshmen who did not demonstrate need for aid received scholarships/grants; average award was $1,763. No-need awards available for academics, art, athletics, leadership, music/drama.

Cumulative student debt: 65% of graduating class had student loans; average debt was $21,998.

FINANCIAL AID PROCEDURES

Forms required: FAFSA.

Dates and Deadlines: Priority date 3/15; no closing date. Applicants notified on a rolling basis starting 4/1.

CONTACT

Louise Janke, Associate Director of Financial Aid
1725 State Street, Cleary Center, La Crosse, WI 54601
(608) 785-8604

University of Wisconsin-Madison

Madison, Wisconsin
www.wisc.edu   Federal Code: 003895

4-year public university in small city.

Enrollment: 28,690 undergrads, 4% part-time. 5,760 full-time freshmen.

Selectivity: Admits 50 to 75% of applicants.

BASIC COSTS (2009-2010)

Tuition and fees: $8,310; out-of-state residents $23,059.

Per-credit charge: $304; out-of-state residents $919.

Room and board: $8,040.

Additional info: Minnesota reciprocity tuition: $380 per-credit-hour.

FINANCIAL AID PICTURE (2008-2009)

Students with need: Out of 3,577 full-time freshmen who applied for aid, 1,861 were judged to have need. Of these, 1,840 received aid, and 453 had their full need met. Average financial aid package met 77% of need; average scholarship/grant was $3,840; average loan was $4,117. For part-time students, average financial aid package was $8,421.

Students without need: 1,346 full-time freshmen who did not demonstrate need for aid received scholarships/grants; average award was $1,933. No-need awards available for academics, alumni affiliation, art, athletics, job skills, leadership, minority status, music/drama, religious affiliation, ROTC, state/district residency.

Scholarships offered: 106 full-time freshmen received athletic scholarships; average amount $21,495.

Cumulative student debt: 49% of graduating class had student loans; average debt was $21,552.

FINANCIAL AID PROCEDURES

Forms required: FAFSA, institutional form.

Dates and Deadlines: No deadline. Applicants notified on a rolling basis starting 4/1; must reply within 9 week(s) of notification.

CONTACT

Susan Fischer, Director Student Financial Aid
Armory & Gymnasium, Madison, WI 53706-1481
(608) 262-3060

University of Wisconsin-Manitowoc

Manitowoc, Wisconsin
www.manitowoc.uwc.edu   Federal Code: 003897

2-year public branch campus and liberal arts college in large town.

Enrollment: 548 undergrads.

BASIC COSTS (2009-2010)

Tuition and fees: $4,579; out-of-state residents $11,563.

Per-credit charge: $178; out-of-state residents $469.

Additional info: Minnesota reciprocity tuition: $178 per-credit-hour.

FINANCIAL AID PICTURE (2008-2009)

Students with need: Need-based aid available for full-time and part-time students. Work study available nights.

Students without need: This college awards aid only to students with need.

FINANCIAL AID PROCEDURES

Forms required: FAFSA.

Dates and Deadlines: Priority date 3/1; no closing date. Applicants notified on a rolling basis starting 5/1; must reply within 2 week(s) of notification.

Transfers: Priority date 5/1; no deadline.

CONTACT

Marilyn Krump, Director of Student Financial Aid
705 Viebahn Street, Manitowoc, WI 54220-6699
(920) 683-4707

University of Wisconsin-Marathon County

Wausau, Wisconsin
www.uwmc.uwc.edu   Federal Code: 003903

2-year public liberal arts college in small city.

Enrollment: 1,382 undergrads.

BASIC COSTS (2009-2010)

Tuition and fees: $4,539; out-of-state residents $11,523.

Per-credit charge: $178; out-of-state residents $469.

Additional info: Minnesota reciprocity tuition: $178 per-credit-hour.

FINANCIAL AID PICTURE (2008-2009)

Students with need: Need-based aid available for full-time and part-time students. Work study available nights.

Students without need: This college awards aid only to students with need.

FINANCIAL AID PROCEDURES

Forms required: FAFSA, institutional form.

Dates and Deadlines: Priority date 4/15; no closing date. Applicants notified on a rolling basis starting 6/1; must reply within 3 week(s) of notification.

CONTACT

Marilyn Krump, Director of Student Financial Aid
518 South Seventh Avenue, Wausau, WI 54401-5396
(715) 261-6235

University of Wisconsin-Marinette
Marinette, Wisconsin
www.marinette.uwc.edu   Federal Code: 003897

2-year public branch campus and liberal arts college in large town.
Enrollment: 220 undergrads.

BASIC COSTS (2009-2010)
Tuition and fees: $4,555; out-of-state residents $11,539.
Per-credit charge: $178; out-of-state residents $469.
Additional info: Minnesota reciprocity tuition: $178 per-credit-hour.

FINANCIAL AID PICTURE (2008-2009)
Students with need: Need-based aid available for full-time and part-time students. Work study available nights.
Students without need: This college awards aid only to students with need.

FINANCIAL AID PROCEDURES
Forms required: FAFSA.
Dates and Deadlines: Priority date 4/15; no closing date. Applicants notified on a rolling basis.

CONTACT
Marilyn Krump, Director of Student Financial Aid
750 West Bay Shore Street, Marinette, WI 54143
(715) 735-4301

University of Wisconsin-Marshfield/Wood County
Marshfield, Wisconsin
www.marshfield.uwc.edu   Federal Code: 003897

2-year public branch campus college in large town.
Enrollment: 670 undergrads.

BASIC COSTS (2009-2010)
Tuition and fees: $4,607; out-of-state residents $11,591.
Per-credit charge: $178; out-of-state residents $469.
Additional info: Minnesota reciprocity tuition: $178 per-credit-hour.

FINANCIAL AID PICTURE (2008-2009)
Students with need: Need-based aid available for full-time and part-time students. Work study available nights, weekends, and for part-time students.
Students without need: This college awards aid only to students with need.
Scholarships offered: Special Entering Scholarships; $1,000; based on academic excellence; 2 awarded. Ken and Ardyce Helting Scholarship; $1,000; priority given to physically challenged or learning disabled; 1 awarded. Valedictorian, Salutatorian and National Merit Finalist and Semi-Finalists; $1,000; ACT of 25 or better. Greenhouse Scholarship; priority to students in Environmental Studies; 1 awarded. Patrice Ptacek Memorial Scholarship; 2 letters of recommendation; 1 awarded. Woman of the Future Scholarship; $1,000; must be full-time female freshman entering sophomore year, well-defined career goals other than nursing; 1 awarded.

FINANCIAL AID PROCEDURES
Forms required: FAFSA.
Dates and Deadlines: Priority date 4/15; no closing date. Applicants notified on a rolling basis starting 5/15; must reply within 3 week(s) of notification.

CONTACT
Marilyn Krump, Director of Student Financial Aid
2000 West Fifth Street, Marshfield, WI 54449
(715) 389-6500

University of Wisconsin-Milwaukee
Milwaukee, Wisconsin
www.uwm.edu   Federal Code: 003896

4-year public university in very large city.
Enrollment: 23,553 undergrads, 12% part-time. 3,945 full-time freshmen.
Selectivity: Admits over 75% of applicants.

BASIC COSTS (2009-2010)
Tuition and fees: $7,702; out-of-state residents $17,431.
Per-credit charge: $287; out-of-state residents $692.
Room and board: $7,890.
Additional info: Minnesota reciprocity tuition: $368 per-credit-hour.

FINANCIAL AID PICTURE (2009-2010)
Students with need: Out of 3,346 full-time freshmen who applied for aid, 2,649 were judged to have need. Of these, 2,516 received aid, and 623 had their full need met. Average financial aid package met 48% of need; average scholarship/grant was $7,270; average loan was $3,605. For part-time students, average financial aid package was $7,447.
Students without need: 5 full-time freshmen who did not demonstrate need for aid received scholarships/grants; average award was $2,191. No-need awards available for academics, art, athletics.
Scholarships offered: 2 full-time freshmen received athletic scholarships; average amount $823.
Cumulative student debt: 67% of graduating class had student loans; average debt was $19,830.

FINANCIAL AID PROCEDURES
Forms required: FAFSA.
Dates and Deadlines: Priority date 3/1; no closing date. Applicants notified on a rolling basis starting 3/1; must reply within 2 week(s) of notification.
Transfers: No deadline. Applicants notified on a rolling basis starting 3/15; must reply within 2 week(s) of notification.

CONTACT
Jane Hojan-Clark, Executive Director of Financial Aid
Box 749, Milwaukee, WI 53201
(414) 229-6300

University of Wisconsin-Oshkosh
Oshkosh, Wisconsin
www.uwosh.edu   Federal Code: 003920

4-year public university in small city.
Enrollment: 10,425 undergrads, 12% part-time. 1,882 full-time freshmen.
Selectivity: Admits over 75% of applicants.

BASIC COSTS (2009-2010)
Tuition and fees: $6,349; out-of-state residents $13,922.
Per-credit charge: $228; out-of-state residents $544.
Room and board: $5,864.
Additional info: Minnesota reciprocity tuition: $239 per-credit-hour.

FINANCIAL AID PICTURE (2008-2009)
Students with need: Need-based aid available for full-time and part-time students.
Students without need: No-need awards available for academics, alumni affiliation, art, leadership, minority status, music/drama, state/district residency.

FINANCIAL AID PROCEDURES
Forms required: FAFSA.
Dates and Deadlines: Priority date 3/15; no closing date. Applicants notified on a rolling basis starting 4/15; must reply within 2 week(s) of notification.
Transfers: Must send financial aid transcript to university.

CONTACT

Beatrice Contreras, Director of Financial Aid

800 Algoma Boulevard, Oshkosh, WI 54901-8602

(920) 424-3377

University of Wisconsin-Parkside

Kenosha, Wisconsin

www.uwp.edu   Federal Code: 005015

4-year public university in small city.

Enrollment: 4,826 undergrads, 24% part-time. 832 full-time freshmen.

Selectivity: Admits 50 to 75% of applicants.

BASIC COSTS (2009-2010)

Tuition and fees: $6,348; out-of-state residents $13,922.

Per-credit charge: $223; out-of-state residents $539.

Room and board: $5,750.

Additional info: Minnesota Reciprocity tuition: $239 per-credit-hour.

FINANCIAL AID PICTURE (2008-2009)

Students with need: Out of 663 full-time freshmen who applied for aid, 523 were judged to have need. Of these, 500 received aid. Need-based aid available for part-time students.

Students without need: No-need awards available for academics, art, athletics, minority status, music/drama, state/district residency.

FINANCIAL AID PROCEDURES

Forms required: FAFSA.

Dates and Deadlines: Priority date 3/15; no closing date. Applicants notified on a rolling basis starting 4/1; must reply within 2 week(s) of notification.

CONTACT

Randall McCready, Director of Financial Aid

PO Box 2000, Kenosha, WI 53141-2000

(262) 595-2574

University of Wisconsin-Platteville

Platteville, Wisconsin

www.uwplatt.edu   Federal Code: 003921

4-year public university in large town.

Enrollment: 6,770 undergrads, 8% part-time. 1,518 full-time freshmen.

Selectivity: Admits over 75% of applicants.

BASIC COSTS (2009-2010)

Tuition and fees: $6,314; out-of-state residents $13,887.

Per-credit charge: $228; out-of-state residents $543.

Room and board: $5,916.

Additional info: Minnesota reciprocity tuition: $239 per-credit-hour. Tri-State Initiative offers Illinois and Iowa students discounted out-of-state rate for select majors.

FINANCIAL AID PICTURE

Students with need: Need-based aid available for full-time and part-time students. Work study available nights, weekends, and for part-time students.

Students without need: This college awards aid only to students with need.

FINANCIAL AID PROCEDURES

Forms required: FAFSA.

Dates and Deadlines: Priority date 3/15; no closing date. Applicants notified on a rolling basis starting 6/1; must reply within 2 week(s) of notification.

CONTACT

Liz Tucker, Director of Financial Aid

One University Plaza, Platteville, WI 53818

(608) 342-1836

University of Wisconsin-Richland

Richland Center, Wisconsin

www.richland.uwc.edu   Federal Code: 003897

2-year public liberal arts college in small town.

Enrollment: 495 undergrads.

BASIC COSTS (2009-2010)

Tuition and fees: $4,747; out-of-state residents $11,731.

Per-credit charge: $178; out-of-state residents $469.

Additional info: Minnesota reciprocity tuition: $178 per-credit-hour.

FINANCIAL AID PICTURE (2009-2010)

Students with need: 14% of average financial aid package awarded as scholarships/grants, 86% awarded as loans/jobs. Need-based aid available for part-time students. Work study available nights, weekends, and for part-time students.

Students without need: This college awards aid only to students with need.

Scholarships offered: Richland Campus Foundation Scholarships available for new, continuing and transfer students.

FINANCIAL AID PROCEDURES

Forms required: FAFSA.

Dates and Deadlines: Priority date 4/15; no closing date. Applicants notified on a rolling basis starting 5/15; must reply within 3 week(s) of notification.

CONTACT

Marilyn Krump, Director of Student Financial Aid

1200 Highway 14 West, Richland Center, WI 53581

(608) 647-6186 ext. 3

University of Wisconsin-River Falls

River Falls, Wisconsin

www.uwrf.edu   Federal Code: 003923

4-year public university and liberal arts college in large town.

Enrollment: 6,044 undergrads, 5% part-time. 1,325 full-time freshmen.

Selectivity: Admits over 75% of applicants.

BASIC COSTS (2009-2010)

Tuition and fees: $6,390; out-of-state residents $13,963.

Per-credit charge: $226; out-of-state residents $542.

Room and board: $5,330.

Additional info: Minnesota reciprocity tuition: $239 per-credit-hour.

FINANCIAL AID PICTURE (2009-2010)

Students with need: 38% of average financial aid package awarded as scholarships/grants, 62% awarded as loans/jobs. Need-based aid available for part-time students. Work study available nights, weekends, and for part-time students.

Students without need: This college awards aid only to students with need.

FINANCIAL AID PROCEDURES

Forms required: FAFSA.

Dates and Deadlines: Priority date 3/15; no closing date. Applicants notified on a rolling basis starting 4/15.

Transfers: No deadline. Applicants notified on a rolling basis starting 4/1.

CONTACT

Barbara Stinson, Director of Financial Aid

410 South 3rd Street, River Falls, WI 54022-5001

(715) 425-3141

PART III: FINANCIAL AID COLLEGE BY COLLEGE

University of Wisconsin-Rock County
Janesville, Wisconsin
www.rock.uwc.edu   Federal Code: 003897

2-year public branch campus and liberal arts college in small city.
Enrollment: 1,171 undergrads.

BASIC COSTS (2009-2010)
Tuition and fees: $4,572; out-of-state residents $11,556.
Per-credit charge: $178; out-of-state residents $469.
Additional info: Minnesota reciprocity tuition: $178 per-credit-hour.

FINANCIAL AID PICTURE (2008-2009)
Students with need: Need-based aid available for full-time and part-time students. Work study available nights, weekends, and for part-time students.
Students without need: This college awards aid only to students with need.

FINANCIAL AID PROCEDURES
Forms required: FAFSA, institutional form.
Dates and Deadlines: Closing date 3/15. Applicants notified on a rolling basis starting 6/1; must reply within 3 week(s) of notification.

CONTACT
Marilyn Krump, Director of Student Financial Aid
2909 Kellogg Avenue, Janesville, WI 53546-5699
(608) 758-6523

University of Wisconsin-Sheboygan
Sheboygan, Wisconsin
www.sheboygan.uwc.edu   Federal Code: 003897

2-year public community and junior college in small city.
Enrollment: 825 undergrads.

BASIC COSTS (2009-2010)
Tuition and fees: $4,545; out-of-state residents $11,529.
Per-credit charge: $178; out-of-state residents $469.
Additional info: Minnesota reciprocity tuition: $178 per-credit-hour.

FINANCIAL AID PICTURE (2009-2010)
Students with need: Need-based aid available for full-time and part-time students.
Students without need: No-need awards available for academics, leadership, music/drama.
Additional info: Scholarship deadline 2/28.

FINANCIAL AID PROCEDURES
Forms required: FAFSA, institutional form.
Dates and Deadlines: Priority date 4/15; no closing date. Applicants notified on a rolling basis starting 6/1; must reply within 2 week(s) of notification.
Transfers: No deadline. Applicants notified on a rolling basis.

CONTACT
Mary Balde, Director of Student Financial Aid
One University Drive, Sheboygan, WI 53081
(920) 459-6633

University of Wisconsin-Stevens Point
Stevens Point, Wisconsin
www.uwsp.edu   Federal Code: 003924

4-year public university in large town.
Enrollment: 8,610 undergrads, 5% part-time. 1,601 full-time freshmen.
Selectivity: Admits 50 to 75% of applicants.

BASIC COSTS (2009-2010)
Tuition and fees: $6,532; out-of-state residents $14,105.
Per-credit charge: $223; out-of-state residents $539.
Room and board: $5,612.
Additional info: Minnesota reciprocity tuition: $239 per-credit-hour.

FINANCIAL AID PICTURE (2008-2009)
Students with need: Out of 1,262 full-time freshmen who applied for aid, 781 were judged to have need. Of these, 735 received aid, and 517 had their full need met. Average financial aid package met 76% of need; average scholarship/grant was $5,386; average loan was $3,777. For part-time students, average financial aid package was $5,851.
Students without need: 116 full-time freshmen who did not demonstrate need for aid received scholarships/grants; average award was $2,519. No-need awards available for academics, alumni affiliation, art, music/drama, ROTC.
Additional info: Tuition discounts offered to qualified residents from other states.

FINANCIAL AID PROCEDURES
Forms required: FAFSA.
Dates and Deadlines: Priority date 5/15; closing date 6/15. Applicants notified on a rolling basis starting 5/1; must reply within 4 week(s) of notification.
Transfers: No deadline.

CONTACT
Paul Watson, Director of Financial Aid
Student Services Center, Stevens Point, WI 54481
(715) 346-4771

University of Wisconsin-Stout
Menomonie, Wisconsin
www.uwstout.edu   Federal Code: 003915

4-year public university in large town.
Enrollment: 7,893 undergrads, 14% part-time. 1,504 full-time freshmen.
Selectivity: Admits over 75% of applicants.

BASIC COSTS (2009-2010)
Tuition and fees: $7,821; out-of-state residents $15,566.
Per-credit charge: $199; out-of-state residents $457.
Room and board: $5,336.
Additional info: Laptop computer included in the cost of tuition. Minnesota reciprocity tuition: $263 per-credit-hour.

FINANCIAL AID PICTURE (2009-2010)
Students with need: Out of 1,262 full-time freshmen who applied for aid, 822 were judged to have need. Of these, 812 received aid, and 435 had their full need met. Average financial aid package met 90% of need; average scholarship/grant was $5,689; average loan was $3,403. For part-time students, average financial aid package was $8,031.
Students without need: 49 full-time freshmen who did not demonstrate need for aid received scholarships/grants; average award was $1,620. No-need awards available for academics.
Scholarships offered: Wisconsin Academic Excellence Scholarship: $2,250; selected by high school. National Merit Finalist Scholarship: $2,000; automatically awarded to NMSQT finalist. National Merit Semifinalist Scholarship: $1,000; automatically awarded to NMSQT semifinalist. Chancellor's Academic Honor Scholarship: $1,000; automatically awarded to top 5% of high school class with ACT of 25 who enroll by July 15.
Cumulative student debt: 78% of graduating class had student loans; average debt was $25,134.

FINANCIAL AID PROCEDURES
Forms required: FAFSA.
Dates and Deadlines: Priority date 3/15; no closing date. Applicants notified on a rolling basis starting 4/1; must reply within 4 week(s) of notification.

CONTACT
Beth Boisen, Director of Financial Aid
1 Clocktower Plaza, Menomonie, WI 54751
(715) 232-1363

University of Wisconsin-Superior
Superior, Wisconsin
www.uwsuper.edu   Federal Code: 003925

4-year public university and liberal arts college in small city.
Enrollment: 2,515 undergrads, 18% part-time. 364 full-time freshmen.
Selectivity: Admits 50 to 75% of applicants.

BASIC COSTS (2009-2010)
Tuition and fees: $6,736; out-of-state residents $14,309.
Per-credit charge: $232; out-of-state residents $548.
Room and board: $5,485.
Additional info: Minnesota reciprocity tuition: $239 per-credit-hour.

FINANCIAL AID PICTURE (2009-2010)
Students with need: Out of 259 full-time freshmen who applied for aid, 198 were judged to have need. Of these, 197 received aid, and 52 had their full need met. Need-based aid available for part-time students.
Students without need: 15 full-time freshmen who did not demonstrate need for aid received scholarships/grants; average award was $1,488. No-need awards available for academics, alumni affiliation, art, leadership, minority status, music/drama, ROTC, state/district residency.
Cumulative student debt: 75% of graduating class had student loans; average debt was $22,516.
Additional info: Tuition Assistance Program (TAP) available to non-resident students on limited basis.

FINANCIAL AID PROCEDURES
Forms required: FAFSA.
Dates and Deadlines: Priority date 4/1; no closing date. Applicants notified on a rolling basis starting 3/15; must reply by 5/1 or within 4 week(s) of notification.
Transfers: No deadline. Applicants notified on a rolling basis starting 3/15; must reply by 5/1 or within 4 week(s) of notification.

CONTACT
Anne Podgorak, Director of Financial Aid
Belknap and Catlin, PO Box 2000, Superior, WI 54880
(715) 394-8200

University of Wisconsin-Washington County
West Bend, Wisconsin
www.washington.uwc.edu   Federal Code: 003897

2-year public branch campus and liberal arts college in large town.
Enrollment: 1,074 undergrads.

BASIC COSTS (2009-2010)
Tuition and fees: $4,618; out-of-state residents $11,602.
Per-credit charge: $178; out-of-state residents $469.
Additional info: Minnesota reciprocity tuition: $178 per-credit-hour.

FINANCIAL AID PICTURE (2008-2009)
Students with need: Need-based aid available for full-time and part-time students. Work study available weekends and for part-time students.
Students without need: No-need awards available for academics.

FINANCIAL AID PROCEDURES
Forms required: FAFSA.

Dates and Deadlines: Priority date 4/15; no closing date. Applicants notified on a rolling basis starting 4/30; must reply within 3 week(s) of notification.
Transfers: No deadline.

CONTACT
Marilyn Krump, Director of Student Financial Aid
400 University Drive, West Bend, WI 53095
(262) 335-5207

University of Wisconsin-Waukesha
Waukesha, Wisconsin
www.waukesha.uwc.edu   Federal Code: 003897

2-year public branch campus and junior college in small city.
Enrollment: 1,819 undergrads, 38% part-time. 813 full-time freshmen.

BASIC COSTS (2009-2010)
Tuition and fees: $4,570; out-of-state residents $11,554.
Per-credit charge: $192; out-of-state residents $483.
Additional info: Minnesota reciprocity tuition: $178 per-credit-hour.

FINANCIAL AID PICTURE (2009-2010)
Students with need: 33% of average financial aid package awarded as scholarships/grants, 67% awarded as loans/jobs. Need-based aid available for part-time students. Work study available nights, weekends, and for part-time students.
Students without need: No-need awards available for academics, art, leadership, minority status, music/drama.
Scholarships offered: University of Wisconsin-Waukesha Scholarship Program; numerous scholarships; amounts vary.

FINANCIAL AID PROCEDURES
Forms required: FAFSA.
Dates and Deadlines: Priority date 4/15; no closing date. Applicants notified on a rolling basis starting 5/15; must reply within 3 week(s) of notification.

CONTACT
Marilyn Krump, Director of Student Financial Aid
1500 North University Drive, Waukesha, WI 53188
(262) 521-5210

University of Wisconsin-Whitewater
Whitewater, Wisconsin
www.uww.edu   Federal Code: 003926

4-year public university in large town.
Enrollment: 9,652 undergrads.

BASIC COSTS (2009-2010)
Tuition and fees: $6,496; out-of-state residents $14,069.
Per-credit charge: $231; out-of-state residents $547.
Room and board: $4,928.
Additional info: Minnesota reciprocity tuition: $239 per-credit-hour.

FINANCIAL AID PICTURE (2009-2010)
Students with need: Need-based aid available for full-time and part-time students. Work study available nights, weekends, and for part-time students.
Students without need: No-need awards available for academics, alumni affiliation, art, leadership, minority status, music/drama, ROTC, state/district residency.

FINANCIAL AID PROCEDURES
Forms required: FAFSA.
Dates and Deadlines: Priority date 3/15; no closing date. Applicants notified on a rolling basis starting 4/1; must reply within 3 week(s) of notification.
Transfers: No deadline. Applicants notified on a rolling basis starting 4/1; must reply within 3 week(s) of notification.

CONTACT
Carol Miller, Director of Financial Aid
800 West Main Street, Whitewater, WI 53190-1790
(262) 472-1130

Viterbo University
La Crosse, Wisconsin
www.viterbo.edu   Federal Code: 003911

4-year private university and liberal arts college in small city, affiliated with Roman Catholic Church.
Enrollment: 2,109 undergrads.
Selectivity: Admits over 75% of applicants.

BASIC COSTS (2009-2010)
Tuition and fees: $20,160.
Per-credit charge: $580.
Room and board: $6,710.
Additional info: Additional fees for some fine arts, dietetics, science courses, and nursing clinicals. Tuition/fee waivers available for minority students.

FINANCIAL AID PICTURE
Students with need: Need-based aid available for full-time and part-time students. Work study available nights, weekends, and for part-time students.
Students without need: No-need awards available for academics, alumni affiliation, art, athletics, leadership, minority status, music/drama, ROTC.
Scholarships offered: Fine arts scholarships: up to $10,000 per year; for incoming full-time freshmen and transfer students talented in areas of art, music or theater. Dr. Scholl Scholarship: full, 4-year tuition; must enroll full-time and maintain 3.5 GPA, 1 awarded. Viterbo University Scholarship: $1,000-$8,000 per year; based on academic history; incoming freshmen and transfers automatically considered; renewable.

FINANCIAL AID PROCEDURES
Forms required: FAFSA, institutional form.
Dates and Deadlines: Priority date 3/15; no closing date. Applicants notified on a rolling basis starting 4/1; must reply within 3 week(s) of notification.

CONTACT
Terry Norman, Director of Financial Aid
900 Viterbo Drive, La Crosse, WI 54601-8804
(608) 796-3900

Waukesha County Technical College
Pewaukee, Wisconsin
www.wctc.edu   Federal Code: 005294

2-year public technical college in large town.
Enrollment: 5,938 undergrads, 59% part-time. 487 full-time freshmen.
Selectivity: Open admission; but selective for some programs.

BASIC COSTS (2009-2010)
Tuition and fees: $3,345; out-of-state residents $4,866.
Per-credit charge: $101; out-of-state residents $152.
Additional info: Materials fees vary by program; minimum $4 per course. $10 per credit fee for online courses.

FINANCIAL AID PICTURE
Students with need: Need-based aid available for full-time students. Work study available nights.
Students without need: No-need awards available for academics.

FINANCIAL AID PROCEDURES
Forms required: FAFSA, institutional form.

Dates and Deadlines: Priority date 3/31; no closing date. Applicants notified on a rolling basis.

CONTACT
Tim Jacobson, Manager/Financial Aid
800 Main Street, Pewaukee, WI 53072
(262) 691-5436

Western Technical College
La Crosse, Wisconsin
www.westerntc.edu   Federal Code: 003840

2-year public community and technical college in small city.
Enrollment: 5,857 undergrads.
Selectivity: Open admission; but selective for some programs.

BASIC COSTS (2009-2010)
Tuition and fees: $3,323; out-of-state residents $4,844.
Per-credit charge: $101; out-of-state residents $152.
Room and board: $4,108.
Additional info: Materials fees vary by program; minimum $4 per course. Tuition/fee waivers available for unemployed or children of unemployed.

FINANCIAL AID PICTURE (2008-2009)
Students with need: Need-based aid available for full-time and part-time students. Work study available nights, weekends, and for part-time students.

FINANCIAL AID PROCEDURES
Forms required: FAFSA, institutional form.
Dates and Deadlines: Priority date 3/1; no closing date. Applicants notified on a rolling basis starting 4/1.

CONTACT
Jerolyn Grandall, Student Financial Services Manager
PO Box 908, La Crosse, WI 54602-0908
(608) 785-9302

Wisconsin Indianhead Technical College
Shell Lake, Wisconsin
www.witc.edu   Federal Code: 011824

2-year public technical college in rural community.
Enrollment: 3,560 undergrads, 53% part-time. 499 full-time freshmen.
Selectivity: Open admission; but selective for some programs.

BASIC COSTS (2009-2010)
Tuition and fees: $3,257; out-of-state residents $4,778.
Per-credit charge: $101; out-of-state residents $152.
Additional info: Materials fees vary by program; minimum $4 per course. $10 per credit fee for online courses.

FINANCIAL AID PICTURE (2008-2009)
Students with need: Need-based aid available for full-time and part-time students. Work study available nights, weekends, and for part-time students.
Students without need: This college awards aid only to students with need.

FINANCIAL AID PROCEDURES
Forms required: FAFSA.
Dates and Deadlines: Priority date 4/1; no closing date. Applicants notified on a rolling basis starting 5/9; must reply by 9/1 or within 4 week(s) of notification.

CONTACT
Terry Klein, Director of Financial Aid
505 Pine Ridge Drive, Shell Lake, WI 54871
(715) 468-2815 ext. 2243

Wisconsin Lutheran College
Milwaukee, Wisconsin
www.wlc.edu   Federal Code: 014658

4-year private liberal arts college in very large city, affiliated with Wisconsin Evangelical Lutheran Synod.

Enrollment: 743 undergrads.

Selectivity: Admits 50 to 75% of applicants.

BASIC COSTS (2009-2010)
Tuition and fees: $21,180.

Per-credit charge: $640.

Room and board: $7,700.

FINANCIAL AID PICTURE (2009-2010)
Students with need: Need-based aid available for full-time and part-time students.

Students without need: No-need awards available for academics, art, leadership, music/drama.

Scholarships offered: Presidential Scholarship: $10,000 ($11,000 if ACT is 30 or greater); based on ACT score of 27 or higher plus top 10% of HS class or 3.7 GPA; no limit on number of awards. Academic Scholarship: $9,000; ACT score of 24 or higher and top 25% of high school class or 3.4 GPA. To qualify, students must be admitted in good standing by May 1.

FINANCIAL AID PROCEDURES
Forms required: FAFSA, institutional form.

Dates and Deadlines: Priority date 3/1; no closing date. Applicants notified on a rolling basis starting 3/15; must reply within 2 week(s) of notification.

Transfers: Transfer scholarship and transfer grant available for qualifying students.

CONTACT
Linda Loeffel, Financial Aid Director
8800 West Bluemound Road, Milwaukee, WI 53226-4699
(414) 443-8856

Wyoming

Casper College
Casper, Wyoming
www.caspercollege.edu   Federal Code: 003928

2-year public community college in small city.

Enrollment: 2,967 undergrads, 31% part-time. 665 full-time freshmen.

Selectivity: Open admission; but selective for some programs and for out-of-state students.

BASIC COSTS (2009-2010)
Tuition and fees: $1,848; out-of-state residents $5,112.

Per-credit charge: $68; out-of-state residents $204.

Room and board: $4,160.

Additional info: Western Undergraduate Exchange students pay $102 per credit-hour.

FINANCIAL AID PICTURE (2009-2010)
Students with need: Need-based aid available for full-time and part-time students. Work study available nights, weekends, and for part-time students.

Students without need: No-need awards available for academics, art, athletics, leadership, music/drama, state/district residency.

FINANCIAL AID PROCEDURES
Forms required: FAFSA.

Dates and Deadlines: Priority date 3/15; no closing date. Applicants notified on a rolling basis starting 4/1.

Transfers: No deadline. Applicants notified on a rolling basis starting 4/1.

CONTACT
Darry Voigt, Director of Financial Aid
125 College Drive, Casper, WY 82601
(307) 268-2510

Central Wyoming College
Riverton, Wyoming
www.cwc.edu   Federal Code: 005018

2-year public community college in large town.

Enrollment: 1,371 undergrads, 36% part-time. 335 full-time freshmen.

Selectivity: Open admission; but selective for some programs.

BASIC COSTS (2010-2011)
Tuition and fees: $2,136; out-of-state residents $5,400.

Room and board: $4,085.

FINANCIAL AID PICTURE (2009-2010)
Students with need: Out of 251 full-time freshmen who applied for aid, 189 were judged to have need. Of these, 186 received aid. Need-based aid available for part-time students.

Students without need: No-need awards available for academics, alumni affiliation, art, athletics, leadership, minority status, music/drama, state/district residency.

Scholarships offered: Honors Scholarships: in-state tuition and general fees plus $300 book stipend; for graduating high school seniors with minimum 3.5 GPA or 25 ACT. Seniors Scholarships: in-state tuition; for graduating high school seniors with 3.0-3.49 GPA or 22 ACT. Full academic scholarships: in-state tuition, general fees, room and board, books and supplies; for Wyoming National Merit finalists.

FINANCIAL AID PROCEDURES
Forms required: FAFSA, institutional form.

Dates and Deadlines: Priority date 4/15; no closing date. Applicants notified on a rolling basis starting 5/1; must reply within 2 week(s) of notification.

CONTACT
Jacque Burns, Director of Financial Aid
2660 Peck Avenue, Riverton, WY 82501
(307) 855-2150

Eastern Wyoming College
Torrington, Wyoming
www.ewc.wy.edu   Federal Code: 003929

2-year public community college in small town.

Enrollment: 722 undergrads, 28% part-time. 199 full-time freshmen.

Selectivity: Open admission.

BASIC COSTS (2009-2010)
Tuition and fees: $2,136; out-of-state residents $5,400.

Per-credit charge: $68; out-of-state residents $204.

Room and board: $3,666.

Additional info: Students from Western Undergraduate Exchange pay $102 per-credit-hour.

FINANCIAL AID PICTURE (2008-2009)
Students with need: Need-based aid available for full-time and part-time students. Work study available nights, weekends, and for part-time students.

Students without need: No-need awards available for academics, alumni affiliation, art, athletics, leadership, music/drama.

Additional info: Installment payment plan on room and board contracts offered.

FINANCIAL AID PROCEDURES

Forms required: FAFSA, institutional form.
Dates and Deadlines: Priority date 3/15; no closing date. Applicants notified on a rolling basis starting 1/1.

CONTACT

Financial Aid Director
3200 West C Street, Torrington, WY 82240
(800) 658-3195 ext. 8325

Laramie County Community College

Cheyenne, Wyoming
www.lccc.wy.edu   Federal Code: 009259

2-year public community college in small city.
Enrollment: 3,424 undergrads, 42% part-time. 344 full-time freshmen.
Selectivity: Open admission; but selective for some programs.

BASIC COSTS (2009-2010)

Tuition and fees: $2,472; out-of-state residents $5,736.
Per-credit charge: $68; out-of-state residents $204.
Room and board: $6,482.
Additional info: Students from Western Undergraduate Exchange schools and Nebraska residents pay $3,288 in tuition and fees per year.

FINANCIAL AID PICTURE (2008-2009)

Students with need: Need-based aid available for full-time and part-time students.
Students without need: No-need awards available for academics, art, athletics, music/drama.

FINANCIAL AID PROCEDURES

Forms required: FAFSA, institutional form.
Dates and Deadlines: Priority date 4/1; no closing date. Applicants notified on a rolling basis starting 6/1; must reply within 2 week(s) of notification.

CONTACT

Dennis Schroeder, Director of Financial Aid
1400 East College Drive, Cheyenne, WY 82007-3299
(307) 778-1215

Northwest College

Powell, Wyoming
www.northwestcollege.edu   Federal Code: 003931

2-year public community college in small town.
Enrollment: 1,851 undergrads.
Selectivity: Open admission; but selective for some programs and for out-of-state students.

BASIC COSTS (2009-2010)

Tuition and fees: $2,172; out-of-state residents $5,436.
Per-credit charge: $68; out-of-state residents $204.
Room and board: $3,916.
Additional info: Students from Western Undergraduate Exchange schools pay $2,352 tuition; $98 per-credit-hour.

FINANCIAL AID PICTURE (2008-2009)

Students with need: Work study available nights.
Students without need: No-need awards available for academics, athletics.
Additional info: Interview, essay recommended for scholarships.

FINANCIAL AID PROCEDURES

Forms required: FAFSA, institutional form.
Dates and Deadlines: Priority date 5/1; no closing date. Applicants notified on a rolling basis starting 5/1; must reply within 2 week(s) of notification.

CONTACT

Tara Piantanida, Director of Financial Aid
231 West 6th Street, Powell, WY 82435
(307) 754-6104

Sheridan College

Sheridan, Wyoming
www.sheridan.edu   Federal Code: 003930

2-year public community college in large town.
Enrollment: 1,916 undergrads, 33% part-time. 431 full-time freshmen.
Selectivity: Open admission; but selective for some programs.

BASIC COSTS (2009-2010)

Tuition and fees: $2,365; out-of-state residents $5,629.
Per-credit charge: $68; out-of-state residents $204.
Room and board: $4,600.

FINANCIAL AID PICTURE (2008-2009)

Students with need: 69% of average financial aid package awarded as scholarships/grants, 31% awarded as loans/jobs. Need-based aid available for part-time students. Work study available nights, weekends, and for part-time students.
Students without need: No-need awards available for academics, art, athletics, leadership, music/drama, state/district residency.
Scholarships offered: Merit scholarships; in-state tuition and fees; must have 25 ACT or 1120 SAT (exclusive of Writing); renewable.

FINANCIAL AID PROCEDURES

Forms required: FAFSA, institutional form.
Dates and Deadlines: Priority date 3/1; no closing date. Applicants notified on a rolling basis; must reply within 3 week(s) of notification.

CONTACT

Randy Thompson, Director of Financial Aid
PO Box 1500, Sheridan, WY 82801-1500
(307) 674-6446 ext. 2100

University of Wyoming

Laramie, Wyoming
www.uwyo.edu   Federal Code: 003932

4-year public university in large town.
Enrollment: 9,586 undergrads, 15% part-time. 1,681 full-time freshmen.
Selectivity: Admits over 75% of applicants.

BASIC COSTS (2010-2011)

Tuition and fees: $3,927; out-of-state residents $12,237.
Per-credit charge: $99; out-of-state residents $376.
Room and board: $8,360.
Additional info: International students must pay an additional $40 fee per semester.

FINANCIAL AID PICTURE (2008-2009)

Students with need: Out of 1,273 full-time freshmen who applied for aid, 744 were judged to have need. Of these, 728 received aid, and 223 had their full need met. Average financial aid package met 34% of need; average scholarship/grant was $3,550; average loan was $2,772. For part-time students, average financial aid package was $6,026.
Students without need: 478 full-time freshmen who did not demonstrate need for aid received scholarships/grants; average award was $5,503. No-need awards available for academics, alumni affiliation, art, athletics, leadership, minority status, music/drama, religious affiliation, ROTC, state/district residency.
Scholarships offered: *Merit:* Western Heritage Scholarship: number awarded and packages vary. President's High School Honor Scholarship: cov-

ers undergraduate fees and tuition; number awarded varies. *Athletic:* 81 full-time freshmen received athletic scholarships; average amount $8,572.
Cumulative student debt: 53% of graduating class had student loans; average debt was $18,760.

FINANCIAL AID PROCEDURES
Forms required: FAFSA.
Dates and Deadlines: Priority date 3/1; no closing date. Applicants notified on a rolling basis starting 3/15; must reply within 3 week(s) of notification.

CONTACT
David Gruen, Director of Student Financial Aid
1000 East University Avenue/Department 3435, Laramie, WY 82071
(307) 766-2116

Western Wyoming Community College
Rock Springs, Wyoming
www.wwcc.wy.edu   Federal Code: 003933

2-year public community college in large town.
Enrollment: 2,553 undergrads, 54% part-time. 260 full-time freshmen.
Selectivity: Open admission; but selective for some programs.

BASIC COSTS (2009-2010)
Tuition and fees: $1,994; out-of-state residents $5,258.
Per-credit charge: $68; out-of-state residents $204.
Room and board: $4,030.

FINANCIAL AID PICTURE (2009-2010)
Students with need: 64% of average financial aid package awarded as scholarships/grants, 36% awarded as loans/jobs. Need-based aid available for part-time students.
Students without need: No-need awards available for academics, art, athletics, music/drama, state/district residency.

FINANCIAL AID PROCEDURES
Forms required: FAFSA.
Dates and Deadlines: Priority date 4/1; no closing date. Applicants notified on a rolling basis starting 2/15; must reply within 2 week(s) of notification.

CONTACT
Stacee Hanson, Financial Aid Director
Box 428, Rock Springs, WY 82902-0428
(307) 382-1643

Part IV

Scholarship Lists

Academic scholarships

Alabama
Alabama State University
Amridge University
Athens State University
Auburn University at Montgomery
Bevill State Community College
Birmingham-Southern College
Bishop State Community College
Calhoun Community College
Central Alabama Community College
Chattahoochee Valley Community College
Enterprise-Ozark Community College
Faulkner University
Gadsden State Community College
George C. Wallace State Community College
    George C. Wallace Community College at
      Dothan
    Wallace State Community College at
      Selma
Huntingdon College
Jacksonville State University
Jefferson Davis Community College
Jefferson State Community College
Judson College
Lurleen B. Wallace Community College
Northeast Alabama Community College
Northwest-Shoals Community College
Oakwood University
Samford University
Snead State Community College
Southeastern Bible College
Spring Hill College
Stillman College
Talladega College
Troy University
Tuskegee University
University of Alabama
University of Alabama
    Birmingham
    Huntsville
University of Mobile
University of Montevallo
University of North Alabama
University of South Alabama
University of West Alabama
Wallace State Community College at Hanceville

Alaska
Alaska Pacific University
University of Alaska
    Anchorage
    Fairbanks
    Southeast

Arizona
Arizona State University
Arizona Western College
Art Center Design College
Cochise College
DeVry University
    Phoenix
Dine College
Eastern Arizona College
Embry-Riddle Aeronautical University: Prescott
    Campus
Grand Canyon University
Mesa Community College
Northern Arizona University
Northland Pioneer College
Pima Community College
Prescott College
Scottsdale Community College
Southwestern College

University of Arizona

Arkansas
Arkansas Northeastern College
Arkansas State University
Arkansas State University
    Beebe
    Mountain Home
Arkansas Tech University
Central Baptist College
Crowley's Ridge College
Ecclesia College
Harding University
Henderson State University
Hendrix College
John Brown University
Lyon College
Mid-South Community College
National Park Community College
North Arkansas College
Northwest Arkansas Community College
Ouachita Baptist University
Philander Smith College
Phillips Community College of the University of
    Arkansas
Rich Mountain Community College
Southeast Arkansas College
Southern Arkansas University
Southern Arkansas University Tech
University of Arkansas
University of Arkansas
    Community College at Batesville
    Community College at Hope
    Fort Smith
    Monticello
    Pine Bluff
University of Arkansas Community College at
    Morrilton
University of Central Arkansas
University of the Ozarks
Williams Baptist College

California
Academy of Art University
Alliant International University
American Academy of Dramatic Arts: West
Art Institute
    of California: Los Angeles
    of California: Orange County
Azusa Pacific University
Bethany University
Bethesda Christian University
Biola University
California Baptist University
California College of the Arts
California Institute of Integral Studies
California Institute of the Arts
California Lutheran University
California Maritime Academy
California Polytechnic State University: San Luis
    Obispo
California State Polytechnic University: Pomona
California State University
    Chico
    Dominguez Hills
    Fresno
    Fullerton
    Long Beach
    Monterey Bay
    Northridge
    San Marcos
    Stanislaus
California State University: Channel Islands

Chaffey College
Chapman University
Claremont McKenna College
Cogswell Polytechnical College
College of the Canyons
College of the Siskiyous
Columbia College
Concordia University
Deep Springs College
    Fremont
    Long Beach
    Pomona
    Sherman Oaks
Dominican University of California
East Los Angeles College
El Camino College
Empire College
Fashion Institute of Design and Merchandising
    Los Angeles
    San Diego
    San Francisco
Fresno Pacific University
Glendale Community College
Golden Gate University
Golden West College
Harvey Mudd College
Holy Names University
Hope International University
Humboldt State University
Humphreys College
King's College and Seminary, The
    The King's College and Seminary
La Sierra University
Life Pacific College
Loyola Marymount University
Marymount College
The Master's College
Mendocino College
Menlo College
Merced College
Mills College
Mount St. Mary's College
Mount San Jacinto College
National Hispanic University
NewSchool of Architecture & Design
Notre Dame de Namur University
Occidental College
Ohlone College
Orange Coast College
Otis College of Art and Design
Pacific States University
Patten University
Pepperdine University
Pitzer College
Point Loma Nazarene University
Riverside Community College
St. Mary's College of California
Samuel Merritt University
San Diego Christian College
San Diego State University
San Francisco Art Institute
San Francisco State University
San Joaquin Delta College
San Jose State University
Santa Clara University
Santa Rosa Junior College
School of Urban Missions: Oakland
Scripps College
Simpson University
Soka University of America
Sonoma State University
Southern California Institute of Architecture
Taft College
University of California
    Berkeley
    Davis
    Irvine
    Los Angeles
    Riverside
    San Diego
    Santa Barbara
    Santa Cruz

University of California: Merced
University of La Verne
University of Redlands
University of San Diego
University of San Francisco
University of Southern California
University of the Pacific
Vanguard University of Southern California
Westmont College
Westwood College of Technology
    Westwood College: Inland Empire
Whittier College
William Jessup University
Woodbury University
Yuba Community College District

Colorado
Adams State College
Arapahoe Community College
Boulder College of Massage Therapy
Colorado Christian University
Colorado College
Colorado Mountain College
Colorado Northwestern Community College
Colorado School of Mines
Colorado State University
Colorado State University
    Pueblo
Colorado Technical University
Community College of Denver
    Westminster
Fort Lewis College
Front Range Community College
Johnson & Wales University: Denver
Mesa State College
Metropolitan State College of Denver
Northeastern Junior College
Otero Junior College
Pueblo Community College
Regis University
Remington College
    Colorado Springs
Rocky Mountain College of Art & Design
Trinidad State Junior College
University of Colorado
    Boulder
    Colorado Springs
    Denver
University of Denver
University of Northern Colorado
Western State College of Colorado
Westwood College: Denver North

Connecticut
Albertus Magnus College
Central Connecticut State University
Eastern Connecticut State University
Fairfield University
Housatonic Community College
Lincoln College of New England: Briarwood
Lincoln College of New England: Suffield
Lyme Academy College of Fine Arts
Mitchell College
Norwalk Community College
Quinnipiac University
Sacred Heart University
Saint Joseph College
Three Rivers Community College
Trinity College
Tunxis Community College
University of Bridgeport
University of Connecticut
University of Hartford
University of New Haven
Wesleyan University
Western Connecticut State University

Delaware
Delaware State University
Goldey-Beacom College
University of Delaware
Wesley College

Wilmington University

District of Columbia
American University
Catholic University of America
Corcoran College of Art and Design
Gallaudet University
George Washington University
Howard University
Trinity Washington University

Florida
Art Institute of Fort Lauderdale
Baptist College of Florida
Barry University
Beacon College
Bethune-Cookman University
Brevard Community College
Broward College
Carlos Albizu University
Central Florida Community College
Chipola College
Clearwater Christian College
    Miramar
    Orlando
Eckerd College
Embry-Riddle Aeronautical University
Embry-Riddle Aeronautical University:
    Worldwide Campus
Flagler College
Florida Agricultural and Mechanical University
Florida Atlantic University
Florida Christian College
Florida College
Florida Gulf Coast University
Florida Institute of Technology
Florida International University
Florida Keys Community College
Florida Southern College
Florida State College at Jacksonville
Florida State University
Gulf Coast Community College
Hillsborough Community College
Hobe Sound Bible College
Hodges University
Indian River State College
International Academy of Design and
    Technology: Tampa
Jacksonville University
Johnson & Wales University: North Miami
Jones College
Lake City Community College
Lake-Sumter Community College
Lynn University
Miami Dade College
New College of Florida
North Florida Community College
Northwest Florida State College
Northwood University
    Florida
Nova Southeastern University
Palm Beach Atlantic University
Palm Beach Community College
Pasco-Hernando Community College
Pensacola Junior College
Polk State College
Ringling College of Art and Design
Rollins College
Saint Leo University
St. Petersburg College
Saint Thomas University
Santa Fe College
Schiller International University
Seminole Community College
South Florida Community College
Southeastern University
State College of Florida, Manatee-Sarasota
Stetson University
Tallahassee Community College
Trinity College of Florida
University of Central Florida
University of Florida

University of Miami
University of North Florida
University of South Florida
University of Tampa
University of West Florida
Warner University
Webber International University

Georgia
Agnes Scott College
Albany State University
Albany Technical College
Andrew College
Armstrong Atlantic State University
    of Atlanta
Athens Technical College
Augusta State University
Berry College
Brenau University
Brewton-Parker College
Clark Atlanta University
Clayton State University
College of Coastal Georgia
Columbus State University
Covenant College
Dalton State College
Darton College
    Alpharetta
    Decatur
East Georgia College
Emmanuel College
Emory University
Fort Valley State University
Gainesville State College
Georgia College and State University
Georgia Highlands College
Georgia Institute of Technology
Georgia Southern University
Georgia Southwestern State University
Georgia State University
Gordon College
Herzing University
Kennesaw State University
LaGrange College
Life University
Macon State College
Medical College of Georgia
Mercer University
Middle Georgia College
Morehouse College
North Georgia College & State University
Oglethorpe University
Oxford College of Emory University
Paine College
Piedmont College
Reinhardt College
Savannah College of Art and Design
Savannah State University
Savannah Technical College
Shorter College
South Georgia College
Southern Polytechnic State University
Spelman College
Toccoa Falls College
Truett-McConnell College
University of Georgia
University of West Georgia
Valdosta State University
Waycross College
Wesleyan College
Young Harris College

Hawaii
Chaminade University of Honolulu
Hawaii Pacific University
Hawaii Tokai International College
University of Hawaii
    Honolulu Community College
    Manoa
    West Oahu

Idaho
Boise Bible College
Boise State University
Brigham Young University-Idaho
College of Idaho
Eastern Idaho Technical College
Idaho State University
Lewis-Clark State College
North Idaho College
Northwest Nazarene University
University of Idaho

Illinois
Augustana College
Aurora University
Benedictine University
Black Hawk College
Blackburn College
Bradley University
Carl Sandburg College
Chicago State University
City Colleges of Chicago
    Kennedy-King College
    Malcolm X College
College of DuPage
College of Lake County
Columbia College Chicago
Concordia University Chicago
Danville Area Community College
DePaul University
    Addison
    Chicago
    Tinley Park
DeVry University: Online
Dominican University
East-West University
Eastern Illinois University
Elgin Community College
Elmhurst College
Eureka College
Governors State University
Greenville College
Harper College
Harrington College of Design
Heartland Community College
Highland Community College
Illinois College
Illinois Eastern Community Colleges
    Frontier Community College
    Lincoln Trail College
    Olney Central College
    Wabash Valley College
Illinois Institute of Art: Schaumburg
Illinois Institute of Technology
Illinois State University
Illinois Wesleyan University
Joliet Junior College
Judson University
Kaskaskia College
Kendall College
Kishwaukee College
Knox College
Lake Forest College
Lake Land College
Lewis University
Lexington College
Lincoln Christian University
Lincoln College
Lincoln Land Community College
Loyola University Chicago
MacCormac College
MacMurray College
McHenry County College
McKendree University
Millikin University
Monmouth College
Moody Bible Institute
Moraine Valley Community College
Morrison Institute of Technology
National-Louis University
North Central College
North Park University

Northeastern Illinois University
Northern Illinois University
Northwestern College
Northwestern University
Oakton Community College
Olivet Nazarene University
Parkland College
Principia College
Quincy University
Rend Lake College
Richland Community College
Robert Morris University: Chicago
Rock Valley College
Rockford College
Roosevelt University
Saint Anthony College of Nursing
St. Francis Medical Center College of Nursing
Saint Xavier University
Sauk Valley Community College
School of the Art Institute of Chicago
South Suburban College of Cook County
Southeastern Illinois College
Southern Illinois University Carbondale
Southern Illinois University Edwardsville
Southwestern Illinois College
Spoon River College
Trinity Christian College
Trinity International University
Triton College
University of Chicago
University of Illinois
    Chicago
    Springfield
    Urbana-Champaign
University of St. Francis
VanderCook College of Music
Waubonsee Community College
West Suburban College of Nursing
Western Illinois University
Wheaton College

Indiana
Ancilla College
Anderson University
Ball State University
Bethel College
Butler University
Calumet College of St. Joseph
DePauw University
DeVry University: Indianapolis
Earlham College
Franklin College
Goshen College
Grace College
Hanover College
Holy Cross College
Huntington University
Indiana Institute of Technology
Indiana State University
Indiana University
    Bloomington
    East
    Kokomo
    Northwest
    South Bend
    Southeast
Indiana University-Purdue University Fort
    Wayne
Indiana University-Purdue University
    Indianapolis
Indiana Wesleyan University
Manchester College
Marian University
Oakland City University
Purdue University
Purdue University
    Calumet
    North Central
Rose-Hulman Institute of Technology
Saint Joseph's College
St. Mary-of-the-Woods College
Saint Mary's College

Taylor University
Trine University
University of Evansville
University of Indianapolis
University of St. Francis
University of Southern Indiana
Valparaiso University
Vincennes University
Wabash College

Iowa
AIB College of Business
Allen College
Briar Cliff University
Buena Vista University
Central College
Clarke College
Coe College
Cornell College
Des Moines Area Community College
Dordt College
Drake University
Ellsworth Community College
Emmaus Bible College
Faith Baptist Bible College and Theological
    Seminary
Graceland University
Grand View University
Grinnell College
Hawkeye Community College
Indian Hills Community College
Iowa Central Community College
Iowa State University
Iowa Wesleyan College
Kaplan University
    Cedar Falls
    Cedar Rapids
    Davenport
    Mason City
Loras College
Luther College
Mercy College of Health Sciences
Morningside College
Mount Mercy College
North Iowa Area Community College
Northeast Iowa Community College
Northwestern College
St. Ambrose University
St. Luke's College
Simpson College
Southeastern Community College
    North Campus
Southwestern Community College
University of Dubuque
University of Iowa
University of Northern Iowa
Upper Iowa University
Vatterott College
Waldorf College
Wartburg College
Western Iowa Tech Community College
William Penn University

Kansas
Allen County Community College
Baker University
Barclay College
Barton County Community College
Benedictine College
Bethany College
Bethel College
Butler Community College
Central Christian College of Kansas
Coffeyville Community College
Colby Community College
Cowley County Community College
Dodge City Community College
Donnelly College
Emporia State University
Fort Hays State University
Friends University
Garden City Community College

Hesston College
Highland Community College
Hutchinson Community College
Johnson County Community College
Kansas City Kansas Community College
Kansas State University
Kansas Wesleyan University
Labette Community College
Manhattan Area Technical College
McPherson College
MidAmerica Nazarene University
Neosho County Community College
Newman University
North Central Kansas Technical College
Ottawa University
Pittsburg State University
Pratt Community College
Seward County Community College
Southwestern College
Sterling College
Tabor College
University of Kansas
University of Kansas Medical Center
University of St. Mary
Washburn University
Wichita State University

Kentucky
Asbury College
Ashland Community and Technical College
Beckfield College
Bellarmine University
Big Sandy Community and Technical College
Bluegrass Community and Technical College
Brescia University
Campbellsville University
Centre College
Clear Creek Baptist Bible College
Daymar College
    Owensboro
Eastern Kentucky University
Georgetown College
Hopkinsville Community College
Kentucky Christian University
Kentucky Mountain Bible College
Kentucky State University
Kentucky Wesleyan College
Maysville Community and Technical College
Mid-Continent University
Midway College
Morehead State University
Murray State University
National College
    Danville
    Florence
    Lexington
    Louisville
    Pikeville
    Richmond
Northern Kentucky University
Owensboro Community and Technical College
St. Catharine College
Somerset Community College
Southeast Kentucky Community and Technical
    College
Spalding University
Spencerian College: Lexington
Sullivan College of Technology and Design
Thomas More College
Transylvania University
Union College
University of Kentucky
University of Louisville
University of the Cumberlands
Western Kentucky University

Louisiana
Baton Rouge Community College
Bossier Parish Community College
Centenary College of Louisiana
Delgado Community College
Dillard University

Grambling State University
Louisiana College
Louisiana State University
    Alexandria
Louisiana State University and Agricultural and
    Mechanical College
Louisiana State University Health Sciences
    Center
Louisiana Tech University
Loyola University New Orleans
McNeese State University
Nicholls State University
Northwestern State University
Our Lady of Holy Cross College
St. Joseph Seminary College
South Louisiana Community College
Southeastern Louisiana University
Southern University and Agricultural and
    Mechanical College
Tulane University
University of Louisiana at Monroe
University of New Orleans

Maine
Bowdoin College
College of the Atlantic
Eastern Maine Community College
Husson University
Maine College of Art
Maine Maritime Academy
New England School of Communications
Saint Joseph's College of Maine
Thomas College
Unity College
University of Maine
University of Maine
    Augusta
    Farmington
    Fort Kent
    Machias
    Presque Isle
University of New England
University of Southern Maine
Washington County Community College
York County Community College

Maryland
Allegany College of Maryland
Baltimore International College
Bowie State University
Capitol College
Carroll Community College
Cecil College
Chesapeake College
College of Notre Dame of Maryland
College of Southern Maryland
Community College of Baltimore County
Coppin State University
DeVry University: Bethesda
Frederick Community College
Frostburg State University
Garrett College
Goucher College
Hood College
Johns Hopkins University
Johns Hopkins University: Peabody
    Conservatory of Music
Loyola University Maryland
Maryland Institute College of Art
McDaniel College
Montgomery College
Mount St. Mary's University
Prince George's Community College
St. Mary's College of Maryland
Salisbury University
Stevenson University
Towson University
University of Maryland
    Baltimore County
    College Park
    Eastern Shore
    University College

Washington Adventist University
Washington Bible College
Washington College
Wor-Wic Community College

Massachusetts
American International College
Anna Maria College
Art Institute of Boston at Lesley University
Assumption College
Atlantic Union College
Babson College
Bard College at Simon's Rock
Bay Path College
Bay State College
Becker College
Benjamin Franklin Institute of Technology
Bentley University
Berkshire Community College
Boston Architectural College
Boston College
Boston University
Brandeis University
Bridgewater State College
Bristol Community College
Bunker Hill Community College
Cape Cod Community College
Clark University
College of the Holy Cross
Curry College
Dean College
Eastern Nazarene College
Elms College
Emerson College
Emmanuel College
Endicott College
Fisher College
Fitchburg State College
Framingham State College
Franklin W. Olin College of Engineering
Gordon College
Hampshire College
Hellenic College/Holy Cross
Holyoke Community College
Laboure College
Lasell College
Lesley University
Marian Court College
Massachusetts College of Art and Design
Massachusetts College of Liberal Arts
Massachusetts College of Pharmacy and Health
    Sciences
Massachusetts Maritime Academy
Merrimack College
Montserrat College of Art
Mount Holyoke College
Mount Wachusett Community College
New England Conservatory of Music
New England Institute of Art
Newbury College
Nichols College
North Shore Community College
Northeastern University
Northern Essex Community College
Pine Manor College
Quinsigamond Community College
Regis College
Simmons College
Smith College
Stonehill College
Suffolk University
Tufts University
University of Massachusetts
    Amherst
    Boston
    Dartmouth
    Lowell
Wentworth Institute of Technology
Western New England College
Wheaton College
Wheelock College
Worcester Polytechnic Institute

Worcester State College
Zion Bible College

Michigan
Adrian College
Albion College
Alma College
Alpena Community College
Andrews University
Aquinas College
Baker College
  of Auburn Hills
  of Cadillac
  of Clinton Township
  of Flint
  of Jackson
  of Muskegon
  of Owosso
  of Port Huron
Bay de Noc Community College
Calvin College
Central Michigan University
Cleary University
College for Creative Studies
Cornerstone University
Davenport University
Delta College
Eastern Michigan University
Ferris State University
Finlandia University
Glen Oaks Community College
Gogebic Community College
Grace Bible College
Grand Rapids Community College
Grand Valley State University
Great Lakes Christian College
Hillsdale College
Hope College
Jackson Community College
Kalamazoo College
Kalamazoo Valley Community College
Kellogg Community College
Kendall College of Art and Design of Ferris
  State University
Kettering University
Kirtland Community College
Kuyper College
Lake Superior State University
Lansing Community College
Lawrence Technological University
Macomb Community College
Madonna University
Marygrove College
Michigan Jewish Institute
Michigan State University
Michigan Technological University
Mid Michigan Community College
Monroe County Community College
Montcalm Community College
Mott Community College
Northern Michigan University
Northwestern Michigan College
Northwood University: Michigan
Oakland Community College
Oakland University
Rochester College
Sacred Heart Major Seminary
Saginaw Valley State University
Schoolcraft College
Siena Heights University
Southwestern Michigan College
Spring Arbor University
University of Detroit Mercy
University of Michigan
University of Michigan
  Dearborn
  Flint
Walsh College of Accountancy and Business
  Administration
Washtenaw Community College
Wayne State University
Western Michigan University

Minnesota
Anoka Technical College
Augsburg College
Bemidji State University
Bethany Lutheran College
Bethel University
Brown College
Carleton College
College of St. Benedict
College of St. Scholastica
College of Visual Arts
Concordia College: Moorhead
Concordia University: St. Paul
Crossroads College
Crown College
Dakota County Technical College
  Edina
Dunwoody College of Technology
Fond du Lac Tribal and Community College
Gustavus Adolphus College
Hamline University
Inver Hills Community College
Itasca Community College
Lake Superior College
Le Cordon Bleu College of Culinary Arts:
  Minneapolis-St. Paul
Macalester College
Martin Luther College
Metropolitan State University
Minneapolis College of Art and Design
Minnesota School of Business: Shakopee
Minnesota State College - Southeast Technical
Minnesota State Community and Technical
  College
Minnesota State University
  Mankato
  Moorhead
National American University
  Bloomington
Normandale Community College
North Central University
North Hennepin Community College
Northland Community & Technical College
Northwestern College
Oak Hills Christian College
Pine Technical College
Rainy River Community College
St. Catherine University
Saint Cloud State University
St. Cloud Technical College
St. John's University
St. Mary's University of Minnesota
St. Olaf College
Southwest Minnesota State University
University of Minnesota
  Crookston
  Duluth
  Morris
  Twin Cities
University of St. Thomas
Winona State University

Mississippi
Alcorn State University
Belhaven University
Blue Mountain College
Copiah-Lincoln Community College
Delta State University
East Central Community College
East Mississippi Community College
Hinds Community College
Holmes Community College
Jackson State University
Jones County Junior College
Meridian Community College
Millsaps College
Mississippi College
Mississippi Delta Community College
Mississippi Gulf Coast Community College
Mississippi State University
Mississippi University for Women
Mississippi Valley State University

Pearl River Community College
Rust College
Tougaloo College
University of Mississippi
Wesley College

Missouri
Avila University
Baptist Bible College
Calvary Bible College and Theological Seminary
Central Methodist University
College of the Ozarks
Columbia College
Conception Seminary College
Cottey College
Crowder College
Culver-Stockton College
  Kansas City
Drury University
East Central College
Evangel University
Fontbonne University
Goldfarb School of Nursing at Barnes-Jewish
  College
Hannibal-LaGrange College
Harris-Stowe State University
Jefferson College
Kansas City Art Institute
Lincoln University
Lindenwood University
Linn State Technical College
Maryville University of Saint Louis
Metropolitan Community College: Blue River
Metropolitan Community College: Longview
Metropolitan Community College: Maple
  Woods
Metropolitan Community College: Penn Valley
Mineral Area College
Missouri Baptist University
Missouri Southern State University
Missouri State University
Missouri State University: West Plains
Missouri Technical School
Missouri Valley College
Missouri Western State University
North Central Missouri College
Northwest Missouri State University
Ozark Christian College
Park University
Research College of Nursing
Rockhurst University
St. Charles Community College
St. Louis Christian College
Saint Louis University
Southeast Missouri State University
Southwest Baptist University
State Fair Community College
Stephens College
Three Rivers Community College
Truman State University
University of Central Missouri
University of Missouri
  Columbia
  Kansas City
  Missouri University of Science and
    Technology
  St. Louis
Washington University in St. Louis
Webster University
Westminster College
William Jewell College
William Woods University

Montana
Dawson Community College
Flathead Valley Community College
Miles Community College
Montana State University
  Billings
  Bozeman
Montana Tech of the University of Montana
Rocky Mountain College

Stone Child College
University of Great Falls
University of Montana
University of Montana: Western

Nebraska
Bellevue University
BryanLGH College of Health Sciences
Central Community College
Chadron State College
Clarkson College
College of Saint Mary
Concordia University
Creative Center
Creighton University
Dana College
Doane College
Grace University
Metropolitan Community College
Mid-Plains Community College Area
Nebraska Christian College
Nebraska Methodist College of Nursing and
  Allied Health
Nebraska Wesleyan University
Northeast Community College
Peru State College
Southeast Community College
Union College
University of Nebraska
  Kearney
  Lincoln
  Omaha
Wayne State College
Western Nebraska Community College
York College

Nevada
  of Las Vegas
DeVry University: Henderson
Sierra Nevada College
Truckee Meadows Community College
University of Nevada
  Las Vegas
  Reno
Western Nevada College

New Hampshire
Chester College of New England
Colby-Sawyer College
Daniel Webster College
Franklin Pierce University
Keene State College
New England College
Plymouth State University
Rivier College
Saint Anselm College
Southern New Hampshire University
Thomas More College of Liberal Arts
University of New Hampshire
University of New Hampshire at Manchester

New Jersey
Berkeley College- Garret Mountain Campus
Bloomfield College
Brookdale Community College
Burlington County College
Caldwell College
Centenary College
The College of New Jersey
College of St. Elizabeth
Cumberland County College
DeVry University: North Brunswick
Drew University
Felician College
Georgian Court University
Kean University
Mercer County Community College
Monmouth University
Montclair State University
New Jersey Institute of Technology
Ocean County College
Passaic County Community College
Ramapo College of New Jersey

Raritan Valley Community College
Richard Stockton College of New Jersey
Rider University
Rowan University
Rutgers, The State University of New Jersey
    Camden Regional Campus
    New Brunswick/Piscataway Campus
    Newark Regional Campus
Saint Peter's College
Salem Community College
Seton Hall University
Somerset Christian College
Stevens Institute of Technology
Union County College
Warren County Community College
William Paterson University of New Jersey

New Mexico
Art Center Design College
Central New Mexico Community College
Clovis Community College
College of Santa Fe
Eastern New Mexico University
Institute of American Indian Arts
Mesalands Community College
Navajo Technical College
New Mexico Highlands University
New Mexico Institute of Mining and Technology
New Mexico Junior College
New Mexico Military Institute
New Mexico State University
New Mexico State University
    Alamogordo
    Carlsbad
Northern New Mexico College
St. John's College
San Juan College
Santa Fe Community College
Southwestern Indian Polytechnic Institute
University of New Mexico
University of the Southwest
Western New Mexico University

New York
Adelphi University
Adirondack Community College
Albany College of Pharmacy and Health Sciences
Alfred University
ASA Institute of Business and Computer Technology
Bard College
Berkeley College
Berkeley College of New York City
Briarcliffe College
Bryant & Stratton Business Institute
    Bryant & Stratton College: Albany
    Bryant & Stratton College: Syracuse
Canisius College
Cayuga Community College
Cazenovia College
City University of New York
    Baruch College
    Brooklyn College
    City College
    College of Staten Island
    Hunter College
    John Jay College of Criminal Justice
    Lehman College
    Medgar Evers College
    Queens College
    York College
Clarkson University
College of Mount St. Vincent
College of New Rochelle
College of Saint Rose
College of Westchester
Columbia University
    School of General Studies
Columbia-Greene Community College
Concordia College

Cooper Union for the Advancement of Science and Art
Culinary Institute of America
Daemen College
DeVry
    College of New York
Dominican College of Blauvelt
Dowling College
Dutchess Community College
D'Youville College
Eastman School of Music of the University of Rochester
Elmira College
Eugene Lang College The New School for Liberal Arts
Excelsior College
Fashion Institute of Technology
Finger Lakes Community College
Five Towns College
Fordham University
Fulton-Montgomery Community College
Globe Institute of Technology
Hartwick College
Hilbert College
Hobart and William Smith Colleges
Hofstra University
Houghton College
Iona College
Ithaca College
Jamestown Business College
Jamestown Community College
Jefferson Community College
Jewish Theological Seminary of America
Keuka College
King's College
Laboratory Institute of Merchandising
Le Moyne College
Long Island Business Institute
Manhattan College
Manhattan School of Music
Manhattanville College
Marist College
Marymount Manhattan College
Medaille College
Mercy College
Metropolitan College of New York
Mohawk Valley Community College
Molloy College
Monroe College
Monroe Community College
Mount Saint Mary College
Nassau Community College
Nazareth College
New York Institute of Technology
New York University
Niagara County Community College
Niagara University
Nyack College
Onondaga Community College
Pace University
Parsons The New School for Design
Paul Smith's College
Polytechnic Institute of New York University
Pratt Institute
Rensselaer Polytechnic Institute
Roberts Wesleyan College
Rochester Institute of Technology
Russell Sage College
Sage College of Albany
Saint Bonaventure University
St. Francis College
St. John Fisher College
St. John's University
St. Joseph's College
St. Joseph's College: Suffolk Campus
St. Lawrence University
St. Thomas Aquinas College
Schenectady County Community College
Siena College
State University of New York
    Albany
    Binghamton

Buffalo
College at Brockport
College at Buffalo
College at Cortland
College at Fredonia
College at Geneseo
College at Old Westbury
College at Oneonta
College at Plattsburgh
College at Potsdam
College of Agriculture and Technology at Cobleskill
College of Agriculture and Technology at Morrisville
College of Environmental Science and Forestry
College of Technology at Alfred
College of Technology at Canton
Farmingdale
Institute of Technology at Utica/Rome
Maritime College
New Paltz
Oswego
Purchase
Stony Brook
Suffolk County Community College
Syracuse University
Tompkins Cortland Community College
Trocaire College
Union College
University of Rochester
Utica College
Vaughn College of Aeronautics and Technology
Villa Maria College of Buffalo
Wagner College
Webb Institute
Wells College
Westchester Community College
Yeshivat Mikdash Melech

North Carolina
Alamance Community College
Appalachian State University
Asheville-Buncombe Technical Community College
Barton College
Beaufort County Community College
Belmont Abbey College
Blue Ridge Community College
Brevard College
Brunswick Community College
Campbell University
Cape Fear Community College
Carolinas College of Health Sciences
Carteret Community College
Catawba College
Catawba Valley Community College
Central Carolina Community College
Central Piedmont Community College
Chowan University
Coastal Carolina Community College
College of the Albemarle
Davidson College
Davidson County Community College
DeVry University: Charlotte
Duke University
Durham Technical Community College
East Carolina University
Elizabeth City State University
Elon University
Fayetteville State University
Forsyth Technical Community College
Gardner-Webb University
Gaston College
Greensboro College
Guilford College
Haywood Community College
High Point University
Isothermal Community College
James Sprunt Community College
Johnson & Wales University: Charlotte
Johnson C. Smith University

Johnston Community College
Lees-McRae College
Lenoir Community College
Lenoir-Rhyne University
Livingstone College
Louisburg College
Mars Hill College
Martin Community College
McDowell Technical Community College
Meredith College
Methodist University
Mid-Atlantic Christian University
Montgomery Community College
Montreat College
Mount Olive College
Nash Community College
North Carolina Agricultural and Technical State University
North Carolina Central University
North Carolina State University
North Carolina Wesleyan College
Peace College
Pfeiffer University
Pitt Community College
Queens University of Charlotte
Randolph Community College
Richmond Community College
Roanoke-Chowan Community College
Rockingham Community College
Rowan-Cabarrus Community College
St. Andrews Presbyterian College
St. Augustine's College
Salem College
Sampson Community College
Sandhills Community College
Shaw University
Southeastern Community College
Stanly Community College
Surry Community College
University of North Carolina
    Asheville
    Chapel Hill
    Charlotte
    Greensboro
    Pembroke
    Wilmington
University of North Carolina School of the Arts
Vance-Granville Community College
Wake Forest University
Wake Technical Community College
Warren Wilson College
Wayne Community College
Western Carolina University
Western Piedmont Community College
Wilkes Community College
Wilson Community College
Wingate University
Winston-Salem State University

North Dakota
Bismarck State College
Dakota College at Bottineau
Dickinson State University
Jamestown College
Lake Region State College
Mayville State University
Minot State University
North Dakota State College of Science
North Dakota State University
Trinity Bible College
University of Mary
University of North Dakota
Williston State College

Ohio
Art Academy of Cincinnati
Art Institute of Cincinnati
Ashland University
Baldwin-Wallace College
Bowling Green State University
Bowling Green State University: Firelands College

Bryant & Stratton College
    Eastlake
Bryant & Stratton College: Cleveland
Capital University
Case Western Reserve University
Cedarville University
Central Ohio Technical College
Central State University
Chatfield College
Cincinnati Christian University
Cincinnati State Technical and Community
    College
Cleveland Institute of Art
Cleveland Institute of Music
Cleveland State University
College of Mount St. Joseph
College of Wooster
Columbus College of Art and Design
Cuyahoga Community College
    Metropolitan Campus
Defiance College
Denison University
    Columbus
Eastern Gateway Community College
Edison State Community College
ETI Technical College of Niles
Franciscan University of Steubenville
Franklin University
God's Bible School and College
Heidelberg University
Hiram College
Hocking College
James A. Rhodes State College
John Carroll University
Kent State University
Kent State University
    Ashtabula
    East Liverpool
    Salem
    Stark
    Trumbull
    Tuscarawas
Kent State University: Geauga
Kenyon College
Kettering College of Medical Arts
Lourdes College
Malone University
Marietta College
Marion Technical College
MedCentral College of Nursing
Mercy College of Northwest Ohio
Miami University
    Hamilton Campus
    Oxford Campus
Mount Union College
Mount Vernon Nazarene University
Muskingum University
Northwest State Community College
Notre Dame College
Oberlin College
Ohio Christian University
Ohio Dominican University
Ohio Northern University
Ohio State University
    Agricultural Technical Institute
    Columbus Campus
    Lima Campus
    Mansfield Campus
    Marion Campus
    Newark Campus
Ohio University
Ohio University
    Southern Campus at Ironton
Ohio Wesleyan University
Otterbein College
Owens Community College
    Toledo
Pontifical College Josephinum
School of Advertising Art
Shawnee State University
Southern State Community College
Stark State College of Technology

Terra State Community College
Tiffin University
Union Institute & University
University of Akron
University of Akron: Wayne College
University of Cincinnati
University of Cincinnati
    Clermont College
    Raymond Walters College
University of Dayton
University of Findlay
University of Northwestern Ohio
University of Rio Grande
University of Toledo
Urbana University
Ursuline College
Walsh University
Wilmington College
Wittenberg University
Wright State University
Wright State University: Lake Campus
Xavier University
Youngstown State University

Oklahoma
Cameron University
Carl Albert State College
Connors State College
DeVry University: Oklahoma City Center
East Central University
Langston University
Mid-America Christian University
Northeastern Oklahoma Agricultural and
    Mechanical College
Northeastern State University
Northwestern Oklahoma State University
Oklahoma Baptist University
Oklahoma Christian University
Oklahoma City Community College
Oklahoma City University
Oklahoma Panhandle State University
Oklahoma State University
Oklahoma State University
    Oklahoma City
Oklahoma Wesleyan University
Oral Roberts University
Redlands Community College
Rogers State University
Rose State College
St. Gregory's University
Seminole State College
Southeastern Oklahoma State University
Southern Nazarene University
Southwestern Christian University
Southwestern Oklahoma State University
Tulsa Community College
University of Central Oklahoma
University of Oklahoma
University of Science and Arts of Oklahoma
University of Tulsa
Western Oklahoma State College

Oregon
Central Oregon Community College
Chemeketa Community College
Clackamas Community College
Clatsop Community College
Concordia University
Corban College
DeVry University: Portland
Eastern Oregon University
Eugene Bible College
George Fox University
Lewis & Clark College
Linfield College
Linn-Benton Community College
Marylhurst University
Mt. Hood Community College
Multnomah University
Northwest Christian University
Oregon College of Art & Craft
Oregon Health & Science University

Oregon Institute of Technology
Oregon State University
Pacific Northwest College of Art
Pacific University
Portland State University
Southern Oregon University
Treasure Valley Community College
Umpqua Community College
University of Oregon
University of Portland
Warner Pacific College
Western Oregon University
Willamette University

Pennsylvania
Albright College
Allegheny College
Alvernia University
Arcadia University
Baptist Bible College of Pennsylvania
Bloomsburg University of Pennsylvania
Bryn Athyn College of the New Church
Bryn Mawr College
Bucknell University
Bucks County Community College
Butler County Community College
Cabrini College
California University of Pennsylvania
Carnegie Mellon University
Cedar Crest College
Central Pennsylvania College
Chatham University
Chestnut Hill College
Cheyney University of Pennsylvania
Clarion University of Pennsylvania
Community College of Allegheny County-
    Allegheny
Community College of Beaver County
Delaware Valley College
DeSales University
    Fort Washington
Dickinson College
Drexel University
Duquesne University
East Stroudsburg University of Pennsylvania
Edinboro University of Pennsylvania
Elizabethtown College
Franklin & Marshall College
Gannon University
Geneva College
Gettysburg College
Grove City College
Gwynedd-Mercy College
Harcum College
Harrisburg Area Community College
Harrisburg University of Science and Technology
Holy Family University
Immaculata University
Indiana University of Pennsylvania
Johnson College
Juniata College
Keystone College
King's College
Kutztown University of Pennsylvania
La Roche College
La Salle University
Lackawanna College
Lafayette College
Lancaster Bible College
Lebanon Valley College
Lehigh Carbon Community College
Lehigh University
Lincoln University
Lock Haven University of Pennsylvania
Lycoming College
Manor College
Mansfield University of Pennsylvania
Marywood University
Mercyhurst College
Messiah College
Millersville University of Pennsylvania
Misericordia University

Montgomery County Community College
Moore College of Art and Design
Moravian College
Mount Aloysius College
Muhlenberg College
Newport Business Institute: Lower Burrell
Northampton Community College
Peirce College
Penn State
    Abington
    Altoona
    Beaver
    Berks
    Brandywine
    DuBois
    Erie, The Behrend College
    Fayette, The Eberly Campus
    Greater Allegheny
    Harrisburg
    Hazleton
    Lehigh Valley
    Mont Alto
    New Kensington
    Schuylkill
    Shenango
    University Park
    Wilkes-Barre
    Worthington Scranton
    York
Pennsylvania College of Technology
Pennsylvania Highlands Community College
Pennsylvania Institute of Technology
Philadelphia Biblical University
Philadelphia University
Point Park University
Robert Morris University
Rosemont College
St. Francis University
Saint Joseph's University
St. Vincent College
Seton Hill University
Shippensburg University of Pennsylvania
Slippery Rock University of Pennsylvania
Susquehanna University
Swarthmore College
Temple University
Thiel College
Thomas Jefferson University: College of Health
    Professions
Triangle Tech
    DuBois
    Pittsburgh
University of Pittsburgh
University of Pittsburgh
    Bradford
    Greensburg
    Johnstown
    Titusville
University of Scranton
University of the Arts
University of the Sciences in Philadelphia
Ursinus College
Valley Forge Christian College
Valley Forge Military Academy & College
Vet Tech Institute
Villanova University
Washington & Jefferson College
Waynesburg University
Westminster College
Westmoreland County Community College
Widener University
Wilkes University
Wilson College
York College of Pennsylvania

Puerto Rico
Inter American University of Puerto Rico
    Aguadilla Campus
    Arecibo Campus
    Bayamon Campus
    San German Campus

National College of Business and Technology:
   Rio Grande
Pontifical Catholic University of Puerto Rico
Turabo University
Universidad del Este
Universidad Metropolitana
Universidad Pentecostal Mizpa
Universidad Politecnica de Puerto Rico
University of Puerto Rico
   Bayamon University College
   Cayey University College
   Humacao
   Utuado
University of the Sacred Heart

Rhode Island
Bryant University
Johnson & Wales University: Providence
New England Institute of Technology
Providence College
Rhode Island College
Roger Williams University
Salve Regina University
University of Rhode Island

South Carolina
Aiken Technical College
Allen University
Anderson University
Charleston Southern University
The Citadel
Clemson University
Coastal Carolina University
Coker College
College of Charleston
Columbia College
Columbia International University
Converse College
Erskine College
Florence-Darlington Technical College
Francis Marion University
Furman University
Greenville Technical College
Horry-Georgetown Technical College
Lander University
Limestone College
Medical University of South Carolina
Morris College
Newberry College
North Greenville University
Presbyterian College
South Carolina State University
Southern Wesleyan University
Spartanburg Methodist College
Tri-County Technical College
University of South Carolina
University of South Carolina
   Aiken
   Beaufort
   Salkehatchie Regional Campus
   Sumter
   Union
   Upstate
Williamsburg Technical College
Winthrop University
Wofford College
York Technical College

South Dakota
Augustana College
Black Hills State University
Dakota State University
Dakota Wesleyan University
Kilian Community College
Mount Marty College
Northern State University
South Dakota School of Mines and Technology
South Dakota State University
Southeast Technical Institute
University of Sioux Falls
University of South Dakota

Tennessee
Aquinas College
Austin Peay State University
Belmont University
Bethel University
Bryan College
Carson-Newman College
Christian Brothers University
Columbia State Community College
Cumberland University
DeVry University: Memphis
Dyersburg State Community College
East Tennessee State University
Fisk University
Free Will Baptist Bible College
Freed-Hardeman University
Jackson State Community College
Johnson Bible College
King College
Lambuth University
Lane College
Lee University
LeMoyne-Owen College
Lincoln Memorial University
Lipscomb University
Martin Methodist College
Maryville College
Memphis College of Art
Middle Tennessee State University
Milligan College
Motlow State Community College
Nashville State Community College
   Nashville
National College of Business & Technology
   National College: Bristol
Northeast State Community College
O'More College of Design
Pellissippi State Community College
Rhodes College
Roane State Community College
Southern Adventist University
Southwest Tennessee Community College
Tennessee State University
Tennessee Technological University
Tennessee Temple University
Tennessee Wesleyan College
Trevecca Nazarene University
Tusculum College
Union University
University of Memphis
University of Tennessee
   Chattanooga
   Knoxville
University of Tennessee Health Science Center
University of the South
Vanderbilt University
Volunteer State Community College
Walters State Community College

Texas
Abilene Christian University
Alvin Community College
Amarillo College
Angelina College
Angelo State University
Austin College
Austin Graduate School of Theology
Baylor University
Brazosport College
Central Texas College
Clarendon College
Coastal Bend College
College of Saint Thomas More
College of the Mainland
Collin County Community College District
Commonwealth Institute of Funeral Service
Concordia University Texas
Dallas Baptist University
East Texas Baptist University
El Paso Community College
Frank Phillips College
Galveston College

Hardin-Simmons University
Hill College
Houston Baptist University
Howard College
Howard Payne University
Huston-Tillotson University
Jacksonville College
Jarvis Christian College
Kilgore College
Lee College
LeTourneau University
Lon Morris College
Lone Star College System
Lubbock Christian University
McMurry University
Midland College
Midwestern State University
Mountain View College
North Central Texas College
North Lake College
Northwest Vista College
Northwood University: Texas
Odessa College
Our Lady of the Lake University of San Antonio
Palo Alto College
Panola College
Prairie View A&M University
Rice University
St. Edward's University
St. Mary's University
Sam Houston State University
San Jacinto College
Schreiner University
South Plains College
South Texas College
Southern Methodist University
Southwestern Adventist University
Southwestern University
Stephen F. Austin State University
Sul Ross State University
Tarleton State University
Tarrant County College
Texarkana College
Texas A&M International University
Texas A&M University
Texas A&M University
   Baylor College of Dentistry
   Commerce
   Corpus Christi
   Galveston
   Kingsville
   Texarkana
Texas Christian University
Texas College
Texas Lutheran University
Texas Southern University
Texas State Technical College
   Waco
   West Texas
Texas State University: San Marcos
Texas Tech University
Texas Tech University Health Sciences Center
Texas Wesleyan University
Trinity University
Trinity Valley Community College
Tyler Junior College
University of Dallas
University of Houston
University of Houston
   Downtown
   Victoria
University of Mary Hardin-Baylor
University of St. Thomas
University of Texas
   Arlington
   Austin
   Brownsville - Texas Southmost College
   Dallas
   El Paso
   Medical Branch at Galveston
   Pan American
   of the Permian Basin

San Antonio
Tyler
University of the Incarnate Word
Vernon College
Victoria College
Wayland Baptist University
West Texas A&M University
Western Technical College
Western Texas College
Wharton County Junior College

Utah
Brigham Young University
College of Eastern Utah
DeVry University: Sandy
Dixie State College of Utah
LDS Business College
Salt Lake Community College
Snow College
Southern Utah University
University of Utah
Utah State University
Utah Valley University
Weber State University
Western Governors University
Westminster College

Vermont
Bennington College
Burlington College
Castleton State College
Champlain College
College of St. Joseph in Vermont
Goddard College
Green Mountain College
Johnson State College
Landmark College
Lyndon State College
Marlboro College
Norwich University
St. Michael's College
Southern Vermont College
Sterling College
University of Vermont
Vermont Technical College

Virginia
Averett University
Blue Ridge Community College
Bluefield College
Bridgewater College
   Richmond
Central Virginia Community College
Christendom College
Christopher Newport University
   Arlington
Eastern Mennonite University
ECPI College of Technology: Virginia Beach
Emory & Henry College
Ferrum College
George Mason University
Germanna Community College
Hampden-Sydney College
Hampton University
Hollins University
J. Sargeant Reynolds Community College-
   Parham Road
James Madison University
Jefferson College of Health Sciences
John Tyler Community College
Liberty University
Longwood University
Lynchburg College
Mary Baldwin College
Marymount University
Mountain Empire Community College
   Bluefield
   Charlottesville
   Danville
   Harrisonburg
   Lynchburg
   Martinsville

Norfolk State University
Northern Virginia Community College-
   Annandale
Old Dominion University
Patrick Henry College
Piedmont Virginia Community College
Radford University
Randolph College
Randolph-Macon College
Regent University
Richard Bland College
Roanoke College
St. Paul's College
Shenandoah University
Southern Virginia University
Southside Virginia Community College- Alberta
Southwest Virginia Community College
Sweet Briar College
University of Mary Washington
University of Richmond
University of Virginia
University of Virginia's College at Wise
Virginia Commonwealth University
Virginia Military Institute
Virginia Polytechnic Institute and State
   University
Virginia State University
Virginia Union University
Virginia Wesleyan College
Virginia Western Community College
Washington and Lee University
Wytheville Community College

Washington
Art Institute of Seattle
Bastyr University
Bellevue College
Big Bend Community College
Centralia College
City University of Seattle
Clark College
Cornish College of the Arts
   Federal Way
Eastern Washington University
Everett Community College
Evergreen State College
Gonzaga University
Grays Harbor College
Northwest College of Art
Northwest Indian College
Northwest University
Olympic College
Pacific Lutheran University
Peninsula College
Pierce College
Saint Martin's University
Seattle Pacific University
Seattle University
Skagit Valley College
South Puget Sound Community College
South Seattle Community College
Trinity Lutheran College
University of Puget Sound
University of Washington
University of Washington Tacoma
Walla Walla University
Washington State University
Wenatchee Valley College
Western Washington University
Whatcom Community College
Whitman College
Whitworth University
Yakima Valley Community College

West Virginia
Alderson-Broaddus College
Bluefield State College
Concord University
Davis and Elkins College
Fairmont State University
Glenville State College
Marshall University

Mountain State University
Ohio Valley University
Potomac State College of West Virginia
   University
Salem International University
Shepherd University
University of Charleston
West Liberty University
West Virginia Business College: Nutter Fort
West Virginia State Community and Technical
   College
West Virginia State University
West Virginia University
West Virginia University at Parkersburg
West Virginia Wesleyan College
Wheeling Jesuit University

Wisconsin
Alverno College
Beloit College
Cardinal Stritch University
Carroll University
Carthage College
College of Menominee Nation
Concordia University Wisconsin
DeVry University: Milwaukee
Edgewood College
Lakeland College
Lakeshore Technical College
Lawrence University
Maranatha Baptist Bible College
Marian University
Marquette University
Mid-State Technical College
Milwaukee Area Technical College
Milwaukee School of Engineering
Moraine Park Technical College
Mount Mary College
Northland College
Ripon College
St. Norbert College
Silver Lake College
University of Wisconsin
   Baraboo/Sauk County
   Eau Claire
   Fond du Lac
   Green Bay
   La Crosse
   Madison
   Marshfield/Wood County
   Milwaukee
   Oshkosh
   Parkside
   Richland
   River Falls
   Rock County
   Sheboygan
   Stevens Point
   Stout
   Superior
   Washington County
   Waukesha
   Whitewater
Viterbo University
Waukesha County Technical College
Wisconsin Lutheran College

Wyoming
Casper College
Central Wyoming College
Eastern Wyoming College
Laramie County Community College
Northwest College
Sheridan College
University of Wyoming
Western Wyoming Community College

Art
scholarships

Alabama
Alabama State University
Athens State University
Auburn University at Montgomery
Birmingham-Southern College
Chattahoochee Valley Community College
Enterprise-Ozark Community College
Faulkner University
Gadsden State Community College
Jacksonville State University
Jefferson State Community College
Judson College
Lurleen B. Wallace Community College
Northeast Alabama Community College
Northwest-Shoals Community College
Samford University
Snead State Community College
Talladega College
Troy University
University of Alabama
University of Alabama
   Birmingham
   Huntsville
University of Montevallo
University of North Alabama
University of South Alabama

Alaska
Alaska Pacific University
University of Alaska
   Fairbanks

Arizona
Arizona State University
Eastern Arizona College
Northern Arizona University
Northland Pioneer College
Pima Community College
University of Arizona

Arkansas
Arkansas Northeastern College
Arkansas State University
Harding University
Henderson State University
Hendrix College
John Brown University
Lyon College
Ouachita Baptist University
Southern Arkansas University
University of Arkansas
University of Arkansas
   Pine Bluff
University of Central Arkansas
University of the Ozarks
Williams Baptist College

California
Academy of Art University
Art Institute
   of California: Orange County
Biola University
California Baptist University
California College of the Arts
California Institute of Integral Studies
California Institute of the Arts
California Lutheran University
California Polytechnic State University: San Luis
   Obispo
California State University
   Chico
   Dominguez Hills
   Fresno

   Long Beach
   Stanislaus
Chapman University
College of the Canyons
College of the Siskiyous
El Camino College
Irvine Valley College
Loyola Marymount University
The Master's College
Otis College of Art and Design
Pepperdine University
Riverside Community College
San Diego State University
San Francisco Art Institute
Santa Rosa Junior College
Sonoma State University
University of California
   Irvine
   Riverside
   San Diego
   Santa Cruz
University of La Verne
University of Redlands
University of Southern California
Westmont College
Whittier College

Colorado
Adams State College
Colorado State University
Colorado State University
   Pueblo
Fort Lewis College
Mesa State College
Metropolitan State College of Denver
Northeastern Junior College
Pueblo Community College
Rocky Mountain College of Art & Design
University of Colorado
   Boulder
   Denver
University of Denver
Western State College of Colorado

Connecticut
Albertus Magnus College
Fairfield University
Lyme Academy of Fine Arts
Mitchell College
Sacred Heart University
University of Connecticut
University of Hartford

Delaware
University of Delaware

District of Columbia
Corcoran College of Art and Design
George Washington University
Howard University

Florida
Barry University
Chipola College
Eckerd College
Edison State College
Flagler College
Florida Agricultural and Mechanical University
Florida International University
Florida Keys Community College
Florida Southern College
Florida State College at Jacksonville
Hillsborough Community College
Jacksonville University

Miami Dade College
North Florida Community College
Northwest Florida State College
Ringling College of Art and Design
Rollins College
St. Petersburg College
Santa Fe College
Seminole Community College
State College of Florida, Manatee-Sarasota
Stetson University
Tallahassee Community College
University of Florida
University of South Florida
University of Tampa
University of West Florida
Warner University

Georgia
Albany State University
Andrew College
Armstrong Atlantic State University
   of Atlanta
Augusta State University
Berry College
Brenau University
Clark Atlanta University
Columbus State University
Covenant College
Darton College
Emmanuel College
Emory University
Gainesville State College
Georgia College and State University
Georgia Highlands College
Georgia Southern University
Kennesaw State University
LaGrange College
Mercer University
Middle Georgia College
Morehouse College
North Georgia College & State University
Piedmont College
Reinhardt College
Savannah College of Art and Design
Shorter College
University of West Georgia
Valdosta State University
Wesleyan College
Young Harris College

Hawaii
Chaminade University of Honolulu
University of Hawaii
   Manoa

Idaho
College of Idaho
Idaho State University
Lewis-Clark State College
North Idaho College
Northwest Nazarene University
University of Idaho

Illinois
Augustana College
Aurora University
Black Hawk College
Bradley University
Carl Sandburg College
College of DuPage
College of Lake County
Columbia College Chicago
Danville Area Community College
DePaul University
Eastern Illinois University
Elgin Community College
Elmhurst College
Eureka College
Greenville College
Harper College
Illinois College
Illinois Institute of Art: Schaumburg
Illinois State University

Illinois Wesleyan University
Judson University
Knox College
Lewis University
Lincoln College
MacMurray College
McKendree University
Millikin University
Monmouth College
North Central College
North Park University
Northeastern Illinois University
Oakton Community College
Olivet Nazarene University
Parkland College
Quincy University
Rend Lake College
Richland Community College
Robert Morris University: Chicago
School of the Art Institute of Chicago
South Suburban College of Cook County
Southeastern Illinois College
Southern Illinois University Edwardsville
Trinity Christian College
University of Illinois
   Chicago
   Springfield
   Urbana-Champaign
University of St. Francis
Waubonsee Community College
Western Illinois University
Wheaton College

Indiana
Anderson University
Bethel College
Franklin College
Goshen College
Grace College
Hanover College
Huntington University
Indiana State University
Indiana University
   Bloomington
   Southeast
Indiana Wesleyan University
Marian University
Oakland City University
St. Mary-of-the-Woods College
Saint Mary's College
Taylor University
University of Evansville
University of Indianapolis
University of St. Francis
University of Southern Indiana
Valparaiso University
Vincennes University
Wabash College

Iowa
Briar Cliff University
Buena Vista University
Central College
Clarke College
Coe College
Cornell College
Dordt College
Drake University
Ellsworth Community College
Graceland University
Grand View University
Iowa Central Community College
Iowa State University
Iowa Wesleyan College
Kirkwood Community College
Luther College
Morningside College
Mount Mercy College
North Iowa Area Community College
Northwestern College
St. Ambrose University
Simpson College

Southeastern Community College
    North Campus
University of Iowa
University of Northern Iowa

Kansas
Allen County Community College
Baker University
Benedictine College
Bethany College
Bethel College
Butler Community College
Coffeyville Community College
Cowley County Community College
Emporia State University
Fort Hays State University
Friends University
Garden City Community College
Hesston College
Highland Community College
Kansas City Kansas Community College
Kansas State University
Kansas Wesleyan University
McPherson College
Neosho County Community College
Newman University
Pittsburg State University
Pratt Community College
University of Kansas
University of St. Mary
Washburn University
Wichita State University

Kentucky
Asbury College
Bellarmine University
Brescia University
Campbellsville University
Eastern Kentucky University
Georgetown College
Kentucky State University
Kentucky Wesleyan College
Midway College
Morehead State University
Murray State University
Northern Kentucky University
Sullivan College of Technology and Design
Thomas More College
Transylvania University
University of Kentucky
University of Louisville
Western Kentucky University

Louisiana
Centenary College of Louisiana
Dillard University
Grambling State University
Louisiana College
Louisiana Tech University
Loyola University New Orleans
McNeese State University
Northwestern State University
University of Louisiana at Monroe

Maine
Maine College of Art
University of Maine
University of Maine
    Machias
    Presque Isle
York County Community College

Maryland
Bowie State University
Carroll Community College
Chesapeake College
College of Notre Dame of Maryland
Goucher College
Maryland Institute College of Art
Montgomery College
Mount St. Mary's University
Salisbury University
Stevenson University

Towson University
University of Maryland
    Baltimore County
    College Park
    Eastern Shore

Massachusetts
Art Institute of Boston at Lesley University
Atlantic Union College
Bay State College
Boston Architectural College
Boston University
Bristol Community College
Cape Cod Community College
Endicott College
Gordon College
Holyoke Community College
Lesley University
Massachusetts College of Art and Design
Massachusetts College of Liberal Arts
Montserrat College of Art
School of the Museum of Fine Arts
Stonehill College
University of Massachusetts
    Amherst
    Lowell

Michigan
Adrian College
Albion College
Alma College
Alpena Community College
Aquinas College
Calvin College
Central Michigan University
College for Creative Studies
Eastern Michigan University
Ferris State University
Glen Oaks Community College
Gogebic Community College
Grand Rapids Community College
Grand Valley State University
Hillsdale College
Hope College
Jackson Community College
Kalamazoo College
Kendall College of Art and Design of Ferris
    State University
Lawrence Technological University
Madonna University
Marygrove College
Michigan State University
Michigan Technological University
Monroe County Community College
Mott Community College
Northern Michigan University
Northwestern Michigan College
Oakland University
Saginaw Valley State University
Siena Heights University
Southwestern Michigan College
Spring Arbor University
University of Michigan
University of Michigan
    Flint
Wayne State University
Western Michigan University

Minnesota
Bemidji State University
Bethany Lutheran College
Bethel University
College of St. Benedict
College of Visual Arts
Concordia College: Moorhead
Concordia University: St. Paul
Gustavus Adolphus College
Hamline University
Minneapolis College of Art and Design
Minnesota State Community and Technical
    College

Minnesota State University
    Mankato
    Moorhead
North Hennepin Community College
Riverland Community College
Saint Cloud State University
St. John's University
St. Mary's University of Minnesota
Southwest Minnesota State University
University of Minnesota
    Twin Cities
Winona State University

Mississippi
Belhaven University
Blue Mountain College
Copiah-Lincoln Community College
Delta State University
East Mississippi Community College
Hinds Community College
Meridian Community College
Millsaps College
Mississippi College
Mississippi State University
University of Mississippi

Missouri
Avila University
College of the Ozarks
Columbia College
Cottey College
Crowder College
Culver-Stockton College
Drury University
East Central College
Evangel University
Fontbonne University
Hannibal-LaGrange College
Jefferson College
Kansas City Art Institute
Lincoln University
Lindenwood University
Maryville University of Saint Louis
Mineral Area College
Missouri Southern State University
Missouri State University
Missouri Western State University
Northwest Missouri State University
Park University
St. Charles Community College
Saint Louis University
Southeast Missouri State University
Southwest Baptist University
State Fair Community College
Truman State University
University of Central Missouri
University of Missouri
    Columbia
    Kansas City
    St. Louis
Webster University
William Jewell College
William Woods University

Montana
Dawson Community College
Montana State University
    Billings
    Bozeman
Rocky Mountain College
University of Great Falls
University of Montana
University of Montana: Western

Nebraska
Central Community College
Chadron State College
Concordia University
Creative Center
Creighton University
Dana College
Doane College
Mid-Plains Community College Area

Nebraska Wesleyan University
Peru State College
University of Nebraska
    Kearney
    Lincoln
    Omaha
Wayne State College
Western Nebraska Community College

Nevada
Sierra Nevada College
Truckee Meadows Community College
University of Nevada
    Las Vegas
    Reno

New Hampshire
Chester College of New England
Colby-Sawyer College
Franklin Pierce University
Keene State College
New England College
University of New Hampshire

New Jersey
Caldwell College
Centenary College
College of St. Elizabeth
Drew University
Georgian Court University
Kean University
Monmouth University
Montclair State University
Richard Stockton College of New Jersey
Rowan University
Rutgers, The State University of New Jersey
    Camden Regional Campus
    New Brunswick/Piscataway Campus
    Newark Regional Campus
Union County College

New Mexico
College of Santa Fe
Eastern New Mexico University
Institute of American Indian Arts
New Mexico Junior College
University of New Mexico

New York
Adelphi University
Alfred University
Canisius College
City University of New York
    Brooklyn College
    College of Staten Island
College of New Rochelle
College of Saint Rose
Daemen College
Fashion Institute of Technology
Hobart and William Smith Colleges
Hofstra University
Houghton College
Jamestown Community College
Manhattanville College
Marymount Manhattan College
Mohawk Valley Community College
Molloy College
Nazareth College
Nyack College
Parsons The New School for Design
Rensselaer Polytechnic Institute
Roberts Wesleyan College
Rochester Institute of Technology
Sage College of Albany
Saint Bonaventure University
St. John's University
School of Visual Arts
State University of New York
    Binghamton
    College at Brockport
    College at Cortland
    College at Fredonia
    College at Geneseo

College at Plattsburgh
College at Potsdam
New Paltz
Purchase
Stony Brook
Suffolk County Community College
Syracuse University
Villa Maria College of Buffalo

North Carolina
Appalachian State University
Barton College
Brevard College
College of the Albemarle
Davidson College
Duke University
East Carolina University
Elon University
Greensboro College
High Point University
Mars Hill College
Meredith College
Mount Olive College
Peace College
Queens University of Charlotte
Rockingham Community College
St. Andrews Presbyterian College
St. Augustine's College
Shaw University
University of North Carolina
    Asheville
    Chapel Hill
    Greensboro
    Pembroke
    Wilmington
University of North Carolina School of the Arts
Wake Forest University
Warren Wilson College
Western Carolina University
Wilkes Community College
Wingate University

North Dakota
Dickinson State University
Jamestown College
Minot State University
North Dakota State University
Trinity Bible College
University of North Dakota

Ohio
Art Academy of Cincinnati
Art Institute of Cincinnati
Ashland University
Bowling Green State University
Bowling Green State University: Firelands
    College
Capital University
Case Western Reserve University
Central State University
Cleveland Institute of Art
Cleveland State University
College of Mount St. Joseph
Columbus College of Art and Design
Cuyahoga Community College
    Metropolitan Campus
Denison University
Kent State University
Kent State University
    Ashtabula
    East Liverpool
    Salem
    Stark
    Trumbull
    Tuscarawas
Kent State University: Geauga
Lourdes College
Marietta College
Miami University
    Oxford Campus
Mount Union College
Muskingum University

Ohio Northern University
Ohio State University
    Agricultural Technical Institute
    Columbus Campus
    Lima Campus
    Mansfield Campus
    Marion Campus
    Newark Campus
Ohio University
Ohio Wesleyan University
Otterbein College
Pontifical College Josephinum
School of Advertising Art
Southern State Community College
University of Akron
University of Akron: Wayne College
University of Cincinnati
University of Dayton
University of Toledo
Ursuline College
Wittenberg University
Wright State University
Wright State University: Lake Campus
Xavier University

Oklahoma
Cameron University
Carl Albert State College
Northeastern Oklahoma Agricultural and
    Mechanical College
Northeastern State University
Northwestern Oklahoma State University
Oklahoma Baptist University
Oklahoma Christian University
Oklahoma City Community College
Oklahoma City University
Oklahoma Panhandle State University
Oklahoma State University
Oral Roberts University
Rogers State University
St. Gregory's University
Southeastern Oklahoma State University
Southwestern Oklahoma State University
Tulsa Community College
University of Central Oklahoma
University of Oklahoma
University of Science and Arts of Oklahoma
University of Tulsa
Western Oklahoma State College

Oregon
Art Institute of Portland
Clackamas Community College
Eastern Oregon University
George Fox University
Lane Community College
Linn-Benton Community College
Oregon College of Art & Craft
Pacific Northwest College of Art
Pacific University
Portland State University
Southern Oregon University
Southwestern Oregon Community College
Western Oregon University

Pennsylvania
Albright College
Arcadia University
Bloomsburg University of Pennsylvania
Bucknell University
California University of Pennsylvania
Carnegie Mellon University
Cedar Crest College
Clarion University of Pennsylvania
Drexel University
East Stroudsburg University of Pennsylvania
Edinboro University of Pennsylvania
Elizabethtown College
Franklin & Marshall College
Immaculata University
Indiana University of Pennsylvania
Juniata College

Kutztown University of Pennsylvania
Lehigh University
Lock Haven University of Pennsylvania
Lycoming College
Manor College
Mansfield University of Pennsylvania
Marywood University
Mercyhurst College
Messiah College
Moore College of Art and Design
Mount Aloysius College
Muhlenberg College
Northampton Community College
Oakbridge Academy of Arts
Point Park University
Rosemont College
Saint Joseph's University
Seton Hill University
Slippery Rock University of Pennsylvania
Temple University
University of the Arts
Ursinus College

Puerto Rico
Humacao Community College

Rhode Island
Rhode Island College
University of Rhode Island

South Carolina
Anderson University
Clemson University
Coastal Carolina University
Coker College
College of Charleston
Columbia College
Converse College
Erskine College
Furman University
Lander University
Limestone College
University of South Carolina
University of South Carolina
    Aiken
Winthrop University

South Dakota
Augustana College
Dakota State University
Dakota Wesleyan University
Mount Marty College
Northern State University
South Dakota State University
University of Sioux Falls
University of South Dakota

Tennessee
Austin Peay State University
Belmont University
Bryan College
Carson-Newman College
Cumberland University
East Tennessee State University
Free Will Baptist Bible College
Freed-Hardeman University
Jackson State Community College
Lambuth University
Lipscomb University
Martin Methodist College
Maryville College
Memphis College of Art
Middle Tennessee State University
Milligan College
Motlow State Community College
Northeast State Community College
Pellissippi State Community College
Rhodes College
Roane State Community College
Southern Adventist University
Tennessee Technological University
Trevecca Nazarene University
Union University

University of Memphis
University of Tennessee
    Chattanooga
    Knoxville
Volunteer State Community College

Texas
Abilene Christian University
Angelina College
Angelo State University
Austin College
Baylor University
Brazosport College
Clarendon College
College of the Mainland
Collin County Community College District
Galveston College
Hardin-Simmons University
Houston Baptist University
Howard College
Howard Payne University
Huston-Tillotson University
Kilgore College
Lee College
Lon Morris College
McMurry University
Midwestern State University
Panola College
Rice University
Richland College
St. Edward's University
Sam Houston State University
San Jacinto College
Schreiner University
South Plains College
Southern Methodist University
Southwestern University
Sul Ross State University
Tarleton State University
Temple College
Texas A&M University
Texas A&M University
    Commerce
    Corpus Christi
Texas Christian University
Texas State University: San Marcos
Texas Tech University
Tyler Junior College
University of Dallas
University of Houston
University of Mary Hardin-Baylor
University of Texas
    Arlington
    Austin
    Brownsville - Texas Southmost College
    El Paso
    Pan American
    of the Permian Basin
    San Antonio
    Tyler
University of the Incarnate Word
Victoria College
Wayland Baptist University
West Texas A&M University
Western Technical College
Western Texas College

Utah
Brigham Young University
College of Eastern Utah
Dixie State College of Utah
Salt Lake Community College
Southern Utah University
University of Utah
Utah State University
Utah Valley University
Weber State University
Westminster College

Vermont
Castleton State College
Goddard College

Green Mountain College
Johnson State College
Landmark College
University of Vermont

Virginia
Averett University
Bluefield College
Christopher Newport University
Eastern Mennonite University
Emory & Henry College
Hollins University
James Madison University
Longwood University
Old Dominion University
Radford University
Randolph College
Southern Virginia University
Sweet Briar College
University of Mary Washington
University of Richmond
University of Virginia's College at Wise
Virginia Commonwealth University
Virginia Intermont College
Virginia Polytechnic Institute and State
    University
Virginia State University

Washington
Art Institute of Seattle
Big Bend Community College
Centralia College
Clark College
Everett Community College
Evergreen State College
Grays Harbor College
Northwest College of Art
Northwest University
Pacific Lutheran University
Saint Martin's University
Seattle Pacific University
Trinity Lutheran College
University of Puget Sound
University of Washington
Washington State University
Western Washington University
Whitman College
Whitworth University

West Virginia
Bluefield State College
Concord University
Davis and Elkins College
Fairmont State University
Marshall University
Shepherd University
West Liberty University
West Virginia University
West Virginia Wesleyan College

Wisconsin
Cardinal Stritch University
Carroll University
Carthage College
Edgewood College
Mount Mary College
Northland College
Ripon College
St. Norbert College
Silver Lake College
University of Wisconsin
    Baraboo/Sauk County
    Eau Claire
    Green Bay
    La Crosse
    Madison
    Manitowoc
    Milwaukee
    Oshkosh
    Parkside
    Richland
    River Falls
    Stevens Point

    Superior
    Waukesha
    Whitewater
Viterbo University
Wisconsin Lutheran College

Wyoming
Casper College
Central Wyoming College
Eastern Wyoming College
Laramie County Community College
Sheridan College
University of Wyoming
Western Wyoming Community College

Athletic scholarships

Archery

Arizona
Dine College M,W

California
College of the Redwoods M

Texas
Texas A&M University W

Badminton

California
Fresno City College M,W

New Jersey
New Jersey Institute of Technology M

Wisconsin
Milwaukee Area Technical College M

Baseball

Alabama
Alabama Agricultural and Mechanical
 University M
Alabama State University M
Auburn University M
Auburn University at Montgomery M
Bevill State Community College M
Central Alabama Community College M
Chattahoochee Valley Community College M
Enterprise-Ozark Community College M
Faulkner State Community College M
Gadsden State Community College M
George C. Wallace State Community College
 George C. Wallace Community College at
 Dothan M
 Wallace State Community College at
 Selma M
Jacksonville State University M
Jefferson Davis Community College M
Jefferson State Community College M
Lawson State Community College M
Lurleen B. Wallace Community College M
Miles College M
Northwest-Shoals Community College M
Samford University M
Selma University M
Shelton State Community College M
Snead State Community College M
Southern Union State Community College M
Spring Hill College M
Troy University M
Tuskegee University M
University of Alabama M
University of Alabama
 Birmingham M
 Huntsville M
University of Mobile M
University of Montevallo M
University of North Alabama M
University of South Alabama M
University of West Alabama M
Wallace State Community College at Hanceville
 M

Arizona
Arizona State University M
Arizona Western College M
Central Arizona College M
Chandler-Gilbert Community College
 Pecos M
Cochise College M
Eastern Arizona College M
GateWay Community College M
Glendale Community College M
Grand Canyon University M
Paradise Valley Community College M
Pima Community College M
Scottsdale Community College M
University of Arizona M

Arkansas
Arkansas State University M
Arkansas Tech University M
Ecclesia College M
Harding University M
Henderson State University M
Lyon College M
North Arkansas College M
Ouachita Baptist University M
Southern Arkansas University M
University of Arkansas M
University of Arkansas
 Fort Smith M
 Little Rock M
 Pine Bluff M
University of Central Arkansas M
Williams Baptist College M

California
Azusa Pacific University M
Bethany University M
Biola University M
California Baptist University M
California Polytechnic State University: San Luis
 Obispo M
California State Polytechnic University: Pomona
 M
California State University
 Chico M
 Dominguez Hills M
 Fresno M
 Fullerton M
 Long Beach M
 Los Angeles M
 Monterey Bay M
 Northridge M
 Sacramento M
 San Bernardino M
 Stanislaus M
Concordia University M
Fresno City College M
Fresno Pacific University M
Grossmont College M
Loyola Marymount University M
The Master's College M
Patten University M
Pepperdine University M
Point Loma Nazarene University M
St. Mary's College of California M
San Diego Christian College M
San Diego State University M
San Jose State University M
Santa Clara University M
Sonoma State University M
Stanford University M
University of California
 Berkeley M

Davis M
Irvine M
Los Angeles M
Riverside M
Santa Barbara M
University of San Diego M
University of San Francisco M
University of Southern California M
University of the Pacific M
Vanguard University of Southern California M
Westmont College M
Yuba Community College District M

Colorado
Colorado Christian University M
Colorado Northwestern Community College M
Colorado School of Mines M
Colorado State University
 Pueblo M
Lamar Community College M
Mesa State College M
Metropolitan State College of Denver M
Northeastern Junior College M
Otero Junior College M
Regis University M
Trinidad State Junior College M
University of Northern Colorado M

Connecticut
Central Connecticut State University M
Fairfield University M
Post University M
Quinnipiac University M
Sacred Heart University M
Southern Connecticut State University M
University of Bridgeport M
University of Connecticut M
University of Hartford M
University of New Haven M

Delaware
Delaware State University M
Delaware Technical and Community College
 Owens M
University of Delaware M
Wilmington University M

District of Columbia
George Washington University M
Georgetown University M
Howard University M

Florida
Ave Maria University M
Barry University M
Bethune-Cookman University M
Brevard Community College M
Central Florida Community College M
Chipola College M
Daytona State College M
Eckerd College M
Edward Waters College M
Embry-Riddle Aeronautical University M
Flagler College M
Florida Atlantic University M
Florida Gulf Coast University M
Florida Institute of Technology M
Florida Memorial University M
Florida Southern College M
Florida State College at Jacksonville M
Florida State University M
Gulf Coast Community College M
Hillsborough Community College M
Indian River State College M
Jacksonville University M
Lake-Sumter Community College M
Lynn University M
Miami Dade College M
North Florida Community College M
Northwest Florida State College M
Northwood University
 Florida M
Nova Southeastern University M

Palm Beach Community College M
Pasco-Hernando Community College M
Pensacola Junior College M
Polk State College M
Rollins College M
Saint Johns River Community College M
Saint Leo University M
St. Petersburg College M
Saint Thomas University M
Santa Fe College M
South Florida Community College M
Southeastern University M
State College of Florida, Manatee-Sarasota M
Stetson University M
Tallahassee Community College M
University of Central Florida M
University of Florida M
University of Miami M
University of North Florida M
University of South Florida M
University of Tampa M
University of West Florida M
Warner University M
Webber International University M

Georgia
Abraham Baldwin Agricultural College M
Albany State University M
Andrew College M
Armstrong Atlantic State University M
Augusta State University M
Brewton-Parker College M
Clark Atlanta University M
Columbus State University M
Covenant College M
Darton College M
Emmanuel College M
Georgia College and State University M
Georgia Institute of Technology M
Georgia Perimeter College M
Georgia Southern University M
Georgia Southwestern State University M
Georgia State University M
Gordon College M
Kennesaw State University M
Mercer University M
Middle Georgia College M
Morehouse College M
Paine College M
Reinhardt College M
Savannah State University M
Shorter College M
Southern Polytechnic State University M
Truett-McConnell College M
University of Georgia M
University of West Georgia M
Valdosta State University M
Young Harris College M

Hawaii
Hawaii Pacific University M
University of Hawaii
 Manoa M

Idaho
College of Idaho M
Lewis-Clark State College M
Northwest Nazarene University M

Illinois
Black Hawk College M
Bradley University M
Carl Sandburg College M
Chicago State University M
College of Lake County M
Danville Area Community College M
Eastern Illinois University M
Elgin Community College M
Highland Community College M
Illinois Central College M
Illinois Eastern Community Colleges
 Lincoln Trail College M
 Olney Central College M

Wabash Valley College M
Illinois Institute of Technology M
Illinois State University M
John A. Logan College M
Judson University M
Kankakee Community College M
Kaskaskia College M
Kishwaukee College M
Lake Land College M
Lewis and Clark Community College M
Lewis University M
Lincoln College M
Lincoln Land Community College M
McHenry County College M
McKendree University M
Moraine Valley Community College M
Morton College M
Northwestern University M
Olivet Nazarene University M
Parkland College M
Quincy University M
Rend Lake College M
Robert Morris University: Chicago M
Saint Xavier University M
Sauk Valley Community College M
South Suburban College of Cook County M
Southeastern Illinois College M
Southern Illinois University Carbondale M
Southern Illinois University Edwardsville M
Southwestern Illinois College M
Spoon River College M
Trinity Christian College M
Trinity International University M
University of Illinois
    Chicago M
    Springfield M
    Urbana-Champaign M
University of St. Francis M
Western Illinois University M

Indiana
Ancilla College M
Ball State University M
Bethel College M
Butler University M
Calumet College of St. Joseph M
Goshen College M
Grace College M
Huntington University M
Indiana Institute of Technology M
Indiana State University M
Indiana University
    Bloomington M
    Southeast M
Indiana University-Purdue University Fort
    Wayne M
Indiana Wesleyan University M
Marian University M
Oakland City University M
Purdue University M
Purdue University
    North Central M
Saint Joseph's College M
Taylor University M
University of Evansville M
University of Indianapolis M
University of Notre Dame M
University of St. Francis M
University of Southern Indiana M
Valparaiso University M
Vincennes University M

Iowa
Briar Cliff University M
Clarke College M
Des Moines Area Community College M
Dordt College M
Ellsworth Community College M
Graceland University M
Grand View University M
Indian Hills Community College M
Iowa Central Community College M

Iowa Lakes Community College- Estherville M
Iowa Wesleyan College M
Iowa Western Community College M
Kirkwood Community College M
Morningside College M
Mount Mercy College M
Muscatine Community College M
North Iowa Area Community College M
Northwestern College M
St. Ambrose University M
Southeastern Community College
    North Campus M
Southwestern Community College M
University of Iowa M
Waldorf College M
William Penn University M

Kansas
Allen County Community College M
Baker University M
Barton County Community College M
Benedictine College M
Bethany College M
Brown Mackie College
    Salina M
Butler Community College M
Central Christian College of Kansas M
Cloud County Community College M
Coffeyville Community College M
Colby Community College M
Cowley County Community College M
Dodge City Community College M
Emporia State University M
Fort Scott Community College M
Friends University M
Garden City Community College M
Hesston College M
Highland Community College M
Hutchinson Community College M
Johnson County Community College M
Kansas City Kansas Community College M
Kansas State University M
Kansas Wesleyan University M
Labette Community College M
MidAmerica Nazarene University M
Neosho County Community College M
Newman University M
Ottawa University M
Pittsburg State University M
Pratt Community College M
Seward County Community College M
Sterling College M
Tabor College M
University of Kansas M
University of St. Mary M
Washburn University M
Wichita State University M

Kentucky
Alice Lloyd College M
Asbury College M
Bellarmine University M
Brescia University M
Campbellsville University M
Eastern Kentucky University M
Georgetown College M
Kentucky State University M
Kentucky Wesleyan College M
Lindsey Wilson College M
Mid-Continent University M
Morehead State University M
Murray State University M
Northern Kentucky University M
Pikeville College M
St. Catharine College M
Union College M
University of Kentucky M
University of Louisville M
University of the Cumberlands M
Western Kentucky University M

Louisiana
Bossier Parish Community College M
Centenary College of Louisiana M
Delgado Community College M
Grambling State University M
Louisiana State University
    Shreveport M
Louisiana State University and Agricultural and
    Mechanical College M
Louisiana Tech University M
McNeese State University M
Nicholls State University M
Northwestern State University M
Southeastern Louisiana University M
Southern University and Agricultural and
    Mechanical College M
Tulane University M
University of Louisiana at Lafayette M
University of Louisiana at Monroe M
University of New Orleans M

Maine
University of Maine M

Maryland
Anne Arundel Community College M
Chesapeake College M
College of Southern Maryland M
Community College of Baltimore County M
Coppin State University M
Garrett College M
Hagerstown Community College M
Harford Community College M
Mount St. Mary's University M
Towson University M
University of Maryland
    Baltimore County M
    College Park M
    Eastern Shore M
Washington Adventist University M

Massachusetts
American International College M
Boston College M
Dean College M
Northeastern University M
Stonehill College M
University of Massachusetts
    Amherst M
    Lowell M

Michigan
Aquinas College M
Central Michigan University M
Davenport University M
Eastern Michigan University M
Glen Oaks Community College M
Grand Rapids Community College M
Hillsdale College M
Kalamazoo Valley Community College M
Kellogg Community College M
Lake Michigan College M
Macomb Community College M
Madonna University M
Michigan State University M
Mott Community College M
Muskegon Community College M
Northwood University: Michigan M
Oakland University M
Rochester College M
Saginaw Valley State University M
Siena Heights University M
Spring Arbor University M
University of Michigan M
Wayne State University M

Minnesota
Concordia University: St. Paul M
Minnesota State University
    Mankato M
Saint Cloud State University M
Southwest Minnesota State University M

University of Minnesota
    Crookston M
    Duluth M
    Twin Cities M
Winona State University M

Mississippi
Alcorn State University M
Belhaven University M
Copiah-Lincoln Community College M
Delta State University M
East Mississippi Community College M
Hinds Community College M
Holmes Community College M
Jackson State University M
Jones County Junior College M
Meridian Community College M
Mississippi Gulf Coast Community College M
Mississippi State University M
Mississippi Valley State University M
Northwest Mississippi Community College M
Southwest Mississippi Community College M
University of Mississippi M
University of Southern Mississippi M

Missouri
Avila University M
Central Methodist University M
College of the Ozarks M
Crowder College M
Culver-Stockton College M
Drury University M
Evangel University M
Hannibal-LaGrange College M
Harris-Stowe State University M
Jefferson College M
Lincoln University M
Metropolitan Community College: Longview M
Metropolitan Community College: Maple
    Woods M
Mineral Area College M
Missouri Baptist University M
Missouri Southern State University M
Missouri State University M
Missouri Valley College M
Missouri Western State University M
North Central Missouri College M
Northwest Missouri State University M
Park University M
Research College of Nursing M
Rockhurst University M
St. Charles Community College M
Saint Louis University M
Southeast Missouri State University M
Southwest Baptist University M
Three Rivers Community College M
Truman State University M
University of Central Missouri M
University of Missouri
    Columbia M
    Missouri University of Science and
        Technology M
    St. Louis M
William Jewell College M
William Woods University M

Montana
Miles Community College M
Montana State University
    Billings M

Nebraska
Bellevue University M
Concordia University M
Creighton University M
Dana College M
Doane College M
Mid-Plains Community College Area M
Peru State College M
University of Nebraska
    Kearney M
    Lincoln M
    Omaha M

Wayne State College M
Western Nebraska Community College M
York College M

Nevada
College of Southern Nevada M
University of Nevada
    Las Vegas M
    Reno M

New Hampshire
Franklin Pierce University M
Southern New Hampshire University M

New Jersey
Bloomfield College M
Brookdale Community College M
Burlington County College M
Caldwell College M
Fairleigh Dickinson University
    Metropolitan Campus M
Mercer County Community College M
Monmouth University M
New Jersey Institute of Technology M
Rider University M
Rutgers, The State University of New Jersey
    New Brunswick/Piscataway Campus M
Saint Peter's College M
Salem Community College M
Seton Hall University M
Sussex County Community College M

New Mexico
Eastern New Mexico University M
New Mexico Highlands University M
New Mexico Junior College M
New Mexico Military Institute M
New Mexico State University M
University of New Mexico M
University of the Southwest M

New York
Adelphi University M
ASA Institute of Business and Computer
    Technology M
Canisius College M
City University of New York
    Queens College M
College of Saint Rose M
Concordia College M
Dominican College of Blauvelt M
Dowling College M
Fordham University M
Globe Institute of Technology M
Hofstra University M
Iona College M
Le Moyne College M
Long Island University
    Brooklyn Campus M
    C. W. Post Campus M
Manhattan College M
Marist College M
Mercy College M
Molloy College M
Monroe College M
Monroe Community College M
New York Institute of Technology M
Niagara University M
Nyack College M
Pace University M
Saint Bonaventure University M
St. John's University M
St. Thomas Aquinas College M
Siena College M
State University of New York
    Albany M
    Binghamton M
    Buffalo M
    Stony Brook M
Wagner College M

North Carolina
Appalachian State University M
Barton College M
Belmont Abbey College M
Brevard College M
Campbell University M
Catawba College M
Chowan University M
Davidson College M
Duke University M
East Carolina University M
Elon University M
Gardner-Webb University M
Guilford Technical Community College M
High Point University M
Lenoir Community College M
Lenoir-Rhyne University M
Louisburg College M
Mars Hill College M
Montreat College M
Mount Olive College M
North Carolina Agricultural and Technical State
    University M
North Carolina State University M
Pfeiffer University M
Pitt Community College M
St. Andrews Presbyterian College M
St. Augustine's College M
Shaw University M
Southeastern Community College M
University of North Carolina
    Asheville M
    Chapel Hill M
    Charlotte M
    Greensboro M
    Pembroke M
    Wilmington M
Wake Forest University M
Western Carolina University M
Wingate University M

North Dakota
Bismarck State College M
Dakota College at Bottineau M
Dickinson State University M
Jamestown College M
Mayville State University M
Minot State University M
North Dakota State University M
University of Mary M
University of North Dakota M
Williston State College M

Ohio
Ashland University M
Bowling Green State University M
Cedarville University M
Clark State Community College M
Cleveland State University M
Kent State University M
Malone University M
Miami University
    Oxford Campus M
Mount Vernon Nazarene University M
Notre Dame College M
Ohio Dominican University M
Ohio State University
    Columbus Campus M
Ohio University M
Shawnee State University M
Tiffin University M
University of Akron M
University of Cincinnati M
University of Dayton M
University of Findlay M
University of Rio Grande M
University of Toledo M
Urbana University M
Walsh University M
Wright State University M
Xavier University M
Youngstown State University M

Oklahoma
Bacone College M
Cameron University M
Carl Albert State College M
Connors State College M
East Central University M
Eastern Oklahoma State College M
Northeastern Oklahoma Agricultural and
    Mechanical College M
Northeastern State University M
Northern Oklahoma College M
Northwestern Oklahoma State University M
Oklahoma Baptist University M
Oklahoma Christian University M
Oklahoma City University M
Oklahoma Panhandle State University M
Oklahoma State University M
Oklahoma Wesleyan University M
Oral Roberts University M
Redlands Community College M
Rogers State University M
Rose State College M
St. Gregory's University M
Seminole State College M
Southeastern Oklahoma State University M
Southern Nazarene University M
Southwestern Oklahoma State University M
University of Central Oklahoma M
University of Oklahoma M
University of Science and Arts of Oklahoma M
Western Oklahoma State College M

Oregon
Blue Mountain Community College M
Chemeketa Community College M
Clackamas Community College M
Concordia University M
Corban College M
Lane Community College M
Linn-Benton Community College M
Mt. Hood Community College M
Oregon Institute of Technology M
Oregon State University M
Portland State University M
Southwestern Oregon Community College M
Treasure Valley Community College M
University of Oregon M
University of Portland M

Pennsylvania
Bloomsburg University of Pennsylvania M
California University of Pennsylvania M
Chestnut Hill College M
Clarion University of Pennsylvania M
Duquesne University M
East Stroudsburg University of Pennsylvania M
Gannon University M
Indiana University of Pennsylvania M
Kutztown University of Pennsylvania M
La Salle University M
Lackawanna College M
Lock Haven University of Pennsylvania M
Mansfield University of Pennsylvania M
Mercyhurst College M
Millersville University of Pennsylvania M
Penn State
    University Park M
Philadelphia University M
Point Park University M
Saint Joseph's University M
Seton Hill University M
Shippensburg University of Pennsylvania M
Slippery Rock University of Pennsylvania M
Temple University M
University of Pittsburgh M
University of the Sciences in Philadelphia M
Villanova University M
West Chester University of Pennsylvania M

Puerto Rico
Inter American University of Puerto Rico
    Aguadilla Campus M

    Bayamon Campus M
    Metropolitan Campus M
    Ponce Campus M
    San German Campus M
Turabo University M
Universidad del Este M
Universidad Metropolitana M
Universidad Politecnica de Puerto Rico M
University of Puerto Rico
    Carolina Regional College M
    Cayey University College M
    Humacao M
    Utuado M

Rhode Island
Bryant University M
Community College of Rhode Island M
University of Rhode Island M

South Carolina
Anderson University M
Charleston Southern University M
The Citadel M
Claflin University M
Clemson University M
Coastal Carolina University M
Coker College M
College of Charleston M
Erskine College M
Francis Marion University M
Furman University M
Lander University M
Limestone College M
Morris College M
Newberry College M
North Greenville University M
Presbyterian College M
Southern Wesleyan University M
Spartanburg Methodist College M
University of South Carolina M
University of South Carolina
    Aiken M
    Sumter M
    Upstate M
Winthrop University M
Wofford College M

South Dakota
Augustana College M
Dakota State University M
Dakota Wesleyan University M
Mount Marty College M
South Dakota State University M
University of Sioux Falls M

Tennessee
Austin Peay State University M
Belmont University M
Bethel University M
Bryan College M
Carson-Newman College M
Chattanooga State Community College M
Christian Brothers University M
Cleveland State Community College M
Columbia State Community College M
Cumberland University M
Dyersburg State Community College M
East Tennessee State University M
Freed-Hardeman University M
Jackson State Community College M
King College M
Lambuth University M
Lee University M
LeMoyne-Owen College M
Lincoln Memorial University M
Lipscomb University M
Martin Methodist College M
Middle Tennessee State University M
Milligan College M
Motlow State Community College M
Roane State Community College M
Southwest Tennessee Community College M
Tennessee Technological University M

Tennessee Temple University M
Tennessee Wesleyan College M
Trevecca Nazarene University M
Tusculum College M
Union University M
University of Memphis M
University of Tennessee
    Knoxville M
    Martin M
Vanderbilt University M
Volunteer State Community College M
Walters State Community College M

Texas
Abilene Christian University M
Alvin Community College M
Angelina College M
Angelo State University M
Baylor University M
Blinn College M
Clarendon College M
Dallas Baptist University M
El Paso Community College M
Frank Phillips College M
Galveston College M
Grayson County College M
Hill College M
Houston Baptist University M
Howard College M
Jarvis Christian College M
Lamar University M
Laredo Community College M
Lon Morris College M
Lubbock Christian University M
McLennan Community College M
North Central Texas College M
Northeast Texas Community College M
Northwood University: Texas M
Odessa College M
Paris Junior College M
Prairie View A&M University M
Ranger College M
Rice University M
St. Edward's University M
St. Mary's University M
Sam Houston State University M
San Jacinto College M
Stephen F. Austin State University M
Tarleton State University M
Texas A&M University M
Texas A&M University
    Corpus Christi M
    Kingsville M
Texas Christian University M
Texas Southern University M
Texas State University: San Marcos M
Texas Tech University M
University of Houston M
University of Texas
    Arlington M
    Austin M
    Brownsville - Texas Southmost College M
    Pan American M
    of the Permian Basin M
    San Antonio M
University of the Incarnate Word M
Vernon College M
Wayland Baptist University M
Weatherford College M
West Texas A&M University M
Western Texas College M
Wharton County Junior College M
Wiley College M

Utah
Brigham Young University M
College of Eastern Utah M
Dixie State College of Utah M
Salt Lake Community College M
Southern Utah University M
University of Utah M
Utah Valley University M

Virginia
Bluefield College M
College of William and Mary M
George Mason University M
James Madison University M
Liberty University M
Longwood University M
Norfolk State University M
Old Dominion University M
Radford University M
St. Paul's College M
University of Richmond M
University of Virginia M
University of Virginia's College at Wise M
Virginia Commonwealth University M
Virginia Intermont College M
Virginia Military Institute M
Virginia Polytechnic Institute and State
    University M
Virginia State University M

Washington
Big Bend Community College M
Centralia College M
Everett Community College M
Gonzaga University M
Grays Harbor College M
Green River Community College M
Lower Columbia College M
Olympic College M
Pierce College M
Saint Martin's University M
Shoreline Community College M
Skagit Valley College M
Spokane Community College M
University of Washington M
Washington State University M
Yakima Valley Community College M

West Virginia
Alderson-Broaddus College M
Bluefield State College M
Concord University M
Davis and Elkins College M
Marshall University M
Ohio Valley University M
Potomac State College of West Virginia
    University M
Salem International University M
Shepherd University M
University of Charleston M
West Liberty University M
West Virginia State University M
West Virginia University M
West Virginia University Institute of Technology
    M
West Virginia Wesleyan College M
Wheeling Jesuit University M

Wisconsin
Cardinal Stritch University M
Milwaukee Area Technical College M,W
University of Wisconsin
    Milwaukee M
    Parkside M
Viterbo University M

Basketball

Alabama
Alabama Agricultural and Mechanical
    University M,W
Alabama State University M,W
Auburn University M,W
Auburn University at Montgomery M,W
Bevill State Community College M,W
Chattahoochee Valley Community College M,W
Enterprise-Ozark Community College M,W
Faulkner State Community College M,W
Faulkner University M,W

Gadsden State Community College M,W
George C. Wallace State Community College
    Wallace State Community College at
        Selma M,W
Jacksonville State University M,W
Jefferson Davis Community College M
Judson College W
Lawson State Community College M,W
Lurleen B. Wallace Community College M,W
Miles College M,W
Northwest-Shoals Community College M,W
Samford University M,W
Shelton State Community College M,W
Snead State Community College M,W
Southern Union State Community College M,W
Spring Hill College M,W
Troy University M,W
Tuskegee University M,W
University of Alabama M,W
University of Alabama
    Birmingham M,W
    Huntsville M,W
University of Mobile M,W
University of Montevallo M,W
University of North Alabama M,W
University of South Alabama M,W
University of West Alabama M,W
Wallace State Community College at Hanceville
    M,W

Alaska
University of Alaska
    Anchorage M,W
    Fairbanks M,W

Arizona
Arizona State University M,W
Arizona Western College M,W
Central Arizona College M,W
Chandler-Gilbert Community College
    Pecos M,W
Cochise College M,W
Eastern Arizona College M,W
Glendale Community College M,W
Grand Canyon University M,W
Mesa Community College M,W
Northern Arizona University M,W
Pima Community College M,W
Scottsdale Community College M,W
University of Arizona M,W

Arkansas
Arkansas State University M,W
Arkansas Tech University M,W
Ecclesia College M,W
Harding University M,W
Henderson State University M,W
John Brown University M,W
Lyon College M,W
North Arkansas College M,W
Ouachita Baptist University M,W
Philander Smith College M,W
Southern Arkansas University M,W
University of Arkansas M,W
University of Arkansas
    Fort Smith M,W
    Little Rock M,W
    Monticello M,W
    Pine Bluff M,W
University of Central Arkansas M,W
Williams Baptist College M,W

California
Azusa Pacific University M,W
Bethany University M,W
Biola University M,W
California Baptist University M,W
California Polytechnic State University: San Luis
    Obispo M,W
California State Polytechnic University: Pomona
    M,W
California State University
    Bakersfield M

Chico M,W
Dominguez Hills M,W
Fresno M,W
Fullerton M,W
Long Beach M,W
Los Angeles M,W
Monterey Bay M,W
Northridge M,W
Sacramento M,W
San Bernardino M,W
Stanislaus M,W
Concordia University M,W
Dominican University of California M,W
Fresno City College M,W
Fresno Pacific University M,W
Grossmont College M,W
Holy Names University M,W
Hope International University M,W
Humboldt State University M,W
Loyola Marymount University M,W
The Master's College M,W
Notre Dame de Namur University M,W
Pepperdine University M,W
Point Loma Nazarene University M,W
St. Mary's College of California M,W
San Diego Christian College M,W
San Diego State University M,W
San Jose State University M,W
Santa Clara University M,W
Sonoma State University M,W
Stanford University M,W
University of California
    Berkeley M,W
    Davis M,W
    Irvine M,W
    Los Angeles M,W
    Riverside M,W
    Santa Barbara M,W
University of San Diego M,W
University of San Francisco M,W
University of Southern California M,W
University of the Pacific M,W
Vanguard University of Southern California
    M,W
Westmont College M,W
William Jessup University M,W
Yuba Community College District M,W

Colorado
Adams State College M,W
Colorado Christian University M,W
Colorado Northwestern Community College
    M,W
Colorado School of Mines M,W
Colorado State University M,W
Colorado State University
    Pueblo M,W
Fort Lewis College M,W
Lamar Community College M
Mesa State College M,W
Metropolitan State College of Denver M,W
Northeastern Junior College M,W
Otero Junior College M,W
Regis University M,W
Trinidad State Junior College M,W
University of Colorado
    Boulder M,W
    Colorado Springs M,W
University of Denver M,W
University of Northern Colorado M,W
Western State College of Colorado M,W

Connecticut
Central Connecticut State University M,W
Fairfield University M,W
Post University M,W
Quinnipiac University M,W
Sacred Heart University M,W
Southern Connecticut State University M,W
University of Bridgeport M,W
University of Connecticut M,W
University of Hartford M,W

University of New Haven M,W

Delaware
Delaware State University M,W
Delaware Technical and Community College
    Stanton/Wilmington M,W
Goldey-Beacom College M,W
University of Delaware M,W
Wilmington University M,W

District of Columbia
American University M,W
George Washington University M,W
Georgetown University M,W
Howard University M,W
University of the District of Columbia M,W

Florida
Ave Maria University M,W
Barry University M,W
Bethune-Cookman University M,W
Brevard Community College M,W
Central Florida Community College M,W
Chipola College M,W
Daytona State College M,W
Eckerd College M,W
Edward Waters College M,W
Embry-Riddle Aeronautical University M
Flagler College M,W
Florida Agricultural and Mechanical University
    M
Florida Atlantic University M,W
Florida College M
Florida Gulf Coast University M,W
Florida Institute of Technology M,W
Florida Memorial University M,W
Florida Southern College M,W
Florida State College at Jacksonville M,W
Florida State University M,W
Gulf Coast Community College M,W
Hillsborough Community College M,W
Indian River State College M,W
Jacksonville University M,W
Lynn University M,W
Miami Dade College M,W
North Florida Community College W
Northwest Florida State College M,W
Nova Southeastern University M,W
Palm Beach Community College M,W
Pasco-Hernando Community College M
Pensacola Junior College M,W
Polk State College M
Rollins College M,W
Saint Johns River Community College M
Saint Leo University M,W
St. Petersburg College M,W
Santa Fe College M,W
State College of Florida, Manatee-Sarasota M
Stetson University M,W
Tallahassee Community College M,W
University of Central Florida M,W
University of Florida M,W
University of Miami M,W
University of North Florida M,W
University of South Florida M,W
University of Tampa M,W
University of West Florida M,W
Warner University M,W
Webber International University M,W

Georgia
Albany State University M,W
Andrew College W
Armstrong Atlantic State University M,W
Augusta State University M,W
Brenau University W
Brewton-Parker College M,W
Clark Atlanta University M,W
Clayton State University M,W
College of Coastal Georgia M
Columbus State University M,W
Covenant College M,W
Darton College W

Emmanuel College M,W
Fort Valley State University M,W
Georgia College and State University M,W
Georgia Institute of Technology M,W
Georgia Perimeter College M,W
Georgia Southern University M,W
Georgia Southwestern State University M,W
Georgia State University M,W
Gordon College M
Kennesaw State University M,W
Mercer University M,W
Middle Georgia College M,W
Morehouse College M
North Georgia College & State University M,W
Paine College M,W
Reinhardt College M,W
Savannah State University M,W
Shorter College M,W
Southern Polytechnic State University M,W
Truett-McConnell College M,W
University of Georgia M,W
University of West Georgia M,W
Valdosta State University M,W

Hawaii
Chaminade University of Honolulu M
Hawaii Pacific University M,W
University of Hawaii
    Hilo M
    Manoa M,W

Idaho
Boise State University M,W
College of Idaho M,W
Idaho State University M,W
Lewis-Clark State College M,W
North Idaho College M,W
Northwest Nazarene University M,W
University of Idaho M,W

Illinois
Black Hawk College M,W
Black Hawk College: East Campus M,W
Bradley University M,W
Carl Sandburg College M,W
Chicago State University M,W
City Colleges of Chicago
    Kennedy-King College M,W
    Malcolm X College M,W
College of Lake County M,W
Danville Area Community College M,W
DePaul University M,W
Eastern Illinois University M,W
Elgin Community College M,W
Highland Community College M,W
Illinois Central College M,W
Illinois Eastern Community Colleges
    Lincoln Trail College M,W
    Olney Central College M,W
    Wabash Valley College M,W
Illinois Institute of Technology M,W
Illinois State University M,W
John A. Logan College M,W
Judson University M,W
Kankakee Community College M,W
Kaskaskia College M,W
Kishwaukee College M,W
Lake Land College M,W
Lewis and Clark Community College M,W
Lewis University M,W
Lincoln College M,W
Lincoln Land Community College M,W
Loyola University Chicago M,W
McHenry County College M,W
McKendree University M,W
Moraine Valley Community College M,W
Morton College M,W
Northwestern University M,W
Olivet Nazarene University M,W
Parkland College M,W
Quincy University M,W
Rend Lake College M,W

Robert Morris University: Chicago M,W
Saint Xavier University M
Sauk Valley Community College M,W
Shawnee Community College M,W
South Suburban College of Cook County M,W
Southeastern Illinois College M,W
Southern Illinois University Carbondale M,W
Southern Illinois University Edwardsville M,W
Southwestern Illinois College M,W
Spoon River College M,W
Trinity Christian College M,W
Trinity International University M,W
University of Illinois
    Chicago M,W
    Springfield M,W
    Urbana-Champaign M,W
University of St. Francis M,W
Waubonsee Community College M,W
Western Illinois University M,W
Wilbur Wright College M,W

Indiana
Ancilla College M,W
Ball State University M,W
Bethel College M,W
Butler University M,W
Calumet College of St. Joseph M,W
Goshen College M,W
Grace College M,W
Huntington University M,W
Indiana Institute of Technology M,W
Indiana State University M,W
Indiana University
    Bloomington M,W
    South Bend M,W
    Southeast M,W
Indiana University-Purdue University Fort
    Wayne M,W
Indiana University-Purdue University
    Indianapolis M,W
Indiana Wesleyan University M,W
Marian University M,W
Oakland City University, M,W
Purdue University M,W
Purdue University
    Calumet M,W
    North Central M
Saint Joseph's College M,W
St. Mary-of-the-Woods College W
Taylor University M,W
University of Evansville M,W
University of Indianapolis M,W
University of Notre Dame M,W
University of St. Francis M,W
University of Southern Indiana M,W
Valparaiso University M,W
Vincennes University M,W

Iowa
AIB College of Business W
Briar Cliff University M,W
Clarke College M,W
Clinton Community College M
Des Moines Area Community College M,W
Dordt College M,W
Drake University M,W
Ellsworth Community College M,W
Graceland University M,W
Grand View University M,W
Indian Hills Community College M
Iowa Central Community College M,W
Iowa Lakes Community College- Estherville
    M,W
Iowa State University M,W
Iowa Wesleyan College M,W
Iowa Western Community College M,W
Kirkwood Community College M,W
Marshalltown Community College M,W
Morningside College M,W
Mount Mercy College M,W
North Iowa Area Community College M,W
Northwestern College M,W

St. Ambrose University M,W
Southeastern Community College
    North Campus M,W
Southwestern Community College M,W
University of Iowa M,W
University of Northern Iowa M,W
Waldorf College M,W
William Penn University M,W

Kansas
Allen County Community College M,W
Baker University M,W
Barton County Community College M,W
Benedictine College M,W
Bethany College M,W
Bethel College M,W
Brown Mackie College
    Salina M,W
Butler Community College M,W
Central Christian College of Kansas M,W
Cloud County Community College M,W
Coffeyville Community College M,W
Colby Community College M,W
Cowley County Community College M,W
Dodge City Community College M,W
Emporia State University M,W
Fort Hays State University M,W
Fort Scott Community College M,W
Friends University M,W
Garden City Community College M,W
Hesston College M,W
Highland Community College M,W
Hutchinson Community College M,W
Johnson County Community College M,W
Kansas City Kansas Community College M,W
Kansas State University M,W
Kansas Wesleyan University M,W
Labette Community College M,W
McPherson College M,W
MidAmerica Nazarene University M,W
Neosho County Community College M,W
Newman University M,W
Ottawa University M,W
Pittsburg State University M,W
Pratt Community College M,W
Seward County Community College M,W
Southwestern College M,W
Sterling College M,W
Tabor College M,W
University of Kansas M,W
University of St. Mary M,W
Washburn University M,W
Wichita State University M,W

Kentucky
Alice Lloyd College M,W
Asbury College M,W
Bellarmine University M,W
Brescia University M,W
Campbellsville University M,W
Eastern Kentucky University M,W
Georgetown College M,W
Kentucky State University M,W
Kentucky Wesleyan College M,W
Lindsey Wilson College M,W
Mid-Continent University M,W
Midway College W
Morehead State University M,W
Murray State University M,W
Northern Kentucky University M,W
Pikeville College M,W
St. Catharine College M,W
Union College M,W
University of Kentucky M,W
University of Louisville M,W
University of the Cumberlands M,W
Western Kentucky University M,W

Louisiana
Bossier Parish Community College M
Centenary College of Louisiana M,W
Delgado Community College M

Dillard University M,W
Grambling State University M,W
Louisiana State University and Agricultural and
    Mechanical College M,W
Louisiana Tech University M,W
Loyola University New Orleans M,W
McNeese State University M,W
Nicholls State University M,W
Northwestern State University M,W
Southeastern Louisiana University M,W
Southern University
    New Orleans M,W
Southern University and Agricultural and
    Mechanical College M,W
Tulane University M,W
University of Louisiana at Lafayette M,W
University of Louisiana at Monroe M,W
University of New Orleans M,W
Xavier University of Louisiana M,W

Maine
University of Maine M,W
University of Maine
    Augusta M,W

Maryland
Allegany College of Maryland M,W
Anne Arundel Community College M,W
Bowie State University M,W
Chesapeake College M,W
College of Southern Maryland M,W
Community College of Baltimore County M,W
Coppin State University M,W
Garrett College M,W
Hagerstown Community College M,W
Harford Community College M,W
Howard Community College M,W
Loyola University Maryland M,W
Morgan State University M,W
Mount St. Mary's University M,W
Towson University M,W
University of Maryland
    Baltimore County M,W
    College Park M,W
    Eastern Shore M,W
Washington Adventist University M,W

Massachusetts
American International College M,W
Assumption College M,W
Bentley University M,W
Boston College M,W
Boston University M,W
College of the Holy Cross M,W
Dean College M,W
Massasoit Community College M
Merrimack College M,W
Northeastern University M,W
Roxbury Community College M
Stonehill College M,W
University of Massachusetts
    Amherst M,W
    Lowell M,W

Michigan
Alpena Community College M,W
Aquinas College M,W
Central Michigan University M,W
Cornerstone University M,W
Davenport University M,W
Delta College M,W
Eastern Michigan University M,W
Ferris State University M,W
Glen Oaks Community College M,W
Gogebic Community College M,W
Grand Rapids Community College M,W
Grand Valley State University M,W
Hillsdale College M,W
Kalamazoo Valley Community College M,W
Kellogg Community College M,W
Kirtland Community College M,W
Lake Michigan College M,W
Lake Superior State University M,W

Lansing Community College M,W
Macomb Community College M,W
Madonna University M,W
Michigan State University M,W
Michigan Technological University M,W
Mott Community College M,W
Muskegon Community College M,W
Northern Michigan University M,W
Northwood University: Michigan M,W
Oakland Community College M,W
Oakland University M,W
Rochester College M,W
Saginaw Valley State University M,W
Siena Heights University M,W
Spring Arbor University M,W
University of Detroit Mercy M,W
University of Michigan M,W
University of Michigan
    Dearborn M,W
Wayne State University M,W
Western Michigan University M,W

Minnesota
Bemidji State University M,W
Concordia University: St. Paul M,W
Minnesota State University
    Mankato M,W
    Moorhead M,W
Saint Cloud State University M,W
Southwest Minnesota State University M,W
University of Minnesota
    Crookston M,W
    Duluth M,W
    Twin Cities M,W
Winona State University M,W

Mississippi
Alcorn State University M,W
Belhaven University M,W
Blue Mountain College M,W
Copiah-Lincoln Community College M,W
Delta State University M,W
East Central Community College M,W
East Mississippi Community College M,W
Hinds Community College M,W
Holmes Community College M,W
Jackson State University M,W
Jones County Junior College M,W
Meridian Community College M,W
Mississippi Gulf Coast Community College M,W
Mississippi State University M,W
Mississippi Valley State University M,W
Northwest Mississippi Community College M,W
Southwest Mississippi Community College
    M,W
Tougaloo College M,W
University of Mississippi M,W
University of Southern Mississippi M,W

Missouri
Avila University M,W
Central Methodist University M,W
College of the Ozarks M,W
Columbia College M,W
Cottey College W
Crowder College W
Culver-Stockton College M,W
Drury University M,W
Evangel University M,W
Hannibal-LaGrange College M,W
Harris-Stowe State University M,W
Jefferson College W
Lincoln University M,W
Metropolitan Community College: Penn Valley
    M
Mineral Area College M,W
Missouri Baptist University M,W
Missouri Southern State University M,W
Missouri State University M,W
Missouri State University: West Plains M
Missouri Valley College M,W
Missouri Western State University M,W

North Central Missouri College M,W
Northwest Missouri State University M,W
Park University M,W
Research College of Nursing M,W
Rockhurst University M,W
Saint Louis University M,W
Southeast Missouri State University M,W
Southwest Baptist University M,W
St. Louis Community College
    Meramec M,W
State Fair Community College M,W
Stephens College W
Three Rivers Community College M,W
Truman State University M,W
University of Central Missouri M,W
University of Missouri
    Columbia M,W
    Kansas City M,W
    Missouri University of Science and
        Technology M,W
    St. Louis M,W
William Jewell College M,W
William Woods University M,W

Montana
Dawson Community College M,W
Miles Community College M,W
Montana State University
    Billings M,W
    Bozeman M,W
Montana Tech of the University of Montana
    M,W
Rocky Mountain College W
University of Great Falls M,W
University of Montana M,W
University of Montana: Western M,W

Nebraska
Bellevue University M
Central Community College M
Chadron State College M,W
College of Saint Mary W
Concordia University M,W
Creighton University M,W
Dana College M,W
Doane College M,W
Mid-Plains Community College Area M,W
Nebraska College of Technical Agriculture M,W
Northeast Community College M,W
Peru State College M,W
University of Nebraska
    Kearney M,W
    Lincoln M,W
    Omaha M,W
Wayne State College M,W
Western Nebraska Community College M,W
York College M,W

Nevada
University of Nevada
    Las Vegas M,W
    Reno M,W

New Hampshire
Franklin Pierce University M,W
Saint Anselm College M,W
Southern New Hampshire University M,W
University of New Hampshire M,W

New Jersey
Bloomfield College M,W
Brookdale Community College M,W
Burlington County College M,W
Caldwell College M,W
Essex County College M,W
Fairleigh Dickinson University
    Metropolitan Campus M,W
Felician College M,W
Georgian Court University W
Mercer County Community College M,W
Monmouth University M,W
New Jersey Institute of Technology M,W
Rider University M,W

Rutgers, The State University of New Jersey
    New Brunswick/Piscataway Campus M,W
Saint Peter's College M,W
Salem Community College M,W
Seton Hall University M,W
Union County College W

New Mexico
Eastern New Mexico University M,W
New Mexico Highlands University M,W
New Mexico Junior College M,W
New Mexico Military Institute M
New Mexico State University M
University of New Mexico M,W
University of the Southwest M
Western New Mexico University M,W

New York
Adelphi University M,W
ASA Institute of Business and Computer
    Technology M,W
Canisius College M,W
City University of New York
    Queens College M,W
Colgate University M,W
College of Saint Rose M,W
Concordia College M,W
Daemen College M,W
Dominican College of Blauvelt M,W
Dowling College M,W
Fordham University M,W
Genesee Community College M,W
Globe Institute of Technology M,W
Hofstra University M,W
Houghton College M,W
Iona College M,W
Le Moyne College M,W
Long Island University
    Brooklyn Campus M,W
    C. W. Post Campus M,W
Manhattan College M,W
Marist College M,W
Mercy College M,W
Molloy College M,W
Monroe College M
Monroe Community College M
New York Institute of Technology M
Niagara County Community College M,W
Niagara University M,W
Nyack College M,W
Pace University M,W
Roberts Wesleyan College M,W
Saint Bonaventure University M,W
St. Francis College M,W
St. John's University M,W
St. Thomas Aquinas College M,W
Siena College M,W
State University of New York
    Albany M,W
    Binghamton M,W
    Buffalo M,W
    Stony Brook M,W
Syracuse University M,W
Wagner College M,W

North Carolina
Appalachian State University M,W
Barton College M,W
Belmont Abbey College M,W
Brevard College M,W
Campbell University M,W
Catawba College M,W
Chowan University M,W
Davidson College M,W
Duke University M,W
East Carolina University M,W
Elizabeth City State University M,W
Elon University M,W
Fayetteville State University M,W
Gardner-Webb University M,W
Guilford Technical Community College M,W
High Point University M,W

Johnson C. Smith University M,W
Lees-McRae College M,W
Lenoir Community College M
Lenoir-Rhyne University M,W
Livingstone College M,W
Louisburg College M,W
Mars Hill College M,W
Montreat College M,W
Mount Olive College M,W
North Carolina Agricultural and Technical State
    University M,W
North Carolina Central University M,W
North Carolina State University M,W
Pfeiffer University M,W
Queens University of Charlotte M,W
St. Andrews Presbyterian College M,W
St. Augustine's College M,W
Shaw University M,W
University of North Carolina
    Asheville M,W
    Chapel Hill M,W
    Charlotte M,W
    Greensboro M,W
    Pembroke M,W
    Wilmington M,W
Wake Forest University M,W
Western Carolina University M,W
Wingate University M,W
Winston-Salem State University M,W

North Dakota
Bismarck State College M,W
Dakota College at Bottineau M,W
Dickinson State University M,W
Jamestown College M,W
Lake Region State College M,W
Mayville State University M,W
Minot State University M,W
North Dakota State College of Science M,W
North Dakota State University M,W
University of Mary M,W
University of North Dakota M,W
Williston State College M,W

Ohio
Ashland University M,W
Bowling Green State University M,W
Cedarville University M,W
Central State University M,W
Cincinnati State Technical and Community
    College M,W
Clark State Community College M,W
Cleveland State University M,W
Columbus State Community College M,W
Edison State Community College M,W
Kent State University M,W
Malone University M,W
Miami University
    Oxford Campus M,W
Mount Vernon Nazarene University M,W
Notre Dame College M,W
Ohio Dominican University M,W
Ohio State University
    Columbus Campus M,W
Ohio University M,W
Owens Community College
    Toledo M,W
Shawnee State University M,W
Southern State Community College M,W
Tiffin University M,W
University of Akron M,W
University of Cincinnati M,W
University of Dayton M,W
University of Findlay M,W
University of Rio Grande M,W
University of Toledo M,W
Urbana University M,W
Ursuline College W
Walsh University M,W
Wright State University M,W
Xavier University M,W
Youngstown State University M,W

Oklahoma
Bacone College M,W
Cameron University M,W
Carl Albert State College M,W
Connors State College M,W
East Central University M,W
Eastern Oklahoma State College M,W
Langston University M,W
Northeastern Oklahoma Agricultural and
    Mechanical College M,W
Northeastern State University M,W
Northern Oklahoma College M,W
Northwestern Oklahoma State University M,W
Oklahoma Baptist University M,W
Oklahoma Christian University M,W
Oklahoma City University M,W
Oklahoma Panhandle State University M,W
Oklahoma State University M,W
Oklahoma Wesleyan University M,W
Oral Roberts University M,W
Redlands Community College M,W
Rogers State University M,W
St. Gregory's University M,W
Seminole State College M,W
Southeastern Oklahoma State University M,W
Southern Nazarene University M,W
Southwestern Oklahoma State University M,W
University of Central Oklahoma M,W
University of Oklahoma M,W
University of Science and Arts of Oklahoma
    M,W
University of Tulsa M,W
Western Oklahoma State College M,W

Oregon
Blue Mountain Community College M,W
Chemeketa Community College M,W
Clackamas Community College M,W
Concordia University M,W
Corban College M,W
Eastern Oregon University M,W
Lane Community College M,W
Linn-Benton Community College M,W
Mt. Hood Community College M,W
Northwest Christian University M,W
Oregon Institute of Technology M,W
Oregon State University M,W
Portland Community College M,W
Portland State University M,W
Southern Oregon University M,W
Southwestern Oregon Community College M,W
Treasure Valley Community College M,W
University of Oregon M,W
University of Portland M,W
Warner Pacific College M,W

Pennsylvania
Bloomsburg University of Pennsylvania M,W
Bucknell University M,W
California University of Pennsylvania M,W
Carlow University W
Chestnut Hill College M,W
Cheyney University of Pennsylvania M,W
Clarion University of Pennsylvania M,W
Community College of Beaver County M
Drexel University M,W
Duquesne University M,W
East Stroudsburg University of Pennsylvania
    M,W
Edinboro University of Pennsylvania M,W
Gannon University M,W
Harcum College M,W
Holy Family University M,W
Indiana University of Pennsylvania M,W
Kutztown University of Pennsylvania M,W
La Salle University M,W
Lackawanna College M,W
Lafayette College M,W
Lehigh University M,W
Lock Haven University of Pennsylvania M,W
Mansfield University of Pennsylvania M,W
Mercyhurst College M,W

Millersville University of Pennsylvania M,W
Penn State
    University Park M,W
Philadelphia University M,W
Point Park University M,W
Robert Morris University M,W
St. Francis University M,W
Saint Joseph's University M,W
Seton Hill University M,W
Shippensburg University of Pennsylvania M,W
Slippery Rock University of Pennsylvania M,W
Temple University M,W
University of Pittsburgh M,W
University of Pittsburgh
    Johnstown M,W
    Titusville M,W
University of the Sciences in Philadelphia M,W
Valley Forge Military Academy & College M
Villanova University M,W
West Chester University of Pennsylvania M,W
Westminster College M,W

Puerto Rico
Bayamon Central University M,W
Inter American University of Puerto Rico
    Aguadilla Campus M,W
    Arecibo Campus M
    Bayamon Campus M,W
    Fajardo Campus M
    Guayama Campus M,W
    Metropolitan Campus M,W
    Ponce Campus M,W
    San German Campus M,W
Turabo University M,W
Universidad del Este M,W
Universidad Metropolitana M,W
University of Puerto Rico
    Bayamon University College M,W
    Carolina Regional College M,W
    Cayey University College M,W
    Humacao M,W
    Ponce M,W
    Utuado M,W
University of the Sacred Heart M

Rhode Island
Bryant University M,W
Community College of Rhode Island M,W
Providence College M,W
University of Rhode Island M,W

South Carolina
Aiken Technical College M
Allen University M,W
Anderson University M,W
Charleston Southern University M,W
The Citadel M
Claflin University M,W
Clemson University M,W
Coastal Carolina University M,W
Coker College M,W
College of Charleston M,W
Columbia College W
Converse College W
Erskine College M,W
Francis Marion University M,W
Furman University M,W
Lander University M,W
Limestone College M,W
Morris College M,W
Newberry College M,W
North Greenville University M,W
Presbyterian College M,W
South Carolina State University M,W
Southern Wesleyan University M,W
Spartanburg Methodist College M,W
University of South Carolina M,W
University of South Carolina
    Aiken M,W
    Upstate M,W
Winthrop University M,W
Wofford College M,W

South Dakota
Augustana College M,W
Black Hills State University M,W
Dakota State University M,W
Dakota Wesleyan University M,W
Mount Marty College M,W
Northern State University M,W
South Dakota School of Mines and Technology
    M,W
South Dakota State University M,W
University of Sioux Falls M,W
University of South Dakota M,W

Tennessee
Austin Peay State University M,W
Belmont University M,W
Bethel University M,W
Bryan College M,W
Carson-Newman College M,W
Chattanooga State Community College M,W
Christian Brothers University M,W
Cleveland State Community College M,W
Columbia State Community College M,W
Cumberland University M,W
Dyersburg State Community College M,W
East Tennessee State University M,W
Freed-Hardeman University M,W
Jackson State Community College M,W
King College M,W
Lambuth University M,W.
Lane College M,W
Lee University M,W
LeMoyne-Owen College M,W
Lincoln Memorial University M,W
Lipscomb University M,W
Martin Methodist College M,W
Middle Tennessee State University M,W
Milligan College M,W
Motlow State Community College M,W
Roane State Community College M,W
Southwest Tennessee Community College M,W
Tennessee State University M,W
Tennessee Technological University M,W
Tennessee Temple University M,W
Tennessee Wesleyan University M,W
Trevecca Nazarene University M,W
Tusculum College M,W
Union University M,W
University of Memphis M,W
University of Tennessee
    Chattanooga M,W
    Knoxville M,W
    Martin M,W
Vanderbilt University M,W
Volunteer State Community College M,W
Walters State Community College M,W

Texas
Abilene Christian University M,W
Angelina College M,W
Angelo State University M,W
Baylor University M,W
Blinn College M,W
Clarendon College M,W
Collin County Community College District M,W
Frank Phillips College M,W
Grayson County College M,W
Hill College M,W
Houston Baptist University M,W
Howard College M,W
Jacksonville College M,W
Jarvis Christian College M,W
Kilgore College M,W
Lamar University M,W
Lee College M
Lon Morris College M,W
Lubbock Christian University M,W
McLennan Community College M,W
Midland College M,W
Midwestern State University M,W
Odessa College M,W
Panola College M,W

Paris Junior College M,W
Prairie View A&M University M,W
Ranger College M,W
Rice University M,W
St. Edward's University M,W
St. Mary's University M,W
Sam Houston State University M,W
San Jacinto College W
South Plains College M,W
Southern Methodist University M,W
Southwestern Assemblies of God University M,W
Stephen F. Austin State University M,W
Tarleton State University M,W
Temple College M,W
Texas A&M University M,W
Texas A&M University
    Commerce M,W
    Corpus Christi M,W
    Kingsville M,W
Texas Christian University M,W
Texas Southern University M,W
Texas State University: San Marcos M,W
Texas Tech University M,W
Texas Woman's University W
Trinity Valley Community College M,W
Tyler Junior College M,W
University of Houston M,W
University of North Texas M,W
University of St. Thomas M
University of Texas
    Arlington M,W
    Austin M,W
    Pan American M,W
    of the Permian Basin M,W
    San Antonio M,W
University of the Incarnate Word M,W
Wayland Baptist University M,W
Weatherford College M,W
West Texas A&M University M,W
Wiley College M,W

Utah
Brigham Young University M,W
College of Eastern Utah M,W
Dixie State College of Utah M,W
Salt Lake Community College M,W
Snow College M,W
Southern Utah University M,W
University of Utah M,W
Utah State University M,W
Utah Valley University M,W
Weber State University M,W
Westminster College M,W

Vermont
St. Michael's College M,W
University of Vermont M,W

Virginia
Bluefield College M,W
College of William and Mary M,W
George Mason University M,W
Hampton University M,W
James Madison University M,W
Liberty University M,W
Longwood University M,W
Norfolk State University M,W
Old Dominion University M,W
Radford University M,W
St. Paul's College M,W
University of Richmond M,W
University of Virginia M,W
University of Virginia's College at Wise M,W
Virginia Commonwealth University M,W
Virginia Intermont College M,W
Virginia Military Institute M
Virginia Polytechnic Institute and State University M,W
Virginia State University M,W
Virginia Union University M,W

Washington
Big Bend Community College M,W
Centralia College M,W
Clark College M,W
Eastern Washington University M,W
Everett Community College M,W
Evergreen State College M,W
Gonzaga University M,W
Grays Harbor College M,W
Green River Community College M,W
Highline Community College M,W
Lower Columbia College M,W
North Seattle Community College M,W
Northwest Indian College M,W
Northwest University M,W
Olympic College M,W
Peninsula College M,W
Pierce College M,W
Saint Martin's University M,W
Seattle Pacific University M,W
Seattle University M,W
Shoreline Community College M,W
Skagit Valley College M,W
Spokane Community College M,W
University of Washington M,W
Washington State University M,W
Western Washington University M,W
Whatcom Community College M,W
Yakima Valley Community College M,W

West Virginia
Alderson-Broaddus College M,W
Bluefield State College M,W
Concord University M,W
Davis and Elkins College M,W
Fairmont State University M,W
Glenville State College M,W
Marshall University M,W
Mountain State University M
Ohio Valley University M,W
Potomac State College of West Virginia University M,W
Salem International University M,W
Shepherd University M,W
University of Charleston M,W
West Liberty University M,W
West Virginia State University M,W
West Virginia University M,W
West Virginia University Institute of Technology M,W
West Virginia Wesleyan College M,W
Wheeling Jesuit University M,W

Wisconsin
Cardinal Stritch University M,W
Marquette University M,W
Silver Lake College M,W
University of Wisconsin
    Green Bay M,W
    Milwaukee M,W
    Parkside M,W
Viterbo University M,W

Wyoming
Casper College M,W
Central Wyoming College M,W
Eastern Wyoming College M,W
Laramie County Community College M
Northwest College M,W
Sheridan College M,W
University of Wyoming M,W
Western Wyoming Community College M,W

Bowling

Arkansas
Arkansas State University W
University of Arkansas
    Pine Bluff W

Connecticut
Sacred Heart University W

Delaware
Delaware State University W

Florida
Bethune-Cookman University W
Webber International University M,W

Illinois
McKendree University M,W
Robert Morris University: Chicago M,W

Indiana
Calumet College of St. Joseph M,W
Indiana Institute of Technology M,W
Marian University M,W
Vincennes University M,W

Iowa
Clarke College M,W
St. Ambrose University M,W

Kansas
Baker University W
Newman University M,W
Wichita State University M,W

Kentucky
Campbellsville University M,W
Pikeville College M,W
St. Catharine College M,W

Louisiana
Southern University and Agricultural and Mechanical College W

Maryland
Bowie State University W
Coppin State University W
Morgan State University W

Michigan
Aquinas College M,W
Davenport University M,W
Saginaw Valley State University M

Mississippi
Jackson State University M,W
Mississippi Valley State University M,W

Missouri
Missouri Baptist University M,W

Nebraska
University of Nebraska
    Lincoln W

New Jersey
Fairleigh Dickinson University
    Metropolitan Campus W

New York
Adelphi University W

North Carolina
Blue Ridge Community College M
Johnson C. Smith University W
Livingstone College M,W
North Carolina Central University M,W
St. Augustine's College W
Shaw University W

Ohio
Urbana University M,W
Ursuline College W

Pennsylvania
Cheyney University of Pennsylvania W

Tennessee
Bethel University M,W
Martin Methodist College M,W

Texas
Prairie View A&M University W
Stephen F. Austin State University W
Texas Southern University W

Virginia
Norfolk State University W

Wisconsin
Viterbo University M,W

Cheerleading

Alabama
Bevill State Community College M,W
Chattahoochee Valley Community College M,W
Faulkner State Community College M,W
Gadsden State Community College W
Northwest-Shoals Community College M,W
Shelton State Community College M,W
Southern Union State Community College M,W
Troy University M,W
University of Alabama M,W
University of Alabama
    Huntsville M,W
University of Mobile M,W

Arizona
Glendale Community College M,W

Arkansas
Lyon College M,W
North Arkansas College W
University of Arkansas M,W
University of Arkansas
    Fort Smith M,W
    Monticello M,W
University of Central Arkansas M,W
Williams Baptist College M,W

California
California Baptist University M,W
Hope International University M,W

Connecticut
Quinnipiac University W

Delaware
Delaware State University W
University of Delaware M,W

Florida
Pensacola Junior College M,W
University of Central Florida M,W
University of Florida M,W
Warner University M,W
Webber International University M,W

Georgia
Albany State University W
Brewton-Parker College M,W
Columbus State University M,W
Georgia Institute of Technology M,W
Gordon College W
Mercer University M,W
Reinhardt College M,W
University of West Georgia M,W

Hawaii
Hawaii Pacific University M,W
University of Hawaii
    Manoa M,W

Idaho
Boise State University M,W
North Idaho College M,W

Illinois
Danville Area Community College W
Kaskaskia College M,W
McKendree University M,W
Northwestern University M,W

Olivet Nazarene University M,W
Rend Lake College W
Robert Morris University: Chicago M,W
University of St. Francis W

Indiana
Ancilla College M,W
Bethel College M,W
Grace College M,W
Indiana Institute of Technology M,W
Indiana Wesleyan University M,W
Marian University M,W
Oakland City University W
University of St. Francis M,W

Iowa
AIB College of Business M,W
Graceland University W
Iowa Western Community College M,W
St. Ambrose University M,W
Waldorf College W
William Penn University W

Kansas
Allen County Community College M,W
Baker University M,W
Barton County Community College M,W
Benedictine College M,W
Bethany College M,W
Central Christian College of Kansas M,W
Coffeyville Community College M,W
Colby Community College M,W
Cowley County Community College M,W
Dodge City Community College M,W
Emporia State University M,W
Fort Scott Community College W
Garden City Community College M,W
Highland Community College M,W
Labette Community College M,W
McPherson College M,W
MidAmerica Nazarene University M,W
Neosho County Community College M,W
Ottawa University M,W
Pittsburg State University M,W
Pratt Community College M,W
Seward County Community College M,W
Southwestern College M,W
Tabor College M,W
Washburn University M,W
Wichita State University M,W

Kentucky
Bellarmine University M,W
Campbellsville University M,W
Kentucky State University W
Murray State University M,W
Pikeville College M,W
St. Catharine College M,W
Union College M,W
University of Louisville M,W
University of the Cumberlands M,W

Louisiana
Bossier Parish Community College M,W
Delgado Community College W
McNeese State University M,W
University of Louisiana at Lafayette M,W
University of Louisiana at Monroe M,W

Maryland
Morgan State University W
University of Maryland
    College Park W

Michigan
Davenport University W
Northwood University: Michigan M,W
University of Detroit Mercy M,W

Mississippi
Copiah-Lincoln Community College M,W
Mississippi Gulf Coast Community College M,W
Northwest Mississippi Community College W

Southwest Mississippi Community College M,W
University of Mississippi M,W

Missouri
Avila University W
Central Methodist University W
Culver-Stockton College M,W
Drury University W
Evangel University M,W
Hannibal-LaGrange College M,W
Harris-Stowe State University M,W
Missouri Baptist University M,W
Missouri Southern State University M,W
Missouri State University: West Plains M,W
Missouri Valley College M,W
Northwest Missouri State University M,W
Southeast Missouri State University M,W
University of Missouri
    Kansas City M,W
William Jewell College M,W

Montana
Rocky Mountain College W

Nebraska
Dana College M,W
Doane College W

Nevada
University of Nevada
    Las Vegas M,W
    Reno M,W

New Mexico
New Mexico Junior College M,W

New York
ASA Institute of Business and Computer Technology W
Hofstra University M,W
Nyack College M,W

North Carolina
Brevard College M,W
Elon University M,W
Gardner-Webb University M,W
Lenoir-Rhyne University M,W
Mars Hill College M,W
Methodist University M,W
Queens University of Charlotte M,W
University of North Carolina
    Wilmington M,W

North Dakota
Williston State College M,W

Ohio
Ashland University W
Kent State University M,W
University of Rio Grande M,W
Urbana University W

Oklahoma
Bacone College M,W
Cameron University M,W
Carl Albert State College W
Eastern Oklahoma State College M,W
Langston University M,W
Northeastern Oklahoma Agricultural and Mechanical College M,W
Northwestern Oklahoma State University M,W
Oklahoma Christian University W
Oklahoma City University M,W
Oklahoma Panhandle State University M,W
Oral Roberts University M,W
Rogers State University M,W
Rose State College M,W
Southeastern Oklahoma State University W
Southern Nazarene University M,W
Southwestern Oklahoma State University M,W
University of Oklahoma M,W

University of Science and Arts of Oklahoma M,W
University of Tulsa M,W
Western Oklahoma State College M,W

Oregon
Southwestern Oregon Community College M,W

Pennsylvania
Kutztown University of Pennsylvania W
Lackawanna College W
Penn State
    University Park M,W
St. Francis University M,W
Seton Hill University M,W
Temple University M,W
West Chester University of Pennsylvania W

Puerto Rico
University of Puerto Rico
    Carolina Regional College M,W
    Cayey University College M,W
    Humacao M,W

South Carolina
Anderson University W
Clemson University M,W
Limestone College M,W
Morris College M,W
Newberry College M,W
North Greenville University M,W
Presbyterian College M,W
Spartanburg Methodist College M,W

South Dakota
Dakota Wesleyan University M,W
University of Sioux Falls W

Tennessee
Bethel University M,W
Cumberland University M,W
Freed-Hardeman University W
King College M,W
Martin Methodist College W
Tennessee Technological University M,W
Tennessee Wesleyan College M,W
Tusculum College W
University of Memphis M,W

Texas
Angelina College W
Baylor University W
Clarendon College M,W
East Texas Baptist University M,W
Houston Baptist University M,W
Howard College M,W
Jacksonville College M,W
Lon Morris College M,W
Lubbock Christian University M,W
Ranger College M,W
St. Edward's University M,W
San Jacinto College M,W
South Plains College M,W
Southern Methodist University M,W
Southwestern Assemblies of God University W
Tarleton State University M,W
Temple College M,W
Texas Southern University M,W
Tyler Junior College M,W
University of Texas
    of the Permian Basin M,W
Western Texas College W

Utah
Brigham Young University M,W
Snow College M,W

Virginia
George Mason University M,W
Liberty University M,W
Old Dominion University M,W
Virginia Intermont College W

Washington
University of Washington M,W

West Virginia
Mountain State University W
University of Charleston M,W

Wyoming
University of Wyoming M,W
Western Wyoming Community College M,W

Cricket

California
College of the Redwoods M

Georgia
College of Coastal Georgia M

Cross-country

Alabama
Alabama Agricultural and Mechanical University M,W
Alabama State University M,W
Auburn University M,W
Bevill State Community College W
Gadsden State Community College W
Jacksonville State University M,W
Miles College M,W
Samford University M,W
Southern Union State Community College M,W
Spring Hill College M,W
Troy University M,W
University of Alabama M,W
University of Alabama
    Birmingham W
    Huntsville M,W
University of Mobile M,W
University of North Alabama M,W
University of South Alabama M,W
University of West Alabama M,W
Wallace State Community College at Hanceville M,W

Alaska
University of Alaska
    Anchorage M,W
    Fairbanks M,W

Arizona
Arizona State University M,W
Central Arizona College M,W
Dine College M,W
GateWay Community College M,W
Glendale Community College M,W
Mesa Community College M,W
Northern Arizona University M,W
Paradise Valley Community College M,W
Pima Community College M,W
Scottsdale Community College M,W
University of Arizona M,W

Arkansas
Arkansas State University M,W
Arkansas Tech University W
Harding University M,W
Henderson State University M,W
Lyon College M,W
Ouachita Baptist University W
Southern Arkansas University W
University of Arkansas M,W
University of Arkansas
    Little Rock M,W
    Monticello W
    Pine Bluff M,W
University of Central Arkansas M,W

California
Azusa Pacific University M,W
Bethany University M,W
Biola University M,W
California Baptist University M,W
California Polytechnic State University: San Luis Obispo M,W
California State Polytechnic University: Pomona M,W
California State University
    Chico M,W
    Dominguez Hills W
    Fresno M,W
    Fullerton M,W
    Long Beach M,W
    Los Angeles M,W
    Monterey Bay M,W
    Northridge M,W
    Sacramento M,W
    Stanislaus M,W
Concordia University M,W
Fresno City College M,W
Fresno Pacific University M,W
Holy Names University M,W
Humboldt State University M,W
Loyola Marymount University M,W
The Master's College M,W
Notre Dame de Namur University M,W
Pepperdine University M,W
Point Loma Nazarene University M,W
St. Mary's College of California M,W
San Diego Christian College M,W
San Diego State University W
San Jose State University M,W
Santa Clara University M,W
Santiago Canyon College M,W
Stanford University M,W
University of California
    Berkeley M,W
    Davis M,W
    Irvine M,W
    Los Angeles M,W
    Riverside M,W
    Santa Barbara M,W
University of San Diego M,W
University of San Francisco M,W
University of Southern California M,W
University of the Pacific W
Vanguard University of Southern California M,W
Westmont College M,W
William Jessup University M,W
Yuba Community College District M,W

Colorado
Adams State College M,W
Colorado Christian University M,W
Colorado School of Mines M,W
Colorado State University M,W
Colorado State University
    Pueblo W
Fort Lewis College M,W
Mesa State College W
Regis University M,W
University of Colorado
    Boulder M,W
    Colorado Springs M,W
University of Northern Colorado W
Western State College of Colorado M,W

Connecticut
Central Connecticut State University M,W
Fairfield University M,W
Post University M,W
Quinnipiac University M,W
Sacred Heart University M,W
Southern Connecticut State University M,W
University of Bridgeport M,W
University of Connecticut M,W
University of Hartford M,W
University of New Haven M,W

Delaware
Delaware State University M,W
Goldey-Beacom College M,W
Wilmington University M,W

District of Columbia
American University M,W
George Washington University M,W
Georgetown University M,W
Howard University M,W

Florida
Bethune-Cookman University M,W
Chipola College W
Embry-Riddle Aeronautical University M,W
Flagler College M,W
Florida Atlantic University M,W
Florida Institute of Technology M,W
Florida Southern College M,W
Florida State University M,W
Jacksonville University W
Nova Southeastern University M,W
Pasco-Hernando Community College W
Saint Leo University M,W
Saint Thomas University M,W
Stetson University M,W
University of Central Florida M,W
University of Florida M,W
University of Miami M,W
University of North Florida M,W
University of South Florida M,W
University of Tampa M,W
University of West Florida M,W
Warner University M,W
Webber International University M,W

Georgia
Albany State University M,W
Andrew College M,W
Augusta State University M,W
Brenau University W
Clark Atlanta University M,W
Clayton State University M,W
Columbus State University M,W
Covenant College M,W
Georgia College and State University M,W
Georgia Institute of Technology M,W
Georgia Southern University W
Georgia Southwestern State University W
Georgia State University M,W
Gordon College M,W
Kennesaw State University M,W
Mercer University M,W
Middle Georgia College M,W
Morehouse College M
Paine College M,W
Reinhardt College M,W
Savannah State University M,W
Shorter College M,W
Truett-McConnell College M,W
University of Georgia M,W
University of West Georgia M,W
Valdosta State University M,W
Young Harris College M,W

Hawaii
Chaminade University of Honolulu M,W
Hawaii Pacific University M,W
University of Hawaii
    Hilo M,W
    Manoa W

Idaho
Boise State University M,W
College of Idaho M,W
Idaho State University M,W
Lewis-Clark State College M,W
Northwest Nazarene University M,W
University of Idaho M,W

Illinois
Bradley University M,W
Chicago State University M,W
College of Lake County M,W
Danville Area Community College M,W
DePaul University M,W
Eastern Illinois University M,W
Illinois Central College M,W
Illinois Institute of Technology M,W
Illinois State University M,W
Judson University M,W
Lewis University M,W
Lincoln College M,W
Loyola University Chicago M,W
McKendree University M,W
Moraine Valley Community College M,W
Morton College M,W
Northwestern University W
Olivet Nazarene University M,W
Rend Lake College M,W
Robert Morris University: Chicago M,W
Saint Xavier University M,W
Sauk Valley Community College M,W
Southern Illinois University Carbondale M,W
Southern Illinois University Edwardsville M,W
Trinity Christian College M,W
University of Illinois
    Chicago M,W
    Urbana-Champaign M,W
University of St. Francis M,W
Waubonsee Community College M,W
Western Illinois University M,W

Indiana
Ball State University W
Bethel College M,W
Butler University M,W
Calumet College of St. Joseph M,W
Goshen College M,W
Grace College M,W
Huntington University M,W
Indiana Institute of Technology M,W
Indiana State University M,W
Indiana University
    Bloomington M,W
Indiana University-Purdue University Fort Wayne M,W
Indiana University-Purdue University Indianapolis M,W
Indiana Wesleyan University M,W
Marian University M,W
Oakland City University M,W
Purdue University M,W
Saint Joseph's College M,W
St. Mary-of-the-Woods College W
Taylor University M,W
University of Evansville M,W
University of Indianapolis M,W
University of Notre Dame M,W
University of St. Francis M,W
University of Southern Indiana M,W
Valparaiso University M,W
Vincennes University M,W

Iowa
Briar Cliff University M,W
Clarke College M,W
Dordt College M,W
Drake University M,W
Ellsworth Community College M,W
Graceland University M,W
Grand View University M,W
Iowa State University M,W
Iowa Wesleyan College M,W
Morningside College M,W
Mount Mercy College M,W
North Iowa Area Community College M,W
Northwestern College M,W
St. Ambrose University M,W
University of Iowa M,W
University of Northern Iowa M,W
William Penn University M,W

Kansas
Allen County Community College M,W
Baker University M,W
Barton County Community College M,W
Benedictine College M,W
Bethany College M,W
Bethel College M,W
Butler Community College M,W
Central Christian College of Kansas M,W
Cloud County Community College M,W
Coffeyville Community College M,W
Colby Community College M,W
Cowley County Community College M,W
Dodge City Community College M,W
Emporia State University M,W
Fort Hays State University M,W
Fort Scott Community College M,W
Garden City Community College M,W
Highland Community College M,W
Hutchinson Community College M,W
Johnson County Community College M,W
Kansas City Kansas Community College M,W
Kansas State University M,W
Kansas Wesleyan University M,W
McPherson College M,W
MidAmerica Nazarene University M,W
Neosho County Community College M,W
Newman University M,W
Ottawa University M,W
Pittsburg State University M,W
Pratt Community College M,W
Southwestern College M,W
Sterling College M,W
Tabor College M,W
University of Kansas M,W
Wichita State University M,W

Kentucky
Asbury College M,W
Bellarmine University M,W
Brescia University M,W
Campbellsville University M,W
Eastern Kentucky University M,W
Georgetown College M,W
Kentucky State University M,W
Kentucky Wesleyan College M,W
Lindsey Wilson College M,W
Midway College W
Morehead State University M,W
Murray State University M,W
Northern Kentucky University M,W
Pikeville College M,W
St. Catharine College M,W
Union College M,W
University of Kentucky M,W
University of Louisville M,W
University of the Cumberlands M,W
Western Kentucky University M,W

Louisiana
Centenary College of Louisiana M,W
Dillard University M,W
Grambling State University M,W
Louisiana State University and Agricultural and Mechanical College M,W
Louisiana Tech University M,W
McNeese State University M,W
Nicholls State University M,W
Northwestern State University M,W
Southeastern Louisiana University M,W
Southern University
    New Orleans M,W
Southern University and Agricultural and Mechanical College M,W
University of Louisiana at Lafayette M,W
University of Louisiana at Monroe M,W
Xavier University of Louisiana M,W

Maine
University of Maine M,W

Maryland
Bowie State University M,W
Coppin State University M,W
Hagerstown Community College M,W
Loyola University Maryland M,W
Morgan State University M,W
Mount St. Mary's University M,W
Towson University M,W
University of Maryland
 Baltimore County M,W
 Eastern Shore M,W
Washington Adventist University M,W

Massachusetts
American International College M,W
Boston College M,W
Boston University M,W
Merrimack College W
Northeastern University M,W
Stonehill College M,W
University of Massachusetts
 Amherst M,W
 Lowell M,W

Michigan
Aquinas College M,W
Central Michigan University M,W
Cornerstone University M,W
Davenport University M,W
Delta College M
Eastern Michigan University M,W
Ferris State University M,W
Grand Rapids Community College M,W
Grand Valley State University M,W
Hillsdale College M,W
Kirtland Community College M,W
Lake Superior State University M,W
Lansing Community College M,W
Macomb Community College M,W
Madonna University M,W
Michigan State University M,W
Michigan Technological University M,W
Mott Community College M,W
Northern Michigan University W
Northwood University: Michigan M,W
Oakland Community College M,W
Oakland University M,W
Saginaw Valley State University M,W
Siena Heights University M,W
Spring Arbor University M,W
University of Detroit Mercy M,W
University of Michigan M,W
Wayne State University M,W
Western Michigan University M,W

Minnesota
Concordia University: St. Paul M,W
Minnesota State University
 Mankato M,W
 Moorhead M,W
Saint Cloud State University M,W
University of Minnesota
 Duluth M,W
 Twin Cities M,W
Winona State University M,W

Mississippi
Alcorn State University M,W
Belhaven University M,W
Blue Mountain College M,W
Delta State University W
Jackson State University M,W
Mississippi State University M,W
Mississippi Valley State University M,W
Tougaloo College M,W
University of Mississippi M,W
University of Southern Mississippi M,W

Missouri
Central Methodist University M,W
Culver-Stockton College M,W
Drury University M,W

Evangel University M,W
Hannibal-LaGrange College M,W
Lincoln University W
Missouri Baptist University M,W
Missouri Southern State University M,W
Missouri State University M,W
Missouri Valley College M,W
Northwest Missouri State University M,W
Park University M,W
Research College of Nursing M,W
Saint Louis University M,W
Southeast Missouri State University M,W
Southwest Baptist University M,W
Stephens College W
Truman State University M,W
University of Central Missouri M,W
University of Missouri
 Columbia M,W
 Kansas City M,W
 Missouri University of Science and
  Technology M,W
William Jewell College M,W
William Woods University M,W

Montana
Flathead Valley Community College M,W
Montana State University
 Billings M,W
 Bozeman M,W
Rocky Mountain College M,W
University of Great Falls M,W
University of Montana M,W

Nebraska
College of Saint Mary W
Concordia University M,W
Creighton University M,W
Dana College M,W
Doane College M,W
University of Nebraska
 Kearney M,W
 Lincoln M,W
 Omaha M,W
Wayne State College M,W

Nevada
University of Nevada
 Las Vegas W
 Reno W

New Hampshire
Southern New Hampshire University M,W
University of New Hampshire M,W

New Jersey
Bloomfield College M,W
Caldwell College W
Fairleigh Dickinson University
 Metropolitan Campus M,W
Felician College M,W
Georgian Court University W
Monmouth University M,W
Rider University M,W
Rutgers, The State University of New Jersey
 New Brunswick/Piscataway Campus M,W
Saint Peter's College M,W
Seton Hall University M,W

New Mexico
Eastern New Mexico University M,W
New Mexico Highlands University M,W
New Mexico Junior College M,W
New Mexico State University M,W
University of New Mexico M,W
University of the Southwest M,W

New York
Adelphi University M,W
Canisius College M,W
City University of New York
 Queens College M,W
Daemen College M,W
Dominican College of Blauvelt W

Fordham University M,W
Hofstra University M,W
Houghton College M,W
Iona College M,W
Le Moyne College M,W
Long Island University
 Brooklyn Campus M,W
 C. W. Post Campus M,W
Manhattan College M,W
Marist College M,W
Mercy College M,W
Molloy College M,W
New York Institute of Technology M,W
Niagara University M,W
Nyack College M,W
Pace University M,W
Roberts Wesleyan College M,W
St. Francis College M,W
St. John's University W
St. Thomas Aquinas College M,W
Siena College M,W
State University of New York
 Albany M,W
 Binghamton M,W
 Buffalo M,W
 Stony Brook M,W
Syracuse University M,W
Wagner College M,W

North Carolina
Appalachian State University M,W
Barton College M,W
Belmont Abbey College M,W
Brevard College M,W
Campbell University M,W
Catawba College M,W
Davidson College M,W
East Carolina University M,W
Elon University M,W
Fayetteville State University M,W
Gardner-Webb University M,W
High Point University M,W
Johnson C. Smith University M,W
Lees-McRae College M,W
Lenoir-Rhyne University M,W
Livingstone College W
Mars Hill College M,W
Montreat College M,W
Mount Olive College M,W
North Carolina Agricultural and Technical State
 University M,W
North Carolina Central University M,W
North Carolina State University M,W
Pfeiffer University M,W
Queens University of Charlotte M,W
St. Andrews Presbyterian College M,W
St. Augustine's College M,W
Shaw University W
University of North Carolina
 Asheville M,W
 Chapel Hill M,W
 Charlotte M,W
 Greensboro M,W
 Pembroke M,W
 Wilmington M,W
Wake Forest University M,W
Western Carolina University M,W
Wingate University M,W
Winston-Salem State University M,W

North Dakota
Dickinson State University M,W
Jamestown College M,W
Minot State University M,W
North Dakota State University M,W
University of Mary M,W
University of North Dakota M,W

Ohio
Ashland University M,W
Bowling Green State University M,W
Cedarville University M,W

Central State University M,W
Cleveland State University W
Kent State University M,W
Malone University M,W
Miami University
 Oxford Campus M,W
Mount Vernon Nazarene University M,W
Notre Dame College M,W
Ohio Dominican University M,W
Ohio University M,W
Shawnee State University M,W
Tiffin University M,W
University of Akron M,W
University of Cincinnati M,W
University of Dayton M,W
University of Findlay M,W
University of Rio Grande M,W
University of Toledo M,W
Urbana University M,W
Ursuline College W
Walsh University M,W
Wright State University M,W
Xavier University M,W
Youngstown State University M,W

Oklahoma
Cameron University M
East Central University M,W
Langston University M,W
Oklahoma Baptist University M,W
Oklahoma Christian University M,W
Oklahoma City University M,W
Oklahoma Panhandle State University M,W
Oklahoma State University M,W
Oklahoma Wesleyan University M,W
Oral Roberts University M,W
Southeastern Oklahoma State University W
Southern Nazarene University M,W
Southwestern Oklahoma State University W
University of Central Oklahoma M,W
University of Oklahoma M,W
University of Tulsa M,W

Oregon
Clackamas Community College M,W
Concordia University M,W
Corban College M,W
Eastern Oregon University M,W
Lane Community College M,W
Mt. Hood Community College M,W
Northwest Christian University M,W
Oregon Institute of Technology M,W
Portland State University M,W
Southern Oregon University M,W
Southwestern Oregon Community College M,W
Treasure Valley Community College M,W
University of Oregon M,W
University of Portland M,W
Warner Pacific College M,W

Pennsylvania
Bloomsburg University of Pennsylvania M,W
California University of Pennsylvania M,W
Chestnut Hill College M,W
Cheyney University of Pennsylvania M,W
Clarion University of Pennsylvania M,W
Duquesne University M,W
East Stroudsburg University of Pennsylvania
 M,W
Edinboro University of Pennsylvania M,W
Gannon University M,W
Holy Family University M,W
Indiana University of Pennsylvania M,W
Kutztown University of Pennsylvania M,W
La Salle University M,W
Lackawanna College M,W
Lock Haven University of Pennsylvania M,W
Mansfield University of Pennsylvania W
Mercyhurst College M,W
Millersville University of Pennsylvania M,W
Penn State
 University Park M,W

Philadelphia University M,W
Point Park University M,W
St. Francis University M,W
Saint Joseph's University M,W
Seton Hill University M,W
Shippensburg University of Pennsylvania M,W
Slippery Rock University of Pennsylvania M,W
Temple University M,W
University of Pittsburgh M,W
University of the Sciences in Philadelphia M,W
Villanova University M,W
West Chester University of Pennsylvania M,W
Westminster College W

Puerto Rico
Bayamon Central University M,W
Inter American University of Puerto Rico
 Aguadilla Campus M,W
 Bayamon Campus M,W
 Guayama Campus M,W
 Ponce Campus M
 San German Campus M,W
Turabo University M,W
Universidad del Este M,W
Universidad Metropolitana M,W
Universidad Politecnica de Puerto Rico M
University of Puerto Rico
 Carolina Regional College M,W
 Cayey University College M,W
 Humacao M,W
 Ponce M,W
 Utuado M,W
University of the Sacred Heart M,W

Rhode Island
Bryant University M,W
Providence College M,W
University of Rhode Island M,W

South Carolina
Anderson University M,W
Charleston Southern University M,W
The Citadel M,W
Claflin University M,W
Clemson University M,W
Coastal Carolina University M,W
Coker College M,W
College of Charleston M,W
Converse College W
Erskine College M,W
Francis Marion University M,W
Furman University M,W
Limestone College M,W
Morris College M,W
Newberry College M,W
North Greenville University M,W
Presbyterian College M,W
South Carolina State University M,W
Southern Wesleyan University M,W
Spartanburg Methodist College M,W
University of South Carolina W
University of South Carolina
 Aiken W
 Upstate M,W
Winthrop University M,W
Wofford College M,W

South Dakota
Augustana College M,W
Black Hills State University M,W
Dakota State University M,W
Dakota Wesleyan University M,W
Mount Marty College M,W
South Dakota School of Mines and Technology M,W
South Dakota State University M,W
University of Sioux Falls M,W
University of South Dakota M,W

Tennessee
Austin Peay State University M,W
Belmont University M,W
Bethel University M,W

Bryan College M,W
Carson-Newman College M,W
Christian Brothers University M,W
Cumberland University M,W
East Tennessee State University M,W
King College M,W
Lee University M,W
LeMoyne-Owen College M
Lincoln Memorial University M,W
Lipscomb University M,W
Middle Tennessee State University M,W
Milligan College M,W
Tennessee Technological University M,W
Tennessee Wesleyan College M,W
Tusculum College M,W
Union University M,W
University of Memphis M,W
University of Tennessee
 Chattanooga M,W
Vanderbilt University M,W

Texas
Abilene Christian University M,W
Angelo State University M,W
Baylor University M,W
Clarendon College M,W
Dallas Baptist University W
Houston Baptist University M,W
Lamar University M,W
Lon Morris College M,W
Midwestern State University W
Northwood University: Texas M,W
Odessa College M,W
Prairie View A&M University M,W
Rice University M,W
Sam Houston State University M,W
South Plains College M,W
Southern Methodist University W
Stephen F. Austin State University M,W
Tarleton State University M,W
Texas A&M University M,W
Texas A&M University
 Commerce M,W
Texas Christian University M,W
Texas Southern University M,W
Texas State University: San Marcos M,W
Texas Tech University M,W
University of Houston M,W
University of North Texas M,W
University of Texas
 Arlington M,W
 Austin M,W
 Pan American M,W
 of the Permian Basin M,W
 San Antonio M,W
University of the Incarnate Word M,W
Wayland Baptist University M,W
West Texas A&M University M,W
Western Texas College M,W

Utah
Brigham Young University M,W
University of Utah W
Utah State University M,W
Utah Valley University M,W
Weber State University M,W

Vermont
University of Vermont M,W

Virginia
Bluefield College M,W
College of William and Mary M,W
George Mason University M,W
Hampton University M,W
James Madison University W
Liberty University M,W
Longwood University M,W
Norfolk State University M,W
Radford University M,W
St. Paul's College M,W
University of Richmond W
University of Virginia M,W

University of Virginia's College at Wise M,W
Virginia Commonwealth University M,W
Virginia Military Institute M,W
Virginia Polytechnic Institute and State
 University M,W
Virginia State University M,W

Washington
Clark College M
Eastern Washington University M,W
Everett Community College M,W
Evergreen State College M,W
Gonzaga University M,W
Highline Community College M,W
Northwest University M,W
Saint Martin's University M,W
Seattle Pacific University M,W
Seattle University M,W
Spokane Community College M,W
University of Washington M,W
Washington State University M,W
Western Washington University M,W

West Virginia
Alderson-Broaddus College M,W
Bluefield State College M,W
Concord University M,W
Davis and Elkins College M,W
Glenville State College M,W
Marshall University M,W
Mountain State University M,W
Ohio Valley University M,W
University of Charleston M,W
West Liberty University M,W
West Virginia University W
West Virginia Wesleyan College M,W
Wheeling Jesuit University M,W

Wisconsin
Cardinal Stritch University M,W
Marquette University M,W
Milwaukee Area Technical College M,W
Silver Lake College M,W
University of Wisconsin
 Green Bay M,W
 Milwaukee M,W
 Parkside M,W
Viterbo University M,W

Wyoming
Sheridan College M,W
University of Wyoming M,W

Diving

Alabama
Auburn University M,W
University of Alabama M,W

Arizona
Arizona State University M,W
Northern Arizona University W
University of Arizona M,W

Arkansas
Ouachita Baptist University M,W
University of Arkansas W

California
California Baptist University M,W
California State University
 Northridge M,W
College of the Redwoods M
San Diego State University W
San Jose State University W
Stanford University M,W
University of California
 Berkeley M,W
 Davis M,W
 Irvine M,W
 Los Angeles M,W

University of San Diego W
University of Southern California M,W

Colorado
Colorado State University W
University of Denver M,W

Connecticut
Central Connecticut State University W
Fairfield University M,W
University of Connecticut M,W

District of Columbia
George Washington University M,W
Howard University M,W

Florida
Florida State University M,W
Indian River State College M,W
University of Florida M,W
University of Miami W

Georgia
Georgia Institute of Technology M,W
Georgia Southern University W
University of Georgia M,W

Hawaii
University of Hawaii
 Manoa M,W

Illinois
Eastern Illinois University M,W
Illinois Institute of Technology M,W
Illinois State University W
Lincoln College M,W
Northwestern University M,W
Robert Morris University: Chicago W
Southern Illinois University Carbondale M,W
University of Illinois
 Chicago M,W
 Urbana-Champaign W
Western Illinois University M,W

Indiana
Ball State University M,W
Indiana University
 Bloomington M,W
Indiana University-Purdue University
 Indianapolis M,W
Purdue University M,W
University of Evansville M,W
University of Notre Dame M,W
Valparaiso University M,W

Iowa
University of Iowa M,W

Kentucky
Asbury College M,W
University of Kentucky M,W
University of Louisville M,W
Western Kentucky University M

Louisiana
University of New Orleans M,W

Maine
University of Maine M,W

Maryland
Loyola University Maryland M,W
Towson University M,W
University of Maryland
 Baltimore County M,W

Massachusetts
Boston College M,W
Boston University M,W
Northeastern University W
University of Massachusetts
 Amherst M,W

Michigan
Eastern Michigan University M,W
Grand Rapids Community College M,W
Grand Valley State University M,W
Hillsdale College W
Michigan State University M,W
Northern Michigan University W
Oakland University M,W
University of Michigan M,W
Wayne State University M,W

Minnesota
Minnesota State University
   Mankato M,W
   Moorhead M
Saint Cloud State University M,W
University of Minnesota
   Twin Cities M,W

Mississippi
Delta State University M,W

Missouri
Drury University M,W
Saint Louis University M,W
University of Missouri
   Columbia M,W

Nebraska
University of Nebraska
   Kearney W
   Lincoln W

Nevada
University of Nevada
   Las Vegas M,W
   Reno W

New Hampshire
University of New Hampshire W

New Jersey
Rider University M,W
Rutgers, The State University of New Jersey
   New Brunswick/Piscataway Campus M,W
Saint Peter's College M,W

New Mexico
University of New Mexico W

New York
Fordham University M,W
Iona College M,W
Marist College M,W
Niagara University M,W
Saint Bonaventure University M,W
St. Francis College M,W
Siena College W
State University of New York
   Binghamton M,W
   Buffalo M,W
   Stony Brook M,W
Syracuse University M,W

North Carolina
Davidson College M,W
East Carolina University M,W
University of North Carolina
   Chapel Hill M,W
   Wilmington M,W

North Dakota
University of North Dakota M,W

Ohio
Ashland University M,W
Cleveland State University M,W
Malone University M,W
Miami University
   Oxford Campus M,W
Notre Dame College W
Ohio University W
University of Akron W

University of Cincinnati M,W
University of Findlay M,W
University of Toledo W
Wright State University M,W

Pennsylvania
Clarion University of Pennsylvania M,W
Drexel University M,W
Gannon University M,W
Indiana University of Pennsylvania M,W
La Salle University M,W
Penn State
   University Park M,W
St. Francis University W
University of Pittsburgh M,W
Villanova University W
West Chester University of Pennsylvania M,W

Rhode Island
University of Rhode Island W

South Carolina
Clemson University M,W
College of Charleston M,W
University of South Carolina M,W

South Dakota
University of South Dakota M,W

Texas
Southern Methodist University M,W
Texas A&M University M,W
Texas Christian University M,W
University of Houston W
University of North Texas W
University of Texas
   Austin M,W

Utah
Brigham Young University M,W
University of Utah M,W

Vermont
University of Vermont W

Virginia
George Mason University M,W
James Madison University W
Old Dominion University M,W
Radford University W
University of Richmond W
University of Virginia M,W
Virginia Military Institute M
Virginia Polytechnic Institute and State
   University M,W

West Virginia
West Virginia University M,W

Wisconsin
University of Wisconsin
   Green Bay M,W
   Milwaukee M,W

Wyoming
University of Wyoming M,W

Equestrian

California
California State University
   Fresno W

Delaware
Delaware State University W

Georgia
University of Georgia W

Indiana
St. Mary-of-the-Woods College W

Kansas
Kansas State University W

Kentucky
Midway College W
Murray State University M,W

Massachusetts
Stonehill College W

Minnesota
University of Minnesota
   Crookston W

Nebraska
Nebraska College of Technical Agriculture M,W

New York
Dowling College W
Vassar College M,W

North Carolina
St. Andrews Presbyterian College M,W

Ohio
Tiffin University M,W

Oklahoma
Oklahoma Panhandle State University M,W
Oklahoma State University W

Oregon
Linn-Benton Community College M,W

Pennsylvania
Seton Hill University W

South Carolina
University of South Carolina W

South Dakota
South Dakota State University W

Texas
Baylor University W
Southern Methodist University W
Texas A&M University W
Texas Christian University W
West Texas A&M University W

Virginia
Virginia Intermont College M,W

Wyoming
Laramie County Community College M,W

Fencing

California
Stanford University M,W

Illinois
Northwestern University W

Indiana
University of Notre Dame M,W

Michigan
University of Detroit Mercy M,W
Wayne State University M,W

New Jersey
Fairleigh Dickinson University
   Metropolitan Campus W
New Jersey Institute of Technology M,W
Rutgers, The State University of New Jersey
   New Brunswick/Piscataway Campus M,W

New York
City University of New York
   Queens College W
St. John's University M,W

Ohio
Cleveland State University M,W

Pennsylvania
Penn State
   University Park M,W
Temple University W

Field Hockey

California
Stanford University W
University of California
   Berkeley W
University of the Pacific W

Connecticut
Fairfield University W
Quinnipiac University W
Sacred Heart University W
Southern Connecticut State University W
University of Connecticut W

Delaware
University of Delaware W

District of Columbia
American University W
Georgetown University W

Illinois
Northwestern University W

Indiana
Ball State University W

Iowa
University of Iowa W

Kentucky
Bellarmine University W
University of Louisville W

Maine
University of Maine W

Maryland
Towson University W
University of Maryland
   College Park W

Massachusetts
American International College W
Boston College W
Boston University W
College of the Holy Cross W
Northeastern University W
Stonehill College W
University of Massachusetts
   Amherst W

Michigan
Central Michigan University W
Michigan State University W
University of Michigan W

Missouri
Missouri State University W
Saint Louis University W

New Hampshire
Franklin Pierce University W
University of New Hampshire W

New Jersey
Monmouth University W
Rider University W
Rutgers, The State University of New Jersey
   New Brunswick/Piscataway Campus W

New York
Adelphi University W
Colgate University W
Hofstra University W
Houghton College W
Long Island University
        C. W. Post Campus W
Siena College W
State University of New York
        Albany W
Syracuse University W

North Carolina
Appalachian State University W
Davidson College W
Duke University W
University of North Carolina
        Chapel Hill W
Wake Forest University W

Ohio
Kent State University W
Miami University
        Oxford Campus W
Notre Dame College W
Ohio University W

Pennsylvania
Bloomsburg University of Pennsylvania W
Drexel University W
East Stroudsburg University of Pennsylvania W
Indiana University of Pennsylvania W
Kutztown University of Pennsylvania W
La Salle University W
Lafayette College W
Lock Haven University of Pennsylvania W
Mansfield University of Pennsylvania W
Mercyhurst College W
Millersville University of Pennsylvania W
Penn State
        University Park W
Robert Morris University W
St. Francis University W
Saint Joseph's University W
Seton Hill University W
Shippensburg University of Pennsylvania W
Slippery Rock University of Pennsylvania W
Temple University W
Villanova University W
West Chester University of Pennsylvania W

Rhode Island
Bryant University W
Providence College W

South Carolina
Limestone College W

Vermont
University of Vermont W

Virginia
College of William and Mary W
James Madison University W
Longwood University W
Old Dominion University W
Radford University W
University of Richmond W
University of Virginia W
Virginia Commonwealth University W

Football (non-tackle)

Alabama
Faulkner University M

Illinois
Olivet Nazarene University M

Michigan
Southwestern Michigan College M,W

New York
State University of New York
        Institute of Technology at Utica/Rome M

Football (tackle)

Alabama
Alabama Agricultural and Mechanical
        University M
Alabama State University M
Auburn University M
Jacksonville State University M
Miles College M
Samford University M
Troy University M
Tuskegee University M
University of Alabama M
University of Alabama
        Birmingham M
University of North Alabama M
University of West Alabama M

Arizona
Arizona State University M
Arizona Western College M
Eastern Arizona College M
Glendale Community College M
Mesa Community College M
Northern Arizona University M
Pima Community College M
Scottsdale Community College M
University of Arizona M

Arkansas
Arkansas State University M
Arkansas Tech University M
Harding University M
Henderson State University M
Ouachita Baptist University M
Southern Arkansas University M
University of Arkansas M
University of Arkansas
        Monticello M
        Pine Bluff M
University of Central Arkansas M

California
Azusa Pacific University M
California Polytechnic State University: San Luis
        Obispo M
California State University
        Fresno M
        Sacramento M
Fresno City College M
Grossmont College M
Humboldt State University M
San Diego State University M
San Jose State University M
Stanford University M
University of California
        Berkeley M
        Davis M
        Los Angeles M
University of Southern California M
Yuba Community College District M

Colorado
Adams State College M
Colorado School of Mines M
Colorado State University M
Colorado State University
        Pueblo M
Fort Lewis College M
Mesa State College M
University of Colorado
        Boulder M
University of Northern Colorado M
Western State College of Colorado M

Connecticut
Sacred Heart University M
Southern Connecticut State University M
University of Connecticut M

Delaware
Delaware State University M
University of Delaware M

District of Columbia
Georgetown University M
Howard University M

Florida
Bethune-Cookman University M
Florida Agricultural and Mechanical University
        M
Florida Atlantic University M
Florida State University M
University of Central Florida M
University of Florida M
University of Miami M
University of South Florida M
Webber International University M

Georgia
Albany State University M
Clark Atlanta University M
Fort Valley State University M
Georgia Institute of Technology M
Georgia Military College M
Georgia Southern University M
Georgia State University M
Morehouse College M
Savannah State University M
Shorter College M
University of Georgia M
University of West Georgia M
Valdosta State University M

Hawaii
University of Hawaii
        Manoa M

Idaho
Boise State University M
Idaho State University M
University of Idaho M

Illinois
Eastern Illinois University M
Illinois State University M
McKendree University M
Northwestern University M
Olivet Nazarene University M
Quincy University M
Saint Xavier University M
Southern Illinois University Carbondale M
Trinity International University M
University of Illinois
        Urbana-Champaign M
University of St. Francis M
Western Illinois University M

Indiana
Ball State University M
Indiana State University M
Indiana University
        Bloomington M
Marian University M
Purdue University M
Saint Joseph's College M
Taylor University M
University of Indianapolis M
University of Notre Dame M
University of St. Francis M

Iowa
Briar Cliff University M
Dordt College M
Ellsworth Community College M
Graceland University M
Grand View University M

Iowa Central Community College M
Iowa State University M
Iowa Wesleyan College M
Morningside College M
North Iowa Area Community College M
Northwestern College M
St. Ambrose University M
University of Iowa M
University of Northern Iowa M
Waldorf College M
William Penn University M

Kansas
Baker University M
Benedictine College M
Bethany College M
Bethel College M
Butler Community College M
Coffeyville Community College M
Dodge City Community College M
Emporia State University M
Fort Hays State University M
Fort Scott Community College M
Friends University M
Garden City Community College M
Highland Community College M
Hutchinson Community College M
Kansas State University M
Kansas Wesleyan University M
McPherson College M
MidAmerica Nazarene University M
Ottawa University M
Pittsburg State University M
Southwestern College M
Sterling College M
Tabor College M
University of Kansas M
University of St. Mary M
Washburn University M

Kentucky
Campbellsville University M
Eastern Kentucky University M
Georgetown College M
Kentucky Christian University M
Kentucky State University M
Kentucky Wesleyan College M
Murray State University M
Pikeville College M
Union College M
University of Kentucky M
University of Louisville M
University of the Cumberlands M
Western Kentucky University M

Louisiana
Grambling State University M
Louisiana State University and Agricultural and
        Mechanical College M
Louisiana Tech University M
McNeese State University M
Nicholls State University M
Northwestern State University M
Southeastern Louisiana University M
Southern University and Agricultural and
        Mechanical College M
Tulane University M
University of Louisiana at Lafayette M
University of Louisiana at Monroe M

Maine
University of Maine M

Maryland
Bowie State University M
Morgan State University M
Towson University M
University of Maryland
        College Park M

Massachusetts
American International College M
Boston College M

Dean College M
Stonehill College M
University of Massachusetts
    Amherst M

Michigan
Central Michigan University M
Eastern Michigan University M
Ferris State University M
Grand Rapids Community College M
Grand Valley State University M
Hillsdale College M
Michigan State University M
Michigan Technological University M
Northern Michigan University M
Northwood University: Michigan M
Saginaw Valley State University M
University of Michigan M
Wayne State University M
Western Michigan University M

Minnesota
Bemidji State University M
Concordia University: St. Paul M
Minnesota State University
    Mankato M
    Moorhead M
Saint Cloud State University M
Southwest Minnesota State University M
University of Minnesota
    Crookston M
    Duluth M
    Twin Cities M
Winona State University M

Mississippi
Alcorn State University M
Belhaven University M
Copiah-Lincoln Community College M
Delta State University M
East Central Community College M
East Mississippi Community College M
Hinds Community College M
Holmes Community College M
Jackson State University M
Jones County Junior College M
Mississippi Gulf Coast Community College M
Mississippi State University M
Mississippi Valley State University M
Northwest Mississippi Community College M
Southwest Mississippi Community College M
University of Mississippi M
University of Southern Mississippi M

Missouri
Avila University M
Central Methodist University M
Culver-Stockton College M
Evangel University M
Lincoln University M
Missouri Southern State University M
Missouri State University M
Missouri Valley College M
Missouri Western State University M
Northwest Missouri State University M
Southeast Missouri State University M
Southwest Baptist University M
Truman State University M
University of Central Missouri M
University of Missouri
    Columbia M
    Missouri University of Science and
      Technology M
William Jewell College M

Montana
Montana State University
    Bozeman M
Montana Tech of the University of Montana M
Rocky Mountain College M
University of Montana M
University of Montana: Western M

Nebraska
Chadron State College M
Concordia University M
Dana College M
Doane College M
Peru State College M
University of Nebraska
    Kearney M
    Lincoln M
    Omaha M
Wayne State College M

Nevada
University of Nevada
    Las Vegas M
    Reno M

New Hampshire
University of New Hampshire M

New Jersey
Monmouth University M
Rutgers, The State University of New Jersey
    New Brunswick/Piscataway Campus M

New Mexico
Eastern New Mexico University M
New Mexico Highlands University M
New Mexico Military Institute M
New Mexico State University M
University of New Mexico M
Western New Mexico University M

New York
ASA Institute of Business and Computer
    Technology M
Long Island University
    C. W. Post Campus M
State University of New York
    Albany M
    Buffalo M
    Stony Brook M
Syracuse University M
Wagner College M

North Carolina
Appalachian State University M
Brevard College M
Catawba College M
Chowan University M
Duke University M
East Carolina University M
Elizabeth City State University M
Elon University M
Fayetteville State University M
Gardner-Webb University M
Johnson C. Smith University M
Lenoir-Rhyne University M
Livingstone College M
Mars Hill College M
North Carolina Agricultural and Technical State
    University M
North Carolina Central University M
North Carolina State University M
St. Augustine's College M
Shaw University M
University of North Carolina
    Chapel Hill M
    Pembroke M
Wake Forest University M
Western Carolina University M
Wingate University M
Winston-Salem State University M

North Dakota
Dakota College at Bottineau M
Dickinson State University M
Jamestown College M
Mayville State University M
Minot State University M
North Dakota State College of Science M
North Dakota State University M
University of Mary M

University of North Dakota M

Ohio
Ashland University M
Bowling Green State University M
Kent State University M
Malone University M
Miami University
    Oxford Campus M
Ohio Dominican University M
Ohio University M
Tiffin University M
University of Akron M
University of Cincinnati M
University of Findlay M
University of Toledo M
Urbana University M
Walsh University M
Youngstown State University M

Oklahoma
Bacone College M
East Central University M
Langston University M
Northeastern Oklahoma Agricultural and
    Mechanical College M
Northeastern State University M
Northwestern Oklahoma State University M
Oklahoma Panhandle State University M
Oklahoma State University M
Southeastern Oklahoma State University M
Southwestern Oklahoma State University M
University of Central Oklahoma M
University of Oklahoma M
University of Tulsa M

Oregon
Eastern Oregon University M
Oregon State University M
Portland State University M
Southern Oregon University M
University of Oregon M

Pennsylvania
Bloomsburg University of Pennsylvania M
California University of Pennsylvania M
Cheyney University of Pennsylvania M
Clarion University of Pennsylvania M
Duquesne University M
East Stroudsburg University of Pennsylvania M
Edinboro University of Pennsylvania M
Gannon University M
Indiana University of Pennsylvania M
Kutztown University of Pennsylvania M
Lackawanna College M
Lock Haven University of Pennsylvania M
Mansfield University of Pennsylvania M
Mercyhurst College M
Millersville University of Pennsylvania M
Penn State
    University Park M
Robert Morris University M
St. Francis University M
Seton Hill University M
Shippensburg University of Pennsylvania M
Slippery Rock University of Pennsylvania M
Temple University M
University of Pittsburgh M
Valley Forge Military Academy & College M
Villanova University M
West Chester University of Pennsylvania M
Westminster College M

Rhode Island
Bryant University M
University of Rhode Island M

South Carolina
Charleston Southern University M
The Citadel M
Clemson University M
Coastal Carolina University M
Furman University M

Newberry College M
North Greenville University M
Presbyterian College M
South Carolina State University M
University of South Carolina M
Wofford College M

South Dakota
Augustana College M
Black Hills State University M
Dakota State University M
Dakota Wesleyan University M
Northern State University M
South Dakota School of Mines and Technology
    M
South Dakota State University M
University of Sioux Falls M
University of South Dakota M

Tennessee
Austin Peay State University M
Bethel University M
Carson-Newman College M
Cumberland University M
Lambuth University M
Lane College M
Middle Tennessee State University M
Tennessee State University M
Tennessee Technological University M
Tusculum College M
University of Memphis M
University of Tennessee
    Chattanooga M
    Knoxville M
    Martin M
Vanderbilt University M

Texas
Abilene Christian University M
Angelo State University M
Baylor University M
Blinn College M
Kilgore College M
Lon Morris College M
Midwestern State University M
Prairie View A&M University M
Rice University M
Sam Houston State University M
Southern Methodist University M
Southwestern Assemblies of God University M
Stephen F. Austin State University M
Tarleton State University M
Texas A&M University M
Texas A&M University
    Commerce M
    Kingsville M
Texas Christian University M
Texas Southern University M
Texas State University: San Marcos M
Texas Tech University M
Trinity Valley Community College M
Tyler Junior College M
University of Houston M
University of North Texas M
University of Texas
    Austin M
West Texas A&M University M

Utah
Brigham Young University M
Dixie State College of Utah M
Snow College M
Southern Utah University M
University of Utah M
Utah State University M
Weber State University M

Virginia
Hampton University M
James Madison University M
Liberty University M
Norfolk State University M
Old Dominion University M

University of Richmond M
University of Virginia M
University of Virginia's College at Wise M
Virginia Military Institute M
Virginia Polytechnic Institute and State
  University M
Virginia State University M
Virginia Union University M

Washington
Eastern Washington University M
University of Washington M
Washington State University M
Western Washington University M

West Virginia
Concord University M
Fairmont State University M
Glenville State College M
Marshall University M
Shepherd University M
University of Charleston M
West Liberty University M
West Virginia State University M
West Virginia University M
West Virginia University Institute of Technology
  M
West Virginia Wesleyan College M

Wyoming
University of Wyoming M

Golf

Alabama
Alabama State University M,W
Auburn University M,W
Central Alabama Community College M
Faulkner State Community College M,W
Faulkner University M,W
Jacksonville State University M,W
Samford University M,W
Spring Hill College M,W
Troy University M,W
University of Alabama M,W
University of Alabama
  Birmingham M,W
University of Mobile M,W
University of Montevallo M,W
University of North Alabama M
University of South Alabama M,W
Wallace State Community College at Hanceville
  M

Arizona
Arizona State University M,W
Chandler-Gilbert Community College
  Pecos M,W
Eastern Arizona College M
GateWay Community College M,W
Glendale Community College M
Grand Canyon University M
Mesa Community College M
Northern Arizona University W
Paradise Valley Community College M,W
Pima Community College M,W
Scottsdale Community College M
University of Arizona M,W

Arkansas
Arkansas State University M,W
Arkansas Tech University M
Harding University M,W
Henderson State University M,W
John Brown University M
Lyon College M
Ouachita Baptist University M
University of Arkansas M,W
University of Arkansas
  Fort Smith M,W
  Little Rock M,W

Monticello M,W
Pine Bluff M,W
University of Central Arkansas M,W

California
California Baptist University M,W
California Polytechnic State University: San Luis
  Obispo M,W
California State University
  Bakersfield M
  Chico M,W
  Dominguez Hills M
  Fresno M,W
  Long Beach M,W
  Monterey Bay M,W
  Northridge M
  Sacramento M,W
  San Bernardino M
  Stanislaus M
Dominican University of California M,W
Fresno City College M,W
Holy Names University M
Loyola Marymount University M
The Master's College M
Notre Dame de Namur University M
Pepperdine University M,W
Point Loma Nazarene University M
St. Mary's College of California M
San Diego State University M,W
San Jose State University M,W
Santa Clara University M,W
Santiago Canyon College M,W
Sonoma State University M
Stanford University M,W
University of California
  Berkeley M,W
  Davis M,W
  Irvine M,W
  Los Angeles M,W
  Santa Barbara M
University of San Diego M
University of San Francisco M,W
University of Southern California M,W
University of the Pacific M
William Jessup University M

Colorado
Adams State College M,W
Colorado Christian University M,W
Colorado State University M,W
Colorado State University
  Pueblo M,W
Fort Lewis College M
Mesa State College M,W
Regis University M,W
Trinidad State Junior College M
University of Colorado
  Boulder M,W
  Colorado Springs M
University of Denver M,W
University of Northern Colorado M,W

Connecticut
Central Connecticut State University M
Fairfield University M,W
Post University M
Sacred Heart University M,W
University of Connecticut M
University of Hartford M,W
University of New Haven M

Delaware
Goldey-Beacom College M
Wilmington University M

District of Columbia
George Washington University M
Georgetown University M,W

Florida
Ave Maria University M,W
Barry University M,W
Bethune-Cookman University M,W

Brevard Community College M
Daytona State College W
Eckerd College W
Embry-Riddle Aeronautical University M,W
Flagler College M,W
Florida Atlantic University M,W
Florida Gulf Coast University M,W
Florida Institute of Technology M,W
Florida Southern College M,W
Florida State University M,W
Jacksonville University M,W
Lynn University M,W
Northwood University
  Florida M,W
Nova Southeastern University M,W
Rollins College M,W
Saint Leo University M,W
Saint Thomas University M
Southeastern University M
Stetson University M,W
University of Central Florida M,W
University of Florida M,W
University of Miami W
University of North Florida M
University of South Florida M,W
University of Tampa M
University of West Florida M,W
Warner University M,W
Webber International University M,W

Georgia
Abraham Baldwin Agricultural College M
Andrew College M,W
Armstrong Atlantic State University M
Augusta State University M,W
Clayton State University M
College of Coastal Georgia M,W
Columbus State University M,W
Covenant College M,W
Darton College M
Georgia College and State University M
Georgia Institute of Technology M
Georgia Southern University M
Georgia Southwestern State University M
Georgia State University M,W
Kennesaw State University M
Mercer University M,W
Paine College M
Reinhardt College M
Shorter College M,W
Truett-McConnell College M,W
University of Georgia M,W
Valdosta State University M
Young Harris College M,W

Hawaii
Chaminade University of Honolulu M,W
Hawaii Pacific University M
University of Hawaii
  Hilo M
  Manoa M,W

Idaho
Boise State University M,W
College of Idaho M,W
Idaho State University W
Lewis-Clark State College M,W
Northwest Nazarene University M
University of Idaho M,W

Illinois
Black Hawk College M
Bradley University M,W
Chicago State University M,W
College of Lake County M,W
Danville Area Community College M
DePaul University M
Eastern Illinois University M,W
Elgin Community College M
Highland Community College M
Illinois Central College M
Illinois State University M,W
John A. Logan College M,W

Kaskaskia College M,W
Kishwaukee College M,W
Lewis and Clark Community College M
Lewis University M,W
Lincoln College M,W
Loyola University Chicago M,W
McKendree University M,W
Moraine Valley Community College M
Northwestern University M,W
Olivet Nazarene University M
Parkland College M
Quincy University M,W
Rend Lake College M,W
Robert Morris University: Chicago M,W
Sauk Valley Community College M
Southern Illinois University Carbondale M,W
Southern Illinois University Edwardsville M,W
University of Illinois
  Springfield M,W
  Urbana-Champaign M,W
University of St. Francis M,W
Waubonsee Community College M
Western Illinois University M,W

Indiana
Ancilla College M,W
Ball State University M,W
Bethel College M
Butler University M,W
Calumet College of St. Joseph M,W
Goshen College M
Grace College M
Huntington University M
Indiana Institute of Technology M,W
Indiana State University W
Indiana University
  Bloomington M,W
Indiana University-Purdue University Fort
  Wayne M,W
Indiana University-Purdue University
  Indianapolis M,W
Indiana Wesleyan University M
Marian University M,W
Oakland City University M,W
Purdue University M,W
Saint Joseph's College M,W
St. Mary-of-the-Woods College W
Taylor University M
University of Evansville M,W
University of Indianapolis M,W
University of Notre Dame M,W
University of St. Francis M,W
University of Southern Indiana M,W
Vincennes University M

Iowa
AIB College of Business M,W
Briar Cliff University M,W
Clarke College M,W
Dordt College M,W
Drake University M,W
Ellsworth Community College M,W
Graceland University M,W
Grand View University M,W
Indian Hills Community College M
Iowa Central Community College M,W
Iowa Lakes Community College- Estherville
  M,W
Iowa State University M,W
Iowa Wesleyan College M,W
Kirkwood Community College M
Marshalltown Community College M,W
Morningside College M,W
Mount Mercy College M
North Iowa Area Community College M,W
Northwestern College M,W
St. Ambrose University M,W
Scott Community College M,W
Southeastern Community College
  North Campus M,W
Southwestern Community College M
University of Iowa M,W

University of Northern Iowa M,W
Waldorf College M,W
William Penn University M,W

Kansas
Allen County Community College M
Baker University M,W
Barton County Community College M,W
Benedictine College M,W
Bethany College M
Bethel College M,W
Central Christian College of Kansas M,W
Coffeyville Community College M,W
Colby Community College M,W
Dodge City Community College M,W
Friends University M
Hutchinson Community College M
Johnson County Community College M
Kansas City Kansas Community College M
Kansas State University M,W
Kansas Wesleyan University M,W
Newman University M,W
Ottawa University M
Pittsburg State University M
Southwestern College M,W
Sterling College M,W
University of Kansas M,W
Washburn University M
Wichita State University M,W

Kentucky
Bellarmine University M,W
Brescia University M,W
Campbellsville University M,W
Eastern Kentucky University M,W
Georgetown College M,W
Kentucky State University M
Kentucky Wesleyan College M,W
Lindsey Wilson College M,W
Morehead State University M
Murray State University M,W
Northern Kentucky University M,W
Pikeville College M,W
St. Catharine College M,W
Union College M
University of Kentucky M,W
University of Louisville M,W
University of the Cumberlands M,W
Western Kentucky University M,W

Louisiana
Centenary College of Louisiana M,W
Grambling State University M
Louisiana State University and Agricultural and
    Mechanical College M,W
Louisiana Tech University M
McNeese State University M,W
Nicholls State University M,W
Southeastern Louisiana University M
Southern University and Agricultural and
    Mechanical College M
Tulane University W
University of Louisiana at Lafayette M
University of Louisiana at Monroe M
University of New Orleans M

Maryland
College of Southern Maryland M,W
Coppin State University M
Harford Community College M
Loyola University Maryland M
Mount St. Mary's University M,W
Towson University M
University of Maryland
    College Park M,W

Massachusetts
Boston College M,W

Michigan
Aquinas College M,W
Cornerstone University M,W
Davenport University M,W

Delta College M,W
Eastern Michigan University M,W
Ferris State University M,W
Grand Rapids Community College M
Grand Valley State University M,W
Kalamazoo Valley Community College M
Kirtland Community College M,W
Lake Superior State University M,W
Lansing Community College M
Madonna University M,W
Michigan State University M,W
Mott Community College M
Muskegon Community College M
Northern Michigan University M
Northwood University: Michigan M,W
Oakland Community College M
Oakland University M,W
Saginaw Valley State University M
Siena Heights University M,W
Spring Arbor University M
University of Detroit Mercy M,W
University of Michigan M,W
Wayne State University M
Western Michigan University W

Minnesota
Concordia University: St. Paul M,W
Minnesota State University
    Mankato M,W
    Moorhead W
Saint Cloud State University M,W
Southwest Minnesota State University W
University of Minnesota
    Crookston M,W
    Twin Cities M,W
Winona State University M,W

Mississippi
Alcorn State University M,W
Belhaven University M,W
Copiah-Lincoln Community College M
Delta State University M
East Mississippi Community College M,W
Jackson State University M,W
Meridian Community College M
Mississippi Gulf Coast Community College M
Mississippi State University M,W
Mississippi Valley State University M,W
Northwest Mississippi Community College M
University of Mississippi M,W
University of Southern Mississippi M,W

Missouri
Avila University W
Central Methodist University M,W
Culver-Stockton College M,W
Drury University M,W
Evangel University M,W
Hannibal-LaGrange College M,W
Lincoln University M,W
Metropolitan Community College: Penn Valley
    M
Missouri Baptist University M,W
Missouri Southern State University M
Missouri State University M,W
Missouri Valley College M,W
Missouri Western State University M
Northwest Missouri State University W
Park University W
Research College of Nursing M,W
Rockhurst University M,W
Southwest Baptist University M
Truman State University M,W
University of Central Missouri M
University of Missouri
    Columbia M,W
    Kansas City M,W
    St. Louis M,W
William Jewell College M,W
William Woods University M,W

Montana
Miles Community College M,W

Montana State University
    Billings M,W
    Bozeman W
Montana Tech of the University of Montana
    M,W
Rocky Mountain College M,W
University of Great Falls M,W
University of Montana W
University of Montana: Western M,W

Nebraska
Chadron State College W
Concordia University M,W
Creighton University M,W
Dana College W
Doane College M,W
Mid-Plains Community College Area M
Nebraska College of Technical Agriculture M,W
Peru State College W
University of Nebraska
    Kearney M,W
    Lincoln M,W
Wayne State College M,W

Nevada
University of Nevada
    Las Vegas M,W
    Reno M,W

New Hampshire
Franklin Pierce University M

New Jersey
Brookdale Community College M
Caldwell College M
Fairleigh Dickinson University
    Metropolitan Campus M,W
Monmouth University M,W
Rider University M
Rutgers, The State University of New Jersey
    New Brunswick/Piscataway Campus M,W
Saint Peter's College M
Salem Community College M
Seton Hall University M,W

New Mexico
New Mexico Junior College M
New Mexico Military Institute M
New Mexico State University M
University of New Mexico M,W
University of the Southwest M,W
Western New Mexico University M,W

New York
Adelphi University M
Canisius University M
College of Saint Rose M
Daemen College M
Dominican College of Blauvelt M
Dowling College M
Hofstra University M,W
Iona College M
Le Moyne College M,W
Long Island University
    Brooklyn Campus M,W
Manhattan College M
Niagara University M
Nyack College M
Pace University M
Saint Bonaventure University M
St. John's University M,W
St. Thomas Aquinas College M,W
Siena College M,W
State University of New York
    Albany W
    Binghamton M
Wagner College M,W

North Carolina
Appalachian State University M,W
Barton College M
Belmont Abbey College M
Brevard College M

Campbell University M,W
Catawba College M,W
Chowan University M
Davidson College M
Duke University M,W
East Carolina University M,W
Elon University M,W
Fayetteville State University M
Gardner-Webb University M,W
High Point University M,W
Johnson C. Smith University M
Johnston Community College M
Lees-McRae College M
Lenoir-Rhyne University M,W
Mars Hill College M
Montreat College M
Mount Olive College M
North Carolina Central University M,W
North Carolina State University M,W
Pfeiffer University M,W
Pitt Community College M
Queens University of Charlotte M,W
St. Andrews Presbyterian College M
St. Augustine's College M,W
University of North Carolina
    Chapel Hill M,W
    Charlotte M
    Greensboro M,W
    Pembroke M,W
    Wilmington M,W
Wake Forest University M,W
Western Carolina University M,W
Wingate University M,W

North Dakota
Dickinson State University M,W
Jamestown College M,W
Minot State University M,W
North Dakota State University W
University of Mary W
University of North Dakota M,W

Ohio
Ashland University M,W
Bowling Green State University M,W
Cedarville University M
Central State University M,W
Cleveland State University M,W
Kent State University M,W
Malone University M,W
Miami University
    Oxford Campus M
Mount Vernon Nazarene University M
Notre Dame College M,W
Ohio Dominican University M,W
Ohio University M,W
Shawnee State University M
Tiffin University M,W
University of Akron M
University of Cincinnati M,W
University of Dayton M,W
University of Findlay M,W
University of Toledo M,W
Urbana University M
Ursuline College W
Walsh University M,W
Wright State University M
Xavier University M,W
Youngstown State University M,W

Oklahoma
Bacone College M,W
Cameron University M,W
East Central University M,W
Northeastern State University M,W
Northwestern Oklahoma State University M,W
Oklahoma Baptist University M,W
Oklahoma Christian University M
Oklahoma City University M,W
Oklahoma Panhandle State University M,W
Oklahoma State University M,W
Oklahoma Wesleyan University M

Oral Roberts University M,W
Redlands Community College W
Rogers State University M,W
Seminole State College M,W
Southern Nazarene University M,W
Southwestern Oklahoma State University M,W
University of Central Oklahoma M,W
University of Oklahoma M,W
University of Tulsa M,W

Oregon
Concordia University M,W
Corban College M,W
Northwest Christian University M,W
Oregon State University M,W
Portland State University M,W
Southwestern Oregon Community College M,W
Treasure Valley Community College M,W
University of Oregon M,W
University of Portland M,W
Warner Pacific College M,W

Pennsylvania
California University of Pennsylvania M,W
Chestnut Hill College M,W
Clarion University of Pennsylvania M
Drexel University M
Duquesne University M
Gannon University M,W
Holy Family University M
Indiana University of Pennsylvania M
Kutztown University of Pennsylvania W
La Salle University M,W
Lackawanna College M,W
Mercyhurst College M,W
Millersville University of Pennsylvania M
Penn State
    University Park M,W
Philadelphia University M
Robert Morris University M,W
St. Francis University M,W
Saint Joseph's University M
Seton Hill University M,W
Temple University M
University of the Sciences in Philadelphia M,W
West Chester University of Pennsylvania M,W

Rhode Island
Bryant University M
University of Rhode Island M

South Carolina
Anderson University M,W
Charleston Southern University M,W
The Citadel W
Clemson University M
Coastal Carolina University M,W
Coker College M
College of Charleston M,W
Erskine College M,W
Francis Marion University M
Furman University M,W
Lander University M
Limestone College M,W
Morris College M
Newberry College M,W
North Greenville University M,W
Presbyterian College M,W
South Carolina State University M,W
Southern Wesleyan University M
Spartanburg Methodist College M,W
University of South Carolina M,W
University of South Carolina
    Aiken M
Winthrop University M,W
Wofford College M,W

South Dakota
Augustana College M,W
Dakota Wesleyan University M,W
Mount Marty College M,W
Northern State University W

South Dakota School of Mines and Technology M,W
South Dakota State University M,W
University of Sioux Falls M,W

Tennessee
Austin Peay State University M,W
Belmont University M,W
Bethel University M,W
Carson-Newman College M
Christian Brothers University M,W
Cumberland University M,W
East Tennessee State University M,W
King College M,W
Lambuth University M,W
Lee University M
LeMoyne-Owen College M,W
Lincoln Memorial University M,W
Lipscomb University M,W
Martin Methodist College M,W
Middle Tennessee State University M,W
Milligan College M
Tennessee Technological University M,W
Tennessee Wesleyan College M,W
Trevecca Nazarene University M,W
Tusculum College M,W
Union University M
University of Memphis M,W
University of Tennessee
    Chattanooga M,W
    Knoxville M,W
    Martin M
Vanderbilt University M,W
Walters State Community College M,W

Texas
Abilene Christian University M
Baylor University M,W
Dallas Baptist University W
Hill College M
Houston Baptist University M,W
Lamar University M,W
Lon Morris College M
Lubbock Christian University M,W
McLennan Community College M
Midland College M
Northwood University: Texas M,W
Odessa College M
Paris Junior College M
Prairie View A&M University M,W
Ranger College M,W
Rice University M
St. Edward's University M,W
St. Mary's University M
Sam Houston State University M,W
Southern Methodist University M,W
Stephen F. Austin State University M,W
Tarleton State University W
Texas A&M University M,W
Texas A&M University
    Commerce M
    Corpus Christi W
Texas Christian University M,W
Texas Southern University M,W
Texas State University: San Marcos M,W
Texas Tech University M,W
Texas Wesleyan University M
Tyler Junior College M,W
University of Houston M
University of North Texas M,W
University of Texas
    Arlington M
    Austin M,W
    Brownsville - Texas Southmost College M,W
    Pan American M,W
    San Antonio M,W
University of the Incarnate Word M,W
Wayland Baptist University M,W
West Texas A&M University M,W

Utah
Brigham Young University M,W
Dixie State College of Utah M
Southern Utah University M
University of Utah M
Utah State University M
Utah Valley University M,W
Weber State University M,W

Virginia
Bluefield College M
College of William and Mary M,W
George Mason University M
Hampton University M,W
James Madison University M,W
Liberty University M
Longwood University M,W
Old Dominion University M,W
Radford University M,W
St. Paul's College M
University of Richmond M,W
University of Virginia M,W
Virginia Commonwealth University M
Virginia Intermont College M
Virginia Military Institute M
Virginia Polytechnic Institute and State University M
Virginia State University M,W
Virginia Union University M,W

Washington
Centralia College W
Eastern Washington University W
Gonzaga University M,W
Grays Harbor College M,W
Green River Community College M
Olympic College M,W
Saint Martin's University M,W
Seattle University M,W
Skagit Valley College M,W
Spokane Community College M,W
University of Washington M,W
Washington State University M,W
Western Washington University M,W

West Virginia
Bluefield State College M
Concord University M
Davis and Elkins College M
Glenville State College M,W
Marshall University M,W
Ohio Valley University M,W
Salem International University M,W
University of Charleston M
West Liberty University M,W
West Virginia University Institute of Technology M
West Virginia Wesleyan College M,W
Wheeling Jesuit University M,W

Wisconsin
Marquette University M
Silver Lake College M,W
University of Wisconsin
    Green Bay M,W
    Parkside M
Viterbo University M,W

Wyoming
Eastern Wyoming College M,W
University of Wyoming M,W

Gymnastics

Alabama
Auburn University W
University of Alabama W

Alaska
University of Alaska
    Anchorage W

Arizona
Arizona State University W
University of Arizona W

Arkansas
University of Arkansas W

California
California State University
    Fullerton W
    Sacramento W
San Jose State University W
Stanford University M,W
University of California
    Berkeley M,W
    Davis W
    Los Angeles W
    Santa Barbara W

Colorado
University of Denver W

Connecticut
Southern Connecticut State University W
University of Bridgeport W

District of Columbia
George Washington University W
Howard University M,W

Florida
University of Florida W

Georgia
University of Georgia W

Idaho
Boise State University W

Illinois
Illinois State University W
University of Illinois
    Chicago M,W
    Urbana-Champaign M,W

Indiana
Ball State University W

Iowa
Iowa State University W
University of Iowa M,W

Kansas
Fort Hays State University M

Kentucky
University of Kentucky W

Louisiana
Centenary College of Louisiana W
Louisiana State University and Agricultural and Mechanical College W

Maryland
Towson University W
University of Maryland
    College Park W
Washington Adventist University M,W

Michigan
Central Michigan University W
Eastern Michigan University W
Michigan State University W
University of Michigan M,W
Western Michigan University W

Minnesota
University of Minnesota
    Twin Cities M,W

Missouri
Southeast Missouri State University W
University of Missouri
    Columbia W

Nebraska
University of Nebraska
        Lincoln M,W

New Hampshire
University of New Hampshire W

New Jersey
Rutgers, The State University of New Jersey
        New Brunswick/Piscataway Campus W

North Carolina
North Carolina State University W
University of North Carolina
        Chapel Hill W

Ohio
Bowling Green State University W
Kent State University W

Oklahoma
University of Oklahoma M,W

Oregon
Oregon State University W
University of Oregon W

Pennsylvania
Penn State
        University Park M,W
Temple University M,W
University of Pittsburgh W
West Chester University of Pennsylvania W

Tennessee
Southern Adventist University M,W

Texas
Texas Woman's University W

Utah
Brigham Young University W
Southern Utah University W
University of Utah W
Utah State University W

Virginia
College of William and Mary M,W

Washington
Seattle Pacific University W
University of Washington W

West Virginia
West Virginia University W

Ice hockey

Alabama
University of Alabama
        Huntsville M

Alaska
University of Alaska
        Anchorage M
        Fairbanks M

Colorado
Colorado College M
University of Denver M

Connecticut
Quinnipiac University M,W
Sacred Heart University M,W
University of Connecticut M,W

Illinois
McKendree University M,W

Indiana
University of Notre Dame M

Maine
University of Maine M,W

Massachusetts
American International College M
Bentley University M
Boston College M,W
Boston University M,W
College of the Holy Cross M
Merrimack College M
Northeastern University M,W
University of Massachusetts
        Amherst M
        Lowell M

Michigan
Davenport University M
Ferris State University M
Lake Superior State University M
Michigan State University M
Michigan Technological University M
Northern Michigan University M
University of Michigan M
Wayne State University W
Western Michigan University M

Minnesota
Bemidji State University M,W
Minnesota State University
        Mankato M,W
Saint Cloud State University M,W
University of Minnesota
        Duluth M,W
        Twin Cities M,W

Nebraska
University of Nebraska
        Omaha M

New Hampshire
New England College M,W
University of New Hampshire M,W

New York
Canisius College M
Clarkson University M,W
Colgate University M,W
Monroe Community College M
Niagara University M,W
Rensselaer Polytechnic Institute M,W
St. Lawrence University M,W
Syracuse University W

North Dakota
Dakota College at Bottineau M
University of North Dakota M,W

Ohio
Bowling Green State University M
Miami University
        Oxford Campus M

Pennsylvania
Mercyhurst College M,W
Robert Morris University M,W

Rhode Island
Providence College M,W

Vermont
University of Vermont M,W

Judo

Puerto Rico
Inter American University of Puerto Rico
        Aguadilla Campus M,W
        Ponce Campus M,W
Turabo University W
Universidad Metropolitana M,W
University of Puerto Rico
        Humacao M,W

Lacrosse

California
Dominican University of California M
Notre Dame de Namur University M
Stanford University M
University of California
        Davis W

Colorado
Fort Lewis College W
Mesa State College M,W
Regis University W
University of Denver M,W

Connecticut
Central Connecticut State University W
Fairfield University M,W
Quinnipiac University M,W
Sacred Heart University M,W
Southern Connecticut State University W
University of Bridgeport W
University of Hartford M
University of New Haven W

Delaware
Delaware Technical and Community College
        Terry M
University of Delaware M,W
Wilmington University W

District of Columbia
American University W
Georgetown University M,W

Florida
Florida Southern College M
Saint Leo University M
University of Florida W

Georgia
Mercer University M,W

Illinois
Northwestern University W

Indiana
Indiana Institute of Technology M,W
University of Notre Dame M,W

Kentucky
Bellarmine University M
University of Louisville W

Maryland
Anne Arundel Community College M,W
Community College of Baltimore County M,W
Harford Community College M,W
Johns Hopkins University M,W
Loyola University Maryland M,W
Mount St. Mary's University M,W
Towson University M,W
University of Maryland
        Baltimore County M,W
        College Park M,W

Massachusetts
American International College M,W
Boston College W
Boston University W
Dean College M,W
Stonehill College W
University of Massachusetts
        Amherst M,W

Michigan
Siena Heights University M,W
University of Detroit Mercy M,W

Minnesota
University of Minnesota
        Duluth M

New Hampshire
Franklin Pierce University M,W
Southern New Hampshire University M,W
University of New Hampshire W

New Jersey
Georgian Court University W
Monmouth University W
Rutgers, The State University of New Jersey
        New Brunswick/Piscataway Campus M,W

New York
Adelphi University M,W
Canisius College M,W
City University of New York
        Queens College W
Colgate University M,W
Dominican College of Blauvelt M,W
Dowling College M
Hofstra University M,W
Iona College W
Le Moyne College M,W
Long Island University
        Brooklyn Campus W
        C. W. Post Campus M,W
Manhattan College M,W
Marist College M,W
Mercy College M,W
Molloy College M,W
Monroe Community College M
New York Institute of Technology M
Niagara University W
Pace University M
St. John's University M
St. Thomas Aquinas College W
Siena College M,W
State University of New York
        Albany M,W
        Binghamton M,W
        Stony Brook M,W
Syracuse University M,W
Wagner College M,W

North Carolina
Catawba College M
Davidson College W
Duke University M
Lees-McRae College M,W
Lenoir-Rhyne University M
Mars Hill College M
Pfeiffer University M,W
Queens University of Charlotte M,W
St. Andrews Presbyterian College M
University of North Carolina
        Chapel Hill M,W
Wingate University M

Ohio
Notre Dame College W
Tiffin University W
University of Cincinnati W
Urbana University W
Walsh University M

Oregon
University of Oregon W

Pennsylvania
Bloomsburg University of Pennsylvania W
Chestnut Hill College W
Drexel University M,W
Duquesne University W
East Stroudsburg University of Pennsylvania W
Gannon University W
Holy Family University W
Indiana University of Pennsylvania W
Kutztown University of Pennsylvania W
La Salle University W
Lehigh University M,W
Lock Haven University of Pennsylvania W
Mercyhurst College M,W
Millersville University of Pennsylvania W

Penn State
University Park M,W
Philadelphia University W
Robert Morris University M,W
St. Francis University W
Saint Joseph's University M,W
Seton Hill University M,W
Shippensburg University of Pennsylvania W
Slippery Rock University of Pennsylvania W
Temple University W
West Chester University of Pennsylvania W

Rhode Island
Bryant University M,W

South Carolina
Erskine College W
Limestone College M,W
Presbyterian College M,W

Tennessee
Tennessee Wesleyan College M
Vanderbilt University W

Vermont
University of Vermont M,W

Virginia
College of William and Mary W
George Mason University W
James Madison University W
Longwood University W
Old Dominion University W
University of Richmond W
University of Virginia M,W
Virginia Military Institute M
Virginia Polytechnic Institute and State
University W

West Virginia
Shepherd University W
West Virginia Wesleyan College W
Wheeling Jesuit University M

Rifle

Alabama
Jacksonville State University M,W

Alaska
University of Alaska
Fairbanks M,W

California
University of San Francisco M,W

Georgia
Columbus State University M,W
Mercer University M
North Georgia College & State University M,W

Kentucky
Morehead State University M,W
Murray State University M,W
University of Kentucky M,W

Michigan
Hillsdale College M,W

Mississippi
University of Mississippi W

Nebraska
University of Nebraska
Lincoln W

Nevada
University of Nevada
Reno M,W

Ohio
University of Akron W

South Carolina
The Citadel M,W

Tennessee
Austin Peay State University W
Bethel University M,W
Tennessee Technological University M,W
University of Memphis M,W
University of Tennessee
Martin M,W

Texas
Texas Christian University W

Virginia
Virginia Military Institute M

West Virginia
West Virginia University M,W

Rodeo

Alabama
Troy University M,W
University of West Alabama M

Arizona
Central Arizona College M,W
Cochise College M
Dine College M,W

Arkansas
Southern Arkansas University M,W
University of Arkansas
Monticello M,W

Colorado
Northeastern Junior College M,W

Idaho
Boise State University M,W

Kansas
Coffeyville Community College M,W
Colby Community College M
Dodge City Community College M,W
Fort Hays State University M
Fort Scott Community College M,W
Garden City Community College M,W
Pratt Community College M,W

Kentucky
Murray State University M,W

Louisiana
McNeese State University M,W

Missouri
Missouri Valley College M,W
Northwest Missouri State University M,W

Montana
Dawson Community College M,W
Miles Community College M,W
Montana State University
Bozeman M,W
University of Montana M
University of Montana: Western M,W

Nebraska
Chadron State College M,W
Nebraska College of Technical Agriculture M,W

New Mexico
Eastern New Mexico University M,W
Navajo Technical College M,W
New Mexico Junior College M,W

North Dakota
Dickinson State University M

Oklahoma
Bacone College M,W
Eastern Oklahoma State College M,W
Northeastern Oklahoma Agricultural and
Mechanical College M,W
Northwestern Oklahoma State University M,W
Oklahoma Panhandle State University M,W
Rogers State University M,W
Southeastern Oklahoma State University M,W
Southwestern Oklahoma State University M,W

Oregon
Blue Mountain Community College M,W
Eastern Oregon University M,W
Treasure Valley Community College M,W

Tennessee
University of Tennessee
Martin M,W

Texas
Clarendon College M,W
Hill College M,W
Howard College M,W
North Central Texas College M
Northeast Texas Community College M,W
Odessa College M,W
Panola College M,W
Ranger College M,W
Sam Houston State University M,W
South Plains College M,W
Tarleton State University M,W
Vernon College M,W
Weatherford College M
Western Texas College M,W
Wharton County Junior College M,W

Utah
Southern Utah University M,W

Wyoming
Casper College M,W
Central Wyoming College M,W
Eastern Wyoming College M,W
Laramie County Community College M,W
Sheridan College M,W
University of Wyoming M,W

Rowing (crew)

Alabama
University of Alabama W

California
California State University
Sacramento W
Humboldt State University W
Loyola Marymount University W
San Diego State University W
Stanford University M,W
University of California
Berkeley M,W
Davis W
Los Angeles M,W
University of San Diego W
University of Southern California W

Connecticut
Fairfield University M,W

Delaware
University of Delaware W

District of Columbia
George Washington University M,W
Georgetown University M,W

Florida
Barry University W
Florida Institute of Technology W
Jacksonville University M,W

Nova Southeastern University W
University of Central Florida W
University of Miami W
University of Tampa W

Indiana
Indiana University
Bloomington W
University of Notre Dame W

Iowa
University of Iowa W

Kansas
Kansas State University W
University of Kansas W

Kentucky
University of Louisville W

Massachusetts
Boston College W
Boston University M,W
Northeastern University M,W
University of Massachusetts
Amherst W

Michigan
Eastern Michigan University W
Michigan State University W
University of Michigan W

Nebraska
Creighton University W

New Jersey
Rutgers, The State University of New Jersey
New Brunswick/Piscataway Campus M,W

New York
Dowling College M,W
Fordham University W
Marist College W
State University of New York
Buffalo W
Syracuse University M,W

North Carolina
Duke University W
University of North Carolina
Chapel Hill W

Ohio
University of Dayton W

Oklahoma
Oklahoma City University M,W
University of Oklahoma W
University of Tulsa W

Pennsylvania
Drexel University M,W
Duquesne University W
Mercyhurst College M,W
Philadelphia University M,W
Robert Morris University W
Saint Joseph's University M,W
Temple University M,W

Rhode Island
University of Rhode Island W

South Carolina
Clemson University W

Tennessee
University of Tennessee
Knoxville W

Texas
Southern Methodist University W
University of Texas
Austin W

Virginia
George Mason University W
Old Dominion University W
University of Virginia W

Washington
Gonzaga University W
University of Washington M,W
Washington State University W
Western Washington University M,W

West Virginia
University of Charleston W
West Virginia University W

Rugby

California
University of California
Berkeley M

Illinois
Eastern Illinois University W

Michigan
Davenport University M

Ohio
Ohio State University
Marion Campus M,W

Pennsylvania
West Chester University of Pennsylvania W

Sailing

California
California State University
Monterey Bay M,W

Skiing

Alaska
University of Alaska
Anchorage M,W
Fairbanks M,W

Colorado
Colorado Mountain College M,W
University of Colorado
Boulder M,W
University of Denver M,W
Western State College of Colorado M,W

Idaho
College of Idaho M,W

Michigan
Michigan Technological University M,W
Northern Michigan University M,W

Minnesota
Saint Cloud State University W
University of Minnesota
Twin Cities M,W

Montana
Montana State University
Bozeman W
Rocky Mountain College M,W

Nevada
Sierra Nevada College M,W

New Hampshire
University of New Hampshire M,W

New Mexico
University of New Mexico M,W

Tennessee
Carson-Newman College M,W

Utah
University of Utah M,W

Vermont
University of Vermont M,W

West Virginia
Davis and Elkins College M,W

Wisconsin
University of Wisconsin
Green Bay M,W

Soccer

Alabama
Auburn University W
Auburn University at Montgomery M,W
Judson College W
Samford University W
Shelton State Community College W
Spring Hill College M,W
Troy University W
University of Alabama W
University of Alabama
Birmingham M,W
Huntsville M,W
University of Mobile M,W
University of Montevallo M,W
University of North Alabama W
University of South Alabama W
Wallace State Community College at Hanceville M

Arizona
Arizona State University W
Arizona Western College M
Chandler-Gilbert Community College
Pecos M,W
Cochise College W
Embry-Riddle Aeronautical University: Prescott Campus M,W
GateWay Community College M
Glendale Community College M,W
Grand Canyon University M,W
Mesa Community College M
Northern Arizona University W
Paradise Valley Community College M,W
Pima Community College M,W
Scottsdale Community College M
University of Arizona W

Arkansas
Arkansas State University W
Harding University M,W
John Brown University M,W
Lyon College M,W
Ouachita Baptist University M,W
University of Arkansas W
University of Arkansas
Little Rock M,W
Pine Bluff W
University of Central Arkansas M,W
Williams Baptist College M

California
Azusa Pacific University M,W
Bethany University M,W
Biola University M,W
California Baptist University M,W
California Polytechnic State University: San Luis Obispo M,W
California State Polytechnic University: Pomona M,W
California State University
Bakersfield M,W
Chico M,W
Dominguez Hills M,W

Fresno W
Fullerton M,W
Los Angeles M,W
Monterey Bay M,W
Northridge M
Sacramento M,W
San Bernardino M,W
Stanislaus M,W
Concordia University M,W
Dominican University of California M,W
Fresno City College M,W
Fresno Pacific University M,W
Grossmont College W
Holy Names University M,W
Hope International University M,W
Humboldt State University M,W
Loyola Marymount University M,W
The Master's College M,W
Notre Dame de Namur University M,W
Pepperdine University W
Point Loma Nazarene University M,W
St. Mary's College of California M,W
San Diego Christian College M,W
San Diego State University M,W
San Jose State University M,W
Santa Clara University M,W
Santiago Canyon College M,W
Sonoma State University M,W
Stanford University M,W
University of California
Berkeley M,W
Davis M,W
Irvine M,W
Los Angeles M,W
Santa Barbara M,W
University of San Diego M,W
University of San Francisco M,W
University of Southern California W
University of the Pacific W
Vanguard University of Southern California M,W
Westmont College M,W
William Jessup University M,W
Yuba Community College District M,W

Colorado
Adams State College M,W
Colorado Christian University M,W
Colorado College W
Colorado School of Mines M,W
Colorado State University
Pueblo M,W
Fort Lewis College M,W
Mesa State College M,W
Metropolitan State College of Denver M,W
Otero Junior College M
Regis University M,W
University of Colorado
Boulder W
Colorado Springs M
University of Denver M,W
University of Northern Colorado W

Connecticut
Central Connecticut State University M,W
Fairfield University M,W
Post University M,W
Quinnipiac University M,W
Sacred Heart University M,W
Southern Connecticut State University M,W
University of Bridgeport M,W
University of Connecticut M,W
University of Hartford M,W
University of New Haven M,W

Delaware
Delaware State University W
Delaware Technical and Community College
Stanton/Wilmington M
Terry M
Goldey-Beacom College M,W
University of Delaware M,W

Wilmington University M,W

District of Columbia
American University M,W
George Washington University M,W
Georgetown University M,W
Howard University M

Florida
Ave Maria University M,W
Barry University M,W
Eckerd College M,W
Embry-Riddle Aeronautical University M,W
Flagler College M,W
Florida Atlantic University M,W
Florida College M,W
Florida Institute of Technology M,W
Florida Southern College M,W
Florida State University W
Jacksonville University M,W
Lynn University M,W
Northwood University
Florida M,W
Nova Southeastern University M,W
Polk State College W
Rollins College M,W
Saint Leo University M,W
Saint Thomas University M,W
Southeastern University M,W
Stetson University M,W
University of Central Florida M,W
University of Florida W
University of Miami W
University of North Florida M,W
University of South Florida M,W
University of Tampa M,W
University of West Florida M,W
Warner University M,W
Webber International University M,W

Georgia
Abraham Baldwin Agricultural College W
Andrew College M,W
Brenau University W
Brewton-Parker College M,W
Clayton State University M,W
Columbus State University W
Covenant College M,W
Darton College M,W
Emmanuel College M,W
Georgia College and State University W
Georgia Military College M,W
Georgia Perimeter College M,W
Georgia Southern University M,W
Georgia Southwestern State University M,W
Georgia State University M,W
Gordon College M,W
Kennesaw State University W
Mercer University M,W
Middle Georgia College M,W
North Georgia College & State University M,W
Reinhardt College M,W
Shorter College M,W
Southern Polytechnic State University M
Truett-McConnell College M,W
University of Georgia W
University of West Georgia W
Young Harris College M,W

Hawaii
Hawaii Pacific University M,W
University of Hawaii
Manoa W

Idaho
Boise State University W
College of Idaho M,W
Idaho State University W
Northwest Nazarene University W
University of Idaho W

Illinois
Bradley University M
College of Lake County M,W
Danville Area Community College M
DePaul University M,W
Eastern Illinois University M,W
Elgin Community College M,W
Illinois Central College M,W
Illinois Institute of Technology M,W
Illinois State University W
Judson University M,W
Kankakee Community College M
Kaskaskia College M,W
Kishwaukee College M
Lewis and Clark Community College M,W
Lewis University M,W
Lincoln College M,W
Lincoln Land Community College M
Loyola University Chicago M,W
McHenry County College M
McKendree University M,W
Moraine Valley Community College M,W
Morton College M
Northwestern University M,W
Olivet Nazarene University M,W
Parkland College M,W
Quincy University M,W
Robert Morris University: Chicago M,W
Saint Xavier University M,W
South Suburban College of Cook County M
Southern Illinois University Edwardsville M,W
Southwestern Illinois College M
Trinity Christian College M,W
Trinity International University M,W
University of Illinois
    Chicago M
    Springfield M,W
    Urbana-Champaign W
University of St. Francis M,W
Waubonsee Community College W
Western Illinois University M,W

Indiana
Ancilla College M
Bethel College M,W
Butler University M,W
Calumet College of St. Joseph M,W
Goshen College M,W
Grace College M,W
Huntington University M,W
Indiana Institute of Technology M,W
Indiana State University W
Indiana University
    Bloomington M,W
Indiana University-Purdue University Fort
    Wayne M,W
Indiana University-Purdue University
    Indianapolis M,W
Indiana Wesleyan University M,W
Marian University M,W
Oakland City University M,W
Purdue University W
Saint Joseph's College M,W
St. Mary-of-the-Woods College W
Taylor University M,W
University of Evansville M,W
University of Indianapolis M,W
University of Notre Dame M,W
University of St. Francis M,W
University of Southern Indiana M,W
Valparaiso University M,W

Iowa
Briar Cliff University M,W
Clarke College M,W
Dordt College M,W
Drake University M,W
Graceland University M,W
Grand View University M,W
Iowa Central Community College M,W
Iowa State University W
Iowa Wesleyan College M,W

Kirkwood Community College M
Morningside College M,W
Mount Mercy College M,W
North Iowa Area Community College M
Northwestern College M,W
St. Ambrose University M,W
Scott Community College M,W
University of Iowa W
University of Northern Iowa W
Waldorf College M,W
William Penn University M,W

Kansas
Allen County Community College M,W
Baker University M,W
Barton County Community College M,W
Benedictine College M,W
Bethany College M,W
Bethel College M,W
Butler Community College W
Central Christian College of Kansas M,W
Cloud County Community College M,W
Coffeyville Community College M,W
Emporia State University W
Friends University M,W
Garden City Community College M,W
Hesston College M
Hutchinson Community College W
Johnson County Community College M
Kansas City Kansas Community College M
Kansas Wesleyan University M,W
MidAmerica Nazarene University M,W
Neosho County Community College M,W
Newman University M,W
Ottawa University M,W
Southwestern College M,W
Sterling College M,W
Tabor College M,W
University of Kansas W
University of St. Mary M,W
Washburn University W

Kentucky
Asbury College M,W
Bellarmine University M,W
Brescia University M,W
Campbellsville University M,W
Georgetown College M,W
Kentucky Wesleyan College M,W
Lindsey Wilson College M,W
Mid-Continent University M
Midway College W
Morehead State University W
Murray State University W
Northern Kentucky University M,W
Pikeville College M,W
St. Catharine College M,W
Union College M,W
University of Kentucky M,W
University of Louisville M,W
University of the Cumberlands M,W

Louisiana
Centenary College of Louisiana M,W
Louisiana College M
Louisiana State University and Agricultural and
    Mechanical College W
McNeese State University W
Nicholls State University W
Northwestern State University W
Southeastern Louisiana University W
Southern University and Agricultural and
    Mechanical College W
University of Louisiana at Lafayette W
University of Louisiana at Monroe W

Maine
University of Maine M,W
University of Maine
    Augusta W

Maryland
Anne Arundel Community College W
Chesapeake College M,W
College of Southern Maryland M,W
Community College of Baltimore County M,W
Hagerstown Community College M,W
Harford Community College M,W
Loyola University Maryland M,W
Mount St. Mary's University M,W
Towson University M,W
University of Maryland
    Baltimore County M,W
    College Park M,W
    Eastern Shore M
Washington Adventist University M,W

Massachusetts
American International College W
Boston College M,W
Boston University M,W
College of the Holy Cross M,W
Dean College M,W
Massasoit Community College M
Merrimack College W
Northeastern University M,W
Stonehill College M,W
University of Massachusetts
    Amherst M,W
    Lowell M,W

Michigan
Aquinas College M,W
Central Michigan University W
Cornerstone University M,W
Davenport University M,W
Delta College M
Eastern Michigan University W
Grand Rapids Community College W
Grand Valley State University W
Kellogg Community College M
Madonna University M,W
Michigan State University M,W
Northern Michigan University W
Northwood University: Michigan M,W
Oakland University M,W
Rochester College M,W
Saginaw Valley State University M,W
Siena Heights University M,W
Southwestern Michigan College M,W
Spring Arbor University M,W
University of Detroit Mercy M,W
University of Michigan M,W
Western Michigan University M,W

Minnesota
Bemidji State University W
Concordia University: St. Paul W
Minnesota State University
    Mankato W
    Moorhead W
Saint Cloud State University W
Southwest Minnesota State University W
University of Minnesota
    Crookston W
    Duluth W
    Twin Cities W
Winona State University W

Mississippi
Alcorn State University W
Belhaven University M,W
Delta State University M,W
East Mississippi Community College M
Hinds Community College M
Holmes Community College M
Meridian Community College M
Mississippi State University W
Northwest Mississippi Community College M,W
Southwest Mississippi Community College
    M,W
University of Mississippi W
University of Southern Mississippi W

Missouri
Avila University M,W
Central Methodist University M,W
Columbia College M
Culver-Stockton College M,W
Drury University M,W
East Central College M
Hannibal-LaGrange College M,W
Harris-Stowe State University M,W
Jefferson College M
Missouri Baptist University M,W
Missouri Southern State University M,W
Missouri State University M,W
Missouri Valley College M,W
Northwest Missouri State University W
Park University M,W
Research College of Nursing M,W
Rockhurst University M,W
St. Charles Community College M,W
Saint Louis University M,W
Southeast Missouri State University W
Southwest Baptist University W
St. Louis Community College
    Meramec M,W
Truman State University M,W
University of Central Missouri W
University of Missouri
    Columbia W
    Kansas City M
    Missouri University of Science and
        Technology M,W
    St. Louis M,W
William Jewell College M,W
William Woods University M,W

Montana
Flathead Valley Community College M,W
Montana State University
    Billings M,W
Rocky Mountain College M,W
University of Great Falls W
University of Montana W

Nebraska
Bellevue University M,W
College of Saint Mary W
Concordia University M,W
Creighton University M,W
Dana College M,W
Doane College M,W
Wayne State College W
Western Nebraska Community College M,W
York College M,W

Nevada
University of Nevada
    Las Vegas M,W
    Reno W

New Hampshire
Franklin Pierce University M,W
Southern New Hampshire University M,W
University of New Hampshire M,W

New Jersey
Bloomfield College M,W
Burlington County College M,W
Caldwell College M,W
Essex County College M
Fairleigh Dickinson University
    Metropolitan Campus M,W
Felician College M,W
Georgian Court University W
Mercer County Community College M,W
Monmouth University M,W
New Jersey Institute of Technology M,W
Rider University M,W
Rutgers, The State University of New Jersey
    New Brunswick/Piscataway Campus M,W
Saint Peter's College W
Salem Community College W
Seton Hall University M,W

Sussex County Community College W

New Mexico
Eastern New Mexico University M,W
New Mexico Highlands University W
University of New Mexico M,W
University of the Southwest M,W

New York
Adelphi University M,W
ASA Institute of Business and Computer
    Technology M
Bryant & Stratton Business Institute
        Bryant & Stratton College: Syracuse M,W
Canisius College M,W
City University of New York
        Queens College M,W
Colgate University M,W
College of Saint Rose M,W
Concordia College M,W
Daemen College M,W
Dominican College of Blauvelt M,W
Dowling College M
Fordham University M,W
Globe Institute of Technology M,W
Hartwick College M
Hofstra University M,W
Houghton College M,W
Iona College M,W
Jamestown Community College M
Le Moyne College M,W
Long Island University
        Brooklyn Campus M,W
        C. W. Post Campus M,W
Manhattan College M,W
Marist College M,W
Mercy College M,W
Molloy College M,W
Monroe Community College M,W
New York Institute of Technology M,W
Niagara University M,W
Nyack College M,W
Pace University W
Roberts Wesleyan College M,W
Saint Bonaventure University M,W
St. Francis College M
St. John's University M,W
St. Thomas Aquinas College M,W
Siena College M,W
State University of New York
        Albany M,W
        Binghamton M,W
        Buffalo M,W
        College at Oneonta M
        Stony Brook M,W
Syracuse University M,W
Wagner College W

North Carolina
Appalachian State University M,W
Barton College M,W
Belmont Abbey College M,W
Brevard College M,W
Campbell University M,W
Catawba College M,W
Chowan University M,W
Davidson College M,W
Duke University M,W
East Carolina University W
Elon University M,W
Gardner-Webb University M,W
High Point University M,W
Lees-McRae College M,W
Lenoir-Rhyne University M,W
Louisburg College M,W
Mars Hill College M,W
Montreat College M,W
Mount Olive College M,W
North Carolina State University M,W
Pfeiffer University M,W
Queens University of Charlotte M,W
St. Andrews Presbyterian College M,W

University of North Carolina
    Asheville M,W
    Chapel Hill M,W
    Charlotte M,W
    Greensboro M,W
    Pembroke M,W
    Wilmington M,W
Wake Forest University M,W
Western Carolina University W
Wingate University M,W

North Dakota
Jamestown College M,W
North Dakota State University W
University of Mary M,W
University of North Dakota W

Ohio
Ashland University M,W
Bowling Green State University M,W
Bryant & Stratton College
    Eastlake M
Cedarville University M,W
Cincinnati State Technical and Community
    College M,W
Cleveland State University M,W
Kent State University W
Malone University M,W
Miami University
    Oxford Campus W
Mount Vernon Nazarene University M,W
Notre Dame College W
Ohio Dominican University M,W
Ohio University W
Shawnee State University M,W
Southern State Community College M
Tiffin University M,W
University of Akron M,W
University of Cincinnati M,W
University of Dayton M,W
University of Findlay M,W
University of Rio Grande M,W
University of Toledo W
Urbana University M,W
Ursuline College W
Walsh University M,W
Wright State University M
Xavier University M,W
Youngstown State University W

Oklahoma
Bacone College M,W
East Central University W
Northeastern Oklahoma Agricultural and
    Mechanical College M,W
Northeastern State University M,W
Northern Oklahoma College M,W
Northwestern Oklahoma State University W
Oklahoma Baptist University M,W
Oklahoma Christian University M,W
Oklahoma City University M,W
Oklahoma State University W
Oklahoma Wesleyan University M,W
Oral Roberts University M,W
Rogers State University M,W
St. Gregory's University M,W
Southern Nazarene University M,W
Southwestern Oklahoma State University M,W
University of Central Oklahoma W
University of Oklahoma W
University of Science and Arts of Oklahoma
    M,W
University of Tulsa M,W

Oregon
Concordia University M,W
Corban College M,W
Eastern Oregon University M,W
Northwest Christian University M,W
Oregon Institute of Technology W
Oregon State University M,W
Portland State University W
Southern Oregon University W

Southwestern Oregon Community College M,W
Treasure Valley Community College M,W
University of Oregon W
University of Portland M,W
Warner Pacific College M,W

Pennsylvania
Bloomsburg University of Pennsylvania M,W
California University of Pennsylvania M,W
Carlow University W
Chestnut Hill College W
Clarion University of Pennsylvania W
Drexel University M,W
Duquesne University M,W
East Stroudsburg University of Pennsylvania
    M,W
Edinboro University of Pennsylvania W
Gannon University M,W
Holy Family University M,W
Indiana University of Pennsylvania W
Kutztown University of Pennsylvania W
La Salle University W
Lackawanna College W
Lafayette College M
Lehigh University M,W
Lock Haven University of Pennsylvania M,W
Mercyhurst College M,W
Millersville University of Pennsylvania M,W
Penn State
    University Park M,W
Philadelphia University M,W
Point Park University M,W
Robert Morris University M,W
St. Francis University M,W
Saint Joseph's University M,W
Seton Hill University M,W
Shippensburg University of Pennsylvania M,W
Slippery Rock University of Pennsylvania M,W
Temple University M,W
University of Pittsburgh M,W
Villanova University M,W
West Chester University of Pennsylvania M,W

Puerto Rico
Inter American University of Puerto Rico
    Aguadilla Campus M
    Bayamon Campus M
    Guayama Campus M
    San German Campus M
Turabo University M
Universidad Metropolitana M,W
University of Puerto Rico
    Carolina Regional College M
    Cayey University College M
    Utuado M

Rhode Island
Bryant University M,W
Community College of Rhode Island M,W
Providence College M,W
University of Rhode Island M,W

South Carolina
Anderson University M,W
Charleston Southern University M,W
The Citadel W
Clemson University M,W
Coastal Carolina University M,W
Coker College M,W
College of Charleston M,W
Columbia College W
Converse College W
Erskine College M,W
Francis Marion University M,W
Furman University M,W
Lander University M,W
Limestone College M,W
Newberry College M,W
North Greenville University M,W
Presbyterian College M,W
South Carolina State University W
Southern Wesleyan University M,W
Spartanburg Methodist College M,W

University of South Carolina M,W
University of South Carolina
    Aiken M,W
    Upstate M,W
Winthrop University M,W
Wofford College M,W

South Dakota
Augustana College W
Dakota Wesleyan University M,W
Mount Marty College M,W
South Dakota State University W
University of Sioux Falls M,W
University of South Dakota W

Tennessee
Austin Peay State University W
Belmont University M,W
Bethel University M,W
Bryan College M,W
Carson-Newman College M,W
Christian Brothers University M,W
Cumberland University M,W
East Tennessee State University M,W
Freed-Hardeman University M,W
King College M,W
Lambuth University M,W
Lee University M,W
Lincoln Memorial University M,W
Lipscomb University M,W
Martin Methodist College M,W
Middle Tennessee State University W
Milligan College M,W
Tennessee Technological University W
Tennessee Temple University M
Tennessee Wesleyan College M,W
Trevecca Nazarene University M,W
Tusculum College M,W
Union University M,W
University of Memphis M,W
University of Tennessee
    Chattanooga W
    Knoxville W
    Martin W
Vanderbilt University W

Texas
Abilene Christian University W
Angelo State University W
Baylor University W
Cedar Valley College M
Dallas Baptist University W
Hill College M,W
Houston Baptist University M,W
Lon Morris College M,W
Midwestern State University M,W
Northwood University: Texas M,W
Prairie View A&M University W
Ranger College M,W
Rice University W
St. Edward's University W
St. Mary's University M,W
Sam Houston State University W
Southern Methodist University M,W
Stephen F. Austin State University W
Texas A&M University W
Texas A&M University
    Commerce W
    Corpus Christi W
Texas Christian University W
Texas Southern University W
Texas State University: San Marcos W
Texas Tech University W
Texas Woman's University W
Tyler Junior College M
University of Houston W
University of North Texas W
University of St. Thomas M
University of Texas
    Austin W
    Brownsville - Texas Southmost College
        M,W

of the Permian Basin M,W
  San Antonio W
University of the Incarnate Word M,W
Wayland Baptist University M,W
West Texas A&M University M,W

Utah
Brigham Young University W
Dixie State College of Utah M,W
University of Utah W
Utah State University W
Utah Valley University W
Westminster College M,W

Vermont
University of Vermont M,W

Virginia
Bluefield College M,W
College of William and Mary M,W
George Mason University M,W
James Madison University M,W
Liberty University M,W
Longwood University M,W
Old Dominion University M,W
Radford University M,W
University of Richmond M,W
University of Virginia M,W
Virginia Commonwealth University M,W
Virginia Intermont College W
Virginia Military Institute M
Virginia Polytechnic Institute and State
  University M,W

Washington
Clark College M,W
Eastern Washington University W
Everett Community College M,W
Evergreen State College M,W
Gonzaga University M,W
Green River Community College M
Highline Community College M,W
Lower Columbia College M,W
Northwest University M,W
Olympic College M,W
Peninsula College M
Pierce College M
Saint Martin's University M,W
Seattle Pacific University M
Seattle University M,W
Shoreline Community College M,W
Skagit Valley College M,W
Spokane Community College W
University of Washington M,W
Washington State University W
Western Washington University M,W
Whatcom Community College M,W
Yakima Valley Community College W

West Virginia
Alderson-Broaddus College M,W
Concord University W
Davis and Elkins College M,W
Marshall University M,W
Mountain State University M,W
Ohio Valley University M,W
Salem International University M,W
Shepherd University M,W
University of Charleston M,W
West Virginia University M,W
West Virginia Wesleyan College M,W
Wheeling Jesuit University M,W

Wisconsin
Cardinal Stritch University M,W
Marquette University M,W
Milwaukee Area Technical College M,W
University of Wisconsin
  Green Bay M,W
  Milwaukee M,W
  Parkside M,W
Viterbo University M,W

Wyoming
Central Wyoming College M,W
Laramie County Community College M,W
University of Wyoming W
Western Wyoming Community College M,W

Softball

Alabama
Alabama State University W
Auburn University W
Bevill State Community College W
Central Alabama Community College W
Chattahoochee Valley Community College W
Enterprise-Ozark Community College W
Faulkner State Community College W
Faulkner University W
Gadsden State Community College W
George C. Wallace State Community College
  George C. Wallace Community College at
    Dothan M
  Wallace State Community College at
    Selma W
Jacksonville State University W
Jefferson Davis Community College W
Jefferson State Community College W
Judson College W
Lurleen B. Wallace Community College W
Miles College W
Northwest-Shoals Community College W
Samford University W
Shelton State Community College W
Snead State Community College W
Southern Union State Community College W
Spring Hill College W
Troy University W
University of Alabama W
University of Alabama
  Birmingham W
  Huntsville W
University of Mobile W
University of North Alabama W
University of West Alabama W
Wallace State Community College at Hanceville
  W

Arizona
Arizona State University W
Arizona Western College W
Central Arizona College W
Chandler-Gilbert Community College
  Pecos W
Eastern Arizona College W
GateWay Community College W
Glendale Community College W
Mesa Community College W
Paradise Valley Community College W
Pima Community College W
Scottsdale Community College W
University of Arizona W

Arkansas
Henderson State University W
Lyon College W
North Arkansas College W
Ouachita Baptist University W
Southern Arkansas University W
University of Arkansas W
University of Arkansas
  Monticello W
  Pine Bluff W
University of Central Arkansas W
Williams Baptist College W

California
Azusa Pacific University W
Bethany University W
Biola University W
California Baptist University W
California Polytechnic State University: San Luis
  Obispo W

California State University
  Bakersfield W
  Chico W
  Dominguez Hills W
  Fresno W
  Fullerton W
  Long Beach W
  Monterey Bay W
  Northridge W
  Sacramento W
  San Bernardino W
  Stanislaus W
Concordia University W
Dominican University of California W
Fresno City College W
Grossmont College W
Holy Names University W
Hope International University W
Humboldt State University W
Loyola Marymount University W
Notre Dame de Namur University W
Patten University W
St. Mary's College of California W
San Diego State University W
San Jose State University W
Sonoma State University W
Stanford University W
University of California
  Berkeley W
  Davis W
  Los Angeles W
  Riverside W
  Santa Barbara W
University of San Diego W
University of the Pacific W
Vanguard University of Southern California W
William Jessup University W
Yuba Community College District W

Colorado
Adams State College W
Colorado Northwestern Community College W
Colorado School of Mines W
Colorado State University W
Colorado State University
  Pueblo W
Fort Lewis College W
Mesa State College W
Otero Junior College W
Regis University W
Trinidad State Junior College W
University of Colorado
  Colorado Springs W
University of Northern Colorado W

Connecticut
Central Connecticut State University W
Fairfield University W
Post University W
Quinnipiac University W
Sacred Heart University W
Southern Connecticut State University W
University of Bridgeport W
University of Connecticut W
University of New Haven W

Delaware
Delaware State University W
Delaware Technical and Community College
  Owens W
  Stanton/Wilmington W
  Terry W
Goldey-Beacom College W
University of Delaware W
Wilmington University W

Florida
Ave Maria University W
Barry University W
Bethune-Cookman University W
Brevard Community College W
Central Florida Community College W
Chipola College W

Daytona State College W
Eckerd College W
Edward Waters College W
Flagler College W
Florida Atlantic University W
Florida Gulf Coast University W
Florida Institute of Technology W
Florida Southern College W
Florida State College at Jacksonville W
Florida State University W
Gulf Coast Community College W
Hillsborough Community College W
Indian River State College W
Jacksonville University W
Lake-Sumter Community College W
Lynn University W
Miami Dade College W
North Florida Community College W
Northwest Florida State College W
Northwood University
  Florida W
Nova Southeastern University W
Palm Beach Community College W
Pasco-Hernando Community College W
Pensacola Junior College W
Polk State College W
Rollins College W
Saint Johns River Community College W
Saint Leo University W
St. Petersburg College W
Saint Thomas University W
Santa Fe College W
South Florida Community College W
State College of Florida, Manatee-Sarasota W
Stetson University W
Tallahassee Community College W
University of Central Florida W
University of Florida W
University of North Florida W
University of South Florida W
University of Tampa W
University of West Florida W
Warner University W
Webber International University W

Georgia
Abraham Baldwin Agricultural College W
Albany State University W
Andrew College W
Armstrong Atlantic State University W
Augusta State University W
Brenau University W
Brewton-Parker College W
Clark Atlanta University W
College of Coastal Georgia W
Columbus State University W
Covenant College W
Darton College W
Emmanuel College W
Georgia College and State University W
Georgia Institute of Technology W
Georgia Perimeter College W
Georgia Southern University W
Georgia Southwestern State University W
Georgia State University W
Gordon College W
Kennesaw State University W
Mercer University W
Middle Georgia College W
North Georgia College & State University W
Paine College W
Reinhardt College W
Shorter College W
South Georgia College W
Truett-McConnell College W
University of Georgia W
University of West Georgia W
Valdosta State University W
Young Harris College W

Hawaii
Chaminade University of Honolulu W
Hawaii Pacific University W
University of Hawaii
    Hilo W
    Manoa W

Idaho
Boise State University W
College of Idaho W
Idaho State University W
North Idaho College W
Northwest Nazarene University W

Illinois
Black Hawk College W
Bradley University W
Carl Sandburg College W
College of Lake County W
Danville Area Community College W
DePaul University W
Eastern Illinois University W
Elgin Community College W
Highland Community College W
Illinois Central College W
Illinois Eastern Community Colleges
    Lincoln Trail College W
    Olney Central College W
    Wabash Valley College W
Illinois State University W
John A. Logan College W
Judson University W
Kankakee Community College W
Kaskaskia College W
Kishwaukee College W
Lake Land College W
Lewis University W
Lincoln College W
Lincoln Land Community College W
Loyola University Chicago W
McHenry County College W
McKendree University W
Moraine Valley Community College W
Morton College W
Northwestern University W
Olivet Nazarene University W
Parkland College W
Quincy University W
Rend Lake College W
Robert Morris University: Chicago W
Saint Xavier University W
Sauk Valley Community College W
Shawnee Community College W
South Suburban College of Cook County W
Southeastern Illinois College W
Southern Illinois University Carbondale W
Southern Illinois University Edwardsville W
Southwestern Illinois College W
Spoon River College W
Trinity Christian College W
Trinity International University W
University of Illinois
    Chicago W
    Springfield W
    Urbana-Champaign W
University of St. Francis W
Waubonsee Community College W
Western Illinois University W

Indiana
Ancilla College W
Ball State University W
Bethel College W
Butler University W
Calumet College of St. Joseph W
Goshen College W
Grace College W
Huntington University W
Indiana Institute of Technology W
Indiana State University W
Indiana University
    Bloomington W

Indiana University-Purdue University Fort
    Wayne W
Indiana University-Purdue University
    Indianapolis W
Indiana Wesleyan University W
Marian University W
Oakland City University W
Purdue University W
Purdue University
    North Central W
Saint Joseph's College W
St. Mary-of-the-Woods College W
Taylor University W
University of Evansville W
University of Indianapolis W
University of Notre Dame W
University of St. Francis W
University of Southern Indiana W
Valparaiso University W

Iowa
Briar Cliff University W
Clarke College W
Dordt College W
Drake University W
Ellsworth Community College W
Graceland University W
Grand View University W
Indian Hills Community College W
Iowa Central Community College W
Iowa Lakes Community College- Estherville W
Iowa State University W
Iowa Wesleyan College W
Iowa Western Community College W
Kirkwood Community College W
Marshalltown Community College W
Morningside College W
Mount Mercy College W
Muscatine Community College W
North Iowa Area Community College W
Northwestern College W
St. Ambrose University W
Southeastern Community College
    North Campus W
Southwestern Community College W
University of Iowa W
University of Northern Iowa W
Waldorf College W
William Penn University W

Kansas
Allen County Community College W
Baker University W
Barton County Community College W
Benedictine College W
Bethany College W
Brown Mackie College
    Salina W
Butler Community College W
Central Christian College of Kansas W
Cloud County Community College W
Coffeyville Community College W
Colby Community College W
Cowley County Community College W
Dodge City Community College W
Emporia State University W
Fort Hays State University W
Fort Scott Community College W
Friends University W
Garden City Community College W
Highland Community College W
Hutchinson Community College W
Johnson County Community College W
Kansas City Kansas Community College W
Kansas Wesleyan University W
Labette Community College W
McPherson College W
MidAmerica Nazarene University W
Neosho County Community College W
Newman University W
Ottawa University W
Pittsburg State University W

Pratt Community College W
Seward County Community College W
Southwestern College W
Sterling College W
Tabor College W
University of Kansas W
University of St. Mary W
Washburn University W
Wichita State University W

Kentucky
Asbury College W
Bellarmine University W
Brescia University W
Campbellsville University W
Eastern Kentucky University W
Georgetown College W
Kentucky State University W
Kentucky Wesleyan College W
Lindsey Wilson College W
Mid-Continent University W
Midway College W
Morehead State University W
Murray State University M,W
Northern Kentucky University W
Pikeville College W
St. Catharine College W
Union College W
University of Kentucky W
University of Louisville M
University of the Cumberlands W
Western Kentucky University W

Louisiana
Bossier Parish Community College W
Centenary College of Louisiana W
Dillard University W
Louisiana State University and Agricultural and
    Mechanical College W
Louisiana Tech University W
McNeese State University W
Nicholls State University W
Northwestern State University W
Southeastern Louisiana University W
Southern University and Agricultural and
    Mechanical College W
University of Louisiana at Lafayette W
University of Louisiana at Monroe W

Maine
University of Maine W

Maryland
Bowie State University W
Chesapeake College W
College of Southern Maryland W
Community College of Baltimore County W
Coppin State University W
Hagerstown Community College W
Morgan State University W
Mount St. Mary's University W
Towson University W
University of Maryland
    Baltimore County W
    College Park W
    Eastern Shore W
Washington Adventist University W

Massachusetts
American International College W
Boston College W
Boston University W
Dean College W
Massasoit Community College W
Merrimack College W
Stonehill College W
University of Massachusetts
    Amherst W
    Lowell W

Michigan
Alpena Community College W
Aquinas College W

Central Michigan University W
Cornerstone University W
Davenport University W
Delta College W
Eastern Michigan University W
Ferris State University W
Glen Oaks Community College W
Grand Valley State University W
Henry Ford Community College W
Hillsdale College W
Kalamazoo Valley Community College W
Kellogg Community College W
Lake Michigan College W
Lake Superior State University W
Madonna University W
Michigan State University W
Mott Community College W
Muskegon Community College W
Northwood University: Michigan W
Oakland Community College W
Oakland University W
Rochester College W
Saginaw Valley State University W
Siena Heights University W
Spring Arbor University W
University of Detroit Mercy W
University of Michigan W
University of Michigan
    Dearborn W
Wayne State University W
Western Michigan University W

Minnesota
Bemidji State University W
Concordia University: St. Paul W
Minnesota State University
    Mankato W
    Moorhead W
Saint Cloud State University W
Southwest Minnesota State University W
University of Minnesota
    Crookston W
    Duluth W
    Twin Cities W
Winona State University W

Mississippi
Alcorn State University W
Belhaven University W
Copiah-Lincoln Community College W
Delta State University W
East Central Community College W
East Mississippi Community College W
Hinds Community College W
Holmes Community College W
Jackson State University W
Jones County Junior College W
Meridian Community College W
Mississippi Gulf Coast Community College W
Mississippi State University W
Mississippi Valley State University W
Northwest Mississippi Community College W
Southwest Mississippi Community College W
University of Mississippi W
University of Southern Mississippi W

Missouri
Avila University W
Central Methodist University W
Columbia College W
Culver-Stockton College W
Drury University W
East Central College W
Evangel University W
Hannibal-LaGrange College W
Harris-Stowe State University W
Jefferson College W
Lincoln University W
Missouri Baptist University W
Missouri Southern State University W
Missouri State University W
Missouri Valley College W

Missouri Western State University W
North Central Missouri College W
Northwest Missouri State University W
Park University W
Research College of Nursing W
Rockhurst University W
St. Charles Community College W
Saint Louis University W
Southeast Missouri State University W
Southwest Baptist University W
St. Louis Community College
    Meramec W
Stephens College W
Three Rivers Community College W
Truman State University W
University of Central Missouri W
University of Missouri
    Columbia W
    Kansas City W
    Missouri University of Science and
        Technology W
    St. Louis W
William Jewell College W
William Woods University W

Montana
Montana State University
    Billings W
University of Great Falls W

Nebraska
Bellevue University W
College of Saint Mary W
Concordia University W
Creighton University W
Dana College W
Doane College W
Mid-Plains Community College Area W
Peru State College W
University of Nebraska
    Kearney W
    Lincoln W
    Omaha W
Wayne State College W
Western Nebraska Community College W
York College W

Nevada
College of Southern Nevada W
University of Nevada
    Las Vegas W
    Reno W

New Hampshire
Franklin Pierce University W
Southern New Hampshire University M,W

New Jersey
Bloomfield College W
Brookdale Community College W
Burlington County College W
Caldwell College W
Fairleigh Dickinson University
    Metropolitan Campus W
Felician College W
Georgian Court University W
Mercer County Community College W
Monmouth University W
Rider University W
Rutgers, The State University of New Jersey
    New Brunswick/Piscataway Campus W
Saint Peter's College W
Salem Community College W
Seton Hall University W

New Mexico
Eastern New Mexico University W
New Mexico Highlands University W
New Mexico State University W
University of New Mexico W
University of the Southwest W
Western New Mexico University W

New York
Adelphi University W
Canisius College W
City University of New York
    Queens College W
Colgate University W
College of Saint Rose W
Concordia College W
Dominican College of Blauvelt W
Dowling College W
Fordham University W
Hofstra University W
Iona College W
Le Moyne College W
Long Island University
    Brooklyn Campus W
    C. W. Post Campus W
Manhattan College W
Marist College W
Mercy College W
Molloy College W
New York Institute of Technology W
Niagara University W
Nyack College W
Pace University W
Saint Bonaventure University W
St. John's University W
St. Thomas Aquinas College W
Siena College W
State University of New York
    Albany W
    Binghamton W
    Buffalo W
    Stony Brook W
Syracuse University W
Wagner College W

North Carolina
Appalachian State University W
Barton College W
Belmont Abbey College W
Brevard College W
Campbell University W
Catawba College W
Chowan University W
East Carolina University W
Elizabeth City State University W
Elon University W
Fayetteville State University W
Gardner-Webb University W
Johnson C. Smith University W
Lees-McRae College W
Lenoir-Rhyne University W
Louisburg College W
Mars Hill College W
Montreat College W
Mount Olive College W
North Carolina Central University W
North Carolina State University W
Pfeiffer University W
Pitt Community College W
Queens University of Charlotte W
St. Andrews Presbyterian College W
St. Augustine's College W
Shaw University W
University of North Carolina
    Chapel Hill W
    Charlotte W
    Greensboro W
    Pembroke W
    Wilmington W
Western Carolina University W
Wingate University W
Winston-Salem State University W

North Dakota
Dakota College at Bottineau W
Dickinson State University W
Jamestown College W
Mayville State University W
Minot State University W
North Dakota State University W

University of Mary W
University of North Dakota W

Ohio
Ashland University W
Bowling Green State University W
Cedarville University W
Cleveland State University W
Kent State University W
Malone University W
Miami University
    Oxford Campus W
Mount Vernon Nazarene University W
Notre Dame College W
Ohio Dominican University W
Ohio University W
Shawnee State University W
Southern State Community College W
Tiffin University W
University of Akron W
University of Dayton W
University of Findlay W
University of Rio Grande W
University of Toledo W
Urbana University W
Ursuline College W
Walsh University W
Wright State University W
Youngstown State University W

Oklahoma
Bacone College W
Cameron University W
Carl Albert State College W
Connors State College W
East Central University W
Eastern Oklahoma State College W
Northeastern Oklahoma Agricultural and
    Mechanical College W
Northeastern State University W
Northern Oklahoma College M,W
Northwestern Oklahoma State University W
Oklahoma Baptist University W
Oklahoma Christian University W
Oklahoma City University W
Oklahoma Panhandle State University M,W
Oklahoma State University W
Rogers State University W
Rose State College W
St. Gregory's University W
Seminole State College W
Southeastern Oklahoma State University W
Southern Nazarene University W
Southwestern Oklahoma State University W
University of Central Oklahoma W
University of Oklahoma W
University of Science and Arts of Oklahoma W
University of Tulsa W
Western Oklahoma State College W

Oregon
Blue Mountain Community College W
Clackamas Community College W
Concordia University W
Corban College W
Eastern Oregon University W
Northwest Christian University W
Oregon Institute of Technology W
Oregon State University W
Portland State University W
Southern Oregon University W
Southwestern Oregon Community College W
Treasure Valley Community College M,W
University of Oregon W

Pennsylvania
Bloomsburg University of Pennsylvania W
California University of Pennsylvania W
Carlow University W
Chestnut Hill College W
Clarion University of Pennsylvania W
Community College of Beaver County W
Drexel University W

East Stroudsburg University of Pennsylvania W
Edinboro University of Pennsylvania W
Gannon University W
Holy Family University W
Indiana University of Pennsylvania W
Kutztown University of Pennsylvania W
La Salle University W
Lackawanna College W
Lock Haven University of Pennsylvania W
Mansfield University of Pennsylvania W
Mercyhurst College W
Millersville University of Pennsylvania W
Penn State
    University Park W
Philadelphia University W
Point Park University W
Robert Morris University W
St. Francis University W
Saint Joseph's University W
Seton Hill University W
Shippensburg University of Pennsylvania W
Slippery Rock University of Pennsylvania W
Temple University W
University of Pittsburgh W
University of the Sciences in Philadelphia W
Villanova University W
West Chester University of Pennsylvania W
Westminster College W

Puerto Rico
Inter American University of Puerto Rico
    Aguadilla Campus M,W
    Bayamon Campus M,W
    Guayama Campus M,W
    Ponce Campus M,W
Universidad del Este M
Universidad Metropolitana W
University of Puerto Rico
    Carolina Regional College W
    Cayey University College M,W
    Humacao W
    Ponce M,W
    Utuado M,W

Rhode Island
Bryant University W
Community College of Rhode Island W
Providence College W
University of Rhode Island W

South Carolina
Aiken Technical College W
Anderson University W
Charleston Southern University W
Claflin University W
Coastal Carolina University W
Coker College W
College of Charleston W
Columbia College W
Erskine College W
Francis Marion University W
Furman University W
Lander University W
Limestone College W
Morris College W
Newberry College W
North Greenville University W
Presbyterian College W
South Carolina State University W
Southern Wesleyan University W
Spartanburg Methodist College W
University of South Carolina W
University of South Carolina
    Aiken W
    Upstate W
Winthrop University W

South Dakota
Augustana College W
Dakota State University W
Dakota Wesleyan University W
Mount Marty College W
Northern State University W

South Dakota State University W
University of Sioux Falls W
University of South Dakota W

Tennessee
Austin Peay State University W
Belmont University W
Bethel University W
Carson-Newman College W
Christian Brothers University W
Cleveland State Community College W
Cumberland University W
Dyersburg State Community College W
East Tennessee State University W
Freed-Hardeman University W
Jackson State Community College W
King College W
Lambuth University W
Lee University W
LeMoyne-Owen College W
Lincoln Memorial University W
Lipscomb University W
Martin Methodist College W
Middle Tennessee State University W
Milligan College W
Motlow State Community College W
Roane State Community College W
Southwest Tennessee Community College W
Tennessee Technological University W
Tennessee Wesleyan College W
Trevecca Nazarene University W
Tusculum College W
Union University W
University of Tennessee
    Chattanooga W
    Knoxville W
    Martin W
Volunteer State Community College W
Walters State Community College W

Texas
Abilene Christian University W
Alvin Community College W
Angelina College W
Angelo State University W
Baylor University W
Blinn College M
Clarendon College W
Frank Phillips College W
Galveston College W
Grayson County College W
Hill College W
Houston Baptist University W
Howard College W
Lon Morris College W
Lubbock Christian University W
McLennan Community College W
Midland College W
Midwestern State University W
Northeast Texas Community College W
Northwood University: Texas W
Odessa College W
Paris Junior College W
Prairie View A&M University W
Ranger College W
St. Edward's University W
Sam Houston State University W
Stephen F. Austin State University W
Tarleton State University W
Temple College W
Texas A&M University W
Texas A&M University
    Kingsville W
Texas Southern University W
Texas State University: San Marcos W
Texas Tech University W
Texas Woman's University W
University of Houston W
University of North Texas W
University of Texas
    Arlington W
    Austin W

of the Permian Basin W
    San Antonio W
University of the Incarnate Word W
Vernon College W
Western Texas College W
Wiley College W

Utah
Brigham Young University W
Dixie State College of Utah W
Salt Lake Community College W
Snow College W
Southern Utah University W
University of Utah W
Utah State University W
Utah Valley University W

Virginia
Bluefield College W
George Mason University W
Hampton University W
James Madison University W
Liberty University W
Longwood University W
Norfolk State University W
Radford University W
St. Paul's College W
University of Virginia W
University of Virginia's College at Wise W
Virginia Intermont College W
Virginia Polytechnic Institute and State
    University W
Virginia State University W
Virginia Union University W

Washington
Big Bend Community College W
Centralia College W
Everett Community College W
Grays Harbor College W
Green River Community College W
Highline Community College W
Lower Columbia College W
Olympic College W
Peninsula College W
Pierce College W
Saint Martin's University W
Seattle University W
Shoreline Community College W
Skagit Valley College W
Spokane Community College W
University of Washington W
Western Washington University W
Yakima Valley Community College W

West Virginia
Alderson-Broaddus College W
Bluefield State College W
Concord University W
Davis and Elkins College W
Glenville State College W
Marshall University W
Ohio Valley University W
Potomac State College of West Virginia
    University W
Salem International University W
Shepherd University W
University of Charleston W
West Liberty University W
West Virginia State University W
West Virginia University Institute of Technology
    W
West Virginia Wesleyan College W
Wheeling Jesuit University W

Wisconsin
Cardinal Stritch University W
University of Wisconsin
    Green Bay W
    Parkside W
Viterbo University W

Squash

Nebraska
University of Nebraska
    Lincoln W

New York
Fordham University M

Swimming

Alabama
Auburn University M,W
University of Alabama M,W

Alaska
University of Alaska
    Fairbanks W

Arizona
Arizona State University M,W
Northern Arizona University M,W
University of Arizona M,W

Arkansas
Henderson State University M,W
Ouachita Baptist University M,W
University of Arkansas W
University of Arkansas
    Little Rock M,W

California
Biola University M,W
California Baptist University M,W
California Polytechnic State University: San Luis
    Obispo M,W
California State University
    Bakersfield M,W
    Northridge M,W
    San Bernardino M,W
Concordia University M,W
Fresno Pacific University M,W
Grossmont College M,W
Loyola Marymount University W
Pepperdine University W
San Diego State University W
San Jose State University W
Stanford University M,W
University of California
    Berkeley M,W
    Davis M,W
    Irvine M,W
    Los Angeles M,W
    Santa Barbara M,W
University of San Diego W
University of Southern California M,W
University of the Pacific M,W
Vanguard University of Southern California
    M,W

Colorado
Adams State College W
Colorado State University W
Mesa State College W
Metropolitan State College of Denver M,W
University of Denver M,W
University of Northern Colorado W

Connecticut
Central Connecticut State University W
Fairfield University M,W
Post University M,W
Sacred Heart University W
Southern Connecticut State University M,W
University of Bridgeport M,W
University of Connecticut M,W

Delaware
University of Delaware W

District of Columbia
George Washington University M,W
Georgetown University M,W
Howard University M,W

Florida
Daytona State College M,W
Florida Atlantic University M,W
Florida Southern College M,W
Florida State University M,W
Indian River State College M,W
Saint Leo University M,W
University of Florida M,W
University of Miami W
University of North Florida W
University of Tampa M,W

Georgia
Brenau University W
Darton College M,W
Georgia Institute of Technology M,W
Georgia Southern University W
University of Georgia M,W

Hawaii
University of Hawaii
    Manoa M,W

Idaho
Boise State University W
College of Idaho M,W

Illinois
Eastern Illinois University M,W
Illinois Institute of Technology M,W
Illinois State University W
Lewis University M,W
Lincoln College M,W
Northwestern University M,W
Robert Morris University: Chicago W
Southern Illinois University Carbondale M,W
University of Illinois
    Chicago M,W
    Urbana-Champaign W
Western Illinois University M,W

Indiana
Ball State University M,W
Indiana University
    Bloomington M,W
Indiana University-Purdue University
    Indianapolis M,W
Purdue University M,W
University of Evansville M,W
University of Indianapolis M,W
University of Notre Dame M,W
Valparaiso University M,W

Iowa
Iowa Central Community College M,W
Iowa State University W
Morningside College M,W
University of Iowa M,W
University of Northern Iowa W

Kansas
University of Kansas W

Kentucky
Asbury College M,W
Campbellsville University W
University of Kentucky M,W
University of Louisville M,W
University of the Cumberlands M,W
Western Kentucky University M,W

Louisiana
Centenary College of Louisiana M,W
Louisiana State University and Agricultural and
    Mechanical College M,W
Tulane University W
University of Louisiana at Monroe M,W
University of New Orleans M,W

Maine
University of Maine W

Maryland
Loyola University Maryland M,W
Mount St. Mary's University W
Towson University M,W
University of Maryland
    Baltimore County M,W
    College Park M,W

Massachusetts
Boston College M,W
Boston University M,W
Northeastern University W
University of Massachusetts
    Amherst M,W
    Lowell M

Michigan
Eastern Michigan University M,W
Grand Rapids Community College M,W
Grand Valley State University M,W
Hillsdale College W
Michigan State University M,W
Northern Michigan University W
Oakland University M,W
University of Michigan M,W
Wayne State University M,W

Minnesota
Minnesota State University
    Mankato M,W
Saint Cloud State University M,W
University of Minnesota
    Twin Cities M,W

Mississippi
Delta State University M,W

Missouri
Drury University M,W
Hannibal-LaGrange College M,W
Missouri State University M,W
Saint Louis University M,W
Stephens College W
Truman State University M,W
University of Missouri
    Columbia M,W
    Missouri University of Science and
      Technology M

Nebraska
College of Saint Mary W
University of Nebraska
    Kearney W
    Lincoln W

Nevada
University of Nevada
    Las Vegas M,W
    Reno W

New Hampshire
University of New Hampshire W

New Jersey
New Jersey Institute of Technology M,W
Rider University M,W
Rutgers, The State University of New Jersey
    New Brunswick/Piscataway Campus M,W
Saint Peter's College M,W
Seton Hall University M,W

New Mexico
New Mexico State University W
University of New Mexico W

New York
Adelphi University M,W
Canisius College W
City University of New York
    Queens College M,W

College of Saint Rose M,W
Fordham University M,W
Iona College M,W
Long Island University
    C. W. Post Campus W
Manhattan College W
Marist College M,W
Monroe Community College M,W
Niagara University M,W
Saint Bonaventure University M,W
St. Francis College M,W
Siena College W
State University of New York
    Binghamton M,W
    Buffalo M,W
    Stony Brook M,W
Syracuse University M,W
Wagner College W

North Carolina
Campbell University W
Catawba College M,W
Davidson College M,W
East Carolina University M,W
Gardner-Webb University M,W
Lenoir-Rhyne University W
Mars Hill College M,W
North Carolina Agricultural and Technical State
    University W
North Carolina State University M,W
Pfeiffer University M,W
University of North Carolina
    Chapel Hill M,W
    Wilmington M,W
Wingate University M,W

North Dakota
University of North Dakota M,W

Ohio
Ashland University M,W
Bowling Green State University W
Cleveland State University M,W
Malone University M,W
Miami University
    Oxford Campus M,W
Notre Dame College W
Ohio University W
University of Akron W
University of Cincinnati M,W
University of Findlay M,W
University of Toledo W
Urbana University M,W
Ursuline College W
Wright State University M,W
Xavier University M,W
Youngstown State University W

Oregon
Oregon State University W

Pennsylvania
Bloomsburg University of Pennsylvania M,W
California University of Pennsylvania W
Clarion University of Pennsylvania M,W
Drexel University M,W
Duquesne University M,W
East Stroudsburg University of Pennsylvania W
Edinboro University of Pennsylvania W
Gannon University M,W
Indiana University of Pennsylvania M,W
Kutztown University of Pennsylvania W
La Salle University M,W
Lock Haven University of Pennsylvania W
Mansfield University of Pennsylvania W
Millersville University of Pennsylvania W
Penn State
    University Park M,W
St. Francis University W
Shippensburg University of Pennsylvania M,W
University of Pittsburgh M,W
Villanova University W
West Chester University of Pennsylvania M,W

Westminster College W

Puerto Rico
Bayamon Central University M,W
Inter American University of Puerto Rico
    Bayamon Campus M,W
Turabo University M,W
University of Puerto Rico
    Cayey University College M,W
    Humacao M,W
University of the Sacred Heart M,W

Rhode Island
Bryant University M,W
University of Rhode Island W

South Carolina
Clemson University M,W
College of Charleston M,W
Limestone College M,W
University of South Carolina M,W

South Dakota
South Dakota State University M,W
University of South Dakota M,W

Tennessee
King College M,W
University of Tennessee
    Knoxville M,W
Vanderbilt University W

Texas
Rice University W
Southern Methodist University M,W
Texas A&M University M,W
Texas Christian University M,W
University of Houston W
University of North Texas W
University of Texas
    Austin M,W
    of the Permian Basin M,W
University of the Incarnate Word M,W

Utah
Brigham Young University M,W
University of Utah M,W

Vermont
University of Vermont W

Virginia
George Mason University M,W
James Madison University W
Radford University W
University of Richmond W
University of Virginia M,W
Virginia Military Institute M
Virginia Polytechnic Institute and State
    University M,W

Washington
Seattle University M,W
University of Washington M,W
Washington State University W

West Virginia
Marshall University W
West Virginia University M,W
West Virginia Wesleyan College M,W
Wheeling Jesuit University M,W

Wisconsin
University of Wisconsin
    Green Bay M,W
    Milwaukee M,W

Wyoming
University of Wyoming M,W

Synchronized swimming

Alabama
University of Alabama
    Birmingham W

California
Stanford University W

New York
Canisius College W

Texas
University of the Incarnate Word W

Table tennis

Puerto Rico
Inter American University of Puerto Rico
    Aguadilla Campus M,W
    Bayamon Campus M,W
    Metropolitan Campus M,W
    Ponce Campus M
Universidad Metropolitana M,W
University of Puerto Rico
    Cayey University College M,W
    Ponce M,W
    Utuado M,W

Tennis

Alabama
Alabama Agricultural and Mechanical
    University M,W
Alabama State University M,W
Auburn University M,W
Auburn University at Montgomery M,W
Central Alabama Community College M,W
Faulkner State Community College M,W
Gadsden State Community College M,W
Jacksonville State University M,W
Judson College W
Samford University M,W
Snead State Community College W
Spring Hill College M,W
Troy University M,W
University of Alabama M,W
University of Alabama
    Birmingham M,W
    Huntsville M,W
University of Mobile M,W
University of Montevallo W
University of North Alabama M,W
University of South Alabama M,W
Wallace State Community College at Hanceville
    M,W

Arizona
Arizona State University W
Eastern Arizona College W
GateWay Community College M,W
Glendale Community College M,W
Grand Canyon University W
Northern Arizona University M,W
Paradise Valley Community College M,W
Pima Community College M,W
Scottsdale Community College M,W
University of Arizona M,W

Arkansas
Arkansas State University W
Arkansas Tech University W
Harding University M,W
Henderson State University W
John Brown University M,W
Ouachita Baptist University M,W

Southern Arkansas University W
University of Arkansas M,W
University of Arkansas
   Fort Smith M,W
   Little Rock M,W
   Pine Bluff M,W
University of Central Arkansas W

California
Azusa Pacific University M
Biola University M,W
California Polytechnic State University: San Luis Obispo M,W
California State Polytechnic University: Pomona M,W
California State University
   Bakersfield W
   Fresno M,W
   Fullerton W
   Long Beach W
   Los Angeles M,W
   Northridge W
   Sacramento M,W
Concordia University M,W
Dominican University of California W
Fresno City College M,W
Fresno Pacific University M,W
Grossmont College M,W
Hope International University M,W
Loyola Marymount University M,W
The Master's College W
Notre Dame de Namur University W
Pepperdine University M,W
Point Loma Nazarene University M,W
St. Mary's College of California M,W
San Diego State University M,W
San Jose State University W
Santa Clara University M,W
Sonoma State University M,W
Stanford University M,W
University of California
   Berkeley M,W
   Davis M,W
   Irvine M,W
   Los Angeles M,W
   Riverside M,W
   Santa Barbara M,W
University of San Diego M,W
University of San Francisco M,W
University of Southern California M,W
University of the Pacific M,W
Vanguard University of Southern California M,W
Westmont College M,W
Yuba Community College District M,W

Colorado
Colorado Christian University M,W
Colorado State University W
Colorado State University
   Pueblo M,W
Mesa State College M,W
Metropolitan State College of Denver M,W
University of Colorado
   Boulder W
University of Denver M,W
University of Northern Colorado M,W

Connecticut
Fairfield University M,W
Quinnipiac University M,W
Sacred Heart University M,W
University of Connecticut M,W
University of Hartford M,W
University of New Haven W

Delaware
Delaware State University M,W
Goldey-Beacom College W

District of Columbia
George Washington University M,W
Georgetown University M,W

Howard University M,W

Florida
Barry University M,W
Bethune-Cookman University M,W
Central Florida Community College W
Eckerd College M,W
Embry-Riddle Aeronautical University M,W
Flagler College M,W
Florida Atlantic University M,W
Florida Gulf Coast University M,W
Florida Institute of Technology M,W
Florida Southern College M,W
Florida State College at Jacksonville W
Florida State University M,W
Hillsborough Community College W
Jacksonville University M,W
Lynn University M,W
Northwood University
   Florida M,W
Nova Southeastern University W
Rollins College M,W
Saint Leo University M,W
Saint Thomas University M,W
Southeastern University W
Stetson University M,W
University of Central Florida M,W
University of Florida M,W
University of Miami M,W
University of North Florida M,W
University of South Florida M,W
University of Tampa W
University of West Florida M,W
Warner University M,W
Webber International University M,W

Georgia
Abraham Baldwin Agricultural College M,W
Albany State University W
Armstrong Atlantic State University M,W
Augusta State University M,W
Brenau University W
Clark Atlanta University W
Clayton State University W
College of Coastal Georgia M,W
Columbus State University M,W
Covenant College W
Emmanuel College M,W
Fort Valley State University M,W
Georgia College and State University M,W
Georgia Institute of Technology M,W
Georgia Perimeter College M,W
Georgia Southern University M,W
Georgia Southwestern State University M,W
Georgia State University M,W
Gordon College W
Kennesaw State University M,W
Mercer University M,W
Morehouse College M
North Georgia College & State University M,W
Reinhardt College M,W
Savannah State University W
Shorter College M,W
South Georgia College W
University of Georgia M,W
Valdosta State University M,W
Young Harris College W

Hawaii
Chaminade University of Honolulu M,W
Hawaii Pacific University M,W
University of Hawaii
   Hilo M,W
   Manoa M,W

Idaho
Boise State University M,W
College of Idaho M,W
Idaho State University M,W
Lewis-Clark State College M,W
University of Idaho M,W

Illinois
Bradley University M,W
Chicago State University M,W
College of Lake County M,W
DePaul University M,W
Eastern Illinois University M,W
Elgin Community College M,W
Illinois State University M,W
Lake Land College M,W
Lewis and Clark Community College M,W
Lewis University M,W
McHenry County College M,W
McKendree University M,W
Moraine Valley Community College M,W
Northwestern University M,W
Olivet Nazarene University M,W
Quincy University M,W
Rend Lake College W
Robert Morris University: Chicago W
Sauk Valley Community College W
Southern Illinois University Carbondale M,W
Southern Illinois University Edwardsville M,W
Southwestern Illinois College M,W
University of Illinois
   Chicago M,W
   Springfield M,W
   Urbana-Champaign M,W
University of St. Francis M,W
Waubonsee Community College M,W
Western Illinois University M,W

Indiana
Ball State University M,W
Bethel College M,W
Butler University M,W
Calumet College of St. Joseph M,W
Goshen College M,W
Grace College M,W
Huntington University M,W
Indiana Institute of Technology M,W
Indiana University
   Bloomington M,W
Indiana University-Purdue University Fort Wayne M,W
Indiana University-Purdue University Indianapolis M,W
Indiana Wesleyan University M,W
Marian University M,W
Oakland City University M,W
Purdue University M,W
Taylor University M,W
University of Evansville W
University of Indianapolis M,W
University of Notre Dame M,W
University of St. Francis W
University of Southern Indiana M,W
Valparaiso University M,W
Vincennes University M

Iowa
Briar Cliff University M,W
Clarke College M,W
Dordt College M,W
Drake University M,W
Graceland University M,W
Iowa State University W
Morningside College M,W
St. Ambrose University M,W
University of Iowa M,W
University of Northern Iowa W

Kansas
Baker University M,W
Barton County Community College M,W
Bethany College M,W
Bethel College M,W
Central Christian College of Kansas M,W
Cowley County Community College M,W
Emporia State University M,W
Fort Hays State University W
Friends University M,W
Johnson County Community College M,W

Kansas State University W
Kansas Wesleyan University M,W
Labette Community College W
Newman University M,W
Seward County Community College M,W
Southwestern College M,W
Sterling College M,W
Tabor College M,W
University of Kansas W
Washburn University M,W
Wichita State University M,W

Kentucky
Asbury College M,W
Bellarmine University M,W
Brescia University M,W
Campbellsville University M,W
Eastern Kentucky University M,W
Georgetown College M,W
Kentucky Wesleyan College W
Lindsey Wilson College M,W
Midway College W
Morehead State University M,W
Murray State University M,W
Northern Kentucky University M,W
Pikeville College M,W
Union College M,W
University of Kentucky M,W
University of Louisville M,W
University of the Cumberlands M,W
Western Kentucky University M,W

Louisiana
Centenary College of Louisiana M,W
Dillard University M,W
Grambling State University M,W
Louisiana State University and Agricultural and Mechanical College M,W
Louisiana Tech University W
McNeese State University W
Nicholls State University M,W
Northwestern State University W
Southeastern Louisiana University W
Southern University and Agricultural and Mechanical College W
University of Louisiana at Lafayette M,W
University of New Orleans M,W
Xavier University of Louisiana M,W

Maryland
College of Southern Maryland M,W
Coppin State University M,W
Loyola University Maryland M,W
Morgan State University M,W
Mount St. Mary's University M,W
Towson University M,W
University of Maryland
   Baltimore County M,W
   College Park W
   Eastern Shore M,W

Massachusetts
Boston College M,W
Boston University W
Merrimack College W
Stonehill College W
University of Massachusetts
   Amherst W
   Lowell W

Michigan
Aquinas College M,W
Davenport University M,W
Eastern Michigan University W
Ferris State University M,W
Grand Rapids Community College M,W
Grand Valley State University M,W
Lake Superior State University M,W
Michigan State University M,W
Michigan Technological University M,W
Muskegon Community College W
Northwood University: Michigan M,W
Oakland Community College W

Oakland University W
Saginaw Valley State University W
Spring Arbor University M,W
University of Detroit Mercy W
University of Michigan M,W
Wayne State University M,W
Western Michigan University M,W

Minnesota
Bemidji State University W
Minnesota State University
    Mankato M,W
    Moorhead W
Saint Cloud State University M,W
Southwest Minnesota State University W
University of Minnesota
    Crookston W
    Duluth W
    Twin Cities M,W
Winona State University W

Mississippi
Alcorn State University M,W
Belhaven University M,W
Copiah-Lincoln Community College M,W
Delta State University M,W
Hinds Community College M,W
Holmes Community College M,W
Jones County Junior College M,W
Meridian Community College M,W
Mississippi Gulf Coast Community College M,W
Mississippi State University M,W
Mississippi Valley State University M,W
Northwest Mississippi Community College M,W
Southwest Mississippi Community College M,W
Tougaloo College M,W
University of Mississippi M,W
University of Southern Mississippi M,W

Missouri
Drury University M,W
Evangel University M,W
Lincoln University W
Missouri Baptist University W
Missouri Southern State University W
Missouri Valley College M,W
Missouri Western State University W
Northwest Missouri State University M,W
Research College of Nursing M,W
Rockhurst University M,W
Saint Louis University M,W
Southeast Missouri State University W
Southwest Baptist University M,W
Stephens College W
Truman State University M,W
University of Missouri
    Columbia W
    Kansas City M,W
    St. Louis M,W
William Jewell College M,W

Montana
Montana State University
    Billings M,W
    Bozeman M,W
University of Montana M,W

Nebraska
Concordia University M,W
Creighton University M,W
University of Nebraska
    Kearney M,W
    Lincoln M,W

Nevada
University of Nevada
    Las Vegas M,W
    Reno M,W

New Hampshire
Franklin Pierce University M,W
Southern New Hampshire University M,W

New Jersey
Bloomfield College M
Caldwell College M
Fairleigh Dickinson University
    Metropolitan Campus M,W
Georgian Court University W
Monmouth University W
New Jersey Institute of Technology M,W
Rider University M,W
Rutgers, The State University of New Jersey
    New Brunswick/Piscataway Campus M,W
Saint Peter's College M,W
Seton Hall University W

New Mexico
New Mexico Military Institute M
New Mexico State University M,W
University of New Mexico M,W
University of the Southwest M,W
Western New Mexico University M,W

New York
Adelphi University M,W
City University of New York
    Queens College M,W
Concordia College M,W
Dowling College M,W
Fordham University M,W
Hofstra University M,W
Le Moyne College M,W
Long Island University
    Brooklyn Campus W
    C. W. Post Campus W
Manhattan College M,W
Marist College M,W
Mercy College M
Molloy College M,W
Niagara University M,W
Pace University M,W
Saint Bonaventure University M,W
St. Francis College M,W
St. John's University M,W
Siena College M,W
State University of New York
    Albany W
    Binghamton M,W
    Buffalo M,W
    Stony Brook M,W
Syracuse University W
Wagner College M,W

North Carolina
Appalachian State University M,W
Barton College M,W
Brevard College M,W
Campbell University M,W
Catawba College M,W
Chowan University M,W
Davidson College M,W
Duke University M,W
East Carolina University M,W
Elon University M,W
Fayetteville State University W
Gardner-Webb University M,W
High Point University M,W
Johnson C. Smith University M,W
Lees-McRae College M,W
Lenoir-Rhyne University M,W
Mars Hill College M,W
Mount Olive College M,W
North Carolina Agricultural and Technical State University M,W
North Carolina Central University M,W
North Carolina State University M,W
Pfeiffer University M,W
Queens University of Charlotte M,W
St. Andrews Presbyterian College W
St. Augustine's College M,W
Shaw University M,W
University of North Carolina
    Asheville M,W
    Chapel Hill M,W

    Charlotte M,W
    Greensboro M,W
    Pembroke W
    Wilmington M,W
Wake Forest University M,W
Western Carolina University W
Wingate University M,W
Winston-Salem State University M,W

North Dakota
University of Mary W
University of North Dakota W

Ohio
Bowling Green State University W
Cedarville University M,W
Central State University M,W
Cleveland State University M,W
Malone University M,W
Miami University
    Oxford Campus W
Notre Dame College M
Ohio Dominican University M,W
Shawnee State University W
Tiffin University M,W
University of Akron W
University of Cincinnati W
University of Dayton M,W
University of Findlay M,W
University of Toledo M,W
Ursuline College W
Walsh University M,W
Wright State University M,W
Xavier University M,W
Youngstown State University M,W

Oklahoma
Bacone College M,W
Cameron University M,W
East Central University M,W
Northeastern State University W
Oklahoma Baptist University M,W
Oklahoma Christian University M,W
Oklahoma State University M,W
Oklahoma Wesleyan University M,W
Oral Roberts University M,W
Seminole State College M,W
Southeastern Oklahoma State University M,W
Southern Nazarene University M,W
University of Central Oklahoma M,W
University of Oklahoma M,W
University of Tulsa M,W

Oregon
Portland State University W
Southern Oregon University W
Treasure Valley Community College M,W
University of Oregon M,W
University of Portland M,W

Pennsylvania
Bloomsburg University of Pennsylvania M,W
California University of Pennsylvania W
Carlow University W
Chestnut Hill College M,W
Clarion University of Pennsylvania W
Drexel University M,W
Duquesne University M,W
East Stroudsburg University of Pennsylvania M,W
Edinboro University of Pennsylvania M,W
Holy Family University W
Indiana University of Pennsylvania W
Kutztown University of Pennsylvania M,W
La Salle University M,W
Mercyhurst College M,W
Millersville University of Pennsylvania M,W
Penn State
    University Park M,W
Philadelphia University M,W
Robert Morris University M,W
St. Francis University M,W
Saint Joseph's University M,W

Seton Hill University M,W
Shippensburg University of Pennsylvania W
Slippery Rock University of Pennsylvania W
Temple University M,W
University of Pittsburgh W
University of the Sciences in Philadelphia M,W
West Chester University of Pennsylvania M,W
Westminster College W

Puerto Rico
Inter American University of Puerto Rico
    Aguadilla Campus M,W
    Bayamon Campus M,W
    San German Campus M,W
Turabo University M,W
Universidad Metropolitana M,W
University of Puerto Rico
    Bayamon University College M,W
    Carolina Regional College M,W
    Cayey University College M,W
    Humacao W
    Ponce M,W
University of the Sacred Heart M

Rhode Island
Bryant University M,W
University of Rhode Island W

South Carolina
Anderson University M,W
Charleston Southern University M,W
The Citadel M
Clemson University M,W
Coastal Carolina University M,W
Coker College M,W
College of Charleston M,W
Columbia College W
Converse College W
Erskine College M,W
Francis Marion University M,W
Furman University M,W
Lander University M,W
Limestone College M,W
Morris College M,W
Newberry College M,W
North Greenville University M,W
Presbyterian College M,W
South Carolina State University M,W
Spartanburg Methodist College M,W
University of South Carolina M,W
University of South Carolina
    Aiken M,W
    Upstate M,W
Winthrop University M,W
Wofford College M,W

South Dakota
Augustana College W
Northern State University W
South Dakota State University M,W
University of Sioux Falls M,W

Tennessee
Austin Peay State University M,W
Belmont University M,W
Bethel University M,W
Carson-Newman College M,W
Christian Brothers University M,W
Cumberland University M,W
East Tennessee State University M,W
King College M,W
Lambuth University M,W
Lee University M,W
LeMoyne-Owen College M,W
Lincoln Memorial University M,W
Lipscomb University M,W
Martin Methodist College M,W
Middle Tennessee State University M,W
Milligan College M,W
Tennessee Technological University M,W
Tennessee Wesleyan College M,W
Tusculum College M,W
Union University M,W

University of Memphis M,W
University of Tennessee
    Chattanooga M,W
    Knoxville M,W
    Martin W
Vanderbilt University M,W

Texas
Abilene Christian University M,W
Baylor University M,W
Collin County Community College District M,W
Dallas Baptist University W
Lamar University M,W
Laredo Community College M,W
Lee College W
Midwestern State University M,W
North Central Texas College W
Prairie View A&M University M,W
Rice University M,W
St. Edward's University M,W
St. Mary's University M,W
Sam Houston State University M,W
Southern Methodist University M,W
Stephen F. Austin State University W
Tarleton State University W
Temple College M,W
Texas A&M University M,W
Texas A&M University
    Corpus Christi M,W
    Kingsville M,W
Texas Christian University M,W
Texas Southern University M,W
Texas State University: San Marcos W
Texas Tech University M,W
Tyler Junior College M,W
University of Houston W
University of North Texas W
University of Texas
    Arlington M,W
    Austin M,W
    Pan American M,W
    San Antonio M,W
University of the Incarnate Word M,W
Weatherford College W

Utah
Brigham Young University M,W
Dixie State College of Utah W
Southern Utah University W
University of Utah M,W
Utah State University M,W
Weber State University M,W

Virginia
Bluefield College M,W
College of William and Mary M,W
George Mason University M,W
Hampton University M,W
James Madison University M,W
Liberty University M,W
Longwood University M,W
Norfolk State University M,W
Old Dominion University M,W
Radford University M,W
St. Paul's College M,W
University of Richmond M,W
University of Virginia M,W
University of Virginia's College at Wise M,W
Virginia Commonwealth University M,W
Virginia Military Institute M
Virginia Polytechnic Institute and State
    University M,W
Virginia State University M,W
Virginia Union University M,W

Washington
Eastern Washington University M,W
Gonzaga University M,W
Green River Community College M,W
Seattle University M,W
Shoreline Community College M,W
Skagit Valley College M,W
Spokane Community College M,W

University of Washington M,W
Washington State University W

West Virginia
Bluefield State College M,W
Concord University M,W
Davis and Elkins College M,W
Marshall University W
Salem International University M
Shepherd University M,W
University of Charleston M,W
West Liberty University M,W
West Virginia University W
West Virginia Wesleyan College M,W

Wisconsin
Marquette University M,W
University of Wisconsin
    Green Bay M,W
    Milwaukee W

Wyoming
University of Wyoming W

Track and field

Alabama
Alabama Agricultural and Mechanical
    University M,W
Alabama State University M,W
Auburn University M,W
Miles College M,W
Samford University M,W
Troy University M,W
University of Alabama M,W
University of Alabama
    Birmingham W
    Huntsville M,W
University of South Alabama M,W
Wallace State Community College at Hanceville
    M,W

Arizona
Arizona State University M,W
Central Arizona College M,W
Glendale Community College M,W
Mesa Community College M,W
Northern Arizona University M,W
Paradise Valley Community College M,W
Pima Community College M,W
Scottsdale Community College M,W
University of Arizona M,W

Arkansas
Arkansas State University M,W
Harding University M,W
University of Arkansas M,W
University of Arkansas
    Little Rock M,W
    Pine Bluff M,W
University of Central Arkansas M,W

California
Azusa Pacific University M,W
Biola University M,W
California Baptist University M,W
California Polytechnic State University: San Luis
    Obispo M,W
California State Polytechnic University: Pomona
    M,W
California State University
    Bakersfield M,W
    Chico M,W
    Dominguez Hills W
    Fresno M,W
    Fullerton M,W
    Long Beach M,W
    Los Angeles M,W
    Northridge M,W
    Sacramento M,W
    Stanislaus M,W

Concordia University M,W
Fresno City College M,W
Fresno Pacific University M,W
Humboldt State University M,W
The Master's College M,W
Pepperdine University W
Point Loma Nazarene University M,W
San Diego State University W
Santa Clara University M,W
Santiago Canyon College M,W
Sonoma State University W
Stanford University M,W
University of California
    Berkeley M,W
    Davis M,W
    Irvine M,W
    Los Angeles M,W
    Riverside M,W
    Santa Barbara M,W
University of Southern California M,W
Vanguard University of Southern California
    M,W
Westmont College M,W
William Jessup University M,W
Yuba Community College District M,W

Colorado
Adams State College M,W
Colorado School of Mines M,W
Colorado State University M,W
Colorado State University
    Pueblo W
Mesa State College W
University of Colorado
    Boulder M,W
    Colorado Springs M,W
University of Northern Colorado M,W
Western State College of Colorado M,W

Connecticut
Central Connecticut State University M,W
Quinnipiac University W
Sacred Heart University M,W
Southern Connecticut State University W
University of Connecticut M,W
University of New Haven M,W

Delaware
Delaware State University M,W
University of Delaware W

District of Columbia
American University M,W
Georgetown University M,W
Howard University M,W

Florida
Bethune-Cookman University M,W
Edward Waters College M
Embry-Riddle Aeronautical University M,W
Florida Agricultural and Mechanical University
    M,W
Florida Atlantic University W
Florida Memorial University M
Florida Southern College M,W
Florida State University M,W
Jacksonville University W
Nova Southeastern University M,W
University of Central Florida W
University of Florida M,W
University of Miami M,W
University of North Florida M,W
University of South Florida M,W
Warner University M,W
Webber International University M,W

Georgia
Albany State University M,W
Clark Atlanta University M,W
Columbus State University M,W
Fort Valley State University M,W
Georgia Institute of Technology M,W
Georgia Southern University W

Georgia State University M,W
Kennesaw State University M,W
Morehouse College M
Paine College M,W
Savannah State University M,W
Shorter College M,W
University of Georgia M,W

Hawaii
University of Hawaii
    Manoa W

Idaho
Boise State University M,W
College of Idaho M,W
Idaho State University M,W
Lewis-Clark State College W
Northwest Nazarene University M,W
University of Idaho M,W

Illinois
Bradley University W
Chicago State University M,W
DePaul University M,W
Eastern Illinois University M,W
Illinois State University M,W
Lewis University M,W
Lincoln College M,W
Loyola University Chicago M,W
McKendree University M,W
Olivet Nazarene University M,W
Rend Lake College M,W
Robert Morris University: Chicago W
Southern Illinois University Carbondale M,W
Southern Illinois University Edwardsville M,W
Trinity Christian College M,W
University of Illinois
    Chicago M,W
    Urbana-Champaign M,W
University of St. Francis M,W
Western Illinois University M,W

Indiana
Ball State University M,W
Goshen College M,W
Grace College M,W
Huntington University M,W
Indiana Institute of Technology M,W
Indiana State University M,W
Indiana University
    Bloomington M,W
Indiana University-Purdue University Fort
    Wayne W
Indiana Wesleyan University M,W
Marian University M,W
Purdue University M,W
Saint Joseph's College M,W
Taylor University M,W
University of Indianapolis M,W
University of Notre Dame M,W
University of St. Francis M,W
Valparaiso University M,W
Vincennes University M,W

Iowa
Briar Cliff University M,W
Clarke College M,W
Dordt College M,W
Drake University M,W
Graceland University M,W
Iowa State University M,W
Iowa Wesleyan College M,W
Morningside College M,W
Mount Mercy College M,W
North Iowa Area Community College M,W
Northwestern College M,W
St. Ambrose University M,W
University of Iowa M,W
University of Northern Iowa M,W
William Penn University M,W

Kansas
Allen County Community College M,W
Baker University M,W
Barton County Community College M,W
Benedictine College M,W
Bethany College M,W
Bethel College M,W
Butler Community College M,W
Cloud County Community College M,W
Coffeyville Community College M,W
Colby Community College M,W
Cowley County Community College M,W
Emporia State University M,W
Fort Hays State University M,W
Friends University M,W
Garden City Community College M,W
Highland Community College M,W
Hutchinson Community College M,W
Johnson County Community College M,W
Kansas City Kansas Community College M,W
Kansas State University M,W
Kansas Wesleyan University M,W
McPherson College M,W
MidAmerica Nazarene University M,W
Neosho County Community College M,W
Ottawa University M,W
Pittsburg State University M,W
Pratt Community College M,W
Southwestern College M,W
Sterling College M,W
Tabor College M,W
University of Kansas M,W
Wichita State University M,W

Kentucky
Bellarmine University M,W
Brescia University M,W
Campbellsville University M,W
Eastern Kentucky University M,W
Kentucky State University M,W
Lindsey Wilson College M,W
Midway College W
Morehead State University M,W
Murray State University W
St. Catharine College M,W
University of Kentucky M,W
University of Louisville M,W
University of the Cumberlands M,W
Western Kentucky University M,W

Louisiana
Grambling State University M,W
Louisiana State University and Agricultural and
   Mechanical College M,W
Louisiana Tech University M,W
McNeese State University M,W
Nicholls State University W
Northwestern State University M,W
Southeastern Louisiana University M,W
Southern University and Agricultural and
   Mechanical College M,W
University of Louisiana at Lafayette M,W
University of Louisiana at Monroe M,W

Maine
University of Maine M,W

Maryland
Bowie State University M,W
Coppin State University M,W
Hagerstown Community College M,W
Morgan State University M,W
Mount St. Mary's University M,W
Towson University M,W
University of Maryland
   Baltimore County M,W
   College Park M,W
   Eastern Shore M,W
Washington Adventist University M,W

Massachusetts
American International College M,W
Boston College M,W
Boston University M,W
Northeastern University M,W
Stonehill College M,W
University of Massachusetts
   Amherst M,W
   Lowell M,W

Michigan
Aquinas College M,W
Central Michigan University M,W
Cornerstone University M,W
Davenport University M,W
Eastern Michigan University M,W
Ferris State University M,W
Grand Rapids Community College M,W
Grand Valley State University M,W
Hillsdale College M,W
Lake Superior State University M,W
Macomb Community College M,W
Michigan State University M,W
Michigan Technological University M,W
Northern Michigan University W
Northwood University: Michigan M,W
Saginaw Valley State University M,W
Siena Heights University M,W
University of Detroit Mercy M,W
University of Michigan M,W
Western Michigan University M,W

Minnesota
Bemidji State University M,W
Concordia University: St. Paul M,W
Minnesota State University
   Mankato M,W
   Moorhead M,W
Saint Cloud State University M,W
University of Minnesota
   Duluth M,W
   Twin Cities M,W
Winona State University W

Mississippi
Alcorn State University M,W
Hinds Community College M
Holmes Community College M
Jackson State University M,W
Jones County Junior College M
Mississippi State University M,W
Mississippi Valley State University M,W
Southwest Mississippi Community College
   M,W
University of Mississippi M,W
University of Southern Mississippi M,W

Missouri
Central Methodist University M,W
Culver-Stockton College M,W
Drury University M,W
Evangel University M,W
Hannibal-LaGrange College M,W
Lincoln University M,W
Missouri Baptist University W
Missouri Southern State University M,W
Missouri State University M,W
Missouri Valley College M,W
Northwest Missouri State University M,W
Park University M,W
Saint Louis University M,W
Southeast Missouri State University M,W
Southwest Baptist University M,W
Truman State University M,W
University of Central Missouri M,W
University of Missouri
   Columbia M,W
   Kansas City M,W
Missouri University of Science and
   Technology M,W
William Jewell College M,W

Montana
Montana State University
   Billings M,W
   Bozeman M,W
University of Montana M,W

Nebraska
Chadron State College M,W
Concordia University M,W
Dana College M,W
Doane College M,W
University of Nebraska
   Kearney M,W
   Lincoln M,W
Wayne State College M,W

Nevada
University of Nevada
   Las Vegas W
   Reno W

New Hampshire
University of New Hampshire M,W

New Jersey
Essex County College M,W
Fairleigh Dickinson University
   Metropolitan Campus M,W
Felician College M,W
Georgian Court University W
Monmouth University M,W
Rider University M,W
Rutgers, The State University of New Jersey
   New Brunswick/Piscataway Campus M,W
Saint Peter's College M,W

New Mexico
Eastern New Mexico University M,W
New Mexico Highlands University W
New Mexico Military Institute M
New Mexico State University W
University of New Mexico M,W
University of the Southwest M,W

New York
Adelphi University M,W
City University of New York
   Queens College M,W
College of Saint Rose M,W
Dominican College of Blauvelt W
Fordham University M,W
Houghton College M,W
Iona College M,W
Long Island University
   Brooklyn Campus M,W
Manhattan College M,W
Marist College M,W
Mercy College M,W
Pace University M,W
Roberts Wesleyan College M,W
St. Francis College M,W
St. John's University M,W
St. Thomas Aquinas College M,W
State University of New York
   Albany M,W
   Binghamton M,W
   Buffalo M,W
   Stony Brook M,W
Syracuse University M,W
Wagner College M,W

North Carolina
Appalachian State University M,W
Brevard College M,W
Campbell University M,W
Davidson College M,W
East Carolina University M,W
Elon University W
Fayetteville State University W
Gardner-Webb University M,W
High Point University M,W
Johnson C. Smith University M,W
Lees-McRae College M,W

Lenoir-Rhyne University M,W
Livingstone College M,W
Mars Hill College M,W
Montreat College M,W
North Carolina Agricultural and Technical State
   University M,W
North Carolina Central University M,W
North Carolina State University M,W
Queens University of Charlotte M,W
St. Augustine's College M,W
Shaw University M,W
University of North Carolina
   Asheville M,W
   Chapel Hill M,W
   Charlotte M,W
   Pembroke M,W
   Wilmington M,W
Wake Forest University M,W
Western Carolina University M,W
Winston-Salem State University M,W

North Dakota
Dickinson State University M,W
Jamestown College M,W
Minot State University M,W
North Dakota State University M,W
University of Mary M,W
University of North Dakota M,W

Ohio
Ashland University M,W
Bowling Green State University W
Cedarville University M,W
Central State University M,W
Kent State University M,W
Malone University M,W
Miami University
   Oxford Campus M,W
Notre Dame College M,W
Ohio University W
Tiffin University M,W
University of Akron M,W
University of Cincinnati M,W
University of Dayton W
University of Findlay M,W
University of Rio Grande M,W
University of Toledo W
Ursuline College W
Walsh University M,W
Wright State University W
Xavier University M,W
Youngstown State University M,W

Oklahoma
Bacone College M,W
Langston University M,W
Oklahoma Baptist University M,W
Oklahoma Christian University M,W
Oklahoma City University M,W
Oklahoma State University M,W
Oklahoma Wesleyan University M,W
Oral Roberts University M,W
Southern Nazarene University M,W
University of Central Oklahoma M,W
University of Oklahoma M,W
University of Tulsa M,W

Oregon
Clackamas Community College M,W
Concordia University M,W
Eastern Oregon University M,W
Lane Community College M,W
Mt. Hood Community College M,W
Northwest Christian University M,W
Oregon Institute of Technology M,W
Portland State University M,W
Southern Oregon University M,W
Southwestern Oregon Community College M,W
Treasure Valley Community College M,W
University of Oregon M,W
University of Portland M,W
Warner Pacific College M,W

Pennsylvania
Bloomsburg University of Pennsylvania M,W
California University of Pennsylvania M,W
Cheyney University of Pennsylvania M,W
Clarion University of Pennsylvania M,W
Duquesne University M,W
East Stroudsburg University of Pennsylvania M,W
Edinboro University of Pennsylvania M,W
Holy Family University M,W
Indiana University of Pennsylvania M,W
Kutztown University of Pennsylvania M,W
La Salle University M,W
Lock Haven University of Pennsylvania M,W
Millersville University of Pennsylvania M,W
Penn State
        University Park M,W
Robert Morris University M,W
St. Francis University M,W
Saint Joseph's University M,W
Seton Hill University M,W
Shippensburg University of Pennsylvania M,W
Slippery Rock University of Pennsylvania M,W
Temple University M,W
University of Pittsburgh M,W
Villanova University M,W
West Chester University of Pennsylvania M,W

Puerto Rico
Bayamon Central University M,W
Inter American University of Puerto Rico
        Aguadilla Campus M,W
        Bayamon Campus M,W
        Fajardo Campus M,W
        Guayama Campus M,W
        Metropolitan Campus M,W
        Ponce Campus M,W
        San German Campus M,W
Turabo University M,W
Universidad del Este M,W
Universidad Metropolitana M,W
University of Puerto Rico
        Bayamon University College M,W
        Carolina Regional College M,W
        Cayey University College M,W
        Humacao M,W
        Ponce M,W
        Utuado M,W
University of the Sacred Heart M,W

Rhode Island
Bryant University M,W
Providence College M,W
University of Rhode Island M,W

South Carolina
Anderson University M,W
Charleston Southern University M,W
The Citadel M,W
Claflin University M,W
Clemson University M,W
Coastal Carolina University M,W
Furman University M,W
Limestone College M,W
Morris College M,W
South Carolina State University M,W
University of South Carolina M,W
University of South Carolina
        Upstate M,W
Winthrop University M,W
Wofford College M,W

South Dakota
Augustana College M,W
Black Hills State University M,W
Dakota State University M,W
Dakota Wesleyan University M,W
Mount Marty College M,W
Northern State University M,W
South Dakota School of Mines and Technology M,W
South Dakota State University M,W

University of Sioux Falls M,W
University of South Dakota M,W

Tennessee
Austin Peay State University W
Belmont University M,W
Bethel University M,W
East Tennessee State University M,W
King College M,W
Lipscomb University M,W
Middle Tennessee State University M,W
Milligan College M,W
Tennessee Technological University W
University of Memphis M,W
University of Tennessee
        Chattanooga M,W
        Knoxville M,W
Vanderbilt University W

Texas
Abilene Christian University M,W
Angelo State University M,W
Baylor University M,W
Dallas Baptist University W
Houston Baptist University M,W
Lamar University M,W
Northwood University: Texas M,W
Prairie View A&M University M,W
Rice University M,W
Sam Houston State University M,W
South Plains College M,W
Stephen F. Austin State University M,W
Tarleton State University M,W
Texas A&M University M,W
Texas A&M University
        Commerce M,W
        Corpus Christi M,W
Texas Christian University M,W
Texas Southern University M,W
Texas State University: San Marcos M,W
Texas Tech University M,W
University of Houston M,W
University of North Texas M,W
University of Texas
        Austin M,W
        Pan American M,W
        San Antonio M,W
University of the Incarnate Word M,W
Wayland Baptist University M,W
Wiley College M,W

Utah
Brigham Young University M,W
Southern Utah University M,W
University of Utah W
Utah State University M,W
Utah Valley University M,W
Weber State University M,W

Vermont
University of Vermont M,W

Virginia
College of William and Mary M,W
George Mason University M,W
Hampton University M,W
James Madison University W
Liberty University M,W
Norfolk State University M,W
Radford University M,W
St. Paul's College M,W
University of Richmond W
University of Virginia M,W
Virginia Commonwealth University M,W
Virginia Military Institute M,W
Virginia Polytechnic Institute and State University M,W
Virginia State University M,W
Virginia Union University M,W

Washington
Clark College M,W
Eastern Washington University M,W

Evergreen State College M,W
Highline Community College M,W
Northwest University M,W
Saint Martin's University M,W
Seattle Pacific University M,W
Seattle University M,W
Spokane Community College M,W
University of Washington M,W
Washington State University M,W
Western Washington University M,W

West Virginia
Alderson-Broaddus College M,W
Glenville State College M,W
Marshall University M,W
Mountain State University M,W
University of Charleston M,W
West Liberty University M,W
West Virginia State University M,W
West Virginia University W
West Virginia Wesleyan College M,W
Wheeling Jesuit University M,W

Wisconsin
Marquette University M,W
Milwaukee Area Technical College M,W
University of Wisconsin
        Milwaukee M,W
        Parkside M,W

Wyoming
University of Wyoming M,W

Volleyball

Alabama
Alabama Agricultural and Mechanical University W
Alabama State University W
Auburn University W
Bevill State Community College W
Central Alabama Community College W
Faulkner State Community College M,W
Faulkner University W
Gadsden State Community College W
Jacksonville State University W
Jefferson Davis Community College W
Judson College W
Lawson State Community College W
Miles College M,W
Northwest-Shoals Community College W
Samford University W
Southern Union State Community College W
Spring Hill College W
Troy University W
Tuskegee University W
University of Alabama W
University of Alabama
        Birmingham W
        Huntsville W
University of Mobile W
University of Montevallo W
University of North Alabama W
University of South Alabama W
University of West Alabama W
Wallace State Community College at Hanceville W

Alaska
University of Alaska
        Anchorage W
        Fairbanks W

Arizona
Arizona State University W
Arizona Western College W
Chandler-Gilbert Community College
        Pecos W
Eastern Arizona College W
Embry-Riddle Aeronautical University: Prescott Campus W

Glendale Community College W
Grand Canyon University W
Northern Arizona University W
Pima Community College W
Scottsdale Community College W
University of Arizona W

Arkansas
Arkansas State University W
Arkansas Tech University W
Harding University W
Henderson State University W
John Brown University W
Lyon College W
Ouachita Baptist University W
Southern Arkansas University W
University of Arkansas W
University of Arkansas
        Fort Smith W
        Little Rock W
        Pine Bluff W
University of Central Arkansas W
Williams Baptist College W

California
Azusa Pacific University W
Bethany University W
Biola University W
California Baptist University M,W
California Polytechnic State University: San Luis Obispo W
California State Polytechnic University: Pomona W
California State University
        Bakersfield W
        Chico W
        Dominguez Hills W
        Fresno W
        Fullerton W
        Long Beach M,W
        Los Angeles W
        Monterey Bay W
        Northridge M,W
        Sacramento W
        San Bernardino W
        Stanislaus W
Concordia University W
Dominican University of California W
Fresno City College W
Fresno Pacific University W
Grossmont College M,W
Holy Names University M,W
Hope International University M,W
Humboldt State University W
Loyola Marymount University W
The Master's College W
Notre Dame de Namur University W
Pepperdine University M,W
Point Loma Nazarene University W
St. Mary's College of California W
San Diego Christian College W
San Diego State University W
San Jose State University W
Santa Clara University W
Sonoma State University W
Stanford University M,W
University of California
        Berkeley W
        Davis W
        Irvine M,W
        Los Angeles W
        Riverside W
        Santa Barbara M,W
University of San Diego W
University of San Francisco W
University of Southern California M,W
University of the Pacific M,W
Vanguard University of Southern California W
Westmont College W
William Jessup University W
Yuba Community College District W

Colorado
Adams State College W
Colorado Christian University W
Colorado Northwestern Community College W
Colorado School of Mines W
Colorado State University W
Colorado State University
    Pueblo W
Fort Lewis College W
Lamar Community College W
Mesa State College W
Metropolitan State College of Denver W
Northeastern Junior College W
Otero Junior College W
Regis University W
Trinidad State Junior College W
University of Colorado
    Boulder W
    Colorado Springs W
University of Denver W
University of Northern Colorado W
Western State College of Colorado W

Connecticut
Central Connecticut State University W
Fairfield University W
Post University W
Quinnipiac University W
Sacred Heart University M,W
Southern Connecticut State University W
University of Bridgeport W
University of Connecticut W
University of Hartford W
University of New Haven W

Delaware
Delaware State University W
Goldey-Beacom College W
University of Delaware W
Wilmington University W

District of Columbia
American University W
George Washington University W
Georgetown University W
Howard University W

Florida
Ave Maria University W
Barry University M,W
Bethune-Cookman University W
Brevard Community College W
Eckerd College M,W
Embry-Riddle Aeronautical University W
Flagler College W
Florida Agricultural and Mechanical University
    W
Florida Atlantic University W
Florida College W
Florida Gulf Coast University W
Florida Institute of Technology W
Florida Memorial University W
Florida Southern College W
Florida State College at Jacksonville W
Florida State University W
Hillsborough Community College W
Indian River State College W
Jacksonville University W
Lake-Sumter Community College W
Lynn University W
Miami Dade College W
Northwood University
    Florida W
Nova Southeastern University W
Palm Beach Community College W
Pasco-Hernando Community College W
Pensacola Junior College W
Polk State College W
Rollins College W
Saint Leo University W
St. Petersburg College W
Saint Thomas University W

South Florida Community College W
Southeastern University W
State College of Florida, Manatee-Sarasota W
Stetson University W
University of Central Florida W
University of Florida W
University of Miami W
University of North Florida W
University of South Florida W
University of Tampa W
University of West Florida W
Warner University M,W
Webber International University W

Georgia
Abraham Baldwin Agricultural College W
Albany State University W
Armstrong Atlantic State University W
Augusta State University W
Brenau University W
Brewton-Parker College W
Clark Atlanta University W
Covenant College W
Fort Valley State University W
Georgia Institute of Technology W
Georgia Southern University W
Georgia State University W
Mercer University W
Paine College W
Savannah State University W
Shorter College W
University of Georgia W
University of West Georgia W
Valdosta State University W

Hawaii
Chaminade University of Honolulu W
Hawaii Pacific University W
University of Hawaii
    Hilo W
    Manoa M,W

Idaho
Boise State University W
College of Idaho W
Idaho State University W
Lewis-Clark State College W
North Idaho College W
Northwest Nazarene University W
University of Idaho W

Illinois
Black Hawk College W
Bradley University W
Carl Sandburg College W
Chicago State University W
College of Lake County W
Danville Area Community College W
DePaul University W
Eastern Illinois University W
Elgin Community College W
Highland Community College W
Illinois Central College W
Illinois Institute of Technology W
Illinois State University W
John A. Logan College W
Judson University W
Kankakee Community College W
Kaskaskia College W
Kishwaukee College W
Lake Land College W
Lewis and Clark Community College W
Lewis University M,W
Lincoln College W
Loyola University Chicago M,W
McHenry County College W
McKendree University W
Moraine Valley Community College W
Morton College W
Northwestern University W
Olivet Nazarene University W
Parkland College W
Quincy University M,W

Rend Lake College W
Robert Morris University: Chicago M,W
Saint Xavier University W
Sauk Valley Community College W
Shawnee Community College W
South Suburban College of Cook County W
Southern Illinois University Carbondale W
Southern Illinois University Edwardsville W
Southwestern Illinois College W
Trinity Christian College W
Trinity International University W
University of Illinois
    Chicago W
    Springfield W
    Urbana-Champaign W
University of St. Francis W
Waubonsee Community College W
Western Illinois University W

Indiana
Ancilla College W
Ball State University M,W
Bethel College W
Butler University W
Calumet College of St. Joseph M,W
Goshen College W
Grace College W
Huntington University W
Indiana Institute of Technology W
Indiana State University W
Indiana University
    Bloomington W
    Southeast W
Indiana University-Purdue University Fort
    Wayne M,W
Indiana University-Purdue University
    Indianapolis W
Indiana Wesleyan University W
Marian University W
Oakland City University W
Purdue University W
Purdue University
    North Central W
Saint Joseph's College W
Taylor University W
University of Evansville W
University of Indianapolis W
University of Notre Dame W
University of St. Francis W
University of Southern Indiana W
Valparaiso University W
Vincennes University W

Iowa
Briar Cliff University W
Clarke College M,W
Clinton Community College W
Des Moines Area Community College W
Dordt College W
Drake University W
Ellsworth Community College W
Graceland University M,W
Grand View University W
Indian Hills Community College W
Iowa Central Community College W
Iowa Lakes Community College- Estherville W
Iowa State University W
Iowa Wesleyan College W
Iowa Western Community College W
Kirkwood Community College W
Morningside College W
Mount Mercy College W
North Iowa Area Community College W
Northwestern College W
St. Ambrose University M,W
Southeastern Community College
    North Campus W
Southwestern Community College W
University of Iowa W
University of Northern Iowa W
Waldorf College W
William Penn University W

Kansas
Allen County Community College W
Baker University W
Barton County Community College W
Benedictine College W
Bethany College W
Bethel College W
Butler Community College W
Central Christian College of Kansas W
Cloud County Community College W
Coffeyville Community College W
Colby Community College W
Cowley County Community College W
Dodge City Community College W
Emporia State University W
Fort Hays State University W
Fort Scott Community College W
Friends University W
Garden City Community College W
Hesston College W
Highland Community College W
Hutchinson Community College W
Johnson County Community College W
Kansas City Kansas Community College W
Kansas State University W
Kansas Wesleyan University W
Labette Community College W
McPherson College W
MidAmerica Nazarene University W
Neosho County Community College W
Newman University W
Ottawa University W
Pittsburg State University W
Pratt Community College W
Seward County Community College W
Southwestern College W
Sterling College W
Tabor College W
University of Kansas W
University of St. Mary W
Washburn University W
Wichita State University W

Kentucky
Asbury College W
Bellarmine University W
Brescia University W
Campbellsville University W
Eastern Kentucky University W
Georgetown College W
Kentucky State University W
Kentucky Wesleyan College W
Lindsey Wilson College W
Mid-Continent University W
Midway College W
Morehead State University W
Murray State University W
Northern Kentucky University W
Pikeville College W
St. Catharine College W
Union College W
University of Kentucky W
University of Louisville W
University of the Cumberlands W
Western Kentucky University W

Louisiana
Centenary College of Louisiana W
Dillard University W
Louisiana State University and Agricultural and
    Mechanical College W
Louisiana Tech University W
McNeese State University W
Nicholls State University W
Northwestern State University W
Southeastern Louisiana University W
Southern University and Agricultural and
    Mechanical College W
University of Louisiana at Lafayette W
University of Louisiana at Monroe W
University of New Orleans W
Xavier University of Louisiana W

Maine
University of Maine W

Maryland
Bowie State University W
College of Southern Maryland W
Community College of Baltimore County W
Coppin State University W
Garrett College W
Hagerstown Community College W
Harford Community College W
Morgan State University W
Towson University W
University of Maryland
    Baltimore County W
    College Park W
    Eastern Shore W

Massachusetts
American International College W
Boston College W
Merrimack College W
Northeastern University W
Stonehill College W
University of Massachusetts
    Lowell W

Michigan
Alpena Community College W
Aquinas College W
Central Michigan University W
Cornerstone University W
Davenport University W
Delta College W
Eastern Michigan University W
Ferris State University W
Grand Rapids Community College W
Grand Valley State University W
Hillsdale College W
Kalamazoo Valley Community College W
Kellogg Community College W
Lake Michigan College W
Lake Superior State University W
Lansing Community College W
Macomb Community College W
Madonna University W
Michigan State University W
Michigan Technological University W
Mott Community College W
Muskegon Community College W
Northern Michigan University W
Northwood University: Michigan W
Oakland Community College W
Oakland University W
Rochester College W
Saginaw Valley State University W
Siena Heights University M,W
Spring Arbor University W
University of Michigan W
University of Michigan
    Dearborn W
Wayne State University W
Western Michigan University W

Minnesota
Bemidji State University W
Concordia University: St. Paul W
Minnesota State University
    Mankato W
    Moorhead W
Saint Cloud State University W
Southwest Minnesota State University W
University of Minnesota
    Crookston W
    Duluth W
    Twin Cities W
Winona State University W

Mississippi
Alcorn State University W
Belhaven University W
Jackson State University W

Mississippi State University W
Mississippi Valley State University W
University of Mississippi W
University of Southern Mississippi W

Missouri
Avila University W
Central Methodist University W
College of the Ozarks W
Columbia College W
Cottey College W
Culver-Stockton College W
Drury University W
East Central College W
Evangel University W
Hannibal-LaGrange College M,W
Harris-Stowe State University W
Jefferson College W
Metropolitan Community College: Longview W
Mineral Area College W
Missouri Baptist University M,W
Missouri Southern State University W
Missouri State University W
Missouri State University: West Plains W
Missouri Valley College M,W
Missouri Western State University W
Northwest Missouri State University W
Park University M,W
Research College of Nursing W
Rockhurst University W
Saint Louis University W
Southeast Missouri State University W
Southwest Baptist University W
Stephens College W
Truman State University W
University of Central Missouri W
University of Missouri
    Columbia W
    Kansas City W
    St. Louis W
William Jewell College W
William Woods University M,W

Montana
Montana State University
    Billings W
    Bozeman W
Montana Tech of the University of Montana W
Rocky Mountain College W
University of Great Falls W
University of Montana W
University of Montana: Western W

Nebraska
Bellevue University W
Central Community College W
Chadron State College W
College of Saint Mary W
Concordia University W
Creighton University W
Dana College W
Doane College W
Mid-Plains Community College Area W
Nebraska College of Technical Agriculture M,W
Peru State College W
University of Nebraska
    Kearney W
    Lincoln W
    Omaha W
Wayne State College W
Western Nebraska Community College W
York College W

Nevada
University of Nevada
    Las Vegas W
    Reno W

New Hampshire
Franklin Pierce University W
University of New Hampshire W

New Jersey
Bloomfield College W
Fairleigh Dickinson University
    Metropolitan Campus W
Georgian Court University W
New Jersey Institute of Technology M,W
Rider University W
Rutgers, The State University of New Jersey
    New Brunswick/Piscataway Campus W
    Newark Regional Campus M
Saint Peter's College W
Seton Hall University W

New Mexico
Eastern New Mexico University W
New Mexico Highlands University W
New Mexico State University W
University of New Mexico W
Western New Mexico University W

New York
Adelphi University W
Canisius College W
City University of New York
    Queens College W
Colgate University W
College of Saint Rose W
Concordia College M,W
Daemen College W
Dominican College of Blauvelt W
Dowling College W
Fordham University W
Genesee Community College W
Globe Institute of Technology W
Hofstra University W
Houghton College W
Iona College W
Le Moyne College W
Long Island University
    Brooklyn Campus W
    C. W. Post Campus W
Manhattan College W
Marist College W
Mercy College W
Molloy College W
New York Institute of Technology W
Niagara University W
Nyack College W
Pace University W
Roberts Wesleyan College W
St. Francis College W
St. John's University W
Siena College W
State University of New York
    Albany W
    Binghamton W
    Buffalo W
    Stony Brook W
Syracuse University W

North Carolina
Appalachian State University W
Barton College W
Brevard College W
Campbell University W
Catawba College W
Chowan University W
Davidson College W
Duke University W
East Carolina University M,W
Elizabeth City State University W
Elon University W
Fayetteville State University W
Gardner-Webb University W
Guilford Technical Community College W
High Point University W
Johnson C. Smith University W
Lees-McRae College M,W
Lenoir Community College W
Lenoir-Rhyne University W
Livingstone College W
Louisburg College W

Mars Hill College W
Montreat College W
Mount Olive College W
North Carolina Agricultural and Technical State
    University W
North Carolina Central University W
North Carolina State University W
Pfeiffer University W
Pitt Community College W
Queens University of Charlotte W
St. Andrews Presbyterian College W
St. Augustine's College W
Shaw University W
Southeastern Community College W
University of North Carolina
    Asheville W
    Chapel Hill W
    Charlotte W
    Greensboro W
    Pembroke W
    Wilmington W
Wake Forest University W
Western Carolina University W
Wingate University W
Winston-Salem State University W

North Dakota
Bismarck State College W
Dakota College at Bottineau W
Dickinson State University W
Jamestown College W
Mayville State University W
Minot State University W
North Dakota State College of Science W
North Dakota State University W
University of Mary W
University of North Dakota W
Williston State College W

Ohio
Ashland University W
Bowling Green State University W
Cedarville University W
Central State University W
Clark State Community College W
Cleveland State University W
Edison State Community College W
Kent State University W
Malone University W
Miami University
    Oxford Campus W
Mount Vernon Nazarene University W
Notre Dame College W
Ohio Dominican University W
Ohio University W
Shawnee State University W
Southern State Community College W
Tiffin University W
University of Akron W
University of Cincinnati W
University of Dayton W
University of Findlay W
University of Rio Grande W
University of Toledo W
Urbana University W
Ursuline College W
Walsh University W
Wright State University W
Xavier University W
Youngstown State University W

Oklahoma
Bacone College W
Cameron University W
East Central University W
Langston University W
Northeastern Oklahoma Agricultural and
    Mechanical College W
Oklahoma City University W
Oklahoma Panhandle State University W
Oklahoma Wesleyan University W
Oral Roberts University W

Redlands Community College W
St. Gregory's University W
Seminole State College M,W
Southeastern Oklahoma State University W
Southern Nazarene University W
University of Central Oklahoma W
University of Oklahoma W
University of Tulsa W

Oregon
Blue Mountain Community College W
Chemeketa Community College W
Clackamas Community College W
Concordia University W
Corban College W
Eastern Oregon University W
Lane Community College W
Linn-Benton Community College W
Mt. Hood Community College W
Northwest Christian University W
Oregon Institute of Technology W
Oregon State University W
Portland State University W
Southern Oregon University W
Southwestern Oregon Community College W
Treasure Valley Community College W
University of Oregon W
University of Portland W
Warner Pacific College W

Pennsylvania
California University of Pennsylvania W
Carlow University W
Chestnut Hill College W
Cheyney University of Pennsylvania W
Community College of Beaver County W
Duquesne University W
Edinboro University of Pennsylvania W
Gannon University W
Harcum College W
Holy Family University W
Indiana University of Pennsylvania W
Kutztown University of Pennsylvania W
La Salle University W
Lackawanna College W
Lehigh University W
Lock Haven University of Pennsylvania W
Mercyhurst College W
Millersville University of Pennsylvania W
Penn State
    University Park M,W
Philadelphia University W
Point Park University W
Robert Morris University W
St. Francis University M,W
Seton Hill University W
Shippensburg University of Pennsylvania W
Slippery Rock University of Pennsylvania W
Temple University W
University of Pittsburgh W
University of the Sciences in Philadelphia W
Villanova University W
West Chester University of Pennsylvania W
Westminster College W

Puerto Rico
Bayamon Central University M,W
Inter American University of Puerto Rico
    Aguadilla Campus M,W
    Bayamon Campus M,W
    Metropolitan Campus M,W
    San German Campus M,W
Turabo University M,W
Universidad del Este M,W
Universidad Metropolitana M,W
University of Puerto Rico
    Bayamon University College M,W
    Carolina Regional College M,W
    Cayey University College M,W
    Humacao M,W
    Ponce M,W
    Utuado M,W

University of the Sacred Heart M,W

Rhode Island
Bryant University W
Community College of Rhode Island W
University of Rhode Island W

South Carolina
Anderson University W
Charleston Southern University W
The Citadel W
Claflin University W
Clemson University W
Coastal Carolina University W
Coker College W
College of Charleston W
Columbia College W
Converse College W
Erskine College W
Francis Marion University W
Furman University W
Lander University W
Limestone College M,W
Morris College W
Newberry College W
North Greenville University W
Presbyterian College W
South Carolina State University W
Southern Wesleyan University W
Spartanburg Methodist College W
University of South Carolina W
University of South Carolina
    Aiken W
    Upstate W
Winthrop University W
Wofford College W

South Dakota
Augustana College W
Black Hills State University W
Dakota State University W
Dakota Wesleyan University W
Mount Marty College W
South Dakota School of Mines and Technology W
South Dakota State University W
University of Sioux Falls W

Tennessee
Austin Peay State University W
Belmont University W
Bethel University W
Bryan College W
Carson-Newman College W
Christian Brothers University W
Cumberland University W
East Tennessee State University W
Freed-Hardeman University W
King College W
Lane College W
Lee University W
LeMoyne-Owen College W
Lincoln Memorial University W
Lipscomb University W
Martin Methodist College W
Middle Tennessee State University W
Milligan College W
Tennessee Technological University W
Tennessee Temple University W
Tennessee Wesleyan College W
Trevecca Nazarene University W
Tusculum College W
Union University W
University of Memphis W
University of Tennessee
    Chattanooga W
    Knoxville W
    Martin W

Texas
Abilene Christian University W
Angelo State University W
Baylor University W

Blinn College W
Clarendon College W
Dallas Baptist University W
Frank Phillips College W
Galveston College W
Hill College W
Houston Baptist University W
Jarvis Christian College W
Lamar University W
Laredo Community College W
Lee College W
Lubbock Christian University W
Midwestern State University W
North Central Texas College W
Panola College W
Paris Junior College W
Prairie View A&M University W
Ranger College W
Rice University W
St. Edward's University W
St. Mary's University W
Sam Houston State University W
Southern Methodist University W
Southwestern Assemblies of God University W
Stephen F. Austin State University W
Tarleton State University W
Temple College W
Texas A&M University W
Texas A&M University
    Commerce W
    Corpus Christi W
    Kingsville W
Texas Christian University W
Texas Southern University W
Texas State University: San Marcos W
Texas Tech University W
Texas Woman's University W
Tyler Junior College W
University of Houston W
University of North Texas W
University of St. Thomas W
University of Texas
    Arlington W
    Austin W
    Brownsville - Texas Southmost College W
    Pan American W
    of the Permian Basin W
    San Antonio W
University of the Incarnate Word W
Vernon College W
Wayland Baptist University W
West Texas A&M University W
Western Texas College W
Wharton County Junior College W
Wiley College W

Utah
Brigham Young University M,W
College of Eastern Utah W
Dixie State College of Utah W
Salt Lake Community College W
Snow College W
University of Utah W
Utah State University W
Utah Valley University W
Weber State University W
Westminster College W

Virginia
Bluefield College W
College of William and Mary W
George Mason University M,W
Hampton University W
James Madison University W
Liberty University W
Norfolk State University W
Radford University W
St. Paul's College W
University of Virginia W
University of Virginia's College at Wise W
Virginia Commonwealth University W
Virginia Intermont College W

Virginia Polytechnic Institute and State University W
Virginia State University W
Virginia Union University W

Washington
Big Bend Community College W
Centralia College W
Clark College W
Eastern Washington University W
Everett Community College W
Evergreen State College W
Gonzaga University W
Grays Harbor College W
Green River Community College W
Highline Community College W
Lower Columbia College W
Northwest University W
Olympic College W
Pierce College W
Saint Martin's University W
Seattle Pacific University W
Seattle University W
Shoreline Community College W
Skagit Valley College W
Spokane Community College W
University of Washington W
Washington State University W
Western Washington University W
Whatcom Community College W
Yakima Valley Community College W

West Virginia
Alderson-Broaddus College W
Bluefield State College W
Concord University W
Davis and Elkins College W
Glenville State College W
Marshall University W
Mountain State University W
Ohio Valley University W
Salem International University W
Shepherd University W
University of Charleston W
West Liberty University W
West Virginia University W
West Virginia University Institute of Technology W
West Virginia Wesleyan College W
Wheeling Jesuit University W

Wisconsin
Cardinal Stritch University M,W
Marquette University W
Milwaukee Area Technical College W
University of Wisconsin
    Green Bay W
    Milwaukee M,W
    Parkside W
Viterbo University W

Wyoming
Casper College W
Central Wyoming College W
Eastern Wyoming College W
Laramie County Community College W
Northwest College W
Sheridan College W
University of Wyoming W
Western Wyoming Community College W

Water polo

Arizona
Arizona State University W

California
California Baptist University M,W
California State University
    Bakersfield W
    Long Beach M,W

Monterey Bay W
Concordia University M,W
Fresno Pacific University M,W
Grossmont College M,W
Loyola Marymount University M,W
Pepperdine University M
San Diego State University W
San Jose State University W
Santa Clara University M,W
Sonoma State University W
Stanford University M,W
University of California
    Berkeley M,W
    Davis M,W
    Irvine M,W
University of Southern California M,W
University of the Pacific M,W

District of Columbia
George Washington University M

Florida
Florida Atlantic University W

Hawaii
University of Hawaii
    Manoa W

Indiana
Indiana University
    Bloomington W

Michigan
University of Michigan W

New York
City University of New York
    Queens College M
Fordham University M
Hartwick College W
Iona College W
Marist College W
St. Francis College M,W
Siena College W
Wagner College W

Pennsylvania
Gannon University M,W
Mercyhurst College M,W

Weight lifting

Puerto Rico
Inter American University of Puerto Rico
    Aguadilla Campus M,W
    Ponce Campus M,W
    San German Campus M,W
Turabo University M,W
Universidad del Este M,W
Universidad Metropolitana M,W
University of Puerto Rico
    Carolina Regional College M,W
    Cayey University College M,W
    Humacao M,W
    Utuado M,W

Washington
Olympic College M,W

Wrestling

Arizona
Arizona State University M
Embry-Riddle Aeronautical University: Prescott
    Campus M
Grand Canyon University M

California
California Baptist University M

California Polytechnic State University: San Luis
    Obispo M
California State University
    Bakersfield M
    Fresno M
    Fullerton M
Fresno City College M
Stanford University M
University of California
    Davis M
    Los Angeles M,W

Colorado
Adams State College M
Colorado School of Mines M
Colorado State University
    Pueblo M
Mesa State College M
University of Northern Colorado M
Western State College of Colorado M

Connecticut
Sacred Heart University M

Delaware
Delaware State University M

District of Columbia
American University M
Howard University M

Florida
University of Tampa M

Idaho
Boise State University M
North Idaho College M

Illinois
Lincoln College M
McKendree University M
Northwestern University M
Rend Lake College M
Southern Illinois University Edwardsville M
University of Illinois
    Urbana-Champaign M
Wilbur Wright College M,W

Indiana
Calumet College of St. Joseph M
Indiana University
    Bloomington M
Purdue University M
University of Indianapolis M

Iowa
Briar Cliff University M
Ellsworth Community College M
Grand View University M
Iowa Central Community College M
Iowa State University M
North Iowa Area Community College M
Northwestern College M
University of Iowa M
University of Northern Iowa M
Waldorf College M
William Penn University M

Kansas
Baker University M
Colby Community College M
Fort Hays State University M
Labette Community College M
Neosho County Community College M
Newman University M
Pratt Community College M

Kentucky
Campbellsville University M
University of the Cumberlands M,W

Maryland
University of Maryland
    College Park M

Massachusetts
American International College M
Boston University M

Michigan
Central Michigan University M
Eastern Michigan University M
Grand Rapids Community College M
Michigan State University M
Muskegon Community College M
University of Michigan M

Minnesota
Minnesota State University
    Mankato M
    Moorhead M
Saint Cloud State University M
Southwest Minnesota State University M
University of Minnesota
    Twin Cities M

Missouri
Hannibal-LaGrange College M
Missouri Baptist University M
Missouri Valley College M,W
St. Louis Community College
    Meramec M
Truman State University M
University of Central Missouri M
University of Missouri
    Columbia M

Montana
University of Great Falls M

Nebraska
Chadron State College M
Concordia University M
Dana College M
University of Nebraska
    Kearney M
    Lincoln M
    Omaha M
York College M

New Jersey
Rider University M
Rutgers, The State University of New Jersey
    New Brunswick/Piscataway Campus M

New York
Hofstra University M
Niagara County Community College M
State University of New York
    Binghamton M
    Buffalo M

North Carolina
Appalachian State University M
Campbell University M
Davidson College M
Duke University M
Gardner-Webb University M
North Carolina Agricultural and Technical State
    University M
North Carolina State University M
University of North Carolina
    Chapel Hill M
    Greensboro M
    Pembroke M

North Dakota
Dickinson State University M
Jamestown College M,W
North Dakota State University M
University of Mary M

Ohio
Ashland University M
Cleveland State University M
Kent State University M
Notre Dame College M
Ohio University M

University of Findlay M

Oklahoma
Bacone College M
Oklahoma City University M,W
Oklahoma State University M
University of Central Oklahoma M
University of Oklahoma M

Oregon
Clackamas Community College M
Oregon State University M
Southern Oregon University M
Southwestern Oregon Community College M

Pennsylvania
Bloomsburg University of Pennsylvania M
Clarion University of Pennsylvania M
Drexel University M
Duquesne University M
East Stroudsburg University of Pennsylvania M
Edinboro University of Pennsylvania M
Gannon University M
Kutztown University of Pennsylvania M
Lehigh University M
Lock Haven University of Pennsylvania M
Mercyhurst College M
Millersville University of Pennsylvania M
Penn State
    University Park M
Seton Hill University M
Shippensburg University of Pennsylvania M
University of Pittsburgh M
University of Pittsburgh
    Johnstown M

Puerto Rico
Inter American University of Puerto Rico
    Bayamon Campus M
    Ponce Campus M,W
University of Puerto Rico
    Bayamon University College M
    Humacao M
University of the Sacred Heart M

Rhode Island
Bryant University M

South Carolina
Anderson University M
The Citadel M
Limestone College M
Newberry College M
Spartanburg Methodist College M

South Dakota
Augustana College M
Dakota Wesleyan University M
Northern State University M
South Dakota State University M
University of Sioux Falls W

Tennessee
Carson-Newman College M
Cumberland University M
King College M,W
University of Tennessee
    Chattanooga M

Utah
Utah Valley University M

Virginia
George Mason University W
Old Dominion University M
University of Virginia M
Virginia Military Institute M
Virginia Polytechnic Institute and State
    University M

Washington
Highline Community College M
Yakima Valley Community College M,W

West Virginia
West Liberty University M
West Virginia University M

Wisconsin
University of Wisconsin
    Parkside M

Wyoming
Northwest College M
University of Wyoming M
Western Wyoming Community College M

Music/drama scholarships

Alabama
Alabama State University
Auburn University at Montgomery
Bevill State Community College
Birmingham-Southern College
Chattahoochee Valley Community College
Enterprise-Ozark Community College
Faulkner University
Gadsden State Community College
Huntingdon College
Jacksonville State University
Jefferson State Community College
Judson College
Lurleen B. Wallace Community College
Northeast Alabama Community College
Northwest-Shoals Community College
Samford University
Snead State Community College
Southeastern Bible College
Talladega College
Troy University
University of Alabama
University of Alabama
    Birmingham
    Huntsville
University of Mobile
University of Montevallo
University of North Alabama
University of South Alabama
University of West Alabama
Wallace State Community College at Hanceville

Alaska
Alaska Pacific University
University of Alaska
    Fairbanks
    Southeast

Arizona
Arizona State University
Eastern Arizona College
Northern Arizona University
Northland Pioneer College
Pima Community College
Southwestern College
University of Arizona

Arkansas
Arkansas Northeastern College
Arkansas State University
Arkansas State University
    Beebe
Arkansas Tech University
Central Baptist College
Crowley's Ridge College
Ecclesia College
Harding University
Henderson State University
Hendrix College
John Brown University
Lyon College
National Park Community College
Northwest Arkansas Community College
Ouachita Baptist University
Phillips Community College of the University of
    Arkansas
Southern Arkansas University
University of Arkansas
University of Arkansas
    Fort Smith
    Monticello
    Pine Bluff
University of Central Arkansas

University of the Ozarks
Williams Baptist College

California
American Academy of Dramatic Arts: West
American Jewish University
Azusa Pacific University
Bethany University
Bethesda Christian University
Biola University
California Baptist University
California Institute of Integral Studies
California Institute of the Arts
California Lutheran University
California Polytechnic State University: San Luis
    Obispo
California State University
    Chico
    Dominguez Hills
    East Bay
    Fresno
    Long Beach
    Stanislaus
Chapman University
College of the Canyons
College of the Siskiyous
Concordia University
Dominican University of California
El Camino College
Fresno Pacific University
Holy Names University
Hope International University
Irvine Valley College
La Sierra University
Loyola Marymount University
The Master's College
Mendocino College
Mills College
Mount San Jacinto College
Notre Dame de Namur University
Occidental College
Pepperdine University
Point Loma Nazarene University
Riverside Community College
San Diego Christian College
San Diego State University
San Francisco Conservatory of Music
Santa Clara University
Santa Rosa Junior College
Shasta Bible College and Graduate School
Simpson University
Sonoma State University
University of California
    Irvine
    Riverside
    San Diego
    Santa Cruz
University of La Verne
University of Redlands
University of San Diego
University of Southern California
University of the Pacific
Vanguard University of Southern California
Westmont College
William Jessup University
Yuba Community College District

Colorado
Adams State College
Colorado Christian University
Colorado State University
Colorado State University
    Pueblo

Fort Lewis College
Mesa State College
Metropolitan State College of Denver
Northeastern Junior College
Pueblo Community College
University of Colorado
    Boulder
    Denver
University of Denver
University of Northern Colorado
Western State College of Colorado

Connecticut
Albertus Magnus College
Fairfield University
Sacred Heart University
University of Bridgeport
University of Connecticut
University of Hartford

Delaware
Delaware State University
University of Delaware

District of Columbia
American University
Catholic University of America
George Washington University
Howard University

Florida
Baptist College of Florida
Barry University
Bethune-Cookman University
Central Florida Community College
Chipola College
Clearwater Christian College
Daytona State College
Eckerd College
Edison State College
Flagler College
Florida Agricultural and Mechanical University
Florida Atlantic University
Florida Christian College
Florida College
Florida Gulf Coast University
Florida International University
Florida Southern College
Florida State College at Jacksonville
Gulf Coast Community College
Hillsborough Community College
Indian River State College
Jacksonville University
Lynn University
Miami Dade College
North Florida Community College
Northwest Florida State College
Nova Southeastern University
Palm Beach Atlantic University
Rollins College
Saint Leo University
St. Petersburg College
Saint Thomas University
Santa Fe College
Seminole Community College
South Florida Community College
Southeastern University
State College of Florida, Manatee-Sarasota
Stetson University
Tallahassee Community College
University of Florida
University of Miami
University of North Florida
University of South Florida
University of Tampa
University of West Florida
Warner University

Georgia
Agnes Scott College
Albany State University
Andrew College
Armstrong Atlantic State University

Augusta State University
Berry College
Brenau University
Brewton-Parker College
Clark Atlanta University
Clayton State University
Columbus State University
Covenant College
Darton College
Emmanuel College
Emory University
Gainesville State College
Georgia College and State University
Georgia Institute of Technology
Georgia Southern University
Gordon College
Kennesaw State University
LaGrange College
Mercer University
Middle Georgia College
Morehouse College
North Georgia College & State University
Oglethorpe University
Paine College
Piedmont College
Reinhardt College
Savannah College of Art and Design
Savannah State University
Shorter College
Spelman College
Toccoa Falls College
Truett-McConnell College
University of West Georgia
Valdosta State University
Wesleyan College
Young Harris College

Hawaii
Hawaii Pacific University
University of Hawaii
    Manoa

Idaho
Boise Bible College
Boise State University
College of Idaho
Idaho State University
Lewis-Clark State College
North Idaho College
Northwest Nazarene University
University of Idaho

Illinois
Augustana College
Aurora University
Benedictine University
Black Hawk College
Bradley University
Carl Sandburg College
College of DuPage
College of Lake County
Columbia College Chicago
Concordia University Chicago
Danville Area Community College
DePaul University
Eastern Illinois University
Elgin Community College
Elmhurst College
Eureka College
Greenville College
Harper College
Illinois Central College
Illinois College
Illinois State University
Illinois Wesleyan University
Judson University
Kishwaukee College
Knox College
Lake Forest College
Lewis University
Lincoln College
McHenry County College

McKendree University
Millikin University
Monmouth College
Moody Bible Institute
North Central College
North Park University
Northeastern Illinois University
Northwestern University
Oakton Community College
Olivet Nazarene University
Parkland College
Quincy University
Rend Lake College
Richland Community College
Rockford College
Roosevelt University
Saint Xavier University
South Suburban College of Cook County
Southeastern Illinois College
Southern Illinois University Edwardsville
Trinity Christian College
Trinity International University
University of Illinois
    Chicago
    Springfield
    Urbana-Champaign
University of St. Francis
VanderCook College of Music
Waubonsee Community College
Western Illinois University
Wheaton College

Indiana
Anderson University
Ball State University
Bethel College
Butler University
DePauw University
Goshen College
Grace College
Hanover College
Huntington University
Indiana Institute of Technology
Indiana State University
Indiana University
    Bloomington
    Southeast
Indiana Wesleyan University
Manchester College
Marian University
Oakland City University
Purdue University
Saint Joseph's College
St. Mary-of-the-Woods College
Taylor University
Trine University
University of Evansville
University of Indianapolis
University of St. Francis
University of Southern Indiana
Valparaiso University
Vincennes University
Wabash College

Iowa
Briar Cliff University
Buena Vista University
Central College
Clarke College
Coe College
Cornell College
Dordt College
Drake University
Ellsworth Community College
Emmaus Bible College
Faith Baptist Bible College and Theological
    Seminary
Graceland University
Grand View University
Iowa Central Community College
Iowa State University
Iowa Wesleyan College

Iowa Western Community College
Kirkwood Community College
Loras College
Luther College
Morningside College
Mount Mercy College
North Iowa Area Community College
Northwestern College
St. Ambrose University
Simpson College
Southwestern Community College
University of Dubuque
University of Iowa
University of Northern Iowa
Waldorf College
Wartburg College
Western Iowa Tech Community College
William Penn University

Kansas
Allen County Community College
Baker University
Barclay College
Benedictine College
Bethany College
Bethel College
Butler Community College
Central Christian College of Kansas
Coffeyville Community College
Colby Community College
Cowley County Community College
Dodge City Community College
Emporia State University
Fort Hays State University
Friends University
Garden City Community College
Hesston College
Highland Community College
Kansas City Kansas Community College
Kansas State University
Kansas Wesleyan University
McPherson College
MidAmerica Nazarene University
Neosho County Community College
Newman University
Ottawa University
Pittsburg State University
Pratt Community College
Southwestern College
Tabor College
University of Kansas
University of St. Mary
Washburn University
Wichita State University

Kentucky
Asbury College
Ashland Community and Technical College
Bellarmine University
Brescia University
Campbellsville University
Centre College
Eastern Kentucky University
Georgetown College
Kentucky Christian University
Kentucky Mountain Bible College
Kentucky State University
Kentucky Wesleyan College
Morehead State University
Murray State University
Northern Kentucky University
Thomas More College
Transylvania University
Union College
University of Kentucky
University of Louisville
Western Kentucky University

Louisiana
Bossier Parish Community College
Centenary College of Louisiana
Delgado Community College

Dillard University
Grambling State University
Louisiana College
Louisiana State University and Agricultural and
    Mechanical College
Louisiana Tech University
McNeese State University
Northwestern State University
Southeastern Louisiana University
Tulane University
University of Louisiana at Monroe
Xavier University of Louisiana

Maine
University of Maine
University of Maine
    Augusta
    Machias
    Presque Isle
University of Southern Maine

Maryland
Bowie State University
College of Notre Dame of Maryland
Goucher College
Hood College
Johns Hopkins University: Peabody
    Conservatory of Music
Montgomery College
Mount St. Mary's University
Salisbury University
Stevenson University
Towson University
University of Maryland
    Baltimore County
    College Park
    Eastern Shore
Washington Adventist University
Washington Bible College

Massachusetts
Anna Maria College
Atlantic Union College
Bay Path College
Boston Conservatory
Boston University
Bristol Community College
Cape Cod Community College
Dean College
Emerson College
Endicott College
Gordon College
Holyoke Community College
Massachusetts College of Liberal Arts
Massachusetts Maritime Academy
New England Conservatory of Music
North Shore Community College
Stonehill College
University of Massachusetts
    Amherst
    Lowell
Western New England College

Michigan
Adrian College
Albion College
Alma College
Alpena Community College
Andrews University
Aquinas College
Calvin College
Central Michigan University
Cornerstone University
Eastern Michigan University
Ferris State University
Glen Oaks Community College
Gogebic Community College
Grace Bible College
Grand Rapids Community College
Grand Valley State University
Great Lakes Christian College
Hillsdale College
Hope College

Jackson Community College
Kalamazoo College
Macomb Community College
Madonna University
Marygrove College
Michigan State University
Michigan Technological University
Monroe County Community College
Mott Community College
Northern Michigan University
Northwestern Michigan College
Oakland University
Rochester College
Saginaw Valley State University
Schoolcraft College
Siena Heights University
Southwestern Michigan College
Spring Arbor University
University of Detroit Mercy
University of Michigan
University of Michigan
    Flint
Wayne State University
Western Michigan University

Minnesota
Augsburg College
Bemidji State University
Bethany Lutheran College
Bethel University
College of St. Benedict
College of St. Scholastica
Concordia College: Moorhead
Concordia University: St. Paul
Crossroads College
Crown College
Gustavus Adolphus College
Hamline University
Itasca Community College
Martin Luther College
Minnesota State Community and Technical
    College
Minnesota State University
    Mankato
    Moorhead
Normandale Community College
North Central University
Northwestern College
Riverland Community College
Saint Cloud State University
St. John's University
St. Mary's University of Minnesota
St. Olaf College
Southwest Minnesota State University
University of Minnesota
    Crookston
    Morris
    Twin Cities
University of St. Thomas
Winona State University

Mississippi
Belhaven University
Blue Mountain College
Copiah-Lincoln Community College
Delta State University
East Mississippi Community College
Hinds Community College
Jackson State University
Meridian Community College
Millsaps College
Mississippi College
Mississippi Gulf Coast Community College
Mississippi State University
Mississippi University for Women
Pearl River Community College
Rust College
University of Mississippi

Missouri
Avila University
Calvary Bible College and Theological Seminary

Central Methodist University
College of the Ozarks
Columbia College
Cottey College
Crowder College
Culver-Stockton College
Drury University
East Central College
Evangel University
Fontbonne University
Hannibal-LaGrange College
Harris-Stowe State University
Jefferson College
Lincoln University
Lindenwood University
Mineral Area College
Missouri Baptist University
Missouri Southern State University
Missouri State University
Missouri Western State University
North Central Missouri College
Northwest Missouri State University
Park University
Rockhurst University
St. Charles Community College
St. Louis Christian College
Saint Louis University
Southeast Missouri State University
Southwest Baptist University
State Fair Community College
Stephens College
Truman State University
University of Central Missouri
University of Missouri
    Columbia
    Kansas City
    Missouri University of Science and
      Technology
    St. Louis
Webster University
Westminster College
William Jewell College
William Woods University

Montana
Dawson Community College
Montana State University
    Billings
    Bozeman
Rocky Mountain College
University of Montana

Nebraska
Central Community College
Chadron State College
College of Saint Mary
Concordia University
Creighton University
Dana College
Doane College
Grace University
Mid-Plains Community College Area
Nebraska Wesleyan University
Northeast Community College
Peru State College
University of Nebraska
    Kearney
    Lincoln
    Omaha
Wayne State College
Western Nebraska Community College
York College

Nevada
Truckee Meadows Community College
University of Nevada
    Las Vegas
    Reno

New Hampshire
Colby-Sawyer College
Keene State College
New England College

Plymouth State University
University of New Hampshire

New Jersey
Bloomfield College
Caldwell College
Centenary College
Drew University
Georgian Court University
Kean University
Montclair State University
Richard Stockton College of New Jersey
Rider University
Rowan University
Rutgers, The State University of New Jersey
    Camden Regional Campus
    New Brunswick/Piscataway Campus
    Newark Regional Campus
Stevens Institute of Technology
William Paterson University of New Jersey

New Mexico
College of Santa Fe
Eastern New Mexico University
New Mexico Highlands University
New Mexico Junior College
University of New Mexico

New York
Adelphi University
Alfred University
Canisius College
City University of New York
    Brooklyn College
    College of Staten Island
    Queens College
College of Saint Rose
Concordia College
Eastman School of Music of the University of
    Rochester
Eugene Lang College The New School for
    Liberal Arts
Five Towns College
Hobart and William Smith Colleges
Hofstra University
Houghton College
Ithaca College
Jamestown Community College
Juilliard School
Manhattan School of Music
Manhattanville College
Mannes College The New School for Music
Marist College
Molloy College
Monroe Community College
Nazareth College
Niagara University
Nyack College
Pace University
Rensselaer Polytechnic Institute
Roberts Wesleyan College
Russell Sage College
Saint Bonaventure University
St. John's University
Skidmore College
State University of New York
    Binghamton
    Buffalo
    College at Cortland
    College at Fredonia
    College at Geneseo
    College at Oneonta
    College at Plattsburgh
    College at Potsdam
    New Paltz
    Purchase
    Stony Brook
Suffolk County Community College
Syracuse University
University of Rochester
Villa Maria College of Buffalo
Wagner College

North Carolina
Appalachian State University
Barton College
Brevard College
Campbell University
Cape Fear Community College
Catawba College
Catawba Valley Community College
Chowan University
College of the Albemarle
Davidson College
East Carolina University
Elon University
Fayetteville State University
Gardner-Webb University
Greensboro College
High Point University
Isothermal Community College
Lees-McRae College
Lenoir-Rhyne University
Livingstone College
Mars Hill College
Meredith College
Methodist University
Mid-Atlantic Christian University
Montreat College
Mount Olive College
North Carolina Agricultural and Technical State
    University
North Carolina Central University
Peace College
Pfeiffer University
Queens University of Charlotte
St. Andrews Presbyterian College
St. Augustine's College
Salem College
Shaw University
Southeastern Community College
University of North Carolina
    Asheville
    Chapel Hill
    Charlotte
    Greensboro
    Pembroke
    Wilmington
University of North Carolina School of the Arts
Wake Forest University
Western Carolina University
Wilkes Community College
Wingate University

North Dakota
Dakota College at Bottineau
Dickinson State University
Jamestown College
Lake Region State College
Mayville State University
Minot State University
North Dakota State College of Science
North Dakota State University
Trinity Bible College
University of Mary
University of North Dakota
Williston State College

Ohio
Ashland University
Baldwin-Wallace College
Bowling Green State University
Bowling Green State University: Firelands
    College
Capital University
Case Western Reserve University
Cedarville University
Central State University
Cincinnati Christian University
Cleveland Institute of Music
Cleveland State University
College of Mount St. Joseph
College of Wooster
Cuyahoga Community College
    Metropolitan Campus

Denison University
God's Bible School and College
Heidelberg University
Hiram College
Kent State University
Kent State University
    Ashtabula
    East Liverpool
    Salem
    Stark
    Trumbull
    Tuscarawas
Kent State University: Geauga
Malone University
Marietta College
Miami University
    Oxford Campus
Mount Union College
Mount Vernon Nazarene University
Muskingum University
Oberlin College
Ohio Northern University
Ohio State University
    Agricultural Technical Institute
    Columbus Campus
    Lima Campus
    Mansfield Campus
    Marion Campus
    Newark Campus
Ohio University
Ohio Wesleyan University
Otterbein College
Pontifical College Josephinum
Southern State Community College
Tiffin University
University of Akron
University of Akron: Wayne College
University of Cincinnati
University of Dayton
University of Findlay
University of Rio Grande
University of Toledo
Urbana University
Walsh University
Wittenberg University
Wright State University
Wright State University: Lake Campus
Xavier University

Oklahoma
Cameron University
Carl Albert State College
Mid-America Christian University
Northeastern Oklahoma Agricultural and
    Mechanical College
Northeastern State University
Northwestern Oklahoma State University
Oklahoma Baptist University
Oklahoma Christian University
Oklahoma City Community College
Oklahoma City University
Oklahoma Panhandle State University
Oklahoma State University
Oklahoma Wesleyan University
Oral Roberts University
Rogers State University
St. Gregory's University
Southeastern Oklahoma State University
Southwestern Christian University
Southwestern Oklahoma State University
Tulsa Community College
University of Central Oklahoma
University of Oklahoma
University of Science and Arts of Oklahoma
University of Tulsa
Western Oklahoma State College

Oregon
Blue Mountain Community College
Clackamas Community College
Concordia University
Corban College

Eastern Oregon University
George Fox University
Lane Community College
Linfield College
Linn-Benton Community College
Multnomah University
Northwest Christian University
Pacific University
Portland State University
Southern Oregon University
Southwestern Oregon Community College
Treasure Valley Community College
University of Oregon
University of Portland
Warner Pacific College
Western Oregon University
Willamette University

Pennsylvania
Albright College
Arcadia University
Baptist Bible College of Pennsylvania
Bloomsburg University of Pennsylvania
Bucknell University
California University of Pennsylvania
Carnegie Mellon University
Cedar Crest College
Clarion University of Pennsylvania
Delaware Valley College
DeSales University
Drexel University
Duquesne University
East Stroudsburg University of Pennsylvania
Edinboro University of Pennsylvania
Elizabethtown College
Franklin & Marshall College
Gannon University
Geneva College
Gettysburg College
Immaculata University
Indiana University of Pennsylvania
Kutztown University of Pennsylvania
Lancaster Bible College
Lebanon Valley College
Lehigh University
Lincoln University
Lock Haven University of Pennsylvania
Lycoming College
Mansfield University of Pennsylvania
Marywood University
Mercyhurst College
Messiah College
Moravian College
Mount Aloysius College
Muhlenberg College
Northampton Community College
Point Park University
St. Francis University
Saint Joseph's University
Seton Hill University
Slippery Rock University of Pennsylvania
Susquehanna University
Temple University
Thiel College
University of the Arts
Ursinus College
Valley Forge Christian College
Valley Forge Military Academy & College
Widener University
Wilkes University
York College of Pennsylvania

Puerto Rico
Humacao Community College
Universidad Politecnica de Puerto Rico
University of Puerto Rico
    Aguadilla
    Humacao

Rhode Island
Rhode Island College
University of Rhode Island

South Carolina
Allen University
Anderson University
Clemson University
Coastal Carolina University
Coker College
College of Charleston
Columbia College
Converse College
Erskine College
Francis Marion University
Furman University
Lander University
Limestone College
Newberry College
North Greenville University
Presbyterian College
Southern Wesleyan University
Spartanburg Methodist College
University of South Carolina
University of South Carolina
    Aiken
Winthrop University
Wofford College

South Dakota
Augustana College
Dakota State University
Dakota Wesleyan University
Mount Marty College
Northern State University
South Dakota State University
University of Sioux Falls
University of South Dakota

Tennessee
Austin Peay State University
Belmont University
Bethel University
Bryan College
Carson-Newman College
Christian Brothers University
Cumberland University
Dyersburg State Community College
East Tennessee State University
Fisk University
Free Will Baptist Bible College
Freed-Hardeman University
Jackson State Community College
Johnson Bible College
King College
Lambuth University
Lee University
LeMoyne-Owen College
Lincoln Memorial University
Lipscomb University
Martin Methodist College
Maryville College
Middle Tennessee State University
Milligan College
Motlow State Community College
Northeast State Community College
Pellissippi State Community College
Rhodes College
Roane State Community College
Southern Adventist University
Southwest Tennessee Community College
Tennessee Technological University
Tennessee Temple University
Tennessee Wesleyan College
Trevecca Nazarene University
Union University
University of Memphis
University of Tennessee
    Chattanooga
    Knoxville
Vanderbilt University
Volunteer State Community College
Walters State Community College

Texas
Abilene Christian University
Angelina College
Angelo State University
Austin College
Baylor University
Brazosport College
Clarendon College
College of the Mainland
Collin County Community College District
Concordia University Texas
Dallas Baptist University
Dallas Christian College
East Texas Baptist University
Frank Phillips College
Galveston College
Hardin-Simmons University
Hill College
Houston Baptist University
Howard College
Howard Payne University
Huston-Tillotson University
Jacksonville College
Kilgore College
Lee College
Lon Morris College
Lubbock Christian University
McMurry University
Midland College
Midwestern State University
Odessa College
Panola College
Paris Junior College
Rice University
Richland College
St. Edward's University
St. Mary's University
Sam Houston State University
San Jacinto College
Schreiner University
South Plains College
Southern Methodist University
Southwestern Adventist University
Southwestern University
Stephen F. Austin State University
Sul Ross State University
Tarleton State University
Temple College
Texas A&M University
Texas A&M University
    Commerce
    Corpus Christi
Texas Christian University
Texas College
Texas Lutheran University
Texas State University: San Marcos
Texas Tech University
Texas Wesleyan University
Trinity University
Tyler Junior College
University of Dallas
University of Houston
University of Mary Hardin-Baylor
University of Texas
    Arlington
    Austin
    Brownsville - Texas Southmost College
    El Paso
    of the Permian Basin
    San Antonio
    Tyler
University of the Incarnate Word
Vernon College
Victoria College
Wayland Baptist University
West Texas A&M University
Western Technical College
Western Texas College
Wharton County Junior College

Utah
Brigham Young University
College of Eastern Utah
Dixie State College of Utah
Salt Lake Community College
Snow College
Southern Utah University
University of Utah
Utah State University
Utah Valley University
Weber State University
Westminster College

Vermont
Castleton State College
Goddard College
Green Mountain College
Johnson State College
Landmark College
Norwich University

Virginia
Averett University
Bluefield College
Bridgewater College
Christopher Newport University
Emory & Henry College
George Mason University
Hampton University
Hollins University
James Madison University
Liberty University
Longwood University
Lynchburg College
Norfolk State University
Old Dominion University
Patrick Henry College
Radford University
Randolph College
Roanoke College
Shenandoah University
Southern Virginia University
Sweet Briar College
University of Mary Washington
University of Richmond
University of Virginia
University of Virginia's College at Wise
Virginia Commonwealth University
Virginia Intermont College
Virginia Polytechnic Institute and State
    University
Virginia State University

Washington
Big Bend Community College
Centralia College
Clark College
Everett Community College
Gonzaga University
Grays Harbor College
Northwest University
Pacific Lutheran University
Pierce College
Saint Martin's University
Seattle Pacific University
Seattle University
Trinity Lutheran College
University of Puget Sound
University of Washington
Walla Walla University
Washington State University
Western Washington University
Whitman College
Whitworth University

West Virginia
Alderson-Broaddus College
Concord University
Davis and Elkins College
Fairmont State University
Glenville State College
Marshall University

Ohio Valley University
Shepherd University
University of Charleston
West Liberty University
West Virginia University
West Virginia Wesleyan College
Wheeling Jesuit University

Wisconsin
Beloit College
Cardinal Stritch University
Carroll University
Carthage College
Concordia University Wisconsin
Edgewood College
Lawrence University
Marquette University
Mount Mary College
Northland College
Ripon College
St. Norbert College
Silver Lake College
University of Wisconsin
    Baraboo/Sauk County
    Eau Claire
    Fond du Lac
    Green Bay
    La Crosse
    Madison
    Manitowoc
    Oshkosh
    Parkside
    Richland
    River Falls
    Rock County
    Sheboygan
    Stevens Point
    Superior
    Waukesha
    Whitewater
Viterbo University
Wisconsin Lutheran College

Wyoming
Casper College
Central Wyoming College
Eastern Wyoming College
Laramie County Community College
Sheridan College
University of Wyoming
Western Wyoming Community College

ROTC scholarships

Air Force ROTC

Alabama
Alabama State University
Auburn University
Auburn University at Montgomery
Birmingham-Southern College
Bishop State Community College
Faulkner University
Huntingdon College
Jefferson State Community College
Miles College
Samford University
Shelton State Community College
Spring Hill College
Stillman College
Troy University
Tuskegee University
University of Alabama
University of Alabama
     Birmingham
University of Mobile
University of Montevallo
University of South Alabama
University of West Alabama

Alaska
Alaska Pacific University
University of Alaska
     Anchorage

Arizona
Arizona State University
Coconino County Community College
DeVry University
     Phoenix
Embry-Riddle Aeronautical University: Prescott
     Campus
Estrella Mountain Community College
GateWay Community College
Mesa Community College
Northern Arizona University
Phoenix College
Pima Community College
Southwestern College
University of Arizona

Arkansas
John Brown University
Northwest Arkansas Community College
University of Arkansas
University of Arkansas
     Fort Smith

California
Biola University
California Baptist University
California Institute of Technology
California Lutheran University
California State University
     Dominguez Hills
     Fresno
     Los Angeles
     Northridge
     Sacramento
     San Bernardino
     San Marcos
Chabot College
Chapman University
Claremont McKenna College
College of San Mateo
College of the Sequoias

Cuyamaca College
De Anza College
Foothill College
Fresno City College
Harvey Mudd College
Holy Names University
Irvine Valley College
Los Angeles City College
Los Angeles Mission College
Loyola Marymount University
Menlo College
MiraCosta College
Mission College
Mount San Antonio College
National University
Occidental College
Ohlone College
Pepperdine University
Pitzer College
Point Loma Nazarene University
Pomona College
Riverside Community College
Sacramento City College
St. Mary's College of California
Samuel Merritt University
San Diego Christian College
San Diego City College
San Diego State University
San Francisco State University
San Jose State University
Santa Clara University
Scripps College
Solano Community College
Sonoma State University
Stanford University
University of California
     Berkeley
     Davis
     Irvine
     Los Angeles
     Riverside
     Santa Cruz
University of Redlands
University of San Diego
University of San Francisco
University of Southern California
University of the Pacific
Vanguard University of Southern California
West Valley College
Westmont College

Colorado
Aims Community College
Arapahoe Community College
Colorado Christian University
Colorado School of Mines
Colorado State University
Community College of Denver
Front Range Community College
Metropolitan State College of Denver
Red Rocks Community College
Regis University
University of Colorado
     Boulder
     Denver
University of Denver
University of Northern Colorado

Connecticut
Capital Community College
Central Connecticut State University
Eastern Connecticut State University
Fairfield University

Quinnipiac University
Southern Connecticut State University
Tunxis Community College
University of Connecticut
University of Hartford
University of New Haven
Wesleyan University
Western Connecticut State University
Yale University

Delaware
Delaware State University
Delaware Technical and Community College
     Stanton/Wilmington
Goldey-Beacom College
University of Delaware
Wilmington University

District of Columbia
American University
Catholic University of America
George Washington University
Georgetown University
Howard University
University of the District of Columbia

Florida
Barry University
Bethune-Cookman University
Brevard Community College
Broward College
Clearwater Christian College
Daytona State College
Eckerd College
Embry-Riddle Aeronautical University
Florida Agricultural and Mechanical University
Florida Atlantic University
Florida College
Florida International University
Florida Southern College
Florida State University
Lynn University
Miami Dade College
Saint Leo University
Santa Fe College
Tallahassee Community College
University of Central Florida
University of Miami
University of South Florida
University of Tampa
University of West Florida
Valencia Community College

Georgia
Agnes Scott College
Clayton State University
Emory University
Georgia Institute of Technology
Georgia State University
Kennesaw State University
Morehouse College
Oglethorpe University
Southern Polytechnic State University
Spelman College
University of Georgia
Valdosta State University

Hawaii
Chaminade University of Honolulu
Hawaii Pacific University
University of Hawaii
     Honolulu Community College
     Leeward Community College
     Manoa
     West Oahu

Idaho
Lewis-Clark State College
Northwest Nazarene University
University of Idaho

Illinois
Elmhurst College
Illinois Institute of Technology
John A. Logan College
Judson University
Lewis University
Lincoln Land Community College
Loyola University Chicago
McKendree University
North Central College
North Park University
Northeastern Illinois University
Northwestern University
Parkland College
Saint Xavier University
Shawnee Community College
Southern Illinois University Carbondale
Southern Illinois University Edwardsville
Southwestern Illinois College
University of Chicago
University of Illinois
     Chicago
     Urbana-Champaign
Wheaton College

Indiana
Bethel College
Butler University
DePauw University
Holy Cross College
Indiana State University
Indiana University
     Bloomington
     South Bend
     Southeast
Indiana University-Purdue University
     Indianapolis
Purdue University
Rose-Hulman Institute of Technology
St. Mary-of-the-Woods College
Saint Mary's College
Trine University
University of Notre Dame
Valparaiso University
Vincennes University

Iowa
Coe College
Drake University
Grand View University
Hawkeye Community College
Iowa State University
Iowa Western Community College
University of Iowa

Kansas
Baker University
Kansas State University
MidAmerica Nazarene University
University of Kansas
University of St. Mary
Washburn University

Kentucky
Asbury College
Bellarmine University
Centre College
Georgetown College
Kentucky State University
Northern Kentucky University
Spalding University
Thomas More College
Transylvania University
University of Kentucky
University of Louisville
Western Kentucky University

Louisiana
Delgado Community College
Dillard University
Grambling State University

Louisiana State University and Agricultural and
    Mechanical College
Loyola University New Orleans
Northwestern State University
Our Lady of Holy Cross College
Our Lady of the Lake College
Southern University
    New Orleans
Southern University and Agricultural and
    Mechanical College
Tulane University
University of New Orleans
Xavier University of Louisiana

Maine
University of Maine
    Augusta
University of Southern Maine

Maryland
Anne Arundel Community College
Bowie State University
Johns Hopkins University
Loyola University Maryland
Prince George's Community College
Salisbury University
Towson University
University of Maryland
    Baltimore County
    College Park

Massachusetts
American International College
Amherst College
Anna Maria College
Assumption College
Babson College
Bay Path College
Becker College
Bentley University
Boston College
Boston University
Brandeis University
Bridgewater State College
Clark University
College of the Holy Cross
Curry College
Eastern Nazarene College
Elms College
Endicott College
Gordon College
Harvard College
Holyoke Community College
Massachusetts College of Pharmacy and Health
    Sciences
Massachusetts Institute of Technology
Massachusetts Maritime Academy
Merrimack College
Middlesex Community College
Mount Holyoke College
Northeastern University
Pine Manor College
Quinsigamond Community College
Salem State College
Smith College
Springfield College
Tufts University
University of Massachusetts
    Amherst
    Boston
    Lowell
Wellesley College
Wentworth Institute of Technology
Western New England College
Westfield State College
Williams College
Worcester Polytechnic Institute
Worcester State College

Michigan
Eastern Michigan University
Finlandia University
Lansing Community College

Lawrence Technological University
Michigan State University
Michigan Technological University
Oakland University
Spring Arbor University
University of Michigan
University of Michigan
    Dearborn
Wayne State University

Minnesota
Anoka-Ramsey Community College
Augsburg College
Bethel University
Century Community and Technical College
College of St. Scholastica
Concordia College: Moorhead
Concordia University: St. Paul
Hamline University
Inver Hills Community College
Macalester College
Minnesota State University
    Moorhead
Normandale Community College
North Central University
North Hennepin Community College
Northwestern College
St. Catherine University
University of Minnesota
    Crookston
    Duluth
    Twin Cities
University of St. Thomas

Mississippi
Belhaven University
Jackson State University
Jones County Junior College
Mississippi College
Mississippi State University
Mississippi University for Women
Northwest Mississippi Community College
University of Mississippi
University of Southern Mississippi

Missouri
Central Bible College
Central Methodist University
Columbia College
Fontbonne University
Harris-Stowe State University
Lincoln University
Saint Louis University
Southeast Missouri State University
St. Louis Community College
    Meramec
Stephens College
University of Central Missouri
University of Missouri
    Columbia
    Missouri University of Science and
        Technology
    St. Louis
Washington University in St. Louis
Webster University
Westminster College
William Woods University

Montana
Montana State University
    Bozeman

Nebraska
Bellevue University
Clarkson College
College of Saint Mary
Concordia University
Creighton University
Dana College
Doane College
Grace University
Nebraska Wesleyan University

University of Nebraska
    Lincoln
    Medical Center
    Omaha
York College

Nevada
University of Nevada
    Las Vegas

New Hampshire
Colby-Sawyer College
Daniel Webster College
Franklin Pierce University
Keene State College
New England College
Plymouth State University
Rivier College
Saint Anselm College
Southern New Hampshire University
University of New Hampshire
University of New Hampshire at Manchester

New Jersey
Brookdale Community College
The College of New Jersey
Fairleigh Dickinson University
    College at Florham
    Metropolitan Campus
Felician College
Kean University
Monmouth University
Montclair State University
New Jersey Institute of Technology
Princeton University
Ramapo College of New Jersey
Raritan Valley Community College
Rutgers, The State University of New Jersey
    Camden Regional Campus
    New Brunswick/Piscataway Campus
    Newark Regional Campus
Saint Peter's College
Stevens Institute of Technology
Union County College
William Paterson University of New Jersey

New Mexico
Central New Mexico Community College
Dona Ana Community College of New Mexico
    State University
New Mexico State University
New Mexico State University
    Alamogordo
University of New Mexico

New York
Adelphi University
Albany College of Pharmacy and Health
    Sciences
Cazenovia College
Clarkson University
College of Mount St. Vincent
College of Saint Rose
Columbia University
Columbia University
    School of General Studies
Cornell University
Dowling College
Elmira College
Fordham University
Hamilton College
Hobart and William Smith Colleges
Hudson Valley Community College
Iona College
Ithaca College
Jewish Theological Seminary of America
Le Moyne College
Manhattan College
Maria College
Mercy College
Mesivta Torah Vodaath Seminary
Monroe Community College
Nazareth College

New York Institute of Technology
New York University
Onondaga Community College
Pace University
Polytechnic Institute of New York University
Rensselaer Polytechnic Institute
Roberts Wesleyan College
Rochester Institute of Technology
Russell Sage College
Sage College of Albany
St. Francis College
St. John Fisher College
St. Joseph's College: Suffolk Campus
St. Lawrence University
St. Thomas Aquinas College
Schenectady County Community College
Siena College
Skidmore College
State University of New York
    Albany
    Binghamton
    College at Brockport
    College at Cortland
    College at Geneseo
    College at Old Westbury
    College at Potsdam
    College of Environmental Science and
        Forestry
    College of Technology at Canton
    Oswego
    Stony Brook
Syracuse University
Union College
University of Rochester
Utica College
Vaughn College of Aeronautics and Technology
Wells College

North Carolina
Belmont Abbey College
Bennett College for Women
Davidson College
Duke University
East Carolina University
Elon University
Fayetteville State University
Gardner-Webb University
Greensboro College
Guilford College
High Point University
Johnson C. Smith University
Meredith College
Methodist University
Mount Olive College
North Carolina Agricultural and Technical State
    University
North Carolina Central University
North Carolina State University
Peace College
Queens University of Charlotte
St. Augustine's College
Shaw University
University of North Carolina
    Chapel Hill
    Charlotte
    Greensboro
    Pembroke
Wingate University

North Dakota
Mayville State University
North Dakota State University
University of North Dakota

Ohio
Baldwin-Wallace College
Bowling Green State University
Capital University
Case Western Reserve University
Cedarville University
Central State University
Cleveland Institute of Art

Cleveland State University
College of Mount St. Joseph
Columbus State Community College
Cuyahoga Community College
    Metropolitan Campus
Heidelberg University
Hocking College
Kent State University
Kent State University
    Stark
    Tuscarawas
Lourdes College
Malone University
Miami University
    Hamilton Campus
    Oxford Campus
Mount Carmel College of Nursing
Mount Union College
Ohio Northern University
Ohio State University
    Agricultural Technical Institute
    Columbus Campus
    Lima Campus
    Mansfield Campus
    Marion Campus
    Newark Campus
Ohio University
Ohio Wesleyan University
Otterbein College
Owens Community College
    Toledo
Tiffin University
University of Akron
University of Akron: Wayne College
University of Cincinnati
University of Cincinnati
    Raymond Walters College
University of Dayton
University of Findlay
University of Toledo
Urbana University
Wilberforce University
Wittenberg University
Wright State University
Xavier University
Youngstown State University

Oklahoma
Langston University
Northeastern Oklahoma Agricultural and
    Mechanical College
Oklahoma Baptist University
Oklahoma Christian University
Oklahoma City University
Oklahoma State University
Oral Roberts University
St. Gregory's University
Southern Nazarene University
University of Oklahoma
University of Tulsa

Oregon
Clackamas Community College
Concordia University
Corban College
George Fox University
Linfield College
Linn-Benton Community College
Oregon State University
Pacific University
Portland State University
University of Oregon
University of Portland
Warner Pacific College
Western Oregon University
Willamette University

Pennsylvania
Bloomsburg University of Pennsylvania
Bryn Athyn College of the New Church
Bryn Mawr College
Cabrini College

California University of Pennsylvania
Carlow University
Carnegie Mellon University
Chatham University
Drexel University
Duquesne University
East Stroudsburg University of Pennsylvania
Eastern University
Keystone College
King's College
La Roche College
La Salle University
Lackawanna College
Luzerne County Community College
Marywood University
Mercyhurst College
Misericordia University
Penn State
    Abington
    Altoona
    Brandywine
    Hazleton
    University Park
    Wilkes-Barre
    Worthington Scranton
Philadelphia Biblical University
Point Park University
Robert Morris University
Rosemont College
Saint Joseph's University
St. Vincent College
Seton Hill University
Swarthmore College
Temple University
Thomas Jefferson University: College of Health
    Professions
University of Pennsylvania
University of Pittsburgh
University of Pittsburgh
    Greensburg
University of Scranton
University of the Sciences in Philadelphia
Valley Forge Military Academy & College
Villanova University
Washington & Jefferson College
West Chester University of Pennsylvania
Widener University
Wilkes University

Puerto Rico
Bayamon Central University
Caribbean University
Inter American University of Puerto Rico
    Aguadilla Campus
    Bayamon Campus
    Fajardo Campus
    Metropolitan Campus
    San German Campus
Pontifical Catholic University of Puerto Rico
Universidad Metropolitana
Universidad Politecnica de Puerto Rico
University of Puerto Rico
    Rio Piedras

South Carolina
Anderson University
Benedict College
Charleston Southern University
The Citadel
Claflin University
Clemson University
College of Charleston
Medical University of South Carolina
Midlands Technical College
South Carolina State University
Southern Wesleyan University
Tri-County Technical College
University of South Carolina
University of South Carolina
    Salkehatchie Regional Campus

South Dakota
Augustana College
Dakota State University
South Dakota State University
University of Sioux Falls

Tennessee
Austin Peay State University
Belmont University
Carson-Newman College
Christian Brothers University
Free Will Baptist Bible College
LeMoyne-Owen College
Lipscomb University
Middle Tennessee State University
Rhodes College
Roane State Community College
Southwest Tennessee Community College
Tennessee State University
Tennessee Technological University
Tennessee Wesleyan College
University of Memphis
University of Tennessee
    Knoxville
Vanderbilt University

Texas
Angelo State University
Austin Community College
Baylor University
College of Saint Thomas More
Concordia University Texas
Dallas Baptist University
Houston Baptist University
Houston Community College System
Lon Morris College
Lubbock Christian University
McLennan Community College
Midwestern State University
North Central Texas College
Our Lady of the Lake University of San Antonio
Rice University
St. Edward's University
St. Mary's University
San Antonio College
San Jacinto College
Southern Methodist University
Tarrant County College
Texas A&M University
Texas Christian University
Texas Lutheran University
Texas State University: San Marcos
Texas Tech University
Texas Wesleyan University
Texas Woman's University
Trinity University
University of Dallas
University of Houston
University of Houston
    Downtown
University of Mary Hardin-Baylor
University of North Texas
University of St. Thomas
University of Texas
    Arlington
    Austin
    Dallas
    El Paso
    San Antonio
University of the Incarnate Word
Wayland Baptist University
Weatherford College

Utah
Brigham Young University
LDS Business College
Salt Lake Community College
University of Utah
Utah State University
Utah Valley University
Weber State University
Westminster College

Vermont
Lyndon State College
Norwich University
St. Michael's College

Virginia
George Mason University
James Madison University
Liberty University
Mary Baldwin College
Piedmont Virginia Community College
University of Virginia
Virginia Military Institute
Virginia Polytechnic Institute and State
    University

Washington
Clark College
Highline Community College
Saint Martin's University
Seattle Pacific University
Seattle University
South Puget Sound Community College
Spokane Community College
University of Washington
University of Washington Bothell
Washington State University

West Virginia
Fairmont State University
Shepherd University
West Virginia University

Wisconsin
Alverno College
Carroll University
Carthage College
Maranatha Baptist Bible College
Marquette University
Milwaukee School of Engineering
University of Wisconsin
    Madison
    Milwaukee
    Stout
    Superior
    Whitewater
Wisconsin Lutheran College

Wyoming
Laramie County Community College
University of Wyoming

Army ROTC

Alabama
Alabama Agricultural and Mechanical
    University
Alabama State University
Auburn University
Auburn University at Montgomery
Birmingham-Southern College
Bishop State Community College
Chattahoochee Valley Community College
Faulkner University
Gadsden State Community College
Huntingdon College
Jacksonville State University
Jefferson State Community College
Judson College
Miles College
Samford University
Shelton State Community College
Spring Hill College
Stillman College
Talladega College
Troy University
Tuskegee University
University of Alabama
University of Alabama
    Birmingham
    Huntsville

University of Mobile
University of Montevallo
University of North Alabama
University of South Alabama

Alaska
University of Alaska
    Anchorage
    Fairbanks

Arizona
Arizona State University
Art Center Design College
Coconino County Community College
Embry-Riddle Aeronautical University: Prescott
   Campus
GateWay Community College
Grand Canyon University
Mesa Community College
Northern Arizona University
Paradise Valley Community College
Phoenix College
Pima Community College
University of Arizona

Arkansas
Arkansas State University
Arkansas State University
    Beebe
    Mountain Home
Arkansas Tech University
Central Baptist College
Henderson State University
Hendrix College
John Brown University
Northwest Arkansas Community College
Ouachita Baptist University
Ouachita Technical College
Philander Smith College
University of Arkansas
University of Arkansas
    Fort Smith
    Little Rock
    Monticello
    Pine Bluff
University of Central Arkansas
Williams Baptist College

California
Azusa Pacific University
Bethany University
Biola University
California Baptist University
California Institute of Technology
California Lutheran University
California Polytechnic State University: San Luis
   Obispo
California State Polytechnic University: Pomona
California State University
    Dominguez Hills
    Fresno
    Fullerton
    Long Beach
    Los Angeles
    Northridge
    Sacramento
    San Bernardino
    San Marcos
Chabot College
Chapman University
City College of San Francisco
Claremont McKenna College
College of San Mateo
Concordia University
Cuyamaca College
De Anza College
Diablo Valley College
Foothill College
Fresno City College
Harvey Mudd College
Holy Names University
Los Angeles City College
Los Angeles Mission College

Loyola Marymount University
Menlo College
Mills College
MiraCosta College
National University
Occidental College
Pepperdine University
Pitzer College
Point Loma Nazarene University
Pomona College
Riverside Community College
Sacramento City College
St. Mary's College of California
Samuel Merritt University
San Diego Christian College
San Diego City College
San Diego State University
San Francisco State University
San Jose State University
Santa Clara University
Scripps College
Simpson University
Sonoma State University
Stanford University
University of California
    Berkeley
    Davis
    Irvine
    Los Angeles
    Riverside
    Santa Barbara
    Santa Cruz
University of La Verne
University of Redlands
University of San Diego
University of San Francisco
University of Southern California
Vanguard University of Southern California
West Valley College
Westmont College
Whittier College

Colorado
Arapahoe Community College
Colorado Christian University
Colorado College
Colorado School of Mines
Colorado State University
Colorado State University
    Pueblo
Colorado Technical University
Community College of Denver
Front Range Community College
Metropolitan State College of Denver
Red Rocks Community College
Regis University
University of Colorado
    Boulder
    Colorado Springs
    Denver
University of Denver
University of Northern Colorado

Connecticut
Capital Community College
Central Connecticut State University
Eastern Connecticut State University
Fairfield University
Post University
Quinnipiac University
Sacred Heart University
Southern Connecticut State University
Trinity College
Tunxis Community College
University of Bridgeport
University of Connecticut
University of Hartford
University of New Haven
Western Connecticut State University
Yale University

Delaware
Delaware State University
University of Delaware
Wesley College
Wilmington University

District of Columbia
American University
Catholic University of America
George Washington University
Georgetown University
Howard University
Trinity Washington University
University of the District of Columbia

Florida
Barry University
Bethune-Cookman University
Brevard Community College
Broward College
Clearwater Christian College
Daytona State College
Eckerd College
Embry-Riddle Aeronautical University
Florida Agricultural and Mechanical University
Florida Atlantic University
Florida College
Florida Institute of Technology
Florida International University
Florida Memorial University
Florida Southern College
Florida State College at Jacksonville
Florida State University
Hillsborough Community College
Miami Dade College
Northwest Florida State College
Pasco-Hernando Community College
Pensacola Junior College
Polk State College
Saint Leo University
Santa Fe College
South Florida Community College
Southeastern University
Stetson University
Tallahassee Community College
University of Central Florida
University of Miami
University of North Florida
University of South Florida
University of Tampa
University of West Florida
Valencia Community College

Georgia
Agnes Scott College
Albany State University
Armstrong Atlantic State University
Augusta State University
Clark Atlanta University
Clayton State University
Columbus State University
Covenant College
East Georgia College
Emory University
Fort Valley State University
Georgia College and State University
Georgia Institute of Technology
Georgia Military College
Georgia Southern University
Georgia State University
Kennesaw State University
Mercer University
Morehouse College
North Georgia College & State University
Paine College
Savannah College of Art and Design
Savannah State University
Southern Polytechnic State University
Spelman College
University of Georgia
University of West Georgia

Hawaii
Chaminade University of Honolulu
Hawaii Pacific University
University of Hawaii
    Honolulu Community College
    Leeward Community College
    Manoa
    West Oahu
    Windward Community College

Idaho
Boise State University
Brigham Young University-Idaho
College of Idaho
Idaho State University
Lewis-Clark State College
North Idaho College
Northwest Nazarene University
University of Idaho

Illinois
Aurora University
Benedictine University
Bradley University
Carl Sandburg College
Chicago State University
DePaul University
Eastern Illinois University
Elmhurst College
Illinois Institute of Technology
Illinois State University
Illinois Wesleyan University
John A. Logan College
Judson University
Kankakee Community College
Kishwaukee College
Lewis and Clark Community College
Lewis University
Lincoln Land Community College
Loyola University Chicago
McKendree University
Monmouth College
North Central College
North Park University
Northeastern Illinois University
Northern Illinois University
Northwestern University
Olivet Nazarene University
Parkland College
Robert Morris University: Chicago
Shawnee Community College
Southern Illinois University Carbondale
Southern Illinois University Edwardsville
Southwestern Illinois College
Spoon River College
University of Chicago
University of Illinois
    Chicago
    Urbana-Champaign
Waubonsee Community College
Western Illinois University
Wheaton College

Indiana
Ball State University
Bethel College
Butler University
DePauw University
Franklin College
Holy Cross College
Indiana State University
Indiana University
    Bloomington
    Kokomo
    Northwest
    South Bend
    Southeast
Indiana University-Purdue University Fort
   Wayne
Indiana University-Purdue University
   Indianapolis
Indiana Wesleyan University

Marian University
Purdue University
Rose-Hulman Institute of Technology
St. Mary-of-the-Woods College
Saint Mary's College
University of Indianapolis
University of Notre Dame
University of Southern Indiana
Valparaiso University
Vincennes University

Iowa
Allen College
Briar Cliff University
Buena Vista University
Clarke College
Coe College
Drake University
Grand View University
Hawkeye Community College
Iowa State University
Iowa Western Community College
Loras College
Morningside College
University of Dubuque
University of Iowa
University of Northern Iowa

Kansas
Baker University
Benedictine College
Kansas State University
MidAmerica Nazarene University
Pittsburg State University
University of Kansas
University of St. Mary
Washburn University

Kentucky
Asbury College
Bellarmine University
Campbellsville University
Centre College
Eastern Kentucky University
Elizabethtown Community and Technical
    College
Georgetown College
Kentucky Christian University
Kentucky State University
Kentucky Wesleyan College
Midway College
Morehead State University
Murray State University
Northern Kentucky University
Pikeville College
Spalding University
Thomas More College
Transylvania University
Union College
University of Kentucky
University of Louisville
University of the Cumberlands
Western Kentucky University

Louisiana
Delgado Community College
Dillard University
Grambling State University
Louisiana College
Louisiana State University
    Alexandria
    Shreveport
Louisiana State University and Agricultural and
    Mechanical College
Louisiana Tech University
Loyola University New Orleans
McNeese State University
Northwestern State University
Our Lady of Holy Cross College
Our Lady of the Lake College
Southeastern Louisiana University
Southern University
    New Orleans

Southern University and Agricultural and
    Mechanical College
Tulane University
University of Louisiana at Lafayette
University of Louisiana at Monroe
University of New Orleans
Xavier University of Louisiana

Maine
Colby College
Husson University
Maine Maritime Academy
New England School of Communications
Saint Joseph's College of Maine
Unity College
University of Maine
University of Maine
    Augusta
University of New England
University of Southern Maine

Maryland
Allegany College of Maryland
Anne Arundel Community College
Bowie State University
Capitol College
College of Notre Dame of Maryland
Coppin State University
Goucher College
Hood College
Johns Hopkins University
Loyola University Maryland
Maryland Institute College of Art
McDaniel College
Morgan State University
Mount St. Mary's University
Prince George's Community College
Salisbury University
Stevenson University
Towson University
University of Baltimore
University of Maryland
    Baltimore County
    College Park

Massachusetts
American International College
Assumption College
Babson College
Bay Path College
Becker College
Bentley University
Boston College
Boston University
Brandeis University
Bridgewater State College
Clark University
College of the Holy Cross
Curry College
Eastern Nazarene College
Elms College
Emmanuel College
Endicott College
Fitchburg State College
Gordon College
Hampshire College
Harvard College
Holyoke Community College
Massachusetts College of Pharmacy and Health
    Sciences
Massachusetts Institute of Technology
Massachusetts Maritime Academy
Middlesex Community College
Mount Holyoke College
Nichols College
Northeastern University
Pine Manor College
Quinsigamond Community College
Regis College
Roxbury Community College
Salem State College
Simmons College

Smith College
Springfield College
Stonehill College
Suffolk University
Tufts University
University of Massachusetts
    Amherst
    Boston
    Dartmouth
Wellesley College
Wentworth Institute of Technology
Western New England College
Westfield State College
Wheaton College
Worcester Polytechnic Institute
Worcester State College

Michigan
Alma College
Calvin College
Central Michigan University
Eastern Michigan University
Ferris State University
Finlandia University
Grace Bible College
Hope College
Kalamazoo College
Kuyper College
Lansing Community College
Michigan State University
Michigan Technological University
Northern Michigan University
Spring Arbor University
University of Michigan
University of Michigan
    Dearborn
Washtenaw Community College
Wayne State University
Western Michigan University

Minnesota
Anoka-Ramsey Community College
Augsburg College
Bethany Lutheran College
Bethel University
College of St. Benedict
Concordia College: Moorhead
Concordia University: St. Paul
Crown College
Gustavus Adolphus College
Hamline University
Inver Hills Community College
Lake Superior College
Macalester College
Minnesota State University
    Mankato
    Moorhead
Normandale Community College
North Central University
North Hennepin Community College
Northwestern College
St. Catherine University
Saint Cloud State University
St. John's University
St. Mary's University of Minnesota
University of Minnesota
    Twin Cities
University of St. Thomas
Winona State University

Mississippi
Alcorn State University
Belhaven University
Delta State University
Hinds Community College
Jackson State University
Millsaps College
Mississippi College
Mississippi State University
Mississippi University for Women
Mississippi Valley State University
Tougaloo College

University of Mississippi
University of Southern Mississippi

Missouri
Avila University
Calvary Bible College and Theological Seminary
Central Bible College
Central Methodist University
College of the Ozarks
Columbia College
Drury University
Evangel University
Fontbonne University
Harris-Stowe State University
Lincoln University
Lindenwood University
Maryville University of Saint Louis
Missouri Baptist University
Missouri State University
Missouri Valley College
Missouri Western State University
Northwest Missouri State University
Park University
Research College of Nursing
Rockhurst University
Saint Louis University
Southwest Baptist University
St. Louis Community College
    Florissant Valley
    Meramec
State Fair Community College
Stephens College
Truman State University
University of Central Missouri
University of Missouri
    Columbia
    Kansas City
    Missouri University of Science and
        Technology
    St. Louis
Washington University in St. Louis
Webster University
Wentworth Military Junior College
Westminster College
William Jewell College
William Woods University

Montana
Montana State University
    Billings
    Bozeman
Rocky Mountain College
University of Montana

Nebraska
Bellevue University
BryanLGH College of Health Sciences
Chadron State College
Clarkson College
College of Saint Mary
Concordia University
Creighton University
Dana College
Doane College
Nebraska Methodist College of Nursing and
    Allied Health
Nebraska Wesleyan University
University of Nebraska
    Kearney
    Lincoln
    Medical Center
    Omaha
Wayne State College
York College

Nevada
College of Southern Nevada
Sierra Nevada College
Truckee Meadows Community College
University of Nevada
    Las Vegas
    Reno

New Hampshire
Colby-Sawyer College
Daniel Webster College
Dartmouth College
Franklin Pierce University
Granite State College
New England College
Plymouth State University
Rivier College
Saint Anselm College
Southern New Hampshire University
University of New Hampshire
University of New Hampshire at Manchester

New Jersey
Bloomfield College
Brookdale Community College
Caldwell College
The College of New Jersey
Fairleigh Dickinson University
    College at Florham
    Metropolitan Campus
Felician College
Kean University
Middlesex County College
Montclair State University
New Jersey Institute of Technology
Princeton University
Raritan Valley Community College
Rider University
Rowan University
Rutgers, The State University of New Jersey
    Camden Regional Campus
    New Brunswick/Piscataway Campus
    Newark Regional Campus
Saint Peter's College
Seton Hall University
Stevens Institute of Technology

New Mexico
Central New Mexico Community College
Dona Ana Community College of New Mexico
    State University
New Mexico Military Institute
New Mexico State University
University of New Mexico

New York
Adelphi University
Albany College of Pharmacy and Health
    Sciences
Alfred University
Canisius College
Cazenovia College
City University of New York
    Baruch College
    Lehman College
    Queens College
Clarkson University
Colgate University
College of New Rochelle
College of Saint Rose
Columbia University
Columbia University
    School of General Studies
Cornell University
Daemen College
Dowling College
D'Youville College
Elmira College
Erie Community College
    City Campus
    North
    South Campus
Finger Lakes Community College
Fordham University
Hamilton College
Herkimer County Community College
Hilbert College
Hobart and William Smith Colleges
Hofstra University
Houghton College

Hudson Valley Community College
Iona College
Ithaca College
Jewish Theological Seminary of America
Le Moyne College
Long Island University
    Brooklyn Campus
    C. W. Post Campus
Manhattan College
Maria College
Marist College
Medaille College
Mercy College
Mohawk Valley Community College
Molloy College
Monroe College
Monroe Community College
Nazareth College
New York Institute of Technology
New York University
Niagara County Community College
Niagara University
Onondaga Community College
Orange County Community College
Pace University
Polytechnic Institute of New York University
Rensselaer Polytechnic Institute
Roberts Wesleyan College
Rochester Institute of Technology
Russell Sage College
Sage College of Albany
Saint Bonaventure University
St. Francis College
St. John Fisher College
St. John's University
St. Lawrence University
Siena College
Skidmore College
State University of New York
    Albany
    Binghamton
    Buffalo
    College at Brockport
    College at Buffalo
    College at Cortland
    College at Fredonia
    College at Geneseo
    College at Old Westbury
    College at Plattsburgh
    College at Potsdam
    College of Agriculture and Technology at
        Morrisville
    College of Environmental Science and
        Forestry
    College of Technology at Alfred
    College of Technology at Canton
    Institute of Technology at Utica/Rome
    Maritime College
    Oswego
    Stony Brook
    Upstate Medical University
Syracuse University
Talmudical Seminary Oholei Torah
Union College
University of Rochester
Utica College
Vaughn College of Aeronautics and Technology
Wagner College
Wells College

North Carolina
Appalachian State University
Belmont Abbey College
Bennett College for Women
Campbell University
Catawba College
College of the Albemarle
Davidson College
Duke University
East Carolina University
Elizabeth City State University
Elon University

Fayetteville State University
Gardner-Webb University
Greensboro College
Guilford College
High Point University
Johnson C. Smith University
Lenoir-Rhyne University
Livingstone College
Louisburg College
Meredith College
Methodist University
Mid-Atlantic Christian University
North Carolina Agricultural and Technical State
    University
North Carolina Central University
North Carolina State University
North Carolina Wesleyan College
Peace College
Pfeiffer University
Pitt Community College
Queens University of Charlotte
St. Augustine's College
Salem College
Shaw University
University of North Carolina
    Chapel Hill
    Charlotte
    Greensboro
    Pembroke
Wake Forest University
Wake Technical Community College
Wingate University
Winston-Salem State University

North Dakota
Mayville State University
North Dakota State University
University of North Dakota

Ohio
Baldwin-Wallace College
Bowling Green State University
Capital University
Case Western Reserve University
Cedarville University
Central State University
Cincinnati State Technical and Community
    College
Cleveland Institute of Art
Cleveland State University
College of Mount St. Joseph
Columbus State Community College
Denison University
DeVry University
    Columbus
Franciscan University of Steubenville
Franklin University
Heidelberg University
Hocking College
John Carroll University
Kent State University
Kent State University
    Stark
    Tuscarawas
Lourdes College
Malone University
Miami University
    Oxford Campus
Mount Carmel College of Nursing
Mount Union College
Notre Dame College
Ohio Dominican University
Ohio Northern University
Ohio State University
    Agricultural Technical Institute
    Columbus Campus
    Lima Campus
    Mansfield Campus
    Marion Campus
    Newark Campus
Ohio University
Ohio Wesleyan University

Otterbein College
Owens Community College
    Toledo
Tiffin University
University of Akron
University of Akron: Wayne College
University of Cincinnati
University of Cincinnati
    Clermont College
    Raymond Walters College
University of Dayton
University of Findlay
University of Toledo
Urbana University
Ursuline College
Wilberforce University
Wittenberg University
Wright State University
Xavier University
Youngstown State University

Oklahoma
Cameron University
Langston University
Northeastern State University
Oklahoma Christian University
Oklahoma City University
Oklahoma State University
Southern Nazarene University
Southwestern Christian University
University of Central Oklahoma
University of Oklahoma

Oregon
Central Oregon Community College
Corban College
Eastern Oregon University
Linn-Benton Community College
Oregon Institute of Technology
Oregon State University
Pacific University
Portland State University
University of Oregon
University of Portland
Warner Pacific College
Western Oregon University
Willamette University

Pennsylvania
Alvernia University
Arcadia University
Baptist Bible College of Pennsylvania
Bloomsburg University of Pennsylvania
Bryn Athyn College of the New Church
Bucknell University
Cabrini College
California University of Pennsylvania
Carlow University
Carnegie Mellon University
Cedar Crest College
Chatham University
Cheyney University of Pennsylvania
Clarion University of Pennsylvania
Community College of Philadelphia
DeSales University
Dickinson College
Drexel University
Duquesne University
East Stroudsburg University of Pennsylvania
Eastern University
Edinboro University of Pennsylvania
Gannon University
Geneva College
Gettysburg College
Harrisburg Area Community College
Indiana University of Pennsylvania
Keystone College
King's College
Kutztown University of Pennsylvania
La Roche College
La Salle University
Lackawanna College

Lafayette College
Lebanon Valley College
Lehigh Carbon Community College
Lehigh University
Lincoln University
Lock Haven University of Pennsylvania
Lycoming College
Mansfield University of Pennsylvania
Marywood University
Millersville University of Pennsylvania
Misericordia University
Moravian College
Muhlenberg College
Neumann University
Penn State
    Abington
    Altoona
    Berks
    Brandywine
    Erie, The Behrend College
    Harrisburg
    Hazleton
    Lehigh Valley
    Mont Alto
    University Park
    Wilkes-Barre
    Worthington Scranton
Pennsylvania College of Technology
Point Park University
Robert Morris University
Rosemont College
St. Francis University
Saint Joseph's University
St. Vincent College
Seton Hill University
Shippensburg University of Pennsylvania
Slippery Rock University of Pennsylvania
Susquehanna University
Swarthmore College
Temple University
University of Pennsylvania
University of Pittsburgh
University of Pittsburgh
    Bradford
    Greensburg
University of Scranton
University of the Sciences in Philadelphia
Valley Forge Military Academy & College
Villanova University
Washington & Jefferson College
Waynesburg University
West Chester University of Pennsylvania
Westminster College
Widener University
Wilkes University
Wilson College
York College of Pennsylvania

Puerto Rico
American University of Puerto Rico
Bayamon Central University
Caribbean University
Inter American University of Puerto Rico
    Aguadilla Campus
    Arecibo Campus
    Bayamon Campus
    Guayama Campus
    Metropolitan Campus
    San German Campus
Pontifical Catholic University of Puerto Rico
Turabo University
Universidad del Este
Universidad Metropolitana
Universidad Politecnica de Puerto Rico
University of Puerto Rico
    Aguadilla
    Arecibo
    Bayamon University College
    Cayey University College
    Ponce
    Rio Piedras
    Utuado

Rhode Island
Brown University
Bryant University
Community College of Rhode Island
Johnson & Wales University: Providence
Providence College
Rhode Island College
Roger Williams University
Salve Regina University
University of Rhode Island

South Carolina
Allen University
Anderson University
Benedict College
Charleston Southern University
The Citadel
Claflin University
Clemson University
Coastal Carolina University
Columbia College
Converse College
Denmark Technical College
Furman University
Lander University
Limestone College
Midlands Technical College
Morris College
Newberry College
North Greenville University
Orangeburg-Calhoun Technical College
Presbyterian College
South Carolina State University
Southern Wesleyan University
Spartanburg Methodist College
Tri-County Technical College
University of South Carolina
University of South Carolina
    Lancaster
    Salkehatchie Regional Campus
    Sumter
    Upstate
Winthrop University
Wofford College

South Dakota
Augustana College
Black Hills State University
Dakota State University
Dakota Wesleyan University
Mount Marty College
National American University
    Rapid City
South Dakota School of Mines and Technology
South Dakota State University
University of South Dakota

Tennessee
Austin Peay State University
Belmont University
Carson-Newman College
Christian Brothers University
Cumberland University
East Tennessee State University
Fisk University
Free Will Baptist Bible College
Jackson State Community College
King College
Lambuth University
LeMoyne-Owen College
Lincoln Memorial University
Lipscomb University
Middle Tennessee State University
Milligan College
Pellissippi State Community College
Rhodes College
Roane State Community College
Southwest Tennessee Community College
Tennessee Technological University
Tennessee Wesleyan College
Trevecca Nazarene University
University of Memphis

University of Tennessee
    Chattanooga
    Knoxville
    Martin
Vanderbilt University
Walters State Community College

Texas
Alvin Community College
Angelina College
Austin Community College
Baylor University
Central Texas College
College of Saint Thomas More
Collin County Community College District
Concordia University Texas
Dallas Baptist University
Del Mar College
El Centro College
El Paso Community College
Houston Baptist University
Houston Community College System
Huston-Tillotson University
Laredo Community College
Lon Morris College
Lubbock Christian University
Mountain View College
Our Lady of the Lake University of San Antonio
Prairie View A&M University
Rice University
St. Edward's University
St. Mary's University
St. Philip's College
Sam Houston State University
San Antonio College
Southern Methodist University
Southwestern Assemblies of God University
Stephen F. Austin State University
Tarleton State University
Tarrant County College
Texas A&M International University
Texas A&M University
Texas A&M University
    Corpus Christi
    Kingsville
Texas Christian University
Texas Lutheran University
Texas Southern University
Texas State University: San Marcos
Texas Tech University
Texas Wesleyan University
Texas Woman's University
University of Dallas
University of Houston
University of Houston
    Downtown
University of Mary Hardin-Baylor
University of North Texas
University of St. Thomas
University of Texas
    Arlington
    Austin
    Brownsville - Texas Southmost College
    Dallas
    El Paso
    Pan American
    San Antonio
University of the Incarnate Word
Wayland Baptist University

Utah
Brigham Young University
Dixie State College of Utah
LDS Business College
Salt Lake Community College
Southern Utah University
University of Utah
Utah State University
Utah Valley University
Weber State University
Westminster College

Vermont
Castleton State College
Champlain College
Johnson State College
Middlebury College
Norwich University
St. Michael's College
University of Vermont
Vermont Technical College

Virginia
Christopher Newport University
College of William and Mary
George Mason University
Hampden-Sydney College
Hampton University
J. Sargeant Reynolds Community College-
    Parham Road
James Madison University
John Tyler Community College
Liberty University
Longwood University
Mary Baldwin College
Marymount University
Norfolk State University
Old Dominion University
Piedmont Virginia Community College
Radford University
Randolph-Macon College
Regent University
Richard Bland College
St. Paul's College
Southern Virginia University
Southside Virginia Community College- Alberta
University of Mary Washington
University of Richmond
University of Virginia
Virginia Commonwealth University
Virginia Military Institute
Virginia Polytechnic Institute and State
    University
Virginia State University
Virginia Union University
Virginia Wesleyan College
Washington and Lee University

Washington
Clark College
    Federal Way
Eastern Washington University
Gonzaga University
Highline Community College
Northwest University
Pacific Lutheran University
Pierce College
Saint Martin's University
Seattle Pacific University
Seattle University
Spokane Community College
Spokane Falls Community College
University of Puget Sound
University of Washington
University of Washington Bothell
Washington State University
Whitworth University

West Virginia
Fairmont State University
Marshall University
University of Charleston
West Liberty University
West Virginia State University
West Virginia University
West Virginia University Institute of Technology

Wisconsin
Alverno College
Carroll University
Carthage College
Edgewood College
Maranatha Baptist Bible College
Marian University

Marquette University
Milwaukee School of Engineering
Mount Mary College
Ripon College
St. Norbert College
University of Wisconsin
    Eau Claire
    Green Bay
    La Crosse
    Madison
    Milwaukee
    Oshkosh
    Parkside
    Platteville
    River Falls
    Stevens Point
    Stout
    Whitewater
Viterbo University
Wisconsin Lutheran College

Wyoming
Laramie County Community College
University of Wyoming

Naval ROTC

Alabama
Auburn University
Stillman College

Arizona
GateWay Community College
Mesa Community College
Pima Community College
Southwestern College
University of Arizona

California
California Maritime Academy
California State University
    San Marcos
Contra Costa College
Diablo Valley College
Foothill College
Fullerton College
Los Angeles City College
Loyola Marymount University
Mission College
National University
Point Loma Nazarene University
Riverside Community College
Sacramento City College
Samuel Merritt University
San Diego Christian College
San Diego State University
San Francisco State University
Sonoma State University
Stanford University
University of California
    Berkeley
    Davis
    Los Angeles
    Santa Cruz
University of Redlands
University of San Diego
University of Southern California

Colorado
Regis University
University of Colorado
    Boulder

Connecticut
Capital Community College
Tunxis Community College

District of Columbia
Catholic University of America
George Washington University
Georgetown University

University of the District of Columbia

Florida
Clearwater Christian College
Embry-Riddle Aeronautical University
Florida Agricultural and Mechanical University
Florida State College at Jacksonville
Florida State University
Jacksonville University
Pasco-Hernando Community College
Tallahassee Community College
University of North Florida
University of South Florida
University of Tampa

Georgia
Armstrong Atlantic State University
Clark Atlanta University
Clayton State University
Georgia Institute of Technology
Georgia State University
Morehouse College
Savannah State University
Southern Polytechnic State University
Spelman College

Hawaii
University of Hawaii
    Hawaii Community College

Idaho
Lewis-Clark State College
University of Idaho

Illinois
Illinois Institute of Technology
Judson University
Lincoln Land Community College
Loyola University Chicago
Northwestern University
Parkland College
Shawnee Community College
University of Illinois
    Chicago
    Urbana-Champaign

Indiana
Indiana University
    South Bend
Indiana University-Purdue University
    Indianapolis
Purdue University
Saint Mary's College
University of Notre Dame

Iowa
Hawkeye Community College
Iowa State University

Kansas
University of Kansas
Washburn University

Louisiana
Dillard University
Louisiana State University and Agricultural and
    Mechanical College
Louisiana Tech University
Loyola University New Orleans
Our Lady of Holy Cross College
Southern University
    New Orleans
Southern University and Agricultural and
    Mechanical College
Tulane University
University of New Orleans
Xavier University of Louisiana

Maine
Husson University
Maine Maritime Academy
University of Maine

University of Maine
    Augusta

Maryland
University of Maryland
    College Park

Massachusetts
Babson College
Becker College
Boston College
Boston University
Clark University
College of the Holy Cross
Harvard College
Massachusetts College of Pharmacy and Health
    Sciences
Massachusetts Institute of Technology
Massachusetts Maritime Academy
Northeastern University
Tufts University
University of Massachusetts
    Boston
Worcester Polytechnic Institute
Worcester State College

Michigan
Eastern Michigan University
Finlandia University
University of Michigan
University of Michigan
    Dearborn

Minnesota
Anoka-Ramsey Community College
Augsburg College
Concordia University: St. Paul
Lake Superior College
Macalester College
Normandale Community College
North Hennepin Community College
University of Minnesota
    Twin Cities
University of St. Thomas

Mississippi
East Mississippi Community College
Tougaloo College
University of Mississippi

Missouri
Columbia College
Lincoln University
Stephens College
University of Missouri
    Columbia
William Woods University

Nebraska
BryanLGH College of Health Sciences
University of Nebraska
    Lincoln
York College

New Hampshire
Rivier College

New Jersey
Montclair State University

New Mexico
Central New Mexico Community College
University of New Mexico

New York
Albany College of Pharmacy and Health
    Sciences
City University of New York
    Queens College
College of New Rochelle
College of Saint Rose
Columbia University
Cornell University

Eastman School of Music of the University of
    Rochester
Fordham University
Hobart and William Smith Colleges
Jewish Theological Seminary of America
Maria College
Mesivta Torah Vodaath Seminary
Molloy College
Monroe Community College
New York University
Rensselaer Polytechnic Institute
Rochester Institute of Technology
Russell Sage College
St. John Fisher College
Siena College
State University of New York
    College at Brockport
    Maritime College
Talmudical Seminary Oholei Torah
Union College
University of Rochester

North Carolina
Belmont Abbey College
Duke University
Guilford College
Lenoir-Rhyne University
North Carolina State University
Peace College
University of North Carolina
    Chapel Hill

Ohio
Cleveland Institute of Art
Cuyahoga Community College
    Metropolitan Campus
Miami University
    Hamilton Campus
    Oxford Campus
Ohio State University
    Agricultural Technical Institute
    Columbus Campus
    Lima Campus
    Mansfield Campus
    Marion Campus
    Newark Campus
University of Cincinnati
    Raymond Walters College

Oklahoma
University of Oklahoma

Oregon
Oregon State University
Warner Pacific College
Western Oregon University

Pennsylvania
Carlow University
Carnegie Mellon University
Chatham University
Drexel University
Duquesne University
Penn State
    University Park
Saint Joseph's University
Swarthmore College
Temple University
Thomas Jefferson University: College of Health
    Professions
University of Pennsylvania
University of Pittsburgh
Villanova University
Widener University

Puerto Rico
Caribbean University
Inter American University of Puerto Rico
    Bayamon Campus
    Ponce Campus
Universidad Metropolitana

South Carolina
The Citadel
Midlands Technical College
University of South Carolina
University of South Carolina
      Salkehatchie Regional Campus

Tennessee
Belmont University
Christian Brothers University
Fisk University
Tennessee Wesleyan College
University of Memphis
Vanderbilt University

Texas
Houston Baptist University
Lon Morris College
Prairie View A&M University
Rice University
Texas A&M University
Texas A&M University
      Galveston
University of Houston
University of Texas
      Austin

Utah
University of Utah
Weber State University
Westminster College

Vermont
Norwich University

Virginia
Hampton University
Mary Baldwin College
New River Community College
Norfolk State University
Old Dominion University
University of Virginia
Virginia Military Institute
Virginia Polytechnic Institute and State
      University

Washington
Seattle Pacific University
Seattle University
Spokane Community College
University of Washington
University of Washington Bothell
Washington State University

Wisconsin
Marquette University
Milwaukee School of Engineering
Mount Mary College
University of Wisconsin
      Madison
Wisconsin Lutheran College

Glossary

Academic Competitiveness Grant. A federal financial aid award to students in their first two years of undergraduate study who are eligible for a Pell Grant and have successfully completed a rigorous high school academic program, as determined by their state or local education agency. The maximum award is $750 for the first year of undergraduate study and $1,300 for the second year, both of which are in addition to the Pell Grant award.

Accelerated program. A college program of study completed in less time than is usually required, most often by attending classes in summer or by taking extra courses during the regular academic terms.

Accreditation. A process that ensures that a college meets acceptable standards in its programs, facilities, and services. Only colleges that are accredited by an agency recognized by the U.S. Department of Education may distribute federal financial aid to their students. Every college described in this book is accredited by such an agency.

Advanced placement. Admission or assignment of a first-year college student to an advanced course in a certain subject on the basis of evidence that he or she has already completed the equivalent of the college's course in that subject.

Advanced Placement Program (AP). An academic program of the College Board that provides high school students with the opportunity to study and learn at the college level. AP offers more than 30 courses and exams in a wide variety of subject areas.

AmeriCorps. A national network of community service programs for which people volunteer and from which they earn an education award that can used to pay for college or pay back student loans.

Articulation agreement. A formal agreement between two higher-education institutions, stating specific policies relating to transfer of credits and recognition of academic achievement in order to facilitate the successful transfer of students without duplication of course work.

Associate degree. A degree granted by a college or university upon completion of a two-year, full-time program of study or its part-time equivalent. In general, the associate of arts (A.A.) or associate of science (A.S.) program is similar to the first two years of a four-year college curriculum. The associate in applied science (A.A.S.) is awarded by many colleges on completion of technological or vocational programs of study.

Award letter. A means of notifying admitted students of the financial aid being offered by the college or university. The award letter provides information on the types and amounts of aid offered, as well as the students' responsibilities, and the conditions governing the awards. Usually the award letter gives students the opportunity to accept or decline the aid offered, and a deadline by which to respond.

Bachelor's degree. A degree received upon completion of a four- or five-year full-time program of study (or its part-time equivalent) at a college or university. The bachelor of arts (B.A.), bachelor of science (B.S.) and bachelor of fine arts (B.F.A.) are the most common such degrees. College catalogs describe the types of degrees awarded in each major.

Bursar. The college official responsible for handling billing and payments for tuition, fees, housing, etc.

Business college. A college that primarily prepares students to work in an office or entrepreneurial setting. The curriculum may focus on management, clerical positions, or both.

Campus-based programs. Federal financial aid programs that are administered directly by the college's financial aid office, which awards these funds to students using federal guidelines. Includes the Federal Supplemental Educational Opportunity Grant Program, Federal Perkins Loan Program and the Federal Work-Study Program.

Candidates' reply date. The date by which admitted students must accept or decline an offer of admission and (if any) the college's offer of financial aid. Most colleges and universities follow the College Board-sponsored Candidates' Reply Date Agreement (CRDA), under which they agree to not require a decision from applicants for admission in the fall semester before May 1. The purpose of this agreement is to give applicants time to hear from all the colleges to which they have applied before having to make a commitment to any of them.

Certificate. An award for completing a particular program or course of study, sometimes given by two-year colleges or vocational or technical schools.

CLEP®. See *College-Level Examination Program.*

College-Level Examination Program (CLEP). Thirty-three examinations — in business, composition and literature, foreign languages, history and social sciences, and science and mathematics — sponsored by the College Board and administered by 1,600 colleges year-round that provide students the opportunity to receive college credit by earning a qualifying score. There are 2,900 colleges that grant credit for passing scores.

Community/junior college. A college offering two-year programs leading to an associate degree. Community colleges are public institutions, while junior colleges are privately operated on a not-for-profit basis. Most two-year colleges offer both vocational programs (also called "career" or "terminal" programs), as well as the first two years of a four-year program ("academic" or "transfer" programs). Students in the vocational program usually go directly into a career after graduation, while students in the academic program usually intend to transfer to a four-year institution or an upper-division college.

Comprehensive fee. If the college combines tuition, fees, room, and board expenses, that single figure is called a comprehensive fee.

Consortium. A group of colleges and universities that share a common geographic location. Consortiums of colleges in the same town often allow students at one institution to take classes at neighboring consortium colleges and use facilities such as libraries at the member colleges. Larger consortiums, at the state or regional level, may offer in-state tuition to out-of-state students.

Cooperative education (co-op). A program in which students alternate class attendance and employment in business, industry, or government. Co-op students are typically paid for their work and may receive academic credit for their participation in the program. Under a cooperative plan, five years are normally required for completion of a bachelor's degree, but graduates have the advantage of about a year's practical work experience in addition to their studies.

Core curriculum. A group of courses, usually in the liberal arts, designated by a college as one of the requirements for a degree. Some colleges have both core-curriculum requirements and general-education requirements.

Cost of attendance. A number of expenses, among them tuition and fees (including loan fees), books and supplies, and the student's living expenses while attending school. The cost of attendance is estimated by the school, within guidelines established by federal regulation. The cost of attendance is compared with the student's expected family contribution to determine the student's need for financial aid.

Coverdell Education Savings Account (ESA). A federal income-tax provision (formerly referred to as the Education IRA) that enables taxpayers to establish a college savings plan. A maximum of $2,000 may be contributed annually to the account, which earns interest and/or dividends on a tax-free basis.

Credit/placement by examination. Academic credit or placement out of introductory courses granted by a college to entering students who have demonstrated proficiency in college-level studies through examinations such as those administered by the College Board's AP and CLEP programs.

Credit Hour. The standard unit of measurement for a college course. Each credit hour requires one classroom hour per week. Most college courses are offered in one to five credit-hour increments. For financial aid purposes, students taking at least 12 credit hours of classes in a semester are considered to be attending the college full-time, and students taking at least six credit hours are considered half-time.

CSS code. A four-digit College Board number that students use to designate colleges or scholarship programs to receive their CSS/Financial Aid PROFILE information. If a college requires financial aid applicants to submit the PROFILE, its CSS code will appear in its description in Part III of this book. A complete list of all CSS codes can also be viewed on the CSS/Financial Aid PROFILE website.

CSS/Financial Aid PROFILE. A Web-based application service offered by the College Board and used by some colleges, universities, and private scholarship programs to award their private financial aid funds. Students complete the online application and supplement, if required. CSS processes and reports the application data to institutions. CSS/Financial Aid PROFILE is not a federal form and may not be used to apply for federal student aid.

Deferred admission. Postponing enrollment, usually for one year, after being accepted for admission by a college.

Dependent student. For federal financial aid purposes, such students are either under the age of 24, attend an undergraduate program, are not married, do not have children of their own, are not orphans or wards of the court, or veterans of the active-duty armed services. The term is used to define eligibility for certain financial aid programs, regardless of whether or not the student lives with a parent, receives financial support from a parent, or is claimed on a parent's tax return. If a student is defined as dependent, parental financial information must be supplied on the Free Application for Federal Student Aid (FAFSA) and on institutional aid applications.

Direct Loan Program. See *Federal Direct Loan Program.*

District. See *In-district tuition.*

Dual enrollment. The practice in which a student enrolls in college courses while still in high school, earning both high school and college credit for his or her work.

Early Action. A nonbinding early decision program in which a student can receive an admission decision from one or more colleges and universities earlier than

the standard response date but is not required to accept the admission offer or to make a deposit before May 1. Compare to *Early Decision*, which is a binding program.

Early action single choice. An early action program in which the student may only apply early action to one college or university.

Early Decision. A binding program where students can receive an admission decision from one college or university before applications are due for regular admission. Participating students commit to enroll at the college if admitted and offered a satisfactory financial aid package.

Elective. A course, not required for one's chosen major or the college's core curriculum, that is selected to fulfill credit hours required for graduation.

Employer tuition assistance. Money that employers offer to employees or their dependents for use in paying education costs. Tuition assistance is considered an outside resource when colleges award financial aid.

Expected family contribution (EFC). The total amount students and their families are expected to pay toward college costs from their income and assets for one academic year. The amount is derived from a need analysis of the family's overall financial circumstances. The *federal methodology* is used to determine a student's eligibility for federal and state student aid. Colleges and private aid programs may use a different methodology to determine eligibility for nonfederal financial aid. Frequently, these private institutions use the *institutional methodology*.

FAFSA. See *Free Application for Federal Student Aid.*

FAFSA on the Web. An electronic option for completing the Free Application for Federal Student Aid (www.fafsa.ed.gov).

Family Educational Rights and Privacy Act (FERPA). A federal law that protects the privacy of student education records. The law applies to all schools that receive funds under an applicable program of the U.S. Department of Education. FERPA gives parents certain rights with respect to their children's education records. These rights transfer to the student when he or she reaches the age of 18 or attends a school beyond the high school level.

Federal code number. A six-digit number that identifies a specific college to which students want their FAFSA information submitted. Each college's federal code appears in its profile in Part III of this book. Formerly known as the Title IV code.

Federal Direct Loan Program. A program that allows participating schools to administer subsidized and unsubsidized Stafford and PLUS loans directly to student and parent borrowers. Direct loans include the subsidized and unsubsidized Federal Stafford Loan, PLUS Loan, and Loan Consolidation programs.

Federal methodology (FM). A need-analysis formula used by colleges and universities to determine students' financial need for the purpose of awarding federal financial aid. Most colleges also use this methodology to determine need for the purpose of awarding their own institutional funds, but some colleges use the *institutional methodology* for that. The federal methodology uses information submitted by students on the FAFSA to assess their ability to pay for college and calculate their expected family contribution.

Federal Parents' Loan for Undergraduate Students (PLUS). A program that permits parents of undergraduate students to borrow up to the full cost of education, less any other financial aid the student may have received.

Federal Pell Grant Program. A federally sponsored and administered program that provides need-based grants to undergraduate students. Congress annually sets the dollar range. As of July 1, 2010, a Pell Grant cannot exceed $5,550 per year. Eligibility for Pell Grants is based on a student's expected family contribution, the total cost of attendance at the college, and whether the student is attending the college full time or part time.

Federal Perkins Loan Program. A federally funded campus-based program that provides low-interest student loans. The maximum amount of loan funds available to an individual for undergraduate education is $27,500. Repayment need not begin until completion of the student's education, and it may be deferred for limited periods of service in the military, Peace Corps or approved comparable organizations. The total debt may be forgiven by the federal

government if the recipient enters a career of service as a public health nurse, law enforcement officer, public school teacher or social worker.

Federal Stafford Loan. A program that allows students to borrow money for educational expenses from banks and other lending institutions (and sometimes from the colleges themselves). Subsidized Stafford loans are offered by colleges based on need. The federal government pays the interest on subsidized loans while the borrower is in college, and repayment does not begin until completion of the student's education. Unsubsidized Stafford loans are non-need based; anyone may apply for one regardless of their ability to pay for college. The interest on unsubsidized loans begins accumulating immediately. For both programs, the amounts that may be borrowed depend on the student's year in school.

Federal student aid. A number of programs sponsored by the federal government that award students loans, grants or work-study jobs for the purpose of meeting their financial need. To receive any federal student aid, a student must demonstrate financial need by filing the Free Application for Federal Student Aid and meet certain other eligibility requirements.

Federal Supplemental Educational Opportunity Grant Program (SEOG). A federal campus-based program that provides need-based grants of up to $4,000 a year for undergraduate study. Each college is given a certain total amount of SEOG money each year to distribute among their financial aid applicants and determines the amount to which the student is entitled.

Federal Work-Study Program. A campus-based financial aid program that allows students to meet some of their financial need by working on- or off-campus while attending school. The wages earned are used to help pay the student's educational costs for the academic year. Job opportunities vary from campus to campus. The time commitment for a work-study job is usually between 10 and 15 hours each week.

Fee waiver. The waiver that significantly reduces the amount a student must pay for an application for admission, application for institutional financial aid, standardized tests or other college-related expenses. Fee waivers are most commonly awarded to low-income students, but are sometimes also awarded to students who are senior citizens or in the military. See also *Tuition and fee waiver*.

Financial aid. Money awarded to students to help them pay for college. Financial aid comes in the form of gifts (scholarships and grants) and self-help aid (loans and work-study opportunities). Most aid is awarded on the basis of financial need, but some awards are non-need based. Both need-based and non-need-based aid may or may not be offered on the additional basis of merit.

Financial aid application form. A form that collects information on the student, his or her income and assets, and (for dependent students) his or her parents' income and assets.

Financial aid award letter. See *Award letter*.

Financial aid package. The total financial aid offered to a student by a college, including all loans, grants, scholarships and work-study opportunities.

Financial aid PROFILE. See *CSS/Financial Aid PROFILE*.

Financial need. The difference between the total cost of attending a college and a student's expected family contribution (EFC). Financial aid grants, loans and work-study will be offered by each college to fill all or a portion of the student's need.

529 Plan. See *Section 529 Plan*.

Fixed interest rate. An interest rate on a loan that is fixed for the lifetime of the loan. Compare to *Variable interest rate*.

For-profit college/university. A higher-education institution not supported by taxes and operated as a for-profit business, either as a publicly traded corporation or as a privately held company. Sometimes referred to as a "proprietary" college.

Free Application for Federal Student Aid (FAFSA). A form completed by all applicants for federal student aid. The FAFSA is also available on the Web, at www.fafsa.ed.gov. In many states, completion of the FAFSA is also sufficient to establish eligibility for state-sponsored aid programs. There is no charge for completing the FAFSA, and you can file it anytime after January 1 of the year for which you are seeking aid (e.g., after January 1, 2011, for the academic year 2011–2012).

Full need. A student's entire financial need at a college. A college that offers a financial aid package covering the complete difference between the cost of attendance and the expected family contribution is "meeting full need." See also *Gapping*.

Full-time status. Enrollment at a college or university for 12 or more credit hours per semester. Students must be enrolled full time to qualify for the maximum award available to them from federal grant programs.

Gapping. A practice by which a college does not meet the full financial need of an admitted student, leaving a gap that must be filled by the student's own financial resources, in addition to the student's expected family contribution.

General education requirements. Courses that give undergraduates a background in all major academic disciplines: natural sciences, social sciences, mathematics, literature, language and fine arts. Most colleges have general education requirements that students complete in their first and second years, giving students a chance to sample a wide range of courses before selecting a major. Some colleges refer to general education courses as the core curriculum; at others, a few courses within the general education requirements are core courses that all students must take.

Gift aid. Financial aid in the form of scholarships or grants that do not have to be repaid.

Grant. A financial aid award given to a student that does not have to be paid back. The terms "grant" and "scholarship" are often used interchangeably to refer to gift aid, but grants tend to be awarded solely on the basis of financial need, while scholarships may require the student to demonstrate merit.

Half-time status. Enrollment at a college or university for at least 6 credit hours per semester, but fewer than the 12 credit hours required to qualify as full time. Students must be enrolled at least half time to qualify for federal student aid loan programs.

Health sciences college. An institution of higher education that primarily prepares students to enter work in a clinic, hospital or private medical practice. For a complete description of health-related fields of study, see the *College Board Book of Majors*.

Independent student. For financial aid purposes, a student who is either age 24 or older, married, a veteran, an orphan, or has legal dependents. Independent students do not need to provide parental information to be considered for federal financial aid programs. However, private institutions may require independent students to provide parental information on their institutional forms in order to be considered for nonfederal sources of funding.

In-district tuition. The tuition charged by a community college or state university to residents of the district from which it draws tax support. Districts are usually individual counties or cities, but sometimes are larger.

Individual Retirement Account (IRA). A retirement account that earns tax-free income. Money withdrawn for college expenses is not charged the penalty that normally would be incurred for withdrawing IRA money before age 59½, but is taxed as regular income.

In-state tuition. The tuition that a public institution charges residents of its state. Some community colleges and state universities charge this rate to students who are not residents of their district, but who are residents of their state.

Institutional form. A financial aid application form custom-made by a particular college or university. Some institutional forms are designed to collect additional information on a family's finances beyond what is collected on the FAFSA, and are required of all financial aid applicants. Others serve specific purposes and are only required from certain students, for example early decision applicants or student athletes.

Institutional Methodology (IM). A need-analysis formula used by some colleges and universities to determine students' financial need and award their own institutional funds. Compared to the *federal methodology*, the IM takes into account a broader and deeper picture of family assets to determine a student's expected family contribution. Most colleges that use the IM collect this additional information through the CSS/Financial Aid PROFILE form, but some collect it using their own customized institutional forms.

International Baccalaureate (IB). A high school curriculum offered by some schools in the United States and other countries. Some colleges award credit for completion of this curriculum. Please visit the organization's website for further information.

Internship. Any short-term, supervised work, usually related to a student's major, for which academic credit is earned. The work can be full time or part time, on or off campus, paid or unpaid. Some majors require the student to complete an internship.

Junior college. See *Community/junior college*.

Lender. An organization authorized to make educational loans to students.

Liberal arts. The study of the humanities (literature, the arts and philosophy), history, foreign languages, social sciences, mathematics and natural sciences. Liberal arts study guides students in developing general knowledge and reasoning ability rather than specific skills.

Liberal arts college. A college that emphasizes the liberal arts in its core curriculum and academic offerings and does not offer vocation or professional programs.

Lifetime Learning Tax Credit. A federal income tax credit of as much as $2,000 per household annually; available to eligible taxpayers based on "out-of-pocket" tuition and fee expenditures, according to income eligibility guidelines.

Major. The subject area in which students concentrate during their undergraduate study. At most colleges, students take one-third to one-half of their courses in the major; the rest of their course work is devoted to core requirements and electives.

Maritime college/institute/academy. An institution of higher education that prepares students to operate commercial shipping or fishing vessels. Upon graduation, students of most maritime academies are commissioned as officers in the United States Merchant Marine, and simultaneously commissioned as officers in the U.S. Navy Reserve.

Master Promissory Note (MPN). A special type of promissory note used to obtain a Federal Stafford loan. The MPN is designated for use as both a single-year and a multi-year note (for four-year and graduate/professional schools). Borrowers can sign a MPN once, the time they first borrow, and then receive additional loans during the same year or in subsequent years without signing an additional note.

Merit aid. Financial aid awarded on the basis of academic qualifications, artistic or athletic talent, leadership qualities, or similar qualities. Most merit aid comes in the form of scholarships. Merit aid may be non-need based, or the merit criteria may be in addition to a requirement that the student demonstrate financial need.

National Science and Mathematics Access to Retain Talent (SMART) Grant. A federal grant program for Pell Grant recipients who are in their third or fourth year of undergraduate study; have declared a major in the sciences, mathematics, engineering, technology or certain foreign languages; and have maintained a GPA of at least 3.0 in that major. The maximum annual award is $4,000, in addition to the student's Pell Grant.

Need analysis. The process of analyzing the student's household and financial information to calculate an EFC and financial need. See also *Federal Methodology, Institutional Methodology*.

Need-analysis form. See *Financial aid application form*.

Need-based aid. Financial aid (scholarships, grants, loans or work-study opportunities) given to students who have demonstrated financial need, calculated by subtracting the student's expected family contribution from a college's total cost of attendance. The largest source of need-based aid is the federal government, but colleges, states and private foundations also award need-based aid to eligible students.

Need-blind admission. The policy of determining whether a student should be admitted to a college without regard to his or her financial need.

Non-need-based aid. Financial aid awarded without regard to the student's demonstrated ability to pay for college. Unsubsidized loans and scholarships awarded solely on the basis of merit are both non-need based. Some financial aid sponsors also offer non-need-based grants tied not to merit, but to other qualities, such as state of residence or participation in ROTC.

Nursing college. An institution of higher education that primarily prepares students to become registered nurses (RNs) or licensed practical nurses (LPNs).

Open admission. The college admissions policy of admitting high school graduates and other adults generally without regard to conventional academic qualifications, such as high school subjects, high school grades and admission test scores. Virtually all applicants with high school diplomas or their equivalent are accepted, although some programs of study may have additional requirements.

Origination fee. A fee charged to a borrower to cover the costs of processing a loan. The origination fee is usually a percentage of the total amount being borrowed. The origination fee for any loan will be disclosed in the promissory note for that loan.

Out-of-state tuition. The tuition a public college or university charges residents of other states.

Outside resources. Student financial aid granted by a source other than the college that the college must take into account when assembling an aid package. Examples of common outside resources include scholarships from private foundations, employer tuition assistance and veterans' educational benefits.

Parents' contribution. The amount a student's parents are expected to pay toward college costs from their income and assets. It is derived from need analysis of the parents' overall financial situation. The parents' contribution and the student's contribution together constitute the total expected family contribution (EFC).

Parents' Loan for Undergraduate Students. See *Federal Parents' Loan for Undergraduate Students.*

Part-time status. Enrollment at a college or university for 11 or fewer credit hours per semester.

Pell Grant. See *Federal Pell Grant Program.*

Perkins Loan. See *Federal Perkins Loan Program.*

PLUS loan. See *Federal Parents' Loan for Undergraduate Students.*

Prepaid tuition plan. See *Section 529 Plans.*

Priority date. The date by which applications for financial aid must be received to be given the strongest possible consideration. The college will consider the financial need of applicants who make the priority date before any other applicants. Qualified applicants who do not make the priority date are considered on a first-come, first-served basis, and are only offered financial aid if (and to the extent to which) the college still has sufficient money left over after all the offers it has made. Can also refer to the priority date for admission applications, where, again, the college will make offers to the priority applicants first, and then consider subsequent applicants on a first-come, first-served basis, making offers only if there is still room in the incoming class.

Private college/university. An educational institution of higher education not supported by public taxes and operated on a not-for-profit basis. May be independent or affiliated with a religious denomination.

PROFILE. See *CSS/Financial Aid PROFILE.*

Promissory note. A binding legal document that a borrower signs to get a loan. By signing this note, a borrower promises to repay the loan, with interest, in specified installments. The promissory note also includes any information about origination fees, grace periods, deferment or cancellation provisions, and the borrower's rights and responsibilities with respect to that loan.

Proprietary college/university. See *For-profit college/university.*

PSAT/NMSQT® (Preliminary SAT/National Merit Scholarship Qualifying Test). A preparatory tool for the SAT that is administered by high schools to sophomores and juniors each year in October. The PSAT/NMSQT® serves as the qualifying test for scholarships awarded by the National Merit Scholarship Corporation.

Public college/university. An institution of higher education supported by public taxes.

Quarter. An academic calendar period of about 12 weeks. Four quarters make up an academic year, but at colleges using the quarter system, students make normal academic progress by attending three quarters each year. In some colleges, students can accelerate their progress by attending all four quarters in one or more years.

Regular admission. At colleges with early action or early decision plans, "regular" admission is the round of admission conducted in January or February, after the early admission rounds.

Renewal FAFSA. A simplified reapplication form for federal student aid. The Renewal FAFSA allows continuing students to update the prior year's FAFSA, rather than completing the entire FAFSA for each award year.

Reserve Officers Training Corps (ROTC). Programs conducted by certain colleges in cooperation with the United States Air Force, Army and Navy reserves. Participating students may receive a merit scholarship while they are in college, and will enter the reserves of their service branch as an officer upon graduation. Naval ROTC includes the Marine Corps. (The Coast Guard and Merchant Marine do not sponsor ROTC programs.) Local recruiting offices of the services themselves can supply detailed information about these programs, as can participating colleges.

Residency requirements. The minimum number of terms that a student must spend taking courses on campus (as opposed to independent study, transfer credits from other colleges or credit-by-examination) to be eligible for graduation. Can also refer to the minimum amount of time a student is required to have lived in-state in order to qualify for the in-state tuition rate at a public college or university.

Rolling admission. An admission procedure by which the college considers each student's application as soon as all the required credentials, such as school record and test scores, have been received. The college usually notifies an applicant of its decision without delay. At many colleges, rolling admission allows for early notification and works much like nonbinding early action programs.

SAR. See *Student Aid Report.*

SAT. A college entrance exam that tests critical reading, writing and mathematics skills, given on specified dates throughout the year at test centers in the United States and other countries. The SAT is used by most colleges and sponsors of financial aid programs.

Satisfactory academic progress. Standards set by a college or university to determine whether a student is meeting sufficient academic standards. The student must achieve these standards to continue to receive financial aid.

SAT Subject Tests. Admission tests in specific subjects given at test centers in the United States and other countries on specified dates throughout the year. The tests are used by colleges for help in both evaluating applicants for admission and determining course placement, and exemption of enrolled first-year students.

Scholarship. A type of financial aid that doesn't have to be repaid. Grants are often based on financial need. Scholarships may be based on need, on need combined with merit, or solely on the basis of merit or some other qualification, such as minority status.

School. In this book, used generically to refer interchangeably to colleges, universities and other institutions of higher education. At some universities, a "school" is a subdivision of the university — for example, the administrative unit that offers nursing courses may be called the "college of nursing" at one institution, and the "school of nursing" at another.

Section 529 Plans. State-sponsored college savings programs commonly referred to as "529 Plans" after the section of the Internal Revenue Code that provides the plan's tax breaks. There are two kinds: Section 529 college savings plans and Section 529 prepaid tuition plans.

Section 529 Prepaid Tuition Plan. State-sponsored plans through which parents can pay in advance for tuition at public institutions in their state of residence.

Self-help aid. Student financial aid, such as loans and work-study jobs, that requires repayment or employment.

Semester. A period of about 16 weeks. Colleges on a semester system offer two semesters of instruction a year; there may also be an additional summer session.

SEOG. See *Federal Supplemental Educational Opportunity Grant.*

Simplified needs test. In Federal Methodology need analysis, the simplified needs test excludes assets from the Expected Family Contribution calculation for low- to moderate-income families who file simplified tax returns (1040A, 1040EZ).

SMART Grant. See *National Science and Mathematics Access to Retain Talent Grant.*

Stafford Loan. See *Federal Stafford Loan Program.*

Student Aid Report (SAR). A report produced by the U.S. Department of Education and sent to students in response to their having filed the Free Application for Federal Student Aid (FAFSA). The SAR contains information the student provided on the FAFSA as well as the federally calculated expected family contribution.

Student expense budget. A calculation of the annual cost of attending college that is used to determine your financial need. Student expense budgets usually include tuition and fees, books and supplies, room and board, personal expenses, and transportation. Sometimes additional expenses are included for students with special education needs, students who have a disability, or students who are married or have children.

Student's contribution. The amount you are expected to pay toward college costs from your income and assets. The amount is derived from a need analysis of your resources. Your contribution and your parents' contribution together compose the total expected family contribution.

Subsidized loan. A loan awarded to a student on the basis of financial need. The federal government or the state awarding the loan pays the borrower's interest while they are in college at least half-time, thereby subsidizing the loan.

Supplemental Educational Opportunity Grant. See *Federal Supplemental Educational Opportunity Grant.*

Taxable income. Income earned from wages, salaries and tips, as well as from interest income, dividends, alimony, estates or trust income, business or farm profits, and rental or property income. Some scholarship awards must be reported as taxable income.

Teacher's college. A college that specializes in preparing students to teach in elementary or secondary schools. Most teacher's colleges offer a curriculum that combines a study of the liberal arts with the study of pedagogy.

Terminal program. An education program designed to prepare students for immediate employment. These programs usually can be completed in fewer than four years beyond high school and are available in most community colleges and trade schools.

Title IV code. See *Federal code number.*

Transfer program. An academic program in a community or junior college primarily for students who plan to continue their studies in a four-year college or university.

Transfer student. A student who has attended another college for any period, which may be defined by various colleges as any time from a single term up to three years. A transfer student may receive credit for all or some of the courses successfully completed before the transfer.

Trimester. An academic calendar period of about 15 weeks. Three trimesters make up one year. Students normally progress by attending two of the trimesters each year and in some colleges can accelerate their progress by attending all three trimesters in one or more years.

Tuition and fee waiver. Some colleges reduce the tuition and/or fees for some categories of students, such as adults, senior citizens or children of alumni.

Two-year college. A college that offers only two years of undergraduate study. See *Community/junior college*; see also *Upper-division college.*

Undergraduate. A student in the freshman, sophomore, junior or senior year of study, as opposed to a graduate student who has earned an undergraduate degree and is pursuing a master's, doctoral or professional degree.

Unmet need. The difference between a specific student's total available resources and the total cost for the student's attendance at a specific institution.

Unsubsidized loan. An education loan that is non-need based and therefore not subsidized by the federal government; the borrower is responsible for accrued interest throughout the life of the loan.

Upper-division college. A college that offers only the junior and senior years of study. Students must complete their freshman and sophomore years at other institutions before entering the upper-division institution to earn their bachelor's degree.

Variable interest rate. An interest rate that changes on an annual basis to better reflect market rates.

Virtual college/university. A degree-granting, accredited institution wherein all courses are delivered by distance learning, with no physical campus.

William D. Ford Federal Direct Loan Program. See *Federal Direct Loan Program.*

Work-study. An arrangement by which a student combines employment and college study. The employment may be an integral part of the academic program (as in cooperative education and internships) or simply a means of paying for college (as in the need-based *Federal Work-Study Program*).

Alphabetical Index of Colleges